INTERNATIONAL WHO'S WHO IN MUSIC VOLUME TWO - POPULAR MUSIC

INTERNATIONAL WHO'S WHO IN MUSIC
VOLUME TWO - POPULAR MUSIC

PUBLISHER:
Nicholas S Law

EDITOR:
Sean Tyler

PRODUCTION MANAGER:
Jocelyn Timothy

EDITORIAL ASSISTANTS:
Barbara Cooper
Janine Lawrence

All communications to: International Biographical Centre,
Cambridge CB2 3QP, England

INTERNATIONAL
WHO'S WHO IN MUSIC
Volume Two - POPULAR MUSIC

SECOND EDITION

1998/99

EDITOR
SEAN TYLER

International Who's Who in Music
Cambridge, England

Distributed exclusively in the United States and Canada by:
Taylor and Francis International Publication Services
1900 Frost Road, Suite 101
Bristol, PA 19007-1598, USA

First Edition
1996
Second Edition
1998

ISBN: 0 948875 97 6

Printed and bound in the United Kingdom by:
MPG Books Limited, Victoria Square, Bodmin, Cornwall PL31 1EG, England.

FOREWORD BY THE EDITOR

For the purposes of compiling the Second Edition of the *International Who's Who in Music Volume Two - Popular Music*, 'popular' music was deemed to include pop, rock, folk, jazz, blues, dance, world and country music, as well as some film and show music, and reducing the wealth of talent currently active in all these areas to approximately five thousand individuals has its obvious pitfalls. There are bound to be numerous artistes whose talents deserve recognition whose details do not appear within this edition, but due to the logistics of the project, and the limitations of time, space and resources, not everyone who could be considered eligible for inclusion appears in the following pages. In addition, certain artists asked not to be included and their wishes have been adhered to. As Compiling Editor, all I could hope to achieve was to include the majority of those whom the reader would expect to find, as well as many of the lesser known, but no less worthy, individuals in the industry, and to offer my apologies to those who do not appear.

As with other IBC titles, all potential biographees were sent a questionnaire to allow accurate and up-to-date information to be supplied first-hand. All such biographees were then sent a typescript of their entry for amendment and approval. However, as is inevitable in such a dynamic and transient industry, a small proportion of individuals considered to be of high reference interest failed to supply such career information, and their profiles were carefully and diligently researched. If errors have occurred, I apologise in advance, and if I am contacted via the publishers, any errors that have inadvertently appeared can be corrected in time for the Third Edition. Similarly, the very nature of the popular music industry means that many of the 'movers and shakers' are from Europe or North America, but I have attempted to represent those involved in Popular Music throughout the world wherever possible, and I shall hope to continue to redress any imbalances in subsequent editions.

Again, it has been a pleasure to be involved in recording the achievements of the talented individuals involved in this exciting industry, from the world-famous and the up-and-coming, to the unsung heroes who work out of the direct glare of the limelight. However, such delight has to be tempered with the sad loss of many wonderful people during the compilation of this volume, who would otherwise have been included in the main text. Among those leading lights who will be sadly missed are: Michael Hutchence; Stephane Grappelli; John Denver; Ronnie Scott; Sonny Bono; Carl Wilson; Floyd Cramer; Carl Perkins; Junior Wells; Ronnie Lane; Jimmy Rogers; Randy California; Luther Allison; Laurindo Almeida; Townes Van Zandt; Irving Caesar; Brian Connolly; Jeff Buckley; Laura Nyro; Fela Kuti; Nusrat Fateh Ali Khan; Glen Buxton; Tony Williams.

My final task is to thank the Publisher, Nicholas Law, for giving me the opportunity and freedom to act as Compiling Editor for this edition, and to Barbara Cooper and Janine Lawrence for the vast quantities of editing required during the preparation of this publication.

Sean Tyler
Compiling Editor

May 1998

INTERNATIONAL BIOGRAPHICAL CENTRE
RANGE OF REFERENCE TITLES

From one of the widest ranges of contemporary biographical reference works published under any one imprint, some IBC titles date back to the 1930's. Each edition is compiled from information supplied by those listed, who include leading personalities of particular countries or professions. Information offered usually includes date and place of birth; family details; qualifications; career histories; awards and honours received; books published or other creative work; other relevant information including postal address. Naturally there is no charge or fee for inclusion.

New editions are freshly compiled and contain on average 80-90% new information. New titles are regularly added to the IBC reference library.

Titles include:

Dictionary of International Biography

Who's Who in Australasia and the Pacific Nations

Who's Who in Western Europe

Dictionary of Scandinavian Biography

International Who's Who in Art and Antiques

International Authors and Writers Who's Who

International Leaders in Achievement

International Who's Who in Community Service

International Who's Who in Education

International Who's Who in Engineering

International Who's Who in Medicine

International Who's Who in Music and Musicians' Directory - Volume One - Classical and Light Classical

International Who's Who in Music - Volume Two - Popular Music

Men of Achievement

The World Who's Who of Women

The World Who's Who of Women in Education

International Youth of Achievement

Foremost Women of the Twentieth Century

International Who's Who in Poetry and Poets' Encyclopaedia

2000 Outstanding People of the 20th Century

Enquiries to:
International Biographical Centre
Cambridge CB2 3QP
England

CONTENTS

A

AAGAARD John, b. 4 Oct 1955, Denmark. Manager. Education: Economics. Career: DJ Club leader, more than 400 DJs, 1983-1994; Manager, producers and DJs, 10 years; Manager of bands, 5 years; Tour productions, 5 years, 1990-1995. Recordings: Producer, bands: Cut'n'Move; Mirah; Teschl. Honours: with Cut'n'Move: 4 Grammy Awards, 1 World Music Award. Hobbies: Badminton; Sailing. Current Management: TG Management, Svendsgade 24, 9000 Aalborg, Denmark.

AALTONEN Juhani "Junnu", b. 12 Dec 1935, Finland. Musician (saxophones, flutes). Musical Education: Flute, Sibelius Academy, Helsinki; Berklee College of Music, Boston, US, 1970. Career: Played with drummer Edward Vesala, 1965-; Played with Arils Andersen's quartet, 1970s; Work in radio, television and studio recordings; Featured soloist, Suomi (jazz suite), Heikki Sarmanto; Crossing, Jukka Linkola; Played in reed section, UMO (New Music Orchestra), 1975-; Former member, jazz rock group Tasavallan Presidentti; Concentrated on flute, as beneficiary of government grant, late 1980s-; Duo with pianist-composer Heikki Sarmanto; Recital of solo improvisations on flute, Tampere Biennale, 1990. Recordings: Several with Arild Andersen, 1970s; Nana, Edward Vesala, 1970; with Heikki Sarmanto: Hearts, 1995; Solo: Springbird, 1979. Honour: Yrjö Award, Finnish Jazz Federation, 1968. Address: Kukintie 10, 01620 Vantaa, Finland.

AALTONEN Tapio "Mongo", b. 14 June 1961, Kiukainen, Finland. Musician (percussion). Musical Education: Sibelius Academy, Helsinki, 1981. Career: Played percussion from age 16; Member, Pori Big Band; Member, Jukka Linkola Octet; Notable player of Latin percussion; Plays with UMO (New Music Orchestra). Address: c/o UMO Jazz Orchestra, Iso Roobertinkatu 23, 00120 Helsinki, Finland.

AARONSON Paul, b. 16 Mar 1955, Queens, New York, USA. Sales and Marketing Director. m. Sharon Stern, 14 Aug 1994. Educaton: BA, University of Florida, 1976; MBA, St John's University, 1981. Career: Salesman, Record Shack, New York, 1978-81; Sales Manager, Important Record Distributors, 1981-86; Owner, One Up Promotions, 1987-90; Director of Marketing, Domino Records, 1991-92; Director, Sales and Marketing, Viceroy Music, 1992. Recordings: with John Mooney: Testimony, 1992; with Cowboy Mouth: Mouthing Off, 1993; with Sunset Heights: Texas Tea, 1994; with Savoy Brown: Bring It Home, 1995; Rattlesnake Guitar, The Music of Peter Green, 1995. Hobbies: Watching and playing basketball. Address: c/o Viceroy Music Group, 547 W 27th Street, 6th Floor, New York, NY 10001, USA.

ABA YAZEED Mohamed Mounir, b. 10 October 1954, Aswan. Singer; Actor. Education: Faculty of Applied Arts (Cinematography). Career: Films, Bitter Day, Sweet Day; An Egyptian Story; Destiny (total of 11 films); Stage: The King is the King; King of the Beggars; Goodnight Egypt; TV film: Tales of the Stranger. Recordings: 11 albums including: Windows; Talk; In the Middle of the Circle; From First Touch. Publications: Windows, 1981; Talk, 1985; In the Middle of the Circle, 1987; From First Touch, 1996. Honour: Second Prize in The Festival of Arab TV, 1995-96. Memberships: Syndicate of Musicians; Syndicate of Actors. Hobby: Music. Address: 13 Fl-Bergass St, Garden City, Cairo, Egypt.

ABADIE Claude, b. 15 Jan 1920, Paris, France. Musician (clarinet); Bandleader. m. Chantal Bertin, 8 Oct 1958, 2 sons, 1 daughter. Education: Engineer. Career: Leader, first

Dixieland Revival Band, France, early 1940s; Modern jazz musician, late 1960s; Leader, own jazz tentette. Recordings: Album: Blues Pour Boris; Revival New Orleans Sur Seine; Vivement Le 15 Novembre. Publications: Le Jazz: Comment Ça Fonctionne, Diaphonie, March 1994. Membership: Union des Musiciens de Jazz. Hobby: Hockey. Address: 16 Domaine des Hocquettes, 92150 Suresnes, France.

ABATÉ Gregory, b. 31 May 1947, Fall River, Massachusetts, USA. Musician (saxophone, flute). m. Denise Marie Forcina, 10 Apr 1988, 2 sons, 1 daughter. Musical Education: Berklee College of Music, Boston. Career: Major tours of US and Europe; Radio appearances on about 200 stations throughout USA; Selmer Saxophone Clinician. Recordings: with Greg Abaté Quartet: Bop City Live At Birdland; Straight Ahead; Bird Lives; with Greg Abaté Quintet: Live At Chans, featuring Richie Cole; Bop Lives with Kenny Barron Trio and Claudio Roditi. Publications: Jazz Times; Penguin Guide To Jazz; Sax Journal; Other trade and national newspapers. Honours: Arts International Grant, 1992. Membership: International Association of Jazz Adjudicators. Current Management: Abby Hoffer Enterprises, 223 East 84th Street, New York, NY 10017, USA; Entertainment Exclusives, 403 Commonwealth, Boston, MA 02215, USA. Address: 14 Blaine Street, Cranston, RI 02920, USA.

ABBEY John E, b. 8 July 1945, London, England. Record Company Executive. Career: Editor and founder, Blues and Soul Magazine, London, 1966-85; President and founder, Contempo Records, London, 1971-78; President and co-founder, Ichiban Records Inc, 1985. Address: c/o Ichiban Records Inc., PO Box 724677, Atlanta, GA 31139, USA.

ABBOTT Gregory Pinero, b. 2 Apr 1957, Manhattan, New York, USA. Singer; Songwriter; Producer; Entertainer. 2 children. Education: BA, Boston University; MA, University of California, San Francisco. Career: Producer, EQ, 1984; 3 years writing songs and novels; Founder, Grabbitt Music Publishing and Music International Records; Involved in Songwriters Summit, Music Speaks Louder Than Words, Russia; Television appearances include: Montreux Festival; Tokyo Music Festival; Top Of The Pops; Chachrina; Fantastico; Johnny Carson; Joan Rivers; Soul Train; Grammy Awards; All My Children; The Magic of Music. Compositions: Songs include: Strong As Steel, for film Taps; Rock You Gently, Jennifer Warnes; Unfinished Business, Ronnie Spector; Everything Is Love, duet with Rosanna, Brazil. Recordings: Shake You Down; I Got The Feeling It's Over; Rhyme And Reason; I'll Prove It To You; One World. Honours: Fastest song to reach 1 million airplays, Shake You Down; Pop Song of the Year, Shake You Down, 1987; Soul Train Awards, Best New Male Singer, Best New Artist; 4 New York Music Awards; 2 Black Gold Awards; R&B Award, Las Vegas; Positive New York Image Award; 2 CEBA Awards; First Prize, Tokyo Music Festival. Memberships: Board of Governors, NARAS; Board of Directors, National Academy of Popular Music; Songwriters Hall of Fame; BMI. Hobbies: Reading; Basketball. Current Management: Drew Levister. Address: Gregory Abbott, c/o Ms Drew Levister, PO Box 68, Bergenfield, NJ 07621, USA.

ABDON Charles Cleveland, b. 27 Jan 1952, Troy, Ohio, USA. Musician (drums). Career: Drummer, various artists including: Margo Smith, 1977-80; Eddie Raven, 1981; Helen Cornelius, 1981-83; Vern Gosdin, 1983; Mel McDaniel, 1983-85; Joe Stampley, 1985-86; Tammy Wynette, 1987-. Membership: AFofM. Address: c/o George Richey Management, 1222 16th Avenue South, Suite 22, Nashville, TN 37212, USA.

ABDUL Paula, b. 19 June 1963, Los Angeles, California, USA. Singer; Dancer; Choreographer. Education: Television and Radio Studies, Cal State, Northridge College. Musical Education: Studied jazz and tap dance. Career: Choreographer, LA Laker basketball cheerleaders; Scenes in films: Bull Durham; Coming To America; Choreographer, pop videos including: The Jacksons and Mick Jagger: Torture; George Michael: Monkey; with Janet Jackson: Nasty; When I Think Of You; What Have You Done For Me Lately; Worldwide performances as singer include: Tours throughout US, UK, Japan and Far East; Prince's Trust Rock Gala, London Palladium, 1989; America Has Heart (earthquake and hurricane benefit concert), 1989; LIFEbeat's Counteraid (AIDS benefit concert), 1993. Recordings: Solo albums: Forever Your Girl (Number 1, US), 1989; Shut Up And Dance (The Dance Mixes), 1990; Spellbound (Number 1, US), 1991; Head Over Heels, 1995; Contributor, Disney charity album For Our Children, 1991; US Number 1 singles include: Straight Up; Forever Your Girl; Cold Hearted; Opposites Attract; Rush Rush; The Promise Of A New Day. Honours: MTV Video Award, Best Choreography, Janet Jackson's Nasty, 1987; Emmy, Best Choreography, for Tracey Ullman Show, 1989; Rolling Stone Awards, including Best Female Singer, 1989; American Music Awards include: Favourite Pop/Rock Female Vocalist, 1989, 1992; Billboard Magazine, Top Female Pop Album, 1990; Grammy, Best Music Video, Opposites Attract, 1991; Star on Hollywood Walk Of Fame, 1993; Humanitarian of the Year, Starlight Foundation, Los Angeles, 1992; Numerous Gold and Platinum discs.

ABDUL-MALIK Ahmed (Sam Gill), b. 30 Jan 1927, New York City, USA. Jazz Musician (bass; ud; lute); Music Educator. Musical Education: African and Middle Eastern music at university. Career: Musician with Art Blakey and Don Byas, 1948; Randy Weston, 1954-57; Thelonius Monk, 1957-58; Herbie Mann, 1961; John Coltrane, 1961; Earl Mines, 1964; Ken McIntyre, 1971; Concerts include: Jazz festivals, Montreux, New York; Tour of South America, 1961; African jazz festival, Tangier, 1972; Tutor, New York University, 1970-; Department of African Studies, Brooklyn College. Honours: BMI Pioneer In Jazz Award, 1985.

ABERCROMBIE John, b. 16 Dec 1944, Portchester, New York, USA. Jazz Musician (guitar). Musical Education: Berklee School Of Music, Boston, USA. Career: Musician with Johnny "Hammond" Smith; Dreams (with Michael and Randy Brecker); Chico Hamilton Band; Gil Evans; Gato Barbieri; Billy Cobham's Spectrum; Founder, own trio Timeless; Founder, trio Gateway (with Jack DeJohnette and Dave Holland), 1975; Leader, own quartet, 1978; Also worked with: Ralph Towner; Michael Brecker; Jan Garbarek; Jack DeJohnette's New Directions; Jan Hammer. Recordings: Albums include: Timeless, 1974; Gateway,1975; Characters, 1977; Night, 1984; Current Events, 1985; Getting There, 1988; While We're Young, 1993.

ABILDGAARD Bertel, b. 2 Apr 1955, Soborg, Denmark. Entertainer; Actor; Songwriter; Musician. m. 14 July 1984, 1 son, 2 daughters. Career: Member, cabaret group, 5XKAJ, 1982-; Main character, Tony, in comedy, Room Service; Many television, radio appearances, radio plays; Solo artist, 1995. Recordings: Kajsynger Pop, 1984; Agte Kærlighed, 1987; Alle Bornene, 1991; Krumme Tær-sang, 1992; Films include: Kajs Fosdeldag, 1990. Honour: Se Og Hors Humor Pris, 1988. Membership: DPA (Danske Populærautorer). Current Management: Erik Morbo/Vagn Moller, Dansk Dirma Og Hotel, Underholding Aps, Rosenparken 81, DK-2670 Greve, Denmark.

ABORG Carl Anders, b. 24 March 1952, Malmö, Sweden. Musician; Journalist; Teacher.

divorced, 2 sons, 1 daughter. Education: University Degree in Ethnology, Swedish and Media Communication: Selftaught Musician. Career: Group, Aston Reymers Rivaler, 1979-85; Television, Own Show, 1981, Nygammalt, 1982; Stage, Roskilde, 1982; Film, Alska mig, 1984; Numerous Radio. Compositions: Sambo; Hall mig hart; Vi bygger om; Rosa-Lill; Grannes Fru. Recordings: With the Group, Aston Reymers Rivaler: Fran Myggjagare till fotrata, 1979; Kraal, 1980; Tval, 1981; Aston!, 1983; I grodornas land, 1984; Masterverk, 1995; With the Group Drompojkarna, Drompojkharna, 1978; With the Group OJJ!600, OJJ!600, 1986. Honours: Munich Youth Prize for Film Animation, 1988. Memberships: MCHK; BMW-Klubben. Address: Olaus Magnus Vag 64, 121 46 Johanneshov, Sweden.

ABRAHAMS Mick, b. 7 Apr 1943, Luton, Bedfordshire, England. Musician (guitar). Career: Guitarist with Neil Christian; Dickie Pride; Toggery Five; McGregor's Engine; Member, Jethro Tull, 1967-69; Concerts include: Support to Pink Floyd, Hyde Park, 1968; Sunbury Jazz And Blues Festival, 1968; Founder, Blodwyn Pig; Solo artiste, 1971-; Financial consultant, 1970s-80s; Reformed Blodwyn Pig, 1989; Recordings include: with Jethro Tull: This Was, 1968; Love Story, 1969; with Blodwyn Pig: Ahead Rings out, 1969; Getting To This, 1970; Solo albums: Mick Abrahams, 1971; A Musical Evening With Mick Abrahams, 1971; At Last, 1982; All Said And Done, 1991. Current Management: Serious Bob Promotions, 250 W 85th Street, Suite 11D, New York, NY 10024, USA.

ACKERMAN William, b. Nov 1949, Germany. Musician (guitar); Composer; Record Company Executive. m. Anne Robinson. Education: Stanford University. Musical Education: Acoustic guitar since age 12. Career: Guitarist, composer, new-age music; Founder, chairman, Windham Hill Productions Inc. including new-age label, Windham Hill Records, 1976-. Compositions: All own records self-composed; Music for Stanford University theatre productions. Recordings: Albums: In Search Of The Turtle's Navel, 1976; It Takes A Year, 1977; Childhood And Memory, 1979; Passage, 1981; Past Light, 1983; Conferring With The Moon, 1986; Imaginary Roads, 1990; Compilation: A Windham Hill Retrospective, 1993; Also producer for: George Winston; Michael Hedges; Alex DeGrassi. Address: Windham Hill Productions Inc, 831 High Street, Palo Alto, CA 94301, USA.

ADA Paul, b. 22 Feb 1962, Istanbul, Turkey. Composer; Singer; Piano; Lyric Writer; Song Writer. Education: Academy of Music of Anderlecht, Brussels; Piano Lessons. Career: Composer and Singer, Rever D'Aventures, Spirou and Fanfasio; cartoon; Working partners: Ralph Benatar, Serge Frances (lyrics), Michel De Neve (producer). Compositions: Songs for Belgian singers Paul Severs; Yasmine Art Sulivan; Caroline Jokris; Maria Mouzon (Africa); Evy Furman (Germany); Garcia del Valle (Spain). Recordings: Maryel Epps: Sing For Me; Curro Savoy: Songs for Whistle (Hollywood); Marc Garcia del Valle: Pienso enti, South America and Spain. Publications: Music of the Ballet; King Solomon and The Queen of Sheba, 1997; Music and Dreams: The Musical, 1995. Honour: Honour Student, Academy of Music. Memberships: Flight Case Music; Recording Student. Hobby: Swimming. Address: Rue Limnander 37, 1070, Brussels, Belgium.

ADAMS Bob, b. 10 Mar 1922, Dalkeith, Scotland. Musician (saxophones, clarinet, bass clarinet, flute). m. Audrey Mason, 30 Apr 1948, 2 sons. Musical Education: Choir boy, Duke of Buccleuch's Private Chapel; Taught by parents. Career: Geraldo Orchestra, 1947-55; Jack Parnell Orchestra, ATV 1956-63; Emigrated to South Africa, 1963-80; MD, Guys and Dolls; Fiddler On

The Roof; Cabaret in Johannesburg; Conductor for many artistes visiting South Africa including: Englebert Humperdinck; Marlene Deitrich; Frankie Laine; Johnny Mathis; Gerry Lewis; Eartha Kitt; Kenneth McKellar. Compositions: Scored 4 films for 20th Century Fox Studios, South Africa; Composition: When I See A Rainbow, chosen for World Song Festival, Tokyo, 1975; Chappells Music and Boosey and Hawkes Music Library. Recordings: Switched On Sax; Let's Party With Bob; Upon A Time; Tales For Children; Membership: Musicians' Union. Hobby: Music. Address: 50 Brick Farm Close, Richmond, Surrey TW9 4EG, England.

ADAMS Bryan, b. 5 Nov 1959, Kingston, Ontario, Canada. Singer; Songwriter; Musician (guitar). Career: International recording artist; Numerous worldwide tours; Album sales exceed 40 million copies to date. Recordings: Albums: Bryan Adams; Cuts Like A Knife; You Want It You Got It; Reckless; Into The Fire; Waking Up The Neighbours; Live! Live! Live!; So Far So Good; 18 Til I Die; Hit singles include: Kids Wanna Rock; Summer Of 69; Heaven; Run To You; Can't Stop This Thing We've Started; It's Only Love (with Tina Turner); Everything I Do, I Do It For You (theme music for Robin Hood-Prince Of Thieves); Have You Ever Really Loved A Woman; I Finally Found Someone, duet with Barbra Streisand. Honours: Longest standing Number 1 in UK singles chart, 16 weeks, Everything I Do, I Do It For You, 1991. Current Management: Bruce Allen Talent, Suite 406, 68 Water Street, Vancouver, British Columbia V6B 1A4, Canada.

ADAMS Oleta, b. Seattle, Washington, USA. Singer. Career: Leader, own trio, 1980s; Cabaret singer, Kansas; Discovered by Tears For Fears, 1985; Singer with Tears For Fears, album and tours, 1987; Solo artiste, 1990-. Recordings: Albums: Circle Of One, 1990; Movin' On, 1995; Singles: Rhythm Of Life, 1990; Get Here, 1991; Tracks with Tears For Fears: Woman In Chains, Badman's Song, on album, The Seeds Of Love, 1987. Current Management: Gallin-Morey Associates, 345 North Maple Drive, Beverly Hills, CA 90210, USA.

ADAMS Stanley, b. 14 Aug 1907, New York, New York, USA. Lyricist. Education: NYU, 1929. Compositions: Lyrics for songs including: There Are Such Things; What A Difference A Day Made; Little Old Lady; La Cucaracha; Contributed songs to films: The Show Is On; A Lady Says Yes; Everyday's A Holiday; Duel In The Sun; Strategic Air Command. Honours include: Presidential Citation, National Federation Music Clubs, 1961; Hon Citizen, State of Tennessee, 1966; Songwriters Hall Of Fame Award for Lifetime Achievement, 1988. Memberships include: AFofM; PRS; Country Music Association; American Guild, Authors and Composers; Director, 1944-, President 1953-80, ASCAP; National Music Council. Address: c/o ASCAP, 1 Lincoln Place, New York, NY 10023, USA.

ADAMSON (William) Stuart, b. 11 Apr 1958, Manchester, England. Singer; Musician (guitar, synthesizer). Career: Member, The Skids; Founder member, Big Country, 1981-; Concerts include: Phoenix Park, Dublin, 1983; Reading Festival, 1983; Pink Pop Festival, Netherlands, 1984; Support to Elton John, Wembley Arena, 1984; Live Aid, Wembley, 1985; Prince's Trust Rock Gala, 1986, 1988, 1990; Golden Rose Festival, Montreux, 1986; Support to Queen, Knebworth Festival, 1986; Support to David Bowie, Glass Spider tour, 1987; Co-headliners with Bryan Adams, Peace Festival, East Berlin, 1988; Soviet Peace Festival, Tallinn, Estonia, 1988; The Big Day, Glasgow, 1990; Heineken Festival, 1995; Acoustic concerts, UK, 1996; Solo appearances: Wet Wet Wet concert, Glasgow, 1989; Appearance, Jerry Lee Lewis concert, London, 1989. Recordings: Albums: The Crossing, 1984; Wonderland, 1984; Steeltown, 1984; The

Seer, 1986; Peace In Our Time, 1988; Through A Big Country - Greatest Hits, 1990; No Place Like Home, 1991; The Buffalo Skinners, 1993; Why The Long Face, 1995; Singles include: In A Big Country, 1983; Chance, 1983; Wonderland, 1984; East Of Eden, 1984; Look Away, 1986; One Great Thing, 1986; King Of Emotion, 1988; I'm Not Ashamed, 1995. Honour: Grammy Nomination, Best New Group, 1984. Membership: Honorary patron, Scottish Prince's Trust, 1988. Current Management: Ian Grant Management, PO Box 107, South Godstone, Redhill, Surrey RH9 8YS, England.

ADDERLEY Nat (Nathaniel), b. 25 Nov 1931, Tampa, Florida, USA. Jazz Musician (trumpet, cornet). Career: Member, Lionel Hampton's Big Band, 1955; Also played with Woody Herman; JJ Johnson; Musician with brother "Cannonball" Adderley, 1958-75; Solo artiste and bandleader; Has also played with Nathan Davis' Paris Reunion Band. Recordings: Albums include: with Cannonball Adderley: Somethin' Else, 1958; In San Francisco, 1960; Them Dirty Blues, 1960; African Waltz, 1961; In New York, 1962; Jazz Workshop Revisited, 1963; Mercy Mercy Mercy, 1967; Accent On Africa, 1968; Solo: Work Song, 1960; The Adderley Brothers In New Orleans, 1962; Don't Look Back, 1976; That's Nat, 1985; Blue Autumn, 1987; Work Songs, 1987; Talkin' About You, 1991.

ADE King Sunny, b. 1 Sept 1946, Oshogbo, Nigeria. Singer. Career: Played with semi-professional juju bands, Nigeria; Lead guitarist, Rhythm Dandies, 1964; Also played with Tunde Nightingale; Formed the Green Spots, 1966; Renamed the African Beats, late 60s; Formed own label, Sunny Alade Records, 1975; Established the Ariya, own juju nightclub, Lagos, Nigeria; Tours include UK, US and Japan; African Beats dissolved; Currently playing in Nigeria, with new group Golden Mercury. Recordings: Numerous albums include: Alanu Loluwa, 1967; Sunny Ade Live Play, 1976; In London, 1977; Festac 77, 1978; The Message, 1981; Ariya Special, 1982; Conscience, 1982; Juju Music, 1982; Synchro System, 1983; Aura, 1984; Otito, 1985; Saviour, 1986; Funmilayo, 1989; Singles include: Challenge Cup, 1967. Address: c/o Atomic Communcations Group, 10553 W Jefferson Blvd, Culver City, CA 90232, USA.

ADEDAYO Shola, b. 27 Apr 1964, Nigeria. Singer. Education: Trained as nurse. Musical Education: Studio programmer. Career: Many ventures with African band Leke Leke, 1990-1993; Member, all-girl dance band Orage. Recordings: Album: with Leke Leke: Leke Leke; Single: with Orage: Body And Soul. Memberships: Musicians' Union; BASCA. Hobbies: Writing lyrics. Current Management: Taurus Records (UK). Address: 23 Blackheath Rise, London SE13 7PN, England.

ADEJUMO Shade, b. 12 Aug 1963, Paddington, London, England. Singer; Songwriter. Career: Backing vocalist with: Carolle Thompson; Lavine Hudson; Take That; Mica Paris; Sting; Yazz; David Grant; Television appearances: Richard Littlejohn Show; Michael Ball Show; The White Room; The South Bank Show; The Brit Awards; Concerts include: Wembley Arena; The Grand; The Marquee; The London Palladium; Radio broadcast: BBC2. Membership: Musicians' Union. Hobbies: Jogging; Reading. Address: 32 Red Post Hill, Herne Hill, London SE24 9JQ, England.

ADKINS Tracey Darcell, b. 13 January 1962, Springhill, Louisiana, USA. 2 daughters. Education: Louisiana Tech University-Petroleum Technology. Career: Hauling Hay; Pipe Fitter; Derrickman in the Old Field; TV Appearances: AM Nashville; CNN; Fox News Channel; Prime Time Country; Talk of the Town; TNN Country News; WNAB Mornings; WGN Morning Show; Good Morning Dallas; Grand Ole Opry; Motion Picture

Appearance: Square Dance, 1986; Motion Picture Soundtrack: Baydu Sunrise, Square Dance, 1986. Recordings: Albums: The New Commitment Quartet, 1979; The Best of the New Commitment Quartet, 1980; Dreamin' Out Loud, 1996. Honours: Peoples Choice Ark-La-Tex, Male Gospel Vocalist of the Year, 1980; Wild Turkey Battle of the Bands, 1985; Terry Award Dance Band of the Year, 1987; Academy of Country Music, New Male Vocalist, 1997. Hobbies: Landscaping; Gardening; Camping; Hunting; Movie Goer; Politics; Civil War Buff. Address: PO Box 121889, Nashville, TN 37212, USA.

ADLER Larry (Lawrence Cecil), b. 10 Feb 1914, Baltimore, Maryland, USA. Musician (harmonica). m. (1) Eileen Walser, 1938 (dissolved 1961), 1 son, 2 daughters, (2) Sally Cline, 1969 (dissolved 1977), 1 daughter. Education: Baltimore City College. Career: Winner, Maryland Harmonica Championship, 1927; Professional musician, 1928-; First UK concert, 1934; First appearance as soloist, Sydney, Australia, 1939; Recitals with dancer Paul Draper, US, 1941-49; Soloist with several US orchestras; Worldwide tours and festivals; Concerts for allied troops, WWII, Korea, Israel; Film appearances: Many Happy Returns, 1933; Music For Millions, 1944; Three Daring Daughters, 1948. Compositions include: Themes & Variations; One Man Show; From Hand To Mouth; Film scores include: Genevieve; King And Country; High Wind In Jamaica; Compositions for television, commercials, stage plays. Recordings include: Larry Adler Live At The Ballroom; Larry Adler Plays Works For Harmonica And Orchestra; The Glory Of Gershwin, 1994. Publications: Articles/reviews for: Sunday Times; Observer; Punch; New Statesman; Spectator; Columnist for: Jazz Express; Jewish Gazette; How I Play, 1937; Larry Adler's Own Arrangements, 1960; Jokes And How To Tell Them, 1963; It Ain't Necessarily So (autobiography), 1985. Honours: Academy Nomination, Best Film Score, Genevieve, 1954; Hon Diploma, Peabody Conservatory of Music, Baltimore, 1986; City College, Baltimore, 1986. Memberships: Equity; Musicians' Union. Hobbies: Tennis; Cycling. Current Management: MBA Literary Agents. Address: 45 Fitzroy Street, London W1P 5HR, England.

ADLER Richard, b. 3 Aug 1921, New York City, USA. Composer; Lyricist; Producer. Career: Collaborator with Jerry Ross, music and lyrics for musicals: Pajama Game, 1954; Damn Yankees, 1955; Composer, lyricist, Kwamina, 1961; Television productions: Little Women, 1959; Gift Of The Magi, 1959; Produced White House shows, salutes and galas for President Kennedy and President Johnson, 1962-65; Composer, lyricist, producer: A Mother's Kisses, 1968; Revival of Pajama Game, 1973; Rex, 1976; Commissions include: Wilderness Suite, for Dept of Interior; The Lady Remembers, Retrospectrum, for Statue of Liberty/Ellis Island; Eight By Adler, for Chicago City Ballet; Chicago (ballet), for City Of Chicago; Fanfare and Overture, US Olympic Festival, for Olympic Committee, 1987. Honours include: Variety Critics Poll Winner, The Pajama Game, 1954; 3 Pulitzer Prize Nominations; Inducted into Songwriters Hall Of Fame, 1984. Memberships: Dramatists Guild; Songwriters Guild Of America; Trustee, John F Kennedy Center For The Performing Arts, 1964-77.

ADOLFSSON Jorgen, b. 14 March 1951, Hallingeberg, Sweden. Musician; Composer. m. Vered Adolfsson Mann, 13 May 1994, 1 son, 1 daughter. Education: Art and Film History, Stockholm University; Classical Violin, 1961-69. Career: Member, Archimedes Badkar, Ramlosa Kvallar, Iskra, Vargavinter, Bitter Funeral Beer Band, Karl Brothers; Performer of Music for Modern Choreographers including Kenneth Kvarnstrom, Cristina Caprioli, Bogdan Szyber, Carina Reich, Greta Lindholm, Efva Lilja; Television and Radio Productions. Compositions:

Grodsymfonin, 1976; Ancient Evenings - Future Mornings, 1984; Exhibo Suite, 1990; Syrinx Svit, 1991; Music in Sand, 1991; Fem Danser, 1995; Digger Dog, 1995. Recordings: With Iskra, Allemansratt, Besvarjelser, Fantasy Music; With Bitter Funeral Beer Band, Bitter Funeral Beer; With Karl Brothers, Air Change; With Vargavinter, S/T, Roster Fran Alla Land; With Archimedes Badkar, II, Tre, Afro 70. Honours: Grand Prix, International Video Danse/Carina Ari, 1992. Memberships: STIM; FSJ; SKAP. Current Management: Musikcentrum, Chapmansgatan 4, SE-11236 Stockholm, Sweden. Address: Selmedalsringen 8 4 tr, 129 36 Hagersten, Sweden.

ADOLFSSON Tommy C, b. 21 October 1953, Ljusdal, Halsingland, Sweden. m. Cecilia Johansson, 1 daughter. Education: Economy College, 1969-72; Development Studies, Sussex University, England, Sweden, Tanzania, Malawi, Zambia, Madagascar, 1976-78; Marketing courses for artists, 1991, 1995. Musical Education: Trumpet Studies, Music School, 1963-70; Trumpet Studies, Stockholm Music Conservatory, 1970-74; Music Studies, England, 1976; Music Studies, Senegal, Tanzania, 1976; Music Studies, Theory and Ensembleplay, Birkagarden Music College, 1980-82; Music Studies, Bali and Java, 1983; Music Studies, India, 1984; Japanese Taiko Drummusic Studies, 1990. Career: Archimedes Bathtube, world music group, 1974-82; ISKRA, free improvised music, 1980-85; Bitter Funeral Beer Band, afro-jazz, 1980-86; Half Nelson, brassband, 1985-88; DAST, Quartet, Southafrican music and poetry, 1985-90; Kenneth Kvarnstrom Danscompany, modern ballet, 1989-91; Swedish Radio jazz group, 1990-94; Peter Bryngelsson Project, 1992; Cristina Caprioli Danscompany, 1992-93; Tuomo Hapaalas Waterorchestra, Stockholm Waterfestival, 1994; Jazz group Krakatau, Finland, 1995-96. Compositions: Wet Fantasy, ISKRA; Three Voices on a White Line; Echoes Beyond Joy and Despair; Baptismal Song; IA; Syrinx Svit, CD, Karl Brothers; Ballet Music: 1989-91: XXX; Exhibo; Trio, Duo, Solo; 1992: Ubergang; Damp; Luege, 1993; Theatre Music: 1996: The Jurt - A Stormy History; The Dolphin. Recordings: Archimedes Bathtube, Three, 1975-78; Bitter Funeral Beer Band, 1981; ISKRA, Fantasies, 1984; Bitter Funereal Beer Band 2, Praise Drumming, 1986; Karl Brothers, Air Change, 1994. Honours: Academy of Art Awards, 1985, 1991, 1993, 1994, 1997; STIM Award, 1995. Memberships: STIM; SAMI; SKAP. Hobbies: Cooking food from different cultures; Travel; Going to modern dance performances. Address: Torkel Knutssonsgatan 39, 2 tr, S-118 49 Stockholm, Sweden.

AERTS Raymond Benedict Charles, b. 12 Apr 1966, Amsterdam, Netherlands. Theatre and Concert Producer; Artist Agent and Manager. m. Sarah Frances Kate Reÿs-Smith, 1 Aug 1992. Education: Marketing Communications. Musical Education: School of Music, piano. Career: with Charles Aerts Theatre Productions International, concert and theatre productions for: Lisa Minelli; Ray Charles; Shirley Bassey; Bold And Beautiful In Concert; Lionel Hampton; Don McLean; Oklahoma!; Elvis; Annie Get Your Gun; Maria de Lourdes; Artists represented include: Charles Aznavour; Gilbert Bécaud; Nana Mouskouri; Julien Clerc; Lionel Hampton; Maria Callas; Don McLean; Shirley Bassey. Honours: with Charles Aerts Theatre Productions International: Ridder, Orde van Oranje Nassau, Netherlands; Chevalier, Ordre des Arts et des Lettres, France; Vecta Member of Honour; Cultural awards and honours from: Brazil; Hungary; Bulgaria; Indonesia. Membership: Vecta. Hobbies: Sports; Film; Music.

AGERSKOV Flemming Michael, b. 29 September 1963, Holstebro, Denmark. 2 daughters. Education: Studied Classical Trumpet, Conservatory in Aarhus, 1983-85; Japanese Music, Kyoto, Japan, 1985-86. Career: Played

with Bob Berg, Jon Balke, Martin France, Joakin Milder, Fredrik Lundin, Thomas Clausen; TV show in Ray Charles. Compositions: Arctic Views; With Closed Eyes. Recordings: CV Joergensen: Sjaelland; Kim Kristensen: A Jazzpar 93 Project on Storyville; Ane Ramlose Sextet: Days Without Make Up. Honour: Trumpet Player of the Year. Address: Holbergsgade 18, 1 TV, 1057 Copenhagen K, Denmark.

AGNEL Sophie, b. 12 July 1964, Paris, France. Jazz Musician (piano). Musical Education: Classical studies; Self-taught jazz. Career: Member, trio with R Wolf and G Etevenard; Festivals: Grenoble; Albi; Instants Chavirés. Recordings: Perigrination, Christian Brazier; Bleu Regard, with Sonny Murray and Razul Siddik. Address: Le Périé Moulard, 81390 Puybegon, France.

AHLIN Tina, b. 6 July 1967, Stockholm, Sweden. Musician (Piano); Singer; Arranger; Composer. Career: Several big Pop Acts and Pop Tours around Scandinavia; Lisa Wilsson, Orup, Tomas Dileva; Musician, lots of records; worked with several TV productions and TV orchestra; Written arrangements to Swedish Radio Symphony Orchestra, Choirs, Big Bands; Work with lots of Jazz and Pop Concerts. Address: Ehrensvardsg 2, 3 tr, 112 35 Stockholm, Sweden.

AHLQUIST Pertti (Pepe) Kalevi, b 4 July 1956, Helsinki, Finland; Vocal; Harmonica; Guitar. m. Ilse Christina Gröndahl, 29 January 1995, 1 son, 1 daughter. Education: Selftaught Musician; Chromatic Harmonica Lessons from George Smith, Los Angeles, 1982. Career: Nothing But the Blues, 30 years; Films: Condition Red (movie), by Mika Kaurismaki, Walt Disney (in Finnish), Aristocats, Toy Story; Music Videos: Back to the River; Bubble Struggle, by M Kauris Maki. Compositions: Stick With the Blues; Raker Village Boogie Comes and Goes; Sip of Tequila; Good Act; Plug Me In; Heikkinen's Barn is Burning; No More Affection; Heal Me With the Blues. Recording: Rocks and Water, 1994. Honour: Jazz Musician of the Year, Finland, 1987. Membership: Finnish Blues Society. Current Management: Rucktops Oy, Tallberginkatu 1 c 84, 00180 Helsinki, Finland. Address: Vaasankatu 2 A 19, 00500 Helsinki, Finland.

AHROLD Robert Liam (Robbin), b. 29 Sept 1943, Washington, USA. Copyright Executive. m. Kyle Warren, 20 Mar 1972, 2 daughters. Education: BSc, Foreign Service School, Georgetown University. Career: Reporter, Time Magazine, 1967-71; Various positions, Home Box Office, including Director, Special Programming; Director, Corporate Public Relations, 1974-82; Producer, Executive producer, Celebration, First pay TV Rock Series, 1975; Vice President, Corporate Relations, RCA Records, 1982-1987; Various pay TV music specials for HBO including: Country In New York, 1976; Vice President, Corporate Relations, Broadcast Music Inc, 1987-. Publications: Editor, publisher, Musicworld (quarterly membership magazine for BMI). Honours: Vice President, Board Of Governors, New York Chapter, NARAS; NATAS; Country Music Association; Gospel Music Association; National Academy Popular Music. Hobbies: Photography; Art; Scuba; Cycling. Address: c/o Broadcast Music Inc, 320 West 57th Street, New York, NY 10019, USA.

AHVENLAHTI Olli, b. 6 Aug 1949, Finland. Composer; Musician (piano, keyboards). Education: Musicology, English Philology, Helsinki University, 1968-73. Musical Education: Piano from age 7; Sibelius Academy from age 11; Berklee College of Music, Boston, US. Career: First jazz concert, Hasse Walli-Make Lievonen Sextet, 1969; Collaborated with Mike Koskinen, Pekka Pöyry, Esko Rsnell; Founding member, The Group, 1970s; Represented Finland, Nordring radio contest; Formed quintet with trumpeter

Markku Johansson, 1970s; Chief conductor, TV1, Finnish Broadcasting Company, 1990-; Pianist, backing singer Vesa-Matti Loiri; Compositions: Composer, arranger for UMO (New Music Orchestra); Music for theatre, film, television dramas; Piece based on texts from Herman Hesse's Glass Bead Game. Honour: Yrjö Award, Finnish Jazz Federation, 1975.

AIREY Don, b. 21 June 1948, Sunderland, England. Musician (Keyboards); Arranger; Conductor. m. Doris, 25 March 1977, 2 sons, 1 daughter. Education: Nottingham University, England; Royal Manchester College of Music. Career: Member of Groups: Colosseum II, 1975-78; Rainbow, 1978-81; Ozzyosbourne, 1982-85; Jethrotull, 1986-87; Whitesnake, 1988-90; Gary Moore Blues Band, 1990-91; Session Player, Arranger, 1992-95; ELO, 1996-97; Conducted winning entry, Eurovision Song Contest. Compositions: Numerous co-writes on various heavy metal albums. Recordings: Down to Earth, Rainbow; Blizzard of Oz, Ozzy Osbourne; Whitesnake 87, Whitesnake; Still Got the Blues, Gary Moore; Variations, Andrew Lloyd Webber; K2, Tales of Triumph and Tragedy, Don Airey. Honour: Eurovision 97. Membership: BASCA; PRS. Hobbies: Cricket; Photography; Football Supporter (Sunderland). Current Management: Sound Evision Enterprises Ltd. Address: 4 Hardwick Road Ind Pk, Gt Gransden, Sandy, Bedfordshire SG19 3BJ, England.

AITKEN Matt, b. 25 Aug 1956. Songwriter; Record Producer. Career: Member, pop band Agents Aren't Aeroplanes, with Mike Stock and Pete Waterman, 1980s; Member, songwriting/production team Stock Aitken Waterman (SAW), 1984-93; Co-founder, PWL label, 1988; Co-producer with Mike Stock, Love This Records, 1994-. Recordings: Albums: Hit Factory, 1987; Hit Factory, Volume 2, 1988; Hit Factory, Volume 3, 1989; The Best Of Stock Aitken And Waterman, 1990; Single: Roadblock, 1987; As co-writer, producer, hit singles include: You Spin Me Round, Dead Or Alive (Number 1, UK), 1984; So Macho, Sinitta, 1986; Respectable, Mel and Kim (Number 1, UK), 1987; Never Gonna Give You Up, Rick Astley, 1987; with Kylie Minogue: I Should Be So Lucky (Number 1, 12 countries), 1988; Got To Be Certain, 1988; The Locomotion, 1988; Hand On Your Heart (Number 1, UK), 1989; Better The Devil You Know, 1990; Other recordings with: Jason Donovan; Sonia; Brother Beyond; Big Fun; Donna Summer; Divine; Hazell Dean. Address: c/o Love This Records, Hundred House, 100 Union Street, London SE1 0NL, England.

AJAO Steven John, b. 1 Oct 1952, Birmingham, England. Musician (blues guitar, saxophone). 1 son. Education: Moseley School of Art, Lanchester Polytechnic (Art). Musical Education: Self-taught. Career: Mainly blues guitarist to 1981; Started to play alto and tenor saxophone; Numerous jazz club appearances; Played with: Red Rodney, Brighton, 1987; Bude Jazz Festival, 1988; Le Puy Peace Festival, 1989; Recorded sessions for Ali Campbell (UB40); Slade; Mickey Greaney. Hobbies: Drawing; Painting; Sculpture. Current Management: Bob Lamb. Address: 122a Highbury Road, Kings Heath, Birmingham B14 7QP, England.

AKCHOTÉ Noel, b. 7 Dec 1968, Paris, France. Musician (guitar, electric, acoustic and prepared). Musical Education: Studies with John Abercrombie; Tal Farlow; Phip Catherine. Career: Played with: Derek Bailey; George Lewis; Tony Hymas; Evan Parker; Tim Berne; Louis Sclavis; Eugene Chadbourne; Wolfgang Puschnig; Daniel Humair; Aldo Romano. Recordings: Soundpage; MAO Red Boot; Mad Nomads, Henri Texier; Lust Corner, with Marc Ribot and C E Chndgourne. Publications: Regular contributor, Jazz Magazine; Cahiers du Cinema. Memberships: SACEM; ADAMI; SPEDIDAM. Hobbies: Radio; Cinema;

Philosophy; Paintings. Current Management: Rectangle/Quentin Rollet. Address: 32 Rue Georges Pitard, 75015 Paris, France.

AKENDENGUE Pierre Claver, b. 25 April 1943, Aouta, Gabon. Psychologist; Musician. m. Michelle Ossoucah, 31 August 1997, 6 sons, 3 daughters. Education: Physiotherapy, 1968-69; PhD, Psychology, Sorbonne, 1987; Musicology; Ethnomusicology. Career: Many Compositions and Recordings; Concerts Worldwide including Africa, Europe, Canada, West Indies, Japan. Compositions: Nandipo Nkere, Powe; Owende; Africa Obota; Awana; Silence; Maladalite; Piroguier Lambarena. Recordings: Nandipo, 1974; Africa Obota, 1976; Awana, 1982; Silence, 1990; Lambarena, 1995; Maladalite, 1995. Honours: Prize, Young Singers, SACEM, 1976; Best Film Music Award, FESCAPO, 1985; RFI Trophy, 1989. Memberships: Founder, Gabonese Association of Artists and Performers. Hobby: Reading. Current Management: Melodie, 50 rue Stendhal, 75020 Paris, France. Address: BP 13, 305 Libreiville, Gabon.

AKHBARI Djalal, b. 29 June 1940, Neishabur. Centour (Santur) Persian and Professeur. m. Parirokh, 2 sons. Education: PhD, Children's Psychology; French Diploma, Persian Classical Music. Career: International professional Musician, talks and interviews on the French Radio (France Musique, France Culture, France Internationale) and also on foreign radios (BBC World Service). Compositions: Disque Arion, CBS, 1981; Cassette Arion, CBS, 1982; Several recordings from different radios; CD arion, 1996; CD Auvidis, 1995. Honour: Choc Award of the world's music magazine, 1995. Hobbies: Music; Composition for centour and voices and different instruments. Address: c/o SADRA, 11 Place G Pompidou, 93160 Noisy Le Grand, France.

AKIYOSHI Toshiko, b. 12 Dec 1929, Dairen, Manchuria, China. Musician (piano); Composer. m. (1) Charlie Mariano; (2) Lew Tabackin. Musical Education: Classically-trained piano; Berklee College Of Music, Boston, USA. Career: Successful jazz pianist, Japan; Recorded for Norman Granz; Moved to USA; Member, various groups including Charlie Mariano; Charles Mingus; Became composer, especially for big bands; Worked with saxophonist (later her husband) Lew Tabackin, Los Angeles, early 1970s; Leader own small group; Subject, documentary film Toshiko Akiyoshi - Jazz Is My Native Language, 1984. Recordings: Toshiko's Piano, 1953; Amazing Toshiko Akiyoshi, 1954; The Toshiko Trio, 1954; Jam Session For Musicians III: The Historic Mocambo Session '54, 1954; Toshiko Her Trio, 1956; Toshiko Her Quartet, 1956; The Many Sides Of Toshiko, 1957; United Nations, 1958; Toshiko Meets Her Old Pals, 1961; Country And Western Jazz Pianos (with Steve Kühn), 1963; Mariano-Toshiko Quartet, 1963; Toshiko Akiyoshi, 1965; Toshiko At The Top Of The Gate, 1968; Toshiko Akiyoshi Quartet Vols I-III, 1970-71; Solo Piano, 1971; Dedications, 1976-77; Plays Billy Strayhorn, 1978; Finesse, 1987; Interlude, 1987; Remebering Bud -Cleopatra's Dream, 1992; Albums with Lew Tabackin: Kogun, 1974; Long Yellow Road, 1974-75; Tales Of A Courtesan, 1975; Road Time, 1976; Insights, 1976; March Of The Tadpoles, 1977; Dedications II, 1977; Live At Newport '77, 1977; Sumi-e, 1979; Farewell To Mingus, 1980; From Toshiko With Love, 1981; Tanuki's Night Out, 1981; European Memoirs, 1982. Address: c/o Thomas Cassidy Inc., 366 Horseshoe Drive, Basalt, CO 81621, USA.

AKKERMAN Jan, b. 24 Dec 1946, Amsterdam, Netherlands. Musician (guitar, lute); Composer; Arranger. Musical Education: Gradutate, Music Lyceum, Amsterdam. Career: Member, groups including: Johnny And The Cellar Rockers, 1958; The Hunters; Brainbox, 1969; Focus, 1969-76; Solo artiste, 1973-; Periodic reunions with Focus; Member, side project

Forcefield, with Ray Fenwick and Cozy Powell, 1988-89. Recordings: Albums: with Focus: In And Out Of Focus, 1971; Moving Waves, 1971; Focus III, 1972; At The Rainbow, 1973; Hamburger Concerto, 1974; Mother Focus, 1975; Solo albums: Profile, 1973; Tabernakel, 1974; Eli, 1977; Jan Akkerman, 1978; Arunjuez, 1978; Live, 1979; 3, 1980; It Could Happen To You, 1985; Can't Stand Noise, 1986; Pleasure Point, 1987; The Noise Of Art, 1990; with Forcefield: The Talisman, 1988; To Oz And Back, 1989; Singles: with Focus: House Of The King, 1971; Hocus Pocus, 1971; Sylvia, 1972. Honours: Melody Maker Poll Winner, Best Guitarist, 1973. Address: c/o Bert Bijlsma, P/A Hamrikkerweg 4, 9943 TB, NW Scheemda, Netherlands.

ALAN Mark, b. 14 Sept 1939, Elizabeth, New Jersey, USA. Personal Manager; Agent. 1 son, 1 daughter. Education: BSc, Masters, Speech and Theatre. Career: Premier Talent Agency, New York City, 1965-68; President, New Beat Management, New York City, 1968-71; Artists included: Tommy James and the Shondells; The Illusion; Robin McNamara; The Sidekicks; Exile; Worked with Jeff Barry and Tommy James; Manager, Andre Cymone; Airkraft; Zwarte; President and owner, National Talent Associates, Minneapolis; President, Mark Alan Agency, 1988-; Manager for Illerazzum, Every Mother's Nightmare and Peter Phippen. Recordings: As manager include: The Dance Electric, Andre Cymone; Did You See Her Eyes, The Illusion; Lay A Little Lovin' On Me, Robin McNamara; with Tommy James: Draggin the Line; Come to Me; Ball and Chain; She; Ball Of Fire; Sweet Cherry Wine; Crimson And Clover; Crystal Blue Persuasion; with Zwarte: Zwarte; Hit the Road; Easy Street; with Peter Phippen: Book of Dreams; Albums: with The Illusion: The Illusion; Together (As a Way of Life); withHow Does It Feel; Tommy James: Crimson and Clover; Best of Tommy James and The Shondells; Travelin'; Tommy James; LP, Tommy James; with Robin McNamara: Lay A Little Lovin' On Me; with Andre Cymone: AC. Address: c/o Mark Alan Agency, PO Box 21323, St Paul, MN 55121, USA.

ALBARN Damon, b. 23 Mar 1968, Whitechapel, London, England. Singer; Songwriter. Education: Drama School, Stratford East, 1 year. Musical Education: Part-time Music course, Goldsmith's College. Career: First solo concerts, Colchester Arts Centre; Member, Blur; Numerous television and radio appearances, include: Later With Jools Holland; Top Of The Pops; Loose Ends, Radio 4; Later With... Britpop Now; Extensive tours, concerts include: Alexandra Palace, Reading Festival, 1993; Glastonbury, 1994; Mile End, 1995. Recordings: Albums: with Blur: Leisure, 1991; Modern Life Is Rubbish, 1993; Parklife, 1994; The Great Escape, 1995; Singles: She's So High, 1990; There's No Other Way, 1991; Bang, 1991; Popscene, 1992; For Tomorrow, 1993; Chemical World, 1993; Sunday Sunday, 1993; Girls And Boys, 1994; To The End, 1994; Parklife, 1994; End Of A Century, 1994; Country House, 1995; The Universal, 1995; Stereotypes, 1996. Honours: Mercury Prize Nomination; Platinum album, Parklife; BRIT Awards: Best Single, Video, Album and Band, 1995; Q Awards, Best Album, 1994, 1995. Current Management: CMO Management, Unit 32, Ransome Dock, 35-37 Parkgate Road, London SW11 4NP, England.

ALBERTO José (José Alberto Justiniano), b. 22 Dec 1958, Santo Domingo, Dominican Republic. Singer; Bandleader. Musical Education: Studied music at Antilles Military Academy, Puerto Rico. Career: Club circuit singer, New York; Recording artiste, 1976-; Known as "El Canario" (The Canary); Member, Típica 73, 1978-81; Bandleader, 1984-; Appearances include: Debut UK performance, with Celia Cruz, 1978; New Orleans Jazz And Heritage Festival, with Celia Cruz, 1990; New York Salsa Festival, Madison

Square Garden, 1990. Recordings: Albums: with Tito Rodríguez II: Curious?, 1976; with Típica 73: Salsa Encendida, 1978; Típica 73 En Cuba - Intercambio Cultural, 1979; Charangueando Con La Típica 73, 1980; Into The 80s, 1981; Solo: Tipicamente, 1984; Canto Canario, 1985; Latino Style, 1986; Sueño Contigo, 1988; Mis Amores, 1989; Dance With Me, 1991. Current Management: Ralph Mercado Management, 568 Broadway, Suite 806, New York, NY 10012, USA.

ALBERTS Al (Al Albertini), b. 19 Aug 1922, Philadelphia, USA. Musician; Television Presenter. m. Stella Zippi, 6 June 1953, 2 sons. Education: BS, Temple University, 1951. Career: Lead singer, The Four Aces, 1946-58, 1975-85; President, Alstel Television Productions Inc, Chester, Pennsylvania, 1958-; Executive producer, television host, Al Alberts Showcase Station, Philadelphia, 1968-; President, Al Alberts Onstage Ltd, Chester, 1988-. Recordings include: It's No Sin; Tell Me Why; Stranger In Paradise; Three Coins In The Fountain; Love Is A Many Splendoured Thing; Mr Sandman; Dream; Heart And Soul; A Woman In Love; Heart Of My Heart; Garden In The Rain; It's A Woman's World; Lazy, Hazy, Crazy Days Of Summer. Honours include: Inducted into Music Hall Of Fame, 1988. Address: Al Alberts Onstage Ltd, 15 E 8th Street, Chester, PA 19013, USA.

ALBINI Steve, b. USA. Vocalist; Musician (guitar); Record Producer. Career: Founder, Big Black, 1982-88; Founder, Rapeman, 1988; Record producer, for artists including The Pixies; The Wedding Present; Tad; The Breeders. Recordings include: Albums: with Big Black: Racer X, 1985; Atomizer, 1986; The Hammer Party, 1986; Sound Of Impact, 1987; Big Black - Live, 1989; Rich Man's Track, 1989; Pigpile, 1992; with Rapeman: Two Nuns And A Pack Mule, 1988; As producer include: Surfer Rosa, The Pixies; Pod, The Breeders; Salt Lick, Tad; Seamonsters, The Wedding Present.

ALBURO Francisco, b. 19 July 1953, Legaspi City, Philippines. Singer; Musician (keyboards); Singer. m. Minerva De Leon, 7 May 1977, 2 sons, 2 daughters. Musical Education: Course, Melody School of Music, Stamford House, London. Career: Formed group, The Spider's Webb (first Phillipino band), 1973; Member, PI Sea Dust, 1976-82; Partime singer, Memoza Club, 1983; Bass guitar, Pula't Asul Band, 1990; Solo singer, 1991-95.

ALESSANDRO b. 26 Nov 1959, Venice, Italy. Singer; Musician (guitar); Entertainer. Education: Cosmologist; Linguist. Career: With Los Primos, tour of Japan, 1988; With Ole, Italy, 1989; Australia; Singapore; Hong Kong; Russia; Canada; Presently touring UK with solo show Passion, Grace, Fire; Television appearances: Wogan; Just For Laughs; Edinburgh Nights; Television commercials: Canale 5. Recordings: Wrote and performed Lorca's Women, for Royal Shakespeare Company; with Los Primos: Paul's Lurking Grapefruit, Latino-comedy. Honours: Time Out Magazine, Pick Of The Fringe, 1989; Winner, Covent Garden Street Festival, 1989; British Gas Best Newcomer, Edinburgh Festival, 1992. Membership: Musicians' Union. Hobbies: Astronomy; Cosmology; Flying; Skiing. Current Management: Wizard Entertainments, 102 Euston Street, London NW1 2HA. Address: 14B Vicarage Grove, London SE5 7LW, England.

ALEXANDER Dennis, b. 7 May 1953, Fyvie, Aberdeenshire, Scotland. Entertainer; Musician (acoustic guitar). m. Isobel, 3 Aug 1974, 1 son, 1 daughter. Education: Member, Ist Purchase and Supply, Hand Promotions Events Management. Musical Education: Self-taught. Career: Lead singer, Crooked Jack; Writer, producer, Crooked Jack's Giant Jeely Piece Show; Appearances, Edinburgh Festival Fringe; Major folk festivals in Scotland. Recordings: Tomorrow Must Wait; The Giant Jeely Piece Show (video); An Audience with Crooked Jack. Membership: Musicians' Union. Hobbies: Running café and joke/fancy dress hire in Kirkcaldy. Current Management: Crooked Jack Promotions. Address: 16 Moray Court, Auchtertool, Kirkcaldy, Fife KY2 5XS, Scotland.

ALEXANDER John Eric, b. 10 Feb 1962, Elizabeth, New Jersey, USA. Composer. m. Ellen Greiss, 3 Aug 1986, 1 son. Education: BFA, Parsons School Of Design, 1983. Career: Associate Producer, Iris Films Inc, New York, 1975-83; Producer, Sam Alexander Productions, New York, 1983-86; John Eric Alexander Music Inc, New York, 1986-. Compositions: Composer, music producer, film soundtracks: The Fly, 1986; Red Heat, 1987; Predator, 1987; The Mosquito Coast, 1987; Witches of Eastwick, 1988; Flatliners, 1990; Lethal Weapon II, 1990; Bird On A Wire, 1990; Die Hard II, 1990; Silence Of The Lambs, 1991; Point Break, 1991; Ricochet, 1991. Honours: Cannes Film Festival Award, Witches Of Eastwick, 1988. Membership: AFofM.

ALEXANDER Van, b. 2 May 1915, New York City, USA. Music Arranger; Composer; Conductor; Author. m. Beth Baremore, 22 Sept 1938, 2 daughters. Education: Columbia University. Musical Education: Studied with Otto Cesana, New York City; with Mario Tedsco, California; (Orchestration, Conducting, Composition). Career: Worked with Chick Webb at The Savoy Ballroom, New York; Benny Goodman; Paul Whiteman; Les Brown; Formed own band, played on radio, The Fitch Bandwagon; Morey Amsterdam's Laugh And Swing Club; Played ballrooms, theatres throughout US, including: New York Paramount, Loews State; Capitol, New York; Earle, Philadelphia; The Stanley, Pittsburg; Arranger/conductor for Dinah Shore; Doris Day; Dean Martin; Gordon and Sheila MacRae; Kay Starr; Peggy Lee; Dakota Staton; Patty Andrews. Compositions include: 22 feature films; Co-writer, arranger, A-Tisket-A-Tasket, hit for Ella Fitzgerald; Hundreds of television segments include: The Wacky World Of Jonathan Winters; Gene Kelly's Wonderful World Of Girls; The Goldiggers Chevy Show; Composer, conductor, NBC's 50th Anniversary Show, A Closer Look; Dom De Luise specials; 1969 Emmy Awards; The Guy Mitchell Show Series; Scoring credits: Hazel; I Dream Of Jeanie; Bewitched; Donna Reed; Dennis The Menace. Recordings: Swing Staged For Stereo; Savoy Stomp; The Last Dance; Numerous albums with Gordon MacRae; Kay Starr; Dakota Staton; Dorothy Kirsten (all on Capitol Records). Publication: First Arrangement (a learning method for the novice arranger). Honours: Irwin Kostal Award, 1995; 3 Emmy Nominations; NARAS Hall Of Fame Award, for A-Tisket-A-Tasket, 1986. Memberships: ASCAP; ASMAC; NARAS; Big Band Academy of America; Academy of Motion Picture Arts and Sciences. Hobbies: Golf; Reading; Watching grandchildren grow up. Address: 10560 Wilshire Blvd, Los Angeles, CA 90024, USA.

ALFORD Clem, b. 2 October 1945, Glasgow, Scotland. Musician. Div. Career: Major Recitals, Radio in India; Toured Europe, Far East, including Japan; Major Concert Appearances with Laxshmi Shankar, Royal Albert Hall; Many Sessions with Major Musical Personalities, Lulu, Maurice Jarre, John Williams. Compositions: The Electronic Sitar of Clem Alford; Magic Carpet; Sangeet Sagar; Pop Explosion, Sitar Style; K.P.M; One More Magic Carpet II; Akasa, Staying On. Recordings: The Electronic Sitar of Clem Alford; Magic Carpet; Sangeet Sagar; Pop Explosion, Sitar Style; K.P.M; One More Magic Carpet II; Monsoon, Akasa, Jewell in the Crown. Publications: The Sitar Manual; The Sitar Book. Honours: Jnr Sangeet Ratnakar, West Bengal; Sangeet Sudhakar, Calcutta; Sur-Mani, Bombay. Memberships: PRS; MCPS; PAMRA; Indian Music Congress. Hobby: Recording. Address: 9 Tavistock Mansions, 16 Tavistock Place, London WC1H 9RA, England.

ALIABADIZADEH Mohammad Hussein, b. 1 May 1952, Tabriz, Iran. Architectural Engineering Educator; Consultant. m. Parvin Godzari-Borhani, 15 Jan 1979, div 1989, 2 s. Education: Maths Dip, Univ Tabriz, 1970. Appointments: Sub-Lt, Iranian Educl Corps, 1972-73; Instr, Coll, Tehran; Archtl Engrng Instr, Fine Arts Fac; Appt to Habitation Admin, 1981-; Engrng Cnslt, 1981-. Publications: Contrb articles to profl jrnls. Memberships: Boy Scout and Intell Serv Copr, Zanjan, 1973; People's Muslim Party, Tabriz, 1979; Fell, Supermarket of Neibor; Jewish Union. Address: Habitation Administration, Talegani Avenue, Tehran, Iran.

ALIFANTIS Nicu, b. 31 May 1954, Braila, Romania. Singer; Composer; Musician (guitar). Career: Wrote music for theatre, 10 film soundtracks; 19 recitals; 5000 concerts, tours: Romania; Bulgaria; Czechoslovakia; Germany; Israel; England; Italy; Hungary; Holland. Recordings: 3 singles; 6 albums; 2 CDs, 1 in France, produced by Radio France International; 8 albums with other singers. Honours: 3 awards, Theatre Music, 1986, 1991, 1993; 1st awards for Singer Of The Year, 1993. Memberships: Romanian Union Of Composers; International Union of Theatre, UNIMA. Hobbies: Autos; Tennis; Books. Current Management: Aurel Mitram, PO Box 26-54, Bucharest, Romania.

ALKER Martin, b. 28 Jan 1969, Darlington, County Durham, England. Singer; Songwriter; Musician (piano, saxophone); Arranger. Musical Education: Graduate diploma, Light Music (GDNSM), Newcastle School of Arts. Career: Formed Big Shot Music (Musical services), 1991; Formed The Groove Company, 1992; Formed Traces of Red, 1996 appearing on The Talent Channel, satellite and cable TV, 1997; Cruised on P&O ships Canberra and Oriana, 1997. Recordings: Albums: Brass arrangements, Plus, Phil Murray, 1991; Solo album: Autograph, 1994 (unreleased); with Traces of Red: Just One of Those Days, CD, 1996. Honours: Variety clubs best showband, The Groove Company, 1993. Current Management: Big Shot Music. Address: 3 Fairview Gardens, Richmond, North Yorkshire DL10 4NP, England.

ALL-STAR FRESH, b. 1 Aug 1965, Amsterdam, Netherlands. Producer; Rapper; Remixer; Composer. Musical Education: Self-taught. Career: Leader, producer, King Bee. Compositions include: (co-writer) Cappella: Move On Baby; Move Your Body; U & Me. Recordings: Back By Dope Demand; Must Be The Music. Honours: Dance Artist Award, 1991, 1992. Hobby: Music. Current Management: Hans Van Pol Management. Address: PO Box 9010, 1006 AA Amsterdam, Netherlands.

ALLEN Anthony Oladipo, b. 20 July 1940, Lagos, Nigeria. Musician (drums); Composer. m. (1) 1 son, 5 daughters, (2) Sylvie Nicollet, 19 Dec 1987, 3 sons. Education: College. Musical Education: Self-taught. Career: Drummer, various groups, 1960-63; Formed Nigerian highlife/jazz group Koola Lobitos, with Fela, 1965; Tour with Nigeria 70, 1969; Band becomes Africa 70, 1970; Formed own group, 1979; Founder, Afrobeat group Mighty Irokos, playing own compositions, 1980; Moved to London, 1984, then Paris, 1986; Played with Amina, tour and album, 1992-94. Recordings: Albums: Jealousy, 1975; Progress, with Fela, 1976; No Accomodation, 1977; No Discrimination, 1979; Nepa, 1985; Afrobeat Express with Cobalt, 1989; Appearances on albums: Oremi, King Sunny Ade; So Hot, Ray Lema; Medecine, Ray Lema; Cithea Live. Memberships: SACEM; SPEDIDAM; ADAMI. Current Management: Sylvie Allen. Address: 5 Place Charles de Gaulle, 92400 Courbevoie, France.

ALLEN David Andrew Wells, b. 1 June 1953, Toronto, Ontario, Canada. Lecturer;

Musician (guitar, bass, classical guitar); Composer. m. 26 May 1975, 2 sons, 1 daughter. Musical Education: Bachelor of Music, Master of Music, Manchester. Career: Concerts as soloist and in duos/trios, 1978-88; Tours and concerts: London; Manchester; Liverpool; Canada, 1981-88; Broadcasts: Radio 3; Granada TV; Lecturer, Popular Music, NEWI Wrexham, 1988-1994; Course Co-ordinator, Performing Arts, Yale College, Wrexham, 1995. Compositions: Sequencing, Theatr Clwyd, 1990; The Roots Of Rhythm, 1993; Theatr Clwyd/BBC Children in Need Commission. Memberships: Musicians' Union; IASPM. Hobbies: Swimming; Gardening; Camping. Address: 31 Birch Hall Lane, Manchester M13 0XJ, England.

ALLEN Duane David, b. 29 Apr 1943, Taylortown, Texas, USA. Singer; Songwriter. m. Norah Lee Stuart, 22 Sept 1969, 2 sons. Education: BS, Music, East Texas University, 1965. Career: Radio disc jockey, Paris, Texas, 1963-65; Lead singer, US gospel/country group Oak Ridge Boys, 1966-; Co-owner, president, Silverline/Goldline Music Publishing; Owner, president, Superior Sound Studios. Compositions: He Did It All For Me; Here's A Song For The Man; How Much Further Can We Go; I Will Follow The Sun. Recordings: Singles include: Praise The Lord And Pass The Soup; I'll Be True To You; Y'All Come Back Saloon; Elvira; Bobbie Sue; Leavin' Louisiana In The Broad Daylight; Trying To Love Two Women; American Made; Make My Life With You; I Guess It Never Hurts To Hurt Sometime; Come On In; Albums include: International, 1971; Light, 1972; Hymns, 1973; Street Gospel, 1973; Gospel Gold Heartwarming, 1974; Oak Ridge Boys, 1974, Super Gold, 1974; Sky High, 1975; Old Fashioned..., 1976; Y'All Come Back Saloon, 1977; Room Service, 1978; The Oak Ridge Boys Have Arrived, 1979; Together, 1980; Greatest Hits, 1980; Fancy Free, 1981; Bobbie Sue, 1982; Oak Ridge Boys Christmas, 1982; Friendship, 1983; American Made, 1983; The Oak Ridge Boys Deliver, 1984; Greatest Hits II, 1984; Step On Out, 1985; Seasons, 1985; Christmas Again, 1986; Where The Fast Lane Ends, 1986; Monongahela, 1987; New Horizons, 1988; American Dreams, 1989; Greatest Hits III, 1989; Unstoppable, 1991; The Long Haul, 1992. Publications: Co-author, The History Of Gospel Music, 1971. Honours: Grammies, 1970-77; 12 Gospel Music Association Dove Awards; American Music Award, Best Country Group of the Year, 1982; Country Music Association Award, Vocal Group of the Year, 1978; Academy of Country Music Awards, Best Vocal Group 1977, 1979; Numerous Gold discs. Memberships: CMA; Gospel Music Association; AFTRA; National Academy Recording Arts and Sciences; Academy Of Country Music. Current Management: Don Light Talent. Address: PO Box 120308, Nashville, TN 37212, USA.

ALLEN Geri, b. 1957, Detroit, Michigan, USA. Jazz Musician (piano). Musical Education: Jazz Studies Degree, Howard University, Washington, 1979; Masters Degree, Ethnomusicology, University of Pittsburgh, 1982; Studied piano with Kenny Barrow. Career: Formed own trio with Ron Carter, Tony Williams; Also played with: Ornette Coleman; Wallace Roney; Jack DeJohnette; Betty Carter; Dave Holland; Marcus Belgrave; Steve Coleman; Lester Bowie. Recordings: The Printmakers; Twilight Time; The Nurturer; Maroons; Twenty One; Etudes And Segments (with Charlie Haden, Paul Motian); Feed The Fire (with Betty Carter, Jack DeJohnette, Dave Holland). Honours: Howard University Alumni Award; SESAE Special Achievement Award; Eubie Blake Award; Downbeat Critics Poll, Talent Deserving Wider Recognition, 1993, 1994. Current Management: Blue Note. Address: 1290 Avenue of the Americas, 35th Floor, New York, NY 10104, USA.

ALLEN Henry Kaleialoha, b. 11 June 1933, Honolulu, HI, USA. Master Artist, Hawaiian Steel Guitar; Recording Artist; Show Producer. m. Sherron Allen, 1971, 1 son, 2 daughters. Education: Studied Jazz, Los Angeles, Music Theory, Composition, Johnny Smith, Alex Keck; Hawaiian Music Institute, Teaching Hawaiian Steel Guitar for County of Maui, Hawaii. Career: Music Parts in Films; Hawaiian Eye; Blue Hawaii; Barnaby Jones; Mama's Family; Regular Guest on Home Shopping Channel Network; QVC and Produces Hawaiian Shows and Music for Their 50th State Tours; Show Producer, own shows; Music is played, Inflight; American Airlines; Opened up Planet Hollywood with Music in Maui, 1995; Own Record Label: Rainbow Records; Albums: Memories of Hawaii; Magic of Steel Guitar; Blue Hawaii. Recordings: Major Compositions: Lahaina; Walking in the Sand; Hookipa (Jazz) Noalani; Koele Mist; We Say Aloha; Goodbye; Lanikai; Hawaii, Islands in the Sky; Kalele; Swinging. Publications: Learning to Play the Hawaiian Way, 1991; Book of Songs - Hawaiian Steel Guitar, 1993. Honours: Awards, State Foundation/Culture and the Arts, 1995, 1996; Master Artist Grants; ASCAP Awards, 1996, 1997; County of Maui Grant for Music Work Musicians Association of Hawaii (Lifetime Member); ASCAP Member; HSGA Member. Hobbies: Jazz; Golf; Wine Tastings; Travel. Current Management: Own Manager, Polynesian Promotions, Rainbow Records. Address: 5161-D, Kohi Street, Lahaina, Maui, Hawaii 96761, USA.

ALLEN Mark, b. 21 Feb 1964, Brighton, Sussex, England. Songwriter; Musician (guitar). Education: BSc Hons, University. Musical Education: Informal. Career: Singer, writer, guitarist with Attacco Decente, 1987-; Tours: UK; Italy; Germany; Radio and television: BBC Radio 1 playlist; MTV; Mavis On 4, documentary about Attacco Decente; Major festival appearances: Edinburgh, Glastonbury. Recordings: Albums: UKA-United Kingdom Of America, 1987; The Baby Within Us Marches On, 1988; Crystal Night, 1994; Singles: The Will Of One, 1988; I Don't Care How Long It Takes, 1989. Memberships: PRS; MCPS; Musicians' Union. Current Management: Born and Bred Management. Address: PO Box 309, Brighton BN2 3SE, England.

ALLEN Peter Raymond, b. 23 November 1954, Newbury, Berkshire, England. m. Petrina, 16 May 1996. Career: Formed Pete Allen Jazz Band, 1978; Regular TV & Radio shows followed including: Pebble Mill at One, BBC TV; Jazzin Around, HTV Series; Most BBC Radio Two Programmes including 5 broadcasts for Friday Night to Music Night & Own Six Week Series for Radio Two. Compositions: Beau Sejour; Mystic Gypsy; St Louis Street Stomp; Riverside Rag; Springtime Swing; Black Lion Rag; At the Upton Mardi Gras. Recordings: Turkey Trot, 1978; Down in Honky Tonk Town, 1979; Gonna Build a Mountain, 1980; Beau Sejour, 1987; Big Chief - Loose Tie, 1996; All Aboard for Alabama, 1997; Oh Play That Thing, 1998; Reeds 'n' Rhythm, 1998. Honours: World Wide All Stars, Sacramento, USA, 1984; Honorary Citizenship of New Orleans, 1992; European Top Eight Jazz Band, Germany. Memberships: Performing Rights Soc; Lions International. Hobbies: Football; Travel. Address: 15 Linsvale Close, Frome, Somerset, BA11 2BR, England.

ALLEN Rick, b. 1 Nov 1963, Sheffield, England. Musician (drums). Career: Drummer, Def Leppard, 1978-; Concerts include: Support tours to Sammy Hagar; AC/DC; Ted Nugent; Reading Rock Festival, 1980; Lost left arm in car crash, 1984; Returns to perform with custom-built electronic drum kit, 1985; Monsters of Rock festivals, including Castle Donington, 1986; Royal Albert Hall, 1989; Freddy Mercury Tribute Concert, Wembley Stadium, 1992; Television interview, Fighting Back, BBC1, 1992. Recordings: Albums: On Through The Night, 1980; High'n'Dry, 1981; Pyromania, 1983; Hysteria, 1987; Adrenalize, 1992; Retroactive, 1993; Vault 1980-95, 1995;

Slang, 1996; Singles include: Photograph; Rock Of Ages; Foolin'; Animal; Pour Some Sugar On Me; Love Bites; Rocket; Let's Get Rocked; Make Love Like A Man; Heaven Is; Two Steps Behind, featured in film soundtrack The Last Action Hero; When Love And Hate Collide. Honours include: American Music Awards: Favourite Heavy Metal Album, Favourite Heavy Metal Artists, 1989. Current Management: Q-Prime Inc. Address: 729 Seventh Avenue, 14th Floor, New York, NY 10019, USA.

ALLEN Steve (Stephen Paul), b. Peterborough, England. Entertainment Agent; Disc Jockey; Radio Presenter. Education: Wisbech Technical College; Leicester College Of Art. Career: Promoter, Entertainment agent, established 1969; Disc jockey, radio presenter, Hereward Radio, CNFM, KLFM, WGMS, 1983-95. Membership: Fellow, Entertainments Agents Association. Hobbies: Golf; Squash; Skiing. Address: 60 Broadway, Peterborough PE1 1SU, England.

ALLEN Terry (Terry L Comp), b. 1 Sept 1947, Niles, Michigan, USA. Entertainer; Vocalist; Musician (bass, rhythm guitar). m. Barbara Sweets, 23 Apr 1995, 4 sons, 4 daughters. Education: Aircraft Maintenance Diploma. Career: Tours USA and Canada, playing private and public clubs and military bases; Numerous television and radio appearances, state and county fairs, 1969-1981; Currently, Director of Marketing for Gf Mac Management Inc. Recordings: CB Duck; A Little Love, 1978; Time Has; Footprints; Good Old Days, 1989. Honours: NE Country Music Hall Of Fame, Achievement and Performance Award, 1987. Hobbies: Horses; Camping; Fishing; Hunting. Current Management: Blackhawk International, Dalton Fuller Management. Address: Rt1 Box 200, Rising City, NE 68658, USA.

ALLMAN Gregg, b. 8 Dec 1947, Nashville, Tennessee, USA. Musician. m. Cher Bono, 1975, (divorced 1979), 1 child. Career: Co-founder, Hour Glass; Support to Eric Burdon and the Animals, 1967; Co-founder, singer, Allman Brothers (with brother Duane), 1969-76, 1978-81, 1989-; Solo artiste, 1973-; Also recorded with wife Cher, 1976-79; Appearances include: Atlanta International Pop Festival, with Jimi Hendrix, Jethro Tull, B B King, Fillmore East, New York, 1971; Mar Y Sol Festival, Puerto Rico, 1972; Watkins Glen Raceway, with Grateful Dead and the Band (largest-ever concert of 600,000), 1973; Knebworth Festival, 1974; New Orleans Jazz & Heritage Festival, 1993; Actor, film Rush, 1991. Recordings: Albums with Hour Glass: Hour Glass, 1967; Power Of Love, 1968; with The Allman Brothers: Allman Brothers Band, 1970; At Fillmore East, 1971; Eat A Peach, 1972; Brothers And Sisters, 1973; Win Lose Or Draw, 1975; The Road Goes On Forever, 1976; Wipe The Windows, Check The Oil, Dollar Gas, 1976; Enlightened Rogues, 1979; Brothers Of The Road, 1981; The Best Of The Allman Band, 1981; Dreams, 1989; Seven Turns, 1989; Shades Of Two Worlds, 1991; Second Set, 1995; Solo albums: Laid Back, 1973; The Gregg Allman Tour, 1974; Playin' Up A Storm, 1977; I'm No Angel, 1987; with Cher: Allman And Woman, 1976; Two The Hard Way, 1977.

ALLOUCHE Joël, b. 6 Nov 1960, Bougie, Algeria. Musician (drums, percussion). m. 24 Dec 1988, 1 son, 1 daughter. Career: Professional with pop bands, singers, 1975-; Jazz, 1980-; Played in Japan; Canada; New York; Africa; England; India; With musicians including: John Suriman; Kenny Whecks; Palle Danielsson; Enrico Rava; Urs Leimgruber; Don Friedman; Maurice Magnoni; Palle Danielsson; Marc Ducret; François Jeanneau; Michel Portal; Michel Marre; Doudou Gouirand; Don Cherry; Antonello Salis; Concerts; festivals with Coincidence, the group of the Llabador brothers; International concerts with trio of guitarist Philippe Caillat, concerts in Berlin; Copenhagen; Hamburg; Hungary; Member,

Reflexionen, 1983; Maurice Magnoni Quintet, 1987; Marc Ducret Trio, 1988; Pandémonium; François Jeanneau Quartet; Michel Portal's New Unit, 1990. Recordings: French Connection, Philippe Caillat, 1981; Fire Brigade, Philippe Caillat, 1982; with J P Llabador: Coincidence, 1984; Brussels, 1987; Forgotten Tales, Doudou Gouirand, with Don Cherry, 1985; with Urs Leimgruber: Reflexionen, 1986; Live, 1986; Remember To Remember, 1987; Andata Senza Ritorno, Maurice Magnoni, 1988; Superbe Déménagement, 1989; Gris, Marc Ducret, 1990; Lato Sensu, Philippe Gareil, 1991; Beatles Stories, Gérard Panseanel/Antonello Salis, 1992; Maloya Transit, François Jeanneau & Trio Tambours, 1992; Paolo Damiani, with Kenny Wheeler, 1992; Nguyên Lê, with Art Lande, Paul McCandless, 1992; Dominique Pifarely, with Ricardo del Fra, F Couturier, 1993; Birds Can Fly, Jean Pierre Llabador, 1995; Orchestra Improvista, Nino Rota-Fellini (Gouvirand, Pansanel), 1995; Tales From Vietnam, Nguyen Lê, 1996. Hobby: Sport. Address: 8 bis Rue du Professeur Lombard, 34000 Montpellier, France.

ALLPASS Soma, b. 9 July 1968, Copenhagen, Denmark. Musician (cello, piano, guitar); Singer; Songwriter; Arranger. Musical Education: Private lessons in Cello playing, 10 years; Royal Academy of Music, Copenhagen, 5 years; Lessons in piano and singing; Selftaught guitar. Career: Cellist and Backing Singer, Trains and Boats and Trains, rock band, 1989-94; Co-arranger, Roskilde Festival, 1992, 1993, 1994; Tours in Denmark, Norway, Sweden, Germany, England, Finland and New York; New Music Seminar, 1992. Compositions: Working on solo CD. Recordings: Trains and Boats and Trains, 1990; Hum, mini LP, 1990; Engulfed, LP, CD, 1991; I Like Cars, single, CD, 1992; Minimal Star, LP, CD, 1992. Honour: Rodovre Music Prize, 1996. Memberships: KODA; Danish Musicians Union. Hobbies: Yoga; Breathing; Favourite Music: Neil Young and Van Morrison. Current Management: Jim Holm, Klarboderne 3, 1001, KBH K, Denmark. Address: Brofogedvej 2, 2th, 2400 KBH NV, Denmark.

ALLWRIGHT (Sydney) Graeme, b. 7 Nov 1926, Lyall Bay, New Zealand. Singer; Author; Composer. m. Catherine Dasté, 8 June 1951, 3 sons, 1 daughter. Education: Short period university. Musical Education: Self-taught. Career: 30 years professional stage work, television, radio; Concerts include: Nyons Festival, Switzerland; Le Printemps de Bourges; Les Francofolies à la Rochelle, France; L'Olympia, Palais des Sports. Recordings: 19 albums. Publications: Songbooks. Membership: SACEM; ADAMI. Hobbies: Woodwork; Gardening. Current Management: Claire Bataille. Address: 13 Place D'Aligre, 75012 Paris, France.

ALMOND (Peter) Marc, b. 9 July 1959, Southport, Merseyside, England. Singer; Lyricist. Education: College, Southport; Fine Arts, Leeds Polytechnic. Career: Member, duo, Soft Cell, 1979-84; Also recorded as Marc and the Mambas; Solo artiste, 1984-; Major concerts include: Future 2 Science Fiction Music Festival, 1980; Terrence Higgins Trust benefit concert, 1990; Red Hot & Dance AIDS benefit concert, Barcelona, 1991; Royal Albert Hall, London; Philharmonic Hall, Liverpool, 1992. Recordings: Singles: with Soft Cell: Singles include: Tainted Love (Number 1, UK), 1981; Bedsitter; Say Hello Wave Goodbye; Torch; Soul Inside; Solo singles include: I Feel Love (medley), with Bronski Beat; Something's Gotten Hold Of My Heart; Jacky; My Hand Over My Heart; The Days Of Pearly Spencer; Adored And Explored; Albums: with Soft Cell: Some Bizarre Album, 1981; Non-Stop Erotic Cabaret, 1981; Non-Stop Ecstatic Dancing, 1982; The Art Of Falling Apart, 1983; As Marc and the Mambas: Untitled, 1982; Torment And Toreros, 1983; This Last Night In Sodom, 1984; As Marc Almond and the Willing Sinners: Vermin In Ermine, 1984; Solo

albums: Mother Fist And Her Five Daughters, 1987; Enchanted, 1990; Tenement Symphony, 1991; 12 Years Of Tears - Live At The Albert Hall, 1993; Fantastic Star, 1996. Honours: Best Selling Selling Of The Year, Tainted Love, 1981; BRIT award, Best British Single, Tainted Love, 1982; Billboard Magazine, New Wave Band Of The Year, 1982.

ALPERT Herb, b. 31 Mar 1935, Los Angeles, California, USA. Musician (trumpet); Songwriter; Arranger; Record Company Executive. m. Lani Hall, 1 son, 2 daughters. Education: University of Southern California. Career: 3 television specials; Leader, own group Tijuana Brass; Multiple world tours; Owner, Dore Records; Manager, Jan And Dean; Co-founder with Jerry Moss, A&M Records (formerly Carnival), 1962-89; Artists have included: The Carpenters; Captain And Tennille; Carole King; Cat Stevens; The Police; Squeeze; Joe Jackson; Bryan Adams. Compositions include: Wonderful World, Sam Cooke (co-writer with Lou Adler). Recordings: The Lonely Bull; A Taste Of Honey; Spanish Flea; Tijuana Taxi; Casino Royale; This Guy's In Love With You (Number 1, UK and US), 1968; Rise (Number 1, US), 1979; Albums include: The Lonely Bull, 1963; Tijuana Brass, 1963; Tijuana Brass Vol 2, 1964; South Of The Border, 1965; Whipped Cream And Other Delights, 1965; Going Places, 1966; SRO, 1967; Sounds Like Us, 1967; Herb Alpert's 9th, 1968; The Best Of The Brass, 1968; Warm, 1969; Rise, 1979; Keep Your Eyes On Me, 1979; Magic Man; My Abstract Heart; Midnight Sun. Honours: Numerous Grammy Awards. Hobbies: Painting; Sculpting. Current Management: c/o Kip Cohen, La Brea Tours, Inc., 1414 Sixth Street, Santa Monica, CA 90401, USA.

ALQUERES Gabriela, b. 1 Sept 1972, Sao Paulo, Brazil. Musician (guitar); Songwriter. m. Pete Whittard, 23 Nov 1992. Musical Education: The Guitar Institute. Career: Played with David McAlmont supporting Cyndi Lauper; Venues played include the Royal Albert Hall; Radio appearances include GLR. Membership: Musicians' Union. Hobby: Aerobics. Address: 7 Cambridge Gardens, Muswell Hill, London N10 2LL, England.

ALTERHAUG Bjorn, b. 3 June 1945, Mo i Rana, Norway. Assistant Professor; Jazz Musician (bass). m. Anne-Lise Alterhaug, 1 Jan 1968, 1 son, 1 daughter. Education: University. Musical Education: Self-taught. Career: Played as jazz soloist with: Ben Webster; Lucky Thompson; Chet Baker; Clark Terry; Numerous television and radio performances; Festival composer, Silver Jubilee of North Norway festival, 1989. Compositions: For big band and symphony-setting. Recordings: Solo albums: Moments, 1979; A Ballad, 1986; Constellations, 1991. Publications: Articles on Improvisation and Communication. Honours: Buddy Award, Norwegian Jazz Federation (highest honour). Memberships: Norwegian Jazz Federation; NOPA. Hobbies: Football; Walking in the mountains. Address: Oysteinsgt 2, 7030 Trondheim, Norway.

ALTMAN John Neville Rufus, b. 5 Dec 1949, London, England. Composer; Conductor; Arranger; Orchestrator; Musician (saxophone). m. Rita Pukacz, 30 Oct 1977, 3 sons, 1 daughter. Education: BA Hons, University of Sussex; Birkbeck College, London. Career: Recorded as keyboard player with Eric Clapton; Sting; Phil Collins; Saxophonist with Muddy Waters; Little Richard; Ben E King; Jimmy Page; John Lennon; Dr John; Slim Gaillard; Musical Director for Van Morrison, late 1970s; Regular conductor, Royal Philharmonic Orchestra. Compositions: Films include: Funny Bones; Bhaji On The Beach; Hear My Song; Bad Behaviour; Devlin; Camilla; Television includes: Peak Practice; Miss Marple; Shadowlands; First And Last; Comic Relief, 1995; By The Sword Divided; Composer, arranger, producer of over 3000 commercials including:

British Airways; AT&T; Pan Am; General Motors; Stella Artois; Rover; Intercity; British Telecom; Films as arranger, orchestrator, conductor include: Monty Python's Life Of Brian; Erik The Viking; Just A Gigolo; Foreign Bodies; The Sheltering Sky; Leon (aka The Professional); Golden Eye. Recordings: Arranger, conductor, producer: Singles: Downtown Train, Rod Stewart; Kissing A Fool; The Ole Devil Called Love, Alison Moyet; Always Look On The Bright Side, Monty Python; Walking In The Air, Aled Jones; Love Is On Our Side, Tom Jones; Albums: Streetfighting Years, Simple Minds; Hey Manhattan, Prefab Sprout; Very Special Season, Diana Ross; It's So Quiet, vocals by Björk; Closing credits, song for film: Innocent Lies, sung by Patricia Kaas. Honours: Anthony Asquith, 1992; BAFTA Nomination; Tric, 1995. Memberships: PRS; ASCAP; BASCA; ASMAC. Hobby: Cricket. Current Management: SDM. Address: 740 N La Brea, Hollywood, CA 90038, USA.

ALU Steve, b. 13 July 1957, Beckenham, Kent, England. Front of House Sound Engineer; Tour Manager; Studio Sound Engineer. Career: 15 years practical experience engineering, production and tour management; Credits: One The Juggler; Air Head; Bolshoi; Eddie And The Hotrods; N-Joi; Senser; OMD; Jason Rebello; Bush Telegraph; Phil Manzanera; Loise Goffin; Royal Festival Ballet; Limelight/Hippodrome clubs; Concorde Agency; Elevator Man. Hobbies: Computers; Videos. Address: Flat F, 78 Deptford High Street, Deptford, London SE8 4RT, England.

AMA Shola, b. Willesden, London, England. Vocalist. Career: Solo recording artiste, 1997-. Recordings include: Debut album: Much Love, 1997; Hit singles: You Might Need Somebody, 1997; You're The One That I Love, 1997; Who's Loving My Baby, 1997; Much Love, 1998. Honours include: Nominated for 3 MOBO Awards, won - Best R'n'B Artist and Best Newcomer, 1997; Nominated, 2 Brit Awards, won - Best Female, 1998. Best Female, 1998. Current Management: 1 2 One Management, 20 Damien Street, London E1 2HX, England. Address: c/o WEA Records, The Warner Building, 28 Kensington Church Street, London W8 4EP, England.

AMADA Maia, b. Scarsdale, New York, USA. Vocalist; Songwriter. m. 6 Jan, 1 daughter. Education; Diploma, Theater Arts Major, Marymount Manhattan College. Musical Education: Jazz and Pop: Arranger, composer Herb Buchanan Eidemiller, 7 years; Classical: Hoff Barthelson School of Music, 3 years. Career: Numerous radio interviews, USA and Japan; Extensive festival touring, USA; Tours as actress, singer: Jesus Christ Superstar; The Me Nobody Knows; Numerous commercials radio and television, English, Spanish. Recordings: Maia Amada Album; Faith Remains; Presently making Spanish record. Honours: Listener's Choice Award, 1995; Most Requested Artist, New York Screen Actors; Largest Christian Radio Station, 970 WWDJ; International Gospel Trailblazers Award, 1995; Most Favorite Mom, Life Time Achievement Award, from My Family Daily. Memberships: Actors Equity Association; AFTRA; ASCAP; Screen Actors Guild. Hobbies: Gardening; Floral arranging; Walking; Playing Kadema; Baking anything. Current Management: Janice Roeg, Joe Boyland. Address: Legend Artist's Management, 120 West 44 Street, Ste 404, New York City, NY 10036, USA.

AMBROSE (Edmund) David, b. 11 Dec 1945, Highgate, London, England. Record Company Executive; Musician (bass). m. Angela, 3 Sept 1975, 2 sons, 1 daughter. Education: Brymshaw College of Art; London College of Printing. Career: Musician with: Shotgun Express; Julie Driscoll; Brian Auger and Trinity; Arthur Brown; Cat Stevens; Numerous television and radio appearances; Concerts include: Royal Albert Hall and Fairfield Hall; Director of Planet 3

Records; Publishing for: Sex Pistols; Vapours; Dexy's Midnight Runners; Duran Duran; Pet Shop Boys; Transvision Vamp; Love City Groove. Recordings: with Shotgun Express: Shotgun Express, 1969; with Brian Auger and The Trinity: Open, 1967; Definitely What, 1968; Steetnoise, 1968; Befour, 1970; Genesis, 1975. Honours: Brightest Hope, Best Record with Brian Auger and The Trinity. Memberships: Chelsea Arts Club; Rye Art Gallery. Hobbies: Sailing; Painting; Songwriting; Tennis. Address: 71 Finlay Street, Fulham, London SW6 6HF, England.

AMENT Jeff. Rock Musician (bass). Career: Musician in Seattle SubPop scene, 1980s; Member, Green River, 1987-89; Mother Love Bone, 1989; Pearl Jam, 1990-; Concerts with Pearl Jam: Support to Alice In Chains, 1991; Lollapalooza Festival 92 tour, 1992; Drop In The Park concert, Seattle, 1992; European tour, 1992; Bridge School Benefit, with Neil Young, Elton John, Sammy Hagar, James Taylor, 1992; Support to Keith Richards & The Expensive Winos, New York, 1992; Concert appearances with Neil Young; Group appearance in film Singles, 1992; Also member, Temple Of The Dog project, 1991. Recordings: Albums: with Green River: Rehab Doll (EP), 1988; with Mother Love Bone: Shine (EP), 1989; Apple, 1990; with Pearl Jam: Ten (Number 2, US), 1991; Vs. (Number 1, US), 1993; Vitalogy, 1994; with Temple Of The Dog: Temple Of The Dog, 1991; Singles: with Pearl Jam: Alive, 1992; Even Flow, 1992; Jeremy, 1992. Honours: American Music Award: Favourite New Artist, 1993; Rolling Stone Readers' Awards, Best New American Band, Best Video, 1993; 4 MTV Awards, 1993; Highest 1-week album sales total in history, Vs., 1993. Current Management: Curtis Management, 417 Denny Way, Ste 200, Seattle, WA 98109, USA.

AMIGO Vicente, b. 25 March 1967, Guadalcanal, Sevilla, Spain. Career: Paris Guitar Festival; International Festival of Cordoba; First on David Bowie Spanish Tour, Ballet Nacional De Espana Tour, USA; L'Ete De Nimes, France; Legends of Guitar Festival, Sevilla; International Guitar Festival, La Habana; Mestres Da Guitarra, Paco De Lucia, John McLaughlin. Compositions: De Mi Corazón Al Aire, 1991; Poeta, Concierto Flamenco Para Un Marinero En Tierra, orchestra; Vivencias Imaginadas, 1995. Honours: Icaro, 1991; Ateneo de Cordoba, 1992; Best Flamenco Guitarist (Guitar Player), 1993. Current Management: Intercambio de Cultura Y Arte (ICARI). Address: Goya, 99 Esc A - 4 Dcha, 28009 Madrid, Spain.

AMIRAHMADI Fred, b. 17 May 1964, Tehran, Iran. Producer. Career: Production work for Columbia Records, Epic Records (UK), France; Signed as artist to Sony Music (Epic), France; EMI Records (UK); Mushroom (Liberation Records), Australia; Appearances at Epic Records Show, with Desire (supporting), July 1994; French TV, radio. Recordings: Producer: A Fair Affair (top 20 hit, France), 1994; Artist: Album: Kind Of Blew; Producer, Composer, Arranger, Artist: Album: Blown. Membership: Musicians Union. Hobbies: Films; Football; Chess. Current Management: Impatient Management. Address: 63 Kensington Mansions, Trebovir Road, London SW5 9ID, England.

AMOS Tori, b. North Carolina, USA. Singer; Songwriter; Musician (piano). Education: Scholarship, Peabody Institute, Baltimore, USA. Musical Education: Church choir, piano from age 4. Career: Singer, piano bars as teenager; Solo recording artiste, 1987-; UK tour, 1991. Recordings: Albums: Y Kant Tori Read, 1988; Me & My Gun (EP), 1991; Little Earthquakes, 1991; Boys For Pele, 1995; Singles include: Cornflake Girl; Caught A Lite Sneeze; Contributor, Tower Of Strength (Leonard Cohen tribute), 1995. Honours include: Q Award, Best New Act, 1992. Current Management: Spivak Entertainment, 11845 W

Olympic Blvd, Suite 1125, Los Angeles, CA 90064, USA.

AMOUROUX Jean-Paul, b. 17 Jan 1948, Aurillac, France. Boogie Woogie Musician (piano). Musical Education: Classical music studies. Career: Paris club work, 1973-; Numerous European Festivals, 1974-; 2 year radio series, history of boogie woogie. Compositions: Over 150 works. Recordings: 25 boogie records, of which one in duo with Milt Buckner, 1976; two on 2 pianos with Willie Mabon, 1979; three on 2 pianos with Memphis Slim, 1981, 1984, 1985; one on 2 pianos with Sammy Price, 1986; one on 3 pianos with Sammy Price and Jay McShann, 1989. Publications: Soul Bag. Honours: Grand Prix, Hot Club of France, 1989. Hobbies: Classical art; American steam trains. Current Management: Timing Show. Address: Timing Show, 62 Allée Sainte-Anne, 93320 Pavillons-sous-Bois, France.

AMSTELL Billy, b. 20 Aug 1911, London, England. Musician (saxophone, clarinet); Composer; Author. m. Tessa, 19 June 1938. Musical Education: 2 Certificates for Piano, Royal College of Music, aged 10. Career: 11 years with Ambrose Orchestra; 2 years with Geraldo Orchestra, radio and records; 8 years with Stanley Black on BBC Radio shows: Much Binding In The Marsh; The Goon Show; Ray's A Laugh; Life With The Lyons; With wife, presented to HRH Princess Anne; Played twice at Buckingham Palace; Sergeant i/c Station Band, RAF Wittering, Lincs. Compositions: At least 30 compositions (Peter Maurice, Music Coy, Keith Prowse, Bosworth). Recordings: Over 1000 with: Ambrose; Geraldo; Stanley Black; Geoff Love; Video: Don't Fuss, Mr Ambrose. Publications: Memoirs: Don't Fuss, Mr Ambrose. Honours: Guild of Freeman of the City Of London; Hon. Citizen of New Orleans (USA). Memberships: Musicians' Union (Hon); PRS; Academy of Songwriters and Authors; Hon. Member of the Clarinet and Saxophone Society of Great Britain; Life Member, Bomber Command Association; Associate Hon. Member, Pathfinders Association. Hobby: Writing for magazines. Address: Billy Amstell, 40 Ebrington Road, Kenton, Harrow, Middlesex HA3 0LT, England.

AMYOT Robert, b. 25 July 1953, Montreal, Canada. French Bagpipes. 2 daughters. Education: Traditional Singing French State Diploma. Career: Played with Jean Blanchard and Evelyne Girardon in Beau-Temps-Sur-La-Province; La Grande Bande De Cornemuse; Le Quintette De Cornemuse; Major folk festivals around the world, St-Chartier, etc; Now playing with Baron Samedi. Compositions: Le Brandevin; Le Loriot De Baltimore; Le Harfang des Neiges; Marie Miville; L'Anniversaire. Recordings: Sur La Vignolon; Trappeur Courtois; Le Grand Festin; La Grande Bande De Cornemuse; Le Quintette De Cornemuse. Publications: Cornemuse; Souffles Infinis Souffles Continus, collection Moda, article, 1991. Honours: First Prize, Cornemuse in Anost, France, 1987; President, St-Chartier Jury, 1990-96. Membership: APMT, France. Hobbies: French Baroque Culture; French Food and Wines. Current Management: Cie du Beau Temps, 20 Cours Suchet, 69002 Lyon, France. Address: Le Bourgeal Dessous, 74130 Brizon, France.

ANCHEV Emil. Vocalist. Founder member, lead vocalist, Concurant, 1986; Numerous concerts, television and radio programmes, Bulgaria. Recordings: Rock For Peace, 1988; Rock Festival In Mitchurin, 1989; The Black Sheep (rock collection), 1992; Something Wet (best-selling album, Bulgaria), 1994; The Best Of Bulgarian Rock, 1995. Honours: First prizes: Top Rock Band, Youth Festival Vidin, 1989; Rock Ring, Sofia, 1990; Top Rock Composition: The Cavalry, 1991; Top Rock Singer, Bulgaria, 1994; Group Of The Year, The Darik Radio Countdown, 1994. Address: 40 St Stambolov Blvd, 1202 Sofia, Bulgaria.

ANDERSEN Arild, b. 27 Oct 1945, Oslo, Norway. Jazz Musician (bass); Bandleader; Composer. Musical Education: Studied with Karel Netolicka and George Russell. Career: Touring musician with George Russell, Jan Garbarek, Karin Krog, Edward Vesala, 1966-73; Also worked with Don Cherry; Stan Getz; Sam Rivers; Paul Bley; Leader, own quartet, 1974; Member, Norwegian quintet Masquelero, 1983-. Compositions include: Sagn (series of works based on traditional folk songs), premiered at Vossajazz Festival, 1990. Recordings: Albums: Clouds In My Head, 1975; Shimri, 1976; Green Shading Into Blue, 1978; Lifelines, 1980; A Molde Concert, 1981; Sagn, 1990; Masquelero, 1983; Bande A Part, 1985; If You Look Far Enough (with Nana Vasconcelos, Ralph Towner), 1993.

ANDERSEN Torfinn Nergaard, b. Norway. Music Co-Executive. Career: Director, Groovy Management; Owner, Record label, Rec 90 (Norway); Manager for Butterfly Garden (Norway). Membership: FONO. Address: Groovy Management, PO Box 1291, N-5001 Bergen, Norway.

ANDERSON Billy (William John), b. 5 Mar 1946, Colinsburgh, Fife, Scotland. Musician (piano accordion); Radio Presenter; Tutor. m. Elizabeth W Hannah, 12 Aug 1966, 3 sons, 1 daughter. Education: Piano-accordion as a boy. Career: Composer; Arranger; Producer; Broadcast with BBC Radio, television, 1969-; Tours: USA; Canada; United Arab Emirates; Oman; Brunei; North Malaysia; Germany; Netherlands; Italy; Australia. Recordings: 7 with Albany (own group), mainly American appearances. Publications: 5 compositions published by the St Andrews Branch, RSCDS. Memberships: Musicians Union; PRS. Hobbies: Walking; MIDI computing. Current Management: Self-managed. Address: 5 Shoolbraids, St Andrews, Fife KY16 8ER, Scotland.

ANDERSON Brett, b. 26 Sept 1967. Singer; Songwriter. Career: Founder member, groups: Geoff, 1985; Suave & Elegant, 1989; Suede, 1989-; Television appearances include: Top Of The Pops, BBC1; BRIT Awards, Alexandra Palace, London, 1993; The Beat, ITV; Later With Jools Holland, BBC2; The Tonight Show, NBC TV; Concerts include: Phoenix Festival; Glastonbury Festival; Tours, Europe, America and Japan; Recordings: Albums: Suede (Number 1, UK), 1993; Dog Man Star, 1994; Singles include: The Drowners; Metal Mickey; Animal Nitrate; Stay Together; Contributor, Shipbuilding, to War Child charity album. Honours include: Mercury Music Prize, 1993; Q Award, Best New Act, 1993. Current Management: Interceptor Enterprises, The Greenhouse, 34-38 Provost St, London N1 7NG, England.

ANDERSON Chris(topher William), b. 22 Sept 1956, Los Angeles, California, USA. Musician (guitar); Singer; Songwriter. m. Sharon Ann Cooper, 11 May 1991, 1 son, 1 daughter. Musical Education: Self-taught. Career: Leader, own Chris Anderson Band; Tours with artists including: Allman Brothers; Stevie Ray Vaughn; Double Trouble; Lynyrd Skynyrd; Bad Company; Government Mule; Outlaws; Marshall Tucker; Charlie Daniels; Wet Willie; Concerts include: Radio City Music Hall; TV: Throw, Fox TV; Commercials: Bush Radio; Budweiser; Videos: Srascle, Outlaws. Recordings: Old Friend, Chris Anderson Band; Trouble On The Tracks, Double Trouble; Right On Time, Grinder Switch; Floyd Miles. Honour: Inducted into Rock And Roll Hall Of Fame. Memberships: AFTRA; AFofM. Hobbies: Motorcycles; Mountain biking. Current Management: Doc Field, Creative Action Music Group. Address: 865 Bellevue Road, Ste E-12; Nashville, TN 37221, USA.

ANDERSON Dave, b. 21 Nov 1949, Essex, England. Musician (bass); Studio Owner; Record

Company Owner; Record Producer and Engineer. 1 son, 2 daughters. Career: Worked with Nick Lowe; Amon Düül II; Hawkwind; Bob Calvert; Groundhogs; Library Music for Chappell Music Publishers. Recordings: Albums with the above artists. Membership: PRS; MCPS; PPL. Hobbies: Flying. Current Management: Self-managed. Address: Foel Studio, Llanfair Caeeinion, Powys SY21 0DS, Wales .

ANDERSON Emma Victoria Jane, b. 10 June 1967, Wimbledon, London, England. Musician (guitar); Songwriter. Education: BA (Hons) Humanities, Ealing College of Higher Education, 1986-90. Career: Bass player, The Rover Girls, 1986-88; Lead guitarist, songwriter, Lush, 1988-; Signed to 4AD Records; Worldwide tours include rock festival tour Lollapalooza, 1992. Recordings: (own compositions) with Lush: Scar (mini-album), 1989; Mad Love (EP), 1990; Single: Sweetness And Light, 1990; Albums: Gala, 1990; Spooky, 1992; Split, 1994. Memberships: PRS; Musicians' Union; PPL. Hobbies: Films; Wine tasting; Sleeping. Current Management: Peter Felstead, CEC Managament; Agent: Mick Griffiths, Asgard. Address: CEC Management, 6 Warren Mews, London W1P 5DJ, England.

ANDERSON Ian, b. 10 Aug 1947, Dunfermline, Scotland. Musician (flute); Vocalist; Record Producer; Engineer. m. Shona Learoyd, 1976, 1 son, 1 daughter. Education: Blackpool College of Art. Career: Founder member, Jethro Tull, 1968-; 40 million records sold in 27 years; Chairman, Ian Anderson Group Cos Ltd, salmon producers, fish processors. Recordings: Albums: This Was, 1968; Stand Up, 1969; Benefit, 1970; Aqualung, 1971; Thick As A Brick, 1972; Living In The Past, 1972; A Passion Play, 1973; Warchild, 1974; The Minstrel In The Gallery, 1975; Too Old To Rock And Roll, Too Young To Die!, 1976; M.U.- The Best Of Jethro Tull, 1976; Repeat: The Best Of Jethro Tull, Volume II, 1977; Songs From The Wood, 1977; Heavy Horses, 1978; Live - Bursting Out, 1978; Stormwatch, 1979; A, 1980; The Broadsword And The Beast, 1982; Under Wraps, 1984; Original Masters, 1985; The Crest Of A Knave, 1987; Twenty Years Of Jethro Tull, 1988; Rock Island, 1989; Catfish Rising, 1991; A Little Light Music, 1992; Roots To Branches, 1995; Solo: Divinities - Twelve Dances With God (for flute and orchestra), 1995. Honours: 47 Gold and 17 Platinum records worldwide, including Thick As A Brick, Living In The Past, Aqualung and M.U.; Gold record, Grammy Award, Best Hard Rock Performance, Crest Of A Knave, 1988. Address: Salamander and Son Music Ltd, 23 Longman Drive, Inverness IV1 1SU, Scotland.

ANDERSON Ian, b. 26 July 1947, Weston-Super-Mare, England. Writer; Broadcaster; Musician (guitar, slide guitar). m. Hanitra Rasoanaivo, 2 May 1990, 1 step-daughter. Musical Education: Self-taught. Career: Solo musician, 1967-72; Member of duo Hot Vultures, 1972-79; English Country Blues Band, 1979-83; Tiger Moth, 1983-89; Editor of Folk Roots Magazine, 1979-; Radio presenter, BBC and ILR, 1984-. Recordings: 5 solo albums include: Stereo Death Breakdown, 1969; 3 albums with Hot Vultures include: Up The Line, 1979; 2 albums with English Country Blues Band, compiled as Unruly, 1993; 2 albums with Tiger Moth, compiled as Mothballs, 1995. Publications: Folk Roots Magazine. Hobbies: Music; Photography. Current Management: Folk Music Services. Address: c/o Folk Music Services, PO Box 337, London N4 1TW, England.

ANDERSON James Noel, b. 23 Dec 1951, Butler, Pennsylvania, USA. Recording Engineer; Producer; Radio Consultant. m. Phoebe Ferguson, 10 Oct 1982, 2 sons. Musical Education: BS, Music Education, Duquesne University, 1973; Postgraduate, 1974; Postgraduate, Eastman School Of Music, 1976; Postgraduate, Audio Engineering, Berlin, 1978. Career: Audio engineer, radio stations, Pittsburgh, Washington, 1973-80; President, James Anderson Audio (radio consultant), New York, 1980; Radio programmes: Taylor Made Piano, with Billy Taylor, 1981; Co-producer, Segovia! (radio documentary), 1983 Television programme: Segovia At The White House, with Andres Segovia, 1980. Recordings: Albums as recording engineer: Live At Fat Tuesdays, Pepper Adams, 1983; Sweet And Lovely, James Moody, 1989; Uptown/Downtown, McCoy Tyner, 1989. Honours include: Emmy Nomination, Segovia At The White House, 1981; Peabody Award, Taylor-Made Piano, 1982; 3 Grammy Award Nominations; EBU Prix Futura Award, 1986. Memberships: Audio Engineering Society; NARAS; Audio Independents in Radio.

ANDERSON Jen, b. 20 June 1959, Adelaide, South Australia. Composer; Performer (Violin). Education: 8th Grade AMEB on Violin. Career: Violinist, Black Sorrows, 1989-92; Composed and performed live with string quartet music score to 1929 silent film, Pandoras Box, 1992; Violinst with Weddings Parties Anything, 1993-97; Composer, Simone de Beauvoir's Babies, TV mini series, 1996. Compositions: Pandoras Box; The Sentimental Bloke. Recordings: Pandoras Box; Seek. Hobbies: Scuba Diving; Short Story; Writing; Films. Address: 13 Victoria Avenue, Albert Park, 3206, Australia.

ANDERSON Jon, b. 25 Oct 1944, Accrington, Lancashire, England. Singer. Career: Member, The Warriors, late 1960s; Co-founder, UK progressive rock group Yes, 1968-80; 1991-; Duo with Vangelis as Jon & Vangelis, 1980-; Concerts include: Support to Cream, Royal Albert Hall, 1968; Support to Janis Joplin, Royal Albert Hall, 1969; Montreux TV Festival, 1969; Support to The Nice, Royal Festival Hall, 1970; Tours, UK and USA, 1970-; Reading Festival, 1975; Evening Of Yes Music, US tour, 1989; Yesshows '91 - Round The World In 80 Dates Tour, 1991. Recordings: Albums: with Yes: Yes, 1969; Time And A Word, 1970; Fragile, 1971; Close To The Edge, 1972; Yessongs, 1973; Tales From The Topographic Oceans, 1973; Relayer, 1974; Yesterdays, 1975; Going For The One, 1977; Tormato, 1978; 90125, 1983; 9012 Live - The Solos, 1986; Union, 1991; Yesstory, 1991; Symphonic Music Of Yes, 1993; History Of The Future, 1993; Open Your Eyes, 1998; with Jon & Vangelis: Short Stories, 1980; Jon & Vangelis, 1980; Private Collection, 1983; The Best Of Jon & Vangelis, 1984; Solo albums: Olias Of Sunbillow, 1976; Song Of Seven, 1980; Animation, 1982; Three Ships, 1985; Change We Must, 1994; The More You Know, 1998; with Anderson Bruford Wakeman Howe: Anderson Bruford Wakeman Howe, 1989; Contributor, Shine, Mike Oldfield; Legend, Tangerine Dream; Wintertime Is On, Whole World Band (proceeds to Down's Syndrome Association, Sickle Cell Society; Singles: with Yes include: Roundabout, 1972; Wondrous Stories, 1977; Owner Of A Lonely Heart (Number 1, US), 1983; Leave It, 1984; with Vangelis: I Hear You Now, 1980; I'll Find My Way Home, 1982; Whatever You Believe, with Steve Harley, Mike Batt (charity single), 1988. Honours: Gold Ticket, Madison Square Garden, 1978; Grammy Award, Best Rock Instrumental Performance, Cinema, 1985. Current Management: Big Bear Management, 9 Hillgate Street, London W8 7SP, England.

ANDERSON Laurie P, b. 5 June 1947, Illinois, USA. Performance Artist; Musician (keyboards, violin). Education: MFA, Columbia University; BA, Barnard College. Career: Major performances: Stories From The Nerve Bible; Voices From The Beyond; Empty Places; Talk Normal; Natural History; United States; Films, videos: Carmen; Personal Service Announcements; Beautiful Red Dress; Talk Normal; Alive From Off Center; What You Mean We?; Language Is A Virus; Home Of The Brave; This Is The Picture; Sharkey's Day; O Superman; Dear Reader; Puppet Motel (CD-Rom), 1995. Recordings include: O Superman, 1981; Big Science, 1982; Mister Heartbreak, 1984; United States Live, 1985; Home Of The Brave, 1986; Strange Angels, 1989; Bright Red, 1994; The Ugly One With The Jewels And Other Stories, 1995; Film scores: Swimming To Cambodia; Monster In A Box. Publications: Stories From The Nerve Bible, 1994; Empty Places; Postcard Book; United States; Words In Reverse. Honours: Distinguished Alumna Award, Columbia School Of The Arts; Honorary Doctorates, Art Institute of Chicago, Philadelphia College Of the Arts. Current Management: Original Artists, 853 Broadway, Suite 1901, New York, NY 10003, USA.

ANDERSON Lynn Rene, b. 26 Sept 1947, Grand Forks, North Dakota, USA. Country Singer. m. (1) Glenn Sutton, 1968, divorced; (2) Harold Stream III, divorced. Career: Former success as horse rider; Singer, recording artist, 1966-; Television appearances include: Lynn Anderson specials; Resident guest, Lawrence Welk Show, 1967-70; Grand Ole Opry; Ed Sullivan Show. Recordings: US Country Number 1 hit singles: Rose Garden; You're My Man; How Can I Unlove You?; Keep Me In Mind; What A Man My Man Is; Other hits include: If I Kiss You (Will You Go Away); That's A No No; Top Of The World; Rocky Top; Encore; Duets include: with Gary Morris: You're Welcome To Tonight; with Ed Bruce: Fool For Each Other; with Billy Joe Royal: Under The Boardwalk; Numerous albums include: Ride Ride Ride, 1967; With Love From Lynn, 1969; No Love At All, 1970; Cry, 1972; Singing My Song, 1973; Smile For Me, 1974; All The King's Horses, 1976; From The Inside, 1978; Lynn Anderson Is Back, 1983; What She Does Best, 1988; Greatest Hits, 1992; Cowboy's Sweetheart, 1993. Honours: Gold discs; Over 700 horse riding trophies. Current Management: Anders Productions. Address: 4925 Tyne Valley Blvd, Nashville, TN 37220, USA.

ANDERSON Moira, b. 5 June 1940, Kirkintilloch, Scotland. Vocalist. Career: Singer, traditional Scottish folk music; Also interpretations of popular standards and light operatic works; Regular UK television appearances, especially religious programmes. Recordings: Numerous albums include: Moira Anderson's Scotland, 1970; This Is Moira Anderson, 1971; The Auld Scotch Songs, 1975; Someone Wonderful, 1978; Golden Memories, 1981; The Love Of God, 1986; A Land For All Seasons, 1988; 20 Scottish Favourites, 1990. Honours: OBE, Services to music industry. Address: c/o International Artistes, Albert House, Albert Street, Chadderton, Greater Manchester OL9 7TR, England.

ANDERSON Stig (Stikkan), b. 25 Jan 1931, Mariestad, Sweden. Music Publisher; Artist Manager; Lyricist. m. Gudrun, 13 Aug 1955, 2 sons, 1 daughter. Education: Graduate, Teacher's High School, Stockholm, 1957. Career: First song published, 1950; Owner, Sweden Music, largest Swedish publishing company in 1960s; Founder, Polar Records; Publisher, manager, lyricist for ABBA; Donated MSEK 42 to Royal Swedish Academy of Music, to establish Stig Anderson Music Prize Fund - The Polar Music Prize, 1 million SEK, 1989. Compositions: Lyrics: Waterloo; Mama Mia; Fernando; Knowing Me, Knowing You. Honours: Honorary Member, Royal Swedish Academy of Music; Trendsetter Award, Billboard Magazine. Memberships: Member of Board, Polygram Records, Sweden. Address: Ulrikagatan 7, S-115 23 Stockholm, Sweden.

ANDERSON Terry Randall, b. 25 Dec 1956, Louisberg, North Carolina, USA. Songwriter; Musician (drums, guitar). m. Grace Brummett, 29 Apr 1989, 1 son. Education: 2 years college, Sandhills Community College, Southern Pines, North Carolina, USA. Career: 2 European tours; Drums with: Don Dixon; Marti Jones. Compositions: Battleship Chains, recorded by Georgia Satellites; I Love You Period; Co-wrote 4 songs on Dan Baird's solo record. Recordings:

Solo record on ESD (Minn, Minn). Membership: ASCAP. Hobbies: Golf; Following UNC (Carolina) basketball; Painting. Current Management: Harry Simmons, Simmons Management. Address: 5214 Western Boulevard, Raleigh, NC 27606, USA.

ANDERSSON G B Benny, b. 16 Nov 1946, Stockholm, Sweden. Composer. m. Mona Nörklit, Dec 1981, 2 sons, 1 daughter. Career: Keyboard player, Songwriter, Abba; Composer: musical, Chess, with Tim Rice, Björn Ulvaeus; Kristina Från Duvemåla, musical based on Vilhelm Moberg's epic novels, Utvandrarna. Recordings: Albums: Waterloo, 1974; Abba, 1976; 8 number 1 in album charts: Greatest Hits, 1976; Arrival, 1976; The Album, 1978; Voulez-Vous, 1979; Greatest Hits Vol 2, 1979; Super Trouper, 1980; The Visitors, 1981 The Singles -The First Ten Years, 1982; also: Thank You For The Music, 1983; Absolute Abba, 1988; Abba Gold, More Abba Gold, 1994. Hobbies: Thoroughbred breeding and racing. Address: Södra Brobänken 41A, 111 49 Stockholm, Sweden.

ANDERSSON Mats Lennart, b. 2 January 1964, Stockholm, Sweden. Drums. Education: Member, bob hund, 1991; More than 250 gigs in Scandinavia; Played at famous Roskilde, Lollipop, Ruisrock, Quartfestivalen and Hultsfred. Compositions: I Stället för Musik: Förvirring, 1996; Düsseldorf, 1996. Recordings: bob hund - bob hund, 1993; bob hund - Edvin Medvind, 7", 1994; Bob Hund - I Stället för Musik: Förvirring, 1996. Publication: Bob Hund - Omslag: Martin Kann, 1996. Honours: Grammy, best live act, 1994; Grammy, best lyrics, 1996. Memberships: STIM; SAMI. Hobbies: Music; Books; Food; Drinking. Address: Box 53045, 400 14, Göteborg, Sweden.

ANDRE Peter, b. 1973, England. Singer. Career: Moved to Australia, aged 10; Solo artiste, 1990-; Australian tours as support act to Madonna and Bobby Brown. Recordings: Albums: Natural, 1996; Time, 1997; Hit Singles: Mysterious Girl; Flava (Number 1, UK); I Feel You (Number 1, UK); Lonely; All About Us; All Night All Right; Collaborations with Coolio, Montell Jordan, Brian McKnight and the Fugees. Honours include: Winner, talent contest to win recording contract, Australia, 1990; Best Selling Single in Australia, 1993; Highest Australian Chart Performer, Most Popular Australian Dance Act, Most Popular Australian Act, Coca Cola Awards, Australia, 1993; Best Australian Pop Dance release, Aria Awards, 1993; Best Selling Independent Single, Mysterious Girl, 1996; Best Selling Independent Album, Natural, 1996; Best International Male Singer, National TV2 Plus, Denmark, 1996; Best Male Singer, TV Hits Magazine, 1996; Best MMale Singer, Best Album Cover, Smash Hits Poll Winners Party, 1996; Best Dude Singer, Capital Slammers, 1996; Best Singer, Best Single, CITV Awards, 1996; Best Male in the Whole World, Otto Award Bravo 1997, Germany; Best Newcomer, Popcorn Awards, Greece, 1997; Best International Artist, Irma's Ireland, 1997; World's Bestselling Australian Artist of the Year, 1996. Address: c/o Sue Harris, Blitz, Edwarebury Farm, Edwarebury Lane, Edgware, Middlesex HA8 8QX, England.

ANDRE Serge Daniel Georges, b. 31 Oct 1956, Versailles, France. Composer; Arranger. m. Erika d'Ambre, 1 son, 4 daughters. Musical Education: Musical Academy; Personal teachers. Career: Band leader, with Christian Delagrange; Numerous appearances on National Radio Networks; arranger for (internationally known singer) Ottawan. Compositions: 200 songs include: Amborah (Ontario); L'Univers de Nerval. Recordings: Albums include: New Age, 1992; Croisés de la Chanson Française; Acticity. Honours: Diploma in arranging, co-sigmataire. Memberships: SACEM. Hobby: Ecology. Current Management: 2MS Productions. Address: 14 Rue de la Mairie, 11170 Moussoulens, France.

ANDREASSEN Preben, b. 23 August 1944, Aalborg, Denmark. Organist; Choir Director. m. 2 sons. Education: Royal Danish Music Academic, Copenhagen; Diploma Degree, Church Organ and Choir Direction, 1974. Career: Concert in Germany, Sweden, Norway, Holland, Greece, USA Los Angeles and Denmark; Television: Danich Channe 1, Before Sunday, 1992, 1993, 1998; Youth Services, 1991, 1995; Christmas Services, 1993; Gospel Services, 1998. Compositions: Choir works at Publisher Edition EGTVED: Before Sunday, 1992; Christmas Songs, 1994; New Danish Hymnbook, 1994; Hymns in different collection. Recordings: Christmas Music, 1982; Before Sunday, MC, VCR; CD Life is Living, 1992; Gospel Music, 1997, 1998. Publications: Brondbyvester Church Organ History, 1987; Christmas Songs, edition EGTVED, 1994. Honour: Intl Choir Fest, Veldhoven, Holland, First Prize, 1989. Memberships: Danich Organist Society; Danich Director Society. Hobby: Wood Carving. Address: Brondbyvester Church as Organist, Pianist, Choir Director and Composer, started in 1975. Address: Kirkebjerg Alle 178, DK-2605, Brondby, Denmark.

ANDREWS Bob "Derwood", b. 17 June 1959, Fulham, London, England. Musician (guitar); Songwriter. Career: Guitarist, punk band Generation X, 1976-79; Formed Empire, early 80s; Formed Westworld, 1986; Tours with Generation X; Westworld; Appeared on Top Of The Pops, and reached Number 11, UK charts, with both bands; Formed Moondogg, 1994; Album due 1995. Recordings: Albums: with Generation X: Generation X; Valley Of The Dolls; Unreleased third album; with Westworld: Where The Action Is; Beatbox Rock'N'Roll; Movers And Shakers; with Empire: Expensive Sound; with Jimmy Pursey: Imagination Camouflage. Membership: PRS. Hobbies: Motorcycles; Speedway; Native American life. Current Management: Moondogg. Address: PO Box 163, Cave Creek, AZ 85331, USA.

ANDREWS Harvey. Singer; Songwriter. Career: Performer, songwriter for over 30 years; Appearances include: 36 major festivals, UK, North America, including 5 Cambridge festivals; Tours throughout Europe; Canada; US; Belize; Played venues throughout UK; Television includes: Old Grey Whistle Test; Rhythm On Two, BBC; Pebble Mill At One; 2 TV specials: The Camera And The Song; The Same Old Smile; 2 specials, Holland and Ireland; Radio includes: John Peel; Stuart Hall; Alan Freeman; Host, Folk On Two, BBC; Music presenter, BBC Radio Stoke. Compositions: Songs covered by artists including: Christy Moore; Mary Hopkin; Max Boyce; Ian MacIntosh; Lyrics used in GCSE English Language examination. Recordings include: Faces And Places; Writer Of Songs; Friends Of Mine; Margarita; Someday; Fantasies From A Corner Seat; Brand New Day; Old Mother Earth; PG; 25 Years On The Road; Spring Again; Snaps (The Family Album). Current Management: c/o Jim McPhee, Acorn Entertainments. Address: Winterfold House, 46 Woodfield Road, Kings Heath, Birmingham B13 9UJ, England.

ANDREWS Julie (Julia Wells), b. 1 Oct 1935, Walton-on-Thames, Surrey, England. Singer; Actress. m. (1) Tony Walton, 10 May 1959, divorced, 1 daughter; (2) Blake Edwards, 1969. Musical Education: Voice lessons with Lillian Stiles-Allen. Career: As actress: Debut, Starlight Roof, London Hippodrome, 1947; Appeared: Royal Command Performance, 1948; Broadway production, The Boy Friend, NYC, 1954; My Fair Lady, 1956-60; Camelot, 1960-62; Putting It Together, 1993; Film appearances include: Mary Poppins, 1964; The Americanization Of Emily, 1964; Torn Curtain, 1966; The Sound Of Music, 1966; Hawaii, 1966; Thoroughly Modern Millie, 1967; Star, 1968; Darling Lili, 1970; The Tamarind Seed, 1973; 10, 1979; Little Miss Marker, 1980; S.O.B., 1981; Victor/Victoria, 1982;

The Man Who Loved Women, 1983; That's Life!, 1986; Duet For One, 1986; Television debut, 1956; Host, The Julie Andrews Hour, 1972-73; Julie (comedy series), ABC-TV, 1992; Television films include Our Sons, 1991. Recordings: Albums: A Christmas Treasure, 1968; The Secret Of Christmas, 1977; Love Me Tender, 1983; Broadway's Fair, 1984; Love Julie, 1989; with Carol Burnett: Julie And Carol At Carnegie Hall, 1962; At The Lincoln Center, 1989; Cast and film soundtracks: My Fair Lady (Broadway cast), 1956; Camelot (Broadway cast), 1961; Mary Poppins (film soundtrack), 1964; The Sound Of Music (film soundtrack), 1965; The King And I (studio cast), 1992. Publications: Mandy (as Julie Edwards), 1971; The Last Of The Really Great Whangdoodles, 1974. Honours: Oscar, Mary Poppins, 1964; Golden Globe Awards, Hollywood Foreign Press Association, 1964, 1965; BAFTA Silver Mask, 1989.

ANDREWS Patti, b. 16 Feb 1920, Minnesota, Louisiana, USA. Singer; Career: Lead singer, vocal group The Andrews Sisters (with sisters Laverne and Maxene), 1938-53; Occasional reunions until Laverne's death, 1967; Solo artiste, 1953-; Film appearances include: Argentine Nights, 1940; Buck Privates; Hollywood Canteen, 1944; Stage appearances include: Broadway musical, Over Here, 1974; Currently singing with Glenn Miller Orchestra. Recordings: Hits include: with The Andrews Sisters: Bei Mir Bist Du Schon; Hold Tight, Hold Tight; Roll Out The Barrel; Boogie Woogie Bugle Boy; Says My Heart; Say Si Si; I'll Be With You At Apple Blossom Time; Three Little Sisters; Strip Polka; Collaborations with: Bing Crosby; Burl Ives; Les Paul; Ernest Tubbs; Carmen Miranda; Solo hit: I Can Dream, Can't I? (Number 1, US), 1949; Albums include: with The Andrews Sisters: Curtain Call, 1956; By Popular Demand, 1957; Dancing Twenties, 1958; The Andrews Sisters Present, 1963; The Andrews Sisters Go Hawaiian, 1965; with Maxene Andrews: Over Here (cast recording), 1974; Numerous compilations and greatest hits collections.

ANDRIES Alexandru Braesti, b, 13 Oct 1954, Brasov, Romania. Singer; Songwriter; Musician (electric guitar, acoustic guitar, keyboards, harmonica); Architect; Lecturer, Institute of Architecture. Education: Graduate, Institute of Architecture, 1980; PhD in progress. Musical Education: Self-taught. Career: Guest, most Romanian jazz festivals including: Sibiu; Costinesti; Cluj; Constanta; Bucharest, 1979-; Tours throughout Romania; Concerts include: Palace Hall, Bucharest; Polivalenta Hall, Bucharest; Special guest, concerts at American Cultural Center, Bucharest; Guest, British Council, 1989; Appearances, most jazz and blues clubs in Romania: Club A, Bucharest; Constanta; Timisoara; Tirgu-Mures; Iasi; Special guest star, Golden Stag Festival, Brasov, Romania, with Kylie Minogue, Dionne Warwick, 1993; Guest, most Romanian radio stations: ProFM; Contact; Total; Independent television stations. Recordings: Albums: Interiors 1, 1984; Interiors 2, 1985; Country And Western Greatest Hits, 1986; Rock'N'Roll, 1987; On Distance, 1988; Three Mirrors, 1989; Censored, 1990; Today, 1991; Appetite Rises Eating, 1992; My She-Neighbours 1, 2, 3, 1992; How Far Away, 1992; Nothing New On The Eastern Front, 1993; Slow Burning Down, 1994; Alexandru Andries, 1994; Hocus Pocus, 1995; Singles: Waiting For Maria, 1990; Wait 'Til Tomorrow, 1992; Dream With Angels, 1994; Video: How Far Away, 1992. Publicatons: Home Alone, short stories, 1992; Waiting For Maria, 1990; Happy Birthday, Mr Dylan, Romanian translations from Bob Dylan's songs, 1991; White Album, 1996; Home, 1996; Ungra, 1996; Silence of the Heart, 1996; Videos: 21 Decembrie 1995/Teatrul Bulandra, 1996; In Concert, 1997. Honours: Voted Best Singer/Songwriter, Vox, Pop, Rock (Romanian musical newspaper), 1990-; Golden Record Award, 1991; Best Singer, 1992;

The Pro FM Contact Radio Awards, Best Singer, Songwriter, 1994. Memberships: Romanian Union of Composers; Romanian Union of Writers; Romanian Union of Architects; The Mickey Mouse Club, 1993. Hobbies: Art shows; Exhibitions of photography and paintings; Films; Theatre; Concerts; Reading. Current Management: Aurel Mitran Management, Calea Victorei 48-50, Sc.B, Apt 73, Sector 1, Bucharest 70102, Romania. Address: Soseaua Stefan Cel Mare 26, Bl. 24A, Apt 26, Sector 2, Bucharest 71158, Romania.

ANDRST Lubos, b. 26 July 1948, Prague, Czech Republic. Musician; Composer. m. 11 July 1974, 1 son. Education: Autodidact. Career: Musician with J Stivin, E Viklicky, R Dasek, M Svoboda, V Misik, M Prokop; Founder, Energit, 1973; Founder, Lubos Andrst Blues Band, 1980. Compositions: Capricornus; November; Ikebana; La Bodeguita Dez Medio; Imprints; Encountering; White Landscape; Follow Your Heart;Europe Blues; Wide - Open Door. Recordings: Energit 1975; Piknik, 1978; Capricornus, 1981; Plus-Minus Blues, 1988; Imprints, 1992; L Andrst With Friends, 1996; L Andrst Acoustic Set, 1996. Publications: Guitar Book - Jazz Rock Blues, 1988; Redaction, 1995. Memberships: Czech Jazz Association; Ochranny svoz Autorsky; OSA. Hobby: Canoeing. Current Management: ARTA Music, Lubzanska 57, 120 00 Praha 2, Czech Republic. Address: Hvozdnice 8, 25205 Praha-Zapad, Czech Republic.

ANDRUSZKOW Life, b. 22 Sept 1955, Copenhagen, Denmark. Singer; Composer; Musician (guitar, multi-instrumentalist). m. 2 children. Education: Private lessons in classical music on trumpet and cornet by conductor Jorgen Clausen and piano by Professor Anker Blyme; Self-taught in pop-rock-avantgarde composition and guitar; Private lessons in vocal by tutor Jens Christian Smith, (Denmark), tutor Ian Adams, (London) and by vario9us tutors at Musicians Institute, London. Career: Performed with pop-rock-bands since 1979 The Law, Art Exist, The Act and Life; Performed on Ringe Festival, 1984 and Roskilde Festival, 1985. Recordings: Own releases: Aubaude Dolorose, maxi-single, 1985; Heaven Cries For No One, video, 1988; Dreams Without Reality, video, 1988; Tones Of An Outsider, novel-video, 1989; Dancing In Burning Silhouettes, video, 1990; Europe After The Rain, CD, 1996; Promises, CD and video, 1998. Composing scores for radio-play: Sincerely, National Radio, 1984; for theatre: Images, Musical, 1986; Film soundtrack: Vertical, 1995; Lyrics for artists Michael Westwood: Bromskij Garden, CD, 1994; Live For It All, CD, 1996; My Living Dawn, CD, 1998. Current management: Out Of Eden Records, Sankt Pauls Gade 42, DK 1313 Copenhagen K, Denmark.

ANGELOPULO Charles, b. 8 Dec 1954, Pretoria, South Africa. Singer; Composer. m. 6 May 1978, 1 son, 1 daughter. Career: Title role, Jesus Christ Superstar, 1990; Lead singer: Web; Cafe Society, Blasé. Compositions: Over 65 recorded and released titles include: Helen Of Troy, The Rock Opera; I Love Africa; Good Time Girls; When You Gonna Love Me; Nothing Anybody Can Say. Honour: Finalist, South African Music Awards, 1995. Memberships: SAMRO; ASAMI. Hobby: Motor sport. Current Management: Self-managed. Address: 433-16th Avenue, Rietfontein, Pretoria 0084, South Africa.

ANGER Darol, b. 7 May 1953, Seattle, Washington, USA. Musician (violin, mandolin, guitar); Publisher; Author; Educator. Education: UC at Santa Cruz. Musical Education: Informal study with David Grisman; David Baker. Career: Member, Montreux Band, 1984; Founding member, David Grisman Quintet (DGQ); Played with artists including Stéphane Grappelli; Bela Fleck; Tony Rice; Mark O'Connor; Vassar Clements; Bill Keith; Richard Greene; Mike Marshall; Tony Trischka; Todd Phillips; Leader,

Turtle Island String Quartet; Co-leader (with Mike Marshall), Psychograss; Featured soloist on film soundtracks, including Best Offer; A Shock To The System; Country; Annual seminars at US colleges; Instructor at Mark O'Connor Fiddle Camps. Numerous recordings include: with Montreux Band: Sign Language; Let Them Say; Montreux Retrospective; with David Grisman: The David Grisman Quintet; Hot Dawg; Acoustic Christmas; with Turtle Island String Quartet: Turtle Island String Quartet; Metropolis; Skylife; On The Town; Spider Dreams; A Night In Tunisia, A Week In Detroit; By The Fireside; with Pyschograss: Like Minds; Anger/Marshall And Psychograss; with Mike Marshall: The Duo; Chiaroscuro; with Barbara Higbie: Tideline; Live At Montreux; Solo albums include: Fiddlistics; Jazz Violin Celebration; Also featured on recordings by: Suzanee Vega; Thomas Dolby; Henry Kaiser; Bela Fleck; Tony Trischka; John Gorka. Publications: Grant Wood And Street Stuff; Songs For Turtle Island; The Turtle Island Workbook; Darol Anger Originals; Fiddle Tunes. Memberships: NARAS; String Chair, International Association of Jazz Educators (IAJE); Sonneck Society. Hobby: Driving. Current Management: BZ Productions, PO Box 19297, Oakland, CA 94619, USA.

ANGUS Colin, b. 24 Aug 1961, Aberdeen, Scotland. Musician. Education: Aberdeen University. Career: Member, Alone Again Or; Founder member, The Shamen, 1986-. Recordings: Albums: Drop, 1987; In Gorbechev We Trust, 1989; Phorward, 1989; En-Tact, 1990; Progeny, 1991; Boss Drum, 1992; SOS, 1993; Axis Mutatis, 1995; Hit singles include: Christopher Mayhen Says, 1987; Jesus Loves Amerika, 1988; Pro Gen, 1990; Move Any Mountain (Pro Gen '91), 1991; Ebeneezer Goode (Number 1, UK), 1992; Destination Eschaton, 1995. Current Management: Moshka Management, PO Box 102, London E15 2HH, England.

ANKA Paul, b. 30 July 1941, Ottowa, Ontario, Canada. Singer; Composer. m. Marie Ann Alison De Zogheb, 16 Feb 1963, 5 daughters. Career: Live and television appearances worldwide, 1956-; Actor, films: Girls Town; The Private Lives Of Adam And Eve; Look In Any Window; The Longest Day. Compositions include: It Doesn't Matter Any More, for Buddy Holly, 1959; Co-writer (with Johnny Carson), Theme for Tonight Show, NBC TV, 1962-; My Way, for Frank Sinatra, 1969; She's A Lady, for Tom Jones, 1971. Recordings: Numerous singles include: Diana; I Love You Baby; You Are My Destiny; Crazy Love; (All Of A Sudden) My Heart Sings; Lonely Boy; Put Your Head On My Shoulder; It's Time To Cry; Puppy Love; My Home Town; Summer's Gone; The Story Of My Love; Tonight My Love Tonight; Dance On Little Girl; Love Me Warm And Tender; A Steel Guitar And A Glass Of Wine; Eso Beso (That Kiss!); Albums include: Paul Anka Sings His Big 15, 1960; Anka At The Copa, 1960; Young Alive And In Love!, 1962; Let's Sit This One Out, 1962; Golden Hits, 1963; Goodnight My Love, 1969; Life Goes On, 1969; Paul Anka, 1972; Jubilation, 1972; Paul Anka Gold, 1974; Feelings, 1975; Times Of Your Life, 1976; The Painter, 1976; The Music Man, 1977; Listen To Your Heart, 1978; Both Sides Of Love, 1978; Walk A Fine Line, 1983; Paul Anka Five Decades, 1992. Membership: BMI. Honours: Numerous BMI Awards, for Most Performed Songs and Over 1 Million Plays; 15 Gold discs; Inducted, Songwriters Hall Of Fame, 1993. Address: c/o Paul Anka Productions, 10573 W Pico Blvd, Suite 159, Los Angeles, CA 90064, USA.

ANNIES Nicholas Charles, b. 23 Jan 1971, Kettering, England. Photographer; Graphic Artist. m. Lauren Kelly Behan, 4 Aug 1996. Musical Educaton: Self-taught. Career: Manager, record labels: Reality Recordings, (circa) 1990; ADI Records, 1991; Paradise Records, 1992; Co-manager, Village Of Experimental Sound

Studios, Cambridge; PA Engineer, including Caister Weekenders, 1987-1991. Recordings: Singles: Armageddon (12"), co-produced by Shades Of Rhythm, 1991; with 39 Orbits: 2 12" releases, 1993-94; Currently working on double album, at Experimental Sound Studios, Cambridge. Publications: Underworld, monthly magazine, Peterborough City, 1990-1993. Memberships: Musicians' Union; Society of Amateur Artists; Media Records Italy. Hobbies: Painting; Making friends.

ANNISETTE (Annisette Hansen), b. 29 Aug 1948, Denmark. Singer; Songwriter; Composer; Lyricist. m. Thomas Koppel, 1971, 2 daughters. Career: Lead Singer, The Savage Rose, 1967-; Numerous tours: Denmark; Europe; USA; Middle East; Newport Festival, 1969; Numerous international television appearances; Title role in her own musical drama with Thomas Koppel, Bella Vita, 1997; Vocal Soloist on the occasion of the 50th Anniversary of Denmark's Liberation from Nazi Army, 1995, in Symphony 2 by Thomas Koppel. Compositions: Several songs, Savage Rose; Lyrics for: Bella Vita, Thomas Koppel, 1993; Symphony No2, Thomas Koppel, 1995; Script for musical drama Bella Vita, 1996-97. Recordings: Savage Rose, 18 albums; Triumph Of Death (ballet), Thomas Koppel, Bella Vita, 1993; Black Angel, 1995;. Honours: Several Grammy nomincations 1989-96; Several Gold, Platinum and Double Platinum Awards, 1968-97; Prize of Honour, Danish Songwriters; Union, 1995; Nomination for Music Award of the Nordic Council, 1996; Grammy, 1996; Memberships: Danish Artist's Union; Danish Jazz, Beat and Folk Authors' Society; Authors' Union. Current Management: South Harbor Productions, Frederikshøj 114, DK 2450 Copenhagen SV, Denmark.

ANSELMO Phil, b. USA. Rock Vocalist; Songwriter. Career: Lead vocalist, lyricist, US heavy rock group Pantera, 1986-; Also, lead vocalist with side-project Down, 1995-. Recordings: Albums: with Pantera: Power Metal, 1988; Cowboys From Hell, 1990; A Vulgar Display Of Power, 1992; with Down: Nola, 1995; Singles with Pantera include: Cowboys From Hell; Mouth For War. Address: c/o Concrete Management, 301 West 31st Street, Suite 11-D, New York, NY 10019, USA.

ANSEMS Tony, b. 9 Mar 1940, Tilburg, Netherlands. Musician (guitar); Songwriter. m. Rita, 8 Apr 1964, 3 sons. Education: American College, Bryn Mawr, Pennsylvania. Career: Guitarist with Breakaway; Songwriter; President, Songwriters of Wisconsin. Compositions: with Danny Mack: Old Rockers Never Die. Memberships: NSA; NAS; ASCAP. Hobby: Football. Address: PO Box 1027, Neenah, WI 54957-1027, USA.

ANSTICE-BROWN Sam, b. 24 July 1963, Sherborne, Dorset, England. Musician (drums); Arranger. Musical Education: BMusic Hons, Berklee College of Music, Boston, USA. Career: Tours, gigs with: Georgie Fame; Barbara Thompson; Mornington Lockett; Guy Barker; Jean Toussaint; Iain Bellamy; Tony Wjan; John Etheridge; Zoot Money; Dick Morissey; Don Weller; Dave Newton; Alan Skidmore; Bobby Wellins. Membership: Musician's Union. Hobbies: Music. Address: 101 Newland, Sherborne, Dorset DT9 3DU, England.

ANT Adam (Stuart Leslie Goddard), b. 3 Nov 1954, Marylebone, London, England. Singer; Songwriter; Actor. Career: Founder, lead singer, Adam And The Ants, 1977-82; Early tours with Siouxsie & The Banshees; X-Ray Spex; Desolation Angels; The Slits; Regular UK tours, 1979-; Solo artiste, 1982-86, 1992-; Appeared at Live Aid, Wembley Stadium, 1985; Numerous television and radio appearances; Member, all-star Peace Choir, 1991; Actor, 15 films, including World Gone Wild; Sunset Heat; Numerous television series including: Northern Exposure; The Equalizer. Compositions: Numerous songs with co-writer Marco Pirroni; Songs covered by: Elastica; Nine Inch Nails. Recordings: Albums: with Adam And The Ants: Dirk Wears White Sox, 1979; Kings Of The Wild Frontier, 1980; Prince Charming, 1981; Solo albums: Friend Or Foe, 1982; Strip, 1983; Vive Le Rock, 1985; Hits, 1986; Manners And Physique, 1990; Wonderful, 1995; Singles include: Ant Music; Dog Eat Dog; Kings Of The Wild Frontier (Number 2, UK); Stand And Deliver (Number 1, UK); Prince Charming (Number 1, UK); Ant Rap (Number 3, UK); Goody Two Shoes (Number 1, UK); Puss In Boots; Apollo 9; Tracks featured on film soundtracks including: Jubilee; Metropolis. Honours: Ivor Novello Award, Songwriters Of Year, with Pirroni, 1982; BRIT Award, Best British Album, Kings Of The Wild Frontier, 1982. Current Management: UK/LA Management. Address: Bugle House, 21a Noel Street, London W1V 3PD, England.

ANTHONY Michael, b. 20 June 1955, Chicago, Illinois, USA. Musician (bass). Career: Member, Snake; Bass player, US rock group Van Halen, 1974-; Support tours with UFO; Santana; Black Sabbath; Regular US and worldwide tours; Major concerts: California Music Festival, 1979; US Festival, 1982; 1983; Monsters of Rock Festival, Castle Donington, 1984; Monsters of Rock US tour (with Metallica, Scorpions), 1988; Texxas Jam, 1988; Co-host, radio show with Sammy Hagar, Radio Westwood One, 1992. Recordings: Albums: Van Halen, 1978; Van Halen II, 1979; Women And Children First, 1980; Fair Warning, 1981; Diver Down, 1982; 1984, 1984; 5150 (Number 1, US), 1986; OU812 (Number 1, US), 1988; For Unlawful Carnal Knowledge (Number 1, US) 1991; Right Here Right Now, 1993; Balance, 1995; Singles include: Your Really Got Me, 1978; Running With The Devil, 1978; Dance The Night Away, 1979; And The Cradle Will Rock, 1980; (Oh) Pretty Woman, 1981; Dancing In The Street, 1982; Jump (Number 1, US), 1984; Panama, 1984; I'll Wait, 1984; Hot For Teacher, 1984; Why Can't This Be Love, 1986; Dreams, 1986; Love Walks In, 1986; When It's Love, 1988; Finish What Ya Started, 1988; Feels So Good, 1989; Poundcake, 1991; Top Of The World, 1991; Right Now, 1992. Honours include: Platinum discs; Grammy Award, Best Hard Rock Performance, 1992; MTV Music Video Awards, 1984, 1992; Band awarded Gold Ticket, Madison Square Garden, 1988; American Music Award, Favourite Album, 1992. Current Management: SRO Management Inc., 189 Carlton Street, Toronto, Ontario M5A 2K7, Canada.

ANTILL Danny Terrance, b. 8 Sept 1959, Johannesburg, South Africa. Musician (keyboards, flute); Producer; Arranger. m. 6 Feb 1982, 1 son, 2 daughters. Musical Education: 8th Grade classical piano, flute (Royal Academy Of Music). Career: Toured with Stingray throughout South Africa; Appeared on National TV 1, 2, 3; Solo piano albums released throughout Europe; Playlisted on German national radio. Recordings: Stingray; Danny Antill, 3 solo albums released throughout Europe; Producer, arranger, 17 Gold records; Composer, theme song for local blockbuster film Boetie Gaan Bordertoe. Honours: 17 Gold records; Top 5 3 years consecutively; South African OKTV Award Nomination, Best Producer, Arranger, Jingle and TV themes writer. Membership: SAMRO. Hobbies: Golf; Fishing; Diving. Current Management: Brettian Productions. Address: Brettian Productions, PO Box 96395, Brixton 2019, Johannesburg, South Africa.

APACHE INDIAN, b. Birmingham, England. Ragga and Bhangra Vocalist. Career: Solo singer, 1992-; International tours include Middle East; India; Japan. Recordings: Albums: No Reservations, 1992; Make Way For The Indian,

1995; Guest vocalist, Wreck Shop, Wreckx'N'Effect, 1993; Solo hit single: Boom-Shack-A-Lack, 1993. Address: c/o Island Records, 22 St Peters Square, London W6 9NW, England.

APELBAUM Morris Moishe, b. 13 July 1957, Haifa, Israel. Producer; Engineer. Married, 1 son. Education: BSc; BA; DipEd; Dip Admin. Recordings: Producer: Oliver Jones: Many Moods; Lights Of Burgundy; Tim Brady: Scenarios; Imaginary Guitars; Inventions; Double Variations. Honours: 3 Juno Nominations; 2 Adisq Nominations; 1 Juno Award. Memberships: CARAS; SOCAN. Current Mamagement: Silent Sound. Address: 3880 Clark Street, Montreal, Quebec H2W 1W6, Canada.

APPLETON Natalie, b. 1974. Singer. Career: Member, female vocal group All Saints, 1995-. Recordings: Singles: Silver Shadow; I Know Where It's At; Never Ever (Number 1, UK); Debut Album: All Saints. Honours include: Brit Award, Best Single. Current Management: John Benson.

APPLETON Nicky, b. 1976. Singer. Career: Member, female vocal group All Saints, 1995-. Recordings: Singles: Silver Shadow; I Know Where It's At; Never Ever (Number 1, UK); Debut album; All Saints. Honours include: Brit Award, Best Single. Current Management: John Benson.

AQUAMANDA (Amanda Greatorex), b. Matlock, Derbyshire, England. Vocalist; Musician (keyboards); Writer; Producer. Education: BA Hons, Fashion Textile Design (Fashion Designer), Leicester. Career: Vocalist, lyricist, Knights Of The Occasional Table; Breathe track on compilation album Shamanarchy In The UK; Album and cover design, Knees Up Mother Earth, 1993; Session on John Peel, 1994; Now solo as Aquamanda; Runs record label Fairy Cake Universe with partner Dr Tony Hare. Compositions: Lyricist, vocalist, composer, Knees Up Mother Earth. Recordings: Album: Knights Of The Occasional Table, 1993; Solo single: Free Your Spirit (12" vinyl), 1995. Memberships: PRS; MCPS; PPL; Musicians' Union. Hobbies: Scuba diving; Tama-Do. Current Management: Self-managed with Dr Tony Hare, FCU Records. Address: Fairy Cake Universe, PO Box LB621, London W1A 5EB, England.

ARAGAO Monique Cavalcanti de, b. 10 Nov 1960, Rio de Janeiro, Brazil. Composer; Musician (piano); Arranger. m. David Ganc, 1 son. Education: BA, Music, University of Rio de Janeiro. Musical Education: Piano with Undine de Mello and Linda Bustani and voice with Carol McDavit, Clarice Szajmbrum. Career: Television: Monique Aragao Special, TVE, 1990; Special, Dentro and Fora do Compasso, TVE, 1994; Guest appearance, New Year's Eve special, TV Globe, 1993; Radio: Radio Roquete Pinto; Radio Mec; Radio Journal do Brasil; Radio Nacional. Recordings: Solo: Monique Aragao, 1991; Canoas, 1993; Ventos do Brasil, 1995; Original soundtracks for theatre, films, ballet. Publications: Coral Hoje; Choral Pieces. Honours: Contests Alcina Navarro, 1970; Liddy Mignone, Lucia Branco, 1976; Sharp Prize, 1992. Membership: AMAR (RJ). Hobbies: Painting; Tap dance. Current Management: Zillion Artistic Productions. Address: Rua São Clemente, no 389/801, Botafogo, Rio de Janeiro, Brazil.

ARAM Vicki, b. 31 Dec 1935, Stanley, County Durham, England. Musician (piano); Vocalist. m. David Wager, 28 Sept 1957, 1 son, 2 daughters. Education: Sunderland Art College. Musical Education: ALCM, aged 15. Career: Successful fashion artist, 1950s-60s; Became professional rehearsal pianist with Dino Shafeek in Action 5; Vocalist, pianist, resident at Mortons, playing to audience including Rod Stewart; David Essex; Marc Bolan; Richard and Grace Jones; Played in many London hotels, jazz venues include: Pizza Express; Pizza On The Park;

Worked with the best jazz musicians; Resident at The Canteen, 1980; Filled in between sets by great American jazz musicians; Now studying astrology and painting idealised style portraits. Address: 43 Baronsmere Road, East Finchley, London N2 9QG, England.

ARCARI Dave, b. 14 Aug 1964, Glasgow, Scotland. Musician (guitar); Producer; Publicist. m. Anne, 5 Feb 1993. Education: FifeCollege. Career: Ex-member, band Summerfield Blues; Numerous live sessions for BBC Radio; Television appearances, European Cable Shows; Member of the Radiotones. Compositions: Ain't Crying, 1993; 24 Hours, 1993; Uncle Jack, 1995; Journeytime is Over, 1997; You Oughta Know, 1997. Recordings: with Summerfield Blues: Devil and The Freightman; Let's Scare The Posh People; Little Miss Behavin'; with Denim Elliots: Gooseberry Rain; with Radiotones: Radiotones. Honours: Scottish Blues Band Of The Year, 1993. Membership: Musicians' Union. Hobbies: Technology; American Roots music. Current Management: Buzz Artist Management, Perth, Scotland. Address: 192 Glasgow Road, Perth PH2 0NA, Scotland.

ARCH David, b. 25 Oct 1962, Watford, England. Composer; Musician (keyboards); Arranger. m. Katherine, 2 Jan 1991, 1 son, 1 daughter. Educaton: King James College, Henley. Musical Education: Guildhall School of Music, GGSM. Career: In NYJO whilst at college; MD for Dash, Hot Shoe Show (Wayne Sleep); Session keyboard player, many films, television, album projects; Started composing, joined Joe And Co, 1988; Writing many television jingles; Now writing, mainly adverts and television music. Compositions: GMTV; Walden; Strange But True; LWT logo; Wipeout; British Airways; Orchestral: Goldeneye; Little Bhudda; Sheltering Sky; Wuthering Heights; Michael Ball albums. Memberships: PRS; MCPS; Association of Professional Composers. Hobbies: Travel; Cars. Current Management: Joe & Co. Address: Denholm House, Pinner Hill, Pinner, Middlesex HAS 3XX, England.

ARCHER Martin Walker, b. 9 Mar 1957, Sheffield, England. Musician (saxophone); Electronics. Education: Law degree, Nottingham University, 1978. Musical Education: Self-taught instrumentalist, composer. Career: Leader, Composer, Hornweb, 1983-1993; Current member, Transient v Resident, Disconnected Bliss; Partner, Discus Record Label. Recordings: Albums: with Hornweb Saxophone Quartet: Kinesis, 1986; Sixteen, 1987; Universe Works, 1989; Solo recordings: Wild Pathway Favourites, 1988; Telecottage, 1995; Compiler of the Network miniatures series: Volume I, 1994; Volume II, 1995. Honours: Wire Magazine World Top 25 album, Wild Pathway Favourites, 1988. Memberships: Sonic Arts Network; Society for Promotion of New Music. Hobbies: Music; Film; Theatre; Fresh air. Current Management: Discus. Address: Discus, PO Box 658, Sheffield S10 3YR, England.

ARCHER Mitchell, b. 29 Sept 1964, Birmingham, England. Musician (drums, percussion). m. Michelle, 16 Apr 1994. Musical Education: Drumtech percussion school, London (advanced concepts and techniques). Career: Currently teaching full-time; Former session musician, based in West Midlands; Studio, live work, various local artists for 15 years, mainly in: UK; Ireland; France; Germany; Spain. Recordings: Bitty McLean: It Keeps Rainin'; Dedicated. Membership: Musicians' Union, teacher/session player. Hobbies: Drumming; Sport. Address: 170 Eachelhurst Road, Walmley, Sutton Coldfield, West Midlands B76 1EL, England.

ARCHER Tasmin Angela, b. 3 Aug 1963, Bradford, England. Singer; Songwriter. Career: Solo artiste, 1992-; Tours of US, UK, Europe.

Recordings: Singles: Sleeping Satellite (Number 1, UK), 1992; In Your Care; Lords Of The New Church; Arriene; Shipbuilding; One More Goodnight With The Boys; Albums: Great Expectations, 1992; Bloom, 1995. Honours: BRIT Award, Best Newcomer, 1993. Membership: Musicians' Union. Hobbies: Reading; Exercise. Current Management: Ian McAndrew, Wildlife Entertainment. Address: 21 Heathmans Road, Parsons Green, London SW6 4TJ, England.

ARDEN-GRIFFITH Paul, b. 18 Jan 1952, Stockport, England. Opera, Music-Theatre, Concert, Cabaret Singer (tenor). Musical Education: Royal Manchester College Of Music; Cantica Voice Studio. Career: Concert, theatre singer, 1971-; Opera singer, 1973-; Major operas include: Midsummer Night's Dream; The Rake's Progress; Of Mice And Men; Carmina Burana; The Barber of Seville; Music, theatre performances include: The Merry Widow; Phantom Of The Opera; The Legendary Lanza; Babes In The Wood; Gilbert and Sullivan to Lloyd Webber- The Great British Musicals; German production of Sunset Boulevard; Concerts, cabarets include: London: Dorchester Hotel; Hyde Park Intercontinental; Picadilly Theatre; The Belfry Club; Savoy Hotel; Tramshed; Theatre Royal Drury Lane; The Limelight Club; Internationally: Wexford (Eire); Hong Kong; Sydney; Singapore; Palm Springs (California); Television appearances include: Wozzeck; A Christmas Carol; The Cleopatras; The Comic Strip; The Bill; Pebble Mill At One; Save The Children Christmas Special. Recordings: Paul Arden Griffith - The Song Is You, 1986; Phantom Of The Opera (original cast album), 1987; An Evening With Alan Jay Lerner, 1987; Minstrel Magic (Black and White Minstrel cast album), 1993; A Minstrel On Broadway, 1994; Encore! - Paul Arden-Griffith In Concert, 1995; The Classic Collection, 1995; Video: On Stage At The Hackney Empire, 1989. Honours: Gwilym Gwalchmai Jones Scholarship For Singing, 1974. Memberships: British Actors Equity Association; Musicians' Union. Hobbies: Travel; Hiking; Swimming; Painting. Current Management: Geoff Stanton, Brunskill Management, UK. Address: c/o Ken Spencer Personal Management, 138 Sandy Hill Road, London SE18 7BA, England.

ARENA Tina. Singer. Career: Albums: Strong as Steel, 1990; Don't Ask, 1995; In Deep, 1997; Other performances include: Nine, 1987; Soul Dynamite, 1989; Joseph and His Amazing Technicolour Dream Coat, 1992; Former Member, Young Talent Time. Recording: Tiny Tina, 1977. Honours: Performer and Rock Performer of the Year MO Awards, 1996; 1995 Aria Best Pop Release, Chains, 1995 Aria Song the Year, Chains; Aria Female Artist of the Year, 1995; Aria Album of the Year, Don't Ask, 1995; Variety Club Entertainer of the Year, 1995; Advance Australia Foundation Award, 1996; APRA Song of the Year, Wasn't It Good, 1996; World Music Award for World's Highest Selling Female Artist, Highest Selling Female Artist in Australian History, 1996. Address: c/o RCM International, Lennox House, 229 Lennox Street, Richmond, Vic 3121, Australia.

ARGENT Rod, b. 14 June 1945, St Albans, Hertfordshire, England. Musician (keyboards); Vocalist. Career: Founder, The Zombies, 1963-69; Founder, own group Argent, 1970s; Also solo artiste and record producer; Appearances include: New York, 1964; UK tour, with Dusty Springfield, The Searchers, 1965; Caravan of Stars US tour, 1965; Production partnerships with Chris White and Peter Van Hooke, 1980s. Recordings: Albums: with the Zombies: The Zombies, 1965; Begin Here, 1965; Odessey And Oracle, 1967; with Argent: Argent, 1970; Ring Of Hands, 1971; All Together Now, 1972; In Deep, 1973; Nexus, 1974; Encore, 1974; Circus, 1975; Counterpoints, 1975; Anthology, 1976; Hold Your Head Up, 1978; Rock Giants, 1982; Music From The Spheres, 1991; Solo: Moving Home, 1978; Ghosts, 1982; Shadowshow, 1985; Red House, 1988; Rescue,

1991; Singles include: with the Zombies: She's Not There (Number 2, US), 1964; Tell Her No, 1965; with Argent: Hold Your Head Up, 1971; God Gave Rock And Roll To You, 1973; Co-producer, debut album by Tanita Tikaram.

ARGÜELLES Julian, b. 28 Jan 1966. Musician (saxophones, various woodwinds); Composer. Musical Education: Studied briefly at Trinity College of Music. Career: Various youth bands; Loose Tubes, including a Proms performance; Mike Gibbs Orchestra; Kenny Wheeler Big Band; Chris McGregor's Brotherhood Of Breath; The Very Big Carla Bley Band; Hermeto Pascoal; Django Bates' Delightful Precipice; Performed Concerto for piano, percussion and saxophone, by Mario Lagina. Recordings: with Julian Argüelles Quartet: Phaedrus; Home Truths; Scapes, 1996; Skull View, 1997; Various recordings with: Steve Argüelles, Django Bates, Kenny Wheeler, Mike Gibbs, Mario Laginha. Honours: Pat Smyth Award; Various BBC Awards; Commission by BBC Radio 3 for Octet. Hobbies: Reading. Current Management: Babel Records. Address: 79B Helix Road, London SW2 2JR, England.

ARMATAGE John Sinclair, 5 August 1929, Newcastle Upon Tyne, England. Musician (drums). m. Ann Johnston, 9 May 1975. Musical Education: Self-taught. Career: Member, Wally Fawkes Band; Bruce Turner Jump Band; Alan Elsdon Band; Pete Allen Band; Terry Lightfoot Band; Tours with Don Byas; Ben Webster; Earl Hines; Red Allen; Pee Wee Russell; Films: Living Jazz; Plenty; Television and radio apppearances. Recordings: Albums with: Bruce Turner; Alan Elsdon; Bud Freeman; Terry Lightfoot. Hobbies: Model railways; Reading; Walking. Current Management: Ann Armatage. Address: 1 Keable Road, Wrecclesham, Farnham, Surrey GU10 4PW, England.

ARMATRADING Joan b. 9 Dec 1950, Basseterre, St Kitts, West Indies. Singer; Songwriter; Musician (guitar). Musical Education: Self-taught piano and guitar. Career: Songwriting, performing partnership, with Pam Nestor, 1969-73; Solo artiste, 1973-; Appearances include: Regular international tours; Concerts include: Prince's Trust Gala, Wembley Arena, 1986; Nelson Mandela's 70th Birthday Tribute, Wembley Stadium, 1988; Numerous world tours, 1973-96. Compositions include: Down To Zero; Willow, 1977. Recordings: Singles: Love And Affection, 1976; Rosie, 1980; Me Myself I, 1980; All The Way From America, 1980; I'm Lucky, 1981; Drop The Pilot, 1983; Perfect Day, 1997; Albums include: Whatever's For Us, 1973; Joan Armatrading, 1976; Show Some Emotion, 1977; Stepping Out, 1979; Me Myself I, 1980; Walk Under Ladders, 1981; The Key, 1983; Track Record, 1983; The Shouting Stage, 1988; The Very Best Of..., 1991; What's Inside, 1995; Film soundtrack, The Wild Geese, 1978. Honour: BASCA Ivor Novello Award for Outstanding Contemporary Collection, 1996. Address: c/o F Winter and Co., Ramillies House, 2 Ramillies Street, London W1V 1DF, England.

ARMSTRONG Bernie, b. 14 May 1959, Windsor, England. Vocalist, Musician (guitar, keyboards); Songwriter. m. Sharon, 20 Dec 1980, 1 son, 1 daughter. Musical Education: Ashford College. Career: Tours: South Australia, Denmark, Sweden, Germany, Netherlands, Belgium, UK, 1980-87; Television: Rock Gospel Show, BBC, 1984, 1985; Crackerjack, Australia, 1980; Songs Of Praise, BBC1, 1994; Heart And Soul series, BBC1, 1994. Recordings: Change Of Heart, 1980; Masks, 1982; New Beginnings, 1983; Open Handed, 1990. Memberships: PRS; MCPS; Musicians' Union. Hobbies: Children; Church and social.

ARMSTRONG Gerry, b. 28 Oct 1929, Detroit, Michigan, USA. Folk Singer; Storyteller. m.

George D Armstrong, 24 Apr 1954, (deceased 1993), 2 daughters. Education: College. Musical Education: The oral tradition. Career: I Come For To Sing, weekly program with Studs Terkel, Big Bill Broonzy and others, 1953-; Folk clubs, festivals, churches, schools, radio and television, films, 1960s-70s; Sometimes play with 3 generations of Armstrong family on stage together, 1990s. Recordings: Simple Gifts, Folkways (now Smithsonian); Wheel Of The Year, Flying Fish (now Rounder); Golden Ring; Five Days Singing, Vol 1 & 2 (Folk-legacy); My Singing Bird (tape); Once Upon a Time..., tape of stories; Music in My Mother's House, CD. Publications: 3 children's books: The Magic Bagpipe; The Boat On The Hill; The Fairy Thorn; Many stories in school readers, Cricket magazine. Memberships: Old Town School Of Folk Music; The Aural Tradition; Sacred Harp Singers. Hobbies: Quilting and other crafts; Cornhusk dolls; Dream catchers; Gods Eyes; Paper pretties. Current Management: Self-managed. Address: 1535 Lake Avenue, Wilmette, IL 60091-1637, USA.

ARMSTRONG Timothy Paul, b. 10 Feb 1961, Birmingham, England. Singer; Songwriter; Recording Artist. 2 sons, 1 daughter. Musical Education: 2 years piano, SC Music. Career: Member, band The Politicians, 1981-86; Appearances: Telethons, 1981-85; Shazam TV Special, 1985; NZ Today, 1992-93. Recordings: Singles: Down In Baghdad, 1983; Energy, 1985; Christmas Day/Photograph, 1986; Albums: Relationships, 1992; Breaking Hearts, 1993; Wondering Why, 1995. Honours: Waikato Rock Awards: Best Male Vocalist, Best Recorded Work. Hobby: Local politics. Current Management: Tim Armstrong. Address: 11 Beatrice Place, Hamilton, New Zealand.

ARNADOTTIR Bergþóra, b. 15 February 1948, Hveragerdi. Musician; Songmaker; Pop Singer. divorced, 1 son, 1 daughter. Career: Saleswoman; Joint-owner, fishing ship, 1971-80; Singer of Folk & Light Music, Output. Compositions include: Hin Mikla Gjöf, 1970; Draumur, 1973; Ljöd an lags, 1982; Synir, 1980; Hljod Streymir Lindin, 1980; Frandi, Pegar Fidlan Pegir, 1973; Prju Ljod Um Litinn Fugl, 1980; Borgarljos, 1982; Modursong, 1983; Gigjan, 1983; Lifsbokin, 1984. Recordings include: I seinna lagi (Delayed), 1987; Landslagid, 1989; Norden synger viser, 1991; Fagra veröld (Beautiful World), 1993; Aldarminning (100 Years' Memory), 1995; Stelpurokk (Girls Rock), 1997. Honours: 3 Month Grant, Ministry of Culture, Iceland, 1983. Memberships: FTT; STEF, 1975-. Address: Under Gyden 22 Torslev, DK 9460 Brovst, Denmark.

ARNESEN Dag S, b. 3 May 1950, Bergen, Norway. Musician (piano); Composer. m. Wenche Gausdal, 17 Oct 1986. Education: Teacher training (Music). Musical Education: Music Conservatory, Bergen, classical piano. Career: Norwegian television (NRV) appearances: with own group: Ny Bris; with project for Vossa Jazz, 8 piece band includes: Elvin Jones, drums, Jon Surman, saxophone, Palle Danielson, bass; with Joe Henderson, Woody Shaw Quintet. Recordings: Albums: Ny Bris, 1982; Renascent, 1984; The Day After, 1990; Photographs, 1992; Movin', 1992. Honours: The Vossa Jazz Prize, 1992; The Grieg Prize, 1994. Memberships: FNJ; NOPA; GRAMART. Hobby: Walking in the mountains. Address: Gutenbergs V6 18, 5035 B6 Sandviken, Norway.

ARNOLD Cheryl Christine, b. 23 Apr 1951, Seattle, Washington, USA. Country Singer. m. 23 June 1979, Michael Stipek, 3 sons (triplets). Education: Washington University, 1970-73. Career: Country singer, 1980-; Support act for country artistes including: Lorrie Morgan, 1982; Hoyt Axton, 1984; Loretta Lynn, 1984; Ricky Nelson, 1985; Johnny Cash, 1988; Reba McEntire, 1989; Glen Campbell, 1990. Memberships: ACM; CMA.

ARNOLD David Michael, b. 21 Apr 1958, Maidstone, Kent, England. Singer; Composer. 1 son. Education: Technical School; Hackney and Hastings Colleges. Musical Education: Self-taught. Career: Various radio appearances, 1980-94; Formed own record label, appearances, 1980-1994; Meridian TV, 1993, 1995. Recordings: High Upon The Rhythm; Hallelujah; Valentine; National Health Tender. Publications: Various (International). Memberships: PRS; MCPS. Hobbies: Art; Poetry; Performance; Writing. Current Management: Happy House; Dead Happy Records. Address: 3B Castledown Avenue, Hastings, East Sussex TN34 3RJ, England.

ARNOLD Eddy (Richard Edward), b. 15 May 1918, Madisonville, Tennessee, USA. Country Singer. m. Sally Arnold, 28 Nov 1941, 1 son, 1 daughter. Education: Self-taught guitar. Career: Member, Pee Wee King's Golden West Cowboys, 1940-43; Radio appearances: WSM Radio, Nashville, as solo artist The "Tennessee Plowboy"; Co-host, Grand Ole Opry, 1943-48; Host, Checkerboard Square, 1947-55; Television appearances: Milton Berle Show, 1949; Host, Eddy Arnold Time, 1950s; Guest on all major shows including Ed Sullivan; Jackie Gleason; Johnny Carson; Dean Martin; TV specials: Profile From The Land, 1968; Kraft Music Hall Specials, 1967-71; Appeared films: Feudin' Rhythm, 1949; Hoedown, 1950: One of first country artists to play Carnegie Hall, 1966; Performed with symphony orchestras of Hartford; Nashville; Memphis, 1960s. Recordings: Record sales total over 80 million (one of most successful artists in history); Over 145 country hits including 21 US Country Number 1s, 1945-55; Hits include: Please Stay Home With Me; That's How Much I Love You; Bouquet Of Roses; Anytime; I'll Hold You In My Heart; Just A Little Lovin' Will Go A Long Way; Cattle Call; Tennessee Stud; What's He Doing In My World?; Make The World Go Away; The Last Word In Lonesome Is Me; Misty Blue; Turn The World Around. Publications: It's A Long Way From Chester Country, 1969. Honours: Inducted into Country Music Hall Of Fame, 1966; Entertainer Of The Year, 1967; Pioneer Award, Academy Of Country Music, 1984; President's Award Songwriter's Guild, 1987. Current Management: Gerald W. Purcell Associates. Address: 964 Second Avenue, New York, NY 10022, USA.

ARNOLD Kristine, b. California, USA. Singer. m. Leonard Arnold, 2 daughters. Career: Member, duo Sweethearts Of The Rodeo with sister Janis Gill; Signed to Columbia Records; Sugar Hill Records; Winners, Wrangler Country Showcase, 1985. Recordings: Sweethearts Of The Rodeo, 1986; Top 20 hits include: Since I Found You; Midnight Girl/Sunset Town; Satisfy You; Chains Of Gold, 1987; Rodeo Waltz, 1993; Video: Things Will Grow. Honours: CMA's Vocal Duo, 9 consecutive years; Music City News Award, Best Vocal Duo; TNN Viewers Choice Award, Favourite Group; NAIRD Award, Best Country Album, 1994. Current Management: M Hitchcock Management. Address: PO Box 159007, Nashville, TN 37214, USA.

ARRIALE Lynne, b. 29 May 1957, Milwaukee, Wisconsin, USA. Composer; Jazz Musician (piano). Musical Education: BMus, MMus, Classical Piano. Career: Tour of Japan with 100 Golden Fingers (featuring 10 great jazz pianists); Tours of Europe and North America with the Lynne Arriale Trio. Recordings: Albums: The Eyes Have It; When You Listen; With Words Unspoken, 1996. Honours: First Prize, Great American Jazz Piano Competition, 1993. Current Management: US: Suzi Reynolds and Associates, 200 Rector Place 7H, New York, NY 10280, USA; Europe: Creative Music Consultants, Edif. Patapata, La Planta, Oficinia 6, 29600 Marbella, Spain.

ARROYO Joe (Alvaro José), b. 1955, Cartagena, Colombia. Singer; Songwriter. Musical Education: Soloist, school choir. Career: Nightclub singer from age 12; Formed La Protesta, 1970; Singer, Fruko Y Sus Tesos, 1971-81; South American and US tours; Numerous hits; Formed own group, La Verdad (15 piece band), 1981-; Concerts include: Empire Leicester Square, London 1992; Founder, own band, Son Caribeno (the Caribbean Sound); Recordings: Hit singles: with Fruko Y Sus Tesos: Manyoma; Tania; El Ausente; with La Verdad: Tumbatecho, 1986; Rebelión (considered all-time Latin classic), UK release 1991; Numerous hit albums with La Verdad include: En Acción; Musa Original; Toque De Clase; Fire In My Mind. Honours: Over 100 music awards; Conga De Oro, Barranquila Carnival; 13 Golden Bongo Awards. Address: c/o Jenny Adlington, World Circuit Records, 106 Cleveland Street, London W1P 5DP, England.

ARTHUR Davey, b. 24 Sept 1954, Edinburgh, Scotland. Musician (multi-instrumentalist); Vocalist. Career: Member, The Buskers; Member, Tam Linn; Appeared at the Cambridge Folk Festival; Later became the Fureys and Davey Arthur, 1980-. Recordings: The Cisco Special, 1960; Songs Of Woody Guthrie, 1961; I Ain't Got No Home, 1962; The Sound Of The Fureys And Davey Arthur, 1981; When You Were Sweet Sixteen, 1982; Steal Away, 1983; In Concert, 1984; Golden Days, 1984; At The End Of A Perfect Day, 1985; The First Leaves Of Autumn, 1986; The Fureys Finest, 1987; The Fureys Collection, 1989; The Scattering, 1989; The Very Best Of, 1991; The Winds Of Change, 1992; Singles include: When You Were Sweet Sixteen, 1981. Current Management: Park Promotions, 20 Raleigh Park Road, North Hinksey, Oxford OX2 9AZ, England.

ARTIST The (Prince Rogers Nelson), b. 7 June 1958, Minneapolis, Minnesota, USA. Singer; Songwriter; Producer. m. Mayté, 1996. Career: Previously billed as Prince, The Artist Formerly Known as Prince (AFKAP) and Symbol; Leader, Prince And The Revolution; Singer, with own backing group the New Power Generation, 1991-; Numerous tours, concerts; Own recording studio and record label, Paisley Park; Currently billed as The Artist. Recordings: Singles include: 1999; Alphabet Street; Controversy; I Could Never Take The Place; If I Was Your Girlfriend; Let's Go Crazy; Little Red Corvette; Purple Rain; Raspberry Beret; Sign O' The Times; U Got The Look; When Doves Cry; Cream; Gold; Albums include: For You, 1978; Dirty Mind, 1979; Controversy, 1979; Prince, 1979; 1999, 1983; Purple Rain, 1984; Around The World In A Day, 1985; Parade, 1986; Sign O' The Times, 1987; Lovesexy, 1988; Batman (soundtrack), 1989; Graffiti Bridge (soundtrack), 1990; Diamond And Pearls (soundtrack), 1991; Come, 1995; The Gold Experience, 1995; As producer: Child Of The Sun, Mayté, 1996. Honours include: Academy Award, Best Original Score, Purple Rain, 1984; 3 Grammy Awards, 1985; BRIT Awards: Best International Male Artist, 1992, 1993, 1995; Q Award, Best Songwriter, 1990. Current Management: Paisley Park Enterprises, 7801 Audoban Road, Chanhassen, MN 55317, USA.

ASHCROFT Richard. Vocalist; Songwriter; Musician (guitar). Career: Vocalist, The Verve; Concerts include: Lollaplooza Tour, US, 1994; UK tours, 1994-95; Support to Oasis, Paris, 1995; Glastonbury Festival, 1995. Compositions include: On Your Own; Drive You Home; History; No Knock On My Door. Recordings: Albums: A Storm In Heaven, 1993; A Northern Soul, 1995; Singles: This Is Music, 1995; On Your Own, 1995, 1995; History, 1995. Current Management: Larrikin Management, 8391 Beverly Blvd #298, Los Angeles, CA 90048, USA.

ASHER James, b. 4 Sept 1950, Eastbourne, Sussex, England. Composer; Producer; Musician (keyboards, drums). Musical Education: Grade VI violin. Career: Sound engineer, R G Jones studio, London. Compositions: Wrote and recorded over 20 albums library music; Films and television include: La Filiere Chinoise, Cinema Euro Group; Gems, Thames Television; The Boat Show, BBC2; The Plant, Screen One; Television station idents for: Central; Granada; MTV, USA; Future TV, Lebanon; European Superchannel; Television themes for: Ulster Television news; Channel 4 rugby programme. Recordings: Single: Peppermint Lump (produced by Pete Townshend); Albums: The Great Wheel; Globalarium (used by The Clothes Show, BBC1); Dance Of The Light; Bush Telegraph; As drummer: Empty Glass, Pete Townshend; Producer for: Ritchie; John "Rabbit" Bundrick; Dream Jungle. Memberships: APC; REPRO. Current Management: Self-managed. Address: 34 Starfield Road, London W12 9SW, England.

ASHER John William, b. 8 July 1927, Ilkeston, Derbyshire, England. Engineer; Lecturer in Mathematics (retired). m. Hazel Lilian, 9 Sept 1950, 4 sons. Education: BSc (Eng), Diploma Maths; Advanced Teachers Certificate. Musical Education: 1 year on violin (pre-war). Career: Played violin, College Orchestra, 1945-48; Clarinetist in Jazz band, 1949-57; Violin and clarinet, pub and dance jobs, 1958-60; Tenor saxophone, with Hi-Fi Rhythm Group, Southampton; Theatre work, shows and dance concerts; Tenor or alto saxophone, big bands; Saxophones, clarinet, jazz clubs; Solo clarinet and first alto sax, military band concerts, including Abbey Gate Players, Colchester. Membership: CASS. Hobbies: Music; Fishing; Gardening; Swimming; Dancing; Going on holiday. Address: Oaklea, New Hall Lane, Mundon, Maldon, Essex CM9 6NY, England.

ASHER Peter, b. 22 June 1944, London, England. Artist Manager; Record Producer; Singer; Musician (guitar). m. Wendy Worth, 20 May 1983, 1 daughter. Education: Philosophy, King's College, London University. Career: Member, duo, Peter and Gordon, 9 top records, 3 Gold discs, 1964-68; Head of A&R, Apple Records, 1968-70; Produced, signed, James Taylor; Founder, Peter Asher Management, USA; Began management, production of Linda Ronstadt; Today represents: Peter Blakeley; Chicano Soul'n Power; Iris DeMent; The Innocence Mission; Little Feat; Kirsty MacColl; Maria Fatal; Mariachi Los Campaneros de Nati Cano; Randy Newman; Over The Rhine; Linda Ronstadt; Laura Satterfield; James Taylor; Williams Brothers; Warren Zevon; Department for management of major record producers, engineers, including Phil Ramone; George Massenburg. Recordings: Albums produced include: with 10,000 Maniacs: In My Tribe, 1987; Blind Man's Zoo, 1989; with Linda Ronstadt: Canciones De Mi Padre, 1987; Cry Like A Rainstorm, Howl Like The Wind, 1989; Frenesi, 1992; with Mary's Danish: American Standard, 1992; with Neil Diamond: The Christmas Album, 1992; The Christmas Album, Volume 2, 1994; with Randy Newman: Faust, 1995; Albums or tracks for: Paul Jones; Barbara Keith; Tony Kosinec; Jo Mama; John Stewart; Kate Taylor; Tony Joe White; Andrew Gold; John David Souther; Bonnie Raitt; Ronin; Cher; Peter Blakeley; Maria Mckee; Williams Brothers; Diana Ross; Julia Fordham; Ringo Starr; Olivia Newton-John; Laura Satterfield. Honours: 31 Gold, 19 Platinum albums, USA; 8 Grammy winning records; 2 Grammys, Producer Of The Year, 1978, 1989. Address: 644 N Doheny Drive, Los Angeles, CA 90069, USA.

ASHFORD Geoff, b. 23 Jan 1949, Leeds, Yorkshire, England. Singer; Songwriter. m. Patricia Harcourt, 2 sons. Musical Education: Private tuition. Career: Played on maiden voyage of Queen Elizabeth II; Played all major cabaret venues in UK, late 1970s - early 1980s; Small part Brideshead Revisited, Granada TV; Played Silk Cut Festival, Wembley, 1986. Recordings:

Charmer, 1974; Rags To Riches (Country hit), 1986; No Such Place As Heaven (Spanish Country hit), 1993. Honours: Winner, TDK, Sealink International, Song Contest, 1985. Memberships: PRS; MCPS. Hobby: Travel. Address: 17 Allerton Grange Way, Leeds LS17 6LP, England.

ASHFORD Nickolas (Nick), b. 4 May 1942, Fairfield, South Carolina, USA. Songwriter; Musician. m. Valerie Simpson, 1974. Career: Member, performing, recording, songwriting duo with Valerie Simpson; Later joined by Jo Armstead. Compositions: Co-writer, Never Had It So Good, Ronnie Milsap; One Step At A Time, Maxine Brown, The Shirelles; Let's Go Get Stoned, Ray Charles; Songs: Ain't No Mountain High Enough; You're All I Need To Get By; Reach Out And Touch Somebody's Hand; Remember Me. Recordings: with Valerie Simpson: Keep It Comin', 1973; Gimme Something Real, 1973; I Wanna Be Selfish, 1974; Come As You Are, 1976; So, So Satisfied, 1977; Send It, 1977; Is It Still Good To Ya?, 1978; Stay Free, 1979; A Musical Affair, 1980; Performance, 1981; Street Opera, 1982; High-Rise, 1983; Solid, 1984; Real Love, 1986; Love Or Physical, 1989; Hit singles: It Seems To Hang On, 1978; Found A Cure, 1979; Solid, 1984. Current Management: Hopsack and Silk Productions, 254 West 72nd Street, Suite 1A, New York, NY 10023, USA.

ASHLEY Steve (Stephen Frank Ashley), b. 9 Mar 1946, Perivale, London, England. Singer; Songwriter; Musician (guitar, bouzouki, harmonica, whistle). m. Elizabeth Mary Holborow, 1 son, 1 daughter. Education: DipAD (Hons), Maidstone. Career: Founder member, Albion Country Band, 1972; Formed Ragged Robin, 1973; Solo tours of Europe and USA; Television and radio appearances, 1974-79, including Family Album (performed with members of Fairport Convention); Peace Songs for CND; Formed Steve Ashley Band, 1983; Tours of Europe, including festivals at Glastonbury, Cambridge and Cropredy. Compositions: Songs: Fire And Wine; The Rough With The Smooth. Recordings: Stroll On, 1974; Speedy Return, 1975; Demo Tapes, 1980; Family Album, 1981; More Demo Tapes, 1983; Mysterious Ways, 1990. Memberships: MCPS; PRS. Hobbies: Painting; Photography. Current Management: Self-managed. Address: 87 Prestbury Road, Cheltenham, Gloucestershire GL52 2DR, England.

ASHTON Bill (William Michael), b. 6 Dec 1936, Blackpool, Lancashire, England. Musician (saxophones, clarinet); Composer; Bandleader; Songwriter; Journalist. Education: St Peter's College, Oxford; Degree, Modern Languages, DipEd. Career: Founder, University Dance Band The Ambassadors; OU Big Band; Founder, secretary, OU Modern Jazz Club; Taught in France, 1960-61; Played US bases with The Stardust Combo, Caveau Des Fouleurs, Chateaudun, France; Worked in Red Bludd's Bluesicians, London; Co-founder with Pat Evans, The London Schools Jazz Orchestra, later renamed The London Youth, then The National Youth Jazz Orchestra (NYJO); Worked full-time with NYJO, 1973-; With NYJO, played worldwide, made numerous television appearances, and recorded over 30 albums; Royal Variety Performance, 1978; Toured twice with Shorty Rogers, John Dankworth, John Williams, and many singers; Formed own publishing company, Stanza Music, 1967; Numerous compositions for NYJO. Honours: MBE; Inter-University Jazz Band Competition Award, 1962; Critics Choice, 1992, 1995; British Jazz Award, Best British Big Band, 1993, 1995; BBC Radio 2 Award, Services to Jazz, 1995; Fellow, Leeds College of Music, 1995. Address: NYJO Records, 11 Victor Road, Harrow, Middlesex HA2 6PT, England.

ASKEM Tracey J, b. 31 May 1970, Slough, England. Musician (saxophones, clarinet, flute, percussion). Musical Education: Graduate diploma in Light Music (Newcastle upon Tyne). Career: Ran 4 piece band The Groove Company with Martin Alker; 8 months on Sealink Ferries; 2 summers in Jersey for holiday camp; Local work for private functions and hotels; Butlins, backing artists including: Little and Large; David Copperfield; Charlie Daze; Soap stars including Coronation Street, Brookside, Emmerdale, 1995; Appeared Grampian TV Scots Away programme; Formed Traces of Red, 1996; Cruised on P&O's SS Canberra and MV Oriana, 1997. Recording: With Traces of Red: Just One of Those Days. Honours: Variety Club Award, Best Band in Jersey, 1993. Membership: Musicians' Union; Hobbies: Sewing; Reading. Address: 39 Meadow Way, Old Windsor, Berkshire SL4 2NX, England.

ASQUITH Stuart Andrew, b. 23 Sept 1971, Wakefield, England. Songwriter; Entertainer; Keyboards. Musical Education: Piano lessons, 4-8 years old; Moved on to keyboard lessons. Career: Made White Label dance record, under name, Mind Vacation, 1992. Changed name of band to: Lost In Process; Made demos, signed to Ouch! Records, 1995. Recordings: Aint We Funky/Sustain The Pressure; Pacemaker/We Can Do This; Rock On; Made In Rio; All recorded 1995. Membership: Musicians Union. Hobbies: Cars; Quad Racing; Socialising; Clubbing. Current Management: Ouch! Records. Address: Ouch! Records, Unit 5, Bowhouse Business Centre, 153-159 Bow Road, London E3 2SE, England.

ASTBURY Ian, b. 14 May 1962, Heswall, Merseyside, England. Vocalist. Career: Founder, Southern Death Cult, 1982; Re-named Death Cult, 1983; Re-named The Cult, 1984-; Headline tours include: UK, Europe, North America, Japan; Also tours with: Bauhaus, 1983; Big Country, 1984; Billy Idol, 1987; Guns N'Roses, 1987; Metallica, 1989; Lenny Kravitz 1991; Major concerts include: Futurama Festival, Leeds, 1983; A Gathering Of The Tribes Festival, California, 1990; Kick Out The Jams Festival, Detroit, 1992; Cult In The Park '92 Festival, Finsbury Park, London, 1992; Guns N' Roses concert, Milton Keynes, 1993. Recordings: Albums: Southern Death Cult, 1983; Dreamtime, 1984; Love, 1985; Electric, 1987; Sonic Temple, 1989; Ceremony, 1991; Pure Cult (Number 1, UK), 1993; The Cult, 1994; Singles include: Fat Man, 1983; Spiritwalker, 1984; She Sells Sanctuary, 1985; Rain, 1985; Love Removal Machine, 1987; Lil' Devil, 1987; Wild Flower, 1987; Fire Woman, 1989; Edie (Ciao Baby), 1989; Sweet Soul Sister, 1990; Wild Hearted Son, 1990. Address: 1880 Century Park East, Suite 900, Los Angeles, CA 90067-1609, USA.

ASTLEY Jon, b. 22 Jan 1951, Manchester, England. Record Producer. 2 daughters. Career: Producer, 1978-; 2 own records released as solo artist, songwriter, 1986, 1988. Recordings: Producer for: The Who; Eric Clapton; Phil Collins; Corey Hart; The Rolling Stones; Debbie Harry; The Eagles; Pete Townsend; LSO and LPO; Own recordings; Remixing and remastering extensive catalogues: The Who; Eric Clapton; Bob Dylan; Joni Mitchell. Memberships: MCPS; PRS. Current Management: A-Sharp Publishing Co. Address: 2 Embankment, Twickenham, TW1 3DH, England.

ASTLEY Rick, b. 6 Feb 1966, Warrington, Cheshire, England. Singer; Songwriter. Career: Drummer, school band, Give Way, 1982; Lead singer, FBI, 1984; Apprenticeship, Stock/Aitken/Waterman, 1985; Tape Operator PWL Studios, 1986; Solo artiste, 1987-; Numerous concerts include: Far East/Australian tour, 1988; Prince's Trust Concert, Royal Albert Hall, 1988; World tour, 1988-89; US tour, 1989. Albums: Whenever You Need Somebody (Number 1, UK), 1987; Hold Me In Your Arms, 1988; Free, 1991; Body And Soul, 1992; Hit singles include: Never Gonna Give You Up (Number 1, UK, US, 15 other countries), 1987; When I Fall In Love, 1987; Together Forever (Number 1, US), 1988; It Would Take A Strong Man, 1988; She Wants To Dance With Me, 1988; Take To Your Heart, 1988; Cry For Help, 1991. Honours: BRIT Award, Best British Single, Never Gonna Give You Up, 1988; 2 Billboard Awards, 1988. Current Management: Tony Henderson Management, 7 Cottingham Grove, Bletchley, Milton Keynes, Buckinghamshire MK3 5AA, England.

ASTON Michael Philip, b. 22 Aug 1957, Bridgend, South Wales. Musician; Artist; Singer. m. Margaret La Guardia, 23 June 1992. Career: Lead vocalist: Gene Loves Jezebel; Toured: USA; Europe; world; MTV Live At Ritz, NY; MTV New Tears Eve Ball; John Peel sessions, UK; Joan Rivers Show (Fox); Television: Japan; Italy; France; Argentina; Songs, various films; Film Role: She's Having My Baby, by John Hughes, 1986. Recordings: Gene Loves Jezebel: Promise; Immigrant; Discover; House Of Dolls; Solo album: Edith Grove, 1995. Publications: Gothic Rock (Black book); Various A-Z Rock. Honours: T J Martel MVP, 1995; Song of Year, Desire, College USA, 1986. Hobbies: Art; Record sleeves; Paintings. Current Management: William Morris (US). Address: 1419 N Hayworth Avenue, Los Angeles, CA 90046, USA.

ATANASSOV Tzvetelin (Elvis), b. 18 Aug 1971, Veliko Tarnovo, Bulgaria. Singer. Musical Education: Music, singing, with personal teacher, B Bogdanov. Career: Began career, 1990-; Concerts include: Show in Memory of Elvis, 1993; Concert, music of 1950s and 60s, 1993; Television Competition (first prize), 1992; Elvis Doubles Competition, Memphis, Tennessee, 1993; Tour, Bulgaria, 1994; Television, radio appearances include: New Year Shows on Bulgarian National television, 1993, 1994. Recordings: Debut album: Memory For Elvis (Most Popular in Billboard Elvis hits), 1993; Own Bulgarian album, 1995. Honours: Peugeot motorcycle (TV Competition) award, Youngest in Elvis Competition; Honoured Citizen, Tupelo, Mississippi, USA. Membership: President, Bulgarian Elvis Fan Club. Hobbies: Cinema; Cars; Ecology; Poetry. Current Management: Musical House Shanson-91. Address: Shanson-91, Liulin-4, bl 414, entr B, ap40, 1359 Sofia, Bulgaria.

ATKINS Bobby Lee, b. 22 May 1933, Surrey County, USA. Musician (guitar); Singer. m. Judy Smit, 4 Apr 1961, 6 sons, 1 daughter. Musical Education: Self-taught. Career: Began with Bill Monroe and the Bluegrass Boys; Played with Charlie Monroe, Flint Hill Playboys; Played with Joe Stone for 15 years; Played with Joe and the Dixie Mountaineers all over USA; Formed own band, Bobby Atkins and The Countrymen, 1967; Rated among the ten best banjo players in the world; Songwriter; Composer; Arranger; Music Publisher, Bob's Special Music Publishing Co; 2 film scores; Performed on stage with: Mac Wiseman; Clyde Moody; Jim Fanes; Radio with: Flatt and Scrugg; Don Reno; Red Smiley. Recordings: 50 albums including: Crimes of the Heart; Gold Hill Gold; The Best of Bobby Atkins, Mark Albin and the Country; The Country Side of Bobby Atkins. Honours: Songwriter of The Year, Hawaii; Represented in Bluegrass Hall Of Fame, Nashville, Tennessee; Top Male Vocal, Top Band, Top Musician; Top Songwriter; Living Legend Award, 1995. Memberships: Country and Bluegrass Music Association; Wall of Fame, New York, New York. Hobbies: Garden; Working in yard. Current Management: c/o Jolene Caudill, 1109 Cleburne Street, Greensboro, NC 27408, USA. Address: PO Box 251, Summerfield, NC 27358, USA.

ATKINS Chet (Chester Burton Atkins), b. 20 June 1924, Luttrell, Tennessee, USA. Musician (guitar); Record Producer; Record Company Executive. Career: Fiddler with the Dixieland Swingers, early 1940s; Recording artist, 1947-; First performance, Grand Ole Opry, 1948; Worked with Maybelle Carter; The Carter Family; Red Souvine; Hank Williams; The Everly Brothers; Producer, talent scout, RCA Records, 1950s;

Worked with: Elvis Presley; Jim Reeves; Don Gibson; Charley Pride; Waylon Jennings; Hank Snow; Jerry Reed; Perry Como. Recordings: Over 100 albums include: Chet Atkins' Gallopin' Guitar, 1953; Chet Atkins In Three Dimensions, 1956; Finger Style Guitar, 1958; Mister Guitar, 1959; Teensville, 1959; Chet Atkins' Workshop, 1960; Down Home, 1961; The Best Of Chet Atkins, 1963; Reminiscing, with Hank Snow, 1964; Chet Atkins Picks On The Beatles, 1965; Me And Jerry, with Jerry Reed, 1970; The Atkins-Travis Traveling Show, 1974; Chester And Lester, with Les Paul, 1975; Chet, Floyd and Danny, with Floyd Cramer, Danny Davis, 1977; Guitar Monsters, with Les Paul, 1978; The First Nashville Guitar Quartet, 1979; The Best Of Chet On The Road...Live, 1980; Reflections, with Doc Watson, 1980; Work It Out With Chet Atkins, 1983; Stay Tuned, 1985; Sails, 1987; Chet Atkins, CGP, 1988; Neck And Neck, with Mark Knopfler, 1992; Sneakin' Around, with Jerry Reed, 1992; Read My Licks, 1994. Honours: Several Grammy Awards; Inducted into Country Music Hall of Fame, 1973; Street in Nashville, and Gretsch guitar both named after him. Current Management: Fred Kewley Management, 1711 18th Avenue S, Suite D-3, Nashville, TN 37212, USA.

ATKINS Malcolm, b. 14 Oct 1956, Deal, Kent, England. Composer. m. Janet Luise Suan, 3 sons. Education: Degree Literature Humanities, Christ Church, Oxford. Musical Education: Self-taught. Career: Performed, recorded with numerous bands; Composer, Shoestring Theatre, 1992-; Tours, Europe, with bands: Dubweiser, Deltones, 1994, 1995; Part-time employment as specialist music teacher by Oxfordshire County Council, 1992-. Compositions: Numerous for amphonic music (sound library) played worldwide; Compositions, recordings for: Dubweiser; Ruthyou Driven (airplay in UK, Europe); Film music includes: Skin (highly acclaimed film, funded by Southern Arts); Theatre music, choral and incidental, for Shoestring Theatre, Agamemnon, Medea, Birds, others. Membership: PRS. Hobbies: Cinema; Computing. Current Management: Self-managed. Address: 41 Bullingdon Road, Oxford, OX4 1QJ, England.

AUBUT Lise, b. 29 Aug 1943, Lévis, Quebec, Canada. Songwriter; Impresario. Education: CEGEP. Career: Songwriter, 15 musical albums and over 150 songs. Compositions include: Hit songs: Paquetville, sung by Edith Butler; Un Million de Fois Je T'aime. Honours: 3 Felix Awards; 3 Platinum discs. Memberships: SPACQ; SODRAC; SACEM. Hobbies: Computers. Current Management: Self-managed. Address: 86 Côte Ste-Catherine, Outremont, Quebec H2V 2A3, Canada.

AUDETTE Matt b. 18 Dec 1956, Bellingham, Washington, USA. Country Recording Artist; Vocalist; Musician (guitar); Songwriter. Musical Education: Self-taught; 1 month private instruction. Career: Resort tours (Coast to Coast, Thousand Trails); TNN, Bittersweet; Rogers Cable, Vancouver; Handicapped Equestrian Fundraiser, Vancouver. Recordings: Tennessee Is Calling Back To Me; Battle Of Armageddon; She Rode Away With His Heart; Sparkle In Your Eye; Bittersweet; 1989-1993. Membership: BMI. Hobbies: Running; Walking; Civil War; Tennis; Instrument construction, radio control flight. Current Management: Self-managed. Address: 3302 Haynie Road, Blaine, WA 98230-9107, USA.

AUDIGANE Raymond-Sean, b. 12 January 1963, Toulon, France. Musician (Three Holes Pipe; Drums; French Horn Pipe). m. Armelle Gauthey, 5 October 1991, 1 son. Education: Fusion Music and Free Music, Traditional Music of Occitanie; Architecture (Plastician); Diplome d'Etat of Traditional Music. Career: Regional and national TV; Region French radio, Radio France; National tour in French with Pedro Aledo, 1989-90; L'Ensemble Méditerranéen with Pedro Aledo,

1991-92; Duo, Contes et Music, with Armelle Audigane, 1992-94; Music Creation, La Fête Des Fous, with Armelle Audigane, regional tour in Provence, 1994; National and regional tours with Rivatge, 1995-96; Cosmophonic, with David rue 1, 1996-97. Recordings: Compact discs: Contes et Musiques de la Mediterranée, 1994; Le Galoubet-Tambourin music from Yesterday and Today, 1995; Diliventi a Rosula, 1996; Cosmophonic, 1997. Memberships: Spedidam; Free Music Improvised Group, GRIM; Regional Mission in Traditional Music and Dance. Current Management: Art Traditional Production. Address: 1764 Avenue du Brusc, 83 140 Six Fours, France.

AUGER Brian Albert Gordon, b. 18 July 1939, London, England. Musician (organ, piano); Composer; Producer. m. Ella Natale, 14 Nov 1968, 1 son, 2 daughters. Musical Education: Mainly self-taught; 1 year, College of Marin, San Francisco, California. Career: Professional musician, 1963-; Performed with: Brian Auger Trinity; Brian Auger's Oblivion Express; Eric Burdon/Brian Auger Band; Worldwide tours; Major television shows in UK; Europe; USA; Japan; Czechoslovakia; Hungary; Greece; Radio appearances worldwide. Recordings: Number 1 single: This Wheel's On Fire, 1968; Albums: Brian Auger Trinity and Julie Driscoll: Open, 1967; Definitely What, 1968; Streetnoise, 1969; Brian Auger Trinity: Befour, 1970: Brian Auger's Oblivion Express: Oblivion Express, 1970; A Better Land, 1971; Second Wind, 1972; Closer To It, 1973; Straight Ahead, 1974; Reinforcements, 1975; Live Oblivion, Volume 1, 1975; Volume II, 1976; Happiness Heartaches, 1977; Encore, 1978; Planet Earth Calling, 1981; Here and Now, 1983; Keys To The Heart, 1987; Eric Burdon/Brian Auger Band: Access All Areas, 1993. Honours: Poll Winner, Jazz Piano and New Star categories, UK Melody Maker magazine, 1963; German Rock and Folk Best Jazz and Best Rock Organist, 1970; Best Jazz Organist, USA Keyboard Magazine, 1976, 1977. Address: c/o Steve Zelenka, Resource Management, 1341 Ocean Avenue #456, Santa Monica, CA 90401, USA.

AUGUSTINE Herbert Joseph, b. 6 Mar 1944, Belmont, Carriacou, Granada, West Indies. Lyric Writer; Vocalist; Musician (bass guitar, rhythm guitar, drums). m. 27 Oct 1983, 2 sons, 4 daughters. Musical Education; Self-taught. Career: 30 years playing; Performances: Netherlands; Denmark; Sweden; BBCTV Look North, early 1970s; Revolver, BBC2, late 1970s; Bubbling Under, Live concert, Leeds University, early 1980s; Big Day Out, Pebble Mill, BBCTV; Radio 1, Janice Long, 1986. Recordings: Socca Music; Loneliness Not Happiness; Keep On Smiling; Pity; Criticise. Hobbies: Listening; Playing; Writing lyrics; Dancing to music. Current Management: Self-managed.

AUSTEN Ed (Edward John Roberts), b. 22 Dec 1942, London, England. Musician (guitar, bass, mandolin); Vocalist. Musical Education: 1 year classical guitar; Then self-taught. Career: Worked with: The Who; Free; Derek and The Dominoes; Eric Clapton; The Hollies; Dave Dee; Cliff Bennett; Robert Fripp; Andy Summers; Many artistes on country music circuit. Membership: Musicians' Union. Hobbies: Martial arts (judo, karate, kendo); Leathercraft; Fishing; Photography. Address: 417 Wimbourne Road East, Ferndown, Dorset BH22 9L2, England.

AUSTIN Patti, b. 10 Aug 1948, California, USA. Singer; Entertainer. Career: Child performer from age 3; Appearances included Sammy Davis Jr television show; Theatre performances: Lost In The Stars; Finian's Rainbow; Tours with Quincy Jones, age 9; Harry Belafonte, age 16; Recording debut, age 17; Singer, television jingles, session work, 1970s; Worked with: Paul Simon; Billy Joel; Frankie Valli; Joe Cocker; George Benson; Roberta Flack; Marshall Tucker; Steely Dan; The Blues Brothers; Continued to work with Quincy

Jones. Recordings: Albums: End Of A Rainbow, 1976; Havana Candy, 1977; Live At The Bottom Line, 1979; Body Language, 1980; Every Home Should Have One, 1981; Patti Austin, 1984; Gettin' Away With Murder, 1985; The Real Me, 1988; Love's Gonna Get You, 1990; Carry On, 1991; Live, 1992; Singles: Family Tree, 1969; Every Home Should Have One; Razzmatazz (with Quincy Jones), 1981; The Dude, 1982; with James Ingram: Baby Come To Me, theme for television series General Hospital (Number 1, US), 1983; Film themes: Two Of A Kind, 1984; Shirley Valentine, 1988; Guest vocalist, album George Gershwin songs, Hollywood Bowl Orchestra, 1992. Honour: Grammy Award, The Dude, 1982.

AUTRY (Orvon) Gene, b. 29 Sept 1907, Tioga, Texas, USA. Country Singer; Musician (guitar); Radio Entertainer; Actor; Broadcasting Executive; Baseball Team Executive. m. (1) Ina Mae Spivey, 1 Apr 1932; (2) Jacqueline Ellam, 1981. Career: Railroad telegraph operator, Oklahoma, 1925; Singer, Tulsa radio station as "Oklahoma Yodeling Cowboy"; Recording artist, 1929-; Radio appearances: National Barn Dance, 1931-34; Host, Conqueror Record Time; Melody Ranch, 1940-56; Actor, 1934-53; 89 film appearances include: In Old Santa Fe; Tumbling Tumbleweeds; President, Flying A Productions; Television productions include: Gene Autry Show, 1950-55; Champion The Wonder Horse; Annie Oakley; The Range Rider; Owner, chairman, California Angels baseball team; Owner, radio stations in Hollywood and Seattle; President, several music and publishing companies. Compositions: Over 200 songs. Recordings: Hits include: That Silver-Haired Daddy Of Mine; Be Honest With Me; Back In The Saddle Again; Goodbye, Little Darlin,' Goodbye; You're The Only Star In My Blue Heaven; Dust; Tears On My Pillow; Be Honest With Me; Tweedle O'Twill; Here Comes Santa Claus; Rudolph The Red-Nosed Reindeer; Frosty The Snowman; Peter Cottontail; Buttons And Bows. Publication: Back In The Saddle Again, with Mickey Herskowitz. Honours: Inducted into Country Music Hall of Fame, 1969; Cowboy Hall Of Fame Of Great Westerners, 1980. Address: c/o California Angels, PO Box 2000, Anaheim, CA 92803, USA.

AVALON Frankie (Francis Avallone), b. 18 Sept 1939, Philadelphia, Pennsylvania, USA. Singer; Musician (trumpet); Actor. m. Kay Avalon, 4 sons, 4 daughters. Career: Began playing trumpet with Rocco and The Saints; Television appearances include: Patti Duke Show; Ed Sullivan Show; Pat Boone Show; Perry Como Show; Milton Berle Show; American Bandstand; Hullaballoo; Steve Allen Show; Dinah Shore Show; Film appearances include: Jamboree, 1957; Guns Of The Timberland, 1960; The Alamo, 1960; Sail A Crooked Ship, 1962; Voyage To The Bottom Of The Sea, 1962; Beach Party, 1963; Bikini Beach, 1964; Muscle Beach Pary, 1964; The Carpetbaggers, 1964; Beach Blanket Bingo, 1965; I'll Take Sweden, 1965; Sergeant Deadhead, 1966; Fireball 500, 1966; How To Stuff A Wild Bikini, 1966; Skidoo, 1968; The Take, 1974; Grease, 1978; Back To The Beach, 1987; Appearances include: Alan Freed's New York Christmas Rock'n'Roll Spectacular, 1959; Saturday Night At The London Palladium, ITV, 1967; American Bandstand's 20th Anniversary Special, ABC, 1973; Easy Does It - Starring Frankie Avalon, CBS, 1976. Recordings include: Dede Dinah, 1957; Venus, 1959; Bobby Sox To Stockings, 1959; A Boy Without A Girl, 1959; Just Ask Your Heart, 1959; Why (Number 1, US), 1960; Albums: Swingin' On A Rainbow, 1960; A Whole Lotta Frankie, 1961. Honours include: Star on Hollywood Walk Of Fame, 1992. Current Management: Fox Entertainment, 1650 Broadway, Suite 503, New York, NY 10019, USA.

AVON Alan, b. 25 Dec 1945, England. Vocalist; Actor; Songwriter. Musical Education: Private Music; Drama Tuition. Career: Backing and session vocalist, London, 1960s; Lead vocalist, Hedgehoppers Anonymous; Toured Europe, Southern Africa, UK, 1965-72; Solo artiste, 1972-; Numerous radio, television, and record apperances; Now presenter, commercial radio. Recordings: Hit single: Good News Week, Hedgehoppers Anonymous, 1965; Compositions featured on other artists' albums. Honours: 3 SARI Awards: Best Male Vocalist; Best Album; Best British Group, 1972. Memberships: Equity; British Academy of Songwriters, Composers and Authors. Hobby: Music. Current Management: Dinosaur Promotions. Address: 5 Heyburn Crescent, Westport Gardens, Stoke On Trent, Staffordshire ST6 4DL, England.

AXELROD John, b. 28 Mar 1966, Houston, Texas, USA. Composer; Conductor; Management. m. Barbara Vandenlinde, 9 June 1992. Education: BA, Harvard University, 1988. Career: A&R, for record labels: RCA/BMG, Atlantic; Music publishing: Rondor Music International; Music supervision: Television Program Enterprises: Entertainment planning: Robert Mondori Wilerry; Management: Iron John Management. Recordings: How Do I Love Thee... Love Songs For The Romantic At Heart. Publications: Music Connection, Billboard Magazine. Memberships: BMI; NARAS; NAS. Hobbies: Wine; Travel; Sports; Piano. Current Management: 11333 Moorpark #177, North Hollywood, CA 91602, USA.

AXLER Arnaud, b. France. Musician (guitar); Educator. Career: Jazz musician, 1979-; Played clubs in Paris; Member of trio with N'Guyen Lé and Serge Merlaud, 1974-84; Performed with Eric Barret; Lionel Belmondo; Pete King; Tony Pagano; Emmanuel Bex, 1984; Formed own big band and Latin ensemble, Som Latinos; Played at festivals: Parthenay; Nantes; Joué-Les-Tours; Educator: Professor of guitar, les Maisons des Jeunes et de la Culture (MJC), 1980-84; Professor, L'Ecole de Jazz Nantes, 1984-90. Membership: Diplome d'Etat De Professeur De Musique Jazz.

AXTON Hoyt Wayne, b. 23 Mar 1938, Duncan, Oklahoma, USA. Singer; Songwriter; Composer; Actor. m. Donna Axton, 2 sons, 1 daughter. Education: Oklahoma State University, 1957-58. Career: Recording artist, 1962-; Film appearances include: Black Stallion, 1980; Junk Man, 1981; Liar's Moon, 1982; Endangered Species, 1983; Gremlins, 1984; Television includes: Dinah Shore Show; The Hoyt Axton Country Western, Boogie Woogie, Gospel Rock and Roll Show; Midnight Special; Johnny Carson Show; Hee Haw; Music Hall America; Nashville On The Road; Barbara Mandrell Show; Dukes Of Hazard; Diff'rent Strokes; Star Search; Nashville Now; Also record producer, music publisher; President, Jeremiah Records, 1979-; Performer, Grand Ole Opry, Nashville, 1974-. Compositions include: Greenback Dollar, Kingston Trio; The Pusher, Steppenwolf; No No Song, Ringo Starr; Joy To The World, Three Dog Night; Never Been To Spain; When The Morning Comes; Boney Fingers; Ease Your Pain; Less Than A Song. Recordings: Numerous albums include: The Balladeer, 1962; Greenback Dollar, 1964; My Griffin Is Gone, 1969; Joy To The World, 1971; Less Than A Song, 1973; Life Machine, 1974; Southbound, 1975; Free Sailin', 1978; Where Did The Money Go, 1980; Everybody's Going On The Road, 1982; Spin Of The Wheel, 1991. Publications: Author, illustrator, Line Drawings, Vols I-V, 1974-78; Songbooks: Life Machine; 1973; Southbound, 1975; Less Than A Song, 1977. Memberships include: CMA; AFofM; AFTRA; Screen Actors Guild; BMI. Address: c/o Hoyt Axton Enterprises, PO Box 976, Hendersonville, TN 37077, USA.

AYERS Ben. Musician (multi-instrumentalist); Songwriter. Career: Musician and singer, Cornershop. Recordings include: Albums: Elvis Sex Change, 1993; Hold On It Hurts, 1994;

Woman's Gotta Have It, 1995; I Was Born For The Seventh Time, 1997; Hit single: Brimful Of Asha (Number 1, UK), 1998. Address: c/o Oasis Productions, 909 Hudson Street, Suite 2, Hoboken, NJ 07030, USA.

AYERS Nigel, b. 3 July 1957, Tideswell, Derbyshire, England. Composer; Visual Artist. Education: BA, Honours, Fine Art, Sculpture, 1977. Musical Education: Self-taught. Career: Founder pioneering multi-media performance group Nocturnal Emissions, 1978; Business ventures: Record labels: Sterile Records, 1978; Earthly Delights, 1987-; Tours: Europe; USA; Canada, including performances with Butch Dance Company: Poppo and the GoGo Boys; Exhibitions of video work in Tate Gallery and ICA, London; Soundtracks for film work by Charlotte Bill. Recordings include: Tissue Of Lies, 1978; Drowning In A Sea Of Bliss, 1982; Viral Shedding, 1983; Befehlsnotstand, 1984; Spiritflesh, 1988; Magnetized Light, 1993; Imaginary Time, 1995. Publications: Network News, Vegetation Flesh, 1995. Honour: Meet The Composer, New York City, 1992. Memberships: MCPS; PRS; PPL. Hobbies: Reading; Walking; Inventing. Current Management: Earthly Delights. Address: PO Box 2, Lostwithiel, Cornwall PL22 OYY, England.

AYERS Roy, b. 10 September 1940, Los Angeles, CA, USA. Vibraphone. m. Argerie J Ayers, 20 July 1973, 2 sons, 1 daughter. Education: Selftaught Musician. Career: Appeared on Mew Griffin Johnny Carson, Jay Leno and most Jazz festivals throughout the world; Live on BBC Hammersmith Odeon London, many times; Live film, Ronnie Scotts Jazz House London. Compositions: Everybody Loves the Sunshine; Running Away; Love Will Bring Us Back; Searching; Most Sampled Composer, by most major Rap Groups, 1988-97. Recordings: Recorded 80 CD's or LP's including: Wayne Henderson, 1980; Music of Many Colors, 1980; Pre-Mixture, 1981; Center of the World, 1981; Feeling Good, 1982; Lots of Love, 1983; Silver Vibrations, 1983; Drivin' On Up, 1983; Lots of Love, 1983; Poo Poo La La, single, 12"; In the Dark, 1984. Publications: Leonard Feather, Encyclopedia of Jazz, 2nd Edition, 1960-65. Honours: New Star on Vibes Downbeat Mag, 1966; American Music Award, 1977; Louis Armstrong Award, 1978; Best Song of Year, Get Money, 1997. Memberships: ASCAP; Local 802; American Federation of Musicians. Hobbies: Plays Chess; Running. Current Management: Roy Ayers, PO Box 1219, New York, NY 10023, USA. Address: PO Box 1219, New York, NY 10023, USA.

AYICK Paul, b. 28 May 1947, Paterson, New Jersey, USA. Musician (trumpet); Composer. m. Rose Marie Kissel, 6 Jan 1984, 1 daughter. Musical Education: NYCOM, 1967-69; NYU, 1969-71. Career: Trumpeter with Ray Fernandez, 1972-75; Hugh Brodie, 1975-78; Leader, Paul Ayick Quintet,1978-88; Co-leader with Ira Sullivan, 1990; Also appeared with: Les Elgant; Ray Anthony; John Spider Martin; Little Anthony; Paul Cohen; Gene Krupa Band. Recordings: Currently recording project for trumpet, synthesiser. Publications: Photographer, contributor, journals and magazines. Membership: AFofM. Hobby: Photography. Current Management: Gemini Productions. Address: 4800 SW 70th Terrace, Davie, FL 33314, USA.

AYRES Mark Richard, b. 28 Dec 1960, London, England. Composer. m. Nicola Jane, 11 Sept 1993, 1 son. Musical Education: BSc Hons, Music, Electronics, University of Keele. Career: Composer of music for films including: The Innocent Sleep; Television including: Doctor Who, BBC TV, 1988-89. Compositions: Soundtracks: The Innocent Sleep, for soprano, orchestra; Doctor Who; Numerous arrangements of film, TV themes, for album release. Memberships: APC (Association Professional Composers); Musicians'

Union; PRS; MCPS. Hobby: Meeting deadlines. Address: London, England.

AYTON Peter Edward, b. 31 Mar 1947, Redcar, England. Musician (double bass, bass guitar). m. Robina Ayton, 1 son, 2 daughters. Education: BSc (Hons) degree. Musical Education: LLCM. Career: Extensive session work in studios; Television and radio appearances; Worked with various major artists including: Nancy Wilson; James Moody; Jimmy Witherspoon; Harry Edison; Louis Stewart; Former visiting lecturer in Music, New College, Durham, and Newcastle College; Tutor, rock and jazz workshops. Membership: Musicians' Union. Address: 7-9 Albany Road, Norton, Stockton-on-Tees, Cleveland TS20 2QX, England.

AZNAVOUR Charles (Varenagh Aznavourian), b. 22 May 1924, Paris, France. Singer; Actor. m. (1) Micheline Rugel, 1946, (2) Evelyene Plessis, 1955, (3) Ulla Thorsel, 1967, 5 children (1 deceased). Education: Ecole Centrale de TSF. Career: Centre de Spectacle, Paris; Jean Dasté Company, 1941; Les Fâcheux, Arlequin, 1944; Numerous film appearances, 1964-; Compositions include: Songs: Il Pleut; Le Feutre Tropez; Jezebel (all recorded by Edith Piaf); Hier Encore (Yesterday When I Was Young); The Old Fashioned Way; She (theme for ITV series, The Seven Faces Of Woman); What Makes A Man; Happy Anniversary. Recordings: Albums include: Charles Aznavour Sings, 1963; Qui, 1964; Et Voici, 1964; Sings His Love Songs In English, 1965; Encore, 1966; De T'Avoir Aimée, 1966; Désormais, 1972; Chez Lui A Paris, 1973; A Tapestry Of Dreams, 1974; I Sing For You, 1975; In Times To Be, 1983. Honours: Chevalier Légion d'Honneur, Des Arts et Lettres; Grand Prix National de la Chanson, 1986. Address: c/o Lévon Sayan, 76-78 Avenue des Champs Elysées, Bureau 322, 75008 Paris, France.

AZRAK Janice, b. 12 Dec 1951, Brooklyn, New York, USA. Record Company Executive. Career: Publicist, MCA Records, New York, 1971-76, SIR Productions, New York, 1976-77; Vice-president, Creative Services/Artist Development, Warner Brothers Records, Nashville, 1977-. Membership: Vice-President, Board Of Directors, Academy of Country Music, 1985-86. Address: c/o Warner Brothers Records, 20 Music Street East, Nashville, TN 37203, USA.

AZZI María Susana, b. 12 Oct 1952, Buenos Aires, Argentina. Social Anthropologist. Education: Licenciada en Ciencias Antropólogicas, Universidad de Buenos Aires, 1987; Columbia University, New York, 1986; MBA, Escuela Superior de Economía y Administración de Empresas, Buenos Aires; Piano Lessons with Teresa Eichelbaum, 1984-92, Vera Anosova, 1992-95. Career: Professor, Board Member, Academia Nacional del Tango, Buenos Aires; Lecturer on the Tango and Astor Piazzolla in Argentina, USA, Europe, Australia, Mexico and Korea; Television and radio appearances in Argentina and UK; Consultant work for: Sony Classical (US), Dance Perspectives Foundation and Metropolitan Museum of Art, Metropolitan Museum of Art, New York; Smithsonian Institution, Washington DC; Fundación Astor Piazzolla and Instituto Nacional de Antropología, Buenos Aires, Argentina. Publications include: Italian Immigration And Their Impact On The Tango In Argentina, 1997; Tango Album by Yo-Yo Ma, 1997; Tango Argentino, 1998; Memberships include: Academia Nacional del Tango; Society for Ethnomusicology; American Anthropological Association; International Council for Traditional Music; International Association for the Study of Popular Music. Hobby: Golf. Address: Posadas 1612 8 piso, Buenos Aires 1112, Argentina.

B

BABCOCK ARNCE Delores Myrtle, b. 3 Oct 1938, Reedsburg, Wisconsin, USA. Musician (guitar). 2 sons, 1 daughter. Education: Matc Reedsburg, Computers. Musical Education: 18 months guitar; 6 months accordion. Career: Performances, airplay of original work, Southern Wisconsin; Participated in opening shows of the Williams and Ree Show, Ho-Chenck Casino. Recordings: I Can Feel You All Over Again, 1995; Over Our Country's Land (dedicated to Oklahoma City tragedy), 1995. Publications: Songwriter of Wisconsin. Honours: Poetry Awards; Poetry, singing; Demo work; Swimming; Walking. Current Management: Circus City Sounds Publishing BMI. Address: Songwriters of WI, PO Box 874, Neemah, WI 5495-0874, USA.

BABULJAK Karel, b. 5 October 1957, Prague, Czech Republic. Musician (Keyboards, Zither); Composer. m. Tereza, 22 June 1996, 2 sons, 1 daughter. Career: Broadrange Musician & Composer, pop music, new age, made demonic experiments; Founder Member of Groups: Relaxace; Ma'ma Bubo; Vopruz; Sajkedelik Sraml Band, 1992; Babalet, Experimental Solo Projects - Firms Bubosound; Sound & Silence; Cooperation with Prague 5. Compositions: A Mass of La'ny; Both Ways; An Organ Meditation; A Man With a Knapsack; A Meeting Silence; Czech Koan. Recordings: Solo Albums: A Man with a Knapsack, 1996; Contributor: Ma'ma Bubo: Ball-Shapedness, 1983-85; Rakish Ma, 1985; Planet Hay, 1985; Babalet-Live, 1987; Relaxace-Dhjana, 1991; Kadael, 1993; Flower Reggae, 1995. Hobbies: Sport; Gardening; Work of all kinds. Current Management: Sound & Silence Lewiathan. Address: Na'drazni 213, 33805 My'to v Cecha'ch, Czech Republic.

BACCHUS Brian Michel, b. 8 Aug 1957, New York, New York, USA. Record Company Executive; Record Producer. Education: AB, Syracuse University, 1980. Career: National Jazz Promotions Co-ordinator, Polygram Records, New York, 1986-87; Manager, National Jazz Promotions, 1987-88; Director, Jazz Promotion, 1988-90; Director, Antilles Records/Island Records, New York, 1990-. Recordings: Producer of albums: Remembrance, The Harper Brothers, 1990; Music Inside, Joyce, 1990; Amazon Secrets, Ricardo Silveira, 1990. Honours: Billboard Award, Top Jazz Album, Remembrance, 1990. Address: c/o Antilles Records, 825 8th Avenue, New York, NY 10019, USA.

BACCHUS Stephen, b. 11 Feb 1959, Toronto, Ontario, Canada. Musician (synthesizers). Musical Education: BFA York University. Career: Composer; Record Label President; Producer. Recordings: Pangaea, 1991; Ancient Mysteries, 1993; Bardo, 1996. Membership: SOCAN. Hobbies: Yoga; Graphic Designer. Current Management: Oasis Productions Ltd. Address: 76 Cadorna Avenue, Toronto, Ontario, M4J 3X1, Canada.

BACH Sebastian (Sebastian Bierk), b. 3 Apr 1968, Bahamas. Rock Vocalist; Lyricist. m. Maria Aquinar, 1992. Lead singer, US rock group Skid Row, 1986-; Major appearances include: Support to Bon Jovi, US tour, 1988; Support to Guns'N'Roses, US tour, 1991; European tour, 1992; US tour, 1992; Earth Pledge Concert, Central Park, New York, 1992; South American tour, 1992; Monsters Of Rock Festival, Castle Donington, 1992; Japanese tour, 1992. Recordings: Albums: Skid Row, 1989; Slave To The Grind (Number 1, US), 1991; B-Sides Ourselves, 1992; Subhuman Race, 1995; Singles: Youth Gone Wild, 1989; 18 And Life, 1989; I Remember You, 1990; Monkey Business, 1991; Slave To The Grind, 1991; Wasted Time, 1991. Honours include: Gold discs; American Music Awards, Favourite New Hard Rock Artist, 1990. Current Management: Doc McGhee, McGhee Entertainment, 8730 Sunset Boulevard, Ste 175, Los Angeles, CA 90069, USA.

BACHARACH Burt, b. 12 May 1928, Kansas City, Missouri, USA. Composer; Arranger; Conductor; Musician (piano). m. (1) Paula Stewart, (2) Angie Dickinson, (3) Carole Bayer Sager, 1982, 1 son, 1 daughter. Musical Education: Composition and Theory, McGill University, Montreal; Music Academy West, Santa Barbara. Career: Jazz musician, 1940s; Accompanist, arranger, conductor, various artists including Vic Damone; Marlene Dietrich; Joel Gray; Steve Lawrence. Compositions: Popular songs, film music and stage musicals; Regular collaborations with Hal David, 1962-70; Carole Bayer Sager, 1981-; Numerous hit songs as co-writer include: with Hal David: The Story Of My Life, Marty Robbins; Magic Moments, Perry Como; Tower Of Strength, Frankie Vaughan; Wives And Lovers, Jack Jones; 24 Hours From Tulsa, Gene Pitney; What The World Needs Now Is Love, Jackie DeShannon; Walk On By; Trains And Boats And Planes; Do You Know The Way To San Jose?; Alfie (all by Dionne Warwick); Anyone Who Had A Heart, Cilla Black; There's Always Something There To Remind Me, Sandie Shaw; Make It Easy On Yourself, Walker Brothers; What's New Pussycat?, Tom Jones; This Guy's In Love With You, Herb Alpert; Raindrops Keep Fallin' On My Head, Sacha Distel; Close To You, The Carpenters; Numerous film scores include: The Man Who Shot Liberty Valence; Wives And Lovers; What's New Pussycat?; Alfie; Casino Royale; Butch Cassidy And The Sundance Kid; with Carole Bayer Sager: Making Love, Roberta Flack; Heartlight, Neil Diamond; That's What Friends Are For, Dionne Warwick And Friends (AIDs charity record); Own My Own, Patti Labelle and Michael McDonald; with Carole Bayer Sager, Peter Allen and Christopher Cross: Arthur's Theme, Christopher Cross. Recordings: Albums include: Hit Maker, 1965; Reach Out, 1967; Make It Easy On Yourself, 1969; Burt Bacharach, 1971; Portrait In Music, 1971; Living Together, 1973; Greatest Hits, 1974; Futures, 1977; Woman, 1979; Publications: Numerous songbooks. Honours: Entertainers Of The Year, with Hal David, Cue Magazine, 1969; 3 Academy Awards; Several Academy Award Nominations; 4 Grammy Awards; 2 Emmy Awards; 1 Tony Award. Address: c/o McMullen And Co, Hollywood, CA, USA.

BACHET Laurent, b. 22 July 1964, Paris, France. Musician (guitar, bass, keyboards). Education: BA (Hons), Communications/Advertising. Career: Touch Sensitive, UK and Canadian tour, 1988, 1989. Recordings: Albums: with Touch Sensitive: Don't Cry, 1988; with Between The Sheets: Whenever, 1993; With Massimo Morsello: Punto Di Non Ritorno, 1995, Poker di Stelle, 1997. Membership: Musician's Union. Hobbies: Languages; Computers; Travel. Address: Flat 4, 13 Beckenham Road, Beckenham, Kent BR3 4PL, England.

BACHMAN Randy, b. 27 Sept 1943, Winnipeg, Manitoba, Canada. Singer; Musician (guitar); Songwriter. Career: Member, Guess Who; Founder member, Brave Belt; Reformed as Bachman-Turner Overdrive, 1972-76; Solo career, 1977-79; Founder member, Ironhorse, 1979; Union, 1981; Solo artist, 1981-; Tours with reformed Guess Who, 1984. Compositions include: You Ain't Seen Nothing Yet. Recordings: with Bachman-Turner Overdrive: Singles: Let It Ride, 1974; Takin' Care Of Business, 1974; You Ain't Seen Nothing Yet (Number 1, US), 1974; Roll On Down The Highway, 1975; Hey You, 1975; Albums: Bachman-Turner Overdrive, 1973; Bachman-Turner Overdrive 2, 1974; Not Fragile (Number 1, US), 1974; BTO As Brave Belt, 1975; Four-Wheel Drive, 1975; Head On, 1976; The Best Of BTO (So Far), 1976; Bachman-Turner Overdrive, 1984; Solo albums: Axe, 1972; Survivor, 1978; Any Road (featuring Neil Young), 1993; with Ironhorse: Ironhorse, 1979; Everything Is Grey, 1979; with Union: on Strike, 1981. Current Management: c/o S.L. Feldman, 1505 W Second Avenue, Suite 200, Vancouver, British Columbia V6H 3Y4, Canada.

BACKER Matthew De Bracey, b. New Orleans, Louisiana, USA. Musician (guitar); Vocalist; Songwriter. m. Elisa Richards, 5 Jan 1994. Education: BA Hons, University of Warwick. Musical Education: Berklee College of Music, Boston, USA. Career: Recordings, performances, television appearances with: Sinéad O'Connor; Elton John; Marcella Detroit; Aimee Mann; Emmylou Harris; Mica Paris; Joe Cocker; Swing Out Sister; Beautiful South; Sarah Jane Morris; Michael Ball; Suzanne Rhatigan; Jools Holland; Soundtrack work for television programmes including Equinox; Cracker; Spitting Image; Knowing Me Knowing You; Rory Bremner; Solo and collaborative singing/songwriting, and session work. Membership: Musicians' Union.

BADLEY Bill, b. Wiltshire, England. Musician (guitar, banjo, mandolin, lute); Vocalist. Education: Medieval Studies, Exeter University. Musical Education: Lute, Royal College of Music. Career: Played with: The Consort Of Musicke; The New London Consort; The Dufay Collective; Own group, Arcadia; Film work includes: Lady Jane; Caravaggio; Member, The Carnival Band, 1984-; First performance, Burnley Canalside Festival, 1984; Play material from: Sweden; Croatia; US; Bolivia; Spain; UK; France; Appearances include: festivals, arts theatres and centres; Barbican Centre; Glasgow Cathedral; Birmingham Symphony Hall; Assistant producer, Thames Television. Recordings include: Album with Maddy Prior: Christmas Carols. Current Management: c/o Jim McPhee, Acorn Entertainments. Address: Winterfold House, 46 Woodfield Road, Kings Heath, Birmingham B13 9UJ, England.

BAEZ Joan, b. 9 Jan 1941, Staten Island, New York, USA. Singer. m. David Harris, 26 Mar 1968, divorced 1974, 1 son. Education: Boston University, 1958; Doctor Humane Letters, Antioch University, 1980; Rutgers University, 1980. Recordings: Albums include: Joan Baez, 1960; Joan Baez, Vol 2, 1961; In Concert, part 2, 1963; 5, 1964; Farewell Angelina, 1965; Noel, 1966; Joan, 1967; Baptism, 1968; Any Day Now, 1968; David's Album, 1969; One Day At A Time, 1969; First Ten Years, 1970; Carry It On (soundtrack), 1971; Ballad Book, 1972; Come From The Shadows, 1972; Where Are You Now My Son?, 1973; Hits - Greatest And Others, 1973; Gracias A La Vida, 1974; Contemporary Ballad Book, 1974; Diamonds And Rust, 1975; From Every Stage, 1976; Gulf Winds, 1976; Blowin' Away, 1977; Best Of, 1977; Honest Lullaby, 1979; Very Early Joan, 1982; Recently, 1987; Diamonds And Rust In The Bullring, 1989; Speaking Of Dreams, 1989; Play Me Backwards, 1992; Rare Live And Classic, 1993; Ring Them Bells, 1995; Gone from Danger, 1997. Publications: Joan Baez Songbook, 1964; Daybreak, 1968; Coming Out (with David Harris), 1971; And Then I Wrote (songbook), 1979; And A Voice To Sing With: A Memoir, 1987. Honours: 8 Gold albums; 1 Gold single; Joan Baez Day In Atlanta, Georgia, 2 Aug 1975; Thomas Merton Award, 1976; Public Service, 3rd Annual Rock Music, 1977; Best Female Vocalist, Bay Area Music, 1978, 1979; ACLU Awards, 1979, 1989; Jefferson Award, 1980; Lennon Peace Tribute, 1982; ADA Award, 1982; Sane Education Fund Peace, 1983; Chevalier, Legion of Honour, France, 1983; Academy Charles Cros (France), 1983; Death Penalty Focus, California, 1992. Memberships include: Founder, Institute Study Nonviolence, 1965; Founder, President, Humanitas International Human Rights Committee, 1979-1992. Address: PO Box 1026, Menlo Park, CA 94026, USA.

BAGGE Nigel, b. 6 June 1953, London, England. Musician (guitarist); Singer; Songwriter. Musical Education: Self-taught. Career: Extensive gigging, bands include: Cold Comfort, 1970s; Highway 61, 1985-90; Duck Soup, 1990-93; Bag Band, 1992-93; Juice On The Loose, 1990; Nicky Moore's Blues Corporation, 1993-; Various session work. Recordings: Albums: Cold Comfort: In The Can; Highway 61: Talk To Me; Further Up The Road; Nicky Moore's Blues Corporation: I Just Got Back; Holding On. Membership: Musicians' Union. Current Management: Steppin' Out Ltd. Address: PO Box 216, Sevenoaks, Kent TN13 3ZT, England.

BAHRI Mamdouh, b. 31 July 1957, Sfax, Tunisia. Musician (guitar). m. Geva Nouyrit, 24 July 1993, 1 son, 1 daughter. Education: Maths, technical studies. Musical Education: Swiss Jazz School; Seminars with Joe Diorio, Jim Hall, John Abercrombie. Career: Festival Jazz D'0-Beziers, 1989; Bastia Festival, 1990; Carthage Music Festival, Tunisia, 1991; New Yok, Blue Note, 1992, 95; Romans Festival, 1993; Pori Jazz Festival, Finland, 1995; Sweet Basil, 1995; Appearances in USA: New York; Alabama; Connecticut; Maryland. Recordings: From Tunisia With Love, The Spirit of Life Ensemble, 1992; Mamoudh Bahri - Nefta, 1993; Inspirations, 1993; Feel The Spirit, 1994; Live At The S Spot, 1995. Memberships: SACEM; SPEDIDAM; ADAMI. Address: 4 Lot Bonnier D'Alco, 34990 Juvignac, France.

BAIKIE Pete, b. 17 Apr 1957, Edinburgh, Scotland. Composer; Writer; Comedian; Musician (guitar); Actor. Education: Edinburgh University. Musical Education: Self-taught. Career: Actor, writer, 4 CH4 television series, Absolutely; Actor, writer, CH4 television series, Squawkie Talkie; Actor, role of Bandleader, Swing Kids (Disney film). Compositions: Television themes for: Vic and Bob's Shooting Stars, BBC2; Absolutely; Squawkie Talkie; Teenage Health Freak, CH4; Radio themes for: Labour Exchange; If You're So Clever; The Preventers, BBC Radio 4. Memberships: Musicians' Union; BASCA. Hobbies: Snorkelling. Current Management: Michael Foster/ICM and Leah Schmidt. Address: Absolutely Productions, 6/7 Fareman Street, London W1V 3AH, England.

BAILEY Derek, b. 29 Jan 1930, Sheffield, Yorkshire, England. Musician (guitar). 1 son. Musical Education: Music with C H C Biltcliffe; Guitar with George Wing, Jack Duarte, and others. Career: Orchestralguitarist, 1951-65; Soloist, 1965-; Performed solo concerts, most of world's cultural centres; Played with most of musicians associated with freely improvised music. Recordings: Recorded over 100 albums on many labels; Recorded with: Company; Cecil Taylor; Han Bennink; Anthony Braxton; Steve Lacey. Publications: Improvisation - Its Nature And Practice. Current Management: Incus Records. Address: 14 Downs Road, London E5 8DS, England.

BAILEY Jim, b. 10 Jan 1948, Philadelphia, USA. Singr; Actor; Entertainer. Musical Education: Voice, piano, Philadelphia Conservatory of Music. Career; Concerts worldwide include: Carnegie Hall, Las Vegas; Top casinos; London Palladium; Specials: Superbowl; Olympics; Peoples Choice Awards; Royal Variety (twice); TV shows: about 40 include: Here's Lucy; Vegas; Rockford Files; Carol Burnett Show; Ed Sullivan; Tonight Show; Des O'Connor; Russell Harty; Pebble Mill. Recordings: Jim Bailey Live At Carnegie Hall; Jim Bailey; Also performed for 3 US presidents. Honours: Las Vegas Entertainer of the Year, 4 times; Peoples Choice Award; IPA Award, 2 times; Many theatre awards. Hobbies: Film and book collector; Pool. Current Management: Stephen Campbell Management. Address: 350 N Crescent Drive, Suite 105, Beverly Hills, CA 90210, USA.

BAILEY Philip, b. 8 May 1951, Denver, Colorado, USA. Vocalist; Musician (percussion); Producer. Career: Musical director, gospel group The Stovall Sisters; Member, Friends And Love; Member, Earth Wind and Fire, 1972-84, 1987-; Solo recording artiste, 1983-86; Peformances include: Opened for Sly and The Family Stone, Madison Square Gardens, 1974; Featured as rock band in film, Shining Star, 1975; Tours, US, Europe, Asia, 1979; Music for UNICEF Concert, UN, New York, 1979; Earth Pledge Concert, Central Park, New York, 1992. Recordings: Albums: Last Days And Time, 1972; Head To The Sky, 1973; Open Our Eyes, 1973; That's The Way Of The World, 1975; Gratitude, 1976; Spirit, 1976; All `N' All, 1978; The Best Of, Vol 1, 1979; I Am, 1979; Faces, 1980; Raise, 1981; Powerlight, 1983; Heritage, 1990; The Wonders Of His Love, 1984; Inside Out, 1986; Triumph, 1986; Wonders Of Love, 1988; Family Affair, 1990; Singles include: Getaway, 1976; Saturday Nite, 1977; Serpentine Fire, 1978; Fantasy, 1978; Got To Get You Into My Life, 1978; September, 1979; Runnin', 1979; Boogie Wonderland, 1979; After The Love Has Gone, 1979; Star, 1979; Let's Groove, 1981; Solo: Easy Lover (duet with Phil Collins, Number 1, UK), 1985. Honours: American Music Awards, Favourite Band, Soul/Rhythm and Blues, 1977, 1979; Grammy, Best R&B Vocal Performance, All `N' All, 1979; After The Love Has Gone, 1980; Best R&B Instrumental, Boogie Wonderland, 1980; Gold Ticket, Madison Square Garden, 1979; MTV Music Video, 1985; Ivor Novello Award, Easy Lover, 1986; Grammy Award, Best Gospel Performance, 1987. Current Management: Bob Cavallo, Third Rail Entertainment. Address: 9169 Sunset Blvd, Los Angeles, CA 90069, USA.

BAILEY Roy, b. 20 Oct 1935, London, England. Folk Singer; Musician (guitar); Academic. m. Val Turbard, 10 Aug 1963, 1 son, 1 daughter. Education: BA Hons, Social Science. Career: Professional singer, 1960-; Radio, television, tours, in: UK; Switzerland; Canada; USA; Australia; Appearances include festivals in: UK; Canada; Switzerland; Belgium; Australia; Professor of Sociology & Social Work, Sheffield Hallam University, 1988. Recordings: Smoke And Dust Where The Heart Should Have Been, 1965; Oats And Beans and Kangaroos, 1966; Cobweb Of Dreams, 1967; Roy Bailey, 1970; That's Not The Way It's Got To Be (with Leon Rosselson), 1975; New Bell Wake, 1976; Love Loneliness And Laundry (with Leon Rosselson) 1977; If I Knew Who The Enemy Was (with Leon Rosselson) 1978; Hard Times, 1982; Freedom Peacefully, 1985; Leaves From A Tree, 1989; Why Does It Have To Be Me, 1990; Never Leave A Story Unsung, 1992; What You Do With What You've Got, 1993; Business As Usual, 1994; Rhythm and Reds (with Band Of Hope), 1994. Publications: Contemporary Social Problems in Britain (with Jock Young), 1973; Radical Social Work (with Mike Brake), 1975; Radical Social Work & Practice (with Mike Brake), 1980; Theory And Practice In Social work (with Phil Lee), 1982. Honours: Fellow, Royal Society Of Arts, 1989; Emeritus Professor, Sheffield Hallam University, 1990. Current Management: Brass Tacks Agency. Address: Orchard House, Hartpury, Gloucester GL19 3BG, England.

BAIN Aly, b. 15 May 1946, Lerwick, Shetland, Scotland. Musician (violin). Musical Education: Began playing aged 11; Taught by Tom Anderson. Career: Member, Boys Of The Lough, 1988; Television includes: Presenter, Down Home, series on spread on fiddle music from Scotland and Ireland to North America, BBC, 1991; Series, The Shetland Set, BBC, 1991. Recordings: Aly Bain-Mike Whelans, 1971; The Silver Bow (with Tom Anderson), 1976; Shetland Folk Fiddling Vol 2 (with Tom Anderson), 1978; Aly Bain, 1985; Down Home Vol 1, 1986; Down Home Vol 2, 1986; Aly Meets The Cajuns, 1988; Lonely Bird, 1992.

BAIYEWU Tunde, b. London, England. Vocalist. Education: Newcastle University. Career: Singer, The Lighthouse Family, 1994-; Television includes: Top Of The Pops. Recordings: Debut album: Ocean Drive, 1995; Singles: Lifted, 1995; Ocean Drive, for film soundtrack Jack And Sarah, 1995. Current Management: Kitchenware, 7 The Stables, St Thomas Street, Newcastle-Upon-Tyne, Tyne And Wear NE1 4LE, England.

BAJTALA Janos, b. 5 Dec 1944, Budapest, Hungary. Singer; Composer; Arranger; Musician (piano). 1 son. Musical Education: Diploma, Jazz Academy, Budapest. Career: Tours with soul bands The Bandwagon, Foundation, 1974; Co-arranger, West End hit musical, The Black Mikado, 1975-76; Tours with reggae group Chosen Few, 1981-88; Tours with Boney M, 1991-; First appearance in 24 years in Hungary, broadcast on national television, 1995. Recordings: Gipsy Girl (own composition), charted in Hungary, 1968; Keyboards, Black Mikado cast album, 1975; Keyboards on album Bad Weathers, Vivian Weathers, 1980; Various recordings with Chosen Few, 1981-88. Honours: First prize, nationwide pop and jazz contest, 1967; Best soloist, Hugarian International Jazz Festival, 1971. Memberships: PRS; Musicians' Union. Hobbies: Computers; Flying. Address: Garden Flat, 34 Hemstal Road, London NW6 2AL, England.

BAKALA Bretislav, b. 18 June 1957, Brno, Czech Republic. Musician (keyboard). m. Marta Srvtova, 8 September 1984, 1 son, 1 daughter. Education: Diploma, College of Technology, Brno, Faculty of Electronics; Folk Art School. Career: Keyboard in Jazz Duo Brno; Good Company - Dancing 19, in Norway, Germany, Switzerland, Mallorca, Austria, 1987-97; Immerwieder, 1 CD, Just Friends, 2 CD, Composer, Keyboards, Sound Studio. Compositions: Warum Lieb'ich Dich Allein; Lift Me Up; You're Crossing My Life; New Day; Zeit, Du Heilst Wunden. Recordings: Immer Wieder, CD, 1994; Just Friends, CD, 1996. Hobbies: Computer; Music; Swimming. Current Management: Good Sound CZ. Address: Za Gymnaziem 2448, 39701 Pisek, Czech Republic.

BAKER Anita, b. 20 Dec 1957, Detroit, USA. Singer. m. Walter Bridgforth, 24 Dec 1988, 1 son. Career: Lead vocalist, soul group Chapter 8, 1976-80; Solo singer, 1983-; Appearances include: Nelson Mandela International Tribute, Wembley, 1990; Radio City Music Hall, 1990; Compositions tour, 1990; Television appearances include: Christmas in Washington, NBC, 1991; A Call To Action In The War Against AIDS, ABC, 1992. Recordings: Albums: with Chapter 8: Chapter 8; Solo albums: The Songstress, 1983; Rapture (Number 1, US R&B chart), 1986; Giving You The Best That I Got (Number 1, US), 1988; Compositions, 1990; Singles: No More Tears; Angel; You're The Best Thing Yet; Sweet Love; Same Ole Love; No One In The World; Just Because; Giving You The Best That I Got; Talk To Me; Also featured on: Rubáiyát (Elektra Records 40th Anniversary compilation), 1990; Barcelona Gold, 1992. Honours: Grammy Awards: 5 consecutive Best Female R&B Vocal Performances, 1987-91; Best R&B Song, Sweet Love, 1987; Giving The Best That I Got, 1989; Best Soul/Gospel Performance, 1988; Soul Train Awards: Best Single, Female, 1987; Best R&B Single, Best R&B Album, Best R&B Song, 1989; American Music Awards: Favourite Female Soul/R&B Artist, 1988, 1990; Favourite Female Soul/R&B Album, 1988; NAACP Image Award, Best Female Artist, 1990. Current Management: Sterling/Winters Co., 1640 Avenue of the Stars, Los Angeles, CA 90067, USA.

BAKER Carroll Anne, b. 4 Mar 1949, Nova Scotia, Canada. Country Singer; Songwriter. Musical Education: Self-taught. Career: UK tour with Slim Whitman; Recorded duets with daughter Candace; Eddie Eastman; Jack Scott; Roger Whittaker; Concert with Canada Pops Orchestra;

Television includes: 3 Carroll Baker super specials, CBC TV; Mini-series, 7 half-hour shows, CBC; Guest appearances: Hee Haw; New Country; Nashville Now; The Tommy Hunter Show; Lifetime; Canada AM; Headlined for Regent Holiday Tours, Carroll Baker's Country Cruise, 1989. Compositions include: I'm An Old Rock And Roller (Dancin' To A Different Beat). Recordings: I Should Have Put A Hold On Love (Canadian Country Number 2), 1990. Honours: Entertainer Of The Year, Country Award, Canada; 3 Platinum, 6 Gold albums; 5 Gold Singles; JUNO Awards: 1975-78; Big Country Awards, 1975-81; 1987; BMI Award, 1977; RPM Programmer Award, 1978, 1981; Procan Award, 1983; 14 consecutive Number 1 singles, Canadian country charts, 1975-81; Top Country Female, Canadian Country Music, 1985; Martin Guitar Award, 1989; Lifetime Achievement, Canadian Country Music Awards, 1991; JUNO Award Nominations, 1974-92; Inductee, Canadian Country Music Hall Of Honour, 1992. Memberships: AFofM; ACTRA; SOCAN. Hobbies: Charities; General home life. Current Management: John Beaulieu, Carroll Baker Enterprises Inc. Address: 210 Dimson Ave, Guelph, Ontario N1G 3C8, Canada.

BAKER Ginger (Peter), b. 19 Aug 1939, Lewisham, London, England. Musician (drums). Career: Drummer with Terry Lightfoot; Acker Bilk; Alexis Korner's Blues Incorporated, 1962; Graham Bond Organisation, 1963; Member, Cream, 1966-68; Blind Faith, 1969; Airforce, 1970-72; Salt (Nigeria); Baker-Gurvitz Army; Energy; Short spells with Atomic Rooster and Hawkwind; Ginger Baker's Nutters; Solo recording artiste, and leader of own trio (with Bill Frisell and Charlie Haden); Collaboration with Masters of Reality, 1993; Performances include: with Cream: Jazz & Blues Festival, Windsor, 1966, 1967; 2 US tours, 1967; Madison Square Garden, New York, 1968; Royal Albert Hall, London, 1968; with Blind Faith: Hyde Park, London, 1969; Madison Square Garden, New York, 1969. Recordings: Albums: with Cream: Fresh Cream, 1967; Disraeli Gears, 1967; Wheels Of Fire, 1968; Goodbye, 1969; The Best Of Cream, 1969; Live Cream, 1970; Live Cream Vol 2, 1972; Heavy Cream, 1972; with Blind Faith: Blind Faith (Number 1, UK and US), 1969; with Airforce: Airforce, 1970; Airforce 2, 1972; Solo: The Best Of, 1973; 11 Sides Of Baker, 1977; From Humble Origins, 1983; Horses And Trees, 1987; In Concert, 1987; African Force, 1980s; In Concert, 1987; Middle Passage, 1992; The Album, 1992; The Alternative Album, 1992; Unseen Rain, 1993; with Ginger Baker Trio: Going Back Home, 1995; Singles with Cream include: I Feel Free, 1967; Strange Brew, 1967; Sunshine Of Your Love, 1968; White Room, 1968. Current Management: Kron Management, 41489 Frontier Road, Parker, CO 80134, USA.

BAKER Kenny, b. 1 March 1921, Withernsea, East Yorkshire, England. m. Susan Mary, 29 April 1974, 1 son. Education: Self-taught Arranger and Composer. Career: Joined Lew Stone, worked with Ambrose Geraldo Jack Hylton, 1939; RAF, 5 years; Joined Ted Heath Orchestra, 1946; Radio Program, BBC with Bakers Dozen, 1952-58; Worked with Jack Parnel at ATV Television; Reformed Bakers Dozen, 1993; Formed Group, The Best of British Jazz, Jazz Soloist. Compositions: Bakerloo Non Stop; Adlib Frolic; Dark Eyes; Trumpet Fantasy; Virtuosity. Recordings: 3 Years of Ted Heath; Bakers Dozen; Date With the Dozen; Bakers 1/2 Dozen; Spectacular Trumpet of Kenny Baker; Phase 4 World of Kenny Baker; The Boss is Home Bakers Dozen. Honour: Gold Badge of Merit, British Academy of Songwriters, Composers and Authors, 1984. Hobbies: Gardening; DIY; Arranging; Composing. Address: 6 Crossbush Road, Felpham, Bognor Regis, West Sussex, PO22 7LS, England.

BAKER Ronald, b. 21 Nov 1968, Baltimore, Maryland, USA. Musician (trumpet); Singer. m.

Patricia Labeau, 26 Feb 1994, 1 daughter. Musical Education; BA, Music Education. Career: Appearances on Radio France; Played in film, Le Nouveau Monde; Opened concerts for: André Ceccarelli; Black Label; Roy Haynes; Benny Waters; Major festivals include: Montlouis; Montpellier; Orléans; Concert at Virgin Megastore. Recordings: Oberlin Jazz Ensemble; Perry-Boulanger Duo; Oppossum Gang. Hobbies: Squash; Juggling. Address: 1 Passage Des Grillons, 37390 La Membrolle, France.

BAKER Toni, b. 24 Feb 1949, Littleborough, Lancashire, England. Musician (keyboards); MD; Arranger. m. Stephanie, 12 Dec 1986, 1 son, 1 daughter. Musical Education: Piano lessons, aged 5-14; Then involved in bands. Career: Played American bases, in soul music apprenticeship; Television shows include: Opportunity Knocks, 1971-76; Formed: Shabby Tiger, pop/rock band; Number 1 hits in Denmark, Netherlands, Belgium; Session work, freelance; Now playing with The Dakotas. Compositions: Eat You Up (Number 3, Japan); 5 album tracks for Shabby Tiger include: Nancy; Shabby Tiger; 20th Century Cowboy. Memberships: Musicians' Union; Equity. Hobbies: Photography; Travelling; Skiing; Being a Dad. Current Management: Freelance Studio Director/Owner. Address: Moose Studio, 12 Milnrow Road, Hollingworth Lake, Littleborough, Lancs OL15 0BS, England.

BALDAN Bebo, b. 16 Apr 1966, Venice, Italy. Musician (drums, percussion, electronics); Composer. Education: College. Musical Education: Studied with Percussione Ricerca Ensemble, Conservatory of Venice. Career: Toured with: Stephen James; Eddy C-Campbell; Tolo Marton; David Torn; Played in: Italy (Interzone Festival, RAI Television, Videomusic TV); France (Sacre du Printemps); England; Switzerland; Brazil; New York (and KPEL Radio, Berkeley, California). Recordings: As composer: Bebo Baldan: Vapor Frames; with Stephen James: Soniasikri-Sub Rosa, 1992; with David Torn: Diving Into The World, 1995; Earthbeat, 1995. Membership: SAE. Hobbies: Ethnic music; Travel. Current Management: Materiali Sonori. Address: Via Trieste 35, 50127 S Giovanni Valdarno, Italy.

BALDOUS Bernard, b. 12 Dec 1951, Montpellier, France. Musician (acoustic bass). Musical Education: Conservatoire de Musique, Montpellier, 1977; Berklee College of Music, Boston, USA, 1979. Career: Plays bass with: R Anouillez; S Baldous; J Blanton; J Benayoun; V Espi-nieto; Fanfan Sanchez; E Goldstein; M Levine; A Marcos; C McBride; J Neves; F Nicolas; J Peiffer; V Perez; P Pellegati; D Ragot; G Reilles; P Rosengoltz; Sega Seck; P Torreglosa; F Urtado; S Wilson; A Woygnet. Compositions: Fantome; Gigi; BB Blues. Recordings: Bernard Baldous Trio, 1993; Concerto for Jazz Band And Symphony Orchestra, 1994; Instant Jazz Quintet, 1995. Membership: Jazz Action Montpellier. Address: 3 Place Coluche, 34670 Baillargues, France.

BALDRY Long John, b. 12 Jan 1941, Haddon, Derbyshire, England. Singer. Career: Member, R&B groups: Cyril Davies' All-Stars; Ramblin' Jack Elliot; Member, Alexis Korner's Blues Incorporated, 1961; Worked with Horace Silver Quintet, Cyril Davies' R&B All-Stars, 1962; Founder, the Hoochie Coochie Men, 1964; UK tour, with Chuck Berry, Moody Blues, 1965; National Jazz And Blues Festival, 1965; Member, Steampacket, 1965-66; Member, Bluesology, 1966-67; Soloist, Rolling Stones '66, 1966; Solo artiste, 1967-; Becomes manager of Stuart A Brown (Bluesology), 1968; First US tour, 1971; Moved to Canada, 1980. Recordings: Hit singles include: Let The Heartaches Begin (Number 1, UK), 1967; When The Sun Comes Shinin' Thru, 1968; Mexico, 1968; It's Too Late Now, 1969; Albums: with Alexis Korner: R&B From The Marquee, 1962; with The Hoochie Coochie Men: Long John's Blues, 1964; Solo: It Ain't Easy, 1971;

Everything Stops For Tea, 1971; Out!, 1979; Silent Treatment, 1986; It Still Ain't Easy, 1991; The Best Of Long John Baldry, 1991. Current Management: S L Feldman, 1505 W Second Avenue, Ste 200, Vancouver, BC V6H 3Y4, Canada.

BALIN Marty (Martyn Jerel Buchwald), b. 30 Jan 1942, Cincinnati, Ohio, USA. Vocalist; Musician (guitar, percussion). m. Karen Deal, 11 Aug 1989, 2 daughters. Education: 2 years, San Francisco State University. Career: San Francisco Town Criers; Founder, vocalist, Jefferson Airplane (later Jefferson Starship / Starship), 1965-71, 1975-80, 1990-; Leader, Balin Solo Band. Film appearances include Gimme Shelter, 1970. All major radio and television shows. Compositions include: Volunteers; It's No Secret; Plastic Fantastic Lover; Young Girl Blues; Miracles; Sunday Blues; Atlanta Lady; Summer Of Love; Solidarity. Recordings: include: Albums: Balin; KBC Band; Lucky; Bodacious DF; Jefferson Airplane Reunion album; Spitfire; Freedom At Point Zero. Honours: Many Gold and Platinum awards. Memberships: American Society of Composers, Authors and Publishers; BMI; SAG; AFTRA. Current Management: Joe Buchwald, Business-Personal Management. Address: PO Box 347008, San Francisco, CA 94134, USA.

BALKE Jon Georg, b. 7 June 1955, Hamar, Norway. Musician (piano, keyboards); Composer. Career: Started professional career with Arild Andersen's quartet, 1974; Tours of Europe; Recordings for ECM Records; Later established as composer for groups such as Oslo 13; Masqualero; Jokleba; Magnetic North Orchestra; Also composer of chamber music and theatre. Recordings: Nonsentration, 1992; Furter, 1994. Honours: Buddy Award, Norwegian Jazz Federation, 1985; Jazz Musician of Year, 1994. Hobbies: Paragliding; Skiing. Current Management: PJP A/S Norway / ECM Records. Address: Hegermannsgt. 15, N-0478 Oslo, Norway.

BALL David, b. Rock Hill, South Carolina, USA. Musician (guitar); Songwriter. Career: Began as bassist, bluegrass, country, swing, classical, Uncle Walt's Band; Moved to Austin Texas, mid 1970s; Moved to Nashville, late 1980s; Television appearances: Live With Regis And Kathie Lee, ABC; Entertainment Tonight; Live From The House Of Blues, WTBS; Late Night With Conan O'Brien, NBC; Politically Correct. Recordings: 4 albums with Uncle Walt's Band; Album: Thinkin' Problem; Singles: Thinkin' Problem; When The Thought Of You Catches Up With Me. Honours: Grammy nomination, Best Male Country Performance; Nominee, Top New Male Vocalist, Academy Of Country Music; 1 of 2 Best New Artists, Reader's Poll, Radio and Records magazine, 1994. Current Management: Dan Goodman Management, Po Box 120775, Nashville, TN 37212, USA.

BALL David, b. 3 May 1959, Blackpool, Lancashire, England. Musician (synthesizer); Composer. m. Ginny. Career: Formed Soft Cell (with Marc Almond), 1979-84; Concerts include: Futurama 2 Festival, Leeds, 1980; UK tours, 1982-84; Member, The Grid, with Richard Norris, 1990-. Composition: Score for stage revival, Suddenly Last Summer, 1983. Recordings: Albums: with Soft Cell: Non-Stop Erotic Cababeret, 1981; Non-Stop Ecstatic Dancing, 1982; The Art Of Falling Apart, 1983; The Last Night In Sodom, 1984; Compilations: The Singles Album, 1986; Memorabilia - The Singles (remixed by Ball), 1991; Hit singles: Tainted Love (Worldwide Number 1), 1981; Bedsitter, 1981; Say Hello Wave Goodbye, 1982; Torch, 1982; What, 1982; Solo album: In Strict Tempo, 1983; Singles with The Grid: Floatation; Beat Called Love. Honours: Billboard Award, New Wave Band Of The Year, 1981; BRIT Award, Best British Single, Tainted Love, 1982.

BALL Kenny Daniel, b. 22 May 1930, Ilford, Essex, England. Jazz Musician (trumpet). m. Michelle, 28 Dec 1984, 1 son, 4 daughters. Career: Played with Charlie Galbraith; Sid Phillip; Eric Delaney; George Chisholm; Terry Lightfoot; Al Fairweather; Formed own dixieland band, Kenny Ball's Jazzmen, 1958-; Film debut, Live It Up (with Gene Vincent), 1963; Film, Trad Dad; TV Appearances: Easy Beat, 3 series; Morcambe and Wise, 6 series; Saturday Night at the Mill, 4 series; Numerous foreign tours; UK concerts with: Acker Bilk; Kenny Baker; Lonnie Donegan; George Chisholm; Played at wedding reception, HRH the Prince and Princess of Wales, 1981. Composition: Midnight in Moscow, arrangement. Recordings: Albums include: Kenny Ball And His Jazzmen, 1961; The Kenny Ball Show, 1962; The Big Ones - Kenny Ball Style, 1963; Jazz Band Ball, 1964; Trubute To Tokyo, 1964; The Sound Of Kenny Ball, 1968; King Of The Swingers, 1969; At The Jazz Band Ball, 1970; Fleet Street Lightning, 1970; Saturday Night With Kenny Ball And His Band, 1970; Pixie Dust (A Tribute To Walt Disney), 1971; My Very Good Friend...Fats Waller, 1972; Have A Drink On Me, 1972; Let's All Sing A Happy Song, 1973; A Friend To You, 1974; Titillating Tango, 1976; In Concert, 1978; Way Down Yonder, 1977; Soap, 1981; Ball, Barber And Bilk Live At The Royal Festival Hall (with Chris Barber and Acker Bilk), 1984; Kenny Ball And His Jazzmen Play The Movie Greats, 1987; On Stage, 1988; Dixie, 1989; Kenny Ball Plays British, 1989; Jazz Classics, 1990; Kenny Ball Now, 1990; The Ultimate! (with Chris Barber and Acker Bilk), 1991; Singles include: Samantha; Midnight In Moscow; March Of The Siamese Children; The Green Leaves Of Summer; Sukiyaki. Honours: 3 Carl Alan Awards; Billboard Best Band. Memberships: PRS; MCPS; BASCA; MU. Current Management: John Martin Promotions. Address: Warmans Farm, Burton End, Stansted, Essex CM24 8UQ, England.

BALL Malcolm, b. 8 Aug 1953, Ilford, England. Musician (percussion, keyboards); Composer. m. Kim Rosamunde Scott, 6 Sept 1980. Musical Education: Royal College of Music, London. Career: Specializing in contemporary music of all kinds; BBC Radio broadcasts with Geoff Warren Quartet for Jazz in Britain, Jazz Today; Arts Council tours of Hungary, Yugoslavia; Workshops with Graham Collier; Head of Percussion, London Borough of Redbridge; Examiner for GSM, London. Compositions: Close Your Eyes and See, for orchestra, 1995; Many used for library music; O-taiko-Do, TerrOR Nova, for percussion ensemble. Recording: Close Your Eyes and See, in New British Music, Vol 1. Publications: Percussive Perspectives (IMP). Honours: Licentiate, Royal Academy of Music, London. Memberships: Royal Society of Musicians of Great Britain; Musicians' Union. Hobbies: Travel; Food. Address: 79 Chalgrove Crescent, Ilford, Essex IG5 0LX, England.

BALL Michael Ashley, b. 27 June 1962, Bromsgrove, Hereford & Worcester, England. Singer; Entertainer. Education: Plymouth College. Musical Education: Guildford School of Acting, 1981-84. Career: The Pirates of Penzance, 1984; Les Miserables, West End, 1985; Phantom of the Opera, West End, 1987; Aspects of Love, West End & New York, 1989-1990; Represented UK, Eurovision Song Contest, 1992; UK tours, 1992, 1993, 1994; Television apperances: Host, own series, Michael Ball, 1993, 1994. Recordings: Michael Ball, 1992; Always, 1993; West Side Story, 1993; One Careful Owner, 1994; The Best Of Michael Ball, 1994. Honours: 4 Gold albums. Hobby: Cars. Current Management: James Sharkey Associates. Address: 21 Golden Square, London W1R 3PA, England.

BALL Tom, b. 24 Oct 1950, Los Angeles, California, USA. Singer; Musician (harmonica, guitar); Writer. m. Laurie Linn, 2 Oct 1983, 1 daughter. Education: Santa Monica College. Career: Singer, harmonica player, Yerba Buena

Blues Band, 1965-67; Freelance musician, 1968-79; Member duo, Tom Ball and Kenny Sultan, 1979-; Business Venture: Good Time Blues Pub (BMI); Studio work on over 40 recordings, films, television shows. Recordings: Albums: Confusion, 1981; Who Drank My Beer, 1983; Bloodshot Eyes, 1986; Guitar Music, 1988; Too Much Fun, 1990; Filthy Rich, 1993; Double Vision, 1996. Publications: Author: Blues Harmonica, 1993; Nasty Blues, 1994; Sonny Terry Licks, 1995. Honours: NARAS MVP Nomination, 1983; Telly Award Winner, 1994. Memberships: NARAS; AFTRA; AFofM; Folk Alliance. Current Management: US Bookings: Clover Creek Artists; International bookings: Mercer Management. Address: PO Box 20156, Santa Barbara, CA 93120, USA.

BALLAMY Iain Mark, b. 20 Feb 1964, Guildford, Surrey, England. Musician (saxophone); Composer. Education: City and Guilds Musical Instrument Technology. Musical Education: Self-taught; Piano lessons as child. Career: Worked with groups include: Loose Tubes; Delightful Precipice; Human Chain; Bill Bruford's Earthworks; Balloon Man; Dewey Redman; Gil Evans; Hermeto Pascoal, 1982-; Karnatica College Of Percussion, Voice Of God; Tours: USA; Canada; Japan; Hong Kong; India; Europe; Scandinavia; Morocco; Turkey; Toronto; Saskatoon; Brecon; Glasgow; Edinburgh; Willisau; Leverkusen; Soho; Cork; Festivals: Berlin; Montreux; Frankfurt; Monterey; Montreal; Copenhagen; Molde; Istanbul; Worldwide television and radio broadcasts. Compositions: Commissions for Apollo Saxophone Quartet, Salford College, Birmingham Jazz. Recordings: All Men Amen; Balloon Man; with Django Bates: Summer Fruits; Winter Truce; 4 albums with Bill Bruford's Enthusiasts. Honours: BT British Jazz Award, 1995; Dankworth Award. Memberships: Musicians' Union; PRS; MCPS; GVL. Hobbies: Metal detecting; Riding. Current Management: Oliver Wendling, Eccentric Management. Address: 29a Connaught Street, London W2 2AY, England.

BALLARD Hank (Henry), b. 18 Nov 1936, Detroit, Michigan, USA. Singer; Songwriter. Career: Lead singer, the Royals (later called the Midnighters), 1953-62; Solo artiste, 1962-; Also worked with James Brown, 1962-. Compositions include: Work With Me, Annie; Finger Poppin' Time; The Twist (also recorded by Chubby Checker), 1960; Recordings: Singles: with the Midnighters: Work With Me, Annie, 1954; Sexy Ways, 1954; Annie Had A Baby, 1955; Annie's Aunt Fanny, 1955; Teardrops On Your Letter, 1959; Finger Poppin' Time, 1960; The Twist, 1960; Let's Go, Let's Go, Let's Go, 1960; The Hoochi-Coochi-Coo, 1961; Let's Go Again, 1961; The Continental Walk, 1961; The Switch-A-Roo, 1961; Albums include: Their Greatest Hits, 1954; The Moidnighters Vol.2, 1957; Great Juke Box Hits, 1958; Singin' And Swingin', 1959; The One And Only, 1960; Mr Rhythm And Blues, 1960; Sing Along, 1961; Let's Go Again, 1961; Jumpin' Hank Ballard, 1962; Twistin' Fools, 1962; Thge Sound 0f 1963, 1963; Stars In Your Eyes, 1964; Those Lazy Days, 1965; Glad Songs, Sad Songs, 1965; You Can't Keep A Good Man Down, 1969; Live At The Palais, 1986; Sexy Ways - The Best Of Hank Ballard & The Midnighters, 1993; Naked In The Rain, 1993. Honours: Inducted into Rock And Roll Hall Of Fame, 1970; Rhythm And Blues Foundation Award, New York, 1990. Address: c/o David Harris Enterprises, 24210 E Fork Road, Ste 9, Star Route 1, Azusa, CA 91702, USA.

BALLARD Kaye, b. 20 Nov 1926, Cleveland, Ohio, USA. Actress; Singer. Career: Television: The Mothers-in-Law; Perry Como Show; Doris Day Show; over 150 performances on the Tonight Show. Films: The Ritz; The Girl Most Likely; House Is Not A Home; Eternity; Which Way To The Front; Modern Love; Tiger Warsaw; Falling In Love Again; Freaky Friday; Concerts include: 2 Royal Command Performances; Hello Dolly;

Nymph Errant; Stage performances include: Nunsense; Gypsy; Annie Get Your Gun; High Spirits; Odd Couple; Ziegfield Follies (touring companies); Top Bananas; Three To Make Ready; Touch And Go; Wonderful Town; She Stoops To Conquer; Golden Apple; Carnival; Molly (Broadway); One woman shows: Working 42nd Street At Last; Hey Ma. Recordings include: Nymph Errant; Songs From Hey Ma; Fanny Brice; Then And Again; Unsung Sondheim. Memberships: SAG; AFTRA; Equity. Current Management: Mark Sendroff c/o Gottlier, Schiff, Bonsee and Sendroff. Address: 555 5th Avenue, New York, NY 10017, USA.

BALLESTER Tony (Antoine), b. 26 June 1953, Montauban, France. Musician (electric acoustic bass); Professor. m. Maguy Piard, 16 Oct 1987, 1 son, 1 stepdaughter. Musical Education: Self-taught. Career: Television with singers: Mireille Mathieu; Gilbert Montagné; Chico And The Gipsys; Concerts, festivals with Manuel Malou include: Whomade; Francofolies; Paleofestival; Bratislava; Ronnie Scott's Jazz; Kenny Clark; Benny Bailey; Harold Danko; Kalil Chahine. Recordings: Graphic and Eric Barret; Seuls Les Tilleuls Mentent, Gilles Grignon; Secret Pleasure, Didier Makaga; Corazon Caliente, Manuel Malou; Music, film: Gazon Maudit. Publications: La Basse Eclectique (method book and CD). Memberships: CIM Paris; Academy Xieme Arrondissement, Paris. Address: Editions Salabert, 22 Rue Chauchat, 75019 Paris, France.

BALLESTRA Frederic, b. 25 Oct 1951, Toulon, France. Editor; Music Journalist. Career: Public Relations; Concert Promoter in France; Editor of NMI; Musik Interactions Magazine. Publications: NMI Musik Interactions. Address: 3 Rue d'Autrechaus, 83000 Toulon, France.

BALTAZANIS Kostas, b. 20 Feb 1965, Patras, Greece. Musician (guitar); Music Educator; Writer. Musical Education: Bachelor of Music, Performance; Professor Music, Berklee College of Music, Boston, USA. Career: Artistic Director, Nakas Conservatory, Athens, Greece; Studio musician, clinician for Berklee College of Music; Writer of music education books. Recordings: 2 forthcoming albums. Publications: Jazz Harmony; Music Theory And Ear Training; Electric Guitar. Address: 25 25th Martiou Str, GR-16233 Athens, Greece.

BANKS Jon, b. 20 July 1962, Bristol, England. Early Musician. m. Rachel Carter, 24 Oct 1992, 1 son. Career: D Phil, 1990: The Motet As A Formal Type In Italy, c.1500, New York, 1992; Joined Dragonfire, 1990; Tours of Canada, Germany, 1990; Founder member, Sirinu; Tours of Turkey, Macedonia, Holland, Belgium, 1991. Recordings: with Dragonfire: A Royal Array, 1990; Crossing The Borders, 1992; A Present From The Past, 1994; with Sirinu: The Frozen Jewel of Potosi, 1992; Bold, Fearless And Rash, 1994; The Cradle Of The Renaissance, 1995. Publications: The Motet As A Formal Type In Italy, c.1500 (New York), 1992. Honour: DPhil (Oxford), 1990. Hobbies: Poetry; Cycling; Camping. Current Management: Seaview. Address: 118 Upper Clapton Road, Clapton, London E5 9JY, England.

BANKS Tony, b. 27 Mar 1950. Musician (keyboards). Career: Musician, Genesis, 1970-; Solo artiste, 1979-; Numerous worldwide tours, include concerts at: Philharmonic Hall, New York; Giants Stadium, New York; Madison Square Gardens, New York; L A Forum; Rainbow Theatre, London; Wembley Arena; World tour, played to 3 million people, 1987. Recordings: Albums with Genesis: Foxtrot, 1972; Selling England By The Pound, 1973; Genesis Live, 1973; The Lamb Lies Down On Broadway, 1974; Trick Of The Tail, 1976; Wind And Wuthering, 1977; Seconds Out, 1977; And Then There Were Three, 1978; Duke, 1980; Abacab, 1981; Three Sides Live, 1982; Genesis, 1983; Invisible Touch, 1986; We Can't

Dance, 1991; Singles with Genesis: Abacab; Follow You Follow Me; Mama; Illegal Alien; Invisible Touch; Land Of Confusion; Tonight Tonight Tonight; That's All; Turn It On Again; Solo albums: A Curious Feeling; The Fugitive; The Wicked Lady; Soundtracks; Bankstatement; Still. Honours: Golden Ticket, Madison Square Gardens, 1986; First group with 5 US Top 5 singles from one album, 1986; Band Of Year, Rolling Stone Readers Poll, 1987. Current Management: Hit And Run Music, 30 Ives Street, London SW3 2ND, England.

BANNISTER Brian. Vocalist; Musician (banjo, mandolin, harmonica). Career: Founder member, Salty Dog; Winner, Birmingham songwriting competition; Performed official Olympic bid record; Resident topical songwriter for John Tainton Show, BBC; Member, The Debonairs, including television and radio appearances; Founder member, Mack And The Boys, 1989; Member, The New Bushbury Mountain Daredevils, 1992-; Work includes: Backing vocalist, Slade album; Producer, songwriter, dance artists. Recordings: With The Debonairs: Hoochey Coochey Man; with Sub Zero: Out Of The Blue; with The Balti Brothers: Balti; with Mack And The Boys: Mack And The Boys; Downtime Love; with The New Bushbury Mountain Daredevils: Bushwacked; The Yellow Album; Bushbury Mountain. Current Management: c/o Jim McPhee, Acorn Entertainments. Address: Winterfold House, 46 Woodfield Road, Kings Heath, Birmingham B13 9UJ, England.

BANNISTER Christopher Philip, b. 19 Oct 1965, Wigan, Lancashire, England. Musical Education: Vocal training, Blackburn Music School. Career: Numerous radio interviews; Airplay on Radio One; Record Of The Week on Radio 2; Various tours. Recordings: Album: Only Human, 1992; Single: We Were Children, 1993. Memberships; PRS; Musicians' Union. Hobbies: Martial Arts; Weight Training; History. Current Management: October Management. Address: 377 Croston Road, Leyland, Lancs PR5 3PL, England.

BANNISTER (Richard) Matthew, b. 16 Mar 1957, Sheffield, England. Broadcast Executive. m. (1) Amanda Gerrard Walker, 1984 (dec'd), 1 daughter, (2) Shelagh Margaret MacLeod, 1989, 1 son. Education: LLB Hons, Nottingham University. Career: Presenter, BBC Radio Nottingham, 1978-81; Reporter, Presenter, Capital Radio, 1981-83; Newsbeat, Radio 1, 1983-85; Deputy Head, Capital Radio, 1985-87; Head, News & Talks, Capital Radio, 1987-88; BBC, 1988-. Managing Editor, Greater London Radio, 1988-91; Project Co-ordinator, Charter Renewal, 1991-93; Programme Strategy Review, 1993; Currently Controller, BBC Radio 1. Hobbies: Rock music; P G Wodehouse first editions. Address: BBC Radio 1, Egton House, Langham Street, London W1A 1AA, England.

BANTON Gary Wayne, b. 2 May 1971, Wimbledon, London, England. Musician (bass guitar); Singer; Royalties Researcher. Education: Kingston College. Career: Appearances as Gene Simmons in Kiss tribute band Dressed To Kill; MTV Feature; European tours; Various radio and television interviews; Official recognition by Kiss and their fans; Also, bassist, backing vocalist in Mystic Game; European tours; Television and radio interviews. Recordings: Mystic Game, 1994. Membership: Musicians' Union. Hobbies: Travel; Collecting record and memorabilia of Kiss and the Doobie Brothers. Current Management: Self-managed.

BANTON Pato (Patrick Murray), b. Birmingham, England. Reggae Singer; Songwriter. Career: Tours throughout US & South America with own 8-piece group The Reggae Revolution; Now solo recording artiste. Recordings: Albums include: Never Give In; Collections; Singles include: Hello Tosh; Baby Come Back, with UB40 (Number 1, UK); Cowboy Song, with Sting; Bubbling Hot. Current Management: Atomic Communications Group, 10553 West Jefferson Blvd, Culver City, CA 90232, USA.

BARBEAU Mark Jerome, b. 20 Sept 1961, San Francisco, California, USA. Event Production; Production Consultant; Screen Writer; Graphic Artist. Education: San Francisco City College. Career: Personal manager for: Anton Barbeau, pop singer; Produced touring scenery for Primus, Fishbone, Babes In Toyland, during Lollapalooza '93 tour; Poster artist for FM Productions on tours for: U2; Pink Floyd; Metallica; Guns N' Roses; ZZ Top; Rolling Stones; Currently Operations Manager, Key Events, and runs own company Runlikehell Productions, San Francisco, focussing on artist management and tour production. Publications: The Art Of Rock, edited by Paul Gruskin. Hobbies: Pool; Bowling; Reading; Travel; Writing fiction. Address: 2269 Chestnut Street #143, San Francisco, CA 94123, USA.

BARBER (Daniel) Chris(topher), b. 17 April 1930, Welwyn Garden City, Hertfordshire, England. Jazz Musician (trombone, trumpet, horn, double bass); Bandleader; Composer. Education: Trombone, bass, Guildhall School Of Music. Career: Leader, various amateur jazz bands; Formed first band with Lonnie Donegan, Monty Sunshine, 1940s; Leader, Chris Barber Jazzband (later changed to Chris Barber Jazz And Blues Band), 1954-; International tours and concerts include: 1954 line-up reformed for 40th Anniversary concerts: Royal Festival Hall, 100 Club, Netherlands, Germany, 1994; Also played with Ken Colyer; Joe Harriott; Wild Bill Davis; Mac Rebenneck; Helped promote US artists in UK, including Brownie McGhee; Muddy Waters; Louis Jordan. Compositions: Numerous works with Richard Hill, including Jazz Elements; Concerto For Jazz Trombone (both premiered in Berlin). Recordings: Numerous albums include: Ragtime, 1960; Getting Around, 1963; Live In East Berlin, 1968; Sideways, 1974; Take Me Back To New Orleans, 1980; Everybody Knows, 1987; Stardust, 1988; Essential Chris Barber, 1990; Get Yourself To Jackson Square, 1990. Honour: OBE, 1991. Current Management: Vic Gibbons, Cromwell Management, 4/5 High Street, Huntingdon, Cambridgeshire PE18 6TE, England.

BARBER Peter George, b. 3 June 1935, Selby, Yorkshire, England. Retired Musician (tenor saxophone). m. Maureen, 7 Dec 1976, 1 son, 1 daughter (from first marriage). Career: Cornet player, Shefford Town Band, 1946; Saxophone, clarinet, REME Staff Band, many radio broadcasts, 1953-56; Skyliners, 1956-60; Leneberge Showband, 1960-70; Johnny Clayton Showband, 1970-75; James Goff Big Band (dedicated to raising funds for charity), 1980-. Membership: Musicians' Union (Gold Card holder). Hobbies: Angling; Gardening; Caravaning. Address: 7 Pulford Road, Leighton Buzzard, Beds LU7 7AB, England.

BARBER Tony, b. 20 Apr 1963, Edmonton, London, England. Musician (guitar, bass, drums, synthesiser); Producer. m. Nathalie, 1 daughter. Musical Education: Self-taught. Career: Musician with Lack Of Knowledge, 1979-1985; Boys Wonder, 1987-88; Buzzcocks, 1992-; Solo recordings as Unit; Appeared on records by other artists, 1986-. Recordings: Sirens Are Back, 1984; Goodbye James Dean, 1987; Trade Test Transmissions, 1993; Twelve Inch Vinyl Sound Recording, 1995; Denim On Ice, 1995; Purple With Red Flashes, 1995. Membership: PRS. Hobby: Football (Latymer Old Boys FC, Data FC). Current Management: c/o Raf Edmonds, Sensei Ltd, New Cavendish Street, London W1, England.

BARBIER Denis, b. 22 Apr 1954, Paris, France. Composer; Musician (flute). 1 daughter. Musical Education: Conservatories, Montreuil, Vincennes. Career: Flute soloist, National French Jazz Orchestra; US tour, with Big Band Lumière, 1991; Tour, Europe, with Gil Evans and Big Band Lumière, 1986; Concerts on Radio France with Lumière; National French Orchestra; Chute Libre; Moravagine; France Culture with Shi Pei Pou (Peking). Compositions include: Music for theatre; Jazz on the Moon, for symphonic orchestra and solo alto saxophone, 1996. Recordings: Sous Le Signe Du Cheval (wind quintet and piano), 1995; Work For 30 Musicians And Rhythm Section In 4 Movements, 1995; Film music: L'Alibi En Or, with Charles Aznavour, 1993; Fausto (A La Mode, USA), 1993; Bosna, 1994; Music for television serial, 1984-; From the Sea to the Land, for two harps, 1996; Television films: Barbe Bleue, with Samy Frey; Jazz records: PRAO with Mino Cinelu and Brothers; Denis Barbier Jazz Group; Chute Libre and Moravagine with Mino Cinelu; National French Jazz Orchestra. Memberships: SACEM; SACD. Hobbies: Kites; Sailing. Current Management: Éditions des Alouettes. Address: 25 Avenue de Wagram, 75017 Paris, France.

BARBIERI Richard, b. 30 Nov 1957. Musician (keyboards). Career: Member, Japan, 1977-83; Member, The Dolphin Brothers (with Steve Jansen), 1987; Member, Rain Tree Crow (with 3 former members of Japan), 1992; UK tours include: Support to Blue Öyster Cult, 1978; Backing musician, No-Man, 1992; Record producer, Swedish group Lustans Lakejer, 1982. Recordings: Albums with Japan: Adolescent Sex, 1978; Obscure Alternatives, 1978; Life In Tokyo, 1979; Quiet Life, 1980; Gentlemen Take Polaroids, 1980; Assemblage, 1981; Tin Drum, 1981; Oil On Canvas, 1983; Exorcising Ghosts, 1984; with The Dolphin Brothers: Catch The Fall, 1987; with Rain Tree Crow: Rain Tree Crow, 1991; with Steve Jansen: Stone To Flesh, 1995. Singles include: The Art Of Parties, 1981; Quiet Life, 1981; Visions Of China, 1981; Ghosts, 1982; Cantonese Boy, 1982; Life In Tokyo, 1982; Night Porter, 1982; Canton, 1982.

BARBOSA Chris. Career: Produced or performed poduction remixes for many artists including: Shannon; Robin Gibb; Billy Idol; George Michael; New Kids on the Block; The Spinners; Lisa Fisher; George Lammond; Nolan Thomas; Andru Donalds; Safire; Cynthia; Judy Torres; Monet; Alisha. Honour: ASCAP Pop Award. Address: CBM Entertainment Corp, 185 Ardsley Loop, Suite 1B, Brooklyn, NY 11239, USA.

BARBOUR Freeland, b. 7 Dec 1951, Edinburgh, Scotland. Musician; Composer; Producer. m. Charlotte Mackintosh, 6 July 1985, 2 daughters. Education: BA Hons (Cantab), English. Career: Member, Silly Wizard, 1975-76; Staff Producer, BBC Radio Scotland, 1981-85; Self-employed, 1985-95; Member, Wallochmor Ceilidh Band, The Occasionals, Spaelimenninir. Compositions: 4 books published. Recordings: 4 solo albums; Numerous recordings as member of Scottish groups. Memberships: PRS; MCPS; Musicians' Union. Current Management: Duncan Hendry. Address: 10 Belmont Street, Aberdeen AB1 1JE, Scotland.

BARCODE, b. 6 Dec 1971, Barcelona, Spain. Programmer; Songwriter; Musician (keyboards, synthesisers). Career: Numerous concerts with band HED include: Phoenix Festival, 1994; Glastonbury Festival, 1995; Les Confort Moderne, 10th anniversay, Poitiers, France, 1995; Strawberry Fayre Festival, Cambridge, 1995; Megatripolis, London, 1995. Recordings: HED: Reigndance, 1994; Reigndance remix, Unity compilation album, 1994; Folklaw, 1995. Membership: Musicians' Union. Hobbies: Juggling; Collecting Town Lego. Current Management: David Crompton, Timebomb. Address: c/o Timebomb, Box No.15, 63 Camden High Street, London NW1 7JL, England.

BARD Alexander, b. 17 Mar 1961, Vaestra Ny, Sweden. Artist; Record Producer; Songwriter. Education: Masters Degree, Economics, Geography. Recordings: with Army of Lovers: Disco Extravaganza, 1990; Massive Luxury Overdose, 1991; The Gods Of Earth And Heaven, 1993; Glory Glamour And Gold, 1994; Les Greatest Hits, 1995; with Vacuum: The Plutonium Cathedral, 1997; Seance At The Chaebol, 1998. Membership: Co-owner, Stockholm Records. Hobbies: Practising Zoroastrian; Internet guru; Breeder of racehorses. Current Management: Tra La La Productions. Address: c/o Tra La La Productions, Naerkesgatan 1, S-11640 Stockholm, Sweden.

BARDY Jean, b. 3 Mar 1957, Soisy, Montmorency, France. Musician (bass, guitar, trumpet); Composer. Musical Education: Conservatoire de Musique d'Eubonne. Career: Professional jazz bass player, playing Be-Bop in clubs including: River Bop; Petit Opportun; Cardinal Paf; Throughout France; Played with artists including: Guy Lafitte; René Urtreger; Martial Solal; Laurent Cugny; Barney Wilen; Laurent De Wilde; Pepper Adams; Steve Grossman; Sonny Stitt; Chet Baker (1 year in France, Europe); Nat Adderley; Johnny Griffin; Harold Danko; Dee Dee Bridgwater. Compositions: Received grant: Léonard de Vinci, from French government to write original music while in the USA. Recordings: Live In Paris, Antoine Hervé; Sud, Antoine Illouz; Naif; Rhythmning, Laurent Cugny, Gil Evans, 1987; Samya Cynthia, François Chassagnite; César Le Chien; Chansons, Jean Bardy, 1991; Anna Livia Plurabelle, André Hodeir. Honours: Prix Django Reinhardt for: Live In Paris; Rhythmning; Prix de l'Academie du Disque. Hobbies: Golf; Tennis. Address; 7 Rue de l'Elysic-Ménilmontant, 75020 Paris, France.

BARE Bobby (Robert Joseph), b. 7 Apr 1935, Ironton, Ohio, USA. Country Singer; Songwriter. Career: Prolific recording artist, 1955-; Club, television and radio station appearances; Television includes: Grand Ole Opry; Host, Bobby Bare and Friends; Film appearance, A Distant Trumpet, 1964. Recordings: Singles include: All American Boy; Detroit City; 500 Miles Away From Home; Miller's Cave; A Dear John Letter; Come Sundown; Please Don't Tell Me How The Story Ends; Marie Laveau; Daddy What If; The Jogger; Tequila Sheila; Numbers; Numerous albums include: Detroit City, 1963; 500 Miles Away From Home, 1963; The Travelling Bare, 1964; Tender Years, 1965; Talk Me Some Sense, 1966; Folsom Prison Blues, 1968; Lincoln Park Inn, 1969; This Is Bare Country, 1970; I'm A Long Way From Home, 1971; What Am I Gonna Do, 1972; Memphis Tennessee, 1973; Lullabys, Legends And Lies,1974; Cowboys And Daddys, 1975; The Winner And Other Losers, 1978; Bare, 1979; Down And Dirty, 1980; Drunk And Crazy, 1980; As Is, 1981; Ain't Got Nothing To Lose, 1982; Bobby Bare - The Mercury Years 1970-72, 1987; Country Store, 1988; with Skeeter Davis: Tunes For Two, 1965; Your Husband, My Wife, 1970; with The Hillsiders: The English Countryside, 1967; with Norma Jean and Liz Anderson: The Game Of Triangles, 1967. Honour: Grammy, Detroit City, 1963. Current Management: Bare Enterprises, PO Box 2422, Hendersonville, TN 37077, USA.

BARE Jon, b. 30 Aug 1953, Santa Monica, California, USA. Producer; Engineer; Musician (guitar); Singer; Writer. Education: Bachelor of Science, University of Southern California Business School. Career: Prominent Los Angeles guitarist, songwriter; 26 songs played on major Los Angeles radio; Guitarist with: Technodudes; Killer Whales; Hula Monsters; Founded Mega Truth Records. Recordings: Albums by: Moonman; Technodudes; Solo album: Follow Your Heart; Killer Whales; Hula Monsters; Shredzilla, with the Killer Whales. Publications: Numerous articles in Recording Magazine. Honours: ASCAP

Special Awards Programme, 1996, 1997. Memberships: NARAS; ASCAP. Address: PO Box 4988, Culver City, CA 90231, USA.

BARKER Aaron G, Snr, b. 3 May 1953, San Antonio, Texas, USA. Songwriter. Compositions: for George Strait: Baby Blue, 1988; Love Without End, 1990; Easy Come, Easy Go, 1990; I Know She Still Loves Me, 1995; I'd Like To Have That One Back, 1995; I Can Still Make Cheyene, 1997; for Doug Supernaw: Honky Tonkin' Fool, 1993; Not Enough Hours, 1995; for Clay Walker: Watch This, 1997. Recording: Feelin' Like Freedom. Honours: Voted Number 1 in all three trades, Cash Box, 1988; Songwriters Award, Music City News, 1990. Memberships: Country Music Association; NSAI; Academy of Country Music. Hobby: Woodwork. Current Management: OTex Music, 1000 18th Avenue South, Nashville, TN 37212, USA.

BARKER Guy, b. 26 Dec 1957, London, England. Jazz Musician (trumpet). Musical Education: Royal College Of Music. Career: Member, National Youth Jazz Orchestra; Major concerts include: Cleveland Jazz Festival, 1978; South Bank Jazz Festival, 1989; Leader, own quintet, UK tour, 1978; Also played with: Gil Evans; John Dankworth; Chris Hunter; Stan Tracey's Hexad; Hubbard's Cubbard; Ornette Coleman; Peter King; Jim Mullen; Jack Sharpe Big Band; Featured soloist, London Symphony Orchestra; Played in backing groups with artists including: Sammy Davis Jr; Mel Tormé; Liza Minnelli; Lena Horne; UK tour with Frank Sinatra, 1991; Far East tour with Georgie Fame; Tribute tours to Chet Baker and Bix Beiderbecke. Recordings: Albums include: Holly J, 1989; Isn't It, 1991; with Hubbard's Cubbard: Hubbard's Cubbard, 1983; Nip It In The Bud, 1985; with Clark Tracey: Suddenly Last Tuesday, 1986; Stiperstones, 1987; with Peter King: Brother Bernard, 1988; Featured on soundtracks: Insignificance, 1985; Absolute Beginners, 1986; The Living Daylights, 1987; Also featured on recordings with Paul McCartney; Grace Jones; Joan Armatrading.

BARKUS Derek Roy, b. 11 June 1952, High Wycombe, Buckinghamshire, England. m. Deborah Leach, 2 Apr 1976, 1 daughter. Education: Gravesend Maritime College. Musical Education: Self-taught. Career: Played on folk circuit, with various bands; Solo work, USA; Television appearance: MTV (USA) with Off The Leash, 1986; Reformed new Off The Leash Band, 1988; Formed blues duet, Juke Boy Barkus and Baldie McGhee, 1994-; British & European tours; Formed Ivy House 1995-. Recordings: Juke Boy Barkus and Baldie McGhee, (14-track blues cassette) 1994; Appeared on: Locked Into Surf, Volume 1, 1994; Volume 2, 1995; Album: Scorching The Blues, 1995. Hobbies: Cooking; Art; Songwriting; Writing. Current Management: Chris Koerner-Davis. Address: Ivy House, 19 The High Street, Benson, Oxford OX10 6RP, England.

BARLOW Eric. Vocalist; Musician (guitar). Musical Education: Classical training. Career: Member, The New Bushbury Mountain Daredevils, 1992-; Backing vocals, Slade; Producer, songwriter for various dance artists; Topical songs for radio. Compositions include: Songs recorded by artists including: Jackie Graham; Asia Blue; Several songs at number 1, Europe and Africa, including: Heartbreaker, Rozalla. Recordings: Solo: You Betta Run; with Rozalla: Heartbreaker; Sunny; The Perfect Kiss; Spirit Of Africa; with Mack And The Boys: The Unknown Legends; with The New Bushbury Mounatin Daredevils: Bushwacked; The Yellow Album; Bushbury Mountain. Current Management: c/o Jim McPhee, Acorn Entertainments. Address: Winterfield House, 46 Woodfield Road, Kings Heath, Birmingham B13 9UJ, England.

BARLOW Gary, b. 20 Jan 1971, Fradham, Cheshire, England. Vocalist; Songwriter. Career: Songwriter, singer, UK all-male vocal group, Take That, 1991-96; Television includes: Take That And Party, C4, 1993; Take That Away documentary, BBC2, 1993; Take That In Berlin, 1994. Recordings: Albums: Take That And Party, 1992; Everything Changes, 1993; Nobody Else, 1995; Greatest Hits, 1996; Hit singles: It Only Takes A Minute, 1992; I Found Heaven, 1992; A Million Love Songs, 1992; Could It Be Magic, 1993; Why Can't I Wake Up With You, 1993; UK Number 1 hits: Pray, 1993; Relight My Fire (with Lulu), 1993; Babe, 1993; Everything Changes, 1993; Sure, 1994; Back For Good, 1995; Never Forget, 1995; How deep Is Your Love, 1996. Publications: Numerous videos, books, magazines. Honours: 7 Smash Hit Awards, 1992; BRIT Award, Best British Single, 1994; BRIT Award Nominations, Best Single, Best Video, 1996. Current Management: c/o Simon Fuller, 19 Management, Unit 32, Ransomes Dock, 35-37 Parkgate Road, London SW11 4NP, England.

BARLOW Thomas, b. 30 Sept 1961, Manila, Philippines. Musician (saxophone). Education: BA Hons, University of Kent; PGCE, De Montfort University. Career: Founder member, The Larks; Aztec Camera, UK, Europe tour, 1988; Tommy Barlow Quartet; Butterfield 8; Founder member, Deptford Dance Orchestra (later Jools Holland Big Band); Matt Bianco; Holly Johnson; Swordfish. Recordings: 3 singles, 1 EP, with The Larks; Recording sessions with: Aztec Camera (Number 3 UK charts), 1988; Jools Holland; Deptford Dance Orchestra; BBC Education Programme; Swordfish. Memberships: Musicians' Union; PRS. Hobbies: Cycling; Basketball. Address: 161A Southampton Way, Camberwell, London SE5 7EJ, England.

BARNACLE Gary, b. 3 Apr 1959, Nicosia, Cyprus. Musician (saxophone, flute); Songwriter. Career: Toured with The Ruts; Elvis Costello; Soft Cell; Marc Almond; Tina Turner; Level 42; Jamiroquai; Played at various Prince's Trust concerts; Nelson Mandela Tribute, Wembley Stadium; Midge Ures's All Star Band; Numerous television, radio appearances in UK and abroad, include 40 Top Of The Pops. Compositions: Co-writer, Jazzmasters album; Space Clav, Jamiroquai; Leisure Process Tracks; Ruts D C tracks. Recordings: Gold and Platinum discs with artists including: Tina Turner (4 albums); Phil Collins; Paul McCartney; David Bowie; The Clash; Swing Out Sister; The Beautiful South; Jamiroquai (2 albums); Björk (2 albums); Soul II Soul; James Brown; Five Star; Yazz; T'Pau (including hit single China In Your Hand); Elvis Costello. Memberships: MCPS; PRS; Musicians' Union; GVL (Germany); SENA (Netherlands). Hobbies: Squash; Football; Collecting old records, films. Address: 160 Queenstown Road, Battersea, London SW8 3QE, England.

BARNACLE Steve, b. 27 Sept 1956, Aldershot, Hampshire, England. Musician (bass guitar, guitar); Composer; Producer. m. Lesley Lacey-Smith, 10 July 1989, 1 son, 2 daughters. Musical Education: Self-taught. Career: Numerous world tours; Most television and radio shows with artists including: Tina Turner; Pete Townshend; Deborah Harry; Spear Of Destiny; Rick Wakeman; Julien Clerc (France only). Compositions: Co-writer, co-producer, Beat Boy album, Visage; Co-writer: Dream City, Samantha Fox; Juanita, Iron Maiden; Numerous writing and production credits. Memberships: PRS; Musicians' Union; MCPS. Hobbies: Reading; Sport; Anything creative. Current Management: Self-managed. Address: 5 York Road, Wimbledon, London SW19 8TP, England.

BARNARD Robert Graeme, b. 24 November 1933, Melbourne, Australia. m. Danielle Ann Barhard, 22 July 1993, 2 sons, 1 daughter. Career: Regular appearances on variety TV;

Co-Compere for ABC-TV Jazz Programme; Featured Soloist, Queensland Symphony Orchestra. Compositions: Many pieces recorded over the years. Recordings: Lord of the Rings, with John Sangster; Many with Graeme Bell; About 300 under own name including: Bob Barnard - With Strings. Honours: Order of Australia, 1990; Advance Australia Award, 1991; Received Prestigeous, MO Award, 1993, 1997. Membership: Professional Musicians Club. Hobby: Golf. Address: 8/9 Hume Street, Crows Nest, Sydney, 2065, Australia.

BARNES Alan Leonard, b. 23 July 1959, Altrincham, Cheshire, England. Musician (saxophones, clarinet, bass clarinet). m. Clare Hirst, 31 July 1995. Musical Education: Leeds Music College, 1977-80, First Class Diploma. Career: Member, Pasadena Roof Orchestra, 1981-83; Tommy Chase Quartet, 1983-86; Jazz Renegades, 1986-89; Humphrey Lyttelton, 1989-93; Currently, leader, Pizza Express, modern jazz quartet; Co-leader, Bruce Adams/Alan Barnes Quintet; Alan Barnes and David Newton Duo. Recordings: Albums: with David Newton: Like Minds; Thirsty Work; with Bruce Adams: Side-Steppin'; Let's Face The Music. Honours: British Jazz Awards, Alto Poll Winner, 1993, 1995; Clarinet Poll Winner, 1994. Current Management: I. Cruikshank, Big Bear. Address: 146 Kings Road, Clapham, London SW4, England.

BARNES Jimmy, b. Scotland. Musician (guitar); Vocalist. Career: Lead singer, Australian group, Cold Chisel, 1979-83; Solo artiste, 1984-; Recordings: with Cold Chisel: Breakfast At Sweethearts, 1979; East, 1980; Circus Animals, 1982; Solo albums: Body Swerve, 1984; Jimmy Barnes, 1985; Freight Train Heart, 1987; Barnestorming, 1988; Two Fires, 1990; Heat, 1993; Psychlone, 1995; Hits: The Best of Jimmy Barnes, 1996. Address: c/o Michael Long Management, P O Box 494, Double Bay 2028, New South Wales, Australia.

BARNHOLDT Ole, b. 14 Feb 1958, Hvorup, Denmark. Composer. Musical Education: Graduate, Film Music Composition, Dick Grove School Of Music, Los Angeles, USA, 1988; Masters degree, Music, University of Aalborg, Denmark, 1990. Career: Scored various film, television, video projects, 1988-. Compositions: For Denmark's Radio Symphony Orchestra: Valley Heart; Siciliano For Maria. Publications: Music Design. Membership: KODA (Denmark). Current Management: Whiteheart Music Limited. Address: Whiteheart Music Limited, 100 Edenbridge Road, Enfield EN1 2HT, England.

BARON Mickie (Michael Dennis Barry Dixon), b. 15 Feb 1952, Chiswick, London, England. Disc Jockey; Presenter; Musician (drums). m. Jennifer Dixon, 25 Aug 1972, 1 son, 2 daughters. Career: Worked for Mike-A-Tone, 1968-69, Harmony Entertainments, 1969-89, owner, 1989-. Recordings: 2 cover songs, 1994. Honours: Best DJ of The Year, Harmony Entertainments, 1985, 1987, 1988. Hobby: Has own farm. Current Management: Harmony Entertainments. Address: 1 Strouds Copse, Garson's Lane, Warfield, Berkshire RG42 6JD, England.

BAROUK Anne, b. 9 Mar 1966, Bordeaux, France. Musician (piano); Composer; Teacher. Education: University: Ethnology. Musical Education: Conservatoire de Bordeaux: classical; CIM (jazz school, Paris); Master of Music, university. Career: Pianist in groups: What Ever (Rhythm & Blues); Kathân Sisters (cabaret duo); Good News Singers (gospel); TAO (big band). Compositions: For cinema (Paulo Films Production); Theatre: Compagnie de Soleil Bleu; Compagnie du Mistral. Memberships: SACEM; UMJ; SACD. Address: 369 Rue des Pyrénées, 75020 Paris, France.

BARRATT Bob, b. 22 Mar 1938, Croydon, Surrey, England. Record Producer. m. Annette Key, 24 Sept 1960, 3 daughters. Musical Education: Self-taught piano. Career: Wrote songs as child; Office boy, EMI Records, 1959; Trained as record producer by Norman Newell and Norrie Paramor; Artist roster included: Max Boyce; Pam Ayres; Wurzels; Basil Brush; King's Singers; Fivepenny Piece; Gene Vincent; Chris Barber; Vince Hill (Edelweiss); Ran own label, Grasmere Records, featuring specialist music, 1984-. Compositions: 300 songs and instrumentals; 5 songs used in films; Many used by recorded libraries; 450 recordings of own compositions made by artists including: Gene Vincent; Dick Haymes; Roger Whittaker; King's Singers; Big Daddy; Brigitte Bardot. Recordings: Produced hundreds of records including: We All Had Doctor's Papers, Max Boyce (number 1 album, UK charts); Combine Harvester, Wurzels (number 1 single, UK charts). Honours: 4 Gold discs, 12 Silver discs; Twice winner of Gibraltar Song Festival, as songwriter. Hobbies: Travel, especially in mountainous regions; Buses and trams. Address: c/o Grasmere Music Ltd, Paramount House, 290-292 Brighton Road, South Croydon, Surrey CR2 6AG, England.

BARREDA Jean-Pierre, b. 29 Sept 1956, Beziers, France. Musician (double bass, 4 and 6 string electric bass). Musical Education: Conservatoire, Montpellier, Stages with NHOP, Gleen Ferris, Bobby Porcelli. Career: Jazz festivals; Tours, Spain, Belgium, England; Plays about 120 concerts annually: clubs, concerts, private functions. Recordings: Album with J P Llabador; Many recordings with singers, jazz groups, and the Salsa from the South of France. Hobbies: Pool; Moto. Address: Le Berlioz, Bat. C, Apt. 60, 42 Avenue de Castelnan, 34000 Montpellier, France.

BARRET Eric, b. 5 May 1959, Le Havre, France. Musician (saxophone); Composer. Career: Played with J P Mas, A Ceccarelli, 1983; Barret, Romano Texier, 1985; Orchestre National de Jazz, 1986; D Humair, 1988; Quartet with M Ducret, 1988; Also played with: A Hervé, R Urtreger, S Swallow, J Griffin, K Wheeler, A Farmer, L Bennett, S Grossman, F Hubbard; Professor, Bagneux Music Conservatory, 1991-; Member, @Roy Haynes 4tet, 1997; Orchestre National de Jazz, 1997. Recordings: Barret, Romano Texier, 1987; Eric Barret Quartet, 1989; L'Echappe Belle, 1992. Publications: Etudes Jazz Pour Saxophone, 2 volumes; Gammes Et Arpèges Pour Le Jazz, 1987. Honour: Boris Vian Price; Bien débuter le saxophone, 1997. Hobbies: Wine; Bicycles; Books; Modern art; Painting; Plants. Current Management: Hélène Manfredi, Atout Jazz. Address: 118 Rue Du Chateau des Rentiers, 75013 Paris, France.

BARRETT Andrew, b. 19 Aug 1953, Oceanside, New York, USA. Musician (keyboards); Arranger; Composer. m. Kathleen Anna McGinley, 22 Sept 1980. Musical Education: Mus B, Indiana University, 1975. Career: Musician, arranger for various artistes including: Diana Ross; Irene Cara; Sister Sledge, 1981-82; Consultant, Cats Shubert Organization, 1982-; Synthesizer consultant, New York stage productions including: Cats, 1987; Me And My Girl, 1987; Les Miserables, 1988; Phantom Of The Opera, 1988; Miss Saigon, 1989. Compositions: Contributor, film soundtracks: Nightmare On Elm Street, Part II, 1987; National Lampoon's Christmas Vacation, 1990; Shattered, 1991. Memberships: ASCAP; NARAS.

BARRETT Brian, b. 9 Feb 1968, Murfreesboro, Tennessee, USA. m. Katrina Startin Barrett. Recording Artist; Songwriter. Education: Hardin-Simmons University, Abilene, Texas. Career: Appearances: Concert of The Age Tour; Television includes: TBN (Gospel America with Pat Boone); Carman's Time 2, TBN; Z-TV; TNN; CCM-TV (Family Channel); ACTS TV Network; Nashville's Talk Of The Town (WTVF CBS Affiliate); Radio: CCM Radio; Dawson McAllister's Praise Him In Your Youth; 20: The Countdown Magazine; The Best Country Countdown. Recordings: Albums: Brian Barrett, 1993; Nailed In Stone, 1995. Honours: Dove Award Nominations, Country Song of Year, Country Album Of Year, 1995; CCM Readers Awards, Favourite Country Artist, Favourite Country Album. Memberships: Gospel Music Association; Alpha Psi Omega (Theatrical Society). Hobbies: Photography; Fishing; Swimming. Current Management: Michael Smith & Associates. Address: 1024 17th Avenue South, Nashville, TN 37212, USA.

BARRETT Carl Tony, b. 2 Mar 1964, Westham Lane, England. Singer; Songwriter; Musician (guitar). Musical Education: Self-taught. Career: Lead singer, lead guitar, songwriter for: Megaton; Electric Samarai; WOT; Visual Thinking; Played many venues, Britain, Europe; Television appearances for Nordoff Robbins Knebworth '90; Radio promotion on Capitol. Recordings: New World's Rising, 1988; Feel The Need For Love, 1990; Major record company interest from songs pending completion, 1995. Membership: Musicians' Union. Hobbies: Travel; Classic motor cycles and cars; Drag racing. Current Management: Moonstar International. Address: 158 Hillyfields, Loughton, Essex IG10 2PZ, England.

BARRETT Mark Vincent, b. 27 Jan 1959, Bishops Stortford, England. Musician (guitar); Sound Engineering. 1 son, 1 daughter. Education: Fine Art Degree, Stourbridge College of Art. Musical Education: Acton Guitar Institute. Career: Member, East Orange, 1983; Q Lazzarus, 1988; Guitarist for Janey Lee Grace; Radio broadcasts: GLR; Regional BBC stations; Various US stations; Major US tour; Television, Tricks and Tracks, BBC. Recordings: with Q Lazzarus: Don't Let Go; Goodbye Horses, from film The Silence Of The Lambs; Mexico 70; Albums: Dust Has Come To Stay; Sing When You're Winning; Singles: Everywhere; Worthless. Membership: Musicians' Union. Hobbies: Drawing and painting; Surfing; White water canoeing. Current Management: Diamond Sounds Management. Address: Fox and Punch Bowl, Burfield Road, Old Windsor, Berkshire, England.

BARRETT Paul, b. 8 Aug 1954, Dublin, Ireland. Producer; Musician Arranger (Keyboards, Brass); Composer. Musical Education: Trinity College, Dublin (Mus B); Royal Irish Academy of Music. Career: Trombone, RTE Symphony Orchestra, 1970-74; Musical Arranger, EMI Records, 1975-76; Keyboards, arranger, composer, trombonist, RTE TV, radio, 1975-89; Founder, bands: Sleepless Knights, 1976-77; Metropolis, 1979-82; Junta, 1982; Founder, STS, 1983; 24 track studio with Fairlight CMI; Performed with artists including: U2; Marianne Faithful; The Edge; Sinead O'Connor; Brian Eno; Tom Robinson; Bono; Hazel O'Connor; Steve Lillywhite; Luka Bloom; Flood; Hothouse Flowers; Bill Whelan; Christy Moore; Now composing film music; Producing records for U2; Hazel O'Connor; Hothouse Flowers; Luka Bloom; Bono; The Stars Of Heaven; Carole King; Coosh; Equation. Recordings: with U2: Desire; Joshua Tree; Unforgettable Fire; Rattle And Hum; Achtung Baby; Night And Day; with Hothouse Flowers: Home; with Hazel O'Connor: Private Wars; with Frank Sinatra and Bono: I've Got You Under My Skin; Contributed to recordings for: Quincy Jones; Frank Sinatra; Jim Sheridan; Stevie Wonder; Marvin Gaye; Johnny Cash; Ray Charles; Leonard Cohen; Willie Nelson. Honours: Platinum discs, Desire; Rattle And Hum; Joshua Tree; Unforgettable Fire; Gold disc, Home. Memberships: PRS; MCPS; AYIC. Hobby: Sailing. Current Management: STS. Address: c/o STS, Ballyward Stud, Oldcourt, Manor Kilbride, Co Wicklow, Ireland.

BARRETT Paul Frank Stalin, b. 14 Dec 1940, Blackwood, Wales. Booking Agent; Promoter; Personal Manager. m. Lorraine Jayne Booth, 27 July 1972, 1 son, 1 daughter. Career: Owner, Paul Barrett Rock 'n' Roll Enterprises; 30 years as promoter, booking agent, personal manager, representing among others: The Jets; Crazy Cavan and the Rhythm Rockers; Sunsets; Freddie 'Fingers' Lee and His Trio; Matchbox; Jean Vincent; Earl Jackson & The Jailbreakers; Screamin' Lord Sutch and the Savages; Wee Willie Harris; The Rimshots; Jack Scott; Tommy Sands; Numerous personal appearances, television, radio; Film appearances: Blue Suede Shoes; Bloody New Year. Recordings: Spirit of Woodstock; I Told You So; Punk; Girl Please Stay; Solo vocals, Superstar, featured on Gold album. Honours: Bop Cat of High Standing, Carl Perkins Fan Club. Memberships: PRS; MCPS. Hobbies: Films; Books; Rock'n'Roll (50s) music. Address: 16 Grove Place, Penarth CF64 2ND, South Wales.

BARRON Andy, b. 4 June 1962, Doncaster, England. Musician (drums). m. Anne Braymand, 22 Aug 1992. Education: College. Musical Education: Privately taught; Doncaster Youth Jazz Orchestra. Career: Played, recorded or toured with Dominic Miller; Nigel Kennedy; Mark King; Mike Lindup; Julia Fordham; Kenny Wheeler; John Scofield; Rick Margitza; Kenny Werner; Stan Sultzman; Marcia Maria; Eurojazz; ORJ (Orchestra Regional de Jazz Rhone Alpes); John Surman; Pierre Drevet; Mario Stantchev; London Contemporary Dance. Memberships: ORJ; AIMRA. Hobbies: Sports. Address: 50 Rue de la Convention, 38200 Vienne, France; Garden Flat 27, Rye Hill Park, London SE15 3JN, England.

BARRON Angela, b. 9 May 1949, Birmingham, England. Composer; Musician; Author; Music Teacher. Education: Moseley School of Art, Birmingham. Musical Education: School of Contemporary Pop and Jazz. Career: Began as freelance percussionist, including work with Birmingham Symphony Orchestra; Theatre, cabaret musician with top entertainers including: Bruce Forsyth; Des O'Connor; Leslie Crowther; Val Doonican. Part-time lecturer, percussion and composition; North Warwickshire and Hinkley College of Technology and Art, Nuneaton, Warwickshire; Well known in the UK for innovative percussion works and master classes featuring percussion. Compositions include: Television signature tunes: Shut That Door (also released as single); Where Are They Now; Commissioned by Chappell Music Library for album, short pieces as jingles, theme, incidental music for television, radio, films (distributed worldwide); Collaboration with Boosey and Hawkes Music Publishers on albums, including album recorded by Royal Philharmonic Orchestra; Also wrote for their educational catalogue under pseudonyms: Chris Barron, Christine Barron. Publications: 2 comprehensive tutors with cassette for Learn As You Play series: Learn As You Play Drums; Learn As You Play Tuned Percussion and Timpani; Learn As You Play Drums Cassette. Memberships: Association of Professional Composers; The British Academy of Songwriters, Composers and Authors. Hobbies: Art; Swimming; Travel. Current Management: Boosey And Hawkes Music Publishers Ltd. Address: 27 Madeira Croft, Coventry, Warwickshire CV5 8NX, England.

BARRON Chris, b. 1968. Vocalist. Musical Education: Music theory, New York's New School College. Career: Founder member, funk/rock group The Spin Doctors, 1988-; Tours, performances include: Horizon Of Blue Developing Everywhere tour, 1992; Saturday Night Live, 1992; MTV Drops The Ball '93, 1992; Late Night Show With David Letterman, CBS TV, 1993. Recordings: Singles include: Little Miss Can't Be Wrong, 1992; Two Princes, 1993; Albums: Homebelly Groove, 1990; Pocket Full Of Kryptonite, 1992; Turn It Upside Down, 1994.

Address: c/o DAS Communications, 83 Riverside Drive, New York, NY 10024, USA.

BARRON Jay, b. 24 Feb 1957, Yokusuka, Japan. Artist Manager; Concert Tour Producer. m. Leann Barron, 2 May 1990, 1 daughter. Career: Artist manager; International concert tour producer, Barron Entertainment. Memberships: CMA; ACM; AFofM; NARAS. Hobby: Collecting antique American Indian Art. Address: Barron Entertainment, 1600 Linden Avenue, Nashville TN 37212, USA.

BARROW Geoff, b. 9 Dec 1971, Walton in Gordano, Bristol, England. Musician (drums); Mixer. Education: Graphic Design. Career: Musician, Portishead; Remixer for Paul Weller; Primal Scream; Ride; Film, To Kill A Dead Man, British Short Film Festival, London, 1994. Compositions include: Someday, on album Homebrew, Neneh Cherry. Recordings: Albums with Portishead: Dummy, 1994; Singles: Numb, 1994; Sour Times, 1994; Glory Box, 1995. Honours: Mercury Music Prize, Best Album, 1995; NME Brat Award, 1995. Current Management: Fruit Management. Address: Unit 104, Saga Centre, 326 Kensal Road, London W10 5BZ, England.

BARRY Daemion, b. 20 Nov 1960, London, England. Musician; Composer. 1 son. Education: First Class Honours, Exeter University. Compositions: Television credits: Signs And Wonders, BBC; The English Wife, Meridian; Chandler And Co, BBC; My Good Friend, Anglia; A Woman's Guide To Adultery, Carlton TV; Friday On My Mind, BBC; Thicker Than Water, BBC; Reportage, BBC2; Go Wild, ITV; Gamesmaster, CH4; The Farm, TVE; Cinema credits: The Duke Of Edinburgh Award Scheme; Commercial: Robinsons Orange Drinks. Honours: BAFTA Award, Best Original Music Score, Friday On My Mind; Golden Gate Award (US), Friday On My Mind. Memberships: PRS; British Songwriters; BAFTA; Groucho. Current Management: Soundtrack Music Management, 22 Ives Street, Chelsea, London SW3 2ND, England.

BARRY James M, b. 16 Jan 1952, Chicago, Illinois, USA. Songwriter. m. Emma Fontes, 1 July 1992, 1 son, 1 daughter. Education: Illinois Wesleyan University, BFA Theatre Cum Laude. Musical Education: Musical Theatre. Compositions: Colors of Grey, for award winning CBS documentary; If I Could Only Say Goodbye, David Hasselhoff, Baywatch; Step By Step, Groove U. Publication: Hear The Quiet. Memberships: EMI Music Publishing; ASCAP; Songwriters Guild Of America. Hobbies: Martial Arts; Skiing; Cooking; Travel. Address: 389 South Many Lakes Drive, Kalispell, MT 59901, USA.

BARRY John (Jonathan Barry Prendergast), b. 3 Nov 1933, York, Yorkshire, England. Film Composer. Career: Leader, John Barry Seven, 1960-62; Composer, film soundtrack music. Recordings: Singles: What Do You Want, Adam Faith (as arranger), 1959; with John Barry Seven: Hit And Miss (theme for Juke Box Jury, BBC), 1960; Walk Don't Run, 1960; As composer: From Russia With Love, Matt Monro, 1963; Goldfinger, Shirley Bassey, 1964; You Only Live Twice, Nancy Sinatra 1967; Down Deep Inside (theme from The Deep), Donna Summer, 1977; Albums (as performer, composer, arranger or conductor): Oh Boy, 1958; Drumbeat, 1959; Beat Girl, 1959; Stringbeat, 1961; Dr No, 1962; Man In The Middle, 1962; It's All Happening, 1963; Zulu, 1963; Elizabeth Taylor In London, 1963; From Russia With Love, 1963; The Man In The Middle, 1964; Sophia Loren In Rome, 1965; King Rat, 1965; Four In The Morning, 1965; Thunderball, 1965; Passion Flower Hotel, 1965; The Wrong Box, 1966; The Chase, 1966; The Quiller Memorandum, 1966; You Only Live Twice, 1967; The Lion In Winter, 1968; On Her Majesty's Secret Service, 1969; Midnight Cowboy, 1969; Diamonds

Are Forever, 1971; Lolita My Love, 1971; Mary Queen Of Scots, 1971; The Persuaders, 1971; Alice's Adventures In Wonderland, 1971; A Doll's House, 1973; The Man With The Golden Gun, 1974; Robin And Marian, 1976; King Kong, 1976; Moonraker, 1979; Frances, 1982; Body Heat, 1983; Out Of Africa, 1985; Jagged Edge, 1985; A View To A Kill, 1985; Peggy Sue Got Married, 1986; Howard The Duck, 1986; The Deep, 1977; The Living Daylights, 1987; Dances With Wolves, 1990; Ruby Cairo; Indecent Proposal; Chaplin; Moviola II - Action And Adventure, 1995. Honours include: Academy Awards: Midnight Cowboy; Born Free; Out Of Africa; Dances With Wolves; Oscar Nomination, Chaplin.

BARSLEY Ronny Laurence, b. 31 Oct 1952, Shortstown, Bedford, England. Musician (drums). m. Tegwen Noelle Morgan, 5 Jun 1976. Musical Education: Les Feast School of Music. Career: Numerous tracks featured on Radio Kent from the Jay Thorne album; Various concerts with the Gil Martin Orchestra backing such artists as Tommy Trinder, Ronnie Carrol, Nicholas Parsons, and Ricky Valance. Recordings: Jay Thorne Synth Sounds; Logo Live; Harlequin - Sounds Of; Cybernetic Loop, featuring Paul Steinhous. Membership: Musicians' Union. Hobbies: Golf; Swimming; Reading. Current Agent: TNB. Address: 109 Ellington Road, Ramsgate, Kent CT11 9TD, England.

BART Lionel, b. 1 Aug 1930, London, England. Composer; Lyricist. Education: St Martin's School of Art. Career: Works include: Lock Up Your Daughters (lyrics), 1959; Fings Ain't Wot They Used To Be (music, lyrics), 1959; Oliver! (music, lyrics, book), 1960; (film), 1968; Blitz! (music, lyrics, direction), 1962; Maggie May (music, lyrics), 1964; Film scores include: Serious Charge; In The Nick; Heart Of A Man; Let's Get Married; Light Up The Sky; The Tommy Steele Story; The Duke Wore Jeans; Tommy The Toreador; Sparrers Can't Sing; From Russia With Love; Man In The Middle; Numerous hit songs. Honours: 3 Ivor Novello Awards, 1957-60; Variety Club Silver Heart for Show Business Personality of The Year, Broadway, 1960; Antoinette Perry Award (Tony), Oliver!, 1962; Gold Disc, Oliver! soundtrack, 1969; Ivor Novello Jimmy Kennedy Award, 1985; Best Original Theme Radio-TV, Ivor Novello Commercial, 1989; Golden Break Award, 1990; Variety Club Silver Heart for Contribution to the World Musical Theatre, 1997. Memberships: PRS; BASCA; SODS. Current Management: ICM. Address: Oxford House, 76 Oxford Street, London W1N OAX, England.

BARTHOLOMEW Simon James, b. 16 Oct 1965, Woolwich, London, England. Musician (rhythm, lead guitar). Education: BA (Hons) Fine Art, Polytechnic of East London. Career: Guitarist, The Brand New Heavies; The Akimbo Band; Session musician for Mother Earth; Jamiroquai; Samuel Purdey; Mr X. Recordings: Albums: with The Brand New Heavies: The Brand New Heavies; The Heavy Rhyme Experience; Brother Sister; Akimbo on Top; Shelter. Honours: Platinum disc, Brother Sister album. Memberships: Musicians' Union; MCPS; PRS. Hobbies: Painting; Filming; Gardening; Design. Current Management: Wildlife Entertainment. Address: Unit F, 21 Heathmans Road, Parsons Green, London, England.

BARTON Bart, b. USA. Songwriter; Record Producer; Manager. m. Pat McKool, 9 Oct 1975. Education: College. Musical Education: Vocal Education; Piano. Career: Songwriter; Record Producer; President, Canyon Creek Records; President, Nashville Bekool Music; Owner, Lemonsquare Music and Friends of the General Music. Recordings: She's Sitting Pretty, Top Record of the Year, Canada, 1989; Also recorded on Super Country 89 Album, one of Top 10 Records of the Year, Canada, 1989; Co-Producer and writer of 4 songs on album A Tribute to the

American Veterans, featuring Charley Pride, Moe Bandy, BJ Thomas, Bobby Bare, Freddie Hart, Billy Walker, Billy Parker, The Kendalls, Johnny Rodriguez, Johnny Paycheck, Jeff Moore, Riders in the Sky and others. Honours: Candian Country Music Association, Outstsanding International Support Award. Memberships: CMA; CCMA; GMA; CARAS; NARAS. Hobby: Geneology. Address: 23 Music Square E, Suite 101, Nashville, TN 37203, USA.

BARTON James L, b. 12 June 1948, Memphis, Tennessee, USA. Musician (trumpet, flugel horn, piccolo trumpet, cornet); Musical Director; Arranger. m. Lorraine McKenna, 8 Dec 1990, 2 sons. Education: MSE, BSE, University of Michigan, Ann Arbor, 1966-72; De Anza College, Cupertino, California, 1974-76; Musical Education: Private instruction with Claude Gordon, 1974-80. Career: Played with The Platters; Little Anthony; The Shirells; Tommy Rowe; K.C. & The Sunshine Band; Bo Diddley; Musicals, London's West End: Cats; Sophisticated Ladies; Grease; Starlight Express; Into The Woods; Also performed in Assassins, Ronnie Scotts, London. Composition: Looking Back, 1989. Honours: John Phillips Sousa Award, 1966, 1969, 1970. Memberships: AFofM; Musicians' Union (UK). Hobbies: Golf; Snooker; Movies. Current Management: Musical Director, West End Theatres, London. Address: Flat 2, 56 Upper Berkeley Street, London W1H 7PP, England.

BARTON Lou Ann, b. 17 Feb 1954, Fort Worth, Texas, USA. Singer. Career: Live concerts for television: MTV; Austin City Limits; Texas Connection; Member of bands: Fabulous Thunderbirds, 1975; Triple Threat Review and Double Trouble (both as lead singer with Stevie Ray Vaughn), 1977-1980; Solo artist, Lou Ann Barton Band, 1981-1995; Featured vocalist with Jimmie Vaughn supporting Eric Clapton, Royal Albert Hall, 1993. Recordings: Old Enough, 1982; Austin Rhythm And Blues Christmas, 1983; Forbidden Tones, 1988; Read My Lips, 1989; Dreams Come True with Angela Strehli, Marcia Ball, 1990. Honours: 4 times winner, Austin Chronicle Music Awards include 3 years Female Vocalist of Year; Inducted Texas Hall Of Fame, 1992. Current Agent: Davis McLarty Agency. Address: PO Box 3156, Austin, TX 78764, USA.

BARTON Tim, b. 27 Mar 1959, Melbourne, Australia. Singer; Musician; Comedian. m. Jane O'Brien, 30 Aug 1992. Musical Education: Grade 5 guitar, Bruce Clarke Jazz School, Australia. Career: Tours: INXS; Men At Work; Midnight Oil; Concerts: Rolf Harris; Yothu Yindi; Jeff St John; Television: Tourala Telefon; Tours: Europe; Australia; Radio: Garry Crowley Show, GLR; Currently touring extensively with Tim Barton's All Star Six. Recordings: with Tim Bartons's All Star Six: T-BASS; Solo: So Called Thing Called Love. Memberships: PRS; Musicians' Union. Hobby: Ceramics. Current Management: Job Management. Address: 71a Penwith Road, London SW18 4PX, England.

BARZEN Dietmar, b. 18 October 1958, Oberhausen, Germany. Producer; Composer. m. 31 May 1994, 1 daughter. Education: Dipl-kfm, Dr rer pol in Business Administration and Marketing; Composer. Compositions: Songs into the Light, Chris Sutton; Friday Night, Kent; Sky High, Far Side Gallery; Piano Dreams, David Warwick; Number One, SES. Recordings: Approximately 150 published and released titles. Publications: Approximately 150 published titles. Membership: Marketing Club. Hobbies: Jogging; Skiing. Address: Mail Box 4502241, 50877 Cologne, Germany.

BASA Andrej, b. 10 Feb 1950, Ljubljana, Croatia. Composer; Musician (keyboards); Producer; Arranger. m. 27 Nov 1977, 1 son. Musical Education: Academy of Music, Ljubljana. Career: Australia; America; Canada; 25 years on television; More than 1200 compositions, 2000 arrangements. Recordings: Suite for orchestra; Music for 3 films; Album: Between The Sky And The Earth (instrumental music); As producer, arranger, sound engineer: over 180 albums with variuos artists. Honours: Eurovision Song Contest, 1993; 6 Festival awards. Membership: HDS, Croatia. Hobby: Yachting. Address: 51215 Kastav, Rubesi 139A, Croatia.

BASIA (Basia Trzetizelewska), b. Warsaw, Poland. Singer; Songwriter. Career: Singer, Matt Bianco, until 1986; Solo artiste, 1986-; Concerts include: Broadway. Recordings: Solo albums: Time And Tide; London, Warsaw, New York; The Sweetest Illusion; Singles: with Matt Bianco: Get Out Of Your Lazy Bed, 1986; Solo singles include: Drunk On Love; Third Time Lucky; Contributor, film soundtrack, Pret-A-Porter. Current Management: BTB Management, PO Box 3509, Westport, CT 06880, USA.

BASSEY Shirley, b. 8 Jan 1937, Tiger Bay, Cardiff, Wales. Singer; Entertainer. m. (1) Kenneth Hume; (2) Sergio Novak. Career: Variety and revue singer, 1950s; Headlined concerts in New York, Las Vegas, early 1960s; Concerts and regular television appearances worldwide; Semi-retirement, 1981-. Recordings: Hit singles include: Banana Boat Song; Kiss Me Honey Honey, Kiss Me; As I Love You (Number 1, UK), 1959; As Long As He Needs Me; Big Spender; You'll Never Know; I'll Get By; (I) Who Have Nothing; Bond film themes: Goldfinger; Diamonds Are Forever; Moonraker; Numerous albums include: The Bewitching Miss Bassey, 1959; Fabulous Shirley Bassey, 1960; Shirley, 1961; Shirley Bassey, 1962; Let's Face The Music, 1962; Shirley Bassey Belts The Best!, 1965; I've Got A Song For You, 1966; Twelve Of Those Songs, 1968; Live At The Talk Of The Town, 1970; Something, 1970; Something Else, 1971; Big Spender, 1971; It's Magic, 1971; What Now My Love, 1971; I Capricorn, 1972; And I Love You So, 1972; Never, Never, Never, 1973; Live At Carnegie Hall, 1973; Broadway, Bassey's Way, 1973; Nobody Does It Like Me, 1974; Good Bad And Beautiful, 1975; Love Life And Feelings, 1976; Thoughts Of Love, 1976; You Take My Heart Away, 1977; The Magic Is You, 1979; As Long As He Needs Me, 1980; As Time Goes By, 1980; I'm In The Mood For Love, 1981; Love Songs, 1982; All By Myself, 1984; I Am What I Am, 1984; Playing Solitaire, 1985; I've Got You Under My Skin, 1985; Sings The Songs From The Shows, 1986; Born To Sing The Blues, 1987; Let Me Sing And I'm Happy, 1988; Her Favourite Songs, 1988; Keep The Music Playing, 1991; Various compilations. Honours include: 20 Gold discs; 14 Silver discs; TV Times Award, Best Female Singer, 1972; Britannia Award, Best Female Solo Singer In The Last 50 Years, 1977; American Guild Of Variety Artists Award, Best Female Entertainer, 1976. Current Management: c/o Stan Scottland, JKES Services, 404 Park Avenue South, 10th Floor, New York, NY 10016, USA.

BATES Alix, b. 5 Mar 1968, Hampton, Twickenham, Middlesex, England. Singer; Actress; Model. Career: Backing singer, major artists; Commercials; Television programmes; Voice overs for animated cartoons; Modelling: hair, cosmetics, clothes, hands. Membership: Musicians' Union. Hobbies: Dancing; Writing; Swimming; Horse riding; Tennis. Current Management: Featured Artists. Address: 21a Lambolle Place, Belsize Park, London NW3, England.

BATES Django Leon, b. 2 Oct 1960, Beckenham, Kent, England. Musician (keyboards, horn); Composer. m. Beverley Hills, 26 Aug 1988 1 son, 1 daughter. Musical Education: CYM/Full time Young Musicians (Morley College); Self-taught jazz. Career: Formed Human Chain, 1981; Co-founder, Loose Tubes, 1983; Formed Delightful Precipice, 1992; Toured over 30 countries with these bands and others: Europe; USA; South America; Japan; Scandinavia; Television includes: 1 In A Million, BBC TV, 1996; Compositions include: Writing commissions for Evelyn Glennie; J McGregor; London Sinfonietta. Recordings: Summer Fruits/Unrest; Autumn Fires/Green Shoots; Winter Truce/Homes Blaze; Spring Is Here/Shall We Dance? Good Evening... Here Is The News; Contributor, All Men Amen, Iain Ballamy, 1995. Publications: Quarterly newsletter, available from management. Honours: 3 UK Wire Awards, All Music, 1987; German Stern Des Jahres, 1993; French Academie Du Jazz, 1994; Danish Jazz Par Nominee, 1996. Hobbies: Compiling 'To Do' lists; Curry; Good books; World news; Beer. Current Management: Peter Luxton, Partnerships. Address: 5 Dryden Street, London WC2E 9NW, England.

BATES Simon Dominic, b. 24 Aug 1964, London, England. Musician (saxophone, clarinet, flute, wind synthesiser, programmer). Musical Education: BA Hons, Colchester Institute; LGSM (Jazz), Guildhall SMD. Career: Yamaha Saxophone; Wind Synthesiser endorsee and clinician; Musician with: Simon Bates Quartet; Sax Appeal; Peter Erskine; Chaka Khan; Lulu; Billy Ocean; D:Ream; Eddie Floyd; Tony Remy; The Great Googly Moogly; The Diplomats; Zig Zag; Dominic King. Recordings: Television, radio, library sessions; Albums and singles with: D:ream; The Diplomats; EKO; Sasha/Brian Transeau. Membership: Musicians' Union. Hobbies: Computing; Jaguar cars; Recorded music; Music programming. Current Management: Self-managed. Address: 1 Erin Close, Bromley, Kent BR1 4NX, England.

BATT Mike, b. 6 Feb 1950. Songwriter; Composer; Producer; Arranger; Singer. Career: Began as A&R man for Liberty/UA Records, producing Groundhogs, Big Joe Williams, leaving to pursue independent career as Artist, Writer Producer; Produced Linda Lewis, Steeleye Span (All Around My Hat), Elkie Brookes (Lilac Wine), David Essex (Oh What a Circus); Wrote, sang and produced The Wombles (8 UK hits, 4 gold albums) and solo albums Schizophonia, Tarot Suite and others. Compositions include: Caravans, film score; Bright Eyes, for Art Garfunkel, (No 1, UK); A Winter's Tale, Dave Essex; I Feel Like Buddy Holly, Alvin Stardust; Please Don't Fall in Love, Cliff Richard; Solo hit singles: Summertime City; The Ride to Agadir; Lady of the Dawn; The Winds of Change; Theatrical project The Hunting of the Snark, starring Cliff Richard, Roger Daltrey, Deniece Williams, John Hurt, Sir John Gielgud, Captain Sensible, Art Garfunkel; Produced Phantom of the Opera list (Steve Harley and Sarah Brightman); Composer of many commissioned pieces, including the opening of the Channel Tunnel for HM the Queen, also for 50th Wedding Anniverdsary of HM the Queen in 1997 a piece for massed bands of the Guards and 100 pipers; Produced and composed Vanessa Mae's album The Violin Player. Memberships: PRS, council; Vice President, BASCA. Address: c/o Artheat Ltd, 7 Strathearn Place, London W2 2NH, England.

BATTEUX Slim, b. 11 July 1949, La Fère, Aisne, France. Backing Singer; Singer; Musician (Hammond B3). Divorced, 2 daughters. Career: Backing singer for: Diane Tell; Eddy Mitchell; Michel Jonasz; Patricia Kaas; Bill Deraime; Johnny Halliday; Jean-Jacques Goldman; Dicks Rivers; Francis Cabrel; Florent Cagny; Hughes Aufrey; Veronique Samson; Percy Sledge; Billy Paul; Recordings with most of the above artists. Recordings include: Ellis Island: Voices Of America; Ray Charles; Gary Christian. Publication: Je parle Sioux-Lakota. Memberships: SPEDIDAM; ADAMI; SACEM. Hobby: Lakota Sioux language of culture. Address: 9 bis, rue Descombes, 75017 Paris, France.

BATTLE Nicholas Nigel, b. 14 Aug 1957, Dartmouth, Devon, England. Music Publisher; Musician; Manager. m. Lynn, 12 Aug 1989. Musical Education: Classical violin, led Sheffield Youth Orchestra; Self-taught guitar, bass, piano. Career: Bass player, After The Fire; Bass player, Writz; Also worked with Godley And Creme, Kajagoogoo; Currently General Manager, Windswept Pacific Music Ltd. Recordings: Songs recorded by Cliff Richard: First Date; Front Page; Producer, Falling In Love Again, Techno Twins; Memberships: PRS; BASCA; MPA Pop Publishers Committee; IPA Council. Hobbies: Family life; Local Church. Address: 27 Queensdale Place, Holland Park, London W11 4SQ, England.

BAUER Johannes, b. 22 July 1954, Halle, East Germany. Musician. Education: Trombone Studies, Berlin, 1971-77. Career: Freelance Improvisational Musician, 1979-; Duo with Barry Gay, Trio with Annick Nozati and Fred Van Hove Doppelmoppel (with Konrad Bauer, Jee Sachse, Uwe Kropinski) Slawterhaus (with Dietmar Diesner, Jon Rose, Peter Hellinger), Ulrich Gumpert Trio, Peter Brötzmann Alara Orchester, März Combe, Tony Oxleys Contemporary Music Ensemble, Globe Unity Orchestra, Derek Baileys Company, Cecil Taylor European Big Band; Leader of Various Workshop Bands. Recordings: Round About Mittweida; ALARM; Nr.12; Cecil Taylor in Berlin '88; Slawterhaus Live a Victoriaville. Address: Dannecker Str 6, Berlin 10245, Germany.

BAUER William Henry (Billy), b. 14 Nov 1915, Bronx, New York, USA. Musician (banjo, guitar). m. Marion V Cos, 15 Mar 1941, 1 son, 1 daughter. Musical Education: Mostly self-taught; Harmony and theory in college. Career: Woody Herman, 1942-45; Lennie Tristano, 1946-49; Teacher, Conservatory of Modern Music, 1946-1949; NBC Staff Musician, 1950-1958; Benny Goodman, 1958; Brussels Worlds Fair, Sherwood Inn, 1960-62; Ice Capades, 1963-67; Broadway Theatre, 1968-69; Billy Bauer Guitar School, 1970-. Recordings: Freelance recording musician for about 10 years; Guitar solos recorded: Blue Mist; Purple Haze; Short Stories; Greenway; Impressions; Pam, for Woody Herman; Marionette; Blue Boy, both for Lennie Tristano; Duet for saxophone and guitar recorded by Lee Konitz. Publications: Jazz Lines, by Lennie Tristano, Lee Konitz, Warne Marsh; Author, Guitar Instructor Series; Sideman: Autobiography of Billy Bauer, 1997. Honours: Metronome All Star Poll, 1947-51; Down Beat Award, 1949-50. Membership: ASCAP. Hobby: Writing instruction books for guitar. Current Management: William H Bauer Inc. Address: 121 Greenway, Albertson, NY 11507-1121, USA.

BAUZA Mario, b. 28 Apr 1911, Havana, Cuba. Musician (clarinet, saxophone, trumpet); Musical Director; Bandleader; Lecturer. Education: Havana Municipal Conservatory, 1927. Career: Bass clarinetist, saxophonist, orchestras in Havana, late 1920s; Saxophonist with Noble Sissle, 1932; Trumpeter with High Clarke and The Missourians, 1932; Chick Webb, 1933-38; Don Redman, 1938; Cab Colloway, 1938-41; Musical Director and Arranger, Machito's Afro-Cuban Orchestra, 1941-75; Musical Director, Mario Bauzá Afro-Cuban Orchestra, 1986-; Lecturer, Jazz History, Smithsonian Institute, Washington, 1981; Caribbean Cultural Center, New York, 1984-. Honours: Mayor's Award, City Of New York, 1984; Grammy Nomination, 1986. Memberships: ASCAP; Broadcast Music Inc. Address: c/o ASCAP, ASCAP Building, One Lincoln Plaza, New York, NY 10023, USA.

BAY Hans Henrik, b. 26 December 1963, Copenhagen, Denmark. Guitar Player; Composer. m. Susanne Bechmann, 1 son, 1 daughter. Education: Rhythmic Music Conservatory, Copenhagen. Career: Tour in Denmark with Jorgen Emborg, 1988-89; Tour in Denmark with Ensemble NEW and Billy Cobham, 1997; Played with James Moody, Ed Neumeister, Jukkis Outtila, Tomas Franck, Bob Rockwell and Jesper Lundgaard. Composition: Crescent 434, 6/8, In the Bar. Recordings: Jorgen Emborg Septet: Keyword, 1989; Ensemble New with Billy Cobham, 1998. Memberships: Danish Music Union; Danish Jazz Beat Autorer. Current Management: Ole Cristensen, vendersgade 28, 7000 Fredericia, Denmark. Address: Bredager 32, 7120 Vejle O, Denmark.

BAYLIS Christopher Edward, b. 7 July 1954, Reading, Berkshire, England. Producer; Musician (guitar). Education: BSc Hons, University of Surrey. Musical Education: Self-taught. Career: Founder member, Siam, 1980; Formed The Guitar Orchestra, 1989; Production credits include: Maddy Prior; Davey Arthur; Automatic Dlamini. Recordings: The Guitar Orchestra, 1991; Interpretations, The Guitar Orchestra, 1994. Memberships: PRS; MCPS; Musicians' Union. Hobbies: Antiques; Furniture design. Current Management: Park Records. Address: 20 Raleigh Park Road, Oxford OX2 9AZ, England.

BAYNE Iain, b. 22 Jan 1960, St Andrews, Fife, Scotland. Musician (drums, percussion, piano). Career: Member, Scottish folk group Runrig, 1980-; International concerts include: Canada, 1987; Support to U2, Murrayfield Stadium, Edinburgh, 1987; Royal Concert Hall, Glasgow; Open-air concert, Loch Lomond. Recordings: Albums: Play Gaelic, 1978; Highland Connection, 1979; Recovery, 1981; Heartland, 1985; The Cutter And The Clan, 1987; Once In A Lifetime, 1988; Searchlight, 1989; The Big Wheel, 1991; Amazing Things, 1993; Transmitting Live, 1995. Current Management: Marlene Ross Management, 55 Wellington Street, Aberdeen AB2 1BX, Scotland.

BAYNHAM Frank, b. 29 May 1942, Warrington, England. Musician (English concertina, bodhran). m. Sherry, 5 Jan 1972, 3 sons. Education: BEd, Hons, Lancaster University, Art, Music. Career: Founder member, Wigan Folk Club; Played solo and with various individuals, bands; Formed current band Kings of Puck, 1993. Honours: Guinness Best Entertainment of Puck Fair, Killorglin, Co. Kerry, Ireland, with Steve Ashton, Dave Mann, 1993. Membership: Musicians' Union. Hobbies: Snooker; Boules; Irish history; Mythology. Current Management: Ricky McCabe Entertainments Ltd. Address: 26 Crosby Road North, Waterloo, Liverpool L22 4QF, England.

BAYSHAM Debbie, b. 5 Feb 1958, Chapeau, Quebec, Canada. Singer. m. Peter Komisar Jr, 1 son, 2 daughters. Musical Education; 4 years classical guitar. Career: Performed coast to coast, Canada; Appeared several major television shows; Host, 3 part variety mini series, CBC Television, Toronto. Recordings: Albums: Time To Move Along; Mixed Emotions. Honours: Winner, Canadian Open Country Singing Contest; CBC TV Contest, Look Out World Here We Come. Membership: AFofM. Hobbies: Cycling; Mending; Craft making. Current Management: Big Peach Records. Address: RR2, Grand Valley, Ontario L0N 1G0, Canada.

BEACHILL Peter C, b. 1 Feb 1961, Barnsley, Yorkshire, England. Musician (trombone). Musical Education: Leeds College of Music. Career: Studio musician; Various television shows: Royal Variety; Barrymore; BAFTA Awards: BBC, LWT Shows; Tours with James Last; Natalie Cole; Shirley Bassey; Pete Townsend; Cliff Richard; Chris Rea. Recordings: Albums with: Paul McCartney; Sting; Pet Shop Boys; Diana Ross; Rod Stewart; James Last; Shirley Bassey; Cliff Richard; Peter Gabriel; Erci Clapton; Grace Jones; Pink Floyd; Led Zeppelin; Pete Townshend. Honour: BBC Don Lusher Trombone Award. Membership: Royal Society of Musicians. Address: 16 Coniston Road, Muswell Hill, London N10 2BP, England.

BEAKER Norman, b. 21 June 1950, Manchester, England. Musician (guitar, piano); Vocalist; Composer; Producer. m. Sept 1977, divorced 1985, 1 son. Musical Education: College of Music (Northern). Career: Concerts with Alexis Korner; Eric Clapton; Jack Bruce; B B King; Lowell Fulson; Graham Bond; Buddy Guy; Television and radio appearances include: Old Grey Whistle Test; The Tube; So It Goes; Radio 1 in Concert; Paul Jones R&B Show Radio 2; Capital Radio with Jack Bruce; First blues band to tour East Germany, 1977. Recordings: Into The Blues - Norman Beaker Band; Modern Days Lonely Nights; I Was Once A Gambler (Phil Guy); Theme music, World In Action; Theme music, Stand Up. Publications: Freelance writer on R&B, various magazines and journals. Honour: Blues Guitarist Of The Year, 1989. Memberships: PRS; MCPS. Hobbies: Tennis; Walking. Current Management: Actual Music. Address: 14 Hawthorn Grove, Heaton Moor, Stockport SK4 4HZ, England.

BEARD Frank, b. 11 June, 1949, Frankston, Texas, USA. Musician (drums). Career: Joined The Warlocks, 1967; Band name changed to The American Blues, 1968; Founder member, ZZ Top, 1970-; Toured regularly, 1970-; Tours include Eliminator tour, 1984; Afterburner tour, 1985-87; Recycler tour, 1990; Rock The Bowl '91, Milton Keynes, 1991. Recordings: Albums include: 2 with The American Blues, 1968; with ZZ Top: ZZ Top's First Album, 1970; Rio Grande Mud, 1972; Tres Hombres, 1973; Fandango, 1975; Tejas, 1977; The Best Of, 1978; Deguello, 1979; El Loco, 1981; Eliminator, 1983; Afterburner, 1985; Recycler, 1990; Greatest Hits, 1992; Antenna, 1994; Singles include: La Grange, 1974; Tush, 1975; Gimme All Your Lovin', 1983; Sharp Dressed Man, 1983; Legs, 1984; Sleeping Bag, 1985; Stages, 1986; Rough Boy, 1986; Velcro Fly, 1986; Doubleback, from film Back To The Future Part III, 1990; Viva Las Vegas, 1992. Honours include: Several MTV Video Awards; ZZ Top Day, Texas, 1991; Silver Clef Award, Nordoff-Robbins Music Therapy Foundation, 1992. Current Management: Lone Wolf Management, PO Box 163690, Austin, TX 78716, USA.

BEARD George Edward, b. 11 June 1937, Islington, London, England. Musician (guitar); Vocalist; Entertainer. m. Miss W M Welch, 21 May 1960, 1 son, 2 daughters. Musical Education: Self-taught. Career: Performances, all types of venue. Recordings: Semi-professional recordings, own compositions. Membership: Musicians' Union. Hobby: Philately. Current Management: GBS Promotions/Go-direct Entertainments. Address: 43 Westwood Road, Hilsea, Portsmouth PO2 9QP, England.

BEARD Susan Stephanie (Sue), b. 25 Feb 1961, London, England. Jazz Singer; Songwriter; Actress; Writer; Stand-up Comic; Musician (piano, oboe, ukelele). Education: Bristol University postgraduate certificate in film. Musical Education: BA Hons, Music, York University, 1983. Career: Comic/satirical jazz singer; Television appearances: Les Dawson Show, BBC1; Pebble Mill, BBC1; The Happening, with Jools Holland, CH4 TV; Numerous radio broadcasts include: Loose Ends; Pick Of The Week, BBC Radio 4; BBC Radio 2; JFM; Many commercial stations; Concerts include: Live at London's Comedy Store; Ronnie Scott's; Pizza On The Park; Astoria; One Woman Show Tour including Edinburgh Festival; Kuala Lumpur; Arezzo, Paris. Compositions: Spooks! (children's musical), 1995; Composer, performer, many topical, satirical and jazz songs for radio, television, live performances. Hobbies: Films; Coaching drama students in singing and performance. Current Management: Nick Young, Crawfords. Address: 2 Conduit Street, London W1R 9TG, England.

BEARDMORE Neil Anthony, b. 10 Nov 1969, Stoke-On-Trent, Staffordshire, England. Singer; Songwriter. Musical Education: Music tech course, Stoke University, 1995. Career: Gigs, Wheatsheaf, Stoke; The Stage, Hanley; Stoke University; Interview with Radio Stoke to promote new single; Children In Need Charity Concert, Stafford University, 1994. Recordings: Singles: In Bed; Believe In Me, 1994. Membership: Musicians' Union. Hobby: Feeding ducks in the park. Address: 24 Daintry Street, Oakhill, Stoke-On-Trent, Staffordshire ST4 5NN, England.

BÉART Guy, b. 16 July 1930, Cairo, Egypt. Singer; Composer; Engineer; Author. 2 daughters. Education: Ecole Nationale des Ponts etChaussées. Career: Cabaret, recitals and concerts, Paris; Author, producer, television series Bienvenue, 1966-72. Compositions: Songs for artists including: Zizi Jeanmaire; Juliette Greco; Patachou, Maurice Chevalier; Film music includes: L'Eau Vive; Pierrot La Tendresse; La Gamberge. Honours: Chevalier, Légion d'Honneur; Officier, Ordre National du Mérite; Commandeur des Arts et des Lettres; Grand Prix, Academy du Disque, 1957; Academy Charles Cros, 1965; Grand Prix de la Chanson, SACEM, 1987; Prix Balzac, 1987. Address: Editions Temporel, 2 Rue du Marquis de Morès, 92380 Garches, France.

BEASLEY Walter, b. California, USA. Musician (alto/soprano saxophones); Songwriter. Career: Jazz Explosion's Just The Sax tour. Recordings: Private Time; Intimacy. Current Management: c/o Preston Powell, Jazzateria Inc, 112 W 72nd Street, #2F, New York, NY 10023, USA.

BEAUMONT Kenneth, b. 24 Oct 1913, Rochdale, Lancashire, England. Bandleader; Singer; Musician (guitar). m. Margaret Dowler Heath, 1 daughter, 1 daughter by previous marriage. Musical Education: Royal Manchester College Of Music. Career: Singer at Gleneagles, Midland, Manchester, with: Henry Hall; Oscar Rabin; Joe Orlando; BBC Dance Orchestra, directed by Billy Ternant; Hungarian Regent Street; Ken Beaumont Sextet, BBC Broadcasts. Recordings: with Blackpool Tower Orchestra (while a student); Billy Ternant Orchestra. Memberships: Musicians' Union; PRS. Hobbies: Reading; Crosswords. Address: Hindhead, Surrey.

BEAUPRE Jhan, b. 29 Apr 1950, Dallas, Texas, USA. Songwriter; Musician (Guitar). m. Joyce Ann Beaupre, 10 Jul 1983, 6 daughters. Education: Degree in Nursing, Southwestern Union College, 1978. Musical Education: Self-taught. Career: Founded The Sound System, age 15; Played with various bands for 7 years; As songwriter, numerous awards and nominations; Business venture, Sound Illusions, promoting and recording new artists and songwriters. Compositions include: She Can Make A Man Cry; A Good Guitar; There's A Flame. Honours: 3 Trail Blazer Award Nominations, Nashville, USA; Semi-finalist, Austin Songwriters; Placed 2 times, Wisconsin Songwriters. Memberships: BMI; Austin Song Writers Group; Secretary, Johnson County Association; Song Writers of Wisconsin; Fort Bend S W Group. Hobbies: Music; Art; Writing. Current Management: Davis and Davis Music, 5755 June Lane, Winston-Salem, NC 27127, USA. Address: 1006 Hyde Park Court, Cleburne, TX 76031, USA.

BEAUSSIER Daniel Gérard Jacques, b. 2 June 1957, Valenciennes, Nord, France. Musician; Composer; Teacher; Producer. m. Aesa Sigurjonsdottir, 22 Aug 1987, 3 sons, 1 daughter. Education: Engineer, ICAM. Musical Education: First prize, CNR, Lille, France. Career: Tour, Europe, with Carla Bley, 1988; with Nana Vasconcellos, Paris Jazz Festival, 1991; Hozan Yamamato, 1995; Monica Passos; Charlélie Couture; Shiro Daimon; Astrolab Collectif; Correspondances with D Beaussier (150 concerts). Recordings: Fleur Carnivore, Carla Bley; Lueurs Bleues, Daniel Goyone, Trilok Gurtu; Sans(e)krit, Daniel Beaussier; Casamento, Monica Passos; Chambre 13, Lydia Domancich. Publications: Analysis of solos in Findings, My Experience With Saxophone, by Steve Lacy. Memberships: UMJ; FNEIJ; IAJS; Director, EDIM, Creative Music School, Paris. Current Management: EDIM Productions. Address: 24 Avenue d'Alembert, 92160 Antony, France.

BEAVERS Les, b. 23 Nov 1934, Manchester, England. Musician (guitar). m. Terry Burton, 23 Jan 1963. Musical Education: Mainly self taught. Career: Played at various ballrooms, 1956-59; Played with BBC Northern Dance Orchestra, 1959-68; Bob Sharples, Thames TV, 1963-78; Appearances on Granada TV and sessions on STV, among others; Also theatre tours. Membership: Musicians' Union. Hobbies: Golf; Trout fishing. Address: 7 Sandown Road, Sunny Bank, Bury, Lancashire BL9 8HN, England.

BEBEK Zeljko, b. 16 Dec 1945, Sarajevo, Croatia. Singer. m. Sandra Bebek, 2 Oct 1982, 2 daughters. Education: University of Civil Rights. Career: Hundreds of concerts and television shows, over 20 years; 2 million recordings; Many concerts of Townsends and Townsends Peoples in Zagreb, Sarajevo; Tours: Europe; USA; Canada. Recordings: (Singing in Croatian language) Bosanac; Selma; Na Zadnjem Sjedistu; Da Je Srece Bilo; Dabogda Te Voda Odnijela; Sta Je Meni Ovo Trebalo; A Svemir Miruje; Odlazim; Tijana. Membership: Hrvatska Glazbewa Unija (HGU). Hobbies: Skiing; Tennis. Current Management: Song Agency, Split, Croatia. Address: Crnciceva 41, 41000 Zagreb, Croatia.

BECK Jeff, b. 24 June, 1944, Surrey, England. Musician (guitar); Composer; Vocalist. Education: Wimbledon Art College. Career: Member, Screaming Lord Sutch; The Tridents; Guitarist, The Yardbirds, 1965-66; Appearances include: Tours with the Kinks, 1965; The Beatles, Paris, 1965; Manfred Mann, 1965; Rolling Stones '66 tour, 1966; Leader, Jeff Beck Group, 1967-; Concerts include: National Jazz And Blues Festival, 1967, 1968; Newport Jazz Festival, 1969; Secret Policeman's Other Ball, London (Amnesty benefit), 1981; Prince's Trust Rock Gala, Royal Albert Hall, 1983; US tour with Stevie Ray Vaughn, 1989. Recordings: Hit singles include: with the Yardbirds: Heart Full Of Soul; For Your Love; Evil Hearted You/Still I'm Sad; Shapes Of Things; Over Under Sideways Down; with Jeff Beck Group: Hi-Ho Silver Lining; Tallyman; Love Is Blue; Albums include: with the Yardbirds: For Your Love, 1965; Having A Rave Up With The Yardbirds, 1965; The Yardbirds with Sonny Boy Williamson, 1966; Yardbirds, 1966; Over Under Sideways Down, 1966; with Jeff Beck Group/solo: Truth, 1968; Beck-Ola, 1969; Rough And Ready, 1971; Jeff Beck Group, 1972; Jeff Beck, Tim Bogert & Carmine Appice, 1973; Blow By Blow, 1975; Wired, 1976; Jeff Beck With The Jan Hammer Group Live, 1977; There And Back, 1980; Flash, 1985; Jeff Beck's Guitar Shop With Terry Bozzio And Tony Hymas, 1989; Crazy Legs, 1993; Contributor, film soundtracks: The Pope Must Die, 1991; Honeymoon In Vegas, 1992; Contributor, Blaze Of Glory, Jon Bon Jovi, 1990; Amused To Death, Roger Waters, 1992; Tribute To Muddy Waters, 1993; Stone Free - A Tribute To Jimi Hendrix, 1993. Honours: Grammy Awards: Best Rock Instrumental Performance, 1986, 1990; BAFTA Award, Best Original Television Music, Frankie's House, with Jed Leiber, 1993. Current Management: c/o Ernest Chapman, Equator Music, 17 Hereford Mansions, Hereford Road, London W2 5BA, England.

BECK Mick, b. 6 Oct 1947, Bournemouth, England. Improviser; Musician (saxophone). m. Marion Carol Rout, 2 Dec 1978. Education: University, Maths, Philosophy. Career: Improvising tours: UK; Netherlands; Germany, 1980-; BBC radio, national, local performances. Recordings: Listen! Feet Packets (14 piece improvising band); Start Moving Earbuds (Something Else). Memberships: Musicians' Union; Performers Rights Society. Address: 78 Kingfield Road, Sheffield S11 9AU, England.

BECKER Irene, b. 30 Mar 1951, Aalborg, Denmark. Musician (piano); Composer. m. Pierre Dorge, 24 Aug 1985. Education: Cand Phil. in Music, University of Copenhagen. Career: Member, Pierre Dorge's New Jungle Orchestra, 1980-; Member, Trio: Dorge, Becker, Carlsen; Performs with singer Sainkho Namtclylak, Austria; Composer, film music. Recordings: Albums: New Jungle Orchestra, 10 albums; Dancing On The Island, Irene Becker and Sainkho. Memberships: DJBFA; Danish Musicians Union. Current Management: Copenhagen Concerts, Holmbladsgade 35, 2300 Copenhagen S, Denmark.

BECKER Jason. Rock Musician (guitar). Musical Education: Classical guitar. Career: Guitarist, US rock group Cacophony (with Marty Friedman), 1986-90; Also solo artiste; Guitarist, David Lee Roth, 1991-. Albums: with Cacophony: Speed Metal Symphony, 1987; Go Off, 1989; Solo: Perpetual Burn, 1988; with David Lee Roth: A Little Ain't Enough, 1991.

BECKER Peter Alexander, b. 20 Sept 1955, Nuneaton, Warwickshire, England. Musician; Engineer; Producer. Education: Qualified Chemical Engineer. Musical Education: Self-taught. Career: Formed electronic duo Eyeless In Gaza, with singer Martyn Bates, 1980; 5 albums for Cherry Red Records UK; Television appearance: Saturday Superstore, 1985; Janice Long Session, Radio 1; Various concert tours, Europe, Scandinavia. Recordings: Eyeless In Gaza: No Noise; Welcome Now; New Risen; for Anne Clark: I Of The Storm. Memberships: MCPS; PRS; Musicians' Union. Hobbies: Music Technology; Teaching computer skills. Current Management: Ambivalent Scale. Address: Ambivalent Scale Recordings, PO Box 3, Nuneaton, Warwickshire CV10 9YT, England.

BECKER Walter, b. 20 Feb 1950, New York, USA. Musician (guitar, bass); Record Producer. 1 son, 2 stepsons. Career: Founder member, Steely Dan, 1972-81, 1993-; Record producer, 1980-; Solo recording artiste; Tours of US; Japan; Europe; Australia. Recordings: Albums: Can't Buy A Thrill, 1973; My Sportin' Life, 1973; Countdown To Ecstacy, 1973; Pretzel Logic, 1974; Katy Lied, 1975; The Royal Scam, 1976; Aja, 1978; Greatest Hits, 1979; Metal Leg, 1980; Gaucho, 1981; Reelin' In The Years, 1985; Do It Again, 1987; Remastered - The Best Of Steely Dan, 1993; Citizen Steely Dan 1972-1980, 1993; Alive In America, 1995; Solo album: 11 Tracks Of Whack, 1995; Singles include: Dallas; Show Biz Wigs; My Old School; Black Friday; Kid Charlemagne; Haitian Divorce; Deacon Blues; FM (No Static At All); Rikki Don't Lose That Number; As producer: Flaunt The Imperfection, China Crisis, 1985; Flying Cowboys, Rickie Jones, 1989; Jazz recordings for: LeeAnn Ledgerwood; Andy Laverne; Jeff Beal; Jeremy Steig; David Kikosi; Lorraine Feather; Sam Butler; Donald Fagen. Honours: Platinum disc; Grammy Award, Aja, 1978; Inducted into Hollywood's Rock Walk, 1993. Current Management: HK Management, 8900 Wilshire Blvd, Ste 300, Beverly Hills, CA 90211, USA.

BECKERS (Ludo) Lazy Lew, b. 27 March 1957, Molenstede, Belgium. Musician (Harmonica). m. 27 March 1981, 1 son, 1 daughter. Education: Selftaught Harmonica; Jazz Theory Lessons, Halewÿnstichting, Antwerp, Belgium. Career: Harmonica Player (sometimes Singer), The Zoots, 1984-86; The Sultans, 1987; Medford Slim Band, 1990-94; Brothers in Blues, 1990-96; European Tours with Zora Young, R L Burnside, Big Lucky Carter, Calvin Jackson.

Recordings: The Zoots and Louisiana Red; The Sultans; Medford Slim Band; P Vansant. Honours: Nominated for W C Handy Award, Category Best Bluesband Foreign (The Zoots), 1987. Membership: SABAM. Hobby: Freelance Journalism. Address: 77 Te Boelaarlei, B-2140 Borgerhout, Belgium.

BECKETT David, b. 11 Jan 1964, London, England. Musician (drums, keyboards); Programmer; Songwriter. Career: Member, Opposition; Member, Josi Without Colours; Tours: UK and Europe, 1978-; Numerous local radio appearances, and Round Table, Radio 1, 1991. Recordings: with Josi Without Colours: Hear The Animals Cry; Children Of The Revolution; Tell Me A Story; Treasure, 1991; Lucy, 1991. Memberships: PRS; Musicians' Union; PPL. Hobbies: New musical equipment; Step aerobics. Current Management: David Rome, Anne-Marie Heighway, Survival. Address: PO Box 888, Maidenhead, Berkshire SL6 2Y2, England.

BECVAR Bruce, b. 22 June 1953, Louisville, Kentucky, USA. Musician (guitar, multi-instrumentalist); Producer. Education: National Outdoor Leadership School. Career: Founded Shining Star Prod's Label; Joined Windham Hill Records for Guitar Sampler 1986; Toured with Winham Hill Summer Concert Series, California; Performance in New York City at Awakening The Soal Conference (Omega Institute) with Derek Chopra, 1995. Recordings: Take It To Heart; The Nature Of Things; Forever Blue Sky; Arriba; Time Dreams; Samadhi; Jiva Mukti; Windham Hill Guitar Sampler 1986. Honour: Handmade guitar displayed, Metropolitan Museum, New York City. Membership: BMI. Hobbies: Self-realization; Meditation; Hiking. Current Management: Gus Swigert Management. Address: 1537 Fourth Street, Suite 197, San Rafael, CA 94901, USA.

BEDER Mark, b. 16 Nov 1959, London, England. Record Producer; Music Publisher; Artist Manager. 1 son, 1 daughter. Career: A&R Dept, Carlin Music Publishers; A&R Manager, Polydor & Virgin Records; Currently Managing Director for Pumphouse Music; Pumphouse Sounds; Pumphouse Songs; FXU Records; Manager of: D:ream; X-Avia; Tri; Siren; D J Peer; Recordings by artists listed above. Honours: Best Newcomers; Best Dance Act; Radio One Tune Of The Year, 1992; Official Labour Party Athem, Things Can Only Get Better. Memberships: PRS; MCPS; MPA; IMF. Hobbies: Music; Fun and games. Address: FXU, G T Studios, 97 Scrubs Lane, London NW10 6QU, England.

BEEBY John, b. 18 Nov 1945, Nuneaton, Warwickshire, England. Musician (guitar); Songwriter; Producer. m. 16 Nov 1974, 1 son. Musical Education: Taught by father. Career: Tour, Germany, 1963-64; The Zephyrs, 1964; Toured with: Del Shannon; Jerry Lee Lewis; Billy Fury; Count Prince Miller, 1968; Tony Gregory; Horace Faith; Television appearances include: Ready Steady Go; Top Of The Pops; Scene At 6.30; Wogan; Pebble Mill; Film appearances: Be My Guest (with Jerry Lee Lewis, Steve Marriot); Primitive London; Ice Cream Dream; Business Ventures: John Beeby's Music Place, 1975; Worked freelance with various artists; Worked with Eurythmics' Dave Stewart as songwriter, producer, 1980s; Co-writer, Dreamtime, with Daryl Hall, 1986; Co-writer, producer, with Brian Hodgson, Why Do I Always Get It Wrong (UK entry, Eurovision Song Contest), Number 2, 1989; Worked in Nashville, USA, with various artists including Robert Ellis Orral, Larry Henley, Roger Cook, 1989. Recordings: She's Lost You, 1964; Wonder What I'm Gonna Do, 1965; A Little Bit Of Soap, 1965; Dreamtime, 1986; Why Do I Always Get It Wrong, 1989; Take A Chance On Me, 1989. Honours: BMI Dreamtime, USA; BMI Dreamtime, UK. Memberships: PRS; BASCA. Address: Crouch End, London N8, England.

BEECHER Franny, b. Philadelphia, Pennsylvania, USA. Musician (guitar). Musical Education: Worked with Benny Goodman. Career: Original member, Bill Haley's Comets, 1952-62; Invented rock'n'roll music; First rock band to headline a film; Worked with Buddy Grecco. Recordings: Rock Around The Clock; See You Later Alligator; Crazy Man Crazy; Shake Rattle And Roll; Rock The Joint; Mabo Rock; Rudy's Rock; Florida Twist; Skinnie Minnie. Publications: Rck Around The Clock; Stage Clear; We're Gonna Party; Never Too Old To Rock. Honours: Best Vocal Group, 1954; Best Instrumental Group, 1956; Best Guitar Player; Rock And Roll Hall Of Fame; Gold Records. Address: Rock It Concerts, Bruno Mefer Platz 1, D-80937 Munich, Germany.

BEGGS Nick, b. 15 December 1961, Winslow, Bucks, England. Musician (Bass Guitar, Chapman Stick); Producer; Writer; Arranger. 1 daughter. Education: Self-taught. Career: Kajagoogoo; Ellis Beggs and Howard Iona; Belinda Carlisle. Compositions: White Feathers; Islands; Crazy People's Right to Speak; Homelands; The Book of Kells; Beyond These Shores. Publication: Too Shy, Kajagoogoo, 1983. Recordings: Bigg Bubbies No Troubles, from LP Homelands by Ellis Beggs and Howard; A Woman and A man, Belinda Carlisle. Memberships: Musicians' Union; MCPS; PPL; PRS. Hobby: Flying Gliders. Address: 61 Atheldene Road, London SW18 3BN, England.

BEIJBOM Lars, b. 1 August 1950, Sweden. Composer; Arranger; Drums. 1 son. Education: Berklee College of Music, composition, arranging diploma, 1975. Career: Composer & arranged music for large number of Radio/TV Programs; Big Bands Symphony Orchestra's, Pop/Rock/Jazz; Played, arranged & composed music for artists including: George Russell, Dorothy Donegan, Tomas Ledin, Maritza Horn, Tre Damer, The Swedish Radio Jazz Group, The Danish Radio Big Band, NDR - band. Compositions: Three for Daniel; The Swinging Triangle; In the Long Run; Eat Your Heart Out; Up Your Alley; The Goose is Out; Sweet Sadness; The Fire Within; Alpha & Omega; 11 Peterborough Street. Recordings: Subway Baby, 1977; White Orange, 1980; Bright Orange - The Goose is Out, 1983; Beijbom Kroner Big Band, Live in Copenhagen, 1996. Memberships: STIM; SKAP; SAMI. Address: Flygelv 4, S-22472 Lund, Sweden.

BELAFONTE Harry (Harold George), b. 1 Mar 1927, Harlem, New York, USA. Singer; Actor; Producer; Human Rights Activist. m. (1) Marguerite, 1948; (2) Julie Robinson, 1957, 1 son, 3 daughters. Education: Dramatic Workshop Of The New School For Social Research. Career: Member, American Negro Theater, late 1940s; Performer, New York clubs, early 1950s; Singer, actor, Broadway, 1953; Recording artist, actor, 1954; Worldwide tours: UK; Europe; USA; Canada; Australia; New Zealand; Jamaica; Cuba; Actor, films: Bright Road, 1952; Carmen Jones (television version), 1955; Island In The Sun, 1957; Odds Against Tomorrow, 1959; Buck And The Preacher, 1971; Uptown Saturday Night, 1974; First Look, 1984; The Player, 1992; Television appearances include: A Time For Laughter, 1967; Harry And Lena (with Lena Horne), 1969; Tonight With Belafonte, 1960; As producer: Strolling Twenties; Beat Street; Producer, stage: To Be Young Gifted And Black, 1969; Performer, co-ordinator, We Are The World, USA For Africa charity recording, 1985. Recordings: Songs include: Banana Boat Song; Matilda; Island In The Sun; Mary's Boy Child; Numerous albums include: Calypso, 1956; Porgy And Bess (with Lena Horne), 1959; Streets I Have Walked, 1963; Don't Stop The Carnival, 1972; Belafonte '89, 1989; Also recorded with Miriam Makeba; Nana Mouskouri. Honours: Tony Award, John Murray Anderson's Almanac, Broadway, 1953; Emmy Award (First black recipient), Tonight With Belafonte, 1960; Grammy Award, We Are

The World, 1985; American Music Award, We Are The World, 1985; Cultural adviser, Peace Corps (first entertainer chosen), 1988; National Conference Of Black Mayors Tribute, 1991; UNICEF's Danny Kaye Award, 1989; Mandela Courage Award (Inaugural presentation), 1990; UNICEF Goodwill Ambassador, 1987. Address: c/o William Morris Agency, 1325 Avenue of the Americas, New York, NY 10019, USA.

BELASCO Pete, b. 1 July 1966, Queens, NY, USA. Vocalist; Songwriter; Saxophonist. m. 3 October 1991, 1 daughter. Education: Rutgers University, New Jersey. Career: Today, show appearance with Kim Carnes. Composition: Lap of Luxury, sung by Diane Wild-Island. Recordings: Debut: Get it Together. Membership: BMI. Current Management: Avenue Management Group, Bruce Garfield, 250 W 57th St Suite 407, New York, NY 10019, USA.

BELCHEV Mikhail Ivanov, b. 13 Aug 1946, Sofia, Bulgaria. Singer; Composer; Lyricist; Musician (guitar); Director. m. Christina Konstantinova Belcheva, 15 Apr 1988, 1 son. Education: Honours degrees in: Mining, Geology Engineering; Theatre Directing; Television Directing. Musical Education: Bodra Smyana Bulgarian National Youth Choir. Career: Solo artiste since 1967-; Tours: Italy, 1970; Spain, 1982; France, 1983; West Berlin, 1986; USA, 1987; Canada, 1988; USSR; Germany; Poland; Czechoslovakia; Romania. Recordings: Albums: Where Are Your Friends, 1972; Counterpart, 1977; Re-Qualification, 1988; Cricket On The Pavement, 1993; Man To Hug (lyrics by Mikhail Belchev) 1994; TV biographical musical films: Where Are You Friends, 1973; Counterpart, 1977. Publications: Poetry: At First Cock-Crow, 1987; A Man To Hug, 1994. Honours: Cyril and Methodius Order Highest degree, Golden Orpheus Festival, many awards; Awards, Bratislava and Sopot Festivals. Memberships: Bulgarian Artiste Association; The Music Author Board Of Directors. Hobbies: Collection of paintings and bronze/brass plastic art works. Current Management: Union Art Foundation. Address: 1408 Sofia, ZK Strelbishte Bl 97, Entr A, Ap 37, Bulgaria.

BELEW Adrian. Musician (guitar); Singer; Songwriter; Producer. Career: Session musician, 1980s; Singer, guitarist, King Crimson, 1981-84, 1993-; Solo artiste, 1982-; Founder, The Bears, 1986; Producer, Jars of Clay, 1966. Recordings: Albums: Solo: Lone Rhino, 1982; Twang Bar King, 1983; Mr Musichead, 1989; Young Lions, 1990; Inner Revolution, 1990; Desire Caught By The Tail, 1991; The Acoustic Adrian Belew, 1995; with King Crimson: Discipline, 1981; Beat, 1982; Three Of A Perfect Pair, 1984; Vroom, 1995; Thrak, 1995; B'Boom, 1995; with The Bears: The Bears, 1987; As session musician: with Laurie Anderson: Mister Heartbreak, 1984; Home Of The Brave, 1986; with David Bowie: Stage, 1978; Lodger, 1979; Another Face, 1981; with Talking Heads: Remain In Light, 1980; The Name Of This Band Is, 1982; with Frank Zappa: In New York, 1978; Sheik Yerbouti, 1979; Yer Are What You Is, 1982; You Can't Do That On Stage Anymore, 1988; The Key, Joan Armatrading, 1983; The Catherine Wheel, David Byrne, 1981; Maybe It's Live, Robert Palmer, 1982; Zoolook, Jean-Michel Jarre, 1984; True Colors, Cyndi Lauper, 1986. Current Management: Umbrella Artists, PO Box 8385, 2612 Erie Avenue, Cincinnati, OH 45208, USA.

BELL Andrew Piran, b. 11 Aug 1970, Cardiff, Wales. Musician (guitar); Songwriter. m. Idha Övelius, 112 Feb 1992. Education: Banbury Art School, 1988-89. Musical Education: Self-taught. Career: Singer, songwriter and lead guitarist, rock band Ride, 1988-; Session musician with Idha, 1992-. Recordings: Nowhere, Ride, 1990; Going Blank Again, Ride, 1992; Carnival Of Light, Ride, 1994; Melody Inn, Idha, 1994.

BELL Andy, b. 25 Apr 1964. Vocalist; Songwriter. Career: Vocalist, Void; Lead vocalist, pop duo Erasure (with Vince Clarke), 1985-; Regular UK and international tours; Performances include: Support to Duran Duran, US tour, 1987; Prince's Trust Rock Gala, NEC Birmingham, 1989; Red Hot And Dance AIDS benefit concert, 1991; Duet with k d lang, BRIT Awards, 1993. Recordings: Albums: Wonderland, 1986; The Circus, 1987; Two Ring Circus, 1987; The Innocents, 1988; Wild!, 1989; Chorus, 1991; Pop! - The First 20 Hits, 1992; I Say I Say I Say, 1994; Erasure, 1995; Numerous hit singles include: Sometimes, 1986; Victim Of Love, 1987; Ship Of Fools, 1988; A Little Respect, 1988; Drama!, 1989; Chorus, 1991; Love To Hate You, 1991; Breath Of Life, 1992; Abba-esque EP (Number 1, UK), 1992; Who Needs Love (Like That) remix, 1992; Stay With Me, 1995; Contributor to: Red Hot & Blue (AIDS benefit record); Tame Yourself (animal rights benefit record). Honours: BRIT Award, Best British Group, 1989; Ivor Novello Award, Most Performed Work of 1990, Blue Savannah, 1991. Address: c/o Mute Records, 429 Harrow Road, London W10 4RE, England.

BELL Chris, b. 26 Aug 1960, London, England. Musician (drums). Career: Joined Thompson Twins, 1979-82; Tour with King Trigger, 1982; Joined Spear Of Destiny, 1982-83; Work with Specimin, 1985; Joined Gene Love Jezebel, 1986-1991; Tour, USA, Japan, 1986; Television includes: MTV Awards, Joan Rivers Show, 1986; Tours: UK/Europe, USA, Japan, South America, UK, 1988; USA, supporting Echo And The Bunnymen, New Order, 1987; USA, Europe, UK, supporting Billy Idol, 1990; USA, 1990; Tours, recordings, television, with Big Country, 1991-92; Tour, recording, Nan Vernon, 1992; Tours with Hugh Cornwall, UK, Europe, 1993; France, 1994; UK, 1994; Live work with Phantom Chords, 1994-95; Various sessions, 1995; Live work with Gene Loves Jezebel, 1995. Recordings: Albums with Thompson Twins: A Product Of, 1981; Set, 1982; Single: In The Name Of Love; Grapes Of Wrath, Spear Of Destiny, 1982; Single: Ain't That Always The Way, Edwyn Collins, 1985; with Gene Loves Jezebel, The Immigrant, 1985; House Of Dolls; Kiss Of Life, 1989; Album with Nan Vernon, 1993; Album with Hugh Cornwall, 1995. Hobby: Checking out places missed when touring. Address: 2 Bolingbroke Road, London W14 0AL, England.

BELL Colin Stewart, b. 11 Sept 1952, Carrickfergus, County Antrim, Northern Ireland. Record Company Executive. Education: BA Hons Drama. Career: Publicist, Rogers and Cowan; Manager, Tom Robinson Band; Head of Press, Phonogram UK Ltd; Joined London Records, 1982, currently Managing Director. Honours: Leslie Perrin P R Award; Music Week Marketing Award. Hobbies: Theatre. Address: 51 Hillgate Place, London SW12 9ES, England.

BELL Dennis Lawrence, b. 4 Dec 1941, New York City, USA. Record Producer; Musician (keyboard); Music Educator; Personal Manager; Arranger; Conductor; Composer. m. Claudette Washington, 28 Apr 1979, 1 son, 3 daughters. Education: Bachelor of Music, NYU; Master of Arts, Composition, Queens College. Musical Education: Piano, arranging, composition, conducting with variety of teachers. Career: Television appearances include: Joan Rivers; BBC, One World One Voice; Top Of The Pops; with U2; Madison Square Garden; Carnegie Hall; Rattle And Hum; Commercials: Pizza Hut with Aretha Franklin; Roy Rogers; Drakes Company; Give Peace A Chance; Keep Rising To The Top; Videos. Recordings: with Tom Browne; Dave Valentine; Doug E; Fresh; U2; Celia Cruz; Give Peace A Chance; Touché; Lee Ritenour; Scrooged film soundtrack. Publication: Music Alive. Honours: Boystown for Public Service; Bronx Boro President's Award for Community Service. Memberships: BMI; National Association

of Jazz Educators. Hobbies: Cooking; Golf. Current Management: City Slicker Productions. Address: PO Box L, Inwood Station, New York, NY 10034, USA.

BELL Eric, b. 3 Sept 1947, Belfast, Northern Ireland. Musician (guitar); Singer; Songwriter. Musical Education: Self-taught. Career: Musician with Van Morrison, Northern Ireland, 1967; Founder member, rock group Thin Lizzy, 1969-74; Co-arranger, Whiskey In The Jar; Television apppearance: Top Of The Pops; Joined Noel Redding Band, 1976-78. Recordings: with Thin Lizzy: Whiskey In The Jar; The Rocker. Honours: Gold album, The Adventures Of Thin Lizzy; Silver single, Whiskey In The Jar. Hobbies: Reading; Listening to music. Address: 115 Pembroke Avenue, Enfield, Middlesex EN1 4EZ, England.

BELL Marc Gordon, b. 20 July 1961, Chelsea, London, England. Musician (guitar); Lead Vocalist; Record Producer; Engineer; Author; Publisher; Studio Owner: Brain Dead; A&R at Candor Records. m. Jane Louise Kingcott, 21 Oct 1982, 1 son, 1 daughter. Education: BEd (hons). Musical Education: Self-taught; Guitar Institute; MIMI (LOCF Level 4). Career: Guitarist with punk band The Straps, 1977; Various bands until 1987; Founder, guitarist. vocalist, The Thamesmead Rollers, 1987; Various live dates, 2 albums; Built own recording studio, Brain Dead, 1992; TMR Lists, 1993-; A&R at Candor Records, 1994-; TMR production, 1994-; Current promoter, Jupiter Joy, television, press, radio, concerts, other acts. Recordings: 3 albums, The Thamesmead Rollers include: Wasted Years, 1992; Too Old To Rock, 1994; Various compilation releases include: Approaching Incandesence; 2 Incandescent Rock EPs; Rock On! features single: Twenty Odd Years; Other acts on album: Slade; The Mission; Current project: Dance Album with Mike Westergaard (ex-The Blesssing). Publications: Author, publisher, The TMR Lists include: TMR A&R List; TMR Venues, Rehearsal Rooms & Studio List; TMR Musical Sevices List; TMR Fanzine List; TMR The List; TMR The Demo Guide. Hobbies: Caving; Rock climbing. Current Management: Candor Management. Address: Marc Bell, TMR Productions, PO Box 3775, London SE18 3QR, England.

BELL Philip, b. 21 May 1965, Finsbury Park, London, England. Musician (guitar, bass). Musical Education: Guitar Institute Of Technology, Wapping, London. Career: Guitarist, Brothers Like Outlaw; European Tour supporting Arrested Development, 1993; Also festivals including: Fest'in Bahia, Salvador, Brazil, 1992; Citta D'ella Musica, Bari, Italy, 1992; Metropolis, Rotterdam, Netherlands, 1992; Jazz In Sardinia, 1992; Radio and television: Chart Show, 1993; BBC Radio 1 session; Member, Vibe Tribe; Concerts include Phoenix Festivals, UK, 1993-94; with The Filberts, Glastonbury Festival, 1993; Television: TXT, 1994; with Leena Conquest; European Tour supporting Bryan Ferry, 1994. Recordings: with Vibe Tribe: Johnny; Our Purpose, 1993; with FM Inc: Call Me Anytime, 1992; Fresh'n'Funky; Chill Me, 1993. Publications: Music Journalist, Sounds, 1980-84. Memberships: Musicians' Union; PRS; MCPS. Hobby: Spiritual development. Address: 17A Northbrook Road, London N22 4YQ, England.

BELLAMY David, b. 16 Sept 1950, Darby, Florida, USA. Vocalist; Songwriter. Career: Played R&B clubs, backing Eddie Floyd, Percy Sledge, Little Anthony and the Imperials; Played throughout Southeast USA, with own band, Jericho; Wrote Spiders and Snakes for Jim Stafford, 3 million sales worldwide; Cut demos with Neil Diamond's band; Formed Bellamy Brothers with brother Howard; Most successful duo in country music history; Tours with Loggins & Messina; Doobie Brothers; Beach Boys; Conway Twitty; Collaborated as songwriter with Costas, Don Schlitz and Bobby Braddock; Formed Bellamy Brothers Records; Initiated annual Snake

Rattle & Roll Jam, 1989, major charity fundraiser. Compositions include: Spiders And Snakes; Sugar Daddy; Do You Love As Good As You Look; Old Hippie; Kids Of The Baby Boom. Recordings: Singles include: Let Your Love Flow, 1976 (Number 1 in charts in ten countries); If I Said You Had A Beautiful Body Would You Hold It Against Me, 1979; Sugar Daddy, Dancin' Cowboys, 1980; Do You Love As Good As You Look, 1981; For All The Wrong Reasons, 1982; Redneck Girl, 1982; When I'm Away From You, 1983; I Need More Of You, 1985; Feelin' The Feelin,' 1985; Too Much Is Not Enough, 1986; Kids Of The Baby Boom, 1986; Crazy From The Heart, 1987; 22 albums, 1976-94. Honours: Platinum albums, UK, Scandinavia; Gold albums, USA, Austria, Germany, UK, Norway, Sweden; Consistently nominated Duo of the Year, CMA, ACM, 1979-; Record of the Year, If I Said You Had A Beautiful Body, England, 1979; Independent Video of Year, Cowboy Beat, CMT. Memberships: ASCAP; AFTRA; AFofM. Hobbies: Collecting Western and Indian artifacts; Travel; Swimming. Current Management: Bellamy Brothers Partners. Address: 13917 Restless Lane, Dade City, FL 33525, USA.

BELLAMY Gary, b. 31 Aug 1957, Hammersmith, London, England. Songwriter; Musician (saxophone); Musical Education: Saxophone tuition with Tim Whithead, Paul Mason. Career: Appearances: Chiltern Radio; Radio One, live interview; Television appearance, Buddy Holly Documentary; Played saxophone for pop group, Did The Earth Move. Recordings: Single: One In A Million. Membership: Musicians' Union. Hobby: Photography. Address: 238 Old Oak Common Lane, London W3, England.

BELLAMY Howard, b. 2 Feb 1946, Darby, Florida, USA. Vocalist; Songwriter. m. Ilona. Career: Played R&B Clubs, backing Eddie Floyd, Percy Sledge, Little Anthony and the Imperials; Played Southeast USA with own band, Jericho; Became Jim Stafford's road manager; Cut demos with Neil Diamond's band; Formed The Bellamy Brothers with brother David; Most successful duo in country music history; Toured USA with Loggins & Messina; Doobie Brothers; Beach Boys; Conway Twitty; 14 number 1 singles in US country charts; Collaborated with Costa, Don Schlitz and Bobby Braddock; Formed Bellamy Brothers Records; Initiated annual benefit concert, Snake Rattle & Roll Jam, 1989, major local charity fundraiser. Recordings: Singles include: Let Your Love Flow, 1976 (Number 1 in charts in ten countries); If I Said You Had A Beautiful Body Would You Hold It Against Me, 1979; Sugar Daddy, 1980; Dancin' Cowboys, 1980; Do You Love As Good As You Look, 1981; For All The Wrong Reasons, 1982; Redneck Girl, 1982; When I'm Away From You, 1983; Old Hippie, 1985; I Need More Of You, 1985; Feelin' The Feelin', 1985; Too Much Is Not Enough, 1986; Kids Of The Baby Boom, 1986; Crazy From The Heart, 1987; You'll Never Be Sorry, 1989; 22 albums, 1976-94. Honours: Consistently nominated Duo of the Year, CMA, ACM, since 1979. Platinum albums, England, Scandinavia; Gold albums, USA, Austria, Germany, UK, Norway, Sweden; Record of the Year, If I Said You Had A Beautiful Body, UK, 1979; Independent Video of 1992, Cowboy Beat, CMT. Memberships: ASCAP; AFTRA; AFofM. Hobbies: Travel; Swimming; Collecting Western & Indian artifacts. Current Mangagement: Bellamy Brothers Partners. Address: 13917 Restless Lane, Dade City, FL 33525, USA.

BELLAMY-LOREN Gina, b. 23 Apr 1957, Dallas, Texas, USA. Record Company Executive; Record Producer; Singer; Songwriter. Education: Graduate, Degree in Geology, University of Texas, Arlington. Musical Education: Classical guitar, voice, music composition. Career: Began recording, singing career, aged 13; Duet concerts with some radio and television appearances; Stand-in actor on television series Dallas; Organized Scootertunes Incorporated, Scooter

Records, Scooter Productions and J B Quantum Music; Participated in the live radio broadcast of Willie Nelson's Farm Aid, 1994. Recordings: True Love Conquers All, Gina Bellamy, 1994; The Fever, The Fever (contemporary Country group), 1995; Feelings of Christmas/Santa's All Star Revue, 1996; Lavender Blue, 1997. Memberships: AFofM; Nashville Songwriters Association International; ASCAP; BMI; AFIM; International Platform Association. Hobbies: Floral design; Gourmet cooking; Travel; Gardening; Studying foreign languages. Current Management: Scootertunes Incorporated. Address: PO Box 610166, Dallas, TX 75261, USA.

BELLE Gloria, b. 9 June 1939, Silver Run, Maryland, USA. Vocalist; Musician (mandolin, guitar, bass, autoharp, banjo, piano). m. Mike Long, 23 Sept 1989. Musical Education: Few lessons, mandolin; Mother taught guitar and piano; Others form records, radio, friends. Career: Age 3, with parents on religious programme, Maryland; 7 years, Cas Walker Show, radio and television, Knoxville, Tennessee; Tour, Japan, with Jimmy Martin Show, 1975; Many guest appearances, with Jimmy Martin Show, Grand Ole Opry; Guest vocalist, Nitty Gritty Dirt Band's multimillion selling album: Will The Circle Be Broken. Recordings: with Johnson Mountain Boys: Love Of The Mountains; with Jimmy Martin And The Sunny Mountain Boys: A Good Hearted Woman; 2 cassettes, 1 compact disc with current band Gloria Belle and Tennessee Sunshine. Honours: Most Versatile Entertainer, First Prize Vocal Category; Fiddler's Convention, Virginia; Most Promising Bass Player, 1971. Memberships: IBMA; Bluegrass Association of North Carolina, South Carolina, Georgia; AFofM. Hobbies: Photography; Gardening; Swimming; Walking; Attending shows by favourite musicians. Address: Gloria Belle and Tennessee Sunshine, 479 Brentlawn Drive, Nashville, TN 37220-2009, USA.

BELLEST Christian, b. 8 Apr 1922, Paris, France. Musician (trumpet); Arranger. m. Sally Pearce, 9 Jan 1962, 1 son. Education: CEP. Musical Education: Musical studies, harmony, counterpoint, fugas. Career: Accompanist, arranger, for singers including Edith Piaf; Yves Montand; Michel Berger; Veronique Sanson; Paul Anka; Television series and films. Recordings with: Django Reinhardt; Aux Combelle; Jazz De Paris; Jacques Helian. Publications: Co-author, Le Jazz for collection Que Sais-Je; Articles for Les Cahiers Du Jazz. Membership: Academie Du Jazz. Hobby: Home studio. Address: 9 Rue Victorien Sardou, 75016 Paris, France.

BELLIS Nigel Gwyn, b. 7 May 1960, Urmston, Manchester, England. Television Producer; Composer. m. Carol Elizabeth Evans, 16 July 1983, 2 sons. Musical Education: Tuition, piano, church organ, clarinet. Career: Played keyboards, sang with a variety of club bands, 1970s, 1980s; Set up 8 track home studio and recorded a range of acts, from solo artistes to choirs; Composed audio/visual production called Visit to Africa; Now, writing TV themes. Compositions: Theme music, 2 war documentaries, also produced: Guns For Malta, HTV Wales, shown internationally; Last Post On River Kwai, Granada TV, 1995. Publications: Former freelance writer for What Keyboard, Electronic Soundmaker. Memberships: Musicians' Union; PRS. Hobby: Travel. Current Management: Self-managed. Address: 67 Church Road, Rhos-On-Sea, Colwyn Bay, Clwyd LL2 8YS, Wales.

BELLOW Roger David, 15 Apr 1950, Chicago, Illinois, USA. Musician (guitar, violin, mandolin, banjo, bass); Teacher. m. Judy Golombeck, 25 Sept 1977, divorced. Education: BA University of Tennessee; Antioch College; Foreign study, Bogotá, Colombia. Musical Education: Old Town School of Folk Music, Chicago. Career: Cas Walker, TV Show,

Knoxville, Tennessee, 1968-70; Kennedy Center Concert, Washington, DC, 1976; Kaustinen International Folk Festival, Finland, 1981; Belize Tour, 1983; University of Chicago, Folk Festival, 1986; Faculty of Augusta Heritage Center, Elkins, W Virginia, 1989-; SC Arts Comm Resident Artist, 1987-; Host, Vintage Country Radio Program, public radio, 1987-; Japan Tour, 1993. Recordings: with Revonah: Get In Line Brother, 1980; with Flying Fish: Success Street, 1988; On The Road To Prosperity, 1991; (Japanese recording) The Bay Quintet, 1993; with Augusta Faculty Band: Zombies Of Swing, 1994. Publications: Research published in Bluegrass Unlimited and Journal of Country Music. Honours: South Carolina Folk Heritage Award, 1995; SC Grant for Research in Country Music. Memberships: AFofM; ROPE (Reunion Of Professional Entertainers). Hobby: Record collecting. Current Management: Town and Country Music. Address: 411 Hibben, Mt Pleasant, SC 29464, USA.

BELMONDO Lionel, b. 19 Aug 1963, Hyères, France. Musician (saxophones, flute). Musical Education: Jazz: Piano and saxophone studies, Conservatory of Toulon. Career: Director, School of Music, Centre Vas; Professor in other schools, 1982-90; Moved to Paris, 1990; Sideman for concerts with Michel Legrand; Phil Woods; Toots Thielemans; Dee Dee Bridgewater; Horace Silver; Lew Tabackin; Own quintet with brother Stéphane; Leader, Belmondo Big Band, with brother Stéphane; Television: Belmondo In Concert, on Jazz 6, at M6, 1995. Recordings include: Belmondo Quintet; For All Friends, Belmondo Quintet; Love And Peace, Dee Dee Bridgewater. Honour: Prix Django Reinhardt, Best French Musician (with brother Stéphane), 1994. Current Management: KSM (Karen Strugg Management). Address: 17 Rue des Ecoles, 75005 Paris, France.

BELMONDO Stéphane, b. 8 July 1967, Hyères, France. Musician (trumpet, flugelhorn). m. Elisabeth Kontomanou (singer), 1 son. Musical Education: Conservatory, Toulon, Marseilles. Career: Member, Big Band Lumiere, conducted by Gil Evans; Sideman and concerts with Michel Legrand Big Band; Chet Baker; Tom Harrell; David Liebman; Dee Dee Bridgewater; Horace Silver; Own quintet with brother Lionel Belmondo; Own Belmondo Big Band, with brother Lionel; Television: Belmondo In Concert, Jazz 6 at M6, 1995. Recordings: Belmondo Quintet JAR; For All Friends, Belmondo Quintet; Sideman: Big Band Band Lumiere with Gil Evans; Love And Peace, Dee Dee Bridgewater. Honour: Django Reinhardt Award, Best French Musician, with brother Lionel, 1994. Current Management: KSM (Karen Strugg Management). Address: 17 Rue des Ecoles, 75005 Paris, France.

BEN Besiakov, b. 27 October 1956, Copenhagen, Denmark. Musician (Piano and Organ). 1 son. Recordings: You Stepped Out of a Dream, CD, 1990; Raney, CD, with Doug Raney, 1996; The Red Light, CD, with Bent Jaedig, 1996; When Granny Sleeps, CD, with Dave Liebman, 1995; Human Beat Boxer, CD, with Niclas Knudsen and Adam Baum, 1997. Honours: Ben Webster Prize, 1990; Jasa Prize, 1993. Membership: Danish Musicians Association. Hobby: Model - flyes. Address: GL Vartov Vej 21, 2900 Hellerup, Denmark.

BENATAR Pat (Patricia Andrzejewski), Brooklyn, New York, USA. Singer. m. (1) Dennis Benatar, 1972, divorced 1979; (2) Neil Geraldo, 20 Feb 1982, 1 daughter. Education: Studied health education. Musical Education: Brief training opera singer. Career: Singer, Holiday Inns, Virginia, 1972-74; Singing waitress in New York Club, Catch A Rising Star; Solo artiste, 1979-. Recordings: Singles include: Heartbreaker; You Better Run; Treat Me Right; Love Is A Battlefield; Hell Is For Children; Invincible (soundtrack to film Legend Of Billie Jean); Hit Me With Your Best

Shot; Sex As A Weapon; We Belong; All Fired Up. Albums include: In The Heat Of The Night, 1979; Crimes Of Passion, 1980; Precious Time, 1981; Get Nervous, 1982; Live From Earth, 1983; Tropico, 1984; Seven The Hard Way, 1985; Wide Awake In Dreamland, 1988; True Love, 1991; Gravity's Rainbow, 1993. Honours: 4 Grammy Awards, Best Female Rock Vocal Performance, 1981-84; Grammy Nomination, Female Rock Vocal Performance, Invincible, 1986; Numerous Gold discs. Current Management: Lookout Management, 2644 30th Street, 1st Floor, Santa Monica, CA 90405, USA.

BENDIX Nicky, b. 22 Mar 1969, Odense, Denmark. Musician (piano, keyboard); Music Teacher; Composer; Arranger. Education: Self-taught; Piano lessons. Career: Started composing and playing at age 15; Performed in Jazz/fusion settings with the Danish Radio Big Band, Rudi Smith, Jorge Degas, Uffe Markussen, Henrik Bolberg and Bent Jædig; Own composition, Suite for Mankind, performed on TV2, Denmark in September 1997; Since 1993 has composed and performed music for contemporary dance and multimedia events; Multimedia performer, The Pillar of Shame, 1997; Composed and recorded the music score for the movie En Sidste gang, by Jesper Bernt. Recordings: Trancework, 1994; with Sunset Yellow: Sunset Yellow, 1995; with Sunzet: Sunzet, 1998. Honour: Jazz Musician of the Year, FYN, Denmark, 1995. Membership: Dansk Musiker Forbund. Hobby: Gardening. Current Management: NB Music. Address: Andekæret 160, 5300 Kekteminde C, Denmark.

BENEDETTI Peter Sergio (Pepe), b. 15 July 1938, Greenock, Scotland. Jazz Blues Singer; Musician (tenor saxophone, clarinet). m. Lorna Magner, 14 Feb 1980, divorced 1983, 1 daughter. Education: College Commerce, 1988-89. Musical Education: Mabel Fletcher School of Music-Drama, Liverpool, 1990. Career: Musician, Robert Bros Circus, 6 months, 1978; Promotional tour, London, Tony Conn Rockabilly Artiste, 1979; Support Jack Bruce Tour, 1985; Played for: The Undertakers, Liverpool, Played 3 day concerts, Hamburg, West Germany, 1990-91; 6 week tour, Sonny Curtis, Denmark, 1991. Compositions: Songwriting: Country/rock; Blues; Rock'n'roll. Honours: Elgin Music Festival (Jazz), Best Male Singer, 1958. Membership: Musicians' Union. Hobbies: Swimming; Photography; Films; Cat shows; Flower shows. Current Management: Rock/Fairisle Music. Address: 212 Blackness Road, Dundee, Tayside DD1 5PC, Scotland.

BÉNEY Jean-Christophe, b. 2 Oct 1969, Boulogne, Billancourt, France. Jazz Musician (saxophone). Musical Education: Conservatoire National Supérieure de Musique, Paris. Career: Le Pom (Scene et Marnaise de Création Musicale); Orchestra co-directed by François Jeanneau; Patrice Caratini; Philippe Macé; Andy Emler; Jean-Christophe Béney Quartet (Pierre de Bethmann, Jules Bikoko; Benjamin Hénocq). Recordings: Hard Scores, Patrice Caratini, 1996; Le Pom, 1997; Sérénade, Philippe Sellam, 1997. Honours: Prix de Soloiste, Concours National de Jazz de la Défense, 1995 Memberships: SACEM; ADAMI; SPEDIDAM. Current Management: C C PRoduction, 70 avenue du 11 novembre, 94170 Le Perreux-sur-Marne, France. Address: 2 Rue Cyrano de Bergerac, 75018 Paris, France.

BENHAM Patrick John, b. 9 Feb 1940, Hove, Sussex, England. Guitar tutor; Composer; Musician (electric and classical guitar). m. (1) Christina Bean, 9 Oct 1964, 4 daughters; (2) Judith Matthews, 7 Aug 1974, 1 son. Musical Education: Private instrumental tutors. Career: Guitar teacher, Spanish Guitar Centre, Bristol and at various schools, 1962-68; Guitar and Jazz tutor, Millfield School, Somerset, 1969-; Backing group for tours by Billy Burden, Keith Harris, Ricky Vallance and others; Many jazz club appearances in Bristol, Bath and throughout the West Country.

Compositions: Jazz pieces include: Pocomolto; Vista Nova; Salsa Surprise; Hopeful Song; Fingerstyle guitar compositions included in Guildhall School of Music and Trinity College Grade Syllabuses. Publications: Mostly Jazz; West Country Sketches; Seven Easy Solos; Three Guitar Solos; Author of The Avalonians, 1993. Honour: Nominated for PEN International Award, 1994. Memberships: Musicians' Union; Society of Authors. Hobbies: Biographical Research; Genealogy. Address: Redmeads, Wagg Drove, Huish Episcopi, Langport, Somerset TA10 9ER, England.

BENHAMOU Lionel, b. 27 Aug 1956, Paris, France. Musician (guitar). m. Helene Ruyer, 30 Oct 1987, 1 son, 1 daughter. Musical Education: Music school, harmony with Mr Weber. Career: Tours with: Gil Evans; Martial Solal; Bernard Lubat; Many festivals in Europe; Plays with Orchestre National de Jazz, directed by Laurent Cugny. Recordings: with Lionel Benhamou Trio: Fruits Cuits, Fruits Crus; 5 albums with Orchestre National de Jazz; Yestenow, conducted by Laurent Cugny; Rhythm a'Ning, with Gil Evans. Publications: 10 Themes et Improvisations Pour Le Saxophone. Membership: UMJ. Hobbies: Computers; Mycology; Cycling. Address: 75 Rue de Turenne, 75003 Paris, France.

BENNETT Allan Charles, b. 12 Mar 1968, London, England. Musician (tenor, soprano saxophones); Singer; Songwriter. 1 daughter. Musical Education: Grade 5 Practical, Grade 5 Theory, Music O Level; Sound Engineering Foundation Course. Career: Waltham Forest Assembly Hall, oboist, Waltham Forest Intermediate Band, 1976; Saxophonist, community reggae band Reality, 1987; Lead saxophonist, reggae band Jimmy Mac, 1991; Polish Club Manchester; Palm Tree Club, Tottenham; Singer, songwriter, saxophonist, Tusu, 1989; Marquee; Porter House, Nottinghamshire; Lead saxophonist, Tribal Union, 1994; Sydenham Wells Park; Amersham Arms the gig; Allan B Promotions and live shows, 1992-; Solo saxophonist, Allan and Lea, 1994; Kingshead Theatre Pub. Recordings: with Jimmy Mac: Little Bit Of Your Time, 1991; with Tusu: August The Two (songs include: Dream Crazy; Catch 66; Fascination); Slipping Away, 1992; Gone To Earth: Be The Dub, 1994; Humanoia: Nothing More, Nothing Less, 1992. Membership: Musicians' Union. Hobbies: Weight training; Swimming; Football; Travel; Sight-seeing; Theatre; Restaurants. Current Management: Self-managed. Address: 22 Gaitskill House, The Drive, Walthamstow, London E17 3DD, England.

BENNETT Brian Laurence, b. 9 Feb 1940, London, England. Musician (drums); Composer. m. Margaret Tuton, 2 sons, 1 daughter. Musical Education: Self-taught. Career: Backed Gene Vincent, Eddie Cochran on tour; Drummer, Cliff Richard and The Shadows, 1961-; Session drummer, 1970s-80s; Composer of film and television music; Arranger, producer; Brian Bennett Band support to Cliff Richard, UK, Japan, USSR, 1970s; Played with Hank Marvin as The Shadows, Knebworth, 1990; UK tour, joined by Hank Marvin, also son Warren Bennett on keyboards. Compositions include: Film themes: Summer Holiday; Wonderful Life; Finders Keepers; The Harpist, 1997; Score: The Boys; Soundtrack: French Dressing; The American Way; Terminal Choice; Television soundtracks: Dallas; Knotts Landing; Ruth Rendell Mysteries; Nomads Of The Wind, BBC2; Pulaski; The Knock; The Sweeney; Minder; Global Sunrise, BBC, 1997; Compositions in music libraries worldwide. Honours: 3 Ivor Novello Awards: Summer Holiday, 1962; 25 Years in British Music, 1983; Best TV Theme, Ruth Rendell Mysteries. Memberships: PRS; MCPS; APC; MPA; SODS. Hobby: Golf. Address: 91 Tabernacle Street, London EC2 4BA, England.

BENNETT Easther. Singer. Career: Singer, UK all-female vocal group Eternal, 1992-. Recordings: Albums: Always And Forever, 1993; Power Of A Woman, 1995; Greatest Hits, 1997; Hit singles: Stay, 1993; Power Of A Woman, 1995; I Am Blessed, 1995; Good Thing, 1996; Angel of Mine, 1997. Honours: BRIT Award Nominations: Best Group, Best Newcomers, Best Album, Best Dance Act, 1995; Best Dance Act, 1996; Smash Hits Award; International Dance Award, Dance Act Of The Year, 1995; Only UK act to have 6 Top 15 hits from debut album.

BENNETT James, b. 27 Apr 1964, Norwich, Norfolk, England. Despatch (lorry loader); Musician. Career: Drummer, Joy, Three In A Thousand; Played live Radio 1 (Norwich Sound City); Slots on national television, local radio stations. Recordings: Joy: Worlds A Beach; Three In A Thousand: Soccer Star, used on England Football Association video.

BENNETT Phil, b. 28 September 1958, Singapore. Singer; Songwriter; Musician (Keyboards). m. Fifi, 4 July 1992. Career: Band Member: Helicopters, mid 1980s; Love Bites, 1990s; Witness, 1997; Support shows with: Duran Duran, Elvis Costello, Joe Jackson, Wreckless Eric, Sandi and the Sunsets, Midnight Oil, Church, Gang Gajang, Models, Jimmy Barnes. Compositions: Eyewitness, 1997; Carved in Stone, 1997. Recordings: Albums: The Helicopters, 1982; Great Moments in Aviation, 1984; Never Seen Eyes, solo, 1990; Kiss the Feet, 1995; Singles: Eyewitness, Lovebites, 1997; Eyewitnes, Witness. Honours: Sonics Magazine on Cue Award, 1990; Australia Day Award, 1993. Membership: Australian Performing Rights Association. Hobbies: Rolling Stones; Rhinos. Current Management: Mischief Management, 8 Michael Court, Shelley 6148, West Australia.

BENNETT Rex, b. 16 December 1920, Victoria, London. Musician (Drums). m. Olive Rosa Bennett, 1 May 1946, 1 daughter. Education: Self-taught. Hobbies: Jazz; Sailing. Recordings: Sandy Shaw; Brotherhood of Man; Crispin St Peter; Ray Conniff in Britain; Singalong with Max; Bring Me Sunshine; Dave Dee Dozy Mick & Tich; Johnathon King; Anita Harris; Everley Bros; Kenny Ball; Acker Bilk; Johnny Halliday; Mike Batt; Harold Geller; Vince Hill; Shirley Bassey; Maynard Ferguson with Strings; Matt Monro; Tony Blackburn; Cliff Richard; George Martin; Madmovies for Bob Monkhouse; Numerous backing tracks for most American jazz musicians. Address: 1 Ellery Close, Cranleigh, Surrey, GU6 8DF, England.

BENNETT Richard, b. 1951, Chicago, IL, USA. Musician (Guitar); Producer; Arranger; Writer. Musical Education: Taught by Forrest Skaggs. Career: Record Producer, Musician - Session and touring; Recording and touring with Neil Diamond in Los Angeles, 1971-88. Recordings: The Red Road, Bill Miller, 1994; Raven In the Snow, Bill Miller, 1995; A Native Suite, Bill Miler, 1995; Kim Richey, Kim Richey, 1995; Silvertone, Steve Earle, 1995; Capitol, High and Dry, Marty Brown; Wild Kentucky Skies, Marty Brown; Cryin', Lovin', Leavin', Marty Brown; Hillbilly Rock, Marty Stuart; Tempted, Marty Stuart; This One's Gonna Hurt You, Marty Stuart; Come on Joe, Jo-El Sonnier; Have A Little Faith, Joe-El Sonnier; Lost and Profound, Lost and Profound; Memory Thieves, Lost and Profound; A Joyful Noise, The Sullivan's; Music Makin' Mama, Jim Silvers; Everybody Knows, Prairie Oyster; Plectrasonics, Nashville Mandolin Ensemble; Sessions: Billy Pilgrim, 1994; Mark Knopfler and Neil Diamond, 1995. Current Management: Dennis Muirhead, Muirhead Management. Address: Muirhead Management, 202 Fulham Road, Chelsea, London SW10 9PJ, England.

BENNETT Vernie, b. 1972. Singer. Education: Studied law. Career: Singer, UK

all-female vocal group Eternal, 1992-. Recordings: Albums: Always And Forever, 1993; Power Of A Woman, 1995; Greatest Hits, 1997; Hit singles: Stay, 1993; Power Of A Woman, 1995; I Am Blessed, 1995; Good Thing, 1996; Angel of Mine, 1997. Honours: BRIT Award Nominations: Best Group, Best Newcomers, Best Album, Best Dance Act, 1995; Best Dance Act, 1996; International Dance Award, Dance Act Of The Year, 1995; Smash Hits Award; Only UK act to have 6 top 15 hits from debut album.

BENNETT Warren, b. 4 July 1962, Palmers Green, London, England. Writer; Record Producer; Singer; Musician (keyboards, guitar). m. Jane Catherine, 18 May 1991, 1 daughter. Career: Hank Marvin UK tour, 1994; Television appearances: Birds Of A Feather; Ruth Rendell Mysteries. Compositions: Songs recorded by: The Shadows; Hank Marvin; Sanctus; Music for films include: American Way; Decadence; Music for television includes: Birds Of A Feather; Close To Home; Numerous commercials; Arranger and writer for Hank Marvin albums: Heartbeat; Into The Light. Recordings: Solo: Secrets Of The Heart; Pathways To Love; Memberships: PRS; MCPS. Hobbies: Tennis; Golf; Wine; Supporting Manchester United Football Club. Address: Waffles Music Ltd, 91 Tabernacle Street, London EC2A 2BA, England.

BENNETT Willie P, b. 26 Oct 1951, Toronto, Ontario, Canada. Songwriter; Musician (harmonica, mandolin, guitar). Musical Education: Self-taught. Career: Radio appearances: CBC Radio National, Toronto: The Entertainers; Morningside; Prime Time; Six Days On the Road; Swingin' On A Star, Murray Mclaughlin; Touch The Earth; CFTO TV: Lifetime; CFPL TV: Morning Break; CBCTV: Ninety Minutes Live, Peter Gzowsky; Festivals: Ontario: Canadian Music; Carlisle Bluegrass; Festival of Friends; Home Country Folk; Mariposa Folk; Northern Lights; Northwinds; Ottawa Folk; Summerfolk; Alberta: Calgary Folk; Edmonton Folk; Northwest Territories: Folk On The Rocks; Saskatchewan: Redberry Folk and Country; British Columbia: Vancouver Folk; Manitoba: Winnipeg Folk. Recordings: As artist: Trying To Start Out Clean; Blackie And The Rodeo King; Hobo's/Taunt; The Lucky Ones; Collectibles; Take My Own Advice; As musician with artists: Fred J Eaglesmith; Robert Atyeo; Joe Hall; The Dixie Flyers. Honours: CCMA Award Song Of the Year: Hello, So Long Goodbye, 1990; CCMA Nomination Special Instrument: Harmonica, 1994. Memberships: AFofM; ACTRA; Canadian Country Music Association. Hobbies: Running; Painting; Travelling. Current Management: Dark Light Music Ltd. Address: 51 Bulwer Street, Toronto, Ontario M5T 1A1, Canada.

BENNETTS Jonathan, b. 24 Apr 1971, Cornwall, England. Rapper; Disc Jockey; Producer. 1 daughter. Career: The Radio 1 Roadshow; Various night spots. Recordings: You've Got To Feel The Rhythm; Energy; Feel So Free. Current Management: Showcase Management International. Address: 27 Rosparuvah Gardens, Heamoor, Penzance, Cornwall TR18 3EB, England.

BENOÎT Blue Boy (Benoît Billot), b. 24 May 1946, Paris, France. Singer; Musician (harmonica, guitar), 2 daughters. Education: Ecole Des Beaux Arts, Paris. Career: Harmonica with: Stevie Wonder; Carol King; James Taylor; Albert King; 1970-1972; Plays with Zachery Richard, 1972; First band: Benoît Blue Boy And The Tortilleurs, 1978. Recordings: Benoît Blue Boy, 1978; Original, 1979; Le Blues Du Vendeur De Blues, 1981; Plaisir Simple, 1982; Tortillage, 1986; BBB et les Toit Cleurs, 1988; Parlez Vouz Français?, 1990; Plus Tard Dans La Soirée, 1992; Couvert De Bleus, 1994. Memberships: SACEM; ADAMI. Hobby: Antiquities. Current Management: Denis

Leblond. Address: c/o Musiques Bleues, 16 Rue Jacquemunt, 75017 Paris, France.

BENSON George, b. 22 Mar 1943, Pittsburgh, Pennsylvania, USA. Musician (guitar); Singer. Career: Session musician, Pittsburgh; Guitarist with Brother Jack McDuff; Session work with Herbie Hancock, Wes Montgomery, 1966; Solo artist, 1966-; Regular worldwide tours; Major concerts include: Rock In Rio Festival, 1983; JVC Jazz Festival, Newport, USA, 1990; North Sea Jazz Festival, Netherlands, 1991; Guitar Legends, Seville, Spain, 1991. Recordings: Singles include: This Masquerade; Nature Boy; Give Me The Night; Love X Love; Turn Your Love Around; On Broadway; Love Ballad; Moody's Mood; In Your Eyes; Love All The Hurt Away (duet with Aretha Franklin); Never Give Up On A Good Thing; The Greatest Love Of All; Lady Love Me; Feel Like Makin' Love; Shiver; Albums: Its Uptown, 1966; Benson Burner, 1966; Giblet Gravy, 1967; Tell It Like It Is, 1969; The Other Side Of Abbey Road, 1970; Beyond The Blue Horizon, 1972; Good King Bad, 1973; Bad Benson, 1974; Supership, 1975; Breezin' (Number 1, US), 1976; Benson And Farrell (with jazz flautist Joe Farrell), 1976; George Benson In Concert - Carnegie Hall, 1977; In Flight, 1977; Weekend In LA, 1978; Livin' Inside Your Love, 1979; Give Me The Night, 1981; George Benson Collection, 1981; In Your Eyes, 1983; 20/20, 1985; The Love Songs (Number 1, UK), 1985; While The City Sleeps, 1986; Collaboration, 1987; Twice The Love, 1988; Tenderly (Number 1, US Jazz chart), 1989; Big Boss Band, 1990; Midnight Moods - The Love Collection, 1991; Love Remembers, 1993; Guest musician, Back On The Block, Quincy Jones, 1991. Honours include: Grammy Awards: Best R&B Instrumental, 1976, 1980; Record of the Year, 1976; Best Pop Instrumental, 1976, 1984; Best R&B Male Vocal Performance, 1978, 1980; Best Jazz Voval Performance, 1980; Best Jazz Instrumental Performance, 1991. Current Management: Ken Fritz Management, 648 N. Robertson Blvd, Los Angeles, CA 90069, USA.

BENSON Jeffrey Scott, b. 1 Sept 1937, London, England. Jazz Musician (tenor saxophone). m. Clare Benson, 11 Apr 1981, 1 son, 3 daughters. Education: South West Essex College. Musical Education: Teachers include Don Rendell, 1960-. Career: Quintet with Dave Gelly, 12 years. Compositions: Co-writer, Genesis Suite, with Matt Hutchinson, performed Round House, 1971; Parson Green played on Radio 1, Humphrey Lyttleton Programme. Publication: Parsons Green. Hobbies: Wine and wine tasting; Teaching saxophone. Address: 96 Ramsden Road, London SW12 8QZ, England.

BENSON Lindy, b. London, England. Artist Manager. Career: Managed Mama's Boys; Now Manager of Celtus. Honours: International Managers Forum; Albemarle Award, Young Manager of the Year, 1997. Memberships: IMF; Equity; BASCA. Hobbies: Reading; Eating good food - strict vegetarian. Current Management: Shamrock Music Ltd, 9 Thornton Place, London W1H 1FG, England.

BENSON Ray, b. 16 Mar 1951, Philadelphia, Pennsylvania, USA. Musician (guitar); Vocalist; Record Producer; Actor; Manager. m. Diane Carr, 27 Mar 1983, 2 sons. Education: 1 year Antioch College. Career: Leader, lead singer, Asleep At The Wheel, for 25 years; Producer, 9 Asleep At The Wheel albums, 1973-93; Also producer for George Strait; Ricky Van Shelton; Sweethearts of the Rodeo; k d lang; Aaron Neville & Rob Wasserman; Bruce Hornsby & Willie Nelson; Darden Smith; Don Walser; 8 film scores; Commercials include: Anheuser-Busch products, Coors, Delta Airlines, Pepsi Cola, Levi's Jeans; Actor, 4 music videos; Numerous television appearances include: Austin City Limits, with band Asleep At The Wheel; Wild Texas Wind; Nashville Now; Johnny Carson; Executive Director and

Co-Producer, Texas Festival, Kennedy Centre, 1991. Recordings: Albums: Coming Right At Ya, 1973; Asleep At The Wheel, 1974; Texas Gold, 1975; The Wheel, 1977; Served Live, 1979; Framed, 1980; Drivin', 1980; Pasture Prime, 1985; Asleep At The Wheel 10, 1987; Western Standard Time, 1988; Keepin' Me Up Nights, 1990; Live & Kickin', 1992; Route 66, 1992; The Swingin' Best Of Asleep At The Wheel, 1992; Tribute To The Music Of Bob Wills and The Texas Playboys, 1993; Still Swingin', 1994; The Wheel Keeps On Rollin'. 1995; Live Back to the Future Now, 1997. Honours: Academy of Country Music Award, 1977; Buddy Award, 1985; 4 Grammy Awards; 3 Grammy Nominations; CMA Nominations, 1975-80, 1994; Western Swing Society Hall of Fame, 1994; Academy Of Country Music Nomination, 1994. Memberships: Trustee, NARAS; Board Member, R&B Foundation. Hobby: Golf. Current Management: Bismeaux Productions, PO Box 463, Austin, TX 78767, USA.

BENSUSAN Pierre, b. 30 Oct 1957, Oran, French Algeria. Musician (guitar); Singer; Composer. m. Doatea Cornu, 22 June 1985, 1 son. Musical Education: Self-taught. Career: Festivals include: Montreux, Nyon, (Switzerland); Musiques Métisses d'Angouleme (France); Jazz Festivals: Montreal; Edmonton (Canada); Brussels; Guitar Festivals: Liege, Grand, (Belgium); Milwaukee (USA); Tel-Aviv (Israel); Paris, Nice (France); Festival Inter-Celtic de Lorient (France); Zenith-Paris (as Jacques Higelin's guest); Boston; Germany (Stockfish tour); Bern; Lanzburg; Eppalinges (Switzerland); Summer Banks Festival, London; Vancouver, Toronto (Canada); Polymusicales de Bollene; Bergamo (Italy); Rotterdam (Netherlands); Flanders Festival, Grand (Belgium); Appeared with or played with artistes including: Suzanne Vega; Jacques Higelin; Paco De Lucia; Carla Bley; Larry Coryell; Philip Catherine; Doc Watson; John Renbourn & David Bromberg; Nana Vasconcelos; Oregon; Uzeb; Taj Mahal; Alan Stivell; Al Stewart; Bobby Thomas; Didier Malherbe. Recordings: Près de Paris; Pierre Bensusan 2; Musiques; Solilai; Spices; Wu Wei; Live an New Morning. Publications: The Guitar Book; Dagad Music; 3 videos: The Guitar of Pierre Bensusan, Vol 1 and 2; Pierre Bensusan in Concert, A World of Celtic Fingerstyle Guitar. Honours: Grand Prix du Disque, Montreux Festival, 1976. Address: B P 232, 02406 Chateau Thierry Cedex, France.

BENTZON Nikolaj, b. 21 Feb 1964, Copenhagen, Denmark. Jazz Musician (piano); Composer. m. Agnethe Koch, 3 July 1993, 1 son, 2 daughters. Musical Education: Performance Diploma, Berklee College of Music, Boston, USA. Career: Member of Danish Radio Jazz Orchestra, 1990-; Leader of Nikolaj Bentzon Trio, 1989; Nikolaj Bentzon & The Scandinavian Connection, 1992-; The Nikolaj Bentzon Brotherhood, 1995; Nikolaj Bentzon Constitution, 1997 with Herbie Hancock Headhunter's rhythm section Paul Jackson (bass) and Mike Clarke (drums); 3 years with Ernie Wilkin's Almost Big Band; Debut performance of Bob Brookmeyer's November Music, written for Nikolaj Bentzon, 24 Nov 1994, Radio House, Copenhagen. Recordings: Albums: with Nikolaj Bentzon Trio: Pianoforte, Between Us, Triskelos, Nexus; 1 album with Nikolaj Bentzon & The Scandinavian Connection; 1 album with Nikolaj Bentzon Brotherhood; 1 album featuring Mike Clark and Paul Jackson; Bentzon album featuring Headhunter greats Paul Jackson, Mike Clarke, 1998. Honours: Best soloist, Dunkerque Jazz Festival, 1983; Jacob Gade Award, 1983; Oscar Peterson Jazz Award, 1985; Danish Society for Jazz, Rock and Folk Music Honorary Award, 1991. Current Management: Anders Tidemann, Word of Mouth. Address: Grundtvigsvej 27B, suite 4mf, DK-1864 Copenhagen, Denmark.

BERAUD Marie Laure, b. 22 Jan 1959, Lyon, France. Singer. 2 sons. Education: Degree Languages and History of Arts, University, Paris.

Career: 4 month tour including France; Belgium; Netherlands; Germany; Switzerland; USA (Ballroom Club, New York), 1992; Television apparences include: Nulle Part Ailleurs, with Antoine de Gaunes, 1992; Recordings: Album: Turbigo 12-12, 1992; Singles: Viens Simon; Les Immortelles; Macadam Ramdam, 1992. Honour: Academie Charles Cros First Album Prize, 1992. Membership: SACEM. Hobbies: Painting; Poetry; Drawings. Current Management: Cyril Prieur, Talent Sorcier. Address: Talent Sorcier, 3 rue des Petites Écuries, 75010 Paris, France.

BERENGUER José, b. 21 Oct 1955, Barcelona, Spain. Musician (guitar). Education: PhD, Clinical Psychology, Medicine. Musical Education: Composer, computer, electroacoustical music. Career: Autumno Musicale, Como, Italy; Internationale Fenienkurse-Danmstadt, Germany; Synthèse, Bourges, France; Festival International de Músicadel Segle XX, Barcelona, Spain; Puntope En Cuentro, Madrid, Spain; Para Lelo Madrid. Recordings: Klängé, 1993; Antropometria Don Quichotte; Spira; Constellacions; Silence. Honours: TIME of CIM/UNESCO; Electroacoustic Music Prize, Bourges. Memberships: Chairman of Ascociacion de Musica Electroacoustica de Espana; Vice-chairman of Associaó Catacana de Compositors; International Electroacoustic Music Academy of Bourges. Current Management: Côchlea. Address: Sardeeva 516 6e 2a, 08024 Barcelona, Spain.

BERG Shelton Glen, b. 18 August 1955, Cleveland, OH, USA. Pianist; Educator; Composer; Arranger. Education: MM, Piano Performance, University of Houston, 1979; BM, Piano Performance, University of Houston, 1977. Career: Chair, Jazz Studies, University of Southern California, 1991-; Composer: Fudge, ABC Television Series, A League of Their Own, CBS Television; Orchestra for Film: Edwards & Hunt; President: International Association of Jazz Education, 1996-98. Compositions: Numerous compositions for Jazz Combos, Chorus & Big Band. Recordings: as Pianist: The Joy, with Bill Watrons; A Time for Love; Space Available. Publications: Jazz Improvisation: The Goal - Note Method, 1989; Numerous articles in Jazz Educators Journal and Piano & Keyboard Magazines. Honours: Finalist, 1988 Grat American Jazz Piano Competition; Commission - Theme Song of 1986 US Olympia Festival. Memberships: IAJÉ; MENC. Current Management: Open Door Management. Address: 3545 Downing Avenue, Glendale, CA 91208, USA.

BERG Terje, b. 24 Jan 1972, Trondheim, Norway. Musician (bass). Education: College. Career: Started Hedge Hog, 1989; Toured Europe, 1994, 1995. Recordings: Erase, 1992; Surprise, 1992; Primal Gutter, 1993; Mercury Red, 1994; Mindless, 1994; The Healing EP, 1995; Thorn Cord Wonder, 1995. Hobby: Paragliding. Current Management: Martin Aam, Hedge Hogment. Address: Hedge Hog, PO Box 683, 7001 Trondheim, Norway.

BERGGREN Jenny, b. Sweden. Singer. Career: Singer, Ace Of Base, 1990-. Recordings: Albums: Happy Nation, 1993; The Bridge, 1995; Singles: Wheel Of Fortune; All That She Wants; Lucky Love; Number 1 records in UK; US; Canada; Australia; New Zealand; Argentina; Israel; Throughout Europe. Honours: Highest-ever worldwide sales for a debut album (Happy Nation, 19 million); Platinum discs worldwide. Current Management: Siljemark Production AB, Gårdsvägen 4, S-17152 Solna, Sweden.

BERGGREN Jonas, b. Sweden. Singer; Songwriter. Career: Singer, Ace Of Base, 1990-. Recordings: Albums: Happy Nation, 1993; The Bridge, 1995; Singles: Wheel Of Fortune; All That She Wants; Lucky Love; Number 1 records in UK; US; Canada; Australia; New Zealand; Israel; Argentina; Across Europe. Honours: Highest-ever worldwide sales for a debut album (Happy Nation, 19 million); Platinum discs worldwide. Current Management: Siljemark Production AB, Gårdsvägen 4, S-171 52 Solna, Sweden.

BERGGREN Malin, b. 1970, Sweden. Singer. Career: Singer, Ace Of Base, 1990-; Recordings: Albums: Happy Nation, 1993; The Bridge, 1995; Singles: Wheel Of Fortune; All That She Wants; Lucky Love; Number 1 records in UK; US; Canada; New Zealand; Australia; Israel; Argentina; Across Europe. Honours: Highest-ever worldwide sales for a debut album (Happy Nation, 19 million); Platinum discs worldwide. Current Management: Siljemark Production AB, Gårdsvägen 4, S-171 52 Solna, Sweden.

BERGH Totti, b. 5 Dec 1935, Oslo, Norway. Musician (tenor, soprano, alto saxophones). m. Laila Dalseth, 1 June 1963, 2 daughters. Career: Jazz artist; Television and radio appearances in Scandinavia; Concerts include: Playboy Jazz Festival; Sacramento Jazz Festival; Caribbean Cruises; Molde Jazz Festival; Oslo Jazz Festival; Jakarta Jazz Festival; Currently fronting own group with singer (wife) Laila Dalseth. Recordings: with Bengt Hallberg's Swinging Swedes: We Love Norway, 1977; with Laila Dalseth/Louis Stewart Quintet: Daydreams, 1984; I Hear A Rhapsody, 1985; with Al Cohn: Tenor Gladness, 1986; with George Masso, Major Holley: Major Blues, 1990; with Plas Johnson: On The Trail, 1992; with Joe Cohn: Remember, 1995; with Laila Dalseth/Philip Catherine Sextet: A Woman's Intuition, 1995.

BERGIN Jimmy, b. 12 June 1955, Dublin, Ireland. Musician; Songwriter (Guitar, Bass, Mandolin, Bazooki, Banjo). Education: Selftaught Guitar, Bass, Mandolin, Bazooki, Banjo. Career: Solo Artist, touring Europe, 1975-78; PTA, backing band for travelling circus touring Europe, 1985-86; Instrumental in forming celtic/punk Psychedelic Band; Toured Eastern Europe, Europe and Scandinavia; TV appearances, Night Hawks, Spanish TV, Kilburn Irish Festival (Channel 4), Southbank Festival (CH4), with Aswad. Compositions: Head Full of Music, 7 Kevins; Sucker for Your Love, 7 Kevins; Hennara Shampoo, TV Ad; McVities, TV Ad. Recordings: Stop the Lights, 7 Kevins, 1991; Sacred Car Bomb, 7 Kevins, 1992; Albums & TV Ads. Membership: PRS; Equity. Hobbies: Cigarettes & Alcohol; Hillwalking; Painting; Pottery. Current Management: Callic Mather, 70A Ivy Road, Cricklewood, London NW2 6SX, England.

BERGMAN Alan, b. Brooklyn, New York, USA. Lyricist; Writer. m. Marilyn Keith, 2 daughters. Musical Education: BA, Music, University of North Carolina. Career: Collaborated with Marilyn Bergman; Michel Legrand; Dave Grusin; Marvin Hamlisch; Henry Mancini; Johnny Mandel; John Williams; David Shire; Neil Diamond; James Newton Howard; Quincy Jones; Lew Spence; Sammy Fain; Billy Goldenberg; Lalo Shifrin; Norman Luboff; Sergio Mendes. Compositions: Songs include: That Face; Yellow Bird; Nice'n'Easy; The Windmills Of Your Mind; The Way We Were; The Summer Knows; What Are You Doing The Rest Of Your Life?; Summer Me, Winter Me; So Many Stars; You Must Believe In Spring; Places That Belong To You; You Don't Bring Me Flowers; Little Boy Lost; In The Heat Of The Night; The Hands Of Time; I Love To Dance; I Believe In Love; Sweet Gingerbread Man; The Last Time I Felt Like This; I'll Never Say Goodbye; Make Me Rainbows; Like A Lover; The Island; All His Children; Marmalade, Molasses And Honey; If We Were In Love; It Might Be You; How Do You Keep The Music Playing; Papa Can You Hear Me? The Way He Makes Me Feel; Ordinary Miracles; Where Do You Start? Most Of All You; The Girl Who Used To Be Me; Broadway scores: Something More; Ballrooom; Film/TV scores: Yentl; Queen Of The Stardust Ballroom; Sybil; TV themes: Maude; Good Times; Alice; Brooklyn Bridge; The Powers That Be. Honours: 3

Academy; 2 Emmy; 2 Golden Globe; 2 Grammy; Inducted into Songwriters Hall Of Fame, 1979. Memberships: ASCAP; AMPAS; Songwriters Guild Of America; Society of Composers and Lyricists. Hobbies: Art and antique collecting; Tennis. Current Management: Gorfaine Scwartz. Address: 3301 Barham Boulevard #201, Los Angeles, CA 90068, USA.

BERGMAN Barry, b. 24 Aug 1944, New York, USA. Artist Manager; Music Publisher. Education: BS, New York University, 1966. Career: Vice President, Marks Music, 1975-79; Vice President, Creative Affairs, United Artists Music, 1979-81; Owner, Barry Bergman Management, 1982-; Elymax Music, 1986-; Artist manager for: Keven Jordan; Marc Ribler; Rob Friedman; Kings Country; Publisher of music by: Cher; Kiss; Michael Bolton. Honour: ASCAP Pop Award, 1989. Memberships: ASCAP; Broadcast Music Inc. Address: Barry Bergman Management, 350 E. 30th Street, Suite 4D, New York, NY 10016, USA.

BERGMAN Marilyn, b. Brooklyn, New York, USA. Lyricist; Writer. m. Alan Bergman, 1 daughter. Education: New York University. Musical Education: High School Of Music & Art. Career: Collaborators: Alan Bergman; Michel Legrand; Dave Grusin; Marvin Hamlisch; Henry Mancini; Johnny Mandel; John Williams; David Shire; Neil Diamond; James Newton Howard; Quincy Jones; Lew Spence; Sammy Fain; Billy Goldenberg; Lalo Schifrin; Norman Luboff; Sergio Mendes. Compositions include: Yellow Bird; Nice'n'Easy; The Windmills Of Your Mind; The Way We Were; The Summer Knows; What Are You Doing For The Rest Of Your Life?; Summer Me Winter Me; So Many Stars; You Must Believe In Spring; Places That Belong To You; You Don't Bring Me Flowers; Little Boy Lost; In The Heat Of The Night; The Hands Of Time; I Love To Dance; I Believe In Love; Sweet Gingerbread Man; The Last Time I Felt Like This; I'll Never Say Goodbye; Make Me Rainbows; Like a Lover; The Island; All His Children; Marmalade, Molasses And Honey; If We Were In Love; It Might Be You; How Do You Keep The Music Playing; Papa Can You Hear Me?; The Way He Makes Me Feel; Ordinary Miracles; Where Do You Start?; Most Of All You; The Girl Who Used To Be Me; Broadway scores: Something More; Ballroom; Film/TV scores, Yentl; Queen Of The Stardust Ballroom; Sybil. Honours include: 3 Academy; 2 Golden Globe; 2 Emmy; 2 Grammy; Inducted into Songwriters Hall Of Fame, 1979; Crystal Award, Women In Film, 1986. Memberships: (Chairman) ASCAP; AMPAS; Society of Composers and Lyricists; Songwriters Guild Of America. Hobbies: Antique and art collecting. Current Management: Gorfaine/Scwartz. Address: 3301 Barnham Boulevard #201, Los Angeles, CA 90068, USA.

BERGMAN Philippe, b. 11 Aug 1960, Brussels, Belgium. Singer. Recordings: Où Les Voyageurs, 1993; Bruits De Coeur, 1995. Current Management: Cyril Prieur, Talent Sorcier. Address: Talent Sorcier, 3 Rue des Petites Écuries, 75010 Paris, France.

BERGSTEIN Scott, b. 8 June 1952, Midland, Michigan, USA. Record Company Executive. m. Elisa Fegarido, 18 Nov 1989, 1 son. Education: BA Communications, American University, Washington DC. Career: Head Buyer, Wherehouse Records; International Operations Manager, Casablanca Records; Director of Artist Development, Allegiance Records; Marketing Manager, Chameleon Music Group; Senior Vice President, Higher Octave Music. Memberships: NARAS; NARM; NAIRD. Address: 23852 Pacific Coast Highway #2C, Malibu, CA 90265, USA.

BERKES Alain (Alain Berques), b. 16 Sept 1955, Saint Maur, France. Singer; Musician (guitar, keyboards); Composer; Arranger. Musical Education: Self-taught; Also has jazz teaching

state diploma. Career: Leader, blues, rock'n'soul band Alain Berkes And Blues Heritage; Session man for commercials and various French artists, including Michel Legrand; Played in many major American blues clubs (B B King's, Buddy Guy's Legends) with Luther Allison and many blues greats. Recordings: Album: The Blues Rocked My Soul; It's About Time, Pat Ramsey (ex-harp player for Johnny Winter). Publications: Monthly columnist, French magazine Guitare Et Claviers. Honour: First prize, Best Composition (Jazz), Concours de la Défense, 1984. Memberships: SACEM; SPEDIDAM. Hobby: Sports; Reading books. Current Management: Blue Line (Paris). Address: 16 Rue Saint Hilaire, 94210 La Varenne, France.

BERLIOZ Gérard, b. 15 Mar 1943, Paris, France. Musician (percussion, tympanon, cymbalum); Music Educator. m. 11 Apr 1964, 1 son, 1 daughter. Musical Education: Prix de Percussion du Mans; Prix de Percussion, Conservatoire National Supérieur de Music de Paris. Career: Professor, several conservatoires in Paris region; Worked with symphony orchestras: Radio-France; Radio-Moscow; Leningrad; Prague; Music Hall concerts at Moulin Rouge; Casino de Paris; Olympia; Theatres, operas, ballet companies include: Paris; Rouen; Vichy; Nice; Toulouse; Grenoble (others in France); Monte Carlo; Canada; Japan; Festivals all over France; International tours with: Mikis Theodorakis; Lorin Maazel; Jerry Lewis (Europe, North Africa, South Africa, USA, Canada, Japan, Thailand, South America, Israel, Australia); Musician accompanying: Claude Bolling; Tom Jones; Ginger Rogers; Ray Charles; Charles Aznavour; Gilbert Bécaud; Mireille Mathieu; Catherine Ribeiro; Music for films, musical comedies and recordings with: Michel Legrand; Maurice Jarre; Claude Nougaro; Mikis Theodakaris; Jean Claude Naude; Guy Defatto; Mireille Mathieu; Catherine Ribeiro. Publications: Director, Percussion Collection; Chronicler, Journal: Tam Tam Percussion; Author, several instruction manuals; Author, numerous articles on percussion. Membership: L'Ordre National Des Musiciens. Hobbies: Collecting drums and percussion instruments.

BERMAN Jeffrey, b. 26 Jan 1954, Brooklyn, New York, USA. Musician (percussion, vibraphone); Composer. m. Susan Powers, 27 Mar 1993. Education: BA Music, York College, New York City. Recordings: As Leader: Things She Said, 1992; Big Black Sun, 1994; Music for documentary film: In Our Water, 1981. Current Management: c/o Palmetto Records, 71 Washington Place, New York City, NY 10011, USA.

BERNARD Alain, b. 8 Sept 1952, Algeria. Jazz Musician (piano, synthesizer). Education: English studies, Paris University, 1971-72. Musical Education: Private lessons until 1985; CIM Diploma, orchestration, arrangement, composition. Career: Musician, 1977-; Sideman for French musicians including: R Guérin; Gérard Badini Swing Machine; Ornicar big-band; American musicians include: F Foster; E L Davis; Joe Henderson; J Newman; Dee Dee Bridgewater; Jazz festivals at Nice and Dresden; Founder, own trio, 1987; Plays in France and Germany. Recordings: Mais Où Est Donc Ornicar, with Joe Henderson; Mr Swing Is Still Alive, Gérard Badini Super Swing Machine; Jazz Cartoon; L'Incroyable Huck. Memberships: SACEM; SPEDIDAM; ADAMI. Address: 91-93 Rue du Plessis-Trévise, 94500 Champigny-Sur-Marne, France.

BERNARD Claude Camille, b. 5 Oct 1945, Paris, France. Musician (alto saxophone); Bandleader. Widower, 2 sons, 2 daughters. Education: Conservatoire Artistique Cardinal Lemoine. Musical Education: Jean Ledieu, Professor, alto saxophone, soloist, Conservatoire National, Nancy. Career: Festivals: Chateauvallon,

1976; Vansovin, 1977; Suse den Netherlands; Yugoslavia, Turkey, 1994; China, Africa, 1995; Played with: Steve Lacy; Michael Smith; Lavelle; Mickey Baker; Wei Wei; Specialises in improvisation, solo and accompanied. Recordings: Quebella Promenade; Brin de Laine; Facett'vega. Publications: Olympic Games Atlanta centennial with Wei Wei and Michael Smith Band, 1996. Memberships: Syndicat des Chefs d'Orchestre; SACEM; SACD; Centre International de Musicotherapie. Address: 48 avenue du Maréchal Foch, 78400 Chatou, France.

BERNASCONI Justin Anthony, b. 29 Sept 1972, Croydon, Surrey, England. Singer; Songwriter; Musician (guitar, keyboards, banjo, bass). Education: Anglia Polytechnic, Cambridge, 2 years music, philosophy. Musical Education: 4 years guitar tuition including advanced guitar lessons with Richard Newman, 2 year foundation course at Anglia Polytechnic, Cambridge. Career: Played Cambridge Folk Festival, 1993, 1994; Appeared as country rock guitarist, Roy Waller's Radio Norfolk Show; Anglia TV featuring The Fen Blows debut album, local news programme. Recordings: Debut album: The Fen Blows, 8 songs on historical events and fables of Cambridgeshire; Composed all own material. Honour: Best Guitarist Award, East Anglian Rock Competition, 1991. Memberships: Musicians' Union; Cambridge Folk Club. Hobbies: Reading; Poetry; Novels; Local History. Current Management: Self-managed. Address: 17 Mill Green, Warboys, Huntingdon, Cambs PE17 25A, England.

BERRI (Rebecca Sleight), b. 3 Aug 1974, York, England. Singer. Musical Education: Hull College of Performing Arts. Career: Television appearances: Top Of The Pops, BBC TV, 1994; The Chart Show, ITV; MTV; Children In Need; Ireland; Radio includes: Several interviews on Irish and Scottish radio during UK tour in 1994; Interviews on City FM, Liverpool, 1995. Recordings: Sunshine After The Rain, with dance outfit New Atlantic, 1994. Membership: Musicians' Union. Hobbies: Dressmaking; Walking; Music. Current Management: Jon Barlow. Address: 3 Beat Music, 58 Wood Street, Liverpool L1 4AQ, England.

BERRY Bill, b. 31 July 1958, Hibbing, Minnesota, USA. Musician (drums). Career: Member, R.E.M., 1980-97; Worldwide tours; Member, side project, Hindu Love Gods, 1986-90. Recordings: Albums: Chronic Town (mini-album), 1982; Murmur, 1983; Reckoning, 1984; Fables Of The Reconstruction, 1985; Life's Rich Pageant, 1986; Dead Letter Office, 1987; Document, 1987; Eponymous, 1988; Green, 1988; Out Of Time, 1991; The Best Of REM, 1991; Automatic For The People, 1992; Monster, 1995; with Hindu Love Gods: Hindu Love Gods, 1990; Singles: with R.E.M.: The One I Love, 1987; Stand, 1989; Orange Crush, 1989; Losing My Religion, 1991; Shiny Happy People, 1991; Near Wild Heaven, 1991; Radio Song, 1991; Drive, 1992; Man On The Moon, 1992; The Sidewinder Sleeps Tonite, 1993; Everybody Hurts, 1993; Crush With Eyeliner; Nightswimming; What's The Frequency Kenneth?; Tracks featured on film soundtracks: Batchelor Party, 1984; Until The End Of The World, 1991; Coneheads, 1993; Recordings with: Indigo Girls; Warren Zevon; Contributor, albums: Tom's Album; I'm Your Fan. Honours: Earth Day Award, 1990; Numerous MTV Music Video Awards; Billboard Awards: Best Modern Rock Artists, Best World Album, 1991; BRIT Awards: Best International Group, 1992, 1993, 1995; Grammy Awards, Best Pop Performance, Alternative Music Album, Music Video, 1992; Atlanta Music Awards: Act Of The Year, Rock Album, Video, 1992; IRMA, International Band Of The Year, 1993; Rolling Stone Critics Awards: Best Band, Best Album, Q Awards: Best Album, 1991, 1992; Best Act In The World, 1991, 1995.

Current Management: REM/Athens Ltd., 250 W Clayton Street, Athens, GA 30601, USA.

BERRY Chuck (Charles), b. 18 Oct 1926, San Jose, California, USA. Rock'n'Roll Singer; Musician (guitar). Career: Member, Johnny Johnson Trio, 1947; Renamed Chuck Berry Trio; Established Berry Park, Wentzville, Missouri (home and country club); Owner, nightclub The Bandstand, St Louis; Hundreds of worldwide concerts including: Newport Jazz Festival, 1958; New York Folk Festival, 1965; Toronto Rock'n'Roll Revival, 1969; UK Rock'n'Roll Revival, Wembley, 1972; White House concert, for President Carter, 1979; 60th Birthday concert, Fox Theatre, St Louis, 1986; Film appearances: Rock Rock Rock, 1956; Jazz On A Summers Day, 1958; Go Johnny Go, 1959; American Hot Wax, 1978; Hail! Hail! Rock'n'Roll!, 1987. Recordings: Numerous albums include: Chuck Berry, 1963; Chuck Berry On Stage, 1963; His Latest And Greatest, 1964; Chuck Berry's Greatest Hits, 1964; St Louis To Liverpool, 1965; Chuck Berry In London, 1965; Chuck Berry's Golden Decade, 1968; Back Home, 1970; St Louis To Frisco To Memphis, 1972; Golden Decade Vol 2, 1973; Motorvatin', 1977; Rock! Rock! Rock'N'Roll, 1980; Chuck Berry - The Chess Box, 1990; Hit singles include: Maybellene, 1955; Roll Over Beethoven, 1956; School Day, 1957; Rock And Roll Music, 1957; Sweet Little Sixteen, 1958; Johnny B Goode, 1958; Memphis Tennessee, 1963; Nadine (Is It You?), 1964; No Particular Place To Go, 1964; You Never Can Tell, 1964; My Ding A Ling, 1972. Publication: Chuck Berry - The Autobiography, 1988. Honours include: Grammy, Lifetime Achievement Award, 1985; Inducted into Rock And Roll Hall Of Fame, 1986; Hollywood Walk Of Fame, 1987; Inducted into Songwriters Hall Of Fame, 1986; Maybellene inducted into NARAS Hall Of Fame, 1988; St Louis Walk Of Fame, 1989; Johnny B Goode, featured on Voyager Interstellar Record, NASA's Voyager satellite, 1989; Roll Over Beethoven inducted into NARAS Hall of Fame, 1990. Current Management: Ira Okun Enterprises, 211 S Beverly Drive, Suite 103, Beverly Hills, CA 90212, USA.

BERRY Dave, b. 6 Feb 1941, Sheffield, England. Vocalist. m. Marthy Van-Lopik, 20 Feb 1967, 1 daughter. Musical Education: Father a semi-professional drummer. Career: Tours with Rolling Stones, 1964-65; Television: Top Of The Pops; Ready Steady Go; Lucky Stars; Song Festival, Knokke, Belgium; Gran Gala, Netherlands; Concert tours, 60's package with other artists, 1985-1995. Recordings: Memphis Tennessee, 1963; Crying Game, 1964; Baby Its You, 1964; This Strange Effect, 1965; Little Things, 1965; Mama, 1966. Honour: Press Prize, Knokke, Belgium. Hobbies: Travel; Hiking. Current Management: Brian Gannon Management. Address: PO Box 106, Rochdale, England.

BERRY Jan, b. 3 Apr 1941, Los Angeles, California, USA. Singer. m. Gertie Filip, 1991. Career: Member, duo Jan and Dean (with Dean Torrence), 1957-66; 1973-; Career interrupted by serious accident, 1966; Performances include: Dick Clark's stage show, Michigan State Fair, with Frankie Avalon, Duane Eddy, The Coasters, 1959; American Bandstand, ABC-TV, 1964; New York, with The Animals, Chuck Berry, Del Shannon, 1964; California Surfer's Stomp Festival, 1973; Subject of biopic, Dead Man's Curve, ABC-TV, 1978. Recordings: Albums: Jan And Dean Take Linda Surfin', 1963; Surf City And Other Swinging Cities, 1963; Drag City, 1964; Dead Man's Curve/The New Girl At School, 1964; The Little Old Lady From Pasadena, 1964; Ride The Wild Surf (film soundtrack), 1964; Command Performance/Live In Person, 1965; Jan And Dean Meet Batman, 1966; One Summer Night - Live, 1982; Various compilations; Singles include: with Jan & Dean: Linda, 1963; Surf City, 1963; Honolulu Lulu, 1963; Dead Man's Curve, 1964; The Little Old Lady (From Pasadena), 1964; Ride The Wild Surf, 1964;

Catch A Wave, 1964; You Really Know How To Hurt A Guy, 1965; Solo albums: Mother Earth, 1972; Don't You Just Know It, 1972; Tinsel Town, 1974. Current Management: Bill Hollingshead Productions, 1720 North Ross Street, Santa Ana, CA 92706, USA.

BERRY John, b. 14 Sept 1959, Aiken, South Carolina, USA. Singer; Songwriter. m. Robin (née Calvert), 2 sons, 1 daughter. Career: Moved to Nashville, 1990; Tours, concerts with own band; Television includes: Music City Tonight; The Ralph Emery Show; CBS This Morning; NBC Weekend Today; Entertainment Tonight; The Road; Exclusively Leeza; Conan O'Brian. Recordings: John Berry, 1995; Standing On The Edge, 1995; O'Holy Night, 1995; Singles: Your Love Amazes Me (Number 1); Standing On The Edge Of Goodbye; I Think About It All The Time; If I Had Any Pride Left At All. Honours include: 2 Gold albums; 1 Platinum album, John Berry, 1995; Platinum single, Your Love Amazes Me; Grammy Awards: Best Male Country Performance, 1995, 1996. Memberships: AFofM; CMA; NARAS; ACM. Hobby: Motorcycles. Current Management: Corlew - O'Grady Management. Address: 1503 17th Avenue South, Nashville, TN 37212, USA.

BERRYHILL Cindy Lee, b. Los Angeles, California, USA. Musician (guitar); Songwriter; Singer. Education: College. Musical Education: Private lessons, classical guitar, age 10. Career: Appearances: USA; England; Ireland; Holland; Belgium, 1988-90; BBC TV Belfast, 1988; Toured USA opening for the Smithereens, 1988, 1994; Mariposa Folk Festival, 1990, 1993; Toured USA headlining, 1994. Recordings: Albums: Who's Gonna Save The World; Naked Movie Star; Garage Orchestra. Hobbies: Books; Recently completed novel. Current Management: Booking Agent: Absolute Artists, Bruce Solar. Address: PO Box 7101, San Diego, CA 92167, USA.

BERRYMAN Peter Anthony, b. 22 June 1945, Redruth, Cornwall, England. Musician (guitar); Composer; Teacher. 2 sons, 1 daughter. Musical Education: Self-taught. Career: Tours with: Famous Jug Band, UK, 1969-71; Mormos, Africa, 1973; Julie Felix, Australasia, UK, 1974; Bridget St John, UK, 1976; Brenda Wootton, UK, France, 1985-90; Blue Ticket, 1987-93; Solo, UK, Europe, 1972-; Radio includes: John Peel; Andy Kershaw, Kaleidoscope, BBC; Television includes: Old Grey Whistle Test, BBC2; Festivals: Cambridge; Hyde Park; Glastonbury; L'Orient; Womad; Guitar teacher, 1982-; Music for Kneehigh Theatre; Theatre Rotto; The Barneys; Tour of UK and Eire with West, 1996; UK tour. duo with Adrian O'Reilly, 1997. Recordings: with Ralph McTell: Spiral Staircase, 1968; with Famous Jug Band: Sunshine Possibilities, 1969; Chameleon, 1970; with Wizz Jones: Legendary Me; Wizz Jones; Magical Flight; Duo with John James: Sky In My Pie, 1971; with Al Stewart: Past, Present and Future; Solo albums: And Guitar; Under A Summer Sky; Compilations: Best Of British Folk; Picture Rags; Guitar Workshop; The Electric Muse. Honour: Winner, International Pan Celtic Song Contest, 1996. Memberships: PRS; Musicians' Union. Hobbies: Walking; Sailing. Current Management: Self-managed. Address: Blue Gates, Lodge Hill, St Blazey Gate, Par, Cornwall PL24 2EF, England.

BERT Eddie, b. 16 May 1922, Yonkers, New York, USA. Musician (trombone). m. Mollie Petrillo, 21 Aug 1940, 3 daughters. Musical Education: Manhattan School of Music, Bachelor and Master of Music. Career: Orchestras include: Illinois Jacquet's Big Band; Thelonius Monk; Charles Mingus; Elliot Lawrence; Lionel Hampton; Stan Kenton; Benny Goodman's Orchestra; Charlie Barnet; Woody Herman; Red Norvo; Broadway shows include: Bye Bye Birdie, 1960; How To Succeed In Business, 1961; Golden Boy, 1964; Pippin, 1972-77; Ain't Misbehavin', 1978-82; Human Comedy, 1984-85; Uptown It's Hot, 1986.

Films: Jam Session With Charlie Barnet Orchestra, 1943; The French Connection; School Daze (Spike Lee), 1987; Television: Dick Cavett Show, 1968-72; Associate Professor, Essex College, 1981-82; Bridgeport University, 1984-86; Tours include: USSR, France, Denmark, 1975; Spain, 1986; Netherlands, 1987; Italy, 1987; Japan, with Walt Levinsky's Great American Swing Band, 1988-89; Five Continents with Gene Harris-Philip Morris Superband, 1989; Performances: Dick Gibson's Jazz Party, Denver, Colorado, 1979, 1981; Florida Jazz Festival, 1981, 1982; Carnegie Hall Jazz Festival, 1980-84. Recordings include: As Eddie Bert: Like Cool, 1955; East Coast Jazz, 1955; Encore, 1955; Musician Of The Year, 1955; Kaleidoscope, 1987; The Human Factor, Eddie Bert Sextet, 1987; Live At Birdland, Eddie Bert Quintet, 1991. Publications: Eddie Bert Trombone Method; Eddie Bert Lead Sheet Book. Honours: Brass Conference Salute, Hotel Roosevelt, New York City, 1990. Membership: NARAS. Hobby: Photography.

BERTHELSEN Claus Gymoese, b. 28 Sept 1958, Copenhagen, Denmark. Songwriter; Author; Singer. 1 daughter. Education: Bachelor of Economics. Musical Education: Copenhagen Boys Choir. Career: Founder, own group Naïve; Several gigs in Denmark including: The Roskilde Festival (twice). Numerous Danish television appearances with Naïve; Actor in Gangway I Tyrol. Compositions: Songs: Carry On; Marble Afternoon. Recordings: Albums: with Naïve: Fish; Careless; Absolution Music. Membership: DJBFA. Hobbies: Writing video screenplays for: Heinrich Von Hinten, underground video team (members include: Henrik Balling; Peter Ravn; Renee Paschburg; Asger G Larsen; Arne Siemsen; Thomas Arnoldi). Current Management: Allan Graunkjaer, Record Music Denmark. Address: Wilkensvej 25, 2000 Frederiksberg, Denmark.

BERTHELSEN Ole, b. 18 Dec 1951, Aalborg, Denmark. Singer; Songwriter. m. Ellen, 18 Dec 1981, 2 sons. Recordings: Altid Vagen Om Natten, 1979; Smid Masken, 1982; Flygtning, 1989; Verden Til Forskel, 1991; Havner Ved Havet, 1993; Basic Needs, 1994. Membership: DJBFA. Current Management: MIS Label, Jellingvet 6, 9230 Svestrup, Denmark.

BERTRAM Dominique, b. 8 Aug 1954, Alger, Algeria. Musician (electric bass). m. Florence Faisan, 6 Nov 1991, 1 son, 1 daughter. Musical Education: Self-taught. Career: Worked with singers: Michael Jonasz; Veronique Sanson; Catherine Lara; Patrick Bruel; Al Jarreau. Recordings: Michael Jonasz; Veronique Sanson; Dominique Bertram: Chinese Paradise, 1985; Bass Now, 1992. Publications: Method Up Bass, 1990; Jouer De La Basse C'Est Facile, 1994. Memberships: SACEM; Spedidam; ADAMI. Hobbies: Cycling; Backgammon. Address: 101 Rue de Mont-Cenis, 75018 Paris, France.

BERTRAM Hans-Dieter "Sherry", b. 20 May 1936, Leipzig, Germany. Musician (drums, percussion). m. Dagmar, 16 Sept 1969, 2 sons. Education: Study of Engineering, Berlin, 1959. Musical Education: Berlin Conservatory, 1959-65. Career: Freelance Musician; Graphic Designer, Moderator for Rias Radio Station, 1957-89; Concerts and recordings, Berlin Philarmonic Orchestra, 1962; Deutsche Oper Berlin, 1962, 1967, 1972, 1993-95; Musicals and music for theatre; Studio musician for television, radio, films, jingles, records, Rias Live Talk Show, 1969-1989; CA 100 Programs; Jazzdrummer with own groups, bigbands; Percussion teacher at Leo-Burchard Music School; Moderator, Jazz Radio Berlin, 1995. Membership: Landesmusikrat Berlin, Jazz Department. Hobbies: Swimming; Cycling; Ice Skating. Current Management: Own agency: Orchester Bertram Gmbtt. Address: Rudolstaedter Strasse 123, 10713 Berlin, Germany.

BERTRAND Plastic, b. 24 Feb 1954, Brussels, Belgium. Singer; Composer; Writer; Producer. m. Evelyne Van Daele, 1979, 1 son, 1 daughter. Musical Education: Conservatoire Royal De Musique de Bruxelles (university level musical High School). Career: Singer, drummer, punk band: Hubble Bubble, 1975; Solo career, 1977-; 8 albums; International tours worldwide; Appears in own television shows: France (TF Jackspot); Italy (Due per tutti); Belgium (Supercool). Recordings: Wrote, produced: Ça Plane Pour Moi; Tout Petite La Planète; Stop Ou Encore; Sentimentale-Moi; Hula Hoop; Slave To The Beat. Honours: 15 Gold, 5 Platinum records worldwide; Billboard Award; Grand Prix de l'Académie Française Du Disque. Membership: SABAM. Hobbies: Antiques. Current Management: MMD, Broodthaers Pierrette. Address: 38 rue Fernand Bernier, 1060 Brussels, Belgium.

BESEMANN Robyn, b. 19 Jan 1954, Reed City, Michigan, USA. Singer; Songwriter; Public Speaker; Author. m. Ivan L Besemann, 1 son, 1 daughter. Career: Gospel recording artist signed with Incubator Records for 2 years; Executive Director, co-founder of LIFE Aerobics, 1980-88; Franklin Graham Crusades; Regular tours. Recordings: In His Name, 1993; For His Glory, 1995. Membership: Gospel Music Association (GMA). Hobbies: Travel; Music; Boating; Going to the coast.

BEST Matthew, b. 26 Jan 1961, London, England. Musician (drums, keyboards); Disc Jockey; Record Producer. Education: West London Institute of HE. Musical Education: Self-taught. Career: Studio drummer, Captain Sensible, 1977-80; Formed Carcrash International, 1983-84; Played live for UK Subs and Anti-Nowhere League; Formed Urban Dogs; Pressure Point (featuring P P Arnold); Simultaneously member of Psychic TV, 1986-; Formed Greedy Beat Syndicate; Play live with techno band Yum Yum. Recordings: 2 albums, Urban Dogs; 12 albums, Psychic TV; 2 albums, Greedy Beat Syndicate. Membership: Musicians' Union. Hobbies: Music; Records; Usual vices associated therewith. Current Management: Colleen Sanders, 1-7 Boundary Row, London SE1, England. Address: 19 Irving Street, London WC2H 7AU, England.

BETTENCOURT Nuno, b. 20 Sept 1966, Azores, Portugal. Musician (guitar); Producer. Career: Member, Sinful; Guitarist, US funk/rock group Extreme, 1985-; Played Boston club circuit, 1985-88; Worldwide appearances include: UK tour, 1991; A Concert For Life, Tribute to Freddie Mercury, Wembley, 1992; American Dream concerts, London, 1992; Support to Bryan Adams, European tour, 1992. Recordings: Singles include: Get The Funk Out, 1991; More Than Words (Number 1, US), 1991; Decadence Dance, 1991; Hole-Hearted, 1991; Song For Love, 1992; Stop The World, 1992; Albums: Extreme, 1989; Extreme II Pornograffitti, 1991; III Sides To Every Story, 1992. Honours: Boston Music Awards: Act Of Year; Outstanding Rock Single, Hole Hearted; Outstanding Pop Single; Outstanding Song/Songwriter, More Than Words; Outstanding Instrumentalist, 1992. Current Management: Andon Artists, 79 Fairview Farm Road, West Redding, CT 06896, USA.

BETTIS John, b. 24 Oct 1946, Long Beach, California, USA. Lyricist. Career: Co-founder, The Carpenters; 38 songs recorded by them, 1970-; Other artists: Michael Jackson; Madonna; Whitney Houston; Diana Ross; 180 million records sold. Compositions include: Top Of The World; Yesterday Once More; Only Yesterday; Goodbye To Love; Human Nature; Crazy For You; Slow Hand; One Moment In Time; When You Tell Me That You Love Me. Honours: Grammy Nomination; Oscar; Golden Globe; Emmy.

BEVAN Bev(erley), b. 24 Nov 1946, Birmingham, England. Musician (drums). Career: Member, groups: Carl Wayne & The Vikings; Denny Laine & The Diplomats; Danny King & The Mayfair Set; Drummer, The Move, 1966-72; Appearances include: National Jazz & Blues Festival, 1966; Support to The Rolling Stones, Paris, 1967; Art Festival Ball, Brighton, 1967; Isle Of Wight Festival, 1968; Reading Festival, 1972; Drummer, Electric Light Orchestra (ELO), 1972-; Concerts include: Heartbeat '86 benefit, Birmingham, 1986; Brief spell, drummer, Black Sabbath, including Reading Festival, 1983; Recordings: Albums: with the Move: Move, 1968; Shazam, 1970; Looking On, 1970; Message From The Country, 1971; Great Move: The Best Of The Move, 1993; with ELO: Electric Light Orchestra, 1972; On The Third Day, 1973; Eldorado, 1974; The Night The Light Went On In Long Beach, 1974; Face The Music, 1975; Olé ELO, 1976; A New World Record, 1976; Out Of The Blue, 1977; Discovery (Number 1, UK), 1979; ELO's Greatest Hits, 1979; Xanadu (film soundtrack), 1980; Time, 1981; Secret Messages, 1983; Balance Of Power, 1986; Greatest Hits, 1989; Electric Light Orchestra, 1991; Singles: with the Move include: I Can Hear The Grass Grow; Flowers In The Rain; Fire Brigade; Blackberry Way (Number 1, UK); Hello Susie; Curly; Brontosaurus; California Man; with ELO: Roll Over Beethoven; Showdown; Can't Get It Out Of My Head; Strange Magic; Evil Woman; Lovin' Thing; Rockaria!; Do Ya; Telephone Line; Turn To Stone; Mr Blue Sky; Wild West Hero; Shine A Little Love; Don't Bring Me Down; Xanadu (Number 1, UK); Hold On Tight; Rock'n'Roll Is King; Calling America; Solo: Let There Be Drums. Honours include: Outstanding Contribution to British Music, Ivor Novello Award, 1979.

BEX Emmanuel Jean, b. 8 June 1959, Caen, France. Musician (Hammond organ). m. Sophie Simon, 31 Aug 1991, 1 son, 1 daughter. Musical Education: Conservatory of Caen; Conservatory of Paris. Career: Member, quintet The Bex'tet, 1991; Sideman with: Babick Reinhardt; Barney Wilen; Philippe Catherine; New Group, Steel Bex, with E Bex and Steel Band, 1997; New Group, Bex Machine, E Bex Quartet, 1997. Recordings: Bex And Jouvelet In Public, 1983; with Ray Lema: Bwana Zoulu, 1987; with Bex, Pino, Teslard: Triple Idiome, 1988; with Xavier Jouvelet: Blues Congo, 1988; with La Bande à Badauld: Vacances Au Soleil, 1988; Caravanserail, 1989; with Bertrand Renaudin: Interplay, 1990; Miscellaneous Song, 1991; with Carl Schlosser: Texas Sound, 1992; with Babick Reinhardt: Histoire Simple, 1992; with Marais, Bex, Romano: Poissons Nageurs, 1993; with Bex'tet: Enfance, 1991; Organique, 1993; Rouge Et Or, 1995; with Barney Wilen: Nitty Gritty, 1993; Steel Bex, Emmanuel Bex, 1996; Due des Lowbards, Christian Escoudé Trio, 1997. Honour: Prix Django Reinhardt, Academy of Jazz, 1995. Current Management: Sophie Simon. Address: 8 Impasse Chanut, 93200 Saint Denis, France.

BHAMRAH Kulwant Singh, b. 11 Feb 1955, India. Bhangra Singer; Songwriter m. Satvinder Bhamrah, 3 Mar 1979, 1 son, 1 daughter. Education: Civil engineer. Musical Education: Hobby developed into profession. Career: Singer, Bhangra Folk Panjabi band Apna Sangeet; Performed in: UK; Kenya; Tanzania; Canada; America; Singapore; India. Television appearances include: BBC; ITV; CH4; TV Asia; Star TV. Appeared on all official Asian broadcasting radio stations. Compositions: Writes own songs. Recordings: Albums include: Toor India; Mera Yaar; Chack Dey Phattay; Desi Rytham; Musicblasters; Mini Blasters; Mister Blasters; Hi-Kiddaw. Honours: Asian Pop Awards, Best Band, 1988; Best Songwriter, 1992; Best Live Band, 1994. Memberships: PRS; MCPS; Musicians' Union; British Actor Equity. Hobbies: Formerly singing; Sport; Television; Keep fit. Current Management: Self-managed. Address: 18 Cubley Road, Hall Green, Birmingham, England.

BHATIA Anjali, b. 15 Oct 1968, Chiswick, London, England. Singer; Musician (guitar, former drummer); Songwriter. Education: Kingsway Princeton College, B-Tec, Art and Design; Goldsmiths College, degree in textiles design, Art and critical theory. Musical Education: Classical guitar training, Grade 4. Career: Festivals: Reading, Phoenix; Radio: 3 John Peel sessions. Recordings: Singles: Supermodel/Superficial; Kenuweehead; f is for fame; Eat The Gems; Album: Chocolate Revenge. Memberships: PRS; Musicians' Union. Hobbies: Art; Food; Travel; Painting. Address: PO Box 1944, London NW10 5PJ, England.

BHEAGLAOICH Seosaimhín Ní, b. West Kerry, Gaeltacht, Ireland. Singer; Broadcaster. Education: BA (Mod) Hons Trinity College Dublin. Career: Presenter, television series The Mountain Lark, RTE; Broadcaster with Raidió-Na-Gaeltachta; Numerous television appearances, RTE, Ireland; Presenter, As I Roved Out, BBC Ulster. Recordings: Solo album: Taobh Na Gréine (Under The Sun), Gael-Linn; Sings title track: Mná Na h-Éireann, on Macalla, all women groups' first album; Also sings on Macalla 2. Hobbies: Travel; Walking. Current Management: Gael-Linn. Address: Gael-Linn, 26 Cearnóg Mhuirfean, Bac 2, Ireland.

BIALEK Robert, b. 27 Mar 1950, Belgium. Artist Manager. 1 daughter. Career: Artist Manager, Robert Bialek Conseils; 25 years in business in France and Europe. Address: 15 rue d'Hauteville, 75010 Paris, France.

BICKERSTETH John Dennis, b. 27 June 1954, Constantine, Cornwall, England. Musician (piano, keyboards); Singer; Composer; Entertainer. Musical Education: Choral Scholar, Truro Cathedral; Organ, piano, John Winter and Guillaume Ormond. Career: Member of: Cruiser; Ian And The Muscletones; The Barneys; Ian Dunlop's Babylon Babies; Daniel Rovai and Friends; Ton and Kirschen Theater (Potsdam); Chip Bray Show (Amsterdam Lido); MD, Back On Stage, UFA Fabrik, Berlin; MD, Stewart and Ross; Live television: Japan; Ireland; Germany. Recordings: Album: Ian and The Muscletones. Membership: Musicians' Union. Hobbies: Jazz; Blues guitar; Classical music; Vintage cars. Address: Tregarth, Bissoe, Truro, Cornwall TR4 8RJ, England.

BICKERTON Wayne, b. 11 July 1941, Rhyl, Wales. Songwriter; Music Publisher; Producer. m. Carole Da-Cliva. Career: Lee Curtis and the All Stars; Pete Best Four; Songwriting in partnership with Tony Waddington, his with: Bing Crosby; Jose Feliciano; The Bachelors; Tom Jones; Andy Williams; Decca Records: Label Manager/A&R Head, Deram; Founder, owner, State Records; Odyssey Group Record Producer (Rubettes, Delegation). Recordings: Sugar Baby Love; Sugar Candy Kisses; I Can Do It; Juke Box Jive; Baby I Know. Honours: Songwriter Of the Year (joint), Ivor Novello Awards, 1975. Memberships: PRS, Chairman, 1993; MCPS; BASCA (UK); ASCAP; BMI (USA). Hobby: Tennis. Address: c/o PRS, Copyright House, 29-33 Berners Street, London W1P 4AA, England.

BICKNELL Robert David, b. 7 December 1957, Jersey, St Helier, Channel Islands. Singing Teacher. Redroofs Theatre School; Goldsmiths University of London. Career: Tosca, Aida, Carmen, Hello Dolly, Rocky Horror Show, Godspell, Many Pantos; TV, Robin Hood, Lenny Henry Show, Doctor Who, Saturday Night Live; TV as Singing Coach, Big Breakfast Show, 16 months; Richard & Judy; Ozone; This Morning; Musical Director, Royal Albert Hall, Wembley Arena. Recordings: Love Can Build a Bridge; Film, The Matchmaker. Contributions to: Daily Mail. Honour: BMus, London. Memberships: Equity; British Voice Association; Incorporated Society of Musicians. Address: 69 Lower Flat, Acre Lane, London SW2 5TN, England.

BIDDLE Elizabeth Rosina, b. 29 Apr 1952, Pontypridd, South Wales. Record Producer; Music Agent; Musician (bassoon). Musical Education: Aberystwth University, BA Hons Music; Guildhall School of Music and Drama, City University, MA Music Performance Studies. Career: Director of Music, Comprehensive School, 1984; Bassoon tutor at Christs Hospital, Horsham, 1984-; Founded Upbeat Management, 1986; Founded Upbeat Recordings, 1989. Recordings: Producer for The Temperance Seven; Terry Lightfoot; Ken Colyer; Carey Blyton. Publications: Writer for Musical Opinion for 3 years. Membership: BACA. Hobbies: Playing bassoon for local operatic societies; Bird watching. Address: 53 The Causeway, Carshalton, Surrey SM5 2LZ, England.

BIET Remi, b. 1 Oct 1958, Dieppe, France. Musician (saxophones, flute). m. Brigitte Tailleux, 2 daughters. Education: Ecole Normale d'Instituteurs. Musical Education: DE and CA of Jazz (self-taught). Career: Tours: USA (New Orleans, San Francisco, Chicago); Italy; Madagascar; Sicily; Germany. Television: Syria; Jordan; France; Italy. Recordings: ONJ: Badault; A Plus Tard, 1991; Mingus, Monk Ellington, 1992; Bouquet Final, 1993. Membership: UMJ. Hobbies: Golf; Chess; Stunt kite. Address: 7 Parc de l'Andelle, 76130 Mt St Aignan, France.

BIG YOUTH Manley Augustus Buchanan, b. February 1955, Jamaica. Reggae Disc Jockey; Record Company Owner. Career: Former cab driver and mechanic; Leading reggae DJ, Kingston, 1970s; Founder, Negusa Nagast and Augustus Buchanan record labels, 1973. Recordings: Albums: Screaming Target, 1973; Reggae Phenomenon, 1974; Dreadlocks Dread, 1975; Natty Cultural Dread, 1976; Hit The Road Jack, 1976; Isaiah First Prophet of Old, 1978; Everybody Skank - the Best of Big Youth, 1980; Some Great Big Youth, 1981; The Chanting Dread Inna Fine Style, 1983; Live at Reggae Sunsplash, 1984; A Luta Continua, 1985; Manifestation, 1988; Jamming In the House of Dread, 1991. Address: c/o Zoe Productions, 450 Broome Street, 8th Floor, New York, NY 10013, USA.

BIJLSMA Bert, b. 26 Feb 1954, Assen, Netherlands. Agent. m. Henriëtte Wolda, 9 July 1987, 1 son, 2 daughters. Education: 2 years study, Geography. Career: Agency for Jan Akkerman, 1980-; Tours with Focus: USA; Japan; Europe; Australia; Bach 300 year Anniversary Berlin; Festival Montreux; Northsea Jazz Festival, The Hague; Parkpop, The Hague; Special: A Touch of Music, for Dutch World Broadcasting Company Recordings: Latest releases: The Noise Of Art; Puccini's Cafe; Blues Hearts. Honour: Number 1 Guitar Player, Melody Maker, 1973. Current Management: Hamrikkerweg 4, 9943 TB Nw Scheemda, Netherlands.

BILA Vera, b. 22 May 1954, Rokycany, Czechoslovakia. 1 son. Career: Appeared on 8pm TV News, France 2, Canal and RAI; Theatre Des Bouffes Du Nord, Paris, France, 6 days; Festivals, Jazz, Montreal, Bourges, Paleo-Nyon, Arezzo, Rennes. Compositions: E Daj Nasval'i on compilation of festivals: Transmusical Rennes, 1996; Arezzo Wave, 1997. Recordings: CDRom Pop, 1996; Kake Kolore, 1998. Publications: Article in Liberation; Article in Les Inrockuptibles. Honour: Record of the Year, 1996. Hobby: Children. Current Management: Jiri Smetana Management, Paris, France. Address: c/o Jiri Smetana, Vinohradska 168, 13000 Prague, Czech Republic.

BILK Acker (Bernard Stanley), b. 28 Jan 1929, Pensford, Somerset, England. Musician (clarinet); Composer; Bandleader. m. Jean, 1 son, 1 daughter. Career: Began playing clarinet in Royal Engineers, 1948; Clarinet, Ken Colyer's Band; Formed Bristol Paramount Jazz Band; Currently freelance artiste; Guest musician on numerous records; Tours worldwide, now with Paramount Jazz Band; Played with Reunion Paramount Jazz Band, Isle of Bute Jazz Festival, 1995; Owner 2 publishing companies. Recordings: Singles include: Somerset; Aria; Stranger On The Shore (Number 1, US and UK, 1961); Albums include: The One For Me; Sheer Magic; Evergreen; Chalumeau-That's My Home; Three In The Morning (with Humphrey Lyttelton, John Barnes, Dave Green, Dave Cliff, Bobby Worth); Giants Of Jazz (with Paramount Jazz Band, Kenny Ball and his Jazzmen, Kenny Baker Don Lusher All Stars); Chris Barber and Acker Bilk, That's It Then!; Clarinet Moods With Acker Bilk, Acker Bilk with string orchestra; Acker Bilk - The Oscars; Clarinet Moods with Acker Bilk; All the Hits and More; The Christmas Album. Hobbies: Painting; Walking. Current Management: Acker's International Jazz Agency. Address: 53 Cambridge Mansions, Cambridge Road, London SW11 4RX, England.

BILLINGTON Scott Thomas, b. 27 Oct 1951, Melrose, Massachusetts, USA. Record Producer; Musician (harmonica). 1 daughter. Career: Produced over 100 albums of roots-orientated music for labels including: Rounder; Columbia; Sire; Real World. Recordings include: Alright Again, Clarence Gatemouth Brown; Pictures And Paintings, Charlie Rich; Voodoo, The Dirty Dozen Brass Band; Turning Point, Buckwheat Zydeco; Johnny Adams, One Foot in the Blues, 1996; Beau Jocque and the Zydeco Hi-Rollers, 1996; Bill Morrissey, You'll Never Get to Heaven, 1996; Ruth Brown, R&B = Ruth Brown, 1997; Irma Thomas, The Story of My Life, 1997; Irma Thomas, Marcia Ball and Tracy Nelson, Sing It!, 1998; Davell Crawford, The B-3 and Me, 1998. Honours: 2 Grammy Awards; 6 Nominations; Grand Prix Du Disque; 2 W C Handy Awards; Producer of the Year, Offbeat Magazine, New Orleans, 1997. Memberships: NARAS; BMI. Address: 47 Forrester Street, Newburyport, MA 01950, USA.

BILOUS Edward. Composer; Conductor. Musical Education: BM, Composition, Manhattan School of Music; MM DMA, Composition, Juillard School. Career: After graduation, joined Juillard School, Music, Drama, Liberal Arts Department, Lincoln Center Institute; Co-chairman of Literature, Music Department at Juillard; Artisitic Director of Music Advancement Program; Director, Consultant of Music Education program by Juillard and Berkley Learning Technologies. Compositions: Film, television music: Sleepaway Camp; Le Bain; Tribeca; Anna Sorror; Urban Fairy Tales; The Last Romantic; Theme for Monaco Film Festival, 1993; Orchestrator, arranger for: Carnegie Hall Tribute to Pete Townshend (with Roger Daltrey, Alice Cooper, Sinead O'Connor, The Spin Doctors, Eddie Vedder). Honours: Joseph Machlis Award for Excellence, Juillard School; Best Public Service Announcement Award (Elephant Slaughter), Cannes, 1989. Current Management: SESAC. Address: 55 Music Sq E, Nashville, TN 37203, USA.

BILY Antonin, b. 7 May 1939, Prague, Czech Republic. Composer; Arranger; Pianist. m. Jitka Bila, 31 August 1972, 2 sons. Education: Conservatory of Prague and J Jezek Conservatory. Career: Pianist & Composer, Traditional Jazz Studio, Prague, 1960-; Teacher & Director, Composer - Conduct Section, J Jezek Conservatory, Prague, 1986-. Compositions: Metamorphoses of Time, 1986; Modus Vivendi, 1991; Fine Stagione; A Town So Strange; On the Seventh Floor. Recordings: CCA 20 albums with traditional Jazz Studio, some recorded with Benny Waters, Tonny Scot, Albert Nicholas, Beryl Breyden. Honours: First awards: Jazz Festival Düsseldorf, 1968; International Contest of Composition for Jazz bigband, Barga, Italy, 1989; Association of Music Artist and Scientists; Czech Music Society; Czech Jazz Society. Hobbies:

Enthnomology; Nature. Current Management: Antonin Bily, Korunni 29, 12000 Praha 2, Czech Republic. Address: Konzervator J Jezka, Rytírska 10, 11000 Praha 1, Czech Republic.

BINDING Philip Robert, b. 20 Mar 1960, Barry, South Wales. Composer; Producer; Writer; Musician (piano-synthesiser). m. Helen Garnett, 23 Nov 1990, 1 daughter. Education: Ravensbourne Art College, 1978-80. Musical Education: Piano, Theory. Career: Sound Engineer, 1980-91; Formed Boom Productions with Simon Moore, producing music for TV, film, 1991. Compositions: TV themes; Incidental music includes Gladiators; International Gladiators; You Bet; Pop Quiz; What's My Line; ITV Sport; Missing; Expert Witness; Strange But True; Beadle's About; Love And Marriage; ITV Promotions. Memberships: Musicians' Union; BASCA; PRS; MCPS. Address: Boom Productions, 5 Clifton Close, Addlestone, Surrey KT15 2EX, England.

BINDZI Lucien, b. Cameroon. Artist Manager; Music Promoter. Education: Industrial Electricity Diploma. Career: Service Leader, Director, Kilo Brother; Rhénaly Péchiney, Alsace; Radio Host and nightclub Disc Jockey, Brittany; Founder, President, producer of shows of African music, dance and culture, Africa Music International, 1986-; Manager, group The Veterans, specialising in traditional Bikutsi music; Numerous tours throughout Africa; Frequent Number 1 hits, African charts. Recordings: Albums with The Veterans include: Min Sounga Mi Kabard, 1975; Me Ne Ngon Oyap, 1983; Wa Dug Ma, 1984; Au Village, 1985; Traditions, 1986; Les Veterans Presentent Ahanda, 1988; Toss Difference, 1993. Address: Africa Music International, 15 Rue Charles Gounod, 56100 Lorient, France.

BIRGÉ Jean-Jacques Gaston, b. 5 Nov 1952, Paris, France. Composer; Musician (synthesizer); Film Director. 1 daughter. Education: IDHEC Diploma, National Film School. Musical Education: Self-taught. Career: Live music on 23 silent films including: Caligari; Fall Of The House Of Usher; Jeanne d'Arc; The Man With The Camera; J'Accuse; Le K (with Richard Bohringer); Il Etait Une Fois La Fête Fotaine. Recordings: Trop D'Adrénaline Nuit, 1977; Rideau!, 1980; A Travail Égal Salaire Égal, 1981; Carnage, 1985; L'Hallali, 1988; Qui Vive?, 1990; Kind Lieder, 1991; Urgent Meeting, 1992; Opération Blow Up, 1993; Sarajevo Suite, 1994; Carton, enhanced CD, 1997. Publication: The Sniper. Honours: Nomination, Victoires de la Musique, for Le K, 1994; British Academy Award for TV Arts, 1994; Video Grand Prix at Locarno Festival for Sarajevo, A Street Under Siege (collective). Membership: Un Drame Musical Instantané. Hobby: Resistance. Address: 134 rue d'Estienne d'Orves, 92140 Clamart, France.

BIRGE Jodle (Birge Lonquist), b. 6 Nov 1945, Sebbersund, Denmark. Musician (guitar). m. Inger-Lise, 1 son, 1 daughter. Education: Butcher. Career: Wembley Arena, London, England; Jonkobing Ice-stadium, Sweden; Tivoli Gardens, Copenhagen, Denmark; Fan Fair, Nashville, USA; Spruce Meadows, Calgery, Canada; Television shows, Denmark; USA; Canada. Recordings: Rigtige Venner (Best Buddies), Platinum disc; Tre Hvide Duer, (Three White Doves), Platinum disc; Tusinde Rode Roser (Garden Full Of Roses), Platinum disc; 82 albums released in Denmark, sales of more than 2 million. Honours: Silver, Gold, Platinum discs. Hobby: Hunting wild animals. Current Management: Calle Nielsen, CB and Ole B Booking Aps, Denmark. Address: Jordsmonnet 4, PO Box 224, 8900 Randers, Denmark.

BIRKBY Peter Richard, b. 30 Nov 1957, England. Composer; Musician (percussion). Musical Education: Leeds College of Music.

Career: BBC Radio; Television from Pebble Mill; Tours with Shirley Bassey; Vic Damone; Gene Pitney; Dave Willets; Jesus Christ Superstar. Recordings: Three Movements for Orchestra, Queen Elizabeth Hall, 1994; With own group, Legends: Special Edition, 1986. Publications: Over 80 pieces for Percussion (solo and ensemble); 6 for Orchestra; 20 for Jazz Orchestra. Memberships: PRS; MCPS; Musicians' Union. Hobbies: Swimming; Cinema. Address: PO Box 7, South Kirkby, Pontefract, West Yorkshire WF9 3XJ, England.

BIRKETT Chris, b. 14 Apr 1953, Aldershot, Hampshire, England. Record Producer; Composer; Musician (guitar); Singer. m. Janet Susan Hewett, 25 Jan 1981, 1 son, 1 daughter. Career: Guitarist with: Ann Peebles; Rufus Thomas; Gene Knight; Love Affair; Singer with Omaha Sherif; Producer: Sinead O'Connor; Buffy Sainte-Marie; Talitha MacKenzie; Television, radio: Wogan; Pebble Mill; BBC News; Radio: Radio1; GLR; Capital. Compositions include: The album: Men From The Sky. Recordings: As producer/mixer/writer: Sinead O'Connor: Nothing Compares 2U; Album: I Do Not Want; Kiss Of Life, Madinka/Put 'Em On Me; Siedah Garrett; Copperhead Road, Steve Earle; with Five Star: Silk & Steel; Luxury Of Life; Love Letters/That Old Devil, Alison Moyet; Nothing But Flowers, Talking Heads; Movements, Osibisa; Johnny Come Lately, Pogues; Also with artists: Sting; Buffy Sainte-Marie; Laurie Freelove; Darden Smith; Cry Sisco; The Bible; Randy Remet; Hernandez; Mango Grove; Mr Big; Ice Cold In Alice; Richard Jon Smith; John Otway; Roman Holiday; Precious Wilson; John Congos; Siobhan McCarthy; Mondino; The Soul Brothers; Talitha MacKenzie; Guo Yue & Joji Hirota. Publications: Articles in Billboard, Studio Engineer. Honours: Ampex Golden Reel Awards: Gold Star and Mango Grove; Platinum discs: Nothing Compares 2U, Sinead O'Connor. Memberships: PRS; MCPS; Musicians' Union. Hobbies: Inventing; Electronics; Building studios; Wine growing. Current Management: Einstein Brothers, Toronto, Canada. Address: Les Mayets, 33220 Riocaud, France.

BIRO Daniel Andrew, b. 29 Jan 1963, Johannesburg, South Africa. Composer; Songwriter; Musician (piano). Musical Education: 8 years, Jazz Conservatory, Monaco; 3 years Nice University, France. Career: As keyboard player, World tours with: The Truth, 1987; Big Bam Boo, 1989; Bandleader, songwriter with L'Orange, 1993-; Arranger, musicals by Henry Lewis include: Joan Of Kent; The End Of The World Show; Co-founder, Lust, multi-arts performance organisation; Business venture, record label, Sargasso Records, (Experimental New Music). Compositions: For dance: Beauty And The Beast, 1992; Desert, 1995; For film: Lessons In How To Wear Red, 1994; Mu, 1995; For lust: Through The Mirror, 1993; The Pinocchio Tapes, 1994; Beba In White, 1995. Recordings: Albums: Soho Square, 1993; The Comparative Anatomy Of Angels, 1996. Memberships: Musicians' Union; SACEM (France); SPNM. Hobbies: Travel; Cinema; Chocolate. Address: 157 Gloucester Place, London NW1, England.

BIROSIK P J, b. 2 Sept 1956, New York, New York, USA. Music Industry Consultant. Education: MA, Columbia, 1977. Career: Formed Musik International Corporation, 1977; Services offered include: Market planning; Media promotion; Media relations; A&R/label development; Previous clients include: Ozzy Osbourne; Black Sabbath; Van Halen; Nils Lofgren; Paul McCartney and Wings; Kiss; Uriah Heep; Blondie; David Soul; Virgin; Lol Creme and Kevin Godley; Fleetwood Mac; Rod Stewart; Stevie Nicks; Herbie Hancock; Sony Records; Guns 'N' Roses; Journey; Japan; David Sylvian; Amii Stewart; Studio 54; The Doobie Brothers; Rickie Lee Jones; Art Of Persuasion; Max Million; Chuck E; New World Music; Earth Wave Productions; New Earth Records.

Publications: Monthly columns is magazines and newspapers. Honours: Gold records, Independent Promotion. Journey: Look Into The Future; Al Wilson: Show And Tell; Nomination, Inland Empire Awards: Best Air Personality, 1976; Billboard Magazine: Best College Station, 1977; 1st Place, Inland Empire Awards: Best Jazz Programming, 1977. Memberships include: Voting member, NARAS, 1980-95; NAIRD, 1994, 1995; Judge, NAIRD Indie Awards, 1993-95; Founder, New Age Music Network; International Platform Association; CMC; IMA; ED; ABA. Hobbies: Monitoring start-up international record companies. Current Management: Musik International. Address: 154 Betasso Road, Boulder, CO 80302, USA.

BIRTLES Gary, b. 10 June 1955, Leicester, England. Musician (saxophone); Singer. 2 sons. Musical Education: Self-taught. Career: Singer, own band, The Swinging Laurels; 2 UK support tours with Culture Club; Saxophone session player for Funboy 3; Member, brass section, The Beautiful South, 1990-; Currently singer, Country/Pop band Yellowbelly. Television appearances include: Top Of The Pops, with Funboy 3 and The Beautiful South. Recordings: Singles: with The Swinging Laurels: Peace Of Mind, 1980; Rodeo, 1982; Lonely Boy, 1983; Zoom, 1984. Membership: PRS. Hobbies: Songwriting; Computers; Tai Chi. Address: 138 Howard Road, Leicester LE2 1XJ, England.

BISHOP David Brian, b. 21 Dec 1958, Plymouth, England. Singer; Songwriter. Career: Written music for commercials; Publishing deal with Carlin Music; Reached Top 20 in Eurovision Song Contest. Recordings: Backing vocals on three tracks on album: Through The Years, Cilla Black. Hobbies: Swimming; Walking. Address: 8 Abbotts Court, Ashbourne Avenue, South Harrow, Middlesex HA2 OLE, England.

BISHOP David Ronald, b. 28 Mar 1960, London, England. Musician (all saxophones, flutes and clarinets). m. Hazel Diane Peat, 23 June 1984, deceased 14 Oct 1993, 1 daughter. Musical Education: National Youth Jazz Orchestra; Self-taught. Career: Worked with various artistes including: Ella Fitzgerald; Stevie Wonder; Sammy Davis; Cliff Richard; Paul McCartney; Liza Minnelli; Roger Daltrey; Dave Gilmour; Wet Wet Wet; Lisa Stansfield; Mel Torme; Nelson Riddle; Henry Mancini; Harry Connick Jr; Stan Tracey; Natalie Cole; Tom Scott; Tom Jones; James Brown; Cher; Take That; Ray Charles; Grace Jones; George Benson; David Sanborn; Van Morrison; Temptations; Swing Out Sister; Daryl Hall; RPO; LSO; BBC Concert Orchestra; Diana Ross; Harry Rabinowitz; Ray Monk; Colin Keyes; John Coleman; Harry (Oasis) Stoneham; 5 Royal Command Performances; Live Aid; Kurd Aid. Honours: UK Yamaha Saxophone Endorsee. Hobbies: Jaguar XK150 DHC (First in Concours, 1995). Address: 27 Radlett Park Road, Radlett, Herts WD7 7BG, England.

BISHOP Michael Joseph, b. 14 June 1951, Santa Monica, California, USA. Recording Engineer; Record Producer. m. Wendy LaTessa, 22 Sept 1979, 2 daughters. Career: Record producer, recording engineer, 1972-. Recordings: As recording engineer: Play That Funky Music, Wild Cherry, 1986; Live At Carnegie Hall, Liza Minnelli, 1987; The Sound Of Music, Cincinnati Pops Orchestra, 1988; Big Band Hit Parade, Dave Brubeck/Cab Calloway/Gerry Mulligan/Doc Severensen, 1988; To Diz with Love, Dizzy Gillespie, 1992; The Great Fantasy Adventure Album, Cincinnati Pops Orchestra, 1995; Seven Steps to Heaven, Ray Brown Trio, 1996; Come On In This House, Junior Wells, 1996; Live at Buddy Guys, Junior Wells, 1997; Copland: Music of America, Cincinnati Pops Orchestra, 1997; Tribute at Town Hall, Oscar Peterson, 1996; So What's New?, Dave Brubeck, 1998. Honours: Grammy Award and Nominations. Membership: Audio Engineering Society; NARAS; MPGA; ASCAP;

AQHA; NRHA. Address: Telarc International Corp, 23307 Commerce Park Road, Cleveland, OH 44122, USA.

BISMUT Michel, b. 20 Apr 1954, Tunis, Tunisia. Composer; Musician (contrebass). m. Agnes Berger, 17 Oct 1992, 1 son, 1 daughter. Engineer, Computer Science and Management. Musical Education: Self-taught; Classic Conservatoire, Avignon-France. Career: Jazz festivals and clubs throughout France; Also UK; Germany; Spain; Israel; Appearances, French local television and national radio. Recordings: Socco, 1991; UR, 1996. Memberships: SACEM (French Composers' Society). Current Management: Condorcet Productions. Address: 21 Rue Tour Gayraud, 34000 Montpellier, France.

BISWAS Kingsuk, b. 12 May 1968, Kingsbury, London, England. Sound Artist. Education: BSc Hons, Geology, UCC; BSc Hons, Environmental Systems, UNL. Career: Singer, guitarist, 1984-90; Session bass, percussion player, 1987-90; Solo performer, soundsystem as Databass/Plantoid Schitzo/Freebass, 1989-92; Recording artist as Young Free Radical, Bedouin Ascent, Ways And Knowing, 1991-; Collaborations with artists including: David Toop; David Moufang; Luke Vibert; K Martin; Peter Khulman. Recordings: Albums include: Music For Particles; Science, Art and Ritual; EPs: Bedouin Ascent; Pavilion Of The New Spirit; Further Self Evident Truths. Memberships: Sound Works Exchange (Shinkansen/Goethe Institute). Current Management: Spacehopper. Address: 30 Tremadoc Road, Clapham, London SW4 7II, England.

BJELLAND Kat, b. Woodburn, Oregon, USA. Vocalist; Musician (guitar). Career: Member, bands with Courtney Love (Hole) and Jennifer (L7); Founder, all-girl rock group Babes In Toyland, 1987-. Recordings: Albums: Spanking Machine, 1990; To Mother (mini-album), 1991; Fontanelle, 1992. Address: c/o Pinnacle Entertainment Inc., 83 Riverside Drive, New York, NY 10024, USA.

BJÖRK (Björk Godmunsdottir), b. 1966. Reykjavik, Iceland. Career: Solo release, aged 11; Singer, various Icelandic groups include: Exodus; Tappi Tikarras; Kukl; Singer, The Sugarcubes, 1987-92; Solo artiste, 1992-; Recent appearances include Reading Festival, 1995. Recordings: Solo albums: Björk, 1977; Debut, 1993; Post, 1995; Hit singles: with The Sugarcubes: Birthday; Solo singles: Army Of Me; Isobel; It's Oh So Quiet; Hyperballad; Other recordings: Gling-Go, Trio Gudmundar Ingolfssonar, 1990; Ex-El, Graham Massey, 1991. Honours: BRIT Award, Best International Female Artist, 1996; Platinum and Gold records. Current Management: One Little Indian, 250 York Road, London SW11 3SJ, England; Insane Artists Management, 7218 ½ Beverly Blvd, Los Angeles, CA 90036, USA.

BJÖRKENHEIM Raoul Melvin, b. 11 Feb 1956, Los Angeles, California, USA. Musician (guitar). m. Päivi Björkenheim (Määttä), 1 son. Musical Education: Helsinki Conservatory, 1977-78; Berklee College of Music, Boston, USA, 1978-81. Career: Founder member, own jazz groups Arbuusi and Roommushklahn, 1980-83; Member, Edward Vesala's Sound and Fury, 1984-86; with Sielun Veljet, 1989; Member, Krakatau, 1987-; Tours throughout Finland with above; Compositions: For big band: Other Places; Some; Primal Mind; For symphony orchestra: Whales; Ballando; For electric guitar orchestra: Apocalypso. Recordings: with Edward Vesala: Bad Luck Good Luck; Kullervo; Lumi; with Krakatau: Ritual, 1988; Alive, 1990; Volition, 1992; Matinale, 1994. Honours: Yrjö Award, Finnish Jazz Federation, 1984; Emma Prize, Best Jazz Record, Volition, 1993. Hobbies: Literature; Photography; Swimming; Walking; Thinking. Current Management: Gunnar Pfabe. Address:

Heinsbergstrasse 30, D-50674 Cologne, Germany.

BJØRNS Siggi, b. 26 June 1955, Iceland. Musician (guitar, harmonica). Musical Education: Self-taught. Career: Former fisherman, 14 years; Professional musician, 1988-; Performed in clubs and halls in more than 20 countries; Television apprences in Denmark and Iceland; Radio broadcasts in Denmark, Iceland, Norway and New Zealand. Compositions: Bubbinn; Kotturinn; Beitningartremmi; One Gentle Touch. Recordings: Albums: Blues On Both Sides, 1993; Live At Sørens, 1993; Bisinn a Trinidad, 1994; Smoke'n'Perfume, 1995; Road, 1998. Memberships: Dansk Musikerforbund (Danish Musicians' Union); KODA. Hobby: Kayaking. Current Management: c/o Bein Leid Ltd, Iceland. Address: Brammersgade 2A-3, 8000 Århus C, Denmark.

BJURSTRÖM Christopher, b. 31 Mar 1954, Lidingö, Sweden. Composer; Musician (piano). 3 daughters. Education: Electronic Engineer. Musical Education: Piano, chamber music. Career: Pianist, accompanied A Papin; E Schwabe; Bjurström Sextet (Jazz); Live music for films: The General; College; Lulu; The Black Pirate; Erotikon; The Thief Of Bagdad. Recordings: Doucement Au Reveil, 1991; Musiques de Films Courts, 1992; Sous L'Etrange Lumière Des Fantômes, 1996. Current Management: Le Bon Alouate, 3 imp Ste Yvonne, 94800 Villejuif, France. Address: Allée des Cormorans, Le Dir, 29280 Locmaria-Plouzane, France.

BLACHMAN Thomas, b. 2 Apr 1963, Copenhagen, Denmark. Musician (drums); Composer; Bandleader; Producer; Label Manager. Musical Education: Jazz Composition, Berklee College of Music, Boston, USA. Career: Co-founder, jazz quintet Page One; Tours of Europe, USA, 1986-1990; Played drums for Lee Konitz, Joe Henderson; Solo artist, 1991-. Recordings: Albums: with Page One: Beating Bop Live, 1988; Live At Ronnie Scott's, 1989; Solo albums: Love Boat, 1991; Blachman Meets Al And Remee, 1994; Blachman Introduces Standard Jazz And Rap Vol.1, Billie Koppel, 1995; Caroline Henderson, 1995. Honours: 3 Grammy Awards, 1991, 1995. Hobby: Swimming. Current Management: Mega Records. Address: Capella India Kaj 1, Frihavnen, 2100 O Copenhagen, Denmark.

BLACK Barry, b. 1 July 1950, Newcastle-upon-Tyne, England. Musician (drums, percussion). m. Barbara Ann, 1 son, 1 daughter. Musical Education: Personal tutors, aged 10-16; Further studies for LTCL, LGSM. Career: Member, John Miles Band, 1973-83; Tours: Europe, US, Canada; Support tours with: Elton John; Fleetwood Mac; Aerosmith; Jethro Tull; Tour with Beckett (later renamed Back Street Crawler); 2 albums, with Splinter; Television appearances: Top Of The Pops; Magpie; Blue Peter; Mike Mansfield television specials; Tonite Show. Compositions: Do It Anyway, John Miles; Madness Money And Music, Sheena Easton; Take My Love And Run, The Hollies. Recordings: All John Miles albums and singles, up to early 1980's. Memberships: PRS; Equity; Musicians' Union.

BLACK Charlie, b. Cheverly, Maryland, USA. Country Music Songwriter. Career: Staff Writer, Terrace Music, Nashville, 1970-; Songwriter, Warner Chappell Music, 1977-88; Own company, Five-Bar-B Songs, 1989-; Songs recorded by: Roy Orbison; Anne Murray; Paul Anka; Dan Seals; Kenny Rogers; K T Oslin; Eddy Raven; Bobby Bare; Bellamy Brothers; Charlie Rich. Compositions: Number 1 Country Hit Singles: Anne Murray: Shadows In The Moonlight; A Little Good News; Blessed Are The Believers; Reba McEntire: You Lie; K T Oslin: Come Next Monday; T G Shepard: Slow Burn; Strong Heart; Bellamy

Brothers: Do You Love As Good As You Look; Tommy Overstreet: I Don't Know You Anymore; Earl Thomas Conley: Honor Bound; Gary Morris: 100% Chance Of Rain. Honours: Country Music Writer Of Year, SESAC, 1979; Country Music Writer Of Year, ASCAP 1983, 1984; Elected to NSAI Songwriters Hall Of Fame, 1991; Grammy Nominations for: A Little Good News; Come Next Monday. Membership: ASCAP Southern Advisory Board. Current Management: Poker Productions. Address: 1618 16th Avenue South, Nashville, TN 37212, USA.

BLACK Cilla (Priscilla White), b. 27 May 1943, Liverpool, Merseyside, England. Singer; Television Host. m. Bobby Willis, 1969. Career: Appearances include: Beatles' Christmas Show, Finsbury Park, London, 1963; Startime Variety Show, 1964; Charity Ball, Mansion House, London, 1964; Royal Variety Show, London Palladium, 1964; Sunday Night At The London Palladium, 1965; Grand Gala du Disques, Amsterdam, 1965; Star Scene '65 Tour, with The Everly Brothers, Billy J Kramer, 1965; Acting roles include: Cameo role, Ferry Cross The Mersey (film), 1964; Work... Is A Four-Letter Word (film), 1967; Way Out In Piccadilly (revue), 1966-67; Television includes: Around The Beatles, ITV, 1964; Several television series, BBC, 1968; Television host: Surprise Surprise; Blind Date (UK's first female game show hostess), 1980s-. Recordings: Singles include: Anyone Who Had A Heart (Number 1, UK), 1964; You're My World (Number 1, UK); It's For You, 1964; You've Lost That Lovin' Feelin', 1965; I've Been Wrong Before, 1965; Love's Just A Broken Heart, 1966; Alfie, 1966; Don't Answer Me, 1966; A Fool Am I, 1966; Step Inside Love, 1968; Surround Yourself With Sorrow, 1969; Conversations, 1969; Something Tells Me (Something's Gonna Happen Tonight), 1970; Albums: Cilla, 1965; Cilla Sings A Rainbow, 1966; Sher-oo, 1968; The Best Of Cilla Black, 1968; Surround Yourself With Cilla, 1969; Sweet Inspiration, 1970; Images, 1971; Day By Day With Cilla, 1973; In My Life, 1974; It Makes Me Feel Good, 1976; Modern Priscilla, 1978; The Very Best Of..., 1983; Surprisingly Cilla, 1983; Love Songs, 1987; Through The Years, 1993. Address: c/o Columbia Records, 10 Great Marlborough Street, London W1V 2LP, England.

BLACK Clint, b. 4 Feb 1962, USA. Singer; Songwriter; Producer. m. Lisa Hartman Black, 20 Oct 1991. Career: Film: Maverick; Television: Wings episode; Halftime performance, Superbowl XXXVIII; Performed National Memorial Day Celebration, Washington DC, 1994. Recordings: Killing Time, 1989; Put Yourself In My Shoes, 1990; The Hard Way, 1992; No Time To Kill, 1993; One Emotion, 1994. Honours: CMA's Horizon Award, 1989; CMA's Top Male Vocalist, 1990; AMA's Favourite New Country Artist, 1990; Music City News: Star Of Tomorrow, Album of the Year, 1990; ACM's Album Of The Year, Single Of The Year; Best New Vocalist; Best Male Vocalist, 1990. Current Management: The Left Bank Organization. Address: 6255 Sunset Blvd #1111, Hollywood, CA 90028, USA.

BLACK Frances, b. 25 June 1960, Dublin, Ireland. Singer. m. Brian Allen, 1 son, 1 daughter. Education: Rathmines College. Career: Member of Arcady, Woman's Heart Tour; Toured with Keiran Goss; Solo career; Tours in USA, Australia, England, Ireland. Recordings: The Black family Album; Arcady: After the Ball; Frances Black and Keiran Goss; Women's Heart Album; Solo: Talk to Me; The Sky Road; Smile on Your Face. Honours: Most Popular Irish Entertainer; National Entertainment Awards, 1995; Best Female, 1995, 1996, IRMA. Current Management: Pat Egan/Brian Allen. Address: c/o Merchants Court, 24 Merchants Quay, Dublin, Ireland.

BLACK Mary, b. 23 May 1955, Dublin, Ireland. Singer. Career: Folk singer, Dublin folk clubs; Member, De Dannan; Also solo career;

Appearance, television series Bringing It All Back Home, with Emmylou Harris, Dolores Keane, Nashville; Also with Van Morrison on Celtic Heartbeat; Tours, USA, UK, Japan. Recordings: Mary Black, 1983; Collected, 1984; Without The Fanfare, 1985; The Black Family, with the Black Family, 1986; By The Time It Gets Dark, 1987; Time For Touching Home (with the Black Family), 1989; No Frontiers, 1989; Babes In The Wood (Number 1, Ireland), 1991; The Best Of Mary Black, 1991; The Collection, 1992; The Holy Ground, 1993; Circus, 1995; Shine, 1997. Honours: Best Female Artist, Irish Rock Music Awards Poll, 1987, 1988. Current Management: Dara Management, Dublin; Big Advance Management, London. Address: c/o Big Advance Management, 12 Oval Road, London NW1 7DH, England.

BLACKMORE Ritchie (Richard Hugh), b. 14 Apr 1945, Weston Super Mare, Avon, England. Rock Musician (guitar); Composer. Musical Education: Thompson School Of Music, 1 year. Career: Musician, toured with: Mike Dee And The Jaywalkers, 1961-62; Screaming Lord Sutch And His Savages, 1962; Gene Vincent; Jerry Lee Lewis; The Outlaws; The Musketeers; The Dominators; The Wild Boys, 1964; Neil Christian's Crusaders; The Roman Empire; Mandrake Root, 1967; Founder member, UK rock group Deep Purple, 1968-75; Founder, Ritchie Blackmore's Rainbow, 1975-84; Reformed Deep Purple, 1984-. Recordings: Albums: with Deep Purple: Shades Of Deep Purple, 1968; The Book Of Taliesyn, 1969; Deep Purple, 1969; Concerto For Group And Orchestra, 1970; Deep Purple In Rock, 1970; Fireball, 1971; Machine Head, 1972; Made In Japan, 1972; Purple Passages, 1972; Who Do You Think We Are?, 1973; Burn, 1974; Stormbringer, 1974; 24 Carat Purple, 1975; Come Taste The Band, 1975; Made In Europe, 1976; Last Concert In Japan, 1977; Perfect Strangers, 1985; House Of Blue Light, 1987; Nobody's Perfect, 1988; Slaves And Masters, 1990; Stranger In Us All, 1995; with Rainbow: Ritchie Blackmore's Rainbow, 1975; Rainbow Rising, 1976; Live On Stage, 1977; Long Live Rock And Roll, 1978; Live In Germany, 1976, 90; Down To Earth, 1979; Difficult To Cure, 1981; Straight Between The Eyes, 1982; Bent Out Of Shape, 1983; Finyl Vinyl, 1986; Blackmore's Night, Shadow of the Moon, 1996. Honours: Grammy Nomination, Best Instrumental, Snowman, 1982; Numerous magazine poll wins, as Best Band; Best Guitarist; Best Album; Best Song. Memberships: ASCAP; BMI; PRS. Hobbies: Football; Seances. Current Management: Carole Stevens at Minstrel Hall Music. Address: PO Box 735, Nesconset, NY 11767, USA.

BLACKSTOCK Narvel Wayne, b. 31 Aug 1956, Fort Worth, Texas, USA. Artist Manager; Entertainment Company Executive. m. Reba McEntire, 3 June 1989, 4 children (3 from previous marriage). Career: Personal Manager: Vice President, Starstruck Entertainment, Nashville, 1988-; Clients include: Reba McEntire; Rhett Atkins; Linda Davis; Brett James; Gary Oliver. Memberships: NARAS; Country Music Association; Academy Of Country Music. Address: Starstruck Entertainment, PO Box 121996, Nashville, TN 37212, USA.

BLACKWELL Chris, b. 22 June 1937, London, England. Record Company Executive. Career: Founder, chairman, Island Records, 1962-; Issued masters from Jamaican producers; Signings to Island include: Jimmy Cliff; Bob Marley; Millie Small (My Boy Lollipop, sold six million copies); Spencer Davis Group; Steve Winwood; John Martyn; Robert Palmer; Nick Drake; Cat Stevens; Free; Mott The Hoople; Spooky Tooth; Fairport Convention. Address: c/o Island Records, 400 Lafayette Street, New York, NY 10003, USA.

BLACKWELL Otis, b. 1931, Brooklyn, New York, USA. Songwriter; Musician. Career: One of major songwriters of rock'n'roll era; Also recording artist. Compositions: for Derek Martin: Daddy Rolling Stone; for Little Willie John: Fever, 1956 (Later hit for Peggy Lee); for Elvis Presley include: All Shook Up (first UK Number 1); Don't Be Cruel, 1956; Paralysed, 1957; Return To Sender, 1962; One Broken Heart For Sale; for Jerry Lee Lewis: Breathless; Great Balls Of Fire, 1958; for Dee Clark: Hey Little Girl; Just Keep It Up, 1959; for Jimmy Jones: Handy Man, 1960; for Cliff Richard: Nine Times Out Of Ten, 1960. Recordings: Album: These Are My Songs, 1978.

BLACKWOOD Sarah, b. Halifax, England. Singer. Career: Singer, Dubstar, 1994-; UK tour, 1996. Recordings: Debut album: Disgraceful, 1995; Singles: Stars, 1995; Not So Manic Now, 1995. Address: c/o Food Records, 43 Brook Green, London W6 7EF, England.

BLADES Jack. Singer; Musician (bass guitar). Career: Member, Night Ranger, 1981-88; Concerts include: supports to Santana; Judas Priest; Doobie Brothers; Member, Damn Yankees, 1989-; US tour with Bad Company, 1990; Member, side project Shaw Blades (with Tommy Shaw), 1995. Recordings: Albums: with Night Ranger: Dawn Patrol, 1982; Midnight Madness, 1983; Seven Wishes, 1985; Big Life, 1987; Man In Motion, 1988; Live In Japan, 1990; with Damn Yankees: Damn Yankees, 1991; Don't Tread, 1992; with Shaw Blades: Hallucination, 1995; Singles: with Night Ranger: Sister Christian; Sentimental Street; with Damn Yankees: Coming Of Age; High Enough; Come Again; Where You Goin' Now; Silence Is Broken, from film Nowhere To Run, 1993. Honours: Motor City Music Award, Outstanding National Rock Pop Single, 1992. Current Management: Madhouse Management, PO Box 15108, Ann Arbor, MI 48106, USA.

BLADES Ruebén, b. 16 July 1948, Panama City, Panama. Singer; Bandleader; Composer; Actor. Education: University of Panama; Harvard Law School, USA. Career: Vocalist, groups Conjunto Latino, Los Salvjes del Ritmo, 1966-69; Lawyer, National Bank Of Panama, 1969-74; Joined Ray Barretto's band, 1974; Renamed Guarare, 1975; Member, Fania All-Stars, 1976-80; Songwriter, numerous Latin artistes, 1970s; Subject of television documentary, The Return Of Rubén Blades, 1986; Leader, group Seis del Solar, 1984-; Film appearances include: Crossover Dreams, 1985; Critical Condition, 1987; The Milagro Beanfield War, 1988; The Lemon Sisters; The Two Jakes; Dead Man Out, 1989. Recordings: Albums included: with Pete Rodríguez, De Panama a Nuevo York, 1970; with Ray Barretto: Barretto, 1975; Barretto Live - Tomorrow, 1976; with Fania All-Stars: Tribute To Tito Rodríguez, 1976; with Larry Harlow: La Raza Latina, 1977; with Louie Ramírez: Louie Ramírez y Sus Amigos, 1978; with Willie Colón: The Good, The Bad, The Ugly, 1975; Metiendo Mano!, 1977; Siembra, 1978; Maestra Vida (parts 1 and 2), 1980; Canciones del Solar de los Arburridos, 1981; The Last Fight, 1982; ; Solo: El Que La Hace La Paga, 1983; Buscando America, 1984; Mucho Mejor, 1984; Crossover Dreams (film soundtrack), 1985; Escenas, 1985; Agua de Luna, 1987; Doble Filo, 1987; Nothing But The Truth, 1988; Antecedente, 1988; Rubén Blades y Son del Solar... Live!, 1990; Caminando, 1991. Honours: Gold discs; Grammy Award, Antecedente, 1988; Grammy Nomination, 1983; ACE Award, Dead Man Out, 1989; Composer Of The Year, Latin NY magazine, 1976. Current Management: Morra, Brezner, Steinberg and Tenenbaum, 345 N Maple Drive, Suite 200, Beverly Hills, CA 90210, USA.

BLAIR Warwick Ian, b. 5 Dec 1965, Christchurch, New Zealand. Composer; Singer; Arranger; Musician (piano). Musical Education: University of Auckland, New Zealand, 1983-87; BMus, 1985; MMus, First class honours, 1987;

Royal Conservatory of the Hague, Netherlands, 1990-92; CertComp, 1992. Career: Moved from classical to pop music with formation of band Glory Box, 1992; Soundtrack work, 1994; Performances with Glory Box include: Meifestival, Kees van Baarenzaal, The Hague, Netherlands, 1992; Goodrich Theatre, London, 1994; South Bank Centre, London, 1994. Film soundtrack: Part of vocal chorus, Stargate, 1994; Multimedia soundtrack, as part of Signpost library, 1995; Computer game soundtrack, Bluey Roo, 1995; with Glory Box: Begin, 1996. Membership: Musicians' Union. Hobby: Arts. Current Management: Self-managed. Address: 23 Fanthorpe Street, Putney, London SW15 1DZ, England.

BLAKE Adam James Wyndham, b. 30 July 1960, Lincoln, England. Singer; Songwriter; Musician (guitar, bass); Teacher. m. Catherine Ramage, 31 Aug 1991, 1 daughter. Musical Education: Self-taught. Career: Played with many groups including: The Cannibals; Treatment; Mumbo-Jumbo; The Hipshakers; Raw, 1976-; Recordings: Restless; Put You Behind Me; Waiting For Love; Even If You Hadn't; Friends. Publications: Blues Guitar Book in preparation, 1995. Memberships: Guild of Electric Guitar Tutors; PRS. Hobbies: Literature; Cinema. Address: 77 Linden Gardens, London W2 4EU, England.

BLAKE Count Richard, b. 15 Apr 1960, London, England. Musician (drums, bass, keyboards). m. Gillian Margaret Blake, 1973, 2 sons. Musical Education: Self-taught. Career: Has played at Glastonbury; Womad Forest Fayre; Strawberry Fayre, Cambridge; Brixton Academy; Club UK; Plymouth Warehouse; Truro City Hall; Tribal Gathering '95; Television: What's Up Doc. Recordings: Alchemy; Tribal Ritural. Membership: Musicians' Union. Hobbies: Walking; Swimming; Cycling; Nature. Address: Higher Trewoofe, Lamorna, Penzance, Cornwall TR19 6PA, England.

BLAKE Ian, b. 9 December 1955, London, England. Composer; Producer; Musician (Woodwinds, Keyboards, Bass). Education: Degree Course, London University; Member of London Boy Singers, 1968-71; Piano, organ, clarinet & lute lessons. Career: Tours & recording with Pyewackett, 1980-88; with Mike Jackson, 1988-93; Backing Musician for June Tabor, Michelle Shocked, Eric Bogle; Musician, National Theatre, London, 1987; Tours with Mellstock Band, 1988; Writer & Musician, The Crusades, Barossa Festival, 1992. Compositions: Persephone, 1995; Spirit of Place, 1996. Recordings: Producer & Musician, Eric Bogles' Small Miracles, 1997; Writer, Producer, Musician, over 20 childrens albums; Contributor, albums by Martin Simpson, Andrew Cronshaw, June Tabor. Publication: The Really Easy Cello Book, 1990. Honours: ARIA Nomination, 1992; Gold Disc, 1995; TDK Talking Book Award Nomination, 1996. Memberships: APRA; Musicians' Union of Australia. Current Management: Serpentine Productions, PO Box 1750, Canberra, ACT 2601, Australia. Address: 4 Rudall Street, Latham, ACT 2615, Australia.

BLAKE Karl Antony, b. 5 Dec 1956, Reading, Berkshire, England. Musician; Filmaker; Lyricist. Education: BA Hons, Fine Art and Mixed Media, 1991-94. Career: Formed Lemon Kittens, 1978; Joined as duo by Danielle Dax, 1979-82; Formed Shock Headed Peters, 1982-87; Formed British Racing Green, 1987; Formed Evil Twin with David Mellor, 1990-; Reformed Shock Headed Peters, 1990-; Currently member of all 3 groups. Recordings: with Lemon Kittens: 2 EPs; 2 albums: We Buy A Hammer For Daddy; The Big Dentist; with Shock Headed Peters: 3 EPs; 4 albums: Not Born Beautiful; Fear Engine; Several Headed Enemy; Fear Engine II; 2 EPs as member, Alternative TV with Mark Perry, 1985-86; Solo: 1

EP, 1 album as The Underneath, 1986-87; 8 short films, poetry in compilation; 2 solo archive albums as Karl Blake. Address: BCM Swarf, London WC1N 3XX, England.

BLAKE Norman, b. 20 Oct 1965, Bellshill, Scotland. Musician (guitar); Vocalist. 1 daughter. Career: Member, The Boy Hairdressers; Founder member, Teenage Fan Club, 1989-. Recordings: Albums: A Catholic Education, 1990; Bandwagonesque, 1991; Thirteen, 1993; Grand Prix, 1995. Address: c/o Creation Records, 109 Regents Park Road, London NW1 8UR, England.

BLANCHARD Pierre, b. 24 May 1956, Saint-Quentin, France. Musician (violin); Composer; Arranger. 1 son. Musical Education: Conservatoire de St Quentin; Université Musicale International de Paris; 6 months study in New York. Career: Lived in Paris, 1977-; Professor CIM, 1979-81; Violinist, Martial Solal's Big Band, 1981-86; Played throughout Europe; Played with Stéphane Grappelli, Antibes and Paris Festivals, 1988; Formed Gulf String, 1989; Director of Jazz class, CNR D'Aubervilliers - La Courneuve, 1992-; Formed Quintette A Cordes de Pierre Blanchard, 1994; Other festivals include: Halle That Jazz, 1993; Presences, 1994; Banlieues Bleues, 1995; Also worked with: Bernard Lubat, Jacques Thollot, Rene Urtreger. Recordings: Solo albums: Each One Teach One, 1985; Music For String Quartet, Jazz Trio, Violin and Lee Konitz, 1987; Gulf String, 1993; 2 albums with Martial Solal Big Band; with Raphael Fays: Voyages, 1988; Gipsy Touch, 1991; with Pierre Michelot: Bass and Bosses, 1989; Other albums with René Urtreger, Eric Le Lann, Post Image, Jazzogene Big Band. Honour: Stéphane Grappelli donated the violin of M Warlop, 1984. Hobbies: Drawing caricatures; Cooking; Travel; Chess. Current Management: Claudette de San Isidoro. Address: 93 bis rue de Montreuil, 75011 Paris, France.

BLANCHARD Terence, b. 13 March 1962, New Orleans, Louisiana, USA. Musician. Education: New Orleans Center of Creative Arts. Career: Numerous concert appearances worldwide; Composer for Films, including: Eve's Bayou; Gia; Free of Eden; Mo' Better Blues; Jungle Fever; Malcolm X; Sugar Hill; Assault at West Point; The Inkwell; Trial By Jury; Crooklyn; The Promised Land; Clockers; Soul of the Game; Get On The Bus; Till There Was You; Four Little Girls; Joined Art Blakey and the Jazz Messengers and toured worldwide, 1982-86; Formed Harrison-Blanchard with Donald Harrison, 1986. Recordings: Terence Blanchard; The Music from Eve's Bayou; Orquestra Was; Jubilant; A Child With the Blues; The Heart Speaks; Mo' Better Blues; Simply Stated; Malcolm X Jazz Suite; Malcolm X The Original Motion Picture Score; The Billie Holiday Songbook; Romantic Defiance; Original Orchestral Score From the Motion Picture Clockers; Dr Jeckyle: Art Blakey & The Jazz Messengers Live at Sweet Basil, 1992; New Year's Eve at Sweet Basil, Art Blakey & The Jazz Messengers, 1992; Art Bleky's Jazz Messengers: Live in Leverkeusen, The Art of Jazz, 1995; Terence Blanchard with Donald Harrison: Discernment, 1986; Crystal Star, 1987; Black Pearl, 1988; New York Second Line, 1994. Publications: Contributor of articles in professional journals and magazines. Honours: Winner, Grand Prix du Disque, 1984; Grammy Nomination, Best Jazz Instrumental Performance by a Group, 1990; Emmy Nomination, Best Original Score for a Documentary, 1995; Grammy Nomination, Best Latin Jazz Performance, 1996. Address: Burgess Management, 3225 Prytania Street, New Orleans, LA 70115, USA.

BLAND Bobby (Robert), b. 27 Jan 1930, Rosemark, Tennessee, USA. Singer. Career: Former valet for B B King, 1949; Member, The Beale Streeters; Gospel and blues vocalist; Early recordings with Ike Turner, 1952; Performances on US R&B circuit, 1957-; Ann Arbor Jazz And Blues Festival, 1973; First UK tour, 1982; Regular tours with B B King, 1990s. Recordings: Hits include: Farther Up The Road, 1957; I'll Take Care Of You, 1960; I Pity The Fool, 1961; Don't Cry No More, 1961; Turn On Your Love Light, 1962; Stormy Monday Blues, 1962; Call Me / That's The Way Love Is, 1963; Sometimes You Gotta Cry A Little, 1963; Ain't Nothing You Can Do, 1964; This Time I'm Gone For Good, 1974; Albums include: Here's The Man, 1962; Call On Me/That's The Way Love Is, 1963; Ain't Nothing You Can Do, 1964; His California Album, 1974; Dreamer, 1974; Together For The First Time... Live (with B B King), 1974; Get On Down With Bobby Bland, 1975; Together Again...Live (with B B King), 1976; Reflections In Blue, 1977; Come Fly With Me, 1978; I Feel Good, I Feel Fine, 1979; You've Got MeLoving You, 1984; Members Only, 1985; After All, 1986; Blues You Can Use, 1988; Midnight Run, 1989. Honour: Inducted into Rock and Roll Hall Of Fame, 1992. Address: It's Happening Now Presents, PO Box 8073, Pittsburg, CA 94565, USA.

BLANDAMER Oscar Stewart Van, b. 8 May 1947, Weymouth, England. Songwriter; Musician (saxophone, guitar). m. Dianne Harrington, 16 July 1966, 1 son, 1 daughter. Musical Education: 1 year saxophone lessons. Career: Member: Orphesians, 1963-66; Jimmy James and the Vagabonds, 1969-72; Curly, 1973-75; Flirtations, Johnny Wakelin, 1976-78; Q-Tips, 1978-81; Adam Ant, 1981-83; Funk Bros., 1984-. Compositions: Darling, recorded by over 30 artists (3 Number 1 singles, US country chart); Songs covered by: Kim Wilde; Q-Tips; Paul Young; Tom Jones; Cliff Richard; Phil Everly. Recordings: with: Status Quo, 1973; Stiff Little Fingers, 1979; Wishbone Ash, 1979; Ray Minnhinnett's Bluesbusters, 1990; Video with Paul McCartney, 1984. Honours: 3 ASCAP Awards. Memberships: Musicians' Union; BASCA; PRS; MCPS. Hobby: Travel. Current Management: Hyperfunk Productions. Address: c/o Hyperfunk Productions, 55 Loudoun Road, St Johns Wood, London NW8 0DL, England

BLANT David, b. 21 Nov 1949, Burton-On-Trent, England. Musician (bass guitar, accordion); Teacher. m. Jennifer Gow, 27 Mar 1971, 1 son, 1 daughter. Musical Education: Dartington College Of Arts. Career: Various bands from age 13; Member of: Yeah Jazz (Indie band); R Cajun and the Zydeco brothers, 1985-; Number of appearances, BBC Radio 2. Recordings: with R Cajun: Pig Sticking; In Arcadia; Out of The Swamp; Don't Leave The Floor; No Known Cure; That Cajun Thing. Memberships: Musicians' Union; PRS. Current Management: Swamp Management. Address: PO Box 94, Derby DE22 1XA, England.

BLATNEY Marek, b. 14 June 1965, Brno, Czech Republic. Musician; Psychologist. m. Radka Pokulilova, 1 March 1997, 1 son. Education: Psychology, University of J E Purkyne, 1988; PhD, 1993. Career: Scientific worker, Academy of Sciences in Brno, 1988-; Leader, rock group Bixley, 1991-. Compositions: Konfrontace; Agon; Play Jazz, play rock, play new music, both with Pavel Blatny; Scenic music to 12 dramas. Address: Traubova 3A, 602 00 Brno, Czech Republic.

BLATNY Pavel, b. 14 Sept 1931, Brno, Czech Republic. m. Danuse Spirková, 19 June 1982, 1 son, 1 daughter. Education: Musicology, University of Brno, 1958; Berklee School of Music, USA, 1968. Career: Composer; Conductor; Pianist; Chief, Music Department, Czech Television, to 1992; Professor, Janácek's Academy, Brno, to 1990. Compositions include: Roll-call; Willow; Christmas Eve; Noonday Witch; Bells; Twelfth Night, based on Shakespeare's play, 1975; Two Movements for Brasses, 1982; Signals for Jazz Orchestra, 1985; Prologue for mixed choir and jazz orchestra, 1984; Per organo e big band, 1983; Ring a Ring o' Roses, for solo piano, 1984. Honours: Prize of Leos Jánácek, 1984; Antiteatro D'Argento for the whole work, Nepal, Italy, 1988. Membership: President, Club of Moravian Composers. Hobby: Write literature (stories). Address: Czech Republic, 62400 Brno, Absolonova 35.

BLATT Melanie, b. 1976. Singer. Career: Founding member, female vocal group All Saints, 1993-. Recordings: Singles: Silver Shadow; I Know Where It's At; Never Ever (Number 1, UK); Debut album: All Saints. Honours include: Brit Award, Best Single. Current Management: John Benson.

BLAZEVIC Kresimir, b. 27 Jan 1958, Slavonski Brod, Croatia. Professor of Literature; Musician (guitar); Composer; Lyricist; Singer; Concert Hall Programme Manager. m. Matea Banoza, 18 May 1991, 1 daughter. Education: University, Ethnology and Literature. Musical Education: Primary musical school, violin, guitar. Career: Over 500 concerts; Over 100 television and radio appearances. Compositions: 60 published works, music and lyrics; Girls in City Clothes, 1996. Recordings: 6 albums with The Animator, latest, The Dream Book; Hit singles include: Summer's Back To Town; I'll Stay Always Young; Summer Rendevous; Angels Asking Us To Take Away Their Wings. Memberships: HGU (Croatian Musical Union); Croatian Composers Society. Address: 10000 Zagreb, Buzanova 14, Croatia.

BLEY Carla Borg, b. 11 May 1938, Oakland, California, USA. Composer; Arranger. m. (1) Paul Bley, 27 Jan 1959, divorced 1967; (2) Michael Mantler, 29 Sept 1967, divorced 1992, 1 daughter. Career: Freelance jazz composer, 1956-; Pianist, Jazz Composers Orchestra, New York, 1964-; European concert tours, Jazz Realities, 1965-66; Founder, WATT, 1973-; Toured Europe with Jack Bruce Band, 1975; Leader, Carla Bley Band, touring USA, Europe, 1977-. Compositions: Composed and recorded: A Genuine Tong Funeral (with Charlie Haden), 1967; Liberation Music Orchestra, 1969; Escalator Over The Hill (opera), 1970-71; Tropic Appetites, 1973; Composer, Chamber Orchestra 3/4, 1974-75; Film score, Mortelle Randonée, 1982. Recordings: Dinner Music, 1976; with The Carla Bley Band: European Tour, 1977; Musique Mecanique, with Nick Mason, 1979; Fictitious Sports, 1980; Social Studies, 1980; Carla Bley Live!, 1981; Heavy Heart, 1984; I Hate To Sing, 1985; Night Glo, 1985; Sextet, 1987; Duets, 1988; Fleur Carnivore, 1989; The Very Big Carla Bley Band, 1991; Go Together, 1993; Big Band Theory, 1993; Songs With Legs (with AndySheppard), 1995; Goes to Church, 1996. Honours include: Guggenheim Fellowship, 1972; Oscar du Disque De Jazz, 1973; Composition grants, 1970s; New York Jazz Award, Arranger, 1979; Grammy Nominations, 1984, 1995; Deutscher Schallplattenpreis, 1985; Downbeat Poll, Best Composer, 1980s; Jazz Times, Composer, 1990; Hi Fi Vision, Jazz Musician of Year, 1990; Prix Jazz Moderne, 1991; Downbeat Poll, Composer/Arranger, 1990-94. Membership: NARAS. Current Management: Watt Works Inc. Address: c/o Watt Works Inc, PO Box 67, Willow, NY 12494, USA.

BLEY Paul, b. 10 Nov 1932, Montreal, Quebec, Canada. Musician (piano, synthesizer); Bandleader; Composer; Record Producer. m. (1) Carla Bley, (2) Annette Peacock. Career: Leader, own trio and quintet (latter included Ornette Coleman, Don Cherry, Charlie Haden, Billy Higgins); Also played with: Pat Metheny; Jaco Pastorius; Charlie Parker; Jackie McLean; Donald Byrd; Art Blakey; Charles Mingus; Bill Evans; Don Ellis; Jimmy Giuffre; John Gilmore; Formed own label, IAI, 1970s. Recordings: Albums include: Introducing Paul Bley, 1954; Paul Bley, 1955; Solemn Meditation, 1958; Footloose, 1963; Barrage, 1965; Closer, 1966; Touching, 1966; Ramblin', 1967; Blood, 1967; Paul Bley In

Haarlem, 1967; Mr Joy, 1968; The Fabulous Paul Bley Quintet, 1969; Paul Bley Trio In Canada, 1969; Ballads, 1970; The Paul Bley Synthesizer Show, 1971; Improvise, 1971; Dual Unity, 1972; Paul Bley And Scorpio, 1973; Open To Love, 1973; Paul Bley/NHOP, 1974; Alone Again, 1975; Copenhagen And Haarlem, 1975; Turning Point, 1975; Virtuosi, 1975; Bley, Metheney, Pastorius, Ditmus, 1975; Japan Suite, 1976; Axis, 1978; Sonor, 1983; Tango Palace, 1983; Tears, 1984; Questions, 1985; Hot, 1986; My Standard, 1986; Fragments, 1986; The Paul Bley Quartet, 1988; Solo, 1988; Solo Piano, 1988; Floater Syndrome, 1989; The Nearness Of You, 1990; Bebop, 1990; Rejoicing, 1990; Blues For Red, 1991; Live At Sweet Basil, 1991; Indian Summer, 1991; Right Time Right Place, 1991; Also recorded with Annette Peacock; Paul Motian; Jesper Lundgaard; Chet Baker; Jimmy Giuffre; Gary Peacock; As producer: albums for artists including Sun Ra; Marion Brown; Sam Rivers.

BLICHFELDT Anders, b. 9 Nov 1963, Copenhagen, Denmark. Singer; Musician (guitarist). m. Marina, 20 Aug 1988, 2 sons. Education: Piano Tuner. Career: Lead singer, Big Fat Snake; Approximately 300 concerts, 1991-94 including Roskilde Festival, 1991, 1994; Midfyn Festival, 1991, 1992, 1994; Skanderborg Festival, 1991, 1992; Several national television and radio shows, 1991-94. Recordings: Big Fat Snake, 1991; Born Lucky, 1992; Beautiful Thing, 1994; Midnight Mission, 1995. Honours: Grammy Nomination, Best Male Vocalist, 1995. Memberships: DJBFA; Dansk Artist Forbund. Hobbies: Friends and family. Current Management: Aarhus Musikkontor. Address: Mindegade 10, DK 8000, Aarhus C, Denmark.

BLIGE Mary J, b. USA. Singer. Career: Solo recording artiste; Support to Jodeci, UK tour, 1995. Recordings: Debut album: My Life, 1994; Single: All Night Long, 1995. Current Management: Steve Lucas Associates, 156 W 56th Street, New York, NY 10019, USA.

BLIZARD H Ralph, b. 5 Dec 1918, Kingsport, Tennessee, USA. Musician (fiddle). 2 sons. Musical Education: Self-taught. Career: Smithsonian Institute Festival; Kingsport Symphony Orchestra; American Festival of Fiddle Tunes; Swannond Gathering, Asheville, North Carolina; Augusta Heritage Festival; Hudson River Clearwater Revival Festival, Croton, New York; Festival, American Fiddle Tunes, Port Townsend, Washington; Tampa Center, Performing Arts, Tampa, Florida; Good Morning America, ABC; PBS Appearances; Charles Karult, Sunday Morning, CBS; Library Of Congress. Recordings: Blizard Train; Ralph Blizard Fiddles; Blue Highway; Green Grass Cloggers: Through The Ears. Honours: Mount Airy Fiddle Championship, 3 years. Membership: Appointed by Governor to Tennessee Arts Committtee, 1987-92. Hobby: Violin making. Address: 1084 State Route #37, Blountville, TN 37617, USA.

BLOCK Uwe, b. 4 July 1946, Bordesholm, Germany. Manager; Publisher. 2 daughters. Career: Artist manager, music publisher, Mainhattan Music Production, Germany. Address: Mainhattan Music Production, Friedrich-Ebert-Str 48, 63179 Obertshausen, Germany.

BLOMSTROM John Paul, b. 19 Apr 1949, Miami, Oklahoma, USA. Artist Agent; Musician (drums). m. Cheryl Ann Byrd, 28 Dec 1978, 1 son, 2 daughters. Career: Artist manager for The Tonyans (family group), 1970's; Vince Vance and the Valiants; Lic and Stiff, 1980; First promoter to bring Pat Benatar to Houston; Also promoter of artists including Muddy Waters; Hall and Oates; Prince; The Police; Agent for artists including Madam X. Publications: Writer for Music News. Memberships: Various. Hobbies: Horse riding; Walking; Baseball; Basketball. Current Management: American Bands Management.

Address: PO Box 840607, Houston, TX 77284-0607, USA.

BLONDIN Ludivine (Josette Edmee), b. 10 Oct 1958, Lyon, France. Actress; Singer; Model. Partner, John Phil Wayne, 1 daughter. Education: Bac+1 (Beaux Arts). Musical Education: Private tuition and school, 6 years. Career: Singer, musical act/films: L'Art de la Fugue with Bernard Haller and Maurice Biraud; William Tell with Will Lyman; Drole D'Endroit Pour Une Rencontre, with Gerard Depardieu; La Petite Maison Dans La Prairie, with Michael Landon; Interview of John Phil Wayne for France 3 TV and TLM TV; Introduction portrait of John Phil Wayne as video. Recordings: Fairy Tales For Fauve; Recording for French radio and television as animator: Les Jeux de 20 Heures; Les Jeux Du Dimanche; La Soupiere a Des Oreilles; Maurice Bejart à Arles. Membership: AZ Production, France. Hobbies: Movies; Modern jazz dancing; Swimming; Painting; Travel; Reading. Current Management: Longsongs Music Ltd, 21-23 Greenwich Market, London SE10 9HZ, England.

BLONDY Alpha, b. 1953, Dimbokoro, Ivory Coast. Reggae Vocalist; Bandleader. Education: Columbia University, USA, 1980-81. Career: Leading West African reggae vocalist and bandleader, 1980s. Recordings: Albums: Jah Glory, 1983; Cocody Rock, 1984; Apartheid Is Nazism, 1985; Jerusalem, 1986; Jah Jah Seh, 1989; Masada, 1992. Address: c/o MA Chetata Management, 105 West 28th Street, 3rd Floor, New York, NY 10001, USA.

BLOOM Eric, b. 1 Dec 1944. Singer; Musician (guitar, keyboards). Career: Singer, guitarist, keyboard player, US rock group Blue Öyster Cult, 1971-; Regular US tours including support to Alice Cooper, 1972; World tour, 1978; Monsters Of Rock Festival, Castle Donington, 1981; UK tour, 1989. Recordings: Albums: Blue Öyster Cult, 1972; Tyranny And Mutation, 1973; Secret Treaties, 1974; Live On Your Feet Or On Your Knees, 1975; Agents Of Fortune, 1976; Spectres, 1978; Some Enchanted Evening, 1978; Mirrors, 1979; Cultosaurus Erectus, 1980; Fire Of Unknown Origin, 1981; ETL (Extra-Terrestrial Live), 1982; The Revolution By Night, 1983; Club Ninja, 1986; Imaginos, 1988; Career Of Evil - The Metal Years, 1990; Singles include: (Don't Fear) The Reaper, 1976; In Thee, 1979; Burnin' For You, 1981; Film soundtrack, Bad Channels, 1992. Honour: Platinum disc, (Don't Fear) The Reaper. Current Management: Steve Schenck, 415 Madison Avenue, New York, NY 10017, USA.

BLOOM Jane Ira, b. 12 Jan 1955, Boston, Massachusetts, USA. Musician (soprano, alto saxphone); Composer. m. Joseph Grifasi, 10 Sept 1984. Education: BA Music, Yale University, 1976. Musical Education: MM, saxophone performance, Yale School of Music, 1977; Saxophone study with Joe Viola. Career: Village Vanguard, New York City, 1983; First musician ever commissioned by NASA Art Program, 1988-89; Town Hall Concert, 1991; Performances, National Air and Space Museum's Einstein Planetarium, 1990, 1992, 1995; CBS jazz recording artist, 1986-89; Performance with orchestra, Lincoln Center's Absolute Concerto, 1993; Carnegie Hall with American Composers Orchestra, 1994; NBC TV film, 1995; Master Classes and Clinics include: New England Conservatory of Music, 1987; Wellesley College, 1988; Yale University, 1988-89; Harvard University, 1988, 1993; New School for Jazz Studies/NYC, 1993; International Association of Jazz Educators, 1992. Compositions: Sixteen Sunsets, 1991; Einstein's Red/Blue Universe, 1994. Recordings: We Are Outline, 1977; Second Wind, 1980; Mighty Lights, 1982; Modern Drama, 1986; Slalom, 1988; Art And Aviation, 1992. Honours: Downbeat International Critics Poll, for soprano saxophone, magna cum laude, Yale University. Membeships: National Space Society; International Association

of Astronomical Artists. Address: New York, NY, USA.

BLUE Barry, b. 4 Dec 1950, London, England. Songwriter; Producer; Singer. m. Lynda Blue, 20 May 1974, 1 son, 2 daughters. Career includes: First television appearance: Stubby Kaye's Silver Star Show, age 11; First major concert: Split Festival, Yugoslavia singing his own composition, 1969; First radio appearance: Bassist, Spice (later became Uriah Heep), John Peel Show; First major tour: Solo artist singer with Queen and Status Quo, 1973; Staff Producer, CBS Records, 1976-; Producer, composer numerous hit records for artists including: Bananarama; Five Star; Heatwave; Diana Ross; Celine Dion; Opened Aosis Recording Studios, where albums produced for artists include: Sinead O'Connor, Bronski Beat, Depeche Mode, Fine Young Cannibals, 1984-88; Owner of Escape Records. Recordings include: Dancin' On A Saturday Night (million seller); Sugar Me, Lynsey De Paul; Boogie Nights, Heatwave; Always And Forever, Heatwave; Over 30 UK Chart singles as singer, producer and writer. Honours: Carl Allan Award, 1973; Producer of The Year, 1977; 6 BMI, ASCAP Awards. Memberships: Councillor, BASCA; PRS. Hobbies: Writing; Lyrics; Computers. Current Management: The Escape Artist Company. Address: PO Box 31, Bushey, Hertfordshire WD2 2PT, England.

BLUE Sam (Simon Blewitt), b. 21 Aug 1959, Newcastle upon Tyne, England. Singer; Songwriter; Casual Actor. 1 son, 1 daughter. Education: Technical College. Career: Backing artists: Lulu; Michael Ball; 1991-93; Giant Killers, 1995; Sang on many television, radio, cinema commercials; Toured Britain, Europe, former Soviet Union, with Ya-Ya, 1987-89; Ultravox, 1993-95; Also television, radio with these groups; Appeared (acting) in Spender, television series; Co-wrote Hollywood Men theme tune for Carlton TV, 1996. Recordings: Emerson single: Something Special, 1984; Lead singer, Ya-Ya album, 1988; Ultravox: Ingenuity, 1994-95; Live, 1995; Eternal 12" single: So Good, 1994; GTS: Tracks From The Dust Shelf, 1995; GTS, Time Stood Still, 1996; Chorus work on Evita, movie and soundtrack; Solo single: For The Life You Don't Yet Know, 1997; Backing Vocalist on Montserrat Caballe album, Friends for Life, 1997. Memberships: PRS; MCPS. Hobbies: Watching and playing football; Golf. Current Management: Agent: Christine Poundford, Hobsons Singers. Address: 62 Chiswick High Road, London W4 1SY, England.

BLUE EAGLE, b. 4 Mar 1962, Philadelphia, Pennsylvania, USA. Singer; Songwriter; Musician; Producer. 1 daughter. Education: Diploma in General Studies from High School. Musical Education: Sang in school choir from elementary school to high school; Self taught. Honour: President Elect for 2 years, All Philadelphia Boys Choir. Memberships: ASCAP; All Philadelphia Boys Choir. Hobbies: Art; Reading. Current Management: Jackie Paul. Address: c/o Jackie Paul, 559 Wanamaker Road, Jenkintown, PA 19046, USA.

BLUEY (Jean-Paul Maunick). Musician; Songwriter; Producer. Career: Leader, Incognito. Recordings: Albums: 100° And Rising, 1995; Singles: Don't Worry About A Thing, 1993; Always There, 1993; Everyday, 1995; As producer, recordings for George Benson; Al Jarreau; Natalie Cole. Current Management: Ricochet, 5 Old Garden House, The Lantern Bridge Lane, London SW11 3AD, England.

BLUMBERG Stuart Lester, b. 27 Oct 1947, Detroit, Michigan, USA. Musician (trumpet). m. Dorothy Ebeling, 1 son. Education: AA, Los Angeles Valley College, 1969; California State University, Northridge. Career: Toured with Don Ellis; Louis Bellson; First trumpet, numerous Broadway performances; Music Contractor,

Shubert Theatre, Los Angeles, 1991; Recorded numerous television and radio commercials, film soundtracks. Recordings: with various artists including: Frank Sinatra; Barbra Streisand; Lou Rawls; Lionel Richie; The Osmonds; Joe Cocker; Dionne Warwick; The Rolling Stones; Barry Manilow; Beach Boys; The Commodores; The Pointer Sisters; Steppenwolf; Jermaine Jackson; Carly Simon; Talking Heads; Air Supply; Blood, Sweat And Tears. Membership: NARAS.

BLUMENTHAL Laurent Pierre, b. 21 Dec 1964, Paris, France. Musician (saxophone). m. Marianne, 11 Aug 1992, 2 daughters. Musical Education: Diploma, CNR Lyons (saxophone, harmony), 1983; 2 months at Eastman School of Music, Rochester, New York, 1986. Career: Concerts and tours: with La Velle & Orj: Tour of USSR, 1991; with Tourmaline: Tour of Quebec, 1991; Festival de Montreal, 1992; with L'Orchestre National de Jazz: Germany; Italy; Portugal; France, 1993-94; with Dimitrinaiditch / Laurent Blumenthal Duo: Tour of Germany, 1995; Played all French jazz festivals, 1990-; Performed with own quintet, septet, and artistes including: Johnny Griffin; Ernie Watts; Michel Colombier; ORJ; Henri Texier; Daniel Humair; Mario Stanchev; L'Orchestre National De Jazz, with Denis Badault (ONJ Badault); Also performed with Tito Puente; Nicole Croisille; Louis Sclavis. Recordings: Il Était Une Fois La Révolution, ORJ, 1988; Shakok, Shakok, 1989; Johnny Griffin et l'ORJ, ORJ, 1990; Sozopol, Mario Stanchev, 1990; Parcours, Aira Works, 1990; Kaleidoscope, Mario Stanchev, 1992; Monk Mingus Ellington, ONJ Badault, 1993; Bouquet Final, ONJ Badault, 1994. Honours: First prize, National Saxophone Competition, 1987; 1st Prize, Festival de Vienne, with Shakok, 1988; First prize, Festival de Sorgues, 1993; Second prize (soloist), Third prize (group), with Dimitri Naiditch, Concours de la Défense, 1993. Hobbies: Tennis; Squash; Swimming. Current Management: Dominique Camard. Address: 12 Rue Justin Godart, 69004 Lyon, France.

BLUNSTONE Colin, b. 24 June 1945, Hatfield, Hertfordshire, England. Singer. Career: Singer, the Zombies, 1963-1967; Solo career, 1969-; Reformed the Zombies, 1991; Appearances include: with The Shangri-Las, The Nashville Teens, US, 1964; with Dusty Springfield, The Searchers, UK 1965; Support to Herman's Hermits, US Caravan Of Stars tour, 1965; Film appearance, Bunny Lake Is Missing, 1966. Recordings: Albums: with the Zombies: The Zombies, 1965; The Zombies - Begin Here, 1965; Odessey And Oracle, 1967; New World, 1991; Solo albums: One Year, 1971; Ennismore, 1973; Journey, 1974; Planes, 1976; Never Even Thought, 1978; Late Nights In Soho, 1979; I Don't Beleive In Miracles, 1982; Sings His Greatest Hits, 1991; Echo Bridge, 1995; Hit singles with the Zombies: She's Not There (Number 2, US), 1964; Tell Her No, 1965; with the Alan Parsons Project: Pyramid, 1978; Eye Of The Sky, 1982; Ammonia Avenue, 1984; Vulture Culture, 1985; Other albums include: Walk On Water, Mae McKenna, 1977; Tarot Suite, Mike Batt, 1979; Exiled, Exiled, 1980; Keats, Keats, 1984. Address: c/o Permanent Records, 22-23 Brook Mews, London W2 3BW, England.

BOB COLOR, b. 20 Aug 1955, Alkmaar, Netherlands. Manager; Singer. Recordings: Albums: Sweat, 1988; Splash Boom Bang, 1990; Xtra Fresh, 1992; Boilin' Up Da Buzz, 1994. Current Management: The Bob Color. Address: Stadhouderskade 61-1, 1072 AC Amsterdam, Netherlands.

BOBBY Marty, b. 4 October 1937, Brugge (Bruges), Belgium. Suffys Nicole, 8 September 1963, 1 son, 1 daughter. Education: Private lessons, Dirigent Pol Horna; Bass Guitar & 1 Year Piano, age of 12 years. Career: Andrex; Ensemble Pol Horna; The Shamrocks; Luc Rène and the Jumps; Own show with the Bobby Marty Dancers,

1980-; Radio's in Belgium & France; TV in France. Compositions: Houtem Mijn Dorpje; De Bruggeling; Adieu Jacques Brel; La Maison Du Bonheur; Mon Amour; Ma Guitare et Quelques Chansons; Une Belle Nuit D'Hiver; Au Rendez-Vous desd Artistesd. Recordings: 18 singles; 1 LP; 2 copilation CD's in France with other French artists. Publications: Flash, own magazine, 1989-. Honours: Golden Record, Rose Des Neiges; Silver Record for Johnny Laat je Jodel nog eens Horen (compilation of Johnny Hoes). Hobbies: All sports especially football; Cycling;Athletics; Travel. Address: Molenwalstraat 8A, 8630 Houtem-veurne,Belgium.

BOBEK Pavel, b. 16 September 1937, Prague, Czech Republic. Singer; Musician. m. Marta Pokorna, 10 October 1978, 1 son, 1 daughter. Education: Architecture, Prague Institute of Technology, 1961; Private Lessons, Piano. Career: Member, Olympic Rock and Roll Group, 1963-66; Actor, The Prague Semafor Theatre, 1967-90; Solo Singer, Founder of Band, 1982-. Recordings: First Singles, 1963; 6 Regular Albums on LP's, MC's and CD's, 1975-93; 7 Compilation Albums on LP's, 1 MC and CD; The Best of Pavel Bobek vol I, vol II. Honours: Platinum Record, 1993. Memberships: OSA; SAI. Hobbies: Aviation; Gardening; Architecture. Current Management: Venkow Records, Ovenecka 6, 170 00 Praha 7, Czech Republic. Address: ul 8 Listopadu 45, 169 00 Praha 6, Czech Republic.

BOBINEC Ivica, b. 16 Sept 1937, Zagreb, Croatia. Radio Station Executive. m. Visnja Kolina, 1 July 1961, 1 son, 1 daughter. Education: Graduated ethnologist, University of Zagreb. Musical Education: Musical Academy, Zagreb. Career: Singer, bass guitar player, Combo 5 (orchestra), 1973-1986; International concert tours across Europe, 1966-69; Split Festival, Zagreb Festival of Popular Music, 1971-77; Radio and television appearances 1958-95, including Eurovision Song Contest, Luxembourg, 1984; Bergen, Norway, 1986; General Manager, Cibona Radio Station. Compositions: Cibona (music and lyrics), anthem of Croatian National Basketball Team, 1990. Recordings: Solo: Pijem Da Zaboravim Nju, 1973. Membership: Glazbena Unija (Music Society of Croatia). Hobby: Tennis. Current Management: Agency Estrada Zagreb, Croatia. Address: Preradoviceva 37, Zagreb, Croatia.

BOCK Jerry (Jerrold Lewis), b. 23 Nov 1928, New Haven, Connecticut, USA. Composer. m. Patricia Faggen, 1950, 1 son, 1 daughter. Education: University of Wisconsin. Career: Composer, scores for high school and college musicals; Author for television, 1951-54; Member, New York board Educiradio broadcasts, 1961-. Compositions: Film score: Wonders Of Manhattan, 1956; Music for show Mr Wonderful, 1956; with Sheldon Harnick: The Body Beautiful, 1958; Fiorello, 1959; Tenderloin, 1960; She Loves Me, 1963; Fiddler On The Roof, 1964; The Apple Tree, 1966; The Rothschilds, 1970; Jerome Robbins Broadway, 1989. Honours: Songwriters Hall Of Fame, 1990; Theatre Hall Of Fame, 1990. Membership: Broadcast Music Inc.

BOCKER Ingemar, b. 6 May 1934, Stockholm, Sweden. Jazz Musician; Transcriber. 1 daughter. Education: Selftaught; Musicology Degree, Stockholm University. Career: Toured Sweden Extensively; Toured American Forces Clubs in West Germany, 1953-55, 1960-62; Toured with Rock and Rhythms Blues Groups; Joined Swedish Folk Rockband Kebnekaise 1972; Archivist, Swedish Centre for Folk Music Research, 1987-. Compositions: Comanche Spring; Ballad of Blackberries and Melon; Galliarde Moderne; Wet Paint. Recordings: Kebnekaise II and III; Electric Mountain. Publications: Lars Gullin 8 Compositions Transcribed by I Bocker, 1998; Several articles in

professional journals and magazines. Memberships: Swedish Jazz Musicians Organization; Lars Gullin Society; SKAP; STIM-NCB. Address: Tensthvagen 94, 16365 Spanga, Sweden.

BODART Jeff, b. 30 Sept 1964, Charleroi, Belgium. Author; Composer; Translator. Education: Humanities, Classics. Musical Education: Piano, at the Academy. Career: Concerts: France; Belgium; Netherlands; Switzerland; Numerous television shows in the above countries. Recordings: Gangsters D'Amour: 2 albums, 1987, 1989; 1 solo album: Du Velo Sans Les Mains, 1994. Memberships: SABAM; UPCACI. Hobby: Music. Current Management: Pierre Mossiat, Templar Music. Address: Templar Music, 412 Avenue de Tervverey, 1150 Brussels, Belgium.

BODDIE Don O'Mar, b. 22 November 1944, St Louis, Missouri, USA. m. Paula R Boddie, 27 July 1991, 4 sons, 2 daughters. Education: BS, Management, 1988; BS, Business Administration, 1988. Musical Education: BA, Music Arts, St Louis Musical Institute, 1968; BA, Music Management, JR College District, St Louis, Missouri, 1974; MBS, Music Production, 1975. Career: Super Sonic Attractions; Stars Spectacular; Salem Spirit Festival. Compositions: Can't Stop the Fire, 1982; Passing Fancy. Recordings: Two Piece Love; True Love; Dreams; Lets Be Lovers; Satisfaction; Legend of O'Mar the Grand Master; Lover Pt 1 and 2. Publications: Lets Be Lovers, 1982, released, 1988; Can't Stop the Fire, 1992; Dreams, 1997. Memberships: Friends of Black Music Society; MAM of Missouri. Hobbies: Martial Arts; Basketball; Recording Productions. Current Management: JD Management Associates, 6112 Hancock, St Louis, MO 63134-2116, USA. Address: 6112 Hancock, St Louis, MO 63134-2116, USA.

BODILSEN Jesper Vejbaek, b. 5 January 1970, Haslev, Denmark. Bass Player (Double Bass/Electric Bass). Education: Rhythmical Diploma Degree, Royal Academy of Music, Aarhus; Played Cornet in Balleskolens Brass Band, 1980-89; Lessons in Big Band Arranging, Line Writing. Appointments: Pori Jazz, Beijing Jazz Festival, Scandinavian Jazz Quartet, 1994; Concerts with Ed Thigpen, Duke Jordan, Janusz Carmello, Bent Jaedig, 1994; James Moody, 1996; Fred Wesley, 1996; Horace Parlan, 1996; Ulf Wakenius, 1997; Tours with Beibom/Kroner Big Band, 1996-97; Katrine Madsen, 1998; Stig Rossen, 1997; Member, Ed Thigpen Trio, 1997; Jazzpar Concerts with Erling Kroner, Dino Saluzzi, 1998. Compositions: Dedication, 1994. Recordings: Contributor, albums: Come Rain Or Come Shine, Hanne Romer, 1994; New Deal, Scandinavian Jazz Quartet, 1994; A Night in Bilbao, Scandinavian Jazz Quartet, 1996; Giving It Away, Helle Hansen, 1995; Red Letter Days, Harvest Moon, 1995; I'm Old Fashioned Katrine Madsen, 1996; Dream Dancing, Katrine Madsen, 1997. Address: Godthaabsvej 36 B, 2 TV, 2000 Frederiksberg, Denmark.

BOGGUSS Suzy Kay, b. 30 Dec 1956, Aledo, Illinois, USA. Country Singer. Education: Art degree. Career: Country singer, 1986-. Recordings: Songs include: I Want To Be A Cowboy's Sweetheart; Night Rider's Lament; I Don't Want To Set The World On Fire; Somewhere Between, 1989; Moment Of Truth, 1990; Aces, 1991; Voices In The Wind, 1992; Other recordings: Happy Trails, with Michael Martin Murphey, 1990; Hopelessly Yours, with Lee Greenwood. Honours: CMA Horizon Award, Most Promising Artist, 1992. Current Management: Morris, Bleisener and Associates, 4155 East Jewel Avenue #412, Denver, CO 80222, USA.

BOGLE Eric, b. 23 Sept 1944, Peebles, Scotland. Songwriter; Musician (guitar). m. Carmel, 29 Jan 1972. Career: Accountant until

1980; Full-time musician, 1980-; Various tours, television appearances. Recordings: The Band Played Waltzing Matilda; The Green Fields Of France/No Man's Land. Publications: 5 songbooks, 12 CDs, 1980-. Honours: United Nations Peace Medal, 1986; APRA Gold Award, 1986; Order Of Australia Medal, 1987. Membership: Full member, APRA. Hobbies: Reading; Television. Current Management: Self. Address: PO Box 529, Magill, Adelaide, South Australia 5072, Australia.

BOGLIUNI Mario, b. 24 May 1935, Svetvincenat-Pula, Croatia. Composer; Musician (piano); Arranger. m. Maria Adler, 24 Aug 1973, 1 son. Musical Education: Conservatorium of Music Art. Career: Concerts and tours, Croatia; European countries; Australia, 1969; USA, 1970; Russia, 1974; Editor, several series on pop music; Compositions for theatre and film. Compositions: Songs: Running Out Of World; Why Do I Love You; Sailors Cha Cha Cha; Three Friends; Serenade. Honours: 25 Croatian and international festival awards. Membership: Music Association of Croatia (DHS). Hobbies: Collector of antiquities; Tennis. Current Management: Mr Finderle Vigor, Agency Adriatic, Opatijska 45, 51000 Rijeka, Croatia. Address: Sestinski Dol 121 A, 41000 Zagreb, Croatia.

BOIC Drazen, b. 11 Apr 1931, Zagreb, Croatia. Musician (piano); Composer; Arranger. m. Anita, 23 Sept 1967, 1 son, 1 daughter. Education: Doctor of Medicine. Musical Education: Secondary Music School, Zagreb. Career: 45 years, love for jazz, playing jazz, commercial music; Leader, own trio, quartet, quintet, sextet; Croatian Zagreb Radio Orchestra, 1954-1958; Playing for US Air Forces, 1957-64; Tours in Russia, 1967-80; Pianist, ballet school, Zagreb, 1980-90; Piano player, Hotel Esplanade, Zagreb, 1980-. Numerous compositions include: Tiho i Mirno; Ljetni Ritam; Anita Fedor; Petra. Membership: Croatian Musicians Union, Zagreb. Hobbies: Photography; Listening to music; Swimming; Eating. Address: Cvijica 17, Zagreb, Croatia.

BOIC Fedor, b. 17 Oct 1968, Zagreb, Croatia. Composer; Producer; Musician (keyboards). Musical Education: Primary, secondary music school, music academy. Career: Playing in theatre, Komedija; With Tereda Kesouija: ITD Band; Aerodrom; Novi Fosili; Many Croatian television and radio shows; Currently playing keyboards in Prijavo Kazaliste; Producer, sound engineer, JM Sound Studio-Zagreb on over 30 LPs for artists including: ITD Band; Jasna Zlokic; Sanja Dolezal; Novi Fosili; Jasmin Stauros; Venera; Vesna Ivic; Duka Caic; Prljavo Kazaliste. Publications: Suzy; Jugoton; Ofej. Honours: 3 Gold records; 1 Gold CD; 10 Silver records; Porin. Memberships: HDS, Croatian Composer Society; HGU, Croatian Musician Society. Hobbies: Reading; Listening to music; Watching films; Bike riding. Current Management: Branko Paic, Crno Bijeli Suijet CBS Croatia. Address: Brace Cvijica 17, 41000 Zagreb, Croatia.

BOJSEN-MOLLER Cai, b. 7 March 1966, Copenhagen, Denmark. Composer; Musician (Drums, Keyboards, Composer). m. Anna Reumert, 20 April 1986, 1 son, 1 daughter. Education: General Certificate of Education A-Level. Musical Education: Copenhagen Boys Choir. Career: Musician, Gangway; Musician for Busstop, Paris-Paris, Naive, Lisa Nilsson and Louise Hoffsten; Composer, Solo Performer, 1990; International concerts in England, Japan and Germany; Performed Roskilde Festival, 1997. Compositions: Solo albums: A Bit of Something, 1997; Super Sonic Jazzy Session, 1998; Singles: A Night in the Pit, 1996; Revert Rhythm, 1996. Recordings: Compilations: Get Lost, 1996; Past, Present and Future, 1997; Further Adventures in Techno Soul, 1998. Publications: Film/Art Videos: Talk Like Whales, 1994; Pets, 1995. Honours: 4 Grammy Awards, Gangway, 1993. Hobbies:

Runner; Japanese Food; Science Fiction Movies; Computer Games; Jazz Music. Current Management: Ferox, Apartment 5, 3 Gatesborough Street, London EC2A 4NS, England. Address: Lundsgade 4A, 2100 O Copenhagen, Denmark.

BOLAM Frank, b. 22 Apr 1949, Glasgow, Scotland. Musician (guitars). m. Jeanette Morrison, 13 May 1967, 1 son, 1 daughter. Musical Education: Studied under Iain McHaffie and Ron Moore, main guitar teachers in Scotland. Career: Professional since age 21; Major productions, theatre, musicals including: Hair, Glasgow Metropole Theatre; West Side Story; Chess; Television appearances include: Ronnie Scott's The Jazz Series; Radio recordings include: The Jazz Train; Extensive professional and session work; Full time teacher, Glasgow schools; Teacher, lecturer, Strathclyde University. Publications: Complete guitar courses (all styles and levels) for exam syllabus for Glasgow and Renfrew Education Department, commissioned by Strathclyde Education Department. Memberships: Glasgow Society of Musicians; Musicians' Union; E15. Hobby: Music. Address: 47 Coltmuir Street, Glasgow G22 6LU, Scotland.

BOLGER Leslie, b. 11 Aug 1947, Liverpool, England. Musician (guitarist); Lecturer. m. Claire Holland, 21 Apr 1970, 3 daughters. Education: Certificate in Education (with distinction), University of Manchester. Musical Education: Studied with world renowned jazz guitarist George Gola, Australia. Career: Jazz performances with artistes including: Martin Taylor; Louis Stewart; Ike Isaacs; Gary Potter; Kenny Baker; Don Rendal; Many television and radio broadcasts; Arranger, Music Adviser, Granada Television; Session guitarist, Arranger, Piccadilly Radio and Radio Merseyside; Backing guitarist for many top cabaret artists including: Russ Abbott; Joe Longthorne; Bob Monkhouse; Vince Hill. Honours: Many first places with honours or distinction for Les Bolger Jazz Guitar Ensemble. Membership: Musicians' Union. Hobbies: Reading; Computer Programming. Current Management: Claire Bolger. Address: 12 Firbank Close, Daresbury View, Runcorn, Cheshire WA7 6NR, England.

BOLLING Claude, b. 10 Apr 1930, Cannes, France. Jazz Musician (piano); Composer; Bandleader; Orchestra Conductor. m. Irène Dervize-Sadyker, 1959, 2 sons. Musical Education: Private teachers including Bob Colin, Earl Hines, Willie The Lion Smith; Maurice Duruflé. Career: As jazz pianist worked with: Dizzy Gillespie; Stéphane Grappelli; Rex Stewart; Roy Eldridge; Sydney Bechet; Albert Nicholas; Lionel Hampton; The Ellingtonians; Carmen McRay; Jo Williams; Formed group Les Parisiennes; Claude Bolling Big Band; Many jazz and variety shows; Crossover music compositions include: Sonatas 1 and 2 for two pianists; Suites for flute, violin, cello, chamber orchestra; Guitar Concerto; Picnic Suite; Toot Suite; More than 100 film soundtrack scores include: Le Jour et l'Heure; Borsalino; Lucky Luke; Le Magnifique; Willie and Phil; California Suite; La Mandarine; L'Homme en Colère; Flic Story; Le Mur de l'Atlantique; On Ne Meurt Que Deux Fois; Television: Jazz Memories; Le Brigades du Tigre; Chantecler. Honours: Gold Records, Canada, USA; Medaille d'Or Maurice Ravel; Officier Arts et Lettres; Chevalier Ordre Nationale du Mérite; Chevalier de la Légion d'Honneur; Los Angeles and New Orleans Honour Citizen; SACEM, Gold Medal and Grand Prix, 1984. Hobbies: Ecology; Model railroading. Address: 20 Avenue de Lorraine, 92380 Garches, France.

BOLO Yammie (Roland Maclean), b. 1970, Kingston, Jamaica. Reggae Vocalist. Career: Began as Singer with Sugar Minott's Youth Promotion sound system; Solo singer, 1985-; Founder, Yam Euphony record label, 1992. Recordings: Numerous singles include: When A Man's In Love, 1985; Jah Made Them All, 1986;

Roots Pon Mi Corner, 1986; Free Mandela, 1987; Ransome of A Man's Life, 1987; Tell Me Why Is This Fussing and Fighting, 1988; Love Me With Feeling, 1989; Poverty and Brutality, 1989; Poor Man's Cry, 1990; Struggle in Babylon, 1990; Turbo Charge, 1991; Blood A Run, 1991; Iniquity Worker, 1991; Jah Jah Loving, 1991; It's Not Suprising, 1992; Joe the Boss, 1992; Be Still, 1992; Revolution; Bowl Mus Fall; Albums: Ransom, 1989; Jah Made Them All, 1989; Who Knows It Feels It, 1991; Up Life Street, 1992; Cool and Easy, 1993; with Lloyd Hemmings: Meets Lloyd Hemmings, 1993. Address: c/o Free World Music Inc, 230 12th Street, Suite 117, Miami Beach, FL 33139-4603, USA.

BOLOGNESI Jacques Philippe Abramo, b. 6 Jan 1947, Gap, France. Musician (trombone, accordion, accordina, piano). Musical Education: Trombone, solfège, CNSM, Paris; Piano, Grenoble. Career: Trombone, accordina, Michel Legrand's Big Band; Trombone with Martial Solal's Big Band; Eddy Louiss; Ivan Julien; Belmondo Big Band; Jean-Jacques Ruhlman; Mico Nissim; Orchestra National de Jazz of France with Antoine Hervé; Bolovaris Group; Accordion, accordina, trombone with Piano Seven. Recordings: Caravansérail; Bolovaris; Paris Sur Valse. Current Management: Alain Brisemontier, Cayamb Productions. Address: Le Moulin 49800 Sarrigne, France.

BOLTON Michael (Michael Bolotin), b. 26 Feb 1953, New Haven, Connecticut, USA. 3 daughters. Singer; Songwriter; Record Producer. Career: Singer, US rock group Blackjack, 1978-82; Collaborator, Glasnost album as member of US songwriting team in Moscow, 1988; Solo recording artiste, formerly under name Michael Bolotin; Appearances include: Support to Heart, US, 1988; Support to Ozzy Osbourne, US, 1988; US tour with Kenny G, 1990; US tour with Celine Dion, 1992; Songwriter for Barbra Streisand, Cher, KISS, Kenny G and Peabo Bryson; World Tour, 1993-95; Christmas in Vienna, 1997; Numerous television appearances include TV special, This Is Michael Bolton, NBC, 1992. Compositions include: How Am I Supposed To Live Without You, Laura Branigan, 1983; I Found Someone, Cher, 1988; Co-writer (with Paul Stanley), Forever, Kiss, 1990; Co-writer (with Bob Dylan), Steel Bars, 1992. Recordings: Singles include: That's What Love's All About, 1987; Dock Of The Bay, 1988; How Am I Supposed To Live Without You, 1990; How Can We Be Lovers, 1990; When I'm Back On My Feet Again, 1990; Georgia On My Mind, 1990; Love Is A Wonderful Thing, 1991; Time, Love And Tenderness, 1991; When A Man Loves A Woman, 1991; Missing You Now, with Kenny G, 1992; Steel Bars, 1992; To Love Somebody, 1993; Drift Away, 1993; Said I Loved You...But I Lied, 1993; A Love So Beautiful, 1995; Can I Touch You...There, 1995; Albums include: Michael Bolton, 1983; Everybody's Crazy, 1985; The Hunger, 1987; Soul Provider, 1989; Time Love And Tenderness (Number 1, US), 1991; Timeless - The Classics (Number 1, US), 1992; The One Thing, 1993; Greatest Hits 1985-1995, 1995; Contributor, Pavarotti And Friends (charity record for Bosnia relief), 1996; Go the Distance, theme from Disney film Hercules; This is the Time - The Christmas Album, 1996. Publication: The Secret of the Lost Kingdom, children's book, 1997. Honours include: New York Music Award, Best R&B Vocalist, 1988; ASCAP Airplay Awards, 1989; Pollstar Tour of the Year, 1990; Grammy Awards: Best Pop Vocal Performance, 1990, 1992; American Music Awards: Favourite Male Pop/Rock Artist, Favourite Album, 1992, 1993; BMI Song Of The Year, 1991; Gold and Platinum discs; Hitmakers Award, National Songwriters Hall of Fame, 1995; Five times winner, BMI Million Peroramcne Song Award. Membership: BMI Current Management: Louis Levin Management, 130 W 57th Street #10-B, New York, NY 10019, USA.

BOLVIG Palle P S, b. 25 Nov 1932, Copenhagen, Denmark. Musician (trumpet, flugelhorn); Composer; Arranger. m. Jytte, 12 July 1969, 1 son, 3 daughters. Musical Education: Private study. Career: Member, Ib Glindemann Orchestra, 1951-61; Member, International Band, Newport Festival, 1958; Member, Danish Radio Big Band, 1964-. Compositions: Easy Mood, 1961; Gosty Day, 1970; Zabacoot, 1970; Portrait Of Cordoba, 1971; Back To Tenderness, 1971; Child Of Pain, 1985. Recordings: Newport International Band, 1958; Brownsville Trolley Line, Danish Radio Big Band, 1969; Ben Webster And The Danish Radio Big-Band, 1970; Thad Jones And The Danish Radio Big-Band, 1978; Ernie Wilkins Almost Big-Band, 1981; Aura, Miles Davis, 1985. Honours: Selected, Newport International Jazz Band, 1958. Memberships: The Danish Trumpet Societies. Hobby: Cycling in the countryside. Current Management: The Danish Radio DR. Address: Danmarks Radio P2 Jazz, 1999 Frederiksberg C, Denmark.

BOM-BANE Jane (Bayley), b. 11 Sept 1953, Leek, Staffordshire, England. Singer; Composer; Lyricist; Musician (harmonium). m. André Schmidt, 20 Dec 1982, divorced, 1 son. Education: BA Hons, French, Cultural Studies, PGCE, English, French, Spanish, Warwick University. Musical Education: History of Music (part of degree); Piano lessons as child. Career: Appearances include: Bracknell Festival, 1993; Edinburgh Fringe Festival, 1994, 1995; Glasgow Mayfest, GFT, 1995; Television and radio includes: Usual Suspects, BBC Radio Scotland, 1994; Don't Look Down, STV, 1994; We Stayed In With Jungr And Parker, BBC Radio 2, 1994; Russian State television. Recordings: Away/Mantovani, The Swinging Cats, 1980; Boy/Yob, The Round-a-way Wrong Chamber, 1984; Solo albums: Round-a-way Wrong Songs, 1993; It Makes Me Laugh, 1995; Soundtrack: The Man From Porlock, 1995. Memberships: Musicians' Union; PRS. Hobbies: Collecting harmoniums; Swimming. Current Management: Round-a-way Wrong Music. Address: PO Box 8416, London SW9 92B, England.

BON JOVI Jon (John Bongiovi), b. 2 Mar 1962, Sayreville, New Jersey, USA. Vocalist; Songwriter; Musician (guitar). m. Dorothea Hurley, May 1989, 1 son, 1 daughter. Career: Singer, local bands: Raze; Atlantic City Expressway; Singer, founder member, US rock group Bon Jovi, 1984-; 40 million albums sold worldwide to date; Numerous worldwide tours, including US, UK, Europe, USSR, South America, Australia, Japan, 1984-; Support tours with Kiss; Scorpions; .38 Special; Headliners, Donington Monsters Of Rock Festival, 1987; Moscow Music Peace Festival, 1989; Numerous television, radio and video appearances worldwide; Own management company, BJM; Own record label Jambco. Recordings: US Number 1 singles include: You Give Love A Bad Name, 1986; Living On A Prayer, 1987; Bad Medicine, 1988; I'll Be There For You, 1989; Solo: Blaze Of Glory, 1990; Numerous other hits include: Wanted Dead Or Alive; Lay Your Hands On Me; Living In Sin; Born To Be My Baby; Keep The Faith; In These Arms; I'll Sleep When I'm Dead; Bed Of Roses; Always; I Believe; Someday I'll Be Saturday Night; This Ain't A Love Song; Lie To Me; These Days; Albums: Bon Jovi, 1984; 7800° Fahrenheit, 1985; Slippery When Wet (13 million copies sold), 1986; New Jersey, 1988; Keep The Faith, 1991; Crossroad (Best Of), 1994; These Days, 1995; Solo album: Blaze Of Glory (film soundtrack, Young Guns II); Contributor, Stairway To Heaven/Highway To Hell charity record, 1989; Two Rooms (Elton John/Bernie Taupin tribute album), 1991. Honours: American Music Awards, Favourite Pop/Rock Band, 1988; Favourite Pop/Rock Single, 1991; Bon Jovi Day, Sayreville, 1989; Silver Clef, Nordoff-Robbins Music Therapy, 1990; All albums Gold or Platinum status; Golden Globe, Best Original Song, Blaze Of Glory, 1991; Oscar Nomination, Blaze Of Glory;

Best Selling Album Of Year, Crossroad, 1994; BRIT Award, Best International Group, 1996. Current Management: c/o Bon Jovi Management, 250 W 57th Street, Ste 603-5, New York, NY 10107, USA.

BONDS Gary "US" (Gary Anderson), b. 6 June 1939, Jacksonville, Florida, USA. Singer; Songwriter; Record Producer. Career: Member, group The Turks; Solo artiste, 1960-; Co-writer, producer with Bruce Springsteen and Steve Van Zandt, 1978-; Appearances include: UK tour, 1962; Richard Nader's second Rock'n'Roll Revival concert, with Bill Haley, Jackie Wilson, 1969; Nuclear Disarmament rally, with Bruce Springsteen, James Taylor, Linda Ronstadt, Jackson Browne, Central Park, New York, 1982; Radio City Music Hall, New York, WCBS Radio's 20th Anniversary Concert, 1992. Recordings: Singles include: New Orleans, 1960; Quarter To Three (Number 1, US), 1961; School Is Out, 1961; Dance Til Quarter To Three, 1961; Dear Lady Twist, 1962; Twist, 1962; Twist Señora, 1962; This Little Girl (written by Bruce Sringsteen), 1981; Out Of Work (also written by Springsteen), 1982; Albums: Dedication, 1978; On The Line, 1982; Standing In The Line Of Fire, 1984; Producer for artistes including: Johnny Paycheck; Z.Z. Hill.

BONE Greg, b. 21 Jan 1962, Hartlepool, England. Musician (guitar). 1 son. Musical Education: Self-taught. Career: Played with Terry Ronald; Support tours with Hall & Oates, 1990; Robert Palmer, 1991; Television: Harry (drama series); Performances with Bros on Wogan; Top of The Pops; Going Live; Polish Music Festival; Radio sessions with One Word and Terry Ronald; Numerous television and radio appearances with Band of Thieves (now known as Thieves Like Us). Recordings: Linda Lewis; DJ Culture; Was It Worth It Singers (Pet Shop Boys); Sting. Albums: Changing Faces, Bros; Confide In Me, Kylie Minogue; Nobody Else, Take That. Remix: Brothers in Rhythm. Membership: Musicians' Union. Hobbies: Music; Cars; Guitars.

BONET Maria Del Mar, b. 27 Apr 1947, Palma, Majorca, Spain. Singer; Songwriter; Musician (guitar). Career: Began singing with Els Setze Jutges, Barcelona, 1967; Performed in: France; Denmark; England; Switzerland; Venezuela; Mexico; Portugal; Poland; Italy; Sweden; Germany; Greece; Tunisia; Netherlands; Belgium; Former USSR; Japan; Annual concerts, Plaça del Rei, Barcelona; Recorded and toured, France and Spain, with Ensemble de Musique Traditionelle de Tunís, 1985; Toured Spain, with Brazilian Milton Nascimiento, 1986; Presented Arenal, with choreographer, dancer, Nacho Duato, 1988; International Peralada Music Festival, 1992; Performed show, The Greece of Theodorakis, 1993; Performed in Cants d'Abelone, 1994; Performed show, Merhaba, Summer Festival, Barcelona, 1994; Edinburgh International Festival, 1995. Recordings include: Maria del Mar Bonet, 1974; A L'Olympia, 1975; Maria del mar Bonet, 1976; Cançons de Festa, 1976; Alenar, 1977; Saba de Terrer, 1979; Quico-Maria del Mar, 1979; Cançons de la Nostra Mediterranea, 1980; L'Aguila Negra, 1981; Jardí Tancat, 1981; Sempre, 1981; Breviari d'Amor, 1982; Maria del Bonet, 1983; Anells d'Aigua, 1985; Gavines i Dragons, 1987; Ben A Prop, 1989; Bon Viatge Faci la Cadernera, 1990; Coreografies, with Nacho Duato, 1990; Ellas, Maria del Mar Bonet Canta a Theodorakis, 1993; Salmaia, 1995; El Cor el Temps, 1997. Publications: Antología de la Nova Cançó Catalana, 1968; Maria del Mar Bonet, 1976; La Nova Cançó, 1976; Tretze que Conten, 1982; Veinte Años de Canción en España, 1984; Una Història de la Cançó, 1987; 25 Anys de Cançó a Mallorca, 1987; Secreta Veu (poems and watercolours), 1987; Maria del Mar Bonet (biography), Joan Manresa, 1994. Honours: Spanish Gold disc, 1971; French Government Charles Cross Academy Award, Best Foreign Record, 1984; Cross Of St George, Catalan

Government Prize, 1984; Catalan Government National Prize, 1992. Memberships: Societat General d'Autors i Editors (SGAE); Associació de Cantants i Intèrprets Professionals en Llangua Catalana (ACIC). Hobbies: Poetry; Writing; Pottery; Painting. Current Management: Jordi de Ramon; Address: Sepúlveda, 147-149 Principal 1a, 08011 Barcelona, Catalonia, Spain.

BONFILS Tony, b. 27 Jan 1948, Nice, France. Musician (bass guitar, double bass); Vocalist. 3 sons, 1 daughters. Education: Licence de Psychologie. Musical Education: Prix de Contre Basse; Medaille de Solfege. Career: Bass player with: Dee Dee Bridgewater; Sacha Distel; Charles Aznavour; Also studio musician.

BONGA Ntshukumo (Ntshuks), 1 Oct 1963, Johannesburg, South Africa. Musician (alto saxophone, clarinet); Engineer. Education: BSc (Hons), Aeronautical Engineering and Design. Musical Education: Self-taught. Career: Appearances include: Reithalle, Berne, Switzerland; Purcell Room, South Bank Centre; London Jazz Festival, 1994; London ICA, 1996; WOMAD Festival, 1997; Performances with Robyn Hitchcock; Radio broadcasts: Interview BBC World Service, Network Africa, 1993; Interview, session, BBC Radio 3, Impressions, 1994; PM Live, Radio South Africa. Recordings: Album: Urban Ritual, Ntshuks Bonga's Tshisa; Moss Elixir, Robyn Hitchcock. Honour: Debut Album, Urban Ritual, voted No 6, Wire magazine Jazz/Improvised Music Poll, 1995. Memberships: Musicians' Union; PRS; London Musicians Collective. Hobbies: Cinema; World travel; Astronomy. Address: 22 Norcott Road, Stoke Newington, London N16 7EL, England.

BONHAM Jason, b. England. Musician (drums, percussion). m. Jan Charteris, 5 May 1990. Musical Education: Played drums from age 4; Taught by father, John Bonham. Career: Member, Airrace, 1984; Founder member, Virginia Wolf, 1986; Worked with members of Led Zeppelin, 1987-88; Concert, Atlantic Records 40th Anniversary concert, Madison Square Garden, 1988; US tour with Jimmy Page, 1988; Founder, own group, Bonham, 1990-. Recordings: Albums: with Airrace: Shaft Of Light, 1984; with Virginia Wolf: Virginia Wolf, 1986; with Jimmy Page: Outrider, 1988; with Bonham: The Disregard Of Timekeeping, 1989; Madhatter, 1992. Current Management: Part Rock Management, Suite 318, 535 Kings Road, London SW10 0SZ, England.

BONNEY Simon, b. 3 June 1961, Sydney, Australia. Singer; Songwriter. m. 15 June 1984, 1 son, 1 daughter. Career: Performed in film Wings Of Desire (Wim Wenders), with Crime and the City Solution; Contributor to film scores: To The Ends Of The World (Wim Wenders); Faraway So Close (Wim Wenders); Gas Food And Lodgings (Alison Anders); Underworld (Roger Christian); Also appeared on MTV Road Hog. Recordings: Albums: with Crime and the City Solution: Room Of Lights; Shine; The Bride Ship; Paradise Discotheque; The Adversary - Live; Solo albums: Forever; Everyman; Also featured on film soundtrack albums: Wings Of Desire; To The Ends Of The World; Faraway So Close; Underworld. Membership: PRS. Current Management: c/o Ted Gardner, Larrkin Management, 8391 Beverly Blvd. #298, Los Angeles, CA 90048, USA.

BONO (Paul Hewson), 10 May 1960, Dublin, Ireland. Singer; Lyricist. m. Alison, 2 daughters. Career: Founder member, lead singer, rock group U2, 1978-; Regular national, international and worldwide tours; Major concerts include: US Festival, 1983; The Longest Day, Milton Keynes Bowl, 1985; Live Aid, Wembley, 1985; Self Aid, Ireland, 1986; A Conspiracy Of Hope (Amnesty International US tour), 1986; Smile Jamaica (hurricane relief concert), 1988; Very Special Arts Festival, White House, 1988; New Year's Eve

Concert, Dublin (televised throughout Europe), 1989; Yankee Stadium, New York (second concert ever), 1992; Group established own record company, Mother Records. Compositions include: Co-writer, Jah Love, Neville Brothers; Lyrics, Misere, Zucchero and Pavarotti; Screenplay, Million Dollar Hotel. Recordings: Albums: Boy, 1980; October, 1981; War (Number 1, UK), 1983; Under A Blood Red Sky, 1983; The Unforgettable Fire (Number 1, UK), 1984; Wide Awake In America, 1985; The Joshua Tree (Number 1, UK and US), 1987; Rattle And Hum, also film (Number 1, US), 1988; Achtung Baby (Number 1, US), 1991; Zooropa (Number 1, UK and US), 1993; Passengers (film soundtrack), with Brian Eno, 1995; Pop, 1997; Hit singles include: Out Of Control (Number 1, Ireland), 1979; Another Day (Number 1, Ireland), 1980; New Year's Day, 1983; Two Hearts Beat As One, 1983; Pride (In The Name Of Love), 1984; The Unforgettable Fire, 1985; With Or Without You (Number 1, US), 1987; I Still Haven't Found What I'm Looking For (Number 1, US), 1987; Where The Streets Have No Name, 1987; Desire (Number 1, UK), 1988; Angel Of Harlem, 1988; When Love Comes To Town, with B B King, 1989; All I Want Is You, 1989; The Fly (Number 1, UK), 1991; Mysterious Ways, 1992; One, 1992; Even Better Than The Real Thing, 1992; Who's Gonna Ride Your Wild Horses, 1992; Stay, 1993; Hold Me, Thrill Me, Kiss Me (from film soundtrack Batman Forever), 1995; Discotheque, 1997; If God Will Send His Angels, 1997 Contributor, Do They Know It's Christmas?, Band Aid, 1985; Sun City, Little Steven, 1985; In A Lifetime, Clannad, 1986; Mystery Girl, Roy Orbison, 1988; Special Christmas, charity album, 1987; Folkways - A Vision Shared (Woody Guthrie tribute), 1988; Live For Ireland, 1989; Red Hot + Blue (Cole Porter tribute), 1990; Tower Of Song (Leonard Cohen tribute), 1995; Pavarotti And Friends, 1996. Honours: Grammy Awards: Album Of The Year, Best Rock Performance, The Joshua Tree, 1987; Best Rock Performance, Desire, 1989; Best Rock Vocal, 1993; BRIT Awards: Best International Group,1988-90; Best Live Act, 1993; World Music Award, Irish Artist Of The Year, 1993; Juno Award, International Entertainer Of The Year, 1993; Q Awards: Best Act In The World, 1990, 1992, 1993; Merit Award, 1994; Numerous poll wins and awards, Billboard and Rolling Stone magazines; Gold and Platinum discs. Current Management: Principle Management, 30-32 Sir John Rogersons Quay, Dublin 2, Ireland.

BONSALL Joseph Sloan Jr, b. 18 May 1948, Philadelphia, Pennsylvania, USA. Singer. m. Barbara Holt, 1969. Career: Member, gospel singing groups, 1966-73; Member, gospel/country group The Oak Ridge Boys, 1973-; Co-owner, Silverline/Goldline Music Publishing. Recordings: Singles: Y'All Come Back Saloon; I'll Be True To You; Leavin' Louisiana In The Broad Daylight; Trying To Love Two Women; Elvira; Bobbie Sue; American Made; Love Song; I Guess It Never Hurts To Hurt Sometime; Come On In; Make My Life With You. Albums: Oak Ridge Boys, 1974; Sky High, 1975; Old Fashioned..., 1976; Live, 1977; Y'All Come Back Saloon, 1977; Room Service, 1978; The Oak Ridge Boys Have Arrived, 1979; Together, 1980; Greatest Hits, 1980; Fancy Free, 1981; Bobbie Sue, 1982; Christmas, 1982; Very Best, 1982; American Made, 1983; The Oak Ridge Boys Deliver, 1983; Friendship, 1983; Greatest Hits II, 1984; Seasons, 1985; Step On Out, 1985; Where The Fast Lane Ends, 1986; Christmas Again, 1986; Monogahela, 1987; New Horizons, 1988; American Dreams, 1989; Greatest Hits III, 1989; Unstoppable, 1991; The Long Haul, 1992. Honours: Numerous Gospel Music Association Dove Awards; Grammy Awards, 1970-77; CMA Vocal Group Of The Year, 1978; ACM Awards, Best Vocal Group, 1979; American Music Award, Best Country Group, 1982; Gold discs. Memberships: Academy Of Country Music; NARAS; AFTRA; Country Music Association. Current Management: Don

Light Talent, PO Box 120308, Nashville, TN 37212, USA.

BONTE Ralph, b. 7 June 1965, Bruges, Belgium. Singer; Musician (Guitar). m. Janne Vergauwe, 28 October 1988, 1 daughter. Education: Psychologist; Selftaught Guitar. Career: Peer, Belgium Rhythm' Blues Festival, 1989; Peer, Belgium Rhythm' N Blues Festival, 1997. Recordings: Hideaway, CD, 1989; Come Inside, CD, 1992; Unable to Label, CD, 1997. Membership: SABAM. Hobby: Luthier. Address: Konijnenpad 17, 8310 Brugge, Belgium.

BOO Betty (Alison Moira Clarkson), b. 6 Mar 1970, Kensington, London, England. Singer. Career: Member, rap group the She-Rockers; Duo, Hit'n'Run; Guest singer with Beatmasters; Solo artiste, 1990-. Recordings: Album: Boomania, 1990; Hit singles: with Beatmasters: Hey DJ (I Can't Dance To That Music You're Playing); Solo: Doin' The Doo, 1990; Where Are You Baby, 1990; Let Me Take You There, 1992; I'm On My Way, 1992. Honours: Numerous dance music awards. Current Management: Big Life Management, 15 Little Portland Street, London W1N 5DE, England.

BOONE Debby (Deborah Ann), b. 22 Sept 1956, Hackensack, New Jersey, USA. Singer; Actress. m. Gabriel Ferrer, 1979, 2 sons, 2 daughters. Career: singer with (father) Pat Boone and family group, 1970-; Recording artist, 1977-; Numerous television appearances include: Sins Of The Past, ABC-TV, 1984; Stage performances: Seven Brides For Seven Brothers, national tour, 1981-82; Sound Of Music, national tour, 1987-88. Publications: Debby Boone - So Far; Bedtime Hugs For Little Ones (children's book), 1988; Co-author, Tomorrow Is A Brand New Day, 1989. Honours: American Music Award, Song Of The Year; Grammy Awards: Best New Artist, 1977; CMA Best New Country Artist, 1977; Singing Star Of Year, AGVA, 1978; Dove Awards, 1980, 1984; Best Inspirational Performance, 1980; Best Gospel Performance, Keep The Flame Burning, 1984; Best New Personality, National Association Theatre Owners. Current Management: c/o Sparrow Communications Group, 101 Winners Circle, Brentwood, TN 37024, USA.

BOONE Pat, b. 1 June 1934, Jacksonville, Florida, USA. Singer; Actor. m. Shirley Foley, 14 Nov 1953, 4 daughters. Education: North Texas State Teachers College; David Liscomb College; Gradute magna cum laude, Columbia, 1958. Career: Appearances include: Ted Mack TV Show, 1953; Arthur Godfrey Show, CBS, 1954-55; Own television show, 1957; Numerous other television appearances include: Moonlighting; Co-host, Wish You Were Here, Nashville Network, 1988-; Film appearances include: Bernadine, 1957; April Love, 1957; Mardi Gras, 1958; Journey To The Centre Of The Earth, 1959; All Hands On Deck, 1961; State Fair, 1962; Main Attraction, 1962; Yellow Canary, 1963; Greatest Story Ever Told, 1965; Perils Of Pauline, 1967; The Cross And The Switchblade, 1971; Owner, Lamb & Lion Records. Publications include: Twixt Twelve And Twenty, 1958; Between You Me And The Gatepost, 1960; The Real Christmas, 1961; Care And Feeding Of Parents, 1967; A New Song, 1971; Joy, 1973; A Miracle A Day Keeps The Devil Away; My Faith, 1976; Pat Boone Devotional Book, 1977; The Honeymoon Is Over, 1977; Together - 25 Years With The Boone Family, 1979; Pray To Win - God Wants You To Succeed, 1980. Honours: Listed in Top Ten Attractions, 1957; Listed in Top Fifteen Namepower Stars, 1959. Current Management: Tim Swift, Cossette Productions. Address: 8899 Beverly Blvd, Los Angeles, CA 90048, USA.

BORENIUS Louis (Andrei Nicholas Tancred Borenius), b. 4 Sept 1949, London, England. Musician (drums, vibes, percussion). m. Suzy Brading, 15 July 1995, 1 son, 1 daughter. Education: Certificate of Education. Musical

Education: Early piano lessons; Mainly self-taught. Career: Tours: Europe, with Sara Jane Morris; East Germany, with John Etheridge and Dick Heckstall-Smith; Granada TV Special with The Republic; Numerous broadcasts with Coup D'Etat. Recordings: Albums with Coup D'Etat: Face To Face; Last Of The Aztecs. Publication: A Musician's Joke Book, 1996. Memberships: Musicians' Union; PRS; MCPS. Hobbies: Fly fishing; Chess. Address: 80 Barnett Road, Holingdean, Brighton BN1 7GH, England.

BORN 2 B (Colin Crook), b. 29 Jan 1971, London, England. Rapper; Producer; Songwriter. Education: Woolwich Polytechnic, 1982-87. Musical Education: Self-taught whilst working for a South London Sound System. Career: Kiss FM Tour, including The Jazz Rap Weekender, London; The Wag Club, London; Juliana's, Istanbul, Turkey; The Brain Club, London, 1990; Interview on ITV London, Thames News programme, 1992; Numerous television appearances on MTV Europe, and in Germany, Turkey and Japan; UK radio appearances on Kiss FM; Capital Radio; Jazz FM, London. Compositions: Kings of the Ring, 1992; Live at Energy Radio Pt 1 & 2, 1997; The Band Played the Boogie/Can We Start Over, 1997. Recordings: Moments In Love, 1990; Aquarian House, 1990; Turkish Delight, 1992; The Band Played The Boogie, 1992-93; Debut album The Last Guv'nor, 1998. Publications: Contributor of numerous articles in the music press. Honour: Official Music Week Top 60 Dance Singles, 1992. Memberships: Musicians' Union; MCPS; Performing Rights Society. Hobbies: Music; Keeping fit; Restaurants; Clubs. Current Management: International Broadcast Music Management (Byron Byrd, UK). Address: The IBM House, 82 Purret Road, Plumstead Point, London SE18 1JP, England.

BORUM Stefan, b. 21 Aug 1954, Viborg, Denmark. Composer; Musician (piano). 2 sons, 1 daughter. Musical Education: 1 term, Creative Music Studio, Woodstock, New York, USA, 1980. Career: Member: Blue Sun, 1975-78; Concerts include: Roskilde Festival, 1977; Member, Lost Kids, 1979-80; Created Sun Quartet; Concerts include: Italian tour, 1984-85; 1st Prize winner, Jazz On The Oder, 1987; Jazz Jamboree, Warsaw, 1987; Autumn Rhythms, Leningrad, 1988; Member, Shades Of Blue, 1987-; Concerts include: Djurs Bluesland, 1988, 1990, 1992; Notoddon Blues Festival, 1991. Recordings: It's All Money Johnny, Blue Sun, 1976; Sun Quartet, Sun Quartet, 1987; On A Mission From Muddy Waters, Shades Of Blue, 1992. Memberships: DMF (Danish Musicians Union); DJFBA.

BOSKOV Ole, b. 31 Aug 1963, Copenhagen, Denmark. Musician (piano, acoustic guitar, keyboards); Vocalist; Songwriter. m. Tina, 5 Sept 1992. Musical Education: Piano lessons for 16 years, organ lessons for 2 years, and guitar lessons for 4 years. Career: Number 1 hit single in Denmark with Danish version of MC Hammer's Can't Touch This; Debut album of own compositions, 1996. Compositions include: Listen To The Wind; Pennsylvania; Going Crazy. Recordings: Backing vocals for Ester Brohus. Solo albums: Listen To The Wind, 1996; Mr Romance, 1998. Membership: Danish Songwriters Guild. Hobbies: Football; Skiing; Spiritual enhancement. Address: Rolfsvej 22 st th, 2000 Frederiksberg, Denmark.

BOSTOCK Chris, b. 23 November 1959, Hillingdon, London, England. Songwriter; Producer; Musician (Bass, Keyboards). Career: Songwriter and Bassist with JoBoxers, 1983-86; 3 hit singles, 1 hit album; Touring in UK, USA, Canada, Australia, New Zealand and with Dave Stewart and Spiritual Cowboys, 1990-92; 2 albums; Touring in Europe; Sessions for OMD, Shakespeare's Sister, Style Council, Sandi Shaw; Produced albums for Savage World, 1993; Clint Bradley, 1997; Film soundtrack, Bad Girl, with

Jane Horrocks, 1992. Compositions: Hit Singles: Just Got Lucky; Johnny Friendly; Is This Really the First Time. Recordings: Just Got Lucky; Johnny Friendly; Is This Really the First Time; Boxerbeat; Spiritual Cowboys and Honest albums by Dave Stewart and the Spiritual Cowboys; Goodbye Cruel World, Shakespeare's Sister; Cafe Bleu, album, Style Council. Memberships: PRS; Musician's Union. Current Management: Groove Management, 6 Cherry Tree Court, Grove Hill, London E18 2JE, England. Address: 6 Cherry Tree Court, 54 Grove Hill, London E18 2JE, England.

BOTH Robert Allen, b. 10 Nov 1952, Montclair, New Jersey, USA. Recording Engineer; Producer; Musician. m. Karen Sue Cody, 2 Mar 1987, 1 son. Education: Art School, Ridgewood. Musical Education: Guitar and piano lessons. Career: A&R, Polydor Records, New York City, 1971-72; A&R Director, Recording engineer, producer, James Brown Enterprises, New York City, 1972-76; Staff engineer, Delta Recording, 1976-77; Staff engineer, Quad Recording, 1979; Owner, Chief engineer, Twain Recordings, New Jersey, 1976-; Audio instructor, Ramapo College of New Jersey, 1993; Audio Instructor, William Paterson University, New Jersey, 1995-; Audio Instructor, County College of Morris, New Jersey, 1997-. Recordings: with The JB's: Doin' It, 1973; with Maceo Parker, US, 1974; with James Brown: Get On The Good Foot, 1972; Reality, 1974; The Payback, 1974; Hell, 1974; Sex Machine Today, 1975; Hot, 1975; with Lyn Collins: Check Me Out, 1975; with The JB's@ Damn Night, 1974; Breakin' Bread, 1974; Hustle with Speed, 1975. Publications: Articles in the music press. Honours: 3 RIAA Gold Records Awards for work with James Brown. Address: Twain Recording, 18 Hiawatha Pass, West Milford, NJ 07480, USA.

BOTSCHINSKY Allan, b. 1940, Copenhagen, Denmark. Musician (trumpet, flugelhorn); Composer. Education: Royal Danish Conservatory at age 14; Studied trumpet under Cecil Collins at the Manhattan School of Music, New York; Private studies of classical composition with Professor Svend Erik Werner and Bo Holten. Career includes: Professional at age 16, playing in leading groups of Copenhagen's Jazz Scene with, among others, Oscar Pettiford, Stan Getz, Dexter Gordon and Ben Webster; Member of Jazz Quintet '60 and the Danish Radio Jazz Group; Played with and conducted The Danish Radio Big Band, whose guest conductors included Thad Jones, Oliver Nelson, Stan Kenton, Dizzy Gillespie, Maynard Ferguson and George Russell; Regular tours and recordings with Peter Herbolzheimer's Rhythm Combination and Brass and Ali Haurand's European Jazz Ensemble and European Trumpet Summit. Compositions: Numerous compositions and arrangements include: Sentiments, prizewinning suite for large orchestra and voice; Exercises For Jazz Orchestra; Synergy, piece for string quartet and jazz quintet; A Jazz Sonata, for trumpet and piano; Jazz-Antiphony, brass octet; Frantasia, piece for solo trumpet and symphony orchestra. Recordings include: Last Summer, 1992; I've Got Another Rhythm, 1995; First Brass; Duologue, with Niels-Henning Ørsted Pedersen. Honours include: Ben Webster Prize, 1983; Special television tribute entitled The Music of Allan Botschinsky, 1984. Address: 64 Gilbey House, 38-46 Jamestown Road, London NW1 7BY, England.

BOTTUM Roddy, b. 1 July 1963, Los Angeles, California, USA. Musician (keyboards). Musical Education: Classically-trained pianist. Career: Member, US rock group Faith No More, 1980-; Appearances include: Brixton, London (recorded for live video), 1990; Reading Festival, 1990; Monsters Of Rock Festivals, Italy and France, 1990; Supported Robert Plant, US, 1990; Day On The Green, San Francisco, 1991; Rock In Rio II Festival, Brazil, 1991; Phoenix Festival, 1993, 1995. Recordings: Singles include: We Care

A Lot, 1988; Epic, 1990; Falling To Pieces, 1990; From Out Of Nowhere, 1990; Midlife Crisis, 1992; A Small Victory, 1992; Everything's Ruined, 1992; I'm Easy, 1993; Albums: Faith No More, 1985; Introduce Yourself, 1987; The Real Thing, 1989; Live At Brixton Academy, 1991; Angel Dust, 1992; King For A Day... Fool For A Lifetime, 1995. Honours: Grammy Nomination, Best Heavy Metal Performance, 1990; Bammy Awards: Outstanding Group, Best Keyboardist, 1991; MTV Video Award, Best Special Effects, 1991; Bay Area Award, Outstanding Keyboardist, 1993. Current Management: Warren Entner Management, 5550 Wilshire Blvd, Ste 302, Los Angeles, CA 90036, USA.

BOUBLIL Alain Albert, b. 5 Mar 1941, Tunis, Tunisia. Author; Dramatist. Career: Author, dramatist and lyricist. Publications: Wrote libretto and lyrics for: La Révolution Française, 1973; Les Misérables, 1980; Abbacadabra, 1984; Miss Saigon, 1989; Le Journal d'Adam et Eve (play), 1994; Martin Guerre, 1996. Honours: 2 Tony Awards, 2 Grammy Awards, 2 Victoire de la Musique Awards, Molière Award (all for Les Misérables); Evening Standard Drama Award (for Miss Saigon); Laurence Olivier Award (for Martin Guerre). Address: c/o Cameron Mackintosh Limited, 1 Bedford Square, London WC1B 3RA, England.

BOUCHEZ Jean-Marc, b. 15 May 1954, Reims, France. Musician (saxophone); Composer. 2 sons. Education: Master of Sciences. Musical Education: Conservatoire; CIM; University of Berkeley, California, USA. Career: Sideman for various French artists: Jessie Garon; Les Forbans; Eddy Louiss Multicolorfanfare; Own recording studio home; Composer of music to images, 10 films for French television and advertisements; One musical comedy "Suzanne". Address: 32 Rue de la Beaune, 93100 Montreuil, France.

BOUDRANT Jean-Claude, b. 9 Mar 1953, Second, France. Musician (piano). m. Carole Guthedel, 3 Sept 1977, 3 sons. Education: University. Musical Education: First prize, piano, 1976. Career: Jazz piano player; Specialist in ragtime and stride piano, Disneyland, Paris, 1992-. Recordings: One record of ragtime music; One record of stride music. Hobby: Piano. Current Management: Self-managed. Address: 32 Grande Rue, 77114 Gouaix, France.

BOULIANE Daniel G, b. 26 Oct 1963, Hull, Quebec, Canada. Producer; Composer; Keyboards; Drums; Vocals; Percussions. m. Lise Roy, 1981, 1 son, 1 daughter. Education: Université du Québec; College Alexandre. Career: Soundtracks for NFB documentaries; Soundtracks for TV series; Soundtracks for Moving the Mountain; Soundtracks for many national ads. Compositions: for Nadia: Free Free; Live on Love; Shine On; Beatman; for Roxxy: Love Set Us Free; I Feel You; For Us to Be; for Nathalie Page: This is the Time. Recordings: New World, 1994; Nomad, 1996; Remember, 1998; Image Compilation, 1992. Publications: Titles of Dak: New World, 1994; Nomad, 1996; Remember, 1998. Honours: Reel Award Nominee, 1992-94; Gémeaux Award Nominee, 1995. Membership: Academic of Canadian Cinema and Television. Hobbies: Astronomy; Fishing; Walking in the woods. Current Management: Dance Music: Promotion Tessier, Instrumentall World Ambiant, OzMoz. Address: D Bouliane, 10 Reinhardt, Hull PQ, J8Y 5V4, Canada.

BOURASSA Francois, b. 26 September 1959, Montreal, Canada. Jazz Musician (piano). Education: Bachelor's Degree, Composition, McGill University; Master's Degree, Jazz, Academic Honours and Distinction in Performance, New England Consevatory of Music, Boston. Career: Concerts in Canada, USA, Europe (France, Belgium, Spain), Korea, Moscow, Mexico; Canadian tours of jazz festivals; Concert

with Dave Brubeck; Celebration of Charles Dutoit's birthday, Radio France, Radio Canada. Compositions: Reflet 1; Jeune Vieux Jeune; Echo. Recordings: Reflet 1, 1986; Jeune Vieux Jeune, 1993; Echo, 1996. Honours: Canada and Québec Arts Council Compositions Grants; Winner, 1985 Montreal International Jazz Festival's Competition. Current Management: Direction D'Artistes Fleming. Address: 5975 Av Du Parc, Montréal, QC, H2V 4H4, Canada.

BOURDE Hervé, b. 12 July 1951, Marseilles, France. Musician (saxophone, flute, piano); Composer. 1 daughter. Career: Tours, France and Europe, 15 years; Concepts for jazz festivals. Recordings: 6 solo records; 10 as soloist, composer. Honours: First prize, City of Marseilles Conservatoire. Memberships: SPEDIDAM; ADAMI. Hobbies: Reading; Cooking; Loving; Music.

BOURGOIN Patrick G, b. 16 Dec 1948, Paris, France. Musician (saxophones, flute, clarinet, EWI). Musical Education: Autodidacte. Career: Has played with many French artists including Gino Vanelli in Paris and Manu Dibango on world tour, 1971-. Recordings include: With many French artists; Music for films; 1 album with Duran Duran. Honour: Nomination for Victoires de La Musique, 1988. Memberships: SACEM; SPEDIDAM. Hobbies: Sport; Photography. Address: 80 Bd Gambetta, 94130 Nogent sur Marne, France.

BOUSSAGUET Pierre-Michel-André, b. 12 Nov 1962, Albi, France. Jazz Musician (string bass player); Composer; Arranger. m. Gil Isabelle, 21 June 1992, 2 daughters. Musical Education: End of Studies Certificate. Career: with Guy Lafitte, 1986-; Tours, worldwide with artists including: Wynton Marsalis; Joe Pass; Didier Lockwood; Monty Alexander. Compositions: Impressions III, Creation for symphonic orchestra and jazz quartet. Recordings: 2 Bass hits (with Ray Brown), 1988-; P Boussaguet Quintet featuring Tom Harrell, 1992. Memberships: SACEM; UMJ. Hobbies: Golf; Aerobatic flying; Wine tasting. Current Management: Beethoven Productions (Switzerland); Jordi Sunol (Spain). Address: 52 Rue Pierre Mourgues, 81000 Albi, France.

BOVA Jeffrey Stephen, b. 22 June 1953, District of Columbia, USA. Musician (keyboards); Composer. Musical Education: Berklee College of Music, 1971-72; Manhattan School of Music, 1972-75. Career: Musician, composer, 1975-; Assistant composer, arranger, Herbie Hancock, 1987-88; Cyndi Lauper, 1987-89; Ryuichi Sakamoto, 1988-89; Musician, composer, Distance, 1988-. Compositions: Composer, arranger, film soundtracks: Colors, 1989; The Handmaid's Tale, 1990; Pretty Woman, 1990. Recordings: Keyboard player on numerous albums including: The Bridge, Billy Joel, 1986; True Colors, Cyndi Lauper, 1986; Love, Aztec Camera, 1987; The Hunger, Michael Bolton, 1987; Cher, Cher, 1987; Foreign Affair, Tina Turner, 1989; Journeyman, Eric Clapton, 1989; Other recordings by Average White Band; Ian Hunter; Robert Hart; Hall and Oates; Mick Jones. Honours: Numerous Platinum discs. Membership: ASCAP.

BOVEE Bob (Robert), b. 17 Feb 1946, Omaha, Nebraska, USA. Musician (guitar, harmonica, banjo, autoharp); Singer. m. Gail A Heil, 8 Dec 1988. Education: BA, History, University of Nebraska, 1969. Career: 6 tours, Western Europe; Regular tours USA, 1971-; Iowa Public TV; Prairie Home Companion; River City Folk; Rural Route 3; Other syndicated radio shows; Festival of American Fiddle Tunes. Recordings: Pop Wagner and Bob Bovee, 1977; The Roundup, 1979; For Old Time's Sake, 1985; Behind The Times, 1986; Come All You Waddies, 1988; Rebel Voices, 1988; Come Over And See

Me, 1991; Rural Route 2, 1996. Publications: Numerous articles, reviews, American traditional music. Memberships: North American Folk Music and Dance Alliance. Hobbies: Reading; Vintage record collecting. Current Management: Self-managed. Address: Bob Bovee and Gail Heil, RT 2 Box 25, Spring Grove, MN 55974, USA.

BOWEN Lorraine, b. 31 Oct 1961, Gloucestershire, England. Musician; Performer; Songwriter. Musical Education: BMus (Hons) Surrey University. Career: Singing teacher to Billy Bragg; Played piano on National television; Songwriter for Loose Ends, BBC Radio 4; Member, group The Dinner Ladies; Writer, singer, The Lorraine Bowen Experience. Compositions: Julie Christie, Crumble Song, Bicycle Adventure, 1995. Recordings: with The Dinner Ladies: These Knees Have Seen The World, 1989; with Billy Bragg: Don't Try This At Home, 1993; with The Lorraine Bowen Experience: Greatest Hits Volume One, 1995. Memberships: Musicians' Union; PRS. Hobbies: Swimming; Coastal Walking. Current Management: Sequin Skirt Management. Address: c/o 6 Stannard Road, London E8 1DB, England.

BOWIE David (David Jones), b. 8 Jan 1947, Brixton, London, England. Singer; Actor. (1) Angela Barnet, divorced, 1 son, (2) Iman, 24 Apr 1992. Career: Solo recording artist, 1970-; Lead singer, Tin Machine, 1989-91; Actor, films, 1976-; World tours, concerts, television and radio appearances, many as Ziggy Stardust and Aladdin Sane; Performances include: Beckenham Free Festival (also organiser), 1969; Glastonbury Festival, 1971; Carnegie Hall, 1972; Royal Festival Hall, 1972; Earls Court, 1973; Madison Square Garden, 1978; Live Aid, Wembley, 1985; Dodger Stadium, Los Angeles, 1990; A Concert For Life (Freddie Mercury Tribute), 1992; Film appearances include: The Man Who Fell To Earth, 1976; Christiane F, 1980; Cat People, 1982; The Hunger, 1983; Merry Christmas Mr Lawrence, 1983; Ziggy Stardust, 1983; Labyrinth, 1986; Absolute Beginners, 1986; The Last Temptation Of Christ, 1988; Theatre includes: The Elephant Man, 1980. Recordings: Numerous solo albums include: David Bowie, 1969; The Man Who Sold The World, 1971; Hunky Dory, 1971; The Rise And Fall Of Ziggy Stardust..., 1972; Aladdin Sane, 1973; Pin-Ups, 1973; Diamond Dogs, 1974; David Live, 1974; Young Americans, 1975; Station To Station, 1976; Let's Dance, 1983; Ziggy Stardust - The Motion Picture, 1983; Scary Monsters; Outside, 1995; with Tin Machine: Tin Machine, 1989; Tin Machine II, 1991; Numerous solo hit singles include: Absolute Beginners; Ashes To Ashes; Blue Jean; China Girl; Diamond Dogs; Fashion; Jean Genie; Let's Dance; The Man Who Sold The World; Life On Mars; Rebel Rebel; Space Oddity; with Bing Crosby: Peace On Earth/Little Drummer Boy; with Mick Jagger: Dancing In The Street; with Queen: Under Pressure; Other projects include: Theme for When The Wind Blows, 1986. Honours include: Music Video Awards; Silver Clef Award for Outstanding Achievement, 1987; Ivor Novello Awards include: Outstanding Contribution To British Music, 1990; Q Magazine Inspiration Award (with Brian Eno), 1995; BRIT Award, Outstanding Contribution To Music, 1996. Current Management: Isolar Enterprises, 641 5th Avenue, Ste 22Q, New York, NY 10022, USA.

BOWIE Lester, b. 11 Oct 1941, Frederick, Maryland, USA. Musician (trumpet). m. Fontella Bass. Career: Trumpeter, R&B bands, St Louis; Involved with Association for the Advancement of Creative Musicians, Chicago; Co-founder, Art Ensemble of Chicago (AEC), 1969; Worked with Archie Shepp; David Murray; Roscoe Mitchell; Also member of groups: Brass Fantasy; Leaders; From The Root To The Source; Fela Kuti's Egypt 80. Recordings: Albums include: Gittin' To Know Y'All, 1969; Fast Last!, 1974; Rope A Dope, 1976; The 5th Power, 1978; African Children, 1978; Works, 1982; The Great Pretender, 1982; All The

Magic, 1983; Twilight Dreams, 1987; Serious Fun, 1989; My Way, 1990; The Fire This Time, 1993; with the Art Ensemble Of Chicago: Numbers 1 And 2, 1967; A Jackson In Your House, 1969; The Spiritual, 1969; Tutankhamun, 1969; People In Sorrow, 1969; With Fontella Bass, 1970; Live, 1970; Phase One, 1971; Fanfare For The Warriors, 1974; Nice Guys, 1978; Full Force, 1980; Among The People, 1981; The Third Decade, 1985; Ancient To The Future, 1987; The Alternate Express, 1989; Eda Wobu, 1991; Dreaming Of The Masters Suite, 1991; with Brass Fantasy: Live At The 6th Tokyo Music Joy '90, 1990. Membership: AACM. Address: c/o Joel Chriss and Co., 300 Mercer Street, Suite 3J, New York, NY 10003, USA.

BOWLS Richard John (Ric), b. 13 July 1950, Rantoul, Illinois, USA. Recording Engineer; Musician (violin, guitar, keyboards). Education: Graduate, University of California, Riverside. Musical Education: Private lessons from age 8; Also played in numerous orchestras. Career: Touring musician, 1975-77; Independent sound engineer, 1977-; Sound engineer, Total Expereince Records, 1986-88; Sound engineer, programmer, MIDI Studio Systems, 1988-; Technical consultant, Music Suite, 1992-; Designer, builder, various recording studios and keyboard systems; Guest speaker, lecturer on Electronic music; Owner/designer, Sendit Electronics; Recording engineer, films: Apocalypse Now; Darkman; Halloweeen; The Fog; Television credits as engineer and/or synth programming include: War & Rememberance; Knots Landing; Dallas; The Incredible Hulk; Little House On The Prairie; Wonder Woman; Love Boat; Hawaii 5-0; Moonlighting; Baywatch; Star Trek-The Next Generation; Mission Impossible; Brady Bunch; Recordings and/or live credits include: Giorgio Moroder (11 albums); Donna Summer (5 albums); Cher; Michael Nesmith; Berlin; Gap Band; Oingo Boingo; Ahmad Jamal; Yarborough And Peoples; ELO; Denice Williams; Earth Wind And Fire; The Crusaders; Frank Zappa; Stephen Stills; Barbra Streisand; George Clinton; David Bowie; Carl Palmer; Jean Luc-Ponty; Aretha Franklin; Peter Frampton; Sly Stone; Tom Jones; Lalo Shifrin; Cityscrapes, film score. Honours: Oscar, Apocalypse Now; Platinum disc, Donna Summer; 2 Gold discs, Cher; Grammy Award, Best Music Video, Michael Nesmith; Emmy Award, Golden Globe, People's Choice Award, all for War & Rememberance, 1989. Membership: NARAS. Current Management: Neil Scotti and Associates. Address: 1722 Rogers Place #25E, Burbank, CA 91504-3668, USA.

BOWMAN Dave, b. 21 Nov 1951, Greensboro, North Carolina, USA. Musician (guitar, keyboard, violin, mandolin). m. 27 Mar 1981, Janet Marie Vanek Bowman, 2 sons, 2 daughters. Education: 1 year, University of North Carolina, Greensboro. Musical Education: Private study from age 8 to the present. Career: Worked with Covenant Players, Los Angeles, musician, actor, singer, 1977-79; Since worked with numerous bands in Arizona, California, Utah; Solo work, Arizona, New Mexico, North Carolina. Recordings: Produced recordings of own music: Songs From Lost Mountain Canyon; On A Christmas So Long Ago. Membership: Gospel Music Association. Hobbies: Hiking; Camping; Fishing; Hunting. Current Management: Bowman Music Services. Address: PO Box 30944, Flagstaff, AZ 86003, USA.

BOWN Alan, b. 21 July 1942, Slough, Berkshire, England. Musician (trumpet); Manager. m. Jean, 7 Mar 1964, 1 son, 1 daughter. Education: S/M/RAF School of Music; RAF bandsman, 1956-60. Career: Started playing with The John Barry Seven; Recorded 5 albums over 10 years with own band The Alan Bown; Tours with: The Who; Yes; Moody Blues; Cream; Television appearances: Top Of The Pops; Ready

Steady Go; Old Grey Whistle Test. Recordings: All compositions on own albums: Live At The Marquee, 1963 (first album); Outward Bown; Listen. Membership: PRS. Hobbies: Music; Bands. Address: 71 Shaggy Calf Lane, Slough, Berks SL2 5HN, England.

BOWN Andrew Steven, b. 27 Mar 1946, City Of London, England. Musician (keyboards, bass guitar, guitar, harmonica); Vocalist. m. Caroline Attard, 4 June 1971, 1 son, 1 daughter. Musical Education: Piano, Grade 6; Recorder to Grade 6. Career: Musician with: The Herd; Status Quo; Pink Floyd; Appearances include: Live Aid; Knebsworth Festival; Prince of Wales Trust; Last Tattoo in Berlin for HM Queen. Compositions: with Status Quo: Burning Bridges; Come On You Reds; Whatever You Want. Recordings: The Herd, Paradise Lost, 1968; The Final Cut, Pink Floyd, 1983; All albums with Status Quo, 1970-; Recordings with other artistes include: Jerry Lee Lewis; Roger Waters; Tim Hardin; Lesley Duncan; Johnny Halliday; Paul McCartney; Wendy James; Dusty Springfield. Honours: Silver Clef, 1981; Ivor Novello Award, 1983; BRIT Award, 1991. Memberships: Musicians' Union; PRS; Equity. Hobbies: Green bowling; Wine; Cooking. Current Management: David Walker, Handle Artistes Ltd. Address: 1 Albion Place, Galena Road, Hammersmith, London W6 0QT, England.

BOX Mick, b. 8 June 1947, Walthamstow, London, England. Vocalist; Musician (guitar); Career: Founder member, UK rock band, Uriah Heep, 1970-; Extensive international tours; First western heavy rock group to perform in Moscow, 1987. Albums: Very 'Eavy, Very 'Umble, 1970; Salisbury, 1971; Look At Yourself, 1971; Demons And Wizards, 1972; The Magician's Birthday, 1972; Uriah Heep Live, 1973; Swwet Freedom, 1973; Wonderworld, 1974; Return To Fantasy, 1975; High And Mighty, 1976; The Best Of Uriah Heep, 1976; Firefly, 1977; Innocent Victim, 1978; Fallen Angel, 1978; Conquest, 1980; Abnominog, 1982; Head First, 1983; Equator, 1985; Anthology, 1986; Live In Moscow, 1988; Raging Silence, 1989; The Uriah Heep Story, 1990; Still 'Eavy, Still Proud, 1990; Different World, 1991; Rarities, 1991; Sea Of Light, 1995.

BOXCAR WILLIE (Lecil Travis Martin), b. 1 Sept 1931, Sterritt, Dallas, Texas, USA. Country Singer; Musician. Career: Recording artist as Marty Martin, 1950s-1975; Billed as Boxcar Willie, 1975-; Concerts include: Grand Ole Opry, 1979; Wembley Country Music Festival, 1979, 1980; Film appearance: Sweet Dreams (film about Patsy Cline). Compositions: Several hundred include: Wabash Cannonball; Kaw-Liga; London Leaves; Wreck Of The Old 97. Recordings: Numerous albums include: Boxcar Willie, 1976; Daddy Was A Railroad Man, 1978; King Of The Road, 1980; Last Train To Heaven, 1982; Live In Concert, 1984; Jesus Makes House Calls, 1988; Spirit Of America, 1991; Several compilations; Other recordings include: with Roy Acuff: Fireball Mail; Streamline Cannonball; with Willie Nelson: Boxcar's My Home; Song Of Songs; Ramblin' In My Shoes, with Hank Williams Jr; We Made Memories, with Penny De Haven; Good Hearted Woman, with Gunter Gabriel. Honours: Music City News, Most Promising Vocalist, 1981. Hobby: Railways. Current Management: The Bobby Roberts Co Inc., PO Box 3007, Hendersonville, TN 37077, USA.

BOY Chrissy (Chris Foreman), b. 8 Aug 1956, London, England. Musician (guitar, keyboards). m. (1) 1976, 1 son, (2) 1992, 1 son. Musical Education: Self-taught. Career: Founder member, group Madness; Numerous appearances on television programmes including Top Of The Pops; Band split in 1987; Became The Madness until 1989; Formed group The Nutty Boys, releasing album Crunch!, 1990. Recordings: with Madness: Baggy Trousers; Our House; Yesterdays Men; with The Nutty Boys: Magic

Carpet; It's OK I'm A Policeman; Pop My Top. Honours: Gold discs; Ivor Novello Award, as songwriter, Our House. Memberships: PRS; VPL; Musicians' Union. Hobbies: Films; Books. Address: c/o PO Box 3087, London NW5 3DZ, England.

BOY GEORGE (George O'Dowd), b. 14 June 1961, Eltham, Kent, England. Singer; Songwriter. Career: Singer, Bow Wow Wow (under name Lieutenant Lush); Founder member, singer, Culture Club, 1982-89; Solo artiste, 1987-; Numerous tours worldwide, including Artists Against Apartheid, 1988. Compositions: Numerous collaborations with John Themis. Recordings: Albums: with Culture Club: Kissing To Be Clever, 1982; Colour By Numbers, 1987; From Luxury To Heartache, 1989; Solo albums: Sold, 1987; Tense Nervous Headache, 1988; High Hat, 1989; Martyr Mantras, 1991; Cheapness And Beauty, 1995; Hit singles with Culture Club: Do You Really Want To Hurt Me; Karma Chameleon; Church Of The Poisoned Mind; Solo singles: Il Adore; The Crying Game (film theme) with Pet Shop Boys, 1992. Publications: Take It Like A Man (autobiography). Current Management: Wedge Music, 63 Grosvenor Street, London W1X 9DA, England.

BOYLAN John Patrick, b., 21 Mar 1941, New York, USA. Record Producer. Education: BA, Bard College. Career: Executive Producer, CBS Records, 1976-80; Vice President, CBS, 1980-86; President, Great Eastern Music Co, 1986-. Recordings: As producer, film soundtracks: Nightshift; Urban Cowboy; Footloose; Born On The 4th Of July; The Simpsons Sing The Blues. Honours: Numerous Platinum and Gold discs. Memberships: NARAS; AFTRA; AFofM. Address: Great Eastern Music Co, 5750 Wilshire Boulevard, Los Angeles, CA 90036, USA.

BOZIC Petar Vedran, b. 21 May 1947, Zadar, Croatia. Musician (Guitars, Piano, Vocals, Harp). m. Majstorovic-Bozic Nada, 9 September 1972, 1 son. Education: Studied Mathematics; Self-taught guitar, bass, harp; Piano, Primary Musical School, 6 years, Secondary Musical School, 4 years. Career: Played piano, amateur groups, 1963; Played guitar professionally, 1965; Played in famous Croatian groups: Gresnici, Roboti, Wheels of Fire, MI, BP Convention, Time, Boomerang, Parni Valjak; Countless stage, TV, radio appearances; Toured all over Europe; Studio Musician, Telephon Blues Band (formerly Call 66). Compositions: Several. Recordings: Studio Musician, recorded over 200 LP's or CD's, 1972-. Membership: HGU. Hobby: Ski Sport Travelling. Address: Livadarskiput 3, 10000 Zagreb, Croatia.

BRACCINI Eric, b. 22 July 1963, Pau, France. Musician (piano, trombone, vibraphone, Hammond organ). m. Florence Lacarce, 4 June 1993, 1 daughter. Education: Doctorate of Oceanology. Musical Education: Graduate of the Conservatory of Pau (Classical). Career: Backing pianist, C Braccini Orchestra, 1976-82; The Gam's, 1983-88; Soloist, 1988-92; Eric Braccini Trio (Jazz), 1993-95. Recordings: Just For Barbara (Jazz), 1995. Membership: UMJ (Jazz Musicians' Union). Hobbies: Funboarding; Skiing. Current Management: Jazzoduc Label. Address: 18 Avenue de l'Eglise St Joseph, 64000 Pau, France.

BRADFIELD Marian, b. 31 Dec 1953, Waterford, Ireland. Singer; Songwriter; Musician (guitar). m. Robert Bradfield, 17 Aug 1974, 2 daughters. Musical Education: Piano, Primary Grade, First Class Honours; Guitar, self-taught. Career: Began career with Young Generation Choir, Waterford; Formed own group Peace; Performed at George Doherty's Folk Club, Donegal; Support concerts with: Mary Black; The Fureys; Davey Arthur; Concert with Sharon Shannon and Mick Hanley, Forum, Waterford, 1994; Performed with Altan, Belfast Festival; Showcase in Austin, Texas; Numerous television

appearances include: Kenny Live, RTE; Bibi Show; Anderson On The Box, BBC; Mike Moloney; Alan Corcoran; Numerous radio appearances on FM 2, BBC Ulster and local radio (Christmas Eve Special). Recordings: Albums: Marian, 1993; Tonight Is Just For Us, 1994. Honours: Hot Press and Smithwick's Nomination, Best Solo Performer, 1993; Voted one of Ireland's Top 10 singers, Hot Press Readers, 1993; IRMA Award Nomination, Tonight Is Just For Us, 1995.

BRADLEY Owen, b. 21 Oct 1915, Westmoreland, Tennessee, USA. Musician (piano, guitar, harmonica); Arranger; Record Producer; Recording Studio Owner. Career: Musician, Ted Weem's dance band; Musical director, orchestra leader, WSM radio, Nashville, 1940-58; Built own recording studio, Nashville, 1952; Other studios include: Quonset hut studio, 1956; Bradley's Barn, 1965; Developed the Nashville Sound with Chet Atkins; Country A&R director, Decca Records, 1958-68; Worked with: Patsy Cline; Red Foley; Brenda Lee; Loretta Lynn. Recordings: Albums include: Christmas Time; Strauss Waltzes; Lazy River; Singin' In The Rain; Cherished Roses; Bandstand Hop; Big Guitar; Paradise Island; Producer for artists including: Ernest Tubb; Kitty Wells; Buddy Holly; Gene Vincent; Johnny Cash; Marty Robbins; k d lang; As session musician (with Chet Atkins): Heartbreak Hotel, Elvis Presley. Honour: Inducted into Country Music Hall Of Fame, 1974.

BRADLEY Stuart, b. 23 Sept 1965, London, England. Musician (6 string fretless bass guitar); Teacher. m. Elizabeth Allen, 1 Apr 1995. Musical Education: Private study with father, Desmond Bradley, aged 4-16 years; Currently studying for LTCL, Trinity College of Music; Studying Composition with John Thomas. Career: Major tours with Take That; Gary Glitter; Roger Taylor; Television and radio appearances include: The Word; 01-For-London; 6 O'Clock News; The Mix, Radio 5; Principal bass instructor, Academy of Contemporary Music until 1996; Member of Examiners Panel, Rockschool. Recordings: Why Can't I Wake Up With You?, Take That; Happiness, Roger Taylor; Piaf, Elaine Page; Up And Over, Edwin Starr. Memberships: Musicians' Union; PAMRA; Rockschool Ltd. Address: 65 Spring Road, Lower Feltham, Middlesex TW13 7JA, England.

BRADY Paul, b. 19 May 1947, Strabane, County Tyrone, Northern Ireland. Folk Singer; Songwriter; Musician (multi-instrumentalist). Career: Member, The Kult; Planxty; Duo with Andy Irvine; Solo artiste, 1978-; Tours, including support to Dire Straits; Eric Clapton; Recent performance, Cambridge Folk Festival, 1995. Compositions: Songs include: Crazy Dreams (recorded by Roger Chapman, Dave Edmunds); Night Hunting Time (recorded by Santana); Steel Claw; Paradise Is Here (both recorded by Tina Turner); Film soundtrack, Cal, with Mark Knopfler; 2 tracks, Luck Of The Draw, Bonnie Raitt, 1991. Recordings: Albums: Andy Irvine/Paul Brady, 1976; The High Part Of The Road (with Tommy Peoples), 1976; Welcome Here Kind Stranger, 1978; Hard Station, 1981; True For You, 1983; Full Moon, 1984; Back To The Centre, 1986; Molloy, Brady, Peoples (with Matt Molloy, Tommy Peoples), 1986; Primitive Dance, 1987; Paradise Is Here, 1989; Trick Or Treat, 1991; Spirits Colliding, 1995; Singles include: Crazy Dreams (Number 1, Ireland); Theme music, UK television series, Faith In The Future, 1995. Current Management: c/o Ed Bicknell, Damage Management, 16 Lambton Place, London W11 2SH, England.

BRADY Philip, b. 4 Mar 1939, Liverpool, England. Singer; Musician (guitar). m. Barbara Ann Shaw, 6 Mar 1942, 1 son, 1 daughter. Musical Education: Self-taught. Career: Tommy Collins tour, Bill Clifton Show, 1963; Ernest Tubb Record Shop, Porter Waggonmaster Show, 1968; Jeannie

Sealey, Hank Cochran tour, Germany; First Country Music Awards Show, Wembley Stadium; Bill Anderson, Loretta Lynn, Conway Twitty, George Hamilton IV; Buck Owens Tour, Liverpool Empire; London Palladium, Country Meets Folk, 1969; Hank Snow, Willie Nelson tour, Liverpool Empire, Bellevue Manchester, Lyceum Ballroom London, 1970; Nightride BBC; Slim Whitman Tour, all ABC theatres nationwide, 1972; Tours: Germany; Italy; Norway; Netherlands; Saudi Arabia. Recordings: Singles: American Sailor At The Cavern/Sidetracked; Little Rosa/One More Time; Rambling Boy; Lonesome For You; Let The Whole World Sing It With Me; Brady Country; Songs Of Nashville; A Little Bit Country; Live At Gunton Hall; Bobby McGee and Other Favourites; 7 albums. Honour: BCMA Award, presented by Roy Orbison, 1970. Membership: Equity. Hobbies: Fishing; Reading. Current Management: Mike Hughes Entertainment. Address: 96 Bold Street, Liverpool, England.

BRAGG Billy, b. 20 Dec 1957. Singer; Songwriter; Musician (guitar). Recordings: Life's A Riot With Spy vs Spy, 1983; Brewing Up With Billy Bragg, 1984; Talking With The Taxman About Poetry, 1986; Back To Basics, 1987; Workers Playtime, 1988; The Internationale, 1990; Don't Try This At Home, 1991. Current Management: Sincere Management. Address: 421 Harrow Road, London W10 4RD, England.

BRAKE Marita, b. Springfield, Illinois, USA. Singer; Songwriter; Musician (guitar). m. Gil Moore, 11 Sept 1982. Education: BS, Theatre, Illinois State University. Musical Education: Private lessons, seminars, workshops. Career: Community concerts tour; Carnegie Hall; Canterbury Festival, Canterbury, England; Television broadcasts on BBC and PBS. Composition: The Marita Brake In Concert Song Book, 1997. Recordings: Albums: The Road I Took To You, 1989; Gypsy Moon, 1996. Publications: Contributor of articles in magazines and reviews. Honours: Performance for Presidential Inauguration, 1997; Woman of Distinction Award for Excellence in the Arts. Memberships: Nashville Songwriters Association; Folk Alliance; Gospel Music Association. Hobbies: Writing; Hiking; Redesigning vintage clothes. Current Management: Community Concerts Inc, New York City. Address: PO Box 501, Normal, IL 61761, USA.

BRAMERIE Thomas, b. 18 Sept 1965, Bergerac, France. Musician (acoustic bass). m. Edith Vuillon, 22 Aug 1992. Musical Education: Various private lessons; Self-taught. Career: Sideman with various international jazz musicians in Europe, 1987-; Played with: Chet Baker; Toots Thielemans; Johnny Griffin; Frank Wess; Tom Harrell; Joshua Redman; European tour, with Jimmy Scott, 1994; Festival appearances: Nice; Montreux; Newport; Northsea; Permanent member, Belmondo Quintet; Michele Hendricks Quintet; Dédé Ceccarelli Quartet; Regular member of Dee Dee Bridgewater's Band, 1997; Several world tours, Japan, Europe, South America, USA, Canada. Recordings: Live In Paris, Teddy Edwards Quartet, 1994; For All Friends, Belmondo Quintet, 1994; From The Heart, Dédé Ceccarelli Quartet, 1996; Ted Nash European Quartet, 1996. Address: 641 East 11th Street #4A, New York, NY 10009, USA.

BRAMLEY Simon T, b. 7 July 1965, Leicester, England. Musician (electric six-string bass). Education: Judge Meadow College; Charles Keene College, Leicester. Musical Education: Played and studied with many local jazz musicians. Career: Has toured with Strop (Acid Jazz Band), Yamanu (Be Bop/Modern) and Afro-Elements (jazz funk); Mr Gone (jazz funk); Radio sessions at Pebble Mill with Yamanu; TV appearances with Strop; 3 Weeks pantomime under John Taylor at Little Theatre, Leicester. Recordings: Numerous recordings with Strop and

Yamanu; Solo as Mr Gone: Looking at the Future in the Rear View Mirror. Memberships: Musicians' Union; Leicester Jazz Alliance; Co-organiser of jazz festivals with Unwind Your Mind Collective; Phoenix Arts and 9-Theatre. Hobbies: Travel; Comedy; Composition; Hitchhiking. Current Management: Internal Bass Records, PO Box 445, Chobham, Surrey GU24 8YQ, England. Address: Flat 2, Sparrow Lodge, 356-360 Humberstone Road, Leicester LE5 0SA, England.

BRANCH Alan, b. 22 Jan 1962, London, England. Sound Engineer; Musician (guitar); Producer; Programmer. m. 4 May 1988, 2 daughters. Education: City & Guilds, and Advanced City & Guilds Carpentry, Lime Grove College. Musical Education: Goldsmiths University, General Musicianship. Career: Live, session guitarist; Student; Tape operator at Topic Records; Engineer at The Works Studio; Engineer at Roundhouse Studios; Chief Engineer, Roundhouse Recording Studios. Recordings: Artists: M People; De La Soul; D:Ream; Jamiroquai; Living Colour; Ruby Turner; Boy George; Omar; On U Sound; Adrian Sherwood; Primal Scream; Lighthouse Family; Eternal; Simply Red; Depeche Mode; Various other artists. Membership: Musicians' Union. Hobbies: Playing music; Family; Computers. Current Management: Self managed. Address: 69 Lateward Road, Brentford, Middlesex TW8 0PL, England.

BRAND Oscar, b. 7 Feb 1920, Winnipeg, Manitoba, Canada. Composer; Folk Singer; Musician (guitar); Writer. m. Karen Grossman, 14 June 1970, 3 sons, 1 daughter. Education: BS Brooklyn College, 1942; Laureate History, Fairfield University, 1974; Musical Education: Self-taught. Career: Presenter, Folksong Festival, New York Public Radio, (oldest continuous radio show in history), 1945-; On credits of 75 documentary films; Hundreds of radio and television shows include: Host, Let's Sing Out, Canadian series; Music Director, Sunday Show, NBC; Exploring; Treasure Chest; Host, composer, First Look; Spirit of '76, NBC; Performer for childen on television, records and film; Member, advisory panel which created television programme Sesame Street; Curator of Songwriters Hall of Fame; President, Gypsy Hill Music; Lecturer on Dramatic Writing, Hofstra University, Hempstead, New York. Compositions include: Songs for: Doris Day; Ella Fitzgerald; Harry Belafonte; The Smothers Brothers; Mormon Tabernacle Choir; Scripted, scored ballets for Agnes DeMille and Michael Bennett; Commercials include: Maxwell House; Oldsmobile; Log Cabin; Rival; Songs in films: The Fox; Sybil; The Long Riders; Blue Chips; Music for: In White America; Score for: How To Steal An Election; Music and lyrics with Paul Nassau for Broadway shows: A Joyful Noise; The Education of Hyman Kaplan; Wrote, scored Kennedy Center's Bicentenniel musical, Sing America Sing; 2 new musicals in progress: Thunder Bay; Fun And Games. Recordings: Over 90 albums, latest being: I Love Cats, 1994; Get A Dog, 1995. Publications: Author, several best-selling books including: When I First Came To This Land; The Ballad Mongers (autobiography); Party Songs; Singing Holidays; Bawdy Songs; Songs Of '76; Western Guitar; Celebrate; Bridge Of Hope. Honours: Laureate, Fairfield University, 1972; Peabody Awards, 1982, 1996; Hon. PhD, University of Winnipeg, 1989; Radio Pioneers of America, 1991; Awards for film credits: Venice, Edinburgh, Golden Reel, Valley Forge, Freedoms Foundation; Scholastic; Golden Lion; Peabody; Ohio State; Edison; Emmy. Memberships: SAG; AFTRA; ACTRA; Dramatists Guild; AFofM. Hobbies: Sailing; Carpentry. Address: 141 Baker Hill, Great Neck, NY 11023, USA.

BRAUN Rick, b. 6 July 1955, Allentown, Pennsylvania, USA. Musician (trumpet); Composer; Producer. m. Laura Hunter, 18 Oct 1992. Musical Education: Eastman School of Music, Rochester, New York. Career; Montreux

Jazz Festival, 1979; 3 world tours with Rod Stewart, 1989-90; 1991-92; 1995; Tonight Show, 1991; Featured soloist with Sade, 1994. Compositions: Co-writer, Here With Me, REO Speedwagon, 1989. Recordings: Intimate Secrets, 1993; Christmas Present, 1994; Nightwalk, 1994; Beat Street, 1995; Featured soloist; Album, Tina Turner, 1994; Born A Rebel, Tom Petty, 1984. Honour: BMI Top 100 Songs Of The Year, Here With Me, 1990. Memberships: BMI; AFofM. Hobbies: Tennis; Skiing; Billiards; Basketball; Woodworking. Current Management: Chapman & Co Management. Address: PO Box 5549, Santa Monica, CA 90409, USA.

BRAXTON Anthony, b. 4 June 1945, Chicago, Illinois, USA. Jazz Musician (alto saxophone, clarinet). Musical Education: Wilson Junior College. Career: Played clarinet and alto saxophone, US Army; Joined musician's co-operative, AACM, Chicago, 1966; Formed own group, The Creative Construction Company (CCC), 1968; Co-founder, Circle (with Chick Corea, Dave Holland, Barry Altschul), 1970; Played in France with various European improvisers; Member, Globe Unity Orchestra; Performed at Derek Bailey's Company Festivals; Performed with own quartet; Duo with drummer Max Roach, 1970s; Teacher, Wesleyan College, Connecticut, 1980s-. Compositions: Approximately 400 include: Series of 12 operas, Trillium; Quartet (London), 1985; Quartet (Birmingham), 1985; Quartet (Willisau), 1991. Recordings: Over 70 albums as bandleader; Appeared on numerous other recordings by artistes including Joseph Jarman; George Lewis; Max Roach; Derek Bailey; Muhal Richard Abrams; CCC; ROVA Saxophone Quartet; London Jazz Composers Orchestra. Publications: Tri-axium Writings, 1985; Composition Notes (5 vols), 1988.

BRAXTON Toni, b. 1969, Philadelphia, Pennsylvania, USA. Vocalist. Career: Member of female vocal group with sisters Tamar, Trin and Tavanda, 1990; Solo recording artiste. Recordings include: Solo albums: Toni Braxton, 1993, Secrets, 1996. Hit singles: Unbreak My Heart; You're Making Me High. Address: c/o Stiefel Entertainment, Suite 6120, 9255 Sunset Blvd, Los Angeles, CA 90069, USA.

BRAZIER Graham Philip (The Brazz), b. 6 May 1952, Auckland, New Zealand. Vocalist; Composer; Musician (guitar, saxophone, harmonica). m. Alexandra, 13 Nov 1993, 1 son, 1 daughter. Musical Education: Self-taught. Career: Appearances, national New Zealand and Australian television on video clips, interviews, Film: Queen City Rocker; Played support to Dire Straits; Eurythmics; Fleetwood Mac; Bryan Ferry; Marianne Faithfull; Canned Heat; Bo Diddley; Gerry Harrison; Many major Australian acts. Recordings: Albums include: 4 Hello Sailor studio albums; 2 solo albums; 1 live album; Numerous compilations, EPs and singles. Honours: Vocalist of Year; Best Song; Runner-up for APRA Silver Scroll 3 times. Membership: APRA (voting member). Hobbies: Reading; Collecting books; Antique curios. Current Management: James Rowe (Strawberry Fields), PO Box, Raglan, New Zealand. Address: 13 Taupata Street, Mt Eden, Auckland 3, New Zealand.

BRAZIER Roy, b. 28 Jan 1965, Walthamstow, London, England. Bandleader; Musician (saxophone, blues harp); Vocalist. Musical Education: Self-taught, alto, tenor saxophones, blues harmonica. Career: Founder member, Darktown, 1987, for parties, functions; Performed for Williams Grand Prix Engineering; Concerts supporting Mud; The Troggs; Desmond Dekker; Jools Holland; Television and video appearances: Ridin' High, Robert Palmer (full length album video); Television commercial for News Of The World, Greystoke Productions; Performed 309 gigs, 1994; Television advertisement for Cross and Blackwell, 1996;

Television appearance on Top Gear, BBC TV, 1997. Recordings: with Darktown: Blues, Jazz and Other Animals. Honours: Voted in Top Ten Blues Harp players, UK, 1995; Certificate of Excellence for Blues Harmonica at the European Harmonica Festival, Germany, 1996. Membership: Musicians' Union. Hobbies: Surfing; Painting; Building classic cars. Address: 227 Monks Walk, Buntingford, Hertfordshire SG9 9DY, England.

BRECHIN Sandy, b. 20 April 1969, Edinburgh, Scotland. Musician; Composer. Education: MA, Languages, Edinburgh University; Private Piano and Accordion Lessons; Selftaught Guitar and Banjo. Career: Many Appearances on BBC Radio Scotland and BBC Television; Scottish Folk Festival Tour with Phil Cunningham and Aly Bain, 1996; Also European Radio and Television Appearances on the Lottery Show Live, 1997; Toured Scandinavia, France, Italy, Germany, Holland. Recordings: Burach - The Weird Set, 1995; Se Elyhou - The First Caul, 1995; Solo Album, Out of His Box, 1996; Born Tired, 1997; Do-re-mi, 1997. Memberships: Musicians Union; MCPS; PRS. Hobbies: Skiing; Diving; Weightlifting; Cooking. Current Management: Tarla, Scotland. Address: 5 The Square, Kirkliston, West Lothian EH29 9AX, Scotland.

BRECKER Michael, b. 29 Mar 1949, Philadelphia, Pennsylvania, USA. Musician (saxophone, horns); Bandleader. Career: Member, Billy Cobham's band, 1970s; Founder, group Dreams; The Becker Brothers (with Randy Brecker); Bandleader, 1987-; Also played with Horace Silver; James Taylor; Yoko Ono; David Sancious; Prolific session musician. Recordings: Albums: with Billy Cobham: Crosswinds, 1974; Total Eclipse, 1974; Shabazz, 1975; A Funky Thide to Sings, 1975; Inner Conflicts, 1978; with The Brecker Brothers: The Brecker Brothers, 1975; Back To Back, 1976; Don't Stop The Music, 1977; Heavy Metal Be-Bop, 1978; Detente, 1980; Straphangin', 1981; Blue Montreux, 1989; Collection, Vol I, 1990; Vol II, 1992; Big Idea, 1992; Return Of The Brecker Brothers, 1992; Out Of The Loop, 1994; Solo albums: City Scape, 1983; Mike Brecker, 1987; Don't Try This At Home, 1989; Now You See It, Now You Don't, 1991; with Randy Brecker: Toe To Toe, 1990; In The Idiom, 1991; Score, 1993; with Herbie Hancock: The New Standard, 1996; Also recorded with numerous artists including: Dreams; Steps Ahead; Charles Mingus; John Lennon; Eric Clapton; Paul Simon; Pat Metheny; John Abercrombie. Current Management: Depth of Field Management, 1501 Broadway, Ste 1304, New Tork, NY 10036, USA.

BRECKER Randy (Randall Edward), b. 27 Nov 1945, Philadelphia, Pennsylvania, USA. Musician (trumpet, saxophone, horns); Arranger. m. Eliane Elias, 1 daughter. Education: Indiana University, 1963-66. Musical Education: Classical trumpet studies at school. Career: Professional trumpeter, 1966-; Prolific freelance musician; Played with: Blood, Sweat And Tears; Horace Silver; Art Blakey; Clark Terry; Janis Joplin; Stevie Wonder; James Brown; Larry Coryell; Billy Cobham; Charles Mingus; Lew Tabakin; Bandleader/arranger, 1975-; Formed Dreams with brother Michael; The Brecker Brothers (also with Michael); Leader, Randy Brecker Band; Arranger for numerous artists include: George Benson; Diana Ross; Chaka Khan; Clinician, National Association of Jazz Educators. Recordings: Albums: with The Brecker Brothers: The Brecker Brothers, 1975; Back To Back, 1976; Don't Stop The Music, 1977; Heavy Metal Be-Bop, 1978; Detente, 1980; Straphangin', 1981; Blue Montreux, 1989; Collection, Vol I, 1990; Collection, Vol 2, 1992; Big Idea, 1992; Return Of The Brecker Brothers, 1992; Out Of The Loop, 1994; Solo albums: Toe To Toe, 1989; In The Idiom, 1991; Live At Sweet Basil, 1992; Score, 1993; with Horace Silver: You Gotta Take A Little Love, 1969; with Billy Cobham: Crosswinds, 1974; Total

Eclipse, 1974; Shabazz, 1975; A Funky Thide To Sings, 1975; Inner Conflicts, 1978; with Charles Mingus: Me, Myself And Eye, 1978; Also on albums by numerous artists including: George Benson; Carla Bley; Eric Clapton; Dire Straits; Billy Joel; Elton John; Rickie Lee Jones; B B King; Manhattan Transfer; John Mayall; Lou Reed; Diana Ross; Todd Rungren; Carly Simon; Paul Simon; Bruce Springsteen; Steely Dan; James Taylor; Tina Turner; Luther Vandross; Steve Winwood; Frank Zappa. Membership: AFofM. Current Management: Depth Of Field Management. Address: 1501 Broadway, Suite 1304, New York, NY 10036, USA.

BRENNAN Dave, b. 24 Dec 1936, Rotherham, England. Bandleader; Musician (banjo, guitar, parade drums); Vocalist; Master of Ceremonies; Broadcaster. m. (1) 2 sons, (2) Val Hudson, 28 Sept 1996. Education: CEng; M I MechE. Career: Own jazz programme, BBC Radio Sheffield, 17 years; Bandleader, 36 years; Leader, Jubilee Jazz Band; Jubilee New Orleans Brass Band; Heritage New Orleans Brass Band; Toured widely including: USSR (twice), Russia and Siberia; Toured Europe with the International Jazz Band, 1997. Recordings: Take Me To The Mardi Gras; Rags, Stomps And Dreamy Melodies; Inn Swinger; Amazing Grace; Bouncing Around; Let's Get This Show On The Road with Alton Purnell; Swinging At Swinden, with Louis Nelson; International Jazz Band; Several recordings with Chris Blount Jazz Band and Ken Colyer. Memberships: Musicians' Union; MI Mech E; Labour Party; SIMA. Hobbies: Record collecting; New Orleans music; Opera; Great singers of the past; Cricket. Address: "Tanglewood", Marcliff Lane, Listerdale, Rotherham S66 2AZ, England.

BRENNAN John Wolf, b. 1954, Dublin, Ireland. Pianist; Composer. Education: Musicology, Film and Literature, University of Fribourg; Piano, Lucerne Conservatory; Organ, Conducting, Academy of School and Church Music; Composition with Karl Berger, CMS Woodstock/New York and James Wilson, Royal Irish Academy of Music, Dublin; Masterclasses with Edison Denisov, Ennio Morricone and Klaus Huber. Career: Member, Swiss composer's group, Groupe Lacroix; Concert tours in Western and Eastern Europe (Russia, Ukraine, Estonia, Hungary), Japan and USA; Performing with international quartet, Pago Libre, with Arkady Shilkloper, Tscho Theissing and Daniele Patumi; Trio Aurealis, with Robert Dick and D Patumi; Minute Age, with Margrit Rieben and Reto Senn; Pipelines, with Hans Kennel; Shooting Stars and Traffic Lights, with Alex Cline, John Voirol, Theissing and D Patumi; Conducted and written for major orchestras. Compositions include: Inside and Outside; Euratorium; Bestiarium; PaniConversations, works for choir; Epithalamium; Chamber Music; Alef Bet - an Oriental Peace Piece; A Golly Gal's Way to Galway Bay; Nearly Charming. Recordings include: Minute Age, 1997; The Science of Sonic Poetry/Entropology, 1998; Subsculpture, 1998; Through the Ear of a Raindrop, 1998; Nisajo, 1998; Projects: Nitty-Gritty Ditties and Nevergreens; Woodwind; Brass Breeze. Honours: Werkjahr, Dienemann Foundation, Lucerne, 1989; Förderpreis, SARNA Jubilee Foundation, 1991; Stipendium of BINZ 39 Art Foundation Zurich, 1993; Prize, National Flute Association, USA, 1993; Award, Jubilee Foundation of Union Bank of Switzerland, 1994; Miglior Disco Del Anno, Jazzpoll of MusicaJazz, Milano, 1994; Album of the Year, Jazzthetik, 1996; Invitation by Hindemith Foundation to write octet, 1997; London Fellowship, Zuger Kulturstiftung Landis & Gyr, 1997. Address: Hofmattstrasse 5, CH-6353 Weggis, Luzern, Switzerland.

BRENNAN Lizzie, b. 12 April 1961, Southampton, England. Singer; Songwriter; Occasional Musician (Guitar). Education: Adelaide College of Music, South Australia, 6 months. Career: Backing Singer and Lead Singer, trios and bands in Perth and Melbourne, Australia, 1986-94; Soloist, World Expo 1988 Brisbane, 4 months; Live television appearance, ITV Telethon, TVS/Meridian, May 1990. Compositions: Never Enough; Into My Life; Not Going Anywhere; View From the Woods; Talk to Me; Need For You. Recordings: Statues in the Park, CD album, 1995; Maxine; Im Not Alone; Live in Mind. Honour: Invited to perform at Composer Exposer, 1997. Membership: Australasian Performing Right Association. Hobbies: Theatre; Films; Bushwalking; Swimming. Current Management: Lavender Music Colonial Surfside, Pacific Highway, Woolgoolga, NSW 2450, Australia.

BRENNAN Maire (Maire Ni Bhraonain), b, 4 Aug 1952, Dublin, Ireland. Vocalist; Musician (harp). Career: Founder member, singer, harpist, folk group Clannad, 1970-; Regular Irish and international tours include: Germany, 1975; US, 1979; Europe, 1983; UK, 1986, 1991; Concerts include: Cambridge Folk Festival, 1991; Scottish Fleadh, Glasgow, 1992; Fleadh '92, Finsbury Park, London, 1992; Royal Albert Hall, 1993; Television includes: Clannad In Donegal, CH4 documentary, 1991; Hostage - Tribute To Brian Keenan, BBC, 1991; The Tonight Show, NBC, 1993. Compositions include: Television and film music: Harry's Game, ITV, 1982 (also used in film soundtrack Patriot Games and Volkswagen television commercial); Robin Of Sherwood, ITV, 1984; The Atlantic Realm, BBC1, 1988. Recordings: Albums: Magical Ring, 1983; Legend, 1984; Macalla, 1986; Sirius, 1987; Atlantic Realm, 1989; Pastpresent, 1989; Clannad The Collection, 1989; Anam, 1993; Banba, 1993; Solo album: Maire, 1992; Singles include: Theme From Harry's Game, 1982; Robin (The Hooded Man), 1984; In A Lifetime, 1986; Both Sides Now, with Paul Young (used in film soundtrack Switch), 1991. Honours: Ivor Novello Award, Best Theme From A Television Or Radio Production, Theme From Harry's Game, 1983; British Academy Award, Best Soundtrack Of Year, Robin Of Sherwood, 1985. Current Management: Upfront Management, 4 Windmill Lane, Dublin 2, Ireland.

BRESLIN Paul, b. 27 June 1950. Singer; Composer; Lyricist; Musician (guitar). m. Cathy Liegeois, 14 Feb 1989, 1 son. Education: Reed College. Musical Education: Self-taught. Career: Bandleader, on stage and live television, for Percy Sledge, 1994-95; Bandleader for Billy Paul, Europe, 1995; Played all major French jazz festivals with Eddy Louiss (Hammond organ). Compositions: Music and lyrics for Ray Charles: Separate Ways; Good Thang. Recordings: Solo albums: Hot Lunch; Rikitikitak; Musician on recordings by: Gilbert Becaud; Serge Ginsbourg; Michel Columbier; Françoise Hardy; Catherine Deneuve; Eddy Louiss; France Gall; Michel Berger. Current Management: Delabel-Chrysalis. Address: 24 Place des Voges, 75003 Paris, France.

BRETECHE Jean Pierre, b. 6 Nov 1946, Nantes, France. Musician (banjo). Education: Philosophy, Fine Arts. Career: Member, 6-piece jazz orchestra 5 Doigts Et Le Pouce Jazz Fanfare, playing New Orleans Jazz music; Regularly accompanies: Bill Coleman; Wallace Davenport; Joe Turner; Michael Silva; Ray Dry Bottom; Appearances include: Jazz Band Ball; Festivals: Saintes et de Luneray; Jazz Mobile de Nice; Casino de Cabourg; Mirabelles, Metz; France A La Voile tour; Tours: Germany; Luxembourg; Italy. Recording: 1 cassette. Address: Les 5 Doigts et le Pouce Jazz Fanfare, 30 Avenue du Docteur Arnold Netter, 75012 Paris, France.

BRETT Martin, b. 29 Mar 1959, Dorking, Surrey, England. Musician (bass guitar, guitar, piano). 2 sons. Musical Education: Self-taught. Career: Bass guitar, Voice Of The Beehive; Worldwide tours; Television includes: 6 Top Of The Pops; Currently in songwriting partnership with VOTB for new album and singles; Formed own music production company (Brett Dempsey Music) with Michael Dempsey (former Cure member); Studio in Sussex; Martin Brett and Michael Dempsey compose for films, television and commercials. Recordings: Albums: Let It Bee; Honey Lingers; Sex And Misery; Singles include: Don't Call Me Baby; Monsters And Angels; Angel Come Down. Memberships: PRS; PAMRA; Musicians' Union; MCPS. Hobby: Work. Current Management: Self-managed. Address: Wimbledon, London SW20, England.

BREWER Neil, b. 15 Jul 1952, Berkhamsted, England. Musician (guitar, bass guitar); Vocalist. Musical Education: Self-taught. Career: Several major tours and radio shows: Television appearance with band Druid, Old Grey Whistle Test, 1975; Currently solo artist, guitarist and lead vocalist, with self-programmed/arranged computerised backing. Recordings: Albums: Toward The Sun, 1975; Fluid Druid, 1976; Druid 1; Singles: Modern Women, Splash; 2 singles, Frame By Frame. Memberships: Musicians' Union; PRS. Hobbies: Music; Life. Address: 45 Melsted Road, Boxmoor, Hemel Hempstead, Hertfordshire HP1 1SX, England.

BREWER Teresa, b. 7 May 1931, Toledo, Ohio, USA. Singer. m. Bob Thiele, 24 Oct 1972, 4 daughters (previous marriage). Career: Played with: Count Basie; Duke Ellington; Benny Carter; Stéphane Grappelli; Earl Hines; Ruby Braff; Dizzy Gillespie; Television appearances: Co-host, Summertime USA, with Mel Tormé, 1953; Co-host, Perry Presents, with Tony Bennett, 1959; Ed Sullivan Show, 39 times; Film appearances include: Those Redheads From Seattle, 1953; Concerts include: Carnegie Hall, New York City, 1978; Montreux Jazz Festival, Switzerland, 1983. Recordings: 75 albums and 125 singles; Recorded over 600 songs; 43 songs in US charts including: Music! Music! Music!; Till I Waltz Again With You; Ricochet; A Sweet Old Fashioned Girl; Let Me Go Lover!; A Tear Fell. Honours: 6 Gold records. Membership: Society of Singers. Current Management: Bob Thiele. Address: c/o Bill Munroe, 584 Prospect Street, New Haven, CT 06511, USA.

BREWIS David, b. 3 June 1957, Sunderland, England. Musician (guitar, bass, keyboards); Record Producer; Songwriter. Musical Education: Newcastle College (diploma). Career: Member, Kane Gang; UK and European tours; Television appearances include Solid Gold (US); Top of the Pops; Whistle Test; The Tube. Recordings: Albums: with the Kane Gang: Bad And Lowdown World; Miracle; Hit singles: Closest Thing To Heaven; Respect Yourself; Gun Law; Smalltown Creed; Motortown; Don't Look Any Further (US Billboard No.1); As Producer: Prefab Sprout albums: Swoon; Life Of Surprises; As Guitarist: Andromeda Heights, Prefab Sprout album; Ocean Drive, Lighthouse Family album. Memberships: PRS; BMI. Hobby: Toy collecting. Address: Soul Kitchens, St Thomas Workshops, Newcastle Upon Tyne NE1 4LE, England.

BREWSTER Cori, b. 1960, Canada. Musician (guitar); Vocalist. Career: Major Canadian festivals, television shows. Recordings: Album: One More Mountain, 1994. Honours: Female Recording Artist Nomination in Alberta, Canada, 1994. Current Management: Horton Management and Publishing. Address: PO Box 48165, 595 Burrard Street, Vancouver, BC V7X 1N8, Canada.

BREZOVSKY Ali, b. 26 February 1940, Slovakia. m. Vlasta Brezovska, 8 Dec 1963, 1 son, 1 daughter. Education: Faculty of Pedagogy, Bratislava, Slovakia. Career: Various projects including scores to Slovak films, Smoliari, 1978; Losers, Zázracny Autobus, 1981; Magic Bus; Scores to theatre plays, many songs (pop and rock) and instrumental compositions. Compositions: Rozpravkovi Stopari, fairy-tale; Hitchhikers, LP, for children; Cengá Do Triedy

(School Bell is Ringing); Let/Flight - Songs for LP of a popular Slovak Rock Group. Recordings: CD, original soundtracks of Ali Brezovsky, 1996. Honours: 3rd Place, International Music Festival, Bratislavska, Lyra, 1974, 1985; Award for Original Soundtrack, 1978; Smoliari; Summer Film Festival. Memberships: Slovak Music Association; Soza/Slovak Union of Authors. Hobbies: Sports; Swimming.

BRIGHT Anna Lia, b. 25 Feb 1952, West Palm Beach, Florida, USA. Songwriter; Singer; Poet. Musical Education: Studied under Napoleon Bright and Bengt Lindskog. Career: Appearances on Danish TV and Radio; Singer in piano bars, clubs, cafés and concert halls in Holland, Spain, Scandinavia and the Canary Islands; Currently Songwriter for various artists; Tours schools with her show Stand Up Poetry (poetry, song and storytelling). Recordings: As songwriter, Wind And Fire, by Frank Ryan, You Better Believe, by Zapp Zapp and Walk The Walk; As singer and songwriter, That's Lambada; To This Planet. Publication: Undiscovered Days, poetry, 1996. Honours: Editors Choice Award for OutstandingAchievement in Poetry, National Library of Poetry, 1997; Honorable Mention for short stories entered in Daily City Short Story Contest. Memberships: KODA; NCB; DJBFA. Hobbies: Music; Hiking. Address: Mosedalvej 9 2 th, 2500 Valby, Copenhagen, Denmark.

BRIMLEY Robert George, b. 11 Mar 1943, Kent, England. Musician (jazz guitar, piano, keyboards). m. Indra, 1989, 2 sons. Education: Technical College. Musical Education: Classical trained, since 9 years of age. Career: Played most jazz venues, jazz festivals. Compositions: Music written for television documentary Corporate Video work; Jingles; Kitty To The Cape; Aldabra Underwater Documentary; Air Ambulance Theme; Lands End Theme; Film including: A Year In Cornwall; Geeyor Tin Mine; Songs Loving You; Love With A Stranger. Memberships: PRS; BASCA; Musicians' Union. Hobbies: Walking; Swimming; Music; Record producer; Studio engineer; Computer programming. Current Management: Cot Valley Music. Address: Cot Valley Lodge, Cot Valley, St Just, Penzance, Cornwall, England.

BRINCK Lars, b. 30 Mar 1957, Copenhagen, Denmark. Musician (keyboards); Composer; Arranger. m. Karen-Lis Kristensen, 18 Aug 1984, 4 sons. Musical Education: Royal Academy of Music, Aarhus, Denmark. Career: Keyboard player for: Arvid Hunter; Gary Snider; Poul Krebs; Jette Torp; Tomas Kellerup; Erik Grip; Lene Siel; Television appearances, Denmark, 1989-91. Recordings with: Arvid Hunter, 1989; Tomas Kellerup, 1990-92; Gary Snider, 1992; Erik Grip, 1993; Lene Siel, 1994; Jette Torp, 1995; Lars Brinck Jam Session, 1997. Publications: Numerous piano teaching manuals. Honours: Royal Academy Annual Award, three times. Memberships: DJBFA; Gramex. Address: c/o LB Productions, Ludvig Holbergsvej 13, 8230 Aabyhoej, Denmark.

BRINK VAN DEN Bert, b. 24 July 1958, Geldrop, Netherlands. m. Medy Doves, 1 s. Education: Private lessons, since age 5 years; Conservatory Utrecht Classical Music, by Herman Uhlhorn; Jazz, selftaught; Composer; Arranger. Teacher, Jazz music at Conservatory, Utrecht; Composer; Arranger; Played with Dee Dee Bridge Water, Toots Thielemans, Denise Jannah, Philip Catherine, Chet Baker, Nat Adderly, Rick Margitza, Charlie Mariano. Composition: Wondering Why. Recordings: Live at Montreal Dee Dee Bridgewater, 1990; Deepest to Dearest, solo album; Hazy Hugs, Amstel Octet with Guest Chet Baker; Denise Jannah Albums. Honour: 1st Prize, International Concours for Visually Handicapped Musicians, Hungary. Current Management: Brink Productions BV, Akkerse Straat 6A, 4061 BH, Ophemert, The Netherlands.

Address: Brink Productions BV, Akkerse Straat 6A, 4061 BH, Ophemert, The Netherlands

BRISLIN Kate (Young), b. 19 Feb 1946, Portsmouth, Ohio, USA. m. (1) Tom Brislin, 8 June 1968; (2) Jody Stecher, 29 July 1987. Education: BA, English, University of Guam. Career: Appearance, Prairie Home Companion, May 1994; As backing singer: Restless Rambling Heart, Laurie Lewis, 1986; Third Annual Farewell Reunion, Mike Seeger, 1994; Pieces Of My Heart, Alice Gerrard, 1994; with Jody Stecher: Going Up On The Mountain, 1976; Rasa, 1980; Out On The Rolling Sea, 1994. Recordings: with Arkansas Sheiks: Whiskey Before Breakfast, 1975; with The Blue Flame Stringband, 1982; with the Any Old Time Stringband, 1978; with Any Old Time: Ladies Choice, 1980; Duets with Jody Stecher: A Song That Will Linger, 1989; Blue Lightning, 1991; Our Town, 1993; Stay Awhile, 1995; Duet with Katy Moffatt: Sleepless Nights, 1996; Heart Songs, 1997. Honour: Grammy Nomination, 1994. Memberships: IBMA; North American Folk Alliance. Hobbies: Knitting; Gardening; Reading. Address: 133 Lake Street, San Francisco, CA 94118, USA.

BRITTON Simon (aka "Balance"), b. 22 Jan 1971, Bristol, England. Record Producer; Re-Mixer; Vocalist; Musician (keyboards). Musical Education: Trained vocalist; Studied classical music. Career: Vocalist under name "Balance", major recording success in Europe; Featured vocalist, several Top 10 UK Dance Music hits; Producer, several Dance Music hits; Featured vocalist with Black Box (major Italian production team). Recordings: Backing vocalist for artists including Tears For Fears; Scritti Politti; Massive Attack. Membership: Musicians' Union. Hobbies: Nightclubs; Producing; Fashion. Current Management: Leisure UK. Address: Suite 404, Victory House, Somers Road North, Portsmouth, Hampshire PO1 1PJ, England.

BRIXVOLD Jakob, b. 30 May 1966, b. Randers, Denmark. Career: Personal Manager, international promoter Off-Beat Productions, Denmark. Address: Off-Beat Productions, Vesterbrogade 149, DK-1620 Copenhagen V, Denmark.

BROCHET Marc, b. 3 Apr 1956, Soissons, Aisne, France. Composer; Musician; Teacher. m. Dominique Hemard, 11 Dec 1981, 1 son, 2 daughters. Musical Education: First Prize d'Harmonie; Orchestration; Conservatoire Superieur de Paris. Career: Concerts with vocal jazz group Vox Office; Festivals include: Nice; Vienna; Tel Aviv; Televised concert for M6; Teacher in musical writings, Conservatoire National d'Enseignement Superieur de Poitiers; Publications for television and radio. Compositions: Music for theatre and dance. Recordings: Boppin' In French, Vox Office. Hobbies: Zen Buddhism; Astrology. Current Management: Hélène Bertrand, 2 Rue Henri Dunant, 60100 Creil, France.

BROCK Dave, b. Isleworth, Middlesex, England. Vocalist; Musician (guitar). Career: Founder member, UK rock group Hawkwind, 1969-; Regular UK and US tours; Concerts include: Glastonbury Fayre, 1971, 1981; Reading Festival, 1975, 1977, 1986; Futurama Festival, Leeds, 1979; Stonehenge Festival, 1981, 1984; Monsters Of Rock, Castle Donington, 1982. Recordings: Albums: Hawkwind, 1970; In Search Of Space, 1971; Doremi Fasol Latido, 1972; Space Ritual, 1973; Hall Of The Mountain Grill, 1974; Warrior On The Edge Of Time, 1975; Astounding Sounds And Amazing Music, 1976; Road Hawks, 1976; Masters Of The Universe, 1977; Quark Strangeness And Charm, 1977; 25 Years On, 1978; PXR-5, 1979; Live 1979, 1980; Levitation, 1980; Sonic Attack, 1981; Church Of Hawkwind, 1982; Choose Your Masques, 1982; Zones, 1983; The Chronicle Of The Black Sword,

1985; Angels Of Death, 1987; Spirit Of The Age, 1988; The Xenon Codex, 1988; Space Bandits, 1990; Stasis, 1990; Electric Tepee, 1992; It Is The Business Of The Future, 1993; The Business Trip, 1994; Singles include: Silver Machine, 1972; Urban Guerilla, 1973. Current Management: Doug Smith Associates, PO Box 2098, London W12 9RZ, England.

BRODERICK Michael, b. 21 Apr 1941, Dumfries, Scotland. Folk Singer; Musician (bohdran). m. Irene Masia, 3 Sep 1976, 1 son, 1 daughter. Career: Founder member of folk group The Whistlebinkies; Appearances include: John Cage's Scottish Circus, 1991; Toured extensively including: France, Germany, Italy, Sweden and China; Played at numerous festivals including Edinburgh International Festival and The Hong Kong Folk Festival; Television appearances: Celtic Weave, 1994; Celtic Connection, 1994. Recordings: The Whistlebinkies 1-5; Anniversary (compilation); Inner Sound. Memberships: Equity; PRS. Hobby: Hill walking. Current Management: Self-managed. Address: Eddie McGuire, 13 Lawrence Street, Glasgow G11 5HH, Scotland.

BRODY Lane (Lynn Connie Voorlas), b. Oak Park, Illinois, USA. Singer; Songwriter. m. Edward H Bayers Jnr, 14 Nov 1994. Musical Education: Private study. Career: Singer; Commercials include: Wrigley's; Johnson Wax; McDonalds; Tours worldwide with: John Anderson; Willie Nelson; Steve Wariner; Tom Bresh; Lee Greenwood; Television appearances: Taxi; Heart Of The City; OSO TV Special; Lee Greenwood TV Special; Today Show; Austin City Limits; Compositions include: Tough Enough; Hottest Night Of The Year, Anne Muray (co-wrote); All The Unsung Heroes; Yellow Rose (co-wrote). Recordings: Tender Mercies theme; The Gift of Life theme; Country Gold soundtrack; Yellow Rose title track; All The Unsung Heroes title song; Tough Enough, title track. Honours include: Academy Award Nomination, Over You; ACM Nomination, Top New Female Vocalist; Emmy Nomination, Gift Of Life; BMI Award, Yellow Rose; American Film Festival Video Documentary of the Year; Numerous awards, Military and Charity organisations. Memberships: SAG; AFTRA; NARAS; CMA; ACM. Hobbies: Gardening; Nutrition; Animals. Current Management: Lane Brody Global Fan Club. Address: PO Box 24775, Nashville, TN 37202, USA.

BROKENSHIRE Frederick, b. 21 Apr 1952, Toronto, Ontario, Canada. Music Industry Executive. 2 sons, 1 daughter. Education: 2 years, Memorial University of Newfoundland. Career: Entered music business, 1972; President, majority shareholder, The Duckworth Group; Atlantica Music & Distribution Ltd; Duckworth Distribution Ltd; Latitude Records Inc; FRB Productions; Wildshore Music Inc; Atlantica Musique et Distribution Ltee; Fred's Records Ltd; Atlantic Canada's leading music companies; Engaged in record production, distribution, artist management, concert promotion, retail, with offices in: St John's; Halifax; Moncton; Toronto; Canada. Memberships: Founding member, president, Music Industry Association, Newfoundland; Director, East Coast Music Association; Member, regional representative, Canadian Country Music Association; Canadian Academy Recording Arts & Sciences; Member, Music Industry Association of Nova Scotia. Hobbies: Sailing; Skiing. Address: The Duckworth Music Group, 198 Duckworth Street, St John's, Newfoundland A1C 1G5, Canada.

BROKOP Lisa, b. 6 June 1973, Surrey, British Columbia, Canada. Singer; Songwriter; Musician (guitar, keyboards). Career: Singer, Rhythm guitarist, keyboardist, Marty Gillan and the Sweetwater Band, 1988; Formed own band, 1989; Toured with Clay Walker and George Strait. Film role: Harmony Cats; Performed CCMA Awards

Show, Canada, and CMA Awards Show Nashville, 1992; Recordings: My Love; Harmony Cats Soundtrack; Every Little Girl's Dream. Honours: Horizon Award (Best New Artist), Gospel Performer of Year, British Columbia Country Music Association (BCCMA), 1990; Princess Margaret Order of Lion, Special Ambassador, 1991; CKWX Songwriter's Contest, 1991; Female Vocalist of Year, BCCMA, 1992; Youth Achievement Award, Vocal Excellence, YTV, 1992; Female Vocalist of Year, International Achievement Award, BCCMA, 1993; Vocal Collaboration Award with Johner Brothers, Saskatchawan Country Music Association, 1994; Worldfest Houston Gold Award, 1994; Female Vocalist of Year, International Achievement Award, Single of Year, BCCMA, 1994. Memberships: SOCAN; CCMA; CMA; ACM; AFofM. Hobbies: Golf; Swimming. Current Management: Mascioli Entertainment Corporation. Address: 11 Music Circle S, 1st Floor, Nashville, TN 37203, USA.

BROM Gustav, b. 22 May 1921, Velké Leváre, Czech Republic. Jazz Band Conductor; Musician (violin, clarinet, saxophone). m. Marie Bromová-Gergelová, 1 son, 1 daughter. Musical Education: Music school; Private study. Career: Jazz band leader, 5 years; 300 concerts home and abroad; Jazz festivals; Rated among 10 best world jazz bands in world. Recordings: 175 albums; About 100 singles; About 30 CDs; 20 own compositions. Publications: My Life With Jazz-band. Honours: Czechoslovak State Award. Hobbies: Sport: Football, hockey, tennis. Address: Preslova 28, 602 00 Brno, Czech Republic.

BROM Rafael, b. 13 Aug 1952, Prague, Czech Republic. Singer; Musician (multi-instrumentalist); Composer; Producer; Performer. Education: Graphic Art; Fine Art; Computer Graphics. Career: Appearances: Radio stations, USA, Canada; 7 albums, 2 singles. Recordings: Albums: Rafael Brom I, 1983; Lord Hamilton-Padre Pio, 1985; Peace Of Heart, 1986; The Sounds Of Heaven, 1989; Dance For Padre Pio, 1991; The True Measure Of Love, 1992; Music For Peace Of Mind, 1993; The Christmas Songs; You'll Never Walk Alone. Membership: ASCAP. Hobbies: Tennis; Videos; Books; Metaphysics; Political Science. Current Management: Cosmotone Records. Address: 3350 Highway 6, Suite 412, Sugarland, TX 77478, USA.

BRON Gerry, b. 1 Mar 1933, London, England. Manager; Producer; Company Director. m. 8 July 1982, 2 sons. Musical Education: Clarinet, Harmony, Composition, Trinity College of Music, London. Career: Family Business, 1949; Manager: Gene Pitney; Manfred Mann; Patrick Lancy; Uriah Heep; Formed Bronze Records, 1971; Built Roundhouse Recording Studios, 1974. Recordings: Productions include: Manfred Mann; Bonzo Dog Doo Dah Band; Colosseum; Gene Pitney; Uriah Heep. Hobbies: Music; Computers; Aviation. Address: 17 Priory Road, London NW6 4NN, England.

BRONZE David, b. 2 Apr 1952, Billericay, Essex, England. Musician (bass). m. Julie, 1 son, 1 daughter. Career: Member of groups: Procul Harum; Robin Trower Band; Dr Feelgood; Art Of Noise; Duane Eddy Band; Barbara Dickson Band; Mickey Jupp Band; Chris Farlowe And The Thunderbirds; Currently with Eric Clapton Band; With Paul Carrack Band. Recordings: As producer, mixer, musician, Down At The Doctors, Dr Feelgood, 1994; On the Road Again, Dr Feelgood, 1996; As musician: From The Cradle, Eric Clapton, 1994; Prodigal Stranger, Procul Harum; with Paul Carrack: Beautiful World, 1997; Gary barlow, 1997; Nik Kershaw, 1997; Eric Bibb, 1997; Eric Clapton, 1997. Many sessions with various artists. Memberships: PRS; Musicians' Union; PAMRA. Address: c/o 107A High Street, Canvey, Essex, England.

BROOKES Bruno, b. 25 Apr 1959, Stoke-on-Trent, Staffordshire, England. Television and Radio Presenter. m. Debbie Brooker, 24 Sept 1994. Career: BBC Radio Stoke, 6 years; BBC Radio 1, 10 years (including The Top 40 Show); Live Aid for Radio 1; Launched Radio 5; Television appearances include: Top Of The Pops; Beat The Teacher; Going Live; I Can Do That; Go Getter; Rock School; Love At First Sight (Sky TV); Wogan; Brit Awards; Pop Quiz; Noel's House Party; Children In Need Telethon; Surprise Surprise; The Generation Game; Celebrity Squares; Krypton Factor; Presenter, Michael Jackson UK Tour; Numerous voice overs, television and radio commercials, including Twix, Nationwide and British Gas; Introduced acts at first Prince's Trust Concert; Charity work including Children In Need, Variety Club of Great Britain, Nordoff-Robbins Music Therapy, and Prince's Trust. Recordings: Shaft, with Five Star; Come Outside, with Sam Fox and Frank Bruno; Let's Dance, with Liz Kershaw; 1 compilation album, Meglomania. Publications: Beat The Teacher; Half A Mind To Scream; What A Week With Bruno Brookes. Honours: Smash Hits Award, Best National DJ, 1989-94; Voted Best DJ, Daily Mirror, Sun, Star, No.1 Magazine, Sony (twice); 40 Gold and Silver records. Hobbies: Angling; Equestrianism; Restoration. Current Management: Susan Shaper (Television); Fox Ltd (other). Address: 101 Shepherds Bush Road, London W6 7LP, England.

BROOKS Anthony Lewis, b. 20 April 1956, Treorchy, Rhondda, Wales. Producer; Composer; Performer. 1 son. Education: Electrical Engineering, Neyland Technical College; Piano, Brass, Percussion, Bass, University of Wales; Music Degree, IRCAM; Sound Design Degree, Institute of Research Computers & Music, Paris. Career: Executives, UK Tours; Artatak, UK Tours, Television and Radio; ICA London Performance, 1975; Europe, USA Tours with Various Groups; Darts 2, UK Tours; Olympic Culture Event, Centre for Performing Arts, Atlanta, 1996; The World Is One Festival, Seoul, 1996; Danish Television, Tony Brooks Is Orchestra Soundscapes; Culture City Europe, Copenhagen, 1996; The Oedipus Production, Seoul, 1997. Compositions: Heaven People; Earth Tribe, 1, 2, & 3. Recordings: Tony Brooks Is Earth Tribe, 1, 2, & 3; Heaven People. Memberships: Danish Music Union; Danish Jazz Beat and Folk Authors; IRCAM, Paris. Hobbies: Golf; Sun and Beach; Beautiful Women. Current Management: Pappagallo, Schleppegrellesgade 8, 8000 Aarhus, Denmark. Address: Heibergsgade 21 kld, 800 Aarhus C, Denmark.

BROOKS Clyde Scott, b. 16 Jan 1948, Milwaukee, USA. Musician (percussion, drums); Record Producer. m. Geri Brooks, 13 May 1988. Musical Education: Berklee College of Music, Boston, 1968-70. Career: Session musician for: Dolly Parton; Kenny Rogers; Ronnie Milsap; Don Henley; Oak Ridge Boys; Johnny Winter; Jerry Lee Lewis; Barbara Mandrell; George Strait; Ted Nugent; Little Richard; B J Thomas. Recordings: Record producer for recordings by: Nancy Brooks; Lynn Anderson; The Headlights; B B Watson; Ronna Reeves. Publication: Author, The Recording Drummer, 1974. Memberships: AFTRA; Country Music Association; AFofM.

BROOKS David John, b. 6 June 1951, Sheffield, England. Singer; Songwriter; Musician (guitar, keyboards). m. Anthia Stephens, 19 Feb 1985. Musical Education: Wells Cathedral School. Career: Opening solo act for many bands on various tours including: Fairport Convention; Georgie Fame; Chris Farlowe; Steve Gibbons Band; Ronnie Lane's Slim Chance. Compositions: Theme and incidental music, BBC television series: The Family, 1974; Story Of Ruth, 1978; Romers Egypt, 1980; Breakaway Girls, 1978; Vox Pop, 1983; One Day, 1988; In Solidarity, 1989; Forty Minutes, 1993; Recordings: Family Theme, 1974; Vox Pop, 1983. Memberships: BASCA;

PRS; Musicians' Union. Hobbies: Cricket; Gardening; Rum. Current Management: Anthia Brooks. Address: 82 Lambton Road, London SW20 0LP, England.

BROOKS David Michael, b. 23 Jan 1972, Doncaster, England. Musician; Songwriter; Singer; Piano; Guitar. Education: Wakefield College for Performing Arts, England; Leeds College of Music, England. Career: Keyboards and Guitar for Nick Van Eede, formally Cutting Crew; Keyboards for Gary Numan; Guitar for German band, Alphaville; Pursuing solo career. Composition: White Lies. Recordings: Gary Numan Live Albums, 1996, 1997. Publication: White Lies, 1992. Address: 28 Sinclair Road, West Kensington, London, W14 0NH, England.

BROOKS Elkie (Elaine Bookbinder), b. 25 Feb 1946, Salford, Manchester, England. Singer. Career: Toured with Eric Delaney Band, 1960s; Joined jazz-rock act Dada (later became Vinegar Joe), 1970-74; Solo artiste, 1974-. Recordings: Albums: Rich Man's Woman, 1975; Two Days Away, 1977; Shooting Star, 1978; Live And Learn, 1979; Pearls, 19081; Pearls II, 1982; Minutes, 1984; Screen Gems, 1984; No More The Fool, 1986; The Very Best Of Elkie Brooks, 1986; The Early Years 1964-1966, 1987; Bookbinder's Kid, 1988; Inspiration, 1989; Round Midnight, 1993; Pearls III, 1993; Circles, 1995; Singles include: Hello Stranger; The Way You Do The Things You Do; Pearl's A Singer, 1977; Sunshine After Rain, 1977; Fool If You Think It's Over, 1982; Nights In White Satin, 1982; No More The Fool, 1986. Address: c/o Barry Collings Entertainments, 21a Clifftown Road, Southend-on-Sea, Essex SS1 1AB, England.

BROOKS (Troyal) Garth, b. 7 Feb 1962, Tulsa, Oklahoma, USA. Country Music Singer; Songwriter; Musician (guitar). m. Sandra Mahl, 1986, 2 daughters. Education: BS, Journalism and Advertising, Oklahoma State University, 1985. Career: Television specials include: This Is Garth Brooks, 1992; This Is Garth Brooks Too!, 1994; Garth Brooks - The Hits, 1995; Best selling country album ever, No Fences (over 13 million copies). Recordings: Albums: Garth Brooks, 1989; No Fences, 1990; Ropin' The Wind, 1991; The Chase, 1992; Beyond The Season, 1992; In Pieces, 1993; The Hits, 1994; Fresh Horses, 1995; Sevens, 1997. Honours: Grammy Award; CMA Horizon Award, Video of the Year, 1990; CMA Awards: Best Single, Best Album 1991; Music City News/TNN Award, Video of Year, 1991; CMA Entertainer of the Year, 1991-92; Numerous ACM Awards include: Music Entertainer of the Year, 1991-94, Best Single 1991, Best Album 1991; ASCAP Voice of Music Award, 1992; 9 People's Choice Awards; Top-selling solo artist in American music history, RIAA. Memberships: Inducted into Grand Ole Opry; ASCAP; CMA; ACM. Hobbies: Horse riding; Sports (hockey, basketball). Current Management: c/o Scott Stern, GB Management Inc., 1111 17th Avenue South, Nashville, TN 37212, USA.

BROOKS Meredith, b. Corvallis, Oregon, USA. Singer; Songwriter; Musician (guitar). Career: Member, all-female group The Graces, 1990; Solo recording artist, 1991-. Recordings include: Debut album: Blurring The Edges, 1997; Hit Single: Bitch, 1997. Current Management: Lori Leve Management, 151 North Almont Drive, Suite 305, Beverly Hills, CA 90211, USA.

BROOKS Nikki (Nichola Jane), b. Bristol, England. Musician (keyboards, bass guitar, clarinet); Vocalist. Education: BPharm, Degree. Musical Education: All grades Theory and Practical, Guildhall School of Music, Associate and Licentiate, London College of Music Diplomas. Career: ECT, Ch4, 1985; Lead vocalist, McCoy, 1985; Lead vocalist, Wild!, 1986-87; Lead and backing vocalist, bass, keyboards in various covers bands; Currently in Adam & The Ants covers band, and session musician; Played with members of: Gillan; Iron Maiden; UFO; Wild Horses; Pat Travers Band; Gary Moore Band; Tours, festivals in UK and Europe; Vocal sessions include: Dreamboys, LA Centrefold Videos; Currently writing material with songwriting partner. Recordings: Wrote and recorded 4 song session for BBC Radio 1 Rock Show (Tommy Vance). Honour: Prize for Grade 3 Guildhall Practical Piano. Membership: Musicians' Union; PRS. Hobbies: Music; Cookery; Films. Address: Flat C, 49 Roxborough Park, Harrow-On-The-Hill, Middlesex HA1 3BA, England.

BROSCH Christopher, b. 9 Apr 1957, Munich, Germany. Promoter; Agent. m. Kerstin Estherr Brosch, 20 June 1991, 1 daughter. Education: German High School degree, 1975; Law studies, Cologne. Career: Freelance tour manager for various German tour promoters, 1980-85; Talent Booker for Peter Rieger Koncertagentur, Cologne, acts include: Peter Gabriel; Joe Cocker; Run-DMC; Beastie Boys; Changed to Hamburg based company, Blinffish Promotion, as talent booker for new bands; Started own company: Bizarre Productions, 1992; Acts promoted include: Beastie Boys; Portishead; Hole; Cocteau Twins; Oasis; Beastie Boys; Portishead; Hole; Foo Fighters; Daft Punk; New talent outdoor festival in the summer. Hobbies: Travel; Golf. Address: Buelaustr 8, 20099 Hamburg, Germany.

BROUDIE Ian, b. 1959. Singer; Songwriter; Musician (guitar); Record Producer. Career: Member, Original Mirrors, late 1970s; Member, Big In Japan, 1977; Member, duo, Care, mid-1980s; Founder, The Lightning Seeds, 1990-; Record producer, 1980s-; Numerous television and radio appearances; Concerts include: Glastonbury Festival, 1995. Recordings: Albums: Cloudcuckooland, 1991; Sense, 1992; Jollification, 1994; Like You Do...The Best Of, 1997; Singles: with The Lightning Seeds: Pure Life; Life Of Riley; Lucky You; Change; Marvellous; Ready Or Not; Singer, songwriter, Three Lions (Official England Squad's Euro '96 theme), with David Baddiel and Frank Skinner (Number 1, UK), 1996; Record producer, numerous artists include: Echo And The Bunnymen; The Fall; Wah!; Icicle Works; The Primitives; Alison Moyet; Frank And Walters; Dodgy; Sleeper. Honour: BRIT Award Nomination, Best British Group, 1996. Current Management: JPR Management, The Powerhouse, 70 Chiswick High Road, London W4 1SY, England.

BROUWER Leovigildo, b. 1939, La Habana, Cuba. Orchestra; Conductor; Composer; Guitarist; Violoncellist; Clarinettist; Pianist; Percussionist. Education: Studied Guitar with Isaac Nicola; Studied at Peyrellade Conservatoire, La Habana; Selftaught, Julliard School of Music, New York; Hartford University. Career: Directed Music Department, Instituto Cubano, 1960; Created the Experimentacion of Sounds with Silvio Rodriguez and Pablo Milanes, 1968; Composed music for more than 100 films all around the world. Compositions: Conductor, Orquesta De Cuba. Honour: Honour Member, Cim of UNESCO, 1987. Current Management: Intercambio De Cultura Y Arte, Goya, 99 Esc A-4 Deha, 28009 Madrid, Spain.

BROWN Alex, b. 17 Jan 1967, Glynde, England. Singer; Musician (piano, trumpet, guitar, drums). Musical Education: Grade 8 trumpet; Music and Drama at college. Career: Lead singer, Macho Frog, 1985-88; UK (South East) tour, 1987; Signed to Brown Bear Records, 1990-; Tours: Austria, Germany, 1991; Belgium, England; Appearances at: Radio 1 FM Roadshows; Atlantic 252 Roadshows; BBC Children In Need Show. Recordings: That's What It Takes, 1993; Supernatural Love, 1994; Life Is Just Worth Living, 1994; Halfway To Heaven, 1994; Too Far Away, 1995; What I Like, 1995; I've Been Missing You, 1995. Memberships: PRS; Musicians' Union; PPL;

VPL; Umbrella. Hobby: Tennis. Current Management: Brown Bear Records. Address: 123A Wilton Road, Victoria, London SW1V 1JZ, England.

BROWN Andy, b. 1 Nov 1968, Auckland, New Zealand. Singer; Songwriter. m. Cherie Katherine Ross. 19 Nov 1994. Career: Mainstage NZ Festival, 1991; Shelterbelt Festival, 1992; New Zealand Tour; Australian Tour, 1993; Parachute Music Festivals, 1992, 1994, 1995; New Zealand tour, 3 months; Tear Fund, Hope and Justice Tour, 1995. Recordings: Albums: Surge, 1991; Nice Moon, 1994. Honours: Nice Moon, 10 Best of '94, Audio Video magazine, NZ. Membership: Australasian Performing Rights Association. Hobby: Watching films. Current Management: Someone Up There Promotions. Address: c/o Kevin & Darlene Adair, 39 Kensington Avenue, Mt Eden, Auckland, New Zealand.

BROWN Angie, b. 13 June 1963, Clapham, London, England. Singer; Actress. Musical Education: Private drama lessons; 4 years intensive singing lessons with Annette Batram. Career: Solo singer; Television appearances include: Jonathan Ross, 1990; America's Top Ten, 1992; Dance Energy, 1993; Top of the Pops, 3 times, 1992-93; Big World Cafe, 1990; The Beat; Dublin Two; Pebble Mill; Currently vocalist of Ramona 55. Composition: Took My Love. Recordings: Singles: Bizarre Inc (Number 2, UK) 1992; I'm Gonna Get You; Took My Love. Album: An Album I Thought I Could Only Dream Of!, with Ramona 55, 1994. Memberships: Equity; Performing Rights Society; Musicians' Union; PAMRA. Hobbies: Driving; Belly Laughing; Red Wine; Smoked Salmon; Cinema; Sauna; Working out. Current Management: Laurie Jay. Address: LJE, 32 Willesden Lane, Kilburn, London NW6 7ST, England.

BROWN Bobby, b. 5 Feb 1969, Roxbury, Massachusetts, USA. Singer. m. Whitney Houston, 18 July 1992, 1 daughter. Career: Founder member, New Edition, 1981-85; Solo artiste, 1985-; Film appearance, Ghostbusters II, 1989; Established Bosstown recording studio and record label. Recordings: Solo albums: King Of Stage, 1986; Don't Be Cruel (Number 1, US), 1989; Dance... Ya Know It!, 1989; Bobby, 1992; B Brown Posse, 1993; NBA Jam Session, 1993; Singles include: Girlfriend, 1986; Girl Next Door, 1987; Don't Be Cruel, 1988; My Prerogative (Number 1, US), 1989; Roni, 1989; Every Little Step, 1989; On Our Own, from film Ghostbusters II, 1989; Rock Wit' Cha, 1989; Humpin' Around, 1992; Good Enough, 1992; Get Away, 1993; That's The Way Love Is, 1993; Two Can Play That Game, 1995; with Glenn Medeiros: She Ain't Worth It (Number 1, US), 1990; Contributor, Voices That Care charity single (for Red Cross Gulf Crisis). Numerous honours include: Regular winner, SKC Boston Music Awards, 1989-; Soul Train Music Award, Best R&B/Urban Contemporary Album of the Year; Regular winner, American Music Awards, 1990-; Grammy, Best Male R&B Vocal Performance, Every Little Step, 1990; Coca-Cola Atlanta Music Award, Outstanding Male Vocalist, 1992. Current Management: Tommy Brown, 2160 North Central Road, Fort Lee, NJ 08014, USA.

BROWN Chris, b. Stockport, Cheshire, England. Recording Engineer; Record Producer. Career: Senior Engineer, Abbey Road Studios, London. Current Management: Townhouse Management. Address: 150 Goldhawk Road, London W12 8HH, England.

BROWN Chris (Christopher M), b. 1 July 1954, Evanston, Illinois, USA. Composer; Producer; Recording Engineer. Musical Education: Oberlin College Conservatory of Music. Career: Long affiliation with Paul Winter and The Winter Consort, 26 albums in nearly 20 years; Several nominated for Grammy Awards; Scores for:

television; film; industrial videos; Recorded, edited or mixed numerous albums, CDs, films and video scores. Recordings include: Prayer for the Wild Things, Paul Winter, 1995. Honour: Grammy Award, 1995. Memberships: NARAS; AFofM. Hobby: Dinghy sailing. Current Management: Image-Net, Goshen, CT, USA. Address: 1401 Rt 35, South Salem, NY 10590, USA.

BROWN Dennis Emanuel, b. 1957, Kingston, Jamaica. Reggae Singer; Record Producer; Record Company Owner. m. Yvonne. Career: Child singer with Studio One record label, age 11; Co-owner and Record Producer, DEB record label; Owner, Yvonne's Special record label. Recordings: Singles: No Man Is An Island; If I Follow My Heart; Money in My Pocket; To the Foundation; Revolution; Big All Round, with Gregory Isaacs; Numerous solo albums include: No Man is an Island, 1970; If I Follow My Heart, 1971; Super Reggae and Soul Hits, 1972; Just Dennis, 1975; West Bound Train, 1977; Visions, 1977; Wolf and Leopards, 1978; Words of Wisdom, 1979; So Long Rastafari, 1979; Joseph's Coat of Many Colours, 1979; 20th Century Dubwise, 1979; Yesterday, Toady and Tomorrow, 1982; Satisfaction Feeling, 1983; The Prophet Rides Again, 1983; Love's Gotta Hold On Me, 1984; Dennis, 1984; Time and Place, 1984; Live at Montreux, 1984; Slow Down, 1985; Revolution, 1985; Spellbound, 1985; Wake Up, 1985; The Exit, 1986; Money in My Pocket, 1986; Hold Tight, 1986; Brown Sugar, 1986; Smile Like an Angel, 1986; In Concert, 1987; Love Has Found Its Way, 1988; Inseparable, 1988; More, 1988; My Time, 1989; Unchallenged, 1990; Ovenproof, 1990; Good Tonight, 1990; Go Now, 1991; Victory is Mine, 1991; Friends for Life, 1992; Some Like It Hot, 1992; Blazing, 1992; Beautiful Morning, 1992; Cosmic Force, 1993; Unforgettable, 1993; Several other compilation albums; Other albums recorded with: Horace Andy, Gregory Isaacs, John Holt, Enos McLeod and Janet Kay. Address: c/o Talent Inc, 1-D Braemar Avenue, Ste 3, Kingston 10, Jamaica.

BROWN Errol, b. 12 Nov 1948, Kingston, Jamaica. Vocalist; Songwriter. Career: Lead vocalist, Hot Chocolate, 1969-87; Solo artiste, 1987-. Compositions: Think About You Children, Mary Hopkin; Bet Yer Life I Do, Herman's Hermits; Hits for Hot Chocolate include: Every 1's A Winner; Girl Crazy; It Started With A Kiss; Tears On The Telephone. Recordings: Albums: with Hot Chocolate: Cicero Park, 1974; Hot Chocolate, 1975; Man To Man, 1976; Hot Chocolate's Greatest Hits, 1976; Every 1's A Winner, 1978; Going Through The Motions, 1979; 20 Hottest Hits, 1979; Class, 1980; Mystery, 1982; Love Shot, 1983; The Very Best Of Hot Chocolate, 1987; Their Greatest Hits, 1993; Solo albums: That's How Love Is, 1989; Secret Rendevous 1992; 30 hit singles with Hot Chocolate include: Love Is Life, 1970; I Believe (In Love), 1971; Brother Louie (Number 1, US), 1973; Emma, 1974; Disco Queen, 1975; A Child's Prayer, 1975; You Sexy Thing, 1976; Don't Stop It Now, 1976; Man To Man, 1976; Heaven In The Back Seat Of My Cadillac, 1976; So You Win Again (Number 1, UK), 1977; Put Your Love In Me, 1977; Every 1's A Winner, 1979; No Doubt About It, 1980; Girl Crazy, 1982; It Started With A Kiss, 1982; Tears On The Telephone, 1983; I Gave You My Heart (Didn't I), 1984. Current Management: Richard Martin Management, Agency House, 6 The Steyne, Worthing, West Sussex BN11 3DS, England.

BROWN Ian, b. 28 Feb 1966, Sale, Lancashire, England. Singer; Songwriter; Musician (bass). Career: Formed Patrol, 1980; Name changed to English Rose, 1983; Becomes the Stone Roses, 1984-; Tours include: UK tour, 1989; European tour, 1989; Japanese tour, 1989; Concert, Alexandra Palace, 1989. Recordings: with the Stone Roses: Albums: The Stone Roses, 1989; Turn Into Stone, 1992; Second Coming,

1994; Singles: Made Of Stone, 1989; Fool's Gold/What The World Is Waiting For, 1989; She Bangs The Drums, 1990; One Love, 1990; I Wanna Be Adored, 1991; Waterfall, 1992; I Am The Resurrection, 1993; Debut solo album: Unfinished Monkey Business, 1998.

BROWN James, b. 3 May 1928, Barnwell, South Carolina, USA. Soul Singer; Broadcasting Executive. m. (1) Deidre Jenkins, (2) Adrienne Brown (deceased 1996). Career: Singer with, then leader of own backing group Famous Flames, 1956-68; Solo performer, recording artist, 1969-; President, JB Broadcasting Ltd, 1968-; James Brown Network, 1968-; Film appearances include: Ski Party, 1964; Come To The Table, 1974; The Blues Brothers, 1980; Concerts include: The Biggest Show Of Stars tour, 1963; The TAMI Show, 1964; Newport Jazz Festival, 1969; Festival Of Hope, Garden City, 1972; Grand Ole Opry, Nashville, 1979; Montreux Jazz Festival, 1981; Coca-Cola Music Festival, Essex, 1992; Pori Jazz, Finland, 1995; Owner, several US radio stations; Co-owner, Brown Stone Records, 1992-. Compositions include: Film scores: Black Caesar, 1972; Slaughter's Big Rip Off, 1972. Recordings: Over 75 albums include: Live At The Apollo, 1963; I Can't Stand Myself, 1968; Hot Pants, 1971; The Payback, 1974; I'm Real, 1988; Universal James, 1992; Hit singles include: Please, Please, Please, 1956; Out Of Sight, 1964; Poppa's Got A Brand New Bag, 1965; I Got You (I Feel Good), 1966; It's A Man's Man's Man's World, 1966; Cold Sweat, 1967; I Got The Feelin', 1968; Say It Loud, 1968; Give It Up Or Turn It Loose, 1969; Get Up, I Feel Like Being A Sex Machine, 1970; Super Bad, 1970; Get On The Good Foot, 1972; Get Up Offa That Thing, 1976; Living In America (used in film Rocky IV), 1986; I'm Real, 1988. Honours: Inducted, Rock'n'Roll Hall Of Fame, 1986; Grammy Awards: Best R&B Recording, 1965; Best R&B Performance, 1987; 44 Gold discs; Award Of Merit, American Music Awards, 1992; NARAS Lifetime Achievement Award, 1992; Lifetime Achievement Trophy, Rhythm & Blues Foundation Pioneer Awards, 1993; Lifetime Achievement Award, National Association of Black Owned Broadcasters' Awards, 1993. Current Management: Brothers Management Associates. Address: 141 Dunbar Avenue, Fords, NJ 08863, USA.

BROWN James Kofi, b. 15 Feb 1949, Kumasi, Kwadaso, Ghana. Musician (guitar); Singer; Composer; Arranger. m. Comfort Peprah Aman Fo, 4 Apr 1992, 3 sons. Musical Education: O Level Music, Ghana; Self-taught. Career: Many concerts in Ghana and 2 in Paris, France; Various radio and television appearances including: TV 5, Radio France International, Radio Africa No 1, Radio GBC 2, Ghana Broadcasting Corporation. Recordings: Time Is So Hard; Riot (That's Too Bad); I'm In The Mood For Love; Life Is A Stage; Be My Girl; I've Found A New Lover (Georgina); Let's Be Together. Honour: Best video clip, festival in Paris, France. Memberships: SACEM; SDRM French Musical Society. Hobbies: Composing; Dancing. Address: 229 Avenue D'Argenteuil, 92270 Bois Colombes, France.

BROWN James Lee, b. 7 Oct 1953, Rocky Mt, North Carolina, USA. Musician (alto, tenor and soprano saxophones, keyboards). m. Angela Y Brown, 8 Aug 1982, 2 sons, 2 daughters. Education: 2 years college. Musical Education: High school band; Peabody study. Career: Appearances: WSMU-TV Nashville, Tennessee; Howard University WHUR-Radio; WEAA Radio Morgan State University. Recordings: Saxophonic Praises; Manifestation. Honours: ASCAP Award for Songwriting. Hobbies: Weightlifting; Jogging; Biking. Current Management: Saxophonic Praises Inc. Address: 4714 Keppler PL, Temple Hills, MD 20748, USA.

BROWN Kevin John, b. 19 July 1960, Nottingham, England. Musician (saxophone).

Career: Member, The Beautiful South; Numerous tours: UK, Ireland, Europe, USA, Canada, Japan, 1989-94; Television appearances: Wogan; Top Of The Pops; The Word; MotorMouth; Dennis Miller Show; Live performances recorded for television/video include: Feile Festival Live, Ireland, 1992, 1994; Bourges Festival Live, France; Live session, The Kelly Show, Ireland; Phoenix Festival, Stratford Upon Avon; Later with Jools Holland; Radio appearances include: Live session, Emma Freud, Radio 1; The Secret Gig, Radio 1. Recordings: Albums: with The Beautiful South: Choke, 1990; 0898, 1992; Carry On Up The Charts, 1994 (Number 1, UK); Rubaiyat (Elektra Records 40th anniversary), 1990; with The Miracle Drug: Imperial 66, 1993; Honours: Platinum Discs, Choke, Carry On Up The Charts; Gold Disc, 0898; Membership: Musicians' Union. Address: 136B Portland Road, Hucknall, Nottingham NG15 7SA, England.

BROWN Lester Valentine, b. 27 Feb 1958, Jamaica. Songwriter, 3 sons, 2 daughters. Musical Education: Singing; Music business training (NBT). Career: Various public appearances, overseas tours (Caribbean); Own independent record label: Black Nation Music Productions. Recordings: I Want You To Want Me, cover of My Love Is True. Membership: Musicians' Union. Hobbies: Music; Songwriting; Performing. Current Management: Broad Lane Music and Artist Management. Address: 14 St Peters House, Cunningham Road, London N15 4DT, England.

BROWN Michael, b. 29 Apr 1968, Grimsby, South Humberside, England. Songwriter; Musician (saxophone, bass guitar, keyboards). Musical Educaton: Self-taught. Career: Saxophonist, Illustrious GY, 1988-93; Signed major recording contract, Arista, 1991; Toured nationally as support act with Arista, 1991; Television appearances on: Going Live (BBC), Mar 1993; Live And Kicking (BBC), 1993; Played acoustically, Steve Wright Show (BBC Radio 1), 1993; Illustrious GY disbanded, 1994; Formed new band: Giant Killers, as songwriter; Signed record contract with MCA, and publishing deal with Windswept Pacific, 1995. Recordings: Illustrious GY: Twenty Questions, 1993; Anytime At All, 1993; I'm Ugly, 1993; Album: No, No, No, 1993. Membership: Musicians' Union. Hobby: Keen football player. Current Management: Jonathon Cooke, Fat Cat Management. Address: 81 Harley House, Marylebone Road, London NW1 5HT, England.

BROWN Norman, b. Shreveport, Louisiana, USA. Musician (guitar). Musical Education: Musicians Institute, Hollywood, California, USA. Career: Worldwide touring, worldwide radio airplay. Recordings: Albums: Just Between Us; After The Storm; Better Days Ahead. Honours: Soul Train Award: Best Jazz Album, BMI, 1995. Current Management: Anchor Entertainment, Bruce Kramer; Agent: Agency For The Performing Arts. Address: c/o Anchor Entertainment, 3522 Moore Street, Los Angeles, CA 90066, USA.

BROWN Robert Jackson, b. 17 Oct 1935, Framingham, Massachusetts, USA. Producer; Composer; Lyricist; Arranger; Singer; Musician (piano, string bass). m. Belva Rousseau, 12 May 1956, divorced 1971, 1 son, 1 daughter. Education: Kimball Union Academy (College Preparation); Colby College. Musical Education: Piano lessons from age 7; Violin, clarinet, voice, music courses, Colby College, Boston Conservatory of Music; Harvard University. Career: Founded Upstarts, vocal/instrumental quintet, 1961; Studio singer, jingle writer, vocal arranger, lounge performer, Boston, 1961-64; New York City, 1964-86; Creative Producer, Mark Century Corporation, New York City, 1966-69; Music Director, Herb Mendelsohn Associates, New York City, 1969-71; President, Creative Director, Hunter Productions Inc; BMK Productions; BMK Records, Inc; Badito

Productions Inc; Owner, Chief Engineer, Brownsound Recording Studios, all in New York City, 1978-83; Formed the Badito Brothers Band, 1974; Lead singer, conductor, music director, The Four Lads vocal group, 1983-86; Lounge performer, Tampa Bay area, Florida, 1986-; Music director, Russ Byrd Music and Entertainment, St Petersburg, Florida, 1989-91; Singer, Pied Pipers vocal group, pianist, Warren Covington Orchestra, 1993-94; Pianist, The Jimmy Dorsey Orchestra, 1995. Publications: Talking To Joscelynne, National Library of Poetry, 1995. Honour: Editor's Choice Award, National Library of Poetry, 1995. Memberships: Screen Actors Guild; American Federation of Television and Radio Artists. Address: PO Box #5253, Largo, FL 33779-5253, USA.

BROWN T Graham (Anthony Graham Brown), b. 1954, Arabi, Georgia, USA. Country Singer; Songwriter. Career: Founder, Rio Diamond, 1976; Founder, T Graham Brown's Rock Of Spam, 1979; Demo singer, Nashville, 1982; Recorded commercials for Budweiser; McDonalds; Solo artiste, 1985-. Recordings: Hit singles: US Country Number 1 hits: Hell Or High Water; Don't Go To Strangers; Darlene; Albums include: I Tell It Like It Used To Be, 1986; Brilliant Conversationalist, 1987; Come As You Were, 1988; Bumper To Bumper, 1990; You Can't Take It With You, 1991. Current Management: Starbound Management, 128 Volunteer Drive, Hendersonville, TN 37075, USA.

BROWN Tony Ersic, b. 11 Dec 1946, Greensboro, North Carolina, USA. Record Company Executive; Songwriter; Producer; Musician (keyboards). m. (1) Janie Breeding (divorced), (2) Gina Morrison, 19 Apr 1979. Career: Songwriter, Silverline Music, 1972; Musician with: Oak Ridge Boys, 1972-75; Elvis Presley, 1975-77; Emmylou Harris, 1977-80; Roseanne Cash, 1980-83; A&R Executive, RCA Records, 1978-84; A&R Executive, MCA Records, 1984-. Recordings: Albums include: with Emmylou Harris: Blue Kentucky Girl, 1979; Christmas Album, 1979; Evangeline, 1981; Cimarron, 1981; White Shoes, 1983; with Guy Clark: Better Days, 1983. Honours: Dove Award, Gospel Music Association, 1972; Grammy Awards, 1980, 1983, 1985; Producer of the Year, NARAS, 1991. Memberships: NARAS; Nashville Entertainment Association; CMA; ACM; Gospel Music Association. Address: c/o MCA Records, 60 Music Square East, Nashville, TN 37203, USA.

BROWNE Jackson, b. 9 Oct 1948, Heidelberg, Germany. Singer; Songwriter; Musician (guitar, piano). Career: Brief spell with Nitty Gritty Dirt Band, 1966; Solo singer, songwriter, musician, 1967-; Tours and concerts with Joni Mitchell; The Eagles; Bruce Springsteen; Neil Young; Major concerts include: Musicians United For Safe Energy (MUSE), Madison Square Garden (instigated by Browne and Bonnie Raitt), 1979; Glastonbury Festival, 1982; Montreux Jazz Festival, 1982; US Festival, 1982; Benefit concerts for: Amnesty International, Chile, 1990; Christie Institute, Los Angeles, 1990; Victims of Hurricane Inki, Hawaii, 1992; Various concerts for other environmental causes; Nelson Mandela Tributes, Wembley Stadium, 1988, 1990; Sang with Bonnie Raitt and Stevie Wonder, memorial service for Stevie Ray Vaughan, Dallas, Texas, 1990; Compositions: Songs recorded by Tom Rush; Nico; Linda Ronstadt; The Eagles; Co-writer with Glenn Frey, Take It Easy. Recordings: Albums: Jackson Browne, 1972; For Everyman, 1973; Late For The Sky, 1974; The Pretender, 1976; Running On Empty, 1978; Hold Out (Number 1, US), 1980; Lawyers In Love, 1983; Lives In The Balance, 1987; World In Motion, 1989; I'm Alive, 1993; Looking East, 1996; Also featured on No Nukes album, 1980; Sun City, Artists United Against Apartheid, 1985; For Our Children, Disney AIDS benefit album, 1991; Singles include: Doctor My Eyes, 1972; Here Come Those Tears Again, 1977;

Running On Empty, 1978; Stay, 1978; That Girl Could Sing, 1980; Somebody's Baby, used in film Fast Times At Ridgemont High, 1982; Tender Is The Night, 1983; You're A Friend Of Mine, with Clarence Clemons, 1986; For America, 1987. Current Management: Donald Miller, 12746 Kling Street, Studio City, CA 91604, USA.

BRUBECK David Warren, b. 6 Dec 1920, Concord, California, USA. Jazz Musician; Composer. m. Iola Whitlock, 1942. 5 sons, 1 daughter. Education: BA, University of Pacific; Composition with Darius Milhaud, Mills College. Career: Leader, Dave Brubeck Octet, Trio, Quartet, 1946-; Formed Dave Brubeck Quartet, 1951; Played colleges, festivals, clubs, symphony orchestras; 3 month tour, Middle East, Europe, for State Department; Frequent tours, Europe, Australia, Japan, USSR. Compositions: Ballets; Points On Jazz; Glances; Orchestral; Elementals; They All Sang Yankee Doodle; Flute And Guitar; Tritonis; Piano; Reminiscences Of The Cattle Country; Four By Four; Oratorios; The Light In The Wilderness; Beloved Son; Voice Of The Holy Spirit; Cantatas; Gates Of Justice; Truth; La Fiesta De La Posada; Chorus And Orchestra; Pange Lingua Mass; To Hope; I See; Satie; Four New England Pieces; Lenten Tryptich; Over 100 jazz compositions include: Blue Rondo A La Turk; In Your Own Sweet Way; The Duke. Numerous recordings. Honours: Honorary doctorates from: University of Pacific; Fairfield University; University of Bridgeport; Mills College; Niagara University; BMI Jazz Pioneer Award, 1985; Compostela Humanitarian Award, 1986; Connecticut Arts Award, 1987; American Eagle Award, National Music Council, 1988; Duke Ellington Fellow, Yale University. Current Management: Derry Music Company. Address: Box 216, Wilton, CT 06897, USA.

BRUCE Hal Nelson, b. 27 May 1952, Halifax, Nova Scotia, Canada. Musician (guitars, piano, harmonica). 1 son, 1 daughter. Education: Career in Cartography (mapping). Musical Education: 28 years experience. Career: Entertained 3 years running on Canadian Country Awards Show; Nominated twice for Canada's Vista Rising Star Award; Opened for Beach Boys 1989, Darlee Beach, Canada, 70,000 people. Recordings: 2 albums. Honours: Male Vocalist of the Year, 1991, Nova Scotia; Winner, talent search, Nova Scotia. Membership: Atlantic Federation of Musicians. Hobbies: White water canoeing; Collecting Beatles memorabilia. Current Management: Self-managed. Address: 18 Bellefontaine Court, Suite 30, Box 5, Dartmouth, Nova Scotia B2Y 3X7, Canada.

BRUCE Jack, b. 14 May 1943, Glasgow, Scotland. Musician (bass); Vocalist. Musical Education: Piano, Royal Scottish Academy of Music. Career: Member, Alexis Korner Blues Incorporated, 1962; Graham Bond Organisation, 1963; John Mayall's Bluesbreakers, 1965; Manfred Mann, 1965-66; Founder member, Cream (with Ginger Baker, Eric Clapton), 1966-68; Solo artiste, 1969-; Played in Tony Williams' Lifetime; Member, West Bruce And Laing; Leader, Jack Bruce and Friends (with Larry Coryell and Mitch Mitchell); Member, John McLaughlin's Mahavishnu Orchestra; Jack Bruce Band; Collaboration with Robin Trower, Bill Lordan, in BLT, 1981; Performances include: with Cream: National Jazz & Blues Festival, Windsor, 1967; Madison Square Garden, 1968; Royal Albert Hall, London, 1968. Recordings: Albums: with Cream: Fresh Cream, 1967; Disraeli Gears, 1967; Wheels Of Fire, 1968; Goodbye, 1969; Live Cream, 1970; Live Cream, Vol 2, 1972; Heavy Cream, 1972; Solo albums: Songs For A Tailor, 1969; Things We Like, 1970; Harmony Row, 1971; Jack Bruce At His Best, 1972; Out Of The Storm, 1974; How's Tricks, 1977; I've Always Wanted To Do This, 1980; Greatest Hits, 1980; Truce, 1982; Automatic, 1987; Willpower, 1989; A Question Of Time, 1990; with West Bruce & Laing: Why

Dontcha, 1972; with Jack Bruce And Friends: Live At The Bottom Line, 1992; Something Els, 1993; Singles: with Cream: Wrapping Paper, 1966; I Feel Free, 1967; Strange Brew, 1967; Sunshine Of Your Love, 1968; Anyone For Tennis (theme for film The Savage Seven), 1968; White Room, 1968. Address: c/o Miracle Prestige International Ltd, London, England.

BRUFORD Bill, b. 17 May 1949, Sevenoaks, Kent, England. Musician (drums, percussion). m. Carolyn, 2 Mar 1973, 2 sons, 1 daughter. Education: Leeds University. Musical Education: Mainly self-taught, some lessons from Lou Pocock, Royal Philharmonic Orchestra. Career: Member of Yes; Genesis; UK; King Crimson; Gong; Sideman to USA and Japanese leaders; Solo career as bandleader with Bruford and Earthworks; Worldwide tours since 1968. Compositions: 122 shared or solo; Writer for BBC TV and Buddy Rich Orchestra. Recordings: Over 50 album releases, 1968-; 9 solo albums. Publications: When In Doubt, Roll; numerous magazine articles. Honours: Modern Drummer Magazine Hall of Fame; Gold records. Memberships: Percussive Arts Society; PRS; BASCA. Hobbies: Family. Current Management: Richard Chadwick, Opium (Arts) Ltd., 49 Portland Road, London W11 4LJ, England.

BRUN Christian, b. 24 Dec 1965, Antibes, France. Musician (guitar); Composer. Education: Masters degree, Physics. Musical Education: Music school, lessons with Tal Farlow. Career: Performances with Lou Bennett; Turk Mauro; Big Band 31 and Dee Dee Bridgewater; Andre Villeger; Daniel Huck; Performed at festivals: Marciac; Albijazz; Jazz sur son 31; Jazz Sous les Pommiers. Recordings: Houseful; Samantha's Dance, with Steve Mabry; Brooklyn Session, with D Kikoski, L Plaxico, T Campbell. Honour: Winner, Radio France Concourse, 1991. Memberships: SACEM; SPEDIDAM. Hobbies: Sailing; Food; Wines; Girls. Address: Les Campanules, 29 Rue des Boulets, 75011 Paris, France.

BRUNBORG Tore, b. 20 May 1960, Trondheim, Norway. Jazz Musician (tenor, soprano saxophone). 1 son, 1 daughter. Education: Music Conservatory in Trondheim. Career: Toured, recorded, with Masqualero, 1982-1992. Compositions: Comission for Vossa Jazz, 1989; Music for big band, small groups. Recordings: 3 recordings with Masqualero; Also with: Bo Stieff; Rita Marcotulli; Jon Balke; Arild Anderson; Anders Jormin; Chick Lyall. Honours: Reenskaugprisen; Spelemannsprisen (3 times with Masqualero). Membership: Norwegian Musicians' Union. Hobbies: Skiing; Cycling. Address: Billingstadveien 52, 1362 Billingstad, Norway.

BRUNEAU Thierry, b. 28 July 1949, Paris, France. Musician (alto saxophone, bass clarinet, bassoon, flute, tenor and baritone saxophones). m. Päivi Hernala, 30 Oct 1971. Education: Anthropology; Ethnomusicology. Musical Education: CIM (jazz school); Private lessons with Allen Eager, Buddy Collette, Chris Woods; Conservatoire of Music (bassoon, flute). Career: Member, Big Bands: Alan Silva Celestrial Communication Orchestra; Laurent Cugny Big Band Lumiere; Quintet with Charles Tyler, 1987; Tours: Scandinavia, 1989-90; Japan, 1989; Europe with local rhythm sections, Mal Waldron, 1988-93; Ken McIntyre, 1990-92, 1996; Anthony Ortega, 1991-92, 1995; Concerts with: Richard Davis, 1990; Dennis Charles, 1994; Also played with: Duke Jordan; Han Bennink; Frank Lowe; Scriptwriter, actor, composer, film Last Date (Hans Hylkema's film about Eric Dolphy); Founder, own record label, Serene, 1989; Released some Eric Dolphy material (the Uppsala Concert); Played festivals at: Turku, Finland; Gothenburg, Sweden; Vienne, Tourcoing, Montpellier, TBB, Jazz Valley (France). Recordings: Live At De Kave, Thierry Bruneau Quartet featuring Mal Waldron; Tribute,

Ken McIntyre/Thierry Bruneau Quintet featuring Richard Davis; Anthony Ortega/Thierry Bruneau - 7 Standards And A Blues, Anthony Ortega. Publication: Book on Eric Dolphy in preparation. Hobbies: Films; Literature; Painting; Photography. Current Management: Self-managed. Address: Saincy, 77510 Bellot, France.

BRUNET Alain, b. 6 Mar 1947, Saint Sorlin, Drome, France. Musician (trumpet). Education: Master, Literature, Musicology. Musical Education: Musicology, Sorbonne University, Paris National Conservatory. Career: Founder, Module, 1974; Founder, Alain Brunet Quartet; Played with: Martial Solal; René Utreger; Jean-Louis Chautemps; Lee Konitz; Sonny Stitt; Georges Wein; Swing Limited Corporation; Machi-oul Big Band; Michel Graillier; Richard Raux; Al Grey; Stéphane Grappelli; Bernard Lubat; Didier Lockwood; Festivals: Vienna, 1983; Paris, 1984; Montpellier, 1988-90; Nevers, 1988; Nice, 1989-90, 1992-93; Montreux, 1992; New Orleans, 1992; Midem, 1993; Halle That Jazz Paris, 1993; Montreal, 1993; Newport, Saratoga, 1993; Invited to numerous international festivals including: East Africa; Tunisia; Greece; Belgium; Germany; Italy; Russia; Poland; Finland; Appearances on French television, 1975-; Hosted with Eve Ruggieri, Musiques Au Coeur (Jazz News), France 2 TV; Adviser to President, 5th TV Channel; Tour, USA includes: Boston, San Francisco, Los Angeles, 1995; Appeared Midem, Cannes, 1994. Recordings: with Machi-oul Big Band, 1975; Module, 1982; Rominus, with Didier Lockwood, 1991; Alain Brunet Plays Serge Gainsbourg, 1993; French Melodies in LA, Alain Brunet, 1995. Membership: SACEM. Current Management: Azimuth, 14 Rue Bleue, 75009 Paris, France.

BRUNK Floyd Dean, b. 18 Oct 1949, Dayton, Ohio, USA. Singer; Songwriter; Electronic technician. m. 24 Apr 1974, 2 sons. Education: Associates degree electronics. Recordings: Singles: Midst Of My Storm, 1992; Somebody Praise Him, 1992; Album: Midst Of My Storm, 1993; Currently working on cassette album. Membership: Gospel Music Association. Hobbies: Golf; Hunting; Fishing; Swimming; Basketball. Address: Rt 2, Box 210, Huntsville, AR 72740, USA.

BRUNNING Bob, b. 29 June 1943, Bournemouth, Dorset, England. Musician (bass); Writer. m. Halina, 8 Aug 1977, 2 sons, 1 daughter. Education: College of St Mark and St John, Chelsea, 3 year course qualified teacher, 1967; Now headteacher. Career: Began in Bournemouth with Tony Blackburn; College band, 1964-67; Fives Company (3 singles); Member, Fleetwood Mac, 1967; Savoy Brown, 1967; Own bands: Brunning Sunflower Blues Band, 1968-71; Tramp, 1971-74; The DeLuxe Blues Band, 1981-95. Recordings: 26 albums with all above, several recordings with visiting blues legends; Latest recording, DeLuxe Blues Band. Publications: Blues: The British Connection; Behind The Mask: Biography of Fleetwood Mac; Blues In Britain: The 50s To The 90s. Hobbies: Travel; Reading. Current Management: BB Management. Address: 55 Cavendish Road, Colliers Wood, London SW19 2ET, England.

BRUNTON Gary, b. 9 Mar 1968, Burnley, Lancashire, England. Jazz Musician (double bass). m. Beatrice Welter, 18 Sept 1993. Education: Modern Languages, Business Studies, University College, Swansea. Musical Education: Bass, double bass, CIM; Classical bass with Thierry Barbé; Private studies with: Henri Texier; Pierre Michelot; Ray Brown; Dave Holland; Gary Peacock, Paris Conservatory. Career: with Upper Space Group: Duc des Lombards; Sunset; Festival de Django Reinhardt, 1995; with Edouard Ferlet Trio: Petit Opportun; Festival de Jazz de Parthenay, 1994; Hotel Adagio; Hotel Lutecia; Trilogie: Salle André Marechal, 1994; with Guitar Hell: Tours, Germany, 1994, 1995; Sunset; Hot

Club de Lyon; La Tour Rose; Performances with: Trio Bojan Zulfikarpasic: Radio France Inter; with Trio Michel Grailler: Le Petit Journal Montparnasse; Le Houdon; with Jonathan Lewis Quartet: Jazz Parade, BBC Radio; Brecon Jazz Festival, Tour, Britain, 1990; Elizabeth Kontamanu Quartet, Rumanian tour, 1992; Stephanie Crawford Quartet; Michelle Hendricks; Paulo Fresu; Stéphane Belmondo; François Théberge; Pete Osbourne; Jeannot Rabeson; Patrice Galas; Philippe Soirat; Simon Goubert; Sangoma Everett; Olivier Hutman; Charles Bellonzi; Craig Handy. Recordings with: Lucide Beausonge; Laure Milena; Bruno Joubrel; Patrick Husson; Commercial television; Film track, Tom Est Tout Seul, La Bande Son, Canal +. Membership: UMJ (Union Musiciens de Jazz). Address: 37 Bld Ornano, 75018 Paris, France.

BRUNTON Richard McNaughton, b. 3 Oct 1949, Newcastle-Upon-Tyne, England. Musician (guitars, keyboards); Composer. 1 son, 2 daughters. Musical Education: Piano lessons age 8-12; Guitar self-taught. Career: Own R&B band, Newcastle, 1964-68; Moved to London, freelance guitarist, 1969; Recorded over 200 records for artists including: Gerry Rafferty; Dr John; Barbara Dickson; Greg Lake; Pete Sinfield; Numerous television and film soundtracks. Recordings include: Still, Pete Sinfield; Night Owl, Snakes And Ladders, Gerry Rafferty; Gold, Heartbeats, Barbara Dickson; Works, Emerson Lake and Palmer; BBC television soundtracks: The Grass Arena; Life And Loves Of A She-Devil. Memberships: Musicians' Union; PRS; BASCA. Hobbies: Electro-mechanical engineering; Aviation.

BRYAN Kelle, b. 1976. Singer. Career: Singer, UK all-female vocal group, Eternal, 1992-. Recordings: Albums: Always And Forever, 1993; Power Of A Woman, 1995; Greatest Hits, 1997; Hit singles: Stay, 1994; Power Of A Woman, 1995; I Am Blessed, 1995; Good Thing, 1996; Angel of Mine, 1997. Honours: BRIT Award Nominations: Best Group, Best Newcomers, Best Album, Best Dance Act, 1995; Best Dance Act, 1996; Smash Hits Award; International Dance Award, Dance Act Of The Year, 1995; Only UK act to have 6 Top 15 hits from debut album. Current Management: First Avenue Management, The Courtyard, 42 Colwith Road, London W6 9EY, England.

BRYANT Colin, b. 20 Nov 1936, Poole, Dorset, England. Musician (clarinet, saxophones). m. (1) 1 son, 2 daughters, (2). Musical Education: Privately taught; Later, Royal Marines School Of Music. Career: Professional musician since leaving school; Principal clarinet, Band of Royal Marines, 1950s; Clarinet saxophone with Nat Gonnells, late 1950s; Toured with Louis Armstrong All Stars, 1962; Tours, performances, throughout Europe; Featured in film with Joe Darensburg (Louis Armstrong's clarinetist); Jazzband leader, The Hot Rhythm Orchestra, Cunard QE2, 1975-1997; Cruises every year for 21 years; Many BBC Radio and ITV performances; Only jazzband invited to play at The Houses of Parliament; Director of Entertainment Agency; Numerous recordings on own Hot Rhythm label. Honours: Melody Maker Poll Winner, Best Jazz Clarinet, 1963. Membership: Musicians' Union. Hobbies: Ships; Birds. Current Management: C B Entertainments. Address: 24 Bushmead Drive, Ringwood, Hants BH24 2HU, England.

BRYANT Dana, b. 2 May 1965, New York City, USA. Spoken word artist. Education: BA, Brandeis University. Career: Jazz festivals: Vienna, 1992; Berlin Jazz, 1992; Brighton Jazz Bop, 1993; Television: The Charlie Rose Show, 1992; Fighting Wordz, MTV, 1992; Spoken Word Unplugged, 1993; The South Bank Show, Ch 4, 1994; The Girlie Show, London, Ch 4, 1996. Recordings: Dominican Girdles Heat, 1993; The Jackal, with Ronnie Jordan (The Quiet Revolution), 1994; Wishing From The Top, 1996.

Publications: Song Of The Siren, 1995. Membership: ASCAP. Current Management: Knitting; Fencing; Cycling. Current Management: Maurice Bernstein, The Groove Academy. Address: c/o The Groove Academy, 62 White Street, Suite 312, New York, NY 10013, USA.

BRYANT David Steve, b. 27 Dec 1921, Chicago, Illinois, USA. Musician (bass). Musical Education: Los Angeles Conservatory, 1947-48; Westlake College of Music, 1952. Career: Bass player, various artistes including: Jimmy Buffett; Sarah Vaughn; Billie Holliday; Gerald Wilson; Louis Jordan; Brook Benton; Lou Rawls; Bassist, Horace Tapscott Orchestra, 1964-; Watts Symphony Orchestra, 1976-80; Leader, own quartet, 1983-84; Music teacher, Los Angeles Board of Education, 1977-80. Membership: AFTRA.

BRYANT Gerry, b. 30 Apr 1965, Portsmouth, England. Musician (bass guitar). Education: Technical Colleges. Career: Bass guitarist, group Mega City Four, touring throughout Europe including Scandinavia, Japan, US and Canada, 1988-; Appeared on Peel Sessions, 1988-93; The Word, Ch4, 1992; Concerts include: Reading Festival, 1990-92; Glastonbury Festival, 1993; Phoenix Festival, 1994. Recordings: with Mega City Four: Tranzophobia, 1988; Who Cares Wins, 1989; Terribly Sorry Bob, 1990; Sebastopol Road, 1992; Inspiringly Titled... (live album), 1992; Magic Bullets, 1993. Publication: Tall Stories And Creepy Crawlies, Mega City Four biography, 1994. Membership: Musicians' Union. Hobbies: Going to concerts; Football; British stately homes and castles; Travel. Current Agent: Paul Bolton, ICM/Fair Warning. Address: The Plaza, 535 Kings Road, London SW10, England.

BRYANT Terl, b. 2 May 1961, Walgrave, Northamptonshire, England. Musician (drums, percussion). m. Juliet, 3 Oct 1992, 1 daughter. Musical Education: Self-taught. Career: Member, group Iona, 1992-; Toured, recorded with artists from UK and USA including: Steve Taylor; Cliff Richard; Darrell Mansfield; Sheila Walsh; Lies Damned Lies; Ben Okafor; Graham Kendrick; Ishmael; Phil and John (The Woodthieves); Iona; Richard Darbyshire; Martin Smith; Noel Richards; Dave Bilbrough; Adrian Snell; Paul Field; Others including 6 years with Peter Murphy (ex-Bauhaus), including 3 albums, extensive tours, USA, Japan, Israel, Europe. Recordings: Love Hysteria, 1987; Deep, 1989; Iona, 1990; Holy Smoke, 1991; Book Of Kells, 1992; Beyond These Shores, 1994; Journey Into The Morn, 1995; Solo: Psalm, 1995. Honours: GMA International Artist Award: The Book Of Kells, 1993. Membership: Musicians' Union. Address: PO Box 5229, Ealing, London W5 2GD, England.

BRYCE Owen, b. 8 Aug 1920, Woolwich, London, England. Musician (trumpet, piano); Writer; Lecturer. m. Iris Edith, 22 Dec 1945, 1 son, 3 daughters. Career: Founder member, George Webb's Dixielanders, many records, broadcasts; Own band, 1956-; Many broadcasts, appearances include Savoy Hotel; Lecturer for many organizations, county councils, colleges, summer schools; First speaker on Jazz on BBC Schools Service; Teacher, pupils include Chris Barber; Humphrey Lyttelton. Publications: Let's Play Jazz 1-4; Book on British Jazz Scene 1942-55, to be published. Honours: Diploma Polish Music Festival; Freeman of New Orleans. Membership: Musicians' Union. Hobbies: Croquet; Stamp collecting. Address: 58 Pond Bank, Blisworth, Northants NN7 3EL, England.

BRYDOY Eivind, b. 20 June 1964, Levanger, Norway. Artist Manager. Education: MBA, Norwegian School of Economics; University of New Orleans; UMIST, Manchester, England. Career: Stageway, 3 years; Controller, Stageway Record Company, 1 year; Agency Dept, Stageway, 2 years; Manager, Artistpartner, own

company, 4 years. Publication: Eureka Collaborative Agreements, 1992. Membership: General Secretary, International Managers Forvum, Norway. Hobby: Sailing. Current Managements of Acts: Cecilia, Ephemera Cornflakes, Baba Nation, Trang Fodsel, Di Derre. Address: Grini Naeringspark 17, 1345 Osteraas, Norway.

BRYNGELSSON Hans Inge Peter, b. 17 September 1955, Vetlanda, Sweden. Musician; Composer. m. Anita Malmguist Bryngelsson, 11 December 1986, 1 son. Education: Vallehilde Folkhojskole Dramatic Institute; Private courses in composition. Career: Leader of the Band Ragnarö, 1972-84, 4 albums; Leader, Triangulus, 1985-89, 2 albums; Guitarsis, Music for 10 guitars, Urban Turban, 1993-; Composed music for film, theatre, expositions, radio & TV. Compositions: Via, 1990; Happy Starr, 1992; Sound of Glass, 1995; Guitarrsis, Music for 10 guitarists; Katabasis, Music for 5 bass instr. Recordings: Ragnarö, 1976; King Tung, 1979; Via, 1990; Urban Turban, 1994; Urban Turban Overtime, 1996; Astro Turf, 1998. Publications: Ode to the Stone, TV-film, 1991; The Other Shore Michael Wiström, TV-film, 1992; Snalast, TV-film, 1997. Honours: 3 grammy nominations in Sweden, 1990, 1993, 1997; STIM's Musical Prize, SKAPs Musical Prize. Memberships: STIM; SKAP; SAMI. Hobbies: Ski vacations; Tennis; Crosswords; Contemporary Art. Current Management: Bryngelsson Musik, Folkungagaton 150, 11630 Stockholm, Sweden. Address: Folkungagatan 150, 11630 Stockholm, Sweden.

BRYSON (Robert) Peabo, b. 13 Apr 1951, Greenville, South Carolina, USA. Soul Singer; Record Producer. Career: Former member, Moses Dillard; Tex-Town Display; Michael Zager's Moon Band, 1976-78; Solo soul artiste, 1979-. Recordings: Albums: Reaching For The Sky, 1978; Crosswinds, 1978; We're The Best Of Friends (with Natalie Cole), 1979; Live - And More (with Roberta Flack), 1980; Paradise, 1980; I Am Love, 1981; Turn The Hands Of Time, 1981; Don't Play With Fire, 1982; Born To Love (with Roberta Flack), 1983; The Peabro Bryson Collection, 1984; Straight From The Heart, 1984; Quiet Storm, 1986; Take No Prisoners, 1987; Positive, 1988; All My Love, 1989; Singles: with Michael Zager's Moon Band: Reaching For The Sky; I'm So Into You; Solo: If Ever You're In My Arms Again, 1984; Duets: Gimme Some Time, with Natalie Cole, 1979; Tonight I Celebrate My Love, with Roberta Flack, 1983; Beauty And The Beast, with Celine Dion, 1992; Other duets with Melissa Manchester; Regina Belle; Contributor, Color And Light - Jazz Sketches On Sondheim, 1995. Current Management: David M. Franklin and Associates, 999 Peachtree Street, Suite 2680, Atlanta, GA 30309, USA.

BRYSON William Shields, b. 10 Nov 1946, Evanston, Illinois, USA. Musician (bass); Singer. m. Anne Jeanine Bailey, 24 July 1976. Career: Bass player, Bluegrass Cardinals; Country Gazette; Doug Dillard Band; The Long Riders with Ry Cooder, 1980-84; The Desert Rose Band, 1984-. Recordings: Albums include: What A Way Earn A Living, Country Gazette, 1977; Long Riders (film soundtrack), Ry Cooder, 1980; Jackrabbit, Doug Dillard, 1980; Home Coming and Family Reunion, The Dillards, 1980; with The Desert Rose Band: The Desert Rose Band, 1987; Running, 1988; Pages Of Life, 1990; True Love, 1991; A Dozen Roses, 1991. Honours: Grammy Nominations, 1987, 1989; ACM Awards: Bass Player of the Year, 1990; Touring Band of the Year, Desert Rose Band, 1988-90. Memberships: Screen Actors Guild; AFTRA; AFofM.

BRZEZICKI Mark, b. 21 June 1957, Slough, Berkshire, England. Musician (drums, percussion). Education: City & Guilds, HNC, Aircraft Engineering, Brooklands Technical College. Career: Member of Big Country, 1981-; Tours include: Fish, 1990-91; Midge Ure, 1991-92; Procul Harum, USA 1991, Europe, 1992; Major concerts include: Mandela Concert, Wembley Stadium, 1989; Annual Princes Trust Rock Galas, 1985-88; Procul Harum European Festivals, 1992; Chieftains, Midge Ure, Roger Daltrey show, 1994; Television appearances include: Children in Need, 1989, BBC; ITV Telethon Live, 1992; BBC Breakfast Time; Phil Collins' This Is Your Life; Appearances with Sting; Nils Lofgren; Procul Harum; The Cult; Tears For Fears; Fish; Midge Ure; Big Country. Recordings include: Albums: 10 with Big Country; 5 with Pete Townshend; 3 with Midge Ure; 4 Prince's Trust Rock Gala Compilations; Also appeared on albums by artists including: Roger Daltrey; Simon Townshend; Procul Harum; Love and Money; The Cult; Fish; Nils Lofgren; Joan Armatrading; Ultravox; Howard Jones; Nik Kershaw; Steve Harley; Go West; Tom Robinson; Played on film soundtracks: Quick Silver Lightning; Rambo 3; Restless Natives; White City. Honours: Invited Special Guest, World Drum Festival, Canada, 1987; 2 Grammy Nominations, 1984; Zildjian Musician Poll, Best Rock/Pop mainstream drummer UK, 1988-90; Making Music Poll, 1988; Pearl Drummers Club, Best UK Rock/Pop drummer, 1990; Princes Trust Award, 1984; Numerous Platinum, Gold and Silver records. Memberships: Prince's Trust; GISM; PRS. Hobby: Boating. Current Management: Ian Grant Management. Address: Owl House, Byers Lane, South Godstone, Surrey RH9 8JL, England.

BUCHANAN Margo, b. 3 Feb 1955, Lanark, Scotland. Vocalist. m. Paul Wickens, 31 Jan 1992. Career: Television: European promotional tour, Billy Idol, 1986; Concert By The Lake, with Eric Clapton, Phil Collins, Steve Winwood, 1988; Amnesty International Concert, with Dave Gilmour, Seal, Tom Jones, 1990; Concert with Billy Bragg, Hugh Cornwall, London Palladium, 1990; The Great Music Experience, with Joni Mitchell, Bob Dylan, Bon Jovi, 1994. Recordings: with Tina Turner: Break Every Rule, 1987; with Mink Deville: Silver Bullets; Recording/writing with Sam Brown: This Feeling; Your Love Is All; It Makes Me Wonder; With A Little Love; As One; with Jools Holland: No-One's To Blame. Memberships: Musicians' Union; Equity. Hobbies: Concerts; Dolls houses; Films; Gardens. Current Management: One Management, 43 St Albans Avenue, London W4 5JS, England.

BUCHWALD Joseph, b. 3 Sept 1917, Cincinnatti, Ohio, USA. Personal Manager. m. 3 Oct 1936, 1 son, 1 daughter. Career: Personal manager. Hobby: Relaxation. Current Management: Self-managed. Address: PO Box 347008, San Francisco, CA 94134, USA.

BUCK Gary Ralph, b. Thessalon, Ontario, Canada. Singer; Record Producer; Songwriter. m. Deb Way, 2 sons, 3 daughters. Career: Singer, most major Country Music television and radio shows, US and Canada; Tours throughout USA, Canada (Calgary Exhibition promotion), England, New Zealand (Miss NZ Pageant); Publisher, composer, songwriter for Calgary's Olympic bid; Music for commercials include: Pepsi, Molson's Export Ale, Kelloggs' Raisin Bran, Mastercard, Ford; Television appearances include: Gary Buck Show, CKCO TV, 1965-67; Host, Maritime Telethon, 3 times; Founder, President, Canadian Country Music Hall of Fame; Manager, Capitol Records Publishing Division, 3 years; Started Broadland Publishing Co; Became Broadlands International Records, 1991; International Director, Country Music Association, Nashville, 10 years; Founding Director, Academy of Country Music Entertainment, now known as Canadian Country Music Association. Literary Agent for Hank Snow; Producer of over 100 albums, launched careers of Wayne Rostad; Family Brown; Dallas Harms; Lee Roy Anderson; Currently producer for Gene Watson; Billie Jo Spears; George Hamilton IV. Honours: Top Male Singer, Canada, 5 times; Top Country Record Producer, 1975; Medal of Merit,

City of Sault Ste Marie, for contributions to music industry, 1990.

BUCK Peter, b. 6 Dec 1956. Musician (guitar); Producer. Career: Member, R.E.M., 1980-; International tours; Also member, side-project, Hindu Love Gods, 1986-90. Recordings: Albums: with R.E.M.: Chronic Town (mini-album), 1982; Murmur, 1983; Reckoning, 1984; Fables Of The Reconstruction, 1985; Life's Rich Pageant, 1986; Dead Letter Office, 1987; Document, 1987; Eponymous, 1988; Green, 1988; Out Of Time, 1991; The Best Of R.E.M., 1991; Automatic For The People (Number 1, UK), 1992; Monster, 1995; with Hindu Love Gods: Hindu Love Gods, 1990; Singles: with R.E.M.: The One I Love, 1987; Stand, 1989; Orange Crush, 1989; Radio Song, 1991; Drive, 1992; Man On The Moon, 1992; The Sidewinder Sleeps Tonite, 1993; Everybody Hurts, 1993; Crush With Eyeliner; What's The Frequency Kenneth?; Nightswimming; Tracks featured on film soundtracks: Batchelor Party, 1984; Until The End Of The World, 1991; Coneheads, 1993; Other recordings: with Indigo Girls; Warren Zevon; Contributor, albums: Tom's Album; I'm Your Fan; Time Inbetween; Producer, albums by Uncle Tupelo; Vigilantes Of Love. Honours: Earth Day Award, 1990; Numerous MTV Music Video Awards; Billboard Awards: Best Modern Rock Artist, Best World Album, 1991; BRIT Awards: Best International Group, 1992, 1993, 1995; Grammy Awards: Best Pop Performance, Alternative Music Album, Music Video, 1992; Atlanta Music Awards: Act Of The Year, Rock Album, Video, 1992; IRMA, International Band Of The Year, 1993; Rolling Stone Critics Awards: Best Band, Best Album, 1993; Q Awards: Best Album, 1991, 1992; Best Act In The World, 1991, 1995. Current Management: REM/Athens Ltd., 250 W Clayton Street, Athens, GA 30601, USA.

BUCKINGHAM Lindsey, b. 3 Oct 1947. Musician (guitar); Singer; Songwriter. Career: Member, rock band Fritz, 1960s; Duo, Buckingham Nicks (with Stevie Nicks), 1971-74; Member, Fleetwood Mac, 1975-87; Solo artiste, 1981-; Appearances include: Regular US tours; Madison Square Garden; US Festival, 1982. Compositions: with Fleetwood Mac: Second Hand News; Tusk; Go Your Own Way; Big Love; Oh Diane. Recordings: Albums: with Buckingham Nicks: Buckingham Nicks, 1973; with Fleetwood Mac: Fleetwood Mac, 1975; Rumours, 1977; Tusk, 1979; Live, 1980; Mirage (also producer), 1982; Tango In The Night, 1987; Solo albums: Law And Order, 1981; Go Insane, 1984; Out Of The Cradle, 1992; Singles with Fleetwood Mac: Over My Head; Rhiannon (Will You Ever Win); Say You Love Me; Dreams; You Make Loving Fun; Tusk; Sara; Think About Me; Trouble; Gipsy. Honours: Grammy Award, Fleetwood Mac, Rumours, 1977; American Music Awards: Favourite Pop/Rock Group, Favourite Album, 1978. Address: c/o Michael Brokaw Management, 2934 Beverly Glen Circle #383, Bel Air, CA 90077, USA.

BUCKLEY Steve, b. 6 Jan 1959, Orpington, Kent, England. Musician (saxophones, bass clarinet, tin whistle). Education: Leeds University degree. Musical Education: Classical clarinet tuition at school. Career: Tours, recordings with Loose Tubes; Delightful Precipice; Human Chain; Numerous television and radio appearances with these bands; Long association with South American, African London-based bands; Own projects include Buckley Batchelor, impro trio with Steve Noble and Oren Marshall. Recordings: Open Letter, Loose Tubes; Third Policeman, Django Bates; Summer Fruits, Delightful Precipice; Winter Truce, Delightful Precipice; Whole And The Half, Buckley Batchelor; Pyrotechnics, Human Chain. Hobbies: Reading; Swimming; Hill walking. Address: 140 Amelia Street, London SE17 3AR, England.

BUDD Stephen, b. 25 Dec 1958, London, England. m. 6 June 1986, 1 daughter. Career: Started Torch Records, age 20, 1979; Signed: The Sound; The Cardiacs; Big Sound Authority; Manager: The Sound, Big Sound Authority; Sally Oldfield, 1980-85; Managed producers, Tony Visconti, Arthur Baker, 1985-88; Started Stephen Budd Management, managing producer: Rapino Brothers; Martyn Ware; Mike Hedges; Mike Vernon; Colin Fairley; Stonebridge; Nick Martinelli; Gus Dudgeon; Rick Nowels; Rafe McKenna, 1988-; Formed Morrison Budd Music Publishing, with partner Bryan Morrison, 1993-. Honours: Numerous Gold, Platinum discs. Memberships: Board member, International Managers Forum; Chairman, Producer Managers Group; REPRO. Hobbies: Eating; Arsenal Football Club. Address: Stephen Budd Management, 109B Regents Park Road, London NW1 8UR, England.

BUDTS Danny, b. 12 May 1958, Wilrijk, Belgium. Production Officer. m. Machteld De Muynck, 6 November 1982, 2 sons. Education: Selftaught guitar, synthesizer, studio equipment, singer, songwriter, composer, producer. Career: Lead Guitar, Cold Turkey, 1970s; Syndromeda, own midi studio, 1990; Different interviews on local radios. Recordings: 6 MC's; 2 full CD's: Mind Trips; Circles of Life; Tracks on: Truth or Dare; Movements; Sequences 14 and 19. Honour: Movements, CD, composition contest, 1997. Hobbies: Music; Music and Music. Current Management: Groove Unlimited, PO Box 2171, 8203 AD, Lelystad, Netherlands. Address: Pastoryveld 28, 2180 Ekeren, Belgie.

BUFFETT Jimmy, b. 25 Dec 1946, Pascagoula, Mississippi, USA. Country Singer; Songwriter. m. Jane Slagsvol, 27 Aug 1977. Education: BS, History, Journalism, University of Southern California, 1969. Career: Former freelance journalist, Inside Sports Outside magazine; Billboard magazine; Solo artiste, 1970s-; Formed Coral Reef Band, 1975. Numerous compositions include: Railroad Lady (recorded by Merle Haggard); He Went To Paris (recorded by Waylon Jennings); Margaritaville; Come Monday; Cheeseburger In Paradise. Recordings: Albums: Down To Earth, 1972; High Cumberland Jubilee, 1972; A White Sport Coat And A Pink Crustacean, 1973; Living And Dying In 3/4 Time, 1974; AIA, 1974; Rancho Deluxe (film soundtrack), 1975; Havaa Daydreaming, 1976; Changes In Latitudes, Changes In Attitudes, 1977; Son Of A Son Of A Sailor, 1978; You Had To Be There, 1978; Volcano, 1979; Coconut Telegraph, 1980; Somewhere Over China, 1981; One Particular Harbour, 1983; Riddles In The Sand, 1984; Last Mango In Paris, 1985; Songs You Know By Heart, 1986; Floridays, 1986; Hot Water, 1988; Off To See The Lizard, 1989; Live Feeding Frenzy, 1991. Publication: Tales From Margaritaville, 1989. Honours: Platinum and Gold discs. Memberships: Honorary director, Greenpeace; Founder member, Cousteau Society. Current Management: Howard Kaufman, HK Management, 8900 Wilshire Blvd, Ste 300, Beverly Hills, CA 90211, USA.

BUHRER Rolf Marcel, b. 28 June 1932, Zurich, Switzerland. Musician (valve-bone, upright string bass). 1 son. Career: Member of bands: Laferrière; Claude Luter; Mixim Saury; Played with: Albert Nicolas; Mezz Mezzrow; Harry `Sweets' Edison; Eddie Davis; Moustache; Tours: France, Germany, North Africa; Numerous recordings. Membership: UMJ (Union Musician de Jazz).

BUIRETTE Michele Jeanne, b. 4 Mar 1949, Boulogne Sur Seine, France. Musician (accordion). 1 daughter. Education: Maitrise de Psychologie. Career: Jazz Festivals: Le Mans; Berlin; Grenoble; Tours, Europe: Germany; Netherlands; Switzerland; Italy; Croatia; Slovenia. Recordings: with Pied de Poule: Indiscretion; Café Noir; Jamais Tranquille!; Solo: La Mise En Plis.

Membership: SACEM. Current Management: Edna Fainaru. Address: 63 Boulevard de Ménilmoutant, 75011 Paris, France.

BUKOVSKY Petr, b. 1 April 1947, Prague, Czech Republic. divorced, 1 son, 1 daughter. Education: Selftaught guitar, piano. Career: Songwriter, Radio, TV, Gramophone Companies (Pop, Rock, Brass and Dance Music), 1970-. Recordings: The Angel Ship, 1970; The Lime, The Lime My, 1974; Today We Will Polka Play to You, 1974; The Easter Rod, 1975; The Gamekeeper's Lodge, 1982; I Know, 1995; Today For the Last Time, 1997; I Can't Call You, 1997. Honours: Today We Will Polka Play to You, 1974; The Easter Rod, 1975. Membership: OSA, Czech Republic. Hobbies: Literature; Music; Sports. Address: Bukovsky Petr, Vitosska 3415/11, 14300 Prague 4, Modrany, Czech Republic.

BULL Irene Sheila, b. 6 May 1953, London, England. Promoter; Songwriter; Publisher. m. 6 May 1972, 3 sons. Education: City & Guilds Catering, Office Skills. Musical education: Self-taught. Career: Co-written songs for 2 musicals including Mayhew's London; Both received television coverage; Head of The New Songwriter's showcase; Head of The Big Break band competition; Co-partner, co-writer, School-Sheet Music; Promote various events include: Country In The City, National Music Day Charity Events and The Kosha Club, Camden; Music Co-ordinator for a youth project; Publishing Sacred Cow and Harmonica Jones; Currently compiling a CD from showcases. Memberships: PRS (writer and publisher); IPA. Hobbies: Study of human psychology; Reading; Crosswords; Cinema; Theatre; Eating out; Debating; Time with family and close friends. Address: Bull-Sheet Music Ltd, c/o 18 The Bramblings, London E4 6LU, England.

BUNDRICK John Douglas (Rabbit), b. 21 Nov 1948, Baytown, Texas, USA. Musician (keyboards, piano, Hammond organ); Composer. m. Susan Elizabeth Vickers, 17 Sept 1989. Musical Education: Piano lessons, age 7; High school and college music. Career: Musical Director, composer, Johnny Nash, Sweden, 1971; Moved to UK, 1971; Member, Free, 1972; Eric Burdon, 1975; Co-founder, Crawler, 1976-79; The Who, 1979-; Concerts include Live Aid Concert, Wembley, 1985; Pete Townshend, US tour, 1993; Roger Daltrey, Carnegie Hall Concert, US tour, 1994; Television: Garth Brooks, BBC TV; Jay Leno Show, Los Angeles; Prolific session musician. Recordings: Numerous albums include: with The Who: Face Dances; Who's Better Who's Best; The Singles; Join Together; Live Aid; with Johnny Nash: I Can See Clearly Now; Celebrate Life; Here Again; My Merry Go Round; with Free: Heartbreaker; Free Story; The Best Of Free; with Pete Townshend: Rough Mix; Empty Glass; Psychoderelict; White City; with Andy Fairweather-Low: La Booga Rooga; Be Bop'N'Holla; with Rabbit: Dream Jungle; Broken Arrows; Dark Saloon; Run For Cover; Same Old Story; Other recordings: Catch A Fire, Bob Marley; Solid Air, John Martyn; Show Some Emotion, Joan Armatrading; Catfish Rising, Jethro Tull; Back Street Crawler, Paul Kossoff; Cosmic Wheels, Donovan; Survivor, Eric Burdon; Highway To The Sun, Snowy White; A Celebration-The Music Of Pete Townshend, Roger Daltrey; She's The Boss, Mick Jagger; Bebop The Future, David Essex; Live At The Albert Hall, David Gilmore; Amused To Death, Roger Waters; Other recordings with artistes including Tom Robinson; Backstreet Crawler; Claire Hamill; Sandy Denny; Suzi Quatro; Toots and the Maytalls; Russ Ballard; Peter Frampton; Hank Wangford; Bill Wyman; Richard Thompson; Barbara Dickson; Boo Hewerdine; Kossoff, Kirke, Tetsu and Rabbit; Film soundtracks: Rocky Horror Picture Show; King Ralph; McVicar; Bad Timing. Memberships: PRS; Musicians' Union. Hobbies: Gardening; Music; Animals. Current Management: Self-managed;

Also David Clayton. Address: c/o David Clayton, 39 Staverton Road, Bilborough, Nottingham NG8 4ET, England.

BUNN Roger, b. Norwich, England. Musician (guitar, bass); Music Organization Executive. Career: Professional musician, 1988-; As musician: Played Star Club, Hamburg, 1960s; Double bass player, Marianne Faithfull; Davy Graham; Guitarist, Roxy Music; Featured, Got To Be Your Lover video, Billy Idol; Double bass player, Chris McGregor band; as Music Organization Executive: President, Music Industry Human Rights Association (MIHRA), Third World fundraising, and combating monopolies in music industry (founded 1994); Founder, Jazz Against Apartheid; Musicians' Emergency Committee; Coordinator, Anti-apartheid Golf Campaign;Coordinator, First British anti-apartheid news team, South Africa, 1988; First man banned by South African minority Government after UN sanctions lifted. Recordings: Solo album: Piece of Mind, 1971. Address: MIHRA, 192 Chiswick Village, London W4 3DG, England.

BURCH Bruce, b. Georgia, USA. Songwriter. m. Cindy. Education: College degree, University of Georgia. Musical Education: Self-taught guitar. Career: Football Coach, Gainsville High School; Signed to Combine Music, Nashville, to develop songwriting, then Famous Music; Co-founder, Burch Brothers Music (with brother David). Compositions: Hits include: Reba McEntire: Rumor Has It; T Graham Brown: The Last Resort; Billy Joe Royal: Out Of Sight and On My Mind; Other songs recorded by: Reba McEntire; Aaron Tippin; George Fox; Dan Seals; Barbara Mandrell; Oak Ridge Boys. Membership: SESAC. Address: c/o SESAC, 55 Music E, Nashville, TN 37203, USA.

BURDON Eric, b. 11 May 1941, Newcastle upon Tyne, England. Vocalist. Education: Newcastle College of Art and Industrial Design. Career: Member, The Pagans; Member, The Animals, 1963-67; Became Eric Burdon & The New Animals, 1968; Eric Burdon And War, 1970; Solo artiste, 1971-; Also, leader, Eric Burdon Band; Tours worldwide; Major concerts include: Monterey Pop Festival, 1967; Reading Festival, 1973; Film appearances: Top Gear, 1965; Stranger In The House, 1967; Joe Vs The Volcano, 1990. Recordings: Albums: with the Animals: The Animals, 1964; Animal Tracks, 1965; The Animals On Tour, 1965; The Best Of The Animals, 1966; The Most Of The Animals, 1966; Animalisms, 1966; Animalization, 1966; Help Me Girl, 1967; When I Was Young, 1967; Best Of (Vol 2), 1967; Winds Of Change, 1967; The Twain Shall Meet, 1968; Every One Of Us, 1968; Love Is, 1969; Before We Were So Rudely Interrupted, 1977; Ark, 1983; Rip It To Shreds, 1984; with Eric Burdon & War: Eric Burdon Declares War, 1970; Black Man's Burdon, 1971; Solo/Eric Burdon Band: Eric Is Here, 1967; Guilty, 1971; Ring Of Fire, 1974; Sun Secrets, 1975; Stop (with Jimmy Witherspoon), 1975; Survivor, 1978; Gotta Find My Baby, 1979; Last Drive, 1980; Live, 1982; Comeback, 1982; I Used To Be An Animal, 1988; Wicked Man (with Jimmy Witherspoon), 1988; Crawling King Snake, 1992. Publication: Autobiography, I Used To Be An Animal, But I'm All Right Now, 1986. Current Management: c/o Denis Vaughan, Bond Street House, 14 Clifford Street, London W1X 2JD, England.

BURFORD Ian James, b. 14 Jan 1963, Leicester, England. Musician (guitar, bass, keyboards); Composer; Tutor of music. m. 15 May 1993, 1 son, 1 daughter. Education: City & Guilds in Mechanical Engineering. Musical Education: Self-taught. Career: Part-tiime College Tutor of music, Founder member, Quasar, 1980; Later, solo artist; Has since worked as Solo Artist on various projects; Engaged in writing and recording New Age music; Performances include The Roadmender, 1997. Recordings: The Industrial

City, 1985; Satalites, 1986; Nowhere To Go, 1986; Strangers, 1986; Fatal Exposure, 1987; Touch Down, 1991; New Age albums: Spirit of the Nile, 1997; Spiritual Journey, 1998. Membership: Musicians' Union. Hobbies: Golf; Visiting craft fairs and steam engine rallies; Family. Current Management: Sandra Higginson-Burford. Address: c/o 52 Greenmoor Road, Leicester LE10 2LT, England.

BURGESS John Edward, b. 8 Mar 1932, London, England. Record Producer; Studio Owner. m. Jean Horsfall, 5 Sept 1964, 3 sons. Career: Press, promotion, publicity, EMI Records, 1951; Production assistant to Norman Newell; Founder member, AIR Group of Companies with George Martin, 1965; AIR Studios opened 1969; Merged with Chrysalis, 1974; Managing Director, Air Studios, Montserrat, West Indies, 1979; Managing Director, Air Studios, London, 1969-90, Lyndhurst, 1990-; Recordings: Producer for: Adam Faith; Manfred Mann; Peter and Gordon; Freddy and the Dreamers; John Barry Seven; Cast albums: Barnum; Guys and Dolls. Address: 2 Sudbury Hill, Harrow on the Hill, Harrow, Middlesex HA1 3SB, England.

BURGESS Tim, b. 30 May 1968, Salford, Manchester, England. Singer. Career: Lead singer, The Charlatans; Sold-out concerts at Manchester Nynex Arena and London Docklands Arena, 1997. Recordings: Albums: Some Friendly, 1990; Between 10th & 11th, 1992; Up To Our Hips, 1994; The Charlatans, 1995; Tellin' Stgories, 1997; Singles include: The Only One I Know; Then; Me In Time; Over Rising; Just When You're Thinkin' Things Over; One to Another; North Country Boy; How High; Tellin' Stories; Honours: Gold, Silver and Platinum discs; Cover version of Time for Living by Sly and the Family Stone on the "Help" Bosnia charity album, 1995; Raised nearly £40,00 for charity Missing Persons Helpline at the Brixton Academy, 1997. Current Management: Steve Harrison Management, 2 Witton Walk, Northwich, Cheshire CW9 5AT, England.

BURGH Steven Lawrence, 17 Dec 1950, Trenton, New Jersey, USA. Record Producer; Musician (guitar). m. Jamie Reisch, 26 Feb 1983, 1 son, 1 daughter. Career: Musician with: Phoebe Snow; Steve Forbert; Billy Joel; Producer, engineer, Baby Monster Studios, New York, 1986-. Recordings: As musician: with Phoebe Snow: Phoebe Snow, 1974; It Looks Like Snow, 1974; Never Letting Go, 1978; with Billy Joel: 52nd Street; with Steve Forbert: Alive In Arrival,1978; Steve Forbert, 1982; Film soundtrack, Tender Mercies, 1982. Honours: Grammy, 52nd Street, 1978; Oscar, Tender Mercies, 1982.

BURLEY Philip George (Pip), b. 31 Dec 1943, Croydon, Surrey, England. Musician (keyboards) Composer; Television Producer. m. Christine Komaromy, 10 June 1974, 3 daughters. Career: Freelance keyboard player, composer, arranger; Played with: Sydney Lipton; Joe Loss; Ken Mackintosh; Cabaret with The Semitones; Television producer, 1987-; Credits include: Darling Buds of May; A Touch Of Frost; Pride of Africa. Compositions: Music for television includes: Musicround; Darling Buds Of May; Numerous commercials and jingles; Score for Romeo And Juliet, 1993; The Comedy Of Errors, 1995. Honours: Ivor Novello Award, 1991. Membership: PRS. Hobbies: Golf; Theatre. Address: Heathwoods, Dorking Road, Tadworth, Surrey KT20 7TJ, England.

BURMAKA Maria, b. 16 June 1970, Kharkiv, Ukraine. m. Dmytro Nebesiftchuk, 27 Nov 1993, 1 daughter. Education: Kharkiv State University. Musical Education: Music School. Career: Won Grand Prix, all Ukrainian festivals: Oberig; Chervona Ruta; Many concerts in Ukraine; Concerts: France; Germany, 1992; Canada; Poland; USA, 1989-93; Songs at MB top national hit parade 7 times, 1993-94. Recordings: Cassette: Don't Blossom Spring, 1990; CD, Maria, 1992; CD: Hope Remains, 1994. Honours: Laureate, Ukrainian festivals, 1989-93; Album, Hope Remains, Best In Ukraine, Council of New Stars Of Old Year Festival, 1993-94. Current Management: Dmytro Nebesijtchuk. Address: Schuseva St 36 #12, 254060 Kiev, Ukraine.

BURN Chris, b. 13 Mar 1955, Epping, Essex, England. Musician (piano). Musical Education: Surrey University, BMus, MMus. Career: UK tours, 1985, 1987, 1990, 1992, 1994; Festivals: Bochum; Berlin: Copenhagen; Ulrichsberg; Cologne; Victoriaville, 1996; Radio 3 broadcasts: 1989, 1992, 1994; WDR-TV, radio. Recordings: A Fountain Replete; Ensemble; A Henry Cowell Concert; Music for Three Rivers. Publications: Various articles. Honours: ACGB, 1988, 1990, 1992, 1994. Membership: PRS. Hobby: 5-a-side-football. Current Management: ACTA. Address: Garden Flat, 33 Grosvenor Road, Wanstead, London E11 2EW, England.

BURNEL Jean-Jacques, b. 21 Feb 1952, London, England. Vocalist; Musician (bass). Education: History degree, Bradford University. Career: Founder member, UK rock group The Stranglers, 1976-; Headline tours, Europe; UK; USA; Canada; International concerts include: Support to Patti Smith, 1976; Climax Blues Band, 1977; Loch Lomond Festival, 1979; Reading Rock Festival, 1983; Alexandra Palace, 1970; Support to Simple Minds, 1991; Dartmoor Prison (first band ever to do so), 1992. Recordings: Albums: Rattus Norvegicus, 1977; No More Heroes, 1978; Black & White, 1978; Live (X Cert), 1979; The Raven, 1979; Themeninblack, 1981; La Folie, 1982; The Collection, 1982; Feline, 1983; Aural Sculpture, 1984; Dreamtime, 1986; All Live And All Of The Night, 1988; 10, 1990; Greatest Hits, 1991; In The Night, 1992; Saturday Night, Sunday Morning, 1993; Solo album: Euroman Cometh, 1979; with Dave Greenfield, Fire And Water, 1983; Hit singles: Peaches, 1977; Something Better Change, 1977; No More Heroes, 1977; Five Minutes, 1978; Nice'n'Sleazy, 1978; Duchess, 1979; Golden Brown (Number 2, UK), 1982; Strange Little Girl, 1982; European Female, 1983; Skin Deep, 1984; Always The Sun, 1986; All Day And All Of The Night, 1987. Honour: Ivor Novello Award, Most Performed Work of 1982, Golden Brown, 1983. Current Management: Mainstreet Management. Address: Ensleigh Cottage, Grenville Road, Ensleigh, Bath, Avon BA1 9BE, England.

BURNETT T-Bone (John Henry), b. 1945, St Louis, Missouri, USA. Musician (guitar); Songwriter; Record Producer; Singer. Career: Touring musician with Delaney & Bonnie; B-52s; Bob Dylan's Rolling Thunder Revue, 1970s; Founder, Alpha Band, 1976-79; Solo recording artiste, 1972, 1980-; Worked with Richard Thompson; Elvis Costello, 1980s. Recordings: Albums: J Henry Burnett, 1972; Truth Decay, 1980; Proof Through The Night, 1983; Behind The Trap Door, 1984; T-Bone Burnett, 1986; The Talking Animals, 1988; with Alpha Band: Alpha Band, 1977; Spark In The Dark, 1977; Statue Makers Of Hollywood, 1978; with Bob Dylan: Hard Rain, 1976; Blowin' In The Wind, 1985; with Los Lobos: How Will The Wolf Survive, 1984; By The Light Of The Moon, 1987; La Pistola Y El Corazon, 1988; with Roy Orbison: In Dreams, 1987; Mystery Girl, 1989; Friends - Black And White Night, 1988; Other recordings with: Willie Dixon; Kinky Friedman; Emmylou Harris; Golden Palaminos; Producer, albums with Bruce Cockburn; Leo Kottke; Bo Deans; Nitty Gritty Dirt Band. Current Management: Addis, Wechsler & Associates. Address: 955 S Carillo Drive, 3rd Floor, Los Angeles, CA 90048, USA.

BURNS Patty, b. 16 August 1967, Köln, Cologne, Germany. Career: Belgian support act for Scorpions; Performing alongside Marillion,

Magnum, Erasure, Kent Festival, England, Sopot Festival, Poland, Bregenz Festival, Austria, Jurmala Festival, Russia. Compositions: Fast Traveller; Too Late; Explode Your Nature; Reach the Sky. Recordings: Just Remember (Trust Me). Recordings: Ready for Duty, CD; Evening News, CD; These Boots, CD. Honours: Winner, Belgian National Rock Meeting; Graduate, Jurmala Festival and Bregenz. Hobbies; Dance; Sport. Current Management: Life for Music, Belgium. Address: 96 Basilique Avenue, 1089 Brussels, Belgium.

BURNS Robert Beverley, b. 16 May 1923, Toronto, Ontario, Canada. Musician (saxophones, clarinets). m. Enid Lambert Burns, 30 Oct 1991, 1 son, 2 daughters. Musical Education: Toronto Conservatory; Tuition with William Matthews ARCM; Hiram and Walter Lear, London, Bournemouth. Career: One of few jazz and classical musicians; RCAF HQ Band, Europe; Returned Canada, 1946; Played with Maynard Ferguson, Ellis McClintock; Mart Kenney, and studio work, Toronto; Returned to England, 1948; Played, recorded with Ted Heath, Ambrose, Lew Stone, Jack Parnell's first band; Theatre, studio freelancing until 1989; Led jazz groups, productions at the National Theatre; Played Triparte by Robert Farnon, commissioned by Musicians' Union for May Day Concert at Festival Hall, Concerto for 3 saxophones played by 1 player; Toured with Tony Bennett, recorded at Albert Hall; Tours, 4 times with Benny Goodman, Ireland, Europe; Soloist, film tracks: The Spy Who Came In From The Cold; Dance With A Stranger; Shot In The Dark; Two For The Road. Compositions: Love theme, I Believe In You; Small jazz groups for Frank Cordell film music. Recordings include: with Benny Goodman: Today; London Date; Directions In Jazz, Bill Le Sage; Great Jazz Solos Revisited, Bernie Cash; As House Band, HMV Studios titles include: When I'm Sixty-Four; Albums with Robert Farnon; Frank Chacksfield; Eric Rogers; Frank Sinatra In London, Robert Farnon; 25 years recording ITV artists including: Lene Horne; Ella Fitzgerald; Peggy Lee; Vic Damone; Vera Lynn; Petula Clark; Barbra Streisand; Also many classical recordings with the four major orchestras; Films and music as soloist with Bill McGuffie; House band with major labels;Albums with The Beatles including solo on When I'm Sixty-Four; Albums with vanessa Redgrave and Noel Coward. Honours: Winner, All Canadian Jazz Poll (saxophone), ARCM. Membership: Musicians' Union, Canada, England. Hobbies: Reading; Music studies; Swimming; Travel. Address: 124 Pearl Street, Sarnia, Ontario N7T 5G5, Canada.

BURNS Robert George Henry, b. 24 Feb 1953, London, England. Musician (bass guitar); Composer; Educator. m. Elizabeth Chennells, 14 Jan 1991, 1 son. Musical Education: Guildhall School of Music and Drama; Brunel University College; Rhodesian College Of Music. Career: Tours, live dates, recordings with: Sam and Dave; Edwin Starr; Lene Lovich; Isaac Hayes; Pete Townshend; Eric Burdon; David Gilmour; Albert Lee; James Burton; Jerry Donahue; Viv Stanshall; Zoot Money; Formed Robert Burns Music, 1987. Compositions: Soundtracks for clients including: Lonrho; Sunday Times; IBM; MTV; P&O. Recordings: Television: Red Dwarf; Mr Bean; 2 Point 4 Children; Alas Smith And Jones; Lenny Henry; Blackadder III; Not The Nine O'Clock News; Three Of A Kind. Publications: The Rock File; Columnist for Bassist and Musician magazines; Syllabus for Trinity/Rockschool graded exams for bass guitar, 1992. Honours: Appointed Principal Examiner, Bass Guitar, Trinity College of Music, 1992; Head, Bass Guitar Studies, BASStech/Thames Valley University, 1994. Hobbies: Cinema; Literature; Music research. Address: Crouch End, London N8, England.

BURONFOSSE Marc, b. 6 May 1963, Soissons, France. Musician (upright acoustic bass). m. Jennifer Forse, 22 May 1993, 1 daughter. Education: 3 year degree, Sound Engineering. Musical Education: Prize, Union Des Conservatoires de Paris. Career: Japanese tour with Las Solistes de Versailles (chamber orchestra); Fellowship to study at the New School of Music, New York; Tour of Central Africa with Sylvain Kassap Quartet; European tours with Sylvain Kassap Quartet and Bojan Z Quartet; Television and radio appearances. Recordings: Sylvain Kassap Quartet Quixote; Bojan Z Quartet. Honours: First prize, Concours de la Défense, 1992; Concours Etrechy, 1995. Memberships: ADAMI; SACEM; SPEDIDAM. Hobbies: Skiing; Cinema. Current Management: Self-managed. Address: 32 bis Avenue Joffre, 94100 St Maur des Fosses, France.

BURRELL Kenny, b. 31 July 1931, Detroit, Michigan, USA. Jazz Musician (guitar). Musical Education: Classical guitar, 1952-53; BMus, Wayne University, Detroit, 1955. Career: Played with Candy Johnson Sextet; Yusef Lateef; Tommy Flanagan; Dizzy Gillespie, 1951; Oscar Peterson Trio, 1955; Hampton Hawes Trio, 1956; Benny Goodman, 1957; Association with organist Jimmy Smith; Recorded with John Coltrane, Sonny Rollins, Coleman Hawkins; Leader, own trio. Recordings: Albums include: The Cats, 1957; Kenny Burrell - John Coltrane, 1958; At The Five Spot Cafe Vol 1, 1959; Midnight Blue, 1960s; Live At The Village Vanguard, 1960s; Guitar Forms, 1965; For Charlie Christian And Benny Goodman, 1967; Handcrafted, 1978; Kenny Burrell In New York, 1981; Night Song, 1982; Listen To The Dawn, 1983; Bluesin' Around, 1984; A La Carte, 1986; Generations, 1987; Blue Lights Vols 1 and 2, 1989; Togethering, 1989; Recapitulation, 1989; Soulero, 1996. Current Management: Tropix International. Address: 163 Third Ave, Suite 206, New York, NY 10003, USA.

BURROUGHS Gary Stuart, b. 3 Apr 1953, Doncaster, England. Musician (drums, percussion, multi-instrumentalist); Singer; Songwriter; Producer; Engineer. m. Lyn Acton, 26 Nov 1976, 1 son. Education: Hull Technical College. Musical Education: Lead tenor, school, 1961; Tenor horn, cornet, Askern Siver Prize Band, 1963; Self-taught drums, 1967. Career: Drummer with: Soul Image; The Pink; Listen; The Weazles; Johnny Duncan and the Bluegrass Boys; Rock and Roll Circus; Rock Orchestrals; Johnny Johnson and the Bandwagon; Snake Eye; The Killers; Jackal; Buster Crab; Sarah Gordans All American Soul Show; Sheer Elegance; Roy Wood - Wizzo; Christie; Nosmo King; Luggage; Export; Earthman Liberation; What Katy Did Next; Tiffanys; Gimmex; Stork Club; Bertice Redding; Lionel Bart; Simon Townshend; Resistdance; Marino; NGO; Naked Orange, 1968-; Fila Brazillia; Tour Manager, Limmie and The Family Cookin', 1976; Sound Engineer, Fairview Music, 1979; Lead singer with: Techno Pop; Marino; Listen; Blitzkrieg; The Weazles; The Choirboys; NGO; Drummer with: American Sweet Sound Tour; Simon Townshend; Support, West Coast Tour, Pretenders; Support, Duran Duran World tour, 1984; Television: Saturday Superstore, BBC1; Lift Off with Aisha; Regional television, BBC2; Televised live concerts: Syracuse, USA; Seattle, USA; Baltimore, USA; Producer for: Smash live, Top Of The Pops, BBC1, 1994; Various radio; Business ventures: DIG for music, Midem, 1991; Wall 2 Wall Records, 1990; Wall 2 Wall Studios, 1992. Recordings: Single: Year Of The Tiger, 1975; Session drummer, vocalist, various singles, albums, 1976-98; As solo artist: Single: Paint It Black, 1980; with Marino: Blues For Lovers, 1991. Honours: Blues Album Of The Year, Paris, France, 1992. Memberships: PRS; Equity. Hobbies: Writing; Walks in the country; Cycling. Current Management: Wall 2 Wall. Address: Wall 2 Wall Studios, PO Box 596, Hull HU5 3XZ, England.

BURROWS Matthew Karl, b. 15 Aug 1971, Croydon, Surrey, England. Musical Director; Producer; Advisor; Musician (keyboards, organ); Singer; Songwriter; Choir Trainer; Location, Studio Recording. Musical Education: Royal School Of Church Music. Career: Started as choirboy, trained, sang with Royal School of Church Music, Southern Cathedral Singers; Organises, runs courses for RSCM; Organist; choir trainer; Wrote songs for, played keyboards, guitar, bass, sang with several gigging bands, also studio work, producing, playing; Company, Tonic Services, currently doing location digital recording work. Memberships: Musicians' Union; Friend of Royal School of Church Music. Hobby: Studying psychology, hypnosis, part-time. Current Management: Tonic Services. Address: 16 Pittsmead Avenue, Hayes, Bromley, Kent BR2 7NL, England.

BURTON Gary, b. 23 Jan 1943, Anderson, Indiana, USA. Jazz Musician (vibraphone, piano). Musical Education: Self-taught piano; Berklee College of Music, Boston. Career: Member, George Shearing's Group, 1963; Played with Stan Getz, 2 years; Formed own bands, 1960s-; Leader, various bands featuring artists including: Larry Coryell; Roy Haynes; Pat Metheny; Eberhard Weber; Also recorded with Stéphane Grappelli; Carla Bley; Keith Jarrett; Chick Corea; Michael Brecker; Peter Erskine; Teacher, Berklee College of Music, 1971-. Recordings include: Albums: Duster, 1967; Lofty Fake Anagram, 1967; Country Roads And Other Places, 1968; Green Apple, 1969; Hotel Hello, 1974; Matchbook, 1974; Dreams So Real, 1975; Easy As Pie, 1980; Picture This, 1983; Real Life Hits, 1984; Whiz Kids, 1986; Times Like These, 1988; Cool Nights, 1990; Six Pack, 1993; with Carla Bley: A Genuine Tang Funeral, 1968; with Stéphane Grappelli: Paris Encounter, 1969; with Keith Jarrett: Gary Burton And Keith Jarrett, 1970; with Eberhard Weber: Ring, 1974; Passengers, 1976; with Chick Corea: Crystal Silence, 1972; Duet, 1978; with Ralph Towner: Slide Show, 1976; with Pat Metheny: Reunion, 1989; with Paul Bley: Right Time Right Place, 1991; with Makoto Ozone: Face To Face, 1995. Current Management: Ted Kurland Associates, 173 Brighton Avenue, Boston, MA 02134, USA.

BURTON Michael Edward, b. 18 Oct 1964, Middleton, Manchester, England. Teacher; Musician (bass guitar). Education: Local colleges. Musical Education: B Mus (hons); ALCM LmusTCL; PGCE; Cardiff University, 1986-89. Career: Bassist, University jazz band, 1987-; Played as part of band for HTV's Telethon, 1988; Freelance session/studio bassist and teacher, 1989-; Entered professional teaching, 1991; Currently music teacher, Ruffwood School, Kirkby, Liverpool; Bassist with Manchester based covers band; Private teacher, bass guitar. Hobbies: Photography; Home wine making. Address: 3 Griffin Street, Sutton, St Helens, Merseyside, England.

BURTON Paddy (Patrick Henry), b. 19 Aug 1961, Stockport, Cheshire, England. Musician (percussion); Musical Instrument Maker (slitdrums, multiplayer giant xylophones). 2 sons. Education: Newcastle University. Career: Musical Director for theatre companies; Performing musician with local bands, 1978-86; Pineapple Agogo, 1986-90; Musician in Residence, City of Edinburgh District Council, 1990-92; Player with Amadeus, 1993-; Jack Drum Arts; Dodgy Clutch; The Fabulous Salami Brothers. Recordings: Trashcan Gamelan Edinburgh, 1992; Black Diamonds, Black Gold, 1993; Fish Xylophone, 1994. Memberships: Musicians' Union; Sound Sense; Equity. Hobbies: Gardening; World travel. Address: 43-44 Gladstone Terrace, Sunniside, Bishop Auckland, County Durham DL13 4LS, England.

BUSH Kate (Catherine), b. 30 July 1958, Bexleyheath, Kent, England. Singer; Songwriter. Education: Voice, dance and mime lessons. Career: Limited live performances include: Tour Of Life, Europe, 1979; Secret Policeman's Third Ball, London, 1987; Television appearances include: Bringing It All Back Home documentary, 1991; Writer, director, actress, film The Line, The Cross And The Curve, 1994. Recordings (mostly self-composed): Albums: The Kick Inside, 1978; Lionheart, 1978; Never Forever (Number 1, UK), 1980; The Dreaming, 1982; Hounds Of Love (Number 1, UK), 1985; The Whole Story (Number 1, UK), 1987; The Sensual World (Number 2, UK), 1989; This Womans Work, 1990; The Red Shoes (Number 2, UK), 1993; Contributor, Games Without Frontiers, Peter Gabriel, 1980; Two Rooms - Celebrating The Songs Of Elton John And Bernie Taupin, 1991; Singles include: Wuthering Heights (Number 1, UK), 1978; The Man With The Child In His Eyes, 1978; Wow, 1979; Breathing, 1980; Babooshka, 1980; Army Dreamers, 1980; Sat In Your Lap, 1981; Running Up That Hill, 1985; Cloudbusting, 1985; Hounds Of Love, 1986; Experiment IV, 1986; Don't Give Up, duet with Peter Gabriel, 1986; This Woman's Work (from film soundtrack She's Having A Baby), 1988; The Sensual World, 1989; Moments Of Pleasure, 1993. Honours: Ivor Novello Awards, Outstanding British Lyric, The Man With The Child In His Eyes, 1979; BRIT Award, Best British Female Artist, 1987. Current Management: c/o Reluctant Management, 10603 Rochester Avenue, Los Angeles, CA 90024, USA.

BUSSCHOTS Patrick Eugéne, b. 18 Dec 1953, Mortsel, Belgium. Managing Director. m. Lydia, 28 Oct 1978, 2 daughters. Education: Jeweller; Various business courses. Career: Retail, wholesale, production, publishing; Currently holding, grouping all activities with ARS Productions. Recordings: with Technotronic: Pump Up The Jam; Material with: Faith No More; Gipsy Kings. Honours: World Music Award, Monte Carlo, 1990. Membership: IFPI. Hobbies: Music; Sports; Outdoor dining. Address: ARS Productions, Singel 5, 2150 Kontich, Belgium.

BUTCHER John Bernard, b. 25 Oct 1954, Brighton, England. Musician (saxophone). Education: PhD, Theoretical Physics. Musical Education: Self-taught. Career: Worked mainly in jazz, late 1970s; Improvisation and new-music, early 1980s; Regular groups include: News From The Shed; Embers; Frisque Concordance; Ensemble; Festival appearances include: Berlin Total Music Meeting; Du Maurier Jazz (Canada); Knitting Factory (New York); Company (London); Head of ACTA Records. Recordings: Fonetiks, 1985; Conceits, 1987; News From The Shed, 1989; Cultural Baggage, 1990; Thirteen Friendly Numbers, 1992; Spellings, 1993; Respiritus, 1995; Concert Moves, 1995. Address: 28 Aylmer Road, London W12 9LQ, England.

BUTINA Roman, b. 5 Aug 1937, Zagreb, Croatia. Musician (organ, keyboards); Composer. m. Ljerka Miladinov, 4 June 1960, 1 son, 1 daughter. Education: Doctor of Medicine. Musical Education: Dip, Intermediate Music School. Career: Member, Dalmatia vocal group, 12 years; Tours former Yugoslavia, Eastern, Western Europe; Leader, organist, The Blue Stars group, 1970-72; Performer, Hammond Organ, Electric Piano, Laguna Hotel, occasionally Zagreb-Intercontinental Hotel, 1973. Compositions recorded and published, numerous popular tunes and songs. Publications: As Editor: With Song Through Zagorje, 1960; Greetings Tyrol, 1969; Ancient Croatian Songs, 1972; World Folk Songs, 1975. Honours: Second Prize, Zagreb Festival, 1971. Memberships: Croatian Composers Association; Union of Artists of Croatia, Zagreb. Hobby: Philately. Address: Turopolska 36, 10000 Zagreb, Croatia.

BUTLER Bernard, b. 1 May 1970, Stamford Hill, London, England. m. Elisa. Musician (guitar, keyboards); Songwriter. Education: History, Queen Mary College, London, 1 year. Musical Education: Studied violin and piano; Self-taught guitar. Career: Member, Suede, 1989-94; Television appearances include: Top Of The Pops, BBC1; BRIT Awards; Later With Jools Holland, BBC2; The Tonight Show, NBC TV; Concerts include Glastonbury Festival; Tours, Europe, America, Japan. Member, duo McAlmont & Butler (with David McAlmont), 1994-95. Recordings: Albums: with Suede: Suede, 1993; Dog Man Star, 1994; with McAlmont And Butler: The Sound Of McAlmont And Butler, 1995; Solo album: People Move On, 1998; Singles include: with Suede: The Drowners; Metal Mickey; Animal Nitrate; So Young; with McAlmont & Butler: Yes, 1995; You Do, 1995; Also recorded with Bryan Ferry; Edwyn Collins; Aimee Mann; Sparks; Eddi Reader; Neneh Cherry. Honours include: Mercury Music Prize, 1993. Current Management: Geoff Travis.

BUTLER Clara G, b. 28 Oct 1938, Greenville, South Carolina, USA. Songwriter; Dancer; Record Company Executive. m. Jojo St Mitchell, 18 May 1993, 1 son, 1 daughter. Education: 1 year college. Musical Education: 7 years with management team and songwriting team. Career: Arthur Murray Dance Awards; Dancing Instructor; CEO of record company, Notary Public; Music publisher and songwriter; Real estate owner; Executive producer of recording artists. Compositions: Songs: I Must Be Gettin' Older Now; It's You Or Me; Executive Producer for groups: Destination Unknown; Safari. Honours: Business Leader; Ballroom Dancing Awards. Memberships: Broadcast Music Inc; Antithesis Music. Hobbies: Reading; Dancing; Cooking; Crafts; Art; Poetry; Antiques. Current Management: The Amethyst Group Ltd. Address: 273 Chippewa Drive, Columbia, SC 29210-6508, USA.

BUTLER Edith, b. 27 July 1942, Paquetville, New Brunswick, Canada. Singer; Musician (guitar). Education: BA, Arts, Pedagogie; MA, Literature. Musical Education: Taught by mother. Career: Tours: Canada; USA; Japan; Olympia Theatre of Paris, France; Place des Arts, Montreal; All major television and radio shows, Canada, France, last 20 years. Recordings: 22 albums; 200 songs. Honours: 3 Platinum records; 3 Gold records; 3 Felix Awards; Nelly Award; Charles-Cros Award. Memberships: SOCAN; SACEM; SODRAC. Hobbies: Gardening; Walking. Current Management: Lise Aubut. Address: 86 Côte Ste-Catherine, Montreal, Quebec H2V 2A3, Canada.

BUTLER Geezer (Terry), b. 17 July 1949, Birmingham, England. Musician (bass). Career: Bass player, UK heavy rock group Black Sabbath, 1967-; Numerous concerts worldwide include: Madison Square Garden, New York, 1975; Live Aid, Philadelphia, 1985. Recordings: Singles include: Paranoid; Iron Man; War Pigs; Never Say Die; Albums: Black Sabbath, 1969; Paranoid, 1970; Masters Of Reality, 1971; Sabbath Bloody Sabbath, 1973; Sabotage, 1975; Technical Ecstasy, 1976; Never Say Die, 1978; Heaven And Hell, 1980; Mob Rules, 1981; Live Evil, 1983; Born Again, 1983; Seventh Star, 1986; The Eternal Idol, 1987; Headless Cross, 1990; Tyr, 1990; Dehumanizer, 1992; Numerous compilations. Current Management: Gloria Butler Management, PO Box 2686, Knowle B94 5NQ, England.

BUTLER Jonathan Kenneth, b. 10 Oct 1961, Cape Town, South Africa. Musician (guitar); Singer; Songwriter. m. Barenese Vanessa, 28 Jan 1983, 2 daughters. Musical Education: Self-taught. Career: 3 month US tour with Whitney Houston; 3 weeks with Eric Clapton, Albert Hall; Extensive touring in own right of USA, Japan, Europe, South America, South Africa; Television: Carson; Jay Leno; David Letterman; Top Of The Pops;

Mandela Birthday Concert, Wembley. Recordings: Introducing Jonathan Butler; Jonathan Butler; More Than Friends; Heal Our Land; Head To Head; EP: Deliverance. Honours: 2 Grammy Nominations; NAACP Award; 5 ASCAP Awards. Memberships: Musicians' Union; PRS; AFTRA. Current Management: Running Dog Management. Address: Minka, Lower Hampton Road, Sunbury, Middlesex TW16 5PR, England.

BUTLER Trixie, b. 6 Jan 1958, Bristol, England. Vocalist. m. Steven Butler, 5 Nov 1993. Career: Singer with various bands, 1989-91; Lead vocalist, Tredegar, with Ray Phillips (ex-Budgie); Lead vocalist, Zue London Band; Tours, all major venues including Marquee; Astoria; Voiceovers, GWR Radio Advertising; Television: Catchphrase; Various compositions, including entry for Song For Europe; Studio work, Koh-sun Recording Studios, Bath; Real World Recording Studios, Bath; The Session Connection, London. Membership: Musicains' Union. Hobbies: Walking the dog; Singing; Driving. Current Management: AU Records Ltd. Address: 8 Woodchester, Chipping Sodbury, Avon BS17 4TZ, England.

BYFORD Bill, b. 24 May 1955, Castleford, West Yorkshire, England. Music Publisher; Songwriter; Musician (guitar). m. Honor Mary Eastwood, 29 Aug 1977, 1 daughter. Education: MA, Film and Media; BEd (Hons). Career: Publisher and Managing Director, Palace of Fun Music, 1980-; Member, songwriter with The Rhythm Sisters, 1986-92; Currently working with Steve Tilston and Maggie Boyle; Featured artist on film soundtracks including: Patriot Games; Before The Fall; Music journalist with NME; Melody Maker; The Guardian, 1973-. Memberships: BASCA; PRS; MPS. Hobby: Leeds United Football Club. Current Management: Palace of Fun Management. Address: 16 Elm View, Huddersfield Road, Halifax, West Yorkshire HX3 0AE, England.

BYRD Charlie, b. 16 Sept 1925, Virginia, USA. Musician. 1 son, 2 daughters. Musical Education: Sophodes Papas, Andre Segovia. Career: Worldwide performances, every kind of venue, including best concert halls. Recordings: Over 100 albums. Honours include: Downbeat Poll; Playboy Poll; Washington College Award. Membership: Musicians' Union. Hobby: Sailing. Current Management: John Gingrich. Address: PO Box 1515, New York, NY 10023, USA.

BYRD Donald, b. Detroit, Michigan, USA. Jazz Musician (trumpet); Educator. Musical Education: Studied trumpet and composition. Career: Recorded with John Coltrane; Sonny Rollins; Art Blakey; Dexter Gordon; Kenny Clarke; Pepper Adams; Educator, Rutgers University and Howard University. Recordings: Long Green, 1955; Two Trumpets, 1956; The Young Bloods, 1956; September Afternoon, 1957; At Newport, 1957; X-tacy, 1957; Jazz Eyes, 1957; Byrd In Paris, Vols 1 & 2, 1958; 10 To 4 At The 5 Spot, 1958; Off To The Races, 1958; Byrd In Flight, 1960; Royal Flush, 1961; Chant, 1961; Groovin' For Nat, 1962; Mustang, 1966; The Creeper, 1967; Electric Byrd, 1970; Black Byrd, 1973; Street Lady, 1974; Steppin' Into Tomorrow, 1975; Places and Spaces, 1975; Caricatures, 1977; Thank You...For F U M L (Funking Up My Life), 1978; Love Byrd, 1981; Words Sounds Colours Shapes, 1982; Harlem Blues, 1987; Getting Down To Business, 1989; with Kenny Clarke: Bohemia After Dark, 1955; with Art Blakey: The Jazz Messengers, 1956; with John Coltrane: Lush Life, 1958; with Dexter Gordon: One Flight Up, 1964; with Kenny Burrell and Herbie Hancock, A New Perspective, 1964. Address: c/o Department Of Music, Rutgers University, New Brusnwick, NJ 08903, USA.

BYRNE David, b. 14 May 1952, Dumbarton, Scotland. Singer; Songwriter; Composer; Film Director; Photographer. m. Adelle Lutz, 1987. Education: Rhode Island School of Design,

1970-71; Maryland Institute College of Art, 1971-72. Career: Co-founder, singer, songwriter, Talking Heads, 1974-88; Recorded 10 albums, numerous worldwide concerts, television and radio appearances; Solo artiste, producer, composer, 1980-; Founder, Luaka Bop record label, 1988; Also artist, stage and lighting designer, album covers/posters designer. Compositions include: Film/stage scores: The Knee Plays, 1984; Alive From Off Center, 1984; Sounds From True Stories, 1986; The Forest, 1986; Something Wild, 1986; The Catherine Wheel, 1988; The Last Emperor, 1988; The Giant Woman And The Lightning Man, 1990; A Young Man's Dream And A Woman's Secret, 1990. Recordings include: with Talking Heads: Talking Heads '77, 1977; More Songs About Buildings And Food, 1978; Fear Of Music, 1979; Remain In Light, 1980; The Name Of This Band Is Talking Heads, 1982; Speaking In Tongues, 1983; Stop Making Sense, 1984; Little Creatures, 1985; True Stories, 1986; Naked, 1988; Popular Favourites - Sand In The Vaseline, 1992; Solo albums: The Forest, 1988; Rei Momo, 1989; Uh-Oh, 1992; David Byrne, 1994; Feelings, 1997; As producer: Mesopotamia, B-52's; Waiting, Fun Boy 3; Elegibo, Margareth Menezes (2 tracks). Honours include: Academy Award, Golden Globe, and Hollywood Foreign Press Association Award, Best Original Score, The Last Emperor, 1987; Film Critics Award, Best Documentary, 1985; MTV's Video Vanguard Award, 1985; Music Video Producers Association, 1992. Memberships: Musicians' Union; Screen Actors Guild. Address: Box 652, Cooper Station, New York, NY 10276, USA.

BYWATER Richard. Musician (string bass). Career: Founder member, Mack And The Boys, tours throughout Europe, 1990-93; Headlined Birmingham's largest ever concert, 100,000 audience; Member, The New Bushbury Mountain Daredevils, 1992-; Backing vocals for Slade; Production, songwriting for dance artists; Topical songs for radio. Recordings: with Mack And The Boys: Mack and The Boys; Downtime Love; The Unknown Legends; with The New Bushbury Mountain Daredevils: Bushwacked; The Yellow Album; Bushbury Mountain. Currnet Management: c/o Jim McPhee, Acorn Entertainments. Address: Winterfold House, 46 Woodfield Road, Kings Heath, Birmingham B13 9UJ, England.

C

CABBLE Lise, b. 10 Jan 1958, Copenhagen, Denmark. Songwriter; Singer; Musician (guitar). Career: Founder member, all-girl punk band Clinic Q, 1981; Founder member, singer, guitarist, songwriter, rock band Miss B Haven, 1986; Tours: England; France; Netherlands; Germany; Denmark. Recordings: with Miss B Haven: Ice On Fire, 1987; On Honeymoon, 1988; Nobody's Angel, 1990; Miss B Haven, 1991; Suk And Stads, 1994. Honours: Danish songwriter and singer awards; Several awards with Miss B Haven. Hobbies: Reading; Backgammon. Current Management: Ernst Mikael Jorgensen, PDH. Address: Katrinebjerg 10, Morkov, Denmark.

CACCI Neil "Guitar Man", (Neil Cacciottolo), b. 9 Nov 1953, Evergreen Park, Illinois, USA. Studio Musician; Arranger; Business Rep. Education: 3 years college, Major, Public Speaking, Business Administration; Music and Journalism. Musical Education: 9 years of Formal Training, Carnevale School of Music, Chicago, DLM, 1990. Career: Prepares budgets, various recording projects; Supervisor, all aspects studio production; Public relations services, major independent artists; Studio musician, involved with recording background music, demo production for song catalogues, commercial recordings; Professional career, 1969-. Recordings: Part Time Love; Rhonda Lee; Bye Bye Baby; Lonely Highway; Loves Touch; Enchanted Meadow; Country Life; The Happy Traveller; Melinda. Publications: The Do's And Don'ts Of The Music Industry. Honours: Honours: CMA Record Promoter and Company of the Year Award, 1992; International Indie Gold Record Awards. Memberships: AFofM; CMA; GMA; NARAS; ASCAP (writer and publisher). Hobbies: Golf; Reading; Cooking. Current Management: Sunset Promotions of Chicago Inc. Address: 14855 S New Van Dyke Road, PO Box 1001, Plainfield, IL 60544, USA.

CACIA Paul Scott, b. 20 June 1956, Santa Ana, California, USA. Musician (trumpet); Bandleader; Producer. m. Janine Cameo, 1978, 2 daughters. Musical Education: Studied with Claude Gordon, 1970-74. Career: Musician with: Calvin Jackson, 1972; Louis Bellson Big Band, 1973; Stan Kenton College Neophonic, 1974; Buddy Miles Express, 1975; Don Ellis Electric Orchestra, 1976; Ray Anthony, 1978; Al Hirt Big Band, 1979; Independent musician and producer, 1979-84; Bandleader, The New Age Orchestra, 1984-; Director, Don Ellis Estate, 1984-87; Lecturer, Besson trumpets, 1984-; Chairman, Stan Kenton Scholar Fund. Recordings: Albums include: Unbelieveable, 1977; Big Band Portrait, 1979; All In Good Time, 1982; Believe It!, Mormon Tabernacle Choir, 1983; Hardcore Jazz, Shelley Manne and Phil Woods, 1986; Alumni Tribute To Stan Kenton, 1987. Membership: AFofM.

CADBURY Richard (Dik) Benjamin, b. 12 June 1950, Selly Oak, Birmingham, England. Musician (bass, guitar); Vocalist; Composer. m. Barbara, 21 Mar 1979, 2 daughters. Musical Education: Violin to Grade 5; School Chorus and Church choral singing; Guitar self-taught. Career: Toured, recorded with Decameron, 1973-76; Member, Steve Hackett (bass and vocals), 1978-80; Tours include: Reading Festival, 1979; UK; Europe; North America, 1980; Owner, Millstream Recording Studio, 1978-88. Compositions include: Saturday, for Third Light (with Dave Bell). Recordings: Albums: Mammoth Special, Decameron; Tomorrow's Pantomime, Third Light; with Steve Hackett: Spectral Mornings, Defector. Memberships: Musicians' Union; PRS. Hobbies: Tending 6 acres of woodland; Playing guitar. Address: c/o Highfield Productions, Stanley Road, Cheltenham, Glos GL52 6PF, England.

CAENS Thierry-Gerard, b. 24 Sept 1958, Dijon, France. Musician (trumpet). m. Noëlle Diebold, 15 Sept 1984, 2 sons, 1 daughter. Musical Education: Paris National Superior Conservatory with Maurice André. Career: Former solo trumpet with Lyon Orchestra; Former solo cornet with Paris Opera Orchestra; Tours of Japan; Creator, William Sheller Trumpet Concerto, Pleyel, Paris, 1992; Soloist, Cyrano, B O Music by Jean-Claude Petit; Duo with Jean Guillou, Organ. Recordings: Tangos And Milongas; Haydn; Bach Brandenburg Concerts; Haydn; Jericho. Publications: Leduc-Hamelle publishers in Paris. Honours: First prize, Paris Conservatory; Victoires de la Musique. Memberships: Artistic Director, Camerata de Bourgogne; Music Festival of Great Wine of Burgundy. Hobbies: Gastronomy; Wine; Films. Current Management: Jacques Thelen; Salle Pleyel. Address: 252 Faubourg St Honoré, 75008 Paris, France.

CAHN Sammy, b. 18 June 1913, New York, New York, USA. Songwriter. m. Career: Songwriter, films, 1940-; Writer for stage shows: Walking Happy; High Button Shoes; Skyscraper; Compositions include: Songs: Love And Marriage; Rhythm In My Nursey Rhymes; Bei Mir Bist Schoen; Until The Real Thing Comes Along; Be My Love; Please Be Kind; I've Heard That Song Before; I'll Walk Alone; Shoe Shine Boy; Victory Polka; Because You're Mine; Let It Snow; It's Magic; Teach Me Tonight; Three Coins In The Fountain; The Tender Trap; All The Way; Call Me Irresponsible. Honours: Inducted into Songwriters Hall of Fame; Emmy Award, Love And Marriage; Academy Awards for: Three Coins In The Fountain; High Hopes; Call Me Irresponsible. Membership: President, Songwriters Hall Of Fame, New York, 1975-. Address: c/o Daniel Howard CPA, 8600 Melrose Avenue, Los Angeles, CA 90069, USA.

CAIN Jonathan, b. 26 Feb 1950, Chicago, Illinois, USA. Musician (keyboards); Songwriter; Producer. Career: Member, The Babys; Member, US rock group Journey, 1981-87; Member, Bad English, 1988-91; Member, Hardline, 1992-; Concerts include: Mountain Aire Festival, 1981, 1986; Support to Rolling Stones, US tour, 1981; Concert, Oakland Alameda County Coliseum, with Santana, The Tubes, Toto, 1982; US tour, supported by Bryan Adams, 1983. Recordings: Albums: with Journey: Escape, 1981; Frontiers, 1983; Raised On Radio, 1986; Greatest Hits, 1989; with Bad English: Bad English, 1989; Backlash, 1991; Singles: with Journey: Still They Ride; Who's Crying Now; Separate Ways (Worlds Apart); Faithfully; After The Fall; Send Her My Love; Be Good To Yourself; Suzanne; Girl Can't Help It; I'll Be Alright; with Bad English: When I See You Smile (Number 1, US) 1990; Straight To Your Heart, 1991. Address: c/o Hemming Morse, 650 California Street, Suite 900, San Francisco, CA 94108, USA.

CAINES Ronald Arthur, b. 13 Dec 1939, Bristol, England. Artist; Musician (saxophonist). m. Susan Weaver, 21 Apr 1958, 1 son, 2 daughters. Education: West of England College of Art. Musical Education: Self-taught, mainly listening to jazz records. Career: Worked extensively in Europe, especially France, Switzerland, UK college circuit; Played in Keith Tippett's Big Band, Ark; Also with: Julie Tippett; Evan Parker, in 1970s; Played improvised and Latin based music, led modern jazz quartet. Compositions included: Northern Hemisphere; Bathers Of Lake Balaton; Isadora; Music for film Laughter In The Dark, 1969. Recordings: Mercator Projected; SNAFU; The World Of East Of Eden. Memberships: PRS; Musicians' Union (Delegate). Hobbies: Travel; Politics. Current Management: Ben Williams, Vital Communications. Address: 15 Highbury Villas, Kingsdown, Bristol B52 8BX, England.

CAIRNS Andy, b. Ireland. Vocalist; Musician (guitar). Career: Singer, musician, Irish rock group Therapy?, 1989-; Appearances include Top Of The Pops, BBC1. Recordings: Albums: Baby Teeth, 1991; Pleasure Death (mini-album), 1992; Nurse, 1993; Troublegum, 1994; Infernal Love, 1995; Semi-Detached, 1998; EPs: Shortsharpshock; Face The Strange; Opal Mantra. Honour: Mercury Music Prize Nomination, 1995. Current Management: DCG Management, 89 Upper Georges Street, Dun Laoghaire, Dublin, Ireland.

CALAZANS Teca, b. 27 Oct 1940, Vitoria, Espirito Santo, Brazil. Composer; Singer. m. Philippe Lesage, 15 June 1991, 1 daughter. Career: Former actress; Moved to France, 1970; Recorded 6 discs, performed at Olympia, with Claude Nougaro, return to Brazil, 1979-88; 5 solo albums, compere television show, 3 years; Appearances include: Festival De Jazz De Vienne, 1991; 60 Villes pour les jeunesses Musicales de France, 1992; Festival de la Guitare, 1992; Festival De Chateauvallon, 1992; Festival de Jazz Zurich au Moods, 1994; Passage Du Nord Ouest, Paris, 1994; Soiree Jazz 94, Nice Jazz Festival, 1995; Guitar master de Pau. 1995. Compositions: Côco Verde; Gabriel; Caíco (sung by Milton Nascimento); Firuliu (sung by Nara Leâo); Atras da luminosidade (sung by Gal Costa). Recordings: Musiques et Chants du Brasil, 1974; Caminho Das Aguas, 1975; Cade O Povo, 1975; Desafio De Viola, 1978; Povo Daqui, 1980; Eu Nao Sou Dos, 1981; Teca Calazans, 1982; Mário Trezentos, 350, 1983; Jardim Exotique, 1983; Mina Do Mar, 1985; Teca Calazans Chante Villa Lobos, 1990; Pizindim, 1991; Intuiçao, 1993; O Samba Dos Bambas, 1994. Hobby: Swimming. Current Management: Rita Sá Rego, Cirandas. Address: 3 Avenue Mathilde, 95210 Sainte-Gratien, France.

CALE J J (John Weldon), b. 5 Dec 1938, Oklahoma City, Oklahoma, USA. Singer; Songwriter; Musician (guitar). Career: Singer, songwriter, pioneer of "Tulsa sound"; Leader, Johnny Cale and the Valentines; Tours with Grand Ole Opry road company; Backing musician to Red Sovine, Little Jimmy Dickens; Studio engineer, guitarist, Los Angeles, 1964; Played with artists including: Leon Russell; Delaney and Bonnie; Built Crazy Mama's recording studio, Nashville, 1972. Compositions include: Most of own recordings; Songs covered by other artists include: After Midnight; Cocaine; I'll Make Love To You (all recorded by Eric Clapton); Call Me The Breeze (Johnny Cash, Lynyrd Skynyrd, The Allman Brothers); Clyde (Waylon Jennings); Bringing It Back (Kansas, Lynyrd Skynyrd); Same Old Blues (Bryan Ferry, Captain Beefheart); Magnolia (Deep Purple, Poco, Chris Smither, Jose Feliciano); The Sensitive Kind (John Mayall, Santana); Film scores include: La Femme De Mon Pote (My Best Friend's Girl), 1984. Recordings: Albums: A Trip Down Sunset Strip (recorded under the name The Leathercoat Minds), 1967; Naturally, 1972; Really, 1973; Okie, 1973; Troubadour, 1976; #5, 1979; Shades (featuring Leon Russell), 1981; Grasshopper, 1982; #8, 1983; Travel Log, 1989; #10, 1992; Closer To You, 1994; Guitar Man, 1996; Producer, albums by John Hammond: Got Love If You Want It; Trouble No More; Contributor, Rhythm Of The Saints, Paul Simon, 1986; The Tractors, The Tractors, 1994. Current Management: Eric Hanson, The Rosebud Agency, PO Box 170429, San Francisco, CA 94117, USA.

CALE John, b. 9 Mar 1942, Garnant, Wales. Vocalist; Musician (bass, keyboards, viola); Record Producer. Musical Education: Classical training. Career: Member, The Dream Academy; Founder member, The Velvet Underground, 1964-68, 1993; Solo artiste, 1970-; Residency, Café Bizarre, Greenwich Village, 1966; House band, Andy Warhol's Factory arts collective, New York, 1966; Reunion, with Lou Reed, Nico, 1972; Reunion with Velvet Underground, European Tour, 1993; Production includes: Nico: The Marble Index, 1969, Desert Shore, 1970, The End, 1974; Iggy Pop: The Stooges, 1969; Patti Smith: Horses,

1975; Jonathan Richman: Modern Lovers, 1975; Squeeze: Squeeze, 1977; Happy Mondays: Squirrel and G Man, 1987; Siouxsie and The Banshees: Rapture, 1995. Recordings: Albums: with The Velvet Underground: The Velvet Underground And Nico, 1967; White Light, White Heat, 1968; Live MCMXCIII, 1993; Solo albums include: Vintage Violence, 1970; Church Of Anthrax, 1971; Academy in Peril, 1972; Paris 1919, 1973; Fear, 1974; June 1 1974, 1974; Slow Dazzle, 1975; Helen Of Troy, 1975; Guts, 1977; Animal Justice, 1977; Sabotage, 1979; Honi Soit, 1981; Music For A New Society, 1982; Caribbean Sunset, 1984; Comes Alive, 1984; Artificial Intelligence, 1985; Words For The Dying, 1989; Fragments of a Rainy Season, 1992; Walking on Locusts, 1996; Dance Music, 1998; with Lou Reed: Songs For Drella, 1990; with Brian Eno: Wrong Way Up, 1991; with Bob Neuwirth: Last Day On Earth, 1994; Film scores: Sid & Nancy, 1982; Paris S'Eveille, 1991; La Naissance de l'Amour, 1993; Antartida, 1995; N'oublie pas que tu vas mourir, 1996; I Shot Andy Warhol, 1997; Eat and Kiss, 1997. Honours: Inducted into Rock'n'Roll Hall Of Fame (with Velvet Underground), 1996; Honor Fellow, Goldsmiths College, London, 1997. Current Management: Firebrand Management, Suite 1.3, 12 Rickett Street, London SW6 1RU, England.

CALHOUN Dave, b. 11 Feb 1969, Whitehaven, Cumbria, England. Musician (guitar); Singer; Songwriter. Musical Education: Self-taught. Career: Played guitar alongside Dave Fenton of The Vapours, 1990; Played with Moondigger at many London venues including the Marquee, 1993-96; Currently writing and recording with Zenshoppers. Recordings: 423, Moondigger, 1993; Guitarist Of The Year Album, 1994; Sorrows Wedding, single, Zenshoppers; Relax, album, Brian Green. Publications: Currently working on two guitar tuition books. Honours: Guitarist of the Year, 1994-95. Memberships: Musicians' Union; PRS; MCPS. Hobby: Carp fishing. Current Management: John Glover, 34 Lotts Road, Chelsea, London SW10, England. Adddress: 15 Broughton Road, Thornton Heath, Surrey CR7 6AG, England.

CALLARD Peter, b. 1 Jan 1971, Hatfield, Hertfordshire, England. Musician (guitar); Teacher; Composer. Musical Education: Musicians Institute, Hollywood, California, USA. Career: Backing musician, QE2, 1991; Artists include: Petula Clark; Lucy Arnaz; Frankie Vaughn; Vince Hill; Shows include: A Chorus Line; Working (UK, US); Smike; The Pajamagame; Tours with: John Burgess Quartet (Europe); National Youth Jazz Orchestra (NYJO); 40 Feet Forward; E P J; Mixed Feelings; Mr President. Honours: Vocational honours; Outstanding Student Of The Year (MI). Membership: Musicians' Union. Hobbies: Cricket; Football; Classical music, opera. Address: c/o 99 Darby's Lane, Oakdale, Poole, Dorset BH15 3EU, England.

CALLE Ed (Eduardo Joaquin), b. 10 Aug 1959, Caracas, Venezuela. Musician (saxophone); Composer; Arranger; Teacher. Education: Senior Mathematics Major. Musical Education: Master's degree Music, University of Miami. Career: Sony recording artist; Recorded and toured with international artistes including Frank Sinatra; Gloria Estefan; Vicki Carr; Julio Iglesias; Arturo Sandoval; Regina Belle. Recordings: Solo albums (original compositions and arrangements): Nightgames, 1985; Double-talk, 1996. Publications: Working on books for the saxophone; Many published arrangements. Membership: NARAS. Hobbies: Athletics; Mathematics; Films; Reading. Current Management: Carl Valldejulli, Turi's Music/Quiet Storm. Address: Turi's Music, 103 Westward Drive, Miami Springs, FL 33166, USA.

CALLIS Jo, b. 2 May 1951, Rotherham, Yorkshire, England. Musician; Songwriter. Education: Edinburgh College of Art. Musical Education: Self-taught. Career: Member of bands including: The Human League; The Rezillos; Shake; Boots For Dancing; Co-writer with many other artistes. Recordings: Albums: with The Human League: Dare; Hysteria; with The Rezillos: Can't Stand The Rezillos; Singles: with The Human League: Don't You Want Me; Open Your Heart; (Keep Feeling) Fascination; Mirror Man; The Lebanon; Louise; with The Rezillos: Top Of The Pops. Honours: ASCAP Awards, Don't You Want Me, (Keep Feeling) Fascination. Membership: BASCA. Hobbies: Collecting old toys; Toy soldiers. Address: 3A Rochester Terrace, Edinburgh EH10 5AA, Scotland.

CÁMARA DE LANDA Enrique Guillermo, b. 3 May 1951, Buenos Aires, Argentina. Enthomusicologist. Education: Degree in Musical Pedagogy, 1977, Degree in Musicology, 1979, Argentinian Catholic University, Buenos Aires; Philosophy Doctorate, University of Valladolid, Spain, 1994. Musical Education: Piano degree, 1972. Career: Currently Professor of Ethnomusiclogy at the Universidad de Valladolid, Spain. Publications: Tango de ida y vuelta, 1992; Argentina: Charnada y chamamé, 1992; Argentina: Carnaval, 1994; L'arrivée du tango en Italie, 1995; Proyecciones de la baguala, 1996; Erkencho, 1995. Memberships: Vice-President, SIbE (Sociedad Ibérica de Etnomusicología); SEdEM (Sociedad Española de Musicología): IASPM; AAM (Asociación Argentina de Musicología). Address: Azorín 5, 4°A, 47005 Valladolid, Spain.

CAMBUZAT François-Régis, b. 15 Sept 1962, Saigon, Vietnam. Singer; Musician (guitar). Career: Average 120 concerts a year, around Europe: France; Germany; Italy; Switzerland; Austria; Spain; Eastern Republics. Recordings: with The Kim Squad: Young Bastards, 1987; Solo: Notre-Dame Des Naufragés, 1988; Uccidamo Kim, 1990; with Il Gram Teatro Amaro: Port-Famine, 1991; Hôtel Brennessel, 1993; with F-R Cambuzat et les Enfants Rouges: Swinoujscie-Tunis, 1995. Membership: SACEM (France). Current Management: Les Enfants Rouges. Address: Le Château, 12260 Salvagnac-Cajarc, France.

CAMERON Chris, b. England. Musician (keyboards); Arranger; Producer. Career: Worked with: Hot Chocolate; Wham!; George Michael (also his musical director); Stevie Nicks; Terence Trent D'Arby; Breathe; Take That; Presumptos Implicados; Pepsi and Shirlie. Current Management: The Liaison And Promotion Co. Address: 70 Gloucester Place, London W1H 3HL, England.

CAMERON John Allan, b. 16 Dec 1938, Inverness, Cape Breton, Nova Scotia. Singer; Songwriter; Musician. Education: BEd, St Francis Xavier University, Antignoish, Nova Scotia, Canada. Career: Professional, 1968; Toured and performed throughout world from Arctic to Middle East; Appeared in Las Vegas and on Grand Ole Opry; Toured with Anne Murray for several years; Hosted TV shows, CBC and CTV Networks. Recordings: Here Comes John Allan Cameron, 1968; Get There By Dawn, 1975; Lord of the Dance, 1977; Weddings, Wakes and Other Things, 1979; Free Born Man, 1987; Good Times, 1990; Wind Willow, 1991; Glencoe Station, 1996. Honours: East Coast Music Association's Lifetime Achievement Award, 1995. Memberships: AFofM; SOCAN. Current Management: Joella Foulds, Rave Entertainment Inc. Address: Rave Entertainment Inc, 363 Charlotte St, Suite 1, Sydney, NS, B1P 1EI, Canada.

CAMERON Kate, b. 14 Nov 1965, Hemel Hempstead, Hertfordshire, England. Singer; Songwriter; Entertainer; Musician (piano, french horn). Musical Education: Theory: Grade V; French Horn: Grade VIII; Piano: Grade VII; O and A Level, Grade A. Career: Lead vocalist, backing vocalist, vocal arranger, writer with GMT, 1990-92; Worked with Doug Wimbish, Bob Jones, John Waddell, Q; Host of Singers Nightclub; Musical Director, Minx, all-female cabaret acapella group, 1993-95; Session singer for artists including Norman Cook, 1994. Recordings: P.A.S.S.I.O.N; Jon Of The Pleased Wimmin, 1995; with Freak Power (backing vocals): Rush; Get In Touch, 1994. Memberships: Musicians' Union; Variety Artiste's Association. Hobbies: Reading; Golf; Badminton; Cooking. Current Management: The Vocal Agency. Address: 43 Windsor Drive, East Barnet, Herts EN4 8UE, England.

CAMILLERI Claude Anthony Paul Francis Xavier, b. 9 Nov 1963, Malta. Audio Engineering And Production Lecturer; Engineering Producer. m. Sharon, 16 June 1988, 1 son, 2 daughters. Education: Maynooth University, Ireland, 1984. Musical Education: Piano and guitar; Synthesis / Music Technology. Career: Considered leading pioneer in training audio engineers and producers, 1986-; Lectures, various universities and colleges worldwide; Founder, Alchemea; Work for Sony; Polygram; Virgin; EMI; Chrysalis; Acid-Jazz; Motor-Germany; Various productions for independent labels. Recordings: Producer for various record labels; Own albums on own label; Various collaborations. Publications: Various papers on production and sound/audio engineering; Two books due for publication in 1996. Honour: National Training Award for Achievements in field of training and education. Memberships: APRS; Producer's Guild. Hobbies: Cooking; Chess; Research; Family. Current Management: c/o Hari Voyantzis, Alchemea Records. Address: The Windsor Centre, Windsor Street, The Angel, Islington, London N1 8QH, England.

CAMILO Michel, b. 4 Apr 1954, Santo Domingo, Dominican Republic. Jazz Musician (piano); Composer; Conductor. m. Sandra Camilo, 22 Feb 1975. Education: Universidad Autonoma de Santo Domingo (VASD). Musical Education: National Conservatory, Dominican Republic; Juillard School Of Music; Mannes School Of Music. Career: Appearances include: Carnegie Hall debut, 1986; Berlin Jazz Festival, 1987; Musical director, Heineken Jazz Festival, Dominican Republic, 1987-; Newport Jazz Festival; North Sea Jazz Festival; Pori Jazz Festival; Grande Parade du Jazz; Copenhagen Jazz Festival; New Orleans Jazz Festival; Madrid and Barcelona Jazz Festivals; San Sebastian and Andorra Jazz Festival; Lugano Jazz Festival; Film: Two Much, 1996. Recordings: Why Not, 1986; Suntan/Michel Camilo in trio, 1987; Michel Camilo, 1988; On Fire, 1991; On The Other Hand, 1991; Rendezvous, 1993; One More Once, 1994; Two Much (soundtrack), 1996; Rhapsody For Two Pianos And Orchestra, 1992. Honours: Emmy Award, 1986; Voted among Top Jazz Artists Of Year, Billboard magazine, 1989, 1991; Honorary Professorship (VASD), 1992; Doctor Honoris Causa (Utesa), 1993. Memberships: AFofM; RMA; American Music Center. Hobbies: Reading; Movies; Computers; Music. Current Management: Sandra Camilo, Redondo Music. Address: PO Box 216, Katonah, NY 10536, USA.

CAMISON Mathias (Mat), b. 5 Aug 1941, Algeria. Composer; Arranger; Musician (keyboards). Musical Education: Conservatory. Career: Musician on tour: All French stars; Artists including Jimmy Cliff; The Four Tops; Film (France): Black And White In Color; Many hits, England, USA as Pepper Box; Television music for: Canal; Sport; Music on France 1; Horses races. Recordings include: Hits with Pepper Box; Love Me Baby, Sheila B Devotion; We've Got A Feeling, with Chris Waddle and B Boli. Honours: Oscar; Molière. Memberships: SACEM; SPEDIMAM; ADAMI. Hobbies: Tennis; Football;

Sailing. Address: 5 Rue de la Tuilierie, 92150 Suresnes, France.

CAMOZZI Christopher Alan, b. 1 May 1957, Burlingame, California, USA. Musician (guitar). Musical Education: Private study. Career: Musician for Michael Bolton tours: Soul Provider; Time, Love and Tenderness; Timeless, The Classics; The One Thing tours; Television: Tonight Show; Arsenio Hall; Billboard Music Awards; American Music Awards; VH-1 Honours; Oprah Winfrey Show; Donahue; NBC TV; Specials; VH2 Unplugged; with Maria Carey: Grammy Awards; Tonight Show. Recordings: with Michael Bolton: Soul Provider; Time, Love And Tenderness; Timeless, The Classics; with Mariah Carey: Mariah Carey; with Barbra Streisand: Greatest Hits and More; with Whitney Houston: I'm Your Baby Tonight. Publications: Guitar Player; Peavey Monitor. Membership: Musicians' Union. Hobby: Golf. Address: 3341 Abbey Lane, Palmdale, CA 93551, USA.

CAMP Manel, b. 20 Apr 1947, Manresa, Barcelona, Spain. Musician (piano); Arranger; Composer; Concert and Recording Director. Musical Education: Professional diploma, piano; Contemporary composition, orchestration, Language and methodology of Jazz, Berklee College of Music, Boston. Career: As solo pianist: International festivals: Grenoble, France; Brirstonas, Lithuania; Cheboksari and Yaroslav, Russia; Buenos Aires, Argentina; Boston, USA; Barcelona, Madrid, San Sebastian and Granada, Spain. Recordings: Minorisa, Fusion; Poesia Secreta; Primer Viatge; La Meva Petita Terra; Escàndols; El Complot Dels Anells; Viu; Ben A Prop; Diàlegs; Ressorgir; Duets; Contrast; Coratge; Rosebud. Publications: Scores of first two albums. Honours: Best Recording Composition, Generalitat de Catalunya, 1985; Best Musical Performance, Radio Nacional, 1988; Best Soloist, International Festival Jazz, San Sebastian, 1986; National Cinematographyc Award, Generalitat, 1992. Current Management: Madma. Address: c/o de la Mel, 23, 2n, 08240 Manresa, Barcelona, Spain.

CAMP Richard, b. 16 Apr 1956, Ipswich, Suffolk, England. Singer; Musician (guitar). Career: Lead singer, guitarist, with Blind Dog Beerbelly Blues Band; Live performances include: Diana Luke Show, Greater London Radio, 1994; Guitarist with groups: Click Click; Savage Bees; World Circus; Eclipse. Recordings: Single: Leave Well Alone, Savage Bees, 1978; EP: Reanimate, Click Click, 1983; Album: Blue Guitar, Blind Dog Beerbelly Blues Band, 1996. Membership: Musicians' Union. Hobbies: Blues history; Guitar collecting; Graphic design; Reading; Socialising. Current Management: Self-managed. Address: PO Box 4039, Dunstable, Bedfordshire LU6 1ZU, England.

CAMPBELL Ali (Alistair), b. 15 Feb 1959, Birmingham, England. Vocalist; Musician (guitar). Career: Member, UK reggae group, UB40, 1979-; Also solo artiste; Concerts include: Tour with the Pretenders, 1980; Support to The Police, Rockatta De Bowl, Milton Keynes, 1980; Nelson Mandela's 70th Birthday Tribute, Wembley Stadium, 1988; Film, Dance With The Devil, 1988; Television film: UB40 - A Family Affair, C4, 1991. Recordings: Albums: with UB40: Signing Off, 1980; Present Arms, 1981; The Singles Album, 1982; UB44, 1982; UB40 Live, 1983; Labour Of Love, 1983; Geffroy Morgan, 1984; Baggariddim, 1985; Rat In The Kitchen, 1986; CCCP - Live In Moscow, 1987; The Best Of UB40 Vol 1, 1987; Labour Of Love II, 1990; Promises And Lies (Number 1, UK), 1993; Solo: Big Love, 1995; Singles include: My Way Of Thinking, 1980; The Earth Dies Screaming, 1980; One In Ten, 1981; Love Is All Is Alright, 1982; Red Red Wine (Number 1, UK), 1983; Please Don't Make Me Cry, 1983; Too Many Rivers To Cross, 1983; Cherry Oh Baby, 1984; If It Happens Again, 1984; I Got You Babe, duet with Chrissie Hynde

(Number 1, UK), 1985; Don't Break My Heart, 1985; Sing Our Own Song, 1986; Rat In Mi Kitchen, 1987; Maybe Tomorrow, 1987; Breakfast In Bed, duet with Chrissie Hynde, 1988; Homely Girl, 1989; Kingston Town, 1990; I'll Be Your Baby Tonight, with Robert Palmer, 1990; The Way You Do The Things You Do, 1990; Here I Am (Come And Take Me), 1991; Can't Help Falling In Love, used in film soundtrack Sliver (Number 1, UK and US), 1993; Higher Ground, 1993; Bring Me Your Cup, 1993. Current Management: David Harper, What Management, 12B South Bar, 1st Floor, Banbury, Oxon OX16 9AA, England.

CAMPBELL David, b. 22 Oct 1969, Glasgow, Scotland. Musician (drums, percussion); Songwriter; Musical Arranger; Producer. Musical Education: Clydebank College. Career: Drummer, percussionist, writer, arranger, producer with: Parksorch, 1987-88; Kiss 'N' Tell, 1988-92; Ragged Laughter, 1992-94; Raglin Street Rattle, 1994-; Concerts and tours include: Beat The Clyde, 1987; Prince of Wales Gala Concert, 1989; Solo American tour of Southern states, 1993; US Coast to Coast tour, 1994; TV Special, Live at The Festival, 1988. Compositions include: Need A Lover, 1992; State Of Confusion, 1993, On Brilliant Wings, 1994, She Called My Name, 1995. Recordings include: Cava Sessions, 1988; The Word Is Out...The Time Is Now, 1992; Raglin Street Rattle, 1995. Honour: Premier Student of The Year, Clydebank College, 1990. Membership: PRS. Hobbies: Photography; Motor sport; World travel. Address: 3 Balfluig Street, Provanhall, Glasgow G34 9PS, Scotland.

CAMPBELL Glen Travis, b. 22 Apr 1936, Delight, Arkansas, USA. Singer; Musician (guitar). Career: Member, Dick Bills Band, 1954; Founder, Glen Campbell And The Western Wranglers, 1958; Session musician, Los Angeles; Replaced Brian Wilson touring with the Beach Boys; Television work; Film appearances include: True Grit, 1969; Norwood, 1970; Duets with Anne Murray, Rita Coolidge, Tanya Tucker; Tours, television appearances, late 1970s. Recordings: Hit singles include: Gentle On My Mind; By The Time I Get To Phoenix; Wichita Lineman; Galveston; Rhinestone Cowboy; Southern Nights; Albums include: Too Late To Worry, Too Late To Cry, 1963; The Astounding 12-String Guitar Of Glen Campbell, 1964; Gentle On My Mind, 1967; By The Time I Get To Phoenix, 1967; Hey Little One, 1968; A New Place In The Sun, 1968; Galveston, 1969; Try A Little Kindness, 1970; Oh Happy Day, 1970; Norwood (soundtrack), 1970; The Last Time I Saw Her, 1971; Anne Murray/Glen Campbell, 1971; I Knew Jesus (Before He Was A Star), 1973; Reunion (The Songs Of Jimmy Webb), 1974; Rhinestone Cowboy, 1975; Bloodline, 1976; Southern Nights, 1977; Basic, 1978; Somethin' About You Baby I Like, 1980; It's The World Gone Crazy, 1981; Old Home Town, 1983; Letter To Home, 1984; Just A Matter Of Time, 1986; No More Night, 1988; Still Within The Sound Of My Voice, 1988; Walkin' In The Sun, 1990; Unconditional Love, 1991. Honours: Grammy, Best Country and Western Recording, Gentle On My Mind, 1967. Current Management: Girsey, Schneider and Co, 10351 Santa Monica Boulevard #300, Los Angeles, CA 90025, USA.

CAMPBELL John, b. 16 Apr 1953, Reigate, Surrey, England. Music Publisher; Artist Manager. m. Sue, 7 Apr 1984. Career: Chairman JC Music; Publisher, Manager for: Richard Feldman; Nick Trevisick; Jeff Paris; Michael Graves; Mike Moran; Artist Manager for: Marcella Detroit; Shakespears Sister; Lena Fiagbe; Oui 3; Clementines; Nut. Recordings: Stay, Shakespears Sister (Number 1, 8 weeks, UK charts); Gotta Get It Right, Lena Fiagbe; I Believe, Marcella Detroit. Memberships: Pegs Club; Liberal Party. Hobby: Fiscal Philosophy. Address: 40 Prebend Mansions, Chiswick High Road, London W4 2LU, England.

CAMPBELL Junior (William), b. 31 May 1947, Glasgow, Scotland. Composer; Arranger; Musician; Singer; Conductor. m. (1) Margaret Hutcheson, 7 Jan 1967, (2) Susan Chibnall, 18 Mar 1989, 1 son, 1 daughter. Musical Education: Studied orchestration, composition, conducting with Eric Gilder and Max Saunders, RCM. Career: Founder member, Gaylords, 1961; Later became Marmalade, many hits, 1968-71; Solo artist, singer, 1972-74; Record producer, songwriter, 1974-80; Produced many artists including Barbara Dickson; Film and television composer including Bafta Award drama: Taking Over The Asylum; Composer on 104 Thomas The Tank Engine Films. Recordings: with Marmalade: Lovin' Things; Obladi Oblada; Reflections On My Life; Rainbow. Solo: Hallalujah Freedom; Sweet Illusion. Memberships: BASCA; PRS; MCPS. Hobbies: Eating out; 2 Labrador dogs; Played showbiz charity football for many years (now retired gracefully); Squash. Current Management: Self-managed. Address: Greyfriars Lodge, Greyfriars Drive, Ascot, Berks SL5 9JD, England.

CAMPBELL Rita, b. 28 Sept 1968, London, England. Singer. Career: Backing singer for: D:ream, Take That tour; Kenny Thomas, UK tour; Act Of Faith; Brand New Heavies, UK tour; Billie Ray Martin; China Black; Carleen Anderson; X-Avia; Ronnie Simon; Bell Curtis; Lisa Stansfield; Swing Out Sister; Dream Academy; Rin Tin Tin; Cindy Jackson; Perception; Television includes: Smash Hits Awards; Dance Energy; In The Air Tonight (Virgin's 21st); Top Of The Pops; The James Whale Show. Recordings: with: Pauline Henry; Sly & Robbie; Bizarre Inc; Odyssey; Act Of Faith; Sid Owen; Eddie Kidd; Dream Academy; Perception; Colour of Love; Brother Beyond; David Dundas; Bell Curtis; Medalling Thieves; Tony Gibber; Cindy Jackson; Johnny Spurling; Commercials: Ribena Spring; Audi; American Airlines; Gordons Gin; Heineken Beer; Pepsi. Membership: Musicians' Union. Hobbies: Films; Photography; Art; Eating out; Travel. Current Management: Hobsons Singers; Session Connection; Simon Harrison, B&H Musician. Address: 21 Ruckholt Close, Leyton, London E10 5NX, England.

CAMPBELL Robin, b. 25 Dec 1954, Birmingham, England. Musician (guitar); Vocalist. Career: Lead guitarist, vocalist, UK reggae group, UB40, 1979-; Concerts include: Tour with the Pretenders, 1980; Support to The Police, Rockatta De Bowl, Milton Keynes, 1980; Nelson Mandela's 70th Birthday Tribute, Wembley Stadium, 1988; Film, Dance With The Devil, 1988; Television film: UB40 - A Family Affair, C4, 1991. Recordings: Albums include: Signing Off, 1980; Present Arms, 1981; The Singles Album, 1982; UB44, 1982; UB40 Live, 1983; Labour Of Love, 1983; Geoffrey Morgan, 1984; Baggariddim, 1985; Rat In The Kitchen, 1986; CCCP - Live In Moscow, 1987; The Best Of UB40, Vol 1, 1987; Labour Of Love II, 1990; Promises And Lies (Number 1, UK), 1993; Singles include: My Way Of Thinking, 1980; The Earth Dies Screaming, 1980; One In Ten, 1981; Love Is All Is Alright, 1982; So Here I Am, 1982; Red Red Wine (Number 1, UK), 1983; Please Don't Make Me Cry, 1983; Too Many Rivers To Cross, 1983; Cherry Oh Baby, 1984; If It Happens Again, 1984; I Got You Babe, duet with Chrissie Hynde (Number 1, UK), 1985; Don't Break My Heart, 1985; Sing Our Own Song, 1986; Rat In Mi Kitchen, 1987; Maybe Tomorrow, 1987; Breakfast In Bed, duet with Chrissie Hynde, 1988; Homely Girl, 1989; Kingston Town, 1990; I'll Be Your Baby Tonight (with Robert Palmer), 1990; The Way You Do The Things You Do, 1990; Here I Am (Come And Take Me), 1991; Can't Help Falling In Love featured in film soundtrack Sliver (Number 1, UK and US), 1993; Higher Ground, 1993; Bring Me Your Cup, 1993. Current Management: David Harper, What Management, 12B South Bar, 1st Floor, Banbury, Oxon OX16 9AA, England.

CAMPBELL Simon John, b. 9 Jan 1958, Bury, Lancashire, England. Musician (guitar); Vocalist; Producer. m. Angela Mary Campbell, 5 Sep 1982, 2 sons. Education: Degree in Chemistry. Musical Education: Self-taught. Career: Tours, 1 single, 1 EP with rock band Whitefire, 1975-81; National tours with R&B band Roadrunner, 1981-85; Tours with pop band Gilt Edge, Cutting Edge, 1985-86; International tours, 1 album with pop band Little Brother, 1986-89; 1 album with Disciples, 1990-92; with The Method, 1992-94; with Simon Campbell Band, 1994-95; Featured artist with The 1995 7. Membership: Musicians' Union. Hobbies: Children; Food and drink. Current Management: Music Business Management. Address: Music Business Management, International House, Drake Street, Rochdale OL16 1PN, England.

CAMPBELL Vivian, b. Belfast, Northern Ireland. Rock Musician (guitar). Career: Guitarist, Dio, 1983-87; Whitesnake, 1987-88; Guitarist, Trinity; Riverdogs; Guitarist, Shadow King, 1991; Def Leppard, 1992-; Major international tours and concerts include Freddie Mercury Tribute Concert, Wembley Stadium, 1992. Recordings: Albums: with Dio: Holy Driver, 1983; The Last In Line, 1984; Sacred Heart, 1985; with Whitesnake: Whitesnake, 1987; with Shadow King: Shadow King, 1991; with Def Leppard: Vault 1980-95, 1995; Slang, 1996; Singles: with Def Leppard: Let's Get Rocked; Make Love Like A Man; Have You Ever Needed Someone So Bad; Stand Up (Kick Love Into Motion); Heaven Is; Tonight; Two Steps Behind, used in film soundtrack The Last Action Hero, 1993; When Love And Hate Collide, 1995; Guest musician, Long Hard Look, Lou Gramm, 1989. Current Management: Q-Prime Inc., 729 Seventh Avenue, 14th Floor, New York, NY 10019, USA.

CAMPI Ray, b. 20 April 1934, New York, New York, USA. Musician (guitar, bass, dobro steel). Education: BFA, University of Texas, Austin, TX, USA, 1957. Career: Austin City Limits, national public TV; Tomorrow Show, NBC TV; Texas Saturday Night, BBC II TV, 1991, BBC Radio, 1977; Echo's Show. Compositions: Rockin' At the Ritz; Caterpillar; A Little Bit of Heartache; Kick Da Bukkit. Recordings: 35 or more CDs and albums on Rollin' Rock Records, 1956-96. Publications: Rolling Stone, 1980; Dynamite, 1995; Now Dig This, 1996. Membership: Austin Federation of Musicians. Hobby: Old car collecting. Current Management: Paul Barrett, Rock 'n' Roll Enterprises. Address: 4814 Rosemont Avenue, La Crescenta, CA 91214, USA.

CANAPE Jean-François, b. 1 Dec 1945, Lagny, France. Jazz Musician (trumpet, key bugle, flute). m. Bathany Jeanne, 26 Mar 1988, 1 son. Musical Education: Versailles Conservatory. Career: Several international festivals and tours: Montreux; Newport; Paris; Berlin; Babylon; Tokyo; Brazaville; India; Boulogne (played with Dave Liebman); Member, Orchestre National de Jazz, 1989-91; Played and composed for cinema, theatre, contemporary and classical music. Recordings: KONPS, Jean-François Canape Trio; Participated in: Jack-Line; Claire, with ONJ; Katchinas, Gerard Marais. Hobbies: Cinema; Fishing. Current Management: Sylvie Caqué. Address: 18 Rue des Plantes, 75014 Paris, France.

CANDOLINI Joel, b. 27 July 1957, Vittel, France. Musician (guitar); Composer; Arranger. m. Catherine L'Hôte, 29 Oct 1983, 1 son, 2 daughters. Musical Education: AIMRA (Lyon, France); CIM (Paris, France). Career: Concerts (solo and sideman); Recordings (sideman); Compositions and arrangements for singers, jazz bands and films. Membership: Union des Musiciens de Jazz (France). Address: 22 La Croisette, 88340 le Val d'Ajol, France.

CANIBOL Heinz, b. 3 July 1951, Gelsenkirchen, Germany. Managing Director. m. Brigitte Canibol, 3 Feb 1984. Education: Degree in Economics. Career: Product Manager and Marketing Director, CBS Records, Germany, 1977-89; Managing Director, Sony Music, Austria, 1989-91; Managing Director and Vice President G/A/S, MCA Music Entertainment, Germany, 1992-. Hobbies: Music; Reading; Gardening. Address: c/o MCA Music Entertainment, Winterhuder Weg 27, D-22085 Hamburg, Germany.

CANN Judith Leonie, b. 3 Apr 1958, Perth, Western Australia. Composer; Musician (keyboard). m. David George Hunt, 14 June 1986, 1 son, 1 daughter. Education: BA degree (majoring in film making); One year at Australian Film and TV school; Exchange student, National Film School, UK. Musical Education: Post-graduate diploma in conducting (Surrey University). Career: Composed, performed synthesized scores and music for use in the film, television, video industry. Recordings: 25 library tracks with Chappell; 175 library tracks with Carlin; Scored music for 1492 The Shattered Utopia (short film); Making Ends Meet; Network Europe; Channel Tunnel videos; Television series: A Tale Of 4 Market Towns; World In Action; Laser, video, fireworks display in China. Publications: Article in APV magazine, Videomaker. Honours: Stemra Award, Netherlands, Most Impressive Use Of Library Music, 1994. Memberships: PRS; Musicians' Union. Hobbies: Drawing; Painting; Gardening. Address: 82 Bushey Hall Road, Bushey, Herts WD2 2EQ, England.

CANNELLI Toni, b. 3 Oct 1957, London, England. Musician (drums); Drum Educator. m. Caroline Goldthorpe, 8 June 1993, 1 daughter. Music Education: Private study with Bob Armstrong. Career: Toured with Gary Boyle and Jim Mullen; Founder, the Drummers Alliance, 1987; Organized three UK drum competitions; Television appearances: Top Of The Pops; Blue Peter (drum demonstration); Also appeared on local BBC TV and Radio. Membership: Musicians' Union. Hobbies: Cycling; Weight training. Address: T. Cannelli, c/o Arbiter Group plc, Wilberforce Road, London NW9 6AX, England.

CANONGE Mario-Laurent, b. 5 September 1960, Fort de France, Martinique. Musician (Piano, Keyboards). 2 daughters. Education: Bachelor Degree in Musicology; Classical Music, Conservatoire Haute de Seine, 2 years. TV: Sur le Pont des Artistes; Rien a Cine, France Inter; Top Live, Europe I; Cerde de Minuit, Pintenne 2; Jazz 6; Jazz a Vienne; Concerts: New Morning, Zenith de Paris; Bataclan; Casino de Paris. Compositions: Pei Mwen Jodi; Pogo; Yélé Congo; L'esé; Palé; Si on sa Révé; Vidé Bo Kay; Echapaya; Dimanoua; Non Muoia; Sé Kon Ca; Bam Ti Bonjou. Recordings: Retour Aux Sources, 1991; Trait D'Union, 1993; Hommage A Marius Cultier, 1994; Aromes Caraibes, 1995. Honours: Best Pianist, Prix de la Défense, 1983; Best Album, Best Composer, SACEM Martinique, 1992-94; Best Album, 1996; Musical Research Prize, 1995. Hobbies: The Sea; Friends; Music. Current Management: c/o Francois Post, Vivienne Sicnasi Promotion, 6 Place George Sand, 91130, Ris Orangis, France.

CANOVILLE Katherine, b. 13 Jan 1965, Hillingdon, Middlesex, England. Company Director; Group Manager. m. Stephen Carrington, 7 July 1995. Career: Concert promoter, 1979-81; Artist Manager, 1981-1995; Managing Director, Buzz Magazine, 1986-1989; Co-founder, Nation Records, 1988; Managing Director, Nation Records, 1990-; Sole Trader, QFM Promotions, 1994. Publications: Ex-writer for Oracle/Teletext World Music Page, until 1992. Membership: BMIA BRIT Award Committee. Hobbies: Music; Computing.

CAPALDI Jim, b. 24 Aug 1944, Evesham, Herefordshire, England. Musician (drums); Vocalist. Career: Member, The Helions; Deep Feeling; Traffic, 1967-69, 1970-74; Also solo artiste. Recordings: Albums: with Traffic: Mr Fantasy, 1968; Traffic, 1968; Solo albums: Oh How We Danced, 1972; Whale Meat Again, 1974; Short Cut Draw Blood, 1976; Fierce Heart, 1983; Some Come Running, 1989; Singles with Traffic include: Paper Sun, 1967; Hole In My Shoe, 1967; Here We Go Round The Mulberry Bush (film title theme), 1967; No Name No Face No Number; Solo single: Love Hurts; Guest, Alone Together, Dave Mason, 1970. Address: c/o Freedom Songs, PO Box 272, London N20 0BY, England.

CAPLIN Arnold Stewart, b. 8 May 1929, New York, USA. Record Company Executive; Record Producer. m. Barbara Stein, 29 June 1950, 2 sons. Career: President, Biograph Records, 1964-; Consultant, advisor, Historic Records. Recordings: Albums: As producer for Thad Jones; George Gershwin; Scott Joplin; James P Johnson; Mel Lewis; Benny Goodman. Honours: Numerous Grammy Nominations, 1967-. Memberships: ASCAP; Broadcast Music Inc; NARAS (fellow); NAIRD; World Jazz Federation. Address: c/o Biograph Records, 35 Medford Street, Somerville, MA 02143-4242, USA.

CAPONE Franco, b. 11 Jan 1968, Rome, Italy. Author; Composer; Musician (guitar); Arranger; Language Teacher. m. Rita Tenan, 7 Sept 1991. Education: Masters Of Arts, Languages; PGCE Education. Career: Founder, French group, Melody, 1987-88; Moved to England, 1989; Worked on first album, 1991; Founded group, Open Arms, 1992; Recorded two albums, tours, Scotland, Ireland, Italy, Belgium, 1992-95; New album due 1996. Recordings: The World My Home, 1991; with Open Arms: Walking With Us, 1992; Back To The World, 1994. Membership: Musicians' Union. Hobbies: Football; Tennis; Chess. Current Management: PPS Communications / Culture-Music, Villaverla, Italy.

CAPONE Philip James, b. 21 May 1960, Eastbourne, East Sussex, England. Musician (guitar); Guitar Teacher. m. Anita Jane Capone, 11 July 1989. Musical Education: Degree, Newcastle College, Newcastle-upon-Tyne; Guildhall School Of Music, London. Career: Toured, recorded with various acts; Session guitarist, Arista Records, mid-1980s; Leader, own band Wild Honey, managed by former Led Zeppelin manager Peter Grant, 1986-87; Currently teaching private school, Hampstead, London, also playing London jazz circuit. Honours: Graduate Diploma Light Music (1st class) Newcastle, LGSM, Guildhall School of Music, London. Membership: Musicians' Union. Hobby: Music. Address: 152 Newport Road, London E10 6PF, England.

CAPTAIN HOLLYWOOD (Tony Harrison), b. 9 Aug 1962, Newark, New Jersey, USA. Singer; Rapper; Producer. Musical Education: Self-taught. Career: Choreographer, major German television programme; Artist, performing and producing: The Mixmaster; Twenty 4 Seven, 1986-1990; Captain Hollywood Project, 1991-. Publications: Grand Piano; I Can't Stand It; More And More. Honours: 14 Gold records; 1 Diamond award; 1 Platinum. Membership: GEMA, Germany. Hobbies: Cars; Basketball. Current Management: Susanne Foecker, D-Town Management. Address: Schündelnhöfe 8, 41751 Viersen, Germany.

CAPTAIN SENSIBLE (Ray Burns), b. Croydon, Surrey, England. Singer; Musician (lead guitar, bass). Musical Education: Self-taught. Career: Invented punk as member of The Damned; Many tours; Numerous television appearances include several on Top Of The Pops. Compositions: Writes most of own material. Recordings: Albums: Solo albums, 1982- including Live At The Milky Way (Amsterdam), 1995;

Meathead, 1995; Singles include: Happy Talk, 1982 (Number 1, UK); Wot, 1982 (Number 1, France, 7 weeks); Glad It's All Over, 1984; Come On Down, 1985; Revolution Now, 1987. Memberships: PRS; Musicians' Union. Hobby: Public transport systems of the world. Current Management: Forward Agency Booking (FAB). Address: Humbug Records, Suite 4N, Leroy House, Essex Road, Islington, London, England.

CARA Irene, b. 18 Mar 1959, Bronx, New York, USA. Singer; Actress; Dancer. Career: Stage appearances: Maggie Flynn, Broadway, 1968; The Me Nobody Knows, 1970; Via Galactica, New York, 1972; Got To Go Disco, 1979; Ain't Misbehavin'; Film appearances: Aaron Loves Angela, 1975; Sparkle, 1976; Fame, 1980; DC Cab, 1980; City Heat, 1984; A Certain Fury, 1985; Busted Up, 1986; Killing 'Em Softly, 1985; The Man In 5-A. Recordings: Singles: Fame (Number 1, UK), 1980; Flashdance... What A Feeling (Number 1, US); Why Me, 1983; Out Here On My Own; Anyone Can See; The Dream, from film DC Cab, 1984; Breakdance, 1984. Honours: Obie Award; Academy Awards: Best Song, Fame; Best Song, Flashdance...What A Feeling. Memberships: Equity; Screen Actors Guild. Address: c/o Talent Consultants International Ltd, 1560 Broadway, Ste 1308, New York, NY 10036, USA.

CARCELES RUIZ Lola, b. 8 June 1960, Murcia, Spain. Singer. m. 25 May 1978, 2 sons, 1 daughter. Musical Education: 5 years at conservatory. Career: Performed throughout Spain, 10 years; Television and radio work; Performed in USA, 1995. Honours: First Prize, Spanish Song Contest. Hobby: Singing. Current Management: Francisco Ferrer Montoya. Address: c/o Augustin Lara N: 10 Piso 5 B, Vistalegre, Murcia, Spain.

CAREY Mariah, b. 22 Mar 1970, Long Island, New York, USA. Singer; Songwriter. m. Tommy Mottola, 5 June 1993. Career: Backing singer, Brenda K Starr, New York, 1988; Solo recording artiste, 1988-; 80 million albums sold to date; Concerts worldwide; Numerous television appearances include: Tonight Show; Arsenio Hall Show; Saturday Night Live; Top Of The Pops; Wogan. Recordings: Albums: Mariah Carey (Number 1, US), 1990; Emotions, 1991; MTV Unplugged EP, 1992; Music Box (Number 1, US and UK), 1993; Merry Christmas, 1994; Daydream (Number 1, UK), 1995; Singles: Vision Of Love; Love Takes Time; Someday; I Don't Wanna Cry; Emotions; Dreamlover; Hero (Number 1, US); Can't Let You Go; Make It Happen; I'll Be There; Open Arms. Honours: 2 Grammy Awards: Best Female Pop Vocal And Best Artist, 1991; Rolling Stone Award, Best Female Singer, 1991; 3 Soul Train Awards, 1991; 6 Billboard Music Awards, 1991-92; 4 American Music Awards, 1992-93; 3 Citations BMI Pop Awards, 1993. Honours include: International Dance Music Award, Best Solo Artist, 1996; Numerous Platinum and Gold records. Current Management: Hoffman Entertainment, 20 W 55th Street, 11th Floor, New York, NY 10022, USA.

CARGILL Rory John, b. 13 May 1955, Toronto, Ontario, Canada. Musician (guitar, keyboards, synthesizer). 2 sons. Career: The Invisible Band, 1981-; Bit of busking, a few free festivals. Recordings: The Invisible Band: Sunburst Earthrise; The Invisible Band, Numbers 1-8, 1981-86; Pan-Dimensional Festival, 1984; Majik Mantra Muzik, 1985; Remembrance, 1985; Remembrance Live, 1985; The Rosetta Stone, 1985, 86; One Day At The Radio Telescope, 1982-84; A Round Trip, 1986; Music For Everyperson, 1986-87; News From Nowhere, 1987; Under These Starry Skies..., 1987-89; 13, 1989; Psychedelic Sam's Synergistic Salad; Tales Of Distant Worlds, 1990; Occam's Razor, 1991; Inner Mind Travel Agency, 1992; Off-Cuts'n'Out-Takes, 1992-93. Membership:

Musicians' Union. Address: 29A Bennerley Road, Battersea, London SW11 6DR, England.

CARLILL Neil William, b. 20 Mar 1967, Ripon, England. Musician. Education: Loughborough University of Technology. Musical Education: Self-taught. Career: Member, band: Delicatessen; TV and radio: Radio 1; Radio 5; Various regional stations, London XFM; Independent radio live concerts; Concerts: Regional, London, UK shows (2 tours); Amsterdam Festival (Paradiso). Recordings: Delicatessen: EP: Inviting Both Sisters Out To Dinner; Singles: C I Kane; I'm Just Alive; Album: Skin Touching Water. Publication: Nervescale magazine. Membership: Musicians' Union. Hobbies: Writing; Various water sports. Current Management: Tony Beard Management. Address: 145A Ladbroke Grove, London W11, England.

CARLISLE Belinda, b. 17 Aug 1958, Hollywood, California, USA. Singer. m. Morgan Mason, 12 Apr 1986, 1 son. Career: Singer, all-girl group The Go-Gos (formerly the Misfits), 1978-85; Numerous tours worldwide; Solo artiste, 1986-94; Support to Robert Palmer, US tour, 1986; Solo tour, US and Canada, 1988; Re-formed Go-Gos, 1994-; Television includes: Late Night With David Letterman; Top Of The Pops; Summer Scene; The O-Zone; Stage performance, Grease, 1983; Film appearance, Swing Shift, 1984; Model, Almay Cosmetics. Recordings: Singles: with The Go-Gos: Our Lips Are Sealed; We Got The Beat; Head Over Heels; The Whole World Lost Its Head; Solo: Mad About You, 1986; Heaven Is A Place On Earth (Number 1, UK and US), 1987; I Get Weak (Number 2, US), 1988; Circle In The Sand, 1988; I Feel Free, 1988; World Without You, 1988; Leave A Light On, 1989; Summer Rain, 1990; Runaway Horses, 1990; We Want The Same Thing, 1990; Live Your Life Be Free, 1991; Albums: with the Go-Gos: Beauty And The Beat (Number 1, US), 1981; Vacation, 1982; Talk Show, 1984; Return To The Valley Of The Go-Gos, 1994; Solo albums: Belinda, 1986; Heaven On Earth, 1988; Runaway Horses, 1989; Live Your Life Be Free, 1991; Greatest Hits, 1992; Contributor, Rainbow Warriors, 1989; Tame Yourself (animal rights benefit album), 1991. Honour: Grammy Nomination, Heaven Is A Place On Earth, 1988. Current Management: c/o Gold Mountain Entertainment, 3575 Cahuenga Blvd West, Los Angeles, CA 90068, USA.

CARLOTTI Jan-Mari, b. 23 June 1948, Meknès, Morocco. Singer; Musician (guitar); Writer; Composer. Education: Medieval History; Ethnology; Sanskrit. Musical Education: Self-taught. Career: Singer, solely in Occitan (Provençal language); Formed Mont Jóia, 1974-83; Solo artist, 1983-; Also worked with Anita/Anita, Michel Marre. Recordings: 5 albums with Mont Jóia; 6 albums as solo artist or in other groups; Latest: Chants des Troubadours, with Michel Marre, 1995. Publications include: Anthologie De La Nouvelle Chanson Occitane, 1984. Honours: Grand Prix, Academie Charles Cros, 1978, 1994; First Prize, International Artist, Turin Folk Competition, 1989; Best Solo Artist, Trad Magazine, 1991. Hobbies: Mediterranean culture; The organisation Rescontres de la Mer. Current Management: Ass Mont Jóia, Ostau de Provença, Parc Jourdan, 13100 Aix, France. Address: 2 bis Imp Fleury-Proudhon, 13200 Arles, France.

CARLYLE Mary Theresa McLeish, b. 18 Mar 1938, Glasgow, Scotland. Musician (piano); Entertainer; Singer; Songwriter. m. Dick Le Claire, 15 Feb 1968, 5 sons. Musical Education: Privately, Frank McLeish (uncle), MA, ARCM; Violet Stewart, LRAM, ARCM. Career: Carroll Levis Discoveries, age 16; Variety; Moss Empires Tour, Scotland; Concert Parties; Rep; Reviews; BBC TV STV Drama, variety; Summer season Jersey's Sunshine Hotel, 1960; Winter, Manchester Clubland; US Forces Club Piani/bar, Frankfurt;

Return Jersey, Formed trio, 1964; Played residencies main hotels, clubs, also solo work; One of original (and current) resident musicians, Blue Note Club, Jersey. Compositions include: Jersey Suite, co-writer, Jack Duff; All I Got Was You; Jersey (all profits to J A Monday Club, childrens charity); I'll Think Of You This Christmas; The Faceless Face; I'll Never Cry; How Can I Write A Song For You? Memberships: Equity; Musicians' Union. Hobbies: Charity work, Jersey Artists Monday Club; Variety Club, Jersey Tent 52; Writing; Composing; Sewing. Current Management: Dick Ray Organisation Ltd, Jersey. Address: 40 Seaton Place, St Helier, Jersey JE2 3QL, Channel Islands.

CARMEN Eric, b. 11 Aug 1949, Cleveland, Ohio, USA. Singer; Songwriter. Musical Education: Classical singing, Cleveland Institute of Music. Career: Singer, various groups, Cleveland, 1960s; Lead singer, The Choir, 1968; Name changed to Raspberries, 1971-75; Solo recording artiste, 1975-80, 1985-; Over 15 million record sales. Recordings include: Albums with: The Raspberries: The Raspberries, 1971; Fresh, 1972; Side 3, 1973; Starting Over, 1975; Solo albums: Eric Carmen, 1975; Boats Against The Current, 1977; Change Of Heart, 1978; Tonight You're Mine, 1980; Eric Carmen, 1985; The Best Of Eric Carmen, 1988; Singles: with The Raspberries: Go All the Way, 1972; Overnight Sensation, 1974; All By Myself (Number 2, US); Never Gonna Fall In Love Again, 1976; Sunrise, 1976; Change Of Heart, 1978; It Hurts Too Much, 1980; I Wanna Hear It From Your Lips, 1985; Hungry Eyes, used in film soundtrack Dirty Dancing, 1988; Make Me Lose Control, 1988; Reason To Try (used for Olympics Games coverage, NBC-TV), 1988. Current Management: QBQ Entertainment Inc., 341 Madison Avenue, 14th Floor, New York, NY 10017, USA.

CARMICHAEL Anita, b. 17 Sept 1964, Upminster, Essex, England. Musician (saxophone, alto); Vocalist. m. Michael Tanousis, 27 Aug 1993, 1 son. Musical Education: Guildhall School of Music. Career: Tours with: The Communards; Jonathan Butler; Fay Weldon; Imagination; M-People; Television, radio: Woman's Hour (BBC Radio 4); BBC World Service; TV: Pebble Mill; Cue The Music; Womens' Jazz Archive (BBC GLR); Concerts: Antibes Festival; Brecon; Glastonbury; Jakarta; Montreux; Ronnie Scott's Club; Jazz Cafe; Red Sea; JVC Capital Jazz; Live TV and BBC Radio 2, 3, 5. Recordings: Live At The Premises (EP), 1993; The Unadulterated, 1994; Plays Dinner Jazz (EP), 1995; Saxotronix, 1995; Lipstick On My Reed, 1996; Video: Sax Skills With Anita Carmichael, 1995. Honours: Wire magazine, Newcomer of the Year, 1987. Memberships: Musicians' Union; PRS; MCPS; Ronnie Scott's. Hobbies: Watching Eastenders; Tennis; Horse riding. Current Management: Saxology Records. Address: 49E St Pauls Road, London N1 2LT, England.

CARMICHAEL Jim, b. 21 Feb 1971, Sevenoaks, Kent, England. Musician (drums); Writer; Producer. Education: Design and Communication; Berklee College of Music, Boston, USA, 1989. Career: Principal percussionist in winning orchestra at National Festival For Youth, 1988; Drummer, acid jazz group, K-Creative, 1991-93; Member, Freak Power. Recordings: with K-Creative: QED, 1992; with Izit: The Whole Affair, 1993; Imaginary Man, 1995; with Freak Power: Drive Thru Booty, 1994; More of Everything for Everybody, 1996; Carmichael's Crunchy Nut Loops, 1997; Mandalay: Empathy, 1998. Address: Flat 1, 88 Beaconsfield Road, Brighton, West Sussex BN1 6DD, England.

CARNEIRO Fernando (Nando), b. 26 June 1953, Belo Horizonte, Brazil. Nora Kholki, 10 July 1997, 2 sons. Musical Education: Classical Guitar; Classical Piano; Composition and Orchestration.

Career: A Barca Do Sol, own group; Recordings with singers: Olivia Byington and Beth Goulart; World tours with E Gismonti, 1986, 1990, 1991, 1993, 1994, 1995, 1996. Compositions: Kiss of the Spider Woman, soundtrack, Co-writer. Recordings: Topazio, Visom; Infancia, Gismonti; Zig-Zag, Gismonti; Glimpse, T Gurtu; Brassileiro, Brassil. Honour: Fiat Prize, Os Povos Da Floresta, 1989. Hobbies: Computer; Internet. Current Management: Maquinando Music. Address: Igarapaua, 59-301 Leblon, Rio De Janeiro, Brazil.

CARNES Kim, b. 20 July 1945, Los Angeles, California, USA. Singer; Songwriter. m. Dave Ellington. Career: Member, New Christy Minstrels, 1960s; Solo artiste; Success as songwriter with husband Dave Ellington. Compositions include: Songs recorded by artists including Frank Sinatra; Barbra Streisand; Kenny Rogers. Recordings: Albums: Rest On Me, 1972; Kim Carnes, 1975; Sailin', 1976; St Vincent's Court, 1979; Romance Dance, 1980; Mistaken Identity, 1981; Voyeur, 1982; Cafe Racers, 1983; Lighthouse, 1986; View From The House, 1988; Gypsy Honeymoon - The Best Of, 1993; Singles: Bette Davis Eyes (Number 1, US); Draw Of The Cards; What About Me (with Kenny Rogers, James Ingram), 1984; Make No Mistake He's Mine (with Barbra Streisand); Speed Of The Sound Of Loneliness (with Lyle Lovett, 1988); Contributor, We Are The World, USA For Africa, 1985. Address: c/o William Morris Agency, 2100 West End Avenue, Suite 1000, Nashville, TN 37203, USA.

CARPENTER Isaac (Ike), b. 11 Mar 1920, Durham, North Carolina, USA. Bandleader; Musician (piano). Education: Duke University, 1941. Career: Pianist, various bands and orchestras, 1938-45; Bandleader, Ike Carpenter Orchestra, 1947-52; Pianist, various groups and residencies, 1952-67; Musical Director, Beverly Styles Music, 1967; Piano restorer, 1974; Musical Director for various artistes including Nat "King" Cole; Sammy Davis Jr; Frankie Laine; Kay Starr; The Andrews Sisters; Host, television show Saturday Date with Ike Carpenter Orchestra.

CARPENTER Mary Chapin, b. 21 Jan 1958, Princeton, New Jersey, USA. Country / Folk Singer; Musician (guitar); Songwriter. Education: Degree, American civilization. Career: Winner, numerous local music competitions; Solo recording artiste, 1986-. Compositions: Songs recorded by Tony Tice; Joan Baez. Recordings: Singles include: Right Now, 1991; I Feel Lucky, 1992; Albums: Home Town Girl, 1987; State Of The Heart, 1989; Shooting Straight In The Dark, 1990; Come On Come On, 1992; Stones In The Road, 1994. Honours: 5 Washington Area Music Awards; CMA Vocalist Of The Year, 1992. Current Management: Studio One Artists, 7010 Westmoreland Avenue #100, Takoma Park, MD 20912, USA.

CARPENTER Richard Lynn, b. 15 Oct 1946, New Haven, Connecticut, USA. Singer; Composer; Arranger; Musician (piano). m. Mary Rudolph, 1984, 2 sons. Career: Co-member, The Carpenters (with sister Karen), 1969-83; Group demise with death of Karen, 1983; Composer, numerous hits; Worldwide tours, countless television, radio appearances; Advisor, television film The Karen Carpenter Story. Recordings: Singles include: Top Of The World; Yesterday Once More; We've Only Just Begun; (They Long To Be) Close To You; Rainy Days And Mondays; Goodbye To Love; Calling Occupants Of Interplanetary Craft; Albums: Offering (aka Ticket To Ride), 1969; Close To You, 1970; Carpenters, 1971; A Song For You, 1972; Now And Then, 1973; Horizon, 1975; A Kind Of Hush, 1976; Live At The Palladium, 1977; The Singles 1974-78; Christmas Portrait, 1978; Made In America, 1979; Voice Of The Heart, 1983; Yesterday Once More, 1984; An Old Fashioned Christmas, 1985; Lovelines, 1990; Christmas Portrait, 1991; From The Top, 1991; Only Yesterday, 1993. Honours:

Numerous gold discs; Group Of Year, 1971; 3 Grammy Awards; American Music Award, 1973; Memberships: ASCAP; National Academy Of Songwriters; NARAS. Hobby: Collecting cars. Address: PO Box 1084, Downey, CA 90240, USA.

CARR Andy, b. 6 Dec 1967, Kirkcaldy, Fife, Scotland. Musician (bass guitar, guitar); Vocalist; Songwriter. Education: Fife College of Further and Higher Education. Musical Education: Self-taught. Career: Lead vocalist and bass guitar with Summerfield Blues with live sessions on Annie Webster Show for BBC Scotland, on BBC Radio Tweed and on various independent radio stations. Recordings: with Summerfield Blues: Devil And The Freightman, Let's Scare The Posh People (EP) and Little Miss Behavin'. Honours: Nominated for Best Blues Album for British Blues Connection, Edinburgh International Festival; Scottish Blues Band of The Year, 1993-94. Memberships: PRS; Musicians' Union. Hobbies: Playwriting; Caving; Socialising. Current Management: Dave Arcari. Address: 192 Glasgow Road, Perth, Scotland.

CARR Budd, b. 5 Sept 1945, Jersey City, New Jersey, USA. Music Supervisor. m. Jeanne, 4 Oct 1970, 2 sons, 1 daughter. Education: BA, MA, University of Illinois. Career: Began as music agent with CMA; Acts handled include: James Taylor; Bob Seger; Blind Faith; Carole King; Crosby Stills and Nash; Moved to IFA, acts handled: Eric Clapton Comeback Tour; Queen; Jefferson Starship; Stephen Stills; Left agency, signed band Kansas; Became personal manager, started management company, 1980; Joined forces with Wil Sharpe in Carr/Sharpe Entertainment Services, 1990; Clients include: Slaughter; Boxing Gandhis; The Buddah Heads; Eric Gales Band; John Wetton; After 25 films as a music supervisor, joined Joel Sill, Windswept Pacific Entertainment, whose catalogue includes: John Mellencamp; Rod Stewart; Willie Nelson; Numerous hits songs of 50s, 60s, 70s; Film credits include: Music consultant: The Terminator, 1984; Return Of The Living Dead, 1985; Music supervisor: Salvador, 1986; Platoon, 1986; Wall Street, 1987; Talk Radio, 1988; Alien Nation, 1988; Born On The Fourth Of July, 1989; Executive Music Producer: The Doors, 1991; JFK, 1991; Heaven And Earth, 1993; Natural Born Killers, 1994; Copycat, 1995; Nixon, 1995. Address: Carr Sharpe Entertainment, 9320 Wilshire Blvd, Suite 200, Beverly Hills, CA 90212, USA.

CARR Ian (Henry Randell), b. 21 Apr 1933, Dumfries, Scotland. Musician (trumpet); Composer; Author; Broadcaster. m. (1) Margaret B Bell, 28 June 1963 (dec 1967), 1 d, (2) Sandra L Major, 9 Dec 1972 (div 1993). Education: BA, Honours, English Language and Literature, King's College, Newcastle-on-Tyne, 1952-56; Early piano lessons; Self-taught as trumpeter and composer. Career: Emcee Five, 1960-62; Rendell-Carr Quintet, 1962-69; Ian Carr's Nucleus, 1969-88; Ian Carr Group, 1989-92; United Jazz and Rock Ensemble, 1975-; Many international radio and television appearances. Compositions: Solar Plexus, 1970; Labyrinth, 1973; Out of The Long Dark, 1978; Awakening, 1980; Old Heartland, 1988; Sounds and Sweet Airs, 1992. Recordings: Numerous professional recordings. Publications: Music Outside, 1973; Miles Davis, A Critical Biography, 1982; Keith Jarrett, The Man and His Music, 1991; Co-author, Rough Guide to Jazz, 1995. Contributions to: Jazz Feature Writer for BBC Music Magazine, 1992-. Honours: Italian Calabria Award for Outstanding Contribution in the Field of Jazz, 1982. Memberships: Royal Society of Musicians of Great Britain; Professor, Guildhall School of Music; PRS; APC. Hobbies: Literature; Art; travel; Swimming. Current Management: Barbara Levy, England. Address: Flat 1, 34 Brailsford Road, London SW2 2TE, England.

CARR Martin, b. Thurso, Scotland. Musician (guitar); Songwriter. Career: Member, The Boo Radleys, 1989-; Televison includes: Top of the Pops; With the Boo Radleys; White Room; The Word. Major Compositions: Lazarus, 1993; Wake Up Boo, 1994; Ride the Tiger, 1995. Recordings: Albums: Ichabod & I, 1989; Everything's Alright Forever, 1992; Giant Steps, 1993; Learning To Walk, 1994; Wake Up, 1995; C'mon Kids, 1996; Hit single: Wake Up Boo, 1995. Publications: Front cover of Melody Maker, 3 times, 1995; Front cover of NME, 1993, 1995. Honours: NME Brat Award, Best Album, 1994; Select Magazine, Best Album of the Year, 1994; Liverpool Echo, Album of the Year, 1995. Current Management: CEC Management, 6 Warren Mews, London W1P 5DJ, England.

CARR Vikki (Florencia Bisenta De Casillas Martinez Cardona), b. El Paso, Texas, USA. Singer; Actress. Career: Appearances include: Television shows with: Dean Martin; Ed Sullivan; Jackie Gleason; Jerry Lewis; Carol Burnett; Bob Hope; Danny Kaye; Glen Campbell; Johnny Carson; Hostess of Tonight Show, several times; 5 TV specials; Concerts in US, Europe, Australia, Japan; Stage actress, South Pacific, Kansas City; Unsinkable Molly Brown, Ohio; I'm Getting My Act Together And Taking It On The Road, St Louis; Hostess, Mrs America Pageant, 1981-87; Mrs World Pageant, 1984-87; Founder and Chairman, Vikki Carr Scholarship Foundation, 1971. Honours: Honorary doctorates: St Edwards University, 1974; University of San Diego, 1975; Woman Of Year, LA Times, 1970; Visiting Entertainer Of Year, Mexico City, 1972; Singer of the Year, American Guild Variety Artists, 1972; Woman Of The World, 1974; Humanitarian Award, Nosotros, 1981; Woman Of The Year, League United Latin American Citizens, 1983; Hispanic Woman Of The Year, 1984; Grammy Award, Best Mexican-American Performance, 1985; Silver Achievement, YWCA, 1989; Golden Eagle, Nosotros, 1989. Current Management: Peter Shukat, 111 W 57th Street, Suite 1120, New York, NY 10019, USA.

CARRACK Paul, b. Sheffield, Yorkshire, England. Vocalist; Songwriter; Musician (keyboards). Career: Member, Ace; Nick Lowe; Squeeze, 1980-81; Member, Mike And The Mechanics, 1986-; Concerts include: Prince's Trust Rock Gala, Birmingham, 1989; Also solo artiste, 1980-; Also worked with: Carlene Carter; John Hiatt; Phil Manzanera; The Pretenders; Roxy Music; Elvis Costello; The Undertones. Recordings: Albums include: with Squeeze: East Side Story, 1981; with Mike And The Mechanics: Mike And The Mechanics, 1986; The Living Years, 1988; Word Of Mouth, 1991; Beggar On A Beach Of Gold, 1995; Hits, 1996; Solo albums: The Nightbirds, 1980; Suburban Voodoo, 1982; One Good Reason, 1987; Ace Mechanic, 1987; Carrack Collection, 1988; Groove Approved, 1989; Carracter Reference, 1991; Blue Views, 1996; Singles include: with Squeeze: Labelled With Love, 1981; with Mike And The Mechanics: Silent Running, 1986; All I Need Is A Miracle, 1986; The Living Years (Number 1, US), 1989; Over My Shoulder, 1995; Solo: How Long?, 1996; Also recorded with Ace and Nick Lowe. Current Management: Hit And Run Music, 30 Ives Street, London SW3 2ND, England.

CARRASCO Joe "King" (Joe Teutsch), b. 6 Dec 1953, Dumas, Texas, USA. Musician (guitar). Divorced, 1 son. Education: University of Texas, 1972; Career: Son of Stiff tour, 1980; Saturday Night Live, 1981; Austin City Limits, 1981. Recordings: 9 albums, 1980-. Honour: Member of Texas Music Hall of Fame. Membership: ASCAP. Hobby: Mexican surfing. Current Management: IKC Productions. Address: Box 12233, Austin, TX 78711, USA.

CARRINGTON Terri Lyne, b, 4 Aug 1965, Medford, Massachusetts, USA. Musician (drums);

Songwriter; Singer. Musical Education: Berklee College of Music, Boston. Career: Original house drummer, Arsenio hall Show; Toured with: Al Jarreau; Herbie Hancock; David Sanborn; Joe Sample; Stan Getz; Wayne Shorter; Gerald Albright; Lalah Hathaway. Compositions: Reach For Your Dreams, for 1996 Olympics; Josa Lee, for Dianne Reeves; Whatcha Gonna Do, Patrice Rushen. Recordings: As a leader: Real Life Story. Honours: Grammy Nomination; Boston Music Award, 1989, 1990. Membership: NARAS. Hobbies: Films; Cooking; Pool. Address: 366 West California Avenue #1, Glendale, CA 91203, USA.

CARROLL Dina, b. Cambridge, England. Singer; Songwriter. Career: Lead vocalist, Quartz, 1990; Solo artiste, 1992-; UK tours, 1993, 1994; Concerts include: Support to Luther Vandross, Wembley, 1993. Compositions: Co-writer with producer, Nigel Lowis. Recordings: Solo albums: So Close, 1993; Hit singles: with Quartz: It's Too Late; Solo: Ain't No Man; Special Kind Of Love; This Time; So Close; Express; Don't Be A Stranger; Perfect Year (written by Andrew Lloyd-Webber). Honours: First-ever million selling debut album for UK female, So Close, 1993; BRIT Award, Best Female Artist, 1994; BRIT Award Nominations: Best Newcomer, 1993; Best Album, 1994; Best Single, 1994; Mercury Music Prize, 1993; 3 International Dance Awards, 1994; Great Britain Variety Award, Best Performing Artist; Silver Clef Award, Best Newcomer, 1994. Current Management: First Avenue Management, The Courtyard, 42 Colwith Road, London W6 9EY, England.

CARRON-SMITH Patricia, b. 3 Apr 1952, Llantrisant, Wales. Singer; Musician. Career: Member, Welsh traditional music group Swansea Jack, 1977-78; Member, Welsh traditional group Calennig, 1978-; Television includes: Torth y Fara, S4C, 1982; Folk On The Move, HTV, 1983; Trade Winds, BBC Wales, 1985; Fastest To Frisco, BBC Wales, 1986; Evening News, Dunedin, New Zealand, 1990; Celtic Magic, HTV, 1990; Gwerin, S4C, 1995. recordings: with Swansea Jack: The Seven Wonders, 1978; with Calennig: Songs And Tunes From Wales, 1980; You Can Take a White Horse Anywhere, 1983; Dyddiau Gwynion Ionawr, 1985; Dwr Glan, 1990; Trade Winds, 1994; Numerous compilations. Memberships: Equity; Musicians' Union; PRS; PAMRA; CDdWC; COTC. Hobbies: Music; Theatre; Travel; Welsh studies. Address: 1 Ty Clwyta Cottages, Cross Inn, Llantrisant Cynon Raf CF72 8AZ, Wales.

CARSON Jeff, b. 16 December 1963, Tulsa, Oklahoma, USA. Singer; Songwriter; Musician (guitar, harmonica). m. Kim Cooper, 14 December 1987. Recordings: Albums: Jeff Carson, 1995; Butterfly Kisses, 1997; Singles: Yeah Buddy, 1995; Not On Your Love, 1995; The Car, 1995; Holdin' On to Something, 1996; That Last Mile, 1996; Do It Again, 1997; Butterfly Kisses, 1997; Here's the Deal, 1997. Honour: Academy of Country Music, Video of the Year, The Car, 1996. Hobbies: Fishing; Hunting; Woodwork; Collecting Police Memorabilia. Current Management: Marv Dennis & Associates. Address: 1002 18th Avenue South, Nashville, TN 37212, USA.

CARSTEA Elena, b. 26 Feb 1963, Agnita, Sibiu County, Romania. Musician (guitar). Musical Education: Classic Singing. Career: Television shows include: Golden Orpheus, 1993; Stars Duel, 1993; Mamaia Festival; Five O'Clock Tea; Golden Stag; Radio and television concerts. Recordings: Your Eyes, 1988; Tomorrow; Some Day, 1990; Ballad For Sandra, 1994. Honours: Public Prize for Composition, Your Eyes, 1983; Best Vocal Soloist of the Year, 1994. Membership: Radio Contact. Hobbies: Parapsychology; Cycling; Men. Current Management: Doru Costea. Address: 61 Buzesti Street A6, 3rd Floor, Ap.18, Sector 1, Bucharest, Romania.

CARTER Benny (Bennett Lester), b. 8 Aug 1907, New York, New York, USA. Musician (saxophone, clarinet, trumpet); Composer; Conductor. Career: Musician, arranger, with bands including: Charlie Johnson, Fletcher Henderson, Chick Webb, Horace Henderson, 1925-32; Leader, own band, 1932-35, 1938-46; Arranger, BBC studio orchestra, 1936-38; Filmappearance: Snows Of Kilimanjaro, 1952; Conductor, workshops, US universities, 1970-; Member, music advisory panel, NEA, 1976-79; Artist in residence, Rutgers University, 1986. Compositions include: Film scores: Stormy Weather, 1943; As Thousands Cheer, 1943; Panic In The Streets, 1950; Snows Of Kilimanjaro, 1952; The Five Pennies, 1959; Guns Of Navarone, 1961; A Man Called Adam, 1966; Buck And The Preacher, 1972; Cosmic Eye, 1985. Recordings: Albums include: Ridin' In Rhythm, 1933; Jazz Giant, 1957; Further Definitions, 1961; The Benny Carter 4: Montreux '77, 1977; Central City Sketches, 1987; In The Mood For Swing, 1987; Over The Rainbow, 1989; All That Jazz, 1990; All Of Me, 1991. Honours include: Silver Award, Esquire, 1943; Gold award, 1946; Grammy Lifetime Achievement Award, 1987; Aggie Award, Songwriters Guild, 1988; Downbeat Awards; ASMAC Golden Score Award. Address: PO Box 870, Hollywood, CA 90028, USA.

CARTER Betty, b. 16 May 1930, Flint, Michigan, USA. Jazz Singer. Career: Singer with jazz musicians including Charlie Parker; Dizzy Gillespie; Buster Williams; Dave Holland; Billy Hart; Cyrus Chestnut; Joined Lionel Hampton as Lorraine Carter; Worked mostly in New York City, including concerts with by Ray Charles; Founder, own record company Bet-Car; Performed, clubs, US and UK, 1980s; Served as bandleader, educator, talent scout; Developed annual jazz showcase Jazz Ahead; Currently touring as Betty Carter & Trio, 1997. Recordings: Numerous including: Albums: Meet Betty Carter And Ray Bryant, 1955; The Bebop Girl, 1955-56; Social Call, 1956; Out There, 1958; Finally, 1959; The Modern Sound Of Betty Carter, 1961; 'Round Midnight, 1963; Inside Betty Carter, 1963; The Betty Carter Album, 1970; Now It's My Turn, 1976; What A Little Moonlight Can Do, 1977; The Audience With Betty Carter, 1979; Whatever Happened To Love?, 1982; Look What I Got, 1988; Droppin' Things, 1990; Feed The Fire, 1994; I'm Yours You're Mine, 1996. Honours: Honorary Doctorate, Williams College, Massachusetts, 1997; American Jazz Masters Fellowship Award, National Council on the Arts. Current Management: Bet-Car Productions, 307 Lake Street, San Francisco, CA 94118, USA.

CARTER (Rebecca) Carlene Smith, b. 26 Sept 1955, Nashville, Tennessee, USA. Country singer; Songwriter. m. (1) Joe Simpkins, divorced, 1 daughter, (2) Jack Routh, divorced, 1 son, (3) Nick Lowe, divorced. Musical Education: Piano lessons; Guitar lessons with Carl Perkins. Career: Country singer, 1974-; Concerts include: Wembley Country Music Family, with Carter family, 1981; Film appearance: Too Drunk To Remember, London Film Festival; Stage performance: Pump Boys and Dinettes, with Kiki Dee, Paul Jones, London, 1985. Compositions: Easy From Now On; Appalachian Eyes; Guardian Angel. Recordings: Albums: Carlene Carter, 1978; Two Sides To Every Woman, 1979; Musical Shapes, 1980; Blue Nun, 1981; C'est Bon, 1983; I Fell In Love, 1990; Little Acts Of Treason, 1995; Contributor, The Junkie And The Juicehead Minus Me, Johnny Cash, 1974; Lost Dogs And Mixed Blessings, John Prine, 1995; Also recorded with members of Squeeze; Dave Edmunds; Kiki Dee; Albert Lee; Jim Kettner. Current Management: Fitzgerald-Hartley Co., 1212 16th Avenue S, Nashville, TN 37203, USA.

CARTER Deana, b. Nashville, Tennessee, USA. Singer; Songwriter; Musician (guitar). Career: UK tour support to Jimmy Nail, 1995.

Recordings: Debut album, Did I Shave My Legs For This?, 1995. Current Management: The Left Bank Organization, 6609 Currywood Drive, Nashville, TN 37205, USA.

CARTER Kent, b. 12 June 1939, Hanover, New Hampshire, USA. m. June 1981, 4 sons. Musical Education: Berklee School of Music, Boston; Private study, piano, cello, bassoon (as child), bass. Career: Participated in October Revolution, New York, early 1960s; Performed with Jazz Composers Guild Orchestra; Toured, recorded with artistes including: Paul Bley; Carla Bley; Michael Mantler; Steve Lacy; Don Cherry; Gato Barbieri; Alan Silva; Mal Waldron; Michael Smith; Bobby Bradford; Max Roach; Enrico Rava; Roswell Rudd; Derek Bailey; John Stevens; Trevor Watts; Steve McCall, 1964-; Member, co-founder, Tok Trio, including tours, Europe and Japan; Member, Steve Lacy Quintet, including tour, USA, 1970-81; Most major European jazz festivals; Radio WDR Köln, Germany; Radio France; Radio RAI, Italy; Founder, leader, chamber group Kent Carter String Trio, with Carlos Zingaro, Francois Dreno; Played major music festivals, Europe; Collaboration with Michala Marcus (dance) in productions including Dance Music Image, 1975-. Compositions include: Collaboration with choreographer Jean Pomares in ballet Paysages Avec Couple. Recordings: Beauvais Cathedral; Kent Carter Solo With Claude Bernard; Suspensions; La Contrebasse. Hobby: Recording. Address: Riviere, 16320 Juillaguet, France.

CARTER Mel, b. 22 Apr 1939, Cincinnati, Ohio, USA. Singer. Musical Education: Cincinnati Conservatory Of Music. Career: Leading soloist, Assistant Director, Greater Cincinnati Youth and Young Adult Choral Union; Moved to Hollywood, 1960; Appearances include: Ciro's, with Dinah Washington; The Crescendo, with Bessie Griffin's Gospel Pearls; Guest on Ed Sullivan Show; Opened at The Flamingo, Las Vegas, with Damita Jo; First hit single led to touring with Dick Clark Caravan of Stars, sharing bill with Sonny and Cher, Tom Jones, others; Headlined nightclubs across USA, Canada; Appearances include: Slate Brothers, Hollywood; Cocoanut Grove; La Fiesta, Mexico; Hotel Americana, New York; Fairmont, Dallas; Played Sportin' Life in concert of Porgy and Bess; Starred in Glitter Palace; Successful actor, films include: Prime Time; No Way Out; Television includes: American Bandstand; Hullaballoo; Tonight Shows; New Love American Style; CHiPs; Many commercials; TV and film soundtracks; Tour of Japan; Engagements: Trump Castle; Taj Mahal; Merv Griffin's Resorts Casino Hotel, Atlantic City; Performance in Fly Blackbird Revisited, early 1990s. Recordings include: Albums: When A Boy Falls In Love; My Heart Sings; Hold Me, Thrill Me, Kiss Me; Enter Laughing; Easy Listening; Be My Love; This Is My Life; Willing; Raise The World/ The Album Of Life - Title Song; Hit singles include: When A Boy Falls In Love, 1963; Hold Me, Thrill Me, Kiss Me, 1965; All Of A Sudden My Heart Sings, 1965; Band Of Gold, 1966; You, You, You, 1966; Take Good Care Of Her, 1966. Honours include: LA Weekly's La Wee Award; NAACP Image Award Nomination, Best Performance in A Musical, Glitter Palace; Grammy Nomination, Willing album; Gold record. Address: c/o Film Artists Associates, 7080 Hollywood Blvd, Suite 704, Hollywood, CA 90028, USA.

CARTER Ronald, b. 4 May 1937, Ferndale, Michigan, USA. Jazz Musician (bass); Educator. m. Janet Hosbrouck, 7 June 1958, 2 sons. Musical Education: BMus, Eastman School Of Music, 1959; MusM, Manhattan School Of Music, 1962. Career: Bass player, college orchestras; Bass player for Chico Hamilton Quintet; Don Ellis; Cannonball Adderley; Thelonious Monk; Eric Dolphy; Miles Davis, 1963-68; Wynton Marsalis; Formed own quartet, 1975; Also prolific freelance musician for numerous artists including George

Benson; Sonny Rollins; VSOP Band (with Herbie Hancock and Tony Williams); McCoy Tyner; Freddie Hubbard; George Duke; Aretha Franklin; Lena Horne; Jazz teacher, universities in Buffalo, St Louis, New York. Recordings: Albums: Out Front, 1966; Uptown Conversation, 1970; Blues Farm, 1973; All Blues, 1974; Magic, 1975; Spanish Blue, 1975; Anything Goes, 1975; Yellow And Green, 1976; Pastels, 1977; Song For You, 1977; Parade, 1979; New York Slick, 1980; Patrao, 1980; Heart And Soul, 1982; Etudes, 1983; Live At Village West, 1984; All Alone, 1989; with Eric Dolphy: Out There, 1960; with Don Ellis: How Time Passes, 1960; with Miles Davis: Seven Steps To Heaven, 1963; Miles In The Sky, 1968; with Herbie Hancock: Maiden Voyage, 1965; Also on numerous recordings by: Roy Ayers; Gato Barbieri; George Benson; Billy Cobham; Chick Corea; Larry Coryell; Miles Davis; Roberta Flack; The Four Tops; Freddie Hubbard; Billy Joel; Quincy Jones; Manhattan Transfer; Diana Ross; Tom Rush; Paul Simon; Grace Slick; Jimmy Smith. Publications: Author, books on jazz and classical bass. Honours: Downbeat Critics Award, International Jazz Bassist Of Year, 1965; Readers Poll Winner, 1973-75, 1983; Detroit Free Press, Jazz Bassist of Decade, 1966; Japan All-Star Jazz Poll Winner, 1969-70; Grammy, Best Jazz Instrumental Composition, 1987. Membership: Jazz Musicians' Association. Current Management: c/o JoAnne Jimenez, The Bridge Agency, 110 Salem Road, Pound Ridge, NY 10576, USA.

CARTER William Tracy, b. 21 Apr 1958, Preston, Lancashire, England. Director; Personal Manager. Musical Education: Piano, keyboards. Career: Stage director, producer, promoter; Tours of USA, Europe; Manager to UK and US artists; Offices in: Nashville, Tennessee; Preston, England; Managing Director, AMC Records; My Mentor Music publishing; Managing Director, Search Music Publishing. Recordings: Album: Long Lonely Road (UK); Girl Ain't One Of The Boys (Nashville). Publications: Davora's Mistress (novel). Memberships: IMF; MCPS; NEA; IPA; NARAS. Hobbies: Networking; Travel; Written word; Humour. Current Management: Michael Freeman, The Pranks, Alison Johnson. Address: Office: PO Box 701, Pilling, Preston, Lancashire PR3 6SJ, England.

CARTHY Eliza Amy Forbes, b. 23 August 1975, Scarborough, England. Musician (Violin); Singer; Folk Singer; Songwriter. Career: Pro, sang with Watersons Cambridge Festival, 1988; Waterdaughters Vancouver Folk Music Festival, 1989; Tours of USA, Australia, England, Germany; TV appearances: Seacombe on Sunday, TV Ballads, London Cable 1, later with Jools Holland; ABC Arts Show, Australia; Mountain Stage, USA. Compositions: By Then; The Wrong Favour; Time In the Sun; Peggy. Recordings: Eliza Carthy and Nancy Kerr, 1993; Waterson: Carthy, 1994; Heat, Light and Sound, 1995; Norma Waterson, 1996; Common Tongue, 1997; Eliza Carthy and the Kings of Calicutt, 1997. Memberships: Musician's Union; PRS; Labour Party. Hobbies: Dying my hair; Clog Dancing; Yoghurt Weaving. Current Management: FAB, 35 Britannia Row, London (Nigel Morton). Address: Hillcrest, Mt Pleasant East, Robin Hood's Bay, Whitby YO22 4RF, England.

CARTHY Martin, b. 21 May 1940, Hatfield, Hertfordshire, England. Vocalist; Musician (guitar). m. Norma Waterson. Career: Member, skiffle group, The Thameside Four; solo folk artiste, 1963-; Resident musician, Troubadour folk club, London; Member, Three City Four; regular recordings, tours, with Dave Swarbrick; Member, Steeleye Span, 1969-72; Member, Brass Monkey; The Watersons; Keith Hancock Band. Recordings: Solo albums: Martin Carthy, 1965; Second Album, 1966; Byker Hill, 1967; But Two Came By (with Dave Swarbrick), 1968; Prince Heathen (with Dave Swarbrick), 1969; Landfall, 1971; This Is

Martin Carthy, 1972; Sweet Wivelsfield, 1974; Shearwater, 1975; Crown Of Horn, 1976; Because It's There, 1979; Out Of The Cut, 1982; Right of Passage, 1989; Life And Limb (with Dave Swarbrick), 1990; Skin And Bone (with Dave Swarbrick), 1992.

CARTWRIGHT Deirdre Josephine, b. 27 July 1956, London, England. Musician (guitar); Composer; Author; Teacher. 1 daughter. Musical Education: Self-taught. Career: Guitar Presenter of both series of BBC TV's Rockschool, shown worldwide; Toured 17 countries with guest stars, national tours with own group Deirdre Cartwright Group, 1994-95; Arts Council tour with her eight-piece band, 1996; Concerts, Germany, Switzerland, 1996-97; Co-runs weekly jazz club, Blow the Fuse, at Vortex, North London; Presents new record releases for Jazz Notes, Radio 3; Advisory Panel, Jazz Services. Recordings: with The Guest Stars: The Guest Stars; Out At Night; Live In Berlin; One Night Stands, as featured artist, jazz compilation; Debut by with The Deirdre Cartwright Group; Play, 2nd solo CD with Steve Lodder, Annie Whitehead, 1998. Publications: Rockschool Books; Rock Guitar Method; The Rockschool Sessions; The Rockfile. Honours: Arts Council Composition Award, 1991; Arts Council funded commission, 1995. Memberships: Musicians' Union; PRS. Hobbies: Music; Walking; Reading; Woodwork; Family. Current Management: Blow The Fuse Records.

CARTY John, b. 7 January 1962, London, England. Musician (Fiddle, Banjo, Flute). m. Maureen Brennan, 23 May 1987, 1 son, 1 daughter. Education: Taught by Brendan Mulkere, Traditional Irish Music. Career: Moved to Ireland, 1991; First album on banjo, 1994, led to 3 album deal; Fiddle release, Last Night's Fun, Multi-instrumentalist playing fiddle, banjo and flute; Leading Member of band, At the Racket. Compositions: Jimmy Batty's, recorded on The Cat That Ate the Candle; Seanamhas Tube Station, recorded on At the Racke. Recordings: The Cat That Ate the Candle, banjo, album, 1994; Last Night's Fun, fiddle, album, 1996; At the Racket, 1997. Current Management: Racket Management. Address: Knockroe, Boyle, Co Roscommon, Ireland.

CASADY Jack (John), b. 13 Apr 1944, Washington DC, USA. Musician (bass). Education: Montgomery College, Maryland. Career: Member, The Triumphs; Member, Jefferson Airplane, 1966-72, 1992; Also member, side project, Hot Tuna, 1968-78; Member, Kantner Balin Casady (KBC) Band, 1985-88, 1992-; Performances include: Berkeley Folk Festival, 1966; Monterey Jazz Festival, 1966; Monterey Pop Festival, 1967; Newport Pop Festival, 1968; Isle Of Wight Festival, 1968; Atlantic City Pop Festival, 1969; Woodstock Music and Art Fair, 1969; Altamont Speedway, with Rolling Stones, 1969; Bath Festival, 1970. Recordings: Albums: with Jefferson Airplane: Jefferson Airplane Takes Off, 1966; After Bathing At Baxter's, 1968; Crown Of Creation, 1968; Volunteers, 1969; Blows Against The Empire, 1970; Bark, 1970; Jefferson Airplane, 1989; Jefferson Airplane Loves You, 1992; with Hot Tuna: Burgers, 1972; The Phosphorescent Rat, 1974; America's Choice, 1975; Yellow Fever, 1975; Hopkorov, 1976; Double Dose, 1977; with KBC Band: KBC Band, 1986; Guest musician: If Only I Could Remember My Name, David Crosby, 1972. Current Management: Bill Thompson Management, 2051 Third Street, San Francisco, CA 94107, USA.

CASEY Albert A, b. 15 Sept 1915, Louisville, Kentucky, USA. Musician (guitar). m. Athena Casey, 18 Sept 1937, 1 son. Musical Education: 2 Years at musical school. Career: Guitarist for artists including: Fats Waller; Teddy Wilson; King Curtis. Honour: Esquire Magazine Award, 1943-44. Membership: AFofM, New York City. Current Management: Al Wolman, New York,

USA. Address: 404 West 54th Street, Apt 3J, New York, NY, USA.

CASEY Harry Wayne, b. 31 Jan 1951, Hialeah, Florida, USA. Musician (keyboards); Vocalist; Producer; Arranger. Career: Founder member (as KC), KC and the Sunshine Band, 1973; Writer, arranger, producer, KC and the Sunshine Band; George McCrae; Career interrupted by severe injuries in car crash, 1982. Recordings: Albums: Do It Good, 1974; KC And The Sunshine Band, 1975; The Sound Of Sunshine, 1975; Part Three, 1976; I Like To Do It, 1977; Who Do Ya Love, 1978; Do You Wanna Go To Party, 1979; Greatest Hits, 1980; Painter, 1981; All In A Night's Work, 1983; The Best Of, 1990; Solo albums: Space Cadet, Wayne Casey/KC, 1981; KC Ten, 1984; US Number 1 hit singles: Get Down Tonight, 1975; That's The Way (I Like It), 1975; Shake Shake Shake, 1976; I'm Your Boogie Man, 1977; Other hits include: Queen Of Clubs; Boogie Shoes; Please Don't Go; Yes I'm Ready, duet with Teri De Sario (Number 2, US). Current Management: Saquier Management. Address: 4770 Biscayne Blvd, Suite 900, Miami, FL 33137, USA.

CASEY Howie (Howard William), b. Liverpool, England. Musician (saxophones). m. Sheila, 19 Sept 1980, 1 daughter. Musical Education: Army Band Kings Regiment; Mostly self-taught. Career: Recording, live concerts with: Paul McCartney; Wings (Over The World), 1975-76, 1980; The Who; ABC; Chuck Berry; Jimmy Ruffin; Cliff Richard; Lee Dorsey; PAL (Plaice, Ashton, Lord); Roy Young Band; Mark Bolan; Les Humphries Singers. Recordings: with Wings: Band On The Run; Wings At The Speed of Sound; Back To The Egg; Wings Over America; Rockestra; Albums with: ABC; Mark Bolan; PAL; Gilbert O'Sullivan; Cliff Richard; Elkie Brooks; Ashton, Gardner, Dyke; The Who. Memberships: PRS; Musicians' Union. Address: 36 R L Stevenson Avenue, Bournemouth, Dorset BH4 8EG, England.

CASH Johnny (John R.), b. 26 Feb 1932, Kingsland, Arkansas, USA. Country Singer; Musician; Songwriter; Entertainer; Actor. m. June Carter, 1968, 1 son, 4 daughters (by previous marriage). Education: HHD, Gardner Webb College, 1971; National University, San Diego, 1975; Career: Composer, solo recording artist, 1955-; Also member of occasional side-project The Highwaymen (with Kris Kristofferson, Waylon Jennings, Willie Nelson), 1985-; Television includes: Johnny Cash Show, 1969-71; Subject of documentaries including: Johnny Cash, The Man, His World, His Music; Johnny Cash At San Quentin; Actor, films: A Gunfight; North And South; Stagecoach; Television films: The Baron And The Kid; The Last Days Of Frank And Jesse; Other television appearances: Columbo; Dr Quinn - Medicine Woman; President, House Of Cash Inc; Songs Of Cash Inc; Vice President, Family Of Man Music Inc. Compositions include: The True West (documentary record); The Gospel Road (co-writer, producer, narrator); Movie soundtracks: I Walk The Line; Little Fauss And Big Halsy. Recordings: Over 150 albums, live recordings and compilations, 1957-; Albums include: The Fabulous Johnny Cash, 1959; Ring Of Fire, 1963; Johnny Cash At Fulsom Prison, 1968; Johnny Cash At San Quentin (Number 1, US), 1969; Hello, I'm Johnny Cash, 1970; Man In Black, 1971; One Piece At A Time, 1976; Water From The Wells of Home, 1988; The Mystery Of Life, 1991; American Recordings, 1994; with The Highwaymen: The Highwayman, 1985; Highwaymen 2, 1990; Hit singles include: I Walk The Line, 1956; There You Go, 1957; Ballad Of A Teenage Queen, 1958; Guess Things Happen That Way, 1958; Ring Of Fire, 1963; A Boy Named Sue, 1969; If I Were A Carpenter (duet with June Carter Cash), 1970; A Thing Called Love, 1972. Publications: Man In Black, 1975; Man In White (novel), 1986. Honours: CMA

Award, Best Album, 1968; Grammy Awards: Best Country Duet (with June Carter Cash), 1968, 1971; Best Country Vocal Performance, 1969, 1970; Best Country Song, 1970, 1986; Best Album Notes, 1969, 1970; Best Spoken Word Recording, 1987; Living Legend Award, 1990; 4 UK Country Music Awards, 1970; Special Award Of Merit, American Music Awards, 1977; LHD (Hon), National University San Diego, 1976; Inducted into Country Music Hall Of Fame, 1980; Aggie Award, Songwriters Guild Of America, 1989; Inducted into Rock'n'Roll Hall Of Fame, 1992. Membership: Country Music Association. Current Management: Artist Consultants Productions, Suite 670, 11777 San Vicente Blvd, Los Angeles, CA 90049, USA.

CASH June Carter, b. 23 June 1929, Maces Springs, Virginia, USA. Singer; Actress. m. Johnny Cash, 1 Mar 1968, 1 son, 6 daughters. Musical Education: Actor's Studio, New York. Career: Singer, Carter family, 1939-43; Carter Sisters, 1943-; Solo artiste; Duo with Johnny Cash, 1963-; Television include: Johnny Cash Show; Grand Ole Opry; Tennessee Ernie Show; Television films: Stagecoach; The Baron; Gospel Road; Road To Nashville; Television special: The Best Of The Carter Family; Television series: Dr Quinn - Medicine Woman (played Dr Ruth); Entertains as singer, actress, musician (guitar, banjo, auto-harp), comedienne. Recordings: Songs include: Baby It's Cold Outside; Music Music Music; Love Oh Crazy Love; Let Me Go Lover; Contributions to recordings by Johnny Cash including: Jackson Duo; If I Were A Carpenter; with Carter family: Wabash Cannon; May the Circle be Unbroken. Publications: Author: Among My Kledaments, 1979; From The Heart, 1987; Wildwood Flower, screenplay, 1990; Mother Maybelle's Cookbook, 1992; Co-author, Ring Of Fire. Honours: HHD (Hon), National University, San Diego, 1977; Civic Award, Nashville Women Executives, 1980; Grammy Awards: Best Country Duo Performance (with Johnny Cash), 1968, 1971; CMA Duet Artists Of The Year, with Johnny Cash; Virginian Of Year, 1989. Memberships: ASCAP; Grand Ole Opry; Country Music Association. Current Management: Lou Robin, Artist Consultants Productions, Suite 670, 11777 San Vicente Blvd, Los Angeles, CA 90049, USA.

CASH Roseanne, b. 24 May 1955, Memphis, Tennessee, USA. Singer. m. Rodney Crowell, 1979, divorced. Education: Drama, Vanderbilt University; Method acting, Lee Strasberg's Institute, Los Angeles. Career: Worked 3 years with (father) Johnny Cash's road show; Worked with Rodney Crowell, Nashville; Recording artiste, 1979-. Recordings: Hit singles include: No Memories Hangin' Round (with Bobby Bare); Couldn't Do Nothin' Right; Take Me Take Me; Never Be You; I Don't Know Why You Don't Want Me (co-written with Rodney Crowell); The Way We Make A Broken Heart; If You Change Your Mind; Rainway Train. Albums include: Roseanne Cash, 1978; Right Or Wrong, 1979; Seven Year Ache, 1981; Somewhere In The Stars, 1982; Rhythm And Romance, 1985; King's Record Shop, 1988; Hits 1979-89, 1989; Interiors, 1990. Honours: Grammy, Best Country Vocal Performance Female, 1985; Top Single Artist Award, Billboard, 1988. Current Management: Side One Management, 1026A Third Avenue, New York, NY 10021, USA.

CASH Tommy, b. 5 Apr 1940, Dyess, Arkansas, USA. Professional Entertainer; Musician (rhythm guitar). m. (1) Barbara Wisenbaker, 18 Aug 1961, 1 son, 1 daughter; (2) Pamela Dyer, 12 Mar 1978. Education: Radio Broadcast School; Real estate school (Realtor); College courses: Tennessee Tech, Vol State. Career: All major country music television shows, many network television programmes; Radio announcer, 1959-64, including: American Forces Network, Germany, 1959-62; Music publisher, 1965-; Professional entertainer, 1965-; Songwriter, songs recorded by: Conway Twitty; Kitty Wells;

Faron Young; Jean Sheppard; Johnny Cash; Loretta Lynn; Music published by Tomcat Music, BMI. Recordings: More than 20 albums, approximately 65 singles, 1965-; Hits include: Six White Horses, 1970; Rise and Shine; That Certain One; So This Is Love; Gypsy Woman; Gospel album: This Happy Heart Of Mine, 1995. Honours: Two BMI Awards for Songwriting, 1965, 1975; Music City News Most Promising Vocalist, 1970. Memberships: AFofM, Nashville; AFTRA, Nashville; National Association of Realtors; ROPE Inc. Hobbies: Golf; Softball; Gardening. Current Management: Joe Taylor, AGN Nashville; Billy Deaton Talent Nashville. Address: Hendersonville, Tennessee, USA.

CASSARD Robert, b. 5 Aug 1961, Grand Rapids, Michigan, USA. Music Producer; Songwriter; Composer; Singer; Musician (multi-instrumentalist). m. Bara Waters, 16 June 1991, 2 sons. Education: University of Michigan; University of Florence, Italy. Musical Education: Extensive study of guitar, double bass, theory and composition. Career: Lead singer, guitarist with various bands, 1972-1978; Solo artist, 1979-; Chief producer (for melodic alternative rock artists), Pentacle Records, 1991-. Compositions: Over 200 published songs. Recordings: Solo albums: Over The Line, 1980; Get This, 1995. Memberships: NARAS; AFofM; AFTRA; ASCAP. Hobbies: Listening; Yoga; Skiing. Current Management: Waters/Cassard Music. Address: PO Box 5055, Laguna Beach, CA 92652, USA.

CASSIDY David, b. 12 Apr 1950, New York, New York, USA. Actor; Singer. Career: Actor, The Partridge Family television series; Lead vocalist, Partridge Family recordings; Solo artiste, 1971-; Actor, Joseph And The Amazing Technicolour Dreamcoat; Lead role, musical, Time, 1987. Recordings: Albums: Cherish, 1972; Could It Be Forever, 1972; Rock Me Baby, 1972; Dreams Are Nothin' More, 1973; Cassidy Live, 1974; The Higher They Climb, 1975; Greatest Hits, 1977; Romance, 1985; His Greatest Hits, Live, 1986; Singles include: with The Partridge Family: I Think I Love You (Number 1, US), 1970; Solo: Cherish (Number 1, US), 1971; Could It Be Forever; How Can I Be Sure? (Number 1, UK); I Am A Clown; Daydreamer/The Puppy Song (Number 1, UK); The Last Kiss. Current Management: c/o Larry Lerner, 20501 Ventura Blvd, Ste 392, Woodland Hills, CA 91364, USA.

CASSWELL Michael, b. 18 June 1966, Romford, Essex, England. Musician (guitar). Education: Art College. Career: Signed to RCA America, album, 1986; MCA Records, 2 albums, 1989; Toured in Brian May Band, Back to the Light tour, 1992. Recordings: Heroes, 1986; Walk On Fire, 1989; Currently writing, producing next Cozy Powell album, release late 1995. Memberships: PRS; Musicians' Union. Hobbies: Cars; Guitars. Current Management: Agent: Session Connection, Brenda Brooker, RAK Records. Address: Angel Cottage, Manor Road, Lambourne End, Romford, Essex RM4 1NH, England.

CASTILLE Patrick, b. 13 Jan 1962, Calais, France. Musician (guitar); Composer; Arranger. Education: Bac D. Musical Education: Graduate with Honours, Guitar Institute of Technology, USA. Career: Tour with De l'Autre Coté de la Rue; Musician with singers: Fred Damiens; Bogdana Shivas; Lionnel Sisti; Studio musician for commercial. Compositions: Television commercial. Recordings: Solo album: Espace Vital. Current Management: SDM. Address: 12 Rue La Condamine, 75017 Paris, France.

CASTLE Pete, b. 25 February 1947, Ashford, Kent, England. Folk Singer; Musician (Guitar); Storyteller. m. Sue Brown, 27 April 1967, 1 son, 1 daughter. Education: Maidstone Technical High School; Bretton Hall College of Education. Career: Organiser of Luton Folk Festival, 1976-78; Solo artist, working at clubs, festivals, in schools and on

community projects, 1978-; Presenter, Chiltern Radio Folk Show, 1981-87; Collaboration with Aroti Biswas, 1987; Mountsorrel Community Play, 1993; Launched the occasional band Popeluc, 1994. Recordings include: Bedfordshire Folk Songs, 1981; Rambling Robin, 1982; Punk's Delight, 1985; One Morning By Chance, 1989; Cottage By the Shore, 1992; Two Tongues One Voice, 1994; Keys of Canterbury, 1994; Maramures Et Cetera, 1994; Falsewaters, 1995; Blue Dor, 1996. Memberships: Musicians' Union; PRS; MCPS; Society for Storytelling. Hobbies: Music; Walking; Cinema. Address: 190 Burton Road, Derby, DE1 1TQ, England.

CATER Pete, b. 8 Feb 1963, Lichfield, Staffordshire, England. Musician (drums); Bandleader; Teacher. Musical Education: Self-taught. Career: Tour worldwide, with Elaine Delmar in Thank You Mr Gershwin; Played with Arturo Sandoval Quintet; Pete Cater Big Band; Freelance session player with: BBC; ITV; C4; BBC Big Band; NYJO; A Ross; Val Doonican; Dave Willetts; S Maughan; Herb Miller Orchestra. Honours: Outstanding drummer, BBC Radio 2 National Big Band Competition, 1980, 1991. Membership: Faculty member, Musician's Institute, London. Address: 59 Boreham Holt, Elstree, Herts WD6 3QQ, England.

CATLEY Bob. Vocalist. Career: Founder member, lead vocalist, UK rock group Magnum, 1972-; Support tours with: Judas Priest; Whitesnake; Blue Öyster Cult; Def Leppard; Own headline tours worldwide. Recordings: Albums: Kingdom Of Madness, 1978; Magnum II, 1979; Marauder, 1980; Chase The Dragon, 1982; The Eleventh Hour, 1983; On A Storyteller's Night, 1985; Vigilante, 1986; Wings Of Heaven, 1988; Goodnight LA, 1990; The Spirit, 1991; Rock Art, 1994; Numerous compilation albums; Singles include: Just Like An Arrow; Days Of No Trust; Rocking Chair; Star Talking Love; It Must Have Been Love; Kingdom Of Madness; On A Storyteller's Night; Midnight.

CATLEY Marc, b. 3 Nov 1959, Birmingham, England. Singer; Songwriter; Musician (guitar). Satirist. Education: Liverpool University; London Bible College. Career: First solo progressive rock album Classical Acoustic Rock, 1986; Numerous radio interviews and airplay in Europe and US; 4 albums, religious satire with band The Flaming Methodists, 1991-; Television and radio appearances include: Granada TV and Radio 4; Formed progressive rock band Paley's Watch, 1993. Composition: Char, 1996. Recordings: Progressive rock albums: with Geoff Mann: The Off The End Of The Pier Show, 1991; Fine Difference, 1992; with Paley's Watch: November, 1994; Satirical albums: Peel Of Hope, 1991; Make The Tea, 1992; Hot Air For Jesus, 1993; No Tomorrow, 1994. Memberships: MCPS; PRS; BASCA; Musicians' Union. Current Management: Plankton Records; Sandcastle Productions. Address: 236 Sebert Road, Forest Gate, London E7 0NP, England.

CATO Pauline, b. 14 Dec 1968, Ashington, Northumberland, England. Musician (Northumbrian pipes, keyboards). Education: BA (Hons) Modern Languages, Sheffield University, 1991; PGCE 1992, Sheffield University. Musical Education: Grade 8 piano; Taught Northumbrian Pipes by Richard Butler, piper to the Duke of Northumberland. Career: Member, Border Spirit, 1988-90; Solo artiste, 1990-94; Cullercoats Tommy (opera), with Northern Sinfonia Orchestra, 1993; Became full-time musician, 1993; Also working in duo with fiddler Tom McConville; Television and radio appearances: Small Folk, YTV/Channel 4, 1989; Several Radio 2/3 features. Recordings: Hindley Steel, Border Spirit, 1988; Solo albums: The Wansbeck Piper, 1992; Changing Tides, 1994; Various recordings as session musician; By Land and Sea, with Tom McConville, 1996. Publication: Pauline Cato's

Northumbrian Choice, with recordings, 1997. Honours: Appointed Piper to Mayor of Gateshead, 1989; Honorary Member, Northumbrian Pipers Society, for Services to Piping; Young Tradition Award Finalist, BBC, 1990; Daily Telegraph Folk Album of the Year, 1996. Address: c/o 122 Osgathorpe Road, Pitsmoor, Sheffield S4 7AS, England.

CATTINI Clem, b. 20 Aug 1937, London, England. Musician (drums). m. Anna, 17 May 1958, 3 daughters. Career: Member, Johnny Kidd and the Pirates; Tornados; Top Of The Pops Orchestra (12 years); Toured with: Sir Cliff Richard; Kids From Fame; Lulu; Grace Kennedy; The Drifters; Liza Minnelli; Sandy Shaw; Tom Jones; Engelbert Humperdinck; Television: Michael Barrymore; Lulu; Michael Jackson; Stevie Wonder; Gladys Knight. Recordings: Johnny Kidd and the Pirates: Please Don't Touch, 1960; Shakin' All Over, 1971; Tornados: Sound Of; Telstar; More Sounds From; Tornado Rock; Away From It All, 1962-64; Everlasting Love; Devil Woman; Musician on: Roy Harper: Folkjokeopus, 1969; Joe Cocker: With A Little Help From My Friends, 1969; P J Proby: 3 Week Hero, 1969; Bee Gees: To Whom It May Concern, 1972; Lou Reed: Lou Reed, 1972; Phil Everly: Phil's Diner, 1974; Recorded with: Kinks; Dusty Springfield; Lulu; Tom Jones; Engelbert Humperdinck; Gene Pitney; Other albums by: Cliff Richard; Hank Marvin; Justin Hayward; Brian Auger; Claire Hamill; Jimmy Page; Albert Lee; John Paul Jones; Played on 42 Number 1s. Honours: Gold Disc, Gold Globe (Telstar); Cup NME Poll Winners (Tornados). Memberships: Musicians' Union; PRS; MCPS. Hobbies: Golf; Football. Address: 15 Blenheim Close, London N21 2HQ, England.

CAUDEL Stephen, b. 29 June 1955, Sheffield, South Yorkshire, England. Composer; Musician (guitar). m. Shelagh Quinn, 17 Dec 1983, 1 son. Musical Education: O Level, A Level Music; Studies Classical, Jazz, Light Music, at City of Leeds College of Music. Career: Numerous television and radio appearances; Concert tours: UK including Royal Albert Hall; Overseas tours including Japan; Compositions: Wine Dark Sea (rock symphony, world premiere, London, 1983); Edel Rhapsody, for Wagner Tuba and Orchestra, (world premiere, Carlisle, 1993). Recordings: Albums: Wine Dark Sea; Bow Of Burning Gold; Impromptu Romance; The Earth In Turquoise; Featured guitarist on Hooked On Classics II, with Royal Philharmonic Orchestra. Memberships: PRS; MCPS; Musicians' Union. Hobbies: Films; Books; Theatrical Magic. Current Management: Mr Laurie Mansfield. Address: International Artistes Limited, Mezzanine Floor, 235 Regent Street, London W1R 8AX, England.

CAUTY Jimmy, b. 1954. Musician (guitar). Career: Co-founder, KLF Communications, with Bill Drummond, 1987-92; Organized music projects under names: JAMs; Disco 2000; The Justified Ancients Of Mu Mu; The Timelords; KLF; Founder, own recording studio, Trancentral, 1988; Appearances include DMC European Convention, Amsterdam, 1990; Film: The White Room, 1988. Recordings: Albums: as JAMs: 1987, 1987; as KLF: The White Room, 1989; Chill Out, 1990; Solo album: Space, 1990; Singles include: as JAMs: Whitney Joins The Jams, 1987; Downtown, 1987; Who Killed The JAMs, 1988; as Disco 2000: I Gotta CD, 1987; Uptight, 1989; as The Timelords: Doctorin' The Tardis (Number 1, UK), 1988; as KLF: Burn The Beat, 1988; What Time Is Love, 1990; 3AM Eternal (Number 1, UK), 1991; Last Train To Trancentral, 1991; as The Justified Ancients Of Mu Mu: It's Grim Up North, 1991; Justified And Ancient, with Tammy Wynette, 1992. Publication: The Manual (guide to getting a hit record), 1988. Honour: BRIT Award, Best British Group (shared with Simply Red), 1992.

CAVALERA Max, b. 4 Aug 1969, Belo Horizonte, Brazil. Rock Musician (guitar,

percussion); Vocalist. m. Gloria Cavalera, 6 June 1993, 1 son. Musical Education: Self-taught. Career: Member, Brazilian heavy rock group Sepultura; Worldwide tours including US, Brazil, Russia, Indonesia; Support tours with The Ramones, Ministry, Ozzy Osbourne; Concerts include: Rock in Rio, Brazil; Hollywood Rock, Brazil; Monsters of Rock Festival, Castle Donington, UK; Dynamo Open Air Festival, Netherlands; Roskilde Festival, Denmark; Television appearances: The Word (UK); MTV Most Wanted (UK). Recordings: Beneath The Remains, 1989; Arise, 1991; Chaos AD, 1993; Roots, 1996; Nativity In Black (Black Sabbath tribute); Virus 100 (Dead Kennedys tribute); Tales From The Crypt (soundtrack). Honours: 2 MTV South America Awards; Best Album, Kerrang! magazine, UK, 1994. Hobbies: Football; Tattoos; Visiting rainforests. Current Management: Gloria Cavalera, Oasis Management, 3010 East Bloomfield, Phoenix, AZ 85032, USA.

CAVALERI Nathan Michael, b. 18 June 1982, Camden, NSW, Australia. Musician (guitar). Education: St Gregory's College, Campbelltown, NSW, Australia. Musical Education: Taught by father. Career: San Francisco Blues Festival, with Albert Collins, 1992; Toured with B B King, special guest, 1995; 25th Birthday for Guitar Player magazine; Kennedy Lifetime Achievement Awards, honouring B B King, 1995; Out In The Green Festival, Zurich, 1995; Tours, with Jimmy Barnes of Diesel, Australia; Appeared on: Arsenio Hall; Inside Edition; Good Morning America; Conan O'Brian; CNN; Hey Hey It's Saturday Australia; Midday Australia; MMM Network; Radio Australia; Camp Nowhere The Film; Baywatch Nights; Australia Music Awards; Entertainment Network Australia; Commercial for MacDonalds with B B King, 1995. Compositions include: Song: Lou's Blues included in Free Willy 2 film soundtrack. Recordings: Albums: Jammin' With The Cats (5 co-written songs), 1994; Nathan (6 co-written songs). Honours: Variety Club, Australia, Young Variety award, 1993; BMW Jazz And Blues Best New Talent, 1993; Young Australian Achiever, 1994. Membership; SAG. Hobbies: Drums; Bodyboarding; Computer Games. Current Management: CAA Agency, Linchpin-Russell Hayward, Los Angeles, California. Address: 2512 Zorada Drive, Los Angeles, CA 90046, USA.

CAVANAUGH Page, b. 26 Jan 1922, Cherokee, Kansas, USA. Musician (piano); Singer; Entertainer. Musical Education: Private teachers. Career: Performed as pianist, vocalist, in films: Record Party, 1947; Romance On The High Seas (2 songs on screen with Doris Day), 1947; A Song Is Born (1 song with Virginia Mayo), 1947; Big City (2 songs with Betty Garret), 1947; Lullaby of Broadway (Song with: Gene Nelson: Zing Went The Strings Of My Heart; with Doris Day and Gene: You're Getting to Be A Habit With Me), 1950. Recordings: Albums: with Michael Feinstein: Crazy Rhythm; Pure Imagination; with Page Cavanaugh Trio: Digital Page: Page One; Page Two, 1993; The Three Bears; All Of Me; Walking My Baby Back Home; Page Cavanaugh Plays For The Cocktail Hour; Something's Happening At Page Cavanaugh's. Memberships: NAOL; Society Of Singers. Hobbies: Cooking; Gardening. Address: 5442 Woodman Avenue, Sherman Oaks, CA 91401, USA.

CAVE Nick, b. Australia. Vocalist; Songwriter; Actor. Career: Member, Birthday Party (formerly Boys Next Door), early 1980s; Founder, Nick Cave And The Bad Seeds; Actor, films include: Wings Of Desire, 1987; Ghosts Of The Civil Dead, 1989. Recordings: Albums: with Birthday Party: Prayers On Fire, 1981; Junkyard, 1982; The Bad Seed/Mutiny, 1989; Hee-Haw, 1989; with The Bad Seeds: From Here To Eternity, 1984; The First Born Is Dead, 1985; Kicking Against The Pricks, 1986; Your Funeral, My Trial, 1986; Tender Prey, 1988; Ghost Of The Civil Dead, 1989; The Good

Son, 1990; Henry's Dream, 1992; Murder Ballads, 1996; Singles: with Birthday Party: Fiend Catcher; Release The Collaborations, with Lydia Lunch And Einsturzende Neubaten; with the Bad Seeds: Tupelo; The Singer; The Mercy Seat; Oh Deanna; The Ship Song; Where The Wild Roses Grow, duet with Kylie Minogue, 1995; Contributor, film soundtrack, Batman Forever, 1995. Publications: And The Ass Saw The Angel (novel), 1989; King Ink (collection of lyrics and verse); King Ink II. Current Management: Roger Jesson at Tender Prey, Studio 4, Ivebury Court, 325 Latimer Road, London W10 6RA, England.

CAZES Henrique, b. 2 Feb 1959, Rio de Janeiro, Brazil. Musician (cavaquinho - small 4-stringed guitar); Producer; Arranger. m. Maria A C L Fernandes, 2 sons. Musical Education: Self-taught acoustic guitar, cavaquinho, banjo; Classes in harmony and arrangement with Ian Guest. Career: Worked with Radames Gnatelli, 7 years; Tours as cavaquinho soloist: Japan, 1985-90; USA, 1988, 1990; Europe, 1993; Founder member, Orchestra Brazilian Strings; Creator, director, Brasília Orchestra; Carrefour Mondial de la Guitare, Martinique. Recordings include: Henrique Cazes, 1988; Henrique Cazes - Tocando Waldir Azevado, 1990; Henrique Cazes - Waldir Azevado, Pixinguinha, Hermeto & Cia, 1992; Cristina Buarque e Henrique Cazes Sem Tostao, 1994; Henrique Cazes & The Guitar Family - Since The Choro Is Choro, 1995. Publications: Text book Escola Moderna de Cavaquinho. Honours: Sharp Awards: 1991, 1992, 1995; Number One Cavaquinho Of The World, Japan, 1990. Membership: AMAR (Brazilian Association of Arrangers and Conductors). Current Management: C Fernandes. Address: Paulo Barreto, No 25/802 Botafogo, 22280-010 Rio de Janeiro, RJ, Brazil.

CECCARELLI Andre, b. 5 Jan 1946, Nice, France. Musician (drums). m. Marcelle Ritling, 8 Apr 1968, 1 son. Musical Education: Music Academy of France. Career: Member, Les Chats Suavages, 1961; Worked with Aime Barelli, Monte Carlo, 1964; Played with Rocky Roberts and the Piranas, 1966-68; Freelance musician, 1968-; Worked with artists including: Brian Auger; Tania Maria; Tina Turner; Michel Legrand; Bireli Lagrene; Mike Stern; Tom Harle. Recordings: with Ceccarelli Trio: Hat Snatcher; Three Around The Floor; with Dee Dee Bridgewater: Keeping Traditions; Love And Peace; with Tina Turner: Love Explosion; with Tania Maria: Live In Copenhagen; with M Portal: Turbulence; Also recorded with: Michel Legrand and Stéphane Grappelli; Aretha Franklin; Tom Harrell and Bob Berg; Paul Mauriat; Bireli Lagrene and NHOP; Enrico Pieranunzi and H Van De Glyn. Honours: Django D'Or, Best Jazz Group, 1993; Victoire de la Musique, Best Jazz Album, 1993; Aigle D'Argent, Nice. Memberships: SACEM; ADAMI; SPEDIDAM. Hobby: Music. Current Management: Isoard Christiane and Sola Thierry. Address: 22 Rue Ernest Revillon, 77630 Barbizon, France.

CECH Christoph, b. 29 June 1960, Vienna, Austria. Composer; Arranger; Musician (keyboards, orchestral percussion). m. Ursula, 5 Mar 1988, 3 sons. Education: Matriculation/studies in Architecture, Technical University, Vienna. Musical Education: Studies in piano, rhythmic, orchestral percussion, jazz theory, composition, Vienna Conservatory. Career: Jazz fairy tale, F F Company & Co (co-composer with Christian Mühlbacher), 1987; TV production, (ORF), 1993; Concert number 1 for piano and orchestra, radio production (ORF), 1994; Suite for doublebass, bass clarinet and 15 players, The Musikvereinshall, Vienna; Teacher (rhythmics), Max Reinhardtseminar (for actors), in many tours with different ensembles. Compositions: Chamber opera, Die Befreiung Des Modulors, State Theatre Schwerin, Germany, 1988; Protophantasm, Concerto Grosso for big band and orchestra; Opera, Aus Allen Blüten Bitternis, Chamber

Opera, Vienna, 1996; B.A.C.H Kantate, Dom St Pölten, 1997. Recordings: with Nouvelle Cuisine Big Band: Flambée, 1988, 1989; Elephant Terrine, 1990; Phrygian Flight, 1994; Ultimate Sentences, 1997; with Striped Roses: Bonsai Beat, 1990; Insection, 1994; Tulpen, 1997; Solo: Mondautos, 1993; with Jubilo Elf: Missing Link, 1991; with Camerata Obscura, Batpulse, 1997; in duo with Bertl Mütter, Lohgesang, 1997. Publication: Keyboard 1-4, 1991. Honours: Stipendium for Composition, City of Vienna, 1987, 1995; First Prize, Kunstpreis Leibnitz, Austria, 1994; State Stipendium, Austrian Republic, 1995. Hobbies: Eating; Drinking; Sleeping. Address: Schottenfeldgasse 61/16, A-1070 Vienna, Austria.

CECH Vladimir, b. 22 Mar 1944, Brno. m. Alena Benesová, 29 Aug 1975, 1 son. Education: Diploma Engineer, Technical University, Brno, 1970; Graduated, Faculty of Musicology and Theatrology, Brno, Masaryka University. Career: Regular programmes on Musical and Theatre Life, Radio Brno; Author, Speaker, public playbacks of classical and pop music. Contributions: Regularly to Brno, Prague, Vienna newspapers, especially Slovo, BT - Rovnist, Opus Musicum. Publications: Regular reports on music life in Czech Republic, Vienna. Honour: Prize, Czech Music Foundation, 1984-90. Hobbies: Travel; Sport. Address: Drobného 16, 602 00 Brno, Czech Republic.

CELLIER Marcel, b. 29 Oct 1925, Zürich, Switzerland. Musical Editor. m. Catherine, 15 May 1953, 3 sons. Education: Studied cello and Ethnomusicology about Eastern Europe. Career: Producer, Radio Suisse Romande, 1961-95, ORTF/Radio France, BR Munich, RDRS Zürich-Berne, WDR Cologne; Producer of 4 sound carriers with Gheorghe Zamfir as well as 4 with Mystère des Voix Bulgares. Recordings: Albanian, Hungarian, Romanian and Bulgarian folk music and vocal art. Honours: Grand Prix et Disque d'or de l'Academie Ch Cros, Paris; Critics Prize, Music Critics of Germany; Grand Prix Audiovisuel de l'Academie Française du Disque; Grammy Award, 1990. Memberships: Rotary; ICTM; Vice-President, GVS Gesellschaft für Volksmusik in der Schweiz. Hobbies: Gypsey music; Improvisations with friends. Address: Rue du Bourg-de-Plait, 1605 Chexbres, Switzerland.

CERMAK Zappa (Johann Leopold), b. 7 July 1949, Heidenreichstein, Austria. Musician (guitar, drums, percussion, harmonica); Vocalist. m. Erika. Education: VSA; HSA; Forestry technician. Career: Began as: Blues Zappa, 1974-76; Original member, Bluespumpm, 1975; Parallel project with Fritz Glatzl as Blues Zappa and Pumpm Fritz (also with Johannes Müller); Major tours, most European countries; Radio, television: Austria; Slovakia; Slovenia; Hungary; Czech Republic. Recordings: with Bluespumpm: Albums: Bluespumpm, 1979; Edlau, 1980; Village, 1981; Live With Friends, 1985; The 5th Ten Years Jubilee, 1987; Live At Utopia, 1988; Live With Friends, 1991; Birthday, 1991; Live In Vienna, 1992; The 5th, 1992; Living Loving Riding, 1994; Singles: Wolfgang Session and Song, 1980; Train And Quick Shoes, 1985; Men From Milwaukee, 1993; with Blues Zappa: Albums: Gitarrero, 1985; Blue Balance, 1987; Glaskar, 1987; Andy Bartosh and Radio 1, 1994; Single: Der Letzte Zug, 1987. Honours: Silbenes Ehrenzeichen, 1992; Third Best Blues Album, Rot-Weis-Role Critics Poll, Live In Vienna, 1992. Memberships: AKM; AUME; LSG. Hobbies: Elephant collecting; Living life. Current Management: Peter Steinbach, RGG Management. Address: Favoritenstr 53/2/6/18, A-1100 Vienna, Austria.

CERVENKOVA Helena, b. 3 March 1937, Slavicin, Czech Republic. Musician (Cimbal). m. Jaroslav Cervenka, 1958, 1 son, 1 daughter. Career: BROLN, radio broadcasting orchestra, Brno, Soloist, Folk Music, 35 years; Presentation of contemporary Czech music - radio, tv. Recordings: Vychodoslovenská Karicka; Romo

Slavonica; Jak Kukacka Kuká; Fantasie; Ked sa Janko na Vojnu Bral. Honours: Festival of Folk Music in Wales, 3rd Prize as Soloist, 1958; Best Soloist of Radio, Czech Repub, 1967. Membership: Cimbal World Association. Address: Lerchova 26, 602 00 Brno, Czech Republic.

CETERA Peter, b. 13 Sept 1944, Chicago, Illinois, USA. Vocalist; Musician (bass). Career: Bassist, The Exceptions; Member, Chicago (formerly Big Thing, Chicago Transit Authority), 1967-85; Solo artiste, 1985-; Regular worldwide tours; Concerts include: Support to Janis Joplin, Jimi Hendrix, 1969; Atlantic Pop Festival, 1969; Isle Of Wight Festival, 1970; First rock group to play Carnegie Hall, New York, 1971; Madison Square Garden, New York, 1977. Compositions include: Wishin' You Were Here; Baby What A Big Surprise; Hard To Say I'm Sorry (co-writer with David Foster); You're The Inspiration (co-writer with David Foster). Recordings: Albums: with Chicago: Chicago Transit Authority, 1969; Chicago II, 1970; Chicago III, 1971; Chicago At Carnegie Hall, 1971; Chicago V, 1972; Chicago VI, 1973; Chicago VII, 1974; Chicago VIII, 1975; Chicago X, 1976; Chicago XI, 1980; Hot Streets, 1978; Chicago 13, 1979; Chicago XIV, 1980; Chicago 16, 1982; Chicago 17, 1984; Chicago 18, 1987; Chicago 19, 1988; Chicago 21, 1991; Various compilations and greatest hits collections; Solo albums: Peter Cetera, 1981; Solitude/Solitaire, 1986; One More Story, 1988; World Falling Down, 1992; One Clear Voice, 1995; Singles: with Chicago: Does Anybody Really Know What Time It Is; Beginnings; Colour My World; If You Leave Me Now (Number 1, US and UK), 1976; Hard To Say I'm Sorry, 1982; Solo singles: Glory Of Love; The Next Time I Fall (duet with Amy Grant); I Wasn't The One Who Said Goodbye (duet with Agnetha Fältskog); One Good Woman; After All (duet with Cher, 1989; Restless Heart; Feels Like Heaven (duet with Chaka Khan); Even A Fool Can See; Contributor, Voices That Care, Gulf Crisis Fund benefit record, 1991. Honours include: Grammy Award, 1977; American Music Award, 1977; Gold Ticket, Madison Square Garden, 1977. Address: c/o Agency for the Performing Arts, 9000 Sunset Blvd 12th Floor, Los Angeles, CA 90069, USA.

CETINIC Meri, b. 15 June 1953, Split, Croatia. Singer; Musician (piano); Composer. 1 daughter. Career: 20 years of singing worldwide, including: USA; Canada; Former USSR; Australia; TV, radio shows; humanitarian concerts; State awards for different ways in music. Recordings: Albums: The Sea; Meri; I'm A Woman; By The Way; Road Dust; Ace; Golden Dreams; Meri (6); Why Do I Love You; Look For Me. Honours: Singer of the Year, 1981-82; 5 Gold albums. Membership: Croatian Composer's Society. Hobbies: Swimming; Home recording. Current Management: ZG Zoe Cetinic, Rendiceva 28, 10000 Zagreb, Croatia. Address: Meri Cetinic, Getaldiceva 27, 58000 Split, Croatia.

CHADWICK James Manfred, b. 16 Oct 1966, Lusaka, Zimbabwe. Jazz Musician (guitar). m. 31 Mar 1995. Education: Shiplake College, Henley-on-Thames. Musical Education: Welsh College of Music and Drama. Career: Appeared on live TV programme Heno in 1993; Member of Enrico Quartet performing at 3 venues in Italy in 1994; Various appearances throughout Britain; Tour of Northern England in 1995. Recording: In The Bag, with James Chadwick Quartet, 1992. Membership: Musicians' Union. Address: 91 Moy Road, Roath, Cardiff CF2 4TE, Wales.

CHADWICK Mark. Vocalist; Musician (guitar); Songwriter. Career: Singer, guitarist, The Levellers, 1990-; Concerts include: Glastonbury Festival, 1992; Regular UK and European concerts; Support to REM, Eastern Europe. Recordings: Singles: 15 Years, 1992; One Way, 1992; Far From Home, 1992; This Garden, 1993; Just The One, 1995; Albums: A Weapon Called

The Word, 1990; Levelling The Land, 1992; Levellers, 1993; Zeitgeist, 1995. Publication: The White Book (directory of action groups). Address: c/o China Records, 111 Frithville Gardens, London W12 7JG, England.

CHALMERS Thomas, b. 4 Dec 1930, Glasgow, Scotland. Musician (saxophone, clarinet, flute). m. Jeanette D McGhee, 21 Dec 1950, 3 sons, 1 daughter. Musical Education: Tutored by member of BBC S V Orchestra. Career: Played with Military Band, 1949-54, Ken Stevens Orchestra, 1960-66, Tommy Sampson Orchestra, 1970-86; Member of Fat Sam's Band, Edinburgh, 1986-96; Freelance musician with Bobby Wishart groups and Strathclyde Youth Jazz Orchestra. Recordings: with Fat Sam's Band: Boogie On Down; Jive On Down; Ring Dem Bells; Fat Sam's Band Live At... Membership: Musicians' Union. Hobbies: Gardening; Walking. Address: 5 Beauly Drive, Craigshill, Livingston, West Lothian EH54 5LG, Scotland.

CHAMBERS Dave, b. 26 Aug 1943, London, England. Musician (saxophone). m. Nellie Verdegaal, 1979, 1 son, 2 daughters. Education: Trained as architect. Musical Education: Self-taught. Career: Worked with Mike Westbrook Brass Band and Concert Orchestra; Julian Bahula's Jazz Africa; Big Chief; OK Band. Recordings: with: Annette Peacock; Mike Westbrook; Julian Bahula; Level 42. Membership: Musicians' Union. Hobbies: Cycling.

CHAMBERS Guy. Producer; Writer; Musician (Keyboards). Career: Jimmy Nail, Robbie Williams, World Party, The Waterboys, Julian Cope, Lemon Trees. Recordings: with Robbie Williams, Cathy Dennis, World Party, Holly Johnson: Blast; Julian Cope: Fried; Lemon Trees. Honours: Musicians' Union; PRS. Current Management: One Management, 43 St Alban's Avenue, London W4 5JS, England.

CHANA Shan, b. 4 Mar 1969, Plymouth, Devon, England. Musician (drums, percussion, latin, timpani). Musical Education: London College of Music, England; GLCM (Hons). Career: West End shows: Crazy For You, Prince Edward Theatre; Grease, Dominion Theatre; Sunset Boulevard, Adelphi Theatre; She Loves Me, Savoy Theatre; Fame, Cambridge Theatre. Recordings: Fame, original cast album, Maison Rouge Studios, London; Major sessions at Snake Ranch Studios, London; CTS Studios, London; Sawmills Studios, Cornwall; ICC Studios, Eastbourne. Honour: Henry Bromley Derry Music Performance Prize, 1990. Membership: Musicians' Union. Hobby: Surfing. Address: 8 Juniper Court, 71 Mulgrove Road, Sutton, Surrey SM2 6LY, England.

CHANDLER Gene (Eugene Dixon), b. 6 July 1940, Chicago, Illinois, USA. Singer. Career: Lead singer, Gene Chandler & The Dukays; Solo artiste. Recordings: Singles include: Duke Of Earl (Number 1, US), 1962; Rainbow, 1963; Man's Temptation, 1963; Just To Be True, 1964; Nothing Can Stop Me, 1965; Groovy Situation, 1970; Albums: The Duke Of Earl, 1962; Just Be True, 1964; The Girl Don't Care, 1967; There Was A Time, 1968; The Two Sides of Gene Chandler, 1969; The Gene Chandler Situation, 1970; Get Down, 1978; When You're Number One, 1979; 80, 1980; Live At The Regal, 1965; Numerous compilations and live albums. Address: 8829 S Bishop, Chicago, IL 60620, USA.

CHANEL Colleen, b. 16 February 1954, Los Banos, California, USA. Recording Artist; Actress. Education: BA, Renaissance History, University of Santa Clara; MBA, Marketing, Management, College of Notre Dame; Licensed in Stocks, Bonds, Options, Commodities, New York Futures, Mutual Funds, Insurance, Real Estate; E F Hutton, Rubloff Investments Training; Hollywood Film School; On Stage Music Productions; California Lawyers for the Arts; Women in Film;

Esoteric Healigh Graduate, International Health Research Network. Career: Stockbroker, Estate Planner, E F Hutton; Mutual Fund Coordinator, Sutro; Investment Analyst, Commerical Real Estate, Rubloff Investments; President, Workshop Leader, Keynote Speaker, Multi-Media Personality, Colleen International; Creative and Business Consultant, Sapphire Productions; Judge, California State Talent Competition; Executive Producer, Enchanté Productions; Independent International Events Travel Agent, World Class Travel Network; Independent Publisher and Writer, Chela Publications. Honours: Wommens Inner Circle of Achievement, American Biographical Institute, 1995; International Woman of the Year in Music, 1995-96. Memberships: International Federation of Festival Organizations; National Association of Female Executives; Writers Connection; Dominican Hospital Guild; California Lawyers for the Arts; Mabel Mercer Foundation; International Health Research Network; Smithsonian Associates; American Film Institute. Address: PO Box 1835, Pebbel Beach, CA 93953, USA.

CHAPIN Tom (Thomas Forbes). b. 13 Mar 1945, Charlotte, North Carolina, USA. Singer; Songwriter; Musician (guitar, banjo, autoharp); Actor. m. Bonnie Chapin, 5 June 1976, 2 daughters, 1 stepson, 1 stepdaughter. Education: College graduate, State University of New York, Plattsburgh. Musical Education: Self-taught. Career: Host, Make A Wish, ABC TV (award-winning children's show), 1971-76; Broadway: Pump Boys and Dinettes, 1983; Host, National Geographic Explorer, TV TBS, 1986-89; Thousands of concerts (mainly in North America) over last 30 years. Recordings: 5 (award-winning) children's recordings: Family Tree; Moonboat; Mother Earth; Billy The Squid; Zag Zig; 5 adult's recordings: Life Is Like That; In The City Of Mercy; Let Me Back Into Your Life; So Nice To Come Home; Join The Jubilee. Publication: Book/cassette: Sing A Whale Song, storybook for children. Honours: Peabody Award, Make A Wish, 1972; Emmy, Make A Wish, 1975; Harry Chapin Award for Contributions to Humanity, NACA, 1990. Memberships: AFofM; SAG; AFTRA; NARAS; NAS. Hobbies: Tennis; Basketball; Reading. Current Management: Sundance Music. Address: Sundance Music, 100 Cedar Street, Suite B-19, Dobbs Ferry, NY 10522, USA.

CHAPMAN Mike, b. 15 Apr 1947, Queensland, Australia. Songwriter. Career: Member, Tangerine Peel; Songwriting partnership with Nicky Chinn; Producer for Blondie hits; Founder, Dreamland label (with Nicky Chinn), 1979-81. Compositions: Hits include: Kiss You All Over, Pat Benatar (Number 1, US); Hot Child In The City, Nick Gilder (Number 1, US); Mickey, Toni Basil (Number 1, US), 1982; Other hits for: Sweet; Gary Glitter; Mud; Suzi Quattro; Smokie; Patti Smith; Lita Ford. Recordings: As producer: with Blondie: Heart Of Glass; The Tide Is High; Sunday Girl; Atomic; Rapture; with The Knack: My Sharona (Number 1, US); Also for Patti Smith; Lita Ford.

CHAPMAN Nigel John, b. 1 Mar 1961, Sheffield, South Yorkshire, England. Musician (piano, keyboards, bass guitar); Teacher. m. Janet Cleminson, 22 July 1988. Musical Education: City of Leeds College of Music. Career: Toured with Harry Beckett, 1984; Appeared on BBC TV programme, Northern Lights, 1985; Radio appearance on Radio Humberside programme, Jazz Weekly, 1990; Toured Russia with Doncaster Youth Jazz Orchestra, 1990. Compositions include: 3 Symphonies; Concertos; Chamber Music. Recording: Whale, with Richard Ingham, 1992. Address: 55 Sunnybank Crescent, Brinsworth, Rotherham, South Yorkshire S60 5JH, England.

CHAPMAN Tracy, b. 30 Mar 1964, Cleveland, Ohio, USA. Singer; Songwriter.

Education: BA, Anthropology and African Studies, Tufts University. Career: Performer on Boston Folk circuit, 1986; Recording artiste, 1987-; Major concerts include: Nelson Mandela 70th Birthday Tribute, Wembley Stadium, 1988; Human Rights Now world tour, with Peter Gabriel, Bruce Springsteen, Sting, Youssou N'Dour, 1988; AIDS benefit concert, Oakland, California, 1989; Nelson Mandela International Tribute, Wembley Stadium, 1990; Martin Luther King Celebration, Minneapolis, 1991; Bill Graham Memorial concert, San Francisco, 1991; Bob Dylan 30th Anniversary celebration, Madison Square Garden, 1992; Farm Aid V with Living Colour's Vernon Reid, 1992; Regular US and UK tours; Television: Motown 30-What's Goin' On, CBS TV, 1990; True Stories - Too White For Me, Ch4, 1992; The Tonight Show, NBC TV, 1992; In Concert, ABC TV, 1992. Recordings: Albums: Tracy Chapman (Number 1, UK and US), 1988; Crossroads (Number 1, UK), 1989; Matters Of The Heart, 1992; New Beginning, 1995; Singles include: Fast Car; Talkin' 'Bout A Revolution; Baby Can I Hold You; Crossroads. Honours: American Music Award, Favourite New Pop/Rock Artist, 1989; BRIT Awards, Best International Artist Female, Best International Newcomer, 1989; Grammy Awards include: Best Female Pop Vocal Performance, Best Contemporary Folk Recording, Best New Artist, 1989; Boston Music Awards include: Best Female Vocalist, Top Song, Rock Album, 1989. Current Management: Gold Mountain Entertainment, Suite 450, 3575 Cahuenga Blvd W, Los Angeles, CA 90068, USA.

CHARBONNIER Vincent, b. 24 Sept 1961, Paris, France. Musician (double bass, bass guitar). Musical Education: Conservatoire National Superieur De Paris. Career: Member, Jacques Loussier Trio; Major baroque orchestras in France, including W Christie, P Herreweghe, M Minkowsky, J C Malgoire; Some jazz groups. Recordings: with Jacques Loussier Trio: Play Bach. Address: 40 Bis rue de Rivoli, 75004 Paris, France.

CHARLES Debbie, b. 9 Aug 1966, London, England. Singer; Songwriter. Career: Backing vocalist with Fine Young Cannibals; Al Green; Bob Geldof; Gabrielle; Alison Moyet; Member, accapella sextet Mint Juleps. Membership: PRS. Hobbies: Writing; Poetry; Swimming. Address: 10 Pemell House, Pemell Close, London E1 4JY, England.

CHARLES Ray (Ray Charles Robinson), 23 Sept 1930, Albany, Georgia, USA. Singer; Musician (piano); Composer. Musical Education: Piano and clarinet, St Augustine's School for Deaf And Blind, Orlando. Career: Blind since age 7 (glaucoma); Member, various groups, Florida; Founder, McSon Trio, 1948; Musical director, Lowell Fulson, 1949-51; Bandleader, own group, 1953-; Concerts include: Newport Jazz Festival, 1958; New York Jazz Festival, 1967; Soul Bowl '69, Houston Astrodome, 1969; Royal Festival Hall, London, 1970; Ann Arbor Jazz & Blues Festival, 1973; Kool Jazz Festival, New York, 1983; John Lennon Tribute Concert, Liverpool, 1990; Playboy Jazz Festival, 1991; Television special, Ray Charles - 50 Years In Music, Fox-TV, 1991; Film appearances: Ballad In Blue, 1964; The Blues Brothers, 1980; Other cameo roles, US television shows: Moonlighting; St Elsewhere; Who's The Boss. Recordings: Singles include: It Should Have Been Me, 1954; Don't You Know, I Got A Woman, 1954; This Little Girl Of Mine, 1954; What'd I Say, 1959; Georgia On My Mind (Number 1, US), 1960; One Mint Julep, 1961; Hit The Road Jack (Number 1, US), 1961; Unchain My Heart, 1962; I Can't Stop Loving You (Number 1, US), 1962; You Don't Know Me, 1962; Take These Chains From My Heart, 1963; Busted, 1963; Cryin' Time, 1966; Seven Spanish Angels, duet with Willie Nelson (US Country Number 1), 1985; I'll Be Good To You, duet with Chaka Khan, 1990; Numerous albums include: Ray Charles,

1957; Ray Charles At Newport, 1958; Soul Brothers (with Milt Jackson), 1959; The Genius Of Ray Charles, 1960; In Person, 1960; The Genius Hits The Road, 1960; Dedicated To You, 1961; Genius + Soul = Jazz, 1961; What'd I Say, 1961; The Genius After Hours, 1961; Ray Charles And Betty Carter, 1961; The Genius Sings The Blues, 1961; Do The Twist, 1962; Modern Sounds In Country And Western Music Vols. 1 and 2, 1962; The Ray Charles Story, 1962; Ingredients In A Recipe For Soul, 1963; Sweet And Sour Tears, 1964; Live In Concert, 1965; Rays Moods, 1966; A Man And His Soul, 1967; Ray Charles Invites You To Listen, 1967; A Portrait Of Ray, 1968; Volcanic Action Of My Soul, 1971; A Message From The People, 1972; Renaissance, 1975; Porgy And Bess (with Cleo Laine), 1976; Heart To Heart, 1980; Friendship, 1985; Back On The Block, 1990; Ray Charles - The Living Legend, 1993; My World, 1993; Strong Love Affair, 1996; Several greatest hits collections; Contributor, We Are The World, USA For Africa, 1985. Membership: Rhythm And Blues Foundation, Washington. Honours include: Numerous Grammy Awards, 1961-; Inducted into Rock'n'Roll Hall Of Fame, 1986; NARAS Lifetime Achievement Grammy Award, 1988; Legend Award, Rhythm & Blues Foundation, 1991; Atlanta Celebrity Walk, 1991; Los Angeles Distinguished Service Medal, 1992; Black History Honoree Award, Los Angeles, 1992; Songwriters Hall Of Fame Lifetime Award, 1993. Address: Ray Charles Enterprises, 2107 Washington Blvd, Los Angeles, CA 90018, USA.

CHARLESON William (Bill), b. 20 June 1940, Oldham, Lancashire, England. Educator; Composer; Arranger; Musician (saxophone). m. Diane Margaret Fox, 18 Aug 1965, 1 son, 1 daughter. Musical Education: Royal Manchester College of Music; University of York; Director of Studies, Leeds College of Music. Career: Appearances with: Ken Mackintosh and Orchestra; BBC Northern Dance Orchestra; BBC Northern Symphony Orchestra; Hallé Orchestra; Royal Liverpool Philharmonic Orchestra; Theatre and cabaret accompanying major British and American artistes; Radio appearances and television sessions for: Granada TV; Yorkshire TV; BBC TV; Consultancy, Open University. Compositions: Jazz compositions for National Youth Jazz Orchestra; Brass Band arrangements, compositions recorded by all major bands. Recordings: with Joe Jackson: Tucker-A Man And His Dream soundtrack. Publications: Jazz Sax 1 (Co-author with J R Brown); Articles for: Crescendo International; British Education Music Journal. Honours: YTV/MU Peter Knight Award, 1989; BBC Rehearsal Band Competition: Arranging Prize, 1989. Membership: PRS. Hobby: Collector of old toys. Address: 144 Sunnybank Road, Mirfield, West Yorkshire WF14 0JQ, England.

CHARLTON Michael Anthony (Mad Dog Santini), b. 27 Feb 1964, South Shields, Tyne And Wear, England. Musician (drums, percussion, keyboards). 1 daughter. Musical Education: BA Hons, Music, University of Northumbria, Newcastle. Career: Television, radio and live appearances include: The Tube; TX45; Mainline; Live 95; Worday Open Air Concert; Gypsies Green Stadium; Metro FM; Wear FM; 7FM; Radio Newcastle; The Riverside; Temple Park Leisure Centre. Recordings: No More War; Is That It; Smooth Funk; Scratch It; Addicted; Devils In Heaven. Memberships: PRS; Musicians' Union; Equity. Hobbies: Volunteer lifeguard; Keep fit. Current Management: Hardy Ismail, Axis Promotions. Address: 55 Marsden Lane, South Shields, Tyne and Wear, England.

CHARMASSON Rémi, b. 3 May 1961, Avignon, France. Musician (guitar). m. Audrey Faure, 22 Sept 1990, 2 daughters. Education: Baccalaureat Philosophy. Musical Education: Gold Medal in Jazz, Avignon Conservatory. Career: Began with André Jaume, Jimmy Giuffre; Played clubs and festivals with: Charlie Mariano; Charles Tyler; Buddy Colette; Dennis Charles; Tony Coe; Freddie Studer; Jean François; Jenny Clarke; Larry Schneider; Randy Kaye; Barry Altschul; Riccardo Del Fra. Recordings: Cinoche, with André Jaume, Rémi Charmasson, Claude Tchamitchian, 1989; Piazza Di Luna, with André Jaume, Rémi Charmasson, Jean-Marc Montera, Fredy Studer, Claude Tchamitchian, Tavagna singers, 1989; FollyFun Music Magic, with Charles Tyler, Rémi Charmasson, Jean Pierre Jullian, Bernard Santacruz, Christian Zagaria, 1990; Caminanado, duo with Claude Tchamitchian, 1990; A Scream For Charles Tyler, with Rémi Charmasson, Dennis Charles, Bernard Santacruz; Casa Blu, with Thierry Maucci; Nemo, trio with F Studer, Jenny Clarke; 10 records in 5 years, 1993; Current recordings with: André Jaume, Charlie Mariano Quintet; A Jaume and Groupes de Gamelans Indonésiens; A Soler and Larry Schneider. Honours: Diapason D'Or, from music newspaper: Diapason. Hobby: Fishing. Current Management: Association Jazz et Musique Improvisée (AJMI), Avignon, France. Address: La Manutention, 4 Rue Scalier Ste Anne, BP 452, 84072 Avignons Cedex, France.

CHASE Katharine Ann, b. 29 April 1963, Ridgecrest, CA, USA. Singer; Songwriter; Musician. Education: BA, Classical Voice, University of California, Los Angeles; Selftaught Bass and Rhythm Guitars. Career: Solo appearances with Hootie and the Blowfish; Mary Lou Lord; Exene Cervankova, Elliot Smith; Co-Founder Spanking Violets, 1992; Founder, Katharine Chase Band, 1994; Cake; The Blasters; Southern Culture on the Skids; Tripping Daisy. Recordings: Loverman, solo album, 1994; Band albums: Spanking Violets, 1994; The Truth, 1995; The Truth, 1997; Contributor, albums: Bigger, Better, Faster, More, 1992; Trinket, 1996; Starene, 1997. Publications: Reviews and Interviews, 1995; San Francisco Chronicle, 1997; Bay Magazine, 1996. Honours: 12 Gold Medals, Regional Texas State Flute Competitions, 1980-86. Memberships: BMI; NARAS. Current Management: Midnight Sun, 382c Union Avenue, Campbell, CA 95008, USA.

CHASSAGNITE François, b. 21 June 1955, Ussel, Correze, France. Musician (trumpet, flugelhorn). Education: Ex-veterinary doctor. Career: Member, Antoine Hervé Big Band; Gerard Badini Big Band; Jean Loup Lognon Big Band; François Jeanneau's Pandemonium; Orchestre National de Jazz; Laurent Cugny Big Band (2 records and a tour in Europe under Gil Evans direction); Festivals Nice, Juan les Pins; Mariac; Paris. Recordings: 2 records with Antoine Hervé; 3 with François Jeanneau; 2 with Laurent Cugny; 1 with G Badini; 1 with Jean Loup Longnon; Several with small combos; 2 with own band Samya Cynthia; Chazzeology. Memberships: SACEM; SPEDIDAM. Hobby: Fly fishing. Current Management: Instant Present; Self-managed. Address: 9 Rue Louis Michel Féraud, 06610 La Gaude, France.

CHASTAIN David T, b. Cincinnati, Ohio, USA. Rock Musician (guitar); Composer. Career: Member, Spike, 1984; Solo artiste, under own name, 1985-; Simultaneous recording projects: Chastain and CJSS (later split, 1987); Predominantly studio recording artist of own works. Recordings: Solo albums: Mystery Of Illusion, 1985; Ruler Of The Wasteland, 1986; The Seventh Of Never, 1987; Instrumental Variations, 1987; The Voice Of The Cult, 1988; Within The Heat, 1989; For Those Who Dare, 1990; with CJSS: World Gone Mad, 1986; Praise The Loud, 1986. Current Management: c/o Leviathon Records, USA.

CHAUDAGNE Remy, b. 26 Aug 1959, Melun, France. Composer; Musician (electric bass). m. Cora, 13 Jan 1994, 1 son. Musical Education: Piano, saxophone, double bass, electric bass.

Career: Tour, France, India, Indonesia, Vietnam, Philippines, Cambodia, Sudan; Performances with: David Liebman; Scott Henderson; F Corneloup; Claude Barthelemy; Andy Sheppard. Compositions: Music for short films, theatre, saxophone quartet, Creation with jazz orchestra (24 musicians) or classical (13 musicians). Recordings: 7 albums as leader, including last in trio with Peter Erskine and Andy Sheppard: 3 Colors. Honours: First Prize, Villembourne Festival, music for film Sem Cor with Katie Adler. Hobby: Family. Current Management: Benoit Lebon. Address: 4B Rue de la Convention, 94270 Kremlin Bicêtre, France.

CHAULK (Lloyd) Wayne, b. 10 June 1950, Corner Brook, Newfoundland, Canada. Composer; Arranger; Musician; Producer. m. Denise, 29 Mar 1975, 1 daughter. Education: Bachelor of Commerce degree; Engineering technician; Real Estate license. Musical Education: Self-taught. Career: Canadian Broadcasting Corporation television features, 1993; Over 20 radio interviews, 1992-93; Music featured on international airlines, worldwide; Music played on over 4,000 US premises and on over 400 radio stations; Over 200 original compositions and 18 CDs produced. Recordings: Albums: Dreamer's Themes, 1991; New Directions and Christmas Keyboards, 1992; No Regrets, 1993; The Christmas to Remember, 1996; Nature's Splendour, 1996; Journey Home, 1997. Honours: Billboard Certificate of Achievement: Your Love Is My Song, 1992; Best Light Rock (Pop) Artist On Record, Aria, 1994, 1995; Albums rated among best instrumentals, Adult Contemporary Music Research Group, US, 1993-94; Juno Award Nomination, Instrumental Artist Of The Year, Canada, 1995. Membership: SOCAN. Hobbies: Golf; Tennis; Nature. Current Management: Self-managed; Distributor, Holborne Distribution Inc, Canada. Address: c/o Ambassador Music, Deer Valley, PO #43029, Calgary, Alberta T2J 7A7, Canada.

CHAUTEMPS Jean-Louis, b. 6 Aug 1931, Paris, France. Musician (saxophone); Composer. Divorced, 1 son, 1 daughter. Education: Philosophy; Musicology. Career: Member, Claude Bolling Orchestra, 1952; Also played with Sydney Bechet; Django Reinhardt; Zoot Sims; Lester Young; Bobby Jaspar; Albert Ayler; Roy Eldridge; Don Byas; European tour with Chet Baker; 3 years as saxphone player, musical arranger, Kurt Edelhagen Orchestra, Cologne, Germany; Played Paris jazz clubs, early 1960s; Played with Kenny Clarke; Martial Solal; Slide Hampton; Eddy Louiss; René Urtreger; Johnny Griffin; Dexter Gordon; Daniel Humair; Composer for films; Teacher, improvisation; Worked with the Ensemble InterContemporain, extensive tours USA with Musique Vivante, early 1970s; Leader, jazz workshop, The Sorbonne, 1975; Founder, Rhizome, 1976; Concerts, tours include Dizzy Gillespie; World premier, Périples For Solo Saxophone by Paul Méfano; Soloist, leader, Albert Mangelsdorff band, 2 years; Member, Martial Solal Big Band; Works for classical and avant garde orchestras; Works with computers and synthesisers; Played at the Guggenheim Museum, New York, with Quatuor de Saxophones, 1987; 3 jazz concerts, Opéra-Bastille, 1992; Also with Ensemble Contrechamps, 1994; Musical director, The Threepenny Opera, Théâtre National de Chaillot, 1995. Compositions: Film music includes Les Coeurs Verts; L'Ombre de la Pomme; Music for theatre, television and film. Recordings: Album: Chautemps, 1988. Honours: Chevalier des Arts et Lettres, Ordre National du Mérite; Prix du Jazz SACEM. Membership: Vice-President de l'Assafra. Hobbies: Music; Computers. Current Management: Agnès Lupovici.

CHECKER Chubby (Ernest Evans), b. 3 Oct 1941, South Carolina, USA. Singer. Career: Television appearances: The Dick Clark Saturday Night Show, ABC-TV, 1960; Ed Sullivan Show, 1961; Ready Steady Go, 1965; Featured in films:

Twist Around The Clock, 1961; Don't Knock The Twist, 1962; Numerous worldwide tours; Featured artist, Dick Clark's Caravan Of Stars, 1961; Performed at Nelson Mandela's 70th Birthday Tribute, Wembley, 1988. Recordings: Singles include: The Twist (Number 1, US), 1960, 1962 (only song ever to reach US Number 1 on two occasions); The Hucklebuck, 1960; Pony Time (Number 1, US), 1961; Dance The Mess Around, 1961; Let's Twist Again, 1961; The Fly, 1961; Jingle Bell Rock, duet with Bobby Rydell, 1961; Twistin' USA, 1961; Slow Twistin', 1962; Teach Me To Twist, duet with Bobby Rydell, 1962; Dancin' Party, 1962; Limbo Rock, 1962; Birdland, 1963; Loddy Lo, 1963; Let's Limbo Some More, 1963; Hooka Tooka, 1964; The Twist (Yo' Twist), with the Fat Boys, 1988; Albums: Twist With Chubby Checker, 1960; It's Pony Time, 1961; For Twisters Only, 1962; Your Twist Party, 1962; Bobby Rydell/Chubby Checker, 1962; For Teen Twisters Only, 1962; Twistin' Round The World, 1962; Don't Knock The Twist (film soundtrack), 1962; All The Hits (For Your Dancin' Party), 1961; Limbo Party, 1963; Chubby Checker's Biggest Hits, 1963; Let's Limbo Some More, 1963; Beach Party, 1963; Chubby Checker In Person, 1963; Chubby Checker's Greatest Hits, 1973; The Change Has Come, 1982. Honours include: Grammy Award, Best Rock And Roll Recording, Let's Twist Again, 1961. Current Management: Twisted Entertainment, 320 Fayette Street, 2nd Floor, Conshohocken, PA 19428, USA.

CHENEOUR (Ian) Paul, b. 19 Apr 1952, Southsea, Hampshire, England. Musician (flute). Musical Education: Guildhall School of Music and Drama, with Professor Rainer Schielein. Career: Member, Dutch Jazz Quintet, France; Leader, own 7 piece group The Cornish Connection; Leader, jazz fusion quartet, Cheneour, 1983-; Leader, The Aeona Flute Quartet, 1991-; Leader, Impromptu, 1993; Freelance musician for films, radios and documentaries; Numerous tours, UK; Europe; Middle East; North America; Canada; Greece, 1997; Masterclasses in Improvisation and Composition, and flute playing; New Duo, Paul Cheneour and Dilly Meah, flutes and tabla, 1997. Recordings: Solo albums: Chenour Live I, 1987; The Time Has Come, 1995; with Impromptu: Sweet Kafka, 1994; Ocean of Dreams, 1996; Reiki Healing Symbols in Sound, 1997. Memberships: Musicians' Union; PRS; MCPS; PPL. Hobbies: Eating; Sleeping. Current Management: Red Gold Music Ltd. Address: 87A Queens Road, East Grinstead, West Sussex RH19 1BG, England.

CHENEVIER Guigou, b. 21 Nov 1955, La Tronche, France. Musician (percussions); Composer. 2 sons. Education: University of Literature. Musical Education: Mostly self-taught, including piano and drum lessons. Career: More than 400 concerts worldwide, include 3 US tours, with Etron Fou Leloublan, 1973-86; Drummer, composer, with Les Batteries; Octavo; Encore Plus Grande; Volapük, 1986-95. Recordings: Demesure Révolutionnaire, Les Batteries; Reedition, Etron Fou LeLoublan, 1991; Des Pieds et Des Mains, Octavo, 1992; Le Diapason Du Père Ubu, 1993; Le Feu Du Tigre, Volapük, 1995. Current Management: Inouï Productions. Address: 3A Maison IV De Chiffre, 26 Rue des Teinturiers, 84000 Avignon, France.

CHER (Cherilyn Sarkisian LaPierre), 20 May 1946, El Centro, California, USA. Singer; Actress; Entertainer. m. (1) Sonny Bono, 1964, divorced, 1 daughter, (2) Gregg Allman, 1975, divorced, 1 son. Career: Worked with Sonny Bono in duo Sonny and Cher, 1964-74; Also solo artiste, 1964-; Performances include: Hollywood Bowl, 1966; Newport Pop Festival, 1968; Television includes: Sonny And Cher Comedy Hour, CBS, 1971; Cher, CBS, 1975-76; Sonny And Cher Show, CBS, 1976-77; Vocalist with rock group Black Rose, including US tour supporting Hall & Oates, 1980; Actress, films: Good Times, 1967; Chastity, 1969; Come Back To The Five And

Dime, Jimmy Dean Jimmy Dean, 1982; Silkwood, 1984; Mask, 1985; The Witches Of Eastwick, 1987; Moonstruck, 1987; Suspect, 1987; Mermaids, 1989. Recordings include: Singles: with Sonny And Cher: I Got You Babe (Number 1, UK and US), 1975; Baby Don't Go, 1965; Just You, 1965; But You're Mine, 1965; What Now My Love, 1966; Little Man, 1966; The Beat Goes On, 1967; All I Ever Need Is You, 1971; A Cowboy's Work Is Never Done, 1972; Solo hit singles include: All I Really Want To Do, 1965; Bang Bang, 1966; Gypsies Tramps And Thieves (Number 1, US), 1971; The Way Of Love, 1972; Half Breed (Number 1, US), 1973; Dark Lady (Number 1, US), 1974; Take Me Home, 1979; Dead Ringer For Love, duet with Meatloaf, 1982; I Found Someone, 1987; We All Sleep Alone, 1988; After All, duet with Peter Cetera (for film soundtrack Chances Are), 1989; If I Could Turn Back Time, 1989; Jesse James, 1989; Heart Of Stone, 1990; The Shoop Shoop Song (from film soundtrack Mermaids) (Number 1, UK), 1991; Love And Understanding, 1991; Oh No Not My Baby, 1992; Walking In Memphis, 1995; Albums: with Sonny and Cher: Look At Us, 1965; All I Really Want To Do, 1965; The Wondrous World Of Sonny And Cher, 1966; Sonny And Cher Live, 1972; Solo albums include: All I Really Want To Do, 1965; The Sonny Side Of Cher, 1966; With Love, 1967; Backstage, 1968; Jackson Highway, 1969; Gypsies Tramps And Thieves, 1972; Foxy Lady, 1972; Greatest Hits, 1974; Stars, 1975; I'd Rather Believe In You, 1976; Take Me Home, 1979; I Paralyze, 1984; Cher, 1988; Heart Of Stone, 1989; Love Hurts, 1991; Cher's Greatest Hits 1965-1992, 1992; It's A Man's World, 1995. Honours include: Oscar, Best Actress, Moonstruck, 1988; Oscar Nomination, Best Supporting Actress, Silkwood, 1984. Current Management: Bill Sammeth Organisation, PO Box 960, Beverly Hills, CA 90213, USA.

CHERONE Gary, b. 24 July 1961, Malden, Massachusetts, USA. Singer; Songwriter. Career: Member, Dream; Singer, funk/rock group Extreme, 1985-; Worldwide appearances include: Regular US tours; American Dream concerts, London, 1992; Concert For Life, Tribute to Freddie Mercury, Wembley, 1992; Support to Bryan Adams, European tour, 1992; Lead singer, Van Halen, 1998-. Recordings: with Extreme: Singles: More Than Words (Number 1, US), 1991; Get The Funk Out, 1991; Decadence Dance, 1991; Hole-Hearted, 1991; Song For Love, 1992; Rest In Peace, 1992; Stop The World, 1992; Albums: Extreme, 1989; Extreme II - Pornograffiti, 1991; III Sides To Every Story, 1992; Waiting For The Punchline, 1994; with Van Halen: 3, 1998. Honours: Winners, MTV Video contest, 1987; Boston Music Awards: Act Of Year; Outstanding Rock Single, Hole-Hearted; Outstanding Pop Single; Outstanding Singer/Songwriter, More Than Words, 1992. Current Management: SRO Management, 189 Carlton Street, Toronto, Ontario M5A 2K7, Canada.

CHESCOE Laurie, b. 18 Apr 1933, London, England. Musician (drums). m. Sylviane Yanou Chescoe, 5 Aug 1960, 1 son, 1 daughter. Musical Education: Tutor. Career: Teddy Layton Band, 1957; Monty Sunshine, 1960; Dick Charlesworth, 1964; Bruce Turner, 1965; Bob Wallis, 1966; Alan Elsdon, 1976 (14 years); Midnite Follies Orchestra, 1978; Alex Welsh Band, 1979; Formed own band, Laurie Chescoe's Good Time Jazz, 1990; Performed at all major festivals, television and radio. Recordings: Albums: 2 with Midnite Follies; 2 with Keith Nicholls; 78s with Eric Allendale New Orleans Knights; Teddy Layton Band; Albums with own band; 3 albums with Benny Walters, Ralph Sutton. Membership: Musicians' Union. Hobbies: DIY; Francophile. Current Management: John Boddy Agency. Address: 10 Southfield Gardens, Twickenham TW1 4SZ, England.

CHESLIN Mat, b. 28 Nov 1970, Wordsley, West Midlands, England. Musician (bass). Career: Founder member, Neds Atomic Dustbin, 1987. Recordings: God Fodder, 1991; Are You Normal?, 1993; Brainbloodvolume, 1995. Membership: Musicians' Union. Hobbies: Football; Squash. Current Management: Paul Bolton, Chris "Tank" Gilks. Address: Stourbridge, West Midlands, England.

CHESTER Johnny, b. 26 December 1941, Melbourne, Victoria, Australia. m. Larraine, 29 September 1964, 3 daughters. Education: Self-taught. Career: TV Host, Teen Scene, ABC TV, 1964-65; TV Host, Country Road, ABC TV, 1977-78; Disc Jockey, Radio 3U2, Melbourne, 1966-69; Presenter, Radio Australia, 1989-91; Toured Australia and New Zealand with The Beatles, 1964; Australia with Kenny Rogers, 1984; Tammy Wynette, 1992; Performed in Vietnam, 1968; with own show, Australia Wide, 1961-. Compositions: World Greatest Mum; My Kind of Woman; Highway 31; I Love You So Rebecca; Lord I'd Forgotten. Recordings: Over 200 song titles released, 1961-. Honours: Male Vocalist of the Year, 1981, 1982, 1983; Australia CM Awards. Memberships: APRA; TSA; CMAA; CMA (US). Hobby: Fishing. Current Management: Ian B Allen, Dynamic Management, PO Box 101, Seaford, Victoria 3198, Australia.

CHEVALLIER D, b. 13 Jan 1969, Ris Orangis, France. Musician (electric and acoustic guitar); Composer. Musical Education: Classical guitar, Conservatoire National De Région de Paris. Career: Concerts, Rome; Berlin; New York; Rochester; Hartford; Richmond; Prague (EBU big band); Paris Jazz Festival; Nord Jazz Festival (Germany); Festival of Montpellier; Festival of Assier; Souillac; Ramatuelle and Montreal Jazz Festival, July 1996. Recordings: Migration, with Daniel Humoir, Yves Robert; Nilxa: State Of Grace; Terre Nova: Danses. Memberships: SACEM; SPEDIDAM. Hobby: Photography. Current Management: Celia Productions. Address: 2 Place Beaumarchais, F-91600 Savigny, S/Orge, France.

CHIARELLI Robert C, b. 13 Jan 1963. Mixer; Remix Producer. Musical Education: University of Miami, Florida. Recordings: Producer and/or Mixer for numerous recordings including: Do You Wanna Ride, Adina Howard; Bootlegs And B-Sides, Lethal Injection, Death Certificate, Ice Cube; Mind, Body And Song, Jade; Truly Blessed, A Little More Magic, Teddy Pendergrass; Make Time For Love, Keith Washington; My World, Ray Charles; U Know (remix), Boyz II Men; Runaway Love, Barcelona Gold, En Vogue; The Truth, Aaron Hall; All The Way, Let's Get Smooth, Calloway; Pronounced Jah-nay, Zhane; UNITY, Queen Latifah; Soundtracks: Jason's Lyric; Streetfighter; Above The Rim; Menace II Society; Mi Vida Loca. Honours: 30 Platinum and Gold discs. Membership: NARAS. Address: 2219 W. Olive Avenue #102, Burbank, CA 91506, USA.

CHIASSON Warren, b. 17 Apr 1934, Cheticamp, Nova Scotia, Canada. Jazz Musician (vibraphone, piano) Composer. Education: St Francis Xavier University, Antigonish, Nova Scotia. Musical Education: Jazz with Lenny Tristano; George Russell; Classical violin lessons for 6 years. Career: George Shearing Quintet, 1959-61, 1972-74; Clubs, concerts, tours with Chet Baker, Tal Farlow, Roberta Flack, 1975-82; Broadway show, Hair (composed the percussion), 1968-72. Compositions: Ultramarine; Bossa Nova Scotia; Bedouin; Hazel Eyes; Bravel; Festival. Recordings: Good Vibes For Kurt Weill; Point Counterpoint; Quartessence; Blues And Jazz, B.B.King. Publications: The Contemporary Vibraphonist. Honours: One of the Top Six Outstanding Jazz Vibraphonists over the last half-century, NY Times, 1989. Memberships: ASCAP; Recording Musicians of America; NARAS. Hobbies: Ice hockey; Classical literature

and poetry; Fine dining. Current Management: Abby Hoffer Enterprises. Address: 223½ E 48th Street, New York, NY 10017, USA.

CHIAVOLA Kathy, b. 7 Mar 1952, Chicago, Illinois, USA. Artist; Vocalist; Musician (guitar). Musical Education: Oberlin Conservatory, BM, MM; Indiana Conservatory, postgraduate work. Career: Sang opera professionally; Moved to Nashville, 1980; Toured with The Doug Dillard Band, Vassar Clements, The Country Gazette; Formed The Lucky Dogs; Toured Eastern Europe with Douglas and Mark O'Connor, USIA tour: The Nashville Masters; UK debut tour, 1993; Voice of State Farm Insurance, television commercial; McDonalds commercial on radio. Recordings: Albums: Labor Of Love, 1990; The Harvest, 1995; Appeared on Emmylou Harris video, Thanks To You; Recorded with: Garth Brooks; Emmylou Harris; Vince Gill; Kathy Mattea; Ricky Skaggs. Honour: Nammie Award, Backup Vocalist of The Year, 1995. Memberships: IBMA; AFofM; AFTRA; NARAS. Hobbies: Gardening; Her dog Lucy; Walking.

CHILD Desmond, b. USA. Songwriter; Record Producer; Musician (keyboards). Career: Formed Desmond Child And Rouge, 1975; Concentrated on songwriting, 1980s. Compositions: Hit songs include: You Give Love A Bad Name, Bon Jovi; Livin' On A Prayer, Bon Jovi; I Was Made For Loving You, Kiss; Other songs for: Cher; Michael Bolton; Alice Cooper; Jimmy Barnes. Recordings: Albums: Desmond Child And Rouge, 1978; Runners In The Night, 1979; Desmond Child Discipline, 1991. Current Management: C Winston Simone Management, 1790 Broadway, 10th Floor, New York, NY 10019, USA.

CHILDS Robert Alexander, b. 23 Apr 1961, London, England. Musician (guitar, steel guitar); Singer; Songwriter; Music Journalist. Career: Member, country band Greta And The Stray Shots; Major concerts: Johnny Cash Show; Americana Fest; Morecombe International Festival; Television: Country By The Sea, BBC; Radio: Live In Concert, BBC Essex. Recordings: Greta And The Stray Shots: EP: Your Foolish Heart, 1988; Albums: Live, 1987; Above and Beyond, 1990; Livewire, 1991; Playtime, 1993; Inclusion of track: I Didn't Mean To Do It, on Declaration of Independence, The Best Of British Country, 1994. Publications: Articles for: Making Music; Country Music Gazette; International Country Music News. Membership: Performing Rights Society. Hobbies: Equestrianism; Motor Racing; Watching TV, video. Current Management: New Cut Records. Address: 40 Fielding Way, Hutton, Essex, England.

CHILDS William Edward, b. 8 Mar 1957, Los Angeles, California, USA. Composer (piano). m. Holly Hamilton, 30 June, 1991, 1 son. Education: University. Musical Education: BM, Composition, University of Southern California (USC). Career: Six years with Freddie Hubbard, 1978-84; Played with J J Johnson, 1977; Played with: Alan Holdsworth; Dianne Reeves; Branford Marsalis; Bobby Hutcherson; Played twice as leader, North Sea Jazz Festival; Twice, Monterey Jazz Festival. Compositions: Two performed by Los Angeles Philharmonic; One for Akron Symphony Orchestra; One (strings, bass, rhythm section), performed at Monterey Jazz Festival, part of commission series; One at Grenoble Jazz Festival. Recordings: Albums: Take For Example This; Twilight Is Upon Us; His April Touch; Portrait Of A Player; I've Known Rivers; Sideman with: Freddie Hubbard; Dianne Reeves; Alan Holdsworth; Eddie Daniels; Kevyn Lettau; Various selections in: New Real Book. Honours: Australian Film Inmstitute nomination: Best Original Score (My Forgotten Man), 1993; Composition Department Award (USC). Hobbies: Basketball; Reading; Aerobic Exercise. Current Management: Open Door Management, 15327 Sunset

Boulevard, Suite 365, Pacific Palisades, CA 90272, USA.

CHILTON John, b. 16 July 1932, London, England. Musician (trumpet); Arranger; Bandleader; Writer. Career: Leader, own band, mid 1950s; Member, arranger, Bruce Turner Jump Band, 1958-63; Played with Alex Welsh and Mike Daniels, early 1960s; Co-leader, the Feetwarmers, late 1960s; Sole bandleader, 1974-; Musical director, George Melly, 1974-; Tours, recordings, broadcasts, as George Melly and John Chilton's Feetwarmers, 1974-; Writer and researcher into jazz history. Publications: Who's Who Of Jazz: Storyville To Swing Street; Louis - The Louis Armstrong Story; Jazz; Billie's Blues, partial biography of Billie Holiday; Historical accounts of: the Jenkins Orphanage bands; McKinney's Cotton Pickers; The Bob Crosby Bobcats; Biographies of: Sidney Bechet; Coleman Hawkins; Louis Jordan; Who's Who of Jazz (Storyville to Swing Street); Who's Who of British Jazz. Current Management: Jack L Higgins, Pear Tree Cottage, Weymarks, Bradwell-On-Sea, Essex CM0 7JB, England.

CHISHOLM George, b. 29 Mar 1915, Glasgow, Scotland. Musician (trombone). Career: Trombonist, bands led by Teddy Joyce and Bert Ambrose; Also played with Benny Carter; Coleman Hawkins; Fats Waller; The Squadronaires; Studio and session musician; Leader, own group The Gentlemen Of Jazz. Recordings: Albums: George Chisholm And His Band, 1956; Stars Play Jazz, 1961; George Chisholm, 1967; Along The Chisholm Trail, 1971; In A Mellow Mood, 1973; Trombone Showcase, 1976; The Swinging Mr C, 1986; That's A-Plenty, 1987; Other recordings with: Sandy Brown; Wild Bill Davison; John Petters; Benny Carter; The Squadronaires. Honours include: OBE, 1984. Address: c/o Wilcox Zodiac Organisation, 1099A Finchley Road, London NW11 0QB, England.

CHIWESHE Stella, b. 8 July 1946, Harare, Zimbabwe. m. (1) 2 daughters, (2) Peter Reich, 27 January 1988. Career: Member, National Dance Company of Zimbabwe, Mbira Soloist, Actress and Dancer, 1981-84; Solotours in Germany, Great Britain & Italy, 1984; Tour through Germany, 1985; Introduction of marimbas for mbira music, 1986; Recording and publication of Ambuya?; Triumphant concert at Hackney Empire, London at Beat Apartheid Road Festival, 1987; European Tour, 1988; Tour in Europe with concerts in Slovenia, Switzerland, Austria, Great Britain, Italy, Poland & Germany, with trio & the Earthquake Band, 1995; Tour in Europe with concerts in the Netherlands, Belgium, Germany, Austria, Hungary, Great Britain and Ireland, 1996; Tour of USA, Netherlands, Germany and Italy, 1998. Compositions: Kasahwa; Chaa!; Nsuzu Chamakuwende; Mapere. Honour: Billboard Music Award, 1993. Membership: GEMA. Hobbies: Travel; Reading; Swimming. Current Management: Alba Kultur-Aktionen, Birgit Ellinghaus. Address: Alba Kulturaktionen, Justinianstr 16, D-50679, Koeln, Germany.

CHODZKO-ZAJKO Maciej, b. 29 Nov 1954, London, England. Computer Engineer. m. Ewa Tymoczko, 17 Sept 1993, 1 daughter. Education: Imperial College. Career: with Millenium Dance Company, 1969-77; Mazury Dance Company, 1975-76, 1979-92; Member and now conductor of J Rumun Memorial Male Voice Choir; Singer for many years; Playing guitar at Polish church services; Various television appearances. Recordings: Backing vocalist, guitarist and arranger, Solidarity Defiant, 1982; Lead vocalist, guitarist and arranger, Ballad Of Janek From Gdynia, 1982. Membership: Musicians' Union. Hobby: Volleyball referee. Address: 17 Claremont Road, Ealing, London W13 0DE, England.

CHOLET Jean-Christophe, b. 11 May 1962, Bühl, Germany. Musician (piano); Composer; Arranger. Divorced. 1 son, 1 daughter. Musical Education: University diploma, piano (schola cantorum), harmony, counterpoint and fugue. Career: Concerts, festivals: Radio France (Paris); Coutances; Couches; Sorgues; Toutplellier; Vienna (Austria); Tous le Savnièr; Worms; Mainz; Bonn; Trier, Germany; Le Havre; Avignon. Recordings: with Odéjy: Osti Natologie; Suite Alpestre; with Mathias Rüegg and Michel Portal: Third Dream. Honours: First Prize, Soloist, Composition and Orchestra, International Festival of Jazz, La Défense, Paris. Membership: Union of Jazz Musicians. Hobbies: Cooking; Wine; Nature; Cinema; Travel. Current Management: Odéjy, Route de St Georges, 8900 Perigny, France. Address: 295 Chemin de la Motte, 45200 Paulcourt, France.

CHOLEWA Tom Mike Werner, b. 4 June 1958, Copenhagen, Denmark. Conductor; Musician (French horn). m. Ellen, 1983, 2 daughters. Musical Education: Degree in Classical Music, Royal Danish Music Academy; French Horn and Musicology, University of Copenhagen. Career: Bandmaster of Zealand Life Regiment, 1989-1996; Freelance conductor and musician; Music Educator. Recording: Conductor, television production Dagen vi aldrig glemmer, with the Danish vocal group Swing Sisters and Band of Zealand Life Regiment. Honour: 2nd Prize, march competition for Prince Joachim, Denmark. Membership: Danish Conductors Association. Address: Folkevej 19, 2820 Gentofte, Denmark.

CHRISTENSEN Nikolaj, b. 19 Feb 1966, Copenhagen, Denmark. Singer; Actor. Career: Major films: Christian, director, Gabrial Axel; Hjerter I Slor, Jesper W Nielsen. Recordings: Piloter, 1990; Jimmy and Vicky, 1991; Hen Over Jorden, 1994; Vi Er På Vej, 1996. Honour: Grammy, Best New Artist, 1990. Membership: DJBFA. Hobbies: Giraffe pictures/paintings. Address: Kick Musik, Energivej 42B, 2750 Ballerup, Denmark.

CHRISTENSEN Thomas Hass, b. 15 Mar 1961, Frederiksberg, Denmark. Musician (saxophone); Composer. Musical Education: Self-taught. Career: Played: 2 weeks, Ronnie Scott's, 1989; Montreal Jazz Festival, with Page One, 1989; Toured with soloists as a sideman. Recordings: with Page One: Beating Bop; Live At Ronnie Scott's; Notes In Time, Thomas Hass; A Matter Of Fact, The End. Honour: The European Jazz Federation Prize, 1977. Memberships: DMF; DJBFA. Address: Sollerod Park, bl 13 no 20, DK-2840 Holte, Denmark.

CHRISTIAN Garry, b. 27 Feb 1955, Liverpool, England. Vocalist. Career: Member, The Christians, 1984-; Appearances include: Liver Aid Ethiopian Famine benefit, Liverpool, 1985; Support to Fleetwood Mac, UK tour, 1988; John Lennon Tribute Concert, Merseyside, 1990; Regular UK and European tours. Recordings: Albums: The Christians (Number 2, UK), 1987; Colour (Number 1, UK), 1990; Happy In Hell, 1992; The Best Of The Christians, 1993; Singles include: Forgotten Town, 1987; Hooverville (They Promised Us The World), 1987; When The Fingers Point, 1987; Ideal World, 1988; Born Again, 1988; Harvest For The World, 1988; Words, 1989; What's In A Word, 1992; The Bottle, 1992; Contributor, Ferry 'Cross The Mersey, Hillsborough football disaster benefit record, 1989. Current Management: Eternal Management, 55 Lark Lane, Liverpool, Merseyside L17 8UW, England.

CHRISTIAN James John, b. Milford, Connecticut, USA. Singer; Songwriter; Musician (guitar, drums, keyboards); Record Producer. Career: Lead singer, LA Rocks; Lead singer, House Of Lords; World tours, opened for acts including: Ozzy Osbourne; Queensrÿche; Cheap Trick; Scorpions; Tesla; Producer, writer, solo musician; Lead singer, tour of Japan with Pata (lead guitarist with Japanese band X), 1993; Opened own recording studio, Bodeo Rodeo Records. Compositions include: Les Ideos Noires, platinum hit single for Julie Masse; Songs for group, Alias. Recordings: 3 albums with House Of Lords include: House Of Lords; Sahara; Solo album: Rude Awakening; Singles include: Can't Find My Way Home; As producer: Album: A Contre Jour, Julie Masse. Current Management: John Dubuque, Dublen Entertainment Group, 330 Merwin Avenue, Unit #F1, Milford, CT 06460, USA.

CHRISTIAN Rick, b. 22 Sept 1951, Romford, Essex, England. Singer; Songwriter; Musician (6 and 12 string guitars). m. Gillian Mary Moore, 11 Apr 1981. Career: Professional musician since 1987; Many radio appearances include: Capital; LBC; BBC and independent local radio stations including Essex, Suffolk, Kent, Bedford, Shropshire; Festivals include: South Downs, Broadstairs; Walton; Co-presenter, Essex Folk, BBC Essex, 1986-1994; Organiser, Maldon Folk Club and Maldon Folk Festival; Supported artists including: Jim Couza; Fred Wedlock; Harvey Andrews; Played charity event alongside Gryff Rhys Jones, 1990; Tours, Denmark, 1994, 1995. Recordings: Albums: Reason Enough, 1983; Looking For Signs, 1990. Publications: Major contributor: Guinness Who's Who Of Folk Music; Guinness Encyclopedia Of Popular Music. Memberships: Musicians' Union; PRS; PPL; EFDSS. Hobbies: Photography; Walking; Swimming; Music. Current Management: MDS Booking, Denmark.

CHRISTIAN Roger, b. 13 Feb 1950, Liverpool, Merseyside, England. Vocalist. Career: Member, The Christians, 1984-87; Solo artiste, 1989-; Appearances include: Liver Aid Ethiopian Famine benefit, Liverpool, 1985; UK tour, 1986. Recordings: with The Christians: The Christians (NUmber 2, UK), 1987; Solo album: Checkmate, 1989; Singles: with The Christians: Forgotten Town, 1987; Hooverville (They Promised Us The World), 1987; When The Fingers Point, 1987; Solo: Take It From Home, 1989. Current Management: Eternal Management, 55 Lark Lane, Liverpool, Merseyside L17 8UW, England.

CHRISTIAN Russell, b. 8 July 1956, Liverpool, Merseyside, England. Vocalist. Career: Member, The Christians, 1984-; Appearances include: Liver Aid Ethiopian Famine benefit, Liverpool, 1985; Regular UK and European tours; Support to Fleetwood Mac, UK tour, 1988; John Lennon Tribute Concert, Merseyside, 1990; Recordings: Albums: The Christians (Number 2, UK), 1987; Colour (Number 1, UK), 1990; Happy In Hell, 1992; The Best Of The Christians, 1993; Singles include: Forgotten Town, 1987; Hooverville, 1987; When The Fingers Point, 1987; Ideal World, 1988; Born Again, 1988; Harvest For The World, 1988; Words, 1989; What's In A Word, 1992; The Bottle, 1992; Contributor, Ferry 'Cross The Mersey, Hillsborough football disaster benefit, 1989. Current Management: Eternal Management, 55 Lark Lane, Liverpool, Merseyside L17 8UW, England.

CHRISTIANE Kelvin, b. 16 Mar 1958, Watford, Hertfordshire, England. Jazz Musician (saxophones, flute, clarinet, keyboards, percussion); Composer. m. Lorraine Cellini, 16 Dec 1989, 1 son. Musical Education: Watford School of Music; City Of Leeds College of Music. Career: Television appearances; Toured Europe with: Afrique, 1980; The Flyers, 1981-84; Various London radio shows during 1995 promoting current album. Recordings: Albums: with Kelvin Christiane Band: Awakening, 1992; Soho, 1993; Great Spirit, 1994; Salute the Sun, 1997. Honours: GDLM. Memberships: Musicians' Union; Jazz Umbrella. Hobbies: Swimming; Running. Address: 78B Avondale Rise, Peckham, London SE15 4AE, England.

CHRISTIE Lou (Lugee Alfredo Giovanni Sacco), b. 19 Feb 1943, Glenwillard, Pennsylvania, USA. Singer; Songwriter; Producer. .. Francesca Winfield, Nov 1971, 1 son, 1 daughter. Musical Education: Studied voice and classical music, with Miss Joliann Williams, 1957-58; Voice, music arranging/production, with Lennie Martin, 1961-62. Career: Leader, The Crewnecks, 1957-58; The Classics, 1959-60; Lugee and the Lions, 1961-62; Sang backgrounds, Marcy Jo, 1961; Solo artist, 1962-; Concerts: Dick Clark Caravan of Stars, 1963-66; First UK tour, 1966; Tour, UK, Germany, Netherlands, 1969; Record Star Show, Wembley, 1970; Cabaret tour, UK, 1970; NME Poll Winners Concert, Wembley, 1970; Club tour, UK, 1972; Tours, USA, 1981-. Television: American Bandstand, 1963-66; Where The Action Is, 1966; Joey Bishop, 1969; Mike Douglas, 1969; The Dating Game, 1969; Top Of The Pops, 1970; Midnight Special, 1974; Entertainment, 1985; Church Street Station, 1986; Nashville Now, 1989. Recordings: The Gypsy Cried, 1962; Two Faces Have I, 1963; Have I Sinned, 1964; Lightnin' Strikes, 1965; Rhapsody In The Rain, 1966; Painter, 1966; Wild Life's In Season, 1966; Don't Stop Me, 1967; Genesis And The Third Verse, 1968; I'm Gonna Make You Mine, 1969; Beyond The Blue Horizon, 1973; Guardian Angels, 1981; Enlightnin'ment, 1988; Glory River: Buddha Years, 1968-1972, 1992; Beyond The Blue Horizon: More Of the Best Of Lou Christie, 1994; Film soundtracks include: Rain Man, 1988; Dutch, 1990; A Home Of Our Own, 1993; Barcelona, 1994; Before Sunrise. Honours: 4 Gold records (USA); BMI Citation, 1966; 1 Gold (Japan), 1971; BMI Award, 1994. Hobby: Painting. Current Management: Steve Harris, Dartmouth Management, 228 West 71st Street #1E, New York, NY 10023, USA.

CHRISTOFIS Lefteris, b. 5 Oct 1964, Athens, Greece. Musician (guitar); Composer; Orchestrator; Tutor. Education: Lyceum of Athens, Greece. Musical Education: BA Hons, Certificate of Credit, Anglia Polytechnic University; Jazz Improvisation in Philippos Nakas Conservatory; Classical guitar in Hellenic Conservatory. Career: Band leader, guitarist, composer, arranger (original music); Concerts in Athens: Anixis Theatre, Rodon Concert Hall, 1988; Petra Amphitheatre with Al'Taba, 1989; Also performed at Mumford Theatre, 1992; Lefteris Christofis with his Cosmic Band: Swan, Orange Club, London; Palataki, Athens, 1994; Radio broadcasts: Diavlos 10, 1989; JFM London, 1994; Jazz FM, Era 2, Athens, 1995-98; Tutor in Music at the Ars Nova Athina. Recordings: Album: Mythoplasia, 1996. Membership: Musicians' Union (UK). Current Management: Eleni Georgiou. Address: Her. Polytechniou 73A, Dasos Haidariou, Athens 124 62, Greece.

CHUCK D (Carlton Ridenhour), b. 1 Aug 1960, Long Island, New York, USA. Rapper. Education: Graphic Design, Adelphi University. Career: Super Special Mix Show, radio WBAU, 1982; Own mobile DJ and concert promotion company, Spectrum City; Founder member, US rap group, Public Enemy, 1984-; Concerts include: Support to the Beastie Boys, US, 1987; Support to LL Cool J, European tour, 1987; Tour Of A Black Planet, 1990; UK tour, 1990; Apocalypse '91 US tour, with Anthrax, 1991; Headliners, The World's Greatest Rap Show, 1992; Madison Square Garden, 1992; Greenpeace Stop Sellafield concert with U2, Manchester, England, 1992; Reading Festival, England, 1992; Support to U2, Zooropa tour, 1992; Manager, promoter, The Entourage (hip-hop venue), Long Island, New York, 1986. Recordings: Albums: Yo! Bum Rush The Show, 1987; It Takes A Nation Of Millions To Hold Us Back, 1988; Fear Of A Black Planet, 1990; Apocalypse '91 - The Enemy Strikes Back, 1991; Greatest Misses, 1992; Muse Sick'n'Hour Mess Age, 1994; Singles include: Rebel Without A Cause; Bring The Noise; Don't Believe The Hype; Night of The Living Baseheads; Fight The Power,

theme for film Do The Right Thing; 911 Is A Joke; Brothers Gonna Work It Out; Can't Do Nuttin For Ya Man; Can't Truss It; Shut 'Em Down; Nighttrain. Honours include: Platinum discs; Best Rap Group, Rolling Stone Readers Picks awards, 1991; Best Rap Album, Soul Train Music Awards, 1992. Current Management: Malik Entertainment, 3 Third Pl., Roosevelt, NY 11575, USA.

CHURCHLEY Richard Allen, b. 13 Nov 1952, Birmingham, England. Songwriter; Singer; Musician (accordion, guitar, mandolin). m. Prue Dobell, 18 Jan 1975, 2 sons. Education: BA, Honours, German, Reading University, England. Career: Appearances with various bands on Folk and acoustic music circuits including: Harry-Ca-Nab; Peaky Blinders; Barker's Knee; Mind Your Own Business; Oh-Cajunal Playboys; Also radio appearances on local radio and BBC Radio 2. Compositions: Various Folk songs. Recordings include: Mega-Maggot, Harry-Ca-Nab, 1990. Membership: Musicians' Union. Hobby: Cricket. Current Management: Ashtree Agency. Address: 1293 Evesham Road, Astwood Bank, Redditch, Worcestershire B96 6AY, England.

CINGL Pavel, b. 1962, Teplice, Czech Republic. Violinist. m. Katerina, 15 July 1989, 2 sons. Education: Conservatory of Jaroslav Jezek, Prague. Career: Support to Alan Stival in Prague; Tours in Germany, Austria, France, Netherlands, Belgium, Denmark; Regular Czech Television and Radio Appearances. Recordings: 16 records with Czech bands. Honours: Several nominations of Rock & Pop Magazine. Hobby: Travel. Current Management: EXUPERY Art Agency, Krizeneckeho nam 322, 15250 Praha 5, Czech Republic. Address: Podlipneho 7, 180 00 Praha 8, Czech Republic.

CISSOKHO Malang, b. 27 May 1962, Thies, Senegal. Musician (Singing; Kora; Guitar; Bass; Percussion); Singer; Songwriter. m. Pirjo Saastamoinen, 24 November 1989, 1 son. Education: Traditional Musicial Education of Mandinko Griot. Career: Kaustinen Folk Music Festival, 1988, 1989, 1995; Jyvaskyla Summer Festival, 1989; Pori Jazz Festival, 1989, 1996; Joensuu Festival, 1994, 1996; Ruisrock, 1996. Compositions: Mun-Mun, 1982; Warale, 1985; Yendi, 1985; Touba, 1985; Foroya, 1997; Kano, 1997; Alimaton Salia, 1990. Recordings: Solo albums: Lotus, 1990; Foroya, 1997; Dialia, 1997; Contributor: Super Etoile II de Dakar: Náteel Weerwi, Piirpanke: Tuku Tuku; Kristian Blak: Addeq; Rinne Radio: Rok; The Cool Sheiks: Serve Cool, Trance Planet Vol 3; J Karjalainen and Electric Sauna: Electric Sauna; Piirpauke: Metamorphosis. Honour: Emma Award, 1996. Membership: Finnish Musician Association. Address: Haapalahdenkatu 5 G44, 00300 Helsinki, Finland.

CLACKETT Matthew James, b. 24 Aug 1972, Dover, Kent, England. Musician (alto, tenor, soprano saxophone). Musical Education: Double music A levels, classical training to age 16. Career: Numerous session appearances and live concerts include: Roachford; Philip Bent; Peter Maas (Freez). Worked in: USA; Canada; Japan. Recordings: Album: Take One, 1989; Second album due release 1995. Membership: Musicians' Union. Hobbies: Motor racing; Travel. Address: 2 Kew Green, Richmond, Surrey TW9 3BH, England.

CLAPTON Eric (Eric Patrick Clapp), b. 30 Mar 1945, Ripley, Surrey, England. Musician (guitar); Singer; Songwriter. m. Patti Boyd, 1979 (divorced); 1 son (deceased). Career: Guitarist with groups: The Roosters, 1963; The Yardbirds, 1963-65; John Mayall's Bluebreakers, 1965-66; Cream, 1966-68; Blind Faith, 1969; Derek and the Dominoes, 1970; Delaney And Bonnie, 1970-72; Solo artiste, 1972-; Concerts include: Concert for Bangla Desh, 1971; Last Waltz concert, The Band's farewell concert, 1976; Live Aid, 1985;

Record series of 24 concerts, Royal Albert Hall, 1991; Japanese tour with George Harrison, 1991; Film appearance: Tommy, 1974. Compositions include: Presence Of The Lord; Layla; Badge (with George Harrison). Recordings include: Albums: Disraeli Gears, 1967; Wheels Of Fire, 1968; Goodbye Cream, 1969; Layla, 1970; Blind Faith, 1971; Concert For Bangladesh, 1971; Eric Clapton's Rainbow Concert, 1973; 461 Ocean Boulevard, 1974; E C Was Here, 1975; No Reason To Cry, 1976; Slowhand, 1977; Backless, 1978; Just One Night, 1980; Money And Cigarettes, 1983; Behind The Sun, 1985; August, 1986; Journeyman, 1989; 24 Nights, 1992; MTV Unplugged, 1992; From The Cradle, 1994; Soundtracks include: Tommy; The Color Of Money; Lethal Weapon; Rush; Hit singles include: I Shot The Sheriff; Layla; Lay Down Sally; Wonderful Tonight; Cocaine; Behind The Mask; Tears In Heaven; Contributed to numerous albums by artists including: Phil Collins; Bob Dylan; Aretha Franklin; Joe Cocker; Roger Daltrey; Dr John; Rick Danko; Ringo Starr; Roger Waters; Christine McVie; Howlin' Wolf; Sonny Boy Williamson; The Beatles: The White Album (listed as L'Angelo Mysterioso). Numerous honours include: 6 Grammy Awards, 1993; Q Magazine Merit Award, 1995. Current Management: Roger Forrester Management, 18 Harley House, Marylebone Road, Regents Park, London NW1 5HE, England.

CLARIN Bjorn A F, b. 15 December 1936. Songwriter; Composer; CD Producer; Television Scriptwriter. m. Marianne, 26 April 1958, 2 sons, 2 daughters. Education: Piano, Flute, Guitar. Career: Over Five Hundred Appearances Mostly in Childrens Programs. Compositions: Over Sixty Songs with Lyrics by Harry Martinson. Recordings: Twenty Five LP and CD Productions of Popular Swedish Music. Honours: Fred Winter Scholarship; Swedish Scholarship of Music. Address: Hampakersvagen 14, 55 339 Lerum, Sweden.

CLARK Anne, b. 14 May 1960, London, England. Poet; Songwriter; Performer. Musical Education: Piano, violin, viola. Career: 10 albums; Major tours, Europe, North America, 1980-; Co-editor, Paul Weller's Riot Stories. Recordings: 10 albums; Singles: Our Darkness; Sleeper In Metropolis; Abuse. Publications: Hard Lines; Notes Taken, Traces Left. Memberships: PRS; MCPS; GVL. Hobbies: Music; Cinema; Reading; Clubbing. Address: 55 Fulham High Street, London SW6 3JJ, England.

CLARK Charles John, b. 19 Aug 1959, Weaverham, Cheshire, England. Producer; Songwriter; Musician (saxophone, keyboards, percussion). Musical Education: Self-taught. Career: Started playing, 1980; Bands include: Pure Motivation; Restriction; with Mad Professor, numerous concerts include: Glastonbury, 1984; First WOMAD; Supports to: Elephant Fayre; Sugar Minott; Eek-A-Mouse; Aguchi; Smith and Mighty; 3pm; Fresh Four; TCP; Tomorrowland; Piston; Session work while living in San Francisco; Several sessions, BBC Radio 1; Television appearances with Restriction; Presently working with Phiber Records; Member, band Transport. Recordings: Writing, production, remix work includes: Restriction; Album: Call Is Strong, Carlton; Smith and Mighty, singles and remixes; Morgan King; Tomorrowland; Transport. Memberships: Musicians' Union; PRS; PAMRA. Hobbies: Writing; Reading; Talking; Design work; Disco dancing. Current Management: Self-managed. Address: Revelstoke Road, Wimbledon Park, London, England.

CLARK Colin, b. 6 June 1953, Hurstpierpoint, England. Vocalist. Musical Education: Self-taught. Career: Apperances on Meridian Television Pier Programme BBC Radio Sussex; Radio Kent; Radio BBC World Service; Radio Huset, Denmark; Mercury; Radio West Point, Denmark, Belgium. Compositions: Black

Train; Trail Of Tears; You Hold The Key To My Heart. Recordings: Songs on forthcoming album: Standing On The Edge Of Lonely; That Numbers Been Changed; You Haunt The Shadows Of My Mind; This Old Honky Tonk; I'm Outta Here; Black Train; Special Kind Of Lady; The Price For Loving You; Boogie Woogie Thang; It's Time I Settled Down. Membership: British Country Music Association. Current Management: Self-managed. Address: c/o Frank Fara, Comstock Records, 10603 N Hayden Road, Suite 114, Scottsdale, AZ 85260, USA.

CLARK Graeme, b. 15 Apr 1966, Glasgow, Scotland. Musician (bass). Career: Member, Wet Wet Wet, 1982-; Performances include: Greenpeace charity concert, Royal Albert Hall, 1986; Support to Lionel Richie, UK tour, 1987; Prince's Trust Rock Gala, Royal Albert Hall, 1988-90; John Lennon Tribute Concert, Merseyside, 1990; Edinburgh Castle, 1992; Live At The Royal Albert Hall 1992, 1993. Recordings: Albums: Popped In Souled Out, 1987; Sgt Pepper Knew My Father, 1988; The Memphis Sessions, 1988; High On The Happy Side, 1992; Wet Wet Wet Live At The Royal Albert Hall, 1993; End Of Part One (Their Greatest Hits), 1993; Picture This, 1995; Singles include: Wishing I Was Lucky, 1987; Angel Eyes (Home And Away), 1988; With A Little Help From My Friends (Number 1, UK), 1988; Temptation, 1988; Sweet Surrender, 1989; Hold Back The River, 1990; Stay With Me Heartache, 1990; Goodnight Girl (Number 1, UK), 1992; More Than Love, 1992; Lip Service, 1992; Shed A Tear, 1993; Love Is All Around (Number 1, UK), 1994; She's All On My Mind, 1995; Julia Said, 1995. Honours include: BRIT Award: Best British Newcomer, 1988. Current Management: The Precious Organisation, The Townhouse, 1 Park Gate, Glasgow G3 6DL, Scotland.

CLARK Guy, b. 6 Nov 1941, Rockport, Texas, USA. Singer; Songwriter. Career: Former photographer; Guest singer, artists including: Emmylou Harris; Rodney Crowell; Steve Earle; Jerry Jeff Walker; Hoyt Axton; Waylon Jennings; Don Everly; Gordon Payne; KT Oslin; Rosanne Cash; Vince Gill; Recent concerts include Cambridge Folk Festival, 1995. Compositions include: LA Freeway, Jerry Jeff Walker; Desperados Waiting For A Train, Tom Rush; Texas 1947, Johnny Cash; The Last Gunfighter Ballad; Virginia's Real; Heartbroke, Ricky Skaggs; Co-writer with Rodney Crowell: The Partner Nobody Chose; She's Crazy For Leavin'. Recordings: Old No 1, 1975; Texas Cookin', 1976; Guy Clark, 1978; The South Coast Of Texas, 1981; Better Days, 1983; Old Friends, 1989. Current Management: Side One Management, 1026a Third Avenue, New York, NY 10021, USA.

CLARK Lenny, b. 3 Mar 1958, Blackmoor, Hampshire, England. Country Singer; Musician (guitar). Harmony Vocalist. Musical Education: Self-taught. Career: Appeared with many of Britain's country bands; Guest on several albums; Backed many visiting artistes from USA; Toured Europe and Far East; Featured on CMR and radio stations nationwide; Currently fronting his 5-piece band, Preacher. Recordings include: Dyin' Ain't Much Of A Living; Preacher. Hobbies: Radio ham (A.Licence); Golf; Photography. Address: 163 Crayford Way, Crayford, Kent DA1 4LG, England.

CLARK Nicholas, b. 13 Apr 1963, Gillingham, Kent, England. Musician (guitar). Education: OND, HND, Business Studies. Musical Education: Guitar Institute, Intermediate. Career: Bands, including sessions: Konstructivitis; Talkies; Elliot Lewis Band; Bazooka Joe. Recordings: Session: Black December, Konstructivitis. Membership: Musicians' Union. Hobbies: Music; Recording. Address: 45 Hazelwood Drive, Maidstone, Kent ME16 0EA, England.

CLARK Petula (Sally Olwen), b. 15 Nov 1934, Epsom, Surrey, England. Singer; Actress.

m. Claude Wolff, 1961, 1 son, 2 daughters. Musical Education: Taught to sing by mother. Career: Stage and screen actress, aged 7; Own radio programme, 1943; Numerous film appearances, 1944-; Films include: Medal For The General, 1944; Here Come The Huggetts, 1948; Finian's Rainbow, 1968; Goodbye Mr Chips, 1969; Stage appearances include: Sound Of Music, 1981; Someone Like You (also writer), 1989; Blood Brothers, Broadway, 1993-; Host, own BBC television series; US television special Petula, NBC, 1968; Solo singing career, 1964-; Sold over 30 million records to date. Recordings: Hit singles include: Ya-Ya Twist, 1960; Downtown (Number 1, US and throughout Europe), 1964; The Other Man's Grass; My Love; I Know A Place; Don't Sleep In The Subway; This Is My Song; Albums: Petula Clark Sings, 1956; A Date With Pet, 1956; You Are My Lucky Star, 1957; Pet Clark, 1959; Petula Clark In Hollywood, 1959; In Other Words, 1962; Petula, 1962; Les James Dean, 1962; Downtown, 1964; I Know A Place, 1965; The New Petula Clark Album, 1965; Uptown With Petula Clark, 1965; In Love, 1966; Hello Paris, Vols I and II, 1966; I Couldn't Live Without Your Love, 1966; Hit Parade, 1967; The Other Man's Grass Is Always Greener, 1968; Petula, 1968; Portrait Of Petula, 1969; Just Pet, 1969; Memphis, 1970; The Song Of My Life, 1971; Warm And Tender, 1971; Live At The Royal Albert Hall, 1972; Now, 1972; Live In London, 1974; Come On Home, 1974. Honours include: 2 Grammy Awards; Grand Prix Du Disque, 1960; More Gold discs than any other UK female artist. Current Management: John Ashby, Hindworth Management Ltd., 235 Regent Street, London W1R 7AG, England.

CLARK Roy Linwood, b. 15 Apr 1933, Meherrin, Virginia, USA. Singer; Songwriter; Musician (guitar, banjo, mandolin). Career: Winner, National Banjo Championship, aged 16; Former professional boxer; Radio appearances include: Ozark Jubilee; Town And Country Time; Television: Guest, Country Style (Washington TV show), 1955; Host of show, early 60s; Actor, The Beverly Hillbillies; Host, television series Swingin' Country; Co-host, Hee Haw, CBS, 1969-; Lead guitarist, Wanda Jackson; Concerts include: Russia, 1976; Concert with Boston Pops Orchestra, 1976; Carnegie Hall, 1977; Film appearances include: Uphill All The Way, 1986; Member, Grand Ole Opry, 1987-; Later involvement in ranching, publishing, advertising, property. Recordings: Albums include: The Lightning Fingers Of Roy Clark, 1962; The Tip Of My Fingers, 1963; Happy To Be Unhappy, 1964; Guitar Spectacular, 1965; Sings Lonesome Love Ballads, 1966; Stingin' Along With The Blues, 1966; Roy Clark, 1966; Live, 1967; Do You Believe This Roy Clark, 1968; In The Mood, 1968; Urban, Suburban, 1968; Yesterday When I Was Young, 1969; The Everlovin' Soul Of Roy Clark, 1969; The Other Side Of Roy Clark, 1970; I Never Picked Cotton, 1970; The Magnificent Sanctuary Band, 1971; The Incredible Roy Clark, 1971; Roy Clark Country!, 1972; Family Album, 1973; Superpicker, 1973; Come Live With Me, 1973; Family And Friends, 1974; The Entertainer, 1974; Roy Clark, 1974; So Much To Remember, 1975; Heart To Heart, 1975; In Concert, 1976; Hookin' It, 1977; My Music And Me, 1977; Labour Of Love, 1978. Honours: CMA Awards: Instrumentalist Of The Year, 1977, 1978, 1980. Address: Roy Clark Productions, 3225 South Norwood, Tulsa, OK 74135, USA.

CLARK Terri, b. 5 Aug 1968, Montreal, Quebec, Canada. Singer; Songwriter; Musician. Career: Tour with George Strait, played dates with Clay Walker and Aaron Tippin, 1994; Performed on Prime Time Country; Recorded At The Ryman; Played on the Grand Ole Opry, 1994; Tour with George Strait, 1996; Tours played to over 1 1/2 million people, 1996; Appearing in Primestar Presents Clay Walker's Four Star Blowout Tour, 1997; Featured Artist, Calgary Stampede; Tours throughout Canada, 1997. Recordings: Better

Things To Do; When Boy Meets Girl; If I Were You; Suddenly Single; Poor Poor Pitiful Me; Emotional Girl; Just the Same; Albums: Terri Clark; Just the Same. Honours: Numerous including: Billboard Music Award, Top New Female Artist, 1995; Nominated Best New Female Vocalist, Academy of Country Music, 1996; Best Female Vocalist, Big Country Awards, 1997; Three Awards, Canadian Country Music Association Awards, 1997. Memberships: AFofM; Broadcast Music Inc; Country Music Association; Academy of Country Music. Hobbies: Working out, physical training. Current Management: Woody Bowles, Woody Bowles Management, 1114 17th Avenue South, Nashville, TN 37212, USA. Address: 5420 Camelot Road, Brentwood, TN 37027, USA.

CLARK W.C., b. 16 Nov 1939, Austin, Texas, USA. Singer; Songwriter; Musician (guitar). 1 son, 1 daughter. Career: Toured with Joe Tex Band, 1960s; Member, Southern Feeling, with Angela Strehli, Denny Freeman; Worked on Triple Threat Revue, with Stevie Ray Vaughan, Lou Ann Barton, Mike Kindred; Support tours to B.B. King; Bobby Bland; Also performed with Albert Collins; Buddy Guy; Johnny Taylor; Lowell Fulsom; Joe Turner; Lou Rawls; Brooks Benton; Freddie King; Alvin Bishop; George Thorogood; James Brown; Matt Murphy; Jimmie Vaughan; Clarence Holliman; Carol Fran; Appeared on Austin City Limits, 1990. Recordings include: Something For Everybody, 1987; Heart Of Gold, 1994; Texas Soul, 1996. Honours: Austin Chronicle Music Awards: Best Blues Band, Best Soul Band; Inducted into Texas Music Hall Of Fame, 1990; W C Handy Award, Best Blues/Soul Album, 1997. Membership: BMI. Current Management: Vicky Gay Moerbe, Crossfire Productions, 1209 Baylor, Austin, Texas, USA.

CLARKE David Roger, b. 28 Jan 1948, Essex, England. Musician (guitar, keyboards); Songwriter; Record Company Owner. m. Patricia, 16 Dec 1966, 1 son, 1 daughter. Education: BSc, MSc, Mathematics. Musical Education: Piano. Career: Joined Sapphires aged 13, 1961; Band renamed Blue Angels, 1963; Major USA, European tours, television appearances, 1975-78; Joined Royal Navy, active service Falkland Islands war, HMS Fearless, retired as Commander, 1979-92; Formed Mouse Records, 1993; Tours: Scandinavia; Germany; New Zealand, 1993-94; Lead vocalist, guitarist, keyboards, principal songwriter, producer on majority of recordings. Recordings: 2 singles as Danny Clyve and the Blue Angels, 1964; Album as Dave Carlsen: Pale Horse, 1974; Lead vocals, as Chester Baynes, hit single, 1972; Producer, Gaylords single: Hit Me With Music, 1974; with Noel Redding Band: 2 singles, 2 albums, 1975-76; Album, 1994; with Jimmy McCulloch and White Line, 2 singles, 1976, album, 1994; Album as Frigate, 1981; 4 releases as Shut Up Frank, with members of: The Kinks; The Animals; Jimi Hendrix Experience, 1993-97; Dream Machine album, 1995. Memberships: PRS; MCPS; PPL; BASCA; PAMRA; Institute of Management. Hobby: Music. Current Management: Mouse Records. Address: 28 Breamore Road, Seven Kings, Essex IG3 9NB, England.

CLARKE Fast Eddie, b. 5 Oct 1950, Isleworth, Middlesex, England. Rock Musician (guitar). Career: Guitarist, Continuous Performance; Guitarist, blues band, Curtis Knight; Guitarist, UK heavy rock group Motörhead, 1976-82; Support to Hawkwind, UK 1977; UK tours, 1978-80; Heavy Metal Barn Dance, Stafford, UK, 1980; Co-founder, Fastway (with Pete Way), 1982-. Recordings: Albums: with Motörhead: Motörhead, 1977; Overkill, 1979; Bomber, 1979; Ace Of Spades, 1980; No Sleep 'Til Hammersmith (Number 1, UK), 1981; Iron Fist, 1982; with Fastway: Fastway, 1983; All Fired Up, 1984; Waiting For The Roar, 1986; The World Waits For You, 1986; Trick Or Treat, 1987; On Target, 1988;

Bad Bad Girls, 1989; Singles: with Motörhead include: Louie Louie; Bomber; No Class; Motörhead; Overkill; Ace Of Spades; Iron Fist; The Golden Years EP; Beer Drinkers And Hell Raisers EP; St Valentine's Day Massacre EP (with Girlschool).

CLARKE George Albert Edward, b. 26 June 1949, Bradford, West Yorkshire, England. Photographer; Musician (guitar); Singer. m. Ann Clarke, seperated, 1 daughter. Musical Education: Night School, Self-taught. Career: Based in West Riding Folk Roots Scene; Performed Mummers plays, including Leeds Folk Festival, 1983; Roadie for band: Iona, concerts: Germany, Italy, tour for Folk Italia, 1983; European tours with Dab Hand; Performed, Dordrechts, shanty festival, 1987; Festivals: Wakefield; Snape; Usually solo, also partnerships: Chris Nelson, accordionist, banjo player; Brian Whitmee, formed West Riding Night Visitors Revivalist Society; Tours with musicians including: Tom McConnville; Gordon Tyrall; Tom Napper; Tony Wilson; Rob Van Sante; Performances throughout England, Scotland, Europe; Traditional, contemporary songs, monologues, humour; Distributor of the Tykes News; Regular contributor, BBC's Folk On The Night Network Radio Programme; Based at Radio Leeds. Recordings: Miners Monday; Suburban Railway Station. Publication: Tykes News. Membership: Musicians' Union. Hobbies: Picture Framing; Tykes News distribution. Current Management: George Clarke. Address: 42 Whitecote Rise, Bramley, Leeds LS13 3LD, England.

CLARKE Herbie, b. 19 Mar 1952, Trinidad. Record Producer; Musician (guitar). 2 sons. Musical Education: Studied classical guitar for 4 years. Career: Guitarist, several pub rock bands including: Mossa; Rednite; Founder, Free Booze Records an indie label, now producing records under same name. Recordings: African Chant; Hit The Floor. Memberships: Musicians' Union; International Managers Forum; PRS; BASCA. Hobbies: Judo; Karate. Address: 39 Birnam Road, Islington, London N4 3LJ, England.

CLARKE Kim Annette, b. 14 Nov 1954, New York, USA. Musician (bass). Education: BA, Communications, CUNY, 1978. Musical Education: BA, Music, Long Island University, 1990. Career: Freelance musician, 1978-; Bass player, Yusef Lateef Quartet; Defunkt; Lester Bowie's Brass Fantasy; George Gruntz; Joe Henderson Quartet; Kit McLure; Also played with: Billy Taylor; Art Blakey; Lionel Hampton; Sarah Vaughn; Branford Marsalis; Betty Carter; Mike Manieri; Robert Palmer.

CLARKE Kory, b. USA. Rock Vocalist; Songwriter. Career: Vocalist, lyricist, US heavy rock group Warrior Soul, 1988-; Tours and concerts include: Support to Metallica, European tour, 1990; Support to Queensryche, Empire tour, 1991; European tour, 1993; UK and European tours, 1995; European festivals, 1995. Recordings: Albums: Last Decade, Dead Century, 1989; Drugs God And The New Republic, 1991; Salutations From A Ghetto Nation, 1992; Chill Pill, 1994; Space Age Playboys, 1995. Current Management: Q-Prime Inc., 729 7th Avenue, 14th Floor, New York, NY 10019, USA.

CLARKE Paul Frazer, b. 25 Sept 1962, Leicester, England. Songwriter; Producer; Musician (keyboards, drums, guitar). Education: Wyggeston Queen Elizabeth I College, Leicester. Career: Recording artist (Epic), UK tours, 1987; with November One, London's Burning (LWT film/series), 1988; Writer, Warner Chappell, 1987-1991; Co-writes with/for Glenn Nightingale; Angie Brown; Rick Astley; Other television appearances include: Rock Goes To College, BBC TV; Wide Awake Club, ITV; Hit Man And Her, LWT. Recordings: Albums: Deja Vu, Magna Charta; Quest For Intelligence, Fast Floor.

Memberships: PRS; MCPS. Hobbies: Football; Cricket; Walking. Current Management: c/o Christian Ulf-Hansen, BMI. Address: 79 Harley House, Marylebone Road, London, England.

CLARKE Sharon D, b. 28 May 1965, London, England. Actress;Vocalist. Career: Performances: First British actress to play The Voice Of Audrey II in The Little Shop Of Horrors, London Bubble Theatre, Leicester Haymarket; The Singing Detective, Dennis Potter, BBC TV; 6 appearances, Top Of The Pops, with Nomad; Guest presenter DJ, Saturday Morning Mayhem; Sunset Radio, Manchester; Princess Of Wales Birthright Charity Trust; Lead vocalist, Royal Albert Hall; Lead vocalist, Stonewall Concert, Royal Albert Hall, 1995; Played opposite Chaka Khan, Mama I Want To Sing, Mama Winter, Cambridge Theatre, London. Recordings: I Wanna Give You (Devotion), Nomad (Number 2, UK charts; Worldwide Number 1 club hit); Happiness, Serious Rope (Number 1 club hit, UK). Honours: Nominations: Manchester Evening News, Best Supporting Performer, A Taste Of Honey, 1989; Laurence Olivier Awards, Best Supporting Performer in a Musical, Once On This Island, 1995. Membership: Equity. Address: 102 Ranelagh Road, Tottenham, London, England.

CLARKE Simon C, b. 9 May 1955, Sheffield, South Yorkshire, England. Arranger; Musician (baritone, tenor, alto, flute, piccolo saxophones). m. Helen Sykes, 20 Aug 1988. Education: BA Hons, York University. Musical Education: Serious flute playing to age 21, switched to saxophone. Career: Tours with Pete Townshend's Deep End, 1985; The Who, 1989-90; The Waterboys, 1990; Eric Clapton, 1993-1995. Hobbies: Marathon running; Claret drinking. Current Management: Self-managed.

CLARKE Stanley, b. 21 July 1951, Philadelphia, Pennsylvania, USA. Musician (bass). Musical Education: Philadelphia Musical Academy. Career: Member, various funk groups; Played jazz with Horace Silver; Joe Henderson; Pharoah Sanders; Chick Corea and Return To Forever Band; Partnership with George Duke. Recordings: Albums: Stanley Clarke, 1974; Journey To Love, 1975; School Days, 1976; Modern Man, 1978; I Wanna Play For You, 1979; Rocks Pebbles And Sand, 1980; Time Exposure, 1984; Find Out, 1985; Hideaway, 1986; Shieldstone, 1987; If This Bass Could Only Talk, 1988; with Pharoah Sanders: Black Unity, 1972; with George Duke: The Clarke/Duke Project, 1981; The Clarke/Duke Project II, 1983; 3, 1990; with Return To Forever: Return To Forever, 1972; with Aziza Mustafa Zadeh: Dance Of Fire, 1995; with Al DiMeola, Jean-Luc Ponty: The Rite Of Strings, 1995. Address: c/o Baker, Winokur, Ryder Public Relations, 405 S. Beverly Drive, 5th Floor, Beverly Hills, CA 90212, USA.

CLARKE Vince, b. 3 July 1960, Basildon, Essex, England. Musician (keyboards, synthesizers); Songwriter. Career: Musician, groups: No Romance In China; Depeche Mode, 1980-81; Yazoo (with Alison Moyet), 1982-83; Erasure (with Andy Bell), 1985-; Support to Duran Duran, US tour, 1987; US tour, 1988; Prince's Trust Rock Gala, Birmingham, 1989. Recordings: Albums: with Depeche Mode: Speak And Spell, 1981; with Yazoo: Upstairs At Eric's, 1982; You And Me Both (Number 1, UK), 1983; with Erasure: Wonderland, 1986; The Circus, 1987; Two Ring Circus, 1987; The Innocents, 1988; Wild!, 1989; Chorus, 1991; Pop! - The First 20 Hits, 1992; I Say I Say I Say, 1994; Erasure, 1995; Singles: with Depeche Mode: New Life, 1981; Just Can't Get Enough, 1981; with Yazoo: Only You, 1982; Don't Go, 1982; The Other Side Of Love, 1983; Nobody's Diary, 1983; with Erasure: Sometimes, 1986; It Doesn't Have To Be, 1987; Ship Of Fools, 1988; Chains Of Love, 1988; A Little Respect, 1988; Drama!, 1989; Blue Savannah, 1990; Chorus, 1991; Love To Hate You, 1991; Breath Of

Life, 1992; Abba-esque EP (Number 1, UK), 1992; Who Needs Love (Like That) remix, 1992; Stay With Me, 1995; Contributor, Red Hot And Blue, AIDS benefit album, 1990; Tame Yourself, animal rights benefit album, 1991. Honours: BRIT Awards: Best British Newcomer, Yazoo, 1983; Best British Group, Erasure, 1989; Ivor Novello Award, Most Performed Work of 1990, Blue Savannah, 1991. Address: c/o Mute Records, 429 Harrow Road, London W10 4RE, England.

CLARKIN Tony. Musician (guitar); Songwriter. Career: Founder member, guitarist, UK rock group Magnum, 1972-; Regular tours include support tours with Judas Priest; Whitesnake; Blue Öyster Cult; Def Leppard; Own headline tours worldwide. Recordings: Albums: Kingdom Of Madness, 1978; Magnum II, 1979; Maurauder, 1980; Chase The Dragon, 1982; The Eleventh Hour, 1983; On A Storyteller's Night, 1985; Vigilante, 1986; Wings Of Heaven, 1988; Goodnight LA, 1990; The Spirit, 1991; Rock Art, 1994; Numerous compilation albums; Singles include: Just Like An Arrow; Days Of No Trust; Rocking Chair; Start Talking Love; It Must Have Been Love; Kingdom Of Madness; On A Storyteller's Night; Midnight.

CLARKSON Ian Christopher, b. 7 May 1964, Ormskirk, Scotland. Musician (trumpet); Vocalist. m. Grazia Bevilacqua, 29 Dec 1993. Musical Education: Self-taught. Career: Front man, vocalist and trumpet, with the Jive Aces; Prior to That, Aces Of Rhythm, The Emperors of Rhythm; Television: Opportunity Knocks, BBC; Monte Carlo TV; Kenny Live RTE (Dublin); Concerts: Royal Albert Hall; Theatre Royal; Many many European tours, at least 250 gigs per year. Compositions: Blues 4 U; Still. Recordings: Album: Jumping With The Aces; Single: Blues 4 U/Heybarberebop. Hobbies: Sports; Films; Dianetics; Spiritual philosophy. Current Management: Jive Aces. Address: St Hill Manor, East Grinstead, West Sussex, England.

CLASTRIER Valentin, b. 14 Feb 1947, Nice, France. Musician. Musical Education: Classical guitar; Singing. Career: Guitar player with Jacques Brel, 1968-69; Guitar, Ricet Barrier, 1975-82; Composer for Hurdy Gurdy (acoustic, electro-acoustic), 1970-; Hurdy Gurdy teacher in training course, Master class, France and abroad. Recordings: Vielle à Roue de l'Imaginaire, 1984; Esprit de la Nuit, 1986; Grands Maîtres de la Vielle à Roue, 1988; Hérésie, 1992; Le Bûcher des Silences, 1994; Palude, 1995. Publication: Anthology For Hurdy Gurdy, 1985. Honours: Chevalier dans L'Ordre des Arts et des Lettres; Grand Prix de l'Académie Charles Cros; Grand Prix Audiovisuel de l'Europe. Address: Gué de la Pierre, 18380 Ennordres, France.

CLAUSEN Thomas, b. 5 Oct 1949, Copenhagen, Denmark. Composer; Musician (piano, keyboards). m. Pi Sveistrup, divorced, 2 daughters. Musical Education: Private lessons; 3 years, Royal Conservatory, Copenhagen. Career: Musician for Dexter Gordon; Palle Mikkelborg; Ben Webster; Jan Garbarek; Leader, own groups 1978-, including Mirror, quartet; Own trio, with NHOP, 1980-83; Trio with Mads Vinding and Alex Riel, 1987-. Compositions: Prism, 1975; Sonata for Oboe, Cello, Harp, 1989; Woods And Lakes, 1993. Recordings: Mirror, 1979; Rain, 1980; The Shadow Of Bill Evans, 1983; She Touched Me, 1988; Piano Music, 1989; Café Noir, 1990; Flowers And Trees, 1991; Psalm, 1995. Honours: Ben Webster Prize, 1989; JASA Prize, 1990; Danish Grammy, 1991. Memberships: KODA; NCB; DJFBA. Hobbies: Family; Nature; Films; Theatre. Address: Rastestedet 5, DK-3500 Værlose, Denmark.

CLAXTON Andrew, b. 22 Jan 1950, London, England. Composer; Musician (keyboards, brass). Musical Education: National Youth Orchestra of Great Britain, 1966-67; Royal Academy of Music

(GRSM, LRAM), 1968-72; University of Reading (ARCM, MMus), 1984-85. Career: Freelance instrumentalist, 1970-; Keyboards/brass in Dead Can Dance, 1987-93; International tour, 1993; Director of Peacock Epoch, 1987-; Regional Contemporary Music Circuit tour, 1988. Compositions: Music for TV, theatre and dance, 1980-; Scores for TV series: Fragile Earth, Dispatches, Secret History, Horizon. Recordings: Albums with Dead Can Dance: Within The Realm Of A Dying Sun, 1987; Toward The Within, 1994; Album with Lisa Gerrard: The Mirror Pool, 1995; Single, with Lisa Gerrard, Sanvean, 1995. Publications: Tuba Technique, University of Reading, 1986. Membership: PCAM. Hobbies: Swimming; Cooking. Current Management: Wendy Gardner, 20 Ladder Hill, Wheatley, Oxon OX33 1SX, England.

CLAYDERMAN Richard (Philippe Pages), b. 1954, Paris, France. Musician (piano); Composer. Musical Education: Paris Conservatory. Career: Former bank clerk; Became successful performer and rcording artist; Played with French pop stars including Johnny Halliday; Michel Sardou; Top album seller, France, South Africa, Japan, early 1980s; Sellout UK concerts, 1982; Numerous television appearances; Concerts include: Japan; Brazil; Australia. Recordings: Albums: Ballade Pour Adeline (The Love Song), 1981; Dreaming (Traumereien), 1981; Dreaming (Traumereien), 3, 1981; Richard Clayderman, 1982; A Comme Amour, 1982; Lettre A Ma Mere, 1982; Musiques De L'Amour, 1982; The Music Of Richard Clayderman, 1983; A Pleyel, 1983; Marriage of Love, 1984; The Music Of Love, 1984; Christmas, 1984; The Classic Touch (with The Royal Philharmonic), 1985; Hollywood And Broadway, 1986; Songs Of Love, 1987; A Little Night Music, 1988; Eleana, 1988; The Love Songs Of Andrew Lloyd Webber, 1989; Together At Last, 1991. Current Management: Gurtman & Mutha Associates, 450 7th Avenue, #603, New York, NY 10123-10101, USA.

CLAYSON Alan, b. 3 May 1951, Dover, Kent, England. Composer; Author; Musician (keyboards; guitar); Vocalist. m. Inese Pommers, 31 July 1979, 2 sons, 1 daughter. Education: Farnborough Technical College; University of Reading. Musical Education: GCE O-Level Music; Otherwise self-taught. Career: Member, Turnpike, 1971-74; Average Joe and the Men in the Street, 1974-75; Billy And The Conquerors, 1972-75; Portsmouth Sinfonia, viola, 1975; Clayson And The Argonauts, 1975-86; Toured UK, Europe, BBC Radio In Concert show, 1977; Solo performer, 1985-; USA debut, 1992; Worked with: Wreckless Eric; Twinkle; Screaming Lord Sutch; Dave Berry's Cruisers. Compositions include: Moonlight Skater with Jim McCarty for Dave Berry and Stairway's Raindreaming album; Sol Nova, 1985; The Landlocked Sailor, for Poacher's Pocket, 1992; Man of the Moment, 1995; Angelette, 1997. Recordings: with The Argonauts: Single, The Taster, 1978; Last Respects (EP), 1982; Album, What A Difference A Decade Made, 1985; Producer, main songwriter, Dave Berry album Hostage To The Beat, 1986; 2 tracks, compilation album Beat Merchants, 1995; Album, Soiree, 1997. Publications: Books: Call Up The Groups! The Golden Age Of British Beat, 1985; Back In The High Life - A Biography of Steve Winwood, 1988; Only The Lonely - The Life And Artistic Legacy Of Roy Orbison, 1989; The Quiet One - A Life Of George Harrison, 1990; Ringo Starr - Straight Man Or Joker, 1991; Death Discs, 1992; Backbeat, with Pauline Sutcliffe, 1994; Aspects Of Elvis (edit) with Spencer Leigh, 1994; Beat Merchants, 1995; Jacques Brel, 1996; Hamburg: The Cradle of British Rock, 1997; Articles for: Record Collector; The Times; Goldmine; Medieval World; The Independent; Folk Roots; Country Music People; Mojo; The Beat Goes On; Gold; The 'Schoolkids' Oz; Discoveries. Membership: PRS. Hobbies: Swimming; Animal welfare; Calligraphy. Address: 18 South Street,

Caversham, Berkshire RG4 8HY, England.

CLAYTON Adam, b. 13 Mar 1960, Chinnor, Oxfordshire, England. Musician (bass). Career: Founder member, bass player, rock group U2, 1978-; Regular national and worldwide tours; Major concerts include: US Festival, 1983; The Longest Day, Milton Keynes, 1985; Live Aid, Wembley, 1985; Self Aid, Dublin, 1986; A Conspiracy Of Hope (Amnesty International Tour), 1986; Smile Jamaica, 1988; Very Special Arts Festival, Washington, 1988; New Year's Eve concert, Dublin (broadcast live to Europe), 1989; Yankee Stadium, New York (second-ever concert there), 1992. Recordings: Albums: Boy, 1980; October, 1981; War (Number 1, UK), 1983; Under A Blood Red Sky, 1983; The Unforgettable Fire (Number 1, UK), 1984; Wide Awake In America, 1985; The Joshua Tree (Number 1, US and UK), 1987; Rattle And Hum, also film (Number 1, US), 1988; Achtung Baby (Number 1, US), 1991; Zooropa (Number 1, UK and US), 1993; Passengers film soundtrack (with Brian Eno), 1995; Pop, 1997; Hit singles include: Out Of Control (Number 1, Ireland), 1979; Another Day (Number 1, Ireland), 1980; New Year's Day, 1983; Two Hearts Beat As One, 1983; Pride (In The Name Of Love), 1984; The Unforgettable Fire, 1985; With Or Without You (Number 1, US), 1987; I Still Haven't Found What I'm Looking For (Number 1, US), 1987; Where The Streets Have No Name, 1987; Desire (Number 1, UK), 1988; Angel Of Harlem, 1988; When Love Comes To Town, with B.B.King, 1989; The Fly (Number 1, UK), 1991; Mysterious Ways, 1992; Even Better Than The Real Thing, 1992; Who's Gonna Ride Your Wild Horses, 1992; Hold Me, Thrill Me, Kiss Me (from film Batman Forever), 1995; Discotheque, 1997; If God Will Send His Angels, 1997. Honours include: Grammy awards: Album Of The Year, 1987; Best Rock Performance, 1987, 1989; Best Rock Vocal, 1993; BRIT Awards: Best International Act, 1988-90; Best Live Album, 1993; World Music Award, 1993; Q Awards: Best Act In The World, 1990, 1992, 1993; Merit Award, 1994; Juno Award, 1993; Gold and Platinum discs. Current Management: Principle Management, 30-32 Sir John Rogersons Quay, Dublin 2, Ireland.

CLAYTON Eddy, b. 6 May 1931, Watford, Hertfordshire, England. Musician (drums); Bandleader. m. Margaret Clayton, 20 Mar 1953, 1 son. Musical Education: Studied with Charles Botterill (drummer with Mantovani). Career: Formed own band at age 14; Member, RAF Skyliners Dance Band, 1949-51; Leader of own Big Band, 1950's-1960's; Currently leader of own quartet performing mainly dance music and jazz. Memberships: Branch Secretary, Jazz Committee Delegate, Vice Chair of District Council, Musicians' Union; ABJM; Film Artists Association. Hobbies: Cars; Caravans. Current Management: Margaret Clayton. Address: Rainbow House, 3 Goodwood Avenue, Watford, Hertfordshire WD2 5LA, England.

CLAYTON Vince, b. 23 July 1942, Clayton, Doncaster, England. Country Singer; Musician (guitar). m. Margaret Neasham, 14 Dec 1963, 2 sons, 1 daughter. Musical Education: Guitar; 3 Grades certificate Piano. Career: Live performance, Radio Hallam; With Pat and Roger Johns, Radio Viking; Radio Humberside. Recordings: My Elusive Dreams; Thirty Nine and Holding; On Pat and Roger John's Country Friends, volume 3. Hobby: Family. Current Management: Self-managed. Address: 48 Briton Street, Thurnscoe, Rotherham, South Yorkshire S63 0HR, England.

CLAYTON-THOMAS David (Thomsett), b. 13 Sept 1941, Surrey, England. Vocalist. Career: Vocalist, Blood Sweat and Tears, 1969-; Performances include: Newport Jazz Festival, 1969; Atlanta Pop Festival, 1969; US State Department sponsored tour, Eastern Europe, 1970; US tour, 1992; Le Festival Les Heros Sont

Immortals, Calais, France; 2 reunion concerts, New York. Recordings: Albums include: with Blood Sweat And Tears: Blood, Sweat & Tears (Number 1, US), 1969; Blood, Sweat And Tears 3 (Number 1, US), 1970; B, S And T - 4, 1971; Mirror Image, 1974; Brand New Day, 1977; Nuclear Blues, 1980; Solo albums: David Clayton-Thomas, 1972; Tequila Sunrise, 1972; Harmony Junction; Singles include: You've Made Me So Very Happy, 1969; Spinning Wheel, 1969; And When I Die, 1969; Hi-De-Ho, 1970; Music for film The Owl And The Pussycat, 1971. Honours: Grammy Awards: Best Album, Best Contemporary Instrumental Performnce, 1970.

CLEGG Johnny, b. 13 July 1953, Rochdale, Lancashire, England. Vocalist; Composer. Education: Social Anthropology, Wits University, South Africa. Career: Moved to South Africa, 1959; Duo, Johnny and Sipho (with Sipho Mchunu), 1972; Founder, sextet Juluka, 1976-85; Tours, UK, Europe and US; Leader, Savuka, 1986; Tours, South Africa and overseas. Recordings: Albums: with Juluka: Universal Men, 1979; African Litany, 1981; Ulshule Bemvelo, 1982; Scatterlings Of Africa, 1982; Work For All, 1983; Musa Ukungilandela, 1984; The Hope Concerts, 1985; Solo: Johnny Clegg Third World Child, 1986; with Savuka: Savuka, 1987; Freedom, 1989; Heat Dust And Dreams, 1993; Hit single: Woza Friday, Juluka, 1978. Current Management: HR Music, 6430 Sunset Blvd, Los Angeles, CA 90028, USA.

CLEMONS Clarence, b. 1 Nov 1942, Norfolk, Virginia, USA. Musician (saxophone) Entertainer. 3 sons. Education: University of Maryland. Musical Education: Music minor, University of Maryland. Career: Member, groups including Bruce Springsteen and E Street Band; Television: Numerous talk shows including David Letterman; Concerts include: Amnesty International tour; Leader, own group West Coast Red Bank Rockers; Films: New York New York; Bill and Ted's Excellent Adventure. Recordings: Solo albums: Rescue, 1981; Night With Mr C, 1983; Hero, 1985; Adventure; Peacemaker, 1995; Get It On, 1995; Peace makers, 1995; Albums with Bruce Springsteen include: Greetings From Astbury Park, 1973; The Wild, The Willing And The E-Street Shuffle, 1973; Born To Run, 1975; Darkness On The Edge Of Town, 1978; The River, 1980; Born In The USA, 1984; Tunnel Of Love, 1987. Honours: Bay Area Music Awards: Outstanding Reed Player, 6 times winner. Membership: Musicians' Union. Hobbies: Fishing; Golf. Current Management: Alan Niven.

CLEVELAND Ashley Alexander, b. 2 Feb 1957, Knoxville, Tennessee, USA. Vocalist; Musician (guitar); Songwriter. m. Kenny Greenberg, 27 Apr 1991, 1 son, 2 daughters. Education: University of Tennessee, Knoxville, 2 years. Musical Education: Self-taught. Career: Featured on US television series The Road; Performed on televised Dove Awards, 1993; Member of John Hiatt's band, 1990-; Performed on Saturday Night Live, David Letterman and Arsenio Hall shows; Appearances in clubs, theatres and festivals. Recordings: Albums: Big Town, 1991; Bus Named Desire, 1993; Lesson Of Love, 1995. Honour: Nashville Area Music Award, Best Contemporary Christian Album, 1995; Grammy Award, Best Contemporary Rock Album, Lesson Of Love, 1996. Memberships: NARAS; GMA; CMA. Hobbies: Children; Gardening; Reading; Cooking. Current Management: Blanton and Harrell Entertainment. Address: 2910 Poston Avenue, Nashville, TN 37203, USA.

CLIFF Jimmy (James Chambers), b. 1948, Jamaica. Reggae Singer; Composer. 1 son. Career: Singer, songwriter, 1960s-; Backing vocalist, London, 1963; Tours worldwide, especially US, Europe, South America, Africa; Concerts include: Montreux Jazz Festival, 1980; World Music Festival, Jamaica, 1982; Rock In Rio

II, Brazil, 1991; Worlds Beat Reggae Festival, Portand, USA, 1992; Actor, films: The Harder They Come (also on film soundtrack), 1972; Bongo Man, 1980; Club Paradise (also on film soundtrack), 1986; Formed own record label, Cliff Records, 1989; Own production company, Cliff Sounds And Films, 1990. Compositions include: You Can Get It If You Really Want, Desmond Dekker; Let Your Yeah Be Yeah, The Pioneers; Trapped, Bruce Springsteen, for USA For Africa album. Recordings: Singles include: Dearest Beverley, 1962; Hurricane Hattie, 1962; Waterfall, 1968; Wonderful World Beautiful People, 1969; Many Rivers To Cross, 1969; Vietnam, 1969; Wild World, 1970; I Can See Clearly Now (featured on film soundtrack Cool Runnings), 1993. Albums: Hard Road, 1967; Jimmy Cliff, 1969; Can't Get Enough, 1969; Wonderful World, 1970; Another Cycle, 1971; The Harder They Come, 1972; Struggling Man, 1974; Follow My Mind, 1975; Give Thanx, 1978; I Am The Living, 1980; Give The People What They Want, 1981; Special, 1982; The Power And The Glory, 1983; Cliff Hanger, 1985; Hanging Fire, 1988; Images, 1990; Breakout, 1992; Contributor, Sun City, Artists Against Apartheid, 1985. Honour: Grammy Award, Best Reggae Recording, 1985; Grammy Nomination, Best Reggae Recording, 1984. Address: c/o DAS Communications, 83 Riverside Drive, New York, NY 10024, USA.

CLIFFORD (Brisley) Grieg, b. 31 Aug 1971, Gillingham, Kent, England. Musician (drums). Education: Diploma, Photography. Career: Drummer with Hit'n'Run, hard rock band, 1989-94; Tours Britain, Europe; Sessions, airplay, most countries; College radio, USA; Album, 1992; Member, If 6 Was 9 (3 piece rock band), first EP released 1995; Many sessions, studio and live work, for many Rock/Funk bands, notably Suicide Ride; Sessions by singer Mark Lehman, include 2 videos for MTV and National TV; Live sessions for Suicide Ride offshoot band: Creed. Recordings: with Hit'n'Run: Hit'n'Run, 1992; Suicide Ride session recordings, 1994; with If 6 Was 9: Out Of The Fire, 1995; Silent Nights; Your Heart Somebody, 1995; Grieg Clifford: Funky Rock Drum Loops. Membership: Musicians' Union. Hobbies: Photography; Art. Current Management: Groovytime Promotions. Address: 23 Harsfold Road, Rustington, West Sussex BN16 2QE, England.

CLIFTON Andrew William, b. 20 May 1954, Hereford, England. Record Company Executive; Music Media Educator; Writer; Broadcaster. Education: Nottingham University, 1973-76; University College Swansea, 1976-77; Cambridge University, 1983-84, 1986-87. Musical Education: University Research Project - Teaching About The Music Industry, 1990-94. Career: Founder, New Leaf Records, 1981; Leaves Music, 1982; Molesworth Label, 1984; Indie 500 Label, 1994; Director, Phonography Foundation, 1994; Popular Music reviewer, columnist, 1973-; Researcher, writer, presenter for college and local radio, 1975-. Publications: Pop Into Class, 1985; The Independent Record Industry Media File, 1992. Memberships: PRS; MCPS; PPL; IASPM (International Association For The Study of Popular Music); AME (Association For Media Education); Sonic Death. Address: 9 Church Road, Conington, Peterborough PE7 3QJ, England.

CLIFTON Bill (William August Marburg), b. 5 Apr 1931, Riderwood, Maryland, USA. Performing Artist; Singer; Musician (guitar, autoharp). m. Trijntje B Labrie, 31 Oct 1978, 4 sons, 6 daughters. Education: Graduate degree, Business Administration, University of Virginia. Career: Extensive work in radio late 1940s to mid 1950s; Recordings 1953-; Organized first all-bluegrass festival, Luray, Virginia, July 4 1961; Founding director, Newport Folk Festival; Compere, weekly BBC Show, Cellar Full of Folk; First bluegrass performer to earn living entirely in Europe, Asia, Africa, Australia, New Zealand. Compositions: Little White-Washed Chimney; Mary Dear; Where The Rainbow Finds Its End; Happy Days (instrumental); Recent albums include: Bill Clifton: The Early Years; Autoharp Centennial Celebration; Where The Rainbow Finds Its End; River Of Memories. Publications: Bill Clifton's 150 Old-time Folk And Gospel Songs. Honours: Award Of Merit, International Bluegrass Music Association, 1992; Preservation Hall Of Greats, SPBGMA, 1993. Memberships: International Bluegrass Music Association; Birthplace of Country Music Alliance. Hobbies: Coin collector (British and American); Camping; Hiking; Cycling. Address: PO Box 69, Mendota, VA 24270, USA.

CLINTON George, b. 22 July 1940, Kannapolis, North Carolina, USA. Singer; Bandleader. 1 son. Career: Founder, leader, The Parliaments, 1950s-; Changed name to Funkadelic, 1969; Parliament/Funkadelic, 1970-; Solo artiste, 1982-; Owner, Bridgeport Music; Regular worldwide concerts and tours; Featured in Graffitti Bridge, Prince, 1990. Recordings: Albums: Funkadelic, 1969; Osmium, 1970; America Eats Its Young, 1972; Cosmic Slop, 1973; Standing On The Verge Of Getting It On, 1974; Chocolate City, 1975; Mothership Connection, 1976; The Clones Of Dr Funkenstein, 1976; Parliament Live/P Funk Earth Tour, 1977; Funkentelechy Vs. The Placebo, 1977; One Nation Under A Groove, 1978; Motor Booty Affair, 1978; Brides Of Funkenstein, 1978; Underjam, 1979; Gloryhallastoopid (Pin The Tale On The Funky), 1979; The Electric Spanking Of War Babies, 1981; Computer Games, 1982; You Shouldn't Nuf Bit, Fish!, 1984; Some Of My Best Friends Are Jokes, 1985; R&B Skeletons In The Closet, 1986; The Cinderella Theory, 1989; Hey Man...Smell My Finger, 1993; Dope Dogs, 1994; The Music Of Red Shoe Diaries, 1995; A Fifth Of Funk, 1995; Mortal Kombat (film soundtrack), 1996; Singles include: One Nation Under A Groove; (Not Just) Knee Deep; Atomic Dog; Walk The Dinosaur, used in film soundtrack Super Mario Brothers. Address: c/o Ciccel Enterprises, Suite 102, 1830 S Robertson Blvd, Los Angeles, CA 90035, USA.

CLIVILLES Robert, b. 1964, New York, USA. Disc Jockey; Record Producer. Education: Business management at college. Career: Disc jockey, member of production team, C & C Music Factory (with the late David Cole); Club DJ, performances worldwide. Recordings: Numerous C & C recordings; Latest projects: Ministry Of Sound Sessions Volume III, 1994; Anything Goes, 1994.

CLOONEY Rosemary, b. 23 May 1928, Maysville, Kentucky, USA. Singer. Career: Early appearances with sister Betty; Joined saxophonist Tony Pastor's band, 1945; Solo recording artiste, 1946-; Films include: The Stars Are Singing, 1953; Here Come The Girls, 1954; Red Garters, 1954; Deep In My Heart, 1954; White Christmas, 1954; Played at Carnegie Hall, 1991. Recordings: Numerous albums include: Deep In My Heart (film soundtrack), 1954; Hollywood's Best, 1955; Blue Rose, 1956; Clooney Times, 1957; Ring A Round Rosie, with the Hi-Lo's, 1957; Swing Around Rosie, 1958; Fancy Meeting You Here, with Bing Crosby, 1958; The Ferrers At Home, 1958; Hymns From The Heart, 1959; Rosemary Clooney Swings Softly, 1960; A Touch Of Tabasco, 1960; Clap Hands, Here Comes Rosie, 1960; Rosie Solves The Swingin' Riddle, 1961; Country Hits From The Past, 1963; Love, 1963; Thanks For Nothing, 1964; That Travelin' Two Beat, 1965; Look My Way, 1976; Nice To Be Around, 1977; Here's To My Lady, 1979; Rosemary Clooney Sings Harold Arlen, 1983; My Buddy, 1983; Rosemary Clooney Sings The Lyrics Of Johnny Mercer, 1987; Rosemary Clooney Sings The Music Of Jimmy Van Heusen, 1987; Show Tunes, 1989; Everything's Coming Up Rosie, 1989; Girl Singer, 1992; Various compilations; Singles include:

You're Just In Love; Beautiful Brown Eyes; Come On - My House; Tenderly; Half As Much (Number 1, UK); Botcha Me; Too Old To Cut The Mustard (with Marlene Dietrich); The Night Before Christmas Song, with Gene Autry; Hey There (Number 1, UK); This Ole House (Number 1, UK); Mambo Italiano; Mangos. Publication: This For Remembrance. Address: c/o Production Central, 3500 West Olive, Suite 1420, Burbank, CA 91505, USA.

CLOUT Tony, b. 25 Feb 1945, Danbury Palace, Chelmsford, England. Arranger; Copyist; Composer; Musician (bass guitar, guitar). m. Julia Anne Lamprell, 15 Aug 1977, 4 sons, 2 daughters. Musical Education: Self-taught. Career: Guitar with Paul Raven (Gary Glitter), 1960; with The Transatlantics, 1965-69; Recorded 6 singles; Television appearances include: 5 o'Clock Club; Thank Your Lucky Stars; BBC Light Programme, Easy Beat; Saturday Club; Bank Holiday Specials with The Beatles; with The Ross Mitchell Band, 1972; with The Ray McVay Band, 1975-83; Television, radio, records, touring, society functions include Prince Charles' 30th Birthday at Buckingham Palace; Musical Director, Circus Tavern cabaret club, Essex, 1983-93; UK Tour with Michael Barrymore, Stutz Bear Cats, Roly Polys, 1985; Arranger, copyist, West End Shows: Blood Brothers; Only The Lonely; Good Rockin' Tonite; Shows for BBC Radio 2, artists including: Charles Augins; Warren Mitchell; Marty Webb; Elaine Page; Chas'n'Dave; Marti Caine; Bobby Crush. Compositions: La Concordia; Paso Doble De Cadiz; Spring's the Time, 1996. Recordings: Singles: Many Things From Your Window; Don't Fight It; Run For Your Life; Albums: Ray McVay dance albums; Pan Pipe Moods; Chas'n'Dave's Street Party albums. Membership: British Music Writer's Council; PaMRA. Hobbies: Steam locomotives; 18th Century architecture; Art; Gardens. Current Management: Self-managed. Address: 36 Shirley Gardens, Hornchurch, Essex RM12 4NH, England.

CLOVER Val (Valerie Ann Cope), b. 17 September 1952, Liverpool, England. Singer; Songwriter; Model; Actress. Education: Selftaught. Career: Joined Girl Trio, The Cheroees, 1968; Lead Singer, The Wheels of Fortune, 1969-70; Joined recording band, Justine, 1970; Concerts include: Earls Court Olympia and Buxton Festival; Appearances on Disco 2 (BBC TV) and Sounds of the Seventies (BBC Radio); Solo career, 1976; Sessions; Voice-overs and numerous TV, film and pop videos as Actress; Rock/Pop Reviewer for Disability Times. Compositions: Co-Writer, single, Don't Make My White Christmas Blue, by Iris Williams, 1982; Co-Writer, Oikotie Sydameen, Scandinavian Triple Platinum Album, Tahtikaaren Taa, by Aikakone, 1995. Recordings: Band Member, Justine, album, 1970; Band Member, Justine, She Brings The Morning With Her, single, 1970. Memberships: PRS; MCPS; NCB; BASCA; Equity. Hobbies: Music; Tennis; Gardening. Current Management: Mouse Records. Address: 28 Breamore Road, Seven Kings, Essex IG3 9NB, England.

COATES Bruce Brian Gilbert, b. 3 July 1972, Birmingham, England. Musician (saxophone - tenor, soprano, melody); Writer; Lecturer. Education: North East Worcestershire College, Bromsgrove. Musical Education: BA Hons, Performing Arts (Music); De Monfort University. Career: Music for Island, dance piece by Jo Walker (with Zo Sosinka and Craig Vear), Phoenix Theatre, Leicester, 1992; Contributed improvisations and ambient sound environment for Modal Spaces - A Sound/Architecture Project, (large-scale musical performance by Andrew Hugill), Queens Building, Leicester, 1994; Performance of Burdocks by Christian Wolff (with Zo Sosinka, Christian Wolff, Dave Smith), 25th Anniversay Concert of the Scratch Orchestra, ICA, 1994; Formed Lusus Naturae, trio with Jamie Smith and Zo Sosinka, 1996. Composition: Solos and Accompaniments, with Lusus Naturae, for improvisers, commission, 1996. Recordings: Sound Score/Tape Collage for She Ain't Jumping Off That Bridge (touring physical theatre piece), Conscious Opera Association, premiered Birmingham Dance Centre, 1994. Publication: Lol Coxhill, Transcending Boundaries, in Rubberneck, 1995; Contributions to: Rubberneck; Jazz on CD; Avant, 1995-. Address: The Octagon, 16 Beeches Farm Drive, Northfield, Birmingham B31 4SD, England.

COATES Donald Denison, b. 23 Mar 1935, Orange, New Jersey, USA. Jazz Musician (piano); Composer. m. (1) Jacqueline Dorsey, divorced, (2) Dorothy Hering, 26 June 1988, 1 daughter. Education: Williams College, 1953-57. Career: Freelance jazz pianist, 1960-82; Played for: Jack Teagarden; Wild Bill Davison; Newport Jazz Festival All-Stars; Eddie Condon; Roy Eldridge; Solo pianist at: Windows On The World, Waldorf Astoria; Musician with vocalists including Maxine Sullivan, 1980-; Music Advisor, Entertainment Development Network, 1987. Compositions: Numerous songs, music for radio and television commercials. Publications: Contributor, articles of jazz instruction and history. Membership: AFofM. Address: 442 W 57th Street, New York, NY 10019, USA.

COBBI Daniel, b. 3 May 1953, Paris, France. Musician (piano); Jazz Composer. 1 daughter. Education: Architecture. Musical Education: Boulogne Conservatory, classical piano studies. Career: Tours, Italy; Spain; Belgium; Switzerland; Television concert, 1988; Many concerts, Radio France; France Musique; France Culture; Free radio's special solo piano; Played in USA, 1978; Many festivals, Europe. Recordings: Music For The Blue Bar, 1980; Eighteen Surprises For Christmas, 1981; Ayanamsa, 1982; Dilation, 1985; For Camille, 1995. Honour: First Command in France of the Culture Ministère, 1982. Hobbies: Astronomy; Spirituality. Address: 27 Avenue d'Italie, 75013 Paris, France.

COBHAM Bill (William Emmanuel) Jr, b. 16 May 1944, Panama. Musician (drums). m. Marcia Ann McCarthy, 1 son, 1 daughter. Education: High School Of Music And Arts, New York, 1962. Career: Musician with: Billy Taylor's New York Jazz Sextet, 1967; Dreams, with Michael and Randy Brecker, 1969; Miles Davis, 1971; John McLaughlin's Mahavishnu Orchestra, 1972; Founder member, Spectrum, 1975-; Prolific recording artist and regular guest musician; Taught at numerous drum clinics; Own television series, Billy Cobham's World Of Rhythm. Recordings: Albums: Spectrum, 1973; Total Eclipse, 1974; Crosswinds, 1974; Shabazz, 1975; A Funky Thide Of Sings, 1975; Life And Times, 1976; Live In Europe, 1976; Magic, 1977; Inner Conflicts, 1978; Simplicity Of Expression, 1978; BC, 1979; The Best Of, 1980; Flight Time, 1982; Observatory, 1982; Smokin', 1983; Warning, 1985; Powerplay, 1986; Picture This, 1987; Best Of, 1986; Stratus, 1988; Billy's Best Hits, 1988; By Design, 1992; with Horace Silver: Serenade To A Soul Sister; with Miles Davis: Directions; Big Fun; Live Evil; Tribute To Jack Johnson; Circle In The Round; On The Cover; with John McLaughlin and Mahavishnu Orchestra: My Goals Beyond; The Inner Mounting Flame; Birds Of Fire; Love Devotion and Surrender; Between Nothingness And Surrender; Electric Guitarist; with Ron Carter: Blues Farm; All Blues; Spanish Blue; Yellow And Green; Also featured on albums by: George Benson; Stanley Clarke; McCoy Tyner; Grover Washington; Larry Coryell; Milt Jackson. Current Management: The Cameron Organization, 2001 W Magnolia Blvd, Burbank, CA 91506, USA.

COBRIN Spencer James, b. 31 Jan 1969, Paddington, London, England. Musician (drums, piano). Musical Education: Private lessons, trumpet, drums, piano. Career: Played London club circuit, 1986-91; International tours as drummer with Morrissey, 1991-; Television performances include: Tonight Show with Johnny Carson; Saturday Night Live; MTV; Tonight Show with Jay Leno; Later With Jools Holland. Recordings: Albums: with Morrissey: Your Arsenal, 1992; Southpaw Grammar, 1995; Videos: Live In Dallas; Malady Lingers On (compilation). Publications: Featured in: Morrissey Shot, by Linder Sterling. Membership: Musicians' Union. Hobbies: Piano; Composition.

COBURN Jewel, b. 4 Mar 1958, Australia. m. Barry Coburn, 19 Sept 1984, 2 sons. Education: College. Career: Singer, RCA and CBS labels, Australia, 1963-82; Actress, Los Angeles; Guest roles include: Bonanza; Mod Squad; Lassie; Night Gallery; Fantasy Island; Films, commercials, 1970-80; Music publisher, 1984-; Hits include: Here In The Real World, Alan Jackson; Something In Red, Lorrie Morgan; I'm Over You, Keith Whitley. Honours: New Country Artist, Billboard Award, 1979. Memberships: CMA; ACM; SOURCE. Hobbies: Cooking; Gardening. Address: 33 Music Square, West Suite 110, Nashville, TN 37203, USA.

COCCIANTE Richard (Riccardo), b. 20 Feb 1946, Saigon, Vietnam. Composer; Singer. m. Catherine Boutet, 8 Oct 1983, 1 son. Musical Education: Self-educated. Career: Solo artiste, 1972-; Regular European tours; Venues include: Piazza della Signoria, Florence, 1983; Gran Teatro La Fenice, Venice, 1988; Sporting Club, Monaco, 1988, 1990, 1995; Vina del Mar Festival, Chile, 1989, 1994; Olympia and Zenith, Paris, 1994; Taj Mahal, Atlantic City, 1995; Collaborated with producers including: Paul Buckmaster; Ennio Morricone; James Newton-Howard; Vangelis; Participated in album World War II, interpreting Michelle with London Symphony Orchestra; Several television, radio appearances worldwide. Compositions: Songs in: Italian (15 albums); French (9 albums); Spanish (9 albums); English (3 albums); Some songs common to all 4 languages. Recordings: Hit Singles: Bella Senz'anima, Italy, 1973; Bella Sin Alma, Spain, Spanish South America; Quand Un Amour, France, Canada, 1974; International Hits: Margherita/Marguerite/Margarita, 1978-79; Coup De Soleil, 1980; Cervo A Primavera/Yo Renacere, 1980; Sincérité/Sincérité/Sinceridad/Sincerity, 1983; Questione di Feeling, duet with Mina, 1985/86; Question De Feeling, duet with Fabienne Thiebeault, 1985/86; Cuestion De Feeling, duet with Melissa, 1985/86; Se Stiamo Insieme, 1991; Pour Elle/ Per Lei/ I'd Fly/ Por Ella, 1993/94. Honours: Rose d'Or Award, 1981; Winner, Sanremo Festival, 1991; Telegatto, 1991; Rino Gaetano Award 2 times; Several Gold, Platinum Records. Hobby: Music. Current Management: Boventeen BV. Address: Information Office, Blue Toon, 4 Rue Chauveau Lagarde, 75008 Paris, France.

COCHRAN Hank, b. 2 Aug 1935, Isola, Mississippi, USA. Songwriter. m. (1) Shirley Kay Foster, 24 July 1954, divorced, 3 sons; (2) Marilyn Jean Seely, 15 June 1969, divorced, 1981; (3) Susan Booth Calder, 18 Aug 1982, 1 stepdaughter. Career: Co-owner, song plugger, writer, Pamper Music Inc, 1950-67; Writer, professional consultant, Tree International, 1967-89; Co-owner, writer, professional consultant, Co-Heart Music Group, 1989-. Compositions include: A Little Bitty Tear, 1961; He's Got You, 1962; Funny Way Of Laughing, 1962; Tears Break Out On Me, 1962; Make The World Go Away, 1963; You Comb Her Hair, 1963; Make The World Go Away, 1963; Don't Touch Me, 1966; It's Not Love But It's Not Bad, 1973; Can I Sleep In Your Arms, 1973; Why Can't He Be You, 1978; Make The World Go Away (sung by Willie Nelson in the film Honeysuckle Rose, 1979); That's All That Matters To Me, 1980; I Fall To Pieces, 1982; What Would Your Memories Do, 1984; The Chair, 1985; Ocean Front Property, 1988; Set 'Em Up Joe, 1989; Who You Gonna Blame It On This Time, 1989; Don't You Ever Get Tired Of Hurting Me, 1989; Right In The Wrong Direction, 1990; Is It Raining At Your House, 1991; I Want To Go With You. Honours: Country Music Association Walkway of Stars, 1967; Nashville Songwriters Association Hall Of Fame, 1974; Betty Clooney Foundation, Singer's Salute to Country Songwriter Award, 1993.

COCKBURN Bruce, b. 1945, Canada. Singer; Songwriter. 1 daughter. Career: Singer, songwriter, reflecting Christian beliefs and environmental issues. Recordings: Albums include: Bruce Cockburn, 1970; High Winds White Sky, 1971; Sunwheel Dance, 1972; Night Vision, 1973; Hand Dancing, 1974; Salt, Sun And Time, 1974; Joy Will Find A Way, 1975; Further Adventures, 1976; In The Falling Dark, 1976; Circles In The Stream, 1977; Dancing In The Dragon's Jaws, 1979; Humans, 1980; Resume, 1981; Inner City Front, 1981; Stealing Fire, 1984; World Of Wonders, 1984; Trouble With Normal, 1985; Rumours Of Glory, 1986; Waiting For A Miracle, 1987; Big Circumstance, 1989; Live, 1990; Nothing But A Burning Light, 1991. Current Management: Finkelstein Management, 151 John Street, Suite 501, Toronto, Ontario M5V 2T2, Canada.

COCKER Jarvis Branson, b. 1964, Sheffield, South Yorkshire, England. Singer; Songwriter. Education: BA, Film studies, St Martin's College of Art, London, 1988-91. Career: Lead singer, Pulp, 1980-; Major concerts include: Headline act, Glastonbury Festival, 1995; Heineken Festival, Leeds, 1995; Television includes: Later With... Britpop Now, BBC2, 1995 Guest presenter, Top Of The Pops, 1995. Recordings: Albums: It, 1983; Freaks, 1986; Separations, 1989 (released 1992); His 'N' Hers, 1994; Different Class, 1995; This Is Hardcore, 1998; Singles: Little Girl (With Blue Eyes); Dogs Are Everywhere (EP); My Legendary Girlfriend; Countdown; OU; Babies; Razzmatazz; Lipgloss, 1994; Do You Remember The First Time?, 1994; Sorted For E's And Whizz, 1995; Disco 2000, 1995; Common People, 1995. Honours: BRIT Award Nomination, Best Group, 1996. Current Management: Rough Trade Management, 66 Golborne Road, London W10 5PF, England.

COCKER Joe, b. 20 May 1944, Sheffield, South Yorkshire, England. Singer; Songwriter. Career: Singer, Northern club circuit with group The Grease Band, 1965-69; Solo artiste, 1968-; Regular worldwide tours; Major concert appearances include: National Jazz And Blues Festival, 1968; Denver Pop Festival, 1969; Newport '69 Festival, 1969; Woodstock Festival (filmed), 1969; Isle Of Wight Festival, 1969; Co-headliner with Beach Boys, Crystal Palace Garden Party, 1972; Prince's Trust Rock Gala, 1988; Nelson Mandela's 70th Birthday Tribute, Wembley Stadium, 1988; Rock In Rio II Festival, 1991; Guitar Legends, Seville, Spain, 1991; Montreux Jazz Festival, filmed for MTV's Unplugged series, 1992; Blues Music Festival, with B.B.King, 1992; Numerous television and radio broadcasts worldwide. Recordings: Hit singles include: With A Little Help From My Friends (Number 1, UK), 1968; Delta Lady, 1969; The Letter, 1970; Cry Me A River, 1970; You Are So Beautiful, 1975; Unchain My Heart, 1987; When The Night Comes, 1990; with Jennifer Warnes: Up Where We Belong (Number 1, US), theme to film An Officer And A Gentleman, 1982; Contributions to film soundtracks include: Edge Of A Dream, for film Teachers, 1984; You Can Leave Your Hat On, for film 9½ Weeks, 1986; Love Lives On, for film Bigfoot And The Hendersons, 1987; (All I Know) Feels Like Forever, for film The Cutting Edge, 1992; Trust In Me, duet with Sass Jordan, for film The Bodyguard, 1992; Albums include: With A Little Help From My Friends, 1969; Joe Cocker, 1970; Mad Dogs And Englishmen, 1970; Cocker Happy, 1971; Something To Say, 1972; I Can Stand A Little Rain, 1974; Jamaica

Say You Will, 1975; Live In Los Angeles, 1976; Stingray, 1976; Joe Cocker's Greatest Hits, 1977; Luxury You Can Afford, 1978; Sheffield Steel, 1982; Civilized Man, 1984; Cocker, 1986; Unchain My Heart, 1987; Nightriding, 1988; One Night Of Sin, 1989; Joe Cocker Live, 1990; Night Calls, 1992; The Legend - The Essential Collection, 1992; Have A Little Faith, 1994; Contributor, Two Rooms (tribute album to Elton John and Bernie Taupin), 1991. Honours: Grammy, Best Pop Vocal Performance, Up Where We Belong, 1983; Academy Award, Best Film Song, Up Where We Belong, 1983; Grammy Nomination, One Night Of Sin, 1989. Current Management: Roger Davies Management, 15030 Ventura Blvd #772, Sherman Oaks, CA 91403, USA.

COHEN Leonard, b. 21 Sept 1934, Montreal, Quebec, Canada. Singer; Songwriter. Education: McGill University. Career: Founder, Country and Western group, The Buckskin Boys, 1951; Novelist; Poet; Solo singer; Subject of BBC documentary. Compositions include: Suzanne; Priests (both recorded by Judy Collins); Sisters Of Mercy; Hey, That's No Way To Say Goodbye; Story Of Isaac; Bird On A Wire. Recordings: Albums: The Songs Of Leonard Cohen, 1968; Songs From A Room, 1969; Songs Of Love And Hate, 1971; Live Songs, 1973; New Skin For The Old Ceremony, 1974; Greatest Hits, 1975; The Best Of Leonard Cohen, 1976; Death Of A Ladies Man, 1977; Recent Songs, 1979; Various Positions, 1985; I'm Your Man, 1988; The Future, 1992; More Best Of, 1997. Publications: Poetry: Let Us Compare Mythologies; Novels: The Favourite Game, 1963; Beautiful Losers, 1966. Honours include: McGill Literary Award for Let Us Compare Mythologies. Current Management: Stranger Music. Address: Suite 91, 419 N Larchmont Blvd, Los Angeles, CA 90004, USA.

COKE Charles M, b. 19 Mar 1943, San Jose, California, USA. Record Producer. 2 sons, 1 daughter. Career: Toured USA for 20 years; Local television and radio shows. Recordings: Producer for: Tiggi Clay; Fizzy Quick; Derrick Hughes; Workforce; Il Big; Bedroom Cowboys; John Payne; CP Salt; NVS; Baby Fat with Big Mitch. Membership: Musicians' Union (local, San Francisco). Hobby: Music. Current Management: Up Front Management. Address: 1906 Seward Drive, Pittsburg, CA 94565, USA.

COKELAERE Laurent, b. 12 July 1957, Suresnes, France. Musician (electric bass). m. Natacha Tuduri, 3 Sept 1988, 1 son. Musical Education: Berklee College of Music, Boston, USA, 1977-78. Career: Sideman with singers (French): Alan Stivell; Jean-Claude Vannier; Century; Michel Fugain; Bill Deraime; Richard Clayderman; Veronique Riviere; Enzo Enzo; Kent; Blues Chris Lancry; J J Milteau. Recordings: Coke Tales, 1983; Minigruel, 1985; Robs, 1984; Le Grand Blues Band, 1992; Coke Tale, Mama Rad Gumbo, 1995. Publications: Stages Bass, 6 volumes Oscar Music, 1988. Current Management: Diploma of Composition, Arrangement, Orchestration, by Ivan Julien, Henri Dutilleux, 1984. Address: 28 Bis Rue Carnot, 92300 Levallois, France.

COLBERT Laurence John, b. 27 June 1970, Kingston, Surrey, England. Musician (drums). Musical Education: Self-taught. Career: Member, Ride; Concerts include: Royal Albert Hall; Reading Festival; Glastonbury; Television includes: The Word; Top Of The Pops; BBC Radio 1 sessions: John Peel; Mark Goodier. Recordings: Nowhere, 1990; Going Blank Again, 1992; Carnival Of Light, 1994. Honours: Silver discs: Nowhere, 1990; Going Blank Again, 1992. Membership: PRS. Hobby: Sailing. Current Management: Dave Newton. Address: PO Box 479, Headington, Oxford OX3 7QW, England.

COLBY Mark Steven, b. 18 Mar 1949, Brooklyn, New York, USA. Musician (saxophone). m. (1) Janet McIntyre, divorced 1970; (2) Mary

Deacon, 21 Apr 1977, 1 son, 3 daughters. Musical Education: MusB, University of Miami, 1972; MusM, 1975. Career: Musician with: Maynard Ferguson, 1975-77; Bob James, 1977-83; Freelance musician, 1980-; Teacher, jazz saxophone, De Paul University, Chicago, 1983-; Clinic musician for Selmer musical instruments, 1987-. Recordings: Solo albums: Serpentine Fire, 1978; One Good Turn, 1979; Mango Tango, 1990; Playground, 1991; Other recordings include: with Bill Wyman: Monkey Grip, 1974; Stone Alone, 1976; Destively Bonaroo, Doctor John, 1974; Real Life Ain't This Way, Jay Ferguson, 1979; Cat In The Hat, Bobby Caldwell, 1980; Marbles, Software, 1981.

COLE B J, b. 17 June 1946, North London, England. Musician (pedal steel guitar); Producer. Career: Musician, Country Music circuit, London, 1964-; Pedal steel guitar player, Cochise; Founder member, producer, Hank Wangford Band; Leading exponent of instrument in UK; Currently prolific session musician and solo artiste; Leader, own group Transparent Music Ensemble. Rcordings: Solo albums: New Hovering Dog, 1972; Transparent Music, 1989; The Heart Of The Moment, 1995; As session musician: Tiny Dancer, Elton John, 1970; Wide Eyed And Legless, Andy Fairweather-Low, 1975; No Regrets, Walker Brothers, 1976; City To City, Gerry Rafferty, 1978; Everything Must Change, Paul Young, 1984; Silver Moon, David Sylvian, 1986; Diet Of Strange Places, k d lang, 1987; Montagne D'Or, The Orb, 1995; Possibly Maybe, Björk, 1995; with Hank Wangford: Hank Wangford, 1980; Live, 1982; Other recordings with: Johnny Nash; Deacon Blue; Level 42; Danny Thompson; Alan Parsons Project; Shakin' Stevens; Beautiful South; John Cale; Echobelly.

COLE Freddy (Lionel F Cole), b. 1931, Chicago, Illinois, USA. Musician (piano); Singer. Musical Education: Roosevelt Institute; Juilliard School Of Music; New England Conservatory. Career: Younger brother of Nat "King" Cole; Performed with numerous jazz musicians, New York, 1950s; Festival performances, US, Japan, Europe. Recordings include: Latest albums: Always, 1995; Circle Of Love, 1996; To the Ends of the Earth, 1997; Contributor, All My Tomorrows, Grover Washington Jr, 1994. Current Management: Maxine S Harvard Unlimited, 7942 West Bell Road, #C5-501, Glendale, AZ 85308, USA.

COLE Gardner, b. 7 Feb 1962, Flint, Michigan, USA. Singer; Musician (keyboards, drums, guitar). Musical Education: 1 year, Berklee College of Music, Boston. Career: 2 solo albums, 1988, 1991; Drummer with ABC; Keyboard player with A-Ha! on Grammies; Toured as opening act for Toni Tony Tone, 1991. Compositions: 60 songs recorded by various artists. Recordings include: Open Your Heart, Madonna, 1987; Most Of All And Everything, Jody Watley, 1991; Barrier, Tina Turner; Tear It Up, Michael McDonald. Honours: BMI Million-Air Award; 3 BMI Pop Awards; 18 Gold and Platinum records. Memberships: AFTRA; SAG. Hobbies: Gardening; Automobile Restoration. Current Management: Bennett Freed, One Love Management. Address: 5410 Wilshire Boulevard, Suite #806, Los Angeles, CA 90036, USA.

COLE Lloyd, b. 31 Jan 1961, Buxton, Derbyshire, England. Singer; Songwriter. Career: Leader, Lloyd Cole and The Commotions, 1984-88; Solo artiste, 1989-. Recordings: Albums: with the Commotions: Rattlesnakes, 1984; Easy Pieces, 1985; Mainstream, 1987; Solo albums: Lloyd Cole, 1989; Don't Get Weird On Me Babe, 1991; Bad Vibes, 1993; Love Story, 1995; Hit singles: Perfect Skin; Brand New Friend; Lost Weekend; Like Lovers Do. Current Management: John Reid Enterprises Ltd., Singers House, 32 Galena Road, London W6 0LT, England.

COLE Natalie Maria, b. 6 Feb 1950, Los Angeles, California, USA. Singer. m. (1) Marvin J Yancy, 30 July 1976, divorced, (2) Andre Fischer, 17 Sept 1989, divorced. Education: BA, Child Psychology, University of Massachusetts, 1972. Career: Stage debut, 1962; Solo recording artist, 1975-; Major concerts worldwide include: Tokyo Music Festival, 1979; Nelson Mandela 70th Birthday Concert, Wembley, 1988; Nelson Mandela tribute, Wembley, 1990; John Lennon Tribute Concert, Liverpool, 1990; Homeless benefit concert with Quincy Jones, Pasadena, 1992; Rainforest benefit concert, Carnegie Hall, 1992; Commitment To Life VI, (AIDs benefit concert), Los Angeles, 1992; Television appearances include: Sinatra And Friends, 1977; Host, Big Break, 1990; Motown 30, 1990; Tonight Show, 1991; Entertainers '91, 1991; Recordings: Hit singles: This Will Be, 1975; Sophisticated Lady, 1976; I've Got Love On My Mind, 1977; Our Love (Number 1, US R&B chart), 1977; Gimme Some Time (duet with Peabo Bryson), 1980; What You Won't Do For Love (duet with Peabo Bryson), 1980; Jump Start, 1987; I Live For Your Love, 1988; Pink Cadillac, 1988; Miss You Like Crazy (Number 1, US R&B charts), 1989; Wild Women Do, from film Pretty Woman, 1990; Unforgettable (duet with father Nat "King" Cole), 1991; Albums: Inseparable, 1975; Natalie, 1976; Unpredictable, 1977; Thankful, 1978; Natalie...Live!, 1978; I Love You So, 1979; Don't Look Back, 1980; Happy Love, 1981; Natalie Cole Collection, 1981; I'm Ready, 1982; Dangerous, 1985; Everlasting, 1987; Good To Be Back, 1989; Unforgettable...With Love (Number 1, US), 1991; The Soul Of Natalie Cole, 1991; Take A Look, 1993; with Peabo Bryson: We're The Best Of Friends, 1980. Honours: Numerous Grammy Awards include: Best New Artist, 1976; Best Female R&B Vocal Performance, 1976, 1977; 5 Grammy Awards for Unforgettable, including Best Song, Best Album, 1992; 5 NAACP Image Awards, 1976, 1988, 1992; American Music Awards: Favourite Female R&B Artist, 1978; Favourite Artist, Favourite Album, 1992; Soul Train Award, Best Single, 1988; Various Gold discs. Memberships: AFTRA; NARAS. Current Management: Dan Cleary Management Associates, Suite 1101, 1801 Avenue Of The Stars, Los Angeles, CA 90067, USA.

COLE Pamela, b. 1 Jan 1959, Edmonton, Alberta, Canada. Musician (bass guitar, acoustic guitar). 1 son, 1 daughter. Education: BA, Criminology. Musical Education: Self-taught. Career: Member, Country band Quickdraw; Performances include: Calgary Stampede, televised on Calgary Cable 10, 1994; Interviewed live, CKUA Radio, Edmonton, Alberta; 3rd place, 4th Annual Country Hootenanny, Claresholm, Alberta; International Country Music Grand Prix, Norway, 1 of 10 finalists with: Next To Nothing, 1995. Recordings: Change Of Heart; Just A Guess; Winning Was The Only Thing; Weekend Cowboy; Next To Nothing. Publications: 2 chapbooks of poetry: In A Corner Of My Room; Between Friends. Honours: Honorable mention from Billboard Magazine for Eye On Me; Alberta Music Project Award, 1992; Winner, 960 CFAC Country Showdown, with band Headin' West. Memberships: SOCAN; ASCAP; ARIA; NCMO 1994. Hobbies: Reading; Walking; Dog training. Address: 5610 Trelle Drive NE, Calgary, AB T2K 3V4, Canada.

COLE Paula, b. 1970, USA. Singer; Songwriter. Education: Berklee College of Music. Career: Singer, Peter Gabriel's Secret World Tour, 1995; Solo Artiste, 1996-. Recordings: Albums: Harbinger, 1996; This Fire, 1997; Hit Single: Where Have All The Cowboys Gone? (EP), 1997. Address: c/o Monterey Peninsula Artists, 509 Hartnell Street, Monterey, CA 93940, USA.

COLEMAN Cy, b. New York, USA. Composer; Producer; Musician (piano); Songwriter. Career: Began performing on piano aged 6; Played New York clubs, 1950s; Composed songs before writing for musical theatre; Began as producer with Barnum, 1980; President, Notable Music Co. Compositions include: Contributions to revues: John Murray Anderson's Almanac; Ziegfeld Follies; Broadway musicals: Wildcat, 1960; Little Me, 1962; Sweet Charity, re-run on Broadway, 1986; Seesaw; On The Twentieth Century; I Love My Wife; Barnum; City Of Angels, 1990; The Will Rogers Follies, 1992; The Life, 1997; Television specials for Shirley MacLaine: If My Friends Could See Me Now; Gypsy In My Soul; Film scores: Father Goose; Power; Garbo Talks; Family Business; Sweet Charity; Songs include: Witchcraft; The Best Is Yet To Come; Hey Look Me Over (from Wildcat); I've Got Your Number (from Wildcat); Real Live Girl (from Little Me); Big Spender (from Sweet Charity); If My Friends Could See Me Now (from Sweet Charity). Honours include: Oscar Nomination, Sweet Charity; 3 Emmys, Shirley MacLaine's Television specials; 2 Grammys: Record Producer, Composer, 1992; 15 Grammy Nominations; Numerous Tony awards, including 6 Tonys, City of Angels, 1990; 6 Tonys, Will Rogers Follies, 1992; Johnny Mercer Award, Songwriters Hall Of Fame; Doctorate, Music, Long Island University, 1994; Irvin Field Humanitarian Award, National Conference, Christians and Jews; Tribute, Avery Fisher Hall. Memberships: Vice President, member, Board of Directors, ASCAP. Address: c/o Notable Music Co Inc, 441 East 57th Street, New York, NY 10022, USA.

COLEMAN George Edward, b. 8 Mar 1935, Memphis, Tennessee, USA. Musician (tenor, alto, soprano saxophones). m. (1) Gloria Bell, 3 Aug 1959, divorced, 1 son, 1 daughter, (2) Carol Hollister, 7 Sept 1985. Musical Education: Self-taught; Privately from older Memphis musicians. Career: Played with: B B King Blues Band, 1952-53; Max Roach Quintet, 1958-59; Miles Davis Quintet, 1963-64; Lionel Hampton 1965-66; Lee Morgan Quintet, 1969; Elvin Jones Quartet, 1970; George Coleman Quartet and Octet, 1971-; NYU, 1984; New School, 1987; LI University, 1987; Consultant, Lenox Jazz School, Massachusetts, 1988. Compositions: 5/4 Thing; You Mean So Much To Me; Blondies Waltz; Amsterdam After Dark; Music in Free Jack. Recordings: My Horns Of Plenty; Live At Yoshi's; Manhattan Panorama; Duo, with Tete Montelui; with Cedar Walton: Eastern Rebellion; with Miles Davis: My Funny Valentine. Honours: International Jazz Critics Poll, 1958; Artist of the Year, Record World Magazine, 1969; Knight of Mark Twain, 1972; AWD Contribution to Music, Beale Street Association, 1977; Tip of the Derby Awards, 1978, 1979; Jazz Audience Award, 1979; Good Note Jazz Award, 1985; Key to City of Memphis, 1991; Grantee, National Endowment for the Arts, 1975, 1985. Hobbies: Body building; Sports. Current Management: Abby Hoffer Enterprises. Address: 223½ E 48th Street, New York, NY 10017, USA.

COLEMAN Jaz (Jeremy), b. Cheltenham, Gloucestershire, England. Singer; Musician (keyboards). Musical Education: Piano lessons; Grade 8 violin; Cathedral choir. Career: Lead singer, keyboard player, UK rock band Killing Joke, 1980-; Numerous tours worldwide, television and radio appearances. Compositions include: 1 symphony. Recordings: Albums with Killing Joke: Killing Joke, 1980; What's This For?, 1981; Revelations, 1982; Fire Dances 1983; Night Time, 1985; Brighter Than A Thousand Suns, 1986; Extremities, Dirt And Various Repressed Emotions, 1990; Pandemonium, 1994; Solo: Outside The Gate, with Anne Dudley, 1988.

COLEMAN Ornette, b. 19 Mar 1930, Fort Worth, Texas, USA. Jazz Musician (saxophone, trumpet, violin); Composer. Musical Education: Lennox School of Jazz; Trumpet and violin studies; Studied theory. Career: Member, bands with Red Connors, 1946; Pee Wee Clayton, 1949; Own Coleman Quartet (Don Cherry, Charlie Haden, Billy Higgins); Residency at Five Spot Café, New York, 1958-63; Trio with David Izenzon and Charles Moffett, 1965; Created own group, Prime Time, mid 1970s-. Albums include: Something Else!, 1958; Tomorrow Is The Question, 1959; The Shape Of Jazz To Come, 1959; Change Of The Century, 1960; This Is Our Music, 1960; Free Jazz, 1961; Ornette!, 1961; Ornette On Tenor, 1961; The Town Hall Concert, 1962, 1963; Chappaqua Suite, 1965; The Great London Concert (aka An Evening With Ornette Coleman), 1966; At The Golden Circle, Volumes 1 & 2, 1966; The Empty Foxhole, 1966; Music Of Ornette Coleman (aka Saints And Soldiers), 1967; New York Is Now, 1968; Love Call, 1968; Ornette At 12, 1969; Crisis, 1969; Friends And Neighbours, 1970; The Art Of Improvisation, 1970; Science Fiction, 1972; Skies Of America, 1972; Twins, 1972; Dancing In Your Head, 1976, 1976; Body Meta, 1976; Paris Concert, 1977; Coleman Classics, Volume One, 1977; Soapsuds (with Charlie Haden), 1977; Broken Shadows, 1982; Opening The Caravan Of Dreams, 1985; Prime Time/Time Design, 1985; Song X (with Pat Metheny), Song X, 1986; In All Languages, 1987; Virgin Beauty, 1988; Live In Milano, 1968, 1989; Jazzbuhne Berlin 88, 1990; Naked Lunch, 1992; Guest musician: Old And New Gospel, Jackie McLean; Tale Of Captain Black, James Blood Ulmer. Address: c/o Monterey International Inc., 200 W Superior, Suite 202, Chicago, IL 60610, USA.

COLEMAN Steve, b. Chicago, Illinois, USA. Jazz Musician (saxophone). Musical Education: Music performance at: Wesleyan University; Chicago Music College. Career: Moved to New York, 1978; Toured USA, Europe with: Slide Hampton; Sam Rivers; Cecil Taylor; Doug Hammond; Formed Steve Coleman and Five Elements, 1982; Formed M-Base. Recordings: Albums: Solo: Motherland Pulse; Five Elements: Black Science; Rhythm People; On The Edge Of Tommorrow; World Expansion; Sine Die; Played on recordings by: Dave Holland; Branford Marsalis; Geri Allen; Cassandra Wilson; Greg Osby. Honours: Regular winner, Downbeat polls. Current Management: SESAC. Address: 55 Music Sq E, Nashville, TN 37203, USA.

COLINET Paul Marie Marcel, b. 27 January 1954, Elisabethville, Belgian Congo. Composer (Classic and Folk); Pianotuner; Violin and Viola Player; Diatonic Accordion. m. Segers Yvonna, 14 August 1982. Education: Private lessons, violin and harmony; Selftaught composition and other instruments (viola, cello, Mandola, Esraj, accordion). Career: Piano Tuner; Orchestra, viola; Chamber Music; Member, Trio Michel Terlinck. Compositions: 2 mandolin concerts; 1 violin concerto; 4 suites, mandolin, solo; 48 diatonic dances for diatonic accordeon. Publications: 37 own editions of own compositions. Honours: First Prize, Instrument Building, Viola d'amore, 1995. Membership: SABAM. Hobbies: Reading; Mushrooms; Instrument Building; Photography; Indian Music; Winemaking. Address: Gustave Fussstraat 37, B-1030 Brussels, Belgium.

COLLAZO Steven André, b. 24 January 1960, Brooklyn, NY, USA. Recording Engineer; Arranger; Composer; Artist; Producer; Keyboardist. m. Linda Susan Dodson, 22 August 1995. Education: Self-taught in Music and Audio Engineering. Career: 9 Piece Band, formed in High School, appeared throughout New York City; Joined Warner Recording Act, Undisputed Truth; Toured USA with Natalie Cole, The Isleys, Smokey Robinson; Toured UK and Europe with Odyssey, 1981; Appeared on TOTP, 1981. Compositions: I've Got to Wonder, 1982; Keep You Comin' Back, 1990s; Do You Right, 1990s; Paradise, 1990s; Waverly Radio, 1997. Recordings: Back to My Roots, classic remake of 80s hit, appeared on CH5 Fives Company, 1997; Producer, several Odyssey classics and new material due for release. Publications: Sound on Sound, 1997; Mentions in SOS; The Mix and Future, demos & progs, 1996, 1997. Honour: Demo Reviews, Sound on Sound, Top Tape, 1997. Memberships: American Society of Composers, Authors and Publishers. Hobbies: Dancing; Board Games Yahtzee; Scrabble. Address: 60 Russell Road, Salisbury, Wiltshire, SP2 7LR, England.

COLLEN Phil, b. 8 Dec 1957, Hackney, London, England. Rock Musician (guitar); Vocalist. Career: Guitarist, Girl, 1979-82; Guitarist, Def Leppard, 1982-; Concerts include: World tour, 1983; Monsters of Rock Festival, Castle Donington, 1986; BRIT Awards, Royal Albert Hall, 1989; Freddie Mercury Tribute Concert, Wembley Stadium, 1992. Recordings: Albums: with Girl: Sheer Greed, 1980; Wasted Youth, 1982; with Def Leppard: Pyromania, 1983; High And Dry, 1984; Hysteria, 1987; Adrenalize, 1992; Retroactive, 1993; Vault 1980-95, 1995; Slang, 1996; Singles include: with Def Leppard: Photograph; Rock Of Ages; Foolin'; Animal; Pour Some Sugar On Me; Armageddon II; Love Bites; Rocket; Let's Get Rocked; Make Love Like A Man; Heaven Is; Two Steps Behind, featured in film soundtrack The Last Action Hero; When Love And Hate Collide. Honours include: American Music Awards: Favourite Heavy Metal Album, Favourite Heavy Metal Artists, 1989. Current Management: Q-Prime Inc., 729 Seventh Avenue, 14th Floor, New York, NY 10019, USA.

COLLIE John Maxwell, b. 21 February 1931, Melbourne, Australia. Trombonist. Divorced, 3 sons, 2 daughters. Career: Band Leader in Melbourne Max Collie Jazz Bandits, then Max Collie Jazz Kings, 1948; Came to England, Joined Melbourne New Orleans Jazz Band, 1962; Joined London City Stompers, 1963; Founder, Max Collie Rhythm Aces, 1966; Played at Festivals, Concerts and Theatres in England, Germany, France, Spain, Denmark, belgium, Holland, Switzerland, Austria, Norway, Sweden, Poland, Yugoslavia, USA, Canada; Several Radio and Television Appearances. Recordings include: Battle of Trafalgar, 1973; World Champions of Jazz, 1976; New Orleans Mardi Gras, 1984; Latest and Greatest, 1993; On Tour in the USA. Honours: Winner, World Championship of Jazz, 1975. Memberships: Musicians Union; MCPS; PRS; PPL. Hobbies: Jazz; Archaeology. Address: 26 Wendover Road, Bromley, Kent, England.

COLLIER Neil Vaughn Robert, b. 25 Apr 1951, Watford, Hertfordshire, England. Record Company Executive. 1 son, 1 daughter. Career: Play Away, BBC TV; Opportunity Knocks; Proprietor, Priory Records. Membership: M Inst M. Hobbies: Football; Cricket. Address: Priory Records, Unit 9B, Upper Wingbury Courtyard, Wingrave, Bucks HP22 4LW, England.

COLLIER Pat, b. 20 October 1951, London, England. Record Producer. m. Jill, 1 son, 2 daughters. Recordings: Wonderstuff, 3 albums; Kingmaker, 2 albums; Soft Boys, several albums; Robyn Hitchcock, several albums; House of Love, Primal Scream; Katrina and the Waves. Current Management: Graham Carpenter, Pachuco Management. Address: Priestlands, Letchmore Heath, Herts, WD2 8EW, England.

COLLIER Tom W, b. 30 June 1948, Puyallup, Washington, USA. Musician (drums, vibraphone); Bandleader. m. Cheryl Zilbert, 31 May 1970, 2 daughters. Education: BA, MusB, University of Washington, 1971. Career: Northwest Jazz Quintet, 1972-80; Freelance musician, various artists including: Bud Shank; Barbra Streisand; Ry Cooder; Sammy Davis Jr; Olivia Newton-John; Paul Williams; Johnny Mathis; Diane Schuur; Earl Hines; The Beach Boys; Jermaine Jackson; Jazz vibraphonist, duo Collier/Dean, 1977-; Director, N W Percussion Institute, Seattle University, 1989-. Recordings: Whistling Midgets, 1981; Illusion, 1987; Pacific Aire, 1991. Publications: Jazz

Improvistion And Ear Training, 1983. Honours: Outstanding Service Award, National Association of Jazz Educators, 1980. Memberships: ASCAP; Percussive Arts Society; National Association of Jazz Educators. Address: University of Washington School Of Music, Seattle, Washington, USA.

COLLING Jonathon, b. 28 May 1968, England. Programmer; Engineer; Record Producer. Education: College; Polytechnic. Career: Record producer, Rumour Records/X-Clusive; All types of dance music, including: house, Euro, jungle; Also jingles for radio/television and radio idents for BBC and local radio. Recordings: Rhythm Nation, 1993; Inner State, 1993; Prohibition Groove, 1994; Music Is My Life; Remixes for X-clusive Records, under name of Proof. Memberships: Musicians' Union; PRS. Hobbies: Badminton; Car maintenance; Music. Current Management: Self-managed. Address: 9 Egerton Road, Hale, Cheshire WA15 8EE, England.

COLLINS Arthur Parker, b. 29 Jan 1951, Stevenson, Ayrshire, Scotland. Singer; Songwriter; Musician (guitar, various instruments). Musical Education: Grade 4 Theory Distinction, SCE Higher Music, Starting HND course leading to degree course. Career: Worked with, influenced, many bands, musicians (pro and amateur); Gigging musician, busker, troubadour, concert and session player. Recordings: Shame On You; Midnight On The Water; Step Out And Take The Odds; In Times Of Trial; Haunted By A Memeory; Green Dragon Lane; Theme For Jacqui; Lost On The River; Linda Anne; Still Waters (Run Deep). Memberships: Musicians' Union; Ex-Songwriters' Association. Hobbies: Social travel; DIY and Construction; Driving; Gardening; Music; Writing.

COLLINS Bootsy (William), b. 26 Oct 1951, Cincinnati, Ohio, USA. Musician (bass). Career: Musician with James Brown's backing group the JBs, 1969-71; Member, George Clinton's Parliament/Funkadelic, 1972-; Also leader, own groups, Bootsy's Rubber Band; Bootzilla Orchestra. Recordings: Albums: with Parliament/Funkadelic: America Eats Its Young, 1972; Cosmic Slop, 1973; Up For The Down Stroke, 1974; Standing On The Verge Of Getting It On, 1974; Chocolate City, 1975; Let's Take It To The Stage, 1975; Mothership Connection, 1976; The Clones Of Dr Funkenstein, 1976; Parliament Live, 1977; Funkentelechy Vs. The Placebo Syndrome, 1977; Player Of The Year, 1978; One Nation Under A Groove, 1978; Motor Booty Affair, 1978; Underjam, 1979; Gloryhallastoopid (Pin The Tale On The Funky), 1979; Trombipulation, 1980; The Electric Spanking Of War Babies, 1981; Computer Games, 1982; Dope Dogs, 1994; Solo: Stretchin' Out, 1976; Ahh... The Name Is Bootsy Baby, 1977; Player Of The Year, 1978; Keepin' Dah Funk Alive 4 1995, 1995; Singles include: Tear The Roof Off The Sucker (Give Up The Funk); Flash Light; One Nation Under A Groove. Address: c/o Bootzilla Productions, PO Box 44158, Cincinnati, OH 45244, USA.

COLLINS Charlie, b. 26 Sept 1952, Sheffield, South Yorkshire, England. Musician (saxophone, clarinet, flute, synthesizer); Composer; Producer. Career: Member, jazz, improvised an dmixed media groups, 1969-; Clock DVA, 1979-81; The Box, 1981-85; The Bone Orchestra, 1985-88; Company Week, 1988; Arts Council Tours, 1988, 1990, 1992; Left Hand Right Hand, 1992-; Solo and production work. Recordings: with Clock DVA: Thirst; White Souls In Black Suits; All recordings with The Box; with Hornweb: Sixteen; with Martin Archer: Wild Pathway Favourites; Telecottage; Left Hand Right Hand; Shockheaded Peters; Ideals Of Freedom, Arts Council Funded Composer, 1990. Address: c/o The Sound Kitchen, 13 Headland Drive, Sheffield S10 5FX, England.

COLLINS Edwyn, b. 1959, Edinburgh, Scotland. Singer. 1 son. Career: Founder, lead singer, Orange Juice (formerly the Nu-Sonics), 1977-1984; Solo artiste, 1985-; International tours, including Europe, Japan, Australia; Phoenix Festival, 1995; Owner, recording studio. Recordings: Albums: with Orange Juice: You Can't Hide Your Love Forever, 1982; Rip It Up, 1982; Texas Fever, 1984; Orange Juice, 1984; The Esteemed Orange Juice, 1992; Ostrich Churchyard, 1992; The Heather's On Fire, 1993; Best Of collections: Solo albums: Hope And Despair, 1989; Hell Bent On Compromise, 1990; Hope And Despair, 1991; Gorgeous George, 1995; I'm Not Following You, 1997; Hit singles with Orange Juice: Rip It Up, 1982; Solo singles: A Girl Like You (Number 1, several countries including UK, France, Netherlands, Australia), 1995; If You Could Love Me, 1995. Honours: BRIT Award Nominations, Best Male Artist, Best Single, 1996. Address: c/o The Agency Group, 370 City Road, London EC1V 2QA, England.

COLLINS Glenn, b. 7 Feb 1968, Emsworth, Hampshire, England. Musician (drums). Career: First drummer, The Auteurs, 18 months; Tour, America, France; Played at: Glastonbury Festival, 1993; Roskilde Festival, Denmark, 1993; Toured UK twice, including support to Suede; Television: Late Show; 2 times, Chart Show; The Beat with Gary Crowley; Radio: Mark Goodier session, Radio 1, 1993; Sheffield Sound City, 1993; Live Broadcast, Radio 1. Honour: Mercury Music Prize Nomination, Top 10 shortlist, 1993. Hobby: New band. Address: 83 Coleridge Road, Crouch End, London N8 8EG, England.

COLLINS Judy Marjorie, b. 1 May 1939, Seattle, Washington, USA. Folk Singer; Songwriter. m. Peter A Taylor, divorced, 1 son. Musical Education: Private piano study with Dr Antonia Brico, 1953-56. Career: Debut as professional folk singer, 1959; Appearances, numerous clubs, US and worldwide; Concerts include: Newport Folk Festival; Worked with: Joni Mitchell; Joshua Rifkin; Stephen Stills; Radio and television include: Judy Collins: From The Heart, HBO special, 1989; Actress, Peer Gynt, New York Shakespeare Festival, 1969; Producer, director, documentary Antonia - A Portrait Of The Woman, 1974. Compositions include: Albatross; Since You've Asked; My Father; Secret Gardens; Born To The Breed; Suite - Judy Blue Eyes. Recordings: Singles include: Both Sides Now, 1968; Amazing Grace, 1971; Send In The Clowns, from musical A Little Night Music, 1975; Albums: A Maid Of Constant Sorrow, 1961; The Golden Apples Of The Sun, 1962; Judy Collins #3, 1964; The Judy Collins Concert, 1964; Judy Collins' 5th Album, 1965; In My Life, 1966; Widlflowers, 1967; Who Knows Where The Time Goes, 1968; Recollections, 1969; Whales And Nightingales, 1970; Living, 1971; Colours Of The Day, 1972; True Stories And Other Dreams, 1973; Judith, 1975; Bread And Roses, 1976; So Early In The Spring (The First Fifteen Years), 1977; Hard Times For Lovers, 1979; The Most Beautiful Songs Of Judy Collins, 1979; Running For My Life, 1980; Time Of Our Lives, 1982; Home Again, 1984; Amazing Grace, 1985; Trust Your Heart, 1987; Trust Your Heart, 1987; Sanity And Grace, 1989; Fires Of Eden, 1991; Just Like A Woman, 1993. Publications: Trust Your Heart (autobiography), 1987; Shameless (novel), 1994. Honours: Grammy, Best Folk Performance,1968; 6 Gold albums; Academy Award Nomination, 1974; Silver Medal, Atlanta Film Festival; Blue Ribbon Award, American Film Festival, New York City; Christopher Award; BMI Performance Award, Both Sides Now, 1990. Current Management: Gurtman & Murtha Associates, 450 7th Avenue, Suite 603, New York, NY 10123-0101, USA.

COLLINS Mike (Michael Edmond), b. 25 July 1949, Manchester, England. MIDI Programmer. Education: MSc (with Distinction), Music Information Technology; BSc Electro-Acoustics with Music. Musical Education: Private tuition by Oliver Hunt, guitar, keyboards. Career: Guitarist, songwriter with jazz-funk band Light Of The World; Top 40 success, Ride The Love Train, 1981; Songwriter, producer, Chappell Music, 1982-83; Dick James Music, 1984-85; Session musician, Top Of The Pops, and other music television shows, 1985-86; MIDI programmer for records and films, 1987-. Recordings: Album: Loops, Music For Multi Media, 1993. Publications: Contributions to: Sound On Sound; Audio Media; Future Music; PCW; Mac World. Memberships: Re-Pro; AES; PRS. Hobbies: Reading; Walking. Address: Flat 1c, 28 Pellatt Grove, Wood Green, London N22 5PL, England.

COLLINS Phil(ip), b. 30 Jan 1951, London, England. Singer;Songwriter; Musician (drums); Record Producer; Actor. m. (1) 1976, divorced, 1 son, 1 daughter, (2) Jill Tavelman, 1984, divorced, 1 daughter. Education: Barbara Speake Stage School. Career: Member, various groups, 1967-70; Drummer, 1970-96, singer, 1975-96, UK group Genesis; Solo recording artiste, 1981-; Numerous worldwide tours, Genesis and solo; Major concerts for charities include Prince's Trust and Live Aid; Record producer for various artists; Film appearances include: Buster, lead role, 1988; Frauds, 1993. Recordings: Albums include: with Genesis: Nursery Crime, 1971; Foxtrot, 1972; Selling England By The Pound, 1973; Genesis Live, 1973; The Lamb Lies Down On Broadway, 1974; A Trick Of The Tail, 1976; Wind And Wuthering, 1977; Seconds Out, 1977; And Then There Were Three, 1978; Duke, 1980; Abacab, 1981; Three Sides Live, 1982; Genesis, 1983; Invisible Touch, 1986; We Can't Dance, 1991; Solo albums: Face Value, 1981; Hello, I Must Be Going, 1982; No Jacket Required, 1985; But Seriously, 1989; Both Sides, 1993; Dance into the Light, 1996; Numerous hit singles include: I Missed Again; In The Air Tonight; You Can't Hurry Love; I Can't Dance; Groovy Kind Of Love; Two Hearts; Easy Lover, with Philip Bailey. Honours include: LVO, 1994; 7 Grammy Awards; 6 Ivor Novello Awards; 4 BRIT Awards; 2 Silver Clef Awards; 2 Variety Club of Great Britain Awards. Membership: Trustee, Prince's Trust. Current Management: Hit And Run Music, 30 Ives Street, London SW3 2ND, England.

COLMAN Stuart, b. 19 Dec 1944, Harrowgate, West Yorkshire, England. Record Producer. m. Janet, 22 Sept 1973, 1 son, 2 daughters. Musician (bass, piano). Career: Producer for: Jeff Beck; The Big Town Playboys; Billy Swan; Cliff Richard; Phil Everly; Duane Eddy; Shakin' Stevens; Little Richard; The Shadows; Gary Glitter; Billy Fury; Kim Wilde; The Hank Wangford Band; Rich Sharp. Publication: They Kept On Rockin'. Honours: Music Week Award, Top Singles Producer, 1981. Memberships: Musicians' Union; Country Music Association, Nashville. Current Management: Dennis Muirhead. Address: Muirhead Management, 202 Fulham Road, London SW10 9PJ, England.

COLQUHOUN Tom, b. 24 Oct 1968, Linwood, Scotland. Musician (guitar). Musical Education: Self-taught. Career: Guitarist, specialising in solo and small group projects; composer and arranger; performances include playing two guitars simultaneously. Composition: Wrote and performed theme music for BBC short film, When I'm 21. Membership: Musicians' Union; SPNM. Hobbies: Reading; Fitness; UFO Research; Music. Address: 14 Barshaw Place, Paisley PA1 3HJ, Scotland.

COLTART Robert Alexander Hendry, b. 20 Dec 1956, West Molesey, Surrey, England. Vocalist; Musician (guitar, bass guitar); Songwriter. m. Angela Gausden, 20 Aug 1983, 1 daughter. Musical Education: Self-taught. Career: Member, Badge, 1972-75; Bass guitar for Peter Noone (Herman's Hermits), 1975; Whispering

Wind, 1976-78; Solo artiste, 1978-80; Life'N'Soul, 1979; Arthur Kay And The Originals, 1980; Vocalist, guitarist, Maroondogs, 1981; Chuck Berry European Tour, 1988; GLR Nina Myskow Show, with Maroondogs, 1989; Mort Shuman Memorial Concert, 1991; Berlin SKA Festival with Arthur Kay, 1995; Backing Chris Andrews, recording with him, 1992-95; Recording and writing with George Williams, 1997. Recordings: Various television and radio commercials; Dark Nights Falling, 1984; Volcanoes, Skatoon Time, 1989; No-One But You; The Chozen I, 1994. Memberships: PRS; MCPS; Musicians' Union. Hobbies: Reading; Walking; Swimming; Football. Current Management: Self-managed; Various agents. Address: 1 Foord Road, Folkstone, Kent CT20 1HH, England.

COLTER Jessi (Miriam Johnson), b. 25 May 1943, Phoenix, Arizona, USA. Singer; Musician (piano); Songwriter. m. (1) Duane Eddy, divorced 1968, (2) Waylon Jennings, 26 Oct 1969, 1 daughter. Career: Church pianist, aged 11; Solo artiste, also with Waylon Jennings, late 1960s-. Compositions include: No Sign Of The Living (recorded by Dottie West); You Hung The Moon; Storms Never Last; Jennifer; Co-writer (with Waylon Jennings), I'm Not Lisa. Recordings: Singles include: Lonesome Road; Guitar On My Mind, with Duane Eddy; I'm Not Lisa; Suspicious Minds; Storms Never Last; The Union Mare And The Confederate Grey; Solo albums: A Country Star Is Born, 1970; I'm Jessi Colter, 1975; Jessi, 1976; Diamond In The Rough, 1976; Mirriam, 1977; That's The Way A Cowboy Rock 'n' Rolls, 1978; Ridin' Shotgun, 1982; Rock'n'Roll Lullaby, 1984; Albums with Waylon Jennings: Wanted - The Outlaws (with Waylon Jennings and Willie Nelson), 1975; White Mansions, 1978; Leather And Lace, 1981; Film soundtrack, The Pursuit Of D B Cooper, 1982. Address: c/o Buddy Lee Attractions, 38 Music Square E #300, Nashville, TN 37203, USA.

COLTRANE Chi, b. 16 Nov 1952, Racine, Wisconsin, USA. Singer; Songwriter; Producer; Musician (multi-instrumentalist). Musical Education: Vocal instruction; Choir and Musical Notation. Career: Las Vegas; Tours throughout USA; Special guest star representing USA at International Song Festival, Rio De Janeiro; Many television appearances USA and Europe including: Tonight Show; Johnny Carson; Merv Griffin; Superstars Of Rock; Numerous television specials, including Chi Coltrane in Concert with the Edmonton Symphony, 1995; Multiple tours of Europe, approximately 300 concerts in one year; Raised money for South American rain forest project; Worked with: Gary Brooker (Procul Harum); Barry McGuire; Jennifer Rush; Nina; Future tours include: USA and Russia. Compositions: Thunder And Lightning; Go Like Elijah; You Were My Friend; Wheel Of Life; Who Ever Told You; Ooh Baby; I'm Gonna Make You Love Me; Recordings: Chi Coltrane, 1972; Let It Ride, 1973; Special Chi Coltrane, 1975; Best Of Chi Coltrane, 1975; Road To Tomorrow, 1977; Silk And Steel, 1981; Ready To Roll, 1983; Chi Coltrane Live, 1982; The Message, 1986; Recording featured in film Beaches. Honours: Gold Hammer, Silver Hammer, Best Female Artist: Germany; Switzerland; Austria; Netherlands. Memberships: AFTRA; AFM; ASCAP; SUISA. Hobbies: Painting (oils, watercolours); Reading; All animals (especially cats, horses); Horse riding; Gymnastics; Dance. Address: Nick Joseph, c/o Stellar Artists Management, 505 South Beverly Drive, Suite 166, Beverly Hills, CA 90212, USA.

COLVILLE (Creighton) Randolph (Victor), b. 23 May 1942, Glasgow, Scotland. Musician (clarinet, saxophone); Composer; Arranger; Musical Director; Teacher. m. Joan Winifred Pym, 23 May 1970, 1 son, 1 daughter. Musical Education: Northern School of Music, 1962-66, appointed to teaching staff, 1966. Career:

Teaching and Freelancing, 1966-75; Permanent Teacher and Conductor, Kent Music School, 1975; Numerous television appearances at home and abroad, including television film Buddy Bolden's Children; Many radio broadcasts for BBC Jazz Club, Jazz Parade, Sounds of Jazz; Frequent engagements as featured soloist at South Bank; Played the Mozart and Brahms Clarinet Quintets at Kenwood House, 1991. Compositions: Mantovani Mix-Up; S'Okay; Fuss Pot. Recordings: Jungle Nights In Harlem, Midnite Follies Orchestra, 1981; Echoes Of The Duke, Humphrey Lyttelton and Helen Shapiro, 1984; The World Of Buddy Bolden, Humphrey Lyttelton, 1986; Hot And Cool, Colville Collection, 1992; Hotter Than That, A Elsdon, 1986; Keepers Of The Flame, A Elsdon, 1994; Various other recordings including with Keith Nichols Groups. Honour: British Jazz Award, Best Clarinettist, 1988. Memberships: Musicians' Union; Performing Rights Society; The British Music Writers Council; The British Jazz Musicians Society. Hobbies: Reading; Travel; Crosswords; Cooking. Current Management: Shirley Walker. Address: 28 Childscroft Road, Rainham, Gillingham, Kent ME8 7SS, England.

COLVIN Shawn, b. 1956, Vermillion, South Dakota, USA. Singer; Songwriter; Musician (guitar). Musical Education: Guitar lessons from age 10. Career: 15 years as bar musician; Touring guitarist with Richard Thompson. Recordings: Albums: Steady On, 1989; Fat City, 1992; Cover Girl, 1994. Honour: Grammy Award, Steady On, 1990. Current Management: AGF Entertainment, 30 West 21st Street, 7th Floor, New York, NY 10010-6905, USA.

COMBELLE Philippe Alix François, b. 14 July 1939, Paris, France. Musician (drums). Françoise Ruiz, 4 May 1964, 1 son, 1 daughter. Education: Postgraduate studies. Musical Education: Studies with father Alix Combelle (Alix Combelle Big Band), piano, saxophone, drums, tabla. Career: Jazz concerts and clubs: Europe; USA; UK; Japan; Africa; Russia; Turkey; Thailand; India; Vietnam; Israel; Martinique; Guadaloupe; Syria; Jordan; Yemen; Oman; Teacher, Marly Conservatory of Music; International Music School, Paris. Recordings: Recorded with: Don Byas; Sonny Criss; Memphis Slim; Willie Dixon; Christian Escoudé; Toots Thielemans; Cat Anderson; Barclay; Buck Clayton; Buddy De Franco; Jimmy Gourley; Marc Johnson; Lavelle; OMD with Ray Brown; Eddie Harris; Guy Lafitte; Alix Combelle; Jimmy Gourley; Rene Mailhes; Bernard Maury Trio; Pierre Michelot; Daniel Colin. Membership: SACEM. Address: 36 Rue Sibuet, 75012 Paris, France.

COMO Perry (Pierino Como), b. 18 May 1913, Canonsburg, Pennsylvania, USA. Singer; Actor. m. Rosbelle Beline, 2 sons, 1 daughter. Career: Singer with Freddy Carlone Band, 1933; Beat The Band radio show, with Ted Weems, 1936-42; International solo artiste, numerous concerts worldwide; Over 60 million records sold to date; Televison host, own shows: Music Hall; Perry Como Show, NBC; Various television specials; Actor, films: Something For The Boys, 1944; Doll Face, 1946; If I'm Lucky, 1946; Words And Music, 1948. Recordings: Numerous albums include: I Believe, 1954; Relaxing With Perry Como, 1955; Dear Perry, 1958; Sing To Me, Mr C, 1961; The Songs I Love, 1963; It's Impossible, 1970; And I Love You So, 1973; Perry, 1974; Especially For You, 1980; So It Goes, 1983; Today, 1987; Numerous greatest hits compilations; Numerous hit singles include: Til The End Of Time; Prisoner Of Love; Surrender; Chi-Baba, Chi-Baba; I Wonder Who's Kissing Her Now; And I Love You So; Catch A Falling Star; Magic Moments; A-You're Adorable; Hello Young Lovers; It's Impossible; Some Enchanted Evening; Hoop-De-Doo; Don't Let The Stars Get In Your Eyes; Wanted; Hot Diggity; Frosty The Snowman. Honours: Best Vocalist, Motion Picture Daily, 1953; Emmy Award; Peabody Award; Christopher

Award; Variety Club Personality of The Year (all 1956); Kennedy Center Award for Lifetime Achievement, 1987; Inducted into Academy of TV Arts and Science Hall Of Fame, 1990. Address: c/o RCA Records, 1540 Broadway, New York, NY 10036, USA.

COMPAGNO Tony, b. 16 Nov 1966, Cork City, Ireland. Singer; Songwriter. Career: Appearances: RTE Cúrsaí; RTE 89FM; Tours, 1989, 1992, 1994; Cork multichannel, video, 1992. Recordings: Debut album: Tony Compagno, 1994; Guest artist to: Jimmy MacCarthy; Hazel O'Connor; Luka Bloom; Cutting Crew; Maura O'Connell; Mary Coughlan; Davy Spillane. Hobbies: Swimming; Listening to music; People. Current Management: Denis Desmond Promotions. Address: Thompson House, MacCurtain St, Cork City, Ireland.

CONLEE John, b. 11 Aug 1946, Versailles, Kentucky, USA. Country Singer; Songwriter. Career: Played guitar on radio, aged 10; Singer, Versailles barbershop group; Disc jockey, Nashville, mid-1970s; Recording artiste, 1978-; Also licensed embalmer, farm owner. Compositions include: Rose-Coloured Glasses; Backside Of Thirty. Recordings: US Country Number 1 hits: Lady Lay Down; Backside Of Thirty; Common Man; I'm Only In It For The Love; In My Eyes; As Long As I'm Rockin' With You; Got My Heart Set On You. Current Management: John Conlee Enterprises Inc., 38 Music Square E #117, Nashville, TN 37203, USA.

CONLEY Earl Thomas, b. 17 Oct 1941, Portsmouth, Ohio, USA. Country Singer; Songwriter; Musician. Career: First artist to have 4 hits from 1 album, 1984; Recorded 18 US Country Number 1 hits. Compositions include: Smokey Mountain Memories, Mel Street; This Time I've Hurt Her More, Conway Twitty. Recordings: US Country Number 1 hits include: Fire And Smoke; Somewhere Between Right And Wrong; Don't Make It Easy For Me, Your Love's On The Line; Angel In Disguise; Holding Her And Loving You; Duets include: Too Many Times, with Anita Pointer; We Believe In Happy Endings, with Emmylou Harris; Albums: Blue Pearl, 1980; Fire And Smoke, 1981; Somewhere Between Right And Wrong, 1982; Don't Make It Easy For Me, 1983; Treadin' Water, 1984; Greatest Hts, 1985; Too Many Times, 1986; The Heart Of It All, 1988; Yours Truly, 1991. Address: c/o Artists International Management Inc., 9850 Sandalfoot Blvd, Suite 458, Boca Raton, FL 33428, USA.

CONNELLY Chris(topher John), b. 11 Nov 1964, Edinburgh, Scotland. Singer; Musician (guitar). Musical Education: Choir, George Heriots School. Career: World tours with Ministry; Revolting Cocks; Solo tours, USA. Recordings: with Ministry: Mind Is A Terrible Thing To Taste; Psalm 69; with Revolting Cocks: Beers, Steers And Queers; Solo: Shipwreck. Memberships: BMI; PRS. Hobbies: Jazz; Thinking; Writing; Staring. Address: Box 472, 1573 N Milwaukee Avenue, Chicago, IL 60622, USA.

CONNICK Harry Jr, b. 11 Sept 1967, New Orleans, Louisiana, USA. Jazz Musician (piano); Singer; Actor. Musical Education: New Orleans Center For The Creative Arts; Studied with Ellis Marsalis; Student, Hunter College, Manhattan School Of Music. Recordings: Albums: Harry Connick Jr, 1987; 20, 1989; When Harry Met Sally (film soundtrack), 1989; We Are In Love, 1990; Blue Light, Red Light, 1991; She, 1994; as Harry Connick Jr Trio: Lofty's Roach Souffle, 1991; 11, 1993; 25, 1993. Contributions to other film soundtracks: Memphis Belle (also actor in film), 1990; Little Man Tate, 1991. Honour: Grammy Award, Male Jazz Vocal Performance, When Harry Met Sally, 1990. Current Management: Wilkins Management, 260 Brookline Street, #200, Cambridge, MA 02139, USA.

CONNIFF Ray, b. 6 Nov 1916, Attleboro, Massachusetts, USA. Musician (trombone); Conductor; Composer; Arranger. Musical Education: Juilliard School of Music; Taught trombone by father. Career: Trombone player, arranger, orchestras of: Bunny Berigan, 1936; Bob Crosby's Bobcats; Artie Shaw, 4 years; Harry James; Arranger, composer, conductor, solo recording artist, 1954-; Worked with Johnny Ray; Rosemary Clooney; Marty Robbins; Guy Mitchell. Recordings include: Lara's Theme, for film Doctor Zhivago, 1965; As composer/arranger: Band Of Gold, Don Cherry, 1954; Numerous hit albums include: S'Wonderful, 1957; Say It With Music, 1960; Memories Are Made Of This, 1961; Somewhere My Love, 1966; Evergreens, 1973; Sentimental Journey, 1978; Amor Amor, 1984; Always In My Heart, 1988; 16 Most Requested Songs, 1993. Address: PO Box 46395, Los Angeles, CA 90046, USA.

CONROY Patricia, b. 30 Jan 1957, Montreal, Quebec, Canada. Songwriter; Singer. Career: Television specials, Canadian networks, TNN; CMT; NCN; CBC. Recordings: Albums: Blue Angel, 1990; Bad Day For Trains, 1992; You Can't Resist, 1994. Honours: CCMA Album of the Year, 1993; CCMA Female Vocalist of the Year, 1994. Membership: AFM. Current Management: Tim Rathert, Tony Gottlieb, Morning Star Management. Address: PO Box 1770, Hendersonville, TN 37075, USA.

CONSTANTIN François, b. 2 Dec 1961, Paris, France. Musician (percussion, drums). m. 10 May 1986, 2 daughters. Musical Education: Normal School Of Music of Paris. Career: In Jazz and others: Lavel; Arturo Sandoval; Francis Lockwood; Veronique Sanson; France Gall; Elsa; Louis Chedid; Johnny Hallyday; Patrick Bruel; Jean-Patrick Capdeviel; Michel Sardoux; Fabian. Recordings: Live records with the above artists; Sessions with Jannick Top; Florent Pagny; Jean Marc Jafet; Own group Latin Jazz. Hobbies: Sports; Judo; Fitness; Humour. Current Management: Self-managed. Address: 53 Rue du Petit Bois, 77200 Torcy, France.

CONSTANTINOU Chris, (Chris De Niro), 20 July 1957, London, England. Musician (bass guitar, guitar, flute); Singer; Actor. Musical Education: Flute, bass at school; Mainly learned playing live. Career: First record with Punk band The Drill and Hollywood Exiles, produced by Chas Chandler, 1976; Joined Adam Ant, as Chris De Niro, 1981-86; Several world tours, playing all major venues; Television appearances include: Saturday Night Live, USA; Solid Gold, USA; American Bandstand; Top Of The Pops; Wogan; Russell Harty; Live Aid; Dick Clarke Show; Formed S.F.Go; Songwriting partnership with Annebella Lwin, ex-Bow Wow Wow singer, with record deal; Singer, writer, own band C.C.Moon Dog; Currently singer/writer, own band, Jackie On Assid; Film appearances: Lead actor, Touch, BBC2; Play Dead, by Danny Cannon; Shopping, by Paul Anderson. Recordings: Drill; Vive Le Rock, Adam Ant; Do What You Do, with Annebella Lwin; Other hit singles and videos. Memberships: PRS; MCPS; Equity; Musicians' Union; AFTRA; PAMRA. Current Management: Jens Hills. Address: Northburgh House, 10 Northburgh Street, London EC1V 0AY, England.

CONWAY Russ (Trevor Herbert Stanford), b. 2 Sept 1925, Bristol, England. Musician (piano); Composer; Entertainer. Education: Commercial College. Career: Royal Naval Service, 1942-46; Merchant Marine Service, 1950-55; Joined Chappels Music Publishers; Accompanist to Dame Gracie Fields; Dorothy Squires; Dennis Lotis; Lita Roza; Joan Regan; Adelaide Hall; Shani Wallis. First solo record, EMI Records, 1957; Regular artist, Billy Cotton television shows, 1959-66; Appearances on all major television shows, including five own series; Subject of This Is Your Life, 1961; Four Summer Seasons, London Palladium; Formed Russ Conway Cancer Fund, produces annual charity galas; Continues to perform regularly. Compositions include: Sidesaddle, 1959. Recordings: 75 singles released; Number 1 singles: Sidesaddle; Roulette; China Tea; 17 Top Twenty records in succession; 41 albums and 35 EPs released; Last 78 rpm ever issued by EMI, Royal Event. Honours: Distinguished Service Medal, 1944; Ivor Novello Award; 1 Platinum, 6 Gold, 2 Silver records (including first Silver record ever issued, Roulette, 1959); Instrumentalist of the Year Trophy, 1959, 1960; Freedom of the City of London, 1996. Memberships: PRS; MCPA; EABF; BASCA; Society of Distinguished Songwriters (SODS), 1996. Hobbies: Swimming; Reading. Address: PO Box 1146, Eastbourne, East Sussex BN22 0AF, England.

CONWAY Tony (James Anthony), b. Bardstown, Kentucky, USA.Entertainment Company Executive. m. Nancy Schaefer, 1976, 1 son, 1 daughter. Education: Graduate, Northwood College, Southern Indiana. Career: Opened first talent agency, Lexington, Kentucky; Moved to Nashville; Agent for Buddy Lee Attractions, Inc, 1975; President, Buddy Lee Attractions, Inc, 1987-; Over 30 clients include: Willie Nelson; Emmylou Harris; Ricky Van Shelton; Clay Walker; Mark Chestnutt; Waylon Jennings; Lorrie Morgan; Handles special event department in offices in Nashville, Kansas City, Los Angeles; Director Services of Main Stage Production Enterprises Inc, producing major events, festivals, state fairs, North America; First agent in Nashville to develop new breed of country acts; Artists signed include: George Strait; Mary Chapin Carpenter; Patty Loveless; Garth Brooks; John Anderson; Sawyer Brown; Talent Coordinator, FarmAid Concerts, Illinois, Texas; Coordinated, booked, Highwayman I and II tours, with: Willie Nelson; Waylon Jennings; Johnny Cash; Kris Kristofferson; Handles international tours for all clients. Honours: CMA Agent Of the Year, SRO Convention, 1990, 1991; Country Agent Of the Year, Performance Magazine Readers Poll, 1992, 1993. Address: 38 Music Square E #300, Nashville, TN 37203, USA.

COODER Ry (Ryland Peter Cooder), b. 15 Mar 1947, Los Angeles, California, USA. Musician (guitar, slide guitar); Composer. Career: Member, Jackie DeShannon's backing group, aged 17; Member: The Risng Sons, 1966; Captain Beefheart's Magic Band, 1967; Session guitar work included: Everly Brothers; Paul Revere and The Raiders; Randy Newman; Rolling Stones; Solo recording artist, 1970-; Formed Little Village with Nick Lowe, John Hiatt, Jim Keltner, 1991; Film music writer, 1980s-. Recordings include: Solo albums: Ry Cooder, 1971; Into The Purple Valley, 1972; Boomer's Story, 1972; Paradise And Lunch, 1974; Chicken Skin Music, 1976; Live Show Time, 1977; Bop Till You Drop, 1979; Why Don't You Try Me Tonight?, 1986; Get Rhythm, 1987; Pecos Bill, with Robin Williams, 1988; Music By Ry Cooder, 1995; with Little Village: Little Village, 1992. Film soundtracks include: Performance Candy; Blue Collar (with Captain Beefheart); Film scores as composer: The Long Riders, 1980; The Border, 1982; Paris Texas, 1985; Alamo Bay, 1985; Crossroads, 1986; Blue City, 1986; Johnny Handsome, 1989; Geronimo, 1993. Honours include: Grammy Award, Best Recording For Children, 1989. Address: c/o Warner Bros Records, 129 Park Street, London W1Y 3FA, England.

COOK David Lynn, b. 11 Nov 1965, Pascagula, Mississippi, USA. Singer; Charity Spokesman; Model. Education: Masters, Business; Doctorate, Child Psychology, Divinty. Musical Education: Masters, Music; Doctorate, Musical Composition. Career: Member, The Cook Family Singers; David L Cook and the Trinidetts; Performs religious songs; Performed at White House for Ronald Reagan, 1986; Appearances in: Japan; Israel; England; Russia; Netherlands; China; Australia; Television apppearances include: 700 Club; Host of The Prestigious Manitoba Awards, 1987, 1988, 1995; Sesame Street; Jerry Lewis Telethon; Night of 100 Stars; Walt Disney World's 35th Anniversary; White House Celebration, 1986. Recordings include: Album: Come Follow Me; Singles: My Song; Lift Him Up. Honours include: 3 Prestigious Manitoba Awards; AMAAA Male Vocalist of Year, 1986-87; AMAAA Composer of Year, 1987-90; ABG Rising Star Award, 1989; 5 Dove Award Nominations, 1995; Numerous Robi Awards, 1986-90; Gospel Music Humanitarian Award, ARAMA, 1995; 4 Gold Albums; Sacred Music USA Award, Contemporary Christian Artist of the Year, 1996. Memberships: GMA; NARAS; CMA; AMARA; SAG; SESAC. Current Management: Daylyn Ware, American Musical Academy Of Arts Assembly. Address: 1336 Cheshire Avenue, Charlotte, NC 28208, USA.

COOK Eddie, b. 18 Apr 1928, Billericay, Essex, England. Publisher; Writer; Musician (saxophone). m. Patricia Mary Beale (deceased), 26 Mar 1955, 1 son, 1 daughter. Musical Education: Taught by mother; Later studied tenor saxophone with Les Evans. Career: Amateur and semi-professional musical work, music industry (buying, selling, repairing musical instruments); Publisher, 1960-; Publisher, Jazz Journal, 1979-; Editor, 1983-. Publications: Jazz Journal International (also numerous earlier non-music publications). Hobbies: Bicycle racing; Playing Jazz; Gardening. Current Management: Self-managed. Address: Jazz Journal Ltd, 1/5 Clerkenwell Road, London EC1M 5PA, England.

COOK Jeff, b. 27 Aug 1949, Fort Payne, Alabama, USA. Vocalist; Musician (guitar). Career: Founder member, country music group Wild Country, 1969-; Changed name to Alabama, 1977-; Worked with Lionel Richie, 1986. Recordings: Albums: Alabama, 1980; My Home's In Alabama, 1980; Feels So Right, 1981; Mountain Music, 1982; The Closer You Get, 1983; Roll On, 1984; 40 Hour Week, 1985; The Touch, 1986; Greatest Hits, 1986; Just Us, 1987; Southern Star, 1989; Pass It On Down, 1990; Greatest Hits Volume 2, 1991; American Pride, 1992; Singles include: I Want To Be With You; Tennessee River; Feels So Right; Love In The First Degree; Pass It On Down. Current Management: Dale Morris And Associates, 818 19th Avenue South, Nashville, TN 37203, USA.

COOK Paul, b. 20 July 1956, London, England. Musician (drums). Career: Drummer, UK punk group, The Sex Pistols, 1975-78; Performances include: First gig, St Martin's School of Art, London, 1975; Screen On The Green Special, London, 1976; 100 Club punk rock festival, 1976; Anarchy In The UK Tour, 1976; Tours, Europe, 1977; US, 1978; Plays dates with Johnny Thunders, 1978; Member band, The Professionals, 1979; Sex Pistols reunion concert scheduled, 1996. Recordings: Albums: Never Mind The Bollocks - Here's The Sex Pistols, 1977; The Great Rock'n'Roll Swindle, 1979; Some Product - Carri On Sex Pistols, 1979; Flogging A Dead Horse, 1980; Kiss This, 1992; Singles: God Save The Queen, 1977; Pretty Vacant, 1977; Holidays In The Sun, 1977; Something Else, 1979; Silly Thing, 1979; C'mon Everybody, 1979; The Great Rock'n'Roll Swindle, 1979; with Steve Jones and Ronnie Biggs: No One Is Innocent (A Punk Prayer By Ronnie Biggs), 1978.

COOKE Paul Anthony, b. 18 Dec 1961, Hull, England. Musician (drums); Singer; Songwriter; Artist Manager. m. Susan Lesley Jarvis, 9 Sept 1991, 2 sons, 1 daughter. Musical Education: Self-taught. Career: Drummer, Pride, 1981-82; Founder member, drummer, Sade, 1982-84; Tours: Danceteria, New York City, 1982; U4, Vienna, 1983; Television and radio appearances include: Switch, 1983; Loose Talk, 1983; Top of the Pops, 1984; Radio 1, Peter Powell Sessions,

1983; Singer, Songwriter, Esposito, 1985-86; Papa Divine, 1987-88; Songwriter, Producer, MBDK, 1989-90; Solo artist, 1991-93; Singer, songwriter, P Eye Eye, 1994; Major concerts include: Esposito, Royal Albert Hall, 1986; Papa Divine, Brighton Pavillion, 1987; Business Ventures: P R Clarke Management; PSP Productions; IVI Records Ltd; IVI Management; Artist Manager for Esposito; Papa Divine; MBDK; Buff Meaba; Proud; P Eye Eye. Compositions: Singles: Co-writer, Smooth Operator and Your Love Is King, Sade; Recordings: Message In A Melody, Esposito, 1986; You Don't Have To Say You Love Me, Paul Cooke, 1991; Emma, Paul Cooke, 1991; Lost At Sea, P Eye Eye, 1994; Album: Diamond Life, Sade, 1984; Honours: BPI Award; Triple Platinum record, Diamond Life, 1984. Memberships: PRS; MCPS. Hobbies: Martial arts; Film making. Current Management: IVI Management. Address: 6 Cheyne Walk, Hornsea, North Humberside HU18 1BX, England.

COOLIDGE Rita, b. 1 May 1944, Nashville, Tennessee, USA. Singer. m. Kris Kristofferson, 1973, divorced 1979. Career: Radio commercials with sister, Memphis, Tennessee; Session singer with artists including Eric Clapton, Stephen Stills, mid-1960s; Tours with Delaney and Bonnie; Leon Russell; Solo artiste, 1970-; UK tour with Kristofferson, including Royal Albert Hall, 1978; Music for UNICEF Concert, New York, 1979. Recordings: Hit singles: Higher And Higher; We're All Alone; The Way You Do The Things You Do; All Time High, theme to film Octopussy; Duets with Kris Kristofferson include: Lovin' Arms; A Song I'd Like To Sing; From The Bottle To The Bottom; Albums: Rita Coolidge, 1971; Nice Feelin', 1971; Lady's Not For Sale, 1972; Fall Into Spring, 1974; It's Only Love, 1975; Anytime Anywhere, 1977; Love Me Again, 1978; Satisfied, 1979; Heartbreak Radio, 1981; Never Let You Go, 1983; Inside The Fire, 1988; Cherokee, 1995; Out of the Blues, 1996; Walela, native American recording, 1997; with Kris Kristofferson: Full Moon, 1974; Breakaway, 1975; Natural Act, 1979. Honours: Grammy Awards: Best Country Duo/Group Vocal Performance, with Kristofferson, 1974, 1975. Current Management: ChoCorp International, 11684 Ventura Boulevard #899, Studio City, CA 91604, USA.

COOLIO (Artis Ivey), b. 1963, Los Angeles, California, USA. Rapper. 5 children. Career: Former fireman; Rapper, from age 15; Member, WC And The Maad Circle; Solo recording artist, 1994-. Recordings: Albums: It Takes A Thief, 1994; Gangsta's Paradise, 1995; Hit singles: Gangsta's Paradise, used in film soundtrack Dangerous Minds (Number 1, UK), 1995; Too Hot, 1996. Honours: BRIT Award Nomination, Best International Male Artist, 1996; International Dance Music Award, Best Rap 12" Single, 1996. Current Management: Powermove, 8489 W 3rd Street, Suite 1007, Los Angeles, CA 90048, USA.

COOMBES Gaz (Gareth). Singer; Musician (guitar). Career: Member, The Jennifers; Lead singer, guitarist, Supergrass, 1994-; Major concerts include: Support to Blur, Alexandra Palace, 1994; UK tour with Shed Seven, 1994; T In The Park Festival, Glasgow, 1995. Recordings: Albums: I Should Coco (Number 1, UK), 1995 In It for the Money, 1997; Singles: Caught By The Fuzz, 1994; Mansize Rooster, 1995; Lenny, 1995; Alright, 1995; Going Out, 1996; Sun Hits the Sky, 1997. Honours: Q Award, Best New Act, 1995; BRIT Award Nominations: Best British Newcomer, Best Single, Best Video, 1996. Current Management: Courtyard Management, 22 The Nursery, Sutton Courtenay, Abingdon, Oxon OX14 4UA, England.

COOPER Alice (Vincent Furnier), b. 4 Feb 1948, Detroit, Michigan, USA. Singer. m Sheryl Goddard, 1 sons, 2 daughters. Career: First to stage theatrical rock concert tours; Among first to film conceptual rock promo videos (pre-MTV);

Considered among originators and greatest hard rock artists; Known as King of Shock Rock; Many film, television appearances. Recordings: Singles include: I'm Eighteen; Poison; No More Mr Nice Guy; I Never Cry; Only Women Bleed; You And Me; Under My Wheels; Bed Of Nails; Albums include: School's Out, 1972; Billion Dollar Babies, 1973; Welcome To My Nightmare, 1976; From The Inside, 1978; Constrictor, 1986; Raise Your Fist And Yell, 1987; Trash, 1988; Hey Stoopid, 1991. Publications: Wrote foreword to short story book: Shock Rock. Honour: Foundations Forum, Lifetime Achievement Award, 1994. Memberships: BMI; NARAS; SAG; AFTRA; AFofM. Hobby: Watching low budget horror films. Current Management: Alive Enterprises. Address: PO Box 5542, Beverly Hills, CA 90211, USA.

COOPER Dorothy, b. 17 Apr 1944, Newcastle-upon-Tyne, England. Vocalist. m. Rob Cooper, 25 May 1970, 1 son, 1 daughter. Education: Neville's Cross College, Durham. Musical Education: Studied with Roy Henderson and John Carol Case. Career: Performed at the Purcell Room and given recitals at many music clubs; Head of Music at various schools, 1967-78; Director of Wavendon Courses, 1980-; Administrator of Guildhall School of Music, Postgraduate Jazz Department; Freelance, manager,education advisor and singer. Honour: ARCM. Membership: Musicians' Union. Hobbies: Aerobics; Gardening. Address: 4 Medland, Woughton Park, Milton Keynes MK6 3BH, England.

COOPER Douglas, b. 3 Sept 1929, Weymouth, Dorset, England. Musician (drums). m. Blanche, 23 Apr 1977, 1 son, 1 daughter. Musical Education: London School Of Music. Career: Worked with: Geraldo; Joe Loss; Tito Burns; Eric Winstone; Edmundo Ross; Paul Fenoulhet; Also worked in USA with Al Grey, Jimmy Forest, Count Basie musicians; Decca sessions for Ray Martin, Norrie Paramour, 1950s; Accompanied many top artists including: Frankie Vaughn; Peter Knight Singers; Matt Monro; Current member, Bournemouth Big Band; Southampton Allstars; Also with own group at local jazz club. Membership: Musicians' Union. Hobby: Golf. Address: 2 Gloucester Street, Weymouth, Dorset DT4 7AP, England.

COOPER Geoffrey Richard, b. 19 Mar 1955, Stoke Newington, London, England. Composer; Musician (drums). 2 daughters. Musical Education: Various private tutors; Hailybury College, Hertfordshire. Career: with Mothers Ruin; Session work includes many radio and television sessions; with Voyeur (unsigned); Sessions for: Kenny Ball; Michael Schenker; Three Degrees; Tim Rice; Mike Berry; Broken English; Member, The Counterfeit Stones, now left to resume session career. Memberships: Musicians' Union; PRS; MCPS. Hobbies: Squash; Cycling; Country walking. Current Management: Self managed. Address: 15 Lilac Road, Hoddesdon, Herts EN11 0PG, England.

COOPER Giles Richard, b. 6 Oct 1968, Amersham, Buckinghamshire, England. Singer; Songwriter; Musician (guitar, bass, keyboards). Career: Live concerts throughout London, include Marquee/100 Club; Various bands include Kindred Spirit; Misbeat; Splinter. Recordings: Painted Sun; That Was The Year That Was; Fly Away; Don't Play Those Games; Minds Eye. Memberships: Musicians' Union; International Songwriters Association; Guild of International Songwriters and Composers. Current Management: A J Promotions. Address: Ground Floor, 108 Inderwick Road, Hornsey, London N8 9JY, England.

COOPER Paul Joseph, b. 27 Dec 1959, Liverpool, Merseyside, England. Musician (bass guitar, guitar). m. Jacqueline Ann Iveson, 5 Aug 1989, 1 son, 1 daughter. Career: Glastonbury

Festival; Royal Albert Hall; Wembley Stadium; London Palladium; Budokan Stadium, Tokyo, Japan; Television and radio: Blue Peter; Kaleidoscope; Radio 4; Newsnight. Recordings: (own composition) All Of The Time, 1983. Hobby: Football. Current Management: Bootleg Beatles.

COOTE Anthony William John, b. 29 Mar 1961, Hilderborough, Kent, England. Musician (guitar, bass guitar); Vocalist. Education: Canterbury College. Musical Education: Kent Music School, guitar, tenor horn. Career: with Ruby Blue: major tours, UK; Television: Rock Steady, C4; James Whale Show (ITV); Daytime Live (BBC1); Garden Party (BBC1); Festivals: Glastonbury; Reading; WOMAD; Rebecca Pidgeon: Recording and touring in USA; Animals That Swim: Recording, touring UK, Europe. Compositions: Down From Above; The Raven. Recordings: Ruby Blue: Down From Above; Virginia Astley: All Shall Be Well; Rebecca Pidgeon: The Raven; Animals That Swim: Workshy; Singles: Ruby Blue: So Unlike Me; Because; Bloomsbury Blue; Stand Together; The Quiet Mind; Primitive Man; Can It Be; John Martyn: Deny This Love; Animals That Swim: Madame Yevonde; Pink Carnations; Videos: Ruby Blue: The Quiet Mind; Primitive Man; Animals That Swim: Madame Yevonde. Membership: Musicians' Union. Hobby: Cycling. Current Management: c/o Elemental Records. Address: 64 Mount Grove Road, London N5 2CT, England.

COPANI Ignacio Anibal, b. 25 Oct 1959, Buenos Aires, Argentina. Musician (guitar, piano); Composer; Singer. m. Nora Krichman, 10 Mar 1981, 3 daughters. Career: Major concerts at main theatres throughout Argentina including: Opera Theatre; Luna Park; Excursionistas Football Stadium; Tours: Argentina; Uruguay; Chile; Colombia; Numerous radio, TV programmes; Own 2 hour daily radio programme. Recordings: Ignacio Copani, 1988; Ya Vendram Temps Mejores, 1989; Copani, 1994; Copani Completo, 1992; Afectos Especiales, 1993; Puerto, 1994; Salvese Quien Pued'a, 1995; Compromiso, 1995. Honours: Nomination: Martin Fiero, 1992; Ace, 1994; Winner, Previsario, 1993; Konex, 1995. Memberships: SADAIC (composers); SADEM (musicians). Hobbies: Computers; Football. Current Management: Nuevo Canto Producciones. Address: 1605 Lavalle St, 4, 8, Buenos Aires, Capital Federal, Argentina.

COPE Julian, b. 21 Oct 1957, Bargoed, Wales. Singer; Musician (guitar, bass); Songwriter. m. Dorian, 2 daughters. Career: Member, The Crucial Tree; Lead singer, musician, Teardrop Explodes, 1978-82; Concerts include: Futurama Festival, Leeds, 1979; Opening of Club Zoo, Liverpool, 1980; Solo artiste, 1983-; Performances include: UK tours, 1987-; Glastonbury Festival, 1987; Phoenix Festival, 1993. Recordings: Albums with Teardrop Explodes: Kilimanjaro, 1980; Wilder, 1981; Singles with Teardrop Explodes include: Treason, 1980; Reward, 1981; Passionate Friend, 1981; Solo albums include: World Shut Your Mouth, 1984; St Julian, 1987; My Nation Underground, 1988; Skellington, 1990; Peggy Suicide, 1991; Jehovah Kill, 1992; Floored Genius, 1992; 20 Mothers, 1995; Solo singles: World Shut Your Mouth, 1986; Beautiful Love, 1991. Publications: Head On (Volume I of autobiography), 1991; Kraut Rock Sampler (Guide to German Music 1968-), 1995; The Modern Antiquarian (due 1996). Current Management: Seb Shelton Management, 13 Lynton Road, London N8 8SR, England.

COPELAND Stewart, b. 16 July 1952, Alexandria, Egypt. Musician (drums, percussion); Singer; Composer. Career: Drummer, Curved Air; Drummer, The Police, 1977-86; Numerous worldwide tours, television and radio appearances with The Police; Founder, Animal Logic with Deborah Holland, Stanley Clarke, 1989. Compositions: Score for films: Rumble Fish; Wall

Steet; Talk Radio; Hidden Agenda; First Power; Men At Work; Ballet: King Lear (for San Francisco Ballet), 1982; Opera: Holy Blood And Crescent Moon, for Cleveland Opera, 1989. Recordings: Hit singles include; With The Police: Walking On The Moon; Message In A Bottle; So Lonely; Roxanne; De Do Do Do De Da Da Da; Every Little Thing She Does; Every Breath You Take; Invisible Sun; Can't Stand Losing You; Don't Stand So Close To Me; Spirits In The Material World; Synchronisity; Albums: with the Police: Outlandos D'Amour, 1977; Regatta De Blanc, 1979; Zenyatta Mondatta, 1980; Ghost In The Machine, 1981; Bring On The Night, 1986; Synchronisity, 1983; Solo album: The Equalizer And Other Cliff Hangers, 1988. Current Management: Firstars, 3520 Hayden Avenue, Culver City, CA 90232, USA.

COPLAND Clive Rowan, b. 6 June 1956, Hampton Court, England. Musician (guitar). m. Linda Copland, 1 son. Musical Education: Grade 3 classical, studied with Andre Edmonds, Kevin Stacey, John Mizarli. Career: First band, London soul band The Strutters, 1974; Later worked with Ray Shields Orchestra; Herb Miller Orchestra (brother of Glen Miller); Now freelance musician. Recordings: Played on film soundtrack to Yanks; Recording sessions with: Hurricane Smith; John Miller; 4 records with Herb Miller. Membership: Association of Motion Picture Sound. Hobbies: Outdoors; Walking; Swimming. Address: 3 Defoe Avenue, Kew, Richmond, Surrey TW9 4DL, England.

COPPEL Michael Henry, b. 1 Oct 1949, Melbourne, Australia. Concert Promoter. m. Michelle Coppel, 15 Feb 1981, 1 son, 3 daughters. Education: Bachelor of Laws (honour), Bachelor of Commerce, Melbourne University. Career: Concerts promoted in last 15 years include: AC/DC, 1981; Narara '83, 3 day Music Festival, Old Sydney Town, 1983; Narara '84, 1984; Whitney Houston tour, 1986; Eurythmics, Revenge Tour, 1987; U2 and B B King, Love Comes To Town Tour, 1989; Tina Turner's Simply The Best Tour, 1993; U2, Zoo TV Tour, 1993; Garth Brooks, 1994; Other tours include: Michael Bolton; UB40; Salt'n'Pepa; Pet Shop Boys; Pantera; Tori Amos, 1994; Janet Jackson Tour, 1995; Alternative Nation, international and Australian alternative music groups, 1995; Tours for The Cranberries; Violent Femmes; Slayer with Biohazard; Jamiroquai; M People; Sheryl Crow, 1995. Honours: Australian Concert Promoter of The Year, 1993, 1994. Membership: EIEA, Executive Councillor. Address: 716-718 High Street, Armadale, Victoria 3143, Australia.

COPPIN Johnny, b. 5 Apr 1946, South Woodford, London, England. Singer; Songwriter; Musician (guitar, piano); Anthologist. m. Gillian Mary Wall, 2 Jun 1990. Education: Diploma in Architecture, Gloucester College of Art and Design, 1971. Musical Education: School choirs; Semi-professional and college rock bands; Self-taught guitar and piano. Career: Lead singer, songwriter with Decameron, 1969-76; Solo performer, 1976-; Support to Jasper Carrott and Gerry Rafferty; Many European festivals and concert tours; Television appearances: Song of Gloucestershire, BBC2, 1986; Stars In A Dark Night, C4, 1990; Songwriters, HTV, 1995; Radio appearances: Kid Jensen Show, BBC Radio 1, 1981; Kaleidoscope Special, BBC Radio 4, 1989; West Country Christmas, BBC Radio 2, 1993. Recordings: 4 albums with Decameron; Solo albums: Roll On Dreamer, 1978; Believe In You, 1979; Everybody Knows, 1982; Forest And Vale And High Blue Hill, 1993; Edge Of Day, with Laurie Lee, 1989; West Country Christmas, 1990; Force Of The River, 1993. Publications: Forest And Vale And High Blue Hill, 1991; Between The Severn And The Wye, 1993. Memberships: BASCA; Equity; PRS; MCPS. Hobbies: Walking; Art; Architecture; Poetry. Current Agent: Brass

Tacks. Address: c/o Red Sky Records, PO Box 7, Stroud, Gloucestershire GL10 3PQ, England.

CORBETT Guy (Heape), b. 29 May 1951, Wigan, England. Musician (bass guitar, guitar, diatonic accordion). m. Emma Clifford-Brown, 30 Sept 1978. Career: Member, bands: Alternative Dance Band (traditional); Les Cloches (traditional); Fatty Black (rock). Membership: Musicians' Union. Address: 1 Warren Crest, Froxfield, Petersfield, Hants GU32 1BL, England.

CORDA Mike, b. 8 July 1921, New York City, USA. Record Company Executive; Composer. m. Helen Marie Wheeler, 7 Dec 1952, 2 daughters. Musical Education: New York College of Music. Career: Bassist, Honolulu Symphony Orchestra, 1945-46; Bassist, original company, Kiss Me Kate, Broadway, 1948-51; Songwriter, various US record companies, 1952-; President, New Horizon Productions, Las Vegas; Record producer, Bluebirds Over The Mountain, Ersel Hickey, 1958; Composer, producer for Mickey Rooney; Robert Goulet; Bill Haley and The Comets; Gloria Lynne; Joe Williams. Membership: ASCAP. Address: Corda Music Inc, 3398 Nahatan Way, Las Vegas, NV 89109, USA.

CORDERO Jorge Luis, b. 12 May 1952, Holguin, Cuba. Singer; Composer; Bandleader. m. Anne Nielsen Cordero, 21 Aug 1976, 1 son, 1 daughter. Education: Technical College. Musical Education: Percussion ISA and AMI. Career: Bandleader, Los Gran Daneses; Concerts, tours include: Germany; Cuba; Poland; Sweden; Norway; Spain; Calle 8 Festival (Miami), 1992; Television and radio, USA, 1993-. Recordings: Que Vida, 1975; Salsa Na'ma, 1981; Diferente, 1988; Rompiendo el Hielo, 1994. Honour: Representing Denmark in Berlin, 1994. Memberships: DMF; DJBFA. Current Management: TTH Records and Management, New York. Address: Mondrupsvej 8, 8260 Viby, Denmark.

CORDIER Thierry, b. 29 May 1963, Mont Saint Martin, France. Writer; Composer; Musician (guitar, keyboards). m. Joël Cordier, 9 Sept 1989, 2 daughters. Musical Education: Self-taught. Career: 1 album with Charles Baudelaire, 1986; 200 concerts in France, Luxembourg, Belgium; 2 hits on compilation Coup de Pauce '95; Television includes: FR3: L'Heure du Ci; Radio includes: France Culture, Fun, Nostalgia. Recordings: Correspondances, 9 hits; Tableau Noir, Charles Baudelaire (dedicated to Les Fleurs Du Mal), 1986; Human; Garcon d'Café; Compilat; Coup d'Pauce '95; Single: Aeroport, 1995. Hobbies: Sport; Jogging. Current Management: Un Poisson Dans L'Desert. Address: 67, Avenue du 8 Mai 45, 54400 Longwy, France.

COREA Chick (Armando Corea), b. 12 June 1941, Chelsea, Massachusetts, USA. Musician (piano); Composer. m. Gayle Moran, 1 son, 1 daughter. Musical Education: Juilliard School Of Music, 1961. Career: Pianist with artistes including: Mongo Santamaria, 1962; Blue Mitchell, 1965; Stan Getz, 1966-68; Miles Davis, 1969-71; Sarah Vaughn, 1970; Founder member, leader, pianist with group, Return To Forever, 1971-; Founder, The Elektric Band, 1986. Recordings: Piano Improvisations 1 & 2; Leprechaun; My Spanish Heart; Mad Hatter; Delphi 1, 2 & 3; Light As A Feather; Romantic Warrior; Hymn Of The Seventh Galaxy; Music Magic; Voyage (with Steve Kujala), 1984; The Chick Corea Akoustic Band, 1989; Elektric Band Inside Out, 1990; Chick Corea Akoustic Band Alive!, 1991; Elektric Band Beneath The Mask, 1991; Time Warp, 1995; Numerous appearances on albums with other groups. Honours include: 9 Grammy Awards; 28 Grammy Nominations; Numerous magazine awards from Downbeat, Keyboard Magazine; Jazz Life Musician Of World, Jazz Forum Music Poll, 1974; Best Electric Jazz group, 1990; Best Acoustic Pianist, 1990; Top Jazz Pianist, 1990. Current

Management: Ron Moss Management, 2635 Griffith Park Blvd, Los Angeles, CA 90039, USA.

CORGAN Billy. Singer; Musician (multi-instrumentalist). Career: Lead singer, Smashing Pumpkins, 1989-; Concerts include: Reading Festival, 1992, 1995. Recordings: Albums: Gish, 1992; Hut Recordings - The Peel Sessions, 1992; Siamese Dream, 1993; Pisces Iscariot, 1994; Mellon Collie & The Infinite Sadness, 1995; Featured on film soundtrack, Singles, 1992. Current Management: Coffer/Gershon Management, 26 Park Road, Bushey, Herts WD2 3EQ, England.

CORKETT Paul Alexander, b. 31 Oct 1964, Hammersmith, London, England. Sound Engineer; Record Producer. m. Rachel, 19 May 1990. Education: Shiplake College. Career: Worked at Jacobs Studio and Trident Studio; Now freelance engineer, producer. Recordings: Albums: As producer: Smart, Sleeper; Time For The Rest Of Your Life, Strangelove; As engineer: Jahova Kill, Julian Cope; Violently Happy, Björk. Current Management: 140dB Management. Address: 1 McCrone Mews, Belsize Village, London NW3 5BG, England.

CORMIER John Paul, b. 23 Jan 1969, London, Ontario, Canada. Musician (Fiddle, Guitar, Banjo, Mandolin); Singer; Songwriter. m. Hilda Chiasson, 1994. Education: Selftaught on guitar, fiddle, banjo, mandolin, dobro, bass and piano. Career: Regular Guest, Up Home Tonight, ATV; Studio, stage and session work with Travis Tritt, Waylon Jennings, Marty Stuart, Carl Perkins and Steve Warner; Major Folk and Celtic Festivals including: Tonder Festival, Denmark; Celtic Connections, Scotland; Celtic Colours, CB-NS; Touring extensively in Canada and US. Compositions: Another Morning; Highland Dream; The Island; Gone; Kelly's Mountain; Long for the Sea. Recordings: Out of the Blue, 1986; North Wind, 1989; The Fiddle Album, 1990; The Gift, 1992; When January Comes, 1993; Lord of the Dance, 1993; Return to the Cape, 1995; Another Morning, 1997. Honours: East Coast Music Award Nomination for Instrumentalist of the Year, Canadian Open Guitar Champion, 1986; Maritime Fiddle Champion, 1995. Memberships: AFofM; SOCAN; CMRRA. Current Management: Max McDonald Rave Entertainment Inc. Address: Rave Entertainment Inc, 363 Charlotte Street, Sydney, Nova Scotia, B1P 1EI, Canada.

CORNELIUS Claes, b. 14 May 1949, Copenhagen, Denmark. A&R Manager; Publisher; Musician (guitar, keyboards). 1 son. Education: Art Academy, Venice, Italy. Musical Education: Piano lessons, various seminars. Career: Professional musician, late 1960s, Italy; Studio session musician; Music publishing, Denmark, early 1970s; With Mega Scandinavia, 1983-. Recordings: Countless studio sessions in Italy including Finardi; Claudio Rocchi; Caterina Caselli; Fausto Leali; Also member of Art Class LP. Honour: Shared Critics Prize for production in Italy. Hobbies: Art installations; Music. Current Management: Mega Scandinavia A/S. Address: Indiakaj 1, DK-2100 Copenhagen O, Denmark.

CORNELIUS Helen Lorene, b. 6 Dec 1941, Hannibal, Missouri, USA. Singer; Songwriter. m. Jerry Garren, 22 June 1981, 2 sons, 1 daughter. Career: Songwriter, 1970-; Recording artist, 1975-80; Television appearances include: Nashville On The Road; Host, Helen Cornelius Show, 1976-; Stage performances: Annie Get Your Gun, US touring production, 1984. Recordings: Hit single: Lying In Love With You, with Jim Ed Brown; Albums include: Helen Cornelius; Born Believer; I Don't Want To Have To Marry You. Honour: CMA Vocal Duo of the Year, 1977. Memberships: Broadcast Music Inc; AFTRA; CMA; National Association of Songwriters; West Coast Academy Of Country

Music. Address: c/o Morningstar Pubic Relations, PO Box 83, Brentwood, TN 32027, USA.

CORNELL Chris, b. USA. Vocalist; Songwriter; Musician (guitar). m. Susan Silver. Career: Vocalist, US heavy rock group Soundgarden, 1984-; Concerts include: Support to Metallica, US, 1991; Support to Guns'n'Roses, US tour, 1991; Lollapalooza II tour, 1992; Reading Festival, 1995; Lollapalooza VI, 1996; Member, tribute group, Temple Of The Dog, 1991; Soundgarden, 1984-97; Began solo career 1997. Recordings: Albums: Ultra Mega OK, 1989; Louder Than Love, 1989; Badmotorfinger, 1991; Superunknown (Number 1, US), 1994; Down on the Upside, 1996; with Temple Of The Dog: Temple Of The Dog, 1991; Singles: Flower; Loud Love; Jesus Christ Pose; Outshined; Black Hole Sun, 1994; Spoonman, 1994; Burden in my Hand, 1996. Address: c/o Susan Silver Management, 207½ First Avenue South, Suite 300, Seattle, WA 98104, USA.

CORNWELL Hugh, b. 28 Aug 1949, London, England. Vocalist; Musician (guitar). Education: Chemistry graduate. Career: Former science teacher; Founder member, UK rock group The Stranglers, 1976-90; Headline tours, Europe; UK; Canada; US; International concerts include: Supports to Patti Smith, 1976; Climax Blues Band, 1977; Loch Lomond Festival, 1979; Reading Rock Festival, 1983, 1987; Alexandra Palace, 1990; Solo artiste, 1991-; Also worked with Roger Cook and Andy West, 1992. Recordings: Albums: Rattus Norvegicus, 1977; No More Heroes, 1978; Black And White, 1978; Live (X Cert), 1979; The Raven, 1979; Themeninblack, 1981; La Folie, 1982; The Collection, 1982; Feline, 1983; Aural Sculpture, 1984; Dreamtime, 1986; All Live And All Of The Night, 1988; 10, 1990; Solo albums: Nosferatu, 1979; Wolf, 1988; Wired, 1993; with Cornwell, Cook and West: C C W, 1992; Singles: with The Stranglers: Peaches, 1977; Something Better Change, 1977; No More Heroes, 1977; Five Minutes, 1978; Nice'n'Sleazy, 1978; Duchess, 1979; Golden Brown (Number 2, UK), 1982; Strange Little Girl, 1982; European Female, 1983; Skin Deep, 1984; Always The Sun, 1986; All Day & All Of The Night, 1987; Solo: One In A Million, 1985; Another Kind Of Love, 1988. Publication: Inside Information. Honours: Ivor Novello Award, Most Performed Work of 1982, Golden Brown, 1983.

CORONADO Gilles, b. 26 Oct 1966, Avignon, France. Musician (guitar); Composer. Education: Superior Technical Brevet of technical drawing. Musical Education: Different School, Banff Jazz Workshop, Canada; Self-taught. Career: Various bands (jazz, funk, rock), South of France; Moved to Paris, 1991; Active member, HASK collective (musicians association, Paris); Founder, leader, quartet Urban Mood; Played various festivals: Germany; Belgium; Portugal; France; Collaborator with Dance Performances, 1993-; Teacher. Recordings: Urban Mood record due 1996. Membership: SACEM. Hobbies: Arts performances; Cooking; Parties; Life. Current Management: Self-managed. Address: Cité Internationale des Arts, 18 Rue de l'Hotel de Ville, 75004 Paris, France.

CORSBY Dave, b. 29 Jun 1938, Hounslow, Middlesex, England. Composer; Arranger; Musician (saxophones; flute; clarinet; keyboards). m. Jill Corsby, 16 Jul 1992. Career: Founder member, Cave Jazz Club, Ramsgate, Kent, 1955; Co-organiser of Thanet Jazz Festival, 1982, 1983; Baritone saxophonist, John Burch Octet, 1986-; Radio, television, film and record sessions; Appeared at Dunkirk Jazzopale, 1994; Hot Club of Lyons, 1995; Arts Council tour with John Burch Octet, 1994-95; Bandleader, Doctor Crotchet's Good Time Jazz (band for functions); Dave Corsby Quartet (modern jazz group); Business ventures: Carpe Diem Arts; Carpe Diem Music; Lincoln Studios. Compositions: The

Subterraneans; Rajans Banquet; Samuel Pepys Jazz Suite; Tale Of Two Cities Jazz Suite (Arts Council Commission); Seven Deadly Sins, jazz musical; The Endeavour Experience, film score, 1994; Cinque Ports Jazz Suite, Sandwich Festival commission, 1997. Recordings: Tale Of Two Cities Jazz Suite; Samuel Pepys Jazz Suite; The Seven Deadly Sins; Roll Call. Memberships: Musicians' Union; Performing Rights Society; Art Pepper Society; Association of British Jazz Musicians. Current Management: Carpe Diem Arts. Address: Lincoln Studios, 8 Lincoln Gardens, Birchington-on-Sea, Kent CT7 9SW, England.

CORTES Joaquim, b. 22 February 1969, Cordoba, Spain. Dancer; Choreographer. Career: Coreography for Carmen, Verona; Participation in Summer Flamenco Festival, Tokyo; Gala Performances, Lincoln Center, New York, USA; Appearance in Don Quijote, Caracas Ballet Company; Performances at the Champs-Elyssée Theater, Paris, 1992; World tours with Joaquin Cortés Flamenco Ballet, with Cibayi and Gipsy Passion. Recording: Gipsy Passion Band, 1997. Hobby: Cinema. Current Management: Pino Sagliocco; PR Press: Macarena Blanchón. Address: Pino Sagliocco Presenta Quintana, 2 7, 9a, 28008 Madrid, Spain.

CORTEZ Alberto (Jose Alberto Garcia Gallo), b. 11 Mar 1940, Rancul, Argentina. Singer; Composer. m. Renee Govaerts, 2 June 1964. Musical Education: Chopin Conservatory, Mendoza, Argentina. Career: Performances include: Teatro de la Zarzuela, Madrid, 1967; Lincoln Center, New York, 1990; Teatro Colon, Buenos Aires, 1992. Compositions: Over 250 songs include: Distancia; Callajero; En Un Rincon Del Alama; El Abuelo; Cuando Un Amigo Se Va; Mi Arbol y Yo; Castillos En El Aire; Eran Tres; Equipaje; A Partir De Mañana. Recordings: Albums: Mr Sucu Sucu, 1960; Welcome To The Latin Club, 1961; Boleros, 1965; Poemas y Canciones, Vol 1, 1967, Vol 2, 1968; El Compositor, El Cantante, 1969; Distancia, 1970; No Soy De Aqui, 1971; Ni Poco... Ni Demasiado, 1973; Como El Ave Solitaria, 1974; A Mis Amigos, 1975; Soy Un Charlatan De Feria, 1976; Pensares y Sentires, 1977; En Vivo Desde Madrid, 1978; A Partir De Mañana, 1979; Castillos En El Aire, 1980; Como El Primer Dia, 1983; Gardel... Como Yo Te Siento, 1984; En Vivo, 1985; Sueños y Quimeras, 1986; Como La Marea, 1987; Almafuerte, 1989; Coincidencias, 1990; Si Vieras Que Facil, 1991; Aromas, 1993; Lo Cortez No Quita Lo Cabral, 1994. Publications: 3 books: Equipaje; Soy Un Ser Humano; Almacen De Almas. Membership: SGAE (Spain). Hobbies: Computers; Football. Current Management: Omar Lauria. Address: c/o Pedro Teixeira 10, 28020 Madrid, Spain.

CORYELL Larry, b. 12 Apr 1943, Galveston, Texas, USA. Musician (guitar); Composer. m. Molly Shueler, 3 Sept 1987, 2 sons, 1 daughter. Education: University of Washington. Musical Education: Studied with Jerry Gray, Leon Bolotine, New York City, 1965. Career: Jazz guitarist, 1966-; Musician with: Chico Hamilton, 1966; Gary Burton, 1967; Founder, fusion band, Free Spirits; Leader, Eleventh House, 1969; Touring solo guitarist, also in duos with: Philip Catherine; Alphonse Mouzon; Steve Kahn; Emily Remier. Recordings: Albums include: Out Of Sight And Sound, 1967; Lady Coryell, 1968; Spaces, 1969; Introducing The 11th House, 1974; The Restful Mind, 1975; Aspects, 1976; Basics, 1976; The Lion And The Ram, 1977; Standing Ovation, 1978; Bolero, 1981; Comin' Home, 1984; A Quiet Day In Spring, 1984; Equipoise, 1986; The Dragon Gate, 1989; Twelve Frets To The Octave, 1991; Fallen Angel, 1992; Dynamics, 1994; Also recordings with Michael Urbaniak, Chet Baker, Gary Burton, Sonny Rollins and Laurindo Almeida. Current Management: Ted Kurland. Address: c/o Ted Kurland Associates, 173 Brighton Avenue, Boston, MA 02167, USA.

COSTEA Constantin, b. 1 Nov 1931, Bucharest, Romania. Writer; Dance, Folklore Researcher; Record Producer. Education: Liceul Teoretic; Liceul Coregrfie; Special Master of Ballet Courses (3 years). Career: Numerous radio and television appearances; Tours, shows: Hungary; Czechoslovakia; Austria; Finland; Germany; France; Netherlands; UK; Sweden; Denmark; Iran. Recordings: As producer, series of 6 albums: Romanian Folk Dances, 1978-82. Publications: Numerous research studies. Membership: ICTM. Address: Bucaresti, 78468 Str, Moldovei, Nr 40, Sect 1, Romania.

COSTELLO Elvis (Declan McManus), b. 25 Aug 1955, London, England. Singer; Songwriter; Musician; Record Producer. m. Cait O'Riordan, 1 child (from previous marriage). Career: Lead singer, Elvis Costello And The Attractions, 1977-; Appearances include: UK tour, 1977; US tour, 1978; Grand Ole Opry, 1981; Royal Albert Hall, with Royal Philharmonic, 1982; Cambridge Folk Festival, 1995; Television includes: Appearance in Scully, ITV drama, 1985; Also worked with The Specials; Paul McCartney; Aimee Mann; George Jones; Roy Orbison; Wendy James; Robert Wyatt; Jimmy Cliff; Co-organiser, annual Meltdown festival, South Bank Centre, London. Compositions include: Alison, 1977; Watching The Detectives, 1977; (I Don't Want To Go To) Chelsea, 1979; Crawling To The USA, 1978; Radio Radio, 1978; Stranger In The House, 1978; Girls Talk, 1979; Oliver's Army, 1979; Boy With A Problem, 1982; Every Day I Write The Book, 1983; Music for television series (with Richard Harvey): G.B.H., 1991; Jake's Progress, 1995; Other songs for artists including Johnny Cash; June Tabor. Recordings: Albums include: My Aim Is True, 1977; This Years Model, 1978; Armed Forces, 1979; Get Happy, 1980; Trust, 1980; Almost Blue, 1981; Taking Liberties, 1982; Imperial Bedroom, 1982; Goodbye Cruel World, 1984; Punch The Clock, 1984; The Best Of, 1985; Blood And Chocolate, 1986; King Of America, 1986; Spike, 1989; Mighty Like A Rose, 1991; My Aim Is True, 1991; The Juliet Letters, with the Brodksy Quartet, 1993; Brutal Youth, 1994; The Very Best Of Elvis Costello And The Attractions, 1995; Kojak Variety, 1995; Deep Dead Blue, Live At Meltdown (with Bill Frisell), 1995. Honours include: BAFTA Award, Best Original Television Music, G.B.H., 1992; MTV Video, Best Male Video, 1989; Rolling Stone Award, Best Songwriter, 1990. Current Management: Jill Taylor, By Eleven Management, 12 Tideway Yard, 125 Mortlake High Street, London SW14 8SN, England.

COTTLE Laurence, b. 16 Dec 1961, Swansea, Wales. Musician (bass guitar). m. Alison Hooper, 16 Apr 1994. Career: Currently touring with Jim Mullen (GTR); Played most jazz festivals with Jim Mullen; Tours with Laurence Cottle Quintet include: America; Cuba; Germany; France; Spain; Italy. Recordings: Solo album: Five Seasons; with Laurence Cottle Quintet: Live At 33, 1995. Membership: Musicians' Union. Address: 1 Harriet Wa;ler Way, Rickmansworth, Hertfordshire WD3 2RT, England.

COULAM Roger Keith, b. 21 Aug 1940, Blackburn, Lancashire, England. Musician (piano, organ, all keyboards). m. Susan Chadwick, 19 Sept 1961, 1 son, 2 daughters. Musical Education: Piano, harmony, London Guildhall School of Music and Drama, LGSM. Career: Backing Helen Shapiro, 1963; Duane Eddy, 1979; Johnny Howard's Band, Radio 1, Easybeat, 1966; Founder member, Blue Mink, 1969-73; Albert Hall Concert; Tour with Booker T and the MG's; Star Cabaret; Talk Of The Town; Television includes: Top Of The Pops; Prominent record, radio, television and film musician, 1966-; Sessions include: Tina Turner; Sammy Davis Jr; The Italian Job; Organist on Je T'Aime. Compositions: Co-writer several Blue Mink album tracks and B sides including chart single Sunday; Library music 1970, used for various radio, film, television series, including: Budgie; Vision On. Recordings: Solo albums: Organ In Orbit, 1966; Blow Hot, Blow Cool, 1969; All Blue Mink recordings, 1969-73. Honours: Silver disc, Melting Pot, Blue Mink. Memberships: Musicians' Union; BMWC; PRS; MCPS; BASCA.

COULOMBE Daniel, b. 11 May 1960, Quebec City, Canada. Music Producer. Education: University Communication. Career: Recording Producer; Remix Engineer; Radio Producer. Recordings: B-52's; Icehouse; Indochine; Mitsou. Hobbies: Mountain biking; Golf; Skiing; Swimming.

COUPLAND Gary, b. 27 Mar 1964, Dumfries, Scotland. Musician (accordion, keyboards). m. Karen Chaisson, 18 Sep 1987, 3 daughters. Education: Dumfries Academy. Musical Education: Napier College, Edinburgh, Scotland. Career: Musical Director with The Singing Kettle, Scotland's Theatre Box Office Record Breakers, London Palladium and Sadler's Wells; 4 series for Children's BBC TV; Folk musician at Cambridge Folk Festival, Stage 1, 1992. Recording: Scottish Tunes. Publications: 6 videos. Honour: BAFTA, Scotland, Best Children's TV Show. Memberships: Musicians' Union; Equity. Address: 12 Stanley Street, Edinburgh EH15 1JJ, Scotland.

COURTOIS Vincent, b. 21 Mar 1968, Paris, France. m. Muriel, 1990, 1 son. Career: Played with: Michel Petrucciani; Niels Lan Doky; Tour with Michel Petrucciani, 1994-95. Recordings for: Khaled N'ssi N'ssi; Philippe Eidel. Recordings: Cello News; Pleine Lune; Pendulum Quartet. Current Management: Laurence Voiturier, Artalent. Address: 15 Passage de la Main d'Or, 75011 Paris, France.

COUSENS Peter William Light, b. 2 November 1955, Tamworth, NSW, Australia. Singer; Actor. m. Suzanne Roylance, 9 December 1984, 3 daughters. Education: National Institute of Dramatic Art Graduate, 1978. Career: Musicals: Camelot (Mordred), with Richard Harris, 1983; Blood Brothers (Eddie), 1987; The Mikado, The Australia Opera, 1986; Les Miserables (Marius), 1989-91; Aspects of Love (Alex), Phantom of the Opera, 1992; Sydney (Raoul), 1993-94; Miss Saigon (Chris), 1995-96; West Side Story (Tony), 1996; London (The Phantom), 1997; Australia Showboat, Ravenal, 1998. Recordings: 1st Album, Corner of The Sky, 1994; 2nd, From a Distance, 1996; International Symphonic Recording Miss Saigon (Chris), 1996; Are We Nearly There Yet, MBF Childrens with Noni Hazelhurst. Honour: Variety Club of Australia Heart Award, 1996. Hobby: Parenting. Current Management: International Casting Service, 147A King Street, Sydney. Address: c/o ICS, 147A King Street, Sydney, 2000, Australia.

COUSIN Andy, b. 28 June 1963, Lincoln, England. Musician (bass guitar); Vocalist. Career: Musician with: All About Eve; The Mission. Recordings: All About Eve: All About Eve, 1988; Scarlet and Other Stories, 1989; Touched By Jesus, 1991; Ultraviolet; Winter Words; Live At Glastonbury; The Mission: Neverland. Address: 65 Vale Road, Finsbury Park, London N4 1PP, England.

COVACI Nicu (Nicolae), b. 19 Apr 1947, Timisoara, Romania. Musician (6 and 12 string guitar); Vocalist. m. (1) 1976-78; (2) 1980-89. Education: High School of Arts; Academy of Arts. Musical Education: 4 years piano and guitar. Career: National Student Festival, Iasi, 1968; National Student Festival, Bucharest, 1969-71; Sopot Festival Poland, 1973; Romanian television: Tops Of The Week; Romanian radio. Recordings: Vremuri (EP), 1968; Floarea Stincilor (EP), 1969; Cei Ce Ne-Au Dat Nume, 1971; Mesteroul Manole (EP), 1973; Mugur De Fluier, 1974; Cantafabule, 1975; Transsylvania, 1980; Symphoenix, 1992; Phoenix-Evergreens, 1995. Honours: First prize, National Student Festival, Iasi, 1968; Awards for:

Composition and Creativity, Bucharest, 1969-71; Originality, Bratislawskalyra, Czechoslovakia, 1973. Memberships: GEMA; OCMR. Hobbies: Painting; Diving; Motorcycles. Current Management: Self-managed. Address: Im Dütetal 2, 49078 Osnabrück, Germany.

COVERDALE David, b. 22 Sept 1949, Saltburn-By-The-Sea, Cleveland, England. Singer; Songwriter. m. Tawny Kitaen, 17 Feb, 1989. Career: Vocalist, Government; Lead singer, UK rock group Deep Purple, 1973-76; Founddr, lead singer, UK heavy rock group Whitesnake, 1977-91; Solo artiste, 1991-; Member, Coverdale/Page, with Jimmy Page, 1993; Regular international tours; Concerts include: Reading Festival, 1979, 1980; Monsters Of Rock, Castle Donington, 1981, 1983, 1990; Texas World Music Festival, 1987; Super Rock '90 Festival, Germany, 1990. Recordings: Albums: with Deep Purple: Burn, 1974; Stormbringer, 1974; 24 Carat Purple, 1975; Come Taste The Band, 1975; with Whitesnake: Whitesnake, 1977; Northwinds, 1978; Trouble, 1979; Ready An' Willing, 1980; Live In The Heart Of The City, 1980; Come An' Get It, 1981; Saints'n'Sinners, 1982; Slide It In, 1984; Whitesnake, 1987; Slip Of The Tongue, 1989; with Coverdale/Page: Coverdale/Page, 1993; Hit singles: with Whitesnake: Fool For Your Loving, 1980 (re-recorded, 1989); Don't Break My Heart Again, 1981; Here I Go Again, 1982 (re-recorded, Number 1, US, 1987); Give Me More Time, 1984; Still Of The Night, 1987; Is This Love, 1987; Give Me All Your Love, 1987; The Deeper The Love, 1990; with Coverdale/Page: Take Me For A Little While, 1993. Current Management: H.K. Management, 8900 Wilshire Blvd #300, Beverly Hills, CA 90211, USA.

COWELL Harry Edmund (Sir), b. 4 Sept 1960, Dorking, Surrey, England. Artist Manager. m. Anita Harriet, 25 Feb 1995, 1 daughter. Career: Management partner of Simon Napier-Bell; Clients include: Yardbirds; Japan; Marc Bolan; Wham!; Recent success with bands: Asia; Ultravox. Recordings include: Hokey Cokey, Captain Sensible, 1994, (for Great Ormond Street Hospital Childrens' Fund). Hobby: Polo. Address: 66 Prince Georges Avenue, West Wimbledon, London SW20 8BH, England.

COX Carl, b. 29 July 1962, Manchester, England. Disc Jockey; Record Producer; Remixer; Record Label Owner. m. Rachel Turner, 19 Mar 1994. Career: DJ, 1980-; Sunrise Rave, 1989; Afterward known as "3 Deck Wizard"; One of top DJs on Rave scene, 1989-93; Signed album deal with Perfecto/BMG, 1991; Presently resident, top UK House/Techno clubs including Cream, Liverpool; Final Frontier, London; Also DJ in Germany; Tours: Australia; US; Japan; France; Switzerland; Austria; Ibiza; Started Ultimate Music Management (managing DJs from around the world), 1993; Started own MMR record label, 1994. Recordings: Own albums: I Want You Forever, 1991; Does It Feel Good To You, 1992; Own record label releases include (own compositions): with Stone Circle: Deep In You; Tonight; with Conquer: Self Destruction; War Path; Solo: Anthemia; Motorway; Det 29-62; Remixed tracks by: Sunscreen; Cuba Gooding; Yello; Stone Roses; Robert Owens; Patti Day; Jam and Spoon. Honours: DJ Magazine, Number 1 Rave DJ, 1992; Stepping Out, Top UK DJ, 1992, 1993; International Dance Awards: DJ Of The Year, 1994, 1995; Frontpage Magazine, Top Overseas DJ, Germany, 1994. Membership: Musicians' Union. Hobby: Work. Address: 49 Highlands Road, Horsham, West Sussex RH13 5LS, England.

COX Deborah, b. 1974, Canada. Singer; Songwriter. Musical Education: Performing Arts School. Career: Singer, commercials and local club circuit, Toronto, age 12; R&B singer, and songwriting partnership with Lascelles Stephens; Tour with Celine Dion; Concerts in Europe; Japan;

Asia. Recordings: Debut album, 1995; Single: Sentimental, 1995. Current Management: c/o Stiletto Entertainment, 5443 Beethoven Street, Los Angeles, CA 90066, USA.

COX Doc, b. 1 July 1946, Sheffield, Yorkshire, England. Singer; Songwriter; Musician (ukelele). Education: Trained as teacher. Musical Education: 8 cello lessons; 3 guitar lessons; Several years with Bert Weedon book. Career: Semi-pro rock'n'roll bands, 1960s, 70s; Top Twenty record, under name of Ivor Biggun (Number 1, Indie-Punk charts), 1978; 2 top 50 placings; Regular on That's Life, BBC TV, lots of BBC Radio. Compositions include: Ketchup Bottle Blues, sung by Marion Montgomery on BBC TV, Radio. Recordings include: The Winker's Song, banned by BBC. Publications: Rock Talk; Newspaper, magazine articles. Honours: Worthing Tourism Promotions Award. Membership: Musicians' Union. Hobbies: Record collecting; Feeding cats. Current Management: Wendy Downes, 96 Broadway, Bexleyheath, Kent DA6 7DE, England.

COX Graham Kenneth, b. 24 November 1965, Hammersmith, London, England. Journalist; Singer; Songwriter; Producer; Manager. Education: Sound Engineer, Detla Akustik & Vibration, Copenhagen. Career includes: Support for Depeche Mode, 1980s'; A Void Citadel Tour, 1980s'; Zenon Tour, Denmark, Infinity Tour, Denmark, late 1980s'; Manager, Suspected Hippies in Transit, Mushroom Season 94 Tour; Singer, Producer, Low Flying Objects, Plant More Trees. Compositions: Plant More Trees; Low Flying Objects; Crazy Horse. Recording: Dragons. Publications: Several articles in professional magazines. Address: Damhusvej 27 st tv, 5000 Odense C, Denmark.

COX Peter, b. 17 Nov 1955. Vocalist; Songwriter; Musician (guitar, keyboards). Career: Songwriting partnership with Richard Drummie, ATV Music; Founder member, duo Go West, 1982-. Compositions include: One Way Street (for film soundtrack Rocky IV). Recordings: Albums: Go West, 1985; Bangs And Crashes, 1986; Dancing On The Couch, 1987; Indian Summer, 1992; Singles: We Close Our Eyes, 1985; Call Me, 1985; Don't Look Down, 1985. Current Management: Blueprint Management, 134 Lots Road, London SW12 0RJ, England.

COX Rachel Elizabeth, b. 15 Apr 1972, British Columbia, Canada. Company Director. m. Carl Cox, 19 Mar 1994. Career: Director of Flying Records UK Ltd, 1990-92; Founder and Director of Ultimate Music Management, 1993-. Address: 49 Highlands Road, Horsham, West Sussex RH13 5LS, England.

COXON Graham Leslie, b. 12 Mar 1969, Rinteln, Germany. Musician (guitar, saxophone). Education: Art and Design Diploma; N Essex School of Art; Goldsmith's College. Musical Education: Saxophone lessons at school. Career: Member, Blur; Television, radio appearances include: Top Of the Pops; Later With Jools Holland; Extensive tours include: Alexandra Palace; Reading Festival, 1993; Glastobury Festival, 1994; Mile End, 1995. Recordings: Blur: Albums: Leisure, 1991; Modern Life Is Rubbish, 1993; Parklife, 1994; The Great Escape, 1995; Singles: She's So High; There's No Other Way; Bang; Popscene; For Tomorrow; Chemical World; Girls And Boys; To The End; Parklife; End Of A Century; Country House; The Universal; Stereotypes. Honours: Mercury Prize Nomination; Platinum Album: Parklife; BRIT Awards: Best Single, Album, Video, Band, 1995; Q Awards, Best Album, 1994, 1995. Current Management: CMO Management, Unit 32, Ransome Dock, 35-37 Parkgate Road, London SW11 4NP, England.

COZENS Chris, b. 3 June 1959, England. Programmer. m. Mel, 5 Nov 1988, 1 daughter.

Musical Education: City Of Leeds College Of Music. Career: Keyboard player; Composed and performed music for new production: The Rise And Fall Of The City Of Mahogany, by Brecht; Spent year in Canada, with own band, Long Distanz; Returned to UK, joined Johnny Mars Band; Worked as arranger, orchestrator, session keyboard player, for: John Parr; Cozy Powell; Jan Akkerman; Barry Humphries; Graham Bonnett; Harry Nilsson; Francis Rossi; Demis Roussos; Jon English; producer Terry Britten. Programmer, musician, recording of Paris, rock opera by Jon English and Dave Mackay, with London Symphony Orchestra, Royal Philharmonic Orchestra, 1989; Toured Australia, MD for Jon English; Co-writer, 2 Australian television series, including All Together Now; Collaborated with Alan Parker, Dave Mackay, on incidental music for scores; Writer, portfolio of library music; Working with Alan Attfield on Facades (musical); Produced, recorded series of albums for Telstar Records under name Project D. Credits include: Films and television: What's Eating Gilbert Grape?; Wild Justice; To Be The Best; Voice of The Heart; Red Fox; Van Der Valk; Minder, by Alan Parker; 99 To 1, by Mike Gibbs; Coasting, West Beach, Making Out, by Dave Mackay; Bullseye; John Du Prez; Composer, incidental music, Children's Ward, 1994; Bridge To The Past, 1994; Music for documentary, Burning Rubber. Recordings include: Album: Synthesiser Greats, 1994. Memberships: PRS; MCPS. Current Management: Soundtrack Music Management. Address: 22 Ives Street, Chelsea, London SW3 2ND, England.

COZENS Spencer James, b. 11 Feb 1965, Weston-Super-Mare, England. Musician (piano, keyboards); Composer; Producer. Musical Education: East Notts Music School; Newark Technical College; Goldsmiths College, 1987-91; B Mus degree. Career: Tours with Julia Fordham; Producing, touring with John Martyn, 1990-; Writer, producer, albums with Miles Bould (percussion) as Peoplespeak; Also with Jacqui McShee (vocals) Gerry Conway (drums), album: About Thyme; Writer, musician with Carol Decker; Toured with Jacqui McShee's Pentangle. Recordings: Albums: with John Martyn: Cooltide (as producer, musician); As Co-producer and Musician: No Little Boy; Couldn't Love You More (as musician); with Steps Ahead: Yin Yang; Albums by: Peoplespeak and About Thyme (as producer, writer, musician); John Martyn, And, co-producer, musician. Memberships: PRS; MCPS; PAMRA. Address: #45 Limehouse Cut, 46 Morris Road, London E14 6NQ, England.

CRACKNELL Sarah, b. 12 Apr 1968, Chelmsford, Essex, England. Singer. Musical Education: Italia Conti Stage School; Drama Studio; Tona De Brett. Career: Singer, St Etienne; Television includes: Top Of The Pops, five appearances; The Word, two appearances; Later With Jools Holland; Concerts include: Glastonbury; Tours of UK; Europe; Japan; US. Recordings: with St Etienne: Albums: Fox Base Alpha; So Tough; You Need A Mess Of Help To Stand Alone; Tiger Bay; Singles: 10 singles in UK Top 40. Honour: Mercury Music Prize, runner-up. Membership: British Actors Equity. Hobbies: Surfing; Snow-boarding. Current Management: Martin Kelly, Heavenly Management. Address: 72 Wardour Street, London W1, England.

CRADDOCK Billy "Crash" (William Wayne), b. 16 June 1939, Greensboro, North Carolina, USA. Singer. Career: Talent shows from age 10; Rock/country recording artiste, 1957-. Recordings: US Country Number 1 hits: Rub It In; Ruby Baby; Broken Down In Tiny Pieces; Other hit singles include: Boom Boom Baby; Knock Three Times; Dream Lover; You Better Move On; Ain't Nothin' Shakin'; I'm Gonna Knock On Your Door; I Cheated On A Good Woman's Love; Sea Cruise; Love Busted; Numerous albums include: I'm Tore Up, 1964; Knock Three Times, 1971; You Better

Move On, 1972; Still Thinkin' About You, 1975; Crash, with Janie Frickie, 1976; Changes, 1980; Back On Track, 1989; Numerous greatest hits compilations. Honours: Cashbox Award, New Find Of Year, 1972. Address: c/o Ace Productions, PO Box 292725, Nashville, TN 37229-2725, USA.

CRAIG David Mark, b. 4 Apr 1969, Leeds, West Yorkshire, England. Musician (guitar); Songwriter. Education: BA Hons Historical Studies (undergraduate). Musical Education: Self-taught. Career: Guitarist with Drill, 1990-91; Television: Elements, Channel 4/Tyne Tees, 1990-91; Skin Down, voted album of the wwek on BBC Network, 1991; Recently formed The Sojourners, 1994. Compositions: Currently writing material with The Sojourners. Recordings: Drill: Skin Down, 1991. Memberships: Musicians' Union. Hobbies: Watching Newcastle United Football Club; Five-a-side football; Reading. Address: 13 St Joseph's Court, Hebburn, Tyne and Wear NE31 2EN, England.

CRAIG Jay, b. 15 Oct 1958, Bellshill, Scotland. Musician (baritone saxophone). Musical Education: Napier College, Edinburgh; Berklee College of Music, Boston, USA. Career: Member, National Youth Jazz Orchestra, 1976-81; Tommy Sampson Orchestra, Glasgow, 1979-82; Buddy Rich Band, 1984-87; BBC Big Band, 1992-; Performances with: Frank Sinatra; Tony Bennett; Sarah Vaughn; Jack Jones; Natalie Cole; Shirley Bassey; Vic Damone; Buddy Greco; Al Martino; Anita O'Day; Syd Lawrence Orchestra; BBC Scottish Radio Orchestra; Various West End shows. Recordings: 4 NYJO albums; with Buddy Rich: Live on King Street, San Francisco, 1985; Live In Leonberg, 1986. Hobby: Making model aeroplanes. Address: 3 Park Way, Ruislip, Middlesex HA4 8PJ, England.

CRANITCH Matt, b. 27 Mar 1948, Cork, Ireland. Traditional Musician (fiddle); Lecturer; Musicologist. m. Liz MacNamara, 17 July 1973, 2 sons. Education: BE (Electrical Engineering), University College, Cork, Ireland. Musical Education: Cork School Of Music, Ireland; BMus, University College, Cork. Career: Numerous concert performances as soloist, with Na Filí, with Any Old Time; Festival appearances include: Belfast; Brest; Cambridge; Clifden; Cologne; Copenhagen; Cork; Cornwall; Derry; Dublin; Exeter; Killarney; Kilkenny; Galway; Inverness; Lenzburg; Loughborough; New York; Norwich; Nyon; Orkney; Paris; Quimper; Rome; Rotterdam; Shetland; Sligo; Swansea; Vienna; Radio and television shows include: Bring Down The Lamp; Cúrsaí; The Humours Of Donnybrook; The Late Late Show; Live From The Cork Opera House; The Pure Drop; As I Roved Out; Bringing It All Back Home; Sult; Geantraí; Lectures, workshops, master-classes in Ireland and abroad; Director, Cork RTC Arts Fest, 1993-95. Recordings include: with Dave Hennessy and Mick Daly: Any Old Time, 1982; Phoenix, 1987; Crossing, 1995; Solo: Éistigh Seal, 1984; Take A Bow, 1992; Give It Stick, 1996; with Dónal Murphy and Tommy O'Sullivan: Sliabh Notes, 1995. Publications: The Irish Fiddle Book, 1988, 3rd edition, 1996. Memberships: Folk Music Society Of Ireland; IrishTraditional Music Archive; Irish Music Rights Organisation. Current Management: Self-managed. Address: Kerry Pike, Co Cork, Ireland.

CRAVEN Beverly, b. 28 June 1963, Sri Lanka. Singer; Songwriter; Musician (piano). Musical Education: Piano lessons. Career: Solo artiste, 1990-; UK tour, 1993. Recordings include: Album: Promise Me, 1990; Single: Promise Me, 1990. Honour: BRIT Award, Best British Newcomer, 1992. Current Management: Blueprint Management, 134 Lots Road, London SW12 0RJ, England.

CRAWFORD Randy (Veronica), b. 18 Feb 1952, Macon, Georgia, USA.Singer. Career:

Singer, 1967-; Appearances include: World Jazz Association tribute concert to Cannonball Adderley, 1968; Montreux Jazz Festival, 1982; 2 concerts with London Symphony Orchestra, Barbican Centre, London, 1988. Recordings: Singles include: Street Life (with The Crusaders), 1979; One Day I'll Fly Away, 1980; You Might Need Somebody, 1981; Rainy Night In Georgia, 1981; Almaz (own composition), 1987; Knockin' On Heaven's Door, used in film soundtrack Lethal Weapon 2, 1989; Guest vocalist, Diamante, Zucchero, 1992; Albums: Everything Must Change, 1976; Miss Randy Crawford, 1977; Raw Silk, 1979; Now We May Begin, 1980; Secret Combination, 1981; Windsong, 1982; Nightline, 1983; Casino Nights (with Al Jarreau), 1983; Miss Randy Crawford - The Greatest Hits, 1984; Abstract Emotions, 1986; The Love Songs, 1987; Rich And Poor, 1989; The Very Best Of, 1993; Don't Say It's Over, 1993; Guest vocalist on albums: Please Don't Touch, Steve Hackett, 1977; Marching In The Streets, Harvey Mason, 1978; Street Life, The Crusaders, 1979; Hard To Hold, Rick Springfield, 1984. Honour: BRIT Award, Best Female Artist, 1982. Current Management: Gross Management Organisation, 930 Third Street, Suite 102, Santa Monica, CA 90403, USA.

CRAWFORD Stephanie, b. 30 Aug 1942, Detroit, Michigan, USA. Singer; Artist; Educator. Education: BA, Fine Arts, Wayne State University, Detroit, Michigan, USA. Musical Education: Barry Harris; Frank Foster, New York City. Career: Plays clubs and festivals including: Crest Jazz Festival; Aix-En-Provence Jazz Festival; Film appearance, La Vie En Rouge, 1995; Voice teacher, Centre d'Informations Musicales; Institut d'Art, Culture et Perception, Paris. Recordings: The Art Of Romance, 1990; A Time For Love, 1991; The Gift, 1992. Honour: Django D'Or, Best Jazz Vocal, 1993. Current Management: Self-managed. Address: 47 Rue Piat, 75020 Paris, France.

CRAY Robert William, b. 1 Aug 1953, Columbus, Georgia, USA. Blues Musician (guitar); Singer; Songwriter. Career: Began playing guitar aged 12; Member, Albert Collins' band, 1973-75; Formed Robert Cray Band, 1975-; Appearances include: Chuck Berry's 60th Birthday Concert, 1986; US tour as Bad Influence, 1987; Support to Tina Turner, European tour, 1987; Support to Eric Clapton, Royal Albert Hall, London, 1990; Concert with Eric Clapton and Stevie Ray Vaughan (his last), East Troy, Wisconsin, 1990; Guitar Legends, Seville, Expo '92, 1991; Tour with B B King, 1992; Festival appearances include: Glastonbury Festival; North Sea Jazz Festival; Newport Jazz Festival; Monterey Jazz Festival; Montreux Jazz Festival; San Francisco Blues Festival; New Orleans Jazz And Heritage Festival; Other concert performances with: The Rolling Stones; Muddy Waters; John Lee Hooker; Willie Dixon; Bonnie Raitt; The Grateful Dead; Film appearances: Animal House; Hail! Hail! Rock And Roll. Compositions: Songs covered by other artists include: Bad Influence, Eric Clapton; Old Love (co-writer with Eric Clapton); Phone Booth, Albert King; Playin' With My Friends, BB King. Recordings: Albums: Who's Been Talking, 1980; Bad Influence, 1983; False Accusations, 1985; Strong Persuader, 1986; Don't Be Afraid Of The Dark, 1988; Midnight Stroll, 1990; I Was Warned, 1992; Shame And A Sin, 1993; Some Rainy Morning, 1995; Singles include: Smoking Gun, 1987; Right Next Door (Because Of Me), 1987; Contributor, recordings by artists including: Albert Collins; Eric Clapton; Tina Turner; BB King; John Lee Hooker; Chuck Berry; Johnny Copeland; The Memphis Horns. Honours include: National Blues Awards, 1983, 1986; NAIRD Award, Best Blues Album, 1985; Grammy Awards, 1985, 1986, 1988; 8 Grammy Nominations; Numerous W.C. Handy Awards, 1984-, including 6 (Best Male Blues Artist, Vocalist of the Year, Single of the Year, Band of the Year, Song of the Year, Best Contemporary Blues Album), 1987; Numerous magazine awards, from Billboard; Downbeat; Rolling Stone; Esquire; Living Blues. Current Management: Eric Hanson, The Rosebud Agency, PO Box 170429, San Francisco, CA 94117, USA.

CREASEY Jason M, b. 23 July 1969, Andover, Hampshire, England. Record Producer; Remixer; Composer; Arranger; Musician. Musical Education: GCE A Level Music and Practical Music; Piano, Grade 8 (Trinity College of Music); Trumpet, Grade 8 (AB). Career: Extensive work in areas of writing, arranging, producing for various artists; Music to film; Keyboards and drum programming; Most recent productions in partnership with Hamish Hutchison (also known as remix duo Hiss and Hum for Absolute Basic Productions). Recordings: Producer (including arranging) for: Chesney Hawkes; Big Fun; Glen Goldsmith; Think 2wice (including writing); Deni Lew (additional production only); Remixer for: PJ and Duncan; Love City Groove; Jack 'n' Chill; Chesney Hawkes. Memberships: PRS; MCPS; Musicians' Union. Address: 7 St John's Street, Aylesbury, Buckinghamshire HP20 1BS, England.

CREME Lol, b. 19 Sept 1947, Manchester, Lancashire, England. Musician (guitar); Vocalist; Songwriter; Producer; Video and Film Director. Education: Graphic design, art college. Career: Founder member, guitarist, songwriter, 10cc, 1972-76; Appearances include: Reading Festival, 1974; Knebworth Festival, 1976; Tours of UK, USA; Producer, songwriter, member, duo Godley and Creme (with Kevin Godley), 1976-; Debut feature film, Howling At The Moon, 1988; Film director, The Lunatic, 1992. Recordings: Albums: with 10cc: Sheet Music, 1974; The Original Soundtrack, 1975; How Dare You?, 1976; with Godley & Creme (mostly self-written and produced): Consequences, 1977; L, 1978; Music From Consequences, 1979; Freeze Frame, 1979; Ismism, 1981; Birds Of Prey, 1983; The History Mix Volume 1, 1985; The Changing Faces Of 10cc and Godley And Creme, 1987; Goodbye Blue Sky, 1988; Hit singles: with 10cc: Donna, 1972; Rubber Bullets, 1973; The Dean And I, 1973; Wall Street Shuffle, 1974; Life Is A Minestrone, 1975; Art For Arts Sake, 1976; I'm Not In Love (Number 1, UK, Number 2, US), 1976; I'm Mandy Fly Me, 1976; Singles: Under Your Thumb, 1981; Wedding Bells, 1981; Cry, 1985; Producer, Long Distant Romancer, Mickey Jupp, 1981; Director, videos including: Every Breath You Take, The Police; Rockit, Herbie Hancock; Feel The Love, 10cc; Relax, Frankie Goes To Hollywood; Two Tribes, Frankie Goes To Hollywood. Honours: Ivor Novello Awards: Best Beat Song, Rubber Bullets, 1974; Most Performed British Work, Best Pop Song, International Hit Of The Year, I'm Not In Love, 1976; 5 MTV Music Video Awards, Rockit, 1984; MTV Video Vanguard Award (shared), 1985.

CRESWELL Guy, 17 May 1963, Bournemouth, England. Musical Entrepeneur; Musician (bass guitar, flute); Vocalist. m. Kate Snoswell. Education: 4 year Engineering diploma. Career: 6 month tour Europe, R&B band, 1983; Move to London, joined Innocent Party, 1984; Nationwide tours with TSB Rockschool teaching Hi tech, 1985-86; Worked as music demonstrator, Roland UK Ltd, 1986-95; Television appearances with: The Sweet; Jools Holland; Midge Ure; Ton Of Joy, 1991-94. Recordings: with Playing For Time: With My Heart, 1990; Six Weeks In July; with Ton Of Joy: Revealed Part 1. Memberships: PRS; Musicians' Union. Hobbies: Mac computers; Reading; Fish keeping. Current Management: Promus Productions. Address: The Barley Mow Centre, 10 Barley Mow Passage, Chiswick, London W4 4PH, England.

CRETU Michael, b. 18 May 1957, Bucharest, Romania. Musician (keyboards); Arranger; Producer; Composer. m. Sandra Lauer, 1988. Musical Education: Piano Lyzeum No 2, Bucharest, 1966; Academy of Music, Frankfurt,

1975. Career: Studio musician, 1978-; Writer, producer, musician, Moti Special; Mike Oldfield; Sylvie Vartan; Sandra, 1985-; Founder member, Enigma, 1990-. Recordings: Albums: Solo album: Legionare, 1983; with Enigma: MCMX aD, 1990; The Cross Of Changes, 1993; 6 albums with Sandra; Singles include: Maria Magdelena, Sandra (Number 1 in 30 countries); C'est Fatale, Sylvie Vartan; Writer, arranger, tracks for film soundtrack Sliver. Honours: Numerous Platinum and Gold discs as producer. Current Management: Nizzari Artist Management, 410 W 25th Street, Suite 5A, New York, NY 10001, USA.

CRIMI Joseph, b. 15 Sept 1962, Mediana, Italy. Musician (guitar, bass); Composer. m. 6 July 1991, 1 son. Musical Education: Conservatoire National Superieur, Paris. Career: Guitarist: Festival Mediterranean; Radio France; International tours with René Bartoli; Bassist: numerous clubs; Festivals: Hyeres; Avignon; Rive de Giers; Crest. Compositions: Theme Et Variations, for violin and piano; Suite, for flute and piano; Triptyque, for guitar and instrumental ensemble. Recordings: Casa Blu; Les Années Divers, T Maucci Quartet, 1992; Big Bang, Joseph Crimi Quintet, 1994. Membership: SACEM. Hobby: Composition.

CRISS Peter (Crisscoula), b. 27 Dec 1947, Brooklyn, New York, USA. Musician (drums); Singer; Songwriter. Career: Founder member, US rock group Kiss, 1973-80; Debut, Academy Of Music, New York, with Blue Öyster Cult; Iggy Pop; Teenage Lust; Tours include UK, 1976; Solo artiste, 1980-82; Member, Balls of Fire. Recordings: Albums with Kiss: Kiss, 1974; Hotter Than Hell, 1974; Dressed To Kill, 1975; Alive, 1975; Destroyer, 1976; The Originals, 1976; Rock And Roll Over, 1976; Kiss Alive II, 1977; Love Gun, 1977; Double Platinum, 1978; Dynasty, 1979; Solo albums: Peter Criss, 1978; Out Of Control, 1980; Let Me Rock You, 1982. Publications: The Kiss Comic Book, Marvel Comics. Honours: Platinum albums; Footprints outside Grauman's Chinese Theatre, Hollywood, 1976; Gold Ticket, Madison Square Garden, New York. Current Management: GHR Entertainment Co., Suite 506, 16601 Ventura Blvd, Encino, CA 91436, USA.

CROCE A J, b. 28 Sept 1971, Bryn Mar, Pennsylvania, USA. Musician (piano); Singer; Songwriter. m. Marlo Gordon, 21 Aug 1994. Musical Education: Self-taught. Recordings: Albums: A J Croce, 1993; That's Me In The Bar, 1995. Memberships: ASCAP; AFTRA; SAG. Current Management: OK Mangement. Address: PO Box 3727, Beverly Hills, CA 90212, USA.

CROISILLE Nicole, b. 9 Oct 1936, Neuilly-Sur-Seine, France. Singer; Actress. Career: Tour with mime artist, Marcel Marceau; Lead role, musical, L'Apprenti Fakir; First record, 1961; Worked in USA with Lester Wilson, Lalo Schiffrin; Un Homme Et Une Femme (A Man And A Woman), 1966; Olympia, Paris, 1976. 1978; Theatre des Champs- Elysées, Paris, 1981; Bataclan, Paris, 1988; Casino de Paris, 1991; Lead role, Hello Dolly, Thèatre du Chatelet, Paris, 1992-93; Actress, Les Miserables du XXe Siècle, 1995. Appearances: Canada; Latin America; Poland; Morocco; New show at Espace Pierre Cardin Theatre, Paris, 1997. Recordings include: Un Homme Et Une Femme; Parlez-Moi De Lui; Femme Avec Toi; T'arrai Voulu Etre Un Artiste; Albums: Croiselle Jazzile; Croiselle Black Et Blanche. Honours: Chevalier des Arts et des Lettres. Membership: SACEM. Hobbies: Dance; Gymnastics; Travel. Current Management: Bertrand Tallec, Showstop Management. Address: 64 Château Trompette, 78950 Gambais, France.

CROISSANT Cecilie, b. 19 May 1958, Oslo, Norway. Musician (keyboards); Pastor. m. John T Croissant, 21 Aug 1982, 2 daughters. Education: 2 years of college; 3 years of Bible College.

Musical Education: Private lessons for 14 years. Career: Extensive travel: Norway; USA; Australia; Europe; Frequent TV and radio appearance in Norway; Soloist, composer, preacher, worship leader; Conducted praise and worship seminars in many countries. Compositions: Majority of songs self-composed. Recordings: Albums: Before You Lord, 1987; Let Your Life Begin, 1994. Hobby: Outings with family. Address: PO Box 55252, Tulsa, OK 74155, USA.

CROKER Brendan, b. 15 Aug 1953, Bradford, Yorkshire, England. Musician (guitar). Education: Studied sculpture, art school. Career: Formed duo, Nev and Norris, with fellow guitarist Steve Phillips; Formed own band, the 5 O'Clock Shadows, early 1980s; Member, Notting Hillbillies (with Mark Knopfler, Guy Fletcher, Steve Phillips), 1990; UK tour, 1990. Recordings: Albums: Close Shave, 1986; Brendan Croker And The 5 O'Clock Shadows, 1989; with the Notting Hillbillies: Missing... Presumed Having, 1990; Guest musician, Ancient Heart, Tanita Tikaram; Singles: That's The Way All My Money Goes, 1986. Current Management: Paul Crockford Management, 56-60 Islington Park Street, London N1 1PX, England.

CROMPHOUT Francis, b. 24 October 1947, Antwerp, Belgium. Singer; Songwriter; Musician (Saxophone, Clarinet, Flute). m. Alejandra Anfossi, 20 January 1994, 1 daughter. Education: University Degree in Romanian Languages, Ghent State University. Career: Several performances in Jazz, Blues and Latin music; Creator and Performer, En Avian La Zizique, song program around Boris Vian; Founder, Band Leader, Cuisine Cajun and Café con Leche; Songwriter, Cuisine Cajun, Café con Leche and Catherine Delasalle; Concerts in Holland, Germany, Belgium; Emmissions in BRTN Radio and the RTBF Television; Major Compositions: Allons au Fais-Do-Do; Le Grand Dérangement, Cofé Bon Dieu, Démarche, (Pigalle). Recording: Le Grand Dérangement, 1996. Publication: Als un pas vernielde stad, poetry, 1978. Honour: Nominee of the CAWAB Award, 1997. Memberships: SABAM, Belgian Association of Authors and Composers; Country and Western Association of Belgium. Hobbies: Journalist for Knack Magazine; Poetry (publication in several literary magazines). Current Management: Berkenhof 7, 9050 Ghent, Belgium. Address: Berkenhof 7, 9050 Ghent, Belgium.

CRONIN Kevin, b. 6 Oct 1951, Evanston, Illinois, USA. Singer; Songwriter. Career: Lead vocalist, US rock group REO Speedwagon, 1972; 1976-; Solo artiste, 1973-76; Regular US and international concerts include: Anti-drug Users Are Losers concert, Miami, 1990. Compositions include: Keep On Loving You; Can't Fight This Feeling; Hard To Believe, for Home Front Trust (for families of Gulf War casualties). Recordings: Albums: with REO Speedwagon: R.E.O. T.W.O, 1972; R.E.O., 1976; REO Speedwagon Live/You Get What You Play For, 1977; You Can Tune A Piano But You Can't Tuna Fish, 1978; Nine Lives, 1979; A Decade Of Rock'N'Roll 1970-80, 1980; Hi Infidelity (Number 1, US), 1981; Good Trouble, 1982; Wheels Are Turning, 1984; Best Foot Forward, 1985; Life As We Know It, 1987; The Hits, 1988; The Earth, A Small Man, His Dog And A Chicken, 1990; A Second Decade Of Rock'N'Roll, 1981-1991, 1991; Hit singles include: Time For Me To Fly, 1978; Keep On Loving You, 1981; Take It On The Run, 1981; Don't Let Him Go, 1981; Keep The Fire Burnin', 1982; I Can't Fight This Feeling (Number 1, US), 1985; One Lonely Night, 1985; That Ain't Love, 1987; In My Dreams, 1987. Honours: Platinum and Gold discs. Current Management: Baruck-Consolo Management, 15003 Greenleaf Street, Sherman Oaks, CA 91403, USA.

CRONK William Henry, b. 28 Aug 1928, Fort Lee, New Jersey, USA. Musician (bass violin, electric bass); Arranger. m. Mary Reisinger, 10

Dec 1947, divorced, 1 son, 1 daughter. Musical Education: Bass, with M. Hinton, G Duvivier, Robert Brennand; Arranging, with Sy Oliver, Hugo Winterhalter. Career: 52nd Street, NYC, with Don Byas, 1945; Tony Pastor, Ray Anthony, Ralph Flanagan, 1946; Joined Tommy Dorsey, 1950; United with Jimmy Dorsey to form The Fabulous Dorseys, 1952; Became associated with Jackie Gleason Show, 1950s; Recorded with: Tommy Dorsey; Jimmy Dorsey; Ray Anthony; Ralph Flanagan; Ray McKinley; Bobby Hackett; Joined Louis Armstrong, early 1960s; Playboy Resort Hotel, New Jersey, 1970s; Playboy In Atlantic City, 1980s; Formed own band for the Meyer Davis Off. Memberships: AFofM (New York and New Jersey). Hobbies: Owning and racing Thoroughbred and Standardbred horses. Current Management: Own company, Bel-Cron Music. Address: William H Cronk Sr, 400 W 43rd Street, Apt 44R, New York, NY 10036, USA.

CROOK Jenny, b. 16 Jan 1971, Bath, Avon, England. Musician (non-pedal harp); Vocalist. Education: BA, Honours, Performance Arts, Middlesex University. Career: Mainly performs as duo with Maclaine Colston (hammered dulcimer, vocals), Folk clubs and Festivals; Television appearances include: Pebble Mill; Summer In The City; Radio appearances in sessions for Folk On 2; Kaleidoscope; Played incidental music, David Attenborough's television series, The Private Life Of Plants, BBC; Played at Barbican Festival. Recordings: Evolving Tradition; Cythara-cythara. Honour: Young Tradition Award Finalist, BBC Radio 2, 1993. Memberships: Musicians' Union; PAN; Clarsach Society. Current Management: Ash Promotions; Mrs Casey Music; Brass Tacks. Address: 41 Bloomfield Park Road, Timsbury, Bath BA3 1LR, England.

CROOK (William) Roger, b. 13 Aug 1942, Forfar, Scotland. Teacher; Semi-professional Singer (tenor); Instrumentalist. m. Nancy, 19 Aug 1968, 1 son, 1 daughter. Musical Education: RSAMD Diplomas: DRSAM (singing teacher); DRSAM (singing performer); ARCM (singing teacher). Career: Broadcasts of Scottish songs, classical material; Leader, Thistle Ceilidh Band; Member, Quatrain; Arranger of Scottish material for voices and orchestra; Musician, accordion, fiddle, piano, for Scottish Dance Bands; Conductor. Recordings: An Evening Of Scottish Songs; An Evening Of Light Music; Songs We Love; Sound Of The Sea. Honours: Officer, St John's Association for Musical Charity Work. Hobbies: Walking; Hospital and Hospice entertaining. Current Management: The Entertainment Company, Edinburgh. Address: 11 Barbour Grove, Dunfermline KY12 9YB, Scotland.

CROSBY David (David Van Cortland), b. 14 Aug 1941, Los Angeles, California, USA. Vocalist; Musician (guitar). m. Jan Dance, 15 May 1987. Career: Member, Les Baxter's Balladeers; The Byrds, 1964-67; Crosby Stills And Nash, 1968-; Also, Crosby Stills Nash and Young; Performances include: with the Byrds: Monterey Pop Festival, 1967; with Crosby Stills and Nash: Woodstock Festival, 1969; Altamont Speedway, with the Rolling Stones, 1969; Royal Albert Hall, 1970; Wembley Stadium, 1974; Anti-nuclear concert, Madison Square Garden, New York, 1979; Peace Sunday concert, Rose Bowl, Pasadena, 1982; Live Aid, Philadelphia, 1985; Madison Square Garden, 1988; Amnesty International benefit, Chile, 1990; Farm Aid IV, 1990; Royal Albert Hall, 1992; Film, No Nukes, 1980; Television: guest, Roseanne, ABC-TV, 1992; The Simpsons, Fox-TV, 1993. Recordings: Albums include: with the Byrds: Mr Tambourine Man, 1965; Turn! Turn! Turn!, 1965; Fifth Dimension, 1966; Younger Than Yesterday, 1967; with Crosby Stills and Nash include: Crosby Stills & Nash, 1969; Déjà Vu, 1970; 4-Way Street, 1971; So Far, 1974; Daylight Again, 1982; What Goes Around, 1983; Allies, 1983; Live It Up, 1990; with Graham Nash: Graham Nash/David Crosby, 1972;

Wind On The Water, 1975; Whistling Down The Wire, 1976; Crosby/Nash Live, 1977; The Best Of, 1978; Solo albums: If Only I Could Remember My Name, 1971; Oh Yes I Can, 1989; Now It's All Coming Back To Me, 1995; Singles include: with the Byrds: Mr Tambourine Man (Number 1, UK and US), 1965; All I Really Want To Do, 1965; Eight Miles High, 1966; 5D (Fifth Dimension), 1966; Mr Spaceman, 1966; So You Want To Be A Rock'n'Roll Star, 1967; with Crosby Stills And Nash: Woodstock, 1970; Teach Your Children, 1970; Ohio, 1970; Just A Song Before You Go, 1977; Wasted On The Way, 1982; Southern Cross, 1982. Honours: Grammy, Best New Artists, Crosby Stills and Nash, 1970; Best International Group, Melody Maker Poll, 1971; MusiCares Man Of The Year, NARAS, 1991. Current Management: Management Network Inc, 14930 Ventura Blvd. #205, Sherman Oaks, CA 91403, USA.

CROSS Christopher (Christopher Geppert), b. 3 May 1951, San Antonio, Texas, USA. Musician (guitar); Vocalist; Songwriter. Career: Member, rock group Flash; Support for acts including Led Zeppelin, Jefferson Airplane, Deep Purple; Formed band for own compositions, 1975; Recording artist, 1978; Own publishing company, Pop'n'Roll, 1978. Compositions include: Co-writer (with Burt Bacharach, Carole Bayer Sager, Peter Allen): Arthur's Theme (Best That You Can Do), for film Arthur, 1981. Recordings: Albums include: Christopher Cross, 1980; Another Page, 1983; Every Turn Of The World, 1985; Back Of My Mind, 1988; Rendezvous, 1992; Window, 1995; Singles include: Ride Like The Wind, 1980; Sailing (Number 1, US), 1980; Never Be The Same, 1980; Say You'll Be Mine, 1981; Arthur's Theme (Number 1, US), 1981; All Right, 1983; No Time To Talk, 1983; Think Of Laura, 1983; A Chance For Heaven (used as swimming theme for Los Angeles Olympics), 1984; Contributor, Pearls - Songs Of Goffin And King, Carole King, 1980; Film soundtrack, Nothing In Common, 1986; As co-producer: Long Time Friends, Alessi Brothers, 1982. Honours: Grammy Awards: Album Of The Year, Christopher Cross; Best New Artist; Record Of The Year, Sailing; Song Of The Year, Sailing; Best Arrangement, Sailing, (all) 1981; Oscar, Best Song From A Film, Arthur's Theme, 1982. Current Management: Baruck/Consolo, 15003 Greenleaf Street, Sherman Oaks, CA 91043, USA.

CROSSLEY Syd, b. 10 Aug 1961, Ilford, East London, England. Musician (saxophones, flute, keyboards, guitars); Vocalist; Programmer. 1 son. Musical Education: Self-taught. Career: Songwriter, saxophone, Bastard Bros Band, 1986; Songwriter, saxophone, lead vocalist, The Never Again With Rob Barham Band, 1987; Vocalist, co-songwriter, saxophone, Trip Cadets, 1988-91; Co-songwriter, saxophone, The Rubber Club, 1991; Co-songwriter, saxophone, Fat Cat Band, 1992-93; Co-songwriter, artist, programmer, Boom Devils, 1994-95; Co-songwriter, programmer, artist, King Kooba Triptet, 1995. Recordings: Life's A Bummer EP, Trip Cadets, 1991; Albums: Saxophonist, Seven, James (Number 1, UK), 1992; Currently completing albums: One Minute Away From Perfection, Boom Devils; The Dub Commander Lands On The Kooba Twins, King Kooba Triptet; King Kooba Triptet EP; Single remix, Utah Saints. Memberships: Musicians' Union; Founder member, The Rubber Club. Hobbies: Inventing instruments; Making sound effects. Current Management: Boom Devil Productions. Address: 236 Canbury Park Road, Kingston upon Thames, Surrey, England.

CROUCHER Piers, b. 1 Nov 1969, Minehead, Somerset, England. Musician (drums, percussion, guitar). Partner, Sadie Doyle. Musical Education: Tommy Cuncliffe, Jersey. Career: Member, Zapf The Band; Air Stream Stream Trailer; The Bar Flies; Summer seasons, Jersey; Lucy And Freud. Recordings: 2 EPs: Lucy And Freud; Field Day. Memberships: Equity; Musicians' Union. Hobbies:

Acting; Television; Motor scooters. Current Management: Robert Smith, Bristol. Address: 16 Poundfield Road, Minehead, Somerset TA24 5EP, England.

CROW Bill, b. 27 Dec 1927, Othello, Washington, USA. Musician (bass). m. Aileen Armstrong, 1965, 1 son. Career: Bassist, various artists including: Stan Getz; Claude Thorhill; Marian McPartland; Gerry Mulligan; Zoot Sims; Bob Brookmeyer; Clark Terry; Benny Goodman; Walter Norris; Peter Duchin; Musician, Broadway shows, 1975-89. Membership: AFofM. Publications: Contributor, The Jazz Review; Jazz Letter; Author: Jazz Anecdotes, 1990. Address: c/o American Federation of Musicians, New York, USA.

CROW Sheryl, b. Feb 1962, Kennett, Missouri, USA. Singer; Songwriter; Musician (guitar). Musical Education: Classical Music degree, Missouri State University; Organ and piano lessons; Self-taught guitar. Career: Backing singer, Michael Jackson tour, 18 months; Also backing singer for Joe Cocker; Rod Stewart; Don Henley; Songwriter, solo performer, mid 1980s-; International concerts and tours with John Hiatt; Crowded House; Big Head Todd; Support tours to Bob Dylan; Eagles, 1994; Joe Cocker, Wembley Arena, 1994; Performed at Woodstock II, 1994. Recordings: Solo album: Tuesday Night Music Club, 1993; Singles include: All I Wanna Do, 1994; Leaving Las Vegas, 1995; Contributor, albums: The End Of Innocence, Don Henley, 1989; Late Night, Neal Schon, 1989; Other recordings by Eric Clapton; Wynnona Judd; Contributor, film soundtracks: Kalifornia, 1994; Leaving Las Vegas, 1995. Honours: 3 Grammy Awards, Tuesday Night Music Club, 1995. Current Management: Weintraub Management, 80 Varick Street #6B, New York, NY 10013, USA.

CROWELL Rodney, b. 7 Aug 1950, Houston, Texas, USA. Country Singer; Songwriter; Musician (guitar); Record Producer. 4 daughters. Career: Member, songwriter, Emmylou Harris' Hot Band, 1974-79; Worked with Willie Nelson; Ry Cooder; Jim Keltner; Solo artiste, and with own band, 1978-. Compositions: 10 US Country Number 1 hits; Songs for Emmylou Harris include: Bluebird Wine, 1974; Till I Gain Control Again, 1975; I Ain't Living Long Like This, 1979; Leaving Louisiana In The Broad Daylight, 1979; 250 versions of own compositions recorded by artists including: Willie Nelson; Foghat; Bob Seger; The Dirt Band; Waylon Jennings; George Jones. Recordings: US Country Number 1 hits include: It's Such A Small World, with Roseanne Cash; I Couldn't Leave You If I Tried; She's Crazy For Leaving; Albums: Ain't Living Long Like This, 1978; But What Will The Neighbours Think, 1980; Rodney Crowell, 1981; Street Language, 1986; Diamonds And Dirt, 1988; The Rodney Crowell Collection, 1989; Keys To The Highway, 1989; Life Is Messy, 1992; Jewel Of The South, 1995; As producer: recordings for: Guy Clark; Albert Lee; Carl Perkins; Jerry Lee Lewis; Bobby Bare; Roseanne Cash; Lari White; Brady Seals; Beth Nielsen Chapman. Honours include: Grammy Award, Best Country Song, After All This Time, 1990. Memberships: CMA; Nashville Songwriters' Association; NARAS. Hobbies: Outdoor activities; Family; Films; Travel; Athletics; Music. Current Management: Gold Mountain Entertainment, Suite 450, 3575 Cahuenga Blvd. West, Los Angeles, CA 90068, USA. Address: c/o Beth Torrell, RC One, PO Box 120576, Nashville, TN 37212, USA.

CRUCIAL BANKIE (Ian Veira), b. 23 Nov 1965, St Kitts, West Indies. Musician (guitar, keyboard); Vocalist. 1 son. Musical Education: Self-taught. Career: Bunny Wailer first Antigua Show; Numerous radio broadcasts; Reggae Sunsplash, with Sagittarius Band, 1986, Stud Band, 1988; Performed with: Leroy Horsemouth Wallace; Jose Whale Brigadier Jerry; Buju Banton; Legendary Bunny Wailer. Recordings: Just A

Sting, 1978; Sweet Reggae Muzik, 1994; Film: Uptown, soundtrack. Publication: The New Music Of Reviews. Membership: ASCAP. Hobbies: Travel; Basketball; Cricket. Current Management: African Shrine Management. Address: 196 4th Avenue, Suite 2L, Brooklyn, NY 11217, USA.

CRUST Geoffrey Leonard, b. 30 Mar 1945, Boston, Lincolnshire, England. Songwriter; Publisher; Musician (guitars, keyboards). m. 5 Oct 1984, 2 daughters. Musical Education: Privately taught, plus cadet musician, as drummer. Career: Songs on Songwriter Round Up albums, 1-4, featuring Ray Jones; Albums: Modern Country Melodies; USA/UK album; Country Headaches. Compositions: 67 published songs, both in UK, USA; Songs on 4 American albums with Music Room Records; Sollie Sunshine Records, USA. Publications: 15A Magazines, Brum Country Magazine, Spain, Denmark. Memberships: PRS; MCPS; TMA; ISA; BCMA; PPL Umbrella. Hobbies: Writing songs, helping new writers, Heartbeat Music Publishing Company. Current Management: Thatch Records (own publishing company and record label). Address: 31 Tower Street, Boston, Lincolnshire, England.

CRUTCHER Johnny, (Isaac John Mark), b. 19 Jun 1934, Bournemouth, Dorset, England. Musician (accordion); Vocalist; Bandleader. m. Valerie Ann Crutcher, 24 Feb 1973. Education: Technical School; FFA; MIMgt; MISM. Musical Education: Private tuition. Career: Bandleader, hotels in UK, 1960-75; Television appearance, 1961; Currently, professional Public Accountant for musicians and some orchestral clients. Address: Units 7 & 8 The Parade, 147 Wareham Road, Corfe Mullen, Wimborne, Dorset BH21 3LA, England.

CRUZ Celia, b. Havana, Cuba. Singer. m. Pedro Knight, 14 July 1962. Education: Teacher training. Musical Education: Classes at National Conservatory of Music, Havana. Career: First prize, Cuban radio talent show; Member, group Gloria Mantecera; Tours, Mexico, Venezuela, with Roderico Neyra's dance troupe, Las Mulatas de Fuego; Lead vocalist, Sonora Matancera, Radio Progreso, 1950; Recording artiste, 1951-; Collaborations with Tito Puente; Johnny Pacheco; Album debut with Fania All Stars, 1975; UK debut, 1976; Tours with Fania All Stars, Africa; Europe; Regular UK appearances with Tito Puente, 1984-; Subject, television documentary My Name Is Celia Cruz, Arena, BBC TV, 1988; Film appearances: Salsa, 1976; The Mambo Kings Play Songs Of Love, 1991. Recordings: Numerous albums include: La Excitante Celia Cruz!, 1968; Etc Etc Etc, 1970; Tremendo Caché, 1975; Azuca Negra, 1993; with Tito Puente: Cuba y Puerto Rico Son, 1966; Son Con Guaguanco, 1966; Quimbo Quimbumbia, 1969; Alma Con Alma, 1971; Algo Especial Para Recordar, 1972; Hoenaje A Beny Moré Vol III, 1985; with Willie Colón: Only They Could Have Made This Album, 1977; Celia y Willie, 1981; The Winners, 1987; with Memo Salamanca: Bravo, 1967; A Ti Mexico, 1968; Serenata Guajira, 1968; Nuevos Exitos de Celia Cruz, 1971; with Johnny Pacheco: Celia And Johnny, 1974; Recordando El Ayer, 1976; Eternos, 1978; De Nuevo, 1985; with Ray Barretto: Tremendo Trio!, 1983; Ritmo En El Corazón, 1988; with Sonora Matancera: Feliz Encuentro, 1982; Live! From Carnegie Hall - 65th Anniversary Celebration, 1989. Honours include: Honorary doctorate, Yale University, 1989; Grammy Award, 1990; Star on Hollywood Walk Of Fame, 1990. Current Management: Ralph Mercado Management, 568 Broadway, Suite 806, New York, NY 10012, USA.

CUGNY Laurent, b. 14 Apr 1955, La Garenne-Colombes, France. Bandleader; Arranger; Musician (piano). m. Philippe Joëlle, 8 Feb 1992, 1 son, 1 daughter. Education: BA, Economics, Cinema. Musical Education: Piano lessons, aged 10-14. Career: Founder, Lumière

Big Band, 1979; European tour, Lumière and Gil Evans, 1987; Director, Orchestre National de Jazz (ONJ), 1994-1997; European tour, ONJ and Lucky Peterson, 1995. Recordings: with Lumière and Gil Evans: Rhythm-A-Ning, 1988; Golden Hair, 1989; with Lumière: Santander, 1991; Dromesko, 1993; with ONJ: Yesternow, 1994; with Abbey Lincoln: A Turtle's Dream, 1995. Publications: Las Vegas Tango - Une Vie De Gil Evans, 1989; Electrique Miles Davis, 1993. Honours: Django Reinhardt Award, Jazz Academy, 1991; Charles-Cros Academy Award, 1991. Hobby: Volleyball. Current Management: Blue Line. Address: 5 Rue Leon Giraud, 75019 Paris, France.

CUILLERIER Philippe "Doudou", b. 5 Sept 1961, Versailles, France. Musician (guitar); Lyricist. Musical Education: Saxophone from age 7; Guitar from age 17; Lessons with Eric Boell, Frederic Sylvestre. Career: Guitar teacher, 1983-; Backing guitarist with: Angelo Debarre; Romane Quintet; Lead guitarist, vocalist with: Fernando Jazz Gang; Little Big Man (blues). Recordings: with Fernando Jazz Gang: Gipsy Violin, Swing Guitars; Gipsy Songs; with Romane Quartet: Quintet. Address: 2 Ruelle des Poulies, 78490 Montfort-l'Amaury, France.

CULLAZ Alby, b. 25 June 1941, Paris, France. Musician (double bass). 1 son, 1 daughter. Musical Education: Classical professors for piano and bass; Self-taught for jazz. Career: Backing for soloists: J Griffin; D Gordon; K Drew; Kenny Clark; H Mobley; Slide Hampton; Philly Joe Jones; Steve Grossman; René Urtreger; Chet Baker; Dee Dee Bridgewater; Alain Jean Marie; Art Farmer; Eric Lelann; Christian Escoude; Jean Luc Pouty; Michel Graillier; Art Taylor. Recordings: The Flip, H Mobley; Reflection, Steve Grosman and Simon Goubert; Duo with Christian Escoude; Jeff Gilson Big Band; Michel Grailler Trio; Christian Escoude Octet; Tac Tic, J.P.Foughet; Recidive, René Urtreger. Honour: Django Reinhardt Prize, 1973. Address: 52 Rue du General Delestraint, 75016 Paris, France.

CULLAZ Pierre Maurice Louis, b. 21 July 1935, Paris, France. Musician (guitar); Teacher. m. Rita Castellano, 24 Feb 1964. Musical Education: Classical, Jazz music, guitar. Career: Studio work; Jazz clubs; Tours with many singers; Contemporary classical music; Currently, extensive teaching, mainly jazz guitar. Publication: A Guitar Method, edited by Alphonse Leduc. Hobbies: Concerts; Theatre; Sports. Address: 1 Rue Charlot, 75003 Paris, France.

CUMMINGS Daniel. Musician (Percussion); Musical Director. 1 son. Career: Dire Straits, On Every Street, Tour, 1991-92; Tina Turner; George Michael; Simply Red, Life, album; Bon Jovi; Sophie B Hawkins; Incognito. Recordings: Albums: Dire Straits, On Every Street, UK No 1; Tina Turner, Foreign Affair, UK No 1; George Michael: Listen Without Prejudice, UK No 1; Careless Whisper, UK No 1; Wham, Make It Big!, UK No 1; Holly Johnson, Blast, UK No 1. Membership:MU. Current Management: One Management, 43 St Alban's Avenue, London W4 5JS, England.

CUMMINS Paul, b. 13 Oct 1953, Portsmouth, Hampshire, England. Artist Manager. m. Janice Bellamy, 25 June 1988. Career: Tour manager, 1975-79; Artists: Talking Heads; Andy Fairweather-Low; Jesse Winchester; XTC; Gallagher and Lyle; Manager, tour manager, Dire Straits, 1979-. Hobbies: Fishing; Walking; Bird spotting; Cooking; Music; Pottery. Address: Damage Management, 16 Lambton Place, London W11 4LQ, England.

CUNNAH Peter, b. 30 Aug 1966, Belfast, Northern Ireland. Singer; Songwriter; Performer; Musician (guitar). Education: York St Art College, University of Ulster. Career: Singer, songwriter with D:ream; Tours and concerts: Support tour

with Take That, UK & Europe; UK, 1993, 1994; Australia, 1994; Gay Pride, London; T In The Park, Glasgow; Fri Rock Festival, Copenhagen; Stonewall, Royal Albert Hall, London; Fleadh Festival, London; Gay Games, New York. Recordings: Albums: D:ream On Vol.1; World, 1995; Singles include: Things Can Only Get Better; Shoot With Me Your Love; The Power (Of All The Love In The World); Remixes for: Deborah Harry; Duran Duran; EMF. Honours: IDA Best Dance Act, 1993. Current Management: Mark Beder, FXU Records, 97A Scrubs Lane, London NW10 6QU, England.

CUNNINGHAM Christopher John, b. 7 Jun 1970, Droylsden, Manchester, England. Musician (acoustic guitar, electric guitar, electronic guitar). Musical Education: Tameside College of Technology. Career: Toured Ireland and Ulster with Indie guitar band, Poors Of Reign; Several appearances, mostly musical and some theatrical, on local and national television including Juice, for Granada TV. Compositions: Over 200 songs written for guitar, bass and drums. Recording: Concerto De Piezo for guitar synthesizer. Membership: Musicians' Union. Hobbies: Theatre; Cinema; Reading. Current Management: James Joseph Cunningham. Address: 37 Wordsworth Avenue, Droylsden, Greater Manchester M43 6GA, England.

CUNNINGHAM Déirdre Mary Gerradine, b. 31 May 1956, Sutton, Surrey, England. Singer; Songwriter; Musician (acoustic guitar). m. Liam Cunningham, July 1977, 1 son. Education: Secretarial. Musical Education: Self-taught. Career: Tours: France; Germany; Netherlands; Ireland; Switzerland; Sweden; Denmark; Finland; Norway; England; Wales; Radio broadcasts: RTE Radio; BBC Radio; First single playlisted on national and local radio; Current album play-listed; Regular appearances on Irish national television, Welsh national television. Recordings: Albums: City of Tribes; Sunny Days; Singles: Take Me For A Fool; Hurry Make Love. Publications: City of Tribes; Sunny Days; Irish Contemporary Songs; In progress, new album Song of the River. Memberships: IASC; ISA; IMRO; MCPS. Hobbies: Mountain walking; Kayaking; Mountain biking; Windsurfing; Basketball; Swimming; Reading. Current Management: Lake Records, Cootehall, Boyle, Co. Roscommon, Ireland.

CUNNINGHAM Philip Martin, b. 27 Jan 1960, Edinburgh, Scotland. Composer; Performer; Music Director; Producer. m. Donna Macrae, 24 Dec 1982, 1 daughter. Musical Education: Private tuition from age 3. Career: Tours of UK, Europe and USA; Music Director of four series, over 4 years, of Talla A' Bhaile, for BBC Scotland; Music Director, Presenter, Hogmonay Live, for BBC, 1991-94; Co-presenter of weekly radio series, Live From The Lemon Tree, for BBC. Compositions: Music for Bill Bryden theatre productions, The Ship and The Big Picnic; Orchestral Suite, premiered 1996; Compositions used for film soundtrack Last Of The Mohicans. Honour: Honorary Citizen, Reading, Pennsylvania, USA. Membership: Musicians' Union. Hobbies: Clay Pigeon shooting; Scuba diving; Golf. Current Management: Donna Cunningham. Address: Cunningham Audio Productions Ltd, Crask of Aigas, By Beauly, Inverness IV4 7AD, Scotland.

CUNNINGHAM Tom, b. 22 June 1965, Glasgow, Scotland. Musician (drums). Career: Member, Wet Wet Wet, 1982-; Performances include: Greenpeace charity concert, Royal Albert Hall, London, 1986; Support to Lionel Richie, UK tour, 1987; Prince's Trust Rock Gala, Royal Albert Hall, 1988-90; John Lennon Tribute Concert, Merseyside, 1990; Children In Need, BBC, 1991; Edinburgh Castle, 1992; Live At The Royal Albert Hall, C4, 1993. Recordings: Albums: Popped In Souled Out, 1987; Sgt Pepper Knew My Father, 1988; The Memphis Sessions, 1988; Holding Back The River, 1989; High On The Happy Side, 1992;

Wet Wet Wet Live At The Royal Albert Hall, 1993; End Of Part One (Their Greatest Hits), 1993; Picture This, 1995; Singles include: Temptation, 1988; With A Little Help From My Friends (Number 1, UK), 1988; Angel Eyes (Home And Away), 1988; Sweet Surrender, 1989; Broke Away, 1989; Hold Back The River, 1990; Make It Tonight, 1991; Goodnight Girl (Number 1, UK), 1992; Lip Service, 1992; More Than Love, 1992; Shed A Tear, 1993; Love Is All Around (Number 1, UK), 1994; She's All On My Mind, 1995; Julia Said, 1995. Honours: BRIT Award: Best British Newcomer, 1988. Current Management: The Precious Organisation, The Townhouse, 1 Park Gate, Glasgow G3 6DL, Scotland.

CUOMO Rivers, b. USA. Singer; Songwriter; Musician (guitar). Career: Singer, songwriter, Weezer. Recordings: Debut album: Weezer - The Album, 1995; Hit single: Undone. Current Management: Third Rail Entertainment, 9169 Sunset Blvd, Los Angeles, CA 90069, USA.

CURNIN Cy, b. 12 Dec 1957, Wimbledon, England. Vocalist. m. Peri, 7 Nov 1985, 2 daughters. Education: Wimbledon College. London. Musical Education: Self-educated. Career: Vocalist with Fixx; US tours throughout 1980s; Tour with The Police, 1983; Appearances on: Saturday Night Live; Old Grey Whistle Test; In Concert (BBC); MTV; VH1. Recordings: Shuttered Room, 1981; Reach The Beach (Platinum US), 1983; Hits include: Stand Or Fall, 1982; Red Skids, 1982; One Thing Leads To Another, 1983; Further albums: Phantoms, 1984; Walkabout, 1986; Calm Animals, 1988; Ink, 1990. Honours: ASCAP; 2 million plays, 1983, 1984. Memberships: PRS; ASCAP. Hobbies: Fishing; Reading. Current Management: Jeff Nebin, USA.

CURRIE Justin, b. 11 Dec 1964, Glasgow, Scotland. Singer;Songwriter; Musician (bass guitar, piano). Career: Founder, Del Amitri, 1981-; Concerts include: UK and international tours; Appearance at Woodstock Festival, 1994. Recordings: Singles: Kiss This Thing Goodbye; Nothing Ever Happens; Move Away Jimmy Blue; Spit In The Rain; Always The Last To Know; Be My Downfall; Here And Now; Roll To Me; Albums: Del Amitri, 1985; Waking Hours, 1989; Change Everything, 1992; Twisted, 1995; Some Other Suckers Parade, 1997. Current Management: JPR Management, The Power House, 70 Chiswick High Road, London W4 1SY, England.

CURSON Theodore, b. 3 June 1935, Philadelphia, Pennsylvania, USA. Musician (trumpet). m. Marjorie Goltry, 1 Apr 1967, 1 son, 1 daughter. Musical Education: Granoff Music Conservatory, Philadelphia, 1952-53. Career: Trumpeter with Charlie Mingus; Max Roach; Philly Joe Jones; Cecil Taylor; Eric Dolphy, 1960-63; Concerts and jazz festivals include: North Sea; Nice; Antibes; Monterey; Newport; Concerts: Europe; USA; India; Middle East; North Africa; Director, Blue Note Open Jam, 1984-; President, Nosruc Publishing Company, 1961-. Recordings include: Plenty Of Horn, 1961; Fire Down Below, 1963; New Thing And Blue Thing, 1965; The Urge, 1966; Ode To Booker Ervin, 1970; Pop Wine, 1972; Quicksand, 1975; Jubilant Power, 1976; Tears For Delphy, 1976; Blue Piccolo, 1976; Flip Top, 1977; Typical Ted, 1977; The Trio, 1979; I Heard Mingus, 1980; Snake Johnson, 1981; 'Round Midnight, 1990; Several film scores. Honours: New Star, Monterey Jazz Festival, 1962; Downbeat Critics Poll Winner, 1966; Readers Poll Winner, 1978; Long Island Musicians Society Award, 1970; Pori City Standard, Finland, 1978. Membership: AFofM.

CURTIS Mac, b. 16 January 1939, Fort Worth, Texas, USA. Singer; Musician (guitar); Songwriter. m. Peggy, 3 March 1967, 3 sons. Education: Graduated, Army Information and Broadcasting School, 1958; Graduated, Anthony School of Real Estate, 1975; Moorpark

Community College Real Estates Course, Moorpark, California, USA, 1975-76; Licensed Real Estate Associate California, 1975-80. Musical Education: Selftaught. Career: Recorded for King records, 1956; Guest, Big D Jambouree and National Radio Show, 1956; Co-star, Alan Feed Rock 'n' Roll Revue, New York, 1956; Toured as Rock 'n' Roll Rockabilly, until 1960; Country Music DJ, Dallas Radio Station; Recorded Country for Epic and GRT Dj Atlanta, Nashville, LA, 1971. Compositions: I'd Run a Mile for Lynn Anderson; Give Us One More Chance. Recordings: The King Original Rockabilly Masters; Blue Jean Heart, CD; The Rollin' Rock series, 3 albums; Rollin' Rock Singles CD, Rollin' Rock Switzerland. Publication: Goldmine Magazine, Vol 9, Issue 10, 1983; We Wanna Boogie, 1988. Honours: Golden Ear Awards, Country Survey News, 1969; ASCAP Chartbuster Award, 1972. Membership: American Society of Composers, Authors and Publishers, 1970-. Hobbies: Music; Writing; International Travel. Current Management: Rock 'n' Roll Enterprises, 16 Grove Place, Penarth, Vale of Glamorgan, CF64 2ND, South Wales.

CURTOLA (Robert Allen) Bobby, b. 14 April 1943, Thunder Bay, Ontario, Canada. Singer; Songwriter. m. Ava, 21 September 1975, 2 sons. Career: Singer, Rock 'n Roll; Co-Host, After Four, TV series, Canada, 1965-66; Own TV series on CTV, Shake, Rock and Roll; Own Christmas Special in Canada; Performer on Bob Hope Show; Guest, numerous national and regional talk and variety specials in Canada and USA; Headlines in Las Vegas for many years. Composition: The Real Thing, 1966. Recordings include: Fortune Teller; Aladdin; 3Rows Over; Corrina. Honours: Winner, Jingle Award for North America; Canada's First RPM Top Male Vocalist Award, 1965; Inducted into Canadian Music Industry Hall of Fame, 1996; Gold record status for 22 singles and 13 albums; Order of Canada, 1998. Memberships: ACTRA; ARIA; AFofM; CARAS; SOCAN. Current Management: Mr Robert Hubbard. Address: Box 5359, Edmonton, Alberta T5P 4C5, Canada..

CUSSON Michel, b. 22 January 1957, Drummondville. Guitarist; Composer. m. Michelle Alie, 2 daughters. Education: College Degree in Pop Music; CEGEP, Drumondville, one session, McGill University Montreal; 4 months at Boston's Berklee College of Music. Career: Composed soundtrack for Omertà, La loi du silence, television series, 1996, 1997, 1998; Composed soundtrack for movies: La Comtesse de Baton Rouge (Amdré Forcier), 1997, and L'Automne Sauvage (Gabriel Pelletier), 1992; Numerous themes for Canadian television shows; Music themes for advertising campaigns; Created jazz-world beat group Michel Cusson and the Wild Unit in 1991 and jazz-fusion group UZEB in 1976. Recordings: 2 albums with Michel Cusson and the Wild Unit; 10 albums wwith UZEB. Honours: Felix Awards, 1983, twice 1984, 1987, 1990, twice 1992; Gemeaux Awards, 1989, 1996, Socan Awards, 1990, 1993, 1995, 1996; Music Plus Award, 1991; Oscar Peterson Trophy, 1991. Address: c/o Productions Flash Rose, 3867 rue Saint Denis, Montreal, Quebec H2W 2M4, Canada.

CYPORYN Dennis, b. 1 Feb 1942, Detroit, Michigan, USA. Musician (banjo); Composer. 1 son, 1 daughter. Education: Oakland University, 2nd Year. Musical Education: Theory. Career: Dennis Cyporyn Band; Composes own music for band; Showcased at Detroit Music Awards, Motor City Music Awards; Won Best Instrumentalist 2 years, also Group Deserving Wider Recognition and Best Folk Group; Currently with Lonesome and Blue, bluegrass band. Recordings: Nashville Alley, 1991; I Must Be Dreaming, 1992; Deja Vu Debut, 1994; Duet to Quintet, 1997. Publications: The Bluegrass Songbook, 1972. Honours: 5 Awards, 12 Nominations, IBMA, MCMA, DMA. Memberships: IBMA; MCMA. Hobby: Sailing.

Address: Krypton Records, PO Box 372, Highland, MI 48357, USA.

CYRKA Jan Josef, b. 31 Oct 1963, Halifax, West Yorkshire, England. Musician (guitar); Composer. Musical Education: Self-taught. Career: Member, Max and the Broadway Metal Choir, 1984; Recording engineer, E-Zee Studios, 1985; Member, Zodiac Mindwarp and the Love Reaction,1986-89; Tours, USA and Canada, supporting Guns N' Roses; Solo artist, 1989-; Session musician, television commercials; Partner, Take It For Granted PR Company; Producer and contributor, cover-mount CD for Guitarist magazine. Composition: Three library albums: Rock Guitar Album, Rock Attitude, Boom; Wrote most of music for BBC Horizon, Great Balloon Race, 1997. Recordings: Max And The Metal Choir, 1985; Tattooed Beat Messiah, Zodiac Mindwarp, 1987; Solo albums: Beyond The Common Ground, 1992; Spirit, 1993; Prickly Pear, 1997; Session guitarist, At This Moment, Tom Jones; Co-producer, All Day Long I Shouted, Carmel. Memberships: Musicians' Union; PRS; MCPS; BMI; Rondor Music; Almo Sounds. Hobbies: Walking; Building and expanding home recording studio. Current Management: Andrew Farrow, Northern Music Company. Address: Cheapside Chambers, 43 Cheapside, Bradford, West Yorkshire BD1 4HP, England.

CYRUS Billy Ray, b. 25 Aug 1961, Flatwoods, Kentucky, USA. Country Singer. Career: Formed own group, Sly Dog, 1983; Worked as car salesman; Solo recording artiste, 1992-. Recordings: Hit singles: Achy Breaky Heart (Number 1, US and UK) 1992; Could've Been Me; Album: Some Gave All (Number 1, US), 1992. Current Management: McFadden Artist Corp. Address: 818 18th Avenue South, Nashville, TN 37203, USA.

CZ, b. 25 June 1969, Charleroi, Belgium. Singer; Guitar; Compositer. Education: Selftaught musician. Career: Many concerts in Belgium and France under name of Candy Stripe, 1989-92, and Bloodminded, 1992-. Recordings: As Above So Below, Candy Stripe, 8 tracks vinyl LP, 1990; Hypocrisy, Blood Minded, 5 tracks tape, 1993; Demons for Tea, Bloodminded, 11 tracks tape, 1996; Rock in Belgium, vol 1, 2 tracks CD compilation, 1996; Rock in Belgium, vol 2, 2 tracks CD compilation, 1997; Bloodyminded CD, to be released 1998. Memberships: SABAM, Brussels, Belgium; Ciney Music Session, Arts Agency, Belgium. Hobbies: Slot Racing; Moolelism. Current Management: PED Records, rue Vertevoie 13A, 5590 Ciney, Belgium. Address: Bloodminded, rue Jean Friot 91, 6180 courcelles, Belgium.

D

D Brenda (Brenda D Boyd), b. 30 Dec 1936, Surrey, England. Vocalist; Actress. m. Jerry Haymes, 1 Aug 1961, 1 son, 1 daughter. Education: Finishing school; Schools of Modelling. Musical Education: Church of England; Self-taught vocalist. Career: Film and television actress; Appearances include original Robin Hood series; Opened in England with Fess Parker as Davy Crockett; Toured USA and Europe; First British female singer to perform Country music on BBC; First British female Country singer to perform at Grand Ole Opry. Recordings: Major songs: Will You Still Love Me Tomorrow; Little Bitty Tear; Love You More Than I Can Say; Just Enough To Keep Me Hanging On. Honours: CMA International Award; Female Vocalist, Art and Entertainment Council; A & E Film Actress Award. Memberships: Screen Actors Guild; Arts and Entertainments Council. Hobbies: Dog breeder, handler; Raises horses. Current Management: Umpire Entertainment Enterprises, J Haymes. Address: 1507 Scenis Drive, Longview, TX 75604, USA.

D'AMBROSIO Joey, b. 1934, Philadelphia, Pennsylvania, USA. Musician (saxophone); Vocalist. Career: Original member, first saxophone, Bill Hailey's Comets, 1953-55; Member, The Jodimans, 1955-58; Invented rock'n'roll; First rock band to headline a film. Recordings: Rock Around The Clock; See You Later Alligator; Crazy Man Crazy; Shake Rattle And Roll; Rock The Joint; Mambo Rock; Rudy's Rock; Florida Twist; Skinny Minny; Let's All Rock Together; Well Now Dig This. Publications: Rock Around The Clock; Stage Clear; We're Gonna Party; Never Too Old To Rock. Honours: Best vocal group of 1953; 150 million records sold by Bill Haley and the Comets; Rock And Roll Hall Of Fame; Gold records. Address: Rock It Concerts, Bruno-Hofer-Platz 1, D-80937 Munich, Germany.

D'ANGELO (Michael Archer), b. 1974, Richmond, Virginia, USA. Singer; Songwriter; Musician (multi-instrumentalist); Producer. Career: Recording artiste, 1992-. Compositions: Co-writer, producer, U Will Know, Black Men United. Recordings: Solo album: Black Sugar, 1995; Single: Brown Sugar. Honours: Harlem Apollo Talent Contest Winner, 3 times. Address; c/o William Morris Agency, 1325 Avenue of the Americas, New York, NY 10019, USA.

D'ARBY Terence Trent, b. 15 Mar 1962, New York, USA. Singer; Songwriter; Producer. 1 daughter. Education: Journalism, University Of Central Florida. Career: Singer, Touch, Germany, 1982; Solo artiste, 1986-; Concerts include: UK tour, support to Simply Red, 1987; Artists Against Apartheid, Royal Albert Hall, 1987; Hardline Introduction, UK tour, 1987; UK tour, support to David Bowie, 1987; US tour, 1988; Nelson Mandela tribute, Wembley, 1990; John Lennon tribute, Liverpool, 1990; Concerts with Bruce Springsteen, New York, 1993; Concerts with Duran Duran, Mexico, 1993; Television includes: Motown 30 - What's Goin' On, CBS, 1990. Recordings: Singles include: If You Let Me Stay, 1987; Wishing Well (Number 1, US), 1987; Dance Little Sister, 1987; Sign Your Name, 1988; Do You Love Me Like You Say, 1993; Delicate (with Des'ree), 1993; She Kissed Me, 1993; Let Her Down Easy, 1993; Holding On To You, 1995; Albums: Introducing The Hardline According To... (Number 1, UK), 1987; Neither Fish Nor Flesh, 1989; Symphony Or Damn - The Tension Inside The Sweetness, 1993; Vibrator, 1995; Contributor track to: Music Of Quality and Distinction Vol 2, British Electric Foundation, 1991. Honours: BRIT Award, Best International Newcomer, 1988; Grammy nomination, Best New Artist, 1988; Platinum disc, Introducing The Hardline, 1988; Grammy Award, Best R&B Vocal Performance,

Introducing, 1989; Best Vocal Performance by Duo or Group, with Booker T and the MG's, 1995. Current Management: Lippman Entertainment, 8900 Wilshire Blvd, Suite 340, Beverly Hills, CA 90211-1906, USA.

D'ARCY Doug, b. 23 Feb 1946, Hull, England. Record Company Executive. m. Catherine Williams, May 1974, 1 son, 1 daughter. Education: Manchester University. Career: Chrysalis Records, 1968-89; Managing Director, Dedicated Records, 1990-95. Hobbies: Tennis; Reading; Painting; Cooking. Address: Dedicated Records, 36 Notting Hill Gate, London W11 3JQ, England.

D'RIVERA Paquito, b. 4 June 1948, Havana, Cuba. Musician (saxophone, clarinet); Bandleader; Composer; Arranger. Career: Performs with Paquito D'Rivera Ensemble and the Caribbean Jazz Project; Conducts Dizzy Gillespie's UN Orchestra; Guest soloist, jazz, classical, Latin/Caribbean music concerts; Television appearances include: CBS Sunday Morning; The David Letterman Show. Compositions: The New York Suite, for saxophone quartet, 1987; Aires Tropicales, for woodwind quintet, 1994; 5 Pieces for brass quintet, 1997. Recordings: Over 20 solo albums, bebop, classical, Latin/Caribbean music. Publications: Music Minus Me instructional tapes, albums; Lessons With the Greats; Jamey Aebersold, Play-along, Vol 77. Honours: Lifetime Achievement Award, Contribution to Latin music, Carnegie Hall; Grammy Award, for Portraits of Cuba, 1997. Current Management: Havana-NY Music Co. Address: PO Box 777, Union City, NJ 07087, USA.

DADAWA (Zhe Zheq), b. 1974, Guangzhou, China. Singer. Career: Solo artist, New Age music; Debut concerts: Midem Asia, Hong Kong, 1995; London Showcase, 1995. Recordings: Albums with He Xuntian: Yellow Child, 1991; Sister Drum, 1995. Address: c/o Warner Records.

DADDY FREDDY (Samuel Small), b. Kingston, Jamaica. Rapper. Career: Television appearances include: Blue Peter; Record Breakers; BBC Summer TV; Big Breakfast; Radio includes: Tim Westwood, BBC Radio 1. Recordings: Albums: Ragamuffin Hip Hop; Ragga House; Pain Killa. Honour: Guinness Book of Records, World's Fastest Rapper. Membership: PRS. Address: c/o 20 Hanway Street, London W1P 9DD, England.

DADSWELL Melvyn John, b. 8 Jan 1946, Uckfield, Sussex, England. Musician (saxophone); Lecturer; Teacher. m. He Feng Qin, 26 Sept 1990, 2 sons, 2 daughters. Education: BA Hons, Exeter University. Musical Education: Self-taught. Career: Began playing jazz, 1959; Teacher, jazz harmony, rhythm to undergraduate music students (privately); Many club concerts and UK tours, with band Anthropology; 3 recordings Devon Air Jazz; Occasional session work; Bath Festival, 1988; Moscow, 1990; Schooled Red Army Orchestra in jazz, 1990-1991. Membership: Musicians' Union. Hobby: Teaching languages: Russian; English; Polish. Current Management: Phil-Seong Huh. Address: Five Poplars, Ford Farm, Chudleigh-Knighton, Newton Abbot, South Devon TQ13 0ET, England.

DAGLEY Christopher, b. 23 June 1971, Solihull, West Midlands, England. Musician (drums). Musical Education: Grade 8 drumming. Career: National Youth Orchestra; BBC Big Band; Various theatre shows; Gemini; Paz; Brian Dee; Various groups. Recordings: 10 albums, NYJO; Dancing In The Park, Paz. Membership: Musicians' Union. Hobby: Weight lifting. Address: 439A Alexandra Avenue, Rayners Lane, Harrow, Middlesex HA2 9SE, England.

DAGNELL John Richard, b. 2 Aug 1956, Oxford, England. Music, Entertainment Promoter;

Record Company Executive; Music Publisher. m. Nicola, 30 July 1983, 1 daughter. Career: Promoted various concert tours by: Maddy Prior; The Carnival Band; Gilbert O'Sullivan. Recordings: Albums: Maddy Prior; Steeleye Span; Gilbert O'Sullivan; Davey Arthur; Guitar Orchestra; Wild Willy Barrett; New recordings by Kathryn Tickell, Pentangle. Memberships: PRS; ILA; PPL. Address: Park Records, PO Box 651, Oxford OX2 9RB, England.

DALGLEISH Lou (Louise), b. 19 Oct 1967, Birmingham, England. Singer-Songwriter; Musician (piano). Musical Education: Grade 8 classical piano and theory. Career: Professional dancer, theatre, film, including Steven Spielberg's Indiana Jones and the Temple of Doom; Singer-Songwriter, including headline residencies at Ronnie Scott's, Birmingham; Support act to Wet Wet Wet, NEC, Birmingham; Bryan Ferry, Dutch tour; Guestings, Brian Kennedy; National radio sessions include BBC TV; Netherlands; Belgium; National television performances include: BBC and ITV (UK); Belgium; Festival appearances: SXSW Austin, Texas, USA; Lowlands, Waterpop, Valkos; Netherlands; Phoenix, England. Recordings: Single: Orange Plane, 1995; Sold Out, 1995; Charlie Girl, 1996; Album: Lou Dalgleish, 1995; Live Album, solo acoustic at Ronnie Scott's, 1997. Memberships: Equity; Musicians' Union. Current Management: c/o Ronnie Scott's Club. Address: c/o Ronnie Scotts, Broad Street, Birmingham B1 2HF, England.

DALLIN Sarah, b. 17 Dec 1961, Bristol, Somerset, England. Singer. Education: London School Of Fashion. Career: Singer, all-girl group Bananarama, 1981-; Performances include: BRIT Awards, Royal Albert Hall, 1988. Recordings: Albums: Deep Sea Skiving, 1983; Bananarama, 1984; True Confessions, 1986; Wow!, 1987; Greatest Hits Collection, 1988; Poplife, 1991; Please Yourself, 1993; Hit singles include: Really Saying Something, 1982; Shy Boy, 1982; Na Na Hey Hey Kiss Him Goodbye, 1983; Cruel Summer, featured in film The Karate Kid, 1983; Robert De Niro's Waiting, 1984; Venus (Number 1, US), 1986; I Heard A Rumour, 1987; Love In The First Degree, 1988; I Want You Back, 1988; Nathan Jones, 1988; Help!, with comedy team French and Saunders, Comic Relief charity single, 1989; Preacher Man, 1991; Long Train Running, 1991; Movin' On, 1992; More More More, 1993; Backing vocalist, It Ain't What You Do, It's The Way That You Do It, Fun Boy Three, 1982; Contributor to: Do They Know It's Christmas?, Band Aid (Ethiopian famine relief), 1984; Let It Be, Ferry Aid (Zeebrugge ferry disaster relief), 1987; Rock The World benefit album, 1990.

DALLIO Patricia, b. 3 Nov 1958, Chaumont, France. Musician (piano); Composer. Career: Tours throughout Europe with Art Zoyd: Concerts include: Berlin; Milan; New York; London, Hong Kong, Adelaide and Yokohama Festivals; Live shows and films include: Nosferatu; Faust; Häxan Composer, Dante theatre, videos. Recordings: Procession; Champs de Mars; La Ronce N'est Pas Le Pire; D'où vient l'eau des puits; Barbe Bleue. Membership: Soundtrack (Composer Association). Address: 11 Rue de la Liberté, 52000 Chaumont, France.

DALSETH Laila, b. 6 Nov 1940, Bergen, Norway. Jazz Singer. m. Totti Bergh, 1 June 1963, 2 daughters. Career: Solo Jazz artist; Television and radio appearances: Scandinavia; Germany; Yugoslavia; England; Scotland; Concerts include: Playboy Jazz Festival; Nice Jazz Festival; Sacramento Jazz Festival; Caribbean Jazz Cruises; Copenhagen Jazz Festival; Molde Jazz Festival; Jakarta Jazz Festival; Currently fronting own group with saxophonist (husband) Totti Bergh. Recordings include: Laila Dalseth/Wild Bill Davidson, 1974; with Bengt Hallberg, Arne Domnerus: Glad There Is You, 1978; with Louis Stewart: Daydreams, 1984; with Red Mitchell

Quartet: Time For Love, 1986; with Al Cohn: Travelin' Light, 1987; with Milt Hinton, Derek Smith, B Rosengarden, B Pizarelli: The Judge And I, 1992; with Joe Cohn, Totti Bergh: Remember, 1995; with Philip Catherine, Egil Kapstad: A Woman's Intuition, 1995. Honours: 3 times Spellemannspris (Norwegian Grammy).

DALTON Lacy J (Jill Byrem), b. 13 Oct 1948, Bloomsburg, Pennsylvania, USA. Country Singer. Career: Club singer, California, 12 years; Singer, psychedelic group Office, under name Jill Croston; Solo artiste, 1979-; Worked with Earl Scruggs, George Jones and Bobby Bare. Recordings: Hit singles: Crazy Blue Eyes; Tennessee Waltz; Hard Times; 16th Avenue; Working Class Man; Albums: As Jill Croston: Jill Croston, 1978; As Lacy J Dalton: Lacy J Dalton, 1979; Hard Times, 1980; Takin' It Easy, 1981; 16th Avenue, 1982; Dream Baby, 1983; Greatest Hits, 1983; Can't Run Away From Your Heart, 1985; Highway Diner, 1986; Blue Eyed Blues, 1987; Survivor, 1989; Lacy J, 1990; Crazy Love, 1991; Chains On The Wind, 1992. Current Management: c/o Aaron Anderson, Lacy J Dalton Enterprises, PO Box 1109, Mount Juliet, TN 37122, USA.

DALTREY David Joseph, b. 30 Dec 1951, London, England. Session Musician (guitar); Guitar Tutor; Composer. m. Helen McIldowie, 20 July 1989. Education: Mid Hertfordshire College. Musical Education: Guildhall School of Music and Drama; Studied with Rogers Covey-Crump; Private studies with Ike Isaacs and Jimmy Page. Career: Recording artist; Worked for BBC; Numerous compositions and recordings for various artists; Currently a session guitarist, tutor and composer. Recordings: Lead vocalist and guitarist, Joseph And The Amazing Technicolour Dreamcoat, 1969, 1971. Memberships: Musicians' Union; ISM. Address: Pilgrims Rest, 34 Guildhall Street, Bury St Edmunds, Suffolk IP33 1QF, England.

DALTREY Roger, b. 1 Mar 1944, Hammersmith, London, England. Singer; Actor. Career: Member, UK rock group the Who, 1964-84; Appearances include: National Jazz and Blues Festivals, 1965, 1966, 1969; Monterey Pop Festival, 1967; Rock At The Oval, 1972; Farewell tour, 1982-83; Live Aid, Wembley, 1985; 25th Anniversary Reunion tour, 1989; Solo artiste, 1984-; Actor in films, including Tommy, 1974; Lisztomania, 1975; The Legacy 1979; McVicar, 1980; Threepenny Opera, 1989. Recordings: Albums: My Generation, 1965; A Quick One, 1966; The Who Sell Out, 1968; Direct Hits, 1968; Tommy (rock opera), 1969; Live At Leeds, 1970; Who's Next, 1971; Meaty Beefy Big And Bouncy, 1971; Quadrophenia, 1973; Odds And Sods, 1974; The Who By Numbers, 1975; The Story Of The Who, 1976; Who Are You, 1978; The Kids Are Alright (film soundtrack), 1979; Face Dances, 1981; Hooligans, 1982; It's Hard, 1982; Rarities Vols 1 and 2, 1983; Once Upon A Time, 1983; The Singles, 1984; Who's Last, 1984; Who's Missing, 1985; Two's Missing, 1987; Who's Better Who's Best, 1988; Joined Together, 1990; 30 Years Of Maximum R&B, 1994; Solo albums: Daltrey, 1973; Ride A Rock Horse, 1975; One Of The Boys, 1977; Best Bits, 1982; If Parting Should Be Painless, 1984; Under A Raging Moon, 1985; I Can't Wait To See The Movie, 1987; Singles include: I Can't Explain, 1965; Anyway Anyhow Anywhere, 1965; My Generation (Number 2, UK), 1965; Substitute, 1966; I'm A Boy (Number 2, UK), 1966; Happy Jack, 1967; Pictures Of Lily, 1967; I Can See For Miles, 1967; Pinball Wizard, 1969; See Me Feel Me, 1970; Won't Get Fooled Again, 1971; Join Together, 1972; Who Are You, 1978; You Better You Bet, 1981; Contributor, Rock And Roll, Rock Aid Armenia, 1991. Honours include: Gold Ticket, Madison Square Garden, 1979; Ivor Novello Award, Outstanding Contribution to British Music, 1982; BRIT Award, Outstanding Contribution to British Music, 1988; Group

inducted into Rock'n'Roll Hall Of Fame, 1990. Current Management: Trinifold Management, 22 Harley Street, Marylebone Road, London NW1 4PR, England.

DALY Stan, b. 27 Nov 1929, Grays Inn Road, London. Jazz Musician (drums); Band leader. m. 3 Aug 1957, 1 son, 3 daughters. Musical Education: Royal Air Force. Career: Played in top dance orchestras of Lou Preager, Frank Weir, Jack Nathan, 1950s-60s; Drummer, Harry Gold's Pieces Of Eight, for 15 years; Broadcasting, television, concerts; Own band Sonny Dee All-Stars playing Chicago/mainstream jazz; Worked on West Coast America with Wild Bill Davison, Dick Cathcart, Eddie Miller, Bob Enevoldson; Played with: Harry Parry's Radio Sextet; Freddy Randall; Pasadena Roof Orchestra; Sandy Brown; Played almost every top international jazz festival worldwide. Recordings: Drummer, many albums. Current Management: Self-managed. Address: 92 Greenway, Totteridge, London N20 8EJ, England.

DAMBRY Stephane, b. 7 Mar 1959, Barentin, France. Singer. Education: Teacher. Musical Education: Self-taught guitarist, singer. Career: Lead singer, Little Big Band, 1987-; Solo artist, 1991-. Compositions: Talk to the Mirror, 1991; The Fatal Glass of Beer, 1994; The Welsh Rare Beat, 1997. Recordings: Talk To The Mirror, 1991; The Fatal Glass Of Beer, 1991; The Welsh Are Beat, 1994; with Little Big Band: Hey! Doc, 1994. Current Management: L'Echo du Kazoo Management. Address: 26 Boulevard Charles De Gaulle, 76140 Petit-Quevilly, France.

DAMEN Paul, b. 26 January, The Netherlands. Musician (Drums). Career: Mid 80s Leading Dutch Top 40 Band accompanying major Dutch Artists, 1989; Toured in Holland, The Trammps; Jimmy Bo Horne; Dutch Group, Haitai; Numerous jingles and commercials (studio) for : Mercedes; SAAB; General Motors; L'Oreal Cosmetics; TV appearances with Gloria Estefan; Toured with popular Dutch Artist Rob Janszen; Toured with International Artist, CB Milton, 1995; National Studio/Session Drummer, currently. Recordings: Promo; Endorser for Remo, Drums and Drumheads. Current Management: De Otter and De Vries, Entertainment Productions BC, Hertogin Juliana Singel 34 055, The Netherlands. Address: Hogehofstraat 26, 5366 CC Megen, Holland.

DAMINESCU Adrian, b. 2 Oct 1956, Timisoara, Romania. Musician (cello, piano, guitar, bass guitar); Vocalist. m. Francis Susan Walker, 30 June 1990, divorced. Musical Education: Department of voice music and composition, Academy of Music. Career: Concerts, tours and recitals throughout Romania; Israel; USSR; Germany; China; Japan; Canada; USA; Czechoslovakia; Television and radio appearances: National Romanian television station; The Stars Duel; 10 weeks in Top 3-2-1; Hit Studio, London 1990; Cable TV; Gloria Hunniford, BBC1; Voice of America; National Radio Station. Compositions: Romania; You're Still Beautiful; Looking In My Teacup; Stop; Pleading For Michael Jackson; I Miss My Home; Final Day; Praying For Mercy; Midnight. Recordings: I Will Love You (Eu Te Voi Iubi); Pieces Of Me (Bucati Din Mine). Publications: Currently writing memoirs: Music And My Life. Honours: Great Prize, Bucharest Festival, 1986; Most Beautiful Voice of the Festival, Bratislava, 1986; 3 times Great Prize winner as singer, Mamaia National Festival, 1986-88; Second Prize, Golden Orpheus Festival, Bulgaria, 1988; 3 Mamaia National Festival Awards as composer: First, 1989; Third, 1991; Second, 1992. Hobbies: Fishing; Painting; Sculpting. Address: Constanta 8700, 45 Gen Manu St, Romania.

DAMMERS Jerry (Gerald Dankin), b. 22 May 1954, Coventry, Warwickshire, England.

Musician (keyboards). Career: Founder member, Coventry Automatics, 1977; Name changed to Coventry Specials, then Special AKA, then the Specials, 1979-; Support to the Clash, UK tour, 1978; Designer, record label 2-Tone, marketed by Chryslis Records, 1979; Kampuchea benefit concert, with the Who, the Pretenders, London, 1979; Film, Dance Craze, 1981; Formed Artists Against Apartheid, 1986; Organizer, Nelson Mandela 70th Birthday Tribute, Wembley, 1990. Recordings: Singles include: Gangsters, 1979; A Message To You, Rudy, 1979; Too Much Too Young, 1980; Do Nothing, 1981; Ghost Town, 1981; Nelson Mandela, 1984; Albums: Specials, 1979; More Specials, 1980; Dance Craze, 1981; In The Studio, 1984; The Specials Singles, 1991; Live - Too Much Young, 1992; Live At The Moonlight Club, 1992.

DAMONE Vic (Vito Farinola), b. 12 June 1928, Brooklyn, New York, USA. Singer; Actor. m. (4)Diahann Carroll, 1 son, 3 daughters. Musical Education: Singing lessons. Career: Winner, Arthur Godfrey's Talent Scouts, CBS, 1946; Singer, La Martinique nightclub, New York; Recording artiste, 1947-; Own CBS radio show, Saturday Night Serenade, late 1940s; Film appearances include: Rich Young And Pretty, 1951; The Strip (featuring Mickey Rooney, Jack Teagarden, Louis Armstrong), 1951; Hell To Eternity; Athena, 1954; Deep In My Heart, 1954; Hit The Deck, 1955; Kismet, 1955; Crash Boat; Own television series, 1956-57; Regular concert tours, UK, US and Australia, 1980s-. Recordings: Albums: Athena (soundtrack), 1954; Rich Young And Pretty (soundtrack), 1955; The Voice Of Vic Damone, 1956; That Towering Feeling, 1956; The Stingiest Man In The World (soundtrack), 1956; The Gift Of Love (soundtrack), 1958; Closer Than A Kiss, 1959; Angela Mia, 1959; This Game Of Love, 1959; On The Swingin' Side, 1961; Linger Awhile With Vic Damone, 1962; Strange Enchantment, 1962; The Lively Ones, 1962; My Baby Loves To Swing, 1963; The Liveliest, 1963; On The Street Where You Live, 1964; You Were Only Fooling, 1965; Stay With Me, 1976; Damone's Feeling 1978, 1979; Now, 1981; Make Somone Happy, 1981; Now And Forever, 1982; Vic Damone Sings The Great Songs, 1983; The Damone Type Of Thing, 1984; Christmas With Vic Damone, 1984; The Best Of Vic Damone, Live, 1989; Various compilations; Hit singles (million sellers): Again; You're Breaking My Heart; On The Street Where You Live; Other hits include: I Have But One Heart; You Do; Tzena Tzena Tzena; Cincinnati Dancing Pig; My Heart Cries For You; My Truly Truly Fair; Here In My Heart; April In Portugal; Eternally; Ebb Tide; On The Street Where You Live; An Affair To Remember; You Were Only Fooling (While I Was Falling In Love). Publications: Recipes For Lovers cookbook. Current Management: c/o Stan Scottland, JKE Services Inc., 404 Park Avenue S, 10th Floor, New York, NY 10016, USA.

DANA (Rosemary Brown), b. 30 Aug 1951, Belfast, Northern Ireland. Singer. Career: Winner, Eurovision Song Contest, with All Kinds Of Everything (Number 1, UK, South Africa, Ireland, Australia), 1970; Over 1 million sales worldwide; Actress, television and pantomime. Recordings: Hit singles: All Kinds Of Everything; Who Put The Lights Out; It's Gonna Be A Cold Christmas; Please Tell Them That I Said Hello; Fairy Tale; Albums: All Kinds Of Everything, 1970; World Of Dana, 1975; Have A Nice Day, 1977; Love Songs And Fairy Tales, 1977; The Girl Is Back, 1979; Totally Yours, 1982; Everything Is Beautiful, 1980; Let There Be Love, 1985; No Greater Love, 1988. Current Management: The Brokaw Company, 9255 Sunset Blvd, Suite 804, Los Angeles, CA 90069, USA.

DANCE Stanley (Frank), b. 15 September 1910, Braintree, England. Reviewer; Writer. m. Helen Oakley, 30 January 1947, 2 sons, 2 daughters. Education: Framlingham College,

1925-28. Career: Reviewer, Jazz Journal, London, 1948-96; Saturday Review, New York City, 1967-72; Music Journal, New York City, 1962-79; Jazz Times, Silver Spring, Maryland, 1980-98. Publications: Editor, Jazz Era, 1961; The World of Duke Ellington, 1970; The Night People, with Dicky Wells, 1971; The World of Swing, 1974; The World of Earl Hines, 1977; Duke Ellington in Person, with Mercer Ellington, 1978; The World of Count Basie, 1980; Those Swinging Years, with Charlie Barnet, 1984. Honour: Deems Taylor Award, American Society of Composers, Authors and Publishers, 1979. Address: 1745 Bittersweet Hill, Vista, CA 92084-7621, USA.

DANDO Evan, b. 4 Mar 1967, USA. Singer; Musician (guitar); Songwriter. Career: Founder member, The Lemonheads, 1986-; Numerous worldwide concerts include: Solo tour, Australia, 1992; Solo acoustic concert, Ronnie Scott's, London, 1992; Reading Festival, 1994. Recordings: Albums: Hate Your Friends, 1987; Creator, 1988; Lick, 1989; Lovey, 1990; It's A Shame About Ray, 1992; Come On Feel The Lemonheads, 1993; Singles include: It's A Shame About Ray; Mrs Robinson (from film soundtrack, 25th Anniversary wide-screen release of The Graduate, 1993); Confetti; Into Your Arms; It's About Time; Contributor, Sweet Relief (Victoria Williams benefit album), 1993. Honour: Boston Music Awards, Outstanding Modern Rock Act, Single Of The Year, 1993. Current Management: Gold Mountain Entertainment. Address: 3575 Cahuenga Blvd W, Ste 450, Los Angeles, CA 90068, USA.

DANE Phil, b. 31 Oct 1961, Leeds, Yorkshire, England. Producer; Engineer; Songwriter. Musical Education: City of Leeds, College of Music. Career: Mixes and/or productions of: Back To The Planet; Bomb The Bass; Boy George; B T: Darkman; D:ream; East 17; Julia Fordham; Innocence; James; Mike Oldfield; Robert Palmer; Diana Ross; Rozalla; Salt 'n' Pepa; Sasha; Utah Saints; Worlds Apart; Yazz; Aswad. Memberships: Musicians' Union; PRS. Hobbies: Motorcycling; Gym training. Current Management: 7 PM. Address: 10 Bathurst Street, London W2 2SP, England.

DANIELS Bob (Robert T Hahn), b. 2 Mar 1959, Milwaukee, Wisconsin, USA. Musician (banjo). m. Denise Blank, 1 son, 2 daughters. Education: College. Musical Education: Various private teachers. Career: Professional musician for 20 years; Played in bands: The Nashville Cats; The Nashtown Ramblers; Backroads; Johnny Rodriguez Backup Band; Played with artists including: Charley Collllins; Bashful Brother Oswald; Earl Scruggs; Jethro Burns; Duane Stuermer; Jack Grassel; Warren Wiegratz; Infamous Ramblin' Rick Trudell; Grand Old Opry, Opry Land, 1976; Broadway production, 1979; Live radio music appearances, WMIL FM 106, late 1980s; Associate songwriter for BMI; Composes for other singers, commercials, theatre. Recordings: Single: Back Home To Yesterday, 1988; Albums: Bob Daniels And A Milwaukee All-Star Pot Pourri, 1990; Bob Daniels, Rick Trudell, Best Banjo, 1995; Bob Daniels, Rick Trudell, Rough Cuts, 1995; Best Banjo, 1995. Honour: Rated by HFR as one of top 5 improvisational 5-string banjo players, USA. Membership: AFofM. Hobby: Fishing. Current Management: D J Blank. Address: 606 W Wisconsin Avenue, Suite 1100, Milwaukee, WI 53203, USA.

DANIELS Charlie, b. 28 Oct 1937, Wilmington, North Carolina, USA. Country Singer; Songwriter; Musician (multi-instrumentalist). Career: Played guitar from age 15; Founder, bluegrass band The Misty Mountain Boys; Changed name to The Jaguars, 1959; Regular session work, Nashville, 1968-; Partnership with Earl Scruggs; Formed Charlie Daniels Band, 1970-; Started Volunteer Jam (became annual

event), 1974; Featured on film soundtrack Urban Cowboy; Recorded film theme for Stroker Ace. Compositions include: It Hurts Me, Elvis Presley, 1964. Recordings: Hit singles include: Uneasy Rider, 1973; The South's Gonna Do It, 1973; The Devil Went Down To Georgia, 1979. Albums: To John, Grease And Wolfman, 1970; Charlie Daniels, 1970; Honey In The Rock, 1973; Way Down Yonder, 1974; Fire On The Mountain, 1975; Nightrider, 1975; Teach Yourself Rock Guitar, 1976; Saddletramp, 1976; High Lonesome, 1976; Volunteer Jam, 1976; Midnight Wind, 1977; Volunteer Jam 3 & 4, 1978; Million Miles Reflections, 1979; Volunteer Jam VI, 1980; Full Moon, 1980; Volunteer Jam VII, 1981; Windows, 1982; A Decade Of Hits, 1983; Me And The Boys, 1985; Powder Keg, 1987; Renegade, 1991; with Bob Dylan: Nashville Skyline, 1969; Self Portrait, 1970; New Morning, 1970; Other recordings with Ringo Starr; Marty Robbins; Hank Williams Jr. Publication: Book of short stories, 1986. Current Management: High Lonesome Management Inc., 17060 Central Pike, Lebanon, TN 37087, USA.

DANIELS Luke, b. 18 Nov 1973, Reading, England. Musician (button accordion). Musical Education: Self-taught. Career: Accordion player with Scarp, formerly with De Danann; Major concerts include: St Chartier Festival, 1993; Philadelphia Festival of Folk Music, 1993; Pebble Mill TV, 1994; Theatre de Ville, Paris, 1995. Compositions include: Musette à Térésa; The Snoring Barber; Wednesday's Tune; Gallowstree Sonata. Recordings: Tarantella. Honours: Young Tradition Award, Folk Musician of the Year, BBC Radio 2, 1992. Hobbies: Literature; Art. Current Management: Acoustics. Address: 2 Stuart Close, Emmer Green, Reading, Berkshire RG4 8RE, England.

DANIELS Maxine (Gladys), b. 2 Nov 1930, Stepney, London, England. Singer. m. Charles Daniels, 8 Jul 1950, 1 daughter. Career: Television appearance on Tonight, with Cliff Mitchelmore, 1956; Toured with Humphrey Lyttelton, Dutch Swing College and Terry Lightfoot; Sang for Metroland Rhythms of Essex, 1994; Currently with Ella Fitzgerald Song Book; Several recordings. Membership: Musicians' Union. Hobbies: Swimming; Reading Science Fiction. Current Management: Jack Higgins. Address: 125 Bellmaine Avenue, Corringham, Stanford-Le-Hope, Essex SS17 7SZ, England.

DANIELZ, b. 25 Nov 1957, Hong Kong. Vocalist; Musician (guitar). Musical Education: Self-taught. Career: Lead guitarist with T Rextasy, T-Rex tribute group; Tours include: UK arena tour as support to Gary Glitter; Tour with Sweet and Slade, Germany, 1995; Japan, 1995; British tour with Sweet, 1997; VH1 shows TRextasy concert footage from Cambridge Corn Exchange Bolan birthday show, 1997; Television appearances: Unplugged, MTV/VH1, 1995; Glam-Doc documentary, Ch4, 1995. Recordings: with T Rextasy: Baby Factory, 1994; Trip And Glide In The Ballrooms Of T Rextasy, 1995 (UK and Japan); Album: Savage Beethoven, 1997; Major record deal in Japan. Publication: Wilderness Of The Mind, biography of Marc Bolan, 1992. Memberships: Musicians' Union; PRS. Hobbies: Rock and Pop Music; Reading; Writing. Current Agent: Len Tuckey, 21 Yew Tree Close, Hatfield Peverel, Near Chelmsford, Essex CM3 2SG, England. Address: 8 Moriaty Close, Holloway, London N7 0EF, England.

DANKO Harold, b. 13 June 1947, Sharon, Pennsylvania, USA. Musician (piano); Composer; Educator. Musical Education: Dana School Of Music, 1965-69; BME, Youngstown State University, Ohio, 1969; Additional studies, Juilliard School of Music, 1970. Career: Tours, concerts and recordings, 1972-; Pianist with various artistes including: Woody Herman; Chet Baker; Thad Jones and Mel Lewis; Lee Konitz; Gerry Mulligan; Leader, Harold Danko Trio, 1980-; Leader, Harold

Danko Quartet, 1990-; Festival appearances include: JVC, New Haven and Clearwater (USA); Montreal (Canada); Metz, TBB and Fort Napoleon (France); Marca and Riva (Italy); Gouvy (Belgium) and North Sea Jazz Festival (Netherlands); Featured artist, Meet The Artist series, Lincoln Center, and Performing Arts Society series, JFK Center; Concert series, Manhattan School of Music, New York funded by NEA fellowship; President, Aaychdee Music; Founder, Jazz Haven (Jazz society); Current music educator, Manhattan School Of Music, New York, Hartt School of Music, Hartford, Connecticut and Neighborhood Music School, New Haven. Compositions include: Tidal Breeze; Alone But Not Forgotten; Ink And Water Suite; Chasin' The Bad Guys; Shorter By Two; Music for theatre and television. Recordings: After The Rain; Tidal Breeze; Alone But Not Forgotten; Mirth Song; Shorter By Two; Next Age; New Autumn; The Feelin' Of Jazz; Tidal Breeze. Publication: Author, The Illustrated Keyboard Series, 1982; Video: Jazz Concepts for Keyboard (Brazil). Honours: Awards from ASCAP and National Association of Concert and Cabaret Acts (NACCA); Outstanding Service to Jazz Education award, International Association of Jazz Educators; Distinguished Alumni award, Youngstown State University; Fellowship, National Endowment for the Arts, 1995. Memberships: AFofM; ASCAP. Hobby: Humour. Address: 172 Alden Avenue, New Haven, CT 06515, USA.

DANKWORTH John Philip William, b. 20 Sept 1927, Walthamstow, London, England. Composer; Musician (saxophone, clarinet). m. Cleo Laine, 18 Mar 1958, 2 sons, 1 daughter. Musical Education: Royal Academy of Music. Career: Involved in post-war development of British Jazz, 1947-60; Formed Jazz orchestra, 1953; Pops Music Director, London Symphony Orchestra, 1985-90; Principal Guest Pops Conductor, San Francisco Symphony Orchestra, 1987-89; Numerous film scores and albums. Compositions: Improvisations (with Matyas Seiber), 1959; Escapade, 1967; Tom Sawyer's Saturday, 1967; String Quartet, 1971; Piano Concerto, 1972; Grace Abounding, 1980; Dialogue And Songs For Colette, starring Cleo Laine, 1980; The Diamond And The Goose, 1981; Reconciliation (for Silver Jubilee of Coventry Cathedral), 1987; Woolwich Concerto (Clarinet Concerto for Emma Johnson), 1995; Dreams '42 (string quartet) for 1997 Kidderminster Festival; Double Vision, 1997 world premiere by BBC Big Band at BBC Proms. Publication: Sax from the Start, 1996. Honours: CBE, 1974; Hon MA, Open University, 1975; Hon MusD, Berklee College of Music, 1982; Hon MusD, York University, 1993; Variety Club of Great Britain Show Business Personality Award, with Cleo Laine, 1977. Membership: Fellow of Royal Academy of Music. Hobbies: Driving; Household maintenance. Current Management: Dankworth Management. Address: The Old Rectory, Wavendon, Milton Keynes MK17 8LT, England.

DANTZLER Russ, b. 5 Dec 1951, Ainsworth, Nebraska, USA. Agent; Artist Manager; Record Producer. Education: Business, University of Nebraska. Career: Began Hot Jazz Management and Production as hobby, to preserve the Swing tradition, 1974; Hot Jazz became full-time career, New York City, 1989; Clients include: Claude "Fiddler" Williams; Earl May; Red Richards; Benny Waters; Al Grey; The Duke's Men with Arthur Baron; Carrie Smith; Bross Townsend; Norris Turney; Ken Peplowski; Bill "Mr Honkey Tonk" Doggett; Contracting work for the Smithsonian Jazz Oral History Department, and Jazz Foundation of America. Recordings: Produced: Claude Williams, Live At J's, Volumes 1 & 2, 1993; Swingtime In New York, with Claude Williams, Sir Roland Hanna, Bill Easley, Earl May, Joe Ascione, 1995. Publications: Columnist, Jam/Jazz Ambassadors Magazine (Kansas City); Scrapple From The Apple, 1993-. Honours: Produced recording placing on critic's polls; Asked to write remembrance of Haywood Henry for the Alabama Jazz Hall of Fame archives. Memberships: Jazz Journalists Association; Kansas City Jazz Ambassadors; American Federation of Jazz Societies; Duke Ellington Society; New York Chapter, National Jazz Service Organization. Hobbies: Photography (credits: Bulletin of the Hot Club of France; New York Times; Downbeat); All music; Travel. Address: Hot Jazz, 328 West 43rd Street, Suite 4F, New York, NY 10036, USA.

DANZIG Glenn. USA. Rock Vocalist. Career: Vocalist, US punk groups, The Misfits; Samhain; Founder, vocalist, Danzig, 1987-. Recordings include: Albums: with the Misfits: Beware, 1979; Walk Among Us, 1982; with Danzig: Danzig, 1988; Danzig II - Lucifage, 1990; Danzig III - How The Gods Kill, 1992; Danzig 4, 1994. Current Management: Big FD Management, 10801 National Blvd, Suite 530, Los Angeles, CA 90064, USA.

DAPOGNY James, b. 3 Sept 1940, Berwyn, Illinois, USA. Musician (piano); Arranger; Bandleader. m. Gail Johnson, 25 Nov 1965. Musical Education: BM Music, 1962; Master of Music, 1963; Doctor of Musical Arts, 1971; Composition, University of Illinois. Career: Performances include: Tours, US, with James Dapogny's Chicago Jazz Band, 1976-. Recordings: with James Dapogny's Chicago Jazz Band: Laughing At Life, 1992; Original Jelly Roll Blues, 1993; Hot Club Stomp, 1995; On The Road, 1996; with James Dapogny's Chicago Jazz Band and the Chenille Sisters: Whatcha Gonna Swing Tonight?, 1992. Publication: Edition Of Music: The Collected Piano Music Of Jelly Roll Morton, 1982. Current Management: Donna Zajonc Management, PO Box 7023, Ann Arbor, MI 48107, USA.

DARLING Helen, b. 5 May, Baton Rouge, Louisiana, USA. Singer; Songwriter. m. Dennis Darling. Education: Bachelor Degree, Organizational Communication, University of Texas, Austin, Texas. Career: Jingle singer, Chicago; Demo singer, Nashville; Female vocalist on Garth Brooks' The Red Strokes; Co-writer with: Bob DiPiero; John Scott Sherill; Karen Staley; Chuck Jones; Michael Omartian. Compositions include: Track for own album, co-written with Tena Clark, Gary Prim: When The Butterflies Have Flown Away. Recordings: Song: It's So Easy, College Vocal Group Album: Ensemble 109; Single; Album, 1995; Helen Darling, 1995. Current Management: Chip Peay, PBH Entertainment.

DAURAT Jean-Sebastien, b. 11 Feb 1961, Neuilly Sur Seine, France. Musician (guitar). 2 sons. Education: 3 years art school. Musical Education: Self-taught, also private lessons. Career: Television: Sideman for H Leonard; Corine Marchand; Maria Glen; Marion Montgomery; Erchy Lawson; Own group, Jazz Oil Quintet; Plays in numerous clubs, Paris (international pop, rock, funk, jazz, Latin jazz); 70 more dates in 1997. Composition: St Emilion, 1997. Recording: On Ne Discute Pas, 1997. Publication: Jazz Hot Magazine, 1997. Hobbies: Writing; Painting; Travel; Cinema; Theatre. Current Management: Jules Music et Cultures Aux Pluriels. Address: 86 Avenue de Gournay, 94800 Villejuif, France.

DAVENPORT Bob, b. 31 May 1932, Newcastle-Upon-Tyne, England. Singer. Education: 4 years, St Martins College of Art, London (sculpture). Career: Member, Bob Davenport & The Rakes; Solo folk artist; Appeared at Newport Folk Festival, with Joan Baez, Phil Ochs, Bob Dylan, Tom Paxton, 1963; Guest on Pete Seegers Central Park and Tanglewood concerts, 1967; Took break from scene, 1980s; Currently singing in clubs. Recordings: Wor Geordie, 1962; The Iron Muse, 1963; Farewell Nancy, 1964; Northumbrian Minstrelcy, 1964; Bob Davenport And The Rakes, 1965; Bob Davenport,

1971; Bob Davenport And The Marsden Rattlers, 1971; Pal Of My Cradle Days, 1974; Down The Long Road, 1975; Postcards Home, 1977; With The Rakes, 1977; The Good Old Way - British Folk Music Today, 1980; Will's Barn, 1990; From The Humber To The Tweed, 1991; With the Rakes, The Rakes, 1976; Guest on albums by David Essex; Mike Harding; Watersons; Flowers And Frolics. Publication: Cuitanovitch's Road To Wigan Pier documentary, for Thames TV. Membership: Equity. Current Management: Self-managed. Address: 14 Calthorpe Street, London WC1X 0JS, England.

DAVERNE Gary Michiel, b. 26 Jan 1939, Auckland, New Zealand. Musical Director; Composer; Educator. Education: Auckland University; Auckland Teachers' College, Dip. Teaching, 1959. Musical Education: Trinity College of Music, London, FTCL (Composition), 1969; LRSM, 1965. Career: Self-employed, international conductor, composer, arranger, record producer, over 20 albums, including 1 Platinum, 2 Gold discs; Conductor of music for television, film, radio; Formerly teacher, economics, accountancy, 1962-77; Composer in Schools, 1978-79; President, Composers' Association, New Zealand, 1979; Musical director, Auckland Symphony Orchestra, 1975; Director of Music, Waitangi Day celebrations (before Queen Elizabeth II). Compositions include: Over 100 pop songs; Operettas; Songs for children; 3 rock operas; Concert accordion music; Many works for orchestra (recorded by NZSO) include: Rhapsody For Accordion and Orchestra; Over 600 television and radio jungles, film soundtracks. Hobbies: Chess; Bridge; Fishing; Films.

DAVEY Rick, b. 11 Jan 1952, Devon, England. Music Publisher; Record Label Owner; Producer. Education: BA Hons Philosophy, London University. Musical Education: ABRSM Grade VIII (Theory). Career: Jazz/blues musician, saxophone and keyboards, since age 15; Music consultant, Tomorrows World, BBC; Artist management for Silver Bullet; Tour manager for Big Youth/Alton Ellis; Studio manager, Machelle Alexander; Acts and labels controlled include: Custers Last Stand Records (Kissing The Pink); Black Cat Records (Jungle/Reggae); Flowsound Ltd publish Zion Train; Terence McKenna (Shamen); KOTOT, Dennis Alcapone; Tour manager, Black Uhuru, Mindlink, Justin Hinds, Jonny Osbourne. Recordings: New Era, on Face movie with Damon Albarn (Blur); Bible and the Gun, Devon Russell; UTE; Black Cat; Tassoulla. Memberships: PRS; MCPS. Current Management: Flowsound Ltd; Black Cat RPM. Address: Unit C, Imperial Works, Perren Street, London NW5 7EE, England.

DAVID Hal. Lyricist. m. Eunice Bernstein, 2 sons. Career: Songwriter, collaborations with Burt Bacharach; Henry Mancini; Joe Rapaso; Record producer for Dionne Warwick. Compositions include: Raindrops Keep Fallin' On My Head; The Look Of Love; What's New Pussycat?; Alfie; Wives And Lovers; It Was Almost Like A Song; What The World Needs Now Is Love; To Love A Child; To All The Girls I've Ever Loved Before (recorded by Julio Iglesias, Willie Nelson); Broadway show, Promises Promises; Films include: April Fools. Honours include: Academy Award, Raindrops Keep Fallin' On My Head; Grammy Award, Promises Promises; Tony Award Nomination: Promises Promises; Inducted into Songwriters Hall Of Fame; Nashville Songwriters Hall Of Fame International; NARM Presidential Award; Creative Achievement Award, B'Nai B'rith. Memberships: ASCAP; Songwriters Guild of America; Lyricists Guild of America; Dramatists Guild; Authors League.

DAVID Joel, b. 22 Dec 1948, Blackburn, Lancashire, England. Musician; Singer; Actor. m. Maureen Seaberg, 10 July 1984. Musical Education: Self-taught. Career: Actor: Brideshead

Revisited, GTV, 1981; Strangers, Granada, 1983; Coronation Street, 1981; 3-4-7-9, GTV; Prime Suspect, GTV, 1989; Nature Of The Beast, British Screen, CH4, 1987; Singer: Victoria Wood Show, GTV; Radio: Live At Golders Green Hippodrome, BBC Radio Two, Live With The BBC Big Band, 1990; Nightride, BBC Radio 2, 1988-91; We'll Meet Again, BBC Radio 2, 1994; The David Jacobs Show, BBC Radio 2; The Charlie Chester Show, BBC Radio Two, 1994-95. Recordings: Old Bones, 1987; Be My Valentine Tonight, 1988; Dance To The End Of Love, 1990; Paws For Love, 1995. Membership: British Actors Equity Association. Hobbies: Eating out; Driving own Rolls Royce; Foreign travel. Current Management: Maureen Seaberg. Address: Old Records, 17 Moor Close, Darwen, Lancashire BB3 3LG, England.

DAVIES Bruce William, b. 25 Nov 1955, Kirkcaldy, Fife, Scotland. Musician; Singer; Songwriter; Entertainer; Radio Presenter. m. (1), 3 sons, (2) Anne, 18 Sept 1993. Musical Education: Briefly at Royal Scottish Academy of Music and Drama. Career: With folk duo Beggars Mantle, 1983-90; Solo artist, 1990-; Television appearances: BBC Network; Scottish Border; Grampian; Ulster; numerous US channels; Performances mainly in Scotland, also: UK; Europe; Africa; USA; Canada; Taking accessible but unique style of folk music to audiences both in and out of the folk field. Recordings: Numerous; 3 albums currently, and one forthcoming in 1998; Numerous recordings as session musician; Arranger and producer for other artists. Hobbies: Music (all aspects); Watching football. Current Management: Rothes Recordings. Address: PO Box 7, Glenrothes, Fife KY6 2TA, Scotland.

DAVIES Helen Margaret, b. 24 November 1950, Aberystwyth, Wales. Musician (harp). m. Palle Mikkelborg, 19 August 1989. Education: BMus, honours, University of Birmingham; Harp, Singing, Piano and Organ Lessons. Career: Solo Harpist, Gothenburg Opera Orchestra, Sweden, 1975-77; Principal Harpist, Irish Radio Orchestra, Dublin, 1977-89; Harp Teacher, Royal Irish Academy of Music, 1983-89; Administrator, Irish Harp Society Summer School, Ireland, 1983-89; Member, Palle Mikkelborg Group, Copenhagen, Denmark, 1989-. Recordings: Contributed to: Granuaile Suite, Shaun Davey, 1986; The Pilgrim, Shaun Davey, 1990; Anything Butggrey, Palle Mikkelborg, 1992; Out to an Other Side, Liam O'Flynn, 1993; The Garden is a Woman, Palle Mikkelborg, 1997. Hobbies: Literature; Mythology; Folk Traditions. Address: Ellegardsvaenge 5B, 2820 Gentofte, Copenhagen, Denmark.

DAVIES Jack Mustafa (John Paul Wynne), b. 15 Sept 1961, Bristol, England. Musician (guitar, piano). m. Saida Rajabali, 6 Oct 1990. Musical Education: Millfield School; University of Newcastle-Upon-Tyne; WCMD. Career: Reynolds Davies Duo, 1985-90; Peccadillo Circus, 1982-1992; Royal Shakespeare Company; Polka Children's Theatre; Harlow Theatrevan, 1986-89; Tres Bon, 1989-90; Presently with Dragonsfire, 1990-. Recordings: Crossing the Borders, 1992; A Present From The Past, 1993. Memberships: Royal Society of Musicians; Musicians' Union; Equity. Address: 27 Sonia Gardens, Neasden, London NW10 1AG, England.

DAVIES Mark John, b. 19 Nov 1969, Ampthill, Bedfordshire, England. Musician (keyboards); Vocalist; Record Producer; Remixer. Education: BA Hons (2:1), German, University of East Anglia, 1988-92. Musical Education: Violin/viola, up to Grade 6, Theory, Grade 4. Career: Keyboards, vocals with Messiah, 1990-; Album released, worked with Ian Astbury (of the Cult) and Precious Wilson; Television includes: 2 appearances Top of The Pops, 1992; O-Zone; 5 times on Radio One Roadshow; Major concerts include: Los Angeles, 1992; Scotland; Guernsey, 1993; London. Recordings: Album: 21st Century

Jesus, 1994; Singles include: There Is No Law (Number 1, USA College Chart), 1991; Temple Of Dreams, 1992; I Feel Love, 1992; Thunderdome, 1994; Creator, with Ian Astbury, Peace And Tranquility; 20,000 Hardcore Members (Number 4, UK Dance Charts), 1990; Law Of The Night, Marc Almond. Membership: Musicians' Union. Hobbies: CAD; Computer games; Football; Herpetology; Skiing; Fashion. Current Management: Stevo Pearce, Some Bizarre. Address: 124 New Bond Street, London W19 9AE, England.

DAVIES Neol Edward, b. 26 Apr 1952, Coventry, England. Songwriter; Musician (guitar); Teacher (guitar). Musical Education: Self-taught. Career: Founded 2 Tone Records with The Specials; Founder member, The Selecter; Tours included: The 2 Tone Tour, 1979; Tours of USA, Europe, Japan, supporting Talking Heads, Blondie, Elvis Costello, The Skatalites, and Prince Buster; Current member, Selecter Instrumental (8-piece instrumental ska band). Television and radio appearances include: Top of the Pops; Old Grey Whistle Test; BBC Radio 1. Recordings: The Selecter; On My Radio; Too Much Pressure; Missing Words; Three Minute Hero; Celebrate The Bullet. Membership: MU. Current Management: Roger Lomas Productions and Management. Address: 35 Dillotford Avenue, Coventry CV3 5DR, England.

DAVIES Noel, b. 18 Dec 1924, Buckley, Flintshire, North Wales. Musician (clarinet, saxophones); Music and Instrument Teacher. m. Edith Mary Edwards, 16 July 1946, 2 sons. Musical Education: Family professional and musical background; Graduate, Stanley Masters School Of Music, Chester. Career: Played in stage bands, theatre orchestra (pit), concert and light orchestras, sound/vision dance, cabaret; Also in music business management, both in UK and abroad, mid 1940s-; Also Stars In Battledress, Central Pool of Artists, world tours; Forces Broadcasting, Radio SEAC, and BFN, Germany; Currently, freelance musician, bandleader, conductor, music industry consultant. Memberships include: Elected representative, Musicians' Union. Hobbies: Music; Some sport; Travel; Current affairs. Current Management: Self-managed. Address: Tamarak, 15 Landon Road, Herne Bay, Kent CT6 6HP, England.

DAVIES Paul Francois William, b. 24 Sept 1953, Epsom, Surrey. Jazz Musician (guitar). Education: St Georges College, Weybridge, Dundee, London University. Musical Education: Self-taught. Career: Participated in dance music for Companies: Perter Goss; Karin Weiner; Jose Cazenave, 1970s; Played with Paul Davies Quartet, clubs: New Morning; Musée de L'Art Moderne; Radio France; France Culture, 1980s; Riot Trio, live record, 1990s. Recordings: Guest soloist, Windows, Jean-Jacques Ruhlmann Big Band; TV series, Novacek; Voices Off, Paul Davies Riot Trio. Memberships: SACEM; SPEDIDAM. Hobby: Reading. Current Management: Palmyre Music Productions. Address: 64 Rue Lepic, 75018 Paris, France.

DAVIES Peter Max Crofts, b. 30 Nov 1950, Salisbury, Wiltshire, England. Luthier; Instrument Designer; Musician (guitar). m. Patricia Anne, 28 Feb 1981, 1 son, 1 daughter. Musical Education: Learned piano as a child; Self-taught on guitar. Career: R & D consultant to: Goodfellow Guitars; Patrick Eggle Guitars, to 1993; Guitar technician to major artists, 1987-; Consultant for care and preservation of Jimi Hendrix' Black Stratocaster guitar; Currently involved in design of new MIDI musical interface, Tonepool; Built guitars for Queen video The Miracle, 1989; Invented Melodic Table and Tonepool instrument, and associated new ways to play and learn music; Currently researching playing techniques for Tonepool and preparing for the manufacture of the instrument. Honours: Bachelor of Arts; Guild of Master Craftsmen Nomination. Hobbies: Music; Blues and

rock guitar; Painting; Writing. Current Management: C-thru Music Ltd. Address: 6 Pleasant Row, Woodford, Kettering, Northamptonshire NN14 4HP, England.

DAVIES Ray, b. 21 June 1944, Muswell Hill, London, England. Singer; Songwriter; Musician (Guitar); Producer. m. 1) Rasa Didztpetris, 12 Dec 1964, 2 daughters, 2) Yvonne, 1 daughter with Chrissie Hynde. Education: Hornsey Art College; Theater Design, Croydon College of Art. Career: Founder, Ray Davies Quartet, aged 16, later named The Ravens; Group became The Kinks, 1963-; UK debut, London, 1963; US debut, Academy of Music, New York, 1965; Concerts and tours worldwide include: Madison Square Garden, New York, 1981; US Festival, San Bernardino, 1981; Earth Day Concert, Foxborough, 1992; Glastonbury Festival, 1993; Royal Albert Hall, 1993. Recordings: Numerous albums include: Kinks, 1964; Kinda Kinks, 1965; Face to Face, 1966; Something Else, 1967; Sleepwalker, 1977; Misfits, 1978; Low Budget, 1979; One for the Road, 1980; Glamour, 1981; Give the People What They Want, 1981; State of Confusion, 1983; Think Visual, 1987; Phobia, 1993; Numerous compilations, live albums and greatest hits collections; Hit Singles: Long Tall Sally, 1964; You Really Got Me, Number 1, UK; All Day and All Of the Night, 1964; Tired of Waiting For You, Number 1, UK, 1965; Everybody's Gonna Be Happy, 1965; Set Me Free, 1965; See My Friend, 1965; Till the End of the Day, 1966; A Well-Respected Man, 1966; Dedicated Follower of Fashion, 1966; Sunny Afternoon, Number 1, UK, 1966; Dead End Street, 1966; Waterloo Sunset, 1967; Autumn Almanac, 1967; Days, 1968; Lola, 1980; Apeman, 1971; Supersonic Rocket Ship, 1972; Come Dancing, 1983. Contributions as songwriter to: The Virgin Soldiers, film soundtrack, 1969; Chorus Girls, play, 1981; Actor, Absolute Beginners, film, 1986. Honours include: Inducted into Rock'n'Roll Hall of Fame, 1990; Ivor Novello Award for Special Contribution to Music, 1990. Address: c/o Asgard, 125 Parkway, London, NW1 7PS, England.

DAVIS Chip. Songwriter; Composer. Career: New Age Music composer; Formed Mannheim Steamroller; Created American Gramaphone record label; Compositions used extensively on television and radio, including: The Today Show; The Rush Limbaugh Show. Compositions: Wrote hit single: Convoy, under pen-name, C W McCall; Series of New Age albums: Fresh Aire 1-7; Music for television documentary: Saving The Wildlife; Several Christmas albums. Hobbies: Nature and Environmental conservation. Current Management: SESAC. Address: 55 Music Sq E, Nashville, TN 37203, USA.

DAVIS Copeland, b, 16 Aug 1950, Orlando, Florida, USA. Pop and Jazz Musician (piano); Entertainer. m. Mary Birt Norman, 23 Aug 1987. Education: BFA, Florida Atlantic University. Musical Education: Degree in Composition, Arranging, BFA. Career: Arranger for The Fifth Dimension; Conductor for Barbara McNair; Arranger, guest artist, Florida Symphonic Pops Orchestra; Television: Tonight Show; Good Morning America; Three Copeland Davis TV Specials; Newly signed with Atlantic Records. Honours: Emmy Nomination: Copeland Davis at Crystal Tree. Membership: BMI. Hobbies: Computers; Cycling. Current Management: Herbert Moon. Address: Bowen Agency, 504 W 168th Street, New York, NY 10032, USA.

DAVIS Daniel, b. 3 Jan 1961, Arlington Height, Illinois, USA. Singer. 1 son. Career: Music City Tonight; Crook and Chase. Recordings: Tyler. Publications: Country Weekly. Membership: CMA. Hobbies: Football; Golf. Current Management: C&M Productions Management Group. Address: 5114 Albert Drive, Brentwood, TN 37027, USA.

DAVIS Eddy Ray, b. 26 Sept 1940, Greenhill, Indiana, USA. Composer; Conductor; Musician.

Education: Purdue University; Chicago University. Musical Education: Cosmopolitan Conservatory; Chicago School Of Music. Career: Appearances include: Mike Douglas Show; Tonight Show; Carnegie Hall; Jazz And Heritage festivals throughout the world including: Japan; Europe; Australia; Russia; Brazil; Records and tours with Woody Allen; Tours with (film star) George Segal; Tours, recordings with Leon Redbone and Tom Waits; Musical Director, Best Of Spike Jones; Makin Whoppee; Warren G; Jazz Leggs. Compositions include: Penny Candy; Play For Me A Love Song; Now I'm Blue. Recordings: Soundtracks: Radio Days; Fried Green Tomatoes (with Patti Labelle); Sophie's Choice. Publications: The Theory Behind Chord Symbols. Honours: First place, Fretts Magazine Poll for Four String Banjo; Award from Berliner Theatretaler. Memberships: The New York Society for the Preservation of Illegitimate Music; The Bunk Project; The New York Banjo Ensemble. Current Management: New York Jazz Productions; Sky King Productions. Address: 260 Fifth Avenue, New York, NY, USA.

DAVIS Jean Michel, b. 2 Mar 1956, Suresnes, Paris, France. Musician (drums, vibraphone, percussion). m. Cynthia Stone, Mar 1985, 1 son, 1 daughter. Musical Education: Conservatoire de Montreuil, Paris; Berklee College of Music, Boston, USA. Career: Drummer, vibraphone player, in clubs: New Morning; Hot Brass; Freelance percussionist playing with: Modulations, (contemporary music ensemble of composer Philippe Durville); Les Primitifs Du Futur; Big bands; Paris opera: Die Soldaten de Zimmerman; Television appearances: Stravinsky's Histoire du Soldat, with the Campagnol theatre troupe (FR3); (France 2); Played with rock group Au Bonheur des Dames, 1997; Studio sessions with various artists; Advertising jingles and cartoon theme tunes. Recordings: Albums with: Les Primitifs Du Futur; The François Fichu Jazz Gang; Cordes Eltames: Accordion Madness; Paris Scat; Aubon heur des Dames, Paris Musette 3. Publications: 10 Études De Vibraphone Jazz (Salabert); Association Française de Percussion. Membership: UMJ (Union des Musiciens De Jazz), France. Hobbies: Family; Hiking. Address: 172 Avenue de Choisy, 75013 Paris, France.

DAVIS Keith, b. 28 Dec 1946, Bristol, England. Musician (guitar, dobro, banjo). m. Susan Carole Wilson, 14 Dec 1984, 1 son. Education: Reading University. Musical Education: Self-taught. Career: Played on national and local radio; Concerts include: Various clubs; Sidmouth International Festival; Burnley National Blues Festival; Warwick Festival; Tutor at London College of Music. Recordings: On The Streets, 1987; Wireless, 1992; Smoke And Mirrors, 1995. Publication: Swagbag Folk Magazine. Memberships: Musicians' Union; Royal Institution of Chartered Surveyors. Current Management: Susie Davis, Ferndale Management. Address: 6 North Street, Downend, Bristol BS16 5SY, England.

DAVIS Lena, b. 8 Mar 1938, London, England. Personal Manager; Songwriter; Publicist. 1 son. Career: Discovered Ricky Valance, had hit with Tell Laura I Love Her, aged 22; Joined Noel Gay Agency as Personal Manager; Later, freelance artist manager. Compositions: Hits for Joe Brown; Kathy Kirby; Polly Perkins; Theme music for BBC TV. Recordings include: Tell Laura I Love Her. Publications: Currently contribute to 5 magazines. Hobbies: Photography; Animals. Address: Cotton's Farmhouse, Whiston Road, Cogenhoe, Northants NN7 1NL, England.

DAVIS Linda Kaye, 26 Nov 1962, Carthage, Texas, USA. VocalEntertainer. m. Lang Jeffrey Scott, 24 Aug 1984, 1 daughter. Career: Opened shows for superstars include: Garth Brooks; George Strait; Currently touring with Reba McEntire's show. Recordings: Duet with Reba

McEntire: Does He Love You; Album: Shoot For The Moon. Honours: CMA Award; Music City News/TNN Award; Grammy. Memberships: ASCAP; CMA; ACM; AFTRA. Hobbies: Being with family; Eating out. Current Management: Starstruck Entertainment, PO Box 121996, Nashville, TN 37212, USA.

DAVIS Mac, b. 21 Jan 1942, Lubbock, Texas, USA. Singer; Songwriter. m. Lisë Kristen Gerard, 1983, 3 sons. Education: Emory University; Georgia State College. Career: Manager, Metric Music, 1966-68; Solo singer, 1969-; Television and film performer, 1978-; Screen performances include: North Dallas Forty, 1979; Cheaper To Keep Her, 1980; The Sting II, 1983. Numerous compositions. Recordings: Albums include: Mac Davis, 1973; Baby Don't Get Hooked On Me, 1973; Forever Lovers, 1978; Thunder In The Afternoon, 1978; Midnight Crazy, 1981; Texas In My Rear View Window, 1981; Soft Talk, 1984; 20 Golden Greats, 1984; Till I Made It With You, 1986. Address: c/o Gallin Morey Associates, 8730 Sunset Blvd, PH West, Los Angeles, CA 90069, USA.

DAVIS Paul, b. 21 Apr 1944, Cumberland, England. Record Producer; Broadcaster; Journalist; Author. m. Hazel, 20 Mar 1965, 1 son, 2 daughters. Career: Presenter/producer, BBC Radio and local radio; Chairman, RTM Radio; Commercial Manager, Word Records; Owner, New Music Enterprises. Recordings: Producer for George Hamilton IV; Wes Davis; Jerry Arhelger. Publications: New Life In Country Music (book); Editor, Publisher, New Music Magazine; Articles, various music and Christian journals. Memberships: MCPS; PRS; European Director, Gospel Music Association. Hobbies: Church Work. Address: Meredale, Reach Lane, Heath And Reach, Bedfordshire LU7 0AL, England.

DAVIS Richard, b. 15 Apr 1930, Chicago, Illinois, USA. Musician (bass); Music Educator. Musical Education: MusB, Vanderbrook College Of Music, 1952; Postgraduate, Manhattan School of Music, 1964-66. Career: Bandleader, own quartet, 1980-; Performed at: Berkeley Jazz Festival; New Orleans Jazz Heritage Festival; Fletcher Henderson Memorial Concert; International tours with: Elvin Jones; Lalo Schrifin; McCoy Tyner; Sun Ra; Archie Shepp; Don Cherry; Associated Professor, Full Tenured Professor of Music, University of Wisconsin, 1976-; Owner, Sympatico Music Publications Inc; Founder, Richard Davis Foundation for Young Bassists. Recordings: Albums: with Richard Davis Quartet: With Understanding, 1975; Epistrophy, 1981; Way Out West, 1981; Harvest, 1988; As One; Other recordings with numerous artist including Janis Ian; Herbie Mann; Van Morrison; Freddie Hubbard; Bo Diddley; Laura Nyro; Melissa Manchester; George Benson; Quincy Jones; Judy Collins; Elvin Jones; Charlie Mingus; Bonnie Raitt; Jimmy Smith; Bruce Springsteen; Loudon Wainwright III; Paul Simon; Carly Simon; Manhattan Transfer. Publications: Author, The Bass Tradition, with M.C. Gridley, 1984; Jazz Styles, 1985; Contributor to numerous journals. Honours: Downbeat Awards: Readers Poll Winner, 1967-72; Critics Poll Winner, 1967-74; ASCAP Popular Award, 1979-83, 1984-85. Memberships: International Composers Society; International Society of Bassists; ASCAP; NARAS; National String Artists; American Jazz Foundation; Screen Actors Guild; National Association Of Jazz Educators. Address: University of Wisconsin, Madison, WI 53706, USA.

DAVIS Skeeter (Mary Frances Penick), b. 30 Dec 1931, Dry Ridge, Kentucky, USA. Singer. Career: Duo, The Davis Sisters, with Betty Jack Davis, on radio, television and recordings, 1949-53; Solo career, 1955-; Worked with Eddy Arnold; Elvis Presley; Regular member, Grand Ole Opry, 1959; Toured extensively, US, Canada, Europe, Far East; Regular performances with

Duke Ellington. Recordings: Hit singles include: I Forgot More Than You'll Ever Know, with Betty Jack Davis; Set Him Free; Can't Help You, I'm Falling Too; My Last Date; The End Of The World; A Dear John Letter, with Bobby Bare; For Loving You, with Don Bowman; Let's Get Together, with George Hamilton IV; Albums include: with The Davis Sisters: Hits, 1952; Jealous Love, 1952; Solo: I'll Sing You A Song..., 1961; Here's The Answer, 1961; The End Of The World, 1961; Cloudy With Occasional Tears, 1963; I Forgot More Than You'll Ever Know, 1964; Written By The Stars, 1965; Sings Buddy Holly, 1967; What Does It Take, 1967; Why So Lonely, 1968; Mary Frances, 1969; Skeeter, 1971; Love Takes A Lot Of My Time, 1971; Foggy Mountain Top, 1971; Sings Dolly, 1972; Bring It On Home, 1972; I Can't Believe That It's All Over, 1973; The Hillbilly Singer, 1973; He Wakes Me With A Kiss Every Morning, 1974; Heartstrings, 1984; Other albums with: Porter Wagoner; Bobby Bare; Don Bowman; George Hamilton IV; NRBQ. Address: c/o Joe Taylor Artist Agency, 2802 Columbine Pl., Nashville, TN 37204, USA.

DAVIS Spencer, b. 17 July 1941, Swansea, Wales. Musician (guitar). Education: Birmingham University. Career: Founder, Spencer Davis Group, 1963-69; Solo artist and duo with Peter Jameson, 1971; Record company executive, Island Records; Played in Blues Reunion, 1988; Reformed Spencer Davis Group, 1990; Film appearances: The Ghost Goes Gear, 1966; Here We Go Round The Mulberry Bush, 1967. Recordings: Albums: with The Spencer Davis Group: Their First LP, 1965; The Second Album, 1966; Autumn 66, 1966; Gimme Some Lovin', 1967; I'm A Man, 1967; Solo albums: It's Been So Long; Mousetrap; Crossfire, 1984; Singles include: with the Spencer Davis Group: I Can't Stand It, 1964; Strong Love, 1965; Keep On Running (Number 1, UK), 1966; Somebody Help Me (Number 1, UK), 1966; When I Come Home, 1966; Gimme Some Lovin', 1966; I'm A Man, 1967; Mr Second Class, 1968. Honour: Carl Alan Award, Most Outstanding Group, 1966. Current Management: Richard Martin Management, Agency House, 6 The Steyne, Worthing, West Sussex BN11 3DS, England.

DAVIS Teresa Jane, b. 8 January 1968, Leeds, West Yorkshire, England. Singer; Musician. Education: Diploma, Wakefield Performing Arts College; Leeds College of Music, Jazz & Light Music. Career: Lead Vocals: Shiva, Album and Live Gigs including Phoenix, 1996, Tribal Gathering, 1996, Northern Exposure, 1996; Featured Artist on Single, Brilliant Feeling, Full Monty All Stars; Backing Vocals: D:ream, Album, World, Featured Artist on Single, Power, 2 UK Headlining Tours, 1 Australian Headlining Tour, Various Television including TOTP, Steve Wright Show; Walkon and Appearances in Eastenders, The Bill, 1991; Backing Singer for Gary Numan, 2 Tours, 1993; Backing Vocals for Lisa Stansfield, ABC, Playing Role of Frida in Bjorn Again, International Tours, 1997-98. Recordings: Lead and Backing Vocals for Sonic R (Sega Game), 1997; Blur, P J Proby/Marc Almond, Album Sigue Sigue Sputnik. Memberships: Equity; Musicians Union; PAMRA. Address: Top Flat, 28 Sinclair Road, West Kensington, London W14 0NH.

DAVISON Peter, b. 26 Oct 1948, Los Angeles, California, USA. Composer; Orchestrator; Conductor; Arranger. m. Iris Pell, 21 Sept 1984, 1 daughter. Musical Education: BA, MA, Music Composition, California State University, Northridge; Film Scoring Workshops, Earle Hagen, BMI; Fred Karlin, ASCAP; Travel to Bali to study Gamelan music. Career: Composed/arranged television series and documentaries, including: Seaquest; Batman - The Animated Series; John Denver Tour Special; Films; Interactive media; Commercials including: Hilton Hotels; India; videos. Recordings: As composer, arranger, producer, artist: Winds Of

Space; Glide - Star Gazer; Forest - Mountain; Traces - Music On The Way; Adagio For Yoga (soundtrack). Memberships: SCL (Society of Composers and Lyricists); ASMA (American Society Music Arrangers); IFP/West; IDA (International Documentary Association).

DAWKES John William, b. 12 Nov 1919, Nottingham, England. Musician (woodwind); Orchestrator. m. Elizabeth, 25 Oct 1947, 1 son. Musical Education: Orchestration, George Evans; Woodwind Technology, Ted Planas. Career: Toured with name bands including: Geo Evans; Teddy Foster; Paul Fenoulhet; Harry Parry; Squadronaires, 1947-51; Resident, London with: Sidney Lipton; Felix King; Staff arranger to music publishers, Bradbury Wood; Performances at West End theatres: Gentlemen Prefer Blondes; How To Succeed In Business; Sail Away; Radio shows: Round The Horne; Take It From Here; BBC radio, television shows, films with: Norman Wisdom; Tony Hancock; Morecambe and Wise; Charles Chaplin; Moved into musical education, setting up and coaching Student Orchestras, later supplying Education Authorities with wind instruments; Formed Wind Instrument businesses of Dawkes Music Ltd; Also Windcraft Ltd, Supplier, Wind Instrument Repair tools and parts to dealers in Common Market, under direction of son Lindsey. Memberships: Hon member, Musicians' Union; ACCS. Hobby: Music.

DAWSON Barry, b. 16 Apr 1929, Rustington, West Sussex, England. Musician (accordion, trumpet); Singer. m. Pamela Douglas ARCM, 27 May 1985, twin daughters. Musical Education: British College of Accordionists, Guildhall SoM (Brass) extra-mural. Career: Rank and file musician with Victor Sylvester, Joe Loss; Television series, Box o' Trix (Jim Dale); Own BBC Childrens' TV spots; Resident, The Mayfair Hotel, London; Boulevard De Paris Restaurant, 2 years solo; Solo spot, Black and White Minstrels, cruising edition; Television: Colditz; BBC Friday Night Music feature, present resident Langham Hilton Russian Bar Restaurant, and other Hilton spots. Recordings: Barry's Bide-A-Wee Band. Publications: Featured writer, Accordion Times, Crescendo International. Memberships: Equity; Musicians' Union. Hobbies: Now relinquished: Sailing; Light aircraft pilot. Current Management: Hilton International Entertainment, 27 Downs Side, Cheam, Surrey SM2 2EH, England. Address: Hill Cottage, 4 Bourne Way, Cheam, Surrey SM1 2EN, England.

DAWSON Dana, b. 1975, New York, USA. Singer. Career: Performed on Broadway, aged 8; Solo artiste, 1993-; Early success in France; Concerts include: Radio 1's Massive Music tour, 1995. Recordings: Debut album: Black Butterfly, 1995; Hit single: 3 Is Family, 1995. Current Management: First Avenue Management, The Courtyard, 42 Colwith Road, London W6 9EY, England.

DAWSON-BUTTERWORTH Russell, b. 14 Mar 1970, Sheffield, England. Composer; Arranger; Musician (keyboards, piano, flute). m. Elizabeth Yvonne Ronald, 2 Jan 1994. Education: University College Salford. Musical Education: Studied electro-acoustic composition gaining BA (Hons) in Band Musicianship, University College, Salford. Career: Started as keyboard player, Sheffield band Midnite; Currently working on solo album. Compositions: Library music and themes for Granada TV, Sky TV. Memberships: British Music Writers Council; PRS; MCPS; Musicians' Union. Hobbies: Motorsport; Photography. Current Management: Self-managed. Address: 247 Carterknowle Road, Sheffield, South Yorks S11 9FW, England.

DAY Doris, b. 3 Apr 1924, Cincinnati, Ohio, USA. Singer; Actress. m. (1) Al Jorden, Mar 1941, divorced 1943, 1 son, (2) George Weilder divorced 1949, (3) Marty Melcher, 3 Apr 1951, deceased

1968. Career: Former dancer, Cincinnati; Singer, shows including: Karlin's Karnival, WCPO-Radio; Bob Hope NBC Radio Show, 1948-50; Doris Day CBS Show, 1952-53; Solo recording artist, 1950-; Actress, numerous films including: Tea For Two, 1950; Lullaby Of Broadway, 1951; April In Paris, 1952; Pajama Game, 1957; Teacher's Pet, 1958; Pillow Talk, 1959; Midnight Lace, 1960; Jumbo, 1962; That Touch Of Mink, 1962; The Thrill Of It All, 1963; Send Me No Flowers, 1964; Do Not Disturb, 1965; The Glass Bottom Boat, 1966; Caprice, 1967; The Ballad Of Josie, 1968; Where Were You When The Lights Went Out, 1968; Own television series, The Doris Day Show, 1970-73; Doris Day And Friends, 1985-86; Doris Day's Best, 1985-86; TV special, The Pet Set, 1972. Honours: Winner (with Jerry Doherty), Best Dance Team, Cincinnati; Laurel Award, Leading New Female Personality In Motion Picture Industry, 1950; Top audience attractor, 1962; American Comedy Lifetime Achievement Award, 1991.

DE BETHMANN Pierre, b. 21 Apr 1965, Boulogne Billancourt, France. Musician (piano). m. Christel Hua, 22 Sept 1990, 2 children. Education: Baccalauréat C (Science), 1982; ESCP (Paris Graduate School of Management), 1987. Musical Education: Classical piano, 1971-87; Private lessons, jazz piano, 1975-; Some self-training; Berklee College of Music, 1989. Career: Management consultant, 1990-94; Professional musician, 1994-; Member, 4 regular groups, including PRYSM, trio with Christophe Wallemme and Benjamin Henocq, 1994; Numerous gigs in most Parisian clubs, various international festivals; Numerous radio and television appearances with PRYSM; Occasionally played with: Vincent Herring; Rick Margitza; Willie Williams; Vanessa Rubin; Sylvain Beuf; Philip Catherine; George Brown; Jean-Loup Longnon; François Jeauneau; François Théberge; Aldo Romano. Recordings: PRYSM, PRYSM, 1995; Quoi de Neuf Docteur, Big Band; La Femme Du Bouc Émissaire; 51 Below, 1996. Honour: First Prize, La Defense National Jazz Contest, 1994. Memberships: SACEM; UMJ (Union des Musiciens de Jazz). Current Management: Renaud di Matteo, Paris. Address: 16 Cité de Trévise, 75009 Paris, France.

DE BURGH Chris (Christopher Davidson), b. 15 Oct 1948, Argentina. Singer; Songwriter. Education: Trinity College, Dublin. Career: Irish tour with Horslips, 1973; Solo artiste, 1974-; Album sales, 35 million to date; Sell-out concerts worldwide; Performances include: Carol Aid, London, 1985; The Simple Truth, benefit concert for Kurdish refugees, Wembley, 1991; Royal Albert Hall, London. Recordings: Singles include: Flying, 1975; Patricia The Stripper, 1976; A Spaceman Came Travelling, 1976; Don't Pay The Ferryman, 1982; High On Emotion, 1984; Lady In Red (Number 1, UK), 1984; Love Is My Decision, theme from film Arthur 2, 1988; Missing You, 1988; Albums: Far Beyond These Castle Walls, 1975; Spanish Train And Other Stories, 1975; At The End Of A Perfect Day, 1977; Crusader, 1979; Eastern Wind, 1980; Best Moves, 1981; The Getaway, 1982; Man On The Line, 1984; The Very Best Of Chris De Burgh, 1985; Into The Light, 1986; Flying Colours, 1988; From A Spark To A Flame - The Very Best Of Chris De Burgh, 1989; High On Emotion - Live From Dublin, 1990; Power Of Ten, 1992. Honours: ASCAP Award, The Lady In Red, 1991; PRS Award, The Lady In Red, 1992. Current Management: Mismanagement, 754 Fulham Road, London SW6 5SH, England.

DE DAVRICHEWY Irakli, b. 1 Feb 1940, Paris, France. Bandleader; Musician (trumpet). 1 son, 2 daughters. Musical Education: Early studies, violin, piano; Self-taught trumpet. Career: Formed first orchestra, 1958; Leader, own groups: The Swing Orchestra; French All-Stars; Jazz Four; Also soloist; Worked as accompanist to: Barney Bigard; Cozy Cole; Arvell Shaw; Claude Hopkins; Wallace Davenport; Christian Morin; Moustache; Numerous television broadcasts for J.C.Averty,

with Victoria Spivey; Edith Wilson; Claude Bolling; Also with the Orchestra of Marc Lafferière; with Moustache et les Petits Français: accompanied Buddy Tate; Harry Edison; Al Grey; Cat Anderson; Jimmy Forrest; Eddie Vinson; Jimmy Witherspoon; Dorothy Donnegan; Played with Lionel Hampton; Dizzy Gillespie; Joe Newman; Jo Jones; Sam Woodyard; Joe Muranyi; Tours: Sweden; Netherlands; Germany; Switzerland; Jazz festivals include: Antibes; Coulombs; Breda; Nice; Andernos; Montauban; Hamburg; Concerts include: First part, Louis Armstrong concert, Palais des Sports, Paris, 1965; Numerous concerts for the Hot Club de France, 1984. Recordings: Abide With Me, Irakli Quartet, 1971; Les Petits Français with G Brassens, 1979; Le Vieux Truc, Raymond Fonsèque, 1984; Mack The Knife, Irakli Swiss All-Stars, 1985; Chicago Southside Sound, Irakli Jazz Four, 1994; Irakli At The Hot Club de Rouen, 1995. Publications: Producer, record and booklets for Media 7: Masters Of Jazz, Louis Armstrong complete and chronological. Honours: Jazz Hot Award, 1959, 1962; Academie du Jazz, 1972. Memberships: President of the Louis Armstrong Association, France; Creation, Paris, Louis Armstrong Square, with City of Paris. Hobbies: Golf; France's leading Louis Armstrong archivist. Address: 10 Avenue Fleury, 92700 Colombes, France.

DE GROOTE Geeraard Albert, b. 3 September 1958, Blankenberge, Belgium. Songwriter; Musician (saxes, guitar, bass); Vocalist. Education: School of Economics, Accounting and Modern Languages; Academy of Music, Bruges; Jazz Studio, Antwerp; Jazz Academy, Knokke-Heist. Career: Studio recordings and TV appearances with various Belgian artists and bands; TV appearances with Tom Robinson; Belgian concerts with Tom Robinson. Compositions: Start Again with Blond. Recordings: with the Belgian Bluesband; Hideaway; Billy Goat Riders; Cly-an and Blond, pop-rock. Hobbies: Literature; Travelling; Cars; Girls; Sport. Address: Westmoere 50, B-8490 Snellegem, Jabbeke, Belgium.

DE GROOTE Patrick, b. 20 Dec 1961, Wilrÿk, Belgium. Promoter; Organizer. Education: Applied Communication Sciences. Musical Education: Solfege. Career: Director, Sfinks Festival; Executive European Forum of Worldwide Music Festivals; Various open air events including: Cultural Capital of Europe, 1993; Antwerp Summer Festival, 1995. Address: J F Willemsstraat 10, B-2530 Boechout, Belgium.

DE JOHNETTE Jack, b. 4 Aug 1942, Chicago, Illinois, USA. Jazz Musician, (piano, drums); Bandleader; Composer. m. Lydia, 8 Sept 1968, 2 daughter. Musical Education: Chicago Conservatory of Music. Career: Performed and recorded with John Coltrane, Thelonious Monk, Miles Davis, Stan Getz, Bill Evans, Herbie Hancock, Betty Carter; currently with Keith Jarrett Trio; Pat Metheny; Gateway Trio with Dave Holland and John Abercrombie; Also leads own group. Composition: Silver Hollow. Recordings: Albums: New Directions Live; Parallel Realities; Earth Walk; Music For The Fifth World; Special Edition; Untitled; Pictures; New Rags; Tin Can Alley; Inflation Blues; Album Album. Honours: Grand Prix Du Disque, Academy of Jazz, Paris, 1978; Best Jazz Album of Year, Album Album; NEA Fellow, 1978; CAPS Composers Grantee, 1980; Winner, Downbeat Readers Poll, 13 consecutive years; Numerous drum magazine awards; Swing Journal Video Award; Honorary Doctorate of Music, Berklee College of Music, 1990. Current Management: Europe: Saudades, A-6200 Rotholz 369A, Austria; USA: Ted Kurland Assoc, 163 Brighton Avenue, Boston, MA 02134, USA.

DE JONGE Jon Colin (aka Jon Veal), b. 5 Jan 1947, Hull, England. Musician (drums, xylophone, timpani). m. Lynette Patricia Long, 22

Dec 1982. Education: BA, Economic History, Exeter University. Musical Education: Self-taught; Courses at Warendon, Barry, Canford. Career: Known as John Veal, 1955-80; Appearances include: Local orchestras, cabaret, theatres, panto, musicals, Hull, York, Ipswich, Derby, Colchester, Swindon; Circus credits: Chipperfields; David Smarts; Gerry Cottle; Ice Show credits: Europe, Holiday On Ice; Blackpool Ice Show, 6 seasons. Publications: A Tale Of Three Piers; Tune Up The Hoover! (Cinema Musicians Tell Their Stories). Memberships: Musicians' Union; British Drummers Association; Percussive Arts Society. Hobbies: Writing history articles (specially social history of music). Address: Flat 4, 91 Lord Street, Blackpool FY1 2DJ, England.

DE JONGH Joeri Alfons Yvon, b. 6 November 1973, Schoten, Belgium. Accordion Player; Composer. Education: Graphic Design; Accordion. Career: Several gigs at Schoten; De Wasserij, theatre play, with over 22 performances. Compositions: Nervoso; Her Farewell; L'Amour A Distance; Em Sesimbra. Recordings: Wijzelf, cassette, 1992; Aangename Kennismaking, cassette, 1994. Publication: Nervoso, 1996. Membership: SABAM. Hobbies: Photography; Local Music, pub & jam sessions. Current Management: Plutostraat 9, B-2900 Schoten, Belgium. Address: Plutostraat 9, B-2900 Schoten, Belgium.

DE LA SIMONE Albin, b. 14 Dec 1970, Amiens, France. Musician (keyboards); Arranger; Composer; Director. Education: Plastic Arts. Musical Education: Self-taught. Career: Jazz festivals: Brecon, Britain; Istanbul, Turkey; Amiens, France; Tours: Morocco; Canada; Spain; Germany; France; United Arab Emirates. Compositions: Composer, director, The Clara Finster Show. Recordings: with André Ceccarelli; G Grignon; Laurent Robin; Tony Ballaster; Own groups: Bonzai Géant; Kifidem. Memberships: SACEM; SPEDIDAM; Editions SALABERT. Hobby: Arts. Address: 6 Rue Berthollet, 75005 Paris, France.

DE MAEYER Marc, b. 23 Apr 1966, Willebroek, Belgium. 1 daughter. Education: Academy of Music, Mechelen, Belgium; Selftaught keyboards. Career: Keyboards and backings in Hardrockband, Rubicon, keyboards and vocals in Flemish Pop Band, Van Gogh; Producer of Demotapes, Prime Mover and Herve and Anton Menke; Writing for Petra, Yasmine and Barbara Dex; TV Appointments: Tien omtezien; BRT, Man bÿt Lond; Radio Appointments: BRT; RSJ. Compositions: Elsje; Jij Bent Voor Mij; Icecubes and Diamonds; Shadow King; Moonlite; Een Nachtje Slapen. Recordings: Alles Draait Om Haar; Vers Bloed, demotape; Prime Mover, demotape. Publication: Alles Draait om Haar, 1994. Honour: Semi-final, Rock in Flanders, 1990. Hobby: Travelling. Address: De Maeyer Marc, Heufstraat 49, BE 3350 Overhespen, Belgium.

DE MASURE Geoffrey, b. 16 May 1969, Tourcoing, France. Musician (trombone). Career: Orchestre National de Jazz (musical director, Denis Badault), 1991-94; Urban Mood; Quadiature. Recordings: 3 CDs: Orchestre National de Jazz; Quad Neuf Docteur; Urban Mood. Membership: Union Musiciens Jazz (UMJ). Address: Les Denizets, 02540 Vendieres, France.

DE MESMAY Benoit, b. 10 Oct 1961, Algeria. Composer; Musician (piano). Education: Licence de Droit. Musical Education: State diploma, professor of jazz. Career: European jazz festivals with Gil Evans; Orchestre National de Jazz; Elizabeth Caumont; John Scofield; Lucky Peterson. Recordings: 2 albums with Elizabeth Caumont; 3 albums with Laurent Cugny, Gil Evans. Address: 9 Rue des Mortes Fontaines, 92370 Chaville, France.

DE RYCKE Herman, b. 20 August 1960, Oudenaarde, Belgium. Musician (Double Bass). m. Maes Riet, 7 January 1989, 1 son. Education: Solfège, Double Bass. Career: Klepper, pop group, 1976-77; Penthouse, pop group, 1979-83; Allan Fawn and The State of the Art, pop group, 1984; Kandahar, pop group, 1983-86; The Peter Band Band, pop group, 1986; Work 4, contemporary jazz, 1987-89; Kalinka Zigeunertrio, gipsy music, 1991; TV: Villatempo (BAT), 1986. Composition: Blue Ballad, jazz. Recordings: Neighbour Fool, single, LP, Penthouse; Light My Fire, single, The Peter Pan Band. Honours: Winner, Humo's Rock Rally, 1986; The Peter Pan Band, 1986; Winner, Knack Rhythm 'n Youth Trophy, 1989. Membership: SABAM. Hobby: Travelling. Address: Hoogmeers 9, 9031 Gent, Belgium.

DE SCHOOLMEESTER Beverley, b. 4 May 1962, Britain. Songwriter; Poet; Musician (bass guitar, piano); Vocalist. Education: National Diploma Business Studies; Student of Scientology. Musical Education: Pianforte to Teaching Standard; Self-taught bassist, vocalist. Career: Solo artist as jazz fusion singer, 1991-; Currently, bass player, backing vocalist for The Dolls, major deal pending; UK nationwide television, radio appearances also in Europe, Indonesia, Singapore, Japan, 1995; Tours: UK; France; Germany; Netherlands; Sweden; Italy; Turkey; Singapore; Indonesia; Ireland. Recordings: 3 EPs; Album: The Dolls: No Shame; Solo material: over 30 tracks written and demoed. Publications: Various poetry in magazines and local press. Memberships: Musicians' Union; London Academy Of Music. Hobbies: Badminton; Martial arts; Swimming; Horse riding; Relaxing on the beach. Current Management: Self-managed. Address: 16 Battle Street, Reading, Berkshire RG1 7NU, England.

DE SMET Francis, b. 3 December 1962, Bruges, Belgium. Musical Supervisor; Musician (Keyboards). Education: Harmony and Piano, Conservatory of Bruges; Electronic Music Composition, Royal Conservatory of Brussels, Academia Chigichiana, 1992. Career: Musical Supervision, Transatlantic Films, Brussels, 1992-. Compositions: Filmtrack of The SexualLife of the Belgians, 1993. Current Management: BVBA De Smet Films, Generaal Lemanlaan 151, BE-8310, Bruges, Belgium. Address: Francis De Smet, Generaal Lemanlaan 151, BE-8310 Bruges, Belgium.

DE VIS Alain, b. 6 September 1953, Brussels, Belgium. Musician (Trumpet; Flugelhorn); Composer; Arranger. m. Nanga Marie-Jeanne, 30 June 1984, 4 sons. Education: Mathematics and Physics; Classical, School in Nivelles, Belgium, 1971. Career: Small commercial bands, 1975; Jazz bands and big bands, 1979; Salsa and Brazilian bands, 1979/80-; Concerts with: Fania All Stars, 1981; Brasil Tropical, shows, in Europe; Salsa De Hoy; Dynamita Salsa. Recordings: Act Big Band, 2nd Album; Many studio sessions for Singers in 1980s. Membership: SABAM, Composer. Current Management: Dynamic Sounds Productions, Rue G Wincqz 24, 7060 Soignies, Belgium. Address: Rue G Wincqz 24, 7060 Soignies, Belgium.

DE VORE David, b. 27 Mar 1943, Hilo, Hawaii, USA. Producer; Engineer. m. Janine, 3 July 1976, 1 daughter. Education: 2 years college, Engineering/Architecture. Career: Producer, Engineer for Fleetwood Mac; Grateful Dead; Santana; Elton John; REO Speedwagon; Ringo Starr; Russ Ballard. Recordings produced include: Don't Let The Sun Go Down On Me; Hot Blooded; Can't Fight This Feeling. Hobbies: Golf; Mountain biking; Rollerblading.

DE VRIES Bert, b. 30 May 1963, Noordbergum, Netherlands. Promotional Manager; Music; Radio; Journalist. m. Hillie Weyer, 9 Aug 1985, 1 son, 1 daughter. Career: Freelance manager for Dutch, French and English bands, 1987-; Writer for regional and national magazines; Producer: Radio pop show, local radio. Hobbies: American and Dutch literature; Family; Music.

DE VRIES Marius, b. 21 Oct 1961, London, England. Producer; Remixer; Songwriter; Musician (keyboards); Programmer; Arranger. m. Felicity, 1 Apr 1989, 1 son, 1 daughter. Education: Peterhouse College, Cambridge. Music Scholarship, St Paul's Cathedral Choir School; Music Scholarship at Bedford School. Career: Two world tours with Blow Monkeys; Musical Director for Rick Astley's tour, 1989; Musical Director for Neneh Cherry, 1991; Television appearances include: South Banks Arts Review; Jonathon Ross; Top Of The Pops; The Word; The Tube; In studio, 1991-; Music Supervisor for Warner Bros The Avengers, 1997-98. Compositions: Co-composer and Co-producer of score for Baz Luhrman's Romeo and Juliet, 1996. Recordings: Albums: with Madonna: Bedtime Stories; with Björk: Debut; Post; with Massive Attack: Protection; with Annie Lennox: Diva, Medusa; with U2: Hold Me Thrill Me Kiss Me Kill Me, Pop; with Robbie Robertson, Contact from the Underground of Red Boy; with Neil Finn, forthcoming untitled album. Publications: Various magazine articles. Memberships: PRS; Musicians' Union. Hobbies: Travel; Reading.

DEACON John, b. 19 Aug 1951, Leicester, England. Musician (bass). Education: First class (hons) degree, Electronics. Career: Bass player, UK rock group, Queen, 1971-; Numerous tours include: UK; US; Australia; Japan; South America; Major concerts include: Rock In Rio Festival, Brazil, 1985; Live Aid, Wembley, 1985; Knebworth Festival, 1986; A Concert For Life, Wembley, 1992. Recordings: Albums include: Queen, 1973; Queen 2, 1974; Sheer Heart Attack, 1974; A Night At The Opera, 1975; A Day At The Races, 1977; Jazz, 1978; Live Killers, 1979; Flash Gordon (film soundtrack), 1980; Greatest Hits, 1981; Hot Space, 1982; The Works, 1984; The Complete Works, 1985; A Kind Of Magic, 1986; Live Magic, 1986; The Miracle, 1989; Innuendo, 1991; Greatest Hits II, 1991; Live At Wembley '86, 1992; Made In Heaven, 1995; Singles include: Killer Queen, 1974; Now I'm Here, 1975; Bohemian Rhapsody (Number 1, UK), 1975; You're My Best Friend, 1976; Somebody To Love, 1977; We Are The Champions, 1977; Bicycle Race, 1978; Don't Stop Me Now, 1979; Love Of My Life, 1979; Crazy Little Thing Called Love, 1979; Save Me, 1980; Play The Game, 1980; Another One Bites The Dust (Number 1, US), 1980; Flash,1981; Under Pressure, with David Bowie (Number 1, UK), 1981; Radio Ga Ga, 1984; I Want To Break Free, 1984; It's A Hard Life, 1984; Hammer To Fall, 1984; One Vision, 1985; A Kind Of Magic, 1986; I Want It All, 1989; Breakthru, 1989; The Invisible Man, 1989; Innuendo (Number 1, UK), 1991; Headlong, 1991; The Show Must Go On, 1991; Heaven For Everyone, 1995; Too Much Love Will Kill You, 1995. Honours include: Britannia Award, 1977; Gold Ticket, Madison Square Gardens, 1978; Ivor Novello Awards: Best Selling British Record, 1976; Outstanding Contribution to British Music, 1987; Silver Clef Award, Nordoff-Robbins Music Therapy Centre, 1984; BRIT Awards: Outstanding Contribution to British Music, 1990; Best British Single, 1991. Current Management: c/o Jim Beach, Queen Productions, 46 Pembridge Road, London W11 3HN, England.

DEAMER Clive, b. 10 Feb 1961, Surrey, England. Musician (drums); Singer. m. Anne Bulhakow, 25 Mar 1995, 1 son. Career: with Hawkwind, Earth Ritual Tour, 1983; Session work includes Van Morrison; Toured with Jerry Lee Lewis; Performed with Eric Clapton; Gary Brooker; Andy Fairweather Low; Jeff Beck; Various television and radio sessions include White Room, with Portishead. Recordings include: Dummy, with Portishead; Crazy Legs, Jeff Beck and the Big Town Playboys; Rust, Kevin Brown. Honours: Platinum disc, Dummy; Mercury Award, 1995. Membership: Musicians' Union. Hobbies: Karate (Shoto-Ryn); Cycling; Cooking; Bonsai trees. Address: 49 First Avenue, Oldfield Park, Bath BA2 3NW, England.

DEAN Elton, b. 28 Oct 1945. Musician (saxello, alto saxophone). m. Marie-Noelle Sala, 16 Jan 1988, 1 daughter. Musical Education: Self-taught. Career: Worked with: Keith Tippett Sextet; Soft Machine, Proms concert, 1970; Brotherhood Of Breath; London Jazz Composer's Orchestra; Carla Bley; Leader, Just Us; EDQ; Own nine-piece group Ninesense, 1975; Elton Dean Quintet, tour of Brazil, British Council, 1986; Leader, various groups including: Unlimited Saxophone Company; In Cahoots; Equip Out; Formed quartet with Howard Riley. Recordings: with Julie Driscoll: Julie Driscoll; with Julie Tippetts: Sunset Glow; with Soft Machine: Third; Fourth; Fifth; with Robert Wyatt: End Of An Ear; with Keith Tippett: I Am There...You Are Here; Dedicated To You...But You Weren't Listening; with Keith Tippett's Centipede: Septober Energy; with Ninesense: Oh! For The Edge; Happy Daze; with Elton Dean Quintet:Boundaries; with Elton Dean and Alan Skidmore: El Skid; with Carla Bley: European Tour; with Dean, Gallivan, Wheeler: The Cheque Is In The Mail; Other recordings include: Elton Dean Duos, Trios, Quartet; Elton Dean's Unlimited Saxophone Company; Elton Dean/Howard Riley Quartet; Elton Dean: The Vortex Tapes; If Dubois Only Knew, with Paul Dunmall duo, 1996; Silent Knowledge, Elton Dean Quintet, 1996; Rumours of an Incident, Quintet with Roswell Rudd, 1997; Bladik, with Mujician and Roswell Rudd, 1997. Address: 7 Farleigh Road, London N16 7TB, England.

DEAN Johnny, b. 1972. Singer; Songwriter. Career: Singer, songwriter, Menswear, 1994-; Television includes: Later With... Britpop Now, 1995; Support tours with: The Charlatans, US; Pulp, Europe; Several headline UK tours; Major concerts include: Heineken Festival, Leeds, 1995. Recordings: Album: Nuisance, 1995; Singles: I'll Manage Somehow, 1995; Daydreamer, 1995. Address: c/o Laurel Records, PO Box 1422, Chancellors House, Chancellors Road, London W6 9SG, England.

DEARIE Blossom, b. 28 Apr 1928, East Durham, New York, USA. Singer; Songwriter; Musician (piano). Musical Education: Piano lessons from age 5; Studied classical music. Career: Joined the Blue Flames, vocal group within the Woody Herman Big Band; Member, The Blue Reys, in the Alvino Rey Band; Moved to Paris, founder member, vocal group, the Blue Stars, 1952; Returned to New York, solo artiste, New York nightclubs; Annual appearances, Ronnie Scott's Club, London, 1966-; Formed own record company, Daffodil Records, 1971; Played Carnegie Hall with Joe Williams, and jazz vocalist Anita O'Day in show the Jazz Singers, 1970s; 6 months a year, The Ballroom, Manhattan, 1983-; Appeared The Pizza On the Park, late 80s/early 90s. Compositions include: I Like You You're Nice; I'm Shadowing You; Hey John. Recordings: Albums include: My Gentleman Friend, 1961; May I Come In?, 1966; The Special Magic Of Blossom Dearie, 1975; My New Celebrity Is You, 1979; Blossom Dearie Sings 1973, 1979; Blossom Dearie Sings 1975, 1979; Winchester In Apple Blossom Time, 1979; May I Come In?, 1981; Blossom Dearie, 1983; Needlepoint Magic, 1988; Featuring Bobby Jasper, 1988; Songs Of Chelsea, 1988; Et Tu Bruce, 1989; Once Upon A Summertime, 1993. Honours: First recipient, Mabel Mercer Foundation Award, 1985. Current Management: F Sharp Productions, Penthouse B, 157 W 57th Street, New York, NY 10019, USA.

DEARNLEY Mark, b. 12 Aug 1957, Barnet, England. Record Producer; Engineer; Musician (keyboards). Education: Southampton University. Musical Education: Piano, Organ. Career: Engineer credits include: AC/DC, 3 albums; Circus of Power; The English Beat, 3 albums; Joan Armatrading; Def Leppard, remix; Producer credits include: The Dog's D'Amour, 3 albums; Steve Jones; Mother Love Bone; The Quireboys; Loudness; Bang Tango; Die Cheerleader; Owen Paul; The Wild Family. Honours: Numerous Platinum, Gold and Silver records. Hobbies: Tennis; Table Tennis. Current Management: Worlds End (America) Inc. Address: 183 N Martel Avenue, Suite 270, Los Angeles, CA 90036, USA.

DEDIC Srdan, b. 13 July 1965, Zagreb, Croatia. Composer; Arranger; Musician (piano). Musical Education: Degree in Composition, Zagreb Academy of Music; Specialisation at l'Universitè des Sciences Humaines de Strasbourg; Sweelinck Conservatorium, Amsterdam. Career: Participated at Gaudeamus Festival (Amsterdam); International Rostum of Composers (Paris); Music Biennale, Zagreb; Performed solo from own compositions: Mouvemente Concertante, with Zagreb Philharmonic; 9 orchestral performances; Over 50 performances in Europe, America, Australia; Writing music for television, theatres, films. Compositions: Snake Charmer, bass clarinet solo, 1986; Beat On, for orchestra, 1988; Canzona, cello, guitar, 1988; Calix, symphonic poem, 1990; At The Party, 1990; Concerto for cello and chamber orchestra; 12 compositions recorded for Croatian Radio; Supercussion album includes composition: At The Party. Publications: Composing Using Music Software (brochure). Honours: First Prize, UNESCO - International Rostrum of Composers, Paris, 1988; Award, student orchestral works, Music Biennale Zagreb, 1989; Winner, Composition Contest, 29th annual Contemporary Music Festival, Indiana State University, 1995. Membership: Croatian Composers Society. Hobby: Music software programming. Current Management: Dr Peter Höhn, Schanze 13, D 57392 Schmallenberg, Germany. Address: Srdan Dedic, Hugo de Grootplein 12, 1052 KW Amsterdam, Netherlands.

DEE Brian, b. 21 Mar 1936, London, England. Musician (piano). m. 28 Dec 1966, to 1982, 1 son, 1 daughter. Musical Education: Local teacher, 6 years. Career: Jazz pianist, late 1950s-; Session musician and accompanist; Extensive BBC radio with trio and many bands; Currently pianist with: Ted Heath Orchestra; Kenny Baker Dozen; Laurie Johnson; Performed at numerous concerts and festivals. Compositions: Background music. Recordings: Featured on approximately 12 albums in 3 years, including own albums. Memberships: PRS; Musicians' Union; BASCA. Hobbies: Watching speedway; Football. Address: 130 Sheering Mill Lane, Sawbridgeworth, Hertfordshire CM21 9ND, England.

DEE Kiki (Pauline Matthews), b. 6 Mar 1947, Bradford, England. Singer. Career: Leader, Kiki Dee band; Recording artist, 1964-; First white artist signed to Tamla-Motown; Cabaret singer, Europe and South Africa; Appearances, London musicals: Pump Boys and Dinettes, 1984; Blood Brothers, 1989; Solo acoustic tour with guitarist Carmelo Uggeri, support to Jools Holland, UK, 1995. Recordings: Albums: I'm Kiki Dee, 1968; Great Expectations, 1971; Loving And Free, 1973; I've Got The Music In Me, 1974; Kiki Dee, 1977; Stay With Me, 1979; Perfect Timing, 1982; Angel Eyes, 1987; Almost Naked, 1995; Singles include: I'm Gonna Run Away From You; Running Out Of Fools; Amoureuse, 1973; I've Got The Music In Me, 1974; How Glad I Am, 1975; Don't Go Breaking My Heart, duet with Elton John (Number 1, UK and US), 1976; Star, 1981. Honours: Olivier Award Nomination, 1989.

DEFRANCO Buddy (Boniface Ferdinand Leonard), b. 17 Feb 1923, Camden, New Jersey, USA. Musician (clarinet); Bandleader. m. Joyce

Yount, 1 son. Musical Education: Mastbaum Music School, Philadelphia. Career: Clarinet/saxophone player with: Johnny Davis Band, 1939; Gene Krupa Orchestra, 1941-42; Tommy Dorsey Orchestra, 1944-48; Count Basie Septet, 1950; Bandleader, Buddy DeFranco Orchestra, 1951; Clarinettist, Jazz At The Philharmonic All-Star Tours, 1952-54; Conductor, Glenn Miller Orchestra, 1966-74; Bandleader, Buddy DeFranco Group, 1974-. Recordings: Albums: Flying Fingers Of Art Tatum and Buddy DeFranco; Cross-Country Suite (with Nelson Riddle); Mr Lucky; Mood Indigo; Chicago Fire (with Terry Gibbs); George Gershwin Songbook (with Oscar Peterson). Publications: Buddy DeFranco on Jazz Improvisation, 1973; Modern Jazz Studies, 1973; Studies For Clarinet, 1973. Honours: Voted Best Jazz Clarinettist, numerous magazine polls; Grammy Award, Cross-Country Suite, 1956. Memberships: Fellow, National Association Jazz Educators; ASCAP; Board of Directors, ClariNetwork, 1980-. Address: c/o Abby Hoffer Enterprises, 223 1/2 E. 48th Street, New York, NY 10017, USA.

DEGRYSE Fabien, b. 6 Nov 1960, Brussels, Belgium. Guitarist; Composer; Teacher. m. Guns Colette, 1985, 2 sons, 2 daughters. Education: Certificate, Berklee College of Music, Boston, USA, 2 years. Career: Played with Zar, 1985-87, including tour in Canada and Belgium; Played with Quadruplex, 1985-92; Concerts with PH Catherine and Toots Thielemans; Played with Panta Rhei including recording of 3 CD's and numerous concerts and festivals between 1994 and 1997, in Europe and Africa; Still plays with L'Ame Des Poetes including Recording of 2 CD's and numerous concerts and festivals and broadcasting in Europe, Africa and Canada, 1994; Tchr, Jazz Guitar, Conservatory of Brussels, Belgium. Recordings: Quadruplex, CD, 1990; Medor Sadness, CD, 1992; Hommage á René Thomas, CD, 1997. Current Management: Rue E Laurent 100, 1420 Braine L'Alleud, Belgique.

DEHAVEN Penny (Charlotte), b. 17 May 1948, Winchester, Virginia, USA. Singer; Actress. Career: As Penny Starr: Singer on Jamboree USA; Name changed to Penny Dehaven; One of first female singers to entertain US troops in Vietnam; Film appearances include: Country Music Story; Travelling Light; Honky Tonk Man. Recordings: Singles: Grain Of Salt; I Feel Fine; Land Mark Tavern (with Del Reeves); We Made Memories (with Boxcar Willie); Albums: Penny DeHaven, 1972; Penny DeHaven, 1984. Film soundtrack, Bronco Billy. Current Management: Morningstar Public Relations, PO Box 83, Brentwood, TN 37027, USA.

DEKKER Desmond (Desmond Dacres), b. 16 July 1941, Kingston, Jamaica. Singer. Career: Solo artiste, also with own group, The Aces, 1963-; Concerts and tours include: Caribbean Music Festivals, Wembley, 1969, 1970; Ethiopian Benefit Concert, London (with Smiley Culture, Lee Perry, Dennis Brown), 1985; Regular international tours. Recordings include: Albums: This Is Desmond Dekker, 1969; Israelites, 1969; Black And Dekker, 1980; Compass Point, 1981; Hit singles: 20 Number 1 recordings in Jamaica; Also: 007 (Shanty Town), 1967; The Israelites (Number 1, UK), 1969; You Can Get It If You Really Want (Number 2, UK), 1970. Honour: First Jamaican artiste to have UK Number 1 record, 1969. Address: c/o Barry Collings Entertainments, 21a Clifftown Road, Southend-on-Sea, Essex SS1 1AB, England.

DEL FRA Riccardo, b. 20 Feb 1956, Rome, Italy. Musician (double bass); Composer. Education: 3 years university, studying Sociology. Musical Education: Double bass, Conservatorio di Frosinone; Private studies; Self-taught guitar. Career: Member, RAI TV Orchestra, Rome; Played with pianist Enrico Pieranunzi; Freelance backing musician, touring with artists in Italy

including: Slide Hampton; Art Farmer; Kai Winding; Played with Chet Baker, trio and quartet (9 years partnership, 12 albums, radio, television and films, tours of Europe and Japan); Freelance work with Johnny Griffin; Toots Thielemans (tours of USA and Japan); Bob Brookmeyer; Also played with Art Blakey and the Jazz Messengers; Kenny Wheeler; Paul Motian; Sonny Stitt; James Moody; Clifford Jordan; Joe Diorio (tours of Italy). Compositions: Silent Call (for jazz quartet and string orchestra); Inner Galaxy (for tenor sax, double bass and four cellos); Aux Fontaines Du Temple (for jazz septet, flutes, harp and string orchestra); Many pieces for different jazz ensembles. Recordings: A Sip Of Your Touch; 12 with Chet Baker include: Chet Sings Again; Mr B; At The Capolinea; Paris Suite, with Bob Brookmeyer; Also recorded with Dominique Pifarely. Honours: Grand Prix FNAC '89, A Sip Of Your Touch, 1989; `Choc' du Monde de la Musique. Hobbies: Reading; Travelling. Current Managment: Helene Manfredi, 118 Rue du Chateau, Des Rentiers, 75013 Paris. Address: 15 Rue des Fontaines du Temple, 75003 Paris, France.

DELAGAYE Freddy, b, 6 June 1944, Eeklo, Belgium. Musician (trumpet); Producer; Impressario. m. Veronica Ng, 7 Mar 1977, 1 son. Education: Economics/languages: Dutch; French; German; English. Musical Education: Music Academy, piano, trumpet. Career: Tour with various bands: Gerry Hayes Orchestra; Bob Azzam Band, from early 60's; With own band the Freddy Delagaye Clan, late 70's-; Numerous concerts and television appearances in most European countries, Middle East, South East Asia, 1980-; MSP (Music and Show Productions), own company in Belgium for television, concerts and special events; Represents: Wall Street Crash; Helen Shapiro; Pasadena Roof Orchestra; Les Bubb. Recordings: Bob Azzam Band: Mustapha; C'est Ecrit Dans Le Ciel; Luna Capresse; Various studio sessions in: Benelux; Scandinavia; France; Germany; Switzerland. Honours: Twice winner: Euro Star Festival, representative of UK Artists: Cantabile, 1987; Fairer Sax, 1988; Award for organizing 100th day festivities, Ghent, Belgium. Membership: BVI (Professional Association Impressarios), Belgium. Hobbies: Director, Big Band; Music for fun; Tennis; Holidays with family, friends. Address: Galgestraat 1, 9970 Kaprijke, Belgium.

DELAKIAN Michel Horen, b. 6 Nov 1957, Saint Etienne, France. Musician (trumpet); Composer. m. Isabelle, 20 Feb 1982, 1 son, 1 daughter. Musical Education: Ecole Nationale de Musique, St Etienne. Career: Member, Claude Bolling Big Band, 1982-; Also played with: Martial Solal, 1983-85; Orchestre National de Jazz, 1986-89; Michel Legrand, 1994-95; Sacha Distel et les Collegiens, 1994-95; Leads own quartet; Television: Musiques Au Coeur, France 2, 1992; Jazz A Juan, 1986; Jazz 6, 1988; Tours include: Africa, 1986; Canada, 1987; USA, 1988, 1989, 1991; Thailand; China, 1994; Mexico, 1995; Turkey, 1995. Recordings: Solo: Biarritz, with Orchestre National De Jazz: 1986; 1987; with Claude Bolling Big Band: Plays Ellington (Volumes 1 & 2); Also recorded with Stephane Grappelli. Publications: Nina, 2 compositions, included in Le Livre Du Jazz En France. Honours: Prix Sidney Bechet, Académie Du Jazz, 1987. Memberships: SACEM; ADAMI; SPEDIDAM. Hobbies: Reading; Travels; Tennis; Swimming. Current Management: Mathilde Creixams Coordination Musicale. Address: 14 Rue Giradon, 75018 Paris, France.

DELANEY Larry (Lawrence), b. 30 Aug 1942, Eastview, Ontario, Canada. Newspaper Editor; Publisher. m. Joanne Bonell, 1 Aug 1964, 1 son, 1 daughter. Education: College. Career: Co-founder, current Editor, Publisher, Country Music News, Canada's national music newspaper, established 1980, providing international exposure and profile for Canadian country music artists and industry. Publications: Country Music News. Honours: 8 times recipient, Canadian Country Music Association: Country Music Person of The Year; Inducted into Builders Category, Canadian Music Hall Of Fame, 1989; Inducted into Canadian Country Music Hall of Honour, 1996. Memberships: CCMA; CMA; CPPA. Hobbies: Vinyl Album Collector. Address: PO Box 7323 Vanier Term, Ottawa, Ont K1L 8E4, Canada.

DELANO Darlene, b. 27 Sept 1955, Hartford, Connecticut, USA. Public Relations Executive; Artist Manager. m. 23 June 1976 to 28 Oct 1983, 1 daughter. Education: BA, University of Connecticut. Career: Publicist for: Carmine Appice; Yngwie Malmsteen; Coma; Management for: The Itch; Naked Rhythm; John Goodwin. Honour: Women In Business Award, 1993. Membership: Licensed Talent Agent, State of Florida. Current Management: Long Distance Entertainment. Address: PO Box 223907, Hollywood, FL 33023, USA.

DELBECQ Benoît Henri André, b. 6 June 1966, St Germain en Laye, France. Composer; Musician (piano, prepared p, synthesisers). Education: Bac (France) A4 + D (Philosophy, Maths, Biology, Physics). Musical Education: Studies at Versailles National Conservatory; Banuff School Of Fine Arts, Canada, 1987, 1990. Career: Major French and European Festivals (Jazz), 1990-; Central African tour, 1994; Canadian tour, 1995; Dutch tour, 1995. Recordings: Paintings, B Dalbecq, 1992; Rhymes, The Recyclers, 1994; Pression, Kartet, 1995. Memberships: SACEM; SACD; SPEDIDAM; ADAMI; Hask Association, Astrolab Association. Current Management: Atralent. Address: 20 Rue de la Jonquière, 75017 Paris, France.

DELGADO Junior (Oscar Hibbert), b. 1958, Kingston, Jamaica. Reggae Singer. Career: School concerts and local talent contests; Singer with Time Unlimited; Solo artist, 1975-; Owner, Incredible Jux record label, Jamaica. Recordings: Singles: with Time Unlimited: Reaction; The Twenty Third Psalm; Numerous solo recordings include: Rasta Dreadlocks; Skanga; Run Baldhead; Thinking; Every Natty; Tition; Devil's Throne; Love Won't Come Easy; Trickster; Armed Robbery; Away With Your Fussing And Fighting; Fisherman Row; Jah Stay; Nine Fence; Poverty; Illegal Gun; Bus I Skull; Raggamuffin Year; Forward Revolution; Hanging Tree; Riot Inna Juvenile Prison; Dubschool; We A Blood. Address: c/o Rick Davey, Unit C, Imperial Works, Perren Street, London NW5 7EE, England.

DELIA (aka Sparrow McShade), b. 14 Nov 1969, London, England.Musician (guitar, flute, drums); Vocalist. Musical Education: Grade 3 flute; GCSE Music; Islington Sixth Form Centre. Career: Member, Mambo Taxi, 1991-95; Extensive English tours; 1 album, 3 singles; Television and radio appearances include: Chart Show, ITV; Local television; BBC Radio 1; GLR; Member, Phantom Pregnancies, 1995-; Scott Bond Commandos, 1995-; Low Down No Goods, 1995-. Recordings: Various split singles and compilation tracks; Latest album: Assassination City, 1995. Publications: But That's Downbeat And Ridiculous Shawn. Honours: Too Pure Awards, 1994. Memberships: PRS; Musicians' Union. Address: c/o Rough Trade Shop, 130 Talbot Road, London W11 1JA, England.

DELL'AMORE Franco, b. 26 Jan 1952, Cesena, Italy. Art Director; Artist Manager. Education: Degree, Political Sciences, Degree in Musicology, University at the Bologna. Musical Education: Degree Musicology/Specialization courses: Musical Philology; Master in Electronic Music. Career: Music Consultant for several cultural institutions; Artistic director, important cultural events, summertime festivals; Italian booking manager, prestigious early music ensembles, world music artists. Publications:

Numerous essays, musicological reviews; Various works on music matters; Currently manager in Italy for Farafina; Terem Quartet; Oumou Sangare; Les Tambours de Bronx; Radio Tarifa; Misia; Les Musiciens du Nil; Alessandro Stradella Cousort; STC. Address: c/o Dell'Amore Management, Via Zefferino Re, 2c 47023 Cesena (Fo), Italy.

DELP Brad, b. 12 June 1951, Boston, Massachusetts, USA. Musician (guitar); Singer. Career: Founder member, US rock group Boston, 1976-; One of most successful debut albums ever (17 million album sales in US alone), 1978; UK tour, 1979; US tour, 1987; Guest with Ringo Starr, 1989; Formed RTZ, 1991; Guest with Nelson, 1991. Recordings: Albums: Boston (Number 1, US), 1976; Don't Look Back (Number 1, US), 1978; Third Stage (Number 1, US), 1986; with RTZ: Return To Zero, 1991; Hit singles: with Boston: More Than A Feeling, 1976; Long Time, 1977; Peace Of Mind, 1977; Don't Look Back, 1978; Amanda, 1986; We're Ready, 1987; Cantcha Say, 1987. Current Management: Boston, PO Box 6191, Lincoln Center, MA 01773, USA. Address: c/o PGE, 244 Pleasant Street, Franklin, MA 02038, USA.

DELS Anita. Singer. Career: Singer, Belgian Dance group 2 Unlimited, 1992-. Recordings: Albums: No Limits, 1993; Real Things, 1994; Hits Unlimited, 1995; Singles: No Limits; Tribal Dance; Let The Beat Control Your Body; The Real Thing; No One. Honours: MTV Award Nominations: Best Dance Act; Best Song, Let The Beat Control Your Body. Current Management: Michel Maartens, CBA Artists, PO Box 1495, 1200 BL Hilversum, Netherlands.

DELVAUX Floch, b. 26 January 1968, Bruxelles, Belgium. Singer; Guitarist; Songwriter. Education: Classical music lessons, Bruxelles; Selftaught guitar. Career: Guitarist and Songwriter, Brain Damage and Depth, 1986-89; Singer and Songwriter, Brain Damage and Death, 1989-92; Singer, Guitarist and Songwriter, Goyasnada, 1990-; Singer, Guitarist and Songwriter, K-02 Office, 1994-. Compositions: Several songs with Goyasnada, some released on several compilations CD; Dreamland, most successful, recorded 1992. Recordings: LP with Brain Damage and Death, 1993, titled, 1986-92; CD album with K-02 Office, 1996, titled Rage Rage Rage. Address: c/o Delvaux Floch, 5 Rue du Pacifique, 1180 Bruxelles, Belgium.

DEMELEMESTER Marc (Rocky) Jean Louis, b. 8 July 1955, Lille Nord, France. Musician (guitar); Singer; Executive Producer. m. Laurence Singery, 10 Dec 1988, 2 sons. Education: Specialized educator for malajusted children diploma. Musical Education: Self-taught. Career: Television show: In Paris, with Eric Burdon, 1977; Palais des Sport, Johnny Halliday, 1982; Zenith, Paris with Johnny Halliday, 1984; Canadian tours with Herbert Leonard, 1986-88; with AMX Group, Olympia, Paris, 1988; Zenith, Paris, with Hubert Felix Thiefaine, 1994; Live concert recordings: Johnny Halliday, Palais des Sport, 1982; Johnny Halliday, Zenith, 1984; John Morgan, 24 Hours in Brittany; Hubert Felix Thiefaine, Zenith, Paris, 1994. Recordings: Singles: 1st, Rocky and AMX 1985; 2nd, Rocky and AMX, 1986; Rocky and AMX, 1988; Album: Dallas Group, 1981. Honours: 2 Gold discs with Dallas Group. Memberships: SACEM (France); SPEDIDEM (Paris). Hobbies: Karate (shotokan); Bike. Current Management: FAM Management, Paris. Address: 3 Rue du 4 Aout, 77200 Torcy, France.

DEML Markus, b. 9 August 1967, Prague, Czechoslovakia. Guitarist; Producer; Songwriter. Education: Musikhochschule, Hamburg (Music University); Guitar Institute of Technologie, Los Angeles. Career: Worldwide & European tours with Saga, John Wetton, Kingdom Come, Rödelheimhartreim - project appearances on MTV's Most Wanted Hangin Out; Rock and Ring,

Montreau Jazz Festival. Compositions: Earth Nation (Thoughts in Past Future); Errorhead, solo project; The Other Side, album. Recordings: Errorhead (The Other Side); Kingdom Come (Twilight Cruiser); Bobby Kimball (Rise Up); Earth Nation (Thoughts in Past Future); Rödelheim HP (Direkt aus Rödelheim); SNAP (Welcome to Tomorrow). Publications: Errorhead, The Other Side, 1998. Memberships: GEMA; GVL. Hobbies: Sports; Music. Address: Alex Merch Music, Trajamstr 18, D-50678, Koeln, address: Koselstr 56, 60318, Frankfurt, Germany.

DEMPSEY Gaylene Katharan, b. 1 Aug 1960, Winnipeg, Manitoba, Canada. Executive Director. m. David Sherman, 10 Apr 1993. Education: Creative Communications (Journalism Major); Managing and Leading in non-profit Sector Certificate, 1995. Career: Editor, Circuit, monthly entertainment paper, 1989-; Editor in Chief, The Insider, monthly entertainment paper, 1990-; Editor, Jazz Winnipeg Festival Programme, 1990-; Volunteer, Winnipeg Folk Festival, 1990-; Executive Director, Manitoba Audio Recording Industry Association (MARIA), 1991-; Represent the Manitoba Music Industry from songwriters to labels; Freelance work. Publications: SOCAN Words and Music, several articles; Grafitti Magazine, several articles. Memberships: FACTOR National Advisory Board; Artspace, Executive Member. Hobbies: Music; Festivals; Theatre; Golf; Travel; Reading Magazines and other non-fiction. Address: #1-242 Spence Street, Winnipeg, Manitoba, R3C 1Y4, Canada.

DEMUS Chaka (John Taylor), b. 1965, West Kingston, Jamaica. Rapper. Career: Rapper, billed as Nicodemus Jr, on various sound systems including Supreme and Jammy's; Changed name to Chaka Demus, 1985; Solo artiste, 1985-91; Rapper, in duo Chaka Demus and Pliers, 1991-. Recordings: Singles: as Chaka Demus: Increase Your Knowledge; One Scotch, One Bourbon, One Beer; 2 Foot Walk; Chaka On the Move; with Chaka Demus and Pliers: Gal Wine; Rough this Year; Love Up the Gal; Without Love; Winning Machine; Worl' A Girls; Murder She Wrote; Tease Me; She Don't Let Nobody; Twist and Shout, number 1, UK, 1993; Albums: Solo: Everybody Loves the Chaka, 1988; The Original Chaka, 1989; with Chaka Demus and Pliers: Gal Wine, 1992; Ruff This Year, 1992; Chaka Demus and Pliers, 1992; Tease Me, 1993; with Shabba Ranks: Rough and Rugged, 1987. Address: c/o Free World Music Inc, 230 12th Street, Suite 117, Miami Beach, FL 33139-4603, USA.

DENCH Ian. Musician (guitar); Songwriter. Career: Member, EMF. Recordings: Albums: Schubert Dip; Stigma; Cha Cha Cha, 1995; Singles: Unbelieveable (Number 1, US); Unexplained (EP); Perfect Day, 1995; I'm A Believer (with Vic Reeves and Bob Mortimer), 1995. Current Management: Bedlam Management, PO Box 3074, London W4 4ZN, England.

DENNARD David Brooks, b. 5 July 1950, Dallas, Texas, USA. Record Company Executive; Musician (bass guitar, guitar, dobro, harmonica). m. Mary Anna Austin, 4 Oct 1980, 2 daughters. Education: Colorado College, Stanford; University of Texas-Austin. Career: CBS/Epic Records recording artist with: Gary Myrick And The Figures; Extensive touring, 1979-1983; President, Owner, Dragon Street Records Inc, 1989-; Director of A&R, Crystal Clear Sound; Director, Steve Records, Dallas. Recordings: with Gary Myrick and the Figures: 2 albums, 2 singles, 7 videos, 250,000 combined sales; Recent releases by Ronnie Dawson, Gene Summers, Scott Whitaker, Buck Jones, Centromatic, Meredith Louise Miller and Pump'n Ethyl. Honours: Award of Excellence, Dallas Society of Visual Communications, 1987; 2 Silver Microphone Awards, 1987; Crystal Award, 1988; Topaz Award, Best Record Company, Steve Records, 1997.

Memberships: NARAS; Texas Music Association, Dallas; Cable Access of Dallas Inc. Hobbies: Swimming; Record collecting; Dogs; Tennis; Gardening. Address: Dragon Street Records Inc, PO Box 670714, Dallas, TX 75367-0714, USA.

DENNEHY Timothy Christopher, b. 29 Dec 1952, Cahersiveen, County Kerry, Ireland. National Teacher; Broadcaster; Singer. m. Máirín, 19 Mar 1976, 2 sons. Musical Education: From oral tradition. Career: Numerous radio appearances, local, national, including own programme on Clare FM: Cuaird An Domhnaigh (Keep in Touch); Television programmes dealing with Irish traditional music; Regular performer at workshops, recitals, concerts throughout Ireland; Founded the Góilin Traditional singers club, with Donall De Barra, Dublin, 1979. Compositions: Many original songs. Recordings: A Thimbleful Of Song; A Winter's Tear - Traditional And Original Songs; Farewell to Miltown Malbay, 1997. Publication: Working on biography of writer Sigerson Clifford. Memberships: IMRO; Cumann Cheoltíre Eireann. Hobbies: Music; Singing; Sport; Reading; Walking. Address: Markham's Cross, Mullagh, Co. Clare, Ireland.

DENNERLEIN Barbara, b. 25 September 1964, Munich, Germany. Jazz Musician; Composer; Producer. m. Andre Baldi. Education: Study of Music Science, Ludwig Maximilian University, Munich; Selftaught Organ Player. Career: Film Music, (title music), Die Partner; WDR/ARD Concerts at all Important Jazz Festivals, Den Haag, New Zealand, Montreal, Vancouver, Toronto, Edmonton, Victoria, Norway, Berlin, Frankfurt; Concerts worldwide, London, Ronnie Scott's, Tokyo, Blue Note, New York, Blue Note, Sweet Basil, Paris. Compositions: 100 pieces on 15 records and CD's. Recordings: Jazz Live, 1983; Orgelspiele, 1984; Bebab, 1985; Tribute to Charlie, 1986; Straight Ahead, 1988; B D Plays Classics, 1988; Live on Tour, 1989; B D Due, 1990; Hot Stuff, 1990; Solo, 1992; That's Me, 1992; Take Off, 1996; Junkanovo, 1997. Honours: Jazz Award for Take Off, 1995, 1997; No 1, DWR Downbeat Critics Poll, 1996; Jazz Award for Junkanoo, 1997; 3 times, Preis der Deutschen Schallplattenkritik. Hobby: Music. Current Management: Newtone Management, Tsingtauer Str 66, 81827 Munchen, Germany. Address: Banhofstr 9B, 85774 Unterfohring, Germany.

DENNIS Cathy, b. 25 Mar 1970, Norfolk, England. Singer; Songwriter. Musical Education: Self-taught. Career: Featured singer, D-Mob, 1989; Solo artiste, songwriter, producer, 1990-; UK Tour; Television appearance: Beverly Hills 90210. Recordings: Solo albums: Move To This; Into The Skyline; Also featured on: A Little Bit Of This A Little Bit Of That, D-Mob, 1989; Looking Through Patient Eyes, PM Dawn. Singles: C'Mon And Get My Love, 1989; Touch Me All Night Long, 1991; Just Another Dream, 1991; Too Many Walls, 1991; Songs on numerous film soundtracks. Honours: Billboard Award, Best New Female Artist; World Music Award, Best International Newcomer; 2 BRIT Awards Nominations; Capital Radio Award, Best Female Artist; SOS Top Woman Award; SE Asia Awards, Top New Artist & Best Song of Year; 5 ASCAP Awards. Membership: ASCAP. Hobbies: Clubbing; Sports racing driving. Current Management: Simon Fuller, 19 Management Ltd (UK); William Morris Agency (US). Address: 19 Management, Unit 32, Ransomes Dock, 35-37 Parkgate Road, London SW11 4NP, England.

DENNIS Jon, b. 27 May 1965, Lewisham, London, England. Singer; Musician (guitar); Songwriter. Education: Leicester University. Career: Lead singer and guitarist with Blab Happy, 1987-93; Slinky, 1994-; Tours with Blab Happy: "Boat" tour, UK, 1991; Support to Kingmaker, "Eat Yourself Whole" UK tour, 1992; Support to Radiohead, "Pablo Money" UK tour, 1993; with Slinky: "Shoot Me Down" tour, 1995. Recordings:

with Blab Happy: EPs: It's Turned Out Nice Again, 1987; Fruits Of Your Labour, 1988; Mad Surge, 1991; Albums: Boat, 1991; Smothered, 1993; Singles: with Blab Happy: Down, 1991; Inside Out, 1992; Tender Hooks, 1993; with Slinky: Shoot Me Down, 1995. Membership: Musicians' Union. Address: 39 Nottingham Road, Leicester LE5 3TT, England.

DENSMORE John, b. 1 Dec 1944, Los Angeles, California, USA. Musician (drums). Education: Physics, Psychology. Career: Member, Psychedelic Rangers, 1965; Member, The Doors, 1966-72; Member, The Butts Band, 1972-; Session, solo work, 1972; Performances include: Northern California Folk-Rock Festival, 1968; Hollywood Bowl, later released as video, 1968; Toronto Rock'n'Roll Revival Show, 1969; Isle of Wight Festival, 1970; Film documentaries: The Doors Are Open, 1968; Feast Of Friends, 1969. Recordings: Albums: The Doors, 1967; Strange Days, 1967; Waiting For The Sun, 1968; Morrison Hotel, 1970; Absolutely Live, 1970; L A Woman, 1971; Other Voices, 1971; Weird Scenes Inside The Gold Mine, 1972; Full Circle, 1972; Live At The Hollywood Bowl, 1987; Singles: Light My Fire (Number 1US), 1967; Love Me Two Times, 1968; Hello I Love You (Number 1 US), 1968; Touch Me, 1969; Love Her Madly, 1971; Riders On The Storm, 1971.

DEPASS Michele Karina, b. 5 Jan 1965, Germany. Vocalist; Songwriter. Musical Education: 1 year MSc course, Composition, General Theory, Voice. Career: Lead vocals, Saxmachine, 1986-88; Lead vocals, The Happy End, 1986-87; Television, radio, UK tour, with Denise Black And The Kray Sisters, 1987; Lead, backing vocals, Luddy Sams and The Deliveries, 1987-88; Lead vocals, Benjamin Zephaniah and The Union Dance Company, 1988; Soundtrack vocals, The Kitchen Child, 1988; Vocals, Haji Ackbar, Pee Wee Ellis, Maceo Parker, 1988; Vocals in Welsh, Sinaid Jones, Si Yn Y Gwnt, 1990; Soundtrack vocals, Prime Suspect, Granada TV, 1992; Backing vocals, 7 Elvis Presley tracks for karaoke, 1994; lead duet vocals, Leo sayer, 1994; Working with T-Rextasy, BV's tribute band to Marc Bolan, 1995; Television include: The Glam Rock Show, Ch4, 1995; Punt And Dennis, BBC1, 1995. Recordings include: Co-writer, vocals, single: Pitter Patter Biscuit, 1989. Membership: Musicians' Union. Hobbies: Horse riding; Stained glass; Travel; Reading; Writing. Address: 13 Tabley Road, Holloway, London N7 0NA, England.

DEPOLO Ozren, b. 13 Mar 1930, Zagreb, Croatia. Musician (saxophones, clarinet, flute); Composer. m. 29 Jan 1959, Ljerka Polak, 2 sons, 1 daughter. Education: Medical Faculty, Zagreb, 1956; Musical Education: Clarinet, Conservatory of Music, Zagreb, graduated 1952. Career: Saxophone soloist, jazz and classical music; Lead alto saxophone, Zagreb Radio-TV big band, 1952-1991; Jazz Small Combos: Zagreb Jazz Quintet, Zagreb Jazz Sextet; Non Convertible International All Styars; International Festival Big Bands: Slide Hampton, Prague, 1978; Clark Terry, 1979; Jerry Mulligan, 1970; Oliver Nelson, Montreux, 1971; EBU (European RTV Union) Big Bands in Copenhagen; Barcelona; Sarajevo; Oslo; Classical Music: First performances, 3 saxophone concertos, Alto Saxophone and Symphony Orchestra: Despalji, 1964; Glazunov, 1968; Odak, 1980; Avantgarde music: Member, Acezantez group, modern music, 1966-1980; Appearances on many Jazz festivals, tours, concerts. Compositions: Music for 53 animated (cartoon) films; 4 films; 3 short documentary films; Music, songs, 5 theatre plays; 2 TV serials; many jazz compositions; songs; Music for children; Arrangements; Orchestrations for popular music. Recordings: Albums: Saxophone concertos; Mistery of Blues. Honours: Josip Slavenski, Musical Achievement. Memberships: Croatian Composers Society; Croatian Musicians' Union.

Hobby: Astronomy. Address: Ljudevita Posavskog 2, 41000 Zagreb, Croatia.

DEQUIDT Loïc, b. 1 May 1973, Arras, France. Jazz Musician (piano). Education: 2 years mathematics, University of Lille. Musical Education: Studies in Italy, with E Rava; F Dandrea; E Pieranunzi. Career: Played with Tommy Smith; Claus Stötter; Daniel Beaussier; Played in Paris; Rome; Brussels; Several festivals, France, Italy; Currently plays with Bruno Tommaso (Italy); Riccardo Delfra; Loïc Dequidt Trio. Radio appearances: France-Musique; France-Inter. Honour: Diploma, Siena Jazz Seminary, Italy. Address: 110 Rue Lepic, 75018 Paris, France.

DERRINGER Rick (Richard Zehringer), b. 5 Aug 1947, Fort Recovery, Ohio, USA. Musician (guitar); Record Producer. Career: Member, The McCoys, late 1960s; Member, Johnny Winter and Edgar Winter groups; Solo artiste, 1974-; Also leader, own group Derringer; Prolific session musician. Recordings: Solo albums: All American Boy, 1974; Spring Fever, 1975; Derringer, 1976; Sweet Evil, 1977; If You Weren't So Romantic, 1978; Guitars And Women, 1979; Face To Face, 1980; Rick Derringer, 1981; Good Dirty Fun, 1983; with Edgar Winter: White Trash, 1971; Road Work, 1972; They Only Come Out At Night, 1973; Shock Treatment, 1974; Jasmine Nightdream, 1975; With Rick Derringer, 1975; with Johnny Winter: Johnny Winter And Rick Derringer, 1971; Johnny Winter Live, 1971; Still Alive And Well, 1973; Saints And Sinners, 1974; John Dawson Winter III, 1974; The Johnny Winter Story, 1980; Lead guitar solo, Eat It, Weird Al Yankovic (parody of Michael Jackson's Beat It), 1984; Also featured on albums by: Air Supply; Donald Fagen; Dan Hartman; Cyndi Lauper; Bette Midler; Meat Loaf; Mason Ruffner; Todd Rundgren; Steely Dan; Bonnie Tyler; Rosie Vela. Current Management: Slatus Management, 208 East 51st Street, New York, NY 10022, USA.

DERUDDER Peter. Musician. Education: Classical, Flute, Uillean, Pipes, Bodhran, Whistles. Career: Group Member, The Swigshift; Dranouter Festival, 1995; Labadoux Festival, 1997; Den Ekster, 1996-97; Paulus Festival, 1997; Sloanthe Festival, 1997; De Brakke Grond, Amsterdam, 1997; National Radio, Radio 1 De Groote Boodschap, and several regional radio and television appearances. Compositions: Jumpin The Fences; Dirty Wally; Friend's Sadness; Something to Fear; Shut the Pub; A Whistler's Wedding. Recordings: 1 CD, Tales From the Great Whiskey Book, 1996. Honours: Government Medal for Flute, 1986; 2nd Place, Youth Soloist Festival, 1986; Finale, Westtalent, 1995. Membership: Volksmuziekfederatie, Belgium. Hobby: Music. Current Management: KAFT Producties, Akkerwindelaan 20, 8791 Beveren-Leie, Belgium. Address: Barrierestraat 49, 8940 Wervik, Belgium.

DERWIG Stijn, b. 22 December 1967, Tilburg, Netherlands. Education: Tilburg Teachers Degree, 1986-92; Tilburg Artist Degree, 1992-94. Career: Willeke, De Musical, Theatre, 1995; A Musical Century, Theatre, 1996; I Got Lyrics, Theatre, 1996; Dutch Students Orchestra, 1996; Der Zigeuner Baron, Theatre, 1997; Atilla, Theatre, 1997; Dutch Students Orchestra, 1998. Compositions: Danceable Ouverture, 1991; The Sounds of Shangha, 1992; Changing Bars, 1994; A Teachers Pension, 1996; Wedding Song, 1997. Recordings: Willeke De Musical, 1996; NTB Education Project, 1997. Membership: NTB Amsterdam. Hobbies: Making own percussion instrument sticks. Current Management: Frankenlaan 28, NL 5037 KJ, Tilburg. Address: Stijn Derwig, Frankenlaan 28, NL-5037 KJ, Tilburg, Netherlands.

DESANDRE-NAVARRE Xavier, b. 11 Oct 1961, Suresnes, Paris. Musician (percussion, drums); Composer. m. Susan Mouget, 5 Sept 1992, 1 daughter. Education: Licence en Sciences-Economiques. Musical Education: Self-taught. Career: Performer, 1989-; Appeared various festivals, radio and television shows, tours; Plays with: Gil Evans; Charlie Haden and Liberation Music Orchestra; Rita Mitsouko; Groove Collective; Orchestre National De Jazz (D Badault); Michel Portal; Iwao Furusawa. Recordings: with Gil Evans; Laurent Cugny Big Band; Orchestre National De Jazz; Alan Stivell; Tribalmopolite Percussion solo (show). Membership: Union des Musiciens de Jazz (France). Hobbies: French cooking; Sailboats. Address: 95 Avenue Jean Lolive, 93500 Pantin, France.

DESEO Csaba, b. 15 Feb 1939, Budapest, Hungary. Musician (Violin). m. Katalin Szony, 1 son. Education: Violin Teacher Diploma, Bartók Conservatory, Budapest, 1961. Career: Member, Hungarian National Philharmonic Orchestra, 1966-; Jazz Soloist, Combo Leader, 4 own LPs, 3 CDs, 1964-. Publications: Monthly jazz-broadcasts in Hungarian Radio; Jazz articles in Hungarian newspapers. Memberships: Hungarian Jazz Federation; Hungarian Composers' Union. Address: Bercsenyi U 36, H-1117 Budapest, Hungary.

DESMARAIS Lorraine, b. 15 August 1956, Montréal, Canada. Jazz Musician (Piano). Education: Master's Degree in Classical Piano, 1979; Jazz education in New York and Boston with Kenny Barron and Charlie Banacas. Career: Toured across Canada (jazz festivals) and US, in Europe (Switzerland), France, Belgium, Denmark, Asia (Indonesia, Philippines); One Woman show, The History of Piano Jazz. Compositions: Sonata for flute and piano. Recordings: Trio Lorraine Desmarais, 1985; Andiamo, 1986; Pianissimo, 1987; Vision, 1991; Lorraine Desmarais, 1995. Honours: Winner, Great American Jazz Piano Competition, Jacksonville, Jazz Festival, Florida, 1986; Winner, Montreal Jazz Festival, 1984; Canada Quebec Arts Council Grants. Current Management: Direction D'Artistes Fleming. Address: 5975 Av Du Parc, Montréal QC, H2V 4H4, Canada.

DETROIT Marcella (Marcy Levy). Singer; Songwriter; Musician (keyboards, guitar, harmonica). Career: Member, Shakespears Sister with Siobhan Fahey, 1988-93; Solo artist, 1993-. Compositions include: Co-writer, Lay Down Sally, hit for Eric Clapton, 1977; Co-writer with Siobhan Fahey, all tracks on album Hormonally Yours, 1992. Recordings: Albums: Sacred Heart, 1989; Hormonally Yours, 1992; Singles: You're History, 1989; Goodbye Cruel World, 1991; Stay (Number 1, UK), 1992; I Don't Care, 1992; Hello (Turn Your Radio On), 1992; My 16th Apology (EP), 1993; Honours: BRIT Award, Best Video, Stay, 1993; Ivor Novello Award, Outstanding Contemporary Song Collection, Hormonally Yours, 1993. Address: c/o John Campbell, 55 Chiswick High Road, London W4 2LT, England.

DEVIC Lino, b. 10 May 1954, Zagreb, Croatia. Musician (fretless bass, piano). Divorced, 2 sons, 1 daughter. Career: Many jazz festivals in former Yugoslavia and Germany; Studio works in France, 1976; Touring Germany with Trini Lopez; Plays with fusion trio, recorded 2 albums, 1994-. Compositions: 25 include: Boulevard Barbes; Blue Duck. Recordings: Drazen Boic Trio: Mirno Itiho (Peaceful And Quiet); LD Experience: LD Experience. Honours: At jazz festivals: Ingolstadt, Germany; Ljubjana; Zagreb; Maribor. Hobby: Walking with my dog. Current Management: A Zaie 39, Panton, Zagreb, Croatia. Address: N Grskovica 58, Zagreb, Croatia.

DEVINE Frank Thomas, b. 24 Nov 1946, Dundee, Scotland. Songwriter; Musician (drums, guitar, mandolin). m. Jacqueline Harper, 12 Jan 1968, 1 son, 1 daughter. Education: Moseley School of Art, Birmingham; Birmingham College of Art. Musical Education: Private drum tuition with Charles Burlison; Self-taught on stringed instruments. Career: Tour of England with Jimmy Cliff; Weekly appearances at the Marquee, London; Played with Blues Hounds and Mike Burney; Television appearance: Ready Steady Go (with the Alpines); Currently songwriter and plays guitar and mandolin. Recording: Limited edition album with Steve Winwood and Dave Mason (prior to formation of Traffic). Membership: Musicians' Union. Hobby: Painting. Address: Milford Hall Cottage, Main Road, Milford, Staffordshire ST17 0UL, England.

DEXTEXTER Even, b. 7 Apr 1971, Ellorio, Vizcaya, Spain. Musician (keyboards, bass, drums); Programmer. Education: University: 2 years of Psychology. Musical Education: 5 years, music and piano studies, Conservatoire of Logrono, La Rioja, Spain, 1982-1987; Career: Member, Dextexter, Nov 1994-; Tours include 2 club tours over London; 3 appearances on Basque, Spanish TV; Currently recording auto-produced and released first single. Membership: Musicians' Union. Hobbies: Personal research in psychoacoustics; Electroacoustics discipline. Current Management: DDT Management. Address: 70 Princes Square, London WL 4NY, England.

DI MEOLA Al, b. 22 July 1954, Jersey City, New Jersey, USA. Jazz Musician (guitar); Composer. Musical Education: Studied with Robert Aslanian; Berklee College of Music, Boston, 1971, 1974. Career: Musician with Barry Miles; Member, Chick Corea's Return To Forever, 1974-76; Solo guitarist, composer, 1976-; Tours as solo artiste; Also toured with acoustic trio (with John McLaughlin and Paco de Lucia); Leader, Al DiMeola Project (musicians include Airto Moreiro), 1985-. Recordings: Albums include: with Return To Forever: Where Have I Known You Before, 1974; No Mystery, 1975; Romantic Warrior, 1976; Best Of, 1980; Solo albums: Land Of Midnight Sun, 1976; Elegant Gypsy, 1977; Casino, 1978; Splendido Hotel, 1979; Electric Rendevous, 1982; Tour De Force Live, 1982; Scenario, 1983; Cielo e Terra, 1983; Soaring Through A Dream, 1985; Tiramu Su, 1988; World Sinfonia, 1990; Heart Of The Immigrants, 1993; Kiss My Axe, 1993; Orange And Blue, 1994; with John McLaughlin and Paco de Lucia: Friday Night In San Francisco, 1980; Passion, Grace And Fire, 1983; with Aziza Mustafa Zadeh: Dance Of Fire, 1995; with Jean-Luc Ponty, Stanley Clarke: The Rite Of Strings, 1996. Current Management: Don't Worry Inc., 111 W 57th Street, Suite 1120, New York, NY 11019, USA.

DIAMOND Jim, b. 28 Sept 1951, Glasgow, Scotland. Singer. Career: Member, bands including Jade; Bandit; PhD; Solo artiste, 1983-. Recordings: Solo albums: Double Crossed, 1985; Desire For Freedom, 1986; Jim Diamond, 1993; Singles include: I Won't Let You Down, PhD, 1982; Solo: I Should Have Known Better (Number 1, UK); Hi Ho Silver, theme song, UK television series Boon. Address: c/o LJE, 32 Willesden Lane, London NW6 7ST, England.

DIAMOND Neil Leslie, b. 24 Jan 1941, Brooklyn, New York, USA. Singer; Composer. m. Marcia Murphey, 1975, 4 children. Education: Pre-med student, New York University. Career: Songwriter for publishing company; Formerly with Bang and MCA Records, 1973-, with Columbia; Record 20 show run at Winter Garden Theatre, 1972; Tours worldwide, include: 2 year, Love In The Round, world tour; Television and radio specials, numerous including: Christmas specials, 1992, 1993; Acted with Sir Laurence Olivier in The Jazz Singer, 1980; Set major box office records world wide; 92 million albums sold. Compositions include: I'm A Believer (number 1 for Monkees); Film scores: Jonathan Livingston Seagull, 1973; Every Which Way But Loose, 1978; The Jazz Singer, 1980. Recordings: Albums include: The Feel Of Neil Diamond, 1966; Just For You, 1967; Shilo, 1970; Velvet Gloves and Spit, 1968; Touching You Touching Me; Stones, 1971; Hot August Nights; Moods, 1972; Jonathan Livingston Seagull, 1973; Serenade, 1974; Beautiful Noise, 1976; Live At The Greek, 1977; I'm Glad You're Here Tonight, 1977; You Don't Bring Me Flowers, 1978; September Morn, 1980; Jazz Singer, 1980; Song Sung Blue, 1982; Headed For The Future, 1986; Hot August Night II, 1987; The Best Years of Our Lives, 1989; Christmas Album, 1992; Greatest Hits 1966-1992, 1992; Up On the Roof - Songs From The Brill Building, 1993; Live In America, 1994; Christmas Album, Vol II, 1994; Tennessee Moon, 1996; Singles include: Sweet Caroline, 1969; Song Sung Blue; Cracklin' Rosie; I Am... I Said. Honours: Platinum, Gold Records; Globe Awards; Grammy, 1973 for: Jonathan Livingston Seagull. Membership: SESAC. Address: c/o Columbia Records, Media Department, 550 Madison Avenue, New York, NY 1002-3211, USA.

DIBANGO Manu, b. 12 Dec 1934, Douala, Cameroon. Musician (saxophone, piano). Musical Education: Classical piano. Career: Moved to Paris, 1949; Then Brussels, Belgium, 1956; Residency at Black Angels Club, Brussels; Joined band led by Joseph Kabsele, African Jazz, 1960; Played with African Jazz in Zaire to 1963; Returned to Cameroon, formed own band, 1963-65; Studio musician, Paris, 1965; Backed visiting black American and African musicians including: Peter Gabriel; Sinead O'Connor; Angélique Kidjo; Geoffrey Oryema; Ray Lema; Touré Kunda; Recording artiste, 1968-. Compositions: Commissioned by President Ahidjo to write patriotic song for Africa Cup football match, 1971. Recordings: Albums: O Boso, 1971; Soma Loba, 1972; Soul Makossa, 1973; Super Kumba, 1974; Manu 76, 1976; Afrovision, 1976; Big Blow, 1976; A L'Olympia, 1977; Ceddo, 1978; Gone Clear, 1980; Ambassador, 1980; Waka Juju, 1982; Deliverence, 1983; Sweet And Soft, 1983; Melodies Africaines Volumes 1 & 2, 1983; Deadline, 1984; Electric Africa, 1985; Afrijazzy, 1986; Negropolitains Vol 2, 1993; Wakafrika, 1994; Hit singles: Soul Makossa (hit in US, Europe, Africa); Wakafika; Big Blow; Sun Explosion; Abele Dance. Publication: Autobiography: Trois Kilos De Café, 1990. Membership: President, Francophone Diffusion. Honours: Gold disc, Soul Makossa; Grammy Award, Best R&B Instrumental Performance Of The Year, 1973. Current Management: IPS Management, 11-13 Rue Mont-Louis, 75011 Paris, France. Address: c/o Francophone Diffusion, 33 Rue du Fbg St Antoine, 75011 Paris, France.

DICK Arthur, b. 4 Aug 1954, Dundee, Scotland. Musician (guitar); Writer; Arranger. Education: First Class Honours, BSc, Liverpool University. Musical Education: Performing Diploma (guitar). Career: Numerous sessions as guitarist; Television appearances: Granada; Yorkshire; Thames; BBC; Central; Radio broadcasts: BBC; Capital; Picadilly, 1980-; MD for: Berni Flint, 1988; Susan Maughan; Recorded sessions for numerous artistes including: Cliff Richard; Paul McCartney; Cilla Black; Barbara Dickson; Formed Tracks Music for production of television and radio soundtracks, 1986; Lecturer, Goldsmith's College (London University); Guitar studies, recording, 1985-; Publications: Numerous for Music Sales Ltd; Works for Eric Clapton; Bon Jovi; Blues and Jazz compilations; Original guitar chord study; Guitar transcriptions of Santana; John Martyn; Robben Ford. Memberships: PRS; Musicians' Union. Hobbies: HiFi; Walking; Swimming; Theatre; Arts; Wine.

DICKINSON (Paul) Bruce, b. 7 Aug 1958, Worksop, Nottinghamshire, England. Singer; Author. Education: Degree, History, Queen Mary College, London University, 1979. Career: Member, groups Speed; Shots; Samson; Lead vocalist, UK heavy rock group Iron Maiden,

1981-93; Regular tours worldwide; Concerts include: Reading Festival, 1982; Monsters Of Rock Festivals, Castle Donington, 1988, 1992; Monsters Of Rock, Germany, 1988; Monsters Of Rock Festival, France, 1992; Super Rock '92, Germany, 1992. Recordings: Albums: with Iron Maiden: The Number Of The Beast, 1982; Piece Of Mind, 1983; Powerslave, 1984; Live After Death, 1985; Somewhere In Time, 1986; Seventh Son Of A Seventh Son, 1988; No Prayer For The Dying, 1990; Fear Of The Dark, 1992; A Real Live One, 1993; A Real Dead One, 1993; Solo albums: Tattooed Millionaire, 1990; Alive In Studio A, 1995; Skunkworks, 1996; Accident of Birth, 1997; Singles include: with Iron Maiden: Run To The Hills; The Number Of The Beast; Flight Of Icarus; The Trooper; 2 Minutes To Midnight; Aces High; Wasted Years; Stranger In A Strange Land; Can I Play With Madness; Evil That Men Do; The Clairvoyant; Bring Your Daughter To The Slaughter (from film A Nightmare On Elm Street 5); Be Quick Or Be Dead; From Here To Eternity; Solo singles: Tattooed Millionaire; All The Young Dudes; Dive! Dive! Dive!; Road to Hell. Publications: Novels: The Adventures Of Lord Iffy Boatrace, 1990; The Missionary Position, 1992. Hobby: Fencing (once rated in UK top 10). Address: c/o Sanctuary Music Management Ltd, 1st Floor Suite, The Colonnades, 82 Bishops Bridge Road, London W2 6BB, England.

DICKSON Barbara (Ruth), b. 27 Sept 1947, Dunfermline, Scotland. Singer; Songwriter; Musician (guitar, piano); Actress. m. Oliver Cookson, 25 Aug 1984, 3 sons. Career: Television appearances include: Two Ronnies; Taggart; Band Of Gold; Own documentaries and most light entertainment shows; UK concert tours, 1977-; Stage performances: John Paul George Ringo & Bert, 1974-75; Blood Brothers, 1982-83, 1993; The 7 Ages of Woman, 1997. Recordings: Hit singles: Answer Me, 1976; Another Suitcase, 1977; Caravans, 1980; January, February, 1980; I Know Him So Well (with Elaine Paige), 1985. Albums include: Barbara Dickson Album, 1980; All For A Song, 1982; Tell Me It's Not True, 1983; Heartbeats, 1984; Barbara Dickson Songbook, 1985; Gold, 1985; The Right Moment, 1986; Coming Alive Again, 1989; Don't Think Twice It's Alright, 1992; Parcel of Rogues, 1994; Dark End Of The Street, 1996. Honours: SWET Award, Blood Brothers; Platinum & Gold albums. Membership: PRS. Hobbies: Walking; Antiques; Collecting paintings; Wine. Current Management: Bernard Theobald. Address: The Coach House, Swinhope Hall, Swinhope, Lincolnshire LN8 6HT, England.

DICKSON Sean, b. 21 Mar 1967, Bellshill, Scotland. Singer; Songwriter; Producer; Musician (guitar). Musical Education: Self-taught. Career: Singer, songwriter, guitarist, producer for The Soup Dragons, 1985-; Worldwide tours; Released 3 albums, 18 singles and 15 videos for The Soup Dragons. Recordings: Singles: I'm Free; Divine Thing; Pleasure; Hang-Ten!; Can't Take No More; Mother Universe; Backwards Dog. Albums: Lovegod; Hotwired; Hydrophonic. Honours: 2 Gold records, 1 Silver record. Memberships: PRS; Musicians' Union. Hobbies: Making videos; Directing films; Collecting records and junk. Current Management: Rick Rogers. Address: Flat 1/L, 160 Great George Street, Hillhead, Glasgow G12 8AH, Scotland.

DIDDLEY Bo (Otha Bates), b. 28 Dec 1928, McComb, Mississippi, USA. Musician (guitar); Singer. Career: Numerous worldwide tours with artists including Ben E King; Ron Wood (as the Gunslingers); Lightnin' Hopkins; The Clash; Major concerts include: Rock'n'Revival, with Jerry Lee Lewis, Little Richard, John Lennon, Toronto, 1969; Hampden Scene '70, with Chuck Berry, Glasgow, 1970; Regular 1950s Rock'n'Roll Revivals concerts, US and UK, 1971-; Jazz & Heritage Festival, New Orleans, 1990; Celebrate The Soul Of American Music Festival, Los Angeles, 1991;

Guitar Legends, Expo '92, Seville, Spain, 1991; Hopefest, annual charity concert for the homeless, Chicago, 1992; Television commercial for Nike, with Bo Jackson, 1989; Films: Sweet Toronto, 1969 (renamed Keep On Rockin', 1972); Let The Good Times Roll, 1973; Trading Places, 1983. Recordings: Albums: Bo Diddley, 1962; Bo Diddley Is A Gunslinger, 1963; Bo Diddley Rides Again, 1963; Bo Diddley's Beach Party, 1964; Two Great Guitars, with Chuck Berry, 1964; Super Blues Band, with Muddy Waters and Little Walter, 1968; Another Dimension, 1971; The London Bo Diddley Sessions, 1973; 20th Anniversary Of Rock'n'Roll, 1976; Hey Bo Diddley, 1986; Live At The Ritz, 1987; Breakin' Through The BS, 1989; Featured on film soundtracks: La Bamba (Number 1, US), 1987; Book Of Love, with Ben E. King, 1991; Singles include: Bo Diddley (R&B Number 2, US); Who Do You Love; Say Man; Road Runner; You Can't Judge A Book By It's Over; Mona; Hey Good Lookin'; Ooh Baby. Honours: Inducted, Rock And Roll Hall Of Fame, 1987; Handprints in Sunset Boulevard's Rock Walk, Los Angeles, 1989. Current Management: Margo Lewis, Talent Source, 1560 Broadway, Suite 1308, New York, NY 10036, USA.

DIDDY (Richard Dearlove), b. 22 Sept 1966, Marston Green, Birmingham, England. Songwriter; Record Producer; Musician (keyboards, guitar); Vocalist; Artist. Career: Pop, dance, singles and remixes. Compositions: Small World; Give Me Love, singles released as Diddy. Recordings: As Remixer, Producer: Blondie: Atomic, 1994; Heart Of Glass, 1995; Rio And Mars: Boy I Gotta Have You; How Deep Is Love; The Tyrell Corporation: Better Days. Membership: Musicians' Union. Hobbies: Watersports; Computers.

DIEUZEY Pierre, b. 31 July 1929, Brignoles, Var, France. Musician (piano); Bandleader. m. Monique Lebland, 21 June 1961, 2 sons, 2 daughters. Education: Engineering School of Mines, Paris. Musical Education: Piano (private school). Career: Nuit de Jazz, Paris - Jeunesse Musicales de France; Several jazz festivals including Tricastin; Labouheyre; St Lizier; Bormes les Mimosas; Cité de la Musique, Paris; Television shows include: Paris Premiere, with J C Averty; Radio appearances include: France Inter; RTL. Recordings: Teppaz Company: Les Capétiens (I-IV); Charleston, Sidney Bechet. Membership: Jazz Club de France. Hobbies: Playing Scrabble; Jogging. Current Management: Projazz. Address: 10 Avenue les 27 Martyrs, 78400 Chatou, Paris, France.

DIFFORD Chris, b. 4 Nov 1954, Greenwich, London, England. Vocalist; Musician (guitar); Songwriter. Career: Founder member, Squeeze, 1974-; Longstanding writing partnership with Glenn Tilbrook; Performances include: Reading Festival, 1978; Dalymount Festival, Dublin, 1980; US tours, 1978-; Jamaica World Music Festival, 1982; Support to Fleetwood Mac, US tour, 1990; Crystal Palace Bowl, London, 1991; Support to Bryan Adams, UK tour, 1992. Compositions include: Songs for Labelled With Love, musical, 1983; Worked with Helen Shapiro; Paul Young; Jools Holland. Recordings: Albums: Squeeze, 1978; Cool For Cats, 1979; Argy Bargy, 1980; East Side Story, 1981; Sweets From A Stranger, 1982; Singles 45 And Under, 1982; Cosi Fan Tutti Frutti, 1985; Babylon And On, 1987; Frank, 1989; A Round And A Bout, 1990; Greatest Hits, 1992; Some Fantastic Piece, 1993; Ridiculous, 1995; with Glenn Tilbrook: Difford And Tilbrook, 1984; Singles include: Take Me I'm Yours, 1978; Cool For Cats, 1979; Up The Junction, 1979; Slap And Tickle; Another Nail In My Heart, 1980; Pulling Mussels From A Shell, 1980; Labelled With Love, 1981; Hourglass, 1987. Current Management: Firstars, 3520 Hayden Avenue, Culver City, CA 90232, USA.

DIGBY Roger, b. 19 Apr 1949, Colchester, Essex, England. Teacher; Musician (concertina).

m. Sian Chatterton. 30 Nov 1985, 2 sons. Education: BA Hons, Bristol University; MA, Carlton University, Ottawa, Canada. Career: Leader, Anglo concertina player, Flowers And Frolics, 10 years; Venues include The Albert Hall, South Bank, Italian Alps; 7 years as co-organiser, acoustic music venue The Empress of Russia, Islington. Recordings: Albums: Bees On Horseback; Sold Out; Wait Till The Work Comes Round (with Bob Davenport). Publications: Numerous reviews. Memberships: Musicians' Union; EFDSS; International Concertina Association. Hobbies: Reading; Cricket; Good beer. Current Management: Self-managed. Address: 3 Wolsey Road, London N1 4QH, England.

DIGITAL Didge, b. 18 May 1955, Shipley, West Yorkshire, England. Musician (keyboard); Programmer. 1 son. Musical Education: Piano lessons from age 6. Career: Keyboard player: FM; Tours with: Meat Loaf; Tina Turner; Bon Jovi; Gary Moore; Gerry and the Pacemakers; Status Quo; Television appearances: Pebble Mill; James Whale Show; Chart Show; Garden Party. Recordings: Albums: FM: Indiscreet; Tough It Out; Takin' It To The Streets; Chris Norman: Jealous Heart. Honours: Second Best Keyboard Player, Metal Hammer, 1987; Fourth Best Keyboard Player, International, 1987. Hobbies: Swimming; Anything to do with Star Trek. Current Management: Flair Management and Agency. Address: 28 Cornmill Lane, Liversedge, Heckmondwike, Yorkshire, England.

DILLARD Doug, b. 6 Mar 1937, East St Louis, Illinois, USA. Career: Formed bluegrass group, The Dillards, with brother Rodney, 1962; Left to form Dillard and Clark with Gene Clark, 1968; Occasional sideline, Dillard-Hartford-Dillard, with brother Rodney and John Hartford. Recordings: Albums: With The Dillards: Back Porch Bluegrass, 1963; The Dillards Live! Almost, 1964; Pickin' And Fiddlin', 1965; with Dillard and Clark: The Fantastic Expedition Of Dillard And Clark, 1968; Through The Morning, Through The Night, 1969; Solo: Dueling Banjos, 1973; You Don't Need a Reason, 1974; Heaven, 1976; with Doug Dillard Band: Jackrabbit, 1997; What's That, 1986; Heartbreak Hotel, 1989.

DILLARD Rodney, b. 18 May 1942, East St Louis, Illinois, USA. Singer; Musician (guitar). Career: Formed bluegrass group, The Dillards, with brother Doug, 1962-; Various line-up changes, but Dillard remained leader of group; Occasional sideline, Dillard-Hartford-Dillard, with brother Doug and John Hartford. Recordings: Albums: Back Porch Bluegrass, 1963; The Dillards Live! Almost!, 1964; Pickin' And Fiddlin', 1965; Wheatstraw Suite, 1969; Copperfields, 1970; Roots And Branches, 1972; Tribute To The American Duck, 1973; The Dillards Versus The Incredible LA Time Machine, 1977; Mountain Rock, 1978; Decade Waltz, 1979; Homecoming and Family Reunion, 1979; I'll Fly Away, 1988; Let It Fly, 1991. Current Management: Keith Case and Associates, 59 Music Square West, Nashville, TN 37203, USA.

DIMATTEO Luis, b. 10 May 1934, Bandonfeol. m. Composer. 1 son, 1 daughter. Education: Studied composition and Bandoneol. Compositions: A Sugerencia Club, 1965; A Sujerencia del Club, 1969; Estudio Para Tres, 1971; Tango en Blue Jeans, 1975; Proceso, 1976; Monologando, 1979; Rumbo al Cenit, 1981; Tango Contemporáneo, 1984; Le Dernier Tango, 1985; Tango, 1987; Por Dentro De Mi, 1988; Del Nuevo Ciclo, 1991; Silvana Deluigi, 1995; Escribo Para Los Angeles, 1997. Address: Jaro Medien, Bismarckstrasse 83, 28203 Bremen, Germany.

DIMOND David, b. 23 Nov 1964, Barking, Essex, England. Freelance Musician (saxophone, clarinet, flute); Music Teacher. Education: BSc Hons, Microbiology, University of Surrey. Musical

Education: Clarinet, flute Grade 8, Royal Schools Of Music; 1 year post-diploma, saxophone (Guildhall School Of Music and Drama). Career: Mainly jazz-based, duos including Duojazz; Quartets, quintets include Jim Mullen quintet; Octets include Caliban; Big bands include: Superjazz, NYJO; Played Ronnie Scott's; Bass Clef; 606 Club; Royal Albert Hall; Festival Hall; Festivals include: Soho Jazz Festival; Edinburgh Festival; Tour with Bondera. Compositions: Over 50. Recordings: Recorded with numerous jazz set-ups as well as for library music, jingles on tenor saxophone. Publications: Article for international journal on acoustics. Hobbies: Painting; Breeding lizards; Reading; Travel. Address: 18 Osborne Road, Dagenham, Essex RM9 5BB, England.

DIO Ronnie James (Ronald Padavona), b. 1940, New Hampshire, USA. Rock Vocalist; Musician (bass, piano, trumpet); Songwriter; Record Producer. m. Wendy Dio. Career: Member, various bands including: The Vegas Kings; Ronnie And The Rumblers; Ronnie And The Redcaps, late 1950s; Singer, musician, Ronnie Dio And The Prophets, 1961-67; Founder, Elf (formerly The Electric Elves), 1967-75; Member, Rainbow, 1975-79; Member, Black Sabbath, 1980-82; Founder member, Dio, 1983-91; Member, Black Sabbath, 1992-93; Also organizer of Hear'N'Aid project (famine relief in Ethiopia), 1986. Recordings: Albums: with Ronnie Dio And The Prophets: Dio At Dominos, 1963; with Elf: Elf, 1972; Carolina County Ball, 1974; Trying To Burn The Sun, 1975; Live, 1976; with Rainbow: Ritchie Blackmore's Rainbow, 1975; Rainbow Rising, 1976; Live On Stage, 1977; Long Live Rock'n'Roll, 1978; with Black Sabbath: Heaven And Hell, 1980; Mob Rules, 1981; Live Evil, 1982; with Dio: Holy Diver, 1983; The Last In Linbe, 1984; Sacred Heart, 1985; Intermission, 1986; Dream Evil, 1987; Lock Up The Wolves, 1990; Other recordings: The Butterfly Ball, Roger Glover, 1975; Hear'N'Aid, 1986; Northwinds, David Coverdale, 1978. Current Management: c/o Wendy Dio, Niji Management, 3633 Lankershim Blvd, Los Angeles, CA 90068, USA.

DION Celine, b. 1968, Charlemagne, Quebec, Canada. Singer. m. Rene Angelil, 17 Dec 1994. Career: Began singing in father's restaurant; Recording artiste, 1979-; Winner, Eurovision Song Contest for Switzerland, 1988; Recorded in French until 1990; 35 million albums sold to date. Recordings: Albums: 9 albums recorded in French (including Tellement J'ai D'Amour; Dion Chante Plamondon; Incognito); Unison, 1990; Celine Dion, 1991; The Colour Of My Love, 1994; D'Eux, 1995; Falling Into You, 1996; Singles: Les Chemins De Ma Maison, 1984; Melanie, 1985; Une Colombe, 1985; Incognito, 1988; Where Does My Heart Beat Now, 1991; The Power Of Love; Think Twice, 1995; Pour Que Tu M'Aimes Encore, 1995; Misled, 1995; Falling Into You, 1996; Beauty And The Beast, duet with Peabo Bryson; When I Feel In Love, from film soundtrack Sleepless In Seattle. Honours: Gala de L'Adisq Awards: Pop Album of Year, 1983; Best Selling Record, 1984, 1985; Best Selling Single, 1985; Pop Song of the Year, 1985, 1988; Female Artist of Year, 1983-85, 1988; Discovery of the Year, 1983; Best Quebec Artist Outside Quebec, 1983, 1988; JUNO Awards: Album of the Year, 1991; Single of the Year, 1993; Female Vocalist of the Year, 1991-93; Journal de Quebec Trophy, 1985; Spectrel Video Award, Best Stage Performance, 1988. Current Management: c/o Rene Angelil, Feeling Productions Inc., 755-2540 Daniel-Johnson, Laval, Quebec H7T 2S3, Canada.

DIRTY PIK, b. 1 September 1961, Tielt, Belgium. Singer; Musician (guitar). 2 daughters. Career: The Dirty Scums, 1981. Recordings: with the Dirty Scums: Dirty Songs, LP, 1985; Martens, single, 1986; Full Speed Ahead!, LP, 1987; 5th Anniversary Gig, tape, 1988; 'Rit 'n Zatte Skit 'N, single, 1988; The Booze and the Chicks, LP, 1989;

The Early Years, tape, 1990; If the Barkeepers are United, tape, 1992; Really High, single, 1993; The Pils Sessions, CD, 1996; Santa Clauz Has Come!, CD, 1997. Hobby: Music - parties. Address: The Dirty Scums, Kapelleweg 10, 8700 Tielt, Belgium.

DISCLEZ Yves, b. 22 Apr 1956, Brussels, Belgium. Writer; Composer; Artist. m. Carine Mairesse, 28 Apr 1990, 1 son, 1 daughter. Musical Education: Music Academy, Ciney, Belgium; Up With People, Tucson, Arizona, as guitar player. Career: 839 shows, USA, 1975-76; Up With People programme; Up With People on tour; Intermission of the Super Bowl, Miami 1976 (Television audience 250,000); Chicago Theatre, 3 days; Civic Center, Long Beach; National Television, USA, 1975-1976. Belgian television: Palmares, 1983; 4 tours, Belgium, 1982-90; Appearances: RTL/TV1, 19 in 1990, 21 in 1991; All national radio. Recordings: Nostalgie, 1983; Compteur A Zero, 1984; J' M'en Fou, 1986; Dazibao, 1989; Conquiatador, 1990; Le Môme de la Bas, 1991; Romanc, 1994. Publications: Nostalgie; J'M'en Fou; Romanc. Honours: Prize of Belgium Artistic Promotion (PAB), 1986; First prize, French Song, Walcourt, Belgium, 1989. Memberships: SABAM (Belgium); Copy Right (Washington, USA). Hobbies: Tennis; Friends; Good wine and good food. Current Management: Mr Patrick Decam, Sony Music (Belgium). Address: 27, Avenue de la Restauration, 5500 Falmagne (Dinant), Belgium.

DISTEL Sacha, b. 29 Jan 1933, Paris, France. Singer; Songwriter; Musician (guitar). m. Francine Breaud, 1963, 2 sons. Career: Professional jazz guitarist, age 16; Worldwide cabaret star; Films: Les Mordus, 1960; Nous Irons A Deauville, 1962; La Bonne Soupe, 1964; Le Voyou, 1970; Sans Mobile Apparent, 1971; Television presenter, France, England, Germany; Co-star, Golden Songs Of The Silver Screen tour; Producer of shows: Sacha Show; Top à Sacha Distel, 1973; Sacha's In Town, 1972; Producer, performer, La Belle Vie, 1984-85. Recordings: Hit singles include: Scoubidou, 1959; Raindrops Keep Falling On My Head, 1970; Albums include: Sacha Distel, 1970; Love Is All, 1976; Forever And Ever, 1978; Golden Hour Of Sacha Distel, 1978; 20 Favourite Love Songs, 1979; From Sacha With Love, 1979; The Sacha Distel Collection, 1980; Move Closer, 1985; More Than More, 1987; Dedications, 1992. Honours include: Best Guitarist, Jazz Hot Magazine, Critics Poll, 1957-59; Chevalier des Arts et des Lettres, 1987; Chevalier de la Legion D'Honneur, 1997. Address: c/o Prosadis, 83 Rue Michel-Ange, 75016 Paris, France.

DISTIN Terry (Terence Alan Hedges), b. 22 Sept 1933, London, England. Musician (drums). m. Margaret Anne Beech, 1 Oct 1960, 1 son, 1 daughter. Education: Clarks College. Musical Education: Mrs Rosie Wright; Harry Hayes (saxophone); Mike Nash (drums). Career: Various bands, trios; Currently, leader, Terry Distin Trio. Memberships: Musicians' Union (Portsmouth); ABJM; Jazz UK. Hobbies: Listening to Music; Walking; Cycling.

DITCHAM Martin Russell, b. 22 Feb 1951, Ilford, Essex, England. Musician (percussion, drums). Musical Education: Studied trumpet, violin, recorder, percussion, at secondary school. Career: World tours with Sade; Chris Rea; Live Aid; Everything But The Girl, US tour; British tours with The Beautiful South. Recordings: All four Sade albums; Last eight Chris Rea albums; Undercover, Rolling Stones; Ross, Diana Ross; Duets, Elton John; 3 albums with Talk Talk; International recordings with: Patricia Kass (France); Westernhagen (Germany); Takanaka (Japan); Presuntas Implicados (Spain). Honours: BPI, ASCAP Awards for Sade, Sweetest Taboo (one of most played songs of year). Memberships: Musicians' Union; PRS. Hobbies: Motor racing; Record collecting. Current Management: Real Life

Ltd. Address: 10 Glyn Mansions, Hammersmith Road, London W14 8XH, England.

DIVLJAN Vladimir, b. 10 May 1958, Belgrade, Yugoslavia. Songwriter; Musician (guitar); Singer; Film Composer; Sound Designer. Education: BSc, Geology, University of Belgrade, 1983; Specialist, Extension Course in Sound Design, AFTRS, Sydney, 1997; Selftaught, guitar, programming. Career: Songwriter, Guitarist & Singer, Belgrade based New Wave Band, Idoli (The Idols), 1980-84, National (Yugoslav) Tours, 1981, 1982, 1983; Songwriter, Solo Performer, Film & TV Composer, Yugoslavia & Australia, 1985-. Compositions: Composed music for features: Six Days in June, 1984; The Rise and Fall of Rock 'N' Roll, 1989; Documentaries: Across Australia, 1993; Heart of the Matter, 1995; You Might as Well Live, 1995. Recordings: Realised 13 albums including: Paket Aranzman, 1981; Odbrana I Poslednji Dani, 1982; Tajni Zivot A P Sandorova, 1988; Odbrana I Zastita, 1996. Honours: Idoli, ranked Fourth Most Promising Group by 8 leading European magazines, 1988; LP, Odbrana I Poslednji Dani, voted Best Yugoslav Rock Record of All Times, 1988; Nomination. Australian Film Institute (AFI) Award, 1997; Quantegy Award for Audio Excellence, AFTRS, 1997. Memberships: Australian Performers Rights Association; Australian Guild of Screen Composers. Current Management: Radio B92, Makedonska 22/V, 11000 Beograd, Yugoslavia. Address: 20/3A Farrell Avenue, Darlinghurst, NSw 2010, Australia.

DIXON Jolyon Keith, b. 6 Dec 1973, Salisbury, Wiltshire, England. Musician (guitar); Singer; Songwriter. Musical Education: Self-taught guitar from age 9; Music A-Level. Career: Tours: Two UK tours backing Toyah Wilcox; Central American tour with Toyah; 2 support tours as: Friday Forever; 2 Heineken Music Festivals; Support to Bryan Ferry, with Scarlet, UK, 1995; Joined as guitarist in Mark Owen's band, and has toured extensively with them; Sold 1 million albums worldwide with Mark Owen; First band to perform in Abbey Road studios since the Beatles; Numerous radio appearances with: Scarlet; Toyah; Television: 3 times, Top Of The Pops; What's Up Doc?; Richard and Judy; Pebble Mill; Parallel Nine. Recordings: Toyah: Take The Leap, 1993; Scarlet: Naked, 1995; Green Man with Mark Owen, 1996; Hit single: Independent Love Song; follow-up singles; Unreleased albums: Voice Of The Beehive: East/West; Judie Tzuke: Duck. Publications: with Mark Owen's band: Child, 1996; Clementine, 1997; I Am What I Am, 1997. Membership: Musicians' Union. Hobbies: Playing guitars; Squash; Producing other acts. Current Management: Friday's Productions. Address: 51A Estcourt Road, Salisbury, Wiltshire, England.

DIXON Willie James, b. 1 July 1915, Vicksburg, Mississippi, USA. Musician; Composer; Record Producer. Career: Founder, Blues Heaven Foundation Inc; Producer, composer, musician, group Chess; Solo recording artist, 1969-; Record producer, T-Bone Burnett, 1988. Compositions include: I'm Your Hoochie Coochie Man; I'm Ready; I Ain't Superstitious; I Can't Quit You Baby; You Can't Judge A Book By Its Cover; You Shook Me; Built For Comfort; Ginger Ale Afternoon (soundtrack); Songs recorded by: The Rolling Stones; Led Zeppelin; Hank Williams Jr; The Doors; Count Basie; Gil Evans; Robert Cray; Oingo Boingo. Recordings: Albums include: Willies Blues (with Memphis Slim), 1959; Boxcar Willie, 1986; Hidden Charms, 1988; Ginger Ale Afternoon, 1989; The Big Three Trio, 1990. Publication: I Am The Blues: The Willie Dixon Story, 1989. Honours: Grammy Award, Hidden Charms, 1989; 6 Grammy Nominations; Inducted, Rock and Roll Hall of Fame. Current Management: Blue Heaven Foundation, 2120 S Michigan Avenue, Chicago, IL 60616, USA.

DIYICI Senem, b. 30 Mar 1953, Istanbul, Turkey. Singer. m. Alain Blesing, 1989, 2 daughters. Musical Education: Istanbul Music Academy, from age of 6. Career: Joined children's choir in Istanbul; 3 albums in Turkey, moved to Germany; Formed several groups, produced 1 album; Arrived in France, in quest for new harmonies and musical crossover; Performs about 100 shows throughout world annually. Recordings: Nar Haniti, 1970; Hatimeyva, 1976; Casino No 1, 1979; Anatoliv, 1986; Takalar, 1989; Geste, 1993; Divan, 1995. Memberships: SACEM; ADATI; SPEDIDAM. Hobbies: Painting; Children. Current Management: Orane Senly, Artalent. Address: Le Village, St Victor de Melcap, F-30500 Saint-Amboix, France.

DOBIE Jonathan, b. 21 March 1956, London, England. Musician. Education: Sociology, Bath University; Private Guitar Lessons; Selftaught Saxophone. Career: Played with Peter Brötzman, Charles Hayward, B-Shops for the Poor; Sonicphonics with Geff Serle, Alexander Alexandrapov, ZGA, Vladimir Miller, Ken Hyder, Scipio; Regular Tours and Festivals, 1989-. Compositions: Halloween Stare; Weimar Years; Sigh. Recordings: Iceberg Principle; Visions and Blue Prints; Plague the Inventor; Wild Goose Chase; Passionate Journey; Signals Through Flames; Dream Photography; Neo Kamikaze Rotator; Spirit of India; Eastern Opus; Staalplaat Cocktail; The Dynamix. Address: No Wave, PO Box 796, London SE20 7UD, England.

DOBRE Liudmila, b. 12 Sept 1941, Chisinau, Moldavia. Agent; Impressario. m. Victor Dobre, 3 Feb 1979, 1 son. Musical Education: 3 years supplementary music school, canto. Career: Worked for the state before the Revolution; Now Managing Director of own agency, with rock, folk, pop and easy listening artistes; Also worked as solo singer and in theatre in Arad, Romania. Hobbies: Pictures; Tourism. Address: West Artistic Agency, Str Grigorescu 7, 2900 Arad, Romania.

DOC MULDOON (Wilbur), b. 24 Apr 1965, Walton, Wakefield, England. Musician (guitar); Vocalist. m. Jane Elaine Donali, 18 Oct 1986, 1 son. Education: Hull College. Musical Education: Self-taught. Career: Lead guitarist, vocalist with Muldoon Brothers; Currently on permanent UK tour; 3 tours, Southern Ireland; RTE TV (Ireland); 2 Danish visits including national TV; 1 visit to Sweden, includes Malmo Festival. Recordings: Album, video: Back O' The Barn; Singles: Cigarettes And Whiskey; Cotton Eyed Joe; Video album: Live At The Frontier. Honours: Best Country Music Newcomer Award, 1993. Membership: Musicians' Union. Hobbies: Soccer; Squash. Current Management: International Artistes Music Ltd. Address: International Artistes Music Ltd, 2 Bond Terrace, Risworth Street, Wakefield WF1 2HW, England.

DOKKEN Don, b. USA. Rock Vocalist. Career: Backing vocalist, Scorpions (recordings unreleased), 1982; Founder, lead singer, rock group Dokken, 1982-88; Solo artiste, 1989-; Worldwide concerts. Recordings: Albums: with Dokken: Breaking The Chains, 1982; Tooth And Nail, 1984; Under Lock And Key, 1985; Back For The Attack, 1987; Beast From The East, 1988; Back On The Streets, 1989; Solo: Up From The Ashes, 1990. Honours: Multi-platinum discs. Current Management: Rick Sales Management, 7144 Senalda Road, Los Angeles, CA 90068, USA.

DOKY Christian Minh, b. 7 February 1969, Glostrup, Denmark. Education: Selftaught. Career: Started on Bass, age 15 (acoustic bass, age 17); Classical piano, age 5-14. Career: Working professionally, age 16, Copenhagen; Moved to New York City, 1988, age 19; Alumni, David Sanborn, Mike Stern, Ryuichi Sahamod; Signed with Blue Note Records, 1995. Compositions: Composed theme for Danish Crownprince Frederiks, 30 year Anniversary Portrait Movie. Recordings: Solo records: Appreciation, 1988; The Sequel, 1989; Letters, 1990; The Toronto Concort, 1990; Paris Nights, 1991; Doky Bros, 1996; Doky Bros 2, 1997; Minh, 1998. Publication: Tunes & Thoughts, 1998. Honour: Simon Spirs Award for Artist of the Year, 1991. Current Management: David Burrell, Tropix, New York City, USA. Address: c/o EMI Records, Vegnmageroade 10, Copenhagen 1120 K, Denmark.

DOKY Niels Lan, b. 3 Oct 1963, Copenhagen, Denmark. Composer; Producer; Jazz Musician (piano). m. Valentine Farlot, 3 June 1989, 1 son, 1 daughter. Musical Education: Degree, Berklee College of Music. Career: Solo artist; Co-leader of Doky Brothers Band (with brother Chris); Tours, concerts, television and radio appearances worldwide with: Randy Brecker; Joe Henderson; Charlie Haden; Jack DeJohnette; John Scofield; Producer for Verve. Recordings: 15 albums as Niels Doky on jazz labels; Publications: Jazz Transcription; Compositions and Improvisations, 1996. Honours: Oscar Peterson Award, 1984; Simon Spies Musik Prize, 1993. Memberships: DJBFA; NCB; KODA. Hobby: Cooking. Current Management: Ron Moss Management, Los Angeles. Address: Norrebrogade 74, 2200 N Copenhagen, Denmark.

DOLBY Ray. Engineer. Education: Physics, London, England. Career: Inventor, Dolby noise-reduction units; Opened laboratory, 1965; Dolby 'A' system sold to recordings studios; Work on noise-reduction for tape cassette and 8-track cartridge led to Dolby 'B' system, 1971; Now adopted worldwide; Adapted for cinema, 1978; Film soundtrack, Star Wars, first to be enhanced by Dolby noise reduction; Dolby systems upgraded for digital recordings, 1991.

DOLBY Thomas (Thomas Morgan Robertson), b. 14 Oct 1958, Cairo, Egypt. Musician (synthesizers); Singer; Songwriter; Programmer; Record Producer. m. Kathleen Beller. Eduucation: Meteorology. Musical Education: Self-taught. Career: Built own synthesizers and PA system; Sound engineer, various groups; Co-founder, Camera Club, 1979; Musician with Lene Lovitch, 1980; Solo recording artiste, 1981-; Musician with David Bowie, Live Aid, Wembley, 1985. Compositions include: New Toy; Film scores include: Howard - A New Breed Of Hero. Recordings: Albums: The Golden Age Of Wireless, 1982; The Flat Earth, 1985; Aliens Ate My Buick, 1988; Astronauts And Heretics, 1992; Singles: Urges; Europa; The Pirate Twins; She Blinded Me With Science; Hyperactive; Contributor, recordings by: Foreigner; Joan Armatrading; M; Stevie Wonder; Grace Jones; Howard Jones; Herbie Hancock; Dusty Springfield; Record producer for artists including: Joni Mitchell; Prefab Sprout. Current Management: Mary Coller Management. Address: 11288 Ventura Blvd, Suite 304B, Studio City, CA 91604, USA.

DOLENZ Mickey (George Michael Dolenz Jr), b. 8 Mar 1945, Tarzana, Los Angeles, California, USA. Musician (drums); Singer; Actor; Producer; Author. m. (1) Samantha Juste, 1968, divorced, (2) Trina Dow, 1977. Education: Architectural Design at Valley College and Los Angeles Technical Institute. Career: Child actor, television series, Circus Boy, 1956-58; Other acting roles in Peyton Place; Route 66; Mr Novak; As musician: Member, The One Nighters; The Missing Links; Member, The Monkees, 1966-70; 1985-91; Actor, Monkees TV series, 1966-68; Other television includes: 33 1/3 Revolutions Per Monkee TV Special, NBC; Film appearance, Head; Stage performances: Remains To Be Seen, 1970; The Point, 1978; Solo artiste, 1971-72; Broadway production of Grease, 1994; Member, Dolenz Jones Boyce And Hart, 1975-76; Also television director, producer, 1977-85; Voiceovers for: My 3 Sons; Scooby Doo; Adam 12; Devlin; Solo artiste, Rockin' Back To The 60s Tour, 1992; Monkees reunion concert, 1997. Recordings: Albums: The Monkees (Number 1, US and UK), 1966; More Of The Monkees (Number 1, US and UK), 1967; Headquarters (Number 1, US), 1967; Pisces, Aquarius, Capricorn and Jones (Number 1, UK); The Birds, The Bees And The Monkees, 1968; Head (soundtrack), 1969; The Monkees Greatest Hits, 1969; The Monkees Present, 1969; Instant Replay, 1969; Changes, 1970; Then And Now, 1986; Poolit, 1987; Hit singles: Last Train To Clarksville (Number 1, US), 1966; I'm A Believer (Number 1, US), 1966; (I'm Not Your Steppin' Stone, 1967; A Little Bit Me, A Little Bit You, 1967; Alternate Title, 1967; Believer (Number 1, US), 1967; Valleri, 1968; Tear Drop City, 1969. Publication: I'm A Beliver: My Life Of Monkees, Music and Madness (autobiography), with Mark Bego. Honours: NARM Awards, Best Selling Group and Album, 1967; Emmy,Outstanding Comedy Series, 1967; 3 BMI Awards, 1968; Monkees Day, Atlanta, 1986; Star on Hollywood Walk Of Fame, 1989. Address: c/o Nationwide Entertainment Services, 2756 North Green Valley Parkway, Suite 449, Las Vegas, NV 89014-2100, USA.

DOMAY Michael, b. 23 Oct 1945, Newcastle-upon-Tyne, England. Medical Laboratory Scientist; Music teacher (guitar, bass, piano); Musician (guitar, bass). m. Stephanie Dennant, 18 Apr 1970, 2 sons, 1 daughter. Education: Salisbury College; Bristol Polytechnic. Musical Education: Vocal training, church choir, 1955-59; Head soloist, 1957-59; Piano and theory training, 1955-60; Guitar (Spanish and electric), bass guitar, self-taught, 1960-. Career: Established rock bands: The Falcons, with Jim Cregan (Rod Stewart); Unit 4, with Greg Lake (Emerson Lake and Palmer) and John Wetton (Asia, King Crimson), 1960-69; Freelance bass guitar, guitar, in dance bands, pit orchestras, cabaret bands, 1970-; Private teacher, guitar, bass guitar, keyboards, piano; 100+ exam successes to date (students include Lydia Cascarino of Dear John; Richard Oakes of Suede). Memberships: Musicians' Union; Registered teacher with Associated Board, Guild Hall, Rock School, REGT; Fellow, Institute of Biomedical Scientists; British Andrology Society; British Electrophoresis Society. Hobbies: Sailing; Art; Music. Current Management: Chris Ferguson Enterprises. Address: 1 Heather Close, Bournemouth, Dorset BH8 0ER, England.

DOMINO (Antoine) Fats, b. 26 Feb 1928, New Orleans, USA. Musician (piano); Singer; Songwriter. Musical Education: Piano lessons with Harrison Verrett. Career: Legendary R&B performer, 1949-; Regular US R&B tours, 1954-; Debut UK performance, 1967; Long-standing partnership with bandleader, arranger, writer Dave Bartholomew; Film appearances: Shake, Rattle & Roll; Jamboree; The Big Beat; The Girl Can't Help It; Any Which Way You Can; Television special, Fats Domino & Friends, 1987. Recordings: Numerous hit singles include: The Fat Man; Every Night About This Time; Goin' Home; Don't You Know; Goin' To The River; Please Don't Leave Me; Ain't That A Shame; You Done Me Wrong; Walking To New Orleans; I'm In Love Again; Blueberry Hill; My Girl Josephine; Valley Of Tears; Blue Monday; Whole Lotta Loving; I Want To Walk You Home; Be My Guest; Albums: Carry On Rockin', 1955; Fats Domino - Rock And Rollin', 1956; This Is Fats Domino!, 1957; Here Stands Fats Domino, 1958; Fabulous Mr D, 1958; Let's Play Fats Domino, 1959; Fats Domino Sings, 1960; I Miss You So, 1961; Twistin' The Stomp, 1962; Just Domino, 1963; Here Comes Fats Domino, 1963; Fats On Fire, 1964; Fats Domino '65, 1965; Getaway With Fats Domino, 1966; Fats Domino, 1966; Stompin' Fats Domino, 1967; Trouble In Mind, Fats Is Back, 1968; Very Best Of, 1970; Sleeping On The Job, 1979; My Blue Heaven, 1990; They Call Me The Fat Man, 1991. Honours: Inducted, Rock And Roll Hall Of Fame, 1986; Grammy, Lifetime

Achievement Award, 1987. Current Management: Al Embry International. Address: PO Box 23162, Nashville, TN 37202, USA.

DONALDSON John, b. 29 June 1955, London, England. Musician (piano); Composer. m. Agatha Coffey, 2 sons, 1 daughter. Musical Education: Anglia University, Cambridge. Career: Lived in USA, 1982-93; Broadcasts with Eddie Henderson, Richie Cole; Live appearances with John Handy, Red Holloway, Bruce Forman, Kitty Margolis; UK concerts with Norma Winstone, Iain Ballamy, Clark Tracey, Dick Pearce, 1993-95. Recordings: Parousia, Paul Contos, 1986; Pan American Suite, with Randy Masters, for film The Situation, 1987; Meeting In Brooklyn with Iain Ballamy, Ray Drummond, Victor Lewis, 1994; Full Speed Sideways, Clark Tracey Sextet, 1995; Big Hits, Dick Pearce Quartet, 1995. Honour: Best Soloist, San Sebastian Jazz Festival, 1980. Memberships: Musicians' Union; PRS. Hobby: Sporran running. Current Management: Eccentric Management. Address: 29A Connaught Street, London W2 2A1, England.

DONALDSON Louis M (Lou), b. 1 Nov 1926, Badin, North Carolina, USA. Jazz Musician (alto saxophone). m. Maker, 1943, 2 daughters. Education: Political Science, North Carolina A&T University. Musical Education: Began clarinet at age 9. Career: Played in Navy band, 1945; Moved to New York, 1950; Played with numerous notable musicians including: Charlie Parker; Sonny Stitt; Bud Powell; Milt Jackson; Philly Joe Jones; Horace Silver; Clifford Brown; Member, Art Blakey's Jazz Messengers; Toured extensively in Europe and Japan. Recordings: Albums: Alligator Boogaloo; New Faces, New Sounds; A Night at Birdland; Her 'Tis Midnight Creeper; Hot Dog; Sassy Soul Strut; Forgotten Man; Birdseed; Caracas; Sweet Papa Lou; Sentimental Journey; with Jimmy Smith: The Sermon. Honours include: Charlie Parker Memorial Medal; Baseball field named in his honour, Badin, North Carolina; Scholarship established in his name, North Caroline A&T University. Current Management: Maxine S Harvard Unlimited. Address: c/o Maxine S Harvard Unlimited, 7942 West Bell Road Ster C-5, Glendale, AZ 85308, USA.

DONE Stephen Edward, b. 13 Oct 1959, Liverpool, Merseyside, England. Musician (guitar); Guitar Teacher; Composer. Education: Hitchin College. Musical Education: Studies of guitar, trombone and composition. Career: Turned professional in 1984; Has worked with artists including: Lol Coxhill; Paul Rutherford; Barry Guy; Eddie Prevost; Leader, own groups: Extet; London Contemporary String Trio. Compositions: Several works for ensembles of various sizes and instrumentation. Recordings: Another Fine Mess, duo with Jon Corbett. Memberships: Musicians' Union; Performing Right Society; Founder member, Action for Creative Music. Hobbies: Literature; Philosophy; Aesthetics; Drinking. Address: 39 Museum Street, London WC1A 1LP, England.

DONEDA Michael, b. 21 Nov 1954, Brive, France. Musician (soprano saxophone). 2 daughters. Musical Education: Self-taught. Career: Improvised music, Europe and Japan. Recordings: On labels in France and Germany. Hobbies: Gardening; Collages.

DONEGAN Lonnie (Anthony), b. 29 Apr 1931, Glasgow, Scotland. Skiffle Musician (guitar, banjo). Career: Musician, jazz bands, 1949-53; Member, Chris Barber's Jazz band, 1954; Leader, Lonnie Donegan Skiffle Group, 1955-; Owner, publishing company, Tyler Music; Regular panelist, New Faces talent show, ITV, 1970s; Semi-retirement, 1976-; Founder, Donegan's Dancing Sunshine, 1986-. Recordings: Singles include: Rock Island Line; Lost John; Skiffle Sesssion; Bring A Little Water Sylvie; Don't You Rock Me Daddy-O; Cumberland Gap (Number 1,

UK); Puttin' On The Style; My Dixie Darling; Jack O'Diamonds; Grand Coolie Dam; Sally Don't You Grieve; Tom Dooley; Does Your Chewing Gum Lose Its Flavour (On The Bedpost Overnight); Fort Worth; Battle Of New Orleans; Sal's Got A Sugar Lip; San Miguel; My Old Man's A Dustman (Number 1, UK); I Wanna Go Home; Lorelei; Lively; Have A Drink On Me; Michael Row The Boat; The Comancheros; The Party's Over; Picka Bale Of Cotton; Albums: Lonnie Donegan Showcase, 1957; Putting On The Style, 1957; A Golden Age Of Donegan, 1962; A Golden Age Of Donegan Vol 2, 1963; Putting On The Style, 1978; Sundown, 1979; Jubilee Concert, 1981; Golden Hour Of Lonnie Donegan, 1991. Honour: First UK act to enter charts at Number 1, My Old Man's A Dustman, 1960. Current Management: Cromwell Management, 4-5 High Street, Huntingdon, Cambs PE18 6TE, England.

DONELLY Tanya, b. 14 July 1966, Newport, RI, USA. Singer; Songwriter; Guitar Player. m. Dean Fisher, 22 September 1996. Career: Founding Member, Throwing Muses,the Breeders Belly; Appearances on David Letterman (USA); The Tonight Show (USA); Conan O'Brien (USA); The Word (England); The Later Show (England); Mark Radcliffe (England); The Black Sessions (France); Support tour to REM. Recordings: with Throwing Muses: Throwing Muses, House Tornado, Hunkpapa, The Fat Skier, Chains Changed, The Real Ramona; with the Breeders: Pod, Safari; with Belly: Slowdust, King; Solo: Lovesongs for Underdogs. Honours: Grammy Nominations for Best Alternative Album, 1993, Best New Artist, 1993. Current Management: Gary Smith, Geronimo Management, 2 Tyler Court, Suite B, Cambridge, MA 02140, USA. Address: 2 Tyler Court, Suite B, Cambridge, MA 02140, USA.

DONENGE Daniel, b. 7 Mar 1966, Sarreguenines, France. Musician. 1 son. Musical Education: Conservatory. Career: Public summer concerts Palavas; Cauron; Grande Motte; Pub café: Avignon/Nîmes; Montpellier; Jazz bar: Ganges. Recordings: Sixun/Uzeb. Membership: Clef de Siol, 34400 Lunel. Hobby: Musique. Current Management: Néant. Address: 7 Rue Chailes Trenet, 34740 Vendargues, France.

DONNELLY Johnny, b. 14 Feb 1972, Dublin, Ireland. Musician (drums). Career: Member, The Saw Doctors; Tours: Ireland; UK; Europe; USA; Canada; Australia: Television and radio appearances include: BBC Late Show; Documentary, Saw Doctors, RTE; Channel 4; BBC Radio 1. Recordings: Albums: If This Is Rock And Roll I Want My Old Job Back; All The Way From Tuam. Honours: Best Band; Best Live Band; Biggest selling single ever in Ireland. Memberships: PRS; Musicians' Union. Hobbies: Running; Walking by the sea. Current Management: Ollie Jennings. Address: 13 St Mary's Terrace, Taylors Hill, Galway City, Ireland.

DONNELLY Kerr (James), sb. 1 May 1964, Glespin, Douglas, Lanarkshire, Scotland. Singer; Songwriter; Entertainer; Musician (rhythm guitar). m. Lynn Fullwood, 20 Apr 1985, 1 son, 2 daughters. Musical Education: Self-taught guitar; CSE Grade 4 Music pass. Career: Vocalist with bands: Legend, 1978; Tennessee Flash Cats, 1982; Crazy Wolf, 1982-87; Kerr Donnelly Band, 1987-; Radio interview on Mick Smiths Country, BBC East Midlands; Songs played on Sky Radio, BBC Scotland and other BBC independent radio sations; Concert: Country In The Park, Donnington, Americana, 1995. Compositions: 185 songs written. Recordings: 6 EPs; Albums: No Help Needed, 1987; EPs: The Early Days, 1992; Haunted Heart, 1992; Rough Cuts, 1995; Country Rocker, 1995. Memberships: PRS; MCPS; ISA (International Songwriters Association). Hobbies: Film;Script-writing; Writing stories; Songwriting; Reading. Current Management: Lindsay White House. Address: L J Promotions, 52 Chatterton

Drive, Baxenden, Accrington, Lancashire BB5 2TD, England.

DONNER Otto, b. 16 Nov 1939, Tampere, Finland. Composer; Musician (trumpet). Musical Education: Sibelius Academy, Helsinki; Studied with Ligeti. Career: Began jazz career, Tampere, late 1950s; Worked at Siemens electronic music studios, Germany; Co-leader, jazz quintet with Christian Schwindt; Worked with American composer Terry Riley; Founder, record label Love Records, 1966-79; Director, Finnish Radio's entertainment section, 1970-74; Leader, The Otto Donner Treatment; Performing new material with own band. Compositions include: Music for numerous Finnish films; Dalens Ande (The Spirit Of The Valley) suite; Pieces for UMO (New Music Orchestra). Recordings: Album: Quintet with Christian Schwindt: Friends And Relatives; with The Otto Donner Treatment: En Soisi Sen Päättyvän, 1970; Kuinka Myohään Valvoo Blues?, 1980. Address: Jomalvik, 10600 Tammisaari, Finland.

DONOHOE David, b. 22 May 1940, Ashton-Under-Lyme, Lancashire, England. Musician (trombone); Bandleader. m. Victoria Hancock, 8 Sept 1962, 2 sons, 2 daughters. Education: Regional College of Art, Manchester (part time). Education: Private tuition, 1 year; Brass Band, 1 year. Career: Concert with Woody Allen (actor, clarinet player), New Orleans Festival, 1971; 6 times guest, radio chat shows; 6 television appearances; Tour of USA with International Band including: Butch Thompson, Sammy Rimmington, 1977; 10 appearances, Ascona Festa, New Orleans Music; Switzerland; 3 tours with bands from New Orleans, Switzerland. Recordings: 10 albums, 6 in own name. Honours: Ambassador of Ninove, Belgium, for services to music, 1989. Membership: Musicians' Union. Hobbies: Running; Researching American Old West; Old films. Current Management: Terry Dash Management, Herts; Plus various in North Of England. Address: 5 Saddleworth Fold, Uppermill, Oldham OL3 6EQ, England.

DONOVAN (Donovan Leitch), b. 10 May 1946, Maryhill, Glasgow, Scotland. Folk Singer; Songwriter. m. Linda Lawrence, Oct 1970, 1 son, 2 daughters. Career: Appearances include: NME Poll Winners Concert, Wembley, 1965; Newport Folk Festival, with Bob Dylan, 1965; Worldwide concerts, tours include: Royal Albert Hall, 1967; National Blues Festival, Windsor, 1967; International Film Festival, Cannes, France, 1968; Woburn Music Festival, 1968; Carnegie Hall, New York, 1968; Bath Festival, 1970; Isle Of Wight Festival, 1970; Tour, Australia and New Zealand, 1975; Edinburgh Festival, 1980; Support to Happy Mondays, Wembley Arena, 1990; UK tour, 1992. Compositions include: Own recorded songs; Songs for film: If It's Tuesday It Must Be Belgium, 1969; The Pied Piper, 1971; Film score, Brother Sun, Sister Moon, 1972. Recordings: Singles include: Catch The Wind, 1965; Colours, 1965; Universal Soldier, 1965; Sunshine Superman, 1966; Mellow Yellow, 1966; There Is A Mountain, 1967; Jennifer Juniper, 1968; Hurdy Gurdy Man, 1968; Atlantis, 1969; Barabajagal (Love Is Hot), with the Jeff Beck Group, 1969; Albums include: What's Bin Did And What's Bin Hid, 1965; Catch The Wind, 1965; Fairy Tale, 1965; Sunshine Superman, 1966; The Real Donovan, 1966; Mellow Yellow, 1967; Universal Soldier, 1967; A Gift From A Flower To A Garden, 1968; Like It Is, Was And Evermore Shall Be, 1968; Donovan In Concert, 1968; Barabajagal, 1969; The Best Of Donovan, 1969; Open Road, 1970; Donovan P Leitch, 1970; HMS Donovan, 1971; Cosmic Wheels, 1973; Essence To Essence, 1974; 7-Tease, 1974; Slow Down World, 1976; Donovan, 1977; Neutronica, 1980; Love Is The Only Feeling, 1980; Lady Of The Stars, 1983; Rising, 1990; Troubadour - The Definitive Collection 1964-76, 1993. Current Management:

Monarch Productions, 8803 Mayne Street, Bellflower, CA 90706, USA.

DONOVAN Jason, b. 1 June 1968, Melbourne, Australia. Singer; Actor. Career: Actor, Australian television series: Skyways, 1979; I Can Jump Puddles, 1979; Neighbours, 1985-89; Heroes, 1988; Shadows Of The Heart, 1988; Stage appearance, lead role, Joseph And The Amazing Technicolour Dreamcoat, London Palladium, 1991-92; Concert tours, Australia; Far East; Europe. Recordings: Albums include: Ten Good Reasons, 1989; Between The Lines, 1990; Joseph And The Amazing Technicolour Dreamcoat. Hit singles include: Nothing Can Divide Us, 1988; Especially For You (duet with Kylie Minogue), 1988; Too Many Broken Hearts, 1989; Sealed With A Kiss, 1989; Everyday, 1989; Hang On To Your Love, 1990; Another Night, 1990; Rhythm Of The Rain, 1990; Doing Fine, 1990; Any Dream Will Do, 1991; Happy Together, 1991; Rough Diamonds, 1994. Honours: Numerous show business awards. Hobbies: Surfing; Biographies. Address: Richard East Productions Pty Ltd, Toorak Road, South Yarra, VIC 3141, Australia.

DONY. Vocalist; Musician (bass); Songwriter; Arranger. Career: Member, Atlas, Bulgaria, 1987-1993; Formed Dony & Momchil, 1993-; Numerous tours, Bulgaria, include Sofia National Theatre (unplugged with National Philharmony), 1995. Recordings: with Atlas: Doll; with Dony & Momchil: CD Albums: The Album!, 1993; The Second One, 1994. Honours: Best Band, Atlas, 1991; Orpheus: Best Single: The Little Prince; Best Video For Duo Or A Group. Address: c/o Union Media, 71 Evl Georgiev Blvd, Sofia 1142, Bulgaria.

DOOMS Bruno Paul, b. 22 October 1976, Leuven, Belgium. Percussion; Drums; Timpani. Education: Yale School of Music, New Haven, Connecticut, USA; Summer schools with Billy Hart. Career: Uitvoerend Musicus, Rotterdam, 1997; Master of Music, Yale School of Music, expected 1999; Several appearances on radio with school bands and on VTM, NED 3; Major stage: Festival of Flandres, Beleuvenissen. Recordings: JP - JF 1990-94; BIYO, 1991; Euregio, 1995; P-J Wagemans, 1996; Belle Epoque, 1996. Honour: Fulbright-Hayes Grant, 1997. Membership: Percussive Arts Society, USA. Current Management: Dooms, Bondgenotenlaan 155, 3000 Leuven, Belgium. Address: Bondgenotenlaan 155, 3000 Leuven, Belgium.

DOONICAN Val (Michael Valentine), b. 3 Feb 1927, Waterford, Ireland. Singer; Musician (guitar, mandolin); Television Presenter. Musical Education: Guitar, mandolin. Career: Member, various Irish bands; Member, vocal group The Four Ramblers; Group had radio series over 2 years, Riders Of The Range, BBC, 1951; Solo artiste, late 1950s-; Television appearances: Beauty Box; Sunday Night At The London Palladium, 1964; Own show, 1964-1988s; Radio includes: Dreamy Afternoon; A Date With Val; Videos, Songs from My Sketchbook - Memories are Made of This; Thank You For The Music, 1993. Recordings: 30 albums include: Val Doonican Rocks But Gently, 1967; Song Sung Blue, 1974; Some Of My Best Friends Are Songs, 1977; By Request, 1987; Singles include: Walk Tall; the Special Years; Elusive Butterfly; What Would I Be; Memories Are Made Of This; If The World Stopped Loving; Morning; If I Knew Then What I Know Now. Publication: Walking Tall The Special Years. Honours: TV Personality Of The Year (3 times). Current Management: Bernard Lee Management. Address: Moorcroft Lodge, Fairleigh Common, Warlingham, Surrey CR3 9PE, England.

DOPOURIDIS Zoe, b. 11 Feb 1952, Lyon, France. Press Promotion Officer. m. Alain Dopouridis, 16 Sept 1983, 4 sons. Education: Baccalauréat B, Ecole Nationale des Beaux-Arts.

Musical Education: Conservatoire, piano. Career: Artists promoted include: Didier Lockwood; Khalil Chahine; Dan Bigras; Sixun; Michel Portal; Jean-Michel Kajdan; Press promotion and Zone Bleue production/concerts. Membership: UNAPC. Address: 57 Boulevard Magenta, 75010 Paris, France.

DORAN Brian John, b. 2 Mar 1965, Croydon, Surrey, England. Singer; Songwriter; Musician (guitar, flute). m. Jane Kendrick, 19 Aug 1994. Education: Diploma in dispensing optics. Musical Education: Grade 8 theory, singing, flute; Self-taught guitar. Career: Lead singer, Orchid Waltz, 1983-86; Played all over England; Acoustic duo Richard III's with Lee Collinson (now popular folk artist); Solo acoustic world tour, 1990-91; Currently solo and session work. Composition: Song: Lady Of The 80s, written for Edinburgh Festival. Recordings: Orchid Waltz; Trident (album not released); Solo album: Acoustics, 1991; Backing vocals, Compassion, Keith Hancock, 1993. Membership: Branch committee member, Musicians' Union. Hobbies: Walking; Cinema; Opera; Theatre. Current Management: 124 Lisbon Avenue, Twickenham, Middlesex TW2 5HN, England.

DORE Michael, b. 7 June 1959, Cleethorpes, Lincolnshire, England. Singer; Musician (piano). Musical Education: Graduate, Guildhall School Of Music and Drama, (GGSM London); Holder of Postgraduate Certificate In Education (PGCE). Career: Member, Swingle Singers, 1981-87; Electric Phoenix; Chameleon; Concert soloist with: BBC Radio 2; London Symphony Orchestra; Los Angeles Philharmonic; Swedish National Radio; Royal Variety Performances; Music Of Andrew Lloyd Webber; Jesus Christ Superstar (Peter); Magic Of The Musicals; Rogers and Hammerstein At The Barbican; Worked for Royal National Theatre, Royal Shakespeare Company; Nederlands Dans Theater; West End credits include: Cats; Starlight Express; Grease; Debuts: Carnegie Hall (New York); Royal Albert Hall Proms, 1994; One Man Show, 1995. Recordings: As session singer: commercials, films, television; Albums: The Musicals with BBC Concert Orchestra; Every Song Has Its Play with Gilbert O'Sullivan (manager); Numerous with Swingle Singers; with Berio: Sinfonia, Canticum. Memberships: British Actors Equity; Musicians' Union. Hobby: Shirley Bassey fan. Current Management: c/o British Actors Equity Association. Address: Guildhouse, Upper St Martins Lane, London WC2H 9EG, England.

DORGE Pierre, b. 28 Feb 1946, Frederiksberg, Denmark. Composer; Conductor; Musician (guitar). m. Irene Becker, 24 Aug 1985. Musical Education: Music, KDAS, College of Copenhagen. Career: Formed own group, Copenhagen Jazz Quintet, 1960; Formed New Jungle Orchestra, 1980; Recorded with: Niels-Henning Orsted Petersen; John Tchicai; Svend Asmussen; Marilyn Mazur; Johnny Dyani; Tours: Europe; US; Canada; Indonesia; Ghana; USSR; Australasia. Composition: Symphony in C, 1994. Recordings include: with New Jungle Orchestra: Pierre Dorge and New Jungle Orchestra, 1982; Brikama, 1984; Even The Moon Is Dancing, 1985; Johnny Lives, 1987; Different Places - Different Bananas, 1989; Peer Gynt, 1989; Live in Chicago, 1991; David Murray and the Jazzpar Prize, 1992; Karawane, 1993; Polar Jungle Orchestra, 1994; Absurd Bird, 1995; Music from the Danish Jungle, 1996; China Jungle, 1997. Honours: Grants, Danish Arts Council; JASA prize, 1985. Hobby: All music. Current Management: Copenhagen Concerts. Address: Holmbladsgade 35, 2300 Copenhagen S, Denmark.

DORONJGA Sinisa, b. 15 Mar 1942, Zagreb, Croatia. Musician; Singer; Entertainer; Actor. m. Bosiljka Kello, 22 Mar 1969, 1 son, 1 daughter. Musical Education: Secondary Music School.

Career: Singer, musician, Bijele Strijele, 1961; World tour, 1968-69; Producer, composer, songwriter, arranger, Suzy record label; Television entertainer. Recordings: Hit album: Domestic songs, Platinum, 1979; 7 Gold albums, 1979-1995; Main songs from albums: Hrvatska Mati; Boze Dragi Sacuvaj Hrvate; Hrvatski Sinovi. Publications: Book, video, Dosel Je Sv Martin (St Martin) traditional ceremony in Croatia. Honours: Croatian Government and Croatan Music AID Awards, Order for a lifetime of music work. Membership: General secretary, Croatian Musicians' Union. Hobbies: Hunting; Fishing; Cooking. Current Management: Simpy and Friends Production and Management. Address: Sinisa Doronjga, Siget 18 b/v, 10020 Zagreb, Croatia.

DORSET Ray. Musician (guitar); Vocalist. Career: Member, Mungo Jerry, 1970-; Appearances include: Hollywood Pop Festival, Staffordshire, 1970; Briefly member, Katmandu, with Peter Green, 1986. Recordings: Albumns: Mungo Jerry, 1970; Electronically Tested, 1971; You Don't Have To Be In The Army To Fight In The War, 1971; Boot Power, 1972; Greatest Hits, 1973; Golden Hour, 1974; Long Legged Woman, 1974; Impala Saga, 1976; Lovin' In The Alleys, Fightin' In The Streets, 1977; File, 1977; Ray Dorset And Mungo Jerry, 1978; Six Aside, 1979; Together Again, 1981; The Early Years, 1992; Solo album: Cold Blue Excursion, 1972; with Katmandu: A Case For The Blues, 1986; Singles include: In The Summertime (Number 1, UK); Baby Jump (Number 1, UK); Lady Rose; You Don't Have To Be In The Army To Fight In The War; Alright Alright Alright, 1973; Longlegged Woman Dressed In Black; As producer: Feels Like I'm In Love, Kelly Marie (Number 1, UK), 1980. Address: c/o Hal Carter Organisation, 101 Hazelwood Lane, London N13 5HQ, England.

DORUZKA Petr, b. 30 October 1949, Prague, Czech Republic. Music Writer; Radio Presenter. m. Jana Doruzková, 5 September 1973, 1 son, 1 daughter. Education: Sound Engineering, Technical University, Prague. Publications: Borderline Music, 1991; Drawer Full of Zappa, 1993. Memberships: World Music Charts Europe; International Association for the Study of Popular Music. Hobby: Yachting. Address: Zeleny Pruh 14, 147 00 Praha 4, Czech Republic.

DOSS Buster (Colonel), b. 4 Feb 1925, Jefferson, Texas, USA. Entertainer; Producer; Writer. m. Barbara Ann Solomon, 14 Apr 1947, 1 son, 1 daughter. Education: College. Musical Education: Began playing: mandolin age 4, guitar, age 5, bass, age 6. Career: Writer, over 500 songs recorded by artists including: Billy Walker; Billy Grammer; Tex Ritter; Marty Robbins; Producer, 1949-, over 2000 albums; Manager, Grand Ole Opry acts; Owned 7 radio stations; 7 newspapers; Owner, record labels; Owner, 3 publishing companies; Co-owner, 7 publishing companies; Owner, Theme Parks: Codyland, Missouri; Six Shooter Junction, Texas; Television shows: Star of The Cactus Kid; Magic on Ed Sullivan Show, Tonight Show; Owned Country Music theatres: Missouri; Harlingen, Texas; Ashdown, Arkansas; Mt Pleasant, Athens; Georgetown, Texas; Winchester (Tennessee); Moved to Shreveport, for Louisiana Hayride, 1948, included Kitty Wells, Elvis Presley, Jim Reeves as an announcer; Numerous appearances, 1949-, Grand Ole Opry. Publications: Owner The Country Gazette. Honours: Over 1000 awards for excellence in show business, including: Pioneer Award and Living Legend, CMA of America. Membership: BMI. Hobby: Writing songs. Current Management: Colonel Buster Doss Presents. Address: 341 Billy Goat Hill Road, Winchester, TN 37398, USA.

DOUCET Michael Louis, b. 14 Feb 1951, LaFayette, Louisiana, USA. Cajun Musician (fiddle, guitar, bass, mandolin, piano). m. Sharon Lee Arms, 14 Feb 1951, 2 sons, 1 daughter.

Education: BS, English Major, Louisiana State University, 1973. Career: First band Coteau dissolved 1977; Formed Beausoleil, 1975; Projects with Savoy-Doucet band and solo work; Performed at Jimmy Carter's inaugural gala, 1977; Worldwide tours with Beausoleil, including Carnegie Hall, New York, 1982; Great American Music Hall, San Francisco, 1988; Numerous television and radio appearances: Austin City Limits; Today Show; Conan O'Brien; Good Morning; Prairie Home Companion. Compositions: Danse De La Vie; Zydeco Gris Gris; L'Ouragon; Music for films: Belizaire The Cajun, 1985; The Big Easy, 1987. Recordings: Solo albums: Beau Solo; Cajun Fiddle; Beausoleil albums include: Bayou Boogie, 1985; Cajun Conja, 1991; Danse De La Vie, 1993; L'Echo, 1994; Mad Reel, 1994; 3 albums with Savoy-Doucet. Honours: Master Folk Musician, Louisiana; National Endowment for the Arts Grant, 1975; 6 Grammy Nominations with Beausoleil; First Clifton Chenier Award, 1990. Hobbies: Chess; Research; French; Poetry. Current Management: The Rosebud Agency. Address: PO Box 170429, San Francisco, CA 94117, USA.

DOUDELLE Jacques, b. 4 July 1949, Paris, France. Musician (soprano and tenor saxophones); Bandleader. Musical Education: Self-taught. Career: Formed Jacques Doudelle Orchestra, Festival du Marais, Paris, 1975; Numerous appearances across France include: Casino de Paris; Marciac Jazz Festival (3 times); Sidney Bechet Night, 1993, 1994; Festivals in Italy; Belgium; Switzerland; Germany; Greece; Turkey; Television: Accords Parfaits, with Pierre Petit; Jazz 6, with Philippe Adler; Sacrée Soirée, with Jean-Pierre Foucault. Compositions include: T'Exagères; Moulin à Légumes; Détournement De Mineur; Coeur De Perles; Film music: Des Enfants Gâtés; Félicité. Recordings: 5 albums, 1978-95; Recordings with Roger Guerin; Jean Lou Longnon; Fabrice Eulry; Sidney Bechet Jr; Honours: Laureate, Concours National de Jazz de la Défense, 1986. Membership: President, Sidney Bechet Academy. Address: Jacques Doudelle Jazz Orchestra, 58 Avenue Philippe de Girard, 93420 Villepinte, France.

DOUGALL David Stuart, b. 19 Feb 1960, Scotland. Musician (guitar, trumpet, piano, bass, guitar, bass voice). m. Maureen, 3 Apr 1982, 1 son, 1 daughter. Education: BSc, Heriot Watt University, 1981. Musical Education: LLCM, Napier University, 1995. Career: Guitarist, Blues Band in Borders; Trumpet, Big Band; Solo classical guitar; Bass voice, Eyemouth Fishermans Choir; Acoustic-classical-electric guitar; Teacher, music groups with special needs people. Membership: Musicians' Union. Address: 12 Church Street, Eyemouth, Berwickshire TD14 5DH, Scotland.

DOUGLAS John Henry, b. 19 June 1920. Composer; Arranger; Conductor. m. Babs, deceased, 1 son, 1 daughter. Education: Selftaught. Career: Pianist, Neville Hughes Sextet, 1939; Formed own RAF dance band; Arranging for many dance bands including: Bert Ambrose, Ted Heath and Edmundo Ros; Staff Arranger to George Elrick; Pianist, Arranger with the Cyril Stapleton Band; Staff Arranger, music publishers, 1948; Scoring and conducting vocal backings for Decca, 1952, first hit was Tex Ritter's High Noon; 1960: Scored and conducted 80 LPs for RCA; Composing and scoring for films; Own BBC Rado programme, Swing Song, ran for 2 years; Arranging, TV shows for international stars including Shirley Jones, Howard Keel, Vera Lynn, Shirley Bassey. Recordings include: It's Magic, CD, cassette. Honours: Melody Maker Jazz Jamboree Award; Gold Disc. Address: 39 Tadorne Road, Tadworth, Surrey KT20 5TF, England.

DOUGLAS Leslie, b. 1 May 1914, London, England. Singer; Bandleader; Songwriter. m. Marian Cherry, 29 Mar 1969, 4 sons, 2 daughters.

Musical Education: Composition, Charles Prentice, Music Bac Percussion, Wag Abbey. Career: Featured singer, radio, and recording bands including: Henry Hall; Carrol Gibbons; Ambrose; Charlie Kunz; Teddy Joyce; Phil Green; Fred Hartley; Joined RAF, 1940; Organiser, director, Bomber Command Dance Band; Tours include: India, Malaysia, Germany; Later bandleader, Leslie Douglas and his Orchestra; Numerous radio broadcasts, variety concerts and ballroom functions. Compositions: Swing Serenade; Oh Miss Muffet; Lead; Little Miss Valentine; Le Touquet; Swinging Inbetween; Old Country; New Boots; One Man Went To Blow; Boys And Girls; Nursery Rhythm. Recordings: As bandleader, and with Carrol Gibbons; Ambrose; Henry Hall. Memberships: PRS; British Academy of Songwriters; Musicians' Union. Hobbies: Gardening; Reading. Current Management: Able Artistes and Associates. Address: 32 Manor Road, Wallington, Surrey SM6 OAA, England.

DOUGLAS Robert James Elliot, b. 13 May 1942, Gifford, East Lothian, Scotland. Musician (Guitar, Banjo). m. Margaret, 18 March 1983, 1 son. Education: Selftaught. Career: Clyde Valley Stompers, 1960-61; It's All Happening, with Tommy Steele and On the Beat, Norman Wisdom; Aley Welsh Band, 1963-82; Newport Jazz Festival, 1966; Freelance, 1982-; Working with Keith Smith, Dave Shepherd, Dig By Fairweather. Recordings: Complete Discography with Pamra; All Aley Welsh LP's; 2 CD's with Great British Jazz Band; 2 CD's recorded in Namburg with Vaché, Brother'/Bob Haggart; Various LPs accompanying American Stars. Honour: British Jazz Award (Guitar), 1992. Membership: Musicians Union Pamra. Hobbies: Golf; Cooking (3 years as Chef). Address: 20 Gillan Way, Houghton Regis, Dunstable, Beds, LU5 5RD, England.

DOWDING Andrew Maurice, b. 23 July 1961, Lowestoft, Suffolk, England. Musician (drums, percussion); Teacher. Musical Education: Self-taught. Career: Toured with Linda Lewis, Ben E King and extensive international tours with Suzi Quatro. Recordings: Played on albums for Wayland and Suzi Quatro. Membership: Musicians' Union. Hobbies: Eating out; Shopping; Relaxation. Address: 9A Ellis Road, Clacton-on-Sea, Essex CO15 1EX, England.

DOWNES David, b. 9 June 1975, Dublin, Ireland. Musical Education: Currently in 3rd year of Music degree, Trinity College, Dublin. Career: Live and television shows for Phil Coulter (including US tour); Eleanor McEvoy and Alan Stivell. Compositions: Numerous soundtracks for RTE TV; Many orchestral works and arrangements. Membership: Irish Musicians' Rights Organisation. Current Management: Real Good Management Ltd. Address: 17 Dame Court, Dublin 2, Ireland.

DOWNES Geoffrey, b. 25 Aug 1952, Stockport, Manchester, England. Musician (keyboards); Songwriter; Record Producer. m. Wenche Steen, 13 Nov 1982, 1 stepson, 2 daughters. Musical Education: City of Leeds College, graduated in Modern Music Studies. Career: Session musician; Jingles composer; Record producer; Best known as artist with: The Buggles; Yes; Asia; First band to sell out 16 consecutive concerts at Madison Square Gardens, with Yes, 1980; First video shown on MTV: Buggles, Video Killed The Radio Star, 1981; First live MTV global satellite broadcast with Asia, from Budokan, Tokyo to 25 million people, 1983; First band to play Moscow Olympic Stadium, 1990; Solo artist, with New Dance Orchestra. Recordings: with Buggles: Age Of Plastic, 1979; Adventures In Modern Recording, 1981; with Yes: Drama, 1980; with Asia: Asia, 1982; Alpha, 1983; Astra, 1985; Then And Now, 1990; Live In Moscow, 1991; Aqua, 1992; Aria, 1994; Arena, 1995; with GTR: GTR, 1986; Geoff Downes with NDO: The Light Program, 1987; Vox Humana, 1993; Evolution,

1995; Various artists: Earthquake, 1989. Honours include: Over 40 Silver, Gold, Platinum discs; with Buggles: Ivor Novello Award Nomination, 1980; NME Award, 1980; Deutsche Gramaphon Award, 1980; with Asia: Billboard, Cashbox and Circus Magazine awards, 1982; FM Magazine Award, 1983; 2 Grammy Nominations; Ampex Gold Reel, 1979, 1980, 1986; Keyboard Magazine Awards, 1980, 1982, 1983; ASCAP Best Rock Song, 1982, 1983. Memberships: PRS; Musicians' Union; ASCAP. Hobbies: Mountain biking; Skiing; English literature. Current Management: Asia Management, Plas Llecha, Llanhennock, Caerleon, Newport, Gwent NP6 1LU, Wales.

DOWNEY Brian, b. 27 Jan 1951, Dublin, Ireland. Musician (drums). Career: Founder member, drummer, rock group Thin Lizzy, 1969-83; Member, Grand Slam (with Thin Lizzy's Phil Lynott), 1984; Regular UK and international appearances with Thin Lizzy include: Reading Festival, 1974, 1975, 1983; Great British Music Festival, London, 1975; World Series Of Rock, Cleveland, 1983; Monsters Of Rock European tour, 1983. Recordings: with Thin Lizzy: Hit singles: Whiskey In The Jar, 1973; Wild One, 1975; The Boys Are Back In Town, 1976; Don't Believe A Word, 1977; Dancin' In The Moonlight, 1977; Rosalie, 1978; Waiting For An Alibi, 1979; Sarah, 1979; Killer On The Loose, 1980; Killers Live EP, 1981; Cold Sweat, 1982; Albums: Thin Lizzy, 1971; Shades Of A Blue Orphanage, 1972; Vagabonds Of The Western World, 1972; Nightlife, 1974; Fighting, 1975; Jailbreak, 1976; Johnny The Fox, 1976; Bad Reputation, 1977; Live And Dangerous, 1978; Black Rose (A Rock Legend), 1979; Chinatown, 1980; The Adventures Of Thin Lizzy, 1981; Renegade, 1981; Thunder And Lightning, 1983; Dedication - The Very Best Of Thin Lizzy, 1991.

DOWNING Will, b. 29 November 1963, Brooklyn, New York, USA. Singer; Vocalist. 1 son, 2 daughters. Education: Virginia Union University. Compositions: That Good Morning Love; Don't Wait For Love; I Can't Make You Love Me; Just A Game. Recordings: Just A Game, early 1980s; Where Is the Love, Top 20, Duet with Mica Paris, 1990.

DOWNS Jeanne, b. 6 Jan 1967, Rustington, Sussex, England. Singer; Songwriter; Television Presenter; Actress; Producer. m. Aron Friedman, 15 May 1993. Musical Education: Arts Education School (Stage School). Career: Continually writing, recording, producing; Developing own music for Manuka, with label deal; Television appearances include: Presenter, Children's ITV, 1989-91; Disney Club; TV Weekly; Ghost Train; MotorMouth; Television commercial voiceovers: Kelloggs Honey Nut Loops; Coco Pops; Ultimate Dance; Kiss FM radio jingles. Recordings: as Jeanne Dee: Simple Solution, 1992; No Life Without Love, 1993; Memberships: Musicians' Union; Pact; PRS; Equity. Hobbies: Television production; Writing; Programme ideas; Tennis. Current Management: Billy Budis, Kudos Management. Address: c/o Kudos Management, Crown Studios, 16-18 Crown Road, Twickenham, Middlesex TW1 3EE, England.

DOWSETT Ian David, b. 30 Sept 1963, Chesterfield, England. Musician (fingerstyle jazz guitar). Musical Education: Classical guitar evening classes, De Bovoir Institute; Jazz and Pop course, Goldsmith's College. Career: Began in Rock and Blues bands, occasional solo gigs, Spanish guitar; Recently playing in duos: saxophone and guitar, 2 guitars; Performances: Union Chapel; Festival Hall Foyer; Conway Hall; Recording for EMI Bachology project, Abbey Road Studio. Hobbies: Gardening; Eastern philosophy. Address: 28 Westpoint, Avondale Square, Old Kent Road, London SE1 5NY, England.

DOY Carl William, b. 6 May 1947, Camberley, Surrey, England. Musician (piano);

Arranger; Composer; Producer. m. Kathleen Mary, 1973, 2 sons. Musical Education: Royal College of Music (Herbert Howells, Eric Harisson). Career: Staff arranger at TVNZ for 15 years; Resident Pianist New Zealand Today and Saturday Live; Arranged, recorded with Dame Kiri Te Kanawa; Played for Gladys Knight and The Pips; Bob Hope; B B King; Shirley Bassey. Recordings: Double album: Piano By Candlelight (Platinum), 1995; Moonlight Piano, USA, Australian release, 1995. Honours: Artistic Award World Song Festival, Los Angeles, 1984; Grand Prix, Pacific Song Contest, 1979; Winner, American Song Festival, 1981. Membership: APRA. Hobbies: Walking; Crosswords. Current Management: Murray Thom. Address: PO Box 35-767, Browns Bay, Auckland 10, New Zealand.

DOYLE Teresa, b. 26 January 1951, Prince Edward Island, Canada. Singer. m. Brett Bunston, 1 son. Education: BA, University of Prince Edward Island, Canada; McGill Conservatory of Music. Career: Performed at festivals and concerts in Japan, Canada, the US and UK; Performed with Chieftains. Recordings: Prince Edward Isle, Adieu; Forerunner; Stowaway; Songs for Lute & Voice; Dance to Your Daddy. Honour: East Coast Music Award, Children's Album of the Year. Membership: American Federation of Musicians. Hobbies: Gardening; Painting. Address: RR #3, Belfast, Prince Edward Island C0A 1A0, Canada.

DOZIER Lamont, b. 16 June 1941, Detroit, Michigan, USA. Composer; Record Producer. Career: Motown artist, 1950s-67; Member, songwriting and production team Holland/Dozier/Holland (with Eddie and Brian Holland), 1963-1973; Co-founder, Invictus and Hot Wax Records, 1967; Resumed solo recording career, 1972-; Founder, own Megaphone label, 1983. Recordings: Solo albums: Out Here On My Own, 1973; Black Bach, 1974; Love And Beauty, 1975; Right There, 1976; Peddlin' Music On The Side, 1977; Bittersweet, 1979; Working On You, 1981; Lamont, 1982; Bigger Than Life, 1983; Solo singles include: Let's Talk It Over, 1960; Why Can't We Be Lovers, 1972; Tryin' To Hold On To My Woman, 1974; Fish Ain't Bitin', 1974; Let Me Start Tonite, 1974; As co-writer/producer: with Marvin Gaye: Can I Get A Witness?; Little Darling; How Sweet It Is; You're A Wonderful One; with Martha and The Vandellas: Heatwave; Quicksand; Nowhere To Run; Jimmy Mack; with the Supremes: You Can't Hurry Love; You Keep Me Hanging On; Love Is Here And Now You've Gone; Where Did Our Love Go?; Baby Love; Come See About Me; Stop! In The Name Of Love; Back In My Arms Again; with the Isley Brothers: This Old Heart Of Mine; Put Yourself In My Place; I Guess I'll Always Love; I Can't Help Myself; (It's The) Same Old Song; Reach Out And I'll Be There; Bernadette; Standing In The Shadows Of Love; Other recordings for artistes including: The Miracles; Kim Weston; Aretha Franklin; Al Wilson; Freda Payne. Address: c/o McMullen & Co., 9744 Wilshire Blvd #301, Beverly Hills, CA 90212-1828, USA.

DR. ROBERT (Bruce Robert Howard), b. 2 May 1961, Norfolk, England. Singer. Career: Former footballer, Norwich City Football Club; Former pop music journalist; Member, The Blow Monkeys, 1984-. Recordings: Albums: Limping For A Generation, 1984; Animal Magic, 1986; She Was Only A Grocer's Daughter, 1987; Whoops There Goes The Neighbourhood, 1989; Choices, 1989; Singles include: Digging Your Scene, 1986; It Doesn't Have To Be This Way, 1987; (Celebrate) The Day After You (featuring Curtis Mayfield), 1987; Slaves No More (featuring Sylvia Tella); Springtime For The World, 1990; Contributor, You Don't Own Me, to soundtrack for film Dirty Dancing; As Dr. Robert: Duet with Kym Mazelle: Wait. Address: c/o Primary Talent, London, England.

DRAGON Daryl, b. 27 Aug 1942, Los Angeles, California, USA. Musician (keyboards); Songwriter. m. Toni Tennille, 14 Feb 1974. Career: Keyboard player, co-writer, The Beach Boys stage band; Member, Natalie Cole's Malibu Music Men; Member, duo Captain & Tennille (with Toni Tennille), 1972-80; Tour with The Beach Boys, 1972; White House Dinner, in honour of Queen Elizabeth II, 1976; The Captain And Tennille, premiere, ABC TV, 1976; Runs Rambo Rec studio, 1979-. Recordings: Albums: with The Captain and Tennille: Love Will Keep Us Together (Number 2, US), 1975; Song Of Joy, 1976; Come In From The Rain, 1977; Captain And Tennille's Greatest Hits, 1978; Dream, 1978; Make Your Move, 1980; Twenty Years of Romance, 1995; Hit singles include: The Way I Want To Touch You, 1975; Love Will Keep Us Together, 1975; Lonely Night (Angel Face), 1976; Muskrat Love, 1976; Shop Around, 1976; Can't Stop Dancin', 1977; You Never Done It Like That, 1979; Do That To Me One More Time (Number 1, US), 1980. Honours: Grammy Award, Record Of The Year, Love Will Keep Us Together, 1976; JUNO Award, Best International Single, Love Will Keep Us Together, 1976. Current Management: c/o Cheri Ingram Co., 3575 Cahuenga Blvd, Suite 600, Los Angeles, CA 90068, USA.

DRAPER Paul, b. Chester, Cheshire, England. Singer. Education: Wrexham Art College. Career: Lead singer, Mansun. Recordings include: Debut album, Attack Of The Grey Lantern, 1997; Singles: Egg Shaped Fred (EP), 1996; Take It Esay Chicken (EP), 1996; Stripper Vicar (EP), 1996; Wide Open Space (EP), 1996. Address: c/o Rock'n'Roll Management, Studio 2, 108 Prospect Quay, Point Pleasant, London SW18 1PR, England.

DREES Michèle Marie, b. Carshalton, Surrey, England. Musician (drums, percussion). Musical Education: GSMD post graduate, advanced jazz course. Career: Marc Almond tour video, television, 1993; Member of houseband, Jonathan Ross TV Show, backing k d lang; Susanne Vega; Mica Paris; Candy Dulfer; Hair, musical, Old Vic, 1993; Freak Power, 1993, 1994; Many jazz concerts, played with: Jean Toussaint; Dill Katz; Tim Whitehead; salsa band Candela; Seal; Eurovision Song Contest; Crystal Aquarium film, CH4, 1995; Marie-Clare D'Ubaldo. Memberships: Musicians' Union; Equity. Hobbies: Guitar; Singing, mainly Brazilian songs. Current Management: Simon Harrison. Address: Lavender Cottage, Love Lane, Kings Langley, Hertfordshire WD4 9HN, England.

DREVER Ivan Cursiter, b. 10 June 1956, Orkney. Singer; Songwriter; Guitar. 2 sons, 2 daughters. Education: Self-taught. Career: Solo/duo work, 6 years; Joined Wolfstone, 1991; Toured America, Canada, Spain, Denmark, Germany and Far East; Networked in appearances with band. Compositions: Many compositions recorded. Recordings: 5 albums with Wolfstone; 3 solo albums; 3 duo albums with Knowe O'Deil. Honours: 2 Gold Discs for albums, Unleashed & The Chase. Memberships: MCPS; PRS. Hobbies: Reading; Sleeping. Address: 10B View Place, Inverness, IV2 4SA.

DREW Martin, b. 11 Feb 1944, Northampton, England. Musician (drums). m. Tessa Denise Rose, 5 Sept 1965, 1 son, 2 daughters. Musical Education: Taught by George Fierstone. Career: Worked with Oscar Peterson, 1974-; Ronnie Scott, 1975-; Played worldwide with many major artists including television, radio, album appearances; Played with: George Coleman; Niels H O Pedersen; James Moody; Dizzie Gillespie; Zoot Sims; Michael Brecker. Recordings: Featured with: Oscar Peterson; Ronnie Scott; Arturo Sandoval; Chucho Valdes; Bill Watrous; Joe Pass; Warren Vache; Dick Morrissey; John Critchinson; Joe Temperley; Tony Lee; Freddy Hubbard; Harry Edison. Honours: 3 times winner, British Jazz

Awards (Drums). Memberships: Musicians' Union; Jazz Umbrella. Hobbies: Cars; Photography.

DREWETT Steve, b. 29 Oct 1954, Islington, London, England. Singer; Songwriter; Musician (guitar). Musical Education: Self-taught. Career: John Peel Sessions, BBC Radio 1; Old Grey Whistle Test, BBC 2; Support tour with Billy Bragg. Recordings: Albums: Beggars Can Be Choosers, 1983; Repercussions, 1985; Kickstarting A Backfiring Nation, 1986; Is Your Washroom Breeding Bolsheviks, 1988; 45 Revolutions Per Minute, 1990. Membership: Musicians' Union. Hobby: Surfing the Internet. Current Management: No Wonder Management. Address: 154 Bishopsfield, Harlow, Essex, England.

DREYER Ole, b. 23 Nov 1961, Copenhagen, Denmark. Personal Manager; Booking Agent. 1 son. Education: Bachelor of Science. Career: Label manager, booking agent, personal manager for many local acts including Miss B Haven; Dizzy Mizz Lizzy; Baal; Strawberry Slaughterhouse. Address: PDH Dansk Musikformidling ApS, Ny Vestergade 7, 1 sal, 1471 Copenhagen K, Denmark.

DROGE Peter, b. 11 Mar 1969, Eugene, Oregon, USA. Singer; Songwriter. Career: Tours supporting Tom Petty; Melissa Etheridge; Sheryl Crowe; Appearance, Late Night With David Letterman; Included on soundtracks for films: Beautiful Girls; Dumb And Dumber; Tour supporting Neil Young. Recordings: Debut album: Necktie Second, 1994; 2nd Album, Find a Door, 1996. Honour: Find a Door voted Most Overlooked Album of the Year, The Rocket, 1996. Membership: ASCAP. Current Management: Curtis Management. Address: 417 Denny Way, Suite 200, Seattle, WA 98109, USA.

DROSSOS Petros, b. 11 June 1966, Athens, Greece. Sound Engineer; Producer. Career: Tape Operator, several Parisian studios, 1986; Assistant Engineer, Polysound Studios, Athens, Greece, 1987; In-house Engineer, Davout Studios, Paris, France, 1988-91; Freelance engineer, music, television, post-production, 1991-. Recordings: Engineer, producer: Single: with Mano Negra: King Kong Five; Albums: Raggabuzzin (French Reggae Compilation); with Rosemary's Babies: Lutte De Classe; Engineer: with Mano Negra: Live à la Cigale (TV programme tracks); with Hector Zazou and Les Polyphonies Corses, Ghetto Youth Progress (French Ragga Hip-Hop Compilation); IAM: Red, Black And Green (maxi-single). Hobby: Drinking Ouzo. Address: 213 Boulevard Davout, 75020 Paris, France.

DRUMMIE Richard. Vocalist; Musician (guitar, keyboards); Songwriter. Career: Songwriting partnership with Peter Cox, ATV Music; Founder member, duo Go West, 1982-. Compositions include: One Way Street (for film soundtrack Rocky IV). Recordings: Albums: Go West, 1985; Bangs And Crashes, 1986; Dancing On The Couch, 1987; Indian Summer, 1992; Singles: We Close Our Eyes, 1985; Call Me, 1985; Don't Look Down, 1985. Current Management: Blueprint Management, 134 Lots Road, London SW12 0RJ, England.

DRUMMOND Bill (William Butterworth), b. 29 Apr 1953, South Africa. Career: Former fisherman, set designer, carpenter, Scotland; Member, Big In Japan, 1977; Co-founder, Zoo Records; Manager, producer, Teardrop Explodes; Echo And The Bunnymen; A&R Executive, WEA Records, 1985; Formed KLF Communications, with Jimmy Cauty; Various recordings as: JMAS, 1987-88; Disco 200, 1987-89; Timelords, 1988; KLF, 1989-92; Justified Ancients Of Mu Mu, 1991-92; DMC European Convention, Amsterdam, 1990; Own studios, Transcentral 1988; Announced departure from music business, 1992. Recordings: Solo albums: The Man, 1986; Bill Drummond, 1987; Albums: The White Room, KLF,

1989; Chill Out, KLF, 1990; Hit singles: Doctorin' The Tardis, The Timelords (Number 1, UK), 1988; What Time Is Love, KLF, 1990; 3am Eternal, KLF (Number 1, UK), 1991; Last Train To Trancentral, KLF, 1991; It's Grim Up North, Justified Ancients Of Mu Mu, 1991; Justified And Ancient, KLF with Tammy Wynette, 1992. Publications: The Manual (guide to having a hit record), 1988. Honours: Gold discs: The White Room, 1991; 3am Eternal, 1991; BRIT Award, Best British Group, KLF (co-winners with Simply Red), 1992.

DRUSKY Roy Frank, b. 22 June 1930, Atlanta, Georgia, USA. Disc Jockey; Country Singer; Songwriter; Television Host. Education: Veterinary medicine, Emory University. Musical Education: Self-taught guitar. Career: Formed Southern Ranch Boys; Radio disc jockey, television announcer, 1950s; Member, Grand Ole Opry, 1958-; Concerts include: Regular UK tours; Wembley Festival; Film appearances: Forty Acre Feud; The Golden Guitar; White Lightning Express; Now involved in production and publishing; Hosts own television programme. Compositions include: Alone With You, Faron Young (US Country Number 1), 1958. Recordings: Hits include: Three Hearts In A Tangle; Second Hand Rose; Yes Mr Peters, duet with Priscilla Mitchell; If The Whole World Stopped Loving; Numerous albums include: Anymore With Roy Drusky, 1961; It's My Way, 1962; Yesterday's Gone, 1964; Country Song Express, 1966; All My Hard Times, 1970; Peaceful Easy Feeling, 1974; This Life of Mine, 1976; Roy, 1981; with Priscilla Mitchell: Love's Eternal Triangle, 1965; Together Again, 1966; We Belong Together, 1968.

DUBOWSKY Jack Curtis, b. 16 Aug 1965, Connecticut, USA. Composer; Arranger; Record Producer; Musician (guitar, bass, piano); Vocalist. Education: Graduate, University of California. Musical Education: Tutored by mother. Career: Radio appearance on German radio, 1990; Recording Technician with Metallica, Live Shit box set, 1994; Actor with Sick And Twisted Players, San Francisco; Currently playing with Snopea Chamber Ensemble. Compositions: The Silver Whistle, chamber opera, 1995; Slave, chamber opera, 1997. Recordings: Diazepam Nights, 1989; Helot Revolt, 1992; Fallout, 1990; Duchampians, 1991; Produced Glen Meadmore's songs for film Hustler White, 1996. Honours: Zellerbach Family Fund Grant, 1997; Friends of the San Francisco Library grant, 1997. Membership: BMI. Hobbies: Skiing; MG maintenance and repair. Current Management: De Stijl Records. Address: PO Box 170206, San Francisco, CA 94117-0206, USA.

DUCAS George, b. 1 Aug 1966, Texas City, Texas, USA. Artist; Singer-Songwriter; Guitarist. Education: BA Economics, Vanderbilt University, Nashville, Tennessee. Career: Moved to Nashville, 1991; Began songwriting and playing local clubs; Signed with Capitol Records, 1994; Television appearances include: CBS This Morning; CNN Showbiz Today; Entertainment Tonight; Good Day New York; Sound FX; FX Breakfast Time; Live From Queens; At The Ryman. Recordings: Singles, videos: Teardrops; Lipstick Promises (Top 10); Hello Cruel World; Kisses Don't Lie; Every Time She Passes By. Memberships: ASCAP; County Music Association. Hobbies: Fitness; Travel; Sports. Current Management: Coast to Coast.

DUCHARME Annette Marie-Jeanne Thérèse, b. 23 Feb, Windsor, Ontario, Canada. Recording Artist; Singer; Songwriter; Musician (guitar, bass, piano, keyboards). Education: BA, Drama, English. Musical Education: Self-taught. Career: Appeared: Peter Czowski show modelling for Evelyn Roth, 1977; Sang, played keyboards, Grade 8 Concert, St Mary's Academy; As lead singer, writer, bass player, toured with Bowers/Ducharme Trio, 1980-81; Keyboards, tour with John Lee Hooker, 1982-83; Opened for Richard Marx with own band, cross-Canada tour,

1989; Own band, opening tour for Larry Gowan, 1994; Sang at Kumbaya Benefits, 1993, 1994; Sang at: Grey Cup Half-time Show, with Tom Cochrane, 1994. Composition: Sinking Like A Sunset, recorded by Tom Cochrane. Recordings: Bowers/Ducharme, 1981; Blue Girl, 1988-89; Sanctuary, 1994; Flowers In The Concrete, 1995. Honours: (West Coast) Caras Award for Most Promising New Artist, 1985; Juno Nomination for Best New Female Singer, 1990; CMPA Award for number 1 Rock Song Of The Year, 1993; SOCAN Award for Pop Song of the Year, 1993; Last two for: Sinking Like A Sunset. Membership; SOCAN. Hobbies: Dancing; Reading poetry; Hiking up mountains; Loves water. Current Management: TKO Management. Address: 1669 East 13th Avenue, Vancouver, BC V5N 2B7 Canada.

DUCHEMIN Philippe, b. 2 Jan 1957, Toulouse, France. Jazz Musician (piano). Musical Education: Self-taught. Career: Played with Kenny Clarke; Lionel Hampton; Ray Brown; Joe Newman; Benny Powell; Wild Bill Davis; Frank Wess; Toured Europe with many French and American musicians, 1985-; Performed at Jazz Festivals with own trio throughout Europe, North Africa, 1990-. Recordings: Middle Jazz Quartet, 1980; Hommage à Count Basie, 1985; François Guin Et Les Four Bones, 1987; with Philippe Duchemin Trio: Alizés, 1990; Live!, 1992; Three Pieces, 1994; Trio with Dominque Vernhes, 1995; with Paris Barcelona: Swing Connection, 1990; Hard Swing, 1991; Wild Cat, 1992; Frank Wess Meets The Paris Barcelona, 1992. Hobby: Cooking. Address: 42 Rue de la Madeleine, 72000 Le Mans, France.

DUCROS Anne, b. 1 Dec 1959, Desures, France. Vocalist. 1 daughter. Musical Education: Boulogne Conservatory. Career: Festivals in France: Aiguillon; Dunkirk; Paris; Andernus; Vienne; Calui; Elsewhere: La Havane; Turin; Milan; Nuremberg; Concerts with Michel Legrand; Clark Terry; Didier Lockwood; Emmanuel Bex. Recordings: Don't You Take Chances, Anne Ducros Quartet; Vendredi 14, with L Strussardi. Honour: 1st Prize, Vocalist, Festival of Dunkirk, 1987; Festival of Vienne, France, 1988. Current Management: Prelude. Address: 50 Rue Bichat, 75010 Paris, France.

DUDGEON Gus. Record Producer. Education: Haileybury and Imperial Service College, Summerhill. Career: Recording engineer, Decca Records, 1960s; Worked with Rolling Stones; Small Faces; Marianne Faithfull; Ten Years After; Founder, own production company, 1968; Worked with The Strawbs; Ralph McTell; Bonzo Dog Doo-Dah Band; Producer for Elton John, 1969-. Recordings: Producer, albums: with Elton John: Elton John; Tumbleweed Connection; Madman Across The Water; Honky Chateau; Don't Shoot Me; Goodbye Yellow Brick Road; Caribou; Captain Fantastic; Rock Of The Westies; Here And There; Blue Moves; Ice On Fire; Leather Jackets; with Elkie Brooks: Pearls; Pearls II; Heart Over Mind, Jennifer Rush; Nonesuch, XTC; 3 albums with Ralph McTell; Joan Armatrading, Joan Armatrading; Ten Years After, Ten Years After; Strawbs, The Strawbs; Brooks: Pearls; Pearls II; Singles include: Don't Go Breaking My Heart, Elton John and Kiki Dee; I've Got The Music In Me, Kiki Dee; Urban Spaceman, Bonzo Dog Doo-Dah Band; Fool If You Think It's Over, Chris Rea; What's In A Kiss, Gilbert O'Sullivan; Menswear, We Love You. Honour: Grammy nomination, 1970, 1974 (x2), 1975 (x2). Membership: Re-Pro. Current Management: c/o Stephen Budd Management, 109B Regents Park Road, London NW1 8UR, England.

DUDLEY Anne. Musician (keyboards); Arranger; Producer; Composer; Songwriter. Career: Pianist, Playschool, BBC TV; Founder member, Art Of Noise, 1984-90; Solo artiste, composer, producer, arranger, 1990-. Compositions include: Television commercials

include: Volvo; Vauxhall Astra; Reebok; Television scores: Jeeves And Wooster; Anna Lee, Crime Traveller. Recordings: Albums: with The Art Of Noise: Albums: (Who's Afraid Of) The Art Of Noise, 1984; In Visible Silence, 1986; Daft, 1987; In No Sense? Nonsense!, 1987; The Best Of The Art Of Noise, 1988; The Ambient Collection, 1990; Solo albums: Songs From The Victorious City, with Jaz Coleman, 1990; Ancient And Modern, 1995; Singles: with The Art Of Noise: Beat Box, 1984; Close To The Edit, 1985; Peter Gunn, with Duane Eddy, 1986; Paranoimia, 1986; Kiss, with Tom Jones, 1988; Art Of Love, 1990; Film themes and scores: include: Buster; Wilt; Say Anything; Mighty Quinn; The Crying Game; The Grotesque (with Sting); Hollow Reed; The Full Monty; Also worked as arranger with: Lloyd Cole; A-Ha; Phil Collins; Rush; Boyzone; Spice Girls. Honours: Grammy, Best Rock Instrumental Performance, Peter Gunn, 1987; Academy Award, Best Original Comedy Score, for The Full Monty, 1998. Current Management: Air Edel, 18 Rodmarton Street, London W1H 3FW, England.

DUFFIN Graeme Ian, b. 28 Feb 1956, Glasgow, Scotland. Musician (guitar). m. Pamela, 15 Apr 1978, 1 son, 1 daughter. Education: HNC, Medical Laboratory Science (Biochemistry). Musical Education: Piano training; Guitar self-taught. Career: Member, folk group New Celeste, 1977-80; Member, Wet Wet Wet, 1985-; Major tours in UK, Europe, USA, Far East and Australia; Live video recorded at Glasgow Green, Edinburgh Castle and Royal Albert Hall. Recordings: Albums: Popped In Souled Out; Holding Back The River; High On The Happy Side; End Of Part One; Picture This; Hit singles include: Wishing I Was Lucky; Sweet Little Mystery; Angel Eyes; A Little Help From My Friends; Goodnight Girl; Love Is All Around (Number 1, 15 weeks, UK charts); Julia Said. Honours: BRITS Award, Best Newcomers, 1987; Award for co-production of Love Is All Around. Current Management: The Precious Organisation, 14/16 Spiers Wharf, Port Dundas, Glasgow, Scotland.

DUFFY Billy, b. 12 May 1959, Manchester, England. Musician (guitar). Career: Guitarist, Theatre Of Hate; The Cult (formerly Southern Death Cult and Death Cult), 1983-; Worldwide tours; Concerts with: Bauhaus; Billy Idol; Big Country; Metallica; Guns N'Roses; Lenny Kravitz; Concerts include: Futurama Festival, Leeds, 1983; A Gathering Of The Tribes, US, 1990; Cult In The Park '92 Festival, Finsbury Park, London, 1992; Guns N' Roses concert, Milton Keynes, 1993. Recordings: Albums: Southern Detah Cult, 1983; Dreamtime, 1984; Love, 1985; Electric, 1987; Sonic Temple, 1989; Ceremony, 1991; Pure Cult, 1993; The Cult, 1994; Singles include: Fat Man, 1983; Spiritwalker, 1984; She Sells Sanctuary, 1985; Rain, 1985; Love Removal Machine, 1987; Lil' Devil, 1987; Wild Flower, 1987; Fire Woman, 1989; Edie (Ciao Baby), 1989; Sweet Soul Sister, 1990; Wild Hearted Son, 1991.

DUFFY Stephen Anthony James, b. 30 May 1960, Birmingham, England. Singer; Songwriter. Education: Birmingham Polytechnic. Career: Founder member, Duran Duran, 1978; Solo artiste, under own name and as Dr Calculus, 1982-; Leader, own group Duffy, 1994-; Founder member, The Lilac Time, 1987-91; Recordings:Albums: Solo: The Ups And Downs, 1985; Because We Love You, 1986; Designer Beatnik (as Dr Calculus), 1986; Music In Colours, with Nigel Kennedy, 1993; with The Lilac Time: The Lilac Time, 1987; Paradise Circus, 1989; And Love For All, 1990; Astronauts, 1991; Duffy, 1995; Singles: Solo: Kiss Me, 1982; Hold It, 1982; Kiss Me (re-release), 1985; Icing On The Cake, 1985; London Girls, 1995; Sugar High, 1995; with The Lilac Time: Return To Yesterday, 1988; Current Management: Self-managed. Address: Box 2, Bromyard, Herefordshire HR7 4UU, England.

DUGMORE Geoff. Drummer; Songwriter; Producer. 1 son. Compositions: The Europeans, Vocabulary LP, Live LP and Recurring Dreams LP; Wildlife, Wildlife LP. Recordings: Played on records for: Deborah Harry; Stevie Nicks, US No 1; Killing Joke; Tina Turner, UK No 1 Foreign Affair; Jeff Beck; Gabrielle, both albums; Art of Noise; Gypsy Kings; Zoe; Rod Stewart; Joan Armatrading; Underworld; Tim Finn; Bob Geldof; Produced records for: Wildlife; Deborah Harry; Belouis; Some; Boss Beat; Sonny Roche; Jason Feddy. Current Management: One Management, 43 St Alban's Avenue, London W4 5JS, England.

DUJMIC Ratko, b. 7 Aug 1954, Zagreb, Croatia. Musician (piano, violin, electronic keyboards). m. Snjezana Simek-Dujmic, 2 Dec 1990, 1 son. Musical Education: Music Academy, Theory of Music and Pedagogy. Career: 4th and 6th places, Eurovision Song Contests, 1987, 1988; Winner, Eurovision song contest, 1989; Sold 38 million recordings; 4 solo television shows; 1 film score, much theatre music; Large number world tours include Opera House, Sydney, Australia. Compositions: About 800 works, many compositions for children and TV Series. Recordings: Around 90, audio and video, worldwide. Honours: All Festivals in former Yugoslavia. Memberships: Union Professional Musicians; Society of Composers, Croatia (DHS). Hobbies: Swimming; Writing poetry. Current Management: Croatia Records; Avet Publishing Company. Address: LL Maksimirsko Naselje I/V, 41000 Zagreb, Croatia.

DUKE George, b. 12 Jan 1946, San Rafael, California, USA. Jazz Musician (keyboards); Composer. Musical Education: Music lessons at school; BMus, San Francisco Conservatory, 1967. Career: Keyboardist, recording artist, 1966-; Accompanist, Dizzy Gillespie, 1965-67; Jean Luc Ponty, 1969; Member, Frank Zappa's Mothers of Invention, 1970-75; Formed jazz-fusion duos with Billy Cobham and Stanley Clarke; Also played with Cannonball Adderley; Bobby Hutcherson; Airto and Flora Purim; John Scofield; Lee Ritenour; Paulinho Da Costa; Major concerts include Nelson Mandela Tribute, Wembley. Recordings: Albums include: Save The Country, 1969; George Duke, 1969; The Inner Source, 1971; Inner Source, 1973; Feel, 1974; Faces In Reflection, 1975; I Love The Blues She Heard Me Cry, 1975; The Aura Will Prevail, 1975; Liberated Fantasies, 1976; Live In Europe, 1976; Solo Keyboard Album, 1976; From Me To You, 1977; Reach For It, 1977; Don't Let Go, 1978; Follow The Rainbow, 1979; Master Of The Game, 1979; A Brazilian Love Affair, 1980; Dream On, 1982; Guardian Of The Light, 1983; Secret Rendezvous, 1984; Thief In The Night, 1988; Night After Night, 1989; George Duke Collection, 1991; Snapshot, 1992; Muir Woods Suite, 1996; Numerous albums with Stanley Clarke include: Clarke Duke Project, 1981; Clarke Duke Project 2, 1982; 3, 1990; with Jean Luc Ponty: Live In LA, 1971; with Frank Zappa: Apostrophe, 1972; Roxy And Elsewhere, 1975; with Billy Cobham: Crosswinds, 1974; Live In Europe, 1976; BC, 1979; with Miles Davis: Tutu, 1986; Also recordings by: Airto; George Benson; Billy Cobham; Aretha Franklin; Freddie Hubbard; Michael Jackson; Al Jarreau; Shalamar. Current Management: Herb Cohen Management. Address: 740 N LaBrea Avenue, Los Angeles, CA 90038, USA.

DULFER Candy, b. Amsterdam, Netherlands. Musician (saxophone). Musical Education: Soprano saxophone from age 7. Career: First recording with father Hans Dulfer, aged 11; Founder, jazz-funk group Funky Stuff, aged 15; Support to Madonna, Dutch tour, 1987; Prince, Dutch tour, 1988; Also played with: Van Morrison; Aretha Franklin; Pink Floyd; Dave Stewart. Recordings: Albums as with Funky Stuff; Solo albums include: Lily Was Here, 1990; Big Girl, 1996; Also featured on We Too Are One, Eurythmics, 1989; Film soundtrack, De Kassiere,

with Dave Stewart, 1990; Singles: with Prince: Party Man; with Dave Stewart: Lily Was Here (Number 1, Netherlands), 1990. Address: c/o Inge Dulfer, PC Hoofstraat 154, 1071 CG Amsterdam, Netherlands.

DUMBRECK Allan M, b. 11 Mar 1961, Edinburgh, Scotland. Music Lecturer; Musician (keyboards). Education: BSc, Electrical Engineering, Edinburgh University. Career: Keyboard player, Big Dish, 1986-87; Horse, 1988-89; Lecturer, Jewel and Esk Valley College, 1986-91; North Glasgow College, 1991-; Established HND Music, Performance and Promotion; NGM Records, 1993; NGM Publishing, 1994. Recordings: The Same Sky, Horse, 1990; Rifferama, Thrum, 1994. Publication: Music Education Directory, editor and compiler. Memberships: Musicians' Union; PRS. Hobby: Property Restoration. Address: c/o North Glasgow College, 110 Flemington Street, Glasgow G21 4BX, Scotland.

DUNBAR Sly (Noel Charles), b. 10 May 1952, Kingston, Jamaica. Reggae Musician (drums); Producer. Career: Played with: The Upsetter; Skin Flesh And Bones; The Revolutionaries; Member, houseband, Channel One label; Member, US rhythm partnership, Sly and Robbie, with Robbie Shakespeare, 1975-; Formed own record label Taxi; Prolific session musician with artistes including: Peter Tosh; Bunny Wailer; Black Uhuru; Grace Jones; Bob Dylan; Ian Dury; Joan Armatrading; Tours with Black Uhuru. Recordings: Solo albums: Simple Sly Man, 1978; Sly Wicked And Slick, 1979; Sly-Go-Ville, 1982; with Sly And Robbie: Sly And Robbie Present Taxi, 1981; A Dub Extravaganza, 1984; Language Barrier, 1985; Sly And Robbie Meet King Tubby, 1985; Reggae Greats, 1985; The Sound Of Taxi, Volume 1, Volume 2, 1986; Rhythm Killers, 1987; Taxi Fare, 1987; Uhuru In Dub, 1987; The Summit, 1988; Hardcore Dub, 1989; Silent Assassin, 1990; Remember Precious Times, 1993. Current Management: Starline Entertainment, 1045 Pomme de Pin Lane, New Port Richey, FL 34655, USA.

DUNCAN Charles Melville, b. 25 Dec 1928, Eltham, London, England. Architect (retired); Semi-pro Musician (tenor saxophone). Widower, 1 daughter. Musical Education: Piano tuition, school; Private accordion tuition; Self-taught saxophone, clarinet. Career: Played with various local jazz bands from age 20; Later, member 2 hotel quartets, 8 years each; Leader, own 9 piece band: The Golden Era jazz Band; Convenor, Annual Jazz Extravaganza, Perth (now in 4th year). Membership: Musicians' Union. Hobbies: Playing saxophone; Arranging for own band; Architecture; Woodwork. Current Management: Self-managed. Address: 120 Burghmuir Road, Perth PH1 1HU, Scotland.

DUNCAN Torey Atkins, b. 5 August 1961, Summerfield, North Carolina, USA. Career: Regular Member, father's band, Bobby Atkins and the Countrymen; Recorded with father on Old Homestead Records, 1974 years; Guest Starred, The Country Side of Bobby Atkins, album. Recordings: Enough to Keep Me Dreaming On; Lost Below Heaven. Address: c/o Bobby Atkins, PO Box 251, Summerfield, NC 27358-0251, USA.

DUNHAM Aubrey, b. Houston, Texas, USA. Singer; Blues Musician (saxophone); Writer; Arranger; Producer. Musical Education: BA, Musical Education, Texas Southern University. Career: Tours, performances with artists including: Wilton Felder; Johnny Clyde Copeland; The O'Jays; The Temptations; Roy Head; Hank Crawford; Leader, own band, Aubrey Dunham and The Party Machine; Writer, arranger, producer. Recordings: Album: Now I'm Singing The Blues, songs include: I Used To Be A Dog (hit single); Shot Gun; I'm Glad About My Good Time. Membership: Houston Blues Society. Hobby:

Teaching music to youth. Current Management: Sirron Kyles, Samuel Rogers and Associates. Address: PO Box 8305, Houston, TX 77288, USA.

DUNKLEY Craig Anthony Spencer, b. 25 Mar 1964, Leicester, England. Musician (percussion). Musical Education: Artist in Education Course at Polytechnic. Career: Two week tour of Russia; Interview on Russian TV; 3 Week tour of Germany; 5 Day tour of Ireland; Local Radio sessions and interviews; Video shown on C4 TV programme, D-Energy. Recording: Album with TYD. Honour: Endorsed by Premier Percussion. Membership: Musicians' Union. Hobbies: Most sports; Travel; Adventure. Current Management: Access to Music; Big Wheel. Address: 86 Hopefield Road, Leicester LE3 2BL, England.

DUNMALL Paul Norman, b. 6 May 1953, South East London, England. Musician (saxophones, woodwind, bagpipes). Musical Education: Clarinet, Blackheath Conservatoire. Career: Tours, Europe with Marsupilami, 1970-71; USA with Blue Aquarius, 1972-74; USA/Europe tour with Johnny Guitar Watson; Tours of Europe in 1980s with: Spirit Level; Tenor Tonic; London Jazz Composers Orchestra; Danny Thompson; Mujician in Russia, 1991. Recordings: Ain't That A Bitch; Johnny Guitar Watson; Mice In The Wallet; Killer Bunnies; Spirit Level; Solo albums: Soliloquy; Folks (Double album); Spiritual Empathy/The Journey, Mujician. Honour: Best Soloist, Dunkirk Jazz Festival, 1979. Memberships: PRS; MCPS. Hobbies: Artwork; Wood engraving; Metal detecting. Current Management: Nod Knowles. Address: Linley House, 1 Pierre Place, Bath, Avon BA1 1JY, England.

DUNN Alan R, b. 19 Oct 1955, Boothstown, Lancashire, England. Musician (accordion, keyboards, tinwhistles). m. Wendy Elizabeth, 6 Jan 1984. Career: Musician for various projects with artistes include: Richard Thompson; Loudon Wainwright III; Bob Geldof; Rolf Harris; Vladimir Asriev; Tour with Toy Dolls, 1997-98. Recordings: Albums: Clannad: Magical Ring, 1983; Lyle McGuiness Band, 1983; Richard Thompson: Across A Crowded Room, 1985; Toy Dolls, One More Megabyte. Address: 10 Holden House, Deptford Church Street, London SE8 45Q, England.

DUNN Gary Michael, b. 7 Mar 1960, Sunderland, England. Musician (guitar). Career: Tours, Europe and USA, including Glastonbury Festival (Pyramid stage); Reading Festival; Appearances at major concert halls including Dominion Theatre; Sadlers Wells; Town and Country Club; Television and radio appearances include: Whistle Test; Jools Holland. Recordings: Albums with: Martin Stephenson and the Dainties: Boat To Bolivia; Gladsome Humour And Blue; Salutation Road And The Boys Heart. Memberships: Musicians' Union; PRS; MCPS. Hobbies: Football; Photography. Address: 280 Fulwell Road, Sunderland SR6 9AP, England.

DUNN Holly Suzette, b. 22 Aug 1957, San Antonio, Texas, USA. Country Singer; Musician (guitar); Songwriter. Education: University. Career: Singer, Freedom Folk Singers, represented Texas, White House bicentennial celebrations; Songwriter with brother Chris Waters, Nashville; Solo artiste, 1986-. Compositions include: Out Of Sight Out Of Mind, recorded by Christy Moore (co-written with brother Chris); An Old Friend, recorded by Terri Gibbs; Love Someone Like Me, recorded by New Grass Revival; That Old Devil Moon, recorded by Marie Osmond; Mixed Emotions, recorded by Bruce Murray. Recordings: Singles: You Really Had Me Going (US Country Number 1); Only When I Love; Strangers Again; That's What Your Love Does To Me; Albums: Holly Dunn, 1986; Cornerstone, 1987; Across The Rio Grande, 1988; The Blue Rose Of Texas, 1989;

Heart Full Of Love, 1990; Milestones, 1991; Getting It Dunn, 1992. Current Management: Refugee Management, 1025 16th Avenue S, #300, Nashville, TN 37212, USA.

DUPONT Hubert, b. 5 May 1959, Versailles, France. Jazz Musician (contrebass); Composer. m. 13 Oct 1990, 1 son. Education: Engineering diploma, INSA (Lyon). Musical Education: Schools; Self-taught; Master classes. Career: Played with: Steve Lacy; Glenn Ferris; Mathieu Michel; Harold Land; Robin Eubanks; Stefano Di Battista; Noël Akchoté; George Brown; Tommy Smith; Steve Potts; Laurent De Wilde; Le Marmite Infernale (ARFI); Mathias Rüegg; Paolo Fresu; Benoit Delbecq; Guillaume Orti. Recordings: Altissimo, Hubert Dupont; Pression, Kartet; A L'Envers, Quoi De Neuf Docteur. Memberships: Collectif HASK; UMJ (Union des Musiciens de Jazz). Hobbies: Bass; Photography; Books; Travel. Current Management: Self-managed. Address: 9 Avenue Pasteur, 93100 Montreuil, France.

DUPREE Cornell, b. 19 Dec 1942, Fort Worth, Texas, USA. Musician (guitar). m. Erma, 23 June 1959, 2 sons, 1 daughter. Education: 1 year college. Musical Education: High School saxophone; Self-taught guitar. Career: Joined King Curtis Band, New York City, 1962, appeared with Jimi Hendrix, Chuck Rainey; Session player, more than 2500 records with artists including: Sam Cooke; Wilson Pickett; Miles Davis; Joe Cocker; Michael Bolton; Mariah Carey; Bonnie Raitt; Toured and recorded with Aretha Franklin, 1967-76; Tours with: Roberta Flack; Joe Cocker; Grover Washington Jr; Currently tours with Herbie Mann and The Deep Pocket Band; Early 70's, teamed with Richard Tee, Steve Gadd to form STUFF, house band for Saturday Night Live. Recordings: King Curtis: Soul Seranade; Brook Benton: Rainy Night In Georgia; Aretha Franklin: Live At Fillmore West; Joe Cocker: Sting Ray; Barbra Streisand: Guilty; Donny Hathaway: Live At the Bitter Inn; Stuff: Stuff. Publications: Coast To Coast; Happy Farms; Southern Comfort. Honours: 2 Grammy Nominations. Memberships: NARA; ASCAP. Hobbies: Sketching; Drawing. Current Management: Fred Hirsch. Address: 696 Barron Avenue, Palo Alto, CA 94306, USA.

DURAL Stanley "Buckwheat" Jr, b. 14 Nov 1947, Lafayette, Louisiana, USA. Musician (zydeco, accordion). m. Bernite Dural. Career: Professional musician from age 9; Formed Buckwheat and the Hitchikers, 1970's; Joined "father of zydeco" Clifton Chenier, 1978-80; Formed Buckwheat Zydeco, 1980; Signed to Island Records, 1987 (first zydeco artist on major record label). Recordings include: Ma 'Tit Fille; What You Gonna Do; Also recorded with artists including: Eric Clapton; Willie Nelson; Dwight Yoakam; Keith Richards. Honours: 4 Grammy Nominations. Current Management: Ted Fox. Address: c/o Ted Fox, PO Box 561, Rhinebeck, NY 12572, USA.

DURBET Thierry, b. 31 Mar 1954, France. Arranger; Musician (keyboards, programming). Musical Education: Orchestral Directory in Conservatoire of Paris. Career: Records arranged for: T Durbet; Axel Bauer; Patricia Kaas; Stephanie De Monaco; Lane Davis; Jeanne Mas; François Feldman; Eddy Mitchell; Gerard Blanc; Corynne Charby; Francis Lalanne; Christophe; Partenaire Particulier. Honours: Prix: Rolf Marbot, 1988; Prix: Vincent Sotto, 1990. Hobbies: Informatique. Address: 234 Rue Championnet, 75018 Paris, France.

DURRANT Bertie (Brian), b. 25 July 1945, Gloucester, England. Jazz Musician (clarinet, soprano, tenor and baritone saxophones, blues harmonica); Vocalist. m. (1) Janice Newman, 1966; m. (2) Diane Thompson, 1976, 2 sons, 1 daughter. Education: Mid-Essex Technical College; University of East London. Musical

Education: Self-taught. Career: Industrial and advertising photographer; Professional musician, 1983-; Founder member, City Vagabonds (prize-winning Essex trad band); Numerous other bands including Tom Collins (4 years); Currently running own name line-up; tours, Europe; North America; Played jazz festivals throughout UK. Membership: Association of British Jazz Musicians. Hobbies: Collecting elderly reed instruments, clocks; Trying not to learn the banjo. Address: 23 Upper Moors, Great Waltham, Essex CM3 1RB, England.

DURRANT Clare Joanne Mary, b. 2 Dec 1962, Southport, England. Musician (keyboards, percussion, violin, guitar); Vocalist. Education: Lancaster University; Salford University College. Musical Education: John Hammond; Tommy Odueso; Wadada; Clare Hogan-Taylor; Salford University College. Career: Keyboard player for Suns of Arqa as Ireti, 1987-; Major concerts include: Womad Festival; Phoenix Festival; Hit The North, BBC Radio session; Set up Ireti Percussion workshops; Formed Otherworld, 1992. Recordings: Album: with Otherworld: Messages; Also tracks licensed for Compilations; with Suns of Arqa as Ireti: Hey Jagunath; Bhoopali (track part of BBC Radio 5 session Hit The North). Hobbies: Art; Designing and making clothes. Current Management: Self-managed. Address: 52 Riverbank Tower, Salford M3 7JY, England.

DURY Ian, b. 12 May 1942, Upminster, Essex, England. Singer; Actor; Composer. Career: Lecturer, Canterbury College of Art, Kent; Formed Kilburn & The High Roads, 1970-75; Ian Dury & The Kilburns, 1975-76; Ian Dury & The Blockheads, 1977-81; Solo artiste, 1977-; Concerts and tours include: Support to The Who, UK tour, 1973; Stiff Live Stiffs UK tour, with Elvis Costello, Nick Lowe, 1977; Support to Lou Reed, US tour, 1978; Annual UK tours, 1978-80; People Of Kampuchea benefit concert, with Paul McCartney, The Who, Robert Plant, London, 1979; The Big One, peace benefit concert, London, 1984; Appearances in films: Number One, 1985; Pirates, 1986; Hearts Of Fire, 1987; Split Second, 1992; Lord Upminster, 1981; BBC TV series: King Of The Ghetto, 1986; Actor, composer, 1987-; Writer of musical Apples, London, 1989. Recordings: Albums: New Boots And Panties, 1978; Do It Yourself, 1979; Lord Upminster, 1981; Juke Box Duries, 1981; 4,000 Weeks Holiday, 1984; Sex And Drugs And Rock And Roll, 1987; Also featured on 1992 - The Love Album, Carter USM, 1992; Singles include: Sex And Drugs And Rock And Roll, 1977; What A Waste, 1978; Hit Me With Your Rhythm Stick (Number 1, UK), 1979; Reasons To Be Cheerful (Part 3), 1979; I Want To Be Straight, 1980; Profoundly In Love With Pandora, theme to television series The Secret Life Of Adrian Mole Aged 13½, ITV, 1985.

DUTOT Pierre, b. 11 June 1946, Caen, France. Musician (trumpet); Trumpet teacher. m. Catherine Groult, 21 June 1975, 1 son, 2 daughters. Education: CAPEPS in EPS; DUEL in Psychology. Musical Education: Premier Prix Conservatoire National Supérieur de Musique, Paris, 1971. Career: Solo trumpeter, National Orchestra of Lyon; Professor, CNSM, Lyon; Solo concert artiste; Tutor, international Master Classes; Member, numerous ensembles: Hexagone; Trompolis; Polygone; Jericho. Recordings: 8 albums as solo artiste; Recordings with: Hexagone; Trompolis; Polygone. Hobbies: Basketball; Skiing; Tennis; Esoterism. Current Management: Kiesgen, Paris. Address: Domaine des Cerisiers, 105 Chemin du Soyard, 69126 Brindas-Lyon, France.

DUVIVIER Jérôme, b. 9 Oct 1965, St Cloud, France. Jazz Singer. Musical Education: Little Singers of Paris; Lessons with Stephanie Crawford, Michelle Hendricks. Career: Concerts in jazz clubs, France: Le Sunset; Le Petit Journal Montparnasse. Recordings: Un Effet Boeuf;

L'Ennui; Courtoisies; Epilogue. Honours: Prix de la SACEM, Crest Festival. Membership: Jazz on the Blocks (French Jazz Singers Association). Address: 29 Rue Basfroi, 75011 Paris, France.

DVORAK Jim, b. 16 Dec 1948, New York City, USA. Musician (trumpet); Composer; Teacher. m. Karen van der Valk, 13 Oct 1995. Musical Education: Eastman School of Music. Career: Regular international jazz festivals and concert tours; Connected with South African musicians, including Brotherhood Of Breath, District Six, Zila, 1970s-80s; Also played with: Dreamtime; In Cahoots; Leader, own band Bardo State Orchestra; Workshop leader with Community Music, London. Compositions include: Score for jazz drama Animal Farm, 1979; Co-writer, score for Kosh Theatre Company's production, The Jago, 1983. Recordings: with District Six: Aguzwakale; Ingoma Yabantwana; Leave My Name At The Door; To Be Free; with Annabel Lamb: Once Bitten; The Flame; When Angels Travel; Brides; Justice; with In Cahoots: Live In Japan; Recent Discoveries; with Research: Laws Of Motion; Social Systems; with Harry Moscoe: Country Boy; Sexy Dancer; Bunny Up, Dreamtime; Innocence, Joe Gallivan; Mama, Mama Quartetto; Gland, Fonolite; Joy, Joy; Thunder In Our Hearts, Jabula; Stanislav Sojka, Stanislav Sojka; Gasoline Band, Gasoline Band; Hat Music, Katie Perks. Honours: Young Jazz Musicians Award, Greater London Arts, 1976; Bachelor of Music. Memberships: Performing Right Society; Composers Guild. Address: 43B Mulkern Road, London N19 3HQ, England.

DVORZAK Zlatko, b. 5 Mar 1939, Zagreb, Croatia. Musician (piano); Composer; Conductor; Arranger; Teacher. m. Gordana Dvorzak, Oct 1970, 1 son, 1 daughter. Musical Education: Zagreb Musical Academy, graduated 1970. Career: Tours of Poland; Bulgaria; Russia; Hungary; Austria; Germany, 1961-76; Played and recorded with: Ernie Wilkins; Clark Terry; Art Farmer; Albert Mangelsdorff; Kai Winding; John Lewis; Bosco Petrovic; Stan Getz; Bud Shank; Al Porcino; Lee Harper; Sal Nistico; Gianni Basso; Ozren Depolo; Dusko Gojkovic; Johnny Griffin; Also performed music for radio and television. Compositions include: Revue; Amoroso; Clarinetorama; Black Street; All That Swing; Discopathia; Fender Express; Mr Hammond; Trumpet Swing; Jazz Concertino for String Quartet and Jazz Sextet; Croatian Folk Motives. Recordings: with BP Convention Big Band: Blue Sunset, 1975; Green Lobster Dream, 1978; Josipa Lisac and BP Convention, 1975; Croatian Big Band, 1977. Honours: First Prize, Contest for Young Pianists, Croatia, 1958; Best Arrangement, Belgrade Pop Festival, 1971. Memberships: Croatian Composers' Society; Orchestras Society; Jazz Club, Zagreb. Hobbies: Painting; Table tennis. Address: Buconjiceva 26, 10000 Zagreb, Croatia.

DWECK Sydney Stevan, b. 28 Dec 1926, New York City, USA. Musician (drums, percussion). 1 son. Education: AA (Hons), Los Angeles Valley College, 1966; BA (Hons), California State Universty at Northridge, 1968; PhD (Hons), University of Southern California, 1978. Career: Freelance drummer and percussionist, Broadway shows including Hello Dolly, Fiddler on the Roof, Kismet, Music Man and Pajama Game; Percussionist, film soundtracks including: The Unsinkable Mollie Brown; Top Banana; The Swinger; Made In Paris; Double Trouble; When The Boys Meet The Girls; Drummer, TV specials including Bob Hope, Perry Como, Fred Astaire, Tony Martin, Tony Bennett, Juliet Prowse, Lucille Ball and Danny Thomas; Musical Director for Liza Minnelli, Debbie Reynolds, Ann Margaret, Joel Grey, Carol Channing and Eleanor Powell. Compositions: Altoon's Dance (musical score), from TV special The Road To Lebanon (with Danny Thomas and Bing Crosby); Command performances for dignitaries including Royal Family of Monaco, 1958, British Royal Family, 1974, US Presidents Kennedy, Johnson, Nixon, Bush and Reagan. Recordings: Recorded with Stan Kenton; Nat King Cole; Freddy Martin; Jack Jones; Liberace. Membership: AFofM. Hobbies: Reading; Gardening; Writing. Address: 1507 Seacrest Drive, Corona Del Mar, CA 92625-1231, USA.

DYENS Roland, b. 19 Oct 1955, Tunis, Tunisia. Musician (guitar); Composer (classic-fusion style). m. Claire Fischbein, 7 Sept 1986, 1 son, 1 daughter. Musical Education: Concert degree, Ecole Normale de Musique de Paris. Career: Concert artist playing throughout world; Guitar festivals include: Nice; Cannes; Paris; Festival du Marais (Paris); Aix En Provence; Radio France Festival, Montpellier; Midem; Printemps de Bourges; Musicora; Carrefour Mondial De La Guitare (Martinique); Liège (Belgium); Arvika (Sweden); Tichy (Poland); Estergom (Hungary); Marktoberdorf (Germany); Classical Guitar Festival of Great Britain; Tours: Middle East; Indonesia; Scandinavia; Poland; Brazil; Numerous television and radio shows; Composer and arranger; Teacher; Member of juries of international contests including Montélimar; Geneva; Fort de France; Bari. Compositions include: Works for guitar solo; 2 octets; Concerto Métis (for guitar and string orchestra); Concerto En Si (for guitar and ensemble of 21 guitars). Recordings: Heitor Villa-Lobos Preludes and Roland Dyens works; Hommage à Brassens with the Enesco Quartet and Roland Dyens works; Ao Vivo (jazz trio); Suite Populaire Brésilienne, Heitor Villa-Lobos (concerto for guitar and string orchestra); French Songs Volumes 1 and 2; Concerto En Si (for guitar and ensemble of 21 guitars). Honours: Grand Prix du Disque, Academie Charles-Cros. Memberships: SACEM; ADAMI.

DYLAN Bob (Robert Allen Zimmerman), b. 24 May 1941, Duluth, Minnesota, USA. Singer; Musician (guitar, piano, harmonica, autoharp); Poet; Composer. Musical Education: Self-taught. Career: Solo folk/rock artist, also performed with The Band; The Traveling Wilburys; Grateful Dead; Songs recorded by estimated 3000 artists, including U2, Bruce Springsteen, Rod Stewart, Jimi Hendrix, Eric Clapton, Neil Young; Numerous tours: USA, Europe, Australia, 1961-; Film appearances include: Pat Garrett and Billy The Kid; Concert For Bangladesh; Hearts Of Fire. Compositions include: Blowin' In The Wind; Like A Rolling Stone; Mr Tambourine Man; Lay Lady Lay; Forever Young; Tangled Up In Blue; Gotta Serve Somebody; Don't Think Twice; It's Alright; A Hard Rain's Gonna Fall; The Times They Are A-Changin'; Just Like A Woman; I'll Be Your Baby Tonight; I Shall Be Released; Simple Twist Of Fate; Paths Of Victory; Dignity. Recordings: Over 40 albums include: The Freewheelin' Bob Dylan, 1964; Bringing It All Back Home, 1965; Highway 61 Revisited, 1965; Blonde On Blonde, 1966; John Wesley Harding, 1968; Nashville Skyline, 1969; Self Portrait, 1970; New Morning, 1970; Before The Flood, 1974; Hard Rain, 1976; Desire, 1976; Street Legal, 1978; Slow Train Coming, 1979; Infidels, 1983; Empire Burlesque, 1985; Knocked Out Loaded, 1986; Down In The Groove, 1988; Biograph (5 record set), 1988; Oh Mercy, 1989; Under The Red Sky, 1990; MTV Unplugged, 1995; with The Band: Planet Waves, 1974; Blood On The Tracks, 1975; with Traveling Wilburys: Traveling Wilburys, 1988; Vol 3, 1990; with Grateful Dead, Dylan And The Dead, 1989; Publications: Tarantula, 1966; Writings And Drawings, 1973; The Songs Of Bob Dylan 1966-75, 1976; Lyrics 1962-85, 1986. Honours include: Honorary D Mus, Princeton University, 1970; Inducted, Rock and Roll Hall of Fame, 1988; Grammy, 1990. Current Management: Jeff Rosen, PO Box 870, Cooper Station, New York, NY 10276, USA.

DYNNESEN Lise Kruuse, b. 24 Dec 1956, Copenhagen, Denmark. Musician (piano, keyboards); Composer (church organ, piano). Education: University studies: Danish Literature; Music. Musical Education: Student, organ, Royal Danish Academy of Music, 1991-. Career: Freelance musician, composer, experimental, rhythmic music scene, Copenhagen, 1978-; Bands include: Primi Band with Marilyn Mazur, 1982-85; Salsanama, 1988-91. Compositions: Sleigh Song - Or Minea's Tale, for organ, 1994. Honours: Scholarships from: The Art Foundation of The Danish State; The Royal Danish Academy of Music; The Society of Danish Jazz Beat Folk Authors (DJBFA). Membership: DJBFA. Hobbies: Skiing; Cycling. Address: Bregnegangen 5, DK-2300 Copenhagen S, Denmark.

DYSON John, b. 11 Mar 1948, Sheffield, England. Musician (keyboards, guitar); Music Producer; Analytical Chemist. Education: Technical college. Musical Education: Self-taught. Career: Formed Wavestar (electronic music), with Dave Ward-Hunt, 1983; Concerts include: UK Electronica '85, Sheffield; Concerts throughout UK; Festivals in France; Record label folded, band split 1988; Formed UK Label Surreal to Real with current partner/director Anthony Thrasher; Played major Dutch Festival, 1990-92; Now established as UK's leading independent label for contemporary instrumental/synthesizer music. Recordings: with Wavestar: Mind Journey; Zenith; Moonwind; Solo: Evolution; Aquarelle; Different Values; Various others for compilation; Wavestar albums re-released on own label. Honours: Voted Best Newcomer, National German Radio E M Show, 1991. Memberships: PRS; MU. Hobbies: Reading science fiction; Films; Driving; Space; Watching Sheffield Wednesday Football Club. Current Management: Surreal To Real. Address: PO Box 33 Evesham, Worcestershire WR11 6UX, England.

DZIUBINSKI Tomasz, b. 17 Sept 1961, Katowice, Poland. Artist Manager; Promoter. m. Mariola Bractawik, 27 Dec 1990, 2 sons. Education: Building Engineer, Technical University. Career: Promoter for: Deep Purple; AC/DC; Metallica; Black Sabbath; Fish; Chris Rea; Europe; Slayer; Paradise Lost; Sepultura; Faith No More; Dr Alban; Biohazard. Recordings: Produced over 20 albums of best Polish heavy metal bands including: Acid Drinkers; Kat; Turbo; Flapjack; Dynamind. Memberships: IFPI; ILMC. Hobbies: Sport; Music. Address: ul Szeligiewicza 8/21, 40-044 Katowice, Poland.

E

EARL SIXTEEN (Earl Daley), b. 9 May 1958, Kingston, Jamaica. Songwriter; Vocalist; Record Producer. Seperated, 2 sons. Musical Education: Self-taught. Career: Producer for L. Perry; Mikey Dread; Derrick Harriott; Neil Frazer; Douglas. Soundtrack of Judge Dread with Left Field's Band; Currently touring with Dreadzone Band; Major Concert, Glastonbury, 1995. Compositions include: Love Is A Feeling, Studio One; Release The Pressure. Recordings include: Holding Back The Years, Simply Red. Honours: Silver disc, Leftfield album. Memberships: PRS; Musicians' Union; MCPS. Hobbies: Writing; Reading; Driving; Swimming. Current Management: Martin Poole. Address: 30 Jackson Road, Holloway, London N7, England.

EARLE Steve, b. 17 Jan 1955, Fort Monroe, Virginia, USA. Singer; Songwriter; Musician (guitar). m. Lou Anne. Career: Bar room musician, Nashville; Solo artiste, with own band The Dukes, 1986-. Compositions include: My Old Friend The Blues, recorded by Janie Frickie; The Devil's Right Hand, recorded by Waylon Jennings; The Rain Came Down, for Farm Aid II benefit concert. Albums: Guitar Town, 1986; Early Tracks, 1987; Exit O, 1987; Copperhead Road, 1988; The Hard Way, 1990; Shut Up And Die Like An Aviator, 1991; Essential Steve Earle, 1993; Train A Comin', 1995; I Feel Alright, 1996; El Corazón, 1997. Current Management: Asgard Management, London, England; Four Twenty Two Management, Nashville, USA. Address: Four Twenty Two Management, 1808 West End Avenue, Suite 1100, Nashville, TN 37203, USA.

EARLY David, b. 6 Apr 1956, Lewisham, London, England. Musician (drums, ethnic hand, atmospheric, percussion). Career: Recording, performance with Mud; Dollar; National Youth Jazz Orchestra; The Nolans; Spitting Image; Sade; Andy White; Maura O'Connell; The Chieftains; Chris Rea; Van Morrison; Mary Black; Kieran Goss and Francis Black; Brian Kennedy; Carmena; Tamalin. Recordings: with Sade: Diamond Life; Promise; with Van Morrison: Avalon Sunset; Enlightenment; Greatest Hits Vol 1; Hymns To The Silence; Live From The Beacon Theatre; Carrying A Torch; Tom Jones/Van Morrison; Francis Black and Kieran Goss; with Tom Moore: Gorgeous And Bright; with Mary Black: The Holy Ground; The Circus. Membership: The Legendary Unknowns. Hobbies: Swimming; Cycling; Papier Maché; My hammock; Heading West. Address: Belfast, Northern Ireland.

EASTON Sheena (Sheena Shirley Orr), b. 27 Apr 1959, Bellshill, Glasgow, Scotland. Singer; Actress. m. Rob Light, 15 Jan 1985. Education: Speech and Drama, Royal Scottish Academy of Music and Drama. Career: Singer, Glasgow club circuit, 1979; Featured in television series The Big Time, BBC1, 1980; Solo recording artiste, 1980-; Concerts and tours worldwide, including: Royal Variety Show, 1980; The Big Day festival, Glasgow, 1990; Television appearances include: TV special, Sheena Easton ...Act 1, NBC, 1983; Actress, Miami Vice, NBC, 1987; Stage debut, Man Of La Mancha, Chicago, then Broadway, 1991-92; Launched own Seven Minute Flat Stomach fitness video. Recordings: Albums: Sheena Easton, 1981; You Could Have Been With Me, 1981; Madness Money And Music, 1982; Best Kept Secret, 1983; A Private Heaven, 1985; Do You, 1985; The Lover In Me, 1989; For Your Eyes Only - The Best Of Sheena Easton, 1989; The Collection, 1989; What Comes Naturally, 1991; No Strings, 1993; Hit singles include: Modern Girl, 1980; Morning Train (9 To 5) (Number 1, US), 1981; One Man Woman, 1981; When He Shines, 1981; For Your Eyes Only, theme music to James Bond film, 1981; We've Got Tonight, duet with Kenny Rogers, 1983; Telefone, 1983; Strut, 1984;

Sugar Walls, 1985; U Got The Look, duet with Prince, 1987; The Lover In Me (Number 2, US), 1989; What Comes Naturally, 1991; Contributor, Voices That Care charity record, 1991; Contributor, film soundtracks: Santa Claus - The Movie, 1985; About Last Night, 1986; Ferngully...The Last Rainforest, 1992. Honours include: Grammy Awards: Best New Artist, 1982; Best Mexican/American Performance, with Luis Miguel, 1985; First artist in history to have Top 5 hits in all major US charts (Pop, R&B, Country, Dance, Adult Contemporary), 1985; Emmy Award, Sheena Easton...Act 1, 1983. Current Management: Harriet Wasserman Management, 15250 Ventura Blvd, Suite 1215, Sherman Oaks, CA 91403-3201, USA.

EASTWOOD Al "Bama", b. 26 Oct 1943, Birmingham, England. Musician (guitar, flute, drums, harmonica); Vocalist. Career: Played drums, rock and roll bands; Member, backing group for Gene Vincent; Television, radio include: Thank Your Lucky Stars; Beat Club, BBC; Jazz FM; John Ciri Show; Paul Jones Show; American radio. Recordings: Album: Seeds; Album and single (own compositions). Honour: Non-drum competitions, Birmingham. Membership: Musicians' Union. Hobbies: Poetry; Classical music; Tai Chi. Address: 104 Maughn Court, Palmerston Road, Acton, London W3, England.

EATON Christopher, b. 16 Sept 1958, Dudley, West Midlands, England. Singer; Songwriter; Musician (keyboards). Musical Education: Grade 6 Piano. Career: Songwriter for: Cliff Richard; Janet Jackson; Amy Grant; Sheena Easton; Patti Austin; Michael Ball; Tours with Amy Grant and Cliff Richard; Performed at Grammy's New York, 1992; Solo recording career, contemporary Christian and pop music. Compositions include: songs for Heat In Motion, Amy Grant (5 million copies sold); Saviours Day, Cliff Richard, (Number 1, UK), 1990. Recordings: Solo albums: Vision; Wonderful World. Honours: Christian Song of the Year, Breath Of Heaven, 1993, USA. Memberships: Musicians' Union; Equity. Hobbies: Tennis; Golf; Country walks; Indian food; Soccer. Current Management: Stuart Ongley, SGO Music. Address: The Old Brewery, Church Street, Tisbury, Wilts, England.

EATON Nigel, b. 3 Jan 1966, Southampton, Hampshire, England. Musician (hurdy-gurdy). Musical Education: Guildhall School Of Music. Career: Member, Blowzabella, 1985-90; Ancient Beatbox, 1990; Whirling Pope Joan, 1993-; Robert Plant and Jimmy Page, 1995-; Also with Howard Skempton: Hurdy-gurdy Concerto; Bournemouth Sinfonietta, 1994; BBC Welsh Symphony, 1992; Films: Aliens; Friends; Harnessing Peacocks; Video: Snub TV, 1989, VHI, 1995. Recordings: 5 albums, Blowzabella; Album: Ancient Beatbox; Spin, Whirling Pope Joan, 1994; Unledded, MTV; No Quarter, Plant and Page, 1995; Sessions for: Marc Almond, 1987; Loreena McKennitt, 1994; Scott Walker, 1995; Gary Kemp, 1995; Solo: Music Of The Hurdy-Gurdy, 1987. Hobby: Sound Engineer. Address: 74 Auckland Road, Crystal Palace, London SE19 2DH, England.

EBB Fred, b. 4 Aug 1936, New York, New York, USA. Songwriter; Lyricist. Education: NYU graduate; Columbia University Masters. Career: Lyrics for: Cabaret; Flora; The Red Menace; Zorba; Happy Time; 70, Girls, 70; Woman Of The Year; The Rink; Kiss Of The Spider Woman; Chicago; The Act; And the World Goes Round. Composition: Steel Pier, 1997. Honours: 3 Tonys; 4 Emmys; 1 Grammy; Songwriters Hall Of Fame; Peabody and Ace Awards. Memberships: BMI Dramatics Guild; AFTRA; Equity. Hobby: Collecting art. Current Management: Sam Cohn, ICM, 40 West 57 Street, New York, USA. Address: 146 Central Park West, New York City, New York, USA.

EBBAGE David, b. 24 May 1942, Bingley, Yorks, England. Conductor; Pianist; Lecturer. m. Avril (Dean). m. 17 October 1964, 1 son, 2 daughters. Education: Trinity College of Music, London, England. Career: Fully qualified Signwriter and artist, 1950-70; Conductor, various orchestras; Founder, SPA Palm Court Orchestra; Pianist, concerts, recitals; Accompanist, with Radio, TV & Video. Compositions: Broadcast 7 CD's; Musical Director, Complete Theatré Company in Opera and Musicals. Honour: Alec Rowley Prize. Memberships: Trinity College Guild; Bill Mayerl & Robert Farnon Society; British Music Society. Hobbies: Swimming; Arranging. Address: The Chalet, 75 Claremont Road, Tunbridge Wells, Kent TN1 1TE, England.

EBBAGE Leonard Charles, b. 21 Aug 1931, Gorleston-on-Sea, England. Bandleader; Musician (keyboards, accordion). m. (1) Hazel Brown 13 June 1953, 3 sons. m (2) Gwen Leach, 1 July 1981, 1 daughter. Musical Education: Piano lessons, 5 years; 2 years working in holiday camps. Career: Broadcast with Hughie Green and Opportunity Knocks; Over 20 full summer seasons for Pontins; Ladbrooks; Holimarine; Warners; Walk-on, BBC and ITV; One of the top sequence dance bands in the country, playing short break dance holidays and sequence festivals all over England. Recordings: Albums: Goody-Goody; 50 Years Of Dancing; Sequence And Party Dances; Say It With Music. Honour: Played for Carl Alan Awards, 1994. Memberships: Musicians' Union; Equity. Hobbies: DIY; Gardening; Big bands. Address: Rosanne, Dyers End, Stambourne, nr Halstead, Essex, England.

ECKERT John Wallace, b. 13 Mar 1939, New York, USA. Musician (trumpet, horns). Musical Education: BA, Music, University of Rochester, 1961. Career: Musician with Stan Kenton; Si Zentner; American Brass Quintet; Buddy Morrow; Maynard Ferguson; Ten Wheel Drive; Deodato; Simon And Garfunkel; Benny Goodman; Gerry Mulligan; Toshiko Akiyoshi Jazz Orchestra, 1984-; American Jazz Orchestra, 1988-; Buck Clayton, 1989-. Recordings: Albums include: Brief Replies, Ten Wheel Drive, 1970; Chris Williamson, Chris Williamson, 1971; Whirlwinds, Deodato, 1974; Concert In Central Park, Simon And Garfunkel, 1981.

ECKERT Vojtech, b. 27 January 1956, Prague, Czechoslovakia. m. Iva Hanusova, 7 March 1997. Education: Faculty of Medicine, Charles University; Private Student of famous Czech Jazzman Karel Velebny. Career: Played piano, from age 4; Multiinstrumentalist, since age 15; Leader of many groups, since age 15; Established top Czech Jazz Trio in Prague, 1983. Compositions: CD Blues; A First Piece; Humoresque From Phillips' Hill; Hammond Intermezzo; Blues for Unknown Queen. Recordings: CD with CSABA DESEO, Magic Violin, 1995; LP Eva Olmerova, 1986; Radio records, 1986-; Svatopluk Košvanec, CD, 1998. Publications: Regular articles from sphere of jazz criticism and education in monthly periodical, Muzikus, 1992-95. Membership: Czech Jazz Society. Hobbies: Volleyball; Geography; History; History of Art; Architecture; Hunting; Fishing; Cooking. Address: MUDr Vojtech Eckert, Balbinova 5, 120 00 Prague 2, Czech Republic.

EDDIE (Jon Edwards), b. 1 Apr 1951, Hampstead, London, England. Musician (drums, percussion). m. Dee Dee, 3 Nov 1989, 1 son, 1 daughter. Musical Education: Studies with Joel Rothman. Career: Member, The Vibrators; Member, The Inmates; Numerous television and radio appearances worldwide, including Top of the Pops. Recordings: Albums: 14 albums with The Vibrators include: Pure Mania; V2 (UK Top 30); Hunting For You; 10 albums with The Inmates include: First Offence (US Top 30); Five; Fast Forward; Singles include: Dirty Water; The Walk; Also recorded with: Chris Spedding; PIL;

Christophe J; Garrie Lammin. Membership: Musicians' Union. Hobbies: Cricket; Travel. Current Management: Self-managed. Address: 16 Crouch Hill, London N4 4AU, England.

EDDY Duane, b. 26 Apr 1958, Corning, New York, USA. Musician (guitar); Songwriter; Record Producer. m. Miriam Johnson, Aug 1961. Career: Bandleader, The Rebels, 1958; Appearances include: UK tour, with Bobby Darin, Clyde McPhatter, Emile Ford, 1960; UK tour, 1967; First Rock'n'Roll Show, London, 1968; US tour, with band including Ry Cooder, 1983; Film appearances; Because They're Young, 1960; The Savage Seven, 1967; Kona Coast, 1967. Recordings: Albums: Have Twangy Guitar Will Travel, 1959; Especially For You, 1959; The Twang's The Thang, 1960; Songs Of Our Heritage, 1960; A Million Dollar's Worth Of Twang, 1961; Girls Girls Girls, 1961; Twistin' And Twangin', 1962; Twangy Guitar - Silky Strings, 1962; Dance With The Guitar Man, 1963; Twanging Up A Storm, 1963; Lonely Guitar, 1963; Duane Eddy, 1986; Twang Twang, 1993; As producer: Star Spangled Springer, Phil Everly, 1973. Singles include: Moving 'n' Groovin'; Rebel Rouser; Ramrod; Cannonball; The Lonely One; Yep!; Forty Miles Of Bad Road; Some Kinda Earthquake; Kommotion; Bonnie Come Back; Pepe; Theme From Dixie; Ring Of Fire; Caravan; The Ballad Of Paladin (theme for television series Have Gun Will Travel); Dance With The Guitar Man; Boss Guitar; Play Me Like You Play Your Guitar. Honours: NME Top Readers Poll Winner, World Musical Personality, 1960; Grammy, Best Rock Instrumental Performance, 1986. Address: c/o Fat City Artists and Management, 1906 Chet Atkins Plaza, Suite 502, Nashville, TN 37205, USA.

EDE Terence Frederick (Terry), b. 4 Aug 1935, London, England. Musician (saxophones, clarinets, flute, oboe). m. Brenda Bonner, 14 Mar 1959, 1 son, 1 daughter. Musical Education: Private, first tuition on piano. Career: Professional freelance player, 1962-; Tours include: Englebert Humperdinck; Jimmy Witherspoon; Larry Williams; Johnny Ray; Well-known teacher both at various schools and privately. Memberships: Musicians' Union; Association of British Jazz Musicians. Hobbies: Music; Motorcycling. Address: 7 Church Farm Lane, Cheam, Surrey SM3 8PT, England.

EDELIN Michel, b. 25 Feb 1941, Paris, France. Musician (jazz flute); Composer. m. Liliane Rouffaud, 6 July 1966, 1 son. Education: Education licence (university) pedagogical. Musical Education: Self-taught. Career: Live concerts recorded by Radio France; Played majority of French stages and major theatres; International festivals include: Montreux; Vienne (France), as guest guest of Dave Valentin Quintet; Nancy Jazz Festival with Barry Altschul, Jiri Stivin; JVC Jazz Festival, Paris; Lausanne; Nimes; Montpellier; Sons D'Hiver; Uzeste Musical, 1997; Plays with Byard Lancaster; Dave Valentin. Recordings: Triode - On N'A Pas Fini D'Avoir Tout Vu, 1972; Michel Edelin/Flutes Rencontre, 1979; Ornithologie/Ornithomagie, 1988; Vu Vol d'Ibis, Michel Edelin Quartet, 1989; Ze Blue Note Opéra - Jazz for quintet and childrens choirs, 1992; Round About Les Parapluies De Cherbourg (from Michel Legrand music film), 1995; Quartet - Déblocage d'Émergence, 1995. Hobby: Music. Current Management: Self-managed. Address: 35 Avenue Benoît Guichon, 94230 Cachan, France.

EDGE (THE) (David Evans), b. 8 Aug 1961, Wales. Musician (guitar); Songwriter. Career: Founder member, guitarist, rock group U2, 1978-; Regular national and worldwide tours; Major concerts include: US Festival, 1983; The Longest Day, Milton Keynes, 1985; Live Aid, Wembley, 1985; Self Aid, Dublin, 1986; A Conspiracy Of Hope (Amnesty International tour), 1986; Smile Jamaica (hurricane relief fundraiser), 1988; Very Special Arts Festival, White House, Washington,

1988; New Year's Eve Concert, Dublin (broadcast live Europe), 1989; Yankee Stadium, New York (second ever concert there). Compositions include: Music to A Clockwork Orange 2004, Royal Shakespeare Company, 1990. Recordings: Albums: Boy, 1980; October, 1981; War (Number 1, UK), 1983; Under A Blood Red Sky, 1983; The Unforgettable Fire (Number 1, UK), 1984; Wide Awake In America, 1985; The Joshua Tree (Number 1, UK and US), 1987; Rattle And Hum, also film (Number 1, US), 1988; Achtung Baby (Number 1, US), 1991; Zooropa (Number 1, US and UK), 1993; Passengers, film soundtrack (with Brian Eno), 1995; Pop, 1997; Hit singles include: Out Of Control (Number 1, Ireland), 1979; Another Day (Number 1, Ireland), 1980; New Year's Day, 1983; Two Hearts Beat As One, 1983; Pride (In The Name Of Love), 1984; With Or Without You (Number 1, US), 1987; I Still Haven't Found What I'm Looking For (Number 1, US), 1987; Where The Streets Have No Name, 1987; Desire (Number 1, UK), 1988; Angel Of Harlem, 1988; When Love Comes To Town, with B.B. King, 1989; All I Want Is You, 1989; The Fly (Number 1, UK), 1991; Mysterious Ways, 1992; Even Better Than The Real Thing, 1992; Who's Gonna Ride Your Wild Horses, 1992; Stay, 1993; Hold Me, Thrill Me, Kiss Me (from film Batman Forever), 1995; Discotheque, 1997; If God Will Send His Angels, 1997; Contributor, Mystery Girl, Roy Orbison, 1988; Red Hot + Blue, 1990; Pavarotti And Friends, 1996. Honours include: Grammy Awards: Album Of The Year, 1987; Best Rock Performance, 1987, 1989; Best Rock Vocal, 1993; BRIT Awards: Best International Act, 1988-90; Best Live Act, 1993; JUNO Award, 1993; World Music Award, 1993; Q Magazine Awards: Best Producer (with Flood, Brian Eno), 1993; Best Act In The World, 1990, 1992, 1993; Merit Award, 1994; Numerous magazine poll wins and awards; Gold and Platinum discs. Current Management: Principle Management. Address: 30-32 Sir John Rogersons Quay, Dublin 2, Ireland.

EDMUNDS Dave, b. 15 Apr 1944, Cardiff, Wales. Singer; Musician (guitar); Record Producer. Career: Member, bands including 99ers; The Raiders; The Image; Member, Love Sculpture, 1968-69; Solo artiste, 1969-1977; Founder, Rockpile, 1977-81; Solo artiste, 1981-; Record producer, 1969-; Built own Rockfield Recording Studios, 1969; Numerous tours include: with Bad Company, US, 1977; with Nick Lowe, 1977, 1978; Elvis Costello, Mink DeVille, 1978; Rock'n'Roll Revue, US tour, 1990; Concerts include: Knebworth Festival, 1978; Concert For Kampuchea, with Wings, Elvis Costello, 1979; Reading Festival, 1982; US Festival, 1982; Princes Trust Rock Gala, Wembley Arena, 1987; John Lennon Tribute Concert, Merseyside, 1990; Television includes: South Bank Show; Blue Suede Shoes, Carl Perkins special, C4; Film appearance: Stardust, 1974. Recordings: Albums: with Love Sculpture: Blues Helping, 1968; Forms And Feeling, 1969; with Rockpile: Tracks On Wax, 1978; Repeat When Necessary, 1979; Seconds Of Pleasure, 1980; Solo: Rockpile, 1972; Subtle As A Flying Mallet, 1975; Get It, 1977; Tracks On Wax, 1978; Twangin', 1981; The Best Of Dave Edmunds, 1982; DE7, 1982; Information, 1983; Riff Raff, 1984; Closer To The Flame, 1990; Singles include: with Love Sculpture: Sabre Dance, 1968; Solo: I Hear You Knocking (Number 1, UK), 1970; Baby I Love You, 1973; Born To Be With You, 1973; I Knew The Bride, 1977; Girls Talk, 1979; Queen Of Hearts, 1979; Singin' The Blues, 1980; The Race Is On, 1981; Contributor, I Fell In Love, Carlene Carter, 1990; Producer for artistes including: Brinsley Schwarz; The Flamin' Groovies; Shakin' Stevens; Stray Cats; Fabulous Thunderbirds; Everly Brothers; Status Quo; k d lang; Music for film soundtracks: Porky's Revenge; Planes, Trains And Automobiles. Current Management: Gold Mountain Entertainment, 3575 Cahuenga Blvd W, Suite 450, Los Angeles, CA 90068, USA.

EDWARDS Bernard, b. 31 Oct 1952, Greenville, North Carolina, USA. Musician (bass); Record Producer. Career: Founder member, Big Apple Band, 1972-76; Became Chic, 1977-; Also recording artiste, record producer. Recordings: Albums: with Chic: C'Est Chic, 1978; Risqué, 1979; Best Of Chic, 1980; Take It Off, 1982; Believer, 1983; Solo: Glad To Be Here, 1985; Freak Out, 1987; Chic-Ism, 1992; Singles: Dance, Dance, Dance, 1978; Everybody Dance, 1978; Le Freak (Number 1, US), 1978; I Want Your Love, 1979; Good Times, 1979; My Forbidden Lover, 1979; My Feet Keep Dancing, 1980; Soup For One, 1982; Jack Le Freak, 1987; Chic Mystique, 1992; As co-producer, writer (with Nile Rodgers) include: Norma Jean, Norma Jean Wright, 1977; He's The Greatest Dancer, Sister Sledge, 1979; We Are Family, Sister Sledge, 1979; Love Somebody Today, Sister Sledge; Diana, Diana Ross, 1980; Upside Down, Diana Ross, 1980; Koo Koo, Debbie Harry, 1981; Why, Carly Simon, 1982.

EDWARDS Bloater B, b. 2 Dec 1971, Aldershot, Hampshire, England. Musician (guitar); Singer (drums, bass, piano). m. Lisa Janine, 29 Apr 1995. Career: Band: Big Boy Bloater And His Southside Stompers; Appearances include: Lyon Jazz Festival; Birmingham Jazz Festival; London's Forum; Hammersmith Palais; Hemsby Rock'n'Roll Festival; Classic Cars, Channel 4 TV; Actor: Let Him Have It; Lipstick On Your Collar; Shine On Harvey Moon. Recordings: Album: (1 track) Haunted Highway; Jump For Joy With The Big Boy (EP), Big Boy Bloater And His Southside Stompers. Membership: Musicians' Union. Hobbies: Writing songs; Touring; Recording. Current Management: Self-managed. Address: Aldershot, Hampshire, England.

EDWARDS Dave, b. 9 Aug 1948, Shrewsbury, England. Music Teacher; Musician (steel pan, guitar). m. Andrea, 28 Dec 1978, 1 son. Musical Education: Shoreditch College of Education, Surrey; Graduate Courses, Wolverhamapton Polytechnic and Northumbria University; Self-taught. Career: Scandinavian tour with Razzle Dazzle Gatemouth Spasm String Band, 1973; Member and Musical Director, Pan L Beaters Steel Band, 1992-96; Television: with North Tyneside Steelband: Boom, 1991; Local news, 1994, 1996; Numerous local radio broadcasts; Freelance Tutor and Workshop Leader, Musical Director for Steel Bands; Teacher, GCSE Music and Music Appreciation. Compositions: Steelband compositions include: Sunshine; Geordie Calypso; Several other steelband compositions and arrangements. Recordings: Some self-promoted recordings. Publications: Steelpan booklet, 1991. Honours: Blood donor (silver). Memberships: Musicians' Union; NUT. Hobbies: Outdoor; Travel; Caravanning; DIY. Current Management: Self-managed. Address: Aynuck's Lodge, 20 Glendale Avenue, Whitley Bay, Tyne and Wear NE26 1RX, England.

EDWARDS David Maurice, b. 29 Apr 1949, Paddock Wood, Kent, England. Musician (bass guitar). m. Michelle, 17 Sept 1976, 2 sons. Musical Education: Self-taught. Career: Played local bands, progressed to West End, London, 1967-; Venues with Sidney Lipton Agency, 1972; Residency with Kingswest, Brighton 1973-80; Currently active on Brighton circuit; Cabaret backing includes: Bruce Forsyth; Vince Hill; Russ Conway; Ronnie Hilton. Membership: Musicians Union. Hobbies: Family. Address: 60 Mill Rise, Westdene, Brighton BN1 5GH, England.

EDWARDS Don, b. 20 Mar 1939, Boonton, New Jersey, USA. Balladeer; Singer; Songwriter; Musician (acoustic guitar, banjo, mandolin). m. Kathy Jean Davis, 7 Jan 1978, 2 daughters. Career: Started as actor, singer, stuntman, Six Flags Over Texas, 1961; First record, 1964; Part owner, White Elephant Saloon, Fort Worth, Texas;

Recognition through Cowboy Poetry Gathering, Elko; Tours USA; Canada; Britain; New Zealand; Europe; Performs solo, with cowboy band, with horse, with cowboy poet Waddie Mitchell as The Bard And The Balladeer; As The Cowboy Jubilee; Musicologist, author on Western and traditional cowboy music; Educational services to universities; Appeared with Fort Worth, Las Vegas and Colorado Springs symphony orchestras. Recordings: Happy Cowboy; America's Singing Cowboy; Songs Of The Cowboy; Guitars And Saddle Songs; Desert Nights And Cowtown Blues; Songs Of The Trail; The Bard And The Balladeer (with Waddie Mitchell); Also recorded on: Other Voices, Other Rooms, Nanci Griffith; The Wild West (soundtrack); How The West Was Swung, Tom Morrell; Ridin' West, Volumes I and II; with Buckaroo: Visions And Voices Of The American Cowboy; A Christmas Tradition; with Michael Martin Murphey: Cowboy Songs; Cowboy Christmas. Publications: Classic Cowboy Songs; Book/tape anthologies: Songs Of The Cowboy; Guitars And Saddle Songs. Honours: Western Heritage Wrangler Award, Outstanding Traditional Music, Cowboy Hall Of Fame, 1992; Western Heritage Wrangler Awards, 1992, 1996. Membership: AFTRA. Hobbies: Ranching; Horses; Antiques; Cowboy, Western collectibles; Vintage instruments. Current Management: Scott O'Malley and Associates. Address: PO Box 9188, Colorado Springs, CO 80932, USA.

EDWARDS Janet, b. Huddersfield, Yorkshire, England. Singer; Musician (piano). Divorced, 2 sons. Education: College of Technology, Huddersfield. Musical Education: Studied piano, with Dr Michael Kruszynski; Piano and song recitals, 1974-; Performed with artists including those from Royal Opera Huse, ENO soloists; Performances: Italy; France; Germany; UK including South Bank, Wigmore Hall; Devised, performed own shows: Sounds Entertaining; I Say I Play; Munich, London, other UK halls; Solo work, classical, popular, theatre, jazz music, in: Europe; Scandinavia; Middle East; Accompanist, assistant musical director, Royal Gala Performance of works by Stephen Sondheim, Theatre Royal Drury Lane; Work as voice coach began Royal Academy of Music, early 1980s; Master class group sessions working with professionals and non-professionals, 1989-; Played: Anna in Girls Were Made To Love And Kiss, West End, 1994; Currently runs professional seminars in auditioning techniques; Course for voice teachers; Workshops; Seminars for general public. Honours: Diploma with distinction, Huddersfield College of Technology; ARCM; LTCL Dip Ed. Hobbies: Tai Chi; Tennis.

EDWARDS Terry David, b. 10 Aug 1960, Hornchurch, Essex, England. Musician (saxophones, trumpet, guitar, piano). Musical Education: BA (Hons), University of East Anglia, 1979-82. Career: Founder member, The Higsons, 1980-86; Co-founder, with Mark Bedford, Butterfield 8, 1988-; Solo artist with and without The Scapegoats, 1991-; Session player with: Gallon Drunk; Julian Cope; Nick Cave and The Bad Seeds; Lush; Tindersticks; Barry Adamson; Test Department; Spiritualized; Moonshake; Farmers Boys; Dept S; Serious Drinking; Yeah Jazz; Alternative TV; Bounty Hunters; Spirea X; Anthony Moore. Recordings: Plays Salutes and Executes, 1993; Terry Edwards Presents No Fish Is Too Weird For Her Aquarium, 1994; I Was Dora Suarez (with Derek Raymond and James Johnston), 1994; My Wife Doesn't Understand Me, 1995. Memberships: Associate member, PRS; MCPS; SPNM. Hobbies: Record buying; Concert-going; Shouting at the television. Address: STIM Records c/o Damaged Goods, PO Box 671, London E17 6NF, England.

EDWINS Myron, b. 4 Jan 1958, Washington, PA, USA. Singer; Musician; Entertainer; Producer (Bass Guitar, Keyboards). Career: Solo artist from 1989-; Tours with The Edwards Generation in Switzerland, Norway, Germany, Japan and Canada; Appeared on TV specials: Mike Douglas in San Francisco, Evening Magazine and Zoom; Business Ventures: MEP; EPB Management, Music publishing; Currently lead singer and keyboardist for R and B group, Movin'. Recordings: Do You Love Me, 1990; Do You Like The Way I Do It, 1991; Love Is, 1993; Let Me Entertain You, 1994; The Best Thing To Do, 1994; I'll See You Again, Myron Edwins, 1995. Hobbies: Video Taping; Swimming; Dancing; Films; Parks and Beaches. Current Management: Entertainment Agency; MEP. Address: Myron Edwins Productions, Box 8442, Pittsburg, CA 94565-8442, USA.

EINARSDOTTER Elise, b. 11 July 1955. Musician (piano). m. Olle Steinholtz, 1 daughter. Musical Education: Diploma of Arranging and Composition, Berklee College of Music, USA, 2 years; Royal Academy of Music, Stockholm, 2 years. Career: Leads, Elise Einarsdotter Ensemble, 1984-; Composes music to lyrics; Writes for choir and orchestra; Tours in Scandinavia, Italy, USA, Sweden, Norway, France, Belgium, Holland, England, Ethiopia and India. Compositions: My Heart; Alexandrinen; Sphinx Acre; Ljus, Dagg, Grönska; Yus Dagg; Eronska, I Live in Music. Recordings: CDs: Sacred Hearts; Secrets of Living; Senses; Rosenäng; Sketches of Roses. Publication: Rosenäng. Honours: Numerous grants and awards; Lo-Kulturpris, 1993. Membership: Swedish Academy of Jazz. Hobbies: Family and Friends; Sailing. Current Management: Mistral Music. Address: Bandyvägen 47, 129 49 Hagersten, Sweden.

EISLER Fil. Artist: Bass & Guitar Player; Producer. Recordings: Robbie Williams; Machine; Imogen Head; Jason Feddy; Ali Thompson and Yazz; Messiah; Galliano; Denzil; Crazy Little Trees. Current Management: One Management Ltd, 43 St Alban's Avenue, London W4 5JS, England.

EJEM Ladislav, b. 18 February 1922, Cernosice, Czechoslovakia. m. Vera Vorlova, 23 March 1949. Education: Conservatoire Prague. Career: Conductor, Na Fidlovacce Theatre; Own orchestra, playing in various places; Piano & Organ Soloist. Compositions: South Bohemia Countryside; Missa Brevis; So As At That Time; Cernosice Polka. Recordings: Tokay Gallop; Red Flower; Renata. Publications: The Ant Suite; The Spanish Suite; The Jubilee March for the Czech Social Democracy Party. Honours: Various honour acknowledgements & prizes. Memberships: Authors' Union; OSA. Hobbies: Study of Ants; Cat Breeding; Books. Address: Zd Lhoty 460, 252 28 Cernosice, Czech Republic.

EKBERG Ulf, b. Sweden. Singer; Songwriter. Career: Singer, Ace Of Base, 1990-. Recordings: Albums: Happy Nation, 1993; The Bridge, 1995; Singles: Wheel Of Fortune; All That She Wants; Lucky Love; Number 1 records in UK; US; Canada; Across Europe; Australia; New Zealand; Israel; Argentina. Honours: Highest-ever worldwide sales for a debut album (Happy Nation, 19 million); Platinum discs worldwide. Current Management: Siljemark Production AB, Gårdsvägen 4, S-171 52 Solna, Sweden.

ELDRITCH Andrew (Andrew Taylor), b. 15 May 1959, England. Singer. Education: Oxford University. Career: Founder member, Sisters Of Mercy, 1980-85; Regular international tours; Concerts include: York Rock Festival, 1984; Royal Albert Hall, London, 1985; Performed as the Sisterhood, 1986; Reforms Sisters of Mercy, 1987-; European tour, 1990; Tune In Turn On Burn Out tour, with Public Enemy, Gang Of Four, Warrior Soul, 1991; Reading Festival, 1991; Support to Depeche Mode, Crystal Palace, 1993. Recordings: Albums: First And Last And Always, 1985; Gift (as the Sisterhood), 1986; Floodland,

1988; Vision Thing, 1990; Some Girls Wander By Mistake, 1992; Greatest Hits, Vol 1, 1993; Singles include: Temple Of Love, 1983; Body And Soul, 1984; Walk Away, 1984; This Corrosion, 1987; Dominion, 1988; Lucretia My Reflection, 1988; More, 1990; Temple Of Love (1992), 1992; Under The Gun, 1993. Current Management: Hard To Handle Management, 640 Lee Road #106, Wayne, PA 19087, USA.

ELFMAN Danny, b. 29 May 1954, USA. Composer; Musician (guitar); Vocalist. Career: Lead singer, songwriter, guitarist, band Oingo Boingo; Compositions: Film scores: Pee-Wee's Big Adventure; Beetlejuice; Batman; Batman Returns; Dick Tracy; Darkman; Edward Scissorhands; Sommersby; Other music for films includes: Weird Science; Ghostbusters II; Something Wild; Television series score: The Simpsons. Recordings: Albums: with Oingo Boingo: Only A Lad, 1981; Nothing To Fear, 1982; Good For Your Soul, 1983; Dead Man's Party, 1985; Boingo, 1986; Skeletons In The Closet, 1989; Dark At The End Of The Tunnel, 1990. Honour: Emmy Nomination, The Simpsons. Current Management: L.A. Personal Development, 950 N. Kings Road, Suite 266, West Hollywood, CA 90069, USA.

ELIS Hefin, b. 4 June 1950, Port Talbot, Wales. Composer; Arranger; Musician (piano, guitar, bass guitar). m. Marian Thomas, 25 July 1981, 2 daughters. Education: University College of Wales, Aberystwyth. Career: Founder member, Welsh language rock band, Edward H Dafis; Recording Engineer, Producer for Sain Records. Composition: I'r Gad. Recording: Ysbryd Y Nos. Memberships: PRS; Musicians' Union. Hobbies: Football; Rugby; Current affairs. Address: Bryn Gellyg, 22 Lon Ddewi, Caernarfon, Gwynedd, Wales.

ELLINGTON Mercer Kennedy, b. 11 Mar 1919, Washington, USA. Musician (trumpet); Bandleader. Musical Education: Columbia University; Juillard School Of Music. Career: Son of Edward "Duke" Ellington; Bandleader until 1949; General Assistant to Duke Ellington, 1955-59; Trumpeter, manager, Duke Ellington Orchestra, 1965-74; Orchestra leader, 1974-. Recording: with Duke Ellington: The Three Black Kings. Publications: Author, Duke Ellington In Person - An Intimate Memoir, 1978. Address: Duke Ellington Orchestra, c/o Ted Schmidt and Associates, 6278 N Federal Highway, Suite 274, Fort Lauderdale, FL 33308, USA.

ELLIOT Sean Andrew, b. 24 Jan 1970, London, England. Musician (guitar); Programming. Musical Education: Private guitar tuition; Part time musicianship, Goldsmiths College. Career: UK circuit tour with: Out Of My Hair; TV Sky Star Search with Earthworks, 1991; Many regional radio appearances and live radio 1, GLR, 1994-95. Recordings: Guitar on: Out Of My Hair; Debut album, 2 singles, 1994-95; Sessions for alternative mixes of Seal's Crazy. Membership: Musiians' Union. Hobbies: Parties; Clubs; Animation and video. Current Management: Space Band Management. Address: 32B Weinster Square London, W2 4NQ, England.

ELLIOTT Anthony (Tony), b. 18 Dec 1963, Liverpool, Merseyside, England. Songwriter; Musician (bass guitar, guitar, piano/keyboard). Musical Education: Self-taught, currently taking musical diploma. Career: Numerous British tours with: 16 Tambourines, 1988-1990; The Tambourines, 1990-1993; Barcelona Olympic Festival with: The Tambourines; Supported, various British tours, 1989-90 (including NEC and Secc): Wet Wet Wet; Squeeze; Hue and Cry; Echo and the Bunnymen; Various appearances national, regional, television, radio. Recordings: Album: 16 Tambourines: How Green Is Your Valley, 1989; Singles: 16 Tambourines: If I Should Stay; How Green Is Your Valley (co-writer); The

Tambourines (EPs): She Blows My Mind; Your So Beautiful; Horizon 7; Sebastiens Men (co-writer). Membership: Musicians' Union. Hobbies: Computer design; Circuit training; Football; Arranging, composing; Socialising; Driving. Address: 210 Mather Avenue, Allerton, Liverpool, Merseyside L18 9TG, England.

ELLIOTT Joe, b. 1 Aug 1959, Sheffield, England. Vocalist. Career; Vocalist, UK rock group Def Leppard, 1977-; Concerts include: Tours supporting Sammy Hagar; AC/DC; Ted Nugent; Reading Rock Festival, 1980; World tour, 1983; Monsters Of Rock Festival, Castle Donington; BRIT Awards, Royal Albert Hall; Freddie Mercury Tribute Concert, Wembley, 1992; Radio includes: Stand-in disc jockey for Simon Bates, BBC Radio 1, 1992. Recordings: Albums: On Through The Night, 1980; High'n'Dry, 1981; Pyromania, 1983; Hysteria, 1987; Adrenalize, 1992; Retroactive, 1993; Vault 1980-95, 1995; Slang, 1996; Singles include: Photograph; Rock Of Ages; Foolin'; Animal; Pour Some Sugar On Me; Hysteria; Armageddon II, 1988; Love Bites; Let's Get Rocked; Make Love Like A Man; Have You Ever Never Needed Someone So Bad; Stand Up (Kick Love Into Motion); Heaven Is; Tonight; Two Steps Behind, featured in film The Last Action Hero; When Love And Hate Collide. Honours include: American Music Awards: Favourite Heavy Metal Album, Favourite Heavy Metal Artists, 1989. Current Management: Q-Prime Inc., 729 Seventh Avenue, 14th Floor, New York, NY 10019, USA.

ELLIS Bobby (Robert), 2 July 1932, Kingston, Jamaica. Musician (trumpet). 4 sons, 3 daughters. Musical Education: At Alpha Boys School, tutor, Raymond Harper, Rueben Delgado. Career: Played with Tony Brown Band; Val Bennett; Luther Williams; Joined The Mighty Vikings, 1962; Played with The Soul Brothers; Lyn Taitt And The Jetts; Billy Vernon; Lance Helwell; The Wailers; Bob Marley And The Wailers (Peace Concert, Jackson 5, Stevie Wonder); Jimmy Cliff (BBC Concert); Toots And The Maytals; Brent Dowe; John Holt; Dennis Brown; The Two Ton Machine; Burning Spear (including Sunsplash Tour); Bunny Wailer (Music City Hall, Madison Square Garden). Compositions: Wrote with Cyrus; Sweet Meat; Up Park Camp; Stormy Weather; Rhythm for reggae hit: Diseases, Michigan & Smiley, 1983-84; Songs: Shaka; Pep-Up; Jiheje Chant; Cutlass; Sounds Of Reggae; Three Finger Jack; Doreth. Recordings: Early records with Burning Spear; Debut solo album: Shaka; All records by Burning Spear; Other recordings by: Herbie Mann; Blazing Horns; Bobby Ellis Meets The Aggravators; Tommy McCook; Numerous singles. Membership: JFM. Hobbies: Football; Cricket; Baseball; Basketball. Address: 13 Savannah Road, Independence City, Gregory Park PO, Saint Catherine, Jamaica, West Indies.

ELLIS John Stewart Maxwell, b. 22 Feb 1945, Lower Slaughter, Gloucestershire, England. Teacher; Head of Music Department, Northcliffe School; Director of Music; Founder, Doncaster Youth Jazz Association. Musical Education: RMSM Kneller Hall, Bretton Hall College. Career: Armed Forces, 1960-72; Brass Teacher, 1972-77; Founder, Director of Music, Doncaster Youth Jazz Association, 1973-, (priority, preparing young musicians for modern profession); Performance tours: Russia; Germany; Poland; Sweden; France; USA; Doncaster Jazz Orchestra first UK band to appear jazz festivals: Montreux, 1979; Nice, 1981; Royal Performance invitations to Buckingham Palace and Windsor Castle, 1991; Numerous television and radio appearances; Currently, band masterclasses and workshops; Jazz panel adjudicator (home and abroad). Recordings: 6 jazz albums, 1979-: Live From Montreux; France...Here Again; A Celebration; A Concert For Friends; You're Nobody Till Somebody Loves You (Second, Jazz Journal International Record Of The Year, 1988); Just For Phil. Honours: MBE, for Services to Education, 1995; European Curriculum

Award, 1992; BBC Big Band Of The Year, 1994; 7 NFMY Outstanding Performance Awards, 1977-87. Memberships: International Association of Jazz Educators (IAJE); Musicians' Union; NUT. Hobbies: Touring France; Reading wine labels (elected to Ordre De Compagnons De Beaujolais, 1994). Current Management: Self-managed. Address: High-Holme, 25 Sandcliffe Road, Wheatley Hills, Doncaster DN2 5NP, England.

ELLIS Paul David, b. 27 Apr 1956, Manchester, England. Composer; Arranger; Producer; Musician (keyboards); Programmer. m. Yasuko Fukuoka, 12 Mar 1993. Education: BA Hons, Fine Art, Sunderland. Musical Education: Self-taught. Career: Tours with Hot Chocolate: Germany, UK, 1983; Middle East, 1984, 1985; Australia, 1986; UK tour with Alison Moyet, 1984; Tours with Billy Ocean: UK, USA, 1986, 1988; Japan, 1986; Japanese tour with Epo, 1988; Software Consultant, Yamaha R&D Centre, London, 1990-. Recordings: Player, arranger, 2 Top 10 albums with Koji Tamaki (Japanese artist); Producer, tours, album, Epo, 1988; Many UK sessions, 1981-90. Membership: Musicians' Union. Hobbies: Literature; Psychology; Travel. Current Management: The Music Network Ltd (own company). Address: 55D Stapleton Hall Road, London N4 3QF, England.

ELLIS Ron, b. 12 Sept 1947, Southport, Lancashire, England. Disc Jockey; Broadcaster; Writer. m. Sue Hargreaves, 5 Aug 1978, 2 daughters. Education: John Moores University, Liverpool. Career: Radio presenter, Dune FM; Promotions Manager, WEA Records; Music Historian and Biographer. Compositions: Hot California Nights, recorded by P J Proby. Recordings: Boys On The Dole (Top 10, New Wave Charts), 1979; New CD from The Johnny Ace Show, forthcoming. Publications: Journal Of A Coffin Dodger; Murder First Glass; Snort Of Kings; Diary Of A Discotheque; Ears of the City, Headline, 1998. Honours: Most Jobs In Britain: Daily Mail, 1976, Sun, 1989. Membership: Crime Writers' Association. Address: 5 Mayfield Court, Freshfield, Liverpool L37 7JL, England.

ELMS Gerald, b. 18 June 1961, London, England. Record Producer. Career: Began with various up and coming bands; Became session musician (keyboards); Currently record producer. Recordings: Latest album by Right Said Fred. Hobbies: Golf. Address: 57 Devereux Road, London SW11 6JR, England.

ELSDON Alan Robert, b. 15 October 1934, Chiswick, London, England. Musician; Trumpet Player; Band Leader; Jazz Vocals; BBC Panelist; Record Reviews. m. June Patricia Elsdon, 21 May 1960, 2 sons. Education: Private tuition with Tommy McQuater; Freddie Staff and Phil Parker. Career: Joined CY Laurie's Band, aged 19 & Graham Stewart 7; Recorded with both groups; Moved to Terry Lightfoot's Band, 1959-61; Formed own group, 1961; Backed many visiting US Musicians including Edmond Hall, Albert Nicholas, Bud Freeman, Wingy Mannone, Warren Vache, Kenny Daverne and Marti Grosz; Broadcasts include Easy Beat Saturday Club; Jazz Club. Recordings: Keepers of the Flame; Hotter Than That, Tape, CD; The Alan Elsdon All Star Jazz Band; Played guest slots over Europe & Middle East, including Germany, Belgium, Holland, Hong Kong. Honours Played in Westminster Abbey at Philip Larkins Funeral; In great demand as Freelance Jazz Trumpeter. Hobby: Golf. Address: 29 Dorchester Road, Northolt, Middlesex UB5 4PA, England.

ELY Joe, b. 9 Feb 1947, Amarillo, Texas, USA. Singer; Songwriter; Musician (guitar). m. Sharon Thompson, 17 Apr 1983, 1 daughter. Musical Education: Self-taught. Career: Concerts include: 8 European tours; David Letterman TV show; Appearances on: Country Music Awards TV; The Road ABC TV Show; 3 Austin City Limits

TV; Radio City Music Hall Madison Square Gardens. Recordings: Joe Ely, 1977; Honky Tonk Masquerade, 1978; Down On The Drag, 1979; Live Shots, 1980; Musta Notta Gotta Lotta, 1981; Hi Res, 1983; Lord Of The Highway, 1987; Dig All Night, 1988; Live At Liberty Lunch, 1989; Love And Danger, 1992; Letter To Laredo, 1995. Honours include: Rolling Stone Top 10 of 70s. Memberships: ASCAP; BMI; NARAS. Hobbies: Billiards; Computers. Current Management: Vector Management, Nashville. Address: 1500 17th Avenue South, PO Box 128037, Nashville, TN 37212, USA.

EMERSON Keith, b. 2 Nov 1944, Todmorden, West Yorkshire, England. Musician (keyboards); Composer. Career: Member, The T-Bones; Emerson Lake & Palmer (ELP), 1970-; Solo artiste; Also recorded as: Emerson Lake And Powell (with Cozy Powell), 1985-86; 3, 1988; Performances include: Isle Of Wight Festival, 1970; Mar-Y-Sol Festival, Puerto Rico, 1972; Film, Pictures At An Exhibition, 1973. Recordings: Albums: Emerson Lake And Palmer, 1970; Tarkus (Number 1, UK), 1971; Pictures At An Exhibition, 1971; Trilogy, 1972; Brain Salad Surgery, 1974; Welcome Back My Friends..., 1974; Works, 1977; Works Volume Two, 1977; Love Beach, 1978; Emerson Lake And Palmer In Concert, 1979; The Best Of Emerson Lake And Palmer, 1979; Emerson Lake And Powell, 1986; To The Power Of Three, 1988; Black Moon, 1992; The Atlantic Years, 1992; Live At The Royal Albert Hall, 1992; Return Of The Manticore, 1993; Solo albums: Inferno; Nighthawks; Best Revenge; Muderock; Singles include: Fanfare For The Common Man, 1977; Solo: Honky Tonk Train Blues, 1976. Address: c/o Premier Talent, L3 East 54th Street, 14th Floor, New York, NY 10022, USA.

EMILIO (Navaira), b. 23 Aug 1962, San Antonio, Texas, USA. Tejano and Country Music Singer. m. Cindy Casias, 29 Nov 1986, 2 sons. Musical Education: Voice Scholarship, Southwest Texas State University, San Marcos. Career: Toured with David Lee Garza, 1985-88; Founder, own group Rio, 1989; Currently solo artiste; Major peformances include: CMA Awards show, 1995; San Antonio Livestock Show and Rodeo, 1994, 1995; Texas State Fair, Cotton Bowl, Dallas, 1995; Houston Livestock Show and Rodeo, with Selena, Houston Astrodome (set concert attendance record for the year), 1995; National Anthem at NBA All-Star Game, 1996; Suuport to Alan Jackson, US tour, 1996; Shared billing with: George Strait; Ricky Van Shelton; Pam Tillis; Vince Gill; Also performed with Dallas and San Antonio Symphony Orchestras. Recordings: Albums: Emilio y Rio, 1989; Sensaciones, 1990; Shoot It, 1991; Unsung Highways, 1992; Emilio Live, 1992; Southern Exposure, 1993; Sound Life, 1994; Life Is Good, 1995; Honours include: 2 Grammy Nominations, Best Mexican-American performance; Numerous Tejano Music Awards including: Male Vocalist of the Year, 4 times; Album of the Year, 6 times; Male Entertainer of the Yera, 7 times; Listed in top 10 New Stars of 1996, County America magazine, 1996. Membership: Tejanos For Children Foundation. Current Management: Stuart Dill, Refugee Management International. Address: 209 10th Avenue South, Suite 347, Nashville, TN 37203, USA.

EMMETT Rik, b. Canada. Musician (guitar); Vocalist. Career: Founder member, Canadian rock group Triumph, 1975-88; Later worked with Lee Aaron. Recordings: Albums: Triumph, 1976; Rock'n'Roll Machine, 1977; Just A Game, 1979; Progressions Of Power, 1980; Allied Forces, 1981; Never Surrender, 1982; Thunder Seven, 1984; Stages, 1985; The Sport Of Kings, 1985; Surveillance, 1987; Classics, 1989. Honour: Toronto Music Award, 1987. Current Management: Randon Entertainment Group, 121 Logan Avenue, Toronto, Ontario M4M 2M9, Canada.

ENGDAHL Elisabeth, b. 17 December 1956, Karlskrona, Sweden. Musician; Composer. m. Thomas Gustafsson, 7 April 1985, 2 daughters. Education: Degree, Afro-American Arrangement, Swedish Academy of Music, 4 years. Career: Orchestral Leader and Performing Musician in a small big band and lady band, 1987-93; Orchestral Leader, Performing House Band Pianist, television show, Good Morning Sweden, 1989-90; Performing Saxophonist, in charge of musical arrangement of a Swedish Talk Show, 1993-95; Concert Performances in Shanghai, China, 1994. Compositions: Musical Score, Kurt Olsson - The Movie About My Life As Myself, 1989; The Love Project Jazz Opera, 1996. Recordings: Musical Arrangements of three records with Kurt Olsson's Lady Band, 1987, 1988, 1990. Memberships: Swedish Popular Music Composers; Swedens Media Composers. Hobby: Family. Address: Landalagangen 5, 411 30 Goteborg, Sweden.

ENGEL Soren Peter Bjarne, b. 6 Apr 1947, Copenhagen, Denmark. Musician (guitar, bass guitar). m. Anne Grethe, 9 May 1991, 1 son. Career: Television appearances in France; Germany; Sweden; Finland; Norway; Denmark; European tours with Bo Diddley; Link Wray; Sonny Terry; Brownie McGee; Delta Cross Band. Recordings: with Delta Cross Band: No Overdubs, 1979; Rave On, 1980; Up Front, 1981; Slide, 1984; Through Times, 1991. with C V Jorgensen: Tidens Tein, 1980; Vinden Vender, 1982. Honours: Several Silver, Gold and Platinum records. Memberships: Danish Artists' Union. Hobbies: Wife; Long walks with dog. Current Management: Århus Musik Kontor.

ENGLAND Ty, b. 5 Dec 1963, Oklahoma City, USA. Singer; Musician (Guitar). m. Shanna Burns England, 3 sons, 1 daughter. Education: Oklahoma State University, USA, 2 years; Graduate, Central State University. Career: Harmony Vocalist and Acoustic Guitarist for former college room-mate Garth Brooks, 6 years; Started solo career, released 2 albums, Ty England, 1995, Two Ways to Fall, 1996. Recordings: Singles: Should've Asked Her Faster; Smoke In Her Eyes; Irresistible You; Albums: Ty England, 1995; Two Ways to Fall, 1996. Honours: National Spokesperson for the Future Farmers, American Alumni Association, 1996-97; Nominee for Star of Tomorrow-Male, TNN/Music City News Awards, 1996-97; Nominee, Performance Magazine, New Country Touring Artist of the Year, 1996. Hobbies: Trailbike Riding; Hunting; Waterskiing. Current Management: Scott Stem, Bob Doyle and Associates. Address: 1111 17th Avenue South, Nashville, TN 37212, USA.

ENO Brian Peter George, b. 15 May 1948, Melton, Suffolk, England. Recording Artist; Record Producer; Musician (keyboards). Recordings: Albums as producer include: with John Cale: Fear, 1974; with Robert Calvert, Lucky Lief And The Longships, 1975; with Michael Nyman: Decay Music, 1976; with Penguin Café Orchestra: Music From The Penguin Café, 19776; with Ultravox: Ultravox, 1977; with Talking Heads: More Songs About Buildings And Food, 1978; Remain In Light, 1980; with Devo: Q- Are We Not Men? A- We Are Devo, 1978; with U2: The Unforgettable Fire, 1984; The Joshua Tree, 1987; Achtung Baby, 1991; Zooropa, 1993; Passengers (film soundtrack), 1995; with Carmel: The Falling, 1986; with Geoffrey Oryema: Exile, 1990; with James: Laid, 1993; Wah Wah, 1994; with Laurie Anderson: Bright Red, 1994; Collaborations include: with Roxy Music: Virginia Plain, 1972; Roxy Music, 1972; For Your Pleasure, 1973; Pyjamarama, 1973; with David Bowie: Low, 1977; Heroes, 1977; Lodger, 1979; As guest musician: Captain Lockheed And The Starfighters, Robert Calvert, 1974; The End, Nico, 1974; The Lamb Lies Down On Broadway, Genesis, 1974; with Phil Mazanera: Diamond Head, 1975; Listen Now, 1977; with John Cale: Slow Dazzle, 1975; Helen Of Troy, 1975; Rain Dances, Camel, 1977;

Exposure, Robert Fripp, 1979; Yellow Rain, The Neville Brothers, 1989; Rattle And Hum, U2, 1989; Mamouna, Bryan Ferry, 1994; with Jah Wobble: Spinner, 1995. Remix productions include: Unbelieveable, EMF, 1992; I Feel You, Depeche Mode, 1993; The River, Geoffrey Oryema, 1993; I'm Only Looking, INXS, 1993; In Your Room, Depeche Mode, 1993; Brian Eno: Box I & Box II, 1993; Introducing The Band, Suede, 1994; 39 Steps, Bryan Ferry, 1994; Protection, Massive Attack, 1994. Honours: Doctor, Technology, University of Plymouth; Ivor Novello Award; 2 Grammy Awards; BRIT Awards: Best Producer, 1994, 1996; Q Magazine Awards: Best Producer (with Flood, The Edge), 1993; Inspiration Award (with David Bowie), 1995;. Memberships: PRS; BASCA. Current Management: Anthea Norman-Taylor, Opal Ltd. Address: 3 Pembride Mews, London W11 3EQ, England.

ENTHOVEN David John, b. 5 July 1944, Windsor, Berkshire, England. Company Director; Artist Manager. Divorced, 1 son, 1 daughter. Career: Founded EG Group of Companies, 1969; Signed: King Crimson; T Rex; Emerson Lake And Palmer; Roxy Music; Founder, IE Management, 1988; Artist Manager for: Bryan Ferry; Massive Attack. Hobby: Motorbikes. Address: IE Management Ltd, 59A Chesson Road, London W14 9QS, England.

ENTWISTLE John, b. 9 Oct 1946, Chiswick, London, England. Musician (bass). Career: Member, UK rock group The Who, 1964-84; Appearances include: National Jazz and Blues Festival, 1965, 1966, 1969; Monterey Pop Festival, 1967; Farewell tour, 1982-83; Live Aid, Wembley, 1985; Reunion tour, 1989. Recordings: Albums: with The Who: My Generation, 1965; A Quick One, 1966; The Who Sell Out, 1968; Direct Hits, 1968; Tommy, 1969; Live At Leeds, 1970; Meaty Beefy And Bouncy, 1971; Who's Next, 1971; Quadrophenia, 1973; Odds And Sods, 1974; The Story Of The Who, 1976; The Who By Numbers, 1975; Who Are You, 1978; The Kids Are Alright (film soundtrack), 1979; Face Dances, 1981; It's Hard, 1982; Hooligans, 1982; Rarities Vols 1 and 2, 1983; Once Upon A Time, 1983; The Singles, 1984; Who's Last, 1984; Who's Missing, 1985; Two's Missing, 1987; Who's Better Who's Best, 1988; Joined Together, 1990; 30 Years Of Maximum R&B, 1994; Solo albums: Smash Your Head Against The Wall, 1971; Wistle Rymes, 1972; Rigor Mortis Sets In, 1973; Too Late The Hero, 1981; Singles include: I Can't Explain, 1965; Anyway, Anyhow, Anywhere, 1965; My Generation, 1965; Substitute, 1966; I'm A Boy, 1966; Pictures Of Lily, 1967; I Can See For Miles, 1967; Pinball Wizard, 1969; See Me Feel Me, 1970; Won't Get Fooled Again, 1971; Join Together, 1972; Who Are You, 1978; You Better You Bet, 1981. Honours include: with the Who: Gold Ticket, Madison Square Garden, 1979; Ivor Novello Award, 1982; BRIT Award, 1988; Inducted into Rock'n'Roll Hall of Fame, 1990. Current Management: Trinifold Management, 22 Harley Street, Marylebone Road, London NW1 4PR, England.

ENYA (Eithne Ni Bhraonain), b. 17 May 1961, Gweedore, County Donegal, Ireland. Singer; Musician (piano, keyboards); Composer. Musical Education: Clasical course; Career: Member, folk group Clannad, 1980-82; Solo artiste, 1988-; 25 million albums sold to date. Compositions: Music for film and television scores: The Frog Prince, 1985; The Celts, BBC, 1987; LA Story, 1990; Green Card, 1990. Recordings: Albums: with Clannad: Crann Ull, 1980; Fuaim, 1982; Solo albums: Watermark, 1988; Shepherd's Moon, 1991; Enya, 1992; The Celts (reissued) 1992; The Book Of Trees, 1996; Singles include: Orinoco Flow (Number 1, UK), 1988; Evening Falls, 1988; Storms In Africa (Part II), 1989; Caribbean Blue, 1991; How Can I Keep From Singing, 1991; Book Of Days, 1992; Anywhere Is, 1995. Honours: Grammy Award, Best New Age Album,

Shepherd's Moon, 1993; IRMA Award, Best Irish Female Artist, 1993. Current Management: Aigle Music, 6 Danieli Drive, Artane, Dublin 5, Ireland.

ERBSEN Wayne, b. 19 Jan 1945, Los Angeles, California, USA. Musician; Publisher; Teacher; Writer; Radio Presenter. m. Barbara Swell, 12 Oct 1982, 1 son, 2 daughters. Education: BA History, UC Berkeley; MA History, University of Wisconsin. Musical Education: Self-taught. Career: Performed USA, 1962-; 2 tours Europe; Taught continuously 1962-; Radio host WCQS, Asheville, 1982-. Recordings: Albums include: Native Ground; Old Time Gospel Instrumentals; Southern Mountain Classics; Southern Soldier Boy; Home Front; Ballads and Songs of the Civil War; Old Time Gospel Favourites; Cowboy Songs of the Wild Frontier; Front Porch Favourites. Publications: Books: Banjo For The Complete Ignoramus; Starting Banjo From Scratch; Front Porch Songs, Jokes and Stories; First place banjo Galax, 1973; First place Chilhowee, Virginia 1973. Hobbies: Music; Writing. Address: Native Ground Music, 109 Bell Road, Ashevlle, NC 28805, USA.

ERDÖS Laurent, b. 30 Mar 1960, Neuilly Sur Seine, France. Musician. Musical Education: Conservatoire de Musique, Paris. Career: Conductor, mambo/cha cha cha big band Mambo Mania. Current Management: Caramba Productions. Address: 7 Place de Seoul, 75014 Paris, France.

ERICSON Peter R, b. 2 July 1950, Uppsala, Sweden. Composer; Producer; Musician (guitar); Singer. m. Nina, 1975, 2 sons, 1 daughter. Education: Journalist's School; English, University; 1 year, St Martins College, Lancaster, England. Musical Education: 1 year, guitar; 4 years, piano. Career: 4 albums with group, Mobben, 1970s; 6 solo albums, 1980s, 1990; Television, radio appearances and regular tours; Currently writing music for major film. Compositions: Music for major Swedish artists including: Monica Zetterlund; Cornelis Vreeswijk. Recordings: 6 solo albums; Many albums as producer. Hobbies: Sailing; Motorcycle riding; Fishing; Travel. Current Management: Hawk Records; Taby, Stockholm, Sweden. Address: Hawk Records, Scandinavian Songs Music Group, Box 109, S-18212 Danderyd, Sweden.

ESCALLE Jean-Louis, b. 3 Mar 1954, Aurimont, Gers, France. Jazz Musician (drums). m. Marie-Jeanne, 24 May 1982, 1 son, 2 daughters. Musical Education: Toulouse Conservatory, 6 years. Career: Jazz sideman, with regional and national jazz musicians, South of France. Recordings: 4 records with regional musicians: J M Pilc; R Calleja; Ch Brun. Hobby: Reading. Address: Orbessan, 32260 Sissan, France.

ESSEX David Albert Cook, b. 23 July 1947, Plaistow, East London, England. Singer; Musician (drums); Actor. Career: 20 British tours; Many world tours; Television appearances include: Top Of The Pops; David Essex Specials; Cher; Johnny Carson; Grammy Awards; Subject, This Is Your Life, 1995; Stage performances include: Jesus, Godspell, 1971-73; Che, Evita, 1978; Lord Byron, Childe Byron, at Young Vic; Fletcher Christian, Mutiny; Films: That'll Be The Day; Stardust; Silver Dream Racer; Wrote most of own recordings. Recordings: 23 UK hit singles, (2 at Number 1), including: Gonna Make You A Star; Hold Me Close; Rock On (Number 1, US); Silver Dream Machine; Winter's Tale; Numerous albums include: Rock On, 1973; David Essex, 1974; All The Fun Of The Fair, 1975; Out On The Street, 1976; Imperial Wizard, 1979; Collection, 1980; Stagestruck, 1982; The Whisper, 1983; Centre Stage, 1986; Touching The Ghost, 1989; Spotlight, 1991; Cover Shot, 1993; Back To Back, 1994; Also appeared on Jeff Wayne's War Of The Worlds (with Richard Burton, Justin Hayward, Phil Lynott), 1978. Honours: Variety Club Of Great Britain, Best Newcomer, 1971; Best

Performer, Evita, 1978; Ambassador, Voluntary Service Overseas. Memberships: American Federation Television; American Screen Actors Guild; Equity-UK. Hobbies: Football; Cricket; Piloting helicopter. Current Management: Derek Bowman, Lamplight Music Ltd; Mel Bush Organisation; Address: 109 Eastbourne Mews, London W2 6LQ, England.

ESSIET Chief Udoh, b. 21 Nov 1959, Ikot Ekpene, Nigeria. Musician (African percussion); Singer; Composer; Bandleader. m. Sherry Margolin, 1 son. Career: In Nigeria until 1983; Performed traditional native music, Highlife music, with Dr Victor Olaiya; Rex Williams; Rex Lawson; Juju (Sunny Ade); Performed Afrobeat music with Fela Anikulapo Kuti, 1978-83; Based in Paris, 1983-; Founded Ghetto Blaster, first part for Fela, James Brown, 1984; Mory Kante; Salif Keita; Formed Afrobeat Blaster, tours in Europe, 1989-. Recordings: with Ghetto Blaster: Preacher Man, 1984; People, 1986; with Salif Keita: Soro; with Sixun, Fela Anikulapo Kuti: ITT; Unknown Soldier; Coffin For Head Of State; Authority Stealing; 2000 Black (with Roy Ayers); with Afrobeat Blaster: No Condition Is Permanent, 1991. Publications; Film: Ghetto Blaster, 1983. Honours: Chief of African Feeling, Amsterdam, 1986. Memberships: SACEM; SPEDIDAM; ADAMI. Hobbies: Cooking African food; Playing with son. Current Management: Self-managed. Address: 19 Rue de Suez, 75018 Paris, France.

ESSING John Leo Thomas, b. 15 August 1964, Stockholm. Musician (guitar, synthesizer, percussion). Education: Self-taught guitar, synthesizer, percussion. Career: Member, bob bund, 1991; More than 250 gigs around Scandinavia; Played at famous Roskilde, Lollipop, Ruisrock, Quartfestivalen and Hultsfred. Compositions: I Stället för Musik, 1996; Düsseldorf, 1996. Recordings: bob hund - bob hund, 1993; bob hund - Edvin Medvind, 1994; bob hund - Omslag: Martin Kann, 1996. Publication: Bob Hund - Omslag: Martin Kann, 1996. Honours: Grammy, best live act, 1994; Grammy, best lyrics, 1996. Memberships: STIM; SAMI. Hobbies: Music; Books; Food; Movies; Drinking. Address: Box 53045, 400 14, Göteborg, Sweden.

ESTEFAN Gloria (Fajado), b. 1 Sept 1957, Havana, Cuba. Singer; Songwriter. m. Emilio Estefan, 1 Sept 1978. Education: BA, Psychology, Univeristy of Miami. Career: Singer, backed by Miami Sound Machine, 1974-; Billed as Gloria Estefan, 1989-; Appearances include: Tokyo Music Festival, Japan, 1985; World tour, 1991; The Simple Truth, benefit concert for Kurdish refugees, Wembley, 1991; White House State Dinner, for President of Brazil, 1991; South American tour, 1992; Royal Variety Performance, London, before Prince and Princess of Wales, 1992; Co-organiser, benefit concert for victims of Hurricane Andrew, Florida, 1992; 45 million albums sold to date. Compositions include: Anything For You; Don't Wanna Lose You; Oye Mi Canto (co-written with Jorge Casas and Clay Ostwald); Cuts Both Ways; Coming Out Of The Dark (co-written with Emilio Estefan and Jon Secada); Always Tomorrow; Christmas Through Their Eyes (co-written with Dianne Warren). Recordings: Albums: Renacer, 1976; Eyes Of Innocence, 1984; Primitive Love, 1986; Let It Loose, 1988; Anything For You (Number 1, UK), 1989; Cuts Both Ways, 1989; Exitos De Gloria Estefan, 1990; Into The Light, 1991; Greatest Hits, 1992; Mi Tierra, 1993; Christmas Through Your Eyes, 1993; Hold Me, Thrill Me, Kiss Me, 1994; Abriendo Puertas, 1995; Also featured on: Jon Secada, Jon Secada (also co-producer), 1991; Til Their Eyes Shine (The Lullaby Album), 1992; Hit singles include: Dr Beat, 1984; Conga, 1986; Hot Summer Nights, used in film soundtrack Top Gun, 1986; Bad Boy, 1986; Words Get In The Way, 1986; Rhythm Is Gonna Get You, 1987; Can't Stay Away From You, 1988; Anything For You (Number 1, US), 1988; 1-2-3, 1988; Oye Mi Canto (Hear My Voice), 1989; Here We Are, 1989; Don't Wanna Lose You, 1989; Get On Your Feet, 1989; Coming Out Of The Dark (Number 1, US), 1991; Remember Me With Love, 1991; Always Tomorrow, 1992; Cuts Both Ways, 1993; Go Away, 1993; Mi Tierra, 1993. Honours: Grand Prize, Tokyo Music Festival, 1985; Numerous Billboard awards, 1986-; American Music Award, Favourite Pop/Rock Duo or Group, 1989; Crystal Globe Award, 21 Club, New York, 1990; Latin Music Award, Crossover Artist Of Year, 1990; Humanitarian Award, B'Nai B'rith, 1992; Desi Entertainment Awards, Performer Of Year, Song Of Year, 1992; Humanitarian Award, National Music Foundation (for helping victims of Hurricane Andrew), 1993. Address: c/o Estefan Enterprises, 555 Jefferson Avenue, Miami Beach, FL 33139, USA.

ESTER Pauline, b. 18 Dec 1963, Toulouse, France. Singer. Musical Education: Private lessons; Different vocal coaches. Career: Tours: France; Belgium; Bulgaria; Canada, Quebec; Opening act, Patrick Bruel tour, 1991; Appearances on all major television and radio shows, France, Canada, Quebec. Recordings: Albums: Le Monde Est Fou, 1990; Je L'Autre Côté, 1992; Singles: Il Fait Chaud; Oui, Je T'Adore; Le Monde Est Fou; Une Fenêtre Ouverte. Honours: France Internationnal, 1991; Trophy Radio, SACEM: Best Song Of Year, 1991; Best New Artist, 1992. Membership: SACEM, 1989. Hobbies: Dance. Current Management: Jean-Claude Camus Production. Address: 6 Rue Daubigny, 75017 Paris, France.

ETHERIDGE John M G, b. 12 Jan 1948, London, England. Musician (guitar). m. Bonnie Bartram, 10 Jan 1973, 1 son, 1 daughter. Education: BA, History of Art, University of Essex. Musical Education: Self-taught. Career: Soft Machine, 1975-79; Stephane Grappelli, 1976-81; Solo tours: Australia; USA; England; 1982-84; MD, Bertice Reading, 1985-90; European tour with Birelli Lagrene, Vic Juris, 1989; European tours with Dick Hextall-Smith (saxophone); Danny Thompson's Whatever, 1989-93; Own Quartet, 1990-; Andy Summers Duo, 1993-; Nigel Kennedy Group, 1993-. Recordings: with Soft Machine: Soft; Alive And Well; Triple Echo; with Stephane Grappelli: At The Winery; Live At Carnegie Hall; with Stephane Grappelli and Yehudi Menuhin: Tea For Two; Strictly For The Birds; with own quartet: Second Vision, 1981; with Vic Juris: Bohemia, 1989; with Dick Hextall-Smith: Obsession Fees, 1990; with Danny Thompson: Elemental, 1991; with Andy Summers: Invisible Threads, 1993; Solo album: Ash, 1994. Publications: The Guitar, OUP, editor, Michael Stimpson; Numerous articles for guitar magazines. Hobbies: Cricket; Walking. Current Management: Dick Turner. Address: Metronome Music, Bath, England.

ETHERIDGE Melissa Lou, b. Leavenworth, Kansas, USA. Singer; Songwriter; Musician (guitar). Musical Education: Berklee College of Music, Boston. Career: Musician, Los Angeles bars, 5 years; Recording artiste, 1988-. Recordings: Albums: Melissa Etheridge, 1988; Brave And Crazy, 1989; Never Enough, 1992; Yes I Am, 1993; Your Little Secret, 1995. Honours: Grammy Nomination, Bring Me Some Water, 1988. Current Management: Bill Leopold, W F Leopold Management, 210 North Pass Avenue, Ste 102, Burbank, CA 91505, USA.

EUBANKS Robin, Jazz Trombonist. Career: Played in bands on Broadway; Appeared in film: Cotton Club; Member, Duke Ellington and Cab Calloway bands; Played on Motown Television special; Played with: Art Blakey; Abdullah Ibrahim; Marvin 'Smitty' Smith; Geri Allen; Dave Holland; Wynford and Branford Marsalis; Steve Coleman; Regular tours: USA; Europe; Japan. Recordings: Different Perspectives; Musician on: Art Blakey: Live At Montreux And Northsea; Not Yet; Kevin Eubanks: Guitarist; Steve Coleman: World Expansion; Sine Die; Marvin 'Smitty' Smith: Keeper Of The Drums; Geri Allen: Open On All Sides; Mark Helias: The Current Set; Herb Robertson: Shades Of Bud Powell; Dave Holland: The Razor's Edge; Branford Marsalis: Scenes In The City. Address: SESAC, 55 Music Square E, Nashville, TN 37203, USA.

EURIPIDES Georganopoulos, b. 12 Dec 1961, Thessaloniki, Greece. Composer; Producer; Musician (keyboards). m. Dr Agnes Leotsakos, 22 Feb 1992, 1 son. Musical Education: ARCM, Dip RCM (Royal College of Music). Career: Writing music for television and video productions; Director, Optimus International Ltd (music production company); Composition, production work in UK, France, Germany, Malta, Greece, Poland. Recordings: Arranger, producer, Hits Of The War Years (Number 4, UK Music Video Charts), 1995. Memberships: BASCA; Musicians' Union; PRS; MCPS. Hobbies: Backgammon. Address: 35 Elm Road, London SW14 7JL, England.

EVANS Cathy, b. Knottingley, West Yorkshire, England. Vocalist; Musician (guitar). Career: Performed with harmony trio, Proper Little Madams, 1980-82; Various television appearances include mini-series, TV South West; Currently with 3 part Acappella group Cattachewdya New Shoes, performing 1920's and 1930's material; Also performing backing vocals. Recordings: Album by Proper Little Madams, 1981; Backing vocalist, Heartache Avenue, The Maisonettes. Membership: Musicians' Union. Address: 39 Porter Road, Derby DE23 6DZ, England.

EVANS Dan (David Rhys), b. 26 May 1956, Middlesbrough, Cleveland, England. Folk Musician (guitar, dulcimer, vocals and poetry). m. Mary Collins, 12 May 1995. Education: BSc, hons, Botany (Dunelm), under David Bellamy. Career: Performing in folk clubs, art centres, theatres, nationwide, for over 20 years; Frequent radio appearances; Television interview and performance; Performed and taught in USA in 1997; One of the leading performers on Appalachian dulcimer in UK, highly respected and innovative guitarist. Recordings: Mini album, Sampler, 1988; Albums: Guardian Spirit (available USA), 1993; Spirit Dancing, 1997. Publications: 5 Poems, Poetry booklet; Other poems published in various anthologies; numerous articles written for folk press; Dulcimer Players News, 1994; frequent appearances in UK dulcimer magazine, Nonsuch. Memberships: PRS; PPL; MCPS; Musicians' Union. Hobbies: Photography; Art. Current Management: DanSing Music. Address: 61 Sillswood, Olney, Bucks MK46 5PN, England.

EVANS David Wyn, b. 29 Jan 1964, Boston, Massachusetts, USA. Multimedia producer. m. Philippa Girling, 18 July 1987, 2 daughters. Education: BSc Hons, Electrical Systems Engineering, University of East Anglia. Career: Multimedia producer, BBC, 1993-; Multimedia producer, freelance 1989-; Clients include: BBC; Harrods; Next; Jaeger; Kingsmill; Marks & Spencer; NCET; SBU; Morgan-Grenfell; SRI; TDK; Dupont; Asahi; Ogilvy and Mather; The Gold Council. Recordings: Produced over £4 million cost CD-ROM and Internet projects, 14 CD-Roms, 1992. Publications: Commex 93 & 94, IEEE, BCS, NCET, BBC. Honours: Certified Apple programmer, developer, 1989. Memberships: Musicians' Union; APRS; IEE; IEEE; BCS. Hobbies: Multimedia performing artist: Grain (alternative pop). Current Management: Kathleen Tobin Sound Advice Ent, 212-80 16th Ave, Bayside, New York, NY 11360, USA. Address: 74 High Street, Wimbledon Village, London SW19 5EG, England.

EVANS Delyth, b. 28 May 1955, Oswestry, Shropshire, England. Musician (celtic harp). m. Nigel Jenkins, 29 June 1982, 2 daughters.

Education: Joint Honours Degree (English, French). Musical Education: Self-taught harpist. Career: Welsh Folk band Cromlech, 1978-1982; Aberjaber, 1982-; Solo work; Tours: UK; Europe. Recordings: Gwlith Y Bore, 1980; Igam Ogam, 1982; Aberjaber, 1985; Aber-Dau-Jaber, 1988; Delta, 1991; Aberjaber - The Perfect Bucket, 1997. Publications: Del Y Delyn, 1994. Address: 124 Overland Road, Mumbles, Swansea SA3 4EU, Wales.

EVANS Frank, b. 1 Oct 1936, England. Jazz Musician (guitar); Arranger. m. Mary, 23 May 1954, 2 sons. Musical Education: Self-taught. Career: Tours with bands; Television: Parkinson (solo); BBC Jazz Club, World Service; Strictly Instrumental, Composed for more than 60 television dramas, documentary films. Recordings: Jazz Tete-á-Tete Tubby Hayes, Tony Coe; Mark Twain Suite (77 records); Noctuary; Soiree; Ballade; Frank Evans For Little Girls; Stretching Forth. Publications: Monthly arrangement of jazz standard for Guitar Techniques. Memberships: PRS; MCPS. Hobby: Snooker. Current Management: Don Percival, Artists Promotion. Address: 9 Holbrook House, Paul's Cray Road, Chislehurst, Kent BR7 6OE, England.

EVANS Lawrence Alan, b. 31 Dec 1958, Bryn Mawr, Pennsylvania, USA. Artist Manager; Producer Manager; Music Publisher. Education: BA, English, University of Texas, Austin, 1983. Career: Manager for engineer and producer Steve Peck, also film actor Charles Gunning; Executive producer, band Argument Clinic, 1994; Business ventures: EuroExport Entertainment Corporation; Tripoli Inferno Music; Raving Cleric Music; RCM Recordings; Cueball Artist Management. Recordings: with Argument Clinic: Bones of Contention, 1989; Unknown Soul, 1992; Argument Clinic, 1994. Memberships: NARAS; ASCAP. Address: EuroExport Entertainment Corporation, PO Box 4735, Austin, TX 78765, USA.

EVANS Lee, b. 7 Jan 1933, New York, USA. Composer; Musician (piano). Education: BA, NYU, 1957; MA, Columbia University, 1958; EdD, 1978. Career: Worked with various artists include: Tom Jones; Cat Stevens; Engelbert Humperdinck; Gilbert O'Sullivan; Professor, Five Towns College, Seaford, 1977-78; President, Piano Plus Inc, 1973-; Leader, Lee Evans Trio, 1966-73; Featured pianist, television specials, The Gershwin Years; Ed Sullivan; Merv Griffin; Performed at 2 White House Command Performances for President Lyndon B Johnson. Publications: Author, series of jazz keyboard books; Contributor to journals. Memberships: ASCAP; AFofM; National Association of Jazz Educators. Address: Piano Plus Inc, New York, USA.

EVANS Tania. Singer. Career: Singer, German dance act Culture Beat, 1990-. Recordings: Singles: Erdbeermund, 1990; I Like You, 1993; Mr Vain (Number 1 throughout Europe, including UK, Germany), 1993; Anything, 1994; World In Your Hands, 1994. Current Management: Pyramid Entertainment Group, Los Angeles, USA. Address: c/o Epic Records, 10 Great Marlborough Street, London W1V 2LP, England.

EVANS Vivian Haydn, b. 18 May 1943, Port Talbot, South Wales. Semi-professional Musician; Shop Assistant; Manager; Mail Order Dealer. Musical Education; Self-taught. Career: Amateur, semi-professional; Songwriter, 1971-; 44 placings in song contests, mainly USA; Poetry, 1989-; Published 54 US magazines; 67 finalist/semi-finalists, US poetry contests; Singer with: The Midnights, 1964-65; The Other Image, 1965; Viv Talbot, 1966; Vivian Evans, 1964-81; Revolutionary Music Council, 1981-; Records on BBC2, ILR Radio, BBC Wales. Recordings: (co-written and sung by himself) In My Direction, 1972, 1981. Publications: Poems in magazines, books; Songwriting success, magazines, newspapers. Honours: 3 first places, US Song

Contests: New York, 1971; Washington DC, 1988; Wisconsin, 1992. Memberships: BASCA; MCPS; PRS; Songwriters of Wisconsin. Hobbies: Church, Sunday School, Youth Club work; Songwriting; Poetry; DIY; Television. Current Management: LOS Records. Address: 19 Connaught Street, Port Talbot SA13 1ET, South Wales.

EVELYN George, b. 15 Jan 1970, England. Musical Education: Drums at High School. Career: Promoter, club: Funky Mule and The Headz Club, Leeds; DJ, under name of E A S E, also: Experience A Sample Expert, Leeds. Recordings: Dextrous; Stating A Fact; Aftermath; EP: A Case Of Funk; Set Me Free; Happiness; Alive; Albums: A Word Of Science; Smokers Delight. Memberships: PRS. Hobbies: Squash; Swimming; Making Music. Current Management: Timebomb, Concorde. Address: 2 Authorpe Road, Leeds LS6 4JB, England.

EVENTHAL Avril, b. 21 May 1947, Liverpool, Merseyside, England. Entertainer; Producer (Honky Tonk piano). m. Philip Howard Eventhal, 12 Aug 1975. Education: Salford Technical College, Sound Engineer. Career: Television appearances: The Gong Show with Frankie Howerd, CH4; My Kind Of People, Michael Barrymore; Support to 3 Degrees, Hippodrome Club, London; Prepared Bad Taste Tour of England, BBC Radio, 1988. Recordings: Paris Is For Lovers; The Man In My Life; You're A Man (Number 10 in Buzzcharts); Yesterday's Lovers; 2 commercial videos: Sex Slaves of New Orleans. Memberships: PRS; BASCA; Equity; MCPS; PPL. Hobbies: Choreography; Photography (modelling). Address: 26 Dovedale Avenue, Prestwich, Manchester M25 0BU, England.

EVERARD Christopher, b. 26 May 1964, Widnes, England. Singer; Songwriter; Musician (guitar, piano). Partner: Karen Halliburton, 2 sons, 2 daughters. Musical Education: Self-taught guitar, piano, songwriting. Career: Hundreds of small venue gigs include Mean Fiddler; Appearance, Granada TV Arts Festival, 1990; Several sessions on local radio. Compositions: Tracks: Just To Survive; The Hunger; Far Over The Fields; Goodnight Angel; Fat Cats. Recording: Debut album released 1995. Publications: Widnes Weekly News; Weekly World. Membership: Musicians' Union. Hobbies: Poetry; Classical music. Current Management: Self-managed.

EVERITT Steven John, b. 7 Dec 1958, Elgin, Scotland. Composer; Programmer. 1 son. Career: Session guitarist, programmer until 1988; Now full time Audio Visual composer. Recordings: Numerous themes, documentary scores. Memberships: MU; PRS. Hobbies: Travel; Music; Cats. Current Management: Atmosphere Music Ltd.

EVERLY Don (Isaac Donald), b. 1 Feb 1937, Brownie, Kentucky, USA. Vocalist; Musician (guitar); Songwriter. m. Adela Everly, 22 Mar 1997. Career: Member, the Everly Brothers (with brother Phil), 1955-73; 1983-; Solo artiste, 1973-83; Performances include: Debut, Grand Ole Opry, 1957; UK tour, supported by Bo Diddley, Rolling Stones, 1963; Represented US, Grand Gala Du Disque, Holland, 1965; Reunion Concert, Royal Albert Hall, 1983; UK tour, 1991; US tour, 1992; Royal Albert Hall, 1993; Televison includes: Everly Brothers Show, ABC TV, 1970. Recordings: Albums include: The Everly Brothers - They're Off And Running!, 1958; Songs Our Daddy Taught Us, 1958; It's Everly Time!, 1960; The Fabulous Style Of The Everly Brothers, 1960; A Date With The Everly Brothers, 1961; Instant Party, 1962; The Golden Hits Of, 1962; The Very Best Of The Everly Brothers, 1964; Gone Gone Gone, 1965; Rock'n'Soul, 1965; In Our Image, 1966; Two Yanks In England, 1966; The Hit Sound Of The Everly Brothers, 1967; The Everly Brothers Sing, 1967; The Everly Brothers Show, 1970; The Everly Brothers Original Greatest Hits, 1970;

Stories We Could Tell, 1972; Pass The Chicken And Listen, 1973; The Very Best Of, 1974; Walk Right Back With..., 1975; Living Legends, 1977; Love Hurts, 1983; The Reunion Concert, 1984; Born Yesterday, 1986; Some Hearts, 1989; Solo albums: Don Everly, 1971; Sunset Towers, 1974; Brother Jukebox, 1977; Singles include: Bye Bye Love; Wake Up Little Susie; All I Have To Do Is Dream (Number 1, US), 1958; Bird Dog; Problems; (Til) I Kissed You; Let It Be Me; Cathy's Clown (Number 1, US), 1960; When Will I Be Loved; So Sad (To Watch Good Love Go Bad); Like Strangers; Walk Right Back (Number 1, UK), 1961; Temptation (Number 1, UK), 1961; Crying In The Rain. Honours: Star on Hollywood Walk Of Fame, 1986; Inducted into Rock'n'Roll Hall Of Fame, 1986; Inducted into Jukebox Legends Hall Of Fame, 1990; Lifetime Achievement Grammy, 1997. Current Management: International Creative Management, 8942 Wilshire Blvd, Beverly Hills, CA 90211, USA.

EVERLY Phil, b. 19 Jan 1939, Chicago, Illinois, USA. Vocalist; Musician (guitar); Songwriter. Career: Member, The Everly Brothers (with brother Don), 1955-73; 1983-; Solo artiste, 1973-83; Performances include: Debut, Grand Ole Opry, 1957; UK tour, supported by Rolling Stones, 1963; Represented US, Grand Gala Du Disque, Holland, 1965; The Reunion Concert, Royal Albert Hall, 1983; UK tour, 1991; US tour, 1992; Royal Albert Hall, 1993; Television includes: The Everly Brothers Show, ABC TV, 1970. Recordings: Albums include: The Everly Brothers - They're Off And Running!, 1958; Songs Our Daddy Taught Us, 1958; It's Everly Time, 1960; The Fabulous Style Of, 1960; A Date With The Everly Brothers, 1961; Instant Party, 1962; Everly Brothers Sing Great Country Hits, 1963; The Very Best Of, 1964; Gone Gone Gone, 1965; Rock'n'Soul, 1965; In Our Image, 1966; Two Yanks In England, 1966; The Everly Brothers Show, 1970; Stories We Could Tell, 1972; Pass The Chicken And Listen, 1973; Living Legends, 1977; The New Album, 1977; The Reunion Concert, 1984; EB 84, 1984; Some Hearts, 1989; Solo albums: Star Spangled Springer, 1973; There's Nothing Too Good For My Baby, 1975; Mystic Line, 1975; Living Alone, 1982; Phil Everly, 1983; Singles include: Bye Bye Love, 1957; Wake Up Little Susie (Number 1, US), 1957; All I Have To Do Is Dream (Number 1, US), 1958; Bird Dog; (Til) I Kissed You; Let It Be Me; Cathy's Clown (Number 1, US); When Will I Be Loved; So Sad (To Watch Good Love Go Bad); Like Strangers; Temptation (Number 1, US); Crying In The Rain; Duets with: Cliff Richard, She Means Nothing To Me, 1983; Nanci Griffith, You Made This Love A Teardrop, 1989. Honours include: Star on Hollywood Walk Of Fame, 1986; Inducted into Rock'n'Roll Hall Of Fame, 1986; Inducted into Jukebox Legends Hall Of Fame, 1990. Address: c/o International Creative Management, 8942 Wilshire Blvd, Beverly Hills, CA 90211, USA.

EVERS Jörg, b. 21 June 1950, Bayreuth, Germany. Composer; Producer; Arranger; Musician (guitar). m. Anna Maria, 18 Mar 1981, 1 son, 1 daughter. Musical Education: Musical Science (Uni München); Richard Strauss Konservatorium München. Career: Tours in Europe with: Embryo; Amon Düül II; Peter Maffay; Pack. Recordings: Claudja Barry: Boogie Woogie Dancin' Shoes; Sylvie Vartan: Disco Queen; Claudja Barry: Down And Counting; Television: Herzblatt; Advertising: McDonalds; Odol; Maggi; Burger King; Löwenbräu; Wrigley's; Reebok; Esso. Honours: Best Composer's Award, 9th Tokyo Music Festival, 1980; NY Clio Award, 1991; Div Platinum, Gold Records. Membership: GEMA. Address: PO Box 1122, 85765 Unterföhring, Munich, Germany.

EWANJE Charles, b. 19 December 1937, Douala, Cameroon. Musician (Guitarist). m. Michelle Lissandre, 12 July 1973, 3 sons, 5 daughters. Education: Bachelor's Degree, Economics, French Baccalaureat. Career: Dance

Band Musician, Guitar, Flute and Arrangements, 1960-72; Classical Guitar Teacher, 1972-76; Artist, Afrcal Classical Guitar, 1977-; Participation in Cameroon and French Televisions. Compositions: Makala Ma Mbasi; African Strings for Luther King; Munenge Mwe o Mboa; Earth Paradise; Esok'am; Longe Lasu. Recordings: Munenge and Esok'am; Ewanje; Longe Lasu. Honours: First Prize of Composition, Guitar Word Thoroughfare, 1982; Arranger Diploma, 1991. Hobbies: Billiards; Chess. Address: 35 Rue Savier, 92240 Malakoff, France.

EWING Thomas D, b. 1 Sept 1946, Columbus, Ohio, USA. Musician (guitar); Singer. m. (1) Margaret Avren, 10 June 1967; (2) Pamela Gwen McReynolds, 12 June 1994, 2 sons, 1 daughter, 1 stepson, 1 stepdaughter. Education: BA, Journalism, BS, Education, The Ohio State University. Musical Education: Self-taught. Career: Earl Taylor and the Stoney Mountain Boys, 1974-77; Bill Monroe and His Blue Grass Boys, 1986-; Tours: USA; Europe; Japan; Carnegie Hall, 1988; WSM Grand Ole Opry; The Nashville Network, television; Appeared in film: High Lonesome Sound. Recordings: Albums: with Earl Taylor: Body And Soul, 1976; with Bill Monroe: Bluegrass '87, 1987; Southern Flavour, 1989; 50 Years at Grand Ole Opry; Cryin' Holy Unto The Lord, 1991; Solo albums: Take Me Home, 1989; Lookin' Out A Window, 1990; It's Good To Be Home, 1992. Publications: 30 Years Ago This Month, Bluegrass Unlimited Magazine. Membership: AFofM. Address: PO Box 1074, Gallatin, TN 37066, USA.

EYDMANN Stuart Anthony, b. 1 May 1953, Dunfermline, Fife, Scotland. Musician (fiddle, concertina); Ethnomusicologist. m. Mairin Downes, 27 July 1991, 1 son, 1 daughter. Education: Diploma, Glasgow School Of Art, 1975; PhD, The Open University, 1995. Career: Performer, various Scottish traditional music groups, 1972-1979; Member, Whistlebinkies, 1980-; Composer, Scottish Circus, including collaborations with John Cage; Worked with: Scottish Chamber Orchestra; Scottish Ballet; Royal Scottish National Orchestra; Yehudi Menuhin, in works by Edward McGuire; Various film scores; Edinburgh International Festival and Festival Fringe; Sessions with The Cutting Crew; Tours: Sweden; France; China; Hong Kong; Holland; Engaged in ethnomusicological research, 1985-. Recordings: As performer, co-writer, co-producer: The Whistlebinkies 3, 1980; The Whistlebinkies 4, 1982; The Whistlebinkies, 1985; The Whistlebinkies Anniversary, 1991; The Whistlebinkies Inner Sound, 1991; As guest: The Music Of Midlothian, 1990. Honours: The Glenfiddich Living Scotland Award, 1984. Memberships: Fellow, Society of Antiquarians of Scotland; Musicians Union; Traditional Music and Song Association of Scotland. Hobbies: Architectural Conservation; Ethnomusicology. Current Management: Jester Management. Address: 41 Hamilton Drive, Glasgow G12 8DW, Scotland.

EYNAUD DE FAY Olivier Georges Alain, b. 28 Apr 1961, Paris, France. Musician (drums). m. Laurence Turreau, 6 May 1988, 1 daughter. Education: BEPC. Musical Education: First Prize, Conservatory, Nice. Career: Casino de Paris; Festival de Carpentras; Antenna 2: Des Enfants Du Roche; FR3; RMC; Palace. Recordings: Abject; Michot Ditin; Matt Boum Boum; Solomon K T; Pasquali; Music, film: Dernier Round; TV Plupité. Publications: Abject; Matt Boum Boum; Pascuali. Membership: Union of Jazz Musicians. Hobbies: Swimming; Cinema. Address: 7 Rue de l'Ecole Polytechnique, 75005 Paris, France.

EYRE Simon James, b. 30 Nov 1964, Sheffield, England. Musician (Guitar, Bass, Vocals). Career: Concert tours with Elaine Page, The Style Council, Womack and Womack; TV appearances with Randy Crawford, Jim Diamond,

Sister Sledge, Second Image and Lenny Henry. Recordings: With Robert Palmer, Shara Nelson, and Errol Brown; Also with The Lighthouse Family for the soundtrack of the film, Jack and Sarah. Memberships: Musicians' Union; Associate Member, PRS. Address: 4 Luffman Road, London SE12 9SX, England.

EZEKE (Ezeke Gray), b. 26 Oct 1943, Jamaica. Singer; Broadcaster; Entertainer; Composer; Caterer. m. Linda Lewis, 11 Oct 1974, 1 son, 1 daughter. Education: Catering, Clarendon College of Further Education, Nottingham. Musical Education: Royal School Of Church Music. Career: Television appearances include Opportunity Knocks; Search For A Star; Nationwide; Pebble Mill At One; Arena; Resident performer, Monte Carlo Sporting Club, 1979-84; Extensive Tours: Europe; Asia; Middle East; Radio Broadcaster, Radio ERI (Cork City, Eire); BBC Radio 3 Counties, 1986; BBC Radio One (Sunshine Show), 1990-1993; BBC Radio One (Ones On One), 1993. Recordings: Sitting In The Moonlight, 1961; Righteous Festival, 1972; Rastaman A Come, 1972; Who's Grovelling Now? (with Tony Greig, England Cricket Captain), 1978; Ragga Ragga 1994; Oh Diana, 1994; Soon You'll Be Gone. Publications: Jakmandora (childrens stories). Honours: Voted Jamaica's Top Entertainer, 1970-75; Sony Awards Certificate; Stanford St Martin Religious Broadcasting, 3rd prize, 1992, 1st Prize, 1994. Membership: Musicians Union. Hobbies: Golf; Swimming; Cooking. Current Management: Habana Productions Ltd. Address: 78 Stanley Gardens, London W3 7SN England.

F

FABBRI Franco, b. 7 Sept 1949, Sao Paulo, Brazil. Musician; Musicologist. m. Monica Silvestris, 31 May 1980, 1 daughter. Education: Chemistry, State University of Milan; Composition, Conservatory Giuseppe Verdi, Milan; Musicology, University of Gothenburg, Sweden. Career: Member, experimental rock group, Stormy Six/Macchina Maccheronica, 1965-82; Freelance writer and lecturer, 1983-85; Consultant to musical institutions in Milan: Musica Nel Nostro Tempo; G Ricordi and Co., (publishers). Recordings: 9 albums with group La Chitarra Rotta: Domestic Flights, 1983; Tempo Rubato, 1983; La Casa Parlante, 1984; Various soundtracks and stage music. Publications: La Musica In Mano, 1978; Elettronica e Musica, 1984; La Musica Che Si Consuma, 1985; Editor, What Is Popular Music?, 1985; Compositore, 1986. Address: Strada Avenue, Torre 1, San Felice, 20090 Segrate, Italy.

FABER Shane, b. 23 Dec 1953, Gainesville, Florida, USA. Producer; Songwriter; Midi Expert; Musician (guitar, keyboards). m. Elizabeth Burkland, 22 May 1994. Musical Education: Bachelor Music/Jazz Guitar, University of Miami, Florida, 1977. Career: Member, Bad Sneakers, 1979-86; Video, Caught in the Act; Moved to New York, 1986; Engineer for: De La Soul; A Tribe Called Quest; Queen Latifah; Brand Nubians; Biz Markie. Compositions: Shine On; Ladies First. Recordings: Producer/mixer of albums: Reachin', Digable Planets; Debut album, Bass Is Base; Singles: Cool Like Dat; Turtle Power, from Teenage Mutant Ninja Turtles soundtrack. Honours: Numerous Golden Reel Awards; 2 Gold albums; 1 Platinum album; 2 Gold singles. Current Management: Sandy Roberton, World's End (America) Management. Address: 183 N Martel Avenue #270, Los Angeles, CA 90036, USA.

FABIANO Roberta Mary, b. 25 June 1952, New York, USA. Musician (guitar); Vocalist; Composer. Musical Education: BA, Composition and Arrangement, Berklee College of Music, Boston, 1975. Career: Guitarist, composer, Lester Lanin and Peter Duchin Orchestras, 1983-84; Doc Pomus, 1984-; Songwriter for Count Basie Band; Performed for HRH Queen Elizabeth, 1985, 1986; Also performed with: Cleo Laine; Melissa Manchester; Al B Sure!; Debbie Gibson; Carol Channing; Gloria Loring; Julia Budd. Recordings include: Working Girl (film soundtrack). Honours: American Song Festival Award, 1982; New York Songwriters Showcase Award, 1984; New York State Senate Achievement Award, 1984. Memberships: AFofM; Songwriters Guild; AFTRA.

FAGAN Donald, b. 10 Jan 1948, Passaic, New Jersey, USA. Vocalist; Musician (keyboards). Career: Member, Steely Dan, 1972-81; Solo artiste, 1981-; Tours worldwide; Organised New York Rock & Soul Revue, New York, USA, 1990, 1991; Music Editor, US film magazine Premiere, 1988. Recordings: Albums: with Steely Dan: Can't Buy A Thrill, 1973; Countdown To Ecstacy, 1973; Pretzel Logic, 1974; Katy Lied, 1975; The Royal Scam, 1977; Aja, 1977; Greatest Hits, 1979; Metal Leg, 1980; Gaucho, 1981; Steely Dan Gold, 1982; Reelin' In The Years, 1985; Do It Again, 1987; Remastered - The Very Best Of Steely Dan, 1993; Citizen Steely Dan - 1972-1980, 1993; Alive In America, 1995; Solo albums: The Nightfly, 1982; Kamakiriad, 1993; Singles include: Do It Again; Reelin'In The Years; Show Biz Kids; My Old School; Black Friday; Do It Again; Haitan Divorce; Deacon Blues; FM (No Static At All); Rikki Don't Lose That Number; Here In The Western World; Hey Nineteen; Time Out Of Mind; Solo singles: True Companion; Century's End, used in film Bright Lights Big City, 1988; I G Y (What A Beautiful World); Tomorrow's Girls; Contributor, Zazu, Rosie Vela, 1987; The New York Rock And Soul Revue - Live At The Beacon, 1992. Honours:

Grammy Award, Best-Engineered Non-Classical Recording, Aja, 1978; Q Inspiration Award, 1993; Inducted into Hollywood's Rock Walk, 1993. Current Management: HK Management, 8900 Wilshire Blvd, Ste 300, Beverly Hills, CA 90211, USA.

FAHEY Siobhan, b. 10 Sept 1957, London, England. Singer; Songwriter. m. Dave Stewart, 1 Aug 1987. Career: Press officer, Decca Records; Singer, Bananarama, 1981-88; Member, Shakespears Sister, with Marcella Detroit, 1988-93. Recordings: Albums: with Bananarama: Deep Sea Skiving, 1983; Bananarama, 1984; True Confessions, 1986; Wow!, 1987; with Shakespears Sister: Sacred Heart, 1989; Hormonally Yours, 1992; Singles include: with Bananarama: Really Sayin' Somethin', 1982; Shy Boy, 1982; Na Na Hey Hey Kiss Him Goodbye, 1983; Cruel Summer, 1983; Robert De Niro's Waiting, 1984; Venus, 1986; I Heard A Rumour, 1987; Love In The First Degree, 1987; with Shakespears Sister: You're History, 1989; Goodbye Cruel World, 1991; Hello (Turn Your Radio On); Stay (Number 1, UK), 1992; My 16th Apology (EP), 1993; Backing vocalist, It Ain't What You Do, It's The Way That You Do It, with Fun Boy Three, 1982; Contributor, Do They Know It's Christmas?, Band Aid (Number 1, UK), 1984; Let It Be, Ferry Aid (Zeebrugge ferry disaster relief), 1987. Honours: BRIT Award, Best Video, Stay, 1993; Ivor Novello Award, Outstanding Contemporary Song Collection, Hormonally Yours, 1993.

FAIRBAIRN Hazel Ann, b. 14 Sep 1965, Amersham, Buckinghamshire, England. Freelance Musician (violin); Teacher. Musical Education: BSc, Honours, Music, City University; PhD, Group Playing in Irish Traditional Music, University of Cambridge. Career: Has played in local traditional Ceili bands in Cambridge busking bands for the last 9 years; Player with Mervyn Afrika's Kaap Finalé; Founder member and fiddle player of Horace X, appearing on Jazz World Stage, Glastonbury, 1994; Amsterdam World Roots Festival, 1995; CD played on national Radio in UK, Croatia and Slovenia, and on the World Service. Recordings: Tout Le Porc Scratchings; Porc Pickings with guitarist Mark Jones; Horace X; Horace X. Publication: Changing Contexts for Traditional Dance Music In Ireland, in Folk Music Journal, 1994. Memberships: Musicians' Union; KHANA. Hobbies: Tang Soo Do, (martial art); Swimming. Current Management: Highfield Management, Cambridge. Address: 1 Wood End Cottages, Grantchester Road, Cambridge CB2 2LJ, England.

FAIRBAIRN Keith, b. 14 Jan 1963, Horsham, Surrey, England. Musician (percussion). Musical Education: Guildhall School of Music. Career: Worked with: Shirley Bassey; Mike Oldfield; Lulu; Judy Tzuke; Madelaine Bell; Vic Damone; Dionne Warwick; Joe Longthorne; Numerous television shows for BBC; LWT; Granada. Recordings: Andrew Lloyd Webber; Jim Steinman; Nick Heyward; Shirley Bassey; Madelaine Bell; Joe Longthorne; Numerous films, shows, library music. Honours: AGSM. Membership: Musicians' Union. Address: 31A St Georges Road, Leyton, London E10 5RH, England.

FAIRLEY Colin. Record Producer; Engineer; Musician (drums). Career: Former drummer; Engineer, Air Studios; Freelance record producer, engineer, 1981-. Recordings: As producer/engineer, albums include: with Nick Lowe: Cowboy Outfit; The Rose Of England; Pinker Than Proud; Blood & Chocolate, Elvis Costello; Wilder, Teardrop Explodes; T-Bird Rhythm, Fabulous Thunderbirds; Sisters, The Bluebells; Gentlemen Take Polaroids, Japan; Welcome To The Cruise, Judie Tzuke; Stop, Sam Brown; Titles, Mick Karn; Porcupine, Echo And The Bunnymen; Singles include: with Madness: It Must Be Love; Grey Day; Driving In My Car; Pills

And Soap, Elvis Costello; Young At Heart, The Bluebells; Quiet Life, Japan; Reward, Teardrop Explodes; Stay With Me 'Til Dawn, Judy Tzuke. Current Management: c/o Stephen Budd Management. Address: 109B Regents Park Road, London NW1 8UR, England.

FAIRWEATHER Digby (Richard John Charles), b. 25 Apr 1946, Rochford, Essex, England. Jazz musician (Trumpet, cornet). Education: Ealing Technical College (1966-68). Musical Education: Self-taught; Trumpet tuition, E M Collier, 1965-6. Career: Semi-professional, 1964-76; Professional, 1977-, played with all major British swing/traditional names; South Bank Concerts, London, 1974-; Own band formed, 1971; BBC Radio Jazz Presenter, 1991-; Re-formed Digby Fairweather's Half Dozen, 1996. Compositions: Songs for Sandy (suite), 1976; Suite for Southwell, 1985; Suite Swinging Southwell, 1987. Recordings: Over 50 as sideman of leader including: A Portrait Of DF; with Stan Barker: Let's Duet, 1986; Squeezin' The Blues Away, 1995; With Nat In Mind, 1995; Solo: The Story So Far, 1995. Publications: How To Play Trumpet, 1985; Jazz-The Essential Companion, 1987; British Co-ordinator, Grove's Dictionary of Jazz, 1988-94; Rough Guide to Jazz, 1995. Honours: Musician of the Year, BBC Jazz Society, 1979; British Jazz Awards, Trumpet, 1992; Services to Jazz, 1993; Freedom Of City of London, 1992; Benno Haussman Award, Services To Jazz, 1993. Memberships: Founder, Association Of British Jazz Musicians; National Jazz Foundation Archive; Musicians' Union (Jazz Section). Hobbies: Jazz; Popular Music; Films. Current Management: Self managed. Address: Westcliff-On-Sea, Essex, England.

FAIRWEATHER-LOW Andy, b. 8 Aug 1950, Ystrad Mynach, Hengoed, Wales. Singer; Musician (guitar). Career: Member, The Taffbeats; The Sect Maniacs; Founder member, Amen Corner, 1966-69; Performances include: Headline act, Pop Proms, Royal Albert Hall, 1969; Solo artiste; Session musician for artists including: Pink Floyd; Roger Waters; Sang with All-Star ARMS band (benefit for research into multiple sclerosis), 1987; Tour with Chris Rea, 1990; Tour with George Harrison, Eric Clapton, Japan, 1991; Member, Eric Clapton's backing band, 1990s; Film appearance, Scream And Scream Again, 1969. Recordings: Albums: with Amen Corner: Round Amen Corner, 1968; Explosive Company, 1969; Solo albums: Beginning From An End, 1971; Spider Jivin', 1974; La Booga Rooga, 1975; Be Bop 'N' Holla, 1976; Mega-Shebang, 1980; with Eric Clapton: Unplugged, 1992; Singles include: Gin House Blues, 1967; World Of Broken Hearts, 1967; Bend Me Shape Me, 1968; High In The Sky, 1968; (If Paradise Is) Half As Nice, 1969; Solo: Natural Sinner, 1970; Reggae Tune, 1974; Wide Eyed And Legless, 1975.

FAITH Adam (Terence Nelhams), b. 23 June 1940, Acton, London, England. Singer; Actor; Producer. Career: Member, skiffle group The Worried Men group, 1957; Solo artiste, 1958-; Residency on Drumbeat, BBC TV, 1959; Film appearances include: Beat Girl, 1960; Never Let Go, 1960; Mix Me A Person, 1962; Stardust, 1974; Yesterday's Hero, 1979; McVicar, 1980; Television acting appearances: Budgie, 1971; Love Hurts, 1991; Alfie, 1992; Now You Know, 1996; Dosh, 1996; A Chorus Line, 1997; Theatre appearances: Billy Liar, 1967; Twelfth Night, 1967; Night Must Fall, 1967; City Sugar, 1976; Musical version, Budgie, 1988; Artist manager for Leo Sayer, 1972-; Owner, Faith Corporation, (financial advice company). Recordings: Singles include: What Do You Want, 1959; Poor Me, 1960; Someone Else's Baby, 1960; Made You, 1960; When Johnny Comes Marching Home, 1960; How About That, 1960; Lonely Pup, 1960; Who Am I, 1961; Don't You Know It, 1961; The Time Has Come, 1961; Lonesome, 1962; The First Time, 1963; We Are In Love, 1964; A Message To Martha, 1964; Albums:

Adam, 1960; Adam Faith, 1962; Faith Alive, 1965; I Survive, 1974; 20 Golden Greats, 1981; Midnight Postcards, 1991; Contributor, Scouse The Mouse (with Ringo Starr, Barbara Dickson), 1977; As producer: Daltry, Roger Daltrey, 1973. Current Management: Alan Field Ltd. Address: 3 The Spinney, Bakers Hill, Hadley Common, Herts EN5 5QJ, England.

FAITHFULL Marianne, b. 29 Dec 1946, Hampstead, London, England. Singer. 1 son. Career: Recording artist, 1964-; Tours, appearances include: UK tour with Roy Orbison, 1965; US tour with Gene Pitney, 1965; Uxbridge Blues and Folk Festival, 1965; Montreux, Golden Rose Festival, 1966; Roger Water's The Wall, Berlin, 1990; Chieftains Music Festival, London, 1991; Acting roles include: I'll Never Forget Whatsiname, 1967; Three Sisters, Chekkov, London, 1967; Hamlet, 1970; Kurt Weill's Seven Deadly Sins, St Ann's Cathedral, New York, 1990; Film appearance, Girl On A Motorcycle, 1968. Recordings: Singles include: As Tears Go By; Come And Stay With Me; This Little Bird; Summer Nights; Something Better/Sister Morphine; The Ballad Of Lucy Jordan; Dreaming My Dreams; Albums: Come My Way, 1965; Marianne Faithfull, 1965; Go Away From My World, 1966; Faithful Forever, 1966; Marianne Faithfull's Greatest Hits, 1969; Faithless, with the Grease Band, 1978; Broken English, 1979; Dangerous Acquaintances, 1981; A Child's Adventure, 1983; Strange Weather, 1987; Blazing Away, 1990; A Secret Life, 1995; Contributor, Lost In The Stars - The Music Of Kurt Weill, 1984; The Bells Of Dublin, The Chieftains, 1992. Publications: Faithfull (ghost written by David Dalton). Honours include: Grammy Nomination, Broken English, 1979. Current Management: Art Collins Management, PO Box 561, Pine Bush, NY 12566, USA.

FAKANAS Viorgos, b. 18 July 1961, Athens, Greece. Composer; Arranger; Musician (bass); Author. m. Nicoletta Pitsikali, 12 June 1992, 1 son. Education: Diploma, Economics (University of Athens). Musical Education: Classical guitar; Classical piano; Self-taught bass. Career: Only Greek correspondant as bass player, Europe, (European Community Youth Jazz Orchestra), 1981-84; Founder, ISKRA (major Greek jazz group), 1984-88; Numerous concerts, Greece and abroad, include: Locabettus Theatre; Herodio, Athens Concert Hall, performed own composition: Topazi, A Composition For Large Strings And Jazz Ensemble; Founder, tutor, Contemporary Music School Of Athens; Numerous TV, radio appearances; Currently leader of own jazz group. Recordings: A New Day, 1986; Horizon, 1989; Parastasis, 1990; Amorosa, 1992; Stand-Art, 1995; Session musician, more than 200 recordings with major Greek artists. Publications: Educational books: For The Bass (vol I, II); Scales Of Modern Music, Jazz Harmony, Modern Counterpoint. Honours: Honoured Member, Greek Radio and TV's Jazz Orchestra. Membership: Member, Hellenic Musician's Union. Hobbies: Football; Theatre; Travel. Current Management: Nicoletta Pitsivalli. Address: 3 L Possidonas St, 18344 Moshato - Athens, Greece.

FALK Leif, b. 18 July 1940, Randers, Denmark. Lecturer; Composer; Musician (drums, keyboards, percussion). m. Ivalo Gilberg, 5 Jan 1962, 1 son, 1 daughter. Education: Teacher. Career: Aarhus Free School, 1965-85; Center of Music and Movement, 1988-95; Member of groups: Blue Sun, 1972-76; Splask, 1972-78; Gnags, 1975-76; Carnival Band, 1982-88; Gumbo, 1988-95; Played at Roskilde Festival, 1974-76. Recordings: Blue Sun, 1973; Gnags, 1975; Splask, 1976; It's All Money Johnny, Blue Sun, 1976; Ymer-Og Fræser Afsted, 1993-94. Honour: Gerlev Prize. Memberships: DMF; DJBFA; Union Of World Music. Hobby: Music. Address: Ormslevbakken 3, 8260 Viby, Denmark.

FALLON Peter Sean, b. 3 June 1968, Reigate, Surrey, England. Record Producer; Songwriter. Musical Education: Piano from age 6. Career: Signed to Big One Records aged 18, 1986; UK Club Promo Tour, signed to Swanyard Records, 1990; Performed at Cesmé 91 Festival in Turkey; Top Of The Pops; Pebble Mill; This Morning, ITV, 1993; BBC Radio 1 Session, 1994. Recordings: with Twin Beat: Let's Pick Up The Pieces, 1988; with Fallon: Get On The Move, 1990; with Technotronic: Get Up Remix, 1991; with Stevie Wonder: You Never Lose Remix, 1991; As writer, producer: with David Hasselhoff: If I Could Only Say Goodbye, 1993; Tighter And Tighter, 1993; with Dannii Minogue: Love And Affection; As writer: with Celine Dion: Don't Turn Away From Me; with Groove U: Step By Step. Memberships: PRS; BASCA; ASCAP. Hobbies: Tennis; Rollerblading; Reading. Current Management: EMI Music Publishing London. Address: C/o Broadhill Recording Studios, Ockley Lane, Keymer, Hassocks, West Sussex BN6 8PA, England.

FÄLTSKOG Agnetha, b. 5 Apr 1950, Sweden. Singer; Actress. m. (1) Bjorn Ulvæus, 1971 (divorced), (2) Tomas Sonnenfeld. Career: Solo recording artist, aged 17; Actress, Jesus Christ Superstar, Sweden; Singer, Abba, 1973-82; Appearances include: Winners, Eurovision Song Contest, 1974; Royal Performance, Stockholm, 1976; Royal Albert Hall, 1977; Worldwide tours; Television: A Gift Of Song - The Music For UNICEF Concert, NBC, 1979; This Is Your Life, Swedish TV, 1986; The Story Of Abba, C4, 1991; Solo artiste, 1982-1990; Films: Abba - The Movie, 1978; As actress: Rakenstam, 1983. Recordings: Albums include: with Abba: Waterloo, 1974; Abba, 1976; Arrival, 1977; The Album, 1978; Voulez-Vous, 1979; Super Trouper, 1980; The Visitors, 1982; Various compilations; Solo: Eleven Women In One Building, 1975; Wrap Your Arms Around Me, 1983; Eyes Of A Woman, 1985; I Stand Alone, 1988; Hit singles include: with Abba: Ring Ring; Waterloo; Mamma Mia; Dancing Queen; Fernando; Money Money Money; Take A Chance On Me; The Name Of The Game; Summer Night City; Chiquitita; Does Your Mother Know?; Gimme Gimme Gimme (A Man After Midnight); The Winner Takes It All; On And On And On; Lay All Your Love On Me; One Of Us; Solo: I Was So In Love (Number 1, Sweden); The Heat Is On; Can't Shake You Loose; I Wasn't The One (Who Said Goodbye). Honours include: Gold discs; Best selling group in pop history, Guinness Book Of Records, 1979; World Music Award, Best Selling Swedish Artist Of Year (with Abba), 1993.

FAME Georgie (Clive Powell), b. 26 Sept 1943, Leigh, Lancashire, England. Singer; Musician (keyboards). Career: Member, Billy Fury's backing group, The Blue Flames, 1961; Band replaced with the Tornados; London residencies, Georgie Fame and the Blue Flames, 1961-63; Tours, concerts television include: UK Tamla Motown Package Tour, 1965; National Jazz And Blues Festival, 1965, 1966; Pop From Britain concert, Royal Albert Hall, 1965; Grand Gala Du Disque, Amsterdam, 1966; Founder, Georgie Fame Band, 1966; Concerts include: International Popular Music Festival, Brazil, 1967; Royal Albert Hall, 1967, 1969; Television series with Alan Price, 1971; Concerts as leader of various groups and ensmebles; Television variety shows and commercials, 1971-; Keyboard player, Van Morrison tour, 1989; International Jazz Festival, Blackpool, 1992; Continues to play on jazz circuit. Recordings: Hit singles: Yeh Yeh (Number 1, UK), 1965; In The Meantime, 1965; Get Away (Number 1, UK), 1966; Sweet Things, 1966; Sunny, 1966; Sitting In The Park, 1967; Because I Love You (own composition), 1967; The Ballad Of Bonnie And Clyde (Number 1, UK), 1968; Peaceful, 1969; Rosetta, with Alan Price, 1971; Albums: Rhythm And Blues At The Flamingo, 1963; Fame At Last, 1964; Sound Venture, 1966; Hall Of Fame, 1967; Two Faces Of Fame, 1967; The Third Face Of

Fame, 1968; Seventh Son, 1969; Fame And Price, Price And Fame Together, 1971; All Me Own Work, 1972; Georgie Fame, 1974; That's What Friends Are For, 1978; Georgie Fame Right Now, 1979; Closing The Gap, 1980; Hoagland, with Annie Ross, 1981; In Goodman's Land, 1983; My Favourite Songs, 1984; No Worries, 1988; Georgie Fame - The First 30 Years, 1989; Cool Cat Blues, 1991; How Long Has This Been Going On, with Van Morrison, 1996; Contributor, Avalon Sunset, Van Morrison, 1989; Contributor, film soundtrack Glengarry Glen Ross, 1992. Address: c/o Brabingers, London, England.

FANFANT Jean-Philippe, b. 27 July 1966, Paris, France. Musician (drums). 1 son. Musical Education: Conservatoire de Musique. Career: Concerts, tours, television with: Angelique Kidjo; Maxime Le Forestier; Mario Canonge (also radio); Mayuko (Montreux Jazz Festival). Recordings with: Mario Cononge; Angelique Kidjo; Julien Clerc; Maxime Le Forestier; Kassav. Address: Paris, France.

FANFANT Thierry, b. 27 March 1964, Paris, France. Musician (Bass Guitar). Education: Diploma of Audiovisual Technician. Musical Education: Selftaught Bass, 1976; Private lessons, 2 years, 1986-87; Course in musical centre, 1 year. Career: Olympia, with Michel Pugain, 1993; Casino de Paris, 1995; France Follies, La Rochelle, 1994, 1995, 1996; France Follies, Montreal; Pantemps de Bourges, 1990, 1991, 1995; Festival Jazz, Nice, 1994; Petit Journal, 1997. Compositions: Don d'organe; Ernest et firmin; Pausove Muen. Recordings: With: Enzo-Enzo; Michel Fugain; Maria Glen; Tuluo De Piscopo; Hajime Mizoguehi; Shukichi Kina; Beethova Obas; Mario Canonge; Taratata; Tery Boise. Honour: Success Prize of the Year, 1994. Hobbies: Photography; Cinema. Address: 3 Allée, Claude Bernard, 93440 Dugny, France.

FARGO Donna (Yvonne Vaughn), b. 10 Nov 1945, Mount Airy, North Carolina, USA. Country Singer; Songwriter. m. Stan Silver. Career: Solo recording artist, 1969-; Numerous television and stage appearances include Country Music Festival, Wembley, 1978. Compositions include: Funny Face, 1972; The Happiest Girl In The Whole USA, 1972; Superman, 1973; You Were Always There, 1973; You Can't Be A Beacon (If Your Light Don't Shine), 1974; That Was Yesterday; Soldier Boy (all US Country Number 1 hits); Members Only (duet with Billy Joe Royal), 1988; Albums include: Winners, 1986. Honours: Billboard, Best New Female Country Artist, 1972; NARM Best Selling Country Artist, 1972-73; ACM Top Female Vocalist, 1972-73; Robert J Burton Award, Most performed country Song, 1972-73; C&W Record of Year on Jukeboxes, 1973; Grammy, Best Female Country Performer, for Funny Face, 1973; Gold discs worldwide. Current Management: c/o Stan Silver, Prima-Donna Entertainment Corp., PO Box 150527, Nashville, TN 37215, USA.

FARLOW Tal(mage) Holt, b. 7 June 1921, Greensboro, North Carolina, USA. Jazz Musician (guitar). m. Tina Zwirlein, 1973. Career: Jazz guitarist with artistes including: Red Norvo; Buddy DeFranco; Artie Shaw; Formed jazz trio, 1956-; Numerous guest appearances and tours, USA, Europe. Recordings: More than 25 albums. Address: c/o Concord Jazz Records, Box 845, 2888 Willow Road, Concord, CA 94522, USA.

FARNELL Thomas, b. 24 Aug 1947, Birmingham, England. Musician (drums). m. 22 Sept 1968, 1 son, 2 daughters. Career: Toured USA extensively with Savoy Brown; Worked with Fairport Convention; Worked with Raymond Frogatt (Top British Country singer). Recordings: Recorded with: Savoy Brown; Fairport Convention; Raymond Froggatt. Honours: Diploma Ed, Percussion. Membership: Musicians' Union. Hobbies: Drum tuition; Session work.

Address: 94 Leasow Drive, Edgbaston, Birmingham B15 2SW, England.

FARNHAM John Peter, b. 1 July 1949. Singer. m. April 1973, 2 sons. Career: Singer; Entertainer; TV Host; Ld Singer, Little River Band, 1982-85; Launched Greenpeace album, Rainbow Warriors, Moscow, 1989. Creative Works: Numerous recordings include: Uncovered, 1980; Whispering Jack, album, 1986; Age of Reason, 1988; Chain Reaction, 1990; Full House Album, 1991; Played Jesus in Jesus Christ Superstar, Jesus Christ Superstar - The Album, 1992; Romeo's Heart, album, 1996. Honours include: Whispering Jack, biggest selling album in Australia by Australian Artist; Australian of Year, 1988; Talk of the Town Tour largest grossing Australian tour, 1994; AO, 1996. Address: c/o Talentworks Pty Ltd, Suite 1, 633 Victoria Street, Abbotsford, Victoria 3067, Australia.

FARRENDEN Shaun, b. 17 Apr 1962, Bishopstoke, England. Musician (didjeridu). Musical Education: Self-taught. Career: Concerts include: Glastonbury Festival; Glastonbury Assembly Rooms. Recordings: Albums: Earth Songs, 1992; Double Spiral, 1994; Yidaki, 1996; With Global: Shamanka; Gig na Gig; Guest musician, Welcome To The Cali, Ron Kavana and the Bucks; Television music for Channel 4. Publications: Earth Vibrations, An Introduction To The Didjeridu. Membership: Musicians' Union. Hobbies: Bridge; Computers; Forest walking; Making didgeridoos. Address: 125 Ashmore Road, London W9 3DA, England.

FARRINGTON Clive, b. 25 Sept 1957, Altrincham, South Manchester, England. Vocalist; Musician (bass guitar, keyboards, programming, drums, percussion). Education: Civil Engineering City and Guilds. Musical Education: A Level Music Theory, Technology. Career: Vocalist, bass guitarist, When In Rome, 2 major US tours, 1985, 1986; Tours: Europe, Brazil, 1992; Remix for Diesel track Man Alive, Australia, 1994; Remix, Chill Factor track One Touch, Australia; Writer, producer, Underground Circus on tracks: Wrapped Around Your Finger; Crazy; Tree Without A Shadow; Remix for Bing Abrahams track One Touch; Currently working with John McGeoch on project Blue, as vocalist, programmer, producer. Recordings: Writer, producer, lead vocalist, album: When In Rome (hit in USA, Europe, South America); Single: The Promise (Number 1, US Dance chart). Memberships: Musicians' Union; PRS (Associate member). Hobbies: Driving; Moto cross; Clothes. Current Management: William Hunt. Address: 68 Neal Street, Covent Garden, London WC2, England.

FARROW Andrew McGregor, b. 24 July 1964, Hamilton, Bermuda. Music Manager; A&R Consultant. Education: Sheffield Polytechnic. Career: Vocalist, Living Dead, 1980-82; Established AMF Music, 1987; Partner, Far North Music, 1988; Proprietor, (renamed) Northern Music Company. Honours: BA (Hons). Hobby: Cycling. Address: Northern Music Company, Cheapside Chambers, 43 Cheapside, Bradford BD1 4HP, England.

FAWCETT David Everington, b. 27 Mar 1938, Watford, Hertfordshire, England. Commercial Manager; Musician (banjo). m. Gloria Ann (née Jeffrey), 1 son, 1 daughter. Career: Television: Winner, with Main Avenue Jazz band, Opportunity Knocks, 1978; Radio broadcasts, with TJ4, Sounds of Jazz, BBC Radio, 1982-85. Recordings: with TJS: Richard Leach's Northside Jazzband. Membership: Musicians' Union. Hobbies: Watford Football Club; Semi-pro football supporter. Address: 31 Langley Road, Watford, Herts WD1 3PR, England.

FEEHAN David, b. 9 Oct 1948, Wellington, New Zealand. Singer; Songwriter; Producer; Vocal Tutor. m. Shelley Catherine Melody, 3 sons.

Education: UE Accountancy Units. Musical Education: Classical to Grade 8, 3 years New Zealand Opera Company. Career: EMI Session vocalist, 1964-70; Lead singer, top New Zealand band Tapestry, 1970-78; Lead singer, Rodger Fox Big Band, 1976-1988; Concerts at Ronnie Scotts, London; Montreux Jazz Festival, Switzerland; Hong Kong; Singapore; New York; Poland; Los Angeles; Sydney; Vancouver; Leader of David Feehan Band, 1988-; Appearances on all major New Zealand television shows and concerts; Played Jesus in Jesus Christ Superstar, 1983. Recordings: with Tapestry: It's Wrong, number 3 hit, 1973; Vocalist on Rodger Fox Big Band albums including: Montreux Live, 1980-; Montreux II Live, 1981; New York Tapes, 1980; Runner-up, Songwriters Contest, San Diego with: Still The One, 1989; 2 solo albums: Ballade, 1986; DF, 1993; Appearances on over 20 other albums. Publications: 2 childrens books due for publication; Writing a vocal technique book. Honours: Finalist, APRA and Best New Artist Awards (Composition); Best Jazz Album Award. Membership: Music tutor at Whitirea Polytechnic, Poriua, New Zealand. Hobbies: Photography; Writing; Squash; Rugby; Rugby League; Community work. Current Management: Tapestry Music Ltd, Box 575 Wellington, New Zealand; The Music Corporation Ltd, Box 68448 Auckland, New Zealand; Thunderbird 9 Productions, 71 Cedar Drive, Paraparaumu, New Zealand.

FEHLING Annika, b. 25 Oct 1962, Gothenburg, Sweden. Singer; Songwriter; Actress; Plays Guitar and Piano. Education: University of Lund, Sweden, 1981-82; Theatre Art School of Skara, 1982-83; State School of Theatre, Malmoe, 1988; Singing and Piano lessons; Selftaught guitar, longterm course in Arranging and Composing, Stockholm, 1993. Career: Mére Ubu in King Ubu, musical; Solo-singer, Duke Ellingtons Sacred Concert; Participated in films, Women on the Roof, Petri Tears; Participating in the Sweden Song Contest, televised, 1998; Concerts with Visby Big Band in Norway, Poland, Rhodes. Recordings: Singles: Oktoberbarn (October Child), 1993; Naren Stjarna Faller (When A Star Falls), 1998; Solo Albums: Jazz Fehlings, 1996; Alskar Du? (Do You Love), 1997. Publication: The Real Swede, 1997. Honours: STIM, Swedens ASCAP Prize, 1992, 1996; State Art Prize, Art Cncl, 1993, 1994; SKAP Prize, 1997. Memberships: STIM; SKAP. Current Management: Musicano Records, c/o Arne Söderquist, Strandg 22 II, 62156 Visby, Sweden. Address: Strandg 22 II, 62156, Visby, Sweden.

FEINSTEIN Michael Jay, b. 7 Sept 1956, Columbus, OH, USA. Singer; Musician (piano); Actor; Musicologist. Career: Archivist, Ira Gershwin, 1977-83; Assistant to Harry Warren, 1979-81; Hotel residencies in US, 1984-89; Accompanist, artistes including Liza Minnelli; Estelle Reiner; Rose Marie; Jessie Matthews; Rosemary Clooney, 1991-; Numerous concerts include: George Gershwin 50th Anniversary celebration, Los Angeles, 1987; Irving Berlin 100th Anniversary celebration, Los Angeles, 1988; Royal Command Performance, London, 1988; Cole Porter 100th Birthday Concert, Carnegie Hall, New York, 1991; Michael Feinstein in Concert- Isn't It Romantic, Broadway/US tour, 1988-89; Stage: Ira Gershwin Centennial, Carnegie Hall, 1996; Television appearances include: Broadway Sings - The Music Of Jule Styne, 1987; George Gershwin Remembered, 1987; Thirtysomething, 1987; Omnibus, 1989; Sing a Song of Hollywood, 1995. Composition: Film score and songs for Get Bruce, 1997. Recordings: Numerous albums include: Pure Gershwin, 1985; Live At The Algonquin, 1986; Michael Feinstein Sings Irving Berlin, 1987; Isn't It Romantic, 1987; Over There -Songs Of War And Peace, 1989; The Mem Album, 1989; Burton Lane Songbook, Vol I, 1990; Jule Styne Songbook, 1991; Pure Imagination, 1991; Jerry Herman Songbook, 1994; Hugh Martin Songbook, 1995; Such Sweet Sorrow, 1995; Nice

Work If You Can Get iT, 1996. Publications: Editor, Ira Gershwin Songbook; Contributor, Washington Post and New York Times; Autobiography, Nice Work If You Can Get It, 1995. Honours: 3 Golden Laurel Awards; San Francisco Council For Entertainment; NYC Seal Of Approval, 1987; Drama Desk Award, 1988; Outer Critics Circle Award, 1988; Doctorate of Fine Arts, California State University at Los Angeles, 1997. Scholarships in his honour established in New York colleges. Membership: ASCAP. Address: 648 North Robertson Blvd, Los Angeles, CA 90069, USA.

FELD Malcolm, b. 7 Sept 1940, London, England. Theatrical Agent; Promoter. m. Georgina Maher, 17 Aug 1989, 2 daughters. Career: Promoted artists in all major venues for 30 years; Joined Issy Bonn Organisation, 1955; Director, Slim Millar Entertainments Agency, late 1960s; Moved to MAM: Created own company: MFA Ltd, late 70's; Expanded as: MFA Casting; MFA Limousine Hire. Hobby: Snooker. Address: 7 The Old Quarry, Woolton, Liverpool L25 6HE, England.

FELDMAN Samuel Leon, b. 14 March 1949, Shanghai, China. Entertainment Company Executive. 1 son, 2 daughters. Career: President, S L Feldman and Associates, a Division of A&F Music Ltd, fully-integrated entertainment company, co-owned with partner Bruce Allen; Management clients include: Bryan Adams, Joni Mitchell, The Chieftains and Sissel; Partner, TMP, largest independent publisher in Canada. Hobbies: Running; Snooker; Golf. Address: #200-1505 West 2nd Avenue, Vancouver, British Columbia V6H 3Y4, Canada.

FELICIANO José, b. 10 Sept 1945, Lares, Puerto Rico. Singer; Musician (guitar, bass, drums, piano, percussion). Career: Moved to New York as child; Performer, English and Latin music, becoming one of most popular artists in Spanish-speaking world and English pop music world; Chosen to sing The Star Spangled Banner, World series baseball, first one to ever stylise it, 1968; Recorded albums in Argentina, Mexico, Venezuela, Italy, USA, Austria; Television show throughout South America; Sang and composed theme music to TV series Chico And The Man; Recording artiste, classical guitar music, English pop, Spanish-language and jazz recordings. Recordings include: The Voice And Guitar Of José Feliciano, 1964; A Bag Full Of Soul, 1965; Feliciano!, 1967; Feliciano 10 To 23, 1969; Alive Alive-O, 1969; Souled, 1969; Fireworks, 1970; That The Spirit Needs, 1971; José Feliciano Sings, 1972; Compartments, 1973; And The Feeling's Good, 1974; Just Wanna Rock'N'Roll, 1974; Sweet Soul Music, 1976; Jose Feliciano, 1980; Escenas De Amor, 1982; Romance In The Night, 1983; Los Exitos De José Feliciano, 1984; The Best Of José Feliciano, 1985; Portrait, 1985; Tu Immenso Amor, 1987; I'm Never Gonna Change, 1989; Steppin' Out, 1990; Latin Street '92, 1992; A Tribute To The Beatles, 1993; Americano, 1996; On Second Thought, 1997; Senor Bolero, 1998; Singles: Light My Fire; Hi Heel Sneakers; The Sun Will Shine. Honours: Six Grammy Awards; Billboard Lifetime Achievement Award' ASCAP Golden Globe Award. Current Management: John Regna, 297-101 Kinderkamack Road, Oradell, NJ 07649, USA.

FELLOUÉ Guillermo, b. 10 Feb 1932, Havana, Cuba. Musician (bugle, trumpet). m. Rosana Fellové, 15 July 1969. Musical Education: Conservatory; Private teachers. Career: Professional from age 13; First trumpet and soloist with leading Cuban singers: Arsenio Rodriguez; Benny More; Soloist with Perez Prado, South America; Tours, Europe, Japan with Havana Cuban Boys of Armando Orefiche; First trumpet and soloist, with the Rosana and Guil Afro-Cuban jazz show, 2 tours Japan; Arrived in Paris aged 19; Played at Moulin Rouge; Casino de Cannes; Palm Beach; First trumpet soloist, Big Band from

Bourdeaux-Aquitane for radio; Casino, Sporting Club, Monte-Carlo, for 7 years; First trumpet, soloist, Bekum=mernis of Luc Le Masne; Television concerts, tours with singer Ellie Medeiros: Japan; New York; Canada; Co-director, Los Salseros. Recordings: with Arseño Rodriguez Conjunto Colonial, Cuba; 3 albums with Bekumernis de Luc Le Masne; Album and single with: Ellie Medeiros; Album: Los Salseros; Single with Pierre Vassiliu. Hobby: Chess. Address: 20 Rue de Rungis, 75013 Paris, France.

FELTHAM Mark, b. 20 Oct 1955, London, England. Musician (harmonica); Composer. m. Susan, 25 June 1994, 1 son. Education: South East London Technical School, Greenwich. Musical Education: Self-taught. Career: Founder member, Nine Below Zero, 1977-82; Harmonica player with Rory Gallagher for last 11 years; Varied studio work including: Georgie Fame, 1984; Godley and Creme (harmonica album), 1986; New Model Army; Deacon Blue, 1988; Texas, 1988; The The, 1989-91; Talk Talk, 1989-92; Joan Armatrading, 1992; Annie Lennox, 1995. Recordings include: Albums: with Nine Below Zero: Packed Fair And Square, 1979; Live At The Marquee, 1980; Don't Point Your Finger, 1981; with Godley and Creme: Goodbye Blue Sky,1986; Other recordings include albums by: Rory Gallagher; Roger Daltrey; Roy Harper; Talk Talk; Paul Young; Telvision documentary scores, live guest appearances. Membership: Musicians' Union. Hobbies: Reading; Sport. Current Management: Session Connection, London SW9, England.

FENDER Freddy (Baldemar G. Huerta), b. 4 June 1937, San Benito, Texas, USA. Singer; Musician (guitar). m. Evangelina Muniz, 10 Aug 1957, 2 sons, 1 daughter. Education: Sociology degree. Career: Solo Country music singer; Founder member, Texas Tornados, 1990; Film appearance: The Milagro Beanfield War, 1987. Recordings: Singles: Don't Be Cruel; Wasted Days Wasted Nights; Before The Next Teardrop Falls (Number 1, US); Secret Love; Vaya Con Dios; You'll Lose A Good Thing; Albums include: Before The Next Teardrop Falls, 1975; Since I Met You Baby, 1975; Are You Ready For Freddy?, 1975; If You're Ever In Texas, 1976; Rock'n'Country, 1976; Don't You Love Me, 1977; Swamp Gold, 1978; The Texas Balladeer, 1979; Tem-Mex, 1979; Together We Drifted Apart, 180; El Major De Freddy Fender, 1986; Crazy Baby, 1987; 16 Greatest Hits, 1993; with Texas Tornados: Texas Tornados, 1990; Zone Of Your Own, 1991; The Freddie Fender Collection, 1991. Honour: Grammy, Outstanding Mexican-American award, 1977. Memberships: CMA; AFTRA; Broadcast Music Inc; AFofM. Current Management: Jim Halsey Co. Address: 3225 South Norwood, Tulsa, OK 74135, USA.

FENGER Sos, b. 2 December 1961, Copenhagen, Denmark. Singer; Songwriter. 1 son. Education: Piano, Guitar and Singing Lessons. Career: Touring with Pop Band, News, early 1980's; Soulband with brother, Love Construction, 1986-89; Solo Career, 1989-; Tour with Doky Brothers and Adam Nussbaum; Recording with Toots Thielemanns and Randy Brecker; Contributor on several Scandinavian Albums. Recordings: Vinterdage, 1989; Sos Fenger on Holiday, 1992; Et Kys Herfra, 1994; Camouflage, 1996; Greatest Hits, 1997. Honours: Female Singer of the Year, 1986, 1990; Grammy Awards; Spies Fondet's Music Award, 1993. Current Management: Annetta Elmo, Holbergsgade 16, Kobenhavn K, Denmark. Address: kanslergade 7, DK-2100, Denmark.

FENTON Graham, b. 28 May 1949, West London, England. Singer. m. Caroline, 25 May 1991. Career: Various bands, 1970s; Matchbox, 1979-86; Television and radio includes over 12 appearances Top Of The Pops; Hits, tours, Germany, Holland, Switzerland, Spain, Austria,

Belgium, Yugoslavia; Television commercial, Japan; Tour with Gene Vincent's Blue Caps, UK and Europe, 1993; Solo tour, television and radio, Australia, 1994; Buddy Holly tribute, Clear Lake, Iowa, USA, 1994; Occasional work with original hit line-up of Matchbox as well as solo work. Recordings: Rockabilly Rebel, (Number 1 hit in many countries); Buzz Buzz A Diddle It; Midnite Dynamoes; When You Ask About Love (Number 4, UK charts); Over The Rainbow; Babes In The Wood; Films: Blue Suede Shoes; Born Too Late (biography). Honours: Gold, Silver, UK, Australia, Finland, Yugoslavia. Membership: Musicians' Union. Hobbies: Record collection (jukeboxes); British motorcycles; American cars; Keeping fit. Current Agent: Paul Barrett, Rock'n'Roll Enterprises. Address: 16 Grove Place, Penarth, South Glamorgan CF6 2LD, South Wales.

FENTON Iris E, b. 24 Mar 1927, Cumberland, Wisconsin, USA. Musician (piano, keyboard); Songwriter. Divorced, 2 daughters. Musical Education: Self-taught, home courses. Career: Writer of lyrics and music to own original songs; Occasional collaborations with another writer; Pop and Country songs; Published records and albums of original songs under label Silver Records, Publishing Company, Lake Silver Music (owner); ASCAP affiliate. Honours: Honorable mention for songs in several contests. Membership: American Society of Composers, Authors, Publishers. Hobbies: Musical pursuits. Address: 412 E Slocumb, Rice Lake, WI 54868, USA.

FENWICK Raymond John, b. 18 July 1946, Romford, Essex, England. Musician (guitar); Record Producer. Musical Education: Guitar lessons; Self taught. Career: Member, The Sydicats, 1965; Marty Wilde, 1965; The Tee Set, 1966; After Tea, 1968; The Spencer Davis Group, 1968-72; Fancy, 1974; The Ian Gillan Band, 1977; Forcefield, 1984-92; Johnny Mars Band, 1990; Concerts include: US tours with The Spencer Davis Group, 1968-72; Fancy, 1974; Butterfly Ball, 1974; Ian Gillan Band, 1977; Japanese tour, 1978; Wizzard's Convention, 1995. Recordings: After Tea, 1968; Magpie, television theme music, 1970s; Bo Diddley sessions, London, 1972; with Fancy: 2 US Top 20 singles: Wild Thing, 1974; Touch Me, 1974; with The Ian Gillan Band: Albums: Live At The Budokan, 1978; Child In Time, 1976; Clear Air Turbulence, 1977; Scarabus, 1977. Memberships: PRS; MCPS; Repro. Hobbies: Record collecting. Current Management: Self-managed: Fenwick Productions. Address: 4 Cassons Close, Weston Hills, Lincolnshire PE12 6DX, England.

FERGUSON David, b. 24 May 1953, London, England. Composer. 1 son. Education: BA Hons, School Of Slavonic and East European Studies, 1971-74. Career: Keyboards, composer with Random Hold, 1978-82; Touring Europe and US with Peter Gabriel; XTC; Orchestral Manoeuvres In The Dark. Compositions: TV series include: Cracker; The Gambling Man; A Fatal Inversion; TV films: Disaster At Valdez; Coded Hostile; Life After Life; Bad Girl. Recordings: Albums: The View From Here; Burn The Buildings; Nine Ways To Win. Membership: Association Of Professional Composers. Current Management: Music For Films. Address: 34 Batchelor Street, London N1 0EG, England.

FERGUSON James Warner, b. 10 Dec 1950, Jefferson City, Missouri, USA. Musician (bass); Singer; Music Educator. m. Assonia Fominya, 27 Sept 1980. Education: B Gen Studies, USC, 1980. Music Education: MusM, 1981. Career: Staff bassist, Brooklyn Academy Of Music, 1978; Bassist, various artists include: Joe Williams; Kenny Burrell; Teddy Wilson; Marion McPartland; Clark Terry; Lew Tabackin; Bill Watrous; Bassist, Crystal Gayle, 1990-; Teacher, Voice, Bellmont College, Nashville, 1983-89. Recordings: As bassist with: Chet Atkins; Stéphane Grappelli; Boots Randolph; Richie Cole; As singer with:

Barbara Mandrell; Don McLean; k d lang; Brenda Lee. Membership: AFTRA.

FERGUSON Maynard, b. 4 May 1928, Montreal, Quebec, Canada. Musician (trumpet); Bandleader. Career: Trumpet player with Boyd Raeburn, Jimmy Dorsey, Charlie Barnet, 1940s; Trumpeter, Stan Kenton Orchestra, 1950-53; Freelance musician, 1953-56; Leader, own 13 piece orchestra, 1957-65; Leader, own sextet, 1965-; Worked with Slide Hampton; Don Sebesky; Bill Chase; Don Ellis; Bill Berry, 1950s-60s. Recordings: Numerous albums include: Sketches On Standards, with Stan Kenton, 1953-55; Dimensions, 1954; Maynard Ferguson Octet, 1955; Around The Horn With Maynard Ferguson, 1955; Maynard Ferguson Conducts The Birdland Dream Band, 1956; Boy With A Lot Of Brass, 1957; A Message From Newport, 1958; Swingin' My Way Through College, 1958; A Message From Birdland, 1959; Plays Jazz For Dancing, 1959; Newport Suite, 1960; Let's Face The Music And Dance, 1960; Straightaway Jazz Themes, 1961; Si! Si!, M F, 1962; Message From Maynard, 1963; The New Sound Of..., 1964; Come Blow Your Horn, 1964; Color Him Wild, 1964; The Blues Roar, 1964; Sis By Sis, 1965; Ridin' High, 1966; Live At Expo '67 Montreal, 1967; M F Horn, 1970; Alive And Well In London, 1971; Magnitude, 1971; M F Horn 2, 1972; M F Horn 3, 1973; M F Horn 4 + 5, Live At Jimmy's, 1973; Chameleon, 1974; Primal Scream, 1975; New Vintage, 1977; Hot, 1977; Carnival, 1978; Uncle Joe Shannon, 1978; Conquistador, 1978; It's My Time, 1980; Hollywood, 1982; Storm, 1982; Live From San Francisco, 1983; High Voltage, 1988; Big Bop Nouveau, 1989; Footpath Cafe, 1993. Honours include: Grammy Nominations, 1978, 1984. Address: c/o Rogers and Cowan PR, 1888 Century Park E, Ste 500, Los Angeles, CA 90067-1709, USA.

FERGUSON Neil, b. 6 Dec 1954, Castleford, Yorkshire, England. Record Producer; Engineer; Musician (guitar, keyboards). m. Helen Mary Ferguson, 11 Dec 1976, 1 son, 1 daughter. Career: Records produced, engineered for: Black Lace; Chumbawamba; Smokie; Credit To The Nation; Chris Norman; Nick Berry; Current member, Chris Norman Band. Recordings: Agadoo; Teenage Sensation; Heartbeat (television theme music); Tubthumping, by Chumbawamba. Memberships: Musicians' Union; PRS. Address: Woodlands Studio, Unit 20, Raglan Works, Methley Road, Castleford WF10 1PW, England.

FERGUSON Sheila Diana, b. 8 Oct 1947, Philadephia, Pennsylvania, USA. Singer; Actress; Author; Presenter. m. Christopher L Robinson, 8 Mar 1980, twin daughters. Career: Lead singer, Three Degrees, 1965-1986; Solo artist; Star of Thames sitcom: Land Of Hope And Gloria, 1990; Cameo roles: French Connection; Sandford And Son; Desmonds; Brookside; Presenter GMTV; BBC, LWT variety shows; Major world tours; West End debut, Always: The Musical, 1997; Grande Theatre, Blackpool, 1996; Ronnie Scott's, 1997; Performed for the armed forces in Bosnia, Germany, Falklands, Cyprus, N Ireland. Recordings: 28 Gold records include: Dirty Old Man; When Will I See You Again; Take Good Of Yourself; T S O P; The Runner; Givin' Up Givin' In; Toast Of Love; Golden Lady Movie. Publications: Soul food: Classic Cuisine Of The American South, 1990. Honours: Tokyo Music Festival; 28 Gold Records; Best Book Of The Year, nominated LA Times, 1991. Memberships: Equity Councilor; Musicians' Union; SAG; AFTRA; Founder Director, PAMRA. Hobbies: Writing; Cooking; Tennis. Current Management: Brian Marshall (Variety); Jean Diamond, London Management (Acting). Address: PO Box 1400, Maidenhead Berkshire, SL6 8LX, England.

FERNANDEZ Michel, b. 14 Mar 1960, Condrieu, France. Musician (saxophone); Composer. m. Maryelle De Paulis, 24 June 1987,

1 daughter. Education: Philosophy, University, France. Musical Education: Conservatory, France. Career: John Tchicai International Orchestra; Trio Soledad; Paco Sanchez Group; Tours, Europe and Africa; Appearances on RFI, Franceculture. Recordings: Soledad, Paris. Memberships: SACEM; ADAMI; SPEDIDAM. Hobby: Philosophy. Current Management: Lionel Valar. Address: Centre Culturel Le Briscope, 69530 Brignais, France.

FERRERA Stephen, b. 26 Dec 1959, Boston, Massachusetts, USA. Producer; Songwriter; Musician; Record Executive. Musical Education: BM, New England Conservatory of Music; MM, Juilliard School of Music. Career: As producer, songwriter, arranger, musical director, musician, worked with: Bob Dylan; Billy Joel; Chaka Khan; Eurythmics; Suzanne Vega; Julian Cope; Shakespears Sister; Shawn Colvin; Tom Jones; Mica Paris; Womack & Womack; Dave Stewart; Currently Head of A&R, The Echo Label. Honours: Platinum and Gold records. Memberships: Musicians' Union; NARAS; ASCAP. Address: The Echo Label, The Chrysalis Building, 13 Bramley Road, London W10 6SP, England.

FERRIS Jim, b. 29 Mar 1955, Coventry, England. Musician (drums); Drum Tutor. m. Janice, 1990. Musical Education: Coventry School Of Music. Career: Member, Coventry Corps of Drums, age 11-16; Appeared Albert Hall aged 15; Supported many television artists in cabaret; Several BBC radio broadcasts, German television, West Country television; Worked in cabaret bands, theatre orchestra, rock bands. Recordings: 2 albums released by AJ's Big Band; Session recording work at studios in London and the Midlands. Publications: Mere Mortals Guide To Drumming, Levels 1-4, 1994-97. Honours: Described as a fantastic drummer, Stage and TV Today. Membership: Musicians' Union. Hobbies: Cars; Writing tutor books, teaching. Current Management: Jim Ferris. Address: Brodick House, 31 Hereford Close, Exmouth, Devon EX8 5QT, England.

FERRONE Stephen, b. 25 Apr 1950, Brighton, West Sussex, England. Musician (drums). 1 son, 1 daughter. Musical Education: Nice Conservatory of Music, France. Career: Played with: Brian Auger; Average White Band; Eric Clapton; Duran Duran; Tom Petty and The Heartbreakers; Chaka Khan; Jeffery Osbourn; George Benson; Anita Baker; Chris Botti; David Bowie; Tribute To Buddy Rich. Recordings: with Average White Band: Cut The Cake; Soul Searching; Person To Person; Journey Man-Unplugged, Eric Clapton; I Feel For You, Chaka Khan; Secret Story, Pat Metheny; Wildflowers, Tom Petty. Membership: ASCAP. Current Management: Steve White (Cavaricci and White). Address: 120 East 56th Street, #1150, New York City, NY 10022, USA.

FERRY Bryan, b. 26 Sept 1945, Washington, County Durham, England. Singer; Songwriter; Musician. 4 sons. Education: Fine Art, Newcastle University. Career: Formed Roxy Music, 1971; Solo artiste, 1973-; Worked with: Brian Eno; Phil Manzanera; Andy Mackay; Steve Ferrone; David Williams; Robin Trower; Pino Palladino; Nile Rodgers; Carleen Anderson; Shara Nelson; Jhelisa; Numerous worldwide tours; Major concerts include: Crystal Palace, 1972; Live Aid, Wembley, 1985; Radio City, New York, 1988; Wembley, 1989; Support tours, Alice Cooper, David Bowie; Television appearances include: Subject of Without Walls documentary, 1992; Videos: New Town (live), 1990; Total Recall (documentary), 1990. Recordings: Singles include: Love Is The Drug, 1975; Dance Away, 1979; Angel Eyes, 1979; Over You, 1980; Jealous Guy, 1981; Slave To Love, 1985; The Right Stuff, 1987; I Put The Spell On You, 1993; Albums: Solo: These Foolish Things, 1973; Another Time Another Place, 1974; Let's Stick Together, 1976;

In Your Mind, 1977; The Bride Stripped Bare, 1978; Boys And Girls, 1985; Bete Noire, 1987; The Ultimate Collection, 1988; Taxi, 1993; Mamounia, 1994; with Roxy Music: Roxy Music, 1972; For Your Pleasure, 1973; Stranded, 1973; Country Life, 1974; Siren, 1975; Viva Roxy Music, 1976; Manifesto, 1979; Flesh And Blood (Number 1, UK), 1980; Avalon, (Number 1, UK), 1982; The High Road (live mini-album), 1983; The Atlantic Years, 1983; Street Life, 1987; Recent compilations include: The Thrill Of It All, 1995; More Than This - The Best Of Roxy Music and Bryan Ferry, 1995. Honours include: Grand Prix Du Disque, Best Album, Montreux Golden Rose Festival, 1973. Current Management: IE Management, 59a Chesson Road, London W14 9QS, England.

FEW Bobby (Robert), b. 21 Oct 1935, Cleveland, Ohio, USA. Musician (piano); Composer. m. 7 July 1972, 1 son, 2 daughters. Musical Education: Cleveland Institute of Music; 2 private teachers. Career: Played vibraphone with Bob Cunningham (cousin); Played with Hyawatha Edmonson; Dick Shelton; Member, Bill Dixon's Free Jazz Workshop, 1958; Worked with Frank Wright; Booker Ervin; Formed own trio; Pianist, musical director, 3 major tours with, Brook Benton; Accompanist, Frank Foster; Roland Kirk; Formed group Center Of The World; Collaboration with Alan Silva's Celestial Communication Orchestra; Member of Steve Lacy's Sextet, tours USA, 1980-; Several solo piano television appearances, Paris; Live concerts, television and radio, France, Japan, Italy, Spain, Morocco. Recordings: Solo albums: Few Coming Thru; More Or Less Few; Continental Jazz Express; Mysteries; With own trio: Bobby Few Trio; with Steve Lacy: The Owl; The Flame; Dreams; Prospectus; Songs; Ballets; Momentum; Brion Gysin Songs; Condor; Live At The Sweet Basil In New York; with Center Of The World Group: Center Of The World; Last Polka In Nancy; Solo And Duets; Uhuru Na Umoja (with Art Taylor); with Albert Ayler: Reevaluations; Music Is The Healing Force; Last album; with Archie Schepp: Coral Rock; Peachin' Can; The In-Between, Booker Erwin; Traffic, Noah Howard; Egyptian Oasis, Talib Kibwe; Indians, Sunny Murray; El Saxofon, Hans Dulfer; What Else Is New, Mike Ellis; Secrets From The Sun, Joe Lee Wilson; Diom Futa, Jo Maka; Flowers Around Cleveland, David Murray 1995. Membership: SACEM. Hobbies: Cycling; Mountain walking. Current Management: Self-managed. Address: 42 Rue Deuingand, 92300 Levallois, France.

FIDRI Ladislav, b. 30 May 1940, Osijek, Croatia. Musician (trumpet); Arranger; Conductor. m. Mia Fidri, 11 Mar 1961, 1 son. Musical Education: Pedagogue Teacher's College of Music. Career: Soloist, Radio-television Big Band, Zagreb, Croatia; Played most jazz festivals, Europe; Member, Gerry Mulligan's International Big Band, Europe; Also played with Clark Terry Big Band; Several times member, EBU Big Bands in Europe. Played, recorded with: Lucky Thompson; Stan Getz; Johnny Griffin; Sou Nistico; Leo Wright; Art Farmer; Albert Mangelsdorf; Kay Winding; Buddy DeFranco; Maynard Ferguson. Publications: Jazz Greetings From The East; Blue Sunset; Nuages. Memberships: HRT Big Band; Croatian Musician Union. Hobbies: Dogs (Golden Retriever); Mushrooms. Current Management: Raimund Frick. Address: Kreuzacker 5, 85049 Ingoldstadt, Germany.

FIELD Lauren Danielle, b. 15 July 1962, London, England. Singer. m. 7 June 1990, Charles Foskett, 1 son. Education: Drama School Diploma. Musical Education: Grade 5 Music Theory; Grade 6 Piano; Voice Theory; Singing. Career: Musical Theatre: Duke Of York's; New End, Hampstead; Recording sessions for many top artists; Television appearances: Top Of The Pops; Pebble Mill; Radio sessions for BBC Radio 2 and local stations; Leader, own 7-piece band; Currently playing London showcases; Opened own school

and workshops for vocal coaching and tuition, 1997; Co-wwriter, co-producer, Joe Cocker, 1997. Memberships: PRS; Equity. Hobby: Songwriting. Current Management: Veracruz Music International. Address: 43 Capron Road, Dunstable, Bedfordshire LU5 5AL, England.

FIGES Kevin John, b. 29 Aug 1964, Portsmouth, England. Jazz, Classical Musician (saxophone); Composer. Education: Honors Degree, Masters Degree, Electrical and Electronic Engineering. Musical Education; Diploma, Classical Saxophone (Guildhall School Music). Career: Performed in own jazz quartet, all major venues, West Country, across UK; Appeared on Radio 2 Jazz Parade; Writes own material for quartet. Honours: South West touring awards, 1994. Membership: Musicians' Union. Hobbies: Walking; Films. Address: 36 Southey Street, Bristol BS2 9RE, England.

FILEK Michal, b. 22 April 1964, Pardubice, Czech Republic. Double Basist; Jazz/Blues Singer; Band Leader - Twin Q, Prague. m. Marie Kurova, 1985, 1 daughter. Education: Jaroslav Jezek's Conservatory, Prague; Summer courses in Frydland; General Double Bass Teachers, Frantisek Uhlir, Jaromir Honzák. Career: Bass Player, Twin Q, Prague, Metropolitan Jazz Band; Jazz-Blues Singer, Twin Q Group; Teacher, state school bass and improvisation; Accompaniment of many prominent soloists and groups. Compositions: Berny Blues; Everywhere is It Good, At Home is My Wife. Recordings: Twin Q and Elena, 1995; Metropolitan Jazz Band, 1996. Membership: Jazz Club Sydney. Hobbies: Lyrics writing; Making of musical instruments. Current Management: Volf Music Centre, Str Mechenická 2556/10, 141 00 Praha 4, Czech Republic. Address: U Hráze 23, 100 00 Prague 10, Czech Republic.

FILT Anni Martensen, b. 23 Nov 1955, Thorsted, Denmark. Singer; Songwriter. m. Klaus Filt, 25 June 1977. Career: Lead singer, Anni and the Countrysun, 1989-1992; Savannah Rose Band, 1992-; Television host, 1991-1993. Recordings: Show Me The Way To Nashville, 1989; Tall Dark Stranger, 1991; Giving It All, 1993; Savannah Rose Band, 1995. Membership: Danish Musicians' Union. Hobbies: Patchwork; Books; Music. Address: Smedevaenget 12, 8464 Galten, Denmark.

FINCH Terry, b. 14 Dec 1964, Lambeth, England. Musician (guitar). Musical Education: Private tuition; West London Institute. Career: Cabaret bands; Function bands; Session work; Cable TV appearance to promote original band. Compositions: Material for bands playing in and around London. Hobbies: Walking; Travel; Reading. Address: 50 Lower Court Road, Epsom, Surrey KT19 8SN, England.

FINLAY Neil M, b. 25 Dec 1955, Hamilton, New Zealand. Musician (electric and acoustic guitar, harmonica). Separated, 2 daughters. Education: Bursary photography. Career: Harmonica player with Brownie McGhee, tours throughout New Zealand; Special guest appearances at folk festivals throughout New Zealand; Appeared with Champion Jack Dupree, Billy Joe Shaver. Recordings: Solo album: Jumping The Tracks; Session work with The Topp Twins; Al Hunter; Patsy Rigger. Membership: Penonport Folk Club. Hobby: Photography. Current Management: Sun Pacific Records. Address: 271 Henderson Valley Road, Auckland, New Zealand.

FINLAYSON Rhonda (Maria Valery Finlayson), b. 28 Aug 1954, Kingston, Jamaica. Semi-professional Singer; Actress; Lyricist; Songwriter. Education: BA, Honours, Creative Arts; Diploma in Careers Guidance and Recreational Arts for Community. Career: Backing singer with Little Douglas Band, 1984; Lead vocalist, Rhonda, 1985-89; Velvet Palm, 1989-. Recordings: Bugs On The Wire, compilation album; 1 track for Radio Lancashire; Black And Strange, Bop cassette tape with Rhonda band. Membership: Musicians' Union. Hobbies: Watching live concerts; Dance events; Dancing; Writing lyrics; Poetry. Address: Flat 87, Lowton Court, Teddington Road, Moston, Manchester M40 0DW, England.

FINN Neil, b. 27 May 1958, Te Awamutu, New Zealand. Singer; Musician (guitar); Songwriter. Career: Member, Split Enz, 1977-85; Founder member, Crowded House, 1985-; Duo with brother Tim, 1995; International concerts include: A Concert For Life, Centennial Park, Sydney, 1992; WOMAD Festival, 1993; Television appearances include: Late Night With David Letterman, NBC; The Tonight Show, NBC; In Concert '91, ABC; Return To The Dome, Ch4; MTV Unplugged; Top Of The Pops, BBC1. Recordings: Albums with Split Enz: Frenzy, 1978; True Colours, 1979; Beginning Of The Enz, 1980; Waita, 1981; Time And Tide, 1982; Conflicting Emotions, 1984; See Ya Round, 1985; History Never Repeats Itself - The Best Of Split Enz, 1993; Oddz & Endz, 1993; Rear Enz, 1993; with Crowded House: Crowded House, 1986; Temple Of Low Men, 1988; Woodface, 1991; Together Alone, 1993; with Tim Finn: Finn, 1995; Singles: with Split Enz include: I See Red; I Got You; History Never Repeats; Six Months In A Leaky Boat; with Crowded House include: Don't Dream It's Over; Something So Strong; Better Be Home Soon; Chocolate Cake; Fall At Your Feet; Four Seasons In One Day; Distant Sun; Nails In My Feet. Honours: Q Awards: Best Live Act (with Crowded House), 1992; Best Songwriter, 1993; OBE, for services to New Zealand, 1993. Current Management: Grant Thomas Management, 3 Mitchell Road, Rose Bay, NSW 2029, Australia.

FINN Tim, b. 25 June 1952, Te Awamutu, New Zealand. Singer; Musician (piano, guitar, drums); Songwriter. Education: Auckland University. Career: Founder member, Split Enz, 1972-85; Solo artiste, 1983-86; Member, Crowded House, 1991; Solo artiste, 1992-; Member, ALT (with Andy White and Liam O'Maonlai), 1994; Duo with brother Neil, 1995; Appearances include: Tours, UK Australia, New Zealand, USA; Television include: Late Night With David Letterman, NBC; The Tonight Show, NBC; In Concert '91, ABC. Recordings: with Crowded House: Woodface, 1991; Solo albums: Escapade, 1983; Big Canoe, 1985; Before & After, 1993; with ALT: Altitude, 1994; with Neil Finn: Finn, 1995; Solo: Tim Finn, 1987; Singles: with Split Enz include: I See Red; I Hope I Never; Dirty Creature; Six Months In A Leaky Boat; with Crowded House: Chocolate Cake; Weather; Fall At Your Feet; Solo: Persuasion; Persuasion; Not Even Close; Many's the Time. Honour: OBE, Services to New Zealand, 1993. Current Management: Grant Thomas Management, 3 Mitchell Road, Rose Bay, NSW 2029, Australia.

FINNEY David Steven, b. 3 June 1963, Stoke Newington, London, England. Writer; Musician; Tutor. m. Anne Catherine, 18 Sept 1988, 1 son, 1 daughter. Musical Education: Self-taught. Career: 5 years, pop/indie band The Company She Keeps; Wide television and radio coverage of first single includes video starring Rick Mayall; Second single became jingle on Garry Davies Show, BBC Radio 1; Solo venture backed by Gerry Cott (formerly Boomtown Rats). Recordings: with The Company She Keeps: What A Girl Wants; The Men Responsible. Publications: Flesh. Honours: Single of The Week, Smash Hits/Record Mirror. Memberships: Musicians' Union; PRS. Hobbies: Reading; Unix computer operating systems; Arsenal Football Club; Own children; Films. Address: 15 River Way, Loughton, Essex IG10 3LJ, England.

FINSTER Clara, b. 10 February 1966, Paris, France. Singer; Actress. Education: BAC A2, Classic Le Hers, Philosophy Degree. Musical Education: Singer Yard, Studio Des Variétes, Paris. Career: Louise, Theatre Du Chatelet; Cabaret Brecht, Theatre De La Main D'Or; Dance in Belgium; Sing Shows at the Bataclan, Bobino, Francofolies and Quebec; TV: Off Voice for Canalt, Radio Canada; Radio: France Culture; France Inter. Compositions: with Salabert Editions. Recordings: with Salabert Editions. Publications: CD, 4 titles, 1994. Hobbies: Dance; Gymnastics; Swimming; Skating. Address: 8 Avenue de la Soeur Rosalie, 75013 Paris, France.

FIONA OF THE SEALS, b. 6 Aug 1958, Seal, Kent, England. Musician (violin); Singer; Writer. m. George Middleton, 2 Aug 1985, 3 daughters. Education: Piano and violin with Gillian Sansom. Career: Debut, London Palladium, 1978; Singer, violinist, plays own compositions to wild seals; UK television appearances include: Really Wild Show; Nature Detectives; Highway; Motormouth; Hume At Large; This Morning. Compositions: Today The Seals; People Of The Sea; Islay Mist. Recordings: Albums: Today The Seals; Serenade To Love. Publications: Seal, 1995; Newspaper and magazine features worldwide including article in Strad. Memberships: Musicians' Union; Performing Rights Society; Society of Authors; Animal Concern. Hobby: Animal Welfare Seal Reserve. Current Management: Roy Stockdill, First Literary Services, 6 First Avenue, Watford WD2 6PZ, England. Address: Kildalton, Isle of Islay, Argyll PA42 7EF, Scotland.

FIRESTAR, b. 18 October 1958, Iserlohn, Germany. Musician (Harp; Flute). 1 son. Education: Degree in Business and Artist Management, Marketing and Public Relations; Grade 12, Royal Conservatory Diploma for Additional Theory, Composition, Copyright and Legal Graduate Courses in Canada. Career includes: 28 years of performance live on television in Canada; Various programs, CBC composing soundtracks for film and television; Performing live on radio. Compositions: 2 albums selfcomposed, published, recorded: Heavenly Angels; Crescent Moon. Recordings: Heavenly Angels, album; Crescent Moon, album. Honours: Many local performance honours, cash money won towards recordings on albums. Memberships: Pacific Music Industry Association; Society of Composers, Authors and Music Publishers of Canada. Hobbies: Composing; Recording; Performing; Travelling; Camping; Swimming; Relaxing. Current Management: Firestar Promotions Inc. Address: PO Box 165, 1896 West Broadway, Vancouver, BC, V6J 1Y9, Canada.

FISH (Derek William Dick), b. 25 Apr 1958, Edinburgh, Dalkeith, Scotland. Vocalist; Lyricist. Career: Member, Stone Dome; Lead singer, lyricist, UK progresssive rock group, Marillion, 1981-88; Regular tours, UK; Europe; US; Concerts include: Theakston Festival, 1982; Reading Festival, 1982, 1983; Nostell Priory Festival, 1982, 1984; Support to Rush, New York City Music Hall, 1983; Milton Keynes Bowl, 1984; Monsters Of Rock Festival, Castle Donington, 1985; Colombian Volcano Appeal Concert, Royal Albert Hall, 1986; Solo artiste, 1988-. Recordings: Albums: with Marillion: Script For A Jester's Tear, 1983; Fugazi, 1984; Real To Reel, 1985; Misplaced Childhood, 1985; Brief Encounter, 1986; Clutching At Straws, 1987; B-Sides Themselves, 1988; Solo albums: Vigil In A Wilderness Of Mirrors, 1990; Internal Exile, 1991; Songs From The Mirror, 1993; Yin, 1995; Yang, 1995; Singles: with Marillion: Market Square Heroes, 1982; He Knows You Know, 1983; Garden Party, 1983; Punch And Judy, 1984; Kayleigh (Number 2, UK), 1985; Lavender, 1985; Heart Of Lothian, 1985; Incommunicado, 1987; Sugar Mice, 1987; Warm Wet Circles, 1987; Solo singles: Shortcut To Somewhere (with Tony Banks), 1986; State Of Mind, 1989; Big Wedge, 1990; A Gentleman's Excuse Me, 1990; Internal

Exile, 1991; Credo, 1991; Just Good Friends (with Sam Brown), 1995.

FISHER Damian Robert, b. 21 Jan 1971, Dartford, Kent, England. Musician (drums). Musical Education: Masterclass Studios, Bob Armstrong. Career: Hank Wangford tour; Only The Lonely (West End Show); The Sound Of Fury (stage show); Bobby Davro Show; Concerts with: The Bert Kaempfert Orchestra; Stutz Bear Cats; Johnny Howard Band; Gerrard Kenny. Membership: Musicians' Union. Hobbies: Drawing; Squash; Golf; Playing The Piano. Address: Flat 5, Duncombe Court, Wingrove Drive, Purfleet, Essex RM19 INF, England.

FISHER James Scott, b. Perth, Australia. Music Company Executive. Career: Television newscaster, presenter of Late Nite Line Up; First presentation as editor, BBC Radio 1 and 2; Artist Liaison, RCA; International General Manager, Motown and Jobette Music, 1976-81; Regional Director, ASCAP, 1981-94; General Secretary, International Managers Forum, 1994-. Hobbies: The Arts; Food; Travel. Address: 14 Ashburn Gardens, London SW7 4DG, England.

FISHER Morgan, b. 1 Jan 1950, London, England. Musician (keyboards). m. Aki Kuniyasu, 26 May 1987. Education: Hendon County Grammar School, 1968. Career: Keyboard player, rock/soul band Love Affair, 1968-70; Leader, progressive rock band Morgan, 1971-2; Keyboard player, rock band Mott The Hoople, 1973-6; Solo recording artist, producer, founder, experimental music label Pipe Records, 1977-81; Keyboard player, rock band Queen, 1982; Solo musician, composer, producer, 1984-. Compositions include: Electronic Music for Institute of Contemporary Art, London, 1971; Numerous film and television soundtracks. Recordings include: Single: Everlasting Love, Love Affair, 1968; Albums: The Hoople, Mott The Hoople, 1972; As producer: Miniatures (concept album) featuring 51 contemporary artists such as Robert Fripp, Michael Nyman, Penguin Cafe Orchestra, The Pretenders, The Damned, XTC, Gavin Bryars, Pete Seeger, George Melly, 1980; Slow Music, 1980; Echoes of Lennon, ambient versions of John Lennon songs, with guest Yoko Ono, 1990. Publications: Far East Tour Diary (account of a tour with a Japanese rock band), 1995. Honours: Two Gold discs and one Silver disc for record sales, Mott The Hoople; Memberships: Phonographic Performance Limited; Performing Rights Society; National Academy of Recording Arts and Sciences; Performing Artists Media Rights Association. Address: 2-9-7 Narita-Higashi, Suginami-ku, Tokyo 167, Japan.

FISHKIN Paul E, b. 29 Apr 1943, Philadelphia, Pennsylvania, USA. Record Company Executive. m. Janis Beckerman, 3 July 1982, 1 son, 1 daughter. Education: BSc Pharmacy (Phila College, Pharmacy and Science). Career: Co-owner, Bearsville Records, with Albert Grossman, 1971-79; Established careers of Todd Rundgren; Foghat; Paul Butterfield; Jesse Winchester; Founder, Modern Records with Danny Goldberg, 1979; Signed and established solo careers of Stevie Nicks and Natalie Cole. Membership: RIAA. Address; 8295 Sunset Boulevard, Los Angeles, CA 90046, USA.

FISK Zebadi (Thomas William Fisk), b. 24 June 1968, Little Thorpe, County Durham, England. Performer (guitar, mandolin); Vocalist; Composer; Teacher. m. Traci Ann Firby, 4 Mar 1989. Career: Lead guitarist, The Rye until 1994; Lead guitarist, Voodoo Guru, 1994-. Recordings: with The Rye: Songs Of Innocence And Experience, 1991; Twist, 1992; Burst, 1993; Flying High, 1994; Even As We Speak, 1994; with Voodoo Guru: Do. Memberships: Musicians' Union; Registry of Music Teachers. Current Management: Tony Davies. Address: PO Box 181, Darlington DL3 6YX, England.

FITZGERALD Cathleen Bernadette Maureen (Cathy), b. 1 Apr 1964, Kitchener, Ontario, Canada. Entertainer; Singer; Artist. Education: 4th year, Bachelor of Arts program, major in Psychology. Career: Performing, 1986-; Involved, several variety/charity events; Prime time country since 1990; Won 3 consecutive championships, Canadian Open Country Singing Competition, Simcoe, Ontario; Several firsts at Ontario Open Singing Competition: Toronto; Ottawa; Many local radio and television programs; Released 2 singles, Canada and Europe, 1992-; Currently working with producer Gary Buck out of Nashville, on first 10 song album to be released, USA, 1995; Single to be released in: USA; Canada; Europe. Honours: Many trophies Canadian singing competitions, 9 first place victories since 1989. Membership: Canadian Country Music Association, 1991-. Hobbies: Reading; Songwriting; Singing. Current Management: Howard Scales, Target Entertainment Group. Address: 100 Denlow Street, Kitchener, Ontario N2B 3T7, Canada.

FITZGERALD Daniel Francis, b. 14 Dec 1955, Cork, Ireland. Record Producer; Sound Engineer. Education: Electronic Technician Certificate, Ireland, NCEA. Musical Education: Self-taught, drums, piano, guitar. Career: Toured with: Mary Black; Nightnoise; Paula Cole. Recordings: Albums include: The Black Family, 1986; Many's The Foolish Youth, The Voice Squad, 1987; By The Time It Gets Dark, Mary Black 1987; Jacket Of Batteries, De Dannann, 1988; Take The Air, Sean Ryan, 1989; No Frontiers, Mary Black, 1989; Horse With A Heart, Altan, 1989; The Red Crow, Altan, 1990; Good People All, The Voice Squad, 1993; A Different Shore, Nightnoise, 1995; Also recorded: Donovan; David Gilmour; Luka Bloom; Christy Moore; Paul Brady; Christy Hennessy; Katell Keinig; Freddie White. Memberships: AES; NARAS; Re-Pro. Current Management: Dennis Muirhead. Address: Muirhead Management, 202 Fulham Road, Chelsea, London SW10 9PJ, England.

FITZGIBBON Martin William, b. 11 May 1950, West Drayton, Middlesex, England. Musician (drums); Singer. m. Frances Trussell, 20 June 1981. Musical Education: National Youth Jazz Association, private tuition. Career: Appearances: Original production, The Rocky Horror Show, London, 1973; BBC radio and television; Major concerts, tours, throughout UK. Recordings: The Rocky Horror Show, original London cast; Moondog Man; The Dockery Boys; Zydcajun Cowboy; Do You Feel Like Dancing. Membership: Musicians' Union. Hobbies: Sleeping; Procrastination. Current Management: Mike Batt Management. Address: PO Box 1862, Bradford On Avon, Wiltshire BA15 1YF, England.

FITZSIMMONS Kevin Robert Mario, b. Glasgow, Scotland. Musician (keyboards, guitar); Conductor; Composer; Screenwriter; Actor; Director. Musical Education: Royal Scottish Academy of Music and Drama, 1972-78; Graduated, London Royal Academy of Music, 1979. Career: Theatre includes: Andrew Lloyd Webber's Jesus Christ Superstar, Evita, Cats, Song and Dance; Anthony Phillips' Alice (founder member/ex of Genesis); Television includes: LWT, The South Bank Show; Own groups: The Little Concert; The 13th Guest; The Trio Of Doom; Film appearances include: Indiana Jones and the Temple of Doom; Deva, 1994; Wasted Youth (also composer), 1994; The Stated Dose (co-writer, composer, actor, director), 1994; Latter three to be premiered, Edinburgh Film Festival, 1995; Film scores include: Hoppla (Special Commendation, Channel 4 Young Film Maker of The Year Award), 1994; Wasted Youth; The Stated Dose; Co-writer, The Enlightening One - The Life Of Ho Chi Minh (forthcoming). Recordings: Marti Webb; Gershwin/Performance albums; Jesus Christ Superstar, 20th Anbniversary Album; K Fz - Film Music (1 and 2). Current Management: TDS

Media/Tutti Sruti Music. Address: 5 East London Street, Edinburgh EH7 4BN, Scotland.

FIX Michael, b. 23 September 1959, Wollongong, NSW, Australia. Musician (guitar); Composer; Performer. m. Susan Jarvis, 4 sons. Education: Diploma of Teaching. Career: Leading Acoustic Guitarist; Sydney Band Hat Trick, 1985-; Working with award-winning singer/songwriter Graeme Connors, touring Australia as Lead Guitarist with Connor's Prodigal Sons band, 1991-95; Recordings: Tantalise, 1992; Fingerpaintings, 1993; The Heart Has Reasons, 1996; Single: Falling, 1996; Video: No Secrets!, 1997; Single: Breakup Breakdown, 1997. Honours: Instrumental of the Year Category, 1994 CMAA Awards; Instrumental of the Year Finalist, 1995, 1996; Nominated Finalist for Instrumental of the Year, 1997. Memberships: APRA; AMCOS. Hobbies: Golf; Reading. Address: Via PO Box 1194, Sunnybank Hills, Qld 4109, Australia. Address: PO Box 1194, Sunnybank Hills, Qld 4109, Australia.

FIXX-IT, b. 1 July 1970, Paramaribo, Surinam. Rapper; Dancer; Dressman; Composer. 1 son. Education: Private dance training and show education. Musical Education: Self-taught. Career: Founder, Twenty 4 Seven, 1988; 3 European major hits; Solo career, 1990-; Male Rapper on Cappella and Anti-Capella songs, 1994-95; Member, Anti-Cappella. Recordings: with Cappella: Move On Baby (co-writer); U & Me (co-writer); Anti-Cappella: Move Your Body. Honours: 3 Golden singles. Membership: FNV Kunstenbond. Hobbies: Music; Child. Current Management: Hans Van Pol Management. Address: PO Box 9010, 1006 AA Amsterdam, Netherlands.

FLACK Roberta, b. 10 Feb 1937, Black Mountain, North Carolina, USA. Singer. m. Stephen Novosel, 1966, divorced 1972. Education: BA, Music Education. Career: Teacher, music and English literature, 1959-67; Recording artist, 1968-; Appearances include: Star, ABC TV Special, The First Time Ever, 1973; Composition: (with Jesse Jackson, Joel Dorn) Go Up Moses; Television theme song Valerie. Recordings: Singles include: The First Time Ever I Saw Your Face, used in film Play Misty For Me, 1972; Where Is The Love, 1973; Killing Me Softly With His Song, 1973; The Closer I Get To You, 1978; Making Love, 1982; Tonight I Celebrate My Love, 1983; Set The Night To Music, 1991; Albums include: First Take, 1970; Chapter Two, 1970; Quiet Fire, 1972; Killing Me Softly, 1973; Feel Like Makin' Love, 1974; Blue Lights In The Basement, 1978; Roberta Flack, 1978; Roberta Flack Featuring Donny Hathaway, 1980; Live And More, 1981; The Best Of Roberta Flack, 1981; I'm The One, 1982; Born To Love, 1983; Hits And History, 1984; Roberta Flack's Greatest Hits, 1984; Roberta Flack, 1985; Oasis, 1989; Roberta, 1995. Honours: Gold record, First Time Ever I Saw Your Face, 1972; Grammy Awards: Best Record, 1972, 1973; Best Pop Vocal Duo, 1972; Best Female Pop Vocal, 1973; Roberta Flack Human Kindness Day, Washington DC, 1972. Current Management: Jerry Kravat Enterprises, 225 Lexington Avenue, Lobby Suite, New York, NY 10016, USA.

FLAHANT Richard, b. 12 Apr 1968, Ipswich, Suffolk, England. Musician (keyboards); Vocalist. Musical Education: Jazz studies, Chichester College of Technology, 1989-90. Career: The Addicts, 1985-; Venues include: 100 Club and The Marquee, 1989-90; Function bands include: Caribbean Cruise; Appearances, Big Breakfast Show, 1986-94; Recording with co-writer Matt Gray on various projects, 1993-; Signed to Albinus Records, 1994. Recordings: Singles: After The Fall, 1994; Meaning Of Our Life, 1995. Memberships: Musicians' Union; PRS. Hobbies: Cycling; Travel; Relaxing. Address: c/o Albinus Records, Coll House, Westgate, Chichester, West Sussex PO20 6QL, England.

FLAHERTY Nicholas Simon, b. 18 Feb 1967, Brewood, Staffordshire, England. Vocalist; Songwriter. Career: Singer, Voodoo Sioux, 1991-; Support tours with Little Angels; Terrorvision; Rockhead; Headline concert, Milton Keynes Day of Rock, 1994; Radio appearances: Radio One session, 1993; Won Radio One Rock War, 1993; Television appearances: Noisy Mothers (interview and video), ITV, 1994; European, UK, Japanese tours, June 1995-. Recordings: Debut album: Skrape, Voodoo Sioux, 1995. Memberships: Musicians' Union; PRS; MCPS. Hobbies: Songwriting; Films; Poetry; Photography. Current Management: c/o Bill Sneyd, White Buffalo, 2 Chillington Close, Cheslyn Hay. Address: 1 Victoria Court, Victoria Road, Shifnal, Shropshire TF11 8AF, England.

FLANAGAN Larry, b. 5 Dec 1953, Detroit, Michigan, USA. Musician (viola, violin). Career: Violist with several orchestras in: Michigan; South Carolina; Ontario, Canada; Violinist/violist for various artists including Natalie Cole; Gladys Knight and the Pips; Melissa Manchester; Barry White; Geri Allen; Isaac Hayes; Sylvia Moy; Concerts include: Montreux Jazz Festival; Detroit Jazz Festival; Film appearance, as fiddler, Disney's Perfect Harmony, 1991; Lecturer, music consultant for schools in Decatur, Georgia.

FLANAGAN Mark "Sonny", b. 27 Oct 1957, Liverpool, England. Musician. Career: Resident musician on BSkyB satellite television; 26 shows, Happening; Don't Forget Your Toothbrush, C4; Occasionally on Later With Jools Holland, BBC2; Recorded songs for film: Roadrunner, with George Harrison; Twice played live on Wogan; Numerous other television, radio, tours. Honours: (as band member) Don't Forget Your Toothbrush, Golden Rose Montreux, 1995. Memberships: Musicians' Union; PAMRA; PRS. Hobbies: Photography; Painting; Yoga. Current Management: Paul Loasby, One Fifteen, Greenwich, London. Address: Helicon Mountain, Halstow Road, Greenwich, London SE3 7LP, England.

FLANZER Richard, b. 30 Feb 1951, New York, USA. Personal Manager; Television Producer; Concert Promoter. m. Janice Rothman, 9 Feb 1990, 2 sons, 1 daughter. Education: Boston University. Career: Clients have included: Roger Daltrey; Manhattan Transfer; Jackson Browne; Dr John; Producer, largest 2 day gross and fastest sell-out in history at Carnegie Hall, Roger Daltrey and Friends, 1994; Producer, largest festival in Florida history (115,000 audience), Florida Sunfest, 1977; Producer, A Day In The Country (first festival ever at Rose Bowl), Pasadena, California; Consultant to Jimi Hendrix Estate; Producer, National Music Critics Awards. Memberships: ASCAP; Chairman, National Critics Awards, 1995. Hobbies: Auto racing; Travel; Tennis. Address: 152 W 57th Street, 40th Floor, New York, NY 10019, USA.

FLASKETT Peter, b. 9 July 1950, Woking, Surrey, England. Guitar Teacher; Musician (guitar, bass guitar). m. Patsy Poley, 24 June 1983. Musical Education: London College of Furniture and Music, 1968-1970. Career: Worked with: Long John Baldry; Screaming Lord Sutch; Tex Withers; Savoy Brown; Jim McCarty (of the Yardbirds); Recorded and toured extensively with: Emile Ford and The Checkmates; The Ramrods; The Flying Tigers; 30 years teaching guitar; 20 years repairing guitars. Recordings: Numerous recordings with Emile Ford; Extensive session work on guitar and bass guitar. Memberships: Institute of Musical Instrument Technology; Musicians' Union. Current Management: Kernow Entertainments, Falmouth, Cornwall. Address: 23 Bridge, St Columb Major, Cornwall.

FLATT Lester, b. 28 June 1914, Overton County, Tennessee, USA. Bluegrass Musician (guitar). Career: Partnership with Earl Scruggs, billed as Flatt and Scruggs, 1945-; Member, Bill

Monroe's Mountain Boys, 1945; Founder member, The Foggy Mountain Boys, 1948-69; Founder member, The Nashville Grass, 1969; Radio includes: WCYB, Virginia; WSM, Nashville; Television appearances: Folk Sound USA. Recordings: Albums include: Foggy Mountain Breakdown, 1975; The Golden Era 1950-1955, 1977; Foggy Mountain Banjo, 1978; 1959-1963, 1992; Singles include: The Ballad Of Jed Clampett (theme song to television show The Beverly Hillbillies); Foggy Mountain Breakdown (used in film Bonnie And Clyde).

FLAVELL Roger Barry, b. 10 Feb 1946, Ruislip, England. Musician (bass guitar); Vocalist. m. Annie Conlon, 31 July 1971, 2 daughters. Musical Education: Self-taught. Career: Magic Roundabout, 1966-68; Sessions, 1969; Geno Washington's Ram Jam Band, 1970; Tommy Hunt Band, 1971-72; Christie, 1973-74; Tommy Hunt Band, 1975; Lonnie Donegan Band, Johnny Wakelin and The Kinshasha Band, 1976; Sessions, 1977-78; Band leader, top cabaret venue, 1978-88; The Byron Band, 1982; Sessions, 1989-95. Compositions include: Music for television: The Animates, co-written with Vic Elmes. Recordings: Albums: Judd, Kris Ife; Live At Wigan Casino, Tommy Hunt; A Sign Of The Times, Tommy Hunt; On The Rocks, Byron Band; Only One, Joe Longthorne; Hold Fast, Roger Flavell; Christie: singles and album. Memberships: PRS; BASCA. Hobbies: Sport parachuting. Address: Marlow, Buckinghamshire, England.

FLAVOR FLAV (William Drayton), b. 16 Mar 1959, Roosevelt, Long Island, USA. Rapper. 3 children. Career: Founder member, US rap group Public Enemy, 1984-; Concerts include: Support to the Beastie Boys, US tour, 1987; Support to LL Cool J, European tour, 1987; UK tour, 1990; Tour Of A Black Planet, 1990; Apocalypse '91 US tour, with Anthrax, 1991; The World's Best Rap Show Ever, 1992; Greenpeace Stop Sellafield concert, with U2, Manchester, 1992; Reading Festival, 1992; Support to U2, Zooropa tour, 1992; MC, The Entourage (hip-hop venue), Long Island, New York, 1986; Solo recording artist, 1993-. Recordings: Yo! Bum Rush The Show, 1987; It Takes A Nation Of Millions To Hold Us Back, 1988; Fear Of A Black Planet, 1990; Apocalypse '91... The Enemy Strikes Back, 1991; Greatest Misses, 1992; Muse Sick'n'Hour Mess Age, 1994; Solo album: Flavor Flav, 1993; Singles include: Rebel Without A Pause; Bring The Noise; Fight The Power, theme for film Do The Right Thing; Don't Believe The Hype; Night Of The Living Baseheads; Black Steel In The Hour Of Chaos; Welcome To The Terrordome; 911 Is A Joke; Brothers Gonna Work It Out; Can't Do Nuttin' For Ya Man; Can't Truss It; Shut 'Em Down; Nighttrain. Honours include: Platinum discs; Rolling Stone Readers Poll, Best Rap Group, 1991; Best Rap Album, Soul Train Music Awards, 1992. Current Management: Malik Entertainment Management, 3 Third Pl., Roosevelt, NY 11575, USA.

FLEA (Michael Balzary), b. 16 Oct 1962, Melbourne, Australia. Musician (bass). Career: First trumpet, Los Angeles Junior Philharmonic; Founder member, Red Hot Chili Peppers, 1983-; Trumpet player, Trulio Disgracias, 1988; Founder, punk band Hate, playing Hollywood clubs, 1988; International tours including US, UK, Europe, Australia, New Zealand; Major appearances include: Lollapalooza Festival tour, 1992; Hollywood Rock Festival, Rio De Janeiro, 1993; Glastonbury Festival, 1993; Television includes: Late Night With David Letterman; Rapido, BBC2; Saturday Night Live; The Word, C4 TV; Top Of The Pops, BBC1; Guest host, The Ben Stiller Show, Fox TV, 1992; Actor, films The Decline Of Western Civilization, 1991; Suburbia, 1991; Motorama, 1992. Recordings: Albums: The Red Hot Chili Peppers, 1984; Freaky Styley, 1985; The Uplift Moto Party Plan, 1987; Mother's Milk, 1989; Blood Sugar Sex Magik, 1991; What Hits?, 1992;

One Hot Minute, 1995; Singles include: Under The Bridge; Breaking The Girl; Give It Away; Soul To Squeeze, from film Coneheads, 1993; Aeroplane, 1996; Contributor, Peace Choir, 1991; Beavis And Butthead Experience, 1993. Honours: MTV Music Video Awards, 1992; Rolling Stone Readers Poll Winner, Best Bassist, 1993; Grammy, Best Hard Rock Song, Give It Away, 1993. Current Management: Lindy Goetz Management, 11116 Aqua Vista #39, Studio City, CA 91602, USA.

FLECK Bela, b. New York City, USA. Musician (banjo); Singer; Composer. Musical Education: Graduate, New York High School of Music and Art, 1976; Studied banjo with Tony Trishka, Erik Darling, Mark Horowitz. Career: Banjo player, composer, 1976-; Played with: Tasty Licks, 1976-79; Spectrum, 1979-81; New Grass Revival, 1982-91; Formed Bela Fleck and the Flecktones, 1989-; Concerts include support to Bonnie Raitt, UK tour; Also recorded solo albums; Studio work, Nashville, with Loretta Lynn; The Statler Brothers; Randy Travis; Television appearances: Hee Haw; Nashville Now; Lonesome Pine Specials. Recordings include: Crossing The Tracks, 1980; Natural Bridge, 1982; Deviation, 1984; Daybreak, 1987; Inroads, with Jerry Douglas, Mark O'Connor, 1987; Places, 1988; Bela Fleck And The Flecktones, 1990; Flight Of The Cosmic Hippo, 1992; UFO TOFU, 1993; Contributor, Hot House, Bruce Hornsby, 1995. Honours: 2 Grammy Award Nominations for instrumental solos; Frets Readers Poll Winner, Top Banjo Player, more than 6 times, 1981-. Current Management: Firstars, 3520 Hayden Avenue, Culver City, CA 90232, USA.

FLEDELIUS Soren, b. 7 February 1969, Vejle, Denmark. Singer; Songwriter; Musician. Education: Higher Business Degree, Horsens Business School, Denmark, 1989; Selftaught Guitar, Bass and Drums. Career: "Voldvo", Denmark Tour 1991; Touring with Stonejuice, 1992-94; Studio Musician for Hege Tokle, Norway, 1995; TouringDenmark with Oktoberdrengene, 1995; Ich Bin So Geil Tour 96, with Halla Da; Halla Da USA Tour, 1996; Appeared in Starship Troopers, Live Concert, Danish National Radio, 1997; Halla Da Denmark Tour, 1997; All Major Festivals. Compositions: Hvorfor Fa'en Skal vi Vare Sa Brune; Von Hinten Fritz; Theme From Shotgunfire Blues. Recordings: Halla Da Albums: Ich Bin So Geil, 1995, Hvorfor Fa'en Skal vi Vare Sa Brune, 1996; Ultra-Brun Edition 2, 1997. Honour: Danish Champion of Rock, 1997. Hobby: Movie Acting. Current Management: Louis Fontaine, World Records. Address: Off-Beat Productions, West End 15, 1661 KBH V, Denmark.

FLEEMAN Jim, b. 21 June 1966, Chesterfield, England. Musician (drums, percussion). Musical Education: City of Leeds College of Music; Guildhall School of Music and Drama. Career: Tour, concerts, with Omar; Dana Bryant, CH4 television pilot; Tour, concerts with Guildhall Jazz Band; Various BBC television and radio appearances; Kenny Wheeler, London concerts; Various theatrical productions; Instrumental tuition and workshops; Lecturer, West London Institute. Recordings: Featured soloist, Essence, Guildhall Jazz Band, 1989; Various commercial, theatrical recordings. Hobbies: Travel; Film; Theatre. Address: 95 Belgrave Road, London SW1V 2BQ, England.

FLEETWOOD Mick, b. 24 June 1942, London, England. Musician (drums). m. (1) Jenny Boyd, (2) Sara Recor, 1988, 2 daughters. Career: Drummer, John Mayall, 1967; Drummer, Fleetwood Mac, 1967-; Appearances include: Tours include: USA; Scandinavia; Europe; Concerts: Fillmore East; Miami Pop Festival Fillmore West, San Francisco; Reading Festival; Tampa Stadium, Florida, with the Eagles; Madison Square Garden; Hollywood Bowl, Los Angeles; US Festival, with Jackson Browne, The Cars, The

Grateful Dead, Eddie Money; The Police; Santana; Talking Heads, 1982; Forms new band, Zoo, signs to Capricorn Records, 1992; Fleetwood Mac reunion, Presidential Inauguration concert, 1993. Film appearance: The Running Man, 1987; Owner, Fleetwoods club, Los Angeles, 1991. Recordings: Albums: Fleetwood Mac, 1968; English Rose, 1969; Pious Bird Of Good Omen, 1969; Then Play On, 1969; Blue Jams At Chess, 1969; Kiln House, 1970; Fleetwood Mac In Chicago, 1971; Black Magic Woman, 1971; Future Games, 1971; Bare Trees, 1972; Penguin, 1973; Mystery To Me, 1973; Heroes Are Hard To Find, 1974; Rumours, 1977; Tusk, 1979; Tango In The Night, 1987; Behind The Mask, 1990; Time, 1995; Solo: The Visitor, 1981; Singles include: Black Magic Woman; Need Your Love So Bad; Albatross; Man Of The World; Over My Head; Rhiannon (Will You Ever Win); Go Your Own Way; Don't Stop; Tusk; Sara; Think About Me; Hold Me; Love In Store; Big Love; Everywhere; As Long As You Follow. Publications: My Life And Times In Fleetwood Mac, 1990. Honours: Favorite Band, Duo Or Group, Pop/Rock, American Music Awards, 1978; Grammy: Album Of The Year, Rumours, 1978; Gold Ticket, Madison Square Garden, 1990; Platinum, Gold discs. Current Management: Courage Management, 2899 Agoura Blvd, Suite 562, Westlake, CA 91361, USA.

FLEMING Kye, b. 9 Oct 1951, Pennsacola, Florida, USA. Songwriter; Publisher. Education: 2 years college. Career: President, Publishing Companies: Dream Catcher Music; Gila Monster Music; Painted Pony Music. Compositions: Co-wrote: Smokey Mountain Rain; Give Me Wings; I Was Country When Country Wasn't Cool; Nobody; Some People's Lives; Years; Sleeping Single In A Double Bed; Roll On Mississippi; Walk The Line (album), Kennedy-Rose. Honours: 2 Grammy Nominations; 43 BMI Awards; 2 CMA Award Mominations; 3 time BMI Songwriter of the Year; NSAI Songwriter of The Year; CMA Triple Play Award. Memberships: NSAI; CMA; BMI. Hobbies: Clay sculpting; Horses; Land sculpting. Current Management: Dream Catcher; Gila Monster Music. Address: 1109 16th Avenue South, Nashville, TN 37212, USA.

FLEMING Mark, b. 6 Jan 1962, Montreal, Canada. Music Publisher; Artist Manager; Film and Television Composer Agent. Education: BA in Political Science and Communications; Legal and Practical Aspects of Recording and Music Publishing, UCLA. Musical Education: Basic Theory, Piano. Career: Manager, Eddie Murphy for Transition Music; Developed Crash Test Dummies, BMG Music Publishing Canada Inc; Own business, MERS Music, publisher, film and television composer agent; Manager for Ian Halperin; Mandela Benefit Concert at Wembley; DJ Ray. Recordings: As producer: Giving You The Best That I Got, Anita Baker; As administrator for: The Bee Gees; Annie Lennox; Dave Stewart; Film soundtrack, Beverly Hills Cop. Memberships: AIMP; SOCAN; BMI. Hobbies: Sports, especially hoops and tennis. Address: 1396 Ste Catherine Street West, Suite 424, Montreal, PQ H3G 1P8, Canada.

FLETCHER Andrew John, b. 8 July 1961, Nottingham, England. Musician (Keyboards). m. Grainne (Mullan), 16 January 1993, 1 son, 1 daughter. Career: Founder Member, Depeche Mode, 1980-. Recordings: 11 Top Ten Singles including: Just Can't Get Enough, 1981; See You, 1982; Everything Counts, 1983; People Are People, 1984; Master and Servant; Enjoy the Silence, 1990; I Feel You, 1993; Condemnation, 1993; In Your Room, 1994; Barrel of a gun, 1997; It's No Good; 11 Top Ten Albums including: Speak and Spell, 1982; A Broken Frame, 1982; Construction Time Again, 1983; Some Great Reward, 1984; The Singles 81-85, 1985; Black Celebration, 1986; Music For the Masses, 1987; 101, 1989; Violator, 1990; Songs Of Faith and

Devotion, 1993; Ultra, 1997. Honours: BPI Brit Award, Enjoy the Silence, 1991. Hobbies: Football; Reading. Current Management: Jonathon Kessler, Baron Inc, 111 West 67th Street, Suite 37F, New York, NY 10023, USA. Address: First Floor, Regent House, 106 Marylebone High Street, London W1M 3DB, England.

FLETCHER Christopher Jeffrey, b. 1 July 1952, Berlin, Germany. Musician (percussion, drums); Vocalist. m. Kate Cochrane, 1 son, 1 daughter. Career: Percussion and backing vocals for many artists 1969-, including: Chris Rea, Road To Hell Tour, 1989-90; Christians, Couler Tour, 1990-91; Beautiful South, 0891 Tour, 1991-92; Judy Tzuke, Wonderland Tour, 1992; Mark Almond, Jaque Tour; Live apperances with: Fergal Sharkey; Roger Chapman; Dusty Springfield; Steve Williams; Cayenne; Paz; Stretch; Morrissey Mullen; The Montellas; Neucleus; Limmy And The Family Cooking; Currently running a 16 piece band of top session players. Recordings: Albums by: Beautiful South; Manfred Mann; Roger Chapman; Cayenne, 2 albums; Paz, 4 albums; Stretch; Morrissey Mullen, 5 albums; John Critchinson; Martin Drew; Peter Green; Molly Duncan; The Montellas; Neucleus; Alan Price. Hobbies: Tennis; Snooker; Comedy; Hang-gliding. Current Management: Chance Management. Address: 106 Cleveland Gardens, London SW13 0AH, England.

FLETCHER Matt James Harry, b. 27 Feb 1968, Lambeth, London, England. Musician (keyboards); Programmer; Engineer; Producer. Education: Goldsmiths College, University of London, BSc Psychology. Career: Keyboards for Bros' TV appearances; Numerous remixes including Shine, by Aswad; Numerous TV commercials and themes; Regular freelance work; Technical advisor to Youth; Signed as Rampage, 1994; Currently writing and producing Betty Boo's 3rd album. Recordings: Top of The Pops theme, 1991-95; One Foot In The Grave, theme remixes; For Rampage: Monkees; Why; Godfather; Album: Priority One; Betty Boo's singles, 1995. Publication: Tuning Your Breakbeat, article, Sound On Sound, May 1993. Honour: D&AD Silver Award, Best TV Soundtrack, Glad, Miller-Lite, 1991. Membership: Musicians' Union. Hobbies: BMWs; Reading; Clubs; Computer programming. Current Management: Jazz Summers, Big Life Management. Address: 15a Little Portland Street, London W1N 5DE, England.

FLICK Vic, b. 14 May 1937, Worcester Park, Surrey, England.Musician (guitar); Composer. m. Judith Mary, 19 May 1960, 1 son, 1 daughter. Education: Graduate diploma. Musical Education: Piano & theory LRAM, guitar. Career: Recorded with most major recordings artistes including: Tom Jones; Nancy Sinatra; Henry Mancini; Engelbert Humperdinck; John Barry; Bee Gees. Compositions: Themes and background music for television, radio and film includes: Music scores for The Europeans; Conquest Of Light, Irish Tourist Board; Commercials: Cheseboro-Ponds; Palitoy; Honours: 2 Royal Command Performances. Memberships: PRS; ASCAP. Hobbies: Sailing; Reading; Writing; Music. Address: PO Box 1913, Santa Monica, CA 90406-1913, USA.

FLINT Keith, Vocalist. Career: Member, The Prodigy, 1990-; Festival appearances include: Glastonbury, 1995, 1997; V97, 1997; Lollapalooza, 1997. Recordings: Albums: Experience, 1992; Music for the Jilted Generation (Number 1, UK), 1994; The Fat of the Land (Number 1, UK), 1997; Hit Singles: Charly, 1991; Everybody In the Place, 1991; Fire, 1992; Out of Space, 1992; Wind It Up, 1993; One Love, 1993; No Good (Start the Dance), 1994; Voodoo People, 1994; Poison, 1995; Firestarter (Number 1, UK), 1996; Breath (Number 1, UK), 1996; Smack My Bitch Up 1997.

Address: c/o XL Recordings, 17-19 Alma Road, London SW18 1AA, England.

FLOREK Jaki, b. Bradford, Yorkshire, England. Vocalist; Lyricist. 2 sons, 1 daughter. Education: Cardiff College of Art. Career: Tours with Shattered Dolls and Adam's Family. Recordings: Singles: with Shattered Dolls: Lipstick Killer (EP); with Adam's Family: Sometimes I Wonder (EP), 1987; Frustration, 1994; Album: with Adam's Family: Disease, 1995, CD, 1997. Memberships: PRS; Musicians' Union. Hobby: Ceramic Artist. Current Management: Loose Records. Address: PO Box 67, Runcorn, Cheshire WA7 4NL, England.

FLORES Remedios (Alendrina De Los Remedios Flores), b. 30 Jan 1952, Ronda, Malaga, Spain. Flamenco Singer. m. Rodrigo Flores, 7 July 1973, 2 sons, 1 daughter. Musical Education: Learned from family. Career: Toured for 20 years with famous guitarist Rodrigo; Under contract to Los Angeles City Schools, presenter, flamenco music. Composed music, National Geographic Special: The Soul Of Spain; State Grants to present Flamenco Song in concert atmosphere; Principle vocalist, El Cid, tablao flamenco, Hollywood (most prestigious flamenco nightclub in world). Recordings: Albums: Flamenco Caravan; Remedios Flores-Gipsy Flamenco Singer; The Gipsy 4; Rumba Festival; Trio Flamenco; Passionate Flamenco Dances; La Familia Flores; Inpiraciones; Flamenco Fantastico (Live); Video: Flamenco Sounds. Honours: Winner, Billboard Magazine Song Contest (Latin Category): Nos Volvemos A Querer. Membership: National Association Female Executives. Hobbies: Swimming; Cooking traditional gypsy/Spanish food. Current Management: Sounds-Vision Music. Address: PO Box 3691, La Mesa, CA 91944, USA.

FLOWERS Herbie, b. 19 May 1938, London, England. Musician (bass guitar, double bass, tuba). m. Ann, 1 Aug 1959, 1 son, 1 daughter. Musical Education: RAF School Of Music. Career: Played tuba in Royal Air Force, 1955-63; Played double bass, Fender bass, London theatre, club, studio circuit; Joined Blue Mink, 1970; Worked for David Bowie, tour of USA, 1974; Member, T-Rex, 2 years; Played on recordings with: Elton John; David Essex; Paul McCartney; Al Kooper; Nilsson; Tom Jones; Tiny Tim; Dusty Springfield; Henry Mancini; George Harrison; Ringo Starr; Formed Sky with John Williams; Tours with Sam Brown; Silvery Moon Band; The Royal Philharmonic Pops Orchestra; Lectures, Fun With Music, East Sussex County Council; Residential week long music courses, RockShops, on University campuses; 3 year teaching post, Bass Studies, Trinity College of Music, London. Recordings: Albums: Transformer, Lou Reed; Diamond Dogs, David Bowie; Burn Down The Mission, Elton John; Rock On, David Essex; Broad Street, Paul McCartney; 10 albums by Sky. Hobbies: Playing double bass with U's, Steve Thompson's Directory; English Jazz Quartet. Address: 15 High Street, Ditchling, East Sussex BN6 8SY, England.

FLOYD Eddie, b. 25 June 1937, Montgomery, Alabama, USA. Singer; Producer; Composer. 6 sons, 2 daughters. Musical Education: Wayne School of Music, Detroit. Career: Founder member, The Falcons, 1954-62; Solo artist, 1962-; Guest singer, The Original Blues Brothers Band, Booker T & the MG's; Worldwide tours with the above; President, Floyd Entertainment Group Inc. Compositions: Songs for Otis Redding, Wilson Pickett, and Sam & Dave, including 634-5789; Ninety-Nine And A Half (Just Won't Do); You Don't Know What You Mean To Me; Knock On Wood. Recordings: With The Falcons: You're So Fine; I Found A Love; Solo albums: Knock On Wood; I've Never Found A Girl; Rare Stamps; You've Got To Have Eddie; California Girl; Down To Earth; Baby Lay Your Head Down; Soul Street; Experience; Try Me; Flashback; Back To The Roots; with the Blues Brothers Band: Live In Montreux; The Red

White & Blues. Honours: Governors Award/Memphis Blues Foundation Inductee, Tennessee; Honourary Lieutenant Colonel, Alabama; President Bush Performance Award; Alabama Hall of Fame Inductee; NAACP BMI 1 Million Performances Award, Knock On Wood; BMI Award. Memberships: BMI. Current Representation: Andy Nazer, Performance Representation. Address: 39 Hopton Road, London SW16 2EH, England.

FLYNN Jerome. Actor; Singer. Career: Actor, UK television series Soldier, Soldier; Singer, duo Robson & Jerome, 1995-. Recordings: Debut album: Robson & Jerome, 1995; Singles: Unchained Melody/White Cliffs Of Dover, 1995; I Believe/Up On The Roof, 1995. Honour: Best selling single of decade to date, Unchained Melody, 1995.

FOAD Paul, b. 26 Sept 1957, Liverpool, England. Musician (guitar); Songwriter; Guitar Teacher. m. Kim Hamilton (singer), 7 May 1994, 1 son, 3 daughters. Musical Education: Birmingham Guitar School, 3 years; Barney Kessel Workshop summer School. Career: With group Au Pairs: BBC TV, Old Grey Whistle Test; BBC Radio 1: 3 John Peel sessions; Janice Long; Kid Jensen session; Local radio; 3 tours, USA; 5 tours, Europe, including Pink Pop, Netherlands; Session guitar for jazz artist Andy Hamilton; Session for local artists; Solo guitar, Birmingahm International Film Festival. Recordings: Au Pairs: (studio albums) Playing With A Different Sex; Sense And Sensibility; (live album) Live In Berlin; 1 radio compilation CD: Equal But Different. Publication: One chapter on Au Pairs in: In The Facists Bathroom, by Greil Marcus. Honour: Songwriters Award, New York's Village Voice, 1980. Memberships: MCPS; PRS; Musicians' Union. Current Management: EMI Publishing; RPM Records. Address: 41 Garfield Road, North Chingford, London E4 7DG, England.

FOGELBERG Dan, b. 13 Aug 1951, Peoria, Illinois, USA. Musician (guitar, piano); Songwriter. Education: University of Illinois. Musical Education: Piano from age 14. Career: Musician, California folk circuit, including tours with Van Morrison, 1971; Recording artiste, 1974-; Support to the Eagles, 1975. Recordings: Singles include: Longer, (Number 2, US), 1980; Same Auld Lang Syne, 1981; Leader Of The Band, 1981; Albums: Home Free, 1973; Souvenirs, 1975; Captured Angel, 1975; Netherlands, 1977; Twin Sons Of Different Mothers, with Tim Weisberg, 1977; Phoenix, 1980; The Innocent Age, 1981; Windows And Walls, 1984; Greatest Hits, 1985; High Country Snows, 1985; Exiles, 1987; The Wild Places, 1990; Dan Fogelberg Live - Greetings From The West, 1991. Current Management: HK Management, 8900 Wilshire Blvd, Suite 300, Beverly Hills, CA 90211, USA.

FOGERTY John, b. 28 May 1945, Berkeley, California, USA. Singer; Composer; Songwriter; Musician (guitar). Career: Member, Blue Velvets, later known as the Golliwogs), 1959-67; Group became Creedence Clearwater Revival, 1967-71; Solo artiste, 1972-. Compositions include: Almost Saturday Night, recorded by Dave Edmunds; Rockin' All Over The World, recorded by Status Quo. Recordings: Albums: with Creedence Clearwater Revival: Creedence Clearwater Revival, 1968; Bayou Country, 1969; Green River, 1969; Willie And The Poor Boys, 1969; Cosmo's Factory, 1970; Pendulum, 1970; Mardi Gras, 1972; Live In Europe, 1973; Live At The Royal Albert Hall, 1980; Solo albums: The Blue Ridge Rangers, 1973; John Fogerty, 1975; Centerfield, 1985; Eye Of A Zombie, 1986; Singles: with the Golliwogs: Don't Tell Me No More Lies; Fight Fire; Walk Upon The Water; with Creedence Clearwater Revival: Suzie Q; I Put A Spell On You; Proud Mary; Green River; Bad Moon Rising; Down On The Corner; Travellin' Band; Up Around The Bend; Looking Out My Back Door; Have You

Ever Seen The Rain; Solo: Bayou, 1973; Hearts Of Stone, 1975; Comin' Down The Road, 1975; The Old Man Down The Road, 1985. Current Management: Wenaha Music Co., PO Box 3513, Granada Hills, CA 91344, USA.

FOLEY Thomas Henry, b. 1 Apr 1961, London, England. Director, React Music Ltd. Career: Editor of Songplugger, 1986-87; Publisher and Editor of Bandit, 1988-90; Personal Assistant to Dave Pearce at Reachin Records up to 1991; Currently, Director of React Music Ltd. Address: 138B West Hill, Putney, London SW15 2UE, England.

FOLLETT Marie-Claire, b. 11 May 1973, Cardiff, Wales. Singer; Songwriter; Actress; Dancer. Education: Brooklands College. Musical Education: Academy of Live and Recorded Arts. Career: Radio broadcasts include: Radio Warsaw, Poland; Thicker Than Water, BBC Radio 2; Television appearances include: Regis and Kathy Lee Show, ABC-TV, US; The Gods Of Olympus, Duals of Honour, Discovery Channel; Concerts in London include: Mean Fiddler; Marquee; Powerhouse; The Orange; Finalist in Yamaha Music Quest; Bands include Subway; Private Life; Nemesis; Fabba-Mania; The Fortune Cookies. Recordings: Spreadeagle; A Guide For The Divorced Child, Jann Turner (film soundtrack); Singles: Cry; Indestructable. Memberships: Musicians' Union; Equity. Current Management: Richard Gillinson. Address: 92 Cheyne Walk, Chelsea, London SW10 0DQ, England.

FOLTAN Pavel, b. 8 May 1957, Benesov Near Prague, Czech Republic. Singer; Songwriter; Musician; Guitar; Violin. m. Jaroslava Foltanova, 1 Apr 1978, 1 son. Education: University JE Purkyne Brno. Career: About 1500 performances, clubs, festivals, concerts, theatres, all Czech important folk-festivals. Compositions: Pijácká; Pruvodce; Posvícení, Jakoby, Nadeláno, Bejvávalo, Prostor pro tebe, Popelnice, Motyl, Vánocní blues, Vyrocní, Osvedcení, Samá voda, Jak to vypadá. Recordings: Solo albums: Old Czech pains; Staré bolesti Ceské, 1992; Double Live, 1996. Publications: Scenic Music: Clowns from Avignon, 1981; Save the Universe, 1982; Minicomedy, 1983; Great Guardian of Herds, 1983; Plays on Interludes, 1984; Gold Chariot, 1985; Mear the Song About That Slaughter, 1985; Absurd Person Singular, 1991; Executive Production: Musicals: Bastard, 1994; Dreams of Midsummer Nights, 1994. Honours: Porta, 1973; Porta, 1975; Academic Festival Wroclaw, 1978; AF Jerevan, 1980; Mohelnice, 1996. Memberships: Dilia; Intergram; OSA, SAI. Current Managements: BABA Agency, Vinohradská 91, CZ-120 00, Prague 2. Address: P Foltan, Vltavska 19, 625 00 Brno, Czech Republic.

FONT-ROUGET Piatuno, b. 31 Dec 1958, Vitry-le-François, France. Singer; Musician (piano, trumpet). Common law wife, Nathalie Olélet, 2 daughters. Musical Education: Self-taught writer and composer. Career: Performed with: Printemps de Bourges; France Inter "Pollen"; Jean Louis Foulquier. Address: 1 Rue Charles Olarchant, 51290 Gigny-Bussy, France.

FONTAINE Bruno, 21 May 1957, Epinal, France. Musician (piano); Conductor; Arranger. M. Fabienne, 26 Aug 1980. Musical Education: First Prize, piano; Chamber music; Accompaniment; Harmony; Conservatoire National Superieur de Paris. Career: Musical direction for: Johnny Halliday; Mylene Farmer; Alaim Chamfort; Julia Migenes; Lambert Wilson; Ute Lemper. Recordings: Production, arrangements, conducting on: Julia Migenes: My Favourite Songs; Ute Lemper: Illusions; City Of Strangers. Honours: Grand Prix Academie Charles Cros, for Illusions, 1993. Current Management: O Gluzman. Address: 40 Rue Folie Régnault, 75011 Paris, France.

FONTANA Wayne (Glyn Ellis), b. 28 Oct 1940, Manchester, Lancashire, England. Career: Founder member, The Jets; The Mindbenders, 1963-1965; Solo artiste, 1965-; Tours include: UK, with Brenda Lee, 1964; UK, supporting Del Shannon, 1965; British Song Festival, Brighton, 1965; Tour, with Herman's Hermits, The Fortunes, Billy Fury, 1965; Swinging '66 Tour, with the Small Faces, 1966; Resident songwriter, Chappell music publishers, 1970-; English Invasion Revival US tour, 1973; Resumed recording career, 1976; Revival tour, 1979; Festival Of The Tenth Summer, Manchester, 1986. Recordings: Albums include: Wayne Fontana And The Mindbenders, 1965; Eric, Rick, Wayne And Bob, 1966; The Mindbenders, 1966; Hit singles: wit The Mindbenders: Um Um Um Um Um Um, 1964; The Game Of Love (Number 2, UK), 1965; Just A Little Bit Too Late; She Needs Love; Solo: Come On Home; Goodbye Bluebird; Pamela Pamela. Address: c/o Barry Collings Entertainments, 21a Clifftown Road, Southend-on-Sea, Essex SS1 1AB, England.

FORCIONE Antonio, b. 2 May 1960, Italy. Musician (guitar); Composer. 1 daughter. Education: Visual Arts, 5 years. Musical Education: Private Jazz and Folk tuition in Italy. Career: Performed in a series of international guitar festivals at Queen Elizabeth Hall and The Royal Festival Hall; Appearances on various radio and television stations including BBC1, ITV, Sky TV, BBC Radio 2 and 4; Tours throughout Europe. Recordings: Albums: Light And Shade, Eurotour, Celebration, 1987; Poema, 1992; Acoustic Revenge, 1993; Live Edinburgh Festival, 1993. Membership: Musicians' Union. Hobbies: Dance; Painting; Acting. Current Management: Robert Masters. Address: Mountfield Court, Dormans Park, East Grinstead, Sussex RH19 39U, England.

FORD Gerry, b. 25 May 1943, Athlone, Eire. Country Music Entertainer; Disc Jockey; Journalist; Singer; Songwriter. m. Joan, 4 Apr 1964, 1 son. Career: Qualified Baker, Confectioner; Served in Edinburgh City Police until 1976; Became professional entertainer, while broadcasting 2 country music programmes for Radio Forth, Edinburgh and performing in clubs; Joined BBC Radio Scotland, Country music presenter, 1978-1993; Own series, BBC Radio 2, 1988-89. Recordings: 15 albums, 1977-; 7 duets with Jean Shepard. Honours: 2 Albums of the Year, 1980; BCM Radio Play Album of the Year, 1991; Presenters Award, 1993; Honorary Citizen, Nashville, Tennessee; 21 appearances, Grand Ole Opry, Nashville; 33 Awards, Male Vocalist, Recording Artiste, various country music clubs and magazines. Address: 13 Winton Park, Edinburgh EH10 7EX, Scotland.

FORD Lita, b. 23 Sept 1959, London, England. Singer; Musician (guitar). m. Chris Holmes (divorced). Original member, all-girl group, The Runaways, 1976-79; Solo artiste, 1980-. Recordings: Albums: with the Runaways: The Runaways, 1976; Queens Of Night, 1977; And Now The Runaways, 1979; Flamin' Schoolgirls, 1980; Solo albums: Out For Blood, 1983; Dancin' On The Edge, 1984; Lita, 1988; Stiletto, 1990; Dangerous Curves, 1991; Hit singles include: Kiss Me Deadly; Close My Eyes Forever (duet with Ozzy Osbourne).

FORD Vince, b. 9 Apr 1962, Newark, Nottinghamshire, England. Singer; Songwriter; Producer; Record Company Executive. m. Julie, 14 Sept 1991, 1 son. Musical Education: None (formal). Career: Formed Capital Queue, 1979; Formed Temper, Temper, 1987; Formed Sheer Bravado Records, 1989. Membership: PRS. Hobbies: Sport; Computers; Photography. Current Management: Self-managed. Address: 7 Backs Close, Waddington, Lincoln LN5 9SG, England.

FORDE Brinsley. Singer; Musician (guitar). Career: Child actor, Here Come The Double Deckers, BBC TV; Founder member, UK reggae group Aswad, 1975-; Performances include: Cliff Richard - The Event, Wembley Stadium, 1989; Nelson Mandela International Tribute concert, Wembley, 1990; Glastonbury Festival, 1990; Reggae Sunsplash US tour, 1991; Heineken Festival, Leeds, 1995; Musician, actor, film Babylon, 1980; Please Sir, Diamonds are Fprever, Leo the Last; Also featured in Bob Marley Tribute, Rapido, BBC2 TV, 1991; Presenter, Soul Vibration, VH-1. Recordings: Singles include: Back To Africa, 1976; Don't Turn Around (Number 1, UK), 1988; Give A Little Love, 1988; Set Them Free, 1988; Beauty's Only Skin Deep, 1989; On And On, 1989; Next To You, 1990; Smile, 1990; How Long (with Yazz), 1993; Dance Hall Mood, 1993; Shine, UK No 5; Albums: Aswad, 1976; Hulet, 1979; New Chapter, 1980; Not Satisfied, 1982; Live And Direct, 1983; Rebel Soul, 1984; To The Top, 1986; Distant Thunder, 1988; Renaissance, 1989; Too Wicked, 1990. Honours include: Reggae Industry Award, Best Group, 1995. Current Management: Hit And Run Music, 30 Ives Street, London SW3 2ND, England.

FORDHAM Julia, b. 10 Aug 1962, Hampshire, England. Singer; Songwriter; Musician (guitar). Career: Began performances own material, folk music clubs, age 14-15; Briefly with National Youth Orchestra; 5 years as backing vocalist; Signed solo record deal, 1987. Recordings include: Albums: Julia Fordham, 1988; Porcelain, 1989; Swept, 1991; Falling Forward, 1994; Fifth album in progress; Hit singles include: Happy Ever After. Honours: Silver Prize, Tokyo Music Festival, 1989; 4 Gold records, Japan. Memberships: Musicians' Union; Equity. Hobbies: Boogie Boarding; Gardening. Current Management: JFD Management. Address: 106 Dalling Road, Hammersmith, London W6 0JA, England.

FORRESTER John, b. 16 Mar 1969, Pembury, Kent, England. Musician (bouzouki, bass, guitar); Vocalist. Career: Vocals, bass, Killing The Rose, 1986-87; Vocals, bass, The Colour Mary, 1988-92; Vocals, bass, bouzouki, Pressgang, 1992-94; Solo artiste, vocals, bouzouki, guitar, 1993; Vocals, bass, WOB, 1993-94; Vocals, bouzouki, bass, Sunspeak, 1995; Tours: with Pressgang: England, France, Germany; with WOB: England, France, Germany, Austria, Holland; Radio: The Colour Mary Live From The Marquee, BBC Radio 1, 1990. Recordings: EPs: with The Colour Mary: Trash And Treasure, 1988; The World Don't Spin, 1989; Black And White, 1990; Sunspeak, 1991; Mindfield, 1992; with Pressgang: Donkey, 1993; Albums: with Pressgang: Burning Boats, 1994; with WOB: Can't Stay Long, 1995; with Sunspeak: album, 1995; Solo: Scars And Memories, 1993; Tales Of Nothing, 1995. Membership: Musicians' Union. Hobbies: Walking; Drinking. Current Management: Cat Records UK; Self-managed. Address: Seaview Studio, 51 Barkham Road, Wokingham, Berkshire RG41 2RG, England.

FORSMAN Ingela "Pling", b. 26 Aug 1950, Stockholm, Sweden. Lyricist; Record Producer; Recording Artist. m. Lars, 1990, 1 son. Education: English, University of Stockholm. Career: Former recording artist with girl group Bambis; Tours: Sweden; Germany; Lyricist, 1971-; 12 years in record business, some as producer; Translated musicals into Swedish: Cats; Grease; Fame; Hair; Also translated songs in films, including: The Little Mermaid; Beauty And The Beast; Hymn for Swedish Hymnbook; Written over 1000 lyrics, most of them recorded. Honours: Swedish Song Contest (Two first places, many in Top 3); SKAP Award. Memberships: STIM; NCB; SKAP. Hobbies: Cooking; Country life. Address: Pling AB, Kungsholms Hamnplan 3, 112 20 Stockholm, Sweden.

FOSKETT Charles A, b. 27 Mar 1949, Newcastle-upon-Tyne, England. Musician (guitar, bass); Composer; Producer. m. Lauren Daniele Field, 7 June 1990, 1 son. Musical Education: Self-taught. Career: Major tours, television and radio sessions including Andy Peebles, BBC; Tyne Tees, Chat Show; Started in Newcastle, played alongside The Animals, 1960s; Put together The Anti Heroin Project, EMI, 1985, 1986, 1987; Wrote, produced double album: It's A Live In World, featuring and bringing together hundreds of big name artists; Worked with: Kim Wilde; Ringo Starr; Precious Wilson; John Cleese; Bonnie Tyler; Elkie Brooks; Daryl Pandy; Cliff Richard; Holly Johnson; Sheila Ferguson; Robin Gibb; Nick Kershaw; Hazel O'Connor. Compositions: Theme music, Strike Command, TV advert, 1996; Theme music, ITV 6-part series, 1997; Theme music, High 5, Channel 4, 1997; Compositions for Sarah Jory, Joe Cocker; I Wanna Be There, Prudential Mexico '97. Recordings: Writer/producer for artists including: Bonnie Tyler; Kim Wlde; Elkie Brooks; Ringo Starr; Holly Johnson; Cliff Richard; Jim Diamond; Sheila Ferguson; Robin Gibb; Nik Kershaw; Hazel Dean; Zak Starkey; Hazel O'Connor; Catherine Zeta-Jones; Produced: Sinitta; Edwin Star; Phil Fearon; John Parr; Mike Peters/Eddie McDonald (The Alarm); Steve Harley; Suggs (Madness); Bucks Fizz; Chas & Dave; Brinsley Ford/Drummie Zeb (Aswad); Nick Heywood; The Icicle Works; Elvis Costello; Thompson Twins; Sarah Jory; Joe Cocker. Honour: Royal Academy Artist. Memberships: PRS; Equity. Hobby: Songwriting. Current Managment: Veracruz Music International. Address: 43 Capron Road, Dunstable, Bedfordshire LU5 5AL, England.

FOSSATI Ramon, b. 14 Sept 1965, Barcelona, Spain. Musician (guitar); Composer; Producer. Career: Creator, co-leader, Paris-Barcelona Swing Connection; Played with Frank Wess; Teddy Edwards; Wild Bill Davis; Performed at Jazz Festival, Birmingham, 1992-94; Terrassa, Spain, 1993-95; Frankfurt, 1995; More than 500 concerts around Europe. Recordings: with the Paris-Barcelona Swing Connection: Hard Swing; Live In Barcelona; with Frank Wess: Frank Wess Meets The Paris-Barcelona Swing Connection; with Wild Bill Davis: Wild Cat. Current Management: Foscar Society. Address: 108 Avenue Roger Salengro, 91600 Savigny Sur Orge, France.

FOSSEN Sverre, b. 4 Oct 1973, Trondheim, Norway. Musician (guitar). Education: College. Career: Joined Hedge Hog, 1990; Several tours, Norway; Toured Europe, 1994, 1995. Recordings: Erase, 1992; Surprise, 1992; Primal Gutter, 1993; Mercury Red, 1994; Mindless, 1994; The Healing EP, 1995; Thorn Cord Wonder, 1995. Publications: Sverre - A Voice From the Gutter, 1994. Membership: Norwegian Association of Musicians. Hobbies: Painting; Football. Current Management: Martin Aam, Hedge Hogment. Address: Hedge Hog, PO Box 683, 7001 Trondheim, Norway.

FOSTER Geoff, b. 5 May 1965, Wimbledon, London, England. Recording Engineer. partner, Dawn Tait, 2 daughters. Education: Marlborough College; Brunel University; Electronics Degree. Career: Worked for Stones Mobile, 1985; Cold Storage Studios, 1986; Air Studios, 1987; Chief Engineer, 1994. Recordings: Film scores: Stargate; Restoration; Romeo and Juliet; Mighty Ducks 3; Don Juan: Demarco; Last of the Dogmen; Mert Wally Sparks; Smilla's Sense of Snow; Photographing Fairies. Recordings: Albums: George Martin; Martin Okasili; John Martyn; Crowded House; Debbie Harry; Hot House; Flowers; Jethro Tull; Park Carrack; Radiohead; The The; Kula Shaker; David Essex; José Carreras; Vanessa-Mae; John Williams. Membership: AMIEE. Current Management: Air Management, Lyndhurst Hall, Lyndhurst Road, London NW3 5NG, England. Address: Air Studios, Lyndhurst Hall, Lyndhurst Road, London NW3 5NG, England.

FOUNTAIN Peter, b. 3 July 1930, New Orleans, LA, USA. Clarinettist. m. Beverly, 27 October 1951, 2 sons, 1 daughter. Career: Operator night club Pete Fountain's New Orleans; Member, Basin Street Six, 1949-54, Lawrence Walk Orchestra, 1957-60; Leader, own group; Appeared in (films), Pete Fountain Sextet, 1962, Pete's Place, 1966, The New Orleans Jazz Museum, 1967; Featured in: PBS spl, Dukes of Dixieland and Friends, 1980; Featured Guest with major orchestras throughout world; Co-author: A Closer Walk: The Pete Fountain Story, 1972; Appeared on Johnny Carson Show, 59 times; Performed for Papal visit, White House for Presidents Eisenhower, Nixon, Ford and Reagan, 1987. Recordings: 85 albums including: The Blues; Down on Rampart Street; Swingin' Blues, 1991; High Society, 1992; Cheek to Cheek, 1993. Honours: 3 Gold Albums; 1 Gold Single (A Closer Walk). Address: 2 Poydras St, New Orleans, LA 70130-1656, USA.

FOWLER Simon, b. Birmingham, England. Vocalist; Songwriter. Career: Lead singer, songwriter, Ocean Colour Scene, 1989-; UK tour, 1996. Recordings: Albums: Yesterday And Today, 1992; Moseley Shoals, 1996; Singles: The Riverboat Song, 1995; You've Got It Bad, 1996. Address: c/o MCA Records, 139 Piccadilly, London W1V 0AX, England.

FOX Angela, b. 31 July 1960, Birkenhead, Cheshire, England. Musician (guitar, dulcimer); Singer. Career: Appearances most folk clubs, festivals, New Zealand; Several radio appearances includes National radio interview, during tour, 1991; Television, 1995. Recordings: 2 solo albums: Takin' A Chance, 1990; Deceptive Love, 1992; Worked on over 50 recording projects as session vocalist, guitarist, arranger, 2nd engineer, producer. Honours: Nominee, New Zealand Music Award. Hobbies: Music; Art. Address: 193 Scenic Drive, Titirangi, Auckland, New Zealand.

FOX George William, b. 23 Mar 1960, Cochrane, Alberta, Canada. Singer; Songwriter. Career: Over 75 TV appearances include: George Fox's New Country, CBC, 1990; Nashville Now, 1991; Newsworld, CBC, 1992; Tommy Hunter Show, 1992; All About Country, 1992; Country Gold, 1992; Canada Day - Seville, Spain, 1992; New Year's Eve Niagara, Baton Broadcasting, 1993; Crook & Chase, TNN, 1993; Sang National Anthem, World Series, Toronto, 1993; Juno Awards, 1989-94, 1996; Rita & Friends, CBC, 1994, 1995; George Fox - Time Of My Life, CBC Special, 1995. Compositions: Angelina, 1988; Mustang Heart, 1993; Breakfast Alone, 1993; Honest Man, 1993; No Hasta La Vista Tonight; 1994; Wear & Tear On My Heart, 1994; What's Holding Me, 1995; First Comes Love, 1995; I Give You My Word, 1997. Recordings: George Fox (Gold), 1988; With All My Might (Gold), 1989; Spice Of Life, 1991; Mustang Heart (Gold), 1993; Time Of My Life (Gold), 1995; Greatest Hits 1987-1997, 1997. Honours: Canadian Country Music Association, Vista Rising Star, 1989; Country Male Vocalist, 1989-93; Juno Awards, Country Male Vocalist Of Year, 1990, 1991, 1992; SOCAN Song Of Year, Clearly Canadian, 1993. Memberships: CARAS; NARAS; CMA; CCMA; ACTRA; AFofM. Hobbies: Hiking; Golf. Address: c/o Balmur Inc., 1105 17th Avenue, Nashville, TN 37212, USA.

FOX Harry, b. 7 May 1941, Munich, Germany. Booking Agent. Career: Booking agent, Harry Fox Agency. Recordings: Juke Box. Publications: Showbusiness Actuel; Stars And Shows. Address: Steinstreet 53, 18667 Munich, Germany.

FOX John (aka David Bell, Peter Balding), b. 30 Apr 1926, Sutton, Surrey, England. Composer; Arranger; Conductor; Musician (piano). m. Joy Devon, 17 May 1980, 2 sons, 1 daughter. Musical Education: Royal College of Music (ARCM); Composition scholarship, Fitznells College of Music. Career: Pianist, arranger, numerous groups; Arranger, conductor, BBC Radio Orchestra, 1960s; Conducted Krakow Radio Symphony Orchestra, recordings, Poland; Broadcasts with John Fox Orchestra and voices; Recorded in London, Customs easy listening music for USA networks, 1970s; Concerts: John Fox Concerts, BBC, Pebble Mill, Musical World of John Fox, Magic of John Fox (London), Numerous String Sound and Romantic Strings, broadcast sessions, 1980s; Also acapella broadcasts with John Fox Singers, Friday Night Is Music Night, BBC Radio; Conductor, arranger, for concerts with vocalist (wife) Joy Devon, Philharmonie Concert Hall, Cologne, Germany; Performed Earth And Space Suite, Huntingdon, England; Owner, publishing company, Coniston Music Publishing. Compositions: Over 1000 published works. Recordings: Memory; Unforgettable Melodies, Nos 1 & 2; Love Is A Many-Splendoured Thing; Whispers Of Love; Pomp & Glory; Heartstrings; Earth And Space; Sailing By; Two's Company; Instrumental Pops (series); John Fox Presents, Vols 1-18; with J F Orchestra And Voices: Gershwin; Here There And Everywhere; with J F Singers: Fairest Isle; Produced (with Joy Devon) albums own material (with large symphony orchestras), Munich, Berlin, Leipzig, London, Yugoslavia, Budapest. Honours: STEMRA Music Award, Netherlands, for Best Film, 1993. Memberships: PRS; MCPS; APC; BASCA. Hobbies: Walking dog; Follower of cricket and rugby; Travel; Swimming. Current Management: Coniston and Sonoton. Address: Coniston Music Publishing Co, 26 Garratts Lane, Banstead, Surrey SM7 2EA, England.

FRAME Roddy, b. 29 Jan 1964, East Kilbride, Scotland. Singer; Songwriter; Musician (guitar). Career: Founder member, Aztec Camera, 1980-; International appearances include: Support to Elvis Costello, US, 1983; The Ritz, New York, 1985; Royal Albert Hall, 1988; Cambridge Folk Festival, 1991; Edinburgh Festival, 1991; Support to Bob Dylan, 1993; Phoenix Festival, 1995. Compositions include: Composed all songs on albums. Recordings: Singles include: Oblivious, 1983; Walk Out To Winter, 1984; How Men Are, 1988; Somewhere In My Heart, 1988; Working In A Goldmine, 1988; Good Morning Britain, 1990; Spanish Horses, 1992; Sun, 1995; Albums: High Land, Hard Rain, 1983; Knife, 1985; Love, 1987; Stray, 1990; Dreamland, 1993; Frestonia, 1995; Contributor to: Red Hot + Blue, 1990; Ruby Trax (duet with Andy Fairweather-Low), 1992. Honours include: Gold Discs: High Land Hard Rain, 1983; Knife, 1985; Platinum disc, Love, 1988. Current Management: Southside Management, 20 Cromwell Mews, London SW7 2JY, England.

FRAMPTON Peter, b. 22 Apr 1950, Beckenham, Kent, England. Musician (guitar); Singer. Career: Member, The Herd; Session musician, Johnny Hallyday; Member, Humble Pie, 1969-71; Solo artiste, 1971-; Performances include: Support to J Geils Band, New York, 1972; Don Kirshner's Second Annual Rock Music Awards, CBS, 1976; Madison Square Garden, New York, 1979; Guitarist, Glass Spider tour, David Bowie, 1987; Tour with Stevie Nicks, 1987; Formed new backing band, Escape, 1990; Appearance, Lynyrd Skynyrd And Friends 20th Anniversary concert, 1993; Film appearance, Sgt Pepper's Lonely Hearts Club Band, 1978. Recordings: Albums with Humble Pie: As Safe As Yesterday Is, 1969; Town And Country, 1969; Humble Pie, 1971; Rock On, 1971; Performance - Rockin' The Fillmore, 1972; Solo albums: Wind Of Change, 1972; Frampton's Camel, 1973; Somethin's Happening, 1974; Frampton, 1974; Frampton Comes Alive, 1976; I'm In You, 1977;

Where Should I Be, 1979; Breaking All The Rules, 1981; The Art Of Control, 1982; Premonition, 1983; Peter Frampton Classics, 1987; New World, 1988; When All The Pieces Fit, 1989; Shine On - A Collection, 1992; Peter Frampton, 1994; Peter Frampton Comes Alive II, 1995; Solo singles include: Show Me The Way, 1976; Baby I Love Your Way, 1976; Signed, Sealed Delivered (I'm Yours), 1977; I Can't Stand No More, 1979; The Bigger They Come, featured in film Harley Davidson & The Marlboro Man, 1991. Honours include: Gold Ticket, Madison Square Gardens, 1979. Address: Firstars, 3520 Hayden Avenue, Culver City, CA 90232, USA.

FRANCE Martin Perry, b. 29 Feb 1964, Rainham, Kent, England. Musician (drums, percussion). Musical Education: Music O Level; 10 year's private study. Career: To date Performed in 36 countries, all usually recorded for television/radio; Featured in various newspapers, music magazines; Performed with many leading jazz musicians; 1994-, working in new quartet led by Kenny Wheeler with John Taylor, Dave Holland. Recordings: First House: Erendira; Cantilena; Iain Bellamy: Balloon Man; All Men Amen; Cleveland Watkiss: Green Chimneys; Julian Argüelles: Phaedrus; Django Bates: Music For The Third Policeman; Summer Fruits And Unrest; Winter Truce And Homes Blaze; Django Bates: Loose Tubes: Loose Tubes Live; Human Chain: Pyrotechnics; Mark Lockheart: Clec; Perfect Houseplants; Billy Jenkins: Aural Art; Sounds Like Bromley; Summer Fest; Eddie Parker: Eddie Parker; Buckley/Batchelor: Whole And The Half; Arguelles, Swallow, Walker and France. Current Management: P Partnerships, 5 Dryden Street, London WC2 9NW. Address: 2 Dewhurst Lane, Wadhurst, E Sussex, England.

FRANCE Nicolas Michael, b. 30 Mar 1956, Standon, Hertfordshire, England. Musician (percussion, drums, piano). m. Billie (Susan Mary) Preston, 21 Oct 1983, 1 son, 2 daughters. Musical Education: Chorister, Ely Cathedral; G Mus Diploma (Music), CCAT, Cambridge. Career: Professional musician, 1980-; Worked with: Tanita Tikaram; Bill Withers; Jackie Graham; Working Week; Mose Allison; Recorded with Pete Townshend; Thomas Dolby; L Shankar; Session player with artists including: Phil Todd; Robbie Macintosh; Snake Davies; Laurence and Richard Cottle; Danny Cummings; Martin Ditcham; Played with jazz artists including: Loose Tubes; Ronnie Scott Quintet; John Taylor; Alan Holdsworth; Jim Mullen; Concerts and tours include: Tours with Loose Tubes, 1983-86; 3 European tours, 3 festivals with Working Week, 1984-87; 2 tours, UK, Europe, 1988-89; Tour, including Montreux and Nice festivals, with Heitor; 3 world tours with Tanita Tikaram, 1990-95. Recordings: with Loose Tubes: Loose Tubes; Delightful Precipice, 1983-85; The Way Through The Woods, Bronte Brothers, 1993; Johnson, The Fat Lady Sings, 1993; with The Working Week: Working Nights; Companeros; Fire In The Mountain; Rodrigo Bay from Absolute Beginners; Fire In The Mountain; Supergrass; Comic Strip Movie (film soundtrack), 1984-87; with Tanita Tikaram: Everybody's Angel; Eleven Kinds Of Loneliness; Lovers In The City, 1990-95. Honour: G Mus, Music diploma. Membership: PRS. Hobbies: Tennis; Cycling.

FRANCES Andrew, b. 17 Mar 1950, New York City, USA. Record Company Executive; Producer; Manager. Education: Graduated NYC's High School of the performing Arts; Bachelor degree, Northwestern University. Career: Worked for labels: MCA; RCA; Millenium; RSO; Founded own labels: Chameleon/Elektra; North South/Atlantic; Grammy Award-winning recordings on own labels; Own management company Adwater and Stir; Artists handled include: David Bowie; Wang Chung; Ruth McCartney; Benny Mardones. Memberships: NARAS; CMA. Hobby: Volleyball. Address: 1303 16th Avenue South, Nashville, TN 37212, USA.

FRANCIS Chris, b. 11 Aug 1948, London, England. Bandleader; Jazz Musician (alto/soprano saxophone, G flute). m. Penny, 1976, 1 son. Education: Manchester and Chelsea Art Schools. Musical Education: Studied privately. Career: Founded Naima, band ranging from trio to fifteen piece, toured Europe, Britain; Founder member, Joy quintet; Recorded with many pop stars, toured with rock bands and folk groups. Recordings: Herm Island Suite, BBC Radio; (session man) Adam Ant: Goody Two Shoes; Numerous broadcasts of own compositions. Honours: Joint winner, GLAA: Young Jazz Musicans Award, 1976. Memberships: Musicians' Union; PRS; MCPS. Hobbies: Painting; Photography; Sailing. Current Management: Art Services. Address: 10a Putney High Street, London SW15 1SL, England.

FRANCIS Connie (Concetta Rosa Maria Franconero), b. 12 Dec 1938, Newark, New Jersey, USA. Singer. Musical Education: Began playing accordion age 4. Career: Professional musician, 1949-; Winner, Arthur Godfrey Talent Show; Recording artiste, 1955-; Charity work for organisations including UNICEF; Entertained US troops, Vietnam, 1960s; Retired from public performance, 1970s; Resumed performances, 1981-; London Palladium, 1989; Las Vegas, 1989. Recordings: Albums include: Who's Sorry Now?, 1958; The Exciting Connie Francis, 1959; My Thanks To You, 1959; Italian Favourites, 1960; Rock'n'Roll Million Sellers, 1960; Country And Western Golden Hits, 1960; Sings Great Jewish Favorites, 1961; Songs To A Swinging Band, 1961; Never On Sunday, 1961; Folk Song Favorites, 1961; Do The Twist, 1962; Second Hand Love And Other Hits, 1962; Country Music Connie Style, 1962; Modern Italian Hits, 1963; In The Summer Of His Years, 1964; Great Country Favourites, with Hank Williams Junior, 1964; A New Kind Of Connie, 1964; Connie Francis Sings For Mama, 1965; Love Italian Style, 1967; Happiness, 1967; My Heart Cries For You, 1967; Hawaii Connie, 1968; Connie And Clyde, 1968; The Wedding Cake, 1969; Connie Francis Sings Great Country Hits, Volume 2, 1973; Sings The Big Band Hits, 1977; I'm Me Again - Silver Anniversary Album, 1981; Connie Francis And Peter Kraus, Volumes 1 & 2, 1984; Country Store, 1988; Various compilations; UK Number 1 singles: Who's Sorry Now; Stupid Cupid; US Number 1 singles: Everybody's Somebody's Fool; My Mind Has A Heart Of Its Own; Don't Break The Heart That Loves You. Current Management: Stan Scottland c/o JKES Services Inc. Address: 404 Park Ave South, 10th Floor, New York, NY 10016, USA.

FRANCIS Panama, Jazz Musician (drums). Career: Orchestras include: Willie Bryant; Panama Francis; Cab Calloway; Duke Ellington; Sy Oliver; New York Jazz; Ray Conniff; Walt Disney World; Panama Francis and His Savoy Sultans; Personal drummer, Dinah Shore; Worldwide concerts include: Carnegie Hall; Lincoln Center; Films, videos: Madonna: Secrets; Lisa Bonet and Mickey Rourke: Angel Heart; Diana Ross and Billy D Williams: Lady Sings The Blues; Gordon Parks: The Learnig Tree; Allan Freed: Rock Around The Clock; Cab Calloway: The Hi-De-Ho-Man; Boogie Woogie. Recordings: Albums: Statemen Of Jazz; Getting In The Groove; Panama Francis and The Savoy Sultans, volumes I and II; Jimmy Witherspoon Meets The Savoy Sultans; Everything Swings; Grooving; The Beat Behind The Million Sellers; Exploding Drums; Tough Talk; Panama Francis All Stars; Studio albums with artists including : Tony Bennett; Little Richard; Lisa Minnelli; Ray Charles; Johnny Mathis; Paul Anka; Sam Cooke; Billie Holiday; Connie Francis; Sarah Vaughn; Nat King Cole; Ella Fitzgerald; Harry Belafonte; The Four Seasons; Dizzy Gillespie; Nancy Wilson; Cab Calloway; Paul Anka; Ray Conniff; Lionel Hampton; Mel Torme; Frankie Avalon; Joan Baez; Hits played on include: Four Season's: Big Girls Don't Cry; Walk Like A Man; Buddy Holly: Peggy Sue; Johnny Mathis: Chances

Are; Tony Bennett: Climb The Highest Mountain; Ray Charles: Drown In My Own Tears; Dinah Washington: What A Difference A Day Makes; Platters: Only You; Paul Anka: Lonely Boy; Connie Francis: Who's Sorry Now; Neil Sadaka: Calendar Girl; Bobby Darien: Splish Splash; James Brown: Prisoner Of Love.

FRANÇOIS Faure, b. 11 Oct 1949, Perigueux, France. Musician (piano). 1 son; 1 daughter. Musical Education: Conservatoire Bordeaux. Career: Festival Radio France de Montpelier, 1986; 1993; Festival d'Apt, 1994; Festival de Nice, 1994. Recordings: Direction Sud Ouest. Current Management: Khat Production. Address: 9, Route du Bazadais, 33650 Cabanac, France.

FRANCOMBE Mark, b. 4 Dec 1963, Ongar, Essex, England. Musician (guitar, bass, keyboards). Education: Portsmouth Art College. Career: Numerous tours of Europe and USA with the Cranes; Also support tour with The Cure, USA and Europe, 1992; Various radio and television appearances include: 2 sessions on John Peel show, BBC Radio 1; MTV; Snub TV, BBC. Recordings: with The Cranes: Self Non Self; Wings Of Joy; Forever Loved. Hobbies: Side project Eardrum; Fire walking. Current Management: Adrian Maddox; Current Agent: AMPI.

FRANKLIN Aretha, b. 25 Mar 1942, Memphis, Tennessee, USA. Singer; Songwriter. m. Glynn Turman, 1978. Career: Recording artist, 1960-; European tour, 1968; Appearances include: Inaugural Eve Gala, Jimmy Carter, Washington DC; Jamaica World Music Festival, 1982; Budweiser Superfest, 1982; Actress, film The Blues Brothers, 1980; Subject, TV specials: Aretha Franklin - The Queen Of Soul, 1988; Aretha Franklin - Duets, 1993. Recordings: Albums include: The Great Aretha Franklin, 1960; The Electrifying Aretha Franklin, 1962; The Tender, The Moving, The Swinging, 1962; Unforgettable - A Tribute To Dinah Washington, 1964; Runnin' Out Of Fools, 1965; Yeah!!!, 1965; Soul Sister, 1966; I Never Loved A Man (The Way I Loved You), 1967; Aretha Arrives, 1967; Aretha: Lady Soul, 1968; Aretha In Paris, 1968; This Girl's In Love With You, 1969; Spirit In The Dark, 1970; Aretha Live At Fillmore West, 1971; Amazing Grace, 1972; Hey Now Hey (The Other Side Of The Sky), 1973; Let Me In Your Life, 1974; With Everything I Feel In Me, 1975; You, 1975; Sweet Passion, 1977; Almighty Fire, 1978; La Diva, 1979; Aretha, 1980; Love All The Hurt Away, 1981; Jump To It, 1982; Get It Right, 1983; Who's Zoomin' Who?, 1985; The First Lady Of Soul, 1986; Aretha, 1987; One Lord, One Faith, One Baptism, 1988; Through The Storm, 1989; What You See Is What You Sweat, 1991; Queen Of Soul, 1993; Greatest Hits 1980-1994, 1994; A Rose Is Still A Rose, 1998; Hit singles include: I Never Loved A Man (The Way I Loved You), 1967; Respect (Number 1, US), 1967; Baby I Love You, 1967; (You Make Me Feel Like A) Natural Woman, 1967; Chain Of Fools, 1968; (Sweet Sweet Baby) Since You've Been Gone, 1968; Think, 1968; I Say A Little Prayer, 1968; Call Me, 1970; Don't Play That Song, 1970; You're All I Need To Get By, 1971; Rock Steady, 1972; Young Gifted And Black, 1972; Day Dreaming, 1972; Until You Come Back To Me, 1974; Sisters Are Doin' It For Themselves, duet with Annie Lennox, 1985; I Knew You Were Waiting For Me, duet with George Michael (Number 1, UK and US), 1987; Through The Storm, duet with Elton John, 1989; Contributor, film soundtracks including: Sparkle, 1976; Jumpin' Jack Flash, 1986; White Men Can't Jump, 1992. Honours include: Aretha Franklin Day, Detroit, 1967; Numerous Grammy Awards, 1968-; American Music Awards; Inducted into Rock'n'Roll Hall Of Fame, 1987; Living Legend Award, NARAS, 1990; Rhythm & Blues Foundation Lifetime Achievement Award, 1992. Current Management: Aretha Franklin

Management, 30150 Telegraph Road, Suite 444, Birmingham, MI 48025, USA.

FRANOLIC Drazen, b. 4 July 1961, Biograd, Croatia. Musician (Arabian lute); Composer. m. Vesna Gorse, 20 June 1992. Career: Member, Franolic-Gorse Duo; Gorse-Franolic Trio; Tao; Concerts: Zagreb; Belgrade; Ljubljana; Sarajevo; Rijeka; Dubrovnik; Italy; Czechoslovakia; Live album recordings, Lisinsui Concert Hall, 1992, 1995. Recordings: with Vesna Gorse: Waterfalls, 1986; New Era Of Instrumental Music, 1990; Wonderland, 1990; Asgard Live, 1993; Just A Music, 1995. Honours: 2 Porin Award Nominations, Asgard Live, 1994. Memberships: Croatian Composers' Society; Croatian Music Union; Amnesty International. Hobby: Films. Current Management: Vesna Gorse. Address: Vankina 3/4, 41020 Zagreb, Croatia.

FRANZEN K B V Hawkey, b. 29 March 1946, Böda, Kalmar, Län, Sweden. Composer; Singer; Songwriter; Artist; Actor (Guitar, Keyboard, Accordion, Ten Sax). Career: Lea Riders Group, 1962-68; Jason's Fleece, 1970-71; Solo Performer, Theatremusic-composer and for radio and TV; Filmmusic, Dom Kallar Oss Mods (They Call Us Misfits). Compositions: LP: Visa Fran Djupvik, 1969; Visa Fran Gungor och Sand, 1970; Visa Fran och Till, 1971; Jason's Fleece, 1970; Visa av och Med, 1972; Smulvisor & Bitlatar, 1981; Det Blaser Pa Manen, 1985 Plötsligt Skulle Vi Skiljas, 1988. Recordings: Lea Riders Group, 1989; Manga Varv Kring Solen, CD, 1996. Honours: Stockholm City; Prize for Best Private Theatre Play, 1969; Konstnärsnämnden, Arts Grants Cttee Schlsps, 1971, 1975, 1985, 1986, 1989, 1990, 1992, 1993, 1996, 1997; STIM, Swedish Performing Rights Society, 1995, 1997. Memberships: Swedish Performing Rights Society; Swedish Society of Popular Music Composers; Swedish Artists and Musicians Interest Organisation; Svenska Teaterförbundet, Swedish Actors Equity Association. Hobbies: Nature; Reading. Current Management: Linnéa Musik Produktion. Address: Nygatan 5 nb, S-599 31 Odeshog, Sweden.

FRATER Josephine, b. 16 May 1963, Glasgow, Scotland. Singer; Composer; Musician (percussion). m. Stephen D Taylor, 6 Sept 1991. Musical Education: Goldsmiths University; Guildhall School of Music and Drama. Career: Joint owner, i.2.i Records with Steve Taylor; Co-run The Runners with Steve Taylor; Appeared on cable TV; Concerts include: Ronnie Scott's; The Jazz Cafe; UK tour; International tour, 1996. Compositions: Hours; Crooked Man; Be Yourself Tonight; Secret World; Journeying. Recordings: Album: Phonetic. Honours: Advanced Certificate Jazz and Pop Music; Postgraduate diploma, Jazz and Studio Music. Memberships: PRS; Musicians' Union. Hobbies: Travel; Gardening; Art; Cycling; Socialising. Address: PO Box 7038, London N3 2HF, England.

FREDERICKX Jan, b. 30 September 1971, Mol, Belgium. Singer; Songwriter; Musician (Bass, Guitar). Education: Ancient Latin and Greek Languages; Psychology; Socio-Cultural Sciences; Classical Guitar, Music Academy, Geel, Belgium, 2 years; Selftaught Bass Guitar. Career: Played in bands including: Hellsaw; MSD; Extreem; Acoustic Grinder; Concerts with: Napalm Death; Extreme Noise Terror; The Varukers; Death; The Gathering; Doom; John Peel-Session, BRTN Session; 3 official live videos, BRTN TV. Compositions: Agathocles: Riek Boois, 1988; Cabbalic Gnosticism, 1988; Disgorge, 1989; Fascination of Mutilation, 1989; If This is Cruel, 1989; Violent Noise Attack, 1990; Blood, 1990; Putrid Offal, 1990; Morbid Organs Mutilation, 1990; Nasum, 1990; Agarchy, 1991; Psycho, 1991; Violent Headache, 1992; Kompost, 1993; Distrust and Abuse, 1993; Nyctophobic, 1993; Man is the Bastard, 1993; Patareni, 1993; Audiorrea, 1993; Social Genocide, 1993; No Use

(Hatred), 1993; Punisher, 1994; Carcass Grinder, 1994; Plastic Grave, 1994; Back to 1987, 1994; Mincemongers in Barna, 194; Unholy Grave, 1996; Praparation H, 1996; Krush, 1996; Excruciating Terror, 1997; Shikabane, 1997; Theatric Symbolisation of Life, 1991; Black Clouds of Determinate, 1994; Black Sharp Daggers, 1995; Thanks for Your Hostility, 1996; Humarrogance, 1997. Honours: BRTN, Session, 1996; John Peel, Session, 1997; Kill Your Idols, CD, Tribute to Agathocles CD. Hobbies: Writing Poetry; Painting; Cooking; Workshops. Current Managements: Agathocles, Asberg 8, 2400 Mol, Belgium. Address: Agathocles, Asberg 8, 2400 Mol, Belgium.

FREDRICKSSON Marie, b. 29 May 1958, Sweden. Singer. 1 daughter. Career: Solo recording artist, 1980s; Formed Roxette with Per Gessle, 1986-; 21 million albums sold, 12 million singles sold worldwide; Appearances in Europe; North America; Central and South America; Television includes: The Tonight Show, NBC TV; MTV Unplugged. Recordings: Albums: Pearls Of Passion, 1986; Look Sharp!, 1988; Joyride, 1991; Tourism, 1992; Don't Bore Us, Get To The Chorus - Roxette's Greatest Hits, 1995; Singles include: The Look (US Number 1), 1989; Listen To Your Heart (Number 1, US), 1989; Dangerous, 1989; Dressed For Success, 1989; It Must Have Been Love, featured in film Pretty Woman (Number 1, US), 1990; Joyride (Number 1, US, Sweden, Germany, Netherlands, Australia, Canada), 1991; Fading Like A Flower (Number 2, US), 1991; The Big L, 1991; Spending My Time, 1991; Church Of Your Heart, 1992; How Do You Do!, 1992; Queen Of Rain, 1992; Almost Unreal, featured in film Super Mario Brothers, 1993; Sleeping In My Car, 1995. Current Management:Rascoff/Zysbalt Organization, 110 W 57th Street, New York, NY 10019, USA.

FREEMAN Bill, b. 10 Dec 1969, Liverpool, England. Musician (guitar); Composer. Musical Education: Sandown College, Liverpool. Career: Tours with band Adam's Family, including headline concerts at the Marquee Club, 1994; Live show for Leicester Cable TV, 1994. Composition: Urban Suite, Classical guitar composition. Recordings: with Adams Family: Singles: Sometimes I Wonder (EP), 1987; Frustration, 1994; Album: Disease, 1995. Memberships: PRS; Musicians' Union. Hobbies: Playing guitar in many different styles. Current Management: Loose Records. Address: PO Box 67, Runcorn, Cheshire WA7 4NL, England.

FREEMAN John David, b. 2 Jan 1955, Jarrow, Tyne and Wear, England. Musician (Bass Guitar); Vocalist; Songwriter; School Teacher. m. Alison Freeman, 11 Aug 1979, 2 sons. Education: Loughborough College of Education. Musical Education: Self-taught. Career: Bass Player, Vocalist and Co-writer of material for band, Havana Fireflies, playing at Glastonbury Festival, 1993 and 1994; Radio appearances include: Johnny Walker Show, and as unsigned band of the week on Steve Wright Show, BBC Radio 1, also airplay of album on GWR Radio; Various television appearances on HTV West shows, Spotlight and First Cut. Recording: Barbed Wire Prophets, by The Havana Fireflies. Membership: Musicians' Union. Hobby: Sport, especially cricket. Address: 40 High Street, Dilton Marsh, Wiltshire, England.

FREEMAN Lisa, b. 27 May 1951, Los Angeles, California, USA. Lyricist; Composer; Conductor; Teacher. m. Svend Garnaes, 4 July 1990, 1 son. Education: College, USA. Musical Education: Conservatory of Music, USA; Music Major, Denmark. Career: Lyricist for Jorgen Emborg; The Danish Radio Big Band; Niels Henning Orsted Pedersen; Niels Lan Doky; Hanne Boel; Composer, Svendborg Theatre; Compositions: Lyrics for albums: Frontlife; Heart Of Matter; Shadow Of Love; Ships In The Night;

Uncharted Land. Publications: Lyrics: Circle Of Songs, with Jorgen Emborg; Summer And Spring, by P Heise. Membership: Danish Jazz Beat and Folk Music Society. Hobbies: Piano and choir arrangements. Current Management: Stunt Records. Address: Klampenborgvej 3, 5700 Svendborg, Denmark.

FREHLEY Ace (Paul), b. 22 Apr 1951, Bronx, New York, USA. Musician (guitar). Career: Member, US rock group Kiss, 1973-82; Numerous US, UK, European and worldwide tours; Left Kiss following serious car accident, 1982; Founder, guitarist, Frehley's Comet, 1987-. Recordings: Albums with Kiss: Kiss, 1974; Dressed To Kill, 1975; Alive!, 1975; Destroyer, 1976; The Originals, 1976; Rock And Roll Over, 1976; Kiss Alive II, 1977; Love Gun, 1977; Double Platinum, 1978; Dynasty, 1979; Kiss Unmasked, 1980; Music From The Elder, 1981; Killers, 1982; Creatures Of The Night, 1982; Solo albums: Ace Frehley, 1978; Trouble Walking, 1989; with Frehley's Comet: Frehley's Comet, 1987; Live + 1, 1988; Second Sighting, 1989; Singles include: Rock'N'Roll All Nite; Beth; Detroit Rock City; Hard Luck Woman; Calling Dr Love; I Was Made For Lovin' You. Honours: Footprints at Grauman's Chinese Theatre, Hollywood, 1976; Gold Ticket, Madison Square Garden, 1979; Gold and Platinum discs. Current Management: The Sewitt Group, 17 Ash Court, Highland Mills, NY 10930, USA.

FRENCH Frank, b. 19 Aug 1952, Oakland, California, USA. Musician (piano); Composer. m. Carolyn Massonneau French, 19 Jan 1991. Education: 4 years college. Musical Education: San Francisco Conservatory of Music; San Francisco State University; Bachelor of Music. Career: Performances in United States, Canada, Europe, Australia; Public radio, television appearances; American and foreign music festival appearances. Compositions: Original compositions featured on La Bamboula, Frontiers; Lacumbia, 1992; Womba Bomba, 1995; Toca con Clave, suite for piano, 1997 Recordings: The Well Tempered Clavier, 48 preludes and fugues, by Bach; Tangos Of Ernesto Nazareth; La Bamboula; More American Souvenirs; Frontiers; (with David Thomas Roberts, Scott Kirby); Terra Verde, new music for piano solo with Scott Kirby and David Thomas Roberts; Creole Music, Piano duets with Scott Kirby; American Originals, music of louis Moreau Gottschalk, for solo piano. Memberships: BMI; Piano Technicians Guild. Hobbies: Brewing beer; Outdoor activities; Hiking and biking. Current Management: Artia Concerts, Sumner, Washington. Address: Frank French, PO Box 4034, Boulder, CO 80306, USA.

FRESU Paolo, b. 10 February 1961, Berchidda, Sardinia, Italy. Musician (Trumpet, Flugelhorn, Arr, Comp). Education: Electronics Expert, Certificate, University/DAMS, Bologna, Italy; Conservatory of Music, Cagliari, Sardinia March Band, 1972-80; Pop Music, 1976-80; Conservatory of Music, Certificate, 1982. Career: Professor, Siena Jazz National Seminars, 1985-; Jazz Univ courses at Terni, 1987-; Winter courses, Siena and sems in Nuoro, 1989-; Guest Soloist, many innovative jazz recording projects; Artistic Director, Time in Jazz Festival in Berchidda, 1988-; Eurojazz Concorso Internazionale per Giovani Musicisti Europei' in Oristano, 1994 & Jazz Seminary in Nuoro, 1989-. Recordings: Ostinato, 1984; Inner Voices, 1986; Live in Montpellier, 1980; Ensalada Mistica, 1994; Mythscapes, 1995; Night on the City, 1995; Wanderlust, 1997. Publications: The first 63 jazz compositions, 1989; 49 compositions, 1996. Honours: Best Italian Musician, 1990; First Italian Young Musician, 1994; Best European Musician, 1996. Hobbies: Literature; Poetry; Design; Movie. Current Management: Pannonica, Albani Vittorio, Bolzano, Italy. Address: PO Box 6, 40047, Riola, Italy.

FREY Glenn, b. 6 Nov 1948, Detroit, Michigan, USA. Musician (guitar); Vocalist. Career: Member, Longbranch Pennywhistle (duo with J D Souther), 1968-71; Founder member, The Eagles, 1971-. Recordings: with Longbranch Pennywhistle: Longbranch Pennywhistle, 1969; with The Eagles: The Eagles, 1972; Desperado, 1973; On The Border, 1974; One Of These Nights (Number 1, US), 1975; Their Greatest Hits 1971-75 (Number 1, US), 1976; Hotel California (Number 1, US), 1978; The Long Run, 1979; Eagles Greatest Hits, Vol 2, 1982; The Best Of The Eagles, 1985; Solo albums: No Fun Aloud, 1982; The Allnighter, 1984; Soul Searchin', 1992; Strange Weather, 1993; Singles include: Witchy Woman, 1972; Peaceful Easy Feeling, 1973; The Best Of My Love (Number 1, US), 1975; One Of These Nights (Number 1, US), 1975; Lyin' Eyes, 1975; Take It To The Limit, 1976; Hotel California (Number 1, US), 1977; Heartache Tonight (Number 1, US), 1979; The Long Run, 1980; I Can't Tell You Why, 1980; Seven Bridges Road, 1981; Solo hits: The Heat Is On (from film Beverly Hills Cop), 1985; You Belong To The City, 1986. Honours: Grammy Awards: Best Vocal Performance, 1976; Record Of The Year, Hotel California, Best Arrangement For Voices, 1978. American Music Awards, Favourite Album, 1977. Current Management: Peter M Lopez, c/o Sumitomo Bank Building, 15250 Ventura Blvd, PH 1220, Sherman Oaks, CA 91403, USA.

FRICK Bob Scott, b. 19 Apr 1940, Indiana, Pennsylvania, USA. Musician (guitar); Vocalist; Producer; Publisher; Minister. m. Ruth Cornman, 13 May 1961, 2 sons. Career: Play guitar, singer, throughout USA, Canada; Produce recordings for many artists; Publisher of hundreds of songs; Also duplicate tapes for many artists; Personal appearances are at churches, fairs; Appearances at Jerry Lewis Telethon; Grand Ole Opry (gospel); Videos on ACTS TV; Jerry Falwell and others. Recordings: Release Me (gospel); I Found Jesus In Nashville (tape and video); The King And I; You And Me Jesus. Publication: Message In Song (songbook). Memberships: ASCAP; BMI. Hobbies: Golf; Woodworking; Loves the water. Current Management: S&S Talent Agency. Address: 404 Bluegrass Avenue, Madison, TN 37115, USA.

FRICKIE Janie (Jane Fricke), b. 19 Dec 1947, South Whitley, Indiana, USA. Country Singer. m. Randy Jackson. Education: University. Career: Session singer, Los Angeles; Member, Lea Jane Singers, Nashville; Uncredited backing voice to Johnny Duncan; Solo recording artiste; Tours with Alabama; Regular session singer; Vocalist with own group Heartache. Recordings: US Country Number 1 hits: Don't Worry 'Bout Me, Baby; He's A Heartache (Looking For A Place To Happen); It Ain't Easy Bein' Easy; Tell Me A Lie; Other singles include: What're You Doing Tonight? Please Help Me I'm Falling; Albums: Singer Of Songs, 1978; Love Notes, 1979; From The Heart, 1980; I'll Need Someone To Hold Me When I Cry, 1981; Nice'n'Easy, with Johnny Duncan, 1980; Sleeping With Your Memory, 1981; It Ain't Easy, 1982; Love Lines, 1983; The First Word In Memory Is Me, 1984; Someone Else's Fire, 1985; Black And White, 1986; After Midnight, 1987; Saddle The Wind, 1988; Labor Of Love, 1989; Janie Fricke, 1991; Numerous recording sessions as backing vocalist include: with Johnny Duncan: Jo And The Cowboy; Stranger; Thinkin' Of A Rendevous; It Couldn't Have Been Any Better; I'll Get Over You, Crystal Gayle; My Way, Elvis Presley; (I'm A) Stand By My Woman Man, Ronnie Milsap; Here's Some Love, Tanya Tucker; I'd Love To Lay You Down, Conway Twitty; Duets include: Till The End, with Vern Gosdin; On My Knees, with Charlie Rich (US Country Number 1); A Place To Fall Apart, with Merle Haggard (US Country Number 1); All I want To Do In Life, with George Jones; The Cowboy And the Lady, Tommy Cash; From Time To Time, with Larry Gatlin; Who Cares?, with Ray Charles. Address:

c/o Janie Frickie Concerts, PO Box 798, Lancaster, TX 75146, USA.

FRIDAY Gavin. Singer; Songwriter. Career: Member, The Virgin Prunes; Solo artiste, 1990-. Compositions: Co-writer, film score: In The Name Of The Father; In production: Passion Of Darkly Noon; Angel Baby. Recordings: Solo albums: Each Man Kills The Thing He Loves, 1990; Adam & Eve, 1992; Shag Tobacco, 1995: Film soundtrack: The Boxer (wth Maurice Seezer), 1998. Address: c/o Island Records, 22 St Peters Square, London W6 9NW, England.

FRIPP Robert, b. 16 May 1946, Wimborne, Dorset, England. Musician (guitar); Composer; Record Producer. m. Toyah Wilcox, 16 May 1986. Career: Member, Ravens; The League Of Gentlemen; Founder member, Giles, Giles And Fripp, which became King Crimson, 1969-84; Regular UK, Europe, US and Far East tours; Collaborations with Brian Eno; The League Of Gentlemen, 1980-81; Solo recording artiste, 1979-; Founder, Guitar Craft guitar school, 1985; Reformed King Crimson, 1993-. Recordings: Albums: with Giles, Giles and Fripp: The Cheerful Insanity Of Giles, Giles And Fripp, 1968; with King Crimson: In The Court Of The Crimson King, 1969; In The Wake Of Poseidon, 1970; Lizard, 1971; Earthbound, 1972; Larks' Tongues In Aspic, 1973; Starless And Bible Black, 1974; Red, 1974; USA, 1975; Discipline, 1981; Beat, 1982; Three Of A Perfect Pair, 1984; Vrooom, 1995; Thrak, 1995; B'Boom, 1995; with Brian Eno: No Pussyfooting, 1975; Evening Star, 1976; with The League Of Gentlemen: The League Of Gentlemen, 1981; God Save The King, 1985; Solo albums: Exposure, 1979; God Save The Queen/Under Heavy Manners, 1980; Let The Power Fall, 1981; Robert Fripp And The League Of Crafty Guitarists, 1986; Network, 1987; Live II, 1990; Show Of Hands, 1991; The Bridge Between, 1995; Soundscapes - Live In Argentina, 1995; with FFWD (Fripp, Fehlman, Weston, Dr Alex): FFWD, 1994; with Andy Summers: I Advance Masked, 1982; Bewitched, 1984; with Toyah: Kneeling At The Shrine, 1986; The Lady And The Tiger, 1987; with David Sylvian: The First Day, 1993; Damage, 1994; Contributor, albums by David Bowie; Peter Gabriel; Daryl Hall; Producer: Gabriel; Hall; Roches; several experimental jazz releases. Current Management: Opium (Arts), 49 Portland Road, London W11 4LJ, England.

FRISCH Albert, b. 27 March 1927, New York, USA. Composer; Pianist; Saxophonist. Career: Saxophonist in nightclubs, on ocean liners & summer resorts; also entertainer, pianist & singer; Writer, weekly column, Music in print, Billboard magazine; Wrote words & music, songs, instrumentals, albums, shows & TV special material; Chief Collaborators: Roy Alfred, Buddy Bernier, Johnny Burke, Sylvia Dee, Buddy Kaye, Larry Kusick, Julian More, Allan Roberts, Al Neiburg, Bernard Spiro, Charles Tobias, Sid Wayne, Fred Wise; Songs & instrumental works: This Is No Laughing Matter; Two Different Worlds; I Won't Cry Anymore; Roses in the Rain; All Over the World; That's What They Meant By the Good Old Summertime; Monte Carlo Melody; Congratulations to Someone; Flowers Mean Forgiveness; The Show Must Go On; Winner Take All; Broadway at Basin Street; What Lies Over the Hill; The Language of Love; Just Married Today; Sipping Cider By the Zuyder Zee; Let It Rain; The Best President We Ever Had (pancho Maximillian Hernandez); The Cool School; The Wonderful World of Christmas; Come On, Come In; Late in December; Starry-Eyed and Breathless; Little Miss Irish; My Mother's Lullaby; She Never Left the Table; April and You; Something for Nothing; Let's Harmonize; Go You Where Go; Tears to Burn; The Same Old Moon; Here Comes That Heartache Again; The Melancholy Minstrel; Now; Palermo; Lovin' Up a Storm The Moment of Truth; Have Have to Believe in Someone; Weep for the Boy; Winter in Miami; Music From Out of Space;

If I'm Elected; Gregory's Chant; It Must Be Emily; Come Back to Rome; Idle Conversation; Always Love Me; I've Got Some Cryin' to Do; All I Get From You are Heartaches; A Chocolate Sundae on a Saturday Night; In Time; Not So Long Ago; My Need For You; He Came on a Long Long Journey; Wherefore Art Thou Romeo; Sweet Brown-Eyed Baby; What More Is There to Say; Give Me the Right; Unafraid; Four Walls, Two Windows, and One Broken Heart; He Cha Cha'd In; After the Fall; No Hard Feelings; Really O, Truly O; Mama, Teach Me to Do the Charleston; Io Canto; You Pass This Way Only Once; People, Places and Things; Fiddle Rock; The Hornet's Nest; Tunes for Muzak; TV Shows: My Love Song to You; Song of the Racoons; Bordello, SHow-Queen's Theatre, London; A Place Like This; Yourself; A Country Bride; Morality; Business Tango; Simple Pleasures; Art Should Be Art; Family Life; If You Should Leave Me; Madame Misia; All the Time in the World; I Love Me; The Way I See It; The Girl in Cabin 54; What Does It Takes; Can-Can Ballet; Hallucination Ballet; Show- Christy; When the Penny Poets Sing; A Somewhere Rainbow; Where's My Rainbow; To Please the Woman in Me; Grain of the Salt of the Earth; Until the Lives of You; Come Out Wherever You Are; Picture Me; The Morning After; It's a Lonesome Thing; All's Fair in Love and War; Great Company; With One Fell Swoop; Beach Ballet; The Heart's Wonder; Down the Hatch; Gallant Little Swearers' Be a Hero. Address: Myra Music Company, 177 White Plains Road - 33F, Tarrytown, NY 10591, USA.

FRISCHMANN Justine Elinor, b. 16 Sept 1966, London, England. Lead Singer; Songwriter. Education: Architecture, London University. Career: Member, Suede, briefly, 1990; Formed Elastica, 1991-; Numerous television and radio appearances include: Later With... Britpop Now, 1995; Tours: UK; USA; Canada; Europe; Concerts include T In The Park Festival, Glasgow, 1995. Recordings: Album: Elastica, 1995; Hit singles: Connection; Waking Up. Current Management: CMO Management. Address: Unit 32, Ransomes Dock, 35-37 Parkgate Road, London SW11 4NP, England.

FRISELL Bill, b. 18 Mar 1951, Baltimore, Maryland, USA. Musician (guitar, banjo, ukulele, bass). Musical Education: North Colorado University, 1969-71; Diploma, arranging, composition, Berklee College Of Music, Boston, 1977. Career: Played with artists including: Eberhard Weber; Mike Gibbs; Jan Garbarek; Charlie Haden; Carla Bley; John Scofield; Member, Power Tools (with Ronald Shannon Jackson, Melvin Gibbs); John Zorn's Naked City; The Paul Bley Quintet (with Paul Bley, Paul Motian, John Surman); Paul Motian Trio (with Paul Motian, Joe Lovano). Recordings: Albums: In Lane, 1983; Rambler, 1985; Lookout For Hope, 1988; Before We Were Born, 1989; Is This You?, 1990; Where In The World?, 1991; Have A Little Faith, 1993; Music From The Films Of Buster Keaton (comprising The High Sign/One Week and Go West), 1995; with Tim Berne: Theoretically, 1984; with John Zorn, George Lewis: News For Lulu, 1987; More News For Lulu, 1992; with Power Tools: Strange Meeting, 1987; with John Scofield: Grace Under Pressure, 1992; with Elvis Costello: Deep Dead Blue, Live At Meltdown, 1995; with Ginger Baker Trio: Going Home Again, 1995. Honour: Harris Stanton Guitar Award. Current Management: Songline/Tone Field Productions, 1649 Hopkins Street, Berkeley, CA 94707, USA.

FRISTORP Goran, . 26 May 1948, Skara, Sweden. m. 1 July 1975, 1 daughter. Education: Conservatory of Gothenbury and Framnas in Ojebyn. Career: Winner, European Song Contest, Sweden, 1973; Many television and radio appearances; 20 LPs and CDs. Compositions: J Belong; Lyrics: Hal David; Music: Goran Fristorp. Recordings: Sings Nils Ferlin; Atersken; Rintniag; Psalmer; Evert Taube; Flickan Från Fjärran.

Publications: Nils Perlin, 1975; Egna Lotar, 1974; Psalmer, 1989; Flickin fran Pistran, 1996. Honours: Evert Taube Prize, 1997; Several Artists Prizes. Memberships: STIM; SKAP; GRAMO (Norway); SAMI. Hobbies: Travelling; Food; Wine. Current Management: Stageway, Bergen Norway. Address: Box 37, 27603, Skillinge, Sweden.

FROSCH Wolfgang, b. 2 July 1960, Knittelfeld, Austria. Musician (bass); Backing Vocalist. m. Maria, 31 Mar 1989, 1 son, 2 daughters. Education: Carpenter. Musical Education: Self-taught, left hand bassist. Career: Member, Blues Pumpm, 1978-; Member, Giant Blonder, 1988-94; Tours, television and radio appearances throughout Europe. Recordings: Albums: with Giant Blonder: Colours Of Rock; with Blues Pumpm: Albums: Bluespumpm, 1979; Edlau, 1980; Village, 1981; Live With Friends, 1985; The 5th Ten Years Jubilee, 1987; Live At Utopia, 1988; Live With Friends, 1991; Birthday, 1991; Live In Vienna, 1992; The 5th, 1992; Living Loving Riding, 1994; Singles: Wolfgang Session And Song, 1980; Men From Milwaukee, 1993. Honours: Silbernes Ehrenzeicher, 1992; Third Best Blues Album Ö3 Rot-Weiss-Rote Critics Poll, Live In Vienna, 1992. Memberships: AKM; AUME; LSG. Hobbies: Children; Music; Reading. Current Management: Peter Steinbach, RGG Management.

FROST Per Christian, b. 30 Oct 1954, Aarhus, Denmark. Musician (guitar, bass guitar); Vocalist. m. Dorthe Th. Holtet, 25 July 1987, 2 sons. Education: 1 year, Art Academy; Musical Education: Self-taught. Career: Member, Gnags, 1974-; Tours: Europe; Africa; India; Cuba; Nicaragua; Numerous television appearances; Also solo artist, guest musician. Recordings: with Gnags, 17 albums; Solo albums: Ned Ad Gaden, 1979; Old Friend's Back, 1990; Breakin' Ice, 1995. Honours: Award of Honour, Danish Musicians' Union, 1988; IFPI Prize, (Danish Grammy), 1990. Memberships: DMF; DJBFA; KODA. Hobbies: Running; Painting. Current Management: Rock On International, Copenhagen, Denmark.

FROST Soren, b. 5 February 1965, Aarhus, Denmark. Musician (drums, percussion). Education: Drummer Collective, 10 Week Certificate Program, New York City, 1988. Career: Played Pop Rock, Jazz and Chorus Line, Sweet Charity Jesus Christ Superstar; Worked with Lillian Boutte, Dr John, Bob Berg, Eliane Elias, Lee Konitz, Bob Brookmeyer, Thad Jones, Slide Hampton, Dee Dee Bridgewater; Many TV and radio shows and tours of Japan, 1990, USSR, 1988, Thailand, 1991, USA, 1997. Recordings: Lillian Boutte: The Jazz Book; The Danish Radio Orchestra: Fusion Symphony; Nikolaj Bentzon: Brotherhood; Jazzgroup 1990 with Bob Berg: Live in Denmark, My Sisters Garden. Honours: Grants from Danish Companies to Go to New York. Current Management: Blegdamsvej 84 5th, DK-2100 Kobenhavn O, Denmark. Address: Blegdamsvej 84 5th, DK 2100 Kobenhavn O, Denmark.

FRUITBAT (Leslie Carter), b. 12 Feb 1958. Career: Founder member (with Jimbob), duo, Carter The Unstoppable Sex Machine (later billed as Carter USM), 1988-; International concerts, including US, Japan. Recordings: Albums: 101 Damnations, 1990; 30 Something, 1991; 1992 - The Love Album, 1992; Post Historic Monsters, 1994; Worry Bomb, 1995; Singles: Sheltered Life; Sherriff Fatman; Rubbish; Anytime, Anyplace, Anywhere; Bloodsports For All; After The Watershed. Current Management: Adrian Boss Promotions, 363-365 Harrow Road, London W9 3NA, England.

FRY Martin, b. 9 Mar 1958, Manchester, Lancashire, England. Singer; Record Producer. Education: English Literature, Sheffield University. Career: Launched fanzine, Modern Drugs, 1979; Lead singer, ABC, 1980-; UK and world tour, 1982; Featured in Julien Temple's film Man Trap, 1983; Subject, BBC documentary, That Was Then, This Is Now, 1990. Recordings: Albums with ABC: The Lexicon Of Love (Number 1, UK), 1982; Beauty Stab, 1983; How To Be A Zillionaire, 1985; Alphabet City, 1987; Up, 1989; Absolutely, 1990; Abracadabra, 1991; Skyscraping, 1997; Singles include: Tears Are Not Enough; Poison Arrow (Number 6, UK); The Look Of Love (Number 4, UK); All Of My Heart (Number 5, UK); That Was Then But This Is Now; Be Near Me; When Smokey Sings; The Night You Murdered Love; One Better World.

FRY Tristan Frederick Allan, b. 25 Oct 1946, London, England. m. Dorothy E Garland, 25 Oct 1993. Musical Education: Taught by Peter Allen, Royal Academy of Music and many amateur orchestras and groups, London. Career: Concerts with Sky in Europe; Australia; Asia; First group to play Westminster Abbey (televised concert); Concerts with Academy of St Martin In The Fields Orchestra around world. Compositions include: Connecting Rooms; Then And Now. Recordings: All Sky singles and albums; 3 recordings, Bartók's 2 piano and percussion concerto; Academy albums include award winning Amadeus; Film score albums include: James Bond, Pink Panther; Also recorded with many artists worldwide. Membership: Royal Society of Musicians.

FUGLER Jon. Vocalist; Musician; Sound Engineer. Founder member, Fluke, 1983-; Concerts include: UK tour, 1994; Glastonbury Festival; Appearances include: Smash Hits Poll Winners Party, with Björk; MTV Awards, with Björk. Recordings: Albums: The Techno Rose Of Blighty, 1991; Out (mini-album); Six Wheels On My Wagon; Oto, 1995; Singles: Thumper; Joni; Slid; Electric Guitar; Groovy Feeling; Bubble; Bullet; Remix, Big Time Sensuality, Björk. Address: c/o Circa Records, Kensal House, 553-579 Harrow Road, London W10 4RH, England.

FUNKEY, b. 20 July 1961, Sint-Niklaas, Belgian. Musician (Synthesizer, Singer). Education: Selftaught. Career: Gigs: debut, Keyboard player and singer, The Soap, 1992; Oortcloud, 1993; Radio: Several times on Bassta, 1995-96; TV: Prettig Gestoord, 1996. Publications: Oortcloud: Raindances, 1995; Colour Dot: Floating Atmospheres, 1997. Honour: Studio Brussels' Candidate for Debut Rock Contest. Memberships: SABAM; ZAMU. Hobby: Internet. Current Management: Higher Grow Productions, Damstraat 2, B9100 Sint-Niklaas, Belgium.

FUREY Eddie, b. 23 Dec 1944, Tipperary, Ireland. Musician (guitar, mandola, mandolin, harmonica, fiddle, bodhran); Vocalist. m. Bibi, 5 children. Career: Member, duo, with brother Finbar, 1960s; Joined Clancey Brothers, US tour, 1969; Member, Tam Linn, with Davey Arthur, Paul Furey; Apperances include: Cambridge Folk Festival; Member, The Fureys and Davey Arthur, 1980. Recordings: Albums: The Sound Of The Fureys And Davey Arthur, 1981; When You Were Sweet Sixteen, 1982; Steal Away, 1983; In Concert, 1984; Golden Days, 1984; At The End Of The Perfect Day, 1985; The First Leaves Of Autumn, 1986; The Fureys Finest, 1987; The Fureys Collection, 1989; The Scattering, 1989; The Very Best Of, 1991; The Winds Of Change, 1992; with Finbar Furey: The Dawning Of The Day, 1970; Singles include: When You Were Sweet Sixteen, 1981; Green Fields of France; Red Rose Cafe. Membership: IMRO. Hobby: Golf. Current Management: Joe McCadden Promotions, Dublin. Address: 19 Stockton Green, Castleknock, Dublin 15, Ireland.

FUREY Finbar, b. 28 Sept 1946, Dublin, Ireland. Musician (uilleann pipes, banjo, whistles, flute); Vocalist. Career: Member, duo with Eddie Furey, 1960s; Played clubs, radio work; Joined Clancey Brothers, US tour, 1969; European tours, 1972; Joined Tam Linn, with Eddie and Paul Furey, Davey Arthur; Appeared at Cambridge Folk Festival; Later became The Fureys and Davey Arthur, 1980-. Recordings: Albums: The Cisco Special, 1960; Songs Of Woody Guthrie, 1961; I Ain't Got No Home, 1962; The Sound Of The Fureys And Davey Arthur, 1981; When You Were Sweet Sixteen, 1982; Steal Away, 1983; In Concert, 1984; Golden Days, 1984; At The End Of A Perfect Day, 1985; The First Leaves Of Autumn, 1986; The Fureys Finest, 1987; The Fureys Collection, 1989; The Scattering, 1989; The Very Best Of, 1991; The Winds Of Change, 1992; with Eddie Furey: The Dawning Of The Day, 1972; Solo album: Love Letters, 1990; Singles include: When You Were Sweet Sixteen, 1981. Address: c/o Joe McCadden Promotions, 19 Stockton Green, Castleknock, Dublin 15, Ireland.

FUREY George, b. 11 June 1951, Dublin, Ireland. Vocalist; Musician (guitar, accordion, mandola, autoharp, whistles). m. Mary, 1972, 3 sons, 3 daughters. Career: Member, The Buskers, 1972; Later became The Furey Brothers; TV appearances in the UK and Ireland. Recordings: Albums: The Cisco Special, 1960; Songs Of Woody Guthrie, 1961; I Ain't Got No Home, 1962; The Sound Of The Fureys And Davey Arthur, 1981; When You Were Sweet Sixteen, 1982; Steal Away, 1983; In Concert, 1984; Golden Days, 1984; At The End Of Perfect Day, 1985; The First Leaves Of Autumn, 1986; The Fureys Finest, 1987; The Fureys Collection, 1989; The Scattering, 1989; The Very Best Of The Fureys And Davey Arthur, 1991; The Winds Of Change, 1992; Singles include: When You Were Sweet Sixteen; I Will Love You (Every Time When We Are Gone); Green Fields of France; Red Rose Cafe. Membership: IMRO. Hobby: Golf. Current Management: Joe McCadden Promotions, Dublin. Address; 19 Stockton Green, Castleknock, Dublin 15, Ireland.

FUREY Paul, b. 6 May 1948, Dublin, Ireland. Musician (accordion, melodeon, concertina, whistles); Vocalist. m. Catherine, 1977, 3 sons. Career: Member, The Buskers (with George Furey, Davey Arthur), 1972; Member, Tam Linn; Appeared at Cambridge Folk Festival; Member, The Fureys and Davey Arthur, 1980-; Mbr, The Furey Brothers; TV appearances in the UK and Ireland. Recordings: Albums: The Cisco Special, 1960; Songs Of Woody Guthrie, 1961; I Ain't Got No Home, 1962; When You Were Sweet Sixteen, 1982; Steal Away, 1983; In Concert, 1984; Golden Days, 1984; At The End Of A Perfect Day, 1985; The First Leaves Of Autumn, 1986; The Scattering, 1989; Various compilations; Singles include: When You Were Sweet Sixteen, 1981; Green Fields of France; Red Rose Cafe. Membership: IMRO. Hobbies: Golf; Reading. Current Management: Joe McCadden Promotions, Dublin. Address: 19 Stockton Green, Castleknock, Dublin 15, Ireland.

FURIC Stephane, b. 15 July 1965, Paris, France. Composer. m. Laurence Horvilleur, 25 July 1992, 2 sons. Musical Education: Diploma in Professional Music, Berklee College of Music, Boston, USA; Private studies with William H Curtis, David Liebman. Career: Concerts including international jazz festivals, tours, radio shows, with Stephane Furic Project (also featuring Chris Cheek, Patrick Goraguer, Jim Black); Hiroshi Minami; Philippe Le Baraillec; Antonio Hart; Guillaume Orti (Europe, USA, Japan); Television shows. Compositions: Kishinev, 1990; Gorag' Rag, 1991; Suite of Dances, 1994; Song of the Open Road, 1994; Song of the Universal, 1994. Recordings: Kishinev, 1991; The Twitter-Machine, 1993; Crossing Brooklyn Ferry, 1995. Memberships: BMI; SACEM (as writer and publisher). Current Management: Limbo Jazz, 505 Bow Street, Elkton, MD 21921, USA. Address: 227 Front Street, Brooklyn, NY 11201, USA.

FYFFE William John Angus, b. 18 Sept 1927, Margate, Kent, England. Musician (piano); Musical Director. m. (1) Michelle Franks, 1951, 1 son, 1 daughter; (2) Sue Addams, 1968, 1 son, 1 daughter; Present partner, Anthea Askey. Education: George Watson's College, Edinburgh. Career: Son of Will Fyffe, comedian, writer of song I Belong To Glasgow; Joined Rank Organisation film studios, 1948; Moved to Chappells as song plugger; A&R, Decca Records; Personal accompanist to artists including: Allan Jones, Josef Locke, Evelyn Laye, Frankie Vaughn, Petula Clark, Ronnie Hilton, 1950s-1970s; Senior MD, Triumph Productions; In Concert act with Anthea Askey; Numerous appearances, television, radio and stage. Compositions: Music score for Glasgow Belongs To Me (working title); Songs include: My September; With A Love Like Ours. Memberships: PRS; BASCA. Hobbies: Photography; Swimming; Travel. Address: Appletree Lodge, Golden Acre, Angmering On Sea, West Sussex BN16 1QP, England.

G

G Kenny (Kenneth Gorelick), b. 1959, Seattle, Washington, USA. Musician (saxophone); Composer. Education: Accounting, University of Washington. Career: European tour with Franklin High School Band, 1974; Musician with Barry White's Love Unlimited Orchestra, 1976; Backing musician, numerous artistes including: Whitney Houston; Natalie Cole; Aretha Franklin; Member, Cold, Bold and Together; Member, jazz fusion group Jeff Lorber Fusion; Solo artiste, 1981-; Regular collaborations with Michael Bolton, including US tour, 1990. Recordings: Solo albums: Kenny G, 1982; G Force, 1983; Gravity, 1985; Duotones, 1986; Silhouette, 1988; Kenny G Live, 1989; Breathless, 1992; with Michael Bolton: Soul Provider, 1989; Time, Love And Tenderness, 1991. Honours: Multi-platinum records. Current Management: Turner Management Group, 3500 W Olive Avenue, Suite 690, Burbank, CA 91505, USA.

GABRIEL (Gabriel J Maciocia), b. 8 Oct 1948, Providence, Rhode Island, USA. Record Producer; Songwriter. Education: Masters Degree, RIC, 1972; Musical Education: Masters in arranging and composition of music. Career: Producer: Budweiser Girls Band (Single of Week, Cashbox Magazine); Produced 18 albums; Produced for Joey Welz of Caprice Records; Also, Four Tops, for Arista, Warner, Slack Records. Recordings: Sexy Lady; Four Tops; Crying Shame; Gloria Gaynor; Elvis Is Smiling. Publications: Whisper Pines (novel). Honours: Single of Week, Nov 1988, Cashbox Magazine. Memberships: BMI; ASCAP. Hobby: Snorkelling. Current Management: Caprice Records, Lititz PA, Joey Welz. Address: 108 Humbert Street, North Providence, RI 02911, USA.

GABRIEL Gilles (Blacky), b. 1 Nov 1946, Clermont Ferrand, France. Musician (drums). Divorced, 1 son, 1 daughter. Musical Education: Self-taught; Percussion, double bass, Music High School, Nancy, 1968-69. Career: First professional appearance, cabaret, Nancy, 1967; Member, Dance Orchestra, 1967-; Appearances include: World Circus Festival, Nancy, 1968; Casinos include: Vichy; Châtel Guyon; Cruise Ships: Massalia; Mermoz (with Isabelle Aubret, Nicole Croisille); Azur; Meridien Hotels: Dakar (with Francis Lemarque); Abu Dhabi; Accompanied Pierre Douglas, Michel Lebb, Monte Carlo (sporting), 1978; Concerts with US musicians: Hal Singer; Benny Waters; John Littleton; Mickey Backer; Stars Of Faith; French musicians: Michel Hausser; Dany Doriz; Laurent Gianez; Françoise Pujol; Eddy Gaddum (Surinam); Member, big bands includng Swing Orchestra; Packard Blues: First sets: Toots Thielemans (Belgium): Mint Julep (UK): Jimmy Johnson (US); Big Wheeler (US); Jaguars; Many concerts in France, Germany, Luxembourg, Belgium; Jazz festivals include: Nancy; Strasbourg; Many concerts with jazzmen in John's Place, Saarbrücken, Germany; with Eddy Gaddum (Jazz Combo) concerts in Luxemburg, Germany, Belgium; Jazz Festival, Luxemburg, 1995; Teacher, music school, private lessons; Leader, Myster Black (jazz), 1989-; Jaguars, 1995. Membership: SLAM. Address: 6 Rue du Maréchal Oudinot, 54000 Nancy, France.

GABRIEL Juan (Alberto Aguilera Valadéz), b. 7 Jan 1950, Parácuaro, Michoacán, Mexico. Singer; Songwriter. Recordings: Singles include: Perdoname (Forgive Me); Lagrimas Y Lluvia (Tears And Rain); La Costumbre (The Habit); Amor Eterno (Eternal Love); Pero Que Necesitad (But The Need); Over 50 albums including: Juan Gabriel En El Palacio De Bellas Artes; Debo Hoceria; Gracias Por Esperar. Current Management: Hauser Entertainment Inc. Address:

PO Box 978, 11003 Rooks Road, Pico Rivera, CA 90660, USA.

GABRIEL Peter, b. 13 Feb 1950, Cobham, Surrey, England. Singer; Songwriter. Career: Founder member, Genesis, 1969-1975; Appearances include: with Genesis: Reading Festival, 1971, 1972, 1973; UK and US tours; Solo artiste, 1975-; Solo appearances include: Worldwide tours; Knebworth II, 1978; Reading Festival, 1979; Inaugurator, WOMAD Festival Bath, 1982-; Amnesty International benefit tour, 1987; Hurricane Irene Benefit, Japan, 1987; Prince's Trust Rock Gala, 1988; Nelson Mandela tribute concerts, Wembley, 1988, 1990; Senegal (with Youssou N'Dour), 1991; The Simple Truth concert for Kurdish refugees, Wembley, 1991. Compositions include: Co-writer: Bully For You, Tom Robinson; Listen To The Radio, Tom Robinson; Animals Have More Fun, Jimmy Pursey; Film scores: Birdy, 1985; Last Temptation Of Christ, 1989. Recordings: Albums with Genesis: From Genesis To Revelation, 1969; Foxtrot, 1972; Genesis Live, 1973; Selling England By The Pound, 1973; Nursery Crime, 1974; The Lamb Lies Down On Broadway, 1974; Solo albums include: 4 albums all entitled Peter Gabriel, 1977-82; Peter Gabriel Plays Live, 1983; So, 1986; Passion, 1989; Shaking The Tree - Sixteen Golden Greats, 1990; Us, 1992; Secret World (interactive CD), 1995; Featured on: All This And World War II, 1975; Exposure, Robert Fripp, 1979; Conspiracy Of Hope (Amnesty International), 1986; Set, Youssou N'Dour, 1989; Exile, Geoffrey Oryema, 1990; It's About Time, Manu Katche, 1992; Until The End Of The World, (soundtrack), 1992; Tower Of Song (Leonard Cohen tribute), 1995; Compiler, Plus From Us, 1993; Singles include: Solsbury Hill; Games Without Frontiers; Shock The Monkey; Sledgehammer; In Your Eyes; Don't Give Up (duet with Kate Bush); Biko; Big Time; Red Rain; Digging In The Dirt; Steam; Blood Of Eden; Kiss That Frog; Contributor, Sun City, Artists United Against Apartheid, 1985; Rainbow Warriors, 1989; Until The End Of The World (soundtrack), 1991; Give Peace A Chance, the Peace Choir, 1991. Honours: Ivor Novello Awards: Outstanding Contribution To British Music, 1983; Best Song, 1987; BRIT Awards: Best British Male Artist, Best British Music Video, Sledgehammer, 1987; Best Producer, 1993; 9 Music Video Awards for Sledgehammer, and Video Vanguard Trophy, 1987; Grammy Awards: Best New Age Performance, 1990; Best Short Form Video, 1993. Address: c/o Real World Inc., Real World Studios, Box, Wiltshire SN13 8PL, England.

GABRIELLE. Singer; Songwriter. Career: Solo recording artiste, 1993-; US tour, 1994; UK Tour, 1996; Performed with Paul Weller. Recordings: Albums: Find Your Way, 1994; New album due 1996; Hit singles: Dreams, 1994; Give Me A Little More Time, 1996. Honour: BRIT Award, Best Newcomer, 1994. Current Management: Johnny Lawes Management, 18 All Saints Road, Unit 8, London W11 1HH, England.

GAGE Peter, b. 31 August 1954, London, England. Musician (Guitar, Keyboards); Producer; Arranger; Programmer; Engineer. m. 1) Elkie Brooks, 2) Ruby James, 15 August 1996. Education: Eltham College, London, England; BSc, Computing, University of Westminster, London. Musical Education: O Level Music; Grade 5 Classical Piano. Career: Formed and Lead, Geno Washington and the Ram Jam Band; Formed Dada and Vinegar Joe; Featuring Robert Palmer and Elkie Brooks; 1973: Musical Director for Elkie Brooks; Commenced Production, Engineering career with Debut LP for Joan Armatrading, 1974; TVs including Best of the Old Grey Whistle Test. Compositions: She's Lost You, for film, Less Than Zero; Hazy Shade of Winter, Bangles; Black Smoke, Calumet, UK Top 20, 1972. Recordings: Back To the Night, Joan Armatrading, album, 1974; Wrecking Crew, album;

Johnny Remember Me, The Meteors, 1985; Live at the Klubfoot, 1985-87. Hobby: Counting money. Current Management: c/o Stamina Management. Address: 47 Prout Grove, London NW10 1PU, England.

GAHAN David, b. 9 May 1962, Epping, England. Musician (Singer). m. 1) Joanne Fox, 4 August 1985, 1 son, 2) Theresa Conroy, 11 April 1992. Career: Founder Member, Depeche Mode, 1980-. Recordings: 11 Top Ten Singles include: Just Can't Get Enough, 1981; See You, 1982; Everything Counts, 1983; People Are People, 1984; Master and Servant, 1984; Enjoy the Silence, 1990; I Feel You, 1993; Condemnation, 1993; In Your Room, 1994; Barrel of A Gun, 1997; It's No Good, 1997; 11 Top Ten Albums include: Speak and Spell, 1981; A Broken Frame, 1982; Construction Time Again, 1983; Some Great Reward, 1984; The Singles 81-85, 1985; Black Celebration, 1986; Music For the Masses, 1987; 101, 1989; Violator, 1990; Songs of Faith and Devotion, 1993; Ultra, 1997. Honour: BPI Brit Award, Enjoy the Silence, 1991. Hobby: Painting. Current Management: Jonathon Kessler, Baron Inc, 111 West 67th Street, Suite 37F, New York, NY 10023, USA. Address: First Floor, Regent House, 106 Marylebone High Street, London W1M 3DB, England.

GALANIN Sergey, b. 16 Nov 1961, Moscow, Russia. Singer; Songwriter; Musician (Guitar, Bass). m. Olga Galanina, 5 Feb 1982, 1 son. Education: Railroad College. Musical Education: Music School. Career: Member of various bands including: Redkaya Ptitsa, Gulliver, Brigada S, Brigadiry Ser'ga; Regular tours in Russia, and appearances at festivals; Concerts in Finland, 1987; Tours of Germany and USA, 1989; Concerts in Poland and Czechoslovakia; Played at Moscow Musik Peace Festival in 1989 with Bon Jovi, Scorpions, Ozzy and others. Recordings: All This Is Rock 'N' Roll, by Brigada S; Rivers, by Brigada S; I Adore Jazz, by Brigada S; Dog's Waitz, by Ser'ga, 1994; Ser'ga, 1995. Hobby: Studio Work. Current Management: Dmitri Griosman. Address: 121309 Moscow, Novozavodskaya Street 27, Russia.

GALLAGHER Benny, b. Largs, Ayrshire, Scotland. Singer; Songwriter; Musician (guitar). Career: Songwriting partnership with Graham Lyle, 1960s-; Member, McGuinness Flint, 1969-71; Folk duo, Gallagher and Lyle, 1972-79; Solo artiste, 1980-. Compositions: Co-writer with Graham Lyle: Mr Heartbreak's Here Instead, Dean Ford; International, Mary Hopkins; for McGuinness Flint: When I'm Dead And Gone; Malt And Barley Blues; for Gallagher and Lyle: Heart On My Sleeve; I Wanna Stay With You. Recordings: Albums: with Gallagher And Lyle: Gallagher & Lyle, 1972; Willie And The Lap Dog, 1973; Seeds, 1973; The Last Cowboy, 1974; Breakway, 1976; Love On The Airways, 1977; Showdown, 1978; Gone Crazy, 1979; Lonesome No More, 1979; The Best Of, 1980; Heart On My Sleeve, 1991; Singles: I Wanna Stay With You, 1976; Heart On My Sleeve, 1976.

GALLAGHER Eve, b. 12 Feb 1956, Sunderland, England. Singer. Education: Drama at College; Language Schools; Swiss Schools. Musical Education: Opera lessons. Career: Actress, singer, various West End musicals include: Hair; Oh Calcutta; Signed by, and co-writer with Boy George, More Protein Records. Recordings: Hit Dance single: Love Come Down, 1991; Album: Woman Can Have It, 1995. Honours: Best Actress in Shakespeare aged 18: Queen Margaret in Richard III. Hobbies: Opera; Biographies; Cooking; Languages. Current Management: Action Artist Management, Förrlibuckstrasse 66, 8005 Zurich, Switzerland. Address: 7 Pepys Court, 84 The Chase, London SW4, England.

GALLAGHER Liam, b. 1972, Burnage, Manchester, England. Vocalist; Musician (guitar, keyboards). m. Patsy Kensit. Career: Founder member, Oasis, 1991-; Support tours with Verve; Concerts include: Glastonbury Festival, 1994; US debut, Wetlands, New York; Earls Court, London (UK's largest-ever indoor concert), 1995; Regular tours, UK, Europe, US. Recordings: Albums: Definitely Maybe, 1994; What's The Story (Morning Glory)?, 1995; Be Here Now, 1997; Singles: Supersonic, 1994; Shakermaker, 1994; Cigarettes And Alcohol, 1994; Live Forever, 1994; Whatever, (Number 3, UK), 1994; Some Might Say (Number 1, UK), 1995; Wonderwall (Number 2, UK), 1995; Roll With It (Number 2, UK), 1995; Don't Look Back In Anger (Number 1, UK), 1996; D'You Know What I Mean, (Number 1, UK), 1997. Honours: BRIT Awards: Best Newcomers, 1995; Best Album, Best Single, Best Video, Best British Group, 1996; BRIT Nominations: Best Group, Best Album; Q Awards: Best New Act, 1994; Best Live Act, 1995. 2 Multi-Platinum albums. Current Management: Ignition, 54 Linhope Street, London NW1 6HL, England.

GALLAGHER Noel, b. 1967, Burnage, Manchester, England. Singer; Songwriter; Musician (guitar). m. Meg Matthews. Career: Roadie, guitar technician, Inspiral Carpets, 1990-93; Member, Oasis, 1991-; Full-time member, 1993-; Debut performance, Boardwalk, Manchester, 1991; Support tours with Verve; Concerts include: Glastonbury Festival, 1994; US debut, Wetlands, New York, 1994; Earl's Court, London (UK's largest ever indoor concert), 1995; Regular tours, UK; Europe; US. Recordings: Albums: Definietely Maybe, 1994; What's The Story (Morning Glory)?, 1995; Be Here Now, 1997; Hit singles: Supersonic, 1994; Shakermaker, 1994; Cigarettes And Alcohol, 1994; Live Forever, 1994; Whatever, (Number 3, UK), 1994; Some Might Say (Number 1, UK), 1995; Wonderwall (Number 2, UK), 1995; Roll With It (Number 2, UK), 1995; Don't Look Back In Anger (Number 1, UK), 1996; D'You Know What I Mean, (Number 1, UK), 1997. Honours: BRIT Awards: Best Newcomers, 1995; Best British Group, Best Album, Best Single, Best Video, 1996; BRIT Nominations: Best Group; Best Album; Q Awards: Best New Act, 1994; Best Live Act, 1995; 2 Multi-Platinum albums; Music Week Award, Top Songwriter, 1996. Current Management: Ignition Management, 54 Linhope Street, London NW1 6HL, England.

GANC David, b. 24 May 1958, Rio De Janeiro, Brazil. Musician (flute and saxophone); Arranger. m. Monique C Aragao, 1 son. Musical Education: Graduate, Music, Federal University of Rio De Janeiro; BA Professor of Music, Berklee College of Music; Flute pro-art Semibars (Odette Ernest Dia), Norton Morozonicz, Federal University of Rio with C Noltzenlogel, Berklee College with Joe Viola, Gary Burton; Harmony with John Neschling. Career: Side musician, recording and playing with artist including: Stevie Wonder (Free Jazz Festival '95); Gal Costa; Simone; Paulo Moura; Luiz Melodia; Nivaldo Ornelas; Elba Ramalho; Geraldo Azevedo; Monique Aragao; Emílio Santiago; Recording musician at Globo TV; Special radio programme with David Ganc Quartet at Radio Mec; Played as guest saxophonist, Brazilian Symphony Orchestra; Also from Brasilia. Recordings: Solo album: Brazilian Ballads, 1996; Solo track at Contemporary Woodwind Brazilian Players, 1994; More than 60 CDs and records, as musician; Recorded for movies, theatre, ballet soundtracks. Hobbies: Literature; Cinema. Current Management: Zillion Prod Art LTDA. Address: R Miguel Couto 134/404, Rio de Janeiro RJ, Brazil.

GANLEY Allan, b. 11 Mar 1931, Tolworth, Surrey, England. Musician (drums); Arranger; Composer. m. June, 15 Aug 1970, 1 daughter. Musical Education: Composing, arranging, Berklee School Of Music, Boston, USA, 1970.

Career: Started 1953, with big bands of Jack Parnell; Ambrose; Geraldo; John Dankworth; Own small band, later joined The Tubby Hayes Quintet; Accompanied many American artistes, including: Stan Getz; Ronnie Scott; Clark Terry; Performed with: Al Haig; Dizzy Gillespie; Bobby Brookmeyer; George Shearing; Peggy Lee; Blossom Dearie; The Pizza Express All-Star Band; Dave Shepherd Quintet; Stephane Grappelli; Carol Kidd; Cleo Laine and John Dankworth; 10 years in Bermuda. Compositions: Composed, arranged and conducted for BBC Radio Orchestra; BBC Radio Big Band; Jack Sharpe Orchestra; Arrangements for Marion Montgomery; Carol Kidd; Elaine Delmar; Georgie Fame. Recordings with: Henry Mancini; Robert Farnon; George Shearing; Yehudi Menuhin; Stephane Grappelli; Nelson Riddle; 2 albums with Scott Hamilton; Recorded in New York with Jim Hall. Honours: Melody Maker Poll winner, several times, 1950s-60s; British Jazz Awards, 1980s, 1990s. Hobbies: Keen tennis player; Studying scores. Address: 5 Asher Drive, Ascot, Berkshire, England.

GANNEY Paul Sefton, b. 11 Feb 1958, Kettering, Northamptonshire, England. Medical Physicist; Musician (bass guitar); Sound Engineer; Producer. m. Mary Blackhurst, 24 July 1983, divorced. Education: MSc (Maths); Certificate Education. Career: First ever Greenbelt Fringe, 1980; Toured with Youth for Christ, 1982, 1983; Crossfire Festival, 1992, 1994; May Day Festival, Hull, 1986-1995; Set up Small And Hairy, 1989; Harland Hamstrings, 1996-. Recordings: Rock, Whitegold, 1992. Membership: Musicians' Union. Hobbies: Recording; PA/lights. Address: 31 Ferry Lane, Woodmansey, North Humberside HU17 0SE, England.

GANNON Oliver, b. 23 March 1943, Dublin, Ireland. Jazz Musician (guitar). m. 14 Feb 1979, 1 son, 1 daughter. Education: 2 years, Engineering, University of Manitoba. Musical Education: BMus, Berklee College of Music, Boston, USA. Career: Lives and performs in Vancouver area; Played at major jazz festivals worldwide including Montreux, Switzerland; Concord, USA; North Sea, Netherlands; Toronto; Quebec; Montreal; Winnipeg; Vancouver; 3 Russian tours with Fraser MacPherson Quartet. Recordings: with Fraser MacPherson: Live At The Planetarium; Live From Montreux; I Didn't Know About You; Indian Summer; Honey And Spice; Encore; In The Tradition; with Ian MacDougall Quartet: Rio; Three; also albums with George Robert Quintet; Pacific Salt; Fred Stride; Gary Guthman; Charles Mountford; Oliver Gannon. Honour: JUNO Award, Best Jazz Album, I Didn't Know About You, 1982. Memberships: SOCAN; Musicians' Association. Hobbies: Golf; Computer programming. Address: 2781 McKenzie Avenue, White Rock, BC V4A 3H5, Canada.

GARBAREK Anja, b. 24 July 1970, Oslo, Norway. Singer; Songwriter. Recordings: Album: Velkommen Inn, including 11 original songs, 1992. Membership: TONO. Current Management: Gunnar Eide A/S. Address: Gunnar Eide A/S, Sonja Henies Plass 2, 0185 Oslo, Norway.

GARBAREK Jan, b. 4 Mar 1947, Norway. Musician (saxophone); Songwriter; Record Producer. Musical Education: Self-taught saxophone. Career: Group with Jon Christensen, Arild Andersen, Terje Rypdal, 1960s; Played with: Keith Jarrett's Belonging, Ralph Towner, 1970s; Leader, own groups, featuring Bill Frisell, Eberhard Weber, Nana Vasconcelos, 1980s; Also played with: Don Cherry; George Russell. Recordings: Esoteric Circle, 1969; Afric Pepperbird, 1971; Triptykon, 1972; Sart, 1972; Dis, 1977; Places, 1978; Photo With, 1979; Eventyr, 1980; Paths, Prints, 1982; Wayfarer, 1983; Works, 1984; It's OK To Listen To The Gray Voice, 1985; All Those Born With Wings, 1986; Legend Of The Seven Dreams, 1988; I Took Up The Runes, 1990; Twelve Moons, 1993; Visible

World, 1996; with Keith Jarrett: Belonging; My Song; Luminesence; Arbour Zena; with Ralph Towner: Solstice; Sounds And Shadows; with George Russell: Othello Ballet Suite; Trip To Prillarguri; Electronic Sonata For Souls Loved By Nature; with L Shankar: Song For Everyone; Art Lande: Red Lanta, 1974; with Bobo Stenson: Witchi-Tai-To, 1974; Dansere, 1976; with Charlie Haden and Egberto Gismonti: Magico, 1980; Folksongs, 1981; with Kjell Johnsen: Aftenland, 1980; with Agnes Buen Garnås: Rosensfole, 1991; with Ustad Fateh Ali Khan: Ragas And Sagas, 1993; with The Hilliard Ensemble: Officium, 1994; with Anouar Brahem, Madar, 1994.

GARBUTT Vin, b. South Bank, Middlesbrough, England. Folk Musician (guitar, tin-whistle); Singer; Songwriter; Humorist. Career: Professional musician, songwriter, 1969-; Appearances include: USA; Canada; Australia; Hong Kong; Indonesia; Europe; New Zealand; Bermuda; Festivals worldwide including: Cambridge; Edinburgh; Wath; Auckland; Fylde; Television show, Small Folk, Yorkshire TV (proceeds to Save The Children Fund). Recordings: Albums include: The Valley Of Tees, 1972; Young Tin Whistle Pest, 1974; King Gooden, 1976; Eston California, 1978; Tossin' A Wobbler, 1978; Little Innocents, 1983; Shy Tot Pommy, 1986; When The Tide Turns, 1989; The South Banker Show, 1991; The Bypass Syndrome, 1992; Bandalised, 1994; Plugged, 1995; Video: The South Banker Show, 1991. Current Management: c/o Jim McPhee, Acorn Entertainments. Address: Winterfold House, 46 Woodfield Road, Kings Heath, Birmingham B13 9UJ, England.

GARCIA Antonio, Associate Professor; Composer. Career: Associate Professor of Music, Northwestern University; Freelance Trombonist, BassTrombonist, Pianist; Scat-Singer with Jazz Bands and Choirs; Adjudicated Festivals and Presented Clinics Internationally, including Music Advocacy and Jazz Pedagogy Workshops for Educators of Canada and Australia. Honour: Excellence in Undergraduate Teaching Award, Northern Illinois University, 1992. Memberships: The Midwest Clinic; Past President, Illinois Unit of IAJE; Past International Co-Chair for Curriculum and for Vocal, Instrumental Integration. Address: Northwestern University School of Music, 1965 Campus Drive South, REG Hall, Evanston, IL 60208-2400, USA.

GARCIA Dean, b. 3 May 1958, London, England. m. J P Fletcher, 1 son, 1 daughter. Career: World tours: Eurythmics; Sinead O'Connor; Television tours: Bryan Ferry; Curve; Own band, radio, television, world touring; Television: Ian Dury; Tour: Japan. Recordings: Albums: Curve: Doppleganger; Cuckoo; Public Fruit; Eurythmics: Touch; Be Yourself Tonight; Mick Jagger: Primitive Cool; Lethal Weapon 1, film soundtrack; Gang Of Four: Tattoo; Ultrasound: Flying Saucer; Last Of England soundtrack (Derek Jarman). Memberships: PRS; Musicians' Union. Hobbies: Animation; Photography; Sampling; Sleeping; Worrying. Current Management: Savidge and Best. Address: 172 Arlington Road, Camden, London NW1, England.

GARCIA Pierre-Louis, b. 6 July 1956, Ménerville, Algeria. Composer; Musician (saxophone, bass clarinet). m. Olivia Hicks, 30 Mar 1993, 2 daughters. Musical Education: Classical saxophone, Conservatoire de Versailles. Career: Concert tour, Germany; Festivals: Nancy; La Seyne; Neufchâtel; Montpellier; Marseille; Concerts in clubs: Sunset; Riverbop; New Morning; Musée d'Art Moderne, Paris; FNAC Tour, France, records promotion; Performance with dancers: Carolyn Carlson; Pierre Doussaint; Radio: Registered concerts for France Musique, France Culture. Compositions: For choreographers Pierre Doussaint, J Patarozzi; For Cineast: Claire Simon. Recordings: Die Grupen,

1984; Pierre-Louis Garcia, 1989. Hobbies: History; Political Science. Current Management: Jean-Louis Lagadou/Agency, Place Chauvier, 83830 Barjemon, France.

GARDEUR Jacques, b. 9 Nov 1953, Paris, France. Musician (guitar); Composer. m. 7 July 1990, 2 sons. Education: University. Musical Education: Study, Music department, Paris 8 University; Master class with: Barre Philips, Charlie Haden; Jose Barrense-Dias. Career: Began career, 1965; Album recorded with choir school; Session man with several blues, jazz and funk music groups, 1975-; Currently plays with Gwendoline Sampe, jazz singer. Compositions: TV film music for Antenne 2 (France TV). Membership: Union des Musiciens de Jazz (UMJ). Hobbies: Sport; Motor racing; Family. Current Management: Mezza-voce. Address: 1 Rue de L'Emaillerie, 93200 St Denis, France.

GARDINER Boris Oliver Patrick, b. 13 Jan 1943, Kingston, Jamaica. Vocalist; Musician (bass, piano, guitar). Divorced, 2 sons, 2 daughters. Musical Education: Self-taught. Career: Lead singer, singing group, The Rhythm Aces, 1960; Kes Chin And Souvenirs Band, 1962; Bassist, vocalist, Carlos Malcolm Afro Jamaican Rhythm Band, 1964; Formed own band, The Boris Gardiner Happening, 1968-82; Performances: USA; Canada; Central America; Caribbean Islands; Bahamas; Guyana; major concerts: Dupon Plaza, Miami; New York Hilton; Playboy Hotel, Jamaica; Sun Splash, Jamaica; The Cat & Fiddle, Nassau, Bahamas; Oslo, Norway; UK; Shared stages with: Jackie Wilson; Brook Benton; Roy Hamilton; The Stylistics; Nina Simone; The Blue Notes; Bob Marley; Radio, TV include: Top Of The Pops, BBC1 TV; France; Spain; Netherlands. Recordings: Elizabethan Reggae, 1970; I Wanna Wake Up With You (Number 1, UK), 1986; You Are Everything To Me, 1986; Studio musician, bass guitar, recordings include: Punky Reggae Party, Bob Marley; Young Gifted And Black, Bob And Marcia; Police And Thieves, Junior Marvin And The Upsetter - Lee Perry. Honours: Best Vocalist, Swing Magazine Awards, 1972; Canadian Reggae Music International Awards, Top Reggae Single, I Wanna Wake Up With You, 1986; Annual Hall Of Fame Award, Excellence In The Arts, Jamaica. Memberships: MCPS; PRS. Hobbies: Dominoes; Backgammon; Watching TV; Fixing Things. Current Management: Self-managed. Address: 2 Solo Way, Queensborough, Kingston 19, Jamaica, West Indies.

GARDNER Jeff, b. 23 Oct 1953, New York, USA. Musician (piano); Composer; Educator. Education: 2 years Harvard University. Musical Education: Study with Hall Overton; Nadia Boulanger; John Lewis; Jaki Byard; Don Friedman; Ivan Tcherepnin. Career: Played in Brazil with Wayne Shorter; Hermeto Pascoal; Pat Metheny; Helen Merrill; Helio Delmiro; Monterey Jazz Festival, with Victor Assis Brasil, Clark Terry, Slide Hampton, 1980; European tours with Steve Lacy and Eddie Harris; Concerts with Gary Peacock; Freddie Hubbard; Piano concerts for French television and radio; Piano Quartet with Martial Solal, Paul Bley, Jaki Byard, 1985; Solo concert tour, Brazil, 1992; Tour, France with Rick Margitza, 1995; Also played with Kenny Wheeler; André Ceccarelli; Paulo Moura; Charlie Mariano; Etta Cameron; Duo with Andrew Schloss, performed IRCAM, Paris; Germany; USA; Worked with soprano S'Ange Susan Belling; Concerts include: October Jazz Festival, Saint Lucia; CMAC, Martinique; Paris Jazz Festival; Madajazzcar Festival, Antananarivo; Tour of Japan, with Lisa Ono, 1996. Recordings: Continuum, trio with Eddie Gomez, Billy Hart; Alchemy, duo with Gary Peacock; Spirit Call; Sky Dance, with Gilberto Gil; Second Home, with Rick Margitza; California Daydream, Kenny Wheeler. Publications: Jazz Piano - Creative Concepts And Techniques; Co-author, Jazz Transcription, with

Niels Lan Doky. Membership: SACEM. Current Management: Lena Michals, 1802 Laurel Canyon Blvd, Los Angeles, CA 90046, USA. Address: 44 Rue Sarrette, 75014 Paris, France.

GARFUNKEL Art (Arthur), b. 5 Nov 1941, Forest Hills, New York, USA. Singer; Actor. m. Kim Cermak, 18 Sept 1988, 1 son. Education: BA, Columbia, 1965; MA, 1967. Career: Member of duo Simon and Garfunkel (with Paul Simon), 1966-70; Appearances with Paul Simon include: Royal Albert Hall, 1967, 1968; Monterey Pop Festival, 1967; Madison Square Garden, 1972; Central Park, New York, 400,000 audience, 1981; Several other reunion tours and benefit concerts; Solo artiste, 1972-; Concerts include: Carnegie Hall, New York, 1981; Sofia, Bulgaria, for 1.4 million people, 1990; Film appearances include: Catch 22, 1970; Carnal Knowledge, 1971; Bad Timing... A Sensual Obsession, 1980; Good To Go, 1986. Recordings: Albums include: with Simon And Garfunkel: Wednesday Morning 3:AM, 1966; Sounds Of Silence, 1966; Parsley Sage Rosemary And Thyme, 1967; Bookends, 1968; The Graduate (soundtrack), 1968; Bridge Over Troubled Water, 1970; The Concert In Central Park, 1972; Greatest Hits, 1972; Solo: Angel Clare, 1973; Breakaway, 1975; Watermark, 1978; Fate For Breakfast, 1979; Scissors Cut, 1981; The Art Garfunkel Album, 1984; The Animals Christmas, 1986; Lefty, 1988; Garfunkel, 1991; Up 'Til Now, 1993; Numerous hit singles include: with Simon and Garfunkel: The Boxer; Bridge Over Troubled Water; Homeward Bound; I Am A Rock; A Hazy Shade Of Winter; Mrs Robinson; 54th Bridge Song; Scarborough Fair; Sound Of Silence; El Condor Pasa (If I Could); Solo: All I Know; I Only Have Eyes For You; Bright Eyes (film theme for Watership Down); My Little Town; Crying In My Sleep. Honours include: Numerous Grammy Awards, for Mrs Robinson, 1969; Bridge Over Troubled Water, 1971; Britannia Award, 1977; Inducted into Rock And Roll Hall Of Fame, 1990. Current Management: Metropolitan Entertainment, PO Box 1566, 7 North Mountain Avenue, Montclair, NJ 07042, USA.

GARLAND Hank "Sugarfoot" (Walter Louis), b. 11 Nov 1930, Cowpens, South Carolina, USA. Jazz and Country Musician (guitar); Songwriter. Musical Education: Self-taught. Career: Session guitarist, Nashville; Played numerous sessions with Elvis Presley, 1958-61; Concerts with Elvis include: Benefit Show, Honolulu, 1961; Moved into country-jazz; Television and radio shows include New York City and Chicago, 1961; Car accident affected playing ability, 1961. Recordings include: Solo albums: The Velvet Guitar Of Hank Garland; Jazz Winds From A New Direction; Unforgettable Guitar; with Elvis Presley: Original 50 Gold Award Hits; Something For Everybody; Elvis Is Back; Elvis Aron Presley; His Hand In Mine; Other recordings include: A Legendary Performer, Jim Reeves; Original Golden Hits, Jerry Lee Lewis; Lonely Weekends, Charlie Rich; Gibson, Guitars, And Girls, Don Gibson; Country Hall Of Fame, Patsy Cline; with Webb Pierce: The Best Of; Western Express; Boogie With A Bullet, Dutch Redita; The Red Foley Story, Red Foley; Also recorded with: Justin Tubb; Patti Page; Grady Martin; Owen Bradley; Autry Inman; Tommy Jackson; Hank Williams Sr; Johnny Horton; Bobby Darrin; The Nashville All-Stars; Various anthologies. Honours: Rock and Roll Hall Of Fame; Gibson Hall Of Fame; Country Music Hall Of Fame. Memberships: BMI; ASCAP. Current Management: Brother Billy. Address: Jacksonville, Florida, USA.

GARLAND Tim (Tim Garland-Waggett), b. 19 Oct 1966, Ilford, Essex, England. Musician (saxophone); Composer. m. Amanda Phillipa Cooper, 28 July 1995. Education: West Kent College. Musical Education: Guildhall School Of Music. Career: Joined Ronnie Scotts Band, aged 23; Started jazz/folk fusion band Lammas; Several UK tours: Radio appearances include: Radio 3,

Lammas with strings; Circle Suite, South Bank; Dankworth Generation Band, Jason Rebello, London Jazz Orchestra. Compositions include: Dance For Human Folk, for big band (recorded by BBC Big Band). Recordings: Lammas: Lammas; Lammas: This Morning; Third album due Nov 1995; Dankworth Generation Band: Nebucadnezzar; Live At Ronnies. Honours: BBC Soloist Award, 1988; British Jazz Awards: Best Ensemble, 1993; BBC Composition Award, 1995. Memberships: PRS; MCPS. Hobbies: Meditation; Folk traditions. Current Management: Judy Greenwall. Address: Lammas, Fl.7, 75 West Hill, London SW15 2UL, England.

GARRETT Kenny, b. 1960, Detroit, Michigan, USA. Musician. Career: Joined The Duke Ellington Orchestra, 1978; Musician, The Mel Lewis Orchestra and the Dannie Richmond's Quintet, 1982; Numerous concerts worldwide; Extensive Tours. Recordings: Black Hope; Triology; Pursuance: The Music of John Coltrane; Songbook; Amandla Dingo; Live Around The World; Miles Davis and Quincy Jones: Live at Montreux; Introducing Kenny Garrett; Prisoner of Love; African Exchange Student. Honours: Named Hot Jazz Artist, Rolling Stone, 1996; Named Alto Saxist of the Year, Down Beat Readers Poll, 1996; Grammy Nomination, Best Jazz Instrumental Performance by a Group, 1997. Address: Burgess Management, 3225 Prytania Street, New Orleans, LA 70115, USA.

GARRETT Peter, b. Australia. Singer. Education: BA, Australian National University; BLLB, University of New South Wales, 1977. Career: Member, Rock Island Line; Lead singer, Midnight Oil, 1976-; Regular tours worldwide including: Earthquake benefit concert, New South Wales (with Crowded House), 1990; Solo performance, Earth Day Sound Action benefit, Foxboro, Massachusetts (with Joan Baez, Steve Miller, The Kinks), 1992; Earth Day Sound Action Benefit, Columbia, 1993; Strong links with ecological groups; Benefit concerts for: Aboriginal Rights Association; Tibet Council; Song proceeds for Deadicated to Rainforest Action Network and Cultural Survival; Protest concert, Exxon Building (Exxon Valdez oil spill), 1990; Ran for Australian Senate, Nuclear Disarmament Party, 1984. Recordings: Albums: with Midnight Oil: Head Injuries, 1979; Bird Noises, 1980; Place Without A Postcard, 1981; Red Sails In The Sunset, 1982; 10, 9, 8, 7, 6, 5, 4, 3, 2, 1, 1983; Diesel And Dust, 1987; Blue Sky Mining, 1990; Scream In Blue - Live Earth, Sun and Moon, 1992, 1993; Breathe, 1996; 20,000 Watt RSL - The Midnight Oil Collection, 1997; Hit single: Beds Are Burning, 1989; Contributor, Artists United Against Apartheid album, 1985; Deadicated (Grateful Dead tribute album), 1991. Honours: 4 Australian Record Industry Association Awards, 1991; Crystal Globe Award, Sony Music, 1991; Gold and Platinum discs. Memberships: Past President, Australian Conservation Foundation, 1987; Board member, Greenpeace International. Current Management: Gary Morris Management, PO Box 186, Glebe, NSW 2037, Australia.

GARRICK Michael, b. Enfield, England. Composer; Pianist; Bandleader; Organist; Teacher; Lyricist. Education: BA, Honours, London; Postgraduate Certificate in Education; Open Fellowship to Berklee College of Music, Boston, Massachusetts, USA. Career: BBC broadcasts, 1960-; Director, Poetry and Jazz in Concert, 1961-69; Director of Travelling Jazz Faculty, Founder, Wavendon Jazz Course; Director, Jazz Academy, Regents College with the Royal Academy of Music; Group Leader of Trio, Sextet, Big Band, ensembles; 1st jazz musician to give concerts on pipe organs at St Paul's Cathedral, 1968; Royal Festival Hall, 1969; Coventry Cathedral, 1973; Guest Conductor, European Community Youth Orchestra. Compositions include: Jazz Praises: Mr Smith's Apocalypse; Judas Kiss; The Hobbit Suite;

Heavenly Bodies; Underground Streams; Faces of Love; Catechism; Zodiac of Angels, orchestra; Carioca Celebration; New Flower of Europe; The Stirring; Romance of the Rose (Rhapsody for jazz violinist and orchestra); Hardy Country, Garrick's Jazz Characters, The Royal Box; For Children: All God's Children; Tree of Dreams; What is Melody?; Norman Gnome and the Rhinoceros; Jazz Curries. Recordings: Poetry and Jazz in Concert (4 volumes); October Woman; Promises; Black Marigolds; Heart is a Lotus; Home Stretch Blues; Troppo; You've Changed; Kronos; Cold Mountain; Anthem; Jazz Praises at St Paul's; A Lady in Waiting; Meteors Close at Hand; Parting is Such; For Love of Duke... and Ronnie. Contributor To: Jazz Now; Times Educational Supplement; The Stage; Piano magazine. Memberships: Royal Society of Musicians; Association of British Jazz Musicians; President, Berkhamsted Jazz Society. Hobbies: Sound Recording; Motorcycling. Current Management: Peter Done, The Old Stables, Romford Road, Pembury, Kent TN2 4AY, England. Address: 12 Castle Street, Berkhamsted, Hertfordshire HP4 2BQ, England.

GARRITY Freddy, b. 14 Nov 1936, Manchester, England. Vocalist. Career: Member, groups The Red Sox; The John Norman Four; The Kingfishers, later changed to Freddy And The Dreamers; Performances include: Cavern Club, with the Beatles, 1962; Royal Albert Hall, 1963; UK tour with Roy Orbison, 1964; Beatles Christmas Show, Hammersmith Odeon, London, 1964; Regular television appearances include: Let's Go; Beat Show; Sunday Night At The London Palladium; Shindig; Hullaballoo; Film appearances: What A Crazy World, 1963; Every Day's A Holiday, 1964; Regular stage and cabaret performances with the New Dreamers, 1968-; Concerts include: The Biggest '60s Party In Town, Olympia Hall, London, 1992; Actor, stage performance, The Tempest, 1988. Address: c/o Jason West Agency, Gables House, Saddlebow, Kings Lynn, Norfolk PE34 3AR, England.

GARTSIDE Green (Green Strohmeyer-Gartside), b. 22 June 1956, Cardiff, Wales. Singer; Songwriter. Education: Leeds Art School. Career: Founder member, Scritti Politti, 1977-; Concerts include: UK tour, support to Joy Division, 1979; Futurma Festival, Leeds, 1979; Montreux Pop Festival, 1988. Compositions: The Sweetest Girl, 1981 (also recorded by Madness); The Perfect Way, 1985 (also recorded by Miles Davis); Love Of A Lifetime, Chaka Khan, 1986; L Is For Lover (co-written with David Gamson), Al Jarreau, 1986. Recordings: Albums: with Scritti Politti: Songs To Remember, 1982; Cupid and Psyche, 1985; Provision, 1988; Singles: Wood Beez (Pray Like Aretha Franklin), 1984; Absolute, 1984; The Word Girl, 1985; The Perfect Way, 1985; Oh Patti, 1988; She's A Woman (with Shabba Ranks), 1991; Contributor, film soundtrack Who's That Girl?; Music Of Quality and Distinction Vol II, British Electric Foundation compilation album. Current Management: c/o Simon Hicks, PO Box 2950, London W11 3ZX, England.

GARVEY Phil, b. 14 Jan 1965, Reading, Berkshire, England. Vocalist; Musician (guitar, percussion). Career: Random Music, 1985-86; Plumbers, 1986-87; Solo folk clubs to 1990; Daisy Telethon Band, 1990; Free Spirits, 1991-94; Misfits Menagerie, 1994-. Compositions: 93 titles include: Would She Dance For Me; Step Out Your Frame; Nobody Fights Time; Here Comes The Twist. Recordings: Dance With Me Daisy (comedy record), 1990; Free Spirits album: Spirited Approach, 1993. Publications: A Good Day To Run Away, short novel, 1994. Membership: Musicians' Union. Hobbies: Writing; Travel; Abstract ideas; Cartoons. Current Management: J Cooper. Address: J Cooper, 44 Springhill Road, Goring, Berkshire RG8 0DA, England.

GARZON Albert, b. 26 Feb 1960, Newburgh, New York, USA. Record Producer; Ragtime Musician (piano); Company President. Education: BS, Fredonia State College, New York. Musical Education: Studied piano; Music Composition; Sound Recording. Career: Produced over 50 albums for artists including: 10,000 Maniacs; Brenda Kahn; Hypnolovewheel; Arson Garden; Antietam; Solo Piano Rags of James Scott; President, Com Four Dustribution, import/exporter of CDs and LPs. Recordings: Music of James Scott. Hobbies: World travel, especially Russia, Africa, Mexico. Address: 7 Dunham Place, Brooklyn, New York, NY 11211, USA.

GATLIN Larry Wayne, b. 2 May 1948, Seminole, Texas, USA. Singer; Songwriter. m. Janis Gail Moss, 9 Aug 1969, 1 son, 1 daughter. Career: Country singer, songwriter, 1971-; Member, Gatlin Brothers. Recordings: Albums: with Gatlin Brothers: Partners; Living In The Land Of Dreams; Cooking Up A Storm; Live At 8pm; Pure'n'Simple; Solo albums include: Houston To Denver; Straight Ahead. Honours: 2 BMI Songwriter Awards for Delta Dirt, 1975; Broken Lady, 1976; 3 ACM Awards, Best Album, Single, Male Vocalist, 1980. Membership: CMA. Address: c/o Gatlin Enterprises, 7003 Chadwick Drive, Suite 360, Brentwood, TN 37027, USA.

GATTO Olivier, b. 22 Jan 1963, Manosque, France. Musician (double bass); Arranger; Composer. m. Lydia Filipovic, 11 Sept 1993. Education: University of Sciences, Bordeaux, France. Education: Berklee College of Music, Boston, USA. Career: Concerts with Joe Henderson Quartet; Billy Cobham Quartet; Ravi Coltrane Quartet; Roy Hargrove and Antonio Hart; Julian Joseph; Ernie Watts; Bill Evans; European tour with John Stubblefield, George Cables and Billy Hart; French television shows, Radio France, Voice of America. Recordings: Album: Here And There (featuring Billy Cobham, George Cables, John Stubblefield), 1996. Hobbies: History; Cooking; Football; Jogging. Current Management: Danielle Gatto. Address: 19 Rue Platon, 33185 Le Haillan, France.

GAUDETTE Claude, b. 15 Oct 1959, Montreal, Quebec, Canada. Composer; Producer; Musician (keyboards). Musical Education: Montreal Conservatory of Music; Dick Grove School of Music, Los Angeles; New York Recording Workshop. Career: Musical Director, France Joli, Yamaha International Song Festival, 1985; Keyboards, David Foster's Super Producer '94 Tour, Japan. Recordings: Producer, writer, musician on albums: The Colour Of My Love, Celine Dion; Belinda, Belinda Carlisle; Everlasting, Good To Be Back, Natalie Cole; Slip Of The Tongue, Whitesnake; also albums by Fiona; Roberta Flack; Sergio Mendes; Eddie Money; Dionne Warwick; Kenny Loggins; Five Star; Little River Band; Smokey Robinson; Martika; Barry Manilow; George Benson; The Commodores. Singles: Mad About You, Belinda Carlisle; Wind Beneath My Wings, Bette Midler; Time Of My Life, Bill Medley and Jennifer Warnes; Make Me Lose Control, Eric Carmen; I Live For Your Love, Pink Cadillac, Natalie Cole; Walk Away, Dionne Warwick; also singles by Sheena Easton; Kenny Loggins; Melissa Morgan; Ziggy Marley; Film soundtracks include: Pretty Woman; Three Men And A Little Lady; Raw Deal; Dirty Dancing; Beaches. Memberships: BMI; NARAS; SCL. Hobbies: Cooking; Water Sports; Golf. Address: 4912 Stern Avenue, Sherman Oaks, CA 91423, USA.

GAUDRY Michel-Marie-Marcel, b. 23 Sept 1928, Eu, France. Divorced, 2 daughters. Musical Education: Piano from ages 5 to 8; Clarinet from 8 to 23, then bass. Career: Jazz music, singers; TV shows; Accompanied Billie Holiday; Carmen McRae; Blues singers; T Flanagan; Sweden; Madagascar; La Reunion; Les Autilles; European Jazz Orchestra (London); Europe; Russia; Japan;

Africa; South America; USA; Canada; England. Recordings: With Duke Ellington; Louis Armstrong; Billy (Strayhorn); Barney Kessel; Bud Powell Trio; Double-Six of Paris; Records with Barbera; G Moustaki; C H Dumont. Honours: Representing France, Big-Band Jazz Europe, London. Hobbies: Drawing; Photography; History.

GAUL Sven H, b. 11 Apr 1953, Flensburg, Germany. Musician (drums); Television Personality. Education: Degree, University of Aarhus in German Language. Appointments: Member, rockband, Taurus, 1974-80; Member, Pop/rockband, TV-2, 1980-; Host, television show, Lul, Lul, Rocken Gaar, 1989; Member, Danish Music Council, 1991-. Recordings: 1 live recording and numerous other releases. Honour: Danish Grammy, 1985. Membership: Danish Musician Union. Hobbies: Film and Design. Address: Arhus Musikkontor, Mindegadelo, 8000 Aarhus, Denmark.

GAY Albert, b. 25 February 1928, London, England. Clarinet; Soprano Sax; Tenor Sax. m. Doreen Gay, 1 September 1983, 1 daughter. Education: Guildhall School of Music. Career: Many broadcasts with Freddy Randall, Alex Welsh, Al Gay Quartet (BBC Jazz Club); Background Music in films: Two Left Feet; L-Shaped Room; TV: Alex Welsh; Bob Wallis; Keith Smith; Harry & Laurie Gold; Jo Daniels Bands. Compositions: South Track for South Bank Show; Band Leader, Queen Mary, 1961. Recordings: CD's: Paul Jones-Elaine Delmar; Ruby Braff, Alex Welsh and Freddy Randall; The World's Greatest Jazz Band, Stockholm. Honour: Nominated Melody Maker and Birmingham Jazz Society. Membership: Musicians' Union. Hobby: Cooking. Current Management: Freelance. Address: Lanterns, North Street, Winkfield, Berks, SL4 4SY, England.

GAYLE Crystal (Brenda Gail Webb), 9 Jan 1951, Paintsville, Kentucky, USA. Country Singer. m. Vassilios (Bill) Gatzimos, 1 son, 1 daughter. Career: Recording artiste with Decca Records, late 1960s; Regular appearances, Jim Ed Brown's television show, The Country Place; Played UK concerts with Kenny Rogers; Loretta Lynn (sister); Appeared at Wembley Country Music Festivals, 1971, 1977, 1979; First US country artist to perform in China, 1979; Contributor, film soundtrack, One From The Heart, 1982. Recordings: Hit singles include: Wrong Road Again; Beyond You; I'll Get Over You; Don't It Make My Brown Eyes Blue; Talking In Your Sleep; Your Kisses Will; Your Own Cold Shoulder; Half The Way; Cry; You And I, with Eddie Rabbitt; Making Up For Lost Time, with Gary Morris; Albums include: Crystal Gayle, 1974; Somebody Loves You, 1975; Crystal, 1976; We Must Believe In Magic, 1977; When I Dream, 1978; I've Cried The Blues Right Out Of My Eyes, 1978; We Should Be Together, 1979; Miss The Mississippi, 1979; A Woman's Heart, 1980; These Days, 1980; Hollywood/Tennessee, 1981; True Love, 1982; One From The Heart, with Tom Waits, 1982; Cage The Sngbird, 1983; Nobody Wants To Be Alone, 1985; Crystal Gayle, 1986; Straight To The Heart, 1986; What If We Fall In Love, 1987; Nobody's Angel, 1988; Ain't Gonna Worry, 1990; Three Good Reasons, 1992. Honours: Female Vocalist of the Year, Academy of Country Music, 1976; Grammy Awards: Beat Female Country Vocal Performance, Best Country Song; Female Vocalist Of The Year, CMA. Current Management: Gayle Enterprises Inc., 51 Music Sq E, Nashville, TN 37203, USA.

GAYLE Michelle, b. 1971, London, England. Singer; Songwriter; Actress. Career: Actress, UK television series: Grange Hill; Eastenders; Solo singer; Concerts include: Radio 1's Massive Music UK tour, 1995. Recordings: Album: Michelle Gayle; Hit singles: Sweetness; Looking Up; Happy Just To Be With You; Contributor, The Gift Of Christmas, Child Liners, 1995. Honours: Smash

Hits Awards; Gold Disc, Michelle Gayle. Current Management: Denis Ingoldsby, First Avenue Management, The Courtyard, 42 Colwith Road, London SW6 1RU, England.

GAYNOR Gloria, b. 7 Sept 1947, Newark, New Jersey, USA. Singer. Career: Singer with the Soul Satisfiers, 1960s; Solo disco music artiste, 1970s-. Recordings: Albums: Never Can Say Goodbye, 1975; Experience Gloria Gaynor, 1976; I've Got You, 1976; Glorious, 1977; Love Tracks, 1979; I Have A Right, 1979; Stories, 1980; I Kinda Like Me, 1981; Gloria Gaynor, 1983; I Am Gloria Gaynor, 1984; The Power Of Gloria Gaynor, 1986; Hit singles: Never Can Say Goodbye, 1974; Reach Out I'll Be There, 1975; I Will Survive (Number 1, US and UK), 1979; I Am What I Am, 1983. Current Management: Cliffside Music Inc., PO Box 374, Fairview, NJ 07022, USA.

GEERS Didier, b. 9 September 1954, Ghent, Belgium. Drums; Percussion; Vocal. m. Naima Barbro Johansson, 10 August 1986, 2 sons, 1 daughter. Education: Ghent Music Conservatoir; Drums and percussion lessons; Vocal coaching by Richard Boone. Career: 32 albums as Contributor: Sammy Rimington Band, Waso Quintet, George Probert, Al Casey, Bill Dillard Earl Warren; 3 Solo Albums: Didier Geers Jazz and Blues Band, 1986-89; Touring with Eddie Burns Guitar (blues); Member of Papa Bue's Viking Jazz Band, Copenhagen-DK, 7 years; Actual with own R & B Group, Virgis. Honour: Golden Mermaid Award, Oostende, 1971. Hobbies: Music; Theater. Current Management: Wim Wigt Productions, Roghorst 303, PO Box 201, 6700 AE, Wageningen, Holland. Address: Didier Geers, Karl Nils väg 15-17, 290 11 Linderöd, Sweden.

GEFFEN David, b. 21 Feb 1943, Brooklyn, New York, USA. Film, Recording and Theatre Executive. Career: Worked at William Morris talent agency, 1964; Launched new film studio with Steven Spielberg, Jeffrey Katzenberg; Co-founder (with Laura Nyro), Tunafish Music Publishing; Joined Ashley Famous Agency; Executive Vice-President, Creative Man, 1968; Co-founder (with Elliot Roberts), Asylum Records and Geffen-Roberts Manufacturing Company, 1970 (later merged with Elektra Records); Vice Chairman, Warner Brothers Pictures, 1975-76; Founder, Geffen Records, Geffen Film Company; Films produced include Little Shop Of Horrors; Beetlejuice; Men Don't Leave; Defending Your Life; Co-producer, musicals: Dreamgirls; Little Shop Of Horrors; Cats; Chess; Founder, DGC record label. Address: c/o Geffen Film Company, 9130 Sunset Boulevard, Los Angeles, CA 90069, USA.

GEILS Jerome, b. 20 Feb 1946, New York, USA. Musician (guitar). Education: Worcester Technical College. Career: Member, The Hallucinations; Founder member, guitarist, The J Geils Blues Band, 1968-85; Appearances include: Fillmore East, New York, with the Allman Brothers, Beach Boys and Mountain, 1971; Mar Y Sol Festival, Puerto Rico, 1972; Pink Pop Festival, Netherlands, 1980; Regular tours, Europe, US, UK; Group disbands, 1985; Concert as Magic Dick/J Geils Blue Time, Paradise Club, Boston, 1992; Television includes: In Concert, ABC TV, 1973; Runs vintage and sports car shop, 1992-. Recordings: Albums: J Geils Band, 1971; The Morning After, 1971; Live, 1971; Bloodshot, 1973; Nightmares..., 1974; Hotline, 1975; Blow Your Face Out, 1975; Monkey Island, 1977; Sanctuary, 1979; Love Stinks, 1980; Freeze Frame (Number 1, US; Number 3, UK), 1982; Showtime!, 1983; You're Getting Even While I'm Getting Odd, 1984; Flashback, 1987; The J Geils Band Anthology: A Houseparty, 1993; Singles include: Looking For Love; Give It To Me; Must've Got Lost; Centrefold (US Number 1, 6 weeks); Angel In Blue; Freeze Frame; I Do; Fright Night, title track for film Fright Night. Honours: Rolling Stone magazine, Most

Promising New Band, 1971; Various Gold discs; Platinum disc for Freeze Frame, 1982.

GELDOF Bob, b. 5 Oct 1954, Dublin, Eire. Vocalist; Songwriter. m. Paula Yates, Aug 1986, 2 daughters. Education: Black Rock College. Career: Journalist, New Musical Express, Melody Maker; Founder member, Boomtown Rats, 1975-84; Organizer, Band Aid Trust (incorporating Live Aid, Band Aid, Sport Aid), for Ethiopian famine relief, 1984-92; Solo artiste, 1986-; International tours, including UK, Europe, US, Japan, Australia; Major concerts include: California Music Festival, 1979; Live Aid, Wembley Stadium, 1985; Freddie Mercury Tribute, Wembley Stadium, 1992; Gosport Festival, 1992; Green Belt Festival, 1992; WOMAD's 10th Birthday, 1992; Film appearances: The Wall, 1982; Number One, 1985; Organizer, Do They Know It's Christmas?, Band Aid, (Number 1, UK), 1984; Participator, We Are The World, USA For Africa, 1984; Organizer, Live Aid concerts, Wembley and Philadelphia (estimated television audience of 2 billion, raising $70 million), 1985; Total of $144 million raised by 1992; Owner, television production company, Planet 24. Recordings: Albums with Boomtown Rats: The Boomtown Rats, 1977; A Tonic For The Troops, 1978; The Fine Art Of Surfacing, 1979; Mondo Bongo, 1981; V Deep, 1982; Solo: Deep In The Heart Of Nowhere, 1986; The Vegetarians Of Love, 1990; The Happy Club, 1993; Singles include: Looking After No 1, 1977; She's So Modern, 1978; Like Clockwork, 1978; Rat Trap (Number 1, UK), 1978; I Don't Like Mondays (Number 1, UK), 1979; Diamond Smiles, 1979; Someone's Looking At You, 1980; Banana Republic, 1980; House On Fire, 1982; Solo: This Is The World Calling, 1987; The Great Song Of Indifference, 1990. Publication: Autobiography, Is That It?, 1987. Honours include: KBE (Hon), 1986; 4 Ivor Novello Awards; Order Of Two Niles, Sudan; Order of Leopold II, Belgium; Irish Peace Prize; UN World Hunger Award; EEC Gold Medal; MTV Video Award, Special Recognition Trophy, 1985; American Music Award, Special Award of Appreciation, 1986; Gold and Platinum discs; Honorary degrees, Kent, London, Ghent Universities. Current Management: Jukes Productions, 330 Harrow Road, London W9 2HP, England.

GENEST Francis, b. 31 Dec 1960, Paris, France. Musician (percussion). Education: Translator, Interpreter, Mastership in English. Musical Education: Self-taught; Worked with Giovanni Hidalgo, Farafina. Career: Performed at many festivals throughout Europe (France, Spain, Belgium, Italy); Several concerts for Radio France and the French Speaking Public Radios Community. Recordings: Albums with the Cache-Cache Trio: L'Océane; Tandems. Honour: First prize, National Jazz Contest with Cache-Cache trio. Membership: Union des Musiciens de Jazz, Paris. Address: La Guéraudière, 37380 Nouzilly, France.

GENTELET Hugues, b. France. Tour Manager; Co-Director. Career: French tour manager for: Whigfield; Reel 2 Reel; A Deva; Rozalla; Dr Alban; Imagination; Boney M; Pasadenas; Kool and The Gang; Numerous other dance acts; Commercial director, Nuits Magiques Production. Address: Nuits Magiques Production, 50 Avenue Du President Wilson, BT 104, 93214 La Plaine St Denis CDX, France.

GENTET Christian, b. 22 Oct 1952, Paris, France. Orchestra Director. m. Marianne Gentet, 15 Sept 1990, 1 daughter. Musical Education: First prize, Conservatory. Career: Director, L'Orchestre de Contrebasses; World tour; Television and radio appearances. Recordings: with L'Orchestre de Contrebasses: Danses Occidentales, 1982; Les Cargos, 1990; Bass, Bass, Bass, Bass, Bass And Bass, 1993; Jeux Dangereux, 1995; Also: Christian Gentet Baixo Acoustico, 1989. Address:

Éditions Musica Guild, 10 Rue Emile Hebert, 37500 Chinon, France.

GENTRY Bobbie (Roberta Lee Streeter), 27 July 1944, Chicasaw County, Mississippi, USA. Singer; Songwriter; Musician (guitar). m. (1) Bill Harrah, (2) Jim Stafford. Education: Philosophy, Music. Career: Recording artiste, 1967-; UK television series, The Bobby Gentry Show, 1969; Retired from performing to look after business interests. Recordings: Hit singles: Ode To Billie Joe (Number 1, US); Let It Be Me, with Glen Campbell; All I Have To Do Is Dream, with Glen Campbell; I'll Never Fall In Love Again, 1969; Albums: Bobbie Gentry And Glen Campbell, 1968; Local Gentry, 1968; Touch 'Em With Love, 1969; I'll Never Fall In Love Again, 1970; Fancy, 1970; Patchwork, 1971; Sittin' Pretty/Tobacco Road, 1971.

GENTRY Teddy, b. 22 Jan 1952, Fort Payne, Alabama, USA. Musician(bass); Vocalist. Career: Founder member, country group Wild Country, 1969; Became Alabama, 1977-; Worked with Lionel Richie, 1986; Recordings: Albums: Alabama, 1980; My Home's In Alabama, 1980; Feels So Right, 1981; Mountain Music, 1982; The Closer You Get, 1983; Roll On, 1984; 40 Hour Week, 1985; The Touch, 1986; Greatest Hits, 1986; Just Us, 1987; Southern Star, 1989; Pass It On Down, 1990; Greatest Hits, Volume 2, 1991; American Pride, 1992; Singles include: I Want To Be With You; My Home's In Alabama; Tennessee River; Feels So Right; Love In The First Degree; Pass It On Down. Current Management: Dale Morris And Associates, 818 19th Avenue South, Nashville, TN 37203, USA.

GENTY Laurent, b. 22 Jan 1958, Rennes, France. Musician (piano). Musical Education: Self-taught; Workshops. Career: Numerous concerts, Britany; Television broadcasts: FR3; Radio Anmoorique. Compositions: Tape: Les Frères de la Cote; CD: Les Portes Du Desert. Hobby: Sailing.

GEORGE Siwsann, b. 2 Apr 1956, Treherbert, Rhondda, Wales. Musician (harp, concertina, guitar, spoons); Teacher; Broadcaster. m. Roger Plater, 29 June 1991, 1 son. Education: Graduate, Aberystwyth University; Welsh College, Music and Drama. Musical Education: Traditional school grounding, mainly self-taught. Career: Lead singer, Mabsant (Welsh roots band), 1980-; Tours: USA; Far East; Western Europe; Latvia; Hungary; British Council; As soloist: UK tour with Ray Fisher and Jo Freya, 1995; Purcell Room, London, 1995; With Robin Williamson, 1996. Recordings: With Mabsant: over a dozen recordings; Solo: Traditional Songs Of Wales, with various musicians accompanying; Several television and film scores; Publications: Mabsant: Book of 54 Welsh Folk Songs. Honours: 3 times Pan Celtic Singing Winner, 1980-1990. Memberships: Musicians' Union; Equity; Welsh Folksong Society. Hobbies: Walking; Yoga. Address: 26 Bassett Street, Abercynon CF45 4SP, Wales.

GERALDO Neil, b. 29 Dec 1955. Musician (guitar); Record Producer. m. Pat Benatar, 20 Feb 1982. Career: Guitarist, Derringer; Guitarist, record producer, Pat Benatar, 1977-. Numerous compositions for Pat Benatar. Recordings: with Pat Benatar: Albums: Crimes Of Passion, 1980; Precious Time, 1981; Get Nervous, 1982; Get Nervous (producer), 1982; Live From Earth, 1983; Tropico, 1984; In The Heat Of The Night, 1985; Seven The Hard Way, 1985; Best Shots, 1987; True Love (producer), 1991; Gravity's Rainbow (co-producer), 1993; Singles include: Heartbreaker; All Fired Up; Treat Me Right; Love Is A Battlefield; Hell Is For Children; Invincible; Hit Me With Your Best Shot; Sex As A Weapon; We Belong; All Fired Up. Current Management: Gold Mountain Management, 3575 Cahuenga Blvd West, Siute 450, Los Angeles, CA 90068, USA.

GERIMON Paul, b. 14 Oct 1954, Dinant, Belgium. Singer-Deep Bass. Education: Classic Humanities, St Paul's College and Dinant's Royal Athenee; Superior Diplomas Violin and Voice; Opera Studio Brussels; Centre de Musique Baroque, Paris. Career: First appearance on Belgian Television singing Spirituals, 1972; Sings Opera, Standards, Original Songs, Musicals, Baroque and Contemporary, 1974-; First part of Kid Creole, with Allez Allez, 1982; Bass Soloist, Opera Royal Wallonie, 1983-86; TV-Radio appearances on Rai, O Globo, Radio France, RTB, WDR, FR3; Regularly invited at Festival D'Aix, TRM, Berlin Philharmonie, Barbican Theatre, Lisbon, Paris, New York; Played part of Don Juan at Theatre, 1990; Tricentenary of La Monnaie, 1995; International tour with R Jacobs and Trisha Brown Company, 1998-99. Recordings: M Kolbe, 1989; Dumont, 1992; WOMA, 1992; Sodoma, 1993; L'Orfeo, 1995; Intra Muros, 1996; Allez Allez, 1997; TV-Films: M Kolbe, 1989; La Vida Breve, 1985. Honours: Orphée D'or, 1991, De L'Académie du Disque, Paris. Membership: Union Des Artistes, Brussels. Hobby: Cycling. Address: Concertbureau Arien, De Boeystraat 6, B-2018 Antwerpen, Belgium.

GERRITSEN Rinus, b. 9 Aug 1946, The Hague, Netherlands. Vocalist; Musician (bass). Career: Founder member, Dutch rock group, Golden Earring, 1961-; Tours, Europe; Canada; US; Support to the Who, European tour, 1972; Support to Rush, 1982. Recordings include: Albums: Just Earrings, 1965; Winter Harvest, 1967; Miracle Mirror, 1968; On The Double, 1969; Eight Miles High, 1970; Golden Earring, 1971; Seven Tears, 1971; Together, 1972; Moontan, 1973; Switch, 1975; To The Hilt, 1975; Rock Of The Century, 1976; Contraband, 1976; Mad Love, 1977; Live, 1977; Grab It For A Second, 1978; No Promises No Debts, 1979; Prisoner Of The Night, 1980; Second Live, 1981; Cut, 1982; N E W S, 1984; Something Heavy Goin' Down, 1984; The Hole, 1986; Face It, 1994; Lovesweat, 1995; Naked II, 1997; with Michel Van Dijk: De G V D Band, 1979; Labyrinth, 1985; Hit singles include: Please Go, 1965; Dong-Dong-Di-Ki-Di-Gi-Dong (Number 1, Netherlands), 1968; Radar Love (Number 1, Netherlands), 1973; Twilight Zone, 1982; When the Lady Smiles, 1984; Turn the World Around, 1989; Temporary Madness, 1991; Another 45 Miles, 1993; Angel, 1995; Burning STuntman, 1997; The Devil Made Me Do It, 1998 Curent Management: Rob Gerritsen, Regentessestraat 29, 2713 EM Zoetermeer, Netherlands.

GERTSMAN Evgeny, b. 22 Jan 1937, Odessa, Russia. Musicologist. m. Lidia Coonizjna, Mar 1974, 2 daughters. Musical Education: Piano, Conservatory, Odessa; Musicology, Institute of Arts, Vladivostock; Post graduate course, theory of music, Musical Academy, Moscow. Career: Lecturer, Institute of Arts, Vladivostock, 1969-78; Member of staff, research, Russian Institute of History of Arts, Saint Petersburg, 1990-. Publications: Ancient Musical Thought, 1986; Byzantine Musicology, 1988; Petersburg Theoretikon, 1994; Music of Ancient Greece And Rome, 1995; Greek Musical Manuscripts In Petersburg, Vol I, 1996; Hymn By Sources Of New Testament, 1996; In Quest Of Chants Of Greek Orthodox Church (Porfiry Uspensky and his collection of Greek Musical Manuscripts), 1996; More than 50 articles on theory and history of Ancient Greek and Byzantine Music. Hobby: Musicology. Address: Russian Institute of History of Arts, Isaakievskaja Square 5, Saint Petersburg 191000, Russia.

GERUP Martin, b. 24 Feb 1960, Himmelev Sogn, Denmark. Singer; Composer, Musician (keyboards). m. Dorte Schou, 13 May 1995, 1 daughter. Musical Education: Danish Conservatory of Jazz, Rock and Latin Music. Career: Roskilde Festival, with Dieters Lieder, 1988; Roskilde Festival, with Flying Fish, 1993; Several radio and television shows. Recordings: with Dieters Lieder: Jeg Ka' Lieder, 1983; Hvorflink Ka' Man Blive?, 1986; with Flying Fish: It's Almost Fairytime, 1993. Memberships: Danish Artists Society; Danish Jazz, Rock and Folk Authors. Hobbies: Fishing; Skiing. Address: Danish Artist Society, Vendersgade 24, 1363, Copenhagen K, Denmark.

GERZINA Igor, b. 23 Feb 1970, Zagreb, Croatia. Musician(saxophone); Composer; Audio Programmer. Education: Center for Education in Culture, Zagreb. Musical Education: Music Academy of University of Zagreb; Berklee Collge of Music, Boston, USA. Career: Member, Croatian Radio Television Big Band; Solo appearance with Zagreb Philharmonic Orchestra, 1993; Croatian TV Festival, 1993; Zagreb Jazz Fair, 1993; International Music Festival, Medugorje, 1994. Recordings: with Soul Fingers: Live In BP Club, 1994; with Ritmo Loco: Za Ljubav Jedne Zene, 1995. Honour: First Prize, Students of Music of Croatia Competition. Membership: Croatian Musicians' Union. Address: Petrinjska 73, 10000 Zagreb, Croatia.

GESSLE Per, b. 12 Jan 1959, Halmstad, Sweden. Musician (guitar); Vocalist: Songwriter. Career: Member, Gyllene Tider; Solo artist and songwriter; Formed Roxette with Marie Fredericksson, 1986-; 35 million albums and 12 million singles sold worldwide by 1997; Tours throughout Europe; US; Central and South America; Asia; Television includes: The Tonight Show, NBC TV; MTV Unplugged, 1993. Recordings: Albums: Pearls Of Passion, 1987; Look Sharp!, 1988; Joyride, 1991; Tourism, 1992; Crash! Boom! Bang!, 1994; Don't Bore Us, Get To The Chorus - Roxette's Greatest Hits, 1995; Balades En Español, 1996 Singles include: The Look (Number 1, US and 22 countries), 1989; Listen To Your Heart (Number 1, US), 1989; Dressed For Success, 1989; Dangerous, 1990; It Must Have Been Love, featured in film Pretty Woman (Number 1, US), 1990; Joyride (Number 1, US, and 18 other countries), 1991; Fading Like A Flower, 1991; The Big L, 1991; Spending My Time, 1991; Church Of Your Heart, 1992; How Do You Do!, 1992; Queen Of Rain, 1992; Almost Unreal, featured in film Super Mario Brothers, 1993; Sleeping In My Car, 1995; You Don't Understand Me, 1996. Honours: Platinum and Gold discs; Grammy Awards; MTV Awards. Current Management: d&d management, Lilla nygatan 19, SE-111 28 Stockholm, Sweden.

GHIGLIONE Bill Barita Daniel, b. 5 July 1947, Nice, France. Composer; Arranger; Musical Director; Musician (keyboards). Education: University Literature Diploma (2nd cycle). Musical Education: Classical piano studies. Career: Tours include: Eddy Mitchell, 1976-77; Claude Nougaro, 1977; Johnny Halliday, 1978-79; Michel Polnareff, Japan (musical director), 1979; Maxime Le Forestier, Europe, 1982-83; Member, Dallas; Performer, theme music, television series Dallas; Producer, composer, Lasya Victory. Recordings: Dallas album, 1981; with Lasya Victory: L'Age D'or, 1989; Tout Ça Nous Fait Mal, 1990; Messie Est De Retour, 1991; Tout S'Arrange, 1992; Mona, 1993; Sound Design, television series Inventions Of Life 3, 1995. Honours: Double Gold Record Award, Dallas theme, 1982; Best French Record of Year, Tout Ça Nous Fait Mal, 1990. Memberships: SACEM; SCPP. Hobbies: Esoterism; Unity of Religions; Peace on Earth. Address: 15 bis rue J J Rousseau, 94200 Ivry/Seine, France.

GIANEZ Laurent (Laurent Gilbert Gianesini), b. 13 May 1942, Moyeuvre-Grande, France. Musician (flute). Musical Education: Diploma, flute, Conservatory, Metz. Career: Member various jazz groups including Duo J M Albertucci-Gianez; Ecaroh (style of Art Blakey); Quartet Gianez (own compositions, Samba music); Annual concert with Archie Shepp and Ted Curson. Recordings: Album with Duo Denis Moog-Gianez: Car La Rouille N'Aura Pas Raison Du Jazz (saxophone, guitar, trumpet); Currently recording own quartet. Membership: SACEM (Paris). Address: 26 Rue de l'Eglise, 57140 Saulny, France.

GIBB Barry Alan Crompton, b. 1 Sept 1946, Douglas, Isle Of Man, England. Singer; Songwriter. m. Linda Gray, 1 Sept 1970, 4 sons, 1 daughter. Career: Formed The Bee Gees, with brothers Robin and Maurice, 1958-69; Reformed group, 1971; Appeared on own weekly television show, Australia; Returned to England; Signed with NEMS Enterprises, 1967; Performed live with Barbra Streisand, One Voice Concert/Video, 1987; Compositions: Co-writer (with brothers), Saturday Night Fever soundtrack, 1977 (40 million copies sold); Producer, co-writer, albums for: Andy Gibb; Barbra Streisand: Guilty; Dionne Warwick: Heartbreaker; Diana Ross: Eaten Alive; Kenny Rogers: Eyes That See In The Dark; Second most Top Ten hits written (after Lennon and McCartney); 5 simultaneous US Top Ten hits written by the Gibb brothers, 1978; Only artists to write and produce 6 consecutive Number 1 singles, 1979; Producer, writer, Grease, for Frankie Valli; Bee Gees songs recorded by artists including: Elvis Presley; Janis Joplin; Andy Williams; Glen Campbell; Rod Stewart; Roberta Flack; Frankie Valli; Michael Bolton. Recordings: Albums include: Bee Gees 1st, 1967; Horizontal And Idea, 1968; Odessa, 1969; Cucumber Castle, 1971; Two Years On, 1971; Trafalgar, 1972; Life In A Tin Can, 1973; Mr Natural, 1974; Main Course, 1975; Children Of The World, 1976; Here At Last...Live, 1976; Saturday Night Fever, 1977; Spirits Having Flown, 1978; Greatest Hits, 1979; Living Eyes, 1980; ESP, 1988; One, 1989; The Very Best Of The Bee Gees, 1990; Tales From The Brothers Gibb (A History In Song 1967-90), 1990; High Civilisation, 1991; You Wouldn't Know, 1992; Size Isn't Everything, 1993; Solo: Now Voyager, 1984; Hawks, 1988; Still Waters, 1997; Singles include: Alone. Honours include: 7 Grammy Awards; Inducted into Songwriters Hall Of Fame, 1994; Inducted in Rock and Roll Hall of Fame, Cleveland; Lifetime Achievement Award, Brit Awards, London; International Artist Award, American Music Awards, Los Angeles. Memberships: Musicians' Union; Equity. Current Management: Left Bank Management, 6255 Sunset Boulevard, 21st Floor, Los Angeles, CA 90028, USA. Address: c/o 1801 Bay Road, Miami Beach, FL 33139, USA.

GIBB Maurice Ernest, b. 22 Dec 1949, Douglas, Isle of Man, England. Singer; Songwriter. m. Yvone Spenceley, 17 Oct 1975, 1 son, 1 daughter. Career: Formed The Bee Gees, with brothers Barry and Robin, 1958-69; Reunited 1971; Performed in Australia during 1960s; Returned to England, signed with NEMS Enterprises, 1967; First US television appearance, American Bandstand, 1967; Compositions: Co-writer (with brothers), Saturday Night Fever soundtrack, (sold 40 million copies), 1977; Co-writer (with brothers), albums for: Andy Gibb; Barbra Streisand: Guilty; Dionne Warwick: Heartbreaker; Diana Ross: Eaten Alive; Kenny Rogers: Eyes That See In The Dark; Co-writer, second most Top 10 hits (after Lennon and McCartney); Only artists to write and produce 6 consecutive Number 1 singles; As producer: Co-producer (with Robin Gibb), Sunrise, Jimmy Ruffin; 3 solo albums for Robin Gibb, 1982, 1984, 1986; Runaway, Carolla (Swedish star), 1986; Writer, producer, A Breed Apart film soundtrack. Recordings: Albums include: Bee Gees 1st, 1967; Horizontal And Idea, 1968; Odessa, 1969; Cucumber Castle, 1971; Two Years On, 1971; Trafalgar, 1972; Life In A Tin Can, 1973; Mr Natural, 1974; Main Course, 1975; Children Of The World, 1976; Here At Last...Live, 1976; Saturday Night Fever, 1977; Spirits Having Flown, 1978; Greatest Hits, 1979; Living Eyes, 1980; ESP, 1988; One, 1989; The Very Best Of The Bee

Gees, 1990; Tales From The Brothers Gibb, A History in Song 1967-1990, 1990; High Civilisation, 1991; You Wouldn't Know, 1992; Tomorrow The World, 1992; Size Isn't Everything, 1993; Still Waters, 1997; Singles include: Alone. Honours include: 6 Grammy Awards; Inducted into Songwriters Hall Of Fame, 1994; Inducted into Rock and Roll Hall of Fame, Cleveland; Lifetime Achievement Award, Brit Awards, London; International Artist Award, American Music Awards, Los Angeles. Memberships: Musicians' Union; Equity. Current Management: Left Bank Management, 6255 Sunset Boulevard, 21st Floor, Los Angeles, CA 90028, USA. Address: c/o 1801 Bay Road, Miami Beach, FL 33139, USA.

GIBB Robin Hugh, b. 22 Dec 1949, Douglas, Isle of Man, England. Singer; Songwriter. m. Dwina Murphy, 31 July 1985, 2 sons, 1 daughters. Career: Formed the Bee Gees with brothers Maurice and Barry, 1958; First single, 1963; Own weekly television show, Australia, 1960s; Moved to England, 1967; First US TV appearance, American Bandstand, 1967; Compositions: Co-wrietr, Saturday Night Fever soundtrack, 1977 (40 million copies sold); Co-writer, albums: Guilty, Barbra Streisand; Heartbreaker, Dionne Warwick; Eaten Alive, Diana Ross; Eyes That See In The Dark, Kenny Rogers; Second only to Lennon & McCartney for most Top 10 hits written; 5 simultaneous US Top 10 hits, 1978; 6 consecutive Number 1 singles, 1979. Bee Gees songs recorded by: Al Green; Elvis Presley; Janis Joplin; Sarah Vaughn; Johnny Mathis; Andy Williams; Glen Campbell; Richie Havens; Jose Feliciano; Rod Stewart; Eric Burdon; Roberta Flack; Nina Simone; Frankie Valli; Michael Bolton. Most covered songs: Massachusetts; Stayin' Alive; To Love Somebody; How Do You Mend A Broken Heart. Recordings: Albums: Bee Gees 1st, 1967; Horizontal And Idea, 1968; Odessa, 1969; Cucumber Castle, 1971; Two Years On, 1971; Trafalgar, 1972; To Whom It May Concern, 1972; Life In A Tin Can, 1973; Mr Natural, 1974; Main Course, 1975; Children Of The World, 1976; Here At Last. Live, 1976; Saturday Night Fever, 1977; Spirits Having Flown, 1978; Greatest Hits, 1979; Living Eyes, 1980; ESP, 1988; One, 1989; The Very Best Of The Bee Gees, 1990; Tales From The Brothers Gibb (A History in Song 1967-90), 1990; High Civilisation, 1991; You Wouldn't Know, 1992; Size Isn't Everything, 1993; Still Waters, 1997; Singles include: Alone; Solo albums: Robin's Reign, 1970; How Old Are You, 1982; Secret Agent, 1984; Walls Have Eyes, 1986. Honours include: 6 Grammy Awards; Inducted into Songwriters Hall of Fame, 1994; Inducted into Rock and Roll Hall of Fame, Cleveland; Lifetime Achievement Award, Brit Awards, London; International Arttist Award, American Music Awards, Los Angeles. Memberships: Musicians' Union; Equity. Current Management: Left Bank Management, 6255 Sunset Boulevard, 21st Floor, Los Angeles, CA 90028, USA. Address: c/o 1801 Bay Road, Miami Beach, Florida 33139, USA.

GIBBONS Beth, b. 4 Jan 1965, Devon, England. Singer; Songwriter. Career: Advertising agency in Bristol; Singer, Portishead. Recordings: Albums: Dummy, 1994; Singles: Numb, 1994; Sour Times, 1994; Glory Box, 1995. Honours: Mercury Music Prize, Best Album, 1995; NME Brat Award, 1995. Current Management: Fruit Management, Unit 104, Saga Centre, 326 Kensal Road, London W10 5BZ, England.

GIBBONS Billy, b. 16 Dec 1949, Houston, Texas, USA. Musician (guitar); Vocalist. Founder member, The Moving Sidewalks, 1968; Founder member, ZZ Top, 1970-; Regular tours and concerts include: Eliminator tour, 1984; Afterburner world tour, 1985-87; Recycler tour, 1990; Rock The Bowl '91, Milton Keynes, 1991. Recordings: Albums: ZZ Top's First Album, 1970; Rio Grande Mud, 1972; Tres Hombres, 1973; Fandango, 1975; Tejas, 1977; Best Of ZZ Top, 1978; Deguello, 1979; El Loco, 1981; Eliminator,

1983; Afterburner, 1985; Recycler, 1990; Greatest Hits, 1992; Antenna, 1994; Contributor, Tribute To Muddy Waters album, 1993; Singles include: La Grange, 1974; Tush, 1975; Gimme All Your Lovin', 1983; Sharp Dressed Man, 1983; Legs, 1984; Sleeping Bag, 1985; Stages, 1986; Rough Boy, 1986; Velcro Fly, 1986; Doubleback, from film Back To The Future Part III, 1990; Viva Las Vegas, 1992. Honours include: Several MTV Music Video Awards; ZZ Top Day, Texas, 1991; Silver Clef Award, Nordoff-Robbins Music Therapy, 1992. Current Management: Lone Wolf Management, PO Box 163690, Austin, TX 78716, USA.

GIBBONS Ian Ronald, b. 18 July 1952, Rochford, Essex, England. Musician (keyboards, accordion). m. Amanda Gaskin, 8 June 1985. Musical Education: Grade 6 Piano accordion. Career: Worked with: The Kinks; Sweet; Roger Chapman; The Crystals; The Shirelles; Dr Feelgood; Eddie and the Hotrods; Chris Farlowe; Kursaal Flyers; The Inmates; Television includes: Top Of The Pops; Saturday Night Live. Recordings: All Kinks albums, 1979-, also single: Come Dancing; Albums with Dr Feelgood and Roger Chapman. Honour: Rock and Roll Hall of Fame, as member of The Kinks. Membership: PRS. Hobbies: Travel; Cinema; Theatre; Horse riding; Car restoration. Current Management: Pete Scarbrow, Pro Active Management. Address: Mushroom Studios, Lubards Farm, Hullbridge Road, Rayleigh, Essex SS6 9QG, England.

GIBBONS Steve, Singer; Songwriter; Musician (guitar). Career: Founder, own R&B band The Steve Gibbons Band, 1971; Tours with The Who, Europe, USA; First foreign act to play in German Democratic Republic. Compositions: Numerous songs recorded by other artists. Recordings: Tulane, (Number 1, UK charts), 1977; Other singles include: Sweetheart; Take Me Home; Eddy Vortex; Get Up And Dance; Loving Me, Loving You; Personal Problem; Albums include: Short Stories, 1971; Any Road Up, 1976; Rolling On, 1977; Caught In The Act, 1977; Down In The Bunker, 1978; Street Parade, 1980; Saints And Sinners, 1981; On The Loose, 1986. Current Management: Jim McPhee, Acorn Entertainments. Address: Winterfold House, 46 Woodfield Road, Kings Heath, Birmingham B13 9UJ, England.

GIBBS Terri, b. 15 June 1954, Augusta, Georgia, USA. Singer; Musician (piano). Career: Gospel singer as teenager; Formed own group, Sound Dimension; Residency in Augusta restaurant, 1975; Recording artist, 1981-. Recordings: Singles: Somebody's Knockin'; Rich Man; Mis'ry River; Somedays It Rains All Day Long; Anybody Else's Heart But Mine; Slow Burning Fire (duet with George Jones); Albums: Somebody's Knockin', 1981; I'm A Lady, 1981; Somedays It Rains All Night, 1982; Over Easy, 1983; Hiding From Love, 1984; Old Friends, 1985. Address: c/o Richard A Barz and Associates, 25 Cobble Creek Drive, RD 1, Box 91, Tannersville, PA 18372, USA.

GIBERT Alain, b. 1 Jan 1947, Langogne, France. Musician (trombone); Composer; Arranger. m. Nadine Faure, 26 Apr 1970, 3 sons. Education: Mathematics. Musical Education: Self-taught. Career: Co-founder, ARFI (Association à la Recherche d'un Folklore Imaginaire); Member, various bands: Marvelous Band; Marmite Infernale; Apollo; Bomonstre. Compositions: Music for Louis Sclavis; Steve Waring; Recordings: L'Age Du Cuivre, Apollo; Trombonist, singer, Chariot D'Or; Pticado; As composer, arranger: Le Roi Demonte; L'Art De La Retraite Sonne. Memberships: SACEM; ARFI. Current Management: ARFI, 13 Rue de l'Arbre Sec, 69001 Lyon, France. Address: Montmorin, 63160 Billom, France.

GIBSON Deborah, b. 31 Aug 1970, Brooklyn, New York, USA. Singer; Songwriter; Pianist;

Actress. Musical Education: Private piano and voice lessons. Career: Youngest performer to have written, performed and produced a number 1 song; Sold over 9 million records worldwide; Starred in Grease, London, West End, 1994. Recordings: Only In My Dreams; Shake Your Love; Out Of The Blue; Foolish Beat; Lost In Your Eyes; Electric Youth; No More Rhyme; Anything Is Possible; Losin' Myself. Honours: ASCAP, Writer of the Year. Current Management: Gibson Management, 300 Main Street #201, Huntington, NY 11743, USA.

GIBSON Don, b. 3 Apr 1928, Shelby, North Carolina, USA. Musician (guitar); Songwriter. Career: Recording artist, 1949-. Compositions include: Sweet Dreams, recorded by Faron Young, Patsy Cline, Emmylou Harris, Roy Buchanan, Reba McIntyre, Elvis Costello; I Can't Stop Loving You, also recorded by Kitty Wells, Ray Charles, Van Morrison; (I'd Be) A Legend In My Time, recorded by Ronnie Milsap; Album of own songs, Roy Orbison Sings Don Gibson, Roy Orbison, 1967; Oh Lonesome Me; Woman (Sensuous Woman). Recordings: Albums include: The King Of Country Soul, 1968; Dottie And Don, with Dottie West, 1969; A Perfect Mountain, 1970; Country Green, 1972; Woman (Sensuous Woman), 1972; Sample Kisses, 1972; Am I That Easy To Forget, 1973; The Two Of Us Together, with Sue Thompson, 1973; Touch The Morning, 1973; Warm Love, with Sue Thompson, 1973; Just Call Me Lonesome, 1973; Snap Your Fingers, 1974; Bring Back Your Love To Me, 1974; Just One Time, 1974; Oh How Love Changes, with Sue Thompson, 1975; Don't Stop Loving Me, 1975; Starting All Over Again, 1978; Look Who's Blue, 1978; Rockin' Rollin' Gibson, Vol 1, 1982; Vol 2, 1982; Don Gibson And Los Indios Tabajaras, 1986; Currents, 1992.

GIBSON Lee, b. 5 Mar 1950, Watford, Hertfordshire, England. Singer. m. Gerry Boyce (musician), 1 Aug 1973, 1 daughter. Education: BA Hons, Humanities. Musical Education: Self-taught. Career: Worked all over Europe with: UMO Danish Orchestra, Helsinki; Danish Radio Band, Copenhagen; Skymasters, Metropol Orchestra, Netherlands; Television appearances in France, Belgium, Italy; Album of television concert with Sarah Vaughn and Francy Boland Band, Dusseldorf; WDR Band, Cologne; Montreux Festival; Over 1,000 BBC solo broadcasts, UK; Film, television includes: The Great Muppet Movie; Privates On Parade; Victor Victoria; Yentl; An American Tale; Willow; Benny Hill Show; Only Fools And Horses; Morecambe And Wise Show; Barrymore, 3 Royal Variety Shows; Concerts include: tours with Syd Lawrence Orchestra; Don Lusher Band; Big Band Specials, BBC Radio Band; Guest appearances with Glen Miller UK Orchestra; Herb Miller Band; Singer, The Music Of Andrew Lloyd Webber, concert for Prince and Princess of Wales at Expo '92, Seville; Singer, UK jazz circuit, including: Barbican; Queen Elizabeth Hall; Festival Hall; Rotherham Arts Centre; Brecon, Southampton Jazz Festivals; Ronnie Scotts; Ruislip Jazz Club; Pizza On The Park. Recordings: Chorale; One World One Peace; You Can See Forever; Never Let Me Go. Publications: Music reviews for The Musician. Honour: Singers Prize, Knikke Festival. Memberships: Musicians' Union; Equity. Hobby: Gourmet food.

GIFFORD Alex, b. 1965. Musician (saxophone, keyboards); Recording Engineer. Career: Musician, brass section with The Stranglers; Sound engineer for The Grid; Member of Propellerheads, with Will White. Recordings: with Propellerheads: Album: Drumsanddecksandrockandroll, 1998; Singles: On Her Majesty's Secret Service (with Shirley Bassey), 1997; Dive, 1997; Take California (EP), 1997; Spybreak (EP), 1997; History Repeating (with Shirley Bassey), 1997; Guest musician on Enlightenment, Van Morrison. Address: c/o Wall of

Sound, Office 3, 9 Thorpe Close, London W10 5XL, England.

GIFT Roland, b. 28 May 1962, Birmingham, England. Singer; Musician (saxophone); Actor. Career: Musician and actor, Hull, 1980s; Singer, Fine Young Cannibals, 1984-; Regular UK and US tours; Film appearances: Group featured in Tin Men, 1987; Actor, films: Sammy And Rosie Get Laid, 1987; Scandal, 1989; Theatre: Romeo, in Romeo and Juliet, UK rep tour, 1990. Recordings: Hit singles: Johnny Come Home, 1985; Suspicious Minds, 1986; Ever Fallen In Love, 1987; She Drives Me Crazy (Number 1, US), 1989; Good Thing (Number 1, US), 1989; Don't Look Back, 1989; Albums: Fine Young Cannibals, 1985; The Raw And The Cooked, 1989; Contributions to film soundtracks: Something Wild, 1986; Tin Men, 1987; Contribution, Red Hot And Blue, 1990. Honours: BRIT Awards, Best British Group, Best British Album, 1990.

GIGOT Raquel, b. 9 November 1965, Ottignies, Belgium. Chromatic and Diatonic Accordions; Composer. Career: Professional Musician, 1990-; Numerous Radio and TV performances in different countries; Studiomusician recording with different artists. Compositions: Bully Wully Jig; Blue Room; Road to Bally Heighue; Rue Des Dunes; Lesidren; Mouse in the Kitchen. Recordings: 1990; Blue Room; Restless Home; Leaving the World Behind; Histoires de Rue; Oceanides; About to Go. Current Management: VZM Orion ASBL, 136 Chaussee De Wemmel, 1090 Brussels, Belgium.

GILBERT Gillian, b. 27 Jan 1961, Manchester, England. Musician (keyboards, guitar). Education: Stockport Technical College, Stockport. Career: Musician, all-girl punk group, The Inadequates; Member, New Order, 1980-; The Other Two, 1991-; Tours: UK; Europe; US; Far East; South America; Australia; New Zealand; Concerts include: Futurama Festival, Leeds, 1982; Glastonbury Festival, 1981, 1987; San Remo Festival, 1988; Reading Festival, 1989; Television includes: Documentary, Celebration, BBC, 1982; Rock Around The Clock, BBC, 1985. Compositions with Stephen Morris include: Numerous tracks for New Order; Television soundtracks: Making Out; Shooting Stars; Reportage. Recordings: Albums with New Order: Movement, 1981; Power Corruption And Lies, 1983; Brotherhood, 1986; Substance, 1987; Technique, 1989; One True Passion, 1990; BBC Radio 1 Live In Concert, 1992; Republic, 1993; with The Other Two: The Other Two And You, 1994; Singles include: with New Order: Ceremony, 1981; Temptation, 1982; Blue Monday, 1983; Confusion, 1983; Thieves Like Us, 1984; Shellshock, 1986; True Faith, 1987; Fine Time, 1988; Round And Round, 1989; World In Motion (with England World Cup Football Squad), 1990; How Does It Feel?, 1992; Regret, 1993; with The Other Two: Tasty Fish, 1991.

GILBERT Grant Mitchell, b. 11 Aug 1957, London, England. Music Producer; Artistic Director; Creative Producer and Coordinator. 1 son, 2 daughters. Musical Education: Implosion at The Roundhouse, Camden Town, 1970-72. Career: Co-founded Torch Song and Guerilla (Productions), W William Orbit and Laurie Mayer, 1983; Founded The Crucial Chemystry Corporation (CCC), 1988; Launched E Zee Possee and Jeremy Healy's DJ career; Set up CCC in Japan introducing British graphic designer Neville Brody and numerous House/Techno artists and DJ's; Co-producer of Glastonbury Festival Green Futures Field, 1993-. Recordings: Torch Song, with William Orbit and Laurie Maye; EZ Posse: Everything Starts with An E; Producer, solar-powered CD, Deep Green: Music to Wake Up, featuring Solar Quest. Honour: Artistic Director of Green Futures Field Gaiasphere Stage, Glastonbury, 1995. Hobbies: Underground comics; Science Fiction; Vegan cooking; Eating;

Developing new musical and creative talent. Current Management: CCC. Address: CCC, PO Box 10, London N1 3RJ, England.

GILBERT Paul, b. USA. Musician (guitar). Career: Guitarist, rock groups: Racer X, 1986-88; Mr Big, 1989-. Recordings: Albums with Racer X: Street Lethal, 1986; Second Heat, 1987; Extreme Volume... Live, 1988; with Mr Big: Mr Big, 1989; Lean Into It, 1991; Singles include: Green-Tinted Sixties Mind; To Be With You. Current Management: Herbie Herbert Management, 2501 3rd Street, San Francisco, CA 94107, USA.

GILBERT Simon, b. 23 May 1965. Musician (drums). Career: Member, Suede, 1991-; Concerts include: Glastonbury Festival, 1993; Tours, UK; Europe; America; Japan; Television appearances include: Top Of The Pops, BBC1; 12th BRIT Awards, Alexandra Palace; The Beat, ITV; Later With Jools Holland, BBC2; The Tonight Show, NBC TV. Recordings: Albums: Suede (Number 1, UK), 1993; Dog Man Star, 1994; Singles include: The Drowners; Metal Mickey; Animal Nitrate; Stay Together. Honours include: Mercury Music Prize, 1993. Current Management: Interceptor Enterprises, The Greenhouse, 34-38 Provost Street, London N1 7NG, England.

GILBERTO Astrud, b. 1940, Bahia, Brazil. m. Joao Gilberto. Career: Singer with husband Joao Gilberto (guitar) and Stan Getz (saxophone); Tours with Stan Getz. Recordings: Albums: The Astrud Gilberto Album, 1965; The Shadow Of Your Smile, 1965; Once Upon A Summertime, 1971; Haven't Got Anything Better To Do, 1968; That Girl From Ipanema, 1977; Best Of, 1982; The Essential Astrud Gilberto, 1984; Look To The Rainbow, 1986; So And So, 1988; with James Last: Plus, 1986; Hit single: The Girl From Ipanema, 1964. Address: c/o Subrena Artist Corp., 330 West 56th Street, Suite 18-M, New York, NY 10019, USA.

GILKYSON Eliza, b. 24 Aug 1950, Hollywood, California. Singer; Musician (piano, guitar); Songwriter. m. Reavis Moore, 23 Aug 1981, 1 son, 1 daughter. Career: Tours with Ladysmith Black Mambazo; Dan Fogelberg; Arlo Guthrie; Andreas Vollenweider; Mary Chapin Carpenter; Television appearances: Austin City Limits; Showtime Concert Special; Film appearances: Two Lane Blacktop; Eight Minutes To Midnight. Composition: Rosie Strike Back, recorded by Roseanne Cash. Recordings: Albums: Pilgrims; Legends Of Rainmaker; Through The Looking Glass; Eolian Minstrel, with Andreas Vollenweider. Hobby: Horse riding. Current Management: Open Door Management. Address: PO Box 9858, Santa Fe, NM 87504, USA.

GILL Andy, b. 1 Jan 1957, Manchester, England. Musician (guitar); Composer. Education: BA Hons, Fine Art, Leeds University. Career: Formed Gang Of Four, 1977. Compositions include: 8 Gang of Four albums; Solo album: Dispossession; Other recordings with: Anthony More; Louise Goffin; The Red Hot Chili Peppers; Almighty Hi Fi; Hugh Cornwell; Terri Nun, Berlin; Television includes: Zero Option, BBC1 (also arranger, producer, recording engineer); Pandora's Box, BBC1, 1992; The Westminster Programme, BBC2, 1992; Westminster Daily, BBC2, 1992; Westminster Live, BBC2, 1993; Scrutiny, BBC, 1993; Films: Karate Kid; Dogs In Space; The Last Of England; Pump Up The Volume; Urgh! A Music War; Requiem Apache; Delinquent (composer, performed as Gang Of Four). Recordings: As performer and producer: with Gang Of Four: Entertainment, 1979; Solid Gold, 1981; Songs Of The Free, 1982; Hard, 1983; Mall, 1991; Shrinkwrapped, 1995; At The Palace (live); Compilation: A Brief History of The 20th Century; As producer: with Red Hot Chili Peppers (Gold disc); What Hits? (Platinum disc); with Busta Jones: Hands Are Shaking; with The Balancing

Act: Curtains; Tracks for: The Most Beautiful Girl; Downey Mildew; Addie Brik; Miracle Legion, for film A Matter of Degrees; with MCD: Tantric Sex Disco, 1995; with Inastella: What Y'Gonna Do, 1995; with The Morgans: Tell Me What You Taste EP; Diversity album in production. Membership: PRS. Hobbies: Tantric Disco; Clay Pigeon shooting. Current Management: Polar Union; Sanctuary Group. Address: The Colonnades, 82 Bishops Bridge Road, London W2 6BB, England.

GILL Janis, b. California, USA. Singer; Musician (guitar). m. Vince Gill, 1 daughter. Musical Education: Studied Music Theory. Career: Member, duo Sweethearts Of The Rodeo with sister Kristine Arnold; Signed to Columbia Records; Sugar Hill Records; Winners, Wrangler Country Showcase, 1985. Recordings: Sweethearts Of The Rodeo, 1986; Top 20 hits include: Since I Found You; Midnight Girl/Sunset Town; Satisfy You; Chains Of Gold, 1987; Rodeo Waltz, 1993; Video: Things Will Grow. Honours: CMA's Vocal Duo, 9 consecutive years; Music City News, Best Vocal Duo; TNN Viewers Choice Award, Favourite Group; NAIRD Award, Best Country Album, 1994. Current Management: M Hitchcock Management. Address: PO Box 159007, Nashville, TN 37214, USA.

GILL Vince (Vincent Grant), b. 5 Apr 1957, Norman, Oklahoma, USA. Country Singer; Musician (guitar); Songwriter. m. Janis Oliver. Career: Member, Mountain Smoke (as a schoolboy); Member, Bluegrass Alliance, 1975-79; Member, Pure Prairie League, 1979-81; Member, Rodney Crowell's band, The Cherry Bombs, 1982; Solo artiste, 1983-. Compositions include: Never Knew Lonely; Look At Us (co-written with Max Barnes). Recordings: Hit singles: When I Call Your Name, duet with Patti Loveless; Pocket Full Of Gold; Liza Jane; Look At Us; I Still Believe In You (US Country Number 1); Take Your Memory With You); Albums: with Pure Prairie League: Can't Hold Back, 1979; Firin' Up, 1980; Something In The Night, 1981; Solo album: Turn Me Loose, 1983; The Things That Matter, 1984; Vince Gill, 1985; The Way Back Home, 1987; When I Call Your Name, 1989; Pocket Full Of Gold, 1991; I Never Knew Lonely, 1992; I Still Believe In You, 1992; The Essential, 1996; Contributor, Patti Loveless albums; On Every Street, Dire Straits. Honours: CMA Single Of The Year, with Patti Loveless; CMA Male Vocalist of Year, 1991, 1992; Song Of The Year, Look At Us, 1992. Current Management: Fitzgerald Hartley Co., 1212 16th Avenue S, Nashville, TN 37203, USA.

GILLAN Ian, b. 19 Aug 1945, Hounslow, London, England. Vocalist. m. Bronwen, 21 Jul 1984, 1 daughter. Career: Lead singer, rock bands: Episode Six; Deep Purple; Gillan; Black Sabbath; Gillan and Glover (with Roger Glover); Singer on over 20 albums, selling in excess of 100 million copies; Numerous worldwide tours, television and radio appearances; Singer, Jesus Christ Superstar. Compositions include: Woman From Tokyo; Smoke On The Water; Black Night; Child In Time. Recordings: Albums include: with Episode Six: Here There and Everywhere, 1966; with Deep Purple: In Rock, 1969; Best Of, 1970; Machine Head, 1972; Who Do We Think We Are, 1973; 24 Carat Purple, 1975; Perfect Strangers, 1984; Purpendicular, 1996; with Gillan: Child In Time, 1976; Gillan, 1978; Mr Universe, 1979; Glory Road, 1980; Future Shock, 1981; Double Trouble, 1981; Magic, 1982; with Black Sabbath: Born Again, 1983; with Gillan and Glover: Accidentally On Purpose, 1988; with Ritchie Blackmore: Rainbow. Current Management: Phil Banfield, Performing Artistes Network. Address: No 1 Water Lane, Camden Town, London NW1 8NZ, England.

GILLESPIE Bobby, b. 22 June 1964, Scotland. Singer. Career: Drummer, Jesus And Mary Chain, 1984; Singer, Primal Scream, 1984-; Performances include: Miners Benefit Trust

Concert, Sheffield Arena, 1992. Recordings: Singles include: All Fall Down, 1985; Crystal Crescent, 1986; Ivy Ivy Ivy, 1989; Loaded, 1990; Come Together, 1990; Higher Than The Sun, 1991; Don't Fight It Feel It, 1991; Dixie-Narco (EP), 1992; Misery, 1995; Albums: Sonic Flower Groove, 1987; Primal Scream, 1989; Screamadelica, 1991; Let Your Dim Lights Shine, 1995; Contributor, Dope Dogs, Parliament/Funkadelic, 1994. Honour: Mercury Music Prize, Screamadelica, 1992. Address: c/o Scream Heights Management.

GILLESPIE Dana, b. 30 March 1949, England. Singer; Songwriter. Recordings: 30 albums released: Foolish Seasons, 1967; Box of Surprises, 1968; Jesus Christ Superstar, 1972; Weren't Born a Man, 1973; Ain't Gonna Play No Fiddle, mojo blues band, 1974; Blue Job, 1982; Solid Romance, 1984; Below the Belt, 1984; It Belongs to Me, 1985; Move You Body close to Me, 1986; I'm a Woman, 1986; Hot News', 1987; Amor, 1990; Blues It Up, 1990; Where Blue Begins, 1991; Boogie Woogie Nights, 1991; Big Boy, with Joachim Palden, 1992; Methods of Release, 1993; Andy Warhol, 1994; Blue One, 1994; One to One, 1995; Hot Stuff, 1995; Have I Got Blues for You, 1996; Mustique Blues Festivals, 1996; Inner View, 1996; Cherry Pie, with Big Jay McNeeley, 1997; Jan Mustique Bluesfest, 1997. Honours: Voted Top British Female Blues Vocalist, 1993, 1994, 1995, 1996.

GILLIS Verna, b. 14 June 1942, New York, USA. Artist Manager; Record Producer. m. Brad Graves, 1 May 1965. Education: PhD,Ethnomusicology. Career: Host, Radio Programme, WBAI, 1975-83; Founder, Director, Soundscape Performance Space, New York City, 1979-85; Record Producer; Artist Manager for: Youssou N'dour, Yomo Toro, Salif Keita, Malouma Mint Maideh, Habib Faye, Ivan Rubenstein-Gillis. Publications: DIW, Live From Soundscape. Honour: Woman of the Year, 1975. Hobbies: Planting; Antiques. Address: 799 Greenwich Street, New York, NY 10014-1843, USA.

GILMOUR David, b. 6 Mar 1946, Cambridge, England. Vocalist; Musician (guitar); Composer. m. Polly Samson, 1994. Career: Member, Pink Floyd, 1968-; Performances include: Rome International Pop Festival, 1968; Hyde Park, London, 1968; Bath Festival, 1970; Montreux Festival, Switzerland, 1971; Pink Floyd Live At Pompeii (recorded for film release), 1972; Knebworth Festival, 1975; Guitarist with Bryan Ferry, Live Aid, Wembley, 1985; Played at Colombian Volcano Appeal, Royal Albert Hall, 1986. Recordings: Albums: A Saucerful Of Secrets, 1968; More (film soundtrack), 1969; Ummagumma, 1969; Atom Heart Mother (Number 1, UK), 1970; Relics, 1971; Meddle, 1971; Obscured By Clouds, 1972; The Dark Side Of The Moon (Number 1, US), 1973; Wish You Were Here, (Number 1, UK and US) 1975; Animals, 1976; The Wall (Number 1, US), 1979; The Final Cut (Number 1, UK), 1983; A Momentary Lapse Of Reason, 1987; The Delicate Sound Of Thunder, 1988; Shine On, 1992; The Division Bell, 1994; Pulse, 1995; Solo albums: David Gilmour, 1978; About Face, 1984; Discovered Kate Bush, Executive Producer for her album The Kick Inside; Played on: Bête Noire, Bryan Ferry; Slave To The Rhythm, Grace Jones; So Red The Rose, Arcadia; Tribute To Muddy Waters; Singles include: Another Brick In The Wall (Number 1, UK and US), 1979; When The Tigers Break Free, 1981; Not Now John, 1983; Learning To Fly, 1987; On The Turning Away, 1987; 1 Slip, 1988; Contributor, film soundtrack of Zabriskie Point, 1970. Honours: Silver Clef Award, Nordoff-Robbins Music Therapy, 1980; MTV Music Video Award, 1988; Ivor Novello Award, Outstanding Contribution To British Music, 1992; Q Award, Best Live Act, 1994; Inducted into Rock and Roll Hall of Fame, 1996; Grammy Award, Producer in Best Instrumental Performance for

Marooned. Current Management: Steve O'Rourke, EMKA Productions Ltd, 43 Portland Road, Holland Park, London W11 4LJ, England.

GILTRAP Gordon, b. 6 Apr 1948, East Peckham, Tonbridge, Kent, England. Musician (guitar). Career: Played college, folk club and university circuit; Regular tours, with Ric Sanders; Solo work; Duets with John Renbourn and Juan Martin. Compositions include: Heartsong, theme to Holiday programme, BBC TV, 1980s; Other television music for: Wish You Were Here; The Open University; Hold The Back Page, 1985. Recordings: Albums: Early Days, 1968; Gordon Giltrap, 1968; Portrait, 1969; Testament Of Time, 1971; Giltrap, 1973; Visionary, 1976; Perilous Journey, 1977; Fear Of The Dark, 1978; Performance, 1980; The Peacock Party, 1981; Live, 1981; Airwaves, 1982; Elegy, 1987; A Midnight Clear, 1988; Gordon Giltrap - Guitarist, 1988; Mastercraftsman, 1989; One To One, with Ric Sanders, 1989; A Matter Of Time, with Martin Taylor, 1991; Compilations: The Very Best Of Gordon Giltrap, 1988; The Best Of Gordon Giltrap - All The Hits Plus More, 1991. Publications: Contributor, Guitarist magazine. Address: c/o NE Music Management, Priory House, 55 Lawe Road, South Shields, Tyne And Wear NE33 2AL, England.

GIMENES Raymond François, b. 12 Dec 1939, Fes, Morocco. Arranger; Conductor; Producer; Musician (guitar); Composer. m. Beatrice Belthoise, 11 Sept 1987, 2 sons, 1 daughter. Education: Sciences at University. Musical Education: First Prize for Violin; Studied harmony, counterpoint, fuga and composition. Career: Backing guitarist for Petula Clark, Dean Martin, Shirley Bassey; Musical Director for Sacha Distel, Henri Salvador, Charles Aznavour; Solo guitarist for Paul Mauriat Orchestra, including US tour, 1971; Japanese tours, 1971, 1986, 1988, 1990. Recordings: 4 albums as leader of Guitars Unlimited; As guitarist: Wings, Michael Colombier; Slide Hampton with Jazz Big Band; Hajime Mizoguchi; Dionne Warwick In Paris. Publication: Orchestration for Paganini's Sonata for Viola and Symphonic Orchestra. Honour: Award for commercial, Radio Spot, 1989. Memberships: SACEM; SPEDIDAM; ADAMI. Hobbies: Computers; Watching tennis. Current Management: Charley Marouani, 37 Rue Marbeuf, 75008 Paris, France. Address: 185 bis Rue Paul Doumer, 78510 Triel sur Seine, France.

GINAPÉ Viviane, b. 30 Apr 1955, Paris, France. Singer. m. Lionel Bouton, 12 Nov 1988. Musical Education: CNRBB, Supérieur. Career: Singer with: Urban/Sax; Claude Bolling; Denis Badault; Yochk 'O Seffer; François Mechali. Recordings: Fraction Sur Le Temps, Urban Sax, 1989; Opéra Jazz François Mechali, L'Archipel, 1995. Current Management: Marc Aubrun. Address: 1 Rue de la Dhuis, 75020 Paris, France.

GINGER, b. South Shields, Tyne And Wear, England. Rock Singer; Songwriter; Musician (guitar). Career: Member, rock groups, The Quireboys; The Throbs; Founder, The Wildhearts, 1991-; Numerous tours, UK; Europe; Ireland; Support tours with Pantera; Manic Steet Preachers; The Almighty; Suicidal Tendencies; Performances include: Monsters of Rock Festival, Castle Donington, 1994; Reading Festival, 1994. Recordings: Albums: with The Quireboys: A Bit Of What You Fancy, 1989; with The Wildhearts: Earth Vs The Wildhearts, 1993; Fishing For Luckies, 1994; P H U Q, 1995; Singles with The Wildhearts: Suckerpunch; Caff Bomb; I Wanna Go Where The People Go; Geordie In Wonderland; Just In Lust; Mondo Akimbo A-Go-Go (EP); Don't Be Happy...Just Worry (EP); TV (EP). Current Management: Tribal Management, 7 Vicarage Road, Wednesbury, West Midlands WS10 9BA, England.

GINMAN Lennart Vidar, b. 2 Mar 1960, Copenhagen, Denmark. Composer; Musician (double bass). m. Lisbeth Maria Hansen, 31 Dec 1987, 2 daughters. Musical Education: Private studies, Copenhagen, New York. Career: Began professional career around 1985; Now one of most sought after bassists in Denmark; Tours with: Kenny Werner; Harry "Sweet" Edison; Al Foster; Lee Konitz; Cæcilie Norby. Recordings: 1991, Lennart Ginman/Kirk Lightsey; Blachman Introduces Standard Jazz & Rap, Thomas Blachman; Cæcilie Norby, Cæcilie Norby; Beatin' Bop, Page One. Honours: Composers Honour Award, 1992, DJBFA. Hobbies: Gardening; Clothes. Address: C F Richsvej 80, 2000 Frederiksberg, Denmark.

GIROT Pierre, b. 11 May 1936, Neuilly, France. Jazz Musician (guitar). m. 30 June 1960, 2 daughters. Musical Education: Academie de Guitare de Paris; Student of Henri Salavador. Career: Accompanied Josephine Baker, Charles Trenet, Worked with jazz artists: Trio Arvanitas; Guy Lafitte; Lou Bennett; Bill Coleman; Hal Singer; International Festivals include: Antibes Juan-les-Pins; Zurich; San Sebastian; Souillac; Marciac; Montpellier; Clermont-Ferrand; French radio and television. Recordings: Jazz and Brazilian guitar with Quatuor Galilé. Publications: Festival 92; Birdy. Honour: Third prize, Festival of Juan-les-Pins, 1960. Memberships: SACEM; SPEDIDAM. Hobbies: Chess; Football. Address: Chemin de Fadat, 19100 Brive, France.

GIUFFRE James P (Jimmy), b. 26 Apr 1921, Dallas, Texas, USA. Musician (saxophones, flutes, clarinet); Composer. m. Juanita Odjenar Giuffre, 22 June 1961. Education: BA North Texas State. Musical Education: Private Studies with Dr Wesley La Violette. Career: Lincoln Center; Carnegie Hall; Numerous European tours; Television and filmscores (art films, 1 feature). Compositions: Four Brothers; Train; The River. Recordings: Free Fall; The Jimmy Giuffre 3. Publications: Jazz Phrasing And Interpretation. Honours: Guggenheim Fellowship, National Endowment Of The Arts. Membership: Broadcast Music Inc. Hobbies: Listening to music. Current Management: Thomas Stowsand/Soudades Tourneen, Austria. Address: A-6200 Rotholz 369, Austria.

GIUSSANI Claudio D C, b. 19 Sept 1969, London, England. Musician (keyboards, percussion- djembe); Programmer; Engineer; Remixer. Education: BEng (Hons) University of Warwick, Coventry, UK. Musical Education: Mostly self-taught, lessons in percussion. Career: Formed band Urban Shakedown (making new breakbeat music), 1990; Formed Union Jack (trance music), 1992, 93; Regular tours, USA; Canada; Russia; Europe; PA in clubs. Recordings: With Urban Shakedown: Some Justice (Top 20 hit); Bass Shake; With Union Jack: Album: There Will Be No Armageddon; Single: Two Full Moons And A Trout. Memberships: PRS; MCPS; PPL. Hobbies: Playing the djembe; Travel. Current Management: Platipus Records.

GJERSTAD Frode, b. 24 Mar 1948, Stavanger, Norway. Musician (saxophone). m. Judith Sorvik, 24 Mar 1983, 1 son, 1 daughter. Career: Worked with: John Stevens; Johnny Dyani; Kent Carter; Billy Bang; Bobby Bradford; Borah Bergman; Derrek Bailey; Paul Rutherford; Terje Isungset; Audun Kleive; Pierre Dorge; Bjorn Kjellemyr. Recordings: Backwards And Forwards, 1983; Okhela, 1984; Ness, 1987; Way It Goes, 1988; Accent, 1989; In Time Was, 1991; Less More, 1992; Enten Eller, 1993; Seeing New York From The Ear, 1995. Hobbies: Reading; Mixing music. Current Management: Circulasione Totale. Address: Gansveien 15, 4017 Stavanger, Norway.

GLADWELL Robert, b. 16 June 1950, Colchester, England. Musician (guitar, bass); Journalist; Luthier. Married, divorced, twice; 4

sons, 1 daughter. Musical Education; Martin Lukins School Of Music (studied guitar). Career: Session guitarist, clinician, worked for Gibson Guitars for 10 years; Own guitar workshop, building, customising guitars; Toured extensively with Steve Harley and Cockney Rebel; Currently touring, recording with Suzi Quatro. Recordings: with Twink: Mr Rainbow, 1990; with Steve Harley: Yes You Can, 1992; Christmas All Stars Album, 1994; with Suzi Quatro: Free The Butterfly, 1995. Publications: Dr Robert column, guitarist magazine, 11 years; Guitar Electronics And Customising, book,1995. Membership: Musicians' Union. Hobbies: History; Listening to music; Instrument restoration. Current Management: Jive Music Management.

GLASSER Adam, b. 20 Sept 1955, Cambridge, England. Musician (keyboards, chromatic harmonica). m. Vivien Roberts, 21 May 1994, 1 daughter. Education: BA (Hons) English and European Literature, Warwick University. Musical Education: Self-taught. Career: MD, The Manhattan Brothers (SA Township legends); Toured, recorded with DuDu Pukwana; Tour and television with Martha Reeves and The Vandellas; Concerts with Jimmy Witherspoon; Appeared in Musicians In Exile, Ch4; SA Blues, BBC2. Recordings: August One on Zila '86 album; Title music for Battle of The Bikes, Ch4, 1994; Talking Woods, with Thebe Lipere; Pedalmarch (for Jazz Sextet) features on continental bike racing in Cycle Sport; Filmscore, The Flood, played harmonica with Toots Thielemans. Honours: Winner, Peter Whittingham Award, Musicians' Benevolent Society, 1997 Memberships: Musicians' Union; Association Internat des Journalistes du Cyclisme. Hobby: Cycling. Address: 88 Upland Road, London SE22 0DE, England.

GLASSON Charlotte, b. 1 Mar 1973, London, England. Musician (saxophones, violin); Composer; Improviser. Musical Education: Music degree, Kingston University; Composition with Michael Finnissy. Career: Own jazz quartet at Ronnie Scotts, Pizza Express; Plays in Divine Comedy; String quartet composition played by LSO; Television appearance with PJ Proby; Vital theatre, Hamlet, Edinburgh Festival, 1995; Worked with many Soul, Pop and Salsa bands. Recordings: Divine Comedy: Casanova; Charlotte Glasson Quartet. Memberships: Musicians' Union. Hobbies: Reading; Travel. Address: 39 Freshfield Road, Brighton, East Sussex BN2 2BJ, England.

GLATZL Friedrich, b. 17 Mar 1956, Gmünd, Austria. Musician (guitar); Backing Vocalist. m. Marianne, 3 Dec 1982, 1 son, 1 daughter. Education: VSA; HSA; Sales Manager. Career: Founder member, Giant Blonder, 1972-83; Guest musician on: Blues Pumpm Live With Friends Tour, 1982; Member: Blues Pumpm, 1983-; Television, radio tours, most of Eastern Europe. Recordings: with Giant Blonder: Giant Blonder; Rock And Blues 2; Single: with Johannes Müller Blues Zappa and Pumpm Fritz: Der Letzte Zug; with Blues Pumpm: Albums: Live With Friends, 1985; The 5th Ten Years Jubilee, 1987; Live At Utopia, 1988; Birthday, 1991; Live In Vienna, 1992; The 5th, 1992; Living Loving Riding, 1994; Singles: Train and Quick Shoes, 1985; Men From Milwaukee, 1993. Honours: Silbernes Ehrenzeichen, 1992; Third Best Blues Album Ö3, Rot-Weiss-Rote Critics Poll, Live In Vienna, 1992. Memberships: ALM; AUME; LSG. Hobbies: Music; Family. Current Management: RGG Management, Peter Steinbach.

GLEESBORG Christian, b. 15 November 1963, Arhus, Denmark. Musician; Singer; Songwriter. 2 sons. Education: Self Taught, Different Classes and Short Courses. Career: Started Playing in Clubs and Festivals, 1986; Formed Duo, Harp & Strings, toured Denmark, 1989-95; Board Member, Danish Folkmusic Association, 1990-; Member of duo, Draught

Baileys. Memberships: Danish Musicians Union. Hobbies: Family; Nature. Address: Saskraenten 95, DK-8260 Viby J, Denmark.

GLEESON David Sean, b. 3 June 1968, Newcastle, Australia. Vocalist. Education: Music, Higher School Certificate. Career: Played with local rock band Aspect, 1985; Played with The Screaming Jets, 1989-; 3 British tours, 2 US tours, 2 European tours; Toured with the Quireboys and Thunder. Recordings: Albums with The Screaming Jets: All For One; Tear Of Thought; The Screaming Jets. Hobbies: Golf; Surfing; Gambling; Beer. Current Management: c/o Aaron Chugg, Grant Thomas Management, PO Box 176, Potts Point, NSW 2011, Australia.

GLEN Alan, b. Wupperthal, Germany. Musician (harmonica). m. Jacqueline Lewis, 31 May 1995, 2 sons. Career: with Nine Below Zero: Sting, tour of Spain, Scandinavia, 1993; Toured with and supported Eric Clapton, Scandinavia, 1993; Royal Albert Hall, 1994; ZZ Top; Joe Cocker, 1994; Alvin Lee, 1994; Played and recorded with: Alannah Myles, Canadian tour, 1994; Alvin Lee, US tour, 1994; Television, radio appearances: USA; Canada; Italy; Sweden; Switzerland; France; Hungary; Austria; Germany; Britain. Compositions: Bad Town Blues, film soundtrack for Circuitry Man II; Another Kind Of Love; It's Nothing New; Recordings: Albums: with Nine Below Zero: Off The Hook, 1993; Best Of Nine Below Zero, 1994; Hot Music For A Cold Night, 1994; Ice Station Zebro, 1995; Singles: with Nine Below Zero: Soft Touch, 1993; Workshy, 1993; with Alannah Myles: Never Loved A Man, 1994; Down By The River, 1995; Live album with Alvin Lee, live Nine Below Zero album, solo harmonica album, all awaiting release. Membership: BASCA. Current Management: Mickey Modern, Arctic King Management. Address: Cambridge House, Card Hill, Forrest Row, East Sussex RH18 5BI, England.

GLENNIE-SMITH Nicholas Hugh, b. 3 Oct 1951, Kingston-On-Thames, England. Composer; Musician (keyboards); Engineer. m. Janet, 21 Dec 1974, 2 sons, 2 daughters. Education: Chorister, New College Oxford. Musical Education: Trinity College, London. Career: Tours with: David Essex; Randy Edelman; Glen Campbell; Classic Rock; Roger Waters, The Wall, Berlin. Compositions: Two if by Sea, 1995; The Rock, 1996; The Preacher's Wife, 1996; Fire Down Below, 1997; Home Alone 3, 1997; The Man in the Iron Mask, 1998. Recordings: Albums: with Cliff Richard: I'm No Hero, 1980; Wired For Sound, 1981; Silver, 1983; with Leo Sayer: Living In A Fantasy, 1980; Strange Day In Berlin, 1983; with Nik Kershaw: Human Racing, 1984; with Tina Turner: Private Dancer, 1984; Break Every Rule, 1986; Foreign Affair, 1989; with The Adventures: Theodore And Friends, 1985; Sea Of Love, 1988; with Beltane Fire: Different Breed, 1986. Also appeared on albums by: Phil Collins; Paul McCartney; Roger Waters; Roger Daltrey; Katrina And The Waves; Five Star; Barbara Dickson; Film soundtracks: The Lion King; K2; Point Of No Return; Calendar Girl; Cool Runnings; House Of The Spirits; I'll Do Anything; Monkey Trouble; Renaissance Man; Beyond Rangoon; Bad Boys; Crimson Tide; 9 Months. Honours: Grammy, as Musician, What's Love Got To Do With It. Memberships: ASCAP; PRS. Current Management: The Kraff Benjamin Agency, Los Angeles, CA, USA. Address: Belle Haven, Rt 4, Box 64c, Scottsville, VA 24590, USA.

GLESS Gilberto, b. 12 Aug 1959, Parral Chihuahua, Mexico. Singer; Voice And Personality Imitator; Entertainer. m. Silvia Hermosillo, 5 Feb 1982, 1 son, 2 daughters. Education: Major, Children's Mental Problems. Musical Education: Voice Education, guitar, piano. Career: Mexican and Latin American theatres, cabaret; Approximately 120 performances a year; Cabaret shows private and companies show. Membership:

Mexican National Actors Association. Hobbies: Jogging; Basketball. Current Management: RAC Producciones SA de CV. Address: Sierra Gorda # 30 Col Lomas De Barrilaco, Mexico DF, Mexico.

GLITTER Gary (Paul Gadd), b. 8 May 1944, Banbury, Oxfordshire, England. Singer; Entertainer; Songwriter. Career: Leader, skiffle group Paul Russell and the Rebels; Worked in Germany as Paul Raven; Relaunched career as glam rock singer Gary Glitter, 1971-; Considerable success in UK, 1970s-; Appearances include: London Rock'n'Roll Festival, Wembley Stadium, 1972; UK tours, 1974-; Charity concert, Theatre Royal, London, 1976; Slough Festival, 1992; Numerous television appearances include: Remember Me This Way (full length movie/documentary), 1973; Presenter, Night Network, 1988; Hyde Park Prince's Trust Concert, 1996; Performed in Quadrophenia with The Who; Toured USA in Quadrophenia with The Who, 1996. Compositions: Numerous hits co-written with Mike Leander. Recordings: Albums: Glitter, 1972; Touch Me, 1973; Remember Me This Way, 1974; Always Yours, 1975; GG, 1975; I Love You Love, 1977; Silver Star, 1978; The Leader, 1980; Boys Will Be Boys, 1984; Leader II, 1991; Numerous compilations; Hit singles include: Rock'n'Roll Part 2 (Number 2, UK), 1972; I Didn't Know I Loved You (Till I Saw You Rock'n'Roll), 1972; Do You Wanna Touch Me (Number 2, UK), 1973; Hello Hello I'm Back Again (Number 2, UK), 1973; I'm The Leader Of The Gang, (Number 1, UK), 1973; I Love You Love Me Love, (Number 1, UK), 1973; Always Yours (Number 1, UK), 1974; Remember Me This Way, 1974; Oh Yes You're Beautiful (Number 2, UK), 1974; Love Like You And Me, 1975; Doin' Alright With The Boys, 1975; Another Rock'n'Roll Christmas, 1984. Publication: Leader - The Autobiography of Gary Glitter, 1991. Honours: Nordoff Robins Lifetime Achievement Award, 1997; BASCA Gold Badge Award, 1997. Current Management: Jef Hanlon Management Ltd. Address: 1 York Street, London W1H 1PZ, England.

GLOCKLER Nigel Ian, b. 24 Jan 1953, Hove, Sussex, England. Musician (drums, percussion). Education; Brighton College. Musical Education: Self-taught. Career: Toyah, 1980-81; Saxon, 1981-87; GTR, 1987-88; Saxon, 1989-; Tours with Toyah, Saxon; Television and radio appearances. Recordings: Albums include: with Toyah: Anthem; with Saxon: The Eagle Has Landed; Power And The Glory; Crusader; Solid Ball Of Rock; Dogs Of War; Forever Free; Rock The Nations; Innocence Is No Excuse; Live albums; with Asia: Aqua; Japanese film soundtrack album; with Steve Howe: Turbulenz; Guitar Speak; with Tony Martin: Back Where I Belong; with Fastway: Bad Bad Girls. Memberships: PRS; MCPS; Musicians' Union. Current Management: Blackmail Management. Address: 60 Cleveland Road, New Malden, Surrey KT3 3QJ, England.

GLOJNARIC Silvestar, b. 2 Dec 1936, Ladislavec, Croatia. m. Ana Jurisic, 7 July 1962, 1 son, 1 daughter. Musical Education: Zagreb Music Academy, Composition and Theory Department. Career: Tours, concerts, Zagreb Jazz Quartet, Europe; Tours with Zagreb Radio Big Band, Europe including Russia; Television, radio appearances with various orchestras as composer, arranger, conductor; Most European Jazz Festivals. Recordings: Zagreb Big Band with: Art Farmer; Slide Hampton; Stan Getz; J Griffin; SFB Big Band, Berlin; NDR Big Band, Hamburg; Ljubljana Big Band; John Lewis, A Mangelsdorf: Animal Dance; Buck Clayton, BJ Turner: Feel So Fine; Georgie Fame. Membership: Croatian Composers' Association. Current Management: Silverstar Glojnaric. Address: Cujetno Naseltje 3, 41430 Samobar, Croatia.

GLOSSOP Mick, b. 18 Mar 1949, Nottinghamshire, England. Record Producer; Engineer. m. Elva Williamson, 1 daughter. Career:

Assistant Engineer and Engineer, various UK and Canadian recording studios, including the Manor and Townhouse Studios to 1979; Freelance producer, 1980-. Recordings: Producer, Engineer of albums: 13 by Van Morrison, including Wavelength, Into The Music, Inarticulate Speech, Sense Of Wonder, No Guru No Teacher No Method, Poetic Champions Compose, Avalon Sunset, Enlightenment, Too Long In Exile, Hymns To The Silence; numerous other albums by: The Skids; Frank Zappa; Camel; The Ruts; Public Image Ltd; The Waterboys; UFO; The Men They Couldn't Hang; The Wonder Stuff; also worked with John Lee Hooker; Magazine; Southern Death Cult; The Alarm; Flesh For Lulu; Vic Reeves (number 1 single Dizzy). Memberships: Re-Pro (UK). Hobbies: Off-roading; Macintosh computers; Flying kites; Family. Current Management: Annie Holloway, c/o The Producers. Address: 45-53 Sinclair Road, London W14 0NS, England.

GLOVER Cory. Singer. Career: Actor, film: Platoon, 1985; Singer, funk rock group Living Colour, 1985-; Tours include: Support to Cheap Trick; Robert Palmer; Anthrax; Billy Bragg; Rolling Stones, Steel Wheels North American Tour, 1989; Miracle Biscuit tour, 1990; Lollapalooza tour, 1991; Stained In The UK tour, 1993; Concerts include: Earth Day concert, Central Park; Reading Festival, 1990; Phoenix Festival, 1993. Recordings: Albums: Vivid, 1988; Time's Up, 1990; Biscuits, 1991; Stain, 1993; Guest on Primitive Cool, Mick Jagger, 1986; Singles include: Cult Of Personality, 1989; Glamour Boys, 1989; Love Rears Its Ugly Head, 1991; Solace Of You, 1991; Leave It Alone, 1993. Honours: Elvis Award, Best New Band, International Rock Awards, 1989; MTV Awards: Best New Artist, Best Group Video, Best Stage Performance, 1989; Grammy Award, Best Hard Rock Performance, Time's Up, 1991; Rolling Stone Critics Poll Winners, Best Band, 1991. Membership: Black Rock Coalition. Address: c/o Jim Grant, Suite 1C, 39A Gramercy Park North, New York, NY 10010, USA.

GLOVER Roger, b. 30 Nov 1945, Brecon, Powys, Wales. Musician (bass); Composer; Record Producer. Career: Founder, The Madisons; Member, Episode Six, including 9 singles, 1966-69; Member, Deep Purple, 1970-73; Record producer, albums for: Nazareth; Status Quo; Judas Priest; Rory Gallagher; Rainbow; Elf; David Coverdale; Pretty Maids; Spencer Davis; Ian Gillan; Rupert Hine; Barbi Benton; Young and Moody; Solo recording artiste; Member, Rainbow, 1979-84; Concerts include: Monsters Of Rock Festival, UK, 1980; Member, Deep Purple, 1984-; Also worked with Ian Gillan; Numerous worldwide tours with the above. Compositions include: The Butterfly Ball (led to book and film), 1974; Co-writer, with Ritchie Blackmore; All Night Long; Can't Happen Here. Recordings: Albums: with Deep Purple: Concerto For Group And Orchestra, 1970; In Rock, 1970; Fireball, 1971; Machine Head, 1972; Made In Japan, 1973; Who Do We Think We Are?, 1973; Perfect Strangers, 1984; House Of Blue Light, 1987; Nobody's Perfect, 1988; Slaves And Masters, 1990; The Battle Rages On, 1993; Purpendicular, 1996; Solo: Elements, 1978; Mask, 1984; with Gillan/Glover: Accidentally On Purpose, 1988; with Rainbow: Down To Earth, 1979; Difficult To Cure, 1981; Straight Between The Eyes, 1982; Bent Out Of Shape, 1983; Finyl Vinyl, 1986; Hit singles: with Deep Purple: Black Night, 1970; Strange Kind Of Woman, 1971; Smoke On The Water, 1973; Knocking At Your Back Door, 1985; with Rainbow: Since You've Been Gone, 1979; All Night Long, 1980; I Surrender, 1981; Can't Happen Here, 1981; Also performed with: Dave Cousins; Andy Mackay; Dan McCafferty. Current Management: Thames Talent, 45 E Putnam Street, Greenwich, CT 06850, USA.

GLYNN Dominic, b. 27 Sept 1960, Cuckfield, West Sussex, England. Composer; Producer. Musical Education: Self-taught. Career: Incidental music: BBC TV's Doctor Who; Space Vets; Various education series; Half of experimental electronic act Syzygy; Appearances London's Kiss FM. Recordings: Theme from Doctor Who, 1986; Numerous albums for Chappell Recorded Music Library; With Syzygy: Morphic Resonance; Terminus. Hobbies: Friends; Clubs; Music. Current Management: Cardinus Management: Address: 57 Farningham Road, Caterham, Surrey, England.

GNATYUK Mikola, b. 14 Sept 1952, Ukraine. Singer. 1 son. Education: Music Institut, Rovno, Ukraine. Musical Education: Numerous television and radio appearances: Moscow; Ukraine; Germany, including: Aein Kessel, Rund; Concerts: Prague; Warsaw; Tours: Russia; Ukraine; Germany. Recordings: Songs: Bazaban; Molinovoi Zvon; Belii Stavni (number 1, Ukraine), 1994; Shas Rikog Pluve; Starenki. Honours: 1st prize, Sopot Festival, Poland; Grand Prix Festival, Dresden. Membership: SVIATO. Hobbies: Visiting son in Germany. Current Management: Mother in Kiev. Address: 252040 Kiev, Vasilkovskai 2A/126, Ukraine.

GOBAC Davor, b. Karlovac, Croatia. Singer; Composer; Entertainer; Actor; Text-writer. m. Deana Pavic, 5 Feb 1994, 1 son. Career: Netherlands tour, 1989; Support to Ramones, Zagreb, Ljubgjana, 1990; Russian tour, 60 concerts, 1991; Toronto, 1993; Germany, Italy, Austria; 3 clips, MTV; Marcel Vanhilt Show; Many television and radio shows, Croatia. Recordings: Godina Zmaja (Year Of Dragon), 1988; Live In Amsterdam, 1989; Sexy Magazin, 1990; Tko Je Ubio Mickey Mousea (Who Killed Mickey Mouse), 1991; Skrebrne Svinje (Silver Pigs), 1993, 1994; Video: Brkiant Video Pop, 1989. Honours: Croatian Film and Video Award, Oktavijan Miletic, 1995. Membership: Hrvatska Glalbena Vnija (Croatian Musicians' Union). Hobbies: Painting; Acting. Address: Sljemeuska 27, 41211 Zapresic, Croatia.

GODDARD Jon, b. 15 May 1955, Suffolk, England. Musician (guitar, keyboards, percussion); Vocalist; Programmer; Composer. m. Catherine Goddard, 27 Dec 1989. Career: Appeared at Womad Festival, Spain; Festival of Arts and Music, Lanzarote; Roskilde Festival, Denmark; Appearances on regional arts television programme and local radio; Tours include: with Wolsey and Eastern Angles Theatre companies. Membership: Musicians' Union. Hobbies: Reading; Walking. Address: Badingham, Suffolk, England.

GODFREY Mary, b. 10 September 1960, Chicago, IL, USA. Singer; Songwriter; Musician (Bass, Guitar). Education: Organ and Bass Guitar lessons; Selftaught guitar. Compositions: Temperature Change, 1990; Hit and Run, 1991; Mine Tonight and Send Me An Angel, 1994; The Edge in the Night, 1995. Recordings: Faces of Emotion: Hot Love, 1987; Back to the Light, 1988; TOC Album, 1989; Solo Recordings: Mary Godfrey, 1991; Contributor: Down O'Keele, backing vocal, 1993. Honours: Chicago Talent Search Winner, 1990; Second Place Lead Vocalist, Chicago Rocker Awards, 1990; Second Place Member, Dunce Category, Chicago Rocker Awards, 1990. Memberships: NARAS, Vice President for WIM (Chicago Outreach Committee, 1989-91); ASCAP; National Academy of Songwriters. Hobbies: Freelance Writer for various magazines; Artist (Acrylic showing at the Ashwell Gallery, Beverly, USA, 1996). Current Management: English Cathy, Transatlantic Management, Box 2831, Tucson, AZ 85702, USA.

GODHOLM Clare, b. 11 July 1955. Music Publisher; Attorney. Education: BA, Barnard College (Columbia University), 1975; JD, Rutgers School of Law, 1978. Career: Pop Music Publisher; Chartered member including Clay Walker, G-Love & Special Sauce, Dandelion, and various European and Asian singles. Membership: Philadelphia Bar Association. Current Management: Stray Dog Music Inc, 303 W Lancaster Avenue, #324, Wayne, PA 19428, USA. Address: 303 West Lancaster Avenue, #324, Wayne, Pennsylvania, 19087, USA.

GODLEMAN Martin John, b. 6 Jan 1958, Hammersmith, London, England. Vocalist; Writer; Musician (drums). Musical Education: BA Hons, Hatfield Polytechnic, 1979; MA, University of Surrey, 1991. Career: Bands: Faut Parler, 5 piece (Serge Gainsbourg jazz band), Mean Fiddler, 1993; Adventures Of Parsley, 5 piece (vocals, percussion), Radio One, Mark Radcliff Show, 1995; Mark Lamarr Show, GLR, 1995; Comedy Cafe Anniverary Show, London, 1995; Adventures of Parsley, Leadline 5 piece (vocals); Big Breakfast TV Show, (Comedy Cafe gig highlights), Ch4, 1995; Edinburgh Fringe (Gilded Balloon), (Adventures of Parsley), 1997. Recordings: Singles: Magpie, Adventures Of Parsley, 1995; Intoxicated Man, Faut Parler, 1996; Minder (Adventures of Parsley), 1997; Albums: Top TV Themes (Adventures of Parsley), 1997. Publication: Chapter in The Power Of The Page, 1993. Memberships: FRA (Royal Academy); Collingwood Athletic Club. Hobbies: Theatre; Running (to half-marathon level); Soccer commentary (with West Ham United Football Club); Songwriting; Production. Current Managment: Norbert J Hetherington Management, 10 Lowfield Road, Acton, London W3 0AY, England.

GODLEY Kevin, b. 7 Oct 1945, Manchester, Lancashire, England. Vocalist; Musician (drums); Songwriter; Producer; Video Director. Career: Founder member, drummer, 10cc, 1972-76; Appearances include: Reading Festival, 1974; Knebworth Festival, 1976; US and UK tours; Producer, songwriter, duo Godley and Creme (with Lol Creme), 1976-; Television includes: One World One Voice, series of programmes, with contributions from artists including: Sting, Peter Gabriel, Lou Reed, Chrissie Hynde, Stewart Copeland; Feature film, Howling At The Moon, 1988. Recordings: Albums: with 10cc: Sheet Music, 1974; Original Soundtrack, 1975; Greatest Hits, 1975; How Dare You?, 1976; with Godley & Creme (mostly self-written and produced): Consequences, 1977; L, 1978; Music From Consequences, 1979; Freeze Frame, 1979; Long Distant Romancer, 1981; Ismism, 1981; Birds Of Prey, 1983; The History Mix, Volume 1, 1985; The Changing Faces Of 10cc and Godley And Creme, 1987; Goodbye Blue Sky, 1988; Singles include: with 10cc: Donna, 1973; The Dean And I, 1973; Rubber Bullets, 1974; Wall Street Shuffle, 1974; Silly Love, 1974; Life Is A Minestrone, 1975; I'm Not In Love (UK Number 1, US Number 2), 1976; Art For Art's Sake, 1976; I'm Mandy Fly Me, 1976; with Godley & Creme: Under Your Thumb, 1981; Wedding Bells, 1981; Cry, 1985; Producer, albums including Long Distant Romancer, Mickey Jupp, 1981; One World One Voice, 1989; Director, videos including: Every Breath You Take, The Police; Rockit, Herbie Hancock; Feel The Love, 10cc; Relax, Frankie Goes To Hollywood; Two Tribes, Frankie Goes To Hollywood. Membership: Co-founder, environmental organisation, ARK. Honours: Ivor Novello Awards: Best Beat Song, Rubber Bullets, 1974; Most Performed British Song, Best Pop Song, International Hit Of The Year, I'm Not In Love, 1976; 5 MTV Video Awards, Rockit, 1984; MTV Video Vanguard Award, 1985.

GOFFEY Danny. Musician (drums). Career: Member, The Jennifers; Drummer, Supergrass, 1994-; Concerts include: Support to Blur, Alexandra Palace; UK tour with Shed Seven, 1994; T In The Park Festival, Glasgow, 1995. Recordings: Albums: I Should Coco (Number 1, UK), 1995; In it for the Money, (No 2, UK); Singles: Caught by the Fuzz, 1994; Mansize Rooster, 1995; Lenny, 1995; Alright, 1995; Going Out, 1996; Sun Hits the Sky, 1997. Honours: Q Award, Best New Act, 1995; BRIT Award Nominations:

Best British Newcomer, Best Single, Best Video, 1996. Current Management: Courtyard Management, 22 The Nursery, Sutton Courtenay, Abingdon, Oxon OX14 4UA, England.

GOHIL Jitesh, b. 3 Apr 1967, Kenya. Record Executive. Education: First Class Degree, Economics, Accounting, Bristol University. Career: Joined Multitone Records, 1988; Multitone developed into largest Asian record label in world, pioneered Bhangra genre; Multitone Records joined BMG Group, 1992; Now Managing Director, Multitone. Address: 1274 Uxbridge Road, Hayes End, Middlesex UB4 8JF, England.

GOLBEY Brian James, b. 5 Feb 1939, Pycombe, Sussex, England. Musician (guitar, fiddle); Vocalist; Journalist. m. (1) 20 Sept 1969, divorced, 2 sons; (2) Sandi Stubbs, 3 May 1980, 1 son; Career: Television with Pete Stanley (partner, 27 years) includes: 3 times Blue Peter; George Hamilton IV shows, BBC2; Many local television appearances; Old Grey Whistle Test; Cajun Moon, 1975; Magpie, ITV, 1969-; Concerts, most theatres include: Wembley Festival Of Country Music, several times; London Palladium; Royal Albert Hall; Recordings for Pye, 1970; Emerald/Decca, 1973-74; Chrysalis, 1975; Waterfront Records, 1979-1980s. Publications: Regular columnist, Country Music People, 1989-; Essay for Aspects of Elvis, 1994. Honours: Billboard; Record Mirror Award, Top UK artist; CMA Award, Top UK Soloist, 1972; BCMA Committee Award for long and continuing service to Country music in Britain, 1993. Membership: PRS. Hobbies: Music; Painting; School activities. Address: 7 Hallcroft Beeston, Nottingham NG9 1E2, England.

GOLD Harry, b. 26 Feb 1907, Dublin, Ireland. Musician (clarinet, all saxophones including bass). m. Margaret (Peggy), 4 Oct 1936, deceased 2 July 1995, 4 sons. Musical Education: London College of Music, Bachelor of Music. Career: Professional, 1923-; Composer, arranger, orchestrator, musical director; Founder, leader, Pieces of Eight Jazz Band; Rhapsody In Green, Radio Telefis Concert Orchestra; Television: Lowest Of The Low. Compositions: Very numerous, about 50 compositions and arrangements published. Publications: Presently writing autobiography. Honours: BBC Special Award; Freeman of City Of London; Derry, Northern Ireland; Blarney, Co Cork. Memberships: Musicians' Union; British Academy of Songwriters, Composers and Authors; PRS. Hobby: Cooking. Address: Flat 126, 53 Foxham Road, London N19 4RR, England.

GOLDBERG Barry, b. 25 Dec 1942, Chicago, Illinois, USA. Musician (piano); Songwriter. m. Gail, 15 May 1971, 1 son. Musical Education: Self-taught. Career: Appeared at Newport Folk Festival with Bob Dylan, 1965; Played at Woodstock and Monterey pop festivals; Has written the score or contributed songs for films: Forrest Gump; Ruby; Flashback; Pow-Wow Highway; Dirty Dancing; Nobody's Fool; Adventures In Babysitting; Studio sessions with: Leonard Cohen; The Byrds; Mitch Ryder; The Ramones; Charlie Musselwhite; Additional associations with: Electric Flag; Bob Crewe; Jimi Hendrix; Gerry Goffin; Neil Young; Solomon Burke; Merry Clayton; Percy Sledge. Recordings: I've Got To Use My Imagination, recorded by Gladys Knight, Joe Cocker and Bobby Blue Bland; It's Not The Spotlight, recorded by Rod Stewart; Sittin' In Circles, recorded by Steve Miller; Additional songs recorded by artists including: Tom Jones; B J Thomas; Manhattan Transfer; Ben E King; The Neville Brothers; Jeff Healey; The Persuasions; Carole King; Junior Walker; Sam Moore. Honour: Pioneer Award, BMI, USA. Memberships: BMI; NARAS; AFofM. Current Management: Christopher Nassif Agency, Joe Schneider, CNA, Century City, Los Angeles, California, USA.

GOLDIE, b. 1966, Wolverhampton, England. Vocalist. Career: Solo vocalist, Jungle music. Recordings: Albums: Goldie Presents Metalheadz: Timeless, 1995; Saturnz Returnz, 1998. Current Management: NUR Entertainment, Canalot Studios, Unit 218A, 222 Kensal Road, London W10 5BN, England.

GOLDMAN Jill Valerie, b. 16 Sept 1945, Nottingham, England. Freelance Showbusinees Writer; Theatre Reviewer; Songwriter; Singer; Poet. m. Richard M Goldman, 8 Aug 1976, 1 son. Education: Secretarial qualifications; Writing and broadcasting courses. Musical Education: Private singing and guitar lessons. Career: Worked at: ATV Music Publishing; British Academy of Songwriters, Composers, Authors; Moved to writing (specialising in profiles of singers, songwriters, writers, actors, film directors), beginning with BASCA magazine; Currently writing musical, showcased Willesden Library Theatre, 1990; Performed own songs, Songwriter venues, festivals; Some acting work. Publications: Contributor, magazines including: Writers' Monthly; The Singer; Writers' News; The Lady; Plays And Players; New Moon; Arts Reviewer, Executive Woman Magazine; Poems in anthologies. Memberships: PRS; British Academy of Songwriters, Composers, Authors; SWWJ (Society of Women Writers and Journalists). Address: Alvia Cottages, 2 Preston Waye, Kenton, Harrow, Middlesex HA3 0Q9, England.

GOLDSBORO Bobby, b. 18 Jan 1941, Marianna, Florida, USA. Musician (guitar); Singer; Songwriter. Career: Guitarist, Roy Orbison, 1960; Solo artiste, 1964-; Later, country artiste, 1980s. Recordings: Hit singles include: See The Funny Little Clown, 1964; Whenever He Holds You; Little Things; Voodoo Woman; It's Too Late; Blue Autumn; Honey (Number 1, US; Number 2, UK), 1968; Watching Scotty Grow; Summer (The First Time); Albums include: Honey, 1968; Today, 1969; Muddy Mississippi Line, 1970; We Gotta Start Lovin', 1971; Come Back Home, 1971; Goldsboro, 1977; Roundup Saloon, 1982; Also numerous compilations. Current Management: Jim Stephany Management, 1021 Preston Drive, Nashville, TN 37206, USA.

GOLDSMITH Harvey, b. 4 Mar 1946, London, England. Chief Executive; Impresario. m. Diana Gorman, 1971, 1 son. Education: Christ's College; Brighton College of Technology. Career: Partner, Big O Posters, 1966-67; Organised first free open-air concert in Parliament Hill Fields with Michael Alfandary, 1968; Opened Round House, Camden Town, 1968, Crystal Palace Garden Party series of concerts, 1969-72; Merged with John Smith Entertainments, 1970; Formed Harvey Goldsmith Entertainments (rock tours promotion company), 1976; Acquired Allied Entertainments Group (rock concert promotions company), 1984; Formed Classical Productions with Mark McCormack, 1986; Promoter and Producer of pop, rock and classical musical events including: Concerts: Bruce Springsteen; The Rolling Stones; Elton john; The Who; Pink Floyd; Opera: Aïda, 1988, Carmen, 1989, Tosca, 1991, Earls Court; Pavarotti at Wembley, 1986; Pavarotti in the Park, 1991; The Three Tenors, 1996; Lord of the Dance, 1996-97; Cirque du Soleil, 1996-97; Music Montserrat at the Royal Albert Hall, 1997. Honour: CBE, 1996. Memberships include: Chairman, Concert Promoters Association, 1986; Chairman, National Music Festival, 1991; Co-Chairman, President's Club, 1994; Vice Chairman, Prince's Trust Action Management Board, 1993; Vice President, REACT, 1989; Vice President, Music Users Council, 1994; Trustee, Band Aid, 1985; Trustee, Life Aid Foundation, 1985; Trustee, Royal Opera House, 1995; Trustee, CST, 1995; British Red Cross Communications Panel, 1992; Prague Heritage Fund, 1994; London Tourist Board, 1994. Address: Allied Entertainments Group Plc, 3-4 Ashland Place, London W1M 3JH, England.

GOLDSMITH Timothy Simon, b. 1 Dec 1962, West London, England. Musician (drums). Career: Tours with: Paul Brady; Tanita Tikaram; Nik Kershaw; Joan Armatrading; Jackie Graham; Television appearances include: Top Of The Pops; Old Grey Whistle Test; Live radio, videos. Recordings include: Albums: Alf, Alison Moyet; Go West, Go West; Track Record, Joan Armatrading. Membership: Musicians' Union. Hobbies: Fishing; Cinema. Address: 343a Upper Richmond Road West, East Sheen, London SW14, England.

GOLT Debbie, b. 2 Apr 1952, London, England. Consultant; Music and Arts Management. 2 daughters. Education: BA Hons, History, York University; PG Diploma, Applied Youth and Community Work, Manchester Polytechnic. Career: Diverse career on alternative/independent circuit; Parallel career in youth work and Arts Management; Ran sound system battles and concerts with Rock Against Racism, 1977-80; Managed major UK based African Band, Taxi Pata Pata (first UK-based African band on RI and Arts Council support); Director, Nyrangongo record label, 1985-90; Co-directed Half The Sky, first women's promotions group promoting female world music; Introduced Oumau Sangare to UK and top television / press coverage; Panelist for RI Sound City, In The City, Umbrella, 1991-93; Set up Eleventh Hour Arts; Co-director, Portobello Jazz; Co-manager, Frank Chickens, 1994-; Manager of Mo Mo, 1997-; Advisor to Frank Chickens, Giffy Naa Diko, Sandika; Co-ordinator, World Music Portobello Festival; Consultant for festivals,m global music, women's music. Publications: Contributor to several publications including Worldbeat; World Music Magazine; The Guardian; Folk Roots; Straight No Chaser, independent catalogue; Published style magazine Topical, 1991-93; Radio programmes on Radio 1, Radio 5 and local radio. Memberships: Women In Music, chair; Sound Sense; IMF. Hobbies: Reading widely; Cultural activities with own children; Art galleries; Gym; Macrobiotic food; Walking in the hills; Wide range of music. Address: Eleventh Hour Arts, 113 Cheesemans Terrace, Star Road, London W14 9XH, England.

GONZALEZ Celina, b. Jovellanos, Cuba. Singer. m. Rentilio Dominguez, Dec 1971, 1 son. Career: Country singer, formerly duo with husband, now with own band Campo Alegre; Daily radio show, Radio Taino, Havana; Regular television appearances include: Palmas y Canas, Cuba; Tours throughout Cuba, Dominican Republic, Columbia; Concerts in New York, and Cali Fest, 1984. Recordings: Hit single: Santa Barbara. Honours: Distinction of National Culture; Egrem Silver disc; 6 Premios Girasoles; Most popular artist in Cuba. Address: c/o World Circuit Records, 106 Cleveland Street, London W1P 5DP, England.

GOOD Bob, b. 9 Sept 1959, Guildford, Surrey, England. Vocalist; Director; Composer; Arranger. m. Alison, 12 Sept 1992. Career: Keyboard player, backing vocalist with: The Smartie People; The Ornaments; Latent Heat; Vocalist with: 13 Feet; The Good Guys; Mixed Blessings; Director of: Sounds Good; Guildford A Cappella; Curtain Raisers; MD, Gooday Productions. Compositions: for Tac-Tix: Whisper On The Street; See The Love; for Bob Terry: Share Another Sunset. Memberships: BASCA; PRS; BABS; Musicians' Union.

GOOD Larry J. Professional Entertainer; Musician (guitar). m.Jennifer, 22 Feb 1985. 1 daughter (by previous marriage). Musical Education: Playing with Grand Ole Opry stars. Career: Shows with major artist including: Charley Pride; Waylon Jennings; Marty Robbins; Roy Acuff; Ray Price; Ernest Tubb; Television appearances: Regular on several local television shows; Ernest Tubb Midnight Jamboree. Recordings: Albums include: Some Old Some

New; As Good As It Gets; Moving Country; Singles include: Raise Your Glass; Long Way To Kansas City. Honour: Nebraska Country Music Hall Of Fame. Hobby: Gardening. Current Management: Lari-Jon Promotions. Address: 325 W Walnut, Rising City, NE 68658, USA.

GOODACRE Tony, b. 3 Feb 1938, Leeds, England. Singer; Entertainer; Musician (guitar). m. (1) Cherry, 18 June 1960, 1 son, 2 daughters; (2) Sylvia, 29 July 1974. Career: First professional engagement, 1956; First recording, 1957; Radio debut, 1958; Formed band Goodacre Country, 1969; Guest, The Arthur Smith Show, USA television, 1973; First appearance, Grand Ole Opry, Nashville, 1977; Wembley Festival, 1982, 1983; Started own Music Publishing Company: Sylvantone Music, 1983; Promoted career of Stu Page, 1984-86; Sarah Jory, 1987-88. Recordings: Albums: Roamin' Round In Nashville, 1974; Grandma's Feather Bed, 1975; Thanks To The Hanks, 1976; Written In Britain, 1977; The Best Of Tony Goodacre, 1978; Mr Country Music, 1978; You've Made My Life Complete, 1979; Recorded Live In Ilkley, 1980; 25th Anniversary, 1981; Red Roses, 1983; Sylvantone Songbook, Volumes 1 & 2, 1984-85; The Tony Goodacre Collection, 1986; Country Favourites, 1988; Something Special, 1989; Livin' On Livin', 1992; 40th Anniversary Album, 1996. Honours: Record Mirror Award, 1973; 3 British Country Music Association Awards, 1982-84; Favourite Male Vocalist in Europe, Country Gazette (Dutch Magazine), 1986; 18 Country Music Club Awards, Top Solo Artist; 3 Country Music Club Awards, Top Duo, with Sarah Jory, 1987. Hobby: Travel. Current Management: Sylvantone Promotions. Address: 17 Allerton Grange Way, Leeds LS17 6LP, England.

GOODFELLOW Adam, b. 27 Oct 1954, Pudsey, Yorkshire, England. Musician; Actor; Editor. m. Heather, 7 June 1975, 1 son, 3 daughters. Career: Wheatstone Bridge, 1972; Pipeline, 1975; Duo with Mark Ostyn: Duplex, appearances Batley Variety Club, Calander, YTV, 1976-83; Single released 1976; 10 years running insurance business, returned to show business, 1993; Performer, Cabaret, Country and Western; Founder, editor, Live On Stage, listings magazine, East Yorkshire; Television appearances as supporting artiste: Emmerdale; Coronation Street; Darling Buds Of May; All Creatures Great And Small; Juliet Bravo; Heartbeat. Current Management: Goodfellow Music and Publications. Address: Yokefleet Lodge, Sandholme, Brough, East Yorkshire HU15 2XP, England.

GOODHEAD David, b. 12 Oct 1963, Burton-Upon-Trent, England. Blues and Rockabilly Musician (guitar). Education: HNC, Electronics and Instrumentation. Career: Played with various bands including Gene Vincent's Blue Caps; Eddie Fontaine; Also appeared in Rock and Roll revival tours. Membership: Musicians' Union. Address: 2 Dorchester Gardens, Westgate, Morecambe, Lancashire LA3 3LS, England.

GOODHIND Frank, b. 3 Oct 1970, Dartford, England. Composer; Musician (keyboards). Musical Education: Self-taught. Career: First appearance, 1977; Second, Elizabeth House, 1989; Performer, programmer, producer with Second Nature, 1991-93; Caprice, 1993-94; La Tour, 1994-95; Composer, 1980-; Business venture, Frank Goodhind Music (personal studio). Recordings: Extravaganza, 1986; The Albatross Waits, 1991; Bugjam, 1995. Membership: Musicians' Union. Address: 18 Eastleigh Road, Barnehurst, Kent DA7 6LU, England.

GOODIER David Charles Gray, b. 11 July 1954, Salisbury, England. Musician (bass guitar fretted/fretless, double bass). Partner, Lynn Thompson, 1 son, 2 daughters. Education: Bachelor of Education (Honours), St Luke's College, Exeter University. Musical Education: Self-taught, studied briefly with Peter Ind and

Rufus Reid. Career: Interests Funk, Fusion, Salsa, Mainstream, Modern and contemporary jazz; Worked in theatre pit bands made radio broadcasts (R3, R2); Television and radio sessions; Many festival appearances: Brecon; Glastonbury; Worked with jazz musicians, including: Guy Barker; Dave De Fries; Tal Farlow; Art Farmer; Slim Gaillard; Dick Morrissey; Gerard Presencer; Don Rendell; Andy Sheppard; Norma Winstone; Often as part of the Dave Gordon Trio with Tony Orrell; Musical Director, Bristol Jazz Workshop, 1991-. Recordings: John Parricelli, Mark Lockheart: Matheran; The Korgis: This World's For Everyone; Brass Reality: For Real. Hobbies: Squash; Badminton; Walking. Current Management: LDT Management.

GOODMAN Clare, b. 19 May 1966, Frimley, Surrey, England. Singer; Dancer. Musical Education: West Street School of Performing Arts. Career: Live: Joseph And The Amazing Technicolour Dreamcoat, UK tour, 1994-95; Appearance with Just Music (for anti-racist alliance) Arafest '94; Films: Frankenstein (Mary Shelley's); The Muppet Christmas Carol; Video: Give Me Just A Little More Time, Kylie Minogue; I've Got A Spell On You, Bryan Ferry; Commercials: Kool-aid; Red Stripe. Membership: Musicians' Union. Hobbies: Painting and drawing; Fashion design; Cycling; Skating; Tennis. Current Management: Pineapple Agency. Address: 29 Womersley Road, Crouch End, Hornsey, London N8 9AP, England.

GOODRICK Mick. Jazz Musician (guitar). Musical Education: BM, Berklee College of Music. Career: Former faculty member, Berklee College Of Music; Faculty member, Jazz Studies, New England Conservatory of Music; Performed and recorded with: Jack DeJohnette; Gary Burton; Paul Motian; Steve Gadd; Pat Metheny; Michael Brecker; Charlie Haden. Recordings: 2 albums with Jack DeJohnette's Special Edition. Publication: Author, The Advancing Guitarist. Address: New England Conservatory of Music, 290 Huntington Avenue, Boston, MA 02115, USA.

GOODRIDGE Walt Frederick Jerome, b. 23 Feb 1966, Jamaica, West Indies. Author; Entrepeneur. Education: BSc, Civil Engineering, Columbia University. Career: Radio disc jockey, 1983-88; Artist manager, 1988-90; Record label President, 1988-93; Writer, 1992-; President, A Company called W. Publications: Rap - This Game Of Exposure (Promoting Your Rap Record/Artist); This Game Of Artist Management (The Success Attitude); The Music Entrepreneur's Calender; The $uccess Diet (A Guide To Higher Living). Memberships: RIAA; NAIRD. Hobbies: Table tennis; Cycling; Listening to music. Address: A Company Called W, PO Box 618, Church Street Station, New York, NY 10008-0618, USA.

GOODWIN Christopher Neil, b. 10 Aug 1962, Oldham, England. Drummer. Education: Graduated from Tameside College. Career: Various TV appearances including a Granada TV special, High And Dry; 2 British tours and a European tour; Appeared in Leeds supporting Happy Mondays; Radio sessions on the Mark Godier and Mark Radcliffe shows. Recordings: Albums: Somewhere Soon, with The High, and Hype, with The High; Singles: Tomorrow's Sunset, with Buzzcocks, and Exiles, with Buzzcocks. Memberships: PRS; Musicians' Union. Hobby: Football. Current Management: Stuart Windsor Inc. Address: 27 Lausanne Road, Withington, Manchester, England.

GOODWIN Len, b. 24 Aug 1940, Sheffield, England. Songwriter; Author. m. Lynne Abbott, 18 Sept 1982, 1 son, 2 daughters. Musical Education: Self-taught. Career: Own songs performed by various artists on Crackerjack, BBC TV; Video Entertainers, Granada Network; Starburst, Granada Network; This Morning, Granada Network; Granada Reports, Granada TV; BBC

Radio 1 and 2, local and independent radio. Compositions: Writing credits on recordings: Good Old Coronation Street; Special Train; This Is A Record Of My Love (Happy Birthday Darling); Here We Are; (England Football Song) Football Anthem; Ain't This A Funny World. Publication: The Money Making Secrets of Successful Songwriters, 1997. Memberships: PRS; MCPS; PPL. Hobbies: Keep fit; Cooking. Current Management: Self-managed, company owned, Tram Promotions/Gable Records. Address: 16 Pendle Court, Astley Bridge, Bolton, Lancashire BL1 6PY, England.

GOODWIN Ronald Alfred, b. 17 Feb 1925, Plymouth, Devon, England. Composer; Conductor. m. Heather Dunsden, 22 Sept 1986, 1 son. Education: Self-taught. Career: Broadcasting and recording, 1950-; Composed 61 feature film scores and many documentaries; Guest Conductor, major orchestras in UK and internationally. Compositions include: Battle of Britain; 633 Squadron; Frenzy; Where Eagles Dare; Those Magnificent Men in Their Flying Machines; Operation Crossbow; The Trap. Recordings: Many soundtrack albums; Numerous recordings as Ron Goodwin and His Orchestra. Honours: 3 Ivor Novello Awards, 1956, 1972, 1994; Gold Disc, 1975; Platinum Disc, 1978; Fellow, City of Leeds College of Music, 1993. Memberships include: Association of Professional Composers; Worshipful Company of Musicians; Young Persons Concert Foundation. Hobbies: Chess; Walking. Current Management: Robert Light Agency, USA. Address: Blacknest Cottage, Brimpton Common, Reading, Berks RG7 4RP, England.

GORCE Partrick, b. 23 May 1962, Alger, Algeria. m. Odile, 24 Apr, 1 son, 1 daughter. Education: Baccalauréat, Music with Mention, 1981. Musical Education: 1st Prize, L'Ecole Superieur de Batterie, Dante Agostini, Paris. Career: Tours, USA; Europe; Performed Paris clubs, Zénith, Olympia, New Morning; Playued with: Ghetto Blaster; Luis Antonio; Jean-Claude Borrelli; Richard Clayderman; TV series; Teacher, Drumming and Traditional Percussion. Compositions: Tambours De La Paix (50 participants). Recordings: African Vibration, Samy Samiamam; Clypso O'Samba, Ile Axe; Travel And See, Nomadic Activities. Honours: Titualire de la Bourse "Lavoisier", Ministry of Foreign Affairs. Membership: SPEDIDAM. Current Management: Self-managed. Address: 21 bis Rue Solferino, 94100 St Maur, France.

GORDON Noah Adrian, b. 19 Sept 1971, Pinckneyville, Illinois, USA. Singer; Writer; Musician (guitar, drums). Education: 14 years; Degree in Electrical Engineering Technology. Musical Education: Self-taught. Career: Charlie Daniels Volunteer Jam, 1992; Nashville Now; Music City Tonight; Country Music Television; The Nashville Network; Nascar Country; Wal-Mart Country Music Across America Tour; TNN Wildhorse Saloon, 1994-95. Recordings: I Need A Break; Patriot Records; Christmas Time In Dixie, Charlie Daniels, 1994-95. Memberships: AFTRA; AFofM. Hobbies: Remote Control Modelling; Racquetball; Tennis. Current Management: Entertainment Artist Inc, 819 18th Ave S, Nashville, TN 37203, USA.

GORDON Robert, b. 4 Oct 1966, Sheffield, England. Music Programmer. 2 daughters. Career: Recording Engineer, Producer. Composition: Track With No Name, The Forgemasters. Recordings: House Arrest, Krush; Wanted, album, Yazz; Track With No Name, The Forgemasters; Rob Gordon Projects, album; Shiftwork, album, The Fall. Honours: Silver Disc, Krush, 1988; Double Platinum Disc, Yazz, 1988. Memberships: PRS; MCPS; PEMRA; PPL; Musicians' Union. Hobbies: Girls; Travelling; Hifi; Electronics; Design; Parties. Address: 18 Talbot Gardens, Sheffield, S2 2TE, England.

GORDON Rod, b. 6 Feb 1934, Flatbush, Alberta, Canada. Songwriter; Recording Artist; Musician (guitar). m. Jennette Richardson, 9 May 1964, 2 sons, 2 daughters. Musical Education: Self-taught. Career: Appeared on GERN-TV, Edmonton, Alberta and CHLT-TV, Sherbrooke, Quebec; Personal radio shows across Canada; Club bookings across Canada. Compositions: 200 compositions including Little Girl. Recordings: 2 singles released. Honour: Certificate of Merit for Outstanding Efforts in Advancement of Country Music. Memberships: Canadian Country Music Association; Country Music Association of Nashville. Hobbies: Fishing; Writing music. Current Management: 21st Century Records. Address: 530 3rd Avenue South No 2, Nashville, TN 37210, USA.

GORDY Berry Jr, b. 28 Nov 1929, Detroit, Michigan, USA. Record Company Executive; Songwriter. m. Grace Eaton, 17 July 1990, 6 children. Career: Owner, record store, Detroit, 1955; Composer and independent producer, late 1950s; Founder, Jobete Music, 1958; Tamla Records, 1959; Motown Record Corporation, 1961-88; Chairman, The Gordy Co; Executive Producer, film Lady Sings The Blues, 1972. Recordings: As composer / producer: Reet Petite, Jackie Wilson; Shop Around, The Miracles; Do You Love Me, The Contours; Try It Baby, Marvin Gaye; Shotgun, Junior Walker And The All-Stars. Honours: American Music Award, Outstanding Contribution to Music Industry, 1975; Inducted into Rock and Roll Hall Of Fame, 1988; NARAS Trustees Award, 1991. Address: Gordy Co, 6255 Sunset Boulevard, Los Angeles, CA 90028, USA.

GORE Lesley, b. 2 May 1946, New York, USA. Singer; Actress. Education: BA, English and American literature, Sarah Lawrence College, Bronxville, New York. Career: Appearances include: Greatest Record Show Of 1963; TAMI Show (released as film Gather No Moss), with Beach Boys, Chuck Berry, Rolling Stones, 1964; Richard Nader's Rock'n'Roll Revival, Madison Square Garden, 1975; Acting debut, The Donna Reed Show, 1966; Also appeared in Batman; Theatrical debut, Half A Sixpence, 1967; Nightclub and stage work, 1970s. Recordings: Albums: I'll Cry If I Want To, 1963; Lesley Gore Sings Of Mixed-Up Hearts, 1964; Boys Boys Boys, 1964; Girl Talk, 1964; The Golden Hits Of Lesley Gore, 1965; My Town, My Guy And Me, 1965; California Nights, 1967; Someplace Else Now, 1972; Love Me By Name, 1975; Singles include: It's My Party (million-selling debut); Judy's Turn To Cry; She's A Fool; You Don't Own Me; That's The Way The Boys Are; Maybe I Know; Sunshine Lollipops And Rainbows; My Town My Guy And Me; California Nights. Current Management: c/o Stan Scottland, JKE Services Inc., 404 Park Avenue S, 10th Floor, New York, NY 10016, USA.

GORE Martin Lee, b. 23 June 1961, London, England. Musician (Singer; Songwriter; Keyboards; Guitar). m. Suzanne (Boisvert), 27 August 1994, 2 daughters. Career: Founder Member, Depeche Mode, 1980-. Compositions: As Depeche Mode's Principal Songwriter since 1982, has written vast majority of songs recorded by the band. Recordings: 11 Top Ten Singles including: Just Can't Get Enough, 1981; See You, 1982; Everything Counts, 1983; People Are People, 1984; Master and Servant; Enjoy the Silence, 1990; I Feel You, 1993; Condemnation, 1993; In Your Room, 1994; Barrel of A Gun, 1994; It's No Good, 1997; 11 Top Ten Albums including: Speak and Spell, 1981; A Broken Frame, 1982; Construction Time Again, 1983; Some Great Reward, 1984; The Singles 81-85, 1985; Black Celebration, 1986; Music For the Masses, 1987; 101, 1989; Violator, 1990; Songs of Faith and Devotion, 1993; Ultra, 1997. Honour: BPI Brit Award, Enjoy the Silence, 1991. Hobbies: Reading; Computer Games. Current Management: Jonathon Kessler, Baron Inc, 111 West 67th Street, Suite 37F, New York, NY 10023,

USA. Address: First Floor, Regent House, 106 Marylebone High Street, London W1M 3DB, England.

GORE Simon Anthony, b. 14 Nov 1962, Bristol, England. Musician (drums). Education: Technical College. Career: Television debut at age 14 on BBC 1; Touring and recording with Andy Sheppard including many television and radio appearances, 1986-91; Currently teaching at several schools in Bristol and The Welsh College of Music and Drama in Cardiff. Recordings: Andy Sheppard, 1987; Introductions In The Dark, 1988; Soft On The Inside, also on video, 1990. Membership: Musicians' Union. Hobby: Cycling. Address: Garden Flat, 6 Goldney Road, Clifton, Bristol BS8 4RB, England.

GORGON James, b. 23 Mar 1963, Peterborough, Cambridgeshire, England. Musician (drums, percussion). Musical Education: Madras College, Pipeband Solo Competitions, private percussion. Career: Tours in USA, Middle East, Germany; 2 festivals, France; Television: Wish You Were Here; Holidays In Scotland, Grampian Television; Appearances at various music festivals; Various radio programme on: BBC Scotland; BBC Radio 2; Local radio. Recordings: with Albany: East West Hame's Best, 1986; Till A' Seas Gang Dry, 1993; Muirhead Accordion Band, 1991; Gathering Of The Clans Tour, 1992; Ted Poletyllo, 1993; with Paul Anderson: In Full Spate, 1994; with The Cutting Edge: Turning The Tide, 1994. Honours: Various Solo Pipeband, Drumming and Drum Corps Awards. Membership: Musicians' Union. Hobbies: Swimming; Squash. Current Management: Ninegates Music, Unit 48, Forum Centre, Dundee, Scotland.

GORHAM Scott, b. 17 Mar 1951, Santa Monica, California, USA. Rock Musician (guitar). Career: Guitarist, pub circuit, with Fast Buck, early 1970s; Guitarist, UK rock group Thin Lizzy, 1974-83; Founder member, 21 Guns, 1992; Appearances with Thin Lizzy include: Reading Festival, 1974, 1975, 1983; Great British Music Festival, London, 1975; World Series Of Rock, Cleveland, 1979; Monsters Of Rock, European tour, 1983; Reunion tribute to Phil Lynott, Self Aid concert, Dublin (with Bob Geldof), 1986. Recordings: with Thin Lizzy: Singles: The Boys Are Back In Town, 1976; Dancin' In The Moonlight, 1977; Rosalie, 1978; Sarah, 1979; Waiting For An Alibi, 1979; Chinatown, 1980; Killer On The Loose, 1980; Killers Live (EP), 1981; Cold Sweat, 1982; Thunder And Lightning, 1983; Albums with Thin Lizzy: Nightlife, 1974; Fighting, 1975; Jailbreak, 1976; Johnny The Fox, 1976; Bad Reputation, 1977; Live And Dangerous, 1978; Black Rose (A Rock Legend), 1979; Chinatown, 1980; Adventures Of Thin Lizzy, 1981; Renegade, 1981; Thunder And Lightning, 1983; Dedication - The Very Best Of Thin Lizzy, 1991; with 21 Guns: 21 Guns, 1992. Address: 49 Oakhill Road, Putney, London SW15, England.

GORME Eydie (Edith), b. 16 Aug 1931, New York, USA. Singer. m. Steve Lawrence, 29 Dec 1957. Career: Toured with Tommy Tucker; Tex Beneke; Night club singer; Recording artiste, 1952-; Own radio show, Cita Con Eydie; Regular shows and recordings with husband Steve Lawrence, 1953-; Member, Steve Allen's Troupe, Tonight Show, 1954; Stage performances: Jerry Lewis Stage Show, Broadway, 1967; Golden Rainbow, Broadway, 1968; Numerous other US stage performances and television specials, including tributes to George Gershwin, Cole Porter, Irving Berlin; Television adaptation, Alice In Wonderland, 1987; Support to Frank Sinatra, Diamond Jubilee world tour, 1991. Recordings: Singles: I've Gotta Crow; Tea For Two; Fini; Too Close For Comfort; Mama Teach Me To Dance; Love Me Forever; You Need Hands; with Steve Lawrence: I Want To Stay Here; I Can't Stop Talking About You; Numerous albums include: Eydie Gorme, 1957; Eydie Swings The Blues,

1957; Eydie In Love, 1958; On Stage, 1959; Eydie Sings Showstoppers, 1959; Eydie In Dixieland, 1960; Come Sing With Me, 1961; I Feel So Spanish, 1962; Blame It On The Bossa Nova, 1963; Let The Good Times Roll, 1963; Amor, 1964; More Amor, 1965; Don't Go To Strangers, 1966; Tonight I'll Say A Prayer, 1970; Toname O Dejame, 1985; Come In From The Rain, 1985; Canta, 1987; with Steve Lawrence: We Got Us, 1960; Cozy, 1961; On Broadway, 1967; What It Was, Was Love, 1969; Real True Lovin', 1969; We Can Make It Together, 1975; Our Best To You, 1977; Alone Together, 1989. Honours: Grammy Awards: We Got Us, 1960; Female Vocalist Of The Year, 1967; 7 Emmy Awards, Steve And Eydie Celebrate Irving Berlin. Address: c/o Premier Artists Services, 1401 University Drive #305, Coral Springs, FL 33071, USA.

GORR Jon Carl, b. 26 Sept 1958, Fredericksburg, Virginia, USA. Composer; Musician (keyboards). Musical Education: Jazz Composition, Chatauqua Institute, 1975; BM, Jazz Composition, Berklee College of Music, 1980. Career: President, Massmedia, 1983-; Songwriter, Cortlem Production, 1983-88; Castle Music, 1984-87; Keyboard player for: I-Tones; Eek-A-Mouse; Mighty Diamonds; Horace Andy, 1980-88; Steve Recker, 1986-87; Bo Diddley, 1987-88; Keyboard player, Gladiators (Europe), 1988-89; Composer, television and film music; Film appearance: Day Of The Dead, 1976; Television appearance: Spenser For Hire, 1987. Recordings: Albums: It's No Lie, 1985; Walk On By, 1985; On The Right Track, 1988. Honours: Boston Music Award, Best Reggae Band, 1987; Beat Magazine Readers Poll, Best Keyboard Player, 1987.

GORRIE Alan, b. 19 July 1946, Perth, Scotland. Singer; Musician (bass). Career: Member, The Vikins, Scotland, 1964-67; Member, Scots of St James, London, 1967-68; Member, Forever More, 1969-71; Member, Brian Auger's Oblivion Express, 1960s; Founder, The Average White Band, 1972-83; Renaissance, 1989; Member, Daryl Hall Band and Hall and Oates, 1993-94; Currently with Average White Band; International performances include: Lincoln Festival, 1972; Support to Eric Clapton, London, 1973; US tours, 1973; The Summer Of 80 Garden Party, Crystal Palace, London, with Bob Marley, Joe Jackson, 1980; Group reformed, 1989. Compositions include: Pick Up the Pieces, 1974; Cut the Cake, 1972, 1975; When Will You Be Mine, 1978; Lets Go Round Again, 1980; Sleepless Nights, 1984; Every Beat of My Heart, 1995. Recordings: Singles include: Pick Up The Pieces (Number 1, US), 1975; Cut The Cake, 1975; Let's Go Round Again, 1980; Albums: Show Your Hand, 1973; Average White Band, 1974; Cut The Cake, 1975; Soul Searching, 1976; Person To Person, 1977; Benny And Us, 1977; Warmer Communications, 1977; Atlantic Family Live at Montreux, 1977; Feel No Fret, 1979; Shine, 1980; Volume VIII, 1980; Cupid's In Fashion, 1982; Sleepless Nights, solo, 1985; Aftershock, 1989; Soul Alone, with Daryl Hall, 1993; Soul Tattoo, 1996. Honours: Grammy Nominations, 1974, 1975, 1978; ASCAP R&B Awards, 1993, 1996; 14 Platinum, Gold and Silver Discs worldwide, 1975, 1976, 1977, 1978, 1980, 1992, 1993. Memberships: PRS; ASCAP. Current management: Average Enterprises, Stamford, CT, USA.Address: c/o Miracle Prestige International, 1 Water Lane, Camden Town, London NW1 8NZ, England.

GORSE Vesna, b. 30 Sept 1961, Skopje, Macedonia. Musician (alto saxophone); Composer; Writer. m. Drazen Franolic, 20 June 1992. Career: Gorse-Franolic duo; Gorse-Franolic trio; Group: Tao; Concerts: Vatroslav Lisinski Concert Hall, Zagreb; Ljubljana; Belgrade; Sarajevo; Dubrovnik; Rijeka; Maribor, Italy; Multi-media festival, Czechoslovakia; Live album recordings at Lisinski. Recordings: with Drazen

Franolic: Waterfalls, 1986; New Era Of Instrumental Music, 1990; Wonderland, 1990; Asgard Live, 1993; Just A Music..., 1995. Honours: 2 Nominations, Porin '94 Awards: Asgard Live. Memberships: Croatian Composers' Society; Croatian Music Union; Amnesty International; World SF. Hobbies: Books; Films. Current Management: Vesna Gorse. Address: Vankina 3, Zagreb, Croatia.

GOSDIN Vern, b. 5 Aug 1934, Woodland, Alabama, USA. Country Singer; Songwriter; Musician (guitars, banjo, mandolin). Career: Member, Gosdin Family (with brothers), radio station, Birmingham, Alabama; Nightclub owner, Chicago, 1956; Member, Golden State Boys, early 1950s; The Hillmen, with Chris Hillman; Session musician, includes Gene Clark, 1966; Owner, glass shop, Atlanta, 1967-76; Solo artiste, and as Gosdin Brothers, 1977-. Compositions include: Someone To Turn To, The Byrds. Recordings: US Country Number 1 hits: I Can Tell By The Way You Dance; Set 'Em Up Joe; Other hits: Hangin' On; Yesterday's Gone; Till The End; Albums: with The Hillmen: The Hillmen, 1969; with The Gosdin Brothers: Gene Clark With The Gosdin Brothers, 1966; Sounds Of Goodbye, 1968; Solo albums: Till The End, 1977; Never My Love, 1978; You've Got Somebody, 1979; Passion, 1981; If You're Gonna Do Me Wrong, Do It Right, 1983; Today My World Slipped Away, 1983; Dream Lady, 1984; There Is A Season, 1984; If Jesus Comes Tomorrow, 1984; Time Stood Still, 1985; Chiseled In Stone, 1988; Alone, 1989; Out Of My Heart, 1991. Address: c/o Kathy Gangwisch and Associates Inc., 207 Westport Road, Suite 202, Kansas City, MO 64111, USA.

GOSS Kieran John, b. 18 May 1962, Newry, Northern Ireland. Songwriter; Singer. Education: LLB, Queen's University, Belfast. Career: Various TV appearances, Ireland; UK; Australia include: Late Late Show; Wogan; Kenny Live; Tours in Ireland; UK; Australia; New Zealand; USA. Recordings: Brand New Star; Frances Black; Kieran Goss; New Day. Honours: Platinum record, Folk Album Of Year In Scotland, for New Day, 1995. Membership: Musicians' Union. Hobbies: Football; Swimming. Current Management: George McCann, SMA Management. Address: 77 Castle Street, Belfast BT1, Northern Ireland.

GOSSARD Stone. Rock Musician (guitar). Career: Member, Green River, 1987-89; Guitarist, Mother Love Bone, 1989; Member, Pearl Jam, 1990-; Member, tribute group Temple Of The Dog, 1991; Formed Shame (renamed Brad), 1993; Concerts with Pearl Jam: Support to Alice In Chains, 1991; Lollapalooza Festival tour, 1992; Group appeared in film Singles, 1992; Drop In The Park concert, Seattle, 1992; Neil Young's Bridge School Benefit, with Elton John, Sammy Hagar, James Taylor, 1992; Concert appearances with Keith Richards; Neil Young. Recordings: with Mother Love Bone: Shine (EP), 1989; Apple, 1990; Albums with Pearl Jam: Ten (Number 2, US), 1992; Vs. (Number 1, US), 1993; Vitalogy, 1994; with Temple Of The Dog: Temple Of The Dog, 1992; with Brad: Shame, 1993; Singles with Pearl Jam: Alive, 1992; Even Flow, 1992; Jeremy, 1992. Honours: Platinum discs; American Music Awards, Favourite New Artist, Pop/Rock and Hard Rock categories, 1993; Rolling Stone Readers' Awards: Best New American Band, Best Video, 1993; 4 MTV Awards, 1993; Highest 1-week album sales total in history, Vs., 1993. Address: c/o Curtis Management, 417 Denny Way, Suite 200, Seattle, WA 98109, USA.

GOTT Karel, b. 14 July 1939, Plzen, Czech Republic. Singer. 2 daughters. Education: Studied under Professor Karenin, Prague Conservatory. Career: Member, Semafor Theatre, Prague, 1963-65; Member, Apollo Theatre, Prague, 1965-67; Freelance artiste, 1967-; Numerous foreign tours; Co-operation with record companies; Founder, chairman, Interpo Foundation, 1993-. Honours: Numerous Golden Nightingale Trophies, annual pop singer poll, 1963-; MIDEM Prize, Cannes, 1967; Music Week, Star Of The Year, 1974, 1975; Artist of Merit, 1982; Gold Aerial, BRT radio station, Belgium, 1984; National Artist, 1985; Polydor Golden Pin, Germany, 1986; Gold discs. Address: Nad Bertramkou 18, 15000 Prague 5, Czech Republic.

GOTT Michael, b. 1 Oct 1960, Weymouth, Dorset, England. Record label executive. Partner, Georgina C Pyle, 2 sons. Career: Label manager, Beat Goes On (BGO) Records. Address: Beat Goes On Records, PO Box 22, Bury St Edmunds, Suffolk IP28 6XQ, England.

GOTT Susan (Susi), b. 4 September 1962, Asheville, NC, USA. Musician (Fiddle); Singer; Songwriter. m. Christian Séguret, 30 September 1990, 1 son, 1 daughter. Education: BA, Environmental Science. Selftaught Musician. Career: Performing, including The Smithsonian National Institute, 1977; The Kennedy Center, with Masters of Bluegrass, 1986; NPR's All Things Considered, 1982; Nashville Networks' Fire on the Mountain; The Knoxville World's Fair, 1982; Sacrée Soirée, Paris, with Hugues Aufray. Compositions: Bound for New Orleans; Dancing Man; Hole in the Deep Blue Sea, with Christian Séguret. Recordings: CMH with Eddie Adcock and Talk of the Town; Cowbell Hollow; A Video Postcard of the Blue Ridge, with David Holt; Talking Feet, with Mike Seeger; Guitars, with Christian Séguret and Thierry Massoulore. Honours: Champion Fiddler, Fiddler's Grove, 1978, 1984; First Place Songwriter, Chris Austin Songwriting Contest, 1996. Memberships: International Bluegrass Music Association; Women in Bluegrass; SACEM. Hobbies: Poetry; Essays; Gardening; Mothering. Current Management: Co-Prod Music. Address: 1 rue du Pourtour, 45340 Auxy, France.

GOUBERT Estelle, b. 12 Feb 1961, Versailles, France. Musician (piano). 1 son, 2 daughters. Musical Education: Conservatory of Versailles. Career: Played with: drummer Aldo Romano; Paco Sery (member of group Sixun); Christian Vander (member of group Magma); Many jazz functions. Recording: Alma Latina, 1983. Address: 49 Bis Rue St Gervais, 95550 Bessancourt, France.

GOUGH Orlando, b. 24 August 1953, Brighton, England. Composer. m. Joanna Osborne, 2 December 1989, 2 sons. Education: Harrow & Oxford. Compositions: Hoovering the Beach, 1979; Buzz Buzz Buzz Went the Honeybee, 1980; Secret Gardens, 1981; New Tactics, 1982; Further and Further into the Night, 1984; Mozart At Palm Springs, 1983-84; Bosendorfer Waltzes, 1985; Weighing The Heart, 1986-87; Goes Without Saying, 1988; Mathematics of a Kiss, 1989; Savage Water, 1989; Currulao, 1989; Late, 1991; Lives of the Great Poisoners, 1991; Slow Walk, Fast Talk, 1992; The Air Shouts, 1992; Earth Bound, 1993; Saeta, 1993; The Empress, 1992-93; Escape at Sea, 1994; On the Rim of the World, 1994, 1997; Badenheim, 1995; People's Century, 1995-97; Sleeping with Audrey, 1996; Hotel, 1996-97; Room of Cooks, 1996-97; Room of Cooks, 1997; Axaxaxas Mlo, 1997. Career: Member of Bands: The Lost Jockey, 1978-82; Man Jumping, 1983-87. Recording: Message From the Border, 1996. Publication: The Complete A Level Maths, 1987. Hobbies: Cooking; Cricket. Current Management: Soundtrack, 22 Ives Street, London, SW3 2ND, England.

GOUIRAND Doudou (Gérard), b. 28 Apr 1940, Menton, France. Musician (alto and soprano saxophones); m. Monica Adrian, 28 Oct 1966, 2 sons, 1 daughter. Education: University degree. Musical Education: 3 years, high school. Career: Various European festivals; Most French jazz festivals; Tours and festivals, Canada; Africa; Scandinavia; Lithuania; Algeria; Middle East; UK (including Pan-Africa Festival, London, 1984); Poland. Recordings: Albums: Islands, with Chris McGregor, 1981; Mouvements Naturels, with J. Dyaui/Pierre Dorge, 1982; Chanting And Dancing, with World Music Company, 1985; Forgotten Tales, with Don Cherry, 1986; Space, with Mal Waldron, 1987; La Nuit De Wounded Knee, 1990; Le Matin D'Un Fauve, with Mal Waldron, 1994; Nino Rota Fellini, W.G.Pansanel, 1995. Hobbies: Music; Films; Reading; Walking; Swimming. Current Management: Opus Productions, Montpellier, France.

GOULDMAN Graham Keith, b. 10 May 1946, Manchester, England. Songwriter; Musician (guitar, bass). m. Gill, 7 Oct 1988, 2 sons, 2 daughters (1 son, 1 daughter, by previous marriage). Career: Many concert tours, television and radio appearances as member of 10cc. Compositions: for The Yardbirds: For Your Love; Heart Full Of Soul; for The Hollies: Bus Stop; Look Thru Any Window; for Herman's Hermits: No Milk Today; Co-wrote for 10cc: Rubber Bullets; Wall Street Shuffle; I'm Mandy Fly Me; Good Morning Judge; I'm Not In Love; Things We Do For Love; Dreadlock Holiday; Co-wrote for Wax: Bridge To Your Heart. Honours: Ivor Novello Awards for: Rubber Bullets; I'm Not In Love; BMI citations for most of the above songs. Memberships: Musicians' Union; PRS; SODS (Society of Distinguished Songwriters). Hobby: Collecting guitars. Current Management: Harvey Lisberg. Address: Harvey Lisberg Associates, 6 Highgate, St Margarets Road, Altrincham, Cheshire WA14 2AP, England.

GOUPY Christian, b. 21 June 1962, Evreux, France. Composer; Musician (piano). Education: Brevet de Technicien Superieur Mechanique et Automatisme. Musical Education: American School of Modern Music; Conservatoire International, Paris. Career: Concerts in France with The Footprints Quintet and The Croco Jazz Big Band; Pianist, Dagorno Restaurant, Paris. Recordings: Escale, Footprints Quintet; Oh Happy Day, Voce Vita Gospel Group; Next To, Croco Jazz Big Band. Publications: Editions Combre, Paris; Quatuors de Saxs. Hobbies: Tennis; Scuba diving. Current Management: Christian Goupy Association Evasion. Address: 18 Impasse St Sébastien, 75011 Paris, France.

GOURDIKIAN Herve, b. 31 Dec 1966, Lyon, France. Musician (saxophones, piano). m. Olga Kroutolapova, 23 Apr 1992, 1 daughter. Musical Education: 2 years at Berklee College of Music, Boston; French Conservaory, Lyon. Tour, Rêve Orange (Liane Foly); Tour, Les Petites Notes (Liane Foly); Concert Place de la Concorde for Liberation of Paris (audience 500,000); TV show: Taratata; Nulle Part Ailleurs with Andoine de Camaes. Recordings: With Liane Foly: Reve Orange; Lumières; Sweet Misery; Also with: Nilda Fernandez; HMF; Mellow Man; Brigitte Fontaine; Mario Stanchen; Liane Foly. Honours: Gold record, Lumières, Liane Foly. Hobby: Crosswords. Address: 258 Avenue Georges Clemenceau, 92000 Nanterre, France.

GOURLEY Sean, b. 12 Dec 1963, Paris, France. Jazz Musician (guitar); Singer. Musical Education: Classical guitar, age 6-14; Jazz harmony, USA, 1983-84; Jazz harmony, with father, Jimmy Gourley and personal coaches. Career: Player, singer, arranger, own band, playing bebop jazz, concerts, clubs; Plays with father Jimmy Gourley in Family Affair Band; Festivals include: Calvi, Corsica; Madagascar (US Embassy); Guitar Masters of Pau, France; Played with: Barney Wilen; Stephanie Crawford; Kim Parker; Also with arrangers Onzy Mathews; Mundell Lowe; Various French musicians. Hobbies: Talking with good friends; Henry Miller's novels. Current Management: Self-managed. Address: 6 Rue Sauffroy, 75017 Paris, France.

GOURLEY Jimmy (James Pasco Jr), b. 9 June 1926, St Louis, Missouri, USA. Musician (guitar); Singer; Composer. Musical Education: Self-taught. Career: Began in Chicago, 1944; Member, Jay Burkhart Orchestra with Sonny Stitt, Gene Ammons, Lou Levy; Member, Jackie Cain, Roy Kral Quintet; Played in Chicago with Chubby Jackson, Anita O'Day, 1951, 1954-57; Worked in Paris with Lester Young, Kenny Clarke, Stan Getz, Stéphane Grappelli, 1957-96. Recordings with: Clifford Brown; Zoot Sims; Bob Brookmeyer; Kenny Clarke; Eddy Louiss; Lou Bennett; Henri Renaud; Lee Konitz; Chubby Jackson; Lester Young; Duke Ellington; Guy Lafitte; Richard Galliano; Own recordings: Jimmy Gourley and the Paris Heavyweights, 1972; Graffitti, 1976; Good News, 1981; Feeling Jazzy, 1983; The Jazz Trio, 1983; The Left Bank Of NY, 1986; Flying The Coop (with Richard Galliano Four), 1991; The Jazz Trio, 1995; Jazz Guitar - Essential Jazz, 1995; Our Delight, 1995; with Stan Getz: Stan Getz, 1958; Live In Europe, 1958; with Stéphane Grappelli: Satin Doll, 1972; Plays Gershwin, 1973; Plays Cole Porter, 1973. Membership: SACEM. Current Management: Self-managed. Address: 114 Ave Anatole France, 94190 Villeneuve St Georges, France.

GOVERT Eddy (Van Mouffaert), b. 15 Jan 1949, Bruges, Belgium. Accordionist; Songwriter; Producer. m. Anneke Van Thorre, 12 Aug 1991, 2 daughters. Musical Education: Muziek Conservatorium, Bruges. Career: Many appearances, band player, 1964-70; Singer, songwriter, as Eddy Govert, 1970-; Solo as international accordion act Le Grand Julot, 1973-; Founded Jump Records and Music, 1975; Professional singer, 1980's. Recordings: with Paul Severs: Ik Ben Verliefd Op Jou, 1971; Love, 1972; with Ronald and Donald: Couac Couac, 1974; with Ricky Gordon: Such A Night; with Margriet Hermans: Don Bosco; Many top 10 hits, 1975-81; as Eddy Govert: Te Kort Van Duur, 1988; Albums: International 1, 1991; International 2, 1993. Belgian Accordion Championship, 1965. Honours: Golden Lion Joepie, 1974; Gold Record, 1974; Cultuurprys Erpe-Mere, 1996. Memberships: SABAM; URADEX, Brussels; ZAMU, Brussels. Hobbies: Walking; Travel; Listening to music. Current Management: Happy Melody VZW. Address: Langemunt 71, G420 Aaigem, Belgium.

GRABOWSKI Stephan A, b. 18 December 1964, Copenhagen, Denmark. Musician; Singer; Composer; Producer; Arranger. 1 daughter. Education: Private Lessons by Hans Fagt, Hanne Bekow; Selftaught on Keyboards and Guitar. Career: Played with Lars H.U.G, 1987-93; Several National Tours; Several Television and Radio Appearances and Gigs in France, Russia, Greenland; With Love Shop, Janes Rejoice, Goldfinger and Special Appearances with Peter Bell, Caroline Henderson, Thomas Di Leva, Elisabeth, Shirtsville, Nina Forsberg. Compositions: Girl in the Ghetto, 1993; Crazy Restless Summer, Who Are You?, 1996; Verden Folo Af Frugt, Gaderne Huisker, 1997. Recordings: Glitter Angels, 1993; Songs For Night Clubs, 1996; Underligere End Kaerlighed, 1997. Honours: Reward, National Arts Trust, 1994, 1996; Numerous Grammy's with Lars H.U.G, 1990-92. Memberships: Artisten; Danish Artist Union; DPA. Hobbies: Travel; Studying Religion and Philosophy. Address: c/o Skriver, Guldbergsgade 12 St Tv, 22000 Kobenhavn N, Denmark.

GRACE Marie Whyte, b. England. Composer; Musician (electronic keyboards, guitar); Singer; Poet. m. twice, single 1986-, 3 sons, 1 daughter. Musical Education: Self-taught. Career: Toured schools, clubs, libraries, playing acoustic guitar solos, reading poetry, singing folksongs in Bedfordshire, 1970s-80s; Performer, keyboards at dinners, matinees, festivals, London, 1990s-; Show, Life's a Gas with Grace; Fundraiser for ChildLine. Compositions: Over 100 instrumentals and ballads; Over 100 poems for adults and children; Programme for children of music, singing, stories, poems, dancing, games, puppets; Currently compiling album of musical stories for children. Publications: 18 anthologies of poetry; The Londonium Bug, book of verse and cartoons, 1997. Honours: Poetry competition winner, 1970; Pictures exhibited; Inducted into the International Poetry Hall of Fame. Memberships: Musicians' Union; Designers and Artists Copyright Society (DACS); ABI; IBC. Address: 56 Warltersville Mansions, Warlterville Road, London N19 3AS, England.

GRACIE Charlie (Charles), b. 14 May 1936, Philadelphia, Pennsylvania, USA. Singer; Musician (Guitar). m. Joan D'Amato, 15 February 1958, 1 son, 1 daughter. Education: Tutored by father, Sam Gracie; Studied Guitar under professional teacher. Career: Youthful Guitar Prodigy, Paul Whiteman TV Teen Show; Played on radio commercials for the Sealtest, Big Top, CBS Program; Headlined, The Alan Freed Show, Brooklyn Paramount, 1957; Ed Sullivan Show; Numerous appearances on American Bandstand TV; Headlined the London Hippodrome and Palladium, 1957; Headlined Yarmouth Rock Festival, England, 1980s; Continues to tour Europe, Italy, Germany, England; Starred in Warner Brothers Rock Movie, Jamboree, 1958. Recordings: Butterfly; Fabulous; I Love You So Much; Albums: Charlie Gracie - The Cameo, 1979; Amazing Gracie, 1982; Charlie Gracie: Live at the Stockton Globe 1957, 1996; It's Fabulous - It's Charlie Gracie, compilation CD, 1996. Honour: Gold Record Award, 3 Million Seller, Butterfly, 1957. Membership: ASCAP. Hobbies: Animals; Ancient European History. Current Management: Paul Barrett R and R Enterprises, 16 Grove Place, Penarth, CF64 2ND, Wales. Address: 820 Edmonds Avenue, Drexel Hill, Pennsylvania, 19026, USA.

GRAHAM Bruce Hebenton, b. 9 Nov 1941, Dundee, Scotland. Musician (multi-instrumentalist); Composer; Author; Entertainer. m. (1) Phyllis Elizabeth McFarlane, 18 Sept 1963, 1 (adopted) daughter, (2) Sharon Belinda Maxim, 7 Apr 1988. Musical Education: Private tuition; Schillinger Course of Composition; Pupil, Henry Nelmes Forbes, ABCA. Career: Session musician; Musical Director, London recording, television and film studios, West End Theatres; Founder, Jingles Records and Jingles Music, 1985; Featured in cabaret, Old Tyme Music Halls, one-man keyboard concerts, 1988; Worked with: Andy Williams; Rock Hudson; Juliet Prowse; Lulu; The Three Degrees; Sacha Distel; Bob Hope; Sir Harry Secombe; Faith Brown; Tommy Steele; Paul Daniels; Cleo Laine and John Dankworth; Matt Monro; Bruce Forsythe; Marti Webb; Richard Chamberlain; Vince Hill; Jimmy Shand; Jeff Wayne; Des O'Connor; Rolf Harris; Val Doonican; Anthony Newley; Helen Reddy; Wayne Sleep; David Hemmings; Michael Crawford; Lionel Blair; Gemma Craven; Tony Basil; Miss World TV Orchestra; Andrew Lloyd Webber; Phil Tate; Ray McVay; Johnny Howard; Ike Isaacs; Geoff Love; Orchestras include: Sydney Thompson's Old Tyme; National Philharmonic; London Concert; BBC Radio; Scottish Radio; Northern Dance; London Palladium; Own small groups. Compositions include: A First Symphony; A Divertimenti For Strings; Reverie For Brass Band; 2 Suites for Large Jazz Orchestra; One-act Ballet; A Musical; Over 300 songs and shorter pieces. Publications: Magazine articles; Music And The Synthesizer, 1969. MembershipS: Musicians' Union; Equity. Hobbies: Magic; Writing; Boating. Address: 25 Milton Road, Wallington, Surrey SM6 9RP, England.

GRAHAME Alan, b. Cornwall, England. Musician (percussion). m. Dulcie Sawyer, 1 son, 2 daughters. Career: Ralph Sharon Sextet, London Jazz Club groups; Jerry Allen Trio: Variety; Music Hall; Freelance studio percussionist; Major tours, UK and Europe with Tom Jones; Shirley Bassey; Perry Como; Englebert Humperdinck; Howard Keel; Radio broadcasts: BBC Radio Orchestra; London Studio Players; Ken Moule Strings; Played with orchestras of: Alec Gould; Ronnie Aldrich; Frank Chacksfield; Cy Payne; Colin Sell; television appearances include: Jerry Allen Trio; Lunch Box, ATV (8 years); BBC Top Of The Pops Orchestra; Benny Hill; Come Dancing; Two Ronnies; Morecombe And Wise; Wogan; Parkinson; Pebble Mill; Miss World; Basil Brush; Crackerjack; Torvil and Dean; Last Of The Summer Wine; Tomorrow's World; Playschool; Record Breakers; With artistes: Tom Jones; Shirley Bassey; Roy Castle; Dionne Warwick; Neil Diamond; Buddy Greco; Richard Clayderman; Demis Roussos; Stylistics; Trini Lopez; Vic Damone. Recordings: With: Tom Jones; Shirley Bassey; Englebert Humperdinck; Matt Monro; Love Affair; White Plains; Brotherhood Of Man; Casuals; 101 Strings; Dana; Lena Zavaroni; Rolf Harris; Frank Pourcell; Jack Emblow; David Essex; Mike Batt; Les Reed; Jeff Wayne; Bee Gees; Peters And Lee; Lena Martell. Publications: Articles in Percussion Press (drums, percussion). Memberships: ISM; Musicians' Union.

GRAILLIER Michel François, b. 18 Oct 1946, Lens, France. Musician (piano, synthesizer). m. Micheline Pelzer, 9 July 1982. Education: Electronic Engineering. Musical Education: Private teacher for 10 years; Self-taught in jazz. Career: Tours with group Magma, 1972-73; Juan-les-Pins Festival, 1977-84; Japan with Chet Baker, 1986; Videos: Candy and Live At Ronnie Scott's with Chet Baker; Liege Jazz Festival, 1992; Radio: MG's trio in 1991-94; Recordings: As leader with: Ad Lib; Fairly; Dream Drops; Others with: Chet Baker; M&B; Al Capolinea; Candy; Chet Sings Again; At Ronnie Scott's; French Ballad; Barney Wilen; Moshi; S Glossman: Born At The Same Time. Honour: Django Reinhardt Prize, France, 1978. Memberships: SACEM; SPEDIDAM; ADAMI. HobbY: Reading. Current Management: Micheline Pelzer. Address: 1 Passage Cottin, 75018 pARIS, France.

GRAMM Lou (Louis Grammatico), b. 2 May 1950, Rochester, New York, USA. Singer; Songwriter. Career: Lead singer, Black Sheep, 1975; Foreigner, 1976-90, 1992-; Regular worldwide tours; Major concerts include: California Jam II, 1978; Reading Festival, 1979; New York State Fair, 1994; Also founder member, Shadow King, 1990-91; Also solo artiste; Recordings: Albums: with Black Sheep, Black Sheep, 1975; Encouraging Words, 1975; with Foreigner: Albums: Foreigner, 1977; Double Vision, 1978; Head Games, 1979; 4 (Number 1, US), 1981; Records, 1983; Agent Provocateur (Number 1, UK), 1984; Inside Information, 1987; The Very Best Of, 1992; The Very Best... And Beyond, 1992; Mr Moonlight, 1994; Solo albums: Ready Or Not, 1987; Long Hard Look, 1989; Hit singles: with Foreigner: Feels Like The First Time, 1977; Cold As Ice, 1977; Long Way From Home, 1978; Hot Blooded, 1978; Double Vision, 1978; Blue Morning Blue Day, 1979; Head Games, 1980; Urgent, 1981; Juke Box Hero, 1981; Waiting For A Girl Like You, 1981; I Want To Know What Love Is (Number 1, US), 1985; That Was Yesterday, 1985; I Don't Want To Live Without You, 1988; Solo: Midnight Blue, 1987; Just Between You And Me, 1990. Address: c/o Dennis Katz, 845 Third Avenue, New York, NY 10022, USA.

GRAMOUN Lélé (Julian Ernest Philéas), b. 28 Feb 1930, Saint Benoit, France. Retired. m. Marie Therèse Votréa, 20 Nov 1956, 3 daughters. Career: France 2 Pollen, RFO; RFI Festival Musique Metisses Angoulême; Festival de Jazz, Reunion des Musique au Zenith. Recordings: Single: Citron Galet, 1977; Album: Namouniman, 1993. Hobbies: Dance; Music; Culture. Current Management: Marcel Willy Phileas. Address: 12

Bis Castor II La Confiance, 97470 Saint Benoit, Ile de la Reunion, France.

GRANAT Endre, b. 3 Aug 1937, Hungary. Musician (violin). m. Mimi, 21 Aug 1993, 1 son. Education: University. Musical Education: Pupil, Joseph Gingold, Jascha Heifetz. Career: Tours: Europe; USA; South America; Asia; Concert master, soloist, major Hollywood films. Honours: Ysaye Award; Grand Prix du Disque. Membership: AFofM. Hobbies: Piloting single engine airplanes; Tennis; Scuba diving. Current Managment: CAMS.

GRANDE Johnny, b. Philadelphia, USA. Musician (piano). Career: Original member, Bill Haley's Comets, 1952-62; Leading innovator of rock'n'roll music; First rock band to headline a film. Recordings: Rock Around The Clock; See You Later Alligator; Crazy Man Crazy; Shake Rattle And Roll; Rock The Joint; Mambo Rock; Rudy's Rock; Florida Twist; Skinny Minnie. Publications: Rock Around The Clock; We're Gonna Party; Never Too Old To Rock. Honours: Best Vocal Group, 1954; Best Instrumental Group, 1956; Rock and Roll Hall Of Fame; Gold Records. Address: Rock It Concerts, Bruno-Hofer Platz 1, D-80937 Munich, Germany.

GRANDJEAN Jacky, b. 12 Feb 1957, Reims, France. Musician (acoustic and electric bass, guitar, drums). m. Corinne Lagoutte, 16 Sept 1986, 1 son. Musical Education: Musical Institute, Reims. Career: Ricard tour; Music for television. Recordings: Meletunetron; Laurent Marc, 1994; Melting Potes, 1995. Memberships: SACEM; SACD; SPEDIDAM. Hobby: Computers. Current Management: Self-managed. Address: 12 Route de Castelmaurou, 31140 Saint Loup Cammas, France.

GRANDMASTER Flash (Joseph Saddler), b. 1 Jan 1958, Barbados, West Indies. Rapper. Career: Mobile DJ, The Bronx, New York; Formed Grandmaster Flash And The 3 MCs, 1977-83; Solo artiste, 1985-; Performed, UK Fresh, Capital Music Festival, Wembley, 1986. Recordings: Albums: The Message, 1982; Greatest Messages, 1984; Solo albums: They Said It Couldn't Be Done, 1985; The Source, 1986; Ba Dop Boom Bang, 1987; Greatest Hits, 1992; Singles: Freedom, 1980; The Adventures Of Grandmaster Flash On The Wheels Of Steel, 1981; The Message, 1982; White Lines (Don't Do It), 1983; Solo: Sign Of The Times, 1985; U Know What Time It Is?, 1987. Address: c/o Richard Walters Entertainment Inc, 421 South Beverly Drive, 8th Floor, Beverly Hills, CA 90212, USA.

GRANFELT Ben Edward, b. 16 June 1963, Helsinki, Finland. Musician (Guitar); Songwriter. m. Nanna Granfelt, 14 January 1997. Musical Education: Selftaught Guitarist, Songwriter. Career: Films: Leningrad Cowboys Meet Moses; Tours in Europe, Scandinavia, England, USA, Australia, Japan, with Leningrad Cowboys, Europe, USA, England; Support to Status Quo, with Gringos Locos; Leningrad Cowboys Meet the Alexandrow Red Army, chorus and ensemble, Live. Recordings: Ben Granfelt: The Truth; Radio Friendly Live; Guitar Slingers: I; Song and Dance; That Little Something; Leningrad Cowboys: We Cum From Brooklyn; Leningrad Cowboys Go Space; Let's Work Together; Russian Red Army Ensemble; Live in Prowinzz; Gringos Locos: Raw Deal; Punch Rock; Gringos Locos. Honour: Pro Musica Award, Gymnasiet Grankulla Samskola. Hobbies: Martial Arts (Karate, Krava Maga, Shootfighting). Current Management: Sprucefield Oy Ltd, Viipurinkatu 8 B 65, 00510 Helsinki, Finland.

GRANT Amy Lee, b. 25 Nov 1960, Augusta, Georgia, USA. Singer; Songwriter. m. Gary W Chapman, 19 June 1982, 1 son, 2 daughters. Education: Furman University; Vanderbilt University. Career: Contemporary Christian (later also pop) singer, songwriter; Began recording career, 1978-; Has sold 18 million records worldwide; First full tour, 1981; Longest tour, Unguarded Tour, 18 months 1985-86; Star of TV Christmas Special: Headin' Home For The Holidays, with Dennis Weaver, Art Garfunkel, Jimmy Webb, 1986. Compositions include: Tender Tennessee Christmas (co-writer). Recordings: 14 recordings include: Amy Grant In Concert Volumes I and II; Age To Age, 1982; A Christmas Album, 1983; Unguarded, 1985; Lead Me On, 1988. Publication: Amy Grant's Heart To Heart Bible Stories, book and cassette. Honours: 5 Grammy Awards; 17 Dove Awards including Artist Of The Year (4 times); Pax Christi, St John's University (First entertainer, third woman to receive this), 1994. Hobbies: Golf; Snow skiing; Painting; Trail riding. Current Management: Blanton/Harrell Entertainment. Address: 2910 Poston Avenue, Nashville, TN 37203, USA.

GRANT Eddy (Edmond Montague Grant), b. 5 Mar 1948, Plaisance, Guyana. Singer; Producer; Musician (multi-instrumental). Career: Member, The Equals; Founder, own production company; Solo artiste, 1977-; Founder, record label Ice Records; Own studio, The Coach House. Recordings: Albums: Message Man, 1977; Walking On Sunshine, 1979; Love In Exile, 1980; Can't Get Enough, 1981; Killer On The Rampage, 1982; Going For Broke, 1984; All The Hits, 1984; File Under Rock, 1988; The Best Of Eddy Grant, 1989; Singles: Living On The Front Line, 1979; Do You Feel My Love, Can't Get Enough Of You; I Don't Wanna Dance (Number 1, UK), 1982; Electric Avenue (Number 2, UK and US), 1983; Gimme Hope Joanna, 1988. Current Management: Metro Management, 24-7 Coda Centre, 189 Munster Road, London SW6 6AW, England.

GRANT Ian Fraser, b. 17 Dec 1950, Lancing, Surrey, England. Artist Management. m. 6 Nov 1975, 1 son, 1 daughter. Musical Education: GCE and Royal Schools Of Music, pianoforte. Career: Manager, acts include: The Stranglers, 1975-80; The Skids, 1980-81; Big Country, 1982-; The Cult, 1985-88; Hazel O'Connor, 1980-81; The Members, 1980-81; Maxi Priest, 1987-1988. Hobbies: Football; Cricket; Horse racing; Gardening; Camping. Address: Ian Grant Management, PO Box 107, South Godstone, Redhill, Surrey RH9 8JL, England.

GRANT Manson, b. 9 Apr 1951, John O'Groats, Scotland. Singer; Musician (keyboards, trumpet, accordion). Education: HNC, Business studies. Musical Education: Piano. Career: Television appearances include: Grampian TV; Channel 4; Holiday Programme, BBC2; Concerts include: CMA Fan Fair, Nashville, Tennessee (representing Scotland); Wembley Country Music Festival, London; Joined Dynamos Band, 1970. Recordings: 14albums/cassettes; 2 CDs; 2 videos. Honours: More than 60 club and theatre awards. Membership: Musicians' Union. Hobbies: Music; Computing. Current Management: R Cameron. Address: Achnaclyth, Tannach, Wick, Caithness KW1 5SF, Scotland.

GRANT Wanda L, b. 6 May 1965, Antigonish, Nova Scotia, Canada. Songwriter. Education: Bachelor, Religious Education. Musical Education: Grade 7, Royal Conservatory. Compositions: Christmas Musicals: I've Been Searchin', 1993; Miracle Morn, 1994; The Fisherman's Trade, Breakin' Tradition, 1996. Honours: Gospel Music Trailblazer Nomination, Airplay International. Membership: Gospel Music Association. Hobby: Painting. Current Management: W L Grant. Address: PO Box 305, Port Hawkesbury, Nova Scotia B0E 2V0, Canada.

GRAY Howard, Record Engineer; Producer; Musician. Career: Engineer to Steve Lillywhite; Independent Producer mid 1980s; Recording artiste with Apollo 440; Numerous remixes/production credits. Recordings: Producer, Mixer, Recording Engineer: Terence Trent D'Arby: Introducing The Hardline; Danny Wilson: Danny Wilson; The Cure: Head On The Door; UB40: Labour Of Love; OMD: Sugar Tax; Scritti Politti: Cupid And Psyche; Tom Verlaine: Cover; Blue Pearl: Naked; Other recordings by: Yazz; Mori Kante; Geoffrey Williams; Kirsty MacColl; Genesis; U2; Duran Duran; Youssou n'Dour; Manic Street Preachers; Skunk Anansie; Siegman; Dust Junkys. Current Management: XL. Address: Studio 7, 27A Pembridge Villas, London W11 3EP, England.

GRAY Les, b. 9 Apr 1946, Carshalton, Surrey, England. Singer. m. Carol, 16 Apr 1980. Musical Education: Self-taught. Career: Member, skiffle and trad jazz bands; Lead singer, Mud, 1967-; Concerts include: Search For Sound, Song Contest Winners, 1967; UK tour supporting Tom Jones, 1973; UK tours, 1974, 1978; Second Hemsby 70s and Glam Rock Weekender (with Glitter Band, Alvin Stardust, ShowaddyWaddy, Sweet, Rubettes, Mungo Jerry), 1991. Recordings: Hit singles with Mud include: Dyna-Mite, 1974; Tiger Feet, (Number 1, UK), 1974; The Cat Crept In, (Number 2, UK), 1974; Rocket, 1974; Lonely This Christmas, (Number 1, UK), 1974; The Secrets That You Keep, (Number 3, UK), 1975; Oh Boy, (Number 1, UK), 1975; L-L-Lucy, 1975; Show Me You're A Woman, 1975; Lean On Me, 1976; Albums: Mud Rock, 1974; Mud Rock Vol 2, 1975; Mud's Greatest Hits, 1975; Use Your Imagination, 1975; Mudpack, 1978; Rock On, 1979; As You Like It, 1979; Mud, 1983; Let's Have A Party, 1991. Memberships: Musicians' Union; Equity; PRS. Hobby: Cooking. Current Management: Sharon Sly. Address: 3 Claremont Road, London N6 5DA, England.

GREBENSCHIKOV Boris Borisovitch, b. 27 Nov 1953, St Petersburg, Russia. Musician (guitar); Singer; Poet; Composer. m. Irina Grebenschiova, 29 May 1992, 1 son, 2 daughters. Education: Leningrad University, Applied Mathematics. Musical Education: Self-taught. Career: Formed Aquarium, 1972; Started recordings (not government approved), 1980; Tapes widely circulated throughout Russia to great success; After Peristroika toured extensively in Russia; Solo album, produced by Dave Stewart, 1988-89; Subject of film: Long Way Home, Granada TV. Recordings: 10 cassette-only albums, 1980-86; Ravnodenstvie, 1987; Radio Silence, 1989; Russian Album, 1992; Rameses The IV Favourite Songs, 1992; Sands Of St Petersburg, 1993; Kostroma Mon Amour, 1994; Navigator, 1995. Publications: Master Bo's Business, 1991; 14 songbooks, 1992; Prose, 1993. Membership: Russian Cinematographer's Union. Hobbies: Painting; Translation of Buddhist texts into Russian (Bardo Guidebook). Address: Flat 3, 2 Marata Street, St Petersburg 191025, Russia.

GREEN Al (Greene), b. 13 Apr 1946, Forrest City, Arkansas, USA. Soul Singer; Songwriter. Career: Founder, The Creations, 1964; Singer, Al Greene & The Soul Mates; Founder, own record label, Hot Line Music Journal, 1967; Performances include: Tokyo Music Festival, Japan, 1978; Nelson Mandela's 70th Birthday Tribute, Wembley, 1988; New Orleans Jazz and Heritage Festivals, 1992; Ann Arbor Blues & Jazz Festival, 1992. Recordings: Albums: Al Green Gets Next To You, 1971; Let's Stay Together, 1972; I'm Still In Love With You, 1972; Green Is Blues, 1973; Call Me, 1973; Livin' For You, 1974; Al Green Explores Your Mind, 1975; Greatest Hits, 1975; Al Green Is Love, 1975; Full Of Fire, 1976; Have A Good Time, 1977; Greatest Hits Volume II, 1977; Truth'n'Time, 1978; The Belle Album, 1978; Cream Of Al Green, 1980; The Lord Will Make A Way, 1980; Higher Plane, 1982; Precious Lord, 1983; I'll Rise Again, 1983; White Christmas, 1983 Going Away, 1986; Soul Survivor, 1987; Hi-Life - The Best Of Al Green, 1988; I Get Joy, 1989;

Greatest Hits, 1991; Al, 1992; Hit singles include: Tired Of Being Alone, 1971; Let's Stay Together (Number 1, US), 1972; Look What You've Done For Me, 1972; I'm Still In Love With You, 1972; You Ought To Be With Me, 1972; Call Me (Come Back Home), 1973; Here I Am (Come And Take Me), 1973; Sha-La-la (Make Me Happy), 1974; L-O-V-E (Love), 1974; Sailin' On The Sea Of Love, duet with Shirley Caesar, 1985; Going Away, 1986; Everything's Gonna Be Alright, 1987; Put A Little Love In Your Heart, duet with Annie Lennox, (used in film Scrooged), 1988; As Long As Were Together, 1989. Honours include: American Music Award, Favourite Soul/R&B Album, 1974; Grand Prize, Tokyo Music Festival, 1978; Al Green Day, Los Angeles, 1978; Soul Train, Best Gospel Recording, 1987; Numerous Grammy awards include: Best Soul Gospel Performances, 1982-85, 1988, 1990; Best Male Soul Performance, 1987. Address: c/o Al Green Music, 3208 Winchester, Memphis, TN 38118, USA.

GREEN Earl Oliver, b. 11 Feb 1945, Kingston, Jamaica. Singer. m. Valerie Jean, 3 Oct 1973, 1 son, 1 daughter. Career: Most major blues festivals in Europe including: Belgium Rhythm and Blues Festival; Nyon Festival; Lugano Festival, Switzerland; Diamond Awards, Antwerp; Radio broadcasts include: Paul Jones Show, BBC Radio 2; GLR; Mary Costello Show; Radio in Netherlands; Television appearances: Spain; Netherlands; Belgium; Switzerland; France; UK, McKewans The Concert, James Whale Show. Recordings: Always Hot, Otis Grand And The Dance Kings; Special Delivery, He Knows The Blues, Otis Grand. Honour: British Blues Connection Nomination, Best Blues Vocalist, 1992-93. Memberships: PRS; Musicians' Union. Hobbies: Gardening; Photography. Current Management: George McFall. Address: 213 Staines Road, Laleham, Middlesex TW18 2R8, England.

GREEN Ian, b. 8 Oct 1969. Producer; Writer; Mixer; Musician (keyboards, bass, drums, guitar). Career: Various television appearances including Wogan and Pebble Mill. Recordings: Voices, Kenny Thomas; Wait For Me, Kenny Thomas; True Spirit, Carleen Anderson; Closer To You, Brand New Heavies; Midnight At The Oasis, Brand New Heavies; Also recordings for Nu Colours; Misty Oldman; Monie Love. Memberships: Musicians' Union; Performing Rights Society. Current Management: BAMN Management. Address: c/o A & M Records, 136-144, New Kings Road, London SW6 4LZ, England.

GREEN Ian Michael, b. 19 Nov 1957, London, England. Musician (percussion, drums). m. Carolyn Margaret Morris, 7 May 1994. Musical Education: Kingsdale, 1968-74. Career: Musician with: Mike Oldfield, 1972-73; Druid, 1977-78; Catherine Howe; Randy Edelman; Lindsey De Paul; Sally Oldfield (Germany), 1978-79; Matt Monroe (London), 1980-81; Michael Crawford, Barnum, TV and radio; Tony Britten; Sammy Davis Jr (Monte Carlo), 1988; Jerry Lee Lewis (Monte Carlo), 1991-92. Recordings: with artistes including: Michael Crawford; Mike Oldfield; Sally Oldfield; Anthony Newley, produced single: What Kind Of Fool Am I?; Film and television: Lace 1 & 2; Lennon The Movie; Casualty; Head Over Heels; Shows: Barnum, 1981; Guys And Dolls, 1987; She Loves Me, 1994; The Snow Queen, 1995; Fame, 1995; Singing In The Rain; Stop The World. Memberships: Musicians' Union; ISM. Hobbies: Writing; Driving. Address: 223 Hayes Lane, Kenley, Surrey CR8 5HN, England.

GREEN Robson. Actor; Singer. Career: Actor, UK television series Soldier, Soldier; Singer, duo Robson & Jerome, 1995. Recordings: Debut album: Robson & Jerome, 1995; Singles: Unchained Melody/White Cliffs Of Dover, 1995; I Believe/Up On The Roof, 1995. Honour: Best

selling single of decade to date, Unchained Melody, 1995.

GREEN Sam, b. 2 January 1960, Melbourne, Australia. Singer; Songwriter (guitar, keyboard). Education: Diploma of Horological Studies; Self-taught various courses. Career: Played live to air with Greenmoss, group, 1979; Played in streets of Europe, 1980; Played with Tome the Poet and street poets, 5 times each week, 1982-86; Players All Are We: Live to air 3 CR, 1994; Live to air Southern FM, 1995; Appeared on Asylum channel 31, 1995; Host of Local and live (7 months), 1995; Appeared new years' night channel 31; Made video played on Rage channel 2, 1996. Compositions: For the Ocean, 1986; Angel of the Morning, 1994. Recordings: live But for Love, 1986; Players All Are We, 1994; I Think Its About Time, 1997. Memberships: APRA; ASA, Full Member; AMCOS Affiliated. Hobbies: Keeping time (clocks & watches). Current Management: B Green Management. Address: 242 Swan Street, Richmond, Victoria 3121, Australia.

GREENSLADE Dave, b. 18 Jan 1943, Woking, Surrey, England. Composer; Musician (keyboards). m. Jan Greenslade, 2 daughters. Career: Keyboard player with Chris Farlowe's The Thunderbirds; Worked with Geno Washington in the Ram Jam Band; Formed Colosseum, with Jon Hiseman; Wrote and co-wrote hit album: Valentyne Suite; Colosseum disbanded 1971; Founder, Greenslade, 1972; Colosseum reformed, reunion tour of Europe and album, 1994; Wrote hit albums, also solo project: Cactus Choir; Wrote television score for BBC series: Gangsters, success led to full time composition. Compositions: Worked on more than 35 drama series, single plays, films, stage plays; Credits include: Kinsey, BBC TV; A Very Peculiar Practice, BBC TV; Wipe Out, Granada TV; Tales Of The Unexpected, Anglia TV; The Detective, BBC TV; Bratt Farrer, BBC TV; Bird Of Prey, BBC TV; The Houseman's Tale, BBC TV; A Family Man, BBC TV; Films: Artemis, BBC Films; Jekyll & Hyde, BBC films; Worked with novelist Terry Pratchett on recording project based on the DiscWorld fantasy novel series. Recordings include: Colosseum: Daughter Of Time; Live; Valentyne Suite; Albums with Greenslade (now re-issued on CD); Cactus Choir; Pentateuch, double album based on illustrations of Patrick Woodroffe; DiscWorld project, 1995; . Honours: Premio Ondas TV Award at Barcelona Film Festival; Won Prix Italia at Palermo; Toyama Prize, Japan. Memberships: Musicians' Union; PRS; MCPS. Current Management: Soundtrack Music Management. Address: 22 Ives Street, Chelsea, London SW3 2ND, England.

GREENWICH Ellie, b. 23 Oct 1940, Brooklyn, New York, USA. Songwriter; Record Producer; Singer. Education: BA, Holfstra University, 1962. Career: Singer, 1958-; Songwriting partnership with Jeff Barry, 1960-67; Founder member, The Raindrops, 1963; Solo artist and songwriter; Performed in revue Leader Of The Pack. Compositions: Hit songs include: Hanky Panky, Tommy James and The Shondells; Da Doo Ron Ron, The Crystals; And Then He Kissed Me, The Crystals; Do Wah Diddy Diddy, The Exciters; Leader Of The Pack, The Shangri-Las; River Deep Mountain High, Ike and Tina Turner; Baby I Love You, The Ronettes; Be My Baby, The Ronettes; Writer, producer, songs recorded by Neil Diamond; Cyndi Lauper; Nona Hendryx. Recordings: Albums: Ellie Greenwich Composes, Produces And Sings, 1968; Let It Be Written, Let It Be Sung, 1973. Honours: 19 BMI Awards; Inducted into Songwriters Hall Of Fame; National Academy of Popular Music Award, 1984. Membership: Songwriters Guild.

GREENWOOD Bernard Paul, b. 21 Apr 1940, Bath, England. Doctor; Musician (saxophone, keyboards). Education: Medicine, London, Oxford; Social Anthropology, Cambridge.

Career: Saxophone player, Chris Farlowe and the Thunderbirds; The Glands; Doctor Kitch; Alkasalsa; Joey The Lips; Jazz Posse; Dicky Pride and the Original Topics; King Cobra and the Rattlesnakes; Tour with Lindsay Kemp. Recordings: Buzz With The Fuzz; Treat Her Right; The Fool; Mr Pitiful (with Chris Farlowe). Publication: Buzz With The Fuzz. Address: Woodcote, Chagford, Devon TQ13 8JF, England.

GREENWOOD Lee Melvin, b. 27 Oct 1942, Southgate, California, USA. Country Singer. m. Melanie Cronk. Recordings: Singles: It Turns Me Inside Out; IOU; Ring On Her Finger, Time On Her Hands; Ain't No Trick; She's Lyin'; Going Going Gone; Fools Gold; with Barbara Mandrell: To Me; It Should Have Been Love By Now; Albums: Inside And Out; Somebody's Gonna Love You; with Barbara Mandrell: Meant For Each Other. Honours: CMA Male Vocalist Of Year, 1983, 1984; ACM Male Vocalist Of Year, 1984; Cash Box Choice Award, 1984; Music City Awards, Best Male Vocalist, 1984, 1985. Hobby: Sport. Address: Lee Greenwood Inc., PO Box 6537, Seiverville, TN 37864, USA.

GREGORY Colin, b. 30 Dec 1961, Radcliffe, Manchester, England. Musician; Songwriter. Education: Lancaster University. Musical Education: Self-taught. Career: Tours of USA, Europe and Japan, 1992; TV and Radio appearances in USA, 1994; UK television appearances include: Snub; The Beat; Northern Routes; The Chart Show; John Craven's Newsround; Look North; Many radio sessions on John Peel, Mark Radcliffe, Janice Long, Mark Goodier and Johnny Walker shows. Recordings: 3 albums in the UK, 2 albums in USA and 2 albums in Japan; 10 UK singles and 8 singles internationally. Memberships: Musicians' Union; PRS. Hobbies: Music; Football; Philosophy. Current Management: Rockmasters Management. Address: Brunswick Studios, 7 Westbourne Grove Mews, London W11 2RU, England.

GREGSON Clive James, b. 4 Jan 1955, Ashton-Under-Lyne, Lancashire, England. Musician; Singer; Songwriter; Record Producer. m. Nancy Ann Kirkland, 6 Nov 1993. Education: Crewe and Alsager College of Education. Musical Education: Mostly self-taught. Career: Founder, leader, Any Trouble, 1976-84; Member, duo, Clive Gregson and Christine Collister, 1985-92; Member, Richard Thompson Band, 1987-92; Solo artist, 1992-. Recordings: with Any Trouble: Where Are All The Nice Girls, 1980; Live At The Venue, 1980; Wheels In Motion, 1981; Any Trouble, 1983; Wrong End Of The Race, 1984; Solo: Strange Persuasions, 1985; Welcome To The Workhouse, 1990; Carousel Of Noise, 1994; People And Places, 1995; I Love this Town, 1996; With Gregson and Collister: Home And Away, 1986; Mischief, 1987; A Change In The Weather, 1989; Love Is A Strange Hotel, 1990; The Last Word, 1992; with Eddi Reader and Boo Hewerdine: Wonderful Lie/Last Night I Dreamt That Somebody Loved Me/Who's Your Jailer Now?, 1993. Memberships: PRS; BASCA; EFDSS; Musicians' Union. Hobbies: Stamp collecting; Ornithology. Current Management: John Martin. Address: Gregsongs, 50 Stroud Green Road, London N4 3EF, England.

GREINKE Arthur Joseph, b. 19 Mar 1963, Milwaukee, USA. Public Relations Executive. Education: BA Mass Communications, Journalism, University of Wisconsin, Milwaukee. Career: Freelance entertainment journalist, Milwaukee, 1981-89; Program coordinator, The Great Circus Parade, Milwaukee, 1985-; Principal Partner, Greinke, Eiers and Associates, Milwaukee, 1985-; Director, Public relations and advertising, Eastside Compact Disc, 1988-; Cooler Music Promotions, USA, Inc, 1990-; Executive Producer (music group), Project Mix, 1985-87. Publications: Articles on national, regional recording industry news to college newspapers, local trades, Rolling Stone magazine; Advertising copy; Rock news scripts for Milwaukee television video show. Memberships; PRSA; IABC, Treasurer, 1989, President, 1990; SPJ; NARAS. Hobbies: Beatles Authority; American Football; Films; Music. Address: 2557C North Terrace Avenue, Milwaukee, WI 53211-3822, USA.

GRESSWELL Steve, b. 20 Jan 1955, Reading, Berkshire, England. Composer; Producer; Musician (keyboards); Programmer. m. Jacqui, 1 Oct 1993, 1 son, 1 daughter. Career: Justin Canns, 1971-76; Scorpio, 1977-81; Steve Gresswell Band, 1981-82; Dream, 1982-84; Poiema, 1984-85; After Dark, 1985; Guardian Angel, 1985-86; Formed own label, Sumo Records, with recording studio, 1988; Video with SG Band: Just For You, 1989; Robin Wilson Productions, 1990; Coalition, 1992-; Compositions: Story Of The Gods, Rock Oratorio. Recordings: with Scorpio: Taking England By Storm, 1977; with Oddjob: Express Yourself, 1977; with Dream: Just For You, 1982; with Poiema: 2 singles from play: Cross Purposes, 1984; with After Dark: Call Of The Wild, 1985; Album: Masked By Midnight, 1985; with SG Band: Just For You (Official Record for Lockerbie Air Disaster Fund), 1989; Producer, single for duo, Vincent, 1989; Composer, musician, engineer, producer, album for Czech rock guitarist Karel Espandr, 1990; Producer, composer, Robin Wilson Project single (fundraising for child with Cerebral Palsy), 1990; Steve Gresswell: Spirit Of Freedom, 1994; Coalition: Rise of the Coalition, 1996, 1997; Steve Cresswell: Visions, 1997; Produced and arranged Brent Morley, Burn, 1997. Memberships: Musicians' Union; PRS; PPL; MCPS; BASCA; BSWC; PAMRA. Hobby: Music. Current Management: Sumo Records. Address: Searles, The Chapel, 26a Munster Road, London SW6 4EN, England.

GREY Carola, b. 5 August 1968, Munich, Germany. Drummer; Composer; Producer. Education: Classical Piano, for 12 years; Masterdegree, Music & Music Education (Jazzdrums). Career: Performed and/or recorded with: Mike Stern, Ravi Coltrane, Benny Green, Craig Handy and others Jazzartists; Drummer for New York based all female gothic rock band, Maria Excommunikata Bandleader, 1989-; Clubs and festivals in Europe, US and Asia (Thailand International Jazz Festival, 1996; Jakarta Jazz Festival, 1995-96; Indian Music Festival Madras, 1996); TV features include: Deutsche Welle, Berlin (Germany); Star TV, (India) WDR, Cologne (Germany), Polish TV. Recordings: Carola Grey, Noisy Mama, 1992; Carola Grey, The Age of Illusion, 1994; Carola Grey, Girls Can't Hit, 1996; Composer, all music for band; Music for minor films and dance theatres: Vox, international cable; MC for the Zildjian Day Berlin, Germany, 1997. Honours: Govt Grant, for extraordinary artists, 1995; Nomination for SWF Jazzprize & Munich Jazz Prize, 1998. Membership: International Drum Organisation. Hobby: Kung-Fu. Current Management: Noisy Mama Productions, Rattenbergerstr 22, 81373, München, Germany.

GRIDLEY Andrew David, b. 3 May 1960, Maldon, Essex, England. Musician (6 and 12 string guitar, keyboards); Singer; Songwriter. Musical Education: Performing Arts at college. Career: Appearances include: Production, London Lights, Ingatestone; Chelmsford Youth Spectacular, Civic Theatre; England Entertains, Clacton, Essex; First EP released Essex Radio, Witham; Live Elvis performance, Southend-On Sea, Cliffs Pavilion; Played guitar for Dr Barnardo's Charity; Accompanied Helen Shapiro on 12 string guitar. Compositions: Forever, 1997; I Want You, 1997; You're Sexy, 1997; Smile on My Pinstripe, 1997. Recordings: Day Through To Night; Leading Lady; Green; Love And Affection; From Me To You; Lonely As A Cloud; Love Can Be; Summer Sun; Take Me; Beautiful; Wild Wild Women; Taking a Chance on Love; I'm a Fool in

Love; Lost in Time (Reflections). Memberships: PRS; BASCA; MCPS. Hobbies: Photography; Walking; Listening to music; Socialising. Address: 17 Coopers Avenue, Heybridge, Maldon, Essex, England.

GRIFFIN Ian, b. 1 Jun 1965, Neath, Glamorgan, Wales. Musician (keyboards, electronic organ, piano). m. Jane Elizabeth Cribb, 2 Sep 1989, 2 daughters. Musical Education: London College of Music. Career: Solo and group musician, 1980-; Television appearances: Young Entertainers, heat winner, BBC1, 1978; Heno, S4C TV, 1991-; Radio appearances include Keyboard, ILR Swansea Sound, 1978-; Keyboard Music, ILR Two Counties, 1987-; Keyboard Magic, BBC West Midlands Radio, 1988-; The Organist Entertains, BBC Radio 2, 1988-; Played at National Keyboard Festivals, 1980-; Opened own sound recording studio, for artists backing, 1989-; Appeared at the Grand Theatre, Swansea, 1993; Formed own cabaret show band, Casual Affair, 1994; Two appearances on HTV Television with Casual Affair, 1996. Recordings: In The Hands Of Ian Griffin, 1986; Introducing Keyklix, 1987; Just Me - Ian Griffin, 1988; Half Way To Paradise, 1995. Honour: Best Keyboard Player Under Age 18, Organ Player and Keyboard Review Readers, 1982; Organist of the Year, Verwood and District Organ Society, 1996. Hobbies: Boats; Sailing. Address: The Studio, 9 Mynachlog Terrace, Pontyberem, Llanelli, Dyfed SA15 5EE, Wales.

GRIFFIN Sid, (Albert Sidney Griffin), b. 18 Sept 1955, Louisville, Kentucky, USA. Musician; Journalist; Record Company Executive. m. Kate St John, 5 May 1993. Education: BA, Journalism, University of South Carolina, 1977. Career: Played with The Frosties, 1973-77; The Unclaimed, 1979-82; The Long Ryders, 1982-87; Soloist and Leader with The Coal Porters; Released various singles, EPs and albums with these bands; Owner, Prima Records Ltd. Recordings: With the Long Ryders: 10-5-60 (EP), 1983; Native Sons, album, 1984; State Of Our Union, 1985; Two-Fisted Tales, 1987; Metallic BO, 1988; Others: Danny And Dusty, The Lost Weekend, 1986; Rebels Without Applause, The Coal Porters, 1992; Land Of Hope And Crosby, The Coal Porters, 1994; Los London, The Coal Porters, 1995; Solo: Little Victories, 1997. Publications: Contributor to Q, Mojo, BAM, and Country Music International magazines. Honour: Honorary Member of Athenaeum Literary Association. Memberships: AFofM; The Paisley Underground. Hobbies: Baseball; Basketball; Drinking in Scotland. Current Management: Pat McGarvey International, London, England. Address: PO Box 2539, London NW3 6DF, England.

GRIFFITH Nanci, b. 6 July 1953, Seguin, Texas, USA. Singer; Songwriter; Musician (guitar). Education: Studied Education, University of Texas. Career: Professional musician, 1977-; Formed backing band, The Blue Moon Orchestra, 1986; Formed own publishing company. Compositions include: Love At The Five And Dime; The Wing And The Wheel; Ford Econoline; Outbound Plane (co-written with Tom Russell). Recordings: There's A Light Beyond These Woods, 1978; Poet In My Window, 1982; Once In A Very Blue Moon, 1984; Last Of The True Believers, 1986; Lone Star State Of Mind, 1987; Little Love Affairs, 1988; One Fair Summer Evening, 1988; Storms, 1989; Late Night Grand Hotel, 1991; Flyer, 1994. Current Management: Vector Management, PO Box 128037, Nashville, TN 37212, USA.

GRIFFITHS Matthew David, b. 6 Mar 1968, Cardiff, Wales. Musician (percussion); Composer. m. Sarah Fisher, 18 Sept 1993. Musical Education: BA, First Class Honours in Performing Arts, specialising in Music, Leicester Polytechnic, 1989. Career: Solo percussion recitals, 1989-; Concerts include: St David's Hall, Cardiff; Cheltenham Town Hall; Bradford Alhambra;

Phoenix Arts, Leicester; Bath Festival; Warwick Festival; Swansea Festival; Chichester Festival; Sounds Like Birmingham; Percussion '90 Festival; Television appearances include: The Clothes Show, BBC1; Heno, Channel 4/S4C; Midlands Today; Radio appearances include: Radio Wales; Radio Leicester; Radio WM; Worked with dance companies in the theatre and for various contemporary music ensembles; Gives workshops, and composer in residence projects in schools, hospitals, prisons and day centres. Compositions: Concerto for Percussion and Embroidery Machine, premiere at Warwick Festival, 1991; Miles Around, with Warwick Festival premiere, 1992; World Of Hospitality, commissioned by Rubbermaid, premiered at Earls Court, 1994. Publication: The North Indian Tabla and Its Use in Modern, Western Music (dissertation), 1989. Honours: ABSA Award, Concerto for Percussion and Embroidery Machine. Memberships: Musicians' Union; Advisor, Arts Council. Hobbies: Vegetarian cooking; Tennis. Address: 15 Bartletts Road, Bedminster, Bristol BS3 3PL, England.

GRIGOROV Robert (Robo), b. 25 September 1964, Bratislava. Singer; Composer. 1 daughter. Education: Film: Fontana Pre Zuzanu 1, actor & singer, 1986; Music for Theatre: Eunuch, 1985; Music for Films: Obyeany Den, 1985; Most, 1993; Touring with own group, Midi, 1982-. Compositions: Robo & Midi, 1985; Mohy, LP, 1986; Olohy, 1984; Cierny Kon, 1989; Chcemja Najst, 1985; Espresso Orient, 1987; Unplugged, 1994; Udychni Reggae, 1995; The Best of Chodci Sveta, 1997. Recordings: About 13 LP's and CD's. Publications: Zuvacka za uchom, 1983; EDO, 1984; Monika, 1985; Dvaja, 1984; Ona Je Madona, 1993. Honours: Bratislavska Lira, 1984, 1985, 1986; Cena Hulobne'ho Fontu, 1985; Diskosla'vik, 1984. Memberships: SOZA; Slovenskyhudobny Fond; Lita. Hobbies: Music (oriental, reggae, classical and ethnology). Address: Stredna 26, 82104 Bratislava, Slovakia.

GRILLO Alex, b. 7 Mar 1956, Fiume-Veneto, Italy. Musician (vibraphone). Musical Education: Conservatory: Percussion, harmony and Orchestration. Career: Jazz concert, Radio France, 1982; Nîmes Jazz Festival, 1985; Duo with Steve Lacy, 1987-88; Orchestra De Nove, Paris, New Morning, Angoulême, 1988; First underwater musician with Michel Redolfi, 1989; Nice, 1989; Brisbane, 1991; Lisbon, 1993; Duo with Terry Riley by satellite, 1993; Duo with Barre Philips, 1994. Recordings: A Table!, 1985; Neuf Pour Neuf, 1988; Mass For Choir and Organ; Music for theatre and ballet, 1990, 1991; Album: Vibraphone Alone, 1993; Sweet Desdemone (rock jazz oratorio), 1995. Publication: C'est Tout Droit (suite for xylophone). Memberships: SACEM; SACD; UMJ. Address: 182 Rue de Charenton, 75012 Paris, France.

GRILLO Carmen, b. 8 August 1954. Musician; Guitar; Vocalist. 1 son. Education: Private instruction & self-taught. Career: with Bill Champlin, Rita Coolidge, Tower of Power. Compositions: One More Day (Chicago 18); Personal Possessions; Who Do You Think You Are; You, Come to a Decision; Soothe You (Tower of Power). Recordings: Tower of Power, with Rita Coolidge, Boz Scaggs, Smokey Robinson, Tom Scott & Helen Reddy. Publications: Guitar Player Magazine. Memberships: AFM; SAG; AFTRA. Hobbies: Tennis; Cooking. Address: Airtight Management, PO Box 113, Winchester Center, CT 06094, USA.

GRIMES Ged, b. 28 Mar 1962, Dundee, Scotland. Musician (bass guitar, upright bass, percussion, keyboards, drum programming); Writer. m. Patricia Colette Boyle, 13 July 1991. Education: Duncan of Jordanstone College of Art. Musical Education: Self-taught. Career: Founder member, Danny Wilson, 1983-90; Tours: USA, UK, Japan; Toured with Eddi Reader, 1994-95;

Television and radio appearances: Montreux Rock Festival; Top Of The Pops; Chart Show; The Late Show; Jools Holland Show; Radio 1 sessions. Recordings: Hit single: Mary's Prayer, 1987. Albums: with Danny Wilson: Meet Danny Wilson, 1987; Be-Bop Mop-Top, 1988; Sweet Danny Wilson, 1991; with Gary Clark: Ten Short Songs About Love, 1993. Memberships: Musicians' Union; PRS; PPL. Hobbies: Food and drink; Travel. Address: c/o 37B Constitution Street, Dundee DD3 6JH, Scotland.

GRIP Erik, b. 2 July 1947, Nykobing, Denmark. Singer; Songwriter; Composer; Musician (guitar, piano). m. Joan Riboe, 2 sons, 1 daughter. Education: Cand Arch. Career: Danish folk singer; General Secretary, Danish Society for Jazz, Rock and Folk Composers (DJBFA), 1976-86. Recordings: 15 albums released. Address: Stationsvej 23, 4320 Lejre, Denmark.

GROBER Jacques, b. 11 Feb 1951, Paris, France. Writer; Composer; Singer. 2 daughters. Education: Baccalaureat, Licence et Maitrise de Russe. Musical Education: with Sarah Gorby. Career: Singer, traditional Yiddish and Russian songs, and own compositions; Appearances in Paris: Theatre 18, Centre Mandapa, TN Chaillot, 1989; Theatre du Tourtour, 1991-92; Bobigny, 1994; Maison de Radio-France, 1995; Other appearances include: Strasbourg, Nancy, Grenoble, Rennes (Festival Tombées de la Nuit); Germany; Zurich; Brussels; Amsterdam. Recordings: Le Paon Doré; Autres Chants Yiddish; Voix du Ghetto (collection). Membership: Animateur Chorale Yiddish. Hobbies: Design; Writing. Address: 58 rue de L'Egalité, Le Verseau 31, 92130 Issy Les Moulineaux, France.

GROCOTT Stephen, b. 21 Feb 1953, London, England. Composer;Musician (guitar, mandolin, harmonium, flowerpots); Vocalist; Teacher. Education: BA Hons, Literature, Kent University. Musical Education: Traditional music, Ireland; Carl Orff Society, England. Career: Television and radio appearances with: The Wise Monkeys, 1990; The Drones, BBC1, 1991; Ch4, Radio 4 and 5, 1995; The Toy Symphony premiered by The Drones at the Purcell Rooms and Norwich Festival. Compositions: Playing With Fire (music for bonfire, pyrotechnics, quartet), 1991; The Toy Symphony (music for toys and instruments) 1992. Recordings: Albums: with The Drones: The Drones, 1992; Giant Bonsai, 1994. Memberships: PRS (associate); Musicians' Union; Carl Orff Society. Hobbies: Thinking; Gardening. Current Management: The Shed Studios.

GROHL Dave, b. 14 Jan 1969. Musician (drums). Career: Member, Dave Bramage Band; Scream; Nirvana, 1990-94; Worldwide appearances include: European tour with Sonic Youth, 1991; Reading Festivals, 1991, 1992;Transmusicales Festival, Rennes, France, 1991; Benefit concert, Washington State Music Coalition, 1992; Benefit concert, Bosnian Women's group, San Francisco, 1993; Member, Foo Fighters, 1994-; Concerts include Reading Festival, 1995. Recordings: Albums: with Nirvana: Nevermind (Number 1, US), 1991; Incesticide, 1993; In Utero (Number 1, UK & US), 1993; Unplugged In New York, 1994; with Foo Fighters: Foo Fighters, 1995; Singles: with Nirvana: Smells Like Teen Spirit, 1991; Come As You Are, 1992; Lithium, 1992; In Bloom, 1992; Oh, The Guilt, 1993; Heart-Shaped Box, 1993; All Apologies, 1993; Contribution to The Beavis And Butthead Experience album, 1993; with Foo Fighters: This Is A Call, 1995; I'll Stick Around, 1995. Honours: 2 MTV Music Video Awards, Smells Like Teen Spirit, 1992; BRIT Award, Best International Newcomer, with Nirvana, 1993; BRIT Award Nomination, Best International Act, Best International Newcomers, with Foo Fighters, 1995. Current Address: Gold Mountain Entertainment, Suite 450, 3575 Cahunega Blvd West, Los Angeles, CA 90068, USA.

GROOM Don, b. 10 Nov 1939, Walthamstow, London, England. Session Musician (drums). m. Lorna Heather, 16 Nov 1963, 1 son, 2 daughters. Musical Education: Music theory, Royal Academy of Music; Drum tuition, Max Abrams, Frank King; Arranging, Berklee School Of Music, Boston. Career: Professional musician, 1960-; Tours in Germany including Hamburg's Top Ten Club and Kaiser Keller; Drummer with: Mike Berry and the Outlaws, 1962; John Leyton; The Crickets, including tours with Bobby Vee, 1962; The Beatles, 2 tours, 1963-64; Rolling Stones tours, 1963-64; Backed Franki Valli and Four Seasons, English tour, 1964; Backed Jet Harris, NME Poll Winners Concert, Wembley. Recordings: with Mike Berry: Don't You Think It's Time; with John Leyton: Son This Is She; Two Sides of John Leyton (album), 1962; with Pinkerton's Assorted Colours: Mirror Mirror. Hobbies: Aviation; Sport.

GROSZ Martin Oliver, b. 28 Feb 1930, Berlin, Germany. Musician (guitar). m. Rachel Whelan, 1956, 2 sons. Education: 2 years at college. Musical Education: Self-taught. Career: Professional musician, 1948-; Recorded under own name in 1950s; Lived in Chicago, 1954-75; Performed with: Village Stompers; Dukes Of Dixieland; Bandleader, Sounds Of Swing, for National public television; New York Jazz repertory group, Soprano Summit, 1975-76. Recordings: Hooray For Bix, Riverside '57, 1975; Let Your Fingers Do The Walking (Guitar Duets), 1978; Swing It; Unsaturated Fats. Publications: Writer on Jazz Guitars and Frank Teschemacher for Time/Life magazines. Honour: Winner, Jazzology Guitar Poll, 1986. Membership: Musicians Union, New York. Hobbies: Designing album and CD covers; Writing arrangements. Current Management: Popinjay Productions, 46 Upper Ritie Street, Piermont, NY 10968, USA.

GRÜB Laura, b. Mexico City, Mexico. Multimedia Composer; Producer; Music Critic. Education: School Of Architecture, UNAM; Executive Program, System Dynamics, Sloan School Of Management. Musical Education: National School Of Music, UNAM; Tchaikovsky Conservatory of Moscow, Composition with Chulaki, and Leman, 1980-83; Berklee College Of Music, 1984-91; Post-graduate research program, Berklee College of Music and MIT. Career: President Laura Grüb Enterprises; President/Founder, Mexican Network International; Lectured at MIT, course opened, based on her symphonic poem, Evocación; Produced Mexican Classical Concerts, Sanders Theatre, Harvard University, Boston Public Library, Carlos Chavez Hall, Oaxtepec Hall; Founded Mexican Classical Concerts and Arts Inc; Television includes: Featured artist/composer, programs on WGBH, WNEV, WGBX, USA; En Vivo, Eco, Hoy Mismo, Mexico; Radio programs Radio Mil, Mexico City; WZLY, USA; Became Kurzwil Artist, 1995; Asked to compose for orchestra and chorus, Princeton Pro Musica, premiere, 1996; Music critic, premieres including: Houston Grand Opera; Philadelphia Orchestra. Address: 235-4 Lucas Lane, Voorhees, NJ 08043, USA.

GRUNTZ George, b. 24 June 1932, Basel, Switzerland. Musician; Composer; Bandleader. Education: Studies, Basel, Zurich. Career: Member, European All-Star Band, Newport International Band, 1958; Appearances at Most Major Jazz Festivals, including: Newport/Kool/JVC, 1958, 1969, 1982, 1984, 1989, 1994; Berlin, Warsaw, Monterey, 1967, 1977, Antibes, Montreux, Pori, Northsea. Several Radio and Television Productions; Accompanied Many US Top Jazz Artists on European Tours; Chief Musical Director, Zurich State Theatre (Schauspielhaus); Program Director, Producer, Berlin Jazz Festival, 1972-94. Compositions include: Spanish Castles; Capricci Cavallereschi; Spring Song; Perambulation I and II; Concerto Sequenzas; Steppenwolf Concorde Suite;

Thundermove, for large orchestra. Honours: Several First Prizes in Many Jazz Festivals; First Prize, Best Performance Award, Japanese Music Critics Association, 1988. Address: Weiherweg 1, 4123 Allschwil, Switzerland.

GRUSIN Dave, b. 26 June 1934, Littleton, Colorado, USA. Composer; Record Producer; Musician (piano, keyboards). Education: University of Colorado. Career: Director of Music, Andy Williams Show, 1959-66; As pianist, played with Art Pepper; Spike Robinson; Terry Gibbs; Benny Goodman; Thad Jones; Carmen McRae; Sarah Vaughan; Arranger for: Phoebe Snow; Peggy Lee; Barbra Streisand; Patti Austin; The Byrds; Grover Washington Jr; Al Jarreau; Donna Summer; Co-founder, owner, GRP Records, with Larry Rosen, 1976-; Client roster includes: Grover Washington Jr; Dizzy Gillespie, Lee Ritenour; ChickCorea; Dianne Schuur; Dave Valentin; Gary Burton; Michael Brecker; Steve Gadd; David Benoit; Don Grusin; Solo pianist, also performs with brother Don Grusin, and jazz-fusion septet NY-LA Dream Band. Compositions: For numerous films including: Three Days Of The Condor; The Graduate; Heaven Can Wait; On Golden Pond; Tootsie; Reds; The Little Drummer Girl; The Goonies; The Milago Beanfield War; The Fabulous Baker Boys; Also television themes: St Elsewhere; Roots; Numerous television films. Recordings: Solo albums: Candy, 1961; The Many Moods Of Dave Grusin, 1962; Kaleidoscope, 1964; Discovered Again, 1976; One Of A Kind, 1977; Dave Grusin and the GRP All-Stars, 1980; Out Of The Shadows, 1982; Mountain Dance, 1983; The NY-LA Dream Band, 1988; Cinemagic, 1987; One Of A Kind, 1988; Migration, 1989; Havana, 1990; The Dave Grusin Collection, 1991; The Gershwin Collection, 1992; Homage To Duke, 1993; with Lee Ritenour: Harlequin, 1984; with Don Grusin: Sticks And Stones, 1988; Also recorded with Billy Joel; Paul Simon; Gerry Mulligan. Honours: Academy Award, Original Score, The Milagro Beanfield War, 1988; 3 Academy Award Nominations. Address: c/o GRP Records, 555 West 57th Street, New York, NY 10019, USA.

GRUZ Sergio, b. 17 Feb 1968, Buenos Aires, Argentina. Musician (piano); Composer. Education: University of Buenos Aires. Musical Education: Jazz music and classical. Career: Festival Des Allumées, 1992; Festivals in France; European Jazz Competition with Sergio Gruz Trio, Germany; Concours National de Jazz à la Défense, Paris; Belgian Jazz Festival. Recordings: Bernardo Baraj Quintet, Argentina, 1992; Tierra del Fuego, France, 1994; Sergio Gruz Trio, France, 1995; Misanthrope, France, 1997. Current Management: Self-managed. Address: 12 Rue du Plateau, 75019 Paris, France.

GRYTT Kajsa, b. 20 June 1961, Stockholm, Sweden. Singer; Songwriter; Musician (Guitar). 1 son. Career: Leader, Tant Strul, punk group. Compositions: Amason, Dunkar varmt, Sucka Migren, Igen, Vand Digbort, Han Sager, Om Du Kunde Semig, Som Om Himlen; Revolution; Visa Horman Alskar. Recordings: Tant Strul; Amason; Ojag Onskar Dig; Historier Fran En Vag; Den Andra Varuden, Kajsa Grytt, Revolution. Publications: Amason, 1983; Dunkar Varmt, 1983; Historier Fran En Vag, 1986; Revolution, 1994. Honours: Skap Stipendie, 1981; Nominated to Swedish Grammy, 1991. Memberships: SKAP; Svenska Musiker Föbundet. Current Management: Warner Chappell.

GUÉRAULT Stéphane, b. 19 Dec 1936, Reims, France. Musician (clarinet, saxophone); Bandleader. m. Isabelle Escoffier, 19 July 1985, 2 daughters. Education: University graduate, Law. Musical Education: Studies with Madame Dussequier. Career: Bandleader; Sideman with: Bill Coleman; Wild Bill Davis; Numerous concerts throughout France; Festival appearances include: Lille; Nice; Marciac. Recordings: with Wild Bill Davis; Bill Coleman; Marc Fosset. Honour: Sidney

Bechet Award, French Musical Academy, 1993. Membership: SACEM. Hobby: Antique cars. Address: 20 Rue Murillo, 75008 Paris, France.

GUILLORY Isaac, b. 27 Feb 1947, Guantanamo Bay, Cuba. Musician (guitar); Singer; Songwriter. m. (1) V M E Thompson, 6 June 1974; (2) V J McMillan, 3 Apr 1993, 2 daughters. Musical Education: Roosevelt University School Of Music, Chicago, Illinois. Career: Recorded and toured with The Cryan Shames, 1967-70; US tours, supporting Jimi Hendrix, Procol Harum, The Byrds, 1967-68; UK debut, Cambridge Folk Festival, 1971; Atlantic recording artist, 1973-75; Recording and touring guitarist for: Al Stewart, Elkie Brooks, Pacific Eardrum, Barbara Dickson, Francis Cabrell, 1975-85; Concerts include: Barbara Dickson band, support to Ray Charles, Royal Albert Hall, 1982; Solo guitarist accompanying Joan Baez, televised concert, MIDEM 1984; Nick Heyward band, support to Wham!, Wembley Stadium, 1986; Started Personal Records, 1986; Exclusively solo artiste, 1986-; Guitar tutor, Guildhall School of Music Summer Course, Barbican, 1988-; Guitar duet with John Renbourn, Europe and US tours, 1992-. Recordings: Solo albums: Side One And Two; Solo; Live; Easy; Slow Down; with The Cryan Shames: A Scratch In The Sky; Synthesis; with Pacific Eardrum: Pacific Eardrum; with Al Stewart: Nostradamus; Past Present And Future; with Peter Sarstedt: A Tall Tree; with Elkie Brooks: Two Days Away; with Donovan: Donovan; with Buggles: Video Killed The Radio Star; with Barbara Dickson: Here We Go Again; with Francis Cabrell: Quelque Un D'Interieur. Publications: Musical author of The Guitar Handbook, with Ralph Denyer. Hobbies: Photography; Electronics. Current Management: Agent: Dave Smith, N E Music. Address: Priory House, 55 Lawe Road, South Shields NE33 2AL, England.

GUIZIEN Christian, b. 8 June 1940, Fougères, France. Musician (trombone); Composer. Divorced, 2 daughters. Education: CEP. Musical Education: Conservatoire de Paris. Career: Musician with: Michel Legrand; Martial Solal; Television, film and radio broadcasts. Hobbies: Music; Computers (Apple, Cubase). Address: 67 Rue Pigalle, 75009 Paris, France.

GULBRANDSSEN Arve, b. 25 Sept 1972, Namsois, Norway. Musician (drums). Education: University, 3 years. Musical Education: 2 years, University of Trondheim. Career: Played various jazz bands like: Fotveita; Smaagnagerne; Joined Hedge Hog, 1993; Toured Europe, 1994, 1995. Recordings: Primal Gutter, 1993; Mercury Red, 1994; Mindless, 1994; The Healing EP; Thorn Cord Wonder, 1995. Membership: Norwegian Association Of Musicians. Current Management: Martin Aam, Hedge Hogment. Address: Hedge Hog, PO Box 683, 7001, Trondheim, Norway.

GULLEY J K (John Kenneth), b. 11 Oct 1954, Toronto, Ontario, Canada. Singer; Songwriter; Producer; Musician (guitar). m. Wilma Schmidt, 1 May 1987, 2 sons, 3 daughters. Musical Education: Self-taught. Career: 15 charted singles; Tours across Canada; USA; Europe; Scandinavia; with Glen Campbell; Billie Jo Spears; Freddie Hart; Michelle Wright; Television appearances: Ronnie Prophet Show, CTV; John Cameron, CBC; Global Easy Country, NCN. Recordings: Dusty Road, 1987; Under Cover, 1987; Blue Jeans Boy, 1990; If She Only Knew Me, 1995. Honours: 5 Nominations, Producer of the Year, CCM; RPM Big Country Awards; Vista Rising Star, CCMA, 1986; SOCAN Song of the Year, Blue Jeans Boy, 1990. Memberships: CCMA; AFofM; CARAS. Hobby: Golf. Current Management: Jerry Renewych, Warner Chappell Music Publishing. Address: #11-333 Sunnidale Road, Barrie, ON L4N 6H5, Canada.

GUMBLEY Christopher James, b. 22 May 1958. Musician (clarinet, saxophones, piano). 1 son. Musical Education: Huddersfield School Of Music, 1976-79. Career: Classical and jazz music; Work includes television, radio, session work, classical recitals, theatre work, international exhibitions; Tours of Europe, Caribbean; Member, Saxtet, resident ensemble at Birmingham Conservatoire; Appeared at Edinburgh Festival; Television and radio: BBC Children In Need; Pebble Mill; Loose Ends, BBC Radio 4; Founded Gumbles Jazz Club, Stafford; Established annual jazz course, Stoke-on-Trent; Music workshops nationwide; Recently worked with the Pasadena Roof Orchestra in Britain, Germany and Abu Dhabi and on the touring Joseph and His Amazing Technicolour Dreamcoat show; Professor of Saxophone, Birmingham Conservatoire. Recordings: with Saxtet: Safer Sax. Publications: Cops Caps and Cadillacs (5 Jazz-rock pieces for clarinet or saxophone and piano); Game Show Addicts, duets. Honours: BA Hons, Music; LTCL (Clarinet Performers). Membership: Musicians' Union. Hobbies: Squash; Aerobics; Badminton; Gardening; Composing. Address: 53 Peel Terrace, Stafford ST16 3HE, England.

GUNDECHA Ramakant, b. 24 November 1962, Vijrin, MP, India. Musicians. m. Mrs Renu Ramakant, 1 son. Education: MA, Music; MCom. Career: Performed Dhrupad Music (vocal), all major festival of India and in Germany, Switzerland, England, France, USA, Norway and Hong Kong. Honours: Ustad Allauddin Khan Fellowship, 1993; Sanskriti Award, 1994. Membership: Multi Arts Complex, Bharat Bhavan, Bhopal, MP, India. Address: Sundaram, 15 Professor Colony Bhopal 462002, Madhya Pradesh, India.

GUNDECHA Umakant, b. 8 May 1959, Vijrin, MP, India. Musicians. m. Aruna Umakant, 1 son, 1 daughter. Education: MA, Music; MA, Economics. Career: Performed Dhrupad Music (vocal), all major festivals of India and in Germany, Switzerland, England, France, USA, Norway and Hong Kong. Honours: Ustad Allauddin Khan Fellowship, 1993; Sanskriti Award, 1994. Membership: Multi Arts Complex, Bharat, Bhavan, Bhopal, MP, India. Address: Sundaram, 15 Professor Colony Bhopal, 462002, Madhya Pradesh, India.

GUNN Andrew David, b. 13 Dec 1974, Paisley, Scotland. Musician (guitar); Songwriter. Education: Charleston Academy, Inverness. Musical Education: Mainly self-taught. Career: Appeared at Pointblank Blues Festival, The Borderline Club, London, 1992; Eddi Reader's Musicality TV show, No Stilletoes, on BBC Radio 1, 2 and 4, Clyde and Forth Radio; Numerous concerts in Scotland. Compositions: Wrote and recorded album, Shades Of Blue, Jumpin' The Gunn, 1992; Many blues-based songs. Memberships: PRS; MCPS; Musicians' Union. Hobby: Swimming. Address: 16A Pict Avenue, Inverness IV3 6LX, Scotland.

GURD Geoffrey Robert, b. 24 Feb 1951, Nottingham, England. Composer; Songwriter; Musician (guitar, keyboards). Education: Manchester University. Musical Education: Self-taught; Film-scoring classes, UCLA. Career: Guitarist, singer with Crystal, The Sadista Sisters, 1975-79; Musical Director, acts including: The Flirtations, Ritz, Love Bandit; Member, The Twentieth Century Saints, 1979-81; Member, The Flying Fratellinis, 1981-82; Chief Sound Engineer, Red Shop Studios, London, 1982-85; Member, Design For Living, 1985-86; Started own production company, 1986; Formed own publishing company, De Mix Music, 1989; Lived in Los Angeles, 1991-93; Started own record label, DiscoVery, 1994. Compositions: As producer: Hold On, Claudia, 1985; Library music album, music for Corporate videos, commercials including: British Airways; Legal & General; Export Financing, 1986; Writer, producer for artists including: Freddie McGregor, Lisa Stansfield, June

Montana, 1986-89; Love Is A House, Force MDs, 1987; Better Be Good Tonight, Nick Kamen, 1988; Music for APV Films, Artworks, ITV; Music for Eye To Eye, BBC TV; Songs for Gina Foster, Chyna, 1989-91; Don't Be A Stranger, Dina Carroll, for So Close album, 1993. Recordings include: Travels Within, Richmond Gurd (duo), 1994. Honours: Quadruple Platinum disc, Don't Be A Stranger. Memberships: BASCA; PRS; Musicians' Union; BMI. Hobbies: Travel; Writing; Learning languages. Current Management: De Mix Music Ltd. Address: De Mix Music Ltd, PO Box 5705, London W10 6WG, England.

GUTHRIE Arlo, b. 10 July 1947, Coney Island, New York, USA. Folk Singer; Songwriter. Career: Appearances on folk circuit include Newport Folk Festival, 1967. Compositions: Alice's Restaurant Massacre; Highway In The Wind; Presidential Rag; Children Of Abraham. Recordings: Albums: Alice's Restaurant, 1967; Arlo, 1968; Running Down The Road, 1969; Alice's Restaurant (soundtrack), 1969; Washington County, 1970; Hobo's Lullaby, 1972; Last Of The Brooklyn Cowboys, 1973; Arlo Guthrie, 1974; Together In Concert (with Pete Seeger), 1975; Amigo, 1976; Outlasting The Blues, 1979; Power Of Love, 1981; Someday, 1986; Son of the Wind, 1992; Arlo Guthrie/Pete Seeger, More Together Again, 1994; Alice's Restaurant The Massacre Revisited, 1995; Mystic Journey, 1996. Address: c/o Rising Son Records, PO Box 657, Housatonic, MA 01236, USA.

GUTHRIE Colin Thomas, b. 16 Apr 1962, Liverpool, England. Musician (guitar). 1 daughter. Musical Education: Self-taught. Career: Semi-professional melodic rock guitarist; Toured Britain with various bands including Gran Torino; Stadium; Cherokee. Compositions: Co-writer, 3 tracks: Take My Heart Away; Somewhere; Out Of The Fire, from album Customized, Gran Torino, 1988; Composer, jingles for local independent radio station. Hobbies: Classical music; Interest in phenomena and the unexplained. Address: 55 Arley Drive, Hough Green, Widnes, Cheshire WA8 9XS, England.

GUTIERREZ Ivan, b. 17 May 1967, New York, NY, USA. Songwriter; Singer; Guitarist. Education: BA, Mathematics, BA, Philosophy, SUNY, Binghamton; MA, Philosophy, University of Wisconsin, Madison; Selftaught guitar; 4 semesters of music theory, SUNY, Binghamton. Career: Extensive stage performances; TV and radio appearances in Czech republic & Slovakia, 1993-; Sporadic stage performances in New York, Wisconsin, Minnesota, USA. Compositions: America; Jaruska; La Violencia; Siendo; Fuego. Recordings: Tres; Vera Bila and Kale, Guest Guitar. Hobbies: Languages; Literature. Address: Zuzana Handuskova,Jugoslavskych Partyzanu 36, 160 00 Prague 6, Czech Republic. Address: Stresovicka 38, 162 00, Prague 6, Czech Republic.

GUTJAHR Michael, b. Mühlacker, Germany. Manager; Singer; Songwriter .m. Andrea Gutjahr, 27 Apr 1990, 1 son. Education: Management, CaroCord Gimbtt Music Company. Musical Education: with Stromberger (music group); Composing and Text. Career: ZDF Volkstumliche Hitparade; ARD Schlagerparade der Volksmusik; MDR, SWF television shows and radio interviews. Compositions include: As lyricist and composer: Jeden Tag Nur Sonnenschein; Das Ist Unser Land; Menschen Helfen Menschen; Frage Nicht; Flieg Vogel Flieg. Recordings: Mitdem Glück Per Du, Stromberger; 5 albums with Stromberger and others. Honours: SDR Golden 7, 1993. Memberships: GEMA; IFPI; GVL. Hobbies: Writing; Nature. Current Management: CaroCord Gmbh, Music Company. Address: CaroCord Gmbh, Aischbühlstr 28, D-75443 Ötisheim, Germany.

GUY Buddy (George), b. 30 July 1936, Lettsworth, Louisiana, USA. Blues Musician (guitar). Career: Played with artists including Slim Harpo; Lightnin' Slim; Member, Rufus Foreman Band; Solo artiste; Member, houseband, Chess Records, including sessions with Muddy Waters; Howlin' Wolf; Musical partnership with Junior Wells; Performances include: Support to Rolling Stones, tour, 1970; Guest, Eric Clapton's Blues Night, Royal Albert Hall, London, 1990. Recordings: Albums: Blues From Big Bill's Copa Cobana, 1963; A Man And The Blues, 1968; This Is Buddy Guy, 1968; Hold That Plane!, 1972; I Was Walking Through The Woods, 1974; Hot And Cool, 1978; Got To Use Your House, 1979; Dollar Done Fell, 1980; DJ Play My Blues, 1982; The Original Blues Brothers - Live, 1983; Ten Blue Fingers, 1985; Live At The Checkerboard, Chicago, 1979, 1988; Breaking Out, 1988; Damn Right I Got The Blues (with Eric Clapton, Jeff Beck, Mark Knopfler), 1991; My Time After Awhile, 1992; Feels Like Rain, 1993; American Bandstand, Vol 2, 1993; with Junior Wells: Buddy And The Juniors, 1970; Buddy Guy And Junior Wells Play The Blues, 1972; Drinkin' TNT And Smokin' Dynamite, 1982; Alone & Acoustic, 1991; Alive In Montreux, 1992; Various compilations; Singles include: First Time I Met The Blues; Stone Crazy. Contributions to Junior Wells: Hoodoo Man Blues; It's My Life Baby. Current Management: The Cameron Organisation Inc., 2001 West Magnolia Blvd, Suite E, Burbank, CA 91506-1704, USA.

H

HACKETT Eric Dexter, b. 13 Apr 1956, Los Angeles, USA. Musician (keyboards). Musical Education; Mus B, University of South California, 1977. Career: Keyboard player with Diana Ross and the Supremes; Talk Back, Forward Motion; Scheme Payne; The Temptations; The Four Tops; Musical Director, Curtis Mayfield, 1977-83; President, Can't Hack It Music, 1978-. Memberships: NARAS; AFofM.

HACKETT Steve, b. 12 Feb 1950, London, England. Musician (guitar). Career; Member, Quiet World; Genesis, 1971-77; Concerts include: Reading Festivals, 1971-73; Regular UK and US tours, 1973-; Lamb World tour, 1974; Film premiere, Genesis In Concert (attended by Princess Anne), 1977; Solo artiste, 1975-; Member, GTR, 1986. Recordings: Albums: with Genesis: Nursery Cryme, 1971; Foxtrot, 1972; Genesis Live, 1973; Selling England By The Pound, 1973; The Lamb Lies Down On Broadway, 1974; A Trick Of The Tail, 1976; Wind & Wuthering, 1977; Seconds Out, 1977; Solo albums: Voyage Of The Acolyte; Please Don't Touch; Spectral Mornings; Defector; Cured; Highly Strung; Bay Of Kings; Till We Have Faces; Blues With A Feeling; Momentum, 1988; Time Lapse, 1992; Guitar Noir, 1993; There are Many Sides to the Night, 1995; Genesis Revisited, 1996; A Midsummer Nights Dream, 1997; with GTR: GTR, 1986. Honour: Ivor Novello Award, 1979. Current Management: Kudos Music, Crown Studios, 16-18 Crown Road, Twickenham, Middlesex TW1 3EE, England.

HADDAWAY Nester Alexander, b. Tobago. Singer; Dancer. Career: Founder, group Elegato, Germany; Solo singer, dance music, 1992-. Recordings: Albums: Haddaway - The Album, 1993; The Drive, 1995; Singles: What Is Love?, 1993; I Miss You, 1994; Rock My Heart, 1994. Address: c/o Coconut Records, Nachtigalenweg 34, 53758 Hennef, Germany.

HADJINEOPHYTOU George Constantinou, b. 28 Oct 1965, London, England. Composer; Musician (bouzouki, saz, lyra). m. Eleni, 23 Oct 1994. Musical Education: GCE O Level, Grade 5 Theory. Career: International Eisteddfod (Wales); BBC World Service, London Greek Radio; Mad About Music, BBC TV. Recordings: Psyche And Eros (animation), Channel 4; Grandmothers Hands (short film for television). Honour: Drama Film Festival (Greece). Mebebrships: PRS; Musicians' Union. Hobbies: Greek folk dancing; Cooking. Address: 10 College Road, Winchmore Hill, London N21 3LL, England.

HADJOPOULOS Sue, b. 26 June 1953, New York, USA. Musician (percussion); Vocalist. Education: BA, Anthroplogy, Columbia University, 1975. Musical Education: Mannes College of Music. Career: Professional percussionist, 1970-; Founder member, female salsa group Latin Fever; Tours include: World tours with Joe Jackson, 1982-83, 1991-; World tour with Simple Minds, 1985-86; True Colors tour with Cyndi Lauper; Support tours with The Who; The Rolling Stones; Performed and recorded as freelance musician with: Laurie Anderson; Mick Jones; Michael Monroe; Laura Nyro; Teena Marie; Percussionist for numerous commercials. Recordings: with Joe Jackson: Night And Day, 1982; Mike's Murder (soundtrack), 1983; Live 1980-1986, 1988; with Simple Minds: Once Upon A Time, 1985; Live In The City Of Light, 1987. Publications: One of Top Latin Percussionists, Modern Drummer Magazine Poll, 1984; Platinum discs with Joe Jackson, Simple Minds. Memberships: AFTRA; ASCAP; NARAS; AFofM; Percussive Arts Society; Recording Musicians Association.

HADLEY Tony (Anthony), b. 2 June 1960, Islington, London, England. Singer. Career: Member, Spandau Ballet, 1979-90; Performances include: Royal Albert Hall, 1983; Royal Festival Hall, 1983; Wembley Arena, 1984; Live Aid, Wembley, 1985. Recordings: Singles include: To Cut A Long Story Short, 1980; The Freeze, 1981; Musclebound, 1981; Chant No. 1 (I Don't Need This Pressure On), 1981; Instinction, 1982; Lifeline, 1982; Communication, 1983; True, 1983; Gold, 1984; Only When You Leave, 1984; I'll Fly For You, 1984; Highly Strung, 1984; Round And Round, 1984; Solo: Lost In Your Love; For Your Blue Eyes Only; The Game Of Love; Albums: Journey To Glory, 1981; Diamond, 1982; Parade, 1984; The Singles Collection, 1985; Through The Barricades, 1986; Heart Like A Sky, 1989; The Best Of Spandau Ballet, 1991; Solo album: Tony Hadley, 1997; Contributor, Do They Know It's Christmas?, Band Aid, 1984. Honours include: BRIT Awards, Sony Trophy For Technical Excellence, 1984.

HADWEN Julie, b. 4 Jan 1965, Reading, Berkshire, England. Singer; Songwriter; Musician (piano, guitar). Musical Education: Private studies, piano, guitar, classical, blues, jazz. Career: Supported Kane Gang on tour, 1984; Montreux Jazz Festival, 1985; British Big Sound Authority tour, 1985; Televison appearances include: The Tube; Old Grey Whistle Test; Top Of The Pops; Wogan; Oxford Road Show; Live radio sessions for Bruno Brookes, Janice Long. Recordings: Albums: An Inward Revolution; Sanctuary; Singles: This House Is Where Your Love Stands; Bad Town; Moving Heaven And Earth; Don't Let Our Love Start A War. Membership: Musicians' Union. Hobbies: Live music; Pscychology; Film; Theatre; Comedy. Current Management: Self-managed. Address: 72 Makepeace Avenue, Highgate, London N6 6HB, England.

HADŽO, (Hadžo Kodžoman) b. 27 January 1967, Zagreb, Croatia. Musician (guitar, bass guitar); Songwriter; Music Writer; Singer. Education: Electrical Engineer; Selftaught Guitar and Bass Guitar. Career: Underground out of Yugoslavia, TV documentary, 1986; J Peel show, radio 1, played Stop the War, Bring the Noiz 7", 1992; Fiju Briju 1, 1993, 3, 1995, 4, 1996, Fijo Brijus, 1997; biggest festivals in Croatia and Salata, 1997; Ecstazy, Berlin, 1990; Zoro, Leipzig, Germany, 1993. Compositions: Obrij me Majko Motornom Pilom, 7", LP, CD; Fuck You All, 1993; Pataren; Šank; Nema Više; MTV. Publications: Croatian Pop/Rock Encyclopedia, 1994; Patareni Tribute, 1996; Patareni Buka, We Can't Be Banned From Here, 1991. Honour: Porin for Best Alternative Album in 1993, Hladno Pivo Džinovski, 1994. Membership: Croatian Musicians Union. Hobbies: Laze Keeping; Dreaming; Listening to Music; Playing; Always being ready to help if needed. Current Management: Jabukaton, B Trenka 9, 10000 Zagreb, Croatia. Address: Davor Kodzoman, Tuskanova 26, 10000 Zagreb, Croatia.

HAGAR Sammy, b. 13 Oct 1947, Monterey, California, USA. Rock Vocalist; Musician (guitar); Songwriter. Career: Singer, bands: Fabulous Castillas; Skinny; Justice Brothers; Dust Cloud; Lead singer, Montrose, 1973-75; Support to The Who, London; Solo artiste, 1975-87; Support to Kiss; Boston; Kansas; One-off project, HSAS (with Neal Schon, Kenny Aaronson and Michael Shrieve), 1984; Lead singer, US rock group Van Halen, 1987-97; Regular US and international tours including Monsters Of Rock US tour, 1988; Co-host, Westwood One radio show with Michael Anthony, 1992. Recordings: with Montrose: Montrose, 1973; Paper Money, 1974; Solo albums: Nine On A Scale Of Ten, 1976; Sammy Hagar Two, 1977; Musical Chairs, 1978; All Night Long-Live, 1978; Street Machine, 1979; Danger Zone, 1979; Loud And Clear, 1980; Standing Hampton, 1982; Rematch, 1982; Three Lock Box, 1983; Live From London To Long Beach, 1983; VOA, 1983; Voice Of America, 1984; Looking Back, 1987; Sammy Hagar, 1987; Red, 1993; with HSAS: Through The Fire, 1984; with Van Halen: 5150 (Number 1, US), 1986; OU812 (Number 1, US), 1988; For Unlawful Carnal Knowledge (Number 1, US), 1991; Right Here Right Now, 1993; Balance, 1995; Singles include: Solo: Your Love Is Driving Me Crazy; I Can't Drive 55; Heavy Metal, film theme from film Heavy Metal; Winner Takes All, from film Over The Top; Give To Live; Eagles Fly; with Van Halen: Why Can't This Be Love, 1986; Love Walks In, 1986; Dreams, 1986; When It's Love, 1988; Finish What Ya Started, 1988; Feels So Good, 1989; Poundcake, 1991; Top Of The World, 1991; Right Now, 1992. Honours: Numerous Platinum discs; Grammy Award, Best Hard Rock Performance, 1992; American Music Award, Favorite Album, 1992; Bay Area Music Awards, Outstanding Male Vocalist, 1992, 1993; MTV Music Video Award, 1992. Hobby: Fast cars. Current Management: SRO Management Inc., 189 Carlton Street, Toronto, Ontario M5A 2K7, Canada.

HAGGARD Merle, b. 6 Apr 1937, Bakersfield, California, USA. Singer; Songwriter. Career: Accompanied Wynn Stewart, 1960; Founder, The Strangers; Successful songwriting and recording career, including 40 US Country Number 1 records. Recordings: Hit singles (own compositions) include: I'm A Lonesome Fugitive, 1966; Okie From Muskogee, 1969; I Take A Lot Of Pride In What I Am; Silver Wings; Today I Started Loving You Again; If We Make It Through December; Poncho And Lefty, with Willie Nelson; Albums include: Just Between The Two Of Us, with Bonnie Owens, 1966; Same Train A Different Time, 1969; The Land Of Many Churches, with Bonnie Owens, Carter Family, 1971; My Love Affair With Trains, 1976; A Taste Of Yesterday's Wine, with George Jones, 1982; Poncho And Lefty, with Willie Nelson, 1983; Heart To Heart, with Leona Williams, 1983; That'e The way Love Goes, 1983; The Epic Collection - Live, 1983; It's All In The Game, 1984; Kern River, 1985; Amber Waves Of Grain, 1985; Out Among The Stars, 1986; A Friend In California, 1986; Seashores Of Old Mexico, 1987; Chill Factor, 1988; 5:01 Blues, 1989; Blue Jungle, 1990; Super Hits, Volume 2, 1994; Super Hits, Volume 3, 1995. Publications: Autobiography, Sing Me Back Home, with Peggy Russell. Current Management: Hag Inc, PO Box 536, Palo Cedro, CA 96073, USA.

HÄGGMAN Ann-Mari (Solveig), b. 19 Sept 1941, Vasa, Finland. Music Organisation Executive. m. Lars-Eric Häggman, 11 Apr 1964, 1 son, 1 daughter. Education: PhD in Ethnomusicology. Career: Researcher and Head of Svenska litteratursällskapets Folkkulturarkiv; Assistant Professor,Department for Folklore, Helsinki University, 1993-1995; Head of the Institute of Finland-Swedish Traditional Music, 1985-. Publications: Magdalena på källebro (The Ballad of Mary Magdalene's Conversion), dissertation; Numerous articles, Cds and films about folk music in Finland. Memberships: Word of Honour of the Finlands svenska spelmansförbund (League of Traditional Musicians); Board Member, Swedish Literature Society; Numerous folk music organisations. Hobbies: Literature; Outdoor life. Address: c/o Finlands svenska folkmusikinstitut, Handelsesplanaden 23A, 65100 Vasa, Finland.

HAGUE Mel (Melvyn Ian), b. 20 Jan 1943, Whiston, South Yorkshire, England. Singer; Entertainer; Songwriter; Musician (guitar). m. Ivy Walton, 6 Aug 1966, 1 son, 1 daughter. Career: Grew up in Canada, 1951-61; Played most UK concert venues, including Wembley Conference Centre; All UK Country music festivals; Several European tours; Appearances: Regional television stations: Country Club, BBC2; Nightride; WSM Nashville radio, television; Much regional radio; Own record label, OGB Records. Recordings: 11 albums (5 on own label), 1974-1996. Publication: Music, book reviewer, Doncaster Entertainer.

Honour: Aria Guitars/Daily Mirror Golden Guitar Award, Top Country Entertainer, 1981. **Memberships:** Performing Rights Society; Equity. **Hobbies:** Writing reviews and stories; Cycling; Snooker and pool; Science Fiction books and films. **Address:** 37 Wroot Road, Finningley Village, Doncaster DN9 3DR, England.

HAIMOVICI Fabien-David, b. 22 Apr 1968, Bordeaux, France. Musician (drums). **Education:** College. **Musical Education:** 4 years in France, drum school; 1 year in Los Angeles, Musicians Institute. **Career:** Played with Bireli Lagrene; Tours all over USA, Europe, Japan; Tour with French artists Jacques Higelin; Nicole Croisille; Tours in Japan, France; Played with international artists in France including Lucky Peterson; Currently plays and records with Coke Tale (comprised of top Paris studio musicians); Recording: Solo rock album. **Honours:** Diploma: Outstanding Student of The Year, Musicians Institute, Los Angeles. **Hobbies:** Wind surfing; Films. **Address:** 16 Rue des cascades, 75020 Paris, France.

HAINES Luke. Singer; Songwriter. **Career:** Member, UK group The Auteurs. **Recordings:** Albums: New Wave, 1993; Now I'm A Cowboy, 1994; After Murder Park, 1996; Singles include: Light Aircraft On Fire, 1995; Back With The Killer Again, 1995. **Honour:** Mercury Prize Nomination, 1993. **Current Management:** Tony Beard, PROD.

HAINES Margaret Ewart Blackwood, b. 28 April 1941, Detroit, MI, USA. m. Peter E Haines, 28 August 1965, 1 son, 1 daughter. **Education:** BA, Elementary Education, Minor in Music, Albion College, Albion, MI, USA; Independent study in composition, theory, harmony, orchestration. **Career:** Marge & Friends, TV program, 1980-83, 1984-85; Featured interviews with leading Christian national and local people, 1980-83. **Compositions:** Love Song: You Are the Love of My Life; Songs of Jesus, songbook, vocal cassette; Cantos de Jesus, 6 Spanish scripture/Worship songs; The Revelation of Jesus Christ!, songbook: Cantata to Revelation. **Recordings:** Songs of Jesus; Are You Ready: 20 Gospel Favorites; The Revelation of Jesus Christ!; Elaine O'Neill: Favorite Hymns. **Publications:** Revelation of Jesus Christ Songbook, 1991, 1994, 1997; Orchestration, 1998; Songs of Jesus Songbook, 1996; Children's Scripture Songbook; Isiah Cantata, forthcoming. **Honours:** Phi Mu Alpha Sinfonia Music Society, 1963; Senior Piano Recital: Albion College, 1963; Grant to study effect of music in teaching retarded children, 1970-71. **Memberships:** National Religious Broadcasters; Christian Copyright Licensing International; ASCAP; American Music Center. **Hobbies:** Music; Composition; Gardening; Piano Composition; Improvising; Arranging; Swimming; Gardening. **Address:** Margaret E Haines, POB 66 85 Crease Road, Budd Lake, NJ 07828, USA.

HAJDOVSKA-TLUSTA Katerina, b. 27 Feb 1953, Prague, Czech Republic. Singer; Musician (percussion); Songwriter. m. Martin Tlusty, 30 Jan 1982, 2 stepdaughters. **Education:** Special Pedagogy, Prague Charles' University. **Career:** FOK, folk-rock; Foersters Choir; J Vycpálek Folklore Music; Ukrainian Folklore Music, Ignis; Prague Madrigals, Chesed, Jewish music; Ester, Jewish music; Music and Musicotherapy Teacher; Czech Radio broadcasts. **Recordings:** Albums: with Ester: To You, Jerusalem; with Chesed: Jewish Feasts in Songs; Jewish Songs Live. **Hobby:** Biblical Study. **Current Management:** K Hajdovská-Tlustá, Michnova 1626, 149 00 Praha 4, Czech Republic.

HAJDOVSKY-POTAPOVIC Alexandr "Lesik", b. 27 Feb 1953, Prague, Czech Republic. m. Miroslava Hajdovska-Vlková, 7 Dec 1973, 2 sons. **Career:** Documentary film music; Advertisement music; Member of Czech television and radio broadcasting groups: FOK, folk rock; Svehlik, rock; Mazelé, rap; Extempore,

rock/humour; Ester, Jewish traditional songs. **Recordings:** Albums: Jizák; Lesik Hajdovsky: Už horí svíce; Lesik Hajdovsky: Manzelé; Prague: Zizkov Kuplets; Svehlík: There's No Time; Ester: To You, Jerusalem. **Honours:** Nomination Award Magazine, 1985, 1988; Mlady svet - Bílá Vrána; Melodie magazine award, 1991. **Membership:** OSA. **Hobby:** Painting pictures. **Current Management:** Katerina Hajdovská-Tlustá, Michnova 1626, 149 00 Prague 4, Czech Republic. **Address:** Brodského 1672, 149 00 Prague 4, Czech Republic.

HAJNALOVA Maria, b. 14 June 1947, Trencin. Singer. m. Jan Hajnal, 14 December 1968, 1 daughter. **Career:** Many radio and TV recordings; Stage Performances; Actress, 1 appearance in film. **Recordings:** Compositions from Jan Hajnal. **Publication:** Lexikon of Pop Music and Jazz in Former CSFR, 1986. **Membership:** Slovak Jazz Society. **Hobbies:** Singing; Cooking; Travel. **Address:** Jaroslavova 12/a, 85101 Bratislava, Slovakia.

HALE Keith, b. 6 Nov 1950, Hull, East Yorkshire, England. Songwriter; Musician (keyboards); Record Producer. 1 daughter. **Musical Education:** Dartington College of Arts, Devon. **Career:** Formed Blood Donor, 1977; Support to J J Burnel on Euroman Tour; Member, Hawkwind, 1980; Left with Ginger Baker, formed Ginger's Nutters, toured Europe, 1981; Member, Toyah's band for Warrior Rock tour, 1982. **Compositions:** It's A Mystery, 1981. **Recordings:** Producer, Toyah's first album Sheep-Farming In Barnet; Other albums include: Zones/Stonehenge, Hawkwind; Toyah On Tour, 1983; Ginger Baker In Concert, 1985. **Memberships:** PRS; MCPS; Musicians' Union. **Hobby:** Reached Scrabble quarter-finals, 1980. **Current Management:** Gems. **Address:** Firs Cottage, 5 Firs Close, London SE23 1BB, England.

HALE Simon B, b. 23 Apr 1964, Birmingham, England. Composer; Arranger; Producer; Musician (keyboards). m. Claire Moore, 15 Oct 1994, 1 son, 1 d. **Musical Education:** A Level Music, Grade VIII piano, violin; Bachelor of Music, Goldsmiths' College, University Of London, 1985. **Career:** Keyboards with Seal: World tour; US Grammy Awards, 1992; Top Of The Pops; Wogan; Live videos; Keyboards with: Howard New; Wendy & Lisa; Tri; Gail Ann Dorsey; Geoffrey Williams; Arranger for: Incognito; George Benson; Yo Yo Honey; Shawn Lee; Maysa Leak; Conductor, MD, concert with Incognito, Royal Festival Hall, 1995; Producer for: 2 albums, Kumiko Yamashita. **Compositions:** George Benson; British Film Institute; Nescafé; Solo album, 1992; String arranger: 100° & Rising, Incognito; String arranger, composer, George Benson; Composer, orchestrator, Tomoyasu Hotei; Solo album: East Fifteen, 1994; Seal, single, EP; BBC TV theme tune The Vote Race, 1992. **Recordings:** String Arranger: Travelling without Moving, Jamiroquai, 1996; Duncan Sheik, 1996; M People, 1997; Brass Arranger, Rat Bat Blue, 1997; Producer/Arranger, forthcoming James Brown live album. **Memberships:** Musicians' Union; PRS; MCPS; Association of Professional Composers. **Hobby:** Cycling. **Current Management:** c/o IRc2 (London) Ltd. **Address:** 1 Star Street, London W2 1QD, England.

HALEY Mark Jonathan, b. 2 Feb 1961, Portsmouth, Hampshire, England. Musician (keyboards, guitar). **Musical Education:** Classical training in piano, guitar, trumpet. **Career:** Began Haley Brothers, 1976; Television appearance, Rund Pop show, East Germany, 1984; Toured with Billy Fury from 1982 until his death; Joined The Monkees comeback tours, 1986-1989; Member, The Kinks, 1989-1993; Current member, The Chaps; Formed new Band, Gorge, 1997; Currently recording new album, On This.. **Recordings:** with Haley Brothers: One Way Love Affair, 1978; What Do You Want To Make Those

Eyes At Me For, 1984; with The Monkees: That Was Then, This Is Now, 1986; with The Kinks: Down All The Days, 1991; with The Chaps: The Collector, 1995. **Honours:** Ivor Novello Award Services To Music (The Kinks). **Memberships:** PRS; Musicians' Union; MCPS. **Hobbies:** Tennis; Golf; Watching West Ham United Football Club. **Current Management:** Markle Rhymes With Sparkle. **Address:** 12, Admiral House, Rivergate, Peterborough PE1 1ES, England.

HALFORD Rob, b. 25 Aug 1951, Birmingham, England. Singer. **Career:** Lead singer, UK heavy rock group Judas Priest, 1974-90; Tours include: Support to Led Zeppelin, US, 1977; Support to Kiss, 1979; Turbo - Fuel For Life tour, 1986; Painkiller tour, US, 1990; US tour, with Alice Cooper, Motörhead, 1991; Concerts, festivals include: Reading Festival, 1976; Monsters Of Rock Festival, Castle Donington, 1980; Heavy Metal Sunday, San Bernadino, California, 1983; Live Aid, Philadelphia, 1985; Founder, lead singer, heavy rock group Fight, 1991-; Appearance as stand-in singer for Black Sabbath, Pacific Amphitheatre, California, 1992. **Recordings:** Albums: with Judas Priest: Rocka Rolla, 1974; Sad Wings Of Destiny, 1976; Sin After Sin, 1977; Stained Class, 1978; Killing Machine, 1978; Unleashed In The East, 1979; British Steel, 1980; Point Of Entry, 1981; Screaming For Vengeance, 1982; Defenders Of The Faith, 1984; Turbo, 1986; Priest Live, 1987; Ram It Down, 1988; Painkiller, 1990; A Touch Of Evil, 1991; Metal Works 1973-93, 1993; with Fight: Fight, 1994; A Small Deadly Space, 1995; Singles include: with Judas Priest: Take On The World; Living After Midnight; Breaking The Law; You've Got Another Thing Coming; Contributor, Stars, Hear'n'Aid (charity record for Ethiopian famine relief), 1986; Singer, with Pantera, for film soundtrack Buffy The Vampire Slayer, 1992. **Current Management:** c/o John Baxter, EMAS, PO Box 55810, Phoenix, AZ 85078, USA.

HALL Brian John, b. 27 Nov 1939, Hoylake, Wirral, England. Musician (guitar, bass). **Career:** Singer, musician with various bands; Solo performer, songwriter, recording service manager. **Compositions:** Amanda, hit for Stuart Gillies, 1973. **Honours:** Golden Note Award; Winner, Opportunity Knocks with song Amanda. **Memberships:** BASCA; PRS; MCPS; Equity. **Hobbies:** Dining out; Table tennis. **Address:** 6 Fieldway, Meols, Wirral, Merseyside L47 9SD, England.

HALL Chris. Musician (accordion, drums); Singer; Agent; Record Company Executive; Journalist; Radio Presenter; Festival Organiser. **Career:** Accordion player, vocalist with R Cajun and The Zydeco Brothers; The Bearcats; Accordian Player with Zydecomotion; Tour organiser, US and UK agent, for Cajun and Zydeco; Writer, co-partner, Cajun Users Manual; Radio presenter, BBC Radio 2; Club organiser, The Swamp Club; Manager, Bearcat Records. **Address:** Swamp, PO Box 94, Derby DE22 1XA, England.

HALL Daryl (Hohl), b. 11 Oct 1949, Pottstown, Pennsylvania, USA. Singer; Musician (guitar); Songwriter. **Education:** Temple University. **Career:** Member, Kenny Gamble & The Romeos; Gulliver; Session singer, Sigma Sounds Studios; Backing singer, The Stylistics; The Delfonics; Member, duo Hall And Oates, with John Oates, 1969-; Concerts worldwide include: Live Aid, Philadelphia, 1985; Rainforest benefit concert, Madison Square Garden, with The Grateful Dead, 1988; Earth Day, Central Park, New York, 1990; USA Harvest National Hunger Relief concert, 1991; The Simple Truth, benefit concert for Kurdish refugees, Wembley, 1991. **Compositions:** Many hit songs co-written with John Oates; Other songs include: Sara Smile; Wait For Me; Kiss On My List (co-written with Janna Allen); One On One; Did It In A Minute (co-written with Sara &

Janna Allen); Foolish Pride; Everything Your Heart Desires; Swept Away, for Diana Ross; Film theme, Ruthless People (co-written with Mick Jagger and Dave Stewart). Recordings: Albums: with Hall And Oates: Whole Oats, 1972; Abandoned Luncheonette, 1974; War Babies, 1974; Daryl Hall And John Oates, 1975; Bigger Than Both Of Us, 1976; No Goodbyes, 1977; Beauty On A Back Street, 1977; Livetime, 1978; Along The Red Edge, 1978; X-Static, 1979; Private Eyes, 1981; H2O, 1982; Big Bam Boom, 1984; Live At The Apollo With David Ruffin And Eddie Kendricks, 1985; Ooh Yeah, 1988; Change Of Season, 1990; The Best Of..., 1991; Solo albums: Sacred Songs, 1980; Three Hearts In The Happy Ending Machine, 1986; Soul Alone, 1993; US Number 1 singles with Hall And Oates: Rich Girl, 1977; Kiss On My List, 1981; Private Eyes, 1981; I Can't Go For That (No Can Do), 1982; Maneater, 1982; Out Of Touch, 1984; Numerous other hit singles. Featured on: Journeyman, Eric Clapton, 1989; Contributor, We Are The World, USA For Africa, 1985; Sun City, Artists Against Apartheid, 1985; The Last Temptation Of Elvis, 1990; Two Rooms - Celebrating The Songs Of Elton John And Bernie Taubin, 1991. Honours include: American Music Awards: Favourite Pop/Rock Duo or Band, 1983-85; 19 US Gold and Platinum discs (most successful duo in US recording history). Current Management: Horizon Entertainment. Address: 130 W 57th Street #12-B, New York, NY 10019, USA.

HALL Gary Martin, b. 29 Nov 1964, Ormskirk, Lancashire, England. Singer; Songwriter; Musicians (guitar). Career: Television appearances: Granada TV, three times; Italian TV; Numerous appearances on radio; Tours of Europe. Recordings: Writer, all songs on albums: Garage Heart, 1989; Wide Open To The World, 1991; What Goes Around, 1993; Twelve Strings and Tall Stories, 1996. Honours: Rising Star Award, BCMA, 1995; Southern Radio Award Nomination, Song Of The Year, 1995. Memberships: PRS; MCPS. Hobby: Music. Address: 10 Rose Terrace, Ashton, Preston, Lancashire PR2 1EB, England.

HALL G P (Graham Peter), b. 15 July 1943, Hampton Hill, England. Artist; Composer; Ambient Sound Sculptures; Musician (saxophone, bass, flamenco guitar, synthesiser, elctric guitar). m. Päivi Annikki Vilkman, 26 June 1987, 4 sons, 2 daughters. Musical Education: Studied flamenco guitar. Career: Member, blues bands, 1960s; Toured Europe, 1962-68; Video: The Estates, 1977; Tour: Estates, 1977; Festivals: France; Germany; Spain; Holland, 1982; North Africa, 1983; Southwest England, 1992; Radio includes: Radio Bristol; Radio Sussex; Radio Mercury; Radio Surrey; Radio Lotus, Denmark; Radio Lux, Ukraine; Television: Wire TV; Germany; Netherlands; Queen Elizabeth Hall, London, 1996; Western Isles tour, 1997. Composition: Commissioned, Sea Sorrow (Isle of Lewis), 1997. Recordings: New Town Suite (The Estates, 1977; Manifestations; Full Moon Over Madrid, 1979; Harbinger, Colours, 1986; Imaginary Seasons, 1992; Slipstreams, Glow, 1994; Shooting Stars, 1995; Eclectic Guitars, 1996; Figments of Imagination, 1996; Mar-Del-Plata, 1997; Recorded 143 titles, all instrumental; Video: Paths Of The Lonely, 1995. Publications: River Flow; Off The Shell; Filmtrax; Prototype; Countdown Productions. Honour: Mercury Music Prize Nomination, Imaginary Seasons, 1992. Memberships: PRS; Musicians' Union. Hobbies: Time with family; Relaxing. Current Management: Imaginary Music. Address: Imaginary Music, 7 Ruxley Close, Wootton, Bassett, Wiltshire SN4 7LB, England.

HALL James S, b. 4 Dec 1930, Buffalo, New York, USA. Musician (guitar). m. Jane Herbert, 9 Sept 1965, 1 daughter. Musical Education: Cleveland Institute of Music. Career: Musician with Chico Hamilton, Jimmy Guiffre Trio, 1957-59; Ella Fitzgerald, 1959-60; Sonny Rollins, 1961-62; Formed Quartet with Art Farmer, 1962-64; Leader, own trio/quartet, 1962-; Concerts include: The White House; Carnegie Hall; Duke Ellington's Birthday Party; Jazz Festivals include: Berlin; Concord; Monterey; Newport; Unbria; Many club appearances in USA, Canada, England, France, Japan; Television appearances worldwide including The Sound of Jazz, CBS; The Tonight Show; Film appearance: Jazz On A Summer's Day, 1958. Recordings: Albums include: with Bobby Brookmeyer and Jimmy Raney: Street Swingers; with Bill Evans: Undercurrent; Intermodulation; with Sonny Rollins: The Bridge; with Art Farmer: Big Blues; with Paul Desmond: Paul Desmond And Friends; Easy Living; with Ron Carter: Alone Together; Live At The Village West; Telephone; with Michel Petrucciani's Power of Three (featuring Jim Hall and Wayne Shorter): Three; Solo, own ensembles: All Across the City; Live At Town Hall, Vols 1 and 2; Subsequently; Youkali; Something Special; Dedications and Inspirations; Other recordings with Red Mitchell; George Shearing; Tom Harrell. Publications: JazzImprovisation-Transcriptions of Jim Hall Solos, 1980; Exploring Jazz Guitar, 1991; Master Sessions with Jim Hall, (instructional video), 1993; Jim Hall-Jazz Guitar Environments, 1994; Honours include: Downbeat Critics Poll Awards, 1963-; Downbeat Reader's Poll Winner, 1965-66; Playboy All-Star Poll Winner, 1968-71; Jazz Magazine Award, Best Performer, 1965-66; Grammy Nominations. Current Management: Mary Ann Topper, Jazz Tree Agency. Address: 648 B'way Suite 703, New York, NY 10012, USA.

HALL Keith Robert, b. 24 Apr 1951, Edgeware, Middlesex, England. Musician (drums). Engaged to marry Titvi Ikäheimo (fashion designer), Dec 1989. Musical Education: Mainly self-taught; Studied with Joe Hodson; Frank King; Joe Morello. Career: Professional musician, 1966-; Founder member, Pickettywitch, 1969-72; Member, Gerry And The Pacemakers, 1973-77; Terry Lightfoot, 1978-84; Musicals: Hair National Tour; 1980; Godspell, 1980; Joseph And The Amazing Technicolour Dreamcoat, 1981; Freelance musician, played with: Kenny Ball; Maxine Daniels; Bertice Redding; Fiona Duncan; Jay McShan; Ellen Rucker; Ritchie Cole, 1984-; Formed jazz-rock fusion band Storm Warning, with Jill Jarman, 1987; Concerts include: Festivals throughout Europe; Toured with Engelbert Humperdinck; with June Harris, 1987-89; Also toured Scandinavia; Worked with: Tom Whittle; Januz Carmello; Al Gray; Spike Robinson; Dick Hestall-Smith, 1990; Moved to Helsinki, 1990; Regular drummer with Antti Sarpila Swing Band; Also worked with: UMO; Espoo Big Band; Pentti Lasanen; Severi Pyysalo; Karita Mattila; Appearances at most Finnish music festivals, and on Finnish television. Recordings: with Pickettywitch: That Same Old Feeling, 1970; Sad Old Kinda Movie, 1970; Baby I Won't Let You Down, 1970; with Gerry And The Pacemakers: Lovely Lady, 1974. Albums: with Pickettywitch: Pickettywitch, 1970; with Storm Warning: Spirit Level, 1988; with Antti Sarpila: Father, Son And Holy Swing, 1993; Chrisse Schwindt Memorial Concert, 1993; Live At Storyville, 1994; with Claus Anderson: Chrisse Schwindt Memorial Concert, 1993; with Swing Gentlemen: Swing Gentlemen's Ball, 1995. Memberships: Musicians' Union; Finnish Drummers Association; Finnish Musicians' Union. Hobbies: Golf; Fishing; Skiing; Chess. Address: Helsinki, Finland.

HALL Martin, b. 26 Apr 1963, Copenhagen, Denmark. Singer; Composer; Musician (multi-instrumentalist). Musical Education: Academy of Piano and Music, Copenhagen; Royal Academy of Fine Arts, Copenhagen. Career: Singer, composer, Ballet Mécanique; Ritual, The World Music Days, Århus Musikhus, 1983; Requiem, The Taksigelses Church, Copenhagen, 1989; Inskription, The Danish National Radio, 1983; Gud Og Grammatik, Danish Academy of Fine Arts, 1984; Current Works, Danish Natonal Radio, 1995. Recordings: Avenues Of Oblivion, 1980; The Icecold Waters Of The Egocentric Calculation, 1981; For, 1982; Ritual, 1983; Apparently All The Same, 1984; Free Force Structure, 1984; Fusion, 1985; Relief, 1985; Warfare, 1985; Treatment, 1985; Cutting Through, 1986; Beat Of The Drum, 1988; Presence, 1988; Surreal Thing, 1989; The Martin Hall Document, 1989; Crush-The Point of No Return Soundtrack, 1989; Prime Material, 1990; Imperfect, 1990; Dreamworld, 1990; Palladium, 1990; The Rainbow Theatre, 1990; Read Only Memory, 1991; Sweet Mystery, 1993; All The Way Down, 1993; Strange Delight, 1993; A Touch Of Excellence, 1993; Angel Of The Night, 1994; Phantasmagoria, 1994; Random Hold, 1996; Testcards 1989-1995, 1997; Performance, 1997. Publications: 4 books; 5 anthologies; 28 albums, magazines, works; The World Days, 1996. Honours: Honorary Award, Danish Association of Composers, 1995; The 3 Year Major Grant, National Fund For The Endowment of the Arts, 1995; Association of Danish Composers (DJBFA); KODA; GRAMEX; NCB. Hobbies: Music; Writing books. Current Management: Motor Danmark. Address: Motor Danmark, Linnésgade 14, DK-1361 CopenhagenK, Denmark.

HALL Terry, b. 19 Mar 1959, Coventry, Warwickshire, England. Singer. Career: Singer, The Special AKA (later as The Specials), 1977; International concerts and tours include: Concert for People of Kampuchea, London, 1979; Founder member, Fun Boy Three, 1980-83; Founder, Colourfield, 1983-1990; Member, Vegas (with Dave Stewart), 1990s; Also solo artiste. Recordings: with The Specials: Singles: Gangsters, 1979; A Message To You Rudy, 1979; Too Much Too Young, 1980; Rat Race, 1980; Stereotype, 1980; Do Nothing, 1981; Ghost Town (Number 1, UK), 1981; Albums: Specials, 1979; More Specials, 1980; Dance Craze (film soundtrack), 1981; with Fun Boy Three: Singles: The Lunatics Have Taken Over The Asylum, 1981; It Ain't What You Do (with Bananarama), 1981; Summertime, 1982; The Telephone Always Rings Twice, 1982; The Tunnel Of Love, 1983; The More I See, 1983; Our Lips Are Sealed, 1983; Albums: Fun Boy Three, 1982; Waiting, 1983; Best Of.., 1984; Solo album: Terry Hall - The Collection, 1993; Home, 1995. Current Management: Asgard Management, 125 Parkway, London NW1 7PS, England.

HALL Thomas James, b. 19 May 1957, Longview, Washington, USA. Record Producer; Sound Engineer. Education: BA, radio and television production, East Washington University, 1980. Career: Producer, sound engineer, Viacom Studios; Logic West Studios; London Bridge Studios; Triad Studios, 1982-. Recordings: As producer/sound engineer: with Queensryche: Queensryche, 1983; Mindcrime Live, 1991; with Kenny G: Kenny G Live, 1990. Address: Triad Studios, 4572 150th Avenue NE, Redmond, WA 98052, USA.

HALL Tom T, b. 25 May 1936, Olive Hill, Kentucky, USA. Songwriter; Singer; Author. Career: Broadcaster, musician, WMOR radio station, Kentucky, with Kentucky Travellers, 1950s-60s; Leader, own touring band The Storytellers; Currently concentrating on novel-writing and composing children's songs. Compositions include: DJ For A Day, Jimmy C Newman; Goodbye Sweetheart, Hello Vietnam, Johnny Wright; Mama Tell 'Em What We're Fighting For, Dave Dudley; Harper Valley PTA, Jeannie C Riley; I Can't Dance, Gram Parsons and Emmylou Harris; Margie's At The Lincoln Park Inn, Bobby Bare; A Week In The County Jail; Pinto The Wonder Horse Is Dead; I Miss A Lot Of Trains; Old Dogs, Children And Watermelon Wine. Albums include: The Storyteller, 1972; The Rhymer And Other Five And Dimers, 1973; For The People In The Last Hard Town, 1973; Country

Is, 1974; Songs Of Fox Hollow, 1974; Faster Horses, 1976; The Magnificent Music Machine, 1976; About Love, 1977; New Train Same Rider, 1978; Places I've Done Time, 1978; Saturday Morning Songs, 1979; Ol' T's In Town, 1979; Soldier Of Fortune, 1980; The Storyteller And The Banjoman (with Earl Scruggs), 1982; In Concert, 1983; World Class Country, 1983; Everything From Jesus To Jack Daniels, 1983; Natural Dreams, 1984; Songs In A Seashell, 1985; Country Songs For Kids, 1988. Publications: The Songwriter's Handbook; The Storyteller's Nashville; The Laughing Man Of Woodmont Cove; Spring Hill (novel). Honour: Grammy Award, Tom T Hall's Greatest Hits. Address: c/o Tom T. Hall Enterprises, PO Box 1246, Franklin, TN 37065, USA.

HALLYDAY Johnny (Jean-Philippe Smet), b. 15 June 1943, Paris, France. Singer; Musician (guitar). m. Sylvie Vartan. Musical Education: Violin lessons. Career: Radio debut, 1960; Film appearance: Les Parisiennes, 1961. Recordings: Numerous albums include: Johnny Hallyday Sings America's Rockin' Hits, 1962; Flagrant Delit, 1975; Drole De Metier, 1986; Trift De Rattles, 1986; Les Grandssuccess De Johnny Hallyday, 1988; La Peur, 1988; La Nuit Johnny (42 CD box set), 1993; Singles include: T'Ai Mer Follement; Let's Twist Again (bilingual version), 1961; If I Were A Carpenter (duet with Emmylou Harris), 1985. Address: c/o 6 Rue Daubigny, 75017 Paris, France.

HALSALL Jennie, b. 23 Jan 1954, London, England. Media Executive; Managing Director. Education: Kilburn Polytechnic, London. Career: Jacksons Advertising Agency; Cue Films Ltd; EMI Records, UK; David Geffen and Elliot Roberts Management, USA; Elektra Asylum Records, USA; Independent PR; Formed own business, Jennie Halsall Consultants (media consultants in Europe and the world outside USA), 1980-. Honours: PR Of The Year, 1980. Hobbies: Tennis; Books; Films; Eating out; Travel; Skiing. Address: 208A King Street, London W6 0RA, England.

HAMILL Andy, b. 25 March 1972, Glasgow, Scotland. Session Musician (Double Bass & Electric Basses). Career: Gigs with American jazz singers, Mark Murphy, Annie Ross and Salena Jones; Played with Chris Bowden at Glastonbury, 1997; Currently recording with pedal steel guitarist BJ Cole and Drum 'n Bass DJ LTJ Bukem. Recordings: Chris Bowden, Time Capsule; 4 Hero, EP Earth Pioneers, CD Two Pages; Trudy Kerr, Sweet Suprise. Membership: Musicians Union. Address: 14A Emu Road, London, SW8 3PR, England.

HAMILTON Andy, b. 1918, Jamaica. Jazz Musician (tenor saxophone). m. Mary, 4 sons, 6 daughters. Career: Moved to Birmingham, 1949; Worked with Jean Toussaint; Mick Hucknall; David Murray; Steve Williamson; Andy Sheppard; Jason Rebello; Bernardo Sassetti; Son, Graeme (trumpet player). Concerts: St Lucia Jazz Festival; Co-producer with Jean Toussaint. Recordings: Albums: Silvershine, 1991; Jamaica By Night, 1993. Current Management: Alan Cross, 120 Lightwoods Road, Bearwood, Birmingham B67 5BE. Address: c/o World Circuit Records, 106 Cleveland Street, London W1P 5DP, England.

HAMILTON Chico (Foreststorn), b. 21 Sept 1921, Los Angeles, California, USA. Jazz Musician (drums); Bandleader. Career: Drummer with: Dexter Gordon, Charles Mingus, Buddy Collette, whilst at school; Lionel Hampton, Slim Gaillard, 1940; Count Basie, Lester Young, late 1940s; Lena Horne, 1948-55; Founder, own quartet, 1955; Own bands (trio, quartet, quintet, octet) featured musicians including: Buddy Collette; Fred Katz; Ron Carter; Jim Hall; Eric Dolphy; Gabor Szabo; Larry Coryell; Eric Gayle; John Abercrombie; Film appearances: Sweet Smell Of Success, 1957; Jazz On A Summer's

Day, 1958; Leader, own group Euphoria, 1980s. Recordings: Numerous albums include: Spectacular, 1955; Sweet Smell Of Success, 1957; Newport Jazz, 1958; The Three Faces Of Chico, 1959; That Hamilton Man, 1959; Passin' Thru, 1962; Man From Two Worlds, 1963; Chic Chic Chico, 1965; The Dealer, 1966; The Further Adventures Of El Chico, 1966; The Gamut, 1967; El Exigente, 1970; Head Hunters, 1974; Peregrinations, 1975; Chico Hamilton And The Players, 1976; Reaching For The Top, 1978; Nomad, 1979; Euphoria, 1986; Reunion, 1989; Chico The Master, 1992; Man From Two Worlds, 1993. Address: Chico Hamilton Productions Inc, 321 E 45th St Penthouse A, New York, NY 10017, USA.

HAMILTON David, 10 Sept 1938, Manchester, England. Broadcaster. Career: Disc Jockey with: BBC Radio 1; BBC Radio 2; Capital Gold; Melody Radio; Shows on many other stations, UK; Television: Host, Pop Music shows, game shows and sports programmes, 1960-. Publication: The Music Game, autobiography. Honour: Best Syndicated Programme, New York Festivals, 1993. Hobbies: Tennis. Current Management: MPC Artists. Address: 15/16 Maple Mews, Maida Vale, London NW6 5UZ, England.

HAMILTON Frank, b. 3 August 1934, New York City, USA. Musician; Singer. m. Mary Hamilton, 5 January 1983, 3 sons, 1 daughter. Education: Los Angeles City College, 1952, 1955, 1966; Roosevelt University, Chicago, 1960-61; Los Angeles Valley College, Van Nuys, 1963-64; Santa Monica City College, 1964-69; California University, Los Angeles, 1970, 1978; Santa Barbara City College, 1974; California University, Northridge, 1978; Georgia University, 1984-87. Career: House Musician, Gate of Horn, Chicago, 1958-62; Newport Folk Music Festival, 1959; With Folk Music Group, The Weavers, Carnegie Hall, Lincoln Center, Forest Hills Stadium, 1963; Concert with Pete Seeger, Abbott Hall, Marble Head, 1984; Meridian Folk Trio, 1986-88. Compositions: We Shall Overcome, 1956; Survival, 1965; The Surfers, 1964; What I Mean, 1965; I Feel It, 1967. Recordings: A Folksingers Folksinger; Frank Hamilton Sings Folksongs; The World of Frank and Valucha; Weavers Reunion at Vanguard Carnegie Hall; Folk Festival at Newport. Publication: Choosing a Guitar Teacher, 1981. Honours: Composition Award, Los Angeles Valley College, 1963. Memberships: Chicago Historical Society; Irish Arts of Atlanta; Founder, Hot Club of Atlanta. Current Management: Frank Hamilton Productions. Address: 852 Cinderella Court, Decatur, GA 30033, USA.

HAMILTON Patrick, b. 16 March 1963, Bruges, Belgium. Producer; Musician (Keyboards); Songwriter. m. Brigitte Vandewalle, 20 November 1987, 2 sons, 1 daughter. Education: Classical Music Degree; Organ and Piano lessons. Career: Played with several well known bands in Belgium; Tour with Johnny Logan, 1990s; Tour in Belgium and The Netherlands for Hammond-organs, 1980s. Compositions: Composed for Sandra Kim, Eurovision contest winner mid 1980s; 2 Lips; Partyzone. Recordings: The Roof, own studio. Address: Sint-Jorisstraat 30, 8730 Beernem, Belgium.

HAMILTON IV George, b. 19 July 1937, Winston-Salem, North Carolina, USA. Singer; Musician; Songwriter. m. Adelaide Peyton, 1958. Eduaction: University of North Carolina. Career: Recording artist, 1956-; Tours with Buddy Holly; Eddie Cochran; Gene Vincent; Broadway appearance with Louis Armstrong; Regular UK appearances include: Wembley Country Music Festival; First country artist to perform in Soviet Union; Occasionally works with son, George Hamilton V. Recordings: Hit singles include: A Rose And A Baby Ruth; If You Don't Know I Ain't Gonna Tell You; Why Don't They Understand; Only One Love; Now And For Always; The Teen

Commandments Of Love (with Paul Anka and Johnny Nash); I Know Where I'm Going; Abilene; Break My Mind; Fort Worth, Dallas Or Houston; She's A Little Bit Country; Albums include: On Campus, 1958; Mister Sincerity, 1965; By George, 1966; Canadian Pacific, 1969; Down Home In The Country (with Skeeter Davis), 1971; Heritage (with The Hillsiders), 1971; Down East Country, 1972; Bluegrass Gospel, 1974; Fine Lace And Homespun Cloth, 1977; Feel Like A Million, 1978; Forever Young, 1979; Cuttin' Across The Country, 1981; One Day At A Time, 1982; Songs For A Winter's Night, 1982; Music Man's Dream, 1984; Hymns Country Style, 1985; A Country Christmas, 1989; American Country Gothic (with the Moody Brothers), 1989; Country Classics (with George Hege Hamilton V), 1992. Honours: International Ambassador Of Country Music, Country Music People magazine, 1974; Trendsetter Award, Billboard magazine, 1975. Current Management: Blade Productions, PO Box 1556, Gainesville, FL 32602, USA.

HAMLISCH Marvin, b. 2 June 1944, New York, USA. Composer; Conductor; Musician (piano); Entertainer. m. Terre Blair, 29 May 1989. Education: Professional Children's School; Queen's College, New York. Musical Education: The Juilliard School, New York. Career: Debut as pianist, Minnesota Orchestra, 1975; Solo concert tours; Conductor of various orchestras throughout US; Principal Pops conductor for: Pittsburgh Symphony Orchestra; Baltimore Symphony Orchestra; Musical director and conductor, Barbra Streisand, 1994. Compositions include: Film scores: The Swimmer, 1968; Take The Money And Run, 1969; Bananas, 1971; The Way We Were, 1974; The Sting (adaptation), 1974; Same Time Next Year, 1979; Starting Over, 1979; Ordinary People, 1980; Seems Like Old Times, 1980; Sophie's Choice, 1982; Film themes for: The January Man; Three Men And A Baby; Little Nikita; The Experts; Popular songs: Sunshine Lollipops and Rainbows; Good Morning America; Nobody Does It Better; Broadway musicals: A Chorus Line, 1975; They're Playing Our Song, 1979; The Goodbye Girl, 1993; Other works: Anatomy Of Peace, Symphony In One Movement, 1991; One Song, for Barcelona Olympics, 1992. Publication: The Way I Was (autobiography), 1992. Honours: 3 Academy Awards; 4 Grammy Awards; 2 Emmy Awards; 1 Tony Award; 3 Golden Globes; Pulitzer Prize, for show A Chorus Line. Membership: ASCAP. Hobby: Loves to travel. Address: c/o Nancy Shear Arts Services, 180 West End Avenue, Suite 28N-P, New York, NY 10023, USA.

HAMMARLUND Jan, b. 17 July 1951, Stockholm, Sweden. Singer; Songwriter; Guitarist; Translator. Education: Private singing lessions, 1981-92. Career: Festivals: Gärdet, Stockholm; Västervik; Roskilde; Midtfyn; Hultsfred; Mariposa; Chile Crea; Tour of England, 1978; California, 1979; Denmark, 1978-86; Chile, 1991; Swedish TV Portrait, 1990. Compositions: Songs: Ville, 1979; Translations of Violeta Parra; Dag Vill Leva I Europa, 1981; Malvina Reynolds. Recordings: 12 LPs, 1972-86; Tusentals Swarnor Over Chile, 1974; Karlek Olh Sang, 1981; Among 6 CDs: Jan Hammarlund, 1972-92; Tvars Over Garn, French cabaret songs, 1995; Om Trädgårdsbevattning, songs by Brecht, 1996. Honours: Awards with Grants: SKAP, 1978; STIM, 1989; Konstnärsnämnden (Artists committee), 1992-96; José Martí Award, 1994. Memberships: STIM; Svenska Teateförbundet, SKAP; Musikcentrum. Hobby: Travel. Address: Skördemane AB, c/o Hammarlund, Vapengatan 22, 12652 Hagersten, Sweden.

HAMMER (Stanley Kirk Burrell), b. 30 Mar 1962, Oakland, California, USA. Rapper; Dancer. Career: Former baseball player; Member, rap duo Holy Ghost Boys; Founder, Bustin Records; Solo artiste (originally as MC Hammer), 1987-; Concerts include: Please Hammer, Don't Hurt 'Em

US tour, 1990; US tour, with Vanilla Ice and En Vogue, 1990; UK and Japan tours, 1991; The Simple Truth (benefit concert for Kurdish refugees), Wembley, 1991; Too Legit To Quit tour, with Boyz II Men, 1992; USA Harvest Hunger Relief Concert, 1992; Kiel Summer Jam, largest rap festival ever, 1992; Television includes: Lou Rawls Parade Of Stars, 1990; Ray Charles, 50 Years In Music Uh-Huh, 1991; Hammer's MTV Birthday Bash, 1992; Hammer From The Heart, CBS, 1992; Hammerman Cartoon series, ABC, 1991; Founder, management, production and video company, Roll-Wit-It Entertainment, 1992. Recordings: Hit singles include: U Can't Touch This, 1990; Have You Seen Her?, 1990; Pray, (Number 2, US), 1990; Here Comes The Hammer, from Rocky V film soundtrack, 1991; Yo! Sweetness, 1991; Addams Groove, from Addams Family film soundtrack, 1992; 2 Legit 2 Quit, 1992; Do Not Pass Me By, 1992; Albums: Feel My Power, 1987; Please Hammer Don't Hurt 'Em (Number 1, US, 10 million copies sold), 1990; Too Legit To Quit, 1991; The Funky Headhunter, 1994. Honours: Several American Music Awards, 1990-91; 3 Grammy Awards, 1991; People's Choice Award, 1991; BRIT Award, Best International Newcomer, 1991; MC Hammer Day declared, Fremont, California, 1991; 2 Bammy Awards, 1991; JUNO Award, International Artist of the Year, 1991; 3 Rolling Stone Readers Poll Wins, 1991; 4 Soul Train Awards, including Sammy Davis Jr Award, 1991-92; 4 NARM Awards, 1991. Current Management: Bust It Management, 80 Swan Way #130, Oakland, CA 94621, USA.

HAMMER Jan, b. 17 Apr 1948, Prague, Czechoslovakia. Musician (keyboards); Composer. Musical Education: Prague Academy of Music and Arts, 1966-68; Berklee College of Music, Boston, USA, 1968. Career: Moved to US, 1968; Jazz musician, 1968-71; Member, John McLaughlin's Mahavishnu Orchestra, 1971-73; Freelance musician and bandleader, 1973-. Compositions: Film scores: A Night In Heaven, 1983; Secret Admirer, 1985; Television series soundtrack: Miami Vice, 1984-. Recordings: Singles: Theme From Miami Vice (Number 1, US), 1985; Crockett's Theme (Number 2, UK), 1987; Solo albums: Like Children, 1974; First Seven Days, 1975; Timeless, 1975; Make Love, 1976; Oh Yeah, 1976; Melodies, 1979; Black Sheep, 1979; Escape From TV, 1987; Snapshots, 1989; Behind The Mind's Eye, 1993; Country And Eastern Music, 1993; with John McLaughlin: Inner Mounting Flame, 1971; Birds Of Fire, 1973; Love Devotion And Surrender, 1973; with Jeff Beck: Wired, 1976; Live With The Jan Hammer Group, 1977; There And Back, 1980; Flash, 1985; with Al Di Meola: Elegant Gypsy, 1977; Splendido Hotel, 1979; Electric Rendezvous, 1982; Tour De Force, 1982; Scenario, 1983; with John Abercombie: Timeless, 1975; Five Years Later, 1982; Other recordings with: Tommy Bolin; Stanley Clarke; Billy Cobham; Steve Lukather; Santana; Jerry Goodman; Neal Schon.

HAMMER Joseph, b. 7 June 1954, San Antonio, Texas, USA. Musician (drums, fairlight); Composer. m. Jacqueline Henry, 28 Feb 1983, 1 son. Musical Education: Drum Instruction, Berklee School of Music; Boston School of Electronic Music. Career: Studio production, 1975-85; Co-production for Daniel Balavoine; Tours, concerts, with Daniel Balavoine, France Gall, Jean-Michel Jarre. Compositions: Summer Dreaming; Love Of A Woman. Recordings: Daniel Balavoine; Jean-Michel Jarre; Jon Anderson; Mick Jagger; Peter Gabriel. Publications: Trophee Sonor, 6-10 Drums. Membership: Institut de Percussions Modernes. Hobby: Fishing. Current Management: La Fretite Studios. Address: La Fretite Studios, 10 Rue Jean Lefevbre, 95530 La Frette, Paris, France.

HAMMETT Barry James, b. 31 Oct 1944, Swansea, Wales. Musician (guitar); Guitar Teacher. m. 16 Mar 1968 to 19 Mar 1978, 2 daughters. Education: Swansea Technical College. Musical Education: Self-taught. Career: Lead guitar, Johnny Kidd and Pirates, 7 years; Swansea Top Rank (resident band), 7 years; P&O Cruises, 14 months with Kiki Dee, Blood Brothers tour; Founder, Fat Barry's Soul Band. Recordings: Numerous radio and TV sessions as featured band, backing musician. Membership: Musicians' Union. Hobby: Arranging music. Address: 52, Ael-y-Bryn, Fforestfarch, Swansea, West Glamorgan, SA5 8JB, Wales.

HAMMETT Kirk, b. 18 Nov 1962, USA. Musician (guitar). Career: Guitarist, Exodus; Joe Satriani; Member, US heavy rock group Metallica, 1983-; Worldwide tours include: Masters Of Puppet world tour, 1986-87; US tour, 1988; Damaged Justice UK tour, 1989; World tour, 1991-; Also tours with Raven; Ozzy Osbourne; Twisted Sister; Motörhead; Major concerts include: Monsters Of Rock Festival, Castle Donington, 1985, 1987, 1991; German Monster Rock festivals, 1987; Monsters of Rock, Europe and US tours, 1988, 1991; Day On The Green, Oakland, 1991. Recordings: Albums: Kill 'Em All, 1983; Ride The Lightning, 1984; Master Of Puppets, 1986; ...And Justice For All, 1988; Metallica (Number 1, US and UK), 1991; Live Shit, 1993; Singles: Garage Days Revisited (EP), 1987; Harvester Of Sorrow, 1988; One, 1989; Enter Sandman, 1991; The Unforgiven, 1991; Nothing Else Matters, 1992; Wherever I May Roam, 1992; Sad But True, 1992; Stone Cold Crazy, track featured on Rubáiyát (Elektra's 40th Anniversary compilation). Honours: Platinum and Gold discs; Grammy Awards: Best Heavy Metal Performance: One, 1989; Stone Cold Crazy, 1991; The Unforgiven 1992; American Music Award, Favourite Heavy Metal Artist, 1993; Bay Area Music Awards: Outstanding Album, 1992; Outstanding Heavy Metal Album, Outstanding Group, Outstanding Guitarist, 1993; Rolling Stone Readers Poll Winners, Best Heavy Metal Band, 1993. Current Management: Q-Prime Inc. Address: 729 7th Avenue, 14th Floor, New York, NY 10019, USA.

HAMMILL Peter. Vocalist; Musician (guitar, piano). Career: Founder member, Van Der Graaf Generator, 1968-72, 1975-78; Also recording artiste. Recordings: Albums with Van Der Graaf Generator: Aerosol Grey Machine, 1968; The Least We Can Do Is Wave To Each Other, 1969; H To He Who Is The Only One, 1970; Pawn Hearts, 1971; Godbluff, 1975; Still Life, 1976; World Record, 1976; Solo albums include: Fool's Mate, 1971; Chameleon In The Shadow Of Night, 1972; The Silent Corner And The Empty Stage, 1974; In Camera, 1974; Nadir's Big Chance, 1975; Sitting Targets, 1981; Enter K, 1982; Black Box, 1983; No Way Out, 1990; The Fall Of The House Of Usher, 1992; The Noise, 1993. Current Management: Gailforce Management, 30 Ives Street, London SW3 2ND, England.

HAMMOND John Paul, b. 13 Nov 1942, New York City, New York, USA. Blues Musician (guitar); Singer. Career: Began playing guitar aged 17; Recording artist, 1962-; UK tours, 1960s; Worked with artists including Duane Allman; JJ Cale; John Lee Hooker; Robbie Robertson; Bill Wyman; Charles Brown; Charlie Musselwhite; Duke Robillard; Host, performer, television documentary The Search For Robert Johnson, 1992. Recordings: Albums: John Hammond; Big City Blues; Country Blues; So Many Roads; Mirrors; I Can Tell; Sooner Or Later; Southern Fried; Source Point; I'm Satisfied; Triumvirate; Can't Beat The Kid; John Hammond Solo; Footwork; Hot Tracks; Mileage; Frogs For Snakes; John Hammond Live; John Hammond Live In Greece; Nobody But You; Got Love If You Want It; Trouble No More; Found True Love; Featured on film soundtracks: Little Big Man, 1971; Matewan, 1987. Honours: Grammy Award, Blues Explosion (with Stevie Ray Vaughan, Koko Taylor), 1985;

Grammy Nominations: Got Love If You Want It, 1992; Trouble No More, 1993. Current Management: Eric Hanson, The Rosebud Agency, PO Box 170429, San Francisco, CA 94117, USA.

HAMPTON Andy, b. 8 May 1958, Sheffield, England. Composer. m. Jennifer Stirling, 22 July 1994, 1 son, 1 daughter. Education: York University, BA Hons. Musical Education: Guildhall, London; LTCL Trinity College, London. Career: Appearance as actor/musician, Lennon, London's West End 1985. Compositions: Themes for: BBC Radio 1; BBC Radio 2; Granada TV; Sky Network; Screensport. Publications: Jazzworks for Clarinet, Saxophone students. Honour: Best Music, National Student Drama Festival, 1979. Memberships: PRS; MCPS; Musicians' Union; BASCA. Hobbies: Sailing; Football. Address: 28 Harold Road, London N8 7DE, England.

HAMPTON Lionel Leo, b. 12 Apr 1913, Birmingham, Alabama, USA. Composer; Conductor; Musician. m. Gladys Riddle, 11 Nov 1936 (deceased). Career: Member, Benny Goodman Quartet, 1936-40; Leader, Lionel Hampton Orchestra (first band to feature electric bass and organ), 1940-; Professor of Music, Howard University, 1981-; Appointed UN Ambassador of Music, 1985; Established Lionel Hampton Jazz Endowment Fund, 1984; Human Rights Commissioner, New York, 1984-86. Compositions: King David Suite (symphonic work), 1953. Recordings: Albums include: Sentimental Journey, 1986; Flying Home, 1991; with Chick Corea: Chick and Lionel Live At Midem, 1972. Honours: Established in his honour: Lionel Hampton School Of Music, University of Idaho, 1987; Lionel Hampton Research Foundation, 1987; Voted into Playboy's All-Stars band, 28 years in succession; Gold Medal, City Of Paris, 1985; Ebony magazine Lifetime Achievement Award, 1979; Numerous Honorary MusD and PhD Mus. Current Management: Jazz One Productions Inc, 44 Rio Vista Drive, Allendale, NJ 07401-1624, USA.

HAMZA Kawkab, b. 1 July 1944, Babylon, Iraq. Composer. Divorced, 1 son, 2 daughters. Musical Education: Fine Art Institute, Baghdad; 5 years, USSR High Institute. Career: Composed first song, 1966, Moved to Syria, 1983, wrote 4 theatre plays, 2 television series; Moved to Detroit, composed for theatre; Now refugee in Denmark, Composing for theatre; Takes part in international musical festivals. Compositions: 6 theatre plays; 4 documentary films; 2 television, music classes; more than 70 songs including: Songs for: Husein Naamah; Fuaad Salim; Saadun Jaber; Anwar Abd Alwahab; Albums: Nehebbkum Wallah Nehebkum; New Babylon Music; Sar Alumur Mahetat. Membership: Danish Society for Jazz, Rock, Folk Composers. Hobbies: Music. Address: Tårnvej 209-2, 2610 Rodovre, Denmark.

HANCOCK Herbie, b. 12 Apr 1940, Chicago, Illinois, USA. Composer; Jazz Musician (piano, synthesizer). m. Gudrun Meixner, 31 Aug 1968, 1 daughter. Education: BA, Grinnell College, Iowa. Musical Education: Manhattan School of Music, New York, 1 year. Career: Chicago Symphony Orchestra, 1952; Miles Davis Quartet, 1963-1968; Television: Coast To Coast (Showtime), Host; Television Scores: Hey, Hey, Hey, It's Fat Albert - Bill Cosby Special; Film Scores: Blow Up, 1966; Death Wish, 1974; A Soldier's Story, 1974; Round Midnight, 1986; Jo Jo Dancer, Your Life Is Calling, 1986; Colors, 1988. Recordings: Taking Off, 1962; Maiden Voyage, 1965; Speak Like A Child, 1967; Headhunters, 1973; Thrust, 1974; Manchild, 1975; VSOP, 1977; Sunlight, 1979; Feets Don't Fail Me Now, 1979; Future Shock, 1983; Sound System, 1984; Perfect Machine, 1988; Tribute To Miles, 1994; Dis Is Da Drum, 1995; The New Standard, 1996; with Miles Davis Quartet: Miles In The Sky; Nefertiti; Sorcerer; ESP; Miles Davis In Concert (My Funny Valentine); In A Silent Way; Jack Johnson; Seven Steps To Heaven; Contributor,

Colour And Light - Jazz Sketches On Sondheim, 1995. Honours: Jay Award, Jazz Magazine, 1963; Downbeat Award, 1967; Several Awards, Black Music Magazine, 1967-71; 5 MTV Awards, including Best Concept Video, Rock It, 1983; 3 Grammy Awards, including Best R&B Instrumental Performance, Rock It, 1983; Oscar, Best Original Score, Round Midnight, 1986; Memberships: AFofM; NARAS; AFTRA; SAG; AMPAS. Hobby: Digital Technology. Current Management: Kushnick Passick Management. Address: 3 East 28th Street, 6th Floor, New York, NY 10016, USA.

HANCOCK Keith, b. 28 Oct 1953, Manchester, England. Singer; Songwriter; Musician (diatonic accordion). m. Janet Karen Wood, 29 Sept 1979, 2 sons. Musical Education: Self-taught. Career: Progressed through English Country dance bands; Began writing, 1984; Toured: Europe; Canada; New Zealand; Hong Kong; Australia; TV Ballads, BBC2, 1995; New Band, KeitH Hancock's Famous Last Words, 1996. Compositions: include best known song Absent Friends. Recordings: This World We Live In, 1985; Madhouse, 1988; Compassion, 1993; Born Blue, 1997. Memberships: Musicians' Union; Equity. Hobbies: Music; Manchester City Football Club. Current Management: Janet Hancock, Spiv Promotions. Address: PO Box 35, SE PDO, Manchester M18 8JY, England.

HANCOCK Robin Jonathon Coventry, b. Croydon, Surrey, England. Record Producer; Musician (guitar). Education: Bsc Electric Engineering, Reading University. Musical Education: Grade 6: Classical guitar. Recordings: Erotica, Madonna; Cyberpunk, Billy Idol; Seal, Seal; Other recordings by Tina Turner; Simple Minds. Hobbies: Skiing; Snowboarding; Windsurfing; Sailing. Current Management: Sarm Productions. Address: 38 Turneville Road, West Kensington, London W14 9PS, England.

HAND Richard, b. 27 Nov 1960, Marsden, Yorkshire, England. Musician (guitar). Musical Education: Open Scholarship to Royal Academy Of Music; Several prizes include: String Players Prize; Julian Bream Prize, Academy's Highest Award. Career: Member, English Guitar Quartet: Tours of Israel; Member, flute and guitar duo: The Lightfingered Gentry; Tours include: Germany; Holland; Gulf States; Egypt; Member, Hand/Dupré Guitar Duo tours: Norway; Poland; India; Bangladesh; Sri Lanka; Philippines; Malaysia; Indonesia; Singapore; Hong Kong; Television, radio appearances worldwide include: BBC Radio 2, 3, 4; Premieres of new works by: Peter Dickinson; Tim Souster; Jonathon Lloyd; David Bedford; Roger Steptoe; Michael Ball; Brian May; Judith Bingham; Wilfred Josephs. Honours: Julian Bream Prize; Associate of Royal Academy Of Music. Memberships: ISM; Musicians' Union. Address: 61 Balcombe Street, Marylebone, London NW1 6HD, England.

HANLEY Ged (formerly Ray Kershwin), b. 22 Mar 1960, Scotland. Musician (guitar, piano); Vocalist. m. Donna Marie Archibald, 25 Nov 1994, 2 sons, 1 daughter. Musical Education: Self-taught. Career: Tours (backing vocals) with Runrig; Wreck On The Highway; BBC appearances and recording. Membership: Musicians' Union. Hobby: Music. Current Management: Self-mangaged. Address: 114 Carnethie St, Rosewall, Midlothian EH24 9AL, Scotland.

HANLON Jef, b. 5 July 1943, Blackpool, England. Artist Manager; Concert Promoter; Agent. m. Alice Welsh, 8 Dec 1973. Career: Guitarist, England and Germany, 1958-64; Personal/tour manager: Wayne Fontana; Herman's Hermits; Extensive world tours, 1964-69; Partner, Billings-Hanlon Management, 1969-73; Clients: Jimmy Ruffin, Kiki Dee, The Hermits; Director, Rock Artist Management Group Of Companies, 1973-76; Clients included: Gary Glitter; The Glitter Band; Bay City Rollers; Barry Blue; Hello; New Seekers; The Damned; Springfield Revival; Director, Derek Block Artists Agency and Derek Block Concert Promotions, 1976-89; Clients included: Duran Duran; UB40; The Police; Tears For Fears; Gary Glitter; The Clash; Ian Dury; Agent for William Morris Agency Inc, (USA), 1977-84; Clients included: Diana Ross; Stevie Wonder; Barry Manilow; Rod Stewart; Concert promotions include: Rod Stewart; Chuck Berry; David Brubeck; Simon and Garfunkel; Stevie Wonder; Bob Hope; Bing Crosby; Duran Duran; Gary Glitter; B B King; Johnny Mathis; The Everly Brothers; Neil Sedaka; The Temptations; Don McLean; Also major tours: Australasia; Japan; Europe; UK; Formed Jef Hanlon Management Ltd, 1990-; Major client: Gary Glitter; Also managed The Wlld Swans; Promoted tours: Bob Hope; Don McLean; Juan Martin's Flamenco Dance Company (Seville); Village People; Bootleg Beatles; Joaquin Cortes. Memberships: President, Agents' Association of Great Britain, 1995-97; Vice-Chairman, International Managers' Forum, 1994-; Member, Concert Promoters' Association. Address: 1 York Street, London W1H 1PZ, England.

HANNAN Neil, b. 12 Aug 1952, Christchurch, New Zealand. Musician (bass). m. Jacqui Fitzgerald, 16 Dec 1993, 1 daughter. Education: University Entrance Exam. Musical Education: 2 years Victoria Unversity, Wellington, New Zealand; Various private tutors from age seven, piano, guitar. Career: Professional musician since age 19; Performed in New Zealand with Randy Crawford, Renee Geyer; Member, popular New Zealand bands: Hello Sailor; Coup d'Etat; Midge Marsden's Country Flyers; Numerous radio programmes and recordings; Professional work in Australia, UK, USA. Recordings: Solo albums: Scoop This Loop; 24 Hour Oasis. Publication: Working on Bass Teaching book. Honour: Single Of Year (with Coup d'Etat), 1981. Memberships: Australasian Peforming Right Association (APRA); Recording Industry Association of New Zealand (RIANZ). Address: 19 Wynyard Road, Mt Eden, Auckland, New Zealand.

HANNAN Patrick Edward Dean, b. 4 Mar 1966, Lymington, Hampshire, England. Musician (drums). 1 daughter. Career: 2 major world tours with the Sundays. Recordings: Albums: with the Sundays: Reading Writing Arithmetic, 1990; Blind, 1992; with Perry Rose: Bright Ring Of The Day, 1995; Singles: with Star 69: Mama Don't Let, 1995; You Are Here, 1995. Honours: Gold and Silver Discs; Gold US Disc. Membership: Musicians' Union. Hobbies: 60s Cars; Golf; Pubs.

HANOT Pierre, b. 25 Mar 1952, Metz, France. Singer; Writer; Composer. Artist. m. Martine Bonici, 28 Feb 1992, 2 daughters. Education: Modern and classical French. Musical Education: Guitar. Career: More than 700 concerts, in clubs, festivals, jails, pubs, cultural centres, 1975-; Dates in: France; Germany; Luxemboug; Belgium; Spain. Recordings: Rock Derivé, 1985; En Un Instant Damnés, 1995. Membership: SACEM. Hobbies: Dogs; Love; Collages. Current Management: Martine Bonici. Address: 8A Place du Temple, 57530 Courcelles Chaussy, France.

HANRAHAN Michael, b. 19 Sept 1958, Ennis, County Clare, Ireland. Songwriter; Musician (guitar); Vocalist. m. Donna Barnes, 3 Sept 1994. Career: Tours worldwide with Stockton's Wing, 1974-94; Performed with Sammy Davis Junior, Dublin; Numerous television, radio shows; Currently touring as solo artist. Compositions: Most successful songs: Beautiful Affair; Walk Away. Recordings: 7 albums with Stockton's Wing; For imminemt release: Someone Like You. Membership: Irish Music Rights Organisation (Board member). Current Management: Kara Hamahoe. Address: 29, St Fintans Villas, Deansgrange, Co. Dublin, Ireland.

HANSEN Annisette, b. 29 August 1948, Copenhagen, Denmark. Singer; Songwriter; Writer. m. Thomas Koppel, 1971, 2 daughters. Career: Numerous tours in Europe, USA, etc; Numerous TV and radio appearances internationally; Newport Jazz Festival, 1969; Montreux Festival and numerous other festivals, 1970-97; Lead character in own musical, Bella Vita, 1997, with Thomas Koppel; Lead Singer, Savage Rose, 1968-. Compositions: Numerous songs recorded by Savage Rose, 1968-98; Musical Bella Vita, with Thomas Koppel, 1996-97; Lyrics for Symphonic Compositions by Thomas Koppel. Recordings: 19 albums with The Savage Rose; Bella Vita, 1995. Honours: Nomination for the Grand Music Award of Nordic Council, 1996; Award of Honour, Danish Songwriters' Association; Grammy, 1996; Numerous awards from Trade Unions and Organisations. Memberships: Danish Artists' Union; DJBFA; KODA; Gramex. Hobby: Painting. Current Management: South Harbur Productions, Frederikshoj 114, 2450 Copenhagen, Denmark.

HANSEN Hanne Wilhelm, b. 23 Jan 1927, Copenhagen, Denmark. Theatre Agent; Artist Manager. Career: Music publisher until 1988; Theatre and artist manager; Chairman of the Wilhelm Hansen Foundation. Address: Gothersgade 11, 1123 Copenhagen K, Denmark.

HANSEN Kai, b. Germany. Vocalist; Rock Musician (guitar). Career: Founder member, German rock band, Helloween, 1984; Numerous tours across Europe; Appearances include: Monsters Of Rock Festival, Castle Donington, 1988; Founder, Gamma Ray, 1989; Extensive tours in Europe and Japan. Recordings: Albums: with Helloween: Helloween (mini-LP), 1985; Walls Of Jericho, 1986; Keeper Of The Seven Kings, Part I, 1987; Part II, 1988; Live In The UK, 1989; with Gamma Ray: Heading For Tomorrow, 1990; Sigh No More, 1991; Also tracks featured on: Death Metal, compilation album, 1984. Current Management: Sanctuary Music (Overseas). Address: 1st Floor Suite, The Colonnades, 82 Bishops Bridge Road, London W2 6BB, England.

HANSON Lloyd A, b. 1 Nov 1964, Fredericton, New Brunswick, Canada. Musician (bass); Record Producer; Recording Engineer. Musical Education: Berklee College of Music, Boston, USA, 1986. Career: Recording career from 1988; Played bass in many jazz, folk, experimental ensembles at major festivals including: Mama's and Papa's, 1987; Harvest Jazz and Blues Festival, with Long John Baldry, 1992; Formed Thrash Peninsula, 1993; Producer, engineer, composer, arranger. Recordings: with Thrash Peninsula: A Different Drummer; A D Shade Café; Thunder God's Wife; with Brent Mason: Down To Heaven; with Ned Landry: Fiddling Champ. Honours: New Brunswick Arts Branch Creation Grant, 1992. Memberships: AFofM; Musicians' Union; SOCAN. Hobbies: Walk average 7 miles a day; Reading spiritual and science; Books; Listening to music. Current Management: Self-managed. Address: 741 McEvoy St, Fredericton, New Brunswick E3A 3B8, Canada.

HANSON Simon, b. 3 Feb 1964, Grantham, Lincolnshire, England. Musician (drums). m. Kath Hanson, 3 Aug 1994. Musical Education: Lincolnshire Youth Orchestra, 1977-80. Career: Drummer/programmer for Rado Science Orchestra; European Tour: Energy Orchard; Full time member, The Blessing; UK, European tours. Recordings: The Blessing: Locust and Wild Honey; Radio Science Orchestra: Arcitec; Film Soundtrack: Tall Story. Publications: Regular columnist, UK Rhythm Magazine, 1994-. Membership: Musicians' Union. Hobby: Water skiing. Current Management: Paul Crockford Management; Agent: Simon Harrison. Address: c/o 8 Kingston Road, Ewell Village, Surrey KT17 2AA, England.

HANZICK Helene Hommel Brincker, b. 18 June 1958, Copenhagen, Denmark. Musician (Bass Guitar); Songwriter; Singer. m. Poul F Hanzick, 15 August 1987. Career: Singer, Mayflowers, band, 1980; Solo Musician, 1981-82; Formed country duo, Twins, with husband; Twins have played all over Denmark and in Norway, Sweden, Holland and Canary Islands; Moved to Sweden, 1994. Compositions: From Alaska to LA, 1989; No Good Full-Time-Cheating, Good-For-Nothing Son-Of-A-Gun, 1991, 1996; Ten Days Together, 1991; She'll Come Again, 1991. Recordings: Champagne and Bourbon, CD, 1989; Days Together, CD, 1991; I Love You/Blue Moon of Kentucky, single, 1986. Honour: Danish Championship in Country Music, 1989. Membership: Danish Musician's Union. Hobbies: Painting; Camping; Old Black-Gunpowder-Weapons. Address: Box 35, 28221 Tyringe, Sweden.

HANZICK Poul Fynbo, b. 22 May 1954, Mariager, Denmark. Musician (Guitar); Singer. m. Helene H B Hanzick, 15 August 1987. Career: Played in several dance and rock bands, 1969-82; Formed the country duo, Twins, with wife Helene; Twins have played all over Denmark and in Norway, Sweden, Holland and Canary Islands; Move to Sweden, 1994. Recordings: I Love You, Blue Moon of Kentucky, single, 1986; Days Together, CD, 1991; Champagne & Bourbon, CD, 1989. Honour: Won Danish Championship in Country Music, 1989. Membership: Danish Musician's Union. Hobbies: Camping; Old Black Gunpowder Weapons; Old American Cars. Current Management: Freelance. Address: Box 35, 28221 Tyringe, Sweden.

HAQUE Asadul, b. 1 March 1930, Pabna, Bangladesh. Retired. m. Firoza Asad, 3 June 1955, 1 son, 1 daughter. Education: Studies of Classical, Semi Classical and Folk Songs. Career: Researcher, National Poet Kazi Nazrul Islam and Classical Music of the Sub-Continent; Music Producer, Radio Pakistan, Karachi, 1963-65, Rawalpindi, 1969-71; Performer, Vocal Songs on Radio and Television. Publications include: Nazrul Sangiter Rupaker, 1990; Nazrul Saralipi, vol 4, 1990; Antaranga Aloke Nazrul O Pramila, 1994; Chalachitrey Nazrul, 1994; Nasruler Hindi Gan, 1995; Amar Surer Jadukar, 1996. Contributions to: Leading Newspapers of Bangladesh and Calcutta. Honours: Sanad E Khidmat, 1st Class, Pakistan Government, 1970; Nazrul award, Churulia Nazrul Academy, West Bengal, 1997. Memberships: Bangla Academy, Dhaka. Hobbies: Research; Writing. Address: 12/D Eastern Housing, Sidheswari, Dhaka 1217, Bangladesh.

HARBO Nils, b. 12 May 1956, Nyborg, Denmark. Musician; Record Producer. m. Ulla Rasmussen, 2 sons. Career: Rock Musician, Guitar Player, 1978-90; Record Producer, var artists, 1990-; Own Projects, Jimi Bikini, Jox, Palle Pirat, A.O; Editor, Danish Music Yearbook. Compositions: Født På Fyn, 1991; Palle Pirat, 1996; Out of Control, 1997; Cant Let Go, 1997. Recording: Palle Pirat. Publications: Improvisation, 1981; Danish Music Yearbook, 1992-98. Memberships: KODA; NCB; DMF; DJBFA. Hobbies: Soccer; Italian Food. Current Management: Techpoint. Address: Birkebakken 8, DK-2500 Valby, Denmark.

HARCOURT Stephen David, b. 30 Nov 1973, Harlow, Essex, England. Musician (guitar); Sequencing. Musical Education: Self-taught. Career: Formed Collapsed Lung, 1992; Several tours, UK and Ireland; Reading Festival; Minor stage, Phoenix Festival; Radio: In Session (Mark Goodier's), Radio 1; Television: Raw Soup, MTV; The Beat. Recordings: Albums: Jackpot Goalie, 1995; Singles: Thundersley Ivacar, 1993; Chainsaw Wedgie, 1993; Down With The Plaid Fad, 1994; Dis-MX, 1994; As G L Stealers: Interactive, 1995. Membership: Musicians' Union; PRS. Hobbies: Membership of Church of the Subgenius; Strange Phenomena (Forteana); Sci-fiction. Current Management: Jim Morewood, ICM, Fair Warning; Wasted Talent. Address: Collapsed Lung Productions, Unit 20, The Fortress, 54-56 Compton Street, London EC1V 0JE, England.

HARDCASTLE Paul, b. 10 Dec 1957, London, England. Musician (keyboards); Composer; Mixer; Record Producer. Compositions: The Wizard (used as Top Of The Pops theme, BBC), 1986; Songwriter, composer for television, including: Themes to BBC series, Supersense & Lifesense; Founder, own record label Fast Forward. Recordings: Hit singles: 19 (Number 1, UK), 1985; Just For Money; Other recordings under pseudonym: Def Boys; Beeps International; Jazzmasters; Kiss The Sky (with Jaki Graham); Latest album: Hardcastle, 1996; Producer for: LW5; Phil Lynott; Carol Kenyon; Remixer for: Third World; Ian Dury.

HARDING Stan, (Walter Stanley), b. 11 Mar 1930, Islington, London, England. Musician (drums); Singer; Songwriter. m. Joyce Matthews, 5 Jun 1954, 2 sons, 1 daughter. Musical Education: Self-taught. Career: Toured American Air Force Bases with Bill Kenyon Combo, 1958-62; Shared billing with Cliff Richard, 1959; Short residency at Royal Garden Hotel; Concert appearances with Jack Emblow; Singer with Billy Smart's Circus; Starred in cabaret at Pizza On The Park; Appearance on Late Night BBC. Composition: Costa Brava, samba for The Polka Dots, 1963, and broadcast by Billy Cotton and Edmundo Ros. Recording: Flying High, with Jack Emblow and Tony Compton. Publication: Costa Brava. Memberships: Musicians' Union; BASCA. Hobbies: DIY; Musical activities; Caravans; Countryside. Address: 9 Lilford Road, Billericay, Essex CM11 1BS, England.

HARDY Françoise, b. 17 Jan 1944, Paris, France. Singer; Author; Lyricist; Actress; Songwriter. m. Jacques Dutronc, 1981, 1 son. Education: Le Bruyère College. Career: Recording artiste, 1962-; Lyricist for artistes including: Julien Clerc; Diane Tell; Alaine Lubrano; Khalil Chanine; Also worked as model and actress. Recordings: Numerous since 1962-; Singles include: Tous Les Garçons Et Les Filles, 1962; All Over The World, 1965. Publications: Le Grande Livre De La Vierge, with B Guenin; Entre Les Lignes Entre Les Signes, with Anne-Marie Simond, 1991; Notes Secrètes, W E Dumont, 1991; Françoise Hardy Présente L'Astrologie Universelle, 1986. Hobby: Reading. Address: 13 Rue Hallé, 75014 Paris, France.

HARKET Morten, b. 14 Sept 1959, Konigsberg, Norway. Singer. Career: Singer with various groups including: Mercy; Laelia Anceps; Souldier Blue; Formed A-Ha with Mags Furuholmen and Pal Waaktaar, 1982; Appearances include: Montreux Pop Festival, 1986; World tour, 1986; Royal Albert Hall, London, 1987; World tour, 1987; Rock In Rio II Festival, 1991; UK tour, 1991; Starred in film Kamilia And The Thief, 1989. Recordings: Albums: Hunting High And Low, 1985; Scoundrel Days, 1986; Stay On These Roads, 1988; East Of The Sun, 1990; Headlines And Deadlines - The Hits Of A-Ha, 1991; Memorial Beach, 1993; Solo album: Wild Seed, 1995; Numerous hit singles include: Take On Me (Number 1, US); The Sun Always Shines On TV (Number 1, UK); Train Of Thought; I've Been Losing You; Cry Wolf; Manhattan Skyline; The Living Daylights (theme music for James Bond film); Stay On These Roads; The Blood That Moves The Body; Touchy!; You Are The One; Crying In The Rain; I Call Your Name; Dark Is The Night; Can't Take My Eyes Off You, for film soundtrack Coneheads; Angel; Solo single: A Kind Of Christmas Card (Number 1, Norway), 1995. Honours: 8 MTV Music Video Awards, for Take On Me and The Sun Always Shines On TV (record number of awards for one act),1986; BMI Award, One Million Broadcast Performances, for Take On Me, 1991; World Music Award, Best Selling Norwegian Artist Of The Year, 1993. Address: c/o Warner Music Norway A/S, Maridalsvn 87B, N-0405 Oslo, Norway.

HARLEY Steve, b. 27 Feb 1951, London, England. Singer. Career: Former journalist; Founder member, Cockney Rebel, 1973-77; 1989-; Solo artiste, 1978-88; Appearances include: Reading Festival, 1974; Support to The Kinks, US, 1975; All Is Forgiven reunion tour, UK, 1989; Heineken Music Big Top, Portsmouth, 1992. Recordings: Albums with Cockney Rebel: Human Menagerie, 1973; The Best Years Of Lives, 1975; Timeless Flight, 1976; Love's A Prima Donna, 1976; Face To Face - A Live Recording, 1977; Greatest Hits, 1988; The Best Of Steve Harley And Cockney Rebel, 1992; Solo albums: Hobo With A Grin, 1978; The Candidate, 1979; Singles: with Cockney Rebel: July Teen, 1974; Mr Soft, 1974; Make Me Smile (Come Up And See Me), 1975; Mr Raffles (Man It Was Mean), 1975; Here Comes The Sun, 1976; Solo: The Phantom Of The Opera (duet with Sarah Brightman), 1986; Contributor, Whatever You Believe, UK TV telethon charity single, 1988. Address: c/o Arctic King Music, Bank Chambers, 4-6 Church Street, Wilmslow, Cheshire SK9 1AU, England.

HARLOW Larry, b. 20 Mar 1939, Brooklyn, New York, USA. Musician (piano); Composer; Arranger; Producer; Conductor. Married 6 times, currently single, 1 son. Education: Masters, Philosophy, New School of Social Research; Institute for Audio Research. Musical Education: BA Music, Brooklyn College. Career: Studied Salsa music, Cuba, 1950s; Helped form Fania All-Stars group, New York; Member Fania All-Stars, 15 years; Produced records for other artists; Touring worldwide with Salsa Orchestra and Latin Legends Band; Tuaght Afro-Cuban music, New York State Schools; Lectures, Yale, Columbia Universities; Producer, star, 3 motion pictures. Established Hot Spots, production company. Compositions: Hommy, Latin Opera; Salsa Suite, La Raza Latima. Recordings: 30 solo albums; 15 albums with Fania All-Stars. Honours: 6 Gold records; 200 record productions; Grammy nomination; ACE Award. Memberships: ASCAP; NARAS; AFofM. Hobbies: Film; Theatre; Sports. Current Management: Latin Legends Inc. Address: 114 W 86th Street, New York City, NY 10024, USA.

HARMÁČEK Vaclav, b. 6 November 1952, Prague, Czech Republic. Musician (clarinet, saxes, viola); Recording Director; Teacher. m. Lenka Stiková, 7 December 1985, 2 daughters. Education: Philosophical Faculty, Charles University, Prague, 1977. Career: Appearance in numerous jazz festivals as Member of various bands and orchestras (notably Prague Big Band, Original Prague Syncopated Orchestra, Causa Bibendi); Several TV and radio appearances in various types of programmes (notably Causa Bibendi or the Reason for a Drink, Czech TV, 1994). Recordings: Contributor, albums of the orchestras: Prague Big Band, 1974-78; Original Prague Syncopated Orchestra, 1979-84; Causa Bibendi - Czech Swingharmonic Orchestra, 1992; Blue World, 1996; Prague Folklore Cymbalon Orchestra, 1975-91. Publication: Editor and Contributor, Small Encyclopaedia of Music, 1983. Hobbies: Sports; Computers; Music; Bandleader of the Causa Bibendi-Czech Swingharmonic Orchestra, The Head of the CB Art Agency. Address: Studentská 2, 160 00 Praha 6, Czech Republic.

HARMAN Buddy, b. 23 Dec 1928, Nashville, Tennessee, USA. Musician (drums). Career: Studio musician, Nashville, 1952-; Thousands of recording sessions with Elvis Presley, records and films. Honours: NARAS Superpicker Awards, 1965-70. Membership: AFofM (executive board of directors, 1981).

HARMAN James Gary, b. 8 June 1946, Anniston, Alabama, USA. Bandleader; Singer; Songwriter; Producer; Musician (harmonica). m. Ella Caroline Harman, 2 sons. Education: Gulf Coast College, University of Florida. Musical Education: Self-taught. Career: Bandleader, Southern dance circuit, 1962-; Recording artist, 1964-; Bandleader, house band Ash Grove Club, Los Angeles, 1970s; International tours; Numerous appearances, television, radio, festivals worldwide; Songs for films. Recordings: Recent albums include: Do Not Disturb, 1991; Two Sides To Every Story, 1993; Cards On The Table, 1994; Back And White, 1995; Other recordings include: So Many Women, Invasion; Kiss Of Fire, The Accused; Jump My Baby (in 3 films). Honours: Nominee, W C Hardy, 7 times; Alabama Music Hall Of Fame. Hobbies: Drag racing, hot rods; Motorcycles; Record collecting. Current Management: Piedmont Talent Booking; Icepick Productions. Address: 5901 Warner Ave, Suite 248, Huntington Beach, CA 92649, USA.

HARMEL Guy, b. 25 Apr 1938, Brussels, Belgium. Singer; Songwriter; Composer. m. 1 son, 1 daughter. Education: Scientific studies and artistic, drawing; Solfeg, violin. Career: 30 years of career, in Belgium and France; Some TV and Radio in Belgium. Compositions: 80 songs. Recordings: 5 albums, 1972-94; 1 CD, 1996. Memberships: SABAM, Belgium; Ministere De La Culture, Belgium. Hobbies: Drawing; Theater. Address: 40 Sart, 4171 Poulseur, Belgium.

HARNICK Sheldon Mayer, b. 30 Apr 1924, Chicago, Illinois, USA. Lyricist. m. (1) Mary Boatner, 1950, (2) Elaine May, 1962, (3) Margery Gray, 1965, 1 son, 1 daughter. Education: Northwestern University. Career: Contributor to revues: New Faces of 1952; Two's Company, 1953; John Murray Anderson's Almanac, 1954; The Shoestring Revue, 1955; The Littlest Revue, 1956; Shoestring 1957, 1957; with composer Jerry Bock: Body Beautiful, 1958; Fiorello, 1959; Tenderloin, 1960; Smiling The Boy Fell Dead (with David Baker), 1961; She Loves Me, 1963; Fiddler On The Roof, 1964; The Apple Tree, 1966; The Rothschilds, 1970; Captain Jinks Of The Horse Marines (opera with Jack Beeson), 1975; Rex (with Richard Rodgers), 1976; Dr Heidegger's Fountain Of Youth (opera with Jack Beeson), 1978; Gold (cantata with Joe Raposo), 1980; Translations: The Merry Widow, 1977; The Umbrellas Of Cherbourg, 1979; Carmen, 1981; A Christmas Carol, 1981; Songs Of The Auvergne (musical; book; lyrics), 1982; The Appeasement of Aeolus, 1990. Address: Kraft, Haiken & Bell, 551 Fifth Avenue, 9th Floor, New York, NY 10176, USA.

HARPER Phillip Melbourne, b. 16 Nov 1970, Islington, London, England. Musician (drums, percussion). Musical Education: GCSE Music, Certificate in music workshop skills. Career: Drummer for Pete Brown (songwriter with Cream); Phil Ryan (ex-keyboard player, Man); The Interceptors UK tour, 1995; Percussionist, Ronnie Laws band, featured guest Jean Carne, Shepherd's Bush Empire; Percussionist, Akwaaba People; Live performance, GLR Radio, 1995; Performances: Ronnie Scott's, 1995; Jazz Café, 1995; Festivals: Hackney Show; Phoenix; Jazz Izz, Highbury Fields, 1995; Live TV (cable channel), 1995; Teacher, drums, percussion, Secondary schools: Highbury Grove; Parliament Hill; Acland Burghley; Islington Sixth form centre; Young Musicmakers (Independent). Membership: Musicians' Union. Address: 27 Approach Close, Spencer Grove, London N16 8UG, England.

HARPER Ray, b. 6 Jan 1961, Copperhill, Tennessee, USA. Singer; Entertainer; Musician (guitar, fiddle, banjo). Education: 4 quarter management course; Other technical courses. Career: Hamby Mt Music Park, Baldwin, Georgia; Many guest appearances, Carl Story Radio Program, WESC, Greenville, South Carolina;

Former member, Carl Storys Rambling Mountaineers; Played shows, festivals across US with audiences up to 10,000; Now performs as Ray Harper and Friends. Recordings: Ray Harper And Friends with Special Guest Carl Story, 1992; Solo: What A Wonderful Saviour Is He, 1994. Memberships: International Bluegrass Music Association; Bluegrass Music Association of Georgia, South Carolina, North Carolina. Hobby: Music. Current Management: Self-managed. Address: 1131 Farrs Bridge Road, Pickens, SC 29671, USA.

HARPER Roy, b. 12 June 1941, Manchester, England. Singer; Songwriter. Career: Busker, played across Europe; Residency, Les Cousins club, London; Solo recording artiste, 1966-. Compositions include: McGoohan's Blues; The White Man; Tom Tiddler's Ground; Hell's Angels; When An Old Cricketer Leaves The Crease; One Of Those Days In England; Watford Gap. Recordings: Albums: The Sophisticated Beggar, 1966; Come Out Fighting Genghis Smith, 1967; Folkjokeopus, 1969; Flat Baroque And Berserk, 1970; Stormcock, 1971; Lifemask, 1973; Valentine, 1974; Flashes From The Archives Of Oblivion, 1974; HQ (aka When An Old Cricketer Leaves The Crease), 1975; Bullingvase, 1977; Harper 1970-1975, 1978; The Unknown Soldier, 1980; Work Of Heart, 1981; Whatever Happened To Jugula, 1985; Born In Captivity, 1985; In Between Every Line, 1986; Descendents Of Smith, 1988; Loony On The Bus, 1988; Once, 1990; Death Or Glory?, 1992. Guest vocalist, Have A Cigar, on album Wish You Were Here, Pink Floyd. Address: c/o Acorn Entertainments, Winterfild House, 46 Woodfield Road, Kings Heath, Birmingham B13 9UJ, England.

HARRELL Bill (George William), b. 14 Sept 1934, Marion, Virginia, USA. Singer; Musician (guitar, mandolin); Songwriter. m. 8 Dec 1959, dec. 14 Dec 1982, 2 sons, 1 daughter. Education: University of Maryland. Musical Education: Self-taught. Career: Television and radio appearances: Monthly, Jimmy Dean Show, ABC Network, 1961-63; Numerous guest spots, Grande Ole Opry, Nashville, Tennessee; 6 months regularly wheeling West Virginia Jamboree; WWVA Radio; The Today Show, NBC, 1985. Honours: Spigma Bluegrass Singer of Year, 1985; Virginia Music Hall Of Fame. Membership: BMI. Hobbies: Fishing; Travel. Current Management: Self-managed, Attoway Music. Address: 938 St George Barber Road, Davidsonville, MD 21035, USA.

HARRIGAN Katie, b. 17 Sept 1963, Irvine, Scotland. Musician (Celtic harp). Education: BA, Honours, French and Spanish, Heriot Watt University, UK; Diplôme in European Politics, College of Europe, Bruges, Belgium. Musical Education: Studied Clarsach (Celtic harp) with Sanchia Pielou and studied piano. Career: Celtic harpist with: Flumgummery, 1981-83; Hamish Moore, including US tour, 1985-86; Ceolbeg, 1988-91; Toured Canada and USA with Vale of Atholl Pipe Band, 1988; Periodically has worked with Billy Ross; Currently, solo harpist. Recordings: Flumgummery One, with Flumgummery, 1982; Not The Bunny Hop, with Ceolbeg, 1990; Celtic Connection, with KPM, 1994. Honours: Solo Clarsach Champion, National MOD, 1980 and 1982; Solo Clarsach Champion, Edinburgh Music Festival, 1981. Membership: Life Member of Clarsach Society. Address: 9 Coleherne Road, London SW10 9BS, England.

HARRIS Dale G, b. 25 Jul 1968. Musician (guitar). Education: Brooklands College, Weybridge, Surrey. Musical Education: West London Institute, Brunel University, Isleworth, Middlesex, England. Career: Guitarist and arranger with Pretty Blue Gun; UK radio airplay on Virgin Radio, BBC Radio 1, and GLR, 1990-93; Guitarist with The Lorne Gibson Trio, 1993-. Recordings: with Pretty Blue Gun: The Only Girl;

Big Blue World. Hobbies: English literature; Weightlifting; Animal welfare. Current Management: Standfast Music. Address: 48 Atney Road, Putney, London SW15 2PS, England.

HARRIS Derrick, b. 12 Oct 1950, Swansea, Wales. Musician (guitar). 1 son. Education: BEd (Hons), Huddersfield. Musical Education: GCLCM, Leeds. Career: Freelance guitarist working mainly in theatre and jazz; Lecturer, guitar, City of Leeds College of Music, 1987-; Appointed External Examiner, Guildhall School of Music, 1994.

HARRIS Eddie, b. 20 Oct 1938, Chicago, Illinois, USA. Jazz Musician (saxophone, reed trumpet, piano); Vocalist; Innovator; Artist. m. Sara Harris, 22 May 1961, 2 daughters. Musical Education: Illinois University; Roosevelt University; Paris Conservatory. Career: Introduced the electric saxophone, 1967; Composer, arranger for Bill Cosby Show and film Pouquoi L'Amerique; Musician, film soundtrack Sharkey's Machine; Soul To Soul; Featured in front of radio band for Swedish, Russian and Danish television; The Tonight Show; The Arsenio Hall; Ebony Music TV Awards; Six videos in Europe (four in Germany, one in Switzerland, one in France); Tours and festivals throughout US and world. Compositions include: Freedom Jazz Dance; Chicago Serenade; Ignominy. Recordings: 4 million sellers: Exodus (first jazz single to sell 1 million copies); Listen Here; Cold Duck Time; Is It In; Recorded more than 80 albums. Publications: Eddie Harris Intervallistic Concept Book; Jazz Licks; 20 Years Of Original Songs; Jazz Astrology And Numerology; Fusionary Jazz Duets; Skips For The Advanced Instrumentalist; The Eddie Harris Fake Book. Honours: United States Patent, reed mouthpiece for trumpet; Inventor, Eddie Harris Attachment for reed trumpet; NARAS award, 1968, 1970; International Fan Club Of America, 1969; Best Selling Jazz album in US, 1968, 1970, 1971; Ebony Music Award, 1975; Gold Disc Award, 1977; BMI Jazz All Stars, 1990; Echo In Harlem, record charts, 1993; Legends Of Jazz Award, 1995. Memberships: AFofM; BMI; AFTRA. Current Management: Y. Marie Management / Vonlo Music. Address: PO Box 7675, Culver City, CA 90233-9998, USA.

HARRIS Elana, b. 13 May 1957, Brighton, Sussex, England. Singer. m. Ciaran McLaughlin, 14 Jan 1987, 1 son, 1 daughter. Education: Foundation Courses in Art and Design, Granville College of Art, Rotherham College of Art, 1972-73. Career: Singing from age 14 in folk clubs; Member, various Sheffield rock bands; Tour with Krakatoa, 1976-77; In house session singer, 1978; Backing vocals for Pete Cox, Surrey Sound Studios; 5 years in residencies, 1978-93; Lead vocalist, Floy Joy, 1983-84; Tours, 1985; Backing vocals in groups: Lip Machine; Zip Codes; The Group on tours, television appearances in Germany and UK, radio in UK; London gigs with Chris Cutler's Almost Blue, Realisation, 1994. Recordings: with Floy Joy: Answer Through Me, 1983; Solo: Come On Rescue Me, 1985; Backing vocals, with That Petrol Emotion: Divine; with Lip Machine: Rocket Love; Our World; Other session work, 1980s-90s. Hobbies: Watching films; Dancing; Walking; Art; Reading. Address: 25 Badsworth Road, Camberwell, London SE5 0JY, England.

HARRIS Emmylou, b. 2 Apr 1947, Birmingham, Alabama, USA. Singer. 2 daughters. Education: UNC, Greensboro. Career: Toured with Fallen Angel Band; Performed across Europe, USA; Recording artist; Appeared in rock documentary, The Last Waltz. Compositions: Songs; Co-writer, co-producer, Ballad Of Sally Rose with Paul Kennerley, 1985. Recordings: No 1 singles include: Together Again, 1975; Two More Bottles of Wine, 1978; Beneath Still Waters, 1979; (Lost His Love) On Our Last date, 1982; To Know Him is to Love Him (Trio), 1987; We believe in Happy Endings (duet with Earl Thomas Conley),

1988; Albums include: Gliding Bird, 1969; Pieces Of The Sky, 1975; Elite Hotel, 1976; Luxury Liner, 1977; Quarter Moon In A Ten-Cent Town, 1978; Blue Kentucky Girl, 1979; Roses in the Snow, 1980; Evangeline, 1981; Cimarron, 1981; Last Date, 1982; White Shoes, 1983; Profile: Best Of Emmylou Harris, 1984; The Ballad Of Sally Rose, 1985; Thirteen, 1986; Trio (with Dolly Parton, Linda Ronstadt), 1987; Angel Band, 1987; Bluebird, 1989; Brand New Dance, 1990; Duets (with Nash Ramblers), 1990; At The Ryman, 1992; Cowgirls Prayer, 1993; Wrecking Ball, 1995; Portraits, 1996; Assisted Gram Parsons on album GP, Grievous Angel, 1973. Honours: 7 Grammy Awards, 1976-95; 27 Grammy Nominations; Female Vocalist of the Year, Country Music Association, 1980; Academy Country Music Award, Album of the Year, 1987. Membership: President, Country Music Foundation, 1983. Address: Monty Hitchcock Management, PO Box 159007, Nashville, TN 37215, USA.

HARRIS George, b. 2 Oct 1946, Nottingham, England. Entertainer; Vocalist; Musician (guitar, synthesizer). Education: Mechanical Engineer; Electronics Test Engineer. Career: Early groups: Country Lanes; Dusty Roads; Member, band Quest; Duos: G&T; City People; Trios: The Spinnets (on Opportunity Knocks); Session work playing throughout England, Spain, Belgium, and on local radio. Membership: Branch Chairman, Musicians' Union. Hobbies: Photography; Motorcycle racing; Woodwork; Oil paintings; Archery. Current Management: Ken Mitchell. Address: Mitchell Music Ltd, 37 Bucks Road, Douglas, Isle Of Man.

HARRIS Kenneth Philip (Kenny), b. 21 May 1927, London, England. Musician (drums); Author. Education: Brooklyn School of Modern Music, USA. Career: Musician on Queen Mary and Mauretania, 1950-53; Played for shows in France and Germany, 1953; Jazz Clubs in London, 1953-56; Emigrated to USA, 1956; Played in Clubs; To Bermuda, 1960; Played in Hotels and worked as Producer, Bermuda Broadcasting Company; To Canada, 1970; Worked for Capitol Records, own Record Company and Producer at Radio Stations, CKNW, CFMI, C-JAZ; Bermuda, 1983; Bermuda Broadcasting Company; Defontes Broadcasting, 1991; To Uk, 1992. Recordings: Ralph Sharon Sextet, 1953; Joe Wylie Trio, 1964; Gene Harris Trio, 1958; Gene Harris Trio, 1959; British Jazz Trio, 1959. Publications: Author, First Call Drummer Don Lamond, 1997; Geraldo's Navy, 1998. Honour: Juno Award, Canadian Academy of Arts & Sciences, 1981. Membership: Society of Composers, Authors and Publishers of Canada. Address: 36, The Maltings, Riverside Way, Brandon, Suffolk, IP27 0BL, England.

HARRIS Paul, m. 9 June 1964, London, England. Singer; Musician (piano); Composer. m. Alison Harris, née Dodd, 3 sons. Education: Kingston Art College. Musical Education: Private tuition from age 7-16; Self-taught, 16 onwards. Career: Appearances: Top Of The Pops, 1995; BBC1 Song For Europe, with co-written entry, Spinning Away; Live radio: Radio 1, Radio 2, London Talkback, Radio Coventry; Live gigs with own band, BFBS Radio (worldwide); County Sound Radio; Eclipse Radio; Tours: UK; Portugal. Compositions: Spinning Away, with M Smith; I Don't Care, with M Smith; It Never Rains, with S Root; The Great Divide, with M Smith, S Root, S Emney. Membership: Musicians' Union. Hobbies: Travel; Weights; Socialising; Giving up smoking. Current Management: Music Business PHD. Address: 21 Walton Street, Walton-On-The-Hill, Tadworth, Surrey KT20 7RR, England.

HARRIS Roland Oliver, b. 6 Apr 1962, Havant, England. Record Producer; Music Recording Engineer. Education: Queen Mary College, University of London. Career: PRT Studios, Recording and Maintenance Engineer; Nova Studios, Chief Engineer, 8 years; Various

freelance recording, arranging, producing work with an emphasis on Sound synchronised to picture; Live sound/production includes: Rata Blanca; Spain, Mexico (Monsters of Rock, Mexico), Rupert Parker, UK and Europe. Recordings: Several albums with Rupert Parker; Various television, theatre recordings with Michael Nyman; 2 albums with Rata Blanca. Membership: Musicians' Union. Current Management: Mabley Street Productions Ltd. Address: Unit 31, Buspace Studios, Conlan Street, London W10 5AP, England.

HARRIS Rolf, b. 30 Mar 1930, Perth, Australia. Entertainer; Singer; Musician (piano, accordion, digeridoo, wobbleboard); Artist. m. Alwen Myfanwy Wiseman Hughes, 1 Mar 1958, 1 daughter. Education: West Australian University. Musical Education: Piano Grade 1, AMEB. Career: International television entertainer, artist and host, Cartoon Time; Animal Hospital; Recordings: Numerous singles include: Tie Me Kangaroo Down Sport; Jake The Peg; Two Little Boys; Stairway To Heaven. Publications: 12 titles including: How To Write Your Own Pop Song. Honours: OBE; AM. Membership: Equity. Hobbies: Wood Carving; Stone Polishing. Current Management: Jan Kennedy, Billy Marsh Associates Ltd. Address: c/o 174-178 North Gower Street, London NW1 2NB, England.

HARRIS Sam, b. 6 Apr 1941, Cushing, Oklahoma, USA. Actor; Singer. Education: UCLA. Career: Concerts and shows include: Carnegie Hall;Universal Amphitheatre, Los Angeles; London's West End; Grease, Broadway; Joseph And The Amazing Technicolour Dreamcoat, National tour; The Life, Broadway; Television includes: Star Search; Night Show; Numerous television specials and national talk shows. Compositions: Musicals: Hurry! Hurry! Hollywood!; Hard Copy; Television sitcom, Down To Earth. Recordings: Sam Harris; Sam-I-Am; Grease; Tribute To Gershwin; Standard Time; Different Stages; The Life. Honours: Drama Desk nomination, Grease; Dramalogue Awards for Hard Copy and Different Hats; Dramalogue Award and Tony, Drama Desk and Outer Critics' Circle nominations for The Life; RIAA Gold Album status for Sam Harris and Sam-I-Am. Hobbies: Gardening; Re-finishing; Furniture. Current Management: Mark Sendroff, 1500 Broadway #200, New York, NY 10036 USA. Address: 250 W 57th Street, Suite 703, New York, NY 10107, USA.

HARRIS Sean. Singer; Songwriter. Career: Founder member, UK rock group Diamond Head, 1977-85; One of leading groups in New Wave Of British Heavy Metal (NWOBHM), UK, 1980s; UK tours, 1980, 1982; Monsters Of Rock Festival, Castle Donington, 1983; Member, Notorious, with Robin George, 1990; Reformed Diamond Head, 1991-; Tours include support to Metallica. Compositions include: In The Heat Of The Night; Am I Evil; Helpless; It's Electric. Albums with Diamond Head: Lightning To The Nations, 1980; (remixed as Behold The Beginning, 1986); Canterbury, 1983; Death And Progress, 1993; with Robin George: Notorious, 1990; Rising Up (mini-album), 1992; Compilation: Am I Evil, 1987.

HARRIS Simon Kenneth, b. 10 Sept 1962, London, England. Creative Director. Career: Record Producer and Remixer with 2 Top 40 Hits; Production Credits include: Derek B, Ambassadors of Funk, Daddy Freddy; Remix Credits include: Stone Roses; James Brown; Tony Toni Tone; Real Thing; DMB; Prince; Steve Silk Hurley; Joyce Simms; Appeared on Top of the Pops, Good Morning, Big Breakfast. Compositions: Bass (How Low Can You Go); Supermario Land, Ambassadors of Funk; Get Ready For This, 2 Unlimited; Here Comes That Sound, Simon Harris. Honour: NME Rap Label of the Year, 1988-89; 50 Most Played Songs, for Get Ready For this, 1996. Memberships: PRS; BMI. Hobbies: Disney Toys; Laser Discs; Films. Current

Management: Chris France, Music of Life. Address: Liscombe Park, Soulbury, LU7 0JL, England.

HARRIS Steve, b. 12 Mar 1957, Leytonstone, London, England. Rock Musician (bass). Career: Member, pub band, Smiler; Founder member, UK heavy rock group Iron Maiden, 1976-; Regular tours worldwide; Concerts include: Reading Festival, 1980, 1982; Monsters Of Rock Festival, Castle Donington, 1988, 1992; Monsters Of Rock, Germany, 1988; Monsters Of Rock, France, 1992; Super Rock '92, Germany, 1992. Recordings: Albums: Iron Maiden, 1980; Killers, 1981; The Number Of The Beast, 1982; Piece Of Mind, 1983; Powerslave, 1984; Live After Death, 1985; Somewhere In Time, 1986; Seventh Son Of A Seventh Son, 1988; No Prayer For The Dying, 1990; Fear Of The Dark, 1992; A Real Live One, 1993; A Real Dead One, 1993; The X-Factor, 1995; Hit singles include: Running Free, 1980; Run To The Hills, 1982; The Number Of The Beast, 1982; Flight Of Icarus, 1983; The Trooper, 1983; 2 Minutes To Midnight, 1984; Aces High, 1984; Wasted Years, 1986; Can I Play With Madness, 1988; Evil That Men Do, 1988; The Clairvoyant, 1988; Infinite Dreams, 1989; Holy Smoke, 1990; Bring Your Daughter To The Slaughter, 1991; Be Quick Or Be Dead, 1992; From Here To Eternity, 1992. Address: c/o Sanctuary Music (Overseas), 1st Floor Suite, The Colonnades, 82 Bishops Bridge Road, London W2 6BB, England.

HARRISON Bobby (Robert), b.23 Dec 1974, Harlow, Essex, England. Musician (guitar); Singer; Songwriter. Musical Education: National Diploma in Pop Music (B-Tec) Harlow College. Career: Playing in 3-piece rock band Baby Paint, currently seeking management, publishing, recording contracts; Featured on local radio numerous times. Recordings: Recorded 2 tracks, Whitfield Street Studios, London (engineered by Will O'Donovan). Honour: Winner, Essex Young Performer Of The Year, 1994. Membership: Musicians' Union. Hobbies: Weight training; Cycling; Walking; Socialising at parties. Address: 24 Tithelands, Harlow, Essex CM19 5NA, England.

HARRISON Gavin, b. 28 May 1963, Harrow, London, England. Musician (drums, bass, keyboards); Composition. Career: Founder member, Dizrhythmia; Worked with: Level 42; Paul Young; Iggy Pop; Eros Ramazotti; Claudio Baglioni; Incognito. Recordings: Albums include: with Sam Brown: Stop, 1988; with Incognito: Inside Life; Always There; Also recorded with: Tom Robinson; Kevin Ayers; Black; Dave Stewart; Paul Young. Publications: Rhythmic Illusions Book; Columns for: Rhythm, Modern Drummer magazines. Hobby: Pole vaulting. Current Management: B & H Management. Address: Lavender Cottage, Love Lane, Kings Langley, Hertfordshire WD4 8EW, England.

HARRISON George, b. 24 Feb 1943, Wavertree, Liverpool, England. Musician (guitar, organ, Indian instruments); Singer; Songwriter. m. (1) Pattie Boyd, 1966, divorced 1977; m. (2) Olivia Arias, 1 son. Career: Member, The Rebels, 1956-58; The Beatles, 1960-70 (formerly as the Quarrymen, 1958-60); Solo artiste, 1970-; Worldwide appearances, 1960-; Residencies include: Hamburg, 1960-62; The Cavern, Liverpool, 1960-61; Co-founder, Apple Corps Ltd, 1968; Organized, performed at Concert For Bangladesh, 1971; Co-founder, Handmade Films; Films include: Time Bandits, 1981; The Long Good Friday, 1982; Water, 1985; Mona Lisa, 1985; Shanghai Surprise, 1986; Founder, Material World Charitable Foundation; Member, The Traveling Wilburys (with Tom Petty, Bob Dylan, Jeff Lynne, Roy Orbison); Japanese tour with Eric Clapton, 1991; Film appearances include: A Hard Day's Night; Help!; Magical Mystery Tour; Let It Be. Compositions: Songs include: Don't Bother

Me; I Need You; If I Needed Someone; I Want To Tell You; Taxman; While My Guitar Gently Weeps; Something; Within You Without You; My Sweet Lord; Give Me Love (Give Me Peace On Earth); All Those Years Ago; Got My Mind Set On You; Recordings: Albums: All Beatles albums and singles; Solo albums include: Wonderwall (film score), 1968; Electronic Music, 1969; All Things Must Pass, 1970; Concert For Bangla Desh, 1972; Living In The Material World, 1973; Dark Horse, 1974; Extra Texture, 1975; Thirty Three And A Third, 1976; George Harrison; Somewhere In England, 1981; Gone Troppo, 1982; Cloud Nine, 1987; Live In Japan, 1992; 3 albums with The Traveling Wilburys. Publication: I Me Mine, 1990. Numerous honours include: MBE. Hobbies: Motor racing; Gardening. Current Management: Morra, Brezner, Steinberg and Tenenbaum, 345 N Maple Drive, Suite 200, Beverly Hills, CA 90210, USA. Address: c/o Hand Made Films, 26 Cadogan Square, London SW1 0SP, England.

HARRISON Sarah Elizabeth, b. 3 Dec 1969, Hampshire, England. Singer; Songwriter; Musician (acoustic guitar). Career: Concerts include: Birmingham University; Portsmouth Guildhall; Mayflower Theatre, Southampton; Sandown Pier, Isle Of Wight; Wedgewood Rooms, Portsmouth; Connaught Rooms, Worthing. Recordings: (all own compositions) No Shame (EP); Album: The Live; Demo: Where Are The Signs. Membership: Musicians' Union. Hobbies: Poetry; Writing; Art; Songwriting; Exercise. Address: 7 Langrish Road, Aldermoor, Southampton SO1 6JF, England.

HARRISON Spencer William, b. 4 July 1968, Shrewsbury, England. Singer; Songwriter; Musician (guitar). m. Amy Bidz, 4 Feb 1994. Musical Education: Self-taught. Career: Formed Savage Penguins, St Louis, Missouri, 1989; Joined as guitarist, Den Of Thieves, 1991; Formed Son Of William, as singer, songwriter, 1992; Incorporated Son Of William Ltd, trading as Berzerker, 1995. Recordings: And The Wolves Devoured The Sun, 1992; Beasts Of Desolation, 1994; Husk, 1995; Knowledge And Oblivion, 1995. Memberships: PRS; MCPS; Gallup RLR. Current Management: Amy Bidz. Address: Berzerker Records, 1 Church Lane, Horbling, Lincs NG34 0PJ, England.

HARRY Deborah Ann, b. 1 July 1945, Miami, Florida, USA. Singer; Songwriter; Actress. Career: Former Playboy bunny waitress; Singer, groups: Wind In The Willows; The Stilettos; Founder, Blondie, 1974-83; Appearances include: New York punk club, CBGBs, 1974; Support to Iggy Pop, US, 1977; Solo recording career, 1981-; Actress, films including: Blank Generation, 1978; The Foreigner, 1978; Union City, 1979; Roadie, 1980; Videodrome; Hairspray; The Killbillies; Intimate Stranger, 1991. Recordings: Hit singles: with Blondie: Denis (Denee), 1978; (I'm Always Touched By Your) Presence Dear, 1978; Picture This, 1978; Hanging On The Telephone, 1978; Heart Of Glass (Number 1, UK), 1979; Sunday Girl (Number 1, UK), 1979; Dreaming, 1979; Union City Blue, 1979; Call Me (Number 1, US and UK), 1980; Atomic, 1980; The Tide Is High (Number 1, UK and US), 1980; Rapture (Number 1, US), 1981; Island Of Lost Souls, 1982; Solo: Backfired, 1981; French Kissin' (In The USA), 1986; I Want That Man, 1989; I Can See Clearly, 1993; Albums with Blondie: Blondie, 1976; Plastic Letters, 1978; Parallel Lines (Number 1, US), 1978; Eat To The Beat (Number 1, UK), 1979; Autoamerican, 1980; The Best Of Blondie, 1981; The Hunter, 1982; Solo albums: Koo Koo, 1981; Rockbird, 1986; Def, Dumb And Blonde, 1989; Debravation, 1993; Compilations: Once More Into The Bleach, 1988; The Complete Picture, 1991; Blonde And Beyond, 1993; Contributor, film soundtracks: American Gigolo, 1980; Roadie, 1980; Scarface; Krush Groove, 1984. Publications: Making Tracks - The Rise Of Blondie (co-written with Chris Stein), 1982. Memberships: ASCAP; AFTRA; Equity; Screen Actors Guild. Current

Management: Overland Productions, 156 W 56th Street, 5th Floor, New York, NY 10019, USA.

HART Angela Ruth, b. 8 Mar 1872, Adelaide, Australia. Singer; Musician. Career: Solo artiste; Also singer with Frente; Australian tour, 1992-93; US tour, 1994; Support to Beautiful South; Crowded House; Counting Crows; They Might Be Giants. Recordings: Marvin - The Album, 1993; Ruby's Arm, Tom Waits Tribute, 1995. Honours: DBL Platinum album, Australia; Gold album, Canada, Indonesia, Phillipines, Malaysia, Thailand. Hobbies: Stained glass; Art.

HART J C, b. 28 Aug 1964, Coventry, England. Musician (guitar). Musical Education: Grade VIII, Violin; Grade V, Piano; 15 Years guitar, mostly self-taught. Career: with Coventry Youth Orchestra, 1977-82, appearing with Nigel Kennedy at Schools Prom in 1982; with Coventry Symphony Orchestra, 1981-83; Warwickshire Symphony Orchestra, 1981-83; Beauchamp Symphonietta, 1981-85; Began teaching guitar, 1991-; Worked with: The Garibaldi Brothers, 1994; Curious Potion, 1994; The Mussolini Brothers, 1994; Steve Jaquar, 1995; Glenn Baker, 1995. Recording: I, by I, 1982. Membership: Musicians' Union. Hobbies: Reading; Walking; Cycling. Address: 23 Langbay Court, Cloister Croft, Walsgrave, Coventry CV2 2AZ, England.

HART Martin, b. 3 January 1939, London, England. m. Glen, 15 August 1965, 1 daughter. Education: Westminster Technical College. Career: John Mayall, Blubs Breakers, 1962-63; Tours with Peanuts Hucko, Harry Edison, Jimmy Witherspoon, 1970-80; Stage Show, Rise & Fall or Little Voices, with Milicent Martin, 1976. Recordings: Crawling Up A Hill, John Mayall; Grace Notes, Garry Potter; The Big Honk, George Ricci. Hobby: Photography. Address: Halcyon, Chapel Hill, Speen, Princess Rinsborough, Bucks HP27 0SL, England.

HARTFORD John, b. 30 Dec 1937, New York City, USA. Singer; Songwriter; Musician (multi-instrumentalist, banjo, guitar, fiddle, dobro). Career: Former employment includes: Sign-painter; Commercial artist; Deckhand; Disc Jockey; Session musician, Nashville, 1960s; Solo artiste, 1966-; Also worked with Dillards, 1977-80. Compositions include: Gentle On My Mind (recorded by over 300 artists including: Glen Campbell; Frank Sinatra; Max Bygraves; Elvis Presley). Recordings: Albums: Looks At Life, 1967; Earthwords And Music, 1967; The Love Album, 1968; Housing Project, 1968; John Hartford, 1969; Iron Mountain Depot, 1970; Aereo Plain, 1971; Morning Bugle, 1972; Tennessee Jubilee, 1975; Mark Twang, 1976; Nobody Knows What You Do, 1976; All In The Name In Love, 1977; Heading Down Into The Mystery Below, 1978; Slumbering On The Cumberland, 1979; You And Me At Home, 1984; Catalogue, 1987; John Hartford, 1988; All In The Name Of Love, 1989; with Doug and Rodney Dillard: Dillard Hartford Dillard, 1977; Permanent Wave, 1980. Honours: Grammy Award, Mark Twang, 1976. Address: c/o Keith Case & Associates, 59 Music Square West, Nashville, TN 37203, USA.

HARVEY PJ (Polly Jean), b. 9 Oct 1969, England. Singer; Songwriter; Musician. Career: Television appearances include: MTV's Most Wanted; 120 Minutes; David Letterman Show; Jay Leno Show; Conan O'Brien Show; Top Of The Pops; The White Room; Later With Jools Holland; Concerts include Glastonbury Festival, 1995; Tours, USA, Europe, Japan, 1995. Recordings: Albums: Dry, 1992; Rid Of Me, 1993; 4 Track Demos, 1993; To Bring You My Love, 1995; Honours: Nominations for awards include: BRIT Award, 1996; BRAT Award, 1996; 2 Grammy Awards, 1996; Danish Grammy, 1995; Mercury Music Prize; MTV Video Awards; Q Awards. Current Management: Principle Management.

Address: 30-32 Sir John Rogersons Quay, Dublin 2, Ireland.

HARVEY Richard John, b. 22 Oct 1960, Birmingham, England. Musician (guitar). m. Laila, 4 Jan 1992. Musical Education: Self-taught. Career: Professional guitarist from age 16; Backing musician, Light Entertainment, cruise ships, cabaret; Lately working as Jazz musician and classical guitarist, West End, London. Membership: Musicians' Union. Hobbies: Wine; Ale; Yoga.

HARVEY Tim, b. 1 Nov 1973, Leeds, England. Musician (bass); Songwriter. Education: BEng, Leeds Met University. Musical Education: Self-taught. Career: Played violin in North Yorkshire Youth Orchestra, 1980-87; Took up bass guitar playing throughout North East England with various jazz and pop bands, 1990-; Studio session work leading to the formation of The Saints, indie pop band. Recordings: Composition and session work for A Dark Affair, 1993; Someone, Toytown, 1994; If I Was Your Father Christmas, Toytown, 1995; I Can Save You (EP), The Saints, 1995. Hobbies: Football; Computer-aided designing; Art. Address: 1 Malpas Road, Northallerton, North Yorkshire DL7 8TJ, England.

HASLAM Annie, b. Bolton, England. Singer; Songwriter. m. Marc I Hoffman, 8 June 1991, divorced. Education: Art College. Musical Education: 9 months opera training with Sybil Knight, London. Career: 65 tours, USA with rock band Renaissance; Tours: Canada; UK; Europe; Middle East; Performances include: Carnegie Hall (New York Philharmonic and Renaissance), 1975; Royal Albert Hall (Royal Philharmonic Orchestra and Renaissance), 1978; Tour of Japan (Annie Haslam Band), 1991; Solo guest with New York Philharmonia Virtuosi, 1986. Recordings: with Renaissance: Prologue, 1972; Ashes Are Burning, 1973; Turn Of The Cards, 1974; Scheherazade And Other Stories, 1975; Live At Carnegie Hall, 1976; Novella, 1977; In The Beginning, 1978; Song For All Seasons, 1978; Azure d'Or, 1979; Camera, Camera, 1981; Timeline, 1983; Tales Of 1001 Nights, Volumes 1-2, 1990; Solo: Annie In Wonderland, 1977; Still Life with Royal Philharmonic Orchestra), 1985; Annie Haslam, 1989; with Annie Haslam's Renaissance: Blessing In Disguise, 1994; Annie Haslam Live in Brazil, 1997; Guest on: Intergalactic Touring Band, 1977; with Mike Read: Betjeman, 1990; with Akio Dobashi: Fox, 1990; with Raphael Rudd: Skydancer, 1991; Guest on: Tales from Yesterday (Yes tribute), 1995; Suppers Ready (Genesis tribute), 1995; with Raphael Rudd, Awakenings, 1996; Renaissance Live at the Royal Albert Hall, with the Royal Philharmonic Orchestra, Vols 1 and 2; Songs from Renaissance Days: Rarities, recorded 1977, 1984. Honours: Silver disc for: Single Northern Lights, 1978; 5th Top Female Singer, Melody Maker, 1978; Silver album, Song For All Seasons. Membership: Equity. Hobbies: Vegetarian cooking; Photography; Active in animal welfare. Current Management: The White Dove Organisation Inc. Address: The White Dove Organisation Inc, P O Box 1157, Doylestown, PA 18901, USA.

HASLAM George, b. 22 Feb 1939, Preston, Lancashire, England. Jazz Musician (baritone saxophone, tarogato). m. Beryl Murphy, 7 Dec 1960, 4 sons, 1 daughter. Education: PhD, Strathclyde University. Musical Education: Some private tuition but mainly self-taught. Career: 2 albums on Spotlite, early 1980s; Extensive work in Eastern Europe; Tour of Mexico; Leader, first British jazz group to play in Cuba, Cervantino Festival, led first British jazz group to play in Cuba, 1986; Founded record label, SLAM, 1989; First British Jazz musician to play in Argentina, 1990; Founder, Oxford Jazz Festival, 1990; Featured in Impressions of George Haslam, BBC Radio 3, 1993; First jazz musician to play in Odessa Opera

House, 1997; Regular tours include: Argentina, Cuba, Hong Kong, Europe; Leads blues and improvisation workshops; The British Saxophone Quartet presents. Recordings under own leadership: Live In Hungary, 1984; The Healing, 1986; 1989 And All That, 1989; The Holywell Concert, 1990; Level Two, 1992; Argentine Adventures, 1994; Waldron-Haslam, 1994; Two New, 1995; Early October, 1995; Argentine Adventures Part 2, 1996; SOLOS East West, 1997. Memberships: Musicians' Union, PRS, MCPS, BASCA. Hobbies: Walking; Reading. Address: 3 Thesiger Road, Abingdon, Oxon OX14 2DX, England.

HASSELL David, b. 26 Nov 1947, Manchester, England. Musician (drums, percussion). m. Valerie, 29 Apr 1967, 1 son, 2 daughters. Musical Education: Private tuition; Studies with Geoff Riley; Jim Blackley; Manik Popatkar; Tony Oxley. Career: Performer, almost every style of music: Jazz; Funk; Rock; Folk; Latin; Show; Cabaret; Symphonic; Session musician for television including: Coronation Street; Brideshead Revisited; Old Grey Whistle Test; Jim'll Fix It; Sunday Night At The London Palladium; Emmerdale Farm; Musician for radio, jingles, records and films; Performed numerous sessions with top artists including: ABBA; The Three Degrees; The Drifters; Cliff Richard; Barbara Dickson; Vince Hill; The Ramones; The Platters; Harold Melvin And The Blue Notes; Les Miserables; Lilly Savage; Maddy Prior; Shirley Bassey; Gloria Gaynor; Bertice Redding; Alan Price; Kiki Dee; Happy Mondays; Sad Cafe; Lisa Stansfield; Roger Whittaker; George Hamilton IV; Mary O'Hara; Moira Anderson; Ute Lemper; Conductors include: Ronnie Hazelhurst; Michel Legrand; Alan Aynsworth; Leader, Apitos, one of UK's foremost Latin American ensembles; Lecturer, Drums and Percussion, Royal Northern College of Music; Royal Academy Of Music, London; Salford College of Technology; Chethams School Of Music; Royal Scottish Academy of Music and Drama; Trinity College. Recordings: Both Hands Free, 1976; with Stan Barker: The Gentle Touch, 1990. Publications: Graded Course For Drum Kit 1-2 (book and tape); Latin Grooves (book and tape), 1994. Memberships: Musicians' Union; NAPT; PAS. Hobbies: Squash; Horse riding; Skiing. Address: 22 Park Road, Timperley, Altrincham, Cheshire WA14 5AU, England.

HASSELQUIST Eric, b. 15 Sept 1965, Stockholm, Sweden. Record Company Executive. Education: Master Degree in Business Economics. Career: Music Manager for Readers Digest Scandinavia, 1990-91; General Manager, Stockholm Records, 1991-. Recording: Impact (EP), Rimshot Party, 1991. Address: PO Box 20504, S-16102 Bromma, Sweden.

HASTINGS Deborah, b. 11 May 1959, Evansville, Indiana, USA. Musician (bass guitar); Photographer. Musical Education: Music, University of Wisconsin. Career: Freelance bass player, 1975-; Photographer, 1976-81; Performed with: Ron Wood; Bo Diddley; Chuck Berry; Jerry Lee Lewis; Ben E King; Little Anthony; Performed at President George Bush Inauguration, with Billy Preston, Dr John, Carla Thomas, Sam Moore, 1979. Publication: Author, Photographers Market, 1981. Address: c/o Talent Source, 1560 Broadway, Suite 1308, New York, NY 10036, USA.

HATCH Tony, b. 30 June 1939, England. Composer; Arranger; Musical Director. m. Jackie Trent, 18 Aug 1967. Musical Education: London Choir School. Career: Band Coldstream Guards, 1959-61; Record Producer, Pye Records, 1961-71; Producer for Petula Clark; Jackie Trent; The Searchers; Musical Director, Carols In The Domain, (Australia) 1984-94. Television: Regular Panelist, New Faces, 1973-78; Films: Travels With My Aunt; Sweeney II. Recordings: Singles: Downtown; Call Me; I Know A Place; Where Are

You Now; Joanna; Don't Sleep In The Subway; I Couldn't Live Without Your Love; Television theme music for Neighbours; Crossroads; Emmerdale; Musical: The Card. Publication: So You Want To Be In The Music Business, 1975. Honours: Several Ivor Novello Awards; ASCAP Awards; BMI Awards. Hobby: Tennis. Current Management: Billy Marsh Associates. Address: 174-178 North Gower Street, London NW1 2NB, England.

HATFIELD Bobby, b. 10 Aug 1940, Beaver Dam, Wisconsin, USA. Singer. Career: Member, The Variations; Formed The Righteous Brothers with Bill Medley, 1962-67; Support to the Beatles, US tour, 1964; Duo continued with Jimmy Walker, 1967-73; Reforms Righteous Brothers with Bill Medley, 1974-; Solo recording artist, 1968-; Appearance on Cheers, 1991. Recordings: Singles include: You've Lost That Lovin' Feelin' (Number 1, UK and US), 1964; Just Once In My Life, 1965; You Can Have Her, 1965; Justine, 1965; Unchained Melody, 1965; Ebb Tide, 1966; You're My Soul And Inspiration, 1966; Solo: Nothing Is Too Good For You, 1969; Rock'n'Roll Heaven, 1974; Albums: You've Lost That Lovin' Feelin', 1965; Some Blue-Eyed Soul, 1965; This Is New!, 1965; Just Once In My Life, 1965; Back To Back, 1965; Soul And Inspiration, 1966; The Best Of The Righteous Brothers, 1966; Go Ahead And Cry, 1966; Sayin' Somethin', 1967; Greatest Hits, 1967; One For The Road, 1968; Re-Birth, 1969; Greatest Hits, Vol 2, 1969; Righteous Brothers Greatest Hits, 1990; The Best Of..., 1990; The Very Best Of..., 1990; Anthology (1962-74), 1990. Address: c/o William Morris Agency.

HATFIELD Juliana, b. 27 July 1967, Wiscasset, Maine, USA. Singer; Songwriter. Musical Education: Berklee School Of Music. Career: Recent concerts include: Reading Festival, 1995. Recordings: Albums: Hey Babe; Forever Baby; Become What You Are; Only Everything; Singles include: Universal Heartbeat. Publication: The Music Of Juliana Hatfield. Membership: AFofM. Hobbies: Ice Skating; Baking. Current Management: c/o Gary Smith, Fort Apache, 2 Tyler Court, Suite B, Cambridge, MA 02140, USA.

HAURAND Ali, b. 15 Nov 1993, Viersen, Germany. Musician (double bass); Teacher. m. Annemarie, Sept 1972, 1 daughter. Musical Education: Studied classical music, Folkwangschool, Essen, Germany. Career: Member, leader, founder, George Maycock Trio, 1967-79; Quintet with Philly Joe Jones, 1968-69; International Jazz Quintet with Jon Eardly, 1969-70; Third Eye, 1970; European Jazz Quintet, 1977; SOH Trio, 1978-84; The Quartet, 1982; European Jazz Ensemble, 1984; Numerous tours and festivals in Europe, USA, Canada and Australia with these and other ensembles featuring: Bobby Jones; Don Byas; Ben Webster; John Handy; Jan Akkerman; John Surman; Gerd Dudek; Joachim Kühn; Enrico Rava; Numerous television and radio appearances including: Jazz At Midnight, German TV, 1991; Talking Jazz, Superchannel, 1993; Over 40 recordings with: The Quartet, European Jazz Ensemble; European Jazz Quintet, 1970-. Honours: European Jazz Poll, Jazz Forum, 7 times. Membership: Jazz Union, Germany. Hobbies: Languages; Paintings, Art. Current Management: K Adenauer Ring 10, D-41747 Viersen, Germany.

HAUSER Tim, b. 1942, New Jersey, USA. Singer; Songwriter. Career: Founder member, singer, Manhattan Transfer, 1971-; Television includes: Mary Tyler Moore Television Special, 1975; Own television show, 1975; Star Parade, Germany; Regular US and European tours; Performed at MIDEM, Cannes, France, 1977. Recordings: Hit singles: Tuxedo Junction; Chanson D'Amour; Birdland; Boy From New York City; Albums include: Junkin' (Unofficial), 1971; Manhattan Transfer, 1975; Coming Out, 1976;

Pastiche, 1978; Live, 1978; Extensions, 1979; Mecca For Moderns, 1981; Best Of Manhattan Transfer, 1981; Bodies And Souls, 1983; Bop Doo-Wop, 1985; Vocalese, 1985; Live, 1987; Brasil, 1988; The Off-Beat Of Avenues, 1991; Contributor, film soundtrack A League Of Their Own, 1992. Honours include: German Grammy, Best New Group, 1975; Numerous Grammy Awards (Best Vocal Arrangement, Best Jazz Fusion Performance, Best Jazz Vocal Performance, Best Pop Vocal Performance, Best Contemporary Jazz Performance), 1980-, including 3 Grammy Awards and 12 Nominations, for Vocalese album, 1985. Address: c/o Columbia Records, 10 Great Marlborough Street, London W1V 2LP, England.

HAUTA-AHO Teppo, b. 27 May 1941, Finland. Composer; Musician (bass). Musical Education: Diploma, Sibelius Academy, 1970; Studied with Professor Frantisek Posta. Career: Bassist, Helsinki Philharmonic, 1965-72; Finnish National Opera, 1975-; Played with numerous artists including: Seppo Paakkunainen, early 1960s; Juhani Vilkki; Kaj Backlund Big Band; Pekka Pöyry quartet; Tuohi Quartet; Leader, own group Kalmisto-Klang; Member, Quintet Moderne, 1980s-; Also classical and chamber musician; Performed at annual festivals, Kuhmo; Currently concentrating on composing; Duos with: singer/pianist Carita Holmström; pianist/composer Eero Ojanen. Compositions include: Fantasy, for trumpet and orchestra; Kadenza, for contrabass, used as set piece in international bass competitions, Munich, 1985, New York, 1990. Honours: Composer's Prize, Royal Academy, Stockholm; First prize, Reine Marie José competition, Geneva, 1986; Winner with Tuohi Quartet, EBU competition for jazz groups, Montreux, 1971. Address: Mechelininkatu 27 B, 00100 Helsinki, Finland.

HAVENS Richie, b. 21 Jan 1941, Brooklyn, New York, USA. Singer. Career: Performances include: Tribute concert to Woody Guthrie, Carnegie Hall, New York, 1968; Miami Pop Festival, 1968; Woodstock Music & Art Fair, Bethel, New York, 1969; Isle Of Wight Festival, 1970; Crystal Palace Garden Party, London, 1972; Stage debut, rock opera, Tommy, 1972; Stonehenge Free Festival, 1977; The Gold Medal Celebration, Carnegie Hall, 1987; Freedom Festival '90, 1990; Troubadours Of Folk Festival, Los Angeles, 1993; Actor, Othello, in Jack Good's Catch My Soul, 1974; Film appearances: Greased Lightning, 1977; Hearts Of Fire, 1987. Current Management: ELD Productions, 123 W 44th Street, Suite 11F, New York, NY 10036, USA.

HAVET Didier, b. 9 Mar 1964, Lille, France. Musician (tuba, bass trombone). m. 12 March 1994, 1 daughter. Musical Education: Lille Conservatory; Paris Conservatory. Career: Member, National Jazz Orchestra, France (ONJ), 1986-94; Worked with orchestras of: Martial Solal; Jean Loup Longnon; Ivan Jullien; Laurent Cugny; Jean Jacques Ruhlman; Luc Le Masne; Marc Steckar; Jean Marc Padovani; Bertrand Reaudin; Gerard Badini; Bass trombone player with Belmondo Big Band; Tour, Europe, with Mingus Big Band of New York, 1994; Paris and Nice Jazz Festival, 1995; Tours, Netherlands; Norway; Finland; Member, Bloc-notes Quintet, Peru and Columbia, 1995; Regular work in traditional jazz and dixieland. Recordings: 5 records with National Orchestra of Jazz, France; Other recordings with: Michel Legrand; Claude Bolling; Julien Clerc; Jacques Higelin; Georges Moustaki; William Sheller. Address: 3 Rue Robert Lavergne, 92600 Asnières, France.

HAWKEN Dominic, b. 19 Apr 1967, Welwyn Garden City, Hertfordshire, England. Songwriter; Musician (keyboards); Multimedia and Internet Consultant. Musical Education: Classically trained pianist to Grade VIII. Career: Session keyboard player, late 80s-early 90s; Performed with Joy

Polloi, Kid Deluxe and Eric and the Good Good Feeling; Now songwriter and record producer with various leading artists; Director, A L Digital Ltd (multimedia and internet technology). Compositions: Co-writer, Stay Another Day, East 17 (Christmas Number 1, UK), 1994; Be There; Let It All Go, East 17, 1994; I remember, East 17, 1995; Don't You Feel So Good, East 17; Someone to Love, East 17, 1995; Cloud 9, Ant and Dec, 1997; Bound, Ant and Dec, 1997. Recordings: Keyboards on album Steam, East 17; Keyboard/remix credits: Shamen; Donna Summer; Malcolm McLaren; Tribe Called Quest; Errol Brown; Kim Mazelle; Hammer; Mike Oldfield; Black Duck; Writing and Production for artists, North South, Alphaville and Shiona; Writing and keyboards on East 17 albums Up All Night, 1995, All Around the World, 1996-97; Writing and Production for Ant and Dec album, The Cult of Ant and Dec, 1997. Publications: Reviews, assessments of digital recording equipment on a regular basis for Audio Media and Sound on Sound magazines. Honours: 2 Ivor Novello Award Nominations, Stay Another Day, 1995. Memberships: BASCA; PRS. Current Management: The Deluxe Corporation. Address: 13 Charnhill Crescent, Bristol BS16 9JU, England.

HAWKINS Screamin' Jay (Jalacy Hawkins), b. 18 July 1929, Cleveland, Ohio, USA. Musician (piano, saxophone). Musical Education: Self-taught. Career: Played piano with artists including: Gene Ammons; Arnett Cobb; Illinois Jacquet; James Moody; Lynn Hope; Count Basie; Member, Tiny Grimes' Rocking Highlanders, 1951; Solo artiste, 1950s; Tours and recordings, 1970s-80s; Founder, The Fuzztones; Film appearances: American Hot Wax; Mystery Train. Recordings: Albums include: At Home With Screamin' Jay Hawkins, 1956; I Put A Spell On You, 1957; The Night & Day Of Screamin' Jay Hawkins, 1965; What That Is, 1969; Screamin' Jay Hawkins, 1970; A Portrait Of A Man & His Woman, 1972; Screamin' The Blues, 1979; Frenzy, 1982; Real Life, 1983; Live, 1985; Feast Of The Mau Mau, 1988; Real Life, 1989; I Is, 1989; Live And Crazy, 1989; I Want To Do It In A Cave!, 1990; Voodoo Jive, 1990; Black Music For White People, 1991; Spellbound 1955-1974, 1991; Screamin' Jay Hawkins 1952-1955, 1991; Stone Crazy, 1993. Address: c/o Jerry Dorn Artist Management, 165 Seaman Avenue, New York, NY 10034, USA.

HAWORTH Bryn, b. 29 July 1948, Blackburn, Lancashire, England. Musician (guitars, especially slide, mandolin); Singer. m. Sally, 22 Jan 1973. Musical Education: Self-taught. Career: Joined Fleur De Lys, motown/soul band, house band for Atlantic Records, late 1960s; Went to California, toured USA in bands including: Jackie Lomax Band; Wolfgang; Returned to England, 1973; Signed to Island Records; Numerous radio and television appearances include: 2 Old Grey Whistle Test; Tours, England Europe, supporting artists including: Traffic; Bad Company; Gallagher & Lyle; Fairport Convention; Worked with musicians including: Chris De Burgh; Marianne Faithfull; John Cale; Ian Matthews; Joan Armatrading; Gerry Rafferty; Cliff Richard (toured with as member of band); Currently leader, The Bryn Haworth Band, extensive tours, UK; Notable exponent slide guitar. Recordings: Albums include: Let The Days Go By, 1974; Sunny Side Of The Street, 1975; Grand Arrival, 1978; Keep The Ball Rolling, 1979; The Bryn Haworth Band Live; 6 Gospel albums include: Gap; Pass It On; Wings Of The Morning; 12 Classics; Mountain Mover; with Gerry Rafferty: On A Wing And A Prayer; Over My Head, 1995. Publication: Bryn Haworth Songbook, Volume One. Hobby: Music. Current Management: Self-managed. Address: PO Box 28, Teddington, Middlesex TW11 0QU, England.

HAY Barry, b. 16 Aug 1948, Fyzlabad, India. Vocalist; Musician(guitar, flute, saxophone). Career: Member, Dutch group, Golden Earring,

1966-; Tours, Europe; Canada; US; Support to the Who, European tour, 1972; Support to Rush, 1982. Recordings: Winter Harvest, 1967; Miracle Mirror, 1968; On The Double, 1969; Eight Miles High, 1970; Golden Earring, 1971; Seven Tears, 1971; Together, 1972; Moontan, 1973; Switch, 1975; To The Hilt, 1975; Rock Of The Century, 1976; Contraband, 1976; Mad Love, 1977; Live, 1977; Grab It For A Second, 1978; No Promises No Debts, 1979; Prisoner Of The Night, 1980; Second Live, 1981; Hole, 1986; face It, 1995; Numerous compilation albums; Solo album: Only Parrots, Frogs And Angels, 1972; Hit singles: Dong-Dong-Di-Ki-Di-Gi-Dong (Number 1, Netherlands), 1968; Radar Love (Number 1, Netherlands), 1973; Twilight Zone, 1982; Lady Smiles. Current Management: c/o Rob Gerritsen, Regentessastraat 29, 2713 EM Zoetmeer, The Netherlands.

HAY Deborah Leigh, b. 30 May 1970, Middlesex, England. Musician (guitar); Singer; Composer; Teacher. m. Wayne Wiggins, 1 daughter. Education: BA Hons, Visual and Performing Arts, Brighton, 1988-91. Musical Education: Junior student, Trinity College of Music, London, 1982-88; MBT, The Playground, London, 1991. Career: Guitarist, Divas Dance Co; Arranger, El Punal Entra En El Corazón, 1991-93; Performed throughout Europe; Concerts include Queen Elizabeth Hall, 1991; Classic FM broadcast, 1993; Mute Opera, 1992-95; Composer, guitarist, Gaudette; Concerts include UK tours. Compositions include: Gaudette, 1992. Recordings: Nothing But Love, 1988; El Punal Entra En El Corazón, 1992; Gaudette, 1993. Honours: Alliance and Leicester Award, El Punal Entra En El Corazón, 1992; Billy Mayerl Award, 1987; Cornelius Cardew Composition Award, Gaudette, shortlisted 1993; South East Arts Award, Mute Opera. Memberships: Musicians' Union; Brighton New Music; Brighton Guitar Orchestra. Hobbies: Reading; Poetry; Painting; Swimming. Current Management: Self-managed. Address: 31 Ashbury Drive, Hawley, Camberley, Surrey GU17 9HH, England.

HAYES Isaac, b. 20 Aug 1942, Covington, Tennessee, USA. Rapper; Arranger; Musician (keyboards, organ). 11 children. Career: Leader, various groups; In-house keyboard player, staff songwriter (with David Porter) for Sam and Dave, Stax Records, 1964; Leader, arranger, Isaac Hayes Movement; Television actor, including Soul Survivors, BBC-TV, 1995; Rockford Files. Compositions include: Film scores: Shaft; Truck Turner; Tough Guys; As co-writer with David Porter: Hold On I'm Coming, Sam and Dave; Soul Man, Sam and Dave; B.A.B.Y., Carla Thomas; I Had A Dream, Johnnie Taylor. Recordings: Albums: Presenting Isaac Hayes, 1967; Hot Buttered Soul, 1969; The Isaac Hayes Movement, 1970; To Be Continued, 1971; Shaft, 1971; Black Moses, 1971; Joy, 1973; Live At The Sahara Tahoe, 1973; Tough Guys, 1974; Truck Turner, 1974; Chocolate Chip, 1975; Use Me, 1975; Disco Connection, 1976; Groove-A-Thon, 1976; Juicy Fruit, 1976; New Horizon, 1977; Man And A Woman, with Dionne Warwick, 1977; New Horizon, 1977; Memphis Movement, 1977; For The Sake Of Love, 1978; Don't Let Go, 1978; Royal Rappin', with Millie Jackson, 1980; And Once Again, 1980; Light My Fire, 1980; A Lifetime Thing, 1981; U Turn, 1986; Isaacs Moods, 1988; Love Attack, 1988; Branded, 1995; Raw And Refined, 1995. Honours: Oscar, Best Original Score, Shaft, 1972; Platinum disc, Hot Buttered Soul. Current Management: Ron Moss Management, 2635 Griffith Park Blvd, Los Angeles, CA 980039, USA.

HAYMES Jerry, b. 30 Aug 1940, Vernon, Texas, USA. Musician (drums, guitar); Vocalist; Actor; Speaker. m. (1) Brenda D, 1 Aug 1961, 1 son, 1 daughter; (2) Joan New, 1 Jan 1987. Education: BSc, Abilene Christian University; Kilgore College Police Academy. Musical

Education: Associate Music, Southern Methodist University. Career: World tours; Performed with Hometown USA Show, World Trade Fair, Berlin, 1961 (first Country show to do so); Performed in Russia at Russian Embassy's request; Armed Forces Radio; Television personality, newsman; Original member, Sun Records Legends Group; Session musician, many hits, various labels. Recordings: Major hits: Rose Marie; Smile Of A Clown; Big Big World; Marry Me; So Fine (Caroline); Let's Have A Party; Party Doll; What Then (gospel hit for Mahalia Jackson). Publications: Southwest Conference Baseball Umpire. Honours: Male vocalist; Bandleader, Video commercial, Gospel Music Association Songwriter Awards. Memberships: AFofM; President, Texas Art and Entertainment Council. Hobbies: Music; Law enforcement; Sport official. Current Management: Umpire Entertainment Enterprises. Address: 1507 Scenic Drive, Longview, TX 75604, USA.

HAYNE Michael (Shane), 22 Nov 1937, Plymouth, England. Vocalist. m. Heather Anne Tarry, 26 June 1971, 1 son, 1 daughter. Education: Warren's College, Plymouth. Career: Lead vocalist, R&B band The Betterdays, 1963-66; Television appearances: Westward TV; TSW; Radio: BBC Plymouth; BBC Radio Devon; Plymouth Sound; Tours throughout UK, 1991-. Recordings: Here Tis; Cracking Up; Aw Shucks; Hush Your Mouth; Don't Want That; Honey What's Wrong; (all 1964-65); EPs: Howl Of The Streets, 1991; Down On The Waterfront, 1992; Here Tis, 1992; No Concessions, 1993; Also featured on compilation albums, Australia, France, USA. Hobbies: 5-a-side football; Cricket; Reading; History. Current Management: Mike Weston. Address: 4 Ashburnham Road, West Park, Plymouth PL5 2LR, England.

HAYNES Kevin, b, 5 Feb 1965, Paddington, London, England. Musician (saxophone, percussion). 1 son. Education: North London College of Performing Arts, 1984-85. Theory, Kingsway College, 1986-87. Career: Concerts; Tours, Oshmare Brazilian Theatre and Dance Companies; Tours with: Steve Williamson, UK; Courtney Pine, UK, Israel, 1990; Own group, UK tour, 1994; Radio: BBC Radio 3 and 4 (Kaleidoscope). Recordings: Albums: Ed Jones: The Home Coming, 1988; Steve Williamson: Waltz For Grace, 1989; with Courtney Pine: Bath Jazz Festival, 1993; Kevin Haynes Group: Eleggra, 1994; Recording track for Bachology, 1995. Membership: Musicians' Union. Current Management: Fish Krish.

HAYNES Warren Dale, b. 6 Apr 1960, Ashville, North Carolina, USA. Singer; Songwriter; Musician (guitar, slide guitarist); Producer. Musical Education: Self-taught (with high school theory course). Career: David Allan Coe, 1980-84; Studio musician, 1984-87; Dickey Betts Band, 1987-89; Allman Bros Band, 1989-; Currently solo artist, member of Government Mule, 1994-; Worldwide tours: Johnny Carson; Jay Lane; Conan O'Brian; David Letterman. Compositions: (co-writer), Two Of A Kind (Workin' On A Full House) for Garth Brooks; True Gravity; A Kind Of A Bird; Recordings: Allman Bros Band albums: Seven Turns; Shades Of Two Worlds; An Evening With...; Where It All Begins; Second Set; Solo album: Tales Of Ordinary Madness. Honours: 2 Grammy Nominations; Allman Bros Band inducted into R&R Hall of Fame, 1995. Memberships: AFTRA; AFofM; BMI. Hobbies: Outdoors; Travel; Musical Activities. Current Management: Doc Field, Creative Action Music; Address: 865 Bellevue Road, Suite E-12, Nashville, TN 37221, USA.

HAYTON William, b. 20 Feb 1969, London, England. Musician (drums, percussion). m. Emilia Hayton, 9 Jan 1992, 1 son, 1 daughter. Musical Education: Graduate Diploma, Jazz and Contemporary Music, Post Graduate Diploma,

Jazz, Contemporary Music, Leeds College Of Music. Career: Played on Radio 2, 3, live and recorded; Tours, Switzerland, Russia, with brass bands; Played all over UK, with Andy Prior Orchestra, including 4 Blackpool summer seasons; Television work includes: Pebble Mill; Good Morning Britain; Primetime; Talking Telephone Numbers; The Generation Game; Granada Tonight; 1 hour Granada television special: A Prior Engagement, also on video; Tour in Madeira; Cabaret work throughout UK and Europe; Aladdin, Cambridge, 1995; Function Band Work, Duncan Norvelle Show, Blackpool, 1996; Peter Pan, Cambridge, 1996; Recordings: with PURR: The Good Times Are Killing Me; with Andy Prior Orchestra: At Last, Alright, OK, You Win; with Hammonds Brass Band: Many Happy Returns, Festivo; with Brighouse And Rastrick Brass Band: B & R For Christmas. Publications: Drumkit Foundation Course, Books 1-3. Honour: College Prize For Kit Drumming, CLCM, 1990-91. Memberships: Hull Music Collective; Musicians' Union. Hobbies: Sports; Arts and Crafts; Star Trek - The Next Generation. Current Management: Self-managed. Address: 51 Cotterdale, Sutton Park Estate, Hull, North Humberside HU7 4AA, England.

HAYWARD (David) Justin, b. 14 Oct 1946, Swindon, Wiltshire, England. Singer; Musician (guitar). Career: Member, The Offbeats; Marty Wilde trio; Singer, The Moody Blues, 1967-74; 1978-; Appearances include: Isle Of Wight Festival, 1969; Royal Albert Hall, 1969; Royal Festival Hall, London, 1970; Carnegie Hall, New York, 1970; Opened own recording studio, London, 1974; Solo recording career, 1974-. Recordings: Singles include: (own composition) Nights In White Satin, 1968; Question; Isn't Life Strange; I'm Just A Singer (In A Rock'n'Roll Band); Gemini Dream; The Voice; Your Wildest Dreams; It Won't Be Easy; Solo: Forever Autumn; Albums: with the Moody Blues: Days Of Future Passed, 1967; In Search Of The Lost Chord, 1968; On The Threashold Of A Dream, 1969; To Our Children's Children, 1969; Caught Live + 5, 1969; A Question Of Balance, 1970; Every Good Boy Deserves Favour, 1971; Seventh Sojourn, 1972; This Is The Moody Blues, 1974; Octave, 1978; Out Of This World, 1979; Long Distance Voyager, 1981; The Present, 1983; Voices In The Sky, 1985; The Other Side Of Life, 1986; Sur La Mer, 1988; Keys Of The Kingdom, 1991; Live At Red Rock, 1993; Solo albums: Blue Jays, with John Lodge, 1975; Songwriter, 1977; Night Flight, 1980; Moving Mountains, 1985; Classic Blue, 1989; Contributor, War Of The Worlds, Jeff Wayne, 1978. Honour: Ivor Novello Award, Outstanding Contribution to British Music (with the Moody Blues), 1985. Address: c/o Bright Music Ltd, 2 Harwood Terrace, London SW6 2AB, England.

HAZELL Patrick James, b. 23 Sept 1945, Burlington, Iowa, USA. Musician (piano, organ, harmonica, drums); Singer; Songwriter. m. Pamela Ann Cummings, 28 Oct 1967, 3 sons, 1 daughter. Education: College Degree. Musical Education: College classes, recording techniques. Career: Professional musician, 1960-; Founder, Mother Blues Band, 1968-70; Founder, Sound Pool, 1972; Member, Rocket 88's; Reformed Mother Blues Band, 1973-83; Solo performer, 1983-; Music instructor, Washington High School, 1987-; Numerous tours, Midwest US and Germany; Concerts supporting: Led Zeppelin; Jefferson Airplane; John Mayall; Robert Cray; Muddy Waters; John Lee Hooker; George Thorogood; Suzy Bogguss; Luther Allison; Asleep At The Wheel; Junior Walker. Recordings: Albums include Band Music, Volume 1, 1975; Volume 2, 1978; Volume 3, 1980; Vicksburg Volume 1, 1981; Volume 2, 1981; Christmas Visions, 1982; Studios Solos, 1985; The New Cool, 1986; Solo Improvisations, 1986; Patrick Hazell-Live!, 1987; Blues Jam, 1988; East Of Midnight, 1989; Nemo's Island, 1989; Mystery Winds, 1989; Santa Was Eating The Christmas Tree/Nicci And The Project,

1989; Tuba And Piano Jam Session, 1990; Blues on the Run, 1995; Patrick Hazell and the Mother Blues Band, 1975-1980, 1996; In The Prairieland, 1996; Dreamcatcher, 1996; Blue Blood, 1997; Soundtracks, 1997; Cityscape Precipice, 1997. Honours: 4 Prairie Sun Awards, Best Rhythm and Blues Band; Memberships: Arts Midwest; Iowa Arts Council; Touring Arts Team Of Iowa. Official endorsee, Hohner Harmonicas. Hobbies: Music. Address: 220 E 17th Street, Washington, IA 52353, USA.

HEALEY Jeff, b. 25 Mar 1966, Toronto, Ontario, Canada. Blues/Rock Musician (guitar, multi-instrumentalist); Singer; Actor. Career: Blind since age 1; Founder, Blue Direction aged 15, Toronto; Played with Albert Collins; Stevie Ray Vaughn; Founder, Jeff Healey Band, 1985; Own record label, Forte, 1985-88; World tour, 1990; Actor, singer, film Roadhouse, 1989. Recordings: Albums: See The Light, 1989; Hell To Pay, 1990; Feel This, 1992; Cover To Cover, 1995; Featured on film soundtrack, Roadhouse, 1989. Address: c/o Forte Records and Productions, 320 Spadina Road, Toronto, Ontario M5R 2V6, Canada.

HEALY Francis, b. 1973, Scotland. Vocalist. Career: Lead singer, Travis, 1990-; Concert performances include support to Oasis, 1997. Recordings include: Debut album: Good Feeling, 1997; Debut single: All I Wanna Do Is Rock. Address: c/o Wildlife Entertainment Ltd, 21 Heathmans Road, London SW6 4TJ, England.

HEALY Jeremy, b. 18 Jan 1962, Woolwich, London, England. Disc Jockey. Career: Formed band Haysi Fantayzee with Kate Garner; 2 hits worldwide; Became scratching-mixing Disc Jockey. Recordings: John Wayne Is Big Leggy, Haysi Fantayzee; Shiny Shiny, Sabres Of Paradise; Everything Starts With An "E", Easy Possee. Honours: Gold album, Haysi Fantayzee; Silver single, John Wayne Is Big Leggy; DJ of the Year, Mixmag, 1995; Most Popular Face, 1995. Membership: PRS. Hobby: Travel. Current Management: Francesca Cutler, Selective Management. Address: 6 Brewer Street, London W1R 3FR, England.

HEAPE Emma A M, b. 16 Dec 1954, Sussex, England. Musician (hurdy gurdy); Singer. m. Guy Corbett Heape, 30 Sept 1978. Musical Education: Studied hurdy gurdy with Nigel Eaton, 1988-93. Career: Member, bands: Les Cloches (traditional); Pure Glass (Rock). Membership: Musicians' Union. Address: 1 Warren Crest, Froxfield, Petersfield, Hampshire GU32 1BL, England.

HEARN Martin Peter, b. 3 Dec 1955, London, England. Musician (drum, percussion); Teacher. m. Noelle Loyd, 16 Aug 1986, 4 sons. Musical Education: National Youth Jazz Association. Career: Worked with: The Drifters; David Soul; Joe Longthorne; Ben E King; Tommy Cooper; Cilla Black; Michael Barrymore; Bob Monkhouse; Joe Longthorne; John Paul James; National Youth Jazz Orchestra; London West End Shows: Cats; Evita; Me And My Girl; Rocky Horror Show; NYSO; North Sea Festival; Montrose Jazz Festival; Pebble Mill; Sunday Sunday; Founder of STIX School Of Rhythm, Music school for the rhythm section of modern music, working bands, 1994. Honours: Rock And Roll Hall Of Fame, with the Drifters, 1985. Memberships: National Youth Jazz Association; NYSO; Musicians' Union; Chamber of Commerce and Trade. Hobbies: Scuba diving; Camping; Photography. Current Management: STIX School of Rhythm, Noëlle Hearn. Address: STIX School of Rhythm, Kings Arm Yard, Church Street, Ampthill, Bedfordshire MK45 2PJ, England.

HEATH Martin, b. 12 Mar 1961, Sussex, England. Record Company Executive. Education: BA Hons. Career: Managing Director, UK-based indie record label Rhythm King Records,

co-founded with Adele Nozedar, 1986; Founder, Renegade Software and Perfect World Programmes. Hobbies: Horse riding; Sailing; Walking; Military history. Address: c/o Rhythm King Records, 121 Salisbury Road, London NW6 6RG, England.

HEATH Rohan Vernon, b. 19 July 1964, Wembley, London, England. Songwriter; Musician (keyboards). Education: BSc, Biology; MSc, Entomology. Musical Education: Grade IX Piano, Victoria College of Music. Career: Keyboards, A Guy Called Gerald, 1990-91; Keyboards, Together, 1991-92; Keyboards, Eek A Mouse, 1992-93; Leader, Urban Cookie Collective, 1993-; Tours include: USA, Canada, Australia, Japan, Singapore, UK, Europe, Israel, Lithuania, Turkey. Compositions: Automatik, A Guy Called Gerald (co-wrote); Urban Cookie Collective hit singles: The Key The Secret; Feels Like Heaven; Sail Away; High On A Happy Vibe; Bring It On Home. Publications: The Phylogenetic Significance Of The Ventral Nervous Chord In Carabid Beetles, Journal of Entomology. Honours: Platinum and Gold discs; Music Week Independent Single, 1994; Perfect 10 Award, Best Live Act, Singapore, 1994. Hobbies: Travel; Music. Current Management: Self-managed. Address: c/o Blitz, Edgeware Bury Farm, Edgeware Bury Lane, Edgeware HA8 8QX, England.

HEATLIE Bob, b. 20 July 1946, Edinburgh, Scotland. Musician (keyboards, saxophone, flute). m. Mary Jane Davie, 3 Mar 1967, 3 sons. Musical Education: Taught by father, Thomas Heatlie. Recordings: Aneka: Japanese Boy, Number 1; Merry Christmas Everyone, Number 1; Cry Just A Little Bit; Many television theme tunes. Honours: 8 Gold discs (singles); 1 Silver and 1 Platinum (albums); 2 ASCAP Awards. Memberships: MCPS; PRS; BASCA. Hobbies: Photography; Drawing. Address: 3 Victoria Street, Edinburgh EH1 2HE, Scotland.

HEATON Paul David, b. 9 May 1962, Birkenhead, Merseyside, England. Singer; Songwriter; Musician. Career: Lead singer, The Housemartins, 1983-88; Released 8 singles (6 Top 20 hits); 3 albums; Founder, The Beautiful South; Releases to date: 14 singles (11 Top 40); 5 albums (All top 5); Concerts include: T In The Park Festival, Glasgow, 1995; McAlpine Stadium, Crystal Palace Stadium, 1997. Recordings: Albums: with the Housemartins: London 0 Hull 4, 1986; The People Who Grinned Themselves To Death, 1987; Now That's What I Call Quite Good, 1988; with the Beautiful South: Welcome To The Beautiful South, 1989; Choke, 1990; 0898, 1992; Miaow, 1994; Blue is the Colour, (No 1, UK); Singles: with the Housemartins: Happy Hour; Think For A Minute; Caravan Of Love; Me And The Farmer; with the Beautiful South: Song For Whoever; I'll Sail This Ship Alone; You Keep It All In; A Little Time (Number 1, UK); My Book; Let Love Speak Up Itself; Old Red Eyes Is Back; We Are Each Other; Bell-Bottomed Tear; Good As Gold; Everybody's Talkin'; Prettiest Eyes; One Last Love Song; Roptterdam; Don't Marry Her; Blackbird on the Wire; Liars Bar. Honours: BPI Awards: Best Newcomers, the Housemartins, 1987; Best Video, A Little Time, The Beautiful South, 1991. Hobbies: Watching and playing football; Writing. Current Management: Self-managed under cooperative agreement. Address: The Beautiful South, PO Box 87, Hull, East Yorkshire HU5 2NR, England.

HECTOR Kevin Jon, b. 17 Jan 1967, Nantwich, Cheshire, England. Producer; Musician (guitar); Electronic artist. Education: Fashion, St Martins. Musical Education: Classical singing; Jazz/classical guitar. Session guitarist, 1983-87; London Club DJ, 1988-; Dance producer, 1990-; Autocreation world tour, 1993; Including live broadcast on Japan TV. Compositions: Miscellaneous dance compositions. Recordings: Mettle, Autocreation. Hobbies: Surfing; Writing.

Address: PO Box 3605, London NW8 0DD, England.

HEDEGAARD Svend, b. 19 December 1959, Sonderborg, Denmark. Musician; Composer. Education: Private Studies and Several Seminars in Composition; Guitar and piano lessons. Career: Guitarist, numerous rock, fusion and jazz bands, 1979-98; Composer, 15 theatre plays, 6 television productions, several major works for different classical ensembles and orchestras in Denmark, 1986-98; Wind O Four, jazz fusion quartet, 1991-. Compositions: Maximal/Minimal, 1991; Some Colours Remain, Some Remind, 1991; Twins Turn, 1996; Efter regnen sas..., 1996; Sangenes Sang, 1997. Recordings: With Wind O Four, Jazz Quartet, 1995, Voices, 1997. Honours: Laurens Bogtman Fondens Haederslegat, 1996; DJBFA, Arbejdslegat, 1997. Memberships: Danish Musicians Union; Danish Jazz, Beat and Folk Music Composers; KODA. Hobbies: Painting; Nature; Music. Address: Romersgade 23 2 tv, 1362 Kobenhavn K, Denmark.

HEDGES Mike. Record Producer. Career: Engineer, Morgan Studios, late 1970s-80s; Founder, Playground Studios, 1980s; Converted Chateau Rouge Motte, Normandy, into full residential studio, 1990. Recordings: Producer, albums include: with Siouxie & The Banshees: Kiss In A Dreamhouse; Hyena; Peep Show; Nocturne; Through The Looking Glass; with Marc Almond: Vermine In Ermine; Stories Of Johnny; A Woman's Story; Mother Fist; with The Beautiful South: Welcome To The Beautiful South; Choke; with The Cure: Three Imaginary Boys; Seventeen Seconds; Faith; Split, Lush; Baby The Stars Shine Bright, Everything But The Girl; Drop, The Shamen; Mask, Bauhaus; Also singles with Wah!; Bauhaus; The Cure; Siouxie & The Banshees; The Creatures; Marc Almond; Everything But The Girl; The Beautiful South. Current Management: c/o Stephen Budd Management, 109B Regents Park Road, London NW1 8UR, England.

HEIL Gail A Ferfecky, b. 20 August 1945, St Louis, Missouri, USA. Musician; Singer. m. Bob Bovee, 8 December 1988. Education: University of Missouri. Career: Regular Tours, USA, 1980-; Iowa Public Television; River City Folk; Rural Route 3; Other Syndicated Radio Shows; Festival of American Fiddle Tunes. Recordings: For Old Time's Sake, 1985; Behind the Times, 1986; Come All You Waddies, 1988; Come Over and See Me, 1991; Rural Route 2, 1996. Honours: Master Fiddler, Iowa State Folk Arts Apprenticeship Program and Minnesota State Folk Arts Apprenticeship Program. Hobby: Gardening. Address: Rt 2 Box 25, Spring Grove, MN 55974, USA.

HEINILA Kari Juhani, b. 31 October 1966, Kiukainen, Finland. Arja Mäkelä, 2 sons, 1 daughter. Education: Classical Piano and Flute in Music School, Saxophone and Improvisation in Sibelius Academy's Jazz Department, 1984-88; Private composing studies, 1993-95. Career: Saxophonist, Umo Jazz Orchestra, 1987-93; Jazz Groups under own name, 1987-; Recordings and concerts with the top names in Finnish Jazz; Performings with such internationally respected Jazz Artists as Billy Hart, Tim Hagans, Vince Mendoza, Anders Jormin and Wayne Krantz; Active Composer in contemporary jazz scene; Regular Techer, Sibelius Academy's Jazz Department, 1993-. Compositions: Frozen Petals; Blue in the Distance; Crossings; Wavestar. Recordings: Espoo Big Band: Grand Mystery; Jarmo Savolainen: Blue Dreams, True Image; Edward Vesala: Lumi; Umo Jazz Orchestra: Selected Standards; Pekka Luukka: Splash of Colors; Jukka Linkola, The Tentet. Honours: BAT-Finland Composition Prize, 1992; Pori Jazz Festival's Artist of the Year Prize, 1995. Address: Hannuksenkuja 4A3, 02270 Espoo, Finland.

HELFER Erwin, b. 20 Jan 1936, Chicago, Illinois, USA. Blues and Jazz Musician (piano); Piano teacher. Musical Education: Mus B American Conservatory of Music; Mus M, Northeastern Illinois University. Career: Annual performances at Chicago Blues Festival; Annual concert tours, Europe, Rolf Schubert Concertburo, Cologne, Germany; Plays in local jazz and blues clubs, Chicago; College tours, USA; Recording artist for Flying Fish; Steeple Chase; Red Beans; CMA. Recordings: Erwin Helfer And Friends On The Sunny Side Of The Street, 1979; Erwin Helfer Plays Chicago Piano, 1986. Honours: Critics Choice Award, Maybee I'll Cry, Downbeat Magazine, 1983; Illinois Arts Council Grant, 1986; Nomination for Jazz Music Award, National Association for Campus Activities. Hobbies: Animals; Transpersonal psychology; Comparative religion; Reading; Gardening. Current Management: Erwin Helfer, 2240 N Magnolia, Chicago, IL 60614, USA.

HELLER Jana Louise Greenberg, b. 18 July 1948, California, USA. Singer; Songwriter; Musician (guitar, dulcimer, piano, celestaphone). m. Michael Heller, 31 Oct 1968. Education: Stephens College, Missouri, University of Southern California, USA; UCLA, Santa Monica City College. Musical Education: 8 years piano. Career: Solo work; Bands: AAAHS; The Phantoms; Concerts, folk, music festivals: UK; US; Poland; Radio: KPFK's Folkscene, Los Angeles, USA; Kroc, USA; Radio Poznan, Poland; BBC Radio II (We Stayed In With Jungr And Parker); GLR Radio; London Talkback Radio; BBC Radio Essex Folkscene. Recordings: Mad Waltzing, 1986; Twist And Turn, 1990; Laughing In Crime, 1995. Honours: American Song Festival, winner lyric division. Memberships: Musicians' Union; PRS. Hobbies: Travel; Writing and illustrating childrens' books; Antique clothing; Horse riding. Current Agent: The Claran Agency, 3 Dorset Road, Ealing, London W5 4HV; Current Management: La Camera Productions Management. Address: 2 Friars Close, Wilmslow, Cheshire SK9 5PP, England.

HELLQUIST Mats, b. 15 May 1964, Stockholm, Sweden. Musician (bass, guitar). 1 son, 2 daughters. Education: Self-taught bass and guitar. Career: Member, bob hund, 1991; More than 250 gigs around Scandinavia; Played at famous Roskilde, Lollipop, Ruisrock Quartfestivalen and Hultsfred. Compositions: I Stället för Musik: Förvirring, 1996, Düsseldorf, 1996. Recordings: bob hund - bob hund, 1993; bob hund - Edvin Medvind, 1994; bob hund - Omslag: Martin Kann, 1996. Honours: Grammy, best live act, 1994; Grammy, best lyrics, 1996. Memberships: STIM; SAMI. Hobbies: Music; Books; Food; Drinking. Address: Box 53045, 400 14 Göteborg, Sweden.

HELLRIEGEL Jan, b. 2 Sept 1967, Auckland, New Zealand. Musician (piano, guitar); Singer; Songwriter; Actor. Education: BA, University of Otago. Musical Education: Classical singing and piano; Rock guitar; University papers. Career: 4 national solo tours, 8 with band; TVNZ Music Awards Television and Film Awards, New Zealand, 1993; Big Day Out Concert, supporting Bavid Byrne, The Cure. Recordings: Singles: The Way I Feel; Manic Is A State Of Mind; Solo albums: It's My Sin, 1993; Tremble, 1995; with Cassandras Ears Band: Private Wasteland (EP), 1990; Your Estimation, 1992 (EP); with Working With Walt: 5 Sides (EP), 1990. Honours: Songwriter of the Year, 1993; Most Promising Female Vocalist, 1993; Nomination, Entertainer of the Year, 1993. Hobbies: Reading; Films; Social Services. Current Management: MGM Management, 9 Dundas Lane, Albert Park, Victoria 3206, Australia.

HELMIS Dimitrios, b. 11 Jan 1962, Pireaus, Greece. Promoter; Agent. 1 son. Career: Owner, Neo Revma International Ltd, 10 years promoting and booking international and local acts in Greece and Balkan area; Hundreds of shows include: Pink Floyd; Michael Jackson; The Scorpions; Stevie Wonder; Guns'n'Roses; Metallica; Philip Glass; Goran Bregovic; Michael Nyman; Neville Brothers. Address: Neo Revma International Ltd, 8 Ainanos Str 104-34, Athens, Greece.

HELSON Robert (Bob), b. 20 Aug 1949, Bristol, England. Music (drums, percussion). Musical Education: Drum lessons with Geoff Smith, 1966-69. Career: Drummer with: Plasma, early 1970's; Bullit, 1974-1990; Appearances with Bullit include: Bracknell Festival, 1986; Le Mans Jazz Festival, 1987; Will Menter's Wind And Fingers, appearing at Bristol Arnolfini and Dunkirk Jazz Festival, 1976; Both Hands Free, 1976-82; Community, appearing at Palais de Beaux Arts, Brussels and Arnolfini, 1980-81; Out Loud, 1984-87; Keith Tippett's Canoe, 1984-85; Currently with rock band RiffRaff; Dance and percussion duet with dancer Beppie Blankert, Bristol Arnolfini, 1981; Broadcasts on BBC Radio 3, Jazz In Britain, with: Both Hands Free, 1979; Steve Mulligan Quartet, 1983, 1984; Out Loud, 1986; Bullit, 1987. Recordings: with Both Hands Free: Use From The Pocket, 1978; Solo percussion improvisations: Noise Reduction, 1979; Will Menter's Community, 1981. Hobbies: Nature; Countryside; Screaming about the mess we're making of this planet. Address: Basement Flat, 34 Cornwallis Crescent, Clifton, Bristol BS8 4PH, England.

HEMMINGS Paul, b. 24 May 1963, Liverpool, England. Musician (guitar, lap steel, mandolin). Education: BA, History and Politics, North Staffs Polytechnic. Career: Guitarist with the La's, 1986-87; Guitarist with The Onset, The Australians, Sensurround, 1988-93; Guitarist, Lightning Seeds, 1994-; Tours: UK; Europe; USA; Various radio sessions; Television appearances include: Danny Baker Show; Music Box; What's Up Doc; Top Of The Pops; German TV. Composition: Co-writer: Saddest Song; Shake, Shake, Shake. Recordings: Albums: Pool Of Life, The Onset, 1988; Timeless Melody, The La's, 1990; Electric Mothers Of Invention, Neuro # Project, 1993; Pool Of Life Revisited, The Onset, 1994. Other recordings: Way Out (EP), The La's, 1987; What You Say (EP), The Onset, 1990; When I Get To Heaven (single), Sensurround, 1993; Lucky You (live single), Lightning Seeds, 1994; With Lightning Seeds, What If; Here Today (live version), Hillsborough Justice Concert, 3 live tracks with Lightning Seeds and Holly Johnson. Honours: Brit Awards, 2 consecutive years. Memberships: Musicians' Union; PRS. Hobbies: Photography; Cinema; The Arts; Sport. Address: Woodcroft, Beaconsfield Road, Liverpool L25 6EJ, England.

HENDERSON Hamish Scott, b. 11 Nov 1919, Blairgowrie, Perthshire, Scotland. Poet; Songwriter. m. Felicity Schmidt, 16 May 1959, 2 daughters. Education: Downing College, Cambridge. Musical Education: With traditional singers, Perthshire and Aberdeenshire. Career: Collection of soldiers songs in WWII, published in Ballads of World War II, 1947; Collection of North-East Scottish folk songs with Alan Lomax, 1951; Joined School of Scottish Studies, Edinburgh University, 1952; Collection of Gaelic and Lowland Scottish Songs and Tales. Compositions: Numerous songs popular with Scottish folk revival include: The Freedom Come'All'Ye; The 51st Highland Division's Farewell To Sicily; The Gillie More; The Men Of Knoydart. Recordings: Album: Freedom Come-All-Ye. Publications: Elegies For The Dead In Cyrenaica, 1948; Alias MacAlias, essays on folklore, 1992; The Armstrong Nose, selected letters, 1996; Gramsci's Prison Letters, 1996. Honour: Somerset Maugham Award, 1949. Memberships: Hon. Member, Saltire Society, Edinburgh; Hon. Member, Folklore Fellows, Helsinki; Hon. Fellow, School of Scottish Studies.

Hobbies: Singing; Songwriting. Address: 20 Melville Terrace, Edinburgh EH9 1LY, Scotland.

HENDERSON Scott, b. 26 Aug 1954, West Palm Beach, Florida, USA. Composer; Musician (guitarist). Education: Florida Atlantic University, 1 year Musicians Institute. Career: Touring, recording, 1981-; 3 years with Jean-Luc Ponty; 1 year, Chick Corea; 4 years, Joe Zawinul; 10 years, Tribal Tech (co-led, Gary Willis). Recordings: Albums: with Tribal Tech: Spears; Dr Hee; Nomad; Tribal Tech; Illicit; Face First; Reality Check; Solo album: Dog Party; with Joe Zawinul: The Immigrants; Black Water; with Chick Corea: Elektrik Band. Publications: The Scott Henderson Guitar Book. Honours: Best Jazz Guitarist, Guitar World magazine, 1990; Guitar Player magazine, 1991; Best Blues Album, Dog Party, Guitar Player magazine, 1994. Hobby: Dogs. Address: 6044 Buena Vista, Los Angeles, CA 90042, USA.

HENDRICKS Michele, b. 27 Sept 1953, New York, USA. Vocalist. m. Pierre Bornard, 28 July 1992. Education: 2 years college. Musical Education: Music major at college. Career: Appearances at: North Sea Festival; Monterey Festival; Montreal Festival; Vienna; Pori; Marciac; Juan Les Pins; Nice; Crest; Mt Fuji; Television: Johnny Carson; Mike Douglas; various local television in Europe, Japan, USA; Has sung with: Jon Hendricks; Buddy Rich; Stan Getz; Count Basie; Bennie Golson; Slide Hampton; George Benson; Al Jarreau; Bobby McFerrin; Roland Hannah; Herbie Hancock; Freddie Hubbard. Recordings: Me And My Shadow; Keepin' Me Satisfied; Carryin' On; Live At Ronnie Scott's With Buddy Rich; Love with Jon Hendricks and Company; The Peacocks with Stan Getz and Jimmy Rowles; Vocal Summit; Santa's Bag; Second Impression; Boppin' At The Blue Note. Honours: Grammy Nomination, Best Jazz Vocal Group, Love. Memberships: ASCAP; Shellrose Music (ASCAP); Jon Hendricks. Hobbies: Cooking; Arranging. Current Management: Pee Bee Jazz, Pierre Bornard. Address: 182 Rue Nationale, 75013 Paris, France.

HENLEY Don, b. 22 July 1947, Linden, Texas, USA. Musician (drums); Vocalist. Career: Member, The Four Speeds, 1963; Member, Shiloh, 1970; Founder member, The Eagles, 1971-; Solo artiste, 1982-; Performances include: California Jam Festival, 1974; Solo appearances; Guest drummer with Guns'N'Roses, American Music Awards, 1989; Indian River Festival, 1991; Madison Square Garden, 1991. Recordings: Albums: with the Eagles: The Eagles, 1972; Desperado, 1973; On The Border, 1974; One Of These Nights (Number 1, US), 1975; Their Greatest Hits 1971-75 (Number 1, US), 1976; Hotel California (Number 1, US), 1977; The Long Run (Number 1, US), 1979; Live, 1980; Eagles' Greatest Hits, Vol 2, 1982; The Best Of The Eagles, 1985; Solo albums: I Can't Stand Still, 1982; Building The Perfect Beast, 1984; The End Of Innocence, 1989; Featured on Leap Of Faith (film soundtrack), 1992; Contributor, Amused To Death, Rogers Waters, 1992; Producer, title track, Tell Me The Truth, Timothy B Schmit, 1990; Singles include: The Best Of My Love (Number 1, US), 1975; One Of These Nights (Number 1, US), 1975; Lyin' Eyes, 1975; Take It To The Limit, 1976; New Kid In Town (Number 1, US), 1977; Hotel California (Number 1, US), 1977; Heartache Tonight (Number 1, US), 1979; Duet with Stevie Nicks: Leather And Lace, 1982; Solo hits: Dirty Laundry, 1983; The Boys Of Summer, 1985. Honours: Grammy Awards: Best Pop Vocal, 1976; Record Of The Year, 1978; Best Rock Vocal, 1986; American Music Awards, 1977, 1981; MTV Music Video Awards, 1985, 1990; People For The American Way's Spirit Of Liberty Award, 1990; Boston Music Awards, Special Recognition Award, 1992. Current Management: c/o Irving Azoff, Revolution, 8900 Wilshire Blvd, Suite 200, Beverly Hills, CA 90211, USA.

HENNES Peter Michael, b. 25 Feb 1954, Great Lakes, Illinois, USA. Musician (guitar, bass); Educator. Education: Wayne State University, 1972; University of Michigan, 1973-74. Musical Education: Professional diploma, Berklee College of Music, Boston, 1978. Career: Musician with numerous artistes including: Frank Sinatra; Liza Minnelli; Perry Como; Anthony Newley; Marvin Hamlisch; Musician, touring stage productions including: Grease; Evita; A Chorus Line; 42nd Street; La Cage Aux Folles; Instructor, Jazz Studies, Georgia State University School Of Music, 1982-88. Membership: AFofM.

HENNING Ann-Marie Elisabeth, b. 2 December 1952, Stockholm, Sweden. Jazz Musician; Composer; Arranger. Education: Royal Academy of Music, Stockholm, 5 years; Berkeley College of Music, Boston, USA, 2 years. Career: Tours in Sweden and Europe with Rockband NQB, 1973-74; Member, Jazzrock Group, Wave Play, 1978; Own Jazz Group, Blue Cluster, 1987; Jazz Festivals, Radio Concerts; Out of Blue Cluster, Formed Red Cluster, 1992; Pianist, Big Band Jatin Dolls, Television, Saturday Night Live Show, Theatre Shows; Accompanist to Musical Artists. Compositions: April Light, for Big Band; The Trees Are Listening; Waltz for Evert; The Rubber Jolly Boat. Recordings: Blue Cluster, 1989; Tidal Dreams, 1997. Publication: Co-Author, The Real Swede. Honours: Swedish Composers Organization Grant, 1987, 1996; Swedish Composers of Popular Music Grant, 1993. Memberships: Swedish Composers Organization; Swedish Composers of Popular Music; Swedish Jazz Musicians Organization. Hobbies: Sailing; Nature. Address: Finnbodav 9B, 131 31 Nacka, Sweden.

HENOCQ Benjamin, b. 1969. Musician (drums). Musical Education: Private lessons, 1976-83; Conservatoire du Centre de Paris, 1983-85; Ecole Agostini, IACP, 1985-87; Private lessons with Daniel Humair; Paul Motian; Keith Copeland. Career: Member, PRYSM; Jean-Christophe Beney Quartet; Jean-Christophe Cholet Quartet; David Patrois Quintet; Philippe Sellam Quintet; Les Standardistes (Funk Octet); Phantastique Orchestre Modulaire; Quoi de Neuf Docteur Big Band; Numerous clubs, Paris; Festivals, France; Played with: Eric Le Lann; Stéphane Belmondo; Robin Eubanks; Glenn Ferris; Tommy Smith; Red Holloway; Rick Margitza; François Janneau; Lionel Belmondo; Sylvain Beuf; Geoffroy de Mazure; Peter Osborne; Olivier Ker-Ourio; Philip Catherine; Louis Winsberg; Harold Land; Laurent de Wilde; Franck Amsallem; Andy Emler; Denis Badault; Wayne Dockery; Henri Texier; Michel Benita; Patrice Caratini; Paul Breslin; Jean-Marc Thorès; KARTET; Teacher, IACP, 1986-88. Recordings: Le Retour, Quoi de Neuf Docteur Big Band, 1991; Hask, KARTET, 1992; En Attendent La Pluie, Quoi de Neuf Docteur Big Band, 1993; AL'Envers, Quoi de Neuf Docteur Big Band, 1994; Pression, KARTET, 1995; La Compil, Instant Charirés, 1995; PRYSM, PRYSM, 1995. Honours: 1st Prize, La Défense National Jazz Contest, 1994; Soloist Award, La Défense National Jazz Contest, 1994. Address: 55 Rue Navier, 75017 Paris, France.

HENRIK Wellejus, b. 15 December 1954, Frederiksberg, Copenhagen, Denmark. Composer; Musician. Education: Private Musical Education. Career: Theatre Music Appearances: En Rede i Traeet, 1983; Det Umuligste Af Alt, 1986; Fra Bord Til Bord, 1987; Hvor Godtfolk Er, 1988; Orla Frösnapper, 1990; Otto Er Et Naesehorn, 1993. Honour: Winner, Music Contest, Young Music Magazine. Membership: Danish Songwriters Guild. Hobbies: Television; Classical music; Reading; Bible reading. Current Management: Radiophelia, 928 MHZ, Box 6, 3100 Hornbaek, Denmark. Address: Sauntevaenget 14B, 3100 Hornbaek, Denmark.

HENRIKSON Richard Ralph, b. 27 Nov 1948, Portland, Oregon, USA. Composer; Lyricist; Musician (violin). Musical Education: BS, Juillard School Of Music, 1972; MusM, 1973. Career: Violinist, various orchestras and chamber ensembles, 1970-; Violinist, Barnum, Broadway, 1980-82; Musical director, musical stage productions include: Singing In The Rain; Sweet Charity; Me And My Girl; Fiddler On The Roof; Les Miserables, 1991-; Musical director, violinist, numerous artistes including: Tom Jones; Billy Ocean; George Benson; Freddie Jackson; Jeffrey Osborne; Stephanie Mills; Gregg Allman; Rick Wakeman; Paul Anka. Recordings: Albums with: Music Minus One; The Tango Project; Hampton String Quartet; Violinist, film soundtracks: The Wiz; Silkwood; The Cotton Club; When Harry Met Sally; Do The Right Thing; Recordings by numerous artistes including: Diana Ross; Sheena Easton; Paul Simon; Billy Cobham; John Sebastian. Memberships: ASCAP; AFofM; NARAS; Recording Musicians of US and Canada. Address: Hampton String Quartet, 344 W 72nd Street, New York, NY 10023, USA.

HENRY Jay Edward, b. 17 Feb 1950, Brooklyn, New York, USA. Record Producer; Sound Engineer. Education: Broadcasting Engineering, Cabrillo College; San Francisco State University. Career: Producer, engineer, Visual Music, 1983-; Secret Society Records, 1986-. Recordings: Albums include: with LL Cool J: Bigger And Deffer, 1987; Walking With A Panther, 1989; with Heavy D: Livin' Large, 1987; with Public Enemy: It Takes A Nation Of Millions, 1987; with Run DMC: Tougher Than Leather, 1988; with Defunkt: Defunkt In America, 1988; with Living Colour: Vivid, 1989. Honours: 5 Gold Reel Awards, Amplex, 1986-89; Numerous Platinum and Gold records; International Producer Award, 1990. Memberships: NARAS; Audio Engineering Society. Address: c/o Visual Music, 753-B Jefferson Avenue, Chula Vista, CA 91910, USA.

HENRY Michael Anthony, b. 10 Mar 1963, London, England. Singer; Composer; Musician (saxophone, clarinet); Arranger; Songwriter. Musical Education: Centre for Young Musicians, 1977-81; Royal College of Music, 1981-85. Singer, writer with Buddy Curtess and The Grasshoppers, 1985-89; Singer and Songwriter with The Flying Pickets, 1991-95; Singer, songwriter, co-producer with Cut 2 Taste, 1994-; Tours include: support to Roy Orbison, 1985; Backing vocalist, Pet Shop Boys, 1989; Flying Pickets, 1991-95; Concerts: Support concerts to: Beach Boys, Wembley, 1986; Bo Diddley, Hammersmith Odeon, 1987; Dr Feelgood, 1987; Glastonbury, main stage, 1987; Television and radio appearances include: The Tube, 1987; Saturday Live, 1987; Ruby Wax, 1988; Meltdown, 1988; BBC1 and C4 Schools workshops, 1991-93; Opera performances, 1991-93; Presenter, Young Musician Of The Year, 1992; Judge, Choir Of The Year, 1993; Concert support, Ray Charles, 1993; Cue The Music, 1995; Support to Michael Jackson, tour, 1997. Compositions: Wind Quartet No 1; Say Ave For Me, for saxophone and piano, performed on BBC Radio 3; Recordings: with Buddy Curtess and the Grasshoppers: Shoobey Baby; Shout; Hello Suzie; Bridge Over Troubled Water; Design For Me; Forever Young, Pretenders, 1992; Sugar Daddy, Billy Bragg, 1996. Other recordings include: Caravan, John Harle, all vocals, 1990; Rain Song, Moodswings, 1990; Real Love, Driza Bone, 1991; The Warning, Flying Pickets, 1993. Publications: 3 Interludes for saxophone and piano. Honours: Dip RCM, ARCM; Winner of composition prizes: Joseph Horowitz; Stanford; Cornelius Cardew; Time Out Magazine Best Live Act, 1986, 1987. Memberships: Musicians' Union; PRS; Equity; Society For Promotion Of New Music (SPNM). Hobbies: X-Men comics; Cryptic crosswords; Dancing; Learning languages. Current Management: Self-managed. Address: 83 Lucien Road, London SW17 8HS, England.

HENSLEY Ken, b. 24 Aug 1945, London, England. Musician (guitar, keyboards); Singer; Record Producer. Career: Musician, singer, Kit And The Saracens; Jimmy Brown Sound; The Gods; Musician, singer, producer, UK rock group Uriah Heep, 1969-80; US rock group Blackfoot, 1981-84; Director, artistic relations, St Louis Music Inc, 1987-. Recordings: Albums: with Uriah Heep: Very 'Umble, Very 'Eavy, 1970; Salisbury, 1971; Look At Yourself, 1971; Demons And Wizards, 1972; Magician's Birthday, 1972; Live, 1973; Sweet Freedom, 1973; Wonderworld, 1974; Return To Fantasy, 1975; Best Of, 1975; High And Mighty, 1976; Firefly, 1977; Innocent Victim, 1978; Fallen Angel, 1978; Conquest, 1980; with Blackfoot: Siogo, 1983; Vertical Smile, 1984. Honours: Gold and Platinum discs. Address: St Louis Music Inc, 1400 Ferguson Avenue, St Louis, MO 63133, USA.

HENSON Joe, b. 18 Sept 1973, London, England. Musician (bass guitar). Career: Played with: Redhead; Marcos d'Cruz & Elio Place; Television: What's That Noise; LWT Arts Festival; Glen Maderos Promo video. Recordings: Debut album: Damage. Address: 7 Clarence Road, Kew, Richmond, Surrey TW9 BNL, England.

HERMAND Charles, b. 23 June 1960, Namur, Belgium. Career: Support tour of Boy George, 1994; Support tour to James Brown in Romania, 1994; Support tour to Magic Platters, 1996-97; Support act to Dave, The Cirque Royal of Brussels, 1997; Popular male singers in french language in Belgium. Recordings: Save Me Now, 1992; Les Petits Pains seventies, 1993; Vague d'Amour, 1993; Les Yeux vers le Ciel, 1994; Trop Fatigué, 1995. Memberships: SABAM, Belgium; Union Professional of Auteursman Compositeurs and Interprets. Hobbies: Specialist about Dolfin's protection over the world. Current Management: Z Comme Ltd Company, Charles Hermand Management, Dijkstraat 24 Box 4, 1780 Wemmel, Belgium.

HERMANS Jozef Eduard, b. 1 Mar 1948, Antwerp, Belgium. Psychologist; Singer; Songwriter. m. Faes Monique, 31 Jan 1998, 1 son, 1 daughter. Education: Psychology; Selftaught Guitar, Banjo, Mandoline, Melodeon. Appointments: Psychologist, City of Antwerp; Member, Flemish Folkgroup, Katastroof; Radio and TV appearances, occasionally. Compositions: More than 100 songs on 13 albums of Katastroof; Met De Wijven Niks As Last; Het Geloof; Paterkesdans; Johnny. Recordings: 12 CDs with Katastroof; 3 CDs with Jos Smos: Jos Smos in het Blote Beestembos, 1996; Smarten en Andere Lappen, 1997; Over Het Geloof, 1998. Publications: Book about reincarnation and regression, forthcoming. Membership: Sabam, Belgium. Hobbies: Reincarnation Therapy; Computers; Photography. Address: Tweelingenstraat 15, 2018 Antwerp, Belgium.

HERMITAGE Richard, b. 20 Oct 1955, London. Agent; Manager; Record Company Executive. Career: Agent, artists included: The Human League; Steel Pulse; ABC; INXS; UB40; Psychedelic Furs; Aswad; Daf; The Art Of Noise; The Residents; Agencies worked at: March Artists; TKA; Asgard; ITB; Fair Warning, 1974-85; Management, artists included: The Human League; Pale Saints; The Darling Buds; Slowdive; The Boo Radleys; Teenage Fanclub; Denim, 1986-93; Currently Manager, management company War Zones; General Manager, record company 4AD, 1994-95. Hobbies: Football; Cricket; Mountaineering. Current Management: War Zones (management). Address: 33 Kersley Road, London N16 0NT, England.

HERRING-LEIGH Judy, b. 3 Oct 1945, Cape Girardeau, Missouri, USA. Concert Artist; Recording Artist; Songwriter; Vocal Music Teacher; Minister of Music; Children's Choir Coordinator. m. Jim Leigh, 1 Oct 1994, 1 son, 1

daughter. Education: Bachelor Music Performance; Master Early Childhood Education. Musical Education: Private Voice, 13 years; 4 year Voice Major, Oklahoma Baptist University; Life Vocal Music Certification grades K-12; Music courses in Master's Program. Career: 26 years in Music Ministry; 5 concert tours, England, also crusades; 6-10 US tours over past 20 years; Recorded 3 albums, 1 live performance tape, 1 gospel songs tape; Musical evangelist, public relations representative for Virginia Baptists; Morningstar album #16 on gospel music charts of Christian Broadcasting Network, April, 1977; Appeared, PTL, CBN, BBC networks, 1978-79; Sang for Governor's Prayer Breakfast, President's Prayer Breakfast, 1980; Minister of Music, 9 churches over 26 years; Music teacher; 10 concert tour, England, Scotland, 1997; Soloist, Good News Mission Trip, Odessa, Ukraine, 1997. Compositions: Morningstar; God's Rose; Suffer The Little Children; The Woman; Brand New Start; Arrangements: Take My Life And Let It Be; Victory In Jesus; I've Been Redeemed. Recordings: Albums: Morningstar; Christmas Means Thinking of Jesus; God's Rose; Tapes: Old Gospel Hymns; Live in Concert; Cherished Moments, 1997; Tribute to Fanny Crosby and George Beverly Shea. Publications: Reflections On God's Rose, article, New Music Magazine, 1979; Experiencing Loss With A Youth Ministry, Equipping Youth Magazine, 1985. Honours: Dimitri Mitropolis Award; Personalities Of The South, 1979; Stylemaker Of The Year, 1979. Memberships: SESAC; Southern Baptist Convention's Music Evangelists, USA; Gospel Music Association, Nashville, Tennessee. Hobbies: Fishing; Water skiing; Composing music. Current Management: Paul Davis, New Music Enterprises UK, Mere Dale, Reach Lane, Leighton Buzzard, Bedfordshire LU7 0AL. Address: PO Box 903, Paris, TN 38242, USA.

HERSH Kristin, b. 7 Aug 1966, Atlanta, Georgia, USA. Musician (guitar); Singer. 3 sons. Musical Education: Self-taught. Career: Singer, Musician, Throwing Muses, 1986-97; Solo Singer/Songwriter, 1994-. Recordings: Albums: Throwing Muses, 1986; Chains Changed, 1987; House Tornado, 1983; The Fat Skier, 1987; Hunkpapa, 1989; The Real Ramona, 1991; Red Heaven, 1992; University, 1995; Hips And Makers, 1994; Limbo, 1996. Membership: AFofM. Current Management: Throwing Music Ltd, 520 Southview Drive, Athens, GA 30605, USA.

HERZHAFT Gerard, b. 8 November 1943, Meyzieu, France. Lise Briere de L'Isle, 27 September 1967, 1 son, 1 daughter. Education: Licence of History, Sorbonne, Paris. Career: Numerous radio broadcasts and TV shows; Musician (blues); Concerts: Blues Passion, Cognac; Thullins Festival; Café Campus (Montreal); Parthenay Blues; Doua De Jazz; Sathonay Blues Festival. Compositions: It It Wasn't For Muddy Waters; Rhone River is Rising; Old Bluesman From Texas; Redneck Blues; My Blues Will. Recordings: 3 recordings; 2 CDs with Herzhaft Bluese; Never Been Plugged; Two Brothers and a Pick. Publications: 15 books publs; Encyclopedia of the Blues; A Long Blues in a Minor; Le Blues; La Country Music; Catfish Blues; John Lee Hooker. Honours: Grand Prix Littéraire de la Ville de Lyon, 1986; Prix Des Auteurs et Ecrivains Lyonnais, 1987; Prix Societe des Gens De Lettres, 1995; Prix Des Lyceens D'Ile De France, 1997. Hobbies: US Films from the 40's & 50's; Travel throughout the world. Address: 57 Rue Florian, 69100 Villeurbanne, France.

HESPEL Olivier, b. 20 August 1964, Paris, France. Musician (guitar); Songwriter; Sound Engineer. Education: Masters in Electronics, University of Paris XI, 1984; Sound Engineering Diploma, Brussels, Belgium; Classical Guitar and Music Theory, Academy of Music, Paris; Private guitar lessons, classical guitar with Olivier Bensa and Jose Leal; Jazz Guitar with Philippe Berthe.

Career: Concerts on France, Belgium, Luxembourg; Guitartist, Vocalist, Songwriter with bands: Parkinson Twist, Paris Jungle Djinns, Only Dry; Guitarist on the feature film, Leon G. Radio appearances on Radio 21, Radio Campus, Radio Judaica, Belgium. Compositions: Free; Falling; Ethan; Rain; Bond Beach. Recording: Free, CD album. Address: 27 Avenue Jean Volders, B-1060 Brussels, Belgium.

HESSION Paul, b. 19 Sept 1956, Leeds, England. Musician (drums). m. Cecilia Jane Charnley, 23 May 1987, 1 son, 1 daughter. Musical Education: Self-taught drummer; Studied instrument technology. Career: Toured Mexico and Cuba with The Siger Band, 1986; Played in Derek Bailey's Company week in London (twice); Duos with Alan Wilkinson on BBC Radio 3, Mixing It; Music for radio play, BBC Radio 4 with Keith Jafrate; Sound symposium, St Johns, Newfoundland, Canada, with Hession, Wilkinson, Fell. Recordings: Album: The Real Case, with Hans-Peter Hiby; Albums with Hession/Wilkinson/Fell: Foom Foom; The Horrors of Darmstadt; with Mick Beck: Start Moving Earbuds. Honours: Jazz bursaries from ACGB, 1986, 1991. Membership: Musicians' Union. Hobby: Art. Address: 41 Hanover Square, Leeds L53 1BQ, England.

HETFIELD James Alan, b. 3 Aug 1963, Los Angeles, California, USA. Musician (guitar); Vocalist. Career: Member, Obsession; Leather Charm; Member, US heavy rock group Metallica, 1981-; Worldwide tours include: Master Of Puppets world tour, 1986-87; US tour, 1988; Damaged Justice tour, UK, 1989; World tour, 1991-; Also tours with Raven; Twisted Sister; Ozzy Osbourne; Motörhead; Major concerts include: Monsters of Rock Festival, Castle Donington, 1985, 1987, 1991; German Monster Rock festivals, 1987; Monsters of Rock Europe, US tours, 1988, 1991; Day On The Green, Oakland, 1991; Freddie Mercury tribute, Wembley, 1992. Recordings: Albums: Kill 'Em All, 1983; Ride The Lightning, 1984; Master Of Puppets, 1986; ...And Justice For All, 1988; Metallica (Number 1, UK and US), 1991; Live Shit, 1993; Singles: Garage Days Revisited (EP), 1987; Harvester Of Sorrow, 1988; One, 1989; Enter Sandman, 1991; The Unforgiven, 1991; Nothing Else Matters, 1992; Wherever I May Roam, 1992; Sad But True, 1992; Stone Cold Crazy, track featured on Rubáiyát (Elektra's 40th anniversary compilation). Honours: Platinum and Gold discs; Grammy Awards: Best Heavy Metal Performance: One, 1989; Stone Cold Crazy, 1991; The Unforgiven, 1992; American Music Award, Favourite Heavy Metal Artist, 1993; Bay Area Music Awards: Outstanding Album, 1992; Outstanding Metal Album, Outstanding Group, 1993; Rolling Stone Readers Poll Winners, Best Heavy Metal Band, 1993. Current Management: Q-Prime Inc. Address: 729 7th Avenue, 14th Floor, New York, NY 10019, USA.

HEURLIN Martin, b. 20 Nov 1963, Frederiksberg, Denmark. Musician (guitar, bass, keyboards); Vocalist; Producer. 3 sons. Musical Education: Self-taught. Career: Founder, rock band Sy-Daff; Member, KB Hallen, 1980; Support act to Sweet, 1982; Played at Roskilde Festival, 1983; Played club circuit in Los Angeles, 1986-88; Guitarist on Danish television for Michael Penn, John Farnham, Anders Glenmark and Tomas Ledin, 1990; Pupil Live, television and radio broadcasts, 1998. Compositions include: TV show theme, Set and Swet; Pupil, Frederik Jorgensen, major hit in Denamrk, 1997. Recordings: Soundtracks for many Danish television documentary programmes, 1990-; Albums with: Sy-Daff, 1982; Mr Man, 1987; James Thomas, 1991; Pupil, 1997; Solo album, 1995. Publication: Pupil: Superglasøjne, 1997. Membership: DJFBA. Current Management: TBA, Strulasgade 14, 2300 Copenhagen S, Denmark. Address: Ryesgade 108B Kld, 2100 Copenhagen Ø, Denmark.

HEWAT Corrina Dawn, b. 21 December 1970, Edinburgh, Scotland. Singer; Musician (Harp, Clarsach); Composer. Education: BA, one year, Performance, Royal Scottish Academy of Music and Drama; Honours Degree, 1st Class, Jazz, Contemporary and Popular Music, City of Leeds College of Music. Career: Band, Bachué Café, formed with David Milligan, 1995; Band, Chantan, formed 1996; Appeared on Taile A Bhaile, BBC 2, Radio 3 and Demo TV; Writing music for audio books, Saltire Society; Teaching, Visiting Tutor, Balnain House, Home of Highland Music, Inverness and Fettes College, Edinburgh; Working with Lammas, Carol Kidd, Seannachie; Commissions: Songs of Redshank, The Highland Festival; Making the Connection, Celtic Connections Festival 1998; Many compositions of a traditional nature recorded. Recordings: Bachué Café, 1996, 1998; Primary Colours, 1997; Contributor: Something Blew, 1995; Northlins, 1995; Volume 4 of Burns' Complete Works, 1998. Honour: Finalist, Young Traditional Musician of the Year, 1995. Memberships: Musicians' Union; Clarsach Society; UKHA; PRS; MCPS; PAMRA. Current Management: Giant Peach, 63 High Street, Dumbarton G82 1LS, Scotland. Address: PO Box 12481, Edinburgh, Scotland, EH3 5YG.

HEWINS Mark Jesson, b. 24 Mar 1955, Hertfordshire, England. Musician (guitar); Composer. m. Yvonne, 23 Sept 1989, 1 daughter. Career: Started as professional guitarist aged 15; Tours, Europe and USA; Played with musicians including: Phil Collins; Julie Felix; Joe Lee Wilson; Long association with Casio as Midi guitarist, leading to compiled sample libraries, supplied accompaniment patterns, demonstration tunes for their keyboards; Introduced Lou Reed to Midi guitar; Midi consultant. Compositions: Over 200 compositions include music for guitar, strings, orchestra. Recordings: Featured on many albums; Solo album: The Electric Guitar; Veritable Centaur, Soft Heap. Publications: Markie's Little Fake Books 1 and 2; Canterbury Tales (relating to Canterbury music scene), published extensively in various journals. Membership: Musicians' Union; PRS; MCPS; British Music Writers Council. Hobbies: Cricket, 1900-1950; Stamps; Photographs. Current Management: Y A Ledley, Musart Services. Address: c/o Musart Services, 81 Knollys Road, London SW16 2JW, England.

HEYWARD Nick, b. 20 May 1961, South London, England. Singer; Musician (guitar); Songwriter. Career: Founder, Haircut 100, 1981-82; Solo artiste, 1983-; Major concerts include: Support to Wham!, The Final farewell concert, Wembley, 1986. Compositions: Most recordings self-written. Recordings: Albums: with Haircut 100: Pelican West (Number 2, UK) 1982; Solo albums: North Of A Miracle, 1983; Postcards From Home, 1986; I Love You Avenue, 1989; The Best Of Nick Heyward And Haircut 100, 1989; From Monday To Sunday, 1993; Tangled, 1995; Hit singles with Haircut 100: Favourite Shirts (Boy Meets Girl), 1981; Love Plus One, 1982; Fantastic Day, 1982; Nobody's Fool, 1982; Solo singles: Whistle Down The Wind, 1983; Take That Situation, 1983; Blue Hat For Blue Day, 1983; Rollerbalde, 1996.

HEYWOOD Brian John, b. 15 Oct 1956, Sydney, Australia. Musician (bass, guitar, acoustic amd electric); Producer. m. Alison Margaret Cowley, 6 Apr 1985, 1 son, 1 daughter. Education: University of New South Wales; University of Surrey. Musical Education: Masters degree, City University. Career: Played with Bluetongue (Sydney); Folk/rock band Cluster Of Nuts; Performed at Sidmouth, Bracknell, Cornwall, Wareham and Godalming Folk Festivals; Benskins Morris, Brunsum Festival, Holland; Current member, folk/rock band Nightwatch; R&B band Innocent Bystander; Joined The Open Road, 1997. Recordings: Fridge In The Fast Lane, Cluster Of Nuts; Radio CIX, Nightwatch and Innocent Bystander; Pantasia Vol 1, Nightwatch;

Nightwatch (EP). Publications: PC Music Handbook; Regular articles, Sound On Sound, audio media. Memberships: Musicians' Union; British Music Writers Council. Hobby: Reading. Current Management: Poke Records. Address: PO Box 649, Dunstable, Bedfordshire LU5 4XD, England.

HIATT John, b. 20 Aug 1952, Indiana, USA. Singer; Songwriter; Musician (guitar). Career: Member, bands: Four Fifths; The White Ducks; Joe Lynch And The Hangmen; Songwriter, Tree Publishing, Nashville, early 1970s; Solo artist, 1974-; Also musician for Sonny Terry and Brownie McGhee; Leon Redbone; Tom Waits; Tours with: Leo Kottke; Southside Johnny and the Astbury Jukes; Edie Brickell; Joined Ry Cooder's backing band, 1981; Concerts include: A Black And White Night, with Roy Orbison, Los Angeles, 1987; Reading Festival, 1988; Roy Orbison Concert Tribute, Universal City, California, 1990; Formed Little Village, with Ry Cooder, Nick Lowe, Jim Keltner, 1992. Compositions include: Thinking Of You, Tracy Nelson; As Sure As I'm Sitting Here, Three Dog Night; Bring Back Your Love To Me, Earl Thomas Conley. Recordings: Albums: Hangin' Round The Observatory, 1974; Overcoats, 1974; Slug Line, 1979; Two Bit Monsters, 1980; All Of A Sudden, 1982; Riding With The King, 1983; Warming Up To The Ice Age, 1985; Bring The Family, 1987; Slow Turning, 1988; Stolen Moments, 1990; Love Gets Strange, 1993; Perfectly Good Guitar, 1993; Walk On, 1995; with Little Village: Little Village, 1992; Featured on: Borderline, Ry Cooder, 1981. Honours: As songwiter: BMI Country Music Award, Bring Back Your Love To Me, Earl Thomas Conley, 1991. Current Management: Side One Management. Address: 1026A Third Avenue, New York, NY 10021, USA.

HIBBERT Frederick (Toots). Vocalist. Career: Lead singer, reggae group The Maytals, later billed as Toots and the Maytals; Leading vocal group in Jamaica, 1960s and 1970s; Film appearance, The Harder They Come. Recordings include: The Sensational; Never Grow Old; Sweet And Dandy; From The Roots; From The Roots; Monkey Man; Funky Kingston; In The Dark; Slatyam Stoot; Reggae Got Soul; Toots Live; Life Could Be A Dream. Hits include: Daddy/It's You (Number 1, Jamaican charts), 1965; 54-46 That's My Number; Do The Reggay; Monkey Man. Honours include: Winners (with the Maytals), Jamaican Festival Song Competition, 1966, 1969 and 1972. Address: c/o Zoe Productions, 450 Broome Street, 8th Floor, New York, NY 10013, USA.

HICKLING Anna Jo, b. 5 Sept 1966, Stockport, Cheshire, England. Singer; Songwriter; Producer; Partner in Record Label. Education: University of Bath. Musical Education: At school: O Level Music; Singing, piano, trumpet tuition; Mostly self-taught; Recording studio engineering course. Career: Backing vocalist for various Manchester bands: Victor Brox; The Glee Company, 1983; Local clubs include Band On The Wall; Writer, lead vocalist Inside Out, 1984; Concerts at The Boardwalk, Manchester; Lead vocalist, Touch Of Spice, 1987; Played Moles Club, Bath; Womad Festival; Various universities, HTV appearance; Invited to play and record at Real World Studios; Backing vocalist, Tammy Payne, UK tour; Also played at Southport Soul Weekender; The Theklar, Bristol; The Underworld, London; Ashton Court Festival. Recordings: Session vocals for: Smith and Mighty; Banderas remix; Startled Insects; Toop (EP); Lead vocals, band member, writing and production work on EPs with: Tommorowland; (Currently) Transport; Remix for single: I Am Free, Morgan King. Memberships: Musicians' Union; PRS; PAMRA. Hobbies: Clothes designing; All kinds of dancing; Experimental cooking; Walking in places of natural beauty. Current Management: Self-managed.

Address: Revelstoke Road, Wimbledon Park, London, England.

HICKS Ivan, b. 6 July 1940, Upper Sackville, New Brunswick, Canada. Musician (fiddle, guitar, mandolin). m. Vivian Paulette Webb, 4 July 1970. Education: Bachelor of Arts; Bachelor of Education; Master of Education. Career: As teenager, formed: The Golden Valley Boys; 1964, began teaching, Salisbury, New Brunswick; Formed: danceband Marshwinds, 1969-89; Formed old time and bluegrass band: Ivan Hicks and Maritime Express, 1979-; Workshops; Teacher fiddling; television appearances include: Up Home Tonight (ATV), 1980's, 8 years; Host, weekly radio show, CFQM Moncton, 1982-95; MC of Maritime Old-Time Fiddling Contest (CBC-TV), 1985-; Concerts: Canada, USA; Entertainer, special occasions; Organizer, promotor, concerts, tours. Compositions include: Apohaqui; Gram Lee's Waltz; Jim, The Fiddle Maker; Marshwinds Waltz; Purple Violet Waltz; Riverview Jig; Maritime 40; Forever Friends; Memories Of Father James Smith; Fiddler's Roast; The MacDonalds Of Highfield; The Fiddler From Douro; Sussex Avenue Fiddlers Two Step. Recordings: The Life and Music of Ivan and Vivian Hicks (video); For You; Shingle The Roof; Old Time Christmas; Fiddlingly Yours; Swinging Fiddles; Purple Violet Fiddling; Friendly Fiddling The Maritime Way; Fiddling For Fun And Friends; The Strength of God's Hand, 1997. Publications: Ivan Hicks Fiddle Tunes and Souvenirs; Ivan Hicks: Fifty Years of Fabulous Fiddle Music by Allison Mitcham, 1996. Honours include: Two-time winner, Maritime Fiddling Contest, 1979-80; Finalist: Canadian Fiddling Contest; 1985; Inducted into New Brunswick Country Music Hall Of Fame; Inducted into North American Fiddlers Hall of Fame, 1990. Memberships include: Canadian Country Music Association; Director, Maritime Fiddlers Association; Director, National Oldtime Fiddlers Association; East Coast Music Association. Hobbies: Promoting old-time fiddle music; Travel; Camping. Address: 157 Sussex Avenue, Riverview, New Brunswick E1B 3A8, Canada.

HICKS Jacqueline (Jacqui), b. 7 July 1966, Pontefract, WestYorkshire, England. Vocalist; Musician (saxophone, flute, clarinet); Songwriter. m. Patrick Hartley. Education: Wakefield District College. Musical Education: City Of Leeds College of Music, 1984-87; Guildhall School Of Music and Drama, 1987-88. Career: 4 years with National Youth Jazz Orchestra; Matt Bianco; Tours: Japan; Indonesia; Europe; Tour with Shakatak, South East Asia; Japan; Also with: John Dankworth; Dick Morrisey; Harry Becket; Don Lusher; Supported George Benson, 1993; Own jazz/funk band, Jacqui Hicks Band. Recordings: Own album: Looking Forward, Looking Back, 1990; with NYJO: Cooking With Gas; Live At Ronnie Scott's; with Matt Bianco: Another Time Another Place; Gran Via. Address: Hemel Hempstead, Hertfordshire, England.

HIGHAM Darrel, b. 5 January 1970, Bedford, England. Musician (Lead Guitar, Double Bass); Singer; Songwriter; Producer. Education: Selftaught. Career: Solo career, Singer, Guitarist with backing band, The Enforcers; Supported Chuck Berry, 1995; Played Lead Guitar for Rocky Burnette, Glen Glenn, Johnny Carroll, Vernon Taylor, Merrill E Moore, Don & Dewey; Toured US, 1992 fronting Eddie Cochran's original backing band, The Kelly Four; Worked in Londons West End, Lead guitar and Singing, Elvis The Musical, 8 months, 1996; TV work includes appearances on Blue Peter, Theatreland; Many radio appearances; Currently tours in UK, throughout Europe and US. Compositions: Prolific Songwriter with over 30 compositions released worldwide. Recordings: 5 solo albums: Mobile Corrosion (Nervous), 1995; Let's Rock Tonight (Fury), 1995; Rockin' At the Coconut Top (Crazy Love), 1996; The Cochran Connection (Rockstar), 1997; Darrel Higham and the Barnshakers

(Gaofin'), 1998; 2 solo EP's; 3 Albums with Bob and the Bearcats; 2 with Johnny Bach and the Moonshine Boozers; 1 with Dave Phillips; 1 with the Blue Devils as Lead Guitarist. Membership: Musicians Union. Address: 18 Biggleswade Road, Upper Caldecote, Beds SG18 9BL, England.

HIGHAM Mike. Programmer. Career: Worked with Seal on Spacejam, film soundtrack, Fly Like An Eagle; Completed work for Tina Turner, Barry White and Boyzone; Other projects include: The Art of Noise, Public Demand, Gary Barlow, Eric Clapton; Clients include: Seal: MTV Unplugged, album; Seal II, album; A Prayer For the Dying 12" remix; Bobby Brown, Every Little Step I Take 12" remix; Tina Turner, Wildest Dreams, album; Ministry of Sound, 6 albums; Whitney Houston, I'm Your Baby Tonight. Address: SARM Productions, SP2 Holdings Ltd, The Blue Building, 42/46 St Luke's Mews, London W11 1DG, England.

HILBORNE Phil, b. 20 Jan 1959, Poole, Dorset, England. Musician (guitar); Journalist; Teacher; Performer; Producer. m. 17 Feb 1977, 2 sons, 1 daughter. Musical Education: Studied with Professor W Grandison, Harpsichordist D Galbraith, Trinity College. Career: Tours, UK, Europe, with Phil Hilborne Band, and Nicko McBrain, Iron Maiden; Many live demonstrations for leading music companies: Gibson; Ampeg; Viger; Paiste; Sonor; Music editor, Guitarist magazine, Rock/Solo Analysis articles, 1985-1995; Music/CD Editor, Guitar Techniques magazine, 1994-. Recordings: Are You Serious?; 'Bout Time, 1993; Guest, John McEnroe, Pat Cash single: Rock And Roll; Angel Easy: Lightning Strikes; Geoff Whitehorn: Big In Gravesend; Maria Kern: Tension and Harmony, 1996; Drome: Overload, 1996; Producer, Playing with Fire, by Dave Kilminster and Fraser T Smith, 1996. Publications: Solo, 1987; Led Zeppelin Off The Record, 1988; Elton John Rockscore, 1991; Editor: Reijo Hittunen's Guitar Chord Method, 1993; Hot Country, by L Hodgson, Produced and engineered, 1997. Contributor to: Jimi Hendrix Electric Gypsy, 1990; Instructional Video: Phil Hilborne Rock Basics, 1992. Membership: Musicians' Union. Hobbies: Music; Golf. Current Management: Phil Hilborne Band Management. Address: Phil Hilborne Band/Widdle Music, PO Box, 1001 Basildon, Essex, SS13 1SR, England.

HILL Beau, b. 25 Sept 1952, Dallas, Texas, USA. Record Producer; Musician (keyboards, guitar). Education: BA, Music and Western European History. Musical Education: Classical training 1958-; Music Major, University of Colorado. Career: Signed as recording artist, Columbia Records, 1978; Chrysalis Records, 1981; BMI writer, 1981-; Producer for Bob Dylan; Eric Clapton; Alice Cooper; Ratt; Warrant; Winger; Europe; Chaka Khan; Fiona; Roger Daltrey; John Miles; Gary Moore; Steve Stevens; Bad Brains. Memberships: NARAS; AES. Hobbies: Scuba diving. Address: c/o Stuart Silfell Esq, 488 Madison Avenue, New York, NY 10023, USA.

HILL Dave, b. 4 Apr 1952, Fleet Castle, Devon, England. Musician (guitar). Career: Member, The Vendors, Wolverhampton, 1965; Member, UK rock group Slade (formerly N'Betweens, Ambrose Slade), 1966-; Currently billed as Slade II; Concerts include: First UK tour, 1972; Fanfare For Europe festival, London Palladium, 1973; Great British Music Festival, 1978; Reading Festival, 1980; Film: Flame, 1974. Recordings: Albums: Beginnings (as Ambrose Slade), 1969; Play It Loud, 1970; Slade Alive, 1972; Slayed, 1973; Sladest, 1973; Old New Borrowed Blue, 1974; Slade In Flame (soundtrack), 1974; Nobody's Fool, 1976; Slade Alive Vol 2, 1978; Return To Base, 1979; Slade Smashes, 1980; Till Deaf Do Us Part, 1981; We'll Bring The House Down, 1981; Slade On Stage, 1982; The Amazing Kamikaze Syndrome, 1983; Slade's Greats, 1984; Rogue's Gallery, 1985; Crackers, 1985; You Boyz Make Big Noize, 1987;

Wall Of Hits, 1991; Keep On Rockin', 1996; UK Number 1 hit singles: Coz I Luv You, 1971; Take Me Bak 'Ome, 1972; Mama Weer All Crazee Now (later recorded by Mama's Boys, Quiet Riot), 1972; Cum On Feel The Noize, 1973; Merry Christmas Everybody, 1973; Other hits: Look Wot You Dun, 1972; Gudbuy T'Jane, 1972; Skweeze Me Pleeze Me, 1973; My Friend Stan, 1973; Everyday, 1974; Bangin' Man, 1974; Far Far Away, 1974; Thanks For The Memory, 1975; In For A Penny, 1975; We'll Bring The House Down, 1981; My Oh My, 1983; Run Run Away, 1984; All Join Hands, 1984. Address: c/o Hal Carter Organisation, London, England.

HILL Dusty, b. 19 May 1949, Dallas, Texas, USA. Musician (bass); Vocalist. Career: Formed The Warlocks, with brother, Rocky, 1967; Renamed American Blues, 1968; Formed ZZ Top, 1970; Regular tours, 1970-; Tours include: Eliminator tour, 1984; Afterburner tour, 1985-87; Recycler tour, 1990; Rock The Bowl '91, Milton Keynes, 1991. Recordings include: Albums: 2 with The American Blues, 1968; with ZZ Top: ZZ Top's First Album 1970; Rio Grande Mud, 1972; Tres Hombres, 1973; Fandango, 1975; Best Of, 1978; Deguello, 1979; El Loco, 1981; Eliminator, 1983; Afterburner, 1985; Recycler, 1990; Greatest Hits, 1992; Antenna, 1994; Singles include: La Grange, 1974; Tush, 1975; Gimme All Your Lovin', 1983; Sharp Dressed Man, 1983; Legs, 1984; Sleeping Bag, 1985; Velcro Fly, 1986; Stages, 1986; Rough Boy, 1986; Doubleback, from film Back To The Future Part III, 1990; Viva Las Vegas, 1992. Honours: Several MTV Video Awards; ZZ Top Day, Texas, 1991; Silver Clef Award, Nordoff-Robbins Music Therapy Foundation, 1992. Current Management: Lone Wolf Management, PO Box 163690, Austin, TX 78716, USA.

HILL Jason, b. 28 Aug 1948, Portsmouth, Hampshire, England. Barn Dance Caller; Musician (guitar, melodeon, autoharp). m. Gwyneth Mair Bound, 22 Feb 1986. Education: University of Keele, 1967-71; Birmingham University, 1990-91. Career: Caller and musician with Oatcake Billy's Ideal Band, 1977-90; Alf Alfa and The Wild Oats, 1991-; Radio broadcast: Shropshire Folk Programme, 1993; Festivals: Potteries Folk Festival, 1991; Crewe and Nantwich Folk Festival, 1992. Recordings: with Alf Alfa: Climbing The Walls, 1995. Memberships: Musicians' Union; English Folk Dance and Song Society. Current Management: Barn Dance Agency Ltd. Address: 62 Beechwood Road, South Croydon, Surrey CR2 0AA, England.

HILL Warren, b. Canada. Musician (alto, soprano saxophone). Musical Education: Berklee College Of Music, Boston. Career: Television appearances including: Tonight Show; Arsenio Hall Show; Unforgettable tour supporting Natalie Cole; Also supported: Ray Charles; Air Supply; Four Play; Worked with: Mitch Malloy; Sheila E; Alex Acuna; Lenny Castro; Jeff Pocaro; Ricardo Silveira. Recordings: Albums: Kiss Under The Moon; Devotion; Performed on: Restless Heart: Tell Me What You Dream (Number 1 Billboard charts); Also The Passion Theme, from Body of Evidence soundtrack; Can't Get You Out Of my Mind, with Aswad and General Levy. Current Management: SESAC. Address: 55 Music Sq E, Nashville, TN 37203, USA.

HILLAGE Steve, b. 2 Aug 1951, England. Musician (guitar). Education: College. Career: Founder member, Khan, 1971-72; Joined Kevin Ayers' touring band Decadence, 1972; Member, Gong, 1972-76; Solo artiste, 1975-; Songwriting partnership with Miquette Giraudy, 1975-; Producer, 1980s-. Albums with Gong: Radio Gnome Invisible - The Flying Teapot, 1973; Angles' Egg, 1973; You, 1974; Solo: Fish Rising, 1975; L, 1976; Motivation Radio, 1977; Green, 1978; Live Herald, 1979; Open, 1979; Rainbow Dome Musick, 1979; For To Next/And Not Or, 1983; System 7, 1991.

HILLARY David, b. 20 May 1965, Witham, Essex, England. Composer. Musical Education: University of Keele. Compositions: Music for Byways: The Icknield Way (television programme); Music for corporate clients Period Of Cosmology, 1993. Recordings: Album: Why This, 1989. Membership: Musicians' Union. Address: Beacon Lodge, Macclesfield Road, Over Alderley, Macclesfield, Cheshire SK10 4UB, England.

HILLERED Eva Karin Maria, b. 4 April 1958, Stockholm, Sweden. Singer; Songwriter; Singing Teacher. m. Peter Ostman, 1 daughter. Education: Drama, music and psychology, University; Choir leader tuition, 1 year; Studied singing, 1 year. Career: Backing Singer, Bob Manning, Py Backman, Eva Dahigren, Anne-Grete Preus, Rolf Wikstrom, Marie Bergman; Toured with Rock Runt Riket, Py Backman, Anne-Grete Preus, Eva Dahigren, Rolf Wikstrom, Riksteaterns Cornelis-show; Own shows in Stockholm. Recordings: Inte Varfor Utan Hur, 1988; Straets langd, 1990; Jag Vet, 1995; Oppningsskedet, 1996. Honours: Noiminated for grammy Award, 1989. Memberships: STIM; SKAP. Hobbies: Travel; Films; Reading; Theatre; Cooking. Current Management: Diva Records, Sweden. Address: Tureholms Gard, S-619 92 Trosa, Sweden.

HILLMAN Chris, b. 4 Dec 1944, Los Angeles, California, USA. Musician (bass, guitar); Songwriter; Singer. Career: Musician, groups: Scottsville Squirrel Barkers; Golden State Boys; The Hillmen; The Byrds, 1964-68; Performances include: Beach Boys Summer Spectacular, 1966; Monterey Festival, 1967; Grand Ole Opry, 1968; Newport Pop Festival, 1968; McGuinn Clark and Hillman (with Gene Clark and Roger McGuinn); The Flying Burrito Brothers; Manassas; Souther Hillman Furay Band; Desert Rose Band. Recordings: Albums with the Byrds: Mr Tambourine Man, 1965; Turn! Turn! Turn!, 1965; Fifth Dimension, 1966; Younger Than Yesterday, 1967; The Notorious Byrd Brothers, 1968; Sweetheart Of The Rodeo, 1968; History Of The Byrds, 1973; The Byrds, 1990; with The Flying Burrito Brothers: The Gilded Palace Of Sin, 1969; Burrito Deluxe, 1970; The Flying Burrito Brothers, 1971; The Last Of The Red Hot Burrito Brothers, 1972; Flying Again, 1975; Airborne, 1976; Close Encounters On The West Coast, 1978; Live In Tokyo, Japan, 1978; Flying High, 1980; Back To The Sweethearts Of The Rodeo, 1988; Southern Tracks, 1990; with Manassas: Manassas, 1972; Down The Road, 1973; with Souther Hillman Furay Band: Souther Hillman Furay, 1974; Trouble In Paradise, 1974; with Desert Rose Band: The Desert Rose Band, 1987; Running, 1988; Pages Of Life, 1990; True Love, 1991; A Dozen Roses, 1991; Life Goes On, 1994; Solo: Slippin' Away, 1976; Singles with the Byrds include: Mr Tambourine Man (Number 1, US), 1965; All I Really Want To Do, 1965; Eight Miles High, 1966; So You Want To Be A Rock'n'Roll Star, 1967. Honour: Inducted into Rock And Roll Hall of Fame, 1991.

HINCHCLIFFE Keith Phillip, b. 4 Jan 1951, Glossop, Derbyshire, England. Musician (guitar); Singer. Education: BA, English, Leicester University; Doctorate in English, Hull University. Career: Several years, Folk and Blues club and concert circuit; Member, Albion Band, 1991-1992; Extensive tuition and workshop experience; Several appearances, BBC Radio, ITV. Recordings: Albums: Carolan's Dream, 1994; The Albion Band: Captured, 1994. Publications: Carolan's Dream, 1995; Original guitar music in Guitar International. Memberships: PRS; Musicians' Union; PAMRA. Hobbies: Reading; Cycling; Hill-walking. Address: 23A Spring Hill, Sheffield S10 1ET, England.

HINCHLIFFE Roger Redman, b. 27 Dec 1944, Springfield, Vermont, USA. Singer; Composer; Translator. m. Karen Soderberg, 30 Sept 1995, 2 daughters. Education: BA, Bowdoin

College, 1966; MBA, Cornell University, 1968; Excellence in Swedish, Stockholm University, 1974; Voice and Theoritical Studies, Glee Club. Career: Ten Tours of USA as solo vocalist, including 80 Concerts in 20 States, 1988-; Guest appearances on Television and Radio in the USA and Sweden. Compositions: Over 30 English Translations and Solo Recordings of Sweden's Greatest Popular Songs; 12 Original Compositions. Recordings: Cantalucha, 1979; Festival Theme, 1980; Swedens Greatest, 1988; Swedes on Love, 1992; Master Olof's Choir, 1994. Publications: Over 100 including: Films Translated from Swedish to English: Three Loves, 1990; Greta Garbo, 1994; Who Killed Olof Palme?, 1995; Jerusalem, 1996; Tattooed Widow, 1997. Honours: 10 Festival Awards for Translations, Cannes, Montreux, 1986-98. Memberships: American Association of Swedens; Compact Disc Association. Hobbies: Tennis; Basketball; Fishing; Diving; Boating. Current Management: c/o RogeRecords, P O Box 414, Cedar Mt, NC 28718, USA. Address: S:t Eriksg 25 1tr, 112 39 Stockholm, Sweden.

HINE Rupert Neville, b. 21 Sept 1947, Wimbledon, England. Record Producer; Musician (multi-instrumentalist); m. Natasha, 1 son. Musical Education: Self-taught. Career: Songwriter for: Tina Turner; Stevie Nicks; Wilson Phillips; Robert Palmer; Dusty Springfield. Recordings: 11 albums: 2 as Quantum Jump; 3 as Thinkman; 6 as Rupert Hine; Producer of 100 albums including: 3 by Tina Turner; 3 by Bob Geldof; 2 by Rush; 4 by The Fixx; 3 by Howard Jones; 3 by Chris De Burgh; Also albums by Stevie Nicks; Numerous film scores and television projects, including One World One Voice featuring: Peter Gabriel; Chrissie Hynde; Suzanne Vega; Lou Reed; Laurie Anderson; Dave Stewart; Sting; Also 300 other musicians from 6 continents. Honours: Producer, Grammy award-winning tracks; Numerous Gold discs. Hobbies: Flying; Classic cars. Current Management: Jukes Productions Ltd. Address: c/o Jukes Productions Ltd, 63 Sutherland Avenue, London W9 2HF, England.

HINKLER Simon Thomas, b. 13 Nov 1959, Sheffield, England. Musician (guitar, keyboards); Producer; Programmer. Musical Education: Self-taught. Career: Multi-instrumentalist with groups Artery and Pulp, 1980-85; Guitarist, The Mission, 1986-90; Worldwide tours (first western band to play Paraguay), numerous television appearances; Programmer, producer, freelance, 1994-. Recordings: Albums: Oceans, 1982; Pulp-it, 1983; Artery Live In Amsterdam, 1985; The Flight Commander, 1985; God's Own Medicine, 1986; The First Chapter, 1987; Children, 1988; Carved In Sand, 1990; Room Full Of This, 1993. Publications: Names Are For Tombstones Baby, 1993. Honours: Gold Discs, all Mission albums. Memberships: Musicians' Union; PRS; PPL. Hobbies: Walking; Films; Computers. Current Management: Curveball Management. Address: PO Box 899, Walkley, Sheffield S6 2YY, England.

HIRABAYASHI Makiko, b. 17 September 1966, Tokyo, Japan. Musician. m. Morten Kargaard Nielsen, 24 September 1990. Education: Music Degree, Berklee College of Music; Major, Piano, Rhythmic Conservatory, Denmark. Career: Performed with Morten Kargaard Group & Sisters, Copenhagen Jazz Festival, 1991-97; Japan Tour with Third Floor Jazz Quartet, 1992, 1993, 1994; Performed, Yokohama Jazz Promenade, 1993, 1994; Performed with Sisters, Stockholm Water Festival, 1996, 1997; Performed with Maravilla, Roskilde Festival, 1997. Recordings: Later Still, 1993; Colour of a Moment, 1996; Elk Dance, 1996; Sa Ka La Musika, 1997; A Story of Multiplicity, 1998; BIMWO Swing, 1998. Honours: 3rd Prize, Best Arrangement, Public Award, Europe Jazz Contest, Belgium, 1995. Address: Linnesgade 33 3tv, 1361 Copenhagen K, Denmark.

HIRD Colin, b. 21 Apr 1964, Sunderland, England. Musician (Bass, Chapman Stick, Keys); Producer. m. Jane Hird, 24 Apr 1991. Musical Education: HND in Music Technology; Studied Bass under Nick Beggs. Career: It's Crucial tour, 1985; McCallum, Left Handed Tour, 1988; TV appearance on BBC 2's Out Of Our Heads, 1988, and ITV's Comedy Bites, 1995 with Morgan Le Fay. Recordings: Left Handed, with McCallum, 1988; Growing Up In Public, with The Flair, 1994. Membership: Musicians' Union. Hobby: Midi Computer Programming. Current Management: Major Management, Blyth, Northumberland, England. Address: 2 Cowpen Road, Blyth, Northumberland NE24 5BS, England.

HIRST Clare, b. 13 Aug 1959, Alston, Cumbria, England. Musician (saxophone); Vocalist; Composer. m. Alan Barnes, 31 July 1995, 1 son. Musical Education: Self-taught, some private tuition. Career: Member, pop band The Bellestars, 1981-86; Played on Live Aid with David Bowie; Toured with The Communards; Sandy Shaw; Iggy Pop; Hazel O'Connor; Maxi Priest; Amazulu; Quireboys. Recordings: All Bellestars recordings; with The Communards: Don't Leave Me This Way; with Clare Hirst Quartet: Tough And Tender, 1995; Singles with The Bellestars include: Iko Iko; Sign Of The Times, 1982. Current Management: c/o 33 Records, 33 Guildford Street, Luton, Bedfordshire, England.

HIRST Willie, b. 2 May 1941, Barnsley, South Yorkshire, England. Bandleader; Musical Director; Arranger; Musician (saxophone, clarinet, flute, recorder). m. Hazel Irene Rainbow, 4 Apr 1966, 2 sons. Musical Education: Huddersfield College Of Music; Bretton Hall College. Career: Musical director, Wakefield Theatre Club, for 15 years; Tours: Bobby Vee; Tony Christie; Marti Caine; Lionel Blair; Concerts: Johnny Mathis; Tony Bennett; Buddy Greco; Victor Borge; Sacha Distell; Tommy Steele; Bruce Forsythe; Matt Monro; Drifters; Des O'Connoer; Bob Monkhouse; Gladys Knight and the Pips; Television appearances: Les Dawson; Three Two One; Play Guitar; Radio: Jimmy Young Show; Late Night Show; Early Breakfast Show. Honours: LRAM (saxophone); ARCM (clarinet); LTCL (recorder); Certificate of Education. Membership: Musicians' Union. Hobbies: Antiques; Cricket; Golf. Current Management: Owner, Maestro Music And Entertainment Agency. Address: Belmont House, 32 Bell Lane, Ackworth, Pontefract, West Yorkshire WF7 7JH, England.

HNILICKA Jaromir, b. 11 February 1932, Bratislava. Composer; Musician. div. 2 daughters. Education: Graduate, State Conservatory for Music. Career: Trumpet Soloist, Gustav Brom Big Band; Composer, Arranger, 1953-. Compositions: Missa Jazz, 1968, 1989. Recordings: Missa Jazz, 1968, 1989. Honours: Prize, Josef Blaha; Prize, Ludek Hulan; Prize, Composers Association. Membership: OSA. Hobbies: Nature; Dogs; Skiing; Cycling; Windsurfing; Good Books. Address: Kupkova 22, 63800 Brno, Czech Republic.

HOBBS Paul Ernest Leonard, b. 28 Dec 1948, Burnt Oak, Edgware, Hendon, England. Musician (drums). m. Sylvia Anne Picton, 25 July 1987, 2 daughters. Musical Education: Self-taught with help from: Buddy Rich; Phil Seamen; Jimmy Blades. Career: Mahogany, Utrecht Railway Museum Performance for Jam, Dutch TV, 1970, 1971; Late Night Line-up, with Marty Wilde, BBC TV, 1970-71; BBC Radio 1 Club. Recordings: Album: Mahogany, produced by Tony Clark, 1969; Mahogany With Marty Wilde, 1970; Bring Back Rock 'n' Roll, Robert Bee Blues Corporation, 1992. Publications: 2 books awaiting publication. Membership: Musicians' Union. Hobbies: Model railway and all main forms of civil transport (UK). Address: 163 Fishermead Boulevard, Fishermead, Milton Keynes, Buckinghamshire, England.

HOBBS Rebecca Ann (Becky), b. 24 Jan 1950, Bartlesville, Oklahoma, USA. Singer; Songwriter. Education: 1 year college, Tulsa University. Musical Education: 6 years piano lessons. Career: Performed in more than 35 countries; Performed on: Hee Haw; Academy Of Country Music Awards Show; Nashville Now; Prime Time Country; Pop! Goes The Country; Staler Bros Show. Compositions: co-wrote Angels Among Us, recorded by Alabama; Co-wrote I Want To Know You Before We Make Love, number 1 country hit for Conway Twitty; Co-wrote, recorded, Jones On The Jukebox; Other songs recorded by: George Jones; Loretta Lynn; Glen Campbell; Emmylou Harris; Helen Reddy; Shirley Bassey. Honours: Most Promising International Act, In Country Music Round-Up, 1989; Top Female On Independent Label, 1994. Memberships: NSAI; AFofM; AFTRA; CMA. Hobbies: Loves cats; Collects antiques; Oil-painting. Address: Becky Hobbs, c/o Beckaroo Music, PO Box 150272, Nashville, TN 37215, USA.

HOBROUGH Mark, b. 11 Sept 1965, Cheshire, England. Record Company Executive; Artist Manager. Education: BA, Honours in Archaeology, Dunelm. Career: Spin Promotions Ltd, 1989; Managing Director, Revolution Promotions and Lemon Records, 1991; Managing Director, Revolution Promotions and Jealous Records; Manager of Sack and Darling Sugar Honey (Revolution Management), 1995. Hobbies: Football; Cricket. Address: 172A Arlington Road, Camden, London NW1 7HL, England.

HODGE Andrew, b. 17 Aug 1966, Ickenham, Middlesex, England. Freelance Musician (bass guitar). m. Susan Louise Jinks (Madeleine Harvey, actress), 27 Sept 1992. Musical Education: Colin Spencer, Classical Guitar Studio, Torquay. Career: Lorna Luft, Dave Willetts Magical World Of The Musicals Tour; Jerry Playle, album promo tour Beyond Silence; Brotherhood Of Man, UK Tour, 1994-95; Home and Away, National Tour. Recordings: Albums: L & A, acoustic; Foreverly Yours; with Dangerously Big: Dangerously Big; with Innocence Lost: Love Is In. Membership: Musicians' Union. Hobbies: Reading; Driving; Walking. Address: 26 The Reddings, Borehamwood, Herts WD6 4ST, England.

HODGE Philip Norman, b. 11 Sept 1953, Aylesbury, Buckinghamshire, England. Musician (keyboards); Computer Engineer. m. Lisa Mary Jane Stacey, 18 June 1994. Musical Education: Piano Grade 6. Career: Semi-pro band: Synthesis, 1970-75; Steve Hillage Band (Virgin), British tour, 1976; American tour, support to ELO, 1977; Hyde Park concert with Queen, 1976; TV: Old Grey Whistle Test, 1976; European TV shows, concerts; Semi-pro bands: Six; As Above So Below; Radio 1, Friday Rock Show; Concert with Dave Stewart, Barbara Gaskin, as keyboard player. Publications: Articles, keyboard reviews, Organ Player Magazine. Hobby: Music. Address: 50 Corbet Ride, Linslade, Leighton Buzzard, Bedfordshire LU7 7SJ, England.

HODGES Chas (Charles Nicholas), b. 28 Dec 1943, Edmonton, London, England. Musician (piano, guitar, bass); Entertainer; Songwriter. m. Joan Adeline Findley, 6 Oct 1966, 2 daughters, 1 son. Musical Education: Self-taught. Career: Turned professional, 1960; Member of bands: Mike Berry and the Outlaws; Cliff Bennett and the Rebel Rousers; Heads, Hands and Feet; Cockney duo Chas and Dave (with Dave Peacock); Worldwide tours; Numerous radio and television appearances. Compositions: Over 300 songs; Biggest hit single Ain't No Pleasin' You, Chas & Dave, co-written with Dave Peacock (Number 1, UK), 1982; Biggest Hit Album/Video: Chas And Dave's Street Party (Number 3, UK), 1995. Recordings: Hit records with all the above artists. Publications: Chas Before Dave, autobiography. Honours: Bass Player of Year, 1962; Over 20 Gold albums and singles. Memberships: PRS; MCPS; Musicians' Union. Current Management: Bob England, Hurricane Entertainments. Address: PO Box 14, Ware, Herts SG1 7SS, England.

HODGSON Lee James, b. 18 May 1961, Chelmsford, England. Musician (guitar, midi); Vocalist; Educator. m. Gloria Maria Ricardo, 20 Aug 1984, 2 sons. Musical Education: Self-taught. Career: Club concerts from age 16; Professional, age 18; Tours with Odyssey, 1980-81; Bobby Thurston, 1980; Television and radio commercial sessions, mid-1980's; Several years with comedy showband Barley; Formed country band Memphis Roots, 1987; Concerts include: Wembley Arena; Royal Albert Hall; Festivals; Columnist, Guitar Techniques magazine; Guitarist magazine; Instructor, Guitar Institute, 1990's. Recordings: Best Of Memphis Roots; Good Noise: The Best of Western Line Dancing Publications: Grade pieces for Rockschool Ltd; Hot Country, guitar tutorial, 1997. Memberships: Musicians' Union; PRS. Hobby: Occasional photography. Address: 2 The Poplars, Pitsea, Basildon, Essex SS13 2ER, England.

HODNETT Paul Joseph, b. 19 July 1966, London, England. Musician (guitar); Songwriter. m. Vikki Kimberley Spencer, 1 July 1995. Education: 2 year catering study. Career: First band: Back Street Jellyroll (blues soul); Joined current band, 1990; Appearances: German TV, played Grosse Freiheit 36, Hamburg; Tour, North Germany; Played Marquee Club, London. Recordings: Debut album, 1993; 3 solo compositions on album. Membership: Musicians' Union. Hobbies: Languages; Travel; Listening to music. Address: 178 Ashley Crescent, London SW11 5QZ, England.

HØEG Thorsten Sehested (Dane T S Hawk), b. 6 Jan 1957, Copenhagen, Denmark. Musician (saxophone); Composer; Writer; Entertainer. Musical Education: Studied with John Tchicai, 1973-78; Courses, private lessons. Career: Member, John Tchicai and the Festival Band, 1975-78; Formed Cockpit Music, 1978; Tours: Scandinavia; Yugoslavia; Czechoslovakia; Switzerland; France; Bandleader, Tapehead, 1981-86; Somesax, 1985-1990; 18 piece bigband, Dane T S Hawk and his Great Mongo Dilmuns; Solo, 1980-; Numerous appearances include: Copenhagen Jazz Festival; Roskilde Festival; Århus Festuge; Pori Jazz Festival, Finland; Gothenburg Book Fair, Sweden; Numerous television and radio appearances; Wrote text and music, 3 plays for Danish Radio. Compositions: Scores to Danish, French dance companies, The Royal Danish Theatre, Billedstofteatret, Denmarks Radio; My River Came Forth In A Flood, 1990; Sweet Devil On The Loose, 1994; I'm 3, 1994; Opera score: Soap Opera (libretti by poet Morti Vizki) 1994; All material for own big band Dane T S Hawk and his Great Mongo Dilmuns. Recordings: Cockpit Music: Transworlds Of Sounds, 1981; Snow Lake City, 1982; Salute For General Wasteland, 1983; Stop/Go, 1985; Hands Up, 1988; Foss/Høeg/Schneidermann/Skeel: How To Play, Volume 3, 1989; Somesax: Flapper, 1990. Publications: Books: Amokoma, 1982; Landskab Ruller Zone, 1983; 1/2 Så Gammel Som Tiden, 1987; Hotel Kontinental I Likvidation, 1990; Gutboy, Autumn, 1995; Numerous contributions to magazines, newspapers. Honours: Several awards and grants for literature and music. Memberships: PEN; DJBFA; DSF. Address: Frederiksbergalle 7, 1621 Copenhagen V, Denmark.

HOFF Jan Gunnar, b. 22 Oct 1958, Bodo, Norway. Musician (piano); Composer. Musical Education: 3 year jazz study, Trondelag Music Conservatory. Career: Debut concert, Harstad Music Festival as solo artist, 1992; Concerts with Jan Gunnar Hoff Group; Concert, Vossa Jazz, Norway, 1995; Molde International Jazzfestival, 1996; Oris London Jazz Festival, Barbican, 1996.

Recordings: Syklus, 1993; Moving, 1995. Honour: The Stubö Prize, 1997. Membership: NOPA (popular composers). Address: Harald Langhellesv. 16B, 8003 Bodo, Norway.

HOFFS Susannah, b. 17 Jan 1959, Los Angeles, California, USA. Singer; Musician (guitar). Education: Graduate, University of California, Berkeley. Career: Founder member, all-female group The Bangles (originally Supersonic Bangs, then The Bangs), 1981-89; Tours and concerts include: Support to The Beat, 1982; Debut UK tour, 1984; World tour, 1986; Support to Simple Minds, Milton Keynes Bowl Pop Festival, 1986; Support to Queen, Ireland, 1986; US tour, 1986; Solo recording career, 1989-; US tour, support to Don Henley, 1991; Actress, The Allnighter, 1986. Recordings: Albums: with The Bangles: The Bangles, 1982; All Over The Place, 1984; Different Light, 1986; Everything, 1988; Bangles' Greatest Hits, 1989; Solo albums: When You're A Boy, 1991; Susannah Hoffs, 1996; Hit singles: Manic Monday, 1986; If She Knew What She Wants, 1986; Going Down To Liverpool, 1986; Walk Like An Egyptian, (Number 1, US), 1986; Hazy Shade Of Winter (used in film soundtrack Less Than Zero), 1988; In Your Room, 1988; Eternal Flame (Number 1, UK), 1989; Be With You, 1989; Solo singles: My Side Of The Bed, 1991; All I Want, 1996. Current Management: c/o Gold Mountain Entertainment, Suite 450, 3575 Cahuenga Blvd. W, Los Angeles, CA 90068, USA.

HOFMAN Jens, b. 28 Apr 1952, Copenhagen, Denmark. Executive Record Producer. Career: Managing Director, Attack Production Company, Denmark; A&R, EMI Medley Records, Polygram Records, Denmark; Executive Producer, Michael Learns To Rock; Sissel Kyrkjebo; Monrad and Rislund; Harvest Moon and Monique. Address: Attack, Rahbeks Alle 32, 1801 Frederiksberg C, Denmark.

HOGARTH Steve, b. 14 May 1959, Kendal, Cumbria, England. Musician; Singer; Songwriter. m. 16 Aug 1980, 1 son, 1 daughter. Career: Singer, groups The Europeans; How We Live; Lead singer, UK progressive rock group, Marillion, 1989-; Tours include: UK, 1991; North America, 1992; South America, 1992; Colaborations with The The, Julian Cope and Toni Childs; World tours with the Europeans; 5 world tours with Marillion. Recordings: Albums: with The Europeans: Vocabulary, 1982; Recurring Dreams, 1984; with Marillion: Season's End, 1989; Holidays In Eden, 1991; A Singles Collection 1982-1992, 1992; Brave, 1994; Afraid Of Sunlight, 1995; This Strange Engine; Solo as H: Ice Cream Genius; Singles: Hooks In You, 1989; Uninvited Guest, 1989; Easter, 1990; Cover My Eyes (Pain And Heaven), 1991; No One Can, 1991; Dry Land, 1991; Sympathy, 1992. Current Management: Hit & Run Music Ltd. Address: 30 Ives Street, London SW3 2ND, England.

HÖGLUND Kjell, b. 8 Dec 1945, Östersund, Sweden. Songwriter; Artist; Musician (guitar). Partner, Margaretha Granström. Education: Bachelor of Arts. Career: 12 albums with own songs; Pioneer of making own records; Legend, Swedish underground music. Compositions include: Songs: Witch-Trial; Smooth Water; Sea of Gennesaret; One Big Strong; One Gets Accustomed; The Last Battle. Recordings: Albums: Wonder, 1971; Flower Season, 1972; Witch-Trial, 1973; Baskervilles Hound, 1974; The Heart Is To The Left, 1975; Dr Jekyll's Will, 1979; The Road Towards Shangri-La, 1980; Signs Of The Times, 1984; Secret Love, 1986; Year of The Serpent, 1989; Höglund Forever, 1992; Incognito, 1995. Publications: Songbook: Burnt Ships, 1987; Novels: Magnum Opus, 1991; The Sicilian Seal, 1997. Honours: Numerous scholarships; Nominated for Swedish Grammy Award, 1992. Hobbies: Pet cat Mirre; Alchemy, Egyptology, Ark of the Covenant. Current Management: Kontur Management, Stockholm, Sweden. Address:

Atlantis Records, Karlbergsvägen 57, 113 35 Stockholm, Sweden.

HOIER Svein, b. 18 Nov 1970, Oslo, Norway. Musician (guitar, keyboard, drummer). Education: 4 years, Trondheim University. Career: Started as drummer: Closet Queens; Joined Hedge Hog, playing guitar, keyboard, sampler, 1994; Toured Europe, 1994, 1995. Recordings: Closet Queens: Closet Queens, 1993; Hedge Hog: Mindless, 1994; The Healing EP, 1995; Thorn Cord Wonder, 1995. Publications: 2 short films released: Smoking; Svein. Honours: Swein, Best Film, Trondheim Film Festival, 1995. Hobbies: Chess; Opera; Poetry. Current Management: Martin Aam, Hedge Hogment. Address: Hedge Hog, PO Box 683, 7001 Trondheim, Norway.

HOLBEK Joachim, b. 12 Nov 1957, Lyngby-Taarbaek, Denmark. Composer; Musician (drums, percussion, piano); m. Lone Nyhuus, 28 May 1988, 1 daughter. Career: Playing professionally, rock and jazz bands, 1975-; First professional composing job, 1979, small theatre in Copenhagen "A Caberet"; 1980-95: 5 plays; 15 ballets; 9 television productions; 8 film scores; Some commercial and radio work; Best known films are: Medea, 1988, by Lars V Trier; Europa, 1990, Lars V Trier; Russian Pizza Blues, 1992, Wikke/Rasmussen; Night Gard, 1994, Ole Bornedal; Kingdom, 1995, Lars V Trier; Film scores: Europa; Pretty Boy; Kingdom. Honours: Robert Awards, Best Danish Film Music, 1992, 1993. Membership: DJBFA (Danish Jazz, Beat Folk Authors). Address: Taarbaek Parcelves 2, 2930 Klampenborg, Copenhagen, Denmark.

HOLDER Noddy (Neville), b. 15 June 1950, Walsall, Warwickshire, England. Vocalist; Songwriter; Musician (guitar). Career: Guitarist, backing vocalist, Steve Brett and The Mavericks; Vocalist, guitarist, UK rock group, Slade (formerly N'Betweens, Ambrose Slade), 1966-91; Concerts include: First UK tour, 1972; Fanfare For Europe festival, London Palladium, 1973; Great British Music Festival, 1978; Reading Festival, 1980; Radio presenter, Picadilly Radio; Film: Flame, 1974. Compositions: Co-writer, all Slade's Top 20 hits, with Jimmy Lea. Recordings: Albums: Beginnings (as Ambrose Slade), 1969; Play It Loud, 1970; Slade Alive, 1972; Slayed, 1973; Sladest, 1973; Old New Borrowed Blue, 1974; Slade In Flame (soundtrack), 1974; Nobody's Fool, 1976; Slade Alive Vol 2, 1978; Return To Base, 1979; Slade Smashes, 1980; Till Deaf Do Us Part, 1981; We'll Bring The House Down, 1981; Slade On Stage, 1982; The Amazing Kamikaze Syndrome, 1983; Slade's Greats, 1984; Rogue's Gallery, 1985; Crackers, 1985; You Boyz Make Big Noize, 1987; Wall Of Hits, 1991; UK Number 1 hit singles: Coz I Luv You, 1971; Take Me Bak 'Ome, 1972; Mama Weer All Crazee Now (later recorded by Mama's Boys, Quiet Riot), 1972; Cum On Feel The Noize, 1973; Merry Christmas Everybody, 1973; Other hits: Look Wot You Dun, 1972; Gudbuy T'Jane, 1972; Skweeze Me Pleeze Me, 1973; My Friend Stan, 1973; Everyday, 1974; Bangin' Man, 1974; Far Far Away, 1974; Thanks For The Memory, 1975; In For A Penny, 1975; We'll Bring The House Down, 1981; My Oh My, 1983; Run Run Away, 1984; All Join Hands, 1984.

HOLDSWORTH Allan, b. Bradford, West Yorkshire, England. Musician (guitar). 1 son, 1 daughter. Musical Education: Self-taught. Career: Tours, television appearances worldwide. Recordings with: Tempest; Soft Machine; Gordon Beck; Allan Holdsworth Band: Sand; Atavachron; Secrets; IOU; Wardenclyffe Tower; Hard Hat Area. Honour: Guitar Hall Of Fame. Hobbies: Cycling; Making beer. Current Management: Marco Polo. Address: 3 The Lilacs, 50 Elm Grove, Hayling Island, Hampshire PO11 9EF, England.

HOLGATE David Edward, b. 19 Apr 1939, Romford, Essex, England. Musician (double bass,

bass guitar). m. Anne Malmström, 1 Apr 1962, 1 son, 1 daughter. Musical Education: Private lessons pianoforte to higher grade RSM. Career: Anglia TV session work for many years include:Crescendo; Miss Anglia; About Anglia; The Mid-day Show; Music Match; BBC Radio One Club; Mr and Mrs; The Seeds Of Love; Beach Boys support group: The Rainbow People. Recordings: Singles include: The Walk'll Do You Good; Dreamtime; The Sailing Song; Rainbows. Membership: Musicians' Union. Hobbies: Sculpture; Computers; French Language. Address: 8 Ash Grove, Norwich NR3 4BE, England.

HOLIDAY Doc (Edward Wohanka), b. 29 Jan 1943, New Jersey, USA. Record Producer; Recording Artist; Record Company Executive. 1 son, 2 daughters. Musical Education: Degrees in Music from Juilliard School Of Music; Berkeley University; University of Miami. Career: Television appearances include: The Tonight Show; American Bandstand; Merv Griffin Show; Joe Franklin Show; Grammy Awards Show; 76 US Country Number 1 hits as a record producer. Recordings include: As recording artist: Expressway To Your Heart; Just My Imagination; Walkin' In Memphis; As producer: Cajun Baby, Hank Williams Jr; Louisiana Man, Doug Kershaw; Mr Jones, Big Al Downing. Honours include: 36 Music Awards; 2 Grammy Awards; ICMA Producer of the Year, 1993-95. Memberships: BMI; ASCAP; SESAC. Hobbies: Fishing; Travel. Address: c/o Doc Holiday Productions, 10 Luanita Lane, Newport News, VA 23606, USA.

HOLLAND Annabel (Annie), b. 26 Aug 1965, London, England. Musician (bass guitar). Career: Member, Elastica; Numerous television and radio appearances; Tours: UK; USA; Canada; Europe. Recordings: Album: Elastica. Current Management: CMO Management. Address: Unit 32, Ransomes Dock, 35-37 Parkgate Road, London SW11 4NP, England.

HOLLAND Brian, b. 15 Feb 1941, Detroit, Michigan, USA. Composer; Record Producer. Career: Lead singer, the Satintones, 1950s; Member, composition and production team Holland/Dozier/Holland (with brother Eddie Holland and Lamont Dozier), 1963; Joined Motown label, 1960s; Co-founder, Invictus and Hot Wax record labels, 1967-75. Recordings: As co-writer, producer: with Marvin Gaye: Can I Get A Witness?; Little Darling; How Sweet It Is (To Be Loved By You); You're A Wonderful One; with Martha And The Vandellas: Heatwave; Quicksand; Nowhere To Run; Jimmy Mack; with Diana Ross and the Supremes: Where Did Our Love Go; Baby Love; Come See About Me; Stop! In The Name Of Love; Back In My Arms Again; You Can't Hurry Love; You Keep Me Hanging On; Love Is Here And Now You're Gone; The Happening; with the Four Tops: Baby I Need Your Loving; I Can't Help Myself; (It's The) Same Old Song; Reach Out I'll Be There; Bernadette; Standing In The Shadows Of Love; with the Miracles: Mickey's Monkey; I'm The One You Need; with the Isley Brothers: This Old Heart Of Mine; Put Yourself In My Place; I Guess I'll Always Love; Other recordings with Aretha Franklin; Kim Weston; Freda Payne; Chairmen Of The Board.

HOLLAND David, b. 5 Apr 1948, Northampton, England. Musician (drums). Musical Education: Self-taught. Career: Member, Pinkerton's Assorted Colours, 1966-1969; Trapeze, 1969-1979; Judas Priest, 1979-1988; Over 20 North American and European tours; Numerous radio and television appearances with the above. Recordings: Albums: with Trapeze, 1970-78: Trapeze; Medusa; You Are The Music We're Just The Band; The Final Swing; Hot Wire; Trapeze; Hold On; Running; with Judas Priest 1980-88: British Steel; Point Of Entry; Screaming For Vengeance; Defenders Of The Faith; Turbo; Priest-Live; Ram It Down; Also featured on: Play

Me Out, Glenn Hughes, 1977; Songwriter, Justin Hayward, 1977; Nightflight, Justin Hayward, 1980. Honours: Over 20 Platinum, Gold, Silver albums with Juads Priest; Crystal Globe Award. Hobbies: Cycling; DIY; Entertaining. Current Management: Kevin Wilson. Address: Studio Y, 7 East Street, Leicester LE1 6EY, England.

HOLLAND Eddie, b. 30 Oct 1939, Detroit, Michigan, USA. Composer; Record Producer. Career: Member, the Fideltones; Member, songwriting and production team Holland/Dozier/Holland (with Brian Holland and Lamont Dozier); Co-writer, producer, numerous records by major Motown artists, including a dozen US number 1 hits, 1963-68; Split from Motown, 1967; Co-founder, Invictus and Hot Wax record labels, 1967-75. Recordings: As co-producer, writer: with Marvin Gaye: Can I Get A Witness?; How Sweet It Is To Be Loved By You; You're A Wonderful One; with Martha And The Vandellas: Heatwave; Quicksand; Nowhere To Run; Jimmy Mack; with Diana Ross and the Supremes: Where Did Our Love Go; Baby Love; Come See About Me; Stop! In The Name Of Love; Back In My Arms Again; You Can't Hurry Love; You Keep Me Hanging On; Love Is Here And Now You're Gone; The Happening; with the Four Tops: Baby I Need Your Loving; I Can't Help Myself; (It's The) Same Old Song; Reach Out I'll Be There; Bernadette; Standing In The Shadows Of Love; with the Miracles: Mickey's Monkey; I'm The One You Need; with the Isley Brothers: This Old Heart Of Mine; Put Yourself In My Place; I Guess I'll Always Love; Other recordings with Freda Payne; Chairman Of The Board; Aretha Franklin; Kim Weston.

HOLLAND Jools (Julian), b. 24 Jan 1958, London, England. Musician (keyboards); Television Presenter. 1 son, 2 daughters. Career: Founder member, pianist, Squeeze, 1974-81, 1985-90; Solo artiste and bandleader: Jools Holland and his Big Band, 1982-84; Jools Holland and his Rhythm And Blues Orchestra, 1991-; Television presenter, music shows: The Tube, C4, 1982-86; Later With Jools Holland, BBC2, 1993-; Various other television specials, including Sunday Night, NBC, 1989. Recordings: Albums: with Squeeze: Squeeze, 1978; Cool For Cats, 1979; Argy Bargy, 1980; Cosi Fan Tutti Frutti, 1985; Babylon And On, 1987; Frank, 1989; Solo albums: A World Of His Own, 1990; The Full Complement, 1991; A To Z Of The Piano, 1992; Live Performance, 1994; Solo Piano, 1994; Sex and Jazz and Rock and Roll, 1996; Lift up the Lid, 1997; Hit singles include: with Squeeze: Take Me I'm Yours, 1978; Cool For Cats, 1979; Up The Junction, 1979; Slap And Tickle, 1979; Another Nail In My Heart, 1980; Pulling Mussels From A Shell, 1980; Hourglass, 1987; 853 5937, 1988. Memberships: Musicians' Union; Equity; Writer's Guild. Hobbies: Jazz and R&B music; Architectural sketching. Current Management: c/o Paul Loasby, One Fifteen, The Gallery, 28-30 Wood Wharf, Horseferry Place, London SE10 9BT, England.

HOLLINGWORTH Roy, b. 12 Apr 1949, Derby, England. Singer; Songwriter; Musician (guitar); Poet; Writer. Education: Nottingham University. Career: Feature writer, critic with Melody maker, London, 1970-74; Editor, Melody Maker, American Bureau, New York, 1973; Session musician, New York, 1973-78; Performance poet, singer, Greenwich Village, New York, 1973-80; American, Canadian tours, Germany, 1995; European Tour, 1997. Recordings: Albums: Guitarist, Electric Shocks, Roger Ruskin Spear, 1973; Solo album: Roy Hollingworth - In The Flesh, 1994. Honour: BBC Radio One, London, Rock Writer Of The Year, 1972. Membership: GEMA, Germany (artists and composers). Hobby: Occultist - Order of Initiates (Bardic). Address: 10 Genoa Avenue, London SW15 6DY, England.

HOLLWEG Rebecca, b. 30 June 1964, London, England. Singer; Songwriter. Education: BA (Hons), French, German, Oxon. Musical Education: Guildhall School of Music and Drama, Jazz Course. Career: Venues include: 606 Club; Vortex; Lyric Hammersmith; Manchester Royal Exchange; Glasgow International Jazz Festival; Pizza Express Jazz Club; Pizza on the Park; Royal Festival Hall Foyer; Barbican Foyer; About to embark on first album project; Radio broadcasts include: BBC Radio 3, Backbeat; BBC Radio Scotland TGIF. Address: 14A Emu Road, London SW8 3PR, England.

HOLMSTED Robert, b. 6 October 1966, Copenhagen, Denmark. Principal Trombonist. Engaged, Julie Praestimark Petersen. Education: Royal Danish Academy of Music; Soloist Class, Academy of Fuenen (Carl Nielsen Academy); Studies in Chicago and London. Career: 2nd Trombonist, Odense Symphony Orchestra, 1992-94; Principal Trombonist, Odense Symphony Orchestra, 1994-95; Principal Trombonist, National Radio Symphony Orchestra of Denmark, 1995-96; Principal Trombonist, Odense Symphony Orchestra, 1996-. Recordings: All Carl Nielsen Symphonies; All Ib Noerholm Symphonies; A Carl Nielsen Record with Lur-Music. Membership: Musical Reunion. Hobbies: Squash and Fitness; Wine Tasting; Travel. Address: Lollandsgade 47, 5000 Odense C, Denmark.

HOLSTEIN Christina Staël von, b. 13 Aug 1969, Lausanne, Switzerland. Singer; Musician (guitar); Lyricist; Composer. Musical Education: Guildhall Singing Grade 5 - Honours. Career: Member, bands The New Quartet; Vers La Flammes; Here Lies A Crime; Paper Fish; Guest vocalist, Wax Club; Jaded Halo; Musicals: West Side Story; Sweeney Todd, The Demon Barber of Fleet Street; The Boyfriend. Recordings: Album: Visitations From A Universal Mind, in progress. Memberships: Musicians' Union; Montessori School, Balderton Street; British School of Complementary Therapists, Harley Street; The Place To Be (charity for children with learning and emotional difficulties). Hobbies: Writing children's stories; Dance; Travel. Address: 44 Palace Gardens Terrace, London W8 4RR, England.

HOLZHAUER Rudy, b. 14 Dec 1951, Hamburg, Germany. Music Publisher; Manager. Career: Live engineer; Studio engineer; Music publisher; Artist manager; Owner, Musikverlag Progressive GmbH. Memberships: GEMA; DMV; DKV. Hobbies: Graphic design; Computing. Current Management: Self-managed. Address: Bramfelder Chaussee 238c, D-22177 Hamburg, Germany.

HOMES Stephen, b. 7 Oct 1955. Flamenco Musician (guitar). 1 daughter. Musical education: Self-taught. Career: Appearances include: Several local television and radio appearances; Solo recitals, art centres, England and Europe; Performances with fusion group Filigree include Commonwealth Institute, London. Recordings: Road To The Sun; Dance On Sand; Albums include many original compositions. Honour: Arts Council Grant to tour Spain, 1986. Hobby: Friends. Current Management: Self-managed. Address: 3 Mitre Court, Norwich NR3 2QB, England.

HONK Jivi (Herbert Gebetsroither), 5 Oct 1957, Linz a.d. Donau, Austria. Musician (guitar, piano); Singer; Songwriter; Performing Artist; Music Publisher; Instrumental Music Teacher. Musical Education: Guitar, piano, voice, theory (jazz), Prayner & Franz Schubert Conservatory, Vienna. Career: Member, US salsa and latin band Obote; Tours of Germany and Netherlands; Founder, Jivi Honk and band, 1983-; 500 live concerts in and around Austria, 1985-; Various own projects include Jivi Honk and the Funkplanet; The Honk Rock Project, 1990; Concerts include: U4, Vienna; Vienna State Opera; Budapest Town Hall; Italian tour, 1989;

Velden; Zürs; Television appearances include: ORF FS1; radio includes: 150 appearances on Austrian public radio and European stations, 1988-; Tokyo FM, 1990-. Recordings: Instrumentals: Lovedancer; Space Me To The Stars, 1988; Sunrider; Vienna Skyline; Moonrider; Highway of Fame; Golden Days, 1993, 1994; Albums: as Jivi Honk: Got My Style, 1990; Sunrider, 1993; Moonrider, 1993; Golden Days, 1994; Live At The Garage, 1995. Memberships: AKM; Austro Mechana; LSG/Östig. Hobbies: Nature; Philosophy; Reading. Current Management: Honk Music, Warner Chappel Group, Austria. Address: Hormayrgasse 3/25, A-1170 Vienna, Austria.

HOOGENDYK Jarmo, b. 28 March 1965, Den Helder, Netherlands. Musician (Trumpet); Teacher, Royal Conservatory, The Hague and Rotterdam Conservatory. Education: Graduate, Royal Conservatory, The Hague, 1989; Private lessons with Woody Shaw, 1987-88. Career: Tours/festival performances with A D Charles McPherson, 1987-89; Teddy Edwards, 1989-90; J J Johnson, Jimmy Heath, 1988; Junior Cook, Art Taylor, Ron Matthews trio; Battles, with A D Freddie Hubbard, 1987; Woody Shaw, 1987, 1988; Clark Terry, Benny Bailey, Lew Soloff; Festivals: Toronto, Montreal, Oakland; Sob's, New York. Compositions: Waltz for Woody; Run For Your Wife; Caught for Speeding; Jungle Fever. Recordings: European Trumpet Summit; Nueva Manteca: Bluesongo; Afrodisia; Let's Face the Music and Dance; Night People; Varadero Bluese; Afro Cuban Sanctus; Ben Van Den Dungen and Jarmo Hoogendÿk Quintet; Double Dutch; Speak Up; Heart of the Matter; Run For Your Wife. Publications: Dutch Playboy Magazine, 1992; Reviews in Downbeat, Latin Beat (USA); Interviews, Holland, Germany. Honours: Nos Meervaart Group Award, 1985; Pall Mall Export Award, 1986. Membership: NTB. Current Management: JWA Jazz & World Music Agency, PO Box 95905, 2509 CX Den Haag, Netherlands.

HOOK Peter, b. 13 Feb 1956, Salford, Lancashire, England. Musician (bass). Career: Member, Joy Division, 1977-80; New Order, 1980-; Revenge, 1990-; Tours: UK; Europe; Australia; New Zealand; Far East; US; South America; Concerts include: Glastonbury Festival, 1981, 1987; Futurama Festival, Leeds, 1982; San Remo Festival, 1988; Reading Festival, 1989. Recordings: Albums: with Joy Division: Unknown Pleasures, 1979; Closer, 1980; Still, 1981; The Peel Sessions, 1988; Also featured on: Short Circuit - Live At The Electric Circus, 1978; with New Order: Movement, 1981; Power Corruption And Lies, 1983; Low Life, 1985; Brotherhood, 1986; Technique, 1989; Republic, 1993; with Revenge: One True Passion, 1990; Singles include: with Joy Division: Love Will Tear Us Apart, 1980; with New Order: Ceremony, 1981; Temptation, 1982; Confusion, 1983; Blue Monday, 1984; Thieves Like Us, 1984; Shellshock, 1986; True Faith, 1987; Fine Time, 1988; Round And Round, 1989; World In Motion (with England World Cup Football Squad), 1990; How Does It Feel?, 1992; Regret, 1993; Ruined In A Day, 1993; Spooky, 1993. Current Management: Spark Management, 100 Wilshire Blvd, Suite 1830, Santa Monica, CA 90064, USA.

HOOKER Jake, b. 5 Mar 1951, New York, USA. Songwriter; Record Producer; Musician (guitar). m. 7 Sept 1994, 1 son, 2 daughters. Musical Education: Self-taught. Career: Wrote No.1 international hit I Love Rock And Roll; Formed UK group The Arrows, 1974. Recordings: I Love Rock And Roll; Destination Unknown (from film soundtrack Top Gun); Sweetest Victory (from film soundtrack Rocky IV); Iron Eagle (from film soundtrack Iron Eagle). Publications: The Arrows Biography. Honours: Several Platinum and Gold records. Memberships: NARAS; BMI; AFofM. Current Management: HEI. Address: 1325 El Hito Circle, Pacific Palisades, CA 90272, USA.

HOOKER John Lee, b. 22 Aug 1917, Clarksdale, Mississippi, USA. Blues Musician (guitar); Singer. Career: Recording artiste, 1948-; Issued about 70 singles under 10 pseudonyms, 1949-54; Debut as radio DJ, Detroit, 1955; Appearances include: Newport Folk Festival, Newport, 1960, 1989; European tour, 1962; Ann Arbor Blues & Jazz Festival, 1970; The Boogie'n'Blues Concert, Carnegie Hall, New York, 1979; All Our Colors - The Good Road Concert benefit, 1992; Film appearance, The Blues Brothers, 1980. Recordings: Albums: Concert At Newport; Live At The Café Au Go-Go, 1966; House Of The Blues, 1967; Hooker'n'Heat, 1971; Endless Boogie, 1971; Never Get Out Of These Blues Alive, 1972; Detroit Special, 1974; Don't Turn Me From Your Door, 1974; The Cream, 1978; The Healer, 1989; Mr Lucky, 1991; Boom Boom, 1992; Chill Out, 1995; Singles include: Crawlin' King Snake; I'm In The Mood; Boom Boom; Dimples; I'm In The Mood (duet with Bonnie Raitt), 1990; Gloria (with Van Morrison), 1993; Contributor, The Iron Man, Pete Townshend, 1989; Got Love If You Want It, John Hammond, 1992; I Heard You Twice The First Time, Branford Marsalis, 1992; Film soundtracks: Blues Brothers, 1980; The Color Purple, 1986. Honours: National Blues Awards, 1990; Soul Beat Awards, 1990; A Tribute To John Lee Hooker, Madison Square Garden, New York, 1990; Inducted into Rock And Roll Hall Of Fame, 1991; Bay Area Music Awards, Outstanding Blues Album, 1992. Address: c/o Rosebud Agency, PO Box 170429, San Francisco, CA 94117, USA.

HOOKER Steve, b. 19 May 1953, Rochford, Essex. Musician (guitar) Singer; Songwriter; Producer. m. (1) 1 son, (2) Elaine, 11 Aug 1992. Education: Southend Art College, Cordwainers, London. Musical Education: Self-taught. Career: The Heat, 1977; Shakers, 1982-87; Jeremy Gluck, 1987; Steve Hooker and Wilko Johnson, (recording project) 1988; Boz and the Bozmen, 1988; Steve Hooker Band, 1989-91; Rumble, 1994; Television includes: Marquee series (Anglia TV); FR3 (France); Several radio appearances; Musical contributor to soundtrack, Burnin' Love, film noir. Compositions include: Elmore Stroll, on Hell for Leather, Rumble, 1996; The Raid, Captain Drugbuster, 1997. Recordings: with The Shakers: Temptation Walk, Catch On; Also featured on: Really Gone, 1984; Wild Heroine, Boz and the Bozmen; Dress in Deadmens Suits, 1988. Publications: Sleeve notes with journalist John Tobler. Honour: Diploma in design of shoe and footwear. Membership: Musicians' Union. Hobby: Collector of Rock'n'Roll and 50's memorabilia. Current Management: NV Records. Address: 149 Lonsdale Road, Southchurch, Southend-on Sea, Essex SS2 4LP, England.

HOOPER Nellee. Record Producer; Arranger. Career: Member, The Wild Bunch Crew; Member, mixing crew Massive Attack; Joined Soul II Soul, offering sound systems services to UK dance clubs, 1985; Residency, Africa Centre, Covent Garden, London; Relocated to Fridge Club, Brixton, 1988; Opened 2 shops, London, 1988; Developed video and film company, fan club, talent agency, record company, 1990-. Recordings include: Albums: with Soul II Soul: Club Classics Volume One, 1989; Volume II - A New Decade, 1990; Volume III - Just Right, 1992; Singles include: Keep On Movin', 1989; Back To Life (However Do You Want Me), 1989; A Dream's A Dream, 1990; Missing You, with Kym Mazelle, 1990; Joy, 1992; Just Right, 1992; Move Me No Mountain, 1992; Wish, 1993; As producer: with Massive Attack: Unfinished Sympathy; Protection; with Madonna: Bedtime Stories; with Björk: Debut; Post; Universal James, James Brown, 1993; As arranger (with Jazzie B): Nothing Compares To U, Sinead O'Connor, 1990 Contributor, Mad About The Mouse (Disney compilation), 1991. Honours include: Platinum discs; Top Dance Sales Artists, Billboard, 1989; 3 American Music Awards, 1990; 4 British DMC Dance Awards, 1990; Grammy

Award, Best R&B Instrumental Performance, 1990; 3 Soul Train Awards, 1990; BMI College Radio Award, Back To Life, 1991; ASCAP Award, Back To Life, 1991; BRIT Award, Best Producer, 1995; BRIT Award Nominations, Best Producer, 1994, 1996.

HOPE-EVANS Peter John, b. 28 Sept 1947, Brecon, Wales. Composer; Performer; Musician (mouth organ, mouth bow, Jews harp). m. Christine Frances Rich, 26 Oct 1973. Education: MA, Romanticism and Modernism, 1991-92. Musical Education: Texas Slim; Maurice Blanchot; Edgar fünf. Career: Played with: Medicine Head; Pete Townshend; Deep End; Ronnie Lane; The Ravishing Beauties; Films: White City, 1986; Mourning; Radio: Strange Navigations (Pirate Radio), 1993-; Embers/descendres/eschenglet, 1994; Classical: 4'33 uncaged (fünf), 1981, 1985, 1989; Multi-media: sigh code: airilicked, 1993; Theatre: La Folie Du Jour, 1989; Manslaughter/Woman's Laughter, 1992. Recordings: New Bottles Old Medicine, 1970; Cassette only series: Elgin Moveme(a)nts; Closer Than Breath (Itself); In The Sacred Cedars; Shadow Of The Object; Theatre: Up Your Ass Solanas, 1992; The Tempest (RSC), 1995. Publications: Harmonica Yoga, 1990; Philosophising With A Harmonica (Back To Nietzsche), 1992. Honours: Prix Italia (music and arts): Strangefish (DV8) 1994. Hobbies: Merdre Sans Tête (performance/study group of the Clown and the Hanged woman in Western Popular Culture). Address: 14 Eastbank Road, Hampton Hill, Middlesex TW12 1RP, England.

HOPKIN Mary, b. 3 May 1950, Pontardawe, Wales. Singer. Career: Winner, talent show, Opportunity Knocks, 1968; First female to top UK charts, 1968; Debut hit, Those Were The Days, also recorded in Spanish, French, German, Italian, Hebrew (sales exceeded 8 million); UK tour, 1969; Backing vocals for various artistes, 1970s; Member, harmony trio, Sundance, 1980; Lead vocalist with Oasis (with Peter Skellern, Julian Lloyd Webber), 1984; Performances include: The Chieftains Music Festival 1991, London Palladium, 1991. Recordings: Albums: Post Card, 1969; Earth Song - Ocean Song, 1971; Those Were The Days, 1972; Spirit, 1991; with Oasis: Oasis, 1984; Singles include: Those Were The Days (Number 1, UK), 1968; Goodbye, 1969; Temma Harbour, 1970; Knock Knock Who's There, UK Eurovision entry, (Number 2, UK), 1970; Think About Your Children; If You Love Me; Contributor, The King Of Elfland's Daughter, 1977; Dylan Thomas' Under Milk Wood, 1988.

HOPKINS Philip Nicholas, b. 5 Feb 1962, Surrey, England. Musician (percussion, chromatic harmonica). m. Barbara Mason, 17 July 1993. Education: MA, Oxford University. Musical Education: Music scholarship, King's School, Canterbury. Career: Sweeney Todd, National Theatre, UK/Europe Tours, 1993-94; London theatre work includes A Little Night Music, National Theatre, 1995; Concert tours, USA with: Phil Coulter; Maura O'Connell; Liam Clancy including Carnegie Hall, New York. Recordings: Television, album work with: Leon Redbone; Phil Coulter; Billy Connolly; The Dubliners; Rory Gallagher; Val Doonican; Television, radio sessions include: Next Of Kin; Men Of The World, BBC1, 1995. Publications: Articles in Modern Drummer, USA. Membership: Musicians' Union. Hobbies: Swimming; Golf. Address: 5 Claygate Road, Dorking, Surrey, England.

HOPPER Hugh, b. 29 Apr 1945, Whitstable, Kent, England. Musician (bass guitar); Composer. 2 daughters. Musical Education: Self-taught. Career: Wilde Flowers; Soft Machine; Isotope; Carla Bley; Robert Wyatt; Own bands. Compositions: Memories, Robert Wyatt and Whitney Houston; Facelift, Soft Machine; Was A Friend, Robert Wyatt. Recordings: Soft Machine 2-6; Hoppertunity Box; 1984; Caveman

2-6; Hoppertunity Box; 1984; Caveman Hughscore; Meccano Pelorus. Publication: Rock Bass Manual. Memberships: Musicians' Union; MCPS; PRS; PAMRA. Hobbies: Cycling; Sailing; Fresh air. Current Management: Euterpe, 61290 Lespesses, France. Address: 29 Castle Road, Whitstable, Kent CT5 2DZ, England.

HOPWOOD Freddy, b. 22 Dec 1948, Lichfield, England. Musician (drums, penny whistle, concertina). m. Beryl Agnes Nutt, 17 May 1974, 2 sons. Education: Uttoxeter and Burton Technical College. Musical Education: Self-taught. Career: Member, Dr Strangely Strange, 1970-71; Television appearances, John Peel session, BBC Radio 1; Member, Sutherland Brothers Band, 1972; Support tours, Free, Mott The Hoople; David Bowie; Performance at Montreux Golden Rose Festival; Television appearances: Switzerland; Denmark; France; Member, R Cajun and the Zydeco Brothers, 1984-97; Numerous television and radio appearances, 1987-97. Recordings: Albums/singles with Sutherland Brothers Band, 1971; Leonard and Squires, 1976; R Cajun and the Zydeco Brothers, 1984-94; Yeah Jazz, 1992; Vice-Bishops Of Uttoxeter, 1995; Big Red Kite, 1996. Hobbies: Cycling; UFOs; Folklore; Musicology. Current Management: Smalltown Records. Address: 17 Colne Mount, Uttoxeter, Staffs ST14 7QR, England.

HORABIN Gren, b. 15 May 1939, Rainhill, Liverpool, England. Senior Lecturer (director of studies); Musician (alto and tenor saxophones, clarinet). m. Catherine Rawlinson, 28 Dec 1968, 1 son. Education: Technical Teachers Certificate. Musical Education: Private tuition, pianoforte, saxophone clarinet; Bandsman in Royal Air Force. Career: Bands include: Leader, alto clarinet, Gren Horabin Combo; Alto saxophone, Band of The Royal Air Force, Bridgnorth; Leader, saxophones, clarinet, Crescendo; Currently tenor clarinet, John Shepherd Combo; Alto, tenor clarinet, Leader, 42nd Street Swing; Jazz, dance gigs, various venues in Midlands with Pete King, Mick Large, Ricky Allan; Allan Billings; various small mainstream groups; Productions include: Lady Audley's Secret; Dirty Work At The Crossroads; Hits From The Blitz; Concert Style In Jazz (with Duncan Swift, Geraint Ellis); Creator, author, original Jazz Studies Units, BTEC National Diploma Level, Kidderminster College, Worcestershire; Senior Lecturer, Director of Studies, Creative Arts & Community Studies, Kidderminster College, retired; Currently leading own band, 42nd Street Swing; Alto, Tenor and Clarinet with John Shepherd Band. Compositions include: Jingle, Calypso Lipstick commercial for Prides Ltd; Classical, modern, theatre and dance. Honours: Skills Assessors and Verifiers Awards. Memberships: Musicians' Union; Association of British Jazz Musicians. Hobbies: Jazz; Music; Golf. Address: 9 Waterlaide Road, Hartlebury, Worcestershire DY11 7TP, England.

HORAN Kevin, b. Dublin, Ireland. m. Yolande Caroline Paris Horan, 20 September 1985, 1 son. Career: Vocals, Guitar in Harp 'N' Drum, 1982-90; Vocal, Guitar in Ash Plant, 1994-; Vocal, Guitar in Trad Lads, 1993-. Recordings: Ashplant, 1985-95; Trad Lads, TLCD 1; Happy Days, 1997. Memberships: DMF; Dansk Musiker Forbund (Danish Musicians Union). Hobbies: Water Skiing; Golf; Badminton. Address: Dalgardsparken 19, 3540 Lynge, Denmark.

HORECKA Hana, b. 22 Dec 1954, Jablonee nad Nisou, Czech. Singer; Songwriter; Musician (guitar). m. Jan Vaculik, 11 August 1994, 2 daughters. School of Arts in Prague. Semafor Theatre, Prague, 1984-85; Fesaci country music group, 1985-89; Sally Rose Band, ladies country music group, 1989; International country music festivals in Europe. Compositions: Oh, Promises; Butterfly Love; Yellow Moon. Recordings: Zenská jak má byt, solo albums, 1992; Tenkrát na západe, 1993; Kovbojská Svatba, 1995; Tráva z

Tennessee, 1990. Membership: Intergram, USA. Current Management: Jan Vaculik, Behounkova 2307, 15500 Praha 5, Czech. Address: Hana Horecká, Behounkova 2307, 15500 Praha 5, Czech Republic.

HORN Shirley, b. Washington, USA. Vocalist; Musician (piano). 1 daughter. Education: Havard University. Career: Concerts include: Lincoln Center, New York, 1989; Blue Note, Tokyo, 1989. Recordings: Albums: Cat On A Hot Fiddle, 1959; Embers And Ashes, 1960; Live At The Village Vanguard, 1961; Loads Of Love, 1963; Shirley Horn With Horns, 1963; Travelin' Light, 1965; For Love Of Ivy, 1968; A Dandy In Aspic, 1968; Where Are You Going?, 1972; A Lazy Afternoon, 1979; All Night Long, 1982; Violets For Your Ears, 1983; The Sentimental Touch, 1985; I Thought About You, 1987; Softly, 1988; Close Enough For Love, 1988; Tune In Tomorrow, 1990; You Won't Forget Me, 1991; Dedicated To You - Tribute To Sarah Vaughn (with Carmen McRae), 1991. Current Management: Sheila Mathis Enterprises, 200 Haven Avenue, Suite 5P, New York, NY 10033, USA.

HORN Trevor, b. 15 July 1949. Record Producer; Record Company Executive; Vocalist; Musician (guitar). m. Jill Sinclair. Career: Session musician, 1970s; Founder, Buggles, 1977-80; Member, Yes, 1980-81; Independent record producer, 1982-; Founder, ZTT Records. Compositions include: Theme music, television series The Tube. Recordings: Albums: with Buggles: The Plastic Age, 1980; with Yes: Drama, 1990; Singles with Buggles: Video Killed The Radio Star (Number 1, UK), 1979; The Plastic Age; Clean Clean; Elstree; I Am A Camera; As producer: Albums include: Welcome To The Pleasure Dome, Frankie Goes To Hollywood, 1984; Lexicon Of Love, ABC, 1982; 90125, Yes, 1983; Seal, Seal, 1991; Tubular Bells II, Mike Oldfield, 1992; Other recordings with Tina Charles; Hans Zimmer; Singles: Relax, Frankie Goes To Hollywood, 1983; Two Tribes, Frankie Goes To Hollywood, 1984; Instinction, Spandau Ballet, 1982; Close (To The Edit), Art Of Noise, 1985; Moments Of Love, Art Of Noise, 1985; Owner Of A Lonely Heart, Yes, 1983. Honours: BRIT Awards: Best British Producer, 1985, 1992; Q Award, Best Producer, 1991. Current Management: Sarm Productions, The Blue Building, 42-46 St Lukes Mews, London W11 1DG, England.

HORNE Lena, b. 30 June 1917, Brooklyn, New York, USA. Singer; Actress. m. Lennie Hayton, 1947 (deceased 1971). Career: Chorus singer, Cotton Club, Harlem, 1934; Singer with Noble Sissle's Society Orchestra, 1935-36; Charlie Barnet, 1940-41; Film appearances: Panama Hattie, 1942; Cabin In The Sky, 1943; Stormy Weather, 1943; Thousands Cheers; I Dood It; Swing Fever; Broadway Rhythm; Two Girls And A Sailor; Ziegfield Follies; Till The Clouds Roll By; Words And Music; Duchess Of Idaho; Meet Me In Las Vegas; Death Of A Gunfighter; The Wiz; Television appearances include: Harry and Lena, 1970; Cosby Show; Sanford And Son; Stage appearances: Dance With Your Gods, Broadway, 1934; Blackbirds Of 1939; Jamaica, Broadway, 1957; The Lady And Her Music, Broadway, 1981; Recent appearances include: JVC Jazz Festival, 1993. Recordings: Hits include: Stormy Weather; Deed I Do; As Long As I Live; Love Me Or Leave Me; Albums include: The Men In My Life, 1989; We'll Be Together Again, 1994; Also recorded with: Cab Calloway; Artie Shaw; Teddy Wilson. Publications: Lena (with Richard Schickel); In Person. Honours include: Tony Award, Distinguished Achievement In The Theatre; Drama Desk Award; New York Drama Critics' Special Award; Handel Medallion, New York City; Emergence Award, Dance Theatre of Harlem; 2 Grammy Awards; NAACP Springarn Award; Honour For Lifetime Contributions To The Arts, 1984; Paul Robson Award, Actor's Equity, 1985;

Honorary doctorate, Harvard University, 1979. Address: c/o Casterbridge Ltd, 1204 Third Avenue, Suite 162, New York, NY 10021, USA.

HORNSBY Bruce Randall, b. 23 Nov 1954, Richmond, Virginia, USA. Musician (piano); Songwriter. m. Kathy Lynn Yankovich, 31 Dec 1983, 2 sons. Musical Education: BA, Music, University of Miami, 1977. Career: Played on over 50 albums for other artists including: Bob Dylan; Grateful Dead; Bonnie Raitt; Don Henley; Bob Seeger; Willie Nelson; Branford Marsalis; Chaka Khan; Squeeze; Robbie Robertson; 8 US top 40 hits (6 as an artist, 2 as a songwriter); Written songs with: Don Henley; Robbie Robertson; Leon Russell; Chaka Khan. Recordings: 5 albums: The Way It Is, 1986; Scenes From the Southside, 1988; A Night On The Town, 1990; Harbour Lights, 1993; Hot House, 1995. Honours: 3 Grammys; 9 Grammy Nominations; 8 times winner, Keyboard Magazine Readers Poll; ASCAP Song Of The Year: The Way It Is, 1987; Album Of The Year: Downbeat Readers Poll: Harbour Lights, 1994; Platinum, Gold albums, worldwide. Memberships: ASCAP; AFofM. Hobbies: Sports (basketball, running); Reading. Current Management: Q-Prime Management, New York. Address: PO Box 3545, Williamsburg, VA 23187, USA.

HORSLEY Richard, b. 5 Jan 1970, Chelmsford, Essex, England. Record Company Executive; Musician (drums); Recording Artist; Producer. Musical Education: 10 years drum tuition. Career: Underground producer, recording artist under name of Timeslip; Numerous remixes; Private commissioned work; Owner, record label, R H Records. Recordings: Kinky & Hypnotiq, 1996. Memberships: PPL; PRS; BASCA. Hobbies: Tennis; Working out; Listening to music. Address: R H Records, Greatworth House, Greatworth, Banbury, Oxon OX17 2DR, England.

HOTATSU Nami, b. 3 September 1969, Tokyo, Japan. Singer; Songwriter; Musician (piano, keyboards, synthesizer, Irish harp). Education: Graduated, Kunitachi College of Music, Tokyo, Japan, 1992; Classical Piano, 4 years old; Musicology, Kumitachi College of Music; Vocal lesson, Japanese Traditional Style and Pop Style. Career: Shu Uemura Make Up Installation, 1992; Eden in the Sky, Yellow, 1993-94; Partheno-Jenesis, Ambient Opera, Tokyo, 1995; Earth Festival, Fili Festival, 1996; Haruomi Hosono and Japanese Sea's Mongoloid, 1996; WaterScape, Nagoya, 1996; Earth Sonic, Tokyo, 1996; The World of Shakespeare, Dramatic Reading, Shakespeare Country Park, Chiba, Japan, 1997. Compositions: Making Sense of Jewel, 1993; Hotatsu-Nami, 1994; Luna Drifting On the Glittering Waves, 1995; Stranger Than Movies, 1997. Recording: Happy Birthday to Me Itaka, 1996. Membership: Japan Soundscape Association. Hobbies: Movies; Books; Cooking; Ecology; Animals. Current Management: Macaroni Tone, #201, 1-5-4 Sakuradai, Nerima-ku, Tokyo 176, Japan. Address: #201, 1-5-4 Sakuradai, Nerima-ku, Tokyo 176, Japan.

HOTTE Kevin Richard, b. 16 Nov 1959, Port Colbourne, Ontario, Canada. Composer; Producer. m. 16 Oct 1982. Education: Graphic Arts, Photography, Niagara College. Musical Education: Privately trained: drums, percussion, keyboards. Career: Owner, Musicom Music Productions; The Sound Kitchen Recording Studio; Creative Images Media; Creative Images, sydicated radio show about photography technique. Compositions: Various radio jingles, corporate video scores. Recordings: Windows (14 song debut album). Memberships: SOCAN; ASCAP. Hobbies: Photography; Martial arts; Motor racing. Current Management: Self-managed. Address: St Catharines, Ontario, Canada.

HOULSTON Robert William, b. 6 July 1955, Wolverhampton, England. Musician Tutor (electric guitar, bass); Vocalist. Education: City and Guilds radio and television. Musical Education: Piano lessons, classical guitar lessons. Career: 25 years live concerts in pubs, clubs, dinner dances; Singer, guitarist, various groups and solo performances; Plays solo, as Daybreak Duo and Daybreak Trio; Teacher, guitar, 7 years. Memberships: Registry of Electric Guitar Tutors; Musicians' Union. Hobbies: Singing and playing various musical instruments; Juggling; Social dancing; Illustrating; Telegraphy amateur radio. Address: 12 Longacres, St Albans, Herts AL4 0DR, England.

HOUSTON Cissy (Emily Drinkard), b. 1933, Newark, New Jersey, USA. Singer. 1 daughter. Career: Member, family gospel group Drinkard Singers; Backing singers for numerous artists including: Wilson Pickett; Solomon Burke; Vocalist, Sweet Inspirations, 1967-70; Prolific session singer. Recordings: Albums: Cissy Houston, 1977; Warning Danger, 1979; Step Aside For A Lady, 1980; Mama's Cooking, 1987; Singles: I'll Be There, 1970; Be My Baby, 1971; Think It Over, 1978; Other albums: with Whitney Houston (her daughter): Whitney Houston, 1985; Whitney, 1987; with Aretha Franklin: Let Me Into Your Life, 1974; Love All The Hurt Away, 1981; Jump To It, 1982; with Van Morrison: Moondance, 1970; No Sheets, 1974; with Diana Ross: Diana's Duets, 1982; Silk Electric, 1982; The Wiz (soundtrack), 1978; with Paul Simon: Paul Simon, 1972; Greatest Hits etc, 1977; with Luther Vandross: Never Too Much, 1981; Forever, For Always, For Love, 1982; Busy Body, 1987; The Night I Fell In Love, 1985; Give Me The Reason, 1987; Other recordings with numerous artists including: Joe Cocker; Judy Collins; Kiki Dee; Jackie De Shannon; Gregg Allman; The Drifters; J Geils Band; Chaka Khan; Don McLean; John Prine; Linda Ronstadt.

HOUSTON Thelma, b. Leland, Mississippi, USA. Singer; Actress. Career: Singer, gospel group the Art Reynolds Singers, late 1960s; Solo artiste, 1969-; Also recorded with Jerry Butler; Actress, films: Death Scream; Norman... Is That You?; The Seventh Dwarf. Recordings: Albums: Sunshower, 1969; Thelma Houston, 1973; Anyway You Like It, 1977; The Devil In Me, 1978; Ready To Roll, 1978; Ride To The Rainbow, 1979; Breakwater Cat, 1980; Never Gonna Be Another One, 1981; I've Got The Music In Me, 1981; Qualifying Heats, 1987; With Jerry Butler: Thelma and Jerry, 1977; Two To One, 1978; Hit single: Don't Leave Me This Way, 1976. Current Management: Gross Management Organization, 930 Third Street, Ste 102, Santa Monica, CA 90403, USA.

HOUSTON Whitney, b. 9 Aug 1963, Newark, New Jersey, USA. Singer. m. Bobby Brown, 18 July 1992, 1 daughter. Musical Education: Singing lessons with mother, Cissy Houston. Career: New Hope Baptist Junior Choir, age 8; Nightclub performances with mother, 1978; Backing vocalist, Chaka Khan and Lou Rawls, 1978; Model, Glamour and Seventeen magazines; Actress, television shows, USA; Solo artiste, 1985-; First US and European tours, 1986; Montreux Rock Festival, 1987; Nelson Mandela Tribute concert, Wembley, 1988; National anthem, Super Bowl XXV, Miami, 1991; Speaker, HIV/AIDs rally, London, 1991; Television specials include: Welcome Home Heroes (return of Gulf troops), 1991; Whitney Houston - This Is My Life, ABC, 1992; Actress, film The Bodyguard, 1992; 87 million albums sold to date. Recordings: Singles include: You Give Good Love, 1985; Saving All My Love For You (Number 1, UK and US), 1985; How Will I Know, 1986; Greatest Love Of All (Number 1, US), 1986; I Wanna Dance With Somebody (Number 1, US and UK), 1987; Didn't We Almost Have It All (Number 1, US), 1987; So Emotional (Number 1, US), 1987; Where Do Broken Hearts Go (Number 1, US), 1988; Love Will Save The Day, 1988; One Moment In Time (Number 1, UK), 1988; I'm Your Baby Tonight (Number 1, US), 1990; All The Man That I Need (Number 1, US), 1991; Miracle, 1991; My Name Is Not Susan, 1991; I Will Always Love You (Number 1 in 11 countries), 1992; I'm Every Woman, 1993; I Have Nothing, 1993; Run To You, 1993; Albums: Whitney Houston, 1985; Whitney, 1987; I'm Your Baby Tonight, 1990; Film soundtrack: The Bodyguard (Number 1 in 20 countries), 1992. Also featured on: Life's A Party, Michael Zager Band; Duet with Teddy Pendergrass, Hold Me, 1984; Duet with Aretha Franklin, It Isn't, It Wasn't, It Ain't Ever Gonna Be, 1989. Honours include: 2 Grammy Awards; 7 American Music Awards; Emmy, 1986; Songwriter's Hall Of Fame, 1990; Longest-ever US Number 1 record (14 weeks), highest-ever US 1-week sales total, second best seller in US ever, all for I Will Always Love You, 1992; Numerous Gold and Platinum discs. Current Management: Nippy Inc., 2160 N Central Road, Fort Lee, NJ 07024, USA.

HOVMAN Klavs, b. 27 Oct 1957, Aarhus, Denmark. Musician (double bass, bass). 1 daughter, 1 son. Career: Member, Savage Rose, 1991-92; Played with numerous jazz/rock bands; Toured with: Ernie Wilkins Almost Big Band; Horace Parlan; Toots Thielemans; Lee Konitz; Svend Asmussen; Bassist with Etta Cameron's jazz and gospel groups, 1980-; Gospel concerts, Europe, 1990's; Member, Marilyn Mazur's groups Future Song and Pulse Unit; Compositions: Music for New Music Orchestra, Copenhagen Jazz Festival Event. Recordings: Album: Baraban, Peter Danemo, 1991; Månebarn, Savage Rose, 1992; Marilyn Mazur's Future Song, 1992; Echoze Of..., Harry Beckett and Pierre Dorge, 1992; Being, Lotte Anker/Mette Peterson Quintet, 1993; Savage Rose 25, Savage Rose, 1993; Gospel Concert, Etta Cameron, 1995; Circular Chant, Marilyn Mazur/Pulse Unit, 1995.

HOWARD Dominic Richard Vincent, b. 3 Dec 1965, Birmingham, England. Musician (bass guitar). m. Lorraine Rogers, 12 May 1995. Education: North East Surrey College of Technology. Musical Education: Self-taught. Career: Televison appearances: with Paul Harris: Top Of The Pops, Song For Europe '95; with B A Robertson: Pebble Mill; Radio appearances: BBC Radio 1, 2; BBC GLR; BBC Southern Counties; BBC Radio Coventry; Mercury; BFBS Worldwide Network. Recordings: Paul Harris: Spinning Away; Lee Collinson: Slip The Driver A Fiver. Membership: Musicians' Union.

HOWARD George Nathaniel, b. 15 Sept 1956, Philadelphia, Pennsylvania, USA. Musician (saxophone). m. Doria Andrea Jones, 28 Sept 1987, 1 daughter. Education: Temple University. Musical Education: Studied bassoon, clarinet, ages 6-15. Career: Two Grammy Nominations; Arsenio Hall Show; Joan Rivers Show; Soul Train; 7 videos Carnegie Hall; Playboy Jazz; Tours with: Grover Washington, 1979. Recordings: Albums: Asphalt Gardens; Steppin' Out; Dancing In the Sun; Love Will Follow; A Nice Place To Be; Reflections; Personal; Love And Understanding; Cross Your Mind; When Summer Comes; A Home Far Away; Working On It. Honours: 2 Grammy Award Nominations; 1 Soul Train Award (inaugural year); 1 BRE. Memberships: AFTRA; AFofM; SAG. Hobbies: Raquet Ball; Billiards; Golf. Current Management: Paul Zukowski. Address: 20750 Ventura Boulevard #160, Woodland Hills, CA 91364, USA.

HOWARD John, b. 9 Apr 1953, Bury, Lancashire, England. Record Company Executive; Musician (keyboards). Education: Art College. Private piano tuition, age 7-16. Career: Songwriter; Singer; Signed to CBS Records, 1973; Moved to Ariola Records with Trevor Horn, 1977; Returned to CBS with Nicky Graham, 1980; Member of Quiz, with Steve Levine and Graham Broad, 1981-83; Label Manager, Conifer Records, 1985; A&R Manager, Pickwick Records, 1986; Strategic Marketing Manager, MCA Records, 1993; A&R Director, Carlton Records, 1995. Recordings: Albums: Kid In A Big World, 1975; On Reflection, 1993; Singles: with Quiz: It's You I Want; And The World; Solo: Nothing More To Say; Songs: Casting Shadows, for film Open Season; with Dave Willetts: Stages of Love; with Stephanie Lawrence: Footlights; with Des O'Connor: Blue Days; International Music Development, Reader's Digest, 1997. Hobbies: Reading biographies; Music; Writing. Address: Reader's Digest, 11 Westferry Circus, Canary Wharf, London E14 4HE, England.

HOWARD Johnny, b. 5 Feb 1931, Croydon, Surrey, England. Bandleader; Musician (saxophone). m. 28 Sept 1970, 1 son, 1 daughter. Musical Education: Private tuition. Career: Professional big band leader, 1959-; Worked Mecca Dancehall circuit until 1967; Radio broadcasts, including 5 years on Easybeat, own lunchtime show, One O'Clock Jump; Television includes: Come Dancing, 1960s-70s; Played corporate and conference engagements, 1980s-90s. Recordings: More than a dozen albums and singles, 1960s-70s; Hit single: Rinky Dink (used by Radio Caroline as theme tune). Honours: Carl Alan Award, Britain's Best Band, 1967. Hobby: Design. Current Management: Fanfare 3000. Address: The Folly, Pinner Hill Road, Pinner, Middlesex HA5 3YQ, England.

HOWARD (Kevin) Robert, b. 31 Oct 1962, Huddersfield, England. Engineering Technician; Semi-Professional Musician (drums). m. Nicola Jane, 24 June 1989, 2 sons. Education: HNC, Industrial Measurement and Control. Musical Education: Studied privately with Geoff Myers, Leeds, from age 13, drums. Career: Les Howard's Northern Dance Orchestra (NDO), 1988-94; Currently with Herb Miller Orchestra, touring Great Britain and Europe, 1996-; Radio appearances: Several on BBC Radio 2, Jazz Parade; Radio 2 Arts Programme; Appearances at many jazz festivals around Britain. Recordings: with Rod Mason's Concept, 1984-88; Alan Skidmore, 1993; Memphis Bell Orchestra, 1995. Membership: Musicians' Union. Hobbies: Shooting; Conservation; DIY (home and cars). Address: 9 Golcar Brow Road, Meltham, Huddersfield, West Yorkshire HD7 3LD, England.

HOWARD Rex, b. 23 July 1930, Thunder Bay, Ontario, Canada. Vocalist; Musician (pedal steel guitar, dobro). m. Candice James, 12 May 1990, 1 son, 2 daughters. Education: 1 year university. Career: Member, Bootleg, support tour with John Anderson; Toured USA, as opening act and steel player and sideman with: Hank Williams Sr; Ernest Tubb; Dave Dudley; Currently performing in Western Canada with the band Saddlestone. Recordings: Little Peg And The Blind Man; A Heartache As Big As Texas; Roadside Ride; If Heaven's Missin' An Angel; An Old Dusty Heartache. Honours: Instrumentalist Of The Year, SCCMA; Male Vocalist Of Year, 1993. Memberships: SOCAN; AFofM; CIRPA. Hobbies: Model ship building; Painting; Creative Art; Songwriting. Current Management: Silver Bow Management. Address: 6260-130-St, Surrey, British Columbia V3X 1R6, Canada.

HOWE Bob, b. 22 December 1956. Musician (Guitars, Harmonica); Singer; Composer. m. Karen Versace, 21 November 1992. Career: Australian Cabaret Artist and Session Musician; Musical Director for Frank Ifield, 1984-88; Guy Mitchell, 1991; Portrayed Paul McCartney, Australian Production of Lennon - The Musical, 1986-87; Toured with Countless Australian Artists, Lucky Starr, Slim Dusty. Compositions: White Man's Blues; Some People Change. Recordings: Contributor to: John Chester Love in the Meantime; Waltzing Matilda, Diana Trask; Cross Country, Sarah Jory; The Fire Still Burns, Frank

Ifield. Publication: Cowboys in Cyberspace, 1997. Honour: Most Popular Guitarist, Musician and Newcomer, Southern Hemisphere Country Music Awards, 1982. Membership: Music Arrangers' Guild of Australia. Hobby: Internet Web-design. Address: PO Box 7341, Bondi Beach, NSW 2026, Australia.

HOWE Brian, b. 22 July 1957, Portsmouth, Hampshire, England. Singer. 1 son, 1 daughter. Career: Member, Ted Nugent Band; Lead singer, rock group Bad Company, 1986-93; US Holy Water tour with Damn Yankees, 1990-91; Last Rebel Here Comes Trouble US Tour, supporting Lynyrd Skynyrd, 1993; Solo Artist, 1993-; Numerous television appearances including: MTV, VH1, Tonight Show, Letterman. Compositions: Co-writer and performer as lead singer on How About That, the #11 Song of All Time in 100 year Billboard Chart Edition in Album Rock. Recordings: Albums: Penetrator, Ted Nugent, 1984; Fame And Fortune, 1986; Dangerous Age, 1988; Holy Water, 1990; Here Comes Trouble, 1992; Best Of Bad Company Live, 1993; Solo album: Tangled in Blue, 1997; Hit Singles include: Shake It Up, 1986; Holy Water, 1990; If You Needed Somebody, 1991; Walk Through Fire, 1991; How About That, 1992; This Could Be The One, 1992. Membership: NARAS, grammy Voting Member. Hobbies: Boating; Football; Portsmouth Football Club supporter. Current Management: TopNotch Entertainment Corp, Box 1515, Sanibel Island, FL 33957-1515, USA.

HOWE Ronald, b. 7 Dec 1957, Leatherhead, Surrey, England. Musician (tenor saxophone). m. Carolanne Edge, 6 July 1989, 1 daughter. Musical Education: Private tuition, adult education, Goldsmith's, London. Career: Concerts, tours with many bands; Large amount of studio work and recording; Toured and recorded with: Fools Can Dance; Worked on Cure album; Worked live with Damned; Currently with The Bucket Band; Videos; Major venues include: Hammersmith Palais; Teaching saxophone (theory, performance, improvisation); Brass/horns arrangement; Music transcription. Recordings: A Night Like This; The Cure; Box Office Poison; Beyond The Twilight Zone; Checkmate; Numerous others. Memberships: Musicians' Union; PAMRA. Hobbies: Ex-powerlifter; Photography; Trees. Current Management: Self-managed. Address: 7 Wentworth, Aurum Close, Horley, Surrey RH6 9BE, England.

HOWE Steve, b. 8 Apr 1947, London, England. Musician (guitar). Career: Member, The Syndicats; The In Crowd; Tomorrow; Bodast; UK progressive rock group Yes, 1970-81; Concerts included: Queen Elizabeth Hall, London; Reading Festival; Madison Square Garden; Asia, 1981-90; Worldwide tours, including Asia In Asia concert, Tokyo, Japan (broadcast by MTV to audience of 20 million), 1983; Member, GTR, 1986-91; Rejoined Yes, 1991-; Concerts include: Yesshows '91 - Round The World In 80 Dates Tour, 1991. Recordings: Albums: with Yes: Time And A Word, 1970; The Yes Album, 1971; Fragile, 1971; Close To The Edge, 1972; Yessongs, 1973; Tales From The Topographic Ocean, 1973; Relayer, 1974; Yesterdays, 1975; Going For The One, 1977; Tormato, 1978; Yesshows, 1981; Union, 1991; Yesstory, 1991; Symphonic Music Of Yes, 1993; History Of The Future, 1993; Open Your Eyes, 1998; with Asia: Asia, 1982; Alpha, 1983; Astra, 1985; with GTR: GTR, 1986: Solo albums: Beginnings, 1975; Steve Howe Album, 1979; Turbulence, 1991; With Anderson Bruford Wakeman Howe: Anderson Bruford Wakeman Howe, 1989; Singles include: with Yes: Roundabout; Wondrous Stories; Going For The One; Brother Of Mine; Lift Me Up; with Asia: Heat Of The Moment; Only Time Will Tell; Don't Cry; with GTR: When The Heart Rules The Mind; The Hunter. Honours: Gold Ticket, Madison Square Garden, with Yes, 1978; Top New Artist, Top Album, with Asia, Billboard magazine, 1982.

Current Management: Tiz Hay Management, 44 Oswald Close, Leatherhead, Surrey KT22 9UG, England.

HOWELL-JONES Richard Mark, b. 18 Apr 1960, Altrincham, Cheshire, England. Actor; Musician (drums, percussion); Singer. Education: Manchester Polytechnic. Musical Education: Self-taught. Career: Drummer, vocalist, with R&B band Flat Hedgehog, 1981-83; Theatre performance band Celebration Of Joe, 1984-85; Roy Woodward Big Band, 1985-87; R&B band The Shades, 1990-91; Television: King Lear, C4, 1983; Dear Ladies, BBC TV, 1984; Films: The Last Meeting, 1996; Currently touring Dusty Pens by Derek Martin. Recording: Celebration Of Joe, with Brian Roberts, 1984. Memberships: Musicians' Union; Equity. Hobbies: Aero-modelling; Reading; Philosophy; Conversation; Computer programming; Keeping fit. Address: 18 Wardle Road, Sale, Cheshire M33 3DB, England.

HOWLETT Liam, Songwriter; Musician. Career: Member, The Prodigy, 1990-; Festival appearances include: Glastonbury, 1995, 1997; V97, 1997; Lollapalooza, 1997. Recordings: Albums: Experience, 1992; Music for the Jilted Generation (Number 1, UK), 1994; The Fat of the Land (Number 1, UK), 1997; Hit Singles: Charly, 1991; Everybody In the Place, 1991; Fire, 1992; Out of Space, 1992; Wind It Up, 1993; One Love, 1993; No Good (Start the Dance), 1994; Voodoo People, 1994; Poison, 1995; Firestarter (Number 1, UK), 1996; Breathe (Number 1, UK), 1996; Smack My Bitch Up, 1997. Address: Glenglye, 205 Vicarage Hill, Benfleet, Essex SS7 1PF, England.

HOYDAL Annika, b. Tórshaun, The Faroe Islands. m. Klaus Lockwood, 25 June 1994. Education: Graduated, Actress, Statens Teaterskole, Copenhagen, Denmark, 1973. Debut: The Faroe Islands, 1966. Career: Freelance Actress and Singer, throughout Scandinavia. Compositions include: Mit Eget Land; Min Krop; Hjemme; Drommen; Bekendelse; Morket; Lammet; Aldan, Draben; Kasper; Til Dans; Tjipp; Munnur; A Palli; A Havi; Morgun; Snigil; Alt; Dulcinea; Hvalspyggja; Taraloppa; Ljós; Kópagents; Dreymahav; Inn Móti Landi; Marmennil; Farin; Sjólátin; Nu Sigla....; Tid; Find en Sten. Recordings include: Til Born og Vaksin, 1975; Annika og Jógvan, 1979; Spor I Sjónum, 1983; Dulcinea, 1991. Honour: Melodi Grand Prix for Faroe Islands, Denmark, 1979. Memberships: Dansk Skuespillerforbund (Actors Association); Danish Jazz Beat and Folk Music Composers Organization; Dansk Solist-Forbund. Address: Admiralgade 22 II tv, 1066 Copenhagen, Denmark.

HRADECKY Emil, b. 25 February 1953, Prague, Czech Republic. Teacher; Composer. m. Alexandra Hradecká, 10 November 1978. Education: Prague Conservatory. Publications: Little Jazz Album; Little Jazz Pieces For 20 Fingers; Dances For The Guitar; Jazz Flute & MC; Jazz Trumpet & MC; Jazz Trombone & MC; Von Blues Bis Disco & MC; Jazz Etudes; Der Kinderkarneval; Kleine Jazz-Stücke Für 20 Finger; Zwei-Seiten Stücke; Klienes Jazz-Album; Tanz-Kompositionen Für Vier Hände; Tänze für Gitarre; Fox-Polka; Swing-Polka; Der Sonnige Rag; We Play The Piano According To The Chord Marks. Honours: Musical Prize, Children's Choirs, Prague, 1995, 1997. Hobby: Sport. Address: Konselská 11, 180 00 Prague 8, Czech Republic.

HUDSON Keith David, b. 26 Sept 1953, Retford, Nottinghamshire, England. Musician (drums, hand percussion); Vocalist. Musical Education: Self-taught; City and Guilds 370, FAETC. Career: Principal drum seat, Butlins Holiday Centres, 1980-82; Soundtrack, The Starlight Boys, BBC Radio 4, 1992; Toured with New Tornadoes; Resident seat with Original Thunderbirds; Toured Russia with Philharmonic

Blues Band; Further Education tutor, Music Departments, Yorkshire and Derbyshire. Recording: Soundtrack, The Starlight Boys. Membership: Musicians' Union. Hobbies: Dog walking; Reading; Theology; Psychology. Address: 70 Cobwell Road, Retford, Nottinghamshire DN22 7DD, England.

HUGGETT Mark J, b. 3 July 1961, Birmingham, England. Musician (drums). Education: BA Fine Art, Reading University. Career: Concerts: Italia '90 (official Irish rock promotion with Pepe jeans); Reading Festival, 1992; Fleadh Festival, 1992; Television and radio includes: BBC2 Taking Liberties; MTV; RTE, Ireland; Dave Fanning, Irish radio; RTI, Italy; Italian radio; Simon Mayo, BBC Radio One. Recordings: Albums: Red Harvest: Strange; Saved; Single: World Won't Listen (playlisted Radio One); Dr Millar and The Cute Hoors: Romance In A Flat (number 12, Irish charts); Currently recording with Chant. Hobbies: Film; Animation. Current Management: Johnny Rogan. Address: 101/103 Devonport Road, Shepherds Bush, London W12 8PB, England.

HUGHES David Alan, b. 25 Apr 1960, Birkenhead, England. Composer; Musician (keyboards); Producer. m. 25 Apr 1984, 1 son, 1 daughter. Musical Education: Self-taught. Career: Worldwide tours, OMD and Thomas Lang; Founder member, electronic duo, Dalek 1; Composer, film scores with composer John Murphy; Television appearances includes: The Tube; Wired; Top Of The Pops; Old Grey Whistle Test. Compositions: Film scores: IlPaladini; CHUD; Hearts And Armour; Film scores with John Murphy: Leon The Pig Farmer; Feast At Midnight; Solitaire For Two; Welcome To The Terrordome; Beyond Bedlam; Body Memories; Dinner In Purgatory; Destroying Angels; Proteus; Giving Tongue; Clockwork Mice; For television: White Men Are Cracking Up; All The President's Women. Recordings: As composer, producer: 4 albums with Thomas Lang. Memberships: Musicians' Union; PRS; BASCA. Hobbies: Football; Computing. Current Management: Soundtrack Music Management. Address: 22 Ives Street, Chelsea, London SW3 2ND, England.

HUGHES David James, b. 1 June 1950, Rotherham, Yorkshire, England. Musician (guitar, cello); Composer; Arranger. Education: Art School, Fine Art, Sir John Cass, Goldsmiths. Musical Education: Self-taught guitar; Cello study with Alfia Bekova. Career: Channel 9 (band); Roy Hill Band; Television, radio, tours: EMI Outbar, TV Pebble Mill At One; 73 childrens shows; Radio One Live. Compositions: Disco Eddy; Away From The Heat; When The Bad Men Come; The Lion Within; Radio One Chart Show (intro music and chart read-out underlay). Honours: Arts Council GLAA Award, Jazz Musician of the Year, 1980. Address: 7A Cleveland Road, London N1 3ES, England.

HUGHES Garry. Producer; Programmer. Career: Work in US producing tracks for The Wilsons forthcoming album; Currently working with Trevor Horn; Recent production work includes: Tina Turner, Unfinished Sympathy (Wildest Dreams), album; Suggs: Cecilia; Camden Town; Selected programming and playing credits: Bjork, Debut Album; Gabrielle, Forget About the World; Charles and Eddie: Would I Lie To You; Duophonic (1st album); Chocolate Milk (2nd album); D Mob: It's Time to Get Funky; Put Your Hands Together; The Way of the World; Come On and get My Love. Address: SARM Productions, SP2 Holdings Ltd, The Blue Building, 42/46 St Luke's Mews, London W11 1DG, England.

HUGHES James William, b. 18 May 1960, Liverpool, England. Musician (drums, percussion); Backing Vocalist. 1 daughter. Musical Education: Studied with Red Carter, Liverpool. Career: Member, Black; Tours of Europe and Japan;

Member, The Darling Buds; Tour of US; Television appearances: Top Of The Pops; Wogan; Jim'll Fix It; The Chart Show; The Roxy; The Tube; Various children's programmes. Recordings: Albums: Wonderful Life, Black; The Darling Buds Of May, two albums. Honour: Gold album, Wonderful Life. Membership: Musicians' Union. Hobbies: Making video films; Making music. Address: 247 Fernhill Road, Bootle, Merseyside L20 0AQ, England.

HULAN Miroslav, b. 23 April 1959, Brno, Czech Republic. Guitar, Mandolin Player. m. Drahomira Spidlikova, 4 July 1981, 2 sons. Debut: With Group Poutnici, 1980. Career: Member, Group Poutnici, 1980-; Duo with Michal Hromcik, 1995-. Composition: Pocta Davidovi. Recordings: Supraphon: Poutnici, 1987; Wayfaring Strangers, 1989; Chromi kone, 1990; The Days of Auld Lang Syne, 1991; Poutnici Live, 1991; GZ: Je to v nas, 1992; UMG: Pisne brnenskych kovboju, 1994; GZ: Co uz je pryc, 1997. Publications: Guitar School for Beginners, 1993; Guitar School for Advanced, 1997. Honour: Best Non-American Bluegrass Recordings, 1989, 1990. Membership: Czech Bluegrass Music Association. Hobbies: Computers; Bikes. Address: Blatnicka 3, 628 00 Brno, Czech Republic.

HULJIC Tonci, b. 29 Oct 1961, Split, Croatia. Composer; Producer. m. Vjekosava Huljic, 5 Sept 1987, 1 son, 1 daughter. Education: Law. Musical Education: High School of Music, piano. Career: Leader, composer, most popular group in Croatia; Magazin; 15 albums (9 million copies sold); 7 major tours; Many television shows; Tours: Russia; USA; Canada; 20 Gold, Platinum, Diamond records with Magazin and other popular Croatian singers; Eurovision Song Contest, 6th Place with song Nostalgia, 1995; Many Grand prix in music festivals, Croatia, 1995-96; European promotion of trilogy; Songs published in Benelux countries, Scandinavia; US; South Africa. Honours: Composer Of The Year, 1988, 1989, 1994; Special Prize for Record Sales. Memberships: Croatian Music Society; President, Croatian Music Union; Croatian Composers Association; Rotary Club. Current Management: Skalind Production, Croatia; Bim, Slavia Publishing, Asse, Belgium.

HUME Alastair Martin Roderick, b. 1 Aug 1958, London, England. Musician (flute, saxophone, keyboards); Arranger; Teacher. m. Vanessa V A Cowlard, 22 July 1989, 1 daughter. Musical Education: Guildhall School of Music and Drama; Homerton College, Cambridge. Career: Cambridge Footlights, 1979; De Blahdeblah Jazz Orchestra, 1979; MD, Littlehampton Community School Big Band, 1982-86; Royal Oman Symphony Orchestra Instructor, 1986-88; Backed Penny Lane and Gordon Scott; Taverners Big Band, German tour, 1983, 1996; MD, Swing Bin and The Liners, 1990-; Tours: Canada, 1991; Lake Geneva, 1994; Lake Garda/Venice, 1996; Brass Roots; Choral conductor, Gli Amici Della Musica, 1977-83; Poole Arts Centre, 10th anniversary concert, 1979. Honours: GGSM Hons; Cert Ed Cantab. Memberships: Musicians' Union. Hobbies: Cricket; Golf; Video; Winemaking; DIY. Address: 3 Donnelly Road, Tuckton, Bournemouth, Dorset BH6 5NW, England.

HUMPERDINCK Engelbert (Arnold George Dorsey), b. 3 May 1936, Madras, India. Singer. m. Patricia Healey, 1963, 2 sons, 1 daughter. Career: Originally billed as Gerry Dorsey; Television includes: Oh Boy, 1950s; Changed name, late 1960s; Own series, The Engelbert Humperdinck Show, 1970; Regular concerts, US and UK. Recordings: Hit singles: Release Me (Number 1, UK), 1967; There Goes My Everything (Number 2, UK), 1967; The Last Waltz, 1967; Other hits include: Am I That Easy To Forget; The Way It Used To Be; Les Bicyclettes De Belsize; A Man Without Love; Winter World Of Love; Albums include: Release Me, 1967; The Last Waltz, 1967; A Man Without Love, 1968; Engelbert, 1969;

Engelbert Humperdinck, 1969; We Made It Happen, 1970; Another Time Another Place, 1971; Live At The Riviera, 1972; Greatest Hits, 1974; Getting Sentimental, 1975; Remember I Love You, 1987; The Engelbert Humperdinck Collection, 1987; Hello Out There, 1992; Golden Love; Ultimate; King Of Hearts; Last Of The Romantics; with Tom Jones: Back To Back, 1993. Honours: Georgie Award, American Guild Of Variety Artists, Best Singer, 1978; Over 50 Gold and 15 Platinum discs. Current Management: 3D Management, PO Box 16817, Beverly Hills, CA 90209-2817, USA.

HUNT Bill, b. 23 May 1947, Birmingham, England. Music Educator; Musician. Musical Education: Birmingham School of Music. Career: Original member, ELO; First ELO tour, Italy; Original member, Wizzard; Compositions: Co-wrote songs for Slade (with Dave Hill). Recordings: First album and single, ELO; First album and hit singles, Wizzard; Various tracks, Slade and Slade II. Honours: Honorary Treasurer, Don Arden Veterans Appreciation Society. Hobbies: River cruisin'; Boozin'. Address: Bromsgrove, Worcestershire, England.

HUNT Brian George Edward, b. 7 June 1937. Singer; Musician. 1 son. Education: Selftaught; Clavissimo Music School, Antwerp, Belgium. Career: Guitarist, Group, The Blue Tones, 1960s'; International Country, Folk, Soft Rock, Ballad Music; Television and Radio in Belgium; Support Act to Steeleye Span and Frank Ifield. Recordings: Louisa From Louisiana; Sing This Song With Me Tonight. Honours: Award, Assistant in the Promotion of Country Music Worldwide, 1981. Memberships: Country Music Association. Hobbies: Old Cars; Reading. Current Management: VAK-Antwerp, Prins Boudewynlaan 166, B-2610 Wilryk, Belgium.

HUNT Kevin Tony, b. 17 Dec 1962, Great Yarmouth, Norfolk, England. Musician (drums). Musical Education: Self-taught. Career: Member, group Runestaff, 1981-86; Released self-titled album and 2 singles; Extensive radio, television and live appearances; Member, Thieving Gypsies, 1991-; Recently changed name to Sliver; Debut single/album, 1996; Extensive work with Princes Trust charity, including work with Phil Collins. Recordings: with Runestaff: Album: Runestaff; Singles: Road To Ruin; Do-It!. Memberships: PRS; MCPS. Hobbies: Travel; Walking; Camping; Coarse fishing. Current Management: Damien Manestar. Address: Centurion Multi-Media Ltd, 39 Arundel Gardens, London W11 2LW, England.

HUNT Max, b. 3 Dec 1966, Newbury, Berkshire, England. Arranger; Producer; Musician (piano, keyboards). Recordings: with New Dawn: Celebrations Of Life; Still Point; Devotion; Storm Life; with Tantalus: Smoking Angels. Memberships: PRS; Musicians' Union. Hobbies: Walking; Alexander technique. Current Management: Mañana Music. Address: 34 Austen Gardens, Newbury, Berks RG14 7UB, England.

HUNT-TAYLOR Amanda. Songwriter. Career: Songwriter with Warner Chappell Music, 1991; Songwriter with Bluewater Music, Nashville, 1996; Co-writer credits with: Rick Giles; Steve Bogard; John Scott Sherrill; Gene Nelson; Kent Robbins; Janis Ian; Rory Bourke. Compositions: Your Love Amazes Me, recorded by John Berry; Tanya Tucker; Andy Childs; Joel Nova; All She Wants, recorded by Rena Gaile; No One Else Like You, recorded by Janis Ian; Able, recorded by Happy Goodmans; Wish I Could Wish On A Star, recorded by Mandy Barnett; A Fire In The Rain, recorded by Doug Supernaw; I Really Do Love You Lovin' Me, recorded by Lori Morgan; Wishing it all away, recorded by Tania Tucker. Honours: For Your Love Amazes Me: SESAC Songwriter of the Year, 1994, SESAC Song of the Year, 1994; Country Grammy Nomination; NSAI Achievement Award, 1995; Music City News Country Songwriters Award, Song of the Year, 1995;

Songwriter of the Year, Music City News Country Song Writers Award Shows, 1995; Song of the Year, Music City News Country Songwriters Award Show; Song of the Year, 2nd Annual Country Radio Music Award Show, 1995; 2 NSAI Awards. Address: PO Box 140494, Nashville, TN 37214, USA.

HUNTER Ian, b. 3 June 1946, Shrewsbury, Shropshire, England. Career: Singer, Mott The Hoople, 1969-74; Solo artiste, 1975-; Performances include: Royal Albert Hall, London, 1971; Woodstock Of The West Festival, Los Angeles, 1972. Recordings: Albums: with Mott The Hoople: Mott The Hoople, 1969; Mad Shadows, 1970; Wild Life, 1971; Brain Capers, 1971; All The Young Dudes, 1972; Rock'n'Roll Queen, 1972; The Hoople, 1974; Mott The Hoople - Live, 1974; Solo albums: Ian Hunter, 1975; All American Alien Boy, 1976; Overnight Angels, 1977; You're Never Alone With A Schizophrenic, 1979; Shades Of Ian Hunter, 1979; Ian Hunter Live/Welcome To The Club, 1980; Short Back And Sides, 1981; All The Good Ones Are Taken, 1983; with Mick Ronson: YUIOrta, 1990. Publication: Diary Of A Rock'n'Roll Star, Ian Hunter.

HUNTER James, b. 2 Oct 1962, Colchester, Essex, England. Singer; Musician (guitar, harmonica); Actor. Career: Formerly performed as, Howlin' Wilf; Television appearances: The Tube, 01 For London, and Wide Angle; Radio guest on Andy Kershaw and Paul Jones shows; Theatre appearance in Buddy; Toured UK, Europe and USA as guest with Van Morrison R&B Revue. Recordings: Albums: Cry Wilf, Howlin' Wilf And The Vee-Jays; A Night In San Francisco, Van Morrison; EP's and mini-albums include: Blue Men Sing The Whites; Shake Your Hips; Six By Six; Days Like This; Duet with Van Morrison. Memberships: Musicians' Union; PRS; Equity. Current Agent: Frank Warren, Matters Musical. Address: Rear of 8 West Street, Dorking, Surrey RH4 1BL, England.

HUNTER Robert (Bob), b. 30 Oct 1936, Corbridge, Northumberland, England. Vocalist; Musician (violin). m. Margaret, 13 Aug 1960, 1 son, 1 daughter. Musical Education: Violin from early age; Studied voice in Royal Engineers Band. Career: Appeared every televised show, The Black And White Minstrels, 1959-; Also radio series with George Mitchell Singers; Now freelance, worked with many groups, radio and television including: The Two Ronnies, various Command Performances; Summer seasons in major resorts with The Black And White Minstrel Show; More recently with The Minstrel Stars; Concerts, cabaret with Original Blend and The Square Pegs, including radio programmes: Friday Night Is Music Night; Round Midnight; Among Your Souvenirs, BBC Radio 2. Recordings: Albums: The Black And White Minstrel Show; Around The World In Song; The Minstrel Stars; Original Blend Entertains. Memberships: Equity; Musicians' Union. Hobbies: Tennis; Table Tennis; Stamp Collecting. Address: 15 Lynwood Road, Ealing, London W5 1JQ, England.

HUNTER Ruby, b. Coorong, South Australia. Singer; Songwriter. Partner, Archie Roach, 5 children. Career: Modern Day Girls tour with band, 1994; Speaker, guest performer, Composing Women's Festival; International Feminist Book Fair, 1994; Sydney Writers Festival, 1995; International tour with Archie Roach, 1995; Television: Corelli (mini-series), ABC TV, 1995. Recordings: Album: Thoughts Within, 1994. Current Management: Julie Hickson. Address: 25 Overend Street, Brunswick, VIC 3056, Australia.

HURLEY Luke, b. 31 Aug 1957, Nyeri, Kenya. Songwriter; Musician (guitar); Performer. m. Jann, 16 May 1992, 1 son, 2 daughters. Education: 1 year university. Musical Education: Self-taught. Career: Major shows since early 1982 specialising in Houseconcerts; Support act for

Michelle Shocked, Marianne Faithfull, New Zealand; Only performer to play live, Radio With Pictures television show; Touring Europe, 1998-99; Invented product for the CD industry. Compositions: Mona Lisa; Fait Accompli; Japanese Overdrive; Greenfields; Precious Time; Missing You; Hungry Gun Song; Information Station. Recordings: Albums: Policestate; Japanese Overdrive; Make Room; First Civilian; Alone in Her Field; Reha; Videos: Japanese Overdrive; Make Room; Mona Lisa. Current Management: Self-managed. Address: PO Box 68087, Newton, Auckland, New Zealand.

HUSBAND Gary, b. 14 June 1960, Leeds, Yorkshire, England. Musician (drums, piano, keyboards). Musical Education: Classical piano. Career: Allan Holdsworth; Jack Bruce Trio; Billy Cobham Band; Gary Moore; Level 42; Gary Husband Group. Compositions: Written for albums by Allan Holdsworth and Level 42. Recordings: Albums include: with Allan Holdsworth: Metal Fatigue, 1985; with Level 42: Staring At The Sun, 1988. Memberships: Musicians' Union; PRS. Hobby: Music. Address: 50B Randolph Avenue, London W9 1BE, England.

HUSBANDS Simon Patrick, b. 2 Feb 1957, Nottingham, England. Musician (keyboards, guitar, bass guitar); Songriter; Programmer; Singer. m. Janet Johnson, 9 July 1994. Education: Newark-Sherwood College. Career: Keyboard player, bass player, singer with band Blue Train; Single All I Need Is You, used in Baywatch television show, 1991; Current solo projects include DIN and UXB. Recordings: Co-producer, album The Business of Dreams; Singles: All I Need Is You (13 weeks, US charts); The Hardest Thing; The Business Of Dreams. Memberships: PRS; Musicians' Union; BMI, USA. Hobbies: Computers; Cinema. Current Management: GOSH! Productions, UK; Gary Heller Management, 11692 Chenault Street #202, Los Angeles, CA 91411, USA. Address: 40 Millicent Road, West Bridgford, Nottingham NG2 7PZ, England.

HUSEIN Hasanefesic, b. 30 Jan 1954, Banja Luka, Croatia. Musician (guitar); Songwriter. m. Viki Peric, 22 Mar 1980, 1 son, 1 daughter. Musical Education: 8 years music school, Zagreb. Career: 20 years on top with own band, Parni Valjek (Steam Roller). Recordings: 15 albums (most of them Platinum). Honours: 7 Porins (Croatian equivalent of Grammy), 1995. Memberships: HGU; HDS. Hobbies: Tennis; Sailing. Current Management: HGU, HDS, Nenas Drobnjak. Address: Zelengaj 67, 10000 Zagreb, Croatia.

HUSSENOT Emmanuel, b. 29 Sept 1951, Saint Cloud, France. Variety Artist; Jazz Musician (cornet, trumpet, saxophone, recorder). 1 daughter. Musical Education: Self-taught. Career: Cornet player, French traditional band, Sharkey & Co; Composer, singer, trumpet, saxophone and recorder player, Orpheon Celesta, 1980-. Recordings: with Sharkey and Co, 1972-78; with Orpheon Celesta: Siphonnée Symphonie; La Prehistoire du Jazz; Best Of. Honours: Prix Sydney Bechet de l'Academie du Jazz, 1990; Grand Prix du Festival d'Humour de Sainy Gervais, 1994; La Vocalise en carton, 1998. Current Management: Blue Line, Paris. Address: 74 Rue Alexandre Guilmant, 92190 Meudon, France.

HUSSEY Wayne, b. 26 May 1959. Musician (guitar); Vocalist. Career: Member, groups Dead Or Alive; The Walkie Talkies; Member, Sisters Of Mercy, 1983-85; Concerts include York Festival, 1984; The Mission, 1986-; Regular UK, European and worldwide tours, including concerts with The Cult and U2; Appearances include: Reading Festival, 1986, 1987, 1989; Lockerbie Air Disaster Fund benefit concert, 1989; Hillsborough football disaster benefit concert, 1989; Finsbury Park,

London, 1991; Off The Street benefit concert, London, 1993. Recordings: Albums: with Sisters Of Mercy: First And Last And Always, 1985; with The Mission: God's Own Medicine, 1986; The First Chapter, 1987; Children (Number 2, UK), 1988; Carved In Sand, 1990; Masque, 1992; Neverland, 1995; Singles: with Sisters Of Mercy: Temple Of Love, 1983; Body & Soul, 1984; Walk Away, 1984; with The Mission: Stay With Me, 1986; Wasteland, 1987; Severina, 1987; Tower Of Strength, 1988; Beyond The Pale, 1988; Butterfly On A Wheel, 1989; Deliverance, 1990; Hands Across The Ocean, 1990; Like A Child Again, 1992.

HUTCHINGS Ashley Stephen, b. 26 Jan 1945, Southgate, Middlesex, England. Musician (bass guitar); Songwriter; Producer; Dancer; Scriptwriter. m. 6 Aug 1971, to 1978, 1 son. Career: Founder member, leading folk-rock groups in England: Fairport Convention, 1967-; Steeleye Span, 1970-; Albion Band, 1972-; Music Director, National Theatre, London, 1977-81; Considered Father of Folk-Rock in Britain by media. Recordings include: Albums: with Fairport Convention: Fairport Convention, 1968; What We Did In Our Holidays, 1969; Unhalfbricking, 1969; Liege And Leaf, 1970; with Steeleye Span: Hark The Village Wait, 1970; Please To See The King, 1971; Ten Man Mop, 1971; with The Albion Band: Battle Of The Field, 1976; Prospect Before Us, 1977; Rise Up Like The Sun, 1978; Albion River Hymns March, 1979; Light Shining Albino, 1984; The Wild Side Of Town, 1987; I Got New Shoes, 1987; Give Me A Saddle I'll Trade You A Car, 1989; 1990, 1990; Acousticity, 1993; Albion Heart, 1995; Solo album: By Gloucester Docks I Sat Down And Wept. Publications: A Little Music, collection of folksongs, tunes and dances. Memberships: PRS; MCPS. Hobbies: Theatre; Music. Current Management: c/o 994 Burnage Lane, Manchester M19 1TD, England. Address: 994 Burnage Lane, Manchester M19 1TD, England.

HUTCHISON Hamish, b. 22 July 1968, Beckenham, Kent. Record Producer; Remixer; Mixing Engineer. Recordings: Producer, numerous acts including: Chesney Hawkes; Big Fun; Glen Goldsmith; Booker Newbury III; Remixer for: PJ and Duncan; China Crisis; Lucianna; Jack 'N' Chill; Chesney Hawkes. Membership: Musicians' Union. Address: c/o Time and Space, PO Box 306, Berkhamsted, Herts HP4 3EP, England.

HUTMAN Olivier, b. 12 Nov 1954, Boulogne, France. Musician (piano); Arranger; Composer. Education: PhD, Ethnology on Urban Music in Ghana. Musical Education: 10 years study, piano, National Conservatory of Music, St Maur. Career: Jazz performer, accompanist for pop singers; Founder, Moravigne, 1975; Member, Chute Libre, 1975-77; Founds own trio, 1983-84; Member Eric Lelann Quartet, 1984-88; Tours, festivals include: Singapore; Bombay; Montreal; Prague; Tokyo, 1991, 93; Newport, USA, 1993; Tahiti, 1995; Martinique, 1994; USA (Boston, San Fransisco, Los Angeles), 1995; Antibes; Nimes; La Reunion; Montreux. Compositions: Composer, arranger in jazz, theatre, films: jingles, music for industrial films, TV documentaries, Long Range Films include: Mon Oncle, 1985; High Speed, 1987; Printemps Perdu, 1990; Ma Soeur Chinoise, 1994; Commissioned by International Musik Fetsival, Davos, to write suite performed by members of New York Philharmonia, 1993. Recordings: with: Moravagine; Chute Libre; J P Debarbat; G Ferris; Eric Lelann; Christian Escoude; Toots Thielemans; C Bellonzi; C Barthelemy; P Delletrz; J P L Labador; S Marc; G Acogny; Abus; Barney Wilen, 1992; A Brunet; M Barrot Quartet; R Galliano; Stephane Grappelli; Luigi Trussardi; Solo: Six Songs, 1984; The Man With The Broken Tooth, trio with Marc Bertaux, Tony Rabeson, 1987; Creole and African music recordings. Honours: Prix Boris Vian, French Academy of Jazz, for Best Record Of The Year, 1983; 2nd European Keyboardist in Jazz, Hot Magazine,

1987; Awards for music for films: Mon Oncle, 1986; Printemps Perdu, 1990. Current Managment: C/o A21 Muth Productions, 14 Rue Bleue, 75009 Paris. Address: 36 Rue de Fontanay, 94300 Vincennes, France.

HUYGEN Michel, 12 Mar 1954, Stanleyville, Zaire. Composer; Producer; Musician (keyboards). Education: University. Musical Education: 4 years notation, self-taught. Career: Founder, group Neuronium, 1976; Concerts, some with visual input from slides (by Tomas C Gilsanz) or lasers, include: Benidorm; Bilbao; Madrid; London; UK Electronica '84; London Planetarium; SIMO; Madrid Planetarium, 1987; Sonar '95, Contemporary Culture Centre, Barcelona, 1995. Recordings: with Neuronium: Quasar 2C361, 1977; Vuelo Quimico, 1978; Digital Dream, 1980; The Visitor, 1981; Chromium Echoes, 1982; Invisible Views, 1983; Heritage, 1984; Alma, 1987; Supranatural, 1987; From Madrid To Heaven, 1988; Numerica, 1989; Olim, 1990; Sybaris, 1991; Extrisimo, 1992; Oniria, 1993; Sonar (live concert), 1996; At First, 1996; Intimo (Definitive Edition), 1996; A Separate Affair (with Vangelis), 1996; Psykya, 1997; Sonar (Live concert), 1997; Solo albums: Absence Of Reality, 1982; Capturing Holograms, 1984; Barcelona 1992, 1986; Elixir, 1989; Intimo, 1990; En Busca Del Misterio, 1992; Musica Para La Buena Mesa, 1994; Infinito, 1994; Astralia, 1995; with other artists: Disc Drive, Tangerine Dream/Neuronium, 1985; The Endless Enigma, with Klaus Schulze, Steve Roach, 1990; Musica Sin Fronteras, with Enya, Mike Oldfield, Ryuichi Sakamoto, Neuronium, 1992; In London (EP), with Vangelis and Neuronium, 1993; Nueva Musica Espanola, with Luis Panigua, David Salvans, 1994; Klem 1994, with Suzanne Ciani, Chris Franke, 1994; e, with Tomas San Miguel, Jordi Sabatés, 1995. Publication: Articles for: Sound On Sound; Audio Media; Keyboard Magazine. Honour: Author, music, CD ROM, Dedicated to Spain, celebrating Spanish Presidency of EEC, 1995. Membership: SGAE (Spanish Society of Composers and Publishers). Hobbies: Computer and synthesizers programming. Current Management: Oniria International, Calle Alzines, 3 St Quirze Parc, 08192 St Quirze dal Vallès, Barcelona, Spain.

HVASS Claus, b. 4 Feb 1959. Composer; Producer; Musician (guitar). m. Birgitte Rode, 14 June 1992, 1 son. Career: Roskilde Festival; Toured England; Concerts: California; France; Norway; Germany; Sweden; Denmark; Grand Prix, Slovenia; National and international television and radio. Composition: Medea. Recordings: with Johnny and The Cold Demons: Paraneuropa; with Walk The Walk: Walk The Walk; Feet On the Ground; Frog Dance. Publications: The International Discography of New Wave, Dansk Rock. Honours: 5 National Music Awards, 1991-95. Membership: DJBFA. Hobbies: Sailsports. Current Management: Zing Zing Musicproduction and Management. Address: Kirkegaardsgade 3, 9000 Aalborg, Denmark.

HYDE Maria Jane, b. 23 Jan 1969, London, England. Singer; Actress. m. Dr Uwe Bodzian, 21 July 1995. Career: Acted: Peppee, in Annie, Victoria Palace, 1980; Ovaltines singing group, 1982; Various TV shows, Childrens Royal Variety Performance, London Palladium; Acted: Pearl, Starlight Express, London, 1985-88; Pearl, Starlight Express, Bochum, West Germany, 1989-91, 1994-95; Assistant Dance and Skate Coach, 1995. Recordings: Albums: Ovaltine Group Album, 1982; Heaven Sent (Number 5, German charts), 1995; Single: Heaven Sent, UK, 1994. Membership: Equity. Current Management: Edward Hyde. Address: Morland House, 11 Woodside Green, London SE25 5EY, England.

HYDE Roger Erik, b. 3 Jun 1951, Hollywood, USA. Composer; Record Producer; Theorist. Musical Education: AB in Music Theory and Composition, UCLA, 1975, with special endorsements in electronic music and composition for film; Studied history of jazz with Paul Tanner (Glen Miller Band), Composition with Gerald Strang, Film scoring with David Raksin, Production with Nik Venet. Career: Folk Scene radio concert, 1970; Series of Los Angeles salon concerts and readings, 1975-76; Director of Washoe Records, producer for Scatman Crothers, 1980-81; Director and Producer, Blue Planet Records, 1985-. Compositions: Our Hearts And Our Hands, song cycle, 1979; Pittsburg; 2811; Symphony à Trois. Recordings: As producer, Scatman Crothers and the Hollywood Radio Hooligans. Publications: Novels: Famous Death, and Weighing Of Secret Burdens; Contributions to The Whole Earth Catalogues. Membership: AES. Hobbies: Kite designing; Scholar. Address: PO Box 91922, Los Angeles, CA 90009, USA.

HYDER Ken, b. 29 June 1946, Dundee, Scotland. Musician (drums); Vocalist. Education: Harris Academy, Dundee. Musical Education: Studied with John Stevens. Career: Moved to London 1970; Formed Celtic-Jazz band, Talisker; Played and recorded with Celtic musicians including Dick Gaughan, then with Tibetan monks, Russian musicians, duo with Tim Hodgkinson, South African musicians, Siberian shamans. Recordings: with Talisker: Dreaming Of Glenisla; Land Of Stone; The Last Battle; The White Light; Humanity; Under The Influence; The Big Team; Fanfare For Tomorrow, with Dick Gaughan; Shams, with Tim Hodgkinson; The Goose, with Hodgkinson, Ponomareva; Piping Hot, with Dave Brooks; The Crux Of The Catalogue, with Tomas Lynch; Hot Sounds From The Arctic, with Vladimir Rezitsky; The Ultimate Gift, Bardo State Orchestra; Urban Ritual, Ntshuks Bonga's Tshisa. Honours: Order Of The Red Banner, Angarsk. Membership: London Musician Collective. Hobbies: Mountain climbing; Travel. Current Management: Oor Wullie Presentations. Address: 69 Ravenslea Road, Balham, London SW12 8SL, England.

HYLAND Brian, b. 12 Nov 1943, New York City, USA. Singer; Musician (guitar, keyboards, bass, harmonica). m. Rosmari Dickey, July 1970, 1 son. Musical Education: Church Choir; Self-taught musician. Career: Television and radio appearances: Host, American Bandstand, 1960-70; Murray The K Show, with Jackie Wilson, 1961; Television special, Japan, 1961; Thank Your Lucky Stars; Jukebox Jury; Saturday Club, UK Radio, 1963; Top Of The Pops, 1975; R&R Palace, Nashville Now, 1988; Numerous tours include: Japan, South America, USA, UK, South East Asia. Recordings: Itsy Bitsy...Polka Dot Bikini, 1960; Let Me Belong To You, 1961; Ginny Come Lately, 1962; Sealed With A Kiss, 1962; Warmed Over Kisses, 1962; The Joker Went Wild, Run Run Look And See, 1966; Tragedy, 1968; Gypsy Woman, 1970. Honours: 3 Gold records; Gee Gee Award, Star of Tomorrow, 16 Magazine, 1961-62. Memberships: AFofM; AGVA; AFTRA; ASCAP. Hobbies: Art; Drawing; Photography; Astronomy; Computers. Current Management: Stone Buffalo. Address: Box 101, Silver Lakes, CA 92342-0101, USA.

HYLAND Vic, b. 7 June 1959, Wilmington, Kent, England. Musician (guitar); Singer; Educator. m. Jane Parker, 28 May 1993, 4 daughters. Musical Education: Studies in classical guitar, Indian music under Helen Lohmueller, Kessel and Lobb. Career: Guitarist, various musical styles from rock and jazz to Indian music; Brief spell playing classical concerts; Worked with Geoff Moore Project, mid-1980s; Established as leading guitar educator in Kent area; Formed Red Touch, late 1980s; Currently with record deal, sponsorship, radio support. Recordings: Grahams Garden; I Don't Care; Before I Made You Cry; Album: Walk On, forthcoming. Publications: Advanced Techniques And Creative Guitar; Self Improvement For Musicians. Memberships: Musicians' Union; Registry Of Electric Guitar

Tutors. Hobbies: Walking; Windsurfing; Reading; Painting. Current Management: RTI. Address: 5 Pleasant Villas, Kent St, Mereworth, Kent ME18 5QN, England.

HYLTON Randall, b. 1 Aug 1946, Christiansburg, Virginia, USA. Stage Performer; Songwriter. m. 5 May 1984, 1 son. Education: BA, Accounting. Musical Education: Self-taught. Career: Full-time solo performer; Stage show includes comedy finger style acoustic guitar, original songs, country, gospel, folk. Recordings: 113 songs recorded by major bluegrass acts include: Lester Flatt; Lewis Famly; Seldom Scene; Bluegrass Cardinals; Doyle Lawson; Country Gentlemen; Ralph Stanley; Gillis Brothers; Larry Sparks; John Starling; Leo Kottke; Kingsmen Quartet; Wendy Bagwell; Primitive Quartet; Vern Gosdin. Honours: Society For The Preservation Of Bluegrass Music In America (SPBGMA): 5 times, Songwriter Of The Year. Membership: SPBGMA. Current Management: Self-managed. Address: PO Box 24533, Nashville, TN 37202, USA.

HYNDE Chrissy, b. 7 Sept 1951, Akron, Ohio, USA. Singer; Musician (guitar); Songwriter. m. Jim Kerr, 1984. Education: Art, Kent State University. Career: Guitarist, group Saturday Afternoon Matinee, 1967; Model, St Martin's School Of Art; Writer, New Musical Express, 1973; Member, groups The Frenchies; Jack Rabbit; Berk Brothers; Founder member, singer, guitarist, The Pretenders, 1978-; Worldwide tours, including UK, US, Far East, Australia; Concerts include: Concert For Kampuchea, London, 1979; Heatwave Festival, Toronto, Canada, 1980; Concerts in Japan, Hong Kong, Australia, 1982; US Festival, San Bernardino, California, 1983; Radio City Music Hall, 1984; Live Aid, Philadelphia, 1985; Nelson Mandela Tribute, Wembley Stadium, 1990; Bob Dylan 30th Anniversary Tribute, Madison Square Garden, 1992. Compositions include: Numerous songs for Pretenders; Private Life, recorded by Grace Jones. Recordings: Albums: Pretenders, 1980; Extended Play (US only), 1981; Pretenders II, 1981; Get Close, 1986; The Singles, 1987; Packed!, 1990; Isle Of View, 1995; Singles include: Stop Your Sobbing, 1979; Kid, 1979; Brass In Pocket (Number 1, UK), 1979; Talk Of The Town, 1980; Message Of Love, 1981; I Go To Sleep, 1981; Back On The Chain Gang (featured in film King Of Comedy), 1983; Learning To Crawl, 1984; I Got You Babe, with UB40 (Number 1, UK), 1985; Don't Get Me Wrong, 1986; Hymn To Her, 1987; Breakfast In Bed, with UB40, 1988; I'm Not In Love (featured in film soundtrack Indecent Proposal); Contributor, Tame Yourself, animal rights album, 1991; Stone Free - A Tribute To Jimi Hendrix, 1993. Honours: Honoured at the People For The Ethical Treatment Of Animals (PETA) 10th Anniversary Humanitarian Awards Gala, 1988. Current Management: Gailforce Management, 30 Ives Street, London SW3 2ND, England.

I

IAN Janis (Janis Fink), b. 7 Apr 1951, New Jersey, USA. Singer; Songwriter; Musician (guitar, piano, French horn); Columnist; Lecturer. Partner, Patricia Snyder. Musical Education: Mainly self-taught, including conducting and orchestration. Career: Solo artiste, 1965-; Debut hit single, Society's Child, featured in Leonard Bernstein's television special, Inside Pop - The Rock Revolution, 1966; Performances include: Royal Festival Hall and Royal Albert Hall, London; Carnegie Hall and Philharmonic Hall, New York; Sydney Opera House; Carre, Amsterdam;Appearances on most major television shows, including 8 times on Tonight Show. Compositions include: Society's Child, 1966; Jesse, recorded by Roberta Flack; At Seventeen, 1976; Fly Too High (co-writer with Giorgio Moroder) for film soundtrack Foxes, 1979; Tattoo; When Angels Cry; Some People's Lives, recorded by Bette Midler; Other compositions recorded by artistes including: Mel Tormé; Dianne Schuur; Chet Atkins; Stan Getz; John Mellencamp; Hugh Masakela. Recordings: Albums: Janis Ian, 1967; A Song for All the Seasons of Your Mind, 1968; The Secret Life Of J Eddy Fink, 1969; Who Really Cares, 1969; Present Company, 1971; Stars, 1974; Between The Lines, (Number 1, US), 1975; Aftertones, 1976; Miracle Row, 1997; Janis Ian, 1978; Night Rains, 1979; Restless Eyes, 1981; Breaking Silence, 1993; Revenge, 1995. Publications: Monthly columnist, The Advocate; Regular columnist, Performing Songwriter Magazine; Book of poetry, 1968. Honours: 2 Grammy Awards, 9 Grammy Nominations; GLCCLA Award for Creative Integrity, 1993; Fisk University Award for Creative Excellence, 1994; Multiple Platinum records worldwide, including Japan, Australia and US. Hobbies: Archaeology; Snorkeling; Reading. Current Management: Simon Renshaw, Senior Management. Address: c/o Janis Ian Subscriber Service, PO Box 121797, Nashville, TN 37212, USA.

IANORA Stèphane, b. 16 Jan 1960, Paris, France. Musician (drums). m. Motomi Ryu, 17 Mar 1989, 2 daughters. Education: University (Japanese Ursus); Graduated (Dev6). Career: Drummer, Bird X funk band, featuring Wally Badatov, 1979; Concerts with William Sheller, 1981-84; Concerts, tours, with: David Koven; Kurim Kalel; Rachid Bahri; Elli Medeiros; Jeanne Mas; World tours with Richard Clayderman, 1989-; Television shows with Vanessa Paradis. Recordings: with William Sheller: J'suis Pas Bien; Civic Olympia, 89; Karim Kalel: P'tite Soeur; David Koven: David Koven; Etè Torride; Marvin; Elli Medeiros: Elli; Jeanne Mas: En Concert; Sheila: Live Olympia 89; Richard Clayderman: English Pop Songs. Hobbies: Tai Chi Chuan; Japanese studies (language and civilisation). Address: 4 Allée des Tilleuls, 94220 Charenton, France.

ICE-T (Tracey Marrow), b. Newark, New Jersey, USA. Rapper; Actor. Career: Innovator of LA Gangsta Rap; Recording artist, 1987-; Rapper, rock group Body Count, 1992; Tours: UK; Europe; US; Canada; South America; Asia; Australia; Middle East; Actor, films include New Jack City; Trespass; Breakin'; Tank Girl; Television includes: Players; Baadasss TV; Owner, Rhyme Syndicate Records; Lecturer and spokesman, major US universities; Also involved in Hands Across Watts and South Central Love, 2 youth intervention programmes. Recordings: Albums: Rhyme Pays; Power; The Iceberg...; Freedom Of Speech - Just Watch What You Say; O.G.- Original Gangster; Home Invasion; Ice VI-Return Of The Real; with Body Count: Body Count; Born` Dead; Also featured on film soundtracks: Colors; Dick Tracy. Publication: The Ice Opinion, 1994. Honours: Best Male Rapper, Rolling Stone Readers Poll, 1992; Grammy Award, Best Rap Song for Back on the Block. Current Management: Rhyme Syndicate Management, 4902 Coldwater Canyon Ave, Sherman Oaks, CA 91423, USA.

IDOL Billy (Willem Wolfe Broad), b. 30 Nov 1955, Stanmore, Middlesex, England. Singer; Musician (guitar); Composer. Career: Lead singer, guitarist, UK punk group Generation X, 1977-81; Solo artiste, 1981-; Worldwide concerts include: Charmed Life Tour, 1990; Rock In Rio II Festival, 1991; Roskilde Festival, Denmark, 1991; Supported Bon Jovi, Milton Keynes Bowl, 1993. Recordings: Albums: with Generation X: Generation X, 1978; Valley Of The Dolls, 1979; Kiss Me Deadly, 1981; Solo albums: Don't Stop, 1981; Billy Idol, 1982; Rebel Yell, 1984; Vital Idol, 1985; Whiplash Smile, 1986; Idol Songs, 1988; Charmed Life, 1990; Cyberpunk, 1993; Solo singles include: Hot In The City, 1982; White Wedding, 1983; Rebel Yell, 1984 (both re-released 1985); Eyes Without A Face, 1984; Flesh For Fantasy, 1984; Catch My Fall, 1984; To Be A Lover, 1986; Don't Need A Gun, 1987; Sweet Sixteen, 1987; Mony Mony (Number 1, US), 1987; Cradle Of Love (Number 2, US), featured in film Adventures Of Ford Fairlane, 1990; LA Woman, 1990; Shock To The System, 1993. Honour: Double Platinum disc, Rebel Yell, 1984. East End Management, 8209 Melrose Avenue, 2nd Floor, Los Angeles, CA 90046, USA.

IGLAUER Bruce, b. 10 July 1947, Ann Arbor, Michigan, USA. Record Company Executive. m. Jo Kolanda, 5 Aug 1995. Education: BA, Lawrence University, Appleton, Wisconsin. Career: Founder, Alligator Records, 1971; President, Alligator Records; Released over 150 contemporary blues recordings. Recordings: Produced almost 100 blues albums including artists: Albert Collins; Koko Taylor; Johnny Winter; Ray Buchanan; Saffire. Publication: Co-founder: Living Blues Magazine. Membership: Founder, Senior Board of Trustees member, National Association of Independent Record Distributors and Manufacturers. Address: PO Box 60234, Chicago, IL 60660, USA.

IGLESIAS Julio (Julio Jose Iglesias de la Cueva), b. 23 Sept 1943, Madrid, Spain. Singer; Songwriter. m. Isabel Preisler, 20 Jan 1971, divorced, 3 sons. Education: Law student, Cambridge University. Musical Education: Learnt to sing in hospital (recovering from car crash). Career: Goalkeeper, Real Madrid junior team; Winner, Spanish Song Festival, Benidorm, 1968; Professional singer, songwriter, 1968-; Winner, Eurovision Song Contest, Netherlands, 1970; Major success in Latin America, 1970s; English Language releases, 1981-; Concerts and television appearances worldwide; In excess of 100 million records sold to date. Compositions include: La Vida Sigue Igual; Mi Amor; Yo Canto; Alguien El Alamo Al Camino; No llores. Recordings: Over 70 albums include: Soy, 1973; El Amor, 1975; A Mis 33 Anos, 1977; De Nina A Miyer, 1981; 1100 Bel Air Lace, 1984; Un Hombre Solo, 1987; Starry Night, 1990; La Carretera, 1995; Also on: Duets (with Frank Sinatra), 1993; Hit singles include: Manuela, 1975; Hey, 1979; Begin The Beguine, 1981; To All The Girls I've Loved Before, duet with Willie Nelson, 1983; My Love, duet with Stevie Wonder, 1988. Publications: Autobiography: Entre El Cielo y El Infernierno, 1981. Honours: Grammy, Best Latin Pop Performance, 1987; Diamond Disc Award, Guinness Book Of Records (most records in most languages), 1983; Medaille de Vermeil de la Ville de Paris, 1983; Eurovision Song Contest Winner, 1970. Membership: Hon member, Spanish Foreign Legion. Address: c/o Anchor Marketing, 1177 Kane Concourse PH, Bay Harbour Island, FL 33154, USA.

IGREC Mario, b. 24 May 1959, Zagreb, Croatia. Musician (guitar); Composer; Arranger; Guitar Teacher. m. Snjezana Drkulec Igrec, 22 Nov 1986, 3 sons. Education: Professor of Philosophy. Musical Education: Conservatory; Degree, jazz guitar. Career: Member, various groups including Zagreb Jazz Portrait; Hot Club Zagreb; Steve Klink Quartet; Mario Igrec Quintet; Pentagon; Good Day; Ritmo Loco; Jazz Big Band HGZ; Big Festival Orchestra; Live concerts and programmes for state television in Slovenia, Austria, Croatia; International jazz festivals include: Croatia; Slovenia; Germany; Hungary. Compositions: Vanova; A Better Tomorrow; Brimbi; Daimonion; Blues No 4; Balrog. Recordings: Moment Notice; Zagreb Jazz Portrait, 1984; with Ritmo Loco: Baila Como Yo, 1992; For A Love Of One Woman, 1995. Honour: Heineken Award for Jazz Band, Croatia, 1995. Memberships: Croatian Music Union (HGU); Jazz Club, Zagreb. Hobbies: Cycling; Table tennis. Current Management: Vesna Vrandecic, Zitnak 1, 41000 Zagreb, Croatia. Address: Mario Igrec, Ozaljska 93, 41000 Zagreb, Croatia.

IMBRUGLIA Natalie, b. 1975, New South Wales, Australia. Singer; Songwriter; Actress. Career: Actress, TV series Neighbours, Australia; Moved to London, 1995; Solo recording artiste, 1997-. Recordings: Debut album: Left Of The Middle, 1997; Hit Single: Torn, 1997. Address: c/o RCA Records, Bedford House, 69-69 Fulham High Street, London SW6 3JW, England.

INABA Kazuhiro, b. 12 June 1960, Osaka, Japan. Musician (5-string banjo, guitar, fiddle). m. Tomoe Mori, 4 June, 1994, 1 son. Education: BA, Kansai University for Foreign Studies. Career: Played with many artists from USA including: Butch Robbins; Larry Stephenson; The Lonesome River Band; Bill Clifton; Producer, Bluegrass concerts; Interpreter, Leon Russell, Japan Tour, 1995. Recordings: Albums: Shore To Shore, 1986; Hard Times Come Again No More, 1989; Goin' Across The Sea, 1993. Publications: Featured articles, Moonshiner magazine, Japan (Bluegrass Journal). Honour: Second place, Bluegrass Banjo, Galax Fiddlers Convention, 1983.Memberships: Musicians' Union, Japan; IBMA (International Bluegrass Music Association), Owensboro, Kentucky. Current Management; Office White Oak. Address: 4-2-16, Nishi-Tezukayama, Sumiyoshi, Osaka 558, Japan.

INDERBERG John Pål, b. 6 Aug 1950, Steinkjer, Norway. Musician (saxophone); Music Professor. m. Kirsten Oxaal, 23 July 1976. Education: University of Trondheim. Career: Played with J Eks; Bob Brookmeyer; Lee Konitz; Warne Marsh; Many albums and tours; EBU Musician, soloist with Symphony Orchestra; Duos with Henning Sommerro; Professor of Music, Music Conservatory, Trondheim, Norway. Recordings: Albums: with Warne Marsh: Sax Of A Kind, 1987; For The Time Being, 1988; with Siri's Svale Band: Blackbird, 1990; with Lee Konitz: Steps Towards A Dream, 1995. Honours: Buddy Award, Norwegian Jazz Federation. Membership: Norwegian Musician Federation. Hobby: Moosehunting. Current Management: Eirik Kvam Olavsfestdagene, Dronnigens Gate 1B, 7011 Trondheim, Norway. Address: Kjopmannsgt 12, 7013 Trondheim, Norway.

INESON Adam Michael, b. 13 Jun 1972, Swindon, Wiltshire, England. Musician (guitar); Composer. Career: Guitarist in several post-punk bands; Currently, guitarist and songwriter for NUB. Recordings: EPs with NUB: Hopper, 1993; Blue Climber, 1995. Hobby: 20th Century Literature. Current Management: SCM Management, c/o Jackass Records. Address: c/o Jackass Records, PO Box 1471, London N5 2LY, England.

INGMAR, b. 31 December 1970, Antwerp, Belgium. Artist; Singer; Songwriter; Musician (Keys). Education: Modern Languages; Basics in Jazz, Jazz Studio, Antwerp. Career: Several national radio appearances; Several major stage live gigs (including one for His Majesty The Former King of Belgium). Compositions: The Quest for Beauty and Truth Continues, 1996; Ramifying Parallels on USA Import Music, 1997.

Recordings: Insanity; Sister Sun; Amour Fatale; Exceptional; Solitude; The Quest; Beyond the Stars; The Dream. Publications: The Quest on Club Excentrique, 1996; Waiting...In These Skies, poem trilogy, 1997. Honour: Laureate in national New Song Contest, SABAM, 1993. Memberships: SABAM, International Copyright Institute; International Writers and Artists Association. Hobbies: Literature; Music; Partying; Kickboxing; Soccer. Address: INGMAR, PO Box 470, 2000 Antwerp 1, Belgium.

INGRAM Charlie Alexander, b. 24 Oct 1972, Cheltenham, England. Musician (guitar, mandolin); Singer. Musical Education: Self-taught. Education: Studying for BA Honours Music Technology, Rose Bruford College. Career: with Eden Burning, touring extensively throughout UK and Europe, 1993-. Recordings: Mirth And Matter, 1994; You Could Be The Meadow (EP), 1994; Be An Angel, 1995; Brink, 1995. Membership: Musicians' Union. Hobbies: Walking; Climbing; Weight training. Address: 9 Wildmoor Lane, Catshill, Bromsgrove B61 0NT, England.

IOMMI Tony, b. 19 Feb 1948, Birmingham, England. Rock Musician (guitar); Composer. Career: Guitarist, UK heavy rock group Black Sabbath, 1967-; Major appearances include: Madison Square Gardens, New York, 1975; Live Aid, Philadelphia, 1985. Recordings: Singles include: Paranoid; Iron Man; War Pigs; Never Say Die; Albums: Black Sabbath, 1969; Paranoid, 1970; Master Of Reality, 1971; Vol 4, 1972; Sabbath Bloody Sabbath, 1973; Sabotage, 1975; Technical Ecstasy, 1976; Never Say Die, 1978; Heaven And Hell, 1980; Mob Rules, 1981; Live Evil, 1983; Born Again, 1983; Seventh Star, 1983; The Eternal Idol, 1987; Headless Cross, 1990; Tyr, 1990; Dehumanizer, 1992; Forbidden, 1995; Numerous compilations. Current Management: Gloria Butler Management, PO Box 2686, Knowle, Birmingham B94 5NQ, England.

IREDALE Simon James, b. 21 Nov 1970, Bradford, West Yorkshire, England. Songwriter; Performer; Musician (Guitar, Keyboards). Musical Education: Grade V, Music and Theory at age 9. Career: Has been in various bands from age 6; Toured Britain with the band, Terrorize and The Love Generation; Currently on tour with the band, Hothead; Radio appearances on Pennine Radio, BBC Radio 1, and BBC GLR programme, Unplugged with Janice Long. Recordings: Numerous recordings, currently with Hothead. Memberships: Musicians' Union; National Band Register. Hobby: Music. Current Management: Calderbank and Clarke Management. Address: 22 Devonshire Road, Chorley, Lancashire, England.

ISAACS Gregory, b. 1951, Kingston, Jamaica. Reggae Singer. Career: Solo singer, 1970s-; Established own African Museum Shop and label, with Errol Dunkley, 1973; Extensive international tours. Recordings: Numerous albums include: Mr Isaacs; Extra Classic; The Early Years; Sly And Robbie Present; The Best Of, Volumes 1 & 2; Cool Ruler; Soon Forward; Lonely Lover; My Number One; Red Roses For Gregory; Taxi Show Case; Night Nurse; Out Deh; Warning; Latest releases: Can't Stay Away, 1992; No Luck, 1993; Private Lesson, 1995; Mr Love, 1995; Memories, 1995. Address: c/o Fantasma Tours International, 2000 S Dixie Highway, West Palm Beach, FL 33401, USA.

ISAACS Jason, b. 30 April 1968, England. Singer; Songwriter; Guitar. m. Marion. Career: Dance Macabre, 1985; The Promise, 1994; Triggerfish, 1996; Solo Artist, 1996-; various radio apps; Various sessions as Backing Vocalist. Compositions: A Girl Called Jesus; Sigh; C-Life; Bike; Funky Chuny; Gun; Only a Northern Band; News; Hold It Down; Who Says I Can; Cornucopia. Recordings: Debut single to be released, 1997, A Girl Called Jesus, 1998. Hobbies: Football; Skiing. Current Management:

Sound Judgement Partnership, 42 Brent Moor Road, Bramhan, Stockport, Cheshire SK7 3PT, England.

ISAAK Chris, b. 26 June 1956, Stockton, California, USA. Singer;Songwriter; Actor. Education: Degree, English and Communication Arts.Career: Singer, 1984-; Extensive international tours include: Turku Festival, Finland, 1993; Support to Tina Turner, US tour, 1993; Television appearances include: The Last Resort; The Tonight Show; Saturday Night Live; Late Show With David Letterman; Actor, films: Married To The Mob, 1988; Wild At Heart, 1989; The Silence Of The Lambs, 1990; Twin Peaks - Fire Walk With Me, 1993; Little Buddha, 1993; Compositions: Music for films: Blue Velvet; Wild At Heart; Music for television: Days Of Our Lives; The Preppie Murder; Private Eye. Recordings: Albums: Silvertone, 1985; Chris Isaak, 1987; Heart Shaped World, 1989; Wicked Game, 1991; San Francisco Days, 1993; Forever Blue, 1995; Singles include: Blue Hotel, 1987; Wicked Game, 1989; Can't Do A Thing (To Stop Me), 1993; San Francisco Days. Honours: International Rock Award, Best Male Vocalist of the Year, 1991; 3 MTV Music Video Awards, Wicked Game, 1991. Current Management: Howard Kaufman, H K Management, 8900 Wilshire Blvd, Suite 300, Beverly Hills, CA 90211, USA.

ISHAM Mark, b. 7 September 1951, NYC, NY, USA. Composer; Producer; Sound Engineer; Jazz Musician (Trumpet). m. Donna Linson, 24 February 1990. Career: Film scores include: Never Cry Wolf, 1983; Mrs Soffel, 1984; The Times of Harvey Milk, 1984; Country, 1984; Trouble in Mind, 1985; The Hitcher, 1986; Made in Heaven, 1987; The Moderns, 1988; The Beast, 1988; Everybody Wins, 1990; Love at Large, 1990; Reversal of Fortune, 1990; Mortal Thoughts, 1991; Crooked Hearts, 1991; Point Break, 1991; Little Man Tate, 1991; Billy Bathgate, 1991; Cool World, 1992; A Midnight Clear, 1992; Of Mice and Men, 1992; The Public Eye, 1992; A River Runs Through It, 1992; Sketch Artist, 1992; Nowhere to Run, 1993; Fire in the Sky, 1993; Made in America, 1993; Short Cuts, 1993; Romeo is Bleeding, 1994; The Getaway, 1994; Quiz Show, 1994; Mrs Parker and the Vicious Circle, 1994; Nell, 1994; Losing Isiah, 1995; The Net, 1995; Home for the Holidays, 1995; Last Dance, 1996; Gotti, 1996; Fly Away Home, 1996; Night Falls on Manhattan, 1997; Afterglow, 1997; The Education of Little Tree, 1997; TV Themes include: Chicago Hope EZ Streets: recordings include (solo) Vapor Drawings, 1983; Castalia, 1988; Tibet, 1989; Mark Isham, 1991; Blue Sun, with Charles Jankel, 1995; Deal It Out, with America, View From the Ground (with Van Morrison), Live at the Belfast Opera House; Into the Music, Inarticulate Speech of the Heart; Common One; Beautiful Vision (with Art Lande); Story of Baku; Eccentricities oe Earl Dant; Rubisa Patrol; Desert Marauders; We Begin (with Group 87); Group 87; A Career In Dada Processing (with the Rolling Stones); Voodoo Lounge (with Bruce Springsteen); Human Touch (with Willie Nelson); Across the Borderline (with Toots Thielmans); Toots. Current Management: Ron Moss Management.

ISLAM Yusuf (formerly Cat Stevens), b. 21 July 1948, London, England. Writer; Director of Production Company. m. Fawzia Mubarik Ali, 7 Sept 1979, 2 sons, 1 dec, 4 daughters. Musical Education: Self-taught. Career: Commenced with release of I Love My Dog, Oct 1966; Achieved international status with multi-platinum sales of albums Tea For The Tillerman, 1970; Teaser And The Firecat, 1971; Following extensive tours, including: Bamboozle, 1974; Majikat, 1976; Numerous television appearances; Decided to retire at summit of popularity in 1978 after embracing Islam. Recordings include: Matthew and Son, 1967; New Masters, 1968; World Of Cat Stevens, 1970; Mona Bone Jakon, 1970; Tea For The Tillerman, 1971; Teaser And The Firecat,

1971; Very Young And Early Songs, US, 1971; Catch Bull At Four, 1972; Foreigner, 1973; Buddha And The Chocolate Box, 1974; View From The Top, 1974; Numbers, 1975; Greatest Hits, 1975; Iztso, 1977; Back To Earth, 1978; Cat's Cradle, 1978; Footsteps In The Dark (Comp), 1984; Classics Vol 24 - Cat Stevens, 1989; Very Best Of Cat Stevens, 1990; As Yusuf Islam: The Life Of The Last Prophet(s), 1995. Publications: Cat Stevens-Definitive Career, Chris Charlesworth; The Boy Who Looked At The Moon, David Evans, 1995. Memberships: Musicians' Union; Member, exclusive club of artists whose composition has been performed more than 2 million times, in US alone (with Morning Has Broken). Hobbies: Swimming; Riding; Reading. Address: c/o Francis Pettican, Westbury Music Consultants, 72 Marylebone Lane, London W1M 5FF, England.

ISLEY Ernie, b. 7 Mar 1952, Cincinnati, Ohio, USA. Musician (guitar, drums). Career: Member, The Isley Brothers with brothers: Rudolph, Ronald, Kelly, Marvin and cousin Chris Jasper, 1969-84; Member, Isley, Jasper, Isley (with Marvin and Chris), 1984-. Recordings: Albums: with The Isley Brothers: The Brothers Isley, 1969; Live At Yankee Stadium, 1969; Givin' It Back, 1971; Brother Brother Brother, 1972; The Isleys Live, 1973; The Isleys Greatest Hits, 1973; Live It Up, 1974; The Heat Is On, 1975; Harvest For The World, 1976; Go For Your Guns, 1977; Forever Gold, 1977; Showdown, 1978; Winner Takes All, 1979; Go All The Way, 1980; Grand Slam, 1981; Inside You; 1981; The Real Deal, 1982; Between The Sheets, 1983; with Isley Jasper Isley: Broadway's Closer To Sunset Boulevard, 1985; Caravan Of Love, 1985; Masterpiece, 1985; Different Drummer, 1987; Solo album: High Wire, 1990; Tracks Of Life (with Marvin and Ronald), 1992; Singles include: with the Isley Brothers: Love The One You're With; Spill The Wine; That Lady; Summer Breeze; Fight The Power; For The Love Of You (Part 1 & 2); Who Loves You Better; Harvest For The World; It's Disco Night (Rock Don't Stop); with Isley, Jasper, Isley: Caravan Of Love. Honours: Inducted into Rock And Roll Hall Of Fame, 1992; Gold Ticket, Madison Square Garden, 1980. Current Management: Ron Weisner Management, 9200 Sunset Blvd, Penthouse 15, Los Angeles, CA 90069, USA.

ISLEY Marvin, b. 1953, Cincinnati, Ohio, USA. Musician (bass, percussion). Career: Member, The Isley Brothers (with brothers, Rudolph, Ronald, Ernie and cousin Chris Jasper), 1969-84; Member, Isley, Jasper, Isley (with Ernie and Chris), 1984-. Recordings: Albums with the Isley Brothers include: The Brothers Isley, 1969; Brother Brother Brother, 1972; The Isleys Live, 1973; The Isley's Greatest Hits, 1973; Live It Up, 1974; The Heat Is On, 1975; Harvest For The World, 1976; Go For Your Guns, 1977; Showdown, 1978; Winner Takes All, 1979; Go All The Way, 1980; Grand Slam, 1981; Inside You, 1981; The Real Deal, 1982; Between The Sheets, 1983; with Isley Jasper Isley: Broadway's Closer To Sunset Boulevard, 1985; Caravan Of Love, 1985; Different Drummer, 1987; Tracks Of Life, (with Ernie and Ronald), 1992; Singles include: It's Your Thing; Love The One You're With; Spill The Wine; Lay-Away; Pop That Thang; That Lady; Summer Breeze; Highway Of My Life; Fight The Power; For The Love Of You; Harvest For The World; It's A Disco Night; Goodnight (It's Time For Love). Honours: Gold Ticket, Madison Square Garden, 1980; Inducted into Rock And Roll Hall Of Fame, 1992. Current Management: Ron Weisner Management, 9200 Sunset Blvd, Penthouse 15, Los Angeles, CA 90069, USA.

ISLEY Ronald, b. 21 May 1941, Cincinnati, Ohio, USA. Singer. Career: Member, gospel group, Isley Brothers, early 1950s; Formed trio with Rudolph and O'Kelly, 1955; First UK tour, 1964; Formed T-Note record label, as producer and writer, 1969; 2 further Isley brothers join, Ernie and Marvin, 1969-84; Group currently billed as The Isley Brothers Featuring Ronald Isley, 1989-. Recordings: Albums: Twist And Shout, 1959; This Old Heart Of Mine, 1966; It's Our Thing, 1969; Givin' It Back, 1971; Brother Brother Brother, 1972; The Isleys Live, 1973; The Isley's Greatest Hits, 1973; Live It Up, 1974; The Heat Is On, 1975; Harvest For The World, 1976; Go For Your Guns, 1977; Forever Gold, 1977; Showdown, 1978; Winner Takes All, 1978; Go All The Way, 1978; Grand Slam, 1978; Inside You, 1978; The Real Deal, 1978; Between The Sheets, 1978; Masterpiece, 1985; Smooth Sailin', 1987; Spend The Night, 1989; Tracks Of Life (with Ernie and Marvin), 1983; Live, 1993; Singles include: Shout; Twist And Shout; Testify; This Old Heart Of Mine; I Guess I'll Always Love You; Behind A Painted Smile; It's Your Thing; I Turned You On; Put Yourself In My Place; Love The One You're With; Spill The Wine; Pop That Thang; Work To Do; That Lady; Summer Breeze; Highway Of Life; Fight The Power; For The Love Of You; Who Loves You Better; Harvest For The World; Livin' In The Life; Goodnight (It's Time For Love); Spend The Night. Honours: Grammy Award, Best R&B Vocal, It's Your Thing, 1969; Inducted into Rock And Roll Hall Of Fame, 1992. Current Management: Ron Weisner Entertainment, 9200 Sunset Blvd, Penthouse 15, Los Angeles, CA 90069, USA.

ISLEY Rudolph, b. 1 Apr 1939, Cincinnati, Ohio, USA. Singer. Career: Member, Isley Brothers, gospel group, early 1950s; Formed trio with brothers Ronald and O'Kelly, 1955-; Formed T-Neck record label, writing, producing, became vice-president, 1969; Group joined by brothers Ernie, Marvin, and cousin Chris Jasper, 1969-84. Recordings: Albums: Shout, 1959; Twist And Shout, 1962; This Old Heart Of Mine, 1966; It's Our Thing, 1969; The Brothers, 1969; Live At Yankee Stadium, 1969; Brother Brother Brother, 1972; The Isleys Live, 1973; The Isley's Greatest Hits, 1973; Live It Up, 1974; The Heat Is On, 1975; Harvest For The World, 1976; Go For Your Guns, 1977; Showdown, 1978; Winner Takes All, 1978; Go All The Way, 1978; Grand Slam, 1981; Inside You, 1981; The Real Deal, 1982; Between The Sheets, 1983; Smooth Sailin', 1987; The Isley Brothers Greatest Hits, 1988; Spend The Night, 1989; Singles include: This Old Heart Of Mine; I Guess I'll Always Love You; Behind A Painted Smile; It's Your Thing; I Turned You On; Put Yourself In My Place; Spill The Wine; Love The One You're With; That Lady; Summer Breeze; What It Comes Down To; Highway Of My Life; For The Love of You (Part 1 & 2); Harvest For The World; It's Disco Night (Rock Don't Stop); Goodnight (Its Time For Love). Honours: Grammy Award, Best R&B Vocal Performance, 1970; Gold Ticket, Madison Square Garden, New York, 1980; Inducted into Rock And Roll Hall Of Fame, 1992. Current Management: Ron Weisner Entertainment, 9200 Sunset Blvd., Penthouse 15, Los Angeles, CA 90069, USA.

IVEY Lee (Carole Lee Ivey), b. Kentucky, North Carolina, USA. Career: Performed with Bobby Atkins; Screenwriter; The Legend of Broken Heart Creek, screenplay, 6 months, 1993; Songwriter. Recordings: Bunnie Mills and Friends, CD; It's Your Lie; Just for Old Times Sake. Address: 4100 N Ohenry Blvd, Lot#158 Greensboro, NC 27405, USA.

IWAN Dafydd, b. 24 Aug 1943, Glanaman, Wales. Welsh Singer-Songwriter; Record Company Director. m. Bethan Jones, 24 Sept 1988, 2 sons (2 sons, 1 daughter from previous marriage). Education: Brynaman, Rhydaman, Bala, University of Wales. Career: Regular stage performances (as solo artist, with folk group, and with own band), 1962-; Regular television appearances, 1965-; Tours: North America; Europe; Celtic countries. Recordings: 11 albums; Songs include: Yma O Hyd; Carlo; Pam Fod Eira'n Wyn; Ai Am Fod Haul; Hawl I Fyw. Publications:

Several song books including: Holl Ganeuon (151 songs). Honours: Honorary member, Gorsedd of Bards. Membership: Equity. Hobbies: Poetry; Sport; Art. Current Management: Sain. Address: Canolfan Sain, Llandwrog, Caernarfon, Gwynedd LL54 5TG, Wales.

J

JACKMAN Frank, b. 1 Apr 1937, Guyana. Musician (steel drums, guitar); Singer. 4 sons, 2 daughters. Musical Education: Private tuition. Career: Danish television and radio appearances; Tours: Sweden, Greece, Denmark; Music teacher, Norway; Professional performer. Recordings: Numerous album releases, 1972-. Memberships: DJBFA; KODA. Hobby: Music. Current Management: Lena McCammon. Address: Hydemorsvej 4, 2730 Herlev, Denmark.

JACKSON Alan Eugene, b. 17 Oct 1958, Newnan, Georgia, USA. Singer; Songwriter. m. Denise Jackson, 12 Dec 1979, 3 daughters. Education: 2 years college. Career: Multi-platinum album sales, over 24 million; Performed before over 3 million fans; Appeared on numerous award shows; Television includes: The Late Show with David Letterman; The Tonight Show; Regis and Kathie Lee. Compositions include: Chattahoochee (Number 1, US). Recordings: Albums: Here In The Real World, 1990; Don't Rock The Jukebox, 1991; A Lot About Livin', 1992; Who I Am, 1994; Greatest Hits Collection, 1995; Everything I Love, 1996. Honours: Academy of Country Music Male Artist Of The Year, 1995; Country Music Association Entertainer Of The Year, 1995. Memberships: ASCAP; NARAS; ACM; CMA. Hobbies: Fishing; Collecting cars and Harley Davidson motorcycles; Boating. Current Management: Chip Peay Entertainment. Address: Alan Jackson Fanclub, PO Box 121945, Nashville, TN 37212-1945, USA.

JACKSON Bob, b. 6 Jan 1949, Coventry, England. Musician (keyboards, guitar); Vocalist; Songwriter. m. Christine, 18 Oct 1980, 2 sons, 1 daughter. Musical Education: Self-taught. Career: Bands: Indian Summer; with Ross: 2 US tours, 1 supporting Eric Clapton, 1974; with Badfinger: UK tour with Man, 1974; 4 US tours, 1982-85; BBC television documentary, 1986; with Dodgers: Various television and radio includes: In Concert, Crackerjack, Supersonic; Scene; David Byron Band; Fortunes. Compositions: Various songwriting deals with Essex, Island, 16 song releases. Recordings: Album/single releases with all the above bands. Memberships: PRS; MCPS; Musicians' Union. Current Management: Brian Yeats. Address: Home Farm House, Canwell, West Midlands B75 5SH, England.

JACKSON Carl Eugene, b. 18 Sept 1953, Louisville, Missouri, USA. Songwriter; Musician (banjo). Career: Musician, Jim and Jesse; The Sullivan Family; Glen Campbell, 1972-84; Songwriter, Glen Campbell Publishing, 1984-87; Ricky Skaggs/Polygram Music Publishing, 1987-90; Famous Music Publishing, 1990-. Compositions: Letter To Home; Little Mountain Church House; Put Yourself In My Place; Breaking New Ground. Recordings: Albums: Roll On, Alabama, 1984; 13, Emmylou Harris, 1987. Honours: IBMA Song Of The Year, Little Mountain Church House, 1990. Memberships: CMA; ACM. Address: Famous Music Publishing, 16 Avenue South, Nashville, TN 37212, USA.

JACKSON Clarence, b. 28 Dec 1923, Green Sea, South Carolina, USA. Recording Artist; Producer; Musician (steel guitar, dobro). m. Carolyn W Jackson, 5 June 1949, 1 son. Education: Clemson College; Coyne Electrical School; Elkin's Radio School. Career: Radio and television personality; Tent, theatre, school and park Country shows; Toured with Western film stars: Al "Lash" Larue; Cowboy Tex Ritter; Shows on US armed forces radio, World War II; Recorded 500 pure dobro guitar tunes (world record for dobroist); PBS radio broadcasting; Traditional music dobro man, comedian. Recordings include: with Sister Foye Turner: Country Gospel; Old Time Country Songs; with Roger Hopkins:

Smokey Mountain Favourites; with Billie and Gordon Hamrick: Gospel Time; with Bernard Sturkie: Gene Autrey Favourites; with Mutt Poston: Favourite Waltzes; James Wall Sings 20 Carter Family Songs; Hoedowns; Hawaiian and Country; Country Get Together; Red White and Country Gospel; with Roy Rea: Dobro Honky-Tonking; with Maggie Country Singers: Country Favourites; Heart Warming Recitations, with C Band; Big John Demarcus: Jimmie Rogers Favourites; The Carolina Boys; 23 guitar instructional videos: How To Play By Ear The Clarence Jackson Way. Publication: Autobiography. Honours: US Air Force; US National Guard; US Army; Country Music Associations. Current Management: Self-managed. Address: 308 Starbright Lane, Moncks Corner, SC 29461, USA.

JACKSON Janet, b. 16 May 1966, Los Angeles, USA. Singer; Actress. m. El DeBarge, 1984 (divorced 1986). Career: First appearance with family singing group The Jacksons, aged 7; Television actress, 1977-81; Appeared in US television series: Good Times, CBS-TV; Diff'rent Strokes; Fame; A New Kind Of Family; Solo recording artiste, 1982-; Concerts and tours include: Rhythm Nation World Tour (US, Europe, Far East), 1990; Film debut, Poetic Justice, 1993. Recordings: Albums: Janet Jackson, 1982; Dream Street, 1984; Control, 1986; Janet Jackson's Rhythm Nation (Number 1, US), 1989; Janet (Number 1, UK and US), 1993; Design Of A Decade 1986-1996, 1995; Hit singles include: What Have You Done For Me Lately, 1986; Nasty, 1986; When I Think Of You (Number 1, US), 1986; Control, 1987; Let's Wait Awhile, 1987; The Pleasure Principle, 1987; Miss You So Much (Number 1, US), 1989; Rhythm Nation, 1990; Escapade (Number 1, US), 1990; Alright, 1990; Come Back To Me, 1990; Black Cat (Number 1, US), 1990; Love Will Never Do (Without You), (Number 1, US), 1991; The Best Things In Life Are Free, duet with Luther Vandross, from film Mo' Money, 1992; That's The Way Love Goes (Number 1, US), 1993; If, 1993; Again (Number 1, US), 1993; Whoops Now, 1995; Scream, 1995; Runaway, 1995; Twenty Foreplay, 1996. Numerous honours include: Billboard Awards, 1986-; American Music Awards, 1987-; Soul Train Awards, 1987-; MTV Video Music Awards, 1987-; Grammy, Best Music Video, Rhythm Nation 1814, 1990; Star on Hollywood Walk Of Fame, 1990; Janet Jackson Week, Los Angeles, 1990; Humanitarian Of The Year Award, Starlight Foundation of Southern California, 1990; Chairman's Award, NAACP Image Awards, 1992; First artist to have seven US Top 5 hits from one album, 1990-91; International Dance Award, Achievement In Dance, 1995. Current Management: Roger Davies Management, 15030 Ventura Blvd #772, Sherman Oaks, CA 91403, USA.

JACKSON Jermaine Lajuan, b. 11 Dec 1954, Gary, Indiana, USA. Singer; Musician (bass); Record Producer. m. Hazel Gordy, 15 Dec 1973. Career: Member, Jackson Five (later The Jacksons), US family singing group. 1969-75; Solo recording artiste, 1972-; Career development of artists including Devo; Michael Lovesmith; Syreeta; Formed own production company, and record label, WORK Records; Producer, US television series The Jacksons - An American Dream, ABC, 1992. Recordings include: Albums: with The Jacksons: Diana Ross Presents The Jackson 5, 1970; ABC, 1970; Third Album, 1970; Christmas Album, 1970; Maybe Tomorrow, 1971; Lookin' Through The Windows, 1972; Skywriter, 1973; Get It Together, 1973; Solo albums: Jermaine, 1972; Come Into My Life, 1973; My Name Is Jermaine, 1976; Feel The Fire, 1977; Let's Get Serious, 1980; Jermaine, 1981; I Like Your Style, 1981; Let Me Tickle Your Fancy, 1982; Jermaine Jackson, 1984; Precious Moments, 1986; Don't Take It Personal, 1990; You Said, 1992; Singles include: Daddy's Home, 1973; Let's Get Serious, 1980; Let Me Tickle Your Fancy, with

Devo, 1982; What Do You Do, 1985; I Think It's Love, 1985; Contributor, film soundtracks: Voyage Of The Rock Aliens, 1985; Perfect, 1985; As record producer: Tracks for Whitney Houston debut album, 1986.

JACKSON Joe, b. 11 Aug 1954, Burton-Upon-Trent, Staffordshire, England. Singer; Songwriter. Musical Education: Violin and piano lessons; S Level, Music; Composition, orchestration, piano and percussion, Royal Collge Of Music, London. Career: Played with Johnny Dankworth; Member, National Youth Jazz Orchestra; Musical director, Coffee & Cream, 1977; Singer, 1978-; Regular UK and international tours, 1978-; Concerts include: The Summer Of '80 Garden Party, with Bob Marley, Average White Band, Crystal Palace, 1980. Compositions include: Film scores: Mike's Murder, 1983; Shijin No Ie (House Of The Poet), 1985; Tucker, 1988. Recordings: Albums: Look Sharp!, 1979; I'm The Man, 1979; Beat Crazy, 1980; Joe Jackson's Jumpin' Jive, 1981; Night And Day, 1982; Big World, 1986; Will Power, 1987; Live 1980/86, 1988; Blaze Of Glory, 1988; Laughter And Lust, 1990; Steppin' Out - The Best Of Joe Jackson, 1990; Night Music, 1994; Hit singles include: Is She Really Going Out With Him?, 1978; It's Different For Girls, 1980; Steppin' Out, 1982. Honour: Grammy Nomination, film score Tucker, 1988. Current Management: C Winston Simone Management, 1790 Broadway, 10th Floor, New York, NY 10019, USA.

JACKSON Kevin, b. 4 October 1970. Singer; Songwriter; Musician (Guitar). m. Jana M, 5 June 1993. Education: Samford University. Career: Jackson Finch Member, 5 years. Compositions: Beyond Complacency, 1993; Singles include: Lift My Eyes; Forever Love. Recordings: Singles include: To Believe; Mile of Me; Only You; Your Grace. Membership: BMI. Hobbies: Water Sports; Gardening. Current Management: The Dupree Co, 130 West 44th Street, New York, NY 10036, USA. Address: PO Box 111863, Nashville, TN 37222, USA.

JACKSON Michael Joseph, b. 29 Aug 1958, Gary, Indiana, USA. m. Lisa Marie Presley, 1994 (divorced 1996). Career: Lead singer, family singing group Jackson Five (later the Jacksons), 1969-75; Solo artist, 1971-; Lengthy world tours, including Bad Tour 1987; Dangerous World Tour, 1992; Film appearances: The Wiz, 1978; Captain Eo, 1986; Moonwalker, 1988; Founder, Heal The World Foundation (children's charity); Owner, ATV Music Company (including rights for John Lennon and Paul McCartney songs); Owner, MJJ record label. Compositions include: Co-writer with Lionel Richie, We Are The World, USA For Africa famine relief single, 1985. Recordings: Albums: with Jackson Five/Jacksons include: Diana Ross Presents The Jackson Five, 1969; ABC, 1970; Third Album, 1970; Goin' Back To Indiana, 1971; Maybe Tomorrow, 1971; Looking Through The Windows, 1972; Farewell My Summer, 1973; Get It Together, 1973; Skywriter, 1973; Dancing Machine, 1974; Moving Violation, 1975; Joyfull Jukebox, Music, 1976; The Jacksons, 1976; Goin' Places, 1977; Destiny, 1978; Triumph, 1980; Boogie, 1980; Live, 1981; Victory, 1984; Solo albums: Got To Be There, 1971; Ben, 1972; Music And Me, 1973; Forever Michael, 1975; The Best Of, 1975; The Wiz (film soundtrack), 1978; Off The Wall, 1979; ET - The Extra Terrestrial (film soundtrack), 1982; Thriller (Number 1 in every Western country), 1982; Bad (Number 1, UK and US), 1987; Dangerous (Number 1, US and UK), 1991; HIStory - Past, Present And Future Book I, 1995; Numerous solo hit singles include: Got To Be There, 1971; Rockin' Robin, 1972; Ain't No Sunshine, 1972; Ben (Number 1, US), 1972; Don't Stop Till You Get Enough (Number 1, US), 1979; Off The Wall, 1979; Rock With You (Number 1, US), 1980; One Day In Your Life (Number 1, UK), 1981; She's Out Of My Life, 1980; The Girl Is Mine, duet with Paul McCartney (Number 1, UK),

1982; Billie Jean (Number 1, US and UK), 1983; Beat It (Number 1, US), 1983; Wanna Be Startin' Somethin', 1983; Human Nature, 1983; Say Say Say, duet with Paul McCartney, 1983; Thriller, 1983; I Can't Stop Loving You (Number 1, UK and US), 1987; Bad (Number 1, US), 1987; The Way You Make Me Feel (Number 1, US), 1988; Dirty Diana (Number 1, US), 1988; Leave Me Alone, 1989; Black And White (Number 1, UK and US), 1991; Remember The Time, 1992; Heal The World, 1992; Give In To Me, 1992; Scream (with Janet Jackson), 1995; You Are Not Alone, 1995; Earth Song, 1995; They Don't Care About Us, 1996; Contributor, recordings by Minnie Ripperton; Carol Bayer Sager; Donna Summer; Paul McCartney. Publications: Moonwalk (autobiography), 1988; Dancing The Dream (poems and reflections), 1992. Honours include: Numerous Grammy Awards, 1980- (including 7 awards, 1984; Song Of The Year, 1986; Legend Award, 1993) Numerous American Music Awards, 1980- (including 11 awards, 1984; Special Award of Achievement, 1989); BRIT Awards: Best International Artist, 1984, 1988, 1989; Artist Of A Generation, 1996; Soul Train Awards, 1988-; MTV Video Vanguard Award, 1988; 2 NAACP Image Awards, 1988; Entertainer of the Decade, American Cinema Awards Foundation, 1990; First recipient, BMI Michael Jackson Award, 1990; 3 World Music Awards, 1993; Most successful album ever, Thriller (50 million copies sold worldwide); Star on Hollywood Walk Of Fame, 1984; Numerous magazine poll wins and awards; Gold and Platinum records. Current Management: Bob Jones, MJJ Productions. Address: 10960 Wilshire Blvd, 2204 Los Angeles, CA 90024, USA.

JACKSON Millie, b. 15 July 1944, Thompson, Georgia, USA. Singer. Career: Professional singer, 1964-; R&B singer, then Country singer; Collaborations with Isaac Hayes. Recordings: Singles include: Ask Me What You Want; Hurts So Good, from film Cleopatra Jones; My Man A Sweet Man; Act Of War, duet with Elton John; Albums: Millie Jackson, 1972; It Hurts So Good, 1973; Caught Up, 1974; Soul Believer, 1974; Still Caught Up, 1975; Best Of Millie Jackson, 1976; Free And In Love, 1976; Lovingly Yours, 1977; Get It Out 'Cha System, 1978; A Moment's Pleasure, 1979; Live And Uncensored, 1980; For Men Only, 1980; Just A Lil' Bit Country, 1981; Live And Outrageous, 1982; Hard Times, 1982; ESP (Extra Sexual Persuasion), 1984; An Imitation Of Love, 1986; The Tide Is Turning, 1988. Current Management: Keishval Enterprises, 133 Cedar Lane, Suite 208, Teaneck, NJ 07666, USA.

JACKSON Milt, b. 1 Jan 1923, Detroit, Michigan, USA. Jazz Musician (vibraphone). m. Sandra Whittington, 18 Jan 1959, 1 daughter. Music Education: Michigan State University, 1957. Career: Played all major concert halls worldwide; Television appearances: Tonight Show; David Frost; Flip Wilson; Today; several specials with Sarah Vaughn and Tony Bennett. Recordings include: Plenty Plenty; Soul Ballads In Blues; Jacksonville; Opus De Jazz; New Sounds In Modern Music; Modern Jazz Quartet; Milt Jackson; Bags & Flute; Bags & Trane; Ballad Artistry; Big Band Bags; Complete Milt Jackson; Opus De Funk; Goodbye; Olinga; Sunflower; Impulse Years; Jazz 'n Samba; Milt Jackson Quintet; Statements; Big Four; Feelings; Live At The Museum Of Modern Art; That's The Way; Soul Believer; Mostly Duke; The Harem; Two Of The Few (with Oscar Peterson); Very Tall. Honours: Awards from Playboy, Down Beat, Jazzmobil, Council of Art and many more; Honorary Doctorate, Berklee College Of Music. Membership: American Guild of Authors & Composers. Hobbies: Billiards; Baking; Cooking. Address: 632 Sunderland Road, Teaneck, NJ 07666, USA.

JACKSON Ronald Shannon, b. 12 Jan 1940, Fort Worth, Texas, USA. Jazz Musician; Bandleader. Career: Musician, Charles Mingus; Betty Carter; Albert Ayler; Ornette Coleman; Cecil Taylor; Bandleader, RSJ and The Decoding Society, 1979-; Musician with Bill Laswell, Bill Frisell, 1980-. Recordings: 12 albums with RSJ and The Decoding Society; Over 40 albums with other artists. Current Management: Worldwide Jazz, 1128 Broadway, Suite 425, New York, NY 10001, USA.

JACKSON Steve. Sound Engineer; Mixer. Recordings: Dire Straits: Brothers in Arms; Money For Nothing; Wet Wet Wet, Holding Back the River; Bryan Adams, So Far So Good; Paul Young, Simply Red, Roachford, James Taylor Quartet, Tori Amos, Sting, Deacon Blue, Capercaillie, Cast, Whipping Boy. Honour: Studio Master Award for Excellence for Homelands by Steve Booker, 1990. Hobby: Sailing. Address: 43 St Alban's Avenue, London W4 5JS, England.

JACKSON Stonewall, b. 6 Nov 1932, Tabor City, North Carolina, USA. Country Singer; Musician (guitar). Musical Education: Self-taught. Career: Member of Grand Ole Opry, 1956; Worked with Ernest Tubb; Recording artist, 1957-. Compositions include: Don't Be Angry, recorded by Daniel O'Donnell; I Washed My Face In Muddy Water; Stamp Out Loneliness. Recordings: Hit singles include: Life To Go, 1958; Waterloo (US Country Number 1), 1959; BJ The DJ (US Country Number 1), 1963; Me And You And A Dog Named Boo, 1971; Numerous albums include: The Dynamic Stonewall Jackson, 1959; Sadness In A Song, 1962; I Love A Song, 1963; Trouble And Me, 1965; The Exciting Stonewall Jackson, 1966; All's Fair In Love 'N' War, 1966; Help Stamp Out Loneliness, 1967; Stonewall Jackson Country, 1967; The Great Old Songs, 1968; Thoughts Of A Lonely Man, 1968; Nothing Takes The Place Of Loving You, 1968; I Pawned My Past Today, 1969; The Old Country Church, 1969; A Tribute To Hank Williams, 1969; The Real Thing, 1970; The Lonesome In Me, 1970; Stonewall Jackson Recorded Live At The Grand Ole Opry, 1971; Waterloo, 1971; Me And You And A Dog Named Boo, 1971; World Of Stonewall Jackson, 1972; Nashville, 1974; Stonewall, 1979; My Favourite Sin, 1980; Stonewall Jackson, 1982; Solid Stonewall, 1982; Greatest Hits, 1982; Alive, 1984; Up Against The Wall, 1984. Address: c/o Ace Productions, PO Box 292725, Nashville, TN 37229-2725, USA.

JACKSON Wanda Lavonne, b. 20 Oct 1937, Maud, Oklahoma, USA. Singer; Songwriter. Career: Toured with Hank Thompson Band; Red Foley; Recording artiste, 1956-; Began recording Christian music, 1970s. Compositions include: Right Or Wrong (hit for Ronnie Dove, George Strait). Recordings: Albums include: Wanda Jackson, 1958; Rockin' With Wanda, 1960; There's A Party Goin' On, 1961; Right Or Wrong, 1961; Lovin' Country Style, 1962; Wonderful Wanda, 1962; Love Me Forever, 1963; Two Sides Of Wanda Jackson, 1964; Blues in My Heart, 1964; Sings Country Songs, 1966; Reckless Love Affair, 1967; You'll Always Have My Love, 1967; The Best Of, 1967; Cream Of The Crop, 1968; The Happy Side Of, 1969; Many Moods Of, 1969; Country!, 1970; Woman Lives For Love, 1970; I've Gotta Sing, 1971; I Wouldn't Want You Any Other Way, 1972; Praise The Lord, 1972; When It's Time To Fall In Love Again, 1973; Country Keepsakes, 1973; Now I Have Everything, 1974; Rock'N'Roll Away Your Blues, 1984; Greatest Country Hits, 1985; Early Wanda Jackson, 1986; Rockin' In The Country, 1990; Singles include: I Gotta Know; Let's Have A Party; In The Middle Of A Heartache. Honours: Twice nominated for Grammy Award. Address: c/o Wanda Jackson Enterprises, PO Box 891498, Oklahoma City, OK 73189-1498, USA.

JACKSON William, b. 18 Feb 1954, York, England. Composer; Arranger; Production; Musician (keyboards, guitar). 1 daughter. Musical Education: Huddersfield School Of Music. Career: Television, radio commercials; Keyboard player, guitarist with Martyn Joseph Band, Magna Carta, UK and Europe; recordings as session player. Memberships: PRS; Musicians' Union. Hobbies: Photography; Sailing. Address: c/o Flat 3, 20 St Andrewsgate, York, Yorkshire, England.

JACOBI Gina, b. 12 December 1962, Hammerdal, Sweden. Composer; Singer; Keyboard Player. 3 daughters. Education: Preschool Teacher, Univ, 2.5 years. Career: Director, 5 projects including music, singing, theatre, choirs with young people; Composed music for theatres, commercial videos; 3 bigger tours after release of albums; 5 videoclips to songs; Appearances in Swedish TV, 20 times; Appearances in Kurdish Satelite. Recordings: Bagateller, Trifles, album, 1985; Tid and Rum, Time and Space, album, 1986; Pa jakt efter solen, Haunting, album, 1988; Ga som pa natar, Walking as Upon, album, 1989; Gare Seretaye, The Kurdish Cassette, album, 1996; Alla ar, Everybody In, album, 1996. Honours: Schlsp from Olof Palmes Fond; Selected as Best Female Artist in Swedish Grammis Galan. Hobbies: Painting own picture in oil and acrylic colours; Writing novels; Writing music for coming album; Working in a music project with refugees, result being recorded and released as cassette in 1998. Address: Gränsg 28, 852 38 Sundsvall, Sweden.

JACOBS David Lewis, b. 19 May 1926, London, England. Broadcaster. m. (1) Patricia Bradlaw, 16 Sept 1949, div 1972, 1 son dec, 3 daughters; (2) Caroline Munro, 1975, dec 1975; (3) Lindsay Stuart Hutcheson, 1 Aug 1979, 1 stepson. Education: Belmont College, London. Career: Royal Navy; Impressionist, Navy Mixture, 1944; Chief Announcer, Radio SEAC, Ceylon; BBC announcer and newsreader; Freelance broadcaster; Radio includes: Housewives Choice; BBC Jazz Club; Pick Of The Pops; Saturday Show Band Show; Any Questions?; Any Answers?; Melodies For You; Founder member, Capital Radio; Own programme, BBC Radio 2, 6 years; Television includes: Juke Box Jury; Top Of The Pops; David Jacobs' Words And Music; Sunday Night With David Jacobs; Where Are They Now?; Whats My Line?; Eurovision Song Contest; A Song For Europe; Miss World; Little Women; Come Dancing; Presents musical concerts and one-man show, An Evening with David Jacobs. Publications: Jacobs Ladder; Caroline; Any Questions? (with Michael Bowen). Honours: 6 Royal Command Performances; Top British DJ, BBC and Radio Luxembourg, 6 years; TV Personality of Year, Variety Club of Great Britain, 1960; BBC Radio Personality of Year, 1975; Sony Gold Award, 1984; Sony Hall of Fame; Richard Martin Award (animal welfare); Honorary Doctorate, Kingston University, 1994; CBE, 1996; Deputy Lieutenant of and for Greater London, 1983; Representative Deputy Lieutenant for the Royal Borough of Kingston-upon-Thames; Honorary Freeman of the Royal Borough of Kingston-upon-Thames, 1997. Memberships include: Vice-President, Stars Organisation for Spastics; Vice-President, Royal Star & Garter Home, Richmond; Vice-President, Kingston Arts Festival; Director, Chairman, Kingston Theatre Trust. Hobbies: Travel; Hotels; Talking; Listening. Current Management: Billy Marsh Associates. Address: 174 North Gower Street, London, NW1 2NB, England.

JACOBS Jon. Engineer; Mixer. Recordings: Engineered, Mixed, Produced: Tom Ribiero, album, 1990; The Slow Club, World of Wonders, album, 1990; Graham Parker, Burning Questions, album, 1992; Mary McLaughlin, Daughter of Lir, 1993; The Pretenders, 1992/93; Wendy James, singles, 1993; The Ya Ya's, See No Rain, single, 1993; Kenji Jammer, album mixed, 1993; Psychedelix, Psychadelix II, album mixed, 1993; Raw, 1993; Planet Claire, After the Fire, album mixed, 1993; Rynten Okazaki, album, 1994; Pacifists, album, 1994; Gota, album, 1995; Rynten

Okazaki, album, soundtrack film, 1994; Psychedelix, 1995; Yuki Saito, album, 1995; Elio, Eat the Phikus, 1996; The Beatles, new singles, 1995-96; Elvis Costello, All This Useless Beauty, 1996; Paul McCartney, album, 1996; The Divine Comedy, live album in production, 1996. Address: Muirhead Management, 202 Fulham Road, Chelsea, London SW10 9PJ, England.

JACOBS Judith (Judy) Kaye, b. 27 Sept 1957, Lumberton, North Carolina, USA. Singer. m. James Eric Tuttle, 24 July 1993. Education: BA, Christian Education, Minor in Music. Musical Education: Production and Arrangement, with Lari Goss, Lee College, Cleveland, Tennessee. Career: Trinity Broadcasting, PTL; Recording artist for New Vision Records with radio airplay all over USA; Performed with Larnelle Harris; Carmen; Brooklyn Tabernacle Choir; Four Him; Major annual tours worldwide. Recordings: For Times Like These, 1993; Once And For All, 1995. Honours: Awarded Distinguished Music Performer, as special guest with Brooklyn Tabernacle Choir. Hobbies: Golf; Whitewater rafting; Raquetball. Current Management: Jamie Tuttle, His Song Ministries. Address: His Song Ministries, Inc, 233½ Broad Street NW, PO Box 0891, Cleveland, TN 37364, USA.

JACOBS Laurie, b. 16 Apr 1950, London, England. Jazz Promoter; Musician (saxophone). m. Ann Cummings, 12 Sept 1974, 3 sons. Education: Medical Graduate, Edinburgh University, 1974. Musical Education: Clarinet, saxophone, Leslie Evans. Career: Founded Peterborough Jazz Club, 1992; Monthly presentations, best in British and American Jazz; As musician, played Dean Street; Pizza Express; Pizza-On-The-Park; Appeared at Soho Jazz Festival. Honour: Peterborough City Leisure Award for Jazz Club, 1996 Membership: Musicians' Union. Hobbies: Art; Sport. Address: 38 Church Street, Werrington, Peterborough, Cambridgeshire PE4 6QE, England.

JACOBSEN Bo, b. 13 Mar 1945, Copenhagen, Denmark. Musician (drums, alto saxophone); Vocalist. 1 son, 1 daughter. Education: Architecture studies, 1966-70; Musical Education: Self-taught. Career: Member, Blue Sun, 1969-75; Osiris (with Lone Kellermann); Nada, 1977-83; Paul Ehlers Quartet, 1985-88; Crescent, 1988-89; Dream City, 1991-; Support tours with Jimi Hendrix; Procul Harum; Dollar Brand; Memphis Slim; Numerous festivals include: Roskilde Festival; Aarhus International Jazz Festival; Midtfyn Festival; Langeland Festival; Djurs Blues Festival. Recordings: with Blue Sun: Peace Be Unto You, 1970; Festival, 1970; Blue Sun, 1971; Blue Sun 73, 1973; with Nada: Nada 1, 1978; Nada 2, 1979; African Flower, 1982; with Dream City: Do The Blues, 1993; Syre, with Dream City, CD, 1996. Memberships: Danish Musicians' Union; DJFBA; KODA; Gramex; NCB. Hobbies: Chess; Country life; Mountain walks; Travel. Current Management: DanArtist, Overgade 41, 5100 Odense, Denmark. Address: Emmelev Kærvej 3, 8500 Grenaa, Denmark.

JACOBSEN Sonia Michelle, b. 5 February 1967, Camden, Australia. Education: Jazz Degree, The New School, Mannes, New York; Musicology Degree, Grenoble & Lyon University, France; Jazz Degree, Chambery Conservatory, France. Career: Co-Leader, Composer, Conductor, Mosaic Orchestra; Composer, Musical Director, No Strings Attached; Leader, Melting Pot. Compositions: Tryzone Suite; Melting Pot. Recordings: Avalanche, 1995; No Strings Attached, 1997. Membership: American Music Center. Current Management: Sun Sounds, PO Box 60, Cold Spring Harbor, NY 11724, USA. Address: 183 Harbor Road, Colo Spring, Harbor, NY 11724, USA.

JACOBSSON (Ruth) Ewa (Maria), b. 8 Dec 1956, Uppsala, Sweden. Composer; Vocalist; Musician (piano). 2 sons. Education: Konstfack, School Of Arts & Handicraft (painting); Stockholm, Sweden; The Royal Academy of Fine Arts (Painting; Mixed Media, Performance); Copenhagen, Denmark. Musical Education: Classical piano, pianist Kerstin Åberg, Uppsala, Sweden; Classical song education, Uppsala, Sweden, Copenhagen, Denmark. Career: Emerald Song, 1985, Concert and television appearances, Stockholm, Sweden; Found Language, 1987, in collaboration with choreographer Jody Oberfelder-Riehm, New York, USA; Die Menschmaschine, in collaboration with composer Morten Carlsen and theatre group Exment, Copenhagen; Voix concert, 1989, Copenhagen; Delta concert and radio appearance, 1991-1992, Copenhagen; Lingua concert, 1993, Copenhagen; Guldbukar concert, 1994, Copenhagen. Compositions: Voix, 1989 (tape, vocal, poem); Détour, 1990 (solo performance, vocal, tape, 8mm film, poem); Delta, choir, words by Martin Sondergaard, 1991-92; Lingua, 1993, (solo performance, tape, vocal, poem, photographic movement); Guldbukar (Golden Belly), 1994, (tape, colour-slides); Anonymous (soloperformance, vocal, tape, photo and objects), 1996; LOGR (soloperformance, vocal, tape, objects, waterfountain Gefjon), 1996; Kongehoved (choir, tape, photo, words by Jens Bjorneboe), 1996; Cold Dews (tape, poem), 1996. Memberships: DJBFA; DICEM (Danish section, International Confederation for Electroacoustic Music); SKRÆP, Experimental Music Forum for Composers. Address: Evens Gate 7, N-0655 Oslo, Norway.

JACQUEMIN André, b. 16 Jan 1952, Hampstead, London, England. Composer; Producer; Musician (bass player). m. 24 Jan 1988, 1 daughter. Musical Education: Guitar course. Career: Joined recording studio as office boy aged 17; Moved to engineering after 9 months; Produced Monty Python's sound, 1972-; Live performances include: Tis-Was; Top of The Pops; Various clubs round UK. Compositions include: Co-writer: Every Sperm Is Sacred (Monty Python's Meaning Of Life); The Brian Song (Monty Python's Life Of Brian). Recordings for: Girlschool; Classix Nouveaux; Powerhouse; Geordie; Mungo Jerry. Publications: Future Music, Home Studio Recording, SEP Studio Sound. Honours: BAFTA Nomination, Most Original Song in a Feature Film, Every Sperm Is Sacred; Over 70 awards for sound production over 25 years. Membership: Re-Pro Producers Guild of Great Britain. Hobbies: Harley-Davidsons; Swimming; Audio production. Current Management: Showcase Management International. Address: c/o Val Risoon, 33 Manarin Place, Grove, Oxfordshire OX12 0QH, England.

JAFET Jean Marc, b. 8 May 1956, Nice, France. Musician (bass). Musical Education: Conservatoire de Musique de Nice. Career: Played with: Didier Lockwood; Toots Thielmans; Christian Escoude; Christian Vander (Magma); Trio Ceccarelli; Richard Galliano; Own band Agora. Recordings: Dolores, Agora; 3 albums with Trio Ceccarelli; 3 albums with Kalil Chahine; Brazilian Witch, Christian Escoude. Publications: Dolores; Hat's Snatcher; L'Arcange. Honours: For Hat's Snatchers, Trio Ceccarelli, Victoires Music 1994. Membership: SACEM. Hobbies: Badminton; Football. Current Management: Marie Poindront. Address: 12 Rue Seuignet, 94370 Sucy Enbrie, France.

JAFFE Jerry, b. 12 Sept 1946, New York City, USA. Artist Manager. m. Celeste Kringer, 9 Oct 1983. Education: PhD Columbia University, New York City, 1972. Career: Manager, artists: Jesus and Mary Chain; Catherine; Course Of Empire; Formerly Saint Etienne; co-manager with Chris Morrison: Dead Or Alive; Midge Ure; John Moore; U S Head; Creation Records, 1992-1994; Formerly Senior Vice-President (Rock Division) and Vice-President Promotion and A&R, Polygram Records, USA; Promotion; Press; Artist development. Address: Management By Jaffe, 1560 Broadway, New York, NY 10036, USA.

JAGGER Mick, b. 26 July 1943, Dartford, Kent, England. Singer; Songwriter. Bianca Pérez Morena de Macias, 1971 (divorced 1979), 1 daughter, (2) Jerry Hall, 1 son, 2 daughters; 1 daughter by Marsha Hunt. Education: London School of Economics. Career: Member, Rolling Stones, 1962-; Numerous tours, concerts include: National Jazz & Blues Festival, Richmond, 1963; Debut UK tour, 1963; Debut US tour, 1964; Free concert, Hyde Park, 1969; Free concert, Altamont Speedway, 1969; Knebworth Festival, 1976; Live Aid, Philadelphia, 1985; Solo tour including Japan, 1988; Steel Wheels North American tour, 1989; National Music Day Celebration Of The Blues, with Gary Moore, 1992; Voodoo Lounge World Tour, 1994-95; Bridges to Babylon Tour, 1997-98; Films include: Ned Kelly, 1970; Performance, 1970; Freejack, 1992; Bent, 1996. Compositions: Co-writer for the Rolling Stones, with Keith Richards (under the psuedonym The Glimmer Twins). Recordings: Albums include: The Rolling Stones, 1964; The Rolling Stones No 2, 1965; Out Of Our Heads, 1965; Aftermath, 1966; Between The Buttons, 1967; Their Satanic Majesties Request, 1967; Beggar's Banquet, 1968; Let It Bleed, 1969; Get Yer Ya-Ya's Out, 1969; Sticky Fingers, 1971; Exile On Main Street, 1972; Goat's Head Soup, 1973; It's Only Rock And Roll, 1974; Black And Blue, 1976; Some Girls, 1978; Emotional Rescue, 1980; Still Life, 1982; Steel Wheels, 1989; Flashpoint, 1991; Stripped, 1995; Bridges to Babylon, 1997 Solo albums: She's The Boss, 1985; Primitive Cool, 1987; Wandering Spirit, 1993; Singles include: It's All Over Now; Little Red Rooster; (I Can't Get No) Satisfaction; Get Off Of My Cloud; Jumping Jack Flash; Let's Spend The Night Together; Brown Sugar; 19th Nervous Breakdown; Harlem Shuffle; Ruby Tuesday; Paint It Black; It's Only Rock'n'Roll; Start Me Up; Undercover Of The Night; Dancing In The Street (with David Bowie). Honours: with Rolling Stones include: Grammy Lifetime Achievement Award, 1986; Inducted into Rock And Roll Hall Of Fame, 1989; Q Award, Best Live Act, 1990; Ivor Novello Award, Outstanding Contribution To British Music, 1991. Current Management: Rupert Loewenstein, 2 King Street, London SW1Y 6QL, England.

JAM Jimmy, b. USA. Record Producer. Career: Joined Terry Lewis' band Flyte Tyme, 1972; Rejoined Flyte Tyme, renamed The Time, 1981-83; Formed (with Terry Lewis) Flyte Tyme Productions, 1982-; Built Flyte Tyme Studios, Minneapolis, 1984; Launched own label (with Terry Lewis), Perspective Records, 1991-; Helped launch new acts including Sounds Of Blackness; Involved with International Association of African American Music (IAAAM), 1990-. Recordings: Producer (with Terry Lewis): Wild Girls, Klymaxx, 1983; Just Be Good To Me, SOS Band, 1983; Heat Of The Heart, Patti Austin; Encore, Cheryl Lynn; I Didn't Mean To Turn You On, Cherelle; Saturday Love, Cherelle and Alexander O'Neal; Runaway, Janet Jackson; The Best Thing In Life Are Free, Janet Jackson and LutherVandross; Albums with Janet Jackson: Control; Rhythm Nation; Janet (all Number 1, US); Other recordings with: Mint Condition; Low Key; George Michael; Karyn White; Boyz II Men; Johnny Gill; Fine Young Cannibals; New Edition; Film soundtrack, Mo' Money. Honours include: R&B Songwriting Awards, American Society of Composers And Publishers, 1989-94.

JAMAL Ahmad, b. 2 July 1930, Pittsburg, Pennsylvania, USA. Musician (piano). Divorced, 1 daughter. Musical Education: Private master classes with Mary Caldwell Dawson and James Miller. Career: George Hudson Orchestra, national tour, 1949; First group, The Four Strings, 1949; Accompanist to The Caldwells, 1950; Trio, The Three Strings, 1950-; Television: The Sound Of Jazz, 1962; Many concert tours (including Philip

Morris); Exclusive Steinway artist, 1960s-; Appeared on film soundtracks: Mash, 1970; Bridges Of Madison County, 1995. Compositions: Comissions: 6 works for Asai Quartet, Yale University, 1994; New Rhumba; Ahmad's Blues; Night Mist Blues; Extensions; The Awakening; Excerpts From The Blues; Tranquility; Manhattan Reflections. Recordings: Over 50 albums include: Poinciana; But Not For Me, (including Bridges of Madison County), 1995. Honours: Man of the Year, Pittsburgh Jay Cee's, 1958; NEA American Jazz Master; Duke Ellington Fellow, Yale University; Pittsburgh Mellon Jazz Festival dedication, 1994; Django D'Or Award, Paris for Essence Part 1, 1996. Hobbies: Resting at home, Upstate New York - being off the road! Current Management: Ellora Management. Address: PO Box 295, Ashley Falls, MA 01222, USA.

JAMES Alex (Stephen Alexander), b. 21 Nov 1968, Bournemouth, Dorset, England. Musician (bass guitar). Education: Goldsmith's College. Musical Education: Violin lessons at school. Career: member, Blur; Television, radio, includes: Top Of The Pops; Later With Jools Holland; Extensive tours include: Alexandra Palace; Reading Festival, 1993; Glastonbury Festival, 1994; Mile End, 1995. Recordings: Blur: Albums: Leisure, 1991; Modern Life Is Rubbish, 1993; Parklife, 1994; The Great Escape, 1995; Singles: She's So High; There's No Other Way; Bang; Popscene; For Tomorrow; Chemical World; Sunday Sunday; Girls And Boys; To The End; Parklife; End Of A Century; Country House; The Universal; Stereotypes. Honours: Mercury Prize Nomination; Platinum Album: Parklife; BRIT Awards, Best Single, Video, Album, Band, 1995; Q Awards, Best Album, 1994, 1995. Current Management: CMO Management, Unit 32, Ransome Dock, 35-37 Parkgate Road, London SW11 4NP, England.

JAMES Etta (Jamesatta Hawkins), b. 25 Jan 1938, Los Angeles, USA. Singer. Career: Performed and recorded with Harvey Fuqua; Muscle Shoals (Chess Records houseband); Solo soul/R&B singer, 1961-; Sang at opening ceremony, Los Angeles Olympics, 1988. Recordings: Albums: At Last!, 1961; Second Time Around, 1961; Etta James, 1962; Etta James Sings For Lovers, 1962; Etta James Top Ten, 1963; Etta James Rocks The House, 1964; Queen Of Soul, 1965; Tell Mama, 1968; Etta James Sings Funk, 1970; Losers Weepers, 1971; Etta James, 1973; Peaches, 1973; Come A Little Closer, 1974; Etta Is Betta Than Evah!, 1978; Deep In The Night, 1978; Changes, 1980; Good Rockin' Mama, 1981; Chess Masters, 1981; Tuff Lover, 1983; R&B Queen, 1986; Blues In The Night, 1986; Late Show, 1986; Her Greatest Sides, Volume I, 1987; R&B Dynamite, 1987; Chicago Golden Years, 1988; On Chess, 1988; Seven Year Itch, 1989; Stickin' To My Guns, 1990; The Right Time, 1992; Time After Time, 1995; Mystery Lady, 1995; I Just Wanna Make Love To You - The Best Of, 1996; Hit singles: All I Could Do Was Cry, 1960; At Last, 1961; I Just Wanna Make Love To You, 1961 (re-released in 1996); Stop The Wedding, 1962; Pushover, 1963; Security, 1967; Tell Mama/I'd Rather Go Blind, 1967; Good Rocking Daddy, 1981. Honour: Grammy Nomination, Etta James, 1973. Current Management: De Leon Artists, 4031 Panama Court, Piedmont, CA 94611, USA.

JAMES Jessica, b. 1 Dec 1981, Los Gatos, California, USA. Singer; Songwriter. Career: Signed to A&M Records, aged 13; Stage performances: Wizard Of Oz; Annie; A Winter's Tale; Sang with local bands, performing with Smokey Robinson, Rodney Dangerfield; Singer, own band, America's Most Wanted Band; Television appearances: Up All Night; Channel 11 Morning News; Arsenio Hall; Subject of documentary, BBC, England; Singer, National Anthem, major US sporting events and Democratic State Convention; Numerous charity functions; Featured soloist, Gospel Choir, First

African Methodist Episcopalian Church, Los Angeles. Membership: SAG (Screen Actor's Guild). Hobbies: Rollerblading; Volleyball; Songwriting. Current Management: Rick Frio. Address: 3050 North Chandelle Road, Los Angeles, CA 90046, USA.

JAMES Mo, b. 16 Mar 1951, Darlington, England. Vocalist; Musician (piano); Radio Producer; Presenter. m. Mike Jowett, 23 July 1983, 1 son, 1 daughter. Musical Education: Northumbria Studio of Music. Career: Lead Singer: White Rabbit, 1968-70; Solo artist; Numerous concert appearances, including Greenbelt Festival, Knebworth; Royal Gospel Gala, Albert Hall; Television appearances: Pebble Mill; TVAM; Rock Gospel Show; Leader, Mo James Soul Band, 1984-90; Solo artiste, 1990-; Producer, presenter, regular talk shows on BBC Radio (North). Recordings: Debut album: More Love, 1982, (with Joe English). Publications: Music reviewer, Crossrhythms magazine. Memberships: Musicians' Union; Association of Christians in Local Broadcasting. Hobbies: Reading; Home and children; Antique and collectors fayres. Current Management: Stanley Joseph, ATS Ltd. Address: 26 St Michael's Road, Headingley, Leeds LS6 3AW, England.

JAMES Rick (James Johnson), b. 1 Feb 1948, Buffalo, New York, USA. Musician; Record Producer. Career: Founder member, Mynah Birds, with Neil Young, Canada, 1965; Signed to Motown Records, Detroit; Producer for: Bobby Taylor; The Spinners; The Marvelettes; Teena Marie; Mary Jane Girls; Founder member, Main Line, London, 1970; Founder, Stone City Band, 1977; US tour with Mary Jane Girls and Stone City Band, 1978; US tour, with Teena Marie, Cameo, Sugarhill Gang. Recordings: Solo albums; Come Get It!, 1978; Bustin' Out Of L Seven, 1978; Fire It Up, 1979; Garden Of Love, 1980; Street Songs (US R&B Number 1), 1981; Throwin' Down, 1982; Cold Blooded, 1983; 17, 1984; The Flag, 1986; Wonderful Rock, 1988; Rhythm And Blues, 1989; with Stone City Band (as producer): In'n'Out, 1980; Boys Are Back, 1981; Out From The Shadow, 1983; Singles: You And I; Mary Jane; Give It To Me Baby (US R&B Number 1); Superfreak Part 1; Cold Blooded (US R&B Number 1); Ebony Eyes (duet with Smokey Robinson); Producer, albums: with Mary Jane Girls: Mary Jane Girls, 1983; Only Four You, 1985; with Teena Marie: Wild And Peaceful, 1979; with Eddie Murphy (also writer/arranger): Party All The Time, 1985. Honours: Grammy Nomination, Street Songs (double Platinum record), 1981; Billboard magazine Poll Winner, Best Black Artiste, Best Black Album, 1981; American Music Award, Best Soul/R&B Album, 1982. Current Management: Richard Walters Entertainment Inc., 421 S Beverly Drive, 8th Floor, Beverly Hills, CA 90212, USA.

JAMES Ruby, b. 23 May 1957, Manchester, Jamaica. Vocalist; Session Singer. Career: Lead Singer, Stax; Recorded with Micky Most, Dick Lehy and other producers; Top Session Singer - George Michael, Boy George, Erasure, Spandau Ballet, Blancmange, James Last Orchestra; Caberet and Sessions; TV Concert; Live Aid with Spandau Ballet. Recording: Locomotion with Ritz. Membership: Musicians' Union and Equity. Current Management: Stamina. Address: Stamina Management, 47 Prout Grove, London NW10 1PU, England.

JAMES Sian, b. 24 Dec 1961, Wales. Folk Singer; Songwriter. m. Gwyn Jones, 2 sons. Education: BMus, Bangor University; Harp lessons, 11 years old; Piano lessons, 6 years old; Violin lessons, 8 years old. Career: Various tours around folk festivals in Brittany, Galicia, Spain, Italy, America, Canada, Ireland, Wales, England, Scotland, 1980-97; Appearances in stage shows for various theatre companies in Wales, 1987-94; Leading role in major film for S4C: Tylluan Wen

(White Owl); Own series on S4C with guests: Capercaillie; Sharon Shannon, Alan Stivel. Recordings: Cysgodion Karma (Shadows of Karma), 1990; Distaw (Silent), 1993; Gweini Tymor (Traditional album), 1996; Di-Gwsg (Sleepless), 1997. Memberships: Equity; PRS; MCPS; PAMRA. Current Management: Sain Records, Llandwrog, Caernaffon, Gwynedd, Wales.

JAMES Sonny (James Loden), b. 1 May 1929, Hackleburg, Alabama, USA. Country Musician (guitar, fiddle). Career: Succesful recording artist, 1953-; Film appearances: Second Fiddle To An Old Guitar; Nashville Rebel; Las Vegas Hillbillies; Hillbilly In A Haunted House. Recordings: 72 US Country chart hits; 23 US Country Number 1's include: You're The Only World I Know; Behind The Tear; Take Good Care Of Her; The Minute You're Gone; A World Of Our Own; I'll Never Find Another You; That's Why I Love You Like I Do; Only The Lonely; It's Just A Matter Of Time; Running Bear; When The Snow Is On The Roses; Is It Wrong (For Loving You)?; Other hit singles include: That's Me Without You; She Done Give Her Heart To Me; For Rent; The Cat Came Back; Young Love; First Date, First Kiss, First Love. Numeorus albums, 1957-; As producer: Paper Roses, Marie Osmond.

JAMES Stafford Louis, b. 24 Apr 1946, Evanston, Illinois, USA. Musician (double bass, piano); Composer. m. Claudine Decouttère, 17 Apr 1992, 1 daughter. Education: Loop College, Chicago; Chicago Conservatory College; Mannes College of Music, New York. Career: Member, Ukrainian National Orchestra, Limberg, 1991; International Congress of Viola D'amore, Europaïsches Musik Festival, Stuttgart, 1988; WDR Radio, Köln, Germany, 1989, 1992, 1994-97; European tours with Stafford James Project (trio) and Stafford James Special Project (quartet), Netherlands; France; Luxembourg; Germany; Italy; Austria; Sicily; Spain; Switzerland; Television: The Days And Nights Of Molly Dodd, 1987; USIA tours: India, Syria, Sudan, Egypt, Morocco, 1984; Argentina, Peru, Chile, Uruguay, Mexico, 1986; Played with: Art Blakey and The Jazz Messengers; Betty Carter; Jimmy Heath; Pharoah Sanders; Woody Shaw; Dexter Gordon; Joe Williams; Mingus Dynasty; Randy Weston; The Gounawas (from Morocco); Teacher, double bass, UN International School, New York, 5 years; New School Of Social Research, New York, 2 years; Privately in Paris, France. Compositions: 150 pieces (many written for double bass as lead melodic voice) including: Les Pyrénées à la Mer; Sonatina (duet for viola d'Amore/contrabass); That's What Dreams Are Made Of; Ethiopia Suite; Bertha Baptist; Game; Teotiuacan; Sashianova; Nighthawk; Blues in The Pockets. Recordings: Music Is The Healing Force Of The Universe, Albert Ayler, 1969; Homecoming, Dexter Gordon, 1976; with Woody Shaw: Little Red's Fantasy Muse, 1975; For Sure, 1980; Night Music, 1980; United, 1980; Stafford James Ensemble. Honours include: Grants from NEA, NYSCA; Gold Medal, Music, Karlstad, Sweden. Memberships: SACEM; BMI; BIMC. Hobbies: Fishing; Model trains; Antiques hunting. Current Management: STAJA Music. Address: 6 Quai des Célestins, 75004 Paris, France.

JAMES Stephen, b. 6 Feb 1956, New York City, USA. Composer; Musician (sarod, violin). m. Judith Papp, 11 Apr 1986. Musical Education: North Indian Classical Music, 1973-83; Shri Vasant Rai, Pandit Ravi Shankar, 1983. Career: Boston MIT; Zakir Hussain and Sitara Devi; New York, Festival of India, Empire State Building; Asia Society and Columbia University; Shri Ram Center, North Delhi India; Franz Liszt Academy, Budapest; Zurich Hallenstadion; Frankfurt Messe Halle; Milan Pallazzrussardi; Appeared at festivals in: Hungary; Italy; France; Switzerland; Germany; Bombay; Delhi Doordashan; Radio and television. Recordings: with Annindo Chatterjee: Raga; Tala;

Makam; with Bill Laswell and Nicky Skopelitis: Axiom; with Bebo Baldan and David Torn: Earth Beat; Diving Into the World. Honours: Bhartiya Vidya Bhavan, New York. Membership: Founder member, Central Europe RIMPA (Ravi Shankar Institute For Music and Performing Arts). Hobby: Music. Current Management: Stress Management. Address: Sabrak u. 3, 1141 Budapest, Hungary.

JAMES Steve, b. 19 Feb 1954, London, England. Record Producer. 1 daughter. Career: Record Producer and engineer, various projects, several years; Early production work includes albums with Toyah; Later credits include Grammy-nominated soundtrack, The Rutles; Monty Python's The Life of Brian, featuring the single Always Look On The Bright Side Of Life; Worked with Angel City, Mental As Anything, The Screaming Jets in Australia, 1988-93; Returned to UK, worked with: Paul Young; Kiki Dee; Peter Skellern; Way Of Thorns. Recordings include: Numerous as producer, co-producer, engineer including: Albums: with Toyah: Sheep Farming In Barnet, 1979; Toyah Toyah Toyah, 1982; with Peter Skellern: Astaire, 1980; The Continental, 1981; Stardust Memories, 1994; with Neil Innes: Off The Record, 1981; with Ginger Baker: Nutters, 1983; with Mental As Anything: Cyclone Raymonde, 1989; with The Screaming Jets: All For One, 1990; Tear Of Thought, 1991; with The Angels: Redback Fever, 1992; with Kiki Dee: Best Of Kiki Dee, 1994; with Paul Young: Acoustic tracks, 1994; Live tracks, 1995; 2 tracks, animated version of Wind In The Willows, Kirsty MacColl and Tim Finn, 1995; Singles include: In The City, The Jam, 1979; Something Else, The Sex Pistols, 1979; Rock And Roll Music, Mental As Anything, 1988; Other recordings with: Shirley Bassey, 1976; Thin Lizzy, 1977; Pat Travers, 1977; Golden Earring, 1978; Ryan Douglas, 1993; Way Of Thorns, 1995; Membership: Producers' Guild. Current Management: Clive Banks. Address: c/o Clive Banks Ltd, 1 Glenthorne Mews, 115a Glenthorne Road, London W6 0LJ, England.

JAMISON Jimi, b. 23 Aug 1951, Durant, Mississippi, USA. Singer; Songwriter; Musician (guitar, piano). m. Deborah Teal, 1 May 1985, 1 son, 2 daughters. Education: University of Memphis, 2 years. Musical Education: High School Choir. Career: Lead singer, major tours with: Target, 1976; Cobra, 1979-82; Survivor, 1983-; Solo artist, 1990-. Numerous television appearances include Solid Gold; MTV guest VJ; American Video Awards, 1986; Compositions: I'm A Fighter; Vital Signs; High On You; I Can't Hold Back; Is This Love; Burning Heart (Rocky IV soundtrack); Moment Of Truth (Karate Kid soundtrack); In Good Faith; When Seconds Count; Rebel Son; The Search Is Over; Too Hot To Sleep; Man Against The World; Rock Hard; When Love Comes Down; Co-writer, I'm Always Here (Baywatch TV theme). Recordings: with Target (2 albums); with Cobra (1 album); with Survivor (6 albums); Lead singer on all tracks; Backing vocals for: ZZ Top; Jeff Healey; Fabulous Thunderbirds; George Thorogood; Colin James; Point Blank; Johnny Diesel; Krokus; De Garmo & Key; Joe Walsh; Gary Chapman; Ten Years After; Rick Vito; Michael Anderson. Honours: Voted in Top 10 Male Vocalists in World, Kasey Kasem Countdown; St Jude Special Olympics Award; Arkansas Governor's Award; Ohio Governor's Award; Tennessee Governor's Award; Numerous Gold & Platinum albums for Survivor, Rocky IV, ZZ Top, and Krokus. Memberships: AFTRA; SAG; NARAS; Grammy Award Committee, 1992. Hobbies: Tennis; Softball; Local and National charities. Current Management: Debbie Jamison, AIM. Address: 4520 Summer Avenue, Suite 155, Memphis, TN 38122, USA; Steve Green, AIM, 9850 Sandlefoot Blvd, Boca Raton, FL 33428, USA.

JAN Hajnal, b. 11 December 1943, Kojice, Slovakia. m. Maria Hajnalova, 14 December 1968, 1 daughter. Education: Piano, Classical Music Degree, Elementary Music School, 10 years; Konzervatorium in Kojice, Piano & Double Bass; Selftaught Composer, with some lessons from best Slovak Composers. Career: Several own TV programs as a Pianist; Numerous recordings in Slovak Radio as a Pianist, Composer, Arranger, Leader, Jazz and higher popular music; Participant of jazz festivals in Europe; Solo performance & small groups - jazz music; Piano Entertainer performance in Amerika, Asia, Europe; Solo piano & 2 pianos perfomances (jazz) on classic music festival in Kojice, 1995. Compositions: Monk's Tatran Dream, 1994; Mosebacke, Early Morning, Geneiro, Home made Blues, many others. Recordings: Slovak Jazz Mainstream, CD, 1994; Samplers from Slovak Jazz Days with Slovak Jazz Quintet. Publications: Recorded in main Czechoslovak Lexikon of Popular Music, 1982-. Honour: First Prize, Frame of the Year, Slovak Music 1996 Competition for Composition: Monk Tatran Dream. Memberships: Slovak Jazz Society; Slovak Music Fond. Hobby: Music. Current Management: Slovak Music Fond Bratislava. Address: Jaroslavova 12/a, 85101 Bratislava, Slovakia.

JANDA Dalibor, b. 21 March 1953, Hranice Na Morave, Czech Republic. Singer; Songwriter; Musician. m. Jirina Jandova, 3 April 1981, 1 son, 1 daughter. Education: Classical Music Degree, 4 year Guitar Studium. Career: Singers in various rock bands, 1969-79; 1st Recording in Radio, 1979; Professional Singer, 1981; 1st single, 1983; 1st LP, named Hurricane, 1985; 2nd LP,MC KDE JSI (Where Are You?), 1987; 3rd album, 1988. Compositions: Ten Fingers for Living; Take Them to Mars, 1988; Dalbiro Janda & Prototype, 1989. Recordings: Jen Ty Samotna A Ja (Only You and Me), 1989; Povidant Spisnickami (Talking with Singing), 1990; Cose Ma'stat (What Was Happened), 1992.Publications: Zlaty Vyber, Gold Best, 1994; Vlasce Nejsou Maty (There is no Maps in Cove), 1995; Krasne Silena (Pretty Crazy), 1996. Honours: Gold Decin Pop Festival, 1985; Gold Nightingale, 1986, 1987, 1988; 6 gold albums, 1 platinn album. Hobbies: Nature; Enthomology; Numsimatic; Arboretum. Current Management: Hurricane Records, songwriter of more than 80 days. Address: Hurikan Records, Kamenicka 39/303, 170 00 Praha 7, Czech Republic.

JANDA Petr, b. 2 May 1952, Prague, Czech Republic. Composer; Musician (guitar); Vocalist. m. (1) Jana, 7 Sept 1966; (2) Martina, 7 Mar 1992, 1 son, 2 daughters. Education: Graduate. Musical Education: Conservatory Jaroslava Jezka, Prague. Career: Leader, famous rock group, Olympic, 32 years, 6 Golden Records. Recordings: Albums: Zelva; Ptak Rosom'k; Prazdniny Na Zemi; Ulice; Jasna Zprava; Okno Me Lasky. Publications: Encyklpedie Ceske Hydby. Honour: Grammy (Olympic), 1993. Membership: OSA. Hobbies: Music; Sport. Current Management: Bestla Pristavni 31, 17000 Prague 7, Czech Republic. Address: Hradec 18, 28167, Czech Republic.

JANIS Conrad, b. 11 Feb 1938, New York City, USA. Jazz Musician (trombone); Actor; Film Director. m. Maria Grimm, 30 Nov 1987. Musical Education: Private tuition, trombone, piano, violin. Career: As actor: Film credits include: Airport '75; Buddy Holly Story, 1977; The Duchess And The Dirtwater Fox, 1976; Mr Saturday Night, 1992; The Feminine Touch, 1995; Television series include: Mork and Mindy; Quark; St Elsewhere; I Bonino; Over 350 starring roles include: Murder She Wrote; Golden Girls; Kojak; Happy Days; Laverne and Shirley; Talk show appearances include: 25 Tonight Shows, with Johnny Carson; 12 times, Mike Douglas; Dinah Shore; Several TV specials; As Jazz musician: Bandleader, Beverly Hills Unlisted Jazz Band; Tailgate Jazz Band; TV Specials: Jerry Lee Lewis Telethon; Bert Convey Special; American Jukebox Special; This Joint Is Jumping; That's A Plenty; Don Lane Show; Concerts include: New York Town Hall, 1962; Phil Academy Of Music, 1955; Carnegie Hall, 1981; Monterey Festival, 1983-87; Victoria BC Terrivic Festival, 1989-93; LA Classic Jazz Festival, 1984-95; Worked with: Roy Eldridge; Henry Red Allen; Wild Bill Davison; Yank Lawson; Claude Hopkins; Coleman Hawkins; Panama Francis; Hot Lips Page; Herbie Hancock; Jimmy McPartland. Recordings: CJ And The Talegate Jazz Band, 1950-58; Jammin' At Rudi's, 1953; with Tony Parenti: A Night At Jimmy Ryan's, 1972; with Conrad Janis And The Beverly Hills Unlisted Jazz Band: Way Down Yonder In Beverly Hills, 1986; America, 1987; This Joint Is Jumpin', with Jack Lemmon, Bea Arthur, Dudley Moore, 1989. Honours: Playboy Poll Nomination, 1960, 1961. Current Management: Maria Janis. Address: 1920 S Beverly Glen, Suite 306, Los Angeles, CA 90025, USA.

JANKE Daniel Jacob, b. 8 September 1957, Edmonton, Alberta, Canada. Composer; Piano; Kora. m. Susan Alton, 31 August 1993, 2 sons. Education: MA, Ethnomusicology. Career: CBC Radio, Two New Hours; BBC, Kaleidoscope and Mixing It; Radio France, La Muse En Circuit. Recordings: Debut, 1984; Big Dance, 1989; In a Room, 1997. Honours: Canada Council B Grant; 1989 Casby Nomination. Membership: Canadian Music Centre, Associate Composer. Hobby: Wilderness Hiking. Current Management: Festival Distribution. Address: PO Box 5381, Whitehorse Yukon, Canada Y1A 4Z2.

JANSCH Bert, b. 3 Nov 1943, Glasgow, Scotland. Vocalist; Musician. Career: Folk musician; Founder member, folk group, Pentangle, 1967-72; 1982-; Also solo artiste. Recordings: Solo albums: Bert Jansch, 1965; It Don't Bother Me, 1965; Jack Orion, 1966; Bert And John (with John Renbourn), 1966; Nicola, 1967; Birthday Blues, 1968; Lucky Thirteen, 1969; Stepping Stones (with John Renbourn), 1969; Rosemary Lane, 1971; Moonshine, 1973; LA Turnaround, 1974; Santa Barbara Honeymoon, 1975; A Rare Conundrum, 1978; Avocet, 1979; Thirteen Down, 1980; Heartbreak, 1982; From The Outside, 1985; Leather Laundrette, 1988; Bert Jansch and Jack Orion, 1993; When The Circus Comes To Town, 1995; Various compilations; with Pentangle: The Pentangle, 1968; Sweet Child, 1968; Basket Of Light, 1969; Cruel Sister, 1970; Reflections, 1971; History Book, 1971; Solomon's Seal, 1972; Open The Door, 1982; Pentangling, 1973; The Pentangle Collection, 1975; Anthology, 1978; The Essential Pentangle Volume 1, 1987; The Essential Pentangle Volume 2, 1987; In The Round, 1988; So Early In The Spring, 1989; One More Road, 1993; People On The Highway 1968-1971, 1993. Current Management: Folklore Inc, 1671 Appian Way, Santa Monica, CA 90401, USA.

JANSEN Steve (Stephen Batt), b. 1 Dec 1959. Musician (drums). Career: Member, Japan, 1977-1983; The Dolphin Brothers (with Richard Barbieri), 1987; Rain Tree Crow (with 3 members of Japan), 1991; Tours include: UK tour supporting Blue Öyster Cult, 1978; Backing musician to No-Man, UK tour, 1991; Abstract Day tour of Japan iwith Jansen, Barbieri and Karn, 1997; Mick Karn Bestial Cluster Tour, Europe, 1994; Yukhiro Takahashi tours of Japan, 1985, 1986, 1998. Recordings: Albums with Japan: Adolescent Sex, 1978; Obscure Alternatives, 1978; Life In Tokyo, 1979; Quiet Life, 1980; Gentlemen Take Polaroids, 1980; Assemblage, 1981; Tin Drum, 1982; Oil On Canvas, 1983; Exorcising Ghosts, 1984; with The Dolphin Brothers: Catch The Fall, 1987; with Rain Tree Crow: Rain Tree Crow, 1991; with Richard Barbieri: Stories Across Borders, 1991; Stone To Flesh, 1995; Other Worlds in a Small Room, 1996; with Richard Barbieri and Mick Karn: Beginning to Melt, 1994; Seal, 1994; with Richard Barbieri and N Takemura: Changing Hands, 1997; with Yukikieu Takahashi: Pulse, 1997; Singles: with Japan: The Art Of Parties, 1981; Quiet Life, 1981; Visions Of

China, 1981; Ghosts, 1982; Cantonese Boy, 1982; Life In Tokyo, 1982; Night Porter, 1982; Canton, 1983. Address: c/o Medium Productions, 74 St Lawrence Road, Upminster, Essex RM14 2UW, England.

JAOJOBY Eusèbe, b. 29 July 1955, Amboangibe, Sambava. Songwriter; Singer; Musician (Guitar). 3 sons, 3 daughters. Education: Diplom of Baccalaureat serie A, 1977; Diploma of Journalism, Internationales Institut für Journalistik von Berlin, 1982; Selftaught guitar; Selftaught singing. Compositions: Samy mandeha samy mitady; Alima; Velono; E,tiako. Recordings: Salegy, 1992; Velono, 1994; E,Tiako, 1997. Publications: Discomad, Songwriter & Singer, 1976. Memberships: Office Malgache du Droits d'Auteur, 1994. Hobbies: Playing music or giving music lessons to my children. Current Management: Mad Minute Music, 5/7 rue Paul Bert, 93400 Saint-Ouen, France. Address: Jaojoby Eusèbe, 349 Cité Ambohipo, 101 Antananarivo, Madagascar.

JARDINE Al, b. 3 Sept 1942, Lima, Ohio, USA. Musician (guitar); Vocalist. Career: Member, the Beach Boys, 1961-62; 1963-; Numerous tours and concerts include: Beach Boys Summer Spectacular, Hollywood Bowl, 1966; London Palladium, 1968; Big Sur Folk Festival, Monterey, 1970; Carnegie Hall, 1971; Royal Festival Hall, London, 1972; Wembley Stadium, 1975, 1980; Knebworth Festival, 1990; Independence Day concert, Washington DC, 1980; Live Aid, Philadelphia, 1985. Recordings: Albums: Surfer Girl, 1963; Little Deuce Coupe, 1963; Shut Down Vol 2, 1964; All Summer Long, 1964; The Beach Boys Concert, 1964; The Beach Boys Christmas Album, 1964; The Beach Boys Today, 1965; Summer Days (And Summer Nights), 1965; Surfin' USA, 1965; Beach Boys Party, 1966; Pet Sound, 1966; The Beach Boys Today, 1966; Smiley Smile, 1967; Wild Honey, 1968; Friends, 1968; Close-Up, 1969; Greatest Hits, 1970; Surf's Up, 1971; Carl and The Passions/So Tough, 1972; Holland, 1973; The Beach Boys In Concert, 1974; Endless Summer, 1974; Spirit Of America, 1975; Good Vibrations - Best Of..., 1975; 15 Big Ones, 1976; The Beach Boys Love You, 1977; LA (Light Album), 1979; Ten Years Of Harmony (1970-1980), 1982; The Very Best Of..., 1983; The Beach Boys (with Stevie Wonder), 1985; Made In The USA, 1986; Still Cruisin', 1989; Summer Dreams, 1990; Summer In Paradise, 1992; Good Vibrations, 1993; Singles include: Surfin' USA; Surfer Girl; Little Deuce Coupe; Fun Fun Fun; I Get Around; When I Grow Up (To Be A Man); Dance Dance; Help Me Rhonda; Barbara Ann; California Girls; God Only Knows; Good Vibrations; Do It Again. Honours include: Inducted into Rock And Roll Hall Of Fame, 1988; Special Award Of Merit, American Music Awards, 1988. Current Management: Elliott Lott, 4860 San Jacinto Circle West, Fallbrook, CA 92026, USA.

JARLETT Dee, b. 28 Oct 1951, Manchester, England. Singer; Musician (guitar); Songwriter. m. John Jarlett, 9 Oct 1977, separated, 2 sons, 1 daughter. Education: DipEd, Teaching Music; RSA Diploma, Teaching Adults. Career: Member, folk duo Orion; UK tours of folk clubs; Numerous local radio appearances; Played film music for Rosie The Great, HTV; Member, Sweet Soul Sisters; Radio appearances: Start The Week, BBC Radio 4; Woman's Hour, BBC Radio 4; BBC Radio 2 arts programme, local radio and HTV. Recordings: with Orion: Jack Orion, 1987; Chicken Soup, 1989; with Sweet Soul Sisters: Live And Lovin' It, 1990; Freshly Squeezed, 1995. Current Management: Maggie Haines, 4 Archfield Road, Cotham, Bristol BS6 6NB, England. Address: 27 Narroways Road, St Werburghs, Bristol BS2 9XB, England.

JARRE Jean-Michel, b. 24 Aug 1948, Lyons, France. Musician (synthesizers, keyboards); Composer; Record Producer. m. Charlotte Rampling, 1977. Musical Education: Piano and guitar from age 5; Conservatoire de Paris, with Jeanine Reuff. Career: Solo debut, Paris Opera, 1971; Youngest composer to appear, Palais Garnier, 1971; Major concerts, often including lasers and fireworks, filmed for video releases include: Beijing, China, 1981; Bastille Day, Place De La Concorde, 1979; Houston, Texas (1.3 million audience), 1986; London Docklands, 1988; La Defense, Paris (2.5 million audience), 1990; Sun City, Johannesburg, South Africa, 1993; Member of jury, First International Visual Music Awards, Midem, France, 1992. Compositions include: Oxygène Part IV, used for several television themes; Ballet and film scores include: Des Garçons Et Des Filles, 1968; Deserted Palace, 1972; Les Granges Brûlées, 1973; La Maladie De Hambourg, 1978; Gallipoli, 1979. Recordings: Albums (all self-composed and produced): Deserted Palace, 1971; Oxygène, 1977; Magnetic Fields, 1981; The Concerts In China, 1982; The Essential Jean-Michel Jarre, 1983; Zoolook, 1984; Rendez-Vous, 1986; In Concert Lyons/Houston, 1987; Revelations (Number 2, UK), 1988; Jarre Live, 1989; Waiting For Cousteau, 1990; Images - The Best Of Jean-Michel Jarre, 1991; Chronologie, 1993; Jaree Hong Kong, 1994. Honours: Grand Prix, Academie Du Disque, Zoolook, 1985; First Western artist to play in China, 1981; Numerous Platinum and Gold discs worldwide. Address: c/o Dreyfus Records, 26 Avenue Kléber, 75116 Paris, France.

JARRE Maurice Alexis, b. 13 Sept 1924, Lyons, France. Composer. m. (1) France Pejot, 1946, 1 son, (2) Dany Saval, 1965, 1 daughter, (3) Laura Devon, 1967, (4) Khong Fui Fong, 1984. Musical Education: Conservatoire National Supéreur de Musique. Career: Musician, Radiodiffusion Française, 1946-50; Director of Music, Théatre National Populaire (TNP), 1950-63. Compositions: Symphonic music; Music for theatre and ballet include: Roland Petit's Notre-Dame de Paris (Paris Opera), 1966; Numerous film scores include: Lawrence Of Arabia, 1963; Dr Zhivago, 1965; Ryan's Daughter, 1970; Shogun, 1980; Doctors In Love, 1982; A Passage To India, 1985; The Mosquito Coast, 1987; Tai-Pan, 1987; Gaby, 1988; Gorillas In The Mist, 1989; Ghost; Dead Poets Society, 1990; Fatal Attraction. Honours: Officer, Légion d'Honneur, Commander des Arts et Lettres; Prix Italia, 1955, 1962; Grand Prix du Disque, Academy Charles Cros, 1962; Hollywood Golden Globe, 1965, 1984; People's Choice Award, 1988. Address: c/o Paul Kohner Inc, 9169 Sunset Boulevard, Los Angeles, CA 90069, USA.

JARREAU Al, b. 12 Mar 1940, Milwaukee, USA. Singer. Education: BS Psychology, Ripon College, 1962; MS Psychology, University of Iowa, 1964. Career: Solo artiste, 1975-. Recordings: Solo albums: We Got By, 1975; Glow, 1976; Look To The Rainbow Live, 1977; All Fly Home, 1979; This Time, 1987; Breaking Away, 1981; Jarreau, 1983; High Crime, 1984; Al Jarreau Live in London, 1985; L Is For Lover, 1986; Heart's Horizon, 1988; Heaven and Earth, 1992; Tenderness, 1994; Best of Al Jarreau, 1996; Also appeared on: I Heard That!, Quincy Jones, 1976; The Love Connection, Freddie Hubbard, 1980; Friends, Larry Carlton, 1983; Two Eyes, Brenda Russell, 1983; Back On The Block, Quincy Jones, 1989. Honours: Grammy Awards: Best Jazz Vocal, Look To The Rainbow, 1977, All Fly Home, 1978, Best Pop Vocal, Breakin' Away, 1981, Best Jazz Vocal, Breakin' Away, 1981, Best R&B Vocal, Male, Heaven and Earth, 1992; Downbeat Reader's Poll Winner, 1977-79. Current Management: Bill Darlington/Marion Wheeler, 1103 11th Street, Santa Monica, CA 90403, USA.

JARRETT Anita, b. 8 Aug 1964, London, England. Vocal; Singer; Songwriter. 1 son, 1 daughter. Career: Television and radio performances Europe; Yo Yo Honey, 1990-92; Solo mini tour, Jamaica, Jan-Mar, 1993. Recordings: Voodoo soul album; Angel; Ghetto Blues; To be released: vocals for Rolling Stone remix; Vocal, Okenfeld Project. Publications: Still Waiting And Persevering To Achieve And Reach the So Called Perfection Of Expression Via The Medium Of Music. Membership: Musicians' Union. Hobbies: Sports design; Swimming; Sauna; Walking; Travel; Reading; Smoking occasionally; Photography; Good food and pampering. Current Management: Trenton, NUR Entertainment. Address: Camelot Studios, Unit 218A, 222 Kensal Road, London W10 5N, England.

JARRETT Keith, b. 8 May 1945, Allentown, Pennsylvania, USA. Musician (piano); Composer. Career: First solo concert, age 7, followed by professional appearances; 2 hour solo concert, own compositions, 1962; Led own trio, Boston; Worked with Roland Kirk; Tony Scott; Joined Art Blakey, 1965; Tours, Europe, with Charles Lloyd, 1966; with Miles Davis, 1970-71; Soloist, leader, own groups, 1969-. Recordings: Personal Mountains; Changeless; Luminessence; Mysteries; Expectations; At The Blue Note - The Complete Recordings. Address: c/o Don Lucoff, D L Media, 270 Park Avenue South, Suite 5C, New York, NY 10010, USA.

JARVIS Jane, b. 31 Oct 1915, Vincennes, Indiana, USA. Musician (piano, organ); Composer; Lyricist. 1 son, 2 daughters. Education: Bachelor Pace University, New York City, New York. Musical Education: Scholarships: Bush Conservatory; Chicago Conservatory; De Paul School of Music. Career: Staff Pianist, WJKS; Featured in High School musicals with Karl Maldin and Red Skelton; Staff musician, WJMJ, Milwaukee and WOC Davenport; Rehearsal Pianist, NBC, New York; Vice President, Muzak Corporation; Lecturer, Yale University; Performed with Clark Terry; Lionel Hampton; Chosen by Smithsonian Institute for Jazz Archives. Compositions: Over 300 original compositions. Recordings: Organ Magic; Cut Glass; LA Jazz Quartet; To Duke; Back To Basics; Statesmen of Jazz; Two-Time (musical). Publications: Various profiles of fellow musicians. Honours: Governor Kentucky for song; Governor Indiana; Made Sagamare Indian Chief; Jane Jarvis Jazz Festival, Tampa, Florida, in her honour. Memberships: ASCAP; NARAS, former Governor. Hobbies: Reading.

JARVIS Toby J, b. 8 May 1965, London, England. Composer; Musician (piano, percussion, samplers, guitar, synthesisers). Career: Arranger, music for films and television; Composed music for television themes and shows, UK, USA; Composed music for over 4000 television commercials worldwide; Wrote, recorded songs for: Maxine Harvey; Hunter (The Gladiators); Georgia Lewis. Compositions: Numerous dance and club hits including Twink Goes Disco and Goin' Outa My Head. Recordings: Loved Up, BBC TV; Schofield's Quest, LWT; Outlaws, BSkyB; Beat That, Channel 4; Super Champs, Thames; British Comedy Awards, LWT; Comedy Club, LWT; Hot House People, BBC. Honours: EDLE Prix De Jeunesse, for Beat That. Memberships: SPAM; Musicians' Union; PRS; Stonewall. Hobbies: Travelling world in search of musical sounds unheard before. Current Management: Mcasso Music Production. Address: 9 Carnaby Street, London W1V 1PG, England.

JAUME Andre, b. 7 Oct 1940, Marseilles, France. Musician (tenor saxophone, bass clarinet, clarinet); Composer. m. Andree Caravaglio, 10 Nov 1979. Musical Education: Conservatoire de Musique, Marseilles. Career: Festival Moers; Patras; Indonesia; USA; Canada; Algeria; Numerous festivals Paris, Radio France; President, label: Celp Musiques. Recordings: sessions with: Charlie Haden; Charlie Mariano; Joe McPhee; Jimmy Giuffre; Java Gamelan. Honours: Diapason d'Or. Membership: SACEM. Hobbies: Travel; Painting; Poetry.

JAY David (Dave) John, b. 13 Nov 1971, Brentwood, Essex, England. Singer; Songwriter; Musician (guitar, keyboard). Musical Education: Self-taught. Education: BA, Politics. Career: Remix work with Vibe Alive Production for London Records and Atlantic Records, USA; Solo and Session work for Mr Exe, Cool Blu, Acorn Arts and various independent labels. Recordings: After The Dance, Austin; Ain't It Rough, The Dave Jay Project; Dedicated To Love, The Journeyman (5 track EP); House Of Love, East 17; Love Is Blind, Echora; Spring Box EP, Dilemma; Change the Style/Windows...., Mighty Alliance. Membership: Musicians' Union. Hobbies: Jogging; Weight-training; Reading. Address: 8 The Meads, Cherry Trees, Ingatestone, Essex CM13 1LX, England.

JAY Martin, b. 27 July 1949, London, England. Singer; Musician (guitar); Writer; Producer. m. Lorraine Jay, 6 Nov 1985, 1 son. Musical Education: Self-taught. Career: Television appearances on Top Of The Pops with 5000 Volts and Enigma; with Cockney Rebel: Yamaha Song Festival, In Concert, LWT; Chile Song Festival. Recordings: with 5000 Volts: I'm On Fire; Dr Kiss Kiss; Medleys with Enigma: Ain't No Stoppin'; I Love Music;Back To The 60's, Tight Fit; Saturday Night Fever "Megamix". Memberships: Musicians' Union; Equity. Hobbies: Tennis; Cricket. Address: 17 Brook Way, Chigwell, Essex IG7 6AW, England.

JAY Michael (Michael Jay Margules), b. 17 Dec 1959, Chicago, Illinois, USA. Songwriter; Record Producer. Education: Lincoln College, Illinois; Illinois State University. Career: A&R for Curtis Mayfield, Curtom Records, Chicago, 1980; Discovered Martika, 1988; Recordings: Producer, Toy Soldiers, Martika; Cross My Heart, Patsy Kensit & Eighth Wonder; Hot Summer Nights, Gloria Estefan (Top Gun soundtrack); The World Still Turns, Kylie Minogue; I Wish The Phone Would Ring, Exposé; The Slightest Touch and If I Say Yes, Five Star; Writer and producer, Shining Through, arranged by Nancy Kerrigan, Olympic Silver Medallist ice-skater. Honours: AMPEX Golden Reel Awards, Silk & Steel and Martika. Memberships: NARAS; BAFTA; BMI. Hobbies: Horse riding; Raquetball; Photography. Current Management: Alan Melina. Address: Shankman DeBlasio Melina, 740 La Brea Avenue, Hollywood, CA 90038, USA.

JAY Robert, b. 15 Nov 1967, Dieren, Netherlands. Musician (guitar); Producer; Artist; Singer. Education: Higher Business Economics and Trade. Musical Education: Conservatory. Career: Schüttorf Open Air Concert; 4 television (national) shows; De 5 Uur show; Glamourland; Actor, television series; Tour manager, clients include: Emmylou Harris; Freddie Fender; Chris Beckers; Ernie Watts; Randy Bernsen; Performed in USA; Canada; Germany; Israel; Egypt; Spain; France; Artists performed with: Hans Dulfer; Candy Dulfer; Jan Akkerman; Adje Vanderberg; Jasper Van't Hof; Joe Sample; Writer for several pop journals; Organiser, music festivals. Membership: EMI Music/Publishing. Hobbies: Cars; Sports; Football; Tennis. Current Management: Frisbee Management. Address: Frisbee Management, PO Box 658, 7500 AR Enschade, Netherlands.

JAZZIE B (Beresford Romeo), b. 26 Jan 1963, London, England. Rapper; Arranger. Career: Formed Soul II Soul, offering sound systems to UK dance clubs; Sunday night residence, Africa Centre, London, 1986; Host, radio show, KISS-FM, 1988; Opened 2 shops, London; Arranger (with Nellee Hooper), Nothing Compares To U, Sinead O'Connor, 1990; Also arranger for Maxi Priest; Neneh Cherry; Fine Young Cannibals; Launched record label Funki Dred, 1991. Recordings: Singles include: Keep On Movin', 1989; Back To Life (However Do You Want Me) (Number 1, UK), 1989; Get A Life, 1989;

A Dream's A Dream, 1990; Missing You (featuring Kym Mazelle), 1990; Joy, 1992; Just Right, 1993; Move Me No Mountain, 1992; Wish, 1993; Love Enuff, 1995; Featured on Give Peace A Chance, The Peace Choir, 1991; Albums: Club Classics Volume One, 1989; Volume II - A New Decade, 1990; Volume III - Just Right, 1993; Best Of, 1994; Volume V - Believe, 1995. Honours include: Billboard Award, Top Dance Sales Artists, 1989; Rolling Stone Award, Best New Foreign Band, 1990; Grammy Awards: Best R&B Performance, Best R&B Instrumental Performance, 1990; 4 British DMC Dance Awards, 1990; 3 American Music Awards, 1990; Soul Train Awards: Best R&B Song, R&B Single, R&B Album, 1990; ASCAP Award, Back To Life, 1991; BMI College Radio Award, Back To Life, 1991; Current Management: Jazz Summers, Big Life Management, 15 Little Portland Street, London W1N 5DE, England.

JEAN-MARIE Alain (Judes), b. 29 Oct 1945, Pointe-A-Pitre, Guadaloupe. Musician (piano). Musical Education: Self-taught. Career: Prix Django Reinhardt, 1979; Concerts with: Chet Baker; Art Farmer; Johnny Griffin; Hal Singer; Slide Hampton; Clark Terry; Records with: Abbey Lincoln; Charles Tolliver. Recordings: Latin Alley, with Niels Henning Orsted Pedersen; The Scene Is Clean, with Aldo Romano, Henri Texier; Biguines Reflections. Honours: Prix Django Reinhardt, Acadimie du Jazz, 1979. Current Management: Martine Palmé, 33 bis Rue Doudeauville, 75018 Paris, France. Address: Chemin Des Cotillons, 95130 Franconville, France.

JEANES Alan LLoyd, b. 22 May 1923, Penarth, South Wales. Composer; Arranger. Musical Education: Jazz Musicianship, Goldsmiths College, London. Career: Founder, former director, University of Greenwich Big Band; Tutor, Jazz Musicianship for various authorities, England and Wales; Arranger for jazz groups. Hobbies: Motoring; Vintage cars; Country inns. Address: 4 Oldfield Road, Bickley, Bromley, Kent BR1 2LF, England.

JEANNEL Didier, b. 24 Feb 1954, Toulouse, France. Musician (guitar, banjo). Career: Jazz musician; Appearances include: Festival Radio France Montpellier; Festival Saint Raphael; Festival de Sorglies (Sorg' Jazz). Recordings: Albums with Calmity Jazz Group. Hobbies: Drawing; Shopping.

JECZALIK Jonathan Edward Stephen, b. 11 May 1955, Banbury, Oxfordshire, England. Musical Director. m. Joanna Louise Hill, 2 daughters. Education: Honours degree, Geography. Musical Education: Self-taught. Career: Programmer, Fairlight CMI; Producer for Pet Shop Boys; Artist with Art of Noise and Art of Silence (current). Recordings: Moments In Love; Beatbox; Close To The Edit; Peter Gunn (Grammy Award winner); Kiss, Tom Jones. Honour: Grammy Award, Best Rock Instrumental, 1986. Membership: Musicians' Union. Hobbies: Clay shooting; Golf; Gardening; Children. Current Management: Self-managed.

JEFFES Simon Harry Piers, b. 19 Feb 1949, Sussex, England. Composer; Musician (various instruments). 1 son. Education: Upper Canada College, Toronto; Grenville College, Bideford, Devon. Musical Education: Guitar with Julian Byzantine; Piano with Dennis Hunt; Musical Godfather, Stephen Dodgson. Career: Founder, Penguin Cafe Orchestra, 1972; Concerts: Europe; USA; Australia; Japan; String arrangements include: Mort Shuman; Caravan; Sid Vicious (My Way); Baaba Maal; Collaborations include: Malcolm McClaren, Ryuichi Sakamoto; Television includes Bank Show, 1987; Ballet Score, Still Life At The Penguin Cafe, for The Royal Ballet, 1988. Recordings: Albums: Music From The Penguin Cafe, 1976; Penguin Cafe Orchestra,

1982; Broadcasting From Home, 1984; Signs Of Life, 1987; When In Rome, 1989; Union Cafe, 1993; Concert Program, 1995; Video/album: Still Life At The Penguin Cafe, 1990. Honours: Silver Star of Bologna. Current Management: 144 Camden High Street, London NW1 0NE, England.

JEFFRIES Peter John Martin, b. 1 Mar 1928, London, England. Composer; Arranger; Musician (piano); Musical Director. m. Pauline Lander, 7 Apr 1955, 1 son, 1 daughter. Musical Education: Eastman School of Music; Private lessons. Career: Pianist, arranger, Phil Tate Orchestra; Arranger, musical director, Philips Records, Pye Records, Decca Records; Radio appearances include: Own broadcasting orchestra, Breakfast special, Radio 2, 1967-72; Accompanist for: Kenny Lynch; Jimmy Tarbuck; Morecambe and Wise; Anne Shelton; Vera Lynn. Compositions: Composer, conductor, 21 film scores, 1966-80; Co-arranger, If My Friends Could See Me Now, Cy Coleman. Memberships: PRS; MCPS; BASCA. Hobby: Golf. Address: Flat 3, 55 High Road, Bushey Heath, Hertfordshire WD2 1EE, England.

JELAVIC Matko, b. 29 Mar 1958, Split, Croatia. Singer; Composer; Musician (drums). m. 31 July 1982, 2 sons. Education: Dipl OECC. Musical Education: Music School (guitar). Career: Drummer, rock band Metak; Drummer in studios; More than 50 albums of different singers and groups; Singer, composer, 1988-; Very successful in Croatia and among Croatians abroad; Biggest concert in Sydney, Australia, audience 10,000 people. Recordings: Album: Dobra Vecer Prijatelji, 1988; (Biggest hit) Majko Stara, 1988; Ljube Ljubavi, 1989; Sretno Ti Bilo Andele, 1990; Matko Jelavic Mix, 1992; Moja Ljubavi, 1993; Pianino, 1995. Honours: 3 Gold albums, rest Silver; Winner, Split Festival, 1988; Most Popular Song Award In Croatia, 1988. Memberships: HGU (Croatian Music Union); DSH (Union of Composers). Hobbies: Basketball; Other popular sports. Current Management: Mr Branko Paic, CBS Zagreb. Address: Dubrovacka 25, Split, Croatia.

JENKINS Billy, b. 5 July 1956, Bromley, Kent, England. Musician (guitar); Bandleader; Composer. Twin daughters. Musical Education: Self-taught guitar; Primary classical violin and piano; Parish choir; Special choirs, Westminster Abbey, St Pauls Cathedral. Career: Burlesque, 1973-77; Numerous tours, UK and Netherlands; Old Grey Whistle Test, BBC TV, 1977; Trimmer and Jenkins, 1979-82; Live From The Comic Strip, 1981; Ginger Baker Band, 1981-; The Voice Of God Collective, 1981-; Many European festival appearances; Mixing It, BBC Radio 3, 1993; Radio 2 Arts Programme, 1995. Recordings: Acupuncture, 1977; Burlesque, 1977; Greenwich, 1985; Uncommerciality, 1986; Wiesen '87, 1986; Scratches Of Spain, 1987; Motorway At Night, 1988; Entertainment USA, 1995. Publications: Articles for Time Out; Making Music; One Two Testing; Musician; Monochrome; Melody Maker; Also: Entertainment USA: The Poems, 1995. Memberships: Right To Peace and Quiet Campaign; Musicians' Union; Performing Rights Society. Hobbies: Motor sports; Slot car racing. Current Management: VOTP Management. Address: PO Box 3162, London SE13 7BE, England.

JENKINS Brian, b. 15 Apr 1949, Birmingham, West Midlands, England. Musician (bass guitar); Haulier. Divorced, 1 daughter. Musical Education: Self-taught. Career: Member, local bands: The Zootcases, 1979; M4, 1980-84; The Flying Bonehead Brothers, 1985-90; Currennt Ed's Kitchen, 1992; TV debut, Sky TV Sport at Coventry City FC, May 1994. Membership: Musicians' Union. Hobbies: Bridge; Golf. Address: 98 Tresillian Road, Exhall, Coventry, Warwickshire CV7 9PW, England.

JENNINGS Waylon Arnold, b. 15 June 1937, Littlefield, Texas, USA. Country Singer; Musician (bass). m. Jessi Colter. Career: Radio DJ, aged 12; Bass player, final Buddy Holly tour; Formed own group, The Waylors, Phoenix, 1964-66; Film appearance, Nashville Rebel; Also recorded as The Highwaymen (with Willie Nelson, Johnny Cash, Kris Kristofferson). Compositions include: You're The One (co-written with Buddy Holly); Television theme, The Dukes Of Hazzard. Recordings: Hit singles include: Anita, You're Dreaming; Love Of The Common People; Only Daddy That'll Walk That Line; MacArthur Park; Luckenbach, Texas; There Ain't No Good Chain Gang (with Johnny Cash); Numerous albums include: Waylon Jennings At JD's, 1964; Don't Think Twice, 1965; Leaving Town, 1966; Nashville Rebel, 1966; The One And Only, 1967; Love Of The Common People, 1967; Hangin' On, 1968; Only The Greatest, 1968; Jewels, 1968; Waylon Jennings, 1969; Ned Kelly (film soundtrack), 1970; Waylon, 1970; Ladies Love Outlaws, 1972; This Time, 1974; Ol' Waylon, 1977; I've Always Been Crazy, 1978; Music Man, 1980; Black On Black, 1982; Waylon And Company, 1983; Will The Wolf Survive?, 1985; A Man Called Hoss, 1987; Full Circle, 1988; The Eagle, 1990; Too Dumb For New York City, Too Ugly For LA, 1992; Waymore's Blues (Part II), 1995; with the Highwaymen: The Highwaymen, 1985; Highwaymen 2, 1990; with Willie Nelson: Waylon And Willie, 1978; WWII, 1982; Take It To The Limit, 1983; Clean Shirt, 1991; with Willie Nelson and Jessi Colter: Wanted - The Outlaws, 1976; with Jessi Colter: White Mansions, 1978; The Pursuit Of DB Cooper (film soundtrack), 1982; with Johnny Cash: Heroes, 1986. Current Management: Waylon Jennings Enterprises, 1117 17th Avenue South, Nashville, TN 37212, USA.

JENSEN Kurt, b. 17 April 1946, Copenhagen, Denmark. Musician; Singer. m. Nan Ehrenstrale, 21 February 1972, 1 daughter. Education: Lithographer. Career: Played in various Danish and Swedish bands, toured with Dave Williams, Kid Sheik Colar, Wild Bill Davidson, Joseph Thomas; Leader, Own Band, Jensens New Orleans Jazz Band, 10 years. Recordings: Jazz Classics & Evergreens, 1996; A Tribute to Kid Thomas, 1997. Membership: Danish Music Union. Address: Bogardsvej 106, 3050 Humlebaek, Denmark.

JENSEN Mark Russell, b. 20 Nov 1959, Eastbourne, England. Composer; Arranger; Conductor; Producer; Recording Artiste. Education: Eastbourne College. Musical Education: Rodney Sadler; John Walker, MA. Arranger, conductor, record producer for singles and albums, 1978-; Recording artiste, 1985-; Composer, arranger, conductor for film, television, theatre, 1992-; Recorded as Spritzo Scaramanga to 1993, as Mark Jensen, 1994-. Compositions: for film/television: The Papermen, 1993; Angleterre Underground, 1994; Caravan To Arcadia, 1995; Monk Dawson, 1995; Famine, 1998; for theatre: Romeo and Juliet, 1993; The Changeling, 1994; The Tempest, 1994; Hamlet, 1995; The Way of Danger (ballet score), 1996. Recordings: as Spritzo Scaramanga, single, 1993. Memberships: Performing Rights Society; British Music Writers Council; Musicians' Union. Address: c/o Zest Zone, 44 Carew Road, Eastbourne, East Sussex BN21 2JN, England.

JENSEN Søren Kjær, b. 1 Dec 1961. Aarhus, Denmark. Musician (bass); Composer; Producer. m. Turid N Christensen, 22 July 1995. Education: University of Aarhus; Studied jazz at the New School for Social Science, New York, USA. Career includes: Teacher, Royal Conservatory of Music, Aalborg; Musik Projekt Aarhus; Space invaders production for Multimedia; Lecturer, Anthropology of Music, University of Aarhus; Musical Director and Producer; Numerous television appearances. Compositions: Numerous works for television, video, film, Planetaria, theme

parks, CD-Roms and CD-I; Producer and co-producer: Waaberi, New Dawn, 1997; Maryam Mursal, 1998. Recordings: Appeared on recordings by many artists including: Maryam Mursal (The Journey), Jacob Haugaard, Evald Krog, Holger Laumanns Orkester, Extrem Normal, Nikos Veropoulos and Bonehead. Honours: Scholarships from: Danish Music Council; Danish Arts Council; Danish Rock Council; Queen Margrethe and Prince Henriks Foundation; European Commission, Innovation Programme; Ministry for the Interior; Danish Cultural Foundation; Awards: Best CD-ROM in Scandinavia, 1997; Industrial Design Award, 1998. Memberships: KODA; NCB; Danish Musicians' Union. Hobbies: Reading; Travel. Current Management: Target Music. Address: Mejlgade 50, 1 tv, DK 8000 Aarhus C, Denmark.

JENSEN Theis Eigil, b. 5 Aug 1938, Copenhagen, Denmark. Singer; Musician (trumpet); Graphic Designer; m. Lesley Celina Geen, 3 June 1961, divorced 1976. Education: Graduate, Graphic Design, Art School, 1959. Career: Member: Louisiana Jazzband, 1952-55; Henrik Johansen's Jazzband, 1955-56; Adrian Bentzon's Jazzband, 1956-63; Co-leader, Theis/Nyegaard Jazzband, 1963-; Tours and festivals: Europe; USA; Argentina; Brazil; Uruguay; Australia; Television and radio appearances: Scandinavia; South America. Recordings: Traditional Jazz, 1964; Theis/Nyegaard Concert At Gothenburg, 1969; Theis/Nyegaard Live At Montmartre, 1972; Papa Bue's Viking Jazz Band Live At Vingården, 1976; Jazztage Hannover, 1977; Jazz For Hatz-Lovers, 1979; Theis Jensen 1956-72, 1980; Mand Mand, 1980; Los Estudiantes Daneses En El Hot Club De Buenos Aires, 1980; Gamle Er Unge, Der Er Blevet Aeldre, 1981; The First 25 Years, 1988; Jorgen Svare Meets Theis Jensen, 1991. Jazz Event, 1992; Theis-Nyegaard Jazzband, Tonight Live, 1996. Publication: Historier Om Theis, 1992. Honour: Jazz Musician of the Year, 1965. Membership: DJBFA. Hobbies: Graphic Design; Jazz Music. Address: Lovenborg Alle 11, DK-4420 Regstrup, Denmark.

JERBIC Zeljko, b. 10 Oct 1954, Koprivnica, Croatia. Record Producer; Teacher. Education: Academy of Pedagogics. Musical Education: High School Of Music. Recordings: As Music and Executive Producer: Damned Die Hard, Phonebox Vandals, 1990; Foxxin, Messerschmitt, 1990; Ikona, Lola V Stain, 1990; 4 x 12", Borghesia, 1991; Mansarda, Lola V Stain, 1992; Asgard Live, Vesna Gorse and Drazen Franolic, 1993; So Shine, Don't, 1995; Ulje Je Na Vodi, Haustor, 1995. Honours: Porin Award Nominations, 1994, 1995. Membership: Croatian Musicians' Union. Address: Attn Mr Zeljko Jerbic, Blind Dog Records, Svilarska 34, 480 00 Koprivnica, Croatia.

JERROLF Mats, b. 28 August 1951, Stockholm, Sweden. Composer; Musician. Education: Archaeology, Etnology, University, 1977. Career: Touring in Sweden; Appearances in Various Folkmusic Programs in Radio. Compositions: Bekannelsen I Logen, 1991; Adjo Till Stockholms Stad, 1993; Krakemala Namdemanlard, 1993; Förskingrarvisan, 1995. Recordings: Skanska Lasses Visor, 1987; Flickan Fran Bellmansro, 1988; Collage, 1990; Haveri, 1993; Namdemans Blandning, 1995. Publications: Birka, 1981; Historisk Malarresa, 1981. Honours: STIM Award, 1991, 1995, 1997; Folk Music Foundation Award, 1992; SKAP Award, 1995. Memberships: SKAP; SAMI. Hobbies: Football; Pubs. Address: Reimersholmsi 8, 117 40 Stockholm, Sweden.

JERVIER Paul Joseph, b. 21 Nov 1966, London, England. Musician (drums); Music Producer. Recordings: 4 UK Number 1 singles with Take That; Other recordings for artists include: Yazz; Eternal; Kaos; Gabrielle; R Kelly. Membership: Musicians' Union. Hobbies: Writing;

Sports; Holidays; DIY; Driving. Address: 108 Perry Rise, London SE23 2QU, England.

JESSE Graham, b. 19 October 1955, Sydney, Australia. m. Peta, 24 May 1986, 1 son, 1 daughter. Education: Sydney Conservatorium of Music to Study Flute; Conservatorium Jazz Course; Studied Saxophone with Dave Liebman & Musical Composition with Ludmilla Uhlehla, New York, 1981-82. Career: Member, Midday Show, live daily TV entertainment programme, 15 years; Toured with Daly Wilson Big Band, Peter Allen, David Atkins; Performed with Sydney Dance Company, James Morrison, Marcia Hines. Compositions: Reflections, CD; In the Company of Women, Sydney Dance Company. Recordings: Leader: Reflections, 1996; Featured Soloist: Tommy Emmanuel: Dare to Be Different; Up From Down Under; Condwangland: Travelling. Honour: Bicentennial Music Week Award, Most Outstanding Studio Musician, 1988. Memberships: Australian Musician's Union; ARRA. Address: 50 Sugarloaf Crescent, Castlecrag, NSW 2068, Australia.

JETT Joan, Vocalist; Musician (guitar). Career: Member, US all-female group, The Runaways, 1976-79; Solo artiste, with own backing band, The Blackhearts, 1979-. Recordings: Albums: with The Runaways: The Runaways, 1976; Queens Of Noise, 1977; Live In Japan, 1977; Solo/with The Blackhearts: Bad Reputation, 1980; I Love Rock'N'Roll, 1981; Album, 1983; Glorious Results Of A Misspent Youth, 1984; Up Your Alley, 1988; Good Music, 1989; Hit List, 1990; Hit single: I Love Rock'n'Roll, 1981. Address: c/o Blackheart Records Group, Suite 6H, 155 East 55th Street, New York, NY 10022, USA.

JEWELL Jimmy, b. 18 Feb 1945, Brierfield, Lancashire, England. Musician (saxophones); Composer; Arranger. m. Mary-Kay Lombardo, 9 Oct 1983, 2 daughters. Musical Education: Largely self-taught. Career: Keef Hartley Band: Woodstock Festival; 4 years touring, recording with Gallagher and Lyle; Original member, Ronnie Lane's Slim Chance; McGuiness-Flint recorded with Joan Armatrading (Love and Affection solo). Recordings: 2 solo albums, jazz fusion, 1977, 1978; Several privately produced tapes, jazz featuring original compositions. Memberships: Musicians' Union; PRS; MCPS. Hobbies: Homebrewing; Winemaking. Address: 105 Britton Street, Gillingham, Kent ME 7 5ES, England.

JIMBOB (James Morrison), b. 22 Nov 1960. Musician. Career: Founder member (with Fruitbat), duo Carter The Unstoppable Sex Machine (later known as Carter USM); International tours, US, Japan. Recordings: 101 Damnations, 1990; 30 Something, 1991; 1992 - The Love Album, 1992; Post Historic Monsters, 1994; Worry Bomb, 1995; Singles: Sheltered Life; Sherriff Fatman; Anytime, Anyplace, Anywhere; Bloodsports For All; After The Watershed. Current Management: Adrian Boss Promotions, 363-365 Harrow Road, London W9 3NA, England.

JIMENEZ-OLARIAGA Marcos Andres, b. 25 Apr 1960, Madrid, Spain. Jazz Musician (piano). 1 daughter. Musical Education: Classical studies, Geneva CPM, with S Risler. Career: Various concerts with saxophonist M Magnoni; Television and radio shows with own band: Chris Cross; Cully Jazz Festival with singer, C Python. Recordings: Albums: Chris Cross; Allastor; Outland Souvenirs; Nirohda. Publications: Helas Moulino, edited in Le Livre du Jazz en France. Honours: Piano certificate with jury congratulations. Membership: AMR, Geneva. Address: 801 Chemin des Broues, F-01220 Divonne, France.

JOEL Billy (William Martin Joel), b. 9 May 1949, Bronx, New York, USA. Musician (piano);

Singer; Songwriter. m. Christie Brinkley, 23 Mar 1989, divorced 1994, 1 daughter. Education: LHD (hon), Fairfield Univesity, 1991; HMD (hon), Berklee College Music, 1993. Career: Popular solo recording artist, 1972-. Compositions include: Just The Way You Are, 1978; Honesty, 1979; We Didn't Start The Fire, 1989; The River Of Dreams, 1994. Albums include: Turnstiles; Streetlife Serenade; The Stranger, 1978; 52nd Street, 1978; Glass Houses, 1980; Songs In The Attic, 1981; Nylon Curtain, 1982; An Innocent Man, 1983; Cold Spring Harbour, 1984; Piano Man, 1984; Greatest Hits, Volumes I & II, 1985; The Bridge, 1986; KOHUEPT-Live In Leningrad, 1987; Storm Front, 1989; River Of Dreams, 1994. Honours: 6 Grammy Awards include: Record of Year, Song of Year, Best Male Vocal Performance, 1978; Best Album, 1979; 10 Grammy Nominations include: Best Song, Record, Producer, Male Vocal Performance of Year; American Music Award, Best Album, 1980; Grammy Legend Award, 1990; Inducted into Songwriters Hall of Fame, 1992; ASCAP Founders Award, 1997; Honorary DHL, Hofstra University, 1997. Hobby: Boating. Address: c/o Maritime Music Inc., 200 West 57th Street, Suite 308, New York, NY 10019, USA.

JOHANSEN Per Oddvar Eide, b. 1 Mar 1968, Oslo, Norway. Musician (drums). Musical Education: Music Gymnasium, Rud High School, 3 years; Studied Jazz at Trondelag Music Conservatory of Music, Trondheim, 3 years. Career: Freelance drummer, mostly Jazz and improvised music; Has toured in Norway and Europe with numerous groups including: Airamero; Kenny Weeler; John Surman; Karin Krog; Nils Petter Molvaer; Jon Christensen; Tore Brunborg; Vigleik Storaas; The Source; Close Erase. Recordings include: Airamero, Airamero; Olemanns Kornett, The Source; This Is You, Jacob Young. Honour: Spellemannsprisen, 1995. Memberships: Norwegian Jazz Federation; Norwegian Musical Union. Hobbies: Animals; Old records and instruments; Vintage drums. Address: Gamleveien 122E, 1350 Lommedalen, Norway.

JOHANSSON Markku, b. 22 Mar 1949, Lahti, Finland. Conductor; Arranger; Composer; Musician (trumpet, flugelhorn). m. Riita Kvitunen, June 1971, 1 son, 1 daughter. Musical Education: Music conservatory in Lahti; Sibelius Academy in Helsinki; Jazz studies in New York, with Thad Jones, Lew Soloff. Career: Radio, television, recording artist, as conductor, arranger, trumpet player; Conductor, UMO Jazz Orchestra, 1992-93; Conductor, Vantaa Pops Orchestra, 1988-. Recordings: Blue Echoes; Tenderly; Exorbitant; Vantaa Pops Orchestra; Umo Jazz Orchestra. Honours: Yrjö Award 1993 (Musician of the Year). Current Management: MJ-Music Oy. Address: Aalto 6 B 18, 02320 Espoo, Finland.

JOHN Elton (Reginald Kenneth Dwight), b. 25 Mar 1947, Pinner, Middlesex, England. Singer; Songwriter; Musician (piano). m. Renate Blauer, 14 Feb 1984, divorced 1988. Musical Education: Piano lessons aged 4; Royal Academy of Music, 1958. Career: Member, Bluesology, 1961-67; Worked at Mills Music Publishers; Solo artiste, 1968-; Long-term writing partnership with Bernie Taupin, 1967-; Partnership wrote for Dick James Music; Founder, Rocket Records, 1973; Own publishing company, Big Pig Music, 1974; Performances include: Wembley Stadium, 1975; First Western star to perform in Israel and USSR, 1979; Live Aid, Wembley, 1985; Wham's farewell concert, Wembley, 1985; Prince's Trust concerts, London, 1986, 1988; Farm Aid IV, 1990; AIDS Project Los Angeles - Commitment To Life VI, 1992; Film appearance, Tommy, 1975. Recordings: Hit singles include: Your Song, 1971; Rocket Man, 1972; Crocodile Rock (Number 1, US), 1973; Daniel, 1973; Saturday Night's Alright For Fighting, 1973; Goodbye Yellow Brick Road, 1973; Candle In The Wind, 1974; Don't Let The Sun Go Down On Me, 1974 (live version with George Michael, Number 1, UK and US, 1991);

Philadelphia Freedom, 1975; Lucy In The Sky With Diamonds (Number 1, US), 1975; Island Girl (Number 1, US), 1975; Pinball Wizard, from film Tommy, 1976; Don't Go Breaking My Heart, duet with Kiki Dee (Number 1, UK and US), 1976; Sorry Seems To Be The Hardest Word, 1976; Song For Guy, 1979; Blue Eyes, 1982; I Guess That's Why They Call It The Blues, 1983; I'm Still Standing, 1983; Kiss The Bride, 1983; Sad Songs (Say So Much), 1984; Nikita, 1986; Sacrifice (Number 1, UK), 1989; True Love (with Kiki Dee), 1993; Made In England, 1995; Contributor, That's What Friends Are For, Dionne Warwick And Friends (charity record), 1986; Albums include: Elton John, 1970; Tumbleweed Connection, 1971; Friends, 1971; 17-11-70, 1971; Madman Across The Water, 1972; Honky Chateau, 1972; Don't Shoot Me, I'm Only The Piano Player, 1973; Goodbye Yellow Brick Road, 1973; Caribou, 1974; Captain Fantastic And The Brown Dirt Cowboy, 1975; Rock Of The Westies, 1975; Here And There, 1976; Blue Moves, 1976; A Single Man, 1978; Lady Samantha, 1980; 21 At 33, 1980; Jump Up!, 1982; Too Low For Zero, 1983; Breaking Hearts, 1984; Ice On Fire, 1985; Leather Jackets, 1986; Live In Australia, 1987; Reg Strikes Back, 1988; Sleeping With The Past, 1989; The One, 1992; Made In England, 1995. Honours include: First album to go straight to Number 1 in US charts, Captain Fantastic..., 1975; Numerous Ivor Novello Awards for: Daniel, 1974; Don't Go Breaking My Heart, 1977; Song For Guy, 1979; Nikita, 1986; Sacrifice, 1991; Outstanding Contribution To British Music, 1986; Star on Hollywood Walk Of Fame, 1975; Madison Square Gardens Honours: Hall Of Fame, 1977; Walk Of Fame (first non-athlete), 1992; American Music Awards: Favourite Male Artist, Favourite Single, 1977; Silver Clef Award, Nordoff-Robbins Music Therapy, 1979; BRIT Awards: Outstanding Contribution To British Music, 1986; Best British Male Artist, 1991; Grammy, Best Vocal Performance By A Group, 1987; MTV Special Recognition Trophy, 1987; Hitmaker Award, National Academy of Popular Music, 1989; Honorary Life President, Watford Football Club, 1989; Inducted into Songwriters Hall Of Fame (with Bernie Taupin), 1992; Q Magazine Merit Award, 1993; Officer of Arts And Letters, Paris, 1993; KBE, 1998. Current Management: John Reid Enterprises Ltd., Singers House, 32 Galena Road, London W6 0LT, England.

JOHN Leee, b. 23 June 1967, Hackney, London, England. Singer; Songwriter; Musician (keyboards); Record Producer; Arranger. Musical Education: Hewanoma Strolling Players; Anna Scher Stage School; Worldwide Productions, New York. Career: Lead singer, Imagination; Backing vocalist, major artists; Concerts include: Prince's Trust Concert (played to Prince and Princess of Wales), Royal Albert Hall; Concerts for: Mandela family; President of Algeria; Princess Caroline, Prince Albert of Monaco; Sellout tours with Imagination, 1982-83. Recordings: with Imagination: Body Talk; Just An Illusion; Music And Lights; Instinctual; Thank You My Love; Flashback; In And Out Of Love; Solo: Let There Be Love (featured with Arthur Baker); The Mighty Power Of Love. Honours: Diamond Award; Gold and Platinum discs worldwide; Blues and Soul Award. Memberships: Musicians' Union; BASCA; PRS; PPL. Hobbies: Writing; Old films; Musicals; Reading; Swimming; Running. Current Management: Johnny X Productions, c/o Gina Smith Management. Address: 22 Croftside, Vigo Village, Kent DA13 0SH, England.

JOHN-PIERRE Linda, b. 2 Mar 1968, London, England. Singer; Entertainer. 1 daughter. Musical Education: Technical singing lessons (breathing). Career: Started singing, aged 16, weddings, private functions; Progressed onto singing competitions; Radio commercials, jingles for Dave Austen (BBC Radio Kent); Appeared on Sky TV talent competitions; Have since teamed up with lyricist/musician Pete Booker, as

songwriters/musicians. Hobbies: Writing songs; Cooking; Socialising; Going to theatre, cinema.

JOHNSON Alastair, b. 1 July 1966, Oxford, England. Recording Engineer; Record Producer; Programmer; Writer. Career: Initially live sound engineer, then house engineer, various UK studios including: Red Bus, Jacobs, Wool Hall, late 1980s; Artist manager, 2 years; Returned to studio as freelance engineer, producer. Recordings: Engineer, albums: First Of A Million Kisses, Fairground Attraction; Extricate, The Fall; Infinity, Donovan. Hobby: Clubbing. Current Management: Strongroom Management. Address: Strongroom Studios, 120 Curtain Road, London EC2A 3PJ, England.

JOHNSON Alison Marie, b. 26 Dec 1966, Staincliffe, West Yorkshire, England. Singer; Songwriter. Musical Education: 5 years brass (trumpet). Career: Professional singer, performer, fronting various bands, 1985-; Pursuing solo career, 1993-; Tours: Spain; UK; USA; Germany; Television and radio include: The Nashville Network; Radio Waky, Luxembourg. Memberships: CMA; NSAI; NEA; ASCAP; PRS; Equity. Hobbies: Songwriting; Horses. Current Management: Tracy Carter Management Ltd. Address: W T House, Pilling, Preston, Lancs PR3 6SJ, England; 9 Music Square South, Suite 366, Nashville, TN 37203, USA.

JOHNSON Brian, b. 5 Oct 1947. Vocalist; Lyricist. Career: Lead singer, UK rock band Geordie; Lead singer, heavy rock group AC/DC, 1980-; Appearances include: Monsters Of Rock Festival, Castle Donington, 1981, 1984; European rock festivals, Switzerland, Hungary, Belgium, Germany, 1991; Concert, Moscow, 1991. Recordings: with Geordie: 3 albums; with AC/DC: Singles include: Back In Black, 1981; You Shook Me All Night Long, 1981; Rock'n'Roll Ain't Noise Pollution, 1981; Let's Get It Up, 1982; For Those About To Rock (We Salute You), 1982; Guns For Hire, 1983; Nervous Shakedown,1984; Shake Your Foundations, 1985; Who Made Who, 1985; That's The Way I Wanna Rock'n'Roll, 1988; Heatseeker, 1988; Thunderstruck, 1990; Moneytalks, 1991; Are You Ready, 1991; Big Gun (used in film The Last Action Hero), 1993; Hard As A Rock, 1995; Albums: Back In Black, 1980; For Those About To Rock (We Salute You), 1981; Flick Of A Switch, 1983; Fly On The Wall, 1985; Who Made Who, 1986; Blow Up Your Video, 1988; The Razor's Edge, 1990; Live, 1992; Ballbreaker, 1995. Current Management: Hard To Handle Management, 640 Lee Road, Ste 106, Wayne, PA 19087, USA.

JOHNSON Derick, b. 7 June 1963, Manchester, England. Musician (bass guitar). 2 sons. Career: Started 52nd Street, 1983-86; Played with Swing Out Sister, 1989-; 4 tours: Italy; Phillipines; Spain; UK; Japan; America; Radio One sessions, Top Of The Pops, Tube, The Word, Pebble Mill. Compositions: That's The Way It Goes; Low Down Dirty Business; Cool As Ice. Recordings: Live album: Swing Out Sister; Get In Touch With Yourself; The Living Return. Membership: Musicians' Union. Hobbies: Electronics; Lovemaking. Current Management: Self-managed. Address: 66 Avebury Road, Boguley, Wytheshowe, Manchester M23 2QE, England.

JOHNSON Henry Joseph Jr, b. 28 Jan 1954, Chicago, Illinois, USA. Jazz Musician (guitar); Vocalist. Education: Indiana University. Musical education: Self-taught (from jazz recordings), Career: Guitarist, for organist Jack McDuff, 1976; Singer, Donny Hathaway, 1977; Pianist, Ramsey Lewis, 1979-82; 1985-; Singer, Joe Williams, 1986-; Saxophonist, Stanley Turrentine, 1995-; Solo artiste, 1987-; Performances include: All jazz festivals including Playboy Jazz Festival; JVC Jazz Festival; North Seas Jazz Festival. Recordings: 5 as solo artiste, include: You're The

One; Future Excursions; New Beginnings; 3 with jazz vocalist, Joe Williams; 6 with pianist, Ramsey Lewis. Honours: Downbeat: CD: You're The One, awarded 5 stars; Billboard Top 100 List, 1986, 87, 88. Memberships: Musicians' Union; AFTRA; NARAS. Hobbies: Recording music; Producing music; Cooking; Reading; Basketball. Current Management: John Levy Enterprises. Address: 2810 W Charleston Blvd G-72, Las Vegas, NE 89102, USA. .

JOHNSON Holly (William Johnson), b. 9 Feb 1960, Liverpool, England. Singer; Songwriter; Author; Artist; Actor. Career: Member, Big In Japan; Founder Member, Frankie Goes to Hollywood, 1980-87; Appearances include: World tours; Montreux Rock Festival, MTV, in the Motion Picture Body Double, 1995, Band Aid single, Hillsborough Justice Concert, 1997; Solo Artist, 1987-; Exhibition of paintings and sculptures, The House of Holly, Cork Street Gallery, London, 1996; Currently performing and producing a new solo album. Recordings: Albums: with Frankie Goes to Hollywood: Welcome to the Pleasuredome, (Number 1, UK), 1984; Liverpool, 1986; Blast (Number 1, UK), 1989; Hollelujah, 1989; Dreams That Money Can't Buy, 1991; Bang! - Greatest Hits of Frankie Goes to Hollywood, 1993; Singles include: Relax, (Number 1, UK), 1984; Two Tribes (Number 1, UK), 1984; The Power of Love (Number 1, UK), 1984; Welcome to the Pleasuredome, 1985; Rage Hard, 1986; Warriors of the Wasteland, 1986; Watching the Wildlife, 1986; Solo singles: Love Train, 1989; Americanos, 1989; Atomic City, 1989; Contributor, Last Temptation of Elvis, compilation album, 1990. Publication: A Bone in My Flute, autobiography, 1994. Honours: Only group to have 2 Platinum singles with first 2 releases, first three singles went to Number 1, UK, 1984; Two BRIT Awards, Best British Single, Best British Newcomer, 1985; Ivor Novello Award, Best Contemporary Song, Two Tribes, 1985. Current Management: Wolfgang Kuhle Artist Management, PO Box 425, London SW6 3TX, England.

JOHNSON John (J J), b. 27 Oct 1951. Newark, Nottinghamshire, England. Musician (drums, keyboards); Vocalist; Producer. Partner, Christine Robertson, 2 sons. Musical Education: Self-taught. Career: Drummer, Wayne County And The Electric Chairs, 1976-80; with Mystere Five; Drums, vocals, Flying Lizards, Thomas Dolby; Skids; Nico; GBM, drums, vocals. Recordings: with The Electric Chairs: The Electric Chairs (EP), 1977; Blatently Offensive (EP), 1978; Albums: The Electric Chairs, 1977; Storm The Gates Of Heaven, 1978; Things Your Mother Never Told You, 1979; 8 singles include: Thunder When She Walks, 1977; Trying To Get On The Radio, 1978; Eddie And Sheena, 1978; Waiting For The Marines, 1979; Berlin, 1979; So Many Ways, 1979; with Mystere 5 singles include: Heart Rules The Head & No Message, 1980; with The Fying Lizards, album: Fourth Wall, 1981; Single: Lovers And Other Strangers; Jungle Line (EP), Thomas Dolby, 1981; Albums: Drama of Exile, Nico; Joy, The Skids, 1981; Ten Thirty On A Summer's Night, Richard Jobson, 1983; with GBM, album: Method In The Madness; Singles: Strange News; Diction And Fiction; Whistling In The Dark, 1983-84. Memberships: Musicians' Union. Hobbies: Swimming; Camping. Address: GBM Productions, 41B Kingsgate Road, London NW6 4TD, England.

JOHNSON Kenny, b. 11 Dec 1939, Halewood, Merseyside, England. Country Music Singer; Songwriter; Musician (guitar). 1 son, 1 daughter. Musical Education: Rock'n'Roll clubs around Liverpool. Career: Leader of group Northwind; 40 years professional; Television appearances throughout UK, Europe and US; Major tours with: Marty Robbins, Billie Jo Spears; Johnny Cash; Major concerts: Rhyman Auditorium, original Grand Ole Opry tour, USA; Grand Ole Opry, Tennessee; Falklands, 3 times;

Belize, twice; Euromasters Festival, Holland; Presenter, weekly radio shows, BBC Radio Merseyside, BBC Northwest; Owner, Stocks Records. Recordings: 16 albums include: Today: City Lights; Today; Summer Nights; Blue Rendezvous. Honours: 2 British Country Music Radio Awards, 1992; CMRU International Publishers Award, 1993; BCMA Award, Best British Male Performer, 1993; Gold Star Award, Netherlands; Best Male Vocalist, Variety Club of Great Britain; 2 MCM Awards. Memberships: Musicians' Union; PRS. Address: 54 Edward Road, Whiston, Merseyside L35 5AJ, England.

JOHNSON Laurie, b. 1927, London, England. Composer. m., 1 daughter. Education: Royal College of Music. Career: Taught at Royal College of Music; Orchestral pieces broadcast by age 20; Composer, arranger, Ted Heath Band and all major bands and orchestras of 1950s; Entered film industry, 1955; Co-owner, film production companies including Gainsborough Pictures, 1979-; Founder, The London Big Band (25 British jazz and orchestral musicians), for concerts and recordings with international star guests, 1994. Compositions include: Lock Up Your Daughters, musical; Pieces of Eight, revue; The Four Musketeers, musical; Scores for over 400 cinema and television films including: Dr Strangelove; First Men In The Moon; The Avengers; The Professionals; The New Avengers; Television themes include: This Is Your Life; World In Action; Whicker's World. Recordings: Synthesis, symphony; The Wind In The Willows, tone poem; Suite for symphonic band (RAF commission for 50th anniversary of Battle of Britain); The Conquistadors, music for Royal occasions; Numerous albums with own studio orchestra. Honours: Various awards and nominations for music scores and record or film productions. Address: The Laurie Johnson Organisation Ltd., 10 College Road, Harrow, Middlesex HA1 1DA, England.

JOHNSON Matt, b. 15 Aug 1961, East London, England. Singer; Songwriter; Musician (guitar); Record Producer. Musical Education: Self-taught. Career: Member, first band Road Star, aged 11; Recording engineer, London, aged 15, 1976; Formed The The, aged 17, 1979; The The, general music collective, over 300 artists to date (including Sinead O'Connor, Jools Holland, Johnny Marr, Neneh Cherry, Zeke Manyika, Warne Livesey), 1979-; Concerts and tours include: Residency at Marquee, London (with Marc Almond, Zeke Manyika), 1983; World tours, 1989-90, 1992-93; Royal Albert Hall, 1990; Headliners, Reading Festival, 1993. Films: Infected (long-form video to accompany album), 1987; The The Versus The World, 1991; From Dusk 'Til Dawn, 1994. Recordings: Albums: Burning Blue Soul, 1981; Soul Mining, 1983; Infected (also film and book), 1987; Mind Bomb, 1989; Dusk, 1993; Solitude, 1994; Hanky Panky, 1995; Singles include: Controversial Subject; Heartland; Infected; Sweet Bird Of Truth; Slow Train To Dawn; Armageddon Days; The Beat(en) Generation; Dogs Of Lust. Publication: Infected (lyrics and paintings), 1987. Honours include: Best Long Form Video, Montreux Film and Music Festival, Infected, 1988; Platinum, Gold or Silver records for all albums. Hobbies: Film making; Photography. Current Management: c/o Fran Musso, REN Management, 1125 Coldwater Canyon, Beverly Hills, CA 90210, USA.

JOHNSON Mike, b. 27 Aug 1965, Grant Pass, Oregon, USA. Musician (guitar, bass); Songwriter; Singer. m. Leslie, 21 Nov 1994. Education: AA. Career: Solo artiste; Basssist, Dinosaur Jnr; Cameo; Appearances in Grace Of My Heart. Recordings: Year Of Monday. Membership: BMI. Hobbies: Drinking; Smoking. Current Management: BYD Management. Address: C/o BYD, 501 N 36th #196, Seattle, WA 98103, USA.

JOHNSON Robb Jenner, 25 Dec 1955, London, England. Singer; Songwriter; Musician (guitar). m. Meeta Kanabar, 22 Aug 1992. Education: BA Hons, MA, English Literature. Career: Folk clubs, 1975-80; Band, Grubstreet, 1980-84; Agit-prop trio, Ministry Of Humour, 1984-86; Solo, then duo with Pip Collings, 1989-94; Solo: Nicaragua TV, Managua Concert for the 10th anniversary of the Revolution, 1989; CH4 documentary, Beyond The Maypole, 1991; Tour of Belgium, 1995; 25th Anniversary, Glastonbury Festival, 1995. Recordings: Albums: Skewed Stewed And Awkward, 1987; Small Town World, 1989; Overnight, 1991; Heart's Desire, 1993; Lack Of Jolly Ploughboy, 1994; This Is The UK Talking, 1994. Publications: Rosa's Lovely Daughters; I Close My Eyes; Boxing Day; Herald Of Free Enterprise. Honours: 1980 Northwest Songwriters Competition. Memberships: Musicians' Union; PRS. Hobbies: Painting; Paris. Address: c/o Rhiannon Records, Freepost LON 6347, London E8 2BR, England.

JOHNSON Stanley Glen, b. 1 Sept 1953, Hillsdale, Michigan, USA. Recording Artist; Artist Manager. m. Jacalyn Joy Ware, 29 Aug 1970, 1 son, 2 daughters. Education: Jackson Community College. Musical Education: Self-taught. Career: Radio in USA; Local church concerts and special fair programmes. Compositions: As songwriter: Hold On; There'll Be Hell To Pay; Not Guilty. Publications: The Singing News; The Gospel Voice; Gospel Music News. Honours: Editors Choice Awards; National Library Of Poetry. Membership: BMI. Hobbies: Songwriting; Poetry; Hunting; Fishing. Current Management: CER Records (USA). Address: 7400 North Adams Road, North Adams, MI 49262, USA.

JOHNSON Wilko, b. 12 July 1947, Canvey Island, Essex, England. Singer; Musician (guitar). m. Irene Knight, 6 Apr 1968, 2 sons. Education: BA Hons, English. Music Education: Self-taught. Career: Guitarist, songwriter, founder member of Dr Feelgood. Played with Ian Dury and The Blockheads, 1980-82; Extensive tours with own band, 1985-. Compositions include: Back in the Night; She Does It Right; Roxette. Recordings: Albums include: Down By the Jetty and Stupidity (with Dr Feelgood); Barbed Wire Blues; Don't Let Your Daddy Know. Memberships: MCPS; PRS. Hobbies: Reading; Astronomy. Current Management: Irene Knight.

JOHNSON Yana, b. 23 Sept 1969, England. Singer; Songwriter. Education: BSc Environmental Control. Musical Education: Grade 1 Classical. Career: Writer, scripts and song material for theatrical productions; Backing vocalist, 291 Talent Show; Worked with Total Contrast; Session work with artists including: Massive Attack; Nenah Cherry; Raw Stylus; Cold Cut; UK Tour with Drizabone. Recordings: Songs: I Do, Total Contrast (on compilation album Full Swing); Believe, Cold Cut; Writer, producer, demo material, I've Found You, Troi. Membership: Musicians' Union. Hobbies: Travel; Fashion; Songwriting; Backing vocals.

JOHNSTON Jim, b. 20 December 1954, Dundalk, Ireland. m. Patricia, 19 June 1981, 1 son, 2 daughters. Education: Primary, Secondary, Teaching Diploma, Saint Patrick's Training College, Drumcondra, Dublin; Tuition in Drums, CCE Dundalk, Fiddle by Mrs Rose O'Connor; Self taught Guitar Harmonica; Matthews School of Irish Dancing. Career: Songwriter & Dancer, Copenhagen Irish Music Festival, 1996; Appeared on RTE TV Live at 3, 1997; Toured Austria with Lá Lugh trad band, 1995; Played support to Don Baker, 1995, Mary Coughlan, 1994, Mick Hanly, 1994, Sonny Condell, 1995, Freddie White, 1996. Compositions: Victory or Defeat; Squeeze Gut Alley Blues; Fairhill-Time Stood Still; It's the Same Sun; The Paragon Seven, 1993. Recordings: The Factories - They're All Closing Down, 1986; Rian An Uaignis, 1993, CD Version, 1996. Publications:

Pléaráca Dhún Dealgan/The Humours of Dundalk - Collection of Folk Songs, 1985. Honours: Men's World Irish Dancing Champion, 1975, 1977, 1979. Membership: Irish Music Rights Organization. Hobbies: Fishing; Reading. Current Management: UAIGNEAS Music. Address: 8 Radharc An Léana (Meadowview), Avondale Park, Dundalk, Co Louth, Ireland.

JOHNSTON Timothy John, b. 12 Nov 1963, Newcastle-Upn-Tyne, England. Musician (drums). Musical Education: 1 year light music course, Newcastle College. Career: Toured extensively with Pauline Murray and The Storm, including full tour supporting The Mission, 1985-; Television and radio appearances with The Light Programme and Swing Palace, 1987-94; Regular appearances at national jazz festivals. Recordings: 2 albums with The Light Programme, 1987, 1989; Album Storm Clouds, 1988; and 2 singles, This Thing Called Love and New Age, with Pauline Murray; 2 albums with Swing Palace, 1991, 1993. Membership: Musicians' Union. Hobbies: Football; Playing guitar. Address: 29 Bolbec Road, Newcastle-upon-Tyne NE4 9EP, England.

JONASSON Jonas, b. 28 August 1967, Angelholm, Sweden. Musician (synthesizer, voloper, melodica). m. Malin Jonasson-Sahlstedt, 16 May 1992, 2 daughters. Education: Selftaught on synthesizer. Career: Member, bob hund, formed in 1991; More than 250 gigs around Scandinavia; Played at famous Roskilde, Lollipop, Ruisrock, Quartfestivalen and Hultsfred. Compositions: I Stället för Musik: Förvirring, 1996; Düsseldorf, 1996. Recordings: bob hund - bob hund, 1993; bob hund - Edvin Medvind, 1994; bob hund - Omslag: Martin Kann, 1996. Publication: Bob Hund - Omslag: Martin Kann, 1996. Honours: Grammy, best live act, 1994; Grammy, best lyrics, 1996. Memberships: STIM; SAMI. Hobbies: Music; Books; Food; Drinking. Address: Box 53045, 400 14, Göteborg, Sweden.

JONES Andy, b. 28 June 1965, Knaphill, England. Musician (guitars, synthesizers, sampling); Producer; Songwriter. Education: BA (Hons), Politics, French Language. Musical Education: Private tuition, most styles of guitar playing. Career: Guitar teacher (private and schools), 1988-; Member, various bands; 6 months nightclub residency; 6 months on cruise ship and gigs for various corps, including BBC; Currently in Cut A Little Life and local radio play received. Recordings: 4 titles published 1992; album featuring songs: Cut A Little Life; Under The Sun; Taste Of Honey; The Veil, 1995; Producer, various artists/writers in private studio. Membership: Musicians' Union. Hobbies: Travel; Dining Out; Shows and concerts; Working with new talent. Current Management: Self-managed. Address: Buttnidge, Odiham, Hants RG29 1JA, England.

JONES Booker T, b. 12 Nov 1944, Memphis, Tennessee, USA. Musician (keyboards); Songwriter; Record Producer. m. Priscilla Coolidge. Career: Session musician, Memphis; Leader, Booker T & The MGs (Memphis Group), 1962-71; Concerts include: Soul Sensation UK Tour, 1967; Monterey Pop Festival, 1967; Solo songwriter and vocalist, 1971-; Reunions with the MGs: Album, 1977; Tours of Europe, US, 1990; Backing band for Neil Young's UK tour, 1993. Compositions include: Film score, Up Tight, 1969; Songwriter, musician with Sam And Dave; Wilson Pickett; Otis Redding; Rufus Thomas. Recordings: Albums: with the MGs: Green Onions, 1964; Hip Hug-Her, 1967; Back To Back, 1967; Doin' Our Thing, 1968; Soul Limbo, 1968; Best Of..., 1968; The Booker T Set, 1969; McLemore Avenue, 1970; Greatest Hits, 1970; Melting Pot, 1971; Union Extended, 1976; Universal Language, 1977; As producer: Stardust, Willie Nelson, 1978; Singles include: Green Onions, 1962 (included in film soundtrack Quadrophenia); Boot-Leg, 1965; Hip Hug-Her, 1967; Groovin', 1967; Soul Limbo,

1968; Hang 'Em High, used as film theme, 1969; Time Is Tight, from film Up Tight, 1969; Melting Pot, 1971. Honours: Rock And Roll Hall Of Fame, Booker T and the MGs, 1992. Address: c/o Concerted Efforts, PO Box 99, Newtonville, MA 02169, USA.

JONES Chris Alan, b. 18 Dec 1966, Reading, England. Musician (drums, percussion). Musical Education: Drum lessons, 1993-. Career: Drummer, Mega City Four, 1987-; 6 albums; Major world tours with each release; Appeared on: Chart Show; The Word; MTV 120 Minutes; Recorded 2 sessions, John Peel Show. Recordings: with Mega City Four: Tranzophobia, 1989; Who Cares Wins, 1990; Terribly Sorry Bob, 1990; Sebastopol Road, 1992; Magic Bullets, 1993; 2 sessions, John Peel Show, album, 1994. Publications: Tall Stories And Creepy Crawlies, by Martin Roach. Membership: Musicians' Union. Hobbies: Teaching drums; Martial arts. Current Management: Paul Bolton: ICM/Fair Warning. Address: 5 Rother Road, Cove, Farnborough, Hampshire GU14 9LP, England.

JONES Davy, b. 30 Dec 1945, Manchester, Lancashire, England. Singer; Actor; Musician (guitar). Career: Member, The Monkees, 1966-70; 1986-89; Actor, The Monkees comedy television series, 1966-68; 33 1/3 Revolutions Per Monkee, TV Special, NBC; Television actor in: June Evening; Coronation Street; Z-Cars; Ben Casey; Farmers Daughter; Trainer; Stage performances include: Oliver; Pickwick; The Point; Founder, Davy Jones Presents record label, 1967; Owner, Zilch Boutique, 1967; Member, Dolenz, Jones, Boyce And Hart, 1975-76. Recordings: Albums: The Monkees (Number 1, US and UK), 1966; More Of The Monkees (Number 1, US and UK), 1967; Headquarters, (Number 1, US), 1967; Pisces, Aquarius, Capricorn and Jones Ltd, 1967; The Birds, The Bees And The Monkees, 1968; Head (soundtrack), 1969; The Monkees Greatest Hits, 1969; The Monkees Present, 1969; Instant Replay, 1969; Then And Now, 1986; Pool It, 1987; Singles; Last Train To Clarksville (Number 1, US), 1966; I'm A Believer (Number 1, US), 1966; (I'm Not Your) Steppin' Stone, 1967; A Little Bit Me, A Little Bit You, 1967; Alternate Title, 1967; Pleasant Valley Sunday, 1967; Daydream Believer (Number 1, US), 1967; Valleri, 1968; Tear Drop City, 1969. Honours: NARM Awards, Best Selling Group, Best Album, 1967; Emmy Award, Outstanding Comedy Series, 1967; 3 BMI Awards, 1968; Monkees Day, Atlanta, 1986; Star on Hollywood Walk Of Fame, 1989. Hobby: Horse-racing. Address: c/o Nationwide Entertainment Services, 2756 North Green Valley Parkway, Suite 449, Las Vegas, NV 89014-2100, USA.

JONES Ed (Edgar Francis), b. 8 July 1961, Amersham, Buckinghamshire, England. Musician (saxophone); Composer. Musical Education: BA Music, Middlesex University. Career: Worldwide tours, television and radio with US3; Incognito; Ed Jones Quartet/Quintet; Teevision appearances include: MTV; CNN; Stations in USA; Europe; Japan; Far East. Recordings: Solo: The Home Coming, 1989; Pipers Tales, 1995; Featured on compilations: Mellow Mahem, 1988; Talkin' Land II, 1993; Bachology, 1995; Other recordings include: Hand On The Torch, US3, 1993; Where One Is, Dick Heckstall-Smith, 1989; New Cool, John Stevens, 1994; Sound Advice, Ron Wallen, 1993; Siren Song, Jessica Lauron, 1994; 100% And Rising, Incognito. Memberships: PRS; MCPS; Musicians' Union. Hobbies: Cooking; The countryside; Literature. Address: Flat C, University House, 16 Victoria Park Square, London E2 9PE, England.

JONES George Glenn, b. 12 Sept 1931, Saratoga, Texas, USA. Country Singer; Musician (guitar). m. Tammy Wynette, 1969-75; Nancy Sepulveda, 1983. Career: Recording artist, 1953-; Worked under names of Johnny Williams, Hank Davis, Glen Patterson; Worked with The Big Bopper; Johnny Preston; Johnny Paycheck;

Recorded duets with Gene Pitney; Melba Montgomery; Tammy Wynette; Elvis Costello; James Taylor; Willie Nelson. Compositions include: The Window Up Above, Mickey Gilley; Seasons Of My Heart, Johnny Cash, Jerry Lee Lewis. Recordings: 150 Country hits include: Why Baby Why; White Lightning; Tender Years; She Still Thinks I Care; You Comb Her Hair; Who Shot Sam?; The Grand Tour; He Stopped Loving Her Today; Recorded over 450 albums; Recent albums include: First Time Live, 1985; Who's Gonna Fill Thier Shoes, 1985; Wine Coloured Roses, 1986; Super Hits, 1987; Too Wild Too Long, 1987; One Woman Man, 1989; Hallelujah Weekend, 1990; You Oughta Be Here With Me, 1990; And Along Came Jones, 1991; Friends In High Places, 1991; Salutes Bob Wills and Hank Williams, 1992; Live At Dancetown USA, 1992; Walls Can Fall, 1992; One; with Tammy Wynette: We Can Go Together, 1971; Me And The First Lady, 1972; Golden Ring, 1976; Together Again, 1980; One, 1995. Address: c/o Nancy Jones, Jones Country, 48 Music Square East, Nashville, TN 37203, USA.

JONES Gordon Thomas, b. 21 Nov 1947, Birkenhead, Merseyside, England. Musician (guitar); Record Company Executive. m. Jackie Jones, 26 May 1984, 1 son. Education: Art College, Edinburgh, Scotland. Career: Founder, Scottish folk band Silly Wizard, recording 9 albums; Founder, partner, Harbourtown Records, producing 36 albums to date including 2 MRA award winners; Toured Europe and USA over 17 years. Recordings: All Silly Wizard albums; Produced most Harbourtown Productions. Honours: 2 MRS Awards as producer; Naird Award as musician, 1986. Memberships include: MCPS; PRS; PPC. Address: PO Box 25, Ulverston, Cumbria LA12 7UN, England.

JONES Grace. Vocalist; Composer; Actress. Career: Film appearances include: Gordon's War; A View To Kill. Recordings: Albums: Portfolio, 1977; Fame, 1978; Music, 1979; Warm Leatherette, 1980; Night Clubbing, 1981; Living My Life, 1982; Island Life, 1985; Slave To The Rhythm, 1985; Inside Story, 1986; Bulletproof Heart, 1990; Singles include: I'm Not Perfect; Love Is A Drug; My Jamaican Guy; Private Life; Pull Up To The Bumper; Slave To The Rhythm. Current Management: Pyramid Entertainment Group (US), 89 5th Avenue, 7th Floor, New York, NY 10003, USA.

JONES Grandpa (Louis Marshall), b. 20 Oct 1913, Niagara, Kentucky, USA. Country Musician (guitar, banjo). m. Ramona Riggins. Career: Radio work: Lum and Abner Show; Boone County Jamboree; Regular performer, Grand Ole Opry, Nashville, 1947; Television includes: Hee-Haw, CBS TV, 1969-; Recordings: Albums: Grandpa Jones Sings His Greatest Hits, 1958; Strictly Country Tunes, 1959; ...Makes The Rafters Ring, 1962; Do You Remember (When Grandpa Jones Sang These Songs), 1963; An Evening With Grandpa Jones, 1963; Yodeling Hits, 1963; Rolling Along With Grandpa Jones, 1963; ...Sings Real Folk Songs, 1964; Other Side Of Grandpa Jones (At Home/On Stage), 1964; ...Remembers The Brown's Ferry Four, 1966; Everybody's Grandpa, 1968; Living Legend Of Country Music, 1969; ...Sings Songs From Hee Haw, 1969; Grandpa Jones Live, 1970; What's For Supper?, 1974; The Grandpa Jones Story (with Ramona Jones and The Brown's Ferry Four), 1976; Old Time Country Music Collection (with Ramona Jones), 1978; Grandpa Jones' Family Album, (with Ramona and their 4 children), 1979; Family Gathering, 1981; The Hee-Haw Gospel Quartet (with Roy Clark, Buck Owens, Kenny Price), 1981; with Brown's Ferry Four: Sacred Songs, 1957; Sacred Songs Volume 2, 1958; 16 Sacred Gospel Songs, 1963; Wonderful Sacred Songs, 1965; Singles include: The All-American Boy; T For Texas. Honour: Inducted into Country Music Hall Of Fame, 1978.

Address: PO Box 916, Hendersonville, TN 37077, USA.

JONES (John) Howard, b. 23 Feb 1955, Southampton, Hampshire, England. Songwriter; Singer; Musician (keyboards, computer); Record Producer. m. Janet Lesley Smith, 25 Oct 1978. Musical Education: Royal Northern College of Music, Manchester. Career: Piano teacher; Solo recording artiste, 1983-; Tours include: US tour, support to Eurythmics, 1984; UK tour, 1984; Live Aid, Wembley Stadium, 1985; Tour, North America, 1992. Recordings: Albums: Human's Lib, 1984; The Twelve Inch Album, 1984; Dream Into Action, 1985; Action Replay, 1986; One To One, 1986; Cross That Line, 1989; The Best Of Howard Jones, 1993; In The Running; Greatest Hits; Working In The Backroom; Live Acoustic America; Angels And Lovers; Singles include: New Song (Number 3, UK), 1983; What Is Love (Number 2, UK), 1984; Hide And Seek, 1984; Pearl In The Shell, 1984; Like To Get To Know You Well, 1984; Things Can Only Get Better, 1985; Look Mama, 1985; Life In One Day, 1985; No One Is To Blame, 1986; All I Want, 1986; You Know I Love You... Don't You?, 1986; Everlasting Love, 1987; The Prisoner, 1989; Lift Me Up, 1992; Contributor, Live-in World (Anti-Heroin Project charity album), 1986; Rubáiyát (Elektra's 40th Anniversary album), 1990. Memberships: ASCAP; PRS. Hobby: Watching Formula One motor racing. Current Management: David Stopps, Friars Management. Address: 33 Alexander Road, Aylesbury, Bucks HP20 2NR, England.

JONES Jack (John Allen Jones), b. 14 Jan 1938, Los Angeles, California, USA. Singer; Actor. Musical Education: Studied singing at high school. Career: Club singer, 1957; Recording artiste, 1962-; Appearances with Jerry Lewis; Bob Hope; Actor, television: The Palace; Funny Face; Love Boat; Condominium; The Comeback; Film appearance: Juke Box Rhythm; Stage performance, Guys And Dolls, US, 1991; Regular concert tours, US and UK. Recordings: Albums include: Call Me Irresponsible, 1963; Wives And Lovers, 1963; Bewitched, 1964; Dear Heart, 1965; My Kind Of Town, 1965; There's Love And There's Love And There's Love, 1965; For The In Crowd, 1966; The Impossible Dream, 1966; Jack Jones Sings, 1966; Lady, 1967; Our Song, 1967; Without Her, 1967; If You Ever Leave Me, 1968; Where Is Love, 1968; A Time For Us, 1969; A Song For You, 1972; Breadwinners, 1972; Together, 1973; Write Me A Love Song Charlie, 1974; Harbour, 1974; The Full Life, 1977; All To Yourself, 1977; I've Been Here All The Time, 1980; Numerous compilations; Hit songs include: Lollipops And Roses, 1961; Wives And Lovers, 1963; Call Me Irresponsible, 1963; The Impossible Dream, 1966; Film music includes: A Ticklish Affair, 1963; Where Love Has Gone, 1964; Love With A Proper Stranger, 1964; Kotch, 1967. Honours: Grammy Awards: Lollipops And Roses, 1962; Wives And Lovers, 1964; Cash Box Award, Most Promising Vocalist, 1962, 1963; Golden Globe Award, film theme for Kotch, 1967. Current Management: Roy Gerber And Associates, 515 N Rexford Drive, Beverly Hills, CA 90210, USA.

JONES John Paul (John Baldwin), b. 3 June 1946, Sidcup, Kent, England. Musician (bass); Producer; Arranger; Composer. Career: Member, UK rock group Led Zeppelin, 1968-80; Also reunion concerts, Live Aid, Philadelphia, 1985; Atlantic's 40th Anniversary concert, Madison Square Gardens, 1988; Producer; Arranger; Session musician; Film score composer; Performances include: Bath Festival, 1969, 1970; Newport Jazz And Blues Festival, 1969; Montreux Jazz Festival, Switzerland, 1970; Madison Square Garden, 1970; Earls Court, 1975; Knebworth Fair, 1979; UNICEF Rock For Kampuchea, 1979; Film appearance, The Song Remains The Same, 1976; Producer for acts including: Butthole Surfers; Stefan Grossman; Ben E King; The Mission; John Renbourn; Arranger for artists including: REM;

Raging Slab. Recordings: Albums: with Led Zeppelin: Led Zeppelin, 1969; Led Zeppelin II (Number 1, US), 1969; Led Zeppelin III (Number 1, US), 1970; Four Symbols (Number 1, UK), 1971; Houses Of The Holy (Number 1, UK), 1973; Physical Graffitti (Number 1, US), 1975; Presence (Number 1, US), 1976; The Song Remains The Same (Number 1, UK), 1976; In Through The Out Door (Number 1, UK) 1979; Contributor to Comin' Atcha, Madeleine Bell, 1973; Singles include: Whole Lotta Love, 1970; Immigrant Song, 1971; Black Dog, 1972; Rock And Roll, 1972. Honours include: Ivor Novello, Outstanding Contribution To British Music, 1977. Current Management: c/o Hip Music Group, 326 N Western Avenue, Suite 150, Los Angeles, CA 90004, USA.

JONES Mick, b. 26 June 1955, Brixton, London, England. Musician (guitar); Record Producer. Career: Guitarist, punk group London SS, 1975; Founder, UK punk group The Clash, 1976-1983; Concerts include: Support to Sex Pistols, Anarchy In The UK tour, 1976; White Riot UK tour, with the Jam, the Buzzcocks, 1977; European Punk Festival, France, 1978; Benefit concert for people of Kampuchea, London (co-headliners with Ian Dury), 1979; Jamaican World Music Festival, 1982; Lochem Festival, Netherlands, 1982; Support to the Who, farewell US tour, 1982; US '83 Festival, 1983; Founder member, Big Audio Dynamite, 1984-90; Later billed as BAD II, then Big Audio; Concerts include: Support to U2, European tour, 1987. Recordings: Singles include: with the Clash: Clash City Rockers, 1978; Tommy Gun, 1979; English Civil War, 1979; I Fought The Law, 1979; London Calling, 1980; Train In Vain (Stand By Me), 1980; Bankrobber, 1980; Know Your Rights, 1982; Rock The Casbah, 1982; Should I Stay Or Should I Go?, 1982; with Big Audio Dynamite: E=MC², 1986; Medicine Show, 1986; Good Morning Britain (co-written with Roddy Frame), 1990; Albums: with The Clash: The Clash, 1977; Give 'Em Enough Rope, 1978; London Calling, 1979; Black Market Clash, 1980; Sandanista!, 1980; Combat Rock, 1982; with Big Audio Dynamite: This Is Big Audio Dynamite, 1986; No. 10 Upping Street, 1986; Tighten Up Vol. '88, 1988; Megatop Phoenix, 1989; Kool Aid, 1990; The Globe, 1991; Higher Power, 1994; F-Punk, 1995; As producer: Spirit Of St Louis, Ellen Foley, 1980; Short Back'n'Sides, Ian Hunter, 1981. Current Management: Overland Productions, 156 W 56th Street, 5th Floor, New York, NY 10019, USA.

JONES Mick, b. 27 Dec 1944, London, England. Musician (guitar); Songwriter; Record Producer. m. Ann. Career: Musician with: Nero and The Gladiators; Johnny Hallyday; Spooky Tooth; Leslie West; Also worked with Otis Redding; Jimi Hendrix; Jimmy Page; Founder member, rock group Foreigner, 1976-; Worldwide appearances include: California Jam II, 1978; Headliners, Reading Festival, 1979; North American tour, 1982; American tour, 1991; New York State Fair, 1994; World Tour, 1994-95; American Tour, 1996. Compositions: Bad Love, recorded by Eric Clapton; Street Thunder, 1984 Olympic Marathon Theme; Numerous tracks for Foreigner, including: Feels Like The First Time; I Want to Know What Love Is; I Don't Want to Live Without You; Dirty White Boy; Waiting For A Girl Like You; That Was Yesterday; Recordings: Albums with Foreigner: Foreigner, 1977; Head Games, 1979; 4 (Number 1, US), 1981; Records, 1982; Agent Provocateur (Number 1, UK), 1985; Inside Information, 1988; Unusual Heat, 1991; The Very Best Of, 1992; The Very Best... And Beyond, 1992; Mr Moonlight, 1994; Solo album: Mick Jones, 1989; As producer: 5150, Van Halen, 1986; Fame and Fortune, Bad Company, 1986; Stormfront, Billy Joel, 1989; In Deep, Tina Arena, 1997; Singles with Foreigner include: Feels Like The First Time, 1977; Cold As Ice, 1977; Long Long Way From Home, 1978; Hot Blooded, 1978; Double Vision, 1978; Blue Morning Blue Day, 1979; Dirty White Boy, 1979; Head

Games, 1979; Urgent, 1981; Juke Box Hero, 1981; Waiting For A Girl Like You, 1982; I Want To Know What Love Is (Number 1, UK), 1985; That Was Yesterday, 1985; I Don't Want To Live Without You, 1988. Honour: Grammy Award, Bad Love, 1989. Current Management: Somerset Songs Publishing Inc, 214 East 70th Street, New York, NY 10021, USA.

JONES Mickey Wayne, b. 10 June 1941, Houston, Texas, USA. Actor; Musician (drums). m. (1) Sandra Davis, 1976; (2) Phyllis Star, 7 June 1980, 1 son, 1 daughter. Education: North Texas State College, 1959-62. Career: Drummer for Trini Lopez, 1957-64; Johnny Rivers, 1964-66; Bob Dylan, 1966-67; Kenny Rogers, 1967-76; Actor, 1976-; Film appearances include: Starman; National Lampoon's Vacation; Stir Crazy; Nadine; The Couch Trip; Television appearances include: V; Mash; The Incredible Hulk; The Colbys; T J Hooker; Numerous other guest roles, commercials, theatre. Albums include: with Trini Lopez: Live At P J's; with Bob Dylan: Blonde On Blonde; with Johnny Rivers: Last Boogie In Paris; Also for Jan and Dean, Kenny Rogers; Singles include: with Johnny Rivers: Maybelline; Mountain Of Love; Secret Agent Man; with Kenny Rogers and The First Edition: Just Dropped In To See What Condition My Condition Was In; Ruby, Don't Take Your Love To Town. Memberships: AFTRA; Screen Actors Guild; AFofM; AGVA; Screen Extras Guild. Hobby: Golf.

JONES Nigel Mazlyn, b. 26 June 1950, Dudley, West Midlands, England. Performer; Songwriter; Musician (acoustic guitar, santor). m. Lynn Coralie Eyers, 15 Apr 1978, divorced 17 Nov 1988, 1 son, 1 daughter. Career: Professional performer, 1975-; Toured folk clubs, colleges; Special guest to Judy Tzuke, Renaissance, national tours; Special guest, Euro Major venue circuit with Barclay James Harvest, 1980; Also, Eurorock circuit, 1984; Glastonbury Festival, 1990; Featured solo on BBC documentary, Festival; Bob Geldof UK tour, 1993; Music used on TV landscape films. Recordings: Albums: Ship To Shore, 1976; Sentinel, 1979; Breaking Cover, 1981; Water From The Well, 1987; Video album: Beyond This Point, 1988; Mazlyn Jones, 1991; Angels Over Water, 1993. Memberships: Musicians' Union; PRS; MCPS. Hobbies: Cliff walking; Sky gazing; Water renovation (wells/springs). Current Management: Isle Of Light. Address: PO Box 1, Polzeath, Cornwall PL32 9RP, England.

JONES Paul, b. 24 Feb 1942, Portsmouth, Hampshire, England. Singer; Musician (harmonica); Composer; Actor; Broadcaster. m. Fiona Hendley, 16 Dec 1984, 2 sons (previous marriage). Education: Edinburgh Academy; Jesus College, Oxford. Musical Education: Cathedral Choir; Self-taught. Career: Lead singer, harmonica player with Manfred Mann; Television includes: Thank Your Lucky Stars; Top Of The Pops; Ready Steady Go; Solo tours of UK, Australia, New Zealand and Europe, 1966-; Theatre: Conduct Unbecoming, London & New York; The Beggar's Opera; Guys and Dolls, National Theatre; Kiss Me Kate, Royal Shakespeare Company; Vocalist, harmonica player with Blues Band, 1979-; Actor, films and television; TV presenter; Radio: Radio 2 Rhythm & Blues, 1985-; JFM radio, 1990-. Compositions include: 54321 (Theme for Ready Steady Go); Songs recorded by: Brian Poole & The Tremeloes; Helen Shapiro; Eric Clapton; Ten Years After. TV and film scores: Intimate Reflections; Fighting Back; The Wednesday Play. Recordings: All Manfred Mann albums to 1966; Blues Band albums include: Bootleg; Ready; Itchy Feet. Publications: Contributions to The Independent on Sunday; Sight and Sound; Tribune. Honours: British Blues Connection, Male Singer, 1990, 1991; Scroll of Honour, 1993. Memberships: Musicians' Union; BACSA; Equity; Hobbies: Reading; Walking; Theatre. Current Management: Chatto and Linnit. Address: c/o

Chatto and Linnit, Prince of Wales Theatre, Coventry Street, London W1V 7FE, England.

JONES Quincy, b. 14 Mar 1933, Chicago, Illinois, USA. Record Producer; Composer; Arranger; Musician (trumpet); Conductor. 5 children. Education: Seattle University. Musical Education: Berklee College Of Music; Boston Conservatory. Career: Trumpeter, arranger, Lionel Hampton Orchestra, 1950-53; Arranger for various singers, orchestra leaders include: Count Basie; Frank Sinatra; Peggy Lee; Dinah Washington; Sarah Vaughn; Trumpeter, Dizzy Gillespie, 1956; Leader, own orchestra, concerts, television appearances, 1960-; Music Director, Mercury Records, 1961; Vice President, 1964. Recordings: Solo albums include: You've Got It Bad Girl, 1973; Walking In Space, 1974; Body Heat, 1974; Mellow Madness, 1975; I Heard That!, 1976; Quintessence, 1977; Sounds And Stuff Like That, 1978; The Dude, 1981; Bossa Nova, 1983; The Q, 1984; Back On The Block, 1989; Producer, video Portrait Of An Album, 1986; Q's Jook Joint, 1995; Music, television series Fresh Prince Of Bel Air, 1990-; Guest musician, albums: with George Benson: Shape Of Things To Come, 1976; Give Me The Night, 1980; with James Ingram: It's Your Night, 1983; Never Felt So Good, 1986; with Michael Jackson: Thriller, 1982; Bad, 1987; Conductor, film music includes: In The Heat Of The Night, 1967; The Slender Thread, 1968; McKenna's Gold, 1968; For The Love Of Ivy, 1968; Banning, 1967; The Split, 1968; Bob And Carol And Ted And Alice, 1969; The Out-Of-Towners, 1970; The Anderson Tapes, 1971; The Hot Rock, 1972; The New Centurions, 1972; The Getaway, 1972; The Wiz, 1978; The Color Purple, 1985. Honours include: Golden Note, ASCAP, 1982; Hon degree, Berklee College, 1983; Over 20 Grammy Awards; Lifetime Achievement, National Academy of Songwriters, 1989; ASMAC Golden Score Award. Address: c/o Quincy Jones Productions, 3800 Barham Blvd #503, Los Angeles, CA 90067, USA.

JONES Rickie Lee, b. 8 Nov 1954, Chicago, Illinois, USA. Singer; Songwriter. Career: Signed to Warner Brothers (after own composition recorded by Loweel George on his album, Thanks I'll Eat Here), 1977; US tour, 1979; Appearance, Saturday Night Live, 1979; Jam session with Bruce Springsteen and Boz Scaggs at Whiskey A Go-Go club, Los Angeles, 1979; Major tour, includes Carnegie Hall, 1979; Singer of ballad for film: King Of Comedy, 1983; The Magazine tour, 1984; Tours, Australia, Europe, UK, Eastern bloc concerts, 1985; Saturday Night Live, NBC TV, 1989; 2 US tours, 1990; Bread And Roses benefit, San Francisco, 1991; US tour, 1991; Appearances at Wiltern Theatre, Los Angeles, 1992; Dominion Theatre, Royal Festiival Hall, London, 1992; The Tonight Show, 1993. Compositions include: Easy Money; The Last Chance; Texaco; Chuck E's In Love (platinum hit record), 1979. Recordings: Albums: Rickie Lee Jones, 1979; Pirates, 1981; Girl At Her Volcano, 1983; The Magazine, 1984; Flying Cowboys, 1989; Pop Pop, 1991; Traffic From Paradise, 1993; Naked Song, 1995; Features on: Duets, Rob Wasserman, 1989; The Bells Of Dublin, The Chieftains, 1991; Joshua Judges Ruth, Lyle Lovett, 1992. Honours: Grammy: Best New Artist, 1979; Rolling Stone Awards, 1979, 1981; Grammy: Best Jazz Vocal Performance, Duo or Group, 1990. Current Management: Gold Mountain Entertainment, Suite 450, 3575 Cahuenga Blvd. W, Los Angeles, CA 90068, USA.

JONES Simeon, b. 10 Mar 1964, London, England. Musician (saxophone, flute, harmonica). 2 sons. Education: BSc English. Career: Tours, television with various name acts including: Gary Glitter; Take That; Bad Manners; Geno Washington; Otis Grand. Recordings: With acts including: Gary Glitter; Take That; Tom Jones; Edwyn Collins; Black; Sam Brown; Shampoo.

Membership; MU. Address: 105 Taybridge Road, London SW11 5PX, England.

JONES Steve, b. 3 May 1955, London, England. Musician (guitar). Career: Guitarist, UK punk group, The Sex Pistols, 1975-78; Performances include: First gig, St Martins School Of Art, London, 1975; Screen On The Green Midnight Special, London, 1976; 100 Club punk rock festival, 1976; Anarchy In The UK Tour, 1976; Tours: Europe, 1977; US, 1978; Winterland Ballroom, San Francisco, 1978; Film: The Great Rock'n'Roll Swindle, 1979; Reunion concert, 1996. Recordings: Albums: Never Mind The Bollocks - Here's The Sex Pistols, 1979; The Great Rock'n'Roll Swindle, 1979; Some Product - Carri On Sex Pistols, 1979; Flogging A Dead Horse, 1980; Kiss This, 1992; Singles: God Save The Queen, 1977; Pretty Vacant, 1977; Holidays In The Sun, 1977; No One Is Innocent (A Punk Prayer By Ronnie Biggs), 1978; Something Else, 1979; Silly Thing, 1978; C'mon Everybody, 1979; The Great Rock'n'Roll Swindle, 1979. Address: c/o Eclipse Entertainment, 100 Wilshire Blvd, Ste 1830, Santa Monica, CA 90028, USA.

JONES Steven Gordon, b. 25 Feb 1966. Musician (drums, percussion). Musical Education: 2 years drum tuition with Roy Bartlett. Career: Member, 60s soul group The Elevators, 5 years; Appeared on stage with group Masque, in Search For A Star; Cabaret backing with Billy Pearce; 1 year with Coventry Youth Jazz Orchestra; Studio work. Honours: Sound engineering with Right Sounds under Barllon Right. Membership: Musicians' Union. Hobbies: Swimming; Model making; Reading; Television; Video. Address: 84 Monks Road, Binley Woods, Coventry CV3 2BY, England.

JONES Tom (Thomas Jones Woodward), b. 7 June 1940, Pontypridd, Wales. Entertainer. m. Melinda Trenchard, 1956, 1 son. Career: Former bricklayer, factory worker, construction worker; Singing debut, aged 3, later sang in clubs, dance halls, with self-formed group The Playboys; Became Tom Jones, 1963; First hit record It's Not Unusual, 1964; Appeared on radio, television; Toured US, 1965; Television show, This Is Tom Jones, 1969-71; Many international hits, albums in Top 10 charts, Europe, USA; Over 30 million discs sold by 1970; Toured continuously, television appearances, 1970s-; Score, musical play Matador; Hit single: A Boy From Nowhere, 1987; Frequent Amnesty International; Simple Truth, 1991; Rainforest Foundation, 1993; Shelter, 1993; Television series: The Right Time, 1992; Glastonbury Festival of Contemporary Performing Arts, 1992; Live stage appearance, Under Milk Wood, Prince's Trust, 1992. Recordings: Hits include: It's Not Unusual, 1964; What's New Pussycat, 1965; Thunderball, 1966; Green Green Grass Of Home, 1966; Delilah, 1968; Love Me Tonight, 1969; Can't Stop Loving You; She's A Lady; Letter To Lucille, 1973; Say You Stay Until Tomorrow, 1976; A Boy From Nowhwere, 1987; It's Not Unusual (reissue), 1987; If I Only Knew, 1994. Albums include: Green Green Grass Of Home, 1967; Delilah, 1968; This Is Tom Jones, 1969; Tom, 1970; I Who Have Nothing, 1970; Close Up, 1972; The Body and Soul Of TJ, 1973; I'm Coming Home, 1978; At This Moment, 1989; After Dark, 1989; The Lead And How To Swing It, 1994. Memberships: SAG; AFTRA: AGVA. Hobbies: Music; History. Current Management: William Morris Agency; Manager: Mark Woodward. Address: Tom Jones Enterprises, 10100 Santa Monica Blvd, Ste 205, Los Angeles, CA 90067, USA.

JONES Tommy, b. 5 Oct 1926, Liverpool, England. Musician (drums); Bandleader; Musical Director. m. Kathy Knight (vocalist), 26 Apr 1954, 3 sons, 1 daughter. Education: College of North East London; Ceddo Film and Television School. Musical Education: Max Abrams (noted drum tutor); Trinity College of Music; London College of

Music. Career: Played, concerts, clubs, broadcasts with bands including: Pete Pitterson Quintet; Cab Quaye Trio; Dill Jones Trio; Jack Butler (US) Band; Leslie "Jiver" Hutchinson Band; Bertie King Band; Dave (Jazz FM) Lee Trio; Tubby Hayes Band; Jimmy Deucher All-Stars; Acker Bilk Band; Major Holly and Rose Murphy (US); Bruce Turner Band; Hutchinson/Henderson Band; Humphrey Lyttleton Band; Mike McKenzie Trio; Joe Harriot Quintet; Shake Keane Quintet; Sliderulers; Tommy Jones Trio; Tommy Eytle Trio; Just Jazz, 1950-; Venues include: Royal Festival Hall, 1953, 1954, 1956; Edinburgh Festival of Jazz, 1958; Les Ambassadeurs Club, 1960; Residency, Lunchtime Jazz, Bishopsgate, 1961; Bix's Club, San Francisco, 1989; Hollywood Savoy Restaurant, Paris, 1990; Films: Blood Orange, 1951; Rough And The Smooth, 1958; Phoenix, 1979; Television includes: TV Series, Crane, 1956; 6.5 Special, BBCTV, 1958; Episode, Danger Man, 1958; Producer, director, Cable Jazz, Cable London TV, 1992; House of Elliott, 1991. Radio includes: Carribean Carnival series, 1955; BBC Jazz Club, 1956, 1958, 1960; Commercial, Smiths Crisps, 1993; Musical Director, Clark Brothers' (US) Dancers, 1966-68. Recordings: Jazz At Club Basie, 1956; In My Condition, Shake Keane Quintet, 1960; With Shake Keane Quintet, 1961. Membership: Musicians' Union. Hobbies: Film and TV Production. Current Management: Ed Jones. Address: 11 Albany Road, London N4 4RR, England.

JONES Wizz, b. 25 Apr 1939, Croydon, Surrey, England. Musician (acoustic guitar); Singer. m. Sandy, 14 Sept 1963, 3 sons, 1 daughter. Career: Began as itinerant busking skiffle/folk singer, late 1950s; Formed bluegrass duo with banjo-picker Pete Stanley, recorded single, album, played Folk Club and College circuit, 1960s; Solo artiste, 1967-; Collaborated with songwriter Alan Tunbridge, guitarist Peter Berryman; Played in group Lazy Farmer with wife Sandy; Appears festivals, tours of acoustic folk and blues circuit, 1990s. Recordings: 11 albums include: The Grapes Of Life, 1988; The Village Thing Tapes, 1993; Late Nights And Long Days (with saxophonist son Simeon); Dazzling Stranger, (first US release), 1995; 2 tracks on Acoustic routes, from BBC TV documentary on Bert Jansch. Memberships: Musicians' Union; PRS. Hobbies: Music and film appreciation; Maintaining old vehicles. Current Management: Sandy Jones. Address: 13 Cheriton Square, London SW17 8AE, England.

JONSSON Wili, b. 27 Mar 1942, Copenhagen, Denmark. Musician (bass, piano). 1 son. Musical Education: Early piano lessons then self taught. Career: Concerts and television appearances with band Gasolin, in Scandinavia, Europe and USA; Touring with singer Sanne Salomensen and other artists. Recordings: Played on 50 recordings over 28 years. Hobby: Music. Address: Dronningensgade 6, 1420 Kobenhavn K, Denmark.

JOOLZ, b. 16 Apr 1966, London, England. Vocalist; Actress; Dancer; Presenter. Musical Education: O Level Music. Career: Session work with artists including: Neneh Cherry; Neil Diamond; Danny Red; Soul II Soul; Tours, worldwide with Soul II Soul, including appearances on children's shows; Member, R&B group Just Good Friends; Supported Glen Jones; H.Town; Silk; Brandy; Keith Sweat; Appeared on Count Prince Miller's Jamaican Independence television special; Cable TV special supporting Don Campbell. Recordings: Looking For An Answer, 1993; The More I Try, Just Good Friends. Membership: Musicians' Union. Hobbies: Reading; Keep fit/dance; Cooking; Going to the theatre; Live shows. Current Management: Phat Management. Address: 35 Tubbs Road, Harlesden, London NW10 4RA, England.

JORDAN Lorraine, b. 22 Nov 1965, Wales. Singer; Songwriter; Musician (guitar, bouzouki). Musical Education: Family influences in Irish music. Career: Singer, guitarist and bouzouki player, bands Mooncoin and Malin Head; Solo artiste, 1991-; Toured Europe and Scandinavia extensively, performing in numerous major folk festivals; Appearances on television and radio; Leader, own band or solo performer. Recordings: Inspiration, 1991 and 1993; Crazy Guessing Games, 1994. Membership: Musicians' Union. Address: Saltire Promotions, Gilkersleugh, Abington, Lanarkshire ML12 6SQ, Scotland.

JORDAN Marc Wallace, b. 6 Mar 1948, New York, USA. Musician (guitar, keyboards); Songwriter; Recording Artist. m. Amy Sky, 31 Jan 1989, 1 son, 1 daughter. Education: University. Musical Education: private guitar and piano lessons. Compositions include: Songs recorded by: Diana Ross (2); Manhattan Transfer (6); Rod Stewart (2); Bette Midler (2); Joe Cocker; Chicago; Kansas; Natalie Cole. Recordings: 7 albums include: Blue Desert, 1979; A Hole In The Wall, 1983; Talking Through Pictures, 1987; Reckless Valentine, 1992. Honours: Juno Award, Producer Of The Year, 1993; 1 Genie Nomination; 2 Juno Nominations. Memberships: AFTRA; ACTRA; AFofM. Hobbies: Riding; Tennis. Current Management: Mogul Ent, Beverly Hills, California, USA. Address: 9744 Wilshire Boulevard, Suite #305, Beverly Hills, CA 90212, USA.

JORDAN Montell, b. 1968, Los Angeles, California, USA. Recording Artist; Producer; Songwriter; Musician (piano, saxophone). Education: BA in Organizational Communication, Pepperdine University, Malibu. Musical Education: Self-taught; Church/gospel background. Career: Budweiser Superfest tour, with Boyz II Men, TLC, Mary J Blige; Television includes: Riki Lake Show; Rolanda Show; The Beat Winter Cooldowns; Host, MTV Jams; Film appearance, The Nutty Professor. Recordings: This Is How We Do It; I Am LV; Jungle Groove (used in film soundtrack Pet Detective); Nutty Professor (film soundtrack); Smooth/Ghetto Life. Honours: Grammy Nomination; 3 MTV Video Award Nominations. Membership: ASCAP. Hobbies: Snowboarding; Wave running; Gym. Current Management: Mad Money Management. Address: 8726 S Sepulveda Blvd, Suite C-161, Los Angeles, CA 90018, USA.

JORDAN Stanley, b. 31 July 1959, Chicago, Illinois, USA. Jazz Musician (guitar, piano). Musical Education: Self-taught guitar; Theory, electronic music and composition, Princetown University. Career: Member, various Chicago groups, 1970s; Regular international jazz festivals, 1976; Musician with Dizzy Gillespie; Benny Carter; Solo recording artist, 1982-; Leading exponent of hammering-on technique. Recordings: Albums: Touch Sensitive, 1982; Magic Touch, 1985; Standards, 1986; Cornucopia, 1990. Address: c/o Mario Tirado, Agency for the Performing Arts, 888 Seventh Avenue, Suite 200, New York, NY 10106, USA.

JORDI Mike, b. 22 July 1964, Roermond, The Netherlands. Education: Classical Guitar, El Guitar, 1989-; Singer, Songwriter, Producer, 1989-; School of Audio Engineering, 1991-92; Basic Musical Education, 1992-93. Career: Suppact for Ten Sharp Concert, Netherlands, 1990; Life Radio Broadcast Show, Night of the Music, Asten, Netherlands, 1990; Radio Appearance, EO Country Show, Alphe A/O Rijn, Netherlands, 1991; Touring with bands, The Disque and Sound Division, 1988-. Compositions: Lady of My Heart, 1992; Message from Jah, 1993; Keep on Going, CD, 1994; You and the Things You Do, 1994. Recording: 5 Jaar Brouwer, CD, 1995. Hobbies: Target Practice; Martial Arts; Cooking; Computers. Current Management: Mike Jordi Productions, Genroyhof 9, 6095 EE Baexem, Holland.

JØRGENS Peter Ole, b. 20 April 1958, Sorgenfri, Denmark. Multi Instrumentalist, mostly percussion including Marimba & Vibe. m. Reneé Paaschburg, 30 May 1992. Education: Classical Percussion with Suzanne Ibstrup, 1970-76, Improvisation with John Tchicai, 1975-77, Percussion with Paul Motian, 1978. Career: John Tchikais Festival Band, 1975-78; Tchikai/Dorge Quarter, 1976-77; Cockpit Music, 1978-; Gronvirke, 1982-83; Global Guaranty Orchestra, 1983-; Clinch, 1987-89; The Wild Mans Band, 1990-; Dog God, 1992-; Sweethearts in a Drugstore, 1996; David Moss/PO Jørgens Duo, 1989-96; Ghost in the Machine, 1989-; Played solo concerts, 1995, Knitting Factory, New York and 1997 at LEM Festival Barcelona; Gefion Calls, 1996, with David Thomas (Pere Ubu), Jørgen Teler and Per Bull Acs, Two Midnight concerts in The Fountain, Gefion, Copenhagen. Compositions include: Soil, 1990; Metal 1-10, 1992; Digital Metal, 1994; Cambodia, 1995; Black Box, 1995; Springtime 1-15, 1996; Somfoni, 1996; The War Kitchen, 1996; The Joy of Feeding Birds, 1997; The Adventure of Hale Bob, 1997. Recordings include: Dog God: Dog God, 1993; Global Guaranty Orchestra, Musical Hair-Splitting in a Remote World, 1993; Wiuf/Jørgens/DeRegt: Catchuptime, 1994; Evan Parker/Ghost in the Machine, 1995; Cockpit Music, The Great Dividing Range, 1996; Dog God: God is Love, 1997; PO Jørgens: The Technology of Touch, 1997; Sweethearts in a Drugstore:, 1997. Honours: 3 Year Grant for Composing From, The Danish Arts Foundation, 1984; One Year Grants, nearly every year, 1982-. Memberships: SKREP (Danish Experimental Composers); DJBFA. Hobbies: Gardening; Literature. Current Management: Ninth World Music. Address: PO Jorgens, Frydenlund, Humlebaekvej 56, 3480 Fredensborg, Denmark.

JORGENSEN Carsten Valentin, b. 9 May 1950, Lyngby, Denmark. Singer; Musician (guitar); Composer; Poet. m. Anne Marie Albrectsen, 27 Jan 1979. Education: Graduate, Art School, 1975. Career: Founder, own band, C V Jorgensen, 1974-; Tours: Denmark, Sweden, Norway, Germany, 1976-; Roskilde Festival, 6 appearances; Television appearances: Numerous C V Jorgensen specials, 1980-94; Danish Live Aid, 1985; Dylan and The Danes, 1991; Leonard Cohen Talkshow, 1992; Performed on films: Kloden Rocker, 1978; Som Et Strejf, 1992; Lyricist/vocalist, film soundtracks: Mig & Charly, 1978; Johnny Larsen, 1979. Recordings: Storbyens Små Oaser, 1977; Tidens Tern, 1980; Lediggang Agogo, 1982; Vennerne & Vejen, 1985; Indian Summer, 1988; Sjælland, 1994. Honours: Poetens Pris (Poets Award), 1989; 2 Grammy Awards, Songwriter of Year, Rock Album of Year, 1991; Prize of Honour, DJBFA; 2 Danish State Art Foundation Awards, 1993, 1994; 4 Grammy Nominations, 1995. Memberships: Nordic Copyright Bureau; KODA; Gramex; DJBFA. Hobbies: Collecting Jazz and Rock Records; Reading Biographies; Wine. Current Management: Rock On. Address: Rådhusstræde 4 A, 1466 Copenhagen K, Denmark.

JORGENSEN Per, b. 9 Sept 1952, Bergen, Norway. Musician (trumpet, guitar, percussion); Vocalist. m. Else Vågen, 8 May 1987, 1 daughter. Education: Pre-school teacher. Musical Education: Self-taught. Career: Freelance musician, 20 years; All major Scandinavian Jazz Festivals with different groups; Tours, concerts in: India; Japan; USA; Germany; Spain; France; Austria; Numerous concerts recorded for television and radio; Jazz visit, teaching and working with Danish musicians, Copenhagen, 1997. Recordings: with Jokleba (trio): On And On; with Jokleba and the Magnetic North Orchestra: Further; with Anders Jormin: Jord; with Marilyn Mazur: Circular Chant; with Tamma (including Don Cherry and Ed Blackwell): Tamma; with Michael Mantler: School of Understanding, 1997; with Sjogren/Voust: The Thule Spirit, 1997. Honours: Vossajazz Prize, 1990; Jazz Musician Of The Year in Norway,

1991. Hobbies: Children; Nature; Drawing. Address: Lia 17, 5280 Dalekvam, Norway.

JORY Sarah Elizabeth, b. 20 Nov 1969, Reading, Berkshire, England. Professional Entertainer; Country Singer; Songwriter. Career: Television appearances include: Opportunity Knocks; Pebble Mill; The South Bank Show; RTE TV Ireland; Ulster TV; Dutch and Belgian TV; Satellite TV worldwide; CBS News America; Anglia TV; East Midlands TV; Concerts: London Palladium; Toured with: Eric Clapton, Glen Campbell and Charley Pride; Broadcasts on BBC Radio 1, 2, 4 and all local radio. Compositions: 4 instrumentals. Recordings: 12 solo recordings; 2 for record company. Honours: 6 British Country Music Awards; 3 European Awards; Many other regional awards. Memberships: PRS; Musicians' Union. Hobbies: Swimming; Cycling; Walking; Listening to music. Current Management: Arthur Jory (personal). Address: 10 Tennyson Road, Balderton, Newark, Notts NG24 3QH, England.

JOSEPH Julian Rapheal Nathaniel, b. 11 May 1966, London, England. Musician (piano); Composer. Musical Education: Classical Composition, Berklee College of Music, Boston, USA. Career: Julian Joseph Weekend, Barbican Centre; Julian Joseph Series, Wigmore Hall; The Proms, Royal Albert Hall, London, 1995; Montreal Jazz Festival. Compositions include: Film score, A Tale Of A Vampire; Commissioned work, Winds Of Change; Orchestral works. Recordings: Albums: The Language Of Truth; Reality; Julian Joseph In Concert At The Wigmore Hall; Universal Traveller, due 1996. Honours: Award to Study at Berklee College of Music; Southern Comfort Award, Best Jazz Group; John Dankworth Award. Memberships: PRS; MCPS; BASCA. Current Management: James Joseph Music Management. Address: 85 Cicada Road, London SW18 2PA, England.

JUB, b. Oxfordshire, England. Musician (double bass); Vocalist. Musical Education: Guildhall School Of Music, London. Career: Bass player, Kreisler String Orchestra; English National Opera; London Festival Ballet; London Contemporary Dance Theatre; Member, The Carnival Band, 1985-; Appearances include: Glasgow Cathedral; Birmingham Symphony Hall; Barbican Centre; Arts centres and theatres; Plays material from: Sweden; Croatia; US; Bolivia; Spain; UK; France. Recordings: Album with Maddy Prior: Christmas Carols. Current Management: C/o Jim McPhee, Acorn Entertainments. Address: Winterfold House, 46 Woodfield Road, Kings Heath, Birmingham B13 9UJ, England.

JUDD Naomi Ellen, b. 1 Nov 1946, Ashland, Kentucky, USA. Singer; Songwriter; Author; Speaker. m. Larry Strickland, 6 May 1989; 2 daughters. Education: RN degree. Member, country music duo The Judds, with daughter Wynonna, 1984-90; Sold 15 million albums; Most succesful duo in country music history. Recordings include: Singles: Had A Dream For The Heart, 1983; Mama He's Crazy, 1984; Why Not Me, 1984; Girls Night Out, 1985; Rockin' With The Rhythm Of The Rain, 1986; Let Me Tell You About Love, 1989; Albums: The Judds, 1984; Why Not Me?, 1985; Rockin With The Rhythm Of The Rain, 1986; Heartland, 1987; Greatest Hits, 1988; River Of Time, 1989; Love Can Build A Bridge, 1990; The Judds Collection, 1991; The Essential, 1996. Publications: Love Can Build A Bridge. Honours: 7 Grammy Awards; 4 Academy Country Music Awards, Best Duet; 3 Country Music Association Awards, Best Vocal Duo; Undefeated, 3 major Country Music Award shows, 8 consecutive years. Hobby: Walking in nature. Current Management: William Morris. Address: The Judd House, 325 Bridge Street, Franklin, TN 37064, USA.

JULES Judge, b. 26 Oct 1965, London, England. Disc Jockey; Record Producer; Remixer; Radio Presenter; A & R. Education: Degree in Law, London School of Economics. Career: Worldwide appearances in over 30 countries; Remixed and produced over 20 top 30 singles, 1994-. Recordings: I Like To Move It, Reel 2 Real; Doop, Doop; Saturday Night, T'empo. Publications: Contributions to The Face, ID, Mix Mag, and DJ Mag. Honours: Best Club DJ, DJ Mag, 1995; Best DJ, London Club Awards, 1995. Membership: Musicians' Union. Hobbies: Current Affairs; Psychology; Law; Football. Current Management: Serious Artist Management. Address: PO Box 13143, London N6 5BG, England.

JULVE SAEZ Maria Isabel, b. 15 Oct 1970, Valencia, Spain. Singer. m. Juan Antonio Sanchez, 16 Dec 1995. Musical Education: Music, rhythm. Career: Appearances, local television (Spain). Recordings: Dedicado A Ti. Hobbies: Dancing; Reading. Current Management: Antonio Egido. Address: Ingeniero Vicente Pichó 4-Bajo, 46020 Valencia, Spain.

JUNGR Barb, b. 9 May 1954, Rochdale, England. Singer; Musician (mandolin, harmonica). Education: BSc, Leeds. Musical Education: Vocal training with S. Elliot, Paul Newnham; Currently studying Ethnomusicology (Masters), Goldsmiths College. Career: Television appearances with Julian Clary in all series of Sticky Moments, Terry and Julian; Radio broadcasts: 5 series, We Stayed In With Jungr And Parker, BBC Radio 2; National tours with Alexei Sayle and Julian Clary. Recordings: 3 Courgettes; Barb; The Stroke; Jungr And Parker. Honour: Perrier Award, 1987. Memberships: PRS; Musicians' Union; Equity; ICTM; Women In Music; Jazz Singers Network. Hobby: Aikido. Current Management: Patrick Hehir. Address: 53 Keyes House, Dolphin Square, London SW1, England.

JURICIC Max Wilson, b. 10 June 1958, Zagreb, Croatia. Musician (guitar); Backing Singer. m. Vanja Matujec, 11 June 1988, 1 son, 1 daughter. Education: Economist. Career: Member, Azra, 1977-78; Film, 1978-86; Le Cinema, 1986; Vjestice, 1989; Ziu Zao, 1995. Recordings: with Film: Film 1; Live Kulusic; Zona Sumraka; Sva Cuda Svijeta; Signali U Noćí; with Le Cinema: Live Kulusic; with Vjestice: Totalno Drukciji Od Drugih; Bez Tisine; Live In Schwarzwald; Djevojke U Ljetnim Haljinama Volim;Kradljivac scra with Vjestice. Honour: Porin 1987, for best album in alternative music. Membership: HGU. Hobbies: Swimming; Skiing. Address: Auzvinkl Tomisalavov trg 19, Zagreb, Croatia.

JUSTICE James Michael, b. 15 Apr 1966, Warwickshire, England. Performer; Composer; Programmer; Musician (guitar, keyboards, drums); Vocalist. m. 4 Jul 1986. Education: Technical College. Musical Education: Classical guitar grades; Sight reading; Digital Technology training. Career: Regular weekly performances around UK; Programming Sequencer for other artists; Music for video production; Run a digital recording studio; Teacher, modern music technology courses. Memberships: Musicians' Union; Equity. Hobby: Music. Current Management: B and M Leisure, Coventry, England; Jade Entertainments, Northampton, England. Address: 1 Foxglove Close, Four Pools, Evesham, Worcestershire WR11 6YU, England.

K

KAAS Patricia, b. 5 Dec 1966, Forbach, France. Singer. Career: Scène de Vie tour, 1990-91 (196 concerts, audience 750,000, 12 countries); Tour de Charme, 1993-94 (145 concerts, audience 600,000, 19 countries). Recordings: Mademoiselle Chante, 1988; Scène De Vie, 1990; Carnet De Scène (double live album) 1991; Je Te Dis Vous, 1993; Tour De Charme, (live album) 1994; More than 8 million albums sold worldwide. Publication: Patricia Kaas-Tour De Charme, 1994. Honours: 6 Victoires de la Musique; 2 World Music Awards. Hobby: Fashion. Current Management: Cyril Prieur, Richard Walter. Address: Talent Sorcier, 3 Rue des Petites Écuries, 75010 Paris, France.

KAASINEN Sari Johanna, b. 15 Sept 1967, Rääkkylä, Finland. Singer; Musician (kanteler); Record Producer. m. Heikki Kemppainen, 21 June 1991, 1 daughter. Musical Education: Master of Music, Sibelius Academy, Helsinki, 1994. Career: Leader, Singer, Värttinä, 1983-96; Tours, Festivals throughout Europe and US include: Kaustingen, Finland, 1985-; WOMAD, UK, 1992; Dranouter, Belgium, 1992; Glastonbury, UK, 1993; Ruisrock, Finland, 1993; Molde Jazz Festival, Norway, 1994; Owner, Producer, Mipu Music; Television appearances: Music From Karelia, Finnish documentary, 1990; Late Late Show, Dublin, 1991; Prize of Europe, 1994; Leading Sirmakka group currently; Persuing solo project; Teacher of Music, Rääkkylä. Compositions: Iro, 1996; Pojaton, 1996; Limoni Ennen, 1996. Recordings: Albums with Värttinä: Värttinä, 1987; Musta Lindu, 1989; Oi Dai, 1991; Seleniko, 1992; Aitara, 1994; Kokko, 1996; With Sirmakka, Tsihi Tsihi, 1997; with Hector Zazou: Songs From The Cold Seas, 1995. Honours: Emma Award, Finland, 1992; State Music Art Prize, 1992; Northern Karelian Music Art Prize, 1992. Membership: Finnish State Music Art Committee, 1995-97. Current Management: Hoedown. Address: Laivurinrinne 2, 00120 Helsinki, Finland.

KABILJO Alfi, b. 22 December 1935, Zagreb, Croatia. m. Katja Kauterna, 11 November 1961, 1 son, 1 daughter. Education: Diploma, Engineering Architecture, Faculty of Architecture, Zagreb, 1964. Career: Professional Composer, Conductor, Arranger, Record Producer; Composer Musicals, Ballets, Film, TV, Chamber, Children; Recorded in Zagreb, Paris, London, Tokyo, Vienna, Ljubljana, Los Angeles. Compositions: Musicals: The Big Race; Yacta Yacta; Shaggy Life; John The Butterfly Boy; Red Island; Marriage License; Emperor Franz Josef in Zagreb; The King is Naked; Balets: Kentaur XII, Pandora's Box; Films: Sky Bandits; Fear; Final Instinct. Recordings: The Big Race; Yacta Yacta; Shaggy Life; Great film Music by Alfi Kabiljo; Sky Bandits; The King is Naked; Emperor Franz Josef in Zagreb; Kentaur XII. Publications: Yacta Yacta, 1972; The King is Naked, 1995; Alfi Kabiljo: Melodite, 1964. Honours: Prin, 1997; Golden Arena for Best Film Score, 1976, 1981. Memberships: Croatian Composers Association, President, 1996-98. Hobbies: Skiing; Tennis. Address: Musical: Tko Pjeva Zlo Ne Misli. Address: 10000 Zagreb, Dvornicceva 29, Croatia, A-1020 Wien, Czerning, 16/7A, Austria.

KADOIC Miro, b. 8 July 1962, Zagreb, Croatia. Musician (altosaxophone, reeds, clarinet, flute). Education: Graduate, University of Zagreb. Musical Education: Music Academy Zagreb, clarinet, studied privately in New York City. Career: Solos, lead alto in Croatian Radio Big Band, 1987-1993; Moved to Slovenia, 1994; Played with Big Band of Radio Slovenia, Ljubljana, 1994; Composer, leads own quartet. Recordings: Album: Dry, with orginal ethno jazz compositions, 1995; Istriana, Axel Moonshine; 50 Years Of The RTV Slovenia Big Band; Pepino Principe, Jazz

Accordion. Memberships: Croatian Music Union; Slovenian Music Union. Hobby: Beer. Current Management: S Limov. Address: Tesovnikova 9, 61000 Ljubljana, Slovenia.

KAGADEEV Andrei, b. 9 July 1961, Moscow, Russia. Songwriter; Musician. m. Tatiana Kagadeeva, 2 March 1985, 1 daughter. Education: Humanitarian University Courses, Technical University of St Petersburg; Guitar Lessons. Career: Songwriter, Composer of the NOM Band; Appearances on Western European Television Channels; Participation in Big Festivals, Les Allummees, Nantes, 1991, Sziget, Budapest, 1995; Concert Tours in Western Europe. Compositions: Films: Masters of the USSR or Ape's Snout, 1994; Made In Europe, (documentary), 1996. Recordings: Albums: Brutto, 1989; To Hell With It, 1991; Superdisc, 1992; Senka-Mosgas, 1994; In the Name of Mind, 1996; Ultracompact, 1996; Live is Game, 1996; Gire, 1997. Honours: Grand Prix, Alternative Video Contest, Exotica 95, Moscow; Best Low Budget Video, Ukrblues, Midem 96 Fair, Cannes, France. Hobbies: Writing Fiction; Art Design; Film Making. Current Management: Agency of Gerhard Busse, St Petersburg, Russia. Address: Bogatyrsky pr 5/1-283, St Petersburg 197348, Russia.

KAJDAN Jean-Michel, b. 16 July 1954, Paris, France. Musician; Song Writer; Singer. Education: Self Taught, Guitar, Bass Guitar. Career: Sideman, Didier Lockwood, Michel Jonasz, Eddy Mitchell, Lionel Ritchie, Eddy Louiss; The Big Blue (film); Subway (film); Taratata, (television with L Ritchie); Taratata (television with D E Mitchell); Montreux Jazz Festival (with Lassy Carlton), 1997. Compositions: The Spy (D Lockwood Album); Spying Taranto; Song for LC. Recordings: Blue Scales; Blue Noise; Fasten Seat Belts; La Mouvellevie. Memberships: SACEM; SPEDIDAM; ADAMI; SACD. Current Management: Maurice Suissa, Suissa Despa Productions. Address: 1 rue du Général de Gaulle, 27500 Pont Audemer, France.

KALASZ Juraj, b. 14 November 1963, Bratislava, Czechoslovakia. m. Dr Krausova Dagmar, 15 December 1990, 1 son. Education: Machine Engineering University, 6 years (Slovak Technological University), Dipl Ing, 1983-89; Studying Double Bass, State Conservatory in Bratislava, 1991-97. Career: First Prof eng, 1987 with local (Bratislava) groups (Exprit, Bratislava Trio), 1991; Just Jazz (tours in Denmark and Czech Republic), 1993; Czechoslovak Quintet (Bratislava Jazz Days Festival); 1995 Tubu (tour in Spain); 1995 Member of Janusz Muniak, Quartet (Cracow, Poland); 1996 Member of Shawn Loescher Trio). Compositions: Tribute to Charlie Parker, recorded for Slovak Radio. Recordings: Czechoslovak Quintet, for Slovak Radio, 1993; Chamber Jazz Trio, 1996. Publication: Walking Double Bass, 1997. Honour: Prize for Outstanding Performance, Zilina Jazz Festival, 1989. Membership: Slovak Jazz Society. Hobbies: Swimming; Books. Address: Rara Musica (Adrian Raiter), Fand Who 1, 81103 Bratislava, Slovakia.

KALOGJERA Niko Nikica, b. 19 May 1930, Beograd, Croatia. Conductor; Composer. m. Ljupka Dimitrovska, 2 Mar 1978, 2 sons, 1 daughter. Education: Medical University. Musical Education: High Music Academy. Career: Chief conductor, Croatian Radio-television Orchestra, International Festival Awards, 28 include: Split 1969; MIDEM, 1969; Athens, 1970; Rio, 1971; Malaga, 1971; Vina Del Mar, 1971; Tokyo, 1971; Dresden, 1972; Eurovision Song Contest, 1989. Compositions: Over 1000 songs on LP, MC, CD, VC (about 400 in foreign countries); Music for theatre, films; Artists: Mireille Mathieu; Claudio Villa; Raymond Lefevre; Tony Christie. Publications: Columnist in many music publications. Membership: Vice-president, Croatian Composers Association. Hobbies:

Comparative Philology; Swimming. Current Management: AVET, Zagreb, Croatia. Address: 10000 Zagreb, Tuskanac 33, Croatia.

KAMAI Allen, b. 6 Dec 1960, Marin County, California, USA. Musician (Bass). Musical Education: College of Marin. Career: Tours with: Oleta Adams; Sheena Easton; Wendy & Lisa; The Rainbirds; Michael Penn; Jude Cole; Ronnie Montrose; Extensive television and video performances in USA; Europe; Canada; Japan. Recordings for/with: Sass Jordan; Curt Smith; Miki Howard; Jeanette Katt; Bronx-Style Bob; Pretty In Pink; The Rainbirds; Chanise Wilson; Wendy & Lisa; Kristian Vigard; Jim Chappell. Honour: Yamaha Soundcheck, Outstanding Bassist, 1987. Hobbies: Mountain biking; Off-road 4x4 racing. Current Management: Doug Buttleman Management. Address: 14625 Dickens #207, Sherman Oaks, CA 91403, USA.

KANE Gregory, b. 11 Sept 1966, Coatbridge, Strathclyde, Scotland. Singer; Lyricist; Composer. Education: Engineering student. Career: Formed Hue And Cry with brother Patrick; Concerts include: Royal Albert Hall; Support to Madonna, Wembley Stadium; Composer for television themes and musical scores. Recordings: Albums: Seduced And Abandoned, 1987; Ordinary Angel, 1988; Bitter Suite, 1989; Remote, 1989; Stars Crash Down, 1991; Labours Of Love, 1993; Showtime!, 1994; Piano And Voice, 1995; Singles: Labour Of Love; Violently; Looking For Linda. Hobbies: Pool; Golf.

KANE Patrick, b. 10 Mar 1964, Coatbridge, Strathclyde, Scotland. Singer; Musician (piano, keyboards); Songwriter; Journalist. Education: Degree, English And Media Studies. Career: Formed Hue And Cry with brother Gregory; Concerts include Royal Albert Hall; Support to Madonna, Wembley Stadium; Also journalist, The Guardian; Radio presenter, Usual Suspects, BBC Radio Scotland; Broadcaster, Radio 4; Rector, Glasgow University. Recordings: Albums: Seduced And Abandoned, 1987; Ordinary Angel, 1988; Bitter Suite, 1989; Remote, 1989; Stars Crash Down, 1991; Labours Of Love, 1993; Showtime!, 1994; Piano And Voice, 1995; Singles: Labour Of Love; Violently; Looking For Linda. Membership: Founder, Artists For An Independent Scotland. Address: c/o BBC Radio Scotland, Queen Margaret Drive, Glasgow G12 8DG, Scotland.

KANE Stevie (Stephen), b. 13 Apr 1961. Musician (fretted and fretless bass, double bass). Career: Tours with The Silencers: Dance To The Holyman European tour, 1992; Seconds Of Pleasure tour, 1993-94; So Be It, 1995; Other concerts include: Rock-Am-Ring, 1993; London Fleah, 1993; St Gallen, 1994; Appearances include: Radio 1 Roadshow, 1993; Free Wheels, 1993; Live Aus Dem Nachtwerk, 1993; Summit In The City, 1993. Recordings: with The Silencers: Seconds Of Pleasure; So Be It. Current Management: Tartan Ghost. Address: 423 Merry Street, Motherwell, Strathclyde ML1 4BP, Scotland.

KANERVA Markku, b. 21 Apr 1965, Finland. Musician (guitar). Musical Education; Studied at The Academy, early 1990s. Career: Played in Summer camps in Oulunkylä Institute, and with music school big band in Vantaa; Soloist with Espoo Big Band; Regular freelance musician with UMO (New Music Orchetsra); Played with various small groups, including Trio Tőykeät (with Iiro Rantala); Severi Pyysalo's The Front. Recordings include: Heavy Jazz, Pekka Pohjola, 1995. Address: Haapaniemenkatu 12 A 87, 00530 Helsinki, Finland.

KANTARDZIJEV-MLINAC Petko, b. 21 Oct 1945, Sofia, Bulgaria. Composer; Sound Engineer; Producer; Musician (piano). m. Mirjana, 15 Aug 1971, 1 daughter. Education: Faculty of

Electronics, 1971. Musical Education: High School For Music, department, Composing and Piano, 1964. Career: Rock musician, 1961-69; Music editor, TV Zagreb, 1969; Rehearser, music, Comedy Theatre, Zagreb: A Man From La Mancha; Fiddler On The Roof; Promises Promises, 1969-71; Radio-television, Zagreb, 1970-89; Music Producer, Suzy Record Company, 1971-72; Sound engineer, Jugoton Record Company, 1974-76; Director, Multimedia Youth Centre, 1987-88; Pianist, 1990-. Compositions: Over 150 compositions and arrangements, pop, easy listening, classical, number recorded for Radio Zagreb and various records. Recordings: As sound engineer: More than 200 soundtracks; films; animations; documentaries; television series; films; 100 albums include: John Luis; Clarck Terry; Sal Nistico; Art Farmer. Honours: First prizes, Best Soundtracks, Yugoslavia, 1982, 1984, 1985, 1986; First prizes, Festivals in: Opatïja, 1968; Zagreb, 1986; Fish Eye animated film, Ottawa, 1981. Memberships: Croatian Composers' Association; Croatian Artist's Association. Hobbies: Playing piano; Tennis; Bridge. Address: Maksimirska 81, 10000 Zagreb, Croatia.

KANTÉ Mory, b. 1950, Kiissidougou, Guinea. Singer; Musician. Recordings: Albums: Ten Cola Nuts, 1986; Akwaba Beach, 1987; Touma, 1990; Nongo Village; Hit single: Yéké-Yéké. Address: c/o Colette De Wouters, 41 Rue de Montmorency, 75003 Paris, France.

KANTNER Paul, b. 12 Mar 1941, San Francisco, California, USA. Musician (guitar). 1 daughter. Education: University of Santa Clara, 1959-61; San Jose State College, 1961-63. Career: Founder member, Jefferson Airplane, 1965-73; Renamed Jefferson Starship, 1974-84; Member, Planet Earth Rock'n'Roll Orchestra, 1984-85; KBC (Kantner Balin Casady) Band, 1985-88; Rejoined Jefferson Airplane (later as Jefferson Starship - The Next Generation), 1989-; Appearances include: Berkeley Folk Festival, 1966; Monterey Jazz Festival, 1966; Monterey Pop Festival, 1967; Newport Pop Festival, 1968; Isle Of Wight Festival, 1968; Atlantic City Festival, 1969; Woodstock Music and Art Fair, 1969; Altamont Speedway, with Rolling Stones, 1969; Bath Festival, 1970; Festival of Hope, 1972; Knebworth, 1978; Free concert, Golden Gate Park, 1989. Recordings: Albums: Jefferson Airplane Takes Off, 1966; Surrealistic Pillow, 1967; After Bathing At Baxter's, 1968; Crown Of Creation, 1968; Bless Its Pointed Little Head, 1969; Blows Against The Empire, 1970; The Worst Of Jefferson Airplane, 1971; Sunfighter, 1972; Long John Silver, 1972; 30 Seconds Over Winterland, 1973; Baron Von Tollbooth And The Chrome Nun, 1973; Dragonfly, 1974; Red Octopus, 1975; Spitfire, 1976; Flight Log (1966-76), 1977; Jefferson Starship Gold, 1979; Freedom At Point Zero, 1980; Modern Times, 1981; Winds Of Change, 1983; Nuclear Furniture, 1984; Jefferson Airplane, 1989; Jefferson Airplane Loves You, 1992; with KBC Band: KBC Band, 1986; Solo: The Planet Earth Rock And Roll Orchestra, 1983; Singles include: Miracles, 1975; With Your Love, 1976; Runaway, 1978; Jane, 1980. Publication: Author, Nicaraguan Diary, 1988. Address: Bill Thompson Management, 2051 Third Street, San Francisco, CA 94107, USA.

KANTONEN Seppo, b. 13 Nov 1963, Kivijärvi. Finland. Musician (piano, keyboards). Musical Education: Sibelius Academy, Helsinki, 1979. Career: Began career playing with Nono Söderberg and Otto Donner Treatment; Pianist with UMO (New Music Orchestra); Pianist with Eero Koivistoinen, 1980s-; Jazz soloist, accompanist, Afro-American tradition; Worked with numerous rock bands including Mustat Lasit, 1980s; Recorded as duo with Jarmo Savolainen. Recordings: Albums: with Jarmo Savolainen: Phases; with Eero Koivistoinen: Dialog, 1995. Honour: Yrjö Award, Finnish Jazz Federation,

1985. Address: Ruusankatu 6 A 18, 00250 Helsinki, Finland.

KAPELLE Frances, b. 21 Aug 1956, London, England. Vocalist. m. Paul Raymond Oldridge, 26 May 1978, divorced, 1 daughter. Education: College. Career: Backing vocalist for singers including: Ian Shaw; Carol Grimes; Brian Kennedy; Mary Coughlan; Preproduction singer, backing vocal arranger, writer with Violet Williams, film soundtrack The Commitments. Recordings: Albums: Junk Puppets, An Emotional Fish (backing vocals); Why Don't They Dance, Carol Grimes. Membership: Musicians' Union. Hobby: Worked with exotic animals (leopards, tigers). Address: Brockton Farm, Egerton Road, Charing Heath, Kent TN27 0AX, England.

KAPHAN Bruce Robert, b. 7 Jan 1955, San Francisco, California, USA. Musician; Producer; Engineer. m. Michele White, 12 Dec 1987. Musical Education: Mostly self-taught. Career: Tours with American Music Club, USA, Western Europe; Television appearances with Jewel (Saturday Night Live and MTV Unplugged), 1997; European and USA tours with David Byrne, including television appearances on the Late Show with David Letterman and Sessions at W 54th St on PBS. Recordings: with John Lee Hooker: Chill Out; with The Black Crowes: Amorica; with Chris Isaak: Forever Blue; with American Music Club: Everclear; Mercury; San Francisco; Black Crowes, Three Snakes and One Charm, Love and Rockets, Sweet FA; Jellyfish, Spilt Milk; Red House Painters, Songs for a Blue Guitar; Francesco di Gregori, Premiere E Lasciare; Susanna Hoffs, Susanna Hoffs; Tara MacLean, Silence; Suzanne Little, Be Here Now; Mark Eitzel, 60 Watt Silver Lining, West. Membership: AFofM. Hobby: Backpacking. Current Management: Self-managed. Address: PO Box 2012, Fremont, CA 94536, USA.

KAPILIDIS Nick, b. 2 Jan 1955, Zanthi, Greece. Musician (drums). m. 1973-1992, 1 son, 1 daughter. Musical Education: Ethnico Conservatory, 4 years piano, 1 year flute, private lessons drums. Career: Jazz festivals, Patea, Athens, Thessaloniki; Live performances with J Stubblefield; D hayes; M Boyd; G Bailey; K Rampton; D Lynch; Y Fakaqnas; L Christofis; TV appearances with many famous Greek composers and singers. Recordings: Electric Jazz Trio, 1990; Flying To The Unknown, M Alexiou, 1995; Oramata, L Christofis, 1996; Forthcoming recording: Serious Fun, with own band. Publications: Book: Modern Greek Odd Rhythms. Membership: Greek Musician's Union. Hobbies: Music; Theatre. Current Management: Self-managed. Address: Markou Botsazi 24, Galatsi 1145, Athens, Greece.

KARN Mick (Anthony Michaelides), b. 24 July 1958, Nicosia, Cyprus. Musician (Bass Guitar). Career: Member, Japan, 1977-82; Support to Blue Öyster Cult, UK tour, 1978; Member, Dali's Car, 1984; Japan reunion, 1989; Member, Rain Tree Crow (with 3 members of Japan), 1991; Backing musician for No-Man, UK tour, 1992; Member, Polytown, 1994; Member, Jansen, Barbieri, Karn (with 2 members of Japan), 1995 Sculptor, exhibition of work, London, 1981, 1992, Japan, 1982, Italy, 1985. Recordings: Albums: with Japan: Adolescent Sex, 1978; Obscure Alternatives, 1978; Life In Tokyo, 1979; Quiet Life, 1980; Gentlemen Take Polaroids, 1980; Assemblage, 1981; Tin Drum, 1981; Oil On Canvas, 1983; Exorcising Ghosts, 1985; Solo albums: Titles, 1982; Dreams Of Reason Produce Monsters, 1987; Bestial Cluster, 1994; The Tooth Mother, 1995; with Dali's Car: The Waking Hour, 1984; with Rain Tree Crow: Rain Tree Crow, 1991; Singles include: with Japan: The Art Of Parties, 1981; Quiet Life, 1981; Visions Of China, 1981; Ghosts, 1982; Cantonese Boy, 1982; Life In Tokyo, 1982; Night Porter, 1982; with Dali's Car: The Judgement is the Mirror, 1984; Solo:

Sensitive, Buoy, 1982; 1987; With Polytown: Polytown, 1994; With Jansen, Barbieri, Karn: Beginning to Melt, 1995; Seed, 1996. Current Management: Medium Productions, 74 Lawrence Road, Upminster, Essex RM14 2UW, England.

KÄRTSY (Kari Hatakka), b. 17 Dec 1967, Helsinki, Finland. Musician; Composer; Lyricist; Singer. Career: European tours, 1993, 1994; Lead singer, Finnish rock band, Waltari, 1994; Roskilde Festival, Denmark, 1994, 1995; Ethno Meets Metal tour with Angelin Tytöt, 1995; European tours, 1995, 1996, 1997. Recordings: Monk Punk, 1991; Torcha!, 1992; So Fine!, 1994; Big Bang, 1995; Yeah! Yeah! Die! Die! Death Metal Symphony in Deep C, 1996; Space Avenue, 1997. Hobbies: Yoga; Swimming; History. Current Management: Focusion/Gunnar Eysel, Postfach 31, 73062 Uhingen, Germany.

KARVONEN Jartsa, b. 27 June 1955, Finland. Musician (drums). Musical Education: Oulunkylä Institute, 1976. Career: Began playing, Rovaniemi, Lapland; Played with bands: Blue Train; Jukka Syrenius Band; Tapiola Big Band, including appearance at Detroit Festival; Played with numerous artists including: Jukka Linkola; Olli Ahvenlahti; Pentti Lahti; Mircea Stan; Regular member, UMO (New Music Orchestra), 1989. Honours: Musician Of The Year, 1989; Voted Best Drummer, Finnish Jazz Federation's magazine JazzIt Readers Poll, 1989. Address: Paraistentie 11 A 6, 00280 Helsinki, Finland.

KASPERSEN Jan Per Sommerfeldt, b. 22 Apr 1948, Copenhagen, Denmark. Musician (piano); Composer; Arranger. 1 son. Career: Musician, European Jazz scene, 1969-; Bandleader, trios up to quintets, using name Space and Rhythm Jazz; Recordings: 18 releases, including Memories Of Monk; Live At Sofie's Cellar; Heavy Smoke; Ballads And Cocktails; Special Occasion Band: Live In Copenhagen Jazz-House; Space And Rhytm Jazz; Joining Forces. Honours: DJBFA Jazz Composer prize, 1987; JASA prize. Memberships: Danish Musicians' Union; Society Of Danish Bandleaders. Current Management: Space And Rhythm Jazz, Danish Music Agency. Address: c/o Space & Rhythm Jazz, Copenhagen, Denmark.

KÄTKÄ Ippe, b. 16 Apr 1948, Finland. Musician (drums); Composer; Record Producer; Theatre Conductor. Formed Ippe Kätkä Band, early 1980s; Appearances include: Turku Festival, 1983; Pori Jazz, 1984; Tampere Jazz Happening, 1984; Concentrated on recording and performing jazz, rock and theatre; Compositions include: Music for stage play by Erkki Lepokorpi. Recordings include: Two-man jazz and poetry with Seppo Pietikäinen. Address: Tallberginkatu 1 C 147, 00180 Helsinki, Finland.

KATKA Ismo (Ippe) Paavo Matias, b. 19 March 1948, Seinajoki, Finland. Composer Producer. Musician (Drums, Keyboards). Divorced, 1990, 2 sons. Education: Selftaught Musician. Career: Local bands, dance, pop, rock, jazz, 1965-; Starboys, Tangopojat, Yahoos, Kari Larne Group, Woodoo, Matthewsd, Kirka & Islanders, Royals, Pekka Pohjola Group, Veltto & Heru, Ippe Kätkä Band, Tampere Jazz Orchestra, Juice Leskinen, Dave Lindholm, Anssi Tikanmäki Film Orchestra, Krakatau, Ismo Alanko, Galaxy (Senea gal); International tours: Pekka Pohjola Group, 1980-82, A T Film Orchestra, 1989-93, Krakatau, 1993-96, Galaxy, 1993-. Compositions: For films, TV, radio, theatre, modern dance ranging from classics through Shakespeare to modern poetry. Recordings: Royals: Spring 76; Out; Live; Pekka Pohjola Group: Kätkävaaran Lohikäärme; Veltto & Heru: Tahdon; Ippe Kätkä Band: Tre Jazz Orchestra: Makumoka; Juice: Minä; Sinä; Dave: Sissi; Sillalla; A T Film Orchestra: Greed@ Krakatau: Matinale; Ismo Alanko: Irti; Taiteilijaelämää; Galaxy: Nobeel. Honours: Several state grants, 1982-; Tampere

City Creative Musician Award, 1989; Critic's Poll, Best Group and Best Album of Year, 1985, 1994; KOURA Award for the best radio programme, 1997. Memberships: ELVIS ry, composers and writers. Hobby: Music. Current MAnagement: Global Music Centre, Mikkolantie 17, Fin 00640 Helsinki, Finland. Address: Tallberginkatu 1c/47, Fin 00180 Helsinki, Finland.

KAUKONEN Jorma, b. 23 Dec 1940, Washington DC, USA. Musician (guitar, dobro, steel guitar); Vocalist. m. Vanessa Lillian, 12 July 1988. Education: BA, Sociology, Santa Clara University; Antioch College. Musical Education: Self-taught; Studied under Ian Buchanan and Rev Gary Davis. Career: Member, The Triumphs; Member, Jefferson Airplane, 1966-72; Member, side project Hot Tuna, 1968-78, 1992-; Jefferson Airplane Reunion, 1989-90; Appearances include: Berkeley Folk Festival, 1966; Monterey Jazz Festival, 1966; Monterey Pop Festival, 1967; Newport Pop Festival, 1968; Isle Of Wight Festival, 1968; Atlantic City Pop Festival, 1969; Woodstock Festival, 1969; Altamont Speedway, with the Rolling Stones, 1969; Bath Festival, 1970. Recordings include: Albums: Jefferson Airplane Takes Off, 1966; After Bathing At Baxter's, 1968; Crown Of Creation, 1968; Bless Its Pointed Little Head, 1969; Volunteers, 1969; Blows Against The Empire, 1970; Long John Silver, 1972; Flight Log (1966-76), 1977; Jefferson Airplane, 1989; Jefferson Airplane Loves You, 1992; with Hot Tuna: First Pull Up Then Pull Down, 1971; Burgers, 1972; The Phosphorescent Rat, 1974; America's Choice, 1975; Yellow Fever, 1975; Hoppkorv, 1976; Double Dose, 1978; 2400 Fulton Street, 1987;Quah; Jorma; Barbeque King; Too Hot To Handle; Land of Heroes, 1995; Jorma Kaukonen Christmas, 1996; Guest musician, If Only I Could Remember My Name, David Crosby, 1972. Current Management: Vanessa Lillian, Gabra Management, 37000 Kingsbury Road, Pomeroy, OH 45769, USA.

KAVANAGH Niamh, b. 13 Feb 1968, Dublin, Ireland. Vocalist; Recording Artist. Musical Education: Voice training, 4 years, Bel canto school. Career: Appearance on Grammies '92, with Commitments, 1992; Television and radio throughout Europe, 1993-; Eurovision Song Contest, 1993. Recordings: Tracks on Commitments soundtracks volumes I & II; Eurovision winner: In Your Eyes, 1993; Debut solo album: Flying Blind, 1995. Honours: Yamaha International Award Of Excellence; Grammy Nomination, with Commitments, 1992; Eurovision Song Contest Winner, In Your Eyes, 1993. Membership: Musicians' Union. Hobbies: Reading; Films; Computers. Current Management: Chris O'Donnell. Address: 62 Ransoms Dock, 35-37 Park Gate Road, London SW11, England.

KAVANAGH Ron, b. Fermoy, County Cork, Ireland. Musician; Producer; Arranger; Songwriter; Composer. Career: Former session musician, producer, arranger; Worked with artists including: Charlie Watts; Richard Thompson; Paddy Moloney; The Pogues; Elvis Costello; Dr John; Clarence Henry; Doug Sahm; Big Jay McNeely; Member, various groups including: Loudest Whisper; Panama Red; Chris Farlowe Band; Identity Kit, with guitarist Ed Deane; Juice On The Loose; In-house bandleader, producer for Ace Records; Member, various bands with Alexis Korner, 1980s; Bees Make Honey; Leader, own band Alias Ron Kavana; 3 support tours with The Pogues; Other projects include: Home Fire; The Bucks; Founder, director, member of LILT (Live Irish Live Trust), non-profit making organisation committed to peace in Northern Ireland; Appearances, songwriter for films including: Ryan's Daughter; Sid And Nancy; Clash Of The Ash, RTE; Hidden Agenda. Compositions include: Co-writer with The Pogues: Young Ned Of The Hill; Every Man Is A King. Recordings: Solo albums: Rollin' & Coasting; Home Fire; with Alias Ron Kavana: Think Like A Hero, 1989; Coming

Days, 1991; Galway To Graceland, 1995; with Loudest Whisper: The Children Of Lire; with Donovan, Liam Og O'Fynn, Philip Donnelly, RTE Chamber Orchestra: The Children Of Lire (re-recorded), 1993; with The Bucks: Dancing To The Ceilli Band, 1995; with LILT: For The Children; Guest musician with The Pogues: Sid And Nancy (soundtrack); Fall From Grace. Honours: Best Live Act In The World, Folk Roots Magazine, 1989-91. Current Management: c/o Jim McPhee, Acorn Entertainments. Address: Winterfold House, 46 Woodfield Road, Kings Heath, Birmingham B13 9UJ, England.

KAY Simon, b. 1 May 1960, London, England. Songwriter; Producer; Musician (keyboards). Career: Keyboard player, Ultramarine; US Tour, Orbital, 1992; Concerts include: Glastonbury Festival; Strawberry Fayre; Radio and television include: Radio 1; Radio 5; 5 Live sessions; MTV Live; Tours with Björk include: USA, Europe, 1993; Britronica; Russian Tour; Glastonbury Festival; Forest Fayre; Megadog, 1994; Formed Exile with partner Tim Ericson; Exile production credits include debut album by Cry. Recordings: with Ultramarine: Album: United Kingdom; Single: Kingdom; Happy Land; Hymn; As producer: Single: with Cry: (It's About) Time For Love. Current Management: MRM. Address: Panther House, 38 Mount Pleasant, London WC1X 0AP, England.

KAYE Hereward Hilken Swain, b. 29 June 1953, Middlesbrough, Cleveland, England. Singer; Songwriter; Composer. m. Patricia Mary Lord, 6 July 1974, 3 sons. Education: Drama College. Musical Education: Self-taught. Career: Member, The Flying Pickets, 4 albums; International tours from Australia to Iceland. Compositions: Moby Dick, Cameron Mackintosh musical, Picadilly Theatre, 1992; Arranger, musical director, Return To The Forbidden Planet; Composer, lyricist, Hell Can Be Heaven, computer game, musical, opening 1996; Composer lyricist, Underworld, musical, opening Seattle, 1998. Honour: Evening Standard Musical Of The Year, Are You Lonesome Tonight (as Musical Director). Membership: PRS. Hobbies: Middlesbrough Football Club; Snooker; Cooking; Writing; Home studio; Songwriting; Partying. Current Management: Sacha Brooks, 55 Greek Street, London W1V 5LR, England. Address: 4 Orchard Road, Linthorpe, Middlesbrough, Cleveland TS5 4PW, England.

KAZAN Paul, b. 9 Apr 1956, Taplow, Buckinghamshire, England. Singer; Musician (piano, violin); composer; Producer. m. Montserrat Arruga, 21 Oct 1994, 1 son. Musical Education: 1 year at Bristol University; Grade VIII Piano; Grade VII violin. Career: Classical background; Settled in Spain, 1976; Session musician, arranger until 1990; Solo artiste, 1990-; Presented first solo album in concert at Barcelona Olympic Games, 1992. Recordings: Albums: Stay, 1992; Miracle Street, 1996. Membership: Spanish Society of Authors (SGAE). Hobbies: Model railways; Travel. Current Management: Oniria International, S L. Address: Alzines, 3, Sant Quirze Park, 08192 Sant Quirze Del Valles, Barcelona, Spain.

KAZASSIAN Hilda, b. 1970, Sofia, Bulgaria. Vocalist; Musician(keyboards, drums, percussion); Composer; Arranger. Musicial Education: Graduate, Academy of Popular Music, Sofia, 1993; Studied percussion in UK and Italy. Career: Hot Jazz debutant; Guest appearances at several jazz festivals; Winner of percussion competitions in Rome and London; Currently working with Acoustic Version (Bulgaria's leading jazz combo); Writes and arranges own compositions. Recordings: Albums: Cover Girl, 1994; Why Not, 1996. Address: c/o Union Media Ltd, 71 Evlogi Georgiev Blvd, Entr. A, Sofia 1142, Bulgaria.

KAZDA Jan, b. 3 October 1958, Prague, Czech Republic. Musician (Bass, Guitar);

Composer; Producer. m. Karen K, 1988, 1 son. Education: Classical Music Degrees; Artists Maturity Degree. Career: Tours with: Ginger Baker, Randy Brecker, Peter Brötzmann, Sonny Sharrock; with own band: Das Pferd and KAZDA, Frankfurt Jazz Festival, Sibiu Jazz Festival (Rumanian), Ruhr-Jazz Leverkusener Jazz Festival; Rockpalast TV HR/WDR TV. Compositions: Composer, 5 CD's with Das Pferd; 2 CD's with KAZDA, 1994-97; 4 CD's with singer Tom Mega, 1988-92. Recordings: Das Pferd, KAZDA, Tom Mega, 1987-97; Recorded with Ginger Baker, Harry Beckett, Randy Brecker, Marilyn Mazur, Ronnell Bey, Frank Wunsch, Nordwestdeutsche Philharmonique (classical orchestra). Address: Dörpfeldstr 41, D-42369 Wuppertal, Germany.

KEAREY Ian, b. 14 Oct 1954, London, England. Singer; Musician (guitar, bass guitar, banjo, mandolin). m. Rebekah Zoob, 19 Apr 1986, 1 son, 1 daughter. Education: University of Kent, Canterbury. Musical Education: Self-taught. Career: Member, Oyster Band, 1976-88; Member, Blue Aeroplanes, 1983-; Producer for: Michelle Shocked; Bootfare; Many television appearances include: Top Of The Pops; Many radio appearances include: Radio 1, Radio 2 sessions; Freelance sessions, 1986-; Member, Heaven Factory, 1990-. Recordings include: with Blue Aeroplanes: Bop Art, 1984; Swagger, 1990; Beatsongs, 1991; Life Model, 1993; Rough Music, 1994; with Oyster Band: Liberty Hall, 1985; Step Outside, 1986; Wide Blue Yonder, 1987; with Gerard Langley: Siamese Boyfriends, 1987; with Heidi Berry: Love, 1991. Publications: Contributor, Folk Roots Magazine, 1984-. Honours: Freedom of the City of Bangor, 1980; Honorary BSC, Indian Institute of Technology, 1986. Membership: Musicians' Union. Hobbies: Cycling; Reading; Collecting music-hall ephemera. Current Management: E Bunbury, RFM. Address: 88 Roundhill Crescent, Brighton, East Sussex BN2 3FR, England.

KEEL Howard (Harold C Leek), b. 13 Apr 1917, Gillespie, Illinois, USA. Singer; Actor. Career: In-house entertainer, Douglas aircraftmanufacturing company; Appeared in musicals: Carousel, 1945; Oklahoma, London; Film appearances: The Small Voice, 1948; Annie Get Your Gun, 1950; Show Boat, 1951; Kiss Me Kate, 1953; Calamity Jane, 1953; Rose Marie, 1954; Seven Brides For Seven Brothers, 1954; Kismet, 1955; Various western movies; US revival tours, 1960s; Regular television appearances, US series Dallas, 1981-; Solo recording artiste, 1984-; Farewell Tour, UK, 1993. Recordings: And I Love You So, 1984; Reminiscing, 1985; The Collection, 1989; The Great MGM Stars, 1991; Close To My Heart, 1991; Various soundtrack albums. Address: c/o Producers Inc., 11806 N 56th Street, Suite B, Tampa, FL 33617, USA.

KEEREMAN Peter, b. 21 August 1968, Brugge, Belgium. Producer; Composer; Pianist. Education: Degree in Music Education, Ghent, Belgium; Graduate, Berklee, College of Music, Music Production and Engineering. Career: Concert tours with Belgian artists; Performances for BRT - Radio & Television. Compositions: Everlasting Love & Revende Hemel (Intersong Primakera), Spaceflight/Snow Flakes; Crazy Comedy Capers (Parsifal). Membership: SABAM Author Organisation. Hobbies: Running; Swimming. Address: Doornstraat 47, 8200 Brugge, Belgium.

KEEZER Geoffrey Graham, b. 20 Nov 1970, Eau Claire, Wisconsin, USA. Jazz Musician (piano); Composer; Arranger. m. Mayumi Tomokane, 23 Apr 1995. Musical Education: 1 year, Berklee College, Boston. Career: Pianist with Art Blakey and the Jazz Messengers, 1989-90; Pianist with Art Farmer, 1991-95; Leader of Geoff Keezer trio and quartet, 1988; Tours: Japan; England; Europe; Russia; Scandinavia;

Canada; Performed: at Lincoln Center; with Carnegie Hall Jazz Orchestra; with Hollywood Bowl Orchestra. Compositions: Many large and small ensemble pieces. Recordings: As leader: Here And Now, 1991; World Music, 1992; Other Spheres, 1993; All For One, with Art Blakey; The Key Players, with The Contemporary Piano Ensemble; Color And Light - Jazz Sketches On Sondheim; Some Of My Best Friends..., with Ray Brown. Membership: BMI; AMRA. Hobbies: Karate; Okinawan weaponry; Japanese language. Address: The Jazz Tree, 648 Broadway, Suite 703, New York, NY 10012, USA.

KEITA Salif, b. 1949, Djoliba, Mali (West Africa). Singer. Career: Japan Tour, 1993; Grande Parade du Jazz de Nice, 1992; WOMAD Festivals: Reading, 1992; Adelaide, 1993; Las Palmas, 1993; Australian tour, 1993; Annual European tour including summer festivals; Montreux Jazz Festivals, 1993, 1995; Canadian tour, 1994; US tour, 1994; African tour, including South Africa, 1994; Parkpop Festival, The Hague, Holland, 1995. Recordings: Soro, 1987; Koyan, 1989; Amen, 1991; Mansa Of Mali, 1994; Folon, 1995. Publications: Video: Noble Of An Outcast. Honours: Chevalier of Arts And Letters, France; Chevalier of Order Of The Nation, Mali; Nominated for US Music Awards: Best World Music Artist, 1992; Grammy. Current Management: Mad Minute Music, Paris, contact Corinne Serres. Address: c/o Mad Minute Music, 5-7 Paul Bert, 93400 St Ouen, France.

KEITH (John) Larry, b. 1 Mar 1955, Hendersonville, North Carolina, USA. Musician (guitar, bass); Vocalist. m. Denna O Nix, 23 Dec 1988, 1 son, 2 daughters. Musical Education: Blue Ridge Community College, Hendersonville, North Carolina. Career: WKIT-WHKP Radio Hendersonville, The Charlie Renfro Concerts, 1980-84; Appearances with: Carl Story and The Ramblin' Mountaineers; The Boys From Indiana; Jim and Jesse and the Virginia Boys; Bill Monroe and The Bluegrass Boys; Doyle Lawson and Quicksilver; Mac Wiseman; Dolly Parton's Premiere Bluegrass Band, Pigeon Forge, Tennessee, 1984-88. Recordings: Albums: First Time Around; On And On; Head Over Heels; Second Time Around; The Old Country Church. Publications; The Bluegrass Newsletter (monthly). Memberships: IBMA; The Bluegrass Music Association of North Carolina, South Carolina, Georgia. Hobbies: Gardening; Classic cars. Current Management: The McMinn Family Band. Address: PO Box 384, Tuxedo, NC 28784, USA.

KEITHLEY Joseph Edward, b. Burnaby, BC, Canada. m. Laura Susan, 2 sons, 1 daughter. Selftaught. Career: 20 years in punk rock band, DOA; Solo acoustic folk act; Appeared in cult films, Terminal City; The Widower. Compositions: 10 albums with DOA. Recordings: Bloodied But Unbound; War on 45; Last Scream of the Missing Neighbours. Publications: Spin, 1985; High Times, 1995; Rolling Stone, 1997. Current Management: Laurie Mercer Management, PO Box 27070, Collingwood PP, Vancouver, BC, Canada.

KELLARD Colin Alan, b. 9 Jan 1941, Bury St Edmunds, Suffolk, England. Insurance Claims Inspector; Musician (banjo, guitar). m. Pamela Randall, 24 Sep 1966, 1 son, 1 daughter. Musical Education: Self-taught. Career: Member of Alvin Roy Saratoga Jazz Band, 1959-63; Tours of Germany, 1961 and 1962; Television appearance: Let's Go, BBC, 1961; Member of Rad Newton Jazz Friends, with various appearances at jazz festivals in UK and Holland, 1987-92; Leader, own Jazz band, 1992-. Recordings: Many recordings with Alvin Roy Saratoga Jazz Band; Own label recordings with Tad Newton Jazz Friends and Colin Kellard Band. Honour: Winner, Soho Fair Jazz Band Contest with Alvin Roy Saratoga Jazz Band, 1960. Hobby: Music. Address: 15 Nathaniel Walk, Tring, Hertfordshire HP23 5DQ, England.

KELLERMANN Lone, b. 20 Mar 1943, Copenhagen, Denmark. Singer. Musical Education: Self-taught. Career: Member of several bands; Numerous film, television, theatre and radio appearances; Many interviews, Scandinavian papers. Recordings: 5 solo albums; Several other recordings. Memberships: DJBFA; Danish Artist Union. Hobby: Having a good time. Current Management: Danish Artist Union. Address: Amagengade 11, 1423 Copenhagen, Denmark.

KELLIE Michael Alexander, b. 24 Mar 1947, Birmingham, England. Musician (drums). m. (1) Apr 1969, 1 daughter, (2) Sept 1997. Musical Education: Self-taught. Career: Original member, Island Records family, 1966-76; Spooky Tooth, 1967 to end; The Only Ones, 1976-81; World tours with above; Recordings with many others; Currently involved in recording new Spooky Tooth album for release in 1998. Recordings: Spooky Two, Spooky Tooth; With A Little Help From My Friends, Joe Cocker; Tommy (film soundtrack), The Who. Memberships: Musicians' Union; PAMRA. Hobbies: Farming; Songwriting. Current Management: Alec Sutton, Attic Music. Address: Attic Music, 19 Holly Road, Edgbaston, Birmingham B16 9NH, England.

KELLY Jeff. Songwriter; Musician (multi-instrumentalist). m. Susanne. Career: Formed the Green Pajamas, 1984-; Also solo artiste. Compositions include: Kim The Waitress, covered by Material Issue and Sister Psychic. Recordings: Albums: with The Green Pajamas: Summer Of Lust, 1984, 1990; Halloween, 1984; Book Of Hours, 1987; November, 1988; Ghosts Of Love, 1990; Solo: Baroquen Hearts, 1985; Coffee In Nepal, 1987, 1991; Portugal, 1990; Twenty Five, 1991; Private Electrical Storm, 1992; Ash Wednesday Rain, 1995; Featured on compilations: Monkey Business, 1986; Splat Sampler, 1988; Time Will Show The Wiser, 1989; The 4th Adventure, 1991. Address: c/o Green Monkey Records, PO Box 31983, Seattle, WA 98103, USA.

KELLY Jon. Record Producer. 3 children. Recordings: Produced Records for: Blue is the Colour, Beautiful South, UK No 1; Deacon Blue; Chris Rea; Kate Bush; The Damned; Jimmy Nail; The Levellers; Fish. Current Management: One Management, 43 St Alban's Avenue, London, W4 5JS, England.

KELLY Juliet, b. 6 May 1970, London, England. Jazz Vocalist. Education: BSc (Hons), Economics; MA, Television Production. Musical Education: Post-graduate Jazz course, Guildhall School of Music and Drama. Career: Part of a cappella Group, Darker Than Blue (formerly Jazz Voices); Performed at Purcell Room, South Bank, part of London Jazz Festival, 1994; Festivals in Germany, 1995; Australia, 1996; Touring with Orphy Robinson, Phoenix Dance Company Project, across UK, including Sadlers Wells, 1995. Membership: Musicians' Union. Hobbies: Travel; Cinema; Reading.

KELLY Mark, b. 9 Apr 1961, Dublin, Ireland. Musician (keyboards). Career: Member, Chemical Alice; UK progressive rock group, Marillion, 1981-; Appearances include: Theakston Festival, 1982; Reading Festival, 1982; Nostell Priory Festival, 1982, 1984; Glastonbury Festival, 1983; Support to Rush, Radio City Music Hall, New York, 1983; Milton Keynes Bowl, 1984; Monsters Of Rock Festival, Castle Donington, 1985; Nelson Mandela Birthday Party with Midge Ure, Wembley Stadium, 1987; Welcome To The Garden Party, Milton Keynes Bowl, 1986. Recordings: Albums: Script For A Jester's Tear, 1983; Fugazi, 1984; Real To Reel, 1984; Misplaced Childhood, 1985; Brief Encounter, 1986; B-Sides Themselves, 1988; The Thieving Magpie, 1988; Season's End, 1989; Holidays In Eden, 1991; A Singles Collection 1982-1992, 1992; Brave, 1994; Afraid Of Sunlight,

1995; This Strange Engine, 1997; Singles include: Market Square Heroes, 1982; He Knows You Know, 1983; Garden Party, 1983; Punch And Judy, 1984; Assassing, 1984; Kayleigh (Number 2, UK), 1985; Lavender, 1985; Heart Of Lothian, 1985; Incommunicado, 1987; Sugar Mice, 1987; Warm Wet Circles, 1987; Freaks, 1988; Hooks In You, 1989; Uninvited Guest, 1989; Easter, 1990; Cover My Eyes (Pain And Heaven), 1991; No One Can, 1991; Dry Land, 1991; Sympathy, 1992. Current Management: Hit And Run Music Ltd., 30 Ives Street, London SW3 2ND, England.

KELLY Paul, b. 23 July 1962, England. Musician (guitar); Songwriter. Career: with groups: East Village; Saint Etienne; UK tours, 1988-90 with East Village; Played with Saint Etienne, 1992-; Tours: UK; Europe; Japan; USA; Festivals: Glastonbury; Roskilde; Hultsfred; Television includes: Top Of The Pops; The Beat; The Word; Later With Jools Holland; Glastonbury, 1994. Recordings: Albums: with East Village: Drop Out; Hot Rod Hotel; BBC Radio 1 session with St Etienne, 1994.

KELLY Roger, b. 3 Apr 1953, Balby, Doncaster, England. Musician (guitar). m. Sabine Kirchner, divorced. Education: BA Hons, Business Studies. Musical Education: Self-taught. Career: Toured with Streetband (with Paul Young); Appeared Top Of The Pops, 1979; Appeared Rock Palast, Germany witj Starry-Eyed And Laughing; Session work with Sandy Shaw in 1980s; Teaching and transcription work also production. Recordings: Albums: Streetband: London; Dilemma; Hit single: Toast (B Side of Hold On) 1979; Co-wrote, produced all album, single material with Paul Young and co-member, John Gifford. Membership: PRS. Hobbies: Guitar playing; Reading; Cycling. Address: 1 Salvington Gardens, Worthing, Sussex, England.

KELSEY Peter R, b. 25 Jan 1949, Lincoln, England. Recording Engineer; Producer. m. Catherine Deguilly, 22 Oct 1985, 2 daughters. Education: BSc Honours degree, Mathematics. Career: Started Trident Studios, London, 1972; Chief Engineer, 1976; Freelance Engineer, 1978; Moved to USA, 1979; Freelance engineer and producer, recordings, film and television music. Recordings: Goodbye Yellow Brick Road, Elton John; Heat Treatment, Graham Parker; Discreet Music, Brian Eno; Dialects, Zawinul; Sans Regrets, Veronique Sanson; Outside From The Redwoods, Kenny Loggins; with Kitaro: Mandala; Heaven and Earth; 7 albums with Jean-Luc Ponty including Mystical Adventures; No Absolute Time; Television: Thirtysomething; Picket Fences; Tekwar; Films: Color Of Night; Best of Best 2; Poison Ivy. Honours: NME Engineering Award, Cafe Jacques, 1976; Emmy Nomination, Kenny Loggins, 1994. Memberships: NARAS; Re-Pro. Hobbies: Reading; Computers; Tennis; Tae Kwon Do. Address: 11022 Haskell Avenue, Granada Hills, CA 91344, USA.

KEMANIS Aina, b. 15 June 1952, Berkeley, California, USA. Singer. Education: Foreign Languages, Music, Diablo Valley College. Career: Sang in Bars, Folk Music, California, 1976-79; Free Jazz with Barre Phillips, 1979-82; Sang in Kitka, Eastern European Women's Chorus, 1987-88; Toured Europe with Barre Phillips, early 1980's; Toured Europe and Scandinavia with Marilyn Mazur, 1988-97; Numerous Radio and TV appearances. Recordings: Journal Violone II, 1979; Music By, 1980; Montsalvat, 1995; Do the Day Over, 1995; Small Labyrinths, 1997. Publication: Compiled traditional Norwegian Music with Hans Wendl for CD, Nordisk Song, 1990. Address: 2726 Dwight Way #8, CA 94704, USA.

KEMP Gary, b. 16 Oct 1959, Islington, London, England. Musician (guitar); Songwriter; Actor. Career: Founder member, Spandau Ballet (originally the Makers), 1979-90; Performances include: Royal Albert Hall, 1982; Royal Festival

Hall, 1982; Wembley Arena, 1984; Live Aid, Wembley, 1985; Solo appearances: Labour Party Red Wedge Tour, 1986; Prince's Trust Rock Gala, 1987; Actor, films: The Krays (with brother Martin), 1988; The Bodyguard, 1992. Compositions: All hit singles by Spandau Ballet. Recordings: Singles include: To Cut A Long Story Short, 1980; The Freeze, 1981; Musclebound, 1981; Chant No. 1 (I Don't Need This Pressure On), 1981; Instinction, 1982; Lifeline, 1982; Communication, 1983; True, 1983; Gold, 1984; Only When You Leave, 1984; I'll Fly For You, 1984; Highly Strung, 1984; Round And Round, 1984; Fight For Ourselves, 1986; Albums: Journey To Glory, 1981; Diamond, 1982; True, 1983; Parade, 1984; The Singles Collection, 1985; Through The Barricades, 1986; Heart Like A Sky, 1989; The Best Of Spandau Ballet, 1991; Solo album: Little Bruises, 1995. Honours include: BRIT Award, Sony Trophy for Technical Excellence, 1984. Current Management: Steve Dagger, Dagger Enterprises, 14 Lambton Place, London W11 2SH, England.

KEMP Martin, b. 10 Oct 1961, Islington, London, England. Education: Acting lessons, Anna Scher's Children's Theatre, 1970. Career: Member, Spandau Ballet, 1979-90; Concerts include: Royal Albert Hall, Sadlers Wells, Royal Festival Hall, London, 1983; Live Aid, Wembley, 1985; TV special, Ibiza 92, 1987; Actor, films: The Krays (with brother Gary), 1988; Waxwork II - Lost In Time, 1992; Actor, television series: Growing Rich, 1991. Recordings: Albums: Journey To Glory, 1981; Diamond, 1982; True, 1983; Parade, 1984; The Singles Collection, 1985; Through The Barricades, 1986; Heart Like A Sky, 1989; The Best Of Spandau Ballet, 1991; Singles include: To Cut A Long Story Short, 1980; The Freeze, 1981; Musclebound, 1981; Chant #1 (I Don't Need This Pressure On), 1981; Paint Me Down, 1981; Instinction, 1982; Lifeline, 1982; Communication, 1983; True (Number 1, UK), 1983; Gold (used for BBC's Olympics coverage, 1984), 1983; Only When You Leave, 1984; Highly Strung, 1984; Round And Round, 1984; Fight For Ourselves, 1986; Contributor, Do They Know It's Christmas?, Band Aid, 1984. Honours include: BRIT Award, Sony Trophy For Technical Excellence, 1984. Current Management: c/o Peters Fraser & Dunlop Artistes, 503/4 The Chambers, Chelsea Harbour, London SW10 0XF, England.

KENDALL Tony (The Essex Man), b. 9 May 1944, Walthamstow, Essex, England. Musician (acoustic bass, guitar, fiddle). m. Carole Anne Bailey, 18 June 1966, 1 daughter. Education: East Ham CAT, London University. Musical Education: Self-taught. Career: Collector, writer, performer, traditional and original songs, County of Essex (500 songs in repertoire); Regular broadcaster for BBC Essex; Appeared at Royal Festival Hall, London Barbican, folk club, history societies nationwide; Musician, Chingford Morrismen, Barnet Fair Ceilidh Band. Recordings: Albums: Rose Of Essex; Closer To The Heartland; An Essex Terret; A Christmas Wassail; A Bicycle Ride With Vaughan Williams, 1995. Memberships: Musicians' Union; PRS; MCPS. Hobbies: Countryside issues; Local history; Campaigner for (sufferer from) ME. Current Management: Stormforce Arts. Address: 18 Edward Avenue, Chingford, London E4 9DN, England.

KENNEDY Peter Douglas, b. 18 Nov 1922, London, England. Ethno-Musicologist. m. Beryl, 3 sons, 1 daughter. Education: Architectural Association School of Architecture, London, 1940-42. Career: Sometimes referred to as Mr Folk; Was main catalyst in post-war Folk Revival in England; North East Area Representative, English Folk Dance & Song Society, 1947-48; Joined BBC Staff, Bristol, 1949; Started mobile recording of traditional folk singers and instrumentalists, Britain and Ireland, 1950-; Leader, own Haymakers Folk Dance band, including Village Barn Dance radio broadcasts, 1951; BBC Folk Music and Dialect Recording

Scheme, with Seamus Ennis, 1952-58; EFDSS staff, London, 1958-68; Established Performers Booking Agency and first Folksong Club in London; Co-organiser, first National Folk Festival, Keele University, 1964, and National Folk Federation, 1965; Degree Lecturer, Folk Studies, Dartington College of Arts, Totnes, Devon, 1969-79; Set up International Folk Archive, 1980; Regular radio and television broadcaster, 1950-70. Recordings: Numerous field recordings of traditional singers and players, customs, dialect and traditions, 1950-; Also recorded many well-known folk performers including Ewan McColl, Bert Lloyd, The Dubliners and the Liverpool Spinners; Recent CDs include: Sea Songs and Shanties; Songs of the Travelling People, 1994; Traditional Songs of Ireland, 1995; Bagpipes of Britain and Ireland, 1996; Traditional Dance Music of Ireland, 1997; English Customs and Traditions, 1997; World Library of Folk and Primitive Music: England and Yugoslavia, 1998. Publications include: The Fiddler's Tunebook, 2 volumes, 1951, 1953; Everybody Swing, Square Dance music, 1952; Editor, UNESCO International Folk Film Directory, 1970; Editor, International Folk Directory, 1973; The Folksongs of Britain and Ireland, 1975; Fiddler's Book of Reels, 1997; Fiddler's Book of Jigs, 1998. Honours: McColvin Award, Outstanding Reference Book of 1975. Memberships: The English Folk Dance and Song Society; The Folklore Society; The Society for Folk-Life Studies. Address: Folk & Blues International Archive, 16 Brunswick Square, Gloucester GL1 1UG, England.

KENNELL Richard W (Rick), b. 8 Nov 1952, Fort Wayne, Indiana, USA. Musician (bass guitar); Recording Artist; Record Producer. m. Leah Marie Waybright, 8 Jan 1976. Education: Indiana University; James Madison University. Recordings: 6 albums currently available: Happy The Man: Happy The Man; Crafty Hands; Better Late; Beginnings; Retrospective; Happy The Man Live; Also: Run Into The Ground. Memberships: ASCAP; NARAS; AES. Hobbies: Basketball; Working in studio. Current Management: The Inner Circle. Address: 77 Tarrytown Road, Suite 201, White Plains, NY 10607, USA.

KENT Rolfe, b. 18 Apr 1963, St Albans, Hertfordshire, England. Composer; Film Composer. Education: BSc Hons, Psychology, Leeds University. Career: Film scores: Final Combination, 1993; Voices From A Locked Room, 1995; Mercy, 1995; Television scores: Big City Metro, 1989; Shalom Joan Collins, CH4, 1989; So Haunt Me, BBC, 1991; Inside Out, 1990; Musicals: Air And Opportunity, 1995. Honours: AICP (American Independent Commecial Producers) Award, Best Music, 1993. Memberships: PRS; AFofM; BMI. Hobbies: Hiking; Watching Sumo wrestling; Travel. Current Management: David May, Santa Monica, California, USA.

KENT Simon Patrick Gilles, b. 20 Feb 1968, Portsmouth, Hampshire, England. Musician (keyboards, guitar); Vocalist. Education: Southampton Institute Of Higher Education. Musical Education: St Johns Cathedral Choir, Pianoforte to Grade 5. Career: Former member, Complex, 1986-1989; Founder, songwriter, lead vocalist, guitarist, keyboard player, Waterfall, 1991; Performed Heineken Festival, 1993; Fuji Television show, 1993; British tour, 1995. Recordings: with Waterfall: Round Inside, 1994; 1000 x Closer (featured track, compilation album: Postcards From The Concrete Nipple), 1994. Membership: Musicians' Union. Hobbies: Cricket; Football; Theatre; Travel; Animals. Current Management: Flamingo Record Management. Address: Highfield House, Danemore Lane, South Godstone, Surrey RH19 8JF, England.

KENYON Duncan, b. 10 Dec 1961, Wembley, Middlesex, England. Rehearsal Studio Owner; Musician (bass guitar, guitar). m. 6 Sept 1991, divorced 1993. Musical Education:

Self-taught from age of 8 years. Career: With French Impression; Toured with The Cool Notes; Support to Rose Royce; Odyssey; German television Oldie Parade with Hello, performed Tell Him and New York Groove; Currently touring with Hello. Recordings: Singles with French Impression: Breaking Love, 1984-5; Get Up And Dance; Currently recording Hello album, and Christmas songs. Memberships: PRS; Musicians' Union. Hobbies: All sports; Social hobbies. Current Management: David Blaylock. Address: 39 Leyton Road, Harpenden, Herts AL5 2JB, England.

KERNON Neil Anthony, b. 13 Sept 1953, London, England. Record Producer; Sound Engineer. m. Kellie O'Neal, 13 July 1991. Career: Recording engineer, Trident Studios, UK, 1971-75; Le Chateau d'Herouville, France, 1975; Startling Studios, UK, 1976-79; Independent producer, USA, 1979-. Recordings: As engineer, producer: Albums with Hall and Oates: Voices, 1980; Private Eyes, 1981; H2O, 1982; Rock'n'Soul Part 1, 1983; Sign In Please, with Autograph, 1984; with Dokken: Under Lock And Key, 1985; Back For The Attack, 1987; Singles: with Hall And Oates: Kiss On My List, 1980; Private Eyes, 1981; I Can't Go For That, 1981; Maneater, 1982. Honours: Platinum and Gold, discs. Hobbies: Sport; Travel; Films. Current Management: Louis Levin Management, 130 W 57th Street, #10B, New York, NY 10019, USA.

KERR Jim, b. 9 July 1959, Glasgow, Scotland. Singer. m. (1) Chrissie Hynde, 1984, divorced, 1 daughter, (2) Patsy Kensit, 1993, divorced, 1 son. Career: Founder, Scottish rock group Simple Minds, 1978-; Worldwide tours and concerts include: WOMAD Festival, Somerset, 1982; Phoenix Park, Dublin, 1983; Support to the Pretenders, US tour, 1984; Live Aid, Philadelphia, 1985; Headliners, Milton Keynes Bowl Pop Festival, 1986; Nelson Mandela 70th Birthday Tribute, 1988; Nelson Mandela - An International Tribute concert, Wembley, 1990. Recordings: Albums: Life In A Day, 1979; Real To Real Cacophony, 1980; Empires And Dance, 1980; Sons And Fascinations, 1981; Sister Feelings Call, 1981; Celebration, 1982; New Gold Dream, 1982; Sparkle In The Rain, 1984; Once Upon A Time, 1985; Live In The City Of Light, 1987; Street Fighting Years, 1989; Themes (4 vols), 1990; Real Life, 1991; Glittering Prize 81-92, 1992; Good News From The Next World, 1995; Neapolis, 1998; Hit singles include: Promised You A Miracle, 1982; Glittering Prize, 1982; Someone Somewhere (In Summertime), 1982; Waterfront, 1983; Speed Your Love To Me, 1984; Up On The Catwalk, 1984; Don't You Forget About Me, used in film Breakfast Club (Number 1, US), 1985; Alive And Kicking, 1985; Sanctify Yourself, 1986; All The Things She Said, 1986; Ghostdancing, 1986; Belfast Child, 1989; This Is Your Land, 1989; Kick It In, 1989; Let There Be Love, 1991; See The Lights, 1991; Stand By Love, 1991; Love Song, 1992. Honours include: Q Award, Best Live Act, 1991. Current Management: Clive Banks, 1 Glenthorne Mews, 115A Glenthorne Road, London W6 0LJ, England.

KERSHAW Andy, b. 9 Nov 1959, Rochdale, England. Broadcaster; Journalist. Education: Leeds University, 1978-82. Career: Broadcaster, BBC Radio One; BBC World Service. Honours: Sony Radio Award, Best Specialist Music Programme, 1987, 1989, 1996. Hobbies: Record collecting; Motorcycling; Travel. Current Management: Sumi Jenner, Sincere Management. Address: Flat B, 6 Bravington Road, London W9 3AH, England.

KERSHAW Martin John, b. 13 July 1944, Shipley, Yorkshire, England. Musician (guitar, banjo, bouzouki, mandolin, ukelele); Composer. Divorced, 1 daughter. Musical Education: Self-taught. Career: Member, number of bands including Manfred Mann; Moved to London, 1966;

Played with: John Dankworth Big Band; Jack Parnell Orchestra; James Last Orchestra; Session guitarist; Guitarist on all 120 Muppet Shows; Television shows, performances include: Perry Como, Michael Jackson; Randy Crawford; Kate Bush; John Denver; Jack Jones; David Essex; David Bowie; Elton John; Buddy Rich; Johnny Cash; Ray Charles; Tom Jones; Glen Campbell; Bing Crosby; Petula Clark; Crystal Gayle; Diana Ross; Dusty Springfield; Andy Williams; Linda Ronstadt; Dizzy Gillespie; Burt Bacharach; Peggy Lee; Perry Como; Julie Andrews; Englebert Humperdinck; Playing featured in films including: Passage To India; Mad Max Thunderdrome; Little Shop Of Horrors; Diamonds Are Forever; Ghandi; You Only Live Twice; Live And Let Die; TV series, Riders; Began composing, 1983-; Recently toured with Sasha Distel. Compositions include: Film: Nightmare Weekend; Commercials include: Sainsbury's; Interflora; Persil; Dulux Paint; Unipart; Boots; TV Themes: Eurosport coverage Olympic Games, 1992; Russell Harty Show; London Programme; Incidental music includes: Prisoner Cell Block H; A Bouquet Of Barbed Wire; Cagney And Lacey; Within These Walls; Promotional videos; Titles for Production Music Libraries include: Bruton; Music House; Peer; Weinberger. Memberships: Musicians' Union; PRS. Hobbies: Fishing; Birdwatching; Current Management: Broadley Music. Address: 1 Bramley Close, Pewsey, Wilts SN9 5HB, England.

KERSHAW Nik (Nicholas David), b. 1 Mar 1958, Bristol, England. Singer; Musician (guitar); Songwriter. m. Sheri. Career: Member, jazz-funk group Fusion; Solo artiste, with backing band The Krew, 1983-. Compositions include: The One And Only, Chesney Hawkes (Number 1, UK), 1991. Recordings: Albums: Human Racing, 1984; The Riddle, 1984; Radio Musicola, 1986; The Works, 1990; The Collection, 1991; Singles: I Won't Let The Sun Go Down On Me (Number 2, UK), 1984; Wouldn't It Be Good, 1984; Guest musician, Nikita, Elton John, 1985.

KERSHAW Steve P, b. 17 Mar 1959, Bradford, Yorkshire, England. Musician (double bass, bass guitar). Education: Bristol University, BA Hons, 1978-81; PhD, 1986. Musical Education: Bass Institute of Technology, Hollywood, California. Career: Member, British Youth Symphony Orchestra, 1978-1982; After Hours; False Idols; Then There Were Six; Claude Bottom And The Lion Tamers; The Honkin' Hep Cats; The Rascals Of Rhythm; Stekpanna; Television: Out West, HTV; ITV Telethon; Film: The Clothes In The Wardrobe; Great Moments in Aviation; Radio: The Usual Suspects; Jungr and Parker At The Edinburgh Festival; Loose Ends; Mary Costello Show; Breakfast Breakout; Honkin' With The Hep Cats At The Edinburgh Festival. Recordings: with After Hours: All Over Town, 1980; with False Idols: Ten Seconds To Midnight, 1981; Centre Of Attention, 1985; Fine Blue Line, 1987; with L'Orange, Si J'Etais Vous, 1991; with The Honkin' Hep Cats: What's The Use?, 1989; Honkin' 'n' Stompin', 1992; Rantin' Ravin' 'n' Misbehavin', 1994; with Stekpanna: Standin' Tall, 1997. Honours: Outstanding Vocational Honours Award, GHS, 1996, Outstanding Student of the Year Award, Fender, 1996, Musicians Institute. Memberships: Musicians' Union; International Society of Bassists. Hobbies: Cricket; Rugby League; Malt Whisky. Current Management: Flat Five Management. Address: 5 Cardwell Crescent, Headington, Oxford OX3 7QE, England.

KERWIN Michael Thomas, b. 19 February 1970, Freiburg, Germany. Producer; Engineer. Education: Honours in Music, Humber College, 1994. Career: Founder, Newmarket Multimedia Recording Studio, 1994; Co-Founder, Limit Records Inc, 1995. Recordings: Producer, Engineer: 30 Odd 6, 1996; Beru's Nephew, 1996; Stone Idols, 1997; Co Producer, Engineer: Woodrow, 1997; The Salads, 1997; Engineer: Sarah Sloan, 1997; Al Connelly, 1996. Current

Management: Last Call Promotions, Unit 5, Newmarket, Ontario, L3Y 3E3, Canada. Address: 312 Maple Street, Newmarket, Ontario L3Y 3K3, Canada.

KESTI Jouni, b. 21 Sept 1946, Oula, Finland. Composer; Musician (percussion); Bandleader. Career: Professional musician, 1966-; Percussionist, Kajaani Big Band, 1979-82; Became full-time composer, 1982-; Leader, Jouni Kesti Ensemble; Performances featured in modern music festivals, Finland, 1983-; Also performed in Sweden and Germany. Compositions include: 5-part composition, Black And Pale Trees, with clarinetists Kari Kriikku and Heikki Nikula, premiered at Audio Box Festival, Italian Study, 1990. Recordings: Albums include: Kollaboratorio, Jouni Kesti Ensemble.

KETCHUM Hal (Michael), b. 1952, Greenwich, New York, USA. Country Singer; Songwriter; Musician (guitar, drums). Career: Drummer, R&B band; Guitarist, blues band; Singer, songwriter, with own band the Alibis, 1987-; Concerts include: Kerville Folk Festival, 1987. Recordings: Albums include: Threadbare Alibi, 1989; Past The Point Of Rescue, 1989; Sure Love, 1992. Current Management: Crowley Artist Management. Address: c/o 602 Wayside Drive, Wimberley, TX 78676, USA.

KHALADJ Madjid, b. 11 Nov 1962, Ghazvin, Iran. Musician (percussion; tombak); Composer. Education: Graduate, School Of Fine Arts, Paris. Musical Education: Graduate, Traditional Academy Of Persian Art Music, Iran. Career: Concerts and radio appearances: Grand Palais, Paris, 1991; Barbad Symposium, Tadjikstan, with Master Shadjarian, 1991; Grande Auditorium de Radio France, with Master Alizadeh, 1992, 1994; Opéra de Lille, 1992; Los Angeles Festival, USA, J Paul Getty Museum, 1993; Théâtre de la Ville, Paris, 1993; Théâtre de la Colline and Radio France, with Master Tala'i, 1994. Recordings: Persian Classical Music, 1992; Persian Art Music, 1992; Iran-The Art Of Tombak, 1993; Music Of Iran, Volumes 1 and 2, 1993; Iranian Music, Improvisations, 1994; Persian Classical Music, 1994; Los Angeles Festival, 1995. Honours: Honoured guest, nominated professor at the Center for Oriental Studies, Paris, Sorbonne Musicology Institute, 1984-. Membership: SACEM. Address: Madjid Khaladj Management, 56, Rue De Sèvres, 92100 Boulogne, France.

KHAN Ali Akbar, b. 14 Apr 1922, Shivpur, Bangladesh. Musician (sarod); Composer. Career: Musician, 1936-; Numerous tours, concerts and major festivals worldwide, 1955-; Founder, Ali Akbar Colleges of Music, Calcutta, India, 1956; San Rafael, California, 1968; Basel, Switzerland, 1982; Collaborations with artists including: Yehudi Menuhin; Ravi Shankar; Duke Ellington; Lecture recitals, major universities, US and Canada; Owner, record company Alam Madina Music Productions; Founder, Ali Akbar Khan Foundation, 1994; MacArthur Foundation Fellowship, 1991. Compositions: Concerti, orchestral pieces and ragas, including Chandranadan; Gauri Manjari; Alamgiri; Medhavi. Recordings include: Legacy, 1996; Passing on the Tradition, 1996. Honours: President of India Award, 1963, 1966; Grand Prix Du Disque, 1968; Hon DLitt Rabindra Bharati University, Calcutta, 1974; Padmabhibhushan Award, 1989; Doctor of Arts, California Institute of Arts, 1991; Kalidas Award, 1992; Bill Graham Lifetime Award, BAM, 1993; Meet the Composer Award, 1996; National Heritage Fellowship, National Endowment for the Arts, 1997; Asian Pantes Ceremony Award, Hall of Fame, Calcutta, 1997. Current Management: Gregory Digiovine, Santana Management, 121 Jordan Street, San Rafael, CA 94901, USA. Address: Ali Akbar College of Music, 215 West End Avenue, San Rafael, CA 94901, USA.

KHAN Chaka (Yvette Stevens), b. 23 Mar 1953, Great Lakes, Illinois, USA. Singer. Career: Member, Afro-Arts theatre, Chicago; Member, groups Shades Of Black; Lock & Chain; Rufus, 1972-1979; Renamed Rufus & Chaka Khan, 1978; Appearances include: Support to Elton John, Wembley, 1975; Rock'n'Bowl, for US Special Olympics, 1977; Solo artiste, 1978-; Concerts and tours include: European tour, 1988; World tour, 1992; A Night On The Town Concert Tour, 1993; Montreux Jazz Festival, 1993; North Sea Jazz Festival, The Hague, 1993; JVC Jazz Festival, Nice, 1993. Recordings: Albums: with Rufus: Rufus, 1979; Rags To Rufus, 1974; Rufusized, 1975; Rufus Featuring Chaka Khan, 1976; Ask Rufus, 1977; Street Player, 1978; Numbers, 1979; Masterjam, 1980; Camouflage, 1981; Party 'Til You're Broke, 1981; Live - Stompin' At The Savoy, 1983; Life Is A Dance - The Remix Project, 1989; Sweet Things - Greatest Hits, 1993; Solo albums: Chaka, 1978; Naughty, 1980; What Cha' Gonna Do For Me, 1981; Chaka Khan, 1983; I Feel For You, 1984; Destiny, 1986; C.K., 1989; The Woman I Am, 1992; Contributor, Echoes Of An Era, Lenny White, 1982; Rock Rhythm And Blues compilation, 1989; Music Of Quality And Distinction compilation, 1991; Hallelujah!, Quincy Jones, 1992; Hot House, Bruce Hornsby, 1995; Hit singles: with Rufus: Tell Me Something Good, 1974; You Got The Love, 1974; Once You Get Started, 1975; Sweet Thing, 1976; Solo singles: I'm Every Woman, 1979; Ain't Nobody, 1983; I Feel For You, 1984; This Is My Night, 1985; Eye To Eye, 1985; Own The Night (used in television series Miami Vice), 1986; Love Of A Lifetime, 1986; Underground, duet with David Bowie, for film Labyrinth, 1986; Feels Like Heaven, duet with Peter Cetera, 1992; Contributor, Dreamland, Joni Mitchell, 1978; Stuff Like That, Quincy Jones, 1978; Higher Love, Steve Winwood, 1986; I'll Be Good To You, Quincy Jones, 1990. Honours: Grammy Awards: Best R&B Vocal Performance, Chaka Khan, Best R&B Performance, Ain't Nobody, Best Vocal Arrangement, Be Bop Medley, 1984; Best Female R&B Vocal Performance, I Feel For You, 1985; Best R&B Performance, The Woman I Am, 1993; Gold discs. Current Management: The Brokaw Company, 9255 Sunset Blvd, Suite 804, Los Angeles, CA 90069, USA.

KHAN Steve Harris, b. 28 Apr 1947, Los Angeles, California, USA. Musician (guitar); Producer. Musical Education: BA, Composition, UCLA. Career: Solo guitarist and prolific session musician. Recordings: Solo albums: Tightrope, 1977; The Blue Man, 1978; Arrows, 1979; Evidence, Best Of, 1980; 1981; Blades, 1982; Eyewitness, 1983; Casa Loco, 1983; Helping Hand, 1987; Local Colour, 1988; Public Access, 1990; Let's Call This, 1991; Crossing Bridges, 1993; Other recordings with numerous artists including: Ashford and Simpson; Patti Austin; George Benson; Michael and Randy Brecker; Billy Cobham; Judy Collins; Larry Coryell; Blood, Sweat and Tears; Luther Allison; Donald Fagen; Aretha Franklin; Billy Joel; Chaka Khan; Kenny Loggins; David Sanborn; Phoebe Snow; Steel Dan; Grover Washington; Bob James. Publications: Wes Montgomery Guitar Folio, 1978; Pat Martino Guitar Solos, 1991; Steve Khan Songbook, 1991. Current Management: Christine Martin Management. Address: 688 Hands Creek Road, East Hampton, NY 11937, USA.

KHOZA Valanga, b. 21 December 1959, Tzaneen, South Africa. Singer; Songwriter; Musician (Kalimba, Guitar, Marimbas, Kora, Mouthharp, M'bira, flute). Education: University of South Africa, Pietersburg; BA, Business Accounting, Goshen University, Indiana, USA. Career: Solo peformance, Hemisphere, 5 piece acapella and percussion; Band Safika, 8 piece; Toured Australia extensively; Support act to Geoffrey Oryema, Lucky Dube, 1996; Lady Smith Black Mambazo, 1995; Soweto String Quartet, 1997; Major festivals all over Australia; Festival of Cultures, Sydney Opera House; Images of Africa,

Festival Copenhagen, Denmark, 6 weeks tour, 1996; ABC Music Deli Program (radio); Jaslyn Halls World Music; Live to air, Australian Broadcasting Commission. Recording: Sebe. Honour: Finalist, Aria Awards World Music Category, 1996. Hobbies: Running; Developing new instruments. Current Managements: KU Promotions, Box 77, Uki, 2484, Australia. Address: Box 77, Uki, 2484, Australia.

KID COCO (Marc Diericx), b. 11 Nov 1964, Ghent, Belgium. Singer; Composer; Musician (guitar, keyboards). Career: Lead vocalist, The Dinky Toys, 1981-1994; Solo artiste, 1995-. Recordings: Albums: with The Dinky Toys: The Colour Of Sex, 1992; Colourblind, 1993; Keep Hope Alive, 1994. Honours: Several Number 1 and Top 10 hits; Platinum album; ZAMU Award, Best Live Performer, 1994. Membership: SABAM/ZAMU. Current Management: Luc Standaert, Tempo Belgium. Address: Krijgslaan 61-9000 Gent, Belgium.

KID CREOLE (August Twelfth Darnell), b. 12 Aug 1950, Bronx, New York, USA. Entertainer; Singer. 4 sons, 3 daughters. Education: BA, Hofstra University. Career: Leader, Kid Creole and the Coconuts; Worldwide tours, 15 years; Member, Dr Buzzard's Original Savannah Band, 3 years; Currently starring, West End Production of Oh What A Night, London. Recordings: Albums include: Tropical Gangsters, 1982; Fresh Fruit In Foreign Places, 1982; Doppelganger, 1983; Cre-ole, 1984. Honours include: BPI Best International Act, Kid Creole, 1982. Memberships: BMI; AFTRA. Hobbies: Rowing; Sailing; Cycling; Antique cars. Current Management: Ron Rainey Management. Address: 315 South Beverly Drive, Suite 206, Beverly Hills, California, USA.

KIEDIS Anthony, b. 1 Nov 1962, Grand Rapids, Michigan, USA. Vocalist. Education: Political Science, UCLA. Career: Founder member, Red Hot Chili Peppers, 1983-; Worldwide tours, including US, UK, Europe, Australia, New Zealand; Major appearances include: Lollapalooza Festival tour, 1992; Glastonbury Festival, 1993; Hollywood Rock Festival, Rio De Janeiro, 1993; Appeared on catwalk, Jean Paul Gaultier fashion benefit, AMFAR AIDS research, 1992; Film appearance, Point Blank, 1991. Recordings: Albums: The Red Hot Chili Peppers, 1984; Freaky Styley, 1985; The Uplift Mofo Party Plan, 1987; Mother's Milk, 1989; Blood Sugar Sex Magik, 1991; What Hits?, 1992; One Hot Minute, 1995; Singles include: Under The Bridge (Number 2, US), 1992; Give It Away, 1992; Breaking The Girl, 1992; Soul To Squeeze, from film Coneheads, 1993; Aeroplane, 1996; Contributor, Give Peace A Chance, Peace Choir, 1990; The Beavis And Butthead Experience, 1993; Featured on film soundtrack, Wayne's World, 1992. Honours: MTV Music Video Awards, 1992; Grammy, Best Hard Rock Song, Give It Away, 1993. Current Management: Lindy Goetz Management, 11116 Aqua Vista #39, Studio City, CA 91602, USA.

KIERAN (Donley), b. 1 Nov 1970, Manchester, England. Disc Jockey; Record Producer; Recording Artist. Musical Education: Self-taught. Career: Promoting Spectrum Oxford; Dance music Disc Jockey at Universe and Fantazia among many others; Recording artist as: Oxide and Hoi Polloi. Membership: Musicians' Union. Hobbies: Walking; Squash; Dancing. Current Management: Adrian Hicks, Equation. Address: 9 Cavell Road, Oxford, England.

KIHN Greg, b. 1952, Baltimore, Maryland, USA. Singer; Songwriter. Career: Backing vocalist with Johnathan Richman; Backed by group Earthquake, 1976; Leader, Greg Kihn Band, 1976-. Recordings: George Kihn, 1976; Greg Kihn Again, 1977; Next Of Kin, 1978; With The Naked Eye, 1979; Glass House Rock, 1980; Rockihnroll, 1981; Kihntinued, 1982; Kihnspiracy, 1983;

Kihntageous, 1984; Citizen Kihn, 1985; Love & Rock'n'Roll, 1986. Current Management: Riot Management, 3210 21st Street, San Francisco, CA 94110, USA.

KILGOUR David Auld, b. 6 Sept 1961, Ranfurly, New Zealand. Musician; Songwriter. Education: University entrance. Career: Member: The Clean; The Great Unwashed and Stephen. Recordings: Solo albums: Here Come The Cars; Sugar Mouth; First Steps and False Alarms. Hobbies: Surfing; Painting. Current Management: c/o Flying Nun Records. Address: Box 677, Auckland, New Zealand.

KILKELLY Frank, b. 17 Sept 1960, Republic of Ireland. Musician (acoustic guitar). Education: BSc, Marketing. Musical Education: Piano lessons, miscellaneous guitar teachers. Career: Regular folk circuit, England; Television includes: Pebble Mill At One, BBC; Anderson On The Box, BBC, Northern Ireland; Kenny Live, RTE, Ireland; Late Late Show, RTE, Ireland; Radio broadcasts: Digby Fairweather's Jazz Notes, BBC2; Anderson's Fine Tunes; Travelling Folk, BBC Scotland. Recordings: Luke Daniels, Tarantella. Hobbies: Music; Non-competitive sports. Current Management: Brass Tacks, Orchard House, Gloucester Road, Hartpury, Gloucestershire GL19 3BG, England.

KIMBALL Bobby (Robert Toteaux), b. 29 Mar 1947, Vinton, Louisiana, USA. Vocalist. Career: Supported acts including: Jackson Browne; Aretha Franklin; Barbra Streisand; Lead vocalist, Toto, 1978-84; Solo artiste, 1984-; Member, Far Corporation. Recordings: Albums: with Toto: Toto, 1979; Hydra, 1979; Turn Back, 1981; Toto IV, 1982; Singles: with Toto: Hold The Line,1979; Georgy Porgy, 1980; 99, 1980; Rosanna, 1982; Make Believe, 1982; Africa (Number 1, US), 1983; I Won't Hold You Back, 1984; with Far Corporation: Stairway To Heaven, 1986; Backing vocalist, albums by Boz Scaggs: Silk Degrees, 1976; Down Two Then Left, 1977. Honours: 6 Grammy Awards with Toto: Best Record, Best Album, Best Producer (Toto), Best Engineered Recording, Best Vocal Arrangement, Best Instrumental Arrangement, 1983. Current Management: Artists International Management, 9850 Sandalfoot Blvd, Suite 458, Boca Raton, FL 33428, USA.

KIMURA Audy, b. 7 Mar 1953, Honolulu, Hawaii. Singer; Songwriter. Education: BBA in Marketing, University of Hawaii, 1975. Career: Recording artist, songwriter, 1984-. Recordings: Albums: Looking For The Good Life, 1983; A Gift Of Song, 1985; Audy In LA, 1989. Honours: Male Vocalist of Year, 1984; Single Of The Year, 1984, 1986, 1990; Most Promising Artist Of Year, 1984; Contemporary Album Of Year, 1984, 1986.

KING B B (Riley), b. 16 Sept 1925, Itta Bena, Mississippi, USA. Singer; Musician (guitar). Musical Education: Self-taught guitar. Career: Performed with the Elkhorn Singers; Played with Sonny Boy Williamson, 1946; Regular broadcast slot, The Sepia Swing Show, Radio WDIA; Averaged 300 performances a year, 1950s-70s; Numerous worldwide tours with wide variety of R&B and pop artistes; Appearances include: Newport Jazz Festival, 1969, 1989; Atlantic City Pop Festival, 1969; Atlanta Pop Festival, 1970; Mar Y Sol Festival, Puerto Rico, 1972; Kool Jazz Festival, New York, 1983; Live Aid concert, Philadelphia, 1985; Benson & Hedges Blues Festival, Dallas, 1989; JVC Jazz Festival, Newport, 1990; Memphis In May Festival, 1991; Montreux Jazz Festival, 1991; San Francisco Blues Festival, 1991; Guitar Legends, Expo '92, Seville, Spain, 1991; Westbury Music Fair, New York, 1993; Pori Jazz, Finland, 1995; Opened B B King's Memphis Blues Club, Memphis, Tennessee, 1991. Recordings: Albums: Completely Well, 1970; The Incredible Soul Of B B King, 1970; Indianola Mississippi Seeds, 1970;

Live In Cook County Jail, 1971; Live At The Regal, 1971; B B King In London, 1971; LA Midnight, 1972; Guess Who, 1972; The Best Of.., 1973; To Know You Is To Love You, 1973; Friends, 1974; Lucille Talks Back, 1975; King Size, 1977; Midnight Believer, 1978; Take It Home, 1979; Now Appearing At Ole Miss, 1980; There Must Be A Better World Somewhere, 1982; Love Me Tender, 1982; Blues'n'Jazz, 1984; Six Silver Strings, 1986; Live At San Quentin, 1991; with Bobby Bland: Together For The First Time - Live, 1974; Together Again - Live, 1976; Hit singles include: Three O'Clock Blues; You Didn't Want Me; Please Love Me; You Upset Me Baby; Sweet Sixteen; Rock Me Baby; The B.B.Jones (used in film soundtrack For The Love Of Ivy); The Thrill Is Gone; Also featured on: Happy Anniversary, Charlie Brown!, 1989; When Love Comes To Town, U2, 1989; Heroes And Friends, Randy Travis, 1990; The Simpsons Sing The Blues, 1990. Honours include: Grammy Awards: Best Male R&B Vocal Performance, 1971; Best Ethnic or Traditional Recording, 1982; Best Traditional Blues Recording, 1984, 1986, 1991, 1992; Inducted into Rock And Roll Hall Of Fame, 1987; Lifetime Achievement Awards include: NARAS, 1988; Songwriters Hall Of Fame, 1990; Gibson Guitars, 1991; Star in Hollywood Walk Of Fame, 1990; MTV Video Award, with U2, 1989; Q Inspiration Award, 1992. Membership: Co-chairman, Foundation For The Advancement Of Inmate Rehabilitation And Recreation. Current Management: Sidney A. Seidenberg Inc., 1414 6th Avenue, New York, NY 10019, USA.

KING Ben E (Benjamin Earl Nelson), b. 28 Sept 1938, Henderson, North Carolina, USA. Singer; Songwriter. Career: Singer, bands including The Four Bs; The Moonglows; The Crowns; Featured vocalist, The Drifters, 1957-60; Solo artiste, 1960-; Cabaret and club circuit, 1968-73; Member, Soul Clan, 1978; Rejoins The Drifters for tours, 1978-; Appearances include: San Remo Festival, Italy, 1964; Prince's Trust Rock Gala, Wembley Arena, 1987; Glastonbury Festival, 1987; Television: UK television debut, Ready Steady Go!, 1964; David Letterman's Sixth Anniversary Special, 1988. Compositions include: Co-writer, There Goes My Baby; Co-writer, Don't Play That Song (also recorded by Aretha Franklin); Stand By Me, later used in: film soundtrack, Stand By Me, 1986; Levi 501 jeans commercial (Number 1, UK) 1987; How Can I Forget. Recordings: Albums: Supernatural, 1975; Let Me Live In Your Life, 1978; Music Trance, 1980; Street Tough, 1981; Stand By Me (The Ultimate Collection), 1987; Dancing In The Night, 1987; Save The Last Dance For Me, 1988; Anthology, 1993; Hit singles include: with The Drifters: There Goes My Baby, (Number 2, US); Dance With Me; True True Love; This Magic Moment; Save The Last Dance For Me (Number 1, US; Number 2, UK); I Count The Tears; Solo: Spanish Harlem; Stand By Me (R&B Number 1, US); Amor; I Who Have Nothing; Seven Letters; Supernatural Thing (R&B Number 1, US); Other recordings: with Average White Band: Benny And Us, 1977; Book Of Love, with Bo Diddley, featured in film Book Of Love, 1991; Guest vocalist, Coast To Coast, Paul Shaffer, 1989. Honours: One Of BMI's Most Performed Songs 1940-90 (over 3 million plays), Stand By Me, 1990. Current Management: Randy Irwin Associates. Address: 7231 Radio Road, Naples, FL 33942, USA.

KING Bob (Robert), b. 2 July 1955, Kilmarnock, Scotland. Musician (guitar). m. Hazel, 30 Mar 1974, 2 sons. Education; Diploma of Higher Education. Career: Appearances most major country music festivals include: Americana, British and Irish Country Music Festival, Worthing; The Inverness Festival Of Country Music. Recordings: Several compositions recorded by artists in Ireland. Honours: Sylvia Saunders Trophy Winner, 1994; Several Act Of The Year Awards throughout career. Memberships: PRS; Equity. Hobby: All aspects of information technology (computers). Address: 10 Hector Road, Longsight, Manchester M13 0QN, England.

KING Carole, b. 9 Feb 1942. Singer; Songwriter. Career: Songwriter in partnership with Gerry Goffin; Worked with artists including: Eric Clapton; Crosby & Nash; Branford Marsalis; David Sanborn; Numerous concerts and tours; Actress in theatre including: Starring role, Mrs Johnstone, Broadway production, Blood Brothers, 1994; Environmental activist for natural forest preservation; Presently studying European traditional music. Compositions: Hit songs include: Will You Love Me Tomorrow; Take Good Care Of My Baby; Go Away Little Girl; The Locomotion; Up On The Roof; Chains; One Fine Day; Hey Girl; I Feel The Earth Move; Natural Woman; Smackwater Jack; You've Got A Friend; Now And Forever (For film, A League Of Their Own); Soundtrack, animated film, Really Rosie. Recordings include: Albums: The City, 1968; Writer, 1970; Tapestry, 1971; Rhymes And Reasons, 1972; Music, 1972; Fantasy, 1973; Wrap Around Joy, 1974; Thoroughbred, 1975; Really Rosie, 1975; Simple Things, 1977; Welcome Home, 1978; Greatest Hits, 1978; Touch The Sky, 1979; Pearls, 1980, 1994; One To One, 1982; Speeding Time, 1983; City Streets, 1989; For Our Children, 1991; A League Of Their Own, 1992; 'Til Their Eyes Shine, 1992; Colour Of Your Dreams, 1993; In Concert, 1994; Time Gone By, 1994 A Natural Woman, 1994. Honours include: Inducted Songwriters' Hall Of Fame, 1987; Rock And Roll Hall Of Fame, 1990; National Academy of Songwriters' Lifetime Achievement Award, 1988; Grammy Awards; Multi-Platinum, Platinum and Gold albums; Academy Award Nomination, Now And Forever. Memberships: AFTRA; AMPAS: NARAS; NAS; SAG; AFofM. Current Management: Lorna Guess. Address: 11684, Ventura Boulevard, #273, Studio City, CA 91604, USA.

KING Eileen Maria Goretti, b. 6 Aug 1959, Bandbridge, Co Down, Northern Ireland. Singer. m. Joe Rafferty, 21 July 1987. Education: College. Career: Television apperances: BBC, UTV, RTE; Concerts include: Wembley Festival; Fanfare Grand Ole Opry, Nashville; Has recorded in Nashville, The Fireside Studios; The Porter Wagoners Studio. Recordings: 6 albums. Honours: Won numerous music awards. Membership: Equity. Hobbies: Cinema; Sport. Current Managment: JR Promotions. Address: 229 Newtownhamilton Rd, Armagh, Co Armagh, Northern Ireland.

KING Evelyn "Champagne", 1 July 1960, Bronx, New York, USA. Singer. Career: Soul/dance music singer, 1977-. Recordings: Albums: Smooth Talk, 1977; Music Box, 1979; Call On Me, 1980; I'm In Love, 1981; Get Loose, 1982; Face To Face, 1983; So Romantic, 1984; A Long Time Coming, 1985; Flirt, 1988; The Best Of, 1990; The Essential Works Of, 1992. Singles include: Shame, 1977; I Don't Know If It's Right, 1979; I'm In Love, 1981; Get Loose, 1982; Face To Face, 1983. Address: c/o Nationwide Entertainment Services, 2756 N. Green Valley Parkway, Ste 449, Las Vegas, NV 89014-2100, USA.

KING Hazel, b. 11 Oct 1948, London, England. Folk Singer; Musician (guitar, concertina). m. Derek Sarjeant, 10 Sept 1977, 1 son, 1 daughter. Education: Wimbledon College of Art; St Martin's School of Art. Musical Education: Trained in various choirs. Career: Resident, 6 years, Surbiton Folkclub; Frequent tours, concerts, festivals, folkclubs, in Britain, Europe, America; National radio, television, film music for America. Recordings: 14 albums for British and German labels. Honours: BA Fine Arts; Winner, National Folk and Beat Final, Hammersmith Town Hall, 1967. Memberships: Musicians' Union; Royal College of Church Music. Hobbies: Painting; Pottery; Travelling. Current Management:

Assembly Artists. Address: 4 Coneygar House, Coneygar Park, Bridport, Dorset DT6 3BA, England.

KING Jonathan, b. 6 Dec 1944, London, England. Singer; Music Journalist; Television Presenter. Education: English, Cambridge University. Career: Occasional recording artist, 1965-; Talent spotter for Decca Records (discovered Genesis, produced their first album); Launched UK Records, 1972; Newspaper and magazine columnist, radio and television presenter, including own show Entertainment USA, BBC, 1980s; Organizer, A Song For Europe (UK's Eurovision Song Contest qualification show), 1995-. Recordings: Solo albums: Or Then Again, 1965; King Size King, 1982; The Butterfly That Stamped, 1989; The Many Faces Of Jonathan King, 1993; Singles include: As Jonathan King: Everyone's Gone To The Moon; Green Is The Grass; It's Let It All Hang Out; Una Paloma Blanca; Wild World; Involved in novelty hits including: Johnny Reggae, The Piglets'; Sugar Sugar, Sakkarin; The Same Old Song, The Weathermen; Leap Up And Down (Wave Your Knickers In The Air), St Cecilia.

KING Mark, b. 20 Oct 1958, Isle Of Wight, England. Vocalist; Musician (bass). Career: Founder member, Level 42, 1980-; Regular international tours, 1983-; Concerts include: Prince's Trust Rock Gala, 1986, 1987, 1989; Crystal Palace Bowl, 1991; Midem Festival, Cannes, France, 1992. Recordings: Albums with Level 42: Level 42, 1981; The Pursuit Of Accidents, 1982; Standing In The Light, 1983; A Physical Presence, 1985; World Machine, 1985; Running In The Family, 1987; Level Best, 1989; Guaranteed, 1991; Solo: Influences, 1984; Hit singles: The Chinese Way, 1983; The Sun Goes Down (Living It Up), 1983; Hot Water, 1984; Something About You, 1985; Leaving Me Now, 1985; Lessons In Love (Number 1 in 8 European countries), 1986; Running In The Family, 1987; To Be With You Again, 1987; It's Over, 1987; Heaven In My Hands, 1988; Tracie, 1988; Guaranteed, 1991. Honours: Making Music magazine poll, Best Bass Player, 1987; BMI Award, 1 million US performances, Something About You, 1991. Current Management: Paul Crockford Management, 56-60 Islington Park Street, London N1 1PX, England.

KING Michael Weston, b. 11 Nov 1961, Derbyshire, England. Singer; Songwriter; Musician (guitar). m. Ann Carter, Aug 1987, 2 sons, 1 daughter. Career: Lead singer, songwriter, Fragile Friends, 1982-87; Solo artist, 1988; Guitarist, Gary Hall and The Stormkeepers, 1989-93; Lead singer, songwriter, The Good Sons, 1993-; UK and European tours; Television appearances on BBC, ITV and RTE, Ireland; Broadcasts on various radio stations including sessions on BBC Radio 1. Recordings: Albums: with Fragile Friends: For Play; with The Stormkeepers: Garageheart; Wide Open To The World; with The Good Sons: Singing The Glory Down, 1995; Singles: with Fragile Friends: Paper Doll; The Novelty Wears Off; with The Stormkeepers: Where The River Meets The Sea (EP); with The Good Sons: The Good Sons (EP), 1994; The Kings Highway, 1996; Wines, Lines and Valentines, 1997; Various songs recorded by other artists: Riding The Range, Townes Van Zandt; Watch My Dreamboats Sail, Tower Of Strength, Carolyn Hester; In Her Father's Bed, Arthur Brown; From These Hills, Carolyn Hester, 1996; Rear View Mirror, Townes van Zandt, 1997; Out of the Blue Vol I, 1995, Vol II, 1996, Vol 3, 1997. Current Management: CMP. Address: 34 Market Street, Southport, Merseyside PR8 1HJ, England.

KING Paul Andrew, b. 20 Jan 1951, Herne Bay, Kent, England. Songwriter; Musician (guitar, piano, keyboards). Musical Education: Guitar, self-taught, late 1960s; Piano Intametzo School Of Music, Canterbury, 1994-. Career: Played guitar in

local MOR band, 1976-79; After band break-up, concentrated on writing; 2 songs published by First Time Music Publishing, UK, 1989-90; Recording sessions, London, 1990-91. Recordings: Like I Never Felt Before, 1990; A Dream To Come True; Where Peaceful Waters Flow, 1991. Membership: Musicians' Union. Hobbies: Reading; Travel; Walking; Cycling. Current Management: Showcase And Management International. Address: 33 Mandarin Place, Grove, Oxfordshire OX12 0QH, England.

KING Pee Wee (Julius Frank Anthony Kuzynski), b. 18 Feb 1914, Milwaukee, Wisconsin, USA. Country Musician (accordion); Songwriter. Career: Member, the King's Jesters, 1932; Toured with Gene Autry, 1934; Member, Autry's Log Cabin Boys, 1935; Became bandleader, renamed the Golden West Cowboys, 1936; Member of Grand Ole Opry, Nashville, 1937-47; Toured extensively with The Grand Ole Opry Camel Caravan, 1941; Film appearances include: Goldmine In The Sky; Own radio and television shows, 1947-62; Worked in Minnie Pearl's Roadshow, 1959-68; Retired from performing, 1969; Director, Country Music Foundation, Nashville; Appeared on Opry's 60th Anniversary Show, 1986. Compositions include: Silver And Gold; Busybody; Changing Partners, Bing Crosby; Bimbo, Jim Reeves. Recordings: Hit singles include: Tennessee Waltz; Tennessee Tears; Tennessee Polka; Slowpoke (Number 1, US). Albums include: Pee Wee King, 1954, 1955; Waltzes, 1955; Swing West, 1958; Back Again, 1964; Country Barn Dance, 1965; Biggest Hits, 1966; The Legendary (Live Transcriptions), 1967; Golden Olde Tyme Dances, 1975; Ballroom King, 1983; Rompin' Stompin' Singin' Swingin', 1984; Hog Wild Too, 1990. Honours: Inducted into Nashville Songwriters Hall Of Fame, 1970; Inducted into Country Music Hall Of Fame, 1974.

KING Peter, b. 1941. Musician (alto saxophone). Career: Played opening night, Ronnie Scott's, 1959; Played, recorded with numerous American artists including: Zoot Sims; Philly Joe Jones; Red Rodney; Nat Adderley; Hampton Hawes; Big bands of Maynard Ferguson, Tubby Hayes; Own quartets, quintets, 1980s; Popular in France, extensive tours; Began with Ben Watt (Everything But The Girl), 1982; Featured soloist, Count Basie Band, 1990; Berlin Jazz Festival with Tete Montoliu, 1990; Partnership with Charlie Watts, appearances include: Ronnie Scott's, London and Birmingham, England; Blue Note, New York; Spiral Hall, Tokyo; Played with Horace Parlan Quartet, 1994; Tour of Spain; Festival, Belgium; Took place of Steve Grussman in quartet at festivals: Molde, Norway; Pori, Finland, 1994; Peter King Quartet, Top Of The Bill, Ronnie Scott's, 1994; with Phil Woods, Jackie McLean, Count Basie Orchestra, Berlin Jazz Festival, 1994; with Rene Urtreger, Middleheim Festival, Belgium, 1994; with George Coleman, Ronnie Scott's, 1995; Adviser, Consultant to Christies Auction House, Sale of Charlie Parkers Grafton Saxophone. Recordings: New Beginning; East 34th Street; Peter King Quintet; Brother Bernard; Peter King In Paris; High Fly; Crusade; Tete Montoliu featuring Peter King; Also featured on four Everything But The Girl albums.

KING AD-ROCK (Adam Horowitz), b. 31 Oct 1966, Manhattan, New York, USA. Rapper; Musician (guitar). Career: Founder member, US rap/rock group Beastie Boys, 1983-; Appearances include: Support to Madonna, Virgin Tour, 1985; Supports to Run DMC, Raisin' Hell Tour, 1986; Coheadliners with Run DMC, Together Forever Tour, 1987; Reading Festival, 1992; Film appearances: Krush Groove; Run DMC's film Tougher Than Leather; Scared Stupid; Acting roles: The Equalizer, TV series; Santa Ana Project; Lost Angels; Roadside Prophets. Recordings: Singles: She's On It; Fight For Your Right To Party; Albums: Licensed To Ill, 1986; Paul's Boutique, 1989; Check Your Head, 1992; Ill

Communication, 1994; Root Down, 1995; The In Sound From Way Out, 1996. Current Management: Gold Mountain Entertainment. Address: 3575 Cahuenga Blvd West, Suite 450, Los Angeles, CA 90068, USA.

KINNAIRD Alison Margaret, b. 30 Apr 1949, Edinburgh, Scotland. Musician (scottish harp, clarsach). m. Robin Morton, 23 Feb 1976, 1 son, 1 daughter. Education: MA, Edinburgh University. Musical Education: Studied Scottish harp with Jean Campbell. Career: Freelance musician, 1971-; Concerts: Edinburgh; London; New York; San Francisco; Hawaii; Tokyo; Berlin; Presenter, The Music Show, Channel 4, 1995. Recordings: The Harp Key, 1978; The Harper's Gallery, 1980; The Harpers Land, 1983; Music In Trust I & II, 1988; The Quiet Tradition, 1989; Mactalla, 1994. Publications: The Harp Key; The Small Harp Tutor; Tree Of Strings (with Keith Sanger). Honours: MTA Music Award, 1983; Living Tradition Award, 1995; MBE for Services to Music and Art, 1997. Membership: Life member, The Clarsach Society. Hobbies: Glass-engraver (other career); Family. Current Management: Robin Morton, Shillinghill, Temple. Address: Shillinghill, Temple, Midlothian EH23 4SH, Scotland.

KINSEY Tony, b. England. Composer; Musician (drums, piano). m. Patricia, 1 daughter. Musical Education: Studied percussion with Bill West, Cozy Cole, Jazz College, New York; Composition, orchestration, arrangement with Bill Russo, Columbia College, Chicago. Career: Professional musician from age 18; Joined John Dankworth, as drummer with Dankworth 7; Preferred drummer in 1960s-70s, for visiting jazz stars including: Osacr Peterson; Ella Fitzgerald; Lena Horne; Sarah Vaughn; Billie Holiday; Ben Webster; Clarke Terry; Musical director, That's Life, BBC TV, 3 years. Compositions include: Films: Souvenir; On The Bridge; Televison: That's Life, BBC; Castle of Adventure, TVS; The John Bird Show, BBC; The Londoners, BBC; A Tribute To Her Majesty; Colour; Four Seasons; Life At The Limit; Two's Company; Over 100 commercials including: Lloyds Bank; Kellogg's Rice Krispies; Danish Bacon; Baby Cham; Domecq; Marshall Cavendish; Raleigh Bicycles; Classical compositions: Pictures; Three Suites For String Quartet; River Thames Suite; Alice Through The Looking Glass. Recordings include: (own compositions) Alice Through The Looking Glass; Classical Lines 1, 2; Time Gentlemen Please; How To Succeed In Business; Jazz At The Flamingo; The Tony Kinsey Quintet; Foursome; Lougerhythms; River Thames Suite; Aspects Of Jazz; Jazz Scenes. Current Management: Soundtrack Music Management. Address: 22 Ives Street, Chelsea, London SW3 2ND, England.

KIPPER (Marc Eldridge), b. 19 Mar 1962, Frimley, Surrey, England. Producer; Arranger; Writer; Musician (guitar, keyboards). Musical Education: Guitar from 9 years old, Jazz and Classical training. Career: Member, One Nation; Toured with: Jeff Beck; The Temptations; Ruby Turner; MD with Beijing Spring; Toured with: Curtis Stigers; Richard Marx; 3 major tours as guitarist for Gary Numan. Recordings: with One Nation: Strong Enough; Big Life Big Tears; Machine and Soul; with David Essex: Back 2 Back. Publication: The Complete Singer, 1995. Membership: PRS. Hobbies: Skiing; Tennis; Motorcycling. Address: East Manor Barn, Manor Yard, Fringford, Bicester, Oxon OX6 9DQ, England.

KIRK Nicholas Kenneth, b. 27 Dec 1945, Bradford, West Yorkshire, England. Musician (New Orleans jazz banjo); Electronics Engineer. Education: BSc, Honours, University of Wales; Postgraduate Diploma in Communications, Southampton University; Postgraduate Diploma in R F and Microwave, Bradford University. Musical Education: Self Taught. Career: Appearances on radio and television Wales with Clive Evans' River City Stompers, 1966-67; Appeared at the Keswick Jazz Festival, Bude Jazz Festival, Marsden Jazz Festival, and at jazz clubs and pubs in Yorkshire, Wales and South of England, with the Dennis Browne Creole Band; Appeared at the 100 Club in London with the New Era Jazzband; Author of British Patent for apparatus for Recording and Replaying Music (The Musical Arranger and Sequencer). Composition: Clouds. Recording: Float Me Down The River, with the Dennis Browne Creole Band, cassette. Memberships: Musicians' Union; Fellow, Royal Microscopical Society. Hobbies: Mountaineering; Languages. Current Management: Self-managed. Address: 36 Kilpin Hill Lane, Staincliffe, Near Dewsbury, West Yorkshire WF13 4BH, England.

KIRKE Simon Frederick, b. 28 July 1949, London, England. Musician (drums, guitar, piano). m. Lorraine Dellac, 15 Dec 1982, 1 son, 3daughters. Musical Education: Self-taught. Career: Member, Black Cat Bones; Free; Bad Company; Performed at 2 Isle of Wight Festivals; Many US tours, 2 world tours; Television: Several Top Of The Pops; Radio includes: John Peel. Compositions: Bad Company with Paul Rodgers; Several songs on Free and Bad Company albums. Recordings: with Black Cat Bones: Barbed Wire Sandwich, 1970; with Free: Tons Of Sobs, 1969; Free, 1969; Fire And Water, 1970; Highway, 1970; Live, 1971; Free At Last, 1972; Heartbreaker, 1972; with Bad Company: Bad Company, 1974; Straight Shooter, 1975; Run With The Pack, 1976; Burning Sky, 1977; Desolation Angels, 1979; Rough Diamonds, 1982; 10 From 6, 1985; Fame And Fortune, 1986; Dangerous Age, 1988; Holy Water, 1990; Here Comes Trouble, 1992; Company Of Strangers, 1995; Hit singles include: with Free: All Right Now; Wishing Well; with Bad Company: Can't Get Enough; Feel Like Making Love. Honours: Gold disc, All Right Now; 12 Gold, Platinum albums with Bad Company. Hobbies: Photography; Tennis; Golf. Address: c/o Alliance Artists Ltd, Ste 220, 3423 Piedmont Road NE, Atlanta, GA 30305, USA.

KIRKPATRICK David Gordon (Slim Dusty), b. 13 June 1927, Kempsey, New South Wales, Australia. Entertainer; Country Singer; Recording Artist. m. Joy McKean, 22 Dec 1951, 1 s, 1 d. Career: Called himself Slim Dusty, 1938; Records first songs: Song for the Aussies; My Final Song, 1942; Record six titles: When the Rain Tumbles Down in July, 1946; Launches Slim Dusty Show, 1954; Showground Ptnrshp w Frankie Foster, 1956-63; The Pub With No Beer, (Australia's first Gold Record Award), 1952; Released first album: Slim Dusty Sings, 1960. Publications: Walk a Country Mile, autobiog w J Lapsley, 1979; Another Day, Another Town, autobiog w Co-auth, 1996; Released 30 albums, titles incl: Slim Dusty Sings, 1960; Walk a Country Mile, 1979; No 50 Gold Anniversary, 1981; Trucks on the Track, 1985; Beer Drinking Songs of Australia, 1986; Neon City, 1987; G'day, 1989; Coming Home, 1990; Two Singers, One Song, 1991; Live into the Nineties, video, 1992; Country Way of Life, 1995; 91 Over 50, 1996; A Time to Remember, 1997; Makin' a Mile, 1997. Honours: MBE, 1970; Australian Record Industry Association Hall of Fame. Memberships: Chairman, Country Music Association of Aust. Hobbies: Fishing, painting, leatherwork. PO Box 115, St Ives, NSW 2075, Australia.

KIRKPATRICK John Hamill, b. 15 Apr 1950, Glasgow, Scotland. Music Workshop Tutor; Trust Chairman. m. Anne, 7 Nov 1970, 2 daughters. Musical Education: Piano and Pipe Band lessons as a child. Career: Teaching guitar, keyboards, for some 22 years; Trust Chairman, of Crisis Limit Promotions, past 10 years; Paisley Community Music Workshops Trust, Music Management, Popular Music. Recordings: Composition of various themes, jingles for local radio, writers workshops, video promotional organizations, community groups. Honour: Training award.

Membership: Musicians' Union. Hobbies: Travel; Performing; Camping. Address: 22A Cedar Avenue, Johnstone, Renfrewshire PA5 9TH, Scotland.

KISSEL Michael Case, b. New York, USA. Musician; Composer; Lyricist; Record Producer. m. Elena Thorton, 29 June 1985. Career: Former bandleader, Los Amigos de Las Americas, Honduras; Musician, composer, producer, vocalist, various artists include: The Drifters; The Pointer Sisters; Gloria Gaynor; Elvin Bishop; Jocelyn Brown; Otis Rush; Ernie Isley; Toots And The Maytals. Recordings: Albums: Surrender, Robin Clark and David Bowie, 1985; Healing Session, Babatunde Olatungi, 1991; Peace Is The World Smiling, Babatunde Olatungi, Pat Seeger, Taj Mahal, 1989; Film soundtracks: In The Blood, 1990; Best Shots, 1990; Pumping Iron II, 1985. Memberships: ASCAP; NARAS; Songwriters Guild; AFofM.

KITCHEN Elizabeth Jane, b. 1 Apr 1959, Rochdale, England. Composer; Arranger; Musician (drums). Musical Education: Studied with: James Blades; Gilbert Webster RNCM. Career: Writes, arranges for television: Playdays; Monster Cafe; Roundabout Stop; Dot Stop; Worked on films/TV: Life And Loves Of A She Devil; King Of The Ghetto; Played with the Blues Band; Barbara Dickson in Blood Brothers; Works with Chickenshed company. Recordings: Freelanced with the Hallé Orchestra; RLPO; Northern Ballet; Opera North; Written many theatre shows: Young Vic; Battersea Arts Centre. Honours: Graduate: RNCM; PRNCM. Memberships: PRS; MCPS. Hobbies: Swimming; Sport; Eating. Address: 1 Warwick Road, London N11 2SA, England.

KITT Eartha Mae, b. 26 Jan 1928, Columbia, South Carolina, USA. Actress; Singer; Entertainer. 1 son. Education: High School Of Performing Arts, New York. Career: Dancer and vocalist, Katherine Dunham Dance Group, 1948; Night club singer, Europe, 1949-; Appearances worldwide; Stage performances: Dr Faust, Paris, 1951; New Faces Of 1952, New York, 1952; Mrs Patterson, Broadway, 1954; Shinbone Alley; The Skin Of Our Teeth; The Owl And The Pussycat; Bunny; The High Bid; Timbuktu, Broadway, 1978; Blues In The Night, 1985; Follies, London, 1988; A Night At The Cotton Club, UK revue tour; Film appearances: New Faces, 1953; Accused, 1957; St Louis Blues, 1957; Mark Of The Hawk, 1958; Anna Lucasta, 1959; Saint Of Devil's Island, 1961; Synanon, 1965; Up The Chastity Belt, 1971; Dragonard; Ernest Scared Stupid, 1991; Boomerang, 1992; Fatal Instinct; Numerous television appearances include: I Spy; Mission Impossible; Played the original Catwoman in Batman series; Living Single; New York Undercover; Jack's Place; Matrix; Subject, documentary All By Myself, 1982; Featured, Unzipped, 1995; International concerts in over 100 countries. Recordings: Numerous albums include: Down To Eartha, 1955; Thursday's Child, 1956; Revisited, 1961; Bad But Beautiful, 1976; At Her Very Best, 1982; C'est Si Bon, 1983; I Love Men, 1984; The Romantic Eartha Kitt, 1984; That Bad Eartha, 1985; In Person At The Plaza, 1988; My Way, 1988; I'm Still Here, 1989; Best Of Eartha Kitt, 1990; Live In London, 1990; Thinking Jazz, 1992; Back In Business, 1994. Publications: Autobiographies: Thursday's Child, 1954; Alone With Me, 1976; Confessions Of A Sex Kitten, 1989. Honours: NANM Woman Of The Year, 1968; Star on Hollywood Walk Of Fame; 2 Tony Award Nominations: Mrs Patterson; Timbuktu; Emmy Award Nomination, I Spy; 3 Grammy Nominations; Academy Award Nomination, Anna Lucasta. Current Management: c/o Stan Scottland, JKE Services Inc., 404 Park Avenue S, 10th Floor, New York, NY 10016, USA.

KJAER Torben Edvard, b. 26 Oct 1946, Gentofte, Denmark. JazzMusician (piano); Composer; Arranger; Conductor; m. Marianne

Kampmann, 28 Sept 1968, 1 son. Musical Education: Theory, Composition, Conducting, Institute Music and Science, University of Copenhagen, 1966-73; Studied with George Russell, 1971; Piano degree, Copenhagen Music Conservatory, 1973; Career: Professional Musician, 1973-; Pianist with: Dexter Gordon; Dizzy Gillespie; Ben Webster; Clark Terry; Al Grey; Roy Eldridge; Red Mitchell; Milton Batiste; Rasheema; Founder, own jazz quartet; Conductor, Danish Radio Jazz Group, 1973-79; Danish Radio Light Orchestra, 1979-88; Danish Radio Big Band; Royal Orchestra; Orchestra Leader, TV Shows, 1986-92; Composer/Arranger for numerous groups including Tritonius (Danish Gospel Choir) and Copenhagen Music Ensemble. Arrangements include: Chamber Version, Candide; Faust, Royal Theatre, Copenhagen; Arranger, musicals including: Guys & Dolls; My Fair Lady; Chicago; Kiss Me Kate; also music for television, radio, film, theatre, cabaret, commercials. Compositions include: Mass Of Piece, 1976; Christmas Oratory, 1981; Concerto Grosso, 1983; David And Batseba, 1985. Recordings include: Whalesongs, 1983; Jazz In Danish, 1988; Tower At The End Of The World, 1988; Stolen Moments, Rasheema, 1995. Honours: Awards, Danish State Fund of Art; Best Popular Composer, 1979. Memberships: Vice President, Danish Jazz, Beat and Folk Music Authors. Address: Skovvej 12, 2820 Gentofte, Denmark.

KJELLEMYR Bjorn, b. 4 Dec 1950, Bamble, Norway. Bassist (Accoustic and Electric). m. Mette Havrewold, 2 sons. Musical Education: Academy of Music, Oslo. Career: European tours mainly with Terje Rypdal, appearing at festivals and other concerts, appearing with Joe Henderson, Chet Baker, and Palle Mikkelborg. Recordings: Chasers, 1986; Blue, 1988; Singles Collection, 1989; If Mountains Could Sing, 1995. Honours: Jazz Musician of The Year, Norway, 1991; Buddy Award, 1995. Current Management: PJP, 5000 Bergen, Norway. Address: Normannsqt 37, 0655 Oslo, Norway.

KJELLERUP Klaus, b. 1954, Copenhagen, Denmark. Composer; Arranger; Record Producer; Musician (guitar, piano, bass). Education: Journalism. Career: Composer of music of major television programmes in Denmark; Concerts and tours with Danish bands Tosedrengene and Danser Med Drenge. Recordings: Various recordings with Tosedrengene and Danser Med Drenge. Membership: Danish Society of Jazz, Beat and Folk Music Authors. Current Management: Sony Music, Copenhagen, Denmark.

KKOSHI Chaz (The Bat), b. 3 Feb 1962, London, England. Record Producer; Musician (keyboards, drums); Vocalist. m. Maria Capsalis, 23 May 1993, 1 daughter. Education: Tottenham Technical College, A Level Technical Drawing. Musical Education: Trinity Musical College Grade 8, pianoforte. Career: Spartacus World Tour, 1982; Hammersmith Odeon, Double Take, Eurovision, 1986; BBC Radio 1 Roadshow, 1992, 1994, 1995; 6 O'Clock Show, LWT, 1991; The Word, 1994; Des O'Connor Show, 1994; Several appearances, Top Of The Pops, 1984-. Recordings: Party 4 The Word, Steve Walsh; Gypsy Kings remix; Four Seasons remix; Awesome - The Singles; Supernatural Love, Alex Brown; Shadows and Elton John compilation; Numerous dance hits. Membership: Musicians' Union. Hobbies: Going to the movies; Spending time with daughter Sophia. Current Management: M&M Management. Address: Owens House, 79 Greenview Drive, Northampton NN2 7LE, England.

KLAKEGG Rune, b. 19 Apr 1955, Skien, Norway. Musician (piano); Composer. m. Kathryn Bresee, 14 Aug 1992, 2 daughters. Musical Education: 2 years study, University of Oslo. Career: Freelance jazz musician, composer, since

late 1970s; Appeared with groups: Cutting Edge; Out To Lunch; Soyr; Rune Klakegg Trio; All major jazz festivals; Arranger, band leader, Van Morrison, Vossajazz, 1988. Recordings: Cutting Edge: CE, 1982; Our Man In Paradise, 1984; Duesenberg, 1986; Out To Lunch: OTL, 1988; Kullboksrytter, 1995; Soyr: Vectors, 1988; Bussene lengter hjem, 1994; Med Kjott og Kjarlighet, 1997; R K Trio: Anaerobics, 1992; Fuzzy Logic: FL, 1996. Honour: NOPA Best Composition of the Year for Pamplemousse, 1995. Memberships: TONO; NOPA. Outdoor activities: Skiing. Address: Ole Bullsgt 45, 0475 Oslo, Norway.

KLASTERKA Zeljen, b. 24 Jan 1958, Zagreb, Croatia. Musician (guitar); Composer; Guitar Teacher. m. Neda Urlicic, 1 July 1995. Education: University graduate. Musical Education: 14 years, graduation, Faculty of Music University, Zagreb. Career: Lead guitarist with Notturno; Ritmo Loco; Patchwork; Studio musician; Classical guitar duet with Milivoj Majdak, Stanko Selak Big Band (orchestra of Music Academy); Music editor, major television show in Croatia: 7 NOC. Recordings: Album: Canto Latino, Patchwork video live concert of Zagreb Bienalle, 1994; Nek'ti Bude Ljubav Sva, Eurovision song contest entry, 5 video spots, Croatian Television. Honours: First Prize, Croatian Contest, Eurovision Song Contest. Memberships: HGU; ZAMP. Hobbies: Sailing; Skiing. Current Management: Neda Urlicic-Klasterka. Address: Davor 3, 10000 Zagreb, Croatia.

KLEIN Harry, b. 25 Dec 1928, London, England. Musician (baritone saxophone). Musical Education: Various teachers including Harry Hayes. Career: Tours with Stan Kenton with groups backing Tony Bennett, Ella Fitzgerald, Aretha Franklin, 1960s-1980s; Now semi-retired doing various solo dates. Recordings: Nemo; Big Ben. Honours: Poll Winner, Melody Maker Poll, 1952-58. Membership: Musicians' Union. Hobby: Music. Address: 8 Bowling Green House, Chelsea, London SW10, England.

KLEMMER John, b. 7 Mar 1956, Chicago, Illinois, USA. Musician (saxophones, flutes, clarinets, kalimba, piano, keyboards, sythesizers, percussion). Musical Education: Interlochen National Music Camp; Private studies, age 5 to mid 20s; Studied, classical saxophone, flute, clarinet; Jazz improvisation with Joseph Daly; Studied composition, arranging, conducting; Private studies, orchestration, film scoring with Albert Harris. Career: Tours with: George Benson; Herbie Hancock; Miles Davis; Weather Report; others; With Don Ellis Orchestra, USA, Europe, England; State Department tour of 11 countries of French West Africa with Oliver Nelson Septet, Impulse Artists on tour; Live Performances, concerts, clubs include: Shellys Manne Hole, The Light House, all major jazz and rock clubs, concert venues, USA; Carnegei Hall; Newport Jazz Festival; Antibes Jazz Festival; Montreux Jazz Festival; Television and radio include: Voice Of America shows; Midnight Special; Rock Concert; Merv Griffin Show; At One With; At One With; Dial M for Music; Live at Tanglewood PBS Special; Kitty Hawk, featuring John Klemmer solo saxophone PBS Special; WWTW presents John Klemmer. Compositions include: Walk In Love, recorded by Manhattan Transfer, Acker Bilk; The Old Man's Tear; Last Summer's Spell; Lost In Love; The Beauty Of Her Soul. Recordings include: Magnificent Madness, 1980; Straight From The Heart, 1980; Finesse, 1981; Hush, 1981; Life, 1981; Music, 1988; TBA, 1996. Honour: Down Beat Magazine International Jazz Critics Poll, Talent Deserving Writer Recognition, 1973. Hobbies: Psycholgy; Poetry; Puppeteering. Current Management: Borman Entertainment, Gary Borman. Address: Sally Poppe 9220 Sunset Blvd, Ste 320, Hollywood, CA 90069, USA.

KLEN Gregory James, b. 9 Feb 1960, Kenosha, Wisconsin, USA. Musician (bass,

keyboards, acoustic guitar); Songwriter. m. Linda Beltran, 7 Apr 1995. Musical Education: Self-taught. Compositions: One Of The Lucky Ones; This Is Goodbye; When The Good Ain't Good Enough; Heartbreak Hall Of Fame. Recordings: Album: Keith Bradford Sings Greg Klen's Best. Publications: Country Western Corner; Co-writer News, Songwriters of Wisconsin. Honours: 2nd Place, Co-writer News Song Contest. Memberships: BMI; Songwriters of Wisconsin. Hobbies: Music; Sports; Pets; Riding my ATV. Address: 225 North St, Box 284, Silver Lake, WI 53170, USA.

KLOOT Per W, b. 19 October 1955, Watermaal, Bosvoorde. Musician; Singer; Guitarist; Producer. m. Ann Vandewalle, 15 August 1993. Education: Atheneum; BITCS, film school. Career: Bands: The Misters, TV, Radio; Lama's: Hit with De Ideale Penis (The Ideal Penis); Solo: 300 gigs in 3 years, 1992-95. Compositions: Candy, duet with Isabelle A; In the Belly, duet with An Pierle; Betrayal, duet with Bea Vanderman. Publication: Muziekrant Oor's Pop Encyclopedie, 10 volumes, 1980-97. Honour: Humo's Rock Rally Finalist Prize for Best Song, Why Do All Those Men, 1986. Memberships: SABAM; ZAMU. Hobby: Basta. Current Management: Backline Productions. Addres: Molenweg 30, 3080 Tervoren, Belgium.

KLUGH Earl, b. 16 Sept 1953, Detroit, Michigan, USA. Musician (guitar). Career: Member, George Benson Group; Chick Corea's Return To Forever; Solo recording artist, 1975-; Performed with numerous artists including George Shearing; Flora Purim; McCoy Tyner; Bob James; Chet Atkins. Recordings: Solo albums include: Earl Klugh, 1976; Living Inside Your Love, 1977; Finger Paintings, 1977; Magic In Your Eyes, 1978; Heart String, 1979; Dream Come True, 1980; Late Night Guitar, 1980; Crazy For You, 1981; Two Of A Kind, 1982; Delta Lady, 1983; Low Ride, 1983; Night Songs, 1984; Wishful Thinking, 1984; Key Notes, 1985; Life Stories; Soda Fountain Shuffle; Whispers And Promises; Solo Guitar; Midnight In San Juan; Best Of Earl Klugh, 1991; with George Benson: White Rabbit; Body Talk; with Al Jarreau: This Time; with Jimmy Buffet: One Particular Harbour; with Jennifer Holliday: Say You Love Me; with McCoy Tyner: Inner Voices; with Flora Purim: Stories To Tell; with Bob James: Touchdown; One On One. Address: EKI, 24225 West Nine Mile Road, Southfield, MI 48034, USA.

KNEPPER James Minter (Jimmy), b. Los Angeles, California, USA. Jazz Musician (trombone). m. Maxine Fields, May 1954, 1 son, 1 daughter. Musical Education: Harmony, Orchestration, LA City and State Colleges. Career: Played with: Charlie Spivak; Charley Parker; Charley Barnet; Charlie Mingus; Benny Carter; Benny Goodman; Thad Jones; Gil Evans; Toshike; Stan Kenton; Woody Herman; Herbie Mann, State Dept tour in Africa, 1960; Mingus Dynasty; Broadway: Funny Girl; On Your Toe (revival); Me Nobody Knows; National Jazz Ensemble; American Jazz Orchestra; Smithsonian Jazz Orchestra; George Grunz Concert Jazz Band; Tony Scott; Joe Albany; Joe Maini; Dean Benedetti. Recordings: Cunningbird; Jimmy Knepper In LA; Dream Dancing; I Dream Too Much; First Place; Mark Master's Jazz Orchestra Plays The Jimmy Knepper Songbook; Primrose Path; Hot Knepper and Pepper; A dozen Mingus albums. Honours: International Critics Poll; Readers Poll of Down Beat Magazine. Membership: AFofM. Address: 11 Bayview Place, Staten Island, NY 10304, USA.

KNIGHT Emrys Glyn, b. 15 June 1951, South Glamorgan, Wales. Musician (lead guitar). Musical Education: Self-taught. Career: Member, Rose Among Thorns; Common Ground; Snatch It Back; Tours, UK and Europe; Numerous television and radio appearances; Concerts and albums with the above; British tours with Ralph McTell; Currently touring with Stone Free (Jimi Hendrix tribute band) in the UK and Europe. Memberships: Musicians' Union; PRS; MCPS. Hobbies: Building guitar amplification; Guitar wiring. Address: 187 College Road, Whitchurch, Cardiff CF4 2NT, Wales.

KNIGHT Gavin, b. 17 Apr 1966, Southampton, Hampshire, England. Musician (drums, percussion); Writer; Producer; Programmer; Arranger; Remixer. Musical Education: Self-taught; Studied with Antony Christmas, 2 years and Albert Cooper, 2 years, Southampton. Career: Drummer with The Shamen, 1991-; Extensive world tours including Europe, Scandinavia, USA, Australia and the Far East; Headlined Glastonbury Festival; Numerous TV appearances worldwide; Drummer, Maroontown, 1993-94; Europeam shows and album recording; Urban Hype, live UK shows, 1992; The Good Strawberries, live UK shows and TV, 1994; Now playing for Marc Almond, major show at the Royal Albert Hall, London, TV appearances and album recording, 1995-; with Victoria Wilson-James, European shows and TV appearances, 1996-; Russian shows with Jam and Spoon, 1997; Remixed, programmed various projects include: The Shamen; Co-writer and Producer, single release, Urban Hype, 1992; Marc Almond; Rhythm programming for album and single, Angelique Kidjo; Victoria Wilson-James; Assisted the Shamen on theme tune, The Ozone, TV programme, 1995; Worked with P J Proby, 1996; Co-Composer, TV programme for Meridian Television, 1996; Co-Member, dance production team, Universal State of Mind, 1996; Rhythm programming for commercial Release, Viva!, 1996. Recordings: Syncronous, Inca, 1994; Tunnel Vision, The Ticket Men, 1995; Co-writer, The Feeling, with Urban Hype, 1992 (released in Japan on compilation album); All Because of You, Universal State of Mind, 1997. Memberships: Musicians' Union; PAMRA. Hobbies: Wining and dining; Socialising; Self-confessed Trekkie. Current Management: Self-managed. Address: c/o The Cottage, 1a Bursledon Road, Hedge End, Southampton, Hampshire SO30 0BP, England.

KNIGHT Gladys, b. 28 May 1944, Atlanta, Georgia, USA. Singer. Career: Singer, Gladys Knight and the Pips, 1957-89; Signed to Motown Records, 1966; Appearances include: Grand Gala Du Disque, Amsterdam, 1969; European tour, 1974; Kool Jazz Festival, San Diego, 1977; London Palladium, 1978; World Music Festival, 1982; Solo artiste, 1989-; Concerts include: Westbury Music Fair, New York, 1992; Television includes: Gladys Knight And The Pips Show, NBC, 1975; Happy New Year America, CBS, 1986; Motown 30 - What's Goin' On, 1990; Ray Charles - 50 Years In Music, Uh-Huh!, 1991; Gladys Knight's Holiday Family Reunion, ABC-TV, 1991; Actress, film Pipe Dreams, 1976; Actress, US sitcoms: Charlie & Co, 1985-86; Guest star, Out All Night, 1989. Recordings: Albums: Everybody Needs Love, 1967; Feelin' Bluesy, 1968; Silk'n'Soul, 1969; Gladys Knight And The Pips' Greatest Hits, 1970; If I Were Your Woman, 1971; Standing Ovation, 1972; Neither One Of Us, 1973; All I Need Is Time, 1973; Imagination, 1974; Anthology, 1974; Knight Time, 1974; Claudine, 1974; A Little Knight Music, 1975; I Feel A Song, 1975; 2nd Anniversary, 1975; The Best Of Gladys Knight And The Pips, 1976; Pipe Dreams, 1976; Still Together, 1977; 30 Greatest, 1977; The One And Only, 1978; About Love, 1980; A Touch Of Love, 1980; Visions, 1983; The Collection - 20 Greatest Hits, 1984; Solo: Good Woman, 1991; Just for You, 1994. Hit singles include: I Heard It Through The Grapevine (Number 2, US), 1967; If I Were Your Woman, 1971; Help Me Make It Through The Night, 1972; The Look Of Love, 1973; Neither One Of Us (Wants To Be The First To Say Goodbye) (Number 2, US), 1973; Midnight Train To Georgia (Number 1, US), 1973; I've Got To Use My Imagination, 1974; Best Thing That Ever Happened To Me, 1974; On And On, 1974; The Way We Were, 1975. Numerous honours

include: Top Female Vocalist, Blues and Soul magazine, 1972; American Music Awards, 1975, 1976, 1984, 1989; Grammy Awards: Best Group Vocal Performance, Best R&B Vocal Performance, 1974; Heritage Award, Soul Train Music Awards, 1988; Honoured, Essence Awards, 1992; NAACP Image Award; Magazine awards from Cashbox, Billboard, Record World, Rolling Stone; Star on Hollywood Walk of Fame, 1995; Gladys Knight and the Pips inducted into Rock 'n' Roll Hall of Fame, 1996; Pinnacle Award, 1998. Current Management: Newman Management Inc, 2110 E Flamingo Road, Ste 300, Las Vegas, NV 89119, USA.

KNIGHT Holly, 24 Sept 1956, New York City, USA. Songwriter; Producer; Musician (keyboards, piano). m. Michael Whitis-Knight, 24 Mar 1990, 2 sons. Musical Education: Classical piano, age 4-14 years. Career: Member, Spider, 2 albums; Member, Device, album 1989; Have written many hits and film songs. Compositions include: for Pat Benatar: Love Is A Battlefield; Invincible; Sometimes The Good Guys Finish First; for Tina Turner: Better Be Good To Me; One Of The Living; The Best; Ask Me How I Feel; Love Thing; Be Tender With Me Baby; You Can't Stop Me Loving You; for Heart: Never; All Eyes; There's The Girl; Tall Dark Handsome Stranger; I Love You; Love Touch, Rod Stewart; Ragdoll, Aerosmith; Change, John Waite; The Warrior, Patti Smyth; Stick To Your Guns, Bon Jovi; Space, Cheap Trick; Pleasure And Pain, the Divinyls; Soul Love, Hall and Oates; Baby Me, Chaka Khan; Just Between You And Me, Lou Gramm; Hide Your Heart, Bonnie Tyler; Turn It On, Kim Wilde; Stiletto, Lita Ford; Hide Your Heart, Kiss; Try A Little Harder, Aaron Neville; It's Over When The Phone Stops Ringing, Patsy Kensit; Wrap Your Arms Around Me, Agnetha Falkstog; Time Waits For No-One, Dusty Springfield; Between Two Fires, Jimmy Barnes; Slow Burn, Ozzy Osbourne; Tracks for: solo album; Spider; Device; A Night In Heaven film soundtrack (with Michael Desbarres). Recordings: Albums include: with Spider: Spider; Between The Lines; with Device: 22B3; Solo: Holly Knight; Honours: 3 Grammies, Best Rock Vocal, Better Be Good To Me; Love Is A Battlefield; One Of The Living. Memberships: ASCAP; Songwriters Guild. Hobbies: Skiing; Travel; Swimming. Address: c/o Fasbender and Associates, 1299 Ocean Avenue, Santa Monica, California, USA.

KNIGHT Larry (aka Fuzzy), b. 21 Oct 1950, St Louis, Missouri, USA. Musician (bass); Singer; Songwriter. m. Aleda Trabue, 26 Oct 1974, 1 daughter. Education: 3 years college. Musical Education: Playing since 3rd grade at school, 1 year St Louis Conservatory of Music. Career: Played with: Albert King; Chuck Berry; Little Milton; Ike Turner, 1964-69; Tim Rose; Delaney-Bonnie and Friends; Peter Kaukenon, 1969-73; Albert Collins, Spirit, 1971-80; The Urge, 1985; Bandleader, Bassist and Lead Vocalist, Blowin' Smoke, R&B band, 1992-98; Tours worldwide over 12 years; Appeared on many US rock shows, also Old Grey Whistle Test, England; Rock Palace, Germany; Recorded over 26 albums; 1 live Spirit album produced by Miles Copeland, Rainbow Theatre, London. Recordings with: Tim Rose; Delaney-Bonnie & Friends; 6 Spirit albums; Peter Kaukenon; Albert Collins; The Urge; Albert Lee; Kaptain Kopter and The Famous Twirlybirds; Randy California; Blowin' Smoke. Honours: Gold disc for Spirit. Memberships: NAMM; VSDA; Musicians' Union. Hobbies: Music; Performing; Acting; Watching sports; Boxing; Football; Singing the blues. Current Management: Lawrence Weisberg, Blowin' Smoke Management and Bookings. Address: 7438 Shoshone Avenue, Van Nuys, CA 91406-2340, USA.

KNOPFLER Mark, b. 12 Aug 1949, Glasgow, Scotland. Musician (guitar); Vocalist; Songwriter; Record Producer. m. Lourdes Salomone, Nov 1983, 2 sons. Education: English Graduate. Career: Former journalist, Yorkshire Evening Post;

Member, Brewer's Droop; Café Racers; Founder member, Dire Straits, 1977-88, 1991-; Worldwide concerts and tours, 1978-; Major concerts include: San Remo Song Festival, Italy, 1981; Live Aid, Wembley, 1985; Princes Trust Rock Gala, Wembley, 1986; Nelson Mandela 70th Birthday Tribute, 1988; Guitarist and vocalist, Eric Clapton US tour, 1988; Nordoff-Robbins charity concert, Knebworth Park, 1990. Numerous compositions include: Private Dancer, Tina Turner, 1985; Setting Me Up, Waylon Jennings, 1984; Co-writer, Money For Nothing, with Sting, 1985; Water Of Love, The Judds, 1989; Film music: Local Hero, 1983; Cal, 1984; The Princess Bride, 1987. Recordings: Albums: with Dire Straits: Dire Straits, 1978; Communique, 1979; Making Movies, 1980; Love Over Gold (Number 1, UK), 1982; Alchemy - Dire Straits Live, 1984; Brothers In Arms (Number 1, 20 countries), 1985; Money For Nothing (Number 1, UK), 1988; On Every Street (Number 1, UK), 1991; On The Night, 1993; with Chet Atkins: Neck And Neck, 1990; with Notting Hillbillies: Missing... Presumed Having, 1990; Solo: Local Hero (film soundtrack), 1983; Cal (film soundtrack), 1984; Golden Heart, 1996; Wag The Dog (film soundtrack), 1998; Hit singles: with Dire Straits: Sultans Of Swing, 1979; Romeo And Juliet, 1981; Tunnel Of Love, 1981; Private Investigations, 1982; Twisting By The Pool, 1983; So Far Away, 1985; Money For Nothing (first video shown on MTV Europe), 1985; Walk Of Life, 1986; Your Latest Trick, 1986; Calling Elvis, 1991; On Every Street, 1992; Solo singles: Going Home (theme from film Local Hero), 1983; Darling Pretty, 1996; Guest on albums including: Slow Train Coming, Bob Dylan, 1979; Solo In Soho, Phil Lynott, 1980; Gaucho, Steely Dan, 1980; Beautiful Vision, Van Morrison, 1982; The Phil Lynott Album, 1982; Boys And Girls, Bryan Ferry, 1985; Down In The Groove, Bob Dylan, 1988; The Shouting Stage, Joan Armatrading, 1988; Land Of Dreams, Randy Newman, 1988; As producer: Infidels, Bob Dylan, 1984; Knife, Aztec Camera, 1984. Honours include: Ivor Novello Awards: Outstanding British Lyric, 1983; Best Film Theme, 1984; Outstanding Contribution to British Music, 1989; Nordoff-Robbins Silver Clef Award, Outstanding Services To British Music, 1985; BRIT Awards: Best British Group, 1983, 1986; Best British Album, 1987; Grammy Awards: Best Rock Performance, Money For Nothing, 1986; Best Country Performance, with Chet Atkins, 1986, 1991; Honorary music doctorate, University of Newcastle Upon Tyne, 1993. Current Management: Ed Bicknell, Damage Management, 16 Lambton Place, London W11 2SH, England.

KNORR Marianne, b. 3 Feb 1949, Copenhagen, Denmark. Folksinger; Guitarist; Actress. m. Preben Friis, 13 May 1989, 2 sons. Education: Danish State Theatre School, 4 years. Musical Education: Studied voice with Jens Chr Schmidt for 12 years. Career: Has appeared at Rimfaxe Theatre, Skagen Festival, Roskilde Festival, in Radio concerts and on Television. Concerts in Denmark, Norway, Sweden, Iceland and Greenland. Recordings: 4 Solo albums: Valmuer Og Jernbeton, Sa Laenge Fuglene Flyver, Sange Af Brecht, and Sommerregn. Memberships: Danish Actors' Association; Danish Society of Jazz and Beat Authors. Address: Strandvejen 138, 5600 Faaborg, Denmark.

KNOX (Ian Milroy Carnochan), b. 4 Sept 1945, London, England. Singer; Musician (guitar, keyboards). Career: Lead singer, songwriter, The Vibrators; Solo artiste, 1983; Singer, songwriter, The Fallen Angels; Member, Urban Dogs. Recordings: with the Vibrators: 11 studio albums; Solo album, 1983; with The Fallen Angels: 3 studio albums; with Urban Dogs: 2 studio albums; with Die Toten Hosen: Baby, Baby; Troops Of Tomorrow. Publications: Currently writing book on The Vibrators (20 years next year). Honours: Gold disc, Baby, Baby (Germany). Memberships: PRS; MCPS. Hobby: Painting.

KNOX Buddy, b. 20 July 1933, Happy, Texas, USA. Entertainer; Musician (guitar). 3 sons, 2 daughters. Education: BBA; BS; MBA. Career: Tour, Shower of Stars, 1957; Ed Sullivan, 1957, 1958; Steve Allen Show, 1958; Movies, Jamboree, Sweet Country Music; Dick Clark's American Bandstand, 1957-65; New York Paramount Christmas Show, 1957; 37 years touring. Recordings: More than 80 include: Party Doll; Hula Love; Rock Your Little Baby To Sleep; Rock House; Lovey Dovey; Ling Ting Tong; Sweet Country Music; My Baby Girl Holly. Publications: Music Is All. Honours: 4 Gold records; 2 Gold albums; 1 platinum album, single. Memberships: BMI; SOCAN; AFofM. Hobbies: Cartooning; Rock sculptures; Writing music. Current Management: Buddy Knox Entertainment Ltd. Address: R3C-10, Evans Road, Armstrong, British Columbia V0E 1B0, Canada.

KNOX Keith, b. 1933, Belper, Derbyshire, England. Record Company Executive; Record Producer; Music Journalist. Education: Southampton University; Brighton College of Advanced Technology. Career: Served with Royal Air Force, 1955-57; Record producer, various recording companies including: Caprice; Storyville; Sonet; WEA; Universal Folk Sounds; Album sleeve note writer; Founder, Executive Producer, own jazz label Silkheart Records, Sweden, 1986-. Recordings: Artists on own label include Steve Lacy; Charles Gayle; David S Ware; Dennis Gonzalez; Matthew Shipp; Booker T Williams; Assif Tsahar; Jim Hobbs; Dennis Charles; Joel Futterman; Alvin Fielder; Rob Brown. Publications: Author, Jazz Amour Affair (The Lars Gullin Story); Contributor, jazz magazines including: Jazz Monthly; Jazz Forum (International Jazz Federation magazine); Jazznews; Articles include: The Parametric Music of Terry Riley, 1967; Relax and Fully Concentrate - the music of Terry Riley; Terry Riley- This Is Our Period. Address: Silkheart Records, Dalagatan 33, S-113 23 Stockholm, Sweden.

KNUDSEN Hans, b. 7 Sept 1950, Copenhagen, Denmark. Musician (piano); Singer; Songwriter. Education: College of Education. Musical Education: Guitar lessons, 1960s; Self-taught piano, 1975-. Career: Former teacher, Music and Biology, 1975-80; Professional musician, 1980-; Worked and toured with leading Danish jazz and blues artists, 1980-83; Member, New Orleans singer Lillian Boutté's band, 1983-90; Leader, own group Hans Knudsen Jumpband, 1990-. Compositions include: Music Is My Life, with Lillian Boutté. Recordings: with Lillian Boutté: Music Is My Life, 1984; Let Them Talk, 1986; with Hans Knudsen Jumpband: So Long John, 1995; Jump In Focus, 1997. Current Management: Self-taught. Address: Kildebakkegårds Allé 92, 1 tv, DK-2860 Soborg, Denmark.

KNUDSEN Kenneth, b. 28 Sept 1946, Copenhagen, Denmark. Composer; Musician (keyboard). m. Christine Heger, 22 Mar 1987, 1 son. Education: Architect, Royal Danish Academy of Fine Arts. Musical Education: Self-taught. Career: Member of jazz/fusion groups: Coronarias Dans, 1969; Secret Oyster, 1976; Anima, 1979; Heart To Heart Trio, 1986; Bombay Hotel, 1988; Special project with Jan Akkerman and Jon Hiseman, 1982; Numerous concerts and television in Scandinavia, Europe, UK, Hong Kong and Japan. Compostions: Film scores; Ballet music for New Danish Dance Theatre and The Royal Danish Ballet; Works for string quartet, cello, piano, choir and electronics; Prizewinning commercials for Carlsberg Breweries. Recordings: I Me Him, 1989; Compacked, 1989; Sounds And Silence, with Palle Mikkelborg, 1994; Appeared on more than 100 records including Garland, Svend Asmussen and L. Subramaniam; It Could Happen To You, Jan Akkerman; Entrance, Heart To Heart, Palle Mikkelborg; Pictures, Heart To Heart, Niels Henning Orsted Pedersen; Aura, Miles Davis;

Anima, Kenneth Knudsen; Honours: Jazz Musician of Year, 1973; Niels Matthiasen Memorial Grant, 1987; Danish State Art Foundation Grant, 1992-94. Membership: Danish Composers Society. Hobbies: Yachting; Visual Arts. Address: Box 51, DK 2840 Holte, Denmark.

KNUDSEN Marius Dahl, b. 30 June 1947, Grinsted, Denmark. Musician (Guitars; Dr; Stringed Instrument; Didgeridoo). m. Lise Jelsbech Knudsen, 14 July 1979, 2 sons, 1 daughter. Education: Classical Guitar, Degree in Music Teaching. Career: Member, Ostjydsk Musikforsyning, 20 years; Danish show-band with numerous appearance on national TV and radio; Stage: Arhus Teater: Rocky Horror Show; Return to the Forbidden Planet; Vejle Teater: Folk Og Rovere; Dansk Spildtid: Elverhoj. Recordings: Det Beskidte Dusin; Aarhus Syncopaterne. Honour: Honorary Member, Danish Musicians' Union, Arets Revykomponist, 1996. Membership: Danish Musicians Union. Current Management: Ostjydsk Musikforsyning, Ved Kirken 2, 8320 Marslet, Denmark. Address: Langballeves 44, 8320 Marslet, Denmark.

KNUDSEN Ole, b. 15 Sept 1943, Koge, Denmark. Music Teacher; Multi-instrumentalist; Singer; Composer. Education: Music Teacher, Teacher training school, 1970. Career: Jazz drummer, 1965-70; Lead singer, guitarist, pianist, percussionist, Danish jazz-rock group: Fujara, 1970-76; Performances: Roskilde Festival, 1971-75; Leader, Arbejdersanggruppen, 1976-82; Freelance jazz-drummer, teacher, 1982-. Recordings: Fujara, 1973; Nattevandring, 1977; Jens Borges Fodselsdag (childrens songs), 1979; Hvor Laenge Skal Vi Vente, 1980; Det Handler Om Kaerlighed, (solo) 1992. Honours: LO (Danish Organisation of Labour) Culture Prize, Arbejdersanggruppen, 1981. Memberships: Danish Jazz Musicians Organisation; Danish Jazz Beat Folkmusic Authors. Hobbies: Football; Tennis.

KNUTSEN Cecilie, b. 9 May 1967, Trondheim, Norway. Singer. Education: Conservatory of Music, Oslo, 3 years; Conservatory of Music, Arhus, Denmark, 3 years. Career: TV Norway, national, 1982; TV Norway, national, 1984, 1995, 1997; TV Denmark, national, 1993; Toured with Deepak Chopra, Louise Hay, Wayne Dyer and Stuart Wilde. Recordings: Voice of the Feminine Spirit, 1994; Violet 19, 1996. Honour: Gold Album, England. Membership: Gramart. Current Management: Eivind Brydoy, Artist Partner as Grini Naering Sparn 17, 1345, Osteraas, Norway. Address: Linderudgrenda 68, Norway.

KOIVISTOINEN Eero, b. 13 Jan 1946, Finland. Composer; Musician (tenor, soprano saxophone). Musical Education: Sibelius Academy, Helsinki, 1968-70, 1973-74; Berklee College of Music, Boston, US, 1971-73. Career: Leader, own quartet; Performed at international jazz competition, Montreux, Switzerland, 1969; Newport Festival, USA; Founder, composer, arranger for UMO (New Music Orchestra), 1975-; Leader, Dialog, 1995-; Established PRO Records Label, 1983; Teaching, 1980s. Compositions include: Ballet, Mother Earth, 1979; Suite, Ultima Thule, represented Finland in Nordring radio competiton, 1981. Recordings: 11 solo albums, 1966-77; Later albums include Pictures In Three Colours (with John Scofield and Jack DeJohnette); Makumoka, Kari Komppa; Ultima Thule, UMO; Dialog, 1995. Honours: First recipient, Yrjö (Georgie) Award, Finnish Jazz Federation, 1967; Best Jazz Ensemble, Montreux Festival, 1969; Best Arranger, Nordring radio competition, Jersey, 1981. Address: Cygnaeuksenkatu 8 B 20, 00100 Helsinki, Finland.

KOJIMA Ian (Koko), b. 28 Dec 1851, Toronto, Canada. Musician (saxophone, Acoustic, electric guitars, keyboards); Composer

(filmscores). m. Anne Peters, 11 Nov 1977, 1 son. Education: 2 years, University of Toronto, Arts. Musical Education: 2 years, Humber College (composition, theory, improvisation). Career: Saxophonist for Stampedes, Ken Tobias; Multi-instrumentalist for: Chris De Burgh; Peter Hoffman; David Hasselhoff. Recordings: Chris De Burgh: Live In Dublin; Filmscore: Circus On The Moon (composer, musician, actor). Publications: Contributions to: Canadian Music. Honours: 5 times Juno Award Nominee. Memberships: Toronto MA; British MU. Hobbies: Golf. Current Management: Ken Thompson Management, Redhead Touring. Address: Thornhill, Ontario, Canada.

KOMPPA Kari, b. 5 Jan 1939, Finland. Composer; Musician (tenor saxophone). Career: Jazz session saxophonist, television conductor, Tampere; Member, Break Big Band, played Pori Festival, 1972; Writer for Radio Jazz Orchestra (became the UMO); Leader, composer, Tampere Jazz Orchestra, 1981-; Represented Finnish Broadcasting Company, throughout Europe, including Nordring Festival, Belgium; EBU Jazz Concert, Pori; Tenor saxophonist, writer for Ippe Kätkä Band, 1980s; Currently, full-time jazz composer; Teacher, Sibelius Academy, Helsinki. Compositions include: Free Aspects, Tampere Jazz Orchestra; Music for Radio Jazz Orchestra; Honours: Winner (with Break Big Band), Finnish Big Band championship, 1973; Winner, EBU orchestral composition contest, Tethys, 1981; Yrjö Award, Finnish Jazz Federation, 1982. Address: Martinlaaksontie 40 F 39, 01629 Vantaa, Finland.

KONTÉ Mamadou, b. June 1945, Tambacunda, Senegal. Music Director, Concert Organizer. 1 son. Career: Founder, Director, Africa Fete Festival, Paris, 1979-; USA, 1993-; Dakar, Senegal, West Africa, 1993-. Honours: Chevalier des Arts et des Lettres, France. Membership: Vice President, de Zoue Franche. Hobbies: Films; Music. Address: Africa Fete, 29 Wagane Diouf, Dakar; 29 Rue Gerna'n Pilou 75010, Paris, France.

KOOPER Al, b. 5 Feb 1944, Brooklyn, New York, USA. Musician (keyboards); Vocalist; Songwriter; Producer. Career: Guitarist, The Royal Teens, 1959; Session musician with artists including: Tom Rush; Peter Paul and Mary, New York; Member, The Blues Project, 1966-67; Concerts include: Monterey International Pop Festival, 1967; Founder member, Blood Sweat & Tears, 1967-68; Producer at Columbia Records; Solo artiste; Established own record label, Sounds Of The Earth (acts included Lynyrd Skynyrd); Founder, Sweet Magnolia, 1970s; Recording artist, computerized soundtrack music. Compositions: with Bobby Brass and Irwin Levine include: This Diamond Ring, Gary Lewis And The Playboys; I Must Be Seeing Things, Gene Pitney; The Water Is Over My Head, The Rocking Berries. Recordings: Albums with The Blues Project: Projections, 1966; Live At Town Hall, 1967; with Blood Sweat & Tears: The Child Is Father To The Man, 1968; Solo albums: Super Session (with Mike Bloomfield and Stephen Stills), 1968; The Live Adventures Of Al Kooper And Mike Bloomfield, 1969; I Stand Alone, 1969; You Never Know Who Your Friends Are, 1969; Kooper Session, 1970; Easy Does It, 1970; Landlord, 1971; New York City (You're A Woman), 1971; A Possible Projection Of The Future, 1972; Naked Songs, 1973; Act Like Nothing's Wrong, 1976; Championship Wrestling, 1982; Guest musician with Bob Dylan: Highway 61 Revisited, 1965; Blonde On Blonde, 1966; New Morning, 1970; Under The Red Sky, 1990; Also featured on: Electric Ladyland, Jimi Hendrix, 1968; Let It Bleed, Rolling Stones, 1969; Producer, recordings by Nils Lofgren; Don Ellis; The Tubes; Green On Red. Publication: Backstage Pass, Al Kooper. Address: c/o Fat City Artists, 1226 17th Avenue S, Suite 2, Nashville, TN 37212, USA.

KOOYMANS George, b. 11 Mar 1948, The Hague, Netherlands. Vocalist; Musician (guitar). Career: Founder member, Dutch rock group Golden Earring, 1961-; Tours, Europe, Canada; US; Suppport to the Who, European tour, 1972; Support to Rush, 1982. Recordings: Albums: Just Earrings, 1965; Winter Harvest, 1967; Miracle Mirror, 1968; On The Double, 1969; Eight Miles High, 1970; Golden Earring, 1971; Seven Tears, 1971; Together, 1972; Moontan, 1973; Switch, 1975; To The Hilt, 1975; Rock Of The Century, 1976; Contraband, 1976; Mad Love, 1977; Live, 1977; Grab It For A Second, 1978; No Promises, No Debts, 1979; Prisoner Of The Night, 1980; Second Live, 1981; Cut, 1982; N E W S, 1984; Something Heavy Goin' Down, 1984; The Hole, 1986; Face It, 1995; Solo albums: Jojo, 1971; Solo, 1987; Numerous compilation albums; Singles: Please Go, 1965; Dong-Dong-Di-Ki-Di-Gi-Dong (Number 1, Netherlands), 1968; Radar Love (Number 1, Netherlands), 1973; Twilight Zone, 1982; Lady Smiles. Current Management: Rob Gerritsen, Regentesstraat 29, 2713 EM Zoetmeer, The Netherlands.

KOPECKY Ladislav, b. 8 April 1944, Prague, Czech Republic. 2 daughters. Education: Economics, Faculty of International Trade, Charles University, Prague. Career: Musician, playing trombone, different bands; Songwriter (lyrics); More than 60 songs broadcasted by Czech TV and Radio; Cooperation with Singer and Songwriter, Petr Ulrych. Compositions: Pojote Dal (Hana Ulrychova); Mec A Preslice; Ententyny; Bylinky; Musical: Nikola Suhaj the robber. Recordings: Songs: Javory (Maple Tree); Jizda Kralu (Ride of the Kings); Trava (Grass); Kridla (Wings); Bylinky (Herbs); Kamen (Stone); Ententyny. Honours: Silver Prize, 1976, Golden Prize, 1980, Bratislavska Lyra Festival; Bronze Prize, 1977, Bronze Prize, 1979, Decinska Kotva Festival. Membership: OSA. Hobbies: Music; Sport (Tennis, Ice Hockey, Ski); Climbing Mountain. Address: Ladislav Kopecky, Ujezd 41, 11800 Prague 1, Czech Republic.

KOPPEL Anders, b. 17 July 1947, Copenhagen, Denmark. Composer; Musician (organ, piano). m. Ulla Lemvigh-Müller, 11 Aug 1969, 1 son, 2 daughters. Musical Education: Clarinet and piano lessons. Career: Child performer, piano and clarinet; Member, Savage Rose, 1967-74; Member, Bazaar, 1975-; Tours: Europe, USA. Compositions: Music for 10 ballets; 200 films and plays; 3 musicals; Piano concerto; Percussion concerto; Marimba concerto; Saxophone concerto; Saxophone quartet; Trio for saxophone, cello, piano; Trio for violin, cello, piano; Toccata for vibes, marimba and orchestra; String Quartet; Partita for chamber ensemble. Recordings: 7 solo albums. Honours: Wilhelm Hansen Prize; several Danish State Art Foundation Awards. Hobby: Family. Current Management: Norsk Musik Forlag A/S (Publisher), Oslo, Norway. Address: Cæciliavej 70, 2500 Valby, Copenhagen, Denmark.

KOPPEL Thomas, b. 24 Apr 1944, Sweden. Musician (piano); Composer; Producer. m. Annisette Hansen, 1971, 2 sons, 2 daughters. Education: Soloist Diploma, Royal Danish Conservatory; Self-taught composer. Career: Debut concert as piano soloist, 1967; Numerous concerts and performances of symphonic works since 7 years of age; Started The Savage Rose, 1967; Numerous international tours and TV and radio appearances since 1968; Newport Festival, 1969; Numerous Scandinavian and European festivals. Compositions: Phrases, 1964; Visions Fugitives, 1965; Ouverture Solebbelle, 1966; Opera, A Mother's Tale, Royal Theatre, 1964; Ballet, Triumph of Death, TV, Royal Theatre, 1970-73; Te Moonchild's Dream, 1991; Symphony No 2, 1995; Musical, Bella Vita, 1996; Musical drama, Mass, 1995. Recordings: 19 albums with The Savage Rose, 1968-98; Recorder concerto,

The Moonchild's Dream, 1994; Ballet, Triumph of Death; Musical drama, Mass, 1995; Bella Vita, 1995. Honours: Carl Nielsen Prize, 1965; Prize, International Compsers Competition, City of Copenhagen 800 Years Anniversary, 1966; Numerous awards from trades unions and organizations; Nominated, Grand Award of the Nordic Council, 1995; H C Lumbye Award, Tivoli Gardens, 1992; Keyboard Player of the Year, 1996; Grammy, 1996. Memberships: Danish Composers' Association; Danish Artists' Union; KODA; NCB; Gramex. Hobby: Photography. Address: H/F Frederikshoj 114, DK 2450 Copenhagen, Denmark.

KORB Ron, b. 7 Sept 1961, Scarborough, Ontario, Canada. Vocalist; Musician (flute, keyboards). Education: Music Bachelor in Performance, University of Toronto. Musical Education: Royal Conservatory of Music. Recordings: Tear Of The Sun, 1990; Japanese Mysteries, 1993; Flute Traveller, 1994; Behind The Mask, 1995; RTHK (radio and television, Hong Kong), Best Original Composition, 1993. Memberships: AFM; SOCAN. Current Management: Oasis Productions Ltd. Address: 76 Cadorna Avenue, Toronto, Ontario M4J 3X1, Canada.

KORJUS Tapio, b. 18 June 1950, Pieksamaki, Finland. Managing Director. m. Eija Savolainen, 7 Dec 1984, 1 daughter. Education: Tampere University. Career: Founder, Rockadillo Management, 1971; Rockadillo Records and Publishing, 1982; Rockadillo Agency, 1983; Zen Master Records and Publishing, 1993; Finnish Music and Media Happening, 1989. Memberships: The Finnish Rock Booking Agents' Association; Finnish Music Publishers Association. Hobbies: Music; Films; Mountain biking. Current Management: Rockadillo. Address: Rockadillo, PO Box 35, 33201 Tampere, Finland.

KOS Lada, b. 12 Nov 1944, Zagreb, Croatia. Singer; Writer; Composer; Arranger; Musician (Violin, Guitar, Piano). Musical Education: Musical Academy for Violin. Career: Solo concerts in Croatia, Barcelona, Paris, Milano, Berlin, Frankfurt, Wien; Tours to Russia, France, Italy, Germany, Austria and Slovenia; TV appearances on RAI, Moscow, St Petersburg, Tallin among others, also on various TV series. Recordings include: Zbog Ljubavi; Covjek Covjeku; Igracica Vjetrova; Music for the Theatre includes: B M Koltés, Roberto Zucco, S Sembera, Hodanje Prugom, E Kisevic, Macak u Trapericama, B Jelusic, Slava Voli Hranislava, V Parun, U Cast Darkerke Djevice Orleanske. Honours: 23 awards for Best Singer, Writer, Composer and Arranger. Membership: Croatian Composers' Society. Hobbies: Fishing; Gardening. Current Management: Best Music, Zagreb, Croatia. Address: Menceticeva 26, 41000 Zagreb, Croatia.

KOS Robert, b. 28 Jan 1954, Connecticut, USA. Personal Manager. m. Debbie Rowell, 27 Aug 1977, 2 daughters. Musical Education: BFA Berklee College of Music. Career: Personal Manager, Metropolitan Entertainment. Address: c/o Metropolitan Entertainment, 7 N Mountain Avenue, Montclair, NJ 07042, USA.

KOSINA Jiri, b. 24 April 1926, Tyniste n Orlicí, Czech Republic. Composer; Conductor. m. Marie Heinevá, 10 April 1971, 1 daughter. Career: Conductor, Opera in Ustí n Labem, Czech Republic; Opava - CR; Bánská Bystrica - Slovakia; Meiningen, Germany; Ceské Budejovice, CR. Compositions: Merry Polka; Recreation Polka; Spring Polka' Monday, Monday; Proc Kalinua. Recordings: Good Morning; Hory,Doly; Jetelícku v Lese; Zertovná; Rychlá; V Udolí. Memberships: Protective Union of Authors; OSA. Hobbies: Music; Travelling. Address: Ceské Budejovice, Puklicova 35, 370 04, Czech Republic.

KOSIORKIEWICZ-KSIEZCKA Jadwiga, b. 16 Mar 1945, Lublin, Poland. Musician (piano, guitar). m. Adam Ksiezycki (deceased 1987), 1 son. Education: Chemist. Career: Pop singer; School organist, for play in church; Composer, poetic lyrics, also sacro-poetry (150 songs, songs for children); Sings in own programme, clubs, churches, for Catholic radio, with poets. Recordings: (Own compositions) Christmas songs; Sacro-songs (singer). Memberships: Polish Authors, Composers; ZAKR; ZAJKS. Hobbies: Poetic lyrics; Swimming.

KOTRUBENKO Viktor, b. 27 November 1948. Composer; Saxophonist. 1 daughter. Education: College of Technology, Electrochemical Faculty; Clarinet, School of Music, Prague. Compositions: Radio Productions Music: Mum, Dad, Sore Made; Film Music: Bohemian Ruby, The Light of Hope, Faul; Music for Television Serials: Rambles Round Bohemia and Moravia; Ecuador. Recordings: The Cat Crawls Through a Hole; Shadow; Virgin Eva; Virgin Bozena and a Little Dog Bobbie; Ballade About a Treefrog or When I Went Water a Little Garden; White Show; Attention Pothole; Accelerate. Publication: secret of the Synthesizers. Honours: Prize, Saxophonist, International Jazz Festival, Prague, 1971; Silver Tablet, 1977; Appreciation for Composition, 1977. Membership: Association of Composers and Scientists. Address: Cerchouska 6, 120 00 Prague 2, Czech Republic.

KOVERHULT Tommy, b. 11 Dec 1945, Stockholm, Sweden. Musician (tenor and soprano saxophone, flute). m. 17 May 1974, divorced, 4 sons, 1 daughter. Education: Franz Schartau's Institute of Commerce, Stockholm. Musical Education: Self-taught. Career: Played in cellar clubs, Stockholm, 1960s; Member, Eje Thelin's Group, with festival appearances in Belgium, 1967; Played in study group with musicians from the Bernt Rosengren Quartet and Maffy Falay's SEVDA, 1967; Member, Jan Wallgren's Quintet, including tour of Germany, 1973; Founder, The Tommy Koverhult Quintet, 1980-89; Freelance musician, 1989-. Compositions: Several by the Tommy Koverhult Quintet. Recordings: with Jan Wellgren: Steel Bend Rock, 1970; Tommy Koverhult With The Jan Wallgren Quintet, 1973; with the Bernt Rosengren Quartet: Improvisations, 1969; Fly Me To The Sun, 1971; Live In Stockholm, Volumes One and Two, 1974; with Lasse Werner: Saxofonsymfoni, 1972; with Maffy Falay and SAVDA: Live At Fregattan, 1973; with own Quintet: Jazz in Sweden '83, 1983; Live At Nefertiti, 1985; Various artists: Notes From Underground, 1973. Honours: Golden Disc Award, Orkester Journalen magazine, 1970; Winner, Orkester Journalen/Tonfallet Readers' Poll, 1983. Hobby: Speedway. Address: Tjustgatan 3, S-118 27 Stockholm, Sweden.

KOZLOWSKI James John ("Koz"), b. 7 Sept 1949, Hartford, Connecticut, USA. Director Artist Development. m. Lula Shepard, 11 June 1994. Education: BSc, Engineering Management, Boston University, 1971; MBA, Human Behaviour, 1973. Musical Education: 5 years lessons, clarinet, alto, tenor saxophones. Career: Managed retail outlet; Started nationally syndicated radio programmes, Rock Around The World and Modern Music; Director of Purchasing, import companies, Peters International, Important Record Distributors; Held position as Label Director, Production Manager, Director Publicity, Director Creative Marketing, Director Artist Management for Relativity Records, Maze and Viceroy Music. Recordings: Project Coordinator, Surfing With The Alien, Joe Satriani; Also for all Viceroy Music acts, including Rattlesnake Guitar - The Music Of Peter Green. Publications: Writer for Creem; Trouser Press; King Biscuit Times; Various freelance publications. Honours: RIAA Gold, Platinum records for Surfing With The Alien, Joe Satriani. Hobbies: Wine; Food; Cooking; Photography;

Sports. Address: 230 East 44th Street #5G, New York, NY 10017, USA.

KRAMER, b. 30 Nov 1958, New York City, USA. Songwriter; Record Producer; Record Label Owner; Performer. m. Shannon, 30 Aug 1982, 1 daughter. Musical Education: Classical organ and singer; Self-taught multi-instrumentalist. Career: Founded/performed in: Gong, 1979; The Chadbournes, 1980-82; The Fugs, 1982-84; Shockabilly, 1982-85; Butthole Surfers, 1985; Half Japanese, 1986-88; BALL, 1987-90; Bongwater, 1987-91; Ween, 1990; Captain Howdy (with Penn Jillette), 1993-; Founder, 3 record labels: Shimmy-Disc, 1987; Kokopop, 1990; Strangelove, 1994. Recordings: Producer for: Palace Songs; New Radiant Storm Kings; Galaxie 500; White Zombie; King Missile; GWAR; Low; Urge Overkill, including track Girl You'll Be A Woman Soon, from Pulp Fiction soundtrack; Maureen Tucker; Daniel Johnston; Jon Spenser; Dogbowl; John Zorn. Hobbies: Fishing; Films. Current Manager: Steve Moir, Santa Monica, California. Address: c/o Shimmy-Disc, Jaf Box 1187, New York, NY 10116, USA.

KRAMER Billy J (William Howard Ashton), b. 19 Aug 1943, Bootle, Lancashire, England. Singer; Musician (guitar). Career: Guitarist, The Phantoms; Singer, The Coasters; Signed by manager Brian Epstein, 1963; Singer with backing group, The Dakotas, 1963-68; Regular UK tours; Appearances include: Star Club, Hamburg, Germany; Mersey Beat Showcase concert, with The Beatles, Gerry And The Pacemakers, 1963; The Beatles Christmas Show, London, 1963; NME Poll Winners Concert, Wembley, with The Beatles, Cliff Richard and the Shadows, Rolling Stones, 1964; Played for HRH Queen Mother, 1964; British Song Festival, 1965; Star Scene 65 tour, with the Everlys, Cilla Black, 1965; Solo career, club tours, 1968-; Appearances include: British Re-Invasion US tour, 1973; Solid Silver Sixties Show tour, with the Searchers, Gerry And The Pacemakers, 1993. Recordings: Albums: Listen To Billy J Kramer, 1963; Little Children, 1964; Best Of Billy J Kramer and the Dakotas, 1993; Singles include: with The Dakotas: Do You Want To Know A Secret? (Number 2, UK), 1963; Bad To Me (Number 1, UK), 1963; I'll Keep You Satisfied, 1963; Little Children (Number 1, UK), 1964; From A Window, 1964; It's Gotta Last Forever, 1965; Trains And Boats And Planes, 1965. Honours: Melody Maker Poll Winner, Best Newcomer, 1963. Address: Ideal Entertainment, 175 Duck Pond Road, Glen Cove, NY 11542, USA.

KRAUSS Alison, b. 1972. Singer; Bluegrass Musician (fiddle).Career: Singer, musician since age 14; Lead singer with backing band Union Station; 3 UK tours. Recordings: 6 albums with Union Station; Solo album: Now That I've Found You, 1995; Singles include: Baby Now That I've Found You; When You Say Nothing At All. Honours: Grammy Award, 1987; Country Music Television, Rising Star of 1995; 4 CMA Awards: Female Vocalist of the Year; Best New Artist; Vocal Event of the Year; Single of the Year, 1995. Address: c/o Keith Case And Associates, 59 Music Square West, Nashville, TN 37203, USA.

KRAVITZ Lenny, b. 26 May 1964, New York, USA. Singer; Musician (piano, guitar); Songwriter; Record Producer. m. Lisa Bonet (divorced). Musical Education: Self-taught. Career: Actor, as teenager; Member, California Boys Choir and Metropolitan Opera; Solo artiste, 1989-; Headline tours, UK, US and worldwide, 1990-; Concerts include: Support to Bob Dylan, New York, 1990; John Lennon Tribute Shows, Tokyo, 1990; Support to the Cult, Toronto, 1991; On-stage with Prince, New York, 1993; World tour, 1993; Glastonbury Festival, 1993; Torhout and Wechter Festival, 1993; Universal Love Tour, 1993; Television includes: Tonight Show; Arsenio Hall Show; Saturday Zoo; Saturday Night Live; Late Show with David Letterman. Recordings: Albums:

Let Love Rule, 1989; Mama Said, 1991; Are You Gonna Go My Way (Number 1, UK), 1993; Circus, 1995; Singles: It Ain't Over Till It's Over (Number 2, US), 1991; Are You Gonna Go My Way, 1993; Believe, 1993; Heaven Help, 1993; Is There Any Love In Your Heart, 1993; Rock'n'Roll Is Dead, 1995; Other recordings include: Use Me, duet with Mick Jagger, Wandering Spirit album, 1993; Film soundtrack, Superfly (with Curtis Mayfield); As producer, songwriter: Be My Baby, Vanessa Paradis, 1992; Justify My Love, Madonna (Number 1, US); Also as co-writer: Line Up, Aerosmith. Current Management: H K Management, 8900 Wilshire Blvd, #300, Beverly Hills, CA 90211, USA.

KRIEF Hervé, b. 3 Aug 1965, Paris, France. Musician (guitar); Singer; Composer; Arranger. Career: 500 concerts, France and abroad. Recordings: Albums: Paris Funk, SAEP, 1988; Comme C'Est Bizarre, SAEP, 1990; Live In Paris, Hervé Krief Big Band, 1991; Barbés Blues, Hervé Krief Blues Trio, 1992; La Dolce Vita, Hervé Krief Big Band, 1994; Paris-Bruxelles, Hervé Krief Blues Trio, 1995. Hobbies: Football; Tennis; Films. Current Management: Gilles Ouakil, BSM Productions. Address: 29 Rue Championnet, 75018 Paris, France.

KRIEGER Robbie, b. 8 Jan 1948, Los Angeles, California, USA. Musician (guitar). Career: Member, The Doors, 1965-72; Member, The Butts Band, 1972-; Also formed Robbie Krieger And Friends; Versions; Performances include: Northern California Folk-Rock Festival, 1968; Hollywood Bowl, later released as a video, 1968; Toronto Rock'n'Roll Revival Show, 1969; Isle Of Wight Festival, 1970; Annual performances, The Love Ride, benefit for Muscular Dystrophy, 1990; Film documentaries: The Doors Are Open, 1968; Feats Of Friends, 1969. Recordings: Albums: The Doors, 1967; Strange Days, 1967; Waiting For The Sun, 1968; Morrison Hotel, 1970; Absolutely Live, 1970; L A Woman, 1971; Other Voices, 1971; Weird Scenes Inside The Gold Mine, 1972; Full Circle, 1972; Best Of The Doors, 1973; Live At The Hollywood Bowl, 1987; Solo: No Habla, 1990; Singles: Light My Fire (Number 1, US), 1967; Love Me Two Times, 1968; Hello I Love You (Number 1, US), 1968; Touch Me, 1969; Love Her Madly, 1971; Riders On The Storm, 1971. Address: c/o Marco Moir Management, 8033 Sunset Blvd, Suite 76, Los Angeles, CA 90046, USA.

KRISTENSEN Paul, b. 21 June 1965, Oslo, Norway. Songwriter; Musician (bass guitar, drums). Education: Graphic Printer. Musical Education: Self-taught. Career: Formed Backstreet Girls, 1984; Tours: Norway; Sweden; Denmark; England; USA, 1987-92; Tour, Norway, with Casino Steel and The Crybabys, 1992. Recordings: Mental Shakedown, 1986; Boogie Till You Puke, 1988; Party On Elm Street, 1989; Coming Down Hard, 1990; Let's Have It, 1992; Live, 1993; Don't Fake It Too Long, 1995; Guest appearances with: Ziggy and The Rhythm Bulldogs; Casino Steel; Comic Messiah; A Technicolour Dream; Also several compilations. Honours: Norwegian Grammy Nominations, 1989, 1990. Memberships: TONO; GRAMO; GRAMART. Hobby: Record collecting. Current Management: Gram Art, Arb Samfunnets Plass 1, 0181 Oslo, Norway.

KRISTIANSEN Morten, b. 4 Apr 1971, Trondheim, Norway. Musician (guitar); Singer. Education: 2 years, University. Career: Started Hedge Hog, 1989; Several tours Norway; Toured Europe, 1994, 1995. Recordings: Erase, 1992; Surprise, 1992; Primal Gutter, 1993; Mercury Red, 1994; Mindless, 1994; The Healing EP, 1995; Thorn Cord Wonder, 1995. Membership: Norwegian Association of Musicians. Hobbies: Rally Car driving. Current Management: Martin Aam, Hedge Hog Management. Address: Hedge Hog, PO Box 683, 7001 Trondheim, Norway.

KRISTINA Sonja, b. 14 April 1949, Brentwood, Essex. Singer; Guitar; Sax; Flute; Piano. m. Stewart Copeland, 16 July 1982, divorced 1992, 3 sons. Education: Selftaught; Extensive music performance studies. Career: Lead Vocalist, Curved Air, rock group; Chrissy, Original London Cast of Hair; Several Fringe Theatre Projects including Shona, directed Claire Davidson; Pentameters Hampstead, 1989. Recordings: Back Street LVV, single, 1971; It Happed Today, single, 1970; 8 albums with Curved Air, 1971-76; Songs From the Acid Folk; Sonja Kristina; Harmonies of Love. Honour: Sounds Poll, Voted Top Female Vocalist, 1971. Memberships: Equity; Musicians Union; AOTOS. Hobbies: Art Teaching; Singing; Theatre; Performance. Current Management: Mystic Records. Address: 226A Haverstock Hill, London NW3 2AE, England. Address: 226A Haverstock Hill, London NW3 2AE, England.

KRISTOFFERSON Kris, b. 22 June 1936, Brownsville, Texas, USA. Singer; Songwriter; Actor. m. (1), 1 son, 1 daughter, (2) Rita Coolidge, 19 Aug 1973, divorced, 1 son; (3) Lisa Meyers, 19 Feb 1983, 2 sons, 1 daughter. Education: PhD, Pomona College; BA, Oxford University, England. Career: Songwriter, 1965-; Solo recording artiste, 1969-; Numerous concerts worldwide, including: Isle Of Wight Festival, 1970; Big Sur Folk Festival, 1971; New York Pop Festival, 1977; UNICEF charity concert, New York, 1978; Farm Aid II, 1987; Bob Dylan Tribute, New York, 1992; Also member of side project The Highwaymen (with Willie Nelson, Johnny Cash, Waylon Jennings), 1985-; Appeared at Farm Aid V, 1992; Actor, 1972-; Film appearances include: Cisco Pike, 1972; Pat Garret And Billy The Kid, 1973; Alice Doesn't Live Here Any More, 1974; The Sailor Who Fell From Grace With The Sea, 1976; A Star Is Born, 1976; Semi-Tough, 1977; Convoy, 1978; Heaven's Gate, 1980; Rollover, 1981; Flashpoint, 1984; Songwriter, 1984; Trouble In Mind, 1985; Big Top Pee Wee, 1988; Millenium, 1989; Christmas In Connecticut, 1992; Numerous appearances, television shows and mini-series. Compositions include: Help Me Make It Through The Night; Me And Bobby McGee, (also recorded by Janis Joplin); Why Me; For The Good Times. Recordings: Albums include: Kristofferson, 1970; The Silver-Tongued Devil And I, 1971; Border Lord, 1972; Jesus Was A Capricorn, 1973; Full Moon, with Rita Coolidge, 1973; Spooky Lady's Sideshow, 1974; Who's To Bless And Who's To Blame, 1975; Breakaway, with Rita Coolidge, 1975; A Star Is Born (soundtrack), 1977; Surreal Thing, 1976; Songs Of Kristofferson, 1977; Easter Island, 1978; Natural Act, with Rita Coolidge, 1979; Shake Hands With The Devil, 1979; Help Me Make It Through The Night, 1980; To The Bone, 1981; The Winning Hand, 1983; Music From Songwriter, with Willie Nelson, 1984; Repossessed, 1986; Third World Warrior, 1990; A Moment Of Forever, 1995; with The Highwaymen: Highwayman, 1985; Highwaymen 2, 1992. Honours: CMA Song Of The Year, Sunday Morning Coming Down, 1970; Grammy Awards: Best Country Song, 1972; Best Country Vocal Performance (with Coolidge), 1973, 1976; Golden Globe, Best Actor, 1976; Inducted into Songwriters Hall Of Fame, 1985; with The Highwaymen: ACM Single Of The Year, Highwayman, 1986; 2 American Music Awards, 1986. Current Management: Rothbaum and Garner, 36 Mill Plain Road, Ste 406, Danbury, CT 06811, USA.

KRIZIC Davor, b. 29 Mar 1966, Zagreb, Croatia. Musician (trumpet, flugelhorn); Composer. Musical Education: Musical High School, Zagreb; 3 years of Jazz Music, University of Graz. Career: Played with: Ernie Wilkins; Ed Thighpen; Bosko Petrovic; Jimmy Woody; David Liebmon; Soloist, Croatian Radio-TV Big Band; Played at Jazz Fair, Zagreb, 1990, 1992-95; Ingolstadt Jazz Festival, 1990; Springtime Jazz Feever, 1995; Many television and radio appearances in Croatia; Greentown Jazz Band

German tour. Compositions: Beleavin'; Some Blues; Urony. Recordings: Albums: with Miro Kadoic: Dry, 1994; with Mia: Ne Ne Ker Se Ne Sme, 1994; with Miljenko Prohaska: Opus 900, 1994; Leader, Boilers Jazz Quartet, Zagreb. Honours: Laureate of the Prize for Best Young Jazz Musician, Jazz Fair, Zagreb, 1990. Memberships: Jazz Club, Zagreb; Croatian Music Union; Croatian Artists Society (ZUH). Hobbies: Cooking; Basketball. Address: Palmoticeva 25, 10000 Zagreb, Croatia.

KROEGHER Freddy, b. 23 Sept 1967, St-Etienne, France. Singer; Composer; Musician (lead guitar, bass); Entertainer. 1 daughter. Musical Education: Studied from 17-20 at AIMRA Jazz School, Lyons, France. Career: Francofolies of La Rochelle, 1993; Festival of Young Creators, Tignes, 1993; National FNAC Tour, special broadcast interview in France-Inter Radio; TV clip video (Killer) 1993; Concerts; Radio appearances; TV interviews, newspapers. Recordings: Albums: Freddy Kroegher: Le Meilleur, 1993; Secoue Ton Seve, 1995; 3 singles; Studio session, backing guitars with: Laoassenko, 1990; Nilda Fernandez, 1991; Jimmy Oihid, 1992; Michel Nouyve, 1993; Gillo Coquard, 1994. Honours: Twice Best Rock Artist, Rhone-Alpes region, France, 1990, 1991; Memberships: RONDOR; SACEM. Hobby: Music. Current Management: Freddy Kroegher Production. Address: Route de Parisièves, 42360 Cottance, France.

KROG Karin, b. 15 May 1937, Oslo, Norway. Jazz Singer. m. Johannes Bergh, 21 Sept 1957, 2 daughters. Education: Business School. Musical Education: Private study with Anne Brown, 1962-69; Ivo Knecevic, 1969-72; Career: Member of Kjell Karlsen Quartet, Frode Thingnaes Quintet and Egil Kapstad Trio; Leader of own groups, 1962-; Worked with Don Ellis; Clare Fischer; Mikkel Flagstad; Einar Iversen; John Surman; Bengt Hallberg; Red Mitchell; Nils Lindberg; Warne Marsh; Richard Rodney Bennett; Founder, First Chairman, Norwegian Jazz Forum, 1965-66; Worldwide live, television and radio appearances include jazz festivals in Antibes, France and Norway, 1965; Warsaw and Prague, 1966; Hamburg and Berlin, 1967; Osaka, 1970; Australia, 1985; Hungary, 1989; USSR, 1990; Djakarta, 1992; Bulgaria, 1994; Umbria (Italy), Bath (England), Sardinia, 1994. Formed Meantime Records, 1987; Compositions include: ballet music for Carolyn Carlson and Lario Ekson; Recordings: By Myself, 1964; Jazz Moments, 1966; Some Other Spring, with Dexter Gordon, 1970; Hi-Fly, with Archie Shepp, 1972; I Remember You, with Red Mitchell and Warne Marsh, 1980; Two Of A Kind, with Beng Hallberg, 1981; Nordic Quartet, with John Surman, Terje Rypdal, Vigleik Storaas, 1995; Compilation: Jubilee, 30 years in recorded music, 1994. Honours: Buddy Award, Norwegian Jazz Foundation, 1965; Down Beat Poll Winner, Talent Deserving Wider Recognition, 1967; Spellemanns Prize, 1974; Grammy, Norway, 1974; Female Singer of the Year, European Jazz Federation, 1975; 2 Swing Journal Awards, Record of the Year, Japan, 1970 and 1978; Oslo Council Artist Award, 1981; Several government grants and scholarships. Memberships: Norwegian Musicians Federation; NOPA. Hobbies: Outdoor life; Sport. Address: Nobelsgate 35, 0268 Oslo, Norway.

KROGH Soren, b. 11 May 1967, Hjorring, Denmark. Songwriter; Singer; Musician (Guitar). m. Kirsten Hoi. Career: Plays 100 gigs a year at music clubs, festivals and radios with band and as solo artiste; Writes own folk-rock songs in Danish; Started playing professionally, 1987. Recordings: Radiosingle, 1997; Indianerdrengen, 1998. Honours: Different scholarships. Memberships: DJBFA; Danish Singer/Songwriter Society. Current Management: Koncertkontoret, Staldgardsgade 39A 1, 7100 Vejle, Denmark. Address: Koncertkontoret, Staldgardsgade 39A 1, Vejle, Denmark.

KRUTILEK Václav, b. 12 Sept 1932, Valasské Mezirící. Composer. m. Frantiska Nemcová, 21 Apr 1956, 1 son, 1 daughter. Musical Education: Selftaught. Career: Children Chorus; Church Chorus; Conductor, Army Chorus; Folk Chorus; Part in Music Band, Wind instruments band. Compositions: MUSIC Without Conductor; Rambling Boots; Music of Czech Mills; The End of Hunting Season; Gentleman on the Road; Moravian Wedding; Under Top Hat; Harvest of Peace. Recordings: 6 songs in 1993; 5 songs, 1994; 11 songs, 1995; 3 songs, 1970. Publications: Music Without Conductor, 1981; With Mother Again; 1984: The End of Hunting Season; Tango Elephantino. Honour: 3rd Prize in state competition, Ostrava, 1974. Membership: Society for Copyrights, Prague, 1967. Hobbies: Music; Sport. Address: Václav Krutilek, Na Vyhlídce 15, 757 01 Valasské Mezirící, Czech Republic.

KRYTOVYCH Ihor, b. Vovchyschovychy reg Lviv. Producer; Manufacturer. m. Maria Pech, 7 Aug 1983. Education: Graduated from Lviv Polytechnic Institute. Musical Education: Drohybych specialized musical school (choir-master). Career: Sound producer for bands: Vatra, 1979; Smerichka, 1980-88; For the Study theatre: Ne Zhurys, 1988; Chairman, Co-operative, Audio Profile, 1989; Director General of joint venture AV Systems, 1991; Renamed Studio Leva, 1993-; Projects on making images, repetoires, advertisements for different bands, singers including Oksana Mocherad; Duet Inessa and Orest; Irchyk; Oleh Yarema; Angelica; Vitaly Sachok; Skriabin; NZ; Tender Blues; Also organized music festivals. Hobbies: Reading spiritual literature. Address: 290000 Lviv, Str Kostiushko 18, Studio Leva, Ukraine.

KUBES Stanislav, b. 4 March 1952, Prague, Czech Republic. Musician (Guitar); Songwriter. m. Marcela, 28 August 1973. Musical Education: Guitar, Public School of Art. Career: The Wizards, 1970; Eminence Group, 1972; Benefit Group, 1973; Respect Group, 1974-75; JIFT Schelinger Group, 1975-81; Tour of Poland with Smokie, 1977; Romance za korunu, Movie, 1975; SLS Group, 1981-85; ETC... Band, 1985-; Support for Rolling Stones, Urban Jungle Tour, Prague, 1990. Compositions: Jsem pry blazen jen, 1978; Vanda a Zanda, LP and TV clip, 1985; Za vodou, CD, MC, 1997; 15 titles published. Recordings: 35 singles, 1975-81; Hrr na ne!, LP, 1975; Nám se Líbí, 1976; SLS, LP, 1982; Coloured Dreams, LP, 1984; ETC..., 1986; ETC...4, 1987; 20 deta duse, LP, CD, 1989; Jen se smej, CD, 1994; ETC... Band, Unplugged Live, CD, 1996; Mésto z périn, CD, 1997. Hobbies: Aeronautics; Cats; Countryside. Current Management: Syrinx, Svornosti 8, 15000 Praha 5, Czech Republic. Address: Mladenovova 3231, CZ 14300 Prague 4, Czech Republic.

KUCERA Josef Simon "Saxophone Joe", b. 8 July 1943, Prague, Czech Republic. All Saxophones; Flute. Career: Framus Five, soul band, Czechoslovakia, 1967-68; Musical, Hair, 1969-70; Duo: Jesse Ballard and Saxphone Joe, 1972-74; Sessions with Alexis Korner, London; Paradise Island Band, Berlin, 1976; Member, Pete "Wyoming" Bender Band, 1980-90; Jazz Festival Karlovy Vary, Czech Republic, 1990, 1993; Japan Tour with Marta Kubisova, 1993. Compositions: Day Dream; Anyway; 1000 Reasons; Waltz for My Friends; Anotherway. Recordings: Control, 1975; Crossroads, 1982; Swindia, 1984; Balance, solo album, 1986; Triangle, Live, 1997. Membership: Rock and Pop Musikerverband. Hobbies: Sailing; Poetry; Painting. Current Management: Events and Arts, H Degner, Grüntenstr 54, 12 107 Berlin, Germany. Address: Koloniestr 28, 13359 Berlin, Germany.

KUHL Ole, b. 30 January 1950, Copenhagen, Denmark. Reed Player; Composer. m. Lena, 12 December 1975, 1 son. Education: Selftaught

Saxophone and Flute; BA, Musicology, 1997. Career: Touring with John Tchicai, 1969-71, Blue Sun, 1971-73, Debbie Cameron, 1981; Leader, Own Band, Natdamperen, 1975-79, Dawn, 1980-86, Diversity, 1997-; Lead Player, Kluvers Big Band, 1983-88. Compositions: Stage Music for Production of Pablo Neruda, Banditten and William Shakespeare's The Tempest. Recordings: Natdamperen: Nat damperen, 1975; Boogieman Eats Frikadeller, 1976; Visions, 1979; With John Tchicai, Blue Sun, 1973-; Gnags, 1974-77; Contemporary Workshop Ensemble, 1997. Memberships: DMF; KODA; GRAMEX; NCB; COPYDAN; DJBFA; MA. Hobby: Meditation. Address: Balagervej 4, 8260 Viby, Denmark.

KUJAHN Lars B, b. 22 June 1958, Denmark. Drummer. Education: Attended Lectures in Rhythms, Istanbul Conservatory, 1988, Cairo, 1989, Casablanca, 1992, Fanoon, 1997. Career: Playing Jazz-Rock in Passengers, Milky Way, 1979-86; Playing Gypsy Music in Svira, 1982-87; Leader of Oriental Mood, 1991; Teacher, Oriental Percussion, 1991-. Compositions: Raqsa Maghzebia, 1992; Yallah Mustagbad, 1992; Macera, 1995; Hobb Harr, 1995; Gediid, 1995; Oriential Moods, 1996; Ahman, 1997; Mapsut, 1997; 12 Ok, 1997. Recordings: Travels, 1994; Oriental Moods, 1996; Oriental Garden, 1996; Ax Kurdistaan, 1996; Côlbanein, 1998; Expoessive Mahala. Memberships: Danish Musicians Union; Danish Rhythmic Composers Organization. Hobby: Travel. Address: Oriental Percussion, Hane Tavsons Gade 17 4 tv, DK 2200 N, Denmark.

KUKKO (Jyrki) Sakari, b. 8 July 1953, Kajaani, Finland. Bandleader; Composer; Arranger; Musician (flute, saxophone, keyboards). m. Marta Cecilia Renza Villanueva, 1981, divorced 1986. Musical Education: Classical music, Sibelius Academy, Helsinki; Jazz with Edward Vesala. Career: Founder, Piirpauke, 1974-; Concerts include: Festivals in Tbilisi; Bombay; Zürich; Paris; Cannes; Barcelona; Concerts, tours with Piirpauke in 30 different countries (4 continents); Also with: Youssou N'Dour; Okay Temiz; Alameda; Aster Aweke; Television and radio appearances worldwide. Compositions: for the Espoo Big Band: Moonlight Caravan; Finnish Characters. Recordings: 20 albums with Piirpauke; 2 solo albums: Will Of The Wisp, 1979; Music For Espoo Big Band, 1989; with Sensation Band Ethiopia '76: Ethiopian Groove; Music for films, theatre, dance. Honours: Yrjö Award, Finnish Jazz Federation, 1976. Hobbies: Different cultures; Yoga; Fishing; Tennis; Palindromes. Current Management: Tapio Korjus, Rockadillo. Address: Sakari Kukko, Koutaniementie 30 A, 87100 Kajaani, Finland; c/o Rockadillo, Keskustori 7 A 11, 33100 Tampere, Finland.

KUKKONEN Jarno, b. 26 July 1964, Nastola, Finland. Musician (guitar). Musical Education: Lessons with Otto Berger, aged 11; Diploma, Sibelius Academy, Helsinki, 1990. Career: Works as jazz guitarist in studios, theatre, and on radio; Also plays with the UMO (New Music Orchestra); Teacher, Sibelius Academy, Helsinki; Compositions performed by the UMO. Address: Sibelius Academy of Music, Töölöntorinkatu 28, 00260 Helsinki, Finland.

KULICK Bruce, b. USA. Musician (guitar). Career: Member, various groups including: Blackjack; Goodrats; Member, US rock group Kiss, 1985-; Appearances include: US tour, with Cheap Trick, 1988; Marquee Club, 1988; US tour, 1990; Revenge '92 Tour, 1992. Recordings: with Kiss: Albums: Asylum, 1985; Crazy Nights, 1987; Smashes Thrashes And Hits, 1988; Hot In The Shade, 1989; Revenge, 1992; Kiss Alive III, 1992; Contributor, Hear'N'Aid (Ethiopian famine relief charity album), 1986; Singles include: Tears Are Falling; Crazy Crazy Nights; Reason To Live; Hide Your Heart; Forever; God Gave Rock And Roll To You, featured in film: Bill And Ted's Bogus

Journey, 1992. Honours: Inducted into Hollywood's Rock Walk, 1993; Kiss Day proclaimed, Los Angeles, 1993. Current Management: Entertainment Services Unlimited, Main Street Plaza 1000, Suite 303, Voorhees, NJ 08043, USA.

KUPPER Eric S, b. 10 July 1962, New York, NY, USA. Producer; Remixer; Musician; Songwriter. m. Gianna F Bavido, 1 son, 1 daughter Education: BA, Music; BA, Theatre and Film, Hunter College, CUNY. Career: Top of the Pops with Frankie Knuckles; Arsenio Hall Show with Rupaul. Compositions include: The Whistle Song, Frankie Knuckles; Imitation of Life. Recordings include: P M Dawn, I'll Be Waiting; Rupaul, Supermodel, album; K-Scope, From the Deep. Memberships: NARAS; ASCAP; AFM. Hobbies: Fishing; Cigars and Pipes; AFM. Current Management: Seven PM.

KUSSIN Al, b. 24 Aug 1952, Edmonton, Canada. Producer; Musician (keyboards). Education: BA; MA, Economics. Musical Education: Grade VII Royal Conservatory, Grade II Theory. Recordings: Lorraine Scott: All Talk; Lorraine Scott, 1995; Party Mix: Party Mix '94; Tropirollo Volumes II-VI; Celine Dion: Unison. Honours: 4 Juno nominations; 4 Platinum records. Memberships: SOCAN; CIRPA; AULA; CARAS. Current Management: Slak Productions. Address: 9 Hector Avenue, Toronto, Ontario M6G 3G2, Canada.

KUVEZIN Albert, b. 27 Nov 1965, Kyzyl, Tuva, Russia. Vocalist; Musician (Marinkhur: ethnic folk string instrument). m. Natalia Toka, 16 Dec 1990, 2 daughters. Musical Education: Kyzyl Musical College; Folk Instrument Class. Career: As member of Yat-Kha: Voice Of Asia Festival (Brian Eno Special Prize), 1990; Sweden, 1991; Siberia Interweek, 1992-94; Berlin Independent Days, 1993; Italy, 1993; WOMAD, 1994; US, 1995. Recordings: Yat-kha, 1993; Huun-Huur-Tu: Go Horses In My Herd. Publications: Numerous in Russian, US, Italian, Scandinavian press. Honours: Voice Of Asia, 1990; Wales Folk Fest, 1992. Hobby: Being out in the country. Current Management: Etz/Artemy Troitsky. Address: PO Box 107, 125212 Moscow, Russia.

KYRKJEBO Sissel, b. 24 June 1969, Bergen, Norway. Singer. m. Eddie Skoller, 21 Aug 1993. Career: Singer, 1985-; Sold 1.5 million discs, Norway, 1986-; Worldwide tours including Scandinavian concerts with Neil Sedaka, 1991; Barcelona Cathedral; Christmas Concert in Vienna with Placido Domingo; Musical Ambassador, singer for Olympic Hymn, Winter Olympic Games, Norway, 1994; Theatre: Maria Von Trapp, Sound of Music; Solveig, Peer Gynt. Recordings: Albums: Sissel, 1986; Glade Jul, 1987; Soria Moria, 1989; Gift of Love, 1992; Innerst I Sjelen, 1994; Hit single: Fire In Your Heart (Olympic Hymn) with Placido Domingo; Honours: Norwegian Grammy; Artist of the Year; H C Andersen Award; Platinum disc, Innerst I Sjelen. Membership: GRAMO. Current Management: c/o Arne Svare, Stageway Impresario A/S, Skuteviksboder 11, 5035 Bergen, Norway.

L

LA PORTE-PITICCO Laurie Margaret, b. 31 Aug 1960, Sudbury, Ontario, Canada. Singer; Songwriter; Musician (rhythm guitar). m. Steve Piticco, 1 son, 1 daughter. Musical Education: Played with musical family from age 15. Career: Rhythm guitarist, singer, songwriter with South Mountain; Television appearances include: Band hosted own series, 4 years, CHRO TV; Tommy Hunter Show; Canadian Country Music Awards Show; Concerts: Support to Vince Gill, Charlie Pride. Compositions: Co-writer: I've Got The Blues, South Mountain (Top 10 hit); Several original songs on South Mountain album: Where There's A Will. Honours: Vista Rising Star Award, CCMA, 1991. Memberships: SOCAN; Canadian Country Music Association. Hobbies: Bible study; Time with children and friends. Current Management: Savannah Music Inc; Agent: Catherine Faint, Stony Plain Records. Address: Box 64, South Mountain, Ontario K0E 1W0, Canada.

LA ROSA Julius, b. 2 Jan 1930, Brooklyn, NY, USA. Singer. m. Rosemary Meyer, 7 Apr 1956, 1 son, 1 daughter. Education: Courses in Italian and Psychology. Career: Has appeared on major Television and on various Radio shows. Recording: Anywhere I Wander; E Cumpari. Memberships: ASCAP; SAG; Actor's Equity. Hobbies: Golf; Chess; Reading; Writing. Current Management: S Rothman. Address: c/o S Rothman, 101 West 57th Street, New York, NY 10019, USA.

LA SALLE Denise, b. 16 July 1941, Mississippi, USA. Vocalist; Songwriter; Publisher. m. James E Wolfe, 16 July, 1977, 1 son, 1 daughter. Career: Dick Clark; Soul Train; Rhythm and Blues Award; Blues Going On; Toured West Africa, 1972; Europe 1974-78; Co-owner, WFKX Radio Station (KIX96 FM), 1984-; Malaco World Tour, 1989; Soul Blues European Tour: France; Italy; England; Austria; Netherlands; Finland; Norway; Sweden, 1993; Owner, Denise La Salle's Chique Boutique and Wigs; Co-owner, The Celebrity Club, Jackson, Tennessee. Recordings: Trapped By A Thing Called Love; Down Home Blues; Married But Not To Each Other; The Bitch Is Bad; Lady In The Street; A Mansize Job; Now Run And Tell That. Publication: Booklet: How To Be A Successful Songwriter. Honours: Jackie Award, Chicago, 1974; BMI Award. Memberships: Founder: National Association For Preservation Of Blues (NAPOB); BMI; NARAS. Hobbies: Cooking; Gardening. Current Management: Roger Redding and Associates Maconga. Address: c/o Denise La Salle, Ordena Entertainment Inc, PO Box 895, Jackson, TN 38302, USA.

LABARRIERE Jacques, b. 29 Nov 1956, Paris, France. Composer; Arranger; Musician (piano). Musical Education: Licence de Musicologie; Prize for harmony, counterpoint. Career: Shows include: Gospel; Cats; Fantasticks; 42nd Street; Trouble in Tahiti; Radio-France broadcast: ACR de France Culture; Concerts: Jazz with Joe Lee Wilson; Anette Lowman; Eric Barret; Philippe Selam; Jean-Louis Mechali; Singers: C Combe; C Magny; Perone. Recordings: Cats; Tie Break, Second Set; Entre 3 and 5. Memberships: SACEM; SACD; ADAMI; SPEDIDAM; SCAM.

LABELLE Patti (Patricia Holt), b. 24 May 1944, Philadelphia, Pennsylvania, USA. Singer; Actress. Founder member, The Blue Belles, 1961; Appearances include: Ready Steady Go, ITV, Thank Your Lucky Stars, ITV, UK tour, 1966; Group name changed to Labelle, 1970-76; Solo artiste, 1976-; Concerts include: Live Aid, JFK Stadium, Philadelphia, 1985; Nelson Mandela International Tribute, Wembley Stadium, England, 1990; Appearance, gospel musical, Your Arm's Too Short To Box With God, Broadway, New York, 1982; Actress, film A Soldier's Story, 1984; Television appearances: Actress, Unnatural Causes, NBC, 1986; Motown 30 - What's Goin' On, CBS, 1990; Arsenio Hall Show special, devoted to Labelle, 1991; Going Home To Gospel With Patti LaBelle, 1991; Own sitcom, Out All Night, NBC, 1992. Recordings: Singles: with Blue Belles: I Sold My Heart To The Junkman, 1962; with LaBelle: Lady Marmalade, 1975; On My Own, duet with Michael McDonald (Number 1, US), 1986; Oh People, 1986; Love Has Finally Come At Last, duet with Bobby Womack; Albums: with LaBelle: LaBelle, 1971; Gonna Take A Miracle, 1971; Moonshadow, 1972; Nightbirds, 1974; Phoenix, 1975; Chameleon, 1976; Solo albums: Patti LaBelle, 1977; Tasty, 1978; It's Alright With Me, 1979; Released, 1977; The Spirit's In It, 1981; I'm In Love Again, 1984; Winner In You, 1986; Be Yourself, 1989; This Christmas, 1990; Burnin', 1991; Live!, 1992; Gems, 1994; Contributor, The Poet II, Bobby Womack, 1984; Good Woman, Gladys Knight, 1990; Hallelujah!, Quincy Jones, 1991; Am I Cool Or What?, 1992; Contributor, film soundtracks: Beverly Hills Cop, 1985; Outrageous Fortune, 1987; Dragnet, 1987; Licence To Kill, 1989; Leap Of Faith, 1992. Honours include: Award Of Merit, Philadelphia Art Alliance, 1986; Lifetime Achievement Award, CORE (Congress Of Racial Equality), 1990; NAACP Entertainer of Year, 1992; American Music Award, Favourite Female R&B/Soul Artist, 1993; Star on Hollywood Walk Of Fame, 1993; Current Management: PAZ Entertainment Co., 2041 Locust Street, Philadelphia, PA 19103, USA.

LACY Steve, b. 1934, New York, USA. Jazz Musician (soprano saxophone). Career: Performed with artists including: Pee Wee Russell; Buck Clayton; Cecil Taylor; Gil Evans Orchestra, 1957; Leader, own groups; Founder, own quartet with Roswell Rudd, early 1960s; Formed sextet, Paris, 1970; Played duets with Mal Waldron, 1979-; Recordings include: Soprano Sax, 1957; Reflections - Steve Lacy Plays Thelonius Monk, 1958; Evidence, with Don Cherry, 1961; Paris Blues, with Gil Evans, Raps, 1977; with Steve Lacy Three: New York Capers, 1979; The Way, 1979; Ballets, 1980; Songs, 1985; Prospectus, 1986; Steve Lacy Two, Five & Six Blinks, 1986; Steve Lacy Nine: Futurities, 1986; Anthem, 1990; with Mal Waldron: Herbe de L'Oubli, 1981; Snake Out, 1981; Let's Call This, 1986; Hot House, 1991. Honours: Downbeat Magazine Poll winner, Best Soprano Saxophonist, several times. Address: 57 rue de Temple, F-75004 Paris, France.

LADINSKY Gary, b. 2 May 1947, Los Angeles, California, USA. Recording Engineer. m. Gina Maria Sodaro, 19 Feb 1972, 2 sons. Education: BA, California State University, Northridge, 1970. Career: Recording engineer, Record Plant, Los Angeles, 1971-75; President, Gary Ladinsky Inc/Design FX Audio, 1979-. Recordings: Engineer, albums by: Lynyrd Skynyrd; Van Morrison; Moody Blues; Cheap Trick; Donna Summer; George Benson; Manhattan Transfer; Mixer, film scores: Ferris Bueller's Day Off, 1987; Trains, Planes and Automoblies, 1987; Naked Gun, 1988. Memberships: NARAS; Audio Engineering Society; Society Professional Audio Recording Services. Address: c/o Design FX Remore Recording, PO Box 491087, Los Angeles, CA 91603, USA.

LADY BO (Peggy), b. 19 July 1940, New York City, USA. Musician (lead guitar); Singer; Dancer; Entertainer; Songwriter; Arranger; Producer; Choreographer. m. Walter Malone, 20 Oct 1968. Education: Complete Performing Arts School, New York. Career: First female guitarist in history of Rock and Roll, Rhythm and Blues, 1957; First female hired, major act, 1959; First female member, original Bo Diddley recording and stage act, 1959; Principle player, protegée of Bo Diddley; The Jewels, leading club band, New York, 1961-67; Backing musician: Chuck Berry, 1971; Richard Berry, 1983; Play: Thunder Knocking on the Door, San Jose Repertory Theatre, 1997; Major concerts: HIC Arena, Hawaii; Monterey Jazz Festival, 1973, 1974; Greek Theater; Circle Star Theater; Ventura County and Nevada State Fair; Monterey Bay Blues Festival, 1994, 1995; Tours: US, Canada, 1965-80s; Europe, 1987; NIKE Endorsement, Bo Knows, 1989; Television: The Jewels, The Mod Mecca TV Special, NYC/BBC, England, 1967; Kenny Rogers, Toronto, 1971; Donnie & Marie, Hollywood, 1976-77; Live Concert, Sweden, 1987; Arts and Entertainment Special, worldwide coverage, 1990; Lady Bo and the BC Horns, South Bay Scene, USA, 1996; Film: The Lost Boys, 1987; Video: I Don't Sound Like Nobody, Bo Diddley with Lady Bo and the Family Jewel, UK, 1992; Flashbacks: Volume One Soul Sensations, 1994; Lady Bo & The BC Horns, Say That You Love Me, 1995. Recordings: Albums: with Bo Diddley: Bo Diddley, 1958; Go Bo Diddley, 1959; Have Guitar, Will Travel, 1960; Bo Diddley In The Spotlight, 1961; Bo Diddley Is A Lover, 1961; Bo Diddley Is A Gunslinger, 1962; Road Runner, 1964; Bo Diddley, 16 All-Time Greatest Hits, 1964; Bo Diddley, The EP Collection, 1992; Bo Diddley, The Chess Years, box set, 1993; with Les Cooper: Wiggle Wobble, 1962, 1988; with Fred Waring Orchestra: The Two Worlds of Fred Waring, 1966; Various artistes: Feeling Happy, 1978; The Doo Wop Era: Harlem, New York, 1987; New York R&B, Harlem Holiday, 1988; King Curtis: Soul Twist and Other Golden Classics, 1988; The Mighty Bo Diddley, Ain't It Good To Be Free, USA, 1984, France, 1988; Lady No & The BC Horns, Shebo-Shebad, 1997; Singles: 19 with Bo Diddley; 8 as the Jewels; Greg and Peg; Peggy and Bob; The Bob Chords Vocal Group. Publications: Listed: The Great Gretsch Guitars Hall Of Fame; She's A Rebel- The History Of Women In Rock'n'Roll, 1992; The Complete Bo Diddley Sessions, by George R White; Bo Diddley Bio, 1995; History Of Doo Wop, The Chicago Scene, 1996; Guitar Player books, 1987, 1990; Suede News, Lady Bo, cover feature, 1997. Honours: Lifetime Achievement Award, South Bay Blues Awards, 1993. Memberships: AFofM; RMA; BMI; ASCAP; AFM Local 153. Current Management: LB-BCH Productions. Address: 14680 Bear Creek Road, Boulder Creek, CA 95006, USA.

LAFFY Stephen, b. 29 May 1953, London, England. Musician; Songwriter; Producer. m. Lynn Heather, 21 Mar 1994, 2 daughters. Musical Education: Self-taught. Career: Performed at Glastonbury Festival; WOMAD; Notting Hill Carnival; Overseas tours, television and radio; Formed own band Rhythm Rising. Recordings: When 2000 Comes, 1995; Don't Go Breaking Down; Carry On; Everybody Needs Someone. Memberships: Musicians' Union; PRS; MCPS. Hobbies: Swimming; Gardening; Reading.

LAFITTE Guy Denis Fernand, b. 12 Jan 1927, Saint-Gaudens, France. Musician (saxophone). m. Dumoulin Colombe, 23 Dec 1985. Education: Ecole de Commerce. Career: Concerts and records with Lionel Hampton; Film music with Duke Ellington, Louis Armstrong, 1963; Concerts with Hank Jones; Bill Coleman; Wild Bill Davis; Clark Terry; Arnett Cobb; Milton Mezzrow; Mady Mesple; Television includes: Vivre 2 Fois, 1976; Pour L'Amour Du Jazz, 1984; Guy Lafitte, 1988; Festivals include: Montreux; Antibes; Montauban; Edinburgh; Barcelona; Nimes; Madrid; Breda; Oslo; Darmstadt; Las Palmas; Palma. Recordings: Latest albums: Guy Lafitte Joue Charles Trenet, 1985; Black And Blue, 1989; Black And Blue, 1990; Other recordings with: Wild Bill Davis, La Velle, Philippe Renault, 1991, Live 93 GL Quartet. Honours: Prix Django Reinhardt, Academie du Jazz, 1954; Golden Disc, Brazil, 1957; Prix Charles Cros; Prix de la Revue Des Arts; Grand Prix Du Disque, Academie di Disque Français, 1957, 1981; Chevalier des Arts et Lettres; Django d'Or, 1996. Membership:

Président d'Honneur de Jazz in Maciac. Hobbies; Trees and nature. Address: Le Serrot, 32420 Tournan, France.

LAHTI Pentti, b. 15 Aug 1945, Finland. Musician (reeds, flutes, saxophones). Career: Musician with Eero Koivistoinen Octet, and Mircea Stan Quartet, early 1970s; Member, Jukka Linkola Octet; Member, UMO (New Music Orchestra); Finnish Broadcasting Company tours to Oslo, 1973; Laren Festival, Holland, 1977; Annual appearance, Pori Festival; Reed player, Wasama Quartet and Ilkka Niemeläinen's Instinct, 1980s. Recording: Solo album: Ben Bay. Honours: Yrjö Award, Finnish Jazz Federation, 1983. Address: Kärpänkuja 8, 04230 Kerava, Finland.

LAIDLAW Raymond Joseph, b. 28 May 1948, Tynemouth, England. Musician (drums). m. Lesley, 9 Apr 1976, 2 sons. Education: Newcastle Art College. Musical Education: Club A GoGo, Newcastle. Career: Drummer, Lindisfarne, 1969-; Now studio owner, music publisher. Compositions: Joint composer: Scotch Mist instrumental (B side of Lindisfarne hit: Meet Me On the Corner). Membership: Musicians' Union. Hobbies: Walking; Talking; Eating; Drinking. Current Management: Lindisfarne Musical Productions. Address: Hi-level Recording, 18 Victoria Terrace, Whitley Bay, Tyne And Wear, England.

LAIDVEE Meelis, b. 10 Jan 1964, Pärnu, Estonia. Musician (keyboards). m. Eve Laidlee (Lublo), 1 Mar 1985, 2 daughters. Musical Education: Private lessons. Career: Concerts, tours, 1978-; Television and radio hitlists with: Provints; Uncle Bella; The Tuberkubited, 1988-. Recordings: 3 abums with The Tuberkuloited. Honours: Radio Top 10 Award, 1994, 1995. Address: PO Box 2225, EE 0035, Tallinn, Estonia.

LAINE Cleo (Clementina Dinah Dankworth), (Dame), b. 28 Oct 1927, Southall, Middlesex, England. Vocalist. m. John Dankworth, 18 Mar 1958, 2 sons, 1 daughter. Career: Vocalist, Dankworth Orchestra, 1953-58; Lead role, Seven Deadly Sins, Edinburgh Festival and Sadlers Wells, 1961; Showboat, 1972; Colette, 1980; Also appeared in A Time To Laugh; Hedda Gabler; The Women Of Troy; The Mystery Of Edwin Drood, Broadway, 1986; Into The Woods, US National Tour, 1989; Numerous television appearances. Recordings include: Feel The Warm; I Am A Song; Live At Melbourne (Gold discs); Best Friends; Sometimes When We Touch (Platinum discs); Most recent recordings: Jazz, 1993; Blue And Sentimental, 1994; Solitude, 1995. Publications: Cleo, autobiography, 1994; You Can Sing If You Want To, 1997. Honours: CBE, 1979; Golden Feather Award, Los Angeles Times, 1973; Edison Award, 1974; Hon MA, Open University, 1975; Singer of the Year, TV Times, 1978; Hon MusD, Berklee College Of Music, 1982; Grammy Award, Best Female Vocalist, 1985; Theatre World Award, 1986; NARM Lifetime Achievement Award, 1990; British Jazz Award, Best Female Vocalist, 1990; Variety Club of Great Britain Show Business Personality of Year, 1977; Hon DA, Luton University, 1994; Hon MusD, York University, 1993; DBE, 1997. Current Management: Dankworth Management. Address: The Old Rectory, Wavendon, Milton Keynes MK17 8LT, England.

LAINE Frankie (Francesco Paolo Lo Vecchio), b. 30 Mar 1913, Chicago, Illinois, USA. Singer; Songwriter. m. Nan Laine, 15 June 1950, deceased 1993, 2 daughters. Musical Education: Studied with Frank Teschemacher. Career: Singer, dance teacher, Merry Garden Ballroom, late 1920s; Dancer, numerous dance marathons; First billed as Frankie Laine, 1938; First record deal, 1946; Sales in excess of 100 million records; Concerts worldwide include: Royal Variety Performance for Queen Elizabeth II, 1954. Film appearances include: When You're Smiling, 1950; Sunny Side Of The Street, 1951; Rainbow Round

My Shoulder, 1952; Bring Your Smile Along, 1955; He Laughed Last, 1956; Performed title songs, films: Gunfight At The OK Corral, 1957; Blazing Saddles, 1974; Featured in The Last Picture Show, 1971; Lemon Popsicle, 1978; Raging Bull, 1980; Television includes: Frankie Laine Time; The Frankie Laine Show; Acted in: Rawhide; Perry Mason; Burke's Law. Compositions: Co-writer: Put Yourself In My Place Baby (with Hoagy Carmichael); It Ain't Gonna Be Like That, with Mel Tormé; Magnificent Obsession (with Freddie Karger); Torchin' with Al Lerner; We'll Be Together Again (with Carl Fischer); Recorded by over 100 artists including Louis Armstrong; Tony Bennett; Ray Charles; Rosemary Clooney; Ella Fitzgerald; Sammy Davis Jr; Jack Jones; Frank Sinatra; Billie Holiday. Recordings: 80 albums and EPs, 1947-; Singles include: Jezebel, 1951; High Noon, 1952; I Believe, 1953; Kid's Last Fight, 1954; Cool Water, 1955; A Woman In Love, 1955; Moonlight Gambler, 1956; Rawhide, 1958; Making Memories, 1971; Lord You Gave Me A Mountain, 1969. Publication: That Lucky Old Son (autobiography), co-author with Joseph Laredo. Address: PO Box 6910, San Diego, CA 92166, USA.

LAINE Reino, b. 11 July 1946, Finland. Musician (drums). Career: Played drums from age 16; Member, quartet with Pekka Pöyry, Montreux, 1968; Played with Eero Koivistoinen, winning group competition, Montreux, 1969; Also appeared at Newport Jazz Festival; Member, Seppo Paakunainen's Conjunto Baron, 1970s; Percussionist, numerous plays at Helsinki City Theatre; Played with major Finnish musicians, also artists including: Dexter Gordon; Clifford Jordan; Charlie Mariano; Appeared with Juhani Aaltonen group, The Finnish Middle-Aged All Stars, Pori Festival, 1985. Member, number of government appointed organizations; Helped increase state support for Finnish jazz. Honour: Yrjö Award, Finnish Jazz Federation, 1981. Memberships: Member of board, Finnish Jazz Federation; Pop Musicians' Union. Address: Hakaniemenranta 26 A 63, 00530 Helsinki, Finland.

LAIZEAU Francois, b. 19 Nov 1955, Paris, France. 1 daughter. Musical Education: Agostini School, 1973-76. Career: Sideman for: Tania Maria; Magma; Eddy Louiss; Michel Legrand; Toots Thielemans; Louis Sclavis; Michel Portal; Dominique Pifarely; Martial Solal; Kenny Wheeler; Claus Stotter. Recordings: Albums with H Kaenzig and K Wheeler; Live At Fat Thursday, Michel Legrand; Eddy Louiss; Nuit Etoilée; 3 recordings with the National Jazz Orchestra. Membership: UMJ. Address: 82 Rue de Rochechouat, 75009 Paris, France.

LAJOIE-DESAVBIN May-Cecile, b. 25 May 1972, Victoria Hospital, Mahe, Seychelles. Research Officer; Languist, Ministry of Education and Culture; Singer, The Waves, band. m. Teddy Desavbin, 6 January 1996, 1 son. Career: Music-Wise, performing in hotels every weekend with band, Waves; Perform for Miss Seychelles Beauty Pageant; Performed for Miss World, Seychelles. Compositions: Lavi Rezete; Only A Dream; Viktorya; Venges-Moi; Ecris-Moi; Nov Devwar; Lot Kote; Konplent Paran; Fer Mwan Oubliye. Recordings: Albums: Lanbeli with the Waves; Victoria, personal album, 1996. Publication: Lavi Rezete, song, 1995. Honours: Media Prizes; Best Singer Award, Radio, 1996; Best Song Award, Radio, 1996; Best Singer Award, People Magazine, 1996; Best Song Award, People Magazine, 1996; Best Band Award, Waves, 1996. Hobbies: Reading; Singing; Swimming. Address: Anse Aux Pins, Mahé, Republic of Seychelles.

LAKE Greg, b. 10 Nov 1948, Bournemouth, Dorset, England. Musician (bass); Vocalist. Career: Member, The Gods, 1968; King Crimson, 1969-70; Emerson Lake And Palmer (ELP),

1970-78; Also as Emerson Lake And Powell (with Cozy Powell), 1985-86, 1992-; Asia, 1983; Festival performances include: Isle Of Wight Festival, 1970; Mar-Y-Sol Festival, Puerto Rico, 1972. Recordings: Albums: with King Crimson: In The Court Of The Crimson King, 1969; In The Wake of Posideon, 1970; with ELP: Emerson Lake And Palmer, 1970; Tarkus (Number 1, UK), 1971; Pictures At An Exhibition, 1971; Trilogy, 1972; Brain Salad Surgery, 1974; Welcome Back My Friends To The Show That Never Ends - Ladies And Gentlemen...Emerson Lake And Palmer, 1974; Works, Volume Two, 1977; Love Beach, 1978; Emerson Lake And Powell, 1986; Black Moon, 1992; Live At The Royal Albert Hall, 1993; Return Of The Manticore, 1993; In The Hot Seat, 1994; Isle of Wight, 1997; Solo albums: Greg Lake, 1981; Manoeuvres, 1983; In Concert on the King Biscuit Flower Hour, 1996; From the Beginning - The Greg lake retrospective, 1997; Singles include: with ELP: Fanfare For The Common Man, 1977; Solo: I Believe In Father Christmas, 1975. Current Management: Booking Agent: Pilato Entertainment, 277 Alexander Street, Suite 813, Rochester, NY 14607, USA. Address: c/o Premier Talent, 3 East 54th Street, 14th Floor, New York, NY 10022, USA.

LALLEMANT Benoît, b. 22 Nov 1952, Paris, France. Musician (double bass, electric bass); Composer; Arranger. m. 10 Sept 1975, 4 daughters. Education: Licence, Dijon and Lyon Universities. Musical Education: First Prize, Musical Conservatory, CNR Dijon; Musicology at university. Career: Concerts and tours, France and Europe; Television and radio; Many jazz festivals, France and Germany; Teacher, music; Founder, Jazz On Music School, Dijon. Compositions: Commercials include: Fiat; CEPME-Kriter; Stage music: Lorca; Le Général Inconnu; Arranger, film La Femme Fardée; Compositions/recordings: Lydia; Bouncing; Communiqué; Valse Triste Et Sentimentale; Road Blues. Honours: Prize, City of Dijon. Membership: Union des Musiciens de Jazz (UMJ). Hobbies: Fine Arts; Skiing. Address: 3 Rue du Chateau d'Eau, 21000 Dijon, France.

LALLET Frederic P, b. 9 July 1960, France. Musician (piano); Vocalist. m. Josephine Giovannai, 1 Apr 1988, 2 sons. Education: BA. Musical Education: Doctor of Music. Career: Concerts in France, Germany and Russia. Recordings: 10 albums. Hobbies: Fishing; Nature. Current Management: Bembule Ministries. Address: PO Box 596, 20189 Ajaccio Cedex, France.

LAMB Andrew John, b. 13 July 1969, North Kensington, London, England. Musician (guitar, bass). Musical Education: Currently studying at the Guitar Institute in London. Career: Member of band Slander; 2 UK tours, 1992-94; Various radio appearances including: Rock Wars, BBC Radio 1; European and American radio. Recordings: Composed and recorded own album with Slander; Various demos with other bands as a studio session musician; Live recordings. Membership: Musicians' Union. Hobbies: Playing guitar; Watching bands; Motorcycling. Address: 24 Rowsley Road, St Annes-on-Sea, Lancashire FY8 2NS, England.

LAMB Paul, b. 9 July 1955, Blyth, Northumberland, England. Musician (harmonica). Divorced, 1 son. Career: Festivals, Europe and UK; Television shows include: Spender, UK; Late Late Show, Ireland; Other shows in Germany; Scandinavia; France; UK; Radio programmes: BBC Radio 2; Jazz FM; Greater London Radio; Radio stations around Europe; Concerts with Mark Knopfler; West End Show: A Slice Of Saturday Night. Recordings: with The Blues Burglars: Breakin In; with Paul Lamb and The King Snakes: Paul Lamb and the King Snakes; Shifting Into Gear; Fine Condition; Harmonica Man; Compilation CDs and box sets: Cooking With The

Blues; Blues Harp Boogie Music Club International; The Deluxe Blues Band, with Big Joe Louis, Otis Grand; Confessin' The Blues; Session work includes: Evil, Lucky Lopez Evans. Publication: Blues In Britain. Honours: First as team in the World Harmonica Championships, Germany; Second as soloist, 1975; Voted Best UK Harmonica Player for 5 years, British and Blues Connection. Memberships: Musicians' Union; NHL; British Blues Connection; PRS. Hobbies: Listening to old blues records; Bird watching. Address: 17 Pollard Road, Whetstone, London, England.

LAMBE Rick, b. 4 Aug 1960, Birmingham, England. Musician (slide guitar, guitars, bass, drums). m. Corinne Croucher, 29 July 1992, 1 son. Musical Education: Grade 5, Electric Guitar; Audio technology course, Kidderminster College, 1996-98. Career: Concerts include: Telford Blues Festival, 1989-90; Played 25 concerts in 1 night for Children In Need charity for BBC; Coventry Blues Festival, 1991; Appeared on BBC show celebrating 21 years of Pebble Mill programme; Appeared as Band Of The Week on John Taynton Show, 1992; Live radio appearances on radio, Children In Need, and Christmas Day radio broadcast; Various sessions for BBC TV; New Year's Eve Concert with Official Receivers Soul Band, Centenary Square, Birmingham performing to over 70,000 people; Recorded an album for local folk hero Gary O'Dea. Recordings: Two Bhangra recordings for Achanak and Ananki; Two tracks on Hazel Dean's album; Abba tribute song forthcoming. Memberships: Musicians' Union; PAMRA. Hobbies: Songwriting; Recording. Current Management: White Lamb. Address: 32 Ombersley Close, Woodrow South, Redditch, Worcestershire B98 7UU, England.

LAMBERT David, b. 3 Dec 1965, Wye, Kent, England. A&R Manager, Club DJ. Education: BA Hons, Social Science, University of Westminster. Career: Helped launch Touch Magazine; Began DJing, 1989; Performing throughout UK and Europe; Head, A&R, Positiva Records. Hobbies: Reading; Swimming; Skiing; Playing guitar; Tennis; Daydreaming. Current Management: DJing: Concorde International Artistes. Address: c/o Positiva, 43 Brook Green, London W6 7EF, England.

LAMBERT Ronnie, (Busker Lambert), b. 3 Oct 1950, Newcastle, England. Singer; Musician (guitar, harmonica); Bricklayer. m. Hazel Welsh, 24 Sept 1974, 1 son, 1 daughter. Career: Rock on the Tyne concert at Gateshead International Stadium, 1981; Appeared as singer on BBCTV 4 times, and on local ITV 4 times; Many radio appearances and interviews on BBC Radio, 1982-94; Metro Radio; Radio Magpie. Recordings: Singles: Home Newcastle, 1981; River Tyne EP, 1982; Goin' Up (Newcastle United official promotional song), 1984; Buildin' Site, 1990; Black And White, 1993, re-recorded 1994; Album: Pure Geordie, 1991. Honour: Newcastle United Football Club play his music at their home games. Memberships: PRS; MCPS; Musicians' Union. Hobbies: Studying Bible; Painting; Songwriting; Crosswords; Newcastle United Football Club supporter. Current Management: QC Entertainment. Address: Newburn Industrial Estate, Newburn, Northumberland, England.

LAMBRECHT Dimitri, b. 9 Apr 1967, Aalst, Belgium. Producer; Composer. Career: 1st Band: PLB System, Concerts in Belgium and France, 1988, 1989; Currently on tour with Natural Born Deejays. Compositions: Singles: For Fun and Jump, 1992; A Good Day, 1996; Sonal Contact and Deejays Mind, 1997; Oxygen, 1998. Recordings: Artificial Defence, 1989; A Good Day, 1996. Hobby: Record collecting. Current Management: King International Service - Leuvensesteenweg 120 A-Diest 3290, Belgium.

LAMMERS MEYER Hermann, b. 7 Dec 1952, Aschendorf, Germany. Musician (pedal steel guitar); Vocalist. m. Anke Barenborg, 21 May 1988, 1 son. Musical Education: Self-teacher. Career: Worked with Clay Baker and the Texas Honky Band; Success of Texas Country Road Show in USA followed by tours of Europe, including UK tour, 1981; Writes and records own songs; Tours with own band The Emsland Hillbillies, all over Europe, UK, US; Solo project: The Honky Tonk Hearts performed for Germany on Euro Country Music Masters TV Show, Netherlands. Recordings include: with Emsland Hillbillies: Albums: Texas Country Road Show, Volumes I, 1979; Volume II, 1981; Texas Lone Star, 1981; Solo: Singles: Moonshine Ladies/Neon Leon, 1987; Southern Comfort/You Ought To Hear Me Cry, 1989; Album: Half My Heart's In Texas, 1989; Above All The Starday Session, Nashville; The End Of Time; The Last Country Song; Duets with: Norma Jean; Kitty Wells; Willie Nelson; Johnny Bush. Honours: Country Album of The Year, GACMA in Germany, 1992. Hobby: Playing steel guitar. Current Management: Desert Kid Records / E L Hillbillies Music, PO Box D-26871 Aschendorf, Germany.

LAMOND George, b. 25 Feb 1967, Georgetown, Washington DC, USA. Recording Artist; Vocalist. m. Oct 1994. Education: New York High School of Art And Design. Musical Education: Various keyboards and Midi courses. Career: Rick Dee's TV Show; CNN Showbiz Today (profile and interview); Entertainment Tonight (profile and interview); No More Games Tour, opened for New Kids On The Block; TV Show, Showtime At The Apollo Theatre. Recordings: Albums: Bad Of The Heart; In My Life; (Spanish) Creo Enti (2 Billboard Top 10 Latin singles); Single: Bad Of The Heart, Top 40, Billboard Chart. Honour: Winter Music Conference, Best Dance 12" Award. Membership: NARAS. Hobbies: Cooking; Paintball; Drawing; Songwriting. Current Management: Chris Barbosa Management. Address: 185 Ardsley Loop, Suite #1B, Brooklyn, NY 11239, USA.

LAMOND Mary Jane, b. 5 Nov 1960, Kingston, Ontario, Canada. Gaelic Singer. Education: Degree in Celtic Studies. Career: Fifth Estate, 1997; Lilith Fair, 1997; Capercaillie UK Tour, 1997; Chieftains Canada Tour, 1997; Hanging Garden Soundtrack, 1997; Contributor: albums: Hi How Are You Today?; Ashley MacIsaac, 1995; Chieftains, 1997. Recording: Bho Thir Nan Craobh, Suas e!. Honours: ECMA Song, Sleepy Maggie, 1997; Much Music Global Groove Video Award, Bog a Lochain, 1997. Memberships: SOCAN; CARAS; ECMA. Current Management: Jones and Co. Address: 5212 Sackville St, Suite 100, Halifax, NS, B3J 1K6, Canada.

LAMONT Duncan, b. 4 July 1931, Greenock, Scotland. Musician (tenor saxophone, woodwinds); Composer. m. Bridget, 20 Feb 1960, 2 sons. Musical Education: Private Study, Glasgow. Career: Started as jazz trumpet player, aged 14; Joined Kenny Graham Afro Cubist Band, age 20; Switched from trumpet to tenor saxophone, played with many Big bands; Studio Jazz player, accompanied major stars including: Frank Sinatra; Bing Crosby; Fred Astaire; Became composer, wrote several suites, success with songs, lyrics, performed by most major singers in England, USA. Compositions include: Songs: Tomorrow's Standards; Best Of Bossa Novas; Summer Sambas; I Told You So, recorded by Cleo Laine; Not You Again, recorded by Cleo Laine and George Shearing; Suites include: The Young Persons Guide To The Jazz Orchestra; Sherlock Holmes Suite (For City of London); The Carnival Of The Animals; Cinderella; Childrens television programmes: Mr Benn; King Rollo; Spot (the dog); Towser; Spot's Magical Xmas (for Disney Studios) 1995. Publications: Tomorrow's Standards. Honours: Tomorrow's Standards, The Music Retailers Association Annual Awards For Excellence, 1995; Best Song Of Year, ASAC,

USA: I Told You So, 1995. Memberships: PRS; ASCAP. Hobby: Practice. Current Management: Bucks Music, 1 Farm Place, London W8 7SX, England. Address: 2 Cadmer Close, New Malden, Surrey KT3 5DG, England.

LAMPRELL Adam Charles, b. 14 June 1965, Sutton, Surrey, England. Musician (guitar). m. Penny Britchfield, 11 June 1994, 1 son. Education: BA Hons, Graphic Design (specializing in Photography). Career: Recording sessions for Michael Prophet and Ricky Tuffy; Joint bandleader, The Scissormen; Worldwide recording, tours, television and radio; Joined Skyscraper, 1995-. Recordings: with The Scissormen: Albums: Nitwit, 1992; Mumbo Jumbo, 1995; Glee (EP), 1997; Skyscraper album, forthcoming; Session, Sylvia Powell album, forthcoming; Sessions for Michael Prophet, Ricky Tuffy, album: Get Ready; Singles include: Kicks; Recording on remixes include: Chaka Demus and Pliers; Freddie McGregor; Lisa Hunt; United Nations; TV commercials. Memberships: Musicians' Union; PRS; MCPS. Hobbies: Football; Reading. Address: 53 Highclere Street, London SE26 4EX, England.

LANDER Judd, b. 1 Mar 1948, Liverpool, England. Session Musician; Actor; Television Producer; Record Company Executive. m. (1) Janine de Wolfe, 3 July 1987, 2 daughters, (2) Danielle, (3) Sienna Tuesday. Career: Member, The Hideaways, 1960s; Moved to London, 1970's; Session musician, CBS Records, 1974; Numerous performances include: The Cavern, Liverpool; Kampuchea charity concert, (with Paul McCartney), 1979; Associate producer, St Lucia Jazz Festival, (with Andy Hamilton), 1991; Floor Director, Brits Music Awards, 1994-95; Television appearances include: Top Of The Pops; The Tube; Old Grey Whistle Test; Wogan; Des O'Connor Show; MTV; Montreux Pop Festival; Producer, television documentary, Jerry Lee Lewis; Concerts: Wembley Stadium; Wembley Arena; Knebworth House; Reading Festival; London Palladium; Royal Albert Hall. Compositions: Resting Rough (film score); Music for The Short Show, LWT. Recordings: Singles: Church Of Poisoned Mind, Karma Chameleon, Culture Club (lead harmonica lines); Albums include: Flowers In The Dirt, Paul McCartney, 1979; Medusa, Annie Lennox, 1995; Session musician for Badfinger; Walker Brothers; Scaffold; Bay City Rollers; Nazareth; Madness; The The; Prefab Sprout; Communards; Mike Oldfield; Dina Caroll; Tina Turner; Kirsty MacColl; Numerous television commercials. Memberships: Musicians' Union; Equity. Hobbies: Clay pigeon shooting; Car renovation; Gardening. Current Management: Charles Armitage, Noel Gay Artists. Address: 6th Floor, 76 Oxford Street, London W1N 0AT, England.

LANDGREN Nils Lennart, b. 15 Feb 1956, Degerfors, Sweden. Trombone Player; Singer; Composer. m. Beatrice Jaras-Landgren, 9 July 1979. Education: College degree; Classical Music degree; Soloist diploma, University of Music in Arvika, Sweden. Career: Professional Trombone Player, age 19; Freelance work in Stockholm, Sweden; Recording and stage performance with all major Swedish artists; Star, Skål, musical, Stockholm, running 2 years; Star, Villon, musical, Stockholm. Compositions: Red Horn, with Bruce Swedien; Aint Nobody, recorded with Maceo Parker; Cheyenne, with Michael Ruff. Recordings: Planet Rock; You're My Number 1; Streetfighter; Miles From Duke, with B A Wallin; Follow You Heart; Ch 2, with Johan Norberg; CH 2 - Two; Ballads; Gotland; Live in Stockholm; Paint It Blue; Swedish Folk Moderne. Honours: 2 Swedish Grammies; German Jazz Award, 1997. Hobby: Wife is my life besides music. Current Management: Walter Brolund Inc, Kungsv 6, 19040, Rosersberg, Sweden. Address: Lillkalmar vägen 100B, 18265 Djursholm, Sweden.

LANDOLL Marie (Mary M), b. Sandusky, Ohio, USA. Singer; Songwriter; Musician (keyboards). Divorced, 3 sons, 1 daughter. Education: Cert instructor, machine shtd (Assoc degree stenography). Musical Education: 1 year vocal, 2 years keyboards, private study. Career: President, secretary, manager, Shooting Stars Variety Band; TV concert, Portside, Toledo, smaller gigs, lodges; Showcasing, Airplay International (live) TNN, 1995; Area TV appearances, touring on church revivals now. Recordings: Just A Faded Memory; Heartbreak, compilation album of crossover Christian music, 1997-98. Publications: Contribution: Lifeboat (short story), Peaceful Thoughts; Contributing writer for Songwriter Monthly magazine. Honours: King Eagle Awards, TNN; Airplay International, 1993-94; King Eagle, Trailblazers, 1994-95; Membership: ASCAP. Hobbies: Helping new artists; Swimming; Films. Address: PO Box 129, Milan, OH 44848, USA.

LANE Jamie, b. 15 Sept 1951, Calcutta, India. Musician (drums); Record Producer; Engineer; Programmer. m. Katerina Koumi, 8 June 1991, 1 daughter. Education: BA Hons, MA, Magdalene College, Cambridge. Musical Education: Self-taught. Career: Member, bands: The Movies, 1976-80; Sniff'n'The Tears, 1980-82; Session drummer, 1982-; Played with: Tina Turner; Mark Knopfler; 10cc; Joan Armatrading; Agnetha; Van Morrison; Randy Newman; Ben E King; Paul Brady; Chage and Aska; Blancmange; Producer for: Microdisney; Railway Children; Pete Townshend; Paul Brady; Falco; Nick Kamen; Hot House; Jackie Quinn; Microgroove; Do Re Mi. Composition: Deep Water, Jackie Quinn. Recordings: As drummer, Living On The Ceiling, Blancmange; As producer: Don't Come To Stay, Hot House; I Promised Myself, Nick Kamen. Membership: Musicians' Union. Hobby: Cricket. Current Management: Stephen Budd Management. Address: 18 Ravenswood Road, London SW12 9PJ, England.

LANE Rick, b. 22 Apr 1953, London, England. Composer; Producer; Musician (keyboards, guitar, bass, percussion); Backing Vocalist. Musical Education: Guildhall Exhibition Scholar. Career: Founder, Rent Boys; Private Lives; 3 tours with The Edgar Broughton Band; Now produces music for film, television, radio, commercials, corporate video, station idents and multimedia. Recordings: with Rent Boys: 2 singles, 1 album; with Private Lives: 3 singles, 2 albums; Over 200 television, cinema, radio commercials, documentary and features for BBC, LWT, Granada, Anglia. Honours: N London Music Festival, Silver Medal; Highly Commended, Roland Syn/Sound, 1992; Creative Circle Nomination, 1993; D and AD Gold Pencil, 1993. Memberships: British Music Writers Council; Society of Producers of Applied Music; Performing Rights Society; MCPS; BASCA; Musicians' Union; Alliance of Composer Organisations; Association of Professional Composers; Composers Guild of Great Britain. Current Management: Nim Nim Musik. Address: Garden Studio, 19 Venetia Road, London W5 4JD, England.

LANE Stevens, b. 7 Nov 1921, Hammersmith, London, England. Semi professional Musician (cornet); Bandleader. Musical Education: Self-taught theory; Cornet teacher, Phil Parker. Career: Leader, own band, The Southern Stompers, 1950-; Re-named Red Hot Peppers, 1985-; Concerts include: Poland; Czechoslovakia; France; Germany; Netherlands; Denmark; Numerous broadcasts, BBC Jazz club; Compositions: Songs and instrumentals written or arranged for the band. Recordings: Albums released on VJM, Major-Minor, Stomp Off and Azure labels. Memberships: Musicians' Union; MCPS; PRS. Hobbies: Shropshire; Medieval churches. Address: 32 Kenton Lane, Harrow, Middlesex HA3 8TX, England.

LANG Andy Lee, b. 26 July 1965, Vienna, Austria. Singer; Entertainer; Musician (piano). Education: Commercial School. Musical Education: Private studies with Grandfather (Music Professor and Conductor). Career: Piano-player of Chuck Berry, European tour, 1992-93; Concerts with: Jerry Lee Lewis; Wanda Jackson; Carl Perkins; The Magic Platters; Fats Domino; Concerts, television and radio shows in: USA; Morocco; France; Switzerland; Germany; Austria. Recordings: Back To Rock'n'Roll, 1990; Rockin' Piano Man, 1991; Back In Town, 1993; That's Entertainment Live, 1994; Rockin' Christmas, 1994. Honours: Golden Microphone, 1991. Membership: Austrian Composer Association. Hobbies: Skiing; Watching television and video. Current Management: Star Box, Angela Kascha. Address: Simmerringer Haide 6/543, A-1110 Vienna, Austria.

lang k d (Kathryn Dawn Lang), b. 2 Nov 1961, Consort, Alberta, Canada. Singer; Composer; Actress. Career: Played North American clubs with own band, 1982-87; Performed at closing ceremony, Winter Olympics, Calgary, 1988; Headlining US tour, 1992; Royal Albert Hall, 1992; Earth Day benefit concert, Hollywood Bowl, 1993; Sang with Andy Bell, BRIT Awards, 1993; Television includes: Late Night With David Letterman; Wogan; The Arsenio Hall Show; The Tonight Show; Top Of The Pops; Subject, South Bank Show documentary, ITV, 1995; Film appearance, Salmonberries, 1991. Recordings: Albums: A Truly Western Experience, 1984; Angel With A Lariat, 1986; Shadowland, 1988; Absolute Torch and Twang, 1990; Ingénue, 1992; Even Cowgirls Get The Blues (soundtrack), 1993; All You Can Eat, 1995; Features on soundtrack to Dick Tracy; Hit singles include: Crying (duet with Barbara Orbison); Constant Craving; The Mind Of Love; Miss Chatelaine; Just Keep Me Moving; If I Were You. Honours: Canadian CMA Awards: Entertainer Of Year, 1989; Album Of Year, 1990; Grammy Awards: Best Female Country Vocal Performance, 1990; Best Pop Vocal, 1993; Album of the Year, Ingénue, 1993; American Music Award: Favourite New Artist, 1993; Songwriter Of The Year, with Ben Lang, 1993; BRIT Award, Best International Female, 1995. Current Management: Bumstead Productions, 140 W 22nd Street, Suite 10-A, New York, NY 10011-2420, USA. Address: c/o Bumstead Productions, PO Box 110, Hoboken, NJ 07030, USA.

LANG Penny, b. 15 July 1942, Montreal, Quebec, Canada. Folk Singer; Songwriter; Musician (guitar). 1 son. Education: 1 year, Sir George Williams University, Montreal. Musical Education: Self-taught (musical family). Career: National Folk Festival, Australia; Philadelphia Folk Festival; Vancouver, Winnipeg, Mariposa Folk Festivals; The Bitter End and Gerdes Folk City, CBGB's, New York; The Riverboat, Yellow Door, Pornographic Onion Coffeehouses, Canada; Caffe Lena, New York; The Folkway, New Hampshire; The Ark, Michigan; Montreal Jazz Festival; Toronto Soul 'n Blues Fest (Harborfront); Music for NFB documentary Marilyn Waring - Who's Counting? Sex, Lies and Global Economics. Compositions: Open Up Our Hearts to See; Ain't Life Sweet; Carry On Children; November Blues; Firewater; Senses Of Your Leave. Recordings: YES!!, 1991; Live (solo), 1992; Carry On Children, 1993; Ain't Life Sweet, 1996. Publications: Lyrics/music, Open Up Our Hearts To See, Sing Out magazine; Articles, reviews for: Toronto Star; Montreal Gazette; Dirty Linen. Honours: Several Canada Council awards for touring, writing, recording; Grant from Quebec Ministère des Affaires Culturelles. Memberships: SOCAN. Hobbies: Gardening; Travel; Nature crafts; Reading. Current Management: Heidi Fleming, Fleming Artists Management. Address: 5975 Avenue du Parc, Montreal, Quebec H2V 4H4, Canada.

LANG Rein, b. 4 July 1957, Tartu, Estonia. Promoter; Broadcaster; Publisher. 1 daughter. Education: Lawyer, Tartu University. Career: Promoter, Rock Summer Festival, 1988-89; Promoter, Song Festivals, 1990-1991; President, Broadcasting Company Trio Ltd, 1991-; President, Estonian Association of Broadcasters. Hobbies: Rotarian. Address: PO Box 3657, Tallinn, EE-0090, Estonia.

LANGBORN Torbjorn, b. 17 May 1955, Stockholm, Sweden. Musician; Composer. 2 daughters. Education: Adolf Fredrik Music School; Musicology, Stockholm University; Piano, Pedagogic, Royal Academy of Music, Stockholm; Salsa and Latin Grove with Bebo Valdez, Sabu Martinez, Wilfredo Stephenson, Amedeo Niccoletti, Don Pancho. Career: Live Gigs, Radio and some Television Appearances Through Sweden, Finland, Poland, Norway; Freelance Pianist, Salsa, Tango and Jazz; Teacher, Improvisation, Afro American and Jazz Theory. Compositions: Sangre nueva; Maldito Primitivo; En Estocolmo no pasa nada; Sad Samba; Salsa; Oiga mi Compadre; Canciones del Alma. Recordings: Hot Salsa - Maldito Primitivo; Hot Salsa Meets Swedish Jazz; Torbjorn Langborn and his Feel Life Orchestra. Memberships: STIM; SAMI; SKAP; Musicians Union. Hobbies: Collecting Music Scores and Books; Bonsai; Vine Tests; Children. Address: Hjalmar Söderbergs Väg 16 D 2tr, 112 52 Stockholm, Sweden.

LAPOUGE Jean, b. 2 Jan 1953, Coutances, Manche, France. Musician (guitar); Composer. m. Marie Christine Tison, 14 Mar 1974, 2 sons. Career: Began as composer; Formed first group, 1970; Professional career, 1972-; Formed Noetra, group of 6 to 9 musicians, 1976-85; Formed duo with Christian Paboeuf, 1986; Duo became quartet, with Mikko Fontaine, Jean-François Bercé, 1989; Tours and recording; Formed Jean Lapouge/Kent Carter duo, 1994; Became quartet, with Pascal Gachet, Lionel Morand, 1995. Recordings: Neuf Songes, Noetra; Hauts Plateaux, with quartet, 1993. Address: 1 Rue Du Plantier, 24000 Perigueux, France.

LARATTA David Ottavio, b. 19 Apr 1970, Saint Denis, France. Musician (bass, drums, trumpet). Education: Arts and Letters (A3). Musical Education: Self-taught. Career: Guest musician, guest Youssou N'Dour, 1990; Francopholies, La Rochelle, France, 1992; Television show, TF1, 1992; 20th Anniversary, Sony France, 1993; Guest, Michel Fugain, 1993; National Concours Jazz in Paris, La Défense, with Used 2b Bop, 1995; Numerous concerts, shows, appearances, throughout France, with various bands; Marcel Sabiani Trio; Lewis Robinson, 1997; Léa loCicero, 1997; Divan du monde, with Cheick Tidiane Seck "Tribute to Fela", 1997. Memberships: SPEDIDAM; SACEM. Hobbies: Drawing; Painting; Football coach (BBES II Dégré). Address: 4 Rue de la République, 93450 L'Ile Saint Denis, France.

LARSEN Jens Kjaer, b. 30 May 1964, Copenhagen, Denmark. Rapper; Singer; Songwriter. m. Camilla Palikaras, 4 August 1997. Education: Selftaught Drummer. Career: Member, Cut 'n' Move Band, Several Television Shows, Tours of Europe, Australia, USA and Asia. Compositions: Get Serious; Spread Love; Give It Up; I'm Alive; 4 Albums. Recordings: Get Serious; Peace Love and Harmony; The Sounds of Now; Into The Zone. Honours: Silver Lion, Germany; 4 Grammies, Denmark. Hobby: Performing. Current Management: TG Management, Denmark. Address: 1120 Kobenhavn K, Copenhagen, Denmark.

LARSEN Jon, b. 7 Jan 1959, Jar, near Oslo, Norway. Musician (guitar); Composer; Record Producer. m. Barbara Jahn, 2 July 1994, 1 stepdaughter. Musical Education: High School of Music; Self-taught. Career: Full-time professional guitarist/composer with Hot Club de Norvège, 1979-; Est Hot Club de Norvège (quartet), 1979; The Django Festival, Oslo, 1980; Hot Club Records, 1982. Recordings: 9 albums with Hot Club de Norvège, 1980-; Produced 105 albums for H C Records: with Chet Baker, Ph Catherine, Warne Marsh, 1982-. Publications: The Vintage Guitars (20 volumes since 1988). Honours: NOPA Composer Of The Year, Norway, 1994. Membership: Composers Society of Norway (NOPA). Hobby: Painting. Current Management: Frost Music Publishing Ltd, Oslo; Hot Club. Address: PO Box 5202, Majorstua, N-0302 Oslo, Norway.

LARSEN Mona Ellinor, b. 31 Aug 1948, Copenhagen, Denmark. Singer; Composer; Lyricist. 1 daughter. Musical Education: Self-taught. Career: Began as nightclub singer, Sweden, 1969; Member, Danish Radio Big Band, 1970's; Tours: Europe; The Far East (with WDR Big Band of Cologne); Worked with: Palle Mikkelborg; Niels Henning Örsted Pedersen; Thomas Clausen; Allan Botschinsky; Thad Jones; Clark Terry; Jukka Linkola; Formed Halberg/Larsen Band with guitarist Poul Halberg, 1980s; Formed Emborg/Larsen Group with pianist Jörgen Emborg, 1991; Tours: UK; France; Italy; Member, Michael Mantler's Octet. Recordings: Ulven Og Högen; Mon Amour; with Halberg/Larsen: Halberg/Larsen; Halberg/Larsen 2; Transit; Halberg/Larsen 4; with Emborg/Larsen Group: Heart Of The Matter; Ships In The Night; with Norma Winstone: Freedom Jazz Dance, 1994; With Michael Mantler's Octet and the Danish Radio Big Band: Cerco Un Paese Innocente, 1994. Membership: The Danish Jazz Association-DDJ. Hobbies: History of Art; Nature. Current Management: The Danish Jazz Association. Address: Kjeld Langes Gade 4A, DK-1367 Copenhagen K, Denmark.

LARSSON Anders, b. 13 Apr 1958, Malmo, Sweden. Manager. Career: Own management for Scandinavian artists, 10 years; Currently, 30 artists in pop, jazz, blues, rock; Name of company: United Stage Production AB. Memberships: Member of Board, Swedish Impressario Association; Swedish Publishers Association. Hobbies: Gardening; Food; Wine. Current Management: United Stage Production AB. Address: PO Box 9174, 200 39 Malmo, Sweden.

LASCELLES Jeremy, b. 14 February 1955, London, England. Managing Director, Chrysalis Music. 1 son, 2 daughters. Career: Artist Management, 1972-75; Tour Management, 1975-79; A&R Consultant, 1979-80, Director of Marketing, 1980-82, Director of A&R, 1982-88, Virgin Records; Managing Director, Ten Records, 1988-92; Offside Productions and Management, 1993-94; Managing Director, Chrysalis Music, 1994-. Hobbies: Football; Cricket; Wine; Food; Film; Travel. Current Management: MD Chrysalis Music. Address: 13 Bramley Road, London W10 6SP, England.

LASSEN Nils, b. 10 March 1960, Denmark. Composer. m. Sisse Lassen, 1 daughter. Career: Composing for Theatre and Film, Denmark and Danish Television, including The Royal Theatre. Compositions: Boy of 1000 Tears, 1997; Riders of Depression, 1997; No Lilacs, No Lillies, No More, 1997. Recordings: Lament for Ronni, 1997; Lost in the Woods, 1997; Most of Us Prefer Not To Think, 1997; Inside/Outside, 1997. Membership: DJBFA. Hobby: Dreaming. Address: Lille Istedgade 5, 1706 Copenhagen V, Denmark.

LAST James (Hans), b. 17 April 1929, Bremen, Germany. Bandleader; Arranger. Career: Member, Radio Bremen Dance Orchestra, 1946; Bandeader, Becker-Last Ensemble, 1948-55; Arranger, radio stations, Polydor Records, 1955; Bandleader, combination of classics, dance, pop and country music, 1965-; Worked with artistes including: Caterina Valente; Astrud Gilberto;

Richard Clayderman; Over 50 million records sold worldwide. Recordings: Numerous albums include: Non Stop Dancing, 1965; This Is James Last, 1967; Hammond A Go Go, 1967; James Last Goes Pop, 1968; Ole, 1973; Country & Square Dance Party, 1974; Ten Years Non Stop Party Album, 1975; Make The Party Last, 1975; Christmas James Last, 1976; In London, 1978; East To West, 1978; Last The Whole Night Long, 1979; Christmas Classics, 1979; Caribbean Nights, 1980; Seduction, 1980; Classics For Dreaming, 1980; Hansimania, 1981; Roses From The South - The Music Of Johan Strauss, 1981; Tango, 1983; Christmas Dancing, 1983; Greatest Songs Of The Beatles, 1983; Games That Lovers Play, 1984; Rose Of Tralee And Other Irish Favourites, 1984; All Aboard With Cap'n James, 1984; In Russia, 1984; In Allgau (In The Alps), 1984; In Scotland, 1985; In Holland, 1987; The Berlin Concert, 1987; Dance Dance Dance, 1987; Flute Fiesta, 1988; By Request, 1988; Plays Bach, 1988; Happy Heart, 1989; Classics By Moonlight, 1990; Together At Last, 1991; Single: The Seduction, used in film American Gigolo, 1981.

LASWELL Bill, b. 14 Feb 1950. Musician (bass, guitar); Record Company Executive; Record Producer. Career: Leader, groups: Material; Curlew; Last Exit; Founder, record labels OAO, Celluloid; Record producer for Herbie Hancock. Recordings: Solo albums: Baselines, 1984; Best Of Bill Laswell, 1985; Point Blank, 1986; Low Life, 1987; Hear No Evil, 1988; with Material: Temporary Music, 1980; Third Power; with Last Exit: The Noise Of Trouble; with Herbie Hancock: Future Shock; with John Zorn and Eugene Chadbourne: The Parachute Years (7-disc set), 1997; Also producer for numerous artistes including: Yoko Ono; Mick Jagger; Gil Scott-Heron; Nona Hendryx; Manu Dibango; PiL; Fela Kuti; Iggy Pop; Motörhead; Laurie Anderson; Afrika Bambaataa; Yellowman. Current Management: AGM (UK), 145A Ladbrooke Grove, London W10 6HJ, England.

LATEEF Yusef (Bill Evans), b. 1920, Chattanooga, Tennessee, USA. Musician (saxophone, flute, oboe); Bandleader; Composer; Educator.Education: MA, Manhattan School Of Music; Postgraduate, University of Massachusetts. Career: Leader, own quartet, New York, 1960; Featured musician with: Charlie Mingus, 1960-61; Babatundi Olatunji, 1961-62; Cannonball Adderley; Bandleader, own group. Compositions include: Do I (Tahira), symphony, recorded with Hambourg Radio Orchestra. Recordings: Albums include: The Boeue Yusef Lateef; The Diverse Yusef Lateef; The Gentle Giant; Hush'n'Thunder; Blues For Orient; Cry-Tender; Eastern Sounds; Expression!; Gentle Giant (with W K Barron); Imagination (with Doug Watkins); Into Something (with Elvin Jones); Live Session, The Many Faces of Yusef Lateef; Plays For Lovers; Sounds Of Yusef; Live At Pep's; Club Date; Little Symphony; Yusef Lateef's Flute Book Of The Blues; Lateef In Nigeria; Jazz For The Thinker. Honour: Grammy Award, Best New Age Performance, 1987. Current Management: Depth of Field Management, 1501 Broadway, Suite 1304, New York, NY 10036, USA.

LATHAM Anthony John Heaton, b. 30 Oct 1940, Wigan, England. University Lecturer. m. Dawn Catherine Farleigh, 10 Nov 1990. Education: BA (Hons) Medieval and Modern History, Birmingham, 1964; PhD African Studies, Birmingham, 1970. Musical Education: Clarinet tuition. Career: Debut, Wigan Jazz Club, 1958; Penn-Latham Quintet, University of Birmingham, 1961-63; Harlech Television, 1967; Axiom Jazz Band, Swansea, 1967-68; J.J.'s Rhythm Aces, Swansea University, 1982-84; Speakeasy Jazz Band, Swansea, 1984-; John Latham's Jazztimers, 1995-; Brecon Jazz Festival, 1986-89, 1991; Cork Jazz Festival, 1987; Birmingham Jazz Festival, 1987, 1988; BBC Wales, 1989, 1990, 1992, 1994; Llangollen Jazz Festival, 1995; Clubs:

Fritzel's; Gazebo; Bonaparte's Retreat; In New Orleans, 1988. Recordings: Blanche Finlay with The Speakeasy Jazzband, 1987; John Latham's Jazz Timers, Sandy's Bar, Cardiff, 1997. Publications: Al Fairweather Discography, 1994; Eurojazz Discographies, No 34; Stan Greig Discography, 1995; Eurojazz Discography, No 42; Sandy Brown Discography, 1997; Eurojazz Discography, No 5; Contributions to: New Orleans Music Vol 2 No 1, 1990; Jazz Journal International, Jan, Sept, 1993, June, 1994, May, 1996; British Jazz Times, Sept-Oct, 1994. Membership: Musicians' Union. HobbY: Trout fishing. Current Management: Self-managed. Address: 2 Church Meadow, Reynoldston, Swansea SA3 1AA, Wales.

LATHAM Warren, b. 17 Sept 1952, Chorley, England. Musician (jass and ragtime percussion, alto saxophone, baritone saxophone); Songwriter. m. Linda Buckley, 14 July 1981, 2 sons, 2 daughters. Career: Percussionist with The Temperance Seven; Lead saxophone player with The Harmony Hounds; Ragtime drumming accompanist for Miss Maureen Dyson, England; Founder musician of Rainbow Gardens Jass Orchestra, Toronto, and Jake's Boathouse/Louisiana Jazzmakers, Toronto, Canada; Alto player with Kid Bastien's Happy Pals, Toronto; Bozo Buttershaw's Hot Potatoes, England; The Society Hot Shots, England; Treasure Island Jazz Band, England; Rhythm Syncopators, England. Recordings: I'm Making Every Move, 1993; I've Got A Spell On You, 1994. Hobbies: Golf; Black and White photography; 1920's Jazz arrangements.

LATTIKAS Urmas, b. 17 Aug 1960, Tapa, Estonia. Composer; Arranger; Conductor; Musician (piano). m. Kaia, 22 Dec 1993, 2 sons. Musical Education: Graduated as composer, Estonian Music Academy, 1977-86; Post-graduate studies, jazz composition, piano, Berklee College of Music, Boston, USA, 1990. Career: Performing artist, founder, leader, own jazz group Urmas Lattikas Quintet; Arranger, jazz, pop, classical styles; Accompanist, numerous vocal and instrumental performances; Extensive club, concert appearances, numerous jazz events, Estonia and abroad; Recordings, appearances, radio and television; Urmas Lattikas Quintet represented Estonian jazz in European Jazz Night television programme; Conducted Estonian song, Eurovision Song Contest, 1994. Compositions: Symphonic, choral, chamber music, film scores; Music for single and album. Recordings: Single: In A Twilight Room; Album: Freedom To Love, Freedom To Lose. Honours: First Prize, U Naissoo composition contest, 1983, 1984; Levi Jaagup Award, Keyboard Player of the Year, 1990. Address: Nurme 26, Tallinn EE 0016, Estonia.

LAUDET Francois, b. 11 November 1958, Paris, France. Drummer. Education: Baccalaureat; Selftaught Drummer. Career: Best Big Band Jazz Drummer in France; Band Leader; Appearances at several Festivals and Television Shows; Replacement of Butch Mills in Count Basie Orchestra in European tour, 1997. Composition: Memphis Belle Blues. Recordings: With: Saxomania, Ellingtomania Ornicar Big Band, Super Swing Machine, Francois Laudet Big Band. Honour: Prix Sydney Bechet, 1994; Académie du Jazz. Membership: Union des Musiciens de Jazz. Hobbies: Flying Planes; Building Plastic Models. Current Management: All Star Productions. Address: 14 rue des Carrieres, 93230 Romainville, France.

LAUDET Philippe, b. 11 Dec 1959, Nanterre, France. Composer; Arranger; Musician (trumpet, piano). m. Catherine Laudet, 19 Dec 1987, 1 son, 2 daughters. Education: Astrophysics, until age 28. Musical Education: Classical piano from age 6-16; Jazz piano from age 10; Jazz trumpet from age 15; Self-taught composer, arranger. Career:

Leader, composer, Ornicar Big Band, 1980-; Played all major jazz festivals in France: Paris; Nice; Salon de Provence; Marciac; Vienne; Trumpet soloist, Tuxedo Big Band, 1992-; Played in Marciac, Coutance, Spain. Recordings: with Ornicar Big Band: Mais Où Est Donc Ornicar?, 1984; Le Retour d'Ornicar, 1986; Jazz Cartoon, 1989; L'Incroyable Huck, 1991; 1 recording with Tuxedo Big Band, 1994; Siesta of the Fiesta, Tuxedo Big Band, 1996; Beautiful Love, Philippe Laudet Quartet, 1996. Honours: Winner, Concours National de la Defense, Paris, with Ornicar Big Band, 1982; Prizes from Academy of Jazz and Hot Club of France, with Tuxedo Big Band, 1994; Hot Club de France, for Siesta at the Fiesta, 1996. Memberships: SACEM; SPEDIDAM; UMJ. Hobby: Astonomy. Current Management: Self-managed. Address: 5 Rue des Eparges, 31500 Toulouse, France.

LAUK Tiit, b. 9 Jan 1948, Tartu, Estonia. Musician (piano, keyboards). m. Eleonora Lauk, 22 Aug 1952, 1 son. Musical Education: Estonian Academy of Music; Pianist, leader, teacher, Jazz Education at Bob Brookmeyer's. Career: Over 35 years as pianist and leader, 15 years, piano and jazz teacher; 3 years as Producer, Musical Programmes, Estonian TV; Director, Estonian Jazz Foundation 1991-; Debut, Gintarine Triuba Festival, Lithuania, 1968; Numerous festivals, solo concerts in former Soviet Union, Europe; Tours with famous Estonian opera singers in Sweden, Finland; Projects with Finnish, Swedish, British, Russian musicians; Numerous recordings, Estonian Radio, Estonian TV, 1972-. Compositions: Over 300 instrumental and vocal arrangements for jazz orchestra/band. Recordings: Numerous recordings since 1970 for Estonian Radio, Estonian Television; MC KohtumispaiK Jazzkaar, 1995; Pendel, 1997. Publications: By The Path Of Estonian Light Music, Lithuania, 1987; Jazz Improvisation. Practical Course For Piano (I Bril), translation into Estonian; Several reviews in several publications in Estonia, Finland, France, Lithuania. Honours: Order of Nicola Rolin (France); Jazzclub du Vallage (France); Jazzclub of Tartu (Estonia). Membership: International Association Of Schools Of Jazz. Hobbies: Riding; Travel. Current Management: Estonian Jazz Foundation. Address: c/o Estonian Jazz Foundation, POB 3641 EE 0090, Viru 16, Tallinn, Estonia.

LAUPER Cyndi (Cynthia Anne Stephanie), b. 22 June 1953, Queens, New York, USA. Singer; Songwriter; Actress. Career: Club singer, Manhattan; Lead singer, Doc West; Member, Flyer, 1974-77; Formed Blue Angel, 1978-79; Solo recording artiste, 1983-; Worldwide tours; Participant, Music Speaks Louder Than Words summit, USSR, 1988; American Music Awards concerts, Tokyo, 1991; Actress, films: Vibes, 1988; Mother Goose Rock'n'Rhyme, Disney Channel, 1990; Paradise Paved, 1990; Off And Running, 1992; Participant, The Wall by Roger Waters, Berlin, 1990. Recordings: Albums: with Blue Angel: Blue Angel, 1980; Solo albums: She's So Unusual, 1983; True Colors, 1986; A Night To Remember, 1989; Music Speaks Louder Than Words, 1990; Hat Full Of Stars, 1993; Hit singles include: Girls Just Want To Have Fun, 1984; Time After Time (Number 1, US), 1984; She Bop, 1984; All Through The Night, 1984; True Colors (Number 1, US), 1986; Change Of Heart, 1987; What's Going On, 1987; I Drove All Night, 1989; The World Is Stone, 1992; That's What I Think, 1993; Contributor, charity records: We Are The World, USA For Africa, 1984; Give Peace A Chance, The Peace Choir, 1991; Put On Your Green Shoes, 1993. Honours: American Video Award, 1984; MTV Music Video Award, 1984; American Music Awards: Favourite Female Artist, Favourite Female Video Artist, 1985; Grammy Award, Best New Artist, 1985. Current Management: Hard To Handle Management, 640 Lee Road, Suite 106, Wayne, PA 19087, USA.

LAURENCE Graham Richard, b. 1 Apr 1964, Croydon, Surrey, England. Songwriter; Musician (guitar). Education: City of London Polytechnic. Musical Education: Goldsmiths University. Career: Guitarist, Danielle Dax, European Tour, 1986; Guitarist/songwriter, Queen B; Appearances: TVAM; Jonathon Ross; Box Office, Radio 1; Radio 1 News; Radio 1 Tour; Recordings: Red Top Hot Shot; I Love You; Satellite; Loving You. Memberships: Musicians' Union; Performing Rights Society. Hobby: Boxing. Current Management: Important Management. Address: Marlow, Bucks, England.

LAURENT Mark, b. 15 Mar 1954, Auckland, New Zealand. Singer; Songwriter; Musician (guitar, harmonica, Rowan lute). m. (1) Adrienne Lovegrove, 5 Feb 1977, 1 son, (2) Brenda Liddiard, 4 Aug 1990. Career: Band or solo performer, playing throughout New Zealand and Australia, 1968-; Studio producer, 1985-; Major tours supporting Larry Norman, 1984; Barry Maguire, 1987; Larbanois Carrero, 1989; Adrian Plass, 1993; Thom Bresh, 1995; Major festivals include: Sweetwaters, 1985; Mainstage, 1987; Jackey's Marsh, Tasmania, 1990; Shelterbelt, 1993; Auckland Folk Festival, 1993-96; Parachute, 1994, 1995; Tahora, 1989-97. Recordings: Mark Laurent, 1982; Kindness In A Strong City, 1986; Songs For Our Friends (collaboration), 1989; Trust, 1992; Heart Attack, 1996; Tahora 21, collaboration, 1997; Songwriter, Producer, musician, other artists' albums. Publications: Perhaps (poetry), 1995; Various articles for music magazines. Membership: Australasian Performing Rights Association. Hobbies: Creative Writing; Walking; Jamming; Films; Friends. Current Management: Self-managed; Distributed by Someone Up There Records. Address: 21 Parkfield Terrace, Grafton, Auckland, New Zealand.

LAURITSEN Joergen, b. 9 August 1966, Svendborg, Denmark. Conductor; Composer; Arranger; Musician. m. Pia Boysen. Education: MA, Music Theory, Conducting, Royal Danish Academy of Music, 1990; MA, Piano, Composition, Rhythmic Music Conservatory, Copenhagen, 1992. Career: All major musicals in Denmark for the last 5 years; Chess in concert with Elaine Page, Tommy Korberg, 1997; Solo with Harolyn Blackwell, 1997; Live Symphonic with Lisa Nilsson, 1988. Compositions: Sarajevo Butterfly; Dance of the Clogs; Songs in the Wind; Mixed Love. Recordings: Mixed Love; Les Miserables. Honours: Danish Ministry of Culture, 1991; Denmark-America Foundation, 1992. Memberships: Danish Society of Jazz, Rock & Folk Composers; Danish Conductors Association. Hobby: Family Life. Address: Kirsten Pilsvej 10, Isal, 2920 Charlottenlund, Denmark.

LAVELLE Caroline. Musician (cello); Vocalist; Songwriter. Career: Leader, all-female trio Electra Strings; Group toured with Nigel Kennedy; As session musician, played with Massive Attack; Peter Gabriel; Ride; The Fall. Recordings: Solo album: Spirit; Solo single: Moorlough Shore; Contributor, Home Of The Whale, Massive Attack; Us, Peter Gabriel.

LAVER Eddie, (Charles Edward Laver), b. 1 Jan 1930, Doncaster, England. Musician (alto saxophone, keyboards); Bandleader. Divorced, 2 sons. Education: HNC in Engineering. Musical Education: Musical family background; Saxophone tuition for 7 years. Career: Own band, The Eddie Laver Showband; Played for dinner dances at Ye Old Hotel Barnry Moor, Retford; Played for P & O Cruises for 12 years including 4 world cruises on the Canberra and Sea Princess; Played at London hotels for 5 years; Played at hotels in Spain for 4 years; Appeared on Radio Sheffield; Played for President Peron of Argentina; Played for Pontins Holidays. Membership: Musicians' Union. Hobbies: Music; Gardening; Flying model aircraft. Current Management: Various. Address: 5 Park

Lane, Westwoodside, Near Doncaster DN9 2EG, England.

LAVIS Gilson, b. 27 June 1951, Bedford, England. Musician (drums, percussion); Songwriter. m. Nicola Mercedes Keller, 10 Nov 1993. Musical Education: Self-taught. Career: Drummer for: The Bo Weavils; Headline News; Springfield Revival; Chris Rea; Squeeze, 1975-91; Pick up drummer, Chuck Berry, Jerry Lee Lewis; Cabaret drummer for artists including: Tommy Cooper; Bob Monkhouse; Lulu; Freddie Starr; David Frost; Engelbert Humperdinck; Currently with Jools Holland and the Rhythm And Blues Orchestra, 1991-; Concerts, tours with: Chris Rea, Europe; Chuck Berry, 2 tours, UK, Europe; Jerry Lee Lewis, UK tour; Squeeze, 20 UK tours, 20-25 US/Canada tours, 1 Australia tour; Jools Holland, 8 UK, 2 Ireland tours; Television includes: with Squeeze: Top Of The Pops; Old Grey Whistle Test; with Jools Holland: Don't Forget Your Toothbrush, CH4, as house band drummer, working with: Jimmy Somerville, Robert Palmer, Cher, Neil Sedaka, Chaka Khan, Lulu, Roger Daltrey, Barry White, Lemmy, Vic Reeves and Bob Mortimer, Roy Wood, Kylie Minogue, Suggs, Kim Wilde, Michelle Gayle; The Happening, BSB/Sky, with artists including: Midge Ure, Mica Paris; Later With Jools Holland, BBC2, with artists including: Dusty Springfield, Sting, Stevie Winwood, Maria Mackee; Houseband drummer, Name That Tune, Channel 5. Compositions: with Jools Holland: Biggy Wiggy; Birdcage Walk. Recordings: Hit singles with Squeeze: Take Me I'm Yours; Cool For Cats; Up The Junction; Pulling Mussels From A Shell; Labelled With Love; Hourglass; Tempted; Another Nail In My Heart; Albums with Squeeze: Squeeze; Argy Bargy; East Side Story; Sweets From A Stranger; Babylon And On; Frank; Play; Greatest Hits. Honours: Gold, Silver, Platinum discs. Hobbies: Ethnic percussion instruments; Home recording studio. Address: One Fifteen Ltd, The Gallery, 28-30 Wood Wharf, Horseferry Place, London SE10, England.

LAW Michael Charles Ewan, b. 30 Mar 1960, Dar Es Salaam, Tanzania. Musician (piano); Singer; Musical Director; Composer; Lecturer. Musical Education: BA Hons, Gonville and Caius College, Cambridge, Choral and Academic Exhibition, 1979-82; Royal College of Music, including 2 years Opera School, 1982-86; LRAM (piano). Career: Musical director, The Piccadilly Dance Orchestra, 1988-; Television appearances include: 4 appearances on Pebble Mill/Daytime Live; Wogan; Radio includes: Radio 2 including Arts Programme, 3 times and VE Day Celebration; Concerts include: Queen Elizabeth Hall, 3 times; Swan Theatre, Stratford-Upon-Avon; In Cabaret (solo), Pizza On The Park; Noel Coward Cabaret, QE2, 1995; Pianist/vocalist for Noel and Gertie, Sheridan Morley at the Mill, Jermyn Street Theatre, 1997. Compositions: Songs recorded include: Play Me An Elegant Song; I'm Singin' A Swing Song Now. Recordings: 4 albums with The Piccadilly Dance Orchestra, 1989, 1993, 1995, 1997. Memberships: PRS; MCPS. Hobbies: Collecting 78 rpm records; Gardening; Art History; Art Deco era generally. Current Management: Alan Bennett. Address: 50 Albert Street, Windsor, Berks SL4 5BU, England.

LAWLESS Jim (Hugh James), b. 18 Feb 1935, Woolwich, London, England. Musician (tuned percussion). m. Carole Ann, 6 Apr 1968, 3 daughters. Education: HNC in Electronics. Musical Education: 3 years piano lessons; 35 years experience. Career: Became professional, joined The Eric Delaney Band on Ronnie Scott's recommendation, 1960; Worked at Hammersmith Palais, Lyceum Empire, Leicester Square, 1963-1965; Freelance session player, records, television, broadcasts, films, 1965; Played jazz, Hollywood Bowl; US tour with George Shearing; US tour with Charlie Watts. Recordings: Recorded with: LSO; Royal Philharmonic; Ted Heath; Jack Parnell; Stéphane Grappelli; Bob Parnow; Joe

Loss; BBC Big Band; George Shearing; Henry Mancini; Mel Tormé; Peggy Lee; Lene Horne; Nelson Riddle; Kiri Te Kanawa; Nearly all 60s, 70s pop stars including Lulu, The Beatles, Tom Jones. Memberships: Musicians' Union; PRS. Hobbies: Squash; Walking dog; Practising. Current Management: 51 Red Lane, Claygate, Surrey KT10 0ES, England.

LAWLEY Yvonne, b. 29 Aug 1954, Telford, Shropshire, England. Vocalist. m. Cliff, 1 July 1995, 2 sons. Career: Sang with semi-pro groups in Shropshire; Break of several years, then solo artiste, 1991; Cabaret/clubland entertainer in The Midlands; Session singer, songwriter demos. Honour: Vocalist Of The Year, Midland Counties Entertainment Secretaries Council, 1993. Current Management: Phil Summers, Abbey Music. Address: 77 Abbey Fields, Telford, Shropshire TF3 2AT, England.

LAWRENCE Andrew (Andy), b. 2 Nov 1954, Swindon, Wiltshire, England. Musician (Trumpeter, Arranger/Composer, Vocalist). 3 daughters. Education: Trumpet lessons, age 11; Brass band training. Career: Professional on British and US soul music scene, 1972-; 5 years touring continent, 1973-78, with Roy Pellett Jazzband; Settled West Berlin, Germany, 1976-; Freelance Studio work, Arranger, Club work, Concerts, TV (SFB, ARD, RTL) and Radio; Moved to Stuttgart, 1983; Lecturer, Instructor, Baden-Würtenberg Youth Jazz Orchestra, 1984; Numerous concert tours with Peanuts Hucko, Ben Waters, George Kelly; Lead for Joe Schwarz Orchestra (5 years); Led large and small own ensembles; Over 120 original compositions, some recorded; Authority on swing music; Currently, much in demand as arranger, soloist and vocalist. Recordings: 14 albums as featured Soloist - one as Leader. Hobbies: Gardening; Walking; Historical literature; Cooking. Current Management: Andy Lawrence, Altenbergstr 32, 70180 Stuttgart, Germany. Address: Altenbergstr 32, 70180 Stuttgart, Germany.

LAWRENCE Denise, b. 15 Feb 1956, Hayes, Middlesex, England. Jazz Vocalist; Bandleader. m. Tony Lawrence, 16 Aug 1985, 2 daughters. Career: Vocalist, bandleader, Denise Lawrence and Storeyville Tickle jazz band, 15 years; Also: Denise Lawrence and Her Trio; Tony Lawrence (husband) as pianist and Musical Director; Most major jazz clubs, festivals, UK, Europe; Compere, co-organiser, residential festivals, various holiday locations; Appears, caberet and theatres; Particular interest, gospel music, hymns, spirituals; Regularly on radio, and television: ITV, BBC, include: Songs Of Praise. Recordings: 10 albums; Let It Shine; Can't Help Lovin' These Men of Mine; Hangin' Around, 1997; Ain't That Good News, 1997; Recording an album, forthcoming. Honours: Best vocalist, UK Jazz Travel Awards, 1994; Let It Shine, Best New Jazz Recording of Year, Der Jazzfreund, German magazine. Membership: Musicians' Union. Hobbies: Cooking (and eating!). Address: 189 Loddon Bridge Road, Woodley, Reading, Berks RG5 4BP, England.

LAWRENCE John, b. 23 Apr 1949, Ilford, England. Guitarist; Photographer. m. Renate Lawrence, Aug 1982, 2 sons. Education: Art College. Musical Education: Self Taught. Career: Played with various blues bands including, Bob Pearce; Touring with Chicago Blues artists Eddie Campbell and Louisiana Red. Membership: Musicians' Union. Hobbies: History; Country Walking. Address: 11 Chapel Crescent, Sholing, Southampton, SO19 8JU, England.

LAWRENCE Peter Raymond, b. 29 Oct 1957, Leamington Spa, England. Producer; Publisher; DJ. 1 daughter. Career: Manager, Our Price Records; Sales Manager, Making Waves Distribution; Owner, Cooking Vinyl Records; Owner, Global Headz; Founder, The Big Chill. Recordings: Producer: Michelle Shocked: Texas

Campfire Tapes. Address: 6 Victoria Road, London N4 3SQ, England.

LAWRENCE Rohn, b. New Haven, Connecticut, USA. Jazz Musician (guitar); Singer. Musical Education: Began playing aged 2; Building guitars aged 9; Played electric guitars aged 13. Career: Played in New Haven funk bands Good News; The Lift; Performed with: Marion Meadows; George Duke; Dianne Reeves; Jonathon Butler; Alex Bugñon; Freddie Jackson; Najee; Moved to Boston, 1993. Recordings: Hanging On A String, 1993. Current Management: Kim Ewing, Atlantic Jazz Publicity.

LAWRENCE Steven, b. 29 Sep 1961, Glasgow, Scotland. Musician (bouzouki, cittern, mandola, dulcimer, percussion); Producer. Education: HNC in Electrical Engineering. Musical Education: Self-taught. Career: Appeared at Celtic Connections Festival, Glasgow, 1993, 1994; Member, Iron Horse; Appearances include: Poland; Eygpt; Tours of Netherlands, Germany, Brittany; Appeared at major European Festivals; National television and radio appearances in Scotland, Poland, Egypt and Sweden; Performed live with Tannas, Anna Murray, Ross Kennedy; Producing and arranging for many artists within traditional music; Composer, theme and incidental music for videos and exhibitions. Recordings: Doll's House, with Marylyn Middleton Pollock, 1992; Thro' Water Earth And Stone, with Iron Horse, 1993; Five Hands High, with Iron Horse, 1994; Coineadh, with Heather Innes, 1994; Gossamer Mansion, with Arran Bede, 1994; Celtic Dawn, with Whirligig, 1995; Voice of the Land, with Iron Horse, soundtrack to BBC Documentary The Gamekeeper, 1995; Summer in Skye, with Blair Douglas, 1996; Into Indigo, with Anne Murray, 1996; Border Ballads, various artists, forthcoming. Honour: Music Retailer's Association Award, Best Folk Album, for Thro' Water, Earth and Stone. Memberships: Musicians' Union; Performing Rights Society. Current Management: KRL Records. Address: c/o KRL Records, 9 Watt Road, Hillington, Glasgow G52, Scotland.

LAWRENCE Syd, b. 26 June 1923, Shotton, Wales. Musician (violin, cornet); Bandleader. Musical Education: Studied violin. Career: Professional musician, 1941-; Member, RAF Middle East Command Dance Orchestra; Also played with Geraldo; Ken MacKintosh; BBC Northern Dance Orchestra, 1953-68; Orchestra leader, Syd Lawrence Orchestra, 1969-. Recordings: Numerous albums include: Something Old Something New, 1973; My Favourite Things, 1973; Singin'n'Swingin', 1975; Disco Swing, 1976; Swing Classics, 1982; Holland Special, 1986; Big Band Swing, 1988. Current Management: Ackers International Jazz Agency, 53 Cambridge Mansions, Cambridge Road, London SW11 4RX, England.

LAWSON David Andrew, b. 22 Aug 1963, Edinburgh, Scotland. Music Teacher; Performer; Composer; Musician (guitar, bass, drums, piano). 1 daughter. Musical Education: ALCM (P). Career: Concerts include: East End Festival, Hackney Empire; Queens Hall, Edinburgh; ICA. Composition: You Rule My World, for Sky TV. Recordings: Album with Simon Smith; Film: A Fist Full Of Fingers. Membership: Musicians' Union; ISM. Hobbies: Chess; Skiing; Swimming. Address: 5 Beecholme Estate, Prout Road, Clapton, London E5 9NS, England.

LAYTON Paul Martin, b. 4 Aug 1947, Beaconsfield, Buckinghamshire, England. Entertainer; Musician (bass guitar). m. Patricia Peters, 14 June 1981, 1 son, 1 daughter. Musical Education: Hendon Music College. Career: Actor, films include: I Could Go On Singing, with Judy Garland; Television includes: Dixon of Dock Green; Emergency Ward 10, 1965-70; Vocalist, bass guitarist, The New Seekers, 1970-; Major world concert tours and television include: The

White House for Nixon; Royal Command; Ed Sullivan. Compositions include: Ride A Horse; Sweet Louise. Recordings: I'd Like To Teach The World To Sing; Never Ending Song Of Love; Circles; You Won't Find Another Fool Like Me; I Get A Little Sentimental Over You; Look What They've Done To My Song Ma; Beg, Steal or Borrow (Eurovision 1972). Honours: Sun Award, Best Vocal Group; Grammy Nomination, 1972. Memberships: Equity; Musicians' Union. Hobbies: Golf; Snooker; Horseriding. Current Management: Hal Carter Organisation. Address: c/o NS (Music) Management Ltd, Norfolk House, Norfolk Road, Rickmansworth, Herts WD3 2RA, England.

LAZAREVITCH Serge, b. 18 Nov 1957, St Germain En Laye, France. Jazz Musician (guitar); Educator. Musical Education: Jazz diploma, Berklee College of Music, Boston, USA. Career: Concerts throughout Europe with various jazz bands; Member, Orchestre National de Jazz, 1989-91; Tours, Europe, Asia; Head opf Jazz Department, Perpignan Conservatory; Clinics, France, Switzerland; Belgium; Germany; Italy. Recordings: CDs: (as leader) Cats Are Welcome, 1987; London Baby, 1989; Walk With A Lion, 1993; Many recordings as sideman. Honours: Choc Of The Month, Record Of The Year, in Jazz Man, for Walk With A Lion. Membership: UMJ (Union des Musiciens de Jazz). Hobbies: Films; Cooking. Address: 7 Rue Durand, 34000 Montpellier, France.

LE Nguyên, b. 14 Jan 1959, Paris, France. Musician (guitar, bass); Synthesizer Programmer; Composer; Arranger. Education: Graduate in Visual Arts; Majored in Philosophy. Musical Education: Self-taught. Career: Co-creator, multi-ethnic band Ultramarine, 1983; Member, National Jazz Orchestra, 1987; Guest soloist, WDR Big Band, with Vince Mendoza, Bob Brookmeyer, 1993; Concerts and tours throughout Europe; Martinique; Ile de la Réunion; Madagascar; Ivory Coast; USA; Canada; North Africa. Recordings: Miracles, 1989; Zanzibar, 1992; Init, 1993; Million Waves, 1995; Tales From Vietnam, 1996; Three Trios, 1997; with Ultramarine: Dé, 1989; Esimala, 1991. Publications: Isoar and Question Mark published in Real Book Volume III. Honours: with Ultramarine: Best World Music Album: 1989; Telerama, 1992; Tales from Vietnam, 1996; Drapson d'Or, choice du monde de la musique; Choice of the Year, 96 Jazzman' 2nd best CD, for Jazzthing. Current Management: Siegfried Loch, ACT Publishing. Address: Gustav Freytag Strasse 10, D-22085 Hamburg, Germany.

LE BON Simon, b. 27 Oct 1958, Bushey, Hertfordshire, England. Vocalist; Lyricist. m. Yasmin Parvanah, 27 Dec 1985, 1 daughter. Education: Birmingham University. Career: Vocalist, Dog Days; Lead vocalist, Duran Duran, 1980-; Arcadia, 1985-86; Performances include: UK tour, supporting Hazel O'Connor, 1980; MENCAP concert, attended by HRH the Prince and Princess of Wales, 1983; Live Aid, Philadelphia, 1985; The Secret Policeman's Third Ball, 1987; An Acoustic Evening With Duran Duran, Birmingham, 1993. Recordings: Albums: with Duran Duran: Duran Duran, 1981; Rio, 1982; Carnival, 1982; Seven And The Ragged Tiger, 1983; Arena, 1984; Notorious, 1986; Big Thing, 1988; Duran Duran (The Wedding Album), 1993; Thank You, 1995; with Arcadia: So Red The Rose, 1985; Singles include: Planet Earth, 1981; Girls On Film, 1981; My Own Way, 1981; Hungry Like A Wolf, 1982; Save A Prayer, 1982; Rio, 1982; Is There Something I Should Know (Number 1, UK), 1983; Union Of The Snake, 1983; Rio, 1984; New Moon On Monday, 1984; The Reflex (Number 1, UK and US), 1984; The Wild Boys, 1984; A View To A Kill, film theme tune (Number 1, US), 1985; Notorious, 1986; Skin Trade, 1987; Meet El Presidente, 1987; I Don't Your Love, 1988; All She Wants, 1989; Do You Believe In Shame, used in film Tequila Sunrise, 1989; Liberty, 1990; Serious,

1990; Ordinary World, 1993; Come Undone, 1993; Too Much Information, 1993; Singles with Arcadia: Election Day, 1985; Goodbye Is Forever, 1986; The Flame, 1986; Contributor, Do They Know It's Christmas?, Band Aid, 1985; Pavarotti And Friends (Bosnia charity record), 1996. Honours: Grammy Awards: Best Video and Best Album, 1984; BRIT Award, Best British Music Video, Wild Boys, 1985; Ivor Novello Award, International Hit Of Year, The Reflex, 1985; Star on Hollywood Walk Of Fame, 1993. Hobby: Sailing. Current Management: The Left Bank Organisation, 6255 Sunset Blvd #1111, Hollywood, CA 90028, USA.

LE DÉLÉZIR Christian Marie André, b. 7 Feb 1958, Auray, France. Musician (flute, alto flute, piano); Improviser; Composer; Arranger; Producer. Musical Education: European Conservatory of Music, Paris; Ecole Normale de Musique, Paris; Berklee College of Music, Boston, USA; Private lessons with Gary Burton, Boston, USA. Career: Improvised solo concerts (flute, alto flute, piano); Group leader (soloist, composer, arranger); Berklee Performance Center; Fine Art Museum, Boston, USA, 1990; Les Tombées de la Nuit, Rennes, France, 1991; Invited as soloist, European Flute Convention, Paris (Jean-Pierre Rampal 70th birthday), 1992; Musicora, Paris, 1994; Invited by Martial Solal to present live solo improvised concert as flutist and pianist, Les Surprises de Martial Solal, France Musique (broadcast by Radio France), Paris, 1996. Recordings: Soloist, composer, arranger, producer; Ftato (music for flute and double bass), 1987; Exaton (music for flute, soprano saxophone, keyboards, bass, drums), with David Liebman, Bob Moses, 1991; ISLE (improvisations, compositions, alto flute, flute), 1994; 23 Improvisations Pour Piano Solo (2 CDs), 1994. Honours: Classical flute award ECM of Paris; Magna Cum Laude, Berklee College; 4 Diapasons for 23 Improvisations Pour Piano Solo. Hobbies: Seaperch fishing; Mathematical games; Walking in the wild. Address: Exaton Records, 9 Avenue Foch, 56400 Auray, France.

LE GAT Gilles, b. 30 Oct 1961, St Jean d'Angeley, France. Musician (guitar); Composer. 1 son. Musical Education: Self-taught; International Music Seminars; Private teacher. Career: Guitar soloist, Orchestre Regional Paton-Chareute, until 1992; Guitarist, sideman with Claude Barthelem tentet, for Tribute To Otis Redding, Patheney Festival, 1995. Recordings: En Avant Two, ORJ Paton Charente. Hobbies: Fishing; Surfing.

LE GENDRE Dominique, b. Trinidad, West Indies. Musician (guitar); Composer. Musical Education: Guitar tuition by Ramon de Herrera, Conservatoire Municipal de Paris XVII; Degree, Musicology, Sorbonne University; Conservatoires: Regional d'Orsay, Municipal de Pars VI; Diploma in Advanced Sound Recording; Production Techniques, Media Production Services; Television: Body of a Poet, Channel 4; 7 Go Mad in Peru, Channel 4, 1995-96; Radio: The Darkest Eye, Hinterlands, Let Them Call it Jazz, Radio 3, 1996; Film: 6th Happiness, directed by Waris Hussein. Compositions: Music for television: The Healer, BBC1; B D Women, C4; Synchro, ITV; Ragga Gyuls D'Bout, Carlton/Arts Council; Booker Prize '93, BBC2; Disabled Lives, BBC2; Kaiso For July, C4; Films: Aliki Ou La Bague Engloutie; La Petite Valse; I Is A Long Memoried Woman; Theatre music includes: Measure For Measure, London Bubble Theatre; Orinoco, National Theatre Studio; Trapped In Time, Avon Touring Theatre Company; Love At A Loss, Wild Iris Theatre; When The Bough Breaks, Theatre Centre; BBC Radio includes: A Midsummer Night's Dream; The Wizard Of Oz; Edward II; Dance music for: The Burial Of Miss Lady, Irie! Dance Company. Recordings: Romeo and Juliet, King John, Twelfth Night, All's Well That Ends Well, The Merchant of Venice, A Midsummer Night's Dream, The Taming of the Shrew; In production: complete plays of

Shakespeare. Honours: Best Performance Art Video (I Is A Long Memoried Woman), New York, 1991; London Fringe Award Nomination, Best Music, 1994. Memberships: PRS; Musicians' Union. Current Management: Soundtrack Music Management. Address: 22 Ives Street, Chelsea, London SW3 2ND, England.

LE MESSURIER James, b. 20 July 1958, Guernsey, Channel Islands. Musician (percussion); Arranger; Bandleader. m. Flavia Chévez De La Cruz, 23 Apr 1994. Musical Education: Bachelor of Music, Major in Professional Music, Berklee College Of Music, Boston, USA. Career: Leader, percussionist, arranger, London based Salsa group La Clave, 1986-; Numerous appearances clubs, festivals: UK; Eire; France; Italy; Holland; Germany; Switzerland; Featured on BBC Radio One, Andy Kershaw Show, 1994; Freelance percussionist, El Sonido de Londres, Alfredo Rodriguez, Orlando Watussi, Adalberto Santiago. Memberships: PRS; Musicians' Union. Address: 38 Forestholme Close, Forest Hill, London SE23 3UQ, England.

LE-VAN Philippe, b. 29 Dec 1959, Marseilles, France. Musician (drums). m. 19 Sept 1987, 1 son, 1 daughter. Education: Pharmacy. Musical Education: Classical piano, drums. Career: Professional musician, 1986-; Freelance musician, Jazz and Latin music; Drum teacher, Tama Paiste; Manager, Ecole de Samba de Marseille. Recordings: Migration, with Gérard Naulet; Raphaele, with M A St Ceran; Hot Game, 1995; Tribute, with Sandy Patton (formerly of Lionel Hampton singers). Hobbies: Fishing; Collecting stones. Address: 13 Avenue Paul Sirvent, 13380 Plan de Cuques, France.

LEA Jimmy, b. 14 June 1952, Wolverhampton, England. Musician (bass, piano, violin); Songwriter; Record Producer. Career: Member, UK rock group Slade (formerly N'Betweens, Ambrose Slade), 1966-91; Concerts include: First UK tour, 1972; Fanfare For Europe festival, London Palladium, 1973; Great British Music Festival, 1978; Reading Festival, 1980; Film appearance: Flame, 1974. Compositions: Co-writer, all Slade's Top 20 singles, with Noddy Holder. Recordings: Albums: Beginnings (as Ambrose Slade), 1969; Play It Loud, 1970; Slade Alive, 1972; Slayed, 1973; Sladest, 1973; Old New Borrowed Blue, 1974; Slade In Flame (soundtrack), 1974; Nobody's Fool, 1976; Slade Alive Vol 2, 1978; Return To Base, 1979; Slade Smashes, 1980; Till Deaf Do Us Part, 1981; We'll Bring The House Down, 1981; Slade On Stage, 1982; The Amazing Kamikaze Syndrome, 1983; Slade's Greats, 1984; Rogue's Gallery, 1985; Crackers, 1985; You Boyz Make Big Noize, 1987; Wall Of Hits, 1991; UK Number 1 singles: Coz I Luv You, 1971; Take Me Back 'Ome, 1972; Mama Weer All Crazee Now (later recorded by Mama's Boys, Quiet Riot), 1972; Cum On Feel The Noize, 1973; Merry Christmas Everybody, 1973; Other hits include: Look Wot You Dun, 1972; Gudbuy T'Jane, 1972; Skweeze Me Pleeze Me, 1973; My Friend Stan, 1973; Everyday, 1974; Bangin' Man, 1974; Far Far Away, 1974; Thanks For The Memory, 1975; In For A Penny, 1975; We'll Bring The House Down, 1981; My Oh My, 1983; Run Run Away, 1984; All Join Hands, 1984; Record producer, UK rock group Chrome Molly.

LEACH Rod (Rodney Christopher), b. 9 Nov 1943, London, England. Composer; Musician (keyboards). m. Anne Leach, 27 June 1969, 2 sons, 2 daughters. Education: BSc in Economics. Musical Education: Grade 6 Merit in Piano; Grade 5 Clarinet. Career: Single album, Standing Before The Gates Of Time, later renamed The Gates Of Time, written, performed, recorded and produced by him using electronic keyboards and synthesizers, and broadcast by Australia Broadcasting Corporation in Adelaide, 1989. Membership: PRS. Hobbies: Composing; Studio performing; Recording; Producing; Historic and

classic sports; Sportsracing; GT Cars. Address: Briar Forge, Vicarage Causeway, Hertford Heath, Hertfordshire SG13 7RT, England.

LEBEUGLE Patricia, b. 19 May 1963, Le Mans, France. Jazz Musician (bass). Musical Education: Self-taught. Career: Played with Walter Bishop; Bob Mover; Bobby Porcelli; Peter Ecklund; Mark Murphy; Ted Brown; European tours with many French and American musicians, 1985-; Jazz festivals throughout Europe with Philippe Duchemin Trio, 1990-; Tour, South Africa, with pianist Jack Van Poll. Recordings: With Philippe Duchemin Trio: Alizés, 1990; Live!, 1992; Three Pieces, 1994; Philippe Duchemin Trio with Dominique Vernhes, 1995. Hobby: Horse riding. Address: Le Boulay, 72440 St Mars de Locquenay, France.

LEBLANC Donald James, b. 7 Mar 1940, Estevan, Saskatchewan, Canada. Musician (guitar, tenor banjo, electric bass); Singer; Composer; Songwriter. Education: BA (English Literature); Bachelor, Business Education (Business Systems); Courses towards Masters Degree in French and Teaching. Musical Education: Self-taught; Now read music. Career: Played local bands in teen years; Played banjo, then lead guitar; Leader, own band Canadian Crescendos, early 60's; Played lead guitar for Bobby Curtola with own television show After Four; Toured extensively in North America; Solo artist, 1976-; Own record companies, Music Machine Records, DJL Records; Publishing company, Don LeBlanc Enterprises. Recordings: Albums: Don LeBlanc And His Guitar, 1977; Beating The Pavement, 1981; Don LeBlanc Country, 1990; Dream and Smile; Singles: How The Worm Turns, 1979; Too Much, 1980; Believe In Magic, 1983; Her Kind Of Love, 1987; How Did She Do It, 1989. Memberships: AFofM; Canadian Country Music Association; Country Music Association, Nashville; SOCAN. Hobby: Classical guitar. Current Management: Music Machine Records. Address: Box 541, Regina, Saskatchewan, Canada.

LEDIN Tomas Jonas Folke, b. 25 Feb 1952, Östersund, Sweden. Artist; Songwriter; Producer. m. Marie Anderson, 22 May 1982, 2 sons. Education: Graduate, Swedish Gymnasium, 1972. Musical Education: Musical Science, Uppsala University, 1977. Career: First album released, 1972; Tours: Sweden & Scandinvia, 1980-; USA, with ABBA; Canada, Europe, 1979; Japan, 1980; Initiated Rocktrain tour, 1981; Toured with the Rocktrain, 1992-93; Appeared on all major television shows, Sweden. Recordings: 18 albums include: Greatest Hits, 1990; Tillfälligheternas Spel, 1990; Du Kan Lita På Mej, 1993. Honours: 2 Grammies, 1991; Rockbjörn Award, 1991, 1992; Måzart prize, 1991; World Music Award, 1992; Represented Sweden, Eurovision Song Contest, 1980; Platinum and Gold discs. Memberships: Board member, SKAP (Swedish Composers Society); Board member, Millesgården's Vänner. Hobbies: Qi Gong; Skiing; Tennis; Diving. Current Management: Jan Beime, Desert Music. Address: Brickebergsvägen 21 A, 701 21 Örebro, Sweden.

LEE Albert, b. 21 Dec 1943, Leominster, Hertfordshire, England. Musician (guitar). Career: Guitarist, Chris Farlowe and The Thunderbirds, 1960s; In-demand session musician; Also member of Country Fever; Member, Poet And The One Man Band (with Chas Hodges of Chas 'n' Dave); Group became Heads Hands and Feet; Member, the Crickets; Emmylou Harris' Hot Band; Touring bands of Eric Clapton; Jackson Browne; Jerry Lee Lewis; Dave Edmunds; Concerts include: Everly Brothers Reunion, Royal Albert Hall, 1983. Recordings: Solo albums: Hiding, 1979; Albert Lee, 1983; Speechless, 1986; Gagged But Not Bound, 1987; Black Claw And Country Fever, 1991; Other recordings: Albums with Eric Clapton: Just One Night, 1980; Another Ticket, 1981; Money And Cigarettes, 1983; with Joe Cocker:

With A Little Help From My Friends, 1969; Stingray, 1976; with The Crickets: Bubblegum, Pop, Ballads And Boogie, 1973; Remnants, 1973; with Dave Edmunds: Repeat When Necessary, 1979; DE7, 1982; with Chris Farlowe: Chris Farlowe And The Thunderbirds, 1966; Stormy Monday, 1966; Out Of The Blue, 1985; with Emmylou Harris: Luxury Liner, 1977; Quarter Moon In A Ten Cent Town, 1978; Blue Kentucky Girl, 1979; Christmas Album, 1979; Roses In The Snow, 1980; Evangeline, 1981; Cimarron, 1981; Ballad Of Sally Rose, 1985; with Head Hands And Feet: Head Hands And Feet, 1971; Tracks, 1972; Old Soldiers Never Die, 1973; with Jimmy Page and John Paul Jones: No Introduction Necessary, 1984; Also recorded on albums with: Chas & Dave; Bobby Bare; Gary Brooker; Teresa Brewer; Guy Clark; Rodney Crowell; Bo Diddley; Lonnie Donegan; Don Everly; Everly Brothers; Nancy Griffith; Jerry Lee Lewis; Jon Lord; Steve Morse; Juice Newton; Dolly Parton; Ricky Skaggs; Shakin' Stevens.

LEE Alvin, b. 19 Dec 1944, Nottingham, England. Musician (guitar, vox); Songwriter. Career: First band: The Jailbreakers, age 13, Became The Jaybirds, then Ten Years After; Moved to London, 1966; Friday residency, Marquee Club, 1968; Fillmore East and West, Woodstock, USA, 1969; Arena dates, 28 tours in 5 years, led to band disbanding, 1976; Solo recordings, collaboration with gospel singer, Mylon Lefevre; Short reunion of Ten Years After, 1988; Returned to solo work. Recordings include: Albums: with Ten Years After: Ten Years After, 1967; Undead, 1968; Ssssh, 1969; Cricklewood Green, 1970; Watt, 1971; A Space In Time, 1971; Alvin Lee And Company, 1972; Rock And Roll Music To The World, 1972; Recorded Live, 1973; Positive Vibrations, 1974; Goin' Home, 1975; Hear Them Calling, 1976; The Classic Performances Of, 1977; Greatest Hits, 1979; Profile, 1980; Portfoloio, 1983; Universal, 1988; About Time, 1989; Texas International Pop Festival, 1992; Pure Blues, 1995; with Mylon Lefevre: On The Road To Freedom; Solo: In Flight, 1974; Pump Iron, 1975; Let It Rock, 1978; Rocket Fuel (& Ten Years Later), 1978; Chrysalis Classics, 1978; Ride On (& Ten Years Later), 1979; Free Fall (Alvin Lee Band), 1980; RX5, 1981; Detroit Deisel, 1986; Zoom, 1992; Nineteen-Ninety-Four, 1993; Live In Vienna, 1994; Guest artist on recordings including: The Session, Jerry Lee Lewis, 1973; Dark Horse, George Harrison, 1974; 20th Anniverary Of Rock And Roll, Bo Diddley, 1976; Revue, Vol 2, Earl Scruggs, 1976; Bull In A Ming Vase, Roy Harper, 1977; Night Of The Guitar Live (1988), 1989; Under No Obligation, Roger Chapman, 1991; 38317, Peter Maffay, 1991. Current Management: Skarda. Address: Bergstrasse 13, 82069 Hohenshäftlarn, Germany.

LEE Brenda (Brenda Lee Tarpley), b. 11 Dec 1944, Lithonia, Georgia, USA. Singer. Career: Solo recording artist, 1950s-1960s; Actress; film The Two Little Bears. Recordings: Hit singles include: Let's Jump The Broomstick; Speak To Me Pretty; One Step At A Time; Rockin' Around The Christmas Tree; I'm Sorry; Thanks A Lot; Too Many Rivers; Losing You; I Wonder; As Usual; Nobody Wins. Albums include: Grandma, What Great Songs You Sang, 1959; Brenda Lee, 1960; This Is Brenda, 1960; Emotions, 1961; All The Way, 1961; Sincerely, 1962; Brenda, That's All, 1962; The Show For Christmas Seals, 1962; All Alone Am I, 1963; Let Me Sing, 1963; By Request, 1964; Merry Christmas From Brenda Lee, 1964; Top Teen Hits, 1965; The Versatile Brenda Lee, 1965; Too Many Rivers, 1965; Bye Bye Blues, 1966; Coming On Strong, 1966; For The First Time (with Pete Fountain), 1968; Johnny One Time, 1969; The Brenda Lee Story, 1974; LA Sessions, 1977; Even Better, 1980; Little Miss Dynamite, 1980; 25th Anniversary, 1984; The Golden Decade, 1985; The Best Of Brenda Lee, 1986; Love Songs, 1986; Brenda Lee, 1991; Guest singer, Shadowland, k d lang, 1988.

Address: c/o Brenda Lee Management, 2174 Carson Street, Nashville, TN 37211, USA.

LEE Crissy, b. 17 June 1943, Colchester, Essex, England. Musician (drums, percussion); Music Teacher. Career: Joined Ivy Benson Dance Band, aged 17, tours worldwide; Appeared with artistes including: Dinah Washington; Frank Sinatra Jr; Fats Domino; Caterina Valente; Tom Jones; Support on The Beatles first Spanish tour; Formed the Crissy Lee Band; Worked alongside: Al Jarreau; Faith Brown; Marion Montgomery; Madeline Bell; Musical Director for guests including: Roy Castle; Ken Dodd; Bob Monkhouse; Launched and managed Koffee & Kreme duo, winners of New Faces television talent show; Other musical projects include Beauty and the Beat, backing band for acts including The Supremes, Johnny Bristol; Sam Dees; Formed The Crissy Lee Big Band (only 17-piece all-female band in Europe); Television appearances include: Barrymore; Wogan; Cilla Black Show; Russell Harty Show; Jack Parnell Big Band Special; Millicent Martin Show; Lady Be Good; Goldeneye; David Frost Chat Show. Recordings: The Beat Chics EP; The Beat Chics: Skinny Mini/Now I Know. Memberships: Equity; Musicians' Union; ABJM (Association of British Jazz Musicians). Hobbies: Sports; Cars; Theatre; Reading; Animal welfare; Eating out. Current Management: Self-managed, 24 Karat Music Ltd. Address: 44 Strawberry Lane, Tolleshunt Knights, Colchester, Eessex CO5 0RX, England.

LEE Eddie, b. 26 Aug 1961, Dublin, Ireland. Musician (bass guitar, double bass); Programmer; Producer. m. Therese O'Loughlin, 17 Feb 1996. Education: BSc, University College, Dublin, 1979. Musical Education: Self-taught. Career: Played or recorded with: Brian Kennedy; Maura O'Connell; Those Nervous Animals; Stockton's Wing; The Pale; Enya; Dolores Keane Band; Katell Keineg; Frances Black; Emmylou Harris (with Dolores Keane); Davy Spillane; A Woman's Heart; Garrett Wall; Speranza; Nine Wassies From Bainne (Irish avant garde group). Recordings include: My Friend John, Those Nervous Animals (co-writer, performer); About Time, Speranza; Solid Ground, Dolores Keane; Tracks on A Womans Heart (biggest selling Irish album ever); Producer, Assassination, Indian; Film appearance with Brian Kennedy, 1995. Memberships: IMRO; PRS; Musicians' Union. Address: Teach Mhuire, Cleveragh Road, Sligo, Ireland.

LEE Geddy (Gary), b. 29 July 1953, Willowdale, Canada. Musician (bass); Vocalist. Career: Member, Canadian rock group Rush, 1969-; Sell-out tours, USA, Canada; UK; Europe; Played on bills with ZZ Top; Areosmith; Kiss; Uriah Heep. Recordings: Albums: Rush, 1973; Fly By Night, 1975; Caress Of Steel, 1975; 2112, 1976; All The World's A Stage, 1976; A Farewell To Kings, 1977; Archives, 1978; Hemispheres, 1978; Permanent Waves, 1980; Moving Pictures, 1981; Exit... Stage Left, 1981; Great White North, 1982; Signals, 1982; Grace Under Pressure, 1984; Power Windows, 1985; A Show Of Hands, 1989; Presto, 1989; Chronicles, 1990; Roll The Bones, 1991; Counterparts, 1993; Singles include: Spirit Of Radio; Tom Sawyer; Vital Signs; New World Man; Closer To The Heart; Countdown; The Big Money; Time Stand Still. Honours: Juno Awards: Most Promising Group, 1975; Best Group, 1978, 1979; Group named Official Ambassadors Of Music, Canadian Government, 1979; Gold Ticket Award, Madison Square Garden, 1991. Current Management: Anthem Entertainment, 189 Carlton Street, Toronto, Ontario M5A 2K7, Canada.

LEE Peggy, b. 26 May 1920, Jamestown, North Dakota, USA. Singer; Actress. m (1) Dave Barbour, 1943, 1 daughter; (2) Brad Dexter, 1955; (3) Dewey Martin, 1956; (4) Jack Del Rio, 1964. Career: Singer, radio station, North Dakota; Singer, Will Osbornes's Band, Chicago; Benny Goodman's Band, 1941-43; Actress, films include:

Mr Music, 1950; The Jazz Singer, 1953; Pete Kelly's Blues, 1955; Researcher, performer, The Jazz Tree Philharmonic Center For Performing Arts, New York, 1963. Compositions: For films: Johnny Guitar; About Mrs Leslie; (cartoon) Tom Thumb; Lyrics for: Lady And The Tramp. Recordings include: Golden Earrings; You Was Right Baby; It's A Good Day; Manana; Is That All There Is; I'm A Woman; There'll Be Another Spring; Seductive; Peggy Lee Sings With Benny Goodman; Peggy Lee Sings The Blues. Publications: Softly With Feeling (verse), 1953. Honours: Grammy Award, Is That All There Is, 1969; Metronome and Downbeat magazine Poll Winner, Best Female Vocalist, 1946; Billboard's Most Popular Vocalist, 1950. Current Management: c/o Stan Scottland, JKE Services Inc., 404 Park Avenue S, 10th Floor, New York, NY 10016, USA.

LEE Philip Robert, b. 8 Apr 1943, London, England. Musician (guitar). m. Doris Anna Zingerli, 31 Mar 1964. Musical Education: Self-taught. Career: First bands: John Williams Big Bands, Graham Collier Septet, 1960s; Henry Lowther, Tony Coe, 1970s; Musician with singers Annie Ross; Marian Montgomery; Sylvia Sims; Norma Winstone; Member, fusion band, Gilgamesh; Played for Americans including Benny Goodman, 1980s; Member, Dardanelle, 1990s. Recordings: Gilgamesh, Gilgamesh; Another Fine Tune You've Got Me Into, Gilgamesh; Twice Upon A Time, Phil Lee - Jeff Clyne; Swingin' In London, Dardanelle; Meteors Close At Hand, Michael Garrick. Memberships: PRS; Musicians' Union. Hobbies: Reading; Walking.

LEE Robert E (Robert Greehy), b. 30 May 1956, Leeds, England. Singer; Musician (drums, guitar, bass, keyboards). Musical Education: Self-taught. Career: Session musician, 1975-79; Member, London Cowboys, 1980-85; Tours: Europe; Japan; USA; Scandinavia; UK; including 2 support tours, Johnny Thunders, 1981, 1982; 2 support tours, Hanoi Rocks, 1982, 1983; Producer, session musician, 1986-; Worldwide television and radio appearances. Recordings: Albums: Animal Pleasure; Tall In The Saddle; Long Time Coming; Dead Or Alive; Singles: Centrefold; Hook; Line And Sinker; Dance Crazy; Let's Get Crazy; Street Full Of Soul. Memberships: MU; MCPS. Hobbies: Reading; Films; Music; Travel; Arts; Photography. Current Management: Wild Card Management Ltd. Address: Acme Studios, 27 Peashill Close, Rawdon, Leeds, Yorks LS19 6EF, England.

LEE Tommy (Thomas Lee Bass), b. 3 Oct 1962, Athens, Greece. Musician (drums). m. (1) Heather Locklear, 1986; (2) Pamela Anderson, 1995. Career: Member, groups Suite 19; Christmas; Founder member, US heavy rock group Mötley Crüe, 1981-; Worldwide concerts include: Tours with: Y&T, 1981, 1982; Kiss, 1983; Ozzy Osbourne, 1984; Iron Maiden, 1984; Cheaap trick, 1986; Theatre of Pain World tour, 1985-86; World tours, 1987, 1989; Major festivals: US Festival, 1983; Monsters of Rock Festival, Castle Donington, 1984; Moscow Music Peace Festival, 1989. Recordings: Albums: Too Fast For Love, 1981; Shout At The Devil, 1983; Theatre Of Pain, 1985; Girls, Girls, Girls (Number 2, US), 1987; Dr Feelgood (Number 1, US), 1989; Decade Of Decadence (Number 2, US), 1991; Til Death Do Us Part, 1994; Singles: Stick To Your Guns, 1981; Looks That Kill, 1984; Too Young To Fall In Love, 1984; Smokin' In The Boys Room, 1985; Home Sweet Home, 1985; You're All I Need, 1987; Dr Feelgood, 1989; Kick Start My Heart, 1990; Without You, 1990; Don't Go Away Mad, 1990; Same Old Situation, 1990; Primal Scream, 1991. Current Management: The Left Bank Organisation, 6255 Sunset Blvd, Ste 1111, Hollywood, CA 90028, USA.

LEE-JAY David, b. 24 Oct 1950, Birmingham, England. Entertainer; Musician (drums, percussion, guitar, bass guitar, ukelele); Sound and Lighting Engineer. m. Sheila Lorraine, 16 Oct 1976. Education: Technical College, Birmingham. Career: Various television and radio appearances; Tours: Europe; Scandinavia; New Zealand; Australia; Various cruises. Recordings: 3 albums with wife, under name Zebedee. Membership: British Equity. Hobbies: Music; Boating; Fishing. Address: c/o Zebedee, Newton Road, Rushden, Northants NN10 0SY, England

LEES John, b. 13 Jan 1947, Oldham, Lancashire, England. Singer; Musician (guitar). Career: Member, Barclay James Harvest (originally the Blues Keepers), 1967-; Regular international tours, UK and Europe, including Free concert, Berlin Wall, 1980. Recordings include: Albums: Barclay James Harvest, 1970; Barclay James Harvest Live, 1974; Time Honoured Ghosts, 1975; Gone To Earth, 1977; Harvest XII, 1978; Eyes Of The Universe, 1980; Turn Of The Tide, 1981; Concert For The Peope, 1981; Ring Of Changes, 1981; Face To Face, 1987; Glasnost, 1988; Welcome To The Show, 1990; Alone We Fly, 1990; The Harvest Years, 1991; The Best Of Barclay James Harvest, 1992. Solo album: A Major Fancy, 1977. Current Management: Handle Artists Management, Handle House, 1 Albion Place, Galena Road, London W6 0QT, England.

LEES Simon (Buggy), b. 16 May 1970, Wolverhampton, England. Musician (guitar); Singer; Songwriter; Entertainer. Education: BTEC ONC at Wulfrun College. Career: Formed Osprey, 1986; Nitebreed, 1990 (support band for The Mock Turtles); Member, The Red House Snakes, 1990; Formed Plain Jain, 1992; Member, Tantrum, 1994; Radio appearances: The Reaper Rock Show, Freedom FM, Chester. Recording: Playing Truant, recorded live at London Music Show, Wembley Conference Centre, 1994. Honour: CD Guitarist of The Year, for Playing Truant, 1994. Membership: Musicians' Union. Hobbies: Cycling; Swimming; Reading. Address: 34 Strathmore Crescent, Wombourne, Wolverhampton, Staffordshire WV5 9AS, England.

LEGGETT Andy, b. 31 Mar 1942, Much Wenlock, England. Musician (saxophone, clarinet, guitar); Songwriter; Arranger. m. Teri Penfold, 5 Sept 1975, 2 sons, 1 daughter. Education: BA, Upper 2nd Class Honours in French, Hull, 1964. Musical Education: School Orchestra. Career: Member of Alligator Jug Thumpers, 1968; Pigsty Hill Light Orchestra, 1970; duo with Pete Finch, 1973; Avon Touring Theatre, 1974; Formed Sweet Substitute, 1975; Later became Musical Director, writer and arranger for them; Toured with: Midnite Follies Orchestra, Pasadena Roof Orchestra, Syd Lawrence, Bob Kerr's Whoopee Band, Temperance Seven; Playing clarinet and saxophone, Rod Mason's Hot Five, 1996-. Compositions: for Sweet Substitute: Tiger Blues, Dear Mr Berkeley, Sleepy Suzie, A Musical Christmas Card; for Henry's Bootblacks: Everyone's Got Horns, New Orleans Feels Like Home, Sugar Makes Your Teeth Fall Out; Co-wrote songs for the play The Godmother, directed by Mel Smith; Music for film, Betjeman Revisited, HTV, 1995. Memberships: Musicians' Union; Associate Member, PRS, MCPS. Address: Rottes 123, Kaarst, Vorst 41564, Germany.

LEGRAND Benjamin, b. 16 Oct 1962, Paris, France. Singer; Musician (piano, drums). m. Tita Gibert, 22 July 1994, 1 daughter. Musical Education: Piano, drums, singing lessons, Paris. Career: Appearances include: Television shows, Paris; Olympia Hall, Paris; Tours: Japan; Tunisia; Belgium; Switzerland; Bobino Music Hall, Paris; Eurodisney concerts; Cannes Jazz Fetsival; Calvi Jazz Festival, Corsica; Radio Shows include France Inter. Recordings: Album with Michel Legrand Big Band; Chansons De Paris (album of French songs); Record of Jazz Trio; Participating in album of French Songs. Publications: Letemps Qui Passe (poetry); La Pensée Universalle.

Memberships: SPEDIDAM; SACEM. Hobbies: Tennis; Long walks. Address: Le Chalet Du Buison, 45240 Marcilly-En-Villette, France.

LEGRAND Michel, b. 24 Feb 1932, Paris, France. Composer; Musician (piano); Conductor; Singer; Arranger. m. Isabelle, 21 Nov 1994, 2 sons, 2 daughters. Musical Education: Paris Conservatoire. Career: Conducted, appeared with Pittsburgh Symphony, The National Symphony Orchestra, Minnesota Orchestra, Buffalo Philharmonic, Symphony Orchestras of Vancouver, Montreal, Atlanta, Denver, New Orleans; Collaborated with Maurice Chevalier, Miles Davis, Kiri Te Kanawa, Johnny Mathis, Neil Diamond, Sarah Vaughn, Stan Getz, Aretha Franklin, Jack Jones, James Galway, Ray Charles, Lena Horne, Barbra Streisand and numerous others. Films: (with Miles Davis) Dingo, 1990; Directed, Cinq Jours En Juin, 1989; Masque de Lune, 1991; Theatre productions, television appearances and film scores including Prêt-à-Porter, 1994. Compositions include: Images; I Was Born In Love With You; I Will Wait For You; Love Makes The Changes; Noelle's Theme; On My Way To You; One At A Time; Once Upon A Summertime; Little Boy Lost; The Summer Knows; Summer Me, Winter Me; Watch What Happens; The Way He Makes Me Feel; What Are You Doing The Rest of Your Life?; The Windmills of Your Mind; You Must Believe In Spring. Recordings include: Erik Satie By Michel Legrand; Four Piano Blues; Michel Plays Legrand. Publication: Michel Legrand Songbook. Honours include: 5 Grammy Awards, 1972-75; 3 Academy Awards, Thomas Crown Affair, 1968; Summer Of '42, 1971; Yentl, 1983; Australian Film Institute Award, Dingo, 1991. Memberships: Songwriters Guild; Dramatists Guild; NARAS; Academy of Motion Arts & Sciences. Current Management: Jim DiGiovanni. Address: 157 West 57th Street, New York, NY 10019, USA.

LEHNERT Miroslav, b. 24 April 1947, Novy Jicin, Czech Republic. Drums; Vocal. m. Jana Lehnertová, 17 November 1994. Musical Education: Private teachers for drums, classical and jazz music, 1975; State examination for professional musicians, highest qualification as drummer and singer. Career: Professional Musician, many night clubs and hotels, 1963-; Military Music, 1967-69; Africa, 1970-72; Ship Around the World, Royal Viking Skg, 1976; About 30 radio recordings. Address: Dlouhá 19, 74101 Novy Jicin, Czech Republic.

LEHRER Tom (Thomas Andrew), b. 9 Apr 1928, New York, USA. Songwriter; Entertainer; Lecturer. Education: BA, Harvard University, 1946; MA, 1947; Postgraduate, 1947-53, 1960-65. Musical Education: Columbia University, 1948-49. Career: Mathematician, Cambridge, Massachusetts, 1953-54; Lecturer in: Business Administration, Harvard, 1962; Education, 1963-66; Political Science, Massachusetts Institute of Technology, 1962-71; Psychology, Wellesley College, 1966; Lecturer, University of California, Santa Cruz, 1972-; Entertainer, nightclubs, 1953-65. Compositions: Numerous songs and songbooks. Recordings: Songs By Tom Lehrer; More Of Tom Lehrer; An Evening Wasted With Tom Lehrer; Tom Lehrer Revisited; That Was The Year That Was. Publications: Songbooks include: Tom Lehrer Songbook, 1964; Tom Lehrer's Second Songbook, 1968; Too Many Songs, 1981; Tomfoolery, 1986. Memberships: ASCAP; AFofM; Maths Association of America.

LEICK Vagn, b. 13 Apr 1939, Lydersholm, Denmark. Composer. Musician (piano). m. Jo Skovsbog, 19 Apr 1985, 2 sons, 1 daughter. Education: PhD, Biochemistry. Musical Education: Private study in Jazz improvisation and composition. Career: Television and radio appearances in Denmark; US; France. Recordings: Twilight; Thing; Jazz Digit. Membership: Danish Society of Jazz, Beat and

Folk Authors. Hobbies: Mountain hiking; Skiing. Current Management: IW Productions. Address: Ved Glyjitotelech 6, 1575 Copenhagen V, Denmark.

LEIGH Joy, b. 23 Apr 1964, Montgomery, West Virginia, USA. Country/Southern Gospel Singer. Divorced. Education: Associate degree, Nursing, West Virginia Institute of Technology. Career: Performed on stage, Grand Ole Opry, Don Reed Talent Competition; Showcase artist, King Eagle Awards Show, Nashville, Tennessee; Headlined Fayette County, West Virginia, Fair, 1994, 1995; Performed at Boone County, West Virginia, Fair, 1994, 1995; Summerville, West Virginia's Suumerfest, 1994; Rotary Club of Montgomery, West Virginia, 1994, 1995. Recordings: What's In It For Me?; Walk Away. Honours: Nomination, Gospel Trailblazer Award, King Eagle Awards Show; Montgomery Rotary Festival Award; United Community Services Entertainment Award. Membership: Gospel Music Association, Nashville, Tennessee. Hobbies: Computers; Reading; Walks through mountains; Playing with my dogs. Current Management: Claudia Johnson, Johnson and Johnson Music Group, PO Box 182 Cannelton, WV 25036, USA. Address: Joy Leigh Enterprises, PO Box 182, Cannelton, WV 25036, USA.

LEINER Boris, b. 28 January 1957, Cakovec, Croatia. Musician; Singer; Drums; Percussions. divorced, 1 daughter. Education: Study, Art Academy, Zagreb; Art University, Utrecht, Holland, 1983-86; Career: Drummer, Singer, Rock Band, Azra, 1977-87; Vjestice, 1987-; Naturalna Mistika, Reggae band, 1983-; Berlin's Band, Love-Sister-Hope, International Tour, 1980-92; European Tour, Vjestice, 1989-90. Compositions: Balkan, 1979; Lijepe Zene Prolaze Kroz Grad, 1980; Provedimo Vikend Zajedno, 1981; Uzas Je Moja Furka, 1981; Klincek Stoji Pod Oblokom, 1983; Totalno Drukciji Od Drugih, 1989. Recordings: Azra-Azra; Suncana Strana Ulice Azra; Ravno Do Dna-Azra Djevojke U Ljetnim Haljinama Volim, Vjestice; Kradljivci SRCA Vjestice, Totalno Drukciji Od Drugih. Publications: Azra I, 1980; Suncana Strana Ulice, 1981; Azra Ravno Do Dna, 1981; Krivo Srastanje, 1984; Totalno Drukciji Od Drugih, 1988; Vjestice, Kradljivci Srca, 1996. Honours: 3 Porin Awards, Cro Music, 1996; Kradljivci Srca, Best Alter, CD; Status Award, Best Drummer, 1996. Memberships: HGU, Croatian Musicians Union; HZSU, Croatian Union of Independent Artists. Hobbies: Yoga; Art Consumer. Current Management: Combat Rock Management, Jurici Tomislavov Trg 19, Zagreb, Croatia. Address: Duzice 23, 1000 Zagreb, Croatia.

LEITNER George, b. 24 Nov 1959, Vienna, Austria. Agent, Manager. m. Dr Brigitte Leitner-Friedrich, 29 Sept 1991. Education: College, South Africa; University, Vienna. Musical Education: piano. Career: 1977, founded Number One Music (with Andreas Eggar); 1980, founded George Leitner Productions, representing: James Brown; Kool and the Gang; Jimmy Cliff; Blood Sweat and Tears; VSOP; The Commodores; George Clinton; others. Publications: Analysis Of The European Music Industry (university thesis). Honours: Mag, Rer Soc Ök. Hobbies: Horseriding; Sailing; Skiing; Tennis. Address: Hütteldorfstr 259, 1140 Vienna, Austria.

LEJEUNE Philippe, b. 6 Feb 1954, Eu, France. Musician (piano). m. Irene, 5 July 1986, 2 sons. Education: DUT, Tech de Co. Musical Education: Conservatoires, Rouen, Reims. Career: Appearances: Detroit Jazz Festival; Festival Radio France; Festival de Jazz de Montauban; Nuits Piano Jazz Lutetia, Paris; Cincinnati Queen City Blues Festival. Recordings: Piano Duet With Memphis Slim, 1980; Live At Blue Moon, 1990; Chicago Non Stop, 1993; 100% Blues and Boogie Woogie, 1996. Memberships: SACEM; SPEDIDAM; ADAMI. Current

Management: Association Jazz Vivant. Address: BP 20, 31921 Toulouse Cedex 9, France.

LEMMY (Ian Kilminster), b. 24 Dec 1945, Stoke-on-Trent, Staffordshire, England. Musician (bass); Vocalist. Career: Member, several groups including: The Rainmakers; The Motown Sect; The Rockin' Vicars; Sam Gopal's Dream; Opal Butterfly; Also road crew member, Jimi Hendrix; Member, UK rock group Hawkwind, 1971-75; Founder, UK heavy rock group Motörhead, 1975-; Regular UK, US and international tours; Major concerts include: Heavy Metal Barn Dance, 1980; Monsters Of Rock Festival, Castle Donington, 1986; Film appearance: Eat The Rich, 1987. Recordings: Albums: with Hawkwind: In Search Of Space, 1971; Doremi Fasol Latido, 1972; Space Ritual, 1973; Hall Of The Mountain Grill, 1974; Warrior On The Edge Of Time, 1975; with Motörhead: Motörhead, 1977; Overkill, 1979; Bomber, 1979; Ace Of Spades, 1980; No Sleep Til' Hammersmith, 1981; What's Words Worth, 1983; Another Perfect Day, 1983; No Remorse, 1984; Orgasmatron, 1986; Rock'n'Roll, 1987; No Sleep At All, 1988; 1916, 1991; March Or Die, 1992; Bastards, 1993; Singles: with Hawkwind: Silver Machine, 1972; Urban Guerilla, 1973; with Motörhead: Motörhead/City Kids, 1977; Louie Louie, 1978; No Class, 1979; Bomber, 1979; The Golden Years (EP), 1980; Beer Drinkers And Hell Raisers, 1980; St Valentine's Day Massacre, with Girlschool, 1981; Iron Fist, 1982; I Got Mine, 1983; Shine, 1983; Killed By Death, 1984; Deaf Forever, 1986; The One To Sing The Blues, 1991; Contributor, Hear'N'Aid, 1987; Let It Be, Ferry Aid, 1987; The Last Temptation Of Elvis, 1990. Current Management: Singerman Entertainment, Penthouse West, 8833 Sunset Blvd, Los Angeles, CA 90069, USA.

LEMPER Ute, b. 4 July 1963, Münster, Germany. Singer; Actress; Dancer. Education: Max-Reinhardt-Seminar, Vienna. Career: Appearances include: Cats, Vienna, 1983; Peter Pan, Berlin; Cabaret, Düsseldorf and Paris; Films include: L'Autrichienne, 1989; Moscou Parade, 1992; Coupable d'Innocence, 1993; Prêt A Porter. Recordings: Albums include: Ute Lemper Sings Kurt Weill, Volume 1, 1988, Volume 2, 1993; Threepenny Opera, 1988; Mahoganny Songspiel, 1989; Illusions, 1992; Espace Indécent, 1993; City Of Strangers, 1995. Honours: Molière Award, 1987; French Culture Prize, 1993. Address: c/o Oliver Gluzman, 40 Rue de la Folie Régnault, 75011 Paris, France.

LENDING Kenn, b. 8 Feb 1955, Copenhagen, Denmark. Musician (guitar); Composer; Songwriter; Vocalist. m. Karina Nevermann, 15 May 1993. Musical Education: Private lessons, music-writing, composing; Classical guitar lessons with Jan Ronnow, Royal Danish Academy of Music. Career: Member, Himmelexpressen, 1972-79; Member, Survivors, 1976-78; Member, Blues Nite, 1977-79; Formed duo with American blues pianist, singer, Champion Jack Dupree, 1979-92; Played over 1000 concerts; Formed Kenn Lending Blues Band, 1980-; Used as backing band by Jan Harrington; Louisiana Red; Jack Dupree; Luther Allison; Support tours, Fats Domino, Germany, 1987; B B King, Netherlands, 1988, Denmark, 1989; Recorded with The Band in Woodstock, 1991; Worked with Lillian Boutté Musicfriends, Spirit of Louisiana Gospel Tour, including Gospel United with Stig Rossen, 1994; Gospel United Tour with Lillian Boutté, 1995. Recordings include: with Kenn Lending Blues Band: Live!, 1981; I'm Coming Home, 1983; Blues For People, 1985; Steamin' Hot, 1988; Diggin' The Blues, 1990; Heartache Motel, 1993; Game of Life, 1995; with Champion Jack Dupree: An Evening With Champion Jack Dupree, 1981; Still Fighting The Blues, 1981; I Had That Dream, 1982; Blues Is Freedom To All, 1987; Back Home In New Orleans, 1990; Forever and Ever, 1991; One Last Time, 1992; After All, 1994; Live Gospel United,

1994; Louisiana Spice: 25 Years of Louisiana Music, various artists, 1995; Gospel United, People Get Ready, 1995; High on the Hog, with The Band, 1996; Also recorded with: Memphis Slim; Louisiana Red; Mickey Baker; Aron Burton; Jan Harrington; Lillian Boutté. Honour: Danish Blues Musician of the Year, 1995. Memberships: The Danish Musicians Union; DJBFA; KODA. Hobbies: Birds (Parakeets); Reading (History, Philosophy, Literature). Current Management: Marsk Music. Address: Kenn Lending, Vendsysselvej 7, DK-2720 Copenhagen-Vanlose, Denmark.

LENGSTRAND Gert O, b. 30 May 1942, Gothenburg, Sweden. Songwriter; Publisher. m. Jeanette, 14 August 1987, 1 son, 4 daughters. Career: Singer, The Streaplers, Swedish pop group, 1957-68; Songwriter, Record Producer, 1969-. Compositions: Hasta La Vista, Silvia, 1974; Eloise, Arvingarna, 1993. Recordings: Diggity Doggerty, 1963; Rockin' Robin, 1965; Mule Skinner Blues, 1964. Honour: Ampex Golden Reel Award, Eloise, 1993. Hobbies: Sport; Music. Current Management: GL-Productions Ltd. Address: GL-Productions Ltd, PO Box 632, S-44217, Kungälv, Sweden.

LENGWINAT Katrin, b. 10 Dec 1960, Berlin, Germany. Musicologist. m. Eduardo Briceño, 16 Apr 1994, 1 son. Education: Bachelor degree; Dr phil, Musicology, Polish and German universities; Studied piano, guitar and folkharp. Career: Musicologist, Academy of Fine Arts, Berlin; Musicologist, FOundation of Ethnomusicology and Folklore, Caracas, Venezuela; Leader for Musicology, Free University of Berlin and Central University of Venezuela; Researcher of folk and popular music in Germany, Venezuela and Peru. Publications: Arpa, Maraca y Buche, 1998; Joropo Central, 1998. Membership: International Council for Traditional Music (ICTM). Address: Apdo post 40.052, 1040 Caracas, Venezuela.

LENNI, b. 17 Apr 41, Stalybridge, Cheshire, England. Musician (saxophone); Vocalist. m. Irene Dale, Mar 1963, 1 son. Musical Education: Theory, Composition, Arrangement. Career: Member, Gladiators, 1959; Corvettes, 1964; St Louis Union, 1965; Tony Christie's Band, 1968-70; Sad Cafe, 1979; Norman Beaker Band, 1986; Look Twice, 1987; Supercharge, 1990; Support tours with Carlos Santana; Toto; Otis Redding; Atlantic Star; Chuck Berry; American Bluesmen: Lowell Fulson; Phil Guy; Larry Garner; Louisianna Red; Johnny Mars; Rockin' Sidney; Also played for: Jack Bruce; Dave Dee; Kiki Dee; Vince Hill; Paul Jones; Lou Rawls; Lisa Stansfield; Alvin Stardust; Herbie Goins; Claire Moore; Gavin Sutherland; Victor Brox; Carl Wayne; When In Rome. Recordings: Sad Cafe (8 albums); Paul Jones R&B Show (3 albums); Norman Beaker Band (3 albums); Judy Boucher (2 albums); Also albums by Cannon & Ball; Magna Carta; Gilbert O'Sullivan; Eric Stewart; 10cc; Featured on television themes and radio commercials. Honours: Gold album, Facades; Silver album, Sad Cafe 4. Memberships: Musicians' Union; PAMRA; MENSA. Hobbies: Writing; Computing; Puzzles. Current Management: Actual Music. Address: 14A Moorside Road, Heaton Moor, Stockport, Cheshire SK4 4DT, England.

LENNON Julian, b. 4 Aug 1963, Liverpool, England. Singer; Songwriter; Musician. Recordings: Albums: Valotte, 1984; The Secret Value Of Daydreaming, 1986; Mr Jordan, 1989; Help Yourself, 1991; Singles include: Valotte; Too Late For Goodbyes; Now You're In Heaven; Salt Water. Address: c/o Solo-ITG Agency, 55 Fulham High Street, London SW6 3JJ, England.

LENNOX Annie, 25 Dec 1954, Aberdeen, Scotland. Singer; Lyricist. m. Rahda Raman, Mar 1984, div. Musical Education: Roy Acady Music. Career: Member, w Dave Stewart, The Catch, 1977; Re-named The Tourists, 1979-80; Formed

Eurhythmics w Dave Stewart, 1980-89; Worldwide concerts incl Nelson Mandela's 70th Birthday Tribute, Wembley, 1988; Solo artiste, 1988-; TV incls: Documentary, Diva, BBC2, 1992; Unplugged concert, MTV, 1992; Actress, film Revolution, 1985; 10 million albums sold to date. Creative works: Rcdngs: w the Tourists: The Tourists; Reality Affect; Luminous Basement; w Eurhythmics: In The Garden, 1982; Sweet Dreams (Are Made Of This), 1983; Touch (Number 1, UK), 1984; 1984 (For The Love Of Big Brother), 1984; Be Yourself Tonight, 1985; Revenge, 1986; Savage, 1988; We Too Are One (Number 1, UK), 1989; Eurhythmics Greatest Hits (Number 1, UK), 1991; Eurhythmics Live 1983-89, 1992; Solo: Diva (Number 1, UK), 1992; Medusa (Number 1, UK), 1995; Contbr: Red Hot And Blue, 1990; Rock The World, 1990; Hit singles incl: w the Tourists: I Only Want To Be With You, 1979; So Good To Be Back Home, 1979; w Eurhythmics: Sweet Dreams (Are Made Of This) (Number 1, US), 1983; Love Is A Stranger, 1983; Who's That Girl?, 1983; Right By Your Side, 1983; Here Comes The Rain Again, 1984; Sex Crime (1984), from film 1984, 1984; Would I Lie To You?, 1985; There Must Be An Angel (Playing With My Heart), (Number 1, UK), 1985; Sisters Are Doing It For Themselves, duet w Aretha Franklin, 1985; It's Alright (Baby's Coming Back), 1986; When Tomorrow Comes, 1986; Thorn In My Side, 1986; Missionary Man, 1986; You Have Placed A Chill In My Heart, 1988; Solo: Put A Little Love In Your Heart, w Al Green, from film soundtrack Scrooged, 1988; Why, 1992; Walking On Broken Glass, 1992; Little Bird/Love Song For A Vampire, from film Bram Stoker's Dracula, 1993; No More I Love You's, 1995; Whiter Shade Of Pale, 1995; Waiting In Vain, 1995; Something So Right, w Paul Simon, 1995; Videos: Eurhythmics Live; Sweet Dreams; Savage. Honours: Grammy Awds; BRIT Awds; Ivor Novello Awds; Rolling Stone Rdrs Poll Winner, Best Fem Singer, 1993. Address: 19 Management, Unit 32, Ransomes Dock, 35-37 Parkgate Road, London SW11 4NP, England.

LEON Craig, b. 7 Jan 1952, Miami, Florida, USA. Producer; Arranger; Composer; Recording Artist. m. Cassell Webb, 10 June, 1984. Recordings: 3 albums as featured artist: Nommos, 1981; Visiting, 1982; Klub Anima Theatre score, 1993; Premiered Bristol Old Vic theatre, 1993; 1 album in collaboration with Arthur Brown: Tape From Atoya, 1981; 5 albums in collaboration with Cassell Webb: Llano, 1985; Thief Of Sadness, 1987; Songs Of A Stranger, 1989; Conversations At Dawn, 1990; House Of Dreams, 1992; Producer, Ramones, 1976; Blondie, 1977; Suicide, 1977; Richard Hell, 1977; Rodney Crowell, 1980; Sir Douglas Quintet, 1980; The Bangles, 1983; The Roches, 1983; Dr and the Medics, 1986; The Pogues, 1986; The Primitives, 1986; Adult Net, 1988; The Fall, 1989-92; Jesus Jones, 1990; New FADS, 1992; Front 242, 1993; Eugenius, 1994; Angel Corpus Christi, 1995; Martin Phillips and the Chills, 1996; Mark Owen, 1996; Cobalt 60, 1996; Psyched Up Janis, 1997. Memberships: British Record Producer's Guild; Nominating Committee, The BRIT Awards. Hobbies: Book and wine collecting. Current Management: SJP/Dodgy Productions, 1 Prince of Wales Passage, 117 Hampstead Road, London NW1 3EF, England.

LEOPOLD Sinisa, b. 16 Apr 1957, Grubisno Polje, Croatia. Music Professor. m. Ljiljana Leopold (Rogic), 22 June 1985, 2 sons. Musical Education: Academy of Music. Career: Chief conductor, HRT Tambura Orchestra, 1985; Lecturer, Academy of Music, University of Zagreb, 1986-; Conductor, Ferdo Livadic Tambura Orchestra, Samobor, 1985. Recordings: Many compositions, arrangements for Tambura Orchestras. Publications: Tambura School T, 1992; Tambura Among Croatians, 1995. Honours: Croatian Discography Award: Porin 95; Many awards at festivals. Memberships: Croatian Sociaety of Composers; Croatian Folklore Society.

Hobbies: Bicycling; Travel. Address: Rapska 37A, 41000 Zagreb, Croatia.

LEPALLEC Bernard, b. 20 Dec 1951, Paris, France. Musician (saxophone). 2 daughters. Education: Doctorate of Philosophy, Sorbonne, Paris. Musical Education: Self-taught. Career: Composer, saxophone player, inprovised music; Member, jazz band Ar Jazz; Playing improvised and celtic traditional music concerts in France; Poland; Italy; Greece. Recordings: Album: Band Ar Jazz, Bernard Lepallec. Membership: SACEM. Hobby: Yachting. Address: 6 Chemin de Goas Meur, 22500 Paimpol, France.

LEROY Christian, b. 23 November 1952. Composer; Musician (pianist). m. Nathalie Cuvelier, 2 sons. Education: General electronic studies; Drums; Also self-taught. Career: Composed works for RTBF Programme 3; Works for theatre plays including Le Monde est Rond, Le Baiser de la Femme Araignée, Le Roi et le Cadavre, The Merchant of Venice; Works with Sanobro Somari, Bram Bogart, Miguel Berrocal and others; Member of Métarythmes de l'Air musical group and Piano Kvartet, group of 4 pianists. Compositions: Le 37 Janvier, opera; Music for Dracula, film of Tod Browning; Music for Robert Flaherty's Nanouk the Eskimo; Images du Tarot, recorded. Recordings: Métarythmes de l'Air; Piano Duet with Fred Von Hove; Phagocyte; 33 Petits Tours; Le Temps Qui Passe; Les Chemins de Lumière; La Roue des Corps; Le Temps des Sabbats; The Merchant of Venice; Mystères d'un Théâtre et d'une Vie. Honours: Prix de Hainaut, 1982; Special Mention for Film Music, Caracas, 1983; Prix de la Presse, SPA Festival. Hobbies: Gardens; Going for walks. Address: 8 Rue des Berceaux, 7061 Castgeau, Belgium.

LESKANICH Katrina, b. 1960, Topeka, Kansas, USA. Singer. Career: Lead singer, Katrina and the Waves, 1982-. Recordings: Albums: Walking On Sunshine, 1983; Katrina And The Waves 2, 1984; Katrina And The Waves, 1985; Break Of Hearts, 1989; Hit singles: Walking On Sunshine, 1985; Going Down To Liverpool (later recorded by the Bangles), 1985; Sun Street, 1986. Address: c/o Jason West Agency, Gables House, Saddlebow, Kings Lynn, Norfolk PE34 3AR, England.

LESLEY Irene, b. Harrow, England. Singer. m. (1) Ralph Monk, 5 Sept 1969, 1 son, 2 daughters; m. (2) Anthony P W Bushe, 1 Aug 1993. Education: RGN; RNT; Cert ED. Musical Education: Stage school: Singing, dance, acting, associated skills. Career: Formerly, nurse, nurse tutor; Singer with own backing band, Hot Toddy, formed 1992; Appearances in numerous clubs, concerts, theatre, tours, festivals, UK, Europe; Session recording works; Support to Moe Brandy; Roy Drusky; Dottsy, UK tour, 1981; Currently working UK, Europe, Ireland. Recordings: Cover Your Tracks, 1993. Membership: Musicians' Union. Hobbies: Guitar; Skiing; Motor racing. Current Management: H T Promotions. Address: Villard, 87370, Bersac sur Rivalier, France.

LESLIE Graeme, b. 9 Jun 1965, Ormskirk, Lancashire, England. Singer; Musician (guitar). Career: Lead singer, guitarist with band Stairway. Recordings: with Stairway: Last Ship Home, 1991; No Rest - No Mercy, 1993. Membership: PRS; Musicians' Union. Hobby: Writing poetry. Current Management: J Nelson. Address: 18 Forest Road, Oldbury, Worcestershire B68 0EE, England.

LESTER Gregory, b. Brighton, England. Musician (guitar). Musical Education: Self-taught; Later, studied classical guitar. Career: Tours, recording and radio/television appearances with: Julia Fordham; Des'ree; Danielle Gaha; John O'Kane; Joe Roberts; Sylvia Powell; Concerts include: with John O'Kane: support to Sting, Soul Cages tour, UK/European legs; with Des'ree: Summer festivals at Wembley Stadium, Old Trafford, Gateshead International; Tour of Japan; Radio and television appearances with the above, and Kindred Spirit; 25th of May; Kim Appleby; Shania Twain; Recordings: Numerous sessions include: Adam F, Aco, The Collective, Sunscream; A Matter Of Time, Sandy Lam; Jimmy Somerville; Gangstarr; Pop Will Eat Itself; Des'ree; Barry Adamson; Peace And Joy, 2 Become 1, Mama, Spice Girls; Love City Groove; Maria Rowe; EYC; London Beat; Nightcrawlers; Freaky Realistic; Sylvia Powell; Dave Stewart; Definition Of Sound; Whitney Houston; Other tracks with artistes including: Joe Roberts; Kylie Minogue; Lush Life; Azizi; Karl Keaton; Monie Love; Atlantique; Workshy; Worlds Apart; Danielle Gaha; Everything But The Girl; Adeva; Tom Robinson; Tyrell Corporation; Alison Limerick; Blade; Live long-play video: Porcélain - Live In Concert, Julia Fordham. Music for television commercials; Television music includes: My Boy, Channel 4; Theme music for The Beat; Painted Lady (Granada TV). Honours: BPI Awards: Platinum, 3, for Spice Girls, Gold, for Kylie Minogue and EBTG, Silver, for Des'ree. Memberships: PRS; Musicians' Union. Address: 18A Southampton Road, London NW5 4HX, England.

LETLEY Matthew, b. 29 Mar 1961, Gillingham, Kent, London. Musician (drums). m. Valerie Hill, 1 May 1982, 2 daughters. Education: Rochester Mathematical School, Kent. Musical Education: Private tuition, Graham Willard, Bob Cleall. Career: Tours, UK or world with: Judie Tzuke, 1983, 1985; Elkie Brooks, 1984; Kim Wilde, 1986; Bob Geldof, 1987-90; A-Ha, 1988-89; David Essex, 1990-97; Vanessa Mae, 1995-97; Hank Marvin, 1997. Membership: Musicians' Union. Address: Cone Tree House, Beckenham, Kent BR3 4DZ, England.

LEURS Lawrence, b. 9 July 1965, Bree, Belgium. Singer; Songwriter; Musician (Guitar). m. Peeters Saskia, 11 June 1994. Education: Licentiate in History, University of Brussels; Degree, Academy of Word and Music Maaseik, Belgium. Recordings: Albums: Ball and Chain, 1989; Trigger Happy, 1990; Major Panic, 1993; Be My Star, 1996. Membership: ZAMU, Union of Musical Artists Belgium. Current Managements: L&S Agency, Postbox, 3800 St Truiden, Belgium. Address: Koningin Astridlaan 37, 3680, Maaseik, Belgium.

LEVAN Christophe, b. 29 Dec 1959, Marseilles, France. Musician (contrabass, bass guitar). 1 son. Education: Dental studies, Marseilles. Musical Education: Self-taught. Career: Concerts with: Michel Legrand; Michel Portal; Chet Baker; Sonny Stitt; Phil Woods; Peter King; Dee Dee Bridgewater; Nicole Croisille; Television and radio broadcasts include: Françaises Variétés et Jazz; Radio France; France Musique. Recordings: About 20 records include: Swinging Marilyn, Gerard Badini Swing Machine; Debussy Meets Mister Swing, Gerard Badini Big Band; Chassaguite Quartet; Johnny Griffin et Hervé Sellin' Sextet; Tribute To Jazz Michel Gaucher. Membership: Syndicate des Musiciens. Hobbies: Fishing; Sculpture; Drawing. Address: 30 Rue de Musselburgh, 94500 Champigny-sur-Marne, France.

LEVIEV Milcho, b. 19 Dec 1937, Plovdiv, Bulgaria. Composer; Musician (piano); Arranger; Conductor. m. Deborah Rothschild, 19 July 1990, 1 daughter. Musical Education: Masters in Composition, Bulgarian State Conservatory, 1960. Career: Conductor, Bulgarian Radio and TV Pop Orchestra, 1962-66; Composer, Bulgarian Feature Film Studios, 1963-69; Arranger, Radio Frankfurt, 1970; Pianist, composer, arranger, Don Ellis Orchestra, Billy Cobham Band, Art Pepper Quartet; Music Director, Lanie Kazan Show; Co-leader, Free Flight quartet; Lecturer, University of Southern California. Compositions: Concerto For Jazz Combo And Strings; Music For Big Band And Symphony Orchestra; Sympho-Jazz Sketches; Orpheus Rhapsody for Piano and Orchestra; The Green House - Jazz Cantata; Film and Theatre Music. Recordings: Over 35 records under own name and over 50 records as a sideman. Honours: Grammy Nomination, Best Vocal Arranger, 1981; Doctor Honoris Causa, Music Academy in Plovdiv, 1995. Memberships: AFofM; NARAS; BMI; GEMA. Hobbies: Swimming; Hiking. Current Management: Deborah Rothschild. Address: 12027 Califa Str, North Hollywood, CA 91607, USA.

LEVY Henry (Hank), b. 27 Sept 1927, Baltimore, Maryland, USA. Teacher; Composer; Arranger. m. Gloria Hidebrand, 14 Aug 1960. Education: BA, Composition. Career: Writer for Don Ellis Band, 1965-78; Writer for Stan Kenton Orchestra, 1968-1979; Compositions found on all Kenton and Ellis recordings; Many concerts with above bands, also Jazz Ensemble for school; Taught jazz courses, Towson State University, 23 years; Clinics all over the country; Commissions to write extended works for symphony orchestra, jazz ensemble. Publications: All music written, orchestrated for Ellis and Kenton and schools; Over 100 pieces published. Honour: Professor Emeritus. Hobby: Golf. Address: 1504 Melton Road, Lutherville, MD 21093, USA.

LEVY Rick, b. 1 November 1949, Allentown, PA, USA. Musician (Guitar); Manager; Songwriter. m. Leiza Levy, 2 December 1991, 1 son. Education: BA, Sociology, University of Pennsylvania, 1971; Education Degree, Moravian College, 1985; Guitar lessons, 5 years; Berklee School of Music, 1 year. Career: Tour US with Jay and The Techniques, 1985-; Manager, Jay and The Techniques; The Box Tops; Performed at Rock 'n' Roll Hall of Fame, September 1996; Pres: Rick Levy Management, Flying Governor Music, Luxury Records. Composition: Rock Roots, History of American Pop Music. Recordings: Love's Just Not For Sale; Ricochet Waltz. Honour: Penna-Broadcasters Association, Rock Roots, Best Single, Children's Program, 1992. Membership: NARAS. Hobbies: Running; Pottery. Current Management: Rick Levy Management, 2356 Commodore's Club Boulevard, St Augustine, FL 32084, USA.

LEWIN Giles, b. Rayleigh, Essex, England. Musician (fiddle, medieval bagpipes, recorders, shawn); Vocalist. Education: Music, Cambridge University. Musical Education: Violin, flute, viol, at school. Career: Member, The Dufay Collective; Plays with: The New London Consort; The Chuckerbutty Ocarina Quartet; Lost Jockey; Afterhours; Music director, The Medieval Players, tours worldwide; Student of Egyptian Fiddle styles and culture; Member, The Carnival Band, 1984-; Appearances include: Glasgow Cathedral; Birmingham Symphony Hall; Barbican Centre; Numerous Arts theatres and festivals; Plays material from: Sweden; Croatia; US; Bolivia; Spain; UK; France. Current Management: c/o Jim McPhee, Acorn Entertainments. Address: Winterfold House, 46 Woodfield Road, Kings Heath, Birmingham B13 9UJ, England.

LEWINSON Stephen Owen Lloyd, b. 19 Feb 1966, Coventry, England. Musician (bass). Education: Accountancy, University level. Career: Tours with: Phil Bent Quartet, 1989; Reggae Philharmonic Orchestra, 1990-91; Courtney Pine, 1991-92; Steve Williamson, 1992; Bomb The Bass, 1992; Tim Finn, 1992; Tom Browne, 1992; Nelson Rangell, 1992; Rebirth Of The Cool, 1992; Juliet Roberts, 1993; Ronny Jordan world tour, 1993-94; Tony Remy, Mica Paris, Boy George, Orphy Robinson, Massive Attack world tour, 1995; Simply Red world tour, 1995-96. Membership: PRS. Current Management: Timeless Music Ltd. Address: 38 Coolhurst Road, London N8, England.

LEWIS David A R, b. 15 Feb 1964, Morecambe, Lancashire, England. Songwriter;

Composer; Musician (guitar). m. Andrea Lewis, 20 Sept 1992. Musical Education: J L Academy. Career: Appearances on National and Granada TV; Single of the Week, Red Rose, Lancashire, Capital; Extensive touring throughout UK; Support to Blur at pop club; Support to Youssou N'Dour, Womad Festival, 1992. Compositions include: Independence Day; The Other Side; This Is England; Sunday; Revolution. Recordings: Jerusalem; Maralyn; Treason. Membership: Musicians' Union. Hobbies: Skiing; Soccer. Current Management: Ice Factory (Management) Co Ltd. Address: Ice Factory (Managament) Co Ltd, c/o John Lewis, 253 Marine Road, Morecambe, Lancashire LA4 4BJ, England.

LEWIS Huey (Hugh Cregg III), b. 5 July 1950, New York, USA. Singer; Musician; Actor; Songwriter. Career: Member, Clover, 1976-79; Founder, Huey Lewis and The News, 1979-; Major concerts include: Over 30 US and Canadian tours; Notable concerts include: Madison Square Gardens, New York, Superdrome, New Orleans, attendance set at numerous venues including: Poplar Creek Amphitheatre, Illinois, Alpine Valley Amphitheatre, Wisconsin, Summerfest, Milwaukee; 7 European tours; 4 Japan Tours; 1 Australia tour; Film appearances: Back to the Futute, 1985; Short Cuts, 1993; Sphere, 1998. Recordings: Albums: with Clover: Clover, 1977; Love on the Wire, 1977; with Huey Lewis and the News: Huey Lewis and the News, 1980; Picture This, 1982; Sports, 1983; Fore!, 1986; Small World, 1988; Hard at play, 1991; Four Chords and Several Years Ago, 1994; Time Flies (Best of), 1996; Singles include: Do You Believe in Love, 1982; Workin' for a Livin', 1982; Heart and Soul, 1983; I Want a New Drug, 1983; The Heart of Rock 'n Roll, 1984; If This Is It, 1984; Walking on a Thin Line, 1984; The Power of Love (No 1, US), 1985; Stuck With You, (No 1 US), 1986; Hip to be Square, 1986; Jacob's Ladder (No 1 US), 1987; Doing It All For My Baby, 1987; I Know What I Like, 1987; Perfect World, 1988; Small World Pt 1 and 2 (featuring Sam Getz), 1988; Give Me the Keys, 1988; Couple Days Off, 1991; It hit Me Like a Hammer, 1991; He Don't Know, 1991; It'a Alright (A capella from People Get Ready, tribute album to Curtis Mayfield), 1993; Some Kind of Wonderful, 1994; But It's Alright, 1994; Little Bitty Pretty One, 1994; Contributor to We Are the World, USA for Africa recording, 1985; Numerous movie videos. Honours: American Music Awards: Favourite Single, 1986, Favourite Band, 1987; Academy Awards, Power of Love, Nominee, song from a movie, 1986; British Music Awards, Best International Group, 1986.

LEWIS Jerry Lee, b. 29 Sept 1935, Ferriday, Louisiana, USA. Singer; Musician (piano); Entertainer. m. 6 times. Career: Appeared on Louisiana Hayride, 1954; Film appearances: Jamboree, 1957; High School Confidential, 1958; Be My Guest, 1965; Concerts include: National Jazz & Blues Festival, 1968; Rock'n'Revival Concert, Toronto, 1969; First appearance, Grand Ole Opry, 1973; Rock'n'Roll Festival, Wembley, 1974; Numerous appearances with own Greatest Show On Earth; Subject of biographical film, Great Balls Of Fire, 1989. Recordings: Hit singles include: Whole Lotta Shakin' Goin' On', 1957; Great Balls Of Fire, 1958; Breathless, 1958; High School Confidential, 1958; What I'd Say, 1961; Good Golly Miss Molly, 1963; To Make Love Sweeter For You, 1969; There Must Be More To Love Than This, 1970; Would You Take Another Chance On Me?, 1971; Me And Bobby Gee, 1972; Chantilly Lace, 1972. Albums include: Jerry Lee Lewis, 1957; Jerry Lee's Greatest, 1961; Live At The Star Club, 1965; The Greatest Live Show On Earth, 1965; The Return Of Rock, 1965; Whole Lotta Shakin' Goin' On, 1965; Country Songs For City Folks, 1965; By Request - More Greatest Live Show On Earth, 1967; Breathless, 1967; Together, with Linda Gail Lewis, 1970; Rockin' Rhythm And Blues, 1971; Sunday Down South, with Johnny Cash, 1972; The Session, with Peter Frampton,

Rory Gallagher, 1973; Jerry Lee Lewis, 1979; When Two Worlds Collide, 1980; My Fingers Do The Talking, 1983; I Am What I Am, 1984; Keep Your Hands Off It, 1987; Don't Drop It, 1988; Great Balls Of Fire! (film soundtrack), 1989; Rocket, 1990; Young Blood, 1995; Many compilations; Contributor, film soundtracks: Roadie, 1980; Dick Tracy, 1990. Honours include: Inducted into Rock'n' Roll Hall Of Fame, 1986; Star on Hollywood Walk Of Fame, 1989. Current Management: Al Embry International, PO Box 23162, Nashville, TN 37202, USA. Address: The Lewis Ranch, Box 384, Nesbit, MS 38651, USA.

LEWIS Laurie, b. 28 Sept 1950, Long Beach, California, USA. Musician (fiddle, guitar, bass); Vocalist; Singer; Songwriter. Musical Education: Traditional knowledge, skills passed on within folk/old time music community in oral tradition. Career: Performing, touring nationally, internationally since early 1970s; Television appearances: Music City Tonight, TNN; The Grand Ole Opry; The American Music Shop; Lonesome Pine Specials, PBS, Later with Jool, BBC; Prairie Home Companion, NPR; Mountain Stage; World Cafe. Recordings: Restless Rambling Heart; Love Chooses You; Singing My Troubles Away; Together (with Kathy Kallick); True Stories; The Oak And The Laurel; Earth & Sky: SOngs of Laurie Lewis. Honours: NAIRD Award, Best Country Album; IBMA Awards, Female Vocalist of The Year, 1992, 1994; Song Of The Year, 1994; Grammy Nomination, Traditional Folk Album, The Oak and the Laurel. Memberships: ASCAP; International Bluegrass Music Association. Hobbies: Running; Riding; River rafting. Current Management: Cash Edwards, Under The Hat Productions. Address: 1121-B Bluebonnet Lane, Austin, TX 78704, USA.

LEWIS Linda, b. 27 Sept 1953, London, England. Singer; Songwriter; Musician (guitar, piano). m. Jim Cregan, 18 Mar 1977 (div), 1 son. Musical Education: Peggy O'Farrels Stage School. Career: Toured with Cat Stevens, Elton John and Richie Havens, 1970's; Appeared at first Glastonbury Festival; Television appearances include: In Concert; Old Grey Whistle Test; Supersonic; Top Of The Pops; numerous others. Recordings: Albums: Say No More; Lark; Fathoms Deep; Not A Little Girl Any More (featuring Luther Vandross, Lowell George, Denise Williams); Woman Overboard; Second Nature, 1995; Whatever, 1998; Also appeared on: Aladdin Sane, David Bowie; Do You Think I'm Sexy, Rod Stewart; recordings by Family and Steve Harley. Honours: Saturday Scene British Pop Award, 1975. Memberships: PRS; Equity. Hobbies: Movies; Reading (biographies, self-awareness); Walking in countryside. Current Management: Don Gallaher Media Management. Address: 26 Weymouth Mews, London W1N, England.

LEWIS Monica, b. 5 May, Chicago, IL, USA. Singer. m. Jennings Lang, 1 Jan 1956. Musical Education: Taught by mother (opera singer) and by father (conductor, composer, pianist). Career: Radio appearances, recording artist, personal appearances, TV shows and films. Recordings: Numerous recordings including, I Wish You Love, 1956. Honour: 1st GRAMMY Award. Address: 1100 Alto Louea Road, Los Angeles, CA 90069, USA.

LEWIS Pamela, b. 23 Nov 1958, Rhinebeck, New York, USA. Public Relations/Marketing Consultant; Media Executive. Education: BA, Wells College. Musical Education: Leadership Music. Career: CEO, founder, PLA Media, Los Angeles, Nashville; NBC Specials: This Is Garth Brooks; This Is Garth Brooks Too; 7-year career as manager to Garth Brooks, including International World Tour, 1993-94. Publications: Dan Rivers Poetry Anthology, American Poetry Anthology. Honours: Pollstar Manager of The Year, 1991, 1992; Performance Manager of Year, 1992, 1993; CMA Manager of Year, 1991.

Hobbies: Gardening; Horseback riding; Canning; Herbal vinegars; Writing; Gourmet cooking; Skiing; Travel. Current Management: Consulting - Winter Harvest Entertainment (Steve Earle). Address: 1303 16th Avenue South, Nashville, TN 37212, USA.

LEWIS Shari, b. 17 Jan 1933, New York, USA. Entertainer, Ventriloquist; Musician (instruments, piano, violin). m. Jeremy P Tarcher, 15 Mar 1958, 1 daughter. Musical Education: Private lessons, piano and voice, High School of Music and Art, New York City; Violin and conducting lessons with Stormy Sacks. Career: Shari Lewis Show, 1960-63; Lamb Chop's Play Along, PBS; Command performances before Queen Elizabeth II, Performances at White House for past 5 Presidents. Recordings: One Minute Bedtime Stories, 1986; Shari On Storyland, 1962; Fun In Shari Land, 1958; Created 24 musical home videos. Publications: Over 60 books; 2 CD-Roms. Honours: 11 Emmys; Gold, New York Film Festival; 8 Parent Choice Awards; A Gemini Award; 3 Grammy Nominations; Peabody Award, 1960; Monte-Carlo Prize - World's Best Television Variety Show, 1963; Kennedy Center Award for Creativity in the Arts, 1983; Recording Industry of America Association certified Gold for 4 A&M videos, 1992; Critics Choice, CD ROM Today, Lamb Chop Loves Music CD-Rom, 1995; Film Advisory Board Award of Excellence, 1996; Distinguished Artist Award, Music Center of Los Angeles Count, 1996. Memberships: Music Educators National Committee; Member of Advisory Council. Current Management: Jim Golden/GTA, 3128 Cavendish, Los Angeles, CA 90064, USA. Address: Shari Lewis Enterprises, 603 Alta Drive, Beverly Hills, CA 90210, USA.

LEWIS Shaznay T, b. 1977. Singer; Songwriter. Career: Founding member, female vocal group All Saints, 1993-. Recordings: Singles: Silver Shadow; I Know Where It's At; Never Ever (Number 1, UK); Debut album: All Saints. Honours include: Brit Award, Best Single. Current Management: John Benson.

LEWIS Terry, b. USA. Record Producer. Career: Founder member, Flyte Time, 1972-; Joined by Jimmy Jam, become backing band for Morris Day, renamed The Time, 1981-1983; Formed Flyte Tyme Productions with Jerry Jam, 1982-; Built Flyte Tyme Studios, Minneapolis, 1984-85; Found own label (with Jerry Jam), Perspective Records, 1991; Helped launch new acts including Sounds Of Blackness; Involved with International Association of African American Music (IAAAM), 1990-. Recordings: As co-producer with Jimmy Jam: Wild Girls, Klymaxx, 1983; Just Be Good To Me, SOS Band, 1983; Heat Of The Heart, Patti Austin; Encore, Cheryl Lynn; I Didn't Mean To Turn You On, Cherelle; Saturday Love, Cherelle and Alexander O'Neal; Runaway, Janet Jackson; The Best Things In Life Are Free Janet Jackson and Luther Vandross; Albums with Janet Jackson: Control; Rhythm Nation; Janet (all Number 1, US); Other recordings with: Mint Condition; Low Key; Sounds Of Blackness; George Michael; Karyn White; Boyz II Men; Johnny Gill; New Edition; Fine Young Cannibals; Film soundtrack, Mo' Money, 1993. Honours include: R&B Songwriting Awards, American Society Of Composers And Publishers, 1989-1994. Address: c/o Perspective Records, 1416 N La Brea Avenue, Hollywood, CA 90028, USA.

LEWIS JR Ramsey E, b. 27 May 1935, Chicago, Illinois, USA. Musician (piano). m. Janet Tamillon, 10 June 1990, 5 sons, 2 daughters (from previous marriage). Education: College, 1955-57. Musical Education: Chicago Musical College, 1955-56. Career: Performed, nightclubs, concerts, festivals, in USA, Canada, Western Europe, Japan, Mexico, The Caribbean, 1957-; Also with symphony orchestras; Host, weekly syndicated radio program; Host 1 hour weekly segment,

BET's Jazz Central. Recordings: Over 60 albums include: The Incrowd, 1965; Sun Goddess, 1974; 3 latest recordings: Ivory Pyramid, 1992; Sky Islands, 1993; Urban Knights, 1995. Honours: Honorary doctorates: Depaul University, 1993; University of Illinois, Chicago, 1995; White House State Dinner Performance, 1995; 3 Grammy Awards; 5 Gold records. Membership: Ravinia Artistic Director, Jazz Series. Hobbies: Reading; Film going. Current Management: Andi Howard, Gardner Howard Ringe Entertainment. Address: 16601 Ventura Boulevard, Suite #506, Encino, CA 91436, USA.

LEYERS Jan, b. 16 May 1958, Antwerp, Belgium. Vocalist; Musician (guitar, bass keyboards); Composer. Career: Soul Sister. Compositions: Billboard Hot Country Chart, 1995; Soulsister - Repertoire, Tom Jones; The Way to Your Heart; That's As Close as I'll Get to Loving You. Recordings: Soulsister: It Takes Two; Heat; Simple Rule; Live Savings; Swinging Like Big Dogs; The Very Best; My Velma: Exposed. Honours: World Music Award, Monaco, 1990; Jozef Platteau, 1991; BMI Country Award, 1996; Golden 006 Award, 1992, 1993. Membership: SABAM. Hobby: Music. Current Management: Johan P Berckmans. Address: Aarschotsesteenweg 245, B-3012, Leuven, Belgium.

LIANA (Liana C Di Marco), b. 25 Mar 1966, Toronto, Ontario, Canada. Singer; Songwriter; Musician (guitar); Multi-media Artist. Education: BA, Social Science, with Honours. Musical Education: Private instruction with leading vocalists and instrumentalists. Career: Played viola in two local orchestras prior to 1986; Solo career as singer, songwriter, 1988-; Business ventures: LCDM Entertainments Productions, music label, and Indie Tips and The Arts, publications. Recordings include: Glitters And Tumbles, 1993; Songs published: Degree In Love; Sweep Me Off My Feet; By My Side; Glitters And Tumbles; You'll Never Know; Boom; Non Fa Differenza Dove Vai; Thinking Of You; Country Funky. Publications: Indie Tips and The Arts. Honours: Awards in Music, Journalism, French and Cinematography. Memberships: CCMA; SAC; Theatre Ontario; UGA. Hobbies: Ceramics; Canvas painting; Collections; Squash; Dance. Current Management: CAG Consultants; LCDM Entertainment. Address: Box 79564, 1995 Weston Road, Weston, Ontario M9N 3W9, Canada.

LIDDIARD Brenda Christine, b. 14 Feb 1950, Essex, England. Writer; Performer; Musician (guitar, mandolin, keyboards). m. Mark Clive Laurent, 4 Aug 1990, 1 stepson, 1 daughter. Musical Education: Piano, to Grade 6. Career: Played in bands, duos, solos, 1978-; Major performances: UN Environmental Song Festival, Bangkok, 1988; Concert For The Living Earth, Auckland, 1989; QE II Arts Council, 6 week New Zealand tour, 1990; Shelterbelt Festival, 1993; Parachute Festival, 1994, 1995; Garth Hewitt, UK support, 1995; Auckland Folk Festival, 1993-95; Session player, recording, concerts. Recordings: Land Of Plenty, Spangled Drongoes, 1985; Songs For Our Friends, with Mark Laurent, 1989; Songs of Protest And Survival, 1991; For The River, Save The Daintree, featured on award winning documentary, Earth First. Honours: Winner, UN Asia Pacific Environmental Song Contest, 1988. Memberships: NZ Composers Foundation; APRA (Australian Performing Rights Society). Hobbies: Gardening; Walking; Reading. Current Management: Mark Laurent, Brenda Liddiard. Address: 21 Parkfield Terrace, Grafton, Auckland, New Zealand.

LIEBMAN David, b. 4 September 1946, Brooklyn, New York, USA. Musician (Saxophone); Composer; Teacher. m. Caris Visentin, 30 October, 1986, 1 daughter. Education: BSc, New York University, USA; Studied with Joseph Allard, Lennie Tristano and Charles Lloyd. Compositions:

200 original compositions. Recordings: On the Corner, Miles Davis; Live at the Lighthouse, Elvin Jones; Lookout Farm, D Liebman; Homage To Coltrane, D Liebman; Long Distance Runner, D Liebman; West Side Story, D Liebman; New Vista, D Liebman. Publications: Developing A Personal Saxophone Sound, 1989; A Chromatic Approach to Jazz, 1991; Self Portrait of a Jazz Artist, 1996; Jazz Connections, Miles Davis and David Liebman, 1996. Honours: Group Deserving of Wider Recognition Downbeat Magazine, 1976; Honorary Doctorate, Sibelius Academy, Helsinki, 1997; Composer Grant, National Endowment of the Arts. Memberships: Artistic Director, International Association of School of Jazz; BMI; SPEDIDAM; Gramex; Naras. Hobby: Reading. Current Management: Artradia Jazz, 34 E 23rd Street, New York, NY, USA. Address: Rd 7, Box 7621G, Stroudsburg, PA 18360, USA.

LIEVEMAA Tommi Tapani, b. 10 Dec 1966, Uusikaupunki, Finland. Musician (electric, acoustic guitar, mandolin). Education: Commercial School, Finland, 1982-86. Musical Education: Jazz, rock guitar, theory studies, Jyvaskyla School Of Music, 1986-89; Jazz Course, Guildhall School Of Music and Drama, London 1993-1994. Career: Constant touring, Finland, with Ohilyönti, 1986-1993; With Dixie Fred, 1987-1992; Tour with Finnish pop star, Katri-Helena, 1992; National Jazz Competition, Finland, with Sale's Promotion, 1986; International Jazz Competition, Spain, Getxo, with John Crawford Group, 1994; Television appearances, Finnish TV, include: Documentary about recording process, Dixie Fried's first album, Channel 1, 1988; Pop Panel, with Dixie Fried, Channel 1, 1988; Nightline, Dixie Fried, Channel 2; Kaikki on Korassa, with Estonian Television, 1990; Haapaves: Folk Festival, Channel 2, 1991; Very many radio appearances. Recordings: Dixie Fried albums: Dixie Fried, 1988; Six Dicks Of Dynamite, 1990; New Deal, 1991; Ohilyonti: OHOH, 1989; Himmeneuva Q, 1989; Sandels On, 1989; Markan Possu, 1990; Soita Soita, 1990; On Karhut Noussect Juhlimaan, 1992; Ankkapaallikko Anna Liisa, 1993; with R Keskinin & Co: Kapteeni, 1993; Charity album, Valaiskoon (with various Finnish stars), 1993; High Register Orchestra, Jühtü, 1993. Honours: First Prize, National Children's Song Contest, Finland, 1990, 1991. Memberships: Musicians' Union, London. Hobbies: Travel; Cooking; Arts. Address: Ylinenkatu 44 A 8, 23500 Uusikaupunki, Finland.

LIFESON Alex, b. 27 Aug 1953, Fernie, Canada. Musician (guitar). Career: Guitarist, founder member, Canadian rock group Rush, 1969-; Concerts include: worldwide tours, 1974-; Sellout concerts include Madison Square Garden, New York; Maple Leaf Gardens, Toronto; Wembley Arena, London; Also member of side-project Victor, 1995-. Recordings: Albums: with Rush: Rush, 1969; Fly By Night, 1975; Caress Of Steel, 1975; 2112, 1976; All The World's A Stage, 1976; A Farewell To Kings, 1977; Archives, 1978; Hemisphere, 1978; Permanent Waves, 1980; Moving Pictures, 1981; Exit... Stage Left, 1981; Great White North, 1982; Grace Under Pressure, 1984; Power Windows, 1985; Hold Your Fire, 1987; A Show Of Hands, 1989; Presto, 1989; Chronicles, 1990; Roll The Bones, 1991; with Victor: Victor, 1996; Singles include: with Rush: Spirit Of Radio; Tom Sawyer; New World Man; Closer To The Heart; Countdown; The Big Money; Time Stand Still. Honours: JUNO Awards: Most Promising Group, 1975; Best Group, 1978-79; Group named Official Ambassadors Of Music, Canadian Government, 1979; Gold Ticket Award, Madison Square Garden, 1991. Current Management: Anthem Entertainment, 189 Carlton Street, Toronto, ON M5A 2K7, Canada.

LIGGINS 'The Legendary' Len, b. 9 Feb 1957, London, England. Singer; Songwriter; Musician (guitar, violin, bass). Education: BA (Hons) Russian Studies, Universiy of Leeds.

Career: Solo artist, 1984-; Lead singer, guitarist for: The Sinister Cleaners, 1984-1987; Lead singer, fiddle, balalaika and sopilka player, Ukrainian line-up of: The Wedding Present, 1987-1989; Lead singer, fiddle player for The Ukrainians, 1991-. Recordings: Solo: A Remedy For Bad Nerves, 1985; The Sinister Cleaners: Lemon Meringue Bedsit, 1985; The Wedding Present: Ukrainski Vistupi V Johna Peela, 1988; The Ukrainians: Pisni Iz The Smiths, 1993; Vorony, 1993; The Ukrainians: Kultura, 1994. Current Management: c/o 23 Lushington Road, London NW10 5UX, England.

LIGHTFOOT Gordon Meredith, b. 17 Nov 1938, Orilla, Ontario, Canada. Singer; Songwriter. m. Elizabeth Moon. Musical Education: Westlake College of Music, Los Angeles, 1958. Career: Singer, songwriter, 1959-; Member, Swinging Singing Eight (square-dance ensemble), Canada; Folk duo Two Tones, 1960; Solo artiste, 1961-; Major concerts include: Town Hall, New York, 1967; Royal Festival Hall, 1969; Bob Dylan's Rolling Thunder Review, 1976; Westbury Music Fair, Westbury, New York, 1989; Carnegie Hall, 1991; Television appearances include: Host, BBC series, 1963; Let's Sing Out, CTV, 1963; Film appearance: Harry Tracy, 1982. Compositions include: Early Morning Rain (recorded by Peter Paul & Mary); Ribbon Of Darkness (Number 1, Country charts, for Marty Robbins); If You Could Read My Mind; Canadian Railroad Trilogy; Sundown; Carefree Highway; Race Among The Ruins; The Wreck Of The Edmund Fitzgerald. Recordings: Albums: Lightfoot, 1965; The Way I Feel, 1967; Did She Mention My Name; Back Here On Earth; Sunday Concert; If You Could Read My Mind, 1971; Summer Side Of Life; Classic Lightfoot, 1971; Don Quixote, 1972; Old Dan's Records, 1972; Sundown, 1974; The Very Best Of..., 1974; Cold On The Shoulder, 1975; Gord's Gold, 1976; Summertime Dream, 1976; Endless Wire, 1978; Dream Street Rose, 1980; The Best Of..., 1982; Shadows, 1982; Salute, 1985; East Of Midnight, 1986; The Original Lightfoot, 1992; Waiting For You, 1993. Honours: Numerous awards include: Order of Canada, 1970; Juno Hall of Fame, 1986; Juno Gold Leaf Awards; Gold and Platinum discs; Canadian Male Artist of Decade, 1980. Current Management: Early Morning Productions, 1365 Yonge Street, Suite 207, Toronto, Ontario M4T 2P7, Canada.

LILLELUND Ole (Billi Skiit), b. 18 Oct 1942, Odense, Denmark. Singer; Lyricist; Teacher; Interpreter; Poet; Actor. Divorced, 1 son, 2 daughters. Education: University teacher, Malay and Nepalese studies, Copenhagen, Yogyakarta and Kathmandu. Musical Education: Self-taught. Career: Videos: Heisse Irma, Billi Skiit, 1985; Live, Infernal Machine, 1989; White Peril, Sound Addicts, 1990. Compositions: Lyrics for singles: Humla Jumla, 1984; Billi Skiit, 1984; Hot Nuts, 1984; Albums: Jaba Jaba, Vincent And His Orchestra, 1990; Room Of Gardenia, Baby Miss Julia, 1995. Recordings: Albums: Collage Lillux, 1985; Secrets, Sound Addicts, 1990; Psyrrealistiske Psalmer, 1994; Ghostriders-When The Spiders Take Over (animation soundtrack), 1995. Publications: Bagdorsenglen (poetry); Auktion Over Van Gogns Ore (poetry). Memberships: DJBFA; Grammex; Koda. Hobbies: Classic Malay studies; Black humour; Zen. Address: Artillerivej 63/37, DK 2300 Copenhagen S, Denmark.

LILLYWHITE Steve, Record Producer. Career: Leading international record producer, 1980-; Currently working with: Bono; Morrissey. Recordings: Produced: Ultravox: Ultravox; Ha Ha Ha; Siouxie And The Banshees: The Scream; XTC: Drums and Wires; Black Sea; Peter Gabriel: Peter Gabriel 3; Psychedelic Furs: Psychedelic Furs; Talk Talk Talk; Joan Armatrding: Walk Under Ladders; The Key; Sleight Of Hand; Big Country: The Crossing; Steeltown; Simple Minds: Sparkle In The Rain; U2: Boy; October; War;

Joshua Tree; Achtung Baby; Talking Heads; Rolling Stones: Dirty Work; Kirsty MacColl: Kite; Electric Landlady; Titanic Days; David Byrne: Rei Momo; The Pogues: If I Should Fall From Grace; Peace And Love; The La's: The La's; Red Hot and Blue (Executive Producer of 1990 AIDS Project including: U2; Annie Lennox; Sinead O'Connor; Neville Bros; Deborah Harry, Iggy Pop); Alison Moyet: Hoodoo; World Party, Bang!; Morrissey: Vauxhall And I; The Dave Matthews Band: Under The Table And Dreaming; Also: Engine; Alley; Marshall Crenshaw; The Smiths; Pretenders; Happy Mondays; David Bowie. Current Mnanagement: XL Talent. Address: Studio 7, 27A Pembridge Villas, London W11 3EP, England.

LIMIC Marin Kresimir, b. 8 Aug 1946, Klis, Split, Croatia. Composer; Musician (piano, keyboard). m. Dubravka Zauhar, 6 Feb 1982, 2 sons. Musical Education: 4 semesters, Music Academy; 3 years of mechanic trade. Career: Over 500 television appearances including: live concerts of group Stijene, 1982-94; Television shows, 1982-83; Live concert, TV Zagreb, 1983; Tonight With You, interview, 1995; Seventh Night, HTV, 1995; Akustkoteka, unplugged concert. Compositions: Songs: Sve Je Neobicno Ako Te Volim; Ima Jedan Svijet; Singing That Rock 'N' Roll; Balkanska Korida; Ja Sam More Ti Si Rijeka; Zaplesimo Kao Nekada; Zbogom Prva Ljubavi. Recordings: 6 singles, 1974-84; Albums: Cementna Prasina (Silver record), 1980-81; Jedanaest I Petnaest (Gold, Silver record), 1982-83; Balkanska Korida; Stijene IV, 1994; Best Of Stijene, 1995. Honours: Gold, Silver discs; Awards from festivals: Zagreb, 1980; Split, 1981, 1982, 1990; Sarajevo, 1981, 1988. Memberships: HDS (Association of Croatian Composers); President, Split Association of Musicians; Vice President, Split Musician Sydicate; Artist-Composer, Republic of Croatia (ZUH Zagreb). Hobbies: Artist; Painter; Sculptor; Soccer player. Current Management: CMA Zagreb. Address: Varos 65, 21231 Klis (Split), Croatia.

LINCE Louis (John Louis James Lince), b. 22 July 1941, St Helens, Lancashire, England. Musician (banjo, guitar); Bandleader. m. Gillian Everil Walker, 9 Dec 1961, 2 daughters. Career: Member, Ken Colyer Allstars, 1976-82; Savoy Jazzmen, 1975-83; Louis Lince's New Orleans Band, 1986-; Founder member, Annie Hawkins' New Orleans Legacy, 1997; Occasional appearances with Jambalaya and Louisiana Joymakers, 1987-; Worked in New Orleans with Tuba Fats' Chosen Few, 1992-95; Lionel Ferbos, 1996, Reginald Koehler, 1996. Recordings: Just A Little While To Stay Here, Ken Colyer Allstars, 1978; You've Got the Right Key, 1979; Savoy Rag, 1981; Jubilee, 1983; Algiers Strut, 1985; Hot At The Dot, 1991; Backstairs Session, 1992; Yearning, 1993; Walking With The King, 1994; More Savoy Jazzmen, 1994; Good Morning to Heaven, 1996; Mardi Gras Parade, 1997. Hobbies: Photography; Reading; Current affairs. Current Management: Hot Jam International. Address: 102A East Hill, Wandsworth, London SW18 2HF, England.

LINDEBORG Britt, b. 22 March 1928, Stockholm, Sweden. Songwriter. Divorced, 1 son, 1 daughter. Education: Private Lessons, Music; Degree, Social Worker, University, 1973. Career: Participated in 12 Swedish Television Trials as Songwriter; Writer of 400 Songs and Lyrics, 30 Songs with Lyrics and Music. Compositions: Judy min vau, 1969; Diggi Loo Diggi Ley, 1984. Recordings: Diggi Loo Diggi Ley; Lucklig a Gatau; Judy min vau; Don't Cry For Me Argentina. Honours: 1st Prize, Eurovision Song Contest, 1969, 1984. Memberships: Swedish Popular Music Authors; Swedish Performing Rights Society. Hobby: Cottage by the sea. Address: Anders Reimers Vag 4, 117 50 Stockholm, Sweden.

LINDELL Tommi Kustaa, b. 21 June 1966, Helsinki, Finland. Musician (keyboards, synthesizer). m. Sari Henttonen, 17 July 1993, 1 daughter. Musical Education: Pop/Jazz Institute, Oulunkylä, Finland. Career: Musician, programmer, producer, for Finnish artistes including: RinneRadio; Timo Turpeinen; Raptori; Neljä Ruusua; Kaivo; Neumann; Tommi Läntinen; Pekka Ruuska; Television: Bandleader, composer, Frank Pappa Show, 1991-94. Recordings: with Lindelltronics: Trendibuumi, 1991; Hello Finland, 1993; with guitarist Vesa Anttila: The Swinghufvuds, 1991; Hits And Other Samples, 1993. Hobby: Science Fiction. Address: Synzataxi, Tehtaankatu 25 C 73, 00150 Helsinki, Finland.

LINDEN Nick, b. 17 Nov 1962, Woolwich, England. Musician (bass, guitar, keyboards). Musical Education: Music O Level. Career: Bass guitar, rock band Terraplane; Signed to Epic Records, 1984-89; Reading Festival, 1982; British tour supporting Meatloaf; Foreigner; ZZ Top; Various video and television appearances. Recordings: Black and White, 1985; Moving Target, 1987. Hobbies: Art; Joinery. Address: 60 Victoria Way, Charlton, London SE7 7NQ, England.

LINDENS Traste, b. 6 May 1960, Gävile, Sweden. Singer. m. Caroline Zielfelt. Education: The Grafic Institut, Stockholm. Career: Band: Traste Linden's Kvintette; Tours: Tågtur, 1987; Never Ending Tour, 1990-93; Festivals: Hultsfred, 1988, 1991; Roskilde, 1992; Storsjeyran, 1992; Television documentary: Traste Linden's Kvintette. Recordings: Traste Linden's Kvintette: Sportfiskarn, 1987; Bybor, 1989; Jolly Bob Gåriland, 1991; Gud Hjåpe, 1992; Utsålt, 1993; Som På Film, 1994; Also; Traste and Superstarana, 1980; Provins, 1985. Honours: Hälsinge Akademins Pris, 1992. Current Management: PO Box 171 80, 104 62 Stockholm, Sweden.

LINDES Hal, b. 30 June 1953, Monterey, California, USA. Composer; Musician (guitar). m. Mary Elizabeth Frampton, 2 Aug 1979, 2 sons, 1 daughter. Education: University of Maryland, USA. Musical Education: Self-taught. Career: Replaced David Knopfler in Dire Straits, 1980; Began Making Movies World Tour playing sellouts in small clubs, ended playing sold-out stadiums; Recorded, toured with band to midway through making Brothers In Arms album, 1985; Also made guest appearances with Tina Turner on release of Private Dancer album; Actor in BBC film: Drowning In The Shallow End, 1989; Began career as film and television composer. Compositions: Television themes include: Between The Lines, BBC; Band Of Gold, Granada; Thieftakers, Carlton; The Guilty, Central; The Trial, BBC; FIA Formula 1 Grand Prix Logo Theme, FIA; Legacy - Great Civilisations Of The World, Central; Into the Land Of Oz, CH4; Joyriders, Granada; Drowning In The Shallow End, BBC; Born Kicking, BBC; Commercials include: Avon; Ford; Kwik Fit; Kelloggs Special K; Johnson & Johnson. Recordings: with Dire Straits: Love Over Gold; Alchemy; Twisting By The Pool; Money For Nothing; Mark Knopfler: Local Hero; with Tina Turner: Private Dancer/Steel Claw; with Kiki Dee: Angel Eyes; with Fish: Vigil In A Wilderness of Mirrors; Hal Lindes: Between The Lines; Senses; Best Of TV Detectives; Best Of German TV Themes; Game Of Hearts-Rugby World Cup Theme. Memberships: PRS; ASCAP; British Equity. Current Management: Joel Roman, William Morris Agency (USA); Seifert Dench Associates; EMI (Music) Publishing Ltd (World). Address: c/o Seifert Dench, 24 D'Arblay St, London W1V 3FH, England.

LINDHOLM Dave (Ralf Henrik), b. 31 Mar 1952, Helsinki, Finland. Singer; Songwriter; Musician (guitar). m. Kirsi Koivunen, 9 Sept 1993, 1 son, 2 daughters. Musical Education: Taught by father and friends. Career:Member of bands:

Ferris; Orfeus; Rock'n'Roll Band; Pen Lee & Co;Bluesounds; 12 Bar; Dave Lindholm and Ganpaza Gypsys; Concerts in most of Europe and Texas, USA; Several blues festivals. Recordings: 34 albums, own music; Some studio sessions with various artists. Hobby Speedway. Current Management: Tiina Vuorinen, Well Done. Address: c/o Well Done, Sorvaajarskatu 9A, 00810 Helsinki, Finland.

LINDSEY Mort, b. 21 Mar 1923, Newark, New Jersey, USA. Conductor; Composer; Orchestrator; Musician (piano). m. Betty J Bonney, 9 Oct 1954, 2 sons, 1 daughter. Education: BA, MA, EdD, Columbia University, New York City. Musical Education: Private study: Tibor Serly; Paul Creston. Career: Staff conductor, NBC; CBS and NBC Networks; Musical Director for: Judy Garland; Barbra Streisand; Merv Griffin; Pat Boone; Musical Director, Merv Griffin Show, 22 years. Recordings: 3 orchestra albums under own name; Film soundtrack albums; Conducted, composed, 8 major films. Publications: Seven Ages Of Man (ballet); Popular songs: Lorna, with Johnny Mercer; Stolen Hours, with Marilyn and Allan Bergmann. Honours: Grammy Award: Judy Garland At Carnegie Hall; Emmy Award: Barbra Streisand in Central Park. Membership: ASCAP; AFofM; Sinfonia; Composers and Lyricists Guild. Hobbies: Oil painting. Equestrian sports. Address: 6970 Fernhill Drive, Malibu, CA 90265, USA.

LINDSTROM Maria, b. 30 August 1953, Stockholm, Sweden. Singer; Songwriter; Musician (Guitar). m. Kjell Andersson, 24 August 1995. Education: Musicology, University of Lund; Music Teacher Exam, 1976. Career: Actress, Musician, Fringe Theatre Group, 1977-88; Freelance, 1988-; Cabaret Artiste, TV. Compositions: More than 100 songs including lyrics and music for stage. Recordings: 1 LP, 1989; 1 CD, 1995; 1 CD, songs by Birger Sjöberg, 1998. Publications: Produced about 15 shows. Honour: Swedish SKAP Prize, 1997. Hobbies: Walking the dog; Cooking; Dreaming of better days. Current Management: Ageta Neumann, Nojesprod AB, Malmo. Address: Sövdeborgsg 33, 216 19 Malmo, Sweden.

LINDUP Mike, b. 17 Mar 1959. Musician (keyboards); Singer. Founder member, Level 42, 1980-; Appearances include: Support to the Police, 1981; Prince's Rock Gala, Wembley Arena, 1986, 1987, 1989; Crystal Palace Bowl, 1991; Midem Festival, Cannes, France, 1992; Regular UK tours. Recordings: Albums: with Level 42: Level 42, 1981; The Pursuit Of Accidents, 1982; Standing In The Light, 1983; True Colours, 1984; A Physical Presence, 1985; World Machine, 1985; Running In The Family, 1987; Staring At The Sun, 1988; Guaranteed, 1991; Solo album: Changes, 1990; Hit singles: The Chinese Way, 1983; The Sun Goes Down (Living It Up), 1983; Hot Water, 1984; Something About You, 1985; Leaving Me Now, 1985; Lessons In Love (Number 1 in 8 countries), 1986; Running In The Family, 1987; To Be With You Again, 1987; It's Over, 1987; Heaven In My Hands, 1988; Tracie, 1989; Guaranteed, 1991. Honours: BMI Award, 1 million US performances, Something About You, 1991. Current Management: Paul Crockford Management, 56-60 Islington Park Street, London N1 1PX, England.

LINKOLA Jukka, b. 21 July 1955, Espoo, Finland. Composer; Musician (piano); Conductor. Musical Education: Sibelius Academy, Helsinki. Career: Has conducted Danish Radio Big Band, Bohuslän Big Band, Oslo Groove Company, Umao Big Band, Prag Radio Big Band, Ljubljana Radio Big Band, Finnish Radio Big Band, Finnish Radio Big Band, helsinki Philharmony, Finnish National Opera Orchestra; Musical Director, Helsinki City Theatre, 1979-90; Currently freelance composer, Jazz, symphony, chamber and theatre music. Compositions include: Ronja The Robber's Daughter (ballet) for Finnish National Opera, premiered 1989; Crossings, for symphony orchestra, 1983; Two trumpet concertos, 1988, 1993; Angelika, opera, 1990; Elina, opera, 1992; String Quartet, 1996; Pegasos, for big band. Recordings: Albums with own octet: Protofunk; Lady In Green; Scat Suite; Ben Bay; with Eija Ahvo: Kuinka Myöhään Valvoo Blues; Crossings and Trumpet Concerto; The Tentet; EQ; Libau; Ronia the Robber's Daughter; Protofunk; Lady in Green; Sketches from Karelia. Honours: Yrjö Award, Finnish Jazz Federation, 1979; Finnish Broadcasting Company, Record Of The Year, with singer Eija Ahvo; First Prize, LUSES competition, 1993; First Prize, Paris Opera Screen, 1993; First Prize, Midem Awards, 1994; First Prize, Concours International de Composition de la Ville du Havre, 1994. Membership: Society of Finnish Composers. Current Management: Syrene Music. Address: c/o Syrene Music, Saarnitie 14 A, 00780 Helsinki, Finland.

LINN Raymond Sayre, b. 20 Oct 1920, Chicago, Illinois, USA. Bandleader; Composer; Musician (trumpet). m. Melinda Baccus, 7 Dec 1977. Career: Trumpeter, various big bands including Jimmy Dorsey, Woody Herman, Tommy Dorsey and Artie Shaw, 1940-45; Bandleader, own group, Ray Linn and Chicago Stompers, 1974-. Recordings with various artists including: Frank Sinatra; Sarah Vaughn; Ella Fitzgerald. Honour: NEA Award, 1981. Memberships: ASCAP; Musicians' Union.

LINNET Anne Kristine, b. 30 July 1953, Aarhus, Denmark. Composer; Musician; Songweiter; Singer. m. Holger Laumann, divorced, 2 sons, 1 daughter. Education: Diploma, Conservatory of Music, Jutland, 1985. Career: Performed in group Tears, 1970; Formed own band Shit & Chanel in 1974, recording 5 albums until 1979; Formed the Anne Linnet Band with Sanne Salomonsen and Lis Soerenson, 1981, touring Scandinavia and Germany; Formed new band Marquis de Sade in 1983; Composed and recorded the musical Berlin '84, 1984; Formed won record company, Pladecompagniet in 1988; Partnership with poet and priest Johannes Moellehave composing music to his poetry; Premiere of musical Krig og Kærlighed (War and Love) in 1990; Currently working on several major classical compositions; Participating in PaPapegoje, an album of children's songs performed by major Danish rock and pop artists; Composer of song for 1995 Eurovision Song Contest to be performed by Ulla Henningsen. Recordings: Anne Linnet Band, 1981; Cha Cha Cha, 1982; Marquis de Sade, 1983; Hvid Magi (White Magic), 1985; En elsker, 1986; Solo: Barndommens Gade, 1986; Jeg er jo lige her (I'm Right Here). 1988; Det' saa dansk, (It is so Typical Danish), 1991; Tal til mig (Talk To Me), 1993; with Johannes Moellehave: Miri Sang (My Song), 1989. Honours: Recipient of numerous Gold and Platinum records. Address: Linnet Songs, Bohlendachvej 45, Holmen, DK-1437 Copenhagen K, Denmark.

LINNMAN Bjorn Olov, b. 15 March 1960, Umea, Sweden. Composer. 1 son. Education: Graduate, Church Music. Career: Sweet Dreams, Mickery Theatre, Amsterdam; Sweet Dreams, Theatre X, Milwaukee, USA; Bjorn Linnman, Swedish Television; Den Halvfardiga Minden, Touring Sweden; Own Church Concerts as Organist and Pianist; Ture Sventon, Swedish Television; Ture Sventon Fallet Isabella, Film. Compositions: Grabbhalvan, Opera; Requieme, for 3 Silos; Ictus, for 4 Percussionists; Linnmania-Marsellaise; Rembrant-Hitzerome. Memberships: Swedish Composers of Popular Music. Current Management: Laguna Opera Concert Inc. Address: Professors Lingan 7, S-10405 Stockholm, Sweden.

LINSTEAD Johannes, b. 6 August 1969, Oakville, Ontario, Canada. Composer; Guitarist; Songwriter. Education: Private Instruction on Flamenco and Classical Guitar; Self Taught Piano. Career: Solo Performer and Band Leader of Instrumental Latin Guitar Music; Theme Music for Television and Films; Contemporary Pop Music Written for Various Solo Artists. Recordings: Sol Luna Tierra; Cleanse; Head is Angry; Alive & Wandering. Honours: Jazz Band Musician of the Year, 1989; Endorsement from Raimundoguitarras of Spain. Memberships: Society of Composers, Authors and Music Publishers, Canada. Hobbies: Kung Fu; Meditation. Current Management: Canadian Music Productions. Address: 1312 Speers Road, Oakville, Ontario L6L 2X4, Canada.

LINTENEN Kirmo, b. 16 May 1967, Finland. Musician (piano). Musical Education: Classical studies with Dmitri Hintze aged 9; Studied piano with Seppo Kantonen, Classical studies with Jouko Laivuori at Sibelius Academy, Helsinki. Career: Works with small jazz groups including: Jari Perkiömäki Quartet; Jukka Perko Quartet; Sonja Lumme Quartet; Leader, own trios or quartets; Regular musician with UMO (New Music Orchestra), 1988-. Compositions include: 2 tracks for Portrait By Heart, album by Jukka Perko. Recordings: Played on UMO recordings. Address: Kustaankatu 6 B 33, 00500 Helsinki, Finland.

LIPA Peter, b. 30 May 1943, Presov, Slovakia. Singer; Songwriter; Bandleader. m. Norina Bobrovská, 7 February 1980, 3 sons, 1 daughter. Education: Technical University, Bratislava, Slovakia; Self-taught guitar; Private lessons, violin, vocal, voice. Career: Bands: Strings, Blues Five, Revival Jazz Band, Blues Band; Peter Lipa Combo; Peter Lipa & Band; Andrej Seban Band; Hundreds of TV and Radio Performances, in Slovak, Czech, German, Hungarian, Polish Radio, TV. Recordings: Moanin'; That's the Way It Is; Naspat Na Stromy; Spirituals; Peter Lipa; (La, La, La) Boogie Up. Honours: Honoured Citizen of Bratislava, 1995; Martonik Annual Jazz Prize, 1995. Membership: President, Slovak Jazz Society; Lions Club International. Hobbies: Swimming; Music. Current Management: East-West Promotion Kuzmanyho 4, 81106, Bratislava, Slovakia. Address: Kuzmanyho 4, 81106 Bratislava, Slovakia.

LIPSON Stephen James, b. 16 Mar 1954, London, England. Record Producer. m. Judy London, 13 Apr 1984. Recordings: Record producer for: Annie Lennox; Simple Minds; Pet Shop Boys; Frankie Goes To Hollywood; Grace Jones; Paul McCartney; Propaganda; Prefab Sprout. Honour: Producer of the Year. Current Management: Zomba Management. Address: 165-167 High Road, London NW10 2SG, England.

LISA Geena (Gina Peeters), b. 20 July 1972, Hamme, Belgium. Singer; Actress. Education: Graphics. Career: Backing vocalist with The Layabouts; The Dinky Toys; Groovemania; Pop In Wonderland, 1988-1994; Solo artiste, 1994-; Television appearances include: A O Tartufo, (BRTN); Luc, (VTM); Tilt (VTM); As actress: Television series Wat Nu Weer? (VTM). Recordings: Shadelahoo, 1994; Lay Me Down, 1995. Membership: SABAM. Hobbies: Reading; Eating out. Current Management: Luc Standaert, Tempo Belgium. Address: Krijgslaan 61, 9000 Gent, Belgium.

LISAK Ivan-Vanja, b. 23 Nov 1941, Zagreb, Croatia. Composer; Musician (piano). m. Ksenija Zivkovic, 27 Mar 1982, 2 daughters. Musical Education: Music Academy, Teacher of Theory. Career: Pop festivals including: Director of oldest festival in Zagreb, 1975-79; Jazz festivals including: Bled 1983; Sofia, 1985; Prague, 1985; Moscow; Kiev; Petrograd, 1986-90; Italy, 1992-94; Tours: Concerts for Croats In Europe, Australia, The Soviet Union, USA; Numerous television and radio appearances, 1962-1995. Recordings: Swing Party I, 1983; II, 1985; III, with Peppino Principe, accordion, 1989; Happy Jazz I, 1991; II, 1994; Cassette: The Tree In The Yard, instrumental. Honours: Festival Awards, 1974, 1979, 1981, 1984. Memberships: Society of Musical Composers; HGU (Croatan Musical Union). Hobbies: Watch collection; Swimming. Address: 35, Marticeva Street, Zagreb 41000, Croatia.

LISBERG Harvey Brian, b. 2 Mar 1940, Manchester, England. Impressario; Artist Manager. m. Carole Gottlieb, 5 Nov 1969, 2 sons. Education: Manchester University. Musical Education: Self-taught piano, guitar. Career: First in discovering: Graham Gouldman; Andrew Lloyd Webber; Tim Rice; Herman's Hermits; Tony Christie; Sad Café; Godley and Creme; 10cc; Currently representing: 10cc; Graham Gouldman; Eric Stewart; George Stiles; Anthony Drewe. Hobbies: Golf; Theatre; Films; Travel. Current Management: Harvey Lisberg Associates. Address: Kennedy House, 31 Stamford Street, Altrincham, Cheshire WA14 1ES, England.

LISKI Jussi, b. 5 July 1960, Finland. Musician (keyboards, bass); Composer. Musical Education: Lessons on piano, violin, guitar; Studied upright bass, Sibelius Academy, Helsinki, 1979-. Career: Electric bass player with progressive rock bands, 1970s; Member, Pekka Pohjola Group; Own group Lentävä Siemen, 1989-; Became Jussi Liski Laboratory; Musical director, actor-singer Taneli Mäkelä. Recordings: Keyboard player, 4 Pekka Pohjola albums.

LISOLO Antoine, b. 15 Nov 1963, Marseilles, France. Musician (drums); Composer. Education: University. Musical Education: Conservatory Diplome. Career: Own band, Antoine Lisolo Barka Concept; Appeared freelance and with own band, concerts: Pakistan; France; Italy; Austria; French radio. Composition: Old Friends, 1996. Recordings: CD: Durance, Alain Soler Quartet with Joe Levano; CD: "A" Production, Antoine Lisolo Barka Concept; Act, Barka Concept. Membership: UMJ (French jazz musicians' union); SACEM, French Jazz Composer's Union). Hobbies: My Life and my wife. Current Management: Chantal Gris, 270 Place Albert, Tanguy 83200, Toulon, France. Address: 10 Boulevard Rey, 13009 Marseilles, France.

LITTLE RICHARD (Richard Penniman), b. 5 Dec 1935, Macon, Georgia, USA. Singer; Musician (piano). Education: Theological college, 1957. Career: R&B singer, various bands; Tours and film work with own band, The Upsetters; Gospel singer, 1960-62; Worldwide tours and concerts include: Star Club, Hamburg, Germany, with Beatles, 1962; European tour, with Beatles, Rolling Stones, 1963; UK tour with Everly Brothers, 1963; Rock'n'Revival Concert, Toronto, with Chuck Berry, Fats Domino, Jerry Lee Lewis, Gene Vincent, Bo Diddley, 1969; Toronto Pop Festival, 1970; Randall Island Rock Festival, with Jimi Hendrix, Jethro Tull, 1970; Rock'N'Roll Spectaculars, Madison Square Garden, 1972-; Muhammad Ali's 50th Birthday; Benefit For Lupus Foundation, Universal City, 1992; Westbury Music Fair, 1992; Giants Of Rock'n'Roll, Wembley Arena, 1992; Film appearances: Don't Knock The Rock, 1956; Mr Rock'n'Roll, 1957; The Girl Can't Help It, 1957; Keep On Rockin', 1970; Down And Out In Beverly Hills, 1986; Mother Goose Rock'n'Rhyme, Disney Channel, 1989. Recordings: Albums: Here's Little Richard, 1957; Little Richard Is Back, 1965; Greatest Hits, 1965; Freedom Blues, 1970; The King Of Rock'n'Roll, 1971; God's Beautiful City, 1979; Lifetime Friend, 1987; Featured on: Folkways - A Vision Shared (Woody Guthrie tribute), 1988; For Our Children, Disney, 1991; Shake It All About, Disney, 1992; Hit singles include: Tutti Frutti, 1956; Long Tall Sally, 1956; The Girl Can't Help It, 1957; Lucille, 1957; She's Got It, 1957; Jenny Jenny, 1957; Keep A Knockin', 1957; Good Golly Miss Molly, 1958; Baby Face, 1959; Bama Lama Bama Loo, 1964. Honours include: Star, Hollywood Walk Of Fame, 1990; Little Richard Day, Los Angeles,

1990; Penniman Boulevard, Macon, named in his honour; Platinum Star, Lupus Foundation Of America, 1992; Grammy Lifetime Achievement Award, 1993.

LITTON Martin, b. 14 May 1957, Grays, Essex, England. Rebekah Morley-Jones, 15 August 1992. Education: BA Hons, Music, Colchester Institute, England, 1978. Career: Pieces of Eight, with Harry Gold, 1980-82; Kenny Ball & His Jazzmen, 1982-84; Tours of Middle East & Russia; Freelance work with many American Musicians, including Bob Wilber, George Masso, Peanuts Hucko, Joe Muranyi, Al Casey, Scott Hamilton; Recorded with Kenny DaVern, Wild Bill Davison, Yank Lawson, Marty Grosz; Work with leading British Musicians includes recordings with Humphrey Lyttleton, Wally Fawkes & Digby Fairweather; Recent tours include Fabulous Fats, with Keith Smith; Frequent performer at London's South Bank Arts Centre. Compositions: Forever Afternoon; Striding Down 52nd Street; Litton on the Keys; Eight Bars - Eight to the Bar; For Rebekah. Recordings: Martin Litton Jazz Piano; Ring Dem Bells. Membership: PRS. Hobbies: Reading & Painting. Address: 7 Bridge Street, Hay-on-Wye, Herefordshire, HR3 5DE, England.

LIVESEY Warne, b. 12 Feb 1959, London, England. Record Producer. m. Barbara, 18 May 1983. Recordings: Producer, albums: Diesel And Dust, Midnight Oil; Blue Sky Mining, Midnight Oil; Infected, The The; Mind Bomb, The The; When The World Knows Your Name, Deacon Blue; Perverse, Jesus Jones; Suddenly Tammy!; Prick; St Julian, Julian Cope; Babe Rainbow, House Of Love; Underdogs, Matthew Good Band; Work, Lovelife, Miscellaneous, by David Devant and his Spirit Wife. Memberships: Musicians' Union. Hobby: Photography. Current Management: John Reid, JPR Management Ltd. Address: The Power House, 70 Chiswick High Road, London W4 1SY, England.

LIVINGSTON Jay, b. 28 March 1915, McDonald, Pennyslvania, USA. Composer; Lyricist; Musician (piano); Arranger. m. Shirley Mitchell, 16 May 1992, 2 daughters. Education: BA, University of Pennsylvania. Musical Education: Orchestration at University of Pennsylvania and UCLA Extension; 10 years of piano lessons. Career: 10 years under contract to Paramount Pictures; Songwriter for other motion picture companies including Warner Bros, MGM, Universal and various independents. Compositions: To Each His Own; Golden Earrings; Buttons And Bows; Tammy; Silver Bells; Mona Lisa; Que Sera Sera; Never Let Me Go. Honours: Three Motion Picture Academy Awards (Oscars), 1948, 1951, 1955. Memberships: ASCAP; Songwriters' Guild of America; Society of Singers; Johnny Mercer Foundation; Motion Picture Academy. Hobby: Travel. Address: c/o ASCAP, 1 Lincoln Plaza, New York, NY 10023, USA.

LIVINGSTONE John Graeme, b. 21 Feb 1951, Nelson, Lancashire, England. Singer; Songwriter; Musician (guitar, auto-harp). Musical Education: Self-taught. Career: Radio airplay; Interviews on Radio Luxembourg; BBC Radio Cumbria. Recordings: Wings Of Fire (EP); Albums: House Full of Strangers; Innocent Bystanders. Memberships: PRS; MCPS. Hobby: Watching motor racing. Current Management: Fair OaksEntertainment. Address: PO Box 19, Ulverston, Cumbria LA12 9TF, England.

LL Cool J (James Todd Smith), b. 14 Jan 1968, St Albans, Queens, New York, USA. Rapper. Career: Began rapping aged 9; Concerts include: Support to Run DMC, Raising Hell tour, 1986; Headliner, Def Jam '87 tour, 1987; Performed at Farm Aid IV, 1990; Budweiser Superfest, 1991; European tour, 1993; Film appearances: Krush Groove, 1985; The Hard Way, 1991; Toys, 1992; Founder, Uncle Records, 1992. Recordings: Singles include: I Can't Live Without My Radio, 1985; I Need Love, 1987; Goin' Back To Cali, 1988; I'm That Type Of Guy, 1989; Around The Way Girl, 1991; How I'm Comin', 1993; Pink Cookies In A Plastic Bag, 1993; Albums: Radio, 1985; Bigger And Deffer, 1987; Walking With A Panther, 1989; Mama Said Knock You Out, 1990; 14 Shots To The Dome, 1993; Mr Smith, 1996; Contributor, King Of Rock, Run DMC, 1985; Simply Mad About The Mouse, 1991. Publication: I Make My Own Rules, autobiography, 1997. Honours: Platinum discs; Soul Train Music Awards: Best Rap Album, Best Rap Single, 1988; MTV Music Video Award, Best Rap Video, 1991; Billboard Top Rap Singles Artist, 1991; Grammy Awards, Best Rap Solo Performance, Mama Said Knock You Out, 1992, Hey Lover, 1996; MTV Video Vanguard Award, 1997. Current Management: Rush Artist Management, 160 Varick Street, New York, NY 10013, USA. Address: LL Cool J and Associates, 186 - 39 Ilion Avenue, St Albans, NY 11412, USA.

LLABADOR Jean-Pierre, b. 15 Dec 1952, Nemours, Algeria. Jazz Musician (guitar); Composer. m. Annie Soulet-Pujol, 28 June 1976, 2 daughters. Education; BA, English; Degrees Philosophy. Musical Education: Conservatoire, France; Los Angeles GIT graduate (2 special awards). Career: Member, various jazz, fusion and rock bands including Coincidence; Johnny Hallyday (tours, radio and television shows, recordings), 1975-85; Lead guitarist, composer, with own bands, 1985-; Many tours, Europe and Africa; International festival appearances include: Nîmes, Montpellier-Radio-France, Nancy Jazz Pulsation, Midem, Barcelona, Laseyne sur Mer, Cardiff, Bath; Numerous radio and television appearances: Radio-France, TF1, FR2, FR3, M6; Artistic Director, OJLR (Region Languedoc Jazz Orchestra). Recordings: Albums (mostly own compostions): French Guitar Connection, quartet (US); 5th Edition, quintet (Germany); Friendship, duo/trio (Germany); Dialogues, OJLR (France); Birds Can Fly, quintet/sextet (France). Memberships: Composer, improviser, SACEM; SPEDIDAM. Hobbies: Family and friends; Books; Music. Current Management: TRIAD Diffusion. Address: 700 Chemin des Mendrous, 34170 Castelnau-Le-Lez, France.

LLACH Lluís, b. 7 May 1948, Girona, Catalonia, Catalan. Singer; Songwriter; Musician (piano, guitar). Career: Singer, songwriter since late 1960's; Pioneer, Nova Cançó (Catalan protest-song movement against General Franco); Member, El Setze Jutges, 1967; Major concerts include: Olympia, Paris, 1973, 1988; Stade de Barcelona, 1985; Edinburgh Arts Festival, 1993. Compositions: Arranger, songwriter on albums by: Teresa Rebull; Francesc Pi De La Serra; Dolors Lafitte; Marina Rossell; Josep Tero; Maria Del Mar Bonet; Joan Americ; Carles Cases. Recordings: Over 25 solo albums, 1967-; Albums include: Viatge a Itaca, 1975; Campanades a Morts, 1977; El Meu Amic el Mar, 1978; Maremar, 1986; Astres, 1987; Geografia, 1988; Un Pont De Mar Blava, 1993; Porrera, 1995; Music for 3 films: Borrasca, 1977; La Forja De Un Rebelde, 1990; El Ladrón De Niños, 1992; Numerous solo singles/EPs, including best known anthem, L'Estaca, 1974. Publications: Poemes i Cançons, 1979; Lluís Llach, 1979; Lluís Llach - Catalogne Vivre, 1979; Un Trobador Per a Un Poble, 1982; Història de Les Seves Cançons Explicada a Josep Maria Espinàs, 1986; La Déraison d'Etat, 1987; La Geografia Del Cor, 1992; Lluís Llach, 1993. Memberships: Societat General d'Autors i Editors (SGAE); Associació de Cantants i Intèrprets en Llengua Catalana (ACIC). Current Management: Andréas Claus. Address: Sepúlveda, 147-149 Principal 1a, 08011 Barcelona, Catalonia, Spain.

LLAMAS Xavier (Zag), b. 19 Dec 1970, Versailles, France. Music Teacher; Musician (guitar); Composer. Education: College. Musical Education: CIM; ASMM: National School, 4th cycle Jazz. Career: Plays regularly in suburban clubs, Paris. Recordings: 2 Tilles CD with RAV'VE (association): Band CM2; DAT 10 Tilles: Band: CM2. Hobbies: Skiing; Hiking; Reading; Cinema. Current Management: Self-managed. Address: 18 Rue de La Providence, 78120 Rambouillet, France.

LLORCA Guy, b. 9 Dec 1950, Koléa, Algeria. Musician (trumpet). Education: BA, 1967. Musical Education: Studies in piano, violin, trumpet. Career: Jazz and improvising music. Hobbies: Painting; Swimming. Current Management: Self-managed. Address: 6 Rue des Islettes, 75018 Paris, France.

LLOYD Andrew Reginald (Popman), b. 2 June 1960, Halesowen, Birmingham, England. Singer; Songwriter; Musician (guitar); Entertainer; Actor; Record Producer. Musical Education: Self-taught. Career: Bands: Mickey Mouse Revival, 1972-76; Andy Lloyd and the Wedge, 1978-79; The Bloomsbury Set, 1980-83; Popman and the Raging Bull, 1986-88; Popman and the Disciple, 1989-93; Radio sessions, Peter Powell, Radio 1, 1981-86; Tours: Judy Tzuke, 1981; Duran Duran, 1982; Various support tours, 1986-92; Headline tour, 1993; Solo acoustic US tour, 1994; Television appearances: Get It Together; Pop 77; Oxford Road Show; Track 1; Razzmatazz. Recordings: Back To School, 1978; It's Up To You, 1978; Living In America, 1979; Letters To Eva, 1979; This Year Next Year, 1981; The Other Side Of You, 1981; Sweet Europeans, 1982; Hanging Around With The Big Boys, Getting Away From It All, Dress Parade, Serenade, 1983; Just Like A Woman, Casual Acquaintance, 1986; Fields In Motion, Hustling Man, 1987; New Feelings, Friends And Lovers, 1988; Pirate, 1989; Girl Of My Best Friend, 1990; Little White Lies, The Same Girl, 1991; Weekend, 1992; Acoustic set, 1994; Plugs Out, 1995. Memberships: MU; Equity; Songwriters Guild; PRS; MLPS. Hobbies: Animal welfare; Gardening; Swimming; Walking; Love; Music. Current Management: Nick Titchener, Don't Panic Promotions. Address: 74 The Archway, Ranelagh Gardens, London SW6 3UH, England.

LLOYD Gary, b. 29 January 1965, Ottawa, Canada. Composer. Education: BA, Mathematics, University of Liverpool Chester College, England, 1986. Career: Ran recording studio, 1987-89; Composition and Soundtrack composer since 1989; Scored music for more than 400 productions including works for TV, film, theatre, contemporary dance, son et lumiere, art installations; First commission Neil Gaiman's Violent Cases, stageplay soundtrack, 1988. Compositions include: A Return To Love, for TV drama, 1994; Ignition, music for Fireworks, 1994; Land of Many Waters, for A/V show and CD release, 1995; Precis for String Orchestra, performed Cholmondeley Castle, Cheshire, England, 1996; The Ghost Tour, filmscore, 1997; Curiously England, documentary, 1997; Alien Blood, filmscore, 1998. Recordings: Albums: The Bridge, with Iain Banks, 1996; Brought to Light, with Alan Moore, 1998. Hobbies: Skateboarding; Mathematics; Films. Current Management: Music for Films, 34 Batchelor Street, Islington, London N1 0EG, England. Address: c/o Gallery Productions, PO Box 1363, Chester, CH2 3WN, England.

LLOYD WEBBER Andrew (Sir), (Baron Lloyd Webber of Sydmonton) b. 22 Mar 1948, London, England. Composer. m. Sarah Jane Hugill, 1971, div 1983, 1 son, 1 daughter, (2) Sarah Brightman, 1984, div 1990, (3) Madeleine Gurdon, 1991, 2 sons, 1 daughter. Education: Magdalen College, Oxford; Royal College of Music, FRCM, 1988. Career: Composer and producer, musicals; Composer, film scores; Deviser, children's board game Calamity! - The International High Risk Insurance Game.

Compositions: Musicals: Joseph And The Amazing Technicolour Dreamcoat (lyrics by Tim Rice), 1968; Jesus Christ Superstar (lyrics by Tim Rice), 1970; Jeeves (lyrics by Alan Ayckbourn), 1975; Evita (lyrics by Tim Rice), 1976; Tell Me On A Sunday (lyrics by Don Black), 1980; Cats (based on poems by T S Eliot), 1981; Song And Dance, 1982; Starlight Express (lyrics by Richard Stilgoe), 1984; The Phantom Of The Opera (lyrics by Richard Stilgoe and Charles Hart), 1986; Aspects Of Love (lyrics by Don Black and Charles Hart), 1989; Sunset Boulevard (lyrics by Don Black and Christopher Hampton), 1993; By Jeeves (lyrics by Alan Ayckbourn), 1996; Whistle Down The Wind (lyrics by Jim Steinman), 1996; Film Scores: Gumshoe, 1971; The Odessa File, 1974; Jesus Christ Superstar, 1974; Others: Requiem, 1985; Variations On A Theme Of Paganini For Orchestra, 1986; Amigos Para Siempre (official theme for 1992 Olympic Games), 1992. Publications: Evita (with Tim Rice), 1978; Cats: The Book of the Musical, 1981; Joseph And The Amazing Colour Dreamcoat (with Tim Rice), 1982; The Complete Phantom of the Opera, 1987; The Complete Aspects of Love, 1989; Sunset Boulevard: From Movie to Musical, 1993; Columnist, the Daily Telegraph. Numerous honours include: 5 Laurence Olivier Awards; 6 Tony Awards; 4 Drama Desk Awards; 3 Grammy Awards; Triple Play Award, ASCAP, 1988; Knighthood, 1992; Praemium Imperiale Award, 1995; Richard Rogers Award, 1996; Oscar, Best Song, (with Tim Rice), 1997. Hobbies: Art; Architecture. Address: 22 Tower Street, London WC2H 9NS, England.

LOANE Cormac, b. 28 Sep 1955, North Shields, England. Musician (saxophone, clarinet); Teacher. m. Amelia Gray, 2 Apr 1994. Musical Education: B.Mus, University of London Goldsmiths' College, London. Career: Member, Last Exit (with Sting), 1974-75; Played with National Youth Jazz Orchestra, 1975-76; Head of Woodwind Teaching, 1984-91, Head of Wind Teaching, 1991-, Birmingham Education Department; Director of Birmingham Schools' Jazz Orchestra, performing with leading jazz musicians including Georgie Fame, Humphrey Lyttelton, Kenny Baker and Don Lusher, 1997-. Publications: Team Woodwind, tutor books. Address: 38 Pine Grove, Lickey, Birmingham B45 8HE, England.

LOCK Eddie, b. 10 February 1969, Bury St Edmonds, England. Musician; Disc Jockey; Producer. m. Maxine, 20 July 1996. Career: Disc Jockey, 1987; Member, Carpe Diem and SMC Project. Recordings: The Buzz; Don't Wanna Be Free; Hypnotic; Music Takes You; Snakecharmer; Space is the Place; Turkish Delight. Memberships: MCPS; BPI; PRS; Music Publishers Association. Hobbies: Football; Drinking; Making Money. Current Management: Plastic Surgery/Mission Control. Address: The Coach House, Mansion Farm, Liverton Hill, Sandway, Maidstone, Kent ME17 2NJ, England.

LOCKETT Peter Robert, b. 8 April 1963, Portsmouth, Hampshire, England. Musician (Percussion). Musical Education: Selftaught; Madras Academy, 1991-93. Career: Live TV work, recording, touring with Kula Shaker; Live TV work and recording with Vanessa Mae; Recording with Björk, Bill Bruford, David Arnold and A R Rahman; Duo concerts at Royal Festival Hall with Joji Hirota; Series on drum programming, The Mix, magazine; World percussion sample CDs for The Mix, magazine; Recorded 2 albums with top Danish guitarist, Henrik Anderson; Recoprdings with Natacha Atlas, Transglobal Underground and on Bond movie Tomorrow Never Dies. Publications: Drum technique articles for Modern Drummer and Rhythmn Magazine. Address: Flat F, 26 Upper Park Road, Belsize Park, London NW3 2UT, England.

LOCKHEART Mark, b. 31 Mar 1961, Hampshire, England. Musician (saxophones, clarinet, flute); Composer. m. Andrea Margo Tosic, 30 July 1985. Musical Education: Trinity College of Music. Career: Saxophone, Loose Tubes, Lysis Steve Berry Trio, 1985-91; Leader, own Perfect Houseplant Group; Co-leader, Matheran; Currently member, Django Bates' Delightful Precipice; Also bands with June Tabor, Billy Jenkins; Session work with Jah Wobble; Prefab Sprout. Recordings: with Perfect Houseplants: Perfect Houseplants, 1993; Clec, 1995; with Matheran: Mark Lockheart-John Paracelli, 1994; with Django Bates: Summer Fruits And Unrest, 1994. Honours: Scottish Arts Commission: Semana Santa, Multi-media Commission, 1991. Hobbies: Travel; Swimming; Tennis; Cinema. Current Management: Eccentric Management. Address: Eccentric Management, 29A Connaught Street, London W2 2AY, England.

LOCKWOOD Didier André Paul, b. 11 Feb 1956, Calais, France. Musician (violin); Jazz Composer. m. Casadesus, 15 Oct 1993, 3 daughters. Education: College. Musical Education: Conservatoire de Calais, (violin, trumpet, piano); École Normale Supérieure de Musique, Paris. Career: First Prize, at Conservatory, age 16; Professional musician with French group, Magma, 1973; Worked with Stéphane Grappelli, 1978; Formed own groups, 1980-; Appearances include: Royal Albert Hall, London, 1979; Carnegie Hall, New York, 1981; 1983; Major jazz festivals; More than 2000 concerts worldwide include Théatre des Champs Elysées, 1993; Peking, 1993. Compositions: Jazz and contemporary music; Violin concerto: Les Mouettes, (with symphony orchestra). Recordings: Recordings: Over 20 include: New World, with Antony Williams (drums), 1981; Live In Montreux, 1982; The Kid; Out Of The Blue, 1986; New York Rendevouz, 1994. Publications: Violin Jazz Method book; 1 song book. Memberships; Blue Note Award, Newy; 2 Victoires de la Musique; Grand Prix, SACEM; Prix Charles Cross; Chevalier des Arts et des Lettres. Hobbies: Painting; Tennis; Football. Current Management: Isoard-Sola. Address: 22 Rue Ernest Revillon, 77630 Barbizon, France.

LOCKWOOD JR, Robert, b. 27 Mar 1915, Turkeyscretch, Arkansas, USA. Musician (guitar). m. Annie Roberts, 13 Sept 1970, 5 sons, 2 daughters. Career: Belgian National Radio; Blues Festival, Peer, July 1994; Helen, Arkansas Blues Festival, Oct 1994; KFFA Radio; WCPN Radio; Lady Luck Casino; Rhythm and Blues, Lula, Mississippi. Recordings: Little Boy Blue; Take A Little Walk With Me, 1948; Something To Do, 1990; Whats The Score?, 1990; Hanged On; Come Day Go Day, 1993; Majors Minors and Ninths, 1993; I Got To Find Me A Woman, 1997. Publications: Volume I Blues; Who, Who, Living, Blues. Honours: W C Handy, 1988; Achievement for Black History, 1994; Blues Hall Of Fame, 1998. Hobbies: Pool And Checkers. Current Management: Agent: Concentrated Efforts Inc; Management: Annie Lockwood. Address: 7203 Lawnview Avenue, Cleveland, OH 44103, USA.

LODGE John Charles, b. 20 July 1945, Birmingham, England. Musician (bass guitar); Vocalist. m. Kirsten, 30 Sept 1968, 1 son, 1 daughter. Education: Birmingham College of Advanced Technology. Musical Education: Self-taught. Career: Member, El Riot and The Rebels; The Carpetbaggers; John Bullbreed; Member, Moody Blues, 1966-; Also solo artiste; Numerous tours, concerts include: Royal Albert Hall; Hollywood Bowl; Isle Of Wight Festival, 1970; Wembley Arena, 1993. Recordings: Albums: In Search Of The Lost Chord, 1968; On The Threshold Of A Dream, 1969; To Our Children's Children, 1969; A Question Of Balance, 1970; Every Good Boy Deserves Favour, 1971; Days Of Future Passed, 1972; Seventh Sojurn, 1972; This Is The Moody Blues, 1974; Blue Jays, 1975; Octave, 1978; Long Distance Voyager, 1981; Voices In The Sky/The Best Of The Moody Blues, 1985; The Other Side Of Life, 1986; Sur La Mer,

1988; Greatest Hits, 1988; Keys Of The Kingdom, 1991; Live At Red Rocks, 1993; Solo: Natural Avenue, 1977 (re-released 1996); Singles include: Nights In White Satin, 1968; Voices in The Sky; Tuesday Afternoon; Ride My See Saw; Isn't Life Strange, 1972; I'm Just A Singer (In A Rock'n'Roll Band), 1973; Gemini Dream, 1981; The Voice; Your Wildest Dreams, 1986. Honours: ASCAP Awards, Singer In A Rock'n'Roll Band; Gemini Dream; 2 Ivor Novello Awards; Outstanding Contribution To British Music, Ivor Novello Awards, 1985. Memberships: PRS; BASCA; Songwriters Guild Of America. Hobbies: Music; Golf. Current Agent: ICM (New York and Los Angeles). Address: c/o Threshold Records Ltd, 53 High Street, Cobham, Surrey KT11 3DP, England.

LOEB Lisa, b. USA. Singer; Musician (guitar); Songwriter. Career: Solo artiste, billed as Lisa Loeb and Nine Stories, 1994-. Recordings: Albums: Tails, 1995; Firecracker, 1998; Singles: Stay (I Missed You), from film soundtrack Reality Bites, 1994; Do You Sleep?, 1995; I Do, 1998. Honours: BRIT Award, Best International Newcomer, 1995. Current Management: Manage This!. Address: c/o Manage This!, 154 w 57th Street # 133, New York, NY 10019, USA.

LOEFFLER Anthony, b. 5 April 1947, Paterson, New Jersey, USA. Musician (guitar); Songwriter. m. 27 April 1968, 1 son, 2 daughters. Education: Psychology major. Musical Education: Self-taught. Career: Festival appearances include: Bay Shore Arts Festival, Long Island, New York, 1986; Rainbow Bash Festival, Sparta, New Jersey, 1993; Cross Rhythms Festival, Devon, UK, 1993, 1996, 1997; Sur Montreau 35th Anniversary Jazz/Rock Festival, Switzerland, 1996; Tours throughout USA; Numerous television and radio apperances. Recordings: 12 albums. Publication: Foundation (the Solid Rock Newsletter). Memberships: Recording Industry Association of America (RIAA); Gospel Music Association; Broadcast Music Inc. Hobby: Music. Current Management: Lord and Associates Music. Address: PO Box 296, 324 Godwin Avenue, Midland Park, NJ 07432, USA.

LOFGREN Nils, b. 21 June 1951, Chicago, Illinois, USA. Musician (guitar); Songwriter; Arranger; Singer. Career: Member, Grin, 1970s; Solo artiste, 1974-; Appearances with Neil Young and Crazy Horse, including Tonight's The Night tour, 1973; Trans tour, 1983; Joined Bruce Springsteen's E Street Band, 1984-; Continues as solo artist. Recordings: Albums: Nils Lofgren, 1975; Back It Up (official bootleg), 1976; Cry Tough, 1976; I Came To Dance, 1977; Night After Night, 1977; Nils, 1979; Night Fades Away, 1981; Wonderland, 1983; Flip, 1985; Code Of The Road, 1986; Silver Lining, 1991; Crooked Lining, 1992; Everybreath, 1994; Damaged Goods, 1995; Acoustic Live, 1997. Current Management: Anson Smith Management, 3 Bethesda Metro Center, Suite 505, Bethesda, MD 20814, USA.

LOGGINS Kenny (Kenneth Clarke), b. 7 Jan 1947, Everett, Washington, USA. Singer; Songwriter; Musician (guitar). m. Eva Ein, 31 Dec 1976 (divorced). Musical Education: Music, Pasadena City College. Career: Member, Gator Creek; Second Helping; Duo, Loggins & Messina (with Jim Messina), 1971-76; Solo artist, songwriter, 1977-; Numerous compositions include: House At Pooh Corner, recorded by Nitty Gritty Dirt Band, 1971; Your Mama Don't Dance, recorded by Loggins & Messina, Elvis Presley, Poison, 1973; Danny's Song, recorded by Annne Murray; Co-writer with Michael McDonald, What A Fool Believes, recorded by Doobie Brothers (Number 1, US), 1979; Co-writer with Melissa Manchester, Whenever I Call Your Friend, 1979. Recordings: Hit singles include: This Is It, 1980; I'm Alright, from film Caddyshack, 1980; Don't Fight It, duet with Steve Perry, 1982; Heart To Heart, 1983; Footloose, from film Footloose (Number 1, US), 1984; Danger Zone, from film

Top Gun (Number 2, US), 1986; Meet Me Half Way, from film Over The Top, 1987; Nobody's Fool, from film Caddyshack 2, 1988; Albums: with Loggins And Messina: Kenny Loggins With Jim Messina Sittin' In, 1971; Loggins & Messina, 1972; Full Sail, 1973; On Stage, 1974; Mother Lode, 1974; So Fine, 1975; Native Sons, 1976; Finale, 1977; The Best Of Friends, 1977; Solo albums: Celebrate Me Home, 1977; Nightwatch, 1978; Keep The Fire, 1979; Kenny Loggins - Alive, 1980; High Adventure, 1982; Footloose, film soundtrack (Number 1, US) 1984; Vox Humana, 1985; Top Gun, film soundtrack (Number 1, US) 1986; Back To Avalon, 1987; Kenny Loggins On Broadway, 1988; Leap Of Faith, 1991; Outside - From The Redwoods, 1993; Contributor, We Are The World, USA For Africa, 1985. Honours: Grammy, Song Of The Year, What A Fool Believes, 1980; Best Pop Vocal Performance, This Is It, 1981; Platinum and Gold discs. Current Management: Next Step, 105 Foothill Road, Ojai, CA 93023, USA.

LOHAN Sinead, b. 21 June 1971, Cork City, Ireland. Singer; Musician. Education: Selftaught Guitar; Piano Lessons. Career: Toured with Womans Heart, Support to Paul Brady, 1995, The Blue Nile, 1996, Joan Baez, 1997; Appearance at Newport Folk Festival, 1997. Compositions include: Who Do You Think I Am; Sailing By; Everything Around Me is Changing; Out of the Woods. Recordings: Who Do You Think I Am; Womans Heart 2. Honours: Triple Platinum; Best Newcomer, Irish National Entertainment Awards. Hobbies: Reading; Walking. Current Management: Pat Egan. Address: c/o Merchants Court 24, Merchants Quay, Dublin 8, Ireland.

LOHRER Eric, b. 15 Feb 1965, Paris, France. Jazz Musician (guitar); Composer. 1 son. Education: Philosophy, Lycée Henri IV; La Sorbonne, Paris. Musical Education: Self-taught. Career: Bandleader for groups Eric Lohrer Trio, Open Air, 1987-93; Red Whale, 1991-95; Olympic Gramofón, solo program based on music of Theolonius Monk, 1995-96; Tours, festivals, France; Europe; Africa; Radio appearances: France Inter; France Musique; Europe 1; Television appearances: FR3; A2. Recordings: Eric Lohrer Trio, 1989; Queekegg, Red Whale, 1991; Dans Le Bleu, Eric Lohrer Trio, 1992; Attitudes, Open Air, 1992; Big One, Jean-Michel Pilc, 1993; Mozol, Red Whale, 1995. Publications: Time And Improvisation In Jazz Music, 1986. Honours: First Prize, soloist and band, Vienna International Jazz Contest, 1987; 2 Band Prizes: La Défense National Jazz Contest, 1988, 1989.Memberships: SACEM; SPEDIDAM. Current Management: Supernova. Address: 94 Rue du Mail, 95310 St Ouen L'Aumône, France.

LOKKE Birgit, b. 11 July 1967, Asserbo, Denmark. School teacher; Musician (drums, percussion). Education: School teacher, Biology, Arts, 1993. Musical Education: Private lessons: Adam Nussbaum; Alex Riel. Career: Television appearance with Savage Rose; Toured with: Embla; Savage Rose; and Palle Daielsson, Larn Jansson, Han Bennink, Alex Riel in: The Big Bang. Composition: Dans Under Broen. Recordings: Savage Rose: Månebarn, 1992. Honours: Highest award, Arts examination. Hobbies: Animals; Plants; Nature.

LOLLIO Lou, b. 30 Dec 1949, West Virginia, USA. Vocals; Musician (guitar, piano); Manager. m. Jean Lollio, 11 Nov 1990. Career: Film: A Star Is Born, 1978; Up In Smoke, 1979; Blues Brothers Movie, 1980; Fantasy Island, 1981; The Mystery Train, Nashville, 1984; Supporting act for Van Halen, 1985; Opening Act for Little Richard, 1984; Buffalo Springfield Revisited Tour, 1986. Recordings: Music producer, Film: LA's Lost Angels, 1969. Publications: Andy Warhol interview. Memberships: Screen Actors Guild (SAG); AFTRA; American Federation of Television and Radio Artistes. Current Management: J Lollio

Management. Address: 505 South Beverley Drive, #327, Beverley Hills, CA 90212, USA.

LOMAS Roger David, b. 8 Oct 1948, Coventry, England. Record Producer. m Linda Lomas, 21 Dec 1966, 2 sons, 1 daughter. Musical Education: Self-taught. Career: Record producer for: The Specials; Bad Manners; The Selecter; Desmond Dekker; The Bodysnatchers; The Modettes; Special-Beat; Selecter Instrumental; Roy Wood. Recordings: 17 hit singles, 10 albums include: with Bad Manners: Can Can; Special Brew; My Girl Lollipop; Walking In The Sunshine; Lip Up Fatty; with The Selecter: On My Radio; Missing Words; Roy Wood, I Wish it Could be Christmas Everyday, live version; 18 hit singles altogether. Honours: Gold and Silver awards for Bad Manners and Selecter albums and singles. Membership: PRS. Hobby: Snooker. Current Management: Self-managed. Address: 35 Dillotford Avenue, Coventry, West Midlands CV3 5DR, England.

LONGNON Jean-Loup, b. 2 Feb 1953, Paris, France. Musician (trumpet, piano); Vocalist; Arranger; Composer; Conductor. Musical Education: Self-taught trumpet, jazz. Career: Trumpet player, various bands and big bands; Soloist or bandleader performing in concerts, recording studios, jazz clubs, master classes, festivals, tours, TV, radio, in France; Throughout Europe; Turkey; Israel; Egypt; Tunisia; Morocco; Reunion Island; Mauritius; US; Cuba (Varandero Festival); Brazil; Played with artists including: Dizzy Gillespie; Stan Getz; Clark Terry; Arturo Sandoval; Martial Solal; Stéphane Grappelli; Didier Lockwood; Michel Petrucciani; Antoine Hervé; Kenny Clarke; Chet Baker; Winton Marsalis; Michel Legrand. Compositions: Torride, Aquarelles, Jazz à Paris, Nathalie... Un Matin; Variations on John Coltrane themes (commissioned by National Jazz Orchestra); Suite for Orchestra on Dizzy Gillespie (commissioned by Michel Legrand for television show Grand Echiquier); Symphonic poem L'Ours (commissioned by Concert Arban brass quintet and Martin Publications); Cyclades suite for jazz solist and symphonic orchestra (commissioned by Musique Française d'Aujopurdhui). Recordings include: Jean-Loup Longnon And His New York Orchestra. Honours: Winner, Festival de la Défense, Paris, 1977; Django Reinhardt Prize; Boris Vian Prize; European Audivisual Grand Prix; Django d'Or, 1995. Membership: SACEM. Hobby: Travel. Current Management: Self-managed. Address: 52 Boulevard Saint Germain, 75005 Paris, France.

LOPEZ Ramon, b. 6 Aug 1961, Alicante, Spain. Musician (drums, tabla). m. Pilar Dominguez, 20 Mar 1992, 1 son. Education: Electronics specialist. Musical Education: Self-taught, drums, 1973-; Tabla student of Krishna Govinda K C (Lucknow, India). Career: Teacher, Indian and modal music, Paris Conservatoire (CNSMDP); Plays with: Claude Tchamitchian; Philippe Deschepper; Enrico Rava; Howard Johnson; Jean-Marc Padovani; Yves Robert; François Cotinaud; Jean-Marc Machado; J F Jenny Clark; Glenn Ferris; Daunik Lazro; Paul Rogers; Sophia Domancich; New groups, Onj 97/2000, National Orchestra of Jazz, conducted by Didier Levallet; Many appearances, Radio France; Television: M6 Jazz 6; Cable Paris Premiere: Capitale Jazz; F3, F3 Region; RTVE (Spain); RTSR (Switzerland); RTBF (Belgium); TRI (Indonesia); WDR (Germany); Druskininkai TV, Baltic TV (Lithuania); Armenia TV. Recordings: Opera (with François Cotinaud), 1993; Princesse, François Cotinaud Quartet, 1990; Face Au Silence, Double Face, 1991; Pyramides (featuring Enrico Rava), 1992; Lousadzak, Claude Tchamitchian Septet, 1994; Portraits, Patrice Thomas Quartet, 1995; With Marc Steckar: Elephant Tuba Horde, 1987; Steckar Trinity, 1988; Tubakoustic, 1989; Jean-Marie Machado; Denis Colin Trio. Publications: La Region Internacional,

17 Aug 1993; Batteur Magazine, no 44, Mar 1992; Informacion de Alicante, Nov 1985; Jan 1986; July 1986; Mar 1990. Memberships: SACEM; SACD; SPEDIDAM; CNSMDP. Hobby: Photography. Current Management: Jazz Bank Ass, Ramon Lopez. Address: 81 Blvd Richard Lenoir, 75011 Paris, France.

LOPEZ Trini, b. 15 May 1937, Dallas, Texas, USA. Singer; Musician (guitar). Career: Nightclub performer, debut appearance, 1967; Recorded for Frank Sinatra, 1963-68; Worldwide entertainer, 1963-; Film roles include: Marriage On The Rocks; A Poppy Is Also A Flower; The Dirty Dozen; Antonio. Television appearances: Adam 12; The Reluctant Heroes; If I Had A Hammer. Recordings include: If I Had A Hammer; Trini Lopez Live At PJ's; More Trini Lopez At PJ's By Popular Demand; Trini Lopez In London; Trini Lopez Now; Trini Lopez Live At Basin Street East; Trini Lopez Greatest Hits; Trini - Transformed By Time; The Best of Trini Lopez. Hit singles include: I'm Coming Home Cindy; Michael; Lemon Tree; Kansas City; If I Had A Hammer; America; La Bamba. Honours: Goodwill Ambassador for US; Honoured by Congress for work in international relations; Gold disc, If I Had A Hammer. Memberships: AFofM; SAG. Hobbies: Tennis; Golf. Current Management: Ray Lawrence Ltd, Studio City, CA, USA. Address: 1139 Abrigo, Palm Springs, CA 92262, USA.

LOPEZ-REAL Carlos Enrique, b. 25 Oct 1969, Nairobi, Kenya. Musician (saxophone); Composer. Education: Psychology, Philosophy, Oxford University. Musical Education: Guildhall School of Music and Drama, post-graduate jazz and studio. Career: Leader, own quartet at festivals including Glastonbury, Oxford; Studied with Jean Toussaint; Played with Django Bates and Norma Winstone; Venues include Barbican Concert Hall; London clubs include Jazz Café, Vortex. Compositions: Folk Song; Para Michele; Mtengene; Soundtracks include film In Profile. Recordings: Dr Dig; Other sessions. Memberships: Musicians' Union; Clarinet and Saxophone Society. Hobbies: Cooking; Film; Travel. Address: 38 Claverley Grove, Finchley, London N3 2DH, England.

LORD Jon, b. 9 June 1941, Leicester, England. Musician (keyboards). Education: Central School of Speech and Drama, London; London Drama Centre. Career: Member, groups including: Artwoods; Flowerpot Men; Founder member, Deep Purple, 1968-76; Member, Paice Ashton Lord, 1976-77; Member, Whitesnake, 1978-84; Also solo recording artiste; Member, Deep Purple, 1984-; Worldwide tours with Deep Purple and Whitesnake; Major concerts include: with Deep Purple: USA; Japan; UK; Australia; Europe; Knebworth Festival; with Whitesnake: Reading Festival, 1979, 1980; Tours with AC/DC, Jethro Tull, USA, 1980; Monsters Of Rock Festival, 1981, 1983. Recordings: All recordings by Deep Purple; Albums: with Ashton And Lord: First Of The Big Bands, 1974; with Paice Ashton Lord: Malice In Wonderland, 1977; with Whitesnake: Trouble, 1978; Lovehunter, 1979; Ready An'Willing, 1980; Live In The Heart Of The City, 1980; Come And Get It, 1981; Saints 'N' Sinners, 1982; Slide It In, 1984; Solo albums: Gemini Suite, 1970; Windows, 1974; Sarabande, 1976; Before I Forget, 1982; Country Diary Of An Edwardian Lady, 1986; Pictured Within, 1997; Also recorded with: Tommy Bolin; Graham Bonnet; Sam Brown; David Gilmour; George Harrison; Alvin Lee; Bernie Marsden; Nazareth; Cozy Powell. Current Management: Thames Talent, 45 E Putnam Avenue, Greenwich, CT 06830, USA. Address: Nr Henley-on-Thames, Oxfordshire, England.

LORING Gloria (Jean), b. 10 Dec 1946, New York, New York, USA. Singer; Songwriter; Actress. m. René Lagler, 20 Dec 1994, 2 sons. Musical Education: Self-taught. Career: 25 years of performances on television; Over 500 appearances as a singer; Over 6 years on "Days Of Our Lives"; Concert appearances in North America and 4 concert tours of Australia. Compositions: Co-writer, television themes, Facts of Life and Diff'rent Strokes; Co-writer, What've You Got To Lose, for feature film Inside Moves. Recordings: 7 albums including Friends And Lovers. Publications: Books: Kids, Food and Diabetes; Parenting A Diabetic Child. Membership: Gold Member, National Academy of Songwriters. Hobby: Gardening. Current Management: Garry George, Suite 500, 9107 Wilshire Boulevard, Beverly Hills, CA 90210, USA. Address: P O Box 1243, Cedar Glen, CA 92321, USA.

LOUIS Eric, b. 28 Oct 1959, Malo Les Bains, France. Musician (trombone); Music Teacher. 1 daughter. Musical Education: Conservatoires de Perpignan, 1978; St Quentin, 1979; Ville De Paris, 1980. Career: Played concerts with: Diana Ross; Charles Aznavour; Jerry Lewis; Lambert Wilson; Julia Migenes-Johnson; Member, jazz groups with: Michel Legrand; Patrice Caratini; Luc Lemasne; Yanko Nilovic; Laurent Cuny; 3 tours Japan with Raymond Lefèvre; Numerous revues and shows include: Cats; 42nd Street; Cabaret; Folies Bergères; Numerous appearances on French television include 4 telethons (1988-94); Several other musical and theatrical works; Performed with Orchestre Philharmonique d'Europe, Orchestre du Luxembourg and various other orchestras; Music teacher in Guéret, 1981-82; Lucé, 1988-89; Gentilly, 1989-90; Chatou, 1991-92. Recordings for: Lisa Minelli; Charles Aznavour; Julia Migenes-Johnson; Pierre Perret; Georges Aperghis; Thomas Fersen; André Hoder. Hobbies: Wine (Bordeaux); Horses. Address: 23 Avenue Gütenberg, 92800 Puteaux, France.

LOUISE (Louise Nurding). Singer. Education: Italia Conti Stage School. Career: Singer, UK all-female vocal group, Eternal, 1992-95; Solo artiste, 1995-. Recordings: Album: with Eternal: Always And Forever, 1993; Solo Albums: Louise, 1996; Woman In Me, 1997; Hit singles: with Eternal: Stay, 1993; Solo hits: Light Of My Life, 1995; In Walked Love, 1996; Arms Around The World, 1997; Let's Go Round Again, 1997. Honours: 4 BRIT Award Nominations; Smash Hits Award. Current Management: First Avenue Management, The Courtyard, 42 Colwith Road, London W6 4EY, England.

LOURAU Julien, b. 2 Mar 1970, Paris, France. Musician (saxophone). 1 daughter. Career: Performed at Marciac Festival; Vienna Festival; Blue Note, New York City; Hot Brass, Paris; Auditorium des Halles, Paris; Festival Banlieues Bleues; Radio-France. Publications: A Turtle's Dream; Abbey Lincoln; Bojan Z Quartet; Julien Lourau Groove Gang. Honours: First prize, soloist, Concours de la Défense, 1993. Current Management: Carine Tedesco, Artalent. Address: 15 Passage de la Main D'Or, 75011 Paris, France.

LOUVIN Charlie, b. 7 July 1927, Alabama, USA. Singer. Career: Appearances include: Nashville Now; Ralph Emery Show; At The Ryman; Grand Ole Opry Live; Backstage At The Opry. Recordings: See The Big Man Cry; Will You Visit Me On Sundays? Cry Myself To Sleep. Honours: Alabama Music Hall Of Fame; Songwriters Hall Of Fame; Grammy Award; 4 Country Music Hall Of Fame Nominations. Memberships: AFofM; AFTRA. Hobbies: Fishing; Golf. Current Management: Susie Reed, Mountain Magic Talent. Address: PO Box 140324, Nashville, TN 37214, USA.

LOVANO Joe, b. 29 Dec 1952, Ohio, USA. Musician (tenor saxophone, clarinet, bass clarinet); Composer. m. Judi Silvano, 30 Sept 1984. Education: Studied with father, Tony Lovano. Musical Education: Berklee College of Music, Boston. Career: Toured with: Woody Herman Big Band; Thad Jones-Mel Lewis Orchestra; John Scofield Quartet; Paul Motian Trio (with Bill Frisell); Formed own bands, tours worldwide. Recordings: Rush Hour; Tenor Legacy; Universal Language Sextet; Recorded with Joshua Redman. Honours: Jazz Artist of The Year, Downbeat Magazine Critics Poll, 1995. Membership: AFofM. Current Management: The Merlin Company. Address: 17609 Ventura Boulevard #212, Encino, CA 91316, USA.

LOVE Courtney, b. 1965. Singer; Musician (guitar); Actress. m. Kurt Cobain, 24 Feb 1992, deceased. 1 daughter. Career: Member, Faith No More, 1 year; Founder, singer/guitarist, Hole, 1991-; Tours include: Support tour to Nine Inch Nails; Reading Festival, 1994, 1995; Film appearances: Straight To Hell; Sid And Nancy; Feeling Minnesota. Recordings: Albums with Hole: Pretty On The Inside, 1991; Live Through This, 1994. Current Management: Q-Prime Inc., 729 7th Avenue, 14th Floor, New York, NY 10019, USA.

LOVE Mike, b. 15 Mar 1941, Baldwin Hills, California, USA. Singer. Career: Member, Beach Boys, 1961-; Own band, Endless Summer, 1981; Numerous tours, concerts, include: The Beach Boys Summer Spectacular, Hollywood Bowl, 1966; UNICEF concert, Paris, 1967; Carnegie Hall, 1971; Royal Festival Hall, London, 1972; Grand Gala Du Disque, Amsterdam, 1972; Wembley Stadium, 1980; Knebworth Festival, 1980; Independence Day concerts, Washington DC, 1980s; Presidential Inaugural Gala, for President Reagan, 1985; Live Aid, Philadelphia, 1985; Tour with Chicago, 1989; Tour, supported by The Everly Brothers, 1991. Compositions include: Co-writer, theme for film: Almost Summer, 1978; Co-writer, song: Rock'n'Roll To The Rescue, 1986. Recordings: Albums Include: Surfin' Safari; Surfer Girl, 1963; Little Deuce Coupe, 1963; Shut Down Vol 2; All Summer Long, 1964; Christmas Album, 1964; The Beach Boys Today!, 1965; Summer Days (And Summer Nights), 1965; Beach Boys Party, 1966; Pet Sounds, 1966; Smiley Smile, 1967; Wild Honey, 1968; Friends, 1968; 20/20, 1969; Sunflower, 1970; Carl And The Passions/So Tough, 1972; Holland, 1973; 15 Big Ones, 1976; The Beach Boys Love You, 1977; MIU, 1978; LA (Light Album), 1980; The Beach Boys, 1985; Still Cruisin', 1989; Two Rooms, 1991; Summer In Paradise, 1992; Numerous compilations; Solo album: Looking Back With Love, 1981; Singles include: Surfin' USA; Fun Fun Fun; I Get Around; When I Grow Up (To Be A Man); Dance Dance Dance; Help Me Rhonda; California Girls; Barbara Ann; Sloop John B; God Only Knows; Good Vibrations; Wouldn't It Be Nice. Honours include: Inducted into Rock And Roll Hall Of Fame, 1988; Special Award Of Merit, American Music Awards, 1988. Current Management: Elliott Lott, 4860 San Jacinto Circle West, Fallbrook, CA 92026, USA.

LOVELESS Patty, b. 4 Jan 1957, Pikeville, Kentucky, USA. Country Singer; Musician (guitar). m. (1) Terry Lovelace, 1976, (2) Emory Gordy Jr, 1989. Career: Summer job singing with the Wilburn Brothers, 1971; Singer, nightclubs and hotels, North Carolina; Moved to Nashville, 1985; Worked with Vince Gill and Emmylou Harris, including CBS' 70th Anniversary of the Grand Ole Opry; Television appearances include: The Tonight Show; Late Night With Conan O'Brian; Good Morning America; ABC In Concert Country; Music City Tonight; The Road; TNN Country News; Grand Ole Opry Live. Recordings: Albums: Only What I Feel, 1992; When Fallen Angels Fly, 1995; The Trouble With The Truth, 1996; Long Stretch of Loneliness, 1998; Singles include: Blame It On Your Heart; Nothin' But The Wheel; You Will; How Can I Help You Can Say Goodbye; You Don't Even Know Who I Am. Honours include: Country Music Awards, 1993, 1995; Country Music Television Award, Female Artist of the Year, 1994; Real Country Listener Award, Female Vocalist of the Year, 1995; Academy of Country Music Award, 1997; Nominations for CMA, ACM and Grammy awards, 1994-. Current Management: Fitzgerald-Hartley Co, 1908 Wedgewood Avenue, Nashville, TN 37212, USA.

LOVEMUSCLE Johnny, b. 3 Apr 1961, Hounslow, England. Record Producer; Writer; Designer; Actor; Singer. Education: Design Degree. Musical Education: Self-taught. Career: Founder, The Rhythm Men, 1982; Founder, The Adventures of Johnny Lovemuscle; Formed partnership with Martin Noakes, as producers for: Gene And Jim Are Into Shakes; Afrikadelic; Little Caesar, 1988; Managed by Pete Waterman; Published by Warner Chappell. Recordings: Shake! (How About A Sampling Gene?); The Whole Of The Moon; Piti Pata; Eez-Zee-Boo-Gie. Honours: BFI Nomination, Best New Act, 1988. Memberships: Musicians' Union; PRS; Equity. Hobbies: Nightclubs; Horseracing. Current Management: Management To The Stars. Address: 28-30 Ecton Road, Addlestone, Surrey KT15 1UE, England.

LOVETT Lyle, b. 1 Nov 1957, Klein, Texas, USA. Singer; Songwriter; Actor. m. Julia Roberts, 27 Jun 1993. Career: Backing vocalist, Nancy Griffith, 1985; Solo singer, songwriter, 1986-; Television appearances include: Late Night With David Letterman, 1992, 1993; The Tonight Show, NBC TV, 1993; Willie Nelson - The Big Six-O, CBS TV, 1993; Regular US tours; Film appearances: The Player, 1992; Short Cuts, 1993. Recordings: Albums: Lyle Lovett, 1986; Pontiac, 1988; Lyle Lovett And His Large Band, 1989; Joshua Judges Ruth, 1992; Leap Of Faith (soundtrack), 1992; I Love Everybody, 1994; Backing vocalist, The Last Of The True Believers, Nanci Griffith, 1985; Great Big Boy, Leo Kottke, 1991; Producer, King Tears, Walter Hyatt, 1990; Contributor, Deadicated (collection of Grateful Dead covers), 1991. Current Management: Vector Management, PO Box 128037, Nashville, TN 37212, USA.

LOVSIN Peter, b. 27 June 1955, Ljubljana, Slovenia. Singer; Songwriter. m. Darija Lovsin, 21 Dec 1980, 1 son, 1 daughter. Education: Faculty for Journalism. Career: Lead singer, punk bands: Pankrti, 1977-87; Sokoli, 1988-93; Currently solo, with support band Vitezi Om'a (The Divers). Recordings: 6 albums with Pankrti; 3 with Sokoli; 2 solo albums. Publications: Poetry: In The Service of Rock'n'Roll. Honours: Croatian Youth Organisation Awards, 1980. Hobbies: Football; Skiing. Current Management: Tales, Lovsin in Ostali. Address: Zadruzna 1, 61000 Ljubljana, Slovenia.

LOWE Christopher Sean, b. 4 Oct 1959, Blackpool, Lancashire, England. Education: Architecture, Liverpool University. Career: Met Neil Tennant, founded West End, renamed Pet Shop Boys, 1981; Granada TV special: Love Me Tender, 1988; Film: It Couldn't Happen Here, 1988; Benefit concert, Picadilly Theatre, 1988; Television: Wogan; Top Of The Pops, 1988; Tour, Hong Kong, Japan, Britain, 1988; USA: With Electronic, Dodgers Stadium; Mayan Theatre, Los Angeles; TV: Arsenio Hall Show, 1990; Performance Tour: Japan; USA; Canada; Europe; UK; Eire, 1991; 2 weeks, Simon Bates Show, Radio One, 1991, 1992; Launched own record label: Spaghetti, 1991; Concert, Heaven Nightclub, 1991; South Bank Show, 1992; Hacienda Club, Manchester, 1992; Roseland, New York, 1992; Opening, Russian MTV, 1993; Songwriter, producer, artists include: Liza Minelli; Dusty Springfield; Patsy Kensit; Boy George; Electronic. Recordings: Albums: Please, 1986; Disco, 1986; Actually, 1987; Introspective, 1988; Behaviour, 1990; Discography, 1991; Very, 1993; Relentless, 1993; Singles: West End Girls (Number 1, UK), 1985; Love Comes Quickly, 1986; Suburbia, 1986; It's A Sin, 1987; with Dusty Springfield: What Have I Done To Deserve This, 1987; Rent, 1987;

Always On My Mind (Christmas Number 1, UK), 1987; Heart, 1988; Domino Dancing, 1988; Left To My Own Devices, 1988; It's Alright, 1989; So Hard, 1990; Being Boring, 1990; Where The Streets Have No Name, 1991; Jealousy, 1991; DJ Culture, 1991; Was It Worth It?, 1991; Can You Forgive Her, 1993; Go West, 1993; Album: Alternative Pet Shop Boys, 1996. Publication: Pet Shop Boys, Literally, 1990. Honours: Ivor Novello Awards, 1987, 1988; BPI Award, Best Single, 1987; Best Group, 1988; Berolina, Germany, 1988. Current Management: Pet Shop Boys Partnership, 8 Pembridge Studios, 27a Pembridge Villas, London W11 3EP, England.

LOWE Jez, b. 14 July 1955, Sunderland, England. Singer; Songwriter; Musician. Education: Sunderland Polytechnic. Career: Professional on folk circuit, 1980-; Toured, mainly Europe, USA; 10 solo albums; Many others as session musician; Solo works and with Bad Pennies. Compositions: for Fairport Convention: London Danny; Back In Durham Jail (10 cover versions); for The Clancy Brothers: Father Mallory's Dance. Publications: Songs Of Jez Lowe, 1988; Songs Of Jez Lowe Vol II. Honours: PRS Composers In Education Award, 1993. Membership: Musicians' Union. Current Management: Lowe Life Music (UK); Nancy Carlin Associates (US). Address: c/o Lowe Life Music, PO Box 25, Horden, Peterlee, County Durham SR8 3YZ, England.

LOWE Nick, b. 24 Mar 1949, Woodchurch, Suffolk, England. Singer; Musician (bass); Record Producer. m. Carlene Carter, 15 Aug 1979. Career: Member, Brinsley Schwarz, 1969-75; Rockpile (with Dave Edmunds), 1977-81; Leader, own band Nick Lowe & The Chaps, 1981; Founder, Little Village (with Ry Cooder, John Hiatt, Jim Keltner), 1992; Appearances include: Support to Van Morrison, 1970; Knebworth Festival, 1978; Support to Blondie, US, 1979; Camridge Folk Festival, 1988, 1995; Film appearance, Stardust, 1974; Documentary, Born Fighters, UK TV, 1979. Recordings: Albums: with Brinsley Schwarz: Brinsley Schwarz, 1970; Despite It All, 1970; Silver Pistol, 1972; Please Don't Ever Change, 1973; Original Golden Greats, 1974; The New Favourites Of Brinsley Schwartz, 1974; Solo albums: Jesus Of Cool, 1978; The Abominable Snowman, 1983; Nick's Knack, 1986; Basher - The Best Of Nick Lowe, 1989; Party Of One, 1990; The Impossible Bird, 1994; with Rockpile: Labour Of Lust, 1979; Seconds Of Pleasure, 1980; with His Cowboy Outfit: Nick Lowe And His Cowboy Outfit, 1984; Rose Of England, 1985; with Little Village: Little Village, 1992; Singles include: I Love The Sound Of Breaking Glass, 1978; Crackin' Up, 1979; Cruel To Be Kind, 1979; Albums as record producer: with Elvis Costello: My Aim Is True, 1977; This Year's Model, 1978; Armed Forces, 1979; Get Happy, 1980; Blood And Chocolate, 1986; with Carlene Carter: Musical Shapes, 1980; Blue Nun, 1981; Also: Chocs Away, Kursaal Flyers, 1975; Malpractice, Dr Feelgood, 1975; Get It, Dave Edmunds, 1976; Rhythm, Fabulous Thunderbirds, 1982; Riding With The King, John Hiatt, 1984; Katydids, Katydids, 1990; Contributor, film soundtracks: Rock'n'Roll High School, 1978; Americathon, 1980. Address: c/o Riviera Global Record Productions, 20 Cromwell Mews, London SW7 2JY, England.

LOWE Robert Christopher, b. 16 Apr 1960, Carshalton, Surrey, England. Musician (drums, percussion, keyboards). m. Julie Ann Burge, 25 Mar 1989. Musical Education: Self-taught. Career: Member, Abbfinoosty; Many concerts and festivals; Local radio airplay; Australian television. Recordings: Album: with Abbfinoosty: Future; The Other Side (EP); Solo project in progress. Membership: Musicians' Union. Hobbies: Art; Nature. Current Management: Self-managed.

LU WIN Annabella (Myant Myant Aye), b. 1966, Rangoon, Burma. Singer. Career: Singer,

Bow Wow Wow, 1980-83; Solo artiste. Recordings: Albums: See Jungle..., 1981; I Want Candy, 1982; When The Going Gets Tough..., 1983; The Best Of Bow Wow Wow, 1989; Singles: C30, C60, C90, Go!; Go Wild In The Country; I Want Candy. Current Management: ESP Management, 888 7th Avenue #2904, New York, NY 10106-0001, USA.

LUBIN Jean-Claude, b. 2 Oct 1935, Paris, France. Musician (piano); Information Scientist. Education: Doctor in Science (Geology). Musical Education: Studying piano classical from 8 to 11 years. Career: Member, various groups, New Orleans, 1953-56; Musician, Paris, with: F Jeanneau; M Saury; A Nicholas; A Reweliotty; Also played with: B Wilen; G Laffite; L Fuentes; J L Chautemps; S Grapelly; J L Ponty; J F Jenny Clarke; A Romano; H Texier; A Lorenzi; D Humair; M Roques; J Griffin; C Baker; D Byrd; L Konitz; D Gordon; G Coleman; J McLean; D Cherry; G Barbieri. Recording: The Fabulous Pescara Jam Session (with C Baker), 1975. Address: Jean-Claude Lubin, 3 Rue d'Alembert, 92130 Issy-Les-Moulineaux, France.

LUCAS David Jonathan, b. 4 Nov 1963, Brentwood, Essex, England. Musician (electric and acoustic guitar, electric and double bass); Vocalist. Musical Education: Self-taught. Career: Double bassist, the Rhythm Doctors, 1994; Tours of Belgium, Netherlands, Germany, Denmark and Canada; Appearances on Canadian and Dutch television, Dutch Radio. Recording: Guitarist, vocalist, The Is, The Is, 1993. Membership: Musicians' Union. Hobbies: Earth mysteries; War gaming; Literature; Art. Current Management: Showcase and Management International. Address: 33 Mandarin Place, Grove, Oxon OX12 0QH, England.

LUKAS Roels, b. 1 December 1957, Gent, Belgium. Teacher; Player, African and Cuban Percussion (Specialty Conga-Drum). m. Mart Vanmechelen, 3 sons. Education: Music, Theater, Dance School, Amsterdam, Netherlands; Instituto Superiore De Arte, La Havana, Cuba. Career: Member, Groups: Wasungu, 1995-96; Un Dia De Ilusion, 1996-; Zunzuncito, 1997-. Recordings: Wasungus Wereldmuziek, 1995; Un Dia De Ilusion, 1997. Publication: Afro-Caraibische Ritmen, 1996. Address: Dolfijnstraat 78, 2018 Antwerpen, Belgium.

LUKATHER Steve, b. 21 Oct 1957, Los Angeles, California, USA. Musician (guitar). Career: Member, Toto, 1978-. Compositions include: Commissioned (with Toto) to write theme for Los Angeles Olympic Games, 1984; Co-writer (with Randy Goodrum), I'll Be Over You, 1986. Recordings: Albums: with Toto: Toto, 1979; Hydra, 1979; Turn Back, 1981; Toto IV, 1982; Isolation, 1984; Dune (film soundtrack), 1985; Fahrenheit, 1986; The Seventh One, 1988; Past To Present 1977-1990, 1990; Kingdom Of Desire, 1992; Singles: with Toto include: Hold The Line, 1979; Georgy Porgy, 1980; 99, 1980; Rosanna, 1982; Make Believe, 1982; Africa (Number 1, US), 1983; I Won't Hold You Back, 1983; I'll Be Over You, 1986; Without Your Love, 1987; Pamela, 1988; Contributor, We Are The World, US For Africa charity single, 1985. Honours: 6 Grammy Awards: Best Record, Best Album, Best Engineered Recording, Best Producer (Toto), Best Vocal Arrangement, Best Instrumental Arrangement, 1983. Address: c/o Fitzgerald-Hartley Co., 50 W Main Street, Ventura, CA 93001, USA.

LULU (Marie Lawrie), b. 3 Nov 1948, Lennox Castle, Scotland. Singer; Entertainer. m. Maurice Gibb (divorced), (2) John Freda, 1976. Career: Singer, Lulu and the Luvvers, 1963-1966; Solo artiste, 1966-; UK tours with: Gene Pitney; Peter & Gordon, Roy Orbison, The Beach Boys, 1965-66; Tour, Poland, with the Hollies, 1966; The Royal Variety Show, 1967, 1981; Host, own variety show, BBC1, 1968; Joint winner for UK (with

France, Netherlands and Spain), Boom-Bang-A-Bang, Eurovision Song Contest, 1969; Berlin Disc Gala, 1971; Film appearance: To Sir With Love, 1966; Theatre and television includes: Guys And Dolls; Song And Dance; The Secret Diary Of Adrian Mole Aged 13½; New record deal and forthcoming album being recorded. Recordings: Albums: To Sir With Love, 1967; New Routes, 1970; The Most Of Lulu, 1971; Take Me To Your Heart Again, 1982; Don't Take Love For Granted, 1978; Lulu, 1981; Independence, 1993; Hit singles include: Shout, 1964; Leave A Little Love, 1965; Try To Understand, 1965; The Boat That I Row, 1967; Let's Pretend, 1967; To Sir With Love, 1967; Me The Peaceful Heart, 1968; I'm A Tiger, 1968; Boom-Bang-A-Bang, 1969; The Man Who Sold The World, 1974; Independence, 1993; I'm Back For More, duet with Bobby Womack, 1993; Guest vocalist, Relight My Fire, Take That (Number 1, UK), 1993. Current Management: Running Dog Management Ltd, PO Box 225, Sunbury-on-Thames, Middlesex TW16 5RT, England.

LUNDEN Petri H, b. 29 Nov 1963, Helsinki. Promoter; Booking Agent; MD. 1 daughter. Career: Breaking the following acts in Scandinavia: Bjoku; Green Day; Nirvana; Offspring; Stereo MC's; Blue Oasis; Prodigy Cranberries; Soul Adylum; Weexer; The Orb; Swedish acts worked with, worldwide: Clawfinger; Cardigans; Popsicle; Stanna Bo. Honours: Most Interesting Promoter of the Year, 1994. Membership: ECPA. Hobbies: Design; Hunting. Address: Box 53045, 40014 Goteborg, Sweden.

LUNDIN Fredrik, b. 7 Apr 1963, Copenhagen, Denmark. Musician (saxophone, flute); Composer; Arranger. m. Trine-Lise Væring, 16 May 1987. Musical Education: Self-taught. Career: Tours across Scandinavia, Europe, as bandleader, 1981-; Recorded with: Paul Bley; Steve Swallow; Bobo Stenson; Palle Danielsson; Joakim Milder; European Youth Orchestra; Bo Stief; Niels Henning Orsted Pedersen; Kenneth Knudsen; Thomas Clausen; Jorgen Emborg; Erling Kroner. Recordings: As bandleader: Twilight Land, 1986; The Cycle, 1987; Pieces Of..., (with Paul Bley), 1990; People Places Times & Faces, (with Palle Danielsson, Kenneth Knudsen, Audun Klieve, Trine-Lise Væring), 1992; With others: Over The Rainbow, Jorgen Emborg & Steve Swallow, 1992; Sounds And Silence, Kenneth Knudsen, 1994; Henrik Metz, NHOP, Fredrik Lundin, 1994. Honours: Sorens Penge; JASA Prize; Hafnia Music Award; Danish Music Council Award; DFBFA Prize of Honour. Membership: Danish Society of Jazz, Beat and Folk Composers. Hobbies: Photography. Address: Ågade 110, 3 th, 2200 Copenhagen N, Denmark.

LUNDSTEN Ralph, b. 6 October 1936, Ersnäs, Sweden. Composer; Filmmaker; Artist; Author; Studio owner. Career: Owner of Andromeda Picture and electronic music studio, including the Love Machine and other invented synthesizers, 1959-; More than 550 opus and 68 records, 12 short films, art exhibitions, a book with CD - Lustbarheter; Work for Opera House in Stockholm in Stockholm and Oslo, the Modern Museum and National Museum in Stockholm, the Louvre and the Biennale in Paris, the Triennale in Milano and the Museum of Contemporary Crafts in New York; Subject of a number of Radio and TV portraits, 1971-98; Special portrait-exhibition at the Music Museum in Stockholm, 1991-92. Compositions include: Nordic Nature Symphony No 1, The Water Sprite; Johannes and the Lady of the Woods; A Midwinter Saga; A Summer Saga; Bewitched; Landscape of Dreams; The Seasons; Erik XIV and Gustav III; Cosmic Love; Ourfather, Nightmare; Horrorscope; Shangri-La; Universe; Discophrenia; Alpha Ralpha Boulevard; Paradise Symphony; The New Age; Pop Age; Music for Relaxation and Meditation; Cosmic Phantazy; The Dream Master; The Gate of Time; The Ages of

Man; Sea Symphony; Mindscape Music; Nordic Light; The Symphony of Light; The Symphony of Love; In Time and Space. Honours: Grand Prix Biennale, Paris, France, 1967; Swedish Film Institute Prize, 1964-67; About 40 other awards for music and film making; Schwingungen Preis, Oscar of Electronic Music, 1997. Address: Frankensburgs väg 1, SE-132 42 Saltsjö-Boo, Sweden.

LUNDSTREM Oleg Leonidovisch, b. 2 Apr 1916, Chita, Siberia, Russia. Composer; Orchestra Leader. Widower. Education: Graduate, musical college, Harbin, China, 1935; High Technical Centre, Faculty of Architecture, Shanghai, 1944; Kazan Conservatory, as composer and symphony conductor, Russia, 1953. Career: Leader, professional jazz band, Shanghai, 1935; Leader, Concert Jazz Orchestra, Moscow, 1956; Film, A Song Without End, 1965; Many appearances on radio and television. Compositions include: Suite on Tatar Folklore, for Symphony Orchestra; Symphony in C Minor; Melody for Violin and Piano; Pieces for jazz big band: Interlude; Mirage; Imprompt; Together Again; Bokhara Ornament; In The Mountains Of Georgia. Recordings: Together Again; Tribute to Jazz Masters; In Swing Time; Nowadays; In A Mellow Tone. Honours: People's Artist Of Russia, 1984; DSc, International Academy of Sciences, San Marino, 1993; Prize of Moscow, for literature and art, 1995; Laureate of the National Musical Prize Ovation, 1996; Order, Services for the Fatherland, III degree, 1996. Memberships: Union of Composers, Russia; Union of Theatre Workers; International Union of Musical Workers. Hobby: Swimming. Cherkisovskaya h 3, B J Apt 49, Moscow 107061, Russia.

LUNGHINI Elsa, b. 20 May 1973, Paris, France. Singer; Actress; Author; Composer. 1 son. Career: Singer: Solo artist, 1986-; European tour and Olympia, Paris, 1990; In duets with Glenn Madeiros: diamond awards, Antwerp, 1988; Actress: Festival de Cannes, for film: Le Retour de Casanova, with Alain Delon, 1991. Recordings: T'en Va Pas (Please Don't Go), 1986; with Glenn Madeiros: Love Always Finds A Reason, 1988; First album: Elsa, 1988; Rien Que Pour Ça, 1990; Dance Violence, 1992. Honours: Gold and Platinum singles and albums; Grand Prix SACEM, 1993. Hobbies: Piano; Dance. Current Management: BMG France/Ariola, 2 Rue des 4 Fils, 75003 Paris, France (Music); Artmedia, 10 Avenue Georges V, 75008 Paris, France (Films).

LUNN John Lawrence, b. 13 May 1956, Scotland. Composer; Musician. m. Sara, 1 son. Education: Glasgow University. Musical Education: Royal Scottish Academy of Music; Electronic Music, Massachusetts Institute of Technology. Career: Formed pop group: Earplay, 1981; Later joined avant garde music group, The Lost Jockey; Developed into: Man Jumping, mid-1980s; Compositions: Films: Four Weddings And A Funeral; The Cormorant, BBC2; The Gift, BBC1; After The Dance, BBC; Other television: Finney, YTV; Hamish McBeth, BBC; The Last Machine, BBC; Beatrix, BBC; Heart Of Shelley, Anglia; The Dance House, BBC2; Focal Point, BBC Scotland; Ballets: Weighing The Heart; Goes Without Saying; In Dream I Loved A Dream; Classical pieces: Le Voyage; Verve; Echoes; Leonce And Elena; Jazz Pointilliste; Strange Fruit; Black and Blue; (opera) Mathematics Of A Kiss. Honours: Scholarship, Scottish Arts Council. Memberships: Musicians' Union; PRS. Current Management: Soundtrack Music Management, 22 Ives Street, Chelsea, London SW3 2ND, England.

LUNT David Brian, b. 3 May 1948, Stockport, England. Musician (bass; guitar). Career: Played with many artists including: Dr John, James Booker, Alexis Korner, Johnny Mars, Victor Brox, Taj Mahal, Jimmy Rogers, Homesick James, Louisiana Red, Cousin Joe Pleasant and Tommy Tucker. Hobby: Electronics. Address: 249

Manchester Road, Heaton Chapel, Stockport, Cheshire SK4 5EB, England.

LÜRSEN Martin, b. 15 June 1949, Hoogwoud, Netherlands. Artist Manager; Record Producer. 1 son. Career: Tour Manager with: Vitesse, 1975-80; Massada, Spargo, Dolly Dots, Mink De Ville, 1980-87; Producer Manager, Live Television shows and festivals, 1987-90; Manager: The Scene, Chris Daniels (US), Jan Rybroek, 1990-. Address: Worldwide Productions Inc, Herculestrat 61, 1973 VN Ymuiden, The Netherlands.

LUSCOMBE Stephen Alfred, b. 29 Oct 1954, Hillingdon, Middlesex, England. Musician (keyboards); Composer; Producer. Musical Education: Self-taught, also pupil of John Steven's Music Workshops, 1971-72. Career: Member, Portsmouth Sinfonia, avant garde orchestra, 1972-74; Member, Spontaneous Music Orchestra, 1972-74; Founder, performer, Music Workshop Miru, 1973-77; Founder, with Neil Arthur, electro-pop duo Blancmange, 1979-86; Numerous tours, television and radio broadcasts, recordings; Co-founder, West India Company, with Pandit Dinesh, 1984-; With artists including: Asha Bhosle; Boy George; Apache Indian; Saeed Jaffrey; La La La Human Steps; Numerous commissions for television, radio, theatre, film productions including National Theatre, 1994; BBC Radio Drama, 1994; Lonely Planet Travel Guide (CH4), 5 programmes, 1995; Music for film Masala, starring Saeed Jaffrey and Zora Seghal, Canada, 1991. Music composition and direction for R National Theatre Production, Wicked Yaar, 1994. Recordings: with Portsmouth Sinfonia: Play The Popular Classics, 1973; Live At The Albert Hall, 1974; with Blancmange: Happy Families, 1982; Mange Tout, 1984; Believe You Me, 1985; Greatest Hits, 1990; Also 8 top 40 singles include: Living On The Ceiling; with West India Company: Ave Maria (EP), 1984; Music From New Demons, 1989; The Art Of Love - Readings From The Kama Sutra, Saeed Jaffrey, 1992; Music From The Lonely Planet, with others, 1995. Memberships: PRS; PPL. Hobbies: Cooking; Walking and climbing; Travel; Gardening. Current Management: Self-managed; Notting Hill Music Ltd. Address: 87 Notting Hill Gate, London W11 3JZ, England.

LUSHER Don, b. 6 Nov 1923, Peterborough, Northamptonshire, England. Musician (trombone); Bandleader. Career: Member, Joe Daniels And His Hot Shots; Joined Lou Preager at Hammersmith Palais; Member, Maurice Winnick's Band, The Squadronaires and the Ted Heath Band; Extensive tours with artists including Frank Sintara, 1960s; Leader, big bands, for television and radio appearances; Educator, USA; Japan; Australia; UK. Recordings: Albums include: Lusher And Lusher And Lusher, 1972; Collection, 1976; Don Lusher Big Band, 1981; Don Lusher Pays Tribute To The Great Bands Volume 2, 1988; Just Good Friends, 1993. Publication: The Don Lusher Book. Current Management: Derek Boulton Management, 76 Carlisle Mansions, Carlisle Place, London SW1P 1HZ, England.

LUTHER Paul James, b. 1 Sept 1974, Salisbury, England. Musician (guitar). Musical Education: 11 years, private tuition, classical guitar. Career: 2 UK tours backing Toyah Wilcox; Concerts for British forces, Belize; Heineken festival concerts, Gateshead, Plymouth, 1994; Member, Scarlet supporting Bryan Ferry, UK tour, 1995; Television: 3 appearances with Scarlet, Top of the Pops; Pebble Mill; Parallel 9; Wot's Up Doc with singer David Dixon. Recordings: with Toyah Wilcox: Take The Leap, 1993; with Scarlet: Naked, 1995; Unreleased: Voice Of The Beehive (as yet untitled); The Friday's Duck; Singles: with Scarlet: Independent Love Song (Top 20, UK charts); I Wanna Be Free. Membership: Musicians' Union. Hobbies: Producing local acts; Squash; Pool; Backgammon. Address: 295 Devizes Road, Salisbury, Wiltshire SP2 9LU, England.

LUUKKA Pekka, b. 1963. Musician (guitar); Bandleader. Musical Education: Degree in Jazz, Sibelius Academy, Helsinki; Working for doctorate. Career: Debut, solist, UMO Jazz Orchestra, 1988; Played in various small bands, including, No Hope Band with Kari Heinilä, Severi Pyysalo; Tour with Jukka Perko, Pekka Pohjola, Kirmo Lintinen, Marko Timonen, 1990; Leader, own band Splash Of Colours; Member, Jari Perkiömäki Trio. Honours: Prizes at: International EU Jazz Competition; Hoilaart Competition, Belgium.

LYDON John (Johnny Rotten), b. 31 Jan 1956, Finsbury Park, London, England. Vocalist. Career: Vocalist, UK punk group the Sex Pistols, 1975-78; Founder, Public Image Limited, 1978-; Performances include: First gig, St Martin's School of Art, London, 1975; Screen on The Green Midnight Special, Islington, London, 1986; Tour, Anarchy In The UK, 1976; Europe, 1977; USA, 1978; Last live show, Winterland Ballroom, San Francisco, 1978; Sex Pistols reunion concert, Finsbury Park, London, 1996; Phoenix Festival, 1996. Recordings: Albums: Never Mind The Bollocks - Here's The Sex Pistols, 1977; The Great Rock'n'Roll Swindle, 1979; Same Product - Carri On Sex Pistols, 1979; Flogging A Dead Horse, 1980; Kiss This, 1992; Singles include: God Save The Queen, 1977; Pretty Vacant, 1977; Holidays In The Sun, 1977; Something Else, 1979; Silly Thing, 1979; C'Mon Everybody, 1979; The Great Rock'n'Roll Swindle, 1979. Current Management: DMA Entertainment, 2029 Century Park East, Suite 600, Los Angeles, CA 90067, USA.

LYLE Graham, b. Largs, Ayrshire, Scotland. Singer; Songwriter; Musician (guitar). Career: Songwriting partnership with Benny Gallagher, 1960s; Member, McGuinness Flint, 1969-71; Folk duo, Gallagher & Lyle, 1972-79; Solo artiste, 1980-. Compositions: Co-writer with Benny Gallagher: Mr Heartbreak's Here Instead, Dean Ford; International, Mary Hopkins; for McGuinness Flint: When I'm Dead And Gone; Malt And Barley Blues; for Gallagher and Lyle: I Wanna Stay With You; Heart On My Sleeve; Co-writer with Terry Britten: What's Love Got To Do With It, Tina Turner; Just Good Friends, Michael Jackson. Recordings: Albums: with Gallagher and Lyle: Gallagher And Lyle, 1972; Willie And The Lap Dog, 1973; Seeds, 1973; The Last Cowboy, 1974; Breakaway, 1976; Love On The Airwaves, 1977; Showdown, 1978; Gone Crazy, 1979; Lonesome No More, 1979; The Best Of, 1980; Heart On My Sleeve, 1991; Singles: I Wanna Stay With You, 1976; Heart On My Sleeve, 1976.

LYNCH Colm, b. 29 Apr 1952, Dublin, Ireland. Musician. 1 son, 1 daughter. Education: Social Pedegog, Denmark. Musical Education: Drums, piano, guitar, through high school: Private tutor in School of Music, Dublin. Career: Successful appearances on RTE (TV, Ireland): Meitheal; Saoire Samhradh; Spin Off; Jimmy Saville show, BBC; Danish radio, television. Compositions: Songwriter in Ireland, Singer/songwriter in UK, wrote hit singles (see Recordings). Recordings: Album: Early One Morning; Hit singles: Violence Has Many Faces; Devil Among The Tailors. Honours: Top Selling Album, 1973; Top Irish Artist, 1973; Best Group. Memberships: KODA (Danish PRS); DJBFA (Danish Society, Jazz, Rock and Folk Composers). Current Management: Self-managed. Address: Mejlgade 89, 8000 Aarhus C, Denmark.

LYNCH Jack (John D.), b. 13 Sept 1930, Duluth, Kentucky, USA. Writer; Singer; Actor; Musician (banjo, guitar, bass, mandolin, violin); Publisher; Producer; Distributor. 1 son. Education: 2 years college; Additional courses. Career: Film appearances: Ernest Goes To Jail; Bluegrass Holiday; Radio show, Jack Lynch Show, WPFB AM Radio, Middletown, Ohio, 10 years; Bandleader; Recording artist, 1963-. Recordings include: 3 albums, first due for release 1996. Publications: Contributor to: Traveling The Highway Home, Professor John Wright, University of Illinois. Honour: Honorable Order, Kentucky Colonels. Memberships: BMI; ASCAP; IBMA (International Bluegrass Music Association). Current Management: Jack Lynch Music Group, Management and Booking. Address: 306 Millwood Drive, Nashville, TN 37217-1604, USA.

LYNGSTAD Frida (Anni-Frid), b. Narvik, Norway. Singer. m. Benny Andersson, 1978 (divorced 1981). Career: Leader, own dance band, Anni-Frid Four; Singer, Abba, 1973-82; Appearances include: Winners, Eurovision Song Contest, 1974; Worldwide tours; Concerts include: Royal Performance, Stockholm, 1976; Royal Albert Hall, 1977; UNICEF concert, New York, 1979; Wembley Arena, 6 sell-out performances, 1979; Reunion with Abba, Swedish TV's This Is Your Life, 1986; The Story Of Abba, C4 TV, 1991; Solo artiste, 1983-; Film: Abba - The Movie, 1977. Recordings: Albums: with Abba: Waterloo, 1974; Abba, 1976; Arrival, 1977; The Album, 1978; Voulez-Vous, 1979; Solo albums: Frida Alone, 1976; Something's Going On, 1982; Shine, 1983; Singles include: Ring Ring; Waterloo; Mamma Mia; Dancing Queen; Fernando; Money Money Money; Knowing Me Knowing You; Take A Chance On Me; The Name Of The Game; Summer Night City; Chiquitita; Does Your Mother Know?; Gimme Gimme Gimme (A Man After Midnight); The Winner Takes All; Super Trouper; On And On And On; Lay All Your Love On Me; When All Is Said And Done; Head Over Heels; Solo: Time (duet with B A Robertson). Honours include: Gold discs; Best-selling group in history of popular music, Guinness Book Of Records, 1979; World Music Award, Best Selling Swedish Artist (with Abba), 1993.

LYNN Loretta (Loretta Webb), b. 14 Apr 1935, Butcher Hollow, Kentucky, USA. Singer. m. Oliver Lynn, 1948, 6 children. Career: Sang local clubs with group The Trailblazers; Regular appearances, Grand Ole Opry; Weekly television show, with the Wilburn Brothers, Nashville; Regular duets with Ernest Tubb and Conway Twitty. Recordings include: 16 Number 1 singles, 60 other hits, 15 number 1 albums; Hit singles include: I'm A Honky Tonk Girl; Success; Before I'm Over You; Blue Kentucky Girl; Don't Come Home A-Drinkin' (With Lovin' On Your Mind); Coal Miner's Daughter; Pregnant Again; Albums include: Loretta Lynn Sings, 1963; Before I'm Over You, 1964; Songs From The Heart, 1965; Blue Kentucky Girl, 1965; Hymns, 1965; I Like 'Em Country, 1966; You Ain't Woman Enough, 1966; Don't Come Home A-Drinkin', 1967; Singin' With Feelin', 1967; Fist City, 1968; Your Squaw Is On The Warpath, 1969; Woman Of The World, 1969; Coal Miner's Daughter, 1971; I Want To Be Free, 1971; Alone With You, 1972; Love Is The Foundation, 1973; They Don't Make 'Em Like Our Daddy, 1974; Home, 1975; Somebody Somewhere, 1976; Out Of My Head And Back In My Bed, 1978; Loretta, 1980; Lookin' Good, 1980; Makin' Love From Memory, 1982; Just A Woman, 1985; with Ernest Tubb: Mr And Mrs Used To Be, 1965; Singin' Again, 1967; If We Put Our Haeds Together, 1969; with Conway Twitty: We Only Make Believe, 1971; Lead Me On, 1971; Lousiana Woman, Misissipp Man, 1973; Country Partners, 1974; Feelins', 1975; United Talent, 1976; Dynamic Duo, 1977; Country Partners, 1974; Honky Tonk Heroes, 1978; Diamond Duets, 1979; Two's A Party, 1981; Making Believe, 1988; Publication: Coal Miner's Daughter (autobiography). Honours include: First woman inducted into Nashville Songwriters International Hall Of Fame; First woman to be voted Country Music Association's Entertainer Of The Year, 1972; CMA Vocal Duo of the Year (with Conway Twitty), 1972. Current Management: Loretta Lynn Enterprises, PO Box 120369, Nashville, TN 37212, USA.

LYNN Vera (Margaret Lewis) (Dame), b. 20 Mar 1917. Singer. m. Harry Lewis, 1941, 1 daughter. Career: Debut performance, 1924; Appeared with Joe Loss, Charlie Kunz, 1935; Ambrose, 1937-40; Applesauce, Palladium, London, 1941; Became known as the Forces Sweetheart, 1939-45; Radio show Sincerely Yours, 1941-47; Tour of Burma, entertaining troops, 1944; 7 Command performances; Appearances, Europe; Australia; Canada; New Zealand; Performed at 50th Anniversary of VE Day Celebrations, London, 1995; Own television shows: ITV, 1955; BBC1, 1956; BBC2, 1970; First British artist to top Hit Parade. Numerous recordings include: Auf Wiederseh'n (over 12 million copies sold). Publication: Vocal Refrain (autobiography), 1975. Current Management: Anglo-American Enterprises, 806 Keyes House, Dolphin Square, London SW1V 3NB, England.

LYNNE Jeff, b. 30 Dec 1947, Birmingham, England. Record Producer; Singer; Songwriter; Musician (guitar); Arranger. Musical Education: Self-taught. Career: Member, Idle Race, 1966-70; Member, The Move, 1970-72; Founder member, The Electric Light Orchestra (ELO), 1972-85; Regular international tours, 1973-; Record producer, 1983-; Formed the Traveling Wilburys (with Bob Dylan, Roy Orbison, George Harrison, Tom Petty), 1988; Also solo artiste. Recordings: Albums include: with ELO (as singer, guitarist, writer and producer): Electric Light Orchestra, 1972; ELO II, 1973; On The Third Day, 1973; Eldorado, 1974; The Night The Light Went On In Long Beach, 1974; Face The Music, 1975; Olé ELO, 1976; A New World Record, 1976; Out Of The Blue, 1977; Discovery, 1979; ELO's Greatest Hits, 1979; Xanadu (film soundtrack), 1980; Time (Number 1, UK), 1982; Secret Messages, 1983; with Traveling Wilburys (also co-writer and co-producer): Traveling Wilburys, Volume 1, 1988; Volume 3, 1991; Solo: Armchair Theatre, 1990; As producer: Information, Dave Edmunds, 1983; Cloud Nine, George Harrison, 1987; Mystery Girl, Roy Orbison, 1988; Full Moon Fever, Tom Petty, 1988; Singles include: with ELO: 10538 Overture; Roll Over Beethoven; Can't Get It Out Of My Head; Evil Woman; Strange Magic; Livin' Thing; Telephone Line; Mr Blue Sky; Sweet Talkin' Woman; Shine A Little Love; Don't Bring Me Down; Xanadu; Hold On Tight; with the Traveling Wilburys: Handle With Care; Solo: Doin' That Crazy Thing; As producer / co-producer: You Got It, Roy Orbison, 1988; Into The Great Wide Open, Tom Petty, 1991; Free As A Bird, The Beatles, 1995; Real Love, The Beatles, 1995. Honours: Nationwide Music Award, Album of the Year, Out Of The Blue, 1978; Ivor Novello Awards: Outstanding Contribution To British Music, 1979; Best Film Song, Xanadu, 1981; Grammy Award, Traveling Wilburys Volume 1, 1989; Grammy Nominations: Best Producer, 1989; Best Song, Learning To Fly (with Tom Petty), 1992; Rolling Stone Award, Best Producer, 1989; BMI Songwriters Award, one million broadcasts of Evil Woman, US, 1992. Memberships: ASCAP; BASCA. Hobbies: Computers; Tennis. Current Management: Craig Fruin. Address: PO Box 1428, Ross, CA 94957-1428, USA.

LYON Steve. Recording Engineer; Producer. Career: Trained under supervision of producer, Glyn Jones, West Sussex studio; Engineer,producer, Virgin Studio Group; Worked at The Townhouse; The Manor; Chief Engineer, Master Control, Los Angeles; Air Studios, London; Freelance, 1988-. Recordings: Albums include: with Depeche Mode: Songs Of Faith And Devotion; Violator; Faith And Devotion - Live; with Wedding Present: George Best; Bizzaro; with Nitzer Ebb: Ebbhead; Other recording sessions: Dedicated, Suzanne Vega; Sowing The Seeds Of Love, Tears For Fears; Rooftops (film), Dave Stewart; Flowers In The Dirt, Paul McCartney; Under Milk Wood, with George Martin; Also recorded with: Berlin; Prefab Sprout; UFO; Labi Siffre; Breathe; The Outfield. Current

Management: c/o Stephen Budd Management, 109B Regents Park Road, London NW1 8UR, England.

LYONS Ken (Tigger), b. 11 Apr 1951, North Allerton, Yorkshire, England. Musician (bass guitar); Songwriter; Composer. m. Linda Fletcher, 19 Apr, 1 daughter. Education: Hammersmith College of Art and Building. Musical Education: Self-taught. Career: with Flesh: Melody Maker Competition Finals, The Roundhouse, 1971; with Hustler: UK Queen Tour, 1974; Status Quo European Tour, 1975; Geordie Scene; Kid Jenson's 45; Radio 1 In Concert; with London club/pub band The Brain Surgeons, 1976-79; with LA band The Shots, 1980-83; KROQ Nick Stavross Show. Compositions include: for Hustler: Get Outta Me House (Get Out Of My House); Little People; for Brian Surgeons: Me And My Guitar; for The Shots: Reject. Memberships: MCPS; PRS. Hobbies: Karate; Clay pigeon shooting; Computer animation. Address: Lion Music, 29 Derby Road, Uxbridge, Middlesex UB8 2ND, England.

LYSDAL Jens, b. 12 Jan 1960, Sweden. Vocalist; Musician (guitar, keyboards); Arranger; Record Producer. Musical Education: Royal Danish Music Conservatory, 1981-85. Career: Backing musician with Superchancen DR (Denmark's radio/television company), backing artists including Pointer Sisters; Donna Summer; Sergio Mendes, 1993; Television show, Meyerheim After 8, backing Lill Lindfors, TV2, 1994; European Song Contest as member of DR Pop-orchestra, DR, 1995; As solo singer and guitarist, Meyerheim After 8, TV 2, 1994; Bent Fabricius Bjerre's 50 year Jubilee Show, DR, 1995; Tjek Ind Hos Mygind, TV 3, 1995; Arranger for symphony orchestra, for Mikael Wiehe; Tamra Rosanes; Majbritte Ulrikkeholm; Peter Busborg; Kirsten Siggaard; Ulla Henningsen; Producer for Kurt Ravn and Rikke Mølgaard. Recordings: Music for A Day In October, Kenneth Madsen film, 1990; Solo album: A Matter of Time; Music for film, The Treasure of the Forest by Nicolas Gaster. Honours: Arnold, for music to commercial, Kim's Peanuts; Winner, Golden Stag, Romania; CD of the Year, 1997. Membership: DJBFA. Current Management: Sundance Records, Havnegade 41, 1058 CPH. Address: Bogevang 30 A, Bureso, 3550 Slangerup, Denmark.

LYTLE Marshall, b. 1933, Old Fort, North Carolina, USA. Musician (upright bass); Vocalist. Married. Career: Original member, Bill Hayley's Comets, 1948-55; Invented rock'n'roll; First rock band to headline a film; Member, The Jodimans, 1955-58. Recordings: Rock Around The Clock; See You Later Alligator; Crazy Man Crazy; Shake Rattle And Roll; Rock The Joint; Mambo Rock; Rudy's Rock; Florida Twist; Skinny Minnie; Let's All Rock Together; Now Dig This. Publications: Rock Around The Clock; Stage Clear; We're Gonna Party; Never Too Old To Rock. Honours: Rock And Roll Hall Of Fame; Gold records; Best vocal group of 1953. Address: Rock It Concerts, Bruno Mefer Platz 1, D-SU937 Munchen, Germany.

LYTTELTON Humphrey Richard Adeane, b. 23 May 1921, Eton, Buckinghamshire, England. Bandleader; Jazz Musician (trumpet); Journalist; Broadcaster; Author. m. (1) Patricia Braithwaite, 1948, divorced, (2) Elizabeth Richardson, 1952, 2 sons, 2 daughters. Education: Camberwell School Of Art. Musical Education: Piano lessons; Self-taught trumpet. Career: Member, George Webb's Dixielanders, 1947; Bandleader, own band, 1948-; Festival appearances include: Nice; Zurich; Montreux; Warsaw; Newcastle; Edinburgh; Glasgow; Recorded and played with artistes including: Sidney Bechet; Buck Clayton; Buddy Tate; Helen Shapiro; Kenny Davern; Jimmy Rushing; Big Joe Turner. Founder, own record label, Calligraph, 1984; Owner, music publishing company Humph Music; Numerous television and radio appearances as musician and presenter;

Compère, BBC radio programmes: Jazz Club;
Jazz Scene; The Best Of Jazz; I'm Sorry I Haven't
A Clue; Freelance music journalist and critic.
Compositions: Numerous original compositions.
Recordings: Numerous albums, 1954-.
Publications: I Play As I Please, 1954; Second
Chorus, 1958; Take It From The Top, 1975; The
Best Of Jazz: Basin Street To Harlem, 1978;
Humphrey Lyttelton's Jazz And Big Band Quiz,
1979; The Best Of Jazz 2: Enter The Giants, 1981;
Why No Beethoven?, 1984; Contributions to:
Melody Maker; Harpers and Queen; Punch; High
Life. Honours: Hon DLitt, Warwick, 1987;
Loughborough, 1988; Hon DMus, Durham, 1989;
Keele, 1992; Honorary Professor of Music, Keele,
1993; Sony Gold Award, radio awards, 1993;
DLitt, University of Hertfordshire, 1995; Waterford
Crystal Award, IEAN, 1996; DArts, De Montfort
University, 1997. Membership: President, Society
For Italic Handwriting. Hobbies: Birdwatching;
Calligraphy. Current Management: Susan Da
Costa, Bull's Head Row, The Green, Surrey, RH9
8DZ, England. Address: BBC Light Music
Department, Broadcasting House, Portland Place,
London W1A 4WW, England.

M

M K SHINE (Mark Lowe), b. England. Singer; Songwriter; Reggae Club Owner. Education: Certificate, Building Construction, College, Jamaica. Musical Education: School Of Music, London. Career: Lead singer, founder, Destiny, with brother, 1986; Played round islands; Played Tokyo, 1989; Solo artist, using name M K Shine, 1991-; 2 week tour, Mexico, special guest at Rock Y Reggae Festival; Television, radio interviews. Recordings: Wild Gilbert, 1988; My Dream, 1994; Simply Magic. Honours: Represented Jamaica, Caribbean Broadcasting Union, 1990. Hobby: Architecture. Current Management: Sirron Kyles, Samuel Rogers And Associates. Address: PO Box 8305, Houston, TX 77288, USA.

MAAETOFT Nils, b. 17 Nov 1950, Vejle, Denmark. Singer; Songwriter; Musician (guitar). Career: Singer, guitarist, main songwriter for Danish rock group The Intellectuals; Wrote, performed, under pseudonym M T Purse; 1992, formed group M T Purse. Recordings: with The Intellectuals: Half A-Live, 1986; Health And Happiness, 1987; as M T Purse: Cross Talk, 1992; Throwing Rocks At The Moon, 1995. Membership: The Danish Society for Jazz Rock Folk Composers. Current Management: c/o Warner/Chappell Music, Denmark. Address: Anker Heegaardsgade 2, DK 1572 Copenhagen, Denmark.

MABUS Joel Dwight, b. 13 Sept 1953, Belleville, Illinois, USA. Singer; Songwriter; Musician (guitar, banjo, fiddle, mandolin). Education: Michigan State University. Musical Education: Self-taught. Career:Vancouver Folk Festival; Philadelphia Folk Festival; Winnipeg Folk Festival; Kerrville Folk Festival; Appearances on: A Prairie Home Companion, American public radio. Recordings: 10 solo recordings include: Promised Land; Flatpick And Clawhammer; Short Stories. Publications: Big Words - The Lyrics Of Joel Mabus. Honours: Detroit Metro Times, Instrumentalist Of The Year. Memberships: AFofM; The Folk Alliance. Hobbies: Fishing; Gardening; Reading. Address: c/o Fossil Records, PO Box 4754, East Lansing, MI 48826, USA.

MABY Graham Geoffrey, b. 1 Sept 1952, Gosport, Hampshire, England. Musician (bass guitar, guitar); Vocalist. m. Mary Beth Bernard, 15 Feb 1987, 2 sons, 1 daughter. Education: 1 year technical college. Musical Education: Self-taught. Career: Performances, live, television, video, with: Joe Jackson; Marshall Crenshaw; Graham Parker; Jules Shear; Garland Jeffreys; The Silos; Freedy Johnston; Darden Smith; Chris Stamey; Peter Holsapple; Delevantes; They Might Be Giants; Henry Lee Summer; Glen Burtnik; Shania Twin; Film: Peggy Sue Got Married, 1986; Tours mainly with Joe Jackson: Europe; North America; Japan; Australia; Laughter And Lust Tour, now on Virgin Video. Recordings: with Joe Jackson: Look Sharp, 1978; I'm The Man, 1979; Beat Crazy, 1980; Jumpin' Jive, 1981; Night And Day, 1982; Mike's Murder, 1983; Body And Soul, 1984; Live '79-84, 1987; Blaze Of Glory, 1989; Laughter And Lust, 1991; Night Music, 1994; with Marshall Crenshaw: Mary Jean And Nine Others, 1987; Good Evening, 1989; My Truck Is My Home, 1994; with Freedy Johnston: Can You Fly, 1991; This Perfect World, 1994; with Chris Stamey: It's Alright, 1987; Fireworks, 1991; with Henry Lee Summer: Henry Lee Summer, 1988; I've Got Everything, 1989; with David Broza: A Time Of Trains, 1993; Second Street, 1994; Little Victories, Darden Smith, 1993; They Might Be Giants, John Henry, 1994; Also with: Patty Smyth; Graham Parker; Jules Shear; Jill Sobule; David Wilcox. Honours: Gold records include: Night And Day; Look Sharp; Body And Soul. Memberships: ASCAP; AFTRA; AFofM. Hobbies: His children; Tennis; Music.

MAC DONNCHA Johnny Mháirtín Learaí, b. 9 Apr 1937, Galway, Ireland. Small Farmer; Craftsman; Singer. Career: Sean-nós singer, Specializing in traditional Irish songs, many from West Connemara; Travelled throughout Ireland as singer; Collects and teaches songs; Winner in Corn Uí Riada, Oirreachtas, Cork, 1985. Recordings: Bruach Na Beirtrí; Cassette, 1988; Album, 1993; Contae Mhuigheo. Honours: Corn Uí Riada, Winner, Cork, 1985. Current Management: Cló Iar-Chonnachta, Indreabhán, Co. Na Gaillimhe.

MACALPINE Tony, b. USA. Rock Musician (guitar, piano). Musical Education: Classical piano. Career: Solo artiste, rock guitarist, 1986-90; Formed MARS, short-lived supergroup, 1987; Founder, Squawk record label; Formed won band MacAlpine, 1990-. Recordings: Albums: Solo artiste: Edge Of Insanity, 1986; Maximum Security, 1987; with MARS: Project Driver, 1987; with MacAlpine: Eyes Of The World, 1990.

MACCOLL Kirsty, b. 10 Oct 1959. Singer; Songwriter. m. Steve Lillywhite, 1984, 2 children. Career: Singer, songwriter, 1976-; Also backing singer on recordings by: Van Morrison; Rolling Stones; Robert Plant; Talking Heads; The Smiths; Morrissey; Simple Minds. Recordings: Albums: Desperate Characters, 1981; Kite, 1989; Electric Landlady, 1991; Singles: There's A Guy Works Down The Chip Shop Swears He's Elvis, 1981; A New England, 1984; Fairytale Of New York, with The Pogues (Number 2, UK), 1987; Walking Down Madison, 1991; Galore - The Best Of Kirsty MacColl, 1995. Current Management: Peter Asher Management, 644 North Doheny Drive, Los Angeles, CA 90069, USA. Address: c/o XL Talent, Studio 7, 27A Pembridge Villas, London W11 3EP, England.

MACDONALD Calum, b. 12 Nov 1953, Lochmaddy, North Uist, Scotland. Musician (drums, percussion). Career: Former member, The Skyvers; Member, Scottish folk group Runrig, 1973-; International concerts include: Canada, 1987; Berlin, 1987; Support to U2, Murrayfield Stadium, Edinburgh, 1987; Concerts at: Royal Concert Hall, Glasgow; Open-air concert, Loch Lomond. Recordings: Albums: Play Gaelic, 1978; Highland Connection, 1979; Recovery, 1981; Heartland, 1985; The Cutter And The Clan, 1987; Once In A Lifetime, 1988; Searchlight, 1989; The Big Wheel, 1991; Amazing Things, 1993; Transmitting Live, 1995. Current Management: Marlene Ross Management, 55 Wellington Street, Aberdeen AB2 1BX, Scotland.

MACDONALD Rod, b. USA. Singer; Songwriter; Musician (guitar, harmonica); Poet; Writer. Education: Law degree, Columbia University. Career: Former writer, Washington Post; Numerous concerts across the USA; Co-organiser, Greenwich Village Folk Festival, New York; Endorsee, Hohner Harmonicas. Recordings: Songs recorded by numerous US artists. Current Management: Jim McPhee, Acorn Entertainments. Address: Winterfold House, 46 Woodfield Road, Kings Heath, Birmingham B13 9UJ, England.

MACDONALD Rory, 27 July 1949, Dornoch, Sutherland, Scotland. Vocalist; Musician (guitar, bass). Career: Founder member, Scottish folk group Runrig, 1973-; International concerts include: Canada; Berlin; Support to Murrayfield Stadium, Edinburgh, 1987; Concerts at: Royal Concert Hall, Glasgow; Open-air concert, Loch Lomond. Recordings: Albums: Play Gaelic, 1978; Highland Connection, 1979; Recovery, 1981; Heartland, 1985; The Cutter And The Clan, 1987; Once In A Lifetime, 1988; Searchlight, 1989; The Big Wheel, 1991; Amazing Things, 1993; Transmitting Live, 1995. Current Management: Marlene Ross Management, 55 Wellington Street, Aberdeen AB2 1BX, Scotland.

MACFARLANE Malcolm Douglas, b. 4 Apr 1961, Edinburgh, Scotland. Musician (guitar); Composer. Musical Education: City of Leeds College of Music, 1983-86. Career: Member, Barbara Thompson's Paraphernalia, 1988-; Several European tours; World tours with Shakatak, 1992-; Formed Mulford/MacFarlane group, 1994; First British tour, 1995. Recordings: with Barbara Thompson's Paraphernalia: Breathless; Everlasting Flame; with Mulford/MacFarlane: Jamming Frequency, 1995. Honours: Eric Kershaw Memorial Prize, Leeds College of Music, 1984-86. Membership: Performing Rights Society. Hobbies: Golf; Hillwalking; Reading. Address: London, England.

MACGOWAN Shane, b. 25 Dec 1957, Kent, England. Musician (guitar); Singer. Career: Member, The Pogues, 1983-90; Support to Elvis Costello, UK tour, 1984; Cambridge Folk Festival, 1985; US tours, 1986, 1988; Self Aid concert, Dublin, 1986; Glastonbury Festival, 1986; Fleadh '91, London, 1991; Chieftains Music Festival, London, 1991; Feile '91,Tipperary, Ireland, 1991; Solo artist, with backing group The Popes, 1993-; Film appearance, Straight To Hell, 1986. Recordings: Albums: with the Pogues: Red Roses For Me, 1984; Rum, Sodomy And The Lash, 1985; If I Should Fall From Grace With God, 1988; Peace And Lore, 1989; Hell's Ditch, 1990; The Best Of The Pogues, 1991; with The Popes: The Snake, 1994; Singles include: with The Pogues: A Pair Of Brown Eyes; Sally Maclennane; Dirty Old Town; Haunted, from film Sid And Nancy; Fiesta; Yeah Yeah Yeah Yeah; Misty Morning, Albert Bridge; Summer In Siam; A Fairytale Of New York (with Kirsty MacColl), 1987; with The Dubliners: The Irish Rover, 1987; Jack's Heroes, 1990; with The Popes: The Church Of The Holy Spook; The Woman's Got Me Drinking; Haunted, duet with Sinead O'Connor, 1995; You're The One, duet with Maire Brennan, for film soundtrack Circle Of Friends, 1995; Contributor, film soundtrack Straight To Hell, 1987; The Last Temptation Of Elvis, Nordoff-Robbins charity record, 1990; Red Hot And Blue, AIDS awareness record, 1990.

MACINTOSH Adrian, b. 7 Mar 1942, Tadcaster, England. Jazz Musician. m. Sheila Christie, 13 Apr 1974. Career: Early work with John Taylor Trio and Norma Winstone; Alan Elsdon Band, 1970; Joined Brian Leakes' Sweet And Sour, 1978; Joined Humphrey Lyttelton's Band, 1982; Work with Helen Shapiro, 1984-; Worked with many leading jazz names including: Sonny Stitt; Teddy Edwards; Jimmy Witherspoon; Harold Ashby; Nat Pierce; Scott Hamilton; Clark Terry; Warren Vache; Kenny Davern; Al Casey. Recordings: Humph and Wally Fawkes, 1983; Humph And Helen Shapiro, 1984; Humph, Al Casey And Kenny Davern, 1984; Humph At The Bulls Head, 1985; Humph And Buddy Tate, 1985; Humph Gigs, 1987; Humph And Lillian Boutté, 1988; Humph At Breda Jazz Festival, 1988; Humph Beano Boogie, 1989; Ken McCarthy Quartet (featuring Dick Pearce); Produced album by Brian Leake's Sweet And Sour, 1993. Memberships: Musicians' Union; Chairman, Association of British Jazz Musicians. Hobby: Long distance walking.

MACK Bobby, b. 19 June 1954, Fort Worth, Texas, USA. Vocalist; Musician (guitar); Music Producer. m. Pat Cullen, 24 May 1994, 1 son, 1 daughter. Education: University of Texas, Austin. Career: Delta Blue Festival, New Orleans Jazz Festival; Tours: Former USSR; Japan; New Zealand; Australia; Scandinavia; Europe; UK. Recordings: Bobby Mack and Night Train Albums include: Say What; Red Hot And Humid; Honeytrap, produced Mississippi Bluesman Willie Foster; I Found Joy, produced Mark Goodwin. Publications: Writer, Texas Blue Magazine. Hobby: Rancher, Wimberley, Texas. Current Management: Hugh Beverton, Albion Management. Address: 881 Lost Creek, Wimberley, TX 78676, USA.

MACK Danny, b. 29 Mar 1943, Harvey, Illinois, USA. Singer; Musician (accordion, drums, trumpet, keyboards); Record Producer; Record Company Executive. m. Caroline Panczyck, 3 Nov 1962, 1 son, 1 daughter. Education: Criminal justice. Musical Education: 15 years private study music instrumental, teaching, theory. Carrer: Bandleader, 1958-; Clubs circuit until 1977; Songwriting career began with first self-penned country recording on K-Ark, 1977; Recorded Fist Full Of Dollars, Nashville, Tennessee; Formed Syntony Publishing BMI and Briarhill Records, 1984; WLS TV, TCI of Indiana; Guest appearances, Sig Sakowitz radio show. Recordings: Jesus Is The Reason For The Season (Number 1 Christmas hit); On The Right Road Again, 1994; Old Rockers Never Die, 1994. Publications: Chicago Tribune; Country and Western Corner; Radio & Record News; Indie Bullet; Star Quest Magazines. Honours: Indie Label Of The Year, Producer Of The Year, CMAA, 1992, 1993, 1994; Honorary Kentucky Colonel; GSCMA Hall Of Fame Nomination; Inspirational Record Of the Year, CMA, USA, 1994; Song Of Year, World Radio Network, Spain, 1994. Memberships: Broadcast Music Inc; NARAS; Lifetime member, Country Music Associations of America. Hobbies: Writing music; Fishing; Vacations in Nevada. Current Management: The Danny Mack Music Group. Address: 3484 Nicolette Drive, Crete, IL 60417, USA.

MACK James Joseph, b. 12 Nov 1971, Kensington, London, England. Musician (percussion). Musical Education: Guildhall School of Music and Drama; West London Institute of Higher Education. Career: Worldwide tours and television appearances with: D:Ream; Des'ree; Lonnie Liston Smith; C J Lewis; Rozalla; NYJO; Skin. Recordings with: D:ream (second album); Skin; NYJO; Various television commercials include: American Express; Maxwell House; John Smiths Bitter. Honours: Performance diploma, Guildhall School of Music and Drama. Membership: Musicians' Union. Hobbies: Good food; Travel; Fitness. Address: 28 Ashburnham Mansions, Ashburnham Road, Chelsea, London SW10 0PA, England.

MACK Warner (McPherson), b. 2 Apr 1938, Nashville, Tennessee, USA. Country Singer; Songwriter; Musician. Career: Performer, radio show, Louisiana Hayride; Successful solo career, late 1950s-; Regular tours, UK country clubs; First country artist to record national commercial for Coca-Cola. Compositions include: Tennessee Born, Mississippi Raised; Is It Wrong (For Loving You)? (US Country Number 1); The Bridge Washed Out. Recordings include: Sitting In An All Night Cafe; Talking To The Walls; How Long Will It Take?; These Crazy Thoughts; He Touched Me; Numerous albums include: The Country Touch, 1966; Drifting Apart, 1967; Love Hungry, 1970; You Make Me Feel Like A Man, 1971; Great Country, 1973; Prince Of Country Blues, 1983; At Your Service, 1984; Several compilation albums. Current Management: Capitol Advertising and Management, 1300 Division Street #200, Nashville, TN 37203, USA.

MACKAY David, b. 11 May 1944, Sydney, Australia. Record Producer; Composer; Musician (Keyboards). m. Brenda Anne Challis, 31 March 1973, 1 son, 1 daughter. Education: St Aloyisious College, Sydney, Australia. Musical Education: Conservatorium of Music, Sydney; Theory, Harmony, Arranging, Piano, Clarinet, privately studied in Melbourne; Modern Arranging, Guitar and Bass. Career: Producer of Records by: Blue Mink; Cliff Richard; New Seekers; Bonnie Tyler; Frankie Miller; Dusty Springfield; Johnny Hallyday; Demis Roussos. Compositions: Theme Punderscores for: TV Programmes: Auf Wiedersehen Pet; Bread; Blott on the Landscape. Honours: Ivor Novello Award for Auf Wiedersehen Pet, 1983; Nomination for BAFTAS, 1984; AKIA Award, Best Cast Album of a Musical 1990.

Memberships: PRS; Repro; BASCA; Professional Composers Guild. Hobbies: Tennis; Football; Golf. Address: Toftrees, Church Road, Woldingham, Surrey CR3 7JH, England.

MACKENZIE Gisèle, b. 1 Oct 1927, Winnipeg, Manitoba, Canada. Singer; Actress. Divorced, 1 son, 1 daughter. Musical Education: Graduate Scholarship School; Royal Conservatory, Toronto, Canada. Career: Your Hit Parade, NBC; Jack Benny Show; Gisèle MacKenzie Show, NBC; Sid Caesar Show. Recordings: Single: Hard To Get (Number 1). Honours: 3 Television Emmy Nominations. Memberships: SAG; AFTRA. Hobbies: Swimming; Cooking; Perfume blending. Current Management: Gold-Marshak. Address: 3500 West Olive, Burbank, CA 91505, USA.

MACKENZIE Henry, b. 15 Feb 1923, Edinburgh, Scotland. Musician (clarinet, saxophone). m. Barbara Holton, 17 Sept 1976. Career: Featured soloist, clarinet, with Ted Heath, 18 years; 4 American tours including 2 at Carnegie Hall, New York, with Ted Heath; Concerts and radio appearances, Billy May and Nelson Riddle; Films with Henry Mancini; Also featured in White Mischief. Recordings include: Appears on: Give My Regards To Broad Street, Paul McCartney; When I'm Sixty-Four, The Beatles. Honours: Melody Maker Poll Winners Recording. Hobbies: Bowls; Watching football. Address: 27 The Glade, Epsom, Surrey KT17 2HN, England.

MACKENZIE Talitha, b. 3 Apr 1956, Oceanside, New York, USA. Instrumentalist; Musician (keyboards); Composer/Arranger; Actress. m. Ian MacKenzie, 6 Sept 1988, 2 sons. Education: Connecticut College, 1974-76. Musical Education: New England Conservatory of Music, Boston, USA; Private study, Classical piano, 1960-78, Classical/Jazz Voice, 1977-80. Career: Concerts include: Ronnie Scott's, London; Chard Festival of Women in Music; WOMAD; Celts in Kent Festival, England; Edinburgh Festival Fringe; Celtic Connections Festival, Glasgow; Folk City, The Bottom Line, New York, USA; Vox Populi, Toronto; Cultures Canada, Ottawa; Winnipeg Folk Festival, Canada; Teatro Campoamor Oviedo; Juntos en Córdoba; WOMEX, Berlin; Melkweg, Amsterdam; Theatre includes: Arts and Parts, Don't Look Down, STV; Ex-S, Ainm a'Ghàidheil, Talla a'Bhaile; Sin Agad E, Brag, BBC Scotland; Global Jukebox, BSB; Radio includes: Nicky Campbell, BBC Radio 1; Mixin It, BBC Radio 3; Women's Hour, BBC Radio 4; Meridian, BBC World Service; All Things Considered, NPR, USA. Recordings: St James Gate, 1985; Shantyman, 1996; Mouth Music, 1990; Sòlas, 1993; Spiorad, 1996; Theatre includes: Réiteach, (Proiseact Naiseanta); Russian Ritual Wedding, Harvard University. Publications: The Triangle Trade-African Influences in the Anglo-American Sea Shanty Tradition, 1984; Song of the Scottish Highlands, Scot, 1985. Honour: Billboard Song Contest for Owen's Boat, 1994. Memberships: Musicians' Union; British Equity. Contact: Donald MacQueen, Winning Promotions, 96/1 South Gyle Wynd, Edinburgh EH12 9HJ, Scotland. Address: 33 Millar Crescent, Edinburgh EH10 5HQ, Scotland.

MACKIE Richard James, b. 6 Jan 1960, Bolton, Lancashire, England. Composer; Artistic Director; Musician (keyboards, saxophone). m. Christine Anne Waterhouse, 20 Apr 1985, 2 daughters. Education: Laban Centre For Movement and Dance. Musical Education: Self-taught. Career: Member of bands including: The Surgical Support Band; The Pharaohs; The Selecter; Extensive tours, UK and Europe; Replacement keyboard player for Madness; Apperances at Montreux Pop Festival and Saturday Night Live in New York; Theatre and radio productions, 1984-; Padmates (produced by Kate Rowland); Zeitgeist Times; Ron Koops Last Roadshow; Many compositions for dance and

dance theatre. Recordings: Albums and single with The Selecter. Hobbies: Cooking; Eating. Current Management: Self-managed. Address: 44 Dallas Road, Lancaster, Lancashire LA1 1TW, England.

MACKINTOSH Andrew Kenneth, b. 20 May 1953, London, England. Musician (saxophone). m. Bonnie Sue 10 Jan 1975, 1 son. Career: Played with: Maynard Ferguson; Buddy Rich; Quincy Jones; James Last; Currently involved in studio work in London. Recordings: Appeared on recordings by: Paul McCartney; Elton John; Bill Wyman; Elaine Paige; Melissa Manchester. Memberships: PRS; Musicians' Union. Hobbies: Music; Golf. Address: 27 Station Road, South Norwood, London SE25 5AH, England.

MACKINTOSH Gregor, b. 20 June 1970, Halifax, West Yorkshire, England. Musician (guitar). M. Mandy Taylor, 5 Aug 1995, 1 daughter. Musical Education: Self-taught. Career: Festivals include: Rockamring; Dynamo; Roskilde; Worldwide tours, television: Channel 4 Special; ITV's Chart Show; MTV; Viva TV; Noisy Mothers; Various radio, television worldwide; Soundtrack for Clarion Audio adverts. Recordings: 5 albums including: Icon; Draconian Times; 3 singles including: The Last Time; Long Form video: Harmony Breaks. Honours: Kerrang, MTV Best video: Embers Fire, 1994. Memberships: PRS; Musicians' Union. Hobbies: Reading; Films. Current Management: Northern Music, Bradford. Address: 43 Cheapside Chambers, Cheapside, Bradford, West Yorkshire, England.

MACKNESS Vanessa, b. Fordingbridge, Christchurch, England. Painter; Vocalist. 1 son, 1 daughter. Education: Degree, fine arts painting, Camberwell School of Art, late 1970s; Post graduate, London University. Musical Education: Playing with artists including Derek Bailey; Barry Guy; Alexander Balanescu; Nishat Khan; Paul Lovens; Phil Minton. Career: Concert tours include: Derek Bailey's Company Week, 1990; 1991; Duo with Barry Guy, Taktlos Festival, Switzerland, 1990; Irma, opera by Tom Phillips, USA, England, 1992; 10th Anniversary Minton-Weston Makhno Project, Bern, Basel, Zürich, Taktlos Festival, Switzerland, 1993; Solo performance, Total Music Meeting, Berlin, 1993; Soloist, Reiner Korff's composition for 35 musicians, Peter Edel Festival, Berlin, 1994; Jazz and More Festival '95, Munich, with Minton/Weston's Natural Formations, 1995; Numerous interviews and recordings for radio include: Music In Our Time, Company With Derek Bailey, Radio 3, 1991; Impressions with Brian Morton, Radio 3, 1992; Trio with Butcher and Durrant, duo with John Butcher, 1996; Television includes 2 appearances Blue Peter; Duo with Phil Minton, 1991. Recordings: 3 CD compilations: Company '91, with Alexander Balanescu, Derek Bailey, Paul Lovens, Paul Rogers, John Zorn, Buckethead; Respirtus, duo with John Butcher. Honours: Awarded funding, concert tour, The Improvised Music Touring Scheme; Art Council Tour of England, with (bassist) Barry Guy, 1990. Membership: PRS. Hobbies: Painting; Going to exhibitions; Theatre; Writing - prose, poetry, free verse; Being with family, lovers and friends. Address: c/o Incus Records, 14 Downs Road, London E5 8DS, England.

MACLEOD James, b. 19 Aug 1974, Sutton Coldfield, West Midlands, England. Musician (guitar); Singer; Composer; Lyricist; Music Teacher. Musical Education: ABRSM Grade 7 Theory, BTec Popular Music Course. Career: Bass guitarist for indie band The Cantels, 1991; Performances include Birmingham Hummingbird Club; Fronted own UK pop band She Chameleon, releasing his compositions on own label, 1992; As guitarist, performed several national BBC Radio sessions and played over 30 sets at Ronnie Scott's Club in Birmingham with Lou Dalgleish Band, 1993; Toured UK universities with Lou

Dalgliesh Band and others, 1993-94; Currently teaching guitar and music theory, working on ambient film music and visuals in studio set up in 1994. Membership: Musicians' Union. Hobbies: Various sports; Reading. Current Management: Pie In The Sky Management. Address: 8 Lincoln Croft, Shenstone, Lichfield, Staffordshire WS14 0ND, England.

MACNEIL Rita, b. 28 May 1944, Nova Scotia, Canada. Singer;Songwriter. 1 son, 1 daughter. Career: Host, one hour weekly CBC TV Music entertainment show; Concert tours, Japan; Australia; UK; Sweden; US; Canada. Recordings: Flying On Your Own, 1986; Reason To Believe, 1988; Now The Bells Ring, 1988; Rita, 1989; Home I'll Be, 1990; Thinking Of You, 1992; Once Upon A Christmas, 1993; Volume 1 - Songs From The Collection, 1994; Porch Songs, 1995; Joyful Sounds: A Seasonal Collection, 1996; Music of a Thousand Nights, 1997. Honours: Order of Canada; 5 Honorary Doctorates; 3 JUNO Awards; 4 Canadian Country Music Awards; 3 Platinum albums; 3 Double Platinum albums; 1 Triple Platinum album; 1 Gold album; 1 Silver album. Memberships: SOCAN; CMA; CARAS; ACTRA; AFofM. Current Management: Lupins Productions. Address: PO Box 183, Sydney, Cape Breton, Nova Scotia B1P 6H1, Canada.

MADDOX Dave Lee, b. 1 Mar 1951, Takoradi, Ghana. Musician (12 string guitar, piano, drums, bass); Vocalist. Musical Education: Self-taught. Career: Tours, Europe and USA; Appeared live on Spectrum, Radio London (first to play live on show). Recordings: Debut album: Superman (as writer, producer). Memberships: BASCA; PRS; BPI. Hobbies: Swimming; Painting; Writing; Watching television. Current Management: 53 Tiverton Road, Edgeware, Middlesex HA8 GBD, England.

MADIOT Thierry, b. 8 Sept 1963, Compiègne, France. Musician (bass and tenor trombone). Musical Education: Trombone with Guy Ferrand, Benny Sluchin; Electroacoustic music. Career: Astrolab, 1991-95; Company Week, London, 1993; Claude Barthelemy Group, 1994-95; Banlieues Bleues, with George Lewis, Evan Parker, Joëlle Leandre, Joel Ryan, R. Barett, 1994; Solo, European Jazz Festival, Le Mans, 1994; Marc Ducret Quintet, 1995. Recordings: Baka Mutz; Lousadzak, C Tchamitchian Septet; Soundpage(s), Noël Akchoté; Ohre Würm; Icis, 10 + Orti. Memberships: SACEM; SPEDIDAM; ADAMI. Hobby: Books. Address: 347 Rue des Pyrénées, 75020, Paris, France.

MADONNA (Madonna Louise Veronica Ciccone), b. 16 Aug 1958, Bay City, Michigan, USA. Singer; Songwriter; Actress. m. Sean Penn, 1985, divorced 1989; 1 d. Education: University Of Michigan, 1976-78. Career: Dancer, New York, 1979; Actress, 1980-; Solo singer, 1983-; Film appearances include: Vision Quest, 1985; Desperately Seeking Susan, 1985; Shanghai Surprise, 1986; Who's That Girl, 1987; Bloodhounds On Broadway, 1990; Dick Tracy, 1990; A League Of Their Own, 1992; Numerous worldwide concerts, 1983-; Major appearances include: Live Aid, Philadelphia, 1985; Don't Bungle The Jungle, ecological awareness benefit, 1989; Television includes: In Bed With Madonna (documentary), 1991; Stage performance, Speed The Plow, Broadway, 1988; Owner, Maverick record label. Compositions include: Co-writer, own hits: Live To Tell; Open Your Heart; Justify My Love; Co-writer, Each Time You Break My Heart, Nick Kamen, 1986. Recordings: Hit singles include: Holiday, 1983; Lucky Star, 1984; Borderline, 1984; Like A Virgin (Number 1, US), 1984; Material Girl, 1985; Crazy For You (Number 1, US), 1985; Angel, 1985; Into The Groove (Number 1, UK), 1985; Dress You Up, 1985; Gambler, 1985; Live To Tell (Number 1, US), 1986; Papa Don't Preach (Number 1, UK and US), 1986; True Blue (Number 1, UK), 1986; Open

Your Heart, 1986; La Isla Bonita (Number 1, UK), 1987; Who's That Girl (Number 1, US and UK), 1987; Causin' A Commotion, 1987; The Look Of Love, 1987; Like A Prayer (Number 1, UK and US), 1989; Express Yourself, 1989; Cherish, 1989; Dear Jessie, 1989; Oh Father, 1990; Keep It Together, 1991; Vogue (Number 1, UK and US), 1991; I'm Breathless, 1991; Hanky Panky, 1991; Justify My Love (Number 1, US), 1991; Rescue Me, 1991; This Used To Be My Playground, 1992; Erotica, 1992; Deeper And Deeper, 1992; Bad Girl, 1993; Fever, 1993; Rain, 1993; Albums: Madonna, 1983; Like A Virgin, 1985; True Blue, 1986; Who's That Girl?, film soundtrack, 1987; You Can Dance, 1988; Like A Prayer, 1989; I'm Breathless, 1990; The Immaculate Collection, 1990; Dick Tracy, film soundtrack, 1990; Erotica, 1992; Bedtime Stories, 1994; Something To Remember, 1995; Evita, film soundtrack, 1996; Ray of Light, 1997. Publications: Sex, 1992. Honours include: Numerous MTV Video Awards, including Vanguard Award, 1986; American Music Awards: Favourite Female Video Artist, 1987; Favourite Dance Single, 1991; Oscar, Best Song, 1991; Juno Award, International Song Of The Year, 1991; Grammy Award, Best Longform Music Video, 1992; Numerous awards from Billboard, Vogue and Rolling Stone magazines. Current Management: DeMann Entertainment, 8000 Beverly Blvd, Los Angeles, CA 90048, USA.

MADS Hansen, b. 24 January 1969, Roskilde, Denmark. Musician; Composer. m. Anne Over, 21 June 1997. Education: Saxophonist, Royal Academy of Music, Aarhus, Denmark, 1992-96; New School, New York, 1996-97; Rhythmic Conservatory, Copenhagen, 1997-98. Career: Copenhagen Jazz Festival with Ten Feet Tall, 1991; Leader, Common Ground, Jazz Festival, Aarhus, Leader, Trio Jazz Mozz, 1993; Member, Mek Pek Partyband, 1995; Own Band, Mediant, 1997. Recordings: Tangokat, with Mek Pek, 1995; Film Music, Wales of the Northsea, 1995; Innovation, 1996; Hej Frede, 1996; Our 15 Minutes, 1997. Address: Strandboulevarden 18 1tv, 2100 Copenhagen, Denmark.

MADSEN Tue, b. 25 January 1969, Hadsten, Denmark. Musician (Guitar); Producer. Career: Playing Guitar for 18 years. Recordings: Pixie Killers: One Size Fits All; Grope: Primates, 1994; Soul Pieces, EP, 1996; The Fury, 1996; Desert Storm, 1997. Honour: Danish Grammy Nominee, 1998. Membership: DMF. Current Management: Diehard, Vindegade 101, 5000 Odensec, Denmark. Address: Terp Skovvej 50, 8260 Vibij, Denmark.

MAEL Ronald, b. 12 Aug 1949, California, USA. Musician (keyboards); Songwriter. Education: BA, Graphic Design, University of California, Los Angeles. Musical Education: Piano lessons, age 6-10; Career: Founder member, Sparks (with brother Russell); Recorded 16 albums; Concert tours: USA; UK; France; Belgium; Netherlands; Sweden; Finland; Canada; Television appearances worldwide. Recordings: 16 albums: Halfnelson (changed to Sparks); A Woofer In Tweeter's Clothing; Kimono My House; Propaganda; Indiscreet; Big Beat; Introducing Sparks; Number One In Heaven; Terminal Jive; Whomp That Sucker; Angst In My Pants; Sparks In Outer House; Pulling Rabbits Out Of A Hat; Music That You Can Dance To; Interior Design; Gratuitous Sax And Senseless Violins. Honours: Various Gold records. Membership: Sons Of The Desert. Current Management: Eric Harle, DEF Management. Address: 21 Premier House, 313 Kilburn Lane, London W9 3EG, England.

MAEL Russell, b. 5 Oct 1956, Santa Monica, California, USA. Singer. Education: Bachelor's Degree. Career: Co-founder, Member, Sparks. Recordings: Albums: Sparks; A Woofer In Tweeters Clothing; Kimono In My House; Propaganda; Indiscreet; Big Beat; Introducing Sparks; Number One In Heaven; Terminal Jive;

Whomp That Sucker; Angst In My Pants; Sparks In Outer Space; Pulling Rabbits Out Of A Hat; Music That You Can Dance To; Interior Design; Gratuitous Sax And Senseless Violins. Membership: ASCAP. Current Management: DEF. Address: Premier House, 313 Kilburn Lane, London W9 3EG, England.

MAGIC Mick (R M Lancaster), b. 21 Apr 1958, Wimbledon, England. Record Company Executive; Musician (guitar, keyboards); Composer. Divorced. Education: Open University. Career: Owner, Music and Elsewhere record label, promoting new bands especially underground bands; Studio work with own band; Appearance on BBC Radio 5. Recordings include: with Magic Moments At Twilight Time: Psychotron O, 1988; Zoen Nostalgia, 1989; White Hawk Atomic, 1992; Creavolution, 1995. Publications: The M and E Newsletter, a three times yearly magazine; M&E Yearbook, annually. Membership: Mensa. Hobbies: Cinema, especially silent movies; Chess. Current Management: Music and Elsewhere. Address: Music and Elsewhere, 6 Farm Court, Farm Road, Frimley, Camberley, Surrey GU16 5TJ, England.

MAGOOGAN Wesley, b. 11 Oct 1951, London, England. Musician (saxophone). m. Marion Willett, 10 Mar 1973, 1 son, 1 daughter (deceased). Musical Education: Royal Academy of Music. Career: Hazel O'Connor; The Beat (also known as The English Beat); Joan Armatrading; Elton John; Billy Ocean; Extensive world tours, 1978-. Recordings: Albums: with O'Connor/Magoogan: Will You; with The Beat: Special Beat Service, 1982; with Hazel O'Connor: Breaking Glass, 1980; Sons And Lovers, 1980; Cover Plus, 1981: with Joan Armatrading: Secret Secrets, 1985; Sleight Of Hand, 1986; Shouting Stage, 1988; 2 albums with Billy Ocean. Membership: Royal Society of Musicians. Hobbies: Reading; Painting. Current Management: Simon Davies. Address: 5 Paddington Street, Marylebone, London W1M 3LA, England.

MAHAL Taj (Henry St Clair Fredericks), b. 17 May 1942, Massachusetts, USA. Composer; Musician. m. Inshirah Geter, 23 Jan 1976. Education: BA, University Massachusetts, Amherst, 1964. Career: Composer, musician, 1964-; Early concerts, Boston; Tours across US; Europe; Africa; Australia; Actor in films: King Of Ragtime; Sounder; Sounder II; Theatre appearance: Mule Bone. Compositions: Taj; Like Never Before; Film soundtracks: Sounder; Sounder II; Brothers; Television shows: Ewoks; The Man Who Broke A Thousand Chains; Brer Rabbit; The Hot Spot. Recordings: Albums: Taj Mahal, 1967; Natch'l Blues, 1968; Giant Step, 1969; The Real Thing, 1971; Happy Just To Be Like I Am, 1971; Recycling The Blues And Other Stuff, 1972; Sounder (film soundtrack), 1972; Ooh So Good'n'Blues, 1973; Mo'Roots, 1974; Music Keeps Me Together, 1975; Satisfied 'n Tickled Too, 1976; Music Fuh Ya, 1977; Brothers (film soundtrack), 1977; Evolution, 1978; Taj Mahal And The International Rhythm Band, 1980; Big Blues, 1990; Mule Bone, 1991; Like Never Before, 1991; An Evening Of Acoustic Music, 1995; Dancing The Blues, 1995; Phantom Blues, 1996. Honours: Best Ethnic Music Award, Brothers, 1979; Bay Area Music Awards, Brothers, 1979. Current Management: Folklore Productions, 1671 Appian Way, Santa Monica, CA 90401, USA.

MAHAR Eric Frederick, b. 11 Jan 1959, Hamilton, Ontario, Canada. Music Producer; Music Consultant; Musician (guitar, banjo, harmonica). m. 11 Jun 1988. Musical Education: Jazz Program, Humber College; Studied classical guitar at University of Toronto. Career: Solo guitarist; Theatre guitarist; R'n'B country guitarist for The Mercey Brothers; Marie Bottrell; Joan Kennedy; Television appearances: Tommy Hunter Show; CCMA Awards Show; Sunshine Country. Recordings: Producer and performer for various record labels. Membership: Musicians' Union. Hobbies: Mountain biking; Skiing; Badminton; Swimming.

MAIDMAN Ian Stuart, b. 24 Jan 1958, Upminster, Essex, England. Record Producer; Songwriter; Musician (multi-instrumentalist). Musical Education: Classical guitar; Piano; Music theory. Career: Producer for: Paul Brady; Pili Pili; Murray Head; Musician, tours with: Joan Armatrading, 1983; Murray Head, 1984–; Paul Brady, 1985–; Penguin Café Orchestra, 1985–; Boy George, 1988-89; David Sylvian, 1988; Currently with: Penguin Café Orchestra; Annie Whitehead; Paul Brady; Murray Head. Compositions: Songwriter, albums by Sam Brown and Boy George. Recordings: Extensive session work includes: Paul Brady; Gerry Rafferty; Joan Armatrading; Shakespears Sister; Boy George; Sam Brown; David Sylvian; Albums include: with Penguin Café Orchestra: When In Rome; with Paul Brady: Back To The Centre; Primitive Dance; with Shakespears Sister: Hormonally Yours. Honour: Back To The Centre, Best Album, Ireland, 1986-87. Memberships: Musicians' Union; PRS; MCPS. Hobbies: Travel; Cats. Current Management: Positive Earth Music. Address: 22 Richford Road, London E15 3PQ, England.

MAITLAND Christopher James, b. 13 May 1964, Cambridge, England. Musician (drums). Career: Original member, Zoom; Drummer for: Richard Barbieri; Phil Watts; Simon May Orchestra; Mark Rattray; Porcupine Tree; Middleman; Don Airey; Noman; Television and radio apperances include: Pebble Mill; The Big E; The Beat; Old Grey Whistle Test; Radio 1; Radio 2; Virgin Radio; Drum kit lecturer, Anglia Polytechnic University, Cambridge. Recordings: with Porcupine Tree: Sky Moves Sideways; Coma Divine; Signify; with Noman: Flowermouth; with Barbieri/Bowness: Flame; with Mark Rattray: Summer Musical Magic. Honour: Best Drummer 1985. Membership: Musicians' Union. Hobby: Shakespearian actor. Address: PO Box 385, Uxbridge, Middlesex UB9 5OZ, England.

MAKAROV Jüri, b. 3 Apr 1959, Tallinn, Estonia. Promoter. m. Tiina Makarov, 3 July 1985, 1 son, 2 daughters. Education: Tallinn Technical University, Economy. Musical Education: Tallinn Music College. Career: Promoter, for: Jethro Tull; Steve Hackett; EMF; Bob Geldof; Procul Harum; Faith No More; The Pogues; Samantha Fox; Bonnie Tyler, 1986–. Current Management: A S Makarov Muusik Management. Address: Regati PSt 1.6 K, EE 0019 Tallinn, Estonia.

MAKEBA Miriam, b. 4 Mar 1932, Johannesburg, South Africa. Vocalist. m. (1) Hugh Masakela, (2) Stokely Carmichael. Career: Member, Cuban Brothers, 1950; Manhattan Brothers, 1950s; Member, touring show, African Jazz and Variety, 1957-59; Musical, King Kong; Starred in semi-documentary film, Come Back Africa; Worked on international club circuit in Europe, South America, Africa; Appearances at jazz festivals include: Montreux; Berlin; North Sea; Unofficial South African representative, Festac '77 festival, Lagos, Nigeria, 1977; Concert with Hugh Masakela, Botswana, 1982; Guest, Graceland tour with Paul Simon, 1987. Recordings include: Albums: The World Of Miriam Makeba; Makeba, 1963; The Click Song, 1965; Pata Pata, 1972; Live At Conakry, 1975; Festac 77, 1978; Greatest Hits From Africa, 1985; Sangoma, 1989; Hit singles: Patha Patha; The Click Song; Malaika. Publication: Makeba, My Story (autobiography), 1989. Honours include: Dag Hammarskjold Peace Prize, 1986. Current Management: Sam Nole Management, 230 Park Avenue, Suite 1512, New York, NY 10169, USA.

MAKEM Tommy, b. 4 Nov 1932, Keady, County Armagh, Ireland. Singer; Actor. m. Mary Shanahan, 21 Sept 1963, 3 sons, 1 daughter. Musical Education: Self-taught. Career: Major concerts: Royal Albert Hall; Carnegie Hall; Lincoln Center; Sydney Opera House; Doothy Chandler Pavilion; Boston Symphony Hall; Tampa Performing Arts Center; Madison Square Gardens; Newport Folkfest's Most Promising Newcomer; Television appearances: Ed Sullivan Show; Arthur Godfrey Show; Johnny Carson Tonight Show; Today Show; Merv Griffin Show; Danny Thomas Show; Entertainment Tonight; Dublin Late Show; BBC Late Show; TV series, US, England and Scotland. Recordings: Four Green Fields; Gentle Annie; Freedom's Sons; Rosie; Sing Me The Old Songs; The Winds Are Singing Freedom; The Winds Of Morning; The Boys Of Killybeg; Lord Nelson; Farewell To Carlingford; Summer Roads; Venezuela; Vancouver; Farewell To Nova Scotia; Sally O; True Love And Time; Better Times. Publications: Tommy Makem's Ireland; The Clancy Brothers And Tommy Makem Songbook; The Tommy Makem Songbook. Honours: Grammy Award; Irish American Top 100 of the Year (5 years); Irish American Hall of Fame. Hobbies: Irish Mythology and History; Photography; Travel. Current Management: Bard Enterprises. Address: 2 Longmeadow Road, Dover, NH 03820, USA.

MAKHENE Blondie Keoagile Gerald, b. 16 Sept 1955, White City Jabavu, Soweto, South Africa. Singer; Musician (guitar, piano). m. Agnes Mary, 18 Dec 1979, 3 daughters. Musical Education: Grade 4. Career: Concert In The Park, 1984; Mandela Welcome Concert, Soweto South Africa, 1990; Black Radio Exclusive Conference, New Orleans, 1992; Africa For Aids Concert, Sun City, South Africa, 1993; Panafest, Ghana, Accra, 1994. Recordings: Weekend Special, Brenda Fassie debut album; Amaquabane featuring Blondie Makhene, 1990; Albums: Elakho Likhona, Pure Gold; Isencane, Platform 1; Amadamara, Freddy Gwala. Honour: Most Outstanding Person, Voice Education Centre, South Africa. Membership: Dorkay House. Hobby: Swimming.

MALACH Bob, b. 23 Aug 1954, Philadelphia, Pennsylvania, USA. Musician (saxophone, flute, clarinet). m. Janine Dreiding, 6 Jan 1981, 1 son, 1 daughter. Musical Education: Study with: Jow Allard; Harold Bennett; Eddie Daniels; David Weber; Keith Underwood. Career: Ben Sidran, 1977; Stanley Clarke, 1977-79; Stevie Wonder, 1980-85; Bob Mintzer, 1983; Horace Silver, 1986; Robben Ford, 1987; Steve Miller Band, 1987; Bill Cosby Show, 1987-92; Mike Stern, 1994. Recordings include: Patti Labelle; Lou Rawls; The O'Jays; The Jackson 5; Soundtrack to Woman In Red (Stevie Wonder); Hoop Dreams; Miles Davis In Montreux; Solo albums: Mood Swing; The Searcher. Publications: Swing Journal; Jazz Life; Ad Lib. Memberships: AFofM; BMI. Hobbies: Darts; Tropical fish; Family life. Current Management: Go Jazz.

MALANIUK Ira, b. 29 Jan 1919, Stanislav, Ukraine. Singer; Professor. m. Dr Ernst Baasch, 1952. Musical Education: Course by Adam Diolur and Anna Bahr-Mildenburg; Studied Summer Academy, Salzburg, Mozarteum. Career: Appearances include: Bayreuth (Brangä in Tristan, Magdelene, in the Meistersingern, Fricke in the Ring Cycle), 1951-53; Covent Garden, London; Grand Opera, Paris; Munich State Opera, 1952; Vienna State Opera, 1956–. Recordings: The Mastersingers; Arabella; Aida; Cosi Fan Tutte; Hochzei. Hobby: Bridge. Address: 1190 Vienna, Reuithlegasse 8/5, Austria.

MALKMUS Stephen, b. USA. Singer; Musician (guitar). Career: Founder, lead singer, rock group Pavement, 1990–; Tours: USA, Europe; Japan; Australia; New Zealand; UK and Ireland including Reading Festival, 1994; Headlined Big Cat Festival Tour, Europe 1995; Lollapalooza Tour, 1995. Recordings: Albums: Slanted And Enchanted, 1992; Westing By Musket And Sextant, 1993; Crooked Rain, 1994; Wowee Zowee, 1995; EPs, singles: Slay Tracks; Perfect Sound Forever; Demolition Plot; Trigger Cut; Watery Domestic. Address: c/o Big Cat Records, PO Box 3074, Chiswick, London W4 4ZN, England.

MALLETT Timmy, b. 18 Oct 1955, Marple, Cheshire, England. Television Presenter; Entertainer; Singer. m. Lynda Bingham, 8 Sept 1990, 1 son. Education: History Degree, Warwick University. Career: BBC Radio Oxford; Piccadilly Radio; Televsion presenter, Wide Awake Club; Wacaday; Utterly Brilliant; Around The World In 80 Seconds; Timmy Stage Show, 1987–; Headlining Pantomimes, 1991-95; Director, Brilliant TV; Producer and Presenter, Timmy Towers, ITV, 1997. Recordings: Singles: Itsy Bitsy Teeny Weeny Yellow Polka Dot Bikini; 7 Little Girls Sitting In The Back Seat, Bombularina (with Andrew Lloyd Webber); Albums: Huggin' And Kissin', 1990; The Bump, MC Mallett, 1991. Publications: How To Be Utterly Brilliant; Utterly Brilliant History Of The World, 1991. Honours: DJ of the Year, 1984; Childrens Television Personality of the Year, 1991. Hobbies: Pinball; Watercolour painting; Travel; Oxford United Football Club. Current Managements: John Mile. Address: Cadbury Camp Lane, Clapton in Gordano, Bristol BS20 9SB, England.

MALLON Peter C, b. 3 February 1936, New York, USA. Concert Producer. m. Cheryl Rae Mallon, 21 September 1991, 1 son, 1 daughter. Education: Student, School of Radio & Television Broadcasting, New York City, 1959; Queens College, New York City, 1960. Career: Actor, Warner Brothers, Hollywood, California, 1958; Promotion Assistant, NBC-TV, New York City, 1960; Promotion Director, CCC Productions Inc, New York City, 1961-65; Executive Vice President, Counterpoint/Concerts Inc, New York City, 1965-94; WRZN Radio, Hernando, Florida, 1994–; Manager, Personal Representative, Gene Krupa, Lee Castle, Jonah Jones, Henny Youngman, 1965–; Vice President, TVI Records Ltd, New York City, 1977-81; Program Director, WNYG-Radio, Babylon, New York, 1983-85; Consultant, WGSM-Radio, Huntington, New York, 1984-87. Honours: 87 Community Service Awards. Hobby: Record Collecting. Address: 8051 Shalom Drive, Spring Hill, FL 34606, USA.

MALLOZZI Charlie, b. Parma, Italy. Record Producer; Mixer; Songwriter. Career: Writer, Producer with Marco Sabiu, known as Rapino Brothers; Moved to London, 1992; Mixer, producer of Pop/Dance music; Member of groups: Tabernacle; Rapination. Recordings: Albums for: Take That; Kylie Minogue; Dannii Minogue; Lulu; Kym Mazelle; Rozalla; Hit singles: Could It Be Magic, Take That; Rhythm Of The Night, Corona; What Is Love, Haddaway; I Know The Lord, Tabernacle; Love Me The Right Way, Rapination & Kym Mazelle; Also produced singles for: Alicia Bridges; Heaven 17; Sparks. Honours: BRIT Award, Single of the Year, Take That; Triple Platinum album, Take That. Current Management: Stephen Budd Management. Address: 109B Regents Park Road, London NW1 8UR, England.

MALMI Jani, b. 1959. Jazz Musician; Record Producer. Musical Education: Originally self-taught; Private study with John Abercrombie and John Scofield. Career: Began playing with various rock bands, 1970s; Bandleader, own quartet; Leader, Jani Malmi trio (with Jorma Ojanperä and Markku Ounaskari). Recordings include: Graffiti, 1988; One Leg Duck, 1995; As producer: Kosketuksia, 1995.

MALMSTEEN Yngwie, b. Sweden. Rock Musician (guitar). Career: Played guitar from age 8; Founder, rock groups Powerhouse; Rising; Lead guitarist, Steeler, Los Angeles, 1983; Lead guitarist, Alcatrazz, 1983-84; Solo artiste, with own band, Rising Force, 1984–. Recordings: Albums: with Steeler: Steeler, 1983; with Alcatrazz: No Parole From Rock'n'Roll, 1984; Live Sentence,

1984; Solo albums: Yngwie Malmsteen's Rising Force, 1984; Marching Out, 1985; Trilogy, 1986; Odyssey, 1988; Live In Leningrad, 1989; Eclipse, 1990; No Mercy, 1992. Current Management: James Lewis Entertainment, 14 Deerfield Lane, Greenwich, CT 06831, USA.

MALONE Tom (aka Bones), b. 16 June 1947, Honolulu, Hawaii, USA.Musician; Arranger; Producer. 2 daughters. Education: BS, Psychology, North Texas State University, 1969. Career: As student played with: Les Elgart; The Supremes; Little Stevie Wonder; Marvin Gaye; The Temptations; Gladys Knight and The Pips; Joined Woody Herman's big band; Tours USA, Europe with: Frank Zappa, 1972; Blood Sweat And Tears, 1973; Billy Cobham, 1975; Joined Gil Evans Orchestra, 1973; Tours, Europe, Japan, Far East; Tour, USA with The Band, appeared in film: The Last Waltz, 1976; Television: Musician, arranger, Saturday Night Live, 1975-85; Musical director, above programme, 1981-85; Played with CBS Orchestra, Late Night With David Letterman, 1993-; Appeared in film The Blues Brothers; Tours with The Blues Brothers Band, 1988-90; Appearing in film, Blues Brothers 2000, 1998. Compositions include: Theme song, Saturday Night Live; Comedy songs for Jim Belushi, Eddie Murphy, Billy Crystal; Arrangements for films: The Blues Brothers; Sister Act; Television: Saturday Night Live; CBS Orchestra. Recordings include: Solo album: Standards Of Living, Tom "Bones" Malone Jazz Septet, 1991; Recorded with artists including: Blues Brothers; Gil Evans Orchestra; Miles Davis And Quincy Jones; Blood, Sweat And Tears; Frank Zappa; Pat Metheny; Cyndi Lauper; Sister Act; Steve Winwood; David Sanborn; James Brown; Spinners; Barry Manilow; Glen Campbell; B B King; Billy Cobham; Lou Reed; Bonnie Tyler; Diana Ross; Carla Bley; Harry Connick Jr; Pink Floyd; Buddy Rich; Woody Herman; J Geils Band; George Benson; Paul Simon; Chaka Khan; Village People; Gloria Gaynor; Carly Simon. Hobbies: Softball; Golf; Homeopathic medicine. Address: c/o Late Show, CBS Orchestra, 1697 Broadway, New York, NY 10019, USA.

MALONE Walter, b. 20 Sept 1946, Pittsburgh, Pennsylvania, USA. Musician (bass player); Singer; Entertainer. m. Peggy Jones, 20 Oct 1968. Career: Principle bassist with Bo Diddley, West Coast, 1970-94; Bassist, Lady Bo, 1969-; Backing musician for: Lightning Hopkins; Richard Berry; Chuck Berry; The Olympics; Concerts include: HIC Arena, 1971; Monterey Jazz Festival, 1973, 1974; Greek Theater, 1976; Boardwalk, 1988; Monterey Blues Festival, 1994, 1995; Tours: East Coast, 1960s; West Coast; Southern; Canada; Pacific Northwest, 1970s; Main Event European, Number 1, 1987; Bo Knows...NIKE Inc, endorsement, 1989; Television: Kenny Rogers, 1971; Donnie And Marie, 1976-77; Live concert, Sweden, 1987; Arts And Entertainment Special, worldwide coverage, 1990; Lady Bo and the BC Horns, South Bay Scene, USA, 1996. Recordings: Albums: The Mighty Bo Diddley; Bo Diddley: Ain't It Good To Be Free, USA, 1984; France, 1988; Lady Bo & The BC Horns; Shebo-Shebad, 1997; Video: I Don't Sound Like Nobody, Bo Diddley with Lady Bo and The Family Jewel, UK, 1992; Flashbacks: Vol One, Soul Sensations, 1994; Say That You Love Me, Lady Bo & The BC Horns, 1997. Publication: Listed: The Complete Bo Diddley Sessions, by George R White, 1993. Memberships: President, RMA of Northern California; President, Professional Musicians of California; Executive Secretary-Treasurer, 1993-, President, 1996-, AFofM Local 153; President, RMA (Recording Musicians Association), Northern California. Address: c/o AFM Local 153, 1445 Koll Circle, Ste 110, San Jose, CA 95112, USA.

MANCHESTER Melissa, b. 15 Feb 1951, Bronx, New York, USA. Singer; Songwriter; Scriptwriter; Actress. Career: Staff writer, Chappell Music; Backing singer, Bette Midler; Solo artiste, 1973-; Actress and scriptwriter. Recordings: Albums: Home To Myself, 1973; Bright Eyes, 1974, 1974; Melissa, 1975; Better Days And Happy Endings, 1977; Singin', 1977; Don't Cry Out Loud, 1978; Melissa Manchester, 1979; For The Working Girl, 1980; Hey Ricky, 1982; Emergency, 1983; Mathematics, 1985; Midnight Blue, 1988; Tribute, 1989; If My Heart Had Wings, 1994; Joy, 1997; Singles: Midnight Blue; Whenever I Call You Friend (co-written with Kenny Loggins), 1978; Dont Cry Out Loud, 1979; You Should Hear How She Talks About You, 1982. Honours: Grammy Award, Best Female Vocalist, 1982; NARAS Governors Award, 1997. Current Management: c/o Kevin DeRemer, Beacon Hill Entertainment, 15882 High Knoll Road, Encino, CA 91436, USA.

MANDRELL Barbara, b. 25 Dec 1948, Houston, Texas, USA. Singer; Musician (guitar). m. Ken Dudney, 1967. Career: Worked with Joe Maphis, Tex Ritter, Las Vegas; Founder member, The Mandrells; Recording artist, 1966; Joined Grand Ole Opry, 1972; Television series, Barbara Mandrell And The Mandrell Sisters, 1980-82. Recordings: Hit singles include: Sleepin' Single In A Double Bed; Years; I Was Country When Country Wasn't Cool; (If Loving You Is Wrong) I Don't Want To Be Right; Til You're Gone; One Of A Kind Pair Of Fools. Albums: Treat Him Right, 1971; A Perfect Match (with David Houston), 1972; The Midnight Oil, 1973; This Time I Almost Made It, 1974; This Is Barbara Mandrell, 1976; Midnight Angel, 1976; Lovers Friends And Strangers, 1977; Love's Ups And Downs, 1978; Moods, 1978; Just For The Record, 1979; Love Is Fair, 1980; Looking Back, 1981; Live, 1981; In Black And White, 1982; He Set My Life To Music, 1982; Spun Gold, 1983; Back To Back (with David Houston), 1983; Clean Cut, 1984; Meant For Each Other (with Lee Greenwood), 1984; Christmas At Our House, 1984; Get To The Heart, 1985; Moments, 1986; Sure Feels Good, 1987; I'll Be Your Jukebox Tonight, 1988; Morning Sun, 1990; No Nonsense, 1991; Key's In The Mailbox, 1991. Current Management: Mandrell Inc., PO Box 800, Hendersonville, TN 37077, USA.

MANGIONE Chuck (Charles Frank), b. 29 Nov 1940, Rochester, New York, USA. Jazz Musician (trumpet); Composer. 2 daughters. Musical Education: MusB, Music Education, Eastman School Of Music, University of Rochester, 1963. Career: Formed Jazz Brothers with Brother Gap, 1958-64; Director, Eastman Jazz Ensemble; Teacher, Eastman School Of Music, 1968-72; Freelance musician with Maynard Ferguson and Kai Winding, 1965; Trumpeter, Art Blakey's Jazz Messengers, 1965-67; Formed Chuck Mangione Quartet, 1968; Guest conductor, Rochester Philharmonic Orchestra, 1970; Numerous concerts worldwide include: Europe; Japan; Australia; South America; Montreal Jazz Festival, 1986; Television appearances include: PBS specials; Grammy Awards Show, 1981; Guest star, Magnum PI; Film appearance: Paradise Blues, 1984. Compositions include: Hill Where The Lord Hides; Land Of Make Believe; Bellavia; Give It All You Got (1980 Winter Olympics theme). Recordings: Albums include: Chuck Mangione Quartet, 1972; Chase The Clouds Away, 1975; Main Squeeze, 1976; Feels So Good, 1977; Children Of Sanchez (film soundtrack), 1978; Fun And Games, 1980; Journey To A Rainbow, 1985; Bellavia, 1986; Classics, Vol 6, 1989. Honours: Most Promising Male Jazz Artist, Record World, 1975; Numerous Gold and Platinum records; Grammy Awards and nominations; Emmy Award, Music Composition and Direction, Give It All You Got, 1980; Numerous Magazine Poll Wins; MusD Hon, 1985; Georgie Award, Instrumental Act Of Year, 1980; Regents Medal Of Excellence, New York State, 1984; Jazz Music Campus Entertainment Award, NACA, 1987. Current Management: c/o Gates Music. Address: Gates Music Inc, 476 Hampton Boulevard, Rochester, NY 14612, USA.

MANGRAM Myles Edwin, b. 30 July 1956, Pueblo, Colorado, USA. Personal Manager; Record Label Executive. m. Chea Rivera, 3 July 1994, 2 sons. Education: BS, Music Science, Master, Businness Administration, Entertainment, Law studies. Musical Education: Classical and Jazz training since age 5. Career: Founder, President, Tri-M Management (personal management company, consulting service); President, Black Lion Records Inc (independent record label); Professor, Music Business Studies; Professional musician and record producer with: Dizzy Gillespie; Tom Scott; Denver Symphony. Recordings: As producer: Alyssa Milano (Gold, Platinum discs); Anita Whitaker. Publications: Research reports, articles for publications include: Optic Music Magazine; Music Connection; Future Systems International. Honours: Outstanding Young Man Of America Award; Colorado Schlars Award; Presidential Scholars Award. Memberships: Conference of Personal Managers; Entertainment Law Society. Hobbies: Hiking; Weight training; Basketball. Address: Myles E Mangram, 5200 White Oak Avenue, #31, Encino, CA 91316, USA.

MANIFOLD Keith, b. 2 Apr 1947, Biggin-By-Hartington, Derbyshire, England. Musician (guitar); Voclaist; Agent; Country Music Consultant. m. Alice Nadin, 21 Nov 1970, 2 daughters. Musical Education: Self-taught. Career: Television performances: Opportunity Knocks - Songwriters; Sing Country; Nationwide; Midlands; Sounds; Grampian Today; Border Today; Sons And Lovers; Radio performances: Radio 2; Local radio; Founder member, North West Promotions. Recordings: 20 albums include: Keith Manifold In Nashville. Honours: Billboard Best Solo Award '75; Nottingham Award For Special Achievement, Numerous Country Music Club Awards. Membership: Equity. Hobbies: Gardening; Snooker. Current Management: Keith Manifold Entertainment Services. Address: Trenton House, 30 Bank Road, Matlock, Derbyshire DE4 3NF, England.

MANIGAT Eval, b. 8 Dec 1939, Haiti. Musician (bass, vibraphone); Composer; Arranger. Divorced, 1 son, 2 daughters. Musical Education: Self-taught. Career: Played with: Tropicana (Haiti); Weber Scott (Haiti); Vaccine; Karen Young Jazz Latin Band; Buzz; Chevere; Founder, band Tchaka; Fronts Many Ways (Latin-jazz ensemble); Appearances include: Montreal Jazz Festival; Ottawa Jazz Festival; Toronto Harbourfront summer festival; SOB, New York City; European tour, 1996. Compositions include: Contredanse, Karen Young, 1988. Recording: Album: Africa, 1994. Honour: Juno Award, Global Recording, Canada, 1994. Hobbies: Computers; Reading; Yoga; Travel. Current Management: Louise Matte. Address: C P 48015, 5678 Ave du Parc, Montreal, Québec H2V 4S8, Canada.

MANILOW Barry (Pinkus), b. 17 June 1946, Brooklyn, New York, USA. Singer; Musician (piano); Songwriter. Education: Advertising, New York City College; Musical Education: NY College Of Music; Juilliard School Of Music. Career: Film Editor, CBS-TV; Writer, numerous radio and television commercials; Member, cabaret duo Jeanne and Barry, 1970-72; MD, arranger, producer for Bette Midler; Solo entertainer, 1974-; Numerous worldwide tours; Major concerts include: Gala charity concert for Prince and Princess of Wales, Royal Albert Hall, 1983; Arista Records 15th Anniversary concert, Radio City Music Hall, 1990; Royal Variety performance, London, 1992; Television film Copacabana, 1985; Numerous television specials and television appearances; Broadway show, Barry Manilow At The Gershwin, 1989; West End musical, Copacabana, 1994. Recordings: Albums include: Barry Manilow, 1973; Barry Manilow II, 1975; Tryin' To Get The Feelin', 1976; This One's For You, 1977; Barry Manilow Live (Number 1, US), 1977; Even Now, 1978; Manilow Magic, 1979;

Greatest Hits, 1979; One Voice, 1979; Barry, 1981; If I Should Love Again, 1981; Barry Live In Britain, 1982; I Wanna Do It With You, 1982; Here Comes The Night, 1983; A Touch More Magic, 1983; Greatest Hits Volume II, 1984; 2.00 AM Paradise Café, 1984; Barry Manilow, Grandes Exitos En Espanol, 1986; Swing Street, 1988; Songs To Make The Whole World Sing, 1989; Live On Broadway, 1990; The Songs 1975-1990, 1990; Because It's Christmas, 1990; Showstoppers, 1991; The Complete Collection And Then Some, 1992; Hidden Treasures, 1993; The Platinum Collection, 1993; Hit singles include: Mandy (Number 1, US), 1975; Could It Be Magic, 1975; I Write The Songs (Number 1, US), 1976; Tryin' To Get The Feelin', 1976; Weekend In New England, 1977; Looks Like We Made It (Number 1, US), 1977; Can't Smile Without You, 1978; Copacabana (At The Copa), from film Foul Play, 1978; Somewhere In The Night, 1979; Ships, 1979; I Made It Through The Rain, 1981; Let's Hang On, 1981; Bermuda Triangle, 1981; I Wanna Do It With You, 1982. Honours: Grammy Awards: Song Of The Year, I Write The Songs, 1977; Best Male Pop Vocal Performance, Copacabana (At The Copa), 1979; Emmy Award, The Barry Manilow Special, 1977; American Music Awards, Favourite Male Artist, 1978-80; Star on Hollywood Walk Of Fame, 1980; Tony Award, Barry Manilow On Broadway show, 1976; Academy Award Nomination, Ready To Take A Chance Again, 1978; Hitmaker Award, Songwriters Hall Of Fame, 1991; Platinum and Gold records. Current Management: Stiletto Entertainment, 5443 Beethoven Street, Los Angeles, CA 90066, USA.

MANLEY Colin William, b. 16 Apr 1942, Liverpool, Merseyside, England. Musician (guitar). m. Sheila Jones, 17 Jan 1972, 1 son, 1 daughter. Musical Education: Self-taught. Career: 1960's tours: Tommy Roe; Gene Pitney; Last Beatles tour of UK with Tommy Quickly; Recent tours with: The Swinging Blue Jeans; Gerry Marsden; The Searchers; London Palladium Orchestra, 2 years; Television appearances: Lift Off, with Remo 4; Top Of The Pops; Ready Steady Go; Crackerjack. Composition: Lies, with Remo 4. Recordings: Wonderwall album (with George Harrison); Smile In Germany, Remo 4. Honours: Third place in first Merseybeat Poll (behind The Beatles and Gerry Marsden); Winner, Best Instrumentalist, Beat Goes On magazine, 1996. Membership: Musicians' Union. Hobbies: Music; Jogging. Current Management: Hal Carter. Address: c/o Hal Carter, 101 Hazelwood Lane, Palmers Green, London N13 5HQ, England.

MANN Jas (Jasbinder), b. 24 April 1970, Dudley, West Midlands, England. Singer; Musician (guitar). Career: Singer, The Sandkings, 1980s; Tours include: Support to Happy Mondays, Stone Roses; Lead singer, Babylon Zoo, 1994-; Concerts include: NME Brats, Midem, 1995; The Night The Earth Stood Still, London, 1995. Recordings: Album: Boy With The X-Ray Eyes, 1996; Singles: Spaceman (International Number 1 hit), 1996; Animal Army, 1996. Honours: Fastest selling debut single since the Beatles, with Spaceman, 1996. Membership: Musicians' Union. Hobbies: Film; Art. Address: c/o Clive Banks, CBL, 1 Glenthorne Mews, 115A Glenthorne Road, London W6 0LJ, England.

MANN Manfred (Michael Lubowitz), b. 21 Oct 1940, Johannesburg, South Africa. Musician (keyboards); Songwriter. Founder member, Mann-Hugg Blues Brothers, 1962; Became Manfred Mann, 1963-69; Concerts include: Brighton Song Festival, 1965; Founder, Emanon, and Manfred Mann Chapter Three, 1969; Manfred Mann Earth Band, 1971-87; National and international tours with Free; Deep Purple; Savoy Brown; Blue Öyster Cult; Concerts include: Pink Pop Festival, Netherlands, 1977; Also taught at Goldsmith's College, London, late 1970s. Recordings: Albums with Manfred Mann: Five Faces Of Manfred Mann, 1964; Mann Made, 1965;

Mann Made Hits, 1966; As Is, 1966; Soul Of Mann, 1967; Up The Junction, 1967; The Mighty Quinn, 1968; This Is Manfred Mann, 1971; Semi-Detached Suburban, 1979; The R&B Years, 1986; The Singles Plus, 1987; The EP Collection, 1989; The Collection, 1990; Ages Of Mann, 1992;2 albums with Manfred Mann Chapter Three; with Manfred Mann's Earth Band: Manfred Mann's Earth Band, 1972; Get Your Rocks Off, 1973; Solar Fire, 1973; The Good Earth, 1974; Nightingales And Bombers, 1975; The Roaring Silence, 1976; The New Bronze Age, 1977; Watch, 1978; Angle Station, 1979; Chance, 1981; Somewhere In Africa, 1983; Budapest, 1983; Criminal Tango, 1986; Masque, 1987; Manfred Mann's Earth Band (13 CD box set), 1992; Solo album: Manfred Mann's Plain Music, 1991; Hit singles include: 5-4-3-2-1 (theme for ITV pop show Ready Steady Go!), 1964; Do Wah Diddy Diddy (Number 1, UK and US), 1964; Come Tomorrow, 1965; Oh No, Not My Baby, 1965; If You Got To Go, Go Now, 1965; Pretty Flamingo (Number 1, UK), 1966; Just Like A Woman, 1966; Semi-Detached Suburban Mr James, 1966; Ha! Ha! Said The Clown, 1967; Mighty Quinn (Number 1, UK), 1968; My Name Is Jack, 1968; Fox On The Run, 1969; Ragamuffin Man, 1969; Joybringer, 1973; Blinded By The Light (Number 1, US), 1976; Davey's On The Road Again, 1978; Runner, 1984; Contributor, film music including: What's New Pussycat?, 1965; Up The Junction, 1968.

MANN Steve, b. 9 Aug 1956, London, England. Musician (guitar, keyboards); Sound Engineer; Record Producer. Education: 1 year university studying electronic engineering. Musical Education: 8 years classical piano, 1 year classical guitar. Career: Joined Liar, toured UK and Europe, 1977; Joined Steve Swindells, appeared on Old Grey Whistle Test, 1980; Formed Lionheart, 1981; Toured UK with Tytan, 1983; Joined MSG, played Monsters of Rock Festival, European and USA tours, 1986; Joined Sweet, 1989; Toured: USA; Canada; Australia; Europe; Russia; Producer, engineer for: Shogun; Tora Tora; MSG; Rough Silk; Letter X; Sweet; Thunderhead; Spice. Compositions: Co-wrote Anytime (Number 2, US AOR charts). Recordings: with Liar: Set The World On Fire, 1978; with Lionheart: Hot Tonight, 1984; with Tytan: Rough Justice, 1985; with MSG: Perfect Timing, 1987; Save Yourself, 1989; with Sweet: A, 1992; Glitz, Blitz And Hits, 1995. Memberships: MCPS; PRS (associate member); Musicians' Union. Hobbies: Computers; Hiking; Photography. Address: c/o Frida Park Studio, 30161 Hannover, Germany.

MANNING Barbara Lynne, b. 12 Dec 1944, San Diego, California, USA. Musician; Songwriter; Singer. Education: 4 years college. Musical Education: Self-taught. Career: Extensive tours, USA, Europe, 1990-. Recordings: 28th Day, 1985; World Of Pooh, 1989; One Perfect Green Blanket, B Manning, 1990; Nowhere, S F Seals, 1994; Truth Walks In Sleepy Shadows, S F Seals, 1995. Honours: SF Goldie; SF Wammie, 1992; Bay Area Music Award, 1996. Hobbies: Listening to records; Gardening. Current Management: Matador, 676 Broadway, New York, NY 10012. Address: P O Box 424762, San Francisco, CA 94142, USA.

MANNING Roger Joseph Jr, b. 27 May 1966, Inglewood, California, USA. Songwriter; Arranger; Record Producer; Musician (keyboards). Musical Education: BMus, Jazz Studies, University of Southern California. Career: Keyboardist, Beatnik Beatch, 1987-89; Keyboardist, songwriter, arranger, Jellyfish, 1990-94; Songwriter, arranger, producer, Imperial Drag, 1995-; Keyboardist, arranger, The Moog Cookbook, 1995-. Recordings: Albums: with Beatnik Beatch: Beatnik Beatch, 1988; with Jellyfish: Bellybutton, 1990; Spilt Milk, 1993; with Imperial Drag: Imperial Drag, 1996; with The Moog Cookbook: The Moog Cookbook, 1996; The Moog Cookbook: Ye Olde Space Bande.. Honours: Best Debut Album, with Beatnick Beatch, 1988; Jellyfish, 1990.

Membership: ASCAP. Hobbies: Collecting 60s and 70s kitch; Vintage keyboards. Current Management: Sharpe Entertainment Services, 683 Palerma Avenue, Pacific Palisades, CA 90272, USA.

MANOURY Olivier, b. 13 July 1953, Tulle, France. Musician (bandoneon); Composer. m. Edda Erlendsdottir, 3 July 1977, 1 son. Education: Fine Arts (painting, sculpture); Literature masters degree, Sorbonne University, Paris. Musical Education: Self-taught. Career: Accompanist to tango singer, Ernesto Rondo; Duo with singer Jorge Chamine; Founder, groups Tangoneon; Tempo di Tango; Duo with pianist Enrique Pascual; Played at Paris Opera; Theatre de Champs Elysées; Stockholm Konserthuset; Trottoirs de Buenos Aires; Jazz club: New Morning; Auditorium des Halles. Recordings: La Cumparsita; Tangoneon; Tangos; Tempo Di Tango. Memberships: SACEM; ADAMI; SPEDIDAM: Academia del Tango. Hobby: Painting. Address: 165 Rue de la Roquette, 75011 Paris, France.

MANOV Dragomir. Musician (guitar). Career: Lead guitarist, Concurent, 1986-; Numerous concerts, TV and radio appearances, Bulgaria. Recordings: Rock For Peace, 1988; Rock Festival In Mitchurin, 1989; The Black Sheep (rock collection), 1992; Something Wet (best-selling album, Bulgaria), 1994; The Best Of Bulgarian Rock, 1995. Honours: First Prizes: Top Rock Band, Vidrin, 1989; Rock ring, Sofia, 1990; Top Rock Composition: The Cavalry, 1991; Group Of The Year, The Darik Radio Countdown, 1994. Address: 40 St Stambolov Blvd, 1202 Sofia, Bulgaria.

MANSON Shirley, b. Scotland. Singer. Career: Singer, Goodbye McKenzie; Angel Fish; Lead singer, Garbage; 2 UK tours. Recordings: Albums: with Garbage: Garbage, 1995; Singles: with Garbage: Vow, 1995; Subhuman, 1995; Queer, 1995; Only Happy When It Rains, 1995; Stupid Girl, 1996. Honours: BRIT Award Nominations: Best International Group, Best International Newcomer, 1996. Current Management: SOS Management, 106 Cleveland Street, London W1 5DP, England.

MANSOUR Ahmad, b. 7 June 1960, Tehran, Iran. Musician (guitar). m. Birgitte Fjord, Dec 1994. Musical Education: Berklee College of Music, Boston, USA. Career: Radio and television: Boston; New York; France; Netherlands; Switzerland; Numerous tours and festivals throughout Europe. Recordings: 6 album releases as bandleader, featuring original compositions. Membership: BMI. Current Management: BMI. Current Management: Jazz Diffusions. Address: 26 Rue des Ponts de Comines, 59800 Lille, France.

MANTELS Viv, b. 31 October 1964, Diest, Belgium. Education: Actress, Singer & Director, Theatre, Music & Film; Singer; Jazz & Classical; Songwriter & Composer, different instruments. Career: Radio (BRTN) Belgium; Film, USA, Worldwide, 1999; TV, Europe, 1998. Compositions: Thinking of You, with Michel Herr; All Night Through, with Mal Waldron; No More Tears, with Mal Waldron. Recordings: Viv Mantels & Mal Waldron Trio, 1989; Alpha & Omega, Eluca, 1984. Memberships: Jazz Educators, USA; National Association Teachers of Singing, USAS; Europe Vrouw & Musiek, Holland. Hobbies: Swimming; Reading; Badminton; Walks (woods). Current Management: Lyons Management, Lorraine Lyons, Essex, England.

MANZAREK Ray, b. 12 Feb 1939, Chicago, Illinois, USA. Musician (keyboards); Producer. Career: Member, The Doors, 1964-72; Northern California Folk-Rock Festival, 1968; Hollywood Bowl (later released as video), 1968; Film documentary, The Doors Are Open, 1968;

Documentary film, The Feast Of Friends, 1969; Toronto Rock'n'Roll Revival Show, 1969; Isle of Wight Festival, 1970; Recordings: Albums: The Doors, 1967; Strange Days, 1967; Waiting For The Sun, 1968; Morrison Hotel, 1970; Absolutely Live, 1970; L A Woman, 1971; Other Voices, 1971; Weird Scenes Inside The Gold Mine, 1972; Full Circle, 1972; Solo: The Golden Scarab, 1975; The Whole Thing Started With R'n'R, 1975; Live At The Hollywood Bowl, 1987; Singles: Light My Fire (Number 1, US), 1967; Love Me Two Times, 1968; Hello I Love You (Number 1, US), 1968; Touch Me, 1969; Love Her Madly, 1971; Riders On the Storm, 1971; Producer for Los Angeles band X. Address: c/o Goldman & Knell, CPA's LLP, 1900 Avenue of the Stars, Suite 1040, Los Anegels, CA 90067, USA.

MAPFUMO Thomas, b. Oct 1945, Marondera, Zimbabwe. Musician (mbira, guitar); Singer; Songwriter. Career: Known as The Lion Of Zimbabwe; Most important figure in local Shona music, 1970s-; Singer, local bands including the Cosmic Dots and the Springfields; Began translating American songs into Shona, early 1970s; Founder, Hallelulah Chicken Run Band, 1973; Researcher, traditional Zimbabwean folk style music; Founder, Pied Pipers Band, 1977; Founder, Acid Band, 1977-; Government banned them from radio, Mapfumo jailed for subversion, 1977; Band renamed Blacks Unlimited, 1978; First tours, Britain, 1984; Europe, 1985. Recordings: Albums: Hokoya!, 1977; Gwindingwe, 1980; Mabesa, 1983; Congress, 1983; The Chimurenga Singles, 1983; Ndangariro, 1984; Mr Music, 1985; Chimurnega For Justice, 1986; Corruphon, 1989; Chamunorwa, 1990; Singles include: Morento; Ngoma Yarira. Address: c/o Free World Music Inc, 230 12th Street, Suite 117, Miami Beach, FL 33139-4603, USA.

MARCHANT Colin, b. 27 November 1937, Batley, England. Musician (drums). m. Joan Marchant, 1 s, 2 d. Education: Music Tuition at school. Career: Touring in 1960's with Gene Vincent, Danny Williams, Dusty Springfield, The Beatles and Rolling Stones; Working and living in Japan, 1968-71, 1972-; Working on Cabaret as back-up Musician. Hobby: Music.

MARGARIT Bernard, b. 19 Feb 1956, Carcassonne, France. Musician (guitar); Composer. 1 son, 1 daughter. Musical Education: Classical guitarist, The Academie, Toulouse. Career: International tours with Johnny Hallyday; Television shows with: Kim Wilde; Eddy Mitchell; Johnny Hallyday; French jazz concert tours with Jean Pierre LLabador; Remy Charmasson; Philippe Petrucciani. Recordings: Various recordings with Johnny Hallyday; Album: Friendship (all original compositions) with jazz guitarist Jean Pierre Llabador. Memberships: SACEM; SPEDIDAM; ADAMI. Hobbies: Sport; Yoga. Current Management: Edma Managements. Address: 13 Rue du Stade, 11300 Limoux, France.

MARGOLIN Bob, b. 9 May 1949, Boston, Massachusetts, USA. Blues Musician (guitar); Writer. Education: Graduated Boston University, 1970. Career: 7 years in Muddy Waters Blues Band; Leader, own blues band, 1980-. Recordings: 4 solo albums; Sideman on 30 albums with other blues players, 1974-96; Albums include: with the Band: The Last Waltz, 1978; with The Nighthawks, 1979; with Muddy Waters: Live At Mr Kellys, 1971; Woodstock Album, 1975; Hard Again, 1977; I'm Ready, 1977; Mississippi Muddy Waters Live, 1977; King Bee, 1980; with Johnny Winter: Nothin' But The Blues, 1977; The Johnny Winter Story, 1980. Publications: Senior writer, regular column for Blues Revue magazine. Current Management: Piedmont Talent, 1222 Kenilworth Avenue, Charlotte, NC 28204, USA.

MARGUET Christophe, b. 14 May 1965, Paris, France. Musician (drums). m. Isabelle, Aug 1992. Musical Education: Self-taught. Career: Played with: Barney Wilen; Vincent Herring; Bud Shank; Alain Jean Marie; Claude Barthélémy; Daunik Lazro; Noël Akchoté; Didier Levallet; Tours: China; Egypt; Syria; Morocco; Cameroon; Own trio with Sebastien Texier (alto sax), Olivier Sens (double bass). Recordings: 2 with Georges Arvanitas: Gershwin; Ellington; Altissimo, Hubert Dupont Sextet; Amazonia, Nicolas Genest; Mr Claude, Claude Barthelemy Quartet, 1997; Resistance Poetique, Christophe Marguet Trio, 1997. Honours: First Prize, Orchestra, First Prize, Composition, Concours de la Défense, 1995; Django d'Or for Resistance Poetique, Best CD of Year, 1997. Hobbies: Music; Painting; Photography; Theatre; Films. Current Management: Self-managed. Address: 25 Rue Jeanne d'Arc, 92600 Asnieres, France.

MARINO Frank, b. Canada. Rock Musician (guitar); Vocalist. Career: Founder, Mahogany Rush, 1970-80; Recorded under own name, 1981-82; Major concerts include: Heavy Metal Holocaust, Port Vale, UK, 1981. Recordings: Albums: with Mahogany Rush: Maxoom, 1971; Child Of The Novelty, 19784; Strange Universe, 1975; Mahogany Rush IV, 1976; World Anthem, 1977; Live, 1978; Tales Of The Unexpected, 1979; What's Next, 1980; Solo: The Power Of Rock'n'Roll, 1981; Juggernaut, 1982; Full Circle, 1986; Double Live, 1988; Also featured on Guitar Speak Vol 2 (compilation album), 1990. Current Management: American Famous Talent Corporation, 816 W Evergreen, Chicago, IL 60622, USA.

MARJORIE-JEAN, b. 12 May 1952, Oakland, California, USA. Vocalist; Actress. Education: BA, Music, University of the Pacific. Broadcasts on music networks include: Waxworks; The Big Band Showcase; Satellite Music Network; International Radio; 3 tours of the Midwest; 2 music videos; 2 West Coast tours; Numerous appearances for the military services; Performances on US Navy ships; 4 East Coast tours; Tour of Philippine nightclubs; Performances for Benefits for the Kevin Collins Foundation; Child Quest International (charities). Recordings: 2 albums; 2 hit singles; 1 Christmas single. Honours: Honorary Member, US Army Pentagon Staff, conferred for contributions during Gulf War, 1991. Memberships: SAG; AFTRA; AGVA; Equity. Current Management: Carmel Artists Management. Address: c/o Carmel Records, PO Box 50353, Palo Alto, CA 94303, USA.

MARKELIUS Nike Maria, b. 29 August 1962, Sweden. Songwriter; Musician; Singer. m. Rolf Markelius, 23 August 1997. Education: Selftaught Drummer; Studied Singing. Career: Drummer, Vocals, Swedish Rock Group, Usch, Tours in Denmark and Sweden, 1979-81; Tant Strul, Scandinavian Tours, 1981-85; Roskilde Festival, Slottspark, Helsingfors, 1985; Songwriter, Solo Performer, Theatre Music; Smisk, Tours in Sweden, 1989-97; Singer, Group, Nike, Tours, 1992-97. Compositions: Hula Hula, 1987; Fandango, 1992; Several Theatre Plays, 1992-96; Music and Lyrics for Solo Album, Nike, 1996. Recordings: With Groups: 3 Singles, 4 Songs, Live Album with Usch, 1979-81; 3 Albums, Amazon, 1993, Jag Önskar Dig, 1994; Samlade Singlar, 1995; Several Singles with Tant Strul, 1981-85; Studio Project, Hula Hula, 1987; Solo Album, Nike, 1996. Honours: Kasper Priset, 1983; Scholarship, SKAP, 1992; Konstnärsnämnden, 1992-93, 1995-96; Stockholm City Artist Grant, 1997. Memberships: STIM; SKAP; SAMI; SMF; Musikcentrum; DIVA. Hobbies: Family; Friends; Running; Boxing; Books; Films. Address: Kattugglevägen 18, 123 52 Farsta, Sweden.

MARKEY Gerry (Gerald Murphy), b. 13 Nov 1963, Liverpool, England. Singer; Songwriter; Actor; Musician (guitar, piano, harmonica). Education: BA Hons, York University; PGCE, London University; AIL, Institute of Linguists.

Musical Education: Self-taught. Career: Extensive tours: Europe; USA; Appeared on BBC TV performing: 95; Granada TV: St Joseph of Paradise Street; The Ballad Of Dixie Dean; Talk To Me; Teacher, Art And Craft Of Songwriting, Liverpool University; Currently Project Coordinator, The European Song Project. Recordings: Oh John, 1984; Sweet Liberty, 1987; Marvellous Marvin Gaye, 1993; Ballad Of Dixie Dean, 1981. Honours: PRS, John Lennon Award, Sweet Liberty, 1987; Second place, National Music Day Songwriter of 1993, Marvellous Marvin Gaye, 1993. Memberships: Musicians' Union; BASCA; Sound Sense; Equity; PRS. Hobbies: Photography; Modern Art; Teaching: Art and Craft of Songwriting. Current Management: Self-managed. Address: The European Song Project, 12 Benson Street, Liverpool L1 2ST, England.

MARKOVIC Milivoje, b. 20 Mar 1939, Zagreb, Yugoslavia. Musician (saxophone, clarinet); Composer; Conductor. Education: Law studies; Jazz Music Degree, Music Academy of Graz, Austria. Career: With Markovic-Gut Sextet performed at the Northsee Jazz Festival and toured Belgium, Germany, Soviet Union, Hungary, Romania, Italy, Turkey, Bulgaria and Cuba; Numerous TV and radio appearances. Compositions include: Otpisani; Ballad in Escutabile; Stemi; YuN QMM; Suze. Recordings include: Markovic-Gut Sextet, 1980, 1981; Clark Terry Live in Belgrade with the Markovic-Gut Sectet, 1982; Message from Belgrade, 1984; Ernie Wilkins in Belgrade with Markovic-Gut Sextet; Machito and His Salsa Big Band. Membership: Composers Union of Yugoslavia, President, 1987-88. Hobby: Radio amateur. Address: Plato Jazz Club, Student TRG, Belgrade, Yugoslavia.

MARKS Roger, b. 20 Feb 1947, Tenby, Wales. Musician (trombone); Jazz Bandleader. m. 1967-87, 2 sons. Musical Education: Honiton Town Band; Later self-taught. Career: Television appearance: Pebble Mill At One, BBC; Southern TV; German, Dutch, Yugoslavian television; Radio broadcast: Jazz Parade, Radio 2. Publication: Roger Marks Discography, 1997. Recordings: Albums: with Rod Mason: Great Having You Around, 1978; After Hours, 1979; Stars Fell On Alabama, 1979; The Last Concert, 1980; Just The Five Of Us, Roger Marks Quartet, 1989; Crazy Rhythm, Roger Marks Quartet and Bruce Turner, 1990; Dixie After Dark, Roger Marks Armada Jazz Band, CD 1994; Plato was a Good Parrot, 1995; Top Marks!, CD, 1996; Jazz Notes, BBC Radio 3, 1997. Honours: City of Plymouth Citation for Outstanding Contribution to the Arts. Membership: ABJM. Hobby: Ex-rugby captain. Current Management: Self-managed. Address: 7 Seven Stars Lane, Tamerton Foliot, Plymouth, Devon, England.

MARKS Toby Anthony, b. 1 Jul 1964, London, England. Musician (guitar, keyboards, electronics, percussion); Composer. Education: University, 1 year. Career: Performed in various bands and concerts in UK and Europe, 1978; Formed, Banco De Gaia (solo electronic project), performing worldwide including Europe, Russia, USA and Japan, 1989-. Recordings: with Banco De Gaia: Maya, 1994; Last Train To Lhasa, 1995. Honour: Mercury Award Nomination, 1994. Memberships: MCPS; PRS; PPL; Musicians' Union. Current Management: Paul West, Space Band Management. Address: c/o Space Band Management, Chancery House, 319 City Road, London EC1V 1LJ, England.

MARLEY Ziggy (David Robert Nesta), b. 17 Oct 1968, Kingston, Jamaica. Singer; Musician (guitar). Career: Leader, Ziggy Marley and the Melody Makers. Recordings: Play The Game Right; Hey World; Conscious Party; One Bright Day; Jahmekya; Joy And Blues; Free Like We Want To Be. Honours: 2 Grammy Awards; NAACP Award; Group are UN Youth Environment

MARLO Clair, b. New York, USA. Singer; Producer; Arranger;Songwriter. m. Alex Baker, 1 Nov 1995, 1 daughter. Musical Education: Berklee College of Music. Career: Tours: US, 1980; US, 1990; Far East, 1994; Television: Here's Johnny, The Philippines. Recordings: Let It Go, 1990; Behaviour Self, 1995; with Liquid Amber: Liquid Amber, 1994; Adrift, 1995; As producer: Just Ahead, Pat Coil, 1993. Honours: 10 songwriting awards. Memberships: ASCAP; NARAS; AIMP; CC; Musicians' Union. Hobbies: Skiing; Boating. Current Management: Mike Gormley, LA Personal Development. Address: 950 N Kings Road #266, West Haywood, CA 90069, USA.

MARMORSTEIN Dan A, b. 3 Nov 1954, Jersey City, New Jersey, USA. Composer; Musician (piano). m. Lone Hoyer Hansen, 29 Dec 1987, 1 stepson, 1 stepdaughter. Education: Brandeis University, 1976; BA, Philosophy, Psychology. Musical Education: Mannes College of Music, New York City, 1981-82; Sweelinck Konservatorium, Amsterdam, 1983-84. Career: Composer of instrumental and vocal music for concert presentation, dance performance, films; Performed at piano in connection with dance concerts and performance art pieces in Netherlands, England, Germany, Denmark, USA; Co-founder, SKRÆP, Danish composers association for the advancement of experimental music. Compositions include: Incidental music for Appolonius of Tyana, 1980; Murmur, for six low-pitched instruments, 1987; Time Out of Mind, incidental music for ballet, 1990; The Lion in Winter/European Sketches, string quartet, 1995. Recordings: Perfo 2, 1984; with Horse Diary: First Gift Of Music, Copenhagen, 1988; The Party Is In Your Head, 1996. Publications: Article in lento/eigenzeit catalogue, published Dortmund, 1994; Candenza article, Jazz Special, Danish Jazz Magazine, 1997; Various reviews in Jazz Special, 1995-97. Honours: Work grants from Danish Art Foundation and DJBFA. Memberships: DJBFA (Danish Jazz Beat and Folk Authors); SKRÆP (Experimental music forum). Hobbies: Photography; Cinematography; Travel; Ping-pong. Address: Murmur Studio, Store Kongensgade 75B, 1264 Copenhagen K, Denmark.

MARR Johnny (John Maher), b. 31 Oct 1963, Ardwick, Manchester, England. Musician (guitar). Career: Founder member, The Smiths, 1982-88; Appearance, John Peel Show, BBC Radio 1, 1983; International tours and concerts; Began playing with Billy Bragg; Brian Ferry; Paul McCartney; Talking Heads; The Pretenders; Played guitar in Midge Ure's band, Nelson Mandela's 70th Birthday Tribute, Wembley, 1988; Member, The The, 1989; Formed Electronic, with Neil Tennant, Bernard Summer, 1990; Worked with Stex, Banderas, 1990. Recordings: Singles include: with the Smiths: Hand In Glove; This Charming Man; What Difference Does It Make; Heaven Knows I'm Miserable Now; William It Was Really Nothing; How Soon Is it Now?; Shoplifters Of The World Unite; Panic; Sheila Take A Bow; Girlfriend In A Coma; with Electronic: Getting Away With It; Get The Message; Feel Every Beat; Disappointed; Albums: with the Smiths: The Smiths, 1984; Meat Is Murder, 1985; The World Won't Listen, 1986; The Queen Is Dead, 1986; Louder Than Bombs, 1987; Strangeways Here We Come, 1987; Best.. 1, Best...II, 1992; with Electronic: Electronic, 1990; Guitarist, Mind Bomb, The The, 1989. Current Managment: Ignition Management, 8A Wyndham Place, London W1H 1PP, England.

MARRE Michel, b. 12 Apr 1946, Rodez, France. Jazz Musician (trumpet). m. D Eynard, 1 son, 1 daughter. Musical Education: Conservatory and Ann Didacre Jazz. Career: Played with Mal Waldron; Don Cherry; Archie Shepp; Joe Lovano; L Texier. Composition: Piece for 450 musicians; Numerous arrangements. Recordings: 17 records; 5 compact discs.

MARS Chris, b. 30 Mar 1965, London, England. Singer; Musician (keyboards, piano, guitar); Musical Education: O Level Music: guitar, piano. Career: A Flock Of Seagulls, USA tour, 1986; Lead singer, The Happening, house band on Sky television, 1990-91; Live broadcast, Greater London Radio, Tim Smith Show, 1991; Solo tour, Norway, Switzerland, Germany, 1994-95. Recordings: Chris Mars (debut album) release due soon. Memberships: Musicians' Union; PRS. Hobbies: Flying aeroplanes; Making music. Address: "00 Cavendish Avenue, Ealing, London W13 0JW, England.

MARS Mick (Bob Deal), b. 3 Apr 1955, Terre Haute, Indiana, USA. Rock Musician (guitar). m. Emi Canyon, 19 Sept 1990. Career: Member, US heavy rock group Mötley Crüe, 1981-; Worldwide concerts include: Tours with: Y&T, 1981, 1982; Kiss, 1983; Ozzy Osbourne, 1984; Iron Maiden, 1984; Cheap Trick, 1986; Theatre of Pain world tour, 1985-86; World tours, 1987, 1989; Major festivals: US Festival, 1983; Monsters of Rock festival, Castle Donington, 1984, 1991; Moscow Music Peace Festival, 1989. Recordings: Albums: Too Fast For Love, 1981; Shout At The Devil, 1983; Theatre Of Pain, 1985; Girls, Girls, Girls (Number 2, US), 1987; Dr Feelgood (Number 1, US), 1989; Decade Of Decadence (Number 2, US), 1991; Till Death Do Us Part, 1994; Singles: Stick To Your Guns, 1981; Looks That Kill, 1984; Too Young To Fall In Love, 1984; Smokin' In The Boys Room, 1985; Home Sweet Home, 1985; You're All I Need, 1987; Dr Feelgood, 1989; Kick Start My Heart, 1990; Without You, 1990; Don't Go Away Mad, 1990; Same Old Situation, 1990; Primal Scream, 1991; Contributor, Stars, Hear'n'Aid charity record, 1985. Honours: Rolling Stone Poll Winners, Best Heavy Metal Band, 1991; American Music Award, Favourite Heavy Metal Album, 1991. Current Management: The Left Bank Organisation, 6255 Sunset Blvd, Ste 1111, Hollywood, CA 90028, USA.

MARSALIS Branford, b. 26 Aug 1960, New Orleans, Louisiana, USA. Jazz Musician (saxophone); Producer; Composer; Actor. Musical Education: New Orleans Centre for Creative Arts; Southern University, Baton Rouge (with Alwin Bastite); Berklee School of Music, Boston. Career: Performed with: Art Blakey; Lionel Hampton; Clark Terry; Bu Blakey; Wynton Marsalis; Herbie Hancock; Sting; Grateful Dead; Albert Collins; Nils Lofgren; Leader of own band with Kenny Kirkland, Jeff Watts, Bob Hurst; Numerous worldwide tours; Major concerts include: Live Aid Concert, London, 1985; Nelson Mandela Concert, London, 1988; Jamaican Hurricane Relief Benefit Concert, Los Angeles, 1990; West Side Story, Aids Project Los Angeles, 1992; Pori Jazz, Finland, 1995; Film roles: School Daze; Throw Mama From The Train; Television and radio appearances include: Bring On The Night, 1985; Host, New Visions, 1987; Story Of A People, Expressions in Black, 1991; Host, Jazzset, radio series, 1992; Co-host, Best of Disney Music, 1992; Music Director, Tonight Show, 1992. Composer and performer on numerous film and television scores; Recordings: Scenes In The City, 1984; Romances For Saxophone, 1986; Bring On The Night, live album, 1986; Royal Garden Blues, 1986; Renaissance, 1987; Random Abstract, 1988; Trio Jeepy, 1989; Crazy People Music, 1990; Music From Mo' Better Blues, 1990; The Beautiful Ones Are Not Yet Born, 1991; I Heard You Twice The First Time, 1992; Bloomington, 1993; Buckshot Le Fonque, 1994. Also performed on albums by Wynton Marsalis and Sting. Honours: 3 Grammy Awards; 7 Grammy Nominations. Current Management: Anne Marie Wilkins, Wilkins Management. Address: 260 Brookline Street, Cambridge, MA 02139, USA.

MARSALIS Wynton, b. 18 Oct 1961, New Orleans, Louisiana, USA. Musician (trumpet). Education: Trained in classical music, Juillard School, New York, USA. Career: Played with New Orleans Philharmonic, age 14; Joined Art Blakey and the Jazz Messengers, 1980; Tour with Herbie Hancock, 1981; Formed own group with brother Branford Marsalis on tenor saxophone, 1982; Leader, Wynton Marsalis Septet; Appearances with New York Philharmonic; Cleveland Orchestra; Los Angeles Philharmonic; London Symphony Orchestra and other major European orchestras; Conductors include: Lorin Maazel; Zubin Mehta; Leonard Slatkin; Esa-Pekka Salonen; Held Saturday Jazz for Young People, Lincoln Centre, New York; Regularly conducts masterclasses in schools and holds private tuition. Compositions include: Blood on the Fields, oratorio; In This House On This Morning, for septet; (At The) Octoroon Ball, for string quartet; Jazz/Syncopated Movements; Jump Start; Sweet Release, with Judith Jamison; Citi Movement/Griot New York, with Garth Fagan. Recordings include: Joe Cool's Blues, Wynton Marsalis Septet and Ellis Marsalis Trio, 1995; In This House On This Morning, 1994; Gabriel's Garden; Jazz for Young People; Jazz/Syncopated Movements, 1997; Jump Start, forthcoming. Honours: Grand Prix du Disque, France; Edison Award, Netherlands; 8 Grammy Awards; Keys to many US cities; Numerous honorary Doctorates from US Univrsities; Named one of the US's Most Influential People; Pulitzer Prize for Music, 1997; Concertos by Haydn, Hummel and Leopold Mozart; Grand Prix Du Disque, France. Address: c/o Shore Fire Media, 193 Joralemon Street, Brooklyn, NY 11201, USA.

MARSDEN Gerry (Gerald), b. 24 Sept 1942, Liverpool, Merseyside, England. Singer; Musician (guitar). m. Pauline Ann, 11 Oct 1965, 2 daughters. Musical Education: Self-taught. Career: 33 years in music; Gerry and the Pacemakers, 1962-; 3 Number 1 hit singles with first 3 records; Numerous concerts and television shows worldwide; West End theatre: Charlie Girl; Pull Both Ends, (5 years). Recordings: Hit singles include: Ferry Cross The Mersey; I Like It; How Do You Do It; I'm The One; Don't Let The Sun Catch You Crying; You'll Never Walk Alone; Albums include: How Do You Like It, 1963; Ferry Cross The Mersey, 1964; Don't Let The Sun Catch You Crying, 1964; Girl On A Swing, 1966; Numerous compilations. Publications: I'll Never Walk Alone (autobiography). Honours: 2 BMI citations; Gold and Silver records; BASCA Gold Badge. Memberships: Musicians' Union; Equity; PRS; Songwriters' Guild. Hobbies: Fishing; Shooting; Boating; Scuba diving. Current Management: Derek Franks Organization/PIP.

MARSH Barbara Lynn, b. Warwick, Rhode Island, USA. Singer; Songwriter; Musician (guitar, piano, mandolin). m. Peter Comley, Divorced 1995, 28 Apr 1984. Education: AA, Pensacola Jr College; BA, Drama, Universty of West Florida. Musical Education: Choral Training, Woodham High Echoes; Certificate of Jazz, Popular Musicianship (studio), Goldsmiths College, London. Career: The Dear Janes, 1992-; Supported the Cranberries, Royal Albert Hall, 1995; Tours: UK, Ireland, Germany, Netherlands, 1993-95; London dates with Robyn Hitchcock, 1996-97; Toured USA with Robyn Hitchcock, 1997; Radio: Woman's Hour; Kaleidoscope; Loose Ends; Johnnie Walker; GLR; Recorded: Dangerous Dangerous Nuts, BBC Screen 2, Crazy For A Kiss; Acting: 2 episodes, Broadway Stories, 1994; Solo work, London, New York (live), 1980-92; Backing vocals, Anthony Thistlethwaite. Recordings: With The DearJanes: Sometimes I, 1994; No Skin, 1996. Publications: Poetry: The Panhandler, Literary Magazine, 1981; Pensacola, Florida, USA; The Auteur, magazine, London, 1992-93. Honours: 3rd Place National Forensics (intercollegiate), Informative Speaking, 1977; Finalist, Informative Speaking, 1978. Memberships: PRS; Musicians' Union; MCPS;

Poetry Society. Hobbies: Poetry; Acting (other professions); Swimming; Water skiing. Current Managment: Steve Weltman Management. Address: 10C Porchester Square, London, W2 6AN, England.

MARSH Henry, b. 8 Dec 1948, Bath, Somerset, England. Composer; Musician (keyboards, guitar). m. Susan Norddahl, 1 Apr 1970, divorced, 2 sons, 1 daughter. Musical Education: O Level Viola; Otherwise self-taught. Career: First group, at Sherborne School (featured future actor Jeremy Irons on drums); Founder member, Sailor, 1970s; First musical, One Last Summer, opened in Atlanta; Currently writing music for television. Recordings: Hit singles with Sailor: Girls Girls Girls; A Glass Of Champagne; Album with Sailor: Trouble - The Third Step. Memberships: PRS; MCPS. Hobbies: Transcendental meditation (for 20 years); Tennis. Current Management: Strawberry Hills Management. Address: The Red Cottage, Rood Ashton, Trowbridge, Wilts BA14 6BL, England.

MARSHALL Christopher William, b. 18 Sept 1956, Calcutta, India. Education: BSc, Hons, Manchester. Musical Education: Piano studies to age 16. Career: Semi-pro until 26; Keyboards with bands: Biddie and Eve; The Next Step; Angie; Started record label, Rhythm Shop Records, 1994. Compositions: Television soundtracks: Ad Armageddon, BBC2; Zapruder Footage, BBC2; Broken Lives, BBC2; The Number 10 Show, Channel 4; Numerous albums library music; Co-writer, Your House Or My House, Samantha Fox, 1989. Recordings: As producer: Tracks by: Demis Roussos; Norman Wisdom; He Ain't Heavy, He's My Brother, Jonathan Paule; Albums: with Tight Fit: Back To The 60's Vol II, III; with Dream On Dream: Strangeways; with Hound Dog and The Megamixers: Junior Party Megamix, 1990. Honours: Gold, Platinum discs: Samantha Fox. Memberships: APRS; Musicians' Union; MCPS; PRS; ANA; PPL. Hobbies: Cricket; Films; Drinking socially. Address: 26 Weiss Road, Putney, London SW15 1DH, England.

MARSHALL Francois L Garcia, b. England. Artist Manager; Arts Critic. Education: BA Honours, Film and Television. Career: Artist manager for Sabbamangalang and Lost Pole Pretensions; Writer, critic of the Arts, music, theatre, film and video. Publications include: Cheshire Magazines; Men; Metropolis. Membership: National Union of Journalists. Hobby: Meditation. Address: c/o Bodō Music Co, 186 Ashley Road, Hale, Altrincham, Cheshire WA15 9SF, England.

MARSHALL Gary Paul, b. 29 Sept 1964, Oswestry, Shropshire, England. Musician (drums, percussion); Teacher. m. Karen Marshall, 1 July 1989. Musical Education: Various private teachers. Career: Work on BBC Radio Oxford Fox FM; BBC Radio Shropshire; Various recording sessions, drum clinics with Lloyd Ryan (teacher of Phil Collins); Colin Woolway (Suzi Quatro, Rocky Horror, Godspell). Publications: Currently working on The Marshall Art Of Drumming. Honours: 5 musical endorsements (via teaching). Memberships: Musicians' Union; NAPT. Hobbies: Sport; Music; Travel. Address: Ruskin House, Ruskin Road, Banbury, Oxfordshire OX16 9HY, England.

MARSHALL Jamie, b. 8 July 1955, Doncaster, Yorkshire, England. Musician (guitar, keyboards); Vocalist; Songwriter; Composer. Partner, Helen Halliday. Education: Business Studies, Honours degree. Musical Education: Self-taught (formal education to O'Level). Career: Over 3000 live concerts in places including: The Marquee Club; The Royal Festival Hall; Live show, Geneva radio to estimated 2 million people; Tour, Top Of The Pops appearance with Don McLean, 1991; Radio 1; Radio 5; Sky TV. Recordings: Album: Even The Strongest Hearts, 1988;

Troubletown (EP), 1990; Third recording in progress. Hobbies: Cooking; Watching sport; Live music; Cinema. Current Management: c/o Thump Thump Music, 1 York Street, London W1H 1PZ, England. Address: Pound Corner, Pound Lane, Windlesham, Surrey GU20 6BP, England.

MARSHALL John Stanley, b. 28 Aug 1941, Isleworth, Middlesex, England. Musician (drums, percussion). m. Maxi Egger. Education: BA (Hons) Psychology, University of Reading. Musical Education: Studied with Jim Marshall; Alan Ganley; Philly Joe Jones. Career: Freelance on London jazz scene; Played with Alexis Korner's Blues Incorporated, 1964; Graham Collier Sextet, 1965-70; Also played with John Surman; John McLaughlin; Dave Holland; Mike Westbrook; Graham Bond Organisation; Joe Harriot; Indo-Jazz Fusions; Keith Tippett's Sextet, Centipede; Alan Skidmore; Founder member, Nucleus, 1969; Montreux Festival (First Prize, 1970); Newport Festival, Village Gate, New York; Regular member, Mike Gibbs Orchestra, early 1970s; Left Nucleus to join Jack Bruce Band, 1971; Joined Soft Machine, 1972; Played with musicians including: Larry Coryell; Gary Burton; Mary Lou Williams; Ronnie Scott; Tubby Hayes; Ben Webster; Milt Jackson; Roy Eldridge; John Taylor; Norma Winstone; Volker Kriegel; Gordon Beck; Charlie Mariano; Jasper van't Hof; Philip Catherine; Joined Eberhard Weber's Colours, 1977-81; Worked with Gil Evans Orchestra; Ian Carr; Kenny Wheeler; Uli Beckerhoff; Anthony Braxton; Manfred Schoof; Joachim Kühn; Michel Portal; John Taylor; Alan Holdsworth; Norma Winstone; Gordon Beck; Jeff Clyne; Arild Anderson; John Abercrombie; John Surman Quartet; Brass Project; Teacher, Jazz Faculty of the Royal Academy of Music, London. Recordings: Over 60 albums include: Elastic Rock, Nucleus, 1970; Harmony Row, Jack Bruce, 1971; Bundles, Soft Machine, 1975; Stranger Than Fiction, John Surman Quartet, 1994. Current Managment: Self-managed. Address: 43 Combemartin Road, London SW18 5PP, England.

MARSHALL Oren Morris, b. 14 June 1966, Geneva, Switzerland. Musician (tuba, recorder, percussion). Musical Education: Oboe, recorder, voice, Purcell School, 1977-79; Tuba, piano, Royal College of Music - JD, 1981-84. Career: Musician with every major orchestra in London, 1985; Jazz big bands include: Loose Tubes, 1984-90; Jazz Warriors, 1986; John Dankworth, 1995; Julian Joseph, 1994-95; Improvised music with: Company '92, with Derek Bailey; Say What Trio, with Steve Noble, Davey Williams, 1991-; Worldwide tours, with London Brass, 1987-; Solo television appearances include: Wogan, BBC, 1987; South Bank Show, ITV, 1988; Performances with the Pan African Orchestra, UK and Ghana, 1991-94. Recordings: 10 albums with London Brass; Other recordings include: Mahler, Symphonies 9 and 10, Frankfurt Radio Orchestra, 1986; The Human Groove, Microgroove, 1988; Solo album: Time Spent At Traffic Lights (all compositions by Oren Marshall), 1995; Noble-Marshall-Buckley, Derek Bailey Trio, 1995; Mike Gibbs Band, 1993. Honours: ARCM (hons), 1983; FTCL, 1984; Shell/LSO Scholarship winner, 1987; Third prize, Geneva International Music Competition, 1991. Hobbies: Dancing; Swimming; Yoga; Drumming; Relaxing.

MARSILI Marco, b. 22 Nov 1968, Milan, Italy. Producer; Composer; Arranger; Remixer; Programmer; Musician (keyboards). Education: Classics, Law. Musical Education: Milan Music School, piano. Career: Producer and remixer for: Riccardo Cocciante; Loredana Berté; Degrees Of Motion; Joe Roberts; Ivan Graziani; Tony Esposito; Ladri Di Biciclette; Patty Johnson; Carol West; Toto Cotugno' Viola Valentino; Dario Gay. Honours: Board of Directors, Association of Italian Phonographics, 1996-. Memberships: SIAE; PPL; VPL; AFI; ANEM; SISC. Hobbies: Collecting concert tickets, badges, CDs. Current

Management: KLF Music SAS. Address: c/o KLF Music SAS, Via Enrico Heine 1, 20141 Milan, Italy.

MARTENS Evert Everardus Antonius Josephus Maria, b. 14 July 1956, Mill & St Hubert. 1 son. Career: Many TV and radio appearances. Compositions: Waltz for Rutger; La Copine; Where's My Key. Recordings: 4 CDs: After You're Gone; Just in Time; La Copine; Way to Go. Honours: First Prize, Capelino, Old Style Jazz Festival Breda, 1990. Memberships: NTB; VAK; SENA; BUMA; STEMRA. Hobbies: Repairing all kinds of things. Address: Sonsbeeksingel 11, 6814 AA Arnhem, The Netherlands.

MARTENS Hervé, b. 11 June 1963, Leuven, Belgium. Keyboard Player. Career: Member of Soulsister, 1989-97. Recordings: Recordings with Bobby Womack and Gibson Brothers. Honour: Best Belgium Band Monte Carlo Award, 1988. Membership: Sabam; Zamu. Hobby: Football. Address: Kerkstraat 12, 3370 Boutersem, Belgium.

MARTIN Barrie, b. 22 May 1944, London, England. Musician (baritone, tenor, alto saxophone). m. Elizabeth Gower, 5 Nov 1976, 1 son, 2 daughters. Musical Education: 5 years with Leslie Evans (private tutor). Career: Member, Quotations, Walker Brothers band for 2-3 years; All concert tours except last; Solo Spot, Sunday Night at London Palladium; Also as guest of Walker Brothers on German TV from Berlin; Played with Jet Harris' band: The Jet Blacks; One Night Stand, with Pete Murray, BBC TV, 1960s; Tours with: Roy Orbison; Brenda Lee; Duane Eddy; Little Richard; Englebert Humperdinck; Geno Washington and The Ram Jam Band; Currently working with Otis Grand and the Big Blues Band. Recordings: Solo, on Walker Brothers EP; Walker Brothers album: Portrait; Atlantic Soul Machine album: Coast To Coast. Membership: Musicians' Union. Hobby: Trying to play piano. Address: 26 Halstow, Queens Crescent, London NW5 4EH, England.

MARTIN Beranger, b. 5 May 1960, Brugge, Belgium. Jazz Musician (Guitar; 2nd Instructor Piano). m. Elsie Tuyaerts, 1988, 2 sons. Education: Jazz School, Dworp, Belgium. Career: On Tour in Sweden with Waso Quartet; with own trio, Beranger Trio; Toured in France, Germany and The Netherlands; Guest Guitar Player in Australia. Compositions: LPs recorded with Gypsy Quintet, Piotto's; CD recorded with Big Band, Arena; Own CD for BRTN, Belgian TV. Recordings: Freelance Guitar Player; Swing-Jazz to Modern-Jazz and Gipsy Jazz; Guest Player on CD's. Publication: Cocktail, 1997. Honour: Jazz-Rally Hasselt, Best Solo Artist, 1990. Hobbies: Music; Sports. Current Management: Kras Artist, Ghent Parcifal, Bruges Booking NTS, Knokke. Address: Sakramentstraat 8, 8300 Knokke-Reist, Belgium.

MARTIN Bill, b. 9 Nov 1938, Glasgow, Scotland. Songwriter; Music Publisher. m. 1972, 1 son, 3 daughters. Musical Education: Royal Scottish Academy Of Music. Career: Tours with The Drifters; Robert Parker; Winner, Eurovision Song Contest with Puppet On A String; Congratulations; All Kinds Of Everything; All Bay City Roller hits including: Shang-A-Lang; Summerlove Sensation; Publisher of: Billy Connolly; Van Morrison; Sky-Songs; Writer, My Boy, for Elvis Presley; Number 1 songs worldwide. Honours: 20 Gold albums; 4 Platinum albums; 3 Ivor Novello Awards; 3 ASCAP Awards. Memberships: BASCA; PRS. Hobbies: Golf; Past Captain RAC, member, St George's Hill. Address: 225 Kensington High Street, London W8 65A, England.

MARTIN Billie Ray, b. Germany. Singer. Career: Singer with Electribe 101; Now solo artiste. Recordings: Album: Deadline For My

Memories, 1995; Singles: with Electribe 101: Talking With Myself, 1990; Solo: Your Loving Arms, 1995; Space Oasis, 1996. Honour: International Dance Music Award, Best New Dance Solo Artist, 1996. Address: c/o Mark Dean, EastWest Records, Electric Lighting Station, 46 Kensington Court, London W8 5DP, England.

MARTIN Clive, b. 21 Mar 1963, London, England. Record Producer; Sound Engineer. Recordings: As Record Producer: Albums: with Reef: Replenish; Puressence album; with Echobelly: Insomniac (EP); with Les Negresses Vertes: Mlah (double Gold disc); Famille Nombreuse (Gold disc); with Hunters and Collectors: Ghost Nation (Platinum disc); As Sound Engineer: Soundtrack, David Byrne's The Last Emperor; with Youssou N'Dour; As Assistant Engineer: Queen; Sting; The Cure; As Assistant to Flood: Jesus and Mary Chain; Matt Johnson; Soft Cell. Honours: Gold and Platinum albums; Oscar, film soundtrack The Last Emperor. Current Management: Caroline Ryan. Address: Estate House, 921A Fulham Road, London SW6 5HU, England.

MARTIN Daniel-John, b. 25 Sept 1965, Congleton, Cheshire, England. Jazz Musician (violin); Composer; Arranger. Musical Education: Schola Cantorum (superieur) American School of Music; Didier Lockwood. Career: Tour with the 11tet de Violon Jazz; Theatre des Champs Elysées, France, Germany; Major French radio shows; TV: Le Cercle de Minuit; First festival, Jazz Violin, with Didier Lockwood; Jazz M6, TV; with Daniel Martin Group: Sunset; Baiser Solé; Petit Journal Montparnasse; Alligators. Recordings with: Onxtet De Violon Jazz; Djeli Moussa (African music); Public Address (rock p-4 mati); Daniel-John Martin Group to be published. Honours: First Prize, Jazz Modern, Jazz Plus, Jazz Hot. Membership: General Secretary, Jazz and Violin Association. Hobbies: Painting; Sculpting.

MARTIN Dey, b. 9 November 1956, Los Angeles, CA, USA. Songwriter; Producer; Musician (Guitar). Musical Education: Composition Degree in Music BM, University of Hawaii; MM, University of California at Irvine, USA. Career: Backing Guitar, Polyphemus, Lollapalloosa Tour, 1995; Producer, Woodpecker, Music West, Vancouver, 1995; Songwriter, Solo Performer, mid 1980s. Compositions: String Quartet, 1978; Three Images, text by EE Cummings for classical guitar, mezzo soprano vocal and piano, 1979; Berlin Wall, 1989. Recording: Mr Monotony, producer. Honour: Young Composers, 1978-80. Membership: ASCAP. Current Management: Naked/Jain Records Inc, PO Box 4132, Palm Springs, CA 92264, USA. Address: 681 E Spencer Drive, Palm Springs, CA 92262, USA.

MARTIN Eric. Singer. Career: Founder member, Eric Martin Band; Lead singer, Mr Big, 1989-; Also member, side project Road Vultures. Recordings: Albums: with Eric Martin Band: Sucker For A Pretty Face, 1983; Eric Martin, 1985; with Mr Big: Mr Big, 1989; Lean Into It, 1991; Singles include: Green-Tinted Sixties Mind; To Be With You. Current Management: Herbie Herbert Management, 2501 3rd Street, San Francisco, CA 94107, USA.

MARTIN Juan, b. 1 Oct 1943, Málaga, Spain. Concert Musician (guitar). m. Helen Foulds, 6 June 1973, 2 sons. Musical Education: Self-taught. Career: Worldwide solo tours; Tours with own Flamenco Dance Company; Played South Bank Centre, and The Barbican, London; Carnegie Hall, and the Lincoln Centre, New York; 18 date tours, including the Barbican, UK, 1993, 1995; Television includes: Wogan; Top Of The Pops; Pebble Mill; Arts programmes. Radio recitals, BBC Radios 1-4; New York WNYC; Boston WGBH. Recordings: Exciting Sound Of Flamenco, 1974; Romance, 1976; Olé Don Juan,

Flamenco en Andalucia, 1977; Picasso Portraits, 1981; Serenade, 1984; Solo album, 1985; Painter In Sounds, 1986; Through The Moving Window, 1988; Andalucian Suites, 1990; Luna Negra, 1993. Publications: El Arte Flamenco de la Guitarra; 5th Edition, La Guitarra Flamenca, video series; Folios: Exciting Sound Of Flamenco; 12 Solos; Andalucian Suites. Memberships: PRS; MCPS. Current Management: Flamencovision, PO Box 508, London N3 3SY, England.

MARTIN Lynne, b. 6 Nov 1957, Bedford, England. Musician (keyboards); Arranger; Musical Director. 1 daughter. Education: College. Musical Education: Sat examinations of Associated Board of Royal Schools of Music. Career: Television appearances: Friday People, Border TV; Look Who's Talking; Laugh-In; Musical Director for numerous summer seasons and pantomimes throughout UK; Personal Musical Director for Derek Batey for 12 years; Also MD for artistes including Max Bygraves; Moira Anderson; Frank Carson. Composition: Theme tune, Friday People, Border TV, 1982. Recordings: Numerous recording sessions. Memberships: Musicians' Union; Equity. Current Management: Ray Cornell Artistes and Productions. Address: Applause House, 56 St Annes Road, Blackpool, Lancashire, England.

MARTIN Marie-Ange, b. 18 Jan 1948, Bois Colombes, France. Jazz Musician (guitar, banjo, cello). Musical Education: Self-taught; 8 years cello study. Career: Played swing and Dixieland music with Benny Waters, Bill Coleman, 1969-76; Bebop and modern jazz, 1976-84; Guitar Institute of Technology, Los Angeles, 1985; Guitarist with own quartet; Banjo player, Hot Kings; Cellist, cello quartet Cellofans, 1986-93; Tours of Asia, Australia, Eastern Europe, with Christian Escoude and Marcel Azzola, 1993-95; Banjo and cello player, Threepenny Opera, 1996. Recordings: Dixieland Parade; Cello Acoustics; Also recording music of Kurt Weil. Honours: Outstanding Award Of The Year, Guitar Institute of Technology, Los Angeles, 1985. Hobbies: Knitting; Cooking; Scrabble; Computer; Gym training. Address: 31 Rue de Fontarabie, 75020 Paris, France.

MARTIN Michael Anthony, b. 9 Nov 1960, London, England. Musician (piano, keyboards). 2 daughters. Musical Education: Post graduate diploma; O'Level Music. Career: Keyboard player for Billy Paul; Aswad; Jean Carne; Cliff Richard; Television: Top Of The Pops; Childrens TV; 3 world tours with Aswad; Montreux Pop Festival; International Aids Day; Nelson Mandela at Wembley. Compositions: Music for BBC, State of Europe. Recordings: Keyboard player: Don't Turn Round, Aswad; Production on Heartbeat, Aswad, Number 1 Japan. Honours: Platinum disc, for album: Rise And Shine, Aswad. Membership: PRS; Musicians' Union. Hobbies: Music; Rollerblading.

MARTIN Millicent, b. Romford, Essex, England. Actress; Singer. m. Marc Alexander, 26 Sept 1977. Career: Side By Side By Sondheim (London, Los Angeles, Broadway); 42nd Street (Broadway, Las Vegas, Los Angeles); The Boyfriend (London, Broadway); King Of Hearts (Broadway); The Card (London); Shirley Valentine; Rise and Fall Of Little Voice; Follies; The Rivals, England and USA; Moon Over Buffalo, USA; Television appearances: Moon And Son; Mainly Millicent; That Was The Week That Was (TW3); Downtown; LA Law; Coach; Upper Hand; Murphy Brown. Recordings: Side By Side; King Of Hearts; Our Man Crighton; Sondheim - A Celebration. Honours: TV Society Medal; Variety Club Award. Hobbies: Cooking; Travel; Animals. Current Management: Sean Diamond, London Management. Address: 2-4 Noel Street, London WC1, England.

MARTIN Neil, b. 10 Dec 1967, Great Britain. Musician (drums). Musical Education: Studied

with: Paul Robinson; Ed Soph; Bob Armstrong. Career: Extensive sessions and television, radio appearances; Jimmy Barnes Psyclone World Tour 95 (including support to The Rolling Stones), venues from 1000-50000 seaters. Compositions: Co-writer, track Stumbling, Psyclone album, Jimmy Barnes. Recordings: Album: Psyclone: Jimmy Barnes. Membership: Musicians' Union. Hobbies: Martial arts; Reading; Listening to music. Address: 2 Waddington Close, Enfield, Middlesex EN1 WB, England.

MARTIN Peter (Philemon Winston), b. 28 Jan 1948, Tuitts Village, Montserrat. Musician (drums, percussion); Vocalist. 2 daughters. Education: Courses in adult education. Musical Education: Self-educated with evening classes. First reggae gigs with Owen Grey, Alton Ellis, small tours of England, early 1970s; Studio musician, mid 1970s; Tours, England, Scotland, Wales, 1980s; Joined Steel and Skin, Art Company, played Danish Festival, 1983; Tour, Sweden, 1984; Recordings, gigs, tours, Europe, West Africa, Scandinavia; Tour with Dr Alban, 1992; Resident in Sweden, 1993; Taught rhythm and dance, Blå Hasten; Production of Benny The Boxer, Theatre X; Played Djembe on dance courses; Joined Afro Tiambo, West African Rhythm and dance group, 1994; Computer course, digital music recording; Sound, lighting engineer, Folkuniversitetet, theatre production, Ritten till havet; Teacher, Malmö Music High School; Television: Old Grey Whistle Test; Opportunity Works; Chinese Detective; WDR Rock Palace; MTV Live; Concerts: Ronny Lane Tour; Style Council Peace Concert, Brixton; Radio: Africa, Sweden, London; Festivals: Hultsfred; Roskilde; Tours/gigs with Jimmy Cliff; Style Council; Papa Dee; Red Mitchell; Eek-A-Mouse; Eddie Grant. Recordings include Dr Alban. Honours: Appearances, before Princess Margaret, London, 1978; Swedish royals, Stockholm, 1992. Memberships: Musicians' Union; Svenska Musik Forbondet. Hobbies: Music; Documentary vidoes; Driving. Current Management: Self-managed. Address: 21 Lavender Grove, Hackney, London E18 3LU, England.

MARTIN Roy, b. 10 July 1961, Liverpool, Merseyside, England. Musician (drums); Drum Tutor. m. Margie Yates, 20 June 1985, 2 daughters. Career: Concet tours: Played for: Modern English, 1986, 1990; Shalom Hanoch, 1987, 1988; Gavin Friday, 1992; Black, 1993; Diesel, 1993. Recordings: Drummer on: Jimmy Barnes: Flesh And Wood; Aretha Franklin: Jimmy Lee; Cock Robin: When Your Heart Is Weak; Black: Black; Film soundtrack (The Christians): Blame It On The Bellboy; Modern English: Pillow Lips; Recorded with: Viv Stanshall; Regina Belle; Billy Brannigan; Shalom Hanoch. Hobby: Sports. Current Management: B & H Management. Address: B & H Management, Lavender Cottage, Love Lane, Kings Langley, Hertfordshire WD4 9HN, England.

MARTIN The Very Reverend Doctor, Vocalist; Musician (guitar); Preacher. Education: Church Of The Eternal Question. Career: Flying Patrol Group, European tour; Glastonbury Festival. Recordings: Albums: Rough Stuff; Half A Mix; Get Heavy. Publications: Prayerbook 1 and 1.1. Membership: Musicians' Union. Current Management: East Coast Road Productions. Address: 61 Abington Avenue, Northampton NN1 4PB, England.

MARTIN Tony, b. 19 Apr 1957, Birmingham, England. Singer; Songwriter. m. Mo, 18 Aug 1990, 2 sons, 1 daughter. Career: First show aged 7; Many local bands; Joined The Alliance, 1983; Signed with Warner Bros publishing, 1984; Released tracks on Bailey Bros Compilation Album; Joined Black Sabbath 1987, 3 albums, 3 world tours; Left Black Sabbath, 1992; Signed with Polydor, 1992, solo album; Rejoined Black

Sabbath, 1993, 2 albums, 2 world tours. Recordings: with Bailey Brothers: Vinyl Frontier; The Talisman; Forcefield II; Valley Of The Kings; Blue Murder; with Black Sabbath: Eternal Idol, 1987; Headless Cross, 1989; Tyr, 1990; Cross Purposes, 1993; Forbidden, 1995; Solo: Back Where I Belong, 1992. Hobby: Life. Current Management: Albert Chapman. Address: Lethal Music UK Ltd, E9 Kenilworth Court, Hagley Road, Birmingham B16 9NU, England.

MARTINO Al, b. 7 Oct 1927, Philadelphia, Pennsylvania, USA. Singer; Entertainer; Actor. m. Judith Stilwell, 10 Dec 1968, 1 son, 2 daughters. Career: Played Johnny Fontaine in The Godfather, 1972; Tours in Australia, Germany, USA and Canada; Played in Godfather I and III yearly. Recordings: Spanish Eyes; Here In My Heart (Number 1, UK charts); Mary In The Morning; I Love You Because; Painted, Tainted Rose; Daddy's Little Girl. Honours: Philadelphia Music Hall of Fame; Gold Disc, Spanish Eyes. Hobby: Cooking.

MARTYN John (Iain McGeachy), b. 11 Sept 1948, New Malden, Surrey, England. Vocalist; Musician (guitar); Lyricist. m. Beverly Kutner (divorced). Career: Duo with wife Beverly; Toured regularly with full-time band. Compositions include: Solid Air; Angeline; May You Never, recorded by Eric Clapton. Recordings: Albums: London Conversation, 1968; The Tumbler, 1968; Stormbringer, 1970; The Road To Ruin, 1970; Bless The Weather, 1971; Solid Air, 1973; Inside Out, 1973; Sunday's Child, 1975; Live At Leeds, 1975; One World, 1977; So Far So Good, 1977; Grace And Danger, 1980; Glorious Fool, 1981; Well Kept Secret, 1982; The Electric John Martyn, 1982; Philentrophy, 1983; Sapphire, 1984; Piece By Piece, 10986; Foundations, 1987; The Apprentice, 1990; Cooltide, 1991; BBC Radio 1 Live In Concert, 1992; Couldn't Love You More, 1992; Live, 1995; The Church With One Bell, 1998. Address: c/o Permanent Records, 22-23 Brook Mews, London W2 3BW, England.

MARUCCI Mathew Roger III (Mat), b. 2 July 1945, Rome, New York, USA. Musician (drums); Producer; Writer; Author. m. Diane Marie, 25 May 1982,1 son, 1 daughter. Education: AAS, Retail Business Management, Auburn Community College, 1965; AA, Music, Sacramento City College, 1973. Career: Recording artist and jazz musician; Applied Music Instructor for American River College, Sacramento; Drummer for major jazz artists including Jimmy Smith, Kenny Burrell, James Moody, Eddie Harris, Les McCann, John Tchicai and Buddy De Franco; Appeared in feature film Uncle Joe Shannon and TV series Fantasy Island; Played on soundtracks for TV; Leader of Trio, Quartet and Quintet. Compositions: Festival; Ulterior Motif; Who Do Voo Doo Suite; Blue Suspension; Danse Desire; Lifeline; Quiescence. Recordings: Who Do Voo Doo, 1979; Lifeline, 1981; Festival, 1982; Extensity, 1982; Avant-Bop, 1983; Body and Soul, 1992; Ulterior Motif, 1998. Publications: Contributor of articles in magazines. Publications: Progressive Studies for Drums, 1971; Progressive Studies in Jazz Drumming; CD Masterclass for Drumset. Membership: Percussive Arts Society. Hobby: Tae Kwon Do. Address: 8216 Northam Drive, Sacramento, CA 95843-4542, USA.

MARVIN Hank (Brian Rankin), b. 28 October 1941, Newcastle-upon-Tyne, England. Musician (Guitar); Songwriter. m. Carole, 2 sons. Career: Lead Guitarist, Cliff Richard's backing group the Drifters, 1958; Group became the Shadows, 1959-. Recordings include: Albums: with the Shadows: The Shadows, Number 1, UK, 1961; Out of the Shadows, Number 1, UK, 1962; The Shadows Greatest Hits, 1963; Dance with the Shadows, 1964; The Sound of the Shadows, 1965; Shadow Music, 1966; Jigsaw, 1967; Established, 1958, 1968; Shades of Rock, 1970; 20 Golden Greats, Number 1, UK, 1977; Thank

You Very Much, 20th Anniversary Reunion Concert, Cliff Richard and the Shadows, 1978; String of Hits, Number 1, UK, 1980; Change of Address, 1980; Hits Right Up Your Street, 1981; XXV, 1983; Moonlight Shadows, 1986; Simply Shadows, 1987; Steppin' To the Shadows, 1989; At Their Very Best, 1989; Reflections, 1990; Themes and Dreams, 1991; Shadows in the Night, 1993; Solo albums: Hank Marvin, 1969; Words and Music, 1982; Into the Light, 1992; Heartbeat, 1993; Hit singles: with the Shadows: Apache, Number 1, UK, 1960; Man of Mystery, 1960; FBI, 1961; Kon-Tiki, Number 1, UK, 1961; The Savage, 1961; Wonderful Land, Number 1, UK, 1962; Guitar Tango, 1962; Dance On, Number 1, UK, 1963; Foot Tapper, Number 1, UK, 1963; Atlantis, 1963; Shindig, 1963; Geronimo, 1963; Stingray, 1965; Don't Make My Baby Blue, 1965; Let Me Be The One, UK's Eurovision Song Contest entry, 1975; Don't Cry For Me Argentina, 1979; Cavatina (Theme From the Deerhunter), 1979; Riders in the Sky, 1980; Living Doll - charity version with Cliff Richard, Number 1, UK, 1986; Contributions to films include: Serious Charge, 1959; The Young Ones, 1961; The Boys, 1962; Summer Holiday, 1963; Wonderful Life, 1964; Finders Keepers, 1966; The Frightened City, 1961; The Deerhunter, 1979; The Third Man, 1981. Honours include: CBS Arbiter Award, for Services to British Music, 1977; with the Shadows: NME Record of the Year, 1960; Gold Disc, Apache, 1962; Ivor Novello Awards: Best Musical Score, 1963; Special Award for 25 Years in the Music Business, 1983; Winners, Split Song Festival, Yugoslavia, 1967. Address: c/o Polydor Records, 72-80 Black Lion Lane, London W6 9BE, England.

MARWICK Gavin, b. 29 Aug 1969, Edinburgh, Scotland. Musician (fiddle). Career: Youngest of family of traditional/folk musicians; Involved in resurgence of Scottish music and dance, 1980s; Numerous television and radio broadcasts; Festivals and extensive tours mainly with Iron Horse, Europe, and (occasionally) US, Africa, 1988-; Composer, television soundtracks; Recording artist and teacher; Recording sessions include: Wolfstone; Talitha MacKenzie; Old Blind Dogs; The Electrics; The Humff Family; Other projects: Twin fiddle-led trio (with members of Old Blind Dogs) Burach. Recordings: with The Iron Horse: The Iron Horse, 1991; Thro Water Earth And Stone, 1993; Five Hands High, 1994; The Gamekeeper, 1995; with Jonny Hardie and Davy Cattanach: Up In The Air, 1995; with Burach: The Weird Set, 1995. Honour: Belhaven Best New Folk Band, Burach, 1995. Memberships: Musicians' Union; PRS. Current Management: Peter Stott. Address: 11 Harling Drive, Troon, Ayrshire KA10 6NF, Scotland.

MARX Richard Noel, b. 16 Sept 1963, Chicago, Illinois, USA. Singer; Songwriter; Record Producer. m. Cynthia Rhodes, 8 Jan 1989, 3 sons. Career: Backing vocalist with Lionel Richie, 1982; Solo artiste, 1986-; Extensive tours throughout US, Europe and Asia; Major concerts include: Farm Aid V, 1992; All-star benefit concert, Pediatric AIDS Foundation, 1992; Television and radio appearances worldwide. Compositions: Co-writer, What About Me?, recorded by Kenny Rogers; Co-writer, album tracks with Chicago; Philip Bailey; Co-writer, co-producer, with Randy Meisner; David Cole; Fee Waybill; Vixen; Poco; Kevin Cronin. Recordings: Hit singles: Don't Mean Nothing, 1987; Should've Known Better, 1987; Endless Summer Nights, 1988; Hold On To The Nights (Number 1, US) 1988; Satisfied (Number 1, US), 1989; Right Here Waiting, (Number 1, US), 1989; Angelia, 1990; Too Late To Say Goodbye, 1990; Children Of The Night, 1990; Hard To Believe, 1991; Keep Coming Back, 1991; Hazard, 1992; Take This Heart, 1992; Chains Around My Heart, 1992; Now And Forever (Number 1, US), 1994; The Way She Loves Me, 1994; Nothing Left Behind Us, 1994; As backing singer: with Lionel Richie: All Night Long; You Are; Running With The Night; Solo albums: Richard Marx, 1987; Repeat

Offender (Number 1, US), 1989; Rush Street, 1991; Paid Vacation, 1994. Honours: Grammy Nominations: Best Rock Vocal Performance, Don't Mean Nothing, 1987; Best Pop Vocal Performance, Right Here Waiting, 1989; Billboard AC Artist of the Year, 1992; First male artist with four Top 3 hits from debut album. Memberships: ASCAP; SAG; AFTRA; AFofM. Hobby: Tennis. Current Management: The Left Bank Organization. Address: 6255 Sunset Blvd #1111, Hollywood, CA 90028, USA.

MARZEC Andrzej, b. 3 Sept 1944, Szczytniki, Poland, Promoter. m. Ewa Olinkiewicz, 31 Mar 1983, 1 son, 1 daughter. Education: Law, Warsaw University. Musical Education: Private lessons on piano. Career: 1969-, Agent for top Polish Rock and Jazz acts: Niemen; Tomasz Stanko; Michal Urbaniak; 1980-, Promoting international acts in Poland including: Kraftwerk; Tangerine Dream; Klaus Schulze; Elton John; Tina Turner; Pat Metheny; Iron Maiden; Depeche Mode; Leonard Cohen; AC/DC; Metallica; David Byrne; Iggy Pop; Bob Dylan; Chris Rea; Jack Bruce; Beastie Boys. Hobbies: Travel; Cycling. Address: Andrzej Marzec Concerts (AMC), Mickiewicza 27/69, 01562 Warsaw, Poland.

MASAKOWSKI Steve, b. 2 Sept 1954, New Orleans, Louisiana, USA. Jazz Musician (guitar). m. Ulrike Sprenger, 22 Mar 1982, 1 son, 1 daughter. Education: Berklee College of Music, Boston. Career: Extensive international travel with Dianne Reeves; Rick Margitza; Astral Project. Recordings: Direct AXEcess; What It Was; Friends; Mars; Appears on 28 albums. Honour: Voted Best Jazz Guitarist in New Orleans, Offbeat Magazine. Current Management: Scott Aiges, Arts International Group. Address: 516 S Rendon Street, New Orleans, LA 70119, USA.

MASCART Vincent, b. 27 July 1971, Villeneuve d'Ascq, France. Musician (saxophone). Musical Education: Medaille D'Or Conservatoire, CNSM Jazz Paris, CIM. Career: Television show N'Oubliez Pas Votre Brosse à Dents (Don't Forget Your Toothbrush); Puzzle; BBCL; Santos Chillemi; Red Whale; Big Band Yock'o Seffer; Big Band Zéphir; Florence Melnotte; Jacques Mahieux. Recordings with: BBCL; Big Band Zéphir; Florence Melnotte; Santos Chillemi. Honours: First Prix de Soloiste, Concours de la Défense, Paris, 1994. Memberships: SPEDIDAM; SACEM. Address: 53 Rue Belliard, 75018 Paris, France.

MASEKELA Hugh Rampolo, b. 4 Apr 1939, Witbank, Johannesburg, South Africa. Musician (trumpet); Bandleader. m. Miriam Makeba, 1964 (divorced). Musical Education: Manhattan School Of Music, New York. Career: Founder, The Merry Makers, 1955-; Joined African Jazz and Variety package tour, 1958; Joined cast of musical, King Kong, 1959; Formed the Jazz Epistles, 1959; Emigrated to USA, 1960; Formed own quartet, 1961; Signed to Motown Records, 1970; Formed Union Of South Africa band, 1970; Played with Fela Kuti; Hedzollah Soundz; Herb Alpert; Major concerts include: Monterey Jazz Festival, 1967; Goin' Home concert, Lesotho, 1980; African Sounds for Mandela concert, Alexandra Palace, 1983; Graceland world tour, with Paul Simon, 1986. Compositions include: Music for Broadway show, Sarafina, 1989. Recordings: Jazz Epistles, 1959; Trumpet Africa, 1962; The Americanization Of Ooga Booga, 1964; The Emancipation Of Hugh Maskela, 1966; Promise Of A Future, 1967; Coincidence, 1967; Maskela, 1968; Reconstruction, 1970; Home Is Where The Music Is, 1972; Your Mama Told You Not To Worry, 1974; I Am Not Afraid, 1974; The Boys Doin' It, 1975; The African Connection, 1975; Colonial Man, 1976; The Main Event, with Herb Alpert, 1978; Herb Alpert/Hugh Maskela, 1979; Home, 1982; Dollar Bill, 1983; Technobush, 1984; Waiting For The Rain, 1985; Tomorrow, 1987; Up Township, 1989; Back To The Future, 1998. Current Management: Sam Nole Management,

230 Park Avenue, Suite 1512, New York, NY 10169, USA.

MASHBURN Robin Arvil (Rob), b. 5 Apr 1942, Andrews, North Carolina, USA. Singer; Songwriter; Musician (guitar, bass). m. Catherine Stears Mashburn, 25 Sept 1982, 2 sons. Musical Education: Self-taught. Career: Grand Ole Opry: Wolftrap; Bele Chere; Tennessee Homecoming - Museum of Appalachia; University of Chicago; Georgia Mountain Fair. Recordings: Albums: The Picker; Another Place Another Time; Brother oF Mine; It's Me Again Lord; Misty Mountain Music; The Picker's Best, CD. Memberships: BMI; Bluegrass Music Association of North Carolina, South Carolina, Georgia. Hobbies: Horseback riding; Fishing; Gardening; Musical instrument repair. Current Management: Catherine Mashburn. Address: PO Box 1318, Andrews, NC 28901, USA.

MASLEN Riz, b. Composer; Programmer; Musician (keyboards); Singer. Career: Keyboard player, Beloved In Europe, 1994; Television apperance: Top Of The Pops, with Future Sound Of London, 1993. Compositions: Small Fish With Spine EP, Stickleback, 1995; 3 tracks, Earthrise album, Instinct, 1995. Membership: Musicians' Union. Hobbies: Mountain biking; Dance. Address: Flat 2, 64 Gloucester Place, London W1H 3HL, England.

MASON Dave, b. 10 May 1947, Worcester, England. Musician (guitar). Career: Guitarist, The Hellions; Road manager, Spencer Davis Group; Founder member (with Steve Winwood), Traffic, 1967-68; Solo artist; Played with Eric Clapton's Derek and The Dominoes, 1970; Moved to US, 1973; Currently recording with Fleetwood Mac. Recordings: Albums: with Traffic: Mr Fantasy, 1968; Solo: Alone Together, 1970; Dave Mason And Cass Elliot, 1971; Headkeeper, 1972; Dave Mason Is Alive!, 1973; It's Like You Never Left, 1973; Dave Mason, 1974; Split Coconut, 1975; Certified Live, 1976; Let It Flow, 1977; Mariposa De Oro, 1978; Old Crest On A New Wave, 1980; with Fleetwood Mac: Time, 1995; Various compilations. Honours include: Gold discs.

MASON Kerry, b. 31 Mar 1968, Dorking, Surrey, England. Singer; Songwriter; Performer. 1 daughter. Musical Education: Singing lessons, Tona De Brett. Career: Singer, band Hed; Played all main festivals including: Glastonbury, Phoenix; 12 years experience; Session singing. Recordings: Singles: Reigndance, 1994; Folklaw, 1995. Membership: Musicians' Union. Hobbies: Books; Music; Parties; Friends and family. Current Management: Timebomb. Address: PO Box No 15, 63 Camden High Street, London NW1 7JL, England.

MASON Nick, b. 27 Jan 1945, Birmingham, England. Musician (drums). Career: Drummer, Pink Floyd, 1965-; Performances include: Rome International Pop Festival, 1968; Hyde Park, London, 1968; Bath Festival, 1970; Montreux Festival, 1971; Knebworth Festival, 1975; Films: Pink Floyd Live At Pompeii, 1972; The Wall, 1982; Autobiographical film, Life Could Be A Dream, 1985. Recordings: Albums: Pipers At The Gates Of Dawn, 1967; A Saucerful Of Secrets, 1968; More (film soundtrack), 1969; Ummagumma, 1969; Atom Heart Mother (Number 1, UK), 1970; Relics, 1971; Meddle, 1971; Obscured By Clouds, 1972; The Dark Side Of The Moon (Number 1, US), 1972; Wish You Were Here (Number 1, UK and US), 1975; Animals, 1976; The Wall, 1979; The Final Cut, 1983; A Momentary Lapse Of Reason, 1987; The Delicate Sound Of Thunder, 1988; Shine On, 1992; The Division Bell, 1994; Pulse, 1995; Solo albums: Nick Mason's Ficticious Sport, 1981; Profiles, 1985; Producer, Music For Pleasure, The Damned, 1977. Honours include: Outstanding Contribution To British Music, 1992. Current Management: Steve O'Rouke, EMKA

Productions Ltd, 43 Portland Road, London W11 4LJ, England.

MASON Pascale, b. 29 October 1961. Singer; Backing Singer. 1 son. Career: Olympia, 1991; Olympia, 1993; Casino de Paris, 1996; Pollen, 1996; Taratata, 1993; Taratata, 1995; Taratata, 1996. Recordings: Live á l'Olympia, 1993; Passer Ma Route, 1995; Auffray Trans Dylan, 1996. Address: 6 rue d'Hautpoul, 75019 Paris, France.

MASSON Laurence, b. 10 May 1966, Chartres, France. Jazz Singer. Education: Faculty of Science. Musical Education: Self-taught. Career: Numerous concerts in France include: Montpellier; Strasbourg; Brive; Also concerts in Guadaloupe; Parisian jazz clubs include: Duc des Lombards; Baiser Salé; Opus Café. Membership: UMJ (Union des Musiciens de Jazz). Hobbies: Painting; Country walks. Current Management: Self-managed. Address: 39 rue Buffon, bât B, 75005 Paris, France.

MASSONI Jean-Francois, b. 23 Nov 1955, Nice, France. Composer. m. Paris, 13 Feb 1993, 1 daughter. Musical Education: Ecole Normale Supérieure de Paris, Conservatoire National; American School of Modern Music. Career: Guitarist in Parisian caberets, from age 20; Arranger, orchestrator; Composer, 1988-; Video composer with companies including: Procitel; Son Et Lumiere; Seriplume; Florida; En Effets; Soundtracks and themes for many television broadcasts: France; Germany; Switzerland; Austria; England; Australia; Japan; Canada; Cable networks; Commercials include: Lancôme; Renoma; Pierre Cardin. Recordings: Solo albums: Endless Journey, 1989; Legend, 1990; Images, 1991; Out Of Space, 1992; The Valley, 1994; Others: Psychomusicale, 1988; Industrialism, 1991; Pastiches, 1992; News, 1994; Mags, 1994; Sabotage; Earth. Honours: Prix du Festival de Biarritz, France. Membership: SACEM. Hobbies: Equitation; Tennis. Current Management: Koka Media, France; As De Coeur Productions, France. Address: Résidence Les Champs Elysées, 9 Rue De Sion, 91000 Evry, France.

MATHIESEN Claus, b. 13 July 1957, Copenhagen, Denmark. Musician (clarinet, recorder). 1 son. Musical Education: Classical education, Copenhagen; Turkish Art Music, Istanbul Conservatory. Career: Musician with Ildfuglen, 1979-83; Kefir, 1983-86; Fuat Saka Band, 1986-; Wild East, 1989-93; Oriental Mood, 1993-; Chochek Brothers, 1994-; All these bands merging Western and Balkan/Middle Eastern music. Recordings: with Fuat Saka Band: Nebengleis, 1989; Askaroz, 1991; Sen, 1994; with Anatolia: Anatolia, 1991; with Oriental Mood: Travels, 1994. Publications: Contributor, Danish National Encyclopedia. Membership: DJBFA. Address: Mariendalsvej 32C, DK 2000 F, Denmark.

MATHIESON Greg, b. 25 Feb 1950, Los Angeles, California, USA. Arranger; Composer; Producer; Musician (keyboards). m. Barbara Price, 9 July 1983, 1 son. Career: Tours: Al Jarreau; Larry Carlton; Abraham Laboriel. Recordings: Baked Potato Super Live; For My Friends; with Al Jarreau: All Fly Home; This Time; Trouble In Paradise; with Bill Champlin: Burn Down The Night; Through It All; with Laura Branigan: Gloria; with Toni Basil: Mickey; with Sheena Easton: Telefone; Strut; Almost Over You; with Donna Summer: MacArthur Park; Heaven Knows; Live & More; with Barbra Streisand: Enough Is Enough; Songbird; Wet; with Abraham Laboriel: Dear Friends; Guidem; Frontline; Koinonia; with Manhattan Transfer: Extensions; Mecca For Moderns; Bodies And Souls; with Lee Ritenour: Banded Together; Earth Run; Collection; with Deniece Williams: When Love Comes; Hot On The Trail; Special Love; From The Beginning; with Rita Coolidge: Ann; with Rickie Lee Jones: Flying Cowboys; with Jimmy Cliff: Peace; with

Steven Bishop: Bowling In Paris; with Umberto Tozzi: Gloria; Notte Rosa; Umberto Tozzi - Live; Le Une Cauzui; Equivacando; with David Hasselhoff: Crazy For You; Keyboard player for: Larry Carlton; Ringo Starr; Joe Cocker; David Foster; Tom Jones; Billy Idol; Julio Iglesias; Nils Lofgren; Simple Minds. Film scores: American Flyer; Unfaithfully Yours; Midnight Express. Honour: One of select few producers to have top 2 singles in same week. Current Management: Wigwam. Address: 3724 Buena Park Drive, Studio City, CA 91604, USA.

MATHIESON Ken, b. 30 June 1942, Paisley, Scotland. Musician (drums, zither); Arranger; Composer. m. with 2 sons, 1 daughter. Musical Education: Self-taught. Career: Freelance musician; 15 year residency in Black Bull Jazz Club, Milngavie, Glasgow; Working and touring with leading UK and US jazz musicians including: George Chisholm; Tommy Whittle; John McLevy; Jack Emblow; Sonny Stitt; Johnny Griffin; Tal Farlow; Played with and written for Fat Sam's Band (Edinburgh-based jazz group touring worldwide), 1985-; Leader, Picante (5 piece Bop and Latin band); Jazz Écosse All-Stars (6-piece Dixieland Band featuring top Scots based players and vocalist Fionna Duncan); Currently setting up joint UK/USA project with USA trombonist Dan Barrett to play at jazz festivals worldwide; Organized first Glasgow International Jazz Festival, 1985; Frequent broadcaster on Jazz and World Music. Recordings: All Fat Sam's records. Hobbies: Writing music; Hill walking. Address: 20 Kylepark Crescent, Uddingston, Glasgow, Scotland.

MATHIEU Jean-François Stanislas, b. 16 Apr 1960, Saint-Denis, France. Musician (drums); Drum Teacher. 1 daughter. Musical Education: First Prize, Ecole Dante Agostini, Paris, 1985. Career: Drum teacher at Le Conservatoire Agréé de Musique et de Danse Clamart, 1986-; Many concerts in Paris and throughout France with various bands, orchestras and singers; Many studio recording sessions; Television appearances on A2 channel, 1986; Drummer, MC Big Band, performed at Le Petit Journal Montparnasse, 1995. Membership: Conservatoire Agréé de Musique et de Danse de Clamart. Hobby: Sports. Address: 116 Bis Rue Pierre Brossolette, 92140 Clamart, France.

MATHIEU Mirielle, b. 24 July 1946, Avignon, France. Singer. Television appearances include: Ed Sullivan TV Show; Andy Williams TV Show; International concerts include: Top Star Festival, 1972. Recordings: Albums: Mirielle Mathieu, 1968; You And I, with Paul Anka, 1979; Les Contes De Cri-Cri, 1985; Recontres De Femme, 1988; Greatest Hits, Vol 1, 1989; Hit singles include: Mon Credo; C'Est Ton Nom; Qu'Elle Est Belle; Funambule; Les Bicyclettes De Belsize.

MATHIS Johnny (John Royce), b. 30 Sept 1935, San Francisco, California, USA. Education: San Francisco State College. Career: Recording artist, 1964-; Tours worldwide. Numerous recordings include: Singles: Wonderful! Wonderful!; Chances Are (Number 1, US), 1957; Someone; The Twelfth Of Never; It's Not For Me To Say; A Certain Smile; Misty; Winter Wonderland; There Goes My Heart; My Love For You; My One And Only Love; Let Me Love You; I'm Stone In Love With You; When A Child Is Born (Number 1, UK), 1976; Too Much, Too Little, Too Late, duet with Deniece Williams, (Number 1, US), 1978; Other duets with Gladys Knight; Natalie Cole; Dionne Warwick; Stephanie Lawrence; Barbara Dickson; Nana Mouskouri. Albums: Johnny Mathis, 1956; Wonderful!, Wonderful!, 1957; Warm, 1957; Good Night, Dear Lord, 1958; Swing Softly, 1958; Open Fire, Two Guitars, 1959; Heavenly, 1959; Faithfully, 1960; Ride On A Rainbow, 1960; Johnny's Mood, 1960; I'll Buy You A Star, 1961; Portrait Of Johnny, 1961; Live It Up,

1962; Rapture, 1962; Johnny, 1963; Romantically, 1963; I'll Search My Heart, 1964; Olé, 1965; Tender Is The Night, 1965; The Wonderful World Of Make Believe, 1965; This Is Love, 1966; The Shadow Of Your Smile, 1966; The Sweetheart Tree, 1967; Up, Up And Away, 1967; Johnny Mathis Sings, 1967; Love Is Blue, 1968; Those Were The Days, 1968; People, 1969; The Impossible Dream, 1969; Raindrops Keep Fallin' On My Head, 1970; The Long And Winding Road, 1970; Close To You, 1970; Love Story, 1970; You've Got A Friend, 1971; In Person, 1972; The First Time Ever I Saw Your Face, 1972; Make It Easy On Yourself, 1972; Me And Mrs Jones, 1973; Killing Me Softly With Her Song, 1973; I'm Coming Home, 1973; Song Sung Blue, 1974; The Heart Of A Woman, 1974; Feelings, 1975; I Only Have Eyes For You, 1976; Sweet Surrender, 1977; When A Child Is Born, 1978; You Light Up My Life, 1978; Mathis Magic, 1979; Different Kinda Different, 1980; Friends In Love, 1982; A Special Part Of Me, 1984; Right From The Heart, 1985; In The Still Of The Night, 1989; How Do You Keep The Music Playing?, 1993; Numerous Greatest Hits, Musical and Christmas compilations. Current Management: Rojon Production Inc., 3500 West Olive, Suite 750, Burbank, CA 91505, USA.

MATOLU-DODE Papy-Tex, b. 28 June 1952, Kinshasa, Zaire. Singer. m. Ekofo-Wando, 21 January 1989, 3 sons, 8 daughters. Education: Itaga College, Kinshasa. Career: Singer, African Choc, 1968; Singer, African Choc (band name changed to Empire Bakuba), 1979-; Player, Etodle Filante, football team. Compositions: Sanda; Karibu; Sanco Yamawa; Welcome in Africa; Music Clarification. Recordings: Bakuba Show; Full Option; Surprise; Livre D'Or; La Belle Etoire. Publications: Sanda, 1973; Karibu, 1985; Bakuba Show, 1988; Full Option, 1997. Honours: Diplome of Performance for Development Initiative, 1995; Apid Certificate of Artistic Merit, 1987; Acknowledgement of Merit, Francophone Counsel of Songs, 1993. Memberships: SONECA; SACEM; SABAM; SUIZA; BURIDA. Hobbies: Cinema; Football; Wrestling. Address: No 69, Rue Luapula, Commune De Kinghasa, RDC.

MATTACKS David, b. 13 Mar 1948, London, England. Musician (drums). m. Caron Woods, 31 Dec 1993. Musical Education: Self-taught. Career: Apprentice piano tuner; Mecca Big Band, 3 years; Played small jazz groups; Joined Fairport Convention, 1969; 7 albums; Tours of: UK; USA; Europe; Antipodes; Japan; Freelance musician, 1974-; Combines freelance work with reformed Fairport Convention, mid 1980s-; International tours include: Europe; USA; Annual Oxfordshire Cropredy Festival; Drums and keyboards in concerts and recordings; Performed with artists including: Jethro Tull; Chris Rea; Joan Armatrading; Sandy Denny; Micky Jupp; Andy Fairweather-Low; Georgie Fame; Nick Heyward; Ashley Hutchings; Ralph McTell; The McGarrigles; The Swingles; Tours in UK, Europe, USA, with Richard Thompson Band, 1994-95; Recorded, played with: Liane Carroll; Everything But The Girl; Week's residency, Ronnie Scott's Club, London, with Liane Carroll Trio; Television and film scores include: Death Wish 2; Green Ice; Give My Regards To Broadstreet; Band of Gold (ITV); Love Hurts (Barbara Dickson); Time Bandits; McVicar; Lisztomania; Hussey; Hearts Of Fire; Shoestring; Fox; Leo Sayer television series; Your Cheatin' Heart; Recordings include: Fairport Convention: Jewel In The Crown, 1995; Also with artists including: Joan Armatrading; Barbara Dickson; Elton John; Paul McCartney; Chris Rea; The Proclaimers; Jimmy Page; Alison Moyet; XTC; Beverley Craven; Richard Thompson; Gary Brooker; Elkie Brooks; John Gorka.

MATTEA Kathy, b. 21 June 1959, Cross Lane, West Virginia, USA. Country Singer; Musician (guitar). m. Jon Vezner. Education: University. Career: Member, Bluegrass group Pennsboro; Tour guide, Country Music Hall Of Fame, Nashville; Singer for demos and commercials; Backing singer, Bobby Goldsboro's roadshow, 1982; Solo recording artiste, mid-80s. Recordings: Singles: Street Talk; Love At The Five And Dime; Goin' Gone; 18 Wheels And A Dozen Roses; Life As We Knew It; Come From The Heart; Burnin' Old Memories; Where've You Been; Ready For The Storm; Albums: Kathy Mattea, 1984; From My Heart, 1985; Walk The Way The Wind Blows, 1986; Untasted Honey, 1987; Willow In The Wind, 1989; Time Passes By, 1991; Lonesome Standard Time, 1992; Only Everything, 1995; Walking Away A Winner, 1995; Ready For The Storm - Favourite Cuts, 1995. Honours: Best Country Song Of Year, Where've You Been. Current Management: Titley And Associates, 706 18th Avenue South, Nashville, TN 37203, USA.

MATTEI Arnaud Pierre Jaen, b. 8 June 1957, Boulogne, Seine, France. Musician (piano); Composer. m. Veronique Baudouin, 30 Dec 1988, 1 son, 1 daughter. Education: Matrise, Economic Sciences. Musical Education: Harmony; Counterpoint; Fugue; Atonal Music; Jazz. Career: Jazz Festivals: Marciac, 1989, 1991, 1993, 1994; Nice, 1994; Vocal Jazz Festival, Crest, 1991, 1992, 1994; Midem, 1992; Sorgues, 1994; Tours, Burkina Faso, 1991; Saudi Arabia, 1994. Recordings: Kamala, Arnaud Mattei Nonet; Smaya Cynthia, François Chamagnite Quartet; The Vth One, Stephane Persiani Quartet. Honours: Prix Boris Vian, Academie du Jazz, 1992. Memberships: SACEM; UMJ. Hobbies: Rollerskating; Skiing; Bonsaï. Current Management: Label La Lichere, Patrick Tandin. Address: 7 Place du Marché Aux Fleurs, 34000 Montpellier, France.

MATTEO Luis Di, b. 10 May 1934, Montevideo, Uruguay. Musician (bandoneon). Musical Education: Conservatory. Career: 30 years professional musician; 5 records released in South America; Four records Europe; 10 European concerts tour; Television appearances in: Netherlands; Sweden; Finland; Germany; Switzerland; Austria. Recording: Album: Del Nuevo Ciclo for Bandoneon and Chamber Orchestra. Hobby: Gardening. Current Management: Jaro Medien. Address: Bismarckstr 83, 28203 Bremen, Germany.

MATTHEWS Donna Lorraine, b. 20 Dec 1971, Newport, Wales. Musician (guitar); Songwriter. Career: Member, Elastica; Numerous television and radio apperances; Tours: UK; USA; Canada; Europe. Recordings: Album: Elastica, 1995. Current Management: CMO Management, Unit 32, Ransomes Dock, Parkgate Road, London SW11 4NP, England.

MATTHEWS Iain, b. 16 June 1946, England. Songwriter; Singer. m. Veronique, 26 Feb 1990, 1 son, 1 daughter. Career: Bands: The Pyramid, 1965; Fairport Convention; Matthews Southern Comfort; Solo, also Plainsong, 1972; Left performing for A&R: Island Records; Windham Hill, early 1980s; Returned to performance, after success at annual Fairport Convention, late 1980s; Moved to Austin, Texas, USA; Reformed Plainsong; Started Hamilton Pool, Singing, songwriting collective, Austin Texas. Recordings: with Fairport Convention: Fairport Convention, 1968; What We Did On Our Holiday, 1968; Unhalfbricking, 1968; Matthews Southern Comfort: Matthews Southern Comfort, 1969; Second Spring, 1970; Later That Same Year, 1970; Best Of Matthews Southern Comfort, 1992; Solo: If You Saw Through My Eyes, 1970; Tigers Will Survive, 1971; Journeys From Gospel Oak, 1972; Valley Hi, 1973; Some Days You Eat The Bear, 1974; Go For Broke, 1976; Hit and Run, 1977; Stealin' Home, 1978; Siamese Friends, 1979; Discreet Repeat, 1980; Spot Of Interference, 1980; Shook, 1983; Walking A Changing Line (The Songs Of Jules Shear), 1988; Pure And Crooked, 1990; Nights In Manhattan, 1991; Orphans And Outcasts, 1991; Live Alone, 1993; Intimate Wash,

1993; The Soul Of Many Places, 1993; Skeleton Keys, 1993; Plainsong: In Search Of Amelia Earhart, 1972; And That's That, 1992; Plainsong On The Air, 1992; Dark Side Of The Room, 1992; Hi Fi: Demonstration Record, 1981; Moods For Mallards, 1982; The Dark Ride, 1994; Camouflage, 1995; God Looked Down, 1996; Nights in Manhattan, 1997. Publication: Its About Time (pictorial biography). Membership: NARAS. Current Management: Frank van den Meijden, Visserslaan 8, 4201-ZJ Copinchem, Netherlands. Address: PO Box 676, Buda, TX 78610, USA.

MATTHEWS Jamie (James Lindsay), b. 15 May 1951, London, England. Musician (harmonicas, ukulele, percussion, jaws harp, whistle); Vocalist. m. Jo Horan, 4 Jul 1990. Musical Education: Church and school choirs; Mainly self-taught. Career: Extensive tours, Far East, late 1960's; Europe and North America, 1980's; Major US tour with Daily Planet, including Telluride Festival, Colorado, 1995. Recordings: Parlour Games, John B Spencer; Sunday Best, John B Spencer; A Month Of Sundays, double album, Johnny G; Clark's Secret, Daily Planet. Honour: Guinness All-Ireland Busking Champion as Gentleman Jamie, 1986. Membership: Musicians' Union. Hobbies: Music; Crosswords. Current Management: Spadger Productions, Orchard House, Hartpury, Gloucester GL19 3BG, England. Address: 5 Cleveland Row, Bathwick, Bath BA2 6QR, England.

MATTHEWS Julie, b. 2 Apr 1963, Sheffield, South Yorkshire, England. Singer; Songwriter; Musician (guitar, piano). Career: 7 years, piano bars throughout Europe, Middle East; Member, Albion Band, 1991-92, 1994-95; Female duo with Pat Shaw; Female duo with Chris While; Toured extensively throughout Europe, Canada; Many radio appearances, sessions; Cambridge, Edmonton festivals, 1995. Compositions include: Song: Thorn Upon The Rose, recorded by Mary Black. Recordings: with Pat Shaw: Lies And Alibis; Compilation: Intuition; with Albion Band: Captured; Albion Heart; Solo album: Such Is Life, 1995; with Chris While: Blue Moon On The Rise (mini-album). Honours: Nominated Rising Star, British Country Music Awards, 1995. Memberships: PRS; MCPS; Musicians' Union. Hobbies: Cycling; Reading; Films. Current Management: Blue Moon Music; Circuit Music. Address: 130 Central Avenue, Southport, Merseyside PR8 3ED, England.

MATTHEWS Phil, b. 13 Jan 1953, Derby, England. Musician (guitar); Songwriter; Record Producer. m. Annette Matthews, 15 Jun 1985, 1 son, 1 daughter. Musical Education: Pete Shepherdson Guitar School. Career: Member, Applause, 1973-78; The Blades, 1978-80; Duo Nova, 1982-86; LAF, 1987-; Host, The Sporting Week Radio Show, Reach FM; Wee Willie Winkie, Guildhall, Derby. Recordings: Slow Dancing, 1990; After Dark, 1991; A Walk In The Sun, 1993; Brief Encounter, 1993; Don't Go Burning Out My Love, 1993; Blues For Kirsty, 1994; Broken Moon, 1994; Summer Rain, 1995; Fragile, 1995; Distant Windows, 1995. Honour: Shortlisted Finalist, Brixton Song Contest, 1993. Membership: Musicians' Union. Hobby: Football commentary for Hospital Radio. Current Management: MW Music. Address: 8 Stanstead Road, Mickleover, Derby DE3 5PP, England.

MATTHEWS Roderick Newton, b. 18 May 1956, London, England. Composer; Musician (guitar); Record Producer. m. Pamela Margaret Johnson, 14 Nov 1992, 1 daughter. Education: Balliol College, Oxford. Musical Education: Grade 1 piano. Career: Produced records for small labels, including Troggs album, 1979-84; Produced for majors, including Roland Rat, Musical Youth, chart entries in Germany, Norway, 1984-86; Remixes include Manfred Mann; Session musician, 1987-92; Writing music for television (commercials, signatures, incidentals) 1988-; MD for Lenny Henry, 1989-91; Also appeared on soundtracks: French and Saunders; Absolutely Fabulous; Alexei Sayle Shows; Lenny Henry; Rory Bremner; Harry Enfield; Girl Friday; Bad News; Blue Peter; Tracy Ullman; Newman and Baddiel; Fry and Laurie. Compositions: Written for 7 series of London's Burning; Newshounds (Screen Two), 1990; The Winston Pom; Funseekers (Comic Strip); Coffee Blues for Lenny Henry (in Lenny Live and Unleashed); Alexai Sayle: Shut Up; The Winjin Pom; Mary Whitehouse Experience, second series; Television commercials for Duracell; Burger King; Twix. Recordings: Played or sung on recordings including: Monkey, George Michael; Don't Make Me Wait, Bomb The Bass; Cross My Heart, Patsy Kensit and Eighth Wonder; ABC; Sinitta; Charles Aznavour; Rick Astley; Pepsi and Shirlee; England Football Squad; Comic Relief. Memberships: PRS; MCPS. Hobbies: Eating and drinking.

MATTHEWS Sarah, b. 22 June 1966, London, England. Singer. Musical Education: Self-taught. Career: Member, Rub Ultra; Radio 1 session; Appearance on Naked City, Ch4; Festivals: Glastonbury; Phoenix, 1994; 4 British tours; Played NME Brats concert; XFM concert broadcast line. Recordings: EPs: Combatstrength Soap, 1994; Korporate Finger Tactic, 1994; Album: Liquid Boots And Boiled Sweets, 1995. Memberships: Musicians' Union; PRS. Hobbies: Hair renovation; Music; Concerts. Current Management: Nick Moore, Splash Management. Address: The Splash Club, 328 Gray's Inn Road, Kings Cross, London W10, England.

MATTHEWS Seán Séamas, b. 28 Nov 1962, London, England. Production Editor (magazine); Musician (repinique, congas, drums). Education: Orpington College; Woolwich College; London College of Printing. Musical Education: London School Of Samba. Career: Played at Womad, Notting Hill Carnival, Edinburgh Festival (including radio appearances). Recordings: with London School Of Samba: Gres, 1992; with Digi-Dub: Lo Pan, 1993; with Three Key Posse: Over The Horizon, 1995. Membership: Musicians' Union; National Union Of Journalists. Hobbies: Leisure; Reading; Cycling. Current Management: Aakashic Records, PO Box 7988, London SE14 5ZD, England.

MAULDIN Jermaine Dupri, b. 23 Sept 1972, Ashville, South Carolina, USA. Producer; Songwriter; Record Company President. Recordings: Warm It Up; Jump; Kris Kross; Understanding; Xscape: Just Kicking It; Funkdafied; Da Brat; Xscape: Feels So Good. Honours: ASCAP: Best Song Of Year, 1993. Current Management: Michael Mauldin. Address: 2849 Piedmont Road, Atlanta, GA 30305, USA.

MAURICE (Glynn) Mike, b. 12 Feb 1937, London, England. Musician (piano, guitar). Record Company Executive; Artist Manager; Promoter. 1 son, 1 daughter. Career: Artist Manager, Purple Dreams; Managing Director, M & M Records; Promoter, Merlin's Cave Nite Club, first Western club, London; Club 21, London; Hangar Lane music venue, London; Originator, Richmont Bingo clubs, Reading; Lilly Road Bingo clubs, London; Auctioneer, Petticoat Lane, 1954-62; Stage act, mind reading and telepathy, 1957-68; Toured Europe, US, Australia, Malaysia, Japan and Israel; Lecturer and demonstrator, clairvoyance, the paranormal and healing, Arthur Findlay College, Stanstead, London, 1968-82; Proprietor, M & M Recording Studios; M & M Video Studio. Recordings: released through M & M Recordings; M & M Records; M & M Video Agency. Publications: Original publisher, free newspapers, 1969; Local Express; Spiritualist News, Vision Journals; Life (biography) due for publication 1997. Hobbies: Football; Dancing; Clubbing. Current Management: M & M Management. Address: 79 Greenview Drive, Northampton NN2 7LE, England.

MAVIAN Robert A. (Gibson Case), b. 29 Oct 1936, New York City, USA. Bluegrass Musician; Performer; Songwriter. m. Barbara Lou Pearson, 18 Aug 1962, 1 son, 1 daughter. Education: Doctorate Degree, Veterinary Medicine and Surgery. Career: Sideman performer with Peter Rowan; John Herald; Hazel Dickens; The Sykes Boys; Member, duo, The Case Brothers - Martin and Gibson; Leader, founder of the Horse Country Bluegrass Band; Performed, World Original WWVA Jamboree, Wheeling West Virginia; WSM Grand Ole Opry, Ryman Auditorium, Nashville, Tennessee; Winnipeg Folk Festival, Canada; Brandy Wine Mountain Music Convention Woodstown, New Jersey; Thomas Point Bluegrass Festival, Brunswick, Maine; Waterloo Bluegrass Festival, Stanhope, New Jersey; Berkshire Mt, Bluegrass Festival, Hillsdale, New York; WKCR-NYC; WFUV-NYC; WFDM-NJ; WHUS-Storrs, CT; WOWL-TV, Florence, Alabama. Recordings: As The Case Brothers - Martin and Gibson, Old Time Duets With Guitar And Mandolin; The Radio Album; Also: Collectors Edition, The Berkshire Mt Bluegrass Festival; Kenneth Brewer And His Melody Kings And Queens; The Cumberland Mountain Boys, single 78 RPM's. Memberships: International Bluegrass Music Association; American Veterinary Medical Association; American Animal Hospital Association; New York State Veterinary Medical Society. Hobbies: Antique cars; Horses; Fine arts and crafts. Current Management: Self-managed. Address: 168 Pines Bridge Road, Ossining, NY 10562, USA.

MAX Buddy (Boris Max Pastuch). Recording Artist; Disc Jockey. Career: America's Singing Flea Market Cowboy; Manager, Singing Flea Market Cowboy, Lecanto, Florida; Kingwood Play Boys Band, performed all over New Jersey, Pennsylvania, New York; Buddy Max Radio Show, WKia, WLBE, WKFL, WINV 1560 AM, AM Radio, Florida; TV: The Buddy Max Show; Country Western Bluegrass Show, 1969-. Recordings include: Buddy Max, 1980; The Great Nashville Star, 1984; The Story Of Freda And Bud; Cowboy Junction Stars, 1985; Tribute to Challenger's Crew of 7, 1986; With Our Friends At Cowboy Junction, 1989; Little Circle B, 1990; Together - Our Masterpiece, 1991; I Love Miss America, 1992; The Life To Fame And Fortune, 1985. Honours: Gold Record, 1995; Inducted into Hall of Fame, 1997; Record John F Kennedy held in Smithsonian Institute, Washington, and Jogn F Kennedy Library, Dallas. Memberships: American Heart Association; American Lung Association; Girl Scouts of America; Citizens Of Citrus County, Florida; Deaf Serv of Citrus County. Hobbies: Farming; Singing; Playing guitar and harmonica. Address: Cowboy Junction Flea Market, Highway 44, Jctn 490, Lecanto, FL 34461, USA.

MAXWELL Thad James, b. 2 July 1945, Brooklyn, New York, USA. Musician (guitar, bass, steel guitar, drums). m. Jeanne Cornell, 1 son, 1 daughter. Education: AA, Glendale College, 1987. Career: Guitarist, drummer, Tarantula, 1969-70; Bassist, various artists including: Ricky Nelson; Arlo Guthrie; Linda Ronstadt; Flying Burrito Brothers, 1970-80; Steel guitarist, guitarist, Mac Davis, 1973-. Recordings include: with Arlo Guthrie: Hobo's Lullabye, 1972; Last Of The Brooklyn Cowboys, 1973; with Tarantula: Tarantula, 1969; Other recordings include: Horizon, The Carpenters, 1975; A Little Warmth, Steve Gillette, 1979; Sweet Country Suite, Larry Murray, 1971; Sierra, Sierra, 1977; Lead Free, B W Stevenson, 1972; Swampwater, Swampwater, 1970; Memberships: AFofM; AFTRA. Hobby: Photography.

MAY Brian, b. 19 July 1947, Twickenham, London, England. Musician (guitar); Singer; Composer; Producer. Education: Astronomy and Physics, Imperial College, London. Musical Education: Self-taught guitar. Career: Guitarist, The Others; Smile; Guitarist, UK rock group Queen, 1970-; Numerous tours include: UK; US; Australia; South America; Japan; Major concerts include: Rock in Rio Festival, Brazil, 1985; Live Aid, Wembley, 1985; Knebworth Festival, 1986; A Concert For Life, Wembley, 1992. Recordings: Albums include: Queen, 1973; Queen 2, 1974; Sheer Heart Attack, 1974; A Night At The Opera, 1975; News Of The World, 1977; Jazz, 1978; Live Killers, 1979; The Game, 1980; Greatest Hits, 1981; Hot Space, 1982; The Works, 1984; The Complete Works, 1985; Live Magic, 1986; The Miracle, 1989; Innuendo, 1991; Greatest Hits II, 1991; Live At Wembley '86, 1992; Made In Heaven, 1995; Solo: Star Fleet Project, 1983; Back To The Light, 1992; Contributions to: Puttin' On The Style, Lonnie Donegan; All American Alien, Ian Hunter; Tribute To Muddy Waters; Singles include: Seven Seas In Rhye, 1974; Killer Queen, 1974; Bohemian Rhapsody (Number 1, UK), 1975; You're My Best Friend, 1976; We Are The Somebody To Love, 1976; We Are The Champions, 1977; Bicycle Race, 1978; Don't Stop Me Now, 1979; Love Of My Life, 1979; Crazy Little Thing Called Love (Number 1, UK), 1979; Save Me, 1980; Play The Game, 1980; Another One Bites The Dust, 1980; Flash, 1981; Under Pressure (with David Bowie), 1981; Radio Ga Ga, 1984; I Want To Break Free, 1984; It's A Hard Life, 1984; One Vision, 1985; A Kind Of Magic, 1986; I Want It All, 1989; Breakthru, 1989; Innuendo (Number 1, UK), 1991; The Show Must Go On, 1991; Headlong, 1991; Heaven For Everyone, 1995; Too Much Love Will Kill You, 1995. Honours include: Ivor Novello Awards: Best Selling British Record, Bohemian Rhapsody, 1976; Outstanding Contribution To British Music, 1987; Gold Ticket, Madison Square Gardens, 1977; Britannia Award, Best British Pop Single 1952-77, 1977; American Music Award, Favourite Single, 1981; Silver Clef Award, Nordoff-Robbins Music Therapy Centre, 1984; BRIT Awards: Outstanding Contribution to British Music, 1990; Best British Single, 1991. Current Management: c/o Jim Beach, Queen Productions, 46 Pembridge Road, London W11 3HN, England.

MAY Simon, b. 15 Aug 1944. Composer. m. Rosie, 1 son, 3 daughters. Musical Education: Choral Scholar, Degree modern languages, Cambridge University. Career: Taught German, French, Music, Kingston Grammar School, 8 years; Following commercial success of stage musical Smike (10,000 performances worldwide, BBC Christmas television production), became full-time composer; Songwriter, record producer, worldwide sales over 15 million, include 10 UK top 20 hits; Songs recorded by: Cliff Richard; Amii Stewart; Nick Berry; The Pointer Sisters; Al Jarreau; Marti Webb; Anita Dobson; The Shadows; Richard Clayderman; Ruby Turner; Jonathan Butler; Stephanie De Sykes; Kate Robbins; Records produced for Amii Stewart include: Knock On Wood (Number 1, US); Light My Fire. Compositions: Film: The Dawning; Television: Eastenders, BBC; Howard's Way, BBC; Trainer, BBC; Elderado, BBC; The Holiday Programme, BBC; The Food And Drink Programme, BBC; Russ Abbot Show; Emergency 999, Tyne Tees; Television Weekly, TVS; Olympic Theme, Thames; The Vet, BBC; People, BBC; Paramedics, BBC; Jobs For The Girls, BBC; The Trial Of James Earl Ray, CH4; Swiss Family Robinson, 1997; Pet Rescue, 1997; Lion Country, 1997. Honours: Novello Award, Every Loser Wins, Nick Berry, 1986; 3 TRIC Awards, Best TV Theme: Eastenders; Howard's Way; Trainer. Memberships: PRS; Songwriters; BASCA; Equity; Musicians' Union. Current Management: Laurelbrook, Ockham Road North, East Horsley, Surrey KT24 6NT, England.

MAY Tina, b. 30 Mar 1961, Gloucester, England. Singer. m. Clark Tracey, 15 June 1989, 1 son. Education: BA Hons, French, University of Wales. Musical Education: Studied singing from age 16, also at University (soprano). Career: Began by tours as singing actress; Then full-time singer; Broadcasts, tours of Australia, Far East, UK, Europe with own quartet. Recordings: Never Let Me Go; Fun; It Ain't Necessarily So; Recordings with own group; Various guest appearances on other recordings. Honours: Worshipful Company of Musicians: Outstanding Jazz Musician, 1993. Memberships: Musicians' Union; Equity; Association of British Jazz Music. Current Management: Europa Jazz Live. Address: 6 Belgrove, Tunbridge Wells, Kent, England.

MAYALL John, b. 29 Nov 1933, Macclesfield, Cheshire, England. Blues Singer; Songwriter; Musician (harmonica). Education: Manchester Art College. Career: Founder, The Blues Syndicate, 1962; John Mayall's Bluesbreakers, (members have included John McVie, Eric Clapton, Peter Green, Jack Bruce, Aynsley Dunbar, Mick Taylor, Mick Fleetwood), 1963-; Major concerts include: Uxbridge Festival, 1965; National Blues Festival, Windsor, 1967; Palm Springs Pop Festival, 1969; Newport Jazz Festival, 1969; Woburn Festival, 1969; Bath Festival, 1969; Regular tours, UK, US, Australia, Europe; Launched own Crusade record label, 1969. Recordings: John Mayall Plays John Mayall, 1965; Blues Breakers, 1966; A Hard Road, 1967; Crusade, 1967; Diary Of A Band, Vols 1 and 2, 1968; Bare Wires, 1968; Looking Back, 1969; Blues From Laurel Canyon, 1969; The Turning Point, 1969; Empty Rooms, 1970; USA Union, 1970; John Mayall - Live In Europe, 1971; Back To The Roots, 1971; Thru The Years, 1971; Memories, 1971; Jazz Blues Fusion, 1972; Moving On, 1972; Down The Line, 1973; Ten Years Are Gone, 1973; The Latest Edition, 1974; New Year New Band New Company, 1975; Time Expired Notice To Appear, 1975; John Mayall, 1976; A Banquet of Blues, 1976; Lots Of People, 1977; Blues Roots, 1978; Bottom Line, 1979; No More Interviews, 1979; Road Show Blues, 1980; Behind The Iron Curtain, 1984; The Power Of The Blues, 1987; Chicago Line, 1988; A Sense Of Place, 1990; Wake Up Call, 1993; Spinning Coin, 1995. Honour: Gold disc, The Turning Point, 1969.

MAYES Ken, b. 11 Jan 1950, Sudbury, Suffolk, England. Country Music Vocalist; Musician (guitar); Bandleader. Education: College of Further Education. Musical Education: Self-taught. Career: Various radio station appearances, UK; UK tours; European tour with Goldrush Country Band; Present band, Kalamazoo. Recordings: with Countryfied; Denver Country Sound; Goldrush; Don't Rock The Jukebox, Kalamazoo; Various sessions. Honours: Marlboro Contest Finalists; Band Of Year Awards. Membership: British Country Music Association. Hobbies: Animals; Relaxing in the sun. Current Management: Self-managed. Address: 4 High View Drive, West Carr Road, Attleborough, Norfolk NR17 1EZ, England.

MAYFIELD Curtis Lee, b. 3 June 1942, Chicago, Illinois, USA. Singer; Musician; Songwriter. Career: Singer with Travelling Soul Spiritualists Church; Founder, Modern Jubilaires; Northern Jubilee Singers; Member, The Impressions, 1958-70; Solo artiste, 1970-; Actor, composer, performer of soundtrack, film Superfly, 1972; Co-founder, record labels Curtom Records Inc, 1968; Conquest, 1993; Crushed and paralysed by lighting rig, outdoor concert, Brooklyn, New York, 1990. Compositions include: Let It Be Me; He Will Break Your Heart; People Get Ready (recorded by numerous artists including Rod Stewart and Aretha Franklin); Love Me. Recordings: with The Impressions: The Impressions, 1963; The Never-Ending Impressions, 1964; Keep On Pushing, 1964; People Get Ready, 1965; The Impressions' Greatest Hits, 1965; One By One, 1965; The Fabulous Impressions, 1967; We're A Winner, 1968; Best Of..., 1968; The Young Mods' Forgotten Story, 1969; Solo albums: Curtis, 1970; Curtis/Live, 1971; Back To The World, 1973; Curtis In Chicago, 1973; Sweet Exorcist, 1974;

Got To Find A Way, 1974; There's No Place Like America Today, 1975; Give, Get, Take And Have, 1976; Never Say You Can't Survive, 1977; Do It All Night, 1978; Heartbeat, 1979; The Right Combination, 1980; Something To Believe In, 1980; Honesty, 1982; Film soundtracks: Superfly (Number 1, US), 1972; Short Eyes, 1977; Featured on Return Of Superfly, 1990. Numerous other retrospective compilations; Singles include: with The Impressions: For Your Precious Love; Gypsy Woman; It's All Right (R&B Number 1, US); Talkin' About My Baby; I'm So Proud; Keep On Pushing; You Must Believe Me; Amen, used in film Lilies Of The Field; People Get Ready; We're A Winner (R&B Number 1, US); Choice Of Colors (R&B Number 1, US); Solo: Move On Up; Freddie's Dead; Superfly. Other recordings as singer, producer include: with Gladys Knight: Claudine; with Aretha Franklin: Sparkle; Almighty Fire; with The Blow Monkeys: Celebrate. Honours: Inducted into Rock And Roll Hall Of Fame, with The Impressions, 1991; Curtis Mayfield Day, Los Angeles, 1991. Current Management: Headline Talent, 1650 Broadway, Suite 508, New York, NY 10019, USA.

MAYOR Simon, b. Sheffield, England. Musician (mandolin, mandocello, guitar, violin). Education: Degree in Russian, Reading University. Career: Live concert, Kaleidoscope, BBC Radio 4; Classic FM; The Pier Show; Meridian TV; Interview, BBC Radio 2; Documentaries, BBC World Service; Two Specials, Singapore TV; Worked as broadcaster, BBC Radio 4, Radio 5; Songs for children's programmes, BBC TV, Radio; Regular international concert touring, includes: Vancouver Festival; Rudolstadt Festival; Return visit to Purcell Room, Londons South Bank Festival. Recordings: The Mandolin Album, 1990; The Second Mandolin Album, 1991; Winter With Mandolins, 1992; The English Mandolin, 1995; Albums feature approximately 50% original compositions. Publications: The New Mandolin (original compositions in music and tablature); Musical Mystery Tour (children's songbook). Memberships: Musicians' Union; Equity; PRS. Hobbies: Fell walking. Current Mnanagement: Self-managed. Address: c/o Acoustics Records, PO Box 350, Reading, Berks RG6 7DQ, England.

MAZETIER Louis, b. 17 Feb 1960, Paris, France. Jazz Musician (piano); Composer. m. Sophie Clement, 1 son, 1 daughter. Education: MD, Radiologist, University. Musical Education: Self-taught. Career: Member, Paris Washboard; Major festivals in France: Antibes; Marciac; Bayonne; Montauban; Festivals in Europe: Breda; Dresden; Plön; Tours, New Zealand; Australia; USA (including Moodus and Santa Rosa Festivals); Argentina; Uruguay; Japan. Recordings: 8 with Paris Washboard; Duet with pianist Francois Rilhac; Duet with pianist Neville Dickie; Solo record; Duet with pianist Bernd Lhotzky. Publications: Many articles, various French Jazz Reviews, mostly about stride piano. Honours: Prix Sidney Bechet; Prix Bill Coleman, Academie de Jazz, 1992. Hobby: Golf. Current Management: Self-managed. Address: 3 rue Larrey, 75005 Paris, France.

MAZUR Marilyn (Marie Douglas), b. 18 Jan 1955, New York City, USA. Composer; Jazz Musician (percussion, drums, piano); Vocalist. 1 son. Musical Education: Degree, Teaching Percusssion, Royal Danish Music Conservatory, 1974-77. Career: Dancer, Creative Dance Theatre, 1971; Formed first band Zirenes, 1973; Played with Six Winds with Alex Riel; Miles Davis, 1985-88; Gil Evans Orchestra, 1986; Wayne Shorter, 1987; Jan Garbarek Group, 1991-; Leader, own projects, Future Song, Pulse Unit, Primi Band; Performed all over the world; Played with Niels Henning Orsted Pedersen; Jasper van't Hof; Andreas Vollenweider; Kenneth Knudsen; Pierre Dorge; numerous others. Compositions: Well Of Clouds, 1982; 30 magiske omkvæd, 1986;

Bydansen (City Dance), 1989; Decemberdanse, 1992; Fjellslottet, 1992. Recordings: Albums include: Clouds, 1982; Rhythm-a-ning (with Gil Evans, Laurent Cugny), 1986; Aura (with Miles Davis, Palle Mikkelborg), 1989; Marilyn Mazur's Future Song, 1992; Jon Balke with Magnetic North Orchestra, 1994; with Pulse Unit: Circular Chant, 1995. Honours: Ben Webster Prize, 1983; Jasa Prize, 1989; HK-Artist of the Year, 1994. Hobbies: Food; Colours; Dancing. Current Management: Hohensee/Bremme, Germany.

MAZZILLO Marc, b. 19 Apr 1957, Tarascon, France. Jazz Musician (drums). Career: Festival Seyne sur Mer; First part of Charlie Hadden concert, 1989; Festival St Chamas, first part of Didier Lockwood concert; Plays regularly in clubs. Recordings: Tacha, Trio Soma, 1990; Autoportrait, Marc Mazzillo Quartet, 1991. Hobby: Playing tablas (Indian percussion). Address: 357 Chemin de la Clément, Les Valayans, 84210 Pernes Les Fontaines, France.

MBANDE Venacio Notico, b, 4 Oct 1928, Chisiko, nr Zavala, Mozambique. Musician (xylophone, timbila); Composer; Performer. m. Alzira. 3 children. Career: Leading musician, Chopi people, in orchestration and xylophone. Leader, Chopi xylophone orchestra, Witwatersrand, South Africa; Demonstrator and lecturer in Chopi music, University of Pennsylvania, USA, 1973. Compositions: Numerous Mgodo xylophone orchestral suites. Recordings: Tapes held by International Library of African Music, Grahamstown, South Africa. Honour: African Arts music competition, for mgodo xylophone suite, USA. Address: c/o Pousada de Zavala, Quissico, Distrito de Inhambane, Mozambique.

MBANGO Charlotte, b. 16 Apr 1960, Douala, Cameroon. Artiste; Singer; Backing Vocalist. m. Mpacko Marcel, 4 Aug 1984, 1 daughter. Musical Education: Solfège; Piano. Career: Tours: Ivory Coast; Cameroon; Gabon; Burkina Faso; Togo; USA; Spain: Barcelona, Madrid, Valencia; London; France; Radio: Africa, France; Television: France, Belgium. Recordings: Nakossa Nostalgie, 1987; Konkai Makossa, 1988; Maloka, 1995; New album in preparation. Honours: Gold Song, Palo Rabanne, 1989; Gold Lion, 1994. Memberships: ADAMI; SACEM; SPEDIDAM; SFA; ACOP: AMF. Hobbies: Cycling; Volleyball; Relaxation. Address: 10 Allée d'Amblonville, 77176 Savigny Le Temple, France.

MCA (Adam Yauch), b. 15 Aug 1967, Brooklyn, New York, USA. Rapper; Musician (bass). m. Iona Skye, 1992. Career: Founder member, US rap/rock group The Beastie Boys, 1983-; Appearances include: Support to Madonna, Virgin Tour, 1985; Supports to Run DMC, Raisin' Hell Tour, 1986, Co-headliners with Run DMC, Together Forever Tour, 1987; Reading Festival, 1992; Made horror film, Scared Stupid; Film apperances: Krush Groove; Run-DMC's film, Tougher Than Leather. Recordings: Singles include: She's On It; Fight For Your Right To Party; Albums include: Licensed To Ill, 1986; Paul's Boutique, 1989; Check Your Head, 1992; Ill Communication, 1994; Root Down, 1995; The In Sound From Way Out, 1996. Current Management: Gold Mountain Entertainment, 3575 Cahuenga Blvd W, Ste 450, Los Angeles, CA 90068, USA.

MCALL Barnaby Jonathon, b. 3 January 1966, Box Hill, Victoria, Australia. Jazz Pianist. Education: Studied Literature, Melbourne University; Graduated, Victorian College of the Arts, Bachelor of Music; Studied in New York City with Barry Harris, Mulgren Miller, Dave Kikoski, Chucho Valdez. Career: Toured Europe, 3 times, playing major festivals including Montreax, North Sea, 1996; Played Blue Note, Tokyo, Japan with the Groove collective; Extensive touring of Italy, Canada; Wrote music for stage show, Solstice, part of Adelaide International Festival. Compositions: Hindered on his way to heaven; Exit, nominated best cd, Aria Awards, 1996. Recordings: Fawx CD's with Vince Jones, writing producing and arranging; Exit, CD. Honours: Best Jazz Composition, APRA, 1993; First Prize, National Jazz Piano Competition, Solo CD Nominated CD of Year, 1996, Aria Awards in Australia. Hobbies: Yoga; Reading; Being here now. Current Management: ELMAC Enterprises, Sydney, Australia. Address: 97 Pembroke Road, Mooroolbark 3138, Victoria, Australia.

MCALMONT David. Singer; Lyricist. Career: Singer, duo Thieves (later as McAlmont), 1993; Member, duo McAlmont and Butler (with Bernard Butler), 1994-95; Appearances include: Phoenix '95 Festival, 1995. Recordings: Albums: with McAlmont & Butler: The Sound Of McAlmont & Butler, 1995; Solo: McAlmont, 1994; Singles: Solo: Either, 1994; with McAlmont & Butler: Yes, 1995; You Do, 1995. Address: c/o MRM Productions, 9-11 Liverpool Road, Islington, London N1 0RP, England.

MCALOON Martin, b. 4 Jan 1962, Durham, England. Composer; Musician (bass); Producer. m. Bernadette McKenna, 1 son. Career: Bass player with Prefab Sprout; Extensive tours: UK; Europe; Japan; Numerous television appearances; Worked with Vince Clark; Fergal Sharkey; Pete Townshend; Stevie Wonder; Thomas Dolby; Andre Crouch Choir; Steve Dolder; Produced Argentinian singer Grassy; Lecturing in production. Recordings: Albums with Prefab Sprout: Swoon, 1984; Steve McQueen, 1985; From Langley Park To Memphis, 1988; Protest Songs, 1989; Jordan - The Comeback, 1990; Life Of Surprises - Best Of Prefab Sprout, 1992; Andromeda Heights, 1997. Current Management: Keith Armstrong, Kitchenware Records. Address: St Thomas Street Stables, Newcastle upon Tyne, England.

MCALOON Paddy (Patrick Joseph). b. 7 June 1957, England. Musician; Singer; Songwriter. Education: BA, English and History, Ushaw College, Co Durham, University of Northumbria. Career: Singer, songwriter, Prefab Sprout; Extensive tours: UK; Europe; Japan; Numerous television appearances. Compositions: Songs covered by Kylie Minogue; Jimmy Nail; The Zombies; Cher; Contributed songs to television series Crocodile Shoes and Where the Heart Is. Recordings: Albums include: Swoon, 1984; Steve McQueen, 1985; From Langley Park To Memphis, 1988; Protest Songs, 1989; Jordan - The Comeback, 1990; Life Of Surprises: Best Of Prefab Sprout, 1992; Andromeda Heights, 1997. Honours: BRIT Award Nomination; Ivor Novello Nomination; BAFTA Nomination. Membership: BASCA. Current Management: Keith Armstrong, Kitchenware Records. Address: St Thomas Street Stables, Newcastle Upon Tyne, England.

MCANDREW Ian, b. 20 Oct 1966, Sudbury, Suffolk, England. Artist Manager. Career: Manager of artists and producers; Founded Wildlife Entertainment, 1986; Manager, Tasmin Archer; The Brand New Heavies; Bomb The Bass; Carleen Anderson; Tim Simenon; Travis; Connor Reeves. Recordings: 13 hits from 14 releases. Honours: 2 Platinum discs; 3 Gold discs; 1 Silver disc. Membership: Council Member, International Managers Forum. Hobbies: Old aeroplanes; Managing artists. Address: Wildlife Entertainment Ltd, 21 Heathmans Road, Parsons Green, London SW6 4TJ, England.

MCATHEY Brent, b. 4 Aug 1967, Calgary, Alberta, Canada. Singer; Songwriter. Career: Performs solo with prerecorded tracks or with 5 piece band in Canada; 7 piece Nashville Band in USA, Europe; Opened for: Joan Kennedy; Dick Damron; Michelle Wright; Prairie Oyster; Television: Capitol Country; Up and Coming; The Breakfast Show; Christmas Special; Radio: Canadian Super Country. Recordings: Brent McAthey, 9 songs composed by McAthey; Waitin' For The Sun, 1994, 3 songs by McAthey, 1 song co-written and duet with Dick Damron, 7 by Nashville Writers; Believe in Me. Publications: The Brent McAthey International Fan Club Newsletter. Honours: Nominated, Alberta Recording Association and Country Music Association of Calgary: 2 times, Most Promising New Artist; 2 times, Top Male Country artist; 2 times, Entertainer Of the Year; 4 times, Top Male Recording Artist; Winner, Alberta's Male Recording Artist of the Year, Alberta Recording Industry Association, 1994-95. Memberships: Country Music Association of Calgary; Alberta Recording Industry Association; Canadian Music Association; CMA, Nashville; Texas Country Music Association; Arts Touring Alliance of Alberta; Canadian Association of Fairs and Exhibitions; Calgary Convention and Visitors Bureau; International Fan Club Organization. Hobbies: Writing; Sports; Motorcycling. Current Management: Box 831, Black Diamond, AB T0L 0H0, Canada.

MCAULEY Jackie, b. Belfast, Northern Ireland. Musician (guitar); Songwriter. Career: Member, Them (with Van Morrison), aged 17; Founder member, Cult; Belfast Gypsies (with brother Pat); Trader Horn; Also solo artiste; Currently member, The Poor Mouth. Compositions: Dear John, recorded by Status Quo (Number 1, UK charts), 1982; 2 Number 1 recordings with the Heptones. Current Management: Jim McPhee, Acorn Entertainments. Address: Winterfold House, 46 Woodfield Road, Kings Heath, Birmingham B13 9UJ, England.

MCAULIFFE Kim, b. England. Singer; Musician (guitar). Career: Founder member, UK all-girl rock band Girlschool, 1978-89; 1992-; Regular tours, including UK tour with Motörhead, 1980. Recordings: Singles: St Valentine's Day Massacre EP, with Motörhead (as Headgirl); Please Don't Touch; Hit'n'Run; C'mon Let's Go; I'm The Leader, with Gary Glitter; Albums: Demolition, 1980; Hit'n'Run, 1981; Screaming Blue Murder, 1982; Play Dirty, 1983; Race With The Devil, 1986; Nightmare At Maple Cross, 1986; Take A Bite, 1988; Cheers You Lot, 1989; Girlschool, 1992.

MCBRIDE Martina, b. 29 July 1966, Medicine Lodge, Kansas, USA. Country Singer. m. John McBride, 1 daughter. Career: Worldwide concert tours. Recordings: Albums: The Time Has Come, 1992; The Way That I Am, 1993; Evolution, 1998. Honours: CMA Video of the Year, 1994; Music Row Industry Awards Breakthrough Video; Billboard Nominations; Nammy Award, Video of the Year; Grammy Nominations, 1994. Address: Bruce Allen Talent, #406-68 Water Street, Vancouver, British Columbia V6B 1A4, Canada.

MCBROOM Amanda, b. 8 Sept 1947, Los Angeles, California, USA. Songwriter; Playwrght; Singer; Actress. m. George Ball, 12 Jan 1974. Education: BA, Drama, University of Texas. Career: Television: Mash; Star Trek; Hawaii 5-0; See-Saw, Broadway; Jacques Brel, Off-Broadway; Several appearances on The Tonight Show; Carnegie Hall; Rainbow And Stars; The Russian Tea Room; Greek Theater; Great American Music Hall; Kennedy Center. Compositions include: The Rose. Recordings: Growing Up In Hollywood Town; West Of Oz; Dreaming; Midnight Matinee; Amanda McBroom Live At Rainbow And Stars; Heartbeats-the cast album. Honours: Grammy Nominations, The Rose, The Portrait; Golden Globe Award, Best Film Song, The Rose, 1980. Memberships: Actors Equity Association; Screen Actors Guild; NAS. Hobbies: Gardening; Cooking; Animal husbandry. Current Management: Garry George Management. Address: 9107 Wilshire Boulevard, Suite 700, Beverly Hills, CA 90210, USA.

MCCANN Peter. Songwriter; Singer. Education: Graduate, Fairfield University, Connecticut, 1970. Career: Signed to Motown Records, 1971; 20th Century Fox Records, 1977

MCCAFFERTY, Dan. Vocalist. Career: Founder member, Scottish rock group Nazareth, 1968-; Regular tours, UK, US, Europe. Recordings: Albums: Nazareth, 1971; Exercises, 1972; Razamanaz, 1973; Loud'N'Proud, 1974; Rampant, 1974; Hair Of The Dog, 1975; Greatest Hits, 1975; Hot Tracks, 1976; Close Enough For Rock'N'Roll, 1976; Playin' The Game, 1976; Expect No Mercy, 1977; No Mean City, 1978; Malice In Wonderland, 1980; The Fool Circle, 1981; 'Snaz, 1981; 2XS, 1982; Sound Elixir, 1983; The Catch, 1984; 20 Greatest Hits, 1985; Play The Game, 1985; Anthology - Nazareth, 1988; The Early Years, 1992; No Jive, 1992; From The Vaults, 1993; Singles include: Broken Down Angel; Bad Bad Boy; This Flight Tonight; My White Bicycle; Love Hurts. Current Management: c/o Variety Artists International Inc, 846 Higuera Street, Suite 5, San Luis Obispo, CA 93403, USA.

MCCANN Eamon, b. Creggan, Omagh, Northern Ireland. Singer; Musician (guitar). m. Margaret, 28 July 1979, 1 son, 3 daughters. Education: FTC; IRTE. Musical Education: Self-taught. Career: Television appearances include: RTE TV: Kenny Live; Live At 3; Its Bibi; Play The Game; Live From The Olympia; Lifelines; The Big Top; Summer Cabaret; Cúrsaí; Country Cool; Winning Streak; A Stretch in the Evening; Southern Nights; The Lyric Board; Anderson On The Box, Breakfast TV, PK to Right, Anderson on the Road, BBC; Kelly, UTV; Scotch 'N' Irish, Grampian Television; Radio appearances: Live on National Music Day, BBC Radio 2, 1994; RTE Radio 1; 2 FM; DTR; BBC Radio Ulster. Recordings: Everything That I Am; Can't Break It To My Heart; Bunch Of Bright Red Roses; Gold In The Mountains; I Give You Music; I've Gone Crazy/Happy Birthday, CD single; Touch Wood, CD album. Publications: Don't Call Me; When You Come To Land; Life After You; Love Is Blind; The Gift Of Love; Bunch Of Bright Red Roses; Everything That I Am; More Than Two Weeks; The Love From Loneliness; Touch Wood; Exactly What I meant; Do I Really Have to Tell You That I Love You; My Home Ireland; I've Gone Crazy; Happy Birthday. Honours: Irish Showcase Award, Best New Male Singer, 1992; Northern Sound Radio, Best Male Singer, 1993; Donegal CMC, Best Male Singer, 1993, 1994; Rehab, Person Of The Year, 1992; Ready Penny Inn, Best Male Singer of New Country, 1994, 1995; Personalities Entertainment Magazine Awards: Best Singer/Songwriter, 1995-96, Best Singer of New Country, 1995-96, Favourite Male Entertainer, 1996-97; Doubla K CMC Band of the Year, Dumfries, Scotland, 1996-97. Memberships: PRS; IMRO. Hobbies: Gaelic football; Basketball; Squash. Current Management: Hilltop Productions. Address: 8 Forthill Road, Enniskillen, County Fermanagh BT74 6AW, Northern Ireland.

MCCANN Les (Leslie Coleman), b. 23 Sept 1935, Lexington, Kentucky, USA. Musician (piano, trumpet, keyboards). m. Charlotte Acentia Watkins, 1 son, 3 daughters. Education: LA City College. Musical Education: Westlake College of Music; LA City College. Career: White House Concert, with Aretha Franklin, 1994; Soul To Soul; African Tour and Movie; Tonight Show; Arsenio Hall Show; ROC, Fox TV; Ed Sullivan Show, CBS; Sunday Morning, CBS; Jazz Central, BET TV; Hands Across America; All major jazz festivals. Recordings: 84 albums; Swiss Movement; Much Les; The Truth; With Lou Rawls: Stormy Monday. Publications: Musican As Artist (paintings). Honours: First person chosen to teach at Harvard University: Artist As Performer. Membership: BMI; ASCAP. Hobbies: Photography; Water Colour Painting; Tennis. Current Management: Fred Hirsch Management. Address: 696 Barron, Palo Alto, CA 94306, USA.

(bought by CBS, 1978); Moved to Nashville, 1985; Association with EMI music publishing; Songs recorded by: Julio Iglesias; Anne Murray; Crystal Gayle; Kenny Rogers; Oak Ridge Boys; Isaac Hayes; K T Oslin; Lynn Anderson; Ricky Nelson; Andy Williams; Paul Anka; Karen Carpenter; Lectures on songwriting for music organizations. Recordings: The Right Time Of The Night, Jennifer Warnes, 1977; She's Single Again, Janie Fricke (Number 1); Nobody Falls Like A Fool, Earl Thomas Conley (Number 1); Treat Me Like A Stranger, Baillie and the Boys; Also sang on Whitney Houston debut album (25 million sales). Honour: Grammy for Kathy Mattea Christmas album. Membership: Vice-president, Nashville Songwriters Association, Co-chair, Legislative committee. Current Management: SESAC. Address: 55 Music Square E, Nashville, TN 37203, USA.

MCCANN Susan, b. 26 Feb 1949, Forkhill, County Armagh, Northern Ireland. Singer. m. Dennis Heaney, 1 Sept 1971, 1 son, 1 daughter. Career: Tours: UK; Ireland; South Africa; USA; Television appearances on: BBC; Network UTV; RTE; SABC. Recordings: 7 albums; 3 videos. Current Management: Dennis Heaney Promotions. Address: Whitehall, Ashgrove Road, Newry, County Down BT34 1QN, Northern Ireland.

MCCARLEY Kevin Paul, b. 19 November 1959, Los Angeles, CA, USA. Singer; Songwriter; Musician (Bass, 12 String-Guitar). Education: BA, Musical Theater Arts; Private teachers, voice; Piano lessons; Selftaught bass and guitar. Career: Member, SAG, over 50 national TV commercials and programs, 1969; Magician and Junior Member, Magic Castle in Hollywood, 1976; 2 world tours with various artists, 1987-91; Performed Rum Tum Tugger, Cats, Denver, 1986. Compositions: Wild Seeds in Wintertime; Give Me What You've Got; The Bridge Across Forever; Downtown Union Station; Always If. Recordings: Blackout, City Lights, 1981; Whips and Kisses, Suki Tawdry, 1991; Winters of The Wild Seed, Kevin McCarley, 1995; Thee Imagine Nation. Publication: Songtalk Magazine, 1994. Memberships: Screen Actors Guild; American Federation of TV and Radio Artists; Broadcast Music Inc. Hobbies: Old movies and records; Being outdoors in nature. Current Management: Rock Goddess Music Management, POB 502, Pacific Palisades, CA 90272-0502, USA. Address: POB 502, Pacific Palisades, CA 90272-0502, USA.

MCCARTNEY Michelle, b. 5 Apr 1960, Paris, France. Singer; Musician (bass guitar). Musical Education: Self-taught bass and rhythm guitar. Career: Pop rock/folk singer; Major tour with Jackie Lomax (legendary blues performer); Television appearances, USA; Many radio interviews in America; Performed at major US Theatres, International Trade Shows; Tours, major US college and university circuit. Recordings: Singles: Everybody Wants My Man; Rocomotion; Money For Honey; Michelle; Billet-Doux; Till I Get You Back. Publication: The Beatles Book, UK fanzine. Honour: Best Dee-Jay Pop Pick in USA, for Till I Get You Back, 1993. Membership: ASCAP. Hobbies: Karting; Songwriting; Reading comic books and biographies; Collecting vinyl records. Current Management: Allstar Management Incorporated. Address: 189 Rue du Temple, 75003 Paris, France.

MCCARTNEY (James) Paul (Sir), b. 18 June 1942, Liverpool, England. Singer; Songwriter; Musician (bass). m. Linda Eastman, 12 Mar 1969, deceased Apr 1998, 1 son, 2 daughters, 1 stepdaughter. Musical Education: Self-taught. Career: Member, The Quarrymen, 1957-59; The Beatles, 1960-1970; Founder, Apple Corporation Limited; Formed MPL Group of Companies, 1970; Founder, group Wings, 1970-81; Solo artiste, 1970-; International tours, concerts, television,

radio and film appearances; Founder, Liverpool Institute of Performing Arts, 1995. Compositions: Co-writer, songs with John Lennon include: Love Me Do; Please Please Me; From Me To You; She Loves You; Can't Buy Me Love; I Want To Hold Your Hand; I Saw Her Standing There; Eight Days A Week; All My Loving; Help!; Ticket To Ride; I Feel Fine; A Hard Day's Night; Yesterday; Eleanor Rigby; Yellow Submarine; Penny Lane; All You Need Is Love; Lady Madonna; Hey Jude; We Can Work It Out; Day Tripper; Paperback Writer; When I'm Sixty-Four; A Day In The Life; Back In The USSR; Hello Goodbye; Get Back; Let It Be; Later compositions include: Band On The Run; Mull Of Kintyre; Coming Up; Ebony And Ivory; No More Lonely Nights; Pipes Of Peace; Other works include: Give My Regards To Broad Street (film score), 1984; Liverpool Oratorio, conducted by Carl Davis, 1991; Standing Stone (orchestral work), commisioned for EMI Centenary celebrations, debut by LSO at Albert Hall, London, 1997. Recordings include: Albums: with the Beatles: Please Please Me, 1963; A Hard Day's Night, 1964; Beatles For Sale, 1964; Help!, 1965; Rubber Soul, 1965; Revolver, 1966; Sgt Pepper's Lonely Hearts Club Band, 1967; Magical Mystery Tour, 1967; The Beatles (White Album), 1968; Yellow Submarine, 1969; Abbey Road, 1969; Let It Be, 1970; with Wings include: Wildlife, 1971; Red Rose Speedway, 1973; Band On The Run, 1973; Venus And Mars, 1975; Wings At The Speed Of Sound, 1976; Wings Over America, 1976; London Town, 1978; Wings Greatest Hits, 1978; Back To The Egg, 1979; Solo albums: McCartney, 1970; Ram, 1971; McCartney II, 1980; Tug Of War, 1982; Pipes Of Peace, 1983; Give My Regards To Broad Street, 1984; Press To Play, 1986; All The Best!, 1987; Flowers In The Dirt, 1989; Tripping The Light Fantastic, 1990; Unplugged, 1991; Choba b CCCP, 1991; Paul McCartney's Liverpool Oratorio, 1991; Off The Ground, 1993; Paul Is Live, 1993. Numerous honours include: MBE, 1965; Numerous Grammy awards; 3 Ivor Novello Awards, including Special Award for International Achievement, 1980; Freeman, City of Liverpool, 1984; Doctorate, University of Sussex, 1988; Guinness Book Of Records Award, most successful composer to date, 1979; Q Merit Award, 1990; Knighthood, 1997. Address: c/o MPL Communications, 1 Soho Square, London W1V 6BQ, England.

MCCARTNEY Robert William (Roy), b. 4 Mar 1958, Belfast, Northern Ireland. Musician (guitar); Singer; Music teacher. m. Susan Edwards, 17 July 1995. Musical Education: GCSE Music; HND, Music Technology (production), July 1994. Career: Solo, pub scene, Belfast, 1981; Lead singer, The Heartbeat City, Belfast clubs, 1984-87; Bluecoat/singer, Pontins, Jersey, Devon, 1988-89; Professional Serenades in and around Newcastle, including 2 radio spots on BBC Newcastle), 1990-94; Presenter/Karaoke compere: Karen Casey Show, Blackpool, 1993; Solo performer, Newcastle club/pub scene, 1991-92; Karaoke spot GMTV, Blackpool, July, 1993; Radio presenter, TVR-FM, Newcastle College, May, June, 1994; Singer, guitar teacher, 1990-. Recordings: Sweet Inspiration, 1991; Traveller, 1994; I'm A Believer (arranged for Newcastle College), 1994. Honours: HND Music (tech) Production, 1994. Membership: Musicians' Union, 1990-94. Hobbies: Learning piano; Running. Current Management: Serenade, Huntingdon Close, Kingston Park, Newcastle, England.

MCCAUSLAND Kelly Edward, b. 10 May 1971, Powell River, British Columbia, Canada. Musician (electric bass, trombone); Composer; Singer. Musical Education: BMus, University of Victoria; Studied trombone with R Williams and T Eadie, and composition with John Celona. Career: Member of University of Victoria Chamber Singers with several concerts in Victoria and a tour of California, recordings played on CFUV. Compositions: Three Shelley Settings for Chorus

a Capella; Airwaves for Wind Ensemble; The Fall Of Hyperion for Chorus, Orchestra and Soloists. Recordings: The Things That You Believe, by Jeremy Greenhouse; Sweetness And Light, by The Utopic Mind Slaves. Honours: Horning Memorial Scholarship; Murray Adaskin Prize. Membership: Victoria Composers Collective. Hobbies: Literature; Sailing; Cooking; Cycling; Swimming; Ecology. Address: No.1 1258 Balmoral Road, Victoria, British Columbia V8T 1B3, Canada.

MCLINTON Delbert Ross, b. 4 Nov 1940, Lubbock, Texas, USA. Singer; Songwriter; Musician (harmonica). m. Wendy Goldstein. Career: Recording artist with The Straightjackets and The Rondelles. Compositions: I Want To Love You; Two More Bottles Of Wine; Giving It Up For Love; B Movie. Recordings: Albums: Victim Of Life's Circumstances, 1975; Genuine Cowhide, 1976; Love Rustler, 1977; Second Wind, 1978; Keeper Of The Flame, 1979; The Jealous Kind, 1980; Plain From The Heart, 1981; Live From Austin, 1989; I'm With You, 1990; Best Of..., 1991; The Great Songs - Come Together, 1995. Honours: In Top 20 Harmonica Players, Rolling Stone magazine, 1985. Membership: BMI. Current Management: Harriet Sternberg Management. Address: 4268 Hazeltine Avenue, Sherman Oaks, CA 91423, USA.

MCCLUSKEY Andy, b. 24 June 1959, Wirral, Cheshire, England. Vocalist. Career: Formed Id, 1977-78; Member, Dalek I Love You, 1978; Co-founder, singer, Orchestral Manoeuvres In The Dark (OMD), 1978-; Tours and concerts include: Tours, Europe, USA, Japan, Australia; Futurama Festival, Leeds, 1979; Supports to Talking Heads, Gary Numan, 1979; Festival of the Tenth Summer, Manchester, 1986; Cities In The Park Festival, Prestwich, 1991; Support to Simple Minds, Milton Keynes Bowl, 1991. Recordings: Singles include: Messages, 1980; Enola Gay, 1980; Souvenir, 1981; Joan Of Arc, 1981; Maid Of Orleans, 1982; Genetic Engineering, 1983; Locomotion, 1984; Talking Loud And Clear, 1984; Tesla Girls, 1984; So In Love, 1985; If You Leave (used in film soundtrack Pretty In Pink), 1986; (Forever) Live And Die, 1986; Dreaming, 1988; Sailing On The Seven Seas, 1991; Pandora's Box, 1991; Stand Above Me, 1993; Dream Of Me, 1993; Albums: Orchestral Manoeuvres In The Dark, 1980; Organisation, 1980; Architecture And Morality, 1981; Dazzle Ships, 1982; Junk Culture, 1984; Crush, 1985; The Pacific Age, 1986; In The Dark - The Best Of OMD, 1988; Sugar Tax, 1991; Liberator, 1993; Contributor, The Message Of Love, Arthur Baker, 1989. Current Management: Direct Management Group, 947 La Cienega Blvd, Ste G, Los Angeles, CA 90069, USA.

MCCLUSKEY John Gerrard, b. 18 Oct 1962, Port Glasgow, Scotland. Musician (bass guitar, acoustic guitar, vocals, harmonica); Songwriter; Vocalist. 2 sons. Musical Education: Self-taught. Career: Numerous concerts in West Scotland area; Played with various rock, blues, folk bands in West Scotland; Solo Singer-Songwriter, 1994-. Compositions: Hard Rain, co-writer with B Turner. Recordings: Overtone 2, with Judy Ferrado Band, 1984; Demos: Standing In The Rain, 1995; Shipwrecks'n'Rum, 1996; Carlton Studio Reels, 1997; Goodbye Halycon Days, 1997. Publication: Produced fanzine Live And Local, 1994. Contributions to: You Don't Have to Be in Harlem - The Story of the Glasgow Apollo by R Leadbetter, 1995.Memberships: Glasgow Songwriters; Musicians' Union. Hobbies: Hillwalking; Fishing; Busking. Current Agent: The Rainman. Address: 22 Slaemuir Avenue, Port Glasgow PA14 6LW, Scotland.

MCCOO Marilyn, b. 30 Sept 1944, Jersey City, New Jersey, USA. Singer. m. Billy Davis Jr, 1969. Career: Member, the Hi-Fis; Vocalist, US harmony group Fifth Dimension (formerly the Versatiles, the Vocals), 1966-75; Appearances include: San Remo Festival, 1967; October Festival, Warsaw, Poland, 1970; Royal Albert Hall, London, 1972; Concert at the White House for President Nixon, 1973; Duo with Billy Davis Jr, 1976-80; Co-host, The Marilyn McCoo and Billy Davis Jr Show, CBS, 1977; Solo artist, 1980-; Television host, Solid Gold, 1980s; Stage performances include: Man Of La Macha; Anything Goes. Recordings: Albums: with Fifth Dimension: Up Up And Away, 1967; The Magic Garden, 1968; Stoned Soul Picnic, 1968; Age Of Aquarius, 1969; Fantastic, 1970; Portrait, 1970; The July 5th Album, 1970; Love's Lines, Angles And Rhymes, 1971; Live!, 1971; Reflections, 1971; Individually And Collectively, 1972; Greatest Hits On Earth, 1972; Living Together, Growing Together, 1973; Earthbound, 1975; Greatest Hits, 1988; with Billy Davis Jr: I Hope We Get To Love In Time, 1977; The Two Of Us, 1977; Marilyn And Billy, 1978; Solo: The Me Nobody Knows, 1990; Singles: with Fifth Dimension: Up Up And Away, 1967; Carpet Man, 1968; Stoned Soul Picnic, 1968; Sweet Blindness, 1968; Aquarius/Let The Sunshine In, based on musical Hair (Number 1, US), 1969; Wedding Bell Blues (Number 1, US), 1969; Save The Country, 1970; One Less Bell To Answer, 1970; Never My Love, 1971; Last Night I Didn't Get To Sleep At All, 1972; If I Could Reach You, 1972; with Billy Davis Jr: You Don't Have To Be A Star (Number 1, US), 1977; Your Love, 1977. Honours: Grammy Awards: 5 awards, 1968; 2 awards, 1970; 1 award (with Billy Davis Jr), 1977; Star on Hollywood Walk Of Fame (with Fifth Dimension), 1991. Current Management: The Sterling/Winters Co., Suite 1640, 1900 Avenue Of The Stars, Los Angeles, CA 90067, USA.

MCCORKLE Susannah, b. 1 Jan 1949, Berkeley, California, USA. Singer. Education: BA, University of California in Italian Literature. Compositions: Translator, 4 Jobim songs. Recordings: 14 CDs: The Music of Harry Warren, 1976; The Songs of Johnny Mercer, 1977; Over the Rainbow, 1981; The People That You Never Get to Love, 1982; Thanks for the Memory, 1984; How Do You Keep the Music Playing, 1985; As Time Goes By, 1987; Dream, 1987; Mo More Blues, 1989; Sabia, 1990; I'll Take Romance, 1992; From Bessie to Brazil, 1993; From Broadway to Bebop, 1994; Easy to Love - Songs of Cole Porter, 1995; Let's Face the Music - Songs of Irving Berlin, 1997; Someone to Watch Over Me, 1998. Publications: O Henry Book of Prize Short Stories, 1975; Author, articles on Ethel Waters and Bessie Smith. Honours: 3 time Award Winner, Stereo Review Album of Year, 1981, 1984, 1988; Singer of Year, LA Times. Memberships: SAG; AFTRA; ASCAP; Songwriters Guild; Society of Singers. Current Management: Dan DiNicola, Susannah McCorkle Music, 41 W 86th Street, #16C, New York City, NY 10024, USA.

MCCOY Jason D, b. 27 Aug 1970, Barrie, Ontario, Canada. Recording Artist; Vocalist; Musician (guitar). Education: Accounting, Georgian College, Barrie, Ontario. Career: Toured Canada extensively as solo recording artist; Appeared on numerous Canadian programmes. Recordings: Greatest Times Of All, 1989; Jason McCoy, 1995. Current Management: Ron Kitchener, RGK Entertainment Group. Address: 32 Triller Avenue, Toronto, Ontario M6K 3B8, Canada.

MCREADY Mike. Rock Musician (guitar). Career: Member, US rock group Pearl Jam, 1990-; Concerts include: Support to Alice In Chains, 1991; Lollapalooza Festival tour, 1992; Drop In The Park concert, Seattle, 1992; Bob Dylan 30th anniversary concert, Madison Square Garden, New York, 1992; Neil Young's Bridge School Benefit, with Elton John, Sammy Hagar, James Taylor, 1992; Support to Keith Richard and The Expensive Winos, New York, 1992; Concert appearances with Neil Young; Also member, tribute group Temple Of The Dog, 1990; Group

appears in film Singles, 1992. Recordings: Temple Of The Dog, 1992; with Pearl Jam: Ten (Number 2, US), 1992; Vs. (Number 1, US), 1993; Vitalogy, 1994; Singles: Alive, 1992; Even Flow, 1992; Jeremy, 199; Contributor, Sweet Relief benefit album, 1993; Film soundtrack, Singles, 1992. Honours: American Music Award, Favourite New Artist, Pop/Rock and Hard Rock categories, 1993; Rolling Stone Readers' Awards, Best New American Band, Best Video, 1993; 4 MTV Awards, 1993; Highest 1-week album sales total in history, Vs., 1993. Current Management: Curtis Management, 417 Denny Way, Ste 200, Seattle, WA 98109, USA.

MCCULLOCH Ian, b. 5 May 1959, Liverpool, Lancashire, England. Vocalist. Career: Founder, the Crucial Three, 1977; Group renamed Echo and The Bunnymen, 1978-88; Major appearances include: Futurama Festival, Leeds, 1979; Daze Of Future Past, Leeds, 1981; WOMAD Festival, 1982; York Rock Festival, 1984; Solo artiste, 1988-; Founder, The Prodigal Sons, 1990; US tour, 1990; Founder, McCulloch's Mysterioso Show, 1992. Recordings: Albums with Echo & The Bunnymen: Crocodiles, 1980; Heaven Up Here, 1981; Porcupine, 1983; Ocean Rain, 1984; Songs To Learn And Sing, 1985; Echo & The Bunnymen, 1987; Solo albums: Candleland, 1989; Mysterio, 1992; Singles include: with Echo And The Bunnymen: The Cutter, 1983; Never Stop, 1983; The Killing Moon, 1984; Seven Seas, 1984; Silver, 1984; Bring On The Dancing Horses, 1985; The Game, 1987; Lips Like Sugar, 1987; People Are Strange, from film The Lost Boys, 1988; Solo: September Song, 1984; Contributor, Last Temptation Of Elvis compilation album, 1990. Address: c/o London Records, PO Box 1422, Chancellors House, Chancellors Road, London W6 9SG, England.

MCDILL Bob (Robert Lee), b. 5 Apr 1944, Beaumont, Texas, USA. Songwriter. m. Nancy Whitsett, 6 Oct 1971, 1 son, 2 daughters. Education; Lamar University, 1962-66. Career: Staff writer, Jack Music, Nashville, 1969-75; Hall Clement Publications, Nashville, 1975-84; Owner, writer, Ranger Bob Music, Nashville, 1984. Compositions: 25 US Number 1 hits include: for Don Williams: Say It Again; She Never Knew Me; Good Ole Boys Like Me; for Ronnie Milsap: Nobody Likes Sad Songs; for Dan Seals: Everything That Glitters; for Mel McDaniel: Baby's Got Her Blue Jeans On; for Waylon Jennings: Amanda. Honours: Distinguished Alumnus Award University, Lamar University, 1989; Composer Of Year, Cash Box magazine, 1979, 1986; Approximately 40 awards from BMI, CMA, Nashville Songwriters Association; 11 ASCAP Awards; 2 Grammy Awards; Top Songwriter, World Record magazine, 1977; Inducted into Nashville Songwriters Association Hall Of Fame, 1985. Memberships: ASCAP; NARAS.

MCDONALD "Country" Joe, b. 1 Jan 1942, El Monte, California, USA. Singer; Musician (guitar). Career: Founder, folk group, Instant Action Jug Band, 1964; Group became Country Joe And The Fish, 1965-70; Concerts with Moby Grape, Howlin' Wolf, Led Zeppelin; Appeared at festivals: Monterey Festival, 1967; Miami Festival, 1968; Woodstock Festival, 1969; New Orleans Pop Festival, 1969; Solo artiste, 1971-; Concerts include: Bickershaw Festival, 1972; Concert with Grateful Dead, Boz Scaggs and Jefferson Starship, Vietnam Veteran's Project, 1982; Maine Arts Festival, 1989; Sporadic line-ups as The All-Star Band, Country Joe And The Fish; Also member, Energy Crisis and Barry Melton Band. Recordings: Albums: with Country Joe And The Fish: Electric Music For The Mind And Body, 1967; I Feel Like I'm Fixin' To Die, 1968; Together, 1968; Here We Are Again, 1969; Tonight I'm Singing For You, 1970; Solo albums: War War War, 1971; Country Joe, 1975; Paradise With An Ocean View, 1975. Address: c/o Tapestry Artists,

17337 Ventura Blvd, Suite 208, Encino, CA 91316-3956, USA.

MCDONALD Alastair, b. 28 October 1941, Glasgow, Scotland. Singer; Musician; Entertainer; Broadcaster. m. Anne, 29 March 1965, 2 sons. Career: Numerous Radio & TV appearances, since 1960s including BBC Scotland's TV; Songs of Scotland; Own series, Alastair; Musical Director & Cameo Actor, BBC Film, The Pinch, 1980. Compositions: Culloden's Harvest. Recordings: Recorded with Major Minor, 1968; Nevis, 1970; Polydor, 1974; Emerald, 1977; Corban Records, 1982-. Honours: Banjo Award, Elgin Jazz Festival, 1962; National Scotstar Award, 1977. Memberships: MCPS; PRS; Equity; ANA. Hobbies: Lifelong passion for traditional stories & songs; Riding motorbike. Address: Corban Records, PO Box 2, Glasgow, G44 3LB, Scotland.

MCDONALD Barry Matthew John, b. 26 July 1955, Sydney, Australia. Student; Researcher; Musician. div. 2 sons, 1 daughter. Education: Diploma, Education, BA, History, Ethnomusicology, PhD, Ethnomusicology, University of New England. Career: Performances at Local Dances, Concerts and National Folk Festivals, 20years; Boradcasts Nationally, Australian Broadcasting Corporation. Recordings: Kind Regards (session musician for Charley Batchelor Album), 1985; Magpie Morning (session musician for Dave de Hugard's CD), 1993; Still A Long Way From Home, 1997; Where The Sun-Lights On the Dew-Drops Shine, 1998. Publications: The Idea of Tradition in the Light of Two Australian Musical Studies, 1996; Tradition As Personal Relationship, 1997. Memberships: International Council for Traditional Music; English Folk Dance and Song Society. Hobby: Motorcycling. Address: 96 Brown Street, Armidale, NSW 2350, Australia.

MCDONALD J Chris, b. 25 Apr 1954, Millington, Tennessee, USA. Musician (trombone); Arranger; Bandleader. m. Brenda Moore, 14 Feb 1988, 1 son. Education; BS, Education, University of Tennessee, 1977. Career: Musical director, arranger, Miss Tennessee Pageant, Jackson, 1977-; Trombonist, Nashville Jazz Machine; Leader, Contraband, 1978-; Conductor, arranger, Brenda Lee, 1982-85. Recordings: Arranger for artists including: Lee Greenwood; Amy Grant; BeBe & CeCe Winans; Kenny Marks; Larnelle Harris. Memberships: ASCAP; AFofM; NARAS.

MCDONALD Michael, b. 2 Dec 1952, St Louis, Missouri, USA. Singer; Musician (keyboards); Songwriter. m. Amy Holland, 1 son. Career: Regular session singer; Member, Steely Dan, 1974; Songwriter, keyboard player, Doobie Brothers, 1975-82; Concerts include: Great American Music Fair, 1975; Day On The Green, 1976; Canada Jam, 1978; Solo artiste, 1982-; Concerts include: Roy Orbison All-Star Benefit Tribute, 1990; Special guest, Tina Turner tour, 1990; Rock'n'Soul Revue, New York, 1991; Benefit concert for family of late Jeff Porcaro (drummer with Toto), 1993. Compositions include: It Keeps You Runnin', Carly Simon, 1976; Co-writer, You Belong To Me, 1978; What A Fool Believes (Number 1, US), 1979; Minute By Minute, 1979; Real Love, 1980; Take It To Heart, 1990; Collaborations with Kenny Loggins; Michael Jackson; Brenda Russell. Recordings: Albums: with The Doobie Brothers: Takin' It To The Streets, 1976; Livin' On The Fault Line, 1977; Minute By Minute (Number 1, US), 1978; One Step Closer, 1980; Solo albums: That Was Then - The Early Recordings Of Michael McDonald, 1982; If That's What It Takes, 1982; No Lookin' Back, 1985; Sweet Freedom, 1986; Take It To Heart, 1990; Blink Of An Eye, 1993; Other recordings (as writer and/or singer) include: Together (film soundtrack), 1979; Christopher Cross, Christopher Cross, 1979; High Adventure, Kenny Loggins, 1982; The Winner In You, LaBelle, 1986; Anywhere You Go, David Pack, 1986;

Decisions, The Winans, 1987; Back Of My Mind, Christopher Cross, 1988; Love At Large (film soundtrack), 1990; The Offbeat Of Avenues, Manhattan Transfer, 1991; Singles include: Let Me Go Love, with Nicolette Larson; I Keep Forgettin' (Every Time You're Near), 1982; Yah Mo B There, with James Ingram, 1984; Sweet Freedom, from film soundtrack Running Scared, 1986; Appeared on: Ride Like The Wind, Christopher Cross, 1979; I'll Be Over You, Toto, 1986. Honours: Grammy Awards: Record of the Year, Song of the Year, Best Pop Vocal Performance, Best Vocal Arrangement, 1979; Ivor Novello Award, Best Film Theme, 1987. Current Management: Howard Kaufman, HK Management, 8900 Wilshire Blvd, Suite 300, Beverly Hills, CA 90211, USA.

MCELHONE Sean, b. 4 Jan 1970, Leeds, Yorkshire, England. Musician (guitar, keyboards). 2 daughters. Musical Education: Self-taught. Career: Television: ITV: Chart Show; Music Box; Radio: Radio 1, session, John Peel; Concerts: Reading Festival; Roundhay Park; Locomotive, Paris; Supported on tour: The Stone Roses; Happy Mondays; Inspiral Carpets. Recordings: One album; Singles: Just Good Friends; Give In; Honesty; Spirit; Don't Fear The Reaper. Membership: Musicians' Union. Current Management: Music; Art; Computers. Address: 37 St Alban Road, Leeds LS9 6LA, England.

MCENTIRE Reba Nell, b. 28 Mar 1955, Chockie, Oklahoma, USA. Singer. m. (1) Charlie Battles, 1976, divorced; (2) Narvel Blackstock, 1989-. Career: Singer with sister and brother as the Singng McEntires, 1972; Solo recording career (over 30 million album sales to date), 1976-; Film appearance, Tremors; 7 members of her band killed in plane crash, 1991. Recordings: Albums: Reba McEntire, 1977; Out Of A Dream, 1979; Feel The Fire, 1980; Heart To Heart, 1981; Unlimited, 1982; Behind The Scenes, 1983; Just A Little Love, 1984; Have I Got A Deal For You, 1985; My Kind Of Country, 1986; Whoever's In New England, 1986; What Am I Gonna Do About You, 1986; The Last One To Know, 1987; So So So Long, 1988; Merry Christmas To You, 1988; Reba, 1988; Sweet Sixteen, 1989; Live, 1989; Rumour Has It, 1990; For My Broken Heart, 1991; It's Your Call, 1992; Read My Mind, 1994; Starting Over, 1995; US Country Number 1 hits: Can't Even Get The Blues; You're The First Time I've Thought About Leaving; How Blue; Somebody Should Leave; Other hit singles include: (You Lift Me) Up To Heaven; Today All Over Again; For My Broken Heart; Whoever's In New England. Current Management: c/o Narvel Blackstock, Starstruck Entertainment, PO Box 121996, Nashville, TN 37212, USA.

MCEVOY Eleanor, b. 22 Jan 1967, Dublin, Ireland. Singer; Songwriter. Musical Education: BA Mod, Music, Trinity College, Dublin. Career: Numerous US and European tours with band; Numerous television appearances. Compositions: Only A Woman's Heart, title track of album. Recordings: Album: Eleanor McEvoy. Honours: Best Solo Artist, Irish Record Industry Awards, 1992; Best Songwriter, Hot Press Award, 1993. Membership: IMRO. Current Management: Real Good Management Ltd. Address: 17 Dame Court, Dublin 2, Ireland.

MCFERRIN Bobby, b. 11 Mar 1950, New York City, USA. Jazz Vocalist; Musician (piano). Musical Education: Piano, Juilliard School; Sacramento State College. Career: Accompanist, pianist, singer, 1970s; Performed with Jon Hendricks, New York, 1979; Appearances include: Kool Jazz Festival, 1981; Solo recording artiste, 1982-. Recordings: Albums include: Bobby McFerrin, 1982; The Voice, 1984; Spontaneous Inventions, 1986; Simple Pleasures, 1988; Medicine Man, 1990. Address: c/o Linda Goldstein, Original Artists, 853 Broadway, Suite 1901, New York, NY 10003, USA.

MCGARRIGLE Anna, b. 1944, Montreal, Quebec, Canada. Musician (keyboards, banjo, guitar, accordian). Vocalist. Career: Singer, performer in both French and English; Member, Mountain City Four, Montreal; Formed duo with sister Kate McGarrigle; Debut UK performance, 1976; Recent appearance, Cambridge Folk Festival, 1995; Barbican, 1996. Compositions: Songs recorded by artists including: Linda Ronstadt; Maria Muldaur; Emmylou Harris. Recordings: Albums include: Kate And Anna McGarrigle, 1976; Dancer With Bruised Knees, 1977; Pronto Monto, 1978; French Record, 1980; Love Over And Over, 1983; Heartbeats Accelerating, 1990; Matapedia, 1996. Address: c/o Concerted Efforts Inc, 59 Parsons Street, West Newton, MA 02165, USA.

MCGARRIGLE Kate, b. 1944, Montreal, Quebec, Canada. Musician (keyboards, guitar); Vocalist. m. Loudon Wainwright III. Career: Singer, performer in both French and English; Member, Mountain City Four, Montreal; Formed duo with sister Anna McGarrigle; UK debut, 1976; Recent cocnert appearance, Cambridge Folk Festival, 1995. Compositions: Songs recorded by artists including: Linda Ronstadt; Maria Muldaur. Recordings: Albums include: Kate And Anna McGarrigle, 1975; Dancer With Bruised Knees, 1977; Pronto Monto, 1978; French Record, 1980; Love Over And Over, 1983; Heartbeats Accelerating, 1990. Address: c/o Concerted Efforts Inc, 59 Parsons Street, West Newton, MA 02165, USA.

MCGARRY David Graham, b. 18 Dec 1955, Stoke-on-Trent, Staffordshire, England. Musician (keyboards). m. 9 May 1981, 2 daughters. Musical Education: Leeds College of Music. Career: Television appearances include: Pebble Mill At One, BBC; Nightride, BBC; ITV Telethon; Toured with Lenny Henry and Ben E King; Musical Director at Alton Towers, 10 years. Recordings: Class, Linda Lewis; Style, Linda Lewis; Dreams Of You, Saxtet. Memberships: Musicians' Union; PRS; British Music Writers Council Section of Musicians' Union. Hobbies: Squash; Chess; Golf; Computers. Address: 8 Castleton Road, Lightwood, Stoke-on-Trent, Staffordshire ST3 7TD, England.

MCGARVEY Patrick James, b. 2 Aug 1971, Belfast, Northern Ireland. Musician (electric bass, guitar). Musical Education: Self-taught initially, basstech, grades 6 and 8 in bass. Career: Bassist, The Coal Porters (Sid Griffin's band), 1993-; Tours: All Europe, USA; Also live shows with Kate St John, 1995; Guitarist, bandleader, The Incredibly Strange Band; Television and radio apperances include: C4, VH1, BBC Radio 1, GLR. Compositions: Featured on albums: All The Colours Of The World; Chasing Rainbows; Santa Mira. Recordings: Land Of Hope And Crosby, The Coal Porters, 1994; Los London, The Coal Porters, 1995. Membership: Musicians' Union. Hobby: Musician. Address: PO Box 2539, London NW3 6DF, England.

MCGEOCH John Alexander, b. 25 Aug 1955, Greenock, Scotland. Musician (guitar, saxophone, keyboards); Composer. m. Denise Dakin, 14 Sept 1988, 1 daughter. Education: BA Hons. Career: Continuous world tours, with various bands for last 18 years; Numerous television shows. Recordings: Albums: with Magazine: Magazine, 1978; Second Hand Daylight, 1979; The Correct Use Of Soap, 1980; with Generation X: Kiss Me Deadly, 1981; with Siouxsie And The Banshees: Kaleidoscope, 1980; Ju Ju, 1981; A Kiss In The Dreamhouse, 1982; with Public Image Ltd: Happy?, 1988; 9, 1989; That What Is Not, 1991; with Visage: Visage, 1980. Membership: PRS. Hobbies: Clay pigeon shooting; Painting. Current Management: William Hunt. Address: 68 Neal Street, Covent Garden, London WC2, England.

MCGINLEY Raymond, b. 3 Jan 1964, Glasgow, Scotland. Vocalist; Musician (guitar). Career: Member, The Boy Hairdressers; Founder member, Teenage Fan Club, 1989-. Recordings: Albums: A Catholic Education, 1990; Bandwagonesque, 1991; Thirteen, 1993; Grand Prix, 1995. Address: c/o Creation Records, 109 Regents Park Road, London NW1 8UR, England.

MCGRATH Bob (Robert Emmet), b. 13 June 1932, Ottawa, Illinois, USA. Vocalist. m. Ann L Sperry, 14 June 1958, 2 sons, 3 daughters. Education: BMus, University of Michigan; Master's Degree, Manhattan School of Music. Career: Performed with: Robert Shaw Chorale; Fred Waring Pennsylvanians; Host for the International Children's Festival at Wolftrap for 10 years; Performed with 100 Symphony Orchestras; Has performed in over 800 concerts in the US, Canada and Japan. Recordings: The Baby Record; Songs And Games For Toddlers; If You're Happy And You Know It Sing Along #1 and #2; Bob's Favourite Street Songs; Sing Me A Story. Publications: I'm A Good Mommy; You're A Good Daddy; Dog Lies; The Shoveller; Me Myself; Sneakers; Uh Oh! Gotta Go. Honours: Honorary Doctorate, Medaille College; Emmanuel Cancer Foundation Tribute; Variety Club Lifetime Honourary Member; Parent's Choice, American Library Association; National Chairperson, UNICEF Day; World Children's Day Foundation, UN General Assembly; Syracuse Symphony Association Achievement Award for Music Education; Canadian Recording Artist Gold Record, 1992, 1993. Current Management: Ken Greengrass, 38 E 57th Street, New York, NY 10022, USA.

MCGREGOR Freddie, b. 1956, Clarendon, Jamaica. Reggae Vocalist; Musician (percussion); Songwriter. Career: Backing singer for ska duo the Clarendons, aged 7; Session drummer and backing singer, 1970s; Lead singer with groups Generation Gap and Soul Syndicate; Solo recording artist, 1980s-. Recordings: Albums include: Mr McGregor; Boby Babylon; Love At First Sight; Big Ship; I Am Ready; Come On Over; Freddie; Across The Border; All In The Same Boat; Freddie McGregor; Rhythm So Nice; Don't Want To Be Lonely; Now; Sings Jamaican; Hard To Get. Address: c/o Jacobson And Colfin PC, 156 Fifth Avenue, Suite 434, New York, NY 10010, USA.

MCGUINN Roger (James McGuinn III), b. 13 July 1942, Chicago, Illinois, USA. Vocalist; Musician (guitar). m. Camilla. Career: Touring musician with: The Limelighters; Chad Mitchell Trio; Judy Collins; Bobby Darin; Founder member, The Byrds, 1964-73; Solo artiste, 1973-; Also member, McGuinn Clark and Hillman (with Gene Clark and Chris Hillman), 1978-79; Performances include: The Beach Boys Summer Spectacular, 1966; Monterey Pop Festival, 1967; Grand Ole Opry, 1968; Newport Festival, 1969; Bath Festival, 1970; Tours with Bob Dylan's Rolling Thunder Revue, 1975; Roy Orbison All-Star Tribute, 1990. Recordings: Albums: with the Byrds: Mr Tambourine Man, 1965; Turn! Turn! Turn!, 1965; Fifth Dimension, 1966; Younger Than Yesterday, 1967; The Notorious Byrd Brothers, 1968; Sweetheart Of The Rodeo, 1968; The Ballad Of Easy Rider, 1970; Untitled, 1970; Byrdmaniax, 1971; Farther Along, 1972; Best Of The Byrds - Greatest Hits Vol 2, 1972; History Of The Byrds, 1973; The Byrds, 1990; Solo albums: Roger McGuinn, 1973; Peace On You, 1974; Cardiff Rose, 1976; Thunderbyrd, 1977; Back From Rio, 1991; with Clark and Hillman: McGuinn Clark & Hillman, 1979; with Hillman: McGuinn/Hillman, 1979; Singles: Mr Tambourine Man (Number 1, US), 1965; All I Really Want To Do; Eight Miles High, 1966; 5D (Fifth Dimension), 1966; So You Want To Be A Rock'n'Roll Star, 1967; Have You Seen Her Face, 1967; I Wasn't Born To Follow. Honour: Inducted into Rock And Roll Hall Of Fame, 1991.

MCHUGH Robert (Bob), b. 20 July 1946, Kearney, NJ, USA. Musician (Piano); Composer. m. Jane Belli, 28 June 1970, 1 son, 1 daughter. Education: BA, Music, Jersey City College; Private Study, Bill Manzi, Morris Nanton, Don Friedman, Hester Randolfi. Career: Performed in documentary, The Art of Worship, produced by Riverside Church, New York City, USA; Appearance on Around New York, WNYC, Concert's at Count Basic Theater, Riverfest, New York Public Library, Lincoln Center. Compositions: Steamboat Ray; Rocky Rog Tune; Bus Boy Circus; Dream Street; Three Greek Dances; Baroque Piece; Buily and The Bean; Uptown. Recordings: Soring on Wings of Ivory and Black; Manhattan Sunrise. Honours: ASCAP Popular Award, every year since 1989. Memberships: ASCAP; NJEA; MTA. Hobbies: Swimming; Walking. Current Management: Manduca Publications, PO Box 10550, Portland, ME 04104, USA. Address: 902 Lincoln Avenue, Pompton Lakes, NJ 07442, USA.

MCKEAN Ian, b. 9 Jan 1958, Hertford, Hertfordshire, England. Musician (guitar). Education: West Surrey College of Art and Design. Musical Education: City Literature Institute (Music Diploma). Career: with Twenty Flight Rockers: Reading Festival, 1986; Numerous live and studio sessions, BBC Radio 1; with Balaam And The Angel: 2 major UK tours, 1988; 4 month tour, US and Canada, 1988; Support to Aerosmith, Belfast and Wembley, 1989. Recordings: Albums: Days Of Madness, 1989; No More Innocence, 1991; Prime Time, 1993; Single: Little Bit Of Love, 1990. Memberships: Musicians' Union; PRS. Hobbies: Music; Art; Reading; Egyptology; General knowledge. Address: 63 Eton Avenue, London NW3 3ET, England.

MCKEE Maria, b. 17 Aug 1964, Los Angeles, California, USA. Singer; Songwriter. Career: Formed duo The Maria McKee Band with half-brother Bryan MacLean, later renamed the Brian MacLean Band; Founder member, Lone Justice; Concerts include: Support tour to U2; Solo artiste, 1987-. Compositions include: A Good Heart, Fergal Sharkey (UK Number 1), 1985. Recordings: Albums: with Lone Justice: Lone Justice, 1985; Shelter, 1987; Solo albums include: You Gotta Sin To Be Saved, 1993; Life Is Sweet, 1996. Current Management: Fabulon Management, 1 McCrone Mews, Belsize Lane, London NW3 5BG, England.

MCKENNA Mae, b. 23 Oct 1955, Coatbridge, Scotland. Singer; Songwriter. m. James Woon, 17 Dec 1977, 1 son. Musical Education: A Level Music, Diploma, Music. Career: Recorded and toured UK and Europe as lead singer with folk rock band Contraband, 1971-75; Sung solo gaelic air on Ultravox tour, 1983; Solo singer, 1985; Backing singer for: Scritti Politti; Blur; Madness; Jason Donovan; Cliff Richard; ABC; Wet Wet Wet; Kylie Minogue; Rick Astley; Donna Summer. Recordings: Solo albums: Mae McKenna; Everything That Touches Me; Walk On Water; Nightfallers; Mirage And Reality; with Contraband: Contraband. Memberships: Musicians' Union; Equity; PRS. Hobby: Hypnosis. Current Management: Keith Harris Music. Address: 204 Courthouse Road, Maidenhead, Berkshire SL6 6HU, England.

MCKENNA Rafe. Record Producer; Engineer; Mixer. Career: Producer, Engineer, Mixer for: David Essex; UFO; Magnum; Buggles; Elkie Brooks; Steve Hackett; Steve Howe; Wishbone Ash; Danny Wilson; Roger Daltrey; Giant; Depeche Mode; Thomas Dolby; Paul McCartney; Spandau Ballet; Gary Glitter. Recordings: Albums: Holy Water, Dangerous Age, Here Comes Trouble, Bad Company; Paid Vacation, Richard Marx; Popped In Souled Out, Wet Wet Wet; Unusual Heat, Foreigner; Bust A Nut, Tesla; UB44, UB40; Singles: Flowers In Our Hair, All About Eve; Sweet Little Mystery, Wet Wet

Wet; Broken Land, Feel The Raindrops, The Adventures; Chant, Absolute Reality, The Alarm; Here I Am, I Got Mine, UB40. Honours: Numerous Platinum and Gold albums. Current Management: Stephen Budd Management, 109B Regents Park Road, London NW1 8UR, England.

MCKENZIE Julia Kathleen, b. 17 Feb 1942, London, England. Actress; Singer. m. Gerald Hjert, 9 Sept 1972. Musical Education: Guildhall School of Music & Drama. Career: Television: Fresh Fields; French Fields; Julia & Company; Maggie And Her; Numerous dramas. Stage: 5 Sondheim musicals; National Theatre; 4 Alan Ayckbourn plays. Recordings: Albums include: The Musicals' Albums; Into The Woods; Side By Side By Sondheim. Publications: Clothes Line. Honours: Swet Awards; Olivier Awards; Evening Standard Award; Emmy; Honorary Fellow of Guildhall. Hobbies: Cooking; Gardening. Current Management: April Young Ltd. Address: April Young Ltd, 11 Woodlands Road, London SW13 0JZ, England.

MCKEOWN Leslie, b. 12 Nov 1955. Singer. Career: Lead singer, Bay City Rollers, 1973-1978; Appearances include: UK tour, 1974; Television series featuring the group, Shang-A-Lang, 1975-77; Saturday Night Variety Show, ABC, 1975; Solo artist, 1978-; Currently tours as Les McKeown's 70s Bay City Rollers. Recordings: with The Bay City Rollers: Hit singles include: Remember (Sha La La), 1974; Shang-A-Lang, 1974; Summerlove Sensation, 1974; All Of Me Loves All Of You, 1974; Bye Bye Baby (Number 1, UK), 1975; Give A Little Love (Number 1, UK), 1975; Money Honey, 1975; Saturday Night (Number 1, US), 1976; I Only Want To Be With You, 1976; It's A Game, 1977; You Make Me Believe In Magic, 1987; Albums: Rollin' (Number 1, UK), 1974; Once Upon A Star (Number 1, UK), 1975; Wouldn't You Like It, 1975; Bay City Rollers, 1976; Rock'N'Roll Love Letter, 1976; Dedication, 1976; It's A Game, 1977; Greatest Hits, 1978; Solo albums include: All Washed Up, 1978. Address: c/o Brian Gannon Management, PO Box 106, Rochdale OL16 4HW, England.

MCKINNA Iain, b. 27 Jan 1955, Kilmarnock, Scotland. Producer; Musician (guitar, bass, keyboards); Songwriter; Recording Engineer; Programmer. 1 son. Career: Recording engineer, 1977-; First production released 1993; Engineer, Bay City Rollers, 1984; Own band The Harmonics; Producer, Solas, Talitha MacKenzie, 1994; Forthcoming album by Mike Heron, due 1996. Concerts include: Guitarist with Flying Colours, Level 42 tour, 1982; Toured with Talitha MacKenzie's band, as guitarist; Support Runrig, 1993; WOMAD '94; Womex, Berlin, 1994; Edinburgh Festival; Also played in Netherlands, Spain, Canada. Recordings: As producer, session musician, computer programmer: Solas, Talitha MacKenzie (Number 12, World Music Charts), 1994; Nectarine No 9; Spoonfed Hybrid. Honour: Best Song, Music In Scotland Trust, with own band The Harmonics, 1993. Memberships: PRS; MCPS. Hobby: Fun. Current Management: Offbeat Scotland. Address: 107 High Street, Royal Mile, Edinburgh EH1 15G, Scotland.

MCLAREN Malcolm Robert Andrew, b. 22 Jan 1946, London, England. Education: Studied Fine Art, University of London. Career: Opened shop on King's Road with Vivienne Westwood (known as Sex), 1972; Created The Sex Pistols, 1974-1979; Managed New York Dolls, USA, 1974; Created The Damned, with Chrissie Hynde; Gave first opportunities to Siouxsie And The Banshees, The Clash; Producer for artistes: Adam And The Ants; Bow Wow Wow; Boy George; Began solo recording career, 1981; Produced rap record, Buffalo Gals; Developed idea of World Music with Duck Rock, 1982; Developed film projects with Steven Spielberg, Hollywood, 1985; Paris album with Catherine Deneuve, 1994; Writing, producing musicals for cinema, stage. Compositions: Music

for advertising including theme for British Airways; Screenplay: The Great Rock'N'Roll Swindle, 1979; Television musical: The Ghosts Of Oxford Street, 1991. Recordings: Albums: Duck Rock, 1982; Fans, 1983; Waltz Darling, 1988; Paris, 1994; Paris The Ambient Album, 1996; Singles: Buffalo Gals, 1981; Double Dutch, 1982; Madam Butterfly, 1983; Deep In Vogue, 1988. Memberships: Musicians' Union; PRS; SAG; SPAM. Address: 61 Rue De Varenne, 75007 Paris, France.

MCLAUGHLIN David Wallace, b. 13 Feb 1958, Washington DC, USA. Musician (guitar, piano, mandolin, violin, bass, drums, percussion, banjo). m. Marilyn Gay Harman, 1 daughter. Musical Education: Private lessons: piano, violin, classical guitar, mandolin. Career: Full time musician, 1978-; Carnegie Hall; Lincoln Centre; White House; Madison Square Garden; Library of Congress; Wolf Trap; Grand Ole Opry; Ambassador Auditorium; Knoxville Worlds Fair; TV appearances: TNN; PBS; CBS; Tours: USA; Canada; England; Africa; India. Recordings: with The Johnson Mountain Boys: Walls Of Time, 1981; Working Close, 1982; Live At The Birchmere, 1983; We'll Still Sing On, 1984; Let The Whole World Talk, 1985; At The Old School House, 1988; Blue Diamond, 1990; Play Requests, 1986; with Crowe and McLaughlin: Going Back On Rounder. Honours: Grammy Nominations, 1990, 1994; Awards from: IBMA; SPBGMA; WAMA. Memberships: IBMA; WAMA; BMI; NARAS. Hobbies: Musical instrument collecting, restoration. Current Management: Shepherd Productions. Address: 18E Monmouth Street, Winchester, VA 22601, USA.

MCLAUGHLIN Dermot, b. 17 Aug 1961, Derry, County Derry, Ireland. Irish Traditional Musician (fiddle). Education: Graduate, Trinity College, Dublin, Early and Modern Irish Language, Literature. Musical Education: Largely self-taught. Career: National Concert Hall, Dublin; Frequent radio and television appearances in Ireland; Concert tours and performances in: Ireland; UK; Europe; Nova Scotia; Record producer for Claddagh Records, specialist Irish label. Publications: Strad, 1991; O Riada Lecture, University College, Cork; Claddagh and Nimbus Records. Honours: Foundation Scholar of Trinity College, Dublin, 1981-86. Membership: Music Officer for the Arts Council, Dublin. Hobbies: Music; Books; Cooking; Plants. Address: c/o The Arts Council, 70 Merrion Square, Dublin 2, Ireland.

MCLAUGHLIN John, b. 4 Jan 1942, Yorkshire, England. Jazz Musician (guitar). Musical Education: Piano and guitar studies. Career: Played with Alexis Korner; Georgie Fame; Graham Bond; Gunter Hampel; Played and recorded with John Surman; Dave Holland; Member, Tony Williams' band, Lifetime, 1969-70; As solo artist, recorded with Charlie Haden; Airto Moreira; Miles Davis; Founder, Mahavishnu Orchestra (with Billy Cobham, Jerry Goodman, Jan Hammer; later with Jean-Luc Ponty, Michael Walden), 1969-; Founder, Shakti, with Indian musicians L. Shankar and Zakir Hussain; Founder, One Truth Band, 1978; Formed trio with Larry Coryell and Paco De Lucia, 1978; Compositions include: Mediterranean Concerto, premiered with Scottish National Orchestra, Glasgow Jazz Festival, 1990. Recordings: Albums include: Solo/Mahavishnu Orchestra: Extrapolation, 1969; Devotion, 1971; My Goals Beyond, 1971; Inner Mounting Flame, 1971; When Fortune Smiles, 1972; Birds Of Fire, 1973; Between Nothingness And Eternity, 1974; Apocalypse, 1974; Visions To The Emerald Beyond, 1975; Inner World, 1976; Electric Guitarist, 1978; Best Of, 1980; Belo Horizonte, 1981; Music Spoken Here, 1983; Live At The Royal Festival Hall, 1990; Greatest Hits, 1991; Que Alegria, 1992; After The Rain, 1995; with Shakti: Shakti With John McLaughlin, 1975; Natural Elements, 1977; with Al Di Meola and Paco De Lucia: Friday Night In San Francisco,

1978; with One Truth Band: Electric Dreams, 1979. Address: c/o Backlash Music Management, 54 Carlton Place, Glasgow G5 9TW, Scotland.

MCLAUGHLIN Mary Theresa, b. 31 Mar 1954, Omagh, Northern Ireland. Singer; Songwriter; Voice Teacher; Special Needs Teacher; Musician (guitar). Education: BA Hons, English Literature, 1975; Post graduate certificate, Education, 1980. Musical Education: Certificate, Music Education (voice), 1995. Career: Several years, British Folk Circuit, including playing with: Anonyme (duo wth Anne Lister); Flash Company (band led by Martin and Jessica Simpson); Began work with own material, with Jon Jacobs, producer; Vocal teacher, special needs teacher. Recordings: Anonyma, 1986; Album: Daughter Of Lir, 1991; Single: Cool Waters (own composition), 1993. Membership: PRS. Address: PO Box 3998, London SE4 2LJ, England.

MCLEAN Don, b. 2 Oct 1945, New Rochelle, New York, USA. Vocalist; Musician (guitar, 5 string banjo); Performer. m. Patricia Shnier, 13 Mar 1987, 1 son, 1 daughter. Education: BBA, Iona College, 1965-68. Musical Education: Self-taught; Also learned from Josh White, Pete Seeger, Brownie McGhee. Career: 12 world tours, 1972-92; Concerts include Carnegie Hall, numerous times; Sydney Opera House; Sydney Entertainment Center; Royal Festival Hall; Royal Albert Hall; Hundreds of solo concerts, USA; Television appearances: The Tonight Show (Johnny Carson); The Smothers Brothers Show; Midnight Special; In Concert; The Great American Dream Machine; Sesame Street; Dinah Shore; Mike Douglas; Merv Griffin; Later, with Bob Costas; 2 BBC television specials (UK): Don McLean at the Royal Albert Hall; Don McLean and Friends; Owner, Benny Bird Co. publishing company. Recordings: 20 albums; Hit singles include: Vincent (Starry Starry Night); American Pie; Castles In The Air; And I Love You So; Crying; Since I Don't Have You; Wonderful Baby. Publications: Numerous song books. Honours: 5 Grammy Nominations; Israel Bonds Award, State of Israel, 1981; Over 40 Gold and Platinum records worldwide. Memberships: ASCAP; BMI; NARAS; AFTRA. Hobbies: Canoeing; Horse riding; Target shooting; Biking. Current Management: Don McLean Music. Address: 1838 Black Rock Turnpike, Fairfield, CT 06430, USA.

MCLEAN Jackie (John Lenwood), b. 17 May 1932, New York City, USA. Musician (alto saxophone); Professor, African American Music. m. Clarice Simmons, 2 sons, 1 daughter. Education: A&T College, Greensboro, North Carolina. Career: Performs regularly nationally at major concert halls; Tours Europe and Japan annually; USIS tour of South African countries: Namibia; Swaziland; Mozambique; Lesotho; South Africa (Johannesburg, Durban, Cape Town). Compositions include: Dig; Little Melonae; Minor March. Recordings include: Rhythm Of The Earth; The Rites Of Passage; Monuments; Contours; Jackie McLean and Co; New Soil. Recordings: Recorded with: Miles Davis; Charles Mingus; Art Blakey and the Jazz Messengers; Dizzy Gillespie. Honours: Voted Number 1 alto saxophonist in Japan, Europe, America; Swing Journal Best Altoist, Downbeat Magazine Critics and Readers Poll, 1993, 1994, 1995; Awarded Officer of the Order of Arts and Letters medal by Jack Lang, Minister of Culture under Francois Mitterand. Hobbies: World history; Boxing. Current Management: Dollie McLean. Address: 261 Ridgefield Street, Hartford, CT 06112, USA.

MCLEOD Rory, b. 23 Jan 1955, London, England. Singer; Songwriter; Poet; Storyteller; Musician (harmonica, guitar, trombone, percussion, tap shoes). 1 son. Career: Former Mexican circus clown and fire-eater; Played harmonica and guitar with Michelle Shocked; Ani Di Franco; Ali Farka Touré; Taj Mahal; Collaborated with Hassan Erraji; Kathryn Tickel;

Paul Rodden; Radio and television appearances: BBC Radio 4 documentary; CH4 TV, After Image singing Farewell Welfare; Scottish Circus Physical Theatre Company as composer, musical director on Hey Big Nose, psychocomedy based on Punch And Judy. Recordings: Albums: Angry Love; Kicking The Sawdust; Footsteps And Heartbeats; Travelling Here; Single: I'm A Rebel Trying To Govern Myself (all self-produced, 1976-92). Publication: Poetry anthology: Apples And Snakes. Honours: Texas Harmonica Champion, 1981; Edinburgh Festival Busker Of The Year. Memberships: Musicians' Union; PRS; MCPS. Address: NE Music, 55 Lawe Road, South Shields, Tyne And Wear NE3 3AL, England.

MCMANUS John Patrick, b. Enniskillen, Northern Ireland. Vocalist; Musician (bass, flute, low whistle, Uilleann pipes, bodhran). Career: First television appearance playing whistle with Matt Molloy of The Chieftains, aged 8; All-Ulster Champion on tin whistle aged 7-12; Formed rock band Mama's Boys with brothers Pat and Tommy and toured the world twice with such acts as: Thin Lizzy, Ratt, Scorpions, Rush, Bon Jovi, Deep Purple, Foreigner, Dio, Gary Moore, Jethro Tull, Status Quo; Numerous television appearances; Disbanded due to Tom McManus'leukaemia, 1993; Tom died 1994; Changed musical director and formed new act Celtus with brother Pat, 1995; Co-wrote Celtus' debut album; Debut performance dates for Celtus as support to Sheryl Crow at Royal Albert Hall, Wolverhampton Civic and Manchester Apollo. Recordings: Official Bootleg; Plug It In; Turn It Up; Mam's Boys; Power and Passion; Growing Up The Hard Way; Live Tonite; Relativity; With Celtus: Moonchild, 1997. Memberships: PRS; Musicians' Union. Hobbies: Shooting footage on video camera; Snooker; Strict vegetarian. Current Management: Lindy Benson, Shamrock Music Ltd., 9 Thornton Place, London W1H 1FG, England.

MCMANUS Pat (Patrick Francis), b. Enniskillen, Northern Ireland. Musician (guitar, fiddle). 1 daughter. Musical Education: 8 honorary exams, Music (Dist) for violin. Career: Played fiddle with the Chieftains on television, aged 7; All-Ulster Champion for several years; All-Ireland Champion, aged 14; Formed rock band Mama's Boys with brothers John and Tommy and toured the world twice with such acts as: Thin Lizzy, Rush, Bon Jovi, Foreigner, Scorpions, Ratt, Deep Purple, Dio, Jethro Tull, Gary Moore, Status Quo; Numerous television appearances; Disbanded due to Tom McManus' leukaemia, 1993; Tom died 1994; Changed musical direction and formed new act Celtus with brother John, 1995; Co-wrote Celtus' debut album with brother John; debut performance dates for Celtus as support to Sheryl Crow at Royal Albert Hall, Wolverhampton Civic and Manchester Apollo. Compositions: Needle in the Groove; Straight Forward; Last Thing at Night; Lonely Soul; Runaway Dreams; 55 compositions published. Recordings: Albums: Official Bootleg; Plug It In; Turn It Up; Mama's Boys; Power and Passion; Growing Up the Hard Way; Live Tonite; Relativity; With Celtus: Moonchild, 1997; Played 4 tracks on Tricky's album, Post Milenium Tension. Memberships: PRS; Musicians' Union. Hobbies: Playing live; Football; Reading; Vegetarian. Current Management: Lindy Benson, Shamrock Music Ltd., 9 Thornton Place, London W1H 1FG, England.

MCMILLAN Tony, b. 19 Apr 1964, London, England. Songwriter; Musician (guitar, bass, drums, piano). m. Sandra Watkins, 9 May 1992, 1 daughter. Musical Education: Self-taught. Career: with The Krewmen: Numerous television, radio, concert tours: Europe: USA; Japan; with Elvis-The Musical, 3 major theatre tours, UK and Canada; Business venture: Tones Music. Recordings: Ramblin/I'm Gonna Get It, 1985; Roll Dem Bones, 1985; What You Are Today/Death Letter Blues, 1985; The Adventures Of The Krewman, 1986; Sweet Dreams, 1987; Into The Tomb, 1987;

Plague Of The Dead, 1988; Curse Of The Graveyard Demon (Compilation), 1988; My Generation (EP), 1988; Do You Wanna Touch (EP), 1988; Power, 1990; Video: Plague Of The Dead, 1990; The Final Adventures, Part 1, 1992; Forbidden Planet (EP), 1992; Live At Billy's Video, 1992; Singled Out, 1994; F A Part II, 1995. Memberships: PRS; Musicians' Union. Hobbies: Computer games; Audio SFX; Star Trek; Sports. Current Management: R McMillan, Tones Music Productions. Address: Tones Music Productions, 4 Milton Close, Basingstoke, Hants RG21 5GU, England.

MCNABB Ian, b. 3 Nov 1962. Singer; Songwriter. Career: Founder member, Icicle Works; Recording debut, 1981; Founder, own record label Troll Kitchen; Solo artiste, 1992-. Recordings: Albums: The Icicle Works, 1984; The Small Price Of A Bicycle, 1985; 7 Singles Deep, 1986; If You Want To Defeat Your Enemy Sing His Song, 1987; Blind, 1987; Permanent Damage, 1990; The Best Of, 1992; Solo: Truth And Beauty, 1992; Head Like A Rock, 1994; Singles include: Nirvana; Birds Fly (Whisper to a Scream); Love Is A Wonderful Colour; Hollow Horse; Understanding Jane.

MCNALLY John, b. 30 Aug 1941, Liverpool, England. Entertainer; Musician (guitar). m. Mary Hollywood, 27 June 1964, 1 son, 1 daughter. Musical Education: Self-taught. Career: Member, The Searchers; Every major media appearance including: Ed Sullivan Show; Royal Variety Show; Palladium Show. Recordings include: Sweets For My Sweet; Needles And Pins; Walk In The Room. Honours: Runners-up to the Beatles in numerous 60s polls. Hobby: Sport. Current Management: Alan Field Ltd. Address: 3 The Spinney, Bakers Hill, Hadley Common EN5 5BY, England.

MCRAE Carmen, b. 8 Apr 1922, New York City, USA. Jazz Singer; Musician (piano); Songwriter. Career: Singer, New York club circuit; Performer with bands led by Benny Carter; Mercer Ellington; Charlie Barnet; Count Basie; Pianist, Minton's Playhouse, early 1950s; International tours, 1960s-. Compositions include: Dream Of Life, Billie Holiday, 1939. Recordings: Albums: Carmen McRae, 1954; By Special Request, 1955; Blue Moon, 1956; After Glow, 1957; Boy Meets Girl, with Sammy Davis Jnr, 1957; Book Of Ballads, 1958; Something To Swing About, 1959; In Person, 1963; Woman Talk, 1965; Portrait Of Carmen, 1967; November Girl, 1970; As Time Goes By, 1973; Carmen McRae, 1977; I'm Coming Home Again, 1978; Two For The Road, 1980; Heat Wave, 1982; Any Old Time, 1986; Fine And Mellow - Live At Birdland West, 1987. Address: c/o De Leon Artists, 4031 Panama Court, Oakland, CA 94611, USA.

MCTELL Ralph, b. 3 Dec 1944, Farnborough, Kent, England. Folk Singer; Songwriter; Musician (guitar). Career: Folk singer, 1960s-; Appearances, UK children's television including: Alphabet Zoo, Tickle On The Turn, 1980s. Compositions include: Streets Of London, 1969; Zimmerman Blues, 1972. Recordings: Albums include: Eight Frames A Second, 1968; Spiral Staircase, 1969; My Side Of Your Window, 1970; Not Till Tomorrow, 1972; Easy, 1973; Streets, 1975; Right Side Up, 1976; Ralph, Albert & Sydney, 1977; Slide Away The Screens, 1979; Love Grows, 1982; Sighs, 1987; Stealin' Back, 1990; The Boy With The Note, 1992; The Silver Celebration, 1992; Sand in Your Shoes, 1995; Hit single: Streets Of London (Number 2, UK), 1974. Current Management: Tickety Boo. Address: 160 Munster Road, London SW6 5RA, England.

MCVICAR Ewan Reynolds, b. 17 Apr 1941, Inverness, Scotland. Songwriter; Singer; Musician (guitar, banjo, autoharp); Author; Poet. m. Linda Rosemary Gammie, 30 Apr 1971. Education: Associate Member, Institute of Bankers in Scotland, 1959; Diploma in Social Work, Glasgow

University, 1975. Career: Founded first folk club in Scotland, 1959; Toured and taught music in USA, 1965-67; Based in Glasgow, singing and writing, 1968-; Tour of Finland, 1980; Wrote show for the Glasgow-Nurnberg Twinning, 1985; Songmaker in Schools Project, 1991-; Mungo 200 Project with Amu Logotse, 1994-95. Compositions: Talking Army Blues, 1959; Wrote 12 songs for The Singing Kettle Show; 20 songs commercially covered by other singers and groups; Shows written include: Salmon Spells; Church Bells; The Fyffes Banana Boat Show. Recordings: Gies Peace, 1987; Produced and released album, I Was Born In Glasgow, 1989. Publications: One Singer One Song, book, 1990; Streets, Schemes And Stages, book, 1991; Cod Liver Oil And The Orange Juice, book, 1993. Honour: Finalist, Songsearch, 1988. Membership: Musicians' Union. Hobby: Music. Current Management: Gallus Music. Address: 84 High Street, Linlithgow EH49 7AQ, Scotland.

MCVIE Christine (Perfect), b. 12 July 1943, Birmingham, England. Musician (keyboards); Singer; Songwriter. m. (1) John McVie, divorced, (2) Eduardo Quintela, 18 Oct 1986. Career: Member, Chicken Shack; Member, Fleetwood Mac, 1970-90; Numerous tours, concerts, television include: US Festival, San Bernadino, California; Shake The Cage tour, Europe, Australia, 1988; Wembley Stadium, with Jethro Tull, Hall & Oates, 1990; The Mask tour, 1990. Compositions include: Don't Stop; You Make Loving Fun. Recordings: Albums with Fleetwood Mac: Future Games, 1971; Bare Trees, 1972; Penguin, 1973; Mystery To Me, 1973; Heroes Are Hard To Find, 1974; Fleetwood Mac, 1975; Rumours, 1977; Tusk, 1979; Fleetwood Mac Live, 1980; Mirage, 1982; Tango In The Night, 1987; Behind The Mask, 1990; Time, 1995; Solo: Christine McVie, 1984; Film soundtrack: A Fine Mess, 1985; Contributor: Law And Order, Lindsey Buckingham, 1981; Rock, Rhythm & Blues, compilation album, 1989; Singles include: The Green Manalishi, 1970; Over My Head, 1976; Rhiannon (Will You Ever Win), 1976; Say You Love Me, 1976; Go Your Own Way, 1977; Dreams, 1977; You Make Loving Fun, 1977; Tusk, 1979; Sara, 1979; Think About Me, 1980; Hold Me, 1982; Gypsy, 1982; Oh Diane, 1983; Big Love, 1987; Little Lies, 1987; Everywhere, 1988; Solo: Got A Hold On Me, 1984; Love Will Show Us How, 1984. Honours: Melody Maker Female Vocalist of the Year, 1969; American Music Awards, Favourite Pop/Rock Group, Favourite Pop/Rock Album, 1978; Grammy, Album Of The Year, Rumours, 1978; Star on Hollywood Walk Of Fame, with Fleetwood Mac, 1979. Current Management: Courage Management, 2899 Agoura Blvd, Suite 562, Westlake, CA 91361, USA.

MCVIE John, b. 26 Nov 1945, London, England. Musician (bass). m. Christine Perfect, divorced. Career: Member, Fleetwood Mac, 1967-; Solo artiste, 1992-; Worldwide appearances include: Windsor Jazz & Blues Festival, 1967; Miami Pop Festival, 1968; Reading Festival, 1970; Bath Festival, 1970; US tour with the Eagles, 1976; US Festival, 1982; Reunion, Presidential Inaugural concert, Maryland, 1993. Recordings include: Albums: with Fleetwood Mac: Fleetwood Mac, 1968; English Rose, 1969; Pious Bird Of Omen, 1969; Then Play On, 1969; Blues Jam At Chess, 1969; Kiln House, 1970; Fleetwood Mac In Chicago, 1971; Black Magic Woman, 1971; Future Games, 1971; Bare Trees, 1972; Penguin, 1973; Mystery To Me, 1973; Rumours, 1977; Tusk, 1979; Tango In The Night, 1987; Behind The Mask, 1990; Time, 1995; Solo album: John McVie's Gotta Band With Lola Thomas, 1992; Singles include: Black Magic Woman; Mr Wonderful; Man Of The World; The Green Manalishi; Rhiannon; Go Your Own Way; Don't Stop; Dreams; You Make Loving Fun; Tusk; Hold Me; Got A Hold On Me; Everywhere; Save Me. Honours: American Music Awards: Favourite

Band, Favourite Album, 1978; Grammy Award: Album Of The Year, Rumours, 1978; Star on Hollywood Walk Of Fame, 1979; Gold Ticket Award, Madison Square Garden, 1990. Address: c/o Ernst and Young LLP, 1999 Avenue of the Stars, Suite 2100, Los Angeles, CA 90067, USA.

MEADE Bazil (Leonard Duncan), b. 4 May 1951, Montserrat, West Indies. Musician (piano, Hammond organ). m. Andrea Encinas, 3 May 1980, 2 sons, 2 daughters. Musical Education: Self-taught in Gospel and R&B. Career: Founder and Principal, London Community Gospel Choir, 1982; Musical Director for numerous concerts including: The London Community Gospel Choir European Tours, 1984-93; Freddie Mercury Tribute Concert, 1991; George Michael UK tour, 1991; HRH Queen Elizabeth's 60th Birthday concert, Royal Opera House; Stevie Wonder, Wembley; Luther Vandross, Royal Albert Hall, 1994; Gloria Gaynor, European Tour, 1994; Also Musical Director for: Amen Corner (theatre production), 1990; Royal Variety television shows for 5 years; Hallelujah Anyhow (film); Rock Gospel (television series); Desmonds (television series); Mama I Want To Sing, 1995. Recordings: with Paul McCartney: Give My Regards To Broadstreet; with The London Community Gospel Choir: Live In Sweden; The London Community Gospel Choir Sings The Gospel Greats; Christmas With The London Community Gospel Choir; Hush And Listen; with Bobby Womack: No Matter How High I Get; Circle Of Life (from Walt Disney's The Lion King). Honours: Greenbelt Award For Services To Gospel Music, 1986; Commonwealth Institute Award For Services To Gospel Music, 1986; BBC Award, Contribution To Gospel Music, 1987. Memberships: Musicians' Union; PRS; MCPS. Hobbies: Football; Cricket; Working out; Wine tasting. Current Management: Choir Connexion. Address: 9 Greenwood Drive, London E4 9HL, England.

MEAT LOAF (Marvin Lee Aday), b. 27 Sept 1951, Dallas, Texas, USA. Entertainer; Singer; Actor. m. Leslie Edmonds, 1975, 2 daughters. Education: University. Career: Appeared in films: The Rocky Horror Picture Show, 1975; Americathon, 1979; Scavenger Hunt, 1979; Roadie, 1980; Dead Ringer, 1981; The Squeeze, 1986; Out Of Bounds, 1986; Motorama, 1990; Gun & Betty Lou's Handbag, 1991; Wayne's World, 1992; Leap Of Faith, 1992; Plays: Hair; Rocky Horror; National Lampoon Show; More Than You Deserve; Rockabye Hamlet; Billy The Kid & Jean Harlow; As You Like It; Othello. Recordings: Hit singles include: Dear Ringer For Love; Bat Out Of Hell; Modern Girl; Two Out Of Three Ain't Bad; You Took The Words Right Out; Rock'n'Roll Mercenaries (with John Parr); I'd Lie For You (And That's The Truth); Not A Dry Eye In The House; Albums include: Featuring Stoney and Meat Loaf, 1970; Free For All (with Ted Nugent), 1976; Bat Out Of Hell, 1977; Dead Ringer, 1982; Midnight At The Lost And Found, 1983; Bad Attitude, 1984; Hits Out Of Hell, 1985; Blind Before I Stop, 1986; Meat Loaf Live, 1987; Bat Out Of Hell II: Back To Hell, 1993; Welcome To The Neighbourhood, 1995; Contributor, Pavarotti And Friends (Bosnia relief charity record), 1996. Honours: Brit Award, 1993; Grammy, 1993. Hobbies: Softball; Golf. Current Management: The Left Bank Organization. Address: 6255 Sunset Boulevard #1111, Hollywood, CA 90028, USA.

MEDLEY Bill, b. 19 Sept 1940, Santa Ana, California, USA. Singer. Career: Member, The Paramours; Founder member, The Righteous Brothers (with Bobby Hatfield), 1962-67, 1974-80; Concerts include: Support to the Beatles, US tour, 1964; Television includes: Shindig!; Scene At 6.30; Ready Steady Go; Discs A Go-Go; Solo career, 1967-73, 1981-; Opened Medleys Club, Los Angeles, 1982; Appearances, Cheers, NBC, 1990; Duet with Jennifer Warnes for film Dirty Dancing, 1987. Returned to performing as Righteous Brothers. Recordings: Singles include:

You've Lost That Lovin' Feelin', later used in film Top Gun (Number 1, UK and US), 1964; Just Once In My Life, 1965; You Can Have Her, 1965; Justine, 1965; Unchained Melody (later used in film Ghost), 1965; Ebb Tide, 1966; (You're My) Soul And Inspiration, 1966; Solo: (I've Had) The Time Of My Life, duet with Jennifer Warnes, for film Dirty Dancing (Number 1, US), 1987; Albums: with the Righteous Brothers: You've Lost That Lovin' Feelin', 1965; Right Now!, 1965; Some Blue-Eyed Soul, 1965; This Is New!, 1965; Just Once In My Life, 1965; Back To Back, 1966; Go Ahead And Cry, 1966; Soul And Inspiration, 1966; The Best Of The Righteous Brothers, 1966; Sayin' Something, 1967; Greatest Hits, 1967; Greatest Hits Vol.2, 1969; Give It To The People, 1974; The Righteous Brothers Greatest Hits, 1990; The Best Of..., 1990; The Very Best Of..., 1990; Anthology (1962-1974), 1990. Solo: 100%, 1968; A Song For You, 1971; Sweet Thunder, 1981; Right Here And Now, 1982; Contributor, film soundtracks: Cobra; Rambo III. Honours: Grammy Award, Best Pop Performance, 1987. Current Management: DBC Management, 131 Spinnaker Court, Marina del Rey, CA 90292, USA.

MEDLEY Sue, b. 19 Aug 1962, Nanaimo, British Columbia, Canada. Recording Artist; Singer; Songwriter. Career: Toured Canada with: Bob Dylan; Dwight Yoakam; Tom Cochrane (as opening act); Television, radio appearances in Canada, including: half hour special, Adrienne Clarkson presents, CBC-TV, spotlights on Much Music. Recordings: Albums: Sue Medley, 1990; Inside Out, 1992; Singles: Dangerous Times; Maybe The Next Time; That's Life; Love Thing; When The Stars Fall; Forget You; Jane's House; Inside Out. Honours: 5 West Coast Music Awards; 2 Juno Awards; 2 Songwriter Awards. Memberships: AFofM; CARAS; SOCAN. Hobbies: Reading; Cycling; Riding. Current Management: Marian Donelly Artist Management. Address: 107 Grenadier Road, Toronto, Ontario M6R 1R1, Canada.

MEDLOCKE Ricky. Rock Musician (guitar); Vocalist. Career: Founder member, US rock group Blackfoot, 1975-85; Numerous tours, US, UK and Europe; Brief reunion, 1990-91. Recordings: Albums: with Blackfoot: No Reservations, 1975; Flying High, 1976; Strikes, 1979; Tomcattin', 1980; Marauder, 1981; Highway Song, Live, 1982; Siogo, 1983; Vertical Smiles, 1984; Medicine Man, 1991; After The Reign, 1994. Current Management: Nalli Productions, 312 Ashley Street, Ann Arbor, MI 48104, USA.

MEIGHU Michael Mark, b. 24 June 1970, Pointe-A-Pierre, Trinidad. Singer; Songwriter. Education: Honours degree, Engineering. Musical Education: Self-taught. Career: Concerts: Tour, New York, Trinidad, 1989; Support to Ani Di Franco, USA, 1994; Radio broadcasts: The Rock Show, Florida, West Indies, 95.1 Radio, FM, 1991. Recordings: Albums: Swords and Plowsheds, 1989; Music Has No Colour, 1991; Play This Loud, 1993; Singles: Love Will Find A Way, 1989; All I See Is Beauty, 1991; Escape Your Mind, 1993. Hobbies: Travel; Volunteer work; Sport; Cycling. Current Management: Mr R Crozier. Address: Crozier Management, 75 Havant Road, Walthamstow, London E17 3JE, England.

MEIKLEJOHN Duncan Warner, b. 16 Dec 1952, Edmonton, Alberta, Canada. Singer; Songwriter; Arranger; Producer; Musician (keyboards, guitars). 3 sons. Musical Education: Royal Conservatory, piano; Private vocal coach. Career: Concert appearances with: Michael Bolton; Sheena Easton; Dudley Moore; The Nylons; David Foster; 1994 Commonwealth Games Ceremonies. Recordings: Song Of Songs; The Best Part (Of You And Me); The Second Time Around; Paradise; Let The Spirit Live On. Honours: Honourable Mentions, Canadian Songwriting Contest. Membership: ACTRA; SOCAN. Hobbies: Art (graphic, sketching); Cars;

Rock Collecting; Softball; Football; Walking. Current Management: Brass Ring Productions, PO Box 1266 Stn A, Kelowna, British Columbia V1Y 7V8, Canada.

MEINE Klaus, b. 25 May 1948, Germany. Singer. Career: Lead vocalist, German heavy rock group The Scorpions, 1971-; Regular worldwide tours; Support tours to Ted Nugent; Bon Jovi; Festivals and major concerts include: World Series Of Rock, Cleveland, Ohio, 1979; US Festival, 1973; Reading Rock Festival, 1973; Rock in Rio, Brazil, 1985; Monsters Of Rock, Germany, 1986; First Western rock band to play former Soviet Union, Leningrad, 1989; Moscow Music Peace Festival, 1989; The Wall, with Roger Waters, Berlin, 1990; MTV New Year's Eve World Party, Berlin, 1990; Invited to meet President Gorbachev, at the Kremlin, 1991. Recordings: Albums: Lonesome Crow, 1972; Fly To The Rainbow, 1974; In Trance, 1975; Virgin Killer, 1976; Taken By Force, 1978; Tokyo Tapes, 1978; Lovedrive, 1979; Animal Magnetism, 1980; Blackout, 1982; Love At First Sting, 1984; World Wide Live, 1985; Savage Amusement, 1988; Best Of Rockers And Ballads, 1989; Hurricane Rock, 1990; Crazy World, 1990; Live Bites, 1995; Hit singles include: There's No One Like You; Can't Live Withou You; Rock You Like A Hurricane; Still Loving You; Rhythm Of Love; Wind Of Change. Honours: ASCAP Award, Wind Of Change, 1993. Current Management: Hard To Handle Management, 1133 Broadway, Suite 1301, New York, NY 10010, USA.

MEISNER Randy, b. 8 May 1946, Scottsbluff, Nevada, USA. Musician (bass); Vocalist. Career: Member, The Dynamics, early 1960s; Member, Soul Survivors (later the Poor); Member, Poco, 1968-69; 1989; The Eagles, 1971-77; Solo artiste, 1977-; Member, Black Tie, 1990-. Recordings: Albums: with The Eagles: The Eagles, 1972; Desperado, 1973; On The Border, 1974; One Of These Nights, 1975; Their Greatest Hits 1971-75 (Number 1, US), 1976; Solo albums: One More Song, 1980; Randy Meisner, 1982; Singles include: Take It Easy, 1972; Witchy Woman, 1972; Peaceful Easy Feeling, 1973; The Best Of My Love (Number 1, US), 1975; One Of These Nights (Number 1, US), 1975; Take It To The Limit, 1976; New Kid In Town (Number 1, US), 1977; Hotel California (Number 1, US), 1977; Life In The Fast Lane, 1977. Honours: Grammy Award, Best Pop Vocal Performance, Lyin' Eyes, 1976; American Music Awards, Favorite Album, 1977; Album Of Year, Their Greatest Hits, National Association of Record Merchandisers, 1977. Address: c/o Geoffrey Blumenauer Artists, 11846 Balboa Blvd, Suite 204, Granada Hills, CA 91344, USA.

MEISSNER Stan, b. 28 Aug 1956, Toronto, Ontario, Canada. Songwriter. Career: Written songs recorded by: Celine Dion; Eddie Money; Rita Coolidge; B J Thomas; Ben Orr (from the Cars); Lee Aaron; Contributing composer for several television shows and films. Recordings: Albums: Dangerous Games, 1984; Windows To Light, 1986; Undertow, 1992. Honours: Gemini Award; Juno Award nomination. Current Management: Meissner Music Productions Inc. Address: 162 Wychwood Avenue, Toronto, Ontario M6C 2T3, Canada.

MELANDER Anders, b. 7 Jan 1948, Stockholm, Sweden. Songwriter; Composer; Musician; Producer. Education: Philosophy and Foreign Languages, University of Lund, Sweden. Career: Band Leader, Bread, 1966-68; Musical Leader, Nationalteatern, 1970-75; Score Composer, SVT, 1976-; Songwriter, various artists; Member of CUE, 1997-. Compositions: Score for SVT WW2 drama serial recorded by Gothenburg Symphony Orchestra, 1994; News Themes for national network TV4, 1990-; Hallå Västindien, Vikingarna, 1981; Speedy Gonzales, Magnus Uggla, 1987. Recordings: Bread: singles

and compilations, including Rough Lover; Nationalteatern: Early albums include: Livet är en fest, 1974; Jack the Ripper; Speedy Gonzales; Bängen Trålar; Solo releases: Good Luck, 1981; Ebba and Didrik, 1990; CUE: #1 hit single: Burnin', 3 Platinum discs, 1997-98. Honours: SKAP Honours, 1984; Grammis Award, 1997. Memberships: Swedish Composers and Authors of Popular Music; Swedish Media Composers. Hobby: Linguistics. Address: Sprängkullsgatan 10 B, S-411 23 Göteborg, Sweden.

MELDER Heinz, b. 16 February 1951, Cologne, Germany. Sound Engineer; Music Producer. m. Anna Maria Melder, 20 November 1976, 1 son. Education: Selftrained Sound Engineer, evening school education. Career: Manager, TMK, Musik Production, 1977-. Recordings: Numerous production in field of German popular music with leading artists. Publications: Eimol Prinz Zo Siu en Kolie Au Rhing. Honours: King Eagle Award, Airplay International Record Label of the Year, 1995-96. Memberships: VDT; IFPI; GVL; GEMA. Hobbies: Music; Travelling with family. Address: TMK, Musik Production, Sebastian Str, 141 50735, Köln, Germany.

MELFI Patrick Joseph, b. 29 Mar 1952, Brooklyn, New York, USA. Composer; Songwriter (piano). 2 sons, 1 daughter. Education: BS Marketing, University of California, Berkeley. Musical Education: Jerry Gladstone School of Lyrics; Geza Wolf, Piano instruction; David Cath Cohen, creative Songwriting Courses; Jamie Faunt's School of Creative Music. Career: Television appearances: All in the Family; Major Motion; Commercials include: Burger King; Xerox Corp; WABC radio; Union Carbide. Compositions: Commercials include: Burger King: Have It Your Way Campaign; Union 76: Spirit of 76. Recordings: (also composed) Ramsey Kearney: Born Loser; You've Won Again; AJ Masters: She's On Her Own Now; Laryn Labeck: The Love In Her Eyes. Memberships: AFofM; ASCAP; BMI; SAG; CMA; ACM. Hobby: Fast cars. Current Management: Starpointe Entertainment Group. Address: 9020 W Rosada, Las Vegas, NV 89129 USA.

MELLE MEL (Melvin Glover). Rapper. Career: Founder member, Grandmaster Flash & The 3 MCs, 1977; Becomes Grandmaster Flash & The Furious Five, 1977-83; Founder, Grandmaster Flash, Melle Mel & The Furious Five, 1987; Recordings: Albums: The Message, 1982; Greatest Messages, 1984; Greatest Hits, 1992; Singles include: Freedom, 1980; The Adventures Of Grandmaster Flash On The Wheels Of Steel, 1981; The Message, 1982; White Lines (Don't Do It), 1983; Beat Street Breakdown Part 1, 1984; We Don't Work For Free, 1984; Sugarhill Work Party, 1984; Pump Me Up, 1985; Vice, featured on soundtrack, Miami Vice, NBC-TV, 1985; Featured on: I Feel For You, Chaka Khan, 1984.

MELLENCAMP John, b. 7 Oct 1951, Seymour, Indiana, USA. Singer; Musician (guitar); Songwriter. m. (1) Priscilla, 1 daughter; (2) Victoria, 2 children; (3) Elaine Irwin, 1 son. Education: Vincennes University. Career: Member, Crepe Soul, 1965; Snakepit Banana Barn, 1966; Glitter-rock group Trash, 1971; Solo artiste, 1975-; Adopted name Johnny Cougar, 1976; Formed The Zone, 1977; Changed name to John Cougar Mellencamp, 1983; Major concerts include: US Festival, 1983; Organiser, inaugural Farm Aid Festival, 1985; Also appeared in Farm Aid II - V, 1986-92; Concert For The Heartland, 1993; Numerous North American tours; Film appearances: Souvenirs, 1990; Falling From Grace (own project), 1992; Exhibition of paintings, 1991. Recordings: Albums: Chestnut Street Incident, 1976; The Kid Inside, 1977; A Biography, 1978; John Cougar, 1979; Nothin' Matters And What If It Did, 1980; American Fool, 1982; Uh-Huh, 1983; Scarecrow, 1985; The Lonesome

Jubilee, 1987; Big Daddy, 1989; Souvenirs (film soundtrack), 1990; Whenever We Wanted, 1991; Human Wheels, 1993; Hit singles: Ain't Even Done With The Night, 1981; Jack And Diane (Number 1, US), 1982; Hurts So Good, 1982; Hand To Hold On To, 1983; Crumblin'Down, 1983; Pink Houses, 1984; Authority Song, 1984; Lonely Ol' Night, 1985; Small Town, 1985; R O C K In The USA, 1986; Paper In Fire, 1987; Cherry Bomb, 1988; Check It Out, 1988; Pop Singer, 1989; Get A Leg Up, 1991; Again Tonight, 1992; Contributor, A Very Special Christmas (charity album), 1987; Folkways - A Vision Shared (Woodie Guthrie tribute), 1988; Film soundtrack, Honeymoon In Vegas, 1992; As producer: Tracks for: Mitch Ryder; The Blasters; James McMurty. Honours: American Music Award, Favourite Male Artist (co-winner), 1983; Nordoff-Robbins Silver Clef, 1991; First US artist to have 2 Top 10 singles and Number 1 album simultaneously, 1982. Current Management: The Left Bank Organisation, 6255 Sunset Blvd, Ste 1111, Hollywood, CA 90028, USA.

MELLY (Alan) George (Heywood), b. 17 Aug 1926, Liverpool, England. Jazz Singer; Critic. m. (1) Victoria Vaughn, 1955, divorced 1962, (2) Diana, 1963, 1 son, 1 stepdaughter. Career: Assistant, London Gallery, 1948-50; Singer, Mick Mulligan's Jazz Band, 1949-61; Cartoon strip writer with Trog, 1956-71; As critic for The Observer: Pop Music, 1965-67; Television, 1967-71; Films, 1971-73; Film scriptwriter, Smashing Time, 1968; Take A Girl Like You, 1970; Singer, John Chilton's Feetwarmers, 1974-; Concerts include: Royal Festival Hall; Royal Albert Hall; Edinburgh Festival; Television includes: Subject, This Is Your Life. Recordings: 30 albums. Publications: I Flook, 1962; Owning Up, 1965; Revolt Into Style, 1970; Flook By Trog, 1970; Rum Bum And Concertina, 1977; The Media Mob (with Barry Fantoni), 1980; Tribe Of One, 1981; Great Lovers, (with Walter Dorin), 1981; Mellymobile, 1982; Scouse Mouse, 1984; It's All Writ Out For You, 1986; Paris And The Surrealists (with Michael Woods), 1991. Honours: Critic Of The Year, IPC National Press Awards, 1970; Fellow, John Moores University; Doctor, Middlesex and Glamorgan University; President, British Humanist Society, 1972-74. Hobbies: Trout fishing; 1920's blues; Collecting modern paintings. Current Management: Jack Higgins. Address: 33 St Lawrence Terrace, London W10 5SR, England.

MENON Brigitte, b. 21 November 1954, Paris, France. Musician (Sitar). m. Menon Indudharan, 1 daughter. Career: Played with Jazz and World Music, toured with Montreux, Saalfelden (North Sea Festival) with Graham Haynes. Recordings: Indian Vibes; Griot's Footsteps. Honours: Radio Nepal Music Competition, 1987, 1988; Laureate of Yehudi Menuhin Association, 1992. Address: 3 rue du President Kennedy, 94220 Charenton Le Pont, France.

MENTER William, b. 13 Dec 1951, Cambridge, England. Musician; Composer; Instrument Maker; Sculptor. m. Annie Kendrick, 30 Mar 1974, 2 sons, 1 daughter. Education: BSc, PhD in Sociology, Bristol University. Musical Education: Self-taught. Career: Numerous concerts at various venues including ICA, Purcell Room, Arnolfini, 1976-; Appearances at Bracknell Jazz Festival, 1986; Le Mans, 1987; Toured Belgium and Netherlands with Overflow and Community, 1985; Exhibitions of his instruments include Crafts Council, Grizedale Forest; Researched Zimbabwean mbira. Recordings: Wind And Fingers, 1976; Both Hands Free, 1978; Community, 1981; Overflow, 1984; Cân Y Graig - Slate Voices, 1990; Strong Winds And Soft Earth Landings, 1994. Publication: The Making of Jazz and Improvised Music - 4 Musicians' Collectives in England and The USA. Honour: Arts Council New Collaborations, 1993. Memberships: Musicians' Union; PRS; MCPS. Current Management:

resOnance. Address: 152 Cheltenham Road, Bristol BS6 5RL, England.

MERCER Frederick William, b. 4 Apr 1920, Deal, Kent, England. Musician (trombone). m. Margaret Staig, 24 Apr 1950. Musical Education: Private teachers and playing experience. Career: Played for various bands and on radio and television shows including: Music While You Work; Northern Variety Orchestra (BBC); Midland Light Orchestra (BBC); Friday Night Is Music Night, early TV show from Alexandra Palace, Music Goes To Town, Simon Dee Show, Lunch Box, and Jerry Allen Big Band. Recordings: Numerous recordings for Teddy Foster; Vic Lewis; Roy Fox; Lou Preager. Publications: Articles for Crescendo magazine. Membership: Musicians' Union, 1943-. Hobbies: Painting; Fly fishing. Address: 61 Charles Road, Solihull, West Midlands B91 1TT, England.

MERCEY Larry Oliver Anthony, b. 12 Dec 1939, Hanover, Ontario, Canada. Recording Artist. m. June, 19 May 1964, 1 son, 1 daughter. Musical Education: Self-taught. Career: Member, The Mercey Brothers, 1957-1990; Solo artist, 1990-; Appeared Grand Ole Opry, Nashville, Tennessee. Recordings: 17 albums, including many number 1 hits; 2 Solo albums. Honours: 7 Juno Awards, Top Country Vocal Group; CF Martin Life Time Achievement Award; Canadian Country Music Awards, Top Vocal Group; Inducted into Canadian Country Hall of Fame, 1990. Hobbies: Golf; Gardening. Current Management: Larry Mercey Productions. Address: 590 Hunters Place, Waterloo, Ontario N2K 3L1, Canada.

MERCHANT Natalie, b. 26 Oct 1963. Singer; Songwriter; Musician (piano); Record Producer. Education: Jamestown Community College. Career: Founder, lead vocalist, 10,000 Maniacs, 1981-92; Concerts include: Tour with REM, US, 1987; Cambridge Folk Festival, 1987, 1988; UK tour, 1987; US tours, 1989, 1992; A Performance For The Planet, Maryland, 1990; Time Capsule Tour, 1990; Earth Day 1991 Concert, Massachusetts, 1991; National Earth Day, Hollywood Bowl, 1993; Television includes: Saturday Night Live; The Tonight Show; Late Night With David Letterman; MTV Drops The Ball '93; MTV's 1993 Rock'n'Roll Inaugural Ball, Washington, 1993; Solo artiste, 1993-. Recordings: Albums: with 10,000 Maniacs: Secrets Of The I Ching, 1983; The Wishing Chair, 1985; In My Tribe, 1987; Blind Man's Zoo, 1989; Hope Chest, 1989; Our Time In Eden, 1992; Solo album: Tigerlily, 1995; Singles include: with 10,000 Maniacs: Like The Weather; What's The Matter Here; These Are Days; Candy Everybody Wants; Few And Far Between; Because The Night; Solo single: Carnival, 1995. Current Management: Jon Landau Management, 40 West Elm Street, Greenwich, CT 06830, USA.

MERCK Alex, b. July 1956, Germany. Publisher; Guitarist; Composer. Education: Economics, Mainz University, Germany; Diploma, Professional Music, Berklec College of Music, Boston; Guitar & Composition Lessons. Career: Live tours with Raoul de Souza & as Solo Artist, 1984-86; Many TV appearances in Germany; Studio recordings, 1985-; TV-film scores, 1987-. Compositions: Molthe; Adios Buenos Aires. Recordings: Doy Days, album, 1986. Publications: Keyboards, Midi, Homgrecording, 1990, 1997. Membership: GEMA. Hobbies: Surfing; Skiing; Sailing. Address: Trujanstr 18, D-50678 Koeln, Germany.

MEREU Jean, b. 19 Feb 1944, St Vallier, France. Musician (trumpet); Composer, Jazz And Improvised Music. m. Chantal Pezet, 12 July 1965, 1 son, 1 daughter. Education: 2 years, Université Lettres. Musical Education: Ecole de Musique St Vallier; Conservatoire Lyon; Private courses. Career: Hot Club de Lyon; ARFI bands: Workshop de Lyon; Le Marmite Infernale; E.

Guijecri; Festin d'Oreilles; Hit Parada; Music for film Battleship Potemkin; Theatre (P. Chereau, M. Marechal, J.Y. Picq); Plays with ARFI bands: Steve Beresford Orchestra; Tony Hymas; Concerts: France; Germany; UK; Austria; Netherlands; Italy; Portugal; Ukraine; Morocco. Recordings with: E. Guijecri; Marmite Infernale; Bandes Dessinées du Spirou; Steve Beresford Orchestra: (Brigitte Bardot songs, Love And Rainy Days with Kasuko Hoki); L'Extraordinaire Jardin de Charles Trenet; Les Fims De Ma Ville; Colette Magny; Michele Bernard; Norbert Stein; T. Hymas. Memberships: ARFI; SACEM; SACD; SPEDIDAM. Hobbies: Cinema; Plastic arts; Gastronomy; Organising concerts. Current Management: ARFI (Association à la Recherche d'un Folklore Imaginaire). Address: 13 Rue de l'Arbre-Sec, 69001 Lyon, France.

MERLE Maurice, b. 27 Apr 1945, Le Puy, France. Musician (alto, soprano saxophone); Composer. m. Martine Lopez, 25 July 1992, 1 son. Education: High School of Trade. Musical Education: Self-taught. Career: Member, ARFI (Lyon); Founder, Workshop de Lyon, concerts throughout Europe; Festivals: Middle East; East Africa; South America; Japan; Canada; US; Member, La Marmite Infernale. Recordings: Chant Bien Fatal, Workshop de Lyon; Gloire A No Heros, Marmite Infernale; Sept Jeunes Et Fieres Maris, Marvelous Band. Memberships: SACEM; SACD; SPEDIDAM. Current Management: ARFI (Lyon). Address: 34 Chemin de Barray, 69530 Brignais, France.

MERRITT Albert Edward, b. 27 May 1929, St Pancras, London, England. Musician (drums); Writer. m. Carole Jean, 24 Mar 1990. Musical Education: Pupil, Eric Delaney, 1946-47. Career: Freelance dance band musician, 1954-68; Including world cruise, 1967; Concentrated on jazz, 1969-; Chas Burchell Quintet, early 1970s-1986; Dave Curtis Trio, 1978-82; Mike Hennessey Chastet, tours: Germany, Austria, Switzerland annually, 1986-97; Also backing musician for Nathan Davis; Clark Terry; Buddy DeFranco; Monty Alexander (one night stands). Recordings: Unsung Hero, Chas Burchell; Shades Of Chas Burchell, Mike Hennessey Chastet; Jumping Jivers; Remembering Dinah - A Salute to Dinah Washington. Publications: Record reviews, Jazz Journal International; Articles, reporting, Jazz Now, California. Membership: Musicians' Union. Hobbies: Studying jazz and its history; Collecting records and CDs; Films (Hollywood); Horse racing. Current Managment: Mike Hennessey (Germany). Address: Bournehurst, Hamm Court, Weybridge, Surrey KT13 8YA, England.

MERRITT Jymie (James Raleigh), b. 3 May 1926, Philadelphia, Pennsylvania, USA. Jazz Musician (bass); Composer. m. (1) Dorothy Small, 1949 (divorced 1977), 5 sons; (2) Ave Maria Davis, 9 Sept 1981. Career: Bass player with Art Blakey and The Jazz Messengers; Gregory and Maurice Hines; Max Roach; Dizzy Gillespie; Lee Morgan; Director, composer, Forerunner Jazz Organization and Orchestra, 1962-.

MERTA Vladimir, b. 20 Jan 1946, Prague, Czech Republic. Singer; Songwriter; Film Director; Composer; Musician (guitar, flute). m. Lucie Lucka, 2 daughters. Education: CVUT, Faculty of Architecture; FAMU - Film Faculty, Academy of Musical Arts, Prague. Musical Education: LSU - People's School of Arts, Prague. Career: Performed at: Roskilde Festival, Denmark, 1988, 1990; Japan, 1991; Vancouver Folk Festival, 1992; Edinburgh Fringe, 1993; More Than Meets The Ear, London; South Bank Centre, London, 1994; Strasbourg, Mittleeuropa; Washington Folk Life Festival; Cheltenham Litterary Festival, 1995; Compositions include: 5 television specials, Thru The Guitar Hole; 1 feature script, Opera In The Wineyard; Music for 15 cartoons; 10 pieces of theatre music. Recordings: Ballade de Prague, 1969; Vladimir Merta Live, Vols I and II, 1989,

1990; Svatky Trpelivosti, Chtit Chytit Vitr, Biti Rublem. 1993; Jewish choir Mispaha, Vols I and II, 1993, 1995; Sefardic Songs (with Jana Lewitova), 1996. Publications: Advantage Server (novel), 1987; Born In The Bohemia (complete lyrics), 1993; Folk Blues Guitar & Harmonica (with 3 hour VHS cassette), 1993; Troubadour In The Age Of Global Village, 1994. Honours: Porta, 1986. Memberships: OSA; INTERGRAM; SAI. Hobbies: Tennis; Downhill skiing; Biking. Current Management: Z Agency, Zdenek Vrestal, Graficka 15, Prague 5, Czech Republic.

MERVILLE François, b. 13 June 1968, Paris, France. Musician (drums, percussion). Musical Education: First Prize of Percusion, National Academy of Music, Paris. Career: Tour, video CD with Ensemble Intercontemporain, conducted by Pierre Boulez, 1991; Played jazz with pianist Jacky Terrasson, 1984; Michel Portal; Martial Solal; J F Jenny Clark; Henri Texier; Richard Galliano; Marc Ducret; Michel Godard; Anthony Ortega; Currently plays in Louis Sclavis Trio; Bojan Zulikarpasic Quartet; Own quintet, with Sebastien Texier, Guillaume Orti, Vincent Segal and François Thuillier, 1995-. Recordings: Sound Pages, Noel Akchoté, 1994; Jade Vision, Trio Olivia, Chevillon, Merville, 1995; Bojan Zulfikarpasic Quartet. Address: 1 ten Rue du Printemps, 78230 Le Pecq, France.

MESSINA Jim, b. 5 Dec 1957, Maywood, California, USA. Musician (guitar, bass); Vocalist; Record Producer; Engineer. Career: Recording engineer, member, Buffalo Springfield, 1968; Poco, 1968-70; Loggins & Messina, 1971-76; Built own studio, Gateway Studios, 1983. Recordings: Albums: with The Jesters: Jim Messina And The Jesters, 1967; The Dragsters, 1967; with Buffalo Springfield: Last Time Around, 1968; with Loggins & Messina: Kenny Loggins With Jim Messina Sittin' In, 1971; Loggins And Messina, 1973; Full Sail, 1973; On Stage, 1974; Mother Lode, 1974; So Fine, 1975; Native Sons, 1976; Solo albums: Finale, 1978; Oasis, 1979; Messina, 1981; One More Mile, 1981; with Poco: Legacy, 1989; Singles include: Your Mama Don't Dance, 1973; Thinking Of You, 1973; My Music, 1973. Current Management: AEG Management, 1025 16th Avenue S, Suite 401, Nashville, TN 37212, USA.

METCALFE Andy, b. 3 Mar 1956, Bristol, England. Musician (bass, keyboards); Producer. m. Lilian Metcalfe, 25 July 1992, 1 son. Education: Sussex University. Musical Eduaction: A-level, degree in Music. Career: 12 albums, many tours with Robyn Hitchcock, 3 of whose albums produced, 1976-94; 3 years, 2 albums with Squeeze, 1985-88; 2 series MD Vic Reeves Big Night Out Channel 4, 1990, 1991. Recordings: Produced: The Reivers; Edge Park; Robyn Hitchcock, 3 albums, 1976-94; Founder member, Soft Boys, 3 albums, 1976-79. Honours: Silver and Platinum discs with Squeeze. Memberships: Musicians' Union (UK); American Musicians' Union. Hobbies: Reading; Crosswords; Walking. Current Management: Peter Jenner, Sincere Management. Address: c/o 421 Harrow Road, London W10 4RD England.

METHENY Pat (Patrick Bruce), b. 12 Aug 1954, Lee's Summit, Missouri, USA. Musician (guitar). Education: University of Miami, Florida. Career: Music Instructor at: University of Miami; National Stage Band Camps, Florida; Berklee College Music, Boston; Guitarist with Gary Burton Quintet; Music director and guitarist, Pat Metheny Group, 1978-; Tours throughout USA; Europe; Canada; Japan; USSR; South America. Compositions: Film scores: The Falcon And The Snowman (with David Bowie), 1984; Twice In A Lifetime, 1985. Recordings: Albums include: Bright Size Life, 1976; Watercolours, 1977; Pat Metheny Group, 1978; New Chautauqua, 1979; American Garage, 1980; As Falls Wichita, So Falls Wichita Falls, 1981; Offramp, 1982; Travels, 1983; Rejoicing, 1983; Works, 1984; First Circle, 1984;

Still Life (Talking), 1987; Works II, 1988; Letter From Home, 1989; Question And Answer (with Roy Haynes and Dave Holland), 1990; Song X (with Ornette Coleman); We Live Here, 1995. Honours include: 5 Grammy Awards, 1982-89; 2 Grammy Nominations, 1980-81; Boston Music Awards: Outstanding Jazz Album, Outstanding Guitarist, Outstanding Jazz Fusion Group, 1986; Magazine Awards and Poll Wins: Downbeat; Jazziz; Guitar Player; Also listed in Guitar Player magazine Gallery of Greats, 1982-86. Address: c/o Ted Kurland Associates, 173 Brighton Avenue, Boston, MA 02134, USA.

METSERS Paul, b. 27 Nov 1945, Netherlands. Singer; Songwriter; Musician (guitar, dulcimer, mandocello). Career: Professional folk musician touring UK, Netherlands, Italy, Japan, Australia and New Zealand, 1980-89; Frequent radio coverage of songs and guest appearances. Compositions include: Farewell To The Gold, sung by various artists including Bob Dylan. Recordings: 5 albums. Publications: Songbook. Honours: Voted in Top 10 of Best Male Folk Artists, Folk On 2 Poll; Featured in Guinness Book of Folk Music. Memberships: Musicians' Union; PRS; MCPS; BASCA. Current Management: P Brocklehurst. Address: Mint Cottage, Gilthwaiterigg Lane, Kendal LA9 6NT, Cumbria.

MEX Paul, b. 25 Nov 1962, St Albans, Hertfordshire, England. Record Producer; Musician. Career: Recording career producing and mixing for numerous artistes; As producer, over 500,000 record sales to credit, including Top 5 UK chart success; Business ventures: State Art; Mex One Recordings; DHE Enterprises. Recordings: with Poison No.9: Lay All Your Love On Me; with United States Of Europe: Free; with Son Of Space: Magic Fly; with Man 2 Man: Malestripper; with Ugly As Sin: Terminal Love. Honours: Silver and Gold discs. Memberships: PRS; MCPS; Musicians' Union. Hobbies: Reading; Keep-fit. Current Management: Mex One Recordings. Address: Lower Ground Floor, 3 Eaton Place, Brighton, East Sussex BN2 1EH, England.

MEYER Björn G, b. 5 Sept 1965, Stockholm, Sweden. Musician (bass guitar, mandola); Composer; Engineer; Record Producer. Career: Member, Hatuey; Tours include Europe, Cuba, 1989-94; Member, Erik Steen Flamenco Fusion; Tours of Europe; Radio and television specials, Sweden, 1992; Member, Milla; Tours, USA and Canada; Radio performances include: VH-1, USA; Much Music, Canada; Music Plus, Canada; Live television, 1994; Preproduction, second album, 1995. Composition: Music to film Vackert Väder, 1996. Recordings: with Hatuey: Songo Mondongo, 1991; La Leyenda, 1993; with Erik Steen Flamenco Fusion: Por Donde Me Leva El Ritmo, 1992; Entre Atardecer y Amanecer, 1995; with Klingström-Bergman: Resfeber, 1995; Klingstrom-Bergman: Sa Länge Skutan Kanga, 1996; En vild och Evig;ängtan, 1997; Erik Steen Flamenco Fusion: Baso La Aurora Boreal, 1997. Honours: Swedish Cultural Council Scholarship for Musicians, Composers, 1992, 1993, 1995. Address: Tomtebogatan 53 #4, 11338 Stockholm, Sweden.

MEYER Patrice, b. 18 December 1957, Saverne, France. Musician. Education: Selftaught Guitar Player. Career: Member, Guitar Player in Hugh Hopper Band, 1989-, in Equip Out with Pip Pyle and Elton Dean; Member, Richard Sinclair's Band. Recordings: Patrice Meyer: Racines Croisées, 1983; Dromadaire Vicmaois, 1986; With Hugh Hopper: Mecano Pelorus, 1989; Carousel, 1994; Hooligan Romantics, 1993. Address: 12 Vieille Route, 77580 Voulangis, France.

MEYERS Ken, b. 20 Aug 1965. Singer; Musician (guitar). Education: University of Lille III, France. Musical Education: Self-taught. Career: Support band for John Mayall; Numerous festivals and concerts; Radio and television appearances:

M6 (television); RFM (radio); Local radio stations. Recordings: Album: Live, 1994. Membership: SACEM. Hobbies: Making life better and the music more beautiful. Current Management: Jivarock, 19 Rue Colbert, 59000 Lille, France.

MICENMACHER Youval, b. 18 Oct 1949, Paris, France. Musician (percussion); Actor. m. Arnelle de Frondeville, 9 Sept 1983, 1 son, 1 daughter. Musical Education: Self-taught from age 12. Career: Co-founder, jazz group, Arcane V; L'Impossible Trio, 1986; Ichthyornis (duo), 1986; Played with: Michel Godard; Philippe Deschepper; Gérard Marais; Vincent Courtois; Louis Sclavis; Mohamad Hamam; Fawzi Al-Aiedy; Djamchid Chémirani; Pierre Seghers; Michel Touraille; Jean-Marc Padovani; Claude Barthélemy; Founder, company Solos Performces; Performances: Peau à Peau, Festival d'Avignon, 1983; Kaddish, Montpellier, 1984; La Braraque Rouge (jazz opera), 1985; Joueurs de Jazz, Festival de Marne-La-Vallée, 1987; Très Horas de Sol (jazz and flamenco), Festival Banlieues Bleues, 1987; Psyché, Opera by Lully, Festival d'Aix En Provence, 1987; Jubal, solo, 1988; Le Rôdeur, Festival de Marne-la-Vallée, tours of France, Austria, Hungary, 1989; Opéra-Goude, with solistes de l'Ensemble Intercontemporain, 1989; Jumelles, opera, 1990; Actor, percussionist, Black Ballad (with Archie Shepp, Dee Dee Bridgewater), 1991; Sud, 1992; Echange, musical, 1992; Around About Bobby, Festival de Banlieues Bleues, 1993; Mister Cendron (jazz opera), 1993; Ma Nuit Chez Lucy, musical, 1994; Hommage à Germaine Dulac, 1994; Numerous festivals with Quartet Opera de Gérard Marais, 1995; The Voice in Upper Galilee Festival, 1995. Recordings: Chants Hébreux D'Orient, 1994; Fera Fera, 1994; Tres Horas De Sol; Le Rodeur; L'Impossible Trio; Nimenio; Est; Lamidbar; Turkish Songs. Hobby: Philosophy. Current Management: Solos Performances. Address: 108 Rue Gambetta, 94120 Fontenay-Sous-Bois, France.

MICHAEL George (Georgios Kyriacos Panayiotou), b. 25 June 1963, Finchley, London, England. Singer; Songwriter; Producer. Career: Singer, The Executive, 1979; Singer, pop duo Wham! with Andrew Ridgeley, 1982-86; Solo artiste, 1986-; Worldwide appearances include: Live Aid, with Elton John, Wembley, 1985; Prince's Trust Rock Gala, 1986; Wham's 'The Final' concert, Wembley, 1986; Nelson Mandela's 70th Birthday Tribute, 1988; Rock In Rio II Festival, Brazil, 1991; A Concert For Life, tribute to Freddie Mercury, Wembley Stadium, 1992; Elizabeth Taylor AIDS Foundation Benefit, Madison Square Garden, New York, 1992; Dispute with Epic record label, and parent company Sony Entertainment, 1992-95; Television special, Aretha Franklin: Duets, 1993. Recordings: Albums: with Wham!: Fantastic (Number 1, UK), 1983; Make It Big (Number 1, UK and US), 1984; The Final, 1986; Solo albums: Faith (Number 1, US), 1987; Listen Without Prejudice, Vol 1, 1990; Contributor, Duets, Elton John, 1991; Two Rooms, 1992; Hit singles include: with Wham!: Wham Rap, 1982; Young Guns (Go For It), 1982; Bad Boys, 1983; Club Tropicana, 1983; Wake Me Up Before You Go Go (Number 1, UK), 1984; Last Christmas, 1984; Careless Whisper (Number 1, US and UK), 1984; Everything She Wants (Number 1, US), 1984; Freedom, 1985; I'm Your Man (Number 1, UK), 1985; The Edge Of Heaven (Number 1, UK), 1986; Solo: A Different Corner (Number 1, UK), 1986; I Knew You Were Waiting For Me, duet with Aretha Franklin, (Number 1, UK), 1987; I Want Your Sex, 1987; Faith (Number 1, US), 1987; Father Figure (Number 1, US), 1988; One More Try (Number 1, US), 1988; Monkey (Number 1, US), 1988; Kissing A Fool, 1988; Praying For Time (Number 1, US), 1990; Freedom 90, 1990; Don't Let The Sun Go Down On Me, duet with Elton John (Number 1, UK and US); Too Funky, 1992; Five Live EP (Number 1, UK), 1993; Somebody To Love, with Queen, 1993; Jesus To A Child (Number 1, UK), 1995;

Contributor, Do They Know It's Christmas?, Band Aid, 1985; Nikita, Elton John, 1985. Publication: Bare, with Tony Parsons (autobiography). Honours include: BRIT Awards: Best British Group, 1985; Outstanding Contribution to British Music, 1986; Best British Male Artist, 1988; Best British Album, 1991; Ivor Novello Awards: Songwriter Of The Year, 1985, 1989; Most Performed Work (Careless Whisper), 1985; Hit Of The Year (Faith), 1989; Grammy, with Aretha Franklin, 1988; Nordoff-Robbins Silver Clef Award, 1989; American Music Awards: Favourite Pop/Rock Male Artist, Soul R&B Male Artist, Favourite Album, 1989; ASCAP Golden Note Award, 1992. Address: c/o Connie Filipello Publicity, 17 Gosfield Street, London W1P 7HE, England.

MICHAEL Sandira, b. 27 Aug 1958, Orotiki, New Zealand. Musician (percussion); Vocalist; Programmer. Musicial Education: Musical tuition with Nemoi Aquam (Speedy). Career: Tours of UK, Europe, with: The Shamen; Loop Guru; Counterfeit Stones; Denise Black and the Kray Sisters; Television and radio with above; Played Phoenix Festival as Sandira; Festivals include: Glastonbury; WOMAD; Reading; Phoenix. Recordings: Singles: Solo: Ishmar Du Bach; Single by Loop Guru, 1995; Also featured on albums by Labi Siffre; Loop Guru. Membership: Musicians' Union. Hobbies: Diving; Gardening; Travel. Current Management: James Clayton. Address: PO Box 9029, London E2 8SU, England.

MICHAEL Shaun, b. 1 Apr 1948, Belfast, Northern Ireland. Singer; Musician (guitar). Divorced, 2 sons. Musical Education: Self-taught. Recordings: Albums: Part Of Your World; Back Home Again; Home I'll Be Achill Island. Honours: British Country Music Association Nomination, 1993. Membership: Equity. Hobbies: Fishing; Golf. Address: Oakfield Cottage, Blagdon Hill, Taunton, Somerset TA3 7SL, England.

MICHAELS Bret, b. 15 Mar 1963, Pittsburgh, Pennsylvania, USA. Singer. Career: Member, US rock groups: the Spectres; Paris; Lead vocalist, US rock group Poison, 1984-; Appearances include: Monsters Of Rock Festival, Castle Donington, 1988, 1990; Solo tour, performing acoustic version of Poison material, 1991; Capitol Record's 50th anniversary gala, Hollywood, 1992; Solo participation, Lynyrd Skynyrd & Friends LYVE concert, Atlanta, 1993; The Tonight Show, NBC TV, 1993, Recordings: Hit singles with Poison: Talk Dirty To Me; I Won't Forget You; Nothin' But A Good Time; Fallen Angel; Your Mama Don't Dance; Unskinny Bop; Every Rose Has It's Thorn; Albums: with Poison: Look What The Cat Dragged In, 1986; Open Up And Say...Aah, 1988; Flesh And Blood, 1990; Swallow This Live, 1991; Guest on album by comedian Sam Kinison, Leader Of The Banned, 1990. Honours include: NARM Award, Best Selling Heavy Metal Album, Flesh And Blood, 1991. Current Management: H K Management, 8900 Wilshire Blvd, Suite 300, Beverly Hills, CA 90211, USA.

MICHAUD François, b. 23 Aug 1965, Québec, Canada. Musician (violin, viola). 1 son. Education: Baccalauréat. Musical Education: Superior School of Music, Québec City; Hull Conservatory. Career: Europa Jazz Festival, Le Mans; TBB Jazz Festival, Boulogne-Billancourt; Music festival, Montpellier-Radio France; Concerts on national radio (Radio France); Accordion International Meeting, Montmagny, Canada; Radio Canada; Yaoundé Jazz Festival, Cameroon. Compositions: Recordings; Theatre; Movies. Recordings: 3 albums with Cordacor String Trio; Cheval Rouge, A Travel For Two (accordion and violin duet). Honours: Best Sonata Player (Junior), Ottawa Music Festival, 1981. Memberships: SACEM; SPEDIDAM; ADAMI. Hobbies: Sports; Cooking; Travel; Going to shows (movies, theatres, concerts). Current Management: Gilles

Fruchaux, Buda Music. Address: 76 Rue Lionel-Royer, 72000 Le Mans, France.

MICHELMORE Guy, b. 27 Aug 1957. Composer. Education: BA Hons, English Language, Literature, Oxford University. Musical Education: Studied mouth organ with Larry Adler. Career: Composer, film and television music including: Eyewitness; Human Animal; 341 - a film for the World Summit for Children. Membership: APC. Address: 35 Binden Road, London W12 9RJ, England.

MICHELUTTI Andrea, b. 20 Sept 1962, Udine, Italy. Musician (drums). m. Amerita Moretti, 2 May 1992. Education: Graduate, Musicology, Bologna University, Italy. Musical Education: Conservatory of Music (percussion), Chatou, France. Career: Worked with: Harry Sweets Edison; Hal Crook; Jimmy Owens; Roger Guerin; Lanfranco Malaguti; Michelle Hendricks; Alain Jean-Marie; Paul Bollenback; Stephanie Crawford; Appearances, jazz festivals, concerts: Italy; France; Switzerland; Austria; Germany; Yugoslavia. Recordings: Orsa Minore, L Malguti Qintet; Tip Of The Hat, La Malaguti Quintet, Sextet. Address: 33 Rue Raymond Queneau, 925 Rueil Malmaison, France.

MICHIELS Paul, b. 15 June 1948, Belgium. Musician (Lead Vocal, Guitar, Keyboards); Composer. Career: Soulsister. Compositions: Soulsister, Repertoire; Changes, Tom Jones; The Way to Your Heart. Recordings: Soulsister: It Takes Two; Heat; Simple Rule; Live Savings; Swinging Like Big Dogs; The Very Best of Paul Michiels: The Inner Child. Honours: Golden 006 Award, 1992, 1993; World Music Award, 1990. Membership: SABAM. Hobby: Music. Current Management: Johan P Berckmans. Address: Aarschotsesteenweg 245, B-3012, Leuven, Belgium.

MIDLER Bette, b. 1 Dec 1945, Paterson, New Jersey, USA. Singer; Actress; Comedienne. m. Martin von Haselberg, 1984, 1 daughter. Education: Theatre studies, University of Hawaii. Career: As actress: Cast member, Fiddler On The Roof, Broadway, 1966-69; Salvation, New York, 1970; Rock opera Tommy, Seattle Opera Company, 1971; Nightclub concert performer and solo artiste, 1972-; Numerous television appearances include: Ol' Red Hair Is Back, NBC, 1978; Bette Midler's Mondo Beyondo, HBO, 1988; Earth Day Special, ABC, 1990; The Tonight Show, NBC, 1991; Now, NBC, 1993; Films include: Hawaii, 1965; The Rose, 1979; Jinxed!, 1982; Down And Out In Beverly Hills, 1985; Ruthless People, 1986; Outrageous Fortune, 1987; Big Business, 1988; Beaches, 1988; Stella, 1990; Scenes From A Mall, 1990; For The Boys (also co-producer), 1991; Hocus Pocus, 1993; Own company, All Girls Productions, 1989-. Recordings: Albums include: The Divine Miss M, 1972; Bette Midler, 1973; Songs For The New Depression, 1976; Broken Blossom, 1977; Live At Last, 1977; Thighs And Whispers, 1979; The Rose, film soundtrack, 1979; Divine Madness, film soundtrack, 1980; No Frills, 1984; Beaches, film soundtrack, 1989; Some People's Lives, 1991; Best Of, 1993; Bette Of Roses, 1995; Singles include: The Rose; Wind Beneath My Wings (Number 1, US), from Beaches soundtrack, 1989; From A Distance, 1991. Publications: A View From A Broad; The Saga Of Baby Divine. Honours: After Dark Award, Performer Of The Year, 1973; Grammy Awards: Best New Artist, 1973; Best Female Pop Vocal Performance, The Rose, 1981; Record Of The Year, Song Of The Year, Wind Beneath My Wings, 1990; Special Tony Award, 1973; Emmy, Ol' Red Hair Is Back, 1978; Golden Globe Awards: The Rose, 1979; For The Boys, 1991; Oscar Nomination, Best Actress, The Rose, 1980; Contributor, We Are The World, USA For Africa, 1985; Oliver And Company, 1988. Address: c/o All Girls Productions, Animation Bldg

#3B-10, 500 South Buena Vista, Burbank, CA 91521, USA.

MIGLIORI Jay, b. 14 Nov 1930, Erie, Pennsylvania, USA. Jazz Musician (saxophone). m. Patti Kleine. Musical Education: Berklee School Of Music, Boston, 1955. Career: Saxophonist with Woody Herman, 1957-59; Saxophonist with Stan Kenton, Gil Evans and Gerald Wilson, 1960; Member, Supersax. Recordings: Studio woodwind player for artistes including Frank Sinatra; The Beach Boys; Lou Rawls; Nelson Riddle; Don Costa. Membership: AFofM. Hobbies: Golf; Freshwater fishing.

MIKA Sophie Michalakoudis, b. 23 November 1964, Brussels, Belgium. m. Jean-Paul Izizaw, 12 September 1997, 1 daughter. Career: Different shows: Vooruit, Gent; Halles of Schaerbeek; Paradox, Antwerpen; 2 video clips; 4 singles; 3 cds. Compositions: MLK; Searching for A Reason; Planet Flanders. Publications: MLK, Martin L King, 1989; Searching for a Reason, 1994; Planet Flanders, compilation, 1996. Honour: SABAM Award, 1986. Hobbies: Nature; Sports; Travel. Current Management: KRAS Agency, Jean Tant, Deinze, Belgium. Address: Mika, Rue Van Soust 120, 1070 BXL, Belgium.

MIKE D (Michael Diamond), b. 20 Nov 1965, New York, USA. Rapper; Musician (drums). Career: Member, the Young And Useless, 1979; Founder, US rap/rock group the Beastie Boys, 1983-; Appearances include: Support to Madonna, Virgin Tour, 1985; Support to Run-DMC, Raisin' Hell Tour, 1986; Co-headliners with Run-DMC, Together Forever Tour, 1987; Reading Festival, 1992; Film appearances: Krush Groove; Scared Stupid; Tougher Than Leather, with Run-DMC. Recordings: Singles: She's On It; Fight For Your Right To Party; Albums: Licensed To Ill, 1986; Paul's Boutique, 1989; Check Your Head, 1992; Ill Communication, 1994; Root Down, 1995; The In Sound From Way Out, 1996. Current Management: Gold Mountain Entertainment, 3575 Cahuenga Blvd W, Ste 450, Los Angeles, CA 90068, USA.

MILENA (Milena Slavova), b. 1966, Sofia, Bulgaria. m. Robert Page-Roberts. Vocalist; Musician (guitar). Songwriter; Lyricist. Career: Member, Review, Bulgaria, 1986-90; Formed own band, 1991-; Best selling female rock singer in Bulgaria; Numerous tours and concerts in Bulgaria and eastern Europe; Currently living and working in London; Writes, plays and sings own compositions with backing band; Only Bulgarian artiste to record album in the UK. Recordings: with Review: Reviwe, 1989; Solo: Ha-ha, 1991; The Scandal, 1993; Sold, 1995. Honours: Seven-times voted First Lady of Bulgarian Rock; Best Female Voice, Bulgarian National Awards (Unison), 1994; Best Album, The Scandal. Address: c/o Union Media Ltd, 71 Evlogi Georgiev Blvd, Entr. A, Sofia 1142, Bulgaria.

MILES Debbie, b. 21 Jul 1970, Ludlow, Shropshire, England. Vocalist. m. Cliff Gottfried, 29 Jun 1994. Musical Education: O Level Music; Grade 7 Piano. Career: Vocal entertainer; Started career at age 15 with the Derek Bruce Showband, Evesham; Remains lead vocalist with the band; Began solo cabaret engagements, 1986; Appeared regularly at many leading UK cabaret venues. Recordings: Holding Out For A Hero; You're The Inspiration; Be My Baby. Membership: Musicians' Union. Hobbies: Exercise (step workouts); Home making; Tenor horn player in Celebration Reed and Brass Band. Current Management: Derek Bruce Entertainment Agency. Address: c/o Derek Bruce Agency, 107 High Street, Evesham, Worcestershire WR11 4EB, England.

MILES Peter, b. 29 Aug 1941, Barking, Essex, England. Jazz Singer. Education: BA Hons, University of London. Musical Education:

Tutor, Mr C Mallett, 1990-; 3 years at Parkshot College, Richmond; Jazz Music. Career: Former actor, television, theatre, radio; Newly emerging artiste of jazz standards; Gigs at Pizza Express, Dean Street, Soho (with Tony Lee Trio and James Pearson Trio); Singer with his own quartet, International Jazz Day Festival, London, 1995, 1996, 1997; Pizza on the Park gig, 1996 and 1997 with own quartet; Gigs, Jazz Bistro, London and at Pizza Express, Kensington; Guest singer in Marion Montgomery and Laurie Holloway Show, Bray with Martin Drew and Jeff Clyne. Memberships: CAA; Musicians' Union; Equity. Hobbies: Swimming; Reading biographies (20th Century); Collecting jazz CDs and cassettes; Going to the movies. Address: 35 Bradley Gardens, Ealing, London W13 8HE, England.

MILLAR John Jhalib, b. 1 July 1951, Belfast, Northern Ireland. Musician (tabla, world percussion). 1 son. Musical Education; Studied at Tabla Alla Rakha Institute Of Music, Bombay, 1979-. Career: First studied tabla, London, 1972; Played with Steve Hillage Band, 1976; Member, Nic Turner's (Hawkwind) Sphynx; Member, Monsoon, 1982-83; Interviewed on Danish radio Copenhagen, 1980; Several compositions, contemporary percussion for major UK modern dance companies; Various sessions for television, dance scores include Chakrada, 1981; Composed with Barrington Pheloung, formed Akasa, 1988; Released 2 singles, 2 promo videos, 1 album, 1990; Guest appearance with Massive Attack, Roxy Club Bologna, Italy, 1995; Joined John Mayers Inov-Jazz Fusions, 1997. Recordings: Ever So Lonely, Monsoon, (Number 12, UK charts), 1982; with Akasa: Kama Sutra, 1989; One Night In My Life, 1990; London Contemporary Dance Theatre, Under The Same Sun, 1983; Union Dance Company, Visions Of Rhythm, 1985. Publications: Currently writing a tabla manual. Honour: Associate member, PRS. Memberships: Musicians' Union; PRS; Mechanical Copyright Protection Society (MCPS). Hobbies: Eastern poetry; Natural walks; Sport. Current Management: Clifton-Wyatt Artistes Management, 1 Poets Road, London N5 2SL, England. Address: 65 Bayham Street, Camden Town, London NW1 0AA, England.

MILLAR Robin, b. 18 Dec 1951, London, England. Record Producer. 1 son, 1 daughter. Education: MA, Cambridge University. Musical Education: A Level Music; Grade 8 guitar. Recordings: As producer, arranger, musician, writer, include: with Lavine Hudson: Abraham, Martin & John, 1991; with Black: Comedy, 1991; I'm Not Afraid; with Latin Quarter and The Bhundu Boys: Radio Africa, 1991; with Patricia Kaas: Je Tu Dis Vous, 1993; Live album, 1994; with Ute Lemper: Espace Indecent, 1994; with Malcolm McLaren: Paris, 1994; with Randy Crawford: Rich And Poor; with The Christians: Ideal World; with The Bhundu Boys: True Jit; with Owen Paul: This Feeling; with Fine Young Cannibals: FYC; with The Style Council: Have You Ever Had It Blue; with Big Country: The Seer; with The Kane Gang: Big Sound Authority; with Everything But The Girl: Love Not Money; Eden; with Tom Robinson: Hope and Glory; with Bluebells: Forever Yours, Forever Mine; with Courtney Pine: Children Of The Ghetto; Artists produced include: Sam Brown; Kate Bush; Wazis Djop; Herbie Hancock; Chris Rea; Juliet Roberts; Wayne Shorter; Jimmy Somerville; Additional production and mixing credits include: Elvis Costello; Wazis Djop; Peter Gabriel; Gary Kemp; Maxi Priest; Gil Scott Heron; Sting; The Special AKA; Tolu; with Sade: Diamond Life (triple Platinum album); Singles: Your Love Is King; Smooth Operator; Sweetest Taboo. When Am I Going To Make A Living (triple Platinum album); Promise; Killer Blow (Absolute Beginners soundtrack). Membership: Re-Pro. Hobbies: Sport; Reading. Current Management: Dennis Muirhead. Address: Muirhead Management, 202 Fulham Road, Chelsea, London SW10 9PJ, England.

MILLER Dominic James, b. 21 Mar 1960, Buenos Aires, Argentina. Musician (guitar); Songwriter. m. 12 Apr 1985, 3 sons, 1 daughter. Musical Education: Berklee College of Music; Guildhall School Of Music. Career: Tours: World Party; Julia Fordham; King Swamp; Sting; Various television and radio appearances; Playing with Sting, touring and broadcasting, 1989-. Compositions include: Co-writer with Sting, Shape Of My Heart, on Ten Summoners Tales album. Recordings: with The Pretenders: Packed; with Phil Collins: But Seriously; with Sting: Soul Cages; Ten Summoners Tales; Fields Of Gold; with Paul Young: Other Voices. Honours: Guitar Album of the Year, Sunday Times, 1983; Played on Sting's and Phil Collins' Grammy Awards. Membership: PRS. Hobbies: Sports fanatic; Family man. Current Management: In Between. Address: 5 Harley Place, London W1 N1HB, England.

MILLER Marcus. Jazz Musician (bass); Record Producer. Career: Recording artiste, worked with Joshua Redman; Lalah Hathaway; M'shell NdegeOcello; Record producer for artists including: Miles Davis; Luther Vandross; Chaka Khan. Recordings: Albums: The Sun Don't Lie; Tales. Current Management: Patrick Rains & Associates, 1543 7th Street, 3rd Floor, Santa Monica, CA 90401, USA.

MILLER Mikel, b. 13 October 1949, Toronto, Ontario, Canada. Singer; Songwriter; Musician (guitar). 1 daughter. Education: Self-taught Guitar. Career: Coffee houses and festivals throughout Canada and the US during the 70's, 80's. Compositions: No More Trains; Hand in the Game; The Kev; Something You Never Knew; Slow Driftin' Song; Pilgrim's Progress; Not Supposed to Be That Way; Stubborn Ghost. Recordings: No More Trains, 6 song demo, lp (vinyl); the key, 10 song CD/cassette both on LEA/JEN Music; Another Day in Paradise a CBC Northern Artist CD, compilation of yukon performers. Publications: Lost Moose Catalogue, record review of No More Trains, 1990. Memberships: Canadian Country Music Association; Folk Alliance. Hobbies: Avid Reader; Music Collector; Mostly Folk. Current Management: LEA/JEN Music, Box 5073, Whitehorse, Yukon Territory, Y1A 4S3, Canada. Address: Box 5073 Whitehorse, Yukon, Y1A 4S3, Canada.

MILLER Ruth, b. 8 May 1962, Newark, Nottinghamshire, England. Songwriter; Singer; Musician (guitar). Education: Degree in Communications; Postgraduate Research. Career: Founder, Rutland Records, 1988; Member of PO!, including BBC Radio 1 session; Member of Ruth's Refrigerator, touring Europe. Recordings: with PO!: Little Stones, 1989; Ducks And Drakes, 1993; Not Marked on the Ordnance Map, 1996; Past Present Tense, 1997; Horse Blanket Weather, 1998; Ruth's Refrigerator: Suddenly A Disfigured Head Parachuted, 1990; A Lizard Is A Submarine On Grass, 1991. Memberships: PRS; MCPS; PPL; Musicians' Union. Hobby: Gardening. Address: c/o Rutland Records, PO Box 132, Leicester LE2 3ZF, England.

MILLER Stephen George, Musician (banjo); Songwriter. Education: BA, Anthropology; BA, Math/Computer Science; MS Computer Science. Musical Education: Self-taught; Reads and writes standard notation and tablature. Career: Played Gaslight Theatre, Tucson, Arizona, 1981; Worked at Lamont Studios, Moody Music Group; Founded Trowbridge Publishing, 1992; Founded The Nashville Folks, 1993; TNN Country News appearance, 1994; Nashville Banner article on own song: The Ballad of O J Simpson. Compositions: Songs: Mass Grass, honorable mention, Jazz/Instructor Category, Louisville, South Carolina; Sunny Summer Blues; Ticklin' The Strings; Jesus Said. Recordings: Album: Sunny Summer Blues, 1992. Publications: Variations On Theme, 1980; Poem: Double-Sided Mirror,

published in Rainbow Wind, 1990. Memberships: AFM Local # 257; Mensa. Hobbies: Nature; Outdoors; Hiking; White-water canoeing; Animals. Current Management: Trowbridge Publishing. Address: P O Box 8563, Hermitage, TN 37076, USA.

MILLER Steve, b. 5 Oct 1943, Milwaukee, Wisconsin, USA. Vocalist; Musician (guitar); Songwriter. Education: Wisconsin University, 1961; Literature, Copenhagen University, Denmark. Musical Education: Guitar with Les Paul, 1948. Career: Member, Marksmen Combo, 1955; The Ardells (became Fabulous Night Train); Worked with Muddy Waters; James Cotton; Howling Wolf; Butterfield Blues Band; Member, World War Three Band (became Goldberg-Miller Blues Band); Founder, the Steve Miller Band, 1966-; Regular international appearances include: San Francisco State College Folk Festival, 1967; Monterey International Pop Festival, 1967; Northern California Folk-Rock Festival, 1968; Hollywood Music Festival, 1970; Knebworth Festival, 1975; Benefit for Texas Special Olympics, Dallas, 1990; Earth Day Sound Action benefit, 1992; All Our Colors - The Good Road benefit concert, California, 1992; Earth Day concert, Hollywood Bowl, 1992; Founder, record label Sailor Records, 1976. Recordings: Albums: with Steve Miller Band: Children Of The Future, 1968; Sailor, 1968; Brave New World, 1969; Your Saving Grace, 1969; Number Five, 1970; Rock Love, 1971; Recall The Beginning...A Journey From Eden, 1972; Anthology, 1972; Fly Like An Eagle, 1977; Book Of Dreams, 1977; Greatest Hits 1974-1978, 1978; Abracadabra, 1982; The Steve Miller Band Live!, 1983; Italian X-Rays, 1984; Living In The 20th Century, 1986; Greatest Hits 1976-86, 1987; Born 2 Be Blue, 1988; The Best Of Steve Miller 1968-1973, 1990; Wide River, 1992; Box Set, 1994; Singles include: The Joker (US number 1), 1974; Take The Money And Run; Rock'n'Me; Fly Like An Eagle; Jet Airliner; Swingtown; Abracadabra. Honours include: Platinum discs; Star on Hollywood Walk Of Fame, 1987. Current Management: Scott Boorey Management, 325 Glen Arms Drive, Danville, CA 94526, USA.

MILLER Bill (William Scott), b. 23 Jan 1955, Neenah, Wisconsin, USA. Entertainer; Musician (guitar, flute). m. Renee Miller, 5 Aug 1978, 2 sons, 1 daughter. Education: College. Career: Tori Amos tour; Television appearances: Good Morning America; Austin City Limits. Recordings: Native Sons; Old Dreams And New Hopes; The Art Of Survival; Loon Mountain Moon; Reservation Road; The Red Road. Hobbies: Camping; Hiking; Fishing. Current Management: Bob Burwell, William Morris Agency. Address: Bob Burwell, 1516 16th Avenue S, Nashville, TN 37212, USA.

MILLS Martin Charles, b. 12 May 1949, Hampton Court, Middlesex, England. Company Director, Group of Music Companies. Partner, Yvonne Damant, 1 son, 1 daughter. Education: BA, Oriel College, Oxford. Career: Owner and Chairman of Beggars Banquet Group of Music Companies. Address: 17-19 Alma Road, London, SW18 1AA, England.

MILLS Mike, b. 17 Dec 1958. Musician (bass). Career: Member, R.E.M., 1980-; International tours; Member, side project, Hindu Love Gods, 1986-90. Recordings: Albums: Chronic Town (mini-album), 1982; Murmur, 1983; Reckoning, 1984; Fables Of The Reconstruction, 1985; Life's Rich Pageant, 1986; Dead Letter Office, 1987; Document, 1987; Eponymous, 1988; Green, 1988; Out Of Time, 1991; The Best Of R.E.M., 1991; Automatic For The People, 1992; Monster, 1995; with Hindu Love Gods: Hindu Love Gods, 1990; Singles: with R.E.M: The One I Love, 1987; Stand, 1989; Orange Crush, 1989; Losing My Religion, 1991; Shiny Happy People, 1991; Near Wild Heaven, 1991; Radio Song, 1991; Drive, 1992; Man On The Moon, 1992; The

Sidewinder Sleeps Tonite, 1993; Everybody Hurts, 1993; Crush With Eyeliner; What's The Frequency, Kenneth?; Nightswimming; Tracks featured on film soundtracks: Batchelor Party, 1984; Until The End Of The World, 1991; Coneheads, 1993; Other recordings with: Warren Zevon; Indigo Girls; Contributor, albums: Tom's Album; I'm Your Fan. Honours: Earth Day Award, 1990; Numerous MTV Music Video Awards; Billboard Awards; Best Modern Rock Artists, Best World Album, 1991; BRIT Awards: Best International Group, 1992, 1993, 1995; Grammy Awards: Best For Performance, Alternative Music Album, Music Video, 1992; Atlanta Music Awards: Act Of The Year, Rock Album, Video, 1992; IRMA, International Band Of The Year, 1993; Rolling Stone Critics Awards: Best Band, Best Album; Q Awards: Best Album, 1991, 1992; Best Act In The World, 1991, 1995. Current Management: REM/Athens Ltd. Address: 250 W Clayton Street, Athens, GA 30601, USA.

MILLSAPS Bill, b. 11 Oct 1948, Snowbird Mountains, North Carolina, USA. Appalachian Mountain Songwriter; Singer; Musician (mandolin, guitar, banjo, fiddle, dobra, bass fiddle). m. Wilma Wakefield, 1 son, 1 daughter. Musical Education: Apprenticed under Carl Story, Kenny Baker, Joe Stuart, Josh Graves. Career: Travelled in over 30 states with Tommy Scott; Appears regularly with The Snowbird Mountain Band; Host of Snowbird Mountain Bluegrass, satellite TV across USA, Canada; Played with Bill Monroe, in: The Father of Blue Grass Music, Original Cinema, 1993; Appeared in: Nell, with Jody Foster Twentieth Century Fox, 1994. Compositions: Bluegrass instrumentals: Slickrock; Nanthala; To The Chief Musician; Suite of his material arranged by Dr Harold Schiffman, for North Carolina Symphony. Recordings include: Legendary Friends Of The Snowbird Mountain Band, with John Hartford, Benny Martin. Memberships: AFofM; IBMA; BMI. Hobbies: Fishing; Photography; Cherokee Indian language. Address: PO Box 85, Robbinsville, NC 28771, USA.

MILNER John D(avid), b. 22 Feb 1959, Hartlepool, England. Musician (drums, piano); Arranger. m. 20 Nov 1982, 2 daughters. Musical Education: Newcastle School of Music. Career: Freelance musician and arranger, many years; Currently runs a jazz orchestra playing the music of Duke Ellington and Charles Mingus; Also involved in Jazz Education. Compositions include: Lady Chatterley's Loofah. Membership: Musicians' Union. Hobby: Cricket. Address: Manifold Valley Hotel, Hulme End, Hartington, near Buxton, Derbyshire SK17 0EX, England.

MILSAP Ronald Lee Milsap, b. 16 Jan 1943, Robbinsville, North Carolina, USA. Country Music Singer; Entertainer. m. F Joyce Reeves, 30 Oct 1965, 1 son. Education: NC Goveernor, Morehead School For The Blind; Young-Harris College, 1964. Musical Education: Violin, piano, guitar, woodwinds, classical music, Morehad School. Career: Numerous television shows, television show themes. Recordings: Albums include: Legend In My Time; I'm A Stand By My Woman Man; Almost Like A Song; There's No Getting Over Me; Lost In The Fifties Tonight; Any Day Now; Pure Love; True Believer; Over 41 Number 1 hits. Publications: Autobiography: Almost Like A Song. Honours: 8 Country Music Association Awards, including Entertainer Of The Year, 1977; 6 Grammy Awards, 1974-; 3 Academy of Country Music Awards; Cashbox Magazine Award, 1981; ASCAP Most Programmed Song Of Year, 1982. Memberships: CMA; NARAS; ACM; AFofM. Hobbies: Ham radio; Collecting old radios; Radio shows; Computers. Current Management: Burt Stein, Gold Mountain Entertainment. Address: 12 Music Circle South, Nashville, TN 37203, USA.

MINNEAR Kerry Churchill, b. 2 Jan 1948, Gloucester, England. Composer; Musician (percussion). m. Lesley Jackson, 16 Apr 1977, 1

son, 2 daughters. Musical Education: Royal Academy of Music. Career: Composer and performer, keyboards and percussion, with Gentle Giant, 1970-80; Several major tours of Europe and North America, also appearances on television and radio; Currently composing for television programmes. Recordings: 12 albums. Publications: The Gentle Giant Magazine. Membership: Musicians' Union. Hobbies: Family; Fitness; Travel. Address: c/o Gentle Giant Magazine, Eidsvolls gt 16, N-7016, Trondheim, Norway.

MINNEBO Stefaan Peter, b. 15 Aug 1958, Ninove, Belgium. Guitar Teacher (Classical, Pop, Jazz); Guitarist; Composer; Arranger. m. Winnie Deleu, 2 Oct 1982, 2 daughters. Education: Classical Guitar Degree, Antwerp Conservatory; Jazz, Arranging and Composing Courses. Career: Concert tours and radio shows with Nobert Detaeye (New Orleans, Blues, Gospel); Symphonic arrangements commissioned by Dirk Brossé, and VRT; Vocal arrangements and compositions. Compositions: Close Friends; String Fever; Arrangements: Vierhoog in de wolken; Het schip. Recordings: as Contributor: Arm in Arm With the Moon, 1990; Jesus on the Main Line, 1995. Honours: BAP Prize, 1993; Laureate, Publisher's Harmonia Contest for Vocal Score. Memberships: ZAMU; SABAM; OVSG Committee for jazz/rock/pop education on music schools. Hobbies: Travelling; Reading. Current Management: Radio Management, Bist 26, B-2610 Wilrijk, Belgium. Address: Mevr Courtmansstraat 7, B-2600 Berchem, Belgium.

MINNELLI Liza May, b. 12 Mar 1946, Los Angeles, California, USA. Singer; Actress; Dancer. m. Peter Allen, 1967 (divorced), (2) Jack Haley Jr, 15 Sept 1974 (divorced), (3) Mark Gero, 4 Dec 1979. Career: Singer and entertainer, stage, film and television; Major appearances include: Best Foot Forward (off-Broadway), 1963; Touring productions: Carnival; The Pajama Game; The Fantasticks; Performed with mother (Judy Garland), London Palladium, 1964; Broadway debut, Flora And The Red Menace, 1965; The Act, 1977; The Rink, 1984; The Ultimate Event, international tour with Frank Sinatra, Sammy Davis Jr, 1988; Film appearances: Charlie Bubbles, 1967; The Sterile Cuckoo, 1969; Cabaret, 1972; Tell Me That You Love Me Junie Moon, 1974; Lucky Lady, 1975; A Matter Of Time, 1976; Silent Movie, 1976; New York, New York, 1977; Arthur, 1981; Arthur 2 - On The Rocks, 1988; Stepping Out, 1991; Television appearances include: Liza With A 'Z', 1972; Goldie And Liza Together, 1980; Baryshnikov On Broadway, 1980; The Princess And The Pea; Showtime, 1983; A Time To Live, 1985; Sam Found Out, 1988. Recordings: Albums include: Liza! Liza!, 1964; It Amazes Me, 1965; There Is A Time, 1966; New Feelin', 1970; Liza With A 'Z', 1972; Liza Minnelli The Singer, 1973; Live At The Winter Garden, 1974; Lucky Lady, 1976; Tropical Nights, 1977; Live At Carnegie Hall, 1987; Live From Radio City Music Hall, 1992; Film and stage soundtracks: Best Foot Forward, 1963; Dangerous Christmas Of Red Riding Hood, 1965; Flora And The Red Menace, 1965; Cabaret, 1972; with Judy Garland: Live At The London Palladium, 1964; with Pet Shop Boys: Results, 1989; Single: Losing My Mind, with Pet Shop Boys, (first UK chart entry), 1989. Honours: Promising Personality Award, 1963; 2 Tony Awards, Best Foot Forward, 1965, The Act, 1977; Academy Award Nomination, 1969; Oscar, Best Actress, Cabaret, 1972; Emmy Award, Lisa With A 'Z', 1972; Golden Globe Award, Best Actress, A Time To Live, 1985. Current Management: Krost/Chapin Management, Penthouse 1, 9911 West Pico Blvd, Los Angeles, CA 90035, USA.

MINOGUE Dannii (Danielle Jane), b. 20 Oct 1971, Melbourne, Victoria, Australia. Singer; Actress; Fashion Designer; Television Presenter. Career: Actress, Australian TV drama series: Skyways, 1978; The Sullivans, 1978; All The Way, 1988; Home And Away, 1989; TV Presenter, Young Talent Time, Australia, 1979-88; New Generation, Australia, USA, 1988; Scoop; It's Not Just Saturday; Dannii on Safari, Disney; Co-host, Big Breakfast, UK, 1993; Fan T.C., UK, 1994; Film appearance: Secrets, 1992. Performances: Royal Children's Variety Performance, 1991; Cesme Festival, Turkey, 1992; Gay Pride Festival, London, 1993, 1994; Promotional tours of Australia, SE Asia, USA and UK. Recordings: Albums: Love And Kisses, 1991. Singles: 10 Top Ten singles, including: Love And Kisses, 1990; This Is It, 1993; Contributor, The Gift Of Christmas, Child Liners, 1995. Honours: Gold discs, UK and Australia; Young Variety Award (Australian Variety Club) 1989. Membership: Australian Actor's Equity, APRA. Address: c/o Terry Blamey Management, PO Box 13196, London SW6 2WA, England.

MINOGUE Kylie (Anne), b. 28 May 1968, Melbourne, Victoria,Australia. Singer; Actress. Career: Actress, Australian television dramas: Skyways, 1980; The Sullivans, 1981; The Henderson Kids, 1984-85;Neighbours, 1986-88; Film appearances: The Delinquents, 1989; Streetfighter, 1994; BioDome, 1995; As singer, biggest selling single of decade in Australia, Locomotion, 1987; Highest UK chart entry for female artist, Locomotion, 1988; Highest debut album chart entry, Australia, UK, Kylie, 1988; First ever artist with 4 Top 3 singles from an album; First female artist with first 5 singles to recieve Silver discs; Performances include: Australian Royal Bicentennial Concert, 1988; John Lennon tribute, Liverpool, 1990; Cesne Music Festival, Turkey, 1992; Sydney Gay Mardi Gras, 1994; Prince's Trust Concert, 1994; T In The Park Festival, Glasgow, 1995; Tours of UK, Europe, Asia, and Australia. Recordings: Albums: Kylie, 1988; Enjoy Yourself, 1989; Rhythm Of Love, 1990; Let's Get To It, 1991; Kylie - Greatest Hits, 1992; Kylie Minogue, 1994. Singles include: Locomotion, 1987; I Should Be So Lucky, 1988; Je Ne Sais Pas Pourquoi, 1988; Especially For You, with Jason Donovan, 1988; Never Too Late, 1989; Confide In Me, 1994; Put Yourself In My Place, 1995; Where Is The Feeling, 1995; Where The Wild Roses Grow (duet with Nick Cave), 1995; Some Kind Of Bliss, 1997. Honours: Numerous Platinum, Gold and Silver discs; 6 Logies (Australia); 6 Music Week Awards (UK); 3 Smash Hits Awards (UK); 3 Australian Record Industry Association Awards; 3 Japanese Music Awards; Irish Record Industry Award; Canadian Record Industry Award; World Music Award; Australian Variety Club Award; MO Award (Australian Showbusiness); Amplex Golden Reel Award; Diamond Award, (Belgium); Woman of the Decade (UK); 25 Top Ten singles worldwide. Address: c/o Terry Blamey Management, PO Box 13196, London SW6 2WA, England.

MINOTT Sugar (Lincoln Minott), b. 25 May 1956, Kingston, Jamaica. Reggae Singer. Career: Billed as one of the African Brothers, 1970s; Success within UK reggae scene; Established own Youth Promotion/Black Roots promotion organisation. Recordings: with the African Brothers: Collectors Item; Numerous solo albums include: Live Loving; Black Roots; Bittersweet; Ghetto-ology; Roots Lovers; Give The People; African Girl; Good Thing Going; With Lots Of Extra; Herbman Hustling; Slice Of The Cake; Wicked A Go Feel It; Leader Of The Pack; Time Longer Than Rope; Sugar And Spice; Them Ah Wolf; Jamming In The Streets; African Soldier; Buy Off The Bar; Ghetto Youth Dem Rising; The Boss Is Back; A Touch Of Class; Run Things. Address: c/o Tempest Entertainment, 245 West 25th Street, New York, NY 10001, USA.

MINTON Philip Watcyn, b. 2 Nov 1940, Torquay, Devon, England. Singer; Improvisor. 1 son, 3 daughters. Career: Performed at most improvised music festivals worldwide, with hundreds of musicians from many countries. Recordings: Songs From A Prison Diary, with Veryan Weston; Ammo, Dadada, with Roger Turner. Honours: Voted Best Singer, Europe Jazz Forum Magazine, 1988. Memberships: LMC; Musicians' Union; PRS; MCPS. Current Management: IMI Bochum, Germany.

MINVIELLE Pierre, b. 30 July 1960, Paris, France. Musician (piano); Composer. Musical Education: Paris (classical) student of Bernard Maury and Andre Hodeir. Career: Played in Printemps de Bourges, 1980; Concerts with Magma, 1981-83; Also plays jazz concerts elsewhere; Radio: France Musique, 1990. Publications: Author, children's book Le Jazz Des Petites Mains (Jazz For Small Hands), Vols I and II. Membership: SACEM (composer, arranger). Hobbies: Sports; Television; Pictures; Reading; Girls. Address: 19 Rue Basse, 78730 St Arnoult en Yvelines, France.

MION Alain, b. 14 Jan 1947, Casablanca, Morocco. Musician (piano); Composer; Singer. m. Mireille Falet, 8 Oct 1971. Career: Co-leader, band Cortex; Solo artist, 1984-; European festivals, clubs, radio and television shows. Recordings: Albums, singles with Cortex: Troupeau Bleu; Mary & Jeff; Les Oiseaux Morts; Volume 2; Devil's Dance and Mary & Jeff Medley; Caribou; Pourquoi; Solo albums, singles: Pheno-Men; No' Mad; Alain Mion In New York, with Marc Johnson and Tom Rainey. Current Management: Rick Brown, C A Management. Address: 8811 Burton Way PH 510, Los Angeles, CA 90048-1945, USA.

MISE Marjan, b. 9 July 1952, Beograd, Croatia. Singer; Musician (drums). m. Dubravka, 22 Dec 1973, 1 son, 1 daughter. Musical Education: Elementary Musical School. Career: 16 years touring ex-USSR; Many performances in Europe; Many international festivals include: Vilach; Bratislava; Golden Orphei; Sopot; Slovenska Popeuka; Portoroz; Split. Recordings: 25 singles; 7 albums; 2 CDs; 2 compilations (in English). Honours: Many Croatian and foreign awards. Membership: Croatian Musical Union. Hobbies: Tennis; Football. Current Management: Croatian Musical Union. Address: Korculanska 6, Zagreb, Croatia.

MISHALLE Luc, b. 6 January 1953. Musician (Saxophones). 1 son. Education: Licenced Law, 1976, University Antwerp. Career: Theatre: Musical Director of Welfare State (GB); Dog Troop (NL); Internationale Nieuwe Scene (B); Music: Marakbar; Blindman Quartet; Galileo's Left Wing. Compositions: Mekove; Urbanized; Akoestisches; Winterverhalen; Metropolis; Webl; Mdawa. Recordings: Marakbar 'Live'; Marockin' Stories; Galileo's Left Wing; Blindman, Poortenbos. Current Management: VZW de Krijtkring, Watermolenstraat 35, 38500 Kortrijk. Address: Lamorinierestr 218, B2018 Antwerp, Belgium.

MITCHELL Alexander, b. 4 Nov 1969, Minster, Kent, England. Musician (guitar, midi programming). Education: Goldsmiths College. Career: Guitarist, Curve, 1991-93; Radio includes: John Peel Sessions for Radio 1; Concerts include: Glastonbury Festival; NME Stage; Major tours: USA; Europe; Japan; UK; Television includes The Beat; Now making Techno music, 2 EPs under name Choob. Recordings: Albums: Doppelganger; Cuckoo; 2 EPs (own compositions): Little Girl; Choobular. Membership: Musicians' Union. Hobbies: DJing Teckno United Systems parties. Current Management: Ms A Law. Address: 60 Crane House, Grummant Road, Peckham, London SE15 5NG, England.

MITCHELL Joni (Roberta Joan Anderson), b. 7 Nov 1943, Fort McLeod, Alberta, Canada. Singer; Songwriter; Musician (piano, guitar, ukelele). m. (1) Chuck Mitchell, 1965 (divorced), (2) Larry Klein, 1982. Education: Alberta College of Art, Calgary, 1962. Career: Duo with Chuck Mitchell, 1965; Solo singer, songwriter, 1966-; Major concerts include: Miami Pop Festival, 1968; Carnegie Hall, New York, 1969; Isle Of Wight Festival, 1970; Tours, US, Europe, with Jackson Browne, 1971; Bob Dylan's Rolling Thunder Revue, 1975; The Last Waltz (The Band's farewell concert), 1976; Playboy Jazz Festival, Hollywood Bowl, 1979; Roger Waters' The Wall, Berlin, 1990; Troubadours Of Folk Festival, 1993; Exhibition of own paintings, Canada In The City exhibition, London, 1990. Compositions include: Urge For Going, Tom Rush; Both Sides Now, Judy Collins; Woodstock, Crosby Still and Nash; This Flight Tonight, Nazareth. Recordings: Albums (own compositions): Joni Mitchell, 1968; Clouds, 1969; Ladies Of The Canyon, 1970; Blue, 1971; For The Roses, 1972; Court And Spark, 1974; Miles Of Aisles, 1974; The Hissing Of Summer Lawns, 1976; Hejira, 1976; Don Juan's Reckless Daughter, 1978; Mingus, 1979; Shadows And Light, 1980; Wild Things Run Fast, 1982; Dog Eat Dog, 1985; Chalk Mark In A Rainstorm, 1988; Night Ride Home, 1991; Turbulent Indigo, 1994; Singles include: Big Yellow Taxi, 1970; You Turn Me On, I'm A Radio, 1997; Help Me, 1974; Free Man In Paris, 1974; Good Friends, duet with Michael McDonald, 1986; Guest vocalist, You've Got A Friend, James Taylor (Number 1, US), 1971. Honours include: Grammy Awards: Best Folk Performance, Clouds, 1970; Best Arrangement (with Tom Scott), 1975; Inducted into Juno Hall Of Fame, 1981; 8 Gold discs. Address: c/o Mind Over Management, 1505 West 2nd Avenue, Suite 200, Vancouver, BC V6H 3Y4, Canada; SL Feldman And Associates, 1505 West 2nd Avenue, Suite 200, Vancouver, BC V6H 3Y4, Canada.

MITCHELL Neil, b. 8 June 1967, Helensborough, Scotland. Musician (keyboards). Career: Member, Wet Wet Wet, 1982-; Performances include: Greenpeace charity concert, Royal Albert Hall, 1986; Support to Lionel Richie, UK tour, 1987; Prince's Trust Rock Gala, London, 1988-90; The Big Day, C4, 1990; Edinburgh Castle, 1992; Nordoff-Robbins Music Therapy Centre, Royal Albert Hall, 1992; Live At The Royal Albert Hall 1992, C4, 1993. Recordings: Albums: Popped In Souled Out, 1987; Sgt Pepper Knew My Father, 1988; The Memphis Sessions, 1988; Holding Back The River, 1989; High On The Happy Side, 1992; Wet Wet Wet Live At The Royal Albert Hall, 1993; Picture This, 1995; Singles include: Wishing I Was Lucky, 1987; Sweet Little Mystery, 1987; Angel Eyes (Home And Away), 1988; Temptation, 1988; With A Little Help From My Friends (Number 1, UK), 1988; Sweet Surrender, 1989; Broke Away, 1989; Hold Back The River, 1990; More Than Love, 1992; Goodnight Girl (Number 1, UK), 1992; Lip Service, 1992; Shed A Tear, 1993; Love Is All Around (Number 1, UK), 1994; She's All On My Mind, 1995; Julia Said, 1995. Honours include: BRIT Award, Best British Newcomer, 1988. Current Management: The Precious Organisation, 14-16 Spiers Wharf, Port Dundas, Glasgow, Scotland.

MITCHELL Susan Mary, b. 27 Mar 1949, Cowbit, Lincolnshire, England. Singer. m. Bruce Robin Mitchell, 2 May 1974, 2 daughters. Musical Education: Grandmother, jazz pianist, teacher from age 4; Classical training age 30, Vaccai method. Career: First solo performance, age 7; Performed pubs, clubs, London, semi-professionally including: Shirley Halls, Canterbury Cathedral; Sang for all major local charities (Epsom and Ewell); Professional singer, all styles (jazz, folk, blues standards, music hall, comic and womens songs), 1990-. Hobby: Oil painting.

MITCHELL-DAVIDSON Paul, b. 29 Dec 1946, Bristol, England. Composer; Arranger; Musician (all guitars, mandolin, banjo). Musical Education: Self-taught. Career: Various bands, 1960s; Monad, 1971-73; Maynard Ferguson Band, US tour, 1972; Paws For Thought, 1974; Freelance session musician, also musical director, radio and television, 1970s-; Played with many top UK and US jazz musicians; Major concert at RNCM, 1995. Compositions: A Good Time Was Had By All; Earthsongs; All About Lions; Gaia; Tapestry; The Bestiary (Jazz Suite); Work for theatre, chamber, choral, orchestral music, jazz, dance, radio, television and commercial recording sessions. Recordings: Out Of My Head; The Joy Of Paranoia, with Lol Coxhill. Honours: BBC Marty Paich Award, 1991-92. Memberships: PRS; APC; BMWC; MCPS; Musicians' Union. Hobby: Reading. Current Management: Self-managed. Address: 25 Bannerman Avenue, Prestwich M25 1DZ, England.

MITON Gilles, b. 3 July 1962, Paris, France. Musician (baritone saxophone, flute). Musical Education: National Conservatory, Versaille, 1980. Career: Television show, with Eddy Mitchell, Ray Charles, Michel Legrand; Played with: Claude Bolling; Michel Legrand; Ornical Band; Arturo Sandoval; Phil Woods; Johnny Griffin; Milky Sax; Lumiere; Laurent Cugny; Super Swing Machine, Gerard Badini; Jean-Loup Longnon; Philippe Baduoin; Antoine Hervé; Quoi de Neuf Doctor; Salena Jones; Dee Dee Bridgewater; Ray Charles; Arthur H; Charles Trenet; Michel Leeb; Le Grand Orchestre du Splendid; Manu Dibango; Sacha Distel; Eddy Mitchell. Recordings: Albums with: Charles Trenet; Le Grand Orchestre Du Splendid; Eddy Mitchell; Michel Legrand; Ornicar; Gerard Badini; Philippe Badouin; Quoi De Neuf Docteur; Salena Jones.

MITSUI Toru, b. 31 March 1940, Saga, Saga, Japan. Music Professor. Education: English Literature and Folklore. Career: Professor and chair, Graduate Program in Music, Kanazawa University, Japan, 1993-; Chairman, International Association for the Study of Popular Music, 1993-97. Publications: The Aesthetics of Rock, 1976; The Michael Jackson Phenomenon, 1985; You Are My Sunshine: The Music and Politics in the American South, 1989. Address: Graduate Program in Music, Kanazawa University, Kanazawa, Ishikawa 920-11, Japan.

MIZRAKI Raf .Musician (drums, percussion, guitar, cello, dulcimer); Vocalist. Education: York University. Career: Plays with: The Dufay Collective; Arab music group, Arabesque; Soul band and various baroque orchestras; Member, The Carnival Band, 1990-; Appearances include: Glasgow Cathedral; Birmingham Symphony Hall; Barbican Centre; Arts theatres throughout UK; Plays material from: France; UK; Spain; Bolivia; US; Croatia; Sweden. Recordings: Album with Maddy Prior: Christmas Carols. Current Management: c/o Jim McPhee, Acorn Entertainments. Address: Winterfold House, 46 Woodfield Road, Kings Heath, Birmingham B13 9UJ, England.

MLINAREC Drago, b. 14 Dec 1942, Zagreb, Croatia. Composer; Musician (guitar); Vocalist; Songwriter. m. Lili Margaretha Gillstadt, 6 July 1982, 1 son, 1 daughter. Education: Chemical technician; Literature, Ethnology (not graduated). Musical Education: Basic Music School, flute. Playing publicly, 1962-; Music for theatre, films, exhibitions; Live performances, radio, TV, concerts, solo, with group. Recordings: 9 solo albums. Honours: Josip Slavenski. Memberships: HDS (Hrvatsko Drusno Skladateya); Matica Hrvatske. Hobbies: Peace; Life. Address: Bijela Gorica, Vinogradsica 3, 41293 Dubravica, Croatia.

MOBERG Sten-Erik "Pyret", b. 20 January 1947, Frösön, Sweden. Composer; Artist; Piano; Guitar. m. Karin Moberg-Hillmann, 2 sons, 1 daughter. Education: Exam, Teachers Training College, 1972; University Studies, Social Science and Pedagogics. Musical Education: Piano, Guitar and Song Studies. Career: The Threaten, TV, Theatre, 1966; The Helper, TV, Film, 1967; Hair, Sweden, Norway, 1968-70; The Diddlers, Tours in Ireland and England, 1966-70; Appearance at Olympia, Paris, 1978; TV appearances and tours in Europe. Compositions: Kärleken Ar Vit (Love is White), various Swedish songs; Another Year of Music; An Irish Saga, symphony. Recordings: Diddlers is Good For You, 1969; Hair, 1969; Kärleken Ar Vit, 1987; Another Year of Music, 1993. Publication: Ett Södermalm Som Gor Dig Varm (A South Part That Makes You Warm), 1987. Honours: STIM Award, 1990; Authors Union, 1991. Memberships: SKAP; STIM; SAMI; Theatre Union. Hobbies: Cinema; Theatre; Football; Pub Sessions. address: Brännkyrkag 75, 118 23 Stockholm, Sweden.

MOBERLEY Gary Mark, b. Sydney, New South Wales, Australia. Musician (keyboards); Composer; Writer; Programmer. Musical Education: Self-taught. Career: Live work/recorded with: The Sweet; John Miles Band; Terence Trent D'Arby; Prefab Sprout; Wet Wet Wet; The Damned; The Wild Bunch; The Alarm; Hipsway; Jodie Watley; Girlschool; Drum Theatre; Sigue Sigue Sputnik; Little Richard; Haywoode; Nicole; Big Country (remix); Loose Ends; The Associates; Talk Talk; Kiki Dee; Band Of Holy Joy; Toni Di Bart; Dangerous Grounds; Funkadelia; Steel Pulse; Trevor Horn; The JBs; ABC; Fine Young Cannibals; Live work with: Bee Gees; Paul Rodgers; Bonnie Tyler; Wilson Pickett; Eddie Floyd; Rufus Thomas; Ben E King; Arthur Conley; 28 European tours; 9 American tours; 3 world tours. Hobbies: Tennis; Cars; Cycling. Address: Flat 4, Grove End House, 150 Grove Terrace, London NW5 1PD, England.

MOBY, b. 11 September 1965, New York, New York, USA. Musician (Guitar, Drums, Keyboards); Producer; Composer; Remixer. Education: University Philosophy Student, University of Connecticut; Private Classical Education, 1976-83. Career: Production & remixes for: Metallica; Smashing Pumpkins; Michael Jackson; Depeche Mode; Soundgarden; Blur; David Bowie; Orbital; Prodigy; Freddie Mercury; Brian Eno; B-52's; Ozzy Osbourne; Guns 'n' Roses; John Lydon; Butthole Surfers; Erasure; Tours: Lollapalooza, 1995; Red Hot Chili Peppers, 1995; Soundgarden, 1996; Big Top, 1997; Prodigy, 1993, 1995; many solo tours. Recordings: Albums: Moby, 1992; Underground, 1993; Move, 1994; Ambient, 1994; Everything is Wrong, 1995; Underwater, 1995; Animal Rights, 1996; Little Idiot, 1996; Collected B-Sides, 1996; I Like to Score, 1997; The End of Everything, 1997; The Dirty Underground, 1997; Singles: That's When I Reach for My Revolver; Come on Baby; Dog Heaven; Why Can't It Stop?; Fucked Up; Higher/Desperate; Into the Blue; Everytime You Touch Me; Feeling So Real; Hymn; Move; UHF; Rock the House; James Bond Theme; Go; Drug Fits the Face; Full movie score: Double Tap, 1997; Movie soundtrakc contributions: Cool World, 1993; Heat, Scream, Joe's APartment, 1996; Tomorrow Never Dies, the Saint, The Jackal, Spawr, 1997; Gattaca, Senseless, 1998. Honours: Eveything Is Wrong, Album of the Year, Spin Magazine, 1995; Top 5 Albums of the Year, Village Voice, Entertainment Weekly & Go; Live Performer in Germany, 1995, Frontpage Magazine. Memberships: BMI; PMRS; AF of M; SAG; AFTRA. Hobby: Tennis. Current Management: c/o Mr Eric Harle, Deutsch-Englische Freundschaft Ltd, 31-33 Ansleigh Place Off Stoneleigh Place, London, W11 4BW, England. Address: c/o Mr Eric Harle, Deutsch-Englische Freundschaft Ltd, 31-33 Ansleigh Place Off Stoneleigh Place, London W11 4BW, England.

MOFFATT Hugh, b. 3 Nov 1948, Fort Worth, Texas, USA. Country Singer; Songwriter; Musician (guitar, trumpet). Education: English degree, Rice University, Houston, Texas. Career: Singer, songwriter, Nashville, 1970s; Recording artist, 1974-; Formed band Ratz, early 1980s. Compositions: Just In Case, recorded by Ronnie

Milsap, 1974; Old Flames Can't Hold A Candle To You (co-writer Pebe Sebert), recorded by Joe Sun, Dolly Parton, Foster And Allen; Wild Turkey (co-writer with Pebe Sebert), recorded by Lacy J Dalton; Love Game, recorded by Jerry Lee Lewis; Praise The Lord And Send Me The Money, recorded by Bobby Bare; Why Should I Cry Over You, (co-writer Ed Penney), recorded by George Hamilton IV; Words At Twenty Paces, recorded by Alabama. Recordings: Putting On The Ratz (EP); Dance Me Outside, (album) duet with Katy Moffatt, 1992; Albums: Loving You, 1987; Troubadour, 1989; Live And Alone, 1991; The Wognum Sessions, 1992; The Life of a Minor Poet, 1996. Address: c/o Criterion Music, 6124 Selma Avenue, Hollywood, CA 90028, USA.

MOFFATT Katherine Louella (Katy), b. 19 Nov 1950, Fort Worth, Texas, USA. Musician (guitar); Vocalist; Songwriter. Education: Sophie Newcomb College, 1968; St John's College, 1969-70. Career: Folk singer, 1967-68; Production assistant, announcer, television stations, 1970; Musician, singer, blues band Corpus Christi, 1970; Solo artiste, 1971-; On concert bills with: Muddy Waters; Everly Brothers; Willie Nelson; Warren Zevon; Musical film roles: Billy Jack; Hard Country; The Thing Called Love; Television and radio includes: Music City Tonight; Texas Connection; Nashville Now; Bobby Bare Show; National Public Radio; E-Town; World Cafe; Mountain Stage. Compositions: The Magic Ring; Kansas City Morning; Gerry's Song; Take Me Back To Texas; (Waiting For) The Real Thing; Didn't We Have Love; Co-writer, Walkin' On The Moon (with Tom Russell). Recordings: Singles include: Take It As It Comes, 1981; Under Loved And Over Lonely, 1983; Albums: Katy; Kissin' In The California Sun; Walkin' On The Moon; The Greatest Show On Earth; A Town South Of Bakersfield; Hearts Gone Wild; Child Bride; Dance Me Outside; Sleepless Nights; Midnight Radio. Honours: Record World Album Award, 1976; Cash Box Single Award, 1976; ACM Nomination, Best New Female Vocalist, 1985; Best Singer-Songwriter, Fort Worth Weekly, 1997. Memberships: AFofM; AFTRA; SAG; NARAS. Address: PO Box 334, O'Fallon, IL 62269, USA.

MOFFETT Johnathan Phillip, b. 17 Nov 1954, New Orleans, Louisiana, USA. Musician (drums); Musical Director; Songwriter. m. Rhonda Bartholomew, 26 June 1976, 1 son, 1 daughter. Career: Drummer for artists including: Patti Austin; Cameo; Lionel Richie; Madonna; Tina Marie; Jermaine Jackson; Major tours and concerts with: The Jacksons, 1979-81, Victory Tour (also as set designer), 1984; Elton John world tours, 1988-89; Madonna, Virgin and Ciao Italia tours; George Michael, Rock In Rio Festival; Musical director for concerts by Jermaine Jackson, Michael Jackson; Numerous television and video appearances with: The O'Jays; Isaac Hayes; The Kane Gang; Cameo. Recordings: Albums include: Silk Electric, Diana Ross, 1982; Victory, The Jacksons, 1984; One More Story, Peter Cetera, 1988; Back To Avalon, Kenny Loggins, 1988; Also recorded with Julian Lennon; Richard Marx; Jody Watley; Chico de Barge.

MOGG Phil, b. 1951, London, England. Rock Vocalist. Career: Founder member, UK rock group UFO, 1969-83; Reformed twice, 1985, 1991; Regular worldwide tours. Recordings: Albums: UFO, 1971; UFO 2 - Flying, 1971; Live In Japan, 1972; Phenomenon, 1974; Force It, 1975; No Heavy Pettin', 1976; Lights Out, 1977; Obsession, 1978; Strangers In The Night, 1979; No Place To Run, 1980; The Wild, The Willing And The Innocent, 1981; Mechanix, 1982; Making Contact, 1982; Headstone, 1983; Misdemeanour, 1985; Ain't Misbehavin', 1988; High Stakes And Dangerous Men, 1992; Hit singles include: Doctor, Doctor; Too Hot To Handle; Lights Out; Rock Bottom. Current Management: Singerman Entertainment, Penthouse West, 8833 Sunset Blvd, Los Angeles, CA 90069, USA.

MOHAMED Pops, b. 10 Dec 1949, Benoni, Johannesburg, South Africa. Musician (piano-synthesiser programming, keyboards, kora, mbira, didgeridu, berimbau, marimba, percussion). Divorced, 2 sons, 1 daughter. Musical Education: Studied Jazz at FUBA, 1979-1984; Studied traditional instruments, 1986-93. Career: Lead guitarist, Les Valiants, 1969-71; Band leader: The Dynamics: El Gringoes; Society's Children; Solo albums, 1975-; Black Disco, 1975; Night Express, 1976; Black Disco 3, 1978; Movement In The City, 1979; Award as original artist for Towntalk Show, 1979; Albums: BM Movement, 1980; Innercity Funk, 1981; Recording Engineer, 1981-87; Record Producer, 1988-95; Own record label Kalamazoo Music, 1993. Compositions: Lolly's Song; A New Hope!, 1995; African Sketches; A New Hope. Recordings: When In New York, 1993. Publications: Kalamazoo Music. Honours: South African OKTV Music Awards Nominations, 1991, 1992. Memberships: Royal Schools and Federated Union Of Black Arts. Hobbies: Traditional music; Squash. Current Management: Kalamazoo Music Productions. Address: 202 Bethlen, 13th Street, Orange Grove, 2192 Johannesburg, Gauteng, South Africa.

MOLDEN Nigel Charles, b. 17 Aug 1948, Oxford, England. Music Company Director. m. Hilary Julia Lichfield, 14 Aug 1971, 3 sons. Education: Bsc (Hons) London University; MSc Brunel University; PhD, Fairfax University. Musical Education: Piano Grade 2. Career: International General Manager, WEA Records, 1971-1980; International Marketing Manager, Thorn EMI Video, 1980-1984; Joint Chief Executive, TKO Magnum Music, 1994-. Honours: Freeman, City of London, 1990. Memberships: FRSA; FCIM; FBIM; FinstD. Address: Ashcombe House, Deanwood Road, Jordans, Buckinghamshire HP9 2UU, England.

MÖLLER Carl, b. 19 Sept 1942, Reykjavik, Iceland. Musician (piano, keyboard); Composer. m. Olof Kristin Magnusdottir, 6 Jan 1979. Education: Private piano lessons with several prominent teachers; Graduate, Reykjavik College of Musicians; Teacher in General Music Education, 1983. Career: Several television and radio appearances with Icelandic singer Haukur Morthens; Appearances on raio and television with own band; Played in all major jazz festivals in Iceland, Norway and London; Currently teaching in the Musical School of Hafnafjordur and the Jazz Department of the FIH School. Compositions: Jazz composition with Icelandic lyric poets and jazz suite, Fourth Dimension; Pslam-Tune with lyrics by Oddson David. Recordings: with sextet Olafs Gauks: Tunes from the Westman Island; Various other recordings. Membership: Musicians' Union of Iceland (FIH). Address: Lambhagi 20, 225 Riftanes, Iceland.

MØLLER Lars Allesø, b. 17 Sept 1966, Copenhagen, Denmark. Musician (tenor saxophone); Composer. Musical Education: Lessons with David Liebman, 5 years; BFA, New School, New York, 1989; Studying composition with Bob Brookmeyer, Rytmekons Conservatory, Copenhagen; Indian classical music studies, New Delhi, 1990-94. Career: Own groups, with Jimmy Cobb, Niels-Henning, Ørsted Pedersen, Billy Hart, Mads Vinding, Alex Riel, Jukkis Outila, Thomas Clausen and John Abercrombie, 1986-91; Concerts in Canada, USA, France, Italy, Sweden, Germany, Norway and India; Television and radio broadcasts in Europe and USA; Featured soloist with Jimmy Cobb Sextet, Hermeto Pascoal Group, European Youth Big Band and European Broadcasting Union Big Band; Also played with Holmes Brothers and various Danish bands such as Sound of Choice Ensemble, with Markus Stockhausen; Played with leading artists including: Lee Konitz, Jimmy Cobb, Adam Nussbaum, Art Blakey, Roy Haynes and David Liebman; Member, Den 3 Vej (composer workshop group); Leader, 18-piece group The Orchestra Big Band, 1997-.

Compositions: Works for small jazz groups, symphony orchestra, chamber orchestra, string quartet, big band and choir. Recordings include: Copenhagen Groove, with Niels-Henning Ørsted Pedersen, 1989; Pyramid, 1993; Cross Current, 1995; Circles, 1996; Colours, with John Abercrombie, 1997. Honours: Honorary prize from Danish Jazz Beat and Folk Authors Society (DJBFA). Address: Valdemarsgade 13 st, tv, DK-1665 Copenhagen V, Denmark.

MOLLISON Deborah, b. 29 May 1958, England. Composer; Musician (piano). m. Gareth Mollison, 3 May 1986. Musical Education: Piano and Composition, Royal Academy Of Music; Master's degree, studied piano with Craig Sheppard, Lancaster University; Film Music course at UCLA; Classical composer; Tutor of Composition, Middlesex University. Compositions: Music for films: Stand Up The Real Glynn Vernon; Go On Make A Wish; Vampires; Television drama, The Gift Of the Nile, Primetime TV; Sleeping With Mickey, BBC2; Before Your Eyes, BBC Wales; The Whistling Boy, BBC Wales; Television documentaries: Treasures At The South Pole, NBC; Thomas Cook On The Nile, Case TV; Connections 2, Discovery Channel; Given Half A Chance, Vanson Wardle Productions; Crossrail, London Transport Authority. Honours: Else Cross Prize, Royal Academy of Music; Song '92 UK Festival. Memberships: PRS; BASCA; Women In Film; Musicians' Union. Current Management: Soundtrack Music Management, 22 Ives Street, Chelsea, London SW3 2ND, England.

MOLLOY Christopher John, b. 20 Mar 1956, Hastings, New Zealand. Artist and Tour Manager. 1 son, 1 daughter. Education: Final year BA, Philosophy, Anthropology. Musical Education: Self-taught. Career: Bass player, punk band The Primmers, New Zealand, 1979; Booking agent, The Harbour Agency, Sydney, 1980-84; Artist and Tour Manager, various artists, Australia, UK, 1984-; Concert co-ordinator, several major outdoor concerts, Australia; Manage artist called Vylinda. Membership: International Managers Forum (London). Hobbies: Guitar; Fishing. Address: 50 Bonnington Square, Vauxhall, London SW8 1TQ, England.

MOLONEY Paddy, b. 1938, Donnycarney, Dublin, Ireland. Folk Musician (uillean pipes, tin whistle). Career: Member, Ceolteoiri Chaulann Folk Orchestra, led by Sean O'Raida, 1950s; Founder member, Irish folk group, The Chieftains, 1964-; Collaborations with classical flute player, James Galway. Recordings: Albums: Chieftains 1, 1964; Chieftains 2, 1969; Chieftains 3, 1971; Chieftains 4, 1973; Chieftains 5, 1975; Women Of Ireland, 1976; Bonaparte's Retreat, 1976; Chieftains Live, 1977; Chieftains 7, 1977; Chieftains 8, 1978; Vol 9, 1979; Boil The Breakfast Early, 1980; Chieftains 10, 1981; The Chieftains In China, 1984; Ballad Of The Irish Horse, 1985; Celtic Wedding, 1987; The Chieftains In Ireland (with James Galway), 1987; Year Of The French, 1988; Irish Heartbeat (with Van Morrison), 1988; A Chieftains Celebration, 1989; Chieftains Collection, 1989; The Celtic Connection - James Galway And The Chieftains, 1990; Bells Of Dublin, 1991; An Irish Evening, 1992; Another Country, 1992; The Celtic Harp (with Belfast Harp Orchestra), 1993; The Fire Aflame (with Sean Keane, Matt Molloy, Liam O'Flynn), 1993. Current Management: S L Feldman and Associates, 1505 West 2nd Street, Suite 200, Vancouver, BC V6H 3Y4, Canada.

MOMCHIL, b. Bulgaria. Musician (keyboards); Vocalist; Songwriter; Arranger. Career: Keyboard player, new wave band Class, -1993; Formed duo, Dony & Monchil, 1993-; Numerous tours, Bulgaria. Recordings: Albums: The Album!, 1993; The Second One, 1994. Honours: Orpheus National Music Awards: Best Single: The Little Prince; Best Video For Duo Or A Group. Address: c/o Union Media, 71 Evl Georgiev Blvd, Sofia 1142, Bulgaria.

MONAGHAN Brendan, b. 3 Apr 1958, Newtownards, County Down, Ireland. Singer; Songwriter; Musician (guitar). m. Valerie McDonnell, 6 Sept 1980, 2 sons, 1 daughter. Musical Education: Basic. Career: Appearances with band The Cattle Company include major country festivals, Europe; Television and radio appearances, Ireland, Europe; USA; Cable television includes: Canada, USA. Composition: I'm Right, You're Wrong, I Win. Recordings: with Cattle Company: Hero (debut album); Love to Be Loved; Featured on album Alive In Belfast; Solo: Sister's Lament; Johnny Got Married. Honours: Top Performance Award, International Country Music Festival, Netherlands; Publishers Award, Ray Shepherd Music, Efforts In Country Music; European Country Music Associations, Best European Group, 1995. Memberships: PRS; International Songwriters Association; BMI, USA. Current Management: David Hull Promotions Ltd, Belfast. Address: 9 Stratford Drive, Bangor, COunty Down BT19 6ZW, Ireland.

MONCK Jack, b. 14 Mar 1950, London, England. Musician (bass guitar); Songwriter. Partner, Belinda Harvey, 2 sons, 1 daughter. Education: Cambridge Technical College. Musical Education: Self-taught. Career: Bass player, Bruno's Blues Band; Concerts with Alexis Korner, tours with Otis Span and Lowell Fulsom, 1968-70; Renamed band Delivery; Moved to Cambridge, played in trio with Fred Frith, Chris Cutker, and band Stars, 1970-73; Moved to London, 1974; Joined Radar Favourites; Bands in London area included: Mike Khan Band; Jon Owen Band; Writing and recording own songs, 1980-81; Concerts, American airbases, 1983; European tour with David Thomas and the Pedestrians, 1984; Formed That Uncertain Feeling, 1985; Band continued as Chan/Monck Group, 1986-87; Formed Relatives, 1988; Co-formed, played in London groups: Don't Let That Horse Eat That Violin; Symphony Sid; Played with Ricky Anderson Band; Tours with Relatives, Netherlands and Belgium, 1989-91; Writing, recording Illuminations, 1992; Formed The Highly Irregulars, 1994; Played in band for Shakers at Nottingham Playhouse. Recordings: Tracks releasd on Variations On A Theme, 1982; Inside The Whale, album of own songs, 1983. Membership: Musicians' Union. Address: Hackney, East London, England.

MONDESIR Michael Trevor Collins, b. 6 Feb 1966, London, England. Musician (bass guitar); Composer. Musical Education: Self-taught. Career: Performed with Django Bates; Billy Cobham; Hermeto Pascoal; Pee Wee Ellis; Lenny White; Neneh Cherry; Jason Rebello; Annette Peacock; Bernard Purdie; Little Axe; Tackhead; Infinitum; Nikki Yeoh. Recordings: Keeping Time, Jason Rebello, 1992; Summer Fruits (And Unrest), Django Bates, 1993; The Traveller, Billy Cobham, 1994; Winter Truce (And Homes Blaze), Django Bates, 1995. Memberships: PRS; Musicians' Union. Hobbies: Cooking; Drawing; Painting; Reading. Address: 97A Hamlets Way, London E3 4TL, England.

MONLEY Julie (Julianne Margaret), b. 1 Mar 1954, Denver, Colorado, USA. Musician; Singer. m. Frederic Desmoulin, 27 Feb 1987, 2 daughters. Musical Education: Private lessons classical jazz. Career: Jazz Valley Festival, MJC club Dunkerque; Radio and television: France Music; Live radio: Vous En Moi; Radio shows in Denver. Honours: Second Prize, Tremplin Jazz, 1995; First Prize, Vocalist Jazz à Vienne, 1996. Membership: Jazz On The Blocks, Paris. Hobby: Painting. Current Management: Self-managed. Address: 69 Blvd Barbes, 75018 Paris, France.

MONRAD Jan, b. 18 Mar 1951, Copenhagen, Denmark. Writer; Composer; Comedian. 1 son, 1 daughter. Musical Education: Teachers Seminarium. Career: Member of band Monrad and Rislund, with Søren Rislund; Several radio and television shows since 1977; Tours of Denmark and Greenland. Compositions: The Championship in Teddybear-Petting, 1993; The Statesman's Funeral, 1994. Recordings: 16 albums with Monrad and Rislund, 1976-; 1991, 1981; Jesus and Jens Vejmand, 1983; Dogstars Hospitalized, 1990; Goodbye Aage, 1994; 18 recordings and 1 video, 1976-. Publications: Black Sketches; Beske Barske Rimom Barn og Andre Kendisser. Honour: Danish Grammy Award, Entertainment Records, 1995. Memberships: DJBFA; Dansk Solistforbund. Hobbies: Old advertisement boards; Tramways. Address: Kongensvej 26, 2000 Frederiksberg, Denmark.

MONTANA Patsy (Rubye B Rose), b. Hot Springs, Arkansas, USA. Musician (violin, guitar). m. Paul E Rose, 3 July 1934, 2 daughters. Musical Education: Violin. Career: Over 50 years touring; Most recent appearances: David Letterman Show, NBC; Women In Country Music, CBS; Tribute To The Cowboys, TNN; BBC, London; WLS Barn Dance (15 years). Recordings: I Want To Be A Cowboy's Sweetheart, first million seller for a woman in country and western music. Honours: Pioneer Award; Cowgirl Hall Of Fame. Memberships: ASCAP; SAG; AFTRA; WMA; AFL. Hobbies: Homemaking; Sewing. Current Management: R B Rose. Address: 21100 Hi-Way 79, Box 147, San Jacinto, CA 92583, USA.

MONTANARO Miqueù (Michel François), b. 13 Aug 1955, Hyères, France. Composer; Musician (flutes, saxophone, accordion, piano); Actor. m. Niké Nagy, 29 Apr 1981, 2 sons, 1 daughter. Education: Teaching diploma. Musical Education: Self-taught; Masters for folk music. Career: First concert, Edinburgh, 1973; Tours, Hungary; Bulgaria; Austria; Italy; Portugal; USA; Indonesia; Algeria; Morocco; Tunisia; West Africa; Television: Hungary; Portugal; France (France 3, Cercle de Minuit, France 2); Radio: France Inter; France Culture; France Musique; Festivals include: Bamako; St Chartier; Nantes; Budapest; Comboscuro; Plays with: B Phillips; Kiss Tamàs; Konomba Traore; A Vitous; P Aledo; G Murphy; Téka; F Frith; Vujicsics; C Tyler; Sebastyén Màrta; P Neveu; Ghymes; F Richard; J Stivin; C Brazier; D Daumas; F Kop; D Regef; C Zagaria; K Ruzicka; Szabados; F Ulihr; P Vaillant; A Gabriel; J Lyonn Lieberman; L Andrst; J N Mabelly; D Phillips; Es Soundoussia; F Gaudé; S Pesce; Hayet Ayad; Christine Wodrascka; Samia Benchikh; Senem Diyici; René Sette; Mathieu Luzi; Nena Venetsanou; Sara Alexander; Michel Bianco; Carlo Rizzo; Corou de Berra; Wayal. Composition: Cri, for symphonic orchestra and traditional instruments, 1997. Recordings: More than 40 include: Albums: Montanaro/Collage, Bonton, 1990; Mesura & Arte del Danzare, 1992; Tenson - La Nef Des Musiques, Bleu Regard, 1993; Vents d'Est/Migrations, 1993; Montanaro/Théâtre, 1994; Galoubet-Tambourin, Musiques d'Hier Et Aujourdhui, 1995; with L'Ensemble Méditerranéen P Aledo: Fusion; D'île En Ile; Tres Corpos Una Alma; Java Sapto Raharjo, 1997; Vents d'Est Ballade pour une Mer qui Chante, 1997. Publications: Video K7 Noir & Blanc with Konomba Traore, CNDP, France. Memberships: ADAMI; SPEDIDAM; SACEM; SFA. Hobbies: Walking; Skiing; Canoeing; Planting trees; Gardening. Current Management: Sylvie Bondier. Address: Grande Fontaine, 83570 Correns, France.

MONTAUT Jean-Marc, b. 19 May 1963, Montauban, France. Jazz Musician (piano). Education: Bac B, Faculté d'Histoire. Musical Education: 3 years classical piano; Self-taught jazz. Career: Concerts with Pierre Boussaguet; Stéphane Belmondo; Jean-Loup Longnon; Daniel Huck; Tuxedo Big Band; Warren Vaché; Principal clubs and festivals; Duet, songwriting partner, Louis Mazetier. Recordings: Blue Stompin Live In Montauban Jazz Festival, 1991; Big Band Turquoise, 1995; Banana Jazz, 1996. Hobbies: Classical and jazz music; Films; Nature; John Williams' music. Address: 24 Rue du Petit Clora, 63400 Chamaliéres, France.

MONTENEGRO Oswaldo, b. 15 Mar 1956, Rio de Janeiro, Brazil. Composer; Singer; Author and Director, Musical Plays; Musician (guitar, piano). 1 son. Education: Communication Course, University of Brazil. Musical Education: Musical Course, University of Rio de Janeiro. Career: Tours, Brazil, 1979-; TV, radio appearances, concerts, Portugal, -1992; Shows in New Jersey; Connecticut; Boston; Miami; Orlando; Mount Vernon; Author and director, musical plays including: Veja Você Brasilia, 1981; Cristal, 1982; A Dança Dos Signos, 1983-87; Os Memestréis, 1985; Aldeia Dos Ventos, 1986; Vale Encantado, 1993; Noturno, 1993; Mayâ, 1992. Compositions include: Bandolins; Lua e Flor; Condor; Seo e Bia; Furtuição; Estrelas; Voz da Tela. Recordings: Trilhas, 1978; Poeta Maldito, Moleque Vadio, 1979; Oswaldo Montenegro Ao Viva, 1980; Asa De Lux, 1981; A Dança Dos Signos, 1982; Cristal, 1983; Os Menestréis, 1984; Drops De Hortelã, 1985; Aldeia Dos Ventos, 1986; Oswaldo Montenegro, 1989; Ao Viva, 1990; Vida de Artista, 1991; Mulungo, 1992; Seu Francisco, 1993; Aos Filhos Dos Hippies, 1995. Honours: 3rd place of honour, with composition, Bandolins, TV Tupi Music Festival, 1979; 1st place of honour, with Agonia, TV Globo Brazilian Popular Music Festival, 1980; Gold Disc, Oswaldo Montenegro, 1989; Platinum disc, Visda de Artista, 1991. Memberships: UBC; SBAT; Warner-Chappell. Hobbies: Movies; Sports. Current Management: Newton Montenegro. Address: R Viscondede Pirajá51, ap 502, Ipanema, Rio de Janeiro, RJ, Brazil.

MONTERA Jean-Marc, b. 6 June 1955, Marseilles, France. Musician (guitar, homemade instruments). 1 son. Musical Education: Self-taught. Career: Festivals (jazz and improvsing music): Rome; LeMans; Ulrichberg; Raab; Münster; Rive de Gier; Grenoble; Banlieues Bleues; Music Action Nancy; Palermo; Lisbon; Ragusa. Recordings include: Hang Around Shout. Memberships: SACEM; GEMA; ADAMI; SPEDIDAM. Current Management: Inclinaison (Marion Piras, Pierre Louis Philippe). Address: 180 Rue de l'Hermitage, 34070 Montpellier, France.

MONTREDON Jean-Claude Pierre, b. 23 Sept 1949, Martinique. Musician (drums); Composer. Musical Education: Self-taught. Career: Member, Frères Bernard Orchestra, Tropicana Orchestra; Drums for Marius Cultier and The Surfs; Formed trio with Alain Jean Marie, Winston Berkley; Performances in Barbados, Trinidad, 1972; Bilboquet, Paris jazz club, French Radio, 1973-75; Founder, Kominkayson, with Richard Raux, Michel Alibo, 1976; Appearances include: Palais de Congrès, Paris; Cultural Center, Martinique, 1976; Played with Didier Levellet Quintet, Chris McGregor, New Morning Jazz Club, Paris, 1977-; Rock concerts with Randy Weston, Claude Sommier, Michel Alibo, 1978-81; Tours, Finland, Sweden, West Africa, with Roland Brival, 1981; Played with Liquid Rock Stonne, Paris; Appearances include France Musique, classical radio station; Sermac Dance Workshop, Martinique, 1983; Jazz Festival, Barbados; Jazz and Folk Festival, Martinique, 1985; Caribbean Jazz Workshop, Berlin; Festival of Trinidad, 1986; Barbados Festival, with West Indies Jazz Band; Caribbean Jazz Workshop, 1987; Olympia, Paris, 1988; Tours, West Indies, South Africa, 1989; Founder, The Musical Corps of Martinique, 1990-94; Currently performs with own band Kominkayson, works with Luther François. Recordings: Malavoi, Tropicana Orchestre; Gisèle Baka; Al Lirvart and Didier Levellet Quintet; Brotherhood Of Breath; Joby Bernabe; Doudou Guirand; 2 albums with The Caribbean Ensemble; West Indies Jazz Band, 1990; 1992; Luther François, 1990. Memberships: SACEM; SPEDIDAM; Congés Spectacle. Hobbies:

Créations; Film music. Address: 131 Rue de Rome, 75017 Paris, France.

MONTROSE Ronnie, b. Colorado, USA. Rock Musician (guitar). Career: Founder, Montrose, 1973-76; Solo artiste, 1976-77; Founder, Gamma, 1978-83; Solo artiste, 1984-. Recordings: Albums: with Montrose: Montrose, 1974; Paper Money, 1975; Jump On It, 1976; Solo albums: Open Fire, 1978; Territory, 1986; Mean, 1987; The Speed Of Sound, 1988; The Diva Station, 1990; with Gamma: 1, 1979; 2, 1980; 3, 1982.

MOODY James, b. 26 March 1925, Savannah, GA, USA. Musician (Tenor, Alto, Soprano, Saxophone, Flute). m. Linda Petersen Moody, 3 April 1989. Education: US Air Force Band Theory, Composition with Dizzy Gillespie, Composition and Theory with Tom McIntosh with Michael Longo. Career: Teachings: Cornell University, Ithaca, New York; Harvard University, Cambridge, Massachusetts; Howard University, Washington, DC; Loyola University, New Orleans, Louisiana; Stanford University, Palo Alto, California; University of Alabama; University of Florida, Gainesville, Florida; Major Performances include: Dizzy Gillespie's 70th Birthday Celebration, televised; Requently appeared in USA, Egypt, Japan, Israel, Canada, Germany including Johnny Carson's Tonight Show and The Ben Sidran Show in New York; Carneo role, Clint Eastwood's film, Midnight in The Garden of Good and Evil; Radio: Voice of America, hosted by Willis Conover, numerous times; Interviews and concerts on many stations in USA and most European countries. Compositions: Moody's Mood for Love; Honey's Tune, with Linda Moody; Look Into My Eyes; It's a One-Way Road; Love, Where Are You?; Never Again; Simplicity and Beauty; The Television Song; You Better Believe It; Everyone Needs It; Coffee Break; He Whispered He Loved Her; Feelin' Low; Love Was the Cause; Put Your Shoes on Baby; I Saw a Flying Saucer; Hey Herbi; Where's Alpert?; Don't Throw Your Back Out-A Whack; Diskom-blu-ba-late Me, Baby; What Do You Do; Moody's Theme; Shake, Rattle and Boogie; Recordings: Moody's Mood for Love, 1951; Last Train from Overbrook, 1958; Sweet and Lovely, 1989; Honey, 1991; Live at the Blue Note, 1995; Young at Heart, 1996; Moody Plays Mancini, 1997; Flute 'N the Blues, Chess; Never Again, Muse; Cookin the Blues, Cadet; Hey - Its James Moody, Argo. Publications include: Jazz Giants: A Visual Retrospective; The Eye of Jazz; Jazz is by Nat Hentoff; Jazz Styles: History and Analysis by Mark C Gridley; The Jazz Years: Earwitness to an Era by Leonard Feather; The Record Collector's Handbook by Alan Leibowitz. Honours include: James Moody Day, 1993; 1996; Jamaica Hall of Fame, 1996; New Jersey Hall of Fame, 1996; International Hall of Fame, 1996; National Endowment for the Arts Jazz Masters Award, 1998. Memberships: National Association of Recording Arts and Sciences, International Association of Jazz Educators; National Jazz Service Organization. Hobbies: Health and Fitness; Tennis; Swimming; Books; Astronomy. Address: 36 Como Street, Romford, Essex RM7 7DR, England.

MOOG Robert Arthur, b. 23 May 1934, Flushing, New York, USA. Music Company Executive; Musical Instrument Designer. m. Shirley Leigh, 15 June 1958, 1 son, 3 daughters. Education: BS Physics, Queens College, 1957; BSEE, Columbia University, 1957; PhD Engineering Physics, Cornell University, 1965. Career: President, Moog Music Inc, 1954-77; President, Big Briar Inc, 1978; Vice President, new product research, Kurzweil Music Systems, 1984-88; Designer, synthisizers, including Moog synthesizer, 1967; Mini-Moog, 1971; Polymoog, 1976; Pedal-operated Taurus system; Memory Moog; Exponents include: Walter Carlos; Keith Emerson; Jan Hammer; Rush. Publications: Contributor, professional journals. Honours:

Honorary doctorates, Lycoming College, 1975; New York Polytechnic University, 1985; NARAS Trustees Award; Trendsetter Award, Billboard Magazine, 1970; Silver Medal, Audio Engineering Society, 1984; Fellow, Audio Engineering Society.

MOONEY Gordon James, b. 27 May 1951, Edinburgh, Scotland. Piper; Musician; Planner; Businessman. m. 17 Ar 1978, 1 son, 1 daughter. Education: BSc Town Planning, Dundee University. Musical Education: Traditional from age 7: Highland bagpipes, border pipes, Northumbrian smallpipes. Career: Concerts include: Edinburgh International Festival; Sanders Tagare, Harvard, Boston; Old Songs Festival, USA; Tacoma University, USA; Quebec Double Reed Convention; Vermont Bagpipe Festival; Television and radio appearances: Border TV; Canadian National Radio; BBC; Radio Scotland; Radio 4; World Service. Recordings: O'er The Border; Global Meditation; Song For Yarrow; Leading Figure, Scottish Music Revival. Publications: 3 collections of music; 1 tutor book. Honours: Scottish Arts Council Award, 1988; Billboard Award, 1993. Memberships: MPRS; President of Lowland and Border Pipes Society. Hobbies: Walking the high places; Archaeology; Building. Current Management: Traditional music. Address: 4 High Street, Melrose, Roxburghshire TD6 4PB, Scotland.

MOONEY Tim, b. 6 Oct 1958, Las Vegas, Nevada, USA. Musician (drums, keyboards, guitar); Songwriter. Education: Self-taught. Career: Member of groups: Sleepers, 1977-79; Negative Trend, 1979-81; Toiling Midgets, 1982-92; American Music Club, 1992-95; Toured with Pearl Jam and Bob Dylan; Various BBC television appearances; Appeared at Reading and Glastonbury festivals. Recordings: with Sleepers: Seventh World, 1978; with Negative Trend: Beach Boulevard, Tooth and Nail, 1979; with Toiling Midgets: Sea Of Unrest, 1982; Deadbeat, 1984; Son, 1992; with American Music Club: Mercury, 1993, San Francisco, 1994; with Li'l Tiger: Live, Work, Know, Growl, 1998. Hobby: Restoring and driving "muscle cars" of the 1960s. Current Management: Bennett Management, 549 14th Avenue, San Francisco, CA 94118, USA.

MOORE Abra, b. 8 June, Mission Bay, CA, USA. Siner; Songwriter; Musician (Guitar). Education: University of Hawaii. Career: Founding Member, Poi Dog Pondering, Solo Artist, toured with Matthew Sweet!, Barenaked Ladies; Medeski, Martin & Wood, Third Eye Blind, Collective Soul, Lilith Fair and Big Head Todd and the Monsters; Appeared in feature films, Slacker and The Newton Boys; Sliding Doors, 1998; TV appearances on VH-1, E!, VH-1 (UK), CNN Showbiz Today; Live with Regis and Kathylee, Fox Live; Appearances on MTI and Westwood One Syndicated Radio. Recordings: Solo albums: Sing, 1995; Strangest Places, 1997; Singles: Four Leaf Clover, 1997; Don't Feel Like Cryin, 1997. Publications: Contributor of national and international music magazines, newspapers and journals. Membership: AFTRA. Current Management: Tim Neece Management, 13101 Highway 71 West, Austin, TX 78736, USA. Address: 13101 Highway 71 West, Austin, TX 78736, USA.

MOORE Becki, b. 21 Apr 1948, Louisa, Virginia, USA. Singer; Songwriter; Entertainer; Fashion Designer. m. Mickey Moore, 17 Jan 1970, 1 son, 1 daughter. Education: BFA Fashion Design, Virginia Commonwealth University. Musical Education: Piano; Guitar; Performance; Voice. Career: As Mickey and Becki Moore, performances: Jesus Northwest; Jesus Orlando; Creation; Fishnet; Television: 700 Club; Ross Bayley Show; 100 Huntley Street (Canada); Joe Franklin Show; I Care, TV Special with Pat Boone; PTL Club Campmeetings. Recordings: Albums include: Everything Is Under Contrrol, Wo Wo, 1976; Studio And Live, 1977; Brand New, 1979;

Love Song For Number Two, 1981; Mickey And Becki Moore, 1984; Keep Me Keeping On, 1991; Tell Me A Story Before I Go To Bed (childrens album), 1987. Membership: SESAC. Current Management: PO Box 777, Trevilians, VA 23170, USA.

MOORE Bob Loyce, b. 30 Nov 1932, Nashville, Tennessee, USA. Musician (bass); Record Producer. Career: Bassist for various artists including: Little Jimmy Dickens, 1949; Red Foley, 1950; Owen Bradley, 1951-66; Elvis Presley, 1963-71; Crystal Gayle, 1982-84; Co-owner, Monument Records, 1961-70; Record producer for Jerry Lee Lewis; George Jones; Johnny Cash; Boxcar Willie; Roy Orbison; President, K&K Productions, 1986-; President, Bob Moore Music, 1963-; Prolific studio musician, over 17,000 recording sessions for artists including: Kenny Rogers; Tammy Wynette; Don McLean; Hank Williams Jr; Tom Jones; Willie Nelson; Dolly Parton; Patsy Cline; Jim Reeves; Frank Sinatra; Simon And Garfunkel; Johnny Cash; Roy Orbison; Conway Twitty; Loretta Lynn; Brenda Lee; Ernest Tubb; Andy Williams; Connie Francis; The Statler Brothers; Clyde McFatter; Marty Robbins; Eddy Arnold; Kitty Wells. Honours: NARAS, Most Valuable Player Awards, 1979-82; Most Recording Session in History; AFofM; Numerous Superpicker Awards. Memberships: AFofM; NARAS.

MOORE Christy, b. 7 May 1945, Dublin, Ireland. Singer; Songwriter; Musician (guitar). Career: Solo folk performer, club circuit, Ireland and England, 1960s; Recording artiste, 1969-; Founder member, Planxty, 1969-75, 1979-80; Involved in Anti-Nuclear Roadshow, mid 1970s; Founder, Moving Hearts, 1981; Solo artiste, 1982-. Recordings: Albums: Paddy On The Road (with Dominc Behan), 1969; Prosperous, 1971; Whatever Tickles Your Fancy, 1975; Christy Moore, 1976; The Iron Behind The Velvet, 1978; Live In Dublin, 1978; The Spirit Of Freedom, 1983; The Time Has Come, 1983; Ride On, 1984; Ordinary Man, 1985; Nice'N'Easy, 1986; Unfinished Revolution, 1987; Voyage, 1989; Smoke And Strong Whiskey, 1991; The Christy Moore Collection, 1991; Live At The Point, 1994; with Planxty: After The Break, 1979; Woman I Loved So Well, 1980. Current Management: Mattie Fox Management, Derynell, Ballinlee, Co. Longford, Ireland.

MOORE Dudley Stuart John, b. 19 Apr 1935. Actor; Composer; Musician (piano). m (1) Suzy Kendall, 1958; m (2) Tuesday Weld, 1975; (3) Brogan Lane, 1988; (4) Nicole Rothschild, 1994. Education: Magdalen College, Oxford. Career: Theatre: Beyond The Fringe, London, 1960-62; Broadway, New York, 1962-64; Play It Again Sam, London, 1970; Behind The Fringe, London, 1972-73; Good Evening Broadway, 1973-74; Royal Command Performance; Tours with own jazz piano trio; Television appearances includes: Not Only...But Also (comedy series with Peter Cook), 1965-70; Goodbye Again; It's Lulu, Not To Mention Dudley Moore; Actor, numerous films including: The Hound Of The Baskervilles; Foul Play; 10; Arthur; Romantic Comedy; Micki And Maude; Best Defense; Santa Claus; Like Father, Like Son; Arthur 2; On The Rocks; Crazy People; Blame It On The Bellboy. Compositions include: Incidental music for Royal Court Theatre productions; Bedazzled; Thirty Is A Dangerous Age Cynthia; The Staircase; Six Weeks. Recordings: Beyond The Fringe And All That Jazz; The Other Side Of Dudley Moore; Today; Dudley Moore Trio Down Under; Dudley Moore And Cleo Laine - Smilin' Through; The Music Of Dudley Moore; Songs Without Words. Publications: Dud And Pete - The Dagenham Dialogues, 1971; Dudley Moore - Offbeat, 1986; The Complete Beyond The Fringe, 1987; Voices Of Survival, 1988. Honours include: Golden Globe Award, Arthur, 1983; Golden Globe Award, Micki And Maude, 1985. Hobbies: Films; Theatre; Music.

Address: c/o Louis Pitt, ICM, 8899 Beverly Boulevard, Los Angeles, CA 90048, USA.

MOORE Gary, b. 4 Apr 1952, Belfast, Northern Ireland. Musician (guitar). Career: Formed Skid Row, 1968; Formed Gary Moore Band, 1973; Guitarist with Thin Lizzy, 1974, 1977-79; Member, Colisseum II, 1975, 1977; Formed G-Force, 1979; Solo career, 1982-; Worked with various artists including: Phil Lynott; Ozzy Osbourne; Albert Collins; Albert King; B B King. Recordings: Singles include: Parisienne Walkways; Over The Hills And Far Away; Cold Day In Hell; Albums: with Skid Row: Skid Row, 1970; 34 Hours, 1971; with Gary Moore Band: Grinding Stone, 1973; with Thin Lizzy: Night Life, 1974; Black Rose, 1978; with Colisseum II: Strange New Flesh, 1975; Electric Savage, 1975; Wardance, 1977; with G-Force: G-Force, 1980; Solo: Back On The Streets, 1978; Corridors Of Power, 1982; Victims Of The Future, 1984; We Want Moore!, 1984; Run For Cover, 1985; Rockin' Every Night, 1986; Wild Frontier, 1987; After The War, 1989; Still Got The Blues, 1990; After Hours, 1992; Blues For Greeny, 1995; Contributor, Tribute To Muddy Waters, 1993. Current Management: Part Rock Management, 53 Kings Road, Suite 318, London SW10 0SZ, England.

MOORE James Kelly, b. 13 Nov 1950, Philadelphia, Pennsylvania, USA. Musician (electric, acoustic and classical guitars, mandolin, dobro, pedal steel guitar, piano, accordion); Vocalist; Composer; Producer. m. Diane Evelyn Moore, 21 July 1993, 1 son. Education: Theatre Lighting Design, Franconia College, University of New Hampshire. Musical Education: Music Theory and Piano, Franconia College; Music Theory, Keyboard Harmony, Guitar and Improvisation, Belmont College, Nashville, Tennessee. Career: 26 years as performer; Major concert appearances include Country Music USA, Opryland Park, with Roy Acuff and Minnie Pearl; Also performed with Pete Seeger, Pumpkin Sail, Soop Clearwater. Compositions: Major works published or recorded include: Sailin' Away; Awaken; Follow My Heart; Celtic Hall; Clearwater; Straight To My Door; Love Isn't Dying Tonight; Shadowland (The Vision Quest); Piper At The Gates Of Dawn; Sing You Lullaby; Daybreak. Recordings: Piper At The Gates Of Dawn, 1987; J Kelly Moore, 1991; Awaken, 1998. Hobbies: Skiing; Sailing; Photography. Current Management: J Kelly Moore Enterprises, PO Box 608, Manchester Center, VT 05255, USA.

MOORE John Arlington, b. 5 Oct 1938, Kingston, Jamaica, West Indies. Musician (trumpet, piano); Entertainer. 3 sons, 1 daughter. Musical Education: Alpha, Jamaica Military Band; Berklee School, Boston, USA. Career: Played with Alpha Boy's Band; J M Band; Mapltoff Poole Band; Thaskatalites; Super Sonics; First tour, with Soul Vendors, England, 1967; with Super Sonic, 1969; Currently travelling world with Solomic Reggerstra. Compositions: Schooling The Duke; Something Special; Tear Up; Ringo; Swing Easy; Rockfoot Rock; Sweet Sugar Candy; Somewhere In time; Where's The Love. Recordings: Album: Something Special; Single: Kibir La Dims. Memberships: Jamaican Federation of Musicians; PRS. Hobbies: Reading; Dancing; Swimming; Conversing. Current Management: Solomic Productions. Address: 173½ Windward Roa Kingston 2, Jamaica, West Indies.

MOORE Malcolm Charles, b. 19 Jan 1971, Chelmsford, Essex, England. Musician (bass guitar, double bassist); Singer; Songwriter. Musical Education: City University, London; Guildhall School of Music. Career: Session bass player with Steve Martland, seen on CH4; BBC Symphony Orchestra; London Sinfonietta; London Philharmonic Orchestra; Tommy Chase Band; Tindersticks; Swordfish (Regular Radio 3 and Jazz FM); New rock/pop band, Felson. Recordings: with Steve Martland: Crossing The Border; Patrol;

with Tindersticks: This Way Up; Horses of Instruction; with Swordfish: Living A Life; Frank and Walters, The Russian Ship. Membership: Musicians' Union. Hobbies: Sport (football, swimming); Comedy. Current Management: Tim Smith, Area 51. Address: 116 Skitts Hill, Braintree, Essex CM7 1AS, England.

MOORE Mickey, b. 9 July 1948, Fort Worth, Texas, USA. Singer; Graphic Designer. m. Becki Moore, 17 Jan 1970, 1 son, 1 daughter. Education: BFA Graphic Design, Commonwealth University. Musical Education: Voice, performance. Career: As Mickey and Becki Moore, performances include: Jesus Northwest; Jesus Orlando; Creation Festival; Fishnet; TV-700 Club; Ross Bagley Show; 100 Huntley Street (Canada); Joe Franklin Show; I Care, TV special with Pat Boone; PTL Club, Campmeeting. Recordings: Albums include: Everything Is Under Control, Wo Wo, 1976; Studio And Live, 1977; Brand New, 1979; Love Song For Number Two, 1981; Mickey And Becki Moore, 1984; Keep The Keeping On, 1991; Tell Me A Story Before I Go To Bed (childrens album), 1987. Membership: SESAC. Current Management: PO Box 777, Trevilians, VA 23170, USA.

MOORE Nicky, b. 21 June 1952, Devon, England. Blues Singer; Musician (guitar, piano, harmonica). m. Maggie Moore, 5 Oct 1974, 4 sons, 1 daughter. Musical Education: Exeter Cathedral/RSCM. Career: Rock bands: Hackensack; Tiger; Samson; Mammoth; Gerry Rafferty; Blues Corporation (current and future); Films: Hearts of Fire; Just Ask For Diamond; Numerous tours, television and radio appearances. Recordings: Tiger: Up The Hard Way; Going Down Laughing; Test Of Time; Before The Storm; Mammoth: Don't Get Mad Get Even; I Just Got Back; Holding On; Numerous singles and videos. Membership: Musicians' Union. Hobby: Music. Current Management: Julia Ficken, Steppin' Out Ltd. Address: PO Box 216, Sevenoaks, Kent TN14 6ZQ, England.

MOORE Sam, b. 12 Oct 1935, Miami, Florida, USA. Singer; Entertainer. m. Joyce McRae, 26 Mar 1982. Career: Singer with Soul duo Sam & Dave; later solo artist; Television appearances include: (Solo) Best of Country; TNN Country News; Entertainment Tonight; Rhythm Country & Blues; Huey Lewis PBS Special; Roots of Country; In Concert Country; Music City Tonight; Good Morning America; Music City Today; Nashville Now; (as Sam and Dave) Ed Sullivan Show; Merv Griffin; Tonight Show; Hollywood Palace; Saturday Night Live; Midnight Special; Bandstand; Mike Douglas Show; Special appearances include: Host, The Pioneer Awards; The George Bush Rhythm & Blues Inaugural Gala; Rhythm Country & Blues, The Concert; Host, Miami Hard Rock Cafe Opening; Videos: Rainy Night In Georgia; Soul Man; Ordinary Man; Hey Joe; Films: One Trick Pony; Tapeheads; Tales Of The City; Soul Man; Command performances for Queen Elizabeth II, England, and US President Jimmy Carter. Recordings: Hit singles include: Soul Man; Hold On I'm Coming; Soul Sister Brown Sugar; Rainy Night In Georgia, duet with Conway Twitty; I Thank You; Something Is Wrong With My Baby; Soothe Me; You Don't Know Like I Know; You Got Me Humming; Soundtracks: White Men Can't Jump; Soul Man; Tapeheads. Guest appearances on: Building The Perfect Beast, Don Henley; Human Touch, Bruce Springsteen. Honours: Numerous Platinum and Gold records; Grammy, Soul Man, 1967; Rhythm & Blues Foundation Pioneer Award, 1991; Rock & Roll Hall of Fame Inductee, 1992; CMA Award Nominee (2 categories), 1994; Two Country Music Association Nominations, 1994; TNN Music City News Nominee, 1995. Memberships: NARAS. Hobbies: Reading; Dogs; Pool; Snooker. Current Management: I'ma Da Wife Enterprises, Inc. Address: 7119 E Shea Blvd, Suite 109-436, Scottsdale, AZ 85254, USA.

MOORE Sarha Caroline, b. 19 June 1954, Croydon, Surrey, England. Musician (saxophone, percussion, pennywhistle); Music Tutor. Education: York University, Mathematics, Music. Musical Education: Oboe, Distinction, Grade 8. Career: Bands include: York Street Band, 1979-83; Featured on Dutch television and Women's Hour, Europe; Orchestra Jazira, 1983-88; Featured on Tyne Tees TV, Sport Aid; Dangerous Designs, 1989-94; Appeared at Camden Jazz Festival; Happy End, 1990-; Appeared at Montreal Jazz Fest, Canada; Mixed Media week with Rhythm Tree, 1990-; Imlatha Dance, 1992-; Lecturer, Goldsmiths College, City Lit; Session work, live and recorded. Recordings: with Julie Dennis: Indiscression In Session, 1985; with Miriam Mackie: Flying High, 1989; with Happy End: Turn Things Upside Down, 1990; Hoofbeat, 1990, 1992; Angels Horns, 1994; World Celebration, 1994. Membership: Musicians' Union. Hobbies: Dancing; Cork flooring. Address: 31 Weymouth Mews, London W1N 3FN, England.

MOORE Thomas Lanning, b. 6 Dec 1943, Los Angeles, California, USA. Songwriter; Philologist; Poet; Translator/Interpreter; Sailor; Teacher. m. Lyubov G Zamytina, 9 Nov 1992, 1 son, 1 daughter. Education: BA University of Claifornia, Los Angeles (magna cum laude), 1969; MA UCLA, 1970. Career: US Navy, (Journalist, 6 months in Vietnam), 1961-65; Singer, songwriter, Ireland, 1971-; Bands: Pumpkinhead, 1973-76; Midnight Well, 1977-78; Train Tu Sliego, 1982-87; Interpreter US Govt, 1987-92; Professor of English, Udmart National University, Izhevisk, Russia. Recordings: Pumpkinhead, 1975; Midnight Well, 1977; Dreamer In Russia; Gorgeous And Bright. Publications: Merit English Grammer, 1985; Quantum Prosody, 1995; 7 Come LL: Mama Needs A New Set Of Days, 1996. Honours: Phi Beta Kappa; BA, Magna cum laude, 1969; Double winner, Second Cavan International Song Contest, 1979. Memberships: MCPS; PRS; IMRO; IASC. Current Management: Madeline Seiler, 5 Wellington Gardens, Oakley Road, Ranelagh, Dublin, Ireland. Address: Cottage A, Pebbly Beach Road, Avalon, Santa Catalina Island, CA 90704, USA.

MOORE Thurston, b. USA. Vocalist; Musician (guitar). Career: Founder member, US rock group Sonic Youth, 1981-; Also spin-off project Ciccone Youth, 1995-; Solo recording artiste, 1995-; Recent concerts include: Lollapalooza Tour (co-headliners with Hole), 1995. Recordings: Albums: Sonic Youth, 1982; Confusion Is Sex, 1983; Kill Yer Idols, 1983; Sonic Death, 1984; Bad Moon Rising, 1985; Evol, 1986; Sister, 1987; Daydream Nation, 1988; Ciccone Youth, 1989; Goo, 1990; Dirty, 1992; Experimental Jet Set, Trash And No Star, 1994; Washing Machine, 1995; Solo album: Psychic Hearts, 1995. Address: c/o Gold Mountain Entertainment, Suite 450, 3575 Cahuenga Blvd. West, Los Angeles, CA 90068, USA.

MOORE Tim, b. 22 May 1958, Sussex, England. Musician (keyboard player); Composer; Producer. m. Venetia, 3 Jan 1987, 2 sons. Musical Education: Piano since age 5, taught by father. Career: with Nik Kershaw: tours, television, videos; concerts include Live Aid, 1985, 1984-86; with Bee Gees: tours, recording, television includes Royal Variety Show, 1990-1993; Tours with: Johnny Hallyday, 1994-95; Saga, 1988; East 17, 1995; Television appearances with Bros; Shakespears Sister. Recordings: Keyboards on albums with Nik Kershaw: The Riddle, 1984; Radio Musicola, 1988; Keyboards/programming on albums with Bee Gees: High Civilization, 1991; Size Isn't Everything, 1993. Membership: Musicians' Union. Hobbies: Pub gigs; Driving; Walking; Working out; Recording at home. Current Agent: Debbie Haxton. Address: The Session Connection, 110-112 Disraeli Road, Putney, London SW15, England.

MOORE Vinnie. Rock Musician (guitar). Musical Education: Jazz guitar. Career: Member, Vicious Rumours, 1985; Solo artiste, 1986-; Guitarist, Alice Cooper, Hey Stoopid tour, 1991. Recordings: Albums: with Vicious Rumours: Soldiers Of The Night, 1985; Solo albums: Mind's Eye, 1986; Time Odyssey, 1988; Meltdown, 1991. Current Management: Frank Solomon Management, PO Box 639, Natick, MA 01760, USA.

MORALES Petra, b. 3 May 1962, Germany. Musician (percussion); Dancer. m. Stéphane Bour, 5 Aug 1989. Education: BAC. Musical Education: BAC; CUBA workshops and studies. Career: Dancer, Eurythmics Tour, 1987-88; European Tours; Radio appearances, Mauritius; 3 month tour, 1993; Cuba tour, 1994; Tours in France, Las Orchidias Del Ritmo, Kathy Kidd Kongo Mambo Project, 1995. Memberships: Musicians' Union, UK; DMV, Germany. Hobbies: Horse riding; Swimming; The beach; Nature. Current Management: ACI. Address: 9 Avenue Alsace Lorraine, 94450 Limeil Brevannes, Paris, France.

MORAN Michael John, b. 18 July 1964, Birkenhead, England. Composer; Producer; Musician (electric guitar, keyboards); Programmer. Musical Education: Diploma, Light Music, Sandown College, Liverpool; BA (Hons) Popular Music and Recording, University College, Salford. Career: Member, 16 Tambourines; Toured with: Squeeze; Hue and Cry; Wet Wet Wet; Tour Manager, 35 Summers tour with EMF; Manager, N-Trust (as Decent Exposure Management); Musical Director, Jungle Book, Redgrave Theatre, Farnham; Sgt Pepper's Magical Mystery Trip, Liverpool Playhouse. Compositions: Co-writer: It's Better To Love; Movies; Language Of Love. Recordings: Album: How Green Is Your Valley, 16 Tambourines; As producer: Quiet Defiance, N-Trust. Singles: with 16 Tambourines: If I Should Stay; How Green Is Your Valley; Memberships: PRS; Musicians' Union; MMIA, committee member; MCPS. Hobbies: Dinghy sailing; Walking; Cinema; Theatre. Current Management: Triple M Productions. Address: 93 Barrington Road, Wavertree, Liverpool L15 3HR England.

MORAN Mike, b. 4 Mar 1948, Leeds, Yorkshire, England. Composer; Musician (piano, clarinet). m. Lynda, 5 Sept 1992, 1 daughter. Musical Education: Royal College Of Music. Career: Musician, arranger, record producer; As musician, arranger, worked with stars including: Paul McCartney; Stevie Wonder; Kate Bush; Paul Simon; Joe Cocker; George Harrison; Gladys Knight; Robert Plant; Cliff Richard; Carly Simon; Julio Iglesias; The Four Tops; Placido Domingo; Jose Carreras; Elvin Jones; Oliver Nelson; Leo Sayer; Lulu; Dusty Springfield; Member of bands: Blue Mink; Stone The Crows; Gillan; Worked with Freddie Mercury; Took part in Wembley tribute to Freddie Mercury, 1994. Compositions include: Film music: Time Bandits; The Missionary; Water; Bloodbath At The House Of Death; Whoops Apocalypse; The Bitch; Top Secret; Deathwish 3; Television music includes: Taggart, STV; Harry's Game, YTV; El CID, Granada; The Contract, YTV; Bookie, STV; Killer, STV; The Racing Game, YTV; The Krypton Factor, Granada; Love Story; The Kenny Everett Show, BBC; The Consultant, BBC; Print Out; Pop Quest, YTV; The Richard And Judy Show, Granada; Commercials include: TV Times; Kentucky Fried Chicken; Halifax Building Society; British Gas; Miss Selfridge; Co-writer, song on Innuendo album, Freddie Mercury; Collaborated on album Barcelona, with Freddie Mercury and Montserrat Caballe; More than 100 songs, recorded by: Freddie Mercury; Queen; George Harrison; Ian Gillan; Maggie Bell; Oliver Nelson; John Kongos; Extreme. Honours: Tric Best Music Award. Memberships: Musicians' Union; PRS. Current Management: Soundtrack Music Management. Address: 22 Ives Street, Chelsea, London SW3 2ND, England.

MORAND Roger, b. 30 September 1958, Nogent sur Marne, France. Musician. m. Christine Chazel, 2 August 1986, 1 son, 1 daughter. Education: Music School, 6 years old; Classical Accordion; Professional 16 years old. Career: Television, MTV, Monte Carlo, FR3, A2, TF1, Arte, M6; Radio, BBC, Radio France, France Culture; Stage, Crawfish Festival, Ugly Day, Cajun Day, Feria de Nimes Jazzavienne, Festival Country, Mirande Nuit Cajun, Playing with Nathan Abshine, John Delajose, Dewey Balfa, Denis Mcgee, Marc Savoy, Corey Harris; Leader, Morand Cajun Band. Recordings: When i'm Up, 1993; Les Blues a Bébè, 1994; Nuit Cajun, 1995; Hey Ariba, 1997. Publications: Contributions to musical journals and magazines. Honour: European Cup, Accordion. Membership: SACEM. Hobby: All About Louisiana. Address: 3 Place du Doyen Gachon, 30610 Sauve, France.

MOREIRA Airto, b. 5 Aug 1941, Itaiopolis, Brazil. Musician (percussion); Bandleader. m. Flora Purim, 19 Mar 1972, 1 daughter. Career: Member, Weather Report, 1971; Partnership with Flora Purim, 1969-; Also worked with Al DiMeola; Currently, bandleader, own Latin fusion group Fourth World. Recordings: Albums: with Weather Report: Weather Report, 1971; Solo/with Flora Purim: Natural Feelings, 1969; Seeds On The Ground, 1970; Free, 1971; Fingers, 1972; Identity, 1975; Promises Of The Sun, 1976; Alue, 1969; San Francisco River, 1972; Deodata/Airto In Concert, 1973; I'm Fine, How Are You, 1977. Address: c/o A-Train Management, PO Box 29242, Oakland, CA 94604, USA.

MORELLINI Richard-Paul, b. 19 May 1949, Casablanca, Morocco. Musician (drums, percussion). m. 2 May 1978, 1 son, 1 daughters. Education; BA, High University. Musical Education: Conservatoire de Strasbourg. Career: Orchestre Symphonique et Lyrique, Nancy; Founder, Co-director, CMCN (Centre Musical Et Creatif, Nancy). Recordings: Erato, with Alain Lomabard; Victoires De la Musique, Marius Constant, 1991. Publications: Drum methodologies: Essential I, Essential II. Current Management: Self-managed. Address: 71 Avenue Anatole France, 54000 Nancy, France.

MORENO Rita (Rosa Dolores Alverio), b. Humacao, Puerto Rico. Actress; Singer; Entertainer. m. Leonard Gordon, 1 daughter. Career: Film, stage, television, concert performer. Films include: The King And I; West Side Story, 1962; Television: Starred in own TV series, sitcom version of 9 To 5; B L Stryker, 1989-90; The Top Of The Heap, Fox Network seies, 1991-92; Cosby Mystery Series, 1994; Performs concerts across USA with symphony orchestras for their Pops series; Performed at President Clinton's Inauguration, 1993; White House, 1993. Recordings include: The Electric Company Album, 1972. Honours: Oscar, West Side Story, 1962; The Golden Globe Award, Golden Apple, John Jefferson Award, Best Actress, Chicago's Theatrical Season, 1968; Grammy, The Electric Company Album, 1972; Tony, The Ritz (Broadway production), 1975; Emmys, The Muppet Show, 1977; Sarah Siddons Award, 1985; Star, Hollywood Walk Of Fame, 1995. Membership: Presidents Committee on the Arts and Humanities. C/o Stan Scotland, JKE Services, 404 Park Ave S, 10th Floor, New York, NY 10016, USA.

MORGAN Charlie, b. 9 Aug 1955, Hammersmith, London, England. Musician (drums, electronic percussion). m. Daniela Francesca James, 6 Oct 1992, 1 daughter. Education: College de Genève. Musical Education: Piano lessons; Classes with James Blades. Career: Mostly freelance, 1973-84; Toured, recorded with Tom Robinson Band, 1979; 2 albums, tours with Judi Tzuke, 1980-81; Numerous recordings for Nick Kershaw, Tracey Ullman, Kate Bush; 14 month world tour, as drummer with Elton John, 1992-93; Tour with Elton John, Billy Joel, USA, 1994-1995; Currently, Elton John World Tour, May 1995-. Compositions: Co-wrote television theme The Bill, ITV. Recordings: Edge Of Heaven, Wham; 2 albums with Tracey Ullman; I Am The Phoenix, Judy Tzuke; Thunderdrome (Mad Max 2), Tina Turner; Iron Man, Pete Townshend; Oasis, Oasis; Out In The Fields, Gary Moore and Phil Lynott; Who's Side Are You On?, Matt Bianco; Rock & Roll Album, Johnny Logan; Human Racing, Nik Kerhsaw; Kane Gang album; Being There, Martyn Joseph; with Elton John: Live In Sydney (with the MSO); Made In England; Silver Bird, Justin Hayward; Go West, Go West; with Chris De Burgh: Spark To A Flame; This Way Up; Magic Ring, Clannad; Golden Days, Bucks Fizz; Theodore And Friends, The Adventures; Lionheart, Kate Bush; Cabaret (Live), Tom Robinson; Linda Thompson album, 1985; Nick Heyward album, 1985; Beverley Craven album tracks, 1991; Tasmin Archer album, 1992; The Glory Of Gershwin, 1994. Memberships: PRS; BASCA; Musicians' Union. Hobby: Motor racing, competed in British Saloons, 1984-86.

MORGAN Dennis William, b. 30 July 1952, Tracy, Minnesota, USA. Songwriter; Music Publisher. m. June Arnold, 27 July 1985. Career: Songwriter, Collins Music, 1969-73; Little Shop of Morgansongs, 1974-. Compositions include: Smoky Mountain Rain, Ronnie Milsap; I Wouldn't Have Missed It For The World, Ronnie Milsap; I Was Country When Country Wasn't Cool, Barbara Mandrell; I Knew You Were Waiting For Me, George Michael and Aretha Franklin; My Heart Can't Tell You Know, Rod Stewart. Honours: 3 Grammy Nominations; Ivor Novello Award; 3 CMA Award Nominations; 43 BMI Awards. Memberships: CMA; Nashville Songwriters Association.

MORGAN Edward Lee (Ed), b. 28 Apr 1941, Noel, Missouri, USA. President, Country Breeze Productions. m. Delores Arneta Shoemake, 1 son, 1 daughter. Musical Education: Self-taught songwriter. Career: Many Number 1 songs on independent charts in America; Songs published by other publishing companies. Compositions include: Shatter Me, recorded by several artists, played worldwide, 1987. Publications: Publish monthly magazine: Midwest Newsbeat, for songwriters and artists. Honours: Golden Cross, for gospel label: Angel Star Records. Memberships: BMI; Midwest Association of Music. Hobbies: Camping; Hunting; Fishing. Current Management: Self-managed. Address: 1715 Marty, Kansas City, KS 66103, USA.

MORGAN H Paul, b. 21 Aug 1958, Southampton, Hampshire, England. Musician (double bass, bass guitar). Musical Education: Studied Jazz and Light Music at Leeds College of Music, 1 year. Career: Member, National Youth Jazz Orchestra, 1980-82; Member, BBC Big Band, 1983-85; Member, Don Lusher Big Band, Alan Barnes Quartet and studio work, 1986. Hobbies: Exploring villages; Playing bass. Address: 56 Franks Avenue, New Malden, Surrey KT3 5DB, England.

MORGAN Jeffrey, b. 20 March 1954, Spokane, Washington, USA. Musician. Education: Liberal Arts, Music, Dance, Theater, Philosophy of Aesthetics; Studied under Don Cherry, Karl Berger, Dumi Mavaieve, Bert Wilson, Robert Gottlieb, Greg Steinke. Career: Concerts and Festivals in Europe and USA; Experimental Theater; Workshops for Sound and Installations. Compositions: Quasar-Mach, 1983; Snake Eyes, 1994; Near Vhana, 1997; Bitin Thru, 1997. Recordings: Quasar-Mach, LP, 1983; Snake Eyes, CD, 1994; Near Vhana, CD, 1997; Bitin Thru, CD, 1997. Honour: British Arts Council Performing Arts Grant, 1992. Membership: GEMA. Address: Lübecker Str 15, 50668 Cologne, Germany.

MORGAN John Marshall, b. 3 May 1958, Clinton, Iowa, USA. Bandleader; Musician (saxophone); Composer; Teacher. m. Nancy Eichman, 15 Mar 1986, 2 sons. Education: 3 Collegiate degrees, Masters. Musical Education: Drake University, Des Moines, Iowa, USA. Career: Sideman/arranger, The Russ Morgan Orchestra, The Don Hoy Orchestra; Leader, The John Morgan Band, 1984-; Saxophone guest artist with Drake Symphony Orchestra, Des Moines Municipal Band; Educator in Drake University Community School, 1986-; Des Moines School District, 1990-. Publications: The Instrumentalist Magazine. Honours: Drake Soloist Artist, 1981, 1987, WO1 Radio; Phi Kappa Lamda; Omicron Delta Kappa; Phi Mu Alpha. Memberships: Macusa (National Association of Composers). Hobbies: Cartooning; Collecting 16mm films (especially Laurel and Hardy).

MORGAN Loretta Lynn, b. 27 June 1959, Nashville, Tennessee, USA. Country Singer. 1 son, 1 daughter. Career: 2 years touring with George Jones; Worked at Opryland, USA aged 18; Acting debut, Proudheart, Nashville Network film; Film, The Enemy Within, ABC-TV; Television includes: Co-host, American Music Awards, 1995; CBS AM; The Ralph Emery Show; Entertainment Tonight; Late Night With David Letterman; 48 Hours; The Tonight Show; CBS 65 Years Of The Grand Ole Opry; Austin City Limits; Hee Haw. Recordings: Albums: Leave The Light On; Something In Red; Watch Me; Merry Christmas From London; War Paint; Greatest Hits, 1995. Honours include: CMA Awards, Vocal Event Of The Year, with Keith Whitley, 1990; Album Of The Year, Common Thread, 1994; TNN/Music City News Awards: Video Collaboration Of The Year, with Keith Whitley, 1991; Female Artist Of The Year, 1994; CMT: Female Vocalist Of The Year, 1992; CMA Nominations, 1990, 1991, 1992; TNN Nominations, 1991, 1992; 1995; ACM Nominations, 1992, 1993. Current Management: Susan Nadler Management. Address: 1313 16th Avenue South, Nashville, TN 37212, USA.

MORGAN Marc, b. 30 April 1962, Huy, Belgium. Singer; Songwriter; Musician (Guitar). Education: Fine Arts Graduate, Saint-Luc Institute, Liège. Career: Debut bands: Objectif lune, mid 80s; Les Révérends Du Prince Albert; Les Tricheurs, 1987; La Variété, 1991; Support tour with Les Innocents, 1993; Francofolies de Montréal, 1994; Francofolies de Spa, 1994, 1996; Festival de Québec, 1994. Compositions: Notre Mystère, Nos Retrouvailles, 1993; Au Train ou Vont Les Choses, 1996; Capable de Tout, 1996. Recordings: with Les Tricheurs, Tendez Vos Lèvres, 1989; with La Variété, Pour La gloire, 1993; Solo: Un Cygne Sur L'Orénoque, 1993; Les Grands Espaces, 1996. Current Management: Double V (Virginie Borgeaud) 2, Rue Navarin, 75009 Paris, France.

MORGAN Tudur, b. 18 May 1958, Bangor, Gwynedd, Wales. Musician (acoustic guitar, bass, keyboards); Vocalist; Producer. m. Annwen Morgan, 18 Oct 1986, 2 daughters. Education: Carmarthen Trinity College. Musical Education: Self-taught. Career: Television and radio appearances: Major television shows in Wales; BBC Pebble Mill; BBC Radio 2; Concerts throughout UK including London Albert Hall; Orkney Islands; Edinburgh Folk Festival and with Ronnie Drew of the Dubliners in Cardiff; Played with many top Welsh performers including Dafydd Iwan; Linda Healy; Plethyn; 4 Yn Y Bar; Mojo and Moniars. Recordings: With numerous artists including: Branwen; Dafydd Iwan; Mojo; 4 Yn Y Bar; Linda Healy; Plethyn; Moniars and Dylan Parry; World Music album for Narada Media. Memberships: MCPS; PRS; Musicians' Union. Hobbies: Music; CDs; Rock and Roll; Cars; Travel. Current Management: Sblash. Address: c/o Sblash, 17 Perth Y Paun, Llangefni, Ynys Mon, Gwynedd LL77 7EX, Wales.

MORGAN Wayne, b. 15 Jan 1970, Warrington, Cheshire, England. Musician (bass guitar). Musical Education: 2 year foundation course. Career: Played in: Pele, 1993-; Supports include: Wet Wet Wet; Iggy Pop; Worked with major producers; Played bass, China Crisis tour. Recordings: 2 Pele albums, produced by Jon Heedy, Simon Vinestock; Various sessions include work for Gary Langan. Membership: Musicians' Union. Hobbies: Running; Football. Current Management: D L Management. Address: No.3 Firshaw Road, Meals, Wirral L47 5BD, England.

MORILLO Erick, b. 26 Mar 1971, New York City, New York, USA. Dance Music Producer. Musical Education: Degree, Center, for Media Arts. Career: Appeared on: MTV Europe's Most Wanted; Top Of The Pops; Zig and Zag's Breakfast Show; Reel 2 Real; Move It World Tour; Numerous television concerts and arena shows. Recordings: Reel 2 Real, featuring The Mad Stuntmen: I Like To Move It; Move It Up; Smooth Touch: Come And Take A Trip; House Of Love/In My House. Honours: Platinum, Gold and Silver albums; International Producer of The Year, Canada, 1994. Hobby: DJing. Address: Positiva Records, PO Box 1ES, London W1A 1ES, England.

MORISSETTE Alanis, b. 1974, Ottawa, Canada. Singer. Career: Solo recording artiste; Appeared on Canadian cable TV, aged 10; Concerts include: Twix Mix Jamboree, with David Bowie, Birmingham NEC, 1995; 16 million albums sold. Recordings: Albums: Alanis, 1991; Now Is The Time, 1992; Jagged Little Pill, 1995; Singles: Fate Stay With Me; You Oughta Know, 1995; One Hand In My Pocket, 1995; Ironic, 1996. Honour: BRIT Award, Best International Newcomer, 1996. Current Management: Third Rail Entertainment, 9169 Sunset Blvd, Los Angeles, CA 90069, USA.

MORRICONE Ennio, b. 11 Oct 1928, Rome, Italy. Composer. Musical Education: Studied trumpet and composition. Career: Composer for radio, television, stage and concerts; Scores for "spaghetti" westerns. Compositions: Scores and arrangements for vocalist Gianni Morandi, 1950s; Arrangement, Ogni Volta, Paul Anka, 1964; Film scores include: Il Federale, 1961; A Fistful Of Dollars (under pseudonym Dan Savio), 1964; Battle Of Algiers, 1966; Big Birds, Little Birds, 1966; 1900, 1976; Exorcist II, 1977; Days Of Heaven, 1978; The Mission, 1986; The Untouchables, 1987; Frantic, 1988; Wolf, 1994; Disclosure, 1995. Recordings: Albums: Moses, 1977; Film Hits, 1981; Chi Mai, 1981; The Mission, 1986; Film Music 1966-87, 1988; Chamber Music, 1988; Frantic, 1988; The Endless Game, 1989; Live In Concert, 1989; Casualties Of War, 1990; The Very Best Of, 1992.

MORRIS Lynn, b. 8 Oct 1948, San Antonio, Texas, USA. Musician (banjo, guitar); Singer. m. Marshall Wilborn, 14 Oct 1989. Education: BA, Art, Colorado College, Colorado Springs, USA. Musical Education: Studied classical and jazz guitar, high school. Career: Began professionally in music, 1972; Performed in Europe; Asia; Canada; USA; Began Lynn Morris Band, 1988; Television appearances: Fire On The Mountain; Reno's Old Time Music Festival; Radio: WWVA on Wheeling Jamboree; WSM Grand Ole Opry, Nashville, Tennessee. Recordings: The Lynn Morris Band; The Bramble And The Rose; Mama's Hand. Honours: Twice, Female Vocalist (Traditional Category), Society for Preservation of Bluegrass Music in America; Twice, National Banjo Champion at Winfield, Kansas. Memberships: IBMA Board of Directors, 6 years; International Bluegrass Music Association; Folk Alliance; Society For The Preservation of Bluegrass Music in America. Hobbies: Animal welfare; Wildlife preservation; Raise cats; Listen to music. Current Management: Mike Drudge, Class

Act Entertainment, PO Box 771, Gallatin, TN 37066, USA.

MORRIS Sarah Jane, b. 21 Mar 1959, Southampton, Hampshire, England. Singer; Songwriter; Actress. m. David J Coulter, 15 Aug, 1992, 1 son. Education: Central School of Speech and Drama for acting training. Career: Lead singer, The Republic, 1980-84; The Happy End, 1984-87; The Communards, 1985-87; Solo career includes 3 albums; Appearances include: Royal Albert Hall; Royal Festival Hall; Wembley Arena; Verona Arena; Venice Opera House; Support act to Simply Red, New Flame tour, 1989; Lead actress in Thin Air, BBC1; Lead Actress in film Expecting, Channel 4. Compositions include: I Am A Woman; Title track for televison series The Mens Room, BBC, 1991-92; Music for film Expecting, Ch4, 1995. Recordings: Don't Leave Me This Way, duet with Jimmy Somerville, (Number 1, UK), 1986; Albums include: Blue Valentine, 1995. Honours: Freedom of the City of Verona; Best Newcomer, Italy, 1989; Nomination, Best Supporting Actress, The Beggars Opera, 1991. Memberships: PRS; MCPS. Hobbies: Walking; Reading; Raising son Otis; Songwriting. Current Management: Self-managed. Address: The Old Post Office, Warton, Warwick CV35 9HX, England.

MORRIS Stephen, b. 28 Oct 1957, Macclesfield, Cheshire, England. Musician (drums). Career: Member, Joy Division, 1977-80; New Order, 1980-; The Other Two, with Gillian Gilbert, 1991-; Tours: UK; Europe; Australia; New Zealand; Far East; US; South America; Concerts include: Glastonbury Fayre, 1981, 1987; Futurama Festival, Leeds, 1982; San Remo Festival, 1988; Reading Festival, 1989. Compositions include: with Gilbert: Numerous tracks for New Order; Television soundtracks: Making Out; Shooting Stars; Reportage. Recordings: Albums: with Joy Division: Unknown Pleasures, 1979; Closer, 1980; Still, 1981; The Peel Sessions, 1988; Also featured on Short Circuit - Live At The Electric Circus, 1978; with New Order: Movement, 1981; Power, Corruption And Lies, 1983; Low Life, 1985; Brotherhood, 1986; Technique, 1989; BBC Radio 1 Live In Concert, 1992; Republic, 1993; with The Other Two: The Other Two And You, 1994; Singles: with New Order: Ceremony, 1981; Temptation, 1982; Confusion, 1983; Thieves Like Us, 1984; Shellshock, 1986; True Faith, 1987; Touched By The Hand Of God, 1987; Fine Time, 1988; Round And Round, 1989; World In Motion, with England World Cup Football Squad, 1990; How Does It Feel?, 1992; Regret, 1993; with The Other Two: Tasty Fish.

MORRISON Mark, b. Leicester, England. Soul Singer. Career: Solo recording artiste, 1994-; Tours include: Support to R Kelly, US tour, 1995; UK tour, 1996. Recordings: Singles: Crazy, 1995; Let's Get Down, 1995; Return Of The Mack, 1995; Album: Return Of The Mack (Number 1, UK), 1996. Current Management: JLM Management, Unit 8, 18 All Saints Road, London W11 1HH, England.

MORRISON Van (George Ivan Morrison), b. 31 Aug 1945, Belfast, Northern Ireland. Singer; Songwriter; Composer; Musician. 1 daughter. Career: Founder, lead singer, Them, 1964-67; Solo artiste, 1967-; Appearances include: Knebworth Festival, 1974; The Last Waltz, The Band's farewell concert, 1976; Played with Bob Dylan, Wembley Stadium, 1984; Self Aid, with U2, Dublin, 1986; Glastonbury Festival, 1987; Prince's Rock Trust Gala, 1989; Performance, The Wall, by Roger Waters, Berlin, 1990; Concert in Dublin, with Bono, Bob Dylan, 1993; Phoenix Festival, 1995. Recordings: Singles include: Gloria; Brown-Eyed Girl; Moondance; Domino; Wild Night; Albums include: Blowin' Your Mind, 1967; Astral Weeks, 1968; Moondance, 1970; His Band And Street Choir, 1973; Tupelo Honey, 1971; St Dominics Preview, 1972; Hard Nose The

Highway, 1973; It's Too Late To Stop Now, 1974; Tb Sheets, 1974; Veedon Fleece, 1974; This Is Where I Came In, 1977; A Period Of Transition, 1977; Wavelength, 1978; Into The Music, 1983; Bang Masters, 1990; Common One, 1980; Beautiful Vision, 1982; Inarticulate Speech Of The Heart, 1983; Live At The Opera House Belfast, 1984; A Sense Of Wonder, 1984; No Guru, No Method, No Teacher, 1986; Poetic Champions Compose, 1987; Irish Heartbeat, 1988; Best Of..., 1990; Avalon Sunset, 1989; Enlightenment, 1990; Hymns To The Silence, 1991; Too Long In Exile, 1993; Best Of..., Vol 2, 1993; Days Like This, 1995; Also recorded on albums: with The Band: Cahoots, 1971; The Last Waltz, 1978; with John Lee Hooker: Folk Blues, 1963; Mr Lucky, 1991; with Bill Wyman: Stone Alone, 1976; with Jim Capaldi: Fierce Heart, 1983; with Georgie Fame: How Long Has This Been Going On, 1996. Honours include: Inducted into Rock And Roll Hall Of Fame, 1993; BRIT Award, Outstanding Contribution to British Music, 1994; Q Award, Best Songwriter, 1995.

MORRISON Will, b. 2 Feb 1968, Tile Hill, Coventry, England. Musician (drums, percussion); Programmer. Education: Coventry University. Musical Education: Coventry School Of Music, Drumtech, London. Career: Tours with Don Mescall supporting: Mary Coghlan; Davey Spillane; David Thomas; Richie Havens; The Dubliners; Festivals with Don Mescall: Phoenix; Larmer Bee; Berlin Music; Radio 1 Roadshows with Faun; Live Radio Sessions on Greater London Radio with: Philip French; Sugartrain; Don Mescall; Television includes: The Happening and Pot Of Gold with Sugartrain; The Big City with Lisa Lamb Quartet. Recordings: State Of The Arts EP; She Don't Know, Faun (featuring John Entwistle, Gordon Giltrap); Album: Here Be Dragons, Gargling With Brains. Publications: Working on drum tuition book: Learning To Read And Write. Membership: Musicians' Union. Hobbies: Fitness; Art; Carpentry; Sailing; Cycling. Current Management: Notes For Notes. Address: 12 The Old Orchard, Solomon Road, Rainham, Kent ME8 8DT, England.

MORRISSEY (Stephen Morrissey), b. 22 May 1959, Daryhulme, Manchester, UK. Singer. Career: Formed The Smiths, 1982; Appearances include: John Peel Show, Radio 1, 1983; Support to Altered Images, 1983; Solo artiste, 1987-. Compositions include: Co-writer (with Johnny Marr), all Smiths hits; Carrying A Torch, recorded by Tom Jones, 1991; Recordings: Singles include: Hand In Glove; This Charming Man; What Difference Does It Make; Heaven Knows I'm Miserable Now; William, It Was Really Nothing; The Boy With The Thorn In His Side; Big Mouth Strikes Again; Panic; Shoplifters Of The World Unite; Sheila Take A Bow; Solo: Everyday Is Like Sunday; Last Of The International Playboys; Ouija Board; November Spawns A Monster; Picadilly Palace; We Hate It When Our Friends Become Successful; You're The One For Me Fatty; Albums: with the Smiths: The Smiths, 1984; Meat Is Murder, 1993; The Queen Is Dead, 1986; The World Won't Listen, 1987; Louder Than Bombs, 1987; Strangeways Here We Come, 1987; Rank, 1988; Best 1, Best II, 1992; Solo albums: Viva Hate, 1988; Bona Drag, 1990; Kill Uncle, 1991; Your Arsenal, 1992; Beethoven Was Deaf, 1993; Vauxhall And I, 1994; Southpaw Grammar, 1995. Honours include: Q Award, Best Songwriter, 1994. Current Management: Stiefel Phillips Entertainment, 9720 Wilshire Blvd, Ste 400, Beverly Hills, CA 90212, USA.

MORROW Ian. Programmer. Career: Worked with Wet Wet Wet on forthcoming album; Commencing production work with Icelandic artist, Suala. Recordings: Wet Wet Wet: Holding Back the River, album, programming; High on the Happy Side, album, programming; Picture This, album, programming; Nightcrawlers, Push the Feeling On, production; Seal, Crazy,

programming. Address: SARM Productions, SP2 Holdings Ltd, The Blue Building, 42/46 St Luke's Mews, London W11 1DG, England.

MORTENSEN Allan, b. 27 Apr 1946, Aarhus, Denmark. Singer; Composer; Actor. m. Titika, Mar 1967, divorced, 1 daughter. Education: Lithographer. Musical Education: Self-taught. Career: Singer, rock group Midnight Sun, 1971; Stage performances include lead parts in: Jesus Christ Superstar, 1972; Hair, 1972; Two Gentlemen Of Verona, 1973; Godspell, 1979; Joseph And The Amazing Technicolour Dreamcoat, 1983; Odysseus, 1983; Tom Parker's Young Messiah, 1986-87; Singer, soul group 2nd Line, 1987-89. Compositions: Musicals: Thor, 1989; The Concert, 1991; The Three Musketeers, 1995. Recordings: Midnight Sun, 1971; Love Ambulance (as singer, composer), 1976; 2nd Line Live, 1988. Honours: The Amber Nightingale, Poland, 1987; Helexpo, Greece, 1991. Membership: Danish Artist Federation. Hobbies: Music; Films. Current Management: Danish Artist Management. Address: Vendersgade 24, 1363 Copenhagen K, Denmark.

MORTON Eddie. Vocalist; Musician (mandolin, accordion, guitar). Career: Member, Sub Zero, 1983; Formed The Trick, 1984; Extensive radio play, BBC1; Hits, Europe and Australia; Worked in production, songwriting with artists including: Phil Lynott; Slade; Ruby Turner; Rozalla; Steve Lillywhite; Roy Harper; Formed own band, 1988; Tours, Europe, UK, USA; Joined The Adventure Babies, 1991; Founder member, The New Bushbury Mountain Daredevils, 1992-; Backing vocals, Slade album; Numerous television and radio performances; Producer, songwriting with dance artists. Recordings: Albums: with Sub Zero: Out Of The Blue; with The Trick: My World; Heart Of Hearts; with Rozalla: Heartbreaker; Sunny; Spirit Of Africa; Perfect Kiss; as Morton: Keeper Of The Light; with Adventure Babies: Adventure Babies; Laugh; Barking Mad; with Mack And The Boys: The Unknown Legends; As Eddie Morton: The Infinite Room; Way Of The World; Black And Blue; with The New Bushbury Mountain Daredevils: Bushwacked; The Yellow Album; Bushbury Mountain. Current Management: c/o Jim McPhee, Acorn Entertainments. Address: Winterfold House, 46 Woodfield Road, Kings Heath, Birmingham B13 9UJ, England.

MORTON Nigel William, b. 23 Nov 1953, Nairobi, Kenya. Manager; Booking Agent; Consultant. M. Hilary Cooper, 26 Nov 1977, divorced, 1 son, 1 daughter. Career: Journalist: Record Mirror; Sounds; Hi-Fi weekly; Booking agent to various acts including: Carmel; Marillion; Wishbone Ash; Jimmy Cliff; Billy Bragg; Angelic Upstarts; Donovan; The Exploited; Pentangle; The Twinkle Brothers, 1978-84; Full time manager: New Model Army, 1982-91; Co-manager: The Almighty, 1987-90; Booking Agent, Consultant, Current clients include: Bruce Cockburn; Kate and Anna McGarrigle; Hot Tuna; The Ukrainians; Porcupine Tree; Test Department, 1992-; Negotiated recording contracts for: New Model Army with: Quiet Records, 1982; Abstract Records, 1983; EMI Records, 1984; Negotiated publishing contracts for New Model Army with: Watteau Music, 1983; Warner-Chappell Music, 1986. Hobbies: Reading; Writing; Music, all forms; Travel; Aircraft History; Cooking. Current Management; Self-managed. Address: Forward Agency Booking, 132 Liverpool Road, London N1 1LA, England.

MORTON Peter Michael, b. 30 July 1964, Leicester, England. Singer; Musician (guitar); Songwriter. Musical Education: Church choir; Busker until 1987. Career: Concerts throughout UK, Europe, North America; British Council Tours, Pakistan, Malaysia; Frequent guest, Folk On 2. Compositions include: Another Train. Recordings: Albums: Frivolrous Love, 1987; One Big Joke, 1988; Urban Folk Vol 1, 1989; Mad World Blues,

1992; Courage, Love, Grace, 1995. Honours: Most Promising Newcomer, Folk Roots Magazine, 1987. Membership: PRS. Hobbies: Reading; Travel. Current Management: Small World Music. Address: PO Box 2259, London E17 4RD, England.

MORYKIT Dmytro, b. 3 Dec 1956, Northampton, England. Composer; Musician (piano, keyboards). m. Elaine Morykit, 2 Nov 1985, 1 daughter. Education: BEd, University of Leicester. Musical Education: Classically trained on Piano from early age to LRAM; Studied with Graham Mayo. Career: Member of the National Student Theatre Company, 1978-80; Composer in Residence; Session musician with various rock bands; Freelance composer and musician. Compositions: Many for film, theatre, dance and public performance including music for The Wasteland by T S Eliot and original music for The Lion The Witch And The Wardrobe by C S Lewis. Publications include: Songs For Piano, 1982; The Enchanted, 1994. Honour: Best Original Music, National Student Drama Festival. Memberships: Musicians' Union; BASCA; Composers' Guild. Hobbies: Music; Reading; Theatre; Cinema; Amateur Dramatics. Current Management: Elaine Morykit. Address: 24 Dundonald Street, Edinburgh EH3 6RY, Scotland.

MOSCA Sal, b. 27 Apr 1927, Mount Vernon, New York, USA. Musician (piano). m. Stella C Di Gregorio, 2 sons, 1 daughter. Musical Education: 3 years New York College of Music and New York University; 8 years Lennie Taistano. Career: Alice Tulley Hall, solo recital; Carnegie Recital Hall, solo recital; Concertgebouw (Netherlands), solo recital; Solo recitals, Rotterdam, Maastricht, The Hague; Philharmonic Hall, West Berlin, with Warne Marsh, Kenny Clark, Eddie Gomez; 5 hour radio interview, WKCR. Recordings: 15 albums with Lee Konitz; Warne Marsh Quartet; Village Vanguard; Zinnia; 3 solo CDs: Interplay; Choice; Wave. Honours: ASCAP Pop Awards. Memberships: ASCAP; AMRA; Local AFofM. Address: 5 South Fifth Avenue, Mount Vernon, NY 10550-3108, USA.

MOSES Jamie (James Michael), b. 30 Aug 1955, Ipswich, Suffolk, England. Musician (guitar, bass guitar, keyboards); Singer; Musical Director. m. Deborah Anne Webb, 30 Aug 1983, 1 son, 1 daughter. Education: Redhill Technical College. Musical Education: Self-taught. Career: Tours with: Brian May; Bob Geldof; Eric Burdon; Broken English; S.O.S Band; Bucks Fizz; The Hollies; Deana Carter; Stage appearances with: Paul Rodgers; Paul McCartney; Steve Lukather; Dave Stewart; Guns'n'Roses; Fish; Chaka Khan; Curtis Stigers; Paul Young; Roger Chapman; Roger Taylor; Extreme; Kiki Dee; Television and radio with artists including: The Pretenders; Olivia Newton-John. Recordings: Brian May Live At Brixton Academy; The Happy Club, Bob Geldof; Comin' On Strong, Broken English; I Used To Be An Animal, Eric Burdon; Various, Paul Young; Do You Really Want Me Back, Broken English; Merlin, Merlin. Memberships: PRS; MCPS; Musicians' Union. Hobbies: Video games; Tennis. Address: 32 William Road, Caterham-On-The-Hill, Surrey CR3 5NN, England.

MOSES Robert (Bob), Jazz Musician (drums, keyboards); Composer; Educator. Career: Leader, bands: Mozamba; Drumming Birds; Founder, owner, Mozown Records, 1975-; Worked with Jack DeJohnette; Keith Jarrett; David Sanborn; Rahsaan Roland Kirk; Gary Burton. Recordings: Albums include: with Larry Coryell: Free Spirit, 1967; Lady Coryell, 1969; with Steve Kuhn: Playground, 1974; Non Fiction, 1978; with David Liebman: Drum Ode, 1975; with Pat Metheny: Bright Size Life, 1975; with Compost: Compost, 1971; Life Is Round, 1973; with Free Spirits: Out Of Sight And Sound, 1967.

MOSLEY Ian, b. 16 June 1953, Paddington, London, England. Musician (drums, percussion). Musical Education: Guildhall School Of Music. Career; Member, Curved Air; Gordon Giltrap Band; Steve Hackett; Member, orchestras for West End musicals: Hair; Jesus Christ Superstar; Member, UK progressive rock group Marillion, 1983-; Tours, UK; Europe; US; Major concerts include: Milton Keynes Bowl, 1984; Nostell Priory Festival, 1984; Monsters Of Rock Festival, Castle Donington, 1985; Colombian Volcano Appeal Concert, Royal Albert Hall, 1986; Welcome To The Garden Party, Milton Keynes Bowl, 1986. Recordings: Albums: with Gordon Giltrap: Peacock Party, 1980; Live, 1981; with Steve Hackett: Highly Strung, 1983; Till We Have Faces, 1984; with Marillion: Fugazi, 1984; Real To Reel, 1984; Misplaced Childhood, 1985; Brief Encounter, 1986; Clutching At Straws, 1987; B-Sides Themselves, 1988; The Thieving Magpie, 1988; Season's End, 1989; Holidays In Eden, 1991; A Singles Collection 1982-1992, 1992; Brave, 1994; Singles with Marillion include: Punch And Judy, 1984; Assassing, 1984; Kayleigh (Number 2, UK), 1985; Lavender, 1985; Heart Of Lothian, 1985; Incommunicado, 1987; Sugar Mice, 1987; Warm Wet Circles, 1987;Freaks, 1988; Hooks In You, 1989; Uninvited Guest, 1989; Easter, 1990; Cover My Eyes (Pain And Heaven), 1991; No One Can, 1991; Dry Land, 1991; Sympathy, 1992; Other recordings with: Sally Oldfield; Darryl Way; Trace; Renaissance; Adrian Snell. Current Management: Hit And Run Music Ltd. Address: 30 Ives Street, London SW3 2ND, England.

MOSS Howard, b. 1 Mar 1975, Luton, Bedfordshire, England. Singer; Songwriter; Musician (guitar). Musical Education: Self-taught. Career: Major concerts commencing 1995; Numerous radio interviews, live acoustic sessions with BBC, RTE; Live television appearances with launch of second single, 1995. Compositions: Numerous. Recordings: Sally Forth (EP), 1994; Album: Tempus Fugit, 1995.

MOSS Mick (Mix), b. 25 May 1953, London, England. Producer; A&R Consultant. Education: BA Hons. Career: Worked with: The Farm; The La's; Elvis Costello; Pete Townshend; Sonya; Racey; The Troggs; Also worked with various members of The Clash; The Christians; Flock Of Seagulls; Icicle Works; Tears For Fears; Suzi Quatro band; Lightning Seeds. Recordings: Producer, Engineer: Singles/EPs: Bread Not Bombs, (benefit single, Campaign Against the Arms Trade), 1986; What's Happening To Our Nation?, L8 Connexion (benefit single for MTUCURC); Free, Live Transmission, 1986; Are U In Pain?, Gaynor Rose Madder, 1987; Fading, Gaynor Rose Madder, 1987; Here Comes The Floor, Benny Profane, 1987; I Love You Liverpool, Steve May, 1988; Worse Year of My Life, Wild Swans, 1989; Soldier On, Wild Swans, 1989; This Is The Age, Pupils of Parkfield School Liverpool, 1989; Post Funk War, 25th Of May, 1989; Cynthia Payne, The Hoovers, 1988; MDM: 4 singles, 2 albums, include: Take What You Want, 1988-94; Awakenings, The Sensies, Oh Father, Ice Factory, 1990; Disease, Adams Family, 1991; Cinemascope, Syndicate, 1994; Greytown, Syndicate, 1995. Publications: Various articles in music magazines. Memberships: PRS; MRF; IMF. Hobbies: Rock'n'Roll lifestyle; Nature; Wildlife; The Planet. Address: PO Box 25, Liverpool L17 8SX, England.

MOST Mickie (Michael Peter Hayes), b. June 1938, Aldershot, Hampshire, England. Record Producer. Career: Toured, recorded as the Most Brothers with Alex Wharton, late 1950s; Solo artiste, South Africa, 1959-63; Producer, UK, 1964-; Head of RAK record label, 1969-; Successful RAK artists included Hot Chocolate; Alexis Korner's CCS; Smokie; Chris Spedding; Kim Wilde; New World; Suzi Quatro; Mud; Television appearances include: Regular panelist,

New Faces, UK television talent show; Presenter, television show, Revolver. Recordings: As producer: The Animals (7 hit singles); Lulu; Terry Reid; Jeff Beck; Donovan; Mary Hopkin; Julie Felix; Johnny Hates Jazz; Perfect Stranger; Also worked with Herman's Hermits; The Nashville Teens. Address: c/o RAK Records, 43 Brook Green, London W6 7EF, England.

MOSUMGAARD Niels Eliot, b. 20 Oct 1961, Aarhus, Denmark. Songwriter; Musician (guitar, saxophone); Vocalist. m. Eva Baadsgaard, 18 May 1991, 2 sons. Musical Education: Self-taught. Career: Songwriter, singer, Lars Liholt Band tour, 1984; Touring Denmark with own band, 1984-; Sideman, saxophone, guitar, blues, calypso and popular bands; Member, Calypsocapellet, 1984-87; Member, Sweethearts, 1989-91; Lyricist for several composers on independent scene in Danish and English; Lyricist for: Bamboo Brothers: Johnny Told Suzi, 1993 (music by Troels Skovgard); Inventor, personal mix of folk, ambient, ethnic and metal called Folkadelic; Working on album: N B Danish Lyrics, 1995.

MOTION David, b. 23 Mar 1959, Hamburg, Germany. Composer. Partner, Vera Hegarty, 1982-. Musical Education: G Gaunt; G Greed; Royal Academy Of Music. Career: Recording engineer, 1982-84; Record producer, 1984-90; Composer. Compositions: Sally Potter's film Orlando; Television: Cardiac Arrest; Commercials: BMW; Ford Mondeo; Frontera; Shell; Johnnie Walker; Tesco; Cable And Wireless; Recordings: as producer: Since Yesterday, Strawberry Switchblade; Lean On Me, Red Box; Carmel; Chara; Toshihiko Takamizawa. Honours: D & AD Silver Award. Hobbies: Food; Wine; Travel; Cycling. Current Management: Bob Last. Address: Holdings Ecosse Ltd, 9/2 Tweeddale Court, 14 High Street, Edinburgh EH1 1TE, Scotland.

MOUCHIQUEL Nirmel, b. 12 Mar 1975, Dijon, France. Musician (clarinets, saxophones). Musical Education: Classical and jazz harmony, chamber music, improvisation, National Conservatory, Dijon (14 years of study). Career: Founder member, Take Five, 1990; Invited by UNESCO Clubs, by Conservatoire of Chenôve; Beaune Theatre; Regional Choir School; Festival Operetta of Lamalou-les-bains (tour); Fourvieres FM radio; France 3 TV, to represent jazz musicians in Burgundy; Founder member, Les Jazzologues, 1995. Compositions: More than 100 compositions: jazz, reggae, jazz-rock, classical, contemporary soul. Recordings: 4 recorded dummies (2 live). Honours: First Prize, clarinet and sight reading, Dijon Conservatory; Musical Theory: Diplôme B, Grade A Pass, International Competition of UFAM. Membership: SACEM. Hobby: Philosophy. Address: 2 Rue du Tire Peseau, 21000 Dijon, France.

MOUFANG David, b. 7 Sept 1966, Heidelberg, Germany. Composer; Producer; Musician (guitar, keyboards, percussion). Career: Runs two record labels with Jonas Grossmanns, Source Records, 1992-, KM 20, 1996-. Recordings: Earth To Infinity, 1992; Big Rooms, Deep Space Network, 1993; Intergalactic Federation, Deep Space Network and Dr Atmo, 1993; Intergalactic Federation 2, 1994; Reagenz, with Jonah Sharp, 1994; View To View, with Rob Gordon, 1994; Kunststoff, 1995; Solitaire, 1995; Koolfang with Pete Namlook, 1995; Koolgang 2, 1995; Traffic (Live '95), Deep Space Network, 1996; Cymbelin, Move D, 1996; RO70/Move D, with Roman Flügel, 1996; Exploring the Psychdelic Landscape, 1996; Lips, with Tobacco Rot, 1997; Deept Space Network Meets Higher Intelligence Agency, 1997; A Day in the Life, 1997; RO70/Move D II, with Roman Flügel, 1997; Conjoint, Berger/Hodge/Moufang/Ruit, 1997; Lost in Music, TV documentary, 1996. Memberships: Sound Works Exchange (sponsored by the Goethe Institute and British Arts Council), 1995.

Current Management: Source Records. Address: Kornmarkt 9, 69117 Heidelberg, Germany.

MOULD Bob, b. 1960, New York, USA. Musician (guitar); Songwriter; Record Producer. Career: Co-founder, lead guitarist, rock group Hüsker Dü, 1979-87; Solo artiste, 1987-92; Solo tour, 1991; Founder, guitarist, Sugar, 1992-. Recordings: Albums: with Hüsker Dü: Land Speed Record, 1981; Everything Falls Apart, 1982; Metal Circus, 1983; Zen Arcade, 1984; New Day Rising, 1985; Candy Apple Grey, 1986; Warehouse - Songs And Stories, 1987; Solo albums: Workbook, 1989; Black Sheets Of Rain, 1990; with Sugar: Copper Blue, 1992; Beaster, 1993; FUEL (File Under Easy Listening), 1994. Current Management: Granary Music, PO Box 4947, Austin, TX 78765, USA.

MOUNSEY Paul Fraser, b. 15 Apr 1959, Irvine, Scotland. Composer; Producer; Arranger; Musician (piano). m. Dorinha Carelli, 8 July 1983. Musical Education: Trinity College Of London: GTCL, FTCL (composition), LTCL (piano). Career: Part-time lecturer: Goldsmith's College, London University, 1984-1985; Songwriter, CBS (Sony) Brazil, 1986-; Producer, arranger, (Sony) Brazil, EMI (Brazil) and Independents, 1987-; Musical Director, Play It Again Studios, Sao Paulo, Brazil, 1989-; Musical Director, Michael Nyman In Brazil, Concert, 1992; Appearances: BBC Radio Scotland, Scot FM, 1994. Recordings: Numerous songs; Soundtrack for mini-series: Procura-se, 1992; La Cigale Et La Fourmi, for soprano, oboe, piano, recorded and broadcast, BBC Radio 3; Nahoo, solo album, UK 1994, USA 1995; Publications: Articles, Brazilian newspapers; Article: Music In Brazil, Contact (British music journal), No 31, Autumn 1987. Address: Iona Records, 27-29 Carnoustie Place, Scotland Street, Glasgow G5 8PH, Scotland; Mesa/Bluemoon Recordings, 209 E Alameda Avenue, Suite 101, Burbank, CA 91502, USA.

MOUSER Richard, b. 4 Jun 1962, Santa Monica, California, USA. Musician (guitar); Record Producer; Engineer; 2 daughters. Musical Education: Theory, Classical Guitar. Career: Support tours with 3 Dog Night; Huey Lewis and the News; Warrant; Michael Schenker Group; Melissa Manchester; Def Leppard; Queensryche; Wrote and produced jingles for numerous commercials. Recordings: Producer, engineer, mixer for albums by: Green Jelly; Corrosion Of Conformity; Lucy's Fur Coat; LSD; The Coup de Grace; Black Market Flowers; The Ex-Idols; Mixed album for: Imperial Tree; Mixed recordings by: Less Than Jake, Insane Clown Posse; Quickspace; Producer, The Generators, Schleprock; Engineer, Clawfinger. Hobbies: Golf; Skiing. Current Management: Tapko Entertainment, 17337 Ventura Boulevard,m Suite 208, Encino, CA 91316, USA.

MOUSKOURI Nana (Joanna), b.13 Oct 1936, Canea, Greece. Singer; Politician. m. George Petsilas, 1 son, 1 daughter. Musical Education: National Conservatory, Athens. Career: Regular European festival performances, late 50s; Regular television appearances, UK; UNICEF Ambassador, 1993-94; Member, European Parliament, 1994-. Recordings: Numerous albums; Hit singles include: Les Enfants du Piree; Weiss Rosen Aus Then; L'Enfant Au Tambour; Parapluies De Cherbourg (duet with Michel Legrand); Guantanamera; Only Love. Honours: Greek Broadcasting Festival Award; Barcelona Festival Award; Several Gold discs, 1959-. Address: 12 Rue Gutenberg, 92100 Boulogne-Sur-Seine, France.

MOWER Mike (Michael Henry), b. 9 June 1958, Bath, England. Composer; Musician (flutes, saxophones). m. Elizabeth Melia, 27 July 1994. Musical Education: Royal Academy of Music, London. Career: Mike Mower Quartet (jazz), frequent broadcasts for BBC Radio, 1980-84;

Wrote arrangements for BBC Radio Orchestra Big Band, 1984-86; Formed Itchy Fingers, jazz saxophone quartet playing his music, won Jazz Sounds '86, 1986-95; Band has toured 42 countries, playing all major European jazz festivals; Currently writes commissions for soloists and ensembles specializing in jazz/classical crossover style. Compositions: Numerous for wind instruments. Recordings: Albums: Producer, writer with Itchy Fingers saxophone quartet: Quark; Teranga; Itchy Fingers Live In Europe; Full English Breakfast; with flute player Kirten Spratt): Doodle And Flight; Triligence (titles taken from jazz sonatas for flute and piano by Mike Mower). Honours: Hon ARAM. Membership: Musicians' Union. Hobbies: Astronomy; Indian food. Address: 56 Lessar Avenue, London SW4 9HQ, England.

MOYET (Genevieve) Alison (Jane), b. 18 June 1961, Billericay, Essex, England. Singer; Songwriter. 1 son, 1 daughter. Education: Musical Foundation, Southend Technical College. Musical Education: Furniture, Musical Instrument Technology. Career: Singer with Yazoo, 1981-83; Solo singer, 1983-. Recordings: Albums: with Yazoo: Upstairs At Eric's, 1982; You And Me Both, 1983; Solo albums: Alf, 1984; Raindancing, 1987; Hoodoo, 1991; Essex, 1994; Singles, 1995. Honours: BRITS Award, Best New Band, Yazoo, 1982; Rock And Pop Award, Best Female Artist, 1982; Brits Awards, Best Female Artist, 1984, 1987; Grammy Nomination, Best Female Rock Vocal Performance, 1992. Hobby: Following Southend United Football Club. Current Management: Motley Music Ltd. Address: 132 Liverpool Road, London N1 1LA, England.

MOYSE Nigel Arthur, b. 26 Feb 1952, Dublin, Ireland. Musician (electric, semi-acoustic, acoustic guitar). m. Elizabeth McColl, 15 June 1974, 1 son, 1 daughter. Education: BA, Natural Sciences, Moderator, Trinity Collge Dublin. Musical Education: Piano, Municipal School of Music (Dublin); Guitar, self-taught, also under Louis Stewart. Career: John Stevens Away and Dance Orchestra; Folkus; Freebop; Ed Speight; Nigel Moyse Quartet; Mike Stock Band; The Flirtations, backing band; Bracknell; Camden; City of London; Sheffield Festivals; Folkus, National tour, 1984; Round House; ICA; Hyde Park; 100 Club; Universities; Clubs; Jazz venues; Jazz in Britain, BBC Radio III; Visiting music teacher, Eton College, Windsor, Berkshire. Compositions: Co-written with Ed Speight: The Dodder Suite, 1980; Complications, 1981; Solo: Tsk Tsk; Ballad For Mick; Martin's Dilemma, 1980; (All performed live and on Jazz In Britain, 1980, 1981). Recordings: Away: Integration, 1980; Mutual Benefit, 1994; Dance Orchestra: Ah, 1978; Some of: Conversation Piece, 1991; A Luta Continua, 1994; Folkus: The Life Of Riley, 1984. Membership: Musicians' Union. Hobbies: Reading; Films; Gardening; Music. Address: Flat 1, 10 Denbeigh Road, Ealing, London W13 8PX, England.

MUBARAK Abdel Aziz el, b. Sudan. Singer; Musician (oud). Musical Education: Institute of Music and Drama, Khartoum. Career: Popular solo artiste; Tours extensively in Africa and Arab States, including: Ethiopia; Somalia; Nigeria; Chad; Cameroon; Egypt; Kuwait; UAE; Member of trio with Abdel Gadir Salim and Mohammed Gubara, UK tour, 1986; Regular television and radio appearances. Recordings: with Abdel Gadir Salim and Mohammed Gubara: The Sounds of Sudan, 1991. Address: c/o World Circuit Records, 106 Cleveland Street, London W1P 5DP, England.

MUES Jan, b. 8 Feb 1955, Leuven, Belgium. Musician (Flugelhorn; Trumpet; Composer; Arranger). m. Marie Paule Branders, 12 Nov 1976, 1 daughter. Education: Painting, Academy Des Beaux Arts, Antwerp, Belgium. Career: Laureate, 11th edition, The European Jazz Contest International, 1989; Soloist, Belgian Jazz Orchestra; Jazz Festival in Milan; Several Belgian Radio and TV appearances; Jazz Middelheim Festival, Antwerp, 1995. Compositions: Mystic Smile; Whippy Lippy; Why Do You Skip So Tippy; Hayday; Who's Watching Who; Lullaby For the Sun; I Hope the Guys Like It; Foolish Enter; Peter's Egg. Recording: Mystic Smile, CD album. Publications: De Koning the Rijk. Honour: Fifth Annually Sabamprice. Membership: SABAM. Hobby: Painting. Current Management: Jan Muës, Mannenberg 70, 3270 Scherpenheuvel, Belgium. Address: Mannenberg 70, 3270 Scherpenheuvel, Belgium.

MUGGLETON Paul Frank, b. 27 Feb 1947, Queen Charlotte, London, England. Record Producer. Partner, Judie Tzuke, 2 sons, 3 daughters. Education: University of Madrid, Faculty of Filosofia Y Leras. Musical Education: Classical guitar, Madrid, 18 months. Career: All major tours with Judie Tzuke including tour of America with Elton John; Played to 450,000, Central Park, New York (with Judy Tzuke); Television includes: Top Of The Pops; many other shows. Recordings: Co-producer with Mike Paxman: All Judi Tzuke albums, 1980-92; Nick Kamen albums; Presently Scarlet. Honours: Song Award, Festival De Malaga, 1970. Memberships: PRS; Musicians' Union. Hobby: Egyptian archaeology (Armana Period). Current Management: Big Ocean Productions. Address: c/o Big Ocean Productions, 42 Princes Road, Weybridge, Surrey KT13 9BH, England.

MUHL Lars, b. 14 November 1950, Aarhus, Denmark. Singer; Songwriter; Musician; Author. Education: Self-taught; Classical Piano, Jutland Conservatory of Music, 2 years. Career: Formed Warm Guns, Released 5 Albums in Europe and Australia, 1978; Solo Career, Released 5 Albums, 1986-; Songwriting for European Artists; Author of 4 Books. Compositions: One More Minute; Open Up My Heart; Regnfang. Recordings: The Glorious Art of Breakin Little Girls Hearts & Blowin Big Boys Brains, 1984; King of Croon, 1988; When Angels Fall, 1990; Kingdom Come, 1993; Mandolina, 1997; The Best of Muhl, 1998. Honours: DJBFA Prize of Honour, 1990; WCM Songwriters Million Certificate, 1996. Memberships: DJBFA; Danish Artists Association. Address: Warner Chappell Music, Anker Heegaardsgade 2, 1572 Copenhagen, Denmark.

MÜHLEIS Daniela, b. 27 Apr 1955, St Gallen, Switzerland. Singer; Musician (guitar, piano). m. Hans Georg Huber, 26 Sept 1986, 1 adopted daughter. Education: Commercial school, commercial association, St Gallen. Musical Education: Music Lessons: guitar, piano. Career: Joined Cargo, 1979; National Country and Western Festival in Zürich, Open-Air Festival, St Gallen, 1981; Swiss finals, European Song Contest; Debut album, 1983; Band renamed Daniela Mühleis and Band, 1984; Successful concerts, Switzerland, Italy; Country Festivals; Swiss television: Sonntagsmagazin, 1989; Holansky kapr Country Music Festival, Prague, 1989; International Country Festival, Geiselwind, 1990; German Cable TV: Offener Kanal Dortmund, 1991; PORTA Country Festival, Czechoslovakia, 1992; International Visagino Country Festival, Lithuania, 1993; Lithuanian television; Swiss TV: Country Roads; Video clip produced in Malta, 1994; Television: Switzerland, Malta; Own radio show in St Gallen, Country Music, 1984-97. Recordings include: Albums: Stage-fright, 1983; Die Sieger des 1 Country und Western Festivals Zürich, 1986; Far Away, 1987; Animals, 1990; Far Away, 1991; Better Life, 1993; Open Minds, 1997. Honours: Winner, Modern Country Music section, Swiss Country Open Air, 1985; SRI Selection, 1997. Memberships: CMA, USA; CMFS, Switzerland; ECMA. Hobby: My dog Snert. Current Management: DMB. Address: Lehnacker 9a, 9033 Untereggen, Switzerland.

MUHLHAUS Doctor John, b. 11 Sept 1947, Redruth, Cornwall, England. Musician (ragtime

guitar, mandolin, bluegrass banjo). Education: MA (Cantab); PhD (Southampton); MIEE. Musical Education: Self-taught on all instruments; Music theory. Career: Folk guitar at university (Cambridge, Southampton); Solo appearances at folk clubs; Formed Now And Then (bluegrass, country, jazz duo), 1981; Edale Bluegrass Festival, 1993; Windsor Arts Festival, 1993. Recordings: Off The Cuff; New Country; British Bluegrass Album Number 1 (1 track on album). Hobbies: World travel; American "muscle" cars; Old films and books. Current Management: Self-managed. Address: Great Bookham, Surrey, England.

MUIRHEAD Dennis Richard, b. 7 Oct 1941, Dubbo, New South Wales, Australia. Lawyer. m. (1) Elizabeth, Dec 1966, 3 sons, (2) Angel, 10 Dec 1988, 1 daughter. Education: Law, University of Adelaide, South Australia. Career: Consultant Lawyer, Simons, Muirhead and Burton; Managing Director, Dennis Muirhead Company Limited, Muirhead Management, 1982-; Management, business, legal services to record producers, engineers, studios, artists, songwriters; Clients include producers: Hugh Padgham (Sting, Paul McCartney, Phil Collins, Melissa Etheridge, Split Enz); Robin Millar (Sade, Fine Young Cannibals); Stuart Colman (Jeff Beck, Billy Sawn); Nick Patrick (Gipsy Kings, Chris Rea); Nicky Graham (Let Loose, PJ And Duncan, Bros); Sun Studio Productions, Memphis; Australian jazz pianist and composer Paul Grabowsky; Missouri rockabilly singer, songwriter Billy Swan. Managing Director, Muirhead Music. Memberships: Chairman, Institute for the Study of Drug Dependence (ISDD); Founding Chairman, Managers Forum (IMF); Country Music Association, Nashville. Hobbies: Music; Motor racing; Keeping fit. Address: 202 Fulham Road, London SW10 9PJ, England.

MULDAUR Maria (Maria Grazia Rosa Domenica d'Avato), b. 12 Sept 1943, Greenwich Village, New York, USA. Singer. m. Jeff Muldaur, divorced 1972. Career: Member, Even Dozen Jug Band (with John Sebastian, Stefan Grossman, Joshua Rifkin, Steve Katz); Jim Kweskin Jug Band; US tour, 1975; European debut, 1975. Recordings: Albums: Maria Muldaur, 1973; Waitress In A Donut Shop, 1974; Sweet Harmony, 1976; Southern Winds, 1978; Open Your Eyes, 1979; Gospel Nights, 1980; There Is A Love, 1982; Sweet And Slow, 1984; Transblucency, 1985; Live In London, 1987; On The Sunny Side, 1991; Louisiana Love Call, 1992; Singles include: Midnight At The Oasis; I'm A Woman. Current Management: Piedmont Talent, 311 Oakdale Road, Charlotte, NC 28216, USA.

MULDOON Mule, (Paul Gerrard), b. 29 Oct 1958, Huddersfield, Yorkshire, England. Musician (bass, guitar); Vocalist. m. C A Nester, 20 May 1995. Career: Own band, Muldoon Brothers; Appeared at many major country festivals throughout Europe; Appearances on British, Irish and Scandinavian television and radio. Compositions: Back O' The Barn; Following The Trail; Brandin' Time. Recording: Back O' The Barn, by Muldoon Brothers. Honour: Most Promising Country Act, 1992. Membership: Musicians' Union. Hobbies: Music; Sport; Writing. Current Management: International Artists Ltd. Address: 17 South Lane, Netherton, Wakefield, West Yorkshire WF4 4LL, England.

MULLEN JR Larry, b. 31 Oct 1961, Dublin, Ireland. Musician (drums). Career: Founder member, drummer, rock group U2, 1978-; Regular national and international tours; Major concerts include: US Festival, 1983; The Longest Day, Milton Keynes, 1985; Live Aid, Wembley, 1985; Self Aid, Dublin, 1986; A Conspiracy Of Hope (Amnesty International Tour), 1986; New Year's Eve concert, Dublin (broadcast live to Europe), 1989. Recordings: Albums: Boy, 1980; October, 1981; War (Number 1, UK), 1983; Under A Blood

Red Sky, 1983; The Unforgettable Fire (Number 1, UK), 1984; Wide Awake In America, 1985; The Joshua Tree (Number 1, UK and US), 1987; Rattle And Hum, also film (Number 1, US) 1988; Achtung Baby (Number 1, US) 1991; Zooropa (Number 1, UK and US), 1993; Passengers (film soundtrack), with Brian Eno, 1995; Pop, 1997; Hit singles include: Out Of Control (Number 1, Ireland), 1979; Another Day (Number 1, Ireland), 1980; New Year's Day, 1983; Two Hearts Beat As One, 1983; Pride (In The Name Of Love), 1984; The Unforgettable Fire, 1985; With Or Without You (Number 1, US), 1987; I Still Haven't Found What I'm Looking For (Number 1, US), 1987; Where The Streets Have No Name, 1987; Desire (Number 1, UK), 1988; Angel Of Harlem, 1988; When Love Comes To Town, with B.B.King, 1989; All I Want Is You, 1989; The Fly (Number 1, UK), 1991; Mysterious Ways, 1992; Even Better Than The Real Thing, 1992; Who's Gonna Ride Your Wild Horses, 1993; Hold Me, Thrill Me, Kiss Me (from film Batman Forever), 1995; Discotheque, 1997; If God Will Send His Angels, 1997. Honours include: Grammy Awards: Album Of The Year, 1987; Best Rock Performance, 1987, 1989; Best Rock Vocal, 1989; BRIT Awards: Best International Group, 1988-90; Best Live Album, 1993; World Music Award, 1993; Juno Award, 1993; Q Awards: Best Act In The World, 1990; 1992; 1993; Merit Award, 1994; Gold and Platinum discs; Numerous magazine awards and poll wins. Current Management: Principle Management, 30-32 Sir John Rogersons Quay, Dublin 2, Ireland.

MÜLLER Anders, b. 2 Feb 1955, Copenhagen, Denmark. Musician (piano, keyboards); Composer; Arranger. m. Anne Macholm, 6 June 1987, 2 sons. Musical Education: Music Graduate, University of Copenhagen; Piano lessons with Ole Kock Hansen. Career: Leader, own jazz trio and quartets, 1975-; Member, orchestras led by Erling Kroner, Leif Johansson, Per Goldschmidt, 1979-92; Co-leader, jazz-rock group, Ariel, 1979-83; Appeared with New Music Orchestra as pianist, 1985, 1992; Conductor, 1990; Composer, 1985, 1988; Also worked with: Thad Jones; Eddie Bert; Red Rodney; Etta Cameron. Compositions: Tashmia; Woody's Blues, recorded by Lee Konitz. Recordings: with Erling Kroner; Leif Johansson; Ariel. Honour: First prize, Dunkerque Jazz Festival, with Soren Bogelund Quartet. Membership: DJBFA. Hobby: Family. Current Management: Mazurka Music. Address: Mazurka Music, Gammel Kongevej 78, 2 tv, 1850 Frederiksberg C, Denmark.

MULLER Ghislain, b. 30 Sept 1950, Roubaix, France. Composer; Musician (vibraphone). 1 son. Education: Arts illustrator, Strasbourg, France. Musical Education: Self-taught. Career: Member, soloist, band Sweet Chorus (with Mandino Reinhardt, Marcel Loeffler); Leader, Vibraphone Special Project; Festivals (mainly with Sweet Chorus) include: Django Reinhardt, Heidelberg; Musica Roma, Italy, 1984; Budapest, National Jazz Festival, 1985; Nîmes Festival, 1986; Chorzow, Poland, 1989; Django Reinhardt, Samois sur Seine, 1990; Nantes, 1990; Strasbourg Tzigan Music Festival, 1991; Banlieues Bleues, Paris, 1993; Estival Jazz Festival, Fribourg, Switzerland, 1993; Alternative Kultur Festival (AAK), Germany, 1993; Seville, 1994; Jazz En Touraine, 1994; Jazz Festival Mulhouse, 1995. Recordings: Transport Terrestre, 1977; Sweet Chorus, 1986; Mandino Reinhardt And Sweet Chorus, 1988; Plan B, 1988; Vibraphone Special Project, with The Brass Gang (recorded in concert), 1995; Patchwork, Sweet Chorus, 1995 (live recording Strasbourg Jazz Festival. Memberships: UMJ (Union Musiciens de France), Paris; Jazz d'Or Festival, Strasbourg, France; Tonight's Episode, with VSP and the Brass Gang. Address: 1 Rue Des Fleurs, 67380 Lingolsheim, France.

MULLIGAN Néillidh (Neil), b. 13 May 1955, Dublin, Ireland. Public Servant; Musician (Uilleann pipes). m. Sandra Ní Gharbháin, 6 Nov 1993, 1 son, 1 daughter. Musical Education: Taught by Tom Mulligan (father) and Leo Rowsome; Self-taught. Career: Played and toured many parts of the world including: Europe; America; New Zealand; Concerts in major cities; Many television and radio appearances home and abroad; Represented Ireland at various International Bagpipe Festivals. Compositions include: Barr Na Cúille; Tom Mulligan's Hornpipe; Wings Of My Soul. Recordings: Albums: Barr Na Cúille, 1991; The Leitrim Thrush, 1997; Guest on other albums. Publications: Contributions, articles to piping publications. Honours: All-Ireland Champion at various age levels. Memberships: Na Píobairí Uilleann; Folk Music Society of Ireland; Irish Traditional Music Archive. Hobbies: Music; Sport; The Irish language and culture. Current Management: Darina Ní Chuinneagáin, Allegro Music Agency. Address: 2 Eachlann Ashington, Bóthar Na Huaimhe, Baile Atha Cliath 7, Éire.

MULLIS Barry Joseph, b. 21 Jun 1964, Ballina, County Mayo, Ireland. Musician (guitar, 5-string banjo); Singer; Songwriter. Musical Education: Self-taught. Career: Played with roots/traditional bands Wholesome Fish, Seven Little Sisters, 1988-; In 1994 formed Red Megaphones playing jazz, blues and roots music; Appeared on Hit The Town, ITV; Travelled across the USA for 6 months playing and jamming with native roots musicians, 1996; Moved to San Francisco and continues to play own brand of progressive roots music with his band Pariah, 1997-. Compositions include: Divide And Rule; The Courtesan. Recordings: Single: with Seven Little Sisters: Daedalus (featuring compositions listed above). Memberships: PRS; MCPS; Musicians' Union. Hobbies: Cooking; Walking; Reading; Cinema; Woodcarving; Furniture design.

MUNDEN David Charles, b. 2 Dec 1943, Dagenham, Essex, England. Musician (drums); Vocalist. m Andrée, 7 Dec 1969, 1 son, 1 daughter. Career: Member, The Tremeloes; Toured worldwide: USA; South America; Australia; New Zealand; Iceland; South Africa; Middle East; Far East; Iceland; Germany; Eastern Bloc countries; Played with Beatles; Rolling Stones; Roy Orbison; Dusty Springfield; Television includes: Ready Steady Go; Top Of The Pops; Sunday Night Live At The Palladium. Recordings: Twist And Shout; Do You Love Me (Number 1, UK), 1963; Someone, Someone; Candy Man; Here Comes My Baby; Silence Is Golden (Number 1, UK); Call Me Number One (Number 1, UK and worldwide); Helule Helule; Even The Bad Times Are Good; My Little Lady; Suddenly You Love Me; Me and My Life; I Shall Be Released; Once on a Sunday Morning; Tremeloes played on Jeff Christie's No 1 hit Yellow River. Publications: Guinness Book Of Hit Records. Honours: Carl Alan Awards. Memberships: Musicians' Union; Equity; PRS. Hobbies: Music; Driving fast cars. Current Management: Stephen Colyer. Address: 25A Cliff Parade, Leigh-On-Sea, Essex SS9 1BB, England.

MUNKGAARD Peer, b. 29 Mar 1965, Vejle, Denmark. Music Teacher; Freelance Musician (viola, violin). Education: Graduate, Esbjerg Kommunale Gymnasium, 1984; Studied viola with Gert Inge Andersson at the Music Academy in Esbjerg, 1987-93. Career: Danced folkdances since 1969; Played folk music (fiddle), 1973-; Danced on television show Les Lanciers, 1983; Danced in and played for numerous folkdance groups including Udöbt on their first tours in England; Danish representative on the Comhaltas Ceoltoiri Eireann European Tour, 1985; Instructor of folk dance and music at seminars, music schools and evening schools; Teacher of viola, violin, cello, chamber music, orchestras and choirs; Member of West Jutland Symphony Orchestra and the Jutland Sinfonietta; Assisted in

various symphony orchestras and Esbjerg Ensemble; Also played in musicals including: The King and I, Showboat and the Phantom of the Opera. Membership: Danish Musicians' Union. Hobbies: Kids; Cats; Cooking; Dancing; Jamming. Current Management: Det Klassiske Koncertbureau, Rorhaven 4, 8900 Randers, Denmark. Address: Peder Skrams Gade 5, II tv, 6700 Esbjerg, Denmark.

MUNNS Heather Shirley (Josephine Lascaux), b. London, England. Singer; Songwriter. Education: Drama, singing, Chichester College. Musical Education: Singing, Grade 6; Drama, 1-8 Guildhall exams; Acting, 1-8 Gold medal LAMDA exams. Career: Member, Disturbed; Concerts in UK and France as Josi (group name Josi Without Colours); Numerous appearances on local radio and BBC Radio 1 Round Table, 1991; Songwriting for current band Josephine. Recordings: with Disturbed: Betrayed; with Josi and The Pussycats: Heroes; with Josi Without Colours: Hear The Animals Cry; Children Of The Revolution; Tell Me A Story; Treasure, 1991; Lucy, 1991. Memberships: PRS; Musicians' Union; PPL. Hobbies: Singing; The sea; Step aerobics. Current Management: David Rome, Anne-Marie Heighway, Survival. Address: PO Box 888, Maidenhead, Berks SL6 2YQ, England.

MUNOZ Michel, b. France. Musician (drums, vibraphone). Musical Education: Classical studies, L'Ecole Nationale De Lorient; Began percussion aged 12; Conservatoire Régional D'Angers et De St Maur des Fosses. Career: Plays with Philharmonic Orchestra in the Loire; Numerous groups in Brittany; Taught percussion, various music schools; Played with Philharmonic Orchestra in Montpellier; Member, various ensembles and groups including: Orchestre de Jazz du Languedoc-Roussillon; Quintet with Jean-Philippe Llabador; Nedjma. Recordings: Mansourah, Nedjma; Dialogues, Orchestre de Jazz du Languedoc-Roussillon.

MUNRO Andrew MacDonald, b. 25 Aug 1950, Aberdeen, Scotland. Songwriter; Children's Musician; One Man Band (drums, guitar, harmonica); Vocalist. m. Morna Gourlay, 5 June 1983, 1 daughter. Education: BSc, Architectural Studies, Edinburgh University. Musical Education: Drum rudiments taught by Willie Lyle, Wick Pipe Band; Self-taught guitar. Career: Drummer, Pipe Band and Dance Band; Session drummer, various artistes including: Pete Atkin, Anika; Anne Lorne Gillies; Musician, actor with Wildcat Stage Productions; Children's entertainer, Mr Boom - Children's One Man Band; 68 television appearances; 28 shows at Glasgow Royal Concert Hall; Tours, UK and abroad, 1985-. Recordings: Soul o' Man, Andy Munro; As Mr Boom: Sing Along With Mr Boom; Dance Along With Mr Boom; Play Along With Mr Boom; Mr Boom Is Over The Moon. Memberships: Musicians' Union; Equity; PRS; MCPS; PPL. Hobbies: Swimming; Touring; Geodesic geometry. Current Management: Self-managed. Address: Lindsaylands Cottage, Biggar ML12 6NR, Scotland.

MUNRO Donnie, b. 2 Aug 1953, Uig, Isle Of Skye, Scotland. Musician (guitar); Art Teacher. m. 1980, 2 son, 1 daughter. Education: DA Hons, Dip Ed. Career: Member, Scottish folk group Runrig; Worldwide tours; Television appearances: Own documentary; Top Of The Pops; TV-AM; Pebble Mill. Recordings: Albums with Runrig: Play Gaelic, 1978; The Highland Connection, 1979; Recovery, 1981; Heartland, 1985; The Cutter And The Clan, 1987; Once In A Lifetime, 1988; Searchlight, 1989; The Big Wheel, 1991; Amazing Things, 1993; Townsmitting Live, 1995. Publications: Going Home - The Runrig Story, Tony Morton. Honours: Rector, Edinburgh University, 1991-94; Dr Honoris Causa, 1994. Membership: Musicians' Union. Current Management: Marlene Ross Management, 55 Wellington Street, Aberdeen AB2 1BX, Scotland.

MUNTON Chris John, b. 6 Sept 1969, Pembury, England. Producer; Songwriter; Musician (guitar, various instruments). Career: Crystal Palace Bowl Concert, with Beep! Beep! and The Giants, 1987; Interviews, Kent Rocks (Radio Kent), Kiss FM, with current band Conscious Pilot, 1995. Recordings: All co-written with Janice Charles: New Age Dawning, 1993; Send Me A Line, 1993; Burning Empire, 1994; I Wonder, 1995. Memberships: Musicians' Union. Hobbies: Ju-jitsu; Martial arts; Film; Meditation; Fitness. Current Management: CSPT Management. Address: CSPT, PO Box 199, Southall, Middlesex UB2 5EY, England.

MURCIA Joey, b. 21 Mar 1948, Brooklyn, New York, USA. Musician (guitar). 1 son. Musical Education: Graduate, Grove School Of Music. Career: Session guitarist, 30 years; Major tours with: Benny Lattimore, support to James Brown, 1975; Bee Gees, Here At Last Tour, 1976, Spirits Having Flown Tour, 1979; Jay Ferguson, support to Foreigner, 1977; Andy Gibb, Shadow Dancing Tour, 1978; Performances with Ann Jillian include: Tahoe, Las Vegas, 1984; Trump Plaza, Atlantic City, 1989, 1990. Compositions: Cozumel, Jay Ferguson, 1978; Jennifer Slept Here, Joey Scarborough, Theme for NBC-TV series, 1985; Ann Jillian, Theme for NBC-TV series, 1990. Recordings: Albums: Clean Up Women, Betty Wright; Rockin Chair, Gwen McCrae; Lattimore III, Benny Lattimore; Monkey Grip Glue, Bill Wyman; Here At Last-Bee Gees Live, Bee Gees; Thunder Island, Jay Ferguson; But Seriously Folks, Joe Walsh; A Luxury You Can Afford, Joe Cocker; Grease, Frankie Valli; Saturday Night Fever, Bee Gees; Restless, Bellamy Brothers; with Andy Gibb: Flowing Rivers; Shadow Dancing; After Dark; Andy Gibb's Greatest Hits; Singles with Andy Gibb: I Just Want To Be Your Everything; Thicker Than Water; Shadow Dancing; Everlasting Love. Honours: 10 Gold Albums, with Bee Gees, Andy Gibb, Joe Walsh. Membership: AFofM, 30 years. Current Management: Have Mercy Music Inc. Address: 2080 W Hillcrest Drive, Suite # 106, Newbury Park, CA 91320, USA.

MURPHY John, b. 4 Mar 1965, Liverpool, England. Composer; Musician (guitar). Career: Session guitarist, worked with members of Japan, Propaganda; While working with Thomas Lang, began collaboration in composition with David Hughes. Compositions: with David Hughes: Films: Leon The Pig Farmer; Solitaire For 2; Clockwork Mice; Welcome To The Terrordome; Beyond Bedlam; A Feast At Midnight; Body Memories; Dinner In Purgatory; Destroying Angels; Proteus; Flame; Giving Tongue; Television: White Men Are Cracking Up, BBC2; All The President's Women; Eunice The Gladiator, CH4; Where The Bad Girls Go, Granada. Memberships: PRS; Musicians' Union. Current Management: Soundtrack Music Management. Address: 22 Ives Street, Chelsea, London SW3 2ND, England.

MURPHY John Paul, b. 4 Mar 1965, Walton, Liverpool, England. Film composer; Musician (piano, guitar). Career: Musician (bass) with: Lotus Eaters; Thomas Lang; Co-wrote songs with both bands; Established Dry Communications Limited (Record Company); Scored nine films to date. Compositions: Co-wrote, orchestrated the films: Leon The Pig Farmer; Dinner In Purgatory; Body Memories; Beyond Bedlam; Welcome To The Terrordome; Solitaire For 2; Feast At Midnight; Clockwork Mice; Proteus; All co-written with David Hughes. Memberships: Musicians' Union; PRS. Hobbies: Screen writing. Current Management: Olav Wyper, Sound Track Music Management. Address: Soundtrack Music Management, 22 Ives Street, Chelsea, London, England.

MURPHY Nicholas, b. 22 Jul 1953, Wallasey, Wirral, England. Musician (keyboards). m. Margaret Murphy, 5 Nov 1991, 2 daughters. Career: Founder member, band Bassheads; Played 187 concerts in 15 months, 1991-92.

Recordings: with Bassheads: Is There Anybody Out There; Who Can Make Me Feel Good; Start A Brand New Life. Memberships: PRS; MCPS; Code of Conduct Member, MCPS. Hobbies: Football; Motor racing. Current Management: Red Parrott Management. Address: 86 Fulham Road, London SW6 3LF, England.

MURPHY Robert Joseph, b. 3 June 1936, Summit, New Jersey, USA. Musician (saxophone, percussion). m. Judith Ann Miller, 3 Aug 1962, 2 daughters. Education: BA, Brown University, 1958; LLB, Stanford University, 1963. Musical Education: Jazz Studies, Deanza College, Cupertino, California, 1972-75. Career: European tour, 1983, 1997; 3 times guest soloist, Kobe Jazz Festival Japan, 1991-93; Ranked number 16 among soprano soloists worldwide, Jazzology Readers Poll, 1985; On faculty of Stanford Jazz Workshop. Compositions: Red Neck Blues, musical condemnation of racism. Recordings: 9 albums with Natural Gas Jazz Band. Publications: Jazz theory text for Stanford jazz workshop. Membership: BMI. Hobby: Music. Current Management: Self-managed. Address: 8 Portola Green Circle, Portola Valley, CA 94028, USA.

MURPHY Terence James, b. 3 Oct 1948, Dublin, Ireland. Musician (mandolin, banjo, guitar); Vocalist. m. Kristina Karlsson, 26 Oct 1991, 1 son, 1 daughter. Musical Education: Provincial High School of Music. Career: Tour of England, 1978; Netherlands, 1979 including television appearance; Tour of Germany with appearances on television and radio folk programmes, 1982; Touring and appearances on TV in Denmark, Sweden and Norway. Recordings: 4 albums with McEwan's Expotit: Hand Across The Water, 1979, McEwans, 1981, Highland Paddy, 1988, and McEwans, 1990; 3 Solo albums: Terry Murphy: A Dubliner In Denmark, 1982, Don't Bury Me 'Til I'm Dead, 1984; Jack Of All Trades, 1986. Memberships: DJBFA; Musicians' Union; Gramex. Hobbies: Aerobics; Swimming; Cycling; Writing poetry. Address: Humlebaekgade 7 4 tv, 2200 Copenhagen, Denmark.

MURRAY Andy, b. 31 July 1952, Isleworth, England. Composer; Songwriter; Musician (guitar, bass, keyboards). Musical Education: University of Sussex; Royal Academy Of Music. Career: Shared music biz/education; Top 20 hit with Piranhas, 1982; Top Of The Pops; Composer, television and video soundtracks; School and college music lecturer, examiner; Advisory consultant, Music Technology in Education. Publications: Music Matters, Notator Software Resource Packs. Honours: BA; LRAM; BBC Song contest winner. Memberships: PRS; Musicians' Union; MANA; NASUWT. Hobby: Cycling. Address: 69 Riley Road, Brighton BN2 4AG, England.

MURRAY Anne, b. 20 June 1946, Springhill, Nova Scotia, Canada. Singer. m. William M Langstroth, 20 June 1975, 1 son, 1 daughter.Education: BPhys, Education, University of New Brunswick, 1966; DLitt (hon), 1978; DLitt (hon), St Mary's University, 1982. Career: Recording artist, 1968-; Worldwide tours; Television appearances: Singer, Singalong Jubilee, local television network; Numerous television specials, 1970-97; Regular guest, Glen Campbell's Goodtime Hour. Recordings: Hits singles: Snowbird, 1970; Danny's Song, 1973; You Needed Me, 1978; He Thinks I Still Care (Number 1, US country chart); Just Another Woman In Love; Could I Have This Dance, from film Urban Cowboy; A Little Good News, 1983; Nobody Loves Me Like You Do, duet with Kenny Loggins (Number 1, US country chart), 1984; Albums: What About Me, 1968; This Was My Way, 1970; Snowbird, 1970; Anne Murray, 1971; Talk It Over In The Morning, 1971; Annie, 1972; Danny's Song, 1973; Love Song, 1974; Country, 1974; Highly Prized Possession, 1974; Together, 1975;

Keeping In Touch, 1976; Let's Keep It That Way, 1977; Hippo In My Tub (children's songs), 1979; New Kind Of Feeling, 1979; I'll Always Love You, 1980; Somebody's Waiting, 1980; Where Do You Go To When You Dream, 1981; The Hottest Night Of The Year, 1982; A Little Good News, 1983; Heart Over Mind, 1985; Something To Talk About, 1986; Songs Of The Heart, 1987; Harmony, 1989; I Will, 1990; Yes I Do, 1991; The Best...So far, 1994; Anne Murray, 1996; An Intimate Evening with Anne Murray, 1997; with Glen Campbell: Anne Murray And Glen Campbell, 1973. Honours: Numerous JUNO Awards, Top Female Vocalist, 1970-81; Grammy, Top Female Vocalist, 1978; Star on Hollywood Walkway Of Stars, 1980; Inducted into Country Music Hall Of Fame; Decorated Companion Order of Canada; Inducted into the Juno Hall of Fame, 1993. Memberships: AFTRA; Association Canadian TV and Radio Artists; Executive member, Canadian Save The Children Fund (Honorary chairwoman, 1978-80). Current Management: Bruce Allen Talent, 68 Water Street, Suite 406, Vancouver, BC V6B 1A4, Canada.

MURRAY Don, b. 3 Feb 1929, Hull, England. Musician (drums). m. Edna Chadwick, 18 Oct 1952, 1 son, 3 daughters. Musical Education: Piano and drums. Career: Started at age 16 doing local gigs; After Army service member of various big bands including Harry Chatterton, Alan Hurst, and Kenny Baker; Also backed David Whitfield, Joe Longthorne and Elizabeth Dawn. Membership: Musicians' Union. Address: 69 Lambwath Road, Hull, Yorkshire HU8 0EZ, England.

MURRAY Ian, b. 17 Jan 1944, Newcastle-upon-Tyne, England. Freelance Musician (drums). m. Ursula Mary Curlé, 5 Jun 1968, 1 son, 4 daughters. Musical Education: Self-taught. Career: Appearances on Border TV and Channel 4 TV; Tour of Ireland; Numerous recordings. Hobbies: Listening to music; Research. Address: 14 Woodlands, Rothbury, Northumberland NE65 7XZ, England.

MURRAY Neil, b. 27 Aug 1950, Edinburgh, Scotland. Musician (bass guitar). Education: London College of Printing. Career: Member, Gilgamesh, 1973; Hanson, 1974; Colosseum II, 1975-76; National Health, 1976-77; Whitesnake, 1978-82; Gary Moore, 1982-83; Whitesnake, 1984-86; Vow Wow, 1987-89; Black Sabbath, 1989-90; Brian May Band, 1992-93; Black Sabbath, 1994-. Recordings: Albums include: with Whitesnake: Trouble, 1978; Lovehunter, 1979; Ready An' Willing, 1980; Live In The Heart Of The City, 1980; Come An' Get It, 1981; Saints An' Sinners, 1982; Slide It In, 1984; Whitesnake 1987, 1987; with Black Sabbath: Tyr, 1990; Forbidden, 1995. Hobbies: Travel, especially in Scottish Highlands. Current Management: Bluefame Ltd. Address: 17 Hereford Mansions, Hereford Road, London W2 5BA, England.

MURRAY Phil, b. 18 Nov 1953, North Shields, England. Writer; Performer. m. Allison Longstaff, 15 Aug 1980, 1 son, 1 daughter. Career: Singer, songwriter with U Boat; Member of Blackie; Actor, television programmes including: Dempsey and Makepeace; Cats Eyes; Les Dawson Show; Many theatre tours; Recently personnel development consultant for a radio show. Recordings: Album: End Of My Time, U Boat; Single: Making A Bad Boy Good, U Boat; Also on albums: Talk Talk; Separate Holiday; Forever Again (love songs). Publications: Books: You Can Always Get What You Want; Before The Beginning Is A Thought; Empowerment, 1995; The 49 Steps to a Bright Life, 1996; Phil Murray Bites on Personal Development, 1997; You and Me Make Three, 1997; Staying Awake Forever, 1997. Memberships: Equity; Musicians' Union; PRS; MCPS; PPS. Hobby: Philosophy studies. Current Management: Perfect Words and Music. Address: Purbeck, Mill Lane, Felbridge, Surrey RH19 2PE, England.

MURRELL David Evan (Dave), b. 22 Jan 1952, London, England. Musician; College Lecturer (music); Arranger. m. Debora Anne Diamond, 5 July 1980, 2 daughters. Education: Art college. Musical Education: Humber College, Toronto, Canada. Career: Solo recordings, sessions, Transatlantic Records; Tours, Canada, USA with: Ken Tobias; Tommy Hunter; Ronnie Prophet; British artists: Psychic TV; Long John Baldry; Zoot Money; MD, arranger, World Of Dance. Recordings: MD, Yamaha Jazz Connection; Film music: Words Of Love, BBC, 1990; Long Way Home, ITV, 1991. Membership: Musicians' Union. Address: 37 Woodland Road, Selsey, Sussex PO20 0AL, England.

MURTO Janne, b. 26 Oct 1964. Musician (saxophone, flutes). Musical Education: Oulunkylä Pop/Jazz Conservatoire, 1982; Jazz Department, Sibelius Academy; Studied musical culture, Cuba. Career: Member, various big bands including Espoo Big Band; Big Bad Family, with Upi Sorvali; UMO Big Band; 10 years with Fiestacita (Afro-Cuban ensemble); Freelance musician for recording studios, radio and theatre; Current member, Paroni Paakunainen's Saxperiment Quartet; Kari Tenaken's Quintet.

MUSTAINE Dave, b. USA. Rock Vocalist; Musician (guitar); Songwriter. Career: Member, Metallica, 1981-83; Founder member, guitarist, songwriter, Megadeth, 1983-; Worldwide tours; Concerts include: Monsters Of Rock Festival, Castle Donington, 1988; Clash Of The Titans Fest (with Slayer, Suicidal Tendencies, Testament), Wembley, 1990; Rock In Rio Festival, Brazil, 1991; Clash Of The Titans, US tour (with Anthrax, Slayer, Alice In Chains), 1991. Recordings: Albums: Killing Is My Business And Business Is Good!, 1985; Peace Sells... But Who's Buying?, 1986; So Far So Good... So What?, 1988; Rust In Peace, 1990; Countdown To Extinction, 1992; Youthanasia, 1994; Hit singles: Wake Up Dead, 1987; Anarchy In The UK, 1988; No More Mister Nice Guy, 1990; Holy Wars, 1990; Hangar 18, 1991; Symphony Of Destruction, 1992; Skin Of My Teeth, 1992; Sweating Bullets, 1993; Other recordings: Contributor, film soundtracks: Super Mario Brothers, 1993; The Last Action Hero, 1993; Contributor, The Beavis And Butthead Experience. Honours include: Doris Day Music Award; Genesis Award. Hobby: Skydiving. Current Management: Lafitte Management, 1333 Ventura Blvd #204, Sherman Oaks, CA 91423, USA.

MWYN Rhys, b. 1 July 1962. Musician (Bass Guitar); Manager. Career: Founding Member, Welsh Bands: Anhrefn; Land of My Mothers; Head of Crai Records. Composition: Tra Di Di, Blue Rose/V2. Recordings: Tra Di Di, Blue Rose/V2; Dis-UK, Blue Rose/V2. Address: Canolfan Sain, Llandwrog, Gwynedd, LL54 5TG, Wales.

MYATT Charlie, b. 24 June 1965, Bristol, England. Booking Agent. Education: Royal Holloway and Bedford New College; Clifton College, Bristol. Career: Six years as agent with: The Levellers; Radiohead; Inspiral Carpets; The La's; Shampoo; Shed Seven; Compulsion; Skunk Anansie; Supergrass; The Bluetones. Address: ITB, 3rd Floor, 27A Floral Street, Covent Garden, London WC2E 9DQ, England.

MYERS James E., b. 26 Oct 1919, Philadelphia, Pennsylvania, USA. Musician (drums); Bandleader; Songwriter; Arranger; Film Producer; Actor; Publisher; Writer. Career: Arranger, conductor, Jimmy DeKnight and his Knights of Rhythm; Actor, over 300 films and television shows; Film producer, The Block; Owner, James E. Myers Enterprises; Chairman, Rock Around The Clock Museum; Discovered artists including: Al Alberts and the Four Aces; Al Martino. Compositions: Over 300 published songs, including Rock Around The Clock, Bill Haley and the Comets. Honours include: Grammy; Inducted, Songwriters Hall Of Fame; Legendary Eagle Award, CMAA; Pioneer Award, Country Music News; Cash Box Record Of The Year; Billboard Triple Crown Award; Legends Awards, Los Angeles, Nashville and Las Vegas; SONA Award; ASCAP Pop Awards; Numerous Presidential, State, City and Congressional citations; Over 100 other awards. Memberships: ASCAP; NMPA; Screen Actors Guild; AFTRA; CMA; SGA; EIA; VFW. Address: James E. Myers Enterprises, 1607 E. Cheltenham Avenue, Philadelphia, PA 19124, USA.

MYLES Heather, b. 31 July 1964, Riverside, California, USA. Singer; Songwriter; Musician (bass). Education; Bachelor, Business Administration. Musical Education: Self taught. Career: Opened for Merle Haggard, 12 times; Charlie Daniels, 30 times; Extensive travel in Europe. Recordings: Albums: Untamed; Just Like Old Times; Sweet Little Dangerous (Live In London). Honours: Picked top 10 in Request Magazine, 1995-96. Hobbies: Horse racing; Restoring cars. Current Management: Clyde Masters, Gehl Group. Address: c/o Gehl Force Management, 1106 18th Avenue South, Nashville, TN 37212, USA.

MYLLÄRI Mika, b. 17 June 1966, Kokkola, Finland. Musician (trumpet); Composer. Musical Education: Jazz Department, Sibelius Academy, 1986; Jazz Composition with Jukka Linkola, 1991. Career: Member, Espoo Big Band; Freelance musician with UMO Big Band; Formed own quintet, playing own material, 1990; Member, 10-man ensemble Zone, 1991-. Honours: Finnish Jazz Federation Award, Band Of The Year, Mika Mylläri Quintet. Address: Dunckerinkatu 4 C 42, 00260 Helsinki, Finland.

MYROL Keith, b. 19 July 1950, Maple Creek, Saskatchewan, Canada. Musician (guitar). m. Trish, 22 Jan 1972, 1 son 1 daughter. Musical Education: Self-taught. Career: The Myrol Brothers; Appearances: Capital Country CFAC TV Calgary; SCMA Awards Show 1990-94; 7 Sunday In the Park concerts; Right Tracks; Gold Rush Cafe; Saskatchewan Showcase Of The Arts; CBC Arts Reel; Project Discovery. Recordings: Albums: The Singles Collection; Raisin' The Roof; Also on: Best Of the West, Volumes I and II, CFAC Country Showdown. Honours: SCMA: Non Touring Band Of The Year. Memberships: CCMA; SCMA Hall Of Fame. Current Management: Self-managed; Agent: Cross Town Entertainment. Address: The Myrol Brothers, Box 969 Outlook, Saskatchewan S0L 2N0, Canada.

MYROL Myles, b. 6 Mar 1957, Maple Creek, Saskatchewan, Canada. Musician (bass guitar). m. Diane, 31 July 1976, 1 son, 1 daughter. Musical Education: Self-taught. Career: The Myrol Brothers; Appearances: Capital Country CFAC TV Calgary; SCMA Awards Show, 1990-94; 7 Sunday In The Park concerts; Right Tracks; Gold Rush Cafe; Sask Showcase Of the Arts; CBC Arts Reel; Project Discovery. Recordings: Albums: The Singles Collection; Raisin' The Roof; Also on: Best Of the West, Volumes I and II, CFAC Country Showdown. Honours: SCMA; Non Touring Band Of the Year. Memberships: CCMA; SCMA Hall Of Fame. Current Management: Self-managed; Agent: Cross Town Entertainment. Address: The Myrol Brothers, Box 969 Outlook, Saskatchewan S0L 2N0, Canada.

MYROL Rick, b. 30 May 1948, Maple Creek, Saskatchewan, Canada. Musician (guitar). m. Violet, 23 Nov 1968, 2 sons. Musical Education: Self-taught. Career: The Myrol Brothers; Appearances: Capital Country CFAC TV Calgary SCMA Awards Show, 1990-94; 7 Sunday In The Park apperances; Right Tracks; Gold Rush Cafe; Saskatchewan Showcase Of the Arts; CBC Arts Reel; Project Discovery. Recordings: Albums: The Singles Collection; Raisin' The Roof; Also on: Best of West, Volumes I and II, CFAC Country Showdown. Honours: SCMA: Non Touring Band

Of The Year. Memberships: CCMA; SCMA Hall Of Fame. Current Management: Self-managed; Agent: Cross Town Entertainment. Address: The Myrol Brothers, Box 969 Outlook, Saskatchewan S0L 2N0, Canada.

N

N'DOUR Youssou, b. 1959, Dakar, Senegal. Musician; Singer; Songwriter. Career: Member, Sine Dramatic, 1972; Orchestre Diamono, 1975; The Star Band (houseband, Dakar nightclub, the Miami Club), 1976-79; Founder, Etoile De Dakar, 1979; Re-formed as Super Etoile De Dakar, 1982-; International tours include support to Peter Gabriel, US tour, 1987. Recordings: Albums: A Abijan, 1980; Xalis, 1980; Tabaski, 1981; Thiapathioly, 1983; Absa Gueye, 1983; Immigres, 1984; Nelson Mandela, 1985; The Lion, 1989; African Editions Volumes 5-14, 1990; Africa Deebeub, 1990; Jamm La Prix, 1990; Kocc Barma, 1990; Set, 1990; Eyes Open, 1992; The Best Of Youssou N'Dour, 1994; The Guide, 1995; Gainde - Voices From The Heart Of Africa (with Yande Codou Sene), 1996; Hit single: Seven Seconds, duet with Neneh Cherry, 1995. Current Management: Soundscape, 799 Greenwich Street, New York, NY 10014, USA.

N-TRANCE (Dale Longworth), 19 June 1966, Middleton, Manchester, England. Musician (keyboards). Musical Education: Degree, Sound recording. Career: Sound engineer, leading PA company, most aspects of live sound (rock and roll, musicals, classical, television); Signed to PWL while working on the Hitman and Her. Recordings: Back To The Bass (unreleased); Set You Free; Turn Up The Power; Set You Free (re-released Number 2, UK). Honours: Best UK Dance Record, 1994; Platinum Disc, 1994; (both for Set You Free). Membership: Musicians' Union. Hobbies: Football (Manchester United); Collecting old MGs. Current Management: All Around The World. Address: All Around The World, 9-13 Penny Street, Blackburn BB1 6HJ, England.

NABORS James Thurston (Jim), b. 12 June 1930, Tuscaloosa, Alabama, USA. Entertainer; Actor; Musician (piano). Education: Business Degree, University of Alabama. Career: The Andy Griffith Show; Gomer Pyle USMC; The Jim Nabors Variety Hour; The Jim Nabors Show (TV); Las Vegas; Reno; Atlantic City; Various personal appearances across country. Recordings: 28 albums, 5 Gold, 1 Platinum. Current Management: William Morris Agency. Address: 151 El Camino, Beverly Hills, CA 91510, USA.

NAGEL Allan, b. 2 December 1967, Copenhagen, Denmark. Musician (Bass guitar); Backing Vocalist. m. Sanne Kejlberg, 23 January 1997, 1 son, 1 daughter. Education: Selftaught. Career: Member, Drive Alive, 1982-92, Skagarack, 1993, Jacob Haugaard, 1992-94, Mek Pek, 1995. Recordings: Jacob Synger; Tangokat; Hej Frede; Hemli Helikopter. Membership: Danish Musicians Organization. Hobbies: Music; Family. Address: Solystgade 61 2 Floor, DK-8000 Arhus C, Denmark.

NAIDENOV Vassil, b. 3 Sept 1950, Sofia, Bulgaria. Singer. Education: Music Academy, Sofia, Bulgaria. Musical Education: Piano. Career: Pop singer, Number 1 in list of Bulgarian National TV and radio for over 10 years; Tours: Germany; Belgium; Canada; Romania; Poland; Cuba; Republics of former USSR; First success with Adaption, 1979. Recordings: 5 albums; 2 singles including Seven Times; Composes most of own material. Honours: Second place, Eurovision, Belgium, 1982; International prizes in Cuba, 1982; USSR; Belgium; Canada; The Golden Orpheus Festival: First prize, 1981; Second prize, 1982; Silver Orpheus, 1983; Prizes for television show, Melody Of The Year, 1979, 1982-84, 1986. Membership: Union Of Bulgarian Musicians. Hobbies: Antiques; Growing flowers. Current Management: Ivailo Manolov. Address: 91-A Vitosha Boulevard, 1408 Sofia, Bulgaria.

NAIL Jimmy (James Michael Aloyisius Bradford), b. 1954, Newcastle-upon-Tyne, England. Singer; Actor. Career: Actor, UK television series, Auf Wiedersehen Pet, ITV; Co-writer, actor, Spender, BBC; Actor, Crocodile Shoes, BBC; Solo recording artiste, 1992-; Own company, Big Boy Productions. Recordings: Singles: Love Don't Live Here Anymore; Ain't No Doubt; Crocodile Shoes; Big River; Albums: Growing Up In Public, 1992; Crocodile Shoes, 1994; Big River, 1995. Honours: Great British Country Music Awards: Best Album, Best Song, 1996. Current Agent: Fairwarning / Wasted Talent, London, England. Address: c/o East West Records, Electric Lighting Station, 46 Kensington Court, London W8 5DP, England.

NAISSOO Tonu, b. 18 Mar 1951, Tallinn, Estonia. Jazz Musician (piano); Composer. m. Kersti Johanson, 8 July 1977, 1 son, 1 daughter. Musical Education: Diplomas: Theory of Music, Tallinn Music School, Estonia, 1970; Composition, Tallinn State Conservatory, Estonia, 1982; Post-graduate studies, Berklee College of Music, Boston, USA (scholarship), 1989-90. Career: Jazz pianist, bandleader (trio, quartet), solo pianist, 1967-; Keyboardist, pop/showgroup Laine, 1972-76; As solo artiste or with Tonu Naissoo Trio/Quartet: Jazz festivals, solo concerts, former Soviet Union, 1978-89; Jazz pianist, sideman, international projects: EBU Big Band, Pori Jazz, Finland, 1985; Trio Eckert-Gaivoronski-Naissoo, Turku Jazz, Finland, 1992; Baltic Trio, Schleswig-Holstein Musik Festival, Germany, 1992; Vladimir Tarasov's Baltic Art Orchestra, Jazz Baltica, 1994; Munster Jazz Festival, Germany, 1994; Pianist, soloist, Alfred Schnittke's First Symphony, Symphony Orchestra of the USSR Ministry of Culture, 1987; Boston Symphony Orchestra, US premiere, 1988; Rotterdam Symphony Orchestra, Netherlands premiere, 1991; Pianist, entertainer, 1991-. Compositions: For films, television, theatre, 1969-; Jazz: First Flight, 1981; A Time There Was, 1983. Recordings: Tonu Naissoo Trio, 1968; Turning Point, 1980; Dedication, 1993. Honour: Music Of The Year, Estonian Radio, 1991. Membership: Estonian Composers' Union, 1984. Hobbies: Architecture; Aviation. Current Management: Jazzkaar Festival Management. Address: Estonian Radio, Jazzkaar, Gonsiori 21, EE 0100 Tallinn, Estonia.

NAPOLEON Marty, b. 2 June 1921, Brooklyn, New York, USA. Musician (piano). m. Marie Giordano, 15 May 1921, 1 son, 1 daughter. Career: Jazz pianist, 1941-; Played with numerous artists including: Gene Krupa; Benny Goodman; Louis Armstrong's All-Stars; Bob Crosby's Bobcats; Red Norvo; Major concerts include: Odessa Jazz Festival, Texas; Berne Jazz Festival; Carnegie Hall (with Frank Sinatra); Command Performance at the White House with Lionel Hampton Sextet; Nice Jazz Festival; North Sea Jazz Festival; Downtown Jazz Festival, Toronto; Film appearances: Glenn Miller Story; All That Jazz; Tootsie; Raging Bull. Numerous recordings with: Charles Barnet; Louis Armstrong; Lionel Hampton. Membership: ASCAP.

NASH Graham, b. 2 Feb 1942, Blackpool, Lancashire, England. Vocalist; Musician (guitar). m. Susan. Career: Touring musician with the Hollies; Member, Crosby Stills and Nash, 1968-; Also Crosby, Stills, Nash and Young; Also solo recording artiste. Performances include: Woodstock Festival, 1969; Altamont Speedway, with the Rolling Stones, 1969; Royal Albert Hall, 1970; Wembley Stadium, 1974; California benefit concerts with Jackson Browne, 1979; Anti-nuclear benefits, Madison Square Garden, 1979; Peace Sunday concert, Rose Bowl, California, 1982; Live Aid, Philadelphia, 1985; Madison Square Garden, New York, 1988; Amnesty International benefit concert, Chile, 1990; Television includes: Presenter, The Inside Track, interview show, cable TV, 1990. Recordings: Albums: with Crosby Stills And Nash: Crosby Stills And Nash, 1969; Déjà Vu, 1970; 4-Way Street, 1971; So Far, 1974; Replay, 1981; Daylight Again, 1982; Allies, 1983; Innocent Eyes, 1986; American Dream, 1989; Live It Up, 1990; Solo albums: Songs For Beginners, 1971; Wild Tales, 1974; Earth And Sky, 1980; with David Crosby: Graham Nash/David Crosby, 1972; Wind On The Water, 1975; Whistling Down The Wire, 1976; Crosby/Nash Live, 1977; The Best Of, 1978; Singles include: Woodstock, 1970; Teach Your Children, 1970; Just A Song Before I Go, 1977; Wasted On The Way, 1982. Honours include: Grammy Award, Best New Artists, 1970. Current Management: Management Network Inc, 14930 Ventura Blvd, #205, Sherman Oaks, CA 91403, USA.

NASH Johnny (John Lester Nash), b. 9 Aug 1940, Houston, Texas, USA. Singer; Actor. Career: Lead soprano, gospel choir; Film appearances include: Take A Giant Step, 1958; Key Witness, 1960; Singer on television variety show and as member, Teen Commandments (with Paul Anka and George Hamilton IV); Solo recording artiste, 1960s-70s; Now involved in recording and production. Recordings: Albums: Hold Me Tight, 1968; Let's Go Dancing, 1969; I Can See Clearly Now, 1972; My Merry-Go-Round, 1973; What A Wonderful World, 1977; Stir It Up, 1981; Johnny Nash, 1985; Here Again, 1986; Tears On My Pillow, 1987; Singles include: Let's Move And Groove Together, 1965; Hold Me Tight, 1969; You Got Soul, 1969; Cupid, 1969; Stir It Up (written by Bob Marley), 1971; I Can See Clearly Now, 1972; There Are More Questions Than Answers, 1972; Tears On My Pillow (Number 1, UK), 1975.

NASH Rob, b. 30 May 1956, Boston, Lincolnshire, England. Vocal Coach; Musician (keyboards, guitar). m. Nic Bagguley, 7 Nov 1989, 3 sons, 1 daughter. Education: Loughborough University. Musical Education: Ely Cathedral Chorister; Cambridge College Of Arts and Technology. Career: Vocal coach to Michael Barrymore, for television series Barrymore; Jeremy Irons, for films The Lion King; Chorus Of Disapproval; Work with Marc Almond; Simon Climie; Dion Estes; Stephanie Lawrence; Colin Blunstone; Nick Cave. Recordings: Work includes: Phantom Of The Opera, A Touch of Music in the Night, Michael Crawford; Weather in the Heart, Carmina; Solo albums: With Love; A Touch Of Music In The Night; Also forthcoming album from Carmina, producer Donal Lunny. Honour: Vivien Ellis Awards, 1990. Memberships: Equity; Musicians' Union. Hobby: Literature. Current Management: Bagmusic. Address: 31 Tyne Street, St Werburgh, Bristol BS2 9UA, England.

NASSIRI Monim, b. 10 December 1972, Boisfort, Belgium. Singer; Songwriter; Producer; Composer. Education: Classical Education of Account. Career: Singer of Phemomene; Composer; Songwriter and Self-Producer; TV: MCM, France; RTL-TVI, Belgium; Popular Radio. Compositions: CD Single of Phemomene: Vis Taule; Prends Le Temps; Histoire D'Amour; Le Weekend. Recordings: Band Album of Phemomene, Vis Tavie, 1996; Arcade Belgium; Prends Le Temps, 1997; Car Music, Belgium; Histoire D'Amour Atoll-emi, France. Memberships: SABAM; SACEM. Hobbies: Writing; Poetry; Dance. Current Management: Moon Production. Address: Rue Du Beguinage 7, 1300 Wavre, Belgium.

NATALIA (Natalia Lapina), b. Nijny Novgorod, Russia. Singer; Film and Television Actress. Education: Academic Theatre of St Petersburg, Russia. Career: European film star prior to recording debut, 1995-; Fluent in 4 languages, Russian, French, German, English; Lead roles, 8 European films, 2 European TV series; Performed as singer, White Nights Festival, Russia, 1995-. Recordings: Albums: Breakin' Through, 1995; Lingerie, 1996. Honours:

Film Awards: Silver Rose of Montreux Award, 1989, 1990; Silver Award, Breakin' Through, 1996. Hobbies: Working out with weights; Aerobics; Dance. Current Management: Topnotch Entertainment Corp. Address: c/o Topnotch Music and Records, Box 1515 Sanibel Island, FL 3957-1515, USA.

NATCH (Ian Mallett), b. 28 Jul 1945, Birmingham, England. Songwriter; Musician (bass guitar). Divorced, 3 sons, 1 daughter. Musical Education: Self-taught. Career: Member, group Renegades; Toured extensively in Finland, Sweden, Germany and Italy; Television appearances in several countries, including San Remo Song Festival, 1966; Currently re-launching career. Recordings: Cadillac, Renegades; Several albums and singles recorded, 1960's; Compilations continue to be released. Publication: Cracking An Ancient Code. Memberships: PRS; MCPS; Songwriting Guild. Hobby: Writing. Address: La Louisiane, 4 Tynedale, Whitby, South Wirral L65 6RB, England.

NAUMOV Julian. Musician (drums). Career: Member, Concurent, 1986-; Numerous concerts, television and radio appearances. Recordings: Rock For Peace, 1988; Rock Festival In Mitchurin, 1989; The Black Sheep (rock collection), 1992; Something Wet (best-selling album, Bulgaria), 1994; The Best Of Bulgarian Rock, 1995. Honours: First Prizes; Top Rock Band, Youth Festival, Vidin, 1989; Rock ring, Sofia, 1990; Top Rock Composition: The Cavalry, 1991; Group Of The Year, The Darik Radio Countdown, 1994. Address: 40 St Stambolov Blvd, 1202 Sofia, Bulgaria.

NAYLOR Martin Howard, b. Ipswich, Suffolk, England. Multimedia Sound Designer; Musician (midi guitar). Musical Education: Self-taught. Career: Successful career on alternative music system, 1979-95; Radio appearances include: Esemble Vibe; Manbru; Virtual tour on the Internet, 1995-2000; Appeared on compilation albums; All records on own label. Compositions: One entered for Cornelius Cardrew Competition; I Desire, used in low budget Sci-fi film. Publications: Technical articles for ST Applications. Memberships: Musicians' Union; AMP. Hobbies: Chess; Chinese Iron Ball direction. Address: 34 Bassingham Road, Wembley, Middlesex HA0 4RL, England.

NAYLOR Patrick, b. 7 July 1966, Hampton, England. Musician (guitar). Education: Degree in Government/Sociology, Essex University. Musical Education: Self-taught. Career: Appeared with bands: Colours; Julian Costello Quintet; Most London Jazz venues; Barbican; Royal Festival Hall; 606 Club; Bass Clef; Performed music for play at Edinburgh Festival. Compositions: Co-composer, Colours, Julian Costello Quintet, forthcoming album. Membership: Musicians' Union. Hobby: Travel. Address: Flat 4, 15 Rugby Street, London WC1N 3QT, England.

NAYLOR Steven J, b. 7 Jun 1949, Woodstock, Ontario, Canada. Composer; Producer. m. Pamela J Ritchie, 2 daughters. Education: BA; BIS. Career: Composer, producer of many scores for theatre, film, television and radio; Member of the Upstream Ensemble; Faculty at Dalhousie University; Producer of various albums. Address: PO Box 3731, Halifax, NS B3J 3K6, Canada.

NEDELCHEV Boyko, b. 24 Apr 1965, Rousse, Bulgaria. Singer; Songwriter; Composer. Career: Singer, songwriter with brother Deyan, 1987-; Appearances include: Festivals: Golden Orpheus, Sunny Beach, Bulgaria, 1990, 1995; Voice Of Asia, International Festival, Kazakhstan, Almati, 1995; First Pop Songs Festival, Cairo, Egypt, 1995; Concerts, television and radio appearances: Bulgaria; Russia; Kazakhstan; Mongolia; Egypt; Italy; Tour, Mediterranean.

Recordings: An Appeal To The World, 1990; Love Game, 1991; Madly In Love, 1993; The Best Of Deyan And Boyko Nedelchev, 1993; Love-Dream; Dedication, 1993; La Mia Musica, 1993; Love For Love, 1994; La Mia Musica, 1994; The Hits Of Deyan And Boyko Nedelchev, 1995; Brothers, 1996. Honours: Music City Hall song festival, Nashville, for song More Than A Hundred Enemies, 1989; Awards at Melody of the Friends Festival, Ulan-Bator, Mongolia, 1990; Audience award, Step To Parnassus, Moscow Festival, 1994; Awards, Golden Orpheus Festival, 1993, 1995; Award at First Pop Songs Festival, Cairo, Egypt, 1995. Membership: FIDOF. Hobbies: Music; Sport; Cinema. Current Management: Self-managed. Address: Lipnik Blvd, 62, Entr G, ap 16, 7005 Rousse, Bulgaria.

NEDELCHEV Deyan, b. 16 Jan 1964, Rousse, Bulgaria. Singer; Songwriter; Composer. Career: Singer, songwriter, composer with brother Boyko, 1987-; Appearances: Golden Orpheus Festival, Sunny Beach, Bulgaria, 1990-95; Many concerts, television appearances and radio broadcasts: Bulgaria; Russia; Kazakhstan; Mongolia; Egypt; Italy; Tour, Mediterranean. Recordings: Albums: An Appeal To The World, 1990; Love Game, 1991; Madly In Love, 1993; The Best Of Deyan and Boyko Nedeltchev, 1993; Love-dream; Dedication, 1993; Love For Love, 1994; La Mia Musica, 1994; The Hits Of Deyan And Boyko Nedelchev, 1995; Brothers, 1996. Honours: Awards received from: Music City Hall song festival, Nashville, for song More Than A Hundred Enemies, 1989; XIVth Melody of the Friends Festival, Ulan-Bator, Mongolia, 1990; Golden Orpheus Festival, Bulgaria, 1993, 1994; Audience Award, Step To Parnassus Festival, Moscow, Russia, 1994; Voice Of Asia Festival, Alamati, Kazakhstan, 1995; Pop Songs Festival, Cairo, Egypt, 1995. Current Management: Self-managed. Address: Lipnik Blvd 62, Entr G, Ap 16, 7005 Rousse, Bulgaria.

NEECE Timothy G, b. 2 Oct 1946, Abilene, Texas, USA. Artist Manager. m. (1) Lynda Hunnicutt, 1 daughter; (2) Deborah Chaffey, 12 June 1988. Education: BA, Business, McMurry University. Musical Education: 8 years experience as musician (drums). Career: Manager, prior to release and through 3 albums for Christopher Cross; Bruce Hornsby and the Range; Charlie Sexton; Manager, Rickie Lee Jones during Flying Cowboys release. Honours: Launched careers of 2 Best New Artist Grammy Award Winners; Many Gold, Platinum awards worldwide for artists managed. Hobby: Golf.

NEERGAARD Niels Erik Kaas, b. 27 May 1946, Denmark. Musician. m. Gitte Neergaard, 21 December 1985, 2 sons, 2 daughters. Education: Trombone, Royal Danish Music Academy, 1969-72; Trombone, Berklee College of Music, 1972-73. Career: Creme Fraiche Big Band, 1978-84; Thad Jones Eclipse, 1980-82; Neergaard-Bissoli Quartet, 1982-; Danish Radio Jazz Group, 1976-82; New Jungle Orchestra. Compositions: Libra; Blues for Cindy Parker Jr; Strunck; Days Gone; Azalea Flying. Recordings: Ambiance; Diferente; Even the Moon is Dancing; Eclipse; Brikama; Creme Fraiche. Memberships: Danish Musicians' Union; Danish Music Teachers Union. Hobbies: Sailing; Bowling. Address: Vodroffsvej 54, 1900 Frederiksberg C, Denmark.

NEGRIJN Thomas, b. 19 Oct 1959, Copenhagen, Denmark. Lead Vocalist; Musician (guitar). Education: Art glazier 7 years. Musical Education: H F Music School in Copenhagen. Career: Own first big band, Simcess, 1985-1992; Played Roskilde Festival, Denmark, 5 times; Midfyn Festival, 6 times, including 2 times on biggest stage for 30,000 - 40,000 people; Many Danish television and radio appearances; Tours: Denmark; Europe; Founder, new band Blink, 1995-; Released EP, toured Denmark, making new album. Recordings: with Simcess: Play With

Your Life, 1988; The House, 1990; with Tam Tam Top: Secrets, 1993; with Blink: Blink, 1994. Honours: Title: Arest John (Lennon) Award, Best Band, Copenhagen, 1987. Membership: Danish Society For Jazz Rock Folk Composers. Hobbies: Sports; Football; Tennis; Basketball; Photography; Nature; Books; Listening to music; Family and friends. Current Management: Off Beat, Norsgade 26-28, 8000 Århus C, Denmark. Address: Hjort Lorenzensgade 6 4tv, 2200 Copenhagen N, Denmark.

NEIL Vince (Vincent Neil Wharton), b. 8 Feb 1961, Hollywood, California, USA. Singer. Career: Singer, Rock Candy; Member, US heavy rock group Mötley Crüe, 1981-92; Worldwide concerts include: Tours with: Y&T, 1981, 1982; Kiss, 1983; Ozzy Osbourne, 1984; Iron Maiden, 1984; Cheap Trick, 1986; Theatre Of Pain World Tour, 1985-86; World tours, 1987, 1989; Major festivals: US festival, 1983; Monsters Of Rock Festival, Castle Donington, 1984; Moscow Music Peace Festival, 1989; Actor, film The Adventures of Ford Fairlane, 1990; Solo artiste, 1992-. Recordings: Albums: with Mötley Crüe: Too Fast For Love, 1981; Shout At The Devil, 1983; Theatre Of Pain, 1985; Girls, Girls, Girls, 1987; Dr Feelgood (Number 1, US), 1989; Decade Of Decadence, 1991; Solo: Exposed, 1993; Carved In Stone, 1995; Singles: with Mötley Crüe: Stick To Your Guns, 1981; Looks That Kill, 1984; Too Young To Fall In Love, 1984; Smokin' In The Boys Room, 1985; Home Sweet Home, 1985; You're All I Need, 1987; Dr Feelgood, 1989; Kick Start My Heart, 1990; Without You, 1990; Don't Go Away Mad, 1990; Same Old Situation, 1990; Primal Scream, 1991; Solo hit: You're Invited But Your Friend Can't Come, from film Encino Man, 1992; Contributor, Stars, Hear'n'Aid, 1985. Honours: Rolling Stone Readers Poll Winners, Best Heavy Metal Band, 1991; American Music Award, Favourite Heavy Metal Album, 1991. Current Management: Burt Stein Entertainment Co., Suite 450, 3575 Cahuenga Blvd W, Los Angeles, CA 90068, USA; Decent Management, 7932 Hillside Avenue, Los Angeles, CA 90046, USA.

NEILL Kevin, b. 25 July 1931, Manchester, England. Musician (lead electric guitar, acoustic guitar, trombone). m. Claire Cregan, 6 Apr 1953, 2 daughters. Career: Johnny Ray tour, 1954; Royal Command Performance, Oh Boy, 1959; Anthony Newley Tour, 1960; Don Lang and Frantic Five; Princess Margaret's state wedding ball, with Joe Loss Orchestra, Buckingham Palace; Accompanied Vera Lynn, Frankie Vaughn; Frankie Laine; Vic Lewis Orchestra; Eric Winstone Orchestra; BBC Northern Variety Orchestra; BBC Midland Orchestra; Karl Denver Trio, 26 years. Compositions: Points North; Singin' And Swingin'. Recordings: Hits with Karl Denver Trio: Whimoweh; Marcheta; Mexicali Rose; Love Me With All Your Heart; Still; Sleepy Lagoon; Just A Little Love; Never Goodbye (Eurovision Song Contest entry); Harry Lime Theme. Honours: Examiner, electric guitar, The London College of Music. Memberships: Vaudeville Golf Society; Variety Club Golf Society. Hobby: Golf. Address: 69 Polefield Road, Blackly, Manchester M9 7EN, England.

NELSON Matthew Edward, b. 20 Mar 1968, Colne, England. Singer; Songwriter. Education: Hotel and Catering Management, Manchester Polytechnic, 1988-89. Career: Lead singer with Milltown Brothers, appearing 5 times on television, touring Britain, USA, Europe and Japan, and appearing at various British Festivals. Compositions: Wrote songs for the BBC TV series, All Quiet On The Preston Front. Recordings: Albums: Slinky; Valve; 5 Singles in UK Top 40. Membership: Performing Rights Society. Hobbies: Golf; Cricket; Football; Rugby; Chinese and Italian cooking; Cycling. Address: Forest House, Forest Lane, Barrowford, Nelson, Lancashire BB9 6QL, England.

NELSON Shara, b. London, England. Singer; Songwriter. Career: Singer, Massive Attack; Solo artiste. Recordings: Album with Massive Attack: Blue Lines; Solo albums: What Silence Knows, 1993; Friendly Fire, 1995; Hit singles: Rough With The Smooth; I Fell. Honours: Mercury Music Prize Nomination, What Silence Knows; BRIT Award Nominations, Best Female Singer, 1994, 1995. Current Management: Def Mix Productions, 938 Broadway, Suite 400, New York, NY 10010, USA.

NELSON Tracy, b. 27 Dec 1944, Madison, Wisconsin, USA. Singer; Musician. Education: 2 years college. Career: Lead singer, Mother Earth, 1968-73; Solo artist, 1965-. Recordings: Albums: with Mother Earth: Living With The Animals, 1968; Make A Joyful Noise, 1969; Mother Earth Presents - Tracy Nelson Country, 1970; Satisfied, 1970; Bring Me Home, 1971; Tracy Nelson / Mother Earth, 1972; Poor Man's Paradise, 1973; Solo albums: Deep Are The Roots, 1965; Tracy Nelson, 1974; Sweet Soul Music, 1975; Time Is On My Side, 1976; Doin' It My Way, 1978; Homemade Songs, 1978; Come See About Me, 1980; In The Here And Now, 1993; I Feel So Good, 1995; Move On, 1996. Honours: Grammy Nomination, with Willie Nelson, 1974; Nashville Music Award, Best Blues Album, 1996; 2 WC Handy Award Nominations, Best Female Vocalist. Hobbies: Gardening; Animals. Current Management: Julie Devereux, Lucks Management, 817 18th Avenue South, Nashville, TN 37203, USA; Agent: Ronnie Narmour, RNA, PO Box 19289, Austin, TX 78760, USA.

NELSON Willie (Hugh), b. 30 Apr 1933, Abbott, Texas, USA. Country & Western Singer; Musician; Songwriter. m. Annie Marie Nelson, 3 sons, 4 daughters. Education: Baylor University. Career: Salesman; Announcer; Host and DJ, Country music shows, Texas; Bass player, Ray Price's band; Formed own band; Appearances, Grand Ole Opry, Nashville, and throughout USA, 1964-; Tours: New Zealand; Australia; USA; Canada; Europe; Japan. Annual 4th of July Picnics throughout USA, 1972-; Performed with: Frank Sinatra; Neil Young; Dolly Parton; Linda Ronstadt; ZZ Top; Waylon Jennings; Film appearances include: Electric Horseman, 1980; Honeysuckle Rose, 1980. Compositions include: Crazy, Number 1 for Patsy Cline; Hello Walls, Number 1 for Faron Young. Recordings: Albums include: The Sound In Your Mind, 1976; The Troublemaker, 1976; Willie Nelson And His Friends, 1976; To Lefty From Willie, 1977; Willie Before His Time, 1978; Wanted/The Outlaw, 1978; The Willie Way, 1978; The Best Of Willie Nelson, 1978; Stardust, 1978; One For The Road, 1979; Willie & Family Live, 1979; Pretty Paper, 1979; Willie Sings Kristofferson, 1979; San Antonio Rose, 1980; Honeysuckle Rose, 1980; Family Bible, 1980; Tougher Than Leather, 1983; City Of New Orleans, 1984; Me And Paul, 1985; Highwayman, 1985; The Promise Land, 1986; Partners, 1986; Island In The Sea, 1987; Seashores Of Old Mexico, 1987; What A Wonderful World, 1988; A Horse Called Music, 1989; Highwayman II, 1990; Born For Trouble, 1990; Clean Shirt Waylon And Willie, 1991; Across The Borderline, 1993; Six Hours At Pedernales, 1994; Healing Hands Of Time, 1994; Just One Love, 1995. Honours: 5 Grammy (NARAS) Awards; 8 CMA Awards; Nashville Songwriters Association, Hall of Fame, 1973; Playboy Hall of Fame, 1983; National Academy of Popular Music, Lifetime Achievement Award, 1983 (fourth-ever recipient); 3 ACM Awards; Tex Ritter Songwriting Award, with Kris Kristofferson, 1984; 25 Platinum and Gold albums. Hobbies: Golf; Running; Swimming; Weight-lifting; Yoga. Current Management: Mark Rothbaum & Associates. Address: c/o Mark Rothbaum & Assocs Inc, PO Box 2689, Danbury, CT 06813-2689, USA.

NERNEY Declan James, b. 20 May 1956, Drumlish, Ireland. Singer; Musician (lead guitar). Career: Played with Gene Stuart plus Brien Coll;

Solo artiste. Career: Played for interval BAA Senior Football Final, Crough Park, Dublin, 1990; 3 US tours, 1995;Australian tour. Recordings: Picture Of My World; Going Places; 3 Way Love Affair; Walking On New Grass; Lucky I Guess; Current release: Part Of The Journey. Honours: 4 Gold discs; Finalist, Person Of The Year, 1994; Band Of The Year, Irish World Awards, 1994. Current Management: Frank Kilbride. Address: Main Street, Edgeworthsown, Co Longford, Ireland.

NESBO Jo, b. Molde, Norway. Singer; Songwriter. Education: MBA (Master of Business Administration). Career: Singer, songwriter, Di Derre; 180 concerts, 1994-95. Recordings: Di Derre: Den Derre (Gold disc, Norway) 1992; Jenter and Sånn (Triple Platinum disc, Norway), 1994. Current Management: Artist Partner AS. Address: Artist Partner As, PO Box 217, 1324 Lysaker, Norway.

NESMITH (Robert) Michael, b. 30 Dec 1942, Houston, Texas, USA. Singer; Songwriter; Musician (guitar); Actor. Career: Folk duo, Mike & John, with John London, 1965; Member, The Monkees, 1966-69; Actor, Monkees television series, 1966-68; 33 1/3 Revolutions Per Monkee (NBC Special); Founder, First National Band, 1970; Reformed as Second National Band, 1972; Founder, President, own Countryside and Pacific Arts Corporation, record labels, 1974; Financed and produced films Repo Man; Elephant Parts; Time Rider. Recordings: Albums with the Monkees: The Monkees (Number 1, US and UK), 1966; More Of The Monkees (Number 1, US and UK), 1967; Headquarters (Number 1, US), 1967; Pisces, Aquarius, Capricorn and Jones Ltd (Number 1, UK), 1967; The Birds, The Bees And The Monkees, 1968; Head (soundtrack), 1969; The Monkees Greatest Hits, 1969; The Monkees Present, 1969; Solo albums: The Wichita Train Whistle Sings, 1968; Magnetic South, 1970; Treason, 1972; And The Hits Just Keep On Comin', 1972; Pretty Much Your Standard Ranch Hash, 1973; The Prison, 1974; From A Radio Engine To The Photon Wing, 1977; Live At The Palais, 1978; Infinite Rider On The Big Dogma, 1979; Listen To The Band, 1997; Hit singles with the Monkees: Last Train To Clarksville (Number 1, US), 1966; I'm A Believer (Number 1, US and UK), 1966; (I'm Not Your) Steppin' Stone, 1967; A Little Bit Me, A Little Bit You, 1967; Alternate Title, 1967; Pleasant Valley Sunday, 1967; Daydream Believer (Number 1, US), 1967; Valleri, 1968; Tear Drop City, 1969; Solo singles: Joanne, 1970; Silver Moon, 1971; Rio, 1977. Publication: The Prison, 1974. Honours include: NARM Awards, Best Selling Group, Best Album, 1967; Emmy Award, Outstanding Comedy Series, 1967; 3 BMI Awards, 1968; Grammy Award, for video Elephant Parts, 1982; Monkees Day, Atlanta, 1986; Star on Hollywood Walk of Fame, 1989. Current Management: Nesmith Enterprises, 11858 La Grange Avenue, Los Angeles, CA 90025, USA.

NESTOROVIC Sascha, b. 27 Aug 1964, Zagreb, Croatia. Musician (saxophone); Composer; Arranger. m. Vlasta Gyrura, 9 Nov 1993. Musical Education: Zagreb Academy of Music. Career: First alto in big band, Croatian State Television; Live concerts with Zagreb Saxophone Quartet, Muscora, Paris; World Saxophone Congress, Pesaro, Italy; Tours with Zagreb Jazz Portrait: Germany; Austria; Italy; France. Recordings: with Zagreb Saxophone Quartet: Croatian Contemporary Music for Saxophones; Zagreb 900; with Slovenian RTV Big Band: Peter Herbolzheimer; Moments Notice, Zagreb Jazz Portrait. Honours: Classical awards: Darko Lukic; Milka Trnina. Memberships: Croatian Musicians' Union; Jazz Club Zagreb. Hobbies: Chess playing; Plants. Current Management: Vesna Vrandecic, Zitnjak 1, 10000 Zagreb. Address: Sascha Nestorovic, Kustossijanska 316, 10000 Zagreb, Croatia.

NETTLETON Christopher, b. 25 Sept 1968, Cardiff, Wales. Singer; Songwriter; Composer; Musician (guitar, keyboards). Musical Education: 8 years, formal piano study; Guitar, self-taught. Career: Played with Hollyweird, 1989-92; Plays with The Nubiles, 1993-; Tours UK, 1994, 1995; Support to: Blur; Elastica; Oasis; Moist; S M A S H. Recordings: 3 singles with The Nubiles: Layabout/Mother and Father, 1995; Without Waking, 1995; Tatjana, 1995. Memberships: Musicians Union; Performing Rights Society. Hobbies: Outdoor pursuits; Arts & Design; Cinema. Current Management: Thirst Music Management. Address: c/o 5 Clare Court, Lime Street, Bedford MK40 1NH, England.

NEUMANN Bob, b. Chicago, Illinois, USA. Producer; Engineer; Musician (keyboards); Electronic Music Composer; Synthesist. m. Carolyn, 28 Mar 1992, 1 daughter. Education: BSc, Electronic Engineering, BSEET. Musical Education: General Music Theory, Organ, Piano Training. Career: 22 years performance experience, Chicago area pop bands; 16 years recording, composition; Currently own and operate Project Studio, Lemont, Illinois. Recordings: 3 albums, 1 dance single released on independent labels; Beatbox-D; Neu Electro; 12" dance single: Juicy. Publications include: Discoveries column, Keyboard Magazine; KLEM. Honours: Discoveries Column Alumni, State Fair, Illinois Awards. Memberships: EARS Society; Chicago BMI. Hobbies: Electronic and dance recording; Composition; Performance; Die-cast miniature vehicle collecting; Aerobic and physical training. Current Management: Neu Electro Productions, USA. Address: PO Box 1582, Bridgeview, IL 60455, USA.

NEVILL Brian Roy, b. 4 Jan 1948, Wuppertal, Germany. Musician (drums, piano). Divorced. Musical Education: Royal Society of Arts School Certificate. Career: Played with Graham Parker; Many recording sessions including The Flying Lizards, 1975-81; Television appearances with Kirsty McColl; Founder member, Shriekback; Member, Pig Bag; Radio and television sessions with Shriekback, Pig Bag; Worked in Brussels for one year; Live work with Virginia Astley, 1982-87; Formed record label, 1989; Recorded and played with numerous blues and rock'n'roll visiting American artists. Recordings: Albums: Lend An Ear, Pigbag; The Best Of, Pigbag; The Infinite, Shriekback; Blues And Stomps, Carl Sonny Leyland; The Panasonics; Eddie Angel's Guitar Party; Big Sixteen, Big Joe Louis and the Blueskings; Laugh It Up, Holly Golightly. Publications: Articles in Goldmine; Sleeve notes to album Soul Classics, The Best Of Bell.Memberships: PRS; MCPS; Musicians' Union. Hobbies: Record collecting; Reading; Travel; Films. Current Management: Self-managed. Address: 6 Lancaster Lodge, 83-85 Lancaster Road, London W11 1QH, England.

NEVILLE Aaron, b. 24 Jan 1941, New Orleans, Louisiana, USA. Vocalist. Career: Singer in various bands with brothers Art, Charles, Cyril; Member, The Neville Sounds, 1962-68; Soul Machine, 1968-1975; The Wild Tchoupitoulas, 1976-77; The Neville Brothers, 1978-; Concerts include: Amnesty International Concert, with Sting, Joan Baez, Peter Gabriel, Bryan Adams, 1986; Nelson Mandela International Tribute Concert, 1990; Jazz & Heritage Festival, New Orleans, 1990; Glastonbury Festival, 1990; Bill Graham Memorial Concert, San Francisco, 1991; Artists Against Homelessness benefit, New Orleans, 1992; Summer Stage 92 concerts, Central Park, New York, 1992; Berloni Foundation leukemia benefit, Modena, Italy, 1992; Commitment To Life AIDS benefit, Los Angeles, 1992; Television includes Saturday Night Live; Late Night with David Letterman; Tonight Show; 48 Hours; Oprah; Actor, films: Everybody's All-American, 1990; Malcolm X, 1992; The Posse, 1993. Recordings: Albums: with the Neville Brothers: The Neville

Brothers, 1978; Fiyo On The Bayou, 1981; Neville-ization, 1984; Treacherous - A History Of The Neville Brothers, 1955-85; Uptown, 1987; Yellow Moon, 1989; Brother's Keeper, 1990; Family Groove, 1992; Solo albums: Warm Your Heart, 1991; The Grand Tour, 1993; Aaron Neville's Soulful Christmas, 1993; The Tattooed Heart, 1995; Also featured on: Cry Like A Rainstorm, Howl Like The Wind, Linda Ronstadt, 1989; Breathless, Kenny G, 1992; Sound Of Love, Ivan Neville, 1992; Film soundtracks: Red Hot + Blue, 1990; The Bodyguard, 1992; Contributor, Tower Of Strength (Leonard Cohen tribute), 1995; Singles include: Tell It Like It Is, (Number 2, US), 1967; Everybody Plays The Fool, 1991; Duets with Linda Ronstadt: Don't Know Much (Number 2, UK & US), 1989; All My Life, 1990. Honours: Grammy Awards: Best Pop Instrumental Performance, Healing Chant, 1990; Best Pop Performance by Duo or Group, Don't Know Much, 1990; All My Life, 1991; Rolling Stone Critics Award, Best Male Singer, 1989, 1990; Downbeat Award, Best Blues/Soul/R&B Group, 1990. Current Management: Bill Graham Management, PO Box 429094, San Francisco, CA 94142, USA.

NEVILLE Alaric James, b. 28 July 1961, Derby, England. Sound Engineer; Record Producer; Musician (guitar). Education: BA Hons Fine Art, Leeds University. Career: Sound engineer to: Oysterband; The Ukrainians; Based at Woodhouse Studios, Hall Place, Leeds. Recordings: Produced artists including Cud; Bridewell Taxis; The Ukrainians; Ringo's High. Membership: Musicians' Union. Current Management: Stolen Sounds. Address: Ivy Cottage, 36 School Lane, Chapel Allerton, Leeds L57 3PN, England.

NEVILLE Art, b. 17 Dec 1937, New Orleans, USA. Musician (piano); Singer. Career: Singer, pianist: The Neville Sound, 1962-68; The Meters, 1968-1977; The Neville Brothers, 1977-; with the Meters: worked with Dr John; Robert Palmer; Labelle; European tour, support to the Rolling Stones, 1975; with the Neville Brothers: Amnesty International Concert, with Joan Baez, Sting, Peter Gabriel, Bryan Adams, 1986; Glastonbury Festival, 1990; Playboy Jazz Festival, 1991; Artists Against Hunger and Homelessness benefit, New Orleans 1992; American Music Festival, 1992; Summer Stage '92 concert series, New York, 1992; Berloni Foundation leukemia benefit concert, Modena, Italy, 1992. Recordings: Albums with the Meters: The Meters, 1969; Look-Ka Py Py, 1970; Rejuvenation, 1974; Fire On The Bayou, 1975; New Direction, 1977; Singles include: Sophisticated Cissy; Cissy Strut; Ease Back; Chicken Strut; Hand Clapping Song; Be My Lady; Albums with The Neville Brothers: The Neville Brothers, 1978; Fiyo On The bayou, 1981; Neville-ization, 1984; Treacherous - A History Of The Neville Brothers, 1987; Yellow Moon, 1989; Brother's Keeper, 1990; Family Groove, 1992; Solo albums: Mardi Gras Rock'n'Roll, 1987; Art Neville - His Speciality Recordings, 1956-58, 1993. Honours: Best Pop Instrumental Performance, Healing Chant, 1990; Rolling Stone Critics Awards, Best Band, 1990. Current Management: Bill Graham Management, PO Box 42094, San Francisco, CA 94142, USA.

NEVILLE Charles, b. 28 Dec 1938, New Orleans, USA. Musician (saxophone). Career: Tours South USA with various blues players, including: Jimmy Reed; Little Walter; Played with Joey Dee & The Starliters, 1962; Member, The Wild Tchoupitoulas, 1976-77; Member, The Neville Brothers, 1977-; Amnesty International Concert, with Sting, Peter Gabriel, Bryan Adams, Joan Baez, 1986; Nelson Mandela Tribute Concert, Wembley, 1990; Glastonbury Festival, 1990; Playboy Jazz Festival, Hollywood, 1991; American Music Festival, 1992; Berloni Foundation's Leukaemia benefit, Modena, Italy, 1992; Summer Stage 92 concerts, New York, 1992. Recordings: The Neville Brothers, 1978;

Neville-ization, 1984; Treacherous: A History Of The Neville Brothers 1955-85, 1987; Yellow Moon, 1989; Brother's Keeper, 1990; Family Groove, 1992; Singles include: Healing Chant; Bird On The Wire; Contribution: In The Still Of The Night, for album: Red Hot + Blue, 1990. Honours: Best Band, Rolling Stone magazine Critics awards, 1989; Grammy: Best Pop Instrumental Performance, Healing Chant, 1990; Downbeat Award, Best Blues/Soul/R&B Group, 1990. Current Management: Bill Graham Management, PO Box 42094, San Francisco, CA 94142, USA.

NEVILLE Cyril, b. 10 Jan 1948, New Orleans, USA. Vocalist; Musician (percussion). Career: Member, The Neville Sounds, 1962-68; Soul Machine, 1968-1975; The Meters, 1975; The Wild Tchouptoulas, 1976; The Neville Brothers, 1977-; Concerts include: Amnesty International Concert, with Joan Baez, Sting, Peter Gabriel, Bryan Adams, 1986; Nelson Mandela Tribute Concert, Wembley, 1990; Glastonbury Festival, 1990; Playboy Jazz Festival, Hollywood, 1991; American Music Festival, 1992; Berloni Foundation leukemia benefit concert, Modena, Italy, 1992. Recordings: Albums: Wild Tchoupitoulas, 1976; The Neville Brothers, 1978; Treacherous - A History Of The Neville Brothers, 1987; Uptown, 1987; Yellow Moon, 1989; Brother's Keeper, 1990; Family Groove, 1992; Singles include: Healing Chant; Bird On The Wire; In The Still Of The Night. Honours: Grammy Award: Best Pop Instrumental Performance, Healing Chant, 1990; Rolling Stone Critics Award, Best Band, 1989. Current Management: Bill Graham Management, PO Box 429094, San Francisco, CA 94142, USA.

NEVIN David Charles, b. 23 Sept 1951, London, England. Musician (multi-instumentalist); Vocalist. Musical Education: Primary and Grammar Schools. Career: Musician for: Unit 4+2; Harmony Grass; Grass; Capability Brown; Sparrow; Divine; Radio and television appearances: Radio 1; Capital Radio; New Faces; Regional Radio; Concerts: Reading Festival; European festivals; Shirley Bassey tour includes Albert Hall. Recordings: Voice, Capability Brown. Publications: Numerous. Memberships: PRS; Musicians' Union; BASCA. Hobbies: Gardening; Cooking; Painting; Tennis. Address: 69 Church Lane, Walthamstow, London E17 9RN, England.

NEWBURY Mickey (Milton J Newbury Jr), b. 19 May 1940, Houston, Texas, USA. Songwriter; Recording Artist. Compositions: Swiss Cottage Place, recorded by Roger Milller; Here Comes The Rain Baby, Eddy Arnold and Roy Orbison; Funny Familiar Forgotten Feelings, Don Gibson and Tom Jones; How I Love Them Old Songs, Carl Smith; Sweet Memories, Willie Nelson; Just Dropped In (To See What Condition My Condition Was In), Kenny Rogers And The First Edition; She Even Woke Me Up To Say Goodbye, Jerry Lee Lewis; San Francisco Mabel Joy, John Denver, Joan Baez, Kenny Rogers; I Dont Think About Her (Him) No More, Don Williams, Tammy Wynette; American Trilogy, Elvis Presley; Makes Me Wonder If I Ever Said Goodbye, Johnny Rodriguez; Blue Sky Shinin', Marie Osmond. Recordings: Albums: Harlequin Melodies, 1968; Mickey Newbury Sings His Own, 1968; Looks Like Rain, 1969; 'Frisco Mabel Joy, 1971; Heaven Help The Child, 1973; Live At Montezuma, 1973; I Came To Hear The Music, 1974; Lovers, 1975; Rusty Tracks, 1977; His Eye Is On The Sparrow, 1978; The Sailor, 1979; After All These Years, 1981; In A New Age, 1988; Sweet Memories, 1988. Honour: Nashville Songwriters International Hall Of Fame, 1980.

NEWCOMB Keith, b. 13 October 1966, Yokosuka, Japan. Music Publishing Executive. Education: BBA, Belmont University, Nashville, Tennessee, USA, 1989. Career: Music Publishing Executive and Consultant, 1987-96; Worked with top songwriters including: Paul Overstreet, Robb Royer, Jimmy Griffin, Stewart Harris, Jim

Weather, Dean McTaggart, Delbert McClinton and others; Investment Broker, JC Bradford and Company, 1996-.

NEWELL Norman, b. 25 Jan 1919, London, England. Lyricist; Former Record Producer. Career: Combined record production and songwriting until 1990; Currently songwriter. Compositions include: More, from film Mondo Cane (over 5,000,000 performances in USA and world hit, over 1,000 recordings); Portrait Of My Love, (world hit). Publications: Many songs. Honours: Academy Nomination for More; Several BMI Awards; Golden Globe Award. Memberships: PRS; BMI; BASCA; MCPS. Hobbies: Theatre. Current Management: Noel Gay Organisation (Charles Armitage). Address: 6th Floor, 76 Oxford Street, London W1R 1RB, England.

NEWLEY Anthony, b. 24 Sept 1931, London, England. Singer; Actor; Songwriter. Education: Italia Conti Stage School. Career: Child actor, films including: The Little Ballerina; Vice Versa; Olver Twist, 1948; Theatre debut, Cranks, 1955; Actor, over 20 films before Idle On Parade, 1959; Doctor Doolittle, 1967; Can Heironymous Merkin Ever Forget Mercy Humppe And Find True Happiness?, 1969; Willy Wonka And The Chocolate Factory (co-written with Leslie Bricusse), 1971; Musicals: Stop The World I Want To Get Off, 1961; The Roar Of The Greasepaint, The Smell Of The Crowd, 1965; The Good Old Bad Old Days, 1972; Returned to England, 1988; West End Revival, Stop the World, 1989; West End appearance, musical version of Scrooge. Compositions: Co-writer with Leslie Bricusse, the above musicals, including hit song: The Candy Man, million seller for Sammy Davis Jr; Lyrics to Goldfinger, 1964. Recordings: Love Is A Now And Then Thing, 1960; Tony, 1961; Stop The World -I Want To Get Off, 1962; Fool Britannia, with Peter Sellers and Joan Collins, 1963; The Roar Of The Greasepaint, The Smell Of The Crowd, 1965; Various compilations; Singles include: I've Waited So Long; Personality; If She Should Come To You; The Heavens Cried; Pop Goes The Weasel; Strawberry Fair; Why (Number 1, UK); Do You Mind (Number 1, UK); What Kind Of Fool Am I?; Once In A Lifetime; Once In A Lifetime; Gonna Build A Mountain; Who Can I Turn To?; A Wonderful Day Like Today; The Joker; Look At That Face; This Dream. Current Management: Peter Charlesworth Ltd. Address: 2nd Floor, 68 Old Brompton Road, London SW7 3LQ, England.

NEWMAN Caleb, b. 14 May 1945, Wales. Singer; Musician (guitar). Divorced, 2 sons, 1 daughter. Musical Education: Self-taught. Career: Host, tribute to Dylan Thomas, Sounds of Britain, HTV; Commissioned to write various pieces for HTV including background music and songs. Recording: Windin Boy (blues album), 1982. Publication: The Cal Newman Chord Dictionary for Left Hand Guitar. Membership: Musicians' Union. Hobby: Guitar. Address: 43 West Lee Apartments, Cambridge Road East, Cardiff CF1 9DT, Wales.

NEWMAN Randy, b. 28 Nov 1943, New Orleans, Louisiana, USA. Singer; Songwriter; Musician (piano); Arranger. m. Gretchen Newman, 1 daughter. Musical Education: Music Composition, UCLA. Career: Staff songwriter, Metric Music, 1962; Became staff arranger, producer, Warner Bros. Records, 1967; Concerts include: Farm Aid, 1985; American Music Festival, Colorado, 1992. Compositions include: They Tell Me It's Summer, The Fleetwoods; I Don't Want To Hear It Anymore, Jerry Butler; I've Been Wrong Before, Cilla Black; Simon Smith And His Amazing Dancing Bear, Alan Price; Nobody Needs Your Love and Just One Smile, Gene Pitney; Mama Told Me (Not To Come), Three Dog Night (Number 1, US); I Think It's Going To Rain Today (also recorded by UB40); I Love L.A. (used to promote 1984 Olympic Games); Songs also recorded by artists including Judy Collins; Harry Nilssen; Manfred Mann; Frankie Laine; Jackie

DeShannon; Walker Brothers; As arranger: Is That All There Is?, Peggy Lee; Film scores: Ragtime, 1982; The Natural, 1984; The Three Amigos, 1986; Awakenings, 1990; Television series Cop Rock, ABC-TV, 1991; Also contributions to soundtracks: Performance; Cold Turkey; Her Alibi; Major League. Recordings: Albums: The Randy Newman Orchestra Plays Music From The Hit Television Series Peyton Place, 1966; Randy Newman, 1968; Twelve Songs, 1970; Randy Newman Live, 1971; Good Old Boys, 1974; Little Criminals, 1978; Born Again, 1979; Trouble In Paradise, 1983; Lonely At The Top, 1987; Land Of Dreams, 1988; Music From The Motion Picture The Paper, 1994; Faust, 1995. Singles include: Short People (Number 2, US), 1978; The Blues, duet with Paul Simon, 1983; Contributor, The Simpsons Sing The Blues, 1990; Film scores: Avalon, 1990; Maverick, 1994; Toy Story, 1995; Michael, 1996; James and the Giant Peach. 1996; 2 stage productions opf Faust, La Jolla Playhouse, 1995, Goodman Theatre, Chicago, 1996. Honours: Oscar Nomination, Best Original Song, 1982; Grammy, Best Instrumental Composition, 1984; Emmy, music for Cop Rock, 1991. Current Management: Cathy Kerr, for Pam Artist Management. Address: 644 N Doheny Drive, Los Angeles, CA 90069, USA.

NEWSTED Jason, b. 4 Mar 1963, Battle Creek, Michigan, USA. Rock Musician (bass). Musical Education: Self-taught. Career: Member, US heavy rock groups: Flotsam and Jetsam; Metallica, 1986-; 750 live appearances with Metallica, 1986-; Concerts include: Freddie Mercury AIDS Tribute, Wembley, 1992; Moscow Monsters of Rock Festival, 1991; Numerous worldwide tours, television and radio appearances. Recordings: with Flotsam And Jetsam: Flotsam And Jetsam, 1986; with Metallica: Garage Days Re-visited; Justice For All; Metallica: Metallica VI; Load. Honours: Grammy Awards, 1990-92; AMAs, 1992; MTV Award, 1992. Memberships: AFofM San Francisco; ASCAP. Hobbies: Mountain biking; Basketball. Current Management: c/o Q-Prime Inc., 729 7th Avenue, 14th Floor, New York, NY 10019, USA.

NEWTON Allen, b. 30 Aug 1950, Fort Worth, Texas, USA. Music Promoter. m. Frances, Apr 1983, 2 daughters. Education: Business degree. Career: 15 years in radio and television; Worked as: Disc jockey; Music and programme director; Station manager; Newscaster; Sales manager; Programme producer; Owner, seven independent record labels and two publishing companies. Honours: Nomination, Promoter Of The Year, MIRL, 1991. Memberships: BMI; ASCAP. Hobbies: Ham and shortwave radio. Address: RT 1, Box 187-A, Whitney, TX 76692, USA.

NEWTON Liz, b. 23 Oct 1956, Birmingham, England. Singer; Musician (harmonica, flute). Education: University and TTC. Career: 12 years classical ballet, contemporary dance training; 14 years travelling Europe in vaudeville duo Liz and Wolf (repertoire includes standards, musical comedy, swing); Now living in France; Vocalist, musician, Liz Newton Swing jazz quartet (with Eric Fairbank, guitar, André Gobbato, contrebass, Michel Martel, drums); Tours of France and Germany. Address: Liz Newton Swing, Figon, 30290 Laudun, France.

NEWTON Tad (Robert Arthur William Newton), b. 25 Jun 1946, Marlborough, Wiltshire, England. Jazz Musician (trombone); Vocalist. m. Anne Marie Newton, 2 Aug 1969, 2 sons, 2 daughters. Education: BA, Honours, University of Southampton. Career: Bandleader, trombonist and vocalist, Tad Newton's Jazzfriends (7-piece dixieland and mainstream jazz band); Concert appearances include: Barbican Centre, Derngate Theatre, Royal Festival Hall, Wembley Conference Centre, major festivals; Also Jazz Promoter and Organiser. Recordings: Basin St To Harlem, 1988; Drivin', 1989; Jumpin' For Joy,

1991; Journey Thru' Jazz, 1994. Membership: Musicians' Union. Hobbies: Jazz; Football; Cinema; Fell walking. Current Management: TNJF Management. Address: 23 Windmill Avenue, Blisworth, Northamptonshire NN7 3EQ, England.

NEWTON (Carson) Wayne, b. 4 Mar 1942, Norfolk, Virginia, USA. Entertainer; Singer; Musician; Actor; Author. m. Kathleen McCrone, 4 Sept 1994, 1 daughter. Musical Education: Self-taught to play 11 instruments (trumpet; piano; guitar; violin; drums; steel guitar; bass; 12 string guitar; valve trombone; dobro guitar, electric guitar). Career: Performances include: Personal television specials; 4th of July concert at Washington monument; USA tours; Total of 2000 television shows and films including: The Lucy Show; Jackie Gleason; Roseanne; Full House. Recordings: Danke Schoen; Red Roses For A Blue Lady; The Letter; Daddy Don't You Walk So Fast; 131 albums released; 300 singles. Publications: Autobiography - Once Before I Go. Honours: Entertainer Of The Year (9 years); Presidential Awards; Ten Outstanding Men Of America. Memberships: AFTRA; SAG; AFofM. Hobbies: Arabian horse breeder; Car collector; Jet pilot. Current Management: Self-managed. Address: 3422 Happy Lane, Las Vegas, NV 89120, USA.

NEWTON-JOHN Olivia, b. 26 Sept 1948, Cambridge, England. Singer; Actress. m. Matt Lattanzi, 1985, 1 daughter. Career: Moved to Australia, aged 5; Singer in folk group as teenager; Local television performer with Pat Carroll; Winner, National Talent Contest, 1964; Singer, actress, 1965-; Represented UK in Eurovision Song Contest, 1974; Music For UNICEF Concert, New York, 1979; Film appearances include: Grease, 1978; Xanadu, 1980; Two Of A Kind, 1983; Own clothing business, Koala Blue, 1984-. Recordings: Albums: If Not For You, 1971; Let Me Be There, 1974; Music Makes My Day, 1974; Long Live Love, 1974; If You Love Me Let Me Know (Number 1, US), 1974; Have You Ever Never Been Mellow, 1975; Clearly Love, 1975; Come On Over, 1976; Don't Stop Believin', 1976; Making A Good Thing Better, 1977; Greatest Hits, 1978; Grease (film soundtrack), 1978; Totally Hot, 1979; Xanadu (film soundtrack), 1980; Physical, 1981; 20 Greatest Hits, 1982; Olivia's Greatest Hits Vol 2, 1983; Two Of A Kind, 1984; Soul Kiss, 1986; The Rumour, 1988; Warm And Tender, 1990; Back To Basics: The Essential Collection 1971-92, 1992; Gaia - One Woman's Journey, 1995; Hit singles include: If Not For You, 1971; What Is Life, 1972; Take Me Home Country Roads, 1973; Let Me Be There, 1974; Long Live Love, 1974; If You Love Me (Let Me Know), 1974; I Honestly Love You (Number 1, UK), 1974; Have You Never Been Mellow (Number 1, US), 1975; Please Mr Please, 1975; Something Better To Do, 1975; Fly Away, duet with John Denver, 1976; Sam, 1977; You're The One That I Want, duet with John Travolta (Number 1, US and UK, third-best selling single in UK), 1978; Summer Nights, duet with John Travolta (UK Number 1, 9 weeks), 1978; Hopelessly Devoted to You (Number 2, UK), 1978; A Little More Love, 1979; Deeper Than The Night, 1979; I Cant Help It, duet with Andy Gibb, 1980; Xanadu, with ELO (Number 1, UK), 1980; Magic (Number 1, US), 1980; Physical (US Number 1, 10 weeks), 1981; Make A Move On Me, 1982; Heart Attack, 1982; Twist Of Fate, from film soundtrack Two Of A Kind, 1983. Honours include: OBE; Grammy Awards: Record of the Year, 1974; Best Country Vocal Performance, 1974; Best Pop Vocal Performance, 1975; Numerous American Music Awards, 1975-77, 1983; CMA Award, Female Vocalist Of Year (first UK recipient), 1975; Star on Hollywood Walk Of Fame, 1981; Numerous other awards from Record World; Billboard; People's Choice; AGVA; NARM; Goodwill Ambassador, UN Environment Programme, 1989. Current Management: Bill Sammeth Organisation, PO Box 960, Beverly Hills, CA 90213, USA.

NGEH Nfor William, b. 24 February 1956, Ndu Nwp, Cameroon. Musician; Singer; Songwriter. 2 sons, 1 daughter. Education: Mighty Flames, 1980; Sonny Okosuns Ozzidi Band, 1983; Ghetto Blaster, France; Mory Kante, 1988-91; Charelie Couture, France, 1991; Mbilia Bel, 1991-92; Manu Dibango, 1995. Compositions: Willy Nfor, Maisha on Dimie Distribution Night/Day France. Recordings: Mory Kante, Yeke Yeke; Manu Dibango Papa Groove; Manu Dibango, Sax & Spirituals; Willy Nfor; Maisha; Lapiro De Mbanga, Ndinga Man. Memberships: SACEM; French Copyrights Organization. Hobbies: Football; Tennis; Pingpong; Composing Music. Address: 71 Rue Pajol, 75018, Paris, France.

NGUYEN Gilbert, b. 10 Oct 1948, Vietnam. Musician (guitar). Musical Education: Modern harmony, Improvisation, Arranging, Orchestration, Berklee Correspondence Course, 1982. Career: Jazz fusion, rock musician; Solo guitarist, Saigon nightclub, Vietnam; Solo guitarist, Orchestre Les Atomes, Metz, 1980-83; Teacher, arranger, guitarist, night club, Paris, 1984-95. Address: 6 Avenue Robert Schuman, 77184 Emerainville, France.

NÍ RIAIN Nóirín, b. 12 June 1951, Limerick, Ireland. Singer; Musician (various Indian drones). m. Mícheál ó Súilleabháin, 27 June 1974, 2 sons. Education: Dip Phil Nul. Musical Education: MA, BMus, Dip, CMSM. Career: Performed UN Conferences in Costa Rica; Rio De Janeiro; Copenhagen; Poland; India; Beijing, China, 1995; Worked with John Cage; Numerous worldwide television and radio appearances; Works extensively in Cathedral of St John the Divine, New York. Recordings: Caoineadh Na Maighdine; Good People All; Vox De Nube; Soundings; Ple Hse Change; Gregorian Chant Experience. Publications: Im Bim Baboro; Stór Amhrán; Gregorian Chant Classics. Honours: MA Hons. Hobbies: Walking; Tennis. Current Management: Chantal Harris, Colin Pagnon, 272 Cathole Road, Litchfield, CT 06759, USA. Address: Dromore House, Newport, Co. Tipperary, Ireland.

NICHOLAS James Hayden, b. 7 May 1956, Hobbs, New Mexico, USA. Musician (guitar); Songwriter. Education: University of Houston, 1975-76. Career: Guitarist, various bands, 1975-86; Lead guitarist, songwriter, Clint Black, 1987-; Guitar technician at: Dale Mullins Studios, Houston, 1977-81; Heck Music Co, 1981-82; Appearances with Clint Black include: Grand Ole Opry; CMA Awards Show; Tonight Show; Arsenio Hall. Compositions include: Better Man; Killing Time; Music City News. Recordings: Albums: with Clint Black include: Killin' Time, 1989; Put Yourself In My Shoes, 1990. Honours: CMA Nomination, Song Of The Years, Better Man, 1990; 2 ACM Nominations, Song Of The Year: Better Man, 1990; Killing Time, 1990.

NICHOLAS Julian Conan, b. 13 January 1965, London, England. Musician (Saxophone); Composer. m. 1 daughter. Education: Hons Degree, York, 1986. Career: Saxophonist with Loose Tubes, 1989-91; Own group, Mountain People, 1989-98; Toured Europe extensively, 1989-98; BAFTA Nominee film score, Fools Gold, Brinksmat Robbery, LWT, 1992; Lecturer and Educationist, Bishop Otter College, West Sussex, 1993-96; Access to Music, 1992-98. Compositions: with W Woolf: A Thousand Ships; Mountain People; Food of Love; A Dawning; Madam, I'm Adam; Dear John. Recordings: Mountain People; RS001; Square Groove; Food of Love; Transformations; Everything You Do To Me. Honours: Twice Winner, Brighton Festival, Zap Award for Jazz, 1989, 1991. Memberships: Musicians' Union; Performing Rights Society. Hobbies: Philosophy; Cooking; Swimming. Current management: Aardvark, 1 Montague Place, Brighton BN2 1JE, England. Address: 8A Powis Square, Brighton, BN1 3HH, England.

NICHOLLS Al (Alan Charles), b. 27 Feb 1957, Wrexham, Wales. Musician (saxophone); Arranger. Musical Education: City of Leeds College of Music. Career: 4 years, Big Town Playboys, 1987-91; Numerous European tours; 2 US tours; Television includes: Jools Holland Happening; Pat Savak Show, USA; 3 years, King Pleasure And The Biscuit Boys, 1991-1994; Elvis: The Musical, Prince of Wales Theatre, West End, 1996; Led own band, Blue Harlem, 1996-; Television includes: What's The Noise; Blue Peter; Ray Gelato Giants, 1994-; Freelance musician. Recordings: Albums: Now Appearing, Big Town Playboys; Don't Mess With The Boogieman, Big Joe Duskin; Live At The Burnley Blues Festival, Champion Jack Dupree; The Full Flavour, Ray Gelato And The Giants; with King Pleasure And The Biscuit Boys: Live At Ronnie Scott's; Blues And Rhythm Revue. Memberships: Musicians' Union; British Music Writers Council. Hobbies: Gastronomy; Hill walking in Wales. Current Management: Self-managed. Address: 23 University Mansions, Putney, London SW15 1EP, England.

NICHOLLS Billy (William Morris), b. 15 Feb 1949, London, England. Singer; Songwriter; Producer. m. Anne Dupée, 2 sons, 1 daughter. Career: Musical director for The Who: Roger Daltrey tour; Pete Townshend Psychoderelict tour; Own solo albums. Compositions: Can't Stop Loving You, Leo Sayer; Without Your Love, Roger Daltrey; Fake It, Pete Townshend; Music for the McVicar film. Recordings: Solo albums: White Horse; Love Songs; Under One Banner. Honours: Ivor Novello Award Nomination. Hobbies: Cooking; Poetry. Address: 16 Park Road, E Twickenham, Middlesex TW1 2PX, England.

NICHOLLS Jonathan Charles, b. 11 Dec 1948, Northampton, England. Bandleader; Compere; Musician (bass guitar). m. Linda Joyce Singleton, 5 Apr 1969, 1 son. Musical Education: Self-taught. Career: Bandleader, top UK showband Mixed Feelings; Performed at leading international venues: New York Hilton; Bahrain Hilton; Gleneagles; Radio interview, The Tunnels Of Arras 1917; Radio performance of play: Voices Of The Fallen, BBC Radio 4. Publications: Cheerful Sacrifice - The Battle Of Arras, 1917, 1992; Play: Voices Of The Fallen, London, 1992-94. Membership: Musicians' Union. Hobbies: History; Rugby Football; Music; France. Address: 64 Wootton Drive, Hemel Hempstead, Herts HP2 6LB, England.

NICKELL Ylonda, b. 27 September 1958, Nopa, California, USA. Alto Saxophonist. m. Richie Cole, 1981, 1 daughter. Career: Performed with: Sonny Stitt, Freddie Hubbard, Mose Allison, Manhattan Transfer, Robert Cray and Willie Nelson; Performed at: Monterey Jazz Festival, Russian River Jazz Festival, Cotati Jazz Festival, Concerts-by-the-Sea, The Jazz Workshop, Roland's, Great American Music Hall, Yoshi's. Compositions: Alto Lady; Minnesota Sax. Current Management: Karen Kindig. Address: Karen Kindig, c/o The Blue Cat Agency, PO Box 399, Novato, CA 94948, USA.

NICKS Stevie (Stephanie), b. 26 May 1948, Phoenix, Arizona, USA. Singer; Songwriter. m. Kim Anderson, 29 Jan 1983, divorced 1984. Career: Member, Fritz (with Lindsey Buckingham); Member, duo Buckingham & Nicks; Member, Fleetwood Mac, 1975-90; Solo artiste, 1981-; Worldwide tours and concerts include: US tour with the Eagles, 1976; US Festival, San Bernardino, California, 1982; Shake The Cage tour, Europe, Australia, 1988; Mask tour, 1990. Compositions include: Rhiannon (Will You Ever Win); Dreams; Sara; Gypsy; Leather And Lace; Edge Of Seventeen; I Can't Wait; The Other Side Of The Mirror; Co-writer with Sandy Stewart: Seven Wonders; If Anyone Falls; Co-writer with Prince: Stand Back. Recordings: Albums: with Lindsey Buckingham: Buckingham Nicks, 1974;

with Fleetwood Mac: Fleetwood Mac (Number 1, US), 1975; Rumours (Number 1, UK and US; 15 million sales), 1977; Tusk (Number 1, UK), 1978; Fleetwood Mac Live, 1980; Mirage (Number 1, US), 1982; Tango In The Night (Number 1, UK), 1987; Greatest Hits, 1988; Behind The Mask (Number 1, UK), 1990; Solo albums: Bella Donna, 1981; The Wild Heart, 1983; Rock A Little, 1985; The Other Side Of The Mirror, 1989; Timespace - The Best Of Stevie Nicks, 1991; Street Angel, 1994; Numerous hit singles include: with Fleetwood Mac: Rhiannon (Will You Ever Win), 1976; Say You Love Me, 1976; Go Your Own Way, 1977; Don't Stop, 1977; Dreams (Number 1, US); You Make Loving Fun, 1977; Tusk, 1979; Sara, 1980; Hold Me, 1984; Oh Diane, 1983; Big Love, 1987; Little Lies, 1987; Everywhere, 1988; Solo: Stop Draggin' My Heart Around, with Tom Petty, 1981; Leather And Lace, duet with Don Henley, 1982; Edge Of Seventeen, 1982; After The Glitter Fades, 1982; Stand Back, 1982; If Anyone Falls, 1983; Talk To Me, 1986; I Can't Wait, 1986; Rooms On Fire, 1989; Also recorded with Kenny Loggins; Richie Vito. Honours: American Music Awards: Favourite Pop/Rock Group, Favourite Pop/Rock Album, 1978; Grammy: Album of the Year, Rumours, 1978; Billboard Awards: Album of the Year, Group of the Year, 1977; Star on Hollywood Hall Of Fame, with Fleetwood Mac, 1979; Gold Ticket, Madison Square Garden, 1990.

NICOL Ken(neth Stephen), b. 27 May 1951, Preston, Lancashire, England. Musician (guitar); Singer; Writer. Musical Education: Self-taught. Career: Signed to CBS Records, 1974; Polydor until 1979; Played lead guitar and recorded with Al Stewart; Appeared live in USA, 1980-88; Currently member, Albion Band; Television appearances include: New Faces; This Morning; Pebble Mill; The Big Breakfast. Recordings: Easy Street, by Nicol and Marsh, 1974, 1976; Under The Glass, 1977; Nicol And Marsh, 1978; Living In A Spanish Town, 1993. Memberships: Musicians' Union; PRS. Hobby: Fly-fishing. Current Management: Ess'ntial Productions. Address: 298 Tag Lane, Ingol, Preston, Lancashire PR2 3UY, England.

NICOL Simon, b. 13 Oct 1950, Muswell Hill, London, England. Folk Musician (guitar, keyboards). Career: Guitarist, founder member, Fairport Convention, 1967-71, 1977-; Founder, guitarist, Albion Country Band, 1971; Appearances include: Royal Albert Hall, 1969; London Palladium, 1970; Tours, festivals, concerts, annual Fairport Convention reunion concerts, 1980-. Recordings: Albums: with Fairport Convention: Fairport Convention, 1968; What We Did On Our Holidays, 1969; Unhalfbricking, 1969; Liege And Lief, 1970; Full House, 1970; Angel Delight, 1971; Babbacombe Lee, 1971; A Bonny Band Of Roses, 1977; Moat On The Ledge, 1982; The Best Of..., 1988; Red And Gold, 1989; Fairport Convention, 1990; Them Five Seasons, 1991; Jewel In The Crown, 1995; with Albion Country Band: Battle Of The Field, 1976; Prospect Before Us, 1977; Rise Up Like The Sun, 1978; Albion River Hymn March, 1979; Light Shining Albino, 1984; Shuffle Off, 1984.

NICOLAS Clovis, b. 13 Mar 1973, Abidjan, Ivory Coast. Musician (acoustic bass). Education: DEVG Philosophy. Musical Education: Jazz and classical music, Conservatoire of Music, Marseilles, 1993. Career: Played with Ted Curson; Peter King; Bobby Porcelli; Sandy Patton and Sara Lazarus, 1994; Plays with many French jazzmen including Jean-Pierre Arnaud; Philippe Renault; Pierre Drevet; Live in Paris, 1996; Played with Brad Mehldau, Belmondo Quintet, Stefano di Batista Quintet, Vincent Herring, Aldo Romano, Laurent de Wilde, Christian Escoude. Composition: Groovy Globy, 1996; Li-Li Smiles Again, 1996; A Romance for JB, 1996. Recordings: Featured on album: Le Collectif Artistique du Cri du Port (Marseilles), 1995; Jean Christope Beney Quartet, 1997. Honours: First

prize, International competition, Jazz Orchestras, Vienne, France, 1995; First Prize, Jazz Class Conservatoire de Marseille, 1996. Hobby: Listening to music. Address: 52 Avenue du Roule, 92200 Neuilly sur Seine, France.

NIEBLA Salvador, b. 28 December 1960, Ceuta, Spain. Drummer; Producer; Composer. Education: Berkle School of Music, Gerona. Career: Olympic Games, Barcelona, 1992; TV 1, Big Band; TV3, Big Band; Tours with Orquesta Mondragon; La Trinca; Max Suwer Tigo; Salvador Niebla Natural Energy; Amargos-Benavent Group; Atila; Orquesta Mirasol. Compositions: J Manuel Serrat; Dyango; Moncho; La Barberia; Carlos Benavent; Sabandenos; J Albert Amargos; J Has Ikitflus; Alameda; Orquesta Mirasol. Memberships: SGAE; AIE; AMJC. Current Management: Odisea Productions. Address: c/ Roselló, 217 2 1a, Barcelona, 08008, Spain.

NIELSEN Billy, b. 28 June 1976, Scarborough, North Yorkshire, England. Musician (guitar); Vocalist; Songwriter. Musical Education: Mainly self-taught. Career: Radio York, 1988; Summer seasons, Scarborough, 1989-90; Yorkshire TV, 1991; Granada TV, 1991; Stage musical: Alas Poor Yorvik, 1992; Guildhall, York, 1992; Dr Rock Show, Radio York, 1993; Performs own songs throughout UK, 1994-. Memberships: Musicians' Union; Group of International Composers and Songwriters. Hobbies: Swimming; Walking; Listening to good music. Current Management: Neal Smith-Amies. Address: 34 Valley Road, Scarborough YO11 2LU, England.

NIELSEN Ditte Marie, b. 22 Oct 1955, Copenhagen, Denmark. Singer; Composer. 1 daughter. Education: Nursery School Teacher course, 3 years. Musical Education: Music Academy, Copenhagen, 1981; Music School, Vestbirk; Private studies with Hanne Boel. Career: Debut at age 13 in Ahus Folkspark, Sweden; Member of various bands including Marie Band, Black Roses, Jazz The Jaguar and Twistor; Performed at Roskilde Festival, 1987; Toured throughout Denmark as soloist, 1990-; Television appearance in 1991; Performed at Ringe Festival, 1992; Performs regularly at Tivoli Vise Vershus Copenhagen. Recording: Dansk/Irish, with Charlie McGettigan, Peter West and others, 1994; Single: Knuste hjerter/Sanger/Lyse Dage, 1995. Membership: Dansk Artistforbund (United Artists of Denmark). Hobbies: Painting; Flying; Nature.

NIELSEN Ib Lund, b. 9 October 1941, Vamdrup, Jylland, Denmark. Musician. m. Inge Holten Nielsen, 19 December 1964, 2 sons. Education: Bass Lessons with John Nielsen; Dr-Radio Symphonic Orchestra, 1967-70. Career: Bass Player in Orchestra with Niels Husum Severel Radio AP; With Quartet, Quintet, Sextet, with the Nielshusum Septet; Bass Player in Leonardo Pedersens Jazz Kapel, 11 Piece Swing Band, 1970-. Compositions: Hic with Stormy's Quartet, 1960; Bass Relief, 1980. Recordings: Lockjaw, Sweets, 1976; Bass Relief, 1980; I Want A Roof, 1994. Honours: With Stormy's Quartet, Winner, Jazz Competition, Denmark, 1960. Memberships: DMF; NDJ. Hobbies: Music; Reading; Theatre. Address: Hvidager 2, 2620 Albertslund, Denmark.

NIELSEN Jens G, b. 1 Aug 1951, Denmark. Musician (drums); Record Producer; Record Company Executive. Career: Member, Gnags; Worldwide tours; Co-founder, Genlyd record label (bought by BMG); A&R Director, BMG, Denmark. Recordings: 20 Gnags albums; Producer, albums for various artists. Honours: Danish Grammy, Mr Swing King, 1990. Current Management: Rock On, Denmark. Address: Rådhusstræde 4a, DK 1466 Copenhagen K, Denmark.

NIELSEN Peter A G, b. 17 Dec 1952, Skjern, Denmark. Singer; Composer. m. Katrine Nyholm, May 1923, 1 son, 1 daughter. Education: Danish

Literature, Aarhus University. Career: Founder, singer, songwriter, Gnags, 1966-. Recordings: Gnags, 20 albums. Honours: Grammy Award, Mr Swing King, 1990. Hobbies: Watching; Listening; Tasting; Touching. Current Management: Rock On, Rådhusstræde 4 A, 1466 Copenhagen, Denmark. Address: Haraldsgade 23, 8260 Viby J, Denmark.

NIELSEN Rick, b. 22 Dec 1946, Rockford, Illinois, USA. Musician (guitar); Vocalist. Career: Member, various bands including Fuse; Sick Man Of Europe; Founder member, US rock group Cheap Trick, 1969-; Appearances include: Concert, Tokyo, 1978; California Music Festival, Los Angeles, 1979; Reading Festival, 1979; UK tour, 1980; Montreux Rock Festival, 1988; US tour with Robert Plant, 1988; US tour with Kiss, 1988; US tour with Heart, 1990; Solo performance, Concerto For Electric Guitar And Orchestra, Michael Kamen, with Rockford Symphony Orchestra, 1993. Recordings: Albums: Cheap Trick, 1977; Heaven Tonight, 1978; Cheap Trick At Budokan, 1979; Dream Police, 1979; Found All The Parts, 1980; All Shook Up, 1980; One On One, 1982; Next Position Please, 1983; The Doctor, 1986; Lap Of Luxury, 1988; Busted, 1990; The Greatest Hits, 1991; Singles include: I Want You To Want Me, 1979; Ain't That A Shame, 1979; Dream Police, 1979; Voices, 1980; Everything Works If You Let It, 1980; If You Want My Love, 1982; Tonight It's You, 1985; Mighty Wings, used in film soundtrack Top Gun, 1986; Ghost Town, 1988; I Can't Stop Falling Into Love, 1990. Hobby: Collecting rare and unusual guitars. Current Management: Ken Adamany Associates, 1818 Parmenter Street, Suite 202, Middleton, WI 53562, USA.

NIEMELÄINEN Ilkka, b. 9 Mar 1956, Finland. Musician (guitar); Composer. Musical Education: Guitar, musical theory, Helsinki Conservatory. Career: Writer, performer, electronic music with Otto Romanowski, Esa Kotilainen, 1970s; Founder, composer, musical director, Wasama Quartet, 1976-85; Concerts included: Ylioppilastalo, Tampere, Finland; Detroit Kool Jazz Festival; Founder, composer, musical director Instinct, 1985-; Represented Finland at EBU Festival, Kristianstad; Numerous concerts in Finland; Founder, trio IN2á3, with Pentti Lahti, Jukka Wasama, 1990. Recordings: Arranger, classical album for saxophonist Pentti Lahti. Address: Haukilahdenrata 21 D, 02170 Espoo, Finland.

NIEWOOD Gerry (Gerard Joseph), b. 6 Apr 1943, Rochester, New York, USA. Musician (woodwind). m. Gurly Hulbert, 2 Mar 1972, 1 son, 1 daughter. Musical Education: BM, Eastman School of Music, 1970. Career: Woodwind player with Chuck Mangione Quartet, 1968-76; Judy Collins, 1977-80; Simon and Garfunkel, 1982-83; Alto saxophonist, Radio City Music Hall, New York, 1979-; Saxophonist with Gerry Mulligan, 1980-; Liza Minnelli, 1984-; Freelance musician, 1986-; Concerts include: Simon and Garfunkel in Central Park, 1982; The Ultimate Event, with Frank Sinatra, Liza Minnelli, Sammy Davis Jr, 1989. Compositions: Floating, 1972; Joy, 1976. Recordings: Slow Hot Wind, 1975; Gerry Niewood and Timepiece, 1977; Share My Dream, 1986; Gerry Niewood/Alone, 1988. Honour: Talent Deserving Wider Recognition, Downbeat Magazine, 1975, 1976. Current Management: Con Sona Music Inc. Address: 228 Bay Avenue, Glen Ridge, NJ 07028, USA.

NIJS Johan Leopold Alice, b. 11 June 1963, Leuven, Belgium. Composer; Musician. m. Buelens Karine, 30 March 1996, 1 daughter. Education: Economic studies; Several degrees, Royal Conservatory of Brussels. Career: Composer, Arranger, De Haske Publications: Clarinet Player, Band of the Royal Air Force, Belgium; Conductor. Compositions: Concert pieces include: Spirit of Life; Fantasy for Band; Reflections, De Haske; Disco Story, De Haske; Celebration Fantasy, De Haske; Explorations, De Haske; The Bermuda Mystery; Overture for Band; Pieces for Band include: In a Holiday Mood; In a Dixie Mood; Mood Romantic; Two Dances for 2 Real Friends; A Holiday Party; Let's Play Dixie; Solo Pieces include: Elegy, piano; Fantaisie Pittoresque, accordion; Epigram, flute; Saxatina, saxophone; Marches include: Admination; Marching for Freedom; On the Beat, De Haske; Doin' Just Fine; Give It a Go. Honours: Composition Prize, France, 1990, Antwerp, 1993, Luxembourg, 1994. Memberships: IMMS; Technical Commission of FEDEKAM, Belgium. Hobbies: Coins; Stamps; Geology; Beer Glasses. Address: St Pauluslaan 8, Vossem Tervuren, 3080, Belgium.

NILES Richard, b. 28 May 1951, Hollywood, California, USA. Composer; Producer; Arranger; Writer. Musical Education: B Mus, Berklee College Of Music, Boston. Career: Arranger for: Paul McCartney; Take That; Tears For Fears; Was Not Was; Swing Out Sister; Grace Jones; Producer for: Pet Shop Boys; Hue And Cry; Pat Metheny; The Troggs; Television: Musical Director for series: David Essex; Leo Sayer; Michael Ball; Ruby Wax (Don't Miss Wax); Numerous television commercials. Compositions: Recorded by: Ray Charles; Bobby Womack; Tina Turner; Hue And Cry; Spike Milligan. Publications: Regular journalist for: Making Music Magazine, London. Honours: Golden Rose Of Montreux, Best Original Film Score for: The Strike. Memberships: Musicians' Union; PRS; Re-Pro. Hobbies: Jungian psychology; Massage; Dating. Address: 34 Beaumont Road, London W4 5AP, England.

NIMMERSJO Conny, b. 20 March 1967, Angelholm, Sweden. Musician (guitar). 1 daughter. Career: Founder member, bob hund, 1991-; Performed more than 250 concerts around Scandinavia; Played at festivals including Roskilde, Lollipop, Ruisrock, Quartfestivalen and Hultsfred. Compositions: I Stället för Musik: Förvirring, 1996; Düsseldorf, 1996. Recordings: with Bob Hund: Bob Hund, 1993, 1994; Edvin Medvind, 1994; I Stället för Musik: Förvirring, 1996; Omslag: Martin Kann, 1996. Honours: Grammy Awards: Best Live Act, 1994, Best Lyrics, 1996. Memberships: STIM; SAMI. Hobbies: Music; Books; Movies; Late night talking; Food; Drinking. Address: Box 53045, S-400 14 Gothenburg, Sweden.

NOBES Roger Michael, b. 26 Dec 1939, Abbots Langley, Hertfordshire, England. Musician (vibraphone, piano, drums); Arranger. m. Maureen Payne, 1 June 1987, 1 daughter. Musical Education: Central School of Music. Career: Numerous national and international tours with The Alex Welsh Band, The Dave Shepherd Quintet; Numerous tours with American artists; Concert performers include: Festival Hall; Barbican Centre; Many radio and television appearances. Recordings: Recorded extensively with many bands and orchestras including The Roger Nobes Quartet. Membership: Musicians' Union. Hobbies: Director of North Hertfordshire Youth Big Band; Cricket. Current Management: Roma Enterprises. Address: 41 Manton Road, Hitchin, Hertfordshire SG4 9NP, England.

NOBLE Douglas, b. 9 July 1964, Edinburgh, Scotland. Guitar Instructor; Freelance Music Journalist. Education: BSc Psychology, Edinburgh University, 1985; Musical Education: ALCM, Classical guitar, London College of Music, 1986; LLCM (TD), Classical guitar, London College of Music, 1987. Career: Freelance music journalist, regular contributor to the Guitar Magazine (UK); Occasional contributor to Guitar Player (US); Bass Player (US); Contributions to several books on the electric guitar; Sleeve notes for several albums; Music Director for Univibes, international Jimi Hendrix magazine; Examiner, Rock School, Trinity College of Music. Publications: Instant Hendrix, book, 1988; Instant Peter Green, book, 1990. Hobbies: Swimming; Tennis; Zen Buddhism. Address: 2F4 99 St Leonard's Street, Edinburgh EH8 9QY, Scotland.

NOBLE Stephen Francis Paterson, b. 26 Mar 1960, Wallingford, Oxfordshire, England. Musician (drums, percussion, musical saw, bugle). Musical Education: Self-taught, still learning. Career: Contemporary Music Network Tour, with Alex Maguire, 1994; Festivals: Glasgow Jazz, 1989-94; New Music America, New York, 1989; Sitges International Dance, 1991; Taklos (Swizz), 1990-92; London Jazz, 1993-94; Television and radio: Featured in On The Edge (series about improvisation), CH4; Live recording from Adrian Boult Hall, Birmingham, broadcast on Radio 3 (Impressions and Midnight Oil), with pianist Alex Maguire; Live broadcasts throughout Europe with various groups. Compositions: Commissioned by South Bank Centre, London to compose music for collaboration with Spanish Dance Company Mal Pelo, 1993. Recordings: Duo with Alex Maguire: Live At Oscar's; (voted one of top jazz albums of 1980s); Once, recordings from Derek Bailey's Company Week, featuring Bailey and Lee Konitz, 1987; The Shakedown Club. Memebrships: Musicians' Union; PRS. Current Management: Ping Pong Productions. Address: 13 Calthorpe Street, London WC1X OJP, England.

NOLAN J William (Bill), b. 13 Nov 1940, Derby, Connecticut, USA. Civil Rights Activist; Musicologist. m. Joan M Owens, 1962, 1 son. Career: Volunteer Radio Broadcaster for WPKN-FM, 1969-; Founder and Executive Director of The Rhythm and Blues Rock 'N Roll Society Inc, 1974; Founder of American Blues Movement, 1975; Volunteer helping Black African-American artists and sustaining music heritage. Address: c/o Rhythm and Blues Rock 'N Roll Society Inc, PO Box 1949, New Haven, CT 06510, USA.

NOLLI Giorgio, b. 5 Feb 1965, Merano, Italy. Musician, (percussion, congas, timbales). Musical Education: Self-taught; Participated in various workshops in the UK. Career: Italian tour, pop band China Boy Hi, 1992; European tour, garage band Nicolette, 1993; Television appearance, James Whale Show, UK, 1993; Japanese tour, jungle group UK Tribe, 1995; Jonathan Ross's Big Big Talent Show, ITV, 1996; The Carmen Miranda Story, Jermyn Street Theatre, 1997. Recordings: Singles: I Want To Be Everything, China Boy Hi, 1992; There Isn't Any Way, China Boy Hi, 1993; Junglites, UK Tribe, 1995; Album: Jungle Soul, UK Tribe, 1995. Membership: Musicians' Union. Hobbies: Travel; Languages; Yoga; Sci-fi. Address: 29 Buckingham Road, Harlesden, London NW10 4RP, England.

NOONE Peter, b. 5 Nov 1947, Davyhulme, Manchester, England. Vocalist. m. Mireille Strasser. Musical Education: Manchester School of Music and Drama, Career: Lead vocalist, Herman's Hermits, 1963-71; Solo artist, 1971-; US tour, 1965; North American tour with the Who, 1967; Madison Square Garden, 1973; Member, The Tremblers, 1980; Actor, film: Mrs Brown You've Got A Lovely Daughter, 1968; Performed, play: The Canterville Ghost, US TV, 1966; Pinocchio, 1968; Business partnership with Graham Gouldman, studio production work, New York boutique, Zoo, 1968; Performed in Pirates Of Penzance, Broadway and London, 1982-83; Video jockey, US Cable TV, 1990s. Recordings: Introducing Herman's Hermits, 1965; Herman's Hermits On Tour, 1965; The Best Of Herman's Hermits, 1965; Hold On!, 1966; Both Sides Of Herman's Hermits, 1966; Volume III, 1968; Mrs Brown You've Got A Lovely Daughter, 1965; Wonderful World, 1965; I'm Henry VIII, I Am, 1965; Just a Little Better, 1965; A Must To Avoid, 1966; No Milk Today, 1966; Dandy, 1966; There's A Kind Of Hush (All Over The World), 1967; Sleepy Joe, 1968; Sunshine Girl, 1968;

Something's Happening, 1969; Years May Come Years May Go, 1970; Solo: Oh You Pretty Thing, 1971. Current Management: DeLauro Management, Suite 1980, 875 Avenue of the Americas, New York, NY 10001, USA.

NORBY Caecilie, b. 9 September 1964, Frederiksberg, Denmark. Singer. Education: SKT Annæ Gymnasium Music School, 1973-80; Music Theatre School, 1 year; Several Music Courses; Private Lessons in Singing and Piano. Career: Different Performing Groups, 1980-81; Lead Singer in the Funk Rock Band, Street Beat, 1981-84; Lead Singer in the recording band, Frontline, 1987; Lead Singer in One Two, together with collegue Nina Forsberg, 1993. Compositions: Several. Recordings: Frontline, 1985; Frontlife, 1986; One Two, 1986; My Corner of the Sky, 1996; Hvide Loegne, 1989; Getting Better, 1993; Caecilie Norby, 1995. Honours: Ben Webster Prize, 1987; Simon Spies Soloist Prize, 1995; 7 Grammy Nominations in Denmark. Memberships: Danish Artist Society; DJBFA. Current Management: PDH Management, Copenhagen, Denmark. Address: Absalonsgade 7A 1Tv, 1658 Copenhagen V, Denmark.

NORCROSS Rick (Richard Charles), b. 23 Mar 1945, Waltham, Massachusetts, USA. Singer; Songwriter; Entertainer; Musician (guitar). Education: BA, Mass Communications, University of South Florida, Tampa, Florida, USA. Career: Solo artiste, 1963-80; 3 tours of England, 1965-75; Lead singer, Rick Norcross and The Nashfull Ramblers Western Swing Band, 1980-; Tours: Central Florida; New England Fair; Festival Circuit; Producer, 35 festivals and special events, 1974-. Recordings: Albums: Nashfull, 1980; Fairly Live, 1983; Tour Du Jour, 1989; You Can't Get There From Here, 1991; Can't Catch A Rambler, 1994; The Legend Of Scratch Leroux, 1995. Publications: Entertainment Editor, The Tampa Times, 1969-74. Honour: Vice President, Yankee Festivals and Events Association. Membership: AFofM. Current Management: Airflyte Productions. Address: 216 Battery Street, Burlington, VT 05401, USA.

NORDENSTAM Stina, b. 4 March 1969, Stockholm, Sweden. Singer; Songwriter. Education: Violin, music theory and classical composition at Nacka Musikskola and Musikkugskolan, Stockholm; Selftaught piano and guitar. Career: Songwriter and performer, early 1980s with group The Flippermen; Performed at Swedish Festivals. Composition: Little Star, 1993. Recordings: Solo albums: Memories Of A Color, 1991; And She Closed Her Eyes, 1993; Dynamite, 1996. Hobbies: Photography; Film; Video Directing. Current Management: Denander and Grahl, Box 4342, S-102 67 Stockholm, Sweden.

NORMAN Chris (Christopher), b. 25 Oct 1950, Redcar, Yorkshire, England. Singer; Songwriter; Musician (guitar). Record Producer. m. Linda Heddle, 16 Mar 1970, 4 sons, 2 daughters. Career: Lead singer, Kindness, Backing group to Peter Noone (ex Herman's Hermits), 1960s; Group later became Smokie, 1970's; Solo artist, 1980's-; Produced number of records. Recordings: Hit singles: If You Think You Know How To Love Me; Living Next Door To Alice; Lay Back In Your Arms; Don't Play Your Rock And Roll To Me; Stumblin' In; Midnight Lady; This Time (We'll Get It Right); Recorded 16 albums. Honours: 3 Bravo Awards, 1976-86; Golden Europa, 1986; CMT Europe, 1994. Memberships: PRS; MCPS; BASCA. Hobbies: Music; Family. Current Agent: Bill Tuckey Music. Address: 20 Tor Bryan, Ingatestone, Essex, England.

NORMAN David, b. 19 May 1962, London, England. Tour/Production Manager; Sound Engineer. m. Suzanne Feit, 18 Oct 1992. Career: Television and live credits include: The Arsenio Hall Show; Late Night with David Letterman Show;

The Jon Stewart Show; MTV Beach House; Top Of The Pops; Showtime at the Apollo; Kenny G 'Breathless' Tour; MTV Japan; The Far East Network; Woodstock, 1994; WOMAD Tour, 1994; Lowlands Festival. Recordings: Engineer on albums: Through The Fire, Peabo Bryson; Zingalamundi, Arrested Development. Hobbies: Reading; Bowling; Computers; Animals. Address: 639 Gardenwalk Boulevard, Suite 1632, College Park, GA 30349, USA.

NORREMOLLE Jens, b. 12 Aug 1956, Vejle, Denmark. Composer; Producer; Musician (keyboards). 1 son. Education: Teacher. Musical Education: Self-taught. Career: Various bands until 1987-; Composer, singer, keyboard player for Singing Zoo; Record producer for Anne Dorte Michelsen and Venter På Far, 1987-1995. Recordings: with Anne Dorte Michelsen: Elskerindens Have; Den Ordlose Time; Min Karriere Som Kvinde (producer, arranger, musician); Also albums with Singing Zoo and Venter På Far. Honours: Best Band, 1988; Musikcafé Prize with Singing Zoo. Membership: DMF; DJBFA. Hobby: Son. Current Management: Warner Chappell, Denmark. Address: Blågårdsgade 17 IV left, 2200 Copenhagen N, Denmark.

NORRIS Richard, b. 23 June 1965, London, England. Musician (keyboards, saxophone, drums); Producer; Remixer. Education: Liverpool University. Career: Member musical duo, The Grid; Met partner Dave Ball, recording Jack The Tab compilation, 1988; Recorded 4 albums, 11 singles; Tours, UK, 1991-; Japan, Thailand, Singapore, New Zealand, Australia, 1995; Producer, remixer, artists including: Pet Shop Boys, Boy George, Marc Almond, Brian Eno, Happy Mondays, 1990-1995. Recordings: Albums: Floatation, Electric Head, 1990; Evolver, Texas Cowboys, 1990; Rollercoaster, Swamp Thing, 1994; Music For Dancing, Diablo, 1995; Recorded with Joe Strummer for Grosse Point Blank movie soundtrack, 1997; Bigg Buddha, Be Here Now, 12". Honours: Silver disc, Swamp Thing, 1994; Platinum disc (Australia), Swamp Thing, 1994. Memberships: PRS; PPL; Musicians' Union. Current Management: Pete Evans, Native Management. Address: Unit 32, Ransome Dock 35-37 Parkgate Road, London SW11 4NP, England.

NORRIS Richard T, b. 9 Feb 1966, Epping, Essex, England. Music Programmer; Writer; Recording Engineer. Career: Programmer, engineer for Bryan Ferry, including albums Taxi, Mamouna, 1990-95; Co-writer with Little Annie, 1989-94; Currently co-writing with Guy Pratt (Pink Floyd) under joint name Deep Cover. Recordings: Albums: Taxi, Bryan Ferry, 1993; Deboravation, Deborah Harry, 1993; Mix-ism, Mad Capsule Markets, 1994; Mamouna, Bryan Ferry, 1994; Grand Central, Deep Cover, from Hackers film soundtrack, 1995. Current Management: This Much Talent, 117 Church Road, Barens, London SW13 9HL, England.

NORRIS Russell Anthony, b. 6 Aug 1971, Walthamstow, London, England. Writer; Producer; Remixer; Musician (keyboards); Insurance Broker. Musical Education: Self-taught. Career: Toured many English dance clubs, 1990-93; Scottish Club Tour, 1992; Appearances on ITV's BPM and Chart Show, and on MTV and Kiss FM. Recordings: Free, X-Static, 1991; The X-Static EP, X-Static, 1992; Global Vibe, X-Static, 1993. Membership: Musicians' Union. Hobbies: Playing and watching football. Current Management: X-Treme Dance. Address: 1 Herbert Gardens, Willesden, London NW10, England.

NOTLEY Wendy, b. 28 Oct 1957, Australia. Singer; Songwriter; Musician (guitar); Teacher. Education: Diploma in Early Childhood Education. Career: Early childhood Teacher and Director, Yinbilliko School, Sydney, Australia; Teaching,

Murawina Aboriginal multi-purpose Education Centre in Redfern, Sydney, for 4 years; Singer, songwriter, guitarist, co-producer, Growin' Up Strong, by Aunty Wendy's Mob; Author, 4 children's books, Teacher's Resource Book and Education Kit. Compositions: Growin' Up Strong; Indigenous; We're Koori Kids; The Wheels On The Holden; Red, Black And Yellow; Wiradjuri And Bundjalung; Until The Fire Is Out; Dreamtime; There Was A Man; Stand Up; Noongar In The Bush; Melaleua; Round The Campfire Tonight; We're Bininj kids. Recording: Growin' Up Strong, Aunty Wendy's Mob. Honour: APRA Award Nomination, children's category, 1996. Membership: Society of Authors. Address: 5/355 Glebe Point Road, Glebe, Sydney, NSW 2037, Australia.

NOVA Aldo, b. Canada. Rock Musician (guitar); Singer. Career: Solo recording artiste, 1980-. Recordings: Albums: Aldo Nova, 1982; Subject, 1984; Twitch, 1985; Blood On The Bricks, 1991; Also featured musician on albums: Bon Jovi, Bon Jovi, 1984; Blaze Of Glory, Jon Bon Jovi, 1991.

NOVOSELIC Kris, b. 16 May 1965, Croatia. Musician (bass). Career: Member, Nirvana, 1987-94; Worldwide tours; Concerts include: Reading Festival, 1991, 1992; Transmusicales Festival, Rennes, France, 1991; Benefit concert, Washington State Music Coalition, 1992; Benefit concert, Tresnjevka Women's Group, Cow Palace, San Francisco, 1993; Founder, Sweet 75, 1995. Recordings: Albums: Bleach, 1989; Nevermind (Number 1, US), 1991; Incesticide, 1993; In Utero (Number 1, UK & US), 1993; Unplugged In New York, 1994; Singles include: Smells Like Teen Spirit, 1991; Come As You Are, 1992; Lithium, 1992; In Bloom, 1992; Oh, The Guilt, 1993; Heart-Shaped Box, 1993; All Apologies, 1993; Track, I Hate Myself And Wanna Die, featured on Beavis & Butthead Experience, 1993. Publication: Come As You Are, Nirvana biography by Michael Azerrad. Honours: Platinum disc, Nevermind; Best Alternative Music Video, Best New Artist Video, Smells Like Teen Spirit, MTV Music Video Awards, 1992; Best International Newcomer, BRIT Awards, 1993.

NOWELS Rick. Songwriter; Record Producer; Musician. Musical Education: Music Major, University of California at Berkeley. Compositions: Madonna, The Power of Good-bye, To Have and Not to Hold, Little Star; Celine Dion, Falling Into You; Robert Miles, One And One; Des'ree, Time, Get a Life; Anita Baker, Body and Soul; Belinda Carlisle, Heaven is a Place on Earth, Circle in the Sand, Leave a Light On, Live Your Life Be Free, In Too Deep, We Want the Same Thing, La Lune, Runaway Horses, Vision of You, Do You Feel Like I Feel?, Stevie Nicks, I Can't Wait, Rooms on Fire, Maybe Love Will Change Your Mind; Roachford, Naked Without You; Kim Wilde, Love is Holy; Rozalla, You Never Love the Same Way Twice; The Corrs, Intimacy; Maria Nayler, Naked and Sacred; As a Producer: Falling Into You, Celine Dion; Heaven on Earth, Runaway Horses, Live Your Life Be Free, Belinda Carlisle; Stevie Nicks, Rock A Little; Then Jericho, Big Area; Des'ree; Crystal Waters; The Corrs; Maria Nayler; Maxi Priest. Honours: Grammy Nomination, Best R&B Song, Anita Baker, 1996; ASCAP Awards; Grammy Award, Album of the Year, Falling Into You by Celine Dion, 1997. Current Management: Stephen Budd. Address: c/o 109 B Regents Park Road, London NW1 8UR, England.

NOYCE Jonathan, b. 15 July 1971, Sutton Coldfield, England. Musician (bass guitar); Composer. m. Sara Joanna King, 15 July 1995. Musical Education: North Herts College, Royal Academy Of Music. Career: with Ian Anderson (Jethro Tull): Tours, USA, Canada, Europe; VH-1 radio broadcast, Secret Life; Television: Pebble Mill; What's Up Doc?; Videos; with C J Lewis: The

White Room; with David Palmer: Concerts in Venezuela; Belgium; Estonia; Romania; Germany; Various concerts and recordings. Recordings: with Take That: Relight My Fire, 1993; with Al Green: Keep On Pushing Love, 1994; with Sister Sledge: Thinking Of You (remix), 1993; with Diana Ross: Love Hangover (remix), 1994; with Joey Negro: Universe Of Love, 1993; with David Palmer: Sgt Pepper. Honours: LRAM, Professional Certificate of Royal Academy Of Music. Membership: Musicians' Union. Hobbies: Cooking; Camel baiting; Shaving. Current Management: Self-managed. Address: 1 Marcus Terrace, Wandsworth, London SW18 2JW, England.

NOYES Cameron George Albert, b. 27 Feb 1965, Edmonton, Alberta, Canada. m. Velveeta Krisp, 1 daughter. Career: Worked in musical or industry capacities with 800 artists including: Faith No More; King Sunny Ade; The Wailers; John Cale; Donovan; SNFU; Dead Kennedys. Recordings: Cable; Don't Care, Didn't Care; Yuppie Flux. Honour: IMBH, Award of Excellence, 1992. Memberships: ARIA; PMIA; OTO. Hobbies: Equestrian; Books; Wine collecting. Current Management: Phantom Product Canada. Address: #104-1540 E 4th Avenue, Vancouver, British Colmubia, Canada.

NOZEDAR Adele, b. 7 Aug 1966, Yorkshire, England. Record Company Executive; Musician (piano, harp). m. Adam Fuest, 1 Aug 1993. Musical Education: Grade B Musical Theory. Career: Managing Director of Rhythm King Records, independent UK label founded in 1986 with Martin Heath; Co-founder of Renegade Software. Honour: Leslie Perrin Award for Public Relations in 1992. Memberships: Musicians' Union; PRS. Hobbies: Stained glass making; Designing; Gilding. Address: c/o Rhythm King Records, 121 Salisbury Road, London NW6 6RG, England.

NUGENT Ted, b. 13 Dec 1949, Detroit, Michigan, USA. Rock Musician (guitar); Singer. Career: Founder, guitarist, The Amboy Dukes, 1966-1975; Solo artiste, 1975-89; Formed Damn Yankees, 1989-; Appearances include: Reading Festival (UK debut), 1976; California Jam II Festival, Los Angeles, 1978; California Music Festival, with Van Halen, Cheap Trick, Aerosmith, 1979; World Series of Rock, Cleveland, with Aerosmith, Journey, Thin Lizzy, 1979; Whiplash Bash, Detroit, 1988; Volunteer Jam XIV, Nashville, 1991; Television includes: Miami Vice, NBC TV, 1984; Late Night With David Letterman, NBC TV, 1991. Recordings: Albums: with The Amboy Dukes: Call Of The Wild, 1973; Tooth Fang And Claw, 1974; Solo albums: Ted Nugent, 1975; Free For All, 1976; Cat Scratch Fever, 1977; Double Live Gonzo, 1978; Weekend Warriors, 1978; State Of Shock, 1979; Scream Dream, 1980; Great Gonzos - The Best Of Ted Nugent, 1981; Intensities In Ten Cities, 1981; Nugent, 1982; Penetrator, 1984; Little Miss Dangerous, 1986; Anthology, 1986; If You Can't Lick 'Em, Lick 'Em!, 1988; Spirit Of The Wild, 1995; with Damn Yankees: Damn Yankees, 1990; Honours: Gold and Platinum discs. Current Management: Madhouse Management. Address: PO Box 15108, Ann Arbor, MI 48106, USA.

NUITTEN Luc Marcel Leo, b. 8 Apr 1956, Wilrijk, Belgium. Impresario. m. Daniela Casagrande, 30 Nov 1992, 1 son. Education: University. Musical Education: Central Examination Board, University Degree. Career: Performing artist for 25 years; Concert organizer for 10 years; Licensed impresario for headline acts at major festivals for 5 years. Publications: Revue. Memberships: SABAM; BVBI. Hobby: Family trips. Address: aa LN International, PB 15 Antwerp 17, B-2018 Antwerp, Belgium.

NUMAN Gary (Gary Webb), b. 8 Mar 1958, Hammersmith, London, England. Singer; Songwriter. Career: Singer, Tubeway Army,

1978-79; Billed as solo artiste, 1979-; Own record label, Numa Records, 1984-87; Extensive tours include: World tour, 1980; Annual UK tours; Regular television appearances. Recordings: Albums: Replicas (Number 1, UK), 1979; The Pleasure Principle (Number 1, UK), 1979; Telekon (Number 1, UK), 1980; Living Ornaments 1979-1980, 1981; Dance, 1981; I Assassin, 1982; New Man Numan - The Best Of Gary Numan, 1982; The Plan, 1984; White Noise Live, 1985; Strange Charm, 1986; Exhibition, 1987; Metal Rhythm, 1988; Skin Mechanic, 1989; Outland, 1991; Machine + Soul, 1992; Best Of 1979-83, 1993; Dream Corrosion, 1994; Exile, 1997; Contributor, Clues, Robert Palmer, 1980; Hit singles include: Are Friends Electric? (Number 1, UK), 1979; Cars (Number 1, UK), 1979; Complex, 1979; We Are Glass, 1980; I Die You Die, 1980; This Wreckage, 1981; She's Got Claws, 1981; Music For Chameleons, 1982; We Take Mystery (To Bed), 1982; White Boys And Heroes, 1982; Warriors, 1983; This Is Love; I Can't Stop; I Still Remember; Cars (E Reg Mix); with Bill Sharpe (Shakatak): Change Your Mind, 1985; New Thing From London Town, 1986.

NUNN Charles David, b. 14 Sept 1954, Stellenbosch, South Africa. Pastor; Musician (pan flute); Singer. m. 8 Jan 1982, 1 son, 2 daughters. Career: Performer, preacher, gospel music, and the Gospel of Jesus Christ; Star of the Week, Afrikaans Stereo; Several radio chat shows. Recordings: 2 albums of pan flute music; 1 album as vocalist. Membership: ASAMI. Hobbies: Photography; Flying; Music. Current Management: Studio Nunn Ministries. Address: PO Box 4292, Secunda 2302, South Africa.

NYA Soleil, b. 24 July 1958, Douala, Cameroon. Artistic Co-ordinator; Musician (guitar); Author; Composer. m. Michèle Frot-Coutaz, 2 sons. Education: Licence Cinema and Audiovisuel; Deug Histoire De L'Art; Deug Musicologie, Paris VIII. Compositions: Yaounde By Night, Pop Mangambe; Que la Paix Rayonn, Devaluation; Toli Toli, Africa Unit; Techno Mangambe, Faux Rendez Vous; Black Pharaoh. Recordings: 3 albums: La Vie Est Un Roman, 1986; Africa Fête, 1989; Toli-Toli, 1998. Membership: SACEM. Hobbies: President, Soleil Pour Tous Association (Cultural & Humanity Association).

NYE Cheryl, b. Montreal, Quebec, Canada. Singer; Songwriter; Musician (keyboards). Musical Education: BFA Music, Voice Major, Concordia University. Career: Sung anthems at: Toronto Skydome; Montreal Forum; Olympic Stadium; Lansdowne Park; Television: CBC; CFCF; Videotron; Télé-Métropole; RDS; CHRO; Radio-Quebec; CFCL-CITO; CHNB-CKNY. Recordings: Singles: Never Give Up On A Dream, 1982; Heartbeat, 1986; Album: Loving You, 1993. Honours: B100 Pepsi Entertainer Award (USA). Memberships: ACTRA; CCMA; SOCAN; CMA. Hobbies: Music; Sports. Current Management: WE Communications. Address: 455 Ballantyne North Montreal West, Quebec H4X 2C8, Canada.

NYS (Magthea) Sandy, b. 30 July 1959, Mechelen, Belgium. Graphic Designer. Education: Graphic Design, Art School. Musical Education: School for Electronic Music: SEM by Joris De Laet, Conservatorium Antwerpen. Career: Tours, Europe, with bands including: Klinik, Hybryds, 1983-; Worldwide radio broadcast, in independent charts. Recordings: Music For Rituals - An Ongoing Musical Spiritual Quest; More than 10 album releases, more than 100 hours music registered at SABAM. Publications: More than 100 pages, official and underground press. Honour: Soundtrack for Aquaria of Antwerp Zoo. Membership: SABAM, Belgian copyright organisation. Hobby: Trying to survive. Current Management: 3riort Vzw. Address: Julian Dillenstr 22, 2018 Antwerp, Belgium.

O

O CONGHAILE Micheál, b. 14 Mar 1962, Galway, Ireland. Writer; Managing Director; Record Company Executive. Education: BA; MA; H Dip In Ed. Musical Education: No formal, expert on Sean-nós (Irish language unaccompanied singing). Career: Author on 6 books in Irish language; Former college lecturer; Founder of Cló Iar-Chonnachta, Ireland's fastest growing traditional music label, 1985; Many national literary awards. Publications: Song collections: Croch Suas É; Up Seanamhach! Memberships: PRS; IMRO. Hobbies: Reading; Sports; The Arts; Travel. Address: Cló Iar-Chonnachta, Indreabhán, Conamara, Co. Galway, Ireland.

O CONLUAIN Proinsias, b. 17 Aug 1919, Benburb, County Tyrone, Ireland. Radio Producer. m. Sheila Murphy, 2 Sept 1947, 1 daughter. Education: Scholarship, Queen's University, Belfast. Career: Scriptwriter, Producer, Radio Éireann, 1947-60; Producer, RTÉ Radio, 1960-83; Numerous radio programmes, popular, folk, traditional music; Series included: The Ballad Tree; The Singer And The Song; Between The Jigs And The Reels; Gold-Dust On The Fiddle; Features, documentaries on traditional singers, musicians, collectors, including: Bunting; Hardebeck; Francis O Neill (The Captain from Chicago); Sam Henry (Coleraine); John Rea The Dulcimer Man (Glenarm); John Maguire (The Rosslea Pad); Robert Cinnamond (Glenavy); Mrs Eileen Keaney (Glenelly and Belfast). Recordings: Robert Cinnamond: You Rambling Boys Of Pleasure, sleeve notes, 1975; Róise na nAmhrán, Songs Of A Donegal Woman, 1994; Songs recorded, Arranmore Island, Co Donegal, 1953; Introductions to Song Translations/Transcriptions. Publications: Articles on traditional music, musicians, in journals including: Irish Folk Music Studies; Dál gCais; The Journal Of Clare, 1986; Dúiche Néill; The Journal Of The O'Neill Country Historical Society (founder, editor). Honours: Jacob's Award, radio, 1979. Memberships: Founder member, Irish Folk Music Society; Board member, Irish Traditional Music Archive, 1993-95. Hobbies: Reading; Research. Address: 75 Blackheath Park, Clontarf, Dublin 3, Ireland.

O CONNOR Martin (Mairtin), b. 28 Mar 1955, Galway, Ireland. Musician (accordion). m. Sietske Van Minnen, 28 Dec 1983, 1 son, 3 daughters. Education: Engineering. Musical Education: Self-taught traditional musician. Career: Tours: America; Europe; Middle East; Hong Kong; Soloist, Bill Whelan's Seville Suite, with RTE Concert Orchestra, World Expo, Seville, 1993; Soloist in Riverdance; Featured in television documentaries: Bringing It All Back Home; River Of Sound. Compositions: Music for 2 short films, many local theatre productions. Recordings: Solo albums: The Connachtman's Rambles; Perpetual Motion; Chatterbox (featuring own compositions). Honours: AIB (Allied Irish Bank) Traditional Musician Of The Year, 1995. Memberships: IMRO; Musicians' Union. Hobbies: Bee-keeping; Golf. Current Management: Annagh Music. Address: Annaghdown Pier, Annaghdown, Co. Galway, Ireland.

O DOCHARTAIGH Seoirse, b. 17 June 1946, Belfast, Northern Ireland. Teacher; Painter; Musician. m. Angela Finan, 4 Aug 1971, 1 son, 1 daughter. Education: BA, Fine Arts. Musical Education: MA by thesis, University College, Cork. Career: Born into musical family, began with singing, later, guitar and tin whistle; Public performances increased 1970s, including television appearances and radio broadcasts; Tours: Germany; France; Netherlands; Ireland; UK; USA. Recordings: Slán Agus Beannacht, 1988; Seoirse O Dochartaigh-Live, 1989; Bláth

Buí, 1992; Amhráin agus Bodhráin, 1994; Oíche Go Maidin, 1994. Publications: Over 50 songs. Honours: Music prizes in the Oireachtas. Memberships: FED; PRS; IMRO; PPI; MCPS. Hobbies: Travel; Musical research. Current Management: Errigal Promotions (Ireland, Germany, USA). Address: Droim Eirc, Baile Dhún na nGall, Co. Dhún na nGall, Éire.

O FARACHÁIN Antaine, b. 6 Feb 1959, Dublin, Ireland. Traditional Singer; Musician. Education: BEd; Selftaught Fiddle. Career: Organiser, Sean-Nós Cois Life Festival; Guest at various music and vocal festivals including Sidmouth Folk Festival, Irishowen Singers Festival, Ennistymon Singers' Festival, Willie Clancy Summer School, Milwaukee Irish Fest; Numerous radio and television appearances: The Pure Drop, Mountain Lark, Fleádh, Tinteán, Late Late Show, Síbín, Eurovision Song Contest Interval Act, 1995. Compositions: Various songs in traditional style, in both Engish and Irish language. Honours: Various prizes at Oireachtas Na Gaeilge (Irish Cultural Festival). Hobbies: Produces radio and television programmes on traditional music; Singing; Folklore. Address: 13 Bóthar Emmet, Cill Mhaighneann, Baile Átha Cliath 8, Dublin, Ireland.

O LAOIRE Liam Lillis, b. 25 July 1961, Donegal, Ireland. Lecturer in Irish, University of Limerick. Education: MA Irish Language, University College, Galway, 1985. Musical Education: Courses in ethnomusicology, University College, Galway; Self-taught traditional singer. Career: Irish poets and musicians tour to Scotland, 1987; Mayfest, Glasgow, 1990, 1991; Winner, Corn Uí Riada (premier Sean-nós competition), 1991, 1994; Milwaukee Irish Fest, 1992; Festival of Lesser Used Languages,Luxembourg, 1992. Recordings: Bláth Gach Géag Dá dTig' CIC075, cassette, 12 songs from Ulster tradition, in Irish. Publications: A Yellow Spot On The Snow, Intro to Homecoming, collection of poetry by Cathal ó Searcaigh CIC, Galway, 1994. Memberships: Folkmusic Society of Ireland; Folklore Society of Ireland; ICTM (UK). Hobbies: Walking; Reading; Singing; Song collecting. Address: Department of Languages, University of Limerick, Ireland.

O'BRIEN Lori, b. 30 Mar 1959, Bridgeport, Connecticut, USA. Singer; Musician (piano, organ); Disc Jockey; Songwriter. m. Frank J O'Brien, 6 July 1980, 2 sons. Education: College graduate. Musical Education: Double major, Music (piano), Theatre. Career: Television appearances include: TBN, Chicago TV 38, GMA convention, Nashville, 1993; Gala concerts, National Anthem singer. Recordings: 4 albums: On With The Show; With Love; Just As You Are; Song Of Light. Memberships: BMI; GMA. Hobbies: Fishing. Address: 180 Red Robin Road, Nougatuck, CT 06770, USA.

O'BRIEN-OLUYEMI Rebecca Jane, b, 4 Jan 1966, Caerphilly, Wales. Vocalist. m. Emmanuel Valentine Oluyemi, 1 Dec 1992. Education: Newham Community College, 1993-94; London Central St Martins School Of Art and Design, 1994-97. Musical Education: Private lessons; Piano theory, 1995; Vocal training course and exam, with John Campbell. Career: Concerts with Thomas The Voice: The Africa Centre; The Bull and Bush; Camden Palace; Backing vocals with Sandra Tavernier. Recordings: Backing vocals, Tell Me Where; Nothing Compares To U; Backing vocals, Time Will Tell, Footsie Drummond; She Move Thru' The Fair, with Thomas The Voice. Membership: Musicians' Union. Hobbies: Music; Art and Design; Dance. Address: 57 Talbot Walk, Church Road, London NW10 9HU, England.

O'CONNELL Carl, b. 24 Feb 1965, Watford, Hertfordshire, England. Musician (keyboards); Programmer. Musical Education: Grade II guitar; Formal jazz tuition. Recordings: Album: Is Nothing Sacred, Love Republic; Several Dox music

albums; Production Assistant, several Mute Records remixes; Charity appearance with East 17. Memberships: Musicians' Union; PAMRA. Current Management: Archangel Music, Ilford. Address: 16 Fortis Green, East Finchley, London N2 9EL, England.

O'CONNOR Gerry, b. 20 July 1960, Tipperary, Ireland. Composer; Musician (banjo, guitar, violin). m. Marie, 13 May 1980, 1 son, 1 daughter. Education: Third level, UCD, Dublin. Musical Education: Self-taught. Career: Solo albums; Member, 4 Men And A Dog; Performances, television, radio: Britain; Europe; Scandinavia; Canada; USA; Australia; Workshop; Festivals; Tutor publications, book, cassette, video. Recordings: Time To Time; Trad At Heart; Funk The Cajun Blues; 4 Men And A Dog: Shifting Gravel; Dr A's Secret Remedies. Publications: 50 Solo's For Tenor Banjo; Tenor Banjo Techniques. Honours: International Radio Festival: Bratislava, 1989; Folk Album of the Year, 1991, (4 Men And A Dog). Memberships: IMRO; PRS; MCPS. Hobbies: Golf; Reading; Athletics. Current Management: Marie O'Connor, 46 Blarney Park, Kimmage, Dublin 12, Ireland; Jim Heaney CBM, 18 Dillons Avenue, Whiteabbey, Co. Antrim BT37 0SX, Northern Ireland.

O'CONNOR Mark, b. Seattle, Washington, USA. Musician (violin, guitar, bass, mandolin). Career: Leader, own group, Nashville Strings; Musician with artistes including: Paul Simon; James Taylor; Dolly Parton; Willie Nelson; Chet Atkins; Randy Travis; Michael Brecker; Concerts include: Barbican Hall (with Yo-Yo Ma); Montreux Jazz Festival; Carnegie Hall, New York. Recordings include: Heroes, 1991; Johnny Appleseed (children's album with Garrison Keillor), 1995; Fiddle Concerto for violin and orchestra, 1995. Honours: Winner, classical guitar competition, aged 11; Country Music Association's Musician Of The Year, 4 times; Grammy Award, New Nashville Cats; Grammy Nomination, Johnny Appleseed. Membership: CMA. Current Management: C M Management, 7957 Nita Avenue, West Hills, CA 91304, USA.

O'CONNOR Sinead, b. 12 Dec 1966, Glenageary, Ireland. Singer; Songwriter; Actress. m. John Reynolds, Mar 1989, 1 son. Musical Education: Dublin College Of Music; Singing lessons with Frank Merriman, Parnell School Of Music, 1992. Career: Solo artiste, Dublin, 1985; Singer, Ton Ton Macoute, 1985; Solo artiste, 1986-; Concerts include: Tours, UK, Europe, USA, 1988; Year Of The Horse World Tour, 1990; Glastonbury Festival, 1990; The Wall Benefit, Berlin, 1990; Amnesty International Benefit, Chile (duet with Peter Gabriel), 1990; Simple Truth Concert (for Kurdish refugees), Wembley, 1991; Bob Dylan 30th Anniversary; As actress: Hush-A-Bye-Baby, C4, Dublin Film Festival, 1990; Ghost Of Oxford Street, C4, 1991; Television documentary: Sinead O'Connor - Coffee and Cigarettes, BBC TV, 1992. Recordings: Singles: Heroine, 1986; Troy, 1987; Mandinka, 1988; Jump In The River, 1988; Nothing Compares To U, 1990; The Emperor's New Clothes, 1990; Three Babies, 1990; My Special Child, 1991; Thief Of Your Heart, 1993; Fire On Babylon, 1994; Thank You For Hearing Me, 1994; Gospel Oak EP, 1997; Albums: The Lion And The Cobra, 1988; I Do Not Want What I Haven't Got, 1990; Am I Not Your Girl, 1992; Universal Mother, 1994; Also featured on: Mind Bomb, The The, 1989; Red Hot + Blue, 1990; Two Rooms - The Songs Of Elton John And Bernie Taupin, 1992; Rising Above Bedlam, Jah Wobble, 1992; Be Still, 1993; Across The Borderline, Willie Nelson, 1993. Honours include: Grammy Award, 1991; Grammy Nomination, 1989; Numerous Music and Video Awards, 1990; 3 MTV Awards, 1990; Billboard Music Award, 1990; BRIT Award, 1991. Current Management: Principle Management. Address: Principle Management, 30-32 Sir John Rogersons Quay, Dublin 2, Ireland.

O'DAY Anita Belle Colton, b. 18 Oct 1919, Chicago, Illinois, USA. Singer. Career: Nightclub entertainer, Chicago, 1939-41; Singer, Gene Krupa's Orchestra, 1941-45; Stan Kenton, 1944; Woody Herman, 1946; Solo artiste, 1947-; Film appearances include: Gene Krupa Story, 1959; Jazz On A Summer's Day, 1960; Zigzag, 1970; Outfit, 1974; Concerts include: 50th Anniversary Concert, Carnegie Hall, 1985. Recordings: Solo albums include: Anita Sings; Pick Yourself Up; An Evening With Anita O'Day; Anita Sings The Winners; Lady Is A Tramp; Travellin' Light; At Mr Kelly's; Other recordings with Gene Krupa and Stan Kenton. Publications: Author: High Times, Hard Times, 1981. Memberships: AFTRA; BMI; Screen Actors Guild. Address: c/o Alan Eichler Associates, 1862 Vista Del Mar Street, Los Angeles, CA 90028-5208, USA.

O'DONNELL Daniel, b. 12 Dec 1961, Kincasslagh, County Donegal, Ireland. Singer. Career: Backing vocalist for sister Margo O'Donnell, early 1980s; Tours, UK and Ireland, 1985-; Concerts include: Carnegie Hall, New York, 1991, 1997, Opera House, Sydney, 1996; Point Theatre, Dublin, NEC, Birmingham, 1997; Own television series, Ireland. Recordings: Albums: Two Sides Of Daniel O'Donnell, 1985; I Need You, 1986; Don't Forget To Remember, 1987; The Boy From Donegal, 1987; From The Heart, 1988; Thoughts Of Home, 1989; Favourites, 1990; The Last Waltz, 1990; The Very Best Of..., 1991; Follow Your Dream, 1992; Chritsmas With Daniel, 1994; Especially For You, 1994; The Classic Collection, 1995; Irish Collection, 1996; Timeless, duet with Mary Duff, 1996; Songs of Inspiration, 1996; I Believe, 1997; Singles: 6 UK Country Number 1 hits; Videos include: Daniel O'Donnell Live In Concert, 1988; Thoughts Of Home, 1989; TV Show Favourites, 1990; An Evening With Daniel O'Donnell, 1990; Follow Your Dream, 1992; Daniel and Friends Live, 1993; Just For You, 1994; The Classic Concert, 1995; Christmas with Daniel, 1996; The Gospel Show, Live at the Point, 1997. Address: c/o Ritz Records, 5/6 Lombard Street East, Dublin 2, Ireland.

O'GRADY Jenny, b. 30 Jan 1949, Loughborough, Leicestershire, England. Singer; Vocal Coach. m. Robert Jolley, 1 son. Musical Education: Royal College of Music, London. Career: Freelance singer, radio, television, film soundtracks, wide variety recordings from Royal Opera House to pop; Also established as leading vocal coach to actors, actresses, musical theatre in London's West End, tours, shows including: Phantom Of The Opera; Cats; Les Miserables; Starlight Express; Joseph; Vocal contractor: West Side Story; Michael Ball recording. Honours: ARCM; LRAM. Memberships: Equity; Musicians' Union. Hobby: Tennis. Address: 2 Queens Road, Barnet, Hertfordshire ENS 4DG, England.

O'GRUAMA Aindrías, b. 9 May 1957, Dun Laoighaire, Ireland. Musician (guitar). Career: Guitar player with The Fatima Mansions; Many BBC radio and television sessions; Support to U2, Zoo TV tour; Tours of USA. MTV appearances. Recordings: Albums: Zerra (produced by Todd Rundgren); My Baby's Arm; Viva Dead Ponies; Valhalla Avenue; Lost In The Former West. Honours: Album Of The Year, Hot Press Critics Poll, 1990. Membership: Musicians' Union. Hobbies: Reading history and philosophy. Current Management: Wasted Talent, ICM. Address: The Plaza, 535 Kings Road, London SW10 0SZ, England.

O'HARA John Mark, b. 28 July 1962, Liverpool, England. Musical Director; Musician (percussion, drums, piano, keyboards). m. Sally Louise Cookson, 29 May 1992, 1 son. Musical Education: Royal Northern College Of Music, GRNCM, PPRNCM. Career: Freelance percussionist for Hallé Orchestra and Royal Liverpool Philharmonic Orchestra; 7 years touring with Ballet Rambert; Theatre work for: Royal Exchange; National Theatre; Lyric Theatre Hammersmith; Musical Director, Bristol Old Vic Theatre Company, 1992. Compositions: Music for most Bristol Old Vic Productions, 1992-; Work performed on BBC Radio 4 and BBC Television. Honours: Major Scholar and Philip Jones Prize at college. Membership: Musicians Union. Hobbies: Squash; Mountain walking; Music. Address: 259 Wick Road, Brislington, Bristol BS4 4HR, England.

O'HIGGINS David Charles, b. 1 Sept 1964, Birmingham, England. Musician (saxophones); Composer. Musical Education: Trumpet, drums, piano, at school; Self-taught saxophone; Studied music, City University, London. Career: Regular working groups: National Youth Jazz Orchestra, 1983-86; Leader, Dave O'Higgins Quartet/Quintet, 1983-; Mezzoforte, 1986-89; Co-leader, Roadside Picnic, 1986-90; Leader, The Gang Of Three, 1987-89; Leader, Dave O'Higgins And The Oblivion Brothers, 1989-91; Cleo Laine and The John Dankworth Quintet; Sax Appeal; Pizza Express Modern Jazz Sextet; Jason Rebello; Jim Mullen Quartet; Itchy Fingers; Clark Tracey Sextet; Martin Taylor's Spirit Of Django; Tours include: Europe, Japan; Cuba; South Africa & Namibia; Tunisia; Sri Lanka; Bangladesh; Venues include: Montreux Jazz Festival, 1989; Havana Jazz Festival, 1993; Several residencies, Ronnie Scott's; New York's Visionez; Television includes: Wogan; Pebble Mill; Jonathon Ross Show; Appearance as busker, Mr Bean; Judge, YTV Young Jazz Musician Of The Year; Many radio broadcasts. Recordings: with NYJO: Full Score; Concrete Cows; With An Open Mind; with Mezzoforte: No Limits; with Roadside Picnic: Roadside Picnic; For Madmen Only; with Jim Mullen: Soundbites; Rule Of Thumb; with Jason Rebello: A Clearer View; with Sax Appeal: Flat Out; Let's Go; with Dave Higgins: All Good Things; Beats Working For A Living; with Clark Tracey: Full Speed Sideways; with Itchy Fingers: Full English Breakfast; with Martin Taylor: Spirit Of Django; with John Dankworth: Live At Ronnie Scott's; with Matt Bianco; Another Time Another Place; with Simon Hale: East Fifteen. Honours: Best New Band, British Jazz Awards, 1988, 1989; Cleo Laine Personal Award, 1990; BT British Jazz Awards, Best Tenor Sax, and Rising Star, 1995.

O'MAONLAI Liam, b. Dublin, Ireland. Singer; Musician (piano).Career: Member, punk group Congress (later became My Bloody Valentine), Dublin; Busker, duo Incomparable Benzini Brothers (with Fiachna O'Brainain), 1985; Founder member, Hothouse Flowers, 1986-. Recordings: Albums: People (Number 2, UK), 1988; Home, 1990; Songs From The Rain, 1993; Singles: Don't Go; I Can See Clearly Now; Give It Up; Movies. Honours: Street Entertainers Of The Year Award, 1985. Current Management: Chris O'Donnell. Address: c/o London Records, PO Box 1422, Chancellors House, Chancellors Road, London W6 9SG, England.

O'NEAL Alexander, b. 14 Nov 1954, Natchez, Mississippi, USA. Singer. Career: Singer, 1972-; Member, Flyte Time; Solo artiste, 1984-; Major concerts worldwide include: Prince's Trust Rock Gala, Birmingham, 1989; Simple Truth, Kurdish refugee benefit concert, Wembley Arena, 1991; World Song-Stylist Live Series, Tokyo, 1991. Recordings: Alexander O'Neal, 1985; Hearsay, 1987; My Gift To You, 1988; Hearsay All Mixed Up, 1988; All True Man (Number 2, UK), 1991; This Thing Called Love - Greatest Hits, 1992; Loves Makes No Sense, 1993; Appeared on Affair, Cherrelle, 1988; Singles include: If You Were Here Tonight, 1985; A Broken Heart Can Mend, 1985; Saturday Love, 1986; Fake (R&B Number 1, US), 1987; Criticize, 1987; The Lovers, 1988; What Can I Say To Make You Love Me, 1988; Christmas Song, 1988; Hitmix, 1989; All True Man, 1990; Sunshine, 1989; What Is This Thing Called Love, 1991; Shame On Me, 1991; Sentimental, 1992; Love Makes No Sense, 1992; In The Middle, 1993; All That Matters To Me, 1993; Duets with Cherrelle: Innocent, 1985; Never Knew Love Like This, 1987. Honour: Platinum disc, Hearsay, 1987; Address: c/o Richard Walters Entertainment, 421 S Beverly Drive, 8th Floor, Beverly Hills, CA 90212, USA.

O'NEILL Bernard Anthony, b. 4 Sep 1961, Dublin, Ireland. Musician (double bass, cello, bass guitar, keyboards). Musical Education: Associate of Royal Irish Academy of Music and Royal College of Music. Career: Teacher, composer, performer; Musical Director for numerous acts including: Rolf Harris; Viv Stanshall; Jon Spencer; Flower Sermon; Aqua Rhythms; Ether; Zumzeaux; Kimbara Brothers; Silly Sisters. Recordings include: with Zumzeaux: Wolf At Your Door, Live In Edinburgh; with Silly Sisters: No More To The Dance; with Andrew Cronshaw: The Language Of Snakes; with Jon Spencer Band: Parlour Games. Hobbies: Photography; Cooking. Current Management: Anne Pomerantz, Aqua Rhythms. Address: 5009 Riviera, Tampa, FL 33609, USA.

O'NEILL John, b. 25 Feb 1955, Romford, Essex, England. Musician (all saxophones, clarinet, flute, piano). m. Sylvie Sims, 26 July 1986, 1 son, 1 daughter. Education: BA Hons, Modern Languages (French, German), Trinity College, Oxford, 1976. Musical Education: PGCE University of Reading, 1984. Career: with group Crosscurrents: BBC Radio 2, 1981; Bracknell Jazz Festival, 1983, 1984; Tour, Germany, Blueprint Jazz Orchestra, 1992; Musical director, arranger, saxophonist, Carlton TV series Shine On Harvey Moon, 1995. Recordings: Albums: The Jazz Method For Saxophone; The Jazz Method For Clarinet; The Jazz Method For Flute; The Jazz Method For Trumpet. Publications: The Jazz Method For Saxophone, 1992; The Jazz Method For Clarinet, 1993; The Jazz Method For Flute, 1994; The Jazz Method For Trumpet (with Steve Waterman), 1995. Memberships: Musicians' Union; Equity. Hobby: Cricket. Current Management: Helen Stafford Management, 14 Park Avenue, Bush Hill Park, Enfield, Middlesex EN1 2HP, England. Address: 103 South View Road, Hornsey, London N8 7LX, England.

O'RIORDAN Dolores, b. 1972, Limerick, Ireland. Singer; Songwriter. m. Don Burton, July 1994. Career: Singer, songwriter, The Cranberries, 1990-; Tours with: Moose; The The; Suede; Duran Duran. Recordings: Albums: Everybody Else Is Doing It, Why Can't We?, 1993; No Need To Argue, 1995; To The Faithful Departed, 1996; Singles: Linger; Zombie; Ode To My Family; I Can't Be With You; Salvation. Current Management: The Left Bank Organisation, 6255 Sunset Blvd, Ste 1111, Hollywood, CA 90028, USA.

O'ROURKE Brian Diarmuid, b. 21 Apr 1948, Co Laois, Ireland. Lecturer; Singer; Songwriter. Education: University College, Galway; University of Paris III. Career: Singing performances at various Irish clubs and festivals; Lecturer on Irish folksong at several venues in Ireland, USA. Recordings: When I Grow Up; Jocoserious songs unaccompanied, 1992. Publications: A Sip From The Honey-pot, 1985; Pale Rainbow, 1990. Membership: IMRO (Provisional member). Hobbies: Reading; Writing. Current Management: Self. Address: 36 Lakeshore Drive, Renmore, Galway, Ireland.

O'SULLIVAN Gilbert (Raymond), b. 1 Dec 1946, Waterford, Ireland. Singer; Musician (piano). Education: Art College, England. Career: Solo recording artiste, 1970-. Recordings: Albums: Himself, 1971; Back To Front, 1972; I'm A Writer Not A Fighter, 1973; Stranger In My Own Backyard, 1974; Greatest Hits, 1976; Southpaw, 1977; Odd Centre, 1980; 20 Golden Hits, 1981; 20 Of The Very Best, 1981; Life And Rhymes, 1982; 20 Golden Pieces Of Gilbert O'Sullivan, 1985; 16 Golden Classics, 1986; Frobisher Drive, 1988; Sounds Of The Loop, 1993; Every Song Has Its

Play, 1995; Singles include: Nothing Rhymed; We Will; No Matter How I Try; Alone Again (Naturally), (Number 1, US); Clair (Number 1, UK), 1972; Get Down (Number 1, UK), 1972; Ooh Baby; Happiness Is Me And You; Christmas Song; I Don't Love You But I Think I Like You; What's In A Kiss? Address: c/o Park Promotions, 20 Raleigh Park Road, North Hinksey, Oxford, Oxon OX2 9AZ, England.

O'TOOLE Gary (Gerald William John), b. 27 Sept 1958, London, England. Musician (drums); Vocalist. Musical Education: On stage, age 4, with parents, playing bass, drums. Career: played with China Crisis; Bucks Fizz; LW5; Papa D; Monroes (Norwegian tours); Orphy Robinson; 25th Of May; Jean Aldebambo; Delfins (Portuguese band); Teaching at drum tech and writing part of curriculum (private lessons, degree level). Recordings: Roland tutorial video for TD7 (electronic kit); with Delfins: Ser Maior (1 track written on album); LW5: with Ripe For The Picking album. Membership: Musicians' Union. Hobby: Mu Gen Do (kickboxing) Instructor. Address: 302 Essex Road, Islington, London N1 3AU, England.

O'TOOLE Steve, b. 4 Apr 1969, Chesterfield, Derbyshire, England. Musician (guitar). Recordings: Pathetic Girlfriend (EP), 1993; Things She Did (EP), 1993; Albums: Wide Open, (US), 1993; Open Wide, 1995. Membership: Musicians' Union. Hobbies include: Football; Wine. Current Management: Chris Carr. Address: 10 Carlyle House, Bethwin Road, London SE5 0XX, England.

OAKENFOLD Paul, b. 1964, London, England. Disc Jockey; Remixer; Recording Artist. Career: Former chef; Began as DJ, Covent Garden, London, 1982; Resident, Heaven Club; Member, Steve Hillage's collective System 7, 1990s; Concerts include support to U2, Naples football stadium, Italy, 1993. Recordings include: JD15 - Paul Oakenfold In the Mix; Remixer, albums on Perfecto label. Honours include: Q Award, Best Producer, 1990. Current Management: 140dB, 1 McCrone Mews, Belsize Lane, London NW3 5BG, England.

OAKEY Philip, b, 2 Oct 1955, Sheffield, South Yorkshire, England. Singer; Musician (synthesizer). Career: Former hospital porter; Lead singer, Human League, 1978-; Concerts include: Support To Siouxsie And The Banshees, UK tour, 1979; Support to Iggy Pop, European tour, 1980; Headline tours, UK, worldwide, 1980-. Recordings: Hit singles include: Sound Of The Crowd, 1981; Love Action, 1981; Open Your Heart, 1981; Don't You Want Me (Number 1, UK and US), 1981; Being Boiled, 1982; Mirror Man, 1982; (Keep Feeling) Fascination, 1983; The Lebanon, 1984; Life On Your Own, 1984; Louise, 1984; Human (Number 1, US), 1986; Only Human, 1994; with Giorgio Moroder: Together In Electric Dreams, for film Electric Dreams, 1984; Albums: Reproduction, 1979; Travelogue, 1980; Dare! (Number 1, UK), 1981; Love And Dancing (remixed mini-album), 1982; Hysteria, 1984; Crash, 1986; Greatest Hits, 1988; Romantic?, 1990; Octopus, 1994. Honours: BRIT Award, Best Newcomer, 1982. Current Management: Huge And Jolly Management, 56-60 Islington Park Street, London N1 1PX, England.

OAKLEY Pete, b. 29 Jun 1962, Burton-on-Trent, Staffordshire, England. Musician (guitar); Singer; Songwriter. m. 12 Apr 1986. Musical Education: Self-taught. Career: Folk/blues guitarist; Many radio and television appearances including: BBC Radio 1, 2 and 5, World Service and European radio stations; Recordings for many local US and Australian radio stations; Tours, 1989-; Owner, 2 music shops, Pete Oakley Music. Recordings: Back Porch Blues; Old Guitars Never Lie; Ghost In The City. Publications: Various magazine contributions. Memberships: British Actors Equity; PRS. Hobbies: Sports cars; Vintage guitars; Fly fishing. Current Management: Pete

Oakley Music. Address: 81 Horninglow Road, Burton-on-Trent, Staffordshire DE14 2PT, England.

OANA Augustin, b. 26 July 1942, Cabesti-Hunedoara, Romania. Folk Singer. m. 28 May 1972, 2 sons. Education: Professional school in construction; Hunedoara Musical Assembly. Career: Several television and radio appearances, including Bucharest radio; Major concerts throughout Romania, and tours of Turkey and Austria; Adapted poems for folk music of region; Participated in many shows and television appearances with Bucharest Radio Orchestra. Recordings: Record of popular music. Address: Str Izvorul Muresului, Nr2 Block A-9, sc-E et4 ap73, Sector 4, Bucharest, Romania.

OATES John, b. 7 Apr 1949, New York, USA. Singer; Songwriter; Musician (guitar). Education: Temple University. Career: Member, The Masters; Gulliver; Member, duo Hall And Oates, with Daryl Hall, 1969-; Appearances worldwide include: Live Aid, Philadelphia, 1985; Rainforest benefit concert, with Grateful Dead, Madison Square Garden, 1988; Earth Day, Central Park, New York, 1990; USA Harvest National Hunger Relief concert, 1991; The Simple Truth, benefit concert for Kurdish refugees, Wembley, 1991. Compositions include: Numerous hit songs co-written with Daryl Hall; Film soundtrack, Outlaw Blues, 1979; Co-writer, Electric Blue, Icehouse, 1988. Recordings: Albums: with Hall And Oates: Whole Oats, 1972; Abandoned Luncheonette, 1974; War Babies, 1974; Daryl Hall & John Oates, 1975; Bigger Than Both Of Us, 1976; No Goodbyes, 1977; Beauty On A Back Street, 1977; Livetime, 1978; X-Static, 1979; Voices, 1980; Private Eyes, 1981; H2O, 1982; Rock'n'Soul (Part 1), 1983; Big Bam Boom, 1984; Live At The Apollo, 1985; Ooh Yeah, 1988; Change Of Season, 1990; Looking Back - The Best Of..., 1991; US Number 1 singles include: Rich Girl, 1977; Kiss On My List, 1981; Private Eyes, 1981; I Can't Go For That (No Can Do), 1982; Maneater, 1982; Out Of Touch, 1984; Numerous other hit singles; Contributor: We Are The World, USA For Africa, 1985; Sun City, Artists Against Apartheid, 1985; The Last Temptation Of Elvis, 1990; Two Rooms - Celebrating The Songs Of Elton John And Bernie Taupin, 1991. Honours include: American Music Awards: Favourite Duo or Band, 1983-85; 19 US Gold and Platinum discs (most successful duo in US recording history). Current Management: Horizon Entertainment, 130 W 57th Street, #12-B, New York, NY 10019, USA.

OBERG Rolf Thomas, b. 15 Mar 1967, Henneborg, Sweden. Vocalist; Musician (melodica, synthesizer). Career: Member, bob hund, 1991-; More than 200 concerts throughout Scandinavia; Played at festivals including Roskilde, Lollipop, Ruisrock, Quartfestivalen and Hultsfred; Member with Magnus Brown of electric and electronic duo, Instant Life. Compositions: I Stället för Musik: Förvirring, 1996; Düsseldorf, 1996. Recordings: with bob hund: bob hund, 1993, 1994; Edvin Medvind, 1994; I Stället för Musik: Förvirring, 1996; Omslag: Martin Kann, 1996; with Instant Life: I Turned My Best Friends into Slaves, CD, 1993; I Made Arrangements for World Peace, 1994. Publication: Omslag: Martin Kann, 1996. Honours: Grammy Awards: Best Live Act, 1994, Best Lyrics, 1996. Memberships: STIM; SAMI. Hobbies: Music; Books; Food; Drinking. Address: Box 53045, S-400 14 Gothenburg, Sweden.

OCASEK Ric (Richard), b. 23 Mar 1949, Baltimore, Maryland, USA. Singer; Songwriter; Musician (guitar); Record Producer. m. Paulina Porizkova, 23 Aug 1989. Founder, singer, guitarist, The Cars, 1976-88; Appearances with the Cars include: Residency, The Rat club, Boston, 1977; European tour, 1978; Concert to 500,000 audience, Central Park, New York, 1979; US Festival, 1982; Founded Synchro Sound recording studio, Boston, 1981; Solo artiste, 1990-; Appearances include Earth Day, Central

Park, New York, 1990. Recordings: Albums with The Cars: The Cars, 1979; Candy-O, 1979; Panorama, 1980; Shake It Up, 1982; Heartbeat City, 1984; The Cars' Greatest Hits, 1985; Door To Door, 1987; Solo albums: Beatitude, 1983; This Side Of Paradise, 1986; Fireball Zone, 1991; Negative Theater, 1993; Hit singles: with the Cars: Just What I Needed, 1978; My Best Friend's Girl, 1978; Good Times Roll, 1979; Touch And Go, 1980; Shake It Up, 1982; Since You're Gone, 1982; You Might Think, 1984; Magic, 1984; Drive, 1984; Hello Again, 1984; Why Can't I Have You?, 1985; Tonight She Comes, 1986; I'm Not The One, 1986; You Are The Girl, 1987; Solo single: Emotion In Motion, 1986; Record producer, artists including: Bad Brains; Black 47; Honours: Rolling Stone Best New Band of the Year, 1979; Grammy Award Nomination, Best New Artist, 1979; MTV Award, You Might Think, 1984. Current Management: Lookout Management, 2644 30th Street, 1st Floor, Santa Monica, CA 90405, USA.

OCEAN Billy (Leslie Charles), b. 21 Jan 1950, Trinidad, WestIndies. Singer; Songwriter. Career: Recording artiste, 1975-; International concerts include: Live Aid, Philadelphia, 1985. Compositions include: Co-writer, own hits: Loverboy; There'll Be Sad Songs; Get Outta My Dreams. Recordings: Albums: Nights (I Feel Like Getting Down), 1981; Inner Feeling, 1982; Suddenly, 1984; Love Zone, 1986; Tear Down These Walls, 1988; Greatest Hits, 1989; Time To Move On, 1993; L.I.F.E, forthcoming. Hit singles include: Love Really Hurts Without You, 1976; Stop Me If You've Heard It Before, 1976; Red Light Spells Danger, 1977; Caribbean Queen (No More Love On The Run), also released as European Queen and African Queen (Number 1, US), 1984; Loverboy, 1985; Suddenly, 1985; When The Going Gets Tough The Tough Get Going, used in film soundtrack The Jewel Of The Nile (Number 1, UK), 1986; There'll Be Sad Songs (To Make You Cry), (Number 1, US), 1986; Love Zone, 1987; Get Outta My Dreams (Get Into My Car) (Number 1, US), 1988. Honours: Grammy Award, Best R&B Performance, 1985; Grammy Nomination, 1986; American Music Awards: Favourite Male Video Artist, Favourite Single, 1988; ASCAP Award for Caribbean Queen, Most Played Song in USA, 1996. Current Management: LJE, 32 Willesden Lane, London NW6 7ST, England.

ODDE SORENSEN Knud, b. 25 Jan 1955, Fröslev, Denmark. Musician (electric bass); Painter; Theatre Designer; Composer; Text Writer. Education: General Certificate of Education, Research Librarian. Career: Member, The Sods, 1977; Name changed to Sort Sol, 1980; Toured: USA, 1982; Russia, 1988; Presently working on music, scenography, and costumes for Danish Royal Ballet production of Hamlet, 1996. Recordings: Minutes To Go, 1979; Under En Sort Sol, 1980; Dagger And Guitar, 1983; Everything That Rises Must Converge, 1987; Flow My Firetear, 1990; Glamourpuss, 1993. Publications: Biography: Knud Odde by Henrik Wivel, 1994. Honours: 3 (local) Grammies, 1991; 5 Grammies in 1994, with Sort Sol. Current Management: Rock On Aps, Rådusstr. 4A, 1466 Copenhagen K, Denmark. Address: PO Box 613, Borups Alle 123, Copenhagen, Denmark.

ODELL Ann Mary, b. 18 Apr 1947, London, England. Musician (keyboards); Vocalist; Arranger. m. Stephen R Spurling, 17 June 1980, divorced 28 Nov 1994, 2 sons. Musical Education: Royal Academy Of Music, 1964-66, LRAM Diploma. Career: Ivy Benson Orchestra; QE2 Maiden Voyage, Anna Dell Trio, 1969; Session musician and arranger, 1972-81; Bryan Ferry World Tour, 1977; BBC Broadcasts, R2 Nightride and Roundabout own band Blue Mink, 1992-94; Television: Top Of The Pops; Les Dawson Show; Little And Large; Currently, running Watermill Jazz Club, Dorking, Surrey; Agency, MIDI recording studio, Take Note Ltd. Recordings: with Blue Mink:

Fruity; Blue Mink; with Bryan Ferry: Another Time, Another Place; In Your Mind; Bride Stripped Bare; Solo: Ann Odell; A Little Taste; Grand Slam, Chopyn; Original Evita album, Jesus Christ Superstar film soundtrack. Honours: 5 Gold discs; Platinum disc; K-Tel Classic Rock Series with LSO. Memberships: PRS; Musicians' Union; Association of British Jazz Musicians. Hobbies: Reading; Collecting jazz recordings; Walks; Travel. Current Management: Take Note Ltd. Address: 24 Dodds Park, Brockham, Betchworth, Surrey RH3 7LD, England.

ODELL Roger Keith, b. 7 Dec 1941, Epping, Essex, England. Musician (drums, percussion); Songwriter. m. Larraine, 18 Nov 1968, 1 son, 1 daughter. Musical Education: Private studies, leading to Grade 8, Guildhall School Of Music, Honours. Career: Toured throughout the world in concert, with numerous appearances on television and radio. Compositions: Contributed to over 20 recordings by Shakatak, as drummer and songwriter; Co-writer, several top 20 UK hits including: Night Birds; Down On The Street. Honours: Tokyo International Song Festival, Silver Prize. Memberships: PRS; International Percussion Society; Professional member, BASCA. Hobbies: Music. Current Management: Les McCutcheon, Skratch Music Ltd. Address: 81, Crabtree Lane, London SW6 6LW, England.

ODGERS Brian Norman (Badger), b. 9 Feb 1942, Forest Gate, London, England. Musician (bass, bass guitar); Teacher of Life, Yoga. m. Jahnet McIlwain, 12 Dec 1976, 4 daughters (3 by previous marriage). Musical Education: Self-taught. Career: Played with: Herbie Hancock; Chick Corea; Freddie Hubbard; Larry Carlton; Van Morrison; Georgie Fame on Herbie's 50th birthday; Television special in Los Angeles; Tours: 2 years Van Morrison; 6 months Andy Williams; 26 years Georgie Fame; 3 years Winifred Atwel; Television, radio appearances over 30 years with most UK and World stars, include: Tom Jones; Englebert Humperdinck; Elton John; Eric Clapton; Cliff Richard; Sarah Vaughn; Shirley Bassey; Neil Diamond; Tony Bennett; Abba; Andre Previn. Recordings: John McLaughlin: Extrapolation; Van Morrison: Enlightenment; Orginal Evita recording with Andrew Lloyd Webber; Roger Daltrey: White Horse; Jimmy Webb: Land's End; Georgie Fame: That's What Friends Are For; Session musician for 20 years; Recorded with almost every artist from rock through jazz to light classical. Honours: Flavour Of The Month Award, 3 times. Membership: Musicians' Union. Hobbies: Sex and drugs and rock'n'roll; All the avenues of the esoteric. Current Management: Self-managed. Address: c/o Ronnie Scotts Club, Frith Street, London W1, England.

OILING Matti, b. 20 Nov 1942, Finland. Musician (drums). Musical Education: State scholarship, to study Latin-American rhythms, 1976. Career: Formed the Happy Jazz Band, 1969; Now playing as Oiling Boiling; Played with brass band Rempsetti, 1980s; Also plays with UHO-Trio; Regular session player; Founded Samba School, Helsinki; Founded own drumming school, 1980; Concerts include: Australia, 1986; California and Hawaii with Richie Cole, 1987; First ever Jazz festival, Jakarta, Indonesia, 1989; Palm Springs, 1989; Opened the Oiling Boiling Jazz & Blues Club, Tallinn, Estonia, 1990. Publications: The Drummer's ABC (first drum tutor in Finnish language), 1969; Volume II, 1975. Honour: Helsinki Medal, 1989. Address: Ristiniementie 40 A 7, 02320 Espoo, Finland.

OJANEN Eero, b. 3 Jan 1943, Finland. Musician (piano); Composer. Career: Played with: Juhani Vilkki's sextet, 1960s; Otto Donner Treatment, 1960s; Pianist, Pekka Pöyry, Montreux Festival, 1968; Concentrated on theatre and film work, 1970s; Currently playing improvised music with Jouni Kesti projects; Accompanist to numerous singers; Member, duo with bass player

Teppo Hauta-Aho. Compositions: Väinämöinen's Music (cantata based on epic Kalevala), Pori Jazz Festival, 1974; Ballet, based on Aleksis Kivi's Seitsemän Veljestä (The Seven Brothers), 1980. Honour: Yrjö Award, Finnish Jazz Federation, 1968. Address: Mechelininkatu 16 A 7, 00100 Helsinki, Finland.

OJANPERÄ Jorma, b. 24 Mar 1961, Alahärmä, Finland. Musician (bass). Musical Education: Studied jazz, Oulunkylä Institute; Helsinki University music department; Sibelius Academy, Helsinki. Career: Performances with The National Theatre and symphony orchestras; Member, Pori Big Band, 1983; Regular bassist, Helsinki clubs: Groovy; Jumo; Orfeus; Played Bengt Hallberg's music, directed by Hannu Hoivula, 1989; Regular appearances at Pori Jazz Festival; Recently member of: The Seppo Kantonene Trio; Markku Johansson Quintet; Also plays with saxophonist Ion Muniz. Address: Rike 24 B, 07700 Koskenkylän Saha, Finland.

OKI Itaru, b. Kobe, Hyogo, Japan. Jazz Musician (trumpet, flugelhorn, flutes). 1 daughter. Career: Ljubljana International Jazz Festival, 1969, 77; Tokyo Jazz Festival, 1969; Tour with Poeters included Japan Festival, England; TV on Arte, Germany; France; Tours include: Japan; Moscow; Austria; Switzerland; Belgium; Netherlands; Germany; England. Recordings: In Japan: Opera Night; Jazz In Tokyo '69; Sirasagi; In France: Perfect Emptiness (with Tchangodei); In Germany: Melusina (with Michel Pilz). Membership: JASRAC (Japan). Address: 17 Rue de la Perle, 69500 Bron, France.

OKIN Earl, b. 31 Jan 1947, Carshalton, Surrey, England. Singer; Songwriter; Musician (guitar, piano, vocal trumpet); Comedian. Education: BA (Philosophy, English Literature), University of Kent, Canterbury. Career: Various television appearances worldwide including Belgium, Germany, Australia, UK; First television appearance, UK, 1959; 13 consecutive years at Edinburgh Festival; Opening act with Paul McCartney and Wings, Van Morrison, Stéphane Grappelli. Compositions: Over 100 various songs; Classical pieces include a string quartet. Recordings: First single: Stop! And You Will Become Aware; 5 album releases. Publications: Various articles, liner notes on opera and jazz. Memberships: PRS; Musicians' Union; British Equity. Hobby: Collecting 78s. Current Management: Spats Music Ltd. Address: 248 Portobello Road, London W11 1LL, England.

OLAWAIYE Fesobi, b. 6 April 1952, Erijiyam Ekiti Ondostate, Nigeria. m. Alix de Brouwer, 1 son, 1 daughter. Education: Commonwealth College, Ilesha-Oyo State, Nigeria. Musical Education: Selftaught Trombonest, Pomgas, Songwriter, Composer. Career: Percussionist, Fela-Kuti, 1977; Trombonist, Fela Amiku Lapo Kuti Band, 1978-, including tour of Europe and Africa. Compositions: Freedom Train; Give and Take; Beginning of the End; Beautiful World; Long Way to Go; Faith. Recordings: Unknown Soldier; Authority Stealing; Solo album Feso Trombone; Freedom Train, 1984; Mini album, Shadow Dance, 1987. Publications: Freedom Train, 1984; Shadow Dance, 1987; Faith, CD, 1997. Membership: Vamu Vzw. Hobby: Sport - Football. Current Management: Kras Artist Buro, Leernsesteenweg 168-9800, Deinze, Belgium. Address: Societe Belge Des Auteurs and Compositeurs and Editeurs, Ruc D'Arlon 75-77, 1040, Brussels, Belgium.

OLDFIELD Michael Gordon, b. 15 May 1953, Reading, Berkshire, England. Musician (multi-instrumentalist); Composer. 3 sons, 2 daughters. Musical Education: Self-taught. Career: 2 World tours, 10 European tours, numerous worldwide television and radio appearances, including premiere concert of Tubular Bells II, Edinburgh Castle, 1992. Recordings: Albums:

Tubular Bells, 1973; Hergest Ridge, 1974; Ommadawn, 1975; Incantations, 1978; Platinum, 1979; QE2, 1980; Five Miles Out, 1982; Crises, 1983; Discovery, 1984; Islands, 1987; Earthmoving, 1989; Amarok; Heavens Open; Tubular Bells II; The Songs Of Distant Earth, 1994; Film score: The Killing Fields. Honours: Grammy Award, Tubular Bells; Ivor Novello Nomination, Moonlight Shadow; BAFTA Nomination, The Killing Fields. Hobbies: Squash; Guinness; Eating out. Current Management: Clive Banks, Clive Banks Ltd., 1 Glenthorne Mews, 115a Glenthorne Road, London W6 0LT, England.

OLDFIELD Sally. Singer; Musician (guitar, keyboards). Recordings: Albums: Water Bearer, 1978; Easy, 1979; Celebration, 1980; Playing In The Flame, 1981; In Concert, 1982; Strange Day In Berlin, 1983; Collection, 1986; Anthology, 1986; Femme, 1988. Current Management: Stephen Budd Management. Address: 109B Regents Park Road, London NW1 8UR, England.

OLIVA Stéphan, b. 7 Jan 1959, Montmorency, France. Jazz Musician (piano); Composer. m. Cathy Frantz, 14 Oct 1982, 1 son. Musical Education: Classical training, Ecole Normale De Musique De Paris. Career: Teacher, performer, Jah, Grim, Ajmi, Roy Hart Theater (France); Concerts in jazz festivals with trios (with drums, bass, violin, saxophone); Selected to Biennale Des Jeunes Createurs D'Europe De La Mediterranée, 1990; Selected to Jeunes Affiches '94, SACEM, 1994; Conferences: History Of Jazz Piano, 1995; Trio Jade Visions, tribute to Bill Evans, 1995. Recordings: with trio: Novembre, 1991; Jade Visions, 1996; Piano solo: Clair Obscur, 1994. Honours: Django D'Or, 1992. Membership: Archipel Mozaïque (Montpellier). Hobbies: Table tennis; Chess; Drawing. Current Management: Michel Lecomte. Address: 2 Rue du Levant, 93100 Montreuil, France.

OLIVER Tim, b. 6 Sept 1959, England. Producer; Engineer. Education: BSc, Hons, Geology; Self-taught guitar and bass guitar. Career: Freelance Engineer, 1981-; Sound Engineering, 1985-; Producer, 1990-; Contributor as writer, Future Music magazine. Recordings: Temper Temper, Temper Temper; Northern Soul, M People; Delightful, Happy Mondays; Definition Of Sound, Definition of Sound; Drawn To The Deep End, Gene. Publications: Regular contributor, Future Music magazine. Hobbies: Photography; Photoshop. Current Management: Isisglow Ltd, The Wool Hall, Castle Corner, Beckington, Somerset, BA3 6TA, England. Address: Tyning Wood, Grace Hill, Frome, Somerset, England.

OLSEN Allan, b. 18 Mar 1956, Frederikshavn, Denmark. Singer; Songwriter. Career: Intensive touring, from mid-seventies; First, solo; 1988-, with own band; All major festivals, Denmark; Touring clubs all: Denmark; Germany; Iceland; All national television programmes in Q' and special portrait features. Recordings: Norlan, 1989; Gaio, 1991; Pindsvin I Pigsko, 1992; Dalton (with colleagues Johnny Madsen and Lars Liholt), 1994: Dubble Live-Rygter Fra Randområderne. Honours: 1 Grammy, 1994; Denmark Labour Union Great Award Of Culture. Memberships: Danish Musicians' Union; DJFBA. Hobby: Bonsai. Current Management: Keiser/Winther Management. Address: Mollevej 35, 9520 Skorping, Denmark.

OLSON Carla Beth, b. 3 July 1952, Austin, Texas, USA. Musician (guitar); Singer; Songwriter. m. Saul Davis, 7 June 1987. Musical Education: Self-taught. Career: Worked with Ry Cooder; Don Henley; Barry Goldberg; Gene Clark; Phil Seymour; Appearances include: Radio City Music Hall, New York; Tours, Europe, Japan; Film soundtrack contributions include: Real Genius; Blue City; Sylvester; Saturday Night Special; A Tiger's Tale. Compositions: Why Did You Stop (recorded by Percy Sledge); Number One Is To Survive (recorded with Gene Clark); Trail Of Tears (co-writer with Eric Johnson); Midnight Mission (recorded with The Textones). Memberships: AFTRA; NARAS; BMI. Hobbies: Foreign languages (Japanese, Italian, French). Current Management: Saul Davis. Address: c/o Saul Davis Management, 11684 Ventura Blvd #583, Studio City, CA 91604, USA.

OLSSON Vagn E, b. 25 Aug 1954, Odense, Denmark. Composer; Musician. Education: MA, Danish and Nordic Literature, University of Copenhagen; Lectures from drummer Paul Motian, and composer/drummer Marilyn Mazur. Career: Member, Group No Knox, 1979; Co-Founder, Dog God, 1993. Compositions include: 7 Shortcuts, for Electric Organ, 1991; 4 Pieces for Mixed Ensemble, 1991; L, 12 Songs for soprano and tenor, 1992; 7 Pieces for woodwind septet, 1992; 4 Short Pieces for symphony orchestra, 1992; U tid, 7 Pieces for solo violin, 1993; 5 Pieces for tenor saxophone, 1993; Piece for boys choir, 1994; 4 1/2 for tenor saxophone, 1995; 2 Songs for Mimi, 1997. Recordings include: Concert Of The Moment, 1980; Nosferatu Festival, 1982; Complication, A Danish Compilation, 1984; Tredive minutter er ikke meget af en dykkers tid, 1985; As She Weeps, 1988; Boogie Stop Shuffle and Brainville, 1990; God Is Love, 1997. Publications: Store forventninger, 1987; Poemer (collection of poems), 1990; Projekt Gadetegn, 1991; Sportsvogn (Sportscar), 1994. Address: Kaalundsgade 5 3th, DK 1664 Copenhagen V, Denmark.

OMA Mra (William G Davenport), b. Philadelphia, Pennsylvania, USA. Jazz Musician (trumpeter). 1 daughter. Education: Commercial business. Musical Education: Granoff School of Music, University of Massachusetts. Career: True France with Archie Shepp; Jazz Festivals: Zurich; Geneva; Village Dewars Jazz Festival, NYC; Major clubs, Paris, include: New Morning; Sunset; Duc des Lombard. Memberships: SACEM; Les Congés; Spectacle. Current Management: Madame Colette Coulon. Address: 105 Blvd Lefevre, 75015 Paris, France.

ONDREICKA Karol Michal, b. 3 Nov 1935, Bratislava, Slovakia. Composer; Arranger; Musician. div, 1 son. Education: Master, Philosophy, Faculty of Arts, Comenius University, Bratislava; Self-taught guitar. Career: Leader, Combo 4, 1961-66, West Coast Jazz Quintet U5, 1975; Colaborated with Quartet pianist Ladislav Gerhardt, 1970-; Tours of Germany, Austria, Netherlands, Luxembourg, Poland, Switzerland and Greece; Performances at International Jazz Festivals in Prague, Bratislava and Athens; Appearances in clubs and festivals with: B Rosengreen, H Sachs, H Beckmann, H Koller, L Harper, K Wheeler, C Mariano, W Lackerschmid and T Küppers. Compositions: The Musical Rabbit, 1974; Music for television series, Boy As Any Other One, 1976; 5-Parts Suite From Our Mountains, 1979; Daddy, Mummy And Me, 1979. Recordings: with Combo 4: Jazz On The Stage, 1962; with the SP Karol Ondreicka Quartet: Reflections, 1965; with the Karol Ondreicka Trio: Slovak Jazz Mainstream, 1994; with Ladislav Gerhardt Quartet: A Sentimental Trumpet, 1970; Bratislava Jazz Days, 1976-82; Why Did We Get Married?, 1978, We Won't Marry Anymore, 1981. Honours: 3 Prizes, Czech Radio Bratislava for Arrangement, 1974, 1975, 1976; Prize, Lifelong Work and Jazz Promotion, Slovak Music Fund, 1990. Memberships: Council, Music Fund, 1990-; Vice President, Slovak Jazz Society, 1990-. Hobby: Science Fiction. Current Management: MIC, Medena 29, 811 02 Bratislava, Slovakia. Address: Azalkova 4, 821 01 Bratislava, Slovakia.

ONO Yoko, b.18 Feb 1933, Tokyo, Japan. Singer; Producer; Actress; Songwriter. m. John Lennon, 20 Mar 1969, deceased, 1 son. Career: Co-host, with John Lennon, Mike Douglas Show, 1972; Producer, film soundtrack, Imagine, 1988. Recordings: Albums with John Lennon/Plastic Ono Band include: Two Virgins, 1968; Life With The Lions, 1969; Wedding Album, 1969; Live Peace In Toronto, 1969; Sometime In New York City, 1972; Double Fantasy, 1980; Collection, 1982; Milk & Honey, 1984; Heart Play - Unfinished Dialogue, 1984; Reflections & Poetry, 1984; Solo albums: Fly, 1971; Feeling The Space, 1973; Approximately Infinite Universe, 1973; Seasons Of Glass, 1981; It's Alright, 1982; Starpeace, 1985; Rising, 1996. Address: c/o The Agency Group Ltd, 1775 Broadway, Suite 433, New York, NY 10019, USA.

OPEKAR Ales, b. 31 Oct 1957, Prague, Czechoslovakia. Musicologist. m. Olga Kovarikova, Dec 1985, 2 daughters. Education: Philosophic Faculty of Charles University, Prague; CSc (equivalent of PhD), Branch of Theory and History of Popular Music. Publications include: Eccentrics In Ground Floor, 1989; Encyclopedia Of Jazz And Modern Popular Music, 1987, revised, 1990. Contributions: Towards the History of Czech Rock Music, 1993; Analysis Of A Rock Album, 1992, 1993; Big Beat Footsteps, 1996, 1998. Memberships: Executive Committee Member, 1993-97, General Secretary, 1995-97, International Association for the Study of Popular Music (IASPM); Association of Musical Artists and Scientists; Union of Authors and Performers (SAI). Address: Institute of Musicology, Puskinovo Nam 9, 1600 Prague 6, Czech Republic.

ORANGE Jason, b. 10 July 1970, Manchester, England. Vocalist. Career: Member, UK all-male vocal group Take That, 1991-96; Television includes: Take That And Party, C4, 1993; Take That Away documentary, BBC2, 1993; Take That In Berlin, 1994. Recordings: Take That And Party, 1992; Everything Changes, 1993; Nobody Else, 1995; Greatest Hits, 1996; Singles: It Only Takes A Minute, 1992; I Found Heaven, 1992; A Million Love Songs, 1992; Could It Be Magic, 1993; Why Can't I Wake Up With You, 1993; UK Number 1 hits: Pray, 1993; Relight My Fire (with Lulu), 1993; Babe, 1993; Everything Changes, 1994; Sure, 1994; Back For Good, 1995; Never Forget, 1995; How Deep Is Your Love, 1996. Publications: Numerous videos, books, magazines. Honours: 7 Smash Hit Awards, 1992; BRIT Award, Best British Single, 1994; BRIT Award Nominations: Best Single, Best Video, 1996. Current Management: Nigel Martin-Smith, 41 South King Street, Manchester M2 6DE, England.

ORCHIN Mark Alan, b. 3 Oct 1957, London, England. Semi-professional Musician (guitar). m. Valerie Orchin, 6 Oct 1979, 1 son, 1 daughter. Career: Lead guitar, late 70s band Possum and various pub, club bands; Currently playing folk/rock, guitar, mandolin with Touchstone; Playing for festivals, theatres, BBC Southern Counties; Duo with singer Bonnie Burden. Recordings: Albums with Touchstone: The Night The Snow Came Down, 1991; One The Rum, 1995; Principal writer of both albums. Membership: Musicians' Union. Hobbies: Tennis; Fishing; Cycling. Current Management: Allwood Music. Address: PO Box 348, Haywards Heath, West Sussex RH17 7RB, England.

ORFORD Tim, b. 10 Mar 1964, Cambridge, England. Sound Engineer; Programmer. Education: BSc Electronic Engineering. Recordings: Dina Carroll; EYC; Young Disciples; Carleen Anderson; Billie Curry; West End; Outlaw Posse; Watergates; Brand New Heavies; S'Express; PJ and Duncan; Sandals; Mary Kiani; Kym Mazelle; Marshall Jefferson; Alex Party; Mike; Rebecca Ryan; Grace; Kicks Like A Mule. Address: The Flat, Thornton, Kingston Hill, Kingston Upon Thames, Surrey KT2 7JX, England.

ORIGJANSKI, b. 13 Nov 1963, Skopje, Macedonia. m. Magda Origjanska, 1 daughter. Career: Member, band Anastasia; Recorded 4 albums; Numerous concerts; Work on film Before The Rain. Recordings: Albums: Ikon; Mansarda; Before The Rain; Melourgia. Honours: Golden Lion Award, Venice, 1994. Hobby: Walking in the mountains. Current Management: Ivo Jankoski. Address: Bukureska 8/2, 91000 Skopje, Macedonia.

ORLANDO Tony (Michael Anthony Orlando Cassivitis), b. 3 Apr 1944, Manhattan, New York, USA. Singer. Career: Demo singer, 1960; Worked for music publishers, 1963-70; Lead singer, trio Dawn (later billed as Tony Orlando and Dawn), 1970-77; Own television series, CBS, 1974-75; Solo artiste, 1977-; Actor, television film: Three Hundred Miles For Stephanie, 1979; Lead role, musical, Barnum, 1981; Dawn reunion, 1990. Recordings: Hit singles with Dawn include: Candida, 1970; Knock Three Times (Number 1, US and UK), 1971; What Are You Doing Sunday, 1971; Tie A Yellow Ribbon Round The Old Oak Tree (Number 1, UK and US), 1973; Say Has Anybody Seen My Sweet Gipsy Rose, 1973; Steppin' Out (Gonna Boogie Tonight), 1974; He Don't Love You (Like I Love You) (Number 1, US), 1975; Look In My Eyes Pretty Woman, 1975; Mornin' Beautiful, 1975; Cupid, 1976; Albums: Candida, 1970; Dawn Featuring Tony Orlando, 1971; Tuneweaving, 1973; Dawn's New Ragtime Follies, 1973; Golden Ribbons, 1974; Prime Time, 1974; Tony Orlando and Dawn II, 1975; He Don't Love You (Like I Love You), 1975; Greatest Hits, 1975; Skybird, 1975; To Be With You, 1976. Honours: American Music Awards: Favourite Single, 1974; Favourite Pop/Rock Group, 1976; Tie A Yellow Ribbon Round The Old Oak Tree named one of BMI's Most Performed Songs, 1940-1990, 1990. Address: c/o William Morris Agency, 1350 Avenue of the Americas, New York, NY 10019, USA.

OROZCO Richard Gomez, b. 5 March 1973, San Antonio, Texas, USA. Singer; Songwriter; Musician. Education: Nuclear Medicine, Biology, Belmont University; Selftaught Guitar. Career: Music City Tonight, 1995; Austin City Limits, 1995. Compositions: Life Is Good; I Wish He Wouldn't Treat Her That Way. Recordings: Buscando Una Estrella, 1996; Don't Try To Find Me, 1998. Hobbies: Basketball; Golf; Cards; Dancing. Current Management: Refugee Management Inc. Address: c/o 209 Tenth Avenue South, Cummins Station, Suite 347, Nashville, TN 37203, USA.

ORR EWING Alastair, b. 28 Nov 1964, Netheravon, England. Musician (harmonica); Teacher. Education: Aberdeen University, 1983-86. Musical Education: Studied under David Michelson, also known as Dr Midnight. Career: Rasp, Rebel Yell, National Student band Final, The Powerhaus, Islington, London, 1993; Glastonbury Cabaret Stage, harmonica duo "et al", theatre stage with Midnight Specials harmonica band, June 1994. Honours: Runner-up, British Harmonica Championships, 1994; Accredited teacher, National Harmonica League. Membership: Musicians' Union. Hobbies: Travel; Sports. Address: 20 Santley Street, London SW4 7BQ, England.

ORRALL Robert Ellis, b. 4 May 1955, Winthrop, USA. Songwriter; Producer; Singer; Musician. Career: Artist, RCA, 1980-84, 1991-93; Giant, 1993-94; Songwriter, Warner Brothers, 1980-84, Zomba, 1987-88, BMG, 1989-91, EMI, 1991-; Producer, Flying Colors, 1991, Orrall and Wright, 1993, Michael Peterson, 1997. Compositions: Next To You, Next To Me, 1990; What's It To You, 1994, 1997; From Here to Eternity, 1997. Recordings: Sweet Nothing, 1979; Fixation, 1981; Special Pain, 1982; Contain Yourself, 1984; Flying Colors, 1991; Orrall and Wright, 1993; Mistakes, 1998. Honours: ASCAP Country Awards, 1990, 1993, 1994; CMA Number

One Awards, 1990, 1993, 1997; CMA Vocal Duo of the Year Finalist, 1994; World Festival Charleston Grand Award, Best Music Video, 1994; ASCAP Pop Award, 1995. Memberships: ASCAP; AFTRA; CMA. Current Management: Alison Averbach Public Relations, 1229 17th Avenue South, Nashville, TN 37212, USA. Address: 35 Music Square East, Nashville, TN 37203, USA.

ORTI Guillaume, b. 8 Dec 1969, Nyons, France. Musician (alto, soprano saxophone). Career: Member, Kartet; Urban Mood; Paintings; Altissimo; Frequent work with theatre and dance companies; Played with Steve Argüelles; Marc Ducret; Aldo Romano; Steve Lacy; Dominique Pifarely; Thierry Madiot; Noël Akchoté; Benoît Delbecq. Recordings: 22 include: Altissimo; With Kartet: Hask; Pression. Membership: Collectif HASK. Address: 4 Rue Bretonneau, 75020 Paris, France.

ORTMANN Carsten, b. 4 Aug 1965, Copenhagen, Denmark. Television Producer; Musician (drums); Singer. Education: MA, Aesthetics and Culture, University of Aarhus; Singing, drumming and piano lessons; Institute of Music, University of Aarhus, 3 years. Career: Drummer in Picnic, 1986-96; Drums and percussion, Hunk Ai, 1986-89; Founder, drummer and singer, Fullface Storband, 1987-89; Drums, percussion and backing vocals, Shirtsville, 1989-91; Percussion and backing vocals, Tintin og Hårtørrerne, 1993-95; Singer, Guttermændene, 1989-. Recordings: with Hunk Ai: Hunk Ai, 1986; Alene Hjemme, 1989; with Picnic: Barking Up the Wrong Tree, 1987; Meat King, 1990; Reverse Ahead, 1992; Leeming Nation, 1995; with Shirtsville: Secrets 3, 1990; Girls Deserve the Best, 1991; with Tintin og Hårtgørrerne: Dance Crazy, 1994; Mad Guppies Fighting the Food Chain, 1995. Hobbies: Karate; Sailing. Address: Nørreallé 30, 2 tv, 8000 Aarhus C, Denmark.

ORTON Kenneth, b. 26 Mar 1934, Bedworth, Warwickshire, England. Musician (all saxophones, woodwind); Teacher; Arranger; Writer. m. Jean Finlay, 1 June 1960, dec7 Dec 1996, 1 daughter. Education: Technical College C&G; Dip Hons, London Art Collge. Musical Education: LLCM TD, London College of Music. Career: Qualified Electrical Engineer, 1955; Army Band, 1955-58; Performed with name Big Bands including: Syd Dean; Ken Turner; Geraldo; Soul Bands include: Ray King; Tours with name artists, 1960s; Formed Don Ellis Connection Big Band, only band dedicated to the late Jazz Star. Compositions: 2 songs, recorded by Ray King; Major work reconstructing Don Ellis scores; Rearrange and set to lyrics (SATB choir) certain Ellis material, establish Don Ellis library in UK, personal interviews with jazz stars; Reconstructed all Ellis 60's vocal arrangements for Karin Krog, and presented concert for Karin Krog, 1994. Publications: Don Ellis' Jazz Journal; Encyclopaedia Of Pop Music; Who's Who In Jazz; Album liner notes; Biography in progress: In Search Of Don Ellis. Hobbies: Siamese cats; Art (painting); Travel in France, USA. Address: 46 Coventry Road, Bedworth, Warwickshire CV12 8NN, England.

ORZABAL Roland, b. 22 Aug 1961, Portsmouth, Hampshire, England. Vocalist; Songwriter; Musician (guitar, keyboards); Record Producer. Career: Member, ska group The Graduate; Founder member, Tears For Fears (with Curt Smith), 1981-; International tours include: Support to Thompson Twins, UK, 1982; UK tour, 1985; US tour, 1990. Compositions include: Everybody Wants To Run The World (amended from hit single), theme for Sport Aid famine relief, 1986; Writer, producer (with Smith), Oleta Adams' album, Circle Of One, 1990. Recordings: Albums: The Hurting, 1983; Songs From The Big Chair, 1985; The Seeds Of Love (Number 1, UK), 1989; Tears Roll Down - Greatest Hits 82-92, 1992; Elemental, 1993; Raoul

And The Kings Of Spain, 1995; Singles include: Pale Shelter, 1982; Mad World, 1982; Change, 1983; Mother's Talk, 1984; Shout (Number 1, US), 1985; Everybody Wants To Rule The World (Number 1, US), 1985; Head Over Heels, 1985; Sowing The Seeds Of Love, 1989; Woman In Chains (featuring Oleta Adams), 1989; Laid So Low, 1992; Breakdown, 1993; Break It Down Again, 1993; Raoul And The Kings Of Spain, 1995; Secrets, 1996. Honours: Smash Hits Award, Most Promising New Act, 1982; BRIT Award, Best British Single, 1985; Ivor Novello Award, Songwriter Of The Year, 1986; BMI Performance awards, Head Over Heels, 1991. Current Management: Debrah Baum, Whirlwind Entertainment, 15025 Greenleaf Street, Sherman Oaks, CA 91403, USA.

OSBORNE Jeffrey, b. 9 Mar 1948, Providence, Rhode Island, USA. Singer; Producer; Songwriter. Career: Singer, LTD (Love Togetherness & Devotion), 1970-82; Solo artiste, 1982-. Recordings: Albums: Jeffrey Osborne, 1982; Stay With Me Tonight, 1983; Don't Stop, 1984; Emotional, 1986; One Love One Dream, 1988; Only Human, 1991; Hit singles include: On The Wings Of Love, 1982; You Should Be Mine, 1986; Love Power (duet with Dionne Warwick), 1990; As singer and producer: Looking For Trouble, Joyce Kennedy, 1984. Current Management: Jack Nelson & Associates, PO Box 3718, Los Angeles, CA 90078-3718, USA.

OSBORNE Joan, b. Anchorage, Kentucky, USA. Singer; Songwriter. Career: Performer, New York blues circuit, 1988; Solo recording artiste; Concerts include: Earth Day Concert with Midnight Oil, New York; Own record label, Womanly Hips Music. Recordings: Debut album: Relish, 1995; Single: One Of Us, 1995. Address: c/o DAS Communications, 83 Riverside, New York, NY 10024, USA.

OSBORNE John Michael, b. 28 Sept 1960, London, England. Agent; Record Company Owner. Education: Royal College of Art. Career: Owner, Slate Records; Own Management Company, John Osborne Management, looking after many top radio DJs. Honours: BEDA DJ of The Year, 1992; Disco International, 1992. Hobbies: Driving; Football; Eating; Theatre. Current Management: John Osborne Management. Address: PO Box 173, New Malden, Surrey KT3 3YR, England.

OSBORNE Pete, b. 15 Sept 1957, London, England. Musician (saxophones: alto, soprano, clarinet) Composer. m. Sally Bowring, 2 Apr 1983. Musical Education: Studied with Professor Malcolm Ellingworth, classical, jazz, clarinet, saxophone. Career: Worked in: England; USA; Denmark; Belgium; Germany; Sweden; Italy; France; Concerts with: Herb Jeffries; Andy Sheppard; John Taylor, 1980; Georgie Fame; Andy Sheppard; Spirit Level, 1985; Bobby Shew; Mark Murphey, 1986; Radio broadcasts: with Rhythm Machine, Nightride, BBC Radio 2, 1987; with Lars Sjosten Trio, Radio Stockholm, 1989; Moved to Paris, concert with Liz McComb, 1991; 2 television shows: Taratata; Cercle De Minuit; 1 radio show, Billy Paul (Me And Mrs Jones), 1994; Concert, Elton John (MCM TV), Paris, 1995. Compositions: Jazz suite for Paris, and 50 original compositions (to be released) for jazz sextet. Recordings: with Billy Joel: Just The Way You Are, 1979; with James Brown: Album and video, 1991; Vanessa Paradis, 1992; Mc Solaar (Caroline Re-mix), 1993; with Cat Stevens: album, 1994; with Abbey Lincoln Trio: title film track, Tom Est Tout Seul, 1994. Honours: Best Saxophone Player, SW England, Bath Evening Chronicle, 1985, 1986, 1987. Memberships: Musicians' Union, London; SACEM, France; SPEDIDAM. Hobbies: Cinema; Swimming; Walking; Chess; Good food; Wine. Current Management: Guy Fletcher. Address: 10 Margaret Street, London W1N 7LF, England.

OSBOURNE Ozzy (John), b. 3 Dec 1948, Aston, Warwickshire, England. Vocalist. m. Sharon Arden, 4 July 1982. Career: Vocalist, Black Sabbath (formerly Earth), 1967-79; Numerous concerts worldwide include: Madison Square Garden, New York, 1975; Reunion concerts include: Live Aid, Philadelphia, 1985; Solo artiste, with own backing band Blizzard Of Ozz, 1979-; US Festival, 1983; Rock In Rio festival, 1984; Monsters of Rock Festival, Castle Donington, 1986; Moscow Music Peace Festival, 1989; No More Tears world tour, 1992; Created highly successful yearly touring festival, Ozz Fest, 1996. Recordings: Hit singles: with Black Sabbath include: Paranoid; Iron Man; War Pigs; Never Say Die; Solo/with Blizzard Of Ozz: Mr Crowley, 1980; Crazy Train, 1980; Bark At The Moon, 1983; So Tired, 1984; Shot In The Dark, 1986; The Ultimate Sin, 1986; Close My Eyes Forever, duet with Lita Ford, 1989; No More Tears, 1991; Perry Mason, 1995; Albums: with Black Sabbath: Black Sabbath, 1969; Paranoid, 1970; Sabbath Bloody Sabbath, 1973; Sabotage, 1975; Technical Ecstasy, 1976; Never Say Die, 1978; Numerous compilations; with Blizzard of Ozz/solo: Blizzards Of Ozz, 1980; Diary Of A Madman, 1981; Talk Of The Devil, 1982; Bark At The Moon, 1983; The Ultimate Sin, 1986; Tribute, 1987; No Rest For The Wicked, 1988; Just Say Ozzy, 1990; No More Tears, 1991; Live & Loud, 1993; Ozzmosis, 1995; The Ozzman Cometh, 1997. Honour: Grammy Award, 1994. Current Management: Sharon Osbourne Management, PO Box 15397, Beverly Hills, CA 90209, USA.

OSLIN K T (Kay Toinette), b. Crossett, Arkansas, USA. Country Music Singer; Songwriter; Actress. Education: Theatre Studies, Lon Morris College, Texas. Career: College drama; Folk singer in Houston; Touring and Broadway productions of: Hello Dolly; Promises, Promises; West Side Story; Began songwriting, 1978; Backing singer for Guy Clark; Signed Elektra Records, 1981; RCA Records, 1986; Fastest selling, highest charting country music debut album by woman (80's Ladies); Television appearances: Johnny Carson; Joan Rivers; Arsenio Hall; Oprah Winfrey; Own television specials; Television acting roles: Paradise; Evening Shade; Poisoned By Love; Film acting: The Thing Called Love; Host of Country Music Aids; Several Television commercials; Benefit concerts, 1993, 1994. Compositions: Songs: Do Ya?; Round The Clock Lovin'; Where Is A Woman To Go; 80's Ladies; Hold Me; Come Next Monday; Younger Men. Recordings: Albums include: 80's Ladies, 1988; This Woman, 1989; Love In A Small Town, 1990 (all million sellers). Honours: 3 Grammy Awards; Best Female Vocalist, CMA, 1988; Song Of The Year, CMA 1988; Best Female Country Vocalist, ACM, 1989. Current Managment: Moress Nanas Shea. Address: 1209 16th Avenue S, Nashville, TN 37212, USA.

OSMAN Mat, b. 9 Oct 1967. Musician (bass). Career: Member, Geoff, 1985; Suave & Elegant, 1989; Suede, 1990-; Concerts include: Glastonbury Festival; Tours, UK, Europe; America; Japan; Television appearances include: Top Of The Pops, BBC1; Later With Jools Holland, BBC2; The Beat, ITV; The Tonight Show, NBC-TV; 12th BRIT Awards, Alexandra Palace, London. Recordings: Suede (Number 1, UK), 1993; Dog Man Star, 1994; Singles include: The Drowners; Metal Mickey; Animal Nitrate; Stay Together. Honours include: Mercury Music Prize, 1993. Current Management: Interceptor Enterprises, The Greenhouse, 34-38 Provost Street, London N1 7NG, England.

OSMOND Donny (Donald Clark), b. 9 Dec 1957, Ogden, Utah, USA. Singer. m. Debra Glenn, 8 May 1978, 3 children. Education: Brigham Young University. Career: Singer with The Osmonds, from age 4, 1963-80; Solo singer, 1971-78, 1988-; Duo with sister Marie; Television includes: Co-star, Donny And Marie TV show,

1976-79; Osmonds Family show, 1980; Film appearance with Marie: Goin' Coconuts, 1978; Head of own television production company Night Star, 1980s; Also satellite television entrepreneur; Stage role, Joseph And His Amazing Technicolour Dreamcoat, Toronto, 1992-93. Recordings include: Singles: with The Osmonds: You Are My Sunshine; One Bad Apple (Number 1, US); Yo-Yo; Down By The Lazy River; Crazy Horses; Goin' Home; Love Me For A Reason (Number 1, UK); Solo: Sweet And Innocent; Go Away Little Girl (Number 1, US); Hey Girl; Puppy Love (Number 1, UK); Too Young; Why; Young Love (Number 1, UK); The Twelfth Of Never (Number 1, UK); I'm In It For Love; Soldier Of Love (Number 2, US); with Marie Osmond: Make The World Go Away; I'm Leaving It All Up To You; Morning Side Of The Mountain; with Dweezil Zappa: Staying Alive, 1991; Albums: Numerous albums with The Osmonds; Solo albums: The Donny Osmond Album, 1971; Too Young, 1972; Portrait Of Donny, 1972; Alone Together, 1973; A Time For Us, 1973; Love Me For A Reason, 1974; Donny, 1974; Discotrain, 1976; Donald Clark Osmond, 1977; Eyes Don't Lie, 1990; with Marie Osmond: I'm Leaving It All Up To You, 1974; Make The World Go Away, 1975; Donny and Marie - Featuring Songs From Their Television Show, 1976; Deep Purple, 1976; Contributor, Voice That Care, American Red Cross charity record. Honour: Georgie Award, Best Vocal Team, with Marie Osmond, 1978; Numerous Gold discs. Current Management: Jill Willis, Renaissance Management, 1571 Lake Lucy Road, Excelsior, MN 55331, USA.

OSMOND Jimmy, b. 16 Apr 1963, Canoga Park, California, USA. Singer; Businessman. Career: Major UK hit with Long-Haired Lover From Liverpool, 1972; Rock impressario and restauranteur; Owner, Oz-Art advertising and design company; Promoter, Prince's Far East Tour; Assistant, Michael Jackson's Bad world tour; Owner, Osmond's family film and video centre, Utah, 1988-. Recordings: Singles: Long-Haired Lover From Liverpool (UK Number 1, 5 weeks), 1972; Tweedle Dee (Number 4, UK), 1973; I'm Gonna Knock On Your Door, 1974; Album: Killer Joe, 1973. Honour: Youngest solo artiste (age 9) to top UK chart, 1972.

OSMOND Marie, b. 13 Oct 1959, Ogden, Utah, USA. Singer. m. (1)Stephen Craig, 1982 (divorced); (2) Brian Blosil, 28 Oct 1986, 1 son, 2 daughters. Career: Member, family singing group The Osmonds, 1966-73; Also solo artiste, 1973-; Member, duo with brother Donny Osmond; Numerous television appearances include: Donny And Marie Show, 1976-79; Osmond Family Show, 1980; Marie, NBC, 1980; Several Osmonds Christmas specials; Film appearance with Donny, Goin' Coconuts, 1978. Recordings: Singles with Donny Osmond: I'm Leaving It All Up To You (Number 2, UK); Morning Side Of The Mountain; Make The World Go Away; Ain't Nothing Like The Real Thing; (You're My) Soul And Inspiration; Solo singles include: Paper Roses (Number 2, UK); Let Me In (Number 2, UK); You're Still New To Me; Albums with Donny Osmond: I'm Leaving It Up To You, 1974; Make The World Go Away, 1975; Donny & Marie - Songs From Their Television Show, 1976; Deep Purple, 1976; Donny & Marie - A New Season, 1977; Winning Combination, 1978; Solo albums include: Paper Roses, 1974; In My Little Corner Of The World, 1974; Who's Sorry Now, 1975; This Is The Way That I Feel, 1977; I Only Wanted You, 1987. Honours: American Music Award, Best Country Band, Duo or Group, with Donny Osmond, 1976; Georgie Award, Best Vocal Team, with Donny Osmond, 1978; Best Country Duo Of Year, with Dan Seals, 1986; Roy Acuff Community Service Award, 1988. Current Management: United Management, Suite 150, 3325 North University Avenue, Provo, UT 84604, USA.

OSTERMANN Flemming, b. 2 June 1947, Aarhus, Denmark. Musician (guitar); Singer; Producer. m. Annette Stenbjoern, 15 Aug 1988, 2 sons, 1 daughter. Education: Associate Professor, Rhythmic Music Conservatory, Copenhagen. Career: Tours with: Savage Rose, 1969-70; Cox Orange, 1972-76; Anne Linnet Band, 1977-80; Billy Cross and All Stars, 1980-95. Recordings: with Savage Rose; Cox Orange; Anne Linnet; Pia Raug; Billy Cross; Jens Rugsted. Publications: Rhythmic Guitar For Beginners, 1995. Memberships: Danish Music Society; DJBFA. Address: Brumleby 325, 2100 Copenhagen O, Denmark.

OTIS Johnny (John Veliotes), b. 28 Dec 1921, Vallejo, California, USA. Musician (drums, piano, vibes); Bandleader; Record Company Owner; Songwriter; Promoter; Radio Disc Jockey; Talent Scout; Author. m. Phyllis Otis, 1941, 5 sons, 3 daughters. Career: Drummer, Count Otis Matthew's West Oakland House Rockers, 1939; Member, Harlan Leonard's Kansas City Rockers, 1943; Founder, Barrelhouse R&B nightclub, Los Angeles (with Bardu Ali), 1948; Founder, California Rhythm & Blues Caravan group; Disc jockey, central Californian radio stations KPFA, KPFB and KFCF, 1950s-; Host, television series, Johnny Otis Show, 8 years; Discovered artists as talent scout including: Esther Phillips; Willie Mae (Big Mama) Thornton; Etta James; Hank Ballard; Jackie Wilson; The Robins (later the Coasters); Owner, Blues Spectrum record label; Played with Big Joe Turner; Louis Jordan; Charles Brown; Joe Liggins; Roy Milton; Lester Young; Illinois Jacquet; Count Basie Orchestra. Compositions include: Every Beat Of My Heart; Mistreatin' Blues; Willie And The Hand Jive; So Fine; Dance With Me Henry (The Wallflower); Double Crossing Blues; Cupid's Boogie; Deceivin' Blues; Gee Baby. Recordings: Harlem Nocturne, 1945; Double Crossing Blues, 1950; Mistreain' Blues, 1950; Cupid's Boogie, 1950; Ma, He's Making Eyes At Me, 1957; Willie And The Hand Jive, 1958; Country Girl, 1968; Spirit Of The Black Territory Bands, 1994; Producer, recordings with Big Mama Thornton, Johnny Ace and Little Richard. Publications: Author: Listen To The Lambs, 1968; Upside Your Head! Rhythm and Blues On Central Avenue, 1993; Colors And Chaos - The Art Of Johnny Otis, 1995; Johnny Otis - Red Beans And Rice And Other Rock & Roll Recipes, 1997. Honours: Grammy Award Nomination, for Spirit of the Black Territory Bands, 1994; Inducted into Rhythm and Blues Hall Of Fame and Rock and Roll Hall Of Fame. Hobbies: Fishing; Growing organic apples (for own brand of fruit juice). Current Management: Terry Gould, 4141 5 Hook Road, Sebastopol, CA 94572, USA. Address: 7105 Baker lane, Sebastopol, CA 95472, USA.

OTWAY John. Singer. Career: Began touring folk circuit with partner, Wild Willy Barrett, 1970-82; Numerous reuunions and splits since; 25 years continuous touring; Television includes: Old Grey Whistle Test; Television commercials for R Whites Lemonade; Danepack Bacon; Radio credits include being banned by Radio 1 for inciting violence, 1981; Concerts include: Reading Festival, 1988; 2000th concert, London Astoria. Recordings: Albums: with Willy Barrett: John Otway and Wild Willy Barrett, 1977; Deep And Meaningless, 1978; Way And Bat, 1980; All Balls And No Willy, 1983; Singles include: with Willy Barrett: Really Free, 1977; Solo: Green Green Grass Of Home, 1980; Headbutts, 1981; Premature Adulation, 1995. Publications: Cor Baby That's Really Me (memoirs), 1990. Current Management: Matters Musical Ltd. Address: The Loft, Rear Of 8 West Street, Dorking, Surrey RH4 1BL, England.

OURS Philippe Paul, b. 2 Sept 1961, Arles, France. Musician (piano); Arranger; Composer. Musical Education: Avignon Conservatory, David Angel Pupil. Career: Played with: Matsakis; Chris Henderson; Mike Ellis; Plamondon; Jimmy Gibson; Roy Robi; Shanna; Ann Carlton; Pianist, Le Restaurant, Paris 8. Recordings: Film music: Intimité, by Dominik Moll; Machine, Etrange Histoire; Patchwork, with Ph D'Ercole. Memberships: UMJ (Union of Jazz Musicians); SACEM. Hobby: Scuba diving. Current Management: Hot Jam International, London, England.

OUZOUNOFF Alexandre, b. 15 Nov 1955, Suresnes, France. Musician (bassoon); Composer. m. 28 Aug 1993, 1 daughter. Musical Education: Student of Maurice Allard. Career: Trio Ozi (with C Villevielle, L Aubert), Festivals: France; Europe, Africa, South Korea; Brazil; Middle East; Russia, 1976-96; Contemporary repertory Constitution; Solo bassoon recitals: Radio France; Centre Pompidou; IRCAM; Festival d'Automne à Paris; INA-GRM; MANCA (Strasbourg; GMEB (Bourges); GRAMW (Lyon); Germany; USA; Italy; Poland, 1979-87; Member, Blue Ensemble, contemporary jazz group (with T Gubitsch, J F Jenny-Clarck, J Schwartz), 1991-94; Appearances, festivals include: De La Butte Montmarte; Estival de Paris; Hyères; Presences 93/Radio France; La Rochelle; Aix En Musique; Heures Musicales de Chatres; Futurs Musiques; D'Automne; Prague; Presence 95/Radio France; Uzès; Breme; Théatre du Châtelet; Moscow-Idaho; Contemporary bassoon masterclasses, France and abroad, 1985-95. Recordings include: Jazz: Palissander's Night, 1988; Sokoa Tanz, 1991; with KOQ Trio: Made In Nigeria, 1993; Contemporary: with Jean Schwartz: Assolutamente, 1990; Canto, 1993; Destroy, 1990; with François Bousch: Espace-Temps, 1992; Classical: Heitor Villa Lobos, Trio d'Anches, 1989; Francis Poulenc, Trio d'Anches, 1991; Etienne Ozi, Trio d'Anches Ozi, 1991; André Caplet/Alberic Magnard, Trio d'Anches Ozi, 1994. Publications: Actually The Bassoon. Honours: First Prize, Music History, CNSM, Paris; Certificate, International Chamber Music Competition, Martigny (Switzerland). Membership: IDRS (International Double Reed Society). Hobby: Cooking. Address: 7 Place Victor Hugo, 94270 Kremlin Bicetre, France.

OVERETT Kelly, b. England. Singer; Dancer. Career: Dancer, SL2; Singer, dance music group, Cappella, 1993-. Recordings: Debut album: U Got To Know, 1994; Singles with Cappella: U Got 2 Know, 1993; U Got To Let The Music (Number 2, UK), 1993; Move On Baby, 1994. Address: c/o Media, 5-7 Mandeville Place, London W1M 5LB, England.

OVERON Geoff(rey John), b. 26 Nov 1953, Leicester, England. Musician (acoustic and electric guitar, bass guitar); Vocalist; Songwriter. Education: De Montfort University. Musical Education: Primarily self-taught with some private tuition. Career: Turned professional in 1978; Played with: Eric Clapton, Muddy Waters' Sideman, Ric Grech, backed Jimmy Witherspoon, jammed with the Van Morrison Band, played at Robert Cray's wedding; Currently, composing, recording and touring with the Geoff Overon Band; Session player, producer and impresario. Compositions: Loving with a Loaded Dice, with Ric Grech; If It Don't Come Easy, with Anthony Thistlethwaite (Waterboys/Saw Doctors). Recordings: Sessions for BBC and Central TV. Honour: Life President, Leicester Rhythm and Blues Society. Memberships: British Music Writers Council; Musician's Union teacher and Registry of Electric Guitar tutors. Hobbies: Classic guitar collecting; Progressive, Blues and Jazz Records. Current Management: GO Productions and Promotions. Address: 12 Somerville Road, Leicester LE3 2ET, England.

OWEN Huw Dylan, b. 20 May 1971, Nantwich, Cheshire, England. Social Worker. Education: Polytechnic of Wales. Career: Lead singer with Y Celtiaid Anhysbus, 1987-89; Lead singer and mandolin player with folk rock group

Gwerinos; Regular appearances on Welsh TV and Radio, 1988-; Lead singer and guitarist with folk punk group Defaid, 1989-92. Compositions: Composed 7 songs on the album Tocio Mogia, Defaid, 1992. Recordings: Tocio Mogia, Defaid, 1992; Di-Didlan, Gwerinos, 1994. Publications: Editor of Welsh language magazines, Defaid and Sothach!. Hobbies: Supporter of Wrexham Football Club; Festival Organiser. Current Management: Adloniant Alffa Entertainment. Address: 1A Maesbrith, Dolgellau, Gwynedd, North Wales.

OWEN Mark, b. 27 Jan 1972. Vocalist; Composer. Career: Member, UK all-male vocal group Take That, 1991-96; Solo artist, 1996-; Television includes: Take That And Party, C4, 1993; Take That Away documentary, BBC2, 1993; Take That In Berlin, 1994; Mark Owen: Green Man documentary, MTV, 1996; Mark Owen Story, Channel 4, 1997; MTV Live and Direct, 1997. Recordings: Albums: Take That And Party, 1992; Everything Changes, 1993; Nobody Else, 1995; Greatest Hits, 1996; Solo Album: Green Man, 1996. Singles: It Only Take A Minute, 1992; I Found Heaven, 1992; A Million Love Songs, 1992; Could It Be Magic, 1993; Why Can't I Wake Up With You, 1993; UK Number 1 hits: Pray, 1993; Relight My Fire (with Lulu), 1993; Babe, 1993; Everything Changes, 1994; Sure, 1994; Back For Good, 1995; Never Forget, 1995; How Deep Is Your Love, 1996; Solo: Child, 1996, Clementine. 1997 (both top 3); I Am What I Am, 1997. Publications: Numerous videos, books, magazines; Mark Owen official magazine. Honours: 7 Smash Hit Awards, 1992; BRIT Award: Best British Single, 1994; BRIT Award Nominations: Best Video, Best Single, 1996; Nominated most stylish male pop star, Elle magazine readers; Best male vocalist, numerous magazines. Memberships: PRS; Equity; MCPS. Current Management: Alex Kadis Management. Address: c/o Basement, 15 Grosvenor Road, London E11 2EW, England.

OWEN Randy, b. 13 Dec 1949, Fort Payne, Alabama, USA. Musician (bass); Vocalist. Career: Founder member, country music group Wild Country, 1969; Changed name to Alabama, 1977-; Worked with Lionel Richie, 1986. Recordings: Albums: Alabama, 1980; My Home's In Alabama, 1980; Feels So Right, 1981; Mountain Music, 1982; The Closer You Get, 1983; Roll On, 1984; 40 Hour Week, 1985; The Touch, 1986; Greatest Hits, 1986; Just Us, 1987; Southern Star, 1989; Pass It Down, 1990; Greatest Hits Volume 2, 1991; American Pride, 1992; Singles: I Want To Be With You; My Home's In Alabama; Tennessee River; Feels So Right; Love In The First Degree; Pass It On Down. Current Management: Dale Morris And Associates, 818 19th Avenue South, Nashville, TN 37203, USA.

OWENS Buck (Alvis Edgar Owens Jr), b. 12 Aug 1929, Sherman, Texas, USA. Country Singer; Songwriter; Musician (guitar). m. Bonnie Campbell, 1 son. Career: Musician, own radio programme with Ray Britten, 1946; Member, Mac's Skillet Lickers; Orange Blossom Playboys; Founder, own band the Schoolhouse Playboys; Session guitarist with artistes including: Sonny James; Wanda Jackson; Gene Vincent; Singer, musician with Tommy Collins; Recording artiste as Buck Owens, 1955-; Co-host, country music variety show Hee Haw, 1969; Retired from performing to run business interests, mid-1970s; Returned to recording and touring, 1988. Compositions include: Together Again, Emmylou Harris; Crying Time, Ray Charles. Recordings: US Country Number 1 hits include: Act Naturally, 1963; Love's Gonna Live Here, 1963; My Heart Skips A Beat, 1964; Together Again, 1964; I've Got A Tiger By The Tail, 1965; Before You Go, 1965; Waitin' In Your Welfare Line, 1966; Think Of Me, 1966; Open Up Your Heart, 1966; Johnny B Goode, 1969; Streets Of Bakersfield, 1988; Over 100 albums include: Under Your Spell Again,

1961; The Instrumental Hits Of Buck Owens And The Buckaroos, 1965; I've Got A Tiger By The Tail, 1965; Carnegie Hall Concert, 1966; Buck Owens In London, 1969; Big In Vegas, 1970; I Wouldn't Live In New York City, 1971; The Songs Of Merle Haggard, 1972; Hot Dog, 1988; Act Naturally, 1989. Address: c/o McFadden Artists, 818 18th Avenue S, Nashville, TN 37203, USA.

OWENS Jimmy (James Robert) Jr, b. 9 Dec 1943, New York, USA. Jazz Musician (trumpet); Composer; Arranger. m. Lola Mae Brown, 18 Mar 1965. Musical Education: MEd, University of Massachusetts, 1975. Career: Musician with Lionel Hampton, 1963-64; Slide Hampton, 1963; Hank Crawford, 1964-65; Charlie Mingus, 1964-65; Thad Jones/Mel Lewis Jazz Orchestra, 1965-66; Duke Ellington, 1968; Count Basie, 1968; Billy Taylor Quintet, David Frost, 1969-72; Worldwide appearances as Jimmy Owens Plus; Panelist, New York State Council of Arts, 1978-81; Director, Jazzmobile Inc, jazz workshops, 1974-90; Blackarts, National Diaspora (board member), 1986-; Faculty member, SUNY, 1981-86; Panelist, National Endowment for Arts, 1972-76; 1990-; Panelist, Ohio Arts Council, 1981-82. Recordings include: Impressions Of The Middle East, Herbie Mann, 1967; Coming At You, Junior Wells, 1968; Zawinul, Joe Zawinul, 1971; Spectrum, Billy Cobham, 1973; Cosmic Vortex, Weldon Irvine, 1974; Sound Of A Drum, Ralph MacDonald, 1976; Inner Conflicts, Billy Cobham, 1978. Honours: Drumbeat Award, Talent deserving wider recognition, 1967; Fellow, National Endowment Arts, 1980; Award for Excellence in Arts, Manhattan Borough, 1986. Memberships: AFofM; BMI; National Jazz Service Organization; Jazz Foundation of America.

P

PAAKKUNAINEN Seppo Toivo Juhani "Baron", b. 24 Oct 1943, Tuusula, Finland. Jazz/Folk Composer; Arranger; Musician (flute, saxophone). m. Ritva Marjatta Ikävalko, 1 son, 1 daughter. Musical Education: Sibelius Academy, Helsinki; Berklee College of Music, Boston, USA. Career: Member, jazz music groups: Pori Jazz; Soulset; Tuohi Quartet; George Gruntz Concert Jazz Band; Braxtonia Project (with Anthony Braxton); Karelia; Worldwide tours, including Norway Winter Olympics, Lillehammer, 1993-94 with artists Nils-Aslak Valkeapää and Juhan Anders Dær; Played with: Most top Finnish Jazz musicians; Charlie Mariano; Mal Waldron; Palle Mikkelborg; First Finnish Jazz musician to play Carnegie Hall, New York; Compositions: Mysterium Sacrum (opera), 1993-94; Amazon, 1994; Numerous works for orchestras, choirs and big bands; Recordings: Albums include: Plastic Maailma, 1971; Unisono, 1975; No Comments, 1975; Kissapa Uu, 1977; Baron Disco-Go, 1978; Kanteletar, 1980; Sami Luondu Golleariisku with Nils-Aslak Valkeapää, 1980; with Karelia: Nunnu, 1971; Tuohihuilu, 1981; Hyvää Joulua, 1981; Maanitus, 1983; Karelia, 1986; Best of Karelia, 1990; Sápmi Lottázan with Nils-Aslak Valkeapää and Ingor Anette Ailu Gaup, 1992; with George Gruntz: George Gruntz Concert Jazz Band, 1981; Theatre, 1984; Dálveleaikkat Wintergames with Nils-Aslak Valkeapää, 1994; Saxperiment, 1997; 2 Compositions (Järvenpää), with Anthony Buxton and Ensemble Braxtonia, 1996. Honours: Gold Medal, Student Youth Festival, 1968; Best Ensemble, Montreux Jazz Competition (with Tuohi Quartet), 1971; Yrjö Award, Finnish Jazz Federation, 1973; Jazz Composer of Year, Helsinki Festival, 1981; Arrangers Prize, Nordring Competition, 1982; Prix Future, West Berlin Festival, 1989. Memberships: Suomen Säveltäjät; ELVIS; Musicians' Union. Hobbies: Finnish Folk Instrument Making; Golf; Books. Address: Katrillipolku 4 A, 04420 Järvenpää, Finland.

PACKHAM Blair James, b. 23 Apr 1959, North Bay, Ontario, Canada. Singer; Songwriter; Composer; Musician (guitar). Education: BA with distinction in English, University of Toronto, Canada. Career: Leader, The Jitters, rock'n'roll group, 1980s; Engineer, live recordings of Bryan Adams, Stevie Ray Vaughn; Television music composer. Compositions: Destiny Ridge; NHL Tonight, World Cup Soccer '94 television series. Recordings: The Jitters; Louder Than Words. Memberships: AFofM; Guild of Canadian Film Composers; Society of Canadian Composers Authors and Publishers. Hobby: Long-distance cycling. Address: 260 Adelaide Street East #131, Toronto, Ontario M5A 1N1, Canada.

PACKHAM Kit (Christopher Stephen), b. 8 June 1953, Bromley, Kent, London. Singer; Musician (saxophone); Songwriter; Writer. Education: BA Fine Art, Maidstone College of Art. Musical Education: Self-taught also tuition from Keith Gemmel, Herman Wilson. Career: Saxophonist with Yakety Yak, 1978-84; Formed own band Kit Packham and the Sudden Jump Band, 1984; Band renamed One Jump Ahead, 1984; Cork Jazz Festival, 1986; Great British R&B Festival, 1994; Radio 2 and GLR appearances; Member, Wolfie Witcher's Brew, 1988-; American Pie Rock'n'Roll Theatre Co, 1992-. Recordings: The Big Ten Inch Record, 1986; On The Shady Side Of The Street, 1989; One Jump Ahead, 1992; with Wolfie Witcher: A Long Way To Tipitana's, 1994. Publications: Articles: Jazz Express; Jazz Musician's Guide; Blueprint. Memberships: Musicians' Union; Equity; British Blues Connection. Hobbies: Birdwatching; Cinema; Country pubs. Current Management: John Boddy. Address: 10 Southfield Gardens, Twickenham, Middlesex TW1 45Z, England.

PACZYNSKI Georges, b. 30 Mar 1943, Grenoble, France. Musician (drums). m. Sophie Tret, 24 Apr 1995, 1 daughter. Musical Education: Self-taught. Career: Represented France, Festival of Montreux, Festival of Zurich, 1968; Broadcast, France Culture, with Black And Blue, 1981; Founded trio with Jean-Christophe Levinson and Jean-François Jenny-Clark, 1984; Une Histoire De La Batterie De Jazz, broadcast, France Culture, 1993; Professor, Conservatoire National de Cergy-Pontoise; Founded new trio with Philippe Macé and Ricardo del Fra, 1996. Compositions: 19 pieces for percussion and piano, Paris, Zurfluh, 1985-97. Recordings: Eight Years Old, 1992; Levin's Song, 1994. Publications: Thesis: Baudelaire Et La Musique, 1973; La Genèse Du Rythme Et L'Anthropologie Gestuelle, 1984; Book: Rythme Et Geste, Les Racines Du Rythme Musical, 1988; Une Histoire De La Batterie, 1997, volume one of three volumes. Honours: Medal of the Society of Encouragement For Progress, 1989. Hobby: Chess. Address: Georges Paczynski, 89 Rue Nationale, 95000 Cergy-Village, France.

PADEN Jyrica, b. 3 Feb 1955, Zagreb, Croatia. Composer; Musician (guitar); Singer. Education: University. Musical Education: 6 years classical guitar in music school. Career: 1000 concerts in various groups, Croatia; 100 television appearances; Tour of former CCCP; Concerts in Netherlands, Germany. Recordings: About 30 albums; 10 hit singles with own group. Honours: Silver and Gold records; First Prize Arena-Fest, Pula. Memberships: HGY (Croatian Music Union); DHS (Composers Union of Croatia). Hobbies: Full-contact sports; Skiing. Current Management: Music Time, Zagreb. Address: Vidriceva 31, 91000 Zagreb, Croatia.

PADEN Tom (Thomas C Paden), b. 13 Oct 1956, Chattanooga, Tennessee, USA. Songwriter; Publisher; Musician (piano). m. Grace Michele Paden, 20 Nov 1993. Education: BS in Business Management, University of Tennessee. Musical Education: Self-taught. Career: Staff writer for Starstruck Writer's Group, Reba McEntire's publishing company. Compositions: Numerous songs include: Same Time Each Year, national theme song for Ducko Unlimited. Recordings: Songs recorded by numerous artists including: Aaron Neville; Tammy Wynette; Restless Heart; Kenny Rogers; Lee Greenwood. Memberships: NARAS; Country Music Association; NSAI. Hobbies: Fishing; Hunting; Photography. Address: 3803 Bedford Avenue, Nashville, TN 37215, USA.

PADGHAM Hugh Charles, b. 15 Feb 1955, London, England. Record Producer; Engineer. Recordings: As producer, engineer, mixer include: with Split Enz: Conflicting Emotions; Time And Tide; with The Police: Synchronicity; Ghost In The Machine; with Phil Collins: Face Value; Hello I Must Be Going; No Jacket Required; But Seriously; with Genesis: Genesis; Invisible Touch; with Sting: Ten Summoner's Tales; The Soul Cages; Fields Of Gold-The Best Of Sting; with Julia Fordham:Porcelain; Swept; with Melissa Etheridge: Yes I Am; Your Little Secret;No One Is To Blame, Howard Jones; Hysteria, Human League; English Settlement, XTC; Between Two Fires, Paul Young: Press To Play, Paul McCartney; Tonight, David Bowie; Two Rooms, Elton John and Bernie Taupin; Walkaway Joe (single), Trisha Yearwood; Clannad, album for release, 1995; Beth Hart Band, album for release, 1996; Engineering/mixing credits include: tracks from World Outside, Psychedelic Furs; Where's The Light, Toni Childs; Just Like Us, Robbie Neville; Nothing Like The Sun, Sting; Love And Affection, Joan Armatrading; Days Of Open Hand, Suzanne Vega; Shakin' The Tree, Youssou N'Dour; The Scattering, Cutting Crew; My Nation Underground, Julain Cope; In The Air Tonight (88 Remix), Phil Collins; Abacab, Genesis; The Third, Peter Gabriel; Black Sea Drums and Wires, XTC; with Hall And Oates: Starting All Over Again; H2O.

Honours: 4 Grammys; Grammy Nominations; Brit Awards; BPI Award Nominations; Music Week Award; TEC Award For Outstanding Creative Achievement. Membership: Re-Pro. Hobby: Motor Racing. Current Management: Dennis Muirhead. Address: Muirhead Management, 202 Fulham Road, Chelsea, London SW10 9PJ, England.

PADOVANI Jean-Marc, b. 2 Feb 1956, Villeneuve les Avignon, France. Musician (saxophone); Composer. m. Françoise Piotelat, 9 Mar 1987, 2 sons. Education: Philosophy. Musical Education: Conservatoire. Career: First part, Miles Davis, 1984; Many tours with his quartet including: France; India; South America; East Europe, 1989-91; Flamenco /Jazz show, Tres Horas de Sol. Recordings: Tres Horas de Sol, 1988; One For Pablo, 1989; Nîmeño, 1990; Sud, 1991; Mingus, Cuernavaca, 1991; Nocturne, 1994. Current Management: Didier Vuillecot, Le Jardin des Délices. Address: 208 Rue de la Convention, 75015 Paris, France.

PAGE Jimmy (James Patrick), b. 9 Jan 1944, Heston, Middlesex, England. Musician (guitar); Songwriter. Career: Member, Neil Christian and the Crusaders, 1959; The Yardbirds, 1966-68; Concerts include: Dick Clark's Caravan Of Stars, US tour, 1966; Rolling Stones '66 tour, 1966; Australia/Far East tour, 1967; Appearance in film Blow-Up, 1967; US and Japan tour, 1968; Founder, The New Yardbirds, 1968; Group becomes Led Zeppelin, 1968-1980; Tours and concerts include: Royal Albert Hall, 1969, 1971; Madison Square Garden, 1970, 1976; Wembley Arena, 1971; Formed Led Zeppelin's own record label, Swan Song, 1974; Guitarist, Honeydrippers (with Robert Plant, Nile Rodgers, Jeff Beck), 1984-85; Guitarist, Coverdale/Page, with former Whitesnake singer David Coverdale, 1993; Guitarist, Page/Plant, with former Led Zeppelin singer, Robert Plant, 1994-. Recordings: Albums: with the Yardbirds: Over Under Sideways Down, 1966; Little Games, 1967; with Led Zeppelin (over 60 million copies sold): Led Zeppelin, 1969; Led Zeppelin II, 1970; Led Zeppelin III, 1970; Led Zeppelin IV, 1971; Houses Of The Holy, 1973; Physical Graffiti, 1975; The Song Remains The Same, 1976; In Through The Out Door, 1979; with Coverdale/Page: Coverdale/Page, 1993; with Page/Plant: No Quarter, 1994; Walking Into Clarksdale, 1998; with The Honeydrippers: Honeydrippers Vol 1, 1985; Contributor, Suicide Sal, Maggie Bell, 1973; Now & Zen, Robert Plant, 1988; As session musician: Here Comes The Night, Them; Shout, Lulu; I Can't Explain, The Who; The Crying Game, Dave Berry; Is It True, Brenda Lee. Honours include: Outstanding Contribution to British Music, 1977; Q Magazine Merit Award (with Led Zeppelin), 1992. Current Management: Trinifold Management, 22 Harley House, Marylebone Road, London NW1 4PR, England.

PAGE Patti (Clara Ann Fowler), b. 8 Nov 1927, Claremore, Oklahoma, USA. Singer. m. Jerry Filiciotto, 12 May 1990, 2 sons, 3 daughters. Career: Discovered by Jack Rael, 1946; Signed to Mercury Records, 1947; Signed to Columbia Records, 1963; Only female artist with hits over 5 decades; Best-selling female artist of all time; 100 million record sales to date. Recordings: 100 albums; 160 singles, including Tennessee Waltz (10 million copies sold, second best selling single ever); Television apperances: Patti Page Oldsmobile Show, NBC; The Big Record, CBS; Patti Page Show, ABC (only musical performer with own series on all 3 US television networks); Actress, Elmer Gantry; Dondi; Boy's Night Out; Stage performances include Annie Get Your Gun. Honours: 14 Gold discs; Hollywood Walk of Fame; Country Music Walkway; Pioneer Award, ACM, 1980; Oklahoma Hall of Fame. Membership: Board of Directors, Academy of Country Music. Hobbies: Tennis; Bridge. Current Management: Jack Rael.

PAGE Stuart, b. 12 May 1954, Leeds, West Yorkshire, England. Musician (guitar); Singer; Songwriter. 2 sons; 1 daughter. Musical Education: Self-taught. Career: Live appearance, Royal Albert Hall; BBC 2 Concert; Radio 2 airplay; Toured with many US country artists, Europe, UK, for last 11 years, including: Billie Jo Spears; James House; Albert Lee. Recordings: Wrote and performed music to ITV series A Brush With Ashley; New album due for release: Can't Sing The Blues. Honours: British Country Music Association, Band of the Year, 3 times. Memberships: PRS; Royal Guild of Songwriters. Hobbies: Motor vehicles; The outdoors. Current Management: Milltown. Address: 26 East Parade, Bedford BD1 5HD, England.

PAGSBERG Mads Jakob, b. 3 November 1970, Copenhagen, Denmark. Conductor; Composer; Musician (bass). Education: Department of Musicology, University of Copenhagen. Career: Bassist, 14 years old; Bassist, Composer, jazz/funk orchestra, MI22; Composer for vocal group, Vox Polish; Own group, MPG. Compositions: With MI22, Hit Me With Your Rhythm, Jamboree, Exit 5, Moonlight Bright; With Vox Polish, Vocal Jazz 'N' Funk. Recordings: Whatever It Is. Membership: Denmark Music Society. Hobby: Judo. Address: Ved Klovermarken 84th, 2300 KBH S, Denmark.

PAICE Ian Anderson, b. 29 June 1948, Nottingham, England. Rock Musician (drums); Writer. m. Jacky, 25 May 1976, 1 son, 2 daughter. Education: Technical College. Musical Education: Self-taught, with father's help. Career: Founder, current member Deep Purple; Major concert headlining California Jam, 1973, to 350,000 people; Also played with Whitesnake and Gary Moore. Recordings: Albums include: Machine Head, 1972; Made In Japan, 1973; Deep Purple In Rock, 1970; Perfect Strangers, 1984; Purpendicular, 1996. Hit singles: include Smoke On The Water; Hush; Highway Star; Child In Time; Perfect Strangers. Honours: Biggest Selling Record Artist in USA, 1973. Hobbies: Fishing; Beer; Football; Cricket; Horse racing. Current Management: Thames Talent, 45 E Putnam Avenue, Suite 116, Greenwich, CT 06830, USA.

PAICH David, b. 25 June 1954, Los Angeles, California, USA. Vocalist; Musician (keyboards). Career: Member, Rural Still Life; Support to artists including: Jackson Browne; Aretha Franklin; Barbra Streisand; Member, Toto, 1978-. Compositions include: Commissioned (with Toto) to write theme for Los Angeles Olympic Games, 1986; Songs include: Africa, co-written with Jeff Porcaro, 1983; Without You Love, 1987. Recordings: Albums: Toto, 1979; Hydra, 1979; Turn Back, 1981; Toto IV, 1982; Isolation, 1984; Dune (film soundtrack), 1985; Fahrenheit, 1986; The Seventh One, 1988; Past To Present 1977-1990, 1990; Kingdom Of Desire, 1992; Singles include: Hold The Line, 1979; Georgy Porgy, 1980; 99, 1980; Rosanna, 1982; Make Believe, 1982; Africa (Number 1, US), 1983; I Won't Hold You Back, 1983; I'll Be Over You, 1986; Without Your Love, 1987; Pamela, 1988; Contributor, We Are The World, USA For Africa charity single, 1985; Backing musician, albums by Boz Scaggs: Silk Degrees, 1976; Down Two Then Left, 1977. Honours: 6 Grammy Awards: Best Record, Best Album, Best Vocal Arrangement, Best Instrumental Arragement, Best Engineered Recording, Best Producer (Toto) 1983. Address: c/o Fitzgerald-Hartley Co., 50 W Main Street, Ventura, CA 93001, USA.

PAIGE Elaine, b. Barnet, England. Singer; Actress. Education: Ada Foster Stage School. Career: Stage appearances include: Hair, West End, London, 1968; Jesus Christ Superstar, 1973; Grease, 1973; Billy, 1974; Lead role of Eva Peron, Evita, 1978; Cats, 1981; Abbacadabra, London, 1983; Chess, 1986; Anything Goes, 1989; Piaf, 1993-94; Sunset Boulevard, 1995. Recordings:

Solo albums include: Elaine Paige, 1982; Stages, 1983; Cinema, 1984; Love Hurts, 1985; Christmas, 1986; Memories - The Best Of Elaine Paige, 1987; The Queen Album, 1988. Honours: Platinum and Gold albums; Society of West End Theatre Award, Best Actress In A Musical, Evita, 1978; Variety Club Awards: Showbusiness Personality of the Year, Recording Artist Of Year, 1986; BASCA Award, 1993. Address: c/o D&J Arlon Enterprises Ltd, Pinewood Studios, Pinewood Road, Iver, Bucks SL10 0NH, England.

PAINE Ed, b. 26 Mar 1949, Chatham, Kent, England. Musician (pedal steel guitar, dobro); Teacher. m. Beverley Paine, 24 May 1980. Education: Technical High School; College. Musical Education: Formal Music Theory; Self-taught on pedal steel guitar and dobro. Career: Club, pub, college, theatre and festival appearances; Live and recorded local radio appearances and regional television appearances; Many recording sessions; Member of Country Cousins; Ned Porridge Band; Pan For Gold; Struck It Rich. Compositions include: The Tear In Daddy's Eye. Recordings: Sessions with many country bands including: Ned Porridge Band; Reg Haynes Outfit; Steve Scott Band; Memphis Roots; Pan For Gold. Membership: Musicians' Union. Hobbies include: Listening to music; Gardening; Photography. Address: Sundown, Lower Hartlip Road, Hartlip, Sittingbourne, Kent ME9 7ST, England.

PAIVINEN Pertti "Pepa", b. 2 June 1955, Vantaa, Finland. Musician (saxophone, multi-instrumentalist). m. Marit Paivinen, 31 Jan 1978, 2 sons, 1 daughter. Education: Flute Study, Vantaa Music Institute, 1967-73; Theory and saxophone, Oulunkyla Pop-Jazz Conservatory, 1975-78. Career: Toured in Europe with Jukka Tolonen Band, 1979-80; Freelance work, television, theatre and teaching, 1980-85; Touring with Edward Vesala Sound and Fury, 1985-; UMO Big Band, 1985-; Saxophone quartet Saxperiment, 1989-; Tour with Anthony Braxton, 1988. Composition: Saxophobia. Recordings: with Jukka Tolonen: Just Those Boys, 1980; with Edward Vesala: Death of Jazz, 1990; Invisible Storm, 1992; Nordic Gallery, 1996; with UMO: UMO Plays the Music of Muhal Abrams, 1986; Selected Standards, 1993; Green And Yellow, 1994; Umo Jazz Orchestra, 1998; with Anthony Braxton: 2 Compositions, 1988; with Saxperiment: Saxperiment, 1997; Pepa Päivinen: Saxigon, 1998. Honour: Pekka Poyry Reward, 1984. Memberships: Finish Saxophone Society. Address: Kitarakuja 2, 01390 Vantaa, Finland.

PALLADINO Pino, b. 17 Oct 1957, Cardiff, Wales. Musician (electric bass guitar). m. Marilyn Roberts, 13 Oct 1992, 1 son, 2 daughters. Musical Education: 1 year classical guitar lessons, age 14. Career: Bass guitar for Paul Young, 1982-87; Recording sessions for artists including: Don Henley; Eric Clapton; Phil Collins; Elton John; Chaka Khan; Jeff Beck; Pete Townshend; Michael McDonald; John McLaughlin; Joan Armatrading. Recordings: No Parlez, Paul Young; Journeyman, Eric Clapton; But Seriously, Phil Collins; Building The Perfect Beast, Don Henley; Sowing The Seeds, Tears For Fears. Publications: Standing In The Shadows Of Motown. Current Management: Keryn Kaplan, Principle Management. Address: 250 West 57th Street, Suite 1502, New York, NY 10019, USA.

PALMER Carl, b. 20 Mar 1950, Handsworth Wood, Birmingham, England. Musician (drums, percussion). m. Maureen Fraser, 4 Mar 1985, 1 daughter. Musical Education: James Blades, Royal Academy; Gilbert Webster, Guildhall. Career: Founder member, Emerson Lake and Palmer (with Keith Emerson, Greg Lake), 1970-81; Founder member, Asia, 1982-86; Numerous worldwide concerts, television, radio appearances; ELP sold 23 million albums to date. Recordings: ELP: Emerson Lake and Palmer,

1970; Tarkus, 1971; Pictures At An Exhibition, 1971; Trilogy, 1972; Brain Salad Surgery, 1973; Welcome My Friends (3 disc set), 1974; Works, 1974; Works Vol II, 1977; Love Beach, 1978; In Concert, 1979; Best Of, 1980; Asia: Asia, 1982; Alpha, 1983; Astra, 1985; Albums with: Atomic Rooster; Arthur Brown; Roger Daltrey; Chris Farlowe; Mike Oldfield; PM; Three; Geno Washington; Solo: Percussion Concerto, 1995. Publications: Applied Rhythms, Carl Palmer. Honours: Playboy Magazine Award, 1977; Hall Of Fame, Modern Drummer Magazine, 1989. Membership: Musicians' Union. Hobbies: Fencing; Indoor bowling. Current Management: Stewart Young, Part Rock Management. Address: 535 Kings Road, Chelsea, London, England.

PALMER Florrie, b. 14 Nov 1947, Broxted, Essex, England. Songwriter; Singer; Musician (Keyboards). 1 son, 1 daughter. Education: Selftaught keyboard player. Compositions: Single: I Get Lonely; Nine to Five, Morning Train; The Heat is On, Agnetha Faltskog, ex-Abba singer; When He Shines; Various album tracks including: Halfway There; The Last One to Leave; I Want to Marry You. Recording: I Get Lonely. Publication: Never Final Till It's Vinyl, 1994. Honours: 9 to 5, Platinum Disc; Ivor Novello Award, Best Lyric of the Year, When He Shines. Membership: PRS. Current Management: Giles Hargreave, Hargreave Music Management, 15-16 Brooks Mews, London, W1Y 1LF, England. Address: 28 Frogge Street, Ickleton, Saffron Walden, CB10 1SH, England.

PALMER Holly, b. 21 July 1970, Los Angeles, California, USA. Singer; Songwriter. Education: Dual Major, Vocal Performance, Music Production, Engineering; BA, Berkley College of Music. Recordings: Holly Palmer, 1996. Memberships: AFTRA; SAG. Current Management: Larry Wanagas. Address: Bumstead Productions, PO Box 110, Hoboken, NJ 07030-0110, USA.

PALMER Ian, b. 3 Mar 1976, Birmingham, England. Musician (drums). Career: Tours: Russia, 1990; USA, 1991; Numerous radio, television sessions; Youngest endorser in world for Yamaha Corporation Sabian Cymbals, Vic Firth drumsticks; Clinic tours for Yamaha Drums and Sabian Cymbals, drums, 1993, 1994, 1995. Publications: Practice Techniques. Honours: BBC Radio Big Band Drummer Of Year, 1992. Memberships: Musicians Union; Percussionists Society. Hobbies: Fitness; Reading. Current Management: Ian Palmer Music. Address: 11A Hartopp Road, Sutton Coldfield, West Midlands, B74 2RQ, England.

PALMER Robert (Alan Palmer), b. 19 Jan 1949, Batley, West Yorkshire, England. Singer; Songwriter. Career: Member, Alan Bown Set; DaDa; Founder, Vinegar Joe, 1971-1974; Solo artiste, 1974-; Member, Power Station, 1985; Regular UK, Europe and US tours; Television appearances include: Arsenio Hall Show; Des O'Connor Tonight; The Tonight Show. Compositions include: Film soundtrack, Sweet Lies, 1987. Recordings: Albums: with Vinegar Joe: Vinegar Joe; Rock'n'Roll Gypsies; Six-Star General; Solo albums: Sneakin' Sally Through The Alley, 1974; Pressure Drop, 1975; Some People Can Do What They Like, 1976; Double Fun, 1978; Secrets, 1979; Clues, 1980; Maybe It's Live, 1982; Riptide, 1985; Heavy Nova, 1988; Addictions Volume 1, 1989; Don't Explain, 1990; Addictions Volume 2, 1992; Ridin' High, 1992; Honey, 1994; The Very Best Of, 1995; with Power Station: The Power Station, 1985; Hit singles include: Every Kinda People, 1978; Bad Case Of Loving You, 1979; Some Guys Have All The Luck, 1982; Addicted To Love (Number 1, US), 1986; Hyperactive, 1986; I Didn't Mean To Turn You On (Number 2, US), 1986; Simply Irresistible (Number 2, US), 1988; She Makes My Day, 1988; Early In The Morning, 1988; I'll Be Your Baby Tonight, with

UB40, 1990; Mercy Mercy Me/I Want You, 1991; with Power Station: Some Like It Hot, 1985; Get It On, 1985; Contributor, film soundtrack, Pretty Woman, 1990; A Matter Of Feel, Brent Bourgeois, 1992. Honours: MTV Music Video Award, Addicted To Love, 1986; Grammy Awards: Best Male Rock Vocal Performance, Addicted To Love, 1987; Simply Irresistible, 1989. Current Management: David Harper, What Management, 12B South Bar, 1st Floor, Banbury, Oxon OX16 9AA, England.

PALMER Tim, b. 4 Oct 1962, North Shields, England. Record Producer; Mixer. m. Nadine Marsh, 31 July 1995, 2 daughters. Career: Assistant, Utopia Studios; Engineer, Producer in England and USA for: Texas; David Bowie; Robert Plant; Pearl Jam; Tears For Fears; numerous others. Recordings: Now & Zen, Shaken & Stirred, Robert Plant; Tin Machine, Tin Machine 2, David Bowie; Elemental, Tears For Fears; Southside, Texas; Carved In Sand, The Mission; Ten, Pearl Jam. Membership: Director, Re-Pro (British Record Producers Guild). Hobby: Music. Current Management: Sandy Roberton, Worlds End Management Inc. Address: 183 N Martel Avenue, Suite 270, Los Angeles, CA 90036, USA.

PALMIERI Edward, b. 15 Dec 1936, Spanish Harlem, New York, USA. Musician (piano). m. 1 July 1955, 1 son, 4 daughters. Musical Education: Piano studies. Career: Played in numerous festivals including: Montreux; North Sea Jazz Festival; Montreal Jazz Festival; Nice Jazz Festival; New Orleans; JVC Festival, New York. Recordings: Albums: La Perfecta; El Molestoso; Lo Que Triago es Sabroso; Enchando Pa'lante; Azucar Pa'Ti; Mambo Con Conga is Mozambique; Palmiere & Tjader; El Sonido Nuevo; Molasses; Palmiere & Tjader: Bamboleate; Champagne; Justicia; Superimposition; Vamonos Pa'l Monte; Harlem River Drive; Live At Sing Sing, Volumes 1 and 2; Sentido; Live At The University Of Puerto Rico; The Sun Of Latin Music; Unfinished Masterpiece; Lucumi Macumba Voodoo; Eddie Palmieri; Palo Pa'Rumba; Solito; La Verdad; Sueno; Llego La India Via Eddie Palmieri; Palmas; Arete; Vortex. Honours: Winner of 5 Grammy Awards. Hobbies: Stickball; Cooking. Current Management: Edward Palmieri II Music Management, 1908 Parker Street, Berkeley, CA 94704, USA.

PANAYI Andy, b. 18 Jan 1964, London, England. Education: Trinity College of Music, London. Career: Teaching: The Brit School, Selhurst, Croydon; The Borough of Waltham Forest: Heathcote Secondary School; Conductor of Bass Tacks Big Band; Conductor, Waltham Forest Junior Orchestra; Intermediate & Advanced Saxophone Choirs, Beginner Flute & Clarinet Choirs; Peripatetic Tuition, Walthamstow Girls Secondary School, Maville Junior School, Willowfield Secondary School, Leytonstone Secondary School, Coppermill Primary School; Kidbrook Secondary School, Ilford Ursuline High School for Girls; Coaching, National Youth Jazz Orchestras; Jazzabelles. Recordings: Thirsty Work; Nebuchadnezzar; Capricorn Rising; Voices of Spring; Concrete Cows; With An Open Mind; Big Band Christmas; Maltese Cross; Unison in All Things; Beasts of Scotland; Full English Breakfast; New Perspectives & Jacqui Dankworth Houseman Settings; Sing the Line; Two: The Matt Wates Sextet; Uschi's House; Blown Away, The Andy Panayi Quartet and others. Honours: Marty Paich Trophy, National Big Band Competitions; John Dankworth Award for Soloist; The Worshipful Company of Musicians of London Jazz Medal, 1994. Address: 58 Lodge Road, Feltwell, Thetford, Norfolk, IP26 4DL, England.

PANIO John, b. 21 Feb 1941, Ituna, Saskatchewan, Canada. Singer. m. Angeline Patron, 2 July 1966, 1 son, 2 daughters. Education: Bachelor of Education. Musical Education: Major in Music. Career: Member of The Panio Brothers; Appearances on CKOS TV, CJGX Radio and Dauphin Radio; Tours of Western Canada. Compositions: Angeline, 1970; The Priest Of Cantor, 1980; Christmas Is Near, 1983. Recordings: Albums: Songs Of Joy, The Panio Brothers, 1971; Songs Of Sentiment, The Panio Brothers, 1972; The Panio Brothers Present Dance Music, 1977; Celebrate Saskatchewan, The Panio Brothers, 1980; Best Of The Panio Brothers, 1987; Vlad Panio Presents Ukranian Country, 1987; Vlad Panio Sings Traditional Ukranian Songs, 1994; Singles: I Once Had A Girl, The Panio Brothers, 1970; Play Oh Gypsy Play, The Panio Brothers, 1970; It's Trudeau, with Father Luzney, 1970; Christmas Is Near, The Singing Gems, 1983. Honour: Outstanding Contribution to Music in Saskatchewan, Saskatchewan Music Educators Association. Membership: Canadian Country Music Association. Hobbies: Musicology; Music Collector. Address: Box 99, Montmartre, Saskatchewan S0G 3M0, Canada.

PAPA DEE (Daniel David Christopher Wahlgren), b. 13 July 1966, Gothenburg, Sweden. Vocalist; Singer; Reggae MC. Musical Education: Church Choirs, Sweden. Career: Tours of Scandinavia with The Stonefunkers, 1987-89; Support to Steel Pulse Tour, USA, 1990; Support act for Ziggy Marley, London, 1991; Roskilde Festival with Papa Levi, 1991; Tour with backing band Protein Bubblers, Scandinavia, Europe, 1992-95. Recordings: Albums: Lettin' Off Steam, 1990; One Step Ahead, 1993; Original Master, 1994; Singles: Let The Music Play, 1988; Competition Is None, 1988; Microphone Poet, 1989; Ain't No Stopping Us, 1990; Beautiful Woman, 1990; Take It Easy, 1991; Ain't No Substitute, 1992; Runaround Girl, 1993; Mr Taxi Driver, 1993; I'd Rather Be With You, 1994; The First Cut Is The Deepest, 1995; Featured on recordings: Tribute To Martin Luther King, 1991; with The Stonefunkers: Hard As Krytonite, 1990; Harder Than Kryptonite, 1991; No Problem '94, 1993; with Dayeene: Big Bad World; with 25th Of May: Go Wild, 1992; with Timebomb Posse: Girls, 1992; with Brooklyn Funk Essentials: Single: The Creator Has A Master Plan, 1994; Album: Cool And Steady And Easy, 1994; with Leftfield: Leftism, 1995; TITIYO: After The Rain, 1991/92; L O V E, 1991/92; My Body Says Yes, 1991/92. Honours: Swedish Dance Music Awards, Hip Hop Album Of The Year, Best Male Vocalist, 1991; Grammy Nomination, 1991; Best Male Vocalist, Best Pop Album, 1995. Membership: Swedish Musicians' Union. Current Management: William Derella, Track Management, NYC. Address: Pontus Pålsson, Backup Production, Knutpunkten 18, S-252 78 Helsinborg, Sweden.

PAPA GEORGE (George Papanicola), b. 9 May 1953, London, England. Songwriter; Blues Musician (guitar). Musical Education: Self-taught since 1964, also live work. Career: Opening act for Tina Turner, Hammersmith Apollo, 1983; Tours: Europe, Texas, Columbia; Appearances and interviews, UA TV (wire cable), 1995; Live radio GLR, local radio Wey-Valley 102-101 6FM. Compositions include: Co-writer with Ian Hunt: Heading South, title track, Ian Hunt; Guilty, for Paul Williams, 1995. Recording: Papa George Live album, 1995. Memberships: Musicians' Union; PRS. Hobbies: Snooker; Cycling; Meditating.

PARDY Richard Alan, b. 17 Apr 1966, Grimsby, Lincolnshire, England. Musician (all saxophones, clarinet, flute, piano); Composer. m. 23 June 1993, 1 son. Musical Education: Grade 8 clarinet, piano, theory; Studied clarinet with Jack Brymer and saxophone with Al Wood; 3 year Jazz/Pop degree course, Leeds, GCLCM; PGCE. Career: Tours include Ben E King, Marty Wilde, Martha Reeves and the Vandellas, Drifters; Tributes to Carpenters, Steely Dan/Donald Fagen, Big Bands/Jazz Combos; Pardy Quintet (appeared at South Bank International Jazz Festival); West

End shows and touring shows in UK, Europe and Worldwide; TV and radio: BBC Radio 1 and 2; Jazz/Capital FM; Pebble Mill; NZ TV; Film: Eyes Wide Shut (Cruise and Kidman), 1997. Recordings: Under the Orange Tree, CD; Session player on advertisement and film music; Featured soloist: Song for the United Nations; Just Can't Give It Up, Nirvana Remix-Hustler's Convention; Blue Lagoon; Living Planet, Lennon. Publication: Development/Evolution of the Big Bands, 1987. Honours: Most improved and promising woodwind student, 1980, 1982. Memberships: CASS; MU. Hobbies: Travel; DIY; Cars; Cycling. Current Management: Richard Pardy Music. Address: 33 Lauderdale Road, Hunton Bridge, Kings Langley, Hertfordshire WD4 8QA, England.

PARFITT Rick (Rick Harrison), b. 12 Oct 1948, Woking, Surrey, England. Musician (guitar); Vocalist. Career: Member, the Highlights; Member, UK rock group Status Quo (originally the Spectres), 1967-; Extensive tours worldwide; Concerts and festivals include: Reading Rock Festival, 1972, 1978, 1987; NEC Birmingham, before Prince and Princess of Wales (televised by BBC), 1982; Milton Keynes Bowl, 1984; Live Aid, Wembley, 1985; Support to Queen, Wembley Stadium, 1986; Knebworth Festival, 1986; Played 4 venues in 12 hours, entered in Guinness Book Of Records, 1991. Recordings: Albums: Pictureque Matchstickable Messages, 1968; Spare Parts, 1969; Ma Kelly's Greasy Spoon, 1970; Dog Of Two Heads, 1971; Piledriver, 1973; Hello, 1973; Quo, 1974; On The Level, 1975; Blue For You, 1976; Status Quo Live!, 1977; Rockin' All Over The World, 1977; If You Can't Stand The Heat, 1978; Whatever You Want, 1979; Just Supposin', 1980; Never Too Late, 1981; 1+9+8+2, 1982; To Be Or Not To Be, 1983; Back To Back, 1983; In The Army Now, 1986; Ain't Complaining, 1988; Rock 'Til You Drop, 1991; Live Alive Quo, 1992; Don't Stop, 1996; Whatever You Want, 1997; Numerous compilations; Hit singles include: Pictures Of Matchstick Men, 1968; Paper Plane, 1973; Caroline, 1973; Break The Rules, 1974; Down Down, 1975; Roll Over Lay Down, 1975; Rain, 1976; Mystery Song, 1976; Wild Side Of Life, 1977; Rockin' All Over The World, 1977; Again And Again, 1978; Whatever You Want, 1979; Living On An Island, 1979; What You're Proposing, 1980; Lies, 1981; Something 'Bout You Baby I Like, 1981; Rock'n'Roll, 1981; Dear John, 1982; Ol' Rag Blues, 1983; A Mess Of The Blues, 1983; Marguerita Time, 1984; Rollin' Home, 1986; In The Army Now, 1986; Burning Bridges, 1989; Anniversary Waltz, 1990. Honours: Silver Clef Award, Nordoff-Robbins Music Therapy Centre, 1981; BRIT Award, Outstanding Contribution To British Music Industry, 1991. Current Management: David Walker, Handle Artists Management, Handle House, 1 Albion Place, Galena Road, London W6 OQT, England.

PARIS Mica (Michelle Warren), b. 1969, London, England. Singer. Career: Singer in church choir, early 1980s; Session singer, notably with Shakatak; Member, gospel group Spirit of Watts; Hollywood Beyond; Solo artiste, 1988-. Recordings: Singles: My One Temptation, 1988; Like Dreamers Do, 1988; Breathe Life Into Me, 1988; Where Is The Love, duet with Will Downing, 1988; Whisper a Prayer, 1993; Stay, 1998; Albums: So Good, 1988; Contribution, 1990; Whisper A Prayer, 1993; Black Angel, 1998.

PARISH Alan Victor, b. 22 Oct 1951, Edmonton, London, England. Musician (drums). Divorced, 2 sons. Education: College. Musical Education: Self-taught, some lessons. Career: Television and radio jingles; Played with Top 40 bands; Currently member of The Hamsters, 8 years; Numerous concerts, television and radio appearances; Toured UK and Europe. Recordings: On all Hamsters albums and video. Hobbies: Watching motor racing. Current Management: Self-managed. Address: 8 Lillyville Walk, Rayleigh, Essex SS6 8UN, England.

PARISH John (Scott Tracey), b. 11 Apr 1959, Yeovil, Somerset, England. Record Producer; Composer; Musician (guitar, drums, percussion); Vocalist. Career: Joined New Wave group Thieves Like Us, 1979; Group disbanded 1981; Founder, singer, guitarist, The Headless Horsemen, under pseudonym Scott Tracey; Frontperson, principal songwriter with experimental West Country band Automatic Dlamini, 1983-92 (with Polly Harvey and Robert Ellis); Began production career specialising in independent guitar groups; Associate lecturer, rock music and recording techniques, Yeovil College, 1991-1994; Played guitar, PJ Harvey World Tour, 1995. Compositions: Two original scores for theatre productions; Two original scores for theatre productions; Music for Dance Hall at Louse Point, with lyrics by PJ Harvey, used for contemporary dance piece, toured Europe 1997. Recordings: Producer, composer, performer with Automatic Dlamini, The D is for Drum, 1988; From a Diva to a Diver, 1992; Producer, composer, performer with PJ Harvey, Dance Hall at Louse Point, 1996; Producer: Kettle, The Chesterfields, 1986; Myth, Becketts, 1991; To Bring You My Love, PJ Harvey, 1995; Orbit, The Harvest Ministers, 1996; Low Estate, 16 Horsepower, 1997; United States, Elliot Green, 1997. Memberships: PRS; Musicians' Union. Current Management: Sincere Management, 6B Bravington Road, London W9 3AH, England.

PARK Graeme, b. 4 Aug 1963, Aberdeen, Scotland. DJ; Remixer; Musician. m. Anne-Marie Curtis. Career: DJ, Garage, Nottingham, 1982; Started Hacienda, Manchester, 1988; Saturday Night resident, Hacienda, 1988-; DJ worldwide including: Australia; South America; USA; Yugoslavia; Iceland. Recordings: Remixed acts including: Brand New Heavies; Inner City; New Order; ABC; Jan Hammer; Eric B. Honours: Dance-Aid DJ of Year, 1991, 1992, 1993. Membership: Musicians' Union. Hobbies: Travel;Photography; Reading; Cooking. Current Management: Cream (DJ); Diesel (remixes, production).

PARKER Alan, b. 26 Aug 1944, England. Composer; Musician (guitar). m. Stephanie, 1 son, 1 daughter. Musical Education: Studied classical guitar with Julian Bream, composition, orchestration, Royal Academy of Music, London. Career: Began as session guitarist, London's leading player, 1960s-70s; Artists worked with included: Stevie Wonder; Frank Sinatra; Elton John; Dusty Springfield; Andy Williams; Tony Bennett; Mick Jagger; David Bowie; Paul McCartney; John Lennon; Jimi Hendrix; John Denver; Johnny Cash; Dame Kiri Te Kanawa; Placido Domingo; Founder member, songwriter, Blue Mink; The Congregation. Compositions: Songs recorded by: Blue Mink; The Congregation; The Walker Brothers; Dusty Springfield; CCS; Arrangements for: Neil Diamond; John Denver; Dusty Springfield; The Walker Brothers; 21 films, 75 television productions include: What's Eating Gilbert Grape; Rhodes, BBC; Up on the Roof, Granada Films; Red Fox, LWT; Jaws 3; To Be The Best; Voice of The Heart; American Gothic; The Glory Boys; Dempsey And Makepeace; Firm Friends; Van Der Valk, Thames TV; Minder, Thames TV; Wild Justice; The Danedyke Mystery, Granada; Mirage; Philby Burgess and McClean; Moody And Peg; Mixed Doubles; Pop Quest, YTV; Children's ITV; Thames News; River Journeys, BBC TV; Commercial jingles include: Kellogg's; Wrangler Jeans; Levi's Jeans; Volkswagen; Heinz; Citröen; Tuborg Lager; Mass performed at the Vatican, 1993; Work for music libraries. Recordings: Hits with Blue Mink and The Congregation; Session guitarist, soundtracks for composers: John Barry; John Williams; Jerry Goldsmith; Lalo Schiffrin. Honour: Ivor Novello. Memberships: PRS; Musicians' Union. Address: Soundtrack Music Management, 22 Ives Street, Chelsea, London SW3, England.

PARKER Brian Thomas, b. 30 Mar 1960, Kent, England. Musician (classical, Spanish guitar, electric guitar, bass all styles, drums); Vocalist; Composer. Education: College of Further Education. Musical Education: Performers course, RCM, London, Junior Exhibitioner, RCM London, aged 14-20. Career: Solo appearances: BBC TV, age 13; Radio 2; Radio Kent; Main support to Frankie Vaughn; Guest soloist with bands of USA national tour; Main support to Semprini; Recitals at the Wigmore Hall, London; Finalist of the Angela Bull Prize, RCM (never previously achieved by a guitarist); Standing ovations in Torremelinos; Rosas; Granada, Spain; Very serious EMI interest, working as Raydio session artist, all styles of music, in studio, live on all guitars, vocals, drummer percussionist in all fields, currently recording on all instruments. Recordings: Live albums with Band of the USA; The Music of Brian Parker: The relaxation albums by Brian Parker; Many recordings for BBC TV and Radio; New albums for release, 1995-96. Honours: Grade 8, FRCM. Membership: Musicians' Union. Hobbies: Keeping fit, weight training; Cars; Making things, especially musical instruments. Address: 54 Tennyson Walk, Northfleet, Kent, England.

PARKER Graham, b. 18 Nov 1950, London, England. Vocalist; Songwriter. Career: Member, R&B groups: The Black Rockers; Deep Cut; Vocalist, Graham Parker & The Rumour, 1975-1980; Solo artiste, 1980-; Concerts include: UK tour, support to Thin Lizzy, 1976; Support to Bob Dylan, 1978; US tour, support to Cheap Trick, 1979; Reading Festival, 1986; Rock'n'roll revue US tour, 1989. Recordings: Albums: with Graham Parker And The Rumour: Howlin' Wind, 1976; Heat Treatment, 1976; Stick To Me, 1977; The Parkerilla, 1978; Squeezing Out Sparks, 1979; The Up Escalator, 1980; The Best Of Graham Parker And The Rumour, 1980; Solo albums: Another Grey Area, 1982; The Real McCaw, 1983; Steady Nerves, 1985; Mona Lisa's Sister, 1988; Human Soul, 1989; Live! Alone In America, 1989; Struck By Lightning, 1991; Burning Questions, 1992; Passion Word - The Graham Parker Anthology 1976-1991, 1993; Singles include: with the Rumour: Silly Thing, 1976; The Pink Parker EP, 1977; Hey Lord Don't Ask Me Questions, 1978; Solo: Temporary Beauty, 1982; Wake Up (Next To You); The Mona Lisa's Sister, 1988; 12 Haunted Episodes, 1995. Address: c/o RCA Records, Bedford House, 69-79 Fulham High Street, London SW6 3JW, England.

PARKER Mick, b. 12 June 1952, London, England. Musician (piano, keyboards, accordion); Composer. m. Angelika Helm, 25 July 1992, 1 son. Education: To degree level. Musical Education: All piano academy grades 1-8. Career: Toured with: Joan Armatrading, 1976-79; Billy Ocean, 1979-80; Linda Lewis, 1980-82; Television with all the above; Touring and recording for Gilbert O'Sullivan as MD, 1991-; Toured Japan with Linda Lewis, 1997. Compositions: Many jingles and film music, includes Merchant Ivory film Heat And Dust, 1985. Compositions: Soundtrack for Thieftakers, ITV, 1996. Recordings: As producer: Single: So Macho, Sinitta, 1986; As arranger: Album: Aqaba Beach, Mory Kante, 1986; As musician: Album: Este Mundo, Gipsy Kings, 1992; with Gilbert O'Sullivan: Sounds Of The Loop, 1992; Live In Japan, 1993; Singer Sewing Machine, Gilbert O'Sullivan, 1996. Honours: Ampex Golden Reel Awards, Sinitta; Azucar Moreno. Memberships: PRS; MCPS; Musicians' Union. Hobbies: Canal boating; Railways. Address: Gateway Studio, Kingston Hill Centre, Surrey KT2 7LB, England.

PARKER Peter Paul, b. 31 Aug 1964, Kingston, Surrey, England. Musician (bass); Songwriter. Musical Education: Basstech College, Acton; Intermediate, Advanced Course. Career: Bassist, Heaven Can Wait, 1982-86; Recorded album, played Hammersmith Palais; Played with Thin Lizzy, Wolverhampton, Phil Lynott Tribute,

1994. Composition: Album, Out of the Blue by Emily's Sister, written, recorded and produced, 1996. Recordings: Garden Of Hope (EP), Afterlife, 1995; Out of the Blue, 1996. Membership: Musicians' Union. Hobbies: Eating; Drinking; Golf; Football; Rugby. Current Management: Metro Music. Address: Metro Music Ltd, PO Box 75, Shepperton, Middlesex TW17 9NA, England.

PARKER Ray Jr, b. 1 May 1954, Detroit, Michigan, USA. Musician (guitar). Career: Member, houseband, 20 Grand Club, late 1960s; Toured with Detroit Spinners; Studio musician for Invicta Wax; Formed Raydio, 1977-; Solo artiste, 1982-. Recordings: Albums: as Raydio: Raydio, 1977; Rock On, 1979; as Ray Parker Jnr & Raydio: Two Places At The Same Time, 1980; A Woman Needs Love, 1981; Solo albums: The Other Woman, 1982; Greatest Hits, 1982; Woman Out Of Control, 1983; Chartbusters, 1984; Sex And The Single Man, 1985; After Dark, 1987; Musician, albums by Stevie Wonder: Talking Book; Innervisions; Singles include: Jack And Jill; A Woman Needs Love (Just Like You Do), 1981; The Other Woman, 1982; Ghostbusters (film theme), 1984. Honour: Grammy Award, Best Pop Instrumental Performance, 1984. Current Management: Joseph Ruffalo Entertainment, 1728 Monte Cielo Court, Beverly Hills, CA 90210, USA.

PARKINSON Bill, b. 28 Nov 1941, Lancaster, England. Musician (guitar); Songwriter; Producer. m. Jennifer, 4 Dec 1965, 2 daughters. Musical Education: Mostly self-taught. Career: The Fourmost; P J Proby; Screaming Lord Sutch; The Savages; Tom Jones backing group: The Squires (3 years); Chuck Berry; Across The Universe-The Beatles; Sammy Davis Jr; Shirley Bassey; Bobby Vee; Petula Clark; Vic Damone; Englebert Humperdinck; Ted Heath Orchestra; Freddy Starr. Compositions: Neil Reid: Mother Of Mine; Jimmy Osmond; Deep Purple: Theme to Mandrake Root. Memberships: PRS; MCPS; Musicians' Union. Hobbies: Water colours and oils (several one-man exhibitions). Address: 2 Beech Place, Epping, Essex CM16 5EJ, England.

PARLETT Michael John, b. 19 July 1963, Bexleyheath, Kent, England. Musician (alto, soprano, tenor, saxophones, flute, percussion, windsynth -WX7). Musical Education: B Mus, Goldsmiths College, London; PGCE, Middlesex University. Career: Broadcasts on Radio 2, 1994; Tours with: Iona; Gail Thompson's Jazz Africa; Appeared on: Dave Taylor, Rock'n'roll Show, Finland; Top Of The Pops; European TV, Netherlands; Recordings: Sessions with: Lulu; Take That; Mica Paris; Eternal; Gabrielle; Yazz; Clive Griffin; Olu; David Grant; The Jones Girls; Currently working on solo album. Honours: Nomination, Arts Foundation Award for Jazz Composition. Membership: Musicians' Union. Hobbies: Practicing; Sport; Running own big band. Current Management: 61 Howland Way, Surrey Quays, London SW16 1HW, England.

PARNELL Jack, b. 6 Aug 1923, London, England. Jazz Musician (drums); Bandleader; Musical Director. Career: Member, Radio Rhythm Club Sextet; Partnership with Vic Lewis as Lewis-Parnell Jazzmen, 1944-46; Member, Ted Heath's Big Band, 7 years; Musical Director, ATV, including Sunday Night At The London Palladium, 1960s; Musical Director, The Muppet Show; Bandleader, UK jazz circuit; Backing musician with touring US musicians, 1970s-. Recordings: Recent albums include: Big Band Show, 1976; Jack Parnell Plays Music Of The Giants, 1975; Braziliana, 1977; 50 Big Band Favourites, 1984.

PARNELL Lee Roy, b. 21 Dec 1956, Abilene, Texas, USA. Country Musician (slide guitar). 1 son, 1 daughter. Musical Education: Self-taught. Career: Ten Feet Tall And Bulletproof tour, with Travis Tritt and Joe Diffie, 1994; Late Show With David Letterman; The TonightShow; Live With Regis and Kathie Lee; Music City Tonight; Happy

New Year America from the House of Blues; Miller Genuine Draft radio commercial; CocaCola Radio commercial; Theme song for "The Road" radio and television programme. Recordings: We All Get Lucky Sometimes; On The Road; Love Without Mercy; Lee Roy Parnell. Honours: CMA Nominations: Horizon Award, 1994; Collaboration, 1995; Grammy Nomination, Best Country Instrumental with Flaco Jiminez, 1996-. Memberships: BMI; ACM; CMA. Hobbies: Songwriting; Working out; Going to pawn shops for collectable guitars. Current Management: Mike Robertson Management. Address: PO Box 120073, Nashville, TN 37212, USA.

PARR John, b. 19 Nov 1957, Nr. Sherwood Forest, Nottinghamshire, England. Singer; Songwriter; Producer. m. Sharon, 29 Aug 1990, 2 sons. Musical Education: Guitar lessons. Career: Tours, 1985-, including support tours with: Tina Turner; Bryan Adams; Toto; Heart; Beach Boys. Recordings: Hit singles: Naughty Naughty; St Elmo's Fire (worldwide Number 1); Rock'N'Roll Mercenaries (with Meatloaf); Paris (with LSO and Philarmonic Choir); Miami Vice; Movie soundtracks: 3 Men And A Baby; Quicksilver; American Anthem; The Running Man; Covers with: Tom Jones; The Monkees; Meatloaf; Roger Daltrey. Honours: Grammy Nomination; ASCAP Award, Most Performed Song; MIDEM Award. Memberships: PRS; MCPS; ASCAP; AFTRA; Equity; Musicians' Union. Current Management: Lou Howson, Bernie Fischbach. Address: Fischbach, 1925 Century Park East, Suite 1260, Los Angeles, CA 90067, USA.

PARRAVANO Beth Amy, b. 5 Apr 1951, Providence, Rhode Island, USA. Singer; Songwriter; Musician (guitar); Performer. m. Tony Parravano, 4 July 1979, 1 son, 1 daughter. Education: College Liberal Arts Degree, Theatre Arts, Music. Musical Education: Private, school instruction. Career: Owner, Peridot Records; Parravano Music (ASCAP); Peridot Now (BMI); Recording artist independent radio country music; Appeared Nashville Gospel Hour; Kid's Break produces own cable TV show: Amy Beth Presents; Opening act various performers; Performs with Joey Welz (original pianist, Bill Haley and The Comets). Recordings: Grandmas Attic, Keith Bradford; The Love That We Share, Lulu Roman; Solo albums: (gospel) Fight The Good Fight; Bankin' On Losin' The Blues. Publications: Poetry chapbook: Heroes And Unsung Heroes. Honours: Grammy Nomination (Universal Love); Nominated first Ballot Dave Award gospel cassette. Memberships: ASCAP; BMI; Country Music Association; IMA; Country Music Showcase International; Greater Southern Country Music Association. Hobbies: Golf; Bicycling. Current Management: Peridot Entertainment. Address: Peridot Music, PO Box 8846, Cranston, RI 02920, USA.

PARRISH Man, b. 6 May 1958, Brooklyn, New York, USA. Producer; Musician (keyboards); Manager. Education: Dramatic Studies, American Academy of Dramatic Arts, New York, 1971. Musical Education: Self-taught. Career: 17 years in music business; Owner, production company, Man Made Productions, 1983-; Partner, Artist Management Company; Manager, Village People, 1988-93; Member of group Man 2 Man. Recordings: Singles: Hip Hop Be Bop, Man Parrish; Male Stripper, Man 2 Man; I Am What I Am, Gloria Gaynor (keyboards); Solo album: Man Parrish, 1983; Producer/writer, approximately 50 recordings, including: Village People; Michael Jackson; Boy George; Gloria Gaynor. Honours: Billboard Award, Dance Artist; Bessie Smith Award. Memberships: ASCAP; National Music Publishers; Harry Fox Agency. Hobbies: Music; Internet. Current Management: AM:PM Entertainment. Address: 415 63rd Street, Brooklyn, NY 11220, USA.

PARRY J Chris, b. 7 Jan 1949, Wellington, New Zealand. Record Company Executive; Record Producer. Divorced, 1 son, 2 daughters.Education: HND Business Studies, 1974; Career: Professional drummer, 1968-71; A&R Manager, Polydor Records, 1974-78; Owner, Fiction Records, 1978-; Managing Director, Fiction Records, Fiction Songs; Managing Director, XFM Radio. Recordings: Albums: In The City, Modern World, All Mod Cons, The Jam; Various recordings, The Cure (as co-producer); Three Imaginary Boys, The Cure (as producer). Membership: BPI; Institute of Marketing. Hobbies: Sailing; Skiing; Horse riding; Scuba-diving. Address: 97 Charlotte Street, London W1 1LB, England.

PARRY Steve, b. 4 Sept 1958, Pontypool, South Wales. Record Company Executive. m. Julia Parry, 20 Mar 1982, 2 daughters. Musical Education: Self-taught guitar; Piano lessons, 2 years. Career: Musician, London, 1978-83; Various groups including Neu Electrikk and The The; Founder, Managing Director, Hwyl Records and Publishing, 1985; Release and promote music, specialising in contemporary instrumental music; Artists including: Gilbert Isbin; Trevor Stainsby; Steve Jadd; Sandor Szabo. Memberships: PRS; PPL. Hobbies: Photography; Study of Celtic Mythology; Climbing mountains; Historical research of churches; Writing Childrens novels. Address: 2 The Square, Yapham, York YO4 2PJ, England.

PARSONS Alan, b. 1948. Musician; Record Producer; Engineer. Career: Former recording engineer, EMI Records; Founder, Alan Parsons Project, 1975-. Recordings: Albums: with Alan Parsons Project: Tales Of Mystery & Imagination, 1976; I Robot, 1977; Pyramid, 1978; Eve, 1979; The Turn Of A Friendly Card, 1980; Eye In The Sky, 1981; Ammonia Avenue, 1983; Vulture Culture, 1984; Stereotomy, 1985; Gaudi, 1987; Instrumental Works - Best Of Alan Parsons Project, 1983; Limelight - Best Of (Vol II), 1988; Recording engineer, artistes including: The Beatles; Wings; Pilot; Cockney Rebel; Al Stewart; Pink Floyd. Address: c/o The Agency, 370 City Road, London EC1V 2QA, England.

PARSONS David John, b. 30 Aug 1962, Colchester, Essex, England. Record Company Executive; Artist Manager; Performer. m. Stephanie Bowyer, 5 Sep 1992, 1 son. Education: BA, Honours; Currently pursuing PhD. Career: Lead vocalist, Splat!, 1981-83; Owner, Ron Johnson Records, 1983-90; Director, Submission Records Limited, 1987-90; Owner, Zung Records, 1994; Director, Too Pye Ahh Records, 1995; Lead vocalist, Chod, 1995; Recordings: 1936, The Ex; Mud On A Colon, Stump; Two Kan Guru, Big Flame; I Am John's Pancreas, A Witness; Dudley Dorite Wristwatch, Chod; Debut album, Wholesome Fish. Honour: Ron Johnson Records, Independent Label of The Year, 1986. Memberships: PRS; MCPS; PPL. Hobby: Aikido. Current Management: Purple Skunk Management. Address: Purple Skunk Management, The Basement, 19 Victoria Parade, Broadstairs, Kent CT10 1QL, England.

PARSONS David Richard, b. 12 Apr 1959, Woking, England. Musician (guitar, violin); Songwriter. 1 son. Musical Education: Violin tuition, Music O Level. Career: Member, Sham 69; Member, The Wanderers, with Stiv Bators on vocals; Arena, TV special with Sham 69. Recordings: Sham 69: Albums: Tell Us The Truth; That's life; Hersham Boys; The Game; Volunteer; Information Libré; Soapy Water and Mr Marmalade; All the singles; The Wanderers: Only Lovers Left Alive, 1981; Solo album: Reconcile. Memberships: PRS; MCPS; Musicians' Union. Hobbies: Tai Chi. Current Management: A & Eye Records. Address: 30 Bois Hall Road, Addlestone, Surrey KT15 2JL, England.

PARTIS Lee Valentine, b. 22 Feb 1954, Romford, Essex, England. Musician (drums); Vocalist; Actor. 1 son. Musical Education: Self-taught. Career: Played with many bands including: Kirsty MacColl; Jah Wobble; Oysterband. Recordings: Numerous albums include: with Oysterband: Deserters, 1992; Holy Bandits, 1993; Trawler, 1994; with Kirsty Macoll: Desperate Character, 1981. Hobbies: Cricket; Tai Chi. Current Management: Forward Management. Address: 132 Liverpool Road, London N1 1LA, England.

PARTON Dolly, b. 19 Jan 1946, Locust Ridge, Tennessee, USA. Country Singer; Actress. m. Carl Dean, 30 May 1966. Career: Singer, local radio, as child; Apperances include: Grand Ole Opry, Nashville, 1968-; Regular on Porter Wagoner Show; Regular recordings with Wagoner, 1967-74; Solo artist, 1969-; Actress, films: 9 To 5, 1980; Best Little Whorehouse In Texas, 1982; Rhinestone, 1984; Steel Magnolias, 1990; Wild Texas Wind, NBC, 1990; Straight Talk, 1992; Host, own television shows, Dolly, 1976, 1987; TV special, Dolly Parton Christmas At Home, ABC, 1990; Owner, Dollywood entertainment complex. Compositions include: I Will Always Love You (also recorded by Whitney Houston, for film The Bodyguard 1992). Recordings: Numerous US Country Number 1 hits include: Joshua, 1970; Jolene, 1974; I Will Always Love You, 1974 (also in 1982); Baby I'm Burnin', 1979; 9 To 5, 1981; Islands In The Stream, with Kenny Rogers, 1983; Think About Love, 1986; To Know Him Is To Love Him, 1987; Yellow Roses, 1989; Albums include: with Porter Wagoner: Just The Two Of Us, 1969; Always, Always, 1969; Porter Wayne And Dolly Rebecca, 1970; Once More, 1970; Two Of A Kind, 1971; Solo albums: My Blue Ridge Mountain Boy, 1969; Joshua, 1973; New Harvest... First Gathering, 1977; Here You Come Again, 1978; Great Balls Of Fire, 1979; Dolly Dolly Dolly, 1980; 9 To 5 And Odd Jobs, 1980; Heartbreak Express, 1982; Best Little Whorehoue In Texas (soundtrack), 1982; Burlap And Satin, 1983; The Great Pretender, 1984; Rhinestone (soundtrack), 1984; Once Upon A Christmas, 1984; Greatest Hits, 1985; Trio (with Linda Ronstadt and Emmylou Harris), 1987; Rainbow, 1988; White Limozeen, 1989; Eagle When She Flies, 1991; Straight Talk (soundtrack), 1992; Slow Dancing With The Moon, 1993; Honky Tonk Angels (with Loretta Lynn and Tammy Wynette), 1993; Contributor, Heroes And Friends, Randy Travis, 1991. Honours include: CMA Awards: Female Vocalist of the Year, 1975, 1976; American Music Awards: Favourite Country Album, 1978; Favourite Country Single, 1984, 1985; Grammy Awards: Best Female Country Artist, 1979; Best Country Vocal Performance, 1982; Top Country Album, 1981; Best Country Vocal, Duo or Group (with Ronstadt and Harris), 1988; ACM Record of the Year, 1983; AMA Best Country Single, 1983. Current Management: Maureen O'Connor, Rogers and Cowan, 10000 Santa Monica Blvd, Los Angeles, CA 90067, USA.

PARTON Stella, b. 4 May 1949, Locust Ridge, Tennessee, USA. Country Singer. Career: Radio debut with sister Dolly Parton, 1955; Featured on soundtrack of Dolly Parton's film Rhinestone; Actress, stage version, The Best Little Whorehouse In Texas. Recordings: Hit singles: I Want To Hold You In My Dreams Tonight; Standard Lie Number 1; Four Little Letters; Albums: I Want To Hold You In My Arms Tonight, 1975; Country Sweet, 1977; Stella Parton, 1978; Love Ya, 1979; So Far... So Good, 1982. Address: c/o Joe Taylor Artist Agency, 2802 Columbine Place, Nashville, TN 37204, USA.

PARTRIDGE Andy, b. 11 Nov 1953, Malta. Musician (guitar); Singer; Songwriter; Record Producer. Career: Guitarist, vocalist, XTC, 1977-; Appearances include: US, Venezuela, SE Asia, Australia; Record as send-up 60s group, The Dukes Of Stratosphear, 1985; XTC work as studio band only, 1987-; Producer, other bands, 1983-. Recordings: Hit singles: with XTC: Making Plans For Nigel, 1979; Sgt Rock (Is Going To Help Me), 1981; Senses Working Overtime, 1982; Albums as XTC: White Music, 1978; Go 2, 1978; Drums And Wires, 1979; Black Sea, 1980; English Settlement, 1982; Waxworks - Some Singles, (1977-1982), 1982; Mummer, 1984; The Compact XTC, 1986; Skylarking, 1986; Chips From The Chocolate Fireball, 1987; Oranges And Lemons, 1989; Nonsuch, 1992; Fossil Fuel, 1996; Solo albums: Takeaway/The Lure Of Salvage, 1980; as The Dukes Of Stratosphear: 25 O'Clock, 1985; Psonic Psunspot, 1987; with Martin Newell: The Greatest Living Englishman, 1993; Through the Hill, with Harold Budd, 1994; As producer: tracks by The Mission; The Lilac Time; Peter Bleevad; Wallflowers; Woodentops. Current Management: Paul Bailey, 61 Kilravock Street, London W10 4HY, England.

PASCOAL Hermeto, b. 22 June 1936, Lagoa da Canoa, Brazil. Multi-instrumentalist; Arranger; Composer. m. Ilza da Silva Pascoal, 30 July 1955, 3 sons, 3 daughters. Musical Education: Self-taught. Career: Accordion, flute, with Quarteto Novo, to 1969; Solo artist, 1970-; Concerts with Hermeto Pascoal Group include Montreux Jazz Festival, 1978; With the Danish Radio Concert Orchestra, Copenhagen, 1989; With Symphonic, Berlin, 1989; Radio Big Band, 1992; with Special Big Band, London, 1994; Tours, Europe, USA; Television, radio: Brazilian TV; Sinfonia do Alto da Ribeira; Sound of Aura with: President Fernando Collor de Melo; Papa Joao Paulo II; Jo Soares; Clovodil; French TV with The Tubes. Recordings: Quarteto Novo, 1967; Hermeto, 1979; A Musica Livre De Hermeto Pascoal, 1973; Slaves Mass, 1976; Zabumbe-bum-a, 1978; Montreux ao Vivo, 1978; Cerebro Magnetico, 1980; Hermeto Pascoal & Grupo, 1982; Lagoa da Canoa Municipalo de Arapiraca, 1984; Brasil Universo, 1986; So Nao Toca Quem Nao Quer, 1987; Por Diferentes Caminhos/Piano solo, 1988; Festa Dos Deuses, 1992. Honours: Best Soloist, Associacao Paulista de Criticos de Arte, Brazil, 1972; Best Group, Brazil, 1988; Best Cover and Best Tune: Pixitotina, Brazil, 1989; Concert of Year and Decade, Guardian, Q Magazine, 1994. Membership: SACEM, France. Hobbies: Playing, making music; Listen to radio (news, football). Current Management: Self-managed. Address: Rua Victor Guisard 333, Jabour, Rio De Janeiro, Brazil.

PASCU Ioan Gyuri, b. 31 Aug 1961, Agnita, Romania. Teacher; Songwriter; Entertainer; Actor; Musician (guitar, drums); Writer; Radio, television producer. m. Daniela Marin, 15 Aug 1993. Education: University of Cluj, Faculty of Philology. Musical Education: Private piano lessons; Self-taught. Career: Member, Divertis Group (humour, political satire shows) since 1990; Many radio and television shows, 1989-1992; Soloist, 1991-; Established the Ioan Gyuri Pascu and The Blues Workers Band; International Jazz and Blues Festivals: Brasov, 1992; Bucharest, 1992; Russe, 1992; Brasov, 1993, 1994; International Rock Festivals: Bucharest, 1993; Dracula, Brasov, 1993; Skip Rock, Bucharest, 1994; International Pop Festival, Golden Stag, Brasov (record debut contest), 1993; Opened the Romanian tours of Beats International, 1993, Asia, 1994; Acted in Unforgettable Summer, by Lucian Pintilie (offically selected for Cannes film festival); TV specials: Stars Duel, 1993; VIP, 1993; Many Divertis Group shows, soloist in musical shows. Compositions: Over 30 songs; Original music for television film: Teapa, 1993; Stars School, 1995. Recordings: It Could Be, 1992; Mixed Grill, 1993; The Machine With Jazzoline, 1994; Video: Divertis Group, 1995. Publications: Short stories in Apostrof (literature magazine), 1990; Cuvantul magazine (serial). Showman of The Year: Pop Rock and Show magazine; Mayor Personality of the Year, 1993; The Song Of the Year, The Songwriter of the Year, Radio Contact, 1994; Record of the Year, Vox, Pop, Rock magazine. Membership: Divertis

Cultural Association. Hobbies: Football; Handball; Tennis; Fishing; Watching action films. Current Management: Daniela Pascu. Address: Sos Viilor Nr 95, Bl 102, Sc4, Ap 113, Sect 5, Cod 75236, Bucharest, Romania.

PASS Liz (Elizabeth Ann), b. Mutare, Zimbabwe. Contemporary Gospel Artist. m. Rev Dr David B Pass, 1 Sept 1973. Musical Education: Bachelor of Music, Voice Performance; BA, Theatre, Communications. Career: Appeared on International TV with song: God Bless Africa; Tours, concerts, television appearances all over Africa, Europe, USA, South America. Recordings: God Bless Africa; Heart Cry For The Earth; Hymns For Africa; Christmas In Africa; African Collection. Publications: 2 songbooks of original songs. Honours: Top voice student, Biola University, 1980. Memberships: ASAMI; SAMRO; SARREL. Hobbies: Wildlife; Conservation; Reading. Current Management: Self-managed. Address: PO Box 387, Pinegowrie, 2123 Johannesburg, South Africa.

PASSARELLA Giancarlo, b. 10 May 1959, Florence, Italy. Rock Manager; Promoter; Music Journalist. Career: Editor, Solid Rock, fortnightly fanzine about Dire Straits, 1983-; Author, 2 books about Mark Knopfler; Works with Italian media, including RAI; Italia Uno; Odeon; Presents and produces rock festivals. Membership: (GGM) Gruppo Giornalisti Musicali. Hobbies: Football; Easy way of life; Cats; Girls. Address: Giancarlo Passarella, c/o Solid Rock, PO Box 35, 50018 Scandicci, Florence, Italy.

PATTON Mike, b. 27 Jan 1968, Eureka, California, USA. Rock Singer. Career: Member, Mr Bungle; Lead singer, US rock group Faith No More, 1988-; Regular international concerts include: Reading Festival, 1990; Support to Robert Plant, 1990; Monsters of Rock European festivals, 1990; Rock In Rio II, Brazil, 1991; Day On The Green, San Francisco, 1991; Phoenix Festival, 1993, 1995. Recordings: Hit singles include: From Out Of Nowhere, 1990; Epic, 1990; Falling To Pieces, 1990; Midlife Crisis, 1992; A Small Victory, 1992; Everything's Ruined, 1992; I'm Easy, 1993; Albums: The Real Thing, 1989; Live At Brixton Academy, 1991; Angel Dust, 1992; King For A Day, Fool For A Lifetime, 1995. Honours: Grammy Nomination, Best Heavy Metal Performance, 1990; Bammy Awards: Outstanding Group, Male Vocalist, 1991. Current Management: Warren Entner Management, 5550 Wilshire Blvd, Ste 302, Los Angeles, CA 90036, USA.

PATTULLO Gordon James, b. 8 Sept 1961, Dundee, Scotland. Musician (accordion). m. June Elspeth McLaren, 17 Oct 1984, 2 sons, 1 daughter. Musical Education: Dundee Accordion School of Music. Career: Concert tours worldwide with Andy Stewart Show, 1977-; Television appearances: 2 series in Andy's Party, Grampian TV; Thingummyjig, STV; Various Hogmanay shows for BBC TV, Grampian and Scottish TV. Compositions include: The Furrows End. Recordings: A Gordon For You; The Northlands; Scotland's Favourite; Here's Tae A Gordon; Accordion Favourites; Scotch On The Box; All The Best; Fair Play; Scottish Accordion Hits; Golden Sound of Scottish Music; A Scottish Celebration. Honour: Junior Accordion Champion of Scotland, 1974. Memberships: Musicians' Union; Equity. Hobbies: Restoring vintage tractors. Address: Hill Cottage, Tullybaccart Farm, Coupar Angus, Blairgowrie, Perthshire PH13 9LA, Scotland.

PAUL Les (Lester Polfus), b. 9 June 1915, Waukesha, Wisconsin, USA. Inventor; Musician (guitar). m. Mary Ford (deceased 1977), 3 sons, 2 daughters. Career: Musician, numerous radio appearances, 1920s-30s; Formed Les Paul Trio, 1936; Recordings and television show with Mary Ford, 1950s; Chet Atkins, 1970s; Television includes: First television broadcast with orchestra, NBC, 1939; Documentary, The Wizard Of

Wankesha, 1980; Concerts include: Jazz At The Philharmonic concert with Nat "King" Cole, 1944; Guitar Legends, Seville, Spain, 1992; Pioneer, multi-track tape recording; Inventor, first 8-track tape recorder; Inventor, sound-on-sound recording; Inventor, designer, Les Paul solid body electric guitar, for Gibson Guitars; Consultant, Gibson Guitar Corporation, Nashville. Recordings include: Lover, 1948; Brazil, 1948; Nola, 1949; Goofus, 1950; Tennessee Waltz, 1950; Little Rock Getaway, 1950; Mockin' Bird Hill, 1951; How High The Moon (Number 1, US), 1951; Smoke Rings, 1952; Tiger Rag, 1953; Vaya Con Dios (Number 1, US), 1954; Albums include: with Mary Ford: New Sound Vols I And II; Les And Mary; Bye Bye Blues; The Hitmakers; Time To Dream; Lover's Luau; Warm And Wonderful; Bouquet Of Roses; Swingin' South; with Chet Atkins: Chester And Lester, 1977; Guitar Masters, 1978; Other recordings with Bing Crosby; Andrews Sisters. Honours: Grammy, Chester And Lester, 1977; Grammy Nomination, Guitar Masters, 1978; Hall Of Fame Award, 1979.

PAUL Lou (Louis Baptist Paul), b. 27 Jan 1936, Portage La Prairie, Manitoba, Canada. Solo Artist; Singer; Musician (guitar, mandolin, banjo). m. Jan Howden-Paul, 1 July 1983, 2 sons, 4 daughters (previous marriage). Musical Education: Self-taught. Career: Canadian Country Music National Finals, 1985; Country Music Week, 1990 Showcase in Edmonton; Performed at Calgary Stampede and Edmonton Klondike; Radio charting in Canada, Europe and Australia. Recordings: Album: This Is Lou Paul; Video: Raisin' Cows and Raisin' Hell. Memberships: CCMA; ARIA; CMA of Canada. Hobbies: Music; Ranching. Current Management: Jan Howden-Paul. Address: RR 1, Clive, Alberta T0C 0Y0, Canada.

PAULIK Dalibor, b. 22 Dec 1953, Zagreb, Croatia. Composer; Musician (piano); Theatre Critic. m. Vesna Paulik, 7 June 1980, 1 son. Education: MSc, Theatrology; Professor, Music theatre. Musical Education: Secondary music school, private music seminars. Career: Croatian and international festivals of popular music; 500 concerts with popular Croatian singers; Music for theatre and television; Festivals in: Ireland; Latin America; Finland; Los Angeles; Croatia (Zagreb, Krapina, Split); Sarjevo; Songs for organisations: Stars of Hope (Sweden); World For Two (UK). Compositions: Over 200 include: Your Face In My Mirror; Goodbye Is Not For You; Love Is A Game; Never In My Life; Memories; The Violin Song; Stars Of Hope; Today I'm Sad My Love; Together Forever; Dancing With The Moonlight. Publications: Scientific publications of HAZU; Who Is Who In Croatia; Directory Of Croatian Composers Society. Honours: 20 at Croatian festivals; 1 in Ireland. Memberships: Croatian Composers Society (FIDOF). Hobbies: Table tennis; Fishing; Collecting theatre publications. Current Management: Damir Gostl, Croatian Music Art. Address: Zerjaviceva 9, Zagreb, Croatia.

PAXTON Glenn G Jnr, b. 7 December 1931, Chicago, IL, USA. Composer. m. Leslie Davis, 12 August 1962, 1 son, 1 daughter. Education: BA, Princeton University, USA, 1953; Studied piano privately; Composition, Chicago Musical College; Orchestration, privately. Career: Composer for Music, Theatre, TV and Film, Concert Hall; Composer (theater productions); First Impressions, 1959; The Adventures of Friar Tuck, 1983; When the Legends Die, film, 1972. Compositions: The Evening Sung, concert pieces, 1981; Walking Home, multimedia, 1991; Prairie Indigo, CD, 1995. Recordings: Vital Signs, TV movies, 1986; Dark Night of the Scarecrow, 1981; Isobel's Choice, 1981; The Two Worlds of Jenny Logan, 1979; The Clone Master, 1978; Charlie and The Great Balloon Chase, 1981; TV Shows: Amazing Stories, 1986; Willa Cather's America, 1976; Qu American Christmas: Words and Music, 1971; The Hill Country: Lyndon Jokuson's Texas,

1967; The Stately Ghosts of England, 1968; New World Visions, 1989. Memberships: ASCAP; American Federation of Musicians. Address: 913 Marco Place, Venice, CA 90291-3919, USA.

PAXTON Tom, b. 31 Oct 1937, Chicago, Illinois, USA. Folk Singer; Songwriter; Author. m. Margaret Ann Cummings, 5 Aug 1963, 3 daughters. Education: BFA, University of Oklahoma, 1959. Career: Folk recording artist, 1962-; Early concerts on Greenwich Village circuit; Worldwide tours and concerts, 1960-; Board of directors, Kerrville Folk Festival, 1990. Compositions include: Lyndon Johnson Told The Nation; Talkin' Vietnam Pot Luck Blues; Leaving London; The Hostage (also recorded by Judy Collins). Recordings: Albums include: Ramblin' Boy, 1964; Ain't That News, 1965; Outward Bound, 1968; Morning Again, 1968; The Things I Notice Now, 1969; Tom Paxton 6, 1970; The Compleat Tom Paxton, 1971; How Come The Sun, 1971; Peace Will Come 1972; New Songs Old Friends, 1973; Something In My Life, 1975; Saturday Night, 1976; Heroes, 1978; Up And Up, 1980; The Paxton Report, 1981; In The Orchard, 1985; One Million Lawyers And Other Disasters, 1985; Even A Gray Day, 1986; And Loving You, 1988; Politics - Live, 1989; Storyteller, 1989. Publications: Ramblin' Boy And Other Songs, 1965; Tom Paxton Anthology, 1971; Politics, 1989; The Authentic Guitar Of Tom Paxton, 1989; The Tom Paxton Children's Song Book, 1990; Author, children's books: Jennifer's Rabbit, 1988; Belling The Cat, 1990; Englebert The Elephant, 1990; Aesop's Fables Retold In Verse, 1988; Androcles And The Lion, 1991. Memberships: ASCAP; AFTRA: AFofM; Screen Actors Guild; World Folk Music Association (Honorary Chairman of Board). Address: c/o Susan Martinez, Martinez Management & Media, PO Box 14901, University Station, Minneapolis, MN 55414, USA.

PAYCHECK Johnny (Donald Eugene Lytle), b. 31 May 1938, Ohio, USA. Singer; Musician (guitar). m. Sharon, 23 Dec 1971, 1 son. Musical Education: Self-taught. Career: Joined George Jones, as bass, steel guitar player, for 6 years, mid-1950s; Worked with country artists including: Faron Young; Ray Price; Porter Wagoner; Hits began 1965; Major success with: Take This Job And Shove It; Concerts, performances include: Carnegie Hall; Wembley Festival, England; Las Vegas; Lone Star, New York City; Television includes: David Letterman Show; Music City Tonight; Nashville Now; Mike Douglas Show; Solid Gold; Major role in film. Compositions include: Apartment #9, Tammy Wynette; Touch My Heart, Ray Price. Recordings: 67 albums; Hit songs include: Don't Take Her She's All I've Got; Someone To Give My Love To; Mr Lovemaker; For A Minute There; A-11; Memory Of A Memory; Outlaw's Prayer; I'm The Only Hell My Mama Ever Raised; Slide Off Your Satin Sheets; Song And Dance Man; Colorado Kool Aid; Old Violin; 11 Months And 29 Days; Don't Monkey With Another Monkey's Monkey; Take This Job And Shove It; Me And The IRS. Honours include: 6 Gold albums, 1 Platinum, 1 double Platinum; Grammy Nominations include: Don't Take Her, She's All I've Got, 1970; Take This Job And Shove It; Lifetime Achievement, BMI; Entertainer Of The Year, Independent Record Labels, 1991. Membership: AFofM. Hobbies: Golf; Fishing. Current Management: Marty Martel, Midnight Special Productions Inc. Address: PO Box 916, Hendersonville, TN 37077, USA.

PAYNE Freda, b. 19 Sep 1945, Detroit, Michigan, USA. Singer; Actress. m. Gregory Abbott, 1 Dec 1976, 1 son. Education: Studied acting with Al Mancini. Musical Education: Detroit Institute of Musical Arts; Piano and Voice tuition. Career: Began singing career at age 17; Toured with Quincy Jones at such theatres as the Apollo in New York City and Regal Theatre in Chicago; Acting debut in the musical Hallelujah Baby, then as Linda in Lost in The Stars, in The Book of Numbers, Daddy Goodness, Ain't Misbehavin' and Sophisticated Ladies; Starred in the television special Freda Payne and The Stylistics, appeared in HBO's The Legendary Ladies of Rock and in the video Soul No 2 America's Music; Hosted her own TV talk show, Today's Black Woman; Has toured in UK, Germany and Japan; Starred in musical, Blues in the Night, 1990-91, and in the musical drama, Jelly's Last Jam by George C Wolf. Recordings include: Albums: Stares And Whispers; Supernatural High; Red Hot; Payne And Pleasure; Out Of Payne Comes Love; Singles: Band Of Gold; Bring The Boys Home; Deeper And Deeper; Cherish What's Dear To You; You Brought The Joy.Honours: 2 Gold Singles; Best Ensemble Performance for Blues In The Night, Drama-Logue Award, 1990; Dame Of Malta, Knights of Malta - The Sovereign Military and Hospital Order of St John of Jerusalem, 1994. Hobbies: Tennis; Fishing; Skiing; Yoga; Healthy Living. Address: 1505 Blue Jay Way, Los Angeles, CA 90069, USA.

PAYNE Les Alexander, b. 22 Aug 1943, Newport, Isle of Wight, England. Singer; Songwriter; Musician (guitar, keyboards). m. (1) Brigitte Jean Wilson, 1965, divorced, 1971, 1 son, (2) Rosalind Jean Butler, 1974, divorced 1993, 2 sons, (3) Pennie Hawkes, 1994, 1 stepson, 1 stepdaughter. Musical Education: Music, choir at school. Career: Concerts supporting artists including: Genesis; Nazareth; Rory Gallagher; Mott The Hoople; 40 date tour with Leo Sayer; Gary Moore; Radio includes: Record of the Week, Radio 1, 1974; Album and single of the week, Capitol; Power Play Luxembourg, 1979; Television includes: Sky; BBC; All ITV regions; Australian documentaries. Recordings: Who Am I?, 1971; I Can't Help To Feel The Love, 1974; Don't Say Goodbye, 1975; Who Do You Love, 1978; By Yourside, 1979; No Money, 1979; Exposure album, 1979; Who Will Be The Winner, (single in Japan), 1982; Single: Can't Cry For You, 1990; Album: 47 Summers. Honours: The Harp Beat Rock Plaque (awarded to musicians who survive without a hit record and who have played more than 5100 concerts). Memberships: PRS; Musicians' Union. Hobbies: Keeping scrap books; Painting; Swimming. Current Management: Self-managed. Address: High Wycombe, Buckinghamshire, England.

PAYNE Steven Ernest, b. 11 Mar 1963, Havant, Hampshire, England. Musician (bass, flute); Recording Engineer; Tutor (Chapman Stick, saxophone, percussion, guitar, keyboards). Education: University of Trent. Musical Education: University of Trent, Chapman Stick workshop group. Career: Bass guitarist: Trevaskis; Chinatown; Bass, flute, saxophone for The Night Watch, 1994; Set up Crimson Studios, Mar 1994; Power FM concert, 1990; Channel 4 Arts programme, 1995. Recordings: (co-writer) The Night Watch: The Bridge Between, 1994; Talking In Whispers, 1995; Solo album: Let There Be Light, 1995. Publications: Contributions to Background magazine; Column in Midmusic, 1993. Membership: Musicians' Union. Hobbies: Teaches martial arts, music, to kids for free. Current Management: Eccentric Ideas, 35 Fortunes Way, Bedhampton, Hants, England. Address: 66 Littlegreen Avenue, Havant, Hants PO9 2LF, England.

PAYTON Nicholas Edward, b. 14 Feb 1972, Birmingham, England. Jazz Musician (saxophone, clarinet). Musical Education: Graduated from Leeds College of Music; Studied with Bob Huber. Career: Lead alto saxophone with the Charleston Chasers; Major concerts at the Southbank Centre, London (International Jazz Orchestra), and The Colston Hall, Bristol; Major jazz festivals in England and Europe include: Edinburgh Festival; The Cork Jazz Festival, Ireland; Also toured USA; Numerous appearances on television and radio; Performed with Bob Huber, Kenny Davern, Spike Robinson, Martyn Grost, Muriel Shane; Co-runs the band Swing Syndicate. Recordings include: Crazy Rhythm, 1988; I'll See You In My Dreams, 1992; Those Charleston Days, 1994; Henderson Stomp, 1994; Pleasure Mad, 1994. Membership: Musicians' Union. Hobbies: Cooking; Study of The Works of Duke Ellington. Address: Halfway House, Grafton Mews, Chipping Campden, Gloucestershire GL55 6BW, England.

PEARSON John, b. 5 Oct 1948, Liverpool, England. Musician (6 and 12 string guitar, mandolin); Singer. m. Kathy Walker, 14 Feb 1976. Career: Television appearances: The Happening, 1991; National radio broadcasts: Paul Jones Blues Show, sessions, 1989, 1992; Major concerts include: Sonny Terry and Brownie McGhee; Alexis Korner; Louisianna Red; Davey Graham; Woody Mann; Jo Anne Kelly; Cephas and Wiggins. Recordings: Solo albums: Drive My Blues Away, 1989; Streamline Train, 1990; Busy Bootin', 1992 (with Roger Hubbard); Grasshoppers In My Pillow, 1995. Honours: British Blues Connection Readers Poll, Best Blues Album Nomination, Busy Bootin', 1993. Current Management: Last Days Recording. Address: PO Box 128, Dover, Kent CT16 2SX, England.

PEART Neil, b. 12 Sept 1952, Hamilton, Ontario, Canada. Musician (drums). Career: Member, Canadian rock group Rush, 1974-; Sell-out tours, US; Canada; UK; Europe. Recordings: Albums: Fly By Night, 1975; Caress Of Steel, 1975; 2112, 1976; All The World's A Stage, 1976; A Farewell To Kings, 1977; Archives, 1978; Hemispheres, 1978; Permanent Waves, 1980; Moving Pictures, 1981; Exit... Stage Left, 1981; Great White North, 1982; Signals, 1982; Grace Under Pressure, 1984; Power Windows, 1985; Hold Your Fire, 1987; A Show Of Hands, 1988; Presto, 1989; Chronicles, 1990; Roll The Bones, 1991; Counterparts, 1993; Solo: Burning For Buddy, 1995; Singles include: Spirit Of Radio; Tom Sawyer; Closer To The Heart; New World Man; The Big Money; Countdown; Time Stand Still. Honours: Platinum discs; Juno Awards: Most Promising Group, 1975; Best Group, 1978, 1979; Group named Official Ambassadors Of Music, Canadian Government, 1979; Gold Ticket, Madison Square Garden, New York, 1991. Current Management: Anthem Entertainment, 189 Carlton Street, Toronto, Ontario M5A 2K7, Canada.

PEDERSEN Karl-Erik, b. 17 Nov 1960, Hobro, Jutland, Denmark. Singer; Songwriter; Musician (guitar, bass); Music Teacher. m. Anne Iben Hansen. Education: University. Career: Member, band Yellow Moon; Played concerts in: Denmark; Sweden; Finland; Iceland; Live concerts, national radio; Compositions: Songwriter for: Nikolaj and Piloterne, 1989; Björn Afzelius (Sweden), 1994; Kim C (Denmark), 1994; Music for films, documentaries with director Ole Henning Hansen. Recordings: Album with Yellow Moon. Memberships: KODA; Danish Jazz Beat & Folk Authors; Danish Musicians' Union. Hobby: Football. Current Management: Finn Thorkildsen, ARTE; Warner/Chappell. Address: Warner/Chappell, Anker Heegårdsgade, 2 st.tv 1572 V, Denmark; ARTE, Hvidkildevej 64, 2400 NV, Denmark.

PEDERSEN Leonardo, b. Copenhagen, Denmark. Musician (saxophone, clarinet, flute); Songwriter. m. Annelise Pedersen, 15 Dec 1972, 1 son, 1 daughter. Education: Self-taught. Career: Formed first jazz band in 1958, becoming Leonardo Pedersen's Jazzkapel; Tours of Germany, Scandinavia, Eastern Europe, England, Italy, Scotland; Performed with numerous leading jazz artists including: Albert Nicolas, Ben Webster, Benny Waters, Al Grey, Bennie Bailey, Harry "Sweets" Edison and Eddie "Lockjaw" Davis; Appearances on national and international television and radio; Also played with: Barbarossa, 1978-88; Van Dango, 1986-89; The Original Danish Polcalypso Orchestra; Recordings: with Leonardo Pedersen's Jazzkapel: Danish

Traditional Jazz, 1963; Leonardo Pedersen's Jazzkapel with Harry "Sweets" Eddison, Eddie "Lockjaw" Davis and Richard Boone, 1977; I Want A Roof, 1994; with Polcalypso: Karlekammeret, 1989, Polcalypso II, 1991; with Hans Knudsen Jumpband: So Long John, 1994; Jump In Focus, 1997; The Original Danish Polcalypso Orchestra featuring James "Jamesie" Brewster, Live, 1996. Current Management: EPC Management, Ørnevej 12, 2 th, 2400 Copenhagen NV, Denmark.

PEDERSEN Torben Evald Dannesboe, b. 15 May 1947, Odense, Denmark. Musician (guitar); Singer. m. Eva Pedersen, 14 Aug 1971, 2 daughter. Education: As Social Worker. Musical Education: Seminars and self-taught. Career: Appearances on local television, at festivals, small music houses and street music. Recordings: Vi Over Bare (We Are Just Trying); Uj Å Cykle (Go On Cycling); Kalanihara (Musicians Adventure); Hilsen Til Vore Born (To Our Children); Vi Rider Mod Vest (We Are Riding Against The West). Memberships: DJBFA; DMF. Hobbies: Photography; Painting; Racing pigeons; Nature. Current Management: VOB Music. Address: VOB Music, O Doensevej 8, 9500 Hobro, Denmark.

PEEL John (John Robert Parker Ravenscroft), b. 30 Aug 1939, Heswall, Cheshire, England. Radio Presenter; Disc Jockey. Career: Radio broadcaster, Texas, Oklahoma and California, 1960s; Broadcaster, own show Perfumed Garden, on pirate radio station, Radio London; Broadcaster, BBC Radio One; Known for promoting new and experimental music. Recordings: Various Peel Sessions recordings taken from own Radio One show, including: Before The Fall; Winters Of Discontent; The New Breed; Too Pure. Address: c/o BBC Radio One, Broadcasting House, London W1A 1AA, England.

PEGG David, b. 2 Nov 1947, Birmingham, England. Musician (bass guitar, mandolin). m. Christine, 12 Dec 1966, 1 son, 1 daughter. Musical Education: Self-taught. Career: Member, bands include The Uglies; The Exception; Way Of Life; Ian Campbell's Folk Group; Joined Fairport Convention, 1969-; Member, Jethro Tull, 1979-95; Co-organizes the Cropredy Music Festival, with wife Chris. Recordings: Numerous albums include: with Fairport Convention: Angel Delight, 1971; Babbacombe Lee, 1971; Rosie, 1973; Nine, 1973; Live Convention, 1974; Rising For The Moon, 1975; Gottle O'Geer, 1976; A Bonny Bunch Of Roses, 1977; Tipplers Tales, 1978; Gladys' Leap, 1985; Five Seasons, 1991; Woodworm Years; Jewel In The Crown; with Jethro Tull: Broadsword And The Beast, 1982; Under Wraps, 1984; Crest Of A Knave, 1987; Rock Island, 1989; Catfish Rising, 1990; Thick As A Brick, 1991; A Little Light Music, 1992; Solo album: The Cocktail Cowboy Goes It Alone, 1984; Other recordings with: Ian Anderson; Sandy Denny; Nick Drake; Bryn Haworth; John Martyn; Ralph McTell; Dave Swarbrick; Richard and Linda Thompson. Honour: Grammy Award, Best Hard Rock Performance, with Jethro Tull, 1989. Membership: PRS. Hobbies: Tennis; Sailing; Walking; Skiing. Address: PO Box 37, Banbury, Oxfordshire OX16 8YN, England.

PELLEN Jacques, b. Apr 1957, Brest, France. Musician (guitar). Education: University. Musical Education: Classical. Career: European tours, 1980-95; Celtic Procession (guest Kenny Wheeler), 1991; Europe Jazz Festival, Le Mans, 1994; Festival Quimper (guest Didier Lockwood), Zénith Paris, with Dan Ar Bras, 1995; Recordings: Celtic Progression; Sorserez (with Riccardo Del Fra). Address: Bertrand Dupond, Ton All, Pouldero Vihan, 56630 Langonned, France.

PELLOW Marti (Mark McLoughlin), b. 23 Mar 1966, Clydebank, Scotland. Singer. Career: Lead singer, Wet Wet Wet, 1982-; Performances include: Royal Albert Hall, Greenpeace charity concert, 1986; Prince's Trust Rock Gala, Royal Albert Hall, London, 1988-90; Nelson Mandela's 70th Birthday Tribute, Wembley, 1988; John Lennon Tribute Concert, Merseyside, 1990; Children In Need, BBC, 1991; Edinburgh Castle, 1992; Nordoff-Robbins Music Therapy Centre benefit, Royal Albert Hall, London, 1992; Live At The Royal Albert Hall 1992, C4, 1993. Recordings: Albums: Popped In Souled Out, 1987; Sgt Pepper Knew My Father, 1988; The Memphis Sessions, 1988; Holding Back The River, 1989; High On The Happy Side, 1992; Wet Wet Wet Live At The Royal Albert Hall, 1993; End Of Part One (Their Greatest Hits), 1993; Picture This, 1995; Singles include: Wishing I Was Lucky, 1987; Sweet Little Mystery, 1987; Angel Eyes (Home And Away), 1988; Temptation, 1988; With A Little Help From My Friends (Number 1, UK), 1988; Sweet Surrender, 1989; Broke Away, 1989; Hold Back The River, 1990; Stay With Me Heartache, 1990; Make It Tonight, 1991; Goodnight Girl (Number 1, UK), 1992; More Than Love, 1992; Lip Service, 1992; Shed A Tear, 1993; Love Is All Around (Number 1, UK), 1994; She's All On My Mind, 1995; Julia Said, 1995. Honours: BRIT Award, Best British Newcomer, 1988. Current Management: The Precious Organisation, 14-16 Spiers Wharf, Port Dundas, Glasgow, Scotland.

PEMELTON Bret. m. Diana Pemelton, 2 sons. Career: Member, Christian pop group Dream of Eden; 2 major tours, USA; Television: CCM-TV, real videos (TBN); Explosion '95 (TBN); Numerous radio appearances. Recordings: 2 Number 1 singles: Wonderful Thing, 1993; Into The Here And Now, 1995. Membership: Gospel Music Association. Current Management: Brian A Mays, BMP Artists Management. Address: PO Box 1703, La Mirada, CA 90637, USA.

PENAVA Pista (Pishta) Gordan, b. 29 Oct 1967, Zagreb, Croatia. Singer; Musician (guitar); Songwriter; Television Host; Radio Disc Jockey; Journalist. Education: Faculty of Political Science, Journalism. Career: Singer, guitar player, Hard Time; Tours: Croatia; Slovenia; France; Appearances on MTV's Headbangers Ball. Recordings: Single cassette, 1992; Album: Kiss My Ass And Go To Hell, 1992; Compilation: Bijeli Put (1 song), 1993; Compilation: Cro Fest '94, Pop rock hit, 1994. Honours: Best Hard Rock Band of Croatia, Hard Time, 1992; Best Video Clip, Hit And Run, 1993. Membership: HGU (Croatian Musician Union); Zamp. Address: Aleja Pomoraca 11, 41000 Zagreb, Croatia.

PENDER Mike (Michael John Prendergast), b. 3 Mar 1942, Liverpool, England. Musician (guitar). Career: Member, lead guitarist, lead vocalist, The Searchers, mid 1960s-; Numerous tours and concerts; Left The Searchers to form Mike Pender's Searchers, 1985. Recordings: Albums: Meet The Searchers, 1963; Sugar And Spice, 1963; Hear! Hear!, 1964; It's The Searchers, 1964; This Is Us, 1964; The New Searchers LP, 1965; The Searchers No 4, 1965; Sounds Like Searchers, 1965; Take Me For What I'm Worth, 1965; Second Take, 1972; Needles And Pins, 1974; The Searchers, 1979; Play For Today, 1981; 100 Minutes Of The Searchers, 1982; The Searchers Hit Collection, 1987; The EP Collection, 1989; 30th Anniversary Collection, 1992; The EP Collection, Vol 2, 1992; UK Number 1 hits: Sweets For My Sweet; Needles And Pins; Don't Throw Your Love Away; Other hit singles include: When You Walk In The Room; Farmer John; Love Potion Number 9; Sugar And Spice; Ain't That Just Like Me; Goodbye My Love; Some Day We're Gonna Love Again; Bumble Bee; He's Got No Love. Current Management: Tony Sherwood Ltd., 5 Castleton Avenue, Carlton, Nottingham NG4 3NZ, England.

PENDERGRASS Teddy (Theodore), b. 26 Mar 1950, Philadelphia, Pennsylvania, USA. Singer; Musician (drums). m. Karen Still, 20 June 1987. Career: Member, Harold Melvin And The Blue Notes, 1969-76; Solo artiste, 1976-; Major appearances include: UK tours, 1981, 1982; Live Aid, JFK Stadium, Philadelphia, 1985; Film debut, Soup For One, 1982. Recordings: Albums: with Harold Melvin: Harold Melvin And The Blue Notes, 1971; Black And Blue, 1975; Wake Up Everybody, 1976; All Their Greatest Hits, 1976; Solo: Teddy Pendergrass, 1977; Life Is A Song Worth Singing, 1978; Teddy, 1979; Teddy Live! (Coast To Coast), 1979; T P, 1980; It's Time For Love, 1981; This One's For You, 1982; Heaven Only Knows, 1983; Love Language, 1984; Workin' It Back, 1985; Greatest Hits, 1987; Joy, 1988; Teddy Pendergrass, 1989; Truly Blessed, 1991; Singles include: with Harold Melvin: I Miss You; If You Don't Know Me By Now; Solo: The Whole Town's Laughing At Me; Close The Door; Turn Off The Lights; Love TKO; Hold Me, duet with Whitney Houston; Love 4 2; Joy; Dream Girl, from film soundtrack Soup For One, 1982; Duet with Lisa Fisher, Glad To Be Alive, from film soundtrack: The Adventures Of Ford Fairlane, 1990; Contributor, Rubáiyát (Elektra's 40th Anniversary compilation), 1990. Honours: Platinum and Gold discs; American Music Award, Favourite Male Soul/R&B Artist, 1979. Current Management: Dream Street Management, 1460 Fourth Street, Suite 205, Santa Monica, CA 90401, USA.

PENDLEBURY Andrew Scott, b. 30 November 1951, Melbourne, Australia. Guitar. Education: Selftaught Guitar. Career: Major Australian Band, The Sports; Recorded 8 albums; Toured England twice; First major tour, Graham Parker and The Rumour; Finished 3 nights at Hammersmith Odeon, London, England. Compositions: Who Listens to the Radio, 1979. Recordings: 8 sports albums; 4 solo albums. Hobbies: Makin' a Livin'. Current Management: Mushroom Records, ABC Music. Address: 34 Wellington Street, Richmond 3121, Melbourne, Victoria, Australia.

PENISTON Cece, b. Dayton, Ohio, USA. Singer; Songwriter. Education: Phoenix College. Musical Education: Vocal lessons with Seth Riggs. Career: Crowned Miss Black Arizona as a student; Guest vocalist with rapper Overweight Pooch; Solo artiste, 1991-; International concerts, Phillipines, Japan, USA, UK, Europe; Tours with: Joe Public; R Kelly; Levert. Recordings: Albums: Finally, 1992; Thought 'Ya Knew, 1994; Hit singles: Finally; We Got A Love Thing; Inside That I Cried; Crazy Love; Keep On Walkin'; I'm In The Mood; Guest voclaist, Female Preacher, Overweight Pooch; Honours: Gold discs, Finally, 1992. Current Management: Devour Management, 4840 Hollow Corner Road #421, Culver City, CA 90230, USA.

PENN Thomas Howard, b. 21 Nov 1954, Cleveland, Ohio, USA. Artist Manager; Concert Promoter. Career: Commenced under name Good Time Productions, 1974; Started out throwing keg parties; Dances and school promotions, progressed to national acts, 1974-; Acts include: Tower of Power; Ronnie Laws and Pressure; George Benson; Side Effect; Karma; Donald Byrd and the Black Byrds; Steel Breeze; Taxi; Curtis Salgado and the Stilletos; Pleasure; U-Krew; Seawind; Shock; Maya; Earth Wind and Fire; Vail Johnson; Alliance with T:T Promotions Inc, Portland, Oregon, 1978-.

PENNANEN Keijo, b. 4 November 1962, Utajärvi, Finland. Guitarist; Guitar Instructor. m. Aija Pennanen, 2 sons. Education: Professional Music Diploma, Berklee College of Music, Boston, USA. Career: Performances as Leader of own groups, 1986-; Jazz Clubs, festivals & radio; Touring, National Jazz Radio feature programmes, 1987, 1991; Fulltime Guitar Instructor, Helsinki's Pop & Jazz Conservatory, 1988-. Recording: Springboard, 1993. Publications: Entering Modal Zone, article; Lick of the Month, 1996. Hobbies: Sports; Ice Hockey. Address: Trumpettitie 8-10 G151, 00420 Helsinki, Finland.

PENNEY John, b. 17 Sept 1968, Birmingham, England. Vocalist; Lyricist. Career: Vocalist, Ned's Atomic Dustbin, 1987-; Various large festivals worldwide include: Reading, 1990, 1991, 1993; Glastonbury, 1992; Phoenix, 1994; Tours: UK (11); Scandinavia (1); Europe (3); USA (9); Australia (3); Japan (3); Television: Top Of The Pops (3 times); The Word (2); The Beat (5); Big Breakfast; Radio sessions: John Peel; Mark Goodyear; Johnnie Walker. Recordings: God Fodder, 1991; Are You Normal?, 1992; 5.22, 1994; Brainbloodvolume, 1995; Long form videos: Nothing Is Cool, 1991; Lunatic Magnets, 1993. Publications: Available For Panto, by Martin Roach, 1994. Honours: Number 1 US Modern Rock Single for Not Sleeping Around, 1993. Membership: Musicians' Union. Hobby: Football. Current Management: Tank Gilks. Address: Floor 4, Sony Music UK, 10 Great Marlborough Street, London, England.

PEPA (Sandra Denton), b. 9 Nov 1969, Kingston, Jamaica. Rapper. Career: Founder member, US female rap duo Salt'N'Pepa, 1985-; Appearances include: Youth Ball, Washington DC, 1993; LIFEBeat AIDS benefit concert, 1993. Recordings: Singles include: My Mike Sounds Nice, 1987; Push It, 1988; Shake Your Thang (It's Your Thing), 1988; Twist And Shout, 1988; Expression, 1990; Do You Want Me, 1991; Let's Talk About Sex, 1991; You Showed Me, 1991; Start Me Up, 1992; Shoop, 1993; Albums: Hot Cool And Vicious, 1987; A Salt With A Deadly Pepa, 1988; Black's Magic, 1990; A Blitz Of Salt 'N' Pepa Hits, 1991; Greatest Hits, 1991; Very Necessary, 1993; Contributor, Backyard, Pebbles, 1991. Honours: Platinum discs. Current Management: CD Enterprises, 105 Duane Street, Suite 46E, New York, NY 10007, USA.

PEPPERELL Giles Henry William, b. 30 Nov 1964, Exeter, Devon, England. Artist Manager; Label Manager; Label Consultant. Career: Fishmonger; Supermarket Management; Special Forces Weapons Specialist; Computer Engineer and Customer Service Manager; Artist Manager with Svengali Management for: The Auranaut; Artist Manager with Power Circle for: Skylab; Annie Williams; The Acoustic Hoods; Label Manager, Plink Plonk Records. Membership: International Managers Forum. Hobbies: Shooting; Scuba; Exotic travel. Address: PO Box 2977, London N1 2SG, England.

PERCIVAL John Graham, b. 7 Mar 1938, Northampton, England. Musician (clarinet, saxophone, musical saw). m. Jane Allsop, 25 Aug 1960, 3 daughters. Musical Education: Self-taught. Career: Appeared on television programmes Opportunity Knocks and Rising Stars, BBC TV; Ran own jazzband, Horace M Smith, 1971-87; Member, Bob Kerr Whoopee Band; Television appearances in Germany, Netherlands, France, Switzerland, Belgium, Sweden, Denmark, Russia. Recordings: as Horace M Smith: Hold That Tiger; with Bob Kerr Whoopee Band: Molotov Cocktails; Happy Daze; Videos: Live At The Half Moon; From Russia With Laughs; Films with Bob Godfrey: French Revolution; Happy Birthday Switzerland. Membership: Musicians' Union. Hobbies: Drawing; Painting; Magic; Old-time radio; Variety. Address: 20 Stoke Road, Blisworth, Northamptonshire NN7 3BZ, England.

PERCIVAL Lynne, b. 24 Nov 1954, Altrincham, Cheshire, England. Teacher; Singer; Musician (guitar, mandolin). Education: Masters Degree in Social Science. Career: Semi-professional singer, guitarist and mandolin player; Member, The Fluence Band, 1988-; Specialising in Irish traditional dance music and song, performing regularly in Northern England, local residencies and ceilidhs; Support to various artists including Dick Gaughan, Maria Tolly and Meliantu; Tours in Brittany, Berlin, Canada, Denmark, Hungary, Scotland and the Isle of Mull; Coordinator of Irish music promotions, Club

Cheoil, Manchester. Recordings: Early singer and songwriter tapes; Goodwill (album of Polish tour), with Wild Bill Flatpick and The Bindle Stiffs, 1987; Children In Need Compilation, 1987; Guesting on various artists recordings, 1991-93. Honour: Voted second folk group in local poll, 1994. Memberships: PRS; Musicians' Union. Hobbies: Travel; Football; Music. Address: 20 Alderfield Road, Manchester M21 9JX, England.

PERCL Ivica, b. 1 Jan 1945, Zagreb, Croatia. Musician (guitar, harmonica). m. Mirjana, 8 Jan 1972, 2 daughters. Musical Education: Music Secondary School. Career: Bass guitarist with groups: Mladi tehnicari, 1962; Kristali, 1963-64; Roboti, 1964-66; First Croatian protest singer, 1966; Festival of Shansone, Zagreb, 1967-71; Concerts include: Bulgaria; Russia; Finland, 1968-71; Playing protest songs, recording for Croatian radio station, Croatian television; Concerts, Boom Festival, 1972-74; Solo, 1979; Concerts on Days Of Croatian Music; Advances in theatre, television as musician. Compositions: Over 200 include: 1966; Postovani profesore; Godine ratne, godine mirne; Izemedu tebe i mene; Kad zatvoris vrata iza sebe. Recordings: 7 singles; 1 album: Stari Pjer, 1967-1975. Honours: Diploma of Soci 69, Russia, 1969; Katom, 1970; Labin, 1970. Memberships: Croatian Association Of Composers; Croatian Music Unit; Professional Association Of Composers; Croatian Music Unit. Hobbies: Painting. Address: Vinogradska 17, Zagreb 41000, Croatia.

PEREIRA Francis Martin Purcell, b. 1 May 1950, Singapore. Producer; Arranger; Musician (Guitar). m. Ann Toh Swee Hua, 1 January 1985. Education: Royal School of Music; Singapore Armed Forces Band (Trombone); Gateway School of Audio Engineering; Selftaught Guitar. Career: Arranger, EMI, Singapore, 1975-83; Television Brunei; Played for Sultan of Brunei, 1985-87; Played for Celia Black, local acts; 1st Asean Festival of Songs, 1986; Director, Shekinah Music Trading, 1992-. Compositions: Local acts; Film Compositions: Eye of the Tiger. Recordings: Guitar Indigo Series; Guitar Latino Series; Guitar Memories; Different Class Harmonica Series; Sax with Love; Dijazz Series; Contemporary Saxophone, vol I/II; Todos Latino; Guitarra Series, Hymns, Asia. Honours: Doctor of Administration & Management Service; Conferred & Awarded by Golden Gates University; Affiliated Member, Ferrum University, Virginia, USA; Ethnic Best Song Composition, 1982. Hobby: Fishing. Current Management: Shekinah Music Trading. Address: Blk 30 #07-17 Kallang Place, Singapore 339159.

PERES Vivian, b. France. Musician (drums). Musical Education: Self-taught. Career: Participated in first Francofolies de la Rochelle; Leader, own group Traction Ailleurs; Worked at Béziers Conservatoire with René Nan; Founder member, La Campagnie du Jazz; Member, quartet Golem; Salsa group with Juan Quintana; Accompanist with numerous singers; Member, Slax; Mezcal Jazz Unit, European tour, 1994; Jazz Festival, Lithuania, 1994; Also performs with groups: Swing; Planete Jazz. Honours: Agfa Song Contest Winner, with group Traction Ailleurs, 1986.

PEREZ Ivan, b. 11 Nov 1964, Orange, France. Musician (guitar); Composer. Education: BPA Floriculture. Musical Education: Conservatoire de Music; Studied improvised music with bassist B Santacruz and saxophonist Andre Jaume. Career: Jazz Festivals: Avignon; Sorgues; Carpentras; Music for Florence Saul contemporary dance company; Member, duo with Frederic Duvivier; Trio with Colin McKellar and Tox Drohead; Trio with Simon Fayolle and Lionel Villard. Address: 80 Rue Henri Durant, 84100 Orange, France.

PEREZ Michel, b. 2 Jan 1946, St Priest, France. Musician (guitar). m. Patricia Van

Ginneken, 31 Dec 1977, 1 son, 2 daughters. Musical Education: Self-taught. Career; Concert 1st part of Miles Davis, Vienne Festival, 1984; Nice Jazz Festival, 1984; Casino de Paris, 1989; Film in concert, Lyon, 1986; Around Midnight (Bertrand Taverner) with Herbie Hancock, Tony Williams, Wayne Shorter; Concert, first part of Zawinul Syndicate, 1992. Recordings: 2 with Speroe: Spheroe, 1976; Primadonna, 1979; Kaleidoscope, 1982; Virgile, 1986; Orange, 1991; Toujours, Ron Carter, 1992; Film: Around Midnight, 1986. Publications: 3 compositions to be published in: Le Livre Du Jazz En France. Address: 19 Rue De La Hacquière Pavillon, No. 68, 91440 Bures Sur Yvette, France.

PERKINS Walter, b. Feb 1932, Chicago, Illinois, USA. Musician (drums). m. Barbara J Henderson, 6 daughters. Musical Education: Cosmopolitan School Of Music, Chicago. Career: Worked in Chicago, Illinois with mmusicians include: Ahmad Jamal; Dinah Washington; Muddy Waters; Memphis Slim; Sara Vaughn; Leader, own group, recorded under name MJT+3; Moved to New York City; Played, toured extensively with Carmen McRae; Played with major artists including: Billie Holiday; Della Resse; Art Farmer; Ernie Wilkins; Roland Kirk; Sonny Rollins; J J Johnson; Sonny Stitt; Teddy Wilson; Billy Taylor; Charles Mingus; Illinois Jacquet; Jimmy Rowe; George Duviver; Errol Garner; Played for King and Queen of England, Palladium, London, England; Numerous teaching jobs include: Public schools, New York; State Hospital; Federal funded, high schools, New York Board of Education system; Currently playing and teaching for Music for Young Audiences; Shared in co-op group with Shaw, Perkins, Holgate, featuring Marilyn Johnson; Performances include: Americana Hotel chain, USA, Caribbean; 2 Club Med resorts (Guadaloupe, Bahamas). Recordings: 40 albums with artists including: Ahmad Jamal; MJT+3; J J Johnson; Sonny Stitt; Sonny Rollins; Lucky Thompson; Art Farmer; Carol Sloan; Carmen McRae; Freda Payne; Josh White; Sunra; Booker Ervin; Yusef Lateef; Ray Bryant; Jaki Byard; Leo Wright; Gigi Gryce; Michael O'Bryant; Richard Williams; Hylton Ruiz; Clark Terry; George Terry; George Shearing; Milt Hinton; Ben Webster; Lightning Hopkins. Honours: US Army, Special Service, Germany; One Hundred Black Businessmens' Award. Hobby: Basketball. Address: 115-21 167th Street, Jamaica, NY 11434, USA.

PERKIÖMÄKI Jari, b. 13 Apr 1961, Finland. Musician (alto saxophone, reeds, flutes). Musical Education: MA, Jazz programme, Sibelius Academy, 1989. Career: Joined Pori Big Band, aged 15; Represented Finland, EBU Big Band, 1981; Conductor, Pori Big Band; Own quartet, appearances included: Tampere Jazz Happening; Pori Jazz Festival; Debrecen Festival, Hungary; Member, Mika Mylläri; As soloist, tours, Sweden and Norway, 1987; As part of Jazz in Joiku project, including Kaamosjazz, Kalottijazz festivals, 1989; Conductor big band, Norway, on Nordic exchange programme, 1990. Compositions include: Music for 2 plays by Ilpo Tuomarila. Honours: Pekka Pöyry Award, 1985; Musician Of The Year, RYTMI magazine, 1985; Thalia Award, for music to play Exit, 1988. Address: Reiherintie 1 H 103, 00870 Helsinki, Finland.

PERKO Jukka, b. 18 Feb 1968, Huittinen, Finland. Musician (alto and soprano saxophone). Musical Education: Saxophone from 1982; Sibelius Academy, 1988. Career: Played Pori Jazz Festival, 1985; Played in Dizzy Gillespie 70th Anniversary Big Band, 1987; Tour with Dizzy Gillespie, 1988; Regular member, UMO (New Music Orchestra), 1989; Formed Jukka Perko Quartet; Finnish Jazz Federation Tour, 1990; Played with Horace Tapscott, Ultra Music Meeting workshop, Pori, 1990; Member, Perko-Pyysalo Poppoo, with Severi Pyysalo. Recording: Albums: Portrait By Heart, Jukka Perko Quartet, 1990;

Uuno Kailas, Perko-Pyysalo Poppoo, 1995. Honour: Yrjö Award, Finnish Jazz Federation, 1989. Address: Minna Canthinkatu 9 A 4, 00250 Helsinki, Finland.

PERONA-WRIGHT Hilary Mary, b. 22 Dec 1947, Godalming, Surrey, England. Musician (guitar, early musical instruments); Vocalist. m. Nigel Perona-Wright, 2 July 1975, 1 son, 1 daughter. Education: Epsom College of Art and Design (qualified with LSIA). Career: Started singing, songwriting at art college; Founder member, Spinning Wheel Folk Group, 1972-82; Founder member, Dragonsfire, 1982; Currently singer, instrumentalist with Dragonsfire, with special responsibility for group's presentation, publicity, costume. Recordings: with Dragonsfire: A Royal Array, 1989; Crossing The Borders, 1992; A Present From The Past, 1994. Membership: Musicians' Union. Hobbies: Book illustration. Current Management: Dragonsfire. Address: 9 Hillside Road, Ashtead, Surrey KT21 1RZ, England.

PERONA-WRIGHT Nigel Guy, b. 31 Aug 1953, Emsworth, Havant, Hampshire, England. Musician (flute, multi-instrument woodwind); Bass Singer; Arranger; Composer. m. Hilary Mary Perona-Wright, 2 July 1975, 1 son, 1 daughter. Education: Choirboy, Westminster Abbey, 1963-67; Whitgift School, Croydon, 1967-72. Musical Education: LRAM; LTCL; LLCM (TD); Royal Academy of Music, 1972-75; Flute with Gareth Morris; Recorder with Christopher Taylor; Singing, privately with Michael Langdon. Career: Bass in choir, Royal Hospital Chapel, Chelsea, 1972-90; Peripatetic flute teacher, East Sussex Council, 1972-80; Croydon Council, 1975-79; Conductor, Sutton Chamber choir, 1977-82; Appointed flute/recorder teacher at City of London Freemen's School, Ashtead (present position), 1979-; Also choirmaster, St George's Church, Ashtead; Member, Spinning Wheel folk group, 1970-82; Founder member, director, Dragonsfire, 1982-. Recordings: With Dragonsfire: A Royal Array; Crossing The Borders; A Present From The Past. Memberships: Royal Society of Musicians; Performing Right Society. Hobbies: Music; Collecting first day cover stamps and Ashtead pottery; Theatre. Current Management: Dragonsfire. Address: 9 Hillside Road, Ashtead, Surrey KT21 1RZ, England.

PERREAU Guy Jocelyn, b. 4 June 1950, Mauritius. m. Michol René, 18 May 1974, 1 son, 1 daughter. Career: Appeared in film Paul Et Virginie, filmed in Mauritius in late 1960s; Mimed One Sega Song; Many TV and radio appearances in both Mauritius, Reunion and also Seychelles; Newspaper appearances. Compositions: Released 2 singles, 1977; Released 7 cassettes, 1991; Released my first compact disc, 16 songs. Recordings: Released 2nd CD, 16 songs; Released 3rd CD, 1997. Honour: Award for Best Entertainer for Radio and TV, Mauritius Broadcasting Corporation, 1974. Memberships: SACEM, France; MASA, Mauritius. Hobbies: Swimming; Jogging; Walking. Address: Anse Aux Pins, Mahé Seychelles, Indian Ocean.

PERRO Juan (Santiago Auseron), b. 25 July 1954, Zaragoza, Spain. Songwriter; Singer. m. Catherine François, 17 Nov 1979. Education: Advanced studies, Philosophy, Madrid, 1972-77, Paris, 1977-78. Career: Songwriter, singer, Radio Futura, 1980-1992; Frequent travels to Cuba, seeking roots of Afro-hispanic son, 1984-; Released historic compilation of traditions Semilla del Son, 1992; Began touring as Juan Perro, with flamenco, jazz, rock musicians, 1993-94; First Juan Perro album, Havana, 1994. Recordings: (as Santiago Auseron) with Radio Futura: La Ley del Desierto, La Ley del Mar, 1984; De Un Pais En Llamas, 1985; La Cancion de Juan Perro, 1987; Escueladecalor, 1989; Veneno En La Piel, 1990; Tierra Para Bailar, 1992; as Juan Perro: Raices Al Viento (including Spanish, Cuban, British

musicians), 1995. Publications: Articles on music, art and philosophy, to newspapers and magazines. Honours: Radio Futura acclaimed as Best Spanish Rock Band of the 1980's (voted by radio stations, rock magazines). Memberships: Spanish Association of Interpreters and Authors; Member, Independent Production Office, Animal Tour. Current Management: Animal Tour. Address: Corazón de Maria, No 2, Ap 230, 28002 Madrid, Spain.

PERRONE Marc, b. 8 Oct 1951, Villejuif (Paris), France. Musician (diatonic accordion). m. Marie Odile Chantran, 27 June 1995. Musical Education: Self-taught. Career: Montparnasse, 1994; Olympia, Paris, 1995; Carnaval de Venise; Numerous foreign tours include: Africa; USA; Canada; South America; Asia; Japan, 1995; Films: La Trace, 1984; Un Dimanche à La Campagne, 1985; Maine Océan, 1986; La Vie Et Rien d'Autre, 1989; L-627, 1992. Recordings: Gabriel Valse, 1974; Perlinpinin, 1974; Rondeaux Et Autres Danses Gasconnes à Samatan, 1976; Accordéons Diatoniques, 1979; Country Dances (Les Lendemains Qui Dansent), 1980; La Forcelle, 1983; La Trace (film score), 1984; Un Dimanche à La Campagne (film score), 1985; Velverde, 1988; Paris Musette, 1990; Cinéma Mémoire, 1993; Paris Musette (Vol 2); Jacaranda, 1995. Honours: Prix de l'Academie Charles Cros for: La Forcelle. Membership: Administration Council of ADAMI. Address: 6 Avenue Parmentier, 75011 Paris, France.

PERRU Marc, b. 25 Nov 1947, Loctudy, France. Musician (guitar). Education: Baccalaureat Philosophie; English, Paris University. Musical Education: 18th Arrondisement of Paris School of Music. Career: Television appearance, Japan, 1969; Founder, Les Jerrys, Brittany, 1970; Paris debut with Cruciferius; Tour, Japan, 1970; Accompanist to Ronnie Bird, 1970; Founder, Nemo; Accompanist to Mort Shuman, stage and studio, 1970; Appeared Top Of The Pops, BBC, 1976; Accompanist to Alan Stivell; World tour; Tour with Mama Béa Tekielski, 1978-79; Met Didier Lockwood, and formed group; Appeared at Riverbop, Paris; Tour, Europe, including Montreux Festival, 1980; Accompanist to Mimi Lorca, also Shiela (studio and TV), 1981-82; Accompanist to Michelle Torr, 1983; Appeared with Quartet, Baiser Salé, Paris, 1983; Toured with Renaud, France, Canada, USSR, 1984-85; Formed blues groups (duo, trio, quartet) with harmonica player Mox Gowland, 1986-88; Debut as soloist, 1990-91; Founder, Quartet Instantané; Accompanist to Alan Simon; Tour, Restaurants du Coeur (Number 1 record, Seychelles), 1993-94. Recordings: Cruciferius, 1968; Nemo I & II, 1974; Marc And Carole, 1977; Live In Montreux, 19077; Enter, 1996. Membership: SACEM. Hobbies: Collages; Poems. Current Management: Arcodam, 1 Rue du Prieuré, (35) Chateaugiron, France. Address: 3 bis Rue Fresnel, 29900 Concarneau, France.

PERRY André, b. 12 Feb 1937, Verdun, Quebec, Canada. Record Company Executive; Record Producer. Divorced, 2 children. Career: Founder, André Perry Productions, 1968-70; Son Québec, 1970-73; Founder, President, Groupe André Perry Inc, 1974-; André Perry Video, 1980-; Founder, on board of directors, Québec Assoc Record and Entertainment Industry; Independent Record Producers Association of Canada; Founder, Le Studio (recording studios); Music coordinator, Montreal Olympic Games, 1976; Record producer for: John Lennon; Charles Aznavour; Wilson Pickett; Numerous Canadian artistes. Memberships: Audio Engineering Society; Pro-Can; Composers, Authors and Publishers Association of Canada; Canadian Recording Industry Association; Societe d'Auteurs, Compositeurs et Editeurs de Musique.

PERRY Joe, b. 10 Sept 1950, Boston, Massachusetts, USA. Musician (guitar). Career:

Lead guitarist, US rock band Aerosmith, 1970-79, 1984-; Leader, Joe Perry Project, 1980-83; Concerts include: Support to the Kinks, Mott The Hoople, 1974; Schaefer Music Festival, Central Park, 1975; Reading Rock Festival, 1977; California Jam II Festival, 1978; Texxas World Music Festival, 1978; Appearance in film: Sgt Pepper's Lonely Heart Club Band, as the Future Villain Band, 1978; California Music Festival, with Van Halen, Cheap Trick, Ted Nugent, 1979; World Series Of Rock, with Journey, Ted Nugent, Thin Lizzy, 1979 Monsters Of Rock Festival, Castle Donington, 1990. Recordings: Albums: Aerosmith: 1973; Toys In The Attic, 1975; Get Your Wings, 1975; Rocks, 1976; Draw The Lion, 1977; Greatest Hits, 1981; Done With Mirrors, 1985; Classic Live!, 1986; Permanent Vacation, 1987; Retrospective Gems, 1988; Pump, 1989; Pandora's Box, 1992; Get A Grip, 1993; with Joe Perry Project: Let The Music Do The Talking, 1980; I've Got The Rock'n'Roll Again, 1981; Once A Rocker, Always A Rocker, 1983; Singles include: Dream On; Draw The Line; Dude (Looks Like A Lady); Love In An Elevator; Janie's Got A Gun; What It Takes; Livin' On The Edge; Eat The Rich; Cryin'; Amazing. Honours include: Grammy Award, 1991; American Music Awards, 1991. Current Management: Magus Entertainment, 584 Broadway, Suite 1009, New York, NY 10012, USA.

PERRY Lee "Scratch" (Rainford Hugh Perry), b. 1936, Hanover, Jamaica. Recording Artist; Record Producer. Career: Also billed as Scratch and the Upsetter; Record scout, 1950s and 1960s; Producer and songwriter for Delroy Wilson, 1963; Debut recording, 1963-; Formed own label, Upsetter, 1968-. Recordings: Albums include: The Upsetter, 1969; Many Moods Of The Upsetter, 1970; Scratch The Upsetter Again, 1970; Prisoner Of Love - Dave Barker Meets The Upsetters, 1970; Africa's Blood, 1972; Battle Axe, 1972; Cloak & Dagger, 1972; Double Seven, 1973; Rhythm Shower, 1973; Blackboard Jungle, 1974; Kung Fu Meets The Dragon, 1974; DIP Presents The Upsetter, 1974; Revolution Dub, 1975; Scratch The Upper Ape, 1976; Jah Lion - Columbia Colly, 1976; Return Of The Super Ape, 1977; Roast Fish, Collie Weed & Corn Bread, 1978; Scratch On The Wire, 1979; Scratch And Company - Chapter 1, 1980; Return Of Pipecock Jackson, 1981; Heart Of The Ark, Volume 1, 1982; Volume 2, 1983; Megaton Dub, 1983; Megaton Dub 2, 1983; History Mystery & Prophecy, 1984; Black Ark In Dub, 1985; Battle Of Armagideon - Millionaire Liquidator, 1986; Time Boom X De Devil Dead, 1987; Satan Kicked The Bucket, 1988; Scratch Attack, 1988; Chicken Scratch, 1989; Build The Ark, 1990; Meets Bullwackie-Satan's Dub, 1990; Meets The Mad Professor, 1990; The Upsetter And The Beat, 1992; Soundz From The Hot Line, 1993; As producer includes: Hurt So Good, Susan Cadogan; Police And Thieves, Junior Marvin; Punky Reggae Party, Bob Marley & The Wailers; Also with Massive Attack; The Clash; The Heptones; Max Romeo; Junior Murvin; David Isaacs; The Untouchables; Junior Byles.

PERRY Steve, b. 22 Jan 1953, Hanford, California, USA. Vocalist. Career: Member, Alien Project; Lead singer, Journey, 1977-87; Solo artiste, 1987-; Concerts include: Regular tours, US, Japan and Europe; World Series of Rock, Cleveland, 1979; Mountain Aire Festival, 1981; Recordings: Albums: with Journey: Journey, 1975; Look Into The Future, 1976; Next, 1977; Infinity, 1978; Evolution, 1979; In The Beginning, 1979; Departure, 1980; Dream After Dream, 1980; Captured, 1981; Escape (Number 1, US), 1981; Frontiers (Number 2, US), 1983; Raised On Radio, 1986; Greatest Hits, 1988; Time 3, 1992; Solo album: Street Talk, 1984; Hit singles: Lovin' Touchin' Squeezin', 1979; Don't Stop Believin', 1981; Who's Crying Now, 1981; Open Arms (Number 2, US), 1982; Separate Ways (World's Apart), 1983; Faithfully, 1983; Send Her My Love,

1983; Only The Young, 1985; Be Good To Yourself, 1986; Tracks for film soundtracks Tron; Vision Quest; Solo singles: Oh Sherrie, 1984; Foolish Heart, 1985; Duet with Kenny Loggins: Don't Fight It, 1982; Contributor, We Are The World, USA For Africa, 1985. Honours: Bay Area Music Awards, Best Vocalist, Best Group, 1987; Numerous Platinum and gold discs. Current Management: Third Rail Entertainment. Address: 10202 Washington Blvd, Tri-Star Bldg 26, Culver City, CA 90203, USA.

PERSSON Nina, b. 1975, Malmo, Sweden. Singer. Career: Singer, The Cardigans; Concerts include: Support to Blur, UK tour, 1995. Recordings: Albums: Emmerdale; Life, 1995; Singles: Sick And Tired, 1995; Carnival, 1995. Honours: Swedish Grammy Nomination, Best Group, 1994; Slitz Magazine, Best Band, 1994. Address: Motor SE, Box 53045, S-400 14 Gothenburg, Sweden.

PESCE Serge, b. 7 September 1959, Nice, France. Musician (guitar); Composer. Musical Education: Self-taught. Career: Performed with: Alan Vitous, Barre Phillips, Miquel Montanaro, Yves Rousguisto, Patrick Vaillant, Alex Grillo, Jean-Louis Ruf; Festival appearances at: Nantes, Toulon, Confolens, Uzeste, Avignon, Parthenay, St Chartier Miskols, Szeged, Hungary. Composition: L'odore del caffe, guitar solo. Recordings: Guitare Attitude; Couples; Le Gaboulet, Tambourin - Ocora Radio France; De vous a moi, Catherine Boulanger; Musique Imaginogène, Pesce et Montanaro; Passages, SP Trio; Tenson, with Alan Vitous and Migueu Montanaro; Silence de faune, with Yves Rousguisto; Amb la doçor, Aguillera, Zagaria. Publications: Yes Bomb'ai. Memberships: SACEM; SPEDIDAM; SACD; SFA. Address: Serge Pesce, Impasse Danzi, 06700 St Laurent du Var, France.

PETEJ Peco Petar, b. 18 Mar 1949, Split, Croatia. Musician (drums, piano). m. Nada Vicic, 12 July 1973, 2 sons. Education: College degree. Musical Education: Academy for Jazz Music and Theatre Arts, Graz, Austria. Career: Delfini, Split, 1972; Played with leading jazz musicians with Hans Koller Free Sound; Member, rock band Time, 1973-79; Moved to Britain, 1974; Played with Jackie McAuley Throat, 1975; The Foundations vocalist Collin Young; Zagreb Jazz scene, TV Big Band, 1979; Returned to London blues scene, 1990; Back to Croatia, war humanitarian work, 1991; Indexi Sarajevo, 1994. Recordings: 2100 recorded minutes for TV Big Band; Recorded over 150 albums with various artists; Original music, theatre play, Hamlet And Tarzan. Honours: Numerous Pop and Rock Festival Awards, jazz fairs, Zagreb, Slovenia, Germany; Original Music Theatre Award, 1994. Memberships: Musicians' Union (UK); Croatian Music Union; Croatian Association of Orchestral Musicians. Hobbies: Cycling; Sailing. Current Management: Vladimir Mihaljek, Croatian Music Art. Address: Ivana Metelka 4, 10000 Zagreb, Croatia.

PETERS Mike, b. 25 Feb 1963, St Asaph, Wales. Musician (guitar); Vocalist. Musical Education: School Bands, Stripey. Career: Lead singer, The Alarm; 6 critically acclaimed worldwide albums; 14 Top 50 singles; Concerts include: Spirit Of '86 (audience of 26,000), UCLA, Los Angeles, worldwide broadcast on MTV. Recordings: Where Were You Hiding When The Storm Broke?; 68 Guns; A New South Wales; Rain In The Summertime. Publications: The Words And Music Of The Alarm. Memberships: Musicians' Union; PRS. Hobbies: Music; Manchester United Football Club. Current Management: Track Artist Management, UK/USA. Address: 7B Holland Road, London W14 8HJ, England.

PETERS Rob, b. 4 Oct 1954, Birmingham, England. Songwriter; Composer; Musician (drums, guitar). Education: Matthew Boulton Technical College, Birmingham; Exeter University; Open University. Career: Member, Dangerous Girls, 1978-82; Everything But The Girl, 1985-87; Ruby Blue, 1987; We'll Always Have Paris, 1990-; Boo Hewerdine, 1992-; Tour Manager, The The, 1989; Tour Manager, The Bible, 1988-94; Recordings: Albums: Nerve Ends, Dangerous Girls, 1982; Fantasy Shift, Here And Now, 1982; Broken Water, Ruby Blue, 1992; Baby The Stars Shine Bright, Everything But The Girl, 1986; Ignorance, Boo Hewerdine, 1991 (co-producer). Honours: Silver Disc, Baby The Stars Shine Bright. Memberships: Musicians' Union; PRS; MCPS; PPL; PAMRA. Hobbies: Cinema; Reading; Watching cricket. Address: PO Box 81, Birmingham B30 2LF, England.

PETERSEN Erik, b. 25 January 1953, Uppsala, Sweden. Musician; Composer; Actor. 2 sons, 1 daughter. Education: Sämus Malmö, Musikhögskolan, Stockholm. Career: Skottes Musikteater, Gävle, 1983-86; Den goda människan i Sezvan, Gävle, Drottningens Juvelsmycke, Dramaten, Den Perfekta Kyssen, Angered, Det Susar i Säven, Stockholm, Oliver Twist, Turteatern, Kärlekens himmelska helvete, Film. Recordings: Den passionerade hästen, 1986; Propeller, 1997. Membership: SKAP. Address: Byfogdevägen 10, 141 39 Huddinge, Sweden.

PETERSEN Kim Lohde, b. 9 April 1960, Copenhagen, Denmark. Singer; Musician (guitar; bass; keyboards). Musical Education: Self-taught. Career: Formed the Pin-Ups, late 70's; Solo artist, as Bravo Dalton, 1984-; Formed Birmingham 6, with former Pin-Ups partner, Mich Hill; Performances include Budapest, 1993; Support tour, Die Krupps, Copenhagen, 1994. Recordings: with The Pin-Ups: Take One, 1982; as Bravo Dalton: Korligheden Lever, 1985; 2 Silhouetter, 1989; with Birmingham 6: Israel, 1992; Contagious, 1994; Mindhallucination, 1994; Love Versus Lust, 1995; Police State, 1995; Assassinate, 1995. Hobbies: Literature; Opera; Wine. Current Management: Hard Records, C F Richsvej 122, 2th, 2000 Frediksberg, Denmark (Europe); Cleopatre Records (USA). Address: 8726 S. Sepulveda Blvd, Ste D-82, Los Angeles, CA 90045, USA.

PETERSON Oscar Emmanuel, b. 15 Aug 1925, Montreal, Quebec, Canada. Jazz Musician (piano). 3 sons, 4 daughters. Musical Education: Studied with Paul de Markey. Career: Weekly radio show; Johnny Holmes Orchestra, Canada, 1944-49; Appeared with Jazz at the Philarmonic, Carnegie Hall, 1949; Worldwide tours 1950-; Leader of own trio, with Ray Brown, Irving Ashby, 1947-; Later with Barney Kessel, Herb Ellis, Ed Thigpen, Sam Jones, Louie Hayes; Concert appearances with Ella Fitzgerald, UK, 1955; Stratford (Ontario) Shakespeare Festival; Newport Jazz Festival. Compositions: Canadiana Suite; Hymn To Freedom; Fields Of Endless Day; City Lights (with Norman McLaren); Begone Dull Care; Salute to Johann Sebastian Bach; Music for films: Big North; Silent Partner. Recordings: with Billie Holiday; Fred Astaire; Benny Carter; Count Basie; Roy Eldridge; Lester Young; Ella Fitzgerald; Joe Pass; Niels Henning Orsted Peterson; Dizzy Gillespie; Harry Edison; Clark Terry. Publications: Jazz Exercises and Pieces; Oscar Peterson New Piano Solos. Honours: Numerous, including 11 Honorary degrees, 1973-94; Edison Award, 1962; Officer, Order of Canada, 1972; Award of Merit, City of Toronto (twice); Companion, Order of Canada, 1984; American Jazz Hall of Fame, 1989; 7 Grammy Awards; 11 Grammy Nominations; Hall of Fame Awards: JUNO, 1982, Contemporary Keyboard, 1983, University of California, Berkeley, 1983; Best Jazz Pianist Award winner: Keyboard (5 times), Playboy (12 times), Downbeat (13 times), Contemporary Keyboard (5 times);

Carnegie Hall Anniversary Medal; Charlie Parker Bronze Medal; Ville de Salon de Provence Medal; Hobbies: Fly-fishing; Astronomy; Photography; Address: Regal Recordings, 2421 Hammond Road, Mississauga, Ontario L5K 1T3, Canada.

PETIT Didier, b. 8 Aug 1962, Reims, France. Musician. 1 son, 1 daughter. Musical Education: 13 years conservatory, 10 years IACP Jazz School. Career: Appeared major French festivals include: Uzest, 38th rugimant Grenoble; Mulouse; Vandoevre; Le Mans; Acier; Rive de Gier; Banlieues Bleues; Sons D'Hivers; Nevers. Recordings: Solo: Sorcier; Trois, Denis Colin Trio; Maryline Crispell Quartet, Paris, 1986. Honours: Artistic Director, record label In Situ. Memberships: SACEM; ADAMI; SPEDIDAM. Hobbies: Reading; Travel. Current Management: Self-managed. Address: 199 Rue Raymond Cosserand, 75014 Paris, France.

PETIT Philippe, b. 23 Nov 1954, Marmande, France. Jazz Musician (guitar); Composer. Musical Education: Bordeaux Conservatory of Music. Career: Tours with Philip Catherine; Tal Farlow; Barney Wilen; Miroslav Vitous; Eliot Zigmund; With own group including: Michel Graillier; Alain Jean Marie; Riccardo Del Fra; Al Levitt; Aldo Romano; J F Jenny-Clark. Compositions: Sigmanialogie 21, for jazz quartet and symphony orchestra, 1985. Recordings: Parfums, 1977; For All The Life, 1979; La Note Bleue, with Barney Wilen, 1986; Impressions Of Paris, with Miroslav Vitous, 1989; Solo: Guitar Reflections, 1991; Standards Recital, with Tal Farlow, 1993; Guitar Attitude, 1996. Membership: SACEM. Hobby: Poetry. Address: 16 Rue Jacquemont, 75017 Paris, France.

PETROV Petar. Musician (bass). Career: Member, Concurent, 1986-; numerous concerts, TV, radio appearances, Bulgaria; Recordings: Rock For Peace, 1988; Rock Festival In Mitcurin, 1989; The Black Sheep (rock collection), 1992; Something Wet (best-selling album, Bulgaria), 1994; The Best Of Bulgarian Rock, 1995. Honours: First Prizes: Top Rock Band, Vidin, 1989; Rock Ring, Sofia, 1990; Top Rock Composition: The Cavalry, 1991; Group Of The Year, The Darik Radio Countdown, 1994. Address: 40 St Stambolov Blvd, 1202 Sofia, Bulgaria.

PETROV Vadim, b. 24 May 1932, Prague, Czech Republic. Composer; Professor of Composition. m. Marta Votápková, 26 June 1954, 1 son, 2 daughters. Education: Graduate, Department of Composition, Academy of Fine Arts, Prague, Czech Republic, 1956. Career: The Giant Mountains Fairy Tales; There Are Some Limits; The Romance of Water Spirit; The Good Old Band; Sonets Chi Seled in Stone; Pax Rerum Optima; The Swans' Lament; The Nightingale and Rose; The Twelve; Johan Doctor Faust Nocturno in G; Burlesque; The Valessian Intermezzo; Song of the Night; The Ditty. Compositions: Melancholical Waltz; Tango Habanero; Scherzo Poetico; Riva Dei Pini; Romans; The Silver Serenade; Russian Evangelium; Song for Jane Eyre; The Autumn Memory; Nigh Tango; Song of Hoping and Belief. Recordings: The Maple Violin; Lucy and Miracles; Anna Snegina; Don Quigxot; Don Jean and others. Publications: Czech and Slovak Composer, 1980; Film and Time, 1983; The Little Czechoslovak Encyclopedia, 1986. Honours: Czech Television, 1997; Svobodné Slovo, Prague, 1997. Hobby: Tourism. Address: Karasovská 833/6, 160 00 Praha 6, Czech Republic.

PETROV Vassil, b. 1964, Sofia, Bulgaria. Musician; Singer. Musical Education: Graduate, Academy of Popular Music, Sofia, 1990. Career: Best-selling Bulgarian pop and jazz star; Numerous jazz, popular music festivals; Best-selling recording artist, Bulgaria; Performances: Helsinki; Oslo; Stockholm;

Belgrade; Winter Olympics, Lillehammer, Norway; Currently working with Villi Kazassyan's Big Band; Acoustic Version (Bulgaria's leading jazz group); Successful concerts with Pleven's Philharmonic Orchestra; Working on albums with composer Vassil Parmakov, lyricist Terry Kaliski; Plays and sings own compositions. Recordings: Only Bulgarian performer to release 3 albums in 1 year: The Other One; Castrol Presents: Vassil Petrov; Duet album with pianist Rumen Toskov; Petrov Sings Parmakoff, 1994. Honours: Number One Male Voice, Bulgaria, First Bulgarian National Music Awards; Orpheus: Best Male Vocalist; Best Hit of the Year; Best Album of the Year: The Other One. Address: C/o Union Media, 71 Evl Georgiev Blvd, Sofia 1142, Bulgaria.

PETROVIC Bosko, b. 18 Feb 1935, Bjelovar, Croatia. Musician (vibraphone); Composer; Record Producer; Author. Divorced, 1 son. Musical Education: Self-taught. Career: Zagreb Jazz Quartet, BP Convention; BP Club All Stars; Over 30 radio and television serials on jazz as author and MC; Over 50 albums as producer; All major jazz festivals. Recordings: With Pain I Was Born, 1965; Swinging East, 1971; Mistery Of Blues, 1974; Stabilisation Blues, with Clark Terry, 1982; Tiffany Girl, 1985; From Moscow To LA, 1986; What's New, with Joe Pass, 1989; Meet Us At The Bar, 1991; Bosko Petrovic Meets James Newton, 1993; Green Mood, 1995. Honours: Annual Award For Music, J Slavenski, 1980; Town of Zagreb Award, 1989; Croatian Grammy Award Pórin, 1995. Membership: Composers Association Of Croatia. Hobbies: Good company; Good books; Lovely wines. Current Management: Jazzette Records. Address: BP Club, Teslina 7, 41000 Zagreb, Croatia.

PETRUCIANNI Louis, b. France. Musician (contrabass). Musical Education: Studies with Chuck Israël, US, 1980. Career: Played with Barre Phillips, 1975-80; European tour with brother Michel Petrucianni; Also played with Lenny White; Trio with brother Michel; Quartet with brother Philippe. Recordings: Solo albums: Loi's Blues; The Librarian; MisterLight; with Tony Petrucianni: Nuages; with Orchestre de Jazz du Languedoc-Rousillon: Dialogues; Recordings with numerous artists including: Bernard Lubat; Lee Konitz; Alain Jean-Marie; Philippe Petit.

PETRUCIANNI Michel, b. 28 Dec 1962, Orange, France. Jazz Musician (piano). Career: Jazz pianist with Clark Terry; Charlie Haden; Freddie Hubbard; Jim Hall; Charles Lloyd. Recordings: Albums include: Live At The Village Vanguard, 1984; Note'N'Notes, 1984; Michel Plays Petrucianni, 1988; Music, 1989; Michel Petrucianni, 1991; Eddy Louiss/Michel Petrucianni, 1995. Honours: Prix Django Reinhardt, French Musician Of Year, 1982. Current Management: Jim Entertainment, USA.

PETRUCIANNI Philippe, b. France. Musician (guitar); Composer. Career: Guitarist from age 8; Member, numerous groups from duos to orchestras; Duo with brother Michel in Philadelphia, 1979; Formed first group with Jeff Gilson, 1980; Also in group with Andy Mackee; Midem '91, with brother Louis; Also played at CMCN; Vittle Guitar Festival; Guitar tutor at IMFP, 1992-. Recordings: The First.

PETTERS John David, b. 13 Apr 1953, Stratford, London, England. Traditional and Swing Jazz Musician (drums); Bandleader. m. Teresa Mellerick, 26 Apr 1980, 2 sons. Musical Education: Self-taught. Career: Formed New Dixie Syncopators, 1976; Worked with John Gill and Ronn Weatherburn, 1977; Joined Ken Sims Dixie Kings, 1979; Formed John Petters Swing Band, 1982; Opened Jazz Club, The Square, Harlow, Essex; American soloists include: Wild Bill Davison; Art Hodes; Kenny Davern; George Masso; Yank Lawson; Slim Gaillard; Al Casey; Billy Butterfield; British stars include: Georgie

Fame; Ken Colyer; Monty Sunshine; Humphrey Lyttelton; Cy Laurie; Maxine Daniels; George Chisholm; Stage shows and concerts include: Queens Of The Blues, 1986; Roarin' 20's Show, 1987; Concerts with Lonnie Donegan; George Chisholm; Yank Lawson; Legends Of American Dixieland, 1988; Swinging Down Memory Lane, 1989; Legends Of British Trad, 1991; This Joint Is Jumpin', 1993; Special Magic Of Benny Goodman, 1994; Boogie Woogie And All That Jazz, 1994; Ran Honky Tonk Train, Severn Valley Railway, 1995; Formed National Traditional Mailing List; Director, Mundesley Jazz Weekeng Festival, 1995; Drum Crazy show and workshops, 1996; Director, This Joint Is Jumping, Blackpool, 1996; Director, first Prestatyn Jazz'n'Swing Forum, 1997; This Is Jazz, festival, Torquay, 1997; Now You Has Jazz Jazz Jazz, Pontins, forthacoming. Recordings include: Live and Swinging, with Kenny Dalvern, 1985; Mixed Salad, with Wally Fawkes, 1986; Together Again, with Art Hodes and Wild Bill Davison, 1988; Swinging Down Memory Lane, with George Chisholm OBE and Maxine Daniels, 1989; Rags Boogie And Swing, with Simon Holliday, 1989; The Legends Of British Trad, 1991; Blowin' A Storm, 1991; This Joint Is Jumping, 1992; Walking With The King, 1994; Boogie Woogie And All That Jazz, with Duncan Swift, 1995; Makin' Whoopee, with John Petters Dixielanders; Swing Band, with Yank Lawson and Kenny Davern, 1996; Bechet Centenary Band, Blame It On The Blues, with Trevor Whiting, John Wurr, Martin Litson, Dave Green, 1997. Publications: History Of Jazz Drumming, Jazz Journal, 1985. Hobby: Amateur radio. Current Management: John Petters Entertainments. Address: PO Box 42, Wisbech, Cambridgeshire PE13 5RJ, England.

PETTY Tom, b. 20 Oct 1953, Gainesville, Florida, USA. Singer; Musician (guitar); Songwriter. Career: Guitarist, with local groups Sundowners; Epics; Mudcrutch, 1971-; Founder, Tom Petty and The Heartbreakers, 1975-; Member, The Traveling Wilburys, with Bob Dylan, George Harrison, Roy Orbison, Jeff Lynne, 1988-; Film appearance: FM, 1978; Regular US and international tours; Concerts include: Knebworth Festival, 1978; Musicians United For Safe Energy (MUSE), Madison Square Garden, 1979; Peace Sunday (Anti-nuclear concert), Pasadena, 1982; US Festival, San Bernardino, 1982; Live Aid, Philadelphia, 1985; Farm Aid, 1985; Tours, Australia, New Zealand, Japan, supporting Bob Dylan, 1986; Amnesty International Concert, 1986; True Confesions Tour with Bob Dylan, 1986; Rock'n'Roll Caravan tour, with Georgia Satellites, 1987; Bob Dylan 30th Anniversary Tribute, 1992. Compositions include: Never Be You, Roseanna Cash (Number 1, US Country chart), 1986. Recordings: Albums: with the Heartbreakers: Tom Petty And The Heartbreakers, 1976; You Gonna Get It!, 1978; Damn The Torpedoes, 1979; Hard Promises, 1981; Long After Dark, 1982; Southern Accents, 1985; Pack Up The Plantation, 1986; Let Me Up (I've Had Enough), 1987; Full Moon Fever, 1989; Into The Great Wide Open, 1991; Greatest Hits, 1993; Take The Highway, 1994; with The Traveling Wilburys: Traveling Wilburys, 1988; Volume 2, 1989; Volume 3, 1990; Solo: Wildflowers, 1994; Hit singles include: Breakdown, 1978; Don't Do Me Like That, 1980; Refugee, 1980; Insider, 1981; You Got Lucky, 1983; Change Of Heart, 1983; Don't Come Around Here No More, 1985; Jammin' Me, 1987; I Won't Back Down, 1989; Runnin' Down A Dream, 1989; Free Fallin', 1989; Learning To Fly, 1991; Too Good To Be True, 1992; Also featured on: Stop Draggin' My Heart Around, Stevie Nicks, 1981; Give Peace A Chance, Peace Choir, 1991; Film theme, Band Of The Hand, with Bob Dylan, 1986. Honours: Gold discs; MTV Music Video Award, Don't Come Around Here No More, 1985. Current Management: East End Management, 8209 Melrose Avenue, 2nd Floor, Los Angeles, CA 90046, USA.

PEWNY Michael, b. 11 Nov 1963, Vienna, Austria. Boogie Woogie and Blues Musician (piano). Education: Master of Business Administration. Musical Education: Private classical education on piano, started playing age 7. Career: First concert, Vienna, 1981; Several radio and television appearances, ORF, Austria; 3 US tours; Festivals include: Blues Spring Festival, Belgium, 1992; Le Nuits Jazz & Boogie Festival, Paris, 1993, 1994. Recordings: Left Hand Roller, featuring Dana Gillespie, 1990; Boogie On My Mind, featuring Sabine Ruzicka, 1992; Vienna Boogie Woogie, featuring Torsten Zwingenberger, 1994. Current Management: Bellaphon Records Company, Grundsteingasse 5, 1160 Vienna, Austria.

PHILLIPPS Martin John James, b. 2 July 1963, Wellington, New Zealand. Songwriter; Performer; Musician (guitar); Vocalist. Musical Education: Self-taught. Career: Member, bands: The Same, 1978-80; The Chills, 1980-92; Tours: Australasia; Europe; USA, late 1980s-early 1990s; Also played with The Clean (reformed); Snapper; Pop Art Toasters; April Fools; Relaunched as Martin Phillipps and The Chills, 1995-. Recordings: The Dunedin Double EP, 1982; The Lost EP, 1984; Albums: Kaleidoscope World (compilation), 1986; Brave Words, 1987; Submarine Bells, 1989; Soft Bomb, 1992; Pop Art Toasters (EP), 1994; Heavenly Pop Hits (Best of...), 1994; Album: Sunburnt, 1996. Honours: New Zealand Music Awards: Top Group, 1987; Top Group, Album, Single, Songwriter, 1990. Hobbies: Record and comic collecting; Film and video watching; The works of Gerry Anderson. Address: PO Box 705, Dunedin Central, New Zealand.

PHILLIPS Bill, b. 29 Aug 1951, Taplow, Berksshire, England. Musician (bass). Divorced, 1 daughter. Career: Many European tours with Glitter; Television: Jools Holland; MTV; The Beat; Raw Soup; Reeves and Mortimer; British tour with: Alvin Stardust; Mud; Glitter Band, 1994-95. Recordings: Denim album: Back In Denim; First single: Shampoo. Membership: Musicians' Union. Hobby: Fishing. Current Management: Hal Carter. Address: 29 Egremont Gardens, Slough, Berkshire, England.

PHILLIPS Dudley, b. 9 June 1960, Maidenhead, Berkshire, England. Musician (electric bass, bass); Composer. Musical Education: Self-taught. Career: Early experience with soul bands; World tour with Womack and Womack, Bill Withers, Mica Paris; Founder member, composer, Perfect Houseplants; Jazz festivals include: Montreux; North Sea; Montreal; Berlin; Numerous television and radio appearances; Projects include: Balanescu Quartet; London Sinfonietta; Orlando Consort; Ernestine Anderson; Ronny Jordan; Dave Valentin; Najma. Compositions include: Sextet for Vanessa Smith, for string quartet, electric bass and percussion. Recordings: 2 albums with Perfect Houseplants; 2 with Orphy Robinson; 2 with June Tabor; Also albums with: Richard Bailey; John Etheridge; Mistura; Colin Towns; Tim Whitehead; Annie Whitehead; Peter Sellars film with Andy Shepherd. Hobbies: Archbishop Mikarios; Lizards; Indian food; Funghi. Address: 64 Weston Park, London N8 9TD, England.

PHILLIPS (Holly) Michelle, b. 4 June 1944, Long Beach, California, USA. Singer; Actress. m. John Phillips, 31 Dec 1962, 2 son, 1 daughter. Musical Education: Voice lessons. Career: Member of The Mamas and the Papas; 2 US tours. Films: Dillinger; Valentino; Bloodline; Let It Ride; Television appearances include: Knots Landing (6 years). Compositions: Co-wrote California Dreamin'; Creque Alley. Recordings: If You Can Believe Your Eyes and Ears; The Mamas and the Papas; Deliver - The Mamas and the Papas. Publications: California Dreamin'. Honours: 4 Gold albums; 1 Grammy. Memberships: NARAS; ACOMPAS. Hobbies: Cooking;

Travelling. Current Management: Ambrosio Mortimer. Address: 9150 Wilshire Boulevard #175, Beverly Hills, CA 90212, USA.

PHILLIPS Jeremy Robin, b. 20 Sep 1958, South London, England. Musician (drums). 1 daughter. Education: History Degree, Polytechnic of Wales, 1981. Musical Education: Self-taught. Career: Member of Pointless Exercise, punk band; Member of Heavy Quartet; Appearances include: 11 Brecon Jazz Festivals, 2 Crawley Inside Out Festivals; Member of Diggers, including 2 Arts Council tours, 1992-93; Worked with HTV and many dance groups including Dance Wales and Paradox Shuffle. Recordings: with Heavy Quartet: Hammer And Sickle, 1986; Bomb, 1988; Poum!, 1989; Screaming, 1990; Short Stories, 1991; with Diggers: Imbolc, 1995. Publication: Rock Music, Techniques and Discography. Memberships: Musicians' Union; PRS; MCPS. Hobby: Computer games. Current Management: Kate Strudwick. Address: 15 Kincraig Street, Roath, Cardiff CF2 3HW, Wales.

PHILLIPS John Keith Andrew, b. 9 June 1961, Darlinghurst, Sydney, Australia. Composer; Producer; Musician (guitar, bass). m. Emily Humphries, 1 son, 1 daughter. Education: Latrobe University, Melbourne, Australia; Self-taught, Guitar, Bass, Programming. Career: Founding Member, Easter, 1983-85; Not Drowning, Waving, 1984-95; Major Film Scores: Body Work, 1988; Proof, 1991; Say A Little Prayer, 1993; Greenkeeping, 1993; That Eye The Sky, 1994; What I Have Written, 1995; River St, 1996; Idiot Box, 1996; The Myth of Finger Prints, 1997; Contributor: Malcolm, 1985. Recordings: Another Pond; Little Desert; Cold and the Crackle; Claim; Tabaran; Circus; Stylin Up, by Christine Anu; Telek, by Telek; World Turning, by Yothu Yindi; Contributor recordings include Archie Roach, Monique Brumby, Hugo Race, Snog, Bloom, Big Bag, Solid. Honours: Aria Award, Proof, film soundtrack CD; Aria Award, Telek, album, 1997; Aria nominations for Not Drowing, Waving. Current Management: Loud & Clear Management, PO Box 276, Albert Park, 2306, Australia.

PHILLIPS Josh, b. 12 Dec 1962. Musician (keyboards). Musical Education: Grade 7 piano, Guildhall School of Music syllabus, 1977. Career: Turned professional, 1982; Tours: Diamond Head, 1983-85; Heatwave, world tour, 1986-88; Big Country, Russia, Estonia, Europe, UK, 1988-90; Midge Ure, Europe, UK, 1991, 1992; Procul Harum, Europe, 1993-94; Steve Roux Band, UK and Europe, 1993-94; Moody Marsden Band, Europe, 1994-95; Gary Brooker All-Star Band Annual Charity Christmas Show, 1990-; Videos: Diamond Head Live; Big Country Live-Russia; Big Country East Berlin; Cliff Richard; Midge Ure; Heatwave; Moody Marsden; Procul Harum; Helen Hofner; Television appearances include: Wogan; Top of the Pops; Wired; Meltdown; Smash Hits Awards; Telethon with Sam Brown, Midge Ure; Various European pop and music shows; Currently recording with Mark Brzezicki, Tony Butler, Steve Roux. Compositions: Incidental television music; Meltdown ITV Rock Music Show; Comment; Music for various commercials. Recordings: Albums with Diamond Head; Heatwave; Big Country; Midge Ure; Pete Townshend; Tim Renwick; Bernie Marsden; Moody Marsden Band; The Hamsters. Current Management: Judy Totton Publicity. Address: EBC House, 1A Ranelagh Gardens, London SW6 3PA, England.

PHILLIPS P J, b. 24 July 1964, London, England. Musician (bass guitar); Vocalist. Musical Education: Self-taught. Career: Worldwide tours include: World tour with Nina Hagen, 1980; Television and radio apperances include: with Taylor Dayne: This Morning, Granada TV; Wogan, BBC TV, 1990; with Curtis Stigers: Wogan; Top Of The Pops, BBC TV (3 times), 1992; with Michael Ball: Top Of The Pops, 1992; with Nina Hagen:

Chameleon Varieté TV show, 1993; with Tom Jones: Top Of The Pops, BBC TV, 1994; Vetton Bass, ZDF TV, 1995; Currently working with Take That. Memberships: Equity; Musicians' Union; PRS; BASCA. Current Agent: Debbie Haxton, The Session Connection. Address: 110/112 Disraeli Road, London SW15 2DX, England.

PHILLIPS Roy, b. 5 May 1941, Parkstone, Poole, England. Musician (keyboards); Singer. Musical Education: Piano lessons (5-10 years). Career: Had own band (trio): The Peddlars, 15 years; Worked Las Vegas, 15 seasons; 12 world tours; Regular television and radio worldwide; Ed Sullivan Show; BBC, ATV (England regularly). Compositions: Wrote complete album: Suite London; Heavy On The Light Side. Recordings: 15 albums; 83 singles; 2 Number 1 hits: Birth; Girlie. Honours: No 1 Keyboards, England, 1971, 1972. Memberships: PRS; Screen Writers Guild; Songwriters Guild. Hobbies: Art; Golf. Current Management: Self-managed. Address: PO Box 10, Paihia, Bay Of Islands, New Zealand.

PHILLIPS Shawn, b. 2 Mar 1943, Fort Worth, Texas, USA. Musician (guitar, keyboards, sitar). 1 daughter. Career: Film appearance, Run With The Wind; Lead singer, Broadway musical, Jesus Christ Superstar; Tours include: South Africa; Quebec; Television includes: 4 appearances Midnight Special, CBS-TV; In Concert, NBC-TV. Compositions include: Co-writer, Sunshine Superman album, with Donovan. Recordings: Albums: Contribution, 1970; Second Contribution, 1971; Collaboration, 1972; Faces, 1973; Furthermore, 1974; Bright White, 1975; Do You Wonder, 1976; Rumplestiltskin's Resolve, 1977; Spaced, 1978; Transcendence, 1980; Best of Shawn Phillips, 1986; Beyond Here Be Dragons, 1988; The Truth If It Kills, 1994; Another Contribution, 1995. Honours: Yamaha World Popular Song Festival; 3 Platinum discs for album Second Contribution. Memberships: SOCAN; BMI. Hobby: Firefighter. Current Mnaagement: Arlo Henning, Lodestone Management. Address: 10920 Irwin Avenue South, Bloomington, MN 55437, USA.

PHILLIPS Steve (Nicholas Stephen), b. 18 Feb 1948, London, England. Singer; Musician (guitar). Partner, Mary Catherine Farrell, 2 daughters. Musical Education: Self-taught. Career: Semi-professional musician, 1961-86; Professional solo artist, 1986-; Also duo with Brendan Croker; Also, member, Notting Hillbillies, 1990. Recordings: The Best of Steve Phillips, 1987; Steel Rail Blues, 1989; with Notting Hillbillies: Missing Presumed Having A Good Time, 1990; Been A Long Time Gone, 1995. Hobby: Landscape painting. Current Management: NEM (UK), Priory House, 55 Lawe Road, South Shields, Tyne & Wear NE33 2AL, England.

PHIPPEN Peter, b. 24 April 1956. Ethnic Flutes from around the world. m. Julie Marie Repaal Phippen, 12 August 1979, 1 son, 1 daughter. Education: Selftaught Musician. Career: Winter Olympics, Lillehammer, Norway, 1994; International Touring, Germany, Austria, Norway, Slovenia; US National Public Radio by Echos-Syndicated, 1965; Radio stations in USA, Wisconsin Public Radio. Compositions: Book of Dreams, album, 1996; Feeding To The Fire; Oh No. Recordings: Book of Dreams; Feed Me To the Fire; In the Red; Oh No. Honours: Eau Claire; Wisconsin Regional Arts Council, USA. Hobbies: Researching folklore of ethnic flutes. Current Management: Mark Alan, PO Box 21323, St Paul, MN 55121, USA. Address: 417 1/2 McDonough, Eau Claire, WI, USA.

PICKERING Mike, b. Manchester, England. Musician (saxophone); Vocalist; Composer; Disc Jockey. Career: Disc Jockey, Manchester clubs; Singer, saxophonist, Quando Quango; Founder member, musician, songwriter, UK dance group M People, 1991-; Major concerts include:

Glastonbury Festival, 1994. Recordings: Albums: Northern Soul, 1992; Elegant Slumming, 1993; Bizarre Fruit, 1994; Bizarre Fruit II, 1995; Hit singles: How Can I Love You More, 1991; One Night In Heaven, 1993; Movin' On Up, 1993; Sight For Sore Eyes, 1994; Itchycoo Park, 1995; Search For The Hero, 1995; Open Your Heart, 1995; Love Rendezvous, 1995. Honours: Mercury Prize, Best Album, Elegant Slumming, 1994; BRIT Awards, Best Dance Act, 1994, 1995. Current Management: RD World Wide Management. Address: 37 Limerston Street, London SW10 0BQ, England.

PICKERING Phil, b. 27 June 1960, Pembury, Kent, England. Musician (bass guitar, didgeridoo, synthesiser). 3 sons, 1 daughter. Musical Education: Guitar tuition as teenager. Career: Webcore; Goat; Tribal Drift; Fun-Da-Mental; Lights In A Fat City; Zuvuya. Recordings include: Vane: Glamourous Boys, 1981; 2 Webcore albums: Webcore, 1987; Webcore Webcore, 1988; 1 Goat album: Goat; Tribal Drift: Like This!, 1992; Medicine Hat, 1992; 2 Zuvuya albums with Terence McKenna: DMT, 1994; Shamania, 1994; Zuvuya: The Goat Faced Girl, 1994; Driving The Monkey Insane, 1994; Moose Jaw, 1994; Away The Crow Road, 1994; The Trance End Of Dreaming, 1994; Turn Around, 1994; 3rd Zuvuya album, 1997. Memberships: PRS; Musicians' Union. Hobbies: Alien Abductions. Current Management: M.E.L.T Music, Lescrow Farm, Fowey, Cornwall PL23 1JS. Address: Delerium Records, PO Box 1288, Gerrards Cross, Bucks SL9 9YB, England.

PICKETT Wilson, b. 18 Mar 1941, Prattville, Alabama, USA. Singer; Musician (guitar). Career: Gospel singer; Lead singer, the Falcons, 1961; Solo artist, 1963-; Recent appearances include: Pori Jazz, Finland, 1995. Recordings: Albums: In The Midnight Hour, 1965; The Exciting Wilson Pickett, 1967; The Sound Of Wilson Pickett, 1967; The Best Of Wilson Pickett, 1967; I'm In Love, 1968; The Midnight Mover, 1968; Hey Jude, 1969; Wilson Pickett In Philadelphia, 1970; The Best Of Wilson Pickett Vol. II, 1971; Mr Magic Man, 1973; Pickett In The Pockett, 1973; A Funky Situation, 1978; I Want You, 1979; The Right Track, 1981; American Soul Man, 1988; Hit singles include: In The Midnight Hour, 1965; Don't Fight It, 1965; 634-5789, 1966; Land Of 1,000 Dances, 1966; Mustang Sally, 1966; Everybody Needs Somebody To Love, 1967; I Found A Love, 1967; Funky Broadway, 1967; Stag-O-Lee, 1967; She's Lookin' Good, 1968; I'm A Midnight Mover, 1968; Hey Jude, 1969; Sugar Sugar, 1970; (Get Me Back On Time) Engine Number Nine, 1970; Don't Let The Green Grass Fool You, 1971; Don't Knock My Love, 1971. Honours: Inducted into Rock And Roll Hall of Fame, 1991. Current Management: Talent Source, 1560 Broadway, Suite 1308, New York, NY 10036, USA.

PICKFORD Andrew Cliffe, b. 22 Oct 1965, Kegworth, Nottinghamshire, England. Musician (electronic keyboards). Musical Education: Self-taught. Career: Solo artist, Electronic music; Concerts include: Derby Cathedral, Derby Assembly Rooms and Guildhall (several times); Radio and television: Interviews and broadcasts on BBC local radio; BBC Radio 1 including John Peel show; Formed Electronic Music and Musicians Association. Recordings: Albums: Replicant, 1993; Terraformer, 1994; Maelstrom, 1995 (all Number 1, Electronic music charts); 2 EP's; Dystopia, 1996; Works Vol 1, Works Vol 2 (both live at Derby), 1997. Memberships: PRS; Past Secretary, EMMA. Hobbies: Esoteric philosophy; Gardening. Current Management: David Shoesmith, Centaur Discs Ltd, 40-42 Brantwood Avenue, Dundee DD3 6EW, Scotland. Address: The Bryans, 89 Dundee Road, West Ferry, Dundee DD5 3LZ, Scotland.

PIERSON Kate, b. 27 Apr 1948, Weehawken, New Jersey, USA. Singer; Musician (organ).

Career: Singer, musician, B-52's, 1976-. Recordings: Albums: B-52's, 1979; Wild Planet, 1980; Mesopotamia, 1982; Whammy!, 1983; Bouncing Off The Satellites, 1986; Cosmic Thing, 1989; Best Of The B-52's - Dance This Mess Around, 1990; Good Stuff, 1992; Singles include: Rock Lobster, 1980; Love Shack, 1989. Current Management: Direct Management Group. Address: Suite G, 947 N La Cienga Blvd, Los Angeles, CA 90069, USA.

PILC Jean-Michel, b. 19 Oct 1960, Paris, France. Musician (piano, keyboards); Composer. m. Musical Education: Self-taught. Career: Played in numerous concerts, festivals, tours to over 40 countries including Africa, Asia, Europe; Sideman with artists including: Roy Haynes Quartet; Jean Toussaint (including Royal Festival Hall, London); Daniel Humair and Jean-François Jenny-Clarke; Michel Portal; Martial Solal; Aldo Romano; André Ceccarelli; Christian Escoude; Rick Margitza; Peter King; George Brown; Dave Liebman; Greg Hutchinson; Harry Belafonte; Leader with: Enrico Rava (trumpet), Marc Ducret (guitar), Mark Mondesir (drums); Composer, leader, arranger playing solo, in duo, trio and big band; Recent European tour, Germany, Switzerland, France; Visit to New York City, 1995. Compositions: Music played throughout Europe, covered by many other artists; Many film scores. Recordings: Electrochoc, 1987; Funambule, 1989; Big One, 1993; For Edith Piaf And Charles Trenet, with Eric Le Lann/Martial Solal, 1989; Prosodie, Aldo Romano, 1995; Life I Want, Jean Toussaint, 1995; From The Heart, André Ceccarelli, 1995; Other recordings with: Elizabeth Kontomanou; Eric Le Lann; J-Loup Longnon. Hobbies: Jogging; Trekking. Current Management: John Waxman Associates, 302 West 12th Street, Suite 10B, New York, NY 10014, USA. Address: 262 Bergen Street #2R, Brooklyn, NY11217, USA.

PILKINGTON Stephen Roy, b. 5 Oct 1946, Bakewell, Derbyshire, England. Music Director; Musician (piano, organ). m. Patricia Anne Wall, 18 July 1970, 1 son, 1 daughter. Musical Education: Royal Manchester College of Music, GRSM; ARMCM; LRAM; ARCO. Career: Music Director, many top star shows including: Royal Shows for Princess Royal, Princess Margaret, 1975-; Music Director for television series; Keyboard backing for television signature tunes and plays; Pianist for Welsh musical programmes. Recordings: Romance, solo piano ballads and orchestra accompaniment; Stephen Pilkington Organ Collection; Backing many Welsh recordings. Membership: Musicians' Union. Hobby: Watching motor racing. Address: Glandwr Onest, Blaenffos, Boncath, Pembrokeshire SA37 0JB, Wales.

PINE Courtney, b. 18 Mar 1964, London, England. Jazz Musician (saxophone). 1 son, 3 daughters. Career: International tours, with own reggae and acoustic jazz bands; Trio (with Cameron Pierre, Talvin Singh) opened for Elton John and Ray Cooper, The Zenith, Paris and Royal Albert Hall, London, European Tour, 1994; Teacher's Jazz European tour, 1996; Support to Cassandra Wilson, US and Canada, 1996; Tours, Japan, South Africa and UK, 1996; Festivals in Europe, Japan, Thailand, 1996; Television appearances; Regular guest, Later With Jools Holland; Black Christmas, Channel 4; The White Room, 1996; Featured Artist on BBC's Perfect Day recording. Recordings include: Albums: Journey To The Urge Within, 1987; Destiny's Song, 1988; The Vision's Tale, 1989; Closer To Home, 1990; Within The Realms Of Our Dreams; To The Eyes Of Creation; Modern Day Jazz Stories', 1996; Underground, 1997; Another Story, 1998; Featured guest on: Wandering Spirit, Mick Jagger; Jazzmatazz, Guru; Jazzmatazz II - The New Reality, Guru; Summertime, track on The Glory of Gershwin (Larry Adler tribute album). Honours: Mercury Music Prize, one of Albums of the Year, 1996; Best Jazz Act, MOBO, 1996, 1997. Current Management: c/o Nikki Neave,

Tickety-Boo, 160 Munster Road, London SW6 5RA, England.

PINKSTON Steven Ray, b. 12 Dec 1960, Columbus, Ohio, USA. Record Producer; Engineer; Songwriter. m. Angie Akin, 30 Oct 1993. Education: Belmont University, Nashville, Tennessee. Career: Concert tours: Linda Ronstadt; Steven Curtis Chapman; Shelley West; The Commodores; Geoff Moore and The Distance; ABC; Amy Grant. Compositions: Cleansing Rain, Kelli Reisen (Number 3, CCM hit). 50 albums include: 4Him; Commissioned; Angelo and Veronica; Brian White; J J Cale; Graham Maw; Videos: 4Him; Commissioned; Harvest; Brian White; Wellington Boone; Grace Lazenby; Becky Tirabassi. Memberships: GMA; NARAS. Address: PO Box 40784, Nashville, TN 37204, USA.

PIRARD Jacques, b. 14 November 1949, Belgium. Musician. m. Garsou Micheline, 26 August 1983, 2 sons. Education: Conservatoire de Musique, Belgium, 9 years; Bass Lessons with Jean-Louis Rassinfosse, Belgium. Career: One Man Show, 1970-86; Double Bass Player in Jazz and Folk Music, 1987-. Hobbies: Nature; Music. Address: Coingsoux 1, 4834 Goe, Belgium.

PITCH Harry, b. 9 May 1925, Hull, Yorkshire, England. Musician (harmonica, trumpet). m. Ruby, 10 June 1946, 1 son, 1 daughter. Musical Education: Self-taught. Career: Session musician; Featured soloist at Sadlers Wells; Royal Festival Hall, with Hans Werner Henze; Barbican Centre with Carl Davis; Television includes: Playing for Last Of Summer Wine, 25 years, Many radio series; Films with: Ron Goodwin; Laurie Johnson; James Horner; Geoff Love; One of the only harmonica players to move successfully from classical to jazz music; Many jazz broadcasts with various groups include Rhythm & Reeds, with Jack Emblow. Compositions: Recorded library music. Recordings: Hits with various artists, throughout 1960s-1980s; Solo albums. Membership: Musicians' Union (Gold Card member). Hobby: Boating. Address: Hunters Moon, Islet Road, Maidenhead, Berks SL6 8HT, England.

PITCHFORD Dean, b. 29 July 1951, Honolulu, Hawaii, USA. Songwriter; Screenwriter; Director. Education: Yale University, 1972. Career: Actor, singer: Godspell, 1971-72; Pippin, 1972-75; The Umbrellas of Cherbourg, 1978; Songwriter, screenwriter, films: Fame, 1980; Footloose, 1984; Sing, 1988; Chances Are, 1989. Compositions: Songs: Fame; Footloose; Let's Hear It For The Boy; You Should Hear How She Talks About You; After All; Almost Paradise; Holding Out For A Hero; All The Man That I Need. Honours: Academy Award, Fame; Golden Globe Award, Fame; 3 Academy Award Nominations. Memberships: BMI; NAS; NARAS. Hobby: Yoga. Current Management: Bob Hohman, c/o Richland, Wunsch, Hohman. Address: 9220 Sunset Boulevard #311, Los Angeles, CA 90069, USA.

PITICCO Steve, b. 6 July 1961, Toronto, Ontario, Canada. Musician (lead guitar). m. Laurie Laporte, 25 Apr 1983, 1 son, 1 daughter. Musical Education: Self-taught, started country music age 15, full time, Grade 9. Career: Performs professionally with Fender Telecaster guitars; Formed own band, South Mountain, 1989; Toured with: Sweethearts of The Rodeo; Marty Stuart; Conway Twitty; Charlie Pride; Played shows supporting: Vince Gill; George Jones; Johnny Cash; Ricky Skaggs; Mid-Canada Television network, with South Mountain, 4 years; Picker, various bands, including South Mountain, on Canadian Country Music Awards' Annual Telecast, 1984-94; Tours in Canada and Europe, 1995. Recordings: 8 albums with South Mountain; Session player on recordings by: Patricia Conroy; Tracy Prescott; Don Neilson. Honours: 7 CCMA Instrumentalist of Year Awards, 1985-94; CCMA

Rising Star Awards, 1991; CCMA Guitar Player Of The Year, 1990-93; Hobbies: Computers; Practising golf shots from own backyard. Current Management: Cathy Faint Entertainment Inc, 430 Signet Drive, Suite C, North York, Ontario M9L 2T6, Canada. Address: Box 64, Lot 7, County Road 1, South Mountain, Ontario K0E 1W0, Canada.

PITMAN Toby John, b. 27 Sep 1971, Crawley, West Sussex, England. Musician (guitar). Musical Education: Graduate Diploma, Guitar Institute of Technology, USA. Career: Appearances on television and radio include: Capital Radio programme, How Do They Do That, BBC, Glam Metal Detectives; Current member, funk/rock band Radio Jim. Recording: Rock Guitar Album. Membership: Musicians' Union. Hobbies: Playing guitar; Live bands; Music; Cooking. Address: c/o E L Seeberg, Acremead, Framfield Road, Blackboys, East Sussex TN22 5LR, England.

PITNEY Gene, b. 17 Feb 1941, Hartford, Connecticut, USA. Singer; Songwriter. Career: Recording artiste, 1959-; Recorded albums in Itlian and Spanish; Regular international tours. Compositions: Songs include: Loneliness, The Kalin Twins; Today's Teardrops, Roy Orbison; Rubber Ball, Bobby Vee; Hello Mary Lou, Ricky Nelson; He's A Rebel, The Crystals; Nessuno Mi Puo Guidicare, second place at San Remo Song Festival, 1966. Recordings: Albums: The Many Sides Of Gene Pitney, 1962; Only Love Can Break A Heart, 1963; Pitney Sings Just For You, 1963; Blue Gene, 1964; Gene Pitney Meets The Fair Young Ladies Of Folkland, 1964; I'm Gonna Be Strong, 1965; George Jones And Gene Pitney, 1965; The Great Songs Of Our Time, 1965; Nobody Needs Your Love, 1966; Young Warm And Wonderful, 1967; Just One Smile, 1967; Pitney Today, 1968; Pitney '75, 1975; Walkin' In The Sun, 1979; Various compilations; Singles include: I Wanna Love My Life Away, 1961; Town Without Pity; The Man Who Shot Liberty Valance; Twenty Four Hours From Tulsa; That Girl Belongs To Yesterday; I'm Gonna Be Strong, 1964; I Must Be Seeing Things, 1965; Looking Through The Eyes Of Love, 1965; Princess In Rags, 1965; Backstage, 1966; Nobody Needs Your Love, 1966; Just One Smile, 1966; Something's Gotten Hold Of My Heart, 1967; Somewhere In The Country; Maria Elena, 1969; Shady Lady, 1970; Blue Angel, 1974; Something's Gotten Hold Of My Heart, with Marc Almond, 1988. Current Management: Duryea Entertainment, 54 Danbury Road, Suite 367, Ridgefield, CT 06877, USA.

PIZZARELLI John "Bucky", b. 9 Jan 1926, USA. Jazz Musician (guitar). m. Ruth Litchult Pizzarelli, 9 Jan 1954, 2 sons, 2 daughters. Musical Education: Studied with Peter and Robert Domenick. Career: Member, Vaughn Monroe Orchestra; White House concerts with Benny Goodman, Frank Sinatra; Staff musician with NBC; ABC; Skitch Henderson, Doc Severinson; Mitch Miller; Concerts and tours with artistes including: George Barnes and Les Paul; Stéphane Grappelli; Skitch Henderson; Bobby Short; Benny Goodman; Zoot Sims; Peter Appleyard; Barney Kessel and Charlie Byrd; Howard Alden; Festivals include: Umbria Jazz Festival; Newport Jazz Festival; Melon Jazz; Dick Gibson's Jazz Parties throughout US; Faculty Member Emeritus, William Paterson College, Wayne, New Jersey. Recordings: Numerous albums include: Green Guitar Blues; Buck Plays Bix; Bucky's Bunch; Cafe Pierre Trio; Love Songs; Solo Flight; with Stéphane Grappelli: All Stars, 1978; Also recorded with: George Barnes; Zoot Sims; Eddie Daniels; Benny Goodman; Joe Venuti.

PLA Roberto Enrique, b. Barranquilla, Columbia. Musician (percussion, timbales, bongos, congas, drums); Bandleader. m. Dominique Roome, 3 Oct 1992. Musical Education; Studied percussion with Pompelio

Rodriguez; National University in Bogota, 1964-. Career: Session musician with artists including Los Ocho De Columbia; Drummer with Orquesto Lucho Bermudez, 1968-78; Tours include Latin America and US; Weekly television appearances, Columbian television; Moved to New York, 1978; Salsa session percussionist, bands including Orquesta La Inspiracion; Moved to London, 1979; Member, jazz-fusion band Cayenne; Founder member, bands including Valdez; Sondido De Londres (co-founder); Roberto Pla Latin Ensemble (12-piece all-star band); Numerous European festivals and television appearances, 1988; Concerts include: Boney M, World tour, 1982; Joe Strummer; Gonzalez, World tour; Arrow, US tour; Radio Futura; Slim Gaillard, Japan and Far East tour, 1987; Alfredo Rodriguez, North African tour; Sonny Southon, Europe, US tours, 1991-92; US3, Europe, Far East tours, 1993; Film apperances include: I Hired A Contract Killer (with Joe Strummer); Eat The Rich (with Motörhead). Recordings: Numerous albums include: Cumbia Dominique, 1990; Recordings with artists including: Kate Bush; M People. Current Management: Salsa Boogie Productions. Address: 153 Shrewsbury Road, London E7 8QA, England.

PLANKA Pavel, b. 29 May 1962, Pilsn, Czech Republic. Musician. Education: Selftaught Drums; Public School of Arts; Prague Conservatoire. Career: Performances with Several Top Czech Ensembles, Jazz, Rock, Pop, Classical, Folk; Support of Rolling Stones, Voodoo Lounge; Numerous Orchestral Music. Recordings: Nerez, Ke zdi, 1990; Tutu, Mr Jazz Man, 1991; Zuzana Navarova, Caribe, 1992; Vitacit, Mate se hnout; Hot line, Still Callin', 1993; Merinsky-Lewitova, Sefardske pisne; Dan Barta Alice, Usta hromu, 1994; Lucie, Cerny kocky mokry zaby; Janek Ledecky, Jenom tak; Michal Pavlicek, Na kloboucku II, 1995; Tresnak-Korman-Koller, Kolaz; Roman Dragoun, Stin my krve; Veleband All Stars Big-Band, 1996; Jarek Nohavica, Divne stoleti; Musical, Hair, 1997. Honour: Prize, Authors Competition, Porta, 1986. Hobbies: Water skiing; Mountain biking; Riding water scooters; Diving. Address: Nahorni 507/3, 182 00 Prague 8, Czech Republic.

PLANT Robert Anthony, b. 20 Aug 1948, West Bromwich, Warwickshire, England. Singer; Songwriter. m. Maureen, 1 son (deceased), 1 daughter. Career: Member, various R&B groups, including Listen; Band Of Joy; Lead singer, UK heavy rock group Led Zeppelin (formerly the New Yardbirds), 1968-80; Appearances include: Carnegie Hall, 1969; Royal Albert Hall, 1969, 1971; Madison Square Gardens, 1970; Knebworth Festival, 1979; Sell-out tours, concerts, worldwide; Rock for Kampuchea concert, London, 1979; Reunion for Live Aid, Philadelphia, 1985; Formed Led Zeppelin's own label Swan Song, 1974; Film: The Song Remains The Same, 1976; Solo artiste, 1980-; Member, The Honeydrippers (with Jimmy Page, Nile Rodgers, Jeff Beck), 1984-85; Currently member of Page/Plant, with Jimmy Page (former Led Zeppelin guitarist), 1994-; Recordings: Albums with Led Zeppelin (over 60 million copies of albums sold): Led Zeppelin I, 1969; Led Zeppelin II, 1969; Led Zeppelin III, 1970; Led Zeppelin IV, 1971; Houses Of The Holy, 1973; Physical Graffiti, 1975; Presence, 1976; The Song Remains The Same, 1976; In Through The Out Door, 1979; Coda, 1983; Remasters, 1993; Solo albums: Pictures At Eleven, 1982; The Principle Of Moments, 1983; Solo albums: Now and Zen, 1988; Manic Nirvana, 1990; with the Honeydrippers: The Honeydrippers Vol 1, 1984; with Page/Plant: No Quarter, 1994; Walking Into Clarksdale, 1998; Contributor: Outrider, Jimmy Page, 1988; Last Temptation Of Elvis (compilation), 1990. Honours include: Ivor Novello Awards, Outstanding Contribution To British Music, 1977; Silver Clef Award, Nordoff-Robbins Music Therapy Foundation, 1990; Q Merit Award (with Led Zeppelin), 1992. Current Management:

Trinifold Management, 22 Harley House, Marylebone Road, London NW1 4PR, England.

PLATT Ted (Edward Stephen Platt), b. 7 Oct 1945, West Yorkshire, England. Musician (guitar, bass); Vocalist; Arranger. 1 daughter. Musical Education: Music College, 1 year; Piano and Guitar Lessons; Arranging Techniques. Career: Tour with Jet Harris, 1963; Contrasts, 1965; Residencies in London, 1966; Resident guitarist and vocalist, Batley Variety Club, 1972-; Musical Director for Freddie Starr for 10 years and for Gene Pitney for 3 years; Rock and Roll Singer with tours of Australia. Recordings: Can't Get You Off Of My Mind; Call Me; Ma He's Making Eyes At Me, by Lena Zavaroni. Memberships: PRS; MCPS; BASCA; Songwriters' Guild. Hobbies: Painting; Reading; Metaphysics; Theology. Current Management: KSP (Leisure) Associates. Address: 19 Hyrst Garth, Batley, West Yorkshire WF1Y 7AD, England.

PLATT Tony, b. 21 January 1952, Yorkshire, England. Record Producer; Engineer. m. Jacqueline, 30 April 1974, 1 son, 1 daughter. Career: Trident Studios, London, England; Assistant Engineer, Island Studios, Basing Street, 1969-70; Recording Engineer for Bob Marley, Toots, Free, etc; Freelance, 1975-; Mutt Lange's Engineer on Highway to Hell, Backin Black, ACDC and Foreigner 4. Recordings include: Producer, Engineer, Marche ou Creve, Trust, 1981; Producer, Engineer, Shock Tactics, Samson, 1981; Producer, Engineer, One Vice at a Time, Krokus, 1982; Producer, Engineer, Another Perfect Day, Motorhead, 1983; Engineer, Co-Producer, Flick of the Switch, AC/DC, 1983; Remix, Producer, All Men Play on Ten, Manowar, 1984; Producer, Engineer, We Want Moore, Gary Moore, 1984; Producer, Engineer, Equator, Uriah Heep, 1984-85; Producer, Engineer, Brave the Storm, Shy, 1985; Producer, Engineer, Nightless City, VowWow, 1985; Producer, Engineer, Live & Dangerous, Krokus, 1986; Producer, Engineer, The Doctor, Cheap Trick, 1986; Producer, Engineer, Wired, Jeff Paris, 1986-87; Producer, BBC-Late Night in Concert, The Cult, 1987; Producer, Engineer, Cold Lake, Celtic Frost, 1988; Producer, Engineer, Love and War, Lillian Axe, 1988-89; Co-Producer, Engineer, Never Turn Your Back on the Blues, Moody Marsden Band, 1991; Producer, Engineer, The Ritual, Testament, 1992; Co-Producer, Engineer, Live in Hell, Moody Marsden Band, 1994; Co-Producer, Green and Blues, Bernie Marsden, 1995; Producer, Engineer, Eternity, Anathema, 1996; Producer, Engineer, Ten, 1997; Producer, Engineer, Mau Mau, 1997; Producer, Mixer, Huge Baby, 1997-98. Publications: Contributer, Music Industry Management and Promotion, by Chris Kemp. Memberships: Re-Pro; PAMRA. Hobbies: Walking; Motor Racing. Current Management: NDM (UK), 2 Bloomsbury Street, London WC1B 3ST, England, and, CMI (USA), 201 E 87th Street, New York, 10128, USA. Address: Inch House, Lower Street, Pury End, Towcester, Northants, NN12 7NS, England.

PLAYFORD Robert, b. 25 Mar 1968, Ware, Hertfordshire, England. Record Producer; Engineer; Programmer; Record Company Executive. Musical Education: Self-taught. Career: Formed Moving Shadow Music, 1990, pioneering and establishing Jungle music; Concerts: Orlando, Los Angeles, New York, 1992; Paris, 1994; Tokyo, US tour, Glastonbury Festival, 1995; Television and radio apperances: The Word; Interviews on Radio 1 (UK); Mars FM (Los Angeles); Radio Nova (Paris). Recordings include: Timeless, Metalheads; New Metalheads album for release 1995; Remixes: Hand Of The Dead Body, Ice-Cube and Scarface; Crazy Bald Heads, Sly and Robbie; Bee Charmer, Ingrid Schroeder. Membership: Musicians' Union. Hobbies: Work; Racing driving; Net-surfing. Address: 55 Conifer Walk, Stevenage, Herts SG2 7QS, England.

PLIERS Everton Banner, b. 1965, Kingston, Jamaica. Disc Jockey; Recording Artist. Career: Recording with Black Scorpio; Recorded for numerous lables including: Pickout; Pioneer Musik; Jammys, Harry J and Studio One; Partner, in duo Chaka Demus and Pliers, 1991-; Recordings: Albums: with Chaka Demus and Pliers: Gal Wine, 1992; Ruff This Year, 1992; Chaka Demus and Pliers, 1992; Tease Me, 1993. Address: c/o Free World Music Inc, 230 12th Street, Suite 117, Miami Beach, FL 33139-4603, USA.

PLIMLEY Paul, b. 16 March 1953, Vancouver, Canada. Composer; Improviser; Pianist; Electronic Music. m. Marlene Madison Plimley, 6 June 1990. Education: Grade Ten Piano, Toronto Conservatory, 1971; Studied with Cecil Taylor, 1979, 1980; Further master classes, Berlin, 1988; Played with finest improvisors in world. Career: 30 min documentary, own music, piano/jazz showcase, Bravo TV; Performances broadcast on French, German and American TV; Numerous radio broadcasts in North America and Europe and Japan; Two residencies, 1989, Banff Centre of the Arts; Two residencies, Western Front Lodge, 1990, 1996; Several European tours. Compositions: Even Daylight; Born Again Needle Dancers; Day and Night Visions of Cassiopeia; Hidden Shades; Parachute 4; Pages From the Diary of Dreams. Recordings: Kaleidoscopes, 1992; Sweet Freedom, Now What, 1994; Everything in Stages, 1995; When Silence Pulls, 1990; Density of the Lovestruck Demons, 1994; Sensology, 1995; Legba Crossing, 1988. Publications: Boogie, Pete and The Senator, Canadian Musicians in Jazz, 1988; Coda Magazine, 1994 Feature article; Adobe Magazine, Best of Show Award, 1996. Honours: Winner, Freddie Stone Award, 1995 for Innovation and Integrity; Silver Prize, CD ROM, New Media Invision, 1996. Memberships: New Orchestra Workshop, Co-Founder, 1977; SOCAN, 1979; National Geographic Society. Hobbies: Writing poetry & comedy; Lifelong student of Finnegans Wake (James Joyce); Pingpong; Technology; History; Politics; Magic. Address: 3016 Waterloo Street, Vancouver BC, V6R 3J6, Canada.

POE David, b. 20 July 1969, Ann Arbor, Michigan, USA. Songwriter; Recording Artist; Singer; Guitarist. m. BS, Mass Communications, Miami University, Oxford. Career: Solo Performer, 1990-; Support Act for: Bob Dylan, Lisa Loeb, Ron Sexsmith, Jonathon Richman; Produced Debut Recording for Melissa Sheehan, Jenifer Jackson. Compositions: Blue Glass Fall; Moon; Reunion, from forthcoming solo debut; Blind Man, co-written with T-Bone Burnett. Recordings: David Poe, 1997; Glass Suit, 1996. Current Management: Pati DeVries, DeVries Entertainment 179 Franklin Street, 5th Floor, New York, N 10013, USA.

POHJOLA Jussi Pekka, b. 13 Jan 1952, Helsinki, Finland. Musician (bass); Composer. 3 sons. Musical Education: Studies in violin and piano, Sibelius Academy, Helsinki. Career: Member of Wigwam; Jukka Tolonen Band; Made In Sweden; UMO; Mike Oldfield, including European tour, 1979; Tours with Pori Big Band, 1980; Founder of several own bands; Tours throughout Scandinavia; Europe; USA; Japan. Compositions: Film music; Theatre music; Arrangements for different artists; One symphony, Sinfonia, 1989. Recordings: 12 solo albums, including Bialoipoikku The Magpie; Urban Tango; Jokamies; Space Waltz; Flight Of The Angel; Heavy Jazz; Numerous recordings with several other artists. Honours: 2 Awards, Best Record of the Year, Finnish Broadcasting Company; Several state artist-grants including 15 year artist-grant. Hobbies: Tennis; Swimming; Golf; Snooker. Current Management: Tapio Korjus, Rockadillo, Keskutori 7 A 11, 33100 Tampere, Finland. Address: Pisanniitty 4 B 14, 02280 Espoo, Finland;

POINTER Anita, b. 23 Jan 1948, East Oakland, California, USA. Singer. Career: Singer, Pointers (with sisters), San Francisco, 1969-71; Recorded as session singers with Boz Scaggs, Elvin Bishop, Taj Mahal, Dave Mason; Member, US female vocal quartet The Pointer Sisters, 1972-78; Continued as trio, 1978-; Concerts include: Midem Festival, 1974, 1993; Grand Ole Opry, 1974; Television includes: 25th Anniversary of American Bandstand, 1977; Welcome Home America! (Gulf forces tribute), 1991. Recordings: The Pointer Sisters, 1973; Live At The Opera House, 1974; Steppin', 1975; Best Of, 1976; Having A Party, 1978; Energy, 1979; Priority, 1979; Special Things, 1980; Black And White, 1981; Jump - The Best Of, 1989; Right Rhythm, 1990; Only Sisters Can Do That, 1993; Solo album: Love For What It Is, 1987; Singles: Yes We Can, 1973; Fairytale, 1974; How Long, 1975; Fire, 1979; He's So Shy, 1980; Slow Hand, 1981; I'm So Excited, 1982; Automatic, 1984; Jump (For My Love), 1984; Neutron Dance (used in film Beverly Hills Cop), 1985; Dare Me, 1985; Be There (used in film Beverly Hills Cop II), 1987; Solo: Duet with Earl Thomas Conley: Too Many Times, 1986; Contributions to: A Very Special Christmas, 1987; Rock Rhythm And Blues, 1989; Am I Cool Or What?, 1991; Charity singles: We Are The World, 1984; Voices That Care, 1991. Honours: Grammy Awards: Best Country Vocal Performance, 1974; Best Performance By Group, Best Vocal Arrangement, 1985; Billboard Awards: Top Dance Single & Album, 1984; American Music Awards: Favourite Soul/R&B Band, 1985; Favourite Soul/ R&B Video, 1985, 1986. Address: c/o The Sterling/Winters Co., Suite 1640, 1900 Avenue of the Stars, Los Angeles, CA 90067, USA.

POINTER June, b. 30 Nov 1953, East Oakland, California, USA. Singer. Career: Singer, Pointers (with sisters), San Francisco, 1969-71; Recorded as session vocalists for Boz Scaggs; Taj Mahal; Dave Mason; Elvin Bishop; Member, US female vocal quartet The Pointer Sisters, 1972-78; Continued as trio, 1978-; Television includes: 25th Anniversary of American Bandstand, 1977; Welcome Home America! (Gulf forces tribute), 1991. Recordings: Albums: The Pointer Sisters, 1973; Live At The Opera House, 1974; Steppin', 1975; Best Of, 1976; Having A Party, 1978; Energy, 1979; Priority, 1979; Special Things, 1980; Black And White, 1981; Greatest Hits, 1982; So Excited, 1982; Break Out, 1984; Contact, 1985; Hot Together, 1986; Serious Slammin', 1988; Jump - The Best Of, 1989; Right Rhythm, 1990; Only Sisters Can Do That, 1993; Solo album: Baby Sitter, 1983; Singles: with the Pointer Sisters: Yes We Can, 1973; Fairytale, 1974; How Long, 1975; Fire, 1979; Jump (For My Love), 1984; Neutron Dance (used in film Beverly Hills Cop), 1985; Dare Me, 1985; Be There (used in film Beverly Cop II), 1987; Contributions to: A Very Special Christmas, 1987; Rock Rhythm And Blues, 1989; Am I Cool Or What?, 1991; Charity singles: We Are The World, 1984; Voices That Care, 1991. Honours: Grammy Awards: Best Country Vocal Performance, 1974; Best Performance by Group, Best Vocal Arrangement, 1985; Billboard Awards: Top Dance Single And Album, 1984; American Music Awards: Favourite Soul/R&B Band, 1985; Favourite Soul/R&B Video, 1985, 1986. Address: c/o The Sterling/Winters Co., Suite 1640, 1900 Avenue of the Stars, Los Angeles, CA 90067, USA.

POINTER Ruth, b. 19 Mar 1946, Oakland, California, USA. Singer. m. Michael Sayles, 8 Sept 1990. Career: Member, US female vocal quartet The Pointer Sisters, 1972-78; Continued as trio, 1978-; Concerts include: Midem Festival, 1974, 1993; Grand Ole Opry, 1974; Television includes: 25th Anniversary Of American Bandstand, 1977; Welcome Home America! (Gulf forces tribute), 1991. Recordings: Albums: The Pointer Sisters, 1973; Live At The Opera House, 1974; Steppin',

1975; Best Of, 1976; Having A Party, 1978; Energy, 1979; Priority, 1979; Special Things, 1980; Black And White, 1981; Greatest Hits, 1982; So Excited, 1982; Break Out, 1984; Contact, 1985; Hot Together, 1986; Serious Slammin', 1988; Jump - The Best Of, 1989; Right Rhythm, 1990; Only Sisters Can Do That, 1993; Hit singles: Yes We Can, 1973; Fairytale, 1974; How Long, 1975; Fire, 1979; He's So Shy, 1980; Slow Hand, 1981; I'm So Excited, 1982; Automatic, 1984; Jump (For My Love), 1984; Neutron Dance (used in film Beverly Hills Cop), 1985; Dare Me, 1985; Be There (used in Beverly Cop II), 1987; Contributor: A Very Special Christmas, 1987; Rock Rhythm And Blues, 1989; Am I Cool Or What?, 1991; Charity singles: We Are The World, 1984; Voices That Care, 1991. Honours: Grammy Awards: Best Country Vocal Performance, 1974; Best Performance By Group, Best Vocal Arrangement, 1985; Billboard Awards: Top Dance Single & Album, 1984; American Music Awards: Favourite Soul/R&B Band, 1985; Favourite Soul/R&B Video, 1985, 1986. Address: c/o The Sterling/Winters Co., Suite 1640, 1900 Avenue of the Stars, Los Angeles, CA 90067, USA.

POINTON Michael, b. 25 April 1941, London, England. Musician; Vocalist; Writer; Broadcaster. Education: Rose Bruford College of Speech and Drama, 1953-57; Private Piano Lessons; Self-taught Trombone. Career: Founded own band, 1950s; Worked with many European New Orleans style groups and American jazzmen and toured many countries; Documentaries for BBC Radio, including Swingtime For Hitler, 1987, Bunk & Bill, 1992, Preservation Hall, 1998. Recordings: Barry Martyn's Band, 1961; Mezz Mezzrow/Cotton City Jazz Band, 1964; Young Olympia Brass Band, 1965; Eagle Brass Band, 1966; European Classic Jazz Band, 1983; British All-Stars, 1993. Membership: Musicians' Union. Hobbies: Literature; Music. Address: 11 Kings Court, Kings Road, Wimbledon, London SW19 8QP, England.

POLAND Chris, b. Dunkirk, New York, USA. Rock Musician (guitar, bass). Career: World tours as member of Megadeth; Tours of USA, Mexico, and Canada as member of Circle Jerks; World tour as member of Damn The Machine; Also worked with Ice T and Industrial Light and Sound. Recordings: Killing Is My Business..., Megadeth; Peace Sells But Who's Buying?, Megadeth; Return To Metalopolis, Chris Poland; Damn The Machine (self-titled); Ice T. Honours: Platinum disc, Peace Sells But Who's Buying?; Gold disc, Killing Is My Business... Memberships: AFTRA; ASCAP; AFofM. Hobbies: Music; Guitars. Current Management: Andy Somers, ICM; Jane Hoffman, Speed Of Sound. Address: Speed Of Sound, 626 Santa Monica Blvd #119, Santa Monica, CA 90401, USA.

POLCER Ed (Edward Joseph), b. 10 Feb 1937, Paterson, New Jersey, USA. Jazz Musician (cornet); Bandleader. m. Judy Jardine, 9 May 1976, 3 sons, 1 daughter. Education: BSE, Engineering, Princeton University. Musical Education: Professor James V Dittamo, Prospect Park, New Jersey. Career: Cornettist, Stan Rubin's Tigertown Five; concerts include: Carnegie Hall, Europe, Prince Rainier, Grace Kelly wedding, 1955-56; Benny Goodman Sextet, 1973; Solo artist, band leader, international Jazz Festival circuit, 1975-; Owner, manager, bandleader, Eddie Condon's NY, 1975-85; Bandleader, 8 major US tours for Columbia Artists, several European tours, 1992-1997; Congressional Ball, White House, by Presidential invitation, 1995; Business ventures: BlewZ Manor Productions, concerts, festivals, recordings. Recordings: Albums include: Ed Polcer-Live In Concert, 1988; with Ed Polcer's All Stars: Coast To Coast-Swinging Jazz, 1990; Some Sunny Day, 1991; Barbara Lea, 1992; A Night At Eddie Condon's, 1992; The Magic Of Swing Street, 1993; A Salute To Eddie Condon, 1993; Jammin' A La Condon, 1994. Publications: Co-editor, Carmina Princetonia - The Songbook

Of Princeton University Centennial Edition, 1968. Membership: President, International Art Of Jazz, 1982-89. Hobbies: Family; Tennis; Marathon walking. Current Management: BlewZ Manor Productions Inc. Address: PO Box 263, Croton-On-Hudson, NY 10520-0263, USA.

PONCHO Ildefonso, b. 30 Oct 1954, Laredo, Texas, USA. Congas Vocalist. m. Stella Martinez, 15 July 1973, 2 sons. Musical Education: Self-taught. Career: Klon; Monterey Jazz Festival; Long Beach Jazz Festival; Playboy Jazz Festival; Jazz Central B E T (58); Japan tour; Europetour. Recordings: 13 CDs released. Publications: Concord Jazz Picante. Honours: Many awards in USA. Hobbies: Fishing; Music. Current Mnagement: Berkeley Agency, Poncho Sanchez Latin Jazz Band. Address: PO Box 59236 Norwalk, CA 90652, USA.

PONOMAREVA Valentina, b. 10 July 1939, Moscow, Russia. m. Konstantin Gogounski, 7 September 1985. Education: Classical Music Degree, Khabarovsk Institute of Arts, vocal & piano. Career: Soloist-Vocalist, Tula Jazz big band conducted by A Kroll, 1967-70; Actress, Singer, Dancer, Moscow Gypsy Theatre Romen, 1971-78; Soloist-vocalist, trio Romen, 1973-84; International concerts with Trio, Romen, 1974-84; Metropolitan Opera, New York, 1976; Midem-76 Festival, Cannes, 1976; Edinburgh International Festival, 1977; National TV and Radio - for all channels in major programs, 1973-; Solo Performer, Russia and international concerts and tours, 1978-; Soviet Avantgarde Jazz Festival in Zurich, 1989; International workshop of free improvised music, Tokyo, Osaka, 1989; Huddersfield Contemporary Music Festival, 1990; Voice Over Festival, London, 1990; International Music Festival in Davos, 1991; Europa Festival Jazz, Italy, 1991; Jazz Summer, 1991; Bolzano, 1991; USA Seven Month Tour: Los Angelos, San Francisco, Chicago, Boston, New York, 1992; Musique Action Nancy, France, 1993. Recordings: Solo: Fortune-teller, 1985; Intrusion, 1988; At Parting I Say, 1989; Temptation, 1989; Don't Rise My Recollection, 1990; Terra Incognita, 1990; Live in Japan, 1991; The Romances of the Friends or Mine, 1992; Dve gitary, 1994; At Parting I Say, 1996; We Strangely Happen to Meet, 1997; The Bird of Sorrow, 1998. Membership: Performing Right Society. Current Management: Valentina Ponomareva Musical Theatre. Address: 14 Malaya Bronnaya Str, Apt 19, Moscow 103104, Russia.

PONOMARYOV Olexander, b. 9 Aug 1973, Khmelnitsky, Ukraine. Singer; Musician (piano). Musical Education: Student, Third course, State Music Academy. Career: Joint concert with Patricia Kaas; Festivals: All-Ukrainian Chervona Ruta, first grant, 1993; International Festival, Slavonic Bazaar, second grant, 1994. Recordings: Album: My Love Has Grey Eyes; Song (same title) nominated for: Best Song of 1994. Publications: Articles on music items, Republican press. Honours: Grants: All Ukrainian Festival, 1993, International Festival, 1994; Best Newcomer, 1993; Best Ukrainian Singer in Popular Music, 1993-94. Hobbies: Dogs; Tennis. Current Management: Oleg Stupka, Kiev, Ukraine. Address: Zarichanska Str 14/1a Ap 35, 280017 Ukraine Khmelnitsky, Ukraine.

PONTIEUX Loic, b. 10 Jun 1967, Harfleur, France. Musician (drums). m. 5 Jan 1994. Musical Education: Conservatoire, 5 years. Career: Drummer with many artists including: Michel Jonasz; Claude Nougaro; Didier Lockwood; Birelli Lagrene; Al Jarreau; Pascal Obispo; Veronique Sanson; Francis Cabrel; Mauranne; Maxime Le Forestier and Bernard Cavilliers. Recordings: Many with various artists including: Didier Lockwood; Bernard Cavilliers; Claude Nougaro; Birelli Lagrene; Solensi; Jean Michel Kajdan; Pascal Obispo; Idrissa Diop; Jean Jacques Milteau. Hobbies: Cinema; Roller skating; Skin diving; Body building; Tennis. Address: 4 bis, rue André Chénier, 92130 Issy les Moulineaux, France.

PONTY Jean-Luc, b. 29 Sept 1942, Avranches, France. Musician (jazz violin, synthesizers); Composer; Bandleader. m. Claudia Bosco, 6 Sept 1966, 2 daughters. Musical Education: Premier Prix (First Prize), violin, Conservatoire National de Musique, Paris. Career: Classical violinist to 1964; Jazz violinist, Europe, 1964-69; Night clubs, music festivals, in collaboration with the George Duke Trio, USA, 1969; Toured with own group, Europe, 1970-72; Moved to USA, 1973; Pioneer electric violin, jazz innovator; Headlined international concerts with own group, 1975-; Music festivals in US include: Meadowbrook; Artpark; Wolf Trap; in Europe: Montreux; North Sea Festival; Paris Jazz Festival; Guest soloist, Montreal Symphony Orchestra, 1984; Toronto Symphony Orchestra, 1986; New Japan Philharmonic, 1987; Television includes: Soundstage; The Tonight Show; Solid Gold; Rock Concert; Fiddlers Three; Appearances in: Europe; Brazil; Chile; Venezuela. Recordings: (own productions) Albums include: Upon The Wings Of Music; Aurora; Imaginary Voyage; Enigmatic Ocean; Cosmic Messenger; Jean-Luc Ponty - Live; Civilised Evil; A Taste For Passion; Mystical Adventures; Individual Choice; Open Mind; Fables; The Gift Of Time; Storytelling; Tchokola (with African musicians); No Absolute Time; The Rite Of Strings (with Stanley Clarke, Al DiMeola); Also recorded with: Elton John; Honky Chateau, 1972; Frank Zappa and the Mothers of Invention, 1973; Mahavishnu Orchestra, 1974-75. Current Management: Bob Zievers, International Creative Management. Address: ICM, 8942 Wilshire Boulevard, Beverly Hills, CA 90211, USA.

POOK Jocelyn, b. 14 February 1960, Birmingham, England. Musician (Viola; Violin); Composer. Education: Performers Diploma, Guildhall School of Music and Drama; Postgraduate Year, GSMD in Orchestral and Early Music Studies. Career: Toured, played live with: The Communards, 1986-89; Lyle Lovett, 1994; The Cranberries, Meatloaf, 1995; Mark Knopfler, 1996; Laurie Anderson, R Yuichi Sakamoto; The Stranglers; Spiritualized, Michael Nyman, 1997; Recordings include: Peter Gabriel; PJ Harvey; Nick Cave; Paul Weller; This Moral Coil; Eddie Reader; Co-Founder, Electra Strings; Performed in several theatre productions, Derek Jarman's Edward II, Midland Bank Advert and regularly with Electra Strings on Later with Jools. Compositions: Composed extensively for theatre, dance and film; Dance productions include: Strange Fish, 1993; MSM, 1994; DV8 Physical Theatre; Deluge, 1995; Covertigo Danse; Blight; Score for Stanley Kubrick's film, Eyes Wide Shut. Recordings: Blow the Wind - Pie Jesu, 1996-97; Deluge, first solo album, 1997. Honour: Prix Italia, Strange Fish, film, 1994. Memberships: Musician's Union; Equity; PRS; MCPS. Current Management: Don Mousseau, 78 Greencroft Gardens, London, NW6 3JQ, England.

POOLE Brian, b. 2 Nov 1941, Barking, Essex, England. Singer. Career: Lead singer, Brian Poole and the Tremeloes, 1961-1966; Appearances include: Tours with artists including: Roy Orbison; The Searchers; Freddie And The Dreamers; Dusty Springfield; PJ Proby; Gerry And The Pacemakers; NME Poll Winners Concert, Wembley, with the Beatles, Cliff Richard, 1964; Solo tour, Scandinavia, 1966; Formed new backing group, The Seychelles, 1969; Left music scene, 1969-88; Reunion with the Tremeloes, 1988; Member, The Corporation, with Reg Presley, Mike Pender, 1989; Appeared at Biggest 60's Party in Town, Olympia, London, 1991; Currently lead singer with Electrix. Recordings: Hit singles include: Twist And Shout, 1963; Do You Love Me? (Number 1, UK), 1963; I Can Dance, 1963; Candy Man, 1964; Someone Someone, 1964; Twelve Steps To Love, 1964; The Three Bells, 1965; I Want Candy, 1965; Good Lovin', 1965. Current Management: Brian Gannon Management, PO Box 106, Rochdale, Lancashire OL16 4HW, England.

POOLE Chris, b. 23 June 1952, New York, USA. Musician (flutes, tenor saxophone); Composer. m. Catherine Dunsmore, 4 Sept 1992. Musical Education: BA, Berklee College of Music, Boston; First woman to complete Berklee's applied music programme; Studied with Gary Burton; Andy McGee; Joe Viola; James Newton. Career: Moved to Denmark from USA, 1975; Performed in jazz and latin bands; Numerous television and radio appearances; Solo performances, 1988-; Writer for theatre, film and modern dance including score for Troll, Norwegian film. Recordings: Chris Poole-Solo Flute, 1990; To The Powers That Be, with Pia Ramusssen, 1993. Honours: Bay Area Critics Award, Best Musical Score For A Drama, The Lady From The Sea, Berkeley Repertory Theater, USA, 1993. Memberships: Danish Musicians' Union; Danish Association of Jazz and Rock Composers; Women In Music. Current Management: Self-managed. Address: Jagvej 229, 1th, 2100 Copenhagen, Denmark.

POOLE Gordon Campbell, b. 8 Dec 1952, Bristol, Avon, England. Showbusiness Agent. m. Jill Hassell, 21 Sept 1974, 1 son. Musical Education: Cathedral School, Wells. Career: Concert promoter, Gordon Poole Agency Ltd; Former disc jockey, Marquee Club, London; Showbusiness agent. Membership: Fellow, Agents Association, Great Britain; Barker, Variety Club of Great Britain. Hobbies: Music; Foreign travel; Reading. Address: Gordon Poole Agency Ltd, The Limes, Brockley, Bristol BS48 3BB, England.

POP Iggy (James Jewel Osterburg), b. 21 Apr 1947, Ypsilanti, Michigan, USA. Singer; Musician (guitar); Actor. Education: University of Michigan. Career: Formed Iguanas, High School band, 1962; Prime Movers, 1966; Concerts in Michigan, Detroit and Chicago; Formed The Stooges (originally the Pyschedelic Stooges), 1967; 3 albums, 1969-73; Solo artiste, 1976-; Collaborations with David Bowie, 1972-; Numerous tours and television appearances; Actor, films including: Sid And Nancy; The Color Of Money; Hardware; Actor, television series, Miami Vice. Compositions include: Co-writer, China Girl, David Bowie. Recordings: Albums: with The Stooges: The Stooges, 1969; Jesus Loves The Stooges, 1977; I'm Sick Of You, 1977; Solo albums: Fun House, 1970; Raw Power, 1973; Metallic KO, 1976; The Idiot, 1977; Lust For Life, 1977; TV Eye Live, 1978; Kill City, 1978; New Values, 1979; Soldier, 1980; Party, 1981; I'm Sick Of You, 1981; Zombie Birdhouse, 1982; I Got The Right, 1983; Blah Blah Blah, 1986; Rubber Legs, 1987; Live At The Whiskey A Go Go, 1988; Death Trip, 1988; Raw Stooges, 1988; Raw Stooges 2, 1988; The Stooges Box Set, 1988; Instinct, 1988; Brick By Brick, 1990; American Caesar, 1994; Naughty Little Doggie, 1996; Contributor, Red Hot And Blue AIDs charity record. Publication: Autobiography, I Need More. Hobbies: Garden; Wife; Pets; Music. Current Management: Art Collins Management, PO Box 561, Pine Bush, NY 12566, USA.

PORCARO Steve, b. 2 Sept 1957, Hartford, Connecticut, USA. Vocalist; Musician (keyboards). Career: Support musician to artists including: Jackson Browne; Aretha Franklin; Barbra Streisand; Member, Toto, 1978-87; Compositions: Commissioned (with Toto) to write theme for Los Angeles Olympic Games, 1984. Recordings: Albums: with Toto: Toto, 1979; Hydra, 1979; Turn Back, 1981; Toto IV, 1982; Isolation, 1985; Dune (film soundtrack), 1985; Singles include: Hold The Line, 1979; Georgy Porgy, 1979; 99, 1980; Rosanna, 1982; Make Believe, 1982; Africa (Number 1, US), 1983; I Won't Hold You Back, 1983; I'll Be Over You, 1986; Without Your Love, 1987; Contributor, We Are The World, USA For Africa charity single, 1985; Backing group, albums by Boz Scaggs: Silk Degrees, 1976; Down Two, 1977. Honours: Grammy Awards: Record of the Year, Album of the Year, Best Vocal Arrangement, Best Instrumental Arrangement, Best Producer (Toto), Best Engineered Recording, 1983. Address: c/o Fitzgerald-Hartley Co., 50 W Main Street, Ventura, CA 93001, USA.

PORTAL Robert, b. 2 Nov 1948, Le Puy 43, France. Musician. Career: Jazz festivals include: Montpellier; Nîmes; Nancy; Rive de Gier; Avignon; Deauville; Samois Sur Seine; Samois sur Seine; Concerts include: Paris: Musée d'Art Moderne; Centre Américain; Maison de Radio France; Also Orléans; Metz; Ris Orangis; Chambry; Le Creusot; Played in various churches; Concerts as duo or quartet with percussionists Ravy and Khalid Kouhen; Conceived and designed the guitar-sarod. Compositions: Theatre music; Film, Hurlements; Music for Rimbaud Je T'Aime; Recordings: Optral; Rashbehari; Musique Pour Enfants; Mélampyre; Solstice; Serre de la Fare; Kalimba; Evanescence. Hobby: Botany. Address: 16 Rue Louis Brioude, 43750 Vals-Pres-Le Puy, France.

PORTASS Nigel John, b. 23 Jan 1943, Wisbech, Cambridgeshire, England. Musician (keyboards, saxophone, drums); Teacher. m. Dorothy Ann, 17 July 1965, 2 sons. Musical Education: Member, backing groups for visiting artistes including Chuck Berry; Gene Vincent; Georgie Fame; Van Morrison; Ronnie Scott; Matt Monro; Music tutor and lecturer at Boston College, 1964. Membership: Music Teachers Association. Hobbies: Travel; Jazz. Address: c/o Portass and Carter Music Shop, 26 Bridge Road, Sutton Bridge, Spalding, Lincolnshire PE12 9UA, England.

PORTEJOIE Philippe René Paul, b. 28 Dec 1956, Niort, France. Musician (saxophone). m. Frederique Lagarde, 15 Sept 1990, 1 son. Musical Education: First Prize, CNSM, Paris. Career: Member duo Portejoie-Lagarde; 2 albums; 100 concerts, France; Italy; Belgium; Norway; Radio: Radio France (France Inter; France Musique); Premier alto saxophone, Big Band with Claude de Bolling. Recordings: 20 recordings include Musique Francaise Du XXe Siècle; Claude Bolling, Stéphane Grappelli; Strictly Classical; Saxomania Et Clark Terry. Honours: Premier Prix d'Honneur à l'Unanité (Concours de Musique d'Ensemble de l'UFAM); Meilleur Formation Française (Musique de Chambre de Paris). Memberships: Yehudi Menuhin Foundation; Professor, Conservatoire Superieur de Paris (CNR). Address: 48 Boulevard Mission Marchand, 92400 Courbevoie, France.

PORTELLI Rose-Marie, b. Toulon, France. Singer; Composer. Musical Education: British and Irish folk music; American Jazz and Blues; Italian Gospel. Career: Appeared at Festival of Traditional Music, Birmingham, England, 1991; Olympia in 1994, Congrès Mondial Acadien, Canada, 1994, Fête de la Musique at American Center in Paris, 1995, Francofolies de la Rochelle, 1995, Disneyland in Paris, 1995; Tour of USA and Canada, 1995. Recordings: Marine Marine, 1993; New album due 1996. Publication: Biography of Canadian singer, Fabienne Thibeau. Honour: First Prize for Interpretation, SACEM, 1992. Membership: SACEM. Hobbies: Surfing; Swimming; Sailing. Current Management: Natasha Grandval, Dolphin Dreams Productions. Address: c/o Dolphin Dreams Productions, 98 Boulevard Poniatowski, 75012 Paris, France.

PORTEOUS Michael Lindsay, b. 2 February 1948, The Mytertoun Menstrie, Clackmannanshire, Scotland. Ethnomusicologist: Jew's Harp Champion. Education: Selftaught in Ethnomusicology, over 30 years playing with Folk Musicians and groups from around the world.

Career: Several television appearances for various companies, and radio including several of own on folk instruments. Compositions: Dunblane, lament cassette; Farewell to Lizziewells. Recordings: Recordings with Heritage, 1978-93; Tell Tae Me, 1993; Greentrax, 1988; Tracks on various CD samplers, 1987-97; Cassettes. Publication: How to Play and Have Fun with the Jew's-Harp, 1990. Honours: Competition Certificates, Traditional Music Song Association, Scotland, 1976-97; Edinburgh Folk Festival, One Man Band Champion, 1982, 1983, 1984. Memberships: MU; The Traditional Music and Song Association of Scotland. Hobby: Making and playing traditional folk instruments. Address: Lindsay Porteous, Tron House, Culross, Fife, KY12 8JG, Scotland.

PORTER Christopher, b. 4 May 1954, Southampton, Hampshire, England. Record Producer. m. Virginia Guarlez, 7 Apr 1977, 2 daughters. Education: Art College. Career: Began as engineer at Good Earth Studios under Tony Visconti, 1980; Early engineering success with Lynx and Junior Giscombe; Long-standing collaboration with George Michael; Co-producer with Tim Simenon for Whycliffe and Zan Jam. Recordings: Producer, Engineer: Singles/tracks include: Take That: Back For Good (Number 1, UK), 1995; Babe; George Michael: tracks for Red Hot And Dance; Elton John: Don't Let The Sun Go Down On Me; Some Other World; Aswad: On And On; Don't Turn Around; Beauty's Only Skin Deep; Wham: Wham Rap; Albums: George Michael: Faith; Listen Without Prejudice, Part 1; Wham!: The Final; Make It Big; Hazel O'Connor, Breaking Glass film soundtrack; Recordings for: Living In A Box; Robbie Nevill; Hall & Oates; Debbie Gibson; Diana Ross; Omar; Breathe; Gary Moore; The Christians; The Alarm; Simple Minds; David Bowie; Dexy's Midnight Runners; Junior Giscombe; Boomtown Rats; Thin Lizzy; A Flock Of Seagulls. Hobbies: Flying; Shooting. Current Management: The Producers. Address: 45-53 Sinclair Road, London W14 0NS, England.

PORTER K C, b. 27 June 1962, Encino, CA, USA. Record Producer; Musician (Keyboards). m. Aimée Porter, 1 daughter. Education: Music Study, CSUN University, 5 years. Career: Producer for Ricky Martin, Selena, Patti Labelle, Ednita Nazario. Compositions: Dondequiera Que Estes; Maria. Recordings for: Boyz II Men; Toni Braxton; Sting; Bon Jovi; Az Yet (Producer of Spanish Crossover Versions). Honours: Many Gold/Platinum Awards; ASCAP/SESAC Writer Awards, 1994. Memberships: SAG; AFTRA; ASCAP; BMI; SESAC; NARAS. Hobbies: Tennis; Swimming; Family Time. Address: 24522 Dry Canyon Cold Creek Road, Calabasas, CA 91302, USA.

PORTER Lisa Jean, b. 4 June 1960, New Orleans, LA, USA. Education: Cornish Music Institute. Career: TV commercials; Opening act on major stages for nationals including: BB King, Kenny G, Elvin Bishop; Voice Overs, Radio, locally. Compositions: CD - Rollercoaster; Land of Lie & Learn & Luv Ya, 2 song demo. Recordings: CD intitled Rollercoaster. Hobbies: Bowling; Swimming. Current Management: Transatlantic Management. Address: 11522 Northup Way, Bellevue, WA 98004, USA.

PORTNOW Neil, b. New York, New York, USA. Career: Professional Musician, played with various bands; Studio Sideman, playing bass and guitar; President, Portnow-Miller Company Inc, own company, 1971; Manager, Talent Acquisition and Development, Screen Gems Publishing Group, 1972; Staff Producer, RCA Records, promoted to Executive Producer, 1977; Senior Vice President, 20th Century Fox Records, 1979; Vice President, Artists and Repertoire, EMI America Records, 1985; Vice President, West Coast Operations for Zomba Group of Companies including: Jive Records; Silvertone Records;

Zomba Music Publishing; Zomba Management; Segue Music; Zomba Music Clearance, Music Supervision, Wired, motion picture, 1988; Music Supervisor for Frank Mancuso Jr's production of Permanent Record, Paramount Pictures, 1987. Memberships: National Trustee, former National Vice President, Board of Trustees, Recording Academy; former Member and Treasurer, Board of Governors, Los Angeles Chapter, National Academy of Recording Arts and Sciences; Advisory Board, Songwriters Resources and Services; Team Captain, Los Angeles City of Hope Music Chapter. Address: Zomba, 9000 Sunset Boulevard #300, Los Angeles, CA 90069 5803, USA.

PORTO José Maria, b. 28 July 1950, Valencia, Spain. Musician (piano); Composer; Arranger. Musical Education: Piano, composition. Career: Local radios and concerts: Spain; USA; Germany; Italy; Argentina. Recordings: Also composer, arranger, producer: Con Tanto Amor, 1994; Las Coasa De La Vida, 1995. Membership: SGAE (Spain). Hobbies: Cinema; Music; Football. Address: Ingeniero Vicente Pichó, 4-Bajo 46020, Spain.

POST Mike, b. San Fernando Valley, California, USA. Composer; Musician (guitar); Producer; Arranger. m. Darla Post, 1 daughter. Career: Founder, Wellingbrook Singers; First Edition; Guitarist with Dick And Dee; Sammy Davis Jr; Dean Martin; Sonny And Cher; Musical Director, Andy Williams Show; Producer, Mac Davis Show. Compositions: Music scores and theme music for numerous television shows including: Rockford Files; LA Law; Hill Street Blues; The A-Team; Magnum PI; Doogie Howser, MD; Quantum Leap; Hardcastle And McCormick; Riptide. Recordings include: As producer and/or arranger: Photograph, Mason Williams; Various albums by Ray Charles; Nine To Five, Dolly Parton; I Could've Been A Sailor, Peter Allen; Greatest American Hero, Joey Scarbury (also as musician and writer), 1981; As musician: All I Really Want To Do, Cher, 1965; Sandman, Herb Pedersen, 1977; Compilations: Television Theme Songs, 1982; Music From LA Law And Otherwise. Honours: Numerous Grammy Awards for: Rockford Files; LA Law; Hill Street Blues; Greatest American Hero. Address: Mike Post Productions, 7007 West Olive Avenue, Burbank, CA 91506, USA.

POTTER (Allen) Dale, b. 28 Apr 1929, Puxico, Missouri, USA. Country Musician (fiddle). 1 son, 1 daughter. Musical Education: Few lessons, fiddle, aged 12. Career: Radio appearances, Poplar Bluff, Missouri, and Blytheville, Arkansas; Played on Grand Ole Opry, 1948-62; Tours with Carl Smith; Webb Pierce; Cowboy Copas; Red Sovine; George Jones; Roger Miller; Played on Phillip Morris country Music Show, with Little Jimmy Dickens, George Morgan; Played throughout Eastern, Western and Southern US; Led 5 piece band, Honolulu, Hawaii, 1970s; Now retired. Compositions: Fiddlesticks Boogie, 1954; Fiddle Patch, 1954; Arrangements: Faded Love; Maidens Prayer; Orange Blossom Special, 1979-80. Recordings: 8 albums; Recorded with Chet Atkins and Country All Stars; Bill Monroe; Ernest Tubb; Hank Williams Sr; Webb Pierce; Red Foley; Carl Smith; Mac Wiseman; Fiddlesticks Boogie And Fiddle Patch, with Chet Atkins and Country All Stars. Honours: Award, Grand Ole Opry, for Outstanding Contribution To Country Music; Inducted into Western Swing Society Hall Of Fame, 1988. Memberships: Musicians' Union; ROPE. Hobbies: Horse riding; Motorcycles. Address: PO Box 351, Puxico, MO 63960, USA.

POTTS Wynne Anne, b. 7 Feb 1966, Blyth, Northumberland, England. Musician (guitar); Vocalist. Education: Cambridge University. Musical Education: Freelance, working experience. Career: Performed with singing,

dancing troupe at The Palladium, London Arena; Television appearance: BBC TV, 1993; Formed band, Mango; Numerous concerts in London; Broadcast on Welsh radio. Compositions: Writer, material for Mango. Publications: Songs published in National Christian Music Songbook. Membership: Musicians' Union. Hobbies: Contemporary and African dance; Swimming in lakes; Hitch-hiking to country; Hanging out in cafés. Address: 13 Cornwall Crescent, London W11 1PH, England.

POUGET Nelly, b. 19 May 1955, Dijon, France. Musician (saxophone); Composer. Education: Classique Conservatoire; School of Art, Beaune. Musical Education: Conservatoire, Dijon. Career: Festivals: Dudelange, Luxembourg; International tours; Television and radio appereances: FR3 TV Bourgogne Franche Comte; RFI Radio Interview; RTL Luxembourg; Radio Monte Carlo, Interview, Los Angeles Trilogy. Recordings: Albums (own compositions): Le Dire, 1991; Le Vivre, 1993; Vidéomusic, Nelly Pouget Quartet Live, 1996; Le Voir, 1997. Honours: Le Dire, four key Review, Telerama. Membership: SACEM France. Hobbies: All Arts; Sculpture; Painting; Cinema; Dance. Current Management: Minuit Regards. Address: Minuit Regards, 56 Rue de la Sablière, 75014 Paris, France.

POULIOT George Stephen, b. 12 June 1954, North Hollywood, California, USA. Record Producer; Sound Engineer; Composer. m. Erica Gardner, 7 May 1989. Education: Sherwood Oaks College. Career: Recording engineer, Steve Pouliot Music, 1979-; Sound engineer for Rita Coolidge and Dwight Yoakam; Compositions: Songwriter for: Micky Martin; Billy Burnett. Recordings: As engineer: Behind The Mask, Fleetwood Mac, 1990; As producer: Rick Vito, 1991; The Honest, 1991. Honours: Grammy, 1978; Gold and Platinum discs. Membership: BMI.

POWELL Claire-Louise, b. Norfolk, England. Singer; Actress; Producer. Career: Lead singer, Pentangle; Lead singer, Sugar Mice; Cabaret at La Parisien; Ma Kindley's Musical Extravaganza; Extensive musicals, film, television, radio and opera Don Giovanni; Director, Osiris Productions; Director, Chucklefactory; Production Executive, Sound Pound; Casting Consultant, Good Vibrations. Recordings: Cabaret Cage; Poison Dwarf; Sacred Songs of Scotland; Rock Opera 1; Soul Sounds, Mellow Yellow. Honours: Le Sarlation, Most Outstanding Female Vocalist, 3 years running. Hobbies: Theatre; Horse riding; Sailing; Tennis. Current Management: Bill Richards Personal Management.

POWELL Don, b. 10 Sept 1950, Bilston, Warwickshire, England. Musician (drums). Career: Member, UK rock group Slade (formerly N'Betweens, Ambrose Slade), 1966-; Concerts include: First UK tour, 1972; Fanfare For Europe festival, London Palladium, 1973; Great British Music Festival, 1978; Reading Festival, 1980; Film appearance: Flame, 1974. Recordings: Albums: Beginnings (as Ambrose Slade), 1969; Play It Loud, 1970; Slade Alive, 1972; Slayed, 1973; Sladest, 1973; Old New Borrowed Blue, 1974; Slade In Flame (soundtrack), 1974; Nobody's Fool, 1976; Slade Alive Vol 2, 1978; Return To Base, 1979; Slade Smashes, 1980; Till Deaf Do Us Part, 1981; We'll Bring The House Down, 1981; We'll Bring The House Down, 1981; Slade On Stage, 1982; The Amazing Kamikaze Syndrome, 1983; Slade's Greats, 1984; Rogue's Gallery, 1985; Crackers, 1985; You Boyz Make Big Noize, 1987; Wall Of Hits, 1991; Keep On Rockin', 1996; UK Number 1 singles: Coz I Luv You, 1971; Take Me Back 'Ome, 1972; Mama Weer All Crazee Now (later recorded by Mama's Boys, Quiet Riot), 1972; Cum On Feel The Noize, 1973; Merry Christmas Everybody, 1973; Other hits: Look Wot You Dun, 1972; Gudbuy T'Jane, 1972; Skweeze Me Pleeze Me, 1973; My Friend Stan, 1973; Everyday, 1974; Bangin' Man, 1974;

Far Far Away, 1974; Thanks For The Memory, 1975; In For A Penny, 1975; We'll Bring The House Down, 1981; My Oh My, 1983; Run Run Away, 1984; All Join Hands, 1984.

POWELL John Derek, b. 13 Sept 1963, Brentwood, Essex, England. Musician (guitar and trumpet); Singer. Musical Education: O and A Level Music. Career: Lead singer, guitarist, Existence, 1980-85; Founder, lead singer, Ten, 1985-. Recordings: with Existence: Fashion Parade, 1981; A Chance Encounter, 1982; with Ten: Work, EP, 1986; Break Down The Walls, 1988. Membership: PRS. Hobbies: Music; Reading; Church Youthwork. Address: The Network, 14 Waverley Road, Steeple View, Laindon, Essex SS15 4HU, England.

POWELLS Jimmy, b. 18 Mar 1947, Arbroath, Scotland. Administrator; Accountant. m. Kathleen Davidson, 2 Dec 1972, 2 sons. Career: Mandolin and guitar player, singer, folk groups: Town Choice; Carterbar; Television appearance: Live French TV with Town Choice. Recording: Mandolin Moments, solo mandolin instrumental album. Honours: Album of the Week, Great North Radio and Great Yorkshire Radio. Membership: Musicians' Union. Hobbies: Junior football with sons; Inventor of Pro-Tactics Professional Football Coaching Board, and Soccer Logic (football board game). Address: 55 Langdale Drive, Cramlington, Northumberland NE23 8EL, England.

POWER Brendan, b. 20 Feb 1956, Mombasa, Kenya. Musician (chromatic and diatonic harmonica). m. Lorraine Power, 26 June 1991. Education: BA, English, Religious Studies; MA, Religious Studies. Musical Education: Self-taught. Career: Top New Zealand session harmonica player; Came to Britain, 1992; In band for Riverdance; Irish TV series: A River Of Sound. Compositions: Jig Jazz; The Real Blues Reel. Recordings: State Of The Harp; Harmonica Nights; Digging In; Harmonica After Hours; New Irish Harmonica; Played on Sting album: Ten Summoners Tales. Publications: Harping On, articles on harmonica playing. Honour: All-Ireland Champion, 1993. Membership: Musicians' Union (UK). Hobbies: Kite flying; Rollerblading. Current Management: John Dunford.

POWER John, b. 1970, Liverpool, England. Vocalist; Musician (bass); Songwriter. Career: Member, The La's, 1991; Vocalist, Cast, 1994-; Concerts include support tours to: Oasis; Supergrass; The Charlatans; Shed Seven; Dodgy. Recordings with Cast: Albums: All Change, 1995; Mother Nature Calls, 1997; Singles: Fine Time, 1995; Alright, 1995; Sandstorm, 1996; Walkaway, 1996; Flying, 1996; Free Me, 1997; Guiding Star, 1997; Live the Dream, 1997; I'm So Lonely, 1997. Honours: BRIT Award Nominations: Best British Newcomer, with the La's 1991; Best British Newcomer, with Cast, 1996. Address: c/o Rock'n'Roll Management, Studio 2, 108 Prospect Quay, Point Pleasant, London SW18 1PR, England.

POWER Niall, b. 14 Nov 1957, Ireland. Musician (drums). m. Michelle, 4 Feb 1991, 1 son. Musical Education: Self-taught drums; 3 years music theory in school. Career: 20 years, professional drummer with various Irish groups, solo artists; Tours with Bob Geldof and The Vegetarians Of Love, 1990-; Hazel O'Connor, live album and tour, 1994; Also: Marianne Faithfull; Johnny Logan; Stepaside. Recordings: with Bob Geldof: Les Enfants Touche, 1985; Happy Club, 1994; with Hazel O'Connor: live album, 1994; Various singles, television themes, jingles. Membership: Musicians' Union. Hobbies: Swimming; Countryside. Current Management: MDO Productions. Address: Northwood Lane, Bewdley, Worcestershire DY12 1AS, England.

POWERS Stephen H, b. 22 Aug 1951, Rockford, Illinois, USA. Record Producer;

Entrepeneur. Education: Massachusetts Institute of Technology. Musical Education: Private tutors. Career: Founder, Manager, Charlotte's Web Performing Arts Center, Rockford, Illinois, 1992-; Founder, President, Mountain Railroad Records Inc., 1974; Producer, over 50 folk, blues, rock, reggae albums; Director of Entertainment, Los Angeles Olympics, 1984; Director, A&R, Capitol Records, Hollywood, 1984-87; Worked with artists including: The Beach Boys; Duran Duran; Duane Eddy; The Eurythmics; Bryan Ferry; Tina Turner; Founder, President, Chameleon Music Group, 1987-1992; Co-founder, CEO, Drive Entertainment Inc, 1993-. Recordings: Producer, Singer In The Storm, Holly Near; 9½ Weeks (soundtrack); Executive Producer, Mad Max III (soundtrack); The Healer, John Lee Hooker (Grammy Award winner), 1991. Honours: Producer Of The Year, Wisconsin Music Awards, 1982; Independent Executive Of The Year, Los Angles Music Council, 1991. Membership: NARAS; National Academy Of Songwriters (Board of Directors); Country Music Association; NAIRD; NARM. Hobbies: Running marathons; Cycling; Basketball; Gardening; Playing guitar. Address: c/o Drive Entertainment Inc, 10351 Santa Monica Blvd, Suite 404, Los Angeles, CA 90025, USA.

POZGAJEC Branko, b. 23 July 1950, Zagreb, Croatia. Vocalist; Musician (flute). m. Margitta Gedo, 16 Apr 1983, 1 son, 1 daughter. Education: Graduate, Economics, university. Musical Education: High Schol Of Music. Career: 25 years, professional singing, playing; 20 years leading Drui Nacin, famous Croatian rock group; More than 1,500 concerts in Croatia and abroad; More than 50 television appearances, all kinds of shows; Numerous radio appearances. Compositions: The Right Words (Prave Rijeci); Dilemas (Dileme); Again (Opet); Ballad Of A Smile (Balada O Osmijehu). Recordings: 5 singles, 3 albums with Drugi Nacin. Memberships: Croatian Composers Union; Croatian Artists Union; Croatian Music Union. Hobbies: Recreative running in natural surroundings. Current Management: Record publisher: Croatia Records, Zagreb Medugorska 61. Address: Belomanastirska 6, 41040 Zagreb, Croatia.

PRATT Guy Adam, b. 3 Jan 1962, London, England. Musician (bass guitar); Record Producer; Songwriter. Musical Education: Self-taught. Career: Tours and television appearances with: Icehouse; Bryan Ferry; Scritti Politti; Pink Floyd; Coverdale/Page; Womack and Womack; Bobby Womack and Jeff Beck; Currently writing stage musical with Gary Kemp. Recordings: with Madonna: Like A Virgin; Hanky Panky; with Robert Palmer: Riptide; Don't Explain; with Bryan Ferry: Beté Noire; Mamounia; with Pink Floyd: The Division Bell; Delicate Sound Of Thunder; Pulse; Ain't No Doubt, Jimmy Nail; Storyville, Robbie Robertson; Power Station, Power Station; History, Michael Jackson; The Orb, The Orb; Communion, Debbie Harry; Toy Matinee, Third Matinee. Honour: Ivor Novello Award Nomination, 1993. Memberships: PRS; Musicians' Union. Hobbies: Art; Cinema; Sailing. Current Management: Paul Toogood. Address: Lancaster House, 14-16 St Marks Road, London W11 1QU, England.

PRESCOTT Peter James, b. 20 Oct 1956, Erith, Kent, England. Singer. m. Wendy Patricia Lewsley, 22 Apr 1978, 2 daughters. Musical Education: Self-taught. Career: Singer for 23 years; 6 albums; Further 7 compilation albums; Appearances on 6 television shows in Europe; Several major festivals, Switzerland and Austria. Recordings: Album with Forcefield (with Cozy Powell, Neil Murray, Ray Fenwick); 2 albums with Paul Sinden; 3 albums with Swiss band Sergeant. Publications: Over 70 songs published. Memberships: Musicians' Union; PRS; MCPS. Hobbies: Running; Sailing; Reading. Address: 157 Bulverhythe Road, St Leonards On Sea, East Sussex TN38 8AF, England.

PRESLEY Reg (Reginald Ball), b. 12 June 1943, Andover, Hampshire, England. Vocalist; Songwriter. Career: Lead singer, The Troggs (formerly The Troglodytes), 1964; Tours, concerts include: Star Scene 66, with Walker Brothers, Dave Dee Dozy Beaky Mick and Tich, 1966; Regular live work, US, UK; Concert for Hillsborough soccer disaster fund, Sheffield, 1989. Compositions include: I Can't Control Myself; With A Girl Like You; Give It To Me; Recordings: Albums: From Nowhere...The Troggs, 1966; Trogglodynamite, 1967; Best Of The Troggs, 1967; Love Is All Around, 1968; The Troggs Tapes, 1972; Vintage Years, 1976; Live At Max's Kansas City, 1980; Athens Andover, 1991; Archeology (1966-1976), 1992; Singles include: Wild Thing (Number 1, US) (later used for Lion Bar commercial); ITV show Gladiators; theme for film Major League), 1966; With A Girl Like You, 1966; I Can't Control Myself, 1966; Any Way That You Want Me, 1967; Give It To Me, 1967; Night Of The Long Grass, 1967; Hi Hi Hazel, 1967; Love Is All Around (Number 1 hit for Wet Wet Wet, used in film 4 Weddings And A Funeral, 1994), 1967; Little Girl, 1968. Current Manangement: Stan Green Management, PO Box 4, Dartmouth, Devon TQ6 0YD, England.

PRESTON Billy, b. 9 Sept 1946, Houston, Texas, USA. Musician (keyboards); Vocalist. Career: Solo singer, keyboard player, 1962-; Keyboard player, Plastic Ono Band (with John Lennon), 1969-71; Backing musician for numerous artists including: The Beatles; Ray Charles; Little Richard; Aretha Franklin; Sam Cooke; Mahalia Jackson; Martha Reeves; Luther Vandross; Stephen Stills; George Harrison; Ringo Starr; The Crusaders; Delaney And Bonnie. Recordings: Singles include: That's The Way (God Planned It), 1969; Will It Go Round In Circles, 1973; Nothing For Nothing, 1974; with The Beatles: Get Back, 1969; Let It Be, 1970; Solo Albums include: Whole New Thing, 1977; Behold, 1979; Fastbreak, 1979; Late At Night, 1979; Billy & Syreeta, 1980; The Way I Am, 1981; Universal Love, 1980; Pressin' On, 1982; The Best Of Billy Preston, 1988; Featured on other albums including: No Reason To Cry, Eric Clapton; Mad Dogs And Englishmen, Joe Cocker; Blood On The Tracks, Bob Dylan; Beat And Soul, Everly Brothers; I Heard That!, Quincy Jones; Sometime In New York City, John Lennon and Yoko Ono. Address: c/o Creative Sound Inc., 22236 #C Boca Rancho Drive, Boca Raton, FL 33428, USA.

PREVOST Edwin John, b. 22 June 1942, Hitchin, Hertfordshire, England. Musician (percussion). m. Jean Kathleen, 3 Aug 1964, 3 sons. Education: BA Hons, History, Philosophy. Musical Education: Self-taught. Career: Tours of USA, 1968, 1972, 1984, 1986, 1992; Festivals: Europe; Russia; Turkey; Lithuania; Czech Republic; Western Europe; Tour, Japan, 1995. Recordings include: with AMM: Ammusic, 1966; Amm-The Crypt, 1968; To Here And Back Again, 1972; It Had Been An Ordinary Enough Day, 1979; Generative Themes, 1983; The Inexhaustible Document, 1987; Newfoundland, 1992; 3CD Retrospective, 1997; Solo: Loci of Change, 1996. Publications: No Sound Is Innocent, 1994. Memberships: Director, London Musicians Collective; Musicians' Union; PRS; PPL. Hobbies: Tai Chi; Golf. Current Management: Matchless Recordings and Publishing. Address: 2 Shetlock's Cottages, Matching Tye, near Harlow, Essex CM17 0QR, England.

PRICE Adrian, b. 11 Mar 1967, Colchester, Essex, England. Musician (drums). m. Joanna Snelling, 17 June 1995. Musical Education: Trinity College of Music, London. Career: Drummer, Scissormen; Live concerts, UK, Europe; Singles promoted on BBC Radio 1, Greater London Radio (GLR); German, French, Eastern European radio; Videos shown on British television and MTV. Recordings: Single: Burst/Sever, Scissormen; Glee (EP), Scissormen; Album: Mumbo Jumbo,

Scissormen. Membership: Musicians' Union; PRS. Hobbies: Travel; Literature; Watersports. Current Management: Diversity, 34B Haven Green, London W5 2NX. Address: c/o Welwyn House, 28 Wash Lane, Clacton, Essex CO15 1DB, England.

PRICE Alan, b. Fatfield, County Durham, England. Formed Alan Price Combo, 1958; Formed the Animals, 1963; Left the Animals, 1965; Formed Alan Price Set, 1965; Formed Alan Price And Friends, 1968-69; Teamed up with Georgie Fame, many television appearances, 1971-1974; Acted in Alfie Darling, 1975; 2 British tours, 1976; Director, Fulham Football Club, 1978; British tour, 1979; Series of shows, BBC2, 1980; Formed own record label Key Records, 1981; Appeared in Andy Capp, Manchester, London, 1982; Reformed Animals, 1983; Tour: Canada; USA; Hawaii; Japan; France; UK; 2 concerts, Royal Albert Hall; Wembley, with The Police, New Year's Eve, 1983; 21st Anniversary Tour, 1986; Travelling Man Tour, 1987; Liberty Tour, 1990-91; Greatest Hits Tour, 1992-93; Current band, Alan Price and the Electric Blues Company. Compositions: include: The House That Jack Built; Jarrow Song; Just For You; Composer, film scores, theatre music, and commercials; Film scores include: O Lucky Man, 1973; The Plague Dogs, 1982; Britannia Hospital, 1982; Whales Of August, 1988; Theatre music: Home, 1970; Early Days, 1980; Musical: Andy Capp, 1982; Television appearances: Turtles' Progress; World's End; Fame Is The Spur; A Night On The Tyne; The Chalk Face. Recordings: Hit singles include: with The Animals: House Of The Rising Sun, 1964; Don't Let Me Be Misunderstood; Gotta Get Out Of This Place; with Alan Price Set: I Put A Spell On You; Hi-Lili Hi-Lo; The House That Jack Built; Don't Stop The Carnival; Simon Smith And His Amazing Dancing Bear; Jarrow Song; Goodnight Irene; Baby Of Mine; Just For You; Albums: Metropolitan Man; Performing Price; Shouts Across The Street; Travelling Man; Liberty; Covers; A Gigster's Life For Me. Honours include: BAFTA Award, 1973; Oscar Nomination, 1973; Inducted into American Rock & Roll Hall of Fame, 1994. Address: Cromwell Management, 4-5 High Street, Huntingdon, Cambs PE18 6TE, England.

PRICE James, b. 20 November 1959, Copenhagen, Denmark. Composer; Orchestrator; Conductor. m. Kirsten, 14 November 1992, 1 son. Musical Education: Composition, Royal Danish Academy of Music, 1979-84. Career: Debut, 1979; Musical Director, Arranger and Pianist; Revues, Veaudevilles, Musicals including Nitouche, Sound of Music, HMS Pinafore, Annie Get Your Gun, Cabaret, Annie; Host in Television show; Around a Piano; Compositions for theater, radio, television, film. Compositions: Ved Frokosten (Opera-Monologue, Royal Theater, 1983); Underscore for TV Serials: Two People in Love; Karrusel; Musicals: Tordenskiold; Livsens Ondskab. Recording: Tordenskiold, 1994. Honours: Wilhelm Hansens Grant, 1992; Revue Composer of the Year, 1983, 1996. Memberships: Danish Songwriters' Guild; Danish Conductors' Society. Hobbies: Cooking; Golf; Fishing. Current Management: Nordiska Strakosch Teater-Förlaget, Gothersgade 11, 4 DK-1123 KBH K. Address: Tesdorpfsvej 65, 2000 F, Denmark.

PRICE Mark, b. 10 Aug 1959, Nelson, Lancashire, England. Musician (drums); Writer; Programmer. m. Lise Regan, 26 Jan 1989, 1 son. Education: BA Honours Graphic Design. Musical Education: Self-taught. Career: Producer/Programmer; Nik Kershaw, 3 world tours; Numerous television appearances and Live Aid; Bryan Ferry; All About Eve: 4 albums and tours; The Cure: album tracks; Julianne Regan: album; Peter Murphy: American tours; Joined Del Amitri, 1997; Currently on World Tour until end of 1998. Compositions: Co-writer, musician, 4 albums: All About Eve; Co-writer album: Never Swallow Stars; Jingles and commercials. Recordings: All About Eve albums: All About Eve;

Scarlet And Other Stories; Touched By Jesus; Ultraviolet. Memberships: Musicians' Union; PRS. Hobby: Football. Current Management: Lise. Address: The Church Studios, 145H Crouch Hill, London N8 9QH, England.

PRICE P J, b. 8 Jul 1964, Houston, Texas, USA. Singer; Songwriter; Musician (guitar, keyboards). 2 sons. Career: Various radio releases; Television appearances: Solo artiste on Entertainment Unlimited; Owner, Priceless Records; Owner, Taste Of Texas Music. Recorded: Album: P J Price, 1994; Singles: Runnin' On Love; What's A Heart Like Yours. Honours: Star of Tomorrow, Airplay International, 1993-94; Best Female Indie and Album of The Year, World Country Music Network, 1994; No.1, GSCMA European Chart, 1995. Memberships: GSCMA; NCMO. Hobbies: Fishing; Photography; Tennis; Writing. Current Management: Priceless Promotions. Address: 111 Pine Valley, Huntsville, TX 77340, USA.

PRICE Ray Noble, b. 12 Jan 1926, Perryville, Texas, USA. Country Singer; Musician (guitar). Career: Appeared as the Cherokee Cowboy, local radio station; Joined the Big D Jamboree, 1949; Member, Grand Ole Opry; Formed own band, The Cherokee Cowboys; Toured extensively, appeared on all major network radio and television shows; Semi-retired, 1973-78; Returned to recording until 1980s; Film appearance, Honkytonk Man. Recordings: Over 100 hit singles; US Country Number 1 hits include: Crazy Arms; My Shoes Keep Walking Back To You; For The Good Times; Release Me (later recorded by Englebert Humperdinck); Other hits: Talk To Your Heart; Don't Let The Stars Get In Your Eyes; Faded Love (duet with Willie Nelson); Numerous albums include: Heart Songs, 1957; Faith, 1960; Night Life, 1964; Born To Lose, 1967; For The Good Times, 1970; This Time Lord, 1974; Help Me, 1977; San Antonio Rose (with Willie Nelson), 1980; Ray Price, 1981; Town And Country, 1981; Tribute To Willie And Kris, 1981; Diamonds In The Stars, 1981; Loving You, 1982; Somewhere In Texas, 1982; Master Of The Art, 1983; Portrait Of A Singer, 1985; Welcome To The Country, 1985; A Revival Of Old Time Singing, 1987; The Heart Of Country Music, 1987; Just Enough Love, 1988; Sometimes A Rose, 1992; Memories That Last (with Faron Young), 1992; Various compilations. Honour: Country Music Hall of Fame, 1996. Current Management: James R Doran, Original Artists Agency. Address: 1031 E Battlefield, Springfield, MO 65807, USA.

PRICE Rick. Singer; Songwriter. Recordings: Heaven Knows, 1992; Tambourine Mountain, 1995. Honours: Apra Award, Song of Year, Heaven Knows, 1992; Australian Music Awards, Song of Year, Walk Away Renee, 1993, Album of Year, Heaven Knows, 1993; Advance Australia Foundation, 1993; Australia Export Award, 1993; Singapore Music Award, Song of Year, Heaven Knows, 1993. Address: c/o RCM International, Lennox House, 229 Lennox Street, Richmond, Victoria 3121, Australia.

PRIDE Charley Frank, b. 18 Mar 1938, Sledge, Mississippi, USA. Musician (guitar); Singer. Career: Former baseball player; Recording artiste, 1965-; First appeared at Grand Ole Opry, 1967; Recordings: 29 US Country Number 1 hits; Singles: The Snakes Crawl At Night; Just Between You And Me; Is Anybody Goin' To San Antone?; Crystal Chandelier; Kiss An Angel Good Mornin'; Albums include: Country Charley Pride, 1966; Songs Of Pride... Charley That Is, 1968; I'm Just Me, 1971; Pride Of America, 1974; Charley, 1975; The Happiness Of Having You, 1975; Sunday Morning With Charley Pride, 1976; She's Just An Old Love Turned Memory, 1977; Someone Loves You Honey, 1978; Burgers And Fries, 1979; You're My Jamaica, 1979; There's A Little Bit Of Hank In Me, 1980; Roll On Mississippi, 1981; Charley Sings Everybody's Choice, 1982; Live,

1982; Night Games, 1983; The Power Of Love, 1984; After All This Time, 1987; I'm Gonna Love Her On The Radio, 1988; Moody Woman, 1989; Amy's Eyes, 1990; Classics With Pride, 1991; Various compilations. Honours include: Grammy, Best Country Record (Male), Just Between You And Me. Current Management: Cecca Productions Inc., 3198 Royal Lane #200, Dallas, TX 75229, USA.

PRIEST Maxi (Max Elliot), b. London, England. Reggae Singer. Career: Former carpenter, builder of sound systems; Tour with UK reggae group Saxon International Sound System; Disc Jockey; Solo artiste. Recordings: Albums: You're Safe, 1985; Intentions, 1986; Maxi, 1987; Bona Fide, 1990; The Best Of Me, 1991; Singles: Strollin' On; In The Springtime; Crazy Love; Some Guys Have All The Luck; Wild World; Close To You.

PRIESTLEY Brian, b. 10 July 1946, Manchester, England. Writer; Musician. Education: BA, Hon, French; Diploma of Education, Leeds University. Publications: Mingus, A Critical Biography, 1982; Jazz Piano, 6 volumes, 1983-90; Charlie Parker, 1984; John Coltrane, 1987; Jazz - The Essential Companion (with Ian Carr and Digby Fairweather), 1987; Jazz on Record, A History, 1988; Jazz - The Rough Guide (with Ian Carr and Digby Fairweather), 1995. Contributions to: Reviews and articles; The Gramophone; New Grove Encyclopedia of Jazz; The Cambridge Companion to the Piano; The International Directory of Black Composers. Literary Agent: Barbara Levy. Address: 120A Farningham Road, Caterham, Surrey CR3 6LJ, England.

PRIESTLEY Mark, b. 13 Jul 1963, Kabwe, Zambia. Musician (saxophone, guitar); Singer; Songwriter. 1 son. Education: BA; MA. Musical Education: Self taught. Career: Various studio session work; Member of Jon Strong Band, From The Underworld, Bassa Bassa, and Dr Fray; Concert appearances include: Glastonbury Festival, 1990; WOMAD Festival, 1990; Edinburgh Fringe Festival, 1991; Live radio sessions on Radio 1. Recordings: with Cassandra Complex, The Word and Kay Field; as Producer: Bassa Bassa album and the forthcoming album, Not In My Back Yard. Membership: Musicians' Union. Current Management: Bassa Bassa Collective. Address: Box 10, Christ Church Mount, Leeds LS12 3NH, England.

PRIESTMAN Henry, b. 21 July 1958, Liverpool, England. Vocalist; Songwriter. Career: Member, The Christians, 1984-; Appearances include: Liver Aid Ethiopian Famine benefit, Liverpool, 1985; Support to Fleetwood Mac, UK tour, 1988; John Lennon Tribute Concert, Merseyside, 1990; Regular UK and European tours; Compositions: Songs recorded by the Christians. Recordings: Albums: The Christians, 1987; Colour (Number 1, UK), 1990; Happy In Hell, 1992; The Best Of The Christians, 1993; Singles include: Forgotten Town, 1987; Hooverville (They Promised Us The World), 1987; When The Fingers Point, 1987; Ideal World, 1988; Born Again, 1988; Harvest For The World, 1988; Words, 1989; The Bottle, 1993; Contributor, Ferry 'Cross The Mersey, Hillsborough football disaster benefit, 1989. Address: c/o Eternal Management, 55 Lark Lane, Liverpool L17 8UW, England.

PRIHA Antero, b. 4 Oct 1965, Finland. Musician (trumpet). Musical Education: Vantaa Music College; Jazz at Sibelius Academy, 1989. Career: Played with Vantaa Orchestra whilst at college; Played in local jazz bands; Member, J Karalainen's Mustat Lasit, 1980s; Hasse Walli's band; Played with Espoo Big Band; UMO Big Band; Big Bad Family; Currently plays with many small bands including Veijonsuo-Priha Quintet. Address: Kasöörinkatu 3 F 122, 00420 Helisnki, Finland.

PRIMORAC Vanja, b. 1 Jan 1966, Zagreb, Croatia. Promoter; Manager; Booking Agent; Producer. 1 son. Education: University of Theatre and Film Art, Political Science. Musical Education: Mid-school, piano. Career: Columnist, musical critic, promotional work, 1985-; Manager, several highly-rated Croatian, Slovenian, American/English artists; producer, manager, first Yugoslavian alternative music festival: Offestum; Work with Siouxie and The Banshees, Laurie Anderson, Tuxedomoon, The Young Gods; First private promoter in ex-Yugoslavia. Honours: Japan Award for Festival Design. Memberships: Croatian (HGU, HGS). Hobbies: Sea-sports; Yachting; Skiing; Books. Current Management: Media Nova Promotions, N L Jain. Address: Via Delle Murina 19, 50053 Empoli (Florence), Italy; Podvrsje 2, Zagreb 41000, Croatia.

PRINCE PICHO (Emmanuel Volel), b. 24 Apr 1942, Port-au-Prince, Haiti. Singer; Actor; Musician (guitar, keyboards). 1 son, 2 daughters. Education: College, Hotel Management. Musical Education: Music studies, New-Sewell Music Conservatory, Washington DC. Career: Appearances include: Cable TV channel 45; Cable TV channel 33; Annual guest at Marvin Gaye Festival, African festival, Washington DC; Perform at benefit for homeless. Recordings: Numerous albums for Henri Debs record company, Guadaloupe, FWI; Also for Marc Recors, New York, USA. Publications: Numerous articles, Montgomery Journal, La Nacíon. Honours: Masons of Washington DC Award. Membership: New Sewell Music Conservatory. Hobbies: Football; Tae-Kwon-Do; Jogging. Current Management: Edwardo Semperegui, Espectaculor Productions. Address: 11212 Grandviewave #111, Wheaton, MD 20902, USA.

PRINE John , b. 10 Oct 1946, Maywood, Illinois, USA. Singer; Songwriter. Career: Began writing folk songs as teenager; Regular on Chicago club circuit, 1970; Recording artiste, 1972-; Founder, president, Oh Boy record label, 1980; US tour supporting Bonnie Raitt, 1991; Summer Stage '92 concert, Central Park, New York, 1992; Cambridge Folk Festival, 1992; Cameo film appearance, Falling From Grace, 1992. Compositions include: Love Is On A Roll, Don Williams (US Country Number 1), 1980; Recordings: Singles include: Take A Look At My Heart, 1992; Albums: John Prine, 1972; Diamonds In The Rough, 1972; Sweet Revenge, 1973; Common Sense, 1975; Prime Prine - The Best Of, 1977; Bruised Orange, 1978; Pink Cadillac, 1979; Storm Windows, 1980; Aimless Love, 1984; German Afternoons, 1986; John Prine Live, 1988; The Missing Years, 1991; A John Prine Christmas, 1993; The John Prine Anthology - Great Days, 1993; Lost Dogs And Mixed Blessings, 1995. Honours include: Grammy Award, Best Contemporary Folk Album, The Missing Years, 1991; Current Management: Al Bunetta Management, 33 Music Square W, Suite 102A, Nashville, TN 37203, USA.

PRIOR Maddy, b. Blackpool, England. Folk Singer; Songwriter. m. Rick Kemp, 2 children. Career: Founder member, lead singer, folk group, Steeleye Span, 1970-; Member, The Carnival Band; Solo artiste, 1978-; Collaborations with Tim Hart, guitarist, and Nick Holland, keyboard player. Recordings: Solo albums: Woman In The Wings, 1978; Changing Winds, 1978; Hooked On Winning, 1982; Going For Glory, 1983; Year, 1994; Hang Up Sorrow And Care, 1996; All albums recorded by Steeleye Span; 4 albums with Tim Hart; Guest vocalist on numerous albums including: Albion River Hymn March, Albion Band, 1979; Shearwater, Martin Carthy, 1972; Too Old To Rock And Roll, Jethro Tull, 1976; Streets, Ralph McTell, 1975; Incantations, Mike Oldfield, 1978; Silly Sisters, June Tabor, 1976; First Light, Richard and Linda Thompson, 1978. Current Management: Jim McPhee, Acorn Entertainments.

Address: Winterfold House, 46 Woodfield Road, Kings Heath, Birmingham B13 9UJ, England.

PRITCHARD Bill (William Frederick), b. 2 Aug 1944, Southampton, Hampshire, England. Jazz Musician (guitar); Teacher. m. 1 July 1972, 1 son, 2 daughters. Education: Technical College, Southampton. Musical Education: Mainly self-taught; Jazz course, Guildhall School of Music, London. Career: Peter Clayton Jazz Program, Radio 2, Sunday Night; Live broadcast 2CR Radio Bournemouth; Jazz on BBC Radio Solent; Chichester Jazz Festival; Bracknell Jazz Festival; Radio Victory Jazz (Portsmouth, Tim Callwer Programme); Festival Hall Foyer with Bassa Rio; 100 Club London. Membership: Musicians' Union. Hobbies: Listening to all kinds of music. Address: 15 Hedgerow Drive, Bitterne, Southampton SO18 5SF, England.

PRITCHARD Peter Andrew, b. 13 Aug 1955, London, England. Musician (bass guitar, double bass). m. Chrystella Maria Nicholas, 6 Oct 1978, 1 son, 1 daughter. Musical Education: Private tuition, Trinity College of Music. Career: Member of Flying Saucers with numerous appearances on German, Dutch and British television and radio; Tours with Chuck Berry, Bill Haley, Scotty Moore, D J Fontana, and The Jordonaires; Film, Blue Suede Shoes. Compositions: 10 compositions. Recordings: Several singles and albums with Flying Saucers; Albums and singles with Avengers; CD with the Jordonaires. Membership: Musicians' Union. Hobbies: Football; Art. Address: 56 King Edwards Road, Edmonton, London N9 7RP, England.

PROBY PJ (James Marcus Smith), b. 6 Nov 1938, Houston, Texas, USA. Singer; Songwriter. Career: Founder, The Moondogs, 1958; Work as demo singer, recording under names: Jett Powers, Orville Wood; Appeared on Beatles TV Special, London, 1964; UK tours, 1965, 1966; Stage performances include: Catch My Soul (rock version of Othello), West End, 1970; Elvis (musical), 1977; Cabaret circuit and recording career continued to 1991. Recordings include: Hold Me, 1964; Together, 1964; Somewhere, 1965; I Apologise, 1965; Let The Water Run Down, 1965; That Means A Lot, 1965; Maria, 1965; You've Come Back, 1966; Niki Hoeky, 1967; Album: I Am PJ Proby, 1965. Honour: Best Musical of the Year, Elvis, 1977.

PROCHAZKA Jiri, b. 23 May 1969, Praha, Czech Republic. Guitar; Keyboards; Drums; Computers; Music Teacher. m. Vladimira Prochazkova, 3 July 1990, 1 daughter. Education: Musical Psychology. Career: Tramp Po Cesku 1-8, video; Unlimited Warriors, videogame. Recording: Unlimited Warriors, videogate. Publication: Unlimited Warriors, videogate. Hobbies: Music; Computers; Swimming. Address: Jiri Prochazka, Hradesínská, 5712409, Praha 10, 101 00, Czech Republic.

PROFESSOR GRIFF (Richard Griffin). Rapper. Career: Member, US rap group Public Enemy, 1984-89; Concerts include: Support to the Beastie Boys, US tour, 1987; Support to LL Cool J, European tour, 1987; Brixton Academy, London, 1990; Solo artiste, 1989-. Recordings: Albums: with Public Enemy: Yo! Bum Rush The Show, 1987; It Takes A Nation Of Millions To Hold Us Back, 1988; Solo album: Pawns In The Game, 1990; Singles: Rebel Without A Pause; Bring The Noise; Don't Believe The Hype; Night Of The Living Baseheads; Black Steel In The Hour Of Chaos; Fight The Power, theme for film Do The Right Thing, 1989; Welcome To The Terrordrome.

PROPHET Ronnie, b. 26 Dec 1928, Hawksbury, Ontario, Canada. Entertainer; Musician (guitar); Singer. m. Glory-Anne, 26 Apr 1986, 2 sons. Career: Duo with wife, Glory-Anne; Ronnie Prophet World Tour; USO tour, England; Germany; Netherlands; Tours with Kenny Rogers;

Johnny Cash; Emmylou Harris; Tammy Wynette; Janie Fricke; Appearances include: Calgary Stampede; Wembley Country Music Festival (7 years); Caesar's Palace, Sands Hotel, Las Vegas; Television appearances include: Johnny Carson Show; Co-host, Canadian Country Music Awards, 1988-1990; Host, Rocky Mountain Inn; Host, Grand Ole Country (6 years); Host, Ronnie Prophet Show; Host, Music Hall America; Host, Ronnie Prophet Entertains. Recordings: 32 albums; The Phantom; No Holiday In LA. Honours: CCMA, 1976, 1980, 1984; Juno Awards, 1977, 1978; TV Country Show Of The Year, Canada, 1977-1980; Angel Award, St Jude Children's Research Hospital; ASCAP Awards for 3 songs as chart records for more than 10 weeks each. Memberships: AFofM; ACTRA; ROPE. Hobbies: Golfing; Fishing; Reading; Films. Current Management: Prophet Productions. Address: 1030 17th Ave S, Nashville, TN 37212, USA.

PROWSE Ian, b. 10 Jan 1967, Ellesmere Port, England. Musician; Songwriter. Career: Seven full headline tours as lead singer, songwriter with: Pele; Support tours with: Del Amitri and the Pogues; Numerous television and live radio appearances; 3 Radio 1 playlists; Composed all three Pele albums. Recordings: Albums: Pele: Fireworks; The Sport Of Kings; Alive, Alive-O. Memberships: PRS; Musicians' Union. Hobbies: Football; Drinking. Current Management: Target Management, London; D L Management, Liverpool. Address: 2 Forge Road, Little Sutton, Wirral, Cheshire L66 3SQ, England.

PSARIS Petros (Pieter Vic), b. 18 May 1949, Rotterdam, The Netherlands. Professor of Music; Concert Singer (Bass Baritone). m. 28 Nov 1988. Education: Private Singing and Music Lessons, 1968-70; Rotterdam Conservatory of Music, 1970-71; Utrecht Conservatory of Music, 1971; Dr of Music, Honorus Causa, International Institute of Missouri, USA, 1988. Career: Singing, Boy-Soprano, Aged 12; Professor Music, Private School of Singing, Houten; Appearances on Swedish TV, 1976, Dutch TV, 1977, 1988, German TV, 1996; Composer of moderate classical expressionistic works; Conductor of male choir, Vianen, Netherlands; Teacher and Conductor, Rotterdam Boys Choir, 1985-89. Recordings: Numerous recordings of both classical music and musicals. Publications: Gezelle's Poetry Set to Music, 1980; 125 Years of Dutch Songs, 1983; Dr René De Clercq: Composer and Music Poet, 1988. Honours: Honorary Freedom of City of Bruges, Belgium, 1980; Knighted, Order of Leopold of Belgium, 1981; Honorary Freedom of Baden Baden, Germany; German Grand Cross and Band, 1982; Golden City Medal of Antwerp, 1987; Freedom and Town Medal of St Niklaas-Waas, Belgium, 1987; Albert Einstein International Academy Bronze Medal for Peace Culture, 3rd Class, 1989; Ehrenurkunde, Internationale Robert Stolz Gesellschaft, Wien, Austria, 1995; Golden Compact Disc, 1996. Hobbies: Painting; Music, particularly piano; Writing of articles and books; Photography.

PUCCI-RIVOLA, Riccardo, b. 22 Sept 1966, Marradi, Florence, Italy. Vocalist; Composer; Performer. Musical Education: Studies in field of experimental singing. Career: Member, vocal trio Trinovox ; Appearances in major TV, radio programs, 1994; Concerts, major German, Swiss, Austrian towns: Berlin, Bremen, Lübeck, Stuttgart, Basel, Vienna, Innsbruck), 1994-95; Soundtrack, radio-play, produced by the Bavarian State Radio, 1995. Recordings: Albums: Incanto, Trinovox, 1994; Voices, Trinovox, Sarband, The Bulgarian Voices, 1994; Earborn, Various Artists And Trinovox, 1995. Honour: Quartetto Cetra '94, Italian National Award for vocal artists, with Trinovox, 1994. Memberships: SIAE; GEMA. Hobbies: Trekking; Cross-country motorcycle racing; Herbal cares. Current Management: Mr Ulrich Balss, Iaro Records, Bremen, Germany.

Address: Iaro Records, Bismarckstr 83, D-28203 Bremen 1, Germany.

PUEYRREDON Cesar, b. 7 July 1952, Buenos Aires, Argentina. Singer; Composer; Musician (keyboards). m. Cecilia Garcia Laborde, 27 Nov 1979, 1 son, 1 daughter. Education: University. Musical Education: Composition, UCA (Universidad Catolica Argentina). Career: Career: Member, group Banana, tours, Argentina, Uruguay, Chile, Paraguay, 1969-84; Tour, Central America, 1977; Solo artiste (as César "Banana" Pueyrredon), tours, Argentina, Uruguay, Paraguay, Chile, Colombia, 1984-; 12 concerts, Teatro Opera, 1989; Opened for Sting, Uruguay, 1990. Recordings include: with Banana: Negra No Te Voyas De Mi Lado, 1971; Conociedote, 1973; Aun Es Tiempo De Souar, 1979; Solo albums: Asi De Simple, 1984; Solo Un Poco Mas, 1985; Esta En Vivo, 1986; Mas Cerca De La Vida, 1987; Ser Uno Mismo, 1988; Tarde O Temprano, 1990; Zo Anos, 1991; Armonia, 1992;. De La Ternura A La Pasión, 1993. Honour: 2 nominations, Premio Prensario, Best TV Musical, for Martin Fierro, 1989; Premio, Santa Clara de Asis. Membership: SADAIC (composers' society). Hobbies: Golf; Football. Current Management: Abraxas Producciones Internacionales. Address: Avda Callao 875 4 H (1023), Buenos Aires, Argentina.

PUOLIS Rolandas, b. 20 Nov 1969, Lithuania. Artist Manager; Broadcaster. Vilnius Technical University. Career: Lithuanian radio and television DJ, 1987-92; Manager, rock group BIX, 1991-. Recordings: Blind Soldiers, Best Record in Lithuania, 1991; Labomba, 1992; Doozgle, Best CD, Lithuania, 1994. Honours: Band Of The Year, 1991, 1992, 1994. Hobby: Hunting. Address: PO Box 552, 2024 Vilnius, Lithuania.

PURIM Flora, b. 6 Mar 1942, Rio De Janeiro, Brazil. m. (1), 1 daughter, (2) Airto Moreira, 19 Mar 1972, 1 daughter. Education: University of California, Long Beach; Graduate, California State University. Recordings: As composer/lyricist with Airto Moreira: Seeds On The Ground, 1970; Natural Feelings, 1969; Free, 1971; Fingers, 1972; Identity, 1975; Promises Of The Sun, 1976; Solo albums: Virgin Land, 1972; Butterfly Dreams, 1973; Stories To Tell, 1974; Open Your Eyes You Can Fly, 1976; 500 Miles High In Montreux, 1976; Encounter, 1977; Nothing Will Be As It Was Tomorrow, 1977; Speed Of Light, 1995; with Chick Corea: Return To Forever, 1972; Light As A Feather, 1973; with Carlos Santana: Welcome, 1973; Borboletta, 1974; with Airto Moreira, Neville Potter: San Francisco River, 1972; with McCoy Tyner: Search for Peace, 1974; with George Duke: Love Reborn, 1973; Feel, 1974; with Airto Moreira: Alue, 1969; with Hermeto Pascoal: We Love, 1970; A Brazilian Love Affair; with Ernie Hood: Mountain Train, 1974; with Duke Pearson: How Insensitive, 1969; It Could Only Happen With You, 1970; with Airto and Deodato: Deodato/Airto In Concert, 1973; That's What She Said, Everyday Every Night, Humble People, 1985; The Magicians; The Sun Is Out, 1987; Producer, with Moreira: I'm Fine How Are You, 1977. Honours include: Downbeat Critics Poll, Established Singer, 1974-76, 1978; Record World, Top Female Jazz Artist, 1974, 1976; Cash Box Award, Top New Female Jazz Artist, 1974; 2 Grammy Nominations, Humble People, 1985; The Magicians. Current Management: A Train Management, PO Box 29242, Oakland, CA 94604, USA.

PYLE Pip, b. 4 Apr 1950, Sawbridgeworth, Hertfordshire, England. Musician (drums); Composer. 1 son, 3 daughters. Education: Bishops Stortford College; Cambridge College of Art. Musical Education: Self-taught. Career: Member, Delivery, 1968-70; Gong, 1970-71; Hatfield And The North, 1972-75; National Health, 1975-80; Soft Heap, 1979-84; L'Equip'out, 1984-95; In Cahoots, 1984-95; Shortwave, 1992-; Gong, 1990-. Recordings: Camembert Electrique, Gong; The Rotters Club, Hatfield And The North;

Of Queues And Cures, National Health; DS Al Coda, National Health; Up, L'Equip'out; Live, Shortwave; Seven Year Itch, Pip Pyle Solo.Memberships: Musicians' Union; MCPS; PRS. Hobby: Cricket. Current Management: Bernard Walbrou, Euterpe, 2 Rue de l'Eglises, 62190 Lespesses, France. Address: 16 bis Rue de General de Gaulle, 94430 Chennevieres, France.

PYYSALO Severi, b. 18 Dec 1967, Finland. Musician (vibes). Musical Education: Sibelius Academy. Career: Began performing, Pori, Finland, 1984; Discovered by Paquito D'Rivera, Sarah Vaughn; Concerts in US include the Village Vanguard; Moved to Helsinki, 1987; Formed group, No Hope Band; Later regrouped as The Front; Member, Perko-Pyysalo Poppoo with Jukko Perko. Recordings include: Uuno Kailas, Perko-Pyysalo Poppoo, 1995. Honours: Yrjö Award, Finnish Jazz Federation, 1988. Address: Museokatu 11 B 45, 00100 Helsinki, Finland.

Q

QUATRO Suzi (Susan Kay), b. 3 June 1950, Detroit, Michigan, USA. Singer; Songwriter; Musician (bass, drums, piano); Actress; Television Presenter. m. (1) Len Tuckey; (2) Rainer Haas, 22 Oct 1992, 1 son, 1 daughter. Career: 30 years as entertainer, 1964-; Numerous worldwide concert tours; Numerous television, stage appearances; Acting, appearing and presenting, including chat show, ITV; Happy Days; Annie Get Your Gun (West End); Wrote and starred in musical about Tallulah Bankhead, "Tallulah Who". Recordings: 16 hit singles include: 48 Crash; Can The Can; Devil Gate Drive; Wild One; Albums include: Suzi Quatro, 1973; Quatro, 1974; Your Mama Won't Like Me, 1975; Aggro Phobia, 1977; If You Knew Suzi, 1978; Suzi And Other 4 Letter Words, 1979; Rock Hard, 1980; Greatest Hits, 1980; Main Attraction, 1982; The Wild One, 1990; Oh Suzi Q, 1990; The Latest and Greatest, 1992. Honours: Numerous Best Female Artist Awards, UK, Europe, Australia, Japan. Hobbies: Swimming; Most sports.

QUAYE Finlay, b. 1974, Edinburgh, Scotland. Singer. Education: BTEC in Music Production, Manchester. Career: Worked with: A Guy Called Gerald; Graham Massey; Rainbow Tribe; Solo artiste, 1996-. Recordings: Album: Maverick A Strike, 1997; Singles: Ultra Stimulation (EP), 1997; Sunday Shining (EP), 1997; Even After All, 1997. Honour: Brit Award, Best Male Solo Artist, 1998. Address: c/o Epic Records, 10 Great Marlborough Street, London W1V 2LP, England.

QUERALT Stephen Paul, b. 4 Feb 1968, Oxford, England. Musician (bass guitar). 1 son. Career: Bass guitarist, rock band Ride; Concerts include: Main support act, Reading Festival, 1992; Television: 3 appearances, Top Of The Pops, BBC; Recorded 2 Top 10 albums and 1 Top 20 album. Recordings: Albums: with Ride: Nowhere, 1991; Going Blank Again, Ride, 1992; Carnival Of Light, Ride, 1994. Current Management: Ben Winchester, Primary Talent. Address: OMC, Suite 1, 2nd Floor, 65 George Street, Oxford OX1 2BE, England.

QUERLIER J, b. 30 July 1946, Tarbes, France. Musician (alto saxophone, soprano saxophone, flute). Education: Chemistry. Musical Education: Certificate, Toulouse Conservatory. Career: Played with Brigitte Fontaine; Jacques Higelin; Christian Escoude; Didier Levallet; Chris MacGregor; Bernard Lubat; René Bottlang; Concerts on Radio France; Festivals at: Antibes; Nîmes; Berlin; Moers; La Haye. Recordings: Christian Escoude Quintet, 1975; Didier Levallet Quintet, 1978; Alan Silva, 1980; Bekummernis Big Band, 1983; René Bottlang, 1991, 93. Membership: UMJ. Hobby: Literature. Address: 22 Rue de Lancry, 75010, Paris, France.

QUEST John A, b. 15 Apr 1919, London, England. Musician (bass, bass guitar). m. Joy Shirley Percy, 28 Dec 1947, 2 sons, 1 daughter. Musical Education: Private tuition. Career: Played with Johnny Denis; Vic Lewis Jazzmen; Vic Lewis Orchestra; Extensive freelance work. Recordings: Numerous recordings with Johnny Denis; Vic Lewis Jazzmen; Vic Lewis Orchestra. Membership: Musicians' Union. Hobbies: Swimming; Golf; Music; Chess. Address: 8 Sunnyside Park, St Ives, Ringwood, Hampshire BH24 2NW, England.

QUIBEL Robert Henri Maurice, b. 12 Oct 1930, Le Havre, France. Musician (double bass); Arranger; Director. m. Madeleine Saumon, 23 Mar 1955, 1 son, 1 daughter. Musical Education: Petit Séminaire de Rouen. Career: Bass player with Benny Bennett; Jacques Helian; Claude Bolling, 1961-63; Backing for various French artistes including: Maurice Fanon; Jacques Martin;

Musical director, director of house band on Dimanche-Matin, weekly French TV programme (France 2), 1980-. Recordings: The Flight Of The Ox-Pecker, Claude Bolling, 1963; Various recordings for children include: Le Petit Ménestral, Lucien Adès; Various title songs and jingles for Dimanche-Matin. Honours: Grand Prix de la Chanson Comique, Les Cuisses de Grenouille by Fernand Raynaud, 1965. Memberships: SACEM; SDRM; SACD. Hobbies: Chess; Bridge; Travel. Address: 2 Rue Ronsard, 95560 Baillet-En-France, France.

QUILLET François "Mr Light", b. 6 May 1959, Paris, France. Composer; Arranger; Musician (piano, keyboards). 1 son, 1 daughter. Education: Musicology, Sorbonne; Schola Cantorum, ENA (École Nouvelle des Arts). Musical Education: Piano with Madame Berger, Maitre Rollay Van Castle; Harmony with Jeanine Rueff (Prix de Rome); Orchestration with Jean Louis Florentz; Arrangement with Ivan Jullien. Career: Member, group Evohé, with V Charbonier, M Goldberg; Also member of groups including Colors And Light; Maggnetick; Provence Brass Band; Musician, actor, film Sandy (with Sandy Stevenson), 1985; Concerts include: First part, Miles Davis, 1987; Betty Carter, Montpellier, 1988; Irakere, with Colors and Light, 1990; Laurie Jam Orchestra, Festival Radio France Montpellier, 1992; Petruciani Quartet, Festival Radio France Montpellier, 1993; Ahmad Jamal and Petrucianni Quartet, 1994; Neville Brothers and Eddy Louiss, 1996; Work with Michel Magne; Bernard Maury; Bob Addrizza; Plays with: P Vassiliu; P Gaillot; R Galiano; D di Piazza; M Barrot; Ivan Jullien; Colors And Light; France (trio), 1995. Compositions: Rap On Jazz; Take No Jazz; Kids; Exit 23; I Got My Reasons; Colors And Light. Recordings: Colors And Light, Colors And Light (with C Flowers); The First, Pettruciani Quartet; Pulsion, M Bachevalier Group; Between You And Me, P Gaillot. Publications: Melody's Universe; Ed. Bable's Dream. Honours: Bac D; Diplôme Superieur Studies of Schola Cantorum, DEUG, Sorbonne. Memberships: IMFP (Institut Musical de Formation Professional); JAM (École Règionale de Jazz Languedoc-Roussillon). Hobbies: Chess; Sport; Philosophy.

QUILLIVIC Jean, b. 10 Jan 1960, Rabat, Morocco. Composer; Musician (saxophone). m. Josiame Robakowski, 2 sons, 2 daughters. Education: BA, Sciences, Brest. Musical Education: MA, BA, Musicology, Paris. Career: CIM School of Jazz, Paris, 1985; First alto saxophone in Pierre Sellin Big Band, 1985-; Formed group Oxyde de Cuivre, 1987; Formed own group Jean Quillivic Quartet, 1988; Concerts in festivals, summer tours, 1989-. Recordings: Prise de Bec, Zap, 1989; La Femme à La Valise, Jean Quillivic Quartet, 1990; En Public Au Fourneau 95, Oxyde de Cuivre, 1995. Membership: SACEM. Current Management: Promoart. Address: B P 27, 29470 Plougastel, Dadulas, France.

QUIN Andrew James, b. 12 Aug 1960, London, England. Composer; Musician (keyboards, percussion); Music Lecturer. m. Anne Perrett, 20 Aug 1983, 1 son, 1 daughter. Education: BA Hons Music, Electronics, Keele University, 1982. Musical Education: Private. Career: 25 albums for Dewolfe, 1984-; Freelance lecturer, Music Technology, universities and conservatories throughout UK; Currently Manchester Metropolitan University; Regular jazz performer in Midlands; Broadcasts in 36 countries, all continents; Television documentary, Quest, 1985. Recordings: Albums: Mirage, 1985; The Cutting Edge, 1987; Four Minus One, 1988; The Corporate Net, 1995; Television themes: Something To Treasure, 1988; Central Weekend, 1985; Scandal, 1988; Commercials: Fairy Snow, 1989; Canderel, 1990; Webster's Bitter, 1991; Lynx Deodorant, 1992. Memberships: Musicians' Union; PRS; APC. Hobbies: Aviation sports;

Badminton; Jazz piano. Current Management: De Wolfe Ltd. Address: De Wolfe Ltd, 80-88 Wardour Street, London W1V 3LF, England.

QUINCY Dave, b. 13 Sept 1939, Battle, Sussex, England. Musician (saxophone); Composer; Music Publisher. m. Patricia Ann (Patti) Quincy, 1 daughter with second wife (3 marriages). Musical Education: Self-taught. Career: First tour, Little Richard, Sam Cooke, 1962; UK tour as member of Jet Harris' group (ex-Shadows); Extensive tours with rock and jazz groups, 1960s; Began recording with band IF, 1969; Material now to be released in compilation album, 1995; Work, tours, recordings, many Jazz Fusion projects. Compositions: Material in IF compilation, 1995. Recordings: IF, Vols 1-4, 1969-72. Memberships: PRS; BASCA; MCPS; Musicians' Union; Jazz Umbrella; Hobbies: Watching cricket; Doing crosswords.

QUINN Edwin Henry, b. 17 Jul 1963, Portsmouth, Hampshire, England. Musician (drums). 1 son, 1 daughter. Musical Education: School lessons, orchestras and bands. Career: Member of Dakinis, with various session work; Drummer, indie band Blow Up, 1990-92; Tours of UK and Paris showcase concerts; Video for single, World, filmed for Music Box, MTV Europe; Currently rehearsing for a musical in Brighton Festival. Recordings: Album: Amazon Eyegasm, 1991; Single: World. Current Management: Sarah Heyworth Independent PR. Address: 67 Cobden Road, Brighton, East Sussex BN2 2TJ, England.

QUINN Eimear, b. 18 December 1972, Dublin, Ireland. Vocalist. Education: Degrees in Town Planning and Music; Piano Lessons; Degree in Music Studies. Career: Lead Voice with Anvna Vocal Group; Vocalist with Anuna, Irish Mediaeval Vocal Group; Sang Lead in London with Riverdance The Show; Toured Australia and Scandinavia as solo act. Recordings: The Voice, Eurovision Winner, 1996; Winter, Fire and Snow, EP, 1996; Caccini's Ave Maria. Honour: Eurovision Song Contest Winner, Oslo, 1996. Current Management: 24 Merchants Quay, Dublin 8, Ireland.

QUINN Mick. Guitarist (bass). Career: Member, Supergrass, 1994-; Concerts include: Support to Blur, Alexandra Palace; UK tour, with Shed Seven, 1994; T In The Park Festival, Glasgow, 1995. Recordings: Album: I Should Coco (Number 1, UK), 1995; In It For The Money (reached No 2), 1997; Singles: Caught By The Fuzz, 1994; Mansize Rooster, 1995; Lenny, 1995; Alright, 1995; Going Out, 1996; Sun Hits The Sky, 1997. Honours: Q Award, Best New Act, 1995; BRIT Award Nominations: Best British Newcomer, Best Single, Best Video, 1996. Current Management: Courtyard Management, 22 The Nursery, Sutton Courtenay, Abingdon, Oxon OX14 4UA, England.

QUINTEN Johan, b. 25 June 1972, Louvain, Belgium. Singer. m. Ilse Theys, 12 August 1995. Career: About 150 gigs in Belgium; 1 gig at local TV; Few presentations on local and national radio. Compositions: Romance; Dislike; End of the Road; Freestyle; No More; Dignity; Middle-Age View; 1.000.000 Bookmaker; Skateboard Yuppies; Song for the Losers. Recordings: Romance, CD; No More, song on compilation; You Gotta Know What You Stand For. Honour: Final of Studio Brussels, Metal Fun Race. Membership: All for Music Member. Hobbies: Reading; Nature; Writing; Youth Care. Current Management: Johan Quinten, Dutselhoek 10, 3220 Holsbeek, Belgium. Address: Dutselhoek, 3220 Holsbeek, Belgium.

R

RABBITT Eddie (Edward Thomas), b. 27 Nov 1944, Brooklyn, New York, USA. Country Singer; Songwriter. Career: Recording artiste, 1964-; Songwriter, co-writer with Even Stevens, David Molloy. Compositions include: Pure Love, Ronnie Milsap (US Country Number 1); Working My Way Up From The Bottom, Roy Drusky; The Sounds Of Goodbye, George Morgan; Love Me And Make It All Better, Bobby Lewis; 3 songs recorded by Elvis Presley: Kentucky Rain; Patch It Up; Inherit The Wind. Recordings: US Country Number 1s: Gone Too Far; Drivin' My Life Away (used in film Roadie); I Love A Rainy Night; Step By Step; Someone Could Lose A Heart Tonight; I Wanna Dance With You; Drinkin' My Baby (Off My Mind); The Wanderer; Other singles include: Six Nights And Seven Days; Bottles; I Just Don't Care No More; You Get To Me; I Just Want To Love You; Suspicions; Film theme, Every Which Way But Loose; Duets include: You And I, with Crystal Gayle; Both To Each Other (Friends And Lovers), with Juice Newton (theme for television series, Days Of Our Lives); Albums: Eddie Rabbitt, 1975; Rocky Mountain Music, 1976; Variations, 1978; Loveline, 1979; Horizon, 1980; Step By Step, 1981; Radio Romance, 1982; Rabbitt Trax, 1986; I Wanna Dance With You, 1988; Jersey Boy, 1990; Ten Rounds, 1991. Current Management: Moress Nanas Entertainment, 12424 Wilshire Blvd, Ste 840, Los Angeles, CA 90025, USA.

RABESON Jean Bernard (Jeanot), b. 20 Aug 1936, Madagascar. Musician (piano). m (1) Jeanne, (2) Lalao, 1 son, 4 daughters. Musical Education: Self-taught. Career: Jazz pianist, French Riviera Jazz Festival, Antibes, 1961; All Indian Ocean Jazz Festival, 1989-; Jazz in Marciac (almost every year with Guy Lafitte Quartet); Jazz at Ramatuelle, 1991. Recordings: Album in San Francisco, 1992; Live in Paris with Turk Mauro (US saxophone player); Under The Magnolias, with Richard Rauk (French saxophone player); Live recording with Guy Lafitte, 1993. Honours: National Order, Madagascar Government, as artiste-musician. Hobbies: Painting (water, pastel, oil), realist style; Bodybuilding; Cycling. Address: 1559 Rue de Bernaü, 94500 Champigny Sur Marne, France.

RABIN Trevor, b. 13 Jan 1954, Johannesburg, South Africa. Musician (guitar, keyboards); Songwriter; Record Producer. m. Shelley May, 17 Aug 1979, 1 son. Musical Education: Orchestration with Walter Mony; 8 years of piano studies. Career: Formed band, Rabbitt, age 14; Several tours, film and television appearances; Moved to England, 1977; Solo artiste, tours and television, 1977-; Member, progressive rock group Yes, 1982-; International concerts include: US tour, 1987; Yesshows tour, 1991; Wembley Arena, 1991. Compositions include: Owner Of A Lonely Heart, Yes (worldwide Number 1 hit); Composer, music for Fair Game. Recordings: Albums: Solo: Trevor Rabin, 1978; Face To Face, 1979; Wolf, 1981; Can't Look Away, 1989; 2 albums with Rabbitt; with Yes: 90125, 1983; 9012 Live - The Solos, 1986; The Big Generator, 1987; Union, 1991; Yesstory, 1991; Hit singles with Yes: Owner Of A Lonely Heart; Leave It; It Can Happen; Rhythm Of Love; Lift Me Up. Publications: Instructional guitar video. Honour: Grammy Award, Best Instrumental Performance, Cinema, 1985. Memberships: AFTRA; Musicians' Union. Current Management: Tony Dimitriades, East End Management. Address: 8209 Melrose Avenue, 2nd Floor, Los Angeles, CA 90046, USA.

RACKLEY Tony, b. 30 Mar 1961, Easley, South Carolina, USA. Singer; Songwriter. m. Emily Elizabeth Collins, 12 Apr 1986, 1 son. Career: Professional songwriter, 1990-; South Carolina Coordinator for Nashville Songwriters Association International (NSAI); Established Flying L Music (publishing), 1993. Recordings: Albums, all original compositions: Winding Road, 1992; Common Ground, due release 1996. Memberships: BMI; IBMA (International Bluegrass Music Association); NSAI (Nashville Songwriters Association International). Hobbies: Farming; Horses; Snow skiing. Current Management: Self-managed (Flying L Music). Address: Flying L Music, 1215 Brown Road, Belton, SC 29627, USA.

RAE Dashiell, b. 10 Jan 1956, New Jersey, USA. Composer; Musician (flute, piano); Vocalist. Musical Education: Eastman School Of Music, New York. Career: Orchestral musician, principal flautist, soloist, New York; Moved to London, 1985; Worked with Julia Fordham (keyboards, flute, backing vocals), 1989-; Worked with: Level 42; The Style Council; Womack & Womack; Midge Ure; Aztec Camera; Paul Young; Became composer film and television music, 1992. Compositions include: Film: Keys; The Queen's House; The Docket Box; The Dream; Television: Hidden Hands; Art And The CIA, CH4; The Dream, BBC Wales; Childrens' Ward, Granada; Last Days At Forchwen, BBC Wales; Touch, BBC Wales; Commercials: Onken Yogurt, 1994; Various: Sky Sport, 1993; Anglia, Survival, 1994; Channel Islands TV News Theme, 1994-; Promos for BBC, ITV; Classical compositions: La Chasse (piano duet); Misere (string orchestra). Recordings include: Solo piano album: Songs Without Words, 1985. Memberships: Musicians' Union; PRS; Equity (UK); AFTRA; ASCAP; Women in Film and TV (UK). Current Management: Soundtrack Music Management, 22 Ives Street, London SW3 2ND, England.

RAESIDE Diane Lesley Cameron, b. Scarborough, Ontario, Canada. Country-Blues Singer. Musical Education: Canadian Academy For The Performing Arts, Ian Garrett. Career: Professional singer from age 18; Concert appearances throughout Ontario, and Zevenbergen Festival, Netherlands, 1995; Television appearance: Be A Star, Nashville Network. Recordings: Album: Crazy Infatuation, 1992; Since You Went Away, 1995; Singles: Turning Into Strangers; Half A Heart; I'll Cry About That Tomorrow; Run For Your Money; Just Another Day; Take Me In Your Arms Tonight; Love Is Where The Good Times Are; Crazy Infatuation; Last Date; Some Rivers Run Dry; Slow Dance; This Time Of Year, Singing Songs Of Love (All-star charity single). Honours: Labatts-Guinness Travel Bursary; Numerous Song Contests; RPM Big Country Award, Outstanding New Artist, 1992. Memberships: Songwriters Association; Canadian Country Music Association. Hobbies: Showdogs; Swimming; Hiking. Address: 23 Timgren Drive, Scarborough, Ontario M1R 3R4, Canada.

RAFFERTY Gerry, b. 16 Apr 1947, Paisley, Scotland. Singer; Songwriter; Musician (guitar). Career: Member, The Humblebums, 1968-70; Founder member, Stealers Wheel, 1972-75; Solo artist, 1978-. Recordings: Albums: with The Humblebums: The New Humblebums, 1969; Open Up The Door, 1970; with Stealers Wheel: Stealers Wheel, 1973; Solo albums: Can I Have My Money Back?, 1971; City To City, 1978; Night Owl, 1979; Snakes And Ladders, 1980; Sleepwalking, 1982; North And South, 1988; Right Down The Line - The Best Of Gerry Rafferty, 1990; A Wing And A Prayer, 1993; Over My Head, 1995; Singles include: with Stealers Wheel: Stuck In The Middle With You, 1973; Solo: Baker Street (Number 2, US), 1978; Right Down The Line, 1978; Home And Dry, 1979; Night Owl, 1980; Days Gone Down (Still Got The Light In Your Eyes), 1980; Get It Right Next Time, 1980; Contributor, film soundtrack Local Hero, with Mark Knopfler, 1983; Producer, Letter From America, The Proclaimers, 1987. Honours: 2 Ivor Novello Awards, Best Song, Best Pop Song, 1979. Address: c/o Asgard Agency, 125 Parkway, London NW1 7PS, England.

RAFFIT Jean-Paul, b. 2 Aug 1964, Patiers, France. Musician (guitar). Education: First year university. Musical Education: 3 years with private guitar teacher. Career: Jazz festivals: Montreal with B Sandoval; Kalamata (Greece) with B Sandoval; Dortmund; Bonn; Frankfurt; Petit Journal; Passage Nordouest; Cartou Cherie; Television: Nulle Part Ailleurs (Canal+) with Eric Lareine; Cercle de Minuit (France 2). Recordings: Albums: with B Sandoval: Camino del Alba, 1992; Caracola, 1993; Vida, 1994; Album with S Lopez, 1993; All The Generics, 1994-95; Graffiti (with 9 original compositions), 1995; Antenne Ouverte A La Conscience (video). Publications: Jean-Paul Raffit, Un Amour de Guitare, 1995; Flash, 1995. Honours: ffff (telerada) for Vida (album with B Sandoval). Memberships: SACEM; SPEDIDAM. Hobbies: Caving; Excursions; Philosophy. Current Management: Michel Guilhem. Address: Plaisance, 09100 Madiere, France.

RAFIATOU Fifi (Rafiatou Bellow-Adjani), b 2 Oct 1963, Atakpame, Togo, Africa. Singer; Composer. 1 son, 1 daughter. Career: Backing singer in Togo; Member, National Presbyterian Choir; International concerts with Papa Wemba; Alpha Blondy; Ossibissa; Miriam Makeba; Masa; Performed at St Martin Black Festival. Compositions: Ibama; Ahe; Ile; Wawa; Ikoule. Publications: Priere Pour La Paix, 1980; Nwassa, 1985; Djofe, 1990; Motus, 1997. Honours: Pan-African Fair of Art and Music Award, 1990; Fisrt Prize, Afrovision, 1991; Spring Festival of Dion-Yang. Memberships: SACEM; ADAMI. Hobbies: Films; Cooking. Current Management: c/o Georges Konila Figah, Discorama Production, BP 12629 Lome, Togo.

RAIMON (Raimon Pelegero Sanchis), b. 2 Dec 1940, Xàtiva, Spain. Singer; Songwriter. m. Annalisa Corti, 22 Aug 1966. Education: University Graduate, Contemporary History. Musical Education: Elemental studies. Career: Tours: France, Mexico; USA; Argentina; Japan; Concerts include: Olympia Theatre, Paris, 1966, 1969, 1974; Teatro Español, Madrid, 1988; Many appearances, Barcelona, Valencia; Television includes: Especial Raimon, TVE, 1984; Raimon previously banned during Franco Dictatorship to 1977; Live broadcast, Festival of La Mercè, Barcelona, 1987; Live recital, Raimon, 30 Anys d'al Vent, Barcelona, TV3, TVE2, 1993. Compositions include: Al Vent; Diguem No; Jo Vinc d'un Silenci; Com Un Puny. Recordings include: Raimon, 1963, 1964; A L'Olympia, 1966; Diguem No, 1971; Catalonian Protest Songs, 1971; T'Adones Amic, 1974; Raimon, 1977; Quan L'Aigua Es Queixa, 1980; Entre La Nota I El So, 1984; Canta Ausiàs March, 1989; Cançons, 1993; Integral, 1993. Publications: Canzoni Contro, 1971; Poemes I Cançons, 1973; Poemas y Canciones, 1976; Les Hores Guanyades, 1983; D'Aquest Viure Insistent, 1986; Les Paraules Del Meu Cant, 1993. Honours include: Grand Prix Francis Carco, Académie Du Disque, Paris, 1967; City of Barcelona Prize, 1982; Fundació Jaume Primer, Barcelona, 1987; Aportació Musical, Valencia, 1993; The Best Show Of The Year, Barcelona, 1994; Premi Nacional De Música, 1993; Grand Prix, Nouvelle Academie Du Disque, Integral Raimon, France, 1994. Current Management: Annalisa Corti. Address: Plaça Bonsuccès, 7 atc 2a, E-08001, Barcelona, Spain.

RAINEY Ron Paul, b. 3 Feb 1946, East Stroudsburg, Pennsylvania, USA. Artist Manager. Career: Concert agent, International Famous Agency (now International Creative Management), New York City, 1969-71; Vice President, concert department, Agency For The Performing Arts, New York City and Los Angeles, 1971-73; Chairman, chief executive officer, Magna Artists Corporation, Los Angeles, 1974-81; President, chief executive officer, Ron Rainey Management Inc, Beverly Hills, California, 1981-. Hobbies: Collecting baseball cards; Fine wines; Antique books; Music memorabilia. Address: 315 S

Beverly Drive, Suite 206, Beverly Hills, CA 90212, USA.

RAITT Bonnie, b. 8 Nov 1949, Burbank, California, USA. Musician (guitar, piano). Education: Radcliffe College. Career: Performer, blues clubs, US East Coast; Concerts include: MUSE concert, Madison Square Garden with Bruce Springsteen, Jackson Browne, Carly Simon, The Doobie Brothers, 1979; Roy Orbison Tribute Concert with artists including: Whoopi Goldberg; kd lang; Bob Dylan; B B King, 1990; Performances with artists including: Stevie Wonder, Bruce Springsteen, Aretha Franklin, Willie Nelson, Elton John. Recordings: Albums include: Bonnie Raitt, 1971; Give It Up, 1972; Takin' My Time, 1973; Streetlights, 1974; Home Plate, 1975; Sweet Forgiveness, 1977; The Glow, 1979; Green Light, 1982; Nine Lives, 1986; Nick Of Time, 1989; The Bonnie Raitt Collection, 1990; Luck Of The Draw, 1991; Road Tested, 1995; Fundamental, 1998. Honours include: 4 Grammy Awards: Album of Year; Best Rock Vocal Performance; Best Female Pop Vocal Performance; Best Traditional Blues Performance (with John Lee Hooker), and numerous nominations. Current Management: Gold Mountain Entertainment. Address: 3575 Cahuenga Blvd W, Suite 450, Los Angeles, CA 90068, USA.

RAITT John Emmet, b. 29 Jan 1917, Santa Ana, California, USA. Actor; Singer. m. Rosemary Kraemer, 2 sons, 1 daughter. Education: BA University of Redlands, California. Musical Education: Private. Career: Oklahoma; Carousel; 3 Wishes For Jamie; Magdelena; Carnival In Flanders; Pajama Game (Broadway and film); Annie Get Your Gun; Zorba; On A Clear Day; Summer Chevy Show; Bell Telephone Hour; 25 Years of Summer Stock; Concerts: A Joyful Noise - Musical Jubilee. Recordings: Oklahoma; Carousel 1945, 1965; Showboat; Highlights Of Broadway; Under Open Skies; Mediterranean Magic; 3 Wishes For Jamie; Annie Get Your Gun. Honours: Hon Dr, University of Redlands and Pepperdine and Boston Conservatory; Theater Hall Of Fame, New York; Hollywood Walk Of Fame. Hobby: Golf. Current Management: James Fitzgerald Ent. Address: 4300 Prominade Way #121 P, Marina Del Rey, CA90292, USA.

RAKSIN David, b. 4 Aug 1912, Philadelphia, Pennsylvania, USA. Composer; Conductor; Author; Professor. m. Joanne Kaiser, 19 Sept 1959, divorced, 2 sons, 1 daughter. Education: University of Pennsylvania. Musical Education: William Happich; Harl McDonald; Isador Freed; Arnold Schoenberg. Career: Went to Hollywood, worked with Charlie Chaplin, music for Modern Times, 1935; Scored over 100 films, including: Laura; The Bad And The Beautiful; Several hundred radio shows; Approximately 400 television programmes; Conducted major orchestras. Compositions: Music from films: Laura; Forever Amber; The Bad And The Beautiful; Composed text and music, conducted premiere of Oedipus Memneitai (Coolidge Commission from Library of Congress). Publications: 7 articles published by Library of Congress; Book Of Songs, 1996. Honours: Career achievement awards from: ASCAP; Composers and Lyricists Guild. Memberships: President, Composers and Lyricists Guild Of America; Board of Directors, ASCAP; President, Society for Preservation of Film Music. Hobby: Researching CD/ROM project Pictures At An Exhibition. Current Management: Shelby Brown. Address: 441 E 57th Street, New York, NY 10022, USA.

RALPH Mark, b. 2 May 1974, Stoke-on-Trent, Staffordshire, England. Musician (guitar). Career: Long term member of Max The Sax, 12-piece jazz funk band; Featured on We Are Family by Sister Sledge, 1993 remixes; Worked with Sure Is Pure, on further dance remixes. Recordings: We Are Family, Sister Sledge; Lost In Music, Sister Sledge; Manha De Brasil, Max The Sax. Hobbies:

Swimming; Squash. Current Management: Nigel Woodcock. Address: 73 Rothesay Avenue, Newcastle-under-Lyme, Staffordshire ST5 2LQ, England.

RALPHES Paul Stuart, b. 23 Feb 1962, Shrewsbury, England. Record Producer; Songwriter; Musician (bass, guitar). m. Rosana Ferrao, 7 Dec 1991. Education: BA in Film, University of Warwick, 1984. Musical Education: Self-taught. Career: Producer, songwriter, musician, Bliss, 1987-1992; Tours with: Van Morrison; Paul Simon; Gipsy Kings; Chris Isaak; Worked with: Rupert Hine; Jon Kelly; John Shaw; Hugh Jones; Currently producer, writer, Duke Baysee. Recordings: As producer, writer, musician: Loveprayer, Bliss, 1989; Change In The Weather, Bliss, 1991; Sugar Sugar, Duke Baysee, 1994; Do You Love Me?, Duke Baysee, 1995. Honours: Best International Act, Bliss, Italy, Brazil, 1989. Memberships: PRS; Musicians' Union. Hobbies: Film; Liverpool Football Club; Travel. Current Management: Thin Men Productions. Address: 14 Hurst Lodge, 25 Coolhurst Road, London N8 8ES, England.

RALPHS Mick, b. 31 Mar 1944, Hereford, England. Musician (guitar); Vocalist. Career: Founder member, Mott The Hoople, 1969-72; Founder member, UK rock group Bad Company, 1973-83; Tour with Dave Gilmour (Pink Floyd), 1983; Solo recording artiste, 1985; Rejoined Bad Company, 1986-; Regular US tours, including Last Rebel Tour, with Lynyrd Skynyrd, 1993. Compositions include: Can't Get Enough; Movin' On; Feel Like Makin' Love (co-writer with Paul Rodgers). Recordings: Albums: with Bad Company: Bad Company, 1974; Straight Shooter, 1975; Run With The Pack, 1976; Burnin' Sky, 1977; Desolation Angels, 1979; Rough Diamonds, 1982; Fame And Fortune, 1986; Holy Water, 1990; Here Comes Trouble, 1992; The Best Of Bad Company Live - What You Hear Is What You Get, 1993; Company Of Strangers, 1995; Solo: Take This, 1983. Honours: Louisiana Colonel, with Bad Company, 1976. Current Management: Legend Artist Management, 120 W 44th Street, Suite 404, New York, NY 10036, USA.

RAMAGE Andrew, b. 24 Sept 1949, Edinburgh, Scotland. Musician (guitar, bass: contra). m. Anita, 11 Apr 1975. Education: Diploma British Display Society, Telford College. Musical Education: Self-taught, traditional Scots/Irish folk music. Career: BBC TV; RME TV; STV; Grampian TV; Tours: Bermuda; Bangladesh; Iceland; Norway; Denmark; Netherlands; Switzerland; Morocco; Ireland; Radio BBC Scotland; Radio Tay; Radio Forth; Radio Moray Firth; Radio Heartland; Radio Clyde. Recordings: Golden Bird Volumes 1 and 2, 1968; Bitter Withy Sampler, 1973; Bridging The Gap, 1983; Two For The Road, 1986; Silver Darlings, 1988; Dancing On A Wave, 1989; Naturally, 1991; Family Ties, 1993; Scotland The Brave, 1995. Honours: RBI, 1970; Glenfarg Quaich, 1980. Membership: Musicians' Union. Hobbies: Wine making; Golf; Bon-Viveur. Current Manager: Self-managed. Address: Sunnyside House, Drunzie, Glenfarg, Perthshire PH2 9PE, Scotland.

RAMIREZ Humberto, b. 31 Jan 1963, San Juan, Puerto Rico. Musician (trumpet); Composer; Producer; Arranger. m. Ivette Maritza Negron, 16 Jan 1988, 1 son, 1 daughter. Education: Escuela Libre de Musica, San Juan, Puerto Rico. Musical Education: Berklee College of Music, Boston, MA, Bachelor of Music. Career: Concerts played at Madison Square Garden; Hollywood Bowl; Miami Arena; Blue Note Jazz Club; Blues Alley; Tours: Spain, Mexico City, USA, Canada and Europe. Recordings: Jazz Project; Aspects; Portrait Of A Stranger; Canciones de Amor. Honours: 5 Gold records; 4 Platinum records; Diplo Award Best Jazz Recording, 1992; TU Musica Award, Best Jazz Recording, 1994, 1995, 1996; 8 Gold and 6 Platinum Records. Memberships: NARAS;

ASCAP. Hobby: Sports. Current Management: Nilpo Music Inc. Address: P O Box 9020924, San Juan, 00902-0924 Puerto Rico.

RAMIREZ Juan, b. 17 Oct 1947, London, England. Flamenco Musician (guitar); Songwriter. m. Marsha, 15 Apr 1972. Musical Education: Studied flamenco guitar, dance accompaniment, Spain and London. Career: Full time 1974-; Formed internationally renowned Viva Flamenco Dance Company, 1976; Performed at Royal Albert Hall; Barbican; Royal Festival Hall, London; Film appearance: The Curse Of The Pink Panther, 1983; World's largest production of Carmen, 1992; Numerous television appearances. Compositions include: Just Love. Recordings: with Marc Almond: The Desperate Hours. Membership: Musicians' Union. Hobbies: Football; Antiques; Art; All types of music. Current Management: Self-managed. Address: 122B Wood Vale, London SE23 3EB, England.

RAMONE Joey (Jeffrey Hyman), b. 19 May 1952, Forest Hills, New York, USA. Vocalist. Career: Founder member, US punk rock group, The Ramones, 1974-; US Festival, 1981; Milton Keynes Bowl, 1985; Artists Against Apartheid, 1985; Film appearances: Punk film, Blank Generation, 1976; Featured in film Rock`n'Roll High School, 1979; Pet Semetary, 1989; Launched festival of new bands, Spring Offense At CBGBS, 1991. Recordings: The Ramones, 1976; Leave Home, 1977; Road To Ruin, 1978; It's Alive, 1979; Rock`n'Roll High School, 1979; End Of The Century, 1980; Pleasant Dreams, 1981; Subterranean Jungle, 1983; Too Tough To Die, 1984; Animal Boy, 1986; Halfway To Sanity, 1982; The Ramones...All The Stuff, 1990; Mondo Bizarro, 1992; Acid Eaters, 1994; Singles include: Sheena Is A Punk Rocker, 1977; Swallow My Pride, 1977; Baby I Love You, 1980. Address: c/o Overland Productions, 156 W 56th Street, 5th Floor, New York, NY 10019, USA.

RAMONE Phil, b. 5 Jan 1939, New York, USA. Record Producer; Musician (violin). m. Apr 1984, 3 sons. Musical Education: Julliard School of Music, New York; Doctor Musicology, Berklee College of Music, Boston; Doctor Musicology, Five Towns College, New York. Career: Founded own studio, A&R Recording, New York, 1961; Theatre credits include: Chicago; Hair; Little Shop Of Horrors; Starlight Express; The Wiz; Film credits include: A Star Is Born; Flashdance; Ghostbusters; Midnight Cowboy; Reds; Yentl; Shampoo. Television credits include: Liza With A Z; Raffi On Broadway; Extreme; Liza Live From Radio Music Hall; The Jim Henson Hour; The Academy Awards; The Grammy Awards; Simon & Garfunkel Concert, Central Park; Show Business. Recordings: As producer: The Stranger, 52nd Street, Glass Houses, Songs From The Attic, Innocent Man, Billy Joel; Flashdance (soundtrack); A Star Is Born, Yentl, Barbra Streisand; One Trick Pony, Still Crazy After All These Years, 50 Ways To Leave Your Lover, Slip Slidin' Away, Paul Simon; Too Late For Goodbyes, Valotte, Julian Lennon; Send In The Clowns, Judy Collins; Alice's Restaurant, Arlo Guthrie; The Look Of Love, Dusty Springfield; Leaving On A Jet Plane, Peter Paul & Mary; Duets I & II, Frank Sinatra; also producer for Elton John; Gloria Estefan; Sinead O'Connor; Barry Manilow; Paul McCartney; Jon Secada; Dionne Warwick; Art Garfunkel; Chicago; Stephen Sondheim. Honours: 8 Grammy Awards; 15 Grammy Nominations; 1 Emmy; Numerous Platinum & Gold albums and singles; TEC Hall Of Fame, 1992; 3M Visionary Award, 1994; Eyes On NY Award, 1994; Rock Walk Award, 1994; Songwriters Hall Of Fame. Memberships: Former President, New York Chapter, NARAS; NATAS; AFTRA;AFofM; ASCAP; BMI; SESAC; SAG. Hobbies: Travel; Reading; Computers; Art collecting; Wine. Current Management: Peter Asher Management. Address: 644 North Doheny Drive, Los Angeles, CA 90069, USA.

RAMPLING Danny, b. 15 July 1961, London, England. Disc Jockey; Record Producer. Career: Broadcaster, BBC Radio 1; Club disc jockey; Record producer for the Millionaire Hippies. Hobbies: Travel; Restaurants; Gym training; Cooking. Address: c/o BBC Radio 1, Broadcasting House, London W1A 1AA, England.

RANADE Ashok Da, b. 25 October 1937. Education: MA, Marathi and English Literature, University of Bombay, India; LLB, University of Bombay. Appointments: Lecturer in English and Marathi, Siddharth College of Commerce and Economics; Director, University Music Centre, Bombay, 1968-83; Associate Director, Archives and Research Centre in Ethnomusicology, American Institute of Indian Studies, 1983-84; Deputy Director, Theatre Research and Ethnomusicology, National Centre for Performing Arts, Bombay, 1984-94. Compositions: Exhibitions: Akar, International Exhibition of Calligraphy, New Delhi, 1988; Discovery of India, Nehru Centre, Bombay, 1989; Plays: Chavata, 1971; Mythmakers, 1971; Sonar Bangla, 1972; Mata Draupadi, 1972; Devajine Karuna Keli, 1973; Sandhyachaya, 1979; Ek Jhunj Varyshi, 1988; Kala Vazir Pandhra Raja, 1992; Tempt Me Not, 1993; Rahile Door Ghar Maze, 1995; Audio Music - Cassettes: Baithakchi Lavani, 1989; Devgani, 1991. Publications: Honours: Degree of Sangeetacharya: Akhil Bharatiya Gandharva Mahavidylaya Mandal, 1976; Adjudged Best Music Direcoer, Ek Jhunj Varyashi, Maharashtra State Competition for Professional Theatre, 1990. Publications: Sangeetache Saundaryashastra, 1971; Lok Sangget Shastra, 1975; Stravinskiche Sangeetik Saundary Ashastra, 1975; On Music and Musicians of Hindoostan, 1984; Marathi Stage Music, 1986; Maharashtra: Art Music, 1989; Keywords and Concepts: Hindustani Classical Music, 1990; Music and Drama in India, 1991; Indology and Ethnomusicology: Contours of Early Indo-British Relationship, 1992; Bhashanrang-Vyasapeeth Anirangpeeth, 1995. Address: 7 Dnyanadevi, Sahitya Sahawas, Kalanager, Kalelkar Marg, Bandra, Mumbai 400051, India.

RANALDO Lee, b. 3 Feb 1956, Glen Cove, New York, USA. Artist; Writer; Musician (bass). Education: BFA SUNY Binghampton: Painting, Cinema, Philosophy. Career: Soloist, performer with Glenn Branca and Rhys Chatham; Founding member, Sonic Youth; Duo performances: spoken word/film/music called Drift, with filmmaker Leah Singer. Recordings: Sonic Youth, 1984; East Jesus; Broken Circle/Spiral Hill; Bad Moon Rising, 1985; Evol, 1986; Sister, 1987; Daydream Nation, 1988; Goo, 1991. Publications: Road movies; Bookstore. Membership: AFofM. Current Management: ICM. Address: PO Box 6179, Hoboken, NJ 07030, USA.

RANDAZZO Teddy, b. 13 May 1935, New York City, USA. Composer; Musician; Actor. m. Rosemary Randazzo, 4 sons, 3 daughters. Musical Education: Private studies. Career: Appeared on Ed Sullivan TV show 7 times, and in 4 films, Rock Rock Rock, The Girl Can't Help It, Mister Rock And Roll, and, Hey, Let's Twist; Appearances at various clubs including: Copa Cabana, Blaisdell Arena, Hawaii, and Araneta Colosseum, Philippines. Recordings: Goin' Out Of My Head; Hurt So Bad; Pretty Blue Eyes; It's Gonna Take A Miracle; I'm On The Outside Looking In; Have You Looked Into Your Heart; Big Wide World; You're So Right For What's Wrong. Membership: BINI. Hobby: Music. Address: 5254 Oak Island Road, Orlando, FL 32809, USA.

RANDOLPH Boots (Homer Louis Randolph), b. 3 June 1927, Paducah, Kentucky, USA. Musician (tenor saxophone). m. Dee Barber, 17 Sept 1947, 1 son, 1 daughter. Musical Education: High School and Army Band. Career: Concerts all over USA and Canada; Most variety television shows, including: Ed Sullivan; Jimmy

Dean; Jackie Gleason; Boston Pops with Arthur Feedler; TNN-Nashville Network. Recordings: Yakety Sax, as composer and musician; Recorded 43 albums. Honours: 8 years Playboy All Star Jazz Poll. Memberships: AFofM; AFTRA. Hobbies: Golf; Snow skiing. Current Management: Gerard W Purcell, New York, New York. Address: 964 Second Avenue, New York, NY 10022-6304, USA.

RANEY Sue, b. 18 June 1939, McPhearson, Kansas, USA. Singer. m. Carmen Fanzone, 14 Dec 1985. Career: Child star, recording debut aged 16; Performed worldwide, with stars including Don Rickles; Dean Martin; Bob Hope; Henry Mancini; Michel Legrand; Guest faculty member, Dick Grove School of Music. Recordings: Over a dozen albums; When Your Lover Has Gone; Songs For a Raney Day; Ridin' High; In Good Compnay; Flight Of Fancy (Lyrics Of Alan & Marilyn Bergman); Dreamsville (The Music of Henry Mancini). Honours: Grammy nominations for 3 albums. Membership: Society Of Singers. Hobbies: Painting; Gardening. Current Management: Jim DiGiovanni, F Sharp Productions Ltd., 157 West 57th Street, New York, NY, USA.

RANKIN Dusty, b. 8 February 1924, Birchip, Victoria, Australia. Singer; Songwriter; Musician; Guitar. m. Mary, 14 May 1957, deceased 1993, 2 daughters. Education: Selftaught. Career: Worked in TV, Melbourne, 1950's; Recorded for Hadley, 1964; Recorded for Selection Records, 1980; Own show, Starnite, throughout Victoria; Toured with Skuthorpe's and Queensland Dild West Rodeos around Australia, 3 times; Toured with Athol McKoy Show, 1962; First Recordings for Columbial EMI Records, 1948. Compositions: Songs released on 13 compilation albums; 2 song albums (books). Recordings: 4 albums: Family Bible; The Country I Love; A Portrait of Dusty Rankin; Sunset Valley Calling; 5 EP's - Red Ding Smooth 'N Country; Dustry Rankin & Bernadette; Intimate Style of Dusty Rankin; Family Bible; 1 cassette, Best of Dusty Rankin. Honours: Won Australian Amateur Hour, 1946; Inducted into Hands of Fame, Tamworth, NSW, 1980; Inducted into Avenue of Honour Bamera, SA, 1985; Golden Guitar, Tambourine Mountain, Queensland, 1988; Inducted into Roll of Renown, Tamworth, NSW, 1996. Membership: Australian Performing Rights Association. Hobbies: Golf; Fishing. Address: PO Box 113, Birchip, Vic 3483, Australia.

RANKIN Mark, b. Glasgow, Scotland. Vocalist. Career: Vocalist, Scottish rock group Gun, 1989-; Concerts include: Support to Rolling Stones, Urban Jungle Tour, Europe, 1990; Support to Simple Minds, 1990; Support to Def Leppard, UK, 1993; International tours as headline act. Recordings: Albums: Taking On The World, 1989; Gallus, 1992; Swagger, 1994; Singles: Better Days, 1989; Shame On You, 1989; Money, 1989; Inside Out, 1990; Word Up, 1994; Don't Say It's Over, 1994. Current Management: G R Management, 974 Pollockshaw Road, Glasgow G41 2HA, Scotland.

RANKS Shabba (Rexton Gordon), b. 17 Jan 1966, Sturgetown, Jamaica. Reggae / Ragga Singer. Career: Club artiste as DJ Don, early 1980s; Solo artiste, mid-1980s; Prolific local recording artiste, Caribbean; Support to Bobby Brown, US, 1992. Recordings: As Raw As Ever, 1991; Rough And Ready Vol 1, 1992; Xtra Naked, 1992; Hit singles: She's A Woman (with Scritti Politti), 1991; Housecall (with Maxi Priest), 1991; Mr Loverman, used in film soundtrack Deep Cover, 1993; Slow And Sexy, 1992; What'cha Gonna Do? (with Queen Latifah), 1993; Family Affair, used in film soundtrack Addams Family, 1993. Honours: Grammy Awards: Best Reggae Album, As Raw As Ever, 1992; Xtra Naked, 1993; 2 Caribbean Music Awards, 1992; 6 International Reggae Awards, 1992. Current Management: Shang Artist Management, 850 7th Avenue, Suite 500, New York, NY 10019, USA

RANSOME Steve, b. 24 Aug 1961, London, England. Musician (keyboards); Composer; Record Producer. m. Shirley Peterson, 8 Apr 1994. Musical Education: Advanced Jazz tuition, Grangewood School in London; Qualified Yamaha Music Teacher. Career: ATV Production Assistant, 1977-78; Played keyboards in various bands at Wembley, Peterborough and Glasgow Festivals; Toured UK, Ireland, Europe and America; Appeared on BBC TV, ITV, MTV, Channel 4 TV and Cable TV; Yamaha demonstration concerts given; Played at Bahai Festivals, the University circuits in Scotland and on most radio stations; Owns recording studio. Compositions include: About 12 television themes and soundtracks; Arranger for 1988 special Olympics theme. Recordings: Single: Peace Moves, worldwide release; Many major artists as production assistant. Publications: Peace Moves; Storming The Gates; Bahai Songbook Volume 1. Memberships: PRS; MCPS; Musicians' Union. Address: Donfield House, Backmill by Turriff, Aberdeenshire AB53 8ET, Scotland.

RANTALA Iiro Emil, b. 19 Jan 1970, Helsinki, Finland. m. Lotta Kuusisto, 12 Aug 1995. Musician (piano). Musical Education: Choirboy, Cantores Minores; Classical piano lessons; Oulunkylän Institute, 1983-; Private lessons with Seppo Kantonen; Manhattan School of Music, New York, 1990-92. Career: Member, jazz groups, Camus Nova; Akimowskaja Brothers & Sisters; Soloist for Upi Sorvali's Big Bad Family; Espoo Big Band; Formed Trio Töykeät, for April Jazz Festival, 1988-; Regulars at JUMO Jazz Club. Recordings include: with Trio Töykeät: Jazzlantis, 1995; with The Tango Kings: The Tango Kings, 1995. Honours include: Prize at Hoilaart Competition, Belgium. Address: Spjutsund 97, 06880 Kärbby, Finland.

RANTAMÄKI Ilkka, b. 1957, Finland. Musician (guitar); Educator. Musical Education: Guitar Institute Of Technology, Hollywood, USA; Studied with Jukka Tolonen. Career: Independent musician; Own record company; Member, various bands: Blues Shakers, 1980s; Blue Blondes (octet); Ilkka Rantamäki Group (quintet); Teacher, Sibelius High School, Helsinki. Recordings include: Crashing, Spacy, Free Mystery, 1994. Address:Huvilakatu 9 A 2, 00150 Helsinki, Finland.

RANUM Jesper, b. 1 Dec 1959, Denmark. Producer; Composer; Musician (electronic instruments); Author. 2 sons. Musical Education: Self-taught. Career: Produced, played and engineered many major Danish albums; Solo album in 1993; Music composed for artists, television, film andcommercials; Owner of 3 recording studio facilities. Recordings: Numerous Danish and some international recordings. Publications: 2 Books on Synthesizers and Midi. Memberships: KODA; GRAMEX; DJBFA; NCB. Address: Ranum Studios, 47 B GL Kongevej, DK-1610 Copenhagen V, Denmark.

RAPHAEL (Rafael Martos), b. Jaen, Spain. Singer. m. Natalia Figueroa, 1972, 2 sons, 1 daughter. Career: First prize, Salzburg Festival (children's singing competition) age 9; Winner, numerous subsequent competitions; Professional debut, Madrid, 1960; Represented Spain, Eurovision Song Contest, 1966, 1967; International concerts, US (including Broadway debut, 1974); USSR; Japan; Australia; Concerts include: 25th Anniversary open air concert, Bernabé Stadium, Madrid, 1985; Film appearances: Cuando Tú Bo Estás; The Hobo. Recordings: Over 200 million records sold; First major recording: Los Hombres Lloran También, 1964. Honours include: First Prize, Salzburg Singing Competition; Numerous Platinum and Gold discs. Address: c/o Arie Kaduri Agency Inc, 16125 NE 18th Avenue, North Miami Beach, FL 33162, USA.

RASE Bill, b. 25 Oct 1926, Long Beach, California, USA. Orchestra Leader. m. Shirley Bishop, 24 Aug 1952, 2 daughters. Education: Sacramento State College. Musical Education: General music courses. Career: Vocalist, Eddie Halter Orchestra, 1946-48; Orchestra leader, Bill Rase Orchestra, 1948-; Over 7500 engagements, backed Bob Hope, Cab Calloway shows; Disc jockey, KCRA Radio-Sacramento: The Bill Rase Show, 1952-64; Producer, host, The Bill Rase Show (talent show), KCRA TV, Channel 3, 9 years, over 500 shows; Children's show host, Bosun Bill & Popeye Show, 4 years, over 2,600 shows; Impersonated Bing Crosby, Network Eddie Cantor Show, 1962; Opened recording video production studio, Bill Rase Productions Inc, 1965-; Vocalist, Rainbow Records, Era Records, Esar Records. Membership: Sacramento Musicians Association. Hobbies: Music; Art. Current Management: Self-managed. Address: 955 Venture Ct, Sacramento, CA 95825, USA.

RASMUSSEN Pia, 10 Nov 1954, Aarhus, Denmark. Musician (piano); Composer; Music Teacher. Education: Cand Phil, Musicology, Copenhagen University. Career: Pianist and composer, all-woman groups Sosterrock and Lilith, 1976-83; Composer for documentaries, films and theatre; Solo concerts, piano, synthesizers, 1991-; Duo with flutist Chris Poole, 1992-. Recordings: Album: To The Powers That Be; Theme song, Nordic Women's Conference, Oslo, 1988. Publications: Blues For Klaver, Vols 1 and 2 (educational books on blues piano). Memberships: DJBFA; Danish Musicians' Union. Address: Skolesvinget 8, DK-8240 Risskov, Denmark.

RATZER Karl, b. 4 July 1950, Vienna, Austria. Musician (guitar); Composer; Singer. Career: Member, C Department, 1969; Gipsy Love, 1970; High Voltage (later known as Rufus And Chaka Khan), USA; Based in USA, 1972-81; Worked with: Chet Baker; Eddie Gomez; Joe Chambers; Steve Gadd; Joe Farrell; Sal Nistico; Bob Mintzer; Johnny Griffin; Clark Terry; Art Farmer; Fritz Baver; Lee Konitz; James Moody; Chaka Khan; Formed band project, Beat The Heat, 1991; Recordings, tours, Europe; Festivals include: Indianapolis; Tampa; Birmingham; Chicago; New York; New Orleans; Atlanta; Played Seventh Avenue Club, New York. Recordings: Live In Paris (I & II), Chet Baker; with Ray Mantilla: Nightbird; Conception; Tune Up; Rainforest, Jeremy Steig; Land Of Dreams, Eddie Lockjaw Davis; Solo albums: In Search Of The Ghost; Street-Talk; Fingerprints; Serenade; Happy Floating; Electric Finger; Dancing On A String; Fool For Your Sake; That's Jazz; Gitarre; Gitarrenfever; Gumbo Dive; Waltz For Ann; Bayou; Coasting. Current Management: Mr Kiss, Agency For Music And Art. Address: Vienna Hilton, Top 1719-1721, Landstrasser Hauptstrasse, A-1030 Vienna, Austria.

RAULIN Francois, b. 17 Mar 1956, Annecy, France. Musician (piano); Composer. 3 sons. Education: Mathematics. Musical Education: Piano lessons from age 9; Self-taught jazz since age 14. Career: Founder, Association Grenoble Espace Musical (AGEM), 1981; Duo with pianist Pascal Lloret, tour, France, 1981; Studied African music, 1980-83; Pianist, La Marmite Infernale, 1982; Tours, France; Festivals include: Paris; Le Mans; Nancy; Milan, 1982; Zürich, 1984; Moers, 1984; Hofheim, 1985; Nickelsdorf, 1986; Tours: Algeria; Germany; Switzerland; Italy; Austria; Member, Louis Sclavis Group, 1985; Festivals worldwide include: All over Europe; Canada; Japan; India; Turkey; Algeria; Mexico; Festival appearances with Claude Barthelemy, Jean-Marc Padovani, 1986; Antoine Herve, 1988; Philippe Deschepper, 1992; Solo performances at festivals including: Grenoble; Lausanne; Geneva; Cologne, 1992-; Tours with trio and quartet. Compositions include: Quelque Chose Du Sud, with Maurice Merle; Battleship Potemkin (film music); with Louis

Sclavis: Chamber Music, 1988; Clarinettes; Indigène, 1989; Duke On The Air, 1990; Face Nord, with Mathilde Monnier's Dance Company, 1991; Vue Sur Tower Bridge (Travelling) (co-writer), 1992; Work for 5 Pianos, 1993; Hit Parada, Jean Mereu, 1993; Les Violences de Rameau, 1993; Music for theatre, film and dance, with Louis Sclavis, J Mereux, A Gibert. Recordings include: Chine; Rouge; First Flush; Duke on The Air. Honours: Winner, Biennale, Barcelona (with Louis Scalvis Quartet), 1988. Current Management: Marion Piras. Montpellier, France. Address: 686 Avenue Saint Jean, 38360 Noyarey, France.

RAUX Richard, b. 17 July 1995, Perigaux, France. Musician (saxophone, flute); Composer; Bandleader. m. Helena, 25 May 1970, 1 son, 1 daughter. Education: Bac Philo; 2 years university. Musical Education: Saxophone, Phil Woods; Flute, Caratgt; Composition, G Russell. Career: Played, recorded with Eddy Louis; Magma; Luther Allisson; Kenny Clarke; Mal Waldron; Charlie Haden; Memphis Slim; Dizzy Gillespie; Festivals, concerts, clubs, Telé France; Nice, 1991, 93; London; Berlin; Jazz teacher, saxophone, flute. Recordings: Feel Good At Last, Richard Raux Quartet; S Murray; Eddy Louis; Album: Under The Magnolias, Richard Raux Quartet, 1989; Album: Live At The Dreyer, Roy Burrowes, Mal Waldron. Hobbies: Movies; Football. Current Management: Self-managed. Address: 2 Chemin Du Mopulin, 95550 Bessancourt, Nr Paris, France.

RAVEN Eddy (Edward Garvin Futch), b. 19 Aug 1944, Lafayette, Louisiana, USA. Musician; Singer; Songwriter. 2 sons. Education: College. Career: Staff writer, La Louisiane, Lafayette; Worked with: Hank Williams Jr; Alabama; Tracy Lawrence; George Strait; Reba McEntire; Alan Jackson; Charlie Daniels; Stevie Ray Vaughn; The Judds; George Jones; Conway Twitty; Merle Haggard; Dolly Parton; Roy Acuff; Barbara Mandrell; Marty Robbins; Television appearances: Co-host, Yesteryear, TNN; Founder, own publishing company. Compositions: Country Green, Don Gibson; Touch The Morning, Don Gibson; Good Morning Country Rain, Jeannie C Riley; Thank God For Kids, Oak Ridge Boys. Recordings: Hit Singles: Bayou Boys; I Got Mexico; Shine Shine Shine; I'm Gonna Get You; Joe Knows How To Live; 'Til You Cry; In A Letter To You; Albums: That Cajun Country Sound, 1969; This Is Eddy Raven, 1976; Eyes, 1979; Desperate Dreams, 1981; Thank God For Kids, 1984; I Could Use Another You, 1984; Love And Other Hard Times, 1985; Right Hand Man, 1986; Temporary Sanity, 1989; Greatest Country Hits, 1990; Right For Flight, 1991; Wild Eyed And Crazy, 1994; 4 Best Of/Greatest Hits compilation albums; 4 Christmas compilation albums. Memberships: ASCAP; BMI; AFTRA; AFofM; Lifetime member, Songwriters Association. Hobbies: Fishing; Cooking; Baseball. Address: PO Box 2476, Hendersonville, TN 37077, USA.

RAWLS Lou, b. 1 Dec 1935, Chicago, Illinois, USA. Singer. Career: Briefly member, gospel group, the Pilgrim Travellers; Solo artiste, 1958-; Also actor; Voiceovers, Budweiser beer commercials. Recordings: Albums: Lou Rawls Sings, 1962; Black And Blue, 1963; Tobacco Road, 1963; Nobody But Lou Rawls, 1965; Lou Rawls And Strings, 1965; Live!, 1966; Soulin', 1966; Merry Christmas Ho! Ho! Ho!, 1967; Feeling Good, 1968; You're Good For Me, 1968; The Way It Was- The Way It Is, 1969; Your Good Thing, 1969; You Made Me So Very Happy, 1970; Bring It On Home To Me, 1970; Natural Man, 1971; Silk And Soul, 1972; All Things In Time, 1976; Unmistakably Lou, 1977; When You Hear Lou, You've Heard It All, 1977; Live, 1978; Let Me Be Good To You, 1979; Sit Down And Talk To Me, 1980; Shades Of Blue, 1981; Now Is The Time, 1982; When The Night Comes, 1983; Close Company, 1984; Love All Your Blues Away, 1986; At Last, 1989; Portrait Of The Blues, 1992;

Greatest Hits In Concert, 1993. Current Management: The Brokaw Co. Address: 9255 Sunset Blvd, Suite 804, Los Angeles, CA 90069, USA.

RAYE Collin (Floyd E. Wray), b. 22 Aug 1960, De Queen, Arkansas, USA. Singer. Musical Education: Self-taught guitar and bass. Career: Television appearances include: 3 Tonight Shows; Street Justice, television series; 3 Regis and Kathy; Kathy Lee Xmas special. Recordings: Platinum albums: All I Can Be; In This Life; Extremes. Memberships: SAG; AFTRA. Hobbies: Boxing. Current Management: Scott Dean Management, 612 Humboldt Street, Reno, NV 89509-1606, USA; William Morris Agency, 2100 West End Avenue, Suite 1000, Nashville, TN 37203, USA.

RAYNAUD Pierre, b. 2 Dec 1954, Mazamet, France. Musician (trumpet). m. Mazamet, 31 Aug 1985, 1 son, 1 daughter. Musical Education: Studies, IACP (Institut Art Culture Perception) Director, Alan Silva Marcial, 1992; Radio France Montpelier, 1993; Big Band 31, Jazz festivals: Toulouse, 1989,90; Paris La Defense, 1988; Albi Jazz, 1988; Nice, Vienna, Nancy Jazz pulsations, 1989. Recordings: Art Mengo: Un 15 Août en Février, 1988; Big Band 31, 1988; Jazz Time Big Band, Hauresala, 1993. Memberships: SACEM; SPEDIDAM.

RAYNER Alison, b. 7 Sept 1952, Bromley, Kent, England. Musician (double and electric bass); Composer. Education: Hammersmith College of Art, London. Musical Education: Self-taught; Early formal education, piano, voice. Career: Recorded, toured with The Guest Stars, 1983-88; Tours included: USA; Europe; Eastern Europe; Middle East; Cyprus; Jazz Festivals include: Berlin; Willisau (Switzerland); Sofia (Bulgaria); Bracknell (England); Brecon (Wales); London International; Own jazz quartet: The Jazz Garden, 1989-93; Currently plays in Deirdre Cartwright Group, 1992-; Diane McLoughlins Giant Steppes, 1992-; Zdravets, 1997-; The Emma Peel Fan Club, 1995-; The Non-Conformists, 1997-; Runs Blow The Fuse Jazz Club, Blow The Fuse Records, Teaches in London. Compositions: On all 3 Guest Stars albums. Recordings: with The Guest Stars: The Guest Stars, 1984; Out At Night, 1985; Live In Berlin, 1987; with Deirdre Cartwright Group: Debut, 1994; Play, 1997; A compilation - One Night Stands: Live At Blow The Fuse, 1994. Memberships: Musicians' Union; PRS; MCPS; Association of British Jazz Musicians. Address: Blow The Fuse Records, 76 Hawksley Road, London N16 0TJ, England.

REA Chris, b. 4 Mar 1951, Middlesbrough, Cleveland, England. Singer; Songwriter; Musician (guitar). m. Joan, 1980. Career: Member, Magdelene, 1973-75; Name changed to The Beautiful Losers, 1975-76; Solo artist, 1977-; Appearances include: Great British Music Festival, Wembley, 1978; Regular UK and European tours. Compositions include: Film score, Soft Top Hard Shoulder, 1993. Recordings: Albums (self-written): Whatever Happened To Benny Santini?, 1978; Deltics, 1979; Tennis, 1980; Chris Rea, 1982; Water Sign, 1983; Wired To The Moon, 1984; Shamrock Diaries, 1985; On The Beach, 1986; Dancing With Strangers (Number 2, UK), 1987; The Best Of Chris Rea - New Light From Old Windows, 1988; The Road To Hell (Number 1, UK), 1989; Auberge (Number 1, UK), 1991; God's Great Banana Skin, 1992; Expresso Logic, 1993; The Very Best Of, 1994; Contributor, Hank Marvin Guitar Syndicate, Hank Marvin, 1977; Duets, Elton John, 1993; Hit singles include: Fool (If You Think It's Over), 1979; I Can Hear Your Heartbeat, 1983; Stainsby Girls, 1985; On The Beach, 1986; Let's Dance, 1987; Driving Home For Christmas, 1988; The Road To Hell (Part 2), 1989; Tell Me There's A Heaven, 1990; Auberge, 1991; Winter Song, 1991; Nothing To Fear, 1992; Julia, 1993; Featured on Do They Know It's Christmas, Band

Aid II (Number 1, UK), 1989. Honours: Grammy Nomination, Fool (If You Think It's Over), 1979; Melody Maker Award, Best Newcomers, with the Beautiful Losers, 1975. Current Management: Real Life Ltd, 122 Holland Park Avenue, London W11 4UA, England.

READER Eddi, b. 29 Aug 1959, Glasgow, Scotland. Singer. 2 sons. Career: Lead singer, Fairground Attraction; Later, solo artiste; Tours: UK; Europe; America; Japan; Television appearances include: Top Of The Pops; Later With Jools Holland. Recordings: Albums: with Fairground Attraction: First Of A Million Kisses; A Fond Kiss; Solo albums: Mirmama; Eddi Reader. Honours: BRIT Awards: Best Single, Best Band, Best British Female Artist. Memberships: Equity; Musicians' Union. Current Management: Douglas Kean, Interface Management. Address: 37 Oxford Gardens, London W4 3BN, England.

READER Mark, b. 21 Mar 1960, Liverpool, England. Musician (guitar); Singer. m. 24 Feb 1986, 1 son. Musical Education; Classical guitar, classical piano with Mrs Watson. Career: Television with Bill Le Sage, Alec Dankworth, Alan Ganley in Body Talk; Composed music for: Bitsa; We Are The Champions; Is That A Fact; Words And Pictures; Guitarist, Liverpool Empire with P J Proby; Now fronting guitarist, singer, Strider. Compositions: for Bitsa: Hurry Up; For We Are The Champions: Hang On Steve, Uphill Champs; for Strider: She's The One; The Loser; Spare Me The Pain; Finding A Way; Seasons With You; UFO. Memberships: Musicians' Union; Equity; PRS (associate member). Hobbies: Archery; Martial arts. Address: 35 Lyra Road, Waterloo, Liverpool L22 0NT, England.

REBELLO Jason Matthew, b. 29 Mar 1969, Carshalton, Surrey, England. Jazz Musician (piano). Musical Education: Degree, Guildhall School of Music and Drama. Career: Concerts with Halle Orchestra; Played with Wayne Shorter, Freddie Jackson, and Mica Paris. Television presenter, Artrageous; Recordings: Albums: A Clearer View; Keeping Time; Make It Real; Last Dance. Honours: The Wire Jazz Album of the Year; Perrier British Jazz Pianist of the Year. Membership: Freemason. Hobbies: Reading; Tennis; Computer games. Current Management: Alex Hardee, Concorde International Artists. Address: 101 Shepherds Bush Road, Hammersmith, London W6 7LP, England.

REDBONE Leon, Vocalist; Musician (guitar). 2 daughters. Career: Performer worldwide, 1973-; Numerous television, film and radio performances, 1976-; Recordings: Albums: On The Track, 1975; Double Time, 1977; Champagne Charlie, 1978; From Branch To Branch, 1981; Red To Blue, 1986; No Regrets, 1988; Christmas Island, 1988, (re-released 1989-91); Sugar, 1990; Up A Lazy River, 1992; Whistling In The Wind, 1994; So Relax, track used in British Rail commercials. Honours: Gold disc, On the Track, 1975; Silver Lion, 1989; London International Advertising Award, 1989. Memberships: AFofM; SAG; AFTRA; Equity. Current Management: Beryl Handler. Address: 2169 Aquetong Road, New Hope, PA 18938-2169 USA.

REDDING Noel David, b. 25 Dec 1945, Folkestone, Kent, England. Musician (bass, rhythm guitar); Vocalist. Education: Art College. Musical Education: Violin lessons at school; Later self-taught. Career: Professional musician aged 17; Guitarist, The Burnettes, The Loving Kind; Bass player, The Jimi Hendrix Experience, 1966-69; Own band, Fat Mattress, 1969-70; Member, Road, 1971; Solo artiste, session musician, 1974-. Recordings: Albums with Jimi Hendrix Experience: Are You Experienced, 1967; Electric Ladyland, 1968; Axis Bold As Love, 1969; Songs include: Little Miss Strange; She's So Fine; Hey Joe; Voodoo Chile; Crosstown Traffic; Foxy Lady; Wind Cries Mary; All Along The Watchtower; with Fat Mattress: Fat Mattress, 1969; Fat Mattress 2, 1970; Road, Road, 1971; with Noel Redding Band: Clonakilty Cowboys, 1975; Blowin', 1976. Publications: Noel Redding's Bass Method Book (tutor); Are You Experienced? (co-author with the late Carol Appleby). Honours: Rock'n'Roll Hall Of Fame Inductee, 1992; Numerous others. Memberships: ASCAP; Equity. Hobbies: Writing; Reading; Television; Restaurants. Current Management: C Carell, 153 W 75th Street #2B, New York, NY 10023, USA. Address: c/o Ardfield PO, Clonakilty, Co. Cork, Ireland.

REDDY Helen, b. 25 Oct 1942, Melbourne, Victoria, Australia. Singer; Actress. m. (1) Jeff Wald, (2) Milton Robert Ruth, 1 son, 1 daughter. Education: UCLA Extension College. Career: Singer, 1966-; Numerous concerts worldwide; Actress, films: Airport, 1975; Pete's Dragon, 1977; Television host, Midnight Special, 1970s; Campaign work for women's political movement and women in prison. Recordings: Albums: I Don't Know How To Love Him, 1971; Helen Reddy, 1971; I Am Woman, 1972; Long Hard Climb, 1973; Love Song For Jeffrey, 1974; Free And Easy, 1974; No Way To Treat A Lady, 1975; Greatest Hits, 1975; Music Music, 1976; Ear Candy, 1977; We'll Sing In The Sunshine, 1978; Live In London, 1979; Reddy, 1979; Take What You Find, 1980; Play Me Out, 1981; Imagination, 1983; Take It Home, 1984; Very Best Of, 1993; Hit singles: I Don't Know How To Love Him, 1971; I Am Woman, 1972; Delta Dawn, 1973; Angie Baby, 1974; I Can't Hear You No More, 1976. Honours: Numerous Gold and Platinum records, LA Times, Woman Of The Year, 1975; NAACP Image Award, 1974; Maggie Award, 1976; Humanitarian Award, B'nai B'rith, 1975. Address: Helen Reddy Inc, 820 Stanford Street, Santa Monica, CA 90403, USA.

REDMOND Melanie, b. 25 Oct 1962, Putney, London, England. Vocalist; Backing Singer; Musician (percussion). m. Brian Tench, 12 July 1993, 2 sons. Career: Backing vocalist for Bob Geldof's Deep In The Heart Of Nowhere Tour, including various TV shows; Backing vocals for Patsy Kensit; Top Of The Pops and various television appearances; World tour with Duran Duran; Big Thing World tour, including Arsenio Hall television appearance, 1988-89; Various live and studio recordings; World tour with The The, The The Versus The World, 1989-90; As solo female singer: video release of live Albert Hall concert, recordings for various singles; Television: Top Of The Pops for Sting; Television commercials for Mazda; Concerts with Adam Ant. Recordings with: Boy George; Apache Indian; Bill Wyman; Georgie Fame. Hobby: Clay pigeon shooting. Current Management: Session Connection (agent). Address: 61 Dysart Avenue, Kingston-Upon-Thames, Surrey KT2 5RA, England.

REECE Alex, b. 18 February 1970, London, England. Compositions: Recorded: Basic Principles, 1995; I Want You, 1995; Chill Pill; Detroit; Jazz Juice; A Nu Era; Touch Me; Pulp Fiction; Ibiza; Jazz Master; UR; Rough Cut; Atlantic Drama; Out of Time; Others; Album: So Far, 1996; Singles: Feel the Sunshine; Candles. Honour: Best Jungle Single, Pulp Fiction, Dance Awards, Kiss FM, 1995. Memberships: PRS; Musicians' Union. Hobbies: Driving; Golf; Snooker computer games; Smoking and drinking; Food. Current Management: Roger Breuer, Stephen King at Ricochet, 5 Old Garden House, The Lanterns, Bridge Lane, Battersea, London SW11 3AD, England.

REED Howard T, b. 4 Feb 1962, Barnsley, Yorkshire, England. Singer; Musician (guitar). m. Margaret Carney, 21 Apr 1994, 1 son, 1 daughter. Musical Education: Self-taught. Career: Member of Rock and Roll group Ouse Brothers; Tours include: USA, 1991; Spain, 1992; Greece, 1993; Solo artist, 1993-94; Currently member of Vinegar Tom. Recordings: Censored, Ouse Brothers, 1992; In Roads, Ouse Brothers, 1993; Cat On A Hot Inn Roof, Vinegar Tom, 1995. Membership: Equity. Hobby: Playing rugby. Current Management: Margaret Reed. Address: 3 Colenso Street, Clementhorpe, York YO2 1AS, England.

REED Jerry (Jerry Hubbard), b. 20 Mar 1937, Atlanta, Georgia, USA. Country Musician (guitar); Singer; Composer; Actor. Career: Session guitarist, Nashville; Solo country artiste, 1967-; Duets with Chet Atkins, 1970s; Regular television appearances with Glen Campbell, 1970s; Film appearances include: W W and The Dixie Dance Kings, 1975; Gator, 1976; Smokey and the Bandit, 1977. Compositions include: Crazy Legs, Gene Vincent; Misery Loves Company, Porter Wagoner; A Thing Called Love, Johnny Cash; Guitar Man, Elvis Presley; Hits include: Amos Moses; When You're Hot, You're Hot; Lord Mr Ford; She Got The Goldmine (I Got The Shaft); Albums include: Tupelo Mississippi Flash, 1967; Alabama Wild Man, 1969; Cookin', 1970; Georgia Sunshine, 1971; When You're Hot, You're Hot, 1971; Ko Ko Joe, 1972; Jerry Reed, 1972; Hot A Mighty, 1973; Lord Mr Ford, 1973; Half And Half, 1974; Red Hot Picker, 1975; Uptown Poker Club, 1975; Smell The Flowers, 1975; Me And Chet, 1976; Eastbound And Down, 1977; Both Barrels, 1978; In Concert, 1980. Address: Jerry Reed Enterprises, PO Box 3586, Brentwood, TN 37024, USA.

REED Leslie David, b. 24 July 1935, Westfield, Woking, Surrey, England. Composer; Arranger; Conductor; Musician (piano). m. June Williams, 21 May 1960, 1 daughter. Musical Education: Personal tutor, age 5; London College of Music exams. Career: Joined John Barry Seven, 1958; Wembley Concerts; Television appearances include: Drumbeat; Oh Boy; Six Five Special; Ready Steady Go (conductor); Gadzooks; Rolf Harris Show; International Pop Proms; New Faces (panellist); Juke Box Jury. Compositions include: It's Not Unusual; The Last Waltz; Delilah; There's A Kind Of A Hush; Love Is All; Tell Me When; Here It Comes Again; I'm Coming Home; Les Bicyclettes De Belsize; 24 Sycamore; Everybody Knows; I Pretend. Recordings include: As arranger, conductor: Green Green Grass Of Home, Tom Jones; You've Got Your Troubles, The Fortunes; Hits recorded by Dave Clark Five; P J Proby; Sammy Davis Jnr; Connie Francis. Honours include: Jimmy Kennedy Award, 1993; Freedom of City Of London, 1994; 110 Gold discs; 10 Ivor Novello awards. Memberships: PRS, Vice President, BASCA; Ambassador, FIDOF. Hobbies: Study of the paranormal; Golf. Current Management: Donna L Ford, Rebecca Music Co Ltd. Address: Terwick Place, Rogate, Nr Petersfield, Hampshire GU31 5BY, England.

REED Lou (Louis Firbank), b. 2 Mar 1943, Freeport, Long Island, New York, USA. Singer; Songwriter; Musician (guitar); Poet; Journalist. m. Sylvia Morales, 14 Feb 1980. Career: Founder member, lead singer, songwriter, Velvet Underground, 1964-1970, 1993-; Tours as part of Andy Warhol's Exploding Plastic Inevitable show; Solo artiste, 1971-93; Appearances include: Montreal World Fair, 1967; Crystal Palace Garden Party, 1973; Reading Festival, 1975; Nelson Mandela - A International Tribute, Wembley Stadium, 1990; John Lennon Tribute Concert, Liverpool, 1990; Glastonbury Festival, 1992; Bob Dylan 30th Anniversary Concert, New York, 1992. Recordings: Albums: with the Velvet Underground: The Velvet Underground And Nico, 1967; White Light, White Heat, 1968; The Velvet Underground, 1969; Loaded, 1970; Solo albums: Lou Reed, 1972; Transformer, 1973; Berlin, 1973; Rock'n'Roll Animal, 1974; Sally Can't Dance, 1974; Lou Reed Live, 1975; Metal Machine Music, 1975; Coney Island Baby, 1976; Rock And Roll Heart, 1976; Walk On The Wild Side - The Best Of Lou Reed, 1977; Street Hassle, 1978; Take No Prisoners, 1979; The Bells, 1979; Growing Up In Public,

1980; Rock And Roll Diary, 1980; The Blue Mask, 1982; Transformer, 1982; Legendary Hearts, 1983; New Sensations, 1984; Mistrial, 1986; Retro, 1989; New York, 1989; Songs For Drella - A Fiction (with John Cale), 1990; Magic And Loss, 1992; Set The Twilight Reeling, 1996; Also appears on: Sun City single, Artists Against Apartheid, 1985; Soul Man (with Sam Moore), theme for film Soul Man, 1987; Duets album, Rob Wasserman, 1988; Victoria Williams benefit album, 1993. Publications include: Between Thought And Expression (poetry), 1992. Honours: Q Magazine Merit Award, 1991; Knight of the Order of Arts and Letters, France, 1992; Inducted into Rock'n'Roll Hall of Fame (with Velvet Underground), 1996. Memberships: AFofM; Screen Actors Guild. Current Management: Sister Ray Enterprises, 584 Broadway, Suite 609, New York, NY 10012, USA.

REESE Della (Deloreese Patricia Early), b. 6 July 1931, Detroit, Michigan, USA. Gospel Singer. m. (1) Vermont Adolphus Bon Taliaferro (divorced), (2) Leroy Basil Gray (divorced), (3) Franklin Thomas Lett Jr. Education: Wayne University. Career: Choir singer, 1938-; Singer with Mahalia Jackson, 1945-49; Clara Ward; Lead singer, Meditation Singers; Erskine Hawkins Orchestra, 1956; Solo artist, 1957-; Organized gospel group at Wayne University; Numerous television appearances include: Jackie Gleason; Ed Sullivan; McCloud; The Love Boat; The A-Team; Charlie & Co; Crazy Like A Fox; MacGyver; Guest host, The Royal Family, 1991; The Tonight Show; Della; Nightmare In Badham County; Ain't Misbehavin'; Blues In The Night; The Last Minstrel Show. Recordings: Singles: And That Reminds Me; In The Still Of The Night; Don't You Know; Not One Minute More; Someday (You'll Want Me To Want You); Bill Bailey; Albums include: Special Delivery, 1961; The Classic Della, 1962; Waltz With Me Della, 1964; Let Me Into Your Life, 1975; The Classical Della, 1980; Della By Starlight, 1982; I Like It Like That, 1984; Sure Like Lovin' You, 1985. Honours: Voted Most Promising Singer Of Year, 1957; Emmy Nomination, Nightmare In Badham County; Grammy Nomination, 1987. Address: c/o William Morris Agency, 1350 Avenue of the Americas, New York, NY 10019, USA.

REEVES Brian Eric, b. 11 Dec 1948, Hammersmith, London, England. Teacher. Partner, Susan Houghton, 1 son. Education: University of Warwick, 978-81; RSA, 1984-86. Career: As rock musician: Guitarist, vocalist, with Bilbo, 1960s; Bishops Wife, 1970s; As folk musician: Guitarist, vocalist with Norman Chop Trio, 1974-77; Ran Royal Oak Folk Club, 1975; Palais De Folk club, 1976-77; Session work with Murray Head, 1975; Chris Rhoman, 1976. Compositions: Hanging On My Wall; Work, co-writer with John Lancaster, recorded 1993; Score with John Lancaster: The Truth Lies In Rostock, CH4, 1993. Recordings: Albums: with John Lancaster: Hokey Cokey 2000; Half A Lifetime. Publications: Various reviews for University of Warwick student magazine. Membership: Musicians' Union. Hobby: Recording. Address: 76 Brookdale Road, London SE6 4JP, England.

REEVES Del (Franklin Delano), b. 14 July 1933, Sparta, North Carolina, USA. Country Singer; Songwriter; Musician (multi-instrumentalist); Artist Manager. Career: Own radio show, aged 12; Own TV show, California, 1950s; Solo recording artiste, 1961-; Regular appearances at Grand Ole Opry, 1958-; Host, numerous TV shows; Film appearances include: Second Fiddle To An Old Guitar; Artist Manager, 1992-; Discovered Billy Ray Cyrus. Recordings: Over 50 country hits include: Girl On A Billboard; Looking At The World Through A Windshield; Good Time Charlies; The Philadelphia Phillies; Duet with Penny DeHaven, Bobby Goldsboro, Billie Jo Spears; Albums include: Girl

On A Billboard, 1965; Mr Country Music, 1966; Our Way Of Life, with Bobby Goldsboro, 1967; Running Wild, 1968; Big Daddy Del, 1970; Friends And Neighbours, 1971; Truckers Paradise, 1973; With Strings And Things, 1975; By Request, with Billie Jo Spears, 1976; Del Reeves, 1979; Baby I Love You, 1988. Address: Joe Taylor Artist Agency, Nashville, TN, USA.

REEVES Martha, b. 18 July 1941, Eufaula, Alabama, USA. Singer; Musician (piano, tambourine). Divorced, 1 son. Career: Began as Martha LaVaille, Blues singer; Lead singer, Martha Reeves and The Vandellas; Recent appearances include: Leeza; Dick Clark Specials; Beverly Sills Special; Motown 25 Special; Dusty Springfield Specials; Ed Sullivan; K T Oslin Show; Dinah Shore; Merv Griffin; Mike Douglas; American Bandstand; Saturday Night Live; Dick Cavett; Flip Wilson; The Legendary Ladies Of Rock And Roll; Music featured in films including: Thelma & Louise; Good Morning Vietnam; Carrie; Tours of USA, other countries; Performances for Charitable organizations include: Arthritis Foundation; Make A Wish Foundation; March Of Dimes; Easter Seals Telethon; Detroit Music Hall; Pat Boone's Telethon; Jerry Lewis' Telethon. Recordings include: Come And Get These Memories, 1963; Love Is Like A Heat Wave, 1963; A Love Like Yours, 1963; Quicksand, 1963; Live Wire, 1964; In My Lonely Room, 1964; Dancing In The Street (Number 1), 1964; Wild One, 1964; Nowhere To Run, 1965; Love (Makes Me Do Foolish Things), 1965; You've Been In Love Too Long, 1965; My Baby Loves Me, 1966; I'm Ready For Love, 1966; Jimmy Mack, 1967; Third Finger, Left Hand, 1967; Honey Chile, 1967. Publications: Dancing In The Street, Confessions Of A Motown Diva; Martha Reeves Exclusive Newsletter. Honours: Soul Of American Music Award, 1992; Rock and Roll Hall Of Fame, 1995; Alabama Music Hall Of Fame, 1995. Membership: AFTRA. Current Management: Publicist: Ann Colding Public Relations. Address: Ann Colding Public Relations, PO Box 1987, Paramount, CA 90723, USA.

REEVES Thomas William Jnr, b. 14 February 1953, Boston, MA, USA. Recording/Live Sound Engineer; Bass Guitar. m. Carol Ann Reeves, 23 January 1998, 1 son, 1 stepdaughter. Education: University of Sound and Engineering, Hollywood, CA at Universal Studios. Career: Owner, Cat's Voice Productions, indie label, Recording Studio, and Disc Jockey Services; Assistant Manager, Wiz and Co, 1988; Disc Jockey, Encore Entertainment, 1989; Producer, Sound Block Studios, 1990; Owner, Reel Adventures II Studio, 1992; Owner, Rahsaan Publisher, Mainiac Music, 1997. Compositions: Protex Blue; Hey Girl; What Do When Want; Clean Shot; Butter Rum; Mangled Ducklings; Hot Moist; Pink and Stinky; Fine and Devine. Recordings: One Groove at a Time, Cleashot; Signature, Paul Wilcox; Moist, Wet and Stinky, The Mangled Ducklings; What Do Woman Want, Grade Ultra. Publications: One Groove at a Time, 1993; Signature, Paul Wilcox, 1997. Honours: Nominated Best Boston Band, 1975, 1980. Memberships: National Association of Music Merchants; American Federation of Musicians. Hobbies: Electronic Music; Bass Guitar; Travel. Current Management: Laite Entertainment, Newburg Port, Massachussetts. Address: 114 Kennebonk Pond Road, Lyman, ME 04002, USA.

REFOY Mark Gerard, b. 3 July 1962, Windsor, Berkshire, England. Songwriter; Musician (guitar). Career: Played guitar, Spacemen 3, 1989; Played guitar, Spiritualized, 1990-94; Musician, singer, songwriter, own band Slipstream; Recordings: Albums as guitarist: Recurring, Spacemen 3; with Spiritualized: Lazer Guided Melodies; Pure Phase; Songwriter, guitarist, Slipstream album. Memberships: Musicians' Union; PRS. Address: c/o Slipstream - Che Trading, PO Box 653, London E18 2NX, England.

REGAN Julianne, b. England. Singer; Musician (bass). Career: Former music journalist; Backing singer, The Mission; Bass player, Gene Loves Jezebel; Lead singer, All About Eve, 1986-. Recordings: with All About Eve: Albums: All About Eve, 1987; Scarlet And Other Stories, 1989; Touched By Jesus, 1991; Ultraviolet, 1992; Winter Words, Hits And Rarities, 1992; Singles: Our Summer, 1987; Flowers In Our Hair, 1987; Martha's Harbour, 1988. Address: c/o Polar Union, 45-53 Sinclair Road, London W14 0NS, England.

REICHE Gerd-Rainer, b. 12 Sept 1956, Bielefeld, Germany. Concert Organizer; Music Publisher. m. Iris, 3 Oct 1986. Education: University of Bielefeld. Career: Member, band Willenlos durch die Nacht (pop music with German text); Booking agent for: PC 69, Bielefeld Club, 1984; Own club, Glashaus, Bad Salzuflen, 1986-89; Konzertburo Reiche, 1986; Elfenbein Entertainment, Bielefeld, 1989; Reichlich Musik Verlag, 1987, Rich Records, 1992. Recordings include: On own label: with Jaywalker: Plug It, 1992; 4 Days In December, 1994. Publications: Texte In Populärer Musik, 1985. Honours: In preparation: Promotion/dissertation, Kabaret Live!. Hobbies: Wife; 3 dogs; Football. Address: Konzertburo Reiche, Elfenbein Entertainment, Niederwall 37-39, 33602 Bielefeld, Germany.

REID Charlie. Singer; Songwriter. Career: Formed The Proclaimers, with twin brother Craig, 1983; Played pubs, Edinburgh, Inverness; UK tour with The Housemartins; Television debut, The Tube, 1987; Signed to Chrysalis Records, 1987; First single Number 3 in charts; 145 performances, 18 countries, 1988-89; Recorded in Nashville, 1991; Song, I'm Gonna Be (500 miles), theme song to film Benny And Joon, 1993; Tour, USA, included Madison Square Gardens, 1993; Tour: Venezuela; Costa Rica; Brazil; Malaysia; Slovakia; Austria; Canada; Germany; Netherlands; Norway. Recordings: (own compositions) Albums: Sunshine On Leith, 1988; This Is The Story, 1994; Hit The Highway, 1994; Singles: Throw The R Away, 1987; Letter From America, 1987; Make My Heart Fly, 1988; I'm Gonna Be (500 Miles), 1988; Sunshine On Leith, 1988; King Of The Road, 1990; Let's Get Married, 1994; What Makes You Cry, 1994; These Arms Of Mine, 1994. Honours: Platinum disc, Sunshine On Leith. Current Management: Braw Music Management. Address: 78 Pentland Terrace, Edinburgh EH10 6HF, Scotland.

REID Junior (Delroy Reid), b. 1965, Kingston, Jamaica. ReggaeSinger; Record Producer. Career: First recording, aged 13; Member, Voice of Progress group; Solo recording artist, early 1980s, and 1989-; Singer, Black Uhuru, 1985-88; Founder, own record label JR Productions and own recording studio; Record producer, leading artists including: Junior Demus, Ninjaman, Dennis Brown and Gregory Isaacs. Recordings: Albums include: with Voice of Progress: Mini-Bus Driver; with Black Uhuru: Brutal; Positive; Solo albums: Boom Shack A Lack; Back To Back; Original Foreign Mind; One Blood; Visa; Hits include: Jailhouse; Sister Dawn; Pallaving Street; Give Thanks And Praise; Boom Shack A Lack; Stop This Crazy Thing (with Coldcut); I'm Free (with the Soup Dragons); One Blood. Honours include: Grammy Nomination, for Black Uhuru album Brutal. Address: c/o Zoe Productions, 450 Broome Street, 8th Floor, New York, NY 10013, USA.

REID Terry (Terrance James), b. 13 Nov 1949, Huntingdon, Cambridgeshire, England. Vocalist; Musician (guitar, piano). 2 daughters. Musical Education: Self-taught. Career: Toured with: The Rolling Stones; The Hollies; Scott Walker; The Small Faces; Paul Jones; Cream; The Beach Boys; Jethro Tull; Del Shannon; Television includes: Whistle Test; Lulu; David Frost. Compositions: Recorded by: Crosby Stills and Nash; Cheap Trick; The Hollies; Arrival.

Membership: PRS. Hobbies: Fishing; Music. Address: 5 Rectory Road, Bluntisham, Huntingdon, Cambs PE17 3LN, England.

REID Vernon, b. England. Musician (guitar). m. Mia McLeod, 6 Apr 1991. Musical Education: Ted Dunbar; Rodney Jones; Manhattan Community College, 2 years. Career: Musician with Defunk; Decoding Society; Founder member, funk rock group Living Colour, 1985-; Tours include: with Rolling Stones, North America, 1989; Miracle Biscuit Tour, US, 1990; Lollapalooza Tour, 1991; Stained In The UK tour, 1993; Concerts include: Host, benefit concert, Black Rock Coalition, Los Angeles, 1989; Earth Day, Central Park, 1990; Reading Festival, 1990; Phoenix Festival, 1993; Photography exhibition, Once Upon A Time, Called Now, Chicago, 1991. Compositions include: Writer, producer, tracks for B B King, 1990. Recordings: Albums: Vivid, 1988; Time's Up, 1991; Biscuits, 1991; Stain, 1993; Contributions to: Primitive Cool, Mick Jagger, 1986; Talk Is Cheap, Keith Richard, 1988; Funk Of Ages, Bernie Worrell, 1988; Singles include: Cult Of Personality, 1989; Glamour Boys, 1989; Love Rears Its Ugly Head, 1991; Solace Of You, 1991; Leave It Alone, 1993. Honours: Elvis Award, Best New Band, International Rock Awards, 1989; MTV Awards, Best New Artist, Best Group Video, Best Stage Performance, 1989; Grammy Award, Best Hard Rock Performance, 1990; Rolling Stone Critics Poll Winners, Best Band, 1991. Membership: Black Rock Coalition. Current Management: Jim Grant, JGM, Suite 1C, 39A Gramercy Park North, New York, NY 10010, USA.

REID Wilson, b. 28 Feb 1961, Accra, Ghana. Singer; Musician (guitar). Education: Qualified teacher. Career: Lead singer, songwriter, Death Bang Party, 1986-94; 2 major UK college tours; Headlined London Town and Country Club, 2 times, 1993; Headlined Marquee Club several times; 2 successful runs, Edinburgh Fringe Festival, 1993, 1994; Appeared on Julian Clary's Best of the Fest, CH4, 1993; Singer and Guitarist with The Tarantinos, completing two nationwide tours. Publication: Thrills, Pills and Backache: The Hank Williams Story, 1995. Honours: Nominated Best Newcomer, Daily Mail, for Edinburgh Fringe, 1993. Memberships: Musicians' Union; Equity. Hobbies: Canoeing; Scuba diving; Salsa dancing. Current Management: DBP Productions. Address: 842 Garratt Lane, London SW17 0NA, England.

REID DICK William F, b. 19 July 1952, London, England. Audio Producer; Engineer. m. Lorna Hewitt, 5 June 1982. Career: CBS Studios, Whitfield Street, West Indies, 1972-73; Ramport Studios, London, 1973-83; Freelance, 1983-95. Recordings: with Thin Lizzy: Jailbreak; Johnny The Fox; Live And Dangerous; with Saxon: Wheels Of Steel; Strong Arm Of The Law; Motörhead: Iron Fist. Honours: 2 Platinum, 5 Gold, 6 Silver albums; Ampex Gold Reel Award. Memberships: Re-Pro; PRS. Hobbies: Tennis; Computers. Address: No 1, 35 Wemyss Road, Blackheath, London SE3 0TG, England.

REIFF Soren, (aka Reiff Jr), b. 22 Oct 1962, Butterup, Denmark. Musician (guitar, keyboard, bass); Producer. Education: Music College, Holstebro, 1982. Career: Toured Europe and USA with different artists and as a solo artist, 1989-98; Guitarist in TV houseband appearing in around 200 talkshows, Meyerheim & Co, 1991-94; Played with Robert Palmer, Randy Crawford, Paul Young, Toots Thielemans, Jamie Walters, Curtis Stigers, Bonnie Tyler, Robin Beck and Suzi Q, 1991-98; Played in houseband on TV show Don't Forget Your Toothbrush, Denmark, 1995; Played in houseband on Safari TV show, 1996; Musical Director of houseband on It's Saturday Night, Denmark, 1997; Appeared on 199 shows with Danish trio, Linie 3, 1997-98. Recordings: Numerous recordings with Tower of Power, Michael Brecker and Madness 4 Real and artists from the UK, Scandinavia, Japan, India and Mexico; Guitar sample CD, 1998. Membership: Board Member, Music Highschool of Jyderup, Denmark, 1998. Current Management: Ballroom.

REINHARDT Babik, b. 8 June 1944, Paris, France. Musician (guitar). Education: Guitar with Milsou. Career: Performed Semi-Professional, 1960's; Performances with Jean-Luc Pnty at Trois Mailletz, Paris, 1965; Regular Concerts and 6 month tour of USA, 1967-72; Performed in Brazil, Turkey, Spain, Sweden, Denmark, Germany, Netherlands; Founder, Trio Gitan, 1986; Frieburg Festival, Germany, 1987. Recordings: Swing 67; Sinti Oun Brazil, 1973; Sur Le Chemin De Mon Pere, 1974; Anniversary Concert, 1983. Address: RIAL Andorra Limited, Avda de Tarragona 24, Andorra la Vella, Principat d'Andorra.

REISIG Bernd, b. 10 Mar 1963, Frankfurt, Germany. Media Manager. Education: Engine Fitter; Children's Male Nurse. Career: Founded concert agency; Artists: Purple Schulz; Bruce Cockburn; Extrabeit, 1984; Founded music publishing agency, 1985; Founded management agency, 1987; Represent artists: Nena; Badesalz; Thomas Koschwitz; Matthias Beltz; Christian Kahrman; Founded RMG Merchandising and RMG Music Entertainment, 1993; Represent artists: Nena; The Stroke; Mellow D; McDowell-Tarr; Dan; Several dance projects; Share in radio station, Radio 01, 1994; Share in advertising agency Koschwitz-Kommunikation; Share in television production company Feedback. Honours: Several Gold records, Grimme-Preis. Memberships: IFPI; GEMA. Hobby: Football. Address: Reisig Media GmbH, Lersnerstrasse 23, 60322 Frankfurt/Main, Germany.

REJHON Marek, b. 3 June 1975, Slany, Czech Republic. Musician; Singer. Education: Jazz courses, Prague Conservatory; Guitar, with Lubos Andrst. Career: Playing Music Clubs, 1994-96; Member of Original Prague Syncopated Orchestra, 1997-; 52 International Music Festival in Marsiac, France; Television and Radio Portraits. Recordings: With OPSO: Walking and Swinging, 1997; Jiri Suchy, 1998. Hobbies: Guitar Making; Collecting jazz recordings. Address: Haskova Street 1178/8, 170 00 Prague 7, Czech Republic.

RENAUD Norman Joseph, b. 11 Aug 1938, Durban, South Africa. Author; Composer; Musician (acoustic, electric guitar, casiotone keyboards, piano, percussion); Singer; Songwriter. 3 sons, 3 daughters. Education: Technical College. Musical Education: City University; The music industry. Career: Radio and television performances, in UK and worldwide; Vocalist and orchestral musician. Recordings: Ballads Standards, Popular styles, Rock'n'Roll; Soul; Dance; Country and Western styles, Popular styles, Jazz, Motown song styles. Publications: Currently compiling own songs and music. Membership: Musicians' Union. Hobbies: Music; Dancing; Television and radio; Films; World of Sport; Songwriting and composing. Current Management: Renaud Durban God Film and Music Record Company. Address: No 17 Corbiere House, 5th Floor, De Beauvoir Estate, Balmes Road, London N1 5SR, England.

RENAULT Nathalie, b. 26 Nov 1966, Paris, France. Musician (banjo). Education: Fine Arts: National Superior Beaux-Arts School Of Paris and University of Arts, Paris. Musical Education: Conservatory of Music, Clamart, Hauts-de-Seine. Career: Concerts: Dixieland Jubilee, Sacramento, USA; International Music Festival, Riga, Lithuania; Centre Cuturel Francais, Skopje, Macedonia; Jazz Festival, Corinth, Greece; Jazz Festival, Parma, Italy; Malmö Festival, Sweden; Cromwell Festival, Upton Upon Severn, UK; Oude Stijl Jazz Festival, Breda, Netherlands; 12 tage Jazz, Frankfurt, Germany; Dixie Jazz Festival, Sargans, Switzerland; Jazz Festival, Vannes; Jazz Band Ball, Paris, France. Recordings: with female jazz (old style) band Certains L'Aiment Chaud (Some Like It Hot): 1 cassette, 1985; 1 cassette, 1991; Album: J'ai Deux Amours, 1995. Honours: Sidney Bechet Prize, Jazz Academy, Paris, France, 1992. Hobby: Sculpture exhibitions, France (mainly Paris). Current Management: Laurent Dalle; Francine Dubettier. Address: c/o Claude Jeantet, 10 Rue Saint Roch, 75001 Paris, France.

RENBOURN John, b. 8 Aug 1944, Marylebone, London, England. Musician (guitar). Education: Kingston Art School. Musical College: Dartington College, Devon. Collaborations with: Bert Jansch; Stefan Groossman; Robin Williamson; Founder, groups Pentangle; John Renbourn Group; Ship Of Fools; Played at Carnegie Hall; New York Town Hall; Central Park Concert; Sydney Opera House; Royal Albert Hall; Festival Hall; Les Cousins. Recordings: Sir Johnalot; Lady And The Unicorn; Black Balloon; Nine Maidens; Wheel of Fortune; Live in America. Publications: Guitar Pieces; Guitar Styles; Medieval Renaissance Anthology. Honours: 2 Grammy Award Nominations. Membership: The Galpin Society. Current Management: Folklore Inc., 1671 Appian Way, Santa Monica, CA 90401, USA.

RENDELL Don, b. 4 Mar 1926, Plymouth, England. Musician (saxophone, flute, clarinet). m. Joan Ruth Yoxall, 27 Mar 1948, 1 daughter. Musical Education: Self-taught (in musical family). Career: Oscar Rabin Band, 1948-49; Founder member, John Dankworth Seven, 1950-53; Ted Heath Orchestra, 1955-56; Stan Kenton, 1956; Own Quartet, Quintet, Sextet, 1957-; Woody Herman Anglo-American Herd, 1959; Recordings with all the above; International jazz festivals: Antibes, 1968; BBC2 TV, Greenwich, 1979; Brecon, 1991; Villeneuve, 1992; Professor, Jazz Saxophone, Guildhall School Music and Drama. Compositions: 100 include: On The Way; Antibes; Euphrates; Calavinas. Recordings: 5 albums as Rendell/Carr 5; Solo albums: Space Walk, 1971; Earth Music, 1979; Don Rendell Big 8: If I Should Lose You, 1992. Publications: Flute Method; Saxophone Selection; Sax Skills (video). Memberships: Founder member, Clarinet and Saxophone Society (CASS); Association of British Jazz Musicians. Hobby: Bible study and teaching. Current Management: Self-managed. Address: 23 Weir Hall Gardens, Edmonton, London N18 1BH, England.

RENLIDEN Ivan, b. 27 September 1936, Sweden. m. Sonja, 27 October 1956, 1 son, 1 daughter. Education: Student, 1956; Academy of Music, Stockholm, Musical Teacher, 1964, Diploma of Piano, 1964. Career: Musical Leader, Arranger and Pianist, major stages in Stockholm; Almost 1000 Radio and TV Programs, losts of recordings with popular Swedish artists. Recordings: Svenska Melodier; Ivan Renliden Spelar Ivan Renliden; Ain't Misbehavin; Spectrum; Ivan Renliden Spelar Chopin. Honour: Cultural Prize of Stockholm, 1975. Memberships: STIM; SAMI. Hobby: Golf. Address: Ullerudsb 79, 12373 Farsta, Sweden.

RENNE Gilles, b. 21 Oct 1964, Arles, France. Musician (guitar); Composer. Education: BA. Musical Education: Graduate, Guitar Institute of Technology, Los Angeles. Career: Professor, CIM, Paris, for Jazz Guitar; Writer, several methods on Jazz Guitar improvisation; Master classes and studio work; French and African television and radio appearances; Concerts in Europe; Africa; Canada; Caribbean; Festivals include: Antibes; Nice; Paris; New York JVC Jazz Festival; Barcelona; Madagascar; Congo; Several tours, Africa, with live recordings. Recordings include: with Sellam-Renne: Rendez-vous, 1990; Vent D'Est, 1992; Afrique (live), 1993; Embrasse-Moi, 1995; Traditional Odysée, 1996; with Bextet: Enfance, 1991; with Big Band Quoi de Neuf Docteur: Le Retour, 1991; En Attendant La Pluie, 1993. Honours: Winner, French Jazz National Contest, Paris, 1984. Hobbies: Sport; Travel.

RENO Mike, b. Canada. Vocalist; Songwriter. Career: Member, Moxy; Founder member, Canadian rock group, Loverboy, 1980-89; Extensive tours, USA, Canada; Support to Def Leppard, European tour, 1988. Compositions: Co-writer, with Bryan Adams, Jon Bon Jovi, Richie Sambora, for Loverboy tracks. Recordings: Albums: Loverboy, 1980; Get Lucky, 1981; Keep It Up, 1983; Lovin' Every Minute Of It, 1985; Wildside, 1987; Big Ones (compilation), 1989; Singles: Turn Me Loose; The Kid Is Hot Tonite; Working For The Weekend; Hot Girls In Love; Lonin' Every Minute Of It. Honours: Multi-platinum records for all 5 studio albums; JUNO Awards: Album of the Year, Loverboy, 1981; Get Lucky, 1982; Single of the Year, Turn Me Loose, 1981; Group Of Year, 1981; 1982; Composer of the Year (with Paul Dean), 1981; Tribute To West Coast Music Awards: Best Group, 1981; 1982; Best Album: 1981, 1982; Song of the Year, The Kid Is Hot Tonite, 1981; Most Promising Act, 1981; International Achievement Award, 1984; Rock Band Of Year, 1981. Current Management: Lou Blair Management Inc. Address: No 407-68 Water Street, Vancouver, British Columbia V6B 1A4, Canada.

RESCALA Tim (Luiz Augusto), b. 21 Nov 1961, Rio de Janeiro, Brazil. Composer; Arranger; Musician (piano). m. Claudia Mele, 24 June 1995, 1 daughter. Musical Education: Piano with Maria Yêda Cadah; Composition with Hans-Joachim Koellreutter, Master's degree at University of Rio de Janeiro. Career: Works with serious music and pop music; Musical producer at TV Globo since 1988. Compositions: Scores for over 50 stage productions; Compositions played in Brazil; France; Canada; Belgium; USA; England; Music for films with director Eduardo Coutinho. Compositions: Music for Berimbuu and Tape, Cliché Music; Slave O Brasil!, Ponto, Linha E Plano. Recordings: Cliché Music (with popular songs and a suite for instruments); Album, Estudio da Glória (electroacoustic music). Honours: First Prize in Villa-Lobos Comp Competition; Mambembe Prize (theatre), 1983, 1993; Prize of Rio de Janeiro Municipality to write an opera. Membership: Estudió da Glória (co-founder). Hobby: Cooking. Address: Estúdio da Gloria, Rua Candido Mendes 53/104, Glória Cep 20.241, Rio de Janeiro, Brazil.

REUBEN Cyril, b. 30 Apr 1930, Bangor, North Wales. Musician (woodwind); Music Shop Retailer. m. Sylvia, 22 Dec 1958, deceased, 1 son, 1 daughter. Musical Education: University College of North Wales. Career: Member, orchestras of: Geraldo; Squadronaires; Jack Parnell; Concerts, tours include: Frank Sinatra; Liza Minelli; Shirley MacLaine; Johnny Mathis; Bing Crosby; Sarah Vaughan; Liberace. Recordings: Records with: The Beatles; The Carpenters; Music for television series include: Thunderbirds; Stingray; Captain Scarlett; Films include: Jesus of Nazareth; Fall Of The Roman Empire; In Hannibals Footsteps. Membership: Musicians' Union. Hobbies: Travel; Driving; Good food. Current Management: Self-managed. Address: Woodwind, Derek Road, Maidenhead, Berkshire SL6 8NT, England.

REVERE Paul, b. 7 Jan 1938, Caldwell, Idaho, USA. Musician; Comic; Businessman. m. Sydney Revere, 1980, 1 son, 1 daughter. Career: Formed Paul Revere And The Raiders, 1960; Television, hosted: Where The Action Is, with Dick Clark, 1965-66; Happening, 1968-69; 2 appearances, Ed Sullivan Show. Recordings: Kicks; Indian Reservation; Just Like Me; Good Thing; Louie Louie; Hungry; Ups And Downs; Him Or Me. Honours: Northwest Music Awards; Hall of Fame; Numerous Gold Records. Current Management: Robert Norman/Fred Lawrence at International Management. Address: 8942 Wilshire Boulevard, Beverly Hills, CA 90211, USA.

REVEY Laurence, b. 22 Dec 1965, Sierre, Switzerland. Education: Lettres and Théâtre.

Musical Education: Classical Singing, Jazz and Studio. Career: Appeared at concert with Bernard Louthiers, 1994; Appeared at concerts in Switzerland, 1995; Belluard-Bolluerk Festival, 1995; Paléo Festival de Nyon, 1995; Music Editing with Petra Gehrmann, Metisse Music, Paris, France. Membership: SUISA. Hobby: Singing. Current Management: L'Agence Marcel Schiess.

REYES Fernando, b. 4 Feb 1939, Conil De La Frontera, Cadiz, Spain. Flamenco Singer; Flamenco Musician (guitar). m. Gillian Carol Hamling, 29 Mar 1975, 1 son, 1 daughter. Musical Education: Private musical tuition, Spain. Career: Performed throughout: Spain; Europe; Canada; USA; Played for Antonio; Paco Romero; The King and Queen of Belgium; Toured with: Los Paraguayos; Performances include: Madison Square Gardens; Palais De Beaux Arts; Royal Albert Hall; Royal Festival Hall; Sadlers Wells; Covent Garden; Queen Elizabeth Hall; Fairfield Hall; Purcell Room; Numerous provincial theatres; Sang in opera Carmen, UK, Germany; Television includes: Opportunity Knocks; Blue Peter; Barrymore; Good Stuff; Film work; Broadcast on Virgin Radio. Compositions: Words and music various songs. Recordings: Albums: Spanish, South American music; Flamenco Songs; Spanish Popular Songs; CDs: Encuentros; Flamenco; Flamenco Gypsy. Honours: Various medals, trophies, awards, flamenco competitions, Spain. Membership: Musicians' Union. Hobby: Gardening. Current Management: Gillian Reyes. Address: 19 Fairmount Road, London SW2 2BJ, England.

REYNOLDS Debbie (Mary Frances), b. 1 Apr 1932, El Paso, Texas, USA. Actress; Singer; Entertainer. m. (1) Eddie Fisher, 26 Sept 1955, divorced, 1959, 1 daughter; m. (2) Harry Karl, 25 Nov 1960, divorced 1973; m. (3) Richard R Hamlett, 1985. Career: Nightclub act, mid 1960s-; Headlines casino circuit, including Reno, Tahoe, Las Vegas, Atlantic City; London Palladium; Tours average 42 weeks a year; Over 30 films include: Three Little Words; Two Weeks With Love; Singin' In The Rain; The Unsinkable Molly Brown; The Tender Trap; Divorce American Style; Theatre includes: Irene, 1973; Annie Get Your Gun; Woman Of The Year, 1983; National tour, The Unsinkable Molly Brown, 1989; Founded Debbie Reynolds Professional Rehearsal Studios, North Hollywood, late 1970s; Currently establishing Hollywood Motion Picture and Television Museum, in the Debbie Reynolds Hollywood Hotel And Casino;. Recordings: Abba Dabba Honeymoon (from Two Weeks With Love); Tammy; 5 videos. Publication: Debbie My Life (co-written with David Patrick Colombia), 1987. Honours include: National Honorary Presented by Girl Scouts USA, 1966-69; Oscar Nomination, The Unsinkable Molly Brown; National Film Award, Humanitarian Award, National Film Society; Celebrity Hall Of Fame Award, National Association for Mental Health; Hollywood Hall Of Fame, Hollywood Historic Trust And Chamber Of Commerce. Memberships: Supporter, fund raiser, Girl Scouts; Founder-president of the Thalians. Address: C/o Stan Scotland, JKE Services, 404 Park Ave S, 10th Floor, New York, NY 10016, USA.

REZNOR Trent, b. USA. Rock Musician; Singer. Career: Founder member, lead vocalist, US rock group Nine Inch Nails, 1989-. Recordings: Albums: Pretty Hate Machine, 1990; Broken (mini-album), 1992; Fixed, 1992; Singles include: Head Like A Hole, 1990; Compiler, film soundtrack Natural Born Killers, 1995. Current Management: John Malm, Conservative Management, 2337 W 11th Street, Ste 7, Cleveland, OH 44113, USA.

RHYS-JONES Merlin, b. 15 June 1958, Brighton, Sussex, England. Musician (guitar); Songwriter; Arranger. Musical Education: Self-taught. Career: Recorded with Lipservice; Toured with Ian Dury and The Music Students, 1983; Ian Dury and The Blockheads, 1992,

1994-95; Ellis, Beggs and Howard, 1989; Television includes: The Tube with Ian Dury; Sight and Sound; Martin Dobson's Main Course, Capital Radio. Recordings: Albums with Ian Dury: 4000 Weeks Holiday; Apples; Bus-Drivers Prayer And Other Stories (includes some co-writes); Warts And Audience (Live Blockheads at Brixton Academy); Several sessions for television shows; Currently teaching at Musicians Institute, Wapping. Memberships: Publishing agreement with Mute Song; Musicians' Union; PRS. Hobbies: Fishing; Theatre. Address: Flat 21, 318 Hornsey Road, London N7 7HE, England.

RIBOT Marc, b. 21 May 1954, Newark, New Jersey, USA. Musician (guitar). Musical Education: Studied with Frantz Casseus. Career: Moved to New York, 1978; Member, Realtones/Uptown Horns Band, 1979-83; Member, John Lurie's Lounge Lizards, 1984-89; Freelance musician, 1989-; Played with Jack MacDuff; Wilson Pickett; Chuck Berry; Solomon Burke; Tom Waits; Elvis Costello. Recordings: Albums: with Tom Waits: Rain Dogs; Big Time; Frank's Wild Years; with John Zorn: Cynical Hysterical Tour; Kristellnacht; with Elvis Costello: Spike; Mighty Like A Rose; Kojak Variety; Numerous solo albums; Also recordings with: The Lounge Lizards; John Lurie; Evan Lurie; Solomon Burke; The Jazz Passengers; David Sanborn; Caetano Veloso; Marianne Faithfull; Laurie Anderson; T-Bone Burnett; Sam Philips. Current Management: Ribot Productions. Address: 151 1st Avenue #88, New York, NY 10003, USA.

RIBOVILLAULT Jean, b. 6 May 1954, St Maur les Fossés, France. Musician; Clown; Composer; Instrument Maker. 3 sons, 2 daughters. Education: Various diplomas, sciences and acoustics. Musical Education: Self-taught. Career: Instrument maker for string instruments; Appearances on Radio France Culture; FR3 Television; Singer, classical concerts; Teacher, popular music; Clown/musician in France, Belgium, Luxemborg, Switzerland; Musical show for pupils in frame of own exhibition of popular musical instruments. Recordings: Les Pays; Les Frères Ribouillault; De l'Arbre à l'Oreille; Chants de Marins Traditionnels des Côtes de France; Epinette des Vosges. Membership: Jeunesse Musicales de France. Current Management: Florence Ribouillault. Address: 1 Rayerand, 88430 Gerbepal, France.

RICE Christopher Patrick, b. 6 Oct 1964, London, England. Musician (4/5 string bass guitar, 6/12 string guitar, keyboard). Musical Education: Tutors for: clarinet, Grade 4/5; saxophone; Graded through Royal School of Music. Career: WMRZ Radio Miami Florida, USA; Belo Jardin radio; Garanhus Difusor radio; 97.7 FM Sao Paulo, Brazil. Recordings: with Deja Vu: Black Angel, 1987; Love Me Tonite, 1988; Away From The Danger (17 of London's Finest album), Perimeter, 1995. Honours: 2 certificates for schools and colleges, playing clarinet and saxophone, 1978, 1979. Hobby: Socialising; Drawing. Address: 435 Devon Mansions, Tooley Street, London SE1 2XJ, England.

RICE Melanie Ailene, b. 4 Nov 1957, Philadelphia, Pennsylvania, USA. Singer; Musical Contractor. Musical Education: Rowan College; BA, Music, University of Delaware. Career: Tours: Opening act for: Joan Rivers; Smokey Robinson; Shecky Greene; David Brenner; Susan Anton; George Kirby; Bobby Vinton; Backing vocalist for: Grover Washington; James Darren; Joe Piscopo; Bobby Rydell; Various Casino Hotel appearances as solo act. Honours: John Phillip Sousa Award. Membership: NACE. Hobby: Golf. Current Management: Melanie Rice Entertainment, Inc. Address: 2511 Huntingdon Pike, Huntingdon Valley, PA 19006, USA.

RICE Tim (Sir) (Miles Bindon), b. 10 Nov 1944, Amersham, Buckinghamshire, England.

Writer; Broadcaster. m. Jane Arterata McIntosh, 1974, div 1990, 1 s, 1 d. Education: Lancing Coll. Appointments: EMI Records, 1966-68; Norrie Paramor Org, 1968-69; Fndr, Dir, GRRR Books Ltd, 1978-, Pavilion Books Ltd, 1981-97. Appearances on TV and radio incl Just A Minute, Radio 4; Creative Works: Lyrics for stage musicals (with Andrew Lloyd Webber): Joseph and the Amazing Technicolour Dreamcoat, 1968; Jesus Christ Superstar, 1970; Evita, 1976; Cricket, 1986; Other musicals: Blondel, w Stephen Oliver, 1983; Chess, w Benny Andersson and Bjorn Ulvaeus, 1984; Tycoon, w Michel Berger, 1992; Sel songs, Beauty and the Beast, w Alan Menken, 1994; Heathcliff, w John Farrar, 1996; King David, w Alan Menken, 1997; Aida, with Elton John, 1998; Lyrics for musical films: Aladdin, w Alan Menken, 1992; The Lion King, w Elton John, 1994, th version, 1997; Lyrics for songs w other compsers incl Paul McCartney, Mike Batt, Freddie Mercury, Graham Gouldman, Marvin Hamlisch, Rick Wakeman, John Barry. Publications: Songbooks from musicals; Guinness Book of Hit Albums, co-auth; Guinness Books of British Hit Singles, co-auth; Fill Your Soul, 1994; Cricket Writer, Natl Newspprs and Cricket Mags. Honours: Oscar, Golden Globe, Best New Song, A Whole New World, 1992, for Can You Feel The Love Tonight, w Elton John, 1994, and for You Must Love Me w Andrew Lloyd Webber, 1996; Gold and platinum records in num countries; 11 Ivor Novello Awds; 2 Tony Awds; 5 Grammy Awds; Kt, 1994. Memberships: Chmn, Stars Org for Spastics, 1983-85; Shaftesbury Ave Centenary Cttee, 1984-86; Pres, Lords Taverners, 1988-90; Dramatists' Saints and Sinners, Chmn, 1990; Cricket Writers; Fndn for Sport and the Arts, 1991-; Garrick Club; Groucho Club; MCC. Hobbies: Cricket; History of Popular Music; Poultry. Address: 31 The Terrace, Barnes, London SW13 0NR, England.

RICHARD Cliff (Harry Webb) (Sir), b. 14 Oct 1940, Lucknow, India. Singer. Career: Leader, Cliff Richard and the Shadows; Later, solo artist; Regular international concert tours, 1958-; Films include: The Young Ones; Expresso Bongo; Summer Holiday; Wonderful Life; Own television show; Frequent television and radio appearances. Recordings: First single, Move It, 1958; Over 100 singles to date; Over 50 albums include: 21 Today, 1961; The Young Ones, 1961; Summer Holiday, 1963; 40 Golden Greats, 1977; Love Songs, 1981; Private Collection, 1988; The Album, 1993 (all Number 1 in UK charts). Publications: Which One's Cliff; Jesus, Me And You; You, Me And Jesus; Mine Forever; Mine To Share; Single-Minded. Honours: OBE, 1980; Knighted, 1995; Numerous music awards. Membership: Equity. Hobbies: Tennis; Gardening. Current Management: Cliff Richard Organisation. Address: c/o PO Box 46c, Esher, Surrey KT10 0RB, England.

RICHARD Marc, b. 22 Nov 1946, Neuilly-Sur-Seine, France. Jazz Musician (saxophone, clarinet); Composer; Arranger. Musical Education: Self-taught musician; 3 years of courses for arrangement. Career: Played cornet with Haricots Rouges, 1963; Played saxophone and clarinet with many different bands including: Irakli; François Biensan; Founder, Anachronic Jazz Band, 1976; Played as sideman in Paris for many years with prominent jazzmen, including: Cab Calloway; Dee Dee Bridgewater; Harry Edison; Teacher, Jazz History, various schools. Recordings: Anachronic Jazz Band, Volume 1, 1977; Volume 2, 1980; Solo recording: After You've Gone. Hobbies: Golf; Cooking. Current Management: Self-managed. Address: 21 Allée de Fontainebleau, 75019 Paris, France.

RICHARD Zachary, b. 8 September 1950. Singer; Songwriter; Poet; Musician (Guitar, Piano, Cajun Accordion, Harmonica). m. Claude Thomas, 11 January 1992. Education: BA, summa cum laude, Tulane University, 1972. Career: Innovator,

Cajun and Zydeco Musical Styles. Recordings: Albums: Bayou des Mystères, 1976; Mardi Gras, 1977; Migration, 1977; Allons Danser, 1978; Live in Montreal, 1979; Vent D'été, 1980; Zack Attack, 1984; Zack's Bon Ton, 1986; Mardi Gras Mambo, 1988; Women in the Room, 1990; Snake Bite Love, 1992; Cap Enragé, 1996; Who Stole My Monkey; Come on Sheila; Cap Enragé; La Ballade de Jean Batailleur. Publications: Poetry: Voyage de Nuit, 1986; Faire Récolte, 1997. Honours: Prix de la Jeune Chanson Francaise, 1980; Prix Miroir de Québec, 1996; Officier de l'Ordre des Arts et Lettres, 1996; 2 Certified Gold Canadian Awards, 1978; Felix de l'ADISQ, 1997; Certified Platinum Canadian, 1997. Current Management: Claude Thomas, PO Box 305, Scott La 70583, 318, 2699926, USA. Address: PO Box 456, Scott La 70583, USA.

RICHARDS Andy. Producer; Programmer; Musician (Keyboards). Career: As Programmer and Keyboard Player has worked with Trevor Horn and Stephen Lipson on many projects including: Frankie Goes to Hollywood, Propoganda, Grace Jones; Other Artists include: George Michael, The Pet Shop Boys, Chris De Burgh, Def Leppard, Wet Wet Wet, Cher, Annie Lennox and Tina Turner; As Producer clients include: Alphaville; Prefab Sprout; The Pet Shop Boys; Fuzzbox; OMD; T'Pau; Dusty Springfield. Address: SARM Management, The Blue Building, 42/46 St Luke's Mews, London W11 1DG, England.

RICHARDS Dick, (Richard Boccelli), b. Philadelphia, Pennsylvania, USA. Musician (drums); Vocalist. Career: Original member, Bill Haley's Comets, 1954-55; Influential in early development of rock'n'roll; First rock band to headline a film; Thgeatre and movie actor (as Richard Boccelli). Recordings: Rock Around The Clock; See You Later Alligator; Crazy Man Crazy; Shake Rattle And Roll; Rock The Joint; Mambo Rock; Rudy's Rock; Florida Twist; Shimmie Minnie. Publications; Rock Around The Clock; Stage Clear; We're Gonna Party; Never Too Old To Rock; Let's All Rock Together; Now Dig This. Honours: Best Vocal group of 1953 Rock And Roll Hall Of Fame; Gold records. Address: Rock It Concerts, Bruno Mefer Platz 1, D-80937 Munich, Germany.

RICHARDS Eric (Thomas), b. 21 July 1953, Alnwick, England. Musician (bass guitar, piano, guitar). 2 daughters. Musical Education: City of Leeds College of Music; BA, Durham University; Jazz and Light Music, Newcastle College of Arts and Technology. Career: with Gloria Gaynor: UK tour, live television; with Dudu Pukwana's Zila: Tours, television and radio: UK, Europe, Africa; UK radio with Lloyd Ryan; Rhythm on Two, with Tony Evans Orchestra. Recordings: with Dudu Pukwana: Live At The 100 Club, 1981; Life In Bracknell and Willisau, 1983; Zila, 1986; Cosmics Chapter 90, 1990; with Lloyd Ryan: Circular Storm, 1989; Four Songs...From Under Mount Nephim, 1997. Publications: The Music Factory (bass guitar instrumental workbooks). Honours: LTCL (flute). Address: Rastenburger Str 17, 44369 Dortmund, Germany.

RICHARDS Keith (Keith Richard), b. 18 Dec 1943, Dartford, Kent, England. Musician (guitar); Vocalist; Songwriter. m. (1) Anita Pallenberg, 1 son, 1 daughter; (2) Patti Hansen, 1983, 2 daughters. Education: Sidcup Art School. Career: Member, The Rolling Stones, 1962-; Co-writer with Mick Jagger, numerous songs (often under psuedonym The Glimmer Twins); Appearances include: First UK tour, 1963; Debut US tour, 1964; Free concert, Hyde Park, 1969; Free concert, Altamont Speedway, 1969; Knebworth Festival, 1976; Played with Chuck Berry, Chicago Blues Festival, 1986; Steel Wheels North American tour, 1989. Recordings: Albums include: The Rolling Stones, 1964; The Rolling Stones No 2, 1965; Out Of Our Heads, 1965; Aftermath, 1966; Between The Buttons, 1967; Their Satanic Majesties

Request, 1967; Beggar's Banquet, 1968; Let It Bleed, 1969; Get Yer Ya-Ya's Out, 1969; Sticky Fingers, 1971; Exile On Main Street, 1972; Goat's Head Soup, 1973; It's Only Rock'n'Roll, 1974; Black And Blue, 1976; Some Girls, 1978; Emotional Rescue, 1980; Still Life, 1982; Steel Wheels, 1989; Flashpoint, 1991; Stripped, 1995; Also: Hail Hail Rock'n'Roll (with Chuck Berry), 1987; Singles include: It's All Over Now; Little Red Rooster; (I Can't Get No) Satisfaction; Jumping Jack Flash; Honky Tonk Women; Harlem Shuffle; Start Me Up; Paint It Black; Angie; Going To A Go-Go; It's Only Rock'n'Roll; Let's Spend The Night Together; Brown Sugar; Miss You; Emotional Rescue; She's So Cold; Undercover Of The Night. Honours: with Rolling Stones include: Grammy, Lifetime Achievement Award, 1986; Inducted into Rock And Roll Hall Of Fame, 1989; Q Award, Best Live Act, 1990; Ivor Novello Award, Outstanding Contribution To British Music, 1991; Songwriters Hall Of Fame, 1993. Current Management: Rupert Loewenstein, 2 King Street, London SW1Y 6QL, England.

RICHARDS Rasheda, b. London, England. Vocalist; Musician. Education: Arts Administrator. Musical Education: Music and voice tutor. Career: European and American tours; Concerts, workshops; Documentary for Arts Council; People Within The Arts Access. Recordings: Releases on UK and Jamaican record labels. Publications: Arts Council; Voice Newspaper; Caribbean Times. Memberships: MCPS; PRS; Musicians' Union. Hobbies: Keep fit; Swimming; Singing classes. Current Management: Miss M Richards. Address: 53 St Joseph's Close, Bevington Road, London W10 5GN, England.

RICHARDS Red (Charles), b. 19 Oct 1912, Brooklyn, New York, USA. Jazz Musician (piano); Vocalist. m. Dorothy, 6 Aug 1942. Musical Education: Studied Classics, 6 years. Career: Played at Savoy Ballroom with Tab Smith, 4 years; Co-leader, Saints and Sinners with Vic Dickenson; Tours as solo artist, trio, quartet: USA; Canada; Europe; Australia; Played with: Sidney Bechet; Muggsy Spanier; Mezz Mezzrow; Frank Sinatra; Wild Bill Davison; Jimmy McPartland. Recordings include: Big Reunion, Fletcher Henderson; Stanley Dances series with Buster Bailey; Dreamy; My Romance; Guest musician, Marion McPartland's Piano Jazz series, Number 11. Honours: Grand Pris Disque de Jazz, Hot Club de France, 1994. Membership: AFofM. Hobbies: Reading; Football; Baseball; Basketball. Current Management: Russ Dantzler, 328 W 44th Street, New York, NY 10036, USA. Address: 3944 Paulding Avenue, Bronx, New York, NY 10466, USA.

RICHARDSON Garth John, b. 23 July 1958, Toronto, Ontario, Canada. Record Producer. m. Jennifer Quinn, 7 Oct 1989, 2 daughters. Musical Education: Fanshawe Music College. Career: Engineer, Canada; Producer, USA; Recordings: Producer for: Rage Against The Machine; L7; The Melvins; Ugly Kid Joe; POL; Engineer for: Red Hot Chili Peppers; Ozzy Osbourne; Kiss; Mötley Crüe; Alice Cooper. Honours: Grammy Nomination, Rage Against The Machine; Judge, JUNO Awards. Hobbies: Hockey; Golf. Current Management: Tap/KO Entertainment. Address: 14839 Huston Street, Sherman Oaks, CA 91403, USA.

RICHARDSON Mark, b. 28 May 1970, Leeds, Yorkshire, England. Rock Musician (drums). Musical Education: Studied with Fred Adamson. Career: Performing from age 6; Member, Little Angels, 1991-94; Support tours: Bryan Adams; Bon Jovi; Van Halen; Toured UK and Europe, including Royal Albert Hall, London 1994; Group disbanded, 1994; Member, b.l.o.w., 1994-. Recordings: with Little Angels: Jam, 1993; Little Of The Past (compilation), 1994; Too Good To Last, 1994; with b.l.o.w: Legalise It EP, 1994; Man And Goat Alike, 1995. Honour: Silver Disc, Jam, 1993.

Membership: Musicians' Union. Hobbies: Golf; Listening to music. Current Management: Kevin Nixon, Trinifold Management. Address: 41 Peasholm Drive, Scarborough, Yorkshire YO12 7NA, England.

RICHEY David Andrew, b. 21 Sept 1965, Edgbaston, Birmingham, England. Musician (guitar); Composer; Actor; Playwright. m. Gillian MacKenzie, 4 June 1988, 1 daughter. Career: Lead guitarist, vocalist with many bands including YZI; Founder member, Aquila; Wayzgoose; Lyra And The Fianna; Created Dave Richey Music, Media Music Production company, 1993; Appeared numerous stage plays, pantomimes; Writer, plays include: The Thorn In The Rose; Directed several plays, wrote and starred in The Parkie; Writer, composer, numerous songs and instrumentals. Memberships: Musicians' Union; SPAM. Hobbies: Computers; Fishing; Walking; Windsurfing; Gardening; Conservation. Current Management: Gill MacKenzie. Address: Sonas, Calgary, Isle Of Mull, Scotland.

RICHIE Lionel, b. 20 June 1949, Tuskegee, Alabama, USA. Singer; Songwriter; Musician (piano); Actor; Record Producer. m. Diane Alexander, 1996. Education: BS, Econs, Tuskegee University, 1971. Career: Member, the Commodores, 1968-82; Support tours with The Jackson 5, 1973; The Rolling Stones, 1975; The O'Jays, 1976; Numerous other concerts; Solo artiste, 1982-; Concerts include: Closing ceremony, Olympic Games, Los Angeles, 1984; Live Aid, Philadelphia, 1985. Compositions: Hits songs with the Commodores: Sweet Love, 1975; Just To Be Close To You, 1976; Easy, 1977; Three Times A Lady (Number 1, US and UK), 1979; Sail On, 1980; Still (Number 1, US), 1980; Oh No, 1981; for Kenny Rogers: Lady (Number 1, US), 1981; for Diana Ross: Missing You, 1984; Solo hits: Endless Love, film theme duet with Diana Ross (Number 1, US), 1981; Truly (Number 1, US), 1982; All Night Long (Number 1, US), 1983; Running With The Night, 1984; Hello (Number 1, US and UK), 1984; Stuck On You, 1984; Penny Lover (co-writer with Brenda Harvey), 1984; Say You Say Me (Number 1, US), 1986; Dancing On The Ceiling, 1987; Love Will Conquer All, 1987; Ballerina Girl, 1987; My Destiny, 1992; Don't Wanna Lose You, 1996; Contributor, We Are The World (co-writer with Michael Jackson), USA For Africa (Number 1 worldwide), 1985; Recordings: Albums with the Commodores: Machine Gun, 1974; Caught In The Act, 1975; Movin' On, 1975; Hot On The Tracks, 1976; Commodores, 1977; Commodores Live!, 1977; Natural High 1978; Greatest Hits, 1978; Midnight Magic, 1979; Heroes, 1980; In The Pocket, 1981; Solo albums: Lionel Richie, 1982; Can't Slow Down, 1983; Dancing On The Ceiling, 1986; Back To Front, 1992; Louder Than Words, 1996. Honours include: ASCAP Songwriter Awards, 1979, 1984-96; Numerous American Music Awards, 1979-; Grammy Awards: Best Pop Vocal Performance, 1982; Album Of The Year, 1985; Producer Of The Year (shared), 1986; Lionel Richie Day, Los Angeles, 1983; 2 NAACP Image Awards, 1983; NAACP Entertainer of the Year, 1987; Oscar, Best Song, 1986; Golden Globe, Best Song, 1986. Current Management: John Reid. Address: 505 S Beverly Drive, Ste 1192, Beverly Hills, CA 90212, USA.

RICHMAN Guy Charles, b. 3 June 1965, Rush Green, England. Musician (drums). m. Alison Murray, 20 June 1994. Musical Education: Taught by Maz Abrams and Bobby Armstrong. Career: Concert dates with Kylie Minogue, 1995; World tours and television appearances with: Black; Patricia Kaas; UK tours with: Joe Longthorne (including television); Sister Sledge; Odyssey; Harold Melvyn. Recordings: with Black; Boy George; Bucks Fizz; Patricia Kaas; Joe Longthorne; Two People; Sister Sledge; Odyssey. Membership: Musicians' Union. Hobby: Badminton. Current Management: Self-managed.

Address: 53 St Marys Lane, Upminster, Essex RM14 2QU, England.

RICHMOND Kim, b. 24 July 1940, Champaign, IL, USA. Musician; Composer; Arranger. m. Chris Zambon, 5 April 1989. Education: Graduate, University of Illinois, 1963; BA, Music Education; BM, Music Compilation. Career: Written and conducted original musical scores for several television series including: Kojak; Harry O; ABC-TV Movie of the Week; Composed new works for concert stage; Arranger, music for singers including: Helen Reddy, Ann Jillian, Buddy Greco and Johnnie Ray, Pat Boone, Dianhann Carroll, Thelma Houston, Jaye P Morgan, Kaye Ballard; Jazz organizations of Stan Kenton, Buddy Rich, Louis Bellson, Stan Getz, Lalo Schifrin; TV Shows: The Donny and Marie Show; Mary Tyler Moore Show; Music Coordinator, CBS-TV, Tony Orlando and Dawn Show, 2 years; Toured with Percy Faith Orchestra in Japan and Australia, several years; Freelance studio work, TV shows, theater orchestras, concerts and other musical activities in Los Angeles; Leader, Conductor, Billy May Band, Los Angeles area; Artist-in-Residence, Australia's University of Sydney Music Conservatorium Jazz Studies Program; Regular Radio Host; Writes articles and reviews for jazz magazines (Saxophone Journal and Jazz Player). Compositions include: All Together; Flapjacks and Maple Syrup; Big Mama Louise; White Tornado; Sojourn; Stupefying Illusions; Portland Stew; Probe; Wind-up; Back a Tad; Osage Autumn; Melon Bells; Old Acquaintances; Chic-a-Brac; Passages; Clear Command; Life Is....; Straining Out Gnats and Swallowing Camels; Nice; Grass of Gethsemane; Gems; Collage in Green; European Icicles; Soft Feelings; Variations; Precious Promises; Big Sur; City of LA. Recordings include: Range; Passages; Thesaurus; Take a Look; Give and Gather; Sacred Addiction; New Beginning; Raisin' the Roof; Something for Nothing; Pastels, Ashes; Bing!; Night Flight to Valhalla; Step on the Gas; Handwrought; On the Move; Disco for Cynthia; One One Home; Fire and Ice; Yesterday and Today; Body and Soul; Hot Nights; Ready For Your Love; Moving On; Children of the World; More Pepper, Shark Bait; Crocodile Tears; New York, New York; On the Move; My Love; The Devil in Me; Come Home to the Father. Publications: Feature Writer for Saxophone Journal and Jazz Player; CD Reviewer in Jazz Player. Memberships: AF of M; ASCAP; ASMAC; International Association Jazz Educators. Hobbies: Computers; Tennis; Hiking; Canoeing. Address: 6248 Rogerton Drive, Hollywood, CA 90068, USA.

RICHRATH Gary, b. 18 Oct 1949, Peoria, Illinois, USA. Musician (guitar); Songwriter. Career: Guitarist, songwriter, US rock group REO Speedwagon, 1971-92; Richrath, 1992-; Live concert, Denver (first stereo concert broadcast), 1981; Anti-drug concert Users Are Losers, Miami, Florida, 1990. Recordings: Albums: with REO Speedwagon: REO Speedwagon, 1971; R.E.O. T.W.O., 1972; Ridin' The Storm Out, 1973; Lost In A Dream, 1974; This Time We Mean It, 1975; R.E.O., 1976; REO Speedwagon Live/You Get What You Play For, 1977; You Can Tune A Piano But You Can't Tuna Fish, 1978; Nine Lives, 1979; A Decade Of Rock'N'Roll 1970-80, 1980; Hi Infidelity, 1981; Good Trouble, 1982; Wheels Are Turning, 1984; Best Foot Forward, 1985; Life As We Know It, 1987; The Hits, 1988; A Second Decade Of Rock'N'Roll 1981-91, 1991; with Richrath: Only The Strong Survive, 1992; Hit singles include: Time For Me To Fly, 1978; Take It On The Run, 1981; Keep On Loving You, 1981; Don't Let Him Go, 1981; Keep The Fire Burnin', 1982; Can't Fight This Feeling (Number 1, US), 1985; That Ain't Love, 1987; In My Dreams, 1987. Honours: Gold, Platinum discs. Current Management: Baruck-Consolo Management, 15003 Greenleaf Street, Sherman Oaks, CA 91403, USA.

RICKFORS Mikael, b. 4 Dec 1948, Sweden. Singer; Musician (guitar, piano); Songwriter. m. Mia, 2 sons, 1 daughter. Career: Concert tours; Television (Europe, USA). Compositions: Yeah Yeah, recorded by Cyndi Lauper; Blue Night, Percy Sledge; Daughter Of The Night, Carlos Santana; The Last Wind, Touch, Carla Olson; Recorded by the Hollies: Don't Leave The Child Alone; They Don't Realise I'm Down. Recordings: Albums: Mikael Rickfors; The Wheel; Tender Turns Tuff; Headhunters; Blue Night; Happy Man Don't Kill. Address: c/o Polygram Records, Stockholm, Sweden.

RIDGELEY Andrew, b. 26 Jan 1963, Windlesham, Surrey, England. Singer; Musician (guitar). Career: Member, The Executive, 1979-80; Member duo, Wham! with George Michael, 1982-86; Most successful English pop group of 1980s; Worldwide tours and concerts include: Club Fantastic Tour, 1983; World tour, 1984; US tour, 1985; First western pop band to play in China, 1985; Farewell concert, 'The Final' concert, Wembley, 1986; Solo artiste, actor and racing driver, 1986-; Performed at Rock in Rio II, with George Michael, 1991. Recordings: Albums with Wham!: Fantastic (Number 1, UK), 1983; Make It Big (Number 1, UK and US), 1984; The Final, 1986; Solo album: Son Of Albert, 1990; Singles include: Young Guns (Go For It), 1982; Wham Rap!, 1982; Bad Boys, 1983; Club Tropicana, 1983; Wake Me Up Before You Go Go (Number 1, UK), 1984; Careless Whisper (Number 1, UK and US); Last Christmas, 1984; Everything She Wants (Number 1, US), 1985; Freedom, 1985; I'm Your Man (UK number 1), 1985; The Edge Of Heaven (Number 1, UK), 1986; Solo single: Shake, 1990. Honours include: BRIT Awards: Best British Group, 1985; Outstanding Contribution To British Music, 1986.

RIDGWAY Stanard, b. 5 Apr 1956, Los Angeles, California, USA. Singer; Songwriter; Composer. m. Pietra Wexstun, 17 May 1981, 1 son. Education: College. Career: Singer, Wall of Voodoo; Television appearances include: The Tube, Top Of The Pops. Compositions: Songs include: Camouflage; The Big Heat; Mexican Radio; Calling Out To Carol. Recordings: with Wall of Voodoo: Wall Of Voodoo, 1979; Dark Continent, 1980; Call Of The West, 1981; Solo recordings: The Big Heat, 1985; Mosquitos, 1990; Party Ball, 1991; Songs That Made This Country Great, 1992. Membership: BMI. Current Management: S.R. Dis-Information. Address: PO Box 9524, Los Angeles, CA 90295-1924, USA.

RIDING Jules, b. 22 May 1949, Cheltenham, Gloucestershire, England. Christian Musician; Singer. m. Lynn Gousmett, 11 May 1980, 2 sons, 2 daughters. Education: First year university, Auckland, New Zealand. Musical Education: Self-taught. Career: Full-time professional, 1988-; Founder, Elkanah School of Music Ministry, 1995. Recordings: Albums: On This Night, 1984; Heartstrings, 1987; Revelation, 1991; Homecoming, 1992; The Fisherman, 1994; Kids Time, 1997. Publications: Don't Let Poor Nellie Starve, poetry, 1975; New Zealand Lamb, poetry, 1981. Honours: New Zealand Music Awards, Gospel Album Of The Year, 1984, 1987. Membership: APRA, New Zealand. Hobbies: Photography; Running. Current Management: Self-managed. Address: Elkanah Music, 37 Gerontius Lane, Snells Beach 1240, New Zealand.

RIDLEY Larry (Laurence Howard II), b. 3 Sept 1937, Indianapolis, Indiana, USA. Musician; Music Educator. m. Magdalena Ridley, 1 daughter. Education: BS, Music Education, Indiana University, 1955-59; New York University, 1971; MA, State University of New York, 1993. Career: Associate Professor of Music, Livingston College of Rutgers University, New Jersey, 1971-; Chairman, Department of Music, Rutgers University, 1972-80; Artist-in-residence, colleges in USA and South Africa; Bandleader, Jazz

Legacy Ensemble; Recordings and international performances with numerous leading musicians including: Dizzy Gillespie; Duke Ellington; Art Farmer; Thelonious Monk; Dinah Washington; Benny Goodman; Dexter Gordon; Benny Carter; Herbie Hancock; Freddie Hubbard; Mercer Ellington; Sonny Rollins; Philly Joe Jones; Jazz Artist-in-Residence, Schomburg Centre/New York Public Library since 1993. Honours: Grammy Nominations, 1983, 1984 with Dameronia; Chairman, Jazz Panel, National Endowment Arts, 1976-78; National co-ordinator, NEA Jazz Artists in School pilot programme, 1978-82; Member, National Association Jazz Educators (advisory board, 1981-); Mid Atlantic Arts Foundation Living Legacy Jazz Award, 1997; Inducted into the International Association of Jazz Educators Hall of Fame, 1998. Address: c/o Rutgers University, Mason Gross School Of Arts (music department), New Brunswick, NJ 08903, USA.

RIDLEY Tim, b. 5 Aug 1967, Portsmouth, Hampshire, England. Teacher; Musician (keyboards, drums, percussion). Musical Education: Royal Academy of Music. Career: Keyboard player, Brotherhood of Man, 1989-; Teacher, drums and percussion, 1989-96, Assistant Master, teaching music and music technology, 1996-, Marlborough College, Wiltshire; Keyboard player, The Sounds Of The Supremes Show, 1993-; Keyboard player, composer, Mentaur. Compositions: Daedalus (musical), 1988; Ongoing film commission; Requiem Mass, 1988. Recordings: Darkness Before Dawn, Mentaur, 1995; Live In Germany, The Sounds Of The Supremes, 1995. Honours: LRAM, 1984; GRSM, 1985. Membership: Rollercoaster Club of Great Britain. Hobbies: Flying (PPL); Music technology; Film and television. Current Management: Videoscope Productions. Address: Marlborough College, Marlborough, Wiltshire SN8 1PA, England.

RIEL Alex, b. 13 Sept 1940, Copenhagen, Denmark. Musician (drums). Musical Education: Private lessons with Borge Ritz; 1 semester with Allan Dawson, Berklee School of Music, Boston, USA. Career: Founder, Alex Riel Trio; Member, Niels Lan Doky Trio; Freelance solo musician. Television appearances with: Nancy Wilson; Manhattan Transfer; Stan Getz; Bill Evans; Eddie Gomez; Toots Thielemans; Gerry Mulligan; Roland Kirk; Niels Henning Orsted Petersen; Played concerts with: John Scofield; Michel Petrucianni; Dizzy Gillespie; Wayne Shorter; Dollar Brand; Archie Shepp; Don Cherry. Videos: Bill Evans Trio in Oslo, 1967; Niels Lan Dorky Trio, Close Encounter, 1992. Recordings include: In A Way, Alex Riel Trio, 1966; Emerge, Alex Riel Trio, 1993; Recorded as guest musician with numerous artistes including: Dexter Gordon; Ben Webster; Gary Burton; Thomas Clausen; Palle Mikkelborg; Karin Krog; Archie Shepp; Toots Thielmans; Jean Luc Ponty; Eddie Lockjaw Davis; Marilyn Mazur; Stéphane Grappelli. Honours: Danish Jazz Musician of Year, 1965; Palace Jazz Award, 1991. Membership: Dansk Musiker Forbund. Hobby: Dogs.

RIENIETS Andrea, b. February 1963, Shepparton, Victoria, Australia. Singer; Songwriter; Composer. Education: BA, Communications; Theatre, Opera Singing, Choir Studies, Jazz Drumming; Selftaught Guitar. Career: 16 scores for stage; Founder Director, Before You Were Blonde, choir, 1991-96; Guest Director, Sing It Up Big, Indigenous Australian Choir, 1997-; Womadelaide, solo performance, 1997. Compositions: Wooden Child, 1996-97; Love of a Lifetime, 1997. Recordings: Fluently Helvetica, debut release; Gorgeous Girl Records, 1996. Current Management: Gorgeous Girl Records. Address: PO Box 10059, Gouger Street, Adelaide, SA 5000, Australia.

RIGBY Paul Julian, b. 21 Dec 1968, Blackburn, Lancashire, England. Musician (drums,

piano); Bandleader. Musical Education: Studied at Salford University, Bretton Hall and University of North Texas, Higher Diploma in Popular Music with Recording, and BA Honours in Popular Music; PGCE. Career: Played with Georgie Fame; Kenny Baker; Mark Nightingale; Bobby Shew; Maynard Ferguson; Appeared in shows and musicals; Toured extensively with Wigan Youth Jazz Orchestra and Northern Jazz Orchestra; Tutor for Lancashire School Jazz Orchestra; Lecturer of Popular Music. Recordings: with Northern Jazz Orchestra; Good News; with Wigan Youth Jazz Orchestra: Aim For The Heart; One More Time; Check It Out. Membership: Musicians' Union. Hobbies: Badminton; Squash; Football. Address:Clairville, Manor Road, Darwen, Lancashire BB3 2SN, England.

RILEY Howard, b. 16 February 1943, Huddersfield, Yorkshire, England. Musician (Piano); Composer. Education: BA, 1964, MA, 1966, University of Wales; MMus, Indiana University, USA, 1967. Career: Festival, Club, TV, Radio appearances as Pianist (solo & group), throughout Europe and USA, 1967-. Recordings: 40 LPs, CDs under own name. Publication: The Contemporary Piano Folio, 1982. Honour: UK/USA Bicentennial Arts Fellowship, 1976. Hobbies: Walking; Reading. Address: Flat 2, 53 Tweedy Road, Bromley, Kent BR1 3NH, England.

RILEY Jeannie C (Jeannie Carolyn Stephenson), b. 19 Oct 1944, Anson, Texas, USA. Singer. m. Mickey Riley, 1 daughter. Recordings: Hit singles: Harper Valley PTA (Number 1, US), 1969; The Girl Most Likely; There Never Was A Time; The Back Side Of Dallas; Things Go Better With Love; The Rib; Good Enough To Be Your Wife; When Love Has Gone Away; Return To Harper Valley. Honours: Grammy Award, 1968; CMA Record Of Year, 1969; Music Operators Of America Award, 1969; Gold disc, Harper Valley PTA (6 million copies sold), 1969. Current Management: Morningstar Public Relations, PO Box 83, Brentwood, TN 37027, USA.

RILEY Teddy, b. 1967. Musician (multi-instrumentalist); Record Producer. Career: Considered pioneer of "New Jack Swing"; Member, groups: Guy; Blackstreet; Musician for various artists including: Kool Moe Dee; Heavy D; Michael Jackson; Roy Brown; Own recording studio, Future Records. Recordings: Over 30 Platinum albums as producer; Albums include: Dangerous, Michael Jackson; Don't Be Cruel, Bobby Brown; Hard Or Smooth, Wreckx'N'Effects; Make It Last Forever, Keith Sweat; Other recordings for: Heavy D; James Ingram; Jazzy Jeff And The Fresh Prince; As musician: U Blow My Mind, Blackstreet, 1995. Current Management: ICM, 40 W 57th Street, New York, NY 10019, USA.

RINNE Tapani, b. 2 Feb 1962, Finland. Musician (saxophones). Musical Education: Recorder, clarinet, saxophones; Sibelius Academy, 1980. Career: Played with: Pori Big Band; Kojo And The Bluesshakers; Edward Vesala's Sound And Fury; Upi Sorvali's Big Bad Family; Leader, own group RinneRadio; Concerts include: Cafe Metropol, Helsinki; Kajaani Festival. Recordings: with RinneRadio include. Address: Porvoonkatu 9 A 9, 00510 Helsinki, Finland.

RINTOUL Laura Jane, b. 3 Oct 1950, Perth, Scotland. Singer; Musician (accordion, recorder). Education: HNC, Napier College, Edinburgh, Scotland. Career: Medical Scientist, then trained in Glasgow from 1985; Concert tour of Japan in 1989; First broadcast on BBC Radio Scotland, 1988 appearing regularly since then; Presenter, local radio, Festival of Remembrance, Perth, 1992; Appeared on Grampian TV, 1994. Recordings: As guest artist on: A Ceilidh From Aberfeldy, and Gather, from the Clan MacGregor Celebration Concerts. Honours: Silver Pendant,

Edinburgh Gaelic MOD, 1987; Gold Medal, Arbroath Music Festival, 1991, Glasgow, 1992; Scots Songs Silver Medal, Perth, 1993. Memberships: Musicians' Union; Perthshire Musical (Competition) Festival Association. Hobbies: Swimming; Charity Work; Scottish Country Dancing; Travel. Address: 18 Low Road, Cherrybank, Perth PH2 0NF, Scotland.

RISDON Ronald Valentine, b. 14 Feb 1950, Dorking, Surrey, England. Artist Manager; Television and Film Producer. m. Jane Risdon, 15 June 1972, 1 son. Musical Education: Self-taught guitar, bass, keyboards. Career: Bassist, then guitarist, with Marjorine, including UK, Europe tours, 1968-; Re-named Jungle Jim, 1972; Tours, North Africa, UK and Europe; Television and radio: Europe, UK, Channel Islands; Manager of various acts including: Tag, Ignorance, Heat featuring T J Felton, Treana, Craig Thomson, actor; Co-owner, production company Everyday Productions. Recordings: Singles: I Live, 1968; Big Fat Orangoman, (Top 20, UK, Number 1, France, Germany); Manager, recording artists 1980-. Memberships: PRS; BASCA. Hobbies: Music; Films; Reading; Travel. Address: Showcase Management International, 33 Mandarin Place, Grove, Oxfordshire OX12 0QH, England.

RISDON Susan Jane, b. 3 Mar 1952, Frimley, Surrey, England. Artist Manager; Television and Film Producer. m. Val Risdon, 15 June 1972, 1 son. Career: Artist promotion and management, USA, UK; Various US, European tours; Radio and television promotions on behalf of artists; Television and film productions, USA, Europe. Recordings: Releases for Tag; Ignorance; Heat featuring T J Felton; Treana; Craig Thomson, actor. Co-owner, production company Everyday Production. Publications: Various magazine articles in USA, Europe. Memberships: PRS; BASCA. Hobbies: Music; Films; Books; Travel. Address: Showcase Management International, 33 Mandarin Place, Grove, Oxon OX12 0QH, England.

RITCHIE Billy (Darrell Jr), b. 11 Sept 1986, High Point, North Carolina, USA. Singer; Songwriter. m. Michelle Ritchie, 6 Sept 1990, 1 daughter. Education: BA, Communications, Gardner-Webb College, 1990. Musical Education: Minor in Music, Gardner-Webb College, 1990. Career: Full time concert artist; Songwriter; Over 500 concerts, 1991-. Recordings: Albums: Stand And Believe, 1992; No Turning Back, 1993; Big Time, 1995. Memberships: Gospel Music Association; BMI. Hobbies: Reading; Writing. Current Management: Darrell Ritchie Concerts. Address: 1071 Colgan Court, Lawrenceville, GA 30244, USA.

RITENOUR Lee, b. 11 Jan 1952, Los Angeles, California, USA. Jazz Musician (guitar). Career: Session player, as Captain Fingers, mid 1970s; Also jazz fusion solo artiste; Played with Herbie Hancock; Steely Dan; Stanley Clarke; Member, Friendship (with Don Grusin). Recordings: Albums: First Course, 1974; Guitar Player, 1975; Captain Fingers, 1975; The Captain's Journey, 1978; Gentle Thoughts, 1978; Sugarloaf Express, 1978; Feel The Night, 1979; Friendship, 1979; Rit, 1981; Rio, 1982; Rit 2, 1983; Banded Together, 1983; On The Line, 1984; Harlequin, with Dave Grusin, 1985; American Flyers, 1986; Earth Run, 1986; Portrait, 1987; Festival, 1988; Wes Bound, 1993; Larry And Lee, with Larry Carlton, 1995. Address: c/o GRP Records, 33 Broadwick Street, London W1V 1FR, England.

RIVERS Johnny, b. 7 Nov 1942, New York, New York, USA. Musician; Singer; Songwriter. Musical Education: Father a musician; Some private lessons; Watched and listened to older professionals. Career: President, top record and publishing company, singer and songwriter by age 25; Started American discotheque craze at

Whiskey A Go Go, Los Angeles, 1963; Appeared La Riviera, with Nancy Wilson, 1966; First rock and roll act to play Copa Cabana, New York; Formed record company, Soul City Records; Currently owner, manager, Rivers Music; Influenced the careers of The Mamas and Papas; Lou Adler; Glen Campbell; Al Wilson; Wolfman Jack; Brought together Hal Blaine, Joe Osborn, Larry Knectel, creators of 1960s-70s West Coast Sound; Special guest on Memphis Horns 25th Anniversary Concert, 1992. Recordings: Hits include: Memphis; Maybelline; Mountain Of Love; Seventh Son; Midnight Special; Secret Agent Man; Poor Side Of Town; Baby, I Need Your Lovin'; Tracks Of My Tears; Summer Rain; Look To Your Soul; Rockin' Pneumonia And The Boogie Woogie Flu; Sea Cruise; Blue Suede Shoes; Help Me Rhonda; Swayin' To The Music (Slow Dancin'); Curious Mind (Um Um Um Um Um Um); As Producer: Jimmy Webb and The Fifth Dimension: Up, Up And Away. Honours: 2 Grammys; BMI Awards. Memberships: BMI; ASCAP; AFTRA; AFofM. Hobbies: Motorcycles; Horses; Songwriting. Current Agents: American Concert And Touring Company, Nashville, Tennessee; Variety Artists, San Luis Obispo, California. Address: Soul City Records Inc, 12358 Ventura Boulevard # 342, Studio City, CA 91604, USA.

RIX (Leon) Luther, b. 11 Feb 1942, Lansing, Michigan, USA. Musician (percussion, drums); Composer. m. Ellen Garrett, 14 May 1973, 1 son. Musical Education: MusB, Indiana University, 1963; Postgraduate, Jordan Conservatory of Music, Indianapolis, 1964-65. Career: Percussionist with Indianapolis Symphony Orchestra, 1965-67; Winter Consort, 1968; Doc Severinsen, 1970; Drummer with Bette Midler, 1971-72; Manhattan Transfer, 1974-75; Mary Travers, 1975-76; Bob Dylan, 1975-76; Leonard Cohen, Laura Branigan, 1976; Peter, Paul and Mary, 1978; Freelance musician, 1979-; Drummer with Rosenhontz, 1986-; Richard Reiter Swing band, 1987-; Crossing Point, 1990-; Musician, shows include: The Wiz; Grease; Barnum; Little Shop Of Horrors. Compositions: Boogaloother, 1972; Like A Beautiful Song, 1980; Tightrope (also arranger), 1969; Compositions recorded by Genya Raven; Buzzy Lindhart; Kaleidoscope. Memberships: ASCAP; AFTRA; BMI; AFofM.

RIZZO Carmen, b. 8 Apr 1964, Akron, Ohio, USA. Record Producer; Engineer. m. 11 Dec 1993. Career: Engineer, mixer, co-writer, programmer, for latest Seal album. Recordings: Albums for: Seal; Prince; Ray Charles; Chris Connelly (Ministry); Wendy And Lisa. Honour: Grammy Nomination. Memberships: ASCAP; NARAS. Current Management: Greg Spotts Management (USA); Worlds End Ltd (England). Address: 421 Hudson Street, Suite #216, New York, NY 10014, USA.

ROACH Archie, b. Australia. Singer; Songwriter. Partner, Ruby Hunter, 5 children. Career: Singer, songwriter; Performed extensively across Australia; Appeared at 3 WOMAdelaide festivals, with Paul Kelly; Frente; Jimmy Barnes; Weddings Parties Anything; Crowded House; Numerous Aboriginal cultural festivals including: Sydney's Survival Day Concerts; Nambundah, New South Wales; Bogong Moth; Brunswick Koori Arts, Victoria; Oyster Cove, Tasmania; Cape York, Queensland; US tour, support to Joan Armatrading and Bob Dylan, 1992; Guest (with Ruby Hunter), Corrobee Festival Festival, Southbank Centre, London, 1993; UK tour, 1993; UK visit with Robin Hitchcock and The Egyptians, 1994; Berlin Independence Festival, 1994; Support to Suzanne Vega, Australia, 1994; Other appearances include AFL Grand Final, 1994; Performed before Prime Minister Paul Keating, football game, Alice Springs. Recordings: Albums: Charcoal Lane, 1990; Jamu Dreaming, 1994. Publications: Anthology of lyrics: You Have The Power, 1994. Current Management: Julie Hickson.

Address: 25 Overend Street, Brunswick, VIC 3056, Australia.

ROACH Max(well Lemuel), b. 10 Jan 1924, Elizabeth City, North Carolina, USA. Jazz Musician (percussion). m. (1) Mildred Wilkinson, 14 Jan 1949 (divorced), 1 son, 1 daughter, (2) Abbey Lincoln, 3 Mar 1963 (divorced). Musical Education: Manhattan School Of Music, New York City; MusD (hon), New England Conservatory of Music, 1982. Career: Jazz percussionist with Charlie Parker, 1946-48; Also played with Thelonious Monk; Bud Powell; Dizzy Gillespie; Sonny Rollins; Eric Dolphy; Co-leader, Max Roach-Clifford Brown Quintet; Appearances include: Paris Jazz Festival, 1949; Newport Jazz Festival, 1972; Producer; Director; Choreographer; Professor of Music, University of Massachusetts, 1973-. Composition: Freedom Now suite. Recordings: Albums include: Percussion Bitter Sweet; It's Time; Drums Unlimited; Speak Brother Speak; The Loadstar; Conservations: Long As Your Living; Survivors; The Long March; Jazz In 3/4 Time; Scott Free; To The Max!, 1991; Max And Dizzy (with Dizzy Gillespie), 1989. Honours: Down Beat Awards: Best Record Of The Year, 1956; Down Beat Poll Winner, 1955, 1957-60, 1984; Metronome Poll Winner, 1951-54. Membership: Organizer, Jazz Artists Guild Inc.; Officier des Arts et des Lettres; Honorary Member, American Academy. Current Management: Max Roach Productions. Address: Suite 14-E, 415 Central Park West, New York, NY 10025, USA.

ROACHFORD Andrew. Vocalist; Musician (keyboards, percussion). Career: Performer, Soho jazz clubs, London, aged 14; Founder, own band Roachford, 1987-; Toured with Terence Trent D'Arby, The Christians, 1988; Recordings: Albums: Roachford, 1988; Get Ready!, 1991; Feel, 1997; Singles include: Cuddly Toy, 1989; Family Man, 1989. Current Management: Pure Management, 6 Chingford Road, London E17 4PJ, England.

ROADHOUSE JOHNNY, b. 13 Jan 1921, Sheffield, Yorkshire, England. Musician (saxophone, woodwind). Divorced, 2 sons, 2 daughters. Musical Education: Self-taught. Career: 35 years BBC Staff Musician (Principal); Freelance Syphony Orchestras: Halle; Liverpool Philharmonic; 30 years in orchestra accompanying television series: Good Old Days; Many tours with top international artists including: Tony Bennett, Vic Damone; Recordings, radio series with Nigel Ogden (Organist Entertains series). Membership: Musicians' Union. Hobbies: Running, organising music shops; Work. Address: 262 Brantingham Road, Manchester M21 0Q2, England.

ROAR Finn, b. 21 July 1937, Kolding, Denmark. Composer; Educator; Musician (piano, saxophone); Singer. m. Gisela Moberg, 8 Apr 1960, 3 sons, 1 daughter. Education: MA, Music, French. Musical Education: Studies with Professor Arne Skjold Rasmussen. Career: Bandleader (FR 5) for radio programmes; Leader and composer, fusion group Beaver Service, 1974-; Television appearances: Denmark, SF; Many concert tours to primary schools (More Jazz To The Children); First director, Danish Conservatory of Jazz, Latin, Rock Music, 1985-88; Festivals in Denmark and France; Co-founder, Radio Jazz; Member of presidency, Rhythmic Folk College. Recordings: Ants In My Ears, 1981; More Jazz To The Children, 1985; U-Spring (concerto for big band), 1990; Black Messiah (oratorio), 1994; Once There Was A Carnival (opera), 1995. Publications: Actual Music, 1975; Have You Heard, 1975; Beaver Service, 1976; From Gregorian Chant To Rock, Western Music History, Blue Book, 1981. Memberships: DJBFA; IAJE. Hobby: Fishing. Current Management: Beaver Records, Copenhagen, Denmark. Address: Udbakken 21, 2750 Ballerup, Denmark.

ROATTA Guillermo, b. 26 Mar 1959, Bogota, Colombia. Musician (drums). Career: Member, bands; Afrodisax; Marc Mangen Trio; Roatta Sextet; Coeur Urbain; Olivier Gatto Quartet; Alex Golino Trio; Bob Scatena Band; Serge Moulinier; Yves Carbonne. Recordings: Afrodisax, 1985; Serge Moulinier Trio (Alba Musica - Conco, to be published), 1995. Current Management: Gautret Agnes. Address: 33 Avenue des Provinces Bat E/@, 33600 Pessac, France.

ROBBINS Dennis Anthony, b. Hazelwood, North Carolina, USA. Musician (guitar). m. Helen Hughs, 2 daughters. Career: US Marines, toured Vietnam, 1968; Joined the Rockets, 1976; Moved to Nashville, record deal on MCA Records, first country album released, 1985; Signed to Warner Brothers with new band, Billy Hill, 1988; first artist signed to Giant Records, 1992; Writer, performer for Warner/Chappell, 1994-. Compositions include: Do You Love Me, Just Say Yes, Highway 101 (Number 1) 1987; Church On Cumberland Road, Shenandoah; Two Of A Kind, Working On A Full House, Garth Brooks; Finally Friday, by both Earl Thomas Connelly, George Jones; Paris Tennessee, Tracy Lawrence; I'm Just A Rebel, by both Confederate Railroad, Joy Lynn White; Home Sweet Home, Dennis Robbins; Film soundtracks: Rolling Dice (used in Pink Cadillac); Looking For A Thing Called Love (used in A Thing Called Love); I Can't Help Myself (used in My Blue Heaven). Recordings: 4 albums, Rockets; Album with Billy Hill, 1988; Albums: Man With A Plan; Born Ready.

ROBERTS Austin. Songwriter; Artist; Producer; Publisher. Career: Approximately 60 hits worldwide including Number 1's (7 in USA); Songs featured, films and television series; Wrote and sang many of the Scooby-Doo songs; Wrote musicals: Damon's Song; Rachinoff; Formed Hot House Music, 1992; Two Top 10 singles as recording artist. Compositions: Hits include: When You Put Your Heart In It; Honor Bound; Strong Heart; IOV; My Night To Howl; Desesperados; You Lie; Songs recorded by: Reba McEntire; Kenny Rogers; Crystal Gayle; Michelle Wright; Lee Greenwood; Oak Ridge Boys; Charley Pride; Lulu; Julio Iglesias; Glen Campbell; Tanya Tucker; Sonny and Cher; Dan Seals; Englebert Humperdinck; Vicky Carr; Loverboy; Billy Crash Craddock; The Osmonds. Honours: 1 Grammy; 3 Grammy Nominations; 3 CMA Nominations; Academy Award Nomination; Golden Globe Nomination; Music City News Award; NSAI Award; ACM Nomination; Numerous ASCAP Airplay Awards; 1 German Grammy; 4 JUNO Awards; SESAC Airplay Award. Current Management: Scramblers Knob Studio. Address: 1000 Scramblers Knob, Franklin, TN 37064, USA.

ROBERTS Graham Andrew, b. 3 Feb 1964, Northampton, England. Musical Education: Royal Academy of Music. Career: Numerous concerts, television, radio, for BBC, ITV, various European stations; Tours, USA, Europe, Far East. Recordings: with Grahamphones: Let's Do It Again, 1990; with Pasadena Roof Orchestra: Breakaway, 1991; with Swing Sisters: Swing, 1992; Take Me Back, 1994; with Tetra Guitar Quartet: By Arrangement, 1993; Pasadena, 1994. Honours: Winner, Julian Bream Guitar Competition, 1988. Current Management: Hothouse Entertainments. Address: 7 Wychwood Close, New Duston, Northampton, England.

ROBERTS J Patricia, b. 17 Feb 1954, Aberdeen, Scotland. Singer; Musician (clarsach, Celtic harp, guitar). Education: Hamilton Academy, 1966-72; BSc, Biology, DipEd, Stirling University, 1977. Musical Education: Studied clarsach with Sanchia Pielou. Career: Teacher and Guidance Counsellor in high school, 1977-94; Appeared at Lorient Folk Festival, 1982-84; Member, folk group Chapter Four, appearing throughout Scotland, 1984-87; Solo artist, 1987-; Radio interviews, Radio Forth; Radio Bretagne; Television appearance: Carols For Christmas, BBC TV, 1994; Currently appearing in castles, stately homes and major hotels in Scotland including Gleneagles, Turnberry and Old Course. Recording: Just As I Am, (mainly traditional Scottish songs with clarsach and guitar accompaniment), 1993. Honours: Academic and Counselling Awards. Membership: Musicians' Union. Hobbies: Mountaineering; Hillwalking; Gardening; Fishing; Photography; Crafts. Address: 113 Lothian Crescent, Causewayhead, Stirling FK9 5SE, Scotland.

ROBERTS Phil, b. 20 May 1951, Portsmouth, Hampshire, England. Songwriter. m. Linda, 7 July 1979, 1 son, 1 daughter. Career: Touring singer, guitarist, 1969-95; Ceased live performance to concentrate on songwriting, 1995. Recordings: Albums: Solo album: Stampede; with Fridge Brothers: Alternate Traumas, 1986; with Panama Red: Back In Town, 1988; Worts And Wonders, 1989; Last Of The Red, 1990. Current Management: GULP Music. Address: 1 Park Cottage, Mayles Lane, Wickham, Hampshire, England.

ROBERTS Rudy, b. 9 Apr 1966, Nantes, France. Rock Musician (guitar). Musical Education: American School Of Modern Music, Paris. Career: Squealer, 1991; French support tour with UDO; Member, Starmania/Tycoon, 1993-95; Solo artist, 1991-; Numerous concerts, France, Belgium, Switzerland, Canada, played to over 1 million people; Played with: Stuart Hamm; Jonathon Mover; Electric guitar teacher, Vitré Conservatory of Music; Demonstrator for Jackson guitars; Hughes and Kettner amplifiers. Recordings: with Squealer: This Is What The World Is About, 1991; with Starmania: Starmania; Solo albums: Passion Colors, 1993; Rudy Roberts Live, 1994. Publications: Instruction video, Plans And Techniques Hard Rock. Honours: Guinness World Record Holder, Non-stop guitar playing (50 hours); 9th Victoires de la Musique Award, Best Live Show, Starmania, 1994. Membership: SACEM; SPEDIDAM. Current Management: Pierrick Morin, Move On Productions. Address: 7 Rue Baudrairie, 35500 Vitré, France.

ROBERTS Stephen, b. 27 Mar 1958, London, England. Musician (drums). m. Philippa Jane, 26 May 1991. Career: 1980, formed legendary New Wave of British Heavy Metal group: Silverwing, with brother Dave; Toured with Diamond Head and Phil Lynott, split 1983; Formed Pet Hate; released 2 albums; Toured USA and Canada; Appeared on C4's ECT; Formed Wild Ones, 1989; Released 1 album; Session musician with Belinda Carlisle and Rick Astley, including appearances on Wogan and at San Remo Festival, 1990; Currently with No Fit State. Recordings: with Silverwing: Rock And Roll Are Four Letter Words, 1980; Sittin' Pretty, 1981; Alive And Kicking, 1982; with Pet Hate: The Bride Wore Red, 1984; Bad Publicity, 1985; with Wild Ones: Writing On The Wall, 1991; with No Fit State: Welcome To..., 1995. Membership: Musicians' Union. Hobby: Gardening. Current Management: Triumphant Productions. Address: 1 Waterloo Street, Stockport SK1 3DB, England.

ROBERTSON Brian, b. 12 Sept 1956, Glasgow, Scotland. Rock Musician (guitar). Career: Guitarist, UK rock group Thin Lizzy, 1974-1978; Concerts include: Regular UK and European tours; Reading Festival, 1974, 1975, 1977; US tour, supporting Bachman-Turner Overdrive, 1976; Briefly with Graham Parker And The Rumour, 1977; Founder, Wild Horses, 1978-81; Guitarist, UK heavy metal group Motörhead, 1982. Recordings: Albums: with Thin Lizzy: Nightlife, 1974; Fighting, 1975; Jailbreak, 1976; Johnny The Fox, 1976; Bad Reputation, 1977; Live and Dangerous (Number 2, UK), 1978; with Motörhead: Another Perfect Day, 1983; Singles: with Thin Lizzy: Still In Love With You, 1975; The Boys Are Back In Town, 1976;

Jailbreak, 1976; Cowboy Song, 1976; Don't Believe A Word, 1977; Dancin' In The Moonlight, 1977; Rosalie, 1978; with Motörhead: I Got Mine, 1983; Shine, 1983. Honour: Gold disc, Jailbreak, 1976.

ROBERTSON Donald Irwin, b. 5 Dec 1922, Beijing, China. Composer; Musician (piano); Singer. m. (1) Ella Lucille Dinning, 2 Aug 1946, divorced, 1 son (deceased), 1 daughter, (2) Irene Symsk, 1 Jan 1962, 2 sons. Education: AA, University of Chicago, 1943. Career: Moved to US, 1927; Freelance songwriter, musician, singer, 1944-. Recordings: Featured on albums by numerous artists including: Elvis Presley; Bob Dylan; Willie Nelson; Dinah Shore; Nat King Cole; Waylon Jennings; Dolly Parton; Perry Como; Eddy Arnold; Roy Clark; Loretta Clark. Honours: Inducted, Walkway of Stars, Country Music Hall of Fame, 1967; 2 BMI Awards, 1954; Billboard Award, 1964; 17 ASCAP Awards, 1955-84; Nashville Songwriters Association International Hall Of Fame, 1972. Memberships: AFTRA; ASCAP; AFofM; NARAS; NSAI; Songwriters Guild Of America.

ROBERTSON Robbie (Jaime), b. 5 July 1944, Toronto, Ontario, Canada. Musician (guitar); Vocalist. Career: Guitarist, singer with The Band (formerly the Hawks), 1964-78; Long association with Bob Dylan; As backing band for Bob Dylan, appearances include: Don't Look Back UK tour, 1965; Royal Albert Hall, 1966; Isle Of Wight Festival, 1969; US tour, 1974; Performances as The Band include: Watkins Glen Festival, with the Grateful Dead, Allman Brothers, 1973; Producer, film The Last Waltz, film of final Band concert, 1977; Film appearance, Solo career, 1978-. Compositions: Much of Band's material including: 4% Pantomime (co-written with Van Morrison); Recordings: Singles: with the Band: The Weight, used in film Easy Rider, 1968; Up On Cripple Creek, 1970; Don't Do It, 1972; Solo singles include: Somewhere Down That Crazy River, 1988; Albums with The Band: The Basement Tapes (with Bob Dylan), 1967; Music From Big Pink, 1968; The Band, 1969; Stage Fright, 1970; Cahoots, 1971; Rock Of Ages, 1972; Moondog Matinee, 1973; Before The Flood (with Bob Dylan), 1974; Northern Lights Southern Cross, 1976; Best Of..., 1976; Islands, 1977; The Last Waltz, 1978; Solo albums: Robbie Robertson, 1987; Storyville, 1991; Music For The Native Americans, 1994; Producer, Beautiful Noise, Neil Diamond, 1976; Contributor, Planet Waves, Bob Dylan, 1974; Beauty, Ryûichi Sakamoto, 1989; Rainbow Warriors, Greenpeace charity album, 1979; Contributor, film soundtracks: Raging Bull; King Of Comedy; The Color Of Money. Honours include: The Band, inducted into Canadian Hall Of Fame, 1989. Current Management: Addis Wechsler & Associates, 955 S Camillo Drive, 3rd Floor, Los Angeles, CA 90048, USA.

ROBIN Thierry, b. 26 Aug 1957, France. Composer; Musician (guitar; ud - oriental lute, bouzouq). Career: French National Scenes including: Théatre de la Ville de Paris; Arabic World Institute; UNESCO; Most European festivals including: Transmusicales; WOMAD; Angoulême; WOMEX; Tours: Europe; USA; Canada; North Africa; Middle East; Appearances include European TV: Arte Megamix, FR3; TVS; France Inter; France Musique; Europe 1. Recordings: Luth et Tablâ, 1985; An Henchoû Treuz, 1990; Trio Erik Marchand, 1991; Gitans, 1993; New album due 1996. Honours: Grand Prix de l'Academie Charles Cros, 1990. Membership: SACEM. Current Management: DIVA-DCM. Address: 3/5 Rue de Metz, 75010 Paris, France.

ROBINSON Barry, b. 10 Sept 1963, Bushey, Watford, Hertfordshire, England. Musical Director; Composer; Conductor; Arranger; Musician (piano, keyboards). Musical Education: Honours Graduate, Composition and arranging, Grove School of Music, Los Angeles. Career: Music for

BBC Television includes: Indie Awards; Come Dancing; Variety Club Awards; Children In Need; The Accountant; Tours with: The Three Degrees; Rose Royce; The Supremes; Kiki Dee; Joe Longthorne; Helen Shapiro; West End Show: Fame. Compositions: Composer, arranger, Midas Touch, game show, Central Television. Membership: PRS. Hobbies: Football; Tennis. Current Management: Emma Darrell, Roger Hancock Ltd. Address: 4 Water Lane, London NW1 8NZ, England.

ROBINSON Chris, b. 20 Dec 1966, Atlanta, Georgia, USA. Rock Singer; Songwriter. Education: Georgia State University. Career: Singer, US rock group The Black Crowes (originally Mr Crowe's Garden), 1989-; Major concerts include: Support tours to Heart, 1990; Robert Plant, 1990; ZZ Top, 1991; Memphis In May Festival, 1991; Monsters of Rock Festival, Castle Donington, 1991; Glastonbury Festival, 1993; Phoenix Festival, 1993. Recordings: Albums: Shake Your Money Maker, 1990; Southern Harmony And Musical Companion, 1992; Amorica, 1995; Singles include: Jealous Again; Hard To Handle; Twice As Hard; She Talks To Angels; Seeing Things; Remedy; Sting Me. Honours: Grammy Nomination, Best New Artists, 1991; Rolling Stone magazine, Best New American Band, Best Male New Singer, 1991. Current Management: Angelus Entertainment, 9016 Wilshire Blvd, Ste 3461, Beverly Hills, CA 90211, USA.

ROBINSON Orphy, b. 13 Oct 1960, London, England. Jazz Musician (vibraphone, drums, percussion, keyboards); Composer. 1 son. Education: Hackney College. Musical Education: Hackney & Islington Youth Band. Career: Played with Savanna; Courtney Pine; Andy Sheppard; Balanescu String Quartet; Mica Paris; David Murray; Jazz Warriors; Lead soloist, Shivanova, 1990-; Solo artiste, 1990-. Recordings: I Can't Turn Away, Savanna; In And Out Of Love, Imagination; Journey To The Urge Within, Courtney Pine; Out Of Many One People, Jazz Warriors; When Tomorrow Comes, The Vibes Describes, Orphy Robinson; Introductions In The Dark, Andy Sheppard; Suite de Lorenzo, Ensemble Bash; Film soundtracks: Men Of The Month; Bloodrights. Honours: British Jazz Awards, Most Promising Newcomer, 1989; Best Miscellaneous Instrumentalist, 1993. Memberships: PRS; Musicians' Union. Hobbies: Cricket; Football; Judo. Address: c/o Coalition Music and Media, Devonshire House, 12 Barley Mow Passage, London W4 4PH, England.

ROBINSON Pat, b. 7 Apr 1948, USA. Songwriter; Singer; Musician (guitar, piano). 2 daughters. Compositions: You Got Away With Love, recorded by Percy Sledge; Civilised Man, Joe Cocker; No Promise No Guarantee, Laura Branigan; Jokers Are Wild, Gene Clark. Membership: BMI. Current Management: Saul Davis. Address: C/o Saul Davis, 11864 Ventura Blvd, #583, Studio City, CA 91604, USA.

ROBINSON Smokey (William), b. 19 Feb 1940, Detroit, Michigan, USA. R&B Soul Singer; Songwriter; Producer. m. Claudette, 7 Nov 1959, 2 children. Career: Singer with The Matadors; Singer with The Miracles, 1954-72; Also billed as Smokey Robinson And The Miracles, 1967-72; Solo artiste, 1973-; Executive producer, composer, film Big Time, 1977; Appearances on television specials: Smokey Robinson 25th Anniversary Special, ABC-TV, 1981; Motown Anniversary special, NBC-TV, 1983; Motown 30 - What's Goin' On, 1990; Aretha Franklin - Duets, 1993. Compositions include: Most recordings with the Miracles until 1968; Other hits include: The Way You Do The Things You Do, The Temptations, 1964; Co-writer, My Guy, Mary Wells (Number 1, US), 1964; My Girl, Temptations (Number 1, US), 1965. Recordings: Albums: The Fabulous Miracles, 1963; The Miracles On Stage, 1963;

Doin' Mickey's Monkey, 1964; Going To A Go-Go, 1966; Make It Happen, 1967; Special Occasion, 1968; Time Out For..., 1969; What Love Has Joined Together, 1970; A Pocketful Of Miracles, 1970; One Dozen Roses, 1971; Flying High Together, 1972; Solo albums: Smokey, 1973; Pure Smokey, 1974; Smokey's Family Robinson, 1976; Deep In My Soul, 1977; Love Breeze, 1978; Smokin', 1979; Where There's Smoke, 1979; Being With You, 1981; Smoke Signals, 1986; One Heartbeat, 1987; Love Songs, 1988; Love, Smokey, 1990; Singles include: with the Miracles: Shop Around, 1961; You've Really Got A Hold On Me, 1963; The Tracks Of My Tears, 1965; Going To A Go-Go, 1966; I Second That Emotion, 1967; If You Can Wait, 1968; Baby Baby Don't Cry, 1969; The Tears Of A Clown (Number 1, US), 1970; Solo: Cruisin', 1980; Being With You (Number 1, UK), 1981; Just To See Her, 1987; Contributor, We Are The World, USA For Africa, 1985; Recorded duets with Barbara Mandrell; Kenny G; Dolly Parton; Rick James. Honours include: Inducted into Rock And Roll Hall Of Fame, 1987; Grammy Award, Best R&B Vocal Performance, 1988; Grammy Living Legend Award, 1989; Inducted into Songwriters Hall Of Fame, 1990; Soul Train Heritage Award, 1991; Motor City Music Award for Lifetime Achievement, 1992. Current Management: Jeff Wald Entertainment, Suite 840, 12424 Wilshire Blvd, Los Angeles, CA 90025, USA.

ROBINSON Tom, b. 1 June 1950, Cambridge, England. Songwriter. 1 son. Career: Joined first band Café Society, London, 1973; Album produced by Ray Davies of The Kinks, 1975; Left Café Society, formed Tom Robinson Band (TRB), 1976; Chart success, concerts for Rock Against Racism, world tours, 1977-78; Formed Sector 27, 1979; US tour with Police, 1981; Lived and worked in East Germany, 1982; Further chart success, 1983-84; Tours of USA, Australia, 1985; Purchased recording studio, 1985; Tours of Japan, Italy, UK 1987; Hit show Private View, Edinburgh Fringe, 1987; Presenter, BBC World Service, Radio 1, 1988; Reformed Tom Robinson Band, 1989; Tours throughout UK, Europe, Canada, USA, Australia, 1991-95; Presenter, BBC Radio 4 series, The Locker Room, 1992-95; Heineken Festival, Leeds, 1995. Compositions include: Co-writer with Peter Gabriel: Bully For You; Merrily Up On High, 1979; Atmospherics- Listen To The Radio, 1983; Co-writer with Elton John: Sartorial Eloquence; Elton's Song; Never Gonna Fall In Love Again, 1979-80; Composed music for More Lives Than One, BBC2 TV, 1985; with Jakko Jakszyk: Hard Cases, Central TV, 1988; Lyrics for It's About Time, Manu Katché, 1991. Recordings: Singles include: 2-4-6-8 Motorway, 1977; Glad To Be Gay, 1978; War Baby, 1983; Atmospherics-Listen To The Radio, 1983; Hard, 1994; Albums include: Café Society, 1975; Power In The Darkness, 1978; TRB Two, 1979; Sector 27, 1981; North By Northwest, 1982; Cabaret 79, 1982; Hope And Glory, 1984; Still Loving You, 1986; We Never Had It So Good (with Jakko Jakszyk) 1990; Living In A Boom Time, 1992; Love Over Rage, 1994; Having It Both Ways, 1996; Holidays in the Sun, 1997. Honours: Gold Winner with You've Got to Hide Your Love Away, UK Sony Awards, 1997. Hobbies: Parenthood; Swimming; Languages; Computers. Address: PO Box 3185, London SW18 3JG, England.

ROCHEMAN Manuel David, b. 23 July 1964, Paris, France. Musician (piano); Composer. m. Beatriz España, 15 Apr 1991, 1 son, 1 daughter. Musical Education: Piano, with Alberto Neuman (CNR de Paris); Jazz with Martial Solal. Career: Appearances with own trio: Radio-France, 1984; Festival de Jazz Paris, 1984, 1986; Montpellier, 1986; Antibes-Juan-Les Pins, 1988; Grande Parade Du Jazz, Nice, 1992; JVC Halle That Jazz, 1992; Auditorium Du Châtelet, 1993; Festival Cervantino and Palacio de Bellas Artes (Mexico), 1993, 1994; Tours: Belgium; Switzerland; East

European countries, 1993-95. Compositions: Concerto for piano and orchestra, 1988; San Felipe, for jazz band and philharmonic orchestra, 1995. Recordings: Trio Urbain, 1989; White Keys, 1992; Tropic City, 1995. Honours: Prix Boris Vian, 1991; Django D'Or, 1992. Memberships: SACEM; SPEDIDAM. Address: 27 Bis Avenue Du Clocher, 93600 Aulnay Sous Bois, France.

RODE Birgitte, b. 26 Feb 1956, Copenhagen, Denmark. Vocalist; Musician (keyboards). m. Claus Hvass, 14 June 1992, 1 son. Musical Education: Academy of Music, Aalborg, Denmark. Career: Roskilde Festival; Tours: UK; California, USA; France; Norway; Germany; Sweden; Denmark; Television appearances: Live Aid; Grand Prix-Slovenia; National and international television and radio. Compositions: Sculptural Music. Recordings: with Johnnny Og De Kolde Dæmoner: Paraneuropa; with Walk The Walk: Walk The Walk; Feet On The Ground; Frog Dance. Publications: The International Discography Of New Wave; Dansk Rock. Honours: 4 National Music Council Awards, 1991-94. Memberships: National Musicians Society; DJBFA. Hobbies: Visual Art and Culture; Sociology. Current Management: Zing Zing Musicproduction and Management. Address: Kirkegaardsgade 3, 9000 Aalborg, Denmark.

RODGERS Nile, b. 19 Sept 1952, New York, USA. Musician (guitar); Record Producer. Career: Member, New World Rising, 1960s; Founder member, Big Apple Band, 1972-76; Became Chic, 1977-; Also solo artiste and record producer; Member, The Honeydrippers, with Robert Plant, Jimmy Page, Jeff Beck; Leader, own trio, Outloud; Co-founder, Ear Candy record label, 1989. Recordings: Albums: with Chic: C'Est Chic, 1978; Risqué, 1979; The Best Of Chic, 1980; Real People, 1982; Take It Off, 1982; Tongue In Chic, 1982; Believer, 1983; Freak Out, 1987; Chic-Ism, 1992; Solo albums: Adventures In The Land Of The Good Groove, 1983; B-Movie Matinee, 1985; Singles include: Dance Dance Dance, 1978; Everybody Dance; I Want Your Love, 1979; Good Times (Number 1, US); My Forbidden Lover; My Feet Keep Dancing, 1980; Soup For One, 1982; Jack Le Freak, 1987; Chic Mystique, 1992; As writer, producer with Bernard Edwards: Norma Jean, Norma Jean Wright, 1977; He's The Greatest Dancer, Sister Sledge, 1979; We Are Family, Sister Sledge, 1979; Love Somebody Today, Sister Sledge, 1979; Upside Down, Diana Ross, 1980; Diana, Diana Ross, 1982; Why, Carly Simon, 1982; Record producer for artists including: David Bowie; Madonna; Duran Duran; Aretha Franklin; Jeff Beck; Mick Jagger; Al Jarreau; Grace Jones; Johnny Mathis.

RODGERS Paul, b. Dec 1949, Middlesborough, Cleveland, England. Singer; Songwriter. Career: Singer, with Roadrunners; Brown Sugar; Founder member, Free, 1968-73; Concerts include: US tour, 1969; Hollywood Music Festival, Staffordshire, 1970; Isle of Wight Festival, 1970; Tours of UK and Japan, 1972; Founder member, singer, Bad Company, 1973-83; Toured worldwide; Played with Eric Clapton, Jimmy Page and Jeff Beck on The Ronnie Lane ARMS appeal concert tour, 1983; Founder member, singer, The Firm, 1984-86; Toured Europe and USA 1985-86; Founder member, singer, The LAW, 1991; Miscellaneous Concerts include: Atlantic Records 40th anniversary party, 1988; Guitar Legends, Expo '92, Seville, Spain, 1992; Gibson Night of 100 Guitars, Wembley, London, 1994; Elvis Tribute, Memphis, 1994; Woodstock '94, USA; Began solo career; Formed new band, Paul Rodgers, 1995-; Toured Europe, USA and Japan. Recordings include: With Free: Albums: Tons of Sobs, 1968; Free, 1969; Fire and Water, 1970; Highway, 1971; Free Live, 1971; Free at Last, 1972; Heartbreaker, 1973; The Free Story, 1973; Best of Free, 1991; Singles: All Right Now; My Brother Jake; Little Bit of Love; Wishing Well; With Bad Company: Albums: Straight

Shooter, 1975; Run With the Pack, 1976; Rough Diamonds, 1982; Singles: Can't Get Enough; Feel Like Making Love; Young Blood; The Firm: Albums: The Firm, 1985; Mean Business, 1986; Singles: Radio-active; All The King's Horses; The Law: Album: The Law, 1991; Single: Laying Down the Law; Solo: Cut Loose, 1983; Live (The Loreley Tapes), 1995; Now, 1997; Hint single, Soul of Love, 1997; Various contributions to compilation albums. Honours: With Free: ASCAP Award; With Bad Company: Grammy Award, 1975; Honorary Colonels of Louisiana 1977. Address: c/o Ramshackle Music Ltd, PO Box 148, Fincham, Norfolk PE33 9HU, England.

RODNEY Godfrey Winston, b. 1 Mar 1945, St Ann's Bay, Jamaica, West Indies. Singer; Songwriter. m. Sonia Marlene Thompson, 13 Sept 1981, 1 son, 3 daughters. Career: Singer, songwriter, reggae group Burning Spear; Career began recording for Studio One label, 1969; Releases for Island Records, 1970s; Toured with bands including: UB40; Talking Heads; The Clash; Tour US from East to West coast; TV appearance Bet, Rockers; Many radio appearances worldwide; Rendered Estimated Prophet on Dedicated, Grateful Dead tribute album, 1991. Recordings: 20 albums include: Burning Spear; Rocking Time; Marcus Garvey; Man In The Hills; Garvey's Ghost; Hail H I M, 1981; Farover, 1982; Resistance, 1984; Mek We Dweet, 1990; Jah Kingdom, 1992; The World Should Know, 1993; Rasta Business, 1995. Honours: 5 Grammy Nominations for Reggae Album of the Year; Musicians Merit Award, Album of the Year, 1990; Martin's International Reggae Award for Most Educational Entertainer of the 1980s, 1991; Album of the Year, Best Arranger (reggae), Caribbean Music Awards; Best Reggae Album, NAIRD Indie Awards, 1992; 4 IRMA Awards, including Best Music Video, 1995; Bob Marley Award Entertainer Of The Year; International Reggae Hall Of Fame; Marcus Garvey Humanitarian Award. Memberships: PRS; ASCAP. Hobbies: Football; Jogging. Current Management: Burning Music Production. Address: 130-34 231th Street, Laurelton, NY 11413, USA.

RODRIGUEZ Arabella Sabina, b. Norfolk, England. Recording and Mixing Engineer. 1 son, 1 daughter. Education: Piano, Harmony, Violin, Flute. Career: Sound Engineer, 1986-. Recordings: Credits as Engineer include: Soul II Soul; Caron Wheeler; Manu Dibango; Angelique Kidjo; D-Influence. Memberships: Repro; PRS; MCPS. Current Management: Stephen Budd Management, 109 B Regents Park Road, London, NW1 8UR, England. Address: 106 Albion Road, London, N16 9AD, England.

ROE (Eileen) Betty, b. 30 July 1930, Kensington, London, England. Accompanist; Singer; Composer; Adjudicator; Teacher. m. John Bishop, 24 May 1954, 1 son, twin daughters. Musical Education: Royal Academy Of Music; Diplomas: ARAM; LRAM; ARCM; FTCL; FRSA. Career: Session singer, London groups, ensembles, opera chorus, 1962-82; Musical Director, London Academy of Dramatic Art (LAMDA), 1968-78; Founded Thames Publishing with husband, 1970; Currently Musical Director, NorthKen Chorale, 1985-; Appears with group: Three's Company Plus; One Woman shows; Conductor, adjudicator, staff summer-schools, music weekends, workshops; Composer, collaborator with librettist Marian Lines. Compositions include: Vocal solos; Choral pieces; Operas; Musical plays; Incidental music; Works for children; Instrumentals; Christmas music. Recordings: Albums: Thomas Hardy And Love; Shakespeare And Love; The Music Tree, solo songs, CD; The Family Tree, vocal music for children, CD. Album of choral music, artists include Trinity College Cambridge Choir; Three's Company Plus; The Allegri Singers. Membership: FRSA. Current Management: John Bishop, 14 Barlby Road, Kensington, London W10 6AR, England.

ROE Tommy, b. 9 May 1942, Atlanta, Georgia, USA. Entertainer; Musician (guitar); Songwriter; Music Publisher. Musical Education: Self-taught. Career: Performances and concerts worldwide; Appearances, all major television and radio shows in 1960's; Sold 40 million records. Recordings: Hit Singles: Sheila; Sweet Pea; Dizzy; Everybody (all Gold discs) Hooray For Hazel; It's Now Winters Day; Jam Up; Jelly Tight. Honours: 4 Gold Singles; Georgy Award; BMI Awards. Memberships: Society of Singers; Academy of Country Music. Hobby: Golf. Current Management: Dave Hoffman. Address: PO Box 26037, Minneapolis, MN 55426, USA.

ROEL (Anne) Charlotte, b. 3 Dec 1964, Copenhagen, Denmark. Vocalist. m. Floyd Adams III, 21 July 1990. Musical Education: Manhattan School Of Music, New York City. Career: Solo performer, 1992-; Concerts: Copenhagen Gospel Rock Festival; Opstand Festival; Glumsö Gospel Festival; Västervik Gospel Festival, Sweden; Performed: Montmartre; Copenhagen Jazz House; Huset; KB Hallen; Radio: Strax, Denmarks National Radio; More Than Music; Tjek Listen; Danish local radio; NIK Kolding; Radio Roskilde; Naestved radio; Copenhagen FM; Radio Ballerup; Swedish radio; KFUM Sweden; Television: KKR/TV Charlotte Roel - A Musical Portrait; Norwegian TV; Hello Norden; Hostess, producer, The Five Blind Boys Of Alabama. Recordings: Single: Perfect Love (Number 1, Denmark), 1994; Debut album, 1995. Membership: DAF (Danish Artist Society). Hobbies: Jazz and Funk Dance; Tennis; Music. Current Management: William B Proven Productions. Address: Nörre Sögade 33 A 1, DK-1370 Copenhagen K, Denmark.

ROESER Donald "Buck Dharma", b. 12 Nov 1947. Musician (guitar); Vocalist. Career: Lead guitarist, vocalist, US rock group Blue Öyster Cult, 1971-; Concerts: US tours, including support to Alice Cooper, 1972; World tour, 1978 Monsters Of Rock Festival, Castle Donington, 1981; UK tour, 1989. Recordings: Singles include: (Don't Fear) The Reaper, 1976. Albums: Blue Öyster Cult, 1972; Tyranny And Mutation, 1973; Live On Your Feet Or On Your Knees, 1975; Agents Of Fortune, 1976; Spectres, 1978; Some Enchanted Evening, 1978; Mirrors, 1979; Cultosaurus Erectus, 1980; Fire Of Unknown Origin, 1981; ETL (Extra-Terrestrial Live), 1982; Club Ninja, 1986; Imaginos, 1988; Career Of Evil- The Metal Years, 1990; Soundtrack, horror film Bad Channels, 1992; Solo album (as Buck Dharma): Flat Out. Honour: Platinum disc, (Don't Fear) The Reaper. Current Management: Steve Schenck.

ROGERS David, b. 3 Jan 1963, Dartford, Kent, England. Composer (keyboards); Programmer; Producer. m. Sue Ward, 21 Nov 1992, 2 sons. Education: First class Honours, Comparative Physiology, London University. Musical Education: Mrs Hoban; Also self-taught. Career: Founder member, Daybreak Productions, 1987; Numerous television, radio appearances including: BBC Radio 1; TV AM; Pebble Mill; Top Of The Pops; Kent Rocks; Noel's House Party; Live And Kicking. Compositions: 346 works published by 1995. Works include: Mr Blobby; Light of Summer; Peanuts; Steady; Blobby - The Album; The Dream; Boing; Probe. Honours: Ivor Novello, Best Selling Song, Mr Blobby, 1993. Memberships: Musicians' Union; PRS. Hobbies: Wildlife; Scuba diving; Travel; Ethnic music. Address: Carlin Music/Destiny Music, Iron Bridge House, Bridge Approach, London NW1 8BD, England.

ROGERS Kenny (Kenneth David), b. 21 Aug 1938, Houston, Texas, USA. Country Singer; Songwriter. m. Wanda Miller. Career: Member, The Scholars, 1955; Founder, Ken-Lee record label (with brother Lelan); Jolly Rogers record label; Bass player, Bobby Doyle Three, 1962; Member, New Christy Minstrels, 1967; Founder member, First Edition, 1967-74; Featured in television films: The Gambler; The Gambler II; The Gambler Returns; Documentary, Kenny Rogers And The American Cowboy. Compositions include: Sweet Music Man, recorded by Billie Jo Spears, Anne Murray, Tammy Wynette, Dolly Parton, Millie Jackson. Recordings: Albums: with First Edition: The First Edition, 1967; The First Editions Second, 1968; The First Edition '69, 1969; Ruby, Don't Take Your Love To Town, 1969; Something's Burning, 1970; Fools (film soundtrack) 1970; Tell It All Brother, 1971; Transition, 1971; The Ballad of Calico, 1972; Backroads, 1972; Monumental, 1973; Rollin', 1974; Solo albums include: Kenny Rogers, 1976; Love Lifted Me, 1976; Daytime Friends, 1977; Every Time Two Fools Collide (with Dottie West) 1978; Love Or Something Like It, 1978; The Gambler, 1978; Kenny, 1978; Gideon, 1980; Share Your Love, 1981; Love Will Turn You Around, 1982; We've Got Tonight, 1983; Eyes That See In The Dark, 1983; What About Me?, 1984; The Heart Of The Matter, 1985; Short Stories, 1986; I Prefer The Moonlight, 1987; Something Inside So Strong, 1989; Some Prisons Don't Have Walls, 1991; Back Home Again, 1992; Albums with The First Edition include: Ruby, Don't Take Your Love To Town, 1969; Something's Burning, 1970; Fools (soundtrack) 1970; Hit singles include: Ruby Don't Take Your Love To Town; Something's Burning; Lucille (Number 1, UK); She Believes Me; You Decorated My Life; Coward Of The County (Number 1, UK); Lady (Number 1, US); I Don't Need You; Morning Desire (US Country Number 1); Tomb Of The Unknown Love (US Country Number 1); Duets include: Don't Fall In Love With A Dreamer, with Kim Carnes; What About Me, with James Ingram and Kim Carnes; Make No Mistake She's Mine, with Ronnie Milsap; We've Got Tonight, with Sheena Easton; Island In The Stream, with Dolly Parton; Contributor, We Are The World, USA For Africa, 1985. Publication; Making It In Music (co-author with Len Epland). Current Management: Kragen And Co., 1112 N. Sherbourne Drive, Los Angeles, CA 90069, USA.

ROGERS Robert, b. 27 Jan 1926, London, England. Bandleader; Musician (guitar); Vocalist. m. Olive, 23 Sept 1950, 1 son. Musical Education: Self-taught. Career: Over 200 TV Tonight shows with Ted Taylor Four; Don Lang's Frantic Five; 6.5 Special; Saturday Club and Country Club on radio; Hundreds of radio shows as Sounds Bob Rogers; Own series, The Towncriers; Things Are Swinging. Recordings: 11 albums; Session guitarist with artists including: John Barry Seven; Adam Faith; Freddy and The Dreamers; Les Reed; Banjo player with artistes including: Mike Daniels Delta Jazzmen; Sid Phillips; Joe Henderson. Hobby: Close harmony vocal groups. Address: 11 Darwin Close, Farnborough Village, Orpington, Kent BR6 7EP, England.

ROGERS Roy, b. 28 July 1950, Redding, California, USA. Producer; Musician (slide guitar). m. Gaynell Toler Rogers, 28 Apr 1984, 1 son, 1 daughter. Education: BA, History, Hayward State University, California. Musical Education: Primarily self-taught. Career: Member, Delta Rhythm Kings; Producer/musician, John Lee Hooker, 1989-; Worldwide tours, major jazz festivals; Numerous television and radio shows including John Lee Hooker special, Rock Steady Late Show, UK; Performed with: Carlos Santana; Miles Davis; Albert Collins; B B King; Bonnie Raitt; Robert Cray; Composition: The Healer, with John Lee Hooker. Recordings: Solo albums: Chops Not Chaps; Slidewinder; Blues On The Range; Slide Zone; Slide Of Hand; Slide Zones; with Norton Buffalo: R&B; Travelin' Tracks; Rhythm and Groove, 1996; Soundtracks: The Hot Spot; One Flew Over The Cuckoo's Nest. Honours: 2 W C Handy Award Nominations; Best Emerging Blues Artist, Jazz Times Critics Poll, 1990; 2 Grammy Nominations; NARAS Award of Recognition. Memberships: AFofM; NARAS; BMI. Hobby: Collecting 78 rpm records. Current Management: Blue Muse Inc. Address: PO Box 598, Novato, CA 94948, USA.

ROKER Ron, b. 23 Jan 1941, Lincoln, England. Composer; Songwriter; Record Producer; Publisher. m. Karol Roker, 7 Sept 1977, 1 son, 1 daughter. Musical Education: Self-taught, keyboards. Career: Founder, lead vocalist, own group, 1960's (with guitarist Albert Lee); Toured, worked with various headliners; Turned to writing and producing; Co-writers include: Gerry Shury; Barry Blue; Lynsey De Paul; Roger Greenaway; Howard Greenfield; Formed own publishing and producing company, Karon Productions. Recordings: Top 10 hits include: Rupert, Jackie Lee; Storm In A Teacup, The Fortunes; Do You Wanna Dance, Barry Blue; Dance Little Lady Dance, Tina Charles; Guilty, The Pearls; US Top 20 hits: Guilty, First Choice; Up In A Puff Of Smoke, Polly Brown; Devils Gun, CJ & Co; Funk Theory, Rokotto and BT Express; Do You Believe In Love At First Sight, Dionne Warwick; Honey Honey, Sweet Dreams. Honours: Composer, Never Giving Up, performed by Sweet Dreams, 1983 Eurovision Song Contest (placed 6th). Memberships: IPA; Term, BASCA Council. Hobbies: Computers; Reading; Football; Cricket. Current Management: Karon Productions. Address: c/o Karon Productions, 20 Radstone Court, Hill View Road, Woking, Surrey GU22 7NB, England.

ROLLINS Henry, b. 13 Feb 1961, Washington DC, USA. Education: American University. Career: Singer, punk rock group, Black Flag, 1981-86; Concerts include: Support tours to The Exploited; The Damned; Christmas On Earth Festival, Leeds; Leader, Henry Rollins Band, 1986-; Regular tours and concerts include: World tour, 1991; Publisher, 1984-; Actor in films including The Chase, 1994 and Johnny Mnemonic, 1995. Compositions include: End To End, 1985; Hallucination Of Grandeur, 1986; Works, 1988; Knife Street, 1989; One From None, 1991; Now Watch Him Die, 1993; Get Him In The Van: On the Road with Black Flag, 1994. Recordings: Albums include: with Black Flag: Everything Went Black, 1982; Damaged, 1982; Slip It In, 1984; Loose Nut, 1985; The Process Of Weeding Out, 1985; In My Head, 1985; Who's Got The Ten, 1986; with Henry Rollins Band: Hot Animal Machine; Drive By Shooting, 1987; Life Time, 1988; Do It, 1989; Hard Volume, 1989; Turned On, 1990; The End Of Silence, 1992; Electro Convulsive Therapy, 1993; The Weight, 1994; Spoken works include: Short Walk On A Long Pier, 1987; Live At McCabe's, 1992; Deep Throat, 1992; The Boxed Life, 1993. Contributions to: Details; Face; Interview; Melody Maker; Sounds; Village Voice. Honour: Grammy Award Nomination, Best Metal Performance, 1995. Current Management: Imago Recording Co., 152 West 57th Street, New York, NY 10019, USA.

ROLLINS (Theodore) Sonny, b. 7 Sept 1930, New York, USA. Jazz Musician (saxophone); Composer. m. Lucille Rollins, 7 Sept 1957. Musical Education: Private music teachers. Career: Modern Jazz innovator; Numerous television appearances including solo saxophone on Tonite Show; Annual concert tours of Europe, Japan, USA by Sonny Rollins and Concert Orchestra, 1973-. Compositions: include Oleo; Doxy; Duke Of Iron; Way Out West; Concerto For Tenor Sax And Orchestra; Soundtrack: Alfie. Publications: Sonny Rollins: Journey Of A Jazzman. Honours: Honorary Doctor of Arts, Bard College; Guggenheim Fellow, 1972; Inducted, several Halls of Fame. Current Management: Ted Kurland Associates; Lucille Rollins. Address: Route 9 G, Germantown, NY 12526, USA.

ROMAN Adam, b. 11 Feb 1966, England. Musician (drums). Education: Wrexham School Of Art. Musical Education: Leeds College Of Music; Graduate diploma, Jazz and Contemporary Music.

Career: Concerts: Dick Morrissey, Martin Taylor, Will Gains, George Hamilton IV; Television and radio: BBC Jazz Parade; Pebble Mill; Tours: 2 times UK; Isle Of Man. Theatre: West End; Whitehall; Theatr Clwyd; English Theatre Frankfurt; German and Swiss tour; Bandleader. Memberships: Musicians' Union; Equity. Hobbies: Writing; Cooking; Socialising; The arts; World music. Address: Flat 2, 440 Upper Richmond Road West, Richmond, Surrey TW10 5DY, England.

ROMAN Lu Lu, b. 6 May 1946, Pilot Point, Texas, USA. Singer; Songwriter. Divorced, 2 sons. Career: Gospel and Country music and contemporary Christian singer; Appearances include: Grand Ole Opry (21 years); One Woman Show, Branson, Missouri, for 3 years; Cast member, television show, Hee-Haw, 1968-; Presidential Inaugural Event for Ronald Reagan, 1980; Featured artist, Bob Hope Charity Benefits, 1988-91; Pat Boone Celebrity Spectacular, 1991; Television includes: The Love Boat; The Tony Orlando Show; The Mike Douglas Show; Sally Jesse Raphael; Nashville Now; The 700 Club; Music City Tonite; Ralph Emory Show; Featured headliner, numerous state fairs. Recordings: Now Let Me Sing, 1974; One Day At A Time, 1975; Love Coming Down, 1976; Lulu's Testimony, 1978; Sing For My Friends, 1979; You Were Loving Me, 1984; Take Me There, 1986; Hymns That Light The Way, 1987; Joy, 1988; Key To The Kingdom, 1990; Best Friend, 1991; King Of Whom I Am; Two More Hands. Honours: Dove Award, Best Album By A Secular Artist, You Were Loving Me, 1985. Memberships: CCMA; GMA. Hobby: Making jewellery. Current Agent: Century II Promotions, PO Box 40707, Nashville, TN 37204-0707, USA; Current Management: Rainey Steele, 1300 Division Street, Suite 206, Nashville, TN 37203, USA.

ROMCESCU Mircea, b. 5 Feb 1957, Bucharest, Romania. Musician (violin, piano, guitar); Songwriter; Vocalist. m. Olimpia Panciu Romcescu, 20 Nov 1986. Musical Education: Special School of Music "George Enesco", 1964-76; Academy of Music "Ciprian Porumbesco", 1976-80. Career: Concerts, tours, television, radio, with own group Academica; Big Band arranging, directing; Film music; Studio musician, producer; Owner, 16 track digital studio; Violin soloist, Academy's Symphony Orchestra, 1980. Recordings: Albums: Academica, 1980; Music Is My Life, 1981; Olimpia, 1983; Words Against Words, 1989; Free, 1993. Honours: Composer Of The Year, 1982; Billboard Song Contest, 3 times. Memberships: Danish Composer's Union; Romanian Composer's Union. Hobby: Sound designing. Current Management: Claes Cornelius, Mega Records. Address: Hyttemestervej 16, Fensmark, 4700 Naestved, Denmark.

ROMCESCU Olimpia Panciu, b. 3 March 1953, Bucharest, Romania. Performer; Lyricist; Entertainer. m. Mircea Romcescu, 20 November 1986. Education: Bucharest, 1960-68; Painting and Drawing, Art School, Bucharest, 1968-71; Arts Popular School, Bucharest, 1973-76. Career: Concert tours in Romania, Germany, Greece, Israel, Scandinavia; Festivals in Poland, Hungary, Germany, Yugoslavia, Czech Republic, Greece, Romania; Television Shows: Cinderella, Beauty in the Sleeping Forest, Popeye the Sailor. Compositions: Lyrics to the album Olimpia, 1983; Just You; Party on my Birthday; Let us Turn Back the Time; We Are no Robots. Recordings: Olimpia, 1983; Running in the Dark, 1991; I've Got to Know, 1991; Can't Believe, 1993; We've Met Incidentally, 1995. Memberships: Danish Music Society; Romanian Lyricist Society. Hobbies: Portrait Drawing and Painting. Current Management: Soul-Mate. Address: Hyttemestervej 16, Fensmark 4700 Naestved, Denmark.

ROMER Hanne, b. 29 July 1949, Copenhagen, Denmark. Composer; Conductor; Musician (guitar, saxophone). 2 daughters. Musical Education: Composing, arranging, conducting, Dick Grove School of Music, Los Angeles, 1983. Career: Founder, singer, guitarist, all-woman rock group, Hos Anna, 1975-81; Hexethyl Big Band, 1978-81; Duo with pianist Marietta Wandell; Conductor, several choirs and big bands; Leader, Nordic All-Women Big Band, 1994-; Tours throughout Denmark and Finland. Compositions: Piano feature, for Danish Radio Light Music Orchestra, 1985; Saxophone Concert, 1987; Several Symphonic poems; Music for string orchestras, choirs, big bands and jazz ensembles. Recordings: 4 albums with Hos Anna; with Marietta Wandall: Akijava, 1990; Ametyst, 1994; with the Nordic All-Women Big Band: Somewhere In Time, 1994; with the Hanne Romer Quartet: Come Rain Or Come Shine, 1994. Address: Amanda Music, Kirkepladsen 8 B, 6200 Aabenraa, Denmark.

ROMMEL Bernd, b. 10 June 1967, Waiblingen, Germany. Musician (drums). m. Monika, 1 daughter. Musical Education; Music High School (MHS, Graz, Austria) with jazz diploma. Career: Several R&B projects throughout Germany including: White Bread; Paddy Corn Band; Member, Lizl, 1990; Member, The Solutions, 1991; Member, Blues Pumpm, 1992. Recordings: with Lizl: Talk About Jobsharing; All Blues Pumpm productions, (1993-) including: Single: Men From Milwaukee, 1993; Album: Living Loving Riding, 1994. Honours: Winner, Bigband Contest Festival with High School Big Band, Graz, Austria. Memberships: AKM; Austromecha; LSG. Hobbies: Eating; Sleeping; Snare drums. Current Management: Peter Steinbach, RGG Music, Favoritenstr. 53/2/6/18, 1100 Vienna, Austria.

ROMO Olle, b. 3 July 1958, Stockholm, Sweden. Programmer; Engineer; Musician (drums). m. Mary Beth Romo, 11 Oct 1991, 1 daughter. Musical Education: Stockholm Music Conservatory. Career: 2 Eurythmics World Tours as drummer; Recording career as drummer, programmer, engineer. Recordings: Albums with Eurythmics; Elton John; Bryan Adams; Mick Jagger; Dave Stewart; Malcolm McLaren; Shakespears Sister. Membership: Musicians' Union. Current Management: Tony Quinn, 7 Hz Productions.

RONCHETTI Francesco, b. 18 Feb 1962, Florence, Italy. Vocalist; Composer; Performer. Education: University, Master degree. Musical Education: DMus, DAMS, University of Bologna, Italy. Career: Member of vocal trio, Trinovox; Appearances on German television and radio, 1994; Concerts in Germany, Switzerland, Austria (Berlin, Lübeck, Stuttgart, Basel, Vienna, Innsbruck), Finland, Italy, 1994-97; Soundtrack for radio play, Bavarian State Radio, 1995; Voice specialist, teacher; Speaker at many international conferences in the field; Collaborations with established American and Italian singers, composers, musical producers. Recordings: Albums: with Trinovox: Incanto, 1994; Voices, (Trinovox, Sarband, The Bulgarian Voices), 1994; Earborn, Trinovox and Various Artists, 1994; Mediterranea, 1997. Publications: Articles: Pop-Rock Singing, in Suonare Uno Strumento, 1989; Tell Me How He Sings..., in Imparerock, 1994. Honours: with Trinovox: Premio Quartetto Cetra, Italian National Award for Vocal Artists, 1994. Memberships: SIAE; GEMA; SIEM; Contemporary A Cappella Society of America. Hobbies: Trekking; Swimming; Rowing; Reading; Writing. Current Management: Ulrich Balss, Jaro Records. Address: Jaro Records, Bismarckstr 83, D-28203 Bremen 1, Germany.

RÖNNBLOM Anders F, b. 9 May 1946, Stockholm, Sweden. Singer; Songwriter; Musician (guitar); Designer. Education: Graduate from College, 1966; Art and Design School, 1972.

Musical Education: Self-taught. Career: First recording in 1959; Played with numerous bands in the 1960's with recordings, 1963-66; Debut album under own name in 1971; Currently 20 albums released. Recordings include: Jag Kysste Henne Våldsamt; Europa Brinner; Det Är Inte Snön Som Faller. Publication: Publishing own magazine, Mac Art & Design. Current Management: Studio Matchbox. Address: c/o Studio Matchbox, Roslagsgatan 11, 11355 Stockholm, Sweden.

RONSTADT Linda, b. 15 July 1946, Tucson, Arizona, USA. Singer. Education: Arizona State University. Career: Sang with sisters in the Three Ronstadts; Founder member, the Stone Poneys; Solo career, 1968-; Performed in operas: The Pirates Of Penzance; La Boheme. Recordings: Hit singles: You're No Good (Number 1, US); I Can't Help It; Somewhere Out There, duet with James Ingram (film theme to An American Tail), 1987; Don't Know Much, duet with Aaron Neville (Number 2, US), 1989. Albums: Hand Sown, Home Grown, 1969; Silk Purse, 1970; Linda Ronstadt, 1971; Don't Cry Now, 1973; Heart Like A Wheel, 1974; Prisoner In Disguise, 1975; Hasten Down The Wind, 1976; Simple Dreams, 1977; Living In The USA, 1978; Mad Love, 1980; Pirates Of Penzance, 1981; Get Closer, 1982; What's New, 1983; Lush Life, 1984; For Sentimental Reasons, 1986; Trio (with Emmylou Harris and Dolly Parton), 1987; Canciones De Mi Padre, 1987; Cry Like A Rainstorm, Howl Like The Wind, 1989; Winter Light, 1994; Feels Like Home, 1995; Compilations include: 5 Stone Poney tracks on Different Drum, 1974. Honours: Grammy Award, Best Female Country Vocal, I Can't Help It. Current Management: Peter Asher Management, 644 N Doheny Drive, Los Angeles, CA 90069, USA.

ROONEY Rick (Hertz Rooney), b. 14 Apr 1952, New Orleans, Louisiana, USA. Producer; Engineer; Publisher. m. Debb Rooney, 04 July 1979, 1 son. Education: North Texas State University, Denton, Texas. Career: Owned and operated live touring sound company for 15 years; Owner: Planet Dallas Recording Studios and Publishing Company, Dallas, Texas; Songs placed with major labels. Recordings: MC 900 Ft; Tripping Daisy; Fu Schnickens; The Blue Johnnies; Gone By Dawn. Memberships: NARRAS; BMI; ASCAP. Hobbies: Spending quality time with family; Biking; Croquet; Badminton. Current Management: Planet Dallas Studios. Address: 3515 Dickason Avenue, Dallas, TX 75219, USA.

ROSA Enrico, b. 18 September 1951, Livorno, Italy. Musician. m. Yrsa Rosa, 29 September 1977, 1 son, 1 daughter. Education: Private Education and Selftaught in Classical and Jazz Field on Guitar. Career: Backing Guitarist, Arranger, Gianni Bella and Marcella (Bella), Italy, 1970-76; Studio Musician, UA and CBS, Milan, 1971-76; Soloist, Creator of Campo Di Marte, 1971; Guitar and Theory Teacher, Esbjerg's Academy of Music, 1984-90; Esbjerg's Guitar and Improvisation Teacher at Koling Music Institute since 1984; Guitar Virtuoso on Danish Television, Musikalske Venner, Musik Jornet; Concert with Ole Kockhansen, Jesper Lundgaard; 10 years of Sans Sousi Theatre. Compositions: Campo Di Marte, 1973; Jazz in the Celler, 1974. Recordings: Campo Di Marte; Jazz in the Celler; Evreka, 1980; Made By Wind, 1982; Scherzo Rosa, 1989. Publications: Baskursus, 1993; Guitar Voicing, 1998; Guitar Versatile, 1998. Memberships: DMF; KODA; GRAMEX. Hobbies: Music; Family Life. Current Management: Bureav'et Aps, Box 152, Rosenvej 1, DK 5750 Ringe, Denmark. Address: Strandvejen 75, 6854 Henne, Denmark.

ROSE Brian. Record Producer; Engineer; Writer. Composition: Crazy Little Trees, 2 EPs. Recordings: Figboy; Roger Waters, Amused to Death, LP; Triggerfish; Toucan. Current

Management: One Management Ltd, 43 St Alban's Avenue, London W4 5JS, England.

ROSE David Richard, b. Chatham, Ontario, Canada. Promoter; Musician (drums). 3 daughters. Education: 3 years study in Electronics. Career: Agent for 3 years; Promoter for 4 years; Owner of promotion company, Rose Concert Productions Inc, producing many concerts including Blue Rodeo, Jefferson Starship, Procol Harum, 54-40; Rusty; King, Cobb Steelie; Change of Heart; Big Sugar; Nazareth. Memberships: CCMA; CARAS; CAE; SOCAN. Hobbies: Live racing; Travel. Address: Rose Concert Productions Inc, Box 23053, London, Ontario N6A 5N9, Canada.

ROSE Dennis Peter, b. 9 Feb 1947, Brooklyn, New York, USA. Musician (guitar, bass, harmonica); Recording Engineer; Producer. Education: High School. Musical Education: Self taught. Career: Session musician for Phil Spector, 1962, on: Bob B Sox & The Blue Jeans; Zip A Dee Do Dah; Albums with: Surf Band: The Centurions; Del-fi: Surfers Pajama Party; Shepard Records: Surf War; Other Surf compilation records; Radio KFWB Surf Battle at Deaville Castle Club, Santa Monica; Number 4, West Coast Battle of the bands, Pismo Beach, California; Second annual Teen-Age Fair, Hollywood Paladium; Backed up: Sonny & Cher; Jimmy Reed; John Lee Hooker; at the Pavilion, Huntington Beach and Marina Palace, Seal Beach; Solo Blues Album Project; Produced, recorded many R&B, Rock, Gospel, Jazz acts at own studio: Golden Goose Recording; Blues Album Project, studio in Costa Mesa, California. Honours: Platinum record: Bullwinkle P11, used for Academy Award winning: Pulp Fiction. Memberships: ASCAP. Hobbies: Oil painting; Reading; Guitar. Address: Golden Goose Productions, 2074 Pomona Avenue, Costa Mesa, CA 92627, USA.

ROSE Michael "Bammie", b. 28 Sept 1942, Jamaica. Musician (flute, tenor, alto, soprano saxophones). m. Cynthia, 1 son, 2 daughters. Musical Education: Self-taught. Career: Cymande, 1973; Paul Simon, 1987; Budely, 1989; Five Guys, 1993; Aswad Jazz Warriors; Jazz Jamaica; Soul II Soul. Recordings: Aswad; Soul II Soul; Jazz Jamaica. Address: 26 Blincoe Close, London SW19 5PP, England.

ROSE W Axl (William Bailey), b. 6 Feb 1962, Lafayette, Indiana, USA. Singer. m. Erin Everly, 28 Apr 1990 (annulled 1991). Career: Member, US heavy rock group Guns'N'Roses, 1985-; Regular international tours include: Support to Iron Maiden, US, 1987, 1988; Mötley Crüe, US, 1987; The Cult, US, 1987; UK tour, 1988; Support to Aerosmith, US, 1988; Get In The Ring tour, with Skid Row, 1991; World tour, 1992; Major concerts include: Monsters Of Rock, Castle Donington, 1988; Farm Aid IV, 1990; Rock In Rio, Brazil, 1991; A Concert For Life (Freddie Mercury Tribute), Wembley, 1992; National Bowl, Milton Keynes, 1993. Recordings: Albums: Appetite For Destruction, 1987; G'N'R Lies (mini-album), 1988; Use Your Illusion I & II (Number 1 and 2, US and UK), 1991; The Spaghetti Incident, 1993; Hit singles: Welcome To The Jungle, 1987; Sweet Child O'Mine (Number 1, US), 1988; Night Train, 1989; Paradise City, 1989; Patience, 1989; Knockin' On Heaven's Door, used in film soundtrack Days Of Thunder, 1990; You Could Be Mine, used in film soundtrack Terminator 2, 1991; Don't Cry, 1991; Live And Let Die, 1991; November Rain, 1992; Yesterdays, 1992; Ain't It Fun, 1993. Honours include: American Music Awards: Favourite Heavy Metal Single, 1989; Favourite Heavy Metal Artists & Album, 1989; Favourite Heavy Metal Artists, 1992; Several MTV Awards; World Music Award, Best Selling Hard Rock Artists Of The Year, 1993; Rolling Stone and Billboard magazine awards. Current Management: Big FD Management, 10801 National Blvd, Ste 530, Los Angeles, CA 90064, USA.

ROSE MARIE (Rose Marie Guy), b. New York City, USA. Performer; Actress; Started in show business aged 3. m. Bobby Guy, 19 June 1946, 1 daughter. Education: 2 yaers college. Career: In Concert: 4 Girls 4; Guest appearances: Dinah Shore; Bob Hope; Milton Berle; Red Skelton; Colgate Comedy Hour; Ed Sullivan; Own coast-to-coast radio show, NBC, aged 6 years; Another coast-to-coast radio show aged 7 years; Broadway shows: Spring in Brazil; Top Banana; Call Me Madam; Personal appearances: Fairmont Hotel (Denver, Dallas, San Francisco, New Orleans), Copacabana, New York; Chez Paree, Chicago; Palmer House, Chicago; Latin Quarter, New York; Ciros, Coconut Grove, Los Angeles. Compositions: Chen A Luna; One Misty Morning; Start Talkin'. Honours: 3 Emmy Nominations; Disney Legend Award; City Of Hope Award; Princess of Radio Award. Recordings: Singles: Chen A Luna; Come Out, Come Out Wherever You Are; Take A Picture Of The Moon; Say That You Were Teasing Me; Albums: Top Banana; Rose Marie Sings Italian; Rose Marie Sings Songs For Single Girls. Membership: ASCAP. Hobbies: Italian cooking; Collector's plates; Decorating. Current Management: Steve LaManna, Epstein-Wyckoff & Associates. Address: 280 South Beverly Drive, Beverly Hills, CA 90212, USA.

ROSELLO Egido, b. 30 Apr 1960, Alcudia de Crespins, Spain. Singer. Musical Education: Music guitar and rhythm. Career: Played on local radios and TV Channels (Spain). Recordings: Chantaje Emocional; Me Dejaste Enamorado El Corazón. Honours: Trophy, Leon and Canals, Spain. Membership: SGAE (Spain). Hobbies: Listening to music; Sports. Current Management: Rosell. Address: Ingenerio Vte Pichó 4-Bajo, 46020 Valencia, Spain.

ROSENTHAL David Michael, b. 1 Jan 1961, New York, USA. Musician (keyboards); Songwriter; Composer; Producer. Musical Education: BA Music, Berklee College of Music, Boston, 1981. Career: Musician with rock group, Rainbow, 1981-84; Little Steven, 1984; Producer, EMI Germany, 1985; Session musician with Cyndi Lauper, 1986-87; Robert Palmer, 1988-89; Music software consultant, Apple Mackintosh. Recordings: As musician: Albums: with Rainbow: Straight Between The Eyes, 1982; Bent Out Of Shape, 1983; Finyl Vinyl, 1984; Personal Attention, with Stacy Lattislaw, 1988; Heaven On Earth, Donna Allen, 1988; Will To Power, Will To Power, 1988; Slip Of The Tongue, Whitesnake, 1989; Passion And Warfare, Steve Vai, 1990; Hit singles include: with Rainbow: Stone Cold, 1982; Street Of Dreams, 1983; I Can't Let You Go, 1983; Baby I Love Your Way, Will To Power, 1988; Let Me Take You Down, Stacy Lattislaw, 1988; Joy And Pain, Donna Allen, 1988. Publications: Contributor, Keyboards magazine; Electronic Musician magazine. Honours: Gold and Platinum discs with Rainbow, Whitesnake, Stve Vai, Will To Power; Grammy Nomination, 1983. Memberships: ASCAP; AFofM.

ROSENTHAL Phil, b. 30 Sept 1948, New Haven, Connecticut, USA. m. Elizabeth Sommers, 4 Sept 1977, 1 son, 1 daughter. Education; BA, English Literature, University of Chicago, 1970. Musical Education: Self-taught. Career: Lead singer, guitarist, bluegrass band The Seldom Scene, including concerts: The White House; The Kennedy Centre; Philadelphia Folk Festival; Prairie Home Companion radio; Many television, radio appearances, 1977-86; Singer, guitarist, banjo player, The Sommers Rosenthal Family Band, 1993-; Founder, President, American Melody Records, 1986-. Recordings: 7 albums, The Seldom Scene, 1977-86; Producer, engineer, 17 albums, 1985-; Solo recordings: Indian Summer, 1978; A Matter Of Time, 1981; Turkey In The Straw, 1985; The Paw Paw Patch, 1987; Chickens In The Garden, 1991; Comin' Round The Mountain, 1994; The Green Grass All Around,

1995; Animal Songs, 1996. Honours: Official Connecticut State Troubadour, 1994; 4 Parents' Choice Awards; 3 American Library Association Awards for solo children's music recordings, 1985-. Membership: International Bluegrass Music Association. Current Management: American Melody. Address: PO Box 270, Guildford, CT 06437, USA.

ROSKO Emperor (Mike Pasternak), b. 26 Dec 1942, Los Angeles, California, USA. Disc Jockey; Broadcaster. Education: 1 year college. Career: Radio Monte Carlo; Europe No 1; Radio Caroline; Radio Luxembourg; France; 208 FM; Radio 1 BBC; Virgin Radio; Many FMs. Honours: Best DJ (UK), Billboard; Top DJ, R&R. Hobby: Cooking. Current Management: Bunny Lewis, 806 Keys House, Dolphin Square, London SW1, England; Radio: Tim Gibson, IBM, The Malting (Anchor House), Hull HU1 3HA, England.

ROSNELL Esko "Raisin", b. 23 June 1943, Pori, Finland. Musician (drums). Career: Drummer with Leo Kähkönen's dance band, 1964; Tour of Soviet Union with band; Played in groups led by: Otto Donner; Pekka Pöyry; Eero Koivistoinen; Played first Montreux Jazz Festival with Esa Pethmen's Quintet, 1967; Appearances with Heikki Sarmanto in: Scandinavia; Yugoslavia; Poland; Czechoslovakia; USA; 2 visits to Cuba in Government's cultural exchange programme; 2 visits to England with UMO (New Music Orchestra); Member, UMO, 1975-; Work in radio, television, theatre, recording studios. Recordings include: To A Finland Station, Dizzy Gillespie; Other recordings with UMO and own quartet. Honour: Best drum solo, Montreux Jazz Festival, 1967. Address: Gyldenintie 14 B, 00200 Helsinki, Finland.

ROSS Andrew David, b. 24 Feb 1960, Bromley, Kent, England. Producer; Songwriter; Musician (guitar). m. Dina Burnstock, 18 Sept 1994. Education: Art School. Musical Education: From father, Ronnie Ross (jazz musician). Career: Formed band Immaculate Fools; Television appearances and tours of UK, Europe, USA; Tours and television appearances with: Howard Jones; Tom Robinson; Basia; Other television broadcasts with: Nik Kershaw; Robert Palmer; Recordings: with Immaculate Fools: Immaculate Fools; Tragic Comedy; Dumb Poet; Another Man's World; The Toy Shop; with Miguel Bosé: The Sign Of Cain; with Howard Jones: Igy; Working In The Back Room; with Tori Amos: Crucify. Memberships: Musicians' Union; PRS; MCPS. Hobby: Flying (anything without an engine). Address: 4 Wellfield Avenue, London N10 2EA, England.

ROSS Brian, b. 13 Feb 1943, Chicago, Illinois, USA. Record Producer; Financier; Musician (keyboards). 2 sons. Education: UCLA (USC Law School). Musical Education: 25 years formal musical education, classically trained. Career: Chairman, CEO, Starborn Records and International Music Commission; Placing talent in over 50 countries worldwide for 30 years; Licensing of masters and music publishing rights to labels and music firms, US and other countries; Produced records for: CBS/Sony; Phonogram; Warner Bros; RCA/BMG; A&M and MCA Record labels. Recordings: Producer, publisher, Music Machine, Talk Talk, 1966; Released childrens' version of We Are The World, written by Michael Jackson, Lionel Richie; Publisher, I'm On Fire, Barry White; Licensed La Bamba, Ritchie Valens. Honours: Gold record, Barry White, The Message Is Love; Grammy Nomination, We Are The World, USA For Africa. Memberships: National Academy Recording Arts And Sciences; AFTRA; Musicians' Union; Japan America Society; Asian Business League. Hobbies: Tennis; Archery (world class archer, Mens Compound Freestyle). Address: 3884 Franklin Avenue, Los Angeles, CA 90027-4661, USA.

ROSS Diana, b. 26 Mar 1944, Detroit, Michigan, USA. Singer; Entertainer; Actress; Fashion Designer. m. (1) Robert Ellis Silberstein, 1971, 3 daughters; (2) Arne Ness, 23 Oct 1985, 1 son. Career: Backing singer, the Temptations, Marvin Gaye, Mary Wells; Lead singer, Diana Ross and The Supremes; Solo artiste, 1969-; Appearances include: Opening ceremonies, Football World Cup, USA, 1994; Rugby World Cup, South Africa, 1995; Film appearances: Lady Sings The Blues, 1972; Mahogany, 1975; The Wiz, 1978; Television specials: An Evening With Diana Ross, 1977; Diana, 1980; Christmas In Vienna, 1992; Business ventures: Diana Ross Enterprises Inc; Anaid Film Productions; RTM Management Corp; Chondee Inc. Recordings: Albums include: Diana Ross, 1970; Lady Sings The Blues, 1972; Touch Me In The Morning, 1973; The Boss, 1979; Why Do Fools Fall In Love?, 1981; Eaten Alive, 1984; Silk Electric, 1982; Chain Reaction, 1986; Ain't No Mountain High Enough, 1989; The Force Behind The Power, 1991; Motown's Greatest Hits, 1992; Live...Stolen Moments, 1993; One Woman - The Ultimate Collection, 1993; The Remixes, 1994; Take Me Higher, 1995. Publication: Secrets Of A Sparrow (autobiography), 1993. Honours include: Citations: Vice-President Humphrey; Mrs Martin Luther King, Rev Abernathy; Billboard award: Record World award, World's Outstanding Singer; Grammy Award, 1970; Female Entertainer Of The Year, NAACP, 1970; Golden Globe, 1972; Antoinette Perry Award, 1977; Nominated Rock and Roll Hall Of Fame, 1988. Address: RTC Management, PO Box 1683, New York, NY 10185, USA.

ROSS Ricky, b. 22 Dec 1957, Dundee, Tayside, Scotland. Singer; Songwriter. Career: Founder member, Deacon Blue, 1985-94; Concerts include: Reading Festival, 1988; John Lennon Tribute Concert, Liverpool, 1990; The Big Day Festival, Glasgow, 1990; Glastonbury Festival, 1990; Currently solo recording artiste. recordings: Albums: with Deacon Blue: Raintown, 1987; When the World Knows Your Name (Number 1, UK), 1989; Ooh Las Vegas, 1990; Fellow Hoodlums, 1991; Whatever You Say, Say Nothing, 1993; New Recordings; Singles include: with Deacon Blue: Dignity, 1987; When Will You Make My Telephone Ring, 1988; Chocolate Girl, 1988; Real Gone Kid, 1988; Wages Day, 1989; Fergus Sings the Blues, 1989; I'll Never Fall In Love Again, 1990; Your Town, 1992; Solo single: Radio On, 1996; Compiler: The Tree and The Fish and The Bird and The Bell (tribute by Glaswegian bands to photographer Oscar Masarovich), 1991; Solo albums: What You Are, 1996; New Recording, 1997. Current Management: CEC Management. Address: 6 Warren Mews, London W1P 5DJ, England.

ROSSELAND Elin, 5 Apr 1959, Oslo, Norway. Singer; Musician (piano). Musical Education: Academy of Music, Oslo. Career: Freelance singer, 1985-; Founder, own group Fair Play; Debut performance, Molde International Jazz Festival, 1985; Concerts include: Tallinn Festival, Estonia, 1990; Molde Festival, with Soyr and Sidsel Endresen project; Soloist, Norwegian and Danish Radio Big Bands; Numerous radio and studio projects; Teacher, University of Music, Oslo; Trondheim Academy of Music, Oslo. Compositions: Several songs for Fair Play; Dans for Soyr; Rouro, composition for 5 voices. Recordings: Albums with Fair Play: Fair Play, 1989; with Soyr: Vectors, 1987; Bussene Lengter Hjem, 1994. Membership: Norwegian Jazz Musicians Society. Address: Oppsalstubben 5B, 0685 Oslo, Norway.

ROSSELL Marina, b. 17 Jan 1954, Barcelona, Spain. Singer. Musical Education: Guitar, Solfege. Career: Professional singer, 1970-; Appearances include: Concerts: Theatre de la Ville, Paris, 1981-87; Festival Tenco, San Remo, Italy, 1982; Moscow, 1985; Bogota, 1988; Festival Utono Musicale, Como, Italy, 1989;

Cuban International Festival, 1994; Concert For Peace, San Sebastian, 1995; International tour, Mexico, Paris, Lisbon, Netherlands, Cuba, Canary Isles, Malaga, Pamplona, Barcelona, Sitges, 1994; Bolivian Pro-Native Concert, 1995; Television includes: TVE (Spanish National TV), 1981; Concert, TVE, 1992; Film: El Vicari d'Olot, 1981; Collaborations with composers including: Georges Moustaki; Tomatito; Antoni Ros Marbà; Manzanita; Maria del Mar Bonet; Joan Bibloni; Pau Riba. Recordings include: Llegendes de Catalunya, 1975; Si Volieu Escolatar, 1977; Penyora, Premio Fotogramas, Vol 1, 1978; Festival Internacional, Vol 1, 1979; Cos Meu Recorda, 1982; Victoria (Banda Sonora Pelicula), 1983; Maremar - Lluis Llach, 1985; Barca del Temps, Disco de Oro, 1986; Les Millors Cançons de Marina Rossell, 1990; Cinema Blau, 1990; Marina, 1993; Gracies (Recopilaciones), 1994; Cinema Blau + La Gavina, 1994. Honours: Silver Shot Award, 1979; Award, Best Catalan record of the Year, R-4, 1981; Best Catalan Record of The Year R-4, for Rosa De Foc (Fire Rose), 1989. Hobbies: Literature; Movies. Current Management: Josep Sanz, JSB Management. Address: c/. Llauder, 161-3er. 2a., 08302 Mataró, Barcelona, Spain.

ROSSELSON Leon, b. 22 June 1934, London, England. Songwriter; Singer; Musician (guitar). m. Rina Picciotto, 27 Sept 1959, 2 daughters. Education: BA Hon Cantab (English Literature). Musical Education: Grade VI Piano. Career: Member, Galliards Folk Group, 1959-61; BBC radio Easy Beat and Saturday Club, solo performer, 1961-; Folk clubs; Arts centres; Universities; Concert halls, including Festival Hall, Royal Albert Hall; Tours: Belgium; Netherlands; Australia; Canada; US; Songs for television programme That Was The Week That Was; Songs for stage production of They Shoot Horses Don't They?, 1973; Television includes: All You Need Is Love; The Oxford Road Show; World Turned Upside Down, singles charts, Billy Bragg, 1985; Ballad Of A Spycatcher, Indie singles charts, 1987. Recordings: Solo albums: Songs For Sceptical Circles, 1967; A Laugh A Song And A Handgrenade, 1968; Hugga Mugga, 1971; That's Not The Way It's Got To Be, 1974; Palaces Of Gold, 1975; Love Loneliness And Laundry, 1976; If I Knew Who The Enemy Was, 1979; For The Good Of The Nation, 1981; Temporary Loss Of Vision, 1984; Bringing The News From Nowhere, 1986; I Didn't Mean It, 1988; Rosselsongs, 1989; Wo Sind Die Elefanten?, 1991; The Happiness Counter, 1992; Intruders, 1995; Perspectives, CD, 1997. Publications: Bringing The News From Nowhere, 125 selected songs, 1993. Memberships: MCPS; PRS; Musicians' Union; Writers' Guild. Hobbies: Theatre; Cinema; Walking; Tennis. Address: 28 Park Chase, Wembley Park, Middlesex HA9 8EH, England.

ROSSI Francis (Mike), b. 29 May 1949, Peckham, London, England. Musician (guitar); Vocalist. Career: Founder member, UK rock group Status Quo, 1967-; Extensive tours worldwide; Concerts, festivals include: British Great Western Festival; Reading Festival, 1972, 1978, 1987; NEC Birmingham, before Prince and Princess of Wales, (televised by BBC); Milton Keynes Bowl, 1984; Live Aid, Wembley Stadium, 1985; Support to Queen, Wembley Stadium, 1986; Played 4 venues in 12 hours, entered in Guinness Book Of Records, 1991. Recordings: Albums: Picturesque Matchsticakble Messages, 1968; Spare Parts, 1969; Ma Kelly's Greasy Spoon, 1970; Dog Of Two Heads, 1971; Piledriver, 1973; Hello, 1973; Quo, 1974; On The Level, 1975; Blue For You, 1976; Status Quo Live!, 1977; Rockin' All Over The World, 1977; If You Can't Stand The Heat, 1978; Whatever You Want, 1979; Just Supposin', 1980; Never Too Late, 1981; 1+9+8+2, 1982; To Be Or Not To Be, 1983; Back To Back, 1983; In The Army Now, 1986; Ain't Complaining, 1988; Rock 'Til You Drop, 1991; Live Alive Quo, 1992; Don't Stop, 1996; Whatever You Want, 1997;

Numerous compilations; Hit singles include: Pictures Of Matchstick Men, 1968; Ice In The Sun, 1969; Paper Plane, 1973; Caroline, 1973; Break The Rules, 1974; Down Down, 1975; Roll Over Lay Down, 1975; Rain, 1976; Mystery Song, 1976; Wild Side Of Life, 1977; Rockin' All Over The World, 1977; Again And Again, 1978; Whatever You Want, 1979; Living On An Island, 1979; What You're Proposing, 1980; Lies, 1981; Rock'n'Roll, 1981; Something 'Bout You Baby I Like, 1981; Dear John, 1982; Ol' Rag Blues, 1983; A Mess Of The Blues, 1983; Marguerita Time, 1984; Rollin' Home, 1986; In The Army Now, 1986; Burning Bridges, 1989; Anniversary Waltz, 1990; Contributor, Do They Know It's Christmas?, Band Aid, 1984. Honours include: Silver Clef Award, Nordoff-Robbins Music Therapy Centre, 1981; BRIT Award, Outstanding Contribution To The British Music Industry, 1991. Current Management: David Walker, Handle Artists Management, Handle House, 1 Albion Place, Galena Road, London W6 0QT, England.

ROSSINGTON Gary, b. 4 Dec 1951, Jacksonville, Florida, USA. Musician (guitar); Songwriter. Career: Musician, US rock group, Lynyrd Skynyrd, 1970-77, 1987-; Rossington-Collins Band (with Allen Collins) later The Rossington Band, 1979-88; US tour, support to The Who, 1973; Knebworth Festival, 1976; Serious injuries in plane crash, 1977; Volunteer Jam Reunion, 1987; Farm Aid V, 1991; 20th Anniversary, Lynyrd Skynyrd & Friends LYVE (pronounced Live), cable Tv pay-per-view performance, 1993; Inaugural Freebird Festival, 1993. Recordings: Albums with Lynard Skynyrd: Pronounced Leh-nerd Skin-Nerd, 1973; Second Helping, 1974; Nuthin' Fancy, 1975; Gimme Back My Bullets, 1976; One More For The Road, 1976; Street Survivors, 1977; Skynyrd's First And Last, 1978; Gold And Platinum, 1980; Best Of The Rest, 1985; Legend, 1987; Southern By The Grace Of God/Lynyrd Skynyrd Tribute Tour, 1988; Lynyrd Skynrd, 1991, 1991; The Last Rebel, 1993; with the Rossington-Collins Band; Anytime Anyplace Anywhere, 1980; This Is The Way, 1981; Love Your Man, 1988; Singles include: Sweet Home Alabama, 1974; Free Bird, 1975; What's Your Name, 1978. Address: c/o Alliance Artists Ltd, 6025 The Corners Parkway, Ste 202, Norcross, GA 30092, USA.

ROTH David Lee, b. 10 Oct 1955, Bloomington, Indiana, USA. Rock Vocalist. Career: Singer, Red Ball Jets; Founder member, US rock group Van Halen, 1975-85; Support tours with UFO; Santana; Black Sabbath; Regular headlining US and worldwide tours; Major concerts include: California Music Festival, 1979; US Festival, 1982, 1983; Monsters Of Rock Festival, Castle Donington, 1984; Solo artiste, 1985-; US tour, 1986; UK tour, 1988; World tour, 1991. Recordings: Albums: with Van Halen: Van Halen, 1978; Women And Children First, 1980; Fair Warning, 1981; Diver Down, 1982; 1984, 1983; Solo albums: Eat 'Em And Smile, 1986; Skyscraper, 1988; A Little Ain't Enough, 1991; Singles with Van Halen include: You Really Got Me, 1978; Running With The Devil, 1978; Dance The Night Away, 1979; And The Cradle Will Rock, 1980; (Oh) Pretty Woman, 1982; Dancing In The Street, 1982; Jump (Number 1, US), 1984; Panama, 1984; I'll Wait, 1984; Hot For Teacher, 1984; Solo: California Girls, 1985; Just A Gigolo/I Ain't Got Nobody, 1985; Yankee Rose, 1986; Goin' Crazy, 1986; Just Like Paradise, 1988; Stand Up, 1988; A Lil' Ain't Enough, 1991. Honours: Numerous Platinum discs; MTV Music Video Award, 1984. Hobby: Mountaineering. Current Management: Diamond Dave Enterprises. Address: c/o Eddie Anderson, 11288 Ventura Blvd, Suite 430, Studio City, CA 91606, USA.

ROTHERY Steve, b. 25 Nov 1959, Brampton, South Yorkshire, England. Musician (guitar). Career: Member, UK progressive rock band, Marillion, 1980-; Tours, UK; Europe; North

America; Major concerts include: Theakston Festival, 1982; Reading Festival, 1982, 1983; Nostell Priory Festival, 1982, 1984; Glastonbury Festival, 1984; Support to Rush, Radio City Music Hall, New York, 1983; Monsters Of Rock Festival, Castle Donington, 1985; Welcome To The Garden Party, Milton Keynes Bowl, 1986. Albums: Script For A Jester's Tear, 1983; Fugazi, 1984; Real To Reel, 1984; Misplaced Childhood, 1985; Brief Encounter, 1986; Clutching At Straws, 1987; B-Sides Themselves, 1988; The Thieving Magpie, 1988; Season's End, 1989; Holidays In Eden, 1991; A Singles Collection 1982-92, 1992; Brave, 1994; Afraid Of Sunlight, 1995; Singles include: Market Square Heroes, 1982; He Knows You Know, 1983; Garden Party, 1983; Punch And Judy, 1984; Assassing, 1984; Kayleigh (Number 2, UK), 1985; Lavender, 1985; Heart Of Lothian, 1985; Incommunicado, 1987; Sugar Mice, 1987; Warm Wet Circles, 1987; Freaks, 1988; Hooks In You, 1989; Uninvited Guest, 1989; Easter, 1990; Cover My Eyes (Pain And Heaven), 1991; No One Can, 1991; Dry Land, 1991; Sympathy, 1992. Current Management: Hit And Run Music Ltd. Address: 30 Ives Street, London SW3 2ND, England.

ROTHSCHILD Michael, b. 7 Aug 1943, Jacksonville, Florida, USA. Record Company Executive. m. Linda Grant, 23 Sept 1993, 1 daughter. Education: BA History, Tulane University, New Orleans, Louisiana. Career: President, Landslide Records, Atlanta, Georgia, 1980-. Recordings: Executive Producer or Producer of albums: Navigator, Paul McCandless; Tore Up, Nappy Brown, Cool On It, Heartfixers; Accept No Substitute, The Bluesbusters; Strange Voices, Colonel Bruce Hampton. Memberships: NARAS; NAIRD. Hobbies: Hiking; Cooking; Fantasy baseball. Address: 1800 Peachtree Street NW, Suite 333, Atlanta, GA 30309, USA.

ROUCAN Jean-Yves, b. 2 June 1962, Neuilly Sur Seine, France. Musician (drums). 1 daughter. Musical Education: CIM, Paris; Berklee School Of Music, Boston, USA. Career: Jazz drummer, Triode, 1986-87; Formed own trio with M Bismut and B Paillard, 1987-; Concerts include: Nîmes Festival, 1988; Béziers Festival, 1989; Radio France Festival, 1991; Radio: France Inter, France Musique, other FM stations, 1992; Television: 4 regional shows, France 3, 1991-92; Worked with: R Beirach; D Liebman's Quest; P Motian; D Holland; B Frisell; J Lovano; D Humair; Currently, freelance jazz drummer, Plays with Passage (big band); Plays with Interplay Collectif, Switzerland. Recordings include: Triode Jazz Quartet; Socco, Trio Paillard-Bismut-Roucan, 1992; With Interplay Collectif: S Duner Project. Honour: First Prize, Concours International de Vienne, France. Hobbies: Gastronomy; Wine. Address: 56 Rue Saint Sebastien, 75011 Paris, France.

ROUGVIE Jeff James, b. 4 Mar 1963, Quincy, Massachusetts, USA. Director of A&R and Special Projects. Education: Art School; Hartford Art School, 1984. Career: Signings: Sugar; Golden Smog; Alejandro Escovedo; Martin Zellar; Morphine; Respoisle for catalogue development: Badfinger; Big Star; David Bowie; Elvis Costello. Hobbies: Collecting antique toys, comic books. Address: Rykodisc A&R, Shetland Park, 27 Congress Street, Salem, MA 01970, USA.

ROUNDS James, b. 16 October 1951, Tokyo, Japan. Musician (Guitar); Songwriter. Education: BA, English, Dickinson College, Carlisle, PA, USA, 1973. Musical Education: Selftaught. Career: Played on stage with John Lee Hooker, Charlie Gracie and others. Compositions: Go Man Go, Charlie Gracie, with the Jordanaires, 1988; Where Everybody Stays, in the film, Liars Club, 1991. Recordings: The Metropolitans, LP, 1996. Honours: Help Heal LA Award, 1992; Music City (Nashville) Award for R&B Category, 1988. Membership: ASCAP Writer and Publisher. Hobbies: Tennis; Surfing. Current Management:

Bristol Music. Address: 515 Rosedale Avenue, Nashville, TN 37211, USA.

ROUSSANOV Christo, b. 7 July 1969, Lovech, Bulgaria. Artist and Concert Manager. Education: Civil Law. Career: Executive Manager, First Private Concert Agency, Julia Christova, 1990-1992; Tour Manager, New Symphony Orchestra, Sofia, 1992-1993; Founder, President, New Music Agency, 1993. Hobby: Fitness. Current Management: New Music Agency. Address: New Music Agency, Nadejda, bl.634, apt.14, Sofia 1231, Bulgaria.

ROUSSIN Didier Jean, b. 1 Nov 1949, St Mandé, France. Musician (classical, electric and acoustic guitars, banjo, dobro, percussion); Writer; Artistic Advisor; Artistic Director; Guitar Teacher. Musical Education: Conservatoire d'Ivry Sur Seine; Brevet d'Enseignement, Ecole Normale de Musique de Paris. Career: Played, recorded with singers: Renaud; Monique Morelli; Gérard Pierron; Backed American jazz accordionists: Art Van Damme, Frank Marocco; Guitarist for Jo Privat, last 13 years; Duo, with jazz accordionist Daniel Colin; Member, several groups including: Dénécheau Jâse Musette; Paris-Musette; Les Primitifs du Futur; Robert Santiago's Latino-Américain; Played or recorded with jazzmen and bluesmen: Georges Arvanitas; Marcel Azzola; Steve Lacy; Bernard Lubat; Jean-Claude Fohrenbach; Pierre Michelot; Jean-Jacques Milteau; Bobby Rangell; Benny Waters; Dominique Pifarely; Co-author, French television documentary Le Blues du Musette (La Sept). Recordings: Juju Doudou, Dominique Cravic; Night And Day Rue de Lappe, with Jo Privat; Jazz Experience; Quel Temps Fait-il à Paris, with Daniel Colin; Dénécheau Jâse Musette à Paris, with Daniel Dénécheau, Robert Santiago. Publications: CD booklets for Musette re-releases; Articles about Musette and jazz accordion in several magazines: Jazz Swing Journal; Modal; Trad Mag; Journal de la Cité de la Musique; Accordéon Magazine; Guitare et Claviers. Co-author, book L'Argot des Musiciens. Honours: Grand Prix du Disque de l'Académie Charles Cros, for Paris Musette Volume I (musician, artistic advisor); Grand Prix de la Littérature Musicale de l'Académie Charles Cros, for Histoires de l'Accordéon, with François Billard. Current Management: Madeleine Juteau, 20, Route de Sorel, 28500 Montreuil, France.

ROWBOTTOM Simon, b. Wallasey, England. Singer. Career: Vocalist, Boo Radleys, 1989-. Recordings: Albums: Ichabod & I, 1989; Everything's Alright Forever, 1992; Giant Steps, 1993; Learning To Walk, 1994; Wake Up, 1995; C'mon Kids, 1996; Solo album under name of Eggman: First Fruits. Honours: Select and NME magazines, Album of the Year, 1993. Current Management: CEC Management, 6 Warren Mews, London W1P 5DJ, England.

ROWE Julian David, b. 30 Nov 1967, Sheffield, South Yorkshire, England. Teacher; Composer; Performer; Musician (piano, bass, drums). Musical Education: BA, Honours in Pop Music and Recording, University College, Salford. Career: Performed in various stage shows: Godspell, 1989; The Whale, 1990; Mike's Place, 1991; Chicago, 1991, 1993; Member, No Man's Band, UK tour, 1992; Sound engineer, live concerts; Producer, No Man's Band album, 1995; Formed Gristle and promotional tour, 1997. Compositions: Composed music for stage shows: The Whale, 1990; Mike's Place, 1991; Pompidou and a Gristle Tray, 1996. Recordings: Stand Back, Misty Blue Halo, 1992; Taz Thurley, 1992; Really Real Reel, 1992; Barbed Wire Glove, 1993; A Patient's Notes, 1993; East Meets West, 1994; Microblitz, 1994. Membership: Musicians' Union. Hobbies: Information technology; Live music; Walking. Current Management: Kidney Bean Managements. Address: 28 Walker Close, Grenoside, Sheffield S35 8SA, England.

ROWLAND Broz (Henry Cottrell Rowland), b. 30 July 1949, Dallas, Texas, USA. Producer; Songwriter; Musician (guitar, bass, keyboards, drums). Education: BA, Communication in the Audio Visual Arts, University of Colorado, 1978. Musical Education: Self-taught. Career: Member, Blue Pearl band, 1978; Formed Alpha Wave, 1980; Member, Modern Kids, 1982; Producer, co-songwriter, Bodyhouse album with Allen Ginsberg, 1986; Formed The Pilots, 1990; Joined Flying Perfect, 1994. Recordings: You Know It's Coming (single and album), Alpha Wave, 1980; Album with Modern Kids, 1982; Co-mixer, Lonnie Hill single, You Got Me Runnin', 1986; Writer, producer, Dreams, Visions And Nightmares, The Pilots, 1992; Producer, co-writer, debut album by Flying Perfect, 1995; Producer, debut solo album, John Guillot (former partner in the Pilots), 1995. Honours: Quarter Finalist, American Song Festival, 1980; KBCO 8th Boulder Music Invitational, 1984; Houston International Film Festival, 1986. Membership: ASCAP. Hobbies: Swimming; Snorkeling; Skiing; Trekking; Travel. Address: High Kite Productions, 1245 Elizabeth Street, Denver, CO 80206, USA.

ROWLAND Kevin, b. 17 Aug 1953, Wolverhampton, West Midlands, England. Vocalist; Musician (guitar). Career: Member, Lacy & The Lovers; The Killjoys; Lead singer, Dexy's Midnight Runners, 1978-; Solo artiste, 1988-. Recordings: Albums: with Dexy's Midnight Runners: Searching For The Young Soul, 1980; Too-Rye-Ay, 1982; Geno, 1983; Don't Stand Me Down, 1985; The Very Best Of Dexy's Midnight Runners, 1991; Solo album: The Wanderer, 1988; Singles: with Dexy's Midnight Runners: Dance Stance; Geno (Number 1, UK), 1980; There There My Dear; Show Me; Come On Eileen (Number 1, UK); Jackie Wilson Said; Let's Get This Straight From The Start; The Celtic Soul Brothers; Because Of You (television theme, Brush Strokes, BBC TV), 1986; Solo: Walk Away, 1988.

ROWLANDS Tom, b. 11 January 1971, England. Musician. Education: Manchester University. Career: Formed First Band, Ariel; Formed, The Dust Brothers with Ed Simons; Member, Chemical Brothers. Compositions: All recorded: Exit Planet Dust, album; Dig Your Own Hole, album (No 1 UK); Block Rockin Beats; Setting Sun; Leave Home. Recordings: Song to the Siren, 1993; 14th Century Sky (EP), 1994; My Mercury Mouth (EP), 1994; Life is Sweet, 1995; Loops of Fury (EP), 1996; Setting Sun, (No 1 UK), 1997; Block Rockin Beats (Number 1, UK), 1997; Electronic Battle Weapons, 1997; Elektrobank, 1997. Honours: Twice Nominated for Brit Awards; Nomination for Mercury Prize, 1997; Grammy Award, 1997. Current Management: Robert Linney. Address: 1 Cowcross Street, London EC1M 6DR, England.

ROWLES Greg, b. 6 Sept 1965, Fredericksburg, Virginia, USA. Entertainer; Musician (guitar, bass guitar, pedal-steel guitar). m. Brandee Ann Courtney, 31 Dec 1992, 1 daughter. Education: Gemanna College Graduate (Business Administration). Career: Performances include: Ed McMahon's Star Search Male Vocalist Champion; Grand Ole Opry Live; Music City Tonight; TNN Country News; Opryland Showpark, 1992-94; Tours, shows with Sammy Kershaw, Martina McBride, 1994-. Compositions: Professional songwriter signed with Music For The Future, 1995-. Honour: Spokesperson in Tennessee for child abuse prevention. Membership: Nashville Union. Hobbies: Golf; Fishing; Camping. Current Management: (Agent) Buddy-Lee Attractions. Address: Williams Bell and Associates, Inc, 707 18th Ave South, Nashville, TN 37203, USA.

ROWLES Jimmy (James George), b. 19 Aug 1918, Spokane, Washington, USA. Musician (piano); Composer. m. Dorothy Jewel Paden, 12 Aug 1941, 1 son, 2 daughters. Education:

Gonzaga University, 1937-38. Career: Pianist with numerous artists and bandleaders, 1940-; Artistes include: Benny Goodman; Lester Young; Billie Holiday; Woody Herman; Les Brown; Tommy Dorsey; Vic Damone; Sarah Vaughn; Henry Mancini; Carmen McRae; Peggy Lee. Compositions: The Peacocks, recorded by Bill Evans and Branford Marsalis (used in film 'Round Midnight), 1986; Compositions for Johnny Mercer. Honours: 5 Grammy Nominations, 1978-82, including The Peacocks, 1978; Peabody Award, 1986. Memberships: AFofM; ASCAP; Songwriters Guild of America; American Guild Authors & Composers.

ROWLES Stacy Amanda, b. 11 Sept 1955, Hollywood, California, USA. Musician (horns). Career: Major concerts: Monterey Jazz Festival, 1973; Wichita Jazz Festival, with Clark Terry All-Star Band, 1975; All-Women's Quintet, US tour, 1985; Charlie Hayden Liberation Orchestra, 1986; Performed at Woody Herman 50th Anniversary Tribute Concert, Hollywood, 1986; Freelance musician, 1987-; Member, Maiden Voyage, all-female jazz orchestra; Performed at Nice Jazz Festival, 1989. Recordings with: Nels Cline; Ray Brown; Donald Bailey; Jimmy Rowles; Sweets Edison. Honours: Best Flugelhorn Soloist, Orange Coast College Jazz Festival, 1973, 1974.

ROWNTREE Dave (David Alexander De Horne), b. 8 May 1964, Colchester, Essex, England. Musician (drums). m. 16 June 1994. Education: HND Computer Science, Woolwich. Musical Education: Lessons in bagpipes, drums. Career: Formed Idle Vice; Played in clubs for 2 years, France; Member, Blur; Extensive television, radio includes: Top Of The Pops; Later With Jools Holland; Concerts include Alexandra Palace; Reading Festival, 1993; Glastonbury Festival, 1994; Mile End, 1995; V97. Recordings: Blur: Albums: Leisure, 1991; Modern Life Is Rubbish, 1993; Parklife, 1994; The Great Escape, 1995; Blur, 1997 Singles: She's So High; There's No Other Way; Bang; Popscene; For Tomorrow; Chemical World; Sunday Sunday; Girls And Boys; To The End; Parklife; End Of A Century; Country House; The Universal; Stereotypes; Beetlebum; Songz; On Your Own; MOR. Honours: Mercury Prize Nomination; 4 Platinum Albums, Parklife; 3 Platinum Albums, The Great Escape; Platinum ALbum, Blur; BRIT Awards: Best Single, Album, Video, Band, 1995; Q Awards, Best Album, 1994, 1995. Current Management: CMO Management, Unit 32, Ransome Dock, 35-37 Parkgate Road, London SW11 4NP, England.

ROYAL Billy Joe, b. 3 Apr 1942, Valdosta, Georgia, USA. Singer. Career: Nightclub singer, Savannah, Georgia; Recording artiste, 1962-. Recordings: Hits include: Down In The Boondocks; I Knew You When; Cherry Hill Park; Burned Like A Rocket; I'll Pin A Note On Your Pillow; I Miss You Already; Members Only, duet with Donna Fargo; Albums: Down In The Boondocks, 1965; Billie Joe Royal, 1965; Hush, 1967; Cherry Hill Park, 1969; Looking Ahead, 1987; The Royal Treatment, 1987; Tell It Like It Is, 1989; Out Of The Shadows, 1990. Current Management: Mark Ketchem Management, 48 Music Square East, Nashville, TN 37203, USA.

ROZALLA, (Rozalla Sandra Miller), b. 18 Mar 1864, Ndola, Zambia. Singer. Career: Support act, Michael Jackson; Support act, Alexander O'Neal; Numerous UK/US television appearances including: Wogan; Big Breakfast; Arsenio Hall. Recordings: Albums: Everybody's Free; Look No Further; Singles:Everybody's Free; You Gotta Have Faith. Honours: Best African Artiste; Diamond Award, Best 12" Single; Silver album, Silver single. Membership: Musicians' Union. Current Management: DMA. Address: c/o Concorde International Artistes, Concorde House, 101 Shepherds Bush Road, London W6 7LP, England.

RUBIE Stephen Mark, b.14 Oct 1952, Marlow, Buckinghamshire, England. Musician (flute, saxophone); Jazz Club Proprietor. Education: University College Hospital, Dental School, London. Musical Education: Flutes with William Bartlett, Principle with BBC Concert Orchestra, Trinity College, London; Jazz theory, harmony, with Peter Ind. Career: Professional freelance, 1974-; Toured Italy, 1975; Peripatetic teacher, 1978-85; Proprietor, 606 Jazz Club, 1976-; Leader, 606 Club Big Band, 1985-90; Bandleader, Jazz/Latin sextet, 1991-; Featured flute player, Julian Joseph Big Band, BBC Prom, live broadcast, 1995; African band, Amabutho, live television in Germany, 1995. Memberships: Musicians' Union; Equity. Hobby: Chess. Address: 10A Stadium Street, London SW10 0PT, England.

RUBIN Rick, b. 10 Mar 1963, Long Beach, New York, USA. Record Producer; Record Company Executive. Education: BFA, New York University, 1985. Career: Owner, founding president, Def Jam Recordings, 1984-88; Def American Recordings, 1988-; Director, co-producer, film Tougher Than Leather, 1987. Recordings include: As producer: Radio, LL Cool J, 1985; License To Ill, Beastie Boys, 1986; Raising Hell, Run DMC, 1986; It Takes A Nation, Public Enemy, 1986; Electric, The Cult, 1987; Blood Sugar Sex Magic, Red Hot Chili Peppers, 1992; Tom Petty, Wildflowers, 1994; One Hot Minute, Red Hot Chili Peppers, 1995. Honours: Numerous Gold and Platinum discs as producer; Rolling Stone Award, Hot Producer Of Year, 1988; Joel Weber Award, New Music Seminar, 1990. Address: c/o American Recordings, 3500 W Olive Avenue, Ste 1550, Burbank, CA 91505, USA.

RUBINI Michel, b. 3 Dec 1942, Los Angeles, California, USA. Musical Director; Composer; Musician; Record Producer. Career: Musical director for: Johnny Mathis, 1968; Nancy Wilson, 1969-70; Producer, arranger for Sonny and Cher, 1971-73; Artist, producer, Motown Records, 1975-78; Worked with numerous artists including: Elvis Presley; John Lennon; Diana Ross; Linda Ronstadt. Compositions: Numerous television and film soundtracks. Recordings: Solo album: Secret Dreams, 1988; As record producer: Stoney End, Barbra Streisand; California Dreamin', Johnny Mathis; All I Never Need Is You, Sonny and Cher; Country Class, Jerry Lee Lewis; So Fine, Loggins and Messina. Honour: BMI Writers Award, 1985. Memberships: BMI; Composers and Lyricists Guild.

RUDD Raphael, Musician; Composer; Songwriter; Arranger. Education: BM, MM, Manhattan School of Music. Career: Orchestrated Final Scene of the Score to the Who Film, Quadraphenia, 1979; Arranged Horns on Pete Townsend's Hit Single, Rough Boys, 1980; Touring Member, Renaissance and Annie Haslam Band as Keyboardist, 1982-92. Recordings: R Rudd: Reflections, 1983; R Rudd: Skydancer, 1991; Raphael Rudd: The Awakening, with Pete Townsend, Phil Collins and Annie Huslam, 1997. Joyfest, 1998. Honours: Artist of the Year, Oakside/Bloomfield Cultural Center, New Jersey, 1996. Membership: American Harp Society. Hobbies: Movies; Classical Music. Current Management: Rob Findlay, Headfirst Management. Address: c/o 1674 Broadway, Suite 7-D, New York, NY 10019, USA.

RUFFIN Bruce, b. 17 Feb 1952, St Catherine, Jamaica, West Indies. Musician (guitar, piano). 3 daughters. Education: Studied for LLB (Law), England. Musical Education: Grade 3 piano. Career: Discovered in Vere John's Talent Contest, Jamaica; Member, The Techniques; Songs inspired by Duke Reid, owner Treasure Isle Label; Formed The Shades, 1969; Joined Inner Circle Band; Concerts include: Support to Stevie Wonder, Carib Theatre, 1969; UK and European tours; Guest of Czechoslovakian Government at Bratislav Song Festival, 1973; Hit single as solo

artist; Television appearance: Top Of The Pops, 1971; Formed Chain Reaction, 1977; Signed to RCA Records, 1979-81; Formed Slick Records and Smash Music, 1980-; Working with Record, Publishing and Management Company, 1982-; Managing Director, Jeunesse Cosmetics Ltd; Yak Yak Babywear Company. Compositions: Hits include: with The Techniques: Love Is Not A Gamble; My Girl; It's You I Love; Run Come Celebrate; Man Of My Word; There Comes A Time; Find Yourself A Fool; Solo: Dry Up Your Tears; Bitterness Of Life; Mad About You; Long About Now; Free The People; with Chain Reaction: Never Lose And Never Win. Recordings: Other hit singles include: as solo artiste: Rain; Candida; with The Techniques: Queen Majesty; You Don't Care; as publisher, Smash Music: Holding On To Love; Fuchi. Memberships: PRS; BASCA; ASCAP; MCPS. Hobbies: Martial arts; Chi Kwang Do. Current Management: BRM Music Consultancy Ltd; BRM Music Publishing Ltd; Genius Management Agency Ltd. Address: 89a High Road, Wood Green, London N22 6BB, England.

RUFFIN Jimmy, b. 7 May 1939, Collinsville, Mississippi, USA. Singer. Career: Session singer, early 1960s; Commercial breakthrough, major US, UK hit, What Becomes Of The Broken-Hearted, 1966. Recordings: Albums: Top Ten, 1967; Ruff'n'Ready, 1969; The Groove Governor, 1970; I Am My Brother's Keeper (with David Ruffin), 1970; Jimmy Ruffin, 1973; Love Is All We Need, 1975; Sunrise, 1980; Singles include: What Becomes Of The Broken-Hearted, 1966; I'll Say Forever My Love; It's Wonderful; Hold On To My Love, 1980; Turn To Me (duet with Maxine Nightingale), 1982; There Will Never Be Another You, 1985. Address: c/o Barry Collings Entertainments, 21a Clifftown Road, Southend-on-Sea, Essex SS1 1AB, England.

RUFFNER Mason, b. 29 Nov 1952, USA. Musician (guitar); Vocalist. Career: Support tours with: U2; Jimmy Page; Ringo Starr; Crosby Stills and Nash. Recordings: Solo albums: Mason Ruffner; Gypsy Blood; Other recordings include: Oh Mercy, Bob Dylan; Acadie, Dan Landis. Hobby: Motorcycles. Current Management: Davis McLarty. Address: Rt 2 Box 592, Wimberley, TX 78676, USA.

RUFFY (Glen) David, b. 23 Mar 1952, York, England. Musician (drums); Programmer; Composer. m. Jennifer, 24 June 1995, 2 daughters. Career: Major tours: Sinead O'Connor; Adam Ant; Aztec Camera; Ruts; Edwyn Collins; Yazz; WaterBoys; World Party; Martin Stephenson; Concerts with Mica Paris; Kirsty MacColl; Prefab Sprout. Recordings include: Ruts: Babylons Burning; In A Rut; West One; Jahwar; Rude Boys; The Crack; Sinead O'Connor: My Special Child; Damn Your Eyes; Year Of The Horse (video). Kirsty MacColl album: Titanic Days; Aztec Camera: Highland; Hard Rain; Knife. Memberships: PRS; MCPS; Musicians' Union. Hobbies: Relaxing; Swimming; Motor Rallying. Current Management: Southside Management; Agent: Grip. Address: 20 Cromwell Mews, London SW7, England.

RUHLMANN Jean-Jacques, b. 18 May 1952, Nogent-le-Rotrou, France. Musician (saxophone, clarinet); Composer. Education: CAPES Musicologie at the Sorbonne. Musical Education: C A Jazz. Career: Played with musicians including: J Thollot; F Jeanneau; J Gilson; E Watson; A Mangelsdorf; A Hervé; Michael O'Neil; B Renaudin; F Moerman; J F Jenny-Clark; Performed at many festivals in France; Belgium; Netherlands; Germany; Colombia; Tunisia; Spain. Recordings: Albums: Evensong, Michael O'Neil; Valses Manouches, with F A Moerman; Ciel De Traine (as a sideman); Windows, J J Ruhlmann Big Band. Current Management: M T Ruhlmann. Address: 3 rue des Poupardieres, 28400 Nogent le Rotrou, France.

RUIZ Fabien, b. 6 Mar 1962, Neuilly, France. Tap-dancer; Hoofer. m. Marguerite de Rohan-Chabot, 25 Jan 1992. Education: Ecole Supérieure de Réalizations Audio-Visuelles. Career: Théâtre de la Ville, Paris; Théâtre Hebertot, Paris; Olympia, Paris; Cirque Royal de Bruxelles; Paramount Theater, Denver; Tel-Aviv Jazz Festival; Engadiner Konzert-Wochen; Festival Mediteraneen; Europa Jazz Festival. Recordings: Un P'tit Air Danc La Tête, TSF; Tomara, Laurence Saltiel; Jazz De J à Z, Philippe Carment; Un Siècle De Jazz, Big-Band Christian Garros. Membership: SPEDIDAM. Hobbies: Cinema; Tennis; Football. Address: 19 Rue de la Bievre, 92340 Bourg-La-Reine, France.

RUNDGREN Todd, b. 2 June 1948, Philadelphia, Pennsylvania, USA. Singer; Songwriter; Musician (guitar); Record Producer. Career: Member, Woody's Truck Stop; Founder member, The Nazz, 1967-70; Solo recording artiste, 1970-; Formed progressive rock group Utopia, 1974-. Recordings: Albums: with The Nazz: Nazz, 1968; Nazz Nazz, 1969; Nazz III, 1970; with Utopia: Todd Rundgren's Utopia, 1974; Another Live, 1975; Ra, 1977; Oops! Wrong Planet, 1977; Adventures In Utopia, 1980; Deface The Music, 1980; Swing To The Right, 1982; Utopia, 1982; Oblivion, 1984; Solo albums: Runt, 1970; The Ballad Of Todd Rundgren, 1971; Something / Anything?, 1972; A Wizard, A True Star, 1973; Todd, 1974; Initiation, 1975; Faithful, 1976; Hermit Of Mink Hollow, 1978; Back To The Bars, 1978; Healing, 1981; The Ever Popular Tortured Artist Effect, 1983; A Cappella, 1985; POV, 1985; Anthology - Todd Rundgren, 1988; Nearly Human, 1989; Second Wind, 1991; Singles, 1995; Record producer, Bat Out Of Hell, Meat Loaf, 1977; Also producer/engineer, recordings by New York Dolls; Grand Funk Railroad; Hall and Oates; XTC; The Band. Current Management: Panacea Entertainment Management. Address: 2705 Glendower Avenue, Los Angeles, CA 90027, USA

RUOCCO Joanne, b. 26 May 1961, New Jersey, USA. Musician (drums, percussion). m. Douglas Newbery, 30 Sept 1989. Education: Graduate, New Jersey. Musical Education: BA, Music, Fine Art, Farleigh Dickenson University, New Jersey. Career: Recordings with: Duke Ellington Orchestra (Mercer Ellington); Chuck Berry; Bobby Womack; J Geils Band; Ron Wood; Hollywood Beyond; Jellybean; Mick Hucknell (Simply Red); The Style Council (Paul Weller). Memberships: Musicians' Union; AFofM. Hobbies: Skiing; Hiking; Swimming; Photography; Travel. Current Management: Independent. Address: 7 Linwood Road, Harpenden, Hertfordshire AL5 1RR, England.

RUPIC Hrvoje, b. 2 Mar 1970, Zagreb, Croatia. Musician (percussion). Musical Education: Latin Percussion, Drum Teaching Studios, London. Career: Concerts, recordings with: Toots Thielmans; Bosko Petrovic; Philippe Catherine; Bob Moover; Gianni Basso; Mind Games; Parni Valjak; Ritmo Loco; Soul Fingers; Patchwork; Dino Dvornik; Numerous appearances major Croatian television and radio shows. Recordings: with Rosko Petrovic and BP Club All Stars: Con Alma; Trilogy; with Mind Games: Pretty Fonky; with Csaba Deseo: The Swinging Violin; with Ritmo Loco: Baila Como Yo; Za Ljubav Jedne Zene; with Soul Fingers: Live in BP Club; with Parni Valjak: Unplugged - Live In ZKM. Membership: HGU, Croatian Musicians Union. Address: TRG Senjskih Uskoka 8, 41000 Zagreb, Croatia.

RUSKIN Tommy, b. 15 July 1942, Kansas City, Missouri, USA. Musician (drums). m. 11 Feb 1963, 1 son. Musical Education: School band and orchestra. Career: Played with: Roy Johnson; Marilyn Maye; Sammy Tucker; Gary Foster; Mike Metheny; Pat Metheny; Julie Turner (wife); Clark Terry; Zoot Sims; Herb Ellis; Carl Fontana; Scott Hamilton; Bill Watrous; Warren Vaché; Jack Sheldon; Jay McShann. Recordings: Mike Metheny: Day in Nightout; Gary Foster: Kansas City Connections; Marlyn Maye: The Second Of Maye; Jay McShann: Warm. Membership: Musicians' Union. Hobbies: Swimming; Walking. Address: 7225 Outlook, Overland Park, KS 66204, USA.

RUSSELL Brenda (Gordon), b. 8 Apr 1949, Brooklyn, New York, USA. Singer; Songwriter; Musician; Producer. m. Brian Russell, 14 Sept 1974, divorced, 1 daughter. Musical Education: Self-taught. Career: Toured with: David Sanborn; Billy Ocean; Jeffrey Osborne; Television appearances: Good Morning America; Today Show; Arsenio Hall; Late Show; British Music Shows, Germany, Sweden; Pat Sajek Show, USA; Toured as singer (pre-solo career) with Mac Davis; Elton John; Television background work: Sonny and Cher Show. Compositions: Songs recorded by: Herb Alpert; Ray Charles; Joe Cocker; Rita Coolidge; Earth Wind and Fire; Roberta Flack; Chaka Khan; Johnny Mathis; Diana Ross; Donna Summer; Dionne Warwick; Oleta Adams; Regina Belle; Peabo Bryson; Alex Bugnon; Don Grusin; Layla Hathaway; George Howard; Bunny Hull; Jermaine Jackson; Walter Jackson; Al Jarreau; Koinonea; Ivan Lins; Byron Miller; Ann Murray; Phil Perry; Anita Pointer; Rufus; Patrice Rushen; Tom Scott; Marilyn Scott; Tavares; Luther Vandross; Tata Vega; Sudao Watanabe; Kirk Whalum; David Williams; Pauline Wilson; Phillipe Wynne. Recordings: Albums: Brenda Russell, 1979; Two Eyes, 1983; Love Life, 1980; Get Here, 1988; Kiss Me With The Wind, 1990; Soul Talkin', 1993; Singles include: So Good So Right; Piano In The Dark. Honours: 3 Grammy Nominations, for Piano In The Dark: Best Pop Female Vocalist, Best Duo or Group, Song of the Year. Hobbies: Artist (charcoal portraits); Making clothes. Current Management: Turner Management Group. Address: 3500 W Olive Suite 770, Burbank, CA 91505, USA.

RUSSELL Devon B (Jones Town King), b. 6 Aug 1948, Jamaica. m. Arden L Russell, 2 sons, 4 daughters. Singer; Musician (guitar); Producer; Songwriter. Career: Lead singer, songwriter, 60s vocal group The Tartans; Tours: UK; Europe; North and South America; Caribbean; Concerts include: Sunsplash, 1979; Fort Clarence, Kingston, 1979; Maastricht, Netherlands, 1980; Espace Bobino, France, 1990; Hummingbird, Birmingham (with Bunny Wailer), 1990; Hackney Empire, London, 1994; Backing vocals for: Max Romeo; The Gladiators; Freddie McGregor; Sugar Minott; Johnny Osbourne; Barry Brown; Jennifer Laura; Nina Soila; Lukie D; Prince Lincoln; Producer, Studio One for: Clement Dodd: Lee Perry; Duke Reid; Television: Jamaica; Germany; Documentary on Jamaican Music; Radio: Radio 1, Andy Kershaw; Capital Radio, David Rodigan; Kiss FM UK; US and French radio. Recordings: Solo: Classic Lovers; Bible And The Gun; Roots Music; Homebound Train; Various artists: Money Sex and Violence; Darker Than Blue - A Tribute To Curtis Mayfield; Something Special; Nitty Gritty, Lukie D; Golden Rule, Lukie D; Roots Classic, Zion Train; Daddy Freddie, General Levy; Prison Life, Earl Smith and Bertram Brown; Hit singles include: Red Bum Ball, with Lloyd Robinson, one of most covered songs ever, 1968; Fattie Bum Bum, 1970; My Woman's Love; People Get Ready; Make Me Believe In You; Thanks And Praise; Jah Holds The Key (Number 1,UK), 1992. Publications: Darker Than Blue - A Tribute To Curtis Mayfield. Honours: National Song Contest Winners, 1979; Award for Contribution to Development Of Young Artists (with Lloyd Robinson). Memberships: PRS; MCPS; PPL. Hobbies: Art; Reading. Address: Prestige Records, 34 James Street, London WC1N 3HB, England.

RUSSELL George Allen, b. 23 June 1923, Cincinnati, Ohio, USA. Composer; Theoritician; Bandleader; Musician (piano). m. Alice Norbury, 4 Aug 1981, 1 son. Education: Wilberforce University High School. Musical Education: Private Study with Stephan Wolpe. Career: Performances with large and small ensembles worldwide, including Tokyo; Paris; London; Scandinavia; Italy; Germany; Portugal; United States; Radio and television: Broadcasts for BBC; Broadcasts in Sweden; Norway; Denmark; Japan; Finland; Germany; Italy; Commissions from National Endowments for the Arts; Massachusetts State Council on the Arts; Swedish Radio; The British Council; Cité de la Musique; Glasgow International Festival; Rocella Ionica; New England Presentors; Relache New Music; Norwegian Cultural Fund; BMI; Bradeis University; Member of faculty, New England Conservatory of Music, 1969-; Seminars and lectures worldwide. Compositions include: African Game; Living Time; Vertical Form VI; All About Rosie; Ezz-Thetic; Stratusphunk; Cubano Be-Cubano Bop; A Bird in Igor's Yard; Uncommon Ground; Listen to the Silence; Time Spiral; Electronic Sonata for Souls Loved by Nature. Honours: MacArthur Foundation Fellow; Guggenheim Fellow; National Endowment for the Arts American Jazz Master; Guardian Milestone Award. Memberships: Member International Society of Contemporary Music; American Federation of Musicians; Foreign Member, Swedish Royal Academy of Music. Current Management: Serious Speakout, Windsor House, 4th Floor, 83 Kingsway, London, WC2B 6SD. Address: c/o Concept Inc, #182, 1770 Massachusetts Avenue, Cambridge, MA 02140, USA.

RUSSELL Graham Cyril, b. 11 June 1950, Nottingham, England. Singer; Musician (piano, guitar); Composer. m. Jodi Varble, 7 June 1986, 1 son, 1 daughter. Musical Education: Self-taught. Career: Singer, Co-founder group, Air Supply, (most successful Australian group); Worldwide tours, 1975-, including China, 1995; Worldwide television and radio appearances. Recordings: 17 albums released; 9 Top 5 songs, US charts; 25 million albums sold to date; Honours: Song of Year, 1980; American Music Awards, Artist of Year, 1980. Memberships: BMI; 2 Million Plays Club. Hobbies: Outdoor Activities; Wildlife. Current Management: Barry Siegel, ICM. Address: 10345 West Olympic Boulevard, Suite 200, Los Angeles, CA 90064, USA.

RUSSELL Jack Patrick, b. 5 Dec 1960, Montebello, California, USA. Vocalist. m. Jana Whisenant, 19 Sept 1991, 1 son. Musical Education: Self-taught. Career: Vocalist with rock group Great White; Support tours with: Whitesnake, UK, 1984; Judas Priest, USA, 1984; Dokken, USA, 1986; Night Ranger, 1987; Ratt, 1987; Twisted Sister, 1987; Whitesnake, 1987-88; Kiss, 1991; Co-headline tour with Tesla, 1989-90; Headline tours USA, 1992-95. Recordings: Albums: Great White, 1984; Shot In The Dark, 1986; Once Bitten, 1987; Recovery Live, 1987; Twice Shy, 1989; Hooked, 1990; Psycho City, 1992; Best Of Great White, 1994; Sail Away, 1994; various live recordings. Honours: Grammy Nomination, Best Hard Rock Performance, 1989. Hobbies: Scuba diving; Fishing; Boating. Current Management: Premier Talent Agency; Wildcat Management. Address: c/o Siegl, Feldstein, Duffin & Vuylstehe, Inc, 10345 W Olympic Boulevard, Los Angeles, CA 90064-2524, USA.

RUSSELL John William Edward, b. 19 Dec 1954, London, England. Improvising Musician (guitar). Musical Education: Private and self-taught. Career: Crossing Bridges, TV, radio include: Channel 4; Radio 3; Radio 4; Local radio. Concerts, festivals, tours include: East, West Europe, North America. Composition: QuaQua. Recordings: 14 albums and CDs. Publications: Essays, interviews in: Musics; Rubberneck; The Wire. Honours: Arts Council development bursary. Membership: London Musicians' Collective. Hobbies: Reading; Gardening. Current

Management: Mopomoso. Address: 23B Charteris Road, London N4 3AA, England.

RUSSELL Kelly, b. 30 Jun 1956, St John's, Newfoundland, Canada. Musician (fiddle, concertina, bouzouki). 1 daughter. Musical Education: Self-taught. Career: Original member of Newfoundland folk and rock groups: Figgy Duff; Wonderful Grand Band; The Plankerdown Band; Owner and Operator of Pigeon Inlet Productions; Researcher and Collector of Newfoundland Folk Music; Teacher of Music. Recordings: Produced over 30 recordings of Newfoundland Folk Music. Honour: Dr Marius Barbeau Medal for Folklore Scholarship, 1997. Address: PO Box 1202, St John's, Newfoundland A1C 5M9, Canada.

RUSSELL Leon (Hank Wilson), b. Lawton, Oklahoma, USA. Musician (guitar, piano, trumpet); Singer. m. Mary McCreary, Jan 1976, 1 son, 1 daughter. Career: Multi-instrumental session musician; Regular member, Phil Spector's Wall Of Sound session crew, 1962; Pianist, television series Shindig!, NBC TV; Built own recording studio, 1967; Appeared in film Mad Dogs And Englishmen, 1970; Played with Bob Dylan; Rolling Stones; Eric Clapton; Major concerts include: Concert For Bangladesh, Madison Square Garden, 1971; New Orleans Jazz & Heritage Festival, 1991; American Music Festival, with Neville Brothers, Randy Newman and Warren Zevon, 1992; Owner, video production company. Compositions include: Co-writer, singer, theme to Flesh And Blood, NBC TV; Delta Lady, recorded by Joe Cocker; A Song For You, recorded by The Carpenters, Donny Hathaway; This Masquerade, recorded by George Benson; Co-writer, Superstar, recorded by The Carpenters. Recordings: Albums: Asylum Choir, 1968; Leon Russell, 1970; Leon Russell And The Shelter People, 1971; Asylum Choir II, 1972; Carney, 1972; Leon Live, 1973; Hank Wilson's Back, 1973; Stop All That Jazz, 1974; Will O'The Wisp, 1975; The Wedding Album, 1976; Make Love To The Music, 1977; Americana, 1978; Willie And Leon (with Willie Nelson), 1979; The Live Album, 1981; Hank Wilson Volume II, 1984; Anything Can Happen, 1992; Singles include: Tight Rope; Bluebird; Lady Blue; Back To The Island; As session musician: A Taste Of Honey, Herb Alpert; Mr Tambourine Man, The Byrds. Honours: Grammy, Record of the Year, This Masquerade, 1976; Several Gold discs.

RUSSELL Mark J. Composer. Education: Honours Degree in Film Music and Composition. m. Joanne Whitworth, 10 May 1997. Career: Joined BBC Television's music department for three years, then left to start own recording studio; As Musican and arranger has worked with Tanita Tikaram, Julia Fordham and acclaimed Chinese flautist Guo Yue, with whom he appeared in concerts throughout Europe and Australia; Writer and presenter of BBC Radio 3's music programme Mixing It which covers jazz through to world music nd experimental techno, drum and bass. Compositions include: Whispers for Chiaroscuro Productions (director Richard Lingard); For television: The Prince of Atlantis (BBC/Canal + Ravensburger); The Peter Principle (Hat Trick/BBC, director, Nick Woods); A Horse's World (Wall To Wall/Channel Four, director, Steve Ruggi); Barnados Children (BBC, director Michael Davies); For Whom The Bull Tolls (Tiger Aspect/Channel Four); Fragile Earth (Channel Four); Love Me Love Me Not (TVS); Comic Relief (BBC, director, Micahel Davies); Crimestoppers (Carlton Television); Poets News (BBC, director, Michael Davies); Granada on Sunday (Granada Television); Dispatches: The Marchioness Tragedy, Dispatches: Lorries, Dispatches: Child Prostitution, Dispatches: Privateers, (Channel Four, director Alex Sutherland); Kingdoms of Survival (Anglia Television); Network First: Going to Chelsea (Hartswood/Carlton, director Michael Davies); Wildlife Showcase (BBC, director Tania Dorrity); Lifeline (BBC); It Happened Next Year (BBC); Style Challenge (BBC); For BBC Radio:

Superman 1, Batman, Spiderman. Independence Day, Superman 2 (all directed by Dirk Maggs, first four recorded and released). Address: c/o Soundtrack Music Management Ltd, 22 Ives Street, Chelsea, London SW3 2ND, England.

RUSSELL Paul Stuart Rupert, b. 13 Feb 1934, Nuthall, Nottingham, England. Musician (drums, New Orleans style). m. June Vivian Hill, 25 Jan 1958, 3 sons, 1 daughter. Education: Leicester School Of Architecture. Musical Education: Study of drumming in New Orleans, casual basis. Career: Member, Mercia Jazz Band (Nottingham), 1954-58; Then musician with various bands: Mike Casimir; Chris Blount; Chris Burke; Spirits Of Rhythm (own band); Oriole Brass Band (own band); Dave Donohoe; Louisiana Joymakers; Worked with Sammy Rimington, accompanied many visiting Americans including: Alton Purnell; Kid Thomas; Louis Nelson; Benny Waters; Herb Hall; Sam Lee; Captain John Handy; Played at Jazz Festivals in New Orleans; Nice; Ascona; Lugano; Milan; Breda; Cork; Gent; Currently with The Teddy Fullick Quintet and the Frank Brooker New Orleans Swingtet. Recordings: With Dave Donahoe, Jimmy Noone Jnr. Memberships: Musicians' Union; ARCUK. Hobbies: Walking; Cycling; DIY; Reconstructing old drums. Address: 105 Kimberley Road, Nuthall, Nottingham NG16 1DD, England.

RUSSELL Steve, b. 12 Apr 1965, Chelmsford, Essex, England. Composer; Musician (guitar, mandolin, charango, balalaika, keyboards); Vocalist. Musical Education: Royal College of Music. Career: Tours include: Switzerland, 1988; UK, 1988-89; Denmark, 1992; Spain, France, 1993. Compositions: Hug, for solo organ; Perplectomy, for trombone and piano; Tug, for 4 part choir; Genus, Nocturne, for piano solo; Numerous guitar solos and songs. Membership: Musicians' Union. Hobby: Art. Address: 97 Lower Anchor Street, Chelmsford, Essex CM2 0AU, England.

RUTHERFORD Mike. b. 2 Oct 1950, Guildford, Surrey, England. Musician (guitar, bass); Record Producer. Career: Musician, Genesis, 1970-; Also solo artiste, 1980-; Founder, producer, Mike and the Mechanics, 1986-; Numerous worldwide tours and major concerts including: Philharmonic Hall, New York; Madison Square Gardens, New York; Giants Stadium, New York; LA Forum. Recordings: Albums: with Genesis: Foxtrot, 1972; Selling England By The Pound, 1973; Genesis Live, 1973; The Lamb Lies Down On Broadway, 1974; Trick Of The Tail, 1976; Wind And Wuthering, 1977; Seconds Out, 1977; And Then There Were Three, 1978; Duke, 1980; Abacab, 1981; Three Sides Live, 1982; Genesis, 1983; Invisible Touch, 1986; We Can't Dance, 1991; with Mike And The Mechanics: Mike And The Mechanics, 1986; The Living Years, 1988; Word Of Mouth, 1991; Beggar On A Beach Of Gold, 1995; Hits, 1996; Solo albums: Small Creep's Day, 1980; Acting Very Strange, 1982; Singles: with Genesis: Abacab; Follow You Follow Me; Mama; Illegal Alien; Invisible Touch; Land Of Confusion; Tonight Tonight Tonight; That's All; Turn It On Again; with Mike And The Mechanics: Silent Running; All I Need Is A Miracle; The Living Years; Over My Shoulder; Also recorded on: Voyage Of The Acolyte, Steve Hackett, 1975; with John Verity: Interrupted Journey, 1983; Truth Of The Matter, 1985. Honours: Golden Ticket, Madison Square Gardens, 1986; First group, 5 Top 5 US singles from 1 album, 1986; Band of the Year, Rolling Stone Readers Poll, 1987. Current Management: Hit And Run Music, 30 Ives Street, London SW3 2ND, England.

RUTHERFORD Paul William, b. 29 Feb 1940, Greenwich, London, England. Musician (trombone, euphonium). Musical Education: RAF Musical Services; Guildhall School of Music Services. Career: 5 years, RAF Music Services; Leading member, avant garde jazz in Uk;

Numerous festivals in UK; International television, radio. Recordings: 3 solo albums; Tony Oxley Sextet; Mike Westbrook Bands; Spontaneous Music Ensemble; Globe Unity Orchestra; London Jazz Composers Orchestra. Honours: Melody Maker Poll, 3 years consecutively. Membership: Musicians' Union. Hobbies: Reading; Politics; Art. Address: Flat 2, 67A Shooters Hill Road, Blackheath, London SE3 7HS, England.

RUTKOWSKI Louise, b. 15 Mar 1964, Paisley, Scotland. Vocalist; Arts Administrator. Musical Education: Self-managed. Career: Worked with: Sunset Gun; This Mortal Coil; The Kindness Of Strangers; Nellee Hooper; Dave Stewart. Recordings: 1 album and 3 singles with Sunset Gun, 1984-86; 2 albums with This Mortal Coil, 1984-86; 1 album with The Kindness Of Strangers, 1990-93. Memberships: Musicians' Union; PRS. Hobbies: Theatre; Concerts; Working out; Art. Current Management: Self-managed, advised by Elliot Davis (manager of Wet Wet Wet). Address: 179 Newlands Road, Glasgow G44 4EU, Scotland.

RUTTEN Leo, b. 25 December 1957, Tongeren, Belgium. Engineer (Playing 2 Row, 3 Row, Melodeon, Bagpipes, Hurdy Gurdy, Flutes, Sax). m. Lieve Veulemans, 9 July 1988, 2 sons, 2 daughters. Education: Industrial Engineer Degree, Khlim Diepenbeek; Selftaught Melodeon; Summer course with Wilfrid Moonen, Riccardo Tesi; Hurdy-Gurdy with Evelyne Girardon. Appointments: Former Hurdy-Gurdy & Melodeon Player with Limburgs Dansorkest, 1984-93; TV Program 'De Milieu-Karavaan', 1987; Concert Zoo Leipzich DDR, 1988; Concert Brin Radio 3, 1993; Concert Festival St Chartier, 1993, France; Former Member, SLEMP; Current Member, Peper and playing with Poescafe, Concert Poescafe Ancienne Belgique, Brussels, 1998. Recordings: Volksmuziek, 1985; Limburgsdans Orkest, 1990; Folk Music from Belgium, 1997; Poescafe, 1997. Compositions: Biesenwals; Wals Voor Mathilde; De Groene Wants; De Gebroken Duimlus; Alvers in De Lucht. Membership: Belgian Bagpipe Player Association. Hobbies: Travelling; Sailing. Address: Rooierheide Straat 11, B3530 Diepenbeek, Belgium.

RYAN Barbara, b. 29 May 1950, Colombo, Sri Lanka. Celtic Musician; Singer. 2 sons. Education: Piano, 1961-64; BA, Languages, George Washington University, 1971; Voice Lessons, 1972-82. Career: Member, Celtic Group, Iona; Solo Performances: VOA, National Geographic Explorer Special '85; Formed Iona in 1986, Venues include: Folger Shakespeare Library, 1983, National Theatre, 1986, Barns of Wolftrap, 1986, Folk Clubs in England; Major US Celtic Festivals; President, Barnaby Productions Inc; Teacher of vocal technique, 1987-98. Recordings: Back to Our Roots, 1992; Holding Our Own, 1994; Nutmeg & Ginger, 1996; Celtic Festival Live! at Oatlands, 1997. Memberships: Folk Alliance; Washington Area Music Association. Hobby: Gardening. Current Management: Barnaby Productions Inc. Address: c/o PO Box 11160, Burke, VA 22009-1160, USA.

RYDELL Bobby (Robert Ridarelli), b. 26 Apr 1942, Philadelphia, Pennsylvania, USA. Singer; Musician (drums). Career: Drummer, Teen Club television show, 3 years; Duo with Frankie Avalon, 1954; Member, Rocco and the Saints; Solo artiste, 18 Top 40 hits, 1959-63; Film appearance, Bye Bye Birdy; Cabaret and club singer. Recordings: Albums include: Rydell At The Copa, 1961; Bobby Rydell/Chubby Checker, 1961; Bobby's Biggest Hits, 1961; All The Hits, 1962; Top Hits Of 1963, 1964; Forget Him, 1964; Singles include: Fatty Fatty; Kissin' Time; Wild One; Sway; Volare; Forget Him. Current Management: Fox Entertainment, 1650 Broadway, Ste 503, New York, NY 10019, USA.

RYDER Shaun, b. 23 Aug 1962, Little Hulton, Lancashire, England. Singer. 1 daughter. Career: Singer, Happy Mondays, 1985-93; Tours, UK, Europe and US; Support tours to: New Order, UK, 1987; Jane's Addiction, US, 1990; Concerts include: Glastonbury Festival, 1990; Great British Music Weekend, Wembley, 1990; Feile Festival, Tipperary, 1990; Cities In The Park Festival, Prestwich, 1990; Featured in film The Ghost Of Oxford Street, C4, 1990; Founder member, Black Grape, 1993-; Concerts include: T In The Park Festival, Glasgow, 1995; Numerous television and radio appearances. Recordings: Albums: with Happy Mondays: Squirrel And G Men 24 Hour Party People Plastic Face Carnt Smile (White Out), 1986; Bummed, 1988; Pills'N'Thrills And Bellyache, 1990; Live, 1991; Yes Please!, 1992; with Black Grape: It's Great When You're Straight... Yeah!, 1995; Singles: with Happy Mondays: Step On, 1990; Kinky Afro, 1990; Judge Fudge, 1991; with Black Grape: Reverend Black Grape, 1995; In The Name Of The Father, 1995. Kelly's Heroes, 1995; Honours: Best Indie Act, DMC World DJ Awards, 1991; BRIT Award Nominations: Best Newcomer, with Happy Mondays, 1991; with Black Grape, 1996. Address: c/o Fairwarning / Wasted Talent, The Plaza, 535 Kings Road, London SW10 0SZ, England.

RYDSKOV Claus, b. 3 Nov 1967, Glostrup, Copenhagen, Denmark.Singer; Songwriter; Musican (guitar, piano); Producer; Recording Engineer. m. Maja K A Rydskov, 16 Aug 1997. Education: Philosophy, University of Copenhagen. Musical Education: Organ lessons, 1978-82; Theory, percussion, piano and clarinet courses, Music School, 1989-94; Private singing lessons, 1989-97; Self-taught guitar. Career: Appearances on national radio and television, Denmark. Compositions include: Music scores for three short films. Recordings include: Claus Rydskov, untitled, 1994. Memberships: Danish Jazz, Beat and Folk Authors (DJBFA); Danish Musicians' Society (DMF). Hobbies: Football; Literature; Art. Current Management: Catharsis Publishing Ltd, Lyovej 4, 1 th, DK-2000 Frederiksberg, Denmark.

RYGERT Göran T, b. 1 May 1935, Tranås, Sweden. m. (1) 2 sons, (2) Janet A Rybka, 19 September 1997. Education: Master of Architecture, Chalmers University of Technology, Göteborg, Sweden; Private, with Torsten Rygert (father), Music Director and Composer. Career: Arranger and Composer, field of song - ballad and folk music; String Bass Musician, Swedish song - ballad artists, in many folk music orchestras, Sweden and USA; Appearances in Swedish, American and Russian Radio and TV; many song festivals; Producer, many song books, Freelance Editor, Warner/Chappell Music Scandinavia AB, Sweden. Compositions: A number of songs with words by Swedish Poets and Writers. Publications: Ölands Folkliga Visor och Melodier Genom Tiderna, 1987; Visor Kring Bordet, 1993; Festvisor, 1994; many other song-books, 1994-97. Honours: Royal Gustav Adolf's Academy Prize, 1991; Kalmar County Council Cultural Award, 1997. Memberships: Honorary Member, Visans Vänner; Swedish Composers of Popular Music; Georgia Music Industry Association; Balalaika and Domra Association of America. Current Management: Composing and arranging. Address: 4390 Ivywood NE, Marietta, Ga 30062, USA.

RYPDAL Terje, b. 23 Aug 1947, Oslo, Norway. Musician (piano, guitar); Composer. m. Elin Kristin Rypdal, 15 June 1988, 3 sons, 1 daughter. Education: Grunnfag in Music, University of Oslo. Musical Education: Composition Studies with Finn Mortensen. Career: Musician with The Vanguards, 1962-67; The Dream, 1967-69; Jan Garbarek Group, 1969-71; Leader, own groups, 1971-. Compositions: 5 symphonies, 2 operas. Recordings: Albums include: Bleak House, 1968; Ved Sorevatn (on album of Baden Baden Free Jazz Meeting), 1969; Terje Rypdal, 1971; What Comes After, 1974; Whenever I Seem To Be Far Away, 1974; Odyssey, 1975; After The Rain, 1976; Waves, 1978; Descendre, 1980; To Be Continued, 1981; Eos, 1984; Chaser, 1986; Works, 1989; Undisonus, 1990; QED, 1993; If Mountains Could Sing, 1995; Nordic Quartet (with John Surman, Karin Krog, Vigleik Storaas), 1995. Honours: Deutscher Schallplattenpreis. Membership: Norwegian Composers Guild. Hobby: Horses. Address: N-6380 Tresfjord, Norway.

S

SAARI Jarmo, b. 1970, Finland. Musician (guitar); Composer. Musical Education: Initially self-taught guitarist; Music theory, other instruments, Espoo Music College. Career: Leader, own bands from age 9; Member, groups ZetaBoo; XL. Compositions: Own works performed by XL and the UMO Big Band. Recordings: Albums: Debut album with ZetaBoo; XLent, XL 1995. Honours: BAT grant for big band work; Items performed by the UMO. Address: Jussaarenkuja 3 B 18, 00840 Helsinki, Finland.

SABIU Marco, b. Forli, Italy. Record Producer; Mixer; Songwriter. Career: Writer, Producer with Charlie Mallozzi, known as Rapino Brothers; Moved to London, 1992; Classically trained pianist; Programmer, mixer, producer of Pop/Dance music. Member of groups: Tabernacle; Rapination. Recordings: Albums for: Take That; Kylie Minogue; Dannii Minogue; Lulu; Kym Mazelle; Rozalla; Hit singles: Could It Be Magic, Take That; Rhythm Of The Night, Corona; What Is Love, Haddaway; I Know The Lord, Tabernacle; Love Me The Right Way, Rapination & Kym Mazelle; I Love My Radio, Taffy; Also singles for: Alicia Bridges; Heaven 17; Sparks. Honours: Brit Award, Single of Year, Take That; Triple Platinum album, Take That. Current Management: Stephen Budd Management. Address: 109B Regents Park Road, London NW1 8UR, England.

SADE (Helen Folasade Adu), 16 Jan 1959, Ibadan, Nigeria. Singer; Songwriter. Education: St Martin's School Of Art, London. Career: Member, Arriva; Member, Pride; Singer, founder, own band, Sade, 1983; Appearances include: Montreux Jazz Festival, 1984; Live Aid, Wembley Stadium, 1985; Film appearance: Absolute Beginners, 1987. Recordings: Singles: with Sade include: Your Love Is King, 1984; Smooth Operator (co-writer), 1984; The Sweetest Taboo, 1986; Never As Good As The First Time, 1986; Love Is Stronger Than Pride, 1988; Paradise, 1988; No Ordinary Love (use in film Indecent Proposal), 1993; Albums: Diamond Life, 1984; Promise, 1985; Stronger Than Pride, 1988; Love Deluxe, 1992; Best Of, 1994; Contributor, film soundtrack Absolute Beginners, 1987. Honours: BRIT Awards: Best British Album, Diamond Life, 1985; Best New Artist, 1986; Black Music Award, 1992. Current Management: Roger Davies Management, 15030 Ventura Blvd, Suite 772, Sherman Oaks, CA 91403, USA.

SAFARI Jean Bosco (Jean Vijdt), b. 10 May 1954, Rwanda. Singer; Songwriter. 1 son, 1 daughter. Career: Band member of A O; Solo artist, originally as Kid Safari; Billed as Jean Bosco Safari, 1995-. Recordings: Wow, 1991; Romantic Heroes, 1993; Little Boy Blue, 1995. Honour: Gold album: Romantic Heroes. Memberships: SABAM; ZAMU. Current Management: Tempo Belgium, Time Lecompte. Address: Krijslaan 61, 9000 Ghent, Belgium.

SAFFRON, b. 1969, Nigeria. Vocalist. Career: Former ballet dancer; Lead singer, N-Joi; Lead singer, Republica, 1994-. Recordings include: with Republica: Album: Republica, 1997; Hit singles: Ready To Go, 1997; Drop Dead Gorgeous, 1997. Address: c/o Rise Management Ltd, 5 Goldhawk Mews, London W12 8PA, England.

SAGER Carole Bayer, b. 1946, New York City, USA. Songwriter; Singer. m. Burt Bacharach. Musical Education: High School of Music and art, New York. Career: Songwriter, 1960s; Recording artiste, 1972-. Compositions: Groovy Kind Of Love (recorded by Patti Labelle, The Mindbenders, Phil Collins); That's What Friends Are For (raised 1 million dollars For AIDS charity, recorded by Dionne Warwick and Friends); Co-writer, Midnight Blue (rcorded by Melissa Manchester); When I Need You (recorded by Leo sayer); They're Playing Our Song, with Marvin Hamlisch; Arthur's Theme, with Burt Bacharach (recorded by Christopher Cross); Nobody Does It Better, Carly Simon (James Bond theme); On My Own, Patti Labelle, Michael McDonald. Recordings: Albums: Carol Bayer Sager, 1977; Too 1978; Sometimes Late at Night, 1981; Singles: You're Moving Out Today; Stronger Than Before (co-written with Bette Midler). Honour: Oscar, Arthur's Theme.

SAGOV Margo Leona, b. 22 Dec 1952, Cape Town, South Africa. Musician (guitar); Singer; Songwriter; Producer; Studio Designer. Education: Registered architect; Studied Architectural Association, London. Career: Founder member, group Amazulu; Guitarist, backing vocalist, 1982-86; Signed to Towerbell Records, 1983; Island Records, 1984-86; Desert Songs, ATV Music Publishing, 1984-89; Toured extensively, UK, Europe; Television appearances include: Top Of the Pops; The Young Ones; Tube; Radio sessions: John Peel; Annie Nightingale; David Jensen. Recordings: with Amazulu: Cairo; Smiley Stylee; Excitable; Moonlight Romance; Don't You Just Know It; Too Good To Be Forgotten; with Clicking The Mouse: I Must Be Dreaming; Numerous sessions include: The Beloved; Zeke Manyika. Memberships: Musicians' Union; Equity; ACTT as sound recordist; ARCUK. Hobbies: Photography; Travel; Cinema; Walking. Current Management: Self-managed. Address: 10 Brookfield Mansions, Highgate West Hill, London N6 6AS, England.

SAHM Doug, b. 6 Nov 1941, San Antonio, Texas, USA. Singer. Career: Recording debut (as Little Doug Sahm), 1955; Lead singer, The Pharoahs, 1958-65; Founder, the Sir Douglas Quintet; Founder, The Honkey Blues Band; Solo artiste; Film appearance, Cisco Pike. Recordings: Hit singles include: with the Sir Douglas Quintet: She's A Mover; The Rains Came; Mendocino. Albums: with Sir Douglas Quintet: Mendocino; Together After Five; Solo: Doug Sahm And Band, 1973; Texas Tornado, 1973; Groovers Paradise, 1974; Texas Rock For Country Rollers, 1976; Live Love, 1977; Hell Of A Spell, 1980; Texas Road Runner, 1986; Live Doug Sahm, 1987; Back To The 'Dillo, 1988; Juke Box Music, 1989; The Texas Tornados, 1990; Zone Of Our Own (as the Texas Tornadoes), 1991; Compilations: Sir Douglas - Way Back When He Was Just Doug Sahm, 1979; Sir Douglas - His First Recordings, 1981; Sir Doug's Recording Trip, 1989; The Best Of Doug Sahm And The Sir Douglas Quintet, 1991; The Last Real Texas Blues Band, 1995. Current Management: Gladrock Artists, 1222 16th Avenue S #21, Nashville, TN 37212, USA.

SAINSBURY Roy, b. 12 Apr 1942, Birmingham, England. Musician (guitar). m. Wendy Sainsbury, 2 sons, 1 daughter. Musical Education: Studied guitar with Reg Bishop and Jack Toogood. Career: Appeared on BBC Radio 2, Night Ride, Jazz Parade; Played with BBC Midland Radio Orchestra and New Millionairs Band; Solo appearances: BBC Radio 2 Arts Programme; Television in Netherlands and Malta. Compositions: Love And Sunshine; Crieff Melody; Wendy's Blues. Recordings: Album: Gentle Guitar. Membership: Musicians' Union. Hobbies: Kart racing; Walking; Travel. Current Management: Norman Phillips Agency, Birmingham, England. Address: 185 Birches Road, Codsall, Wolverhampton WV8 2JW, England.

SAINT-PIERRE Martin, b. 5 Aug 1945, Las Flores, Argentina. Composer; Musician (percussion). 1 son, 2 daughters. Education: Teacher. Musical Education: Studied in Brazil, Spain, Italy, Africa. Career: Moved from Buenos Aires to Paris, 20 years ago. Career: Opera Comique, Paris, Radio France; Ircam; Festivals all over the world, including: South America; Senegal; Uganda; Kenya; Missions ethnomusicals; Films: Dust; Special sounds, Stargate; Numerous concerts, France. Recordings: Solo: La Terre Des Quatre Coins; L'Incroyable Histoire d'un Tambour et Sa Memoire. Honours: Laureat Yehudi Menuhin Foundation. Memberships: La Terre des Quatre Coins; Percussion Sans Frontières. Current Management: Victoria Bengolea. Address: 116 Rue des Pyrénées, 75020 Paris, France.

SAINTE-MARIE Buffy, b. 20 Feb 1941, Saskatchewan, Canada. Singer; Songwriter; Musician (keyboards, guitar, mouthbow, computer). 1 son. Education: PhD, Fine Arts, University of Massachusetts (undergraduate, Philosophy). Musical Education: Self-taught. Career: Solo concerts worldwide, 1963-; Symphony concerts with: Calgary Symphony; National Arts Centre Orchestra; Vancouver Opera Symphony; Toured with various bands major cities, hundreds of Indian reservations, indigenous area worldwide. Recordings: 19 albums include: Coincidence And Likely Stories, 1992; Up Where We Belong, 1996. Honours: Academy Award as songwriter, Up Where We Belong, from film An Officer And A Gentleman; Billboard Best New Artist, 1964; Premico Award, Italy, 1972; Queen Elizabeth Jubilee Medal; Academy Award, 1981; Charles De Gaulle Grand Prix, Best International Artist, 1994; Saskatchewan Lifetime Achievement Award, 1994; Canada JUNO Hall of Fame, 1995. Memberships: ASCAP; AFofM. Hobbies: Digital music; Digital painting. Current Management: Jack Lentz, Einstein Brothers. Address: 20 Duncan Street, Toronto, Ontario M5H 3G8, Canada.

SAKAMOTO Ryûichi, b. 17 Jan 1952, Tokyo, Japan. Musician; Composer; Actor. m. Akiko Yano, 1979. Musical Education: Composition and electronic music, Tokyo College of Arts; Masters degree, 1976. Career: Founder, Yellow Magic Orchestra, 1978; Worked with David Sylvian, 1982-83; Solo recording artist, composer, 1982-; Actor, films including Merry Christmas Mr Lawrence, 1983; Worked with leading musicians including Adrain Belew; Andy Partridge; Iggy Pop; Brian Wilson; Thomas Dolby; Robbie Robertson; Conductor, arranger, music for Olympic Games opening ceremony, Barcelona, Spain, 1992. Albums: B-2 Unit, 1980; Hidariudeno (A Dream Of The Left Arm), 1981; Merry Christmas Mr Lawrence (film soundtrack), 1983; Coda, 1983; Ongaku Zukan (A Picture Book Of Music), 1984; Esperanto, 1985; Miraiha Yarô (A Futurist Chap), 1986; Media Bahn Live, 1986; Oneamisno Tsubasa (The Wings Of Oneamis), 1986; Illustrated Musical Encyclopedia, 1986; Neo Geo, 1987; The Last Emperor (film soundtrack), with David Byrne, Cong Su, 1987; Playing The Orchestra, 1988; Tokyo Joe, 1988; Sakamoto Plays Sakamoto, 1989; Grupppo Musicale, 1989; Beauty, 1989; Heartbeat, 1991; Neo Geo, with Iggy Pop, 1992; Sweet Revenge, 1994; Singles include: Bamboo Houses, with David Sylvian, 1982; Forbidden Colours, with David Sylvian, 1983; Field Work, with Thomas Dolby, 1986. Publications: Otowo Miru, Tokiwo Kiku (Seeing Sound and Hearing Time), with Shôzo Omori; Seldom-Illegal; Contributor, Album, Public Image Limited; Esperanto, Arto Lindesy. Honours: Academy Award, The Last Emperor, 1987. Current Management: David Rubinson Management, PO Box 411197, San Francisco, CA 94141, USA.

SALIM Abdel Gadir, b. Kordofan Province, Sudan. Singer; Musician (oud); Teacher. Musical Education: Institute for Music and Drama, Khartoum. Career: Headmaster in Chad; Regular national television and radio appearances popularizing traditional folk music; UK tour with Abdel Aziz el Mubarak and Mohammed Gubara, 1986. Recordings: with Mubarak and Gubara: The Sounds Of Sudan, 1991. Address: c/o World Circuit Records, 106 Cleveland Street, London W1P 5DP, England.

SALISBURY Malcolm John, b. 14 Aug 1952, Shropshire, England. Musician (bass guitar, six string guitar); Film Maker. m. Pam Moore, 7 Aug 1992. Education: HND Design/Communications. Career: 2 years with Pony Express, 1960s; Member, various bands, 1960s-70s; Currently organiser of Ironbridge Music Festival, which plays host to many bluegrass, cajun and roots artists from all over the world. Recordings: National and international video packages. Memberships: BBMA; EFDSS; NAFA. Hobby: Ki Aikido. Current Management: Self-managed. Address: 9 St Lukes Road, Doseley, Telford TF4 3BE, England.

SALLEY Jerry, b. Tennessee, USA. Singer; Songwriter; Producer. m. 3 daughters. Career: Regular performer, Nashville Showcase Circuit; 5 appearances, Grand Ole Oprey; Regular television appearances; Over 100 songs commercially recorded; Staff writer, Warner Chappell; Instructor, music business, Belmont University; Frequent panelist in music industry forums. Compositions: I Fell In The Water, John Anderson (Top 5); Breakin' New Ground, Wild Rose (Top 10); His Strength Is Perfect, Stephen Curtis Chapman; Songs for: Patty Loveless; The Hutchins; Woody Lee; Rhonda Vincent. Honours: Dove Award, for His Strength Is Perfect, 1990; Four Dove Award Nominations; 4 SESAC National Performance Activity Awards. Memberships: Gospel Music Association; Country Music Association; Nashville Songwriter's Association; SESAC. Current Management: SESAC. Address: 55 Music Sq E, Nashville, TN 37203, USA.

SALMINEN Simo, b. 16 Dec 1956, Finland. Musician (trumpet, flugelhorn). Career: Played with: Tapiola Big Band; Paradise (dance orchestra); UMO (New Music Orchestra); Went to US, 1978; Played with Thad Jones/Mel Lewis band; Buddy Rich; Machito; Eddie Palmieri; Gladys Knight And The Pips; 1 year in Broadway show; Returned to Finland, 1983; Teacher, Oulunkylä Jazz and Pop Institute; Played in UMO; Led UMO in performance of music of Bob Moses, 1984; Leader, Arctic Big Band, 1987-. Recordings: Albums with: Espoo Big Band; UMO; Mel Lewis; Buddy Rich. Address: Hämeentie 72 A 7, 00550 Helsinki, Finland.

SALMINEN Teemu, b. 5 June 1953, Finland. Musician (tenor saxophone, clarinet, reeds, flutes). Musical Education: Clarinet, flute, Sibelius Academy, 1974-78; Studied with Steve Grossman, New York, 1974-78; Studied with Bob Berg, 1982. Career: Member, Tapiola Big Band, as baritonist; Toured Scandinavia and played in London; Joined UMO (New Music Orchestra) and the Jukka Linkola Octet, 1976; Performed at festivals worldwide including: Detroit; Copenhagen; Stockholm; twice at Pori Jazz; Leader, Salminen trio and quartet, early 1980s; Represented Finland, EBU Big Band, London, 1982. Address: Tollinpolku 1 B, 00410 Helsinki, Finland.

SALT (Cheryl James), 28 Mar 1969, Brooklyn, New York, USA. Rapper. 1 daughter. Career: Formed US female rap duo Salt 'N' Pepa, 1985-; Performances include: Youth Ball, Washington DC, 1993; LIFEBeat AIDS benefit concert, 1993. Recordings: Hit singles include: My Mike Sounds Nice, 1987; Push It, 1988; Shake Your Thang (It's Your Thing), 1988; Twist And Shout, 1988; Expression, 1990; Do You Want Me, 1991; Let's Talk About Sex, 1991; You Showed Me, 1991; Start Me Up, 1992; Shoop, 1993; Albums: Hot Cool And Vicious, 1987; A Salt With A Deadly Pepa, 1988; Blitz Of Salt And Pepa Hits, 1991; Greatest Hits, 1991; Very Necessary, 1993; Contributor, Backyard, Pebbles, 1991. Honours: Platinum discs. Current Management: CD Enterprises, 105 Duane Street, Suite 46E, New York, NY 10007, USA.

SALT Jack (John Robert), b. 30 Jan 1920, Stafford, England. Musician (alto, baritone saxophones, clarinet, violin, viola). m. Katherine Barbara Barnard, 19 Aug 1948, 4 sons. Musical Education: Private tuition. Career: Sandy Powell

Road Show, 1941; Alan Green, 1942; Waldini Gypsy Band, including Ensa overseas tour of War Zones: Nort hAfrica; Middle East; Far East; Europe, 1943-49; Wally Fry, 1949; Don Rico, 1952; Benny Freedman, 1953-63; Model Railways specialist, 1957-94; Television and radio broadcasts: BBC; All India Radio; Radio Solent; Radio Victory; Southern TV; Currently, Havant Symphony Orchestra. Publications: Featured in Frontline Theatre, Waldini; Mentioned in Life and Death of Peter Sellers, Evans. Honours: Italy Star; Burma Star; 1939/45 War and Victory Medals. Memberships: Musicians' Union; National Federation of Musical Societies. Hobby: Chamber Music. Address: 171 Fratton Road, Portsmouth, Hampshire PO1 5ET, England.

SALUT Christian "Ton-Ton", b. 2 Feb 1953, Montauban, France. Jazz Musician (drums, percussion). 1 daughter. Education: Literature, University of Toulouse. Musical Education: Certificate of Completion, Drummers Collective, New York City. Career: Founder, Ton-Ton Quartet, 1980-84; Accompanist for soloists including: Sonny Stitt; Siegfried Kessler; Guy Lafitte; Michel Roques; Founder, Drumpact, 1986-; Tours: Germany; Switzerland; Austria; Netherlands; Denmark; Spain; Africa (Cameroon, Nigeria); Festivals with Drumpact include: Hyères; Madrid; Berlin; Marciac; Visits and concerts, Boston, New York; Tour with Drumpact and Ballet-Theatre Le Baobab, of Yaoundé; Freelance musician with Christian Escoudé; Jack Walrath; Glenn Ferris; Hein Van de Geyn; Also played with: Magali Piétri; Yéko-Lé-Bop; Black'n'Blue; Big Band 31 (including festivals: Vienna, Nice, Ramatuelle, Tarbes); Concerts, tours with: Christian Escoudé; Lou Bennett; Tony Pagnao; Jay Cameron; Daniel Huck; Peter King; Ted Curson; Eric Lelann; Andrew White; Turk Mauro; Jazz teacher, Conservatoire National de Région de Toulouse; Festival of Saint-Louis, Senegal, 1997-98. Composition: Creation for a Double Trio, in festival, Jazz sur Son 31, 1997. Recordings: with Drumpact: Journey Into The World; Percussion Unlimited; New Music; with Big Band 31: Big Band; Billie; Nobody Knows, with Magali Pietri; Mauresaca, 1993; Samantha's Dance, Steve Mabry, 1993; Ali-Aba, 1993; Abdu Salim Qintet, 1995; Street Music, Sonny Simmons, 1997; Don't Stop the Carnival, Hip Jazz Trio, 1997. Honour: Nominated to: Victoires de la Musique (Jazz). Membership: UMJ (Union of Jazz Musicians). Hobby: Literature. Current Management: Jazz Unit. Address: 8 Rue Lakanal, 31000 Toulouse, France.

SALUZZI Dino, b. Campo Tanta, Argentina. Musician (Bandoneon, Flute); Composer. Career: Several European, US and South American Tours including with George Gruntz, Mark Egan, Charlie Haden, Palle Mikkelbourg, Bob Moses and Enrico Rava. Recordings: Kultrum; Once Upon a Time; Volver; Andina. Current Management: Karen Kindig, c/o Blue Cat Agency, PO Box 399, Novato, CA 94948, USA.

SALWAY Colin James, b. 13 July 1960, London, England. Singer; Musician (trumpet). m. Jackie Carole Linger, 20 Nov 1979, 2 sons, 1 daughter. Musical Education: Currently in year II, Bsc Hons, Music, City University. Career: Bass singer with The Metrotones; 7th Hemsby Rock'n'Roll Festival, 1991; 2nd Rock'n'Roll stage show, Wembley, 1991; 8th Hemsby Rock'n'Roll Festival, 1992; TV documentary, Chrome Icons (Vamp films), 1993. Recordings: Singles: Possibility, 1991; Don't Take Your Love, 1992; Albums: Zoom Boom Zing, 1992; Compilation Albums: Lordy Hoody, 1992; Rock'n'Roll At The Turn Of The Century. Membership: Musicians Union. Hobbies: Cycling; Tennis; Football; Reading. Current Management: Paul Solomons. Address: 25 Marlborough Hill, Harrow HA1 1TX, England.

SAMBORA Richie, b. 1 July 1959. Musician (guitar); Singer; Songwriter. Career: Guitarist, US rock group Bon Jovi, 1983-; Appearances include: Regular worldwide tours; Donington Monsters Of Rock Festival, 1987; Moscow Music Peace Festival, 1989; Solo US tour, 1991; Solo appearance, Late Night With David Letterman, 1991; Solo performance, KISS Radio's 13th Anniversary Concert, Massachusetts, 1992; Numerous hit compositions with Jon Bon Jovi and Desmond Child. Recordings: Singles include: with Bon Jovi: You Give Love A Bad Name; Livin' On A Prayer; Wanted Dead Or Alive; Bad Medicine; Born To Be My Baby; I'll Be There For You; Miracle; Bed Of Roses; In These Arms; I'll Sleep When I'm Dead; I Believe; These Days; Solo: The Wind Cries Mary (featured in film The Adventures Of Ford Fairlane); Ballad Of Youth; Albums with Bon Jovi: Bon Jovi, 1984; 7800° Fahrenheit, 1985; Slippery When Wet, 1986; New Jersey, 1988; Keep The Faith, 1992; Crossroads, 1994; These Days, 1995; Solo albums: Stranger In This Town, 1991; Contributor to Tribute To Muddy Waters album, 1993; Undiscovered Soul, 1998. Honours include: Best Stage Performance, MTV Music Video awards, 1987; All Bon Jovi albums Gold or Platinum status. Current Management: Bon Jovi Management, 250 West 57th Street, Suite 603-5, New York, NY 10107, USA.

SAMPKOPF Kjell, b. 6 May 1952, Bærum, Norway. Composer; Percussionist. m. Mona Wladerhaug, 23 July 1994, 1 son. Education: Diploma in Composition, 1977, Degree in Percussion, 1978, Norwegian State Academy of Music; Studied jazz vibraphone at the Berklee College of Music, Boston, Massachusetts, 1979. Career: Timpanist, Trondheim Symphony Orchestra, Norway, 1974-75; Freelance Percussionist with the Norwegian Opera Orchestra and the Oslo Philharmonic Orchestra, 1975-82; Teacher of Percussion, East Norway Conservatory, 1979-85; Head of Percussion Department, 1988-, currently Professor, Norwegian State Academy of Music. Compositions: Associations, for large orchestra with live electronics and 4-channel tape, 1940; Invention No 5, for solo percussion and electronics, 1981; Aqua, for tape and two percussionists, 1986; Tide, for 5 tapes, 1990; Harstad, for symphonic band and percussion solist, 1991; Did You Sing This For Grieg?, electroacoustic, 1993; Mårådalen Walk, electroacoustic, 1994; Bergen, for woodwind quintet and two percussion players, 1996. Recordings: Invention No 5; On The Way; Because Of GH; Intention, solo percussion with electronics; Asphyxy; Positive Frustrations; Waltz Around The Circle; Intention; Blues Extract (with Sandvika Stornad); Aqua (with Rob Waring Duo); Did You Sing This For Grieg?, electroacoustic; Self-Portrait; Invention No 3, solo piece for snare drum; Tokke Kraftverk; Mårådalen Walk, electroacoustic. Publications: Practical Drum Method, Volume 1a, 1981. Honours: Concours International de Composition de la Ville du Havre, Special Mention of the Jury for Harstad. Memberships: Vice-President, Society of Norwegian Composers, 1988-90; President of the Board, Norwegian Music Information Centre, 1994-95. Address: Rudshagen 8, N-3430 Spikkestad, Norway.

SAMMES Michael William, b. 19 Feb 1928, Reigate, England. Singer. Founder, Mike Sammes Singers. Career: Principally providing vocal backing for hundreds of major artistes on records and television, plus Mike Sammes Singers solo albums; Radio includes: Sammes Songs series, BBC Radio 2. Publications: Three Piece Suite For Strings; Autobiography: Backing Into The Limelight. Honours: BASCA Gold Badge; Wavendon Vocal Ensemble of the Year, 1990. Memberships: PRS; MCPS; BASCA. Hobby: Writing music. Address: 1 Orchard Road, Reigate, Surrey RH2 0PA, England.

SAMUEL Julie, b. 15 May 1949, London, England. Music Manager. Widow, 1 daughter. Musical Education: Italia Conti Stage School, London. Career: Began as actress, singer, 1962; Appeared in over 100 television shows, 10 films, numerous stage plays; Started Music Management, 1980; Now Artist manager for rock group Mexico 70; Sarah Cracknell (vocalist with Saint Etienne); Janey Lee Grace (recording artist, television presenter, DJ for Virgin Radio); Donna Air, Janey Hoy, Vicky Taylor (vocal act from Byker Grove). Honours: Silver discs, So Tough; Fox Base Alpha; Platinum album, Smash Hits '91. Membership: IMF. Hobbies: Swimming; Films; Travel. Address: Diamond Sounds Music Management, The Fox and Punchbowl, Burfield, Old Windsor, Berks Sl4 2RD, England.

SAMUELS Elaine Mary, b. 17 Sept 1962, Hampton, Middlesex, England. Singer; Songwriter; Folk Blues and Bluegrass Musician (guitar, banjo, cittern, dulcimer, bodhran). m. Michael Paul Samuels, 23 July 1982, 1 son. Education: Electrical Engineering Degree. Career: Featured on HTV singing own songs; Appearances: Wire TV; BBC radio stations: Kent; Cambridge; Essex; Oxford; Suffolk; Kingston FM; Wey Valley Radio; Atlantis Radio, Belgium; Played at: Barbican; Marquee; Weavers; Half Moon; Mean Fiddler; Tour throughout UK, including Glastonbury, 1995. Recordings: Albums: Solo: Obsession; Reach Out For Me; Blue Skies; Dragonfire; with Now And Then: New Country; Best Of British Bluegrass, Volume 1. Honours: Second place, Leicester's Live At The Y (song competition). Membership: Musicians' Union. Hobbies: Canoeing; Art; Sport; Youth work. Address: 55C Sheen Road, Richmond, Surrey TW9 1YH, England.

SANBORN David, b. 30 July 1945, Tampa, Florida, USA. Musician (alto saxophone). Career: Member, Paul Butterfield group; Leading session player with artists including: David Bowie; James Taylor; Stevie Wonder; Albert King; Solo recording artiste, 1975-. Recordings: Albums: Taking Off, 1975; David Sanborn, 1976; Promise Me The Moon, 1977; Heart To Heart, 1978; Hideaway, 1980; Voyeur, 1981; As We Speak, 1982; Backstreet, 1983; Straight To The Heart, 1984; Double Vision (with Bob James), 1986; A Change Of Heart, 1987; Close Up, 1988; Another Hand, 1991; Upfront, 1992; Hearsay, 1994; Pearls, 1995; Songs From The Night Before, 1996; Honours: Grammy Award, Voyeur, 1982. Address: c/o Patrick Rains and Associates, 1543 7th Street, 3rd Floor, Santa Monica, CA 90401, USA.

SANBOWER Jack Douglas, b. 14 Sept 1960, Waynesboro, Pennsylvania, USA. Bluegrass Musician (banjo, guitar, bass). m. Albina Marie, 19 Feb 1983, 1 son, 1 daughter. Education: AA Degree Data Processing. Musical Education: Self-taught. Career: Performed at Bluegrass festivals, USA, include: Gettysburg, Pennsylvania; Bass Mountain, North Carolina; Lazy River, New York; Wind Gap, Pennsylvania; Wellsboro, Pennsylvania. Recordings: Four Leaf Clover Breakdown, 1983; Before The Weekend's Over, 1986; Jack In the Box, 1989; Traveling Down This Lonesome Road, 1991; Just Monkeyin' Around, 1990; Throwing Caution To The Wind, 1991; Finger Pickin' For Supper, 1992; Let Loose, 1993; Thinking Of Old Memories, 1994. Memberships: International Bluegrass Music Association; Tri-State Bluegrass Association. Hobbies: Computers; Fishing; Couch potato. Current Management: Self-managed. Address: 14461 Edgemont Road, Smithsburg, MD 21783, USA.

SANCHEZ David (Jose David Sanchez De Leon), b. 3 Sept 1968, Hato Rey, Puerto Rico. Jazz Musician (tenor/soprano saxophones). Education: Psychology, University of Puerto Rico. Musical Education: Rutgers University. Career: Member, Eddie Palmieri Group, 1988-90; Member, Dizzy Gillespie and the United Nation

Orchestra, 1991; Performances include: Live The Future - An Evening with Dizzy Gillespie and Miriam Makeba, 1991; Member, Phillip Morris Super Band, 1992; Slide Hampton and the Jazz Masters, 1992-; Roy Hargrove's Crisol, 1997; Also appeared on CNBC television, 1995. Recordings: To Bird With Love, 1992; The Departure, 1994; Sketches Of Dreams, 1995; Street Scenes Bird Songs, 1997. Memberships: AFofM; BMI. Hobbies: Films; Multicultural music research. Current Management: Charismic Productions, 2604 Mozart Place W., Washington, DC 20009, USA.

SANCHEZ Paco, b. 7 June 1956, Murcia, Spain. Musician (drums). Education: University of Human Sciences. Musical Education: Paris VII Conservatory. Career: Played with the International Orchestra of Tchicai John in Denmark and Morocco; Played in West Africa; Benin; Festival of Brazzville, Bangui; Trio Soledad, France. Recordings: Soledad, with Carlos Acciari and Michel Fernandez. Honours: First Excellency Prize. Membership: SACEM. Current Management: RDC Records. Address: 16 Rue Du Transvaal, 75020 Paris, France.

SANDERS Kevin Bruce, b. 22 May 1962, Torquay, Devon, England. Freelance Musician (double bass, bass guitar); Arranger. m. 6 June 1987, 1 daughter. Education: College. Musical Education: Private classical double bass tuition. Career: Started with Dennis Rowland Trio; Later joined Lawrie Dixon Trio; Since worked with: Mornington Lockett; Kathy Stobart; Don Weller; Michael Hashim; Tony Lee; Stan Grieg; Worked with Dave Thompson Quartet, 1992-94; Lectured in bass studies at Dartington College of Arts; Runs successful 7-piece soul and blues review Rhythm Machine and contemporary jazz ensemble. Recordings: Rayas Pictures, 1992. Honours: Musicians' Union Award, Most Promising Bass Player, 1984. Membership: Musicians' Union. Hobbies: Cooking; Motorcycling. Current Management: Bette Holman (For Rhythm Machine); Music à La Carte Ent. Services (for self). Address: 30 Elm Park, Paignton, Devon TQ3 3QH, England.

SANDERS Steve, b. Richland, Georgia, USA. Singer; Musician (guitar); Songwriter. m. Janet Sanders (divorced). Career: Guitarist, singer, Oak Ridge Boys, 1987-; Film appearance: Hurry Sundown, 1967; Television appearances include: Gunsmoke; Noon Wine; Appeared in Broadway production The Yearling. Compositions include: Live In Love, 1982. Address: c/o Don Light Talent, Nashville, USA.

SANDERS Tim Bryan, b. 16 Apr 1962, Stoke-on-Trent, Staffordshire, England. Singer; Songwriter. m. Jynine James, 1 May 1993, 3 sons. Education: Music and Law Studies at Cauldon College. Musical Education: Guitar tuition; Private tuition for music reading, Cauldon College. Career: Formed the City Zones in 1979; Re-formed in 1992; Appeared in BBC Radio live sessions; Appeared on television with Toyah; Supported many early 1980's artists; Actor, Joy Swift's original Murder Weekends, German Satellite TV and BBC TV, 1990-91. Recordings: La Maison De l'Amour, The City Zones, 1992; Live At The BBC, The City Zones, 1992; Born To Win; Knock Me Down Pick Me Up; Pain Of Love; When I Dream; Spoils Of Humanity; Past Shadows. Publications: Collections of works. Honours: Presentation Disc for sales of La Maison De l'Amour and Pain of Love (released by Jynine James and Peter Frampton), Mr and Mrs Music Publishing, 1992, 1993. Memberships: PRS; Guild of International Songwriters. Hobbies: Badminton; Listening to music. Current Management: Fast Tracks Records; Mr and Mrs Music Publishing; Joy Swift. Address: c/o Fast Tracks Records, Golden Gate Centre, Gainge Road, Towyn, Abergele, Clwyd LL22 9HU, North Wales.

SANDKE Randy, b. 23 May 1949, Chicago, Ilinois, USA. Composer; Arranger; Musician (trumpet). m. Karen Kelly, 15 September 1990. Education: University of Chicago Lab School; Indiana University; Studied TPT with Renold Shilke, Vince Penzerella; Arranging with Oliver Nelson; Composing with Henry Brant and Easley Blackwood. Career: TPT with Benny Goodman, 1985-86, with Buck Clayton, 1986-90; Concord Recording Artist, 1993-; Written several suites for Carnegie Hall Jazz Band; Performed on soundtracks of 3 Woody Allen films. Compositions: Orphic Mystery, 1997; Overture For the Year 2000, 1997. Recordings: NY Stories, 1986; I Hear Music, 1993; Get Happy, 1994; The Chase, 1995; Calling All Cats, 1996; Awakening, 1997. Publications: Introduction to Metatonal Music, 1997; Bix Beiderbecke From a Musician's Perspective, 1998; Annual Review of Jazz Studies. Memberships: National Academy of Recording Arts and Sciences Inc; IAJRC; Musicians Union Local 802. Address: 213 1/2 Bergen Street, Brooklyn, New York, 11217, USA.

SANDOVAL Arturo, b. 6 Nov 1949, Artemisia, Cuba. Musician (trumpet); Professor. m. Marianela, 17 Oct 1975, 1 son. Musical Education: National Music Institute, Havana, Cuba. Career: Full Professor (tenure), Florida International University; Musician; Appearances: with Irakere, 1972-81; World tours, 1980-; United Nations Band; Sandoval Group, 1981; Dizzy Gillespie, 1987-91; Television includes: Super Bowl Halftime Event, 1995; King Orange Disney New Year's show, 1995; Tonight Show; David Letterman; Arsenio Hall; HBO; CNN; Summit Of The Americas, Grammy Awards; Oscar Awards with Celine Dion. Recordings: Live At Royal Festival Hall, Dizzy Gillespie; Danzón; Flight To Freedom; Dream Come True; I Remember Clifford; Latin Train; The Classical Album; Swinging; Sandoval's Hot House; Perez Family soundtrack; Mambo Kings Soundtrack. Publications: Hal Leonard 4 Trumpet Method Books. Honours: Grammy, Best Latin Album, Irakere II; Danzon; 11 Grammy Nominations; 2 Billboard International Jazz, Jazz Central Station Best Latin Jazz Artist Award; Disney Music Hall Of Fame, 1994; 4 Scholarships given in his name at various USA universities. Memberships: ITG; IAJE; NARAS. Hobby: Baseball. Current Management: Carl Valldejuli, Turi's Music Ent Inc. Address: 103 Westward Drive, Miami Springs, FL 33166, USA.

SANDREN Heikki, b. 1 June 1960, Finland. Musician (drums). Musical Education: Clarinet and drums; Sibelius Acadmey, Helsinki. Career: Began in music shop, early 1980s; Became professional musician; Member, Pekka Toivanen quartet; Played for Severi Pyysalo's No Hope Band; Stayed with Pyysalo's reformed band The Front; Played on tour with leading Finnish trumpeter Markku Johansson. Address: Lönnrotinkatu 23 B 31, 00120 Helsinki, Finland.

SANDS Colum, b. 26 May 1951, Newry, Ireland. Singer; Songwriter; Musician. m. Barbara Wendel, 3 May 1978, 3 sons, 1 daughter. Career: Tours with Sands Family, 1972-, USA (including Carnegie Hall), Canada, Ireland, England, Germany, Belgium, France, Spain, Portugal, Netherlands, Switzerland, Austria, Italy, Poland, Luxembourg. Compositions: Solo albums: Unapproved Road, 1981; March Ditch, 1989; All My Winding Journeys, 1996; Songs include: Whatever You Say, Say Nothing; Almost Every Circumstance; The Man with the Cap; Looking the Loan of a Spade. Honour: Living Tradition Award, Glasgow, 1996. Memberships: PRS; MCPS. Current Management: Spring Records. Address: 50 Shore Road, Rostrevor, County Down, BT34 3EW, Ireland.

SANDS Tommy, b. 19 December 1945, Mayobridge, Co Down, Northern Ireland. Singer; Songwriter; Musician (Guitar, Whistle, Banjo,

Bodhran). m. Katrine Bescond, 1 son, 1 daughter. Education: Latin, Philosophy, Newry St Colman's College, St Patrick's Carlow. Career: Began playing with Sands Family, first album, 1968; Concerts, Carnegie Hall, New York, USA, 1972; Federick Palast, Berlin, 1974; Moscow Olympic Stadium, solo; Numerous world tours including appearances with Miriam Makeba; Harry Belafonte; Pete Seeger; Mikis Theodorakis. Compositions: There Were Roses; Daughters and Sons; Dresden; Music of Healing, with Pete Seeger; Sudako and 1000 Paper Cranes; Sarajevo, with Vedran Smailovic and Joan Baez. Recordings: 5 solo albums: Singing of the Times, 1985; Beyond the Shadows, 1992; Down By Bendys Lane, 1993; Hedges of County Down, 1994; The Hearts A Wonder, 1995; 20 albums with the Sands Family. Publication: Tommy Sands Songbook, 1986. Honours: Best Irish Single of the Year, There Were Roses, 1986; Living Tradition Award, 1995. Memberships: PRS; MCPS; MIMA. Hobbies: Sport; Community Work. Current Management: Katrine Bescond, Spring Records. Address: 50 Shore Road, Rostrevor, County Down, BT34 3AA, Northern Ireland.

SANGARE Oumou, b. 1968, Bamako, Mali. Singer; Songwriter. m. Ousmane Haidara, 1 child. Career: Began singing age 5; First performance, Stade des Omnisports, age 6; Member, National Ensemble of Mali, Djioliba percussion, 1986-89; Solo artiste, with own backing group, 1989-; Concerts: Regular tours, West Africa; Europe; First US concert, 1994; Radio includes: BBC Radio 1 session, Andy Kershaw; Television includes: The Late Show, BBC2; Campaigner, Women's Rights, Mali. Recordings: Moussolou (Women), 1990; Ko Sira (Marriage Today); New album being recorded, (provisional title, Inshallah); Also recording with Ali Farka Touré. Honours: Best Selling African Album of Year, Moussolou, 1990; European World Music Album of the Year, Ko Sira, 1993; Performance of the Year, 1993; Numerous African Music Awards. Current Management: Wim Westerweldt. Address: c/o World Circuit Records, 106 Cleveland Street, London W1P 5DP, England.

SANGER Keith, b. 13 Jul 1943, United Kingdom. Musicologist. m. Bella Lab, 31 May 1968. Education: Nautical Studies; Sciences; Medical Technologist. Career: Health Service. Publication: Co-author, Tree Of Strings, a history of the harp in Scotland; About 40 articles; Papers on subjects of piping and harping. Memberships: The Piobaireachd Society; Cumann Cheol Tire Eireann; The Lowland and Borders Pipers' Society. Hobbies: Research in piping and harping in Scotland and Ireland. Address: 11 Greenhill Place, Edinburgh EH10 4BR, Scotland.

SANLUCAR Manolo, b. 24 Nov 1943, Sanlucar De Barrameda, Cadiz, Spain. Composer; Musician (Flamenco Guitar). Education: Learnt to play guitar with father (famous Flamenco Guitarist). Career: Musical Director, Sevillanas A Carlos Saura, film; La Gallarda, Rafael Alberti. Compositions: Medea, composed for Ballet Nacional De Espana; Tauromagia; Solea. Honours: Prize Spanish Guitarist, Recor World, USA, 1978; First Prize, Mundial Competition of Guitar, Italy, 1972. Current Management: Intercambio De Cultura Y Arte. Address: Goya 99, Esc A - 4 Dcha, 28009 Madrid, Spain.

SANQUEST Nick, b. 20 Dec 1956, Cork, Ireland. Musician (guitar, bass guitar); Singer; Writer. m. Maria, 13 Aug 1988, 1 daughter. Musical Education: Self-taught. Career: Radio appearances and concerts with group Capricorn; Support tours to artists including Dollar; Solo singer and songwriter on London circuit. Memberships: PRS; BASCA; Equity; Musicians' Union. Hobbies: Tennis; Reading. Current Management: Self-managed. Address: c/o 6 Camden Terrace, London NW1 9BP, England.

SANSOM Frank Roger Charles, b. 3 Dec 1946, London, England. Company Director. m. Frances Sansom, 27 Mar 1976, 2 sons, 1 daughter. Education: Christopher Wren, Gloucestershire and Wimbledon College of Art. Musical Education: Jack Jackson: Ready Steady Go; 6 5 Special. Career: Art Director, B&C Records, 1971; Marketing Director, Charisma Records, 1973-78; Management, 1979-81; Set up First Bill Ltd (First Independent Tele-Sales Team), 1981; First Strike, 1985; Sold companies to Stylus Music, 1987; TV Marketing Consultant, 1987-90; Managing Director, shareholder, Pulse Records launched 1990-1995. Membership: BPI. Hobbies: Swimming; Horse racing; Football; Rugby. Address: 53A Hereford Road, Bayswater, London, W2 5BB, England.

SANTAMARIA Mongo (Ramón), b. 7 Apr 1927, Havana, Cuba. Bandleader. Career: Played with first charanga band, led by Gilberto Valdés; Also played with Pérez Prado; Tito Puente, 1951-57; Formed own charanga and Latin fusion groups; Developed artists including Chick Corea; La Lupe; Herbert Laws; Marty Sheller. Recordings: Albums include: Changó, 1955; Yambú, 1958; Concert On The Campus, 1960; Our Man In Havana, 1960; Live And Direct, 1960; Más Sabroso, 1962; Viva Mongo!, 1962; Go, Mongo!, 1962; Mongo Introduces La Lupe, 1963; Mongo At The Village Gate, 1963; Mongo Explodes, 1964; El Pussy Cat, 1965; La Bamba, 1965; Hey! Let's Party, 1966; El Bravo!, 1966; Mongo Santamaria, Explodes At The Village Gate, 1967; Soul Bag, 1968; Stone Soul, 1969; Workin' On A Groovy Thing, 1969; Feelin' Alright, 1970; Mongo '70, 1970; Mongo At Montreux, 1971; At Yankee Stadium, 1974; Dawn (Amanecer), 1977; Red Hot, 1979; Mambo Show, 1990; Live At Jazz Alley, 1990; Other recordings with: Tito Puente; Cal Tjader; Joe Loco; Bob James and Charlie Palmieri; Toots Thielemans and Dizzy Gillespie; Justo Betancourt; Fania All Stars. Honours: Grammy Award, Dawn (Amanecer), 1977. Current Management: Jack Hooke, 568 Broadway, Suite 806, New York, NY 10012, USA.

SANTANA Carlos, b. 20 July 1947, Autlan de Navarro, Mexico. Musician (guitar); Vocalist. m. Deborah, Apr 1973. Career: Played Tijuana nightclubs; Recorded with Mike Bloomfield and Al Kooper; Founder, Santana Blues Band, 1966; Played club circuit, San Francisco; Major concerts include: Woodstock, 1969; Texas International Pop Festival, 1969; Bath Festival, 1970; Crystal Palace Garden Party, 1977; California Jam II, audience of 250,000, 1978; US Festival, 1982; Support to Bob Dylan, Europe, 1983; Live Aid, Philadelphia, 1985; Peace Concert, Moscow, 1987; Freedom World Tour, 1987; Rock In Rio II Festival, Brazil, 1991; Laughter, Love And Music memorial concert, San Francisco, 1991; Performed/recorded with: Buddy Miles; McCoy Tyner; Jose Feliciano; Herbie Hancock; Wayne Shorter and Alice Coltrane; Aretha Franklin; Producer, music for La Bamba, 1986; Founder, own record company Guts And Grace, 1989. Recordings: Albums include: Santana, 1969; Abraxas, 1971; Santana III, 1971; Carlos Santana And Buddy Miles, Live!, 1972; Caravanserai, 1972; Love Devotion Surrender, with Mahavishnu John McLaughlin, 1973; Welcome, 1973; Santana's Greatest Hits, 1974; Illuminations, with Alice Coltrane, 1974; Borboletta, 1974; Amigos, 1976; Festival, 1977; Moonflower, 1977; Inner Secrets, 1978; Orness/Silver Dreams - Golden Reality, 1979; Marathon, 1980; Zebop!, 1981; Havana Moon, 1983; Beyond Appearances, 1985; Blues For Salvador, 1987; Viva Santana, 1988; Spirits Dancing In The Flesh, 1990; Milagro, 1992; Sacred Fire, 1993; Brothers, 1994; Dance Of The Rainbow Serpent (box set), 1995; Contributor, The Live Adventures Of Al Kooper And Mike Bloomfield, 1969; Featured on: The Healer, John Lee Hooker, 1989; Tribute To Muddy Waters, 1993; Singles include: Evil Ways, 1970; Black Magic Woman, 1971; Oye Como Va, 1971;

Everybody's Everything, 1971; She's Not There, 1977; Stormy, 1979; Winning, 1981; Hold On, 1982. Honours: Grammy Award, Best Rock Instrumental Performance, 1989; Bay Area Music Awards: Outstanding Guitarist, 1992; Musician Of The Year, 1993; Legend Award, Nosotros Golden Eagle Awards, 1992; Gold Medal Award, 1977; Numerous Gold discs. Current Management: Santana Management. Address: P O Box 10348, San Rafael, CA 94912-0348, USA.

SANTOS Alejandro, b. 11 April 1956, Buenos Aires, Argentina. Musician (Flute); Composer. 2 sons, 2 daughters. Education: Berklee College of Music; Juan José Castro Conservatory. Career: Performances at: Mar del Plata International Jazz Festival, Hatch Shell, La Pena; Various other venues in US, Europe and South America; Several TV appearances in US and South America. Recordings: Candombe de Parque Chacabuco; 5 Carnavales 4; Night Reflections. Current Management: Karen Kindig. Address: c/o Blue Cat Agency, PO Box 399, Novato, CA 94948, USA.

SAPP Dean, b. 5 Aug 1950, Wilmington, USA. Musician (banjo, guitar, fiddle, mandolin, dobro, bass, auto harp, dulcimer, peddle steel). m. Linda R Dubree, Nov 1985, 1 son, 1 daughter. Musical Education: Musical family background. Career: 9 recorded projects being played in: Japan; Germany; USA; Canada; Australia; England. Recordings: Albums: Can't You Hear Me Calling; Hard Times Have Been Here; Last Public Hanging; Long Black Veil; Tears Of Joy; Above The Dixie Line; You've Never Had The Blues. Membership: IBMA. Hobby: Antique cars. Current Management: Old Train Music. Address: 2711 Augustine Herman Highway, Chesapeake City, MD 21915, USA.

SAPUNDZIJEV Mary, b. 16 Feb 1965, Melbourne, Victoria, Australia. Musicologist; Musician (piano). Musical Education: Piano lessons; MA (Music Major), 1986, BA Hons (Music), 1988, PhD (Music), 1997, Monash University. Career: Pianist, Accompanist, Musicologist, Dancer and Choreographer; Artistic Director, Folk dance company, 1977-92; Film appearance, The John Sullivan Story, 1979; Stage appearances, Sale of the Century, 1983-86; Production Assistant, ethnic radio, Victoria; Dancer and Co-organiser of cultural festivals throughout Australia, including Multicultural Arts festival, Victoria, and Miss Yugoslav of Australia. Publications: Politics in Music - Music of Politics: The Choral Miniature Repertoire of First Generation Macedonian Composers, forthcoming. Honours: Shared Ernst Morawetz Prize for Music, Monash University Music Department, 1987; Australian Postgraduate Research Award, 1988-1991; Various certificates, tokens and awards from ethnic artistic associations throughout Australia. Memberships: Australian Music Centre; Australian Musicological Society; International Council for Traditional Music; International Musicological Society; Board Member, Multicultural Arts Vic, 1984-89; Artistic Director, Yugoslav Cultural Artistic Association, Melbourne, 1984-92. Hobbies: Composition: Songwriting; Arranging. Address: 11 Anne Street, North Blackburn, Victoria 3130, Australia.

SARA K, b. 16 May 1956, Dallas, Texas, USA. Singer; Songwriter; Musician (4 string guitar). Education: Art, music studies. 1 daughter. Career: Chesky recording artist; PBS Radio Australia; Mountain Stage; US and international airplay. Recordings: Gypsy Alley; Closer Than They Appear; Play On Words; Fourth album in progress. Honours: Gypsy Alley, received 8 awards from New Mexico Music Industry Coalition including Best Album, 1990; Audio-Ohr award, Grammy, Play On Words album, 1994. Hobbies: Hiking; Skiing; Windsurfing; Painting; Being mom. Current Management: Chesky Records, New

York, New York. Address: PO Box 696, Ruidoso, NM 88345, USA.

SARIC Stanko, b. 26 June 1960, Stitar, Croatia. Musician (tambura - national instrument). m. Verca Saric (Salopek), 10 Nov 1984, 1 son, 1 daughter. Education: Engineer of Architecture. Musical Education: Self-taught. Career: Appearances with group: Zlatni Dukati (Golden Coins), in biggest concert halls in Croatia; Tours all around the world: USA; Canada; Australia; Western Europe. Recordings: Patriotic songs: Don't Touch My Fields; Croatia In Me; Singing The Song About Croatia; Other popular songs: Crying Because of You; Tena; Marijana; High Road; Anica; To Whom Could I Give My Young Years; 13 albums; Christmas Songs; Classical Music. Honours: 10 Golden Records, many other awards. Membership: Croatian Musical Union. Hobby: Horse riding. Current Management: Josip Ivanovic. Address: Zlatni Dukati, Zatisje 8E, 41000, Zagreb, Croatia.

SARJEANT Derek, b. 7 June 1932, Chatham, Kent, England. Folk Singer; Musician (concertina, guitar, trumpet). m. (1) Diane Doherty, 23, Sept 1966, 2 sons, (2) Hazel King, 10 Sept 1977, 1 son, 1 daughter. Education: Kingston College. Career: Member, jazz bands, leader, Golden Gate Jazzmen, 1950s; Pioneer, British Folk revival, 1960s; Organiser, one of Britain's largest Folk clubs, Surbiton and Kingston for 14 years; Assisted with Organisation of English Folk Dance and Songs Society's First Folk Festival, 1965; Radio and television, all British stations including: Hootenanny Show; Folk In Focus; Television commercials on all British independent channels, also USA; Tours solo, also with wife, Hazel: Folk clubs, concerts, festivals in UK, Europe, America; Work as session musician; Teaches Folk guitar at Adult Education Centre. Recordings: 24 albums, British and German labels. Publications: Books with records: How Do You Do, stages 1-5 (English Folksongs For German Schools). Honours: First English Folk singer booked in Dublin Folkclub, 1962; Melody Maker Folk Medal of Year, Best First Record, Derek Sarjeant Sings English Folksongs, 1962; Represented Britain, British Week, Stockholm, Sweden, 1968; Membership: Musicians' Union. Hobbies: Collecting old musical instruments; Photography. Current Management: Assembly Artistes. Address: 4 Coneygar House, Coneygar Park, Bridport, Dorset DT6 3BA, England.

SARJEANT Hazel, b. 11 Oct 1948, London, England. Folk Singer; Musician (guitar, concertina). m. Derek Sarjeant, 10 Sept 1977, 1 son, 1 daughter. Education: Wimbledon College Of Art; St Martin's College Of Art; BA (Fine Arts). Musical Education: Trained in various choirs. Career: Resident singer, Surbiton Folkclub, 6 years; Frequent tours, concerts, festivals, folkclubs, UK, Europe and US; National radio and television; Film music for US. Recordings: 14 albums, cassettes, UK and German labels. Honour: National Folk and Beat Final, Hammersmith Town Hall, 1967. Memberships: Musicians' Union; Royal College of Church Music. Hobbies: Painting; Pottery; Travel. Current Management: Assembly Artists, 4 Coneygar House, Coneygar Park, Bridport, Dorset DT6 3BA, England.

SARMANTO Heikki, b. 22 June 1939, Finland. Composer; Musician (piano). Musical Education: Music and language, Helsinki University and Sibelius Academy, 1962-64; Lessons with Margaret Chaloff, Berklee College of Music, Boston, US, 1968-71. Career: Regular visits to East Coast of US; Own ensemble became UMO (New Music Orchestra); Played Jazz Mass, Newport Festival, 1979. Compositions include: New Hope Jazz Mass (premiered in New York); Jazz Mass; Jazz opera; Songs to words by Finnish poets including: Edith Södergran; Laura Vita; Eino Leino; 3 suites for solists: Maija

Hapuoja; Juhani Aaltonen; Pekka Sarmanto; Suomi, suite for jazz ensemble and strings; Passions Of Man, ballet suite; Music for radio stories by Robert Shure: Man With A Sax; Felix The Great; Hearts (commissioned by WHO), 1995. Honours include: First prize, Jazz composition contest, Minneapolis, 1961; Yrjö Award, Finnish Jazz Federation, 1970. Address: Kankurinkatu 8 B 14, 00150 Helsinki, Finland.

SARMANTO Pekka, b. 15 Feb 1945, Finland. Musician (bass). Musical Education: Sibelius Academy. Career: One of Finland's most recorded artists; Played with: Eero Koivisoinen, 1965-; Long term partnership playing with brother Heikki Sarmanto; Played at The Groovy Club, with artists including: Benny Carter; Toots Thielmans; Clifford Jordan; Joe Newman; Bob Berg; Tom Harrell; Member of UMO (New Music Orchestra), 1975-; Accompanist to numerous visiting foreign musicians; Festival appearances include: Warsaw; London; Paris; Newport; Montreal; Soloist, performance Heikki Sarmanto's suite, Song For My Brother, 1982; Duo with Juhani Aaltonen, 1980s. Recordings include: To A Finland Station, with Dizzy Gillespie and Arturo Sandoval, 1982. Honour: Yrjö Award, Finnish Jazz Federation, 1978. Address: Albertinkatu 5 B 27, 00150 Helsinki, Finland.

SAROSI Bálint, b. 1 January 1925, Csikrákos, Harghita, Romania. Ethnomusicologist. m. Benkö Jolán, 18 October 1952, 2 daughters. Education: PhD, University; Composition and Musicology, Liszt Ferenc High School of Music, Budapest, Hungary. Career: Research Fellow, Institute for Musicology, Budapest, 1956-; Director, Ethnomusicological Section, 1974-, retired, 1988; Lectures on folk music, Hungarian Radio, weekly program, 1969-87; Guest Professor, University of Innsbruck, 1985-86, University of Göttingen, 1989, 1994; Invited Lecturer, most countries of Europe and USA, Japan, Armenia and Samarkand, Jerusalem. Recordings: Hungarian Instrumental Folk Music, 3 discs, 1980; Anthology of Hungarian Folk Music V and VI, 1993, 1995. Publications: Die Volksmusikinstrumente Ungarus, 1967; Gypsy Music, 1978; Folk Music, 1986; Amagyar népzene, 1996. Honours: Erkel Prize, 1976; Order of Labour, Golden Degree, 1988; Middle Cross of the Order of Hungarian Republic, 1995. Membership: Executive Board, International Council for Traditional Music, 1978-91. Address: Aldás u 11, H-1025 Budapest, Hungary.

SARPILA Antti Juhani, b. 11 June 1964, Helsinki, Finland. Jazz Musician (clarinet, saxophones). m. Minna Sarpila, 23 Apr 1994, 2 sons. Musical Education: Studied with Bob Wilber. Career: Leader, own band Antti Sarpila Swing Band; Attended Dick Gibson Jazz Party, 1982; Played with musicians including: Zoot Sims; Frank Wess; Marshall Royal; Buddy Tate; Concerts include: Benny Goodman Memorial Concert, Carnegie Hall, 1988; Royal Ellington Concert, Royal Festival Hall, London, 1989; Antti Sarpila Swing Band 10th Anniversary Concert, 1992; Guest apperance, Count BasieOrchestra, 1995; Antti Sarpila 15th Anniversary Concert, 1997. Recordings include: The Original Antti Sarpila, 1990; Moments Like This: Antti Sarpila Meets Bob Wilber, 1991; Antti Sarpila Swing Band 10th Anniversary, 1992; Tribute To Coleman Hawkins, 1994; Buck Clayton Remembered, 1995; Antti Sarpila Swing Band 15th Anniversary, 1997. Honour: Voted Best Musician in Finland, 1993. Membership: TEOSTO (Composers' Society). Hobbies: Watercolour painting; Ornithology. Current Management: Self-managed. Address: Museokatu 26 A 14, 00100 Helsinki, Finland.

SARSTEDT Peter, Folk Singer; Songwriter. m. Joanna. Recordings: Albums: Peter Sarstedt, 1969; PS..., 1979; Up Date, 1981; Asia Minor, 1987; Never Say Goodbye, 1987; with Eden Kane & Robin Sarstedt: Worlds Apart Together, 1973; Singles: I Am A Cathedral; Where Do You Go To

My Lovely (Number 1, UK), 1969; Frozen Orange Juice, 1969; Beirut; Love Among The Ruins, 1982. Address: c/o Jason West Agency, Kings Lynn, Norfolk, England.

SARTORIUS Paula, b. 18 Feb, New York, USA. Artist Manager. Education: BA, Fordham University. Career: Artist Manager, Side One Management, for: Los Lobos; Luscious Jackson.

SASSETTI Bernardo, b. 24 June 1970, Lisbon, Portugal. Musician (piano); Jazz Composer. Musical Education: Graduate, Lisbon Academy of Music. Career: Played with major jazz names including: John Stubblefield; Andy Sheppard; Frank Lacy; Al Grey; Art Farmer; Kenny Wheeler; Freddie Hubbard; Paquito d'Rivera; Benny Golson; Eddie Henderson; The United Nation Orchestra; Concerts in France; Spain; Italy; USA; South Africa; UK, including Ronnie Scott's, London. Recordings: Album: Salssetti, 1995. Honours: Various local awards. Membership: Member, Professor, Jazz School of HCP, Lisbon. Current Management: Paulo Santos Gil. Address: Rua Das Pracas, 66-1-DRT-1200, Lisbon, Portugal.

SATRIANI Joe, b. Long Island, New York, USA. Musician (guitar, banjo, harmonica); Educator. Career: Founder member, The Squares; Member, Greg Kihn Band; Solo artiste, 1984-; UK tour, 1995; Guitar tutor to rock musicians Steve Vai, Kirk Hammett. Recordings: with Greg Kihn Band: Love & Rock'N'Roll, 1986; Solo: Joe Satriani (EP), 1984; Not Of This Earth, 1986; Surfing With The Alien, 1987; Dreaming II, 1988; Flying In A Blue Dream, 1990; Joe Satriani, 1995. Honours: Several Grammy Awards. Current Management: Bill Graham Management. Address: PO Box 429094, San Francisco, CA 94142-9094, USA.

SAUNDERS Cameron, b. 18 Feb 1973, Cuxhaven, England. m. Louise Latham, 22 May 1994. Education: BA (Hons), Social Anthropology, King's College, Cambridge. Career: New Atlantic (1989-1993); Extensive tours, UK, especially Scotland; Television: Hitman And Her, 1992; Top Of The Pops, 1992; Radio: BBC Radio 1; Capital Radio; World Service; Interviews; Debut broadcast, Radio Berlin International (club of). Recordings: I Know; Into The Future; Take Off Some Time. Honours: Scottish Clubscene 1992: Best Newcomer, Runner-up best dance band. Memberships: Musicians' Union; PRS. Hobbies: DJing; Clubbing; Reading. Current Management: Self-managed. Address: 16 Shirdley Crescent, Ainsdale, Southport PR8 3RR, England.

SAUNDERS Eddie (Edward John), b. 6 July 1965, London, England. Lead Vocalist; Composer; Lyricist; Musician (percussion, various other instruments). Musical Education: Self-taught. Career: Founder member, lead vocalist, Push; Lead and back-up vocals, Groove Nation; Extensive live appearances UK, Europe; Live work with the above, also: Reuben Wilson (Push was his UK pick-up band); Omar; Leon Ware; Jo Cang; Boogie Back All Stars; Support to Curtis Mayfield; Airto and Flora Purim; Maceo Parker; Average White Band. Recordings: Traffic, track on Acid Jazz And Other Illicit Grooves compilation (first ever Acid Jazz record), 1988; Further recordings with Push; Talbot/White; Jo Cang; Galliano; Groove Nation; Memberships: PRS; Musicians' Union; MCPS. Hobbies: Sunshine; Travel; Languages; Food and Wine; Philosophy; Fitness; Annoying People. Current Management: Represented by Alexis Grower, McGrath & Co. Address: 18 Dartmouth Park Avenue, London NW5 1JN, England.

SAUNDERS Gerry (Gerald Ivor Ewart), b. 3 Nov 1929, Plymouth, Devon, England. Music (percussion). Radio Presenter; Writer. Career: ENSA, 1943-45; Theatre Pit, 1945-47; RAF, 1947-49; Big band/Orchestra tours, 1949-55;

Magazine proprietor, broadcasting, writing, 1955-65; Jazz club proprietor (6 clubs), music/stage producer, jazz tours, 1965-80; Musical/stage tours, writing, band management, broadcasting, 1980-93; National Executive, South East District Council; Chairman Bournemouth Branch, Musicians' Union; Radio presenter; Writer; Jazz tours, 1980-. Publications: Playtime Entertainment Newspaper; Editor and Publisher, Secretary, Editor, Video Record. Membership: National Executive Musicians' Union; Chairman, British Citizens Band Confederation; Chief Executive, National Citizens Band Confederation; Chairman, Bournemouth Branch, Musicians' union; Director, Coastal Radio, community radio station. Hobbies: Leader, Just Jazz orchestra; Ham radio; Video photography; Neighbourhood Watch co-ordinator; Dorset Watch Liaison Group; Radio historian; After Dinner speaker; Jazz lecturer; Local charities support. Address: 12 Lincoln Avenue, Springbourne, Bournemouth, Dorset BH1 4QS, England.

SAUNDERS Mark, b. 20 Mar 1959, Basingstoke, Hampshire, England. Mixing Engineer; Record Producer. Recordings: Albums: Raw Like Sushi; Neneh Cherry; Wild, Erasure; Maxinquaye, Tricky; Singles: with The Cure: Lullaby; Lovesong; with The Farm: Groovy Train; with Lisa Stansfield: This Is The Right Time. Address: The Smoothside Organisation, Ashbank, Heyford Road, Middleton Stoney, Oxfordshire OX6 8SH, England.

SAUNDERS Roger, b. 9 Mar 1947, Barking, Essex, England. Musician (guitar, piano). Musical Education: Self-taught. Career: Television includes: Top Of The Pops; Jonathon Ross; Concerts include: Wembley Stadium; Wembley Arena; Tours throughout US, including Madison Square Gardens, New York; Middle East including Dubai, Bahrain; Europe including Germany, France, Italy, Spain, Norway, Denmark, Sweden, Finland; Concerts with: Medicine Head; Gary Glitter; Peter Skelton; Duane Eddy; Chicken Shack; Numerous recordings; Over 600 songs published. Memberships: PRS; MCPS; Songwriters Guild; Musicians' Union. Hobby: Music. Current Management: Self-managed. Address: Barking, Essex, England.

SAVAGE Rick, b. 2 Dec 1960, Sheffield, England. Rock Musician (bass); Vocalist. Career: Bass player, UK rock group Def Leppard, 1977-; International concerts include: Support tours with Sammy Hagar; AC/DC; Ted Nugent; Reading Rock Festival, 1980; World tour, 1983; Monsters of Rock Festival, Castle Donington, 1986; World tour, 1988; Freddie Mercury Tribute Concert, Wembley, 1992. Recordings: Albums: On Through The Night, 1980; High'n'Dry, 1981; Pyromania, 1983; Hysteria, 1987; Adrenalize, 1992; Retroactive, 1993; Vault 1980-95, 1995; Slang, 1996; Singles include: Photograph; Rock Of Ages; Foolin'; Animal; Pour Some Sugar On Me; Love Bites; Rocket; Make Love Like A Man; Let's Get Rocked; Stand Up (Kick Love Into Motion); Heaven Is; Two Steps Behind, featured in film soundtrack The Last Action Hero; When Love And Hate Collide. Honours include: American Music Awards: Favourite Heavy Metal Album, Favourite Heavy Metal Artists, 1989. Current Management: Q-Prime Inc. Address: 729 Seventh Avenue, 14th Floor, New York, NY 10019, USA.

SAVANNAH Jonn, b. 13 Jan 1957, Nairobi, Kenya. Musician. m. Marie. Education: 1 year college. Musical Education: Grade 4 piano. Career: Toured with: Tina Turner; Squeeze; Van Morrison; Session work; Number 3 hit, Germany, 1984; Signed publishing deal with EMI UK, 1994. Recordings: The Catch: 25 Years (Number 3, Germany). Memberships: BASCA; Musicians' Union; MCPS. Hobbies: Motorbikes; Gardening. Address: Little Barn, Plaistow Road, Loxwood, West Sussex RH14 0SX, England.

SAVOLAINEN Jarmo Tapio, b. 24 May 1961, Iisalmi, Finland. Composer; Musician (piano, keyboards). m. Helena Haaranen, 1 daughter. Musical Education: Jazz and composition studies, Berklee College of Music, Boston, USA. Career: Member, various groups including: Finnforest; Blue Train; Formed own nine-piece ensemble and quartet; Duos with Make Lievonen, 1988; Seppo Kantonen, 1990; Major jazz festivals worldwide, including Jukkis Uotila Quintet, Paris, 1984; EBU Big Band, Pori Jazz, 1985; Kalott Jazz & Blues Festival, 1995; Television appearances on many European national networks. Compositions: Music for big bands, theatre and films. Recordings: Blue Dreams, 1987; Songs For Solo Piano, 1990; First Sight, 1992; True Image, 1995. Honour: Jazz Musician of The Year, Finland, 1994. Membership: Finnish Light Music Composers. Hobbies: Food; Cooking. Current Management: Self-managed. Address: Porvoonkatu 17 B 25, 00150 Helsinki, Finland.

SAYER Ron James, b. 24 Oct 1970, Wisbech, Lincolnshire, England. Musician (guitar, bass); Vocalist; Songwriter; Teacher. Career: Bassist, composer with Monster; Played live concert broadcast on Friday Rock Show, Radio 1; Sound City 1992; Toured supporting: Quireboys; Skin; Mr Big; L7; Mini-tour with Monster and Supercircus, including Royal Standard, London; Currently guitarist with Spider Murphy. Recordings: Radio broadcast concert included: So Here It Is; Innocence; What Would U Do; My Mind's Treasure; released on Rock The Canary album. Memberships: Musicians' Union; PRS; Guild of International Songwriters and Composers (GISC). Hobbies: Performing live and recording with Spider Murphy. Current Management: Self-managed, with Charlotte Joyce, singer in Spider Murphy. Address: 18 Munhaven Close, Mundesley, Norwich, Norfolk NR11 8AR, England.

SCABIES Rat (Chris Miller), b. 30 July 1957, Kingston Upon Thames, Surrey, England. Musician (drums). Career: Member, groups Rat; London SS; Member, UK punk rock group, The Damned, 1976-77; Appearances include: Mont de Marsan punk festival, France, 1976; Support to Sex Pistols, Anarchy In The UK Tour, 1976; First UK punk band to play US, 1977; Member, the White Cats, 1978; Rejoined the Damned, 1979-89; Regular international concerts include: Christmas On Earth Festival, Leeds, 1981; Farewell tour UK, 1989; UK reunion tour, 1991; Member, side project Naz and the Nomads, 1988; Recordings: Albums with the Damned: Damned, Damned, Damned, 1977; Music For Pleasure, 1977; Machine Gun Etiquette, 1979; The Black Album, 1980; The Best Of, 1981; Strawberries, 1982; Phantasmagoria, 1985; Anything, 1986; Light At The End Of The Tunnel, 1987; with Naz and the Nomads: Give Daddy The Knife, Cindy, 1988; Singles with The Damned: Love Song, 1979; Smash It Up, 1979; Grimly Fiendish, 1985; The Shadow Of Love, 1985; Is It A Dream, 1985; Eloise, 1986; Gigolo, 1987; Alone Again Or, 1987.

SCAGGS Boz, b. 8 June 1944, Ohio, USA. Musician (guitar); Singer. Career: Member, groups The Marksmen; The Ardells; Formed R&B group, The Wigs; Folk-singer in Europe, successful in Sweden; Joined Steve Miller Band, 1967; Solo artiste, 1968-. Recordings: Albums: Boz, 1966; Boz Scaggs, 19069; Moments, 1971; Boz Scaggs And Band, 1971; My Time, 1972; Slow Dancer, 1974; Silk Degrees, 1976; Two Down Then Left, 1977; Middle Man, 1980; Hits!, 1980; Other Roads, 1988; Hit singles include: Lowdown (Number 3, US); What Can I Say?; Lido Shuffle. Current Management: HK Management, 8900 Wilshire Blvd, Suite 300, Beverly Hills, CA 90211, USA.

SCARTH Andrew. Record Producer. Recordings: Recordings for: Levellers; Heather Nova; Blameless; Skunk Anansie; Killing Joke; Mundy; Credit to the Nation; Addict; Underworld;

Mainstream; Diamond Head; Bad Company. Current Management: One Management Ltd, 43 St Alban's Avenue, London W4 5JS, England.

SCAVONE Sam John, b. 12 July 1926, New York, USA. Musician (trumpet). m. (1) Esther Scavone, divorced 1961, 1 son, 1 daughter, (2) Marion Scavone, 1965, divorced 1973, 1 son, 1 daughter. Musical Education: Hartnet School Of Music, 1948-50. Career: Trumpeter, jazz groups, 1943-; Played with numerous artists including: Buddy Morrow; Woody Herman; Tito Puente; Xavier Cugat; Sammy Kaye; Tex Beneke; Charlie Spivak; Les Elgart.

SCHACK Michael E K, b. 11 May 1966, St Miklaas, Belgium. Musician (Drummer); Songwriter. Education: Economics, Degree in Marketing; Selftaught Drummer. Career: Blue Blot, 1987; Drummer, with Clouseau, 1995-97; Roland Demoband, 1992; Blue Blot Tour, 1992-94; Groovemania and Clouseau, 1995; Demonstrator, Sabian - Vic Firth Endorser - Slingerland Clinician, 1997. Compositions: Blue Blot: Pretty Good; New Blunk; Groovemania: Posativity; Mich van Hautem, Jacky; Beasone. Recordings: Blue Blot Albums, 1990-94; Orphan; September Rain; De 7 Drumzonden; Live for Life, 1993; Drum Editor, Meetmusic, 1992-97. Honour: Drumvideo of the Year, 1996. Membership: SABAM, Uradex, Zamu, Belgium. Current Management: King IS, Leuvensesteemweg 120A, 3290 Diest, Belgium. Address: Lage Vosbergstraat 76, B-2840 Rumst, Belgium.

SCHAFFER Jan E T, b. 24 Sept 1945, Stockholm, Sweden. Musician. Education: University. Career: Professional from 1970-; Played on records with Abba (27 numbers); 10 solo albums (1 with Toto); Many television programmes. Compositions: About 120. Recordings: Hallmans Affair; Bersellii; Park And Electric Banana Band. Publications: Play Guitar, with R Gustavsson. Memberships: STIM; SAMI. Hobbies: Skiing; Diving. Address: Dr Abrahamsu 43, 16152 Bromma, Sweden.

SCHELL Daniel (Schellekens), b. 5 Apr 1944, Brussels, Belgium. Composer; Musician (Chapman Stick). m. Claudia Wester, 28 Apr 1995, 1 son, 2 daughters. Education: Engineer, University of Brussels; MSc Ope Res, London School Of Economics. Musical Education: Solfege; Harmony; Composition; Guitar, Academy d'Uccle. Career: Member, group COS, 1970-83; Member, Ensemble Karo, 1985-; Founder, Tap Seminar, Chapman Stick; Teacher of Indian music, Académie d'Anderlecht, Brussels. Recordings: Pasiones, 1980; If Windows They Have, 1990; Gira Girasole Materiali Sonori, 1995; Hygiène De L'Assassin (opera), 1995. Publications: My Space My Time; Practice Of Indian Music. Hobbies: Table tennis; Biking. Current Management: Clic Music. Address: Groenstraat 51, B-1750 Lennik, Belgium.

SCHELLEKENS Marc, b. 10 April 1967. Audio Engineer; Producer; Composer. Education: Audio Engineer, specialization: Acoustics, Psycho-Acoustics, Digital Signal Processing; Degree in Musicology. Compositions: Soundtrack Animation Film, Heresy, 1994; Mult Soundtracks for Company Video's, 1995, 1996; Soundtrack, De Dulle Griet, 1997. Recordings: Quod Erat Demonstrandum, CD, 1997; Tangens Immortalis, CD, 1997. Memberships: AES; SABAM. Address: Fort V Straat 12, B-2650 Edegem, Belgium.

SCHENKER Michael, b. 10 Jan 1955, Savstedt, Germany. Musician (guitar). Career: Founder, German heavy rock group The Scorpions, 1971-; Member, UFO, 1973-78; Rejoined Scorpions, 1979; Formed own band, The Michael Schenker Group, later called MSG, 1979-; Contributor, Contraband recording project (with members of Shark Island, Vixen, Ratt, LA Guns), 1991. Recordings: Albums: with the Scorpions:

Lonesome Crow, 1972; Lovedrive, 1979; with UFO: Phenomenon, 1974; Force It, 1975; No Heavy Pettin', 1976; Lights Out, 1977; Strangers In The Night, 1977; Obsession, 1978; with MSG: The Michael Schenker Group, 1980; MSG, 1981; One Night At Budokan, 1982; Assault Attack, 1982; Built To Destroy, 1983; Rock Will Never Die, 1984; Perfect Timing, 1987; Save Yourself, 1989; Never Ending Nightmare, 1992; with Contraband: Contraband, 1991.

SCHENKER Rudolph, b. 31 Aug 1948, Germany. Musician (guitar); Songwriter. Career: Founder member, German heavy rock group The Scorpions, 1971-; Worldwide tours; Concerts include: Support to Ted Nugent, US, 1979; World tour, 1982; Support to Bon Jovi, US, 1984; Leningrad, Russia, 1989; Festivals include: World Series Of Rock, Cleveland, Ohio, 1979; Reading Rock Festival, 1983; US Festival, 1983; Rock In Rio, Brazil, 1985; Moscow Music Peace Festival, 1989; Roger Waters' The Wall spectacular, Berlin, 1990; Invited to meet President Gorbachev at the Kremlin, 1991. Recordings: Albums: Lonesome Crow, 1972; Fly To The Rainbow, 1974; In Trance, 1975; Virgin Killer, 1976; Taken By Force, 1978; Tokyo Tapes, 1978; Lovedrive, 1979; Animal Magnetism, 1980; Blackout, 1982; Love At First Sting, 1984; World Wide Live, 1985; Savage Amusement, 1988; Best Of Rockers And Ballads, 1989. Hurricane Rock, 1990; Crazy World, 1990; Face The Heat, 1993; Live Bites, 1995; Singles include: Can't Live Without You; No One Like You; Still Loving You; Rhythm Of Love; Wind Of Change. Current Management: McGhee Entertainment, 9145 Sunset Blvd, Suite 100, Los Angeles, CA 90069, USA.

SCHIFRIN Lalo, b. 21 June 1932, Buenos Aires, Argentina. Musician (piano, keyboards); Composer; Educator; Arranger. Education: Sociology, Law, University. Musical Education: Classical piano; Studied with Olivier Messiaen, Paris Conservatoire. Career: Represented Argentina, Paris International Jazz Festival, 1955; Founded Argentina's first big band; Played with Dizzy Gillespie, including European tour with Jazz At The Philharmonic Ensemble, 1960-62; Also played with Quincy Jones; Jimmy Smith; Tutor, Composition, University of California, Los Angeles, 1968-71. Compositions: 2 suites for Dizzy Gillespie: Gillespiana; New Continent; Film music includes: The Cincinnati Kid, 1965; Bullitt, 1968; Dirty Harry, 1971. Recordings: Albums include: New Fantasy, 1966; Towering Toccata, 1977; Black Widow, 1976; Free Rides, 1979; Guitar Concerto, 1985; Anno Domini, 1986; Mission - Anthology, 1994; with Jimmy Smith: Verve Jazz, 1972; The Cat Strikes Again, 1980; with Eddie Harris: Bossa Nova, 1962; with Quincy Jones: Plays Hip Hits, 1963; with Paul Horn: Dream Machine, 1978. Address: c/o Peter Levinson Communications Inc., 1650 Broadway, Suite 1206, New York, NY 10019, USA.

SCHLUETER Hazel Ann, b. 3 Dec 1945, New Orleans, Louisiana, USA. Musician (mandolin, guitar, autoharp, radio producer); Singer. m. Larry Schlueter, 2 Apr 1965, 1 son. Education: Cornell University, St John's College. Career: Played bass, mandolin, singer for Dr Bill C Malone and the Hill Country Ramblers; Formed Hazel And The Delta Ramblers, bluegrass band and played New Orleans Jazz and Heritage Festival, 1977-; Produced radio shows for WWHOZ radio station, 1981-. Recordings: Hazel And The Delta Ramblers: Live At The 1992 New Orleans Jazz and Heritage Festival, 1992. Hobbies: Running; Walking; Biking; Gardening. Address: 1120 Bourdeaux Street, New Orleans, LA 70115, USA.

SCHMIDT Bjarne Gregers, b. 3 November 1957, Copenhagen, Denmark. Tenor Banjo; Irish Bouzouki; Guitar. Musical Education: Piano lessons; Sound Engineering Course, 1996; Musical Studies, Ireland. Career: Foxhunters,

band, Skagen Festival, 1986; Live appearance, Danish Radio, 1987, 1989, 1991, 1992, 1996, 1997; Scandinavian Tour with Irish topacts, Mary Bergin and Mick Conneely Gin Whistle and Fiddle, 1991; Live at TV-Stop, 1993, Telemark Festival Norway, 1997. Compositions: The Moth in the Lampshade; Happy Days, 1997. Recordings: Same Old Story, contributor, 1990; Folkmusic in Denmark 1, 1992; Folkmusic in Denmark 2, 1993; Trad Lads, Happy Days, 1997; Eck D'Ville, Contributor, 1997; Folkmusic of Denmark, 1997. Publications: Trad Lads, Happy Days, 1997; Eck D'Ville, 1997. Hobbies: Readings; Travels. Current Management: Martin O'Hare, Selvedje Allé 19, 2500 Valby, Denmark.

SCHMIT Timothy B, b. 30 Oct 1947, Sacramento, California, USA. Career: Member, folk trio, Tim, Tom & Ron, 1962; Member, groups: The Contenders; New Breed; Glad; Member, Poco, 1970-77; Member, The Eagles, 1977-. Recordings: Albums: with Poco: Poco, 1970; Deliverin', 1971; From The Inside, 1971; A Good Feelin' To Know, 1973; Crazy Eyes, 1973; Seven, 1974; Cantamos, 1974; Head Over Heels, 1975; The Very Best Of Poco, 1975; Poco Live, 1976; Rose Of Cimarron, 1976; Indian Summer, 1977; With The Eagles: The Long Run (Number 1, US), 1979; Live, 1980; Eagles Greatest Hits, 1982; The Best Of The Eagles, 1985; Solo albums: Playin' It Cool, 1981; Timothy B, 1987; Singles include: Heartache Tonight (Number 1, US), 1979; I Can't Tell You Why, 1980; Seven Bridges Road, 1981. Honours: Grammy Award, Best Rock Vocal Performance, Heartache Tonight, 1980; American Music Awards, Favourite Band, Favourite Album, 1981. Address: c/o William Morris Agency, 1350 Avenue of the Americas, New York, NY 10019, USA.

SCHNEIDER John, b. 8 Apr 1954, Mount Kisco, New York, USA. Singer; Actor. Career: Performed in musicals since age 14; Actor, televison series The Dukes Of Hazzard, 1979-85; Country artiste, 1981-89; Actor, television series, Grand Slam, 1990-. Recordings: Hits: US Country Number 1 hits include: I've Been Around Enough To Know; Country Girls; What's A Memory Like You (Doing In A Love Like This)?; You're The Last Thing I Needed Tonight; Albums: Now Or Never, 1981; Dukes Of Hazzard cast album, 1982; Quiet Man, 1982; If You Believe, with Jill Michaels, 1983; Too Good To Stop Now, 1984; Trying To Outrun The Wind, 1985; A Memory Like You, 1986; Take The Long Way Home, 1986; You Ain't Seen The Last Of Me, 1987. Current Management: Lee S. Mimms And Associates, 2644 E Chevy Chase Drive, Glendale, CA 91206, USA.

SCHNEIDER Maria, b. 27 November 1960, Windom, Minnesota, USA. Education: BM, Theory & Composition, University of Minnesota; Studied, University of Miami; Master in Jazz and Contemporary Media, Eastman School of Music. Career: Led own orchestra, Maria Schneider Jazz Orchestra, New York, 1993-, performing weekly; Conducted jazz orchestras throughout Sweden, Norway, Finland, Germany, Denmark, Holland, France, Spain & Italy. Compositions: El Viento, Carnegie Hall Jazz Orchestra, 1994; Scenes from Childhood, Monterey Jazz Festival, 1995. Recordings: Evanescence; Coming About. Honours: Evanescence, Nominated for 2 Grammy Awards, 1995, 1997; Jazztimes and Downbeat Critics, Nominated for Copenhagen's Jazzpar Prize, 1995. Address: 50W 72nd St #510, New York, NY 10023, USA.

SCHOELINCK Roland, b. 3 January 1951, Anderlues, Hainaut, Belgium. Lefevre Chantal, 2 sons, 1 daughter. Education: Self-educated composer. Career: Director, private music school; Composer, Arranger and Performer, jazz, classical and popular music and studio work; Works: Ballet music, Arranger and Composer for Gerard Corbiau's film, L'année de l'éveil. Compositions:

Toots Concerto, harmonica and symphony orchestra; Safety First, official safety hymn; Complicity, flute, piano (jazzy); 1 Symphony; 1 Symphony Poem; 1 String Quartet; 1 Wind Quintet; Pieces for Solo Piano. Recordings: Safety First; Dolphin Tears; Complicity; Toots Concerto. Publications: Sur La Voie de l'improvisation, 1996; Easy to Write, 1997; Petit Livre de Jazz, 1 and 2, 1997; Complicity, 1997; 26 Airs de Gilles, piano. Memberships: Belgians Composers Union; SABAM; Administration, Thieusies Village de la Musique. Address: 6 Chemin Brulotte, B7063, Neufvilles, Belgium.

SCHOLZ Drazen, b. 25 June 1961, Zagreb, Croatia. Musician (drums). m. 28 June 1986, 1 daughter. Career: Promise Of Spring; Parliament; Film: Some Like It Hot; Le Cinema; Parni Valjak (Steam Roller). Recordings: with Parni Valjak: Live In ZKM (Unplugged); Parni Valjak - All 15 Years (3 LPs live), 1990; Dream Hunters, 1990; Awakenings, 1994. Honours: 7 Porin Awards (Croatian equivalent of Grammy) with Parni Valjak. Membership: HGU (Croatian Music Union). Hobby: Films. Current Management: Nenad Drobnjak, Miramarska 15b, Zagreb, Croatia. Address: Laginjina 9, 41000 Zagreb, Croatia.

SCHOLZ Tom, 10 Mar 1947, Toledo, Ohio, USA. Singer; Musician. Education: Masters, Mechanical Engineering, Massachusetts Institute of Technology. Career: Founder, rock group Boston, 1976; UK tour, 1979; 7 year absence from recording; US tour, 1987. Recordings: Albums: Boston (Number 1, US), 1976; Don't Look Back (Number 1, US), 1978; Third Stage (Number 1, US), 1986; Walk On, 1994; Greatest Hits, 1997; Singles include: More Than A Feeling, 1976; Long Time, 1977; Peace Of Mind, 1977; Don't Look Back, 1978; Amanda (Number 1, US), 1986; We're Ready, 1987; Can'tcha Say, 1987. Hobbies: Aviation; Inventing (holds numerous patents), including Rockman mini-amplifier. Honours: Platinum and Gold discs; Best-selling debut album all-time, 16 million copies. Address: c/o Boston, PO Box 6191, Lincoln Center, MA 01773, USA.

SCHON Neal, b. 27 Feb 1954, San Mateo, California, USA. Musician (guitar); Vocalist. Career: Guitarist with Carlos Santana; Founder, Azteca; Founder member, US rock group Journey, 1973-87; Member, HSAS, 1984; Bad English, 1988-91; Hardline, 1992-; Partnership with Jan Hammer, 1981-82. Recordings: with Santana: Santana, 1972; with HSAS: Through The Fire, 1984; with Jan Hammer: Untold Passion, 1981; Here To Stay, 1982; with Bad English: Bad English, 1989; Backlash, 1991; Solo: Beyond The Thunder, 1995; Hit singles include: with Journey: Who's Crying Now; Don't Stop Believin'; Open Arms; Separate Ways (Worlds Apart); After The Fall; Send Her My Love; Suzanne; Be Good To Yourself; with Bad English: When I See You Smile (Number 1, US), 1990; Straight To The Heart, 1991. Current Management: Bill Thompson Management. Address: 2051 3rd Street, San Francisco, CA 94107, USA.

SCHÖNBERG Claude-Michel, b. 6 July 1944, France. Composer. m. Béatrice Szabo, 1979, 1 son, 1 daughter. Career: Record Producer for EMI France; Composer, songs and musicals, 1967-. Compositions: Musicals include: La Révolutions Française, 1973; Les Misérables, 1980-84; Miss Saigon, 1985-86. Honours: Tony Awards; Grammy Awards; Evening Standard Awards.

SCHOUW Henrik, b. 17 September 1944, Copenhagen, Denmark. Musician (Piano). m. Tommi Björno Schouw, 10 June 1990, 1 son, 1 daughter. Education: Selfmade Pianist. Education: Provides easy listening on Soft Solo Piano; Over 600 popular tunes on soft solo piano, cassettes, CDs; Pianist in most exclusive restaurants and hotels; Songwriter; Composer. Recordings: CD production: Soft Solo Piano Music, 1990; Live

Piano Music d'Angleterre, 1992; Soft Piano Music, 1995; 60 Christmas Songs on Soft Piano, 1996; After Eight...., 1997. Address: Bülowsvej 5, DK-1870 Frederiksberg C, Copenhagen, Denmark.

SCHREURS Dirk, b. 23 May 1966, Neerpelt, Belgium. Professor of Jazz/Popular Music; Professor Pianist, The Brussels Royal Conservatory. m. Vera Kerckhoven, 28 July 1990. Education: Master Degree in Arts and Humanities, University of Louvain; Master Degree in Teaching; Assistant, Faculty of Arts, University of Louvain; Master Classes with John Abercrombie & Dave Kikoski, Trilok Gurtu. Career: Keyboardist with Real Deal, DSWB 4, Jan Mues Quartet, Jive Talk, Marco Ruggiero Band; Appearances on Belgian Radio and TV. Compositions: Over 200 compositions & arrangements in various styles. Recordings: Flexibility, 1992; Beyond Ballads, 1993; From Blues to Funk, 1995; The Joy of Rhythm 'N Jazz, 1996. Publications: Author, Jazzics; A Book on Jazz Theory, Analysis and Improvisation, 1993. Honours: Touch Down, composition selected for publication, 1994-95. Memberships: SABAM; ZAMU; Zavelhof Cultural Society. Hobbies: Playing Rhodes; Hammond Organ. Current Management: Dirk Schreurs, Don Boscostraat 98, 3940, Hechtel, Belgium.

SCHULDINER Chuck, b. USA. Rock Musician (bass, guitar); Vocalist. Career: Founder member, heavy rock group Death (formerly known as Mantas), 1983-; Considered originators of Death Metal genre; Tours include: European tour, 1992. Recordings: Albums: Scream Bloody Gore, 1987; Leprosy, 1988; Spiritual Healing, 1990; Human, 1992; Fate - The Best Of Death, 1992; Individual Thought Patterns, 1993.

SCHULTZ Debra Kay, b. 30 Oct 1955, Holden, West Virginia, USA. Gospel Singer. m. Robert A Schultz, 13 Dec 1974, 2 sons. Musical Education: Vocal lessons, Robert Turner; Several years of piano. Career: Appearances, gospel concerts, Gospel TV stations, throughout USA; Radio stations internationally. Recordings: Radio singles: Lord You're My Strength, 1991; Don't Lift The Anchor, 1992; I Just Found Jesus, 1993. Honours: King Eagle Award, Christian Female Artist of the Year, Airplay International, 1994-95. Membership: Gospel Music Association (GMA). Hobbies: Making crafts; Writing; Travel. Address: PO Box 88 Rt 17, Sharples, WV 25183, USA.

SCHULTZ Eric, b. 11 Sept 1960, Los Angeles, California, USA. Musician (guitar, electric bass); Composer; Arranger; Teacher. Education: BA, Humanities, California State University, Northridge, USA. Musical Education; Composition, California State University, Northridge; Guitar studies with Ralph Towner; Joe Diorio; John Abercrombie; Ron Escheté. Career: Professional jazz player, 1982; Resident Paris, 1986-; Worked regularly with some of greatest drummers in jazz: Oliver Johnson; Barry Altschul; Sunny Murray; Frank Butler; Alan Jones; Peter Perfido; ESP with Paul Carman, 1984-85; Onzy Matthews Quartet, Peter Perfido/Andy Laster Group; Eric Schultz Trio (with Oliver Johnson, Jack Gregg), 1991-; Eric Schultz Nonet; Jean Michel Couchet/Eric Schultz Quartet, 1993-; Eric Schultz Space And Time Ensemble, 1995; Viviane Ginapé/Eric Schultz duo. Recording: Eric Schultz Space And Time Ensemble, 1995; Release due, 1996. Membership: SACEM. Current Management: Space And Time Productions. Address: 8 Rue de la Pompe, 94410 St Maurice, France.

SCHULTZ Irma, b. 1 October 1965, Stockholm, Sweden. Singer; Songwriter; Actress. Education: Special Music School, 6 years; Drama School, 4 years. Career: Tours of Sweden and Many Television Shows; Background Vocals on 40 Albums in Sweden; Actress in The Black Rider by Waits, Wilson and Bourroughs at the Royal Dramatic Theatre; 10 Television Productions,

Leading Role in Kvällspressen, 1992; 3 Movies for Cinema. Compositions: Stureplan; Precis som du; Andas Fritt. Recordings: Da Staden Vaknat, 1989; Irma, 1991; Tröst för Stygga Barn, 1993; Andas Fritt, 1995; A Bird That Whistles, Songs of Joni Mitchell, 1996. Honour: Scholarships, STIM, SKAP; Grammy Award, Best Female Artist in Sweden, 1989. Current Management: Sony Music AB, Box 20037, S-16102 Bromma, Sweden. Address: Erstagatan 20, 116 36 Stockholm, Sweden.

SCHUUR Diane. Singer. m. Dave Schuur. Career: Performances include: White House; Monterey Jazz Festival; Hollywood Bowl; Tours: Europe; Japan; Far East; South America. Recordings: Albums: Pilot Of My Destiny, 1983; Schuur Thing, 1985; Timeless, 1986; Diane Schuur and The Count Basie Orchestra, 1987; Talkin' About You, 1988; Pure Schuur (Number 1, Billboard contemporary jazz chart), 1991. Honours: Grammy Awards: Best Female Jazz Vocal, Timeless, 1986; Diane Schuur and the Count Basie Orchestra, 1987. Current Management: Paul Cantor Enterprises, 33042 Ocean Ridge, Dana Point, CA 92629-1708, USA.

SCLAVIS Louis, b. 2 Feb 1953, Lyon, France. Musician (clarinets, saxophones). 1 son. Musical Education: Clarinet studies at Lyon Conservatory, 1962-. Career: Played with: Michel Portal; Chris McGregors's Brotherhood Of Breath; Henri Texier; Cecil Taylor; Many other leading European musicians; Several performances with dancer and choreographer Mathilde Monnier. Recordings: Clarinettes, 1984; Chamber Music, 1987; Chine, 1987; Ellington On The Air, 1990; Rouge, 1991; Acoustic Quartet, 1993; Green Dolphin Street, 1995; Carnet Des Routes, 1995. Honours: Prix Django Reinhardt, 1988; British Jazz Award, 1990-91. Current Management: Marion Piras, Inclinaisons, 180 Rue de l'Hermitage, 34070 Montpellier, France.

SCOCCO Mauro, b. 11 September 1962, Stockholm, Sweden. Artist; Composer. Career: Sales in Scandinavia: 600,000 albums; 4 Swedish Grammies; numerous other awards. Recordings: Sarah, single, topped every list in Sweden. Hobby: Harley Davidson Motorcycles. Current Management: Diesel Music. Address: Diesel Music, Blasieholmsg 2a, 1148 Stockholm, Sweden.

SCOFIELD John, b. 26 Dec 1951, Ohio, USA. Jazz Musician (guitar); Composer. Musical Education: Berklee College Of Music, Boston. Career: Began playing in local R&B groups; Solo artiste, 1970s-; Played with Billy Cobham; Gary Burton; Dave Liebman; Charlie Haden; Jack DeJohnette; McCoy Tyner; Marc Johnson; French National Orchestra; Mike Gibbs Orchestra; Member, Miles Davis' group, 1983-85. Recordings: Albums include: John Scofield Live, 1977; Rough House, 1978; Who's Who, 1979; Bar Talk, 1980; Shinola, 1981; Out Like A Light, 1981; Electric Outlet, 1984; Still Warm, 1987; Blue Matter, 1987; Loud Jazz, 1987; Flat Out, 1989; Pick Hits Live, 1989; Time On My Hands, 1990; Slo Sco, 1990; Meant To Be, 1991; Blue Matter, 1991; Grace Under Pressure, 1992; What We Do, 1993; with Miles Davis: Decoy, 1984; You're Under Arrest, 1985; Star People, 1989; Groove Elation, 1996; with Herbie Hancock: The New Standard, 1996; Also recorded with Gerry Mulligan; Chet Baker; John Abercrombie. Current Management: Ted Kurland Associates, 173 Brighton Avenue, Boston, MA 02134, USA.

SCOTT Al. Record Producer. Career: Musician, Recording, session work; Live Sound for: The Jam' Little Feat; Fleetwood Mac; Composer and arranger; Record producer, with close links with Vinyl Solution. Recordings: Albums: The Levellers: Levelling The Land; Cud: Slip Away; Dogs D'Amour: Uncharted Heights Of Disgrace; Oyster Band: Holy Bandits; Tom

Robinson: Love Over Rage; Cherry Bombz: Live; Derek B: Bullet From A Gun; Bomb The Bass: Love So True; Betty Boo: Where Are You Baby; Eddie Grant: Gimme Hope Joanna; Eric B and Rakim: Paid In Full; Other artists including: Mae; Suicide Twins; Bizarre Inc; Gunshot; War; Catch My Soul. Current Management: XL Talent. Address: Studio 7, 27A Pembridge Villas, London W11 3EP, England.

SCOTT Clive Kenneth, b. 24 Feb 1945, Coventry, England. Musician (keyboards); Producer; Writer. m. Ann Constance, 18 June 1994, 1 son. Musical Education: Church choir to pop groups. Career: Keyboard player, co-writer for Jigsaw, 1968-81; Independent writer producer. Recordings: with Apollo 100: Joy; with Candlewick Green and St Etienne: Who Do You Think You Are; with Jigsaw: Sky High; with Bad Boys Inc: Walking On Air. Publications: Music for video and film includes Shape Challenge fitness videos. Honours: Gold discs, Sky High; Ivor Novello Certificate of Honour. Memberships: Songwriters Guild; PRS. Hobbies: House renovation. Current Management: Chas Peate, Belsize Music. Address: 29 Manor House, Marylebone Road, London NW1 5NP, England.

SCOTT David Andrew, b. 20 Aug 1964, Falkirk, Scotland. Musician (guitar; keyboards); Vocalist. m. Julie Parker, 19 Aug 1989. Education: Graphics, Falkirk College; Glasgow School of Art. Career: Appeared on Indie compilation, 1984; Other recordings as Chewy Raccoon and Hearts And Minds; Film and television commissions; Founder, My Dark Star record label to release records by The Pearlfishers, 1991-; Major concert appearances include: Scottish Fleadh, 1992; T In The Park, Glasgow, 1994; Celtic Connections, Royal Concert Hall, 1995. Recordings: Sacred (EP), The Pearlfishers, 1991; Hurt (EP), The Pearlfishers, 1991; Za Za's Garden, The Pearlfishers, 1994. Memberships: PRS; Musicians' Union. Hobbies: Painting; Cooking. Current Management: My Dark Star Records. Address: PO Box 1, Glasgow G3 6TZ, England.

SCOTT Hammond, b. 15 May 1950, Alexandria, Louisiana, USA. Record producer; Attorney. Education: Doctor of Law. Career: Co-owner, Black Top Records Inc (internationally distributed and recognized blues, R&B and roots label); Produced over 100 albums; Served as personal manager of blues artist Clarence "Gatemouth" Brown, 1970's; Former writer, Living Blues Magazine; Hosted radio show on WWOZ FM, New Orleans, for 5 years; Produced recordings by R&B artists including: Solomon Burke; Maria Muldaur; Earl King; Snooks Eaglin; Bobby Parker; Neville Brothers; Anson Funderburgh and the Rockets, Former Prosecutor, District Attorneys Office of Harry Connick Sr. Honours: Numerous W C Handy Awards, Grammy Award nominations. Hobbies: Vintage arts collector and restorer; Vintage watch collector. Address: 5340 Camp Street, New Orleans, LA 70115, USA.

SCOTT Malcolm, b. 20 Aug 1964, San Francisco, California, USA. Musician (drums, percussion, guitar); Songwriter; Singer. m. Dominique Atkins, 26 Aug 1994. Musical Education: Berkshire Centre Performing Arts; Musicians Institute, London. Career: Musician for: The Cure; Pretenders; Belinda Carlisle; Buddy Curtiss; McAlmont; Jimmy Nail; Vanessa Mae; Skunk Anansie; Take That; Michelle Gayle; Grace. Recordings: Lovesongs End, Grace. Membership: Musicians' Union. Hobbies: Football; Television; Family and friends. Current Management: Agent: Session Connection; Management: Mickey Curbishley. Address: 16 Lynfield Court, 161 Devonshire Road, London SE23 3ND, England.

SCOTT Matthew, b. 19 September 1956, Cliveden, Berkshire, England. Composer;

Conductor; Musician (Keyboard). Education: Guildhall School of Music and Drama, London; City University, London; New York University, New York, USA; Brecht Archiv, Berlin, Germany. Career: Music Director, Royal National Theatre, 1981-87; Music, many for productions including: Animal Farm; Ting Tang Mine; Fathers and Songs; Member of The Wrestling School, 1988-; Freelance Composer, 1987-; Member, The Lost Jockey, band, 1981-85. Compositions: Drop the Dead Donkey; Floodtide; Underworld; Lord of Misrule; Eleven Men Against Eleven; Medics; King Leek; Have You Seen This Girl (Opera with Peter Terson). Memberships: Groucho Club; Association of Professional Composers; LSFO. Hobbies: Reading; Hillwalking; Clay Shooting. Current Management: Soundtrack Music Associates, 22 Ives Street, London SW3 2ND, England. Address: 22 Holly Grove, London SE15 5DF, England.

SCOTT Matthew James, b. 11 Oct 1967, London, England. Musician (piano); Composer. Musical Education: Self-taught. Career: Resident pianist, The Vortex, 1994-1995; Regular appearances on London jazz/pop circuit, London jazz festivals, 1994-95; Clubs include: The 606; The Orange; The King's Head, Upper Street; Chat's Palace. Compositions: L'Esquisse, film soundtrack, 1995; Trio for strings, 1995. Recordings: Album: Improvisations For Solo Piano, 1995; Standards, 1995. Hobbies: Hedonism; Lunacy. Current Management: Paddy French. Address: 249 Goswell Road, London EC1V 7JD, England.

SCOTT Mike, b. 14 Dec 1958, Edinburgh, Scotland. Singer;Songwriter; Musician (guitar). Musical Education: Self-taught. Career: Lead singer, groups: Another Pretty Face, 1979-81; The Red And The Black, 1982; The Waterboys, 1983-93; Solo artiste, 1994-; Tours, UK, US and Japan, 1995; Glastonbury Festival, 1995; UK, Europe, Japan, 1997. Recordings: Albums: with The Waterboys: A Pagan Place, 1984; This Is The Sea, 1985; Fisherman's Blues, 1988; Room To Roam, 1990; The Best of The Waterboys, 1991; Dream Harder, 1993; Secret Life of the Waterboys, 1994; Solo albums: Bring 'Em All In, 1995; Still Burning, 1997. Publications: Jungleland, 1977-80. Honours: Ivor Novello Award for composition, The Whole Of The Moon, 1992. Current Management: Strawberry Management Ltd, 112 Maxwell Avenue, Glasgow G61 H11, Scotland.

SCOTT Mike, b. 14 May 1962, Johnson City, Tennessee, USA. Musician (guitar, banjo, mandolin, bass); Songwriter; Singer; Entertainer; Producer; Music Publisher; Record Label Owner. m. Brenda Marshall, 13 Apr 1995, 2 sons. Education: Business Management, Marketing Education. Musical Education: Private instruction, age 10. Career: Began performing (aged 10), 1972; Performances include: Grand Ole Opry, debut with Jim & Jesse And The Virginia Boys, 1983-86; Founded own band, Mike Scott And The All-American Band, 1986-; Plays bluegrass, gospel and acoustic country music; Tours include: USA; Canada, Nova Scotia; 2 Wembley Music tours in Europe (including: London; Belfast; Vienna; Zurich; Frankfurt), 1983; 1985; Southern Africa (Zambia, Lesotho, Malawi), 1986; Played banjo for Danny Davis and the Nashville Brass, 1996; Television includes: 60th Anniversary Tribute to Grand Ole Opry, CBS, 1986 (Photo of cast displayed in Country Music Hall of Fame foyer, Nashville, Tennessee); New Country, TNN; Nashville Now (with Ralph Emory), TNN; Grand Ole Opry Live, TNN; Austin City Limits, PBS; European TV, London, South Africa, BBC; Voice of America, worldwide radio program, Washington DC; Various radio and syndicated networks; Songwriter with wife Brenda Marshall. Recordings: Solo: Classics For Banjo, 1983; with Mike Scott and the All-American Band: American Virtue, 1988; Acoustic Country (with Emmylou Harris), 1992; Good Life, 1998. Publication: The Mike

Scott Banjo Instruction Book. Honours: First band to receive full lifetime sponsorship (by the owner, Henry Juskerwich), from Gibson Instruments USA, 1986; Acoustic Band Of The Year, Metro Music Awards, 1990. Memberships: AFofM; IBMA (International Bluegrass Music Association); BMI (affiliated writer). Current Management: Creative Encounters / C. Michael Scott Productions. Address: PO Box 575, Hendersonville, TN 37077, USA.

SCOTT Rick, b. 14 July 1948, New Jersey, USA. Singer; Songwriter; Actor; Musician (dulcimer, whimmydiddle, guitar, trombone, tuba, Japanese flute). Musical Education: Self-taught. Career: Pied Pumkin String Ensemble, 1975-1976; Pied Pear, 1976-1983; Rick Scott Band, 1985-1986; Concert tours throughout Canada, USA, Australia, Asia as solo family performer; Starred, numerous stage plays, musicals including: Barnum (title role); The Late Blumer and Angry Housewives. Recordings: 10 recordings including 3 albums for children; The Electric Snowshoe, 1989; Rick Around the Rock, 1992; Philharmonic Fool, 1995. Honour: Juno Award nominee, 1996. Memberships: AFofM; SOCAN; ACTRA; Canadian Actors Equity. Current Management: Ms Valley Hennell, Manager. Address: 2736 W 13 Avenue, Vancouver, BC V6K 2T4, Canada.

SCOTT Toni Lee, b. 15 Jan 1933, San Francisco, California, USA. Singer. m. Angelo Ligi, 26 Dec 1989. Career: Professional singer, from age 14; Member, Bob Scobey's Band; Bob Crosby's Band; Television shows: This Is Your Life; Johnny Carson; Steve Allen; Tennessee Ernie Ford; Mike Douglas; Radio shows across the country; Clubs include: Stardust, Las Vegas; Riviera, Las Vegas; Roundtable, New York; Mr Kelly's, Chicago; Sherman House, Chicago; Mr T's, Chicago; Pigalle, Chicago; Cafe Continental, Chicago; Memory Lane, Los Angeles; Purple Onion, San Francisco; Other appearances include: Chicago Tribune Music Festival, Chicago; Codac Benefit, Phoenix. Recordings: Albums: San Francisco; Goody Goody; Something's Always Happening On The River, 1959; Volume Lonely, 1963; Songs Of My Friends, 1996. Publications: A Kind Of Loving, (autobiography). Honours: Fade To Gold Award, Entertainer Of The Year - Cerbral Palsy; Woman Of The Year, Heart Association. Memberships: Society of Singers; Women In Music Business. Hobbies: Swimming; Cooking. Current Management: (agent) Prince SF Prod; Management; Terri Tilton Management. Address: 6 Haverhill Court, Novato, CA 94947, USA.

SCOTT Tony, b. 3 Oct 1973, Paramaribo, Surinam. Rapper; Dancer; Singer; Composer. Musical Education: Self-taught. Career: First hit and recording, 1987; 10 Top 10 hits; Currently working with Candy Dulfer. Recordings: Pick Up The Pieces, 1987; Top 10 hit singles: The Chief, 1988; That's How I'm Living, 1988; Gangster Boogie, 1989; Get Into It, 1990; Greenhouse Effect, 1991; The Bigband, 1992; Love And Let Love, 1992. Honours: Dance Artist Award, 1989, 1990; 5 Golden singles. Membership: FNV Kunstenbond. Hobby: Music. Current Management: Hans Van Pol Management. Address: PO Box 9010, 1006 AA Amsterdam, Netherlands.

SCOTT-HERON Gil, b. 1 Apr 1949, Chicago, Illinois, USA. Singer; Songwriter. Education: Lincoln University, Pennsylvania, USA. Career: Co-founder, The Midnight Band, 1972-; Major concerts include: Phoenix Festival, 1995. Compositions include: The Revolution Will Not Be Televised, Labelle; Home Is Where The Hatred Is, Esther Phillips. Recordings: Albums: Small Talk At 125th And Lenox, 1970; Pieces Of A Man, 1971; Free Will, 1972; Winter In America, 1974; The Revolution Will Not Be Televised, 1974; The First Minute Of A New Day, 1975; From South Africa To South Carolina, 1975; It's Your World, 1976;

Bridges, 1977; Secrets, 1978; The Mind Of Gil Scott-Heron, 1979; 1980, 1980; Real Eyes, 1980; Reflections, 1981; Moving Target, 1982; The Best Of Gil Scott-Heron, 1984; Amnesia Express, 1990; Singles include: The Bottle, 1973; Johannesburg, 1976; B-Movie, 1982. Publications: Author, novels: The Vulture; The Nigger Factory; Book of poetry.

SCOTTI Bernard, b. 1 Sept 1955, Constantine, France. Musician (guitar); Songwriter. m. Danielle Torres, 22 July 1980, 1 daughter. Education: Self-taught. Career: Concerts and jazz festivals, France and Europe; Concerts on French television and radio. Recordings: Albums: Mademoiselle Swing Quartet; Trio Anacord: Flame in Jazz. Memberships: SACEM; SPEDIDAM. Address: 77 Fbg de Rochebelle, 30100 Ales, France.

SCREECHY Jah (Elton Loye Sinclair), b. 9 Feb 1958, Jamaica. Vocalist; Disc Jockey. Education: College diploma; City & Guilds. Career: Mechanical Engineering; Television appearances: Top Of The Pops; Radio 1 Road Show, Margate; Ritzy Night Club, Streatham; Stage shows and persoanl appearances, England, France and Germany. Recordings: Walk And Skank, 1984; Shadow Move, Hop Scotch, 1985; On A Ragga Tip, 1992. Memberships: Musicians' Union; PRS. Hobbies: Weight training; Martial arts. Current Management: James Augustus (Jessus). Address: Oxford House Studio, Oxford House, Derbyshire Street, Bethnal Green, London E2, England.

SCRUGGS Earl, b. 6 Jan 1924, Cleveland County, North Carolina, USA. Country Musician (banjo). Career: Member, Bill Monroe's Bluegrass Boys, 1944-48; Co-founder, Flatt & Scruggs show with Lester Flatt, 1948; Regular radio and television appearances include: Folk Sound USA; Concerts include: Newport Folk Festival, 1960; Leader, Earl Scruggs Revue, 1969-; Concerts include: Wembley Country Music Festival, 1972. Composition: Foggy Mountain Breakdown. Recordings include: Foggy Mountain Breakdown, from film Bonnie And Clyde; The Ballad Of Jed Clampett, theme for television series The Beverly Hillbillies; Albums: with Earl Scruggs Revue: include: Duelling Banjos, 1973; Family And Friends, 1972; Anniversary Special Vol.I, 1975; Family Portrait, 1976; Bold And New, 1978; Today And Forever, 1979; Top Of The World, 1983; Several collections of Flatt and Scruggs. Publications: Author, Earl Scruggs And The 5-String Banjo. Honours include: Artist of the Year, Hi-Fi Institute, 1975; Citation of Merit Country Music Association nomination, Best Country Instrument Group, 1975; Best Country Instrumental Group, Billboard Magazine, 1975; Certificate of Appreciation, Governor of Tennessee, 1978; Earl Scruggs Day, for contribution to American Music, 1980; Gibson Hall of Fame, 1981; Country Music Association Hall of Fame, 1985; Honorary Member, Lieutenant Governors Staff, State of Tennessee, 1987; Order of the Long Leaf Pine Award, Governor of North Carolina, 1988; Hall of Honour, International Bluegrass Music Association, 1991; National Medal of Arts, presented by George Bush, 1992. Memberships: Country Music Association; Current Management: Louise Scruggs, PO Box 66, Madison, TN 37116, USA.

SCUSSEL Gianpiero, b. 29 Nov 1933, Milan, Italy. Music and Video Consultant. Musical Education: Tuition in Trumpet. Career: Director, A&R, EMI Records. Recordings: Several million records produced. Membership: Technical Consulting Tribunale of Milan. Hobbies: Sailing; Fishing; Tennis. Current Management: Sorpasso Edizioni Musicali Srl. Address: Piazza Carlo Mirabello No 1, 20149 Milan, Italy.

SEAL (Henry Samuel), b. 19 Feb 1963, Paddington, London, England. Singer; Songwriter. Career: Singer, Adamski, 1990; Solo artiste, 1991-; Concerts and tours: Red Hot and Dance,

AIDS benefit concert, London, 1991; Amnesty International's Big 30, 1991; Freddie Mercury Tribute, A Concert For Life, Wembley, 1992; Support to Rolling Stones, 1994. Recordings: Solo albums: Seal (Number 1, UK), 1991; Hit singles: Killer, with Adamski (Number 1, UK), 1990; Solo singles: Crazy (Number 2, UK), 1991; Future Love Paradise, 1991; The Beginning, 1991; Prayer For The Dying, 1994; Kiss From A Rose, 1995; If I Could, 1995; I'm Alive, 1995; Featured on film soundtracks: Toys, 1991; Indecent Proposal, 1993. Honours: Ivor Novello Award, Best Contemporary Song, Killer, 1991; Q Award, Best New Act, 1991; Variety Club of Great Britain's Recording Artist Of 1991; BRIT Awards: Best Male Artist, Best British Album, Best British Video, 1992; 4 Grammy Awards, including Best Record, Best Song, 1996; Grammy Nominations, 1992, 1995; Ivor Novello Awards: Best Contemporary Song, International Hit Of The Year, Crazy, 1992. Current Management: Third Rail Entertainment, 9169 Sunset Blvd, Los Angeles, CA 90069, USA.

SEALS Dan, b. 8 Feb 1950, McCamey, Texas, USA. Country Singer; Songwriter. Career: Partnership with John Ford Coley, 1967-80; Originally billed as Southwest FOB, then as England Dan and John Ford Coley; Solo artiste, 1980-. Recordings: As England Dan and John Ford Coley: Hit singles include: I'd Really Love To See You Tonight; Nights Are Forever Without You; Albums: Smell Of Incense (as Southwest FOB), 1968; England Dan and John Ford Coley, 1971; Fables, 1971; I Hear The Music, 1976; Nights Are Forever, 1976; Dowdy Ferry Road, 1977; Some Things Don't Come Easy, 1978; Dr Heckle and Mr Jive, 1978; Just Tell Me If You Love Me, 1980; Solo hits include: Meet Me In Montana, with Marie Osmond (US Country Number 1), 1985; Bop; Everything That Glitters (Is Not Gold); You Still Move Me; I Will Be There; Three Time Loser; One Friend; Addicted; Big Wheels In The Moonlight; Albums: Stones, 1980; Harbinger, 1982; Rebel Heart, 1983; San Antone, 1984; Won't Be Blue Anymore, 1985; On The Front Line, 1986; Rage On, 1988; On Arrival, 1990; Walking The Wire, 1992. Current Management: Morningstar Management, PO Box 1770, Hendersonville, TN 37077, USA.

SEALS Troy, b. 16 Nov 1938, Big Hill, Kentucky, USA. Songwriter; Musician (guitar). m. Jo Ann Campbell. Career: Guitarist, club bands, Ohio, 1960s; Formed duo with Jo Ann Campbell; Moved to Nashville as songwriter; Session guitarist and solo artiste. Compositions: There's A Honky Tonk Angel (Who'll Take Me Back In), recorded by Elvis Presley, Conway Twitty (US Country Number 1); Pieces Of My Life, recorded by Elvis Presley; We Had It All (co-written with Donnie Fritts), recorded by Rita Coolidge, Brenda Lee, Scott Walker, Waylon Jennings; Feeling (co-written with Will Jennings and Don Goodman), recorded by Loretta Lynn and Conway Twitty (US Country Number 1); Storms (co-written with Max Barnes), recorded by Randy Travis; Seven Spanish Angels (co-written with Eddie Setser), recorded by Willie Nelson and Ray Charles (US Country Number 1). Recordings: Solo albums include: Now Presenting Troy Seals, 1973; Troy Seals, 1976.

SEALY Denice, b. 25 Nov 1964, London, England. Backing Vocalist. Musical Education: Vocal Studies, University of East London. Career: Greenbelt Christian Festival, with Bryan Powell, 1989-91; Hammersmith Odeon, with Jennifer Holliday, 1993; EMI Music Conference, with Kenny Thomas, 1993; Wembley Arena, with Dina Carroll, 1993; with Carleen Anderson, UK tour, 1993; Motor Traders Awards, 1995; with D C Lee, UK promo tour, 1995; Television: The Beat; The Late Show, 1993; Virgin Records Music Anniversary, 1994; Pebble Mill, 1995; Backing vocals, World (Pentecostal Conference), Jerusalem, Israel, 1995. Recordings: Albums: I Think Of You, Bryan Powell, 1992; Michelle Gayle,

1993; Nu Inspirational Album, Soul Stirrings. Membership: Musicians' Union. Hobbies: Tap dancing; Theatre; Gospel concerts; Tennis. Current Management: c/o Mixed Music Ltd. Address: 2 The Spinney, Dyke Road Avenue, Hove, Sussex BN3 6QT, England.

SEAMONE Joyce Evelyn, b. 21 May 1946, Bridgewater, Nova Scotia, Canada. Singer; Songwriter; Entertainer. m. Gerald Ivan Seamone, 12 Sep 1964, 3 daughters. Career: Toured Canada, early 1970's; Television appearances, Countrytime, Canadian National TV show; Headliner, exhibitions and clubs in Eastern Canada; Currently performing in Eastern Canada. Recordings: Testing 1-2-3, 1972; Merry Christmas From Joyce Seamone, 1972; Stand By For A Special Announcement, 1973; I Can See It In His Eyes, 1976; The Other Side Of Me, 1994; Instructional Line, Dance video, 1995. Honours: Gold Record, Testing 1-2-3, 1973; CHFX-FM, Country Music Hall of Fame, Halifax, Nova Scotia, Canada. Memberships: CCMA; SOCAN; ECMA; MIANS; SAC. Hobby: Reading. Current Management: Gerald Seamone. Address: RR2 New Germany, Nova Scotia B0R 1E0, Canada.

SEARLE Richard, b. 28 July 1963, South East London, England. Musician (bass guitar). Career: Co-founder, member, Doctor And The Medics; Television includes: 5 appearances, Top Of The Pops; Film: Maid To Order; Soundtrack for another film; Left group after 8 years; Joined Boys Wonder; Co-founder, Corduroy, 1992-. Recordings: with Doctor And The Medics: Spirit In The Sky (Number 1, UK); 5 other singles; 2 EPs, 2 albums; with Corduroy: 4 singles; 4 albums, co-writer, all albums. Honours: Gold Amplex Award; Silver Disc, Spirit In The Sky; Silver disc, Corduroy. Memberships: Musicians' Union; PRS. Hobbies: Cartoonist; Mountain biking; Illustration. Current Management: Martin Bartlett; Pete Elliot, Primary Talent Agents. Address: MBM, PO Box 47, Bromley, Kent BR1 8DQ, England.

SEBASTIAN John, b. 17 Mar 1944, New York, USA. Singer; Musician (guitar, harmonica, autoharp). Career: Founder member, The Lovin' Spoonful, 1965-1968; Appearances include: UK tour, 1966; Beach Boys Summer Spectacular, Anaheim, 1966; State Fairs tour, 1966; Solo artiste, 1969-; Appearances include: Woodstock Festival, 1969; Isle Of Wight Festival, 1970; Tours as one-man show, 1970s; Session musician for artistes including: Stephen Stills; Rita Coolidge; Everly Brothers; Host, The Golden Age Of Rock'N'Roll, A&E cable channel, 1991; Actor, episode, Married With Children, Fox TV, 1992. Compositions include: Music for television and films: Welcome Back, for Welcome Back, Kotter, ABC TV, 1976; The Care Bears; Strawberry Shortcake; The Jerk II, NBC TV. Recordings: Albums: with The Lovin' Spoonful: Do You Believe In Magic, 1965; Daydream, 1966; What's Shakin', 1966; Hums Of The Lovin' Spoonful, 1966; The Best Of The Lovin' Spoonful, 1967; Everything Playing, 1968; The Best Of The Lovin' Spoonful Vol. 2, 1968; Solo albums: John B Sebastian, 1970; John Sebastian Live, 1970; Cheapo Cheapo Productions Present, 1971; The Four Of Us, 1971; The Tarzana Kid, 1974; Welcome Back, 1976; Tar Beach, 1993; Hit singles include: with Lovin' Spoonful: Do You Believe In Magic, 1965; You Didn't Have To Be So Nice, 1966; Daydream, 1966; Did You Ever Have To Make Up Your Mind, 1966; Summer In The City (Number 1, US), 1966; Rain On The Roof, 1966; Nashville Cats, 1967; Darling Be Home Soon, 1967; Six O'Clock, 1967; She's Still A Mystery, 1967; Money, 1968. Current Management: Firstars, 3520 Hayden Avenue, Culver City, CA 90232, USA.

SEBASTIAN Mark Douglas, b. 20 Feb 1951, New York City, USA. Performer; Songwriter; Screenwriter; Film Producer; Musician (guitar, bass, keyboards). Education: Kim Stanley Drama Study. Musical Education: Piano study, New York.

Career: Performances: New York clubs: Gaslight; Wetlands; Lone Star; Theatre Music: La Mama; Television: Solid Gold; Cheers; Wizards and Warriors; Los Angeles clubs: The Strand; Wadsworth Theatre; Also performing member, Second City Imperor (Santa Monica group). Compositions: Summer In The City (Lovin' Spoonful, 1966), song co-written with (brother) John Sebastian and Steve Boone, used in film Die Hard - With A Vengeance, 1996. Honours: 3 Gold records. Memberships: BMI; ASCAP; SAG; AFTRA. Address: c/o BMI, Los Angeles, California, USA.

SECADA Jon, b. 10 Apr 1961, Havana, Cuba. Vocalist; Songwriter; Producer. Musical Education: Master's degree, Jazz Vocal Performance, University of Miami. Career: Central and South America Tour, 1994; US Tour, 1995; World Cup, 1994; X-Mas in Washington, 1994; National Anthem World Series, 1992; Grease, Broadway, 1995; Lifebeat concert, 1994. Recordings: Albums: Jon Secada, 1992; Heart Soul And A Voice, 1994; Si Te Vas, 1994; Frank Sinatra Duets II: The Best Is Yet To Come, 1994. Honours: Grammy: Best Latin Pop Album: Otro Dia Mas Sin Verte, 1992; Alumnus of Distinction, University of Miami. Membership: National Academy of Recording Arts and Sciences. Hobbies: Exercising; Playing tennis; Watching sports. Current Management: William Morris Agency, 151 El Camino Drive, Beverly Hills, CA 90212, USA; Estefan Enterprises, 6205 Bird Road, Miami, FL 33155, USA.

SECK Cheick Amadou Tidiane, b. 11 Dec 1953, Segou, Mali. Musician (keyboards, African percussion); Vocalist. 1 son. Education: BEPC, Diplome Institut National des Arts. Musical Education: Lear Organ and Solfege in church. Career: Concert with Jimmy Cliff, 1977; African and European tours with The Ambassadors of Mali and Salif Keita; World Tour with Amina, 1992-93; Printemps de Bourges Festival; Television Show: Taratata; Cercle De Minuit; Nulle Part Ailleurs, France. Recordings: Salif Keita: Soro; Amen; Graham Haynes: The Griots Footstep; Joe Zawinul: Next; Hank Jones, Cheick Tidiane Seck: My People; The Madenkas. Honours: Emission: Pollen by Jean Louis Foulquier; Articles: Liberation/Bingo. Honours: Gold record in Greece: Ioni, Heleni Dinou; First Prize, for film soundtrack Laada. Memberships: SACEM; SPEDIDAM. Hobbies: Table tennis; Football; Films; Painting. Current Management: Jacques Sajuan, Polygram Music, 20 Rue des Fosses St Jacques, 75005 Paris, France.

SEDAKA Neil, b. 13 Mar 1939. Singer; Songwriter. m. Leba Margaret Strassberg, 11 Sept 1962, 1 son, 1 daughter. Musical Education: Graduate, Juilliard School of Music. Career: Solo performer, worldwide, 1959-; Television apperances include: NBC-TV Special, 1976. Compositions include: Breaking Up Is Hard To Do; Stupid Cupid; Calendar Girl; Oh! Carol; Stairway To Heaven; Happy Birthday Sweet Sixteen; Laughter In The Rain; Bad Blood; Love Will Keep Us Together; Solitaire; The Hungry Years; Lonely Night (Angel Face). Recordings: Albums include: In The Pocket; Sedaka's Back; The Hungry Years; Steppin' Out; A Song; All You Need Is The Music; Come See About Me; Greatest Hits, 1988; Oh! Carol And Other Hits, 1990; Timeless, 1992. Honours: Songwriters' Hall Of Fame, 1980; Platinum album, Timeless, 1992; Numerous Gold records; Various industry awards. Memberships: AGVA; AFofM; AFTRA. Address: c/o Neil Sedaka Music, 201 East 66th Street, Suite 3N, New York, NY 10021, USA.

SEDGLEY Nicholas, b. 27 Jan 1969, Margate, Kent, England. Singer; Songwriter; Musician (acoustic and slide guitar). m. Caroline, 1 Oct 1992. Musical Education: Self-taught; Began on ukelele age 4 years (from a musical family). Career: Regular concerts, all Southern England;

Featured/reviewed all local newspapers, music magazines; Airplay all local radio stations including BBC Radio Kent; 6 original songs, May 1993; 8-9 Show on Nicky Leigh, former stage name, 1993; Now mainly acoustic singer/songwriter and composer with a large catalogue of songs. Compositions: Catalogue of original material for future albums; Theme tunes. Recordings: Working on CD, Songwriter's Cut, forthcoming. Membership: Musicians' Union. Hobbies: Music. Current Management: JMS, UK. Address: 80 Sweyn Road, Cliftonville, Margate, Kent CT9 2DD, England.

SEDGWICK Amanda, b. 7 Oct 1970, Stockholm, Sweden. Musician; Songwriter; Composer. Education: Royal Swedish University College of Music, Stockholm. Career: Toured Sweden; Appeared on Swedish Television and Radio, including Live Broadcasts. Compositions: Volt, 3 movement suite for jazz group, string quartet and woodwinds. Recordings: Volt, 1996; Contributor to So Many Stars, 1996 and Kalabra, 1997. Honours: Debut of the Year, Swedish National Radio. Memberships: Swedish Society of Popular Music Composers; Swedish Performing Rights Society. Address: Stromkarlsvagen 74, 167 62 Bromma, Sweden.

SEEGER Michael, b. 15 Aug 1933, New York, New York, USA. Singer; Musician; Folklorist. m. (1) Marjorie L Ostrow, 20 Dec 1960, divorced, 3 children, (2) Alice L Gerrard, 16 Aug 1970, divorced, (3) Alexia Smith, 27 Aug 1995. Career: Founder member, New Lost City Ramblers, 1958-; Strange Creek Singers, 1968-76; Bent Mountain Band, 1981; Guest lecturer, English department, University of California, Fresno, 1974; Performs Appalachian vocal and instrumental music in variety of styles, radio, TV, USA and abroad; Numerous record albums and documentary recordings from traditional folk musicians and dancers. Honours: First prize, banjo, Galax Virginia Old Time Fiddlers Convention, 1958; National Endowment for the Arts grantee, 4 times; Visiting scholar, Smithsonian Institute, 1983, Guggenheim Fellow, 1984; 3 Grammy Nominations, Best Traditional Folk Album, 1986, 1991, 1994; Ralph J Gleason Memorial Award Rex Foundation, 1994. Current Management: Josh Dunson, 520 S Clinton Street, Oak Park, IL 60304-1111, USA. Address: PO Box 1592, Lexington, VA 24450-1592, USA.

SEEGER Peggy, b. 17 June 1935, New York, USA. Singer; Songmaker; Musician (guitar, piano, 5-string banjo, autoharp, Appalachian dulcimer, English concertina). m. Ewan MacColl, 25 Jan 1978, 2 sons, 1 daughter. Education: Radclyffe College, Musical Education: Radclyffe College. Career: Concerts include: (in USA) Boston Orchestra Hall; Carnegie Hall; Australia; New Zealand; Canada; UK; Sweden; Soviet Union; France; Belgium; Netherlands; Many television and radio appearances; Tours since 1955. Compositions: Ballad Of Springhill; Gonna Be An Engineer. Recordings: 18 solo albums; Major participation in over 100 other albums. Publications: Peggy Seeger Songbook: Forty Years of Songmaking; with Ewan MacColl: Travellers' Songs Of England and Ireland; Doomsday In The Afternoon; Solo: The Essential Ewan Macoll Songbook. Honours: Italia Prize for participation in BBC radio-ballad: Singing The Fishing. Memberships: Musicians' Union; USA and UK. Hobbies: Travel; Environmental work; Reading; Sports. Current Management: Josh Dunson. Address: c/o Dunson, 520 S Clinton, Oak Park, IL 60304, USA.

SEEGER Pete, b. 3 May 1919, New York, USA. Folk Musician (banjo, guitar); Composer. m. Toshi, 20 July 1943, 1 son, 2 daughters. Education: Harvard College, 1936-38. Career: Folk singer/musician for 56 years; Worldwide tours across 35 countries; Collaborated on anti-Facist and labour songs; National Director, People's

Songs Inc, 1945; Formed the Weavers, 1948; appeared, until blacklisted from, on national radio and television networks; Assisted Newport Folk Festivals; Produced educational short films, Folklore Research Films; TV and film appearances: To Hear My Banjo Play, 1946; Rainbow Quest, 1965; Tell Me That You Love Me, Junie Moon, 1970. Compositions include: Turn, Turn, Turn; Where Have All The Flowers Gone; If I Had A Hammer (with Lee Hays); Kisses Sweeter Than Wine (with the Weavers); Also popularized Guantanamera, We Shall Overcome. Publications: American Folk Ballads, 1961; The Bells Of Rhymney, 1964; How To Play The Five String Banjo, Henscratches And Flyspecks, 1973; The Incompleat Folksinger (with Charles Seeger), 1973; The Foolish Frog, 1973; Where Have All The Flowers Gone (autobiography), 1993; Co-writer with Robert Reiser: Abiyoyo, 1983; Carry It On, 1986; Everybody Says Freedom, 1990; Honours: Westchester People's Action Committee, Peace and Justice Award to Toshi and Peter Seeger, 1990; NEA National Medal Of Arts, 1994; Kennedy Center Honours, 1994. Membership: AFofM. Hobby: Axe chopping. Current Management: Harold Leventhal. Address: Room 1218, 250 W 57th Street, New York, NY 10107, USA.

SEGER Bob, b. 6 May 1945, Dearborn, Missouri, USA. Singer; Songwriter; Musician (keyboards). Career: Member, The Town Criers; Doug Brown & The Omens, 1965-66; Leader of own bands: The Last Heard, 1966-67; The Bob Seger System, 1967-70; The Silver Bullet Band, 1976-; Regular US tours. Recordings: Albums: Ramblin' Gamblin' Man, 1969; Noah, 1970; Mongrel, 1970; Brand New Morning, 1971; Smokin' OP's, 1972; Back In '72, 1973; Seven/Contrasts, 1974; Beautiful Loser, 1975; Live Bullet, 1976; Night Moves, 1977; Stranger In Town, 1978; Against The Wind (Number 1, US), 1980; Nine Tonight, 1981; The Distance, 1983; Like A Rock, 1986; The Fire Inside, 1991; Greatest Hits, 1995; It's A Mystery, 1995; Hit singles include: Ramblin' Gamblin Man, 1969; Katmandu, 1975; Night Moves, 1977; Mainstreet, 1977; Still The Same, 1978; Hollywood Nights, 1978; We've Got Tonight, 1979; Fire Lake, 1980; Against The Wind, 1980; You'll Accomp'ny Me, 1980; Tryin' To Live My Life Without You, 1981; Shame On The Moon (Number 2, US), 1983; Even Now, 1983; Roll Me Away, 1983; American Storm, 1986; Like A Rock, 1986; Shakedown (Number 1, US), from film soundtrack Beverley Hills Cop II, 1987; The Real Love, 1991; It's A Mystery, 1995; Also contributor to film soundtracks: Risky Business, 1983; Teachers, 1984; Miami, for television series Miami Vice, 1986; A Very Special Christmas benefit album, 1987; Let It Roll, Little Feat, 1988. Honours: Numerous Platinum discs; Grammy Award, Best Rock Performance, 1981; Star on Hollywood Walk Of Fame, 1988; Governors Award, NARAS, 1992; Motor City Music Awards, Musician of the Year, Outstanding National Rock'n'Pop Album, 1992. Current Management: Punch Enterprises, 567 Purdy, Birmingham, MI 48009, USA.

SEGLEM Karl, b. 8 July 1961, Ardalstangen, Norway. Musician (tenor saxophone); Composer; Arranger. Musical Education: Private lessons, 2 years music study at Scandinavian High School. Career: Toured Norway and abroad with jazz bands, 1985-; Now one of foremost saxophone players, Norway; Now working with own music based on Norwegian folk music; Numerous television and radio appearances; Concert tours: USA; Japan; Poland; Germany. Recordings: with Isglem: Poems For Trio; Sogn-A-Song; with Utla: To Steg; Juv; Brodd; Solo album: Rit and Tya. Memberships: TONO; NOPA; GRAMO; FONO; Norwegian Musician Association. Hobbies: Food; Nature. Address: Kongens Gate 16, N-0153 Oslo, Norway.

SEINE Johannes Hendricus, b. 30 Mar 1946, Amsterdam, Netherlands. Managing Director; Artist Manager; Agent. m. Annette Washington, 17 Dec 1971, 2 sons. Career: Manager, Amsterdam bands, 1964; Producer Dutch radio 3 Vara Drive-in show, 1969; Producer, Radio Northsea Mobile Show, 1972; Managing Director, Europop; Manager, agent for: American Gipsy; Lois Lane; Boney M; Doop; Tours organized with: Divine; Inner Circle; Latoya Jackson; Tower Of Power; Capella; Prodigy. Hobbies: Tennis; Football. Current Management: Europop. Address: Gaelstraat 1b, 2013 CE Haarlem, Netherlands.

SELIGMAN Matthew, b. 14 July 1955, Cyprus. Musician (bass guitar). Career: The Soft Boys, 1979-80; The Thompson Twins, 1981-82; Thomas Dolby, 1982-84; Toured USA, Europe, with Thomas Dolby, 1984; Performed at Live Aid with David Bowie, 1985; Session bassist, London, 1986-94; Radio Science Orchestra, 1994-95. Compositions: Co-writer of: The Brightest Star; Now And Forever; Motorcycle; Neon Sisters; Slipping You The Midnight Fish; Daddy; Stabbed In The Heart Again. Recordings: English Garden, Bruce Woolley And The Camera Club, 1979; Drip Dry Zone, SW9, 1980; with The Soft Boys: Underwater Moonlight, 1980; Lope At The Hive, 1981; Invisible Hits, 1983; The Soft Boys 1979-81, 1994; Black Snake Diamond Rock, Robyn Hitchcock, 1981; In The Name Of Love, The Thompson Twins, 1982; Magic's Wand, Whodini, 1982; with Thomas Dolby: Blinded By Science, 1982; The Flat Earth, 1983; Retrospectacle, 1994; A Moral Tale, Sophie Cherie, 1983; Absolute Beginners, David Bowie, 1985; Dancing In The Street, David Bowie and Mick Jagger, 1985; Be My Enemy, The Waterboys, 1986; with Transvision Vamp: Tell That Girl To Shut Up, 1988; Baby I Don't Care, 1989; with Morrissey: Yes I Am Blind, 1989; East West, 1989; Build It Up, June Mitchell, 1989; April Moon, Sam Brown, 1990; with Sinead O'Connor: The Value Of Ignorance, 1989; Fire On Babylon, 1994; China, Tori Amos, 1991; with The Stereo MCs: Elevate My Mind, 1990; All Night Long, 1992; The End, 1992; Nan Vernon: Manta Ray, 1994; with The Radio Science Orchestra: Theme From The Electronic City; The Architect; Beachcombing Man; The Brightest Star, 1995; As Producer: Crazy, The Pop Guns, 1991; Membership: Musicians' Union. Hobbies: Writing; Reading; Tennis; The night sky. Address: 68 Highbury Hill, London N5 1AP, England.

SELLAM Philippe, b. 24 Oct 1960, Algeria. Musician (saxophone). Musical Education: Self-taught. Career: Concerts with: John Scofield; Gil Evans; European Union Radio Big Band; Michel Portal; Many tours, Africa. Recordings: with Gil Evans; French National Jazz Orchestra; Michel Legrand; 3 records with own band African Project. Honour: Best Soloist, Concours National De Jazz De Paris La Defense, 1987. Hobby: Sport.

SELLAR Gordon Maxwell, b. 13 June 1947, Glasgow, Scotland. Musican (bass guitar, guitar). m. Julie, 22 Mar 1975, 1 son, 1 daughter. Career: Band member: Beggars Opera; Tony Crane; Huckleberry; The Alex Harvey Band; The Denny Laine Band; The Freddie Starr Band, 1994. Compositions: Featured on 2 Gordon Neville albums. Recordings include: Robson and Jerome, 1995. Membership: Musicians' Union. Address: 2 Clewer Court Road, Clewer Village, Windsor, Berks SL4 5JD, England.

SELLERS Joey Elton, b. 5 May 1962, Phoenix, Arizona, USA. Musician (trombone); Composer. Education: BS, Music Education, State University, Arizona. Musical Education: Studied improvisation with Warne Marsh; Chuck Mahronic; Bobby Shew; Gary Foster. Career: Merv Griffin with Side Street Strutters, 1984; US Presidents dinner, 1986; Numerous radio broadcasts; Brass quintets, I & II, St Louis Brass; Trombone with

California Arts Trombone Quartet. Recordings: Joey Sellers Jazz Aggregation: Something For Nothing; Pastels, Ashes; Malby/Sellers Quartet: Cosas; Kim Richmond/Clay Jenkins Ensemble: Range; Commission for Gil Evans Fellowship: Seeds; Trumpet Summit for Summit Records featuring: Bobby Shew; Alan Vizzetti; Vince D'Marino. Honours: Gil Evans Fellowship in Jazz Composition. Memberships: BMI; AFofM. Hobbies: Marathon running; Basketball; Philosophy. Current Management: Walrus Publishing; Balquidder Music. Address: 4243 E 5th Street #1, Long Beach, CA 90814, USA.

SELWYN Esmond Wayne, b. 19 Feb 1948, London, England. Musician (guitar). m. Veronica, 27 July 1975, dec, 3 sons. Education: BA Hons, Kings, London, German with French. Musical Education: Personal tuition from master musicians: Ivor Mairants; Tal Farlow. Career: Professional musician from age 12; Varied career especially in Jazz includes: Private party, Frank Sinatra, Savoy Hotel, 1975; Malta Jazz Festival, opposite Chick Corea and Elvin Jones, 1993; Tour with Salena Jones, Thailand, 1994. Recordings: Matt Bianco: Tequila; Melanie Marshall: Cocktail; Robin Jones Quartet: Eye Of The Hurricane; Don Rendell. Publications: Jake Lee Arrives; The Jakes Progress; Included in Guildhall Guitar Syllabus. Membership: Musicians' Union. Hobby: Tai Chi (qualified instructor). Address: Min Y Dyffryn, The Green, Gresford, Wrexham, Clwyd LL11 7BB, Wales.

SENFLUK Jerry (Jaromir), b. 17 March 1946, Prague, Czechoslovakia. Jazz Musician (Clarinet). m. Jirina, 7 June 1973, 1 son. Education:. Piano & Elementary Theory of Music, 1952-60; Clarinet, by Mr Karel Dlouhy, 1969-61; Intonation, 1959-61; Conservatoire in Prague, 1961-67. Career: Frequent bookings in West Germany, worked with a band accompanying Freddie Kohlman, and with Savoy Gang, swing quartet, 1975-77; Founded Hallmark Swingtet, Berlin, 1979-84; West End venues and composing, London, England, 1985-90; With pianist Mick Pyne, guitarist Nils Solberg, double bassist John Rees-Jones and drummer Rex Bennett, formed Capital Swing, 1991; Yves "Little Fats" Guyot and Eric Luter, residencies at Hotel Ermitage Golf near Gstaad, Switzerland, 1991-94; Radio Appearances: BBC2, Jazz Parade, 1993; BBC 2, Jazz Notes, 1994. Compositions: Pas De Chat; Air Condition Breakdown; Recordings: From East to West, 1974; We Swing - Take It From Me, 1995; Swing Express, 1997. Memberships: Musicians' Union; Association of British Jazz Musicians. Hobbies: Civil Air Transport; Fauna and Flora; Chess; Literature; History. Address: 280 Lordship Lane, Dulwich, London SE22 8LY, England.

SENIOR Russell, b. 18 May 1961, Sheffield, England. Musician (guitar, violin). 1 son, 1 daughter. Education: BSc, Business Administration, Bath University. Career: Worked as Antique Dealer; Member of group Pulp, 1983-97; Currently working as musical consultant/producer. Honour: Mercury Music Prize Nomination; Ivor Novello Award; Brat Awards. Hobby: Cooking. Current Management: Julia Trace & Co, 15 Pratt Mews, Camden, London NW1 0AD, England.

SEPE Daniele, b. 17 Apr 1960, Naples, Italy. Musician (wind instruments). Musical Education: Graduated, flute, Conservatorio Sanpietro A Masella, Naples. Career: Formed group, Gruppo Operaio 'E Zezi Di Pomigliano; Appeared festivals: Rennes, Martigues, Bonn, 1976; Played at festivals including: Les Allummes, Nanates; Vignola; Atina; Ravenna; Horizontal Radio Linz; Rai Stereonette; Audio Box; DOC; Radiotresuite. Compositions include: Arrangements for groups including: Little Italy; Bisca; Walhalla; Degrado; Music for theatre, ballet, cinema. Recordings: Malamusica, 1983; L'Uscita dei Gladiatori, 1991;

Plays Standards And More, 1991; Vite Perdite, 1993; Spiritus Mundi, 1995. Publications: L'Italia Del Rock; Encyclopedia Del Rock. Honour: Academia International Del Tango. Hobbies: Good music; Good eating. Current Management: Roberto Balassoue. Address: Daniele Sepe, Via Manzoni 191, 80123 Naples, Italy.

SERGENT Carole, b. 22 Jan 1962, Montargis, Loiret, France. Singer; Entertainer; Author; Composer; Actress. 1 daughter. Musical Education: CIM; ARIAM. Career: Festivals: Jacques Brel; Jazz Amiens; Jazz Montlouis; Printemps Bourges; Choralies; Jazz Paris; Tourtour Paris; Jazz Sous Les Pommiers; Estival; France Television 2; MCM Telsat; 1988-; 673rd concert, 1997. Recordings: Albums: Chant Du Corps, 1994; Cherche Passion, 1997. Honours: Ellipse d'Or Canal, 1992. Membership: SACEM. Current Management: J Fallot. Address: 45 Rue Jussieu, 78150 Le Chesnay, France.

SERMILÄ Jarmo Kalevi, b. 16 Aug 1939, Hämeenlinna, Finland. Composer; Musician (trumpet, flugelhorn). m. Ritva, 6 Nov 1962. Education: Studied with Frantisek Kovaricek, Prague; Master's degree, University of Helsinki, 1975. Musical Education: Composer's diploma, Sibelius Academy, 1975. Career: Worked for Finnish Broadcasting Company (YLE); Director, YLE Experimental Studio, 1973-79; Jazz improvising on trumpet, 1970s; Played with Czech artists, Emil Vicklicky, Rudolf Dasek; Artistic Director, Time of Music Festival, late 1980s-. Compositions: Avant-garde, electro-acoustic music; Music for chamber groups; Ballets and orchestral works. Recordings: Quattro Rilievi Condine; At Bizarre Exits; Random Infinities. Honours: Janacek Medal, 1978; Music Reward of the City of Hämeenlinna, 1981; Smetana Medal, 1984; State Grant for Composing, 1990-. Membership: Finnish Composers' Society. Address: Niittykatu 7 A 7, 13100 Hämeenlinna, Finland.

SERRANITO Victor Monge, b. 1944, Madrid, Spain. Musician (Flamenco Guitar). m. Victoria, 2 sons, 1 daughter. Education: Selftaught. Recordings: 32 albums and CDs. Honour: Golden Medal of Madrid City (first living flamenco player to receive this award), 1997. Hobby: Tennis. Address: Pascal Lair, RIAL Andorra Ltd. Address: RIAL Andorra Ltd, Avda de Tarragona 24, Andorra La Vella, Principat d'Andorra.

SERVI Jo, b. 17 May 1970, Aylesbury, Buckinghamshire, England. Vocalist; Actor. Career: Session singer, 1988-; Steel pan player, singer, Radcliffe Rollers Steel Band; Television: Saturday Superstore, 1986; Barrymore, 1993; Performed Tommy, Marquee, with the Who, 1993; Backing vocalist, duo, Sister-Brother; Lead singer, keyboards, The Bizz, 1993; Wind Parade, 1994; Joined Southlanders vocal quartet, 1995. Memberships: Musicians' Union; Equity. Current Management: Richard Starnowski Casting; Jackie Palmer Agency. Address: 2 Bateman Drive, Brookhurst, Aylesbury, Buckinghamshire WP21 8AF, England.

SEVERINSEN Doc (Carl H), b. 7 July 1927, Arlington, Oregon, USA. Musician; Music Director. m. Emily Marshall, 1980, 2 sons, 3 daughters. Career: Musician with: Ted Fio Rito, 1945; Charlie Barnet, 1947-49; Also with Tommy Dorsey; Benny Goodman; House band, Steve Allen Show, NBC, 1954-55; NBC Orchestra for Tonight Show, 1962-; MD, 1967-; Partner, Severinsen-Akwright Co. Recordings: Albums: Brass Roots, 1971; Facets, 1988; Night Journey. Current Management: Brentwood Management Group, 11812 San Vicente Boulevard #200, Los Angeles, CA 90049, USA.

SEVERSON Paul Thomas, b. 18 Aug 1928, Fargo, North Dakota, USA. Composer; Arranger; Musician (piano, trombone). Educator. m. (1)

Shirley Jean Thompson, div, 1 son, 1 daughter, (2) Karen Louise Schwankel, 1 son. Education: BMus, 1950, MusM, 1951, Northwestern University, Evanston, Illinois, USA. Career: Performed with various orchestras including Stan Kenton Orchestra, Hal McIntyre Orchestra, Chicago Theatre Orchestra and Chicago Civic Symphony, 1951-54; Performed with artists including Stan Getz, Dizzy Gillespie, Louis Armstrong, Zoot Simms, Art Van Damme, Ella Fitzgerald and Al Hirt; Solo trombonist and arranger, CBS Studios, 1954-62; Composer, arranger, producer, Dick Marx Associates, 1962-73; President, Severson Enterprises, 1975-84; Director, Musical Industry programme, Moorhead (Minnesota) State University, 1984-91; Leader, Great American Ballroom Band, 1980-91; Music Director, Red River Dance and Performing Co, 1980-96; Leader, Paul Severson and Friends Jazz Quintet, 1995-; Leader, composer, arranger, Pianist, Mood Indigo orchestra, 1996-. Compostions: Over 3000 compositions and arrangements in the broadcast and publishing media; Music for commercials including Chevrolet, McDonalds, Kelloggs, Sears and Wrigley; 4 network television themes; 22 music scores for films. Recordings: Albums: with Paul Severson Quintet and Septet. Publication: Co-author, Brass/Wind Artistry - Know Your Instrument, Know Your Mind. Honours: Hollywood Advertising Club Grand Slam Award, 1965; Silver medal, Advertising Federation, 1988; 15 Clio Awards; Outstanding Advisor Award, Moorhead State University. Hobbies: Fishing; Hiking; Playing bridge; Tennis. Address: PO Box 535, Ranier, MN 56668-0535, USA.

SEXTON Charlie, b. 11 August 1968, San Antonio, Texas, USA. Singer; Songwriter; Musician (Guitar). Career: Toured with David Bowie, numerous appearances with Letterman, Conan O'Brien; Acted in Thelma & Louise; Last Ride, with Mickey Rourke and Lori Singer; Recorded with Steve Earle. Compositions: Contributed to film soundtracks: Thelma & Louise, True Romance, Beverly Hills Cop II, Air America. Recordings: Solo Artist: Pictures for Pleasure, 1985; Charlie Sexton, 1989; Arc Angels, 1992; Under the Wishing Tree, 1995; Contributions on albums, as Member of the band, by Bob Dylan, Kon Henley, Keith Richards, Ron Wood. Current Management: Tim Neece Management, 13101 Highway 71 West, Austin, TX 78736, USA. Address: 13101 Highway 71 West, Austin, TX 78736, USA.

SEXTON Will, b. 10 August 1970. Guitarist. Career: Bassist for WC Clark Bires Band, performed & recorded with Stevie Ray Vaughan, Speedy Spaks, Joe Ely, Stephen Stills, Waylon Jennings, Steve Earle; Frontman for the Kill; Member of the Sexton Sextet. Current Management: Tim Neece Management, 13101 Highway 71 West, Austin, TX 78736, USA. Address: 13101 Highway 71 West, Austin, TX 78736, USA.

SEYMOUR Patrick, b. 11 Dec 1958, Reading, Berkshire, England. Composer; Musician (keyboard); Producer. Musical Education: BA Music, Oxford University. Career: Songwriter, film composer; World tours with The Eurythmics, 1986, 1989. Compositions: Film scores: Parallel Lives; Chantilly Lace; The Flat; The Johnsons; Co-writer, film score: No Worries; Co-writer: Revival, When Tomorrow Comes, Eurythmics; You're History (Shakespears Sister). Recordings: Keyboard player on albums withEurythmics: Revenge; We Two Are One; with The Pretenders: Get Close; Other albums by: Mick Jagger; Bob Dylan. Current Management: Anxious Music Limited. Address: 147 Crouch Hill, London N8 9QH, England.

SFECI Paolo, b. 15 May 1955, Zagreb, Croatia. Musician (drums). m. Gordana Farkas, 2 daughters. Career: Groups: Aerodrom; Parni Valjak; Boa. Recordings: 1 album with Aerodrom; 14 albums with Parni Valjak; 4 albums with Boa.

Honours: President, Croatian Musicians' Union; Memberships: EC, Croatian Performers Rights Collecting Society); EC, Porin Music Awards; Croatian Musicians' Union. Address: Al V Ruzdjaka 37, 10000 Zagreb, Croatia.

SHACKLETON Danny J, b. 7 Apr 1966, Wegberg, Germany. Engineer; Producer; Programmer; Writer; Musician (keyboards). Education: 4 years art college. Musical Education: Self-taught. Career: Freelance engineer, producer, studios throughout UK, for several years; Programmed for various projects including specialist jazz ventures, library music; Taught Music Technology to A Level; Various chart entries for albums, singles; Major jazz pieces due completion, July, 1995; Various dance projects, 1995. Membership: Musicians' Union. Current Management: Fairview Music. Address: c/o Fairview Studio, Willerby, Hull HU10 6DP, England.

SHAFRANOV Vladimir "Vova", b. 1948, Leningrad, Russia. Musician (piano). Musical Education: Piano, violin lessons from age 4; Piano diploma, Rimsky-Korsakov Conservatory, 1962. Career: Played with various bands throughout USSR; Became Israeli citizen, 1973; Became Finnish citizen, 1980-; Worked in Finnish jazz trios with Eero Koivistoinen; Represented Finland at Middleheim Festivals, Belgium, 1978; Ljubljana, 1979; Lived and worked in New York, 1983-; Performed duos, trios in local clubs with American jazz artists including : Ron Carter; Eddie Gomez; Mark Johnson; Al Foster; Mel Lewis. Recording: Album with Al Foster and George Moraz.

SHAKESPEARE Robbie, b. 27 Sept 1953, Kingston, Jamaica. Reggae Musician (bass); Producer. Career: Member, US rhythm partnership, Sly And Robbie, with Sly Dunbar, 1975-; Prolific session musician with artists including: Peter Tosh; Bunny Wailer; Black Uhuru; Grace Jones; Bob Dylan; Ian Dury; Joan Armatrading; Formed own label, Taxi; Tours with Black Uhuru. Recordings: Sly And Robbie Present Taxi, 1981; A Dub Extravaganza, 1984; Language Barrier, 1985; Sly And Robbie Meet King Tubby, 1985; Reggae Greats, 1985; The Sound Of Taxi, Volume 1, 1986; Volume 2, 1986; Rhythm Killers, 1987; Taxi Fare, 1987; Uhuru In Dub, 1987; The Summit, 1988; Hardcore Dub, 1989; Silent Assassin, 1990; Remember Precious Times, 1993. Current Management: Starline Entertainment, 1045 Pomme de Pin Lane, New Port Richey, FL 34655, USA.

SHALIT Jonathan Sigmund, b. 17 Apr 1962, London, England. Career: Saatchi and Saatchi; Sigmund Shalit and Associates. Recordings: Devised and presented The Glory Of Gershwin, featuring Larry Adler, produced by George Martin, guest performances include: Peter Gabriel; Sting; Elton John; Carly Simon; Elvis Costello; Cher; Kate Bush; Bon Jovi. Publications: Me And My Big Mouth, Larry Adler; Walking On Air, Trevor Jones. Membership: International Managing Forum. Hobbies: Triathlon; Sailing. Address: Cambridge Theatre, Seven Dials, Covent Garden, London WC2H 9HU, England.

SHANK Bud (Clifford), b. 27 May 1926, Dayton, Ohio, USA. Musician (alto saxophone). m. Linda Alexander Shank, 14 May 1994. Education: 3 years, University of North Carolina. Musical Education: UNC; Private studies, New York, Los Angeles. Career: Played in big bands of Charlie Barnet, late 1940s; Stan Kenton, late 1950s; with Howard Rumsey's Lighthouse All Stars, also trumpet ace Shorty Rogers, 1950s; Club, university, festival apppearances, North and South America, Europe, Japan, studio work, 1960s-70s; Formed world renowned LA Four, with Ray Brown, Jeff Hamilton, Laurindo Almeida, recordings, tours, 1970s-80s; Performed with orchestras including: Royal Philharmonic; New American Jazz; Gerald Wilson Big Band; Stan Kenton's

Neophonic; Duke Ellington; Created multi-media jazz performance The Lost Cathedral; Expanded Bud Shank Jazz Workshop and festival in Port Townsend, Washington; Works with sextet and quartet worldwide; Collaborated with koto player Kimio Eto and sitar player Ravi Shankar. Recordings: 126 as leader or co-leader, many others as sideman/featured artist; Also classical works by: Bach; Faure; Debussy; Ravel; Scriabin; Several scores for films and television. Publications: Autobiography in progress; Quarterly newsletter, Budnotes. Honours: Multiple Playboy Poll; NARAS; Theme International. Memberships: ASCAP; IAJE. Hobbies: F1 and Indy racing; Vintage car racing; Reading; Dining out. Current Management: Linda Alexander Shank. Address: PO Box 948, Port Townsend, WA 98368, USA.

SHANKAR Ravi, b. 7 Apr 1920, Varansi, India. Musician (sitar). m. Sukanya, 23 Jan 1989, 1 son, 2 daughters. Musical Education: Studied under Ustad Allaudin Khan of Maihar. Career: International career as solo sitarist; Former director of music, All-India Radio; Founded National Orchestra, All India Radio; Founder, Director, Kinnara School of Music, Bombay, 1962, Los Angeles, 1967; Concerts worldwide (except East and South Africa); Major festivals include: Edinburgh; Woodstock; Monterey. Compositions include: 2 Concertos, sitar and orchestra, 1971, 1981; Film scores: Pather Panchali; Charlie; Chappaqua; Ghandhi; Music for television production, Alice In Wonderland; Opera-ballet, Ghanashayam, 1989. Recordings: Over 50 albums include: Concertos 1 and 2 for Sitar and Orchestra, Raga Jageshwari, 1981; Homage To Mahatma Ghandhi, 1981; West Meets East (with Yehudi Menuhin and others). Publications: My Music My Life (autobiography), 1968. Honours: Fellow, Sangeet Natak Academy, 1976; Padma Vibushan, 1981; Elected to Rajya Sabha (Indian Upper House), 1986; Magisaysay; Grand Prize, Fukuoka, Japan; 12 honorary doctorates worldwide. Hobby: Reading. Address: Unit 2, 39 Tadema Road, London SW10 0PY, England.

SHANNON Sharon, b. 1968, Corofin, County Clare, Ireland. Traditional Musician. Education: German and Irish, Cork University. Career: Musician with the Waterboys, Room To Roam tour and album; Also played with Adam Clayton; Van Morrison; Sinead O'Connor; Dennis Bovell; Solo recording artiste, 1991-; Regular festival appearances including Glastonbury, Cambridge and Isle of Wight; Tours of US, Europe, Australia, New Zealand, Hong Kong, Japan. Recordings: Albums: Sharon Shannon, 1991; Out The Gap, 1994; Each Little Thing, 1997. Address: c/o Top Floor Management, 7-9 Sweetman's Avenue, Blackrock, County Dublin, Ireland.

SHANTZ Corry-Lynn, b. 18 July 1972, Edmonton, Alberta, Canada. Freelance Promoter. Musical Education: Associate of Applied Arts degree, Music promotion, marketing. Career: Promotion Coordinator for concert with internationally acclaimed gospel group The Total Experience Gospel Choir, and Grammy Award nominee, Esther Little Dove John. Honours: Award of Merit for Achievement in Promotions. Memberships: CCMA; ARIA. Hobbies: Golf; Music collection; Curling; Old film collection. Current Management: Corshan Productions. Address: 529 Beacon Hill Drive, Fort McMurray, Alberta T9H 2R4, Canada.

SHAPER Harold David (Hal), b. 18 July 1931, Cape Town, South Africa. Author; Composer; Music Publisher. m. Pippa Marsh, 1 son, 3 daughters. Education: Attorney-at-Law, Cape Bar, 1955. Career: Founder, Sparta Florida Music Group and Prestige Records Ltd, London; Writer of many Hollywood film songs. Compositions include: Softly as I Leave You (Frank Sinatra and Elvis Presley); Adaptation and libretto of opera La Bohème: Noir. Publications: A Prince of Liars, poetry; Book and lyrics of musical

opera Cyrano, 1996; Wrote poetic epitaph on Enoch Sontonga's National Monument; Contributed to President Mandela's Heritage Day tribute Speech. Honours: British Academy Awards for musicals Treasure Island and Great Expectations; Freedom of the City of London, 1989; Lord of Stoke Bruerne. Memberships: Queens Club; Hurlingham; Chelsea Arts; Memorial Society; British Academy of Songwriters, Composers and Authors. Hobbies: Songwriter memorabilia; Golf; Tennis; Chess; Poker. Address: Waterlane House, Wynberg Park, Cape Town, South Africa.

SHAPIRO Helen, b. 28 Sept 1946, Bethnal Green, London. Singer. Musical Education: Vocal lessons, Maurice Berman Singing Academy, London. Career: Solo recording artiste, aged 14; Numerous radio and television appearances by age 15; Tours worldwide including: UK, supported by the Beatles, 1963; UK/Ireland, with The Beach Boys, 1967; Far East, 1964; Poland, 1965; Concerts include: Concerts with own band, 1963-98; British Song Festival, Brighton, 1966; Gospel concert with Cliff Richard, Royal Albert Hall, 1991; Humph'n'Helen Show with Humphrey Lyttelton, 1984-98; Solid Silver Sixties Tour with The Searchers and Swinging Blue Jeans, 1998; Gospel concerts in UK and Europe; Television includes: Sunday Night At The London Palladium; Thank Your Lucky Stars; Subject of This Is Your Life, ITV, 1995; Film appearance: It's Trad Dad, 1962; Play It Cool, 1992; Theatre includes: I'll Get My Man, 1967; West End musicals: The French Have A Song For It; Oliver; Theatre: Cabaret, 1982; Goose Pimples, 1982; Ello Ello Ello, 1982; One For The Road, 1985; Seesaw, 1987; Numerous pantomimes as principal boy. Recordings: Albums: Tops With Me, 1962; It's Trad, Dad (film soundtrack), 1962; Helen's Sixteen, 1963; Helen Hits Out, 1964; All for the Love of Music, 1978; Straighten Up And Fly Right, 1983; Echoes of the Duke, 1985; Humph'n'Helen, 1990; The Pearl, 1990; Helen Shapiro 25th Anniversary Album, 1991; Kadosh, 1992; Nothing But The Best, 1995; The Essential Helen Shapiro, 1997; Enter Into His Gates, 1997; The Best of the 80's, 1997; Humph'n'Helen Mark II, 1998; Helen Shapiro at Abbey Road, 1998; Contributor, Echoes Of The Duke, with Humphrey Lyttelton, 1985; Hit singles include: Don't Treat Me Like A Child, 1961; You Don't Know (Number 1, UK), 1961; Walkin' Back To Happiness (Number 1, UK), 1961; Tell Me What He Said (Number 2, UK), 1962; Little Miss Lonely, 1962. Publication: Walking Back to Happiness, autobiograpby, 1993. Honour: NME Reader's Poll Winner, Best British Female Singer, 1961; 1 Gold Discs, 3 Silver Discs; BASCA Gold Badge of Merit, 1991. Current Management: John Robert Williams Productions. Address: PO Box 423, Chislehurst, Kent BR7 5TU, England.

SHARDA Anju, b. 17 Mar 1969, Perivale, Middlesex, England. Singer; Songwriter. Education: BA Hons, Communication Studies. Musical Education: A level Music; Grade 8 violin. Career: Member, Cardiff-based trio Banana Cat (later Glorious), 1991; Television: Band appeared on Rough Mix, 1992; Dance Energy, BBC2, 1993; Left Glorious, 1993; Co-writing deal with Simon and Diamond Dougal, 1994; Co-writing deal with Jon Moss (ex-Culture Club), 1995. Recordings: Backing vocals, album: The Lick, Definition Of Sound, 1992. Memberships: Musicians' Union; PRS. Hobbies: Swimming; Cooking; Drinking. Current Management: Sue Carling. Address: 13 Elvendon Road, London N13 4SJ, England.

SHAW Ian, b. 2 June 1962, North Wales. Jazz Singer; Musician (piano, trumpet). Musical Education: 8 piano grades (Trinity College of Music); BMus, King's College, London. Career: Plays regularly Ronnie Scott's London; Tours, UK, Europe; Worked with Kenny Wheeler; John Taylor; Carol Grimes; Ruby Turner; Mari Wilson; TV includes: Top of the Pops; Pebble Mill; Jools

Holland's The Happening; The Jack Dee Show; The Late Show; Radio: Kaleidoscope; Nicky Campbell (Radio One); Major US Tour, 1997. Recordings: Lazy Blues Eyes, album of jazz love songs with Carol Grimes, 1990; Ghostsongs, Live at Ronnie Scott's, 1992; Zebra, guest singer with Yello, 1994; Taking It To Hart, a tribute to Rodgers and Hart, 1995; Famous Rainy Day, 1996; The Echo of a Song, 1996. Publications: Making It In The Music Business, 1993. Honours: Perrier Award, Edinburgh, 1991; Nominated 5 times Best Jazz Singer, British Jazz Awards; British Jazz Awards nominee, 1997. Membership: Equity. Hobbies: Cooking; Animals; Drawing; Reading. Current Management: Viva Voce - Darren Crowdy. Address: 111 Sciarappa St, #6, Cambridge, MA 02141, USA.

SHAW Paul John, b. 20 Feb 1962, Dartford, Kent, England. Composer; Musician (keyboards, guitar); Programmer; Producer. m. Jacqueline Ives (Shaw), 2 July 1994. Musical Education: Self-taught. Career: Started business, Daybreak Productions, with David Rogers, 1987; Success with library music ever since; Regular CD-I and CD-Rom work; Conferences, television and radio including: Mr Blobby; BBC Radio; BBC Pebble Mill; Top Of The Pops; Live and Kicking; House Party. Compositions: 345 published works co-written with David Rogers; Mostly library music (production): Peanut Vendor, 1987; Mr Blobby, 1995; Light Of Summer, 1995; Mr Blobby, The Album, 1995-96. Publications: Various interviews in industry publications; PRS yearbooks. Honours: Ivor Novello, Best Selling Song, 1993; Various corporate awards for Mr Blobby. Memberships: Musicians' Union; PRS. Hobbies: Wildlife; Sport; Motor racing. Address: Carlin Music/Destiny Music, Iron Bridge House, Bridge Approach, London NW1 8BD, England.

SHAW Sandie (Sandra Goodrich), b. 1947, Dagenham, Essex, England. Singer; Songwriter; Record Producer. m. (1) Jeff Banks; (2) Nik Powell. Education: Pschyodynamic Psychology, university. Career: International recording artist, singer, composer and producer; numerous hit singles, over 30 years; Winner, Eurovision Song Contest, 1967; Semi-retirement during 1970s; Relaunched music career with Morrissey, 1984; Numerous concerts, television and radio appearances worldwide; Founder, Arts Clinic, psychological counsellor, writer and lecturer. Compositions: Numerous collaborations with Chris Andrews. Recordings: Hit singles include: (There's) Always Something There To Remind Me; Long Live Love; Message Understood; Girl Don't Come; Tomorrow; Nothing Comes Easy; Puppet On A String; Monsieur Dupont; Hand In Glove (with Morrissey and The Smiths); Most 1960s hits self-produced; Latest album: Nothing Less Than Brilliant - The Best Of Sandie Shaw. Publications: The World At My Feet (partly autobiographical); Stress In Rock Musicians: The Phenomena of Fame and its Psychological Effect on the Developmental Process of Artists. Honours: Eurovision Song Contest Winner, Puppet On A String, 1967; International Ambassador for Women Aid, United Nations, 1985; Professor of Music, Royal Society of Musicians, 1998. Membership: Royal Society of Musicians. Hobbies: Painting; Jigsaw puzzles; Collecting faerie and angel images; Devout Buddhist. Address: c/o Negus-Fancey Co., 78 Portland Road, London W11 4LQ, England.

SHAW Tommy. Musician (guitar); Singer; Songwriter. Career: Guitarist, Styx, 1975-89; Damn Yankees, 1989-; Also member of side project Shaw Blades (with Jack Blades), 1995; Worldwide tours and concerts. Recordings: Albums: with Styx: Crystal Ball, 1976; The Grand Illusion, 1977; Pieces Of Eight, 1978; Cornerstone, 1979; Paradise Theater (Number 1, US), 1980; Kilroy Was Here, 1983; Caught In The Act, 1984; with Damn Yankees: Damn Yankees, 1990; Don't Tread, 1992; with Shaw Blades: Hallucination,

1995; Singles: with Styx: Sail Away; Babe (Number 1, US); The Best Of Times; Too Much Time On My Hands; with Damn Yankees: Coming Of Age; High Enough; Come Again; Where You Goin' Now; Silence Is Broken, from film Nowhere To Run, 1993. Honours: Motor City Music Award, Outstanding National Rock/Pop Single, 1992. Current Management: Madhouse Management, PO Box 15108, Ann Arbor, MI 48106, USA.

SHEARING George Albert, b. 13 Aug 1919, London, England. Musician (piano); Composer. m. Beatrice Bayes, 1 May 1941 (divorced), 1 daughter, (2) Eleanor Geffert. Education: Linden Lodge School for the Blind, London. Career: Musician with Harry Parry; Stéphane Grappelli; Leader, own quintet, with members including Gary Burton, Joe Pass, Cal Tjader; Later played in trio, duo and as solo artiste; Played with Marian McPartland; Hank Jones; Peggy Lee; Carmen McRae; Frequent collaborations with Mel Tormé; Appearances at: London Symphony Pops Concerts, 1986, 1987; London Palladium, 1987; Concord Jazz Festival, Japan, 1987; Vice President, Shearing Music Corporation. Compositions: Numerous popular songs including Lullaby Of Birdland. Recordings: Singles: September In The Rain; Lullaby Of Birdland; Let Their Be Love (with Nat "King" Cole); Numerous albums include: Latin Escapade, 1956; Velvet Carpet, 1956; Black Satin, 1957; Burnished Brass, 1957; White Satin, 1960; The Shearing Touch, 1960; Satin Affair, 1961; Jazz Concert, 1963; My Ship, 1974; The Way We Are, 1974; Continental Experience, 1975; 500 Miles High, 1977; On Target, 1979; On A Clear Day, 1980; Bright Dimensions, 1984; Grand Piano, 1985; More Grand Piano, 1986; Breakin' Out, 1987; Piano, 1989; with Peggy Lee: Americana Hotel, 1959; with Stéphane Grappelli: The Reunion, 1976; with Carmen McRae: Two For The Road, 1980; with Marian McPartland: Alone Together, 1981; with Mel Tormé: An Evening With Mel Tormé And George Shearing, 1982; Top Drawer, 1983; An Elegant Evening, 1986; with Barry Tuckwell: George Shearing And Barry Treadwell Play The Music Of Cole Porter, 1986; with Hank Jones: The Spirit Of 1761, 1989. Honours: Voted Top English Pianist, 1941-47; Winner, All-American Jazz polls; American Academy Of Achievement, Golden Plate Award, 1968. Memberships: BMI; Board directors, Guide Dogs For The Blind, San Rafael, Hadley School for the Blind, Winnetka, Illinois. Current Management: Joan Shulman. Address: 103 Avenue Road, Suite 301, Toronto, ON M5R 2G9, Canada.

SHEEHAN Billy, b. Musician (bass). Career: Founder member, rock group Talas, 1980-83; Bass player, David Lee Roth, 1985-88; Founder member, Mr Big, 1989-. Recordings: Albums: with Talas: Talas, 1980; Sink Your Teeth Into That, 1982; Live Speed On Ice, 1983; The Talas Years, 1990; with David Lee Roth: Eat 'Em And Smile, 1986; Skyscraper, 1988; with Mr Big: Mr Big, 1989; Lean Into It, 1991; Singles include: with Dave Lee Roth: Yankee Rose; Goin' Crazy; Just Like Paradise; with Mr Big:Green-Tinted Sixties Mind; To Be With You. Current Management: Herbie Herbert Management, 2501 3rd Street, San Francisco, CA 94107, USA.

SHEHAN Steve, b. 18 Jan 1957, Fort Eustis, Virginia, USA. Composer; Musician (percussion, bass). Education: Swedish Teaching Certificates. Musical Education: Kenny Clarke School; Classical piano, Balinese gamelan. Career: Concerts and recordings with: John McLaughlin, 1981; Yves Montand, 1982; Alan Stivell, 1982; Magma, 1984; Michael Jonasz, Veronique Samson, 1984; Kim Wilde, 1984; Richard Horowitz, 1985-92; Gipsy Kings, 1987-89; Amina, 1987; Leonard Bernstein, Carnegie Hall, 1989; Peter Gabriel's band and Akiro Inoué, 1989; Les Polyphonies Corses, 1989-90; Paco de Lucia's band, 1991; David Sylvian, Jon Hassel, John Cage, Manu Dibango, 1991-92; Film music with:

Elliot Goldenthal, 1991; Gabriel Yared (L'Amant); Several fashion shows, as composer and performer; Own publishing and production and record label: Dakota Music, Safar Production Inc. Recordings: Impressions de Voyages, 1984; Arrows, 1989; Assouf, with Baly Otmani Touareg, 1994; Figaro Si!, with D Figaro, 1995; Indigo Dreams, 1995; Safar - A Journey, 1995; Bye Bye, original film score, 1995; Recordings in: Amazonia; Indonesia; Ethiopia; Egypt; North Africa; Senegal; Spain. Membership: SACEM. Hobbies: Private pilot (multi and single engined); Ethno travelling; Recording. Current Management: c/o Sabbah -Safar Production Inc. Address: 18 Rue Charles de Montesquieu, 92160 Antony, France.

SHELDON Kenny, b. 1 May 1923, Berlin, Germany. Orchestra Leader; Conductor; Master of Ceremonies; Musician (trumpet, piano, drums, vibraphone). m. Rita Sheldon, 21 Feb 1961. Education: College, New York City; New York University; Columbia University & CCNY. Musical Education: Private study, Berlin; Manhattan School of Music, New York; Juillard, New York. Career: Entertainer in nightclubs, resorts, country clubs, colleges, hotels; Worldwide tours with Dance Orchestra and Swing Jazz band; Starred, Stars & Styles, New York City; Television: Quantum Leap; Peaceable Kingdom; Composer, arranger, for own Ballroom Dance Orchestra. Recordings: Album: Dance Around the World with Kenny Sheldon Orchestra; Producer: Theme From Love Story, with Andy Williams. Honours: Plaques from various Mayors and City Councils, USA. Memberships: AFofM; Beverly Hills Chamber of Commerce. Hobbies: Electronic engineering; Ballroom dancing; Volleyball; Tennis. Current Management: Kenny Sheldon Orchestras and Entertainment. Address: 1420 North Fuller Avenue, Suite 304, Los Angeles, CA 90046, USA.

SHEPARD Leslie Alan, b. 21 June 1917, London, England. Writer; Folklorist. Wife deceased, 1 daughter. Career: Commercial, 1923-41; Documentary film technician, production manager, director, producer of documentary films, 1942-57; Studied Indian music in Indan, 1958-59; Folk Music Collector, 1959; Production controlling officer central office of information, 1960-62; Editor, researcher, University Books, New York, Gale Research Company, Detroit, 1965-90; Publications: Author of Books on Street Ballads: The Broadside Ballad, 1962; John Pitts, Ballad Printer Of Seven Dials, London, 1969; The History Of Street Literature, 1973; Author, Editor, of various books on Indian religion, occultism and parapsychology; Editor, reprint programmes, written new introductions for some 70 reprints; Editor, Encyclopaedia Of Occultism And Parapsychology, 1st, 2nd editions, 3rd edition 2 volumes, 1991; 2 record albums with notes, Vox Humana: Alfred Wolfsohn's Experiments In Extension Of Human Vocal Range; Yoga Vedanta: Documentary Of Life In An Indian Ashram. Memberships: English Folk Dance and Song Society; Folk Music Society of Ireland; International Council For Traditional Music; Ephemera Society, London. Address: 1 Lakelands Close, Stillorgan, Blackrock, Co. Dublin, Ireland.

SHEPHERDSON Paul, b. 23 June 1941, Hull, England. Musician (drums); Drama Teacher; Director, Drama and Stage Musicals. m. Sandra Nicholl, 13 July 1963, 1 son, 1 daughter. Musical Education: Piano, 5 years; Self-taught drums. Career: Member, Mike Peters Florida Jazz Band; Supporting Kenny Ball Band; Roy Williams; Terry Lightfoot Band; Backing residental musician to most cabaret acts including: Marti Caine; The Nolans; Norman Collier; Faith Brown; Currently, own band with Martin Jones. Compositions: Co-writer, various musicals for local performance. Membership: Musicians' Union. Hobby: Greek holidays. Address: 73 The Wolds, Castle Park, Cottingham, Nr Hull HU16 5LQ, England.

SHEPPARD Andy, b. 20 Jan 1957, Bristol, Avon, England. Jazz Musician (soprano saxophone). Musical Education: Clarinet, saxophone, flute and guitar. Career: Musician with: Sphere; Klaunstance; Lumiere (French Big Band); Urban Sax; Paul Dunmall; Keith Tippett; Leader, own band, 1987; Founder, Soft On The Inside Big Band, 1990; Founder, Co-motion, 1991-. Recordings: Albums: Andy Sheppard, 1987; Introductions In The Dark, 1989; Soft On The Inside, 1990; 66 Shades Of Lipstick (with Keith Tippett), 1990; In Co-Motion, 1991; Inclassifiable (with Nana Vasconcelos and Steve Lodder), 1995; Songs With Legs (with Carla Bley), 1995; with Sphere: Spere, 1988; Present Tense, 1988; Guest musician with Judy Tzuke: Ritmo, 1983; Turning Stones, 1989. Current Management: Serious Speakout, 42 Old Compton Street, London W1V 5PB, England.

SHERRY Rachel Patricia, b. 16 Mar 1960, Nottingham, England. Musician (harp); Vocalist. m. John Byron, 25 Sep 1993. Musical Education: Birmingham University; Royal Academy of Music. Career: Appearances at Purcell Room and Queen Elizabeth Hall; Concert tours to France, Italy, Spain and throughout UK; Numerous television appearances as actress, singer and harpist; 4 programmes of music for harp and voice for BBC Radio and numerous broadcasts with BBC Singers. Recording: Rachel Sherry - Voice And Harp; New album due for release, 1996. Publications: Folksongs For Voice And Harp, in preparation. Memberships: Musicians' Union; Equity. Current Management: Alexander Personal Management. Address: 16 Roughdown Avenue, Hemel Hempstead, Hertfordshire HP3 9BN, England.

SHERWOOD John Torrance, b. South Africa. Composer; Producer; Musician (guitar); Engineer. Education: Architectural Association of Architecture. Musical Education: Studied classical guitar with Patrick Bashford and Hector Quine. Compositions: Soundtracks: Rumours Of Rain, CH4, 1992; Spoilt For Choice, BBC2, 1993; Trouble, CH4, 1993. Recordings: Albums: As guitarist with Haysi Fantayzee: Battle Hymns For Children Singing; As engineer with P M Dawn: Of The Heart Of The Soul And Of The Cross; Single: Set Adrift On Memory Bliss; As engineer: Project One and Irresistible Force: Outlaw Posse: My Afro's On Fire. Honours: Gold records for PM Dawn: Set Adrift On Memory Bliss; Of The Heart Of The Soul And Of The Cross. Memberships: Musicians' Union; PRS. Current Management: Paradox Productions. Address: PO Box 3083, London N1 8NZ, England.

SHEVLIN Anne-Marie Antoinette (Xuereb), b. 13 June 1964, Tunisia, North Africa. Singer; Songwriter; Musician (piano); Businesswoman. 2 sons, 1 daughter. Musical Education: Studied classical music with tenor Ivor Evans; Piano grades; Currently taking studio sound audio engineering diploma; Studied dancing and acting. Career: Dancer, pantomimes; Backing singer, various sessions; Frontwoman, composer, band, Natalie West and the Banknotes; Then solo artiste. Recordings include: Houndog; As songwriter: Right On The Edge; Wild Woman. Memberships: Musicians' Union; PRS; BASCA; Equity. Hobbies: Tennis; Reading; Walking. Current Management: Simon Harrison, B&H Musicians; Personal Manager: Lawrence Hall, Althorn Cottage, Althorn Farm, Latchingdon, nr. Chelmsford, Essex, England. Address: Lavender Cottage, Love Lane, Kings Langley, Hertfordshire WD4 9HN, England.

SHEYTANOV Jean, b. 16 July 1959, Bourgas, Bulgaria. Composer; Arranger; Musician (piano, synthesiser, guitar, computers). m. Anna Karabadjakova, 14 May 1983, 1 daughter. Education: College. Musical Education: Musical Academy. Career: Young competition, Bulgarian song; Television: Good Morning; Music, Music;

Musical emissions; Competition for Bulgarian Song: Golden Orpheus; Radio, top emissions, 2 times first place, 1 second place; Music for pantomime: 45 minutes, Faith And Heresy. Recordings: 2 singles; 1 album: Gallant Man. Publications: Many song s for Bulgarian singers. The spectacle: Faith And Heresy. Honours: 2 first places, radio; 1 second place, 1 third place: Golden Orpheus, 1992. Memberships: Union of Bulgarian Composers, 1986-; Society of Musical Authors, 1992-. Hobbies: Dealer in pictures, silver; Football. Current Management: Maxim Hristov. Address: Obelia 2, bl 225 Vh V, Sofia, Bulgaria; Ljuben Caralov 36, Bourgas, Bulgaria; Sozopol ul, Apolonia 12, Bulgaria.

SHIJI (Awoyinka), b. 23 Oct 1969, London, England. Singer; Songwriter; Musician (keyboards, percussion). Education: BEng (hons), Mechanical Engineering; MSc, Product Design. Career: Finalist, Sony Dance Music Search, 1993; Concerts: Ronnie Scotts, 1995; Orange, 1995; WKD, 1995. Recordings: Facets (Debut EP). Memberships: MCPS; PRS; Musicians' Union. Hobbies: Singing; Collecting jazz records. Current Management: Ivy Records. Address: 15 Reynardsons Court, High Road, London N17 9HX, England.

SHILKLOPER Arkady, b. 17 October 1956, Moscow, Russia. Musician (horn). m. Olga Goloborodko, 22 July 1981, 1 son, 1 daughter. Education: Moscow Gnesin Institut, 1976-81. Career: Bolschoj Theater Orchestra, 1978-85; Moscow Philharmonic Orchestra, 1985-89; Freelance Musician (Jazz, Classik, Folk), since 1990; Hornplayer (also Alphorn, Corno du Caccio); Jazz Podium; Jazz Time; Jazz Kwadrat. Recordings: On major record labels. Memberships: International Horn Society. Address: Osennij Boulevard 6-526, Moscow, 121609, Russia.

SHINKARUK Irina Volodimirivna, b. 31 July 1979, Fastiv, Kiev, Ukraine. Singer. Education: Musical College, Zhitomyr-city, Ukraine,1995-97; Zhitomir State Pedagogical Institute, 1995-. Career: Film: Cheremhove Vihola, 1993; Tours of Ukraine, 1994; Concert of The Prizewinners, at International Competition: The Voice of Asia, 1994; Tours: France; Germany; Hungary, other countries, 1994; Television show: Ukraine, Spring, Slavutich (commemorating Chernobyl), 1995. Compositions: Mermaid's Week, 1993; I'm Like A Bird, 1996. Recordings: I'm Like A Bird (14 Songs of the Period), 1993; The Fifth Season Of The Year (The Season Of Love), 1995; Step Towards the Summer, 1996; Best composition: The Moon Talisman (Misyachniy Oberig). Publications: The Stars Of Chervona Ruta Academy, 1993. Honours: First Prize: Chervona Ruta, 1993; Grand Prize, International Festival, Bilostotsky Malvi, Poland, 1993; Diploma FIDOF vth International Festival, The Voice of Asia, 1994; The Best Singer, nominated to Magic Rock, Festival Of New Stars of The Old Year, 1994. Membership: FIDOF. Hobby: Ukrainian folklore, especially Ukrainian legends, ancient Christian and BC rituals. Current Management: Vlodimir Shinkaruk. Address: 102 B Ten Str, Apt 65, Zhitomir 262024, Ukraine.

SHIPSTON Roy, b. 25 Aug 1951, London, England. Musician (keyboards); Vocalist; Composer; Arranger; Record Producer. m. Julia Diane Twigg, 23 Nov 1968, div 1994, 1 son, 1 daughter. Musical Education: ABRSM Finals: Theory Of Music, Pianoforte. Career: Music journalist, Disc and Music Echo, 1969-71; Musician, 1971-; Member, Formerly Fat Harry; Leader, own bands: Rococo; The Brats; Future; Performed on nearly 30 albums; Sessions with Peter Green; Carl Palmer (ELP); Mike Harrison (Spooky Tooth); Chris Thompson; Peter Cox (Go West); Jake Sollo (Osibisa); Biddu; Jim Diamond; Now member, First Light; Co-owner, The Mill Recording Studios, Cookham, Berkshire; 1989-94; Clients included: Elton John; George Harrison;

Chris Rea; Clannad. Honours: 2 BASF/Studio Master Awards; Music Week Top European Engineer Award; 3M Award. Memberships: PRS; Musicians' Union. Current Management: Rococo Productions. Address: 2 Selwyn Court, Church Road, Richmond, Surrey TW10 6LR, England.

SHIPTON Russ, b. 22 Feb 1946, Manchester, England. Musician; Guitar Teacher; Writer. Education: BA Economics. Musical Education: Self-taught. Publications: Tutor books including: The Complete Guitar Player; Russ Shipton's Rock and Pop Guitar; Russ Shipton's Keyboard and Piano Course; Russ Shipton's Music Course: Guitar, Keyboards. Address: 35 Tadmor Street, London W12 8AH, England.

SHIPWAY Nigel Howard, b. 29 Mar 1953, Reading, Berkshire, England. Musician (percussion, timpani, mallets). Musical Education: Studied percussion, composition with James Blades, Royal Academy of Music; Reg Barker, principal percussionist, Royal Opera House; Studied with Bobby Christian, USA. Career: Film appearances: Hunchback; The Wall; Return To Oz; Musical performances: Principal percussionist, National Symphony Orchestra, for 21 years; Academy of St Martins in the Fields; English Chamber Orchestra; Cats, New London Theatre, 13 years; Played on film scores: The Far Pavilions; Knight's Move; The Tall Guy; Morons From Outer Space; The Honorary Consul; The Killing Fields; Appearances with: The Moody Blues; Pink Floyd; Bob Geldof; Gene Pitney; Dionne Warwick; Bob Hoskins; Jose Carreras; Kiri Te Kanawa; Placido Domingo; Frankie Laine; The Pointer Sisters; Billy Daniels. Compositions: 44 studies for timpani; Style Studies For Xylophone; Concert Marimba Etude. Recordings: Over 1000 listings with: National Symphony Orchestra; English Chamber Orchestra; Royal Opera House Orchestra; Alyn Ainsworth Orchestra; Ron Goodwin Orchestra. Publications: Articles: Talking Drums; Percussive Notes. Honours: President (UK Chapter), Percussive Arts Society; Royal Society of Musicians. Memberships: Bonsai growing; Reading; Cookery; DIY; Photography; Historical research. Current Management: Lindsay Music Entertainments. Address: 23 Hitchin Street, Biggleswade, Bedfordshire SG18 8AX, England.

SHOCKED Michelle, b. 24 Feb 1962, Dallas, Texas, USA. Singer; Songwriter; Musician (guitar). m. 4 July 1992. Education: BSc, University of Texas, Austin. Career: Worldwide tours, 1987-; Concerts include: Heineken Festival, Leeds, 1995. Recordings: Short Sharp Shocked, 1988; Captain Swing, 1989; Arkansas Traveller, 1992; Kind Hearted Woman, 1994. Honours: Grammy Nominations, 1988, 1992; Brit Award Nomination, 1988. Membership: NARAS; Rhythm & Blues Foundation. Hobbies: Politics; Community Activities. Current Management: Peter Paterno, King, Purtich, Holmes, Paterno, Berliner, 2121 Avenue of the Stars, 22nd Floor, Los Angeles, CA90067, USA. Address: 828 Royal Street #520, New Orleans, LA 70116, USA.

SHORE Dinah (Frances Rose), b. 1 Mar 1921, Winchester, Tennessee, USA. Singer; Television Presenter. m. (1) George Montgomery, 5 Dec 1943 (divorced 1962), 1 son, 1 daughter; m (2) Maurice Smith, 26 May 1963 (divorced 1964). Education: BA, Vanderbilt University, 1939. Career: Professional singer, 1938-; Entertained Allied troops, ETO, 1944; Star, radio programmes: Eddie Cantor; Proctor and Gamble; Star, television shows for: General Foods, 1941; Chevrolet, 1951-61; Film appearances include: Thank Your Lucky Stars, 1943; Make Mine Music, 1946; Follow The Boys, 1963; Oh! God, 1977; Hostess, own television shows: Dinah's Place, NBC, 1970-74; Dinah!, CBS, 1974-79; Dinah! And Friends, 1979-; A Conversation With Dinah, TNN, 1989-; Television appppearance, Hotel, 1987. Publication: Someone's In The Kitchen With Dinah, 1971. Honours: New Star Of Radio, 1940;

Motion Picture Daily Fame's Radio Poll, Best Female Vocalist, 1941-61; Michael Award, Best Female Vocalist, Radio and TV, 1950-52; Billboard Awards: Favourite Female Vocalist On Records, 1947; Favourite Popular Female Singer In Radio, 1949; Gallup Poll, America's Best Known And Favourite Female Vocalist, 1950-51; 10 Emmy Awards, 1954-76; Peabody Award, 1958; Sylvania Award, 1958. Address: c/o Triad Artists, Los Angeles, USA.

SHORROCK Glenn, b. 30 July 1944, Rochester, Kent, England.Vocalist. Career: Vocalist, Little River Band (formerly Mississippi), 1975-83; 1988-; Also solo artiste. Recordings: Albums: Little River Band, 1975; After Hours, 1976; Diamantina Cocktail, 1977; Sleeper Catcher, 1978; First Under The Wire, 1979; Backstage Pass, 1980; Time Exposure, 1981; Greatest Hits, 1982; Monsoon, 1988; Too Late To Load, 1989; Get Lucky, 1990. Current Management: Talentworks Pty Ltd, Suite 1a, 663 Victoria Street, Abbotsford, VIC 3067, Australia.

SHORTER Wayne, b. 25 Aug 1933, Newark, New Jersey, USA. Musician (saxophone). Education: BA, New York University, 1956. Career: Saxophonist with: Art Blakey, 1959-63; Miles Davis, 1964-70; Weather Report, 1970-86; Solo artiste, 1962-; Recent appearances include: London Jazz Festival, 1995. Recordings: Solo albums: Freeform, 1962; Search For A New Land, 1964; Night Dreamer, 1964; Some Other Stuff, 1964; Ju Ju, 1987; Speak No Evil, 1965; All Seeing Eye, 1966; Adam's Apple, 1967; Schizophrenia, 1968; Odyssey Of Iska, 1970; Super Nova, 1970; Shorter Moments, 1972; Wayne Shorter, 1974; Moto Grosso Felo, 1975; Native Dancer, 1975; The Soothsayer, 1980; Etcetera, 1981; Wayning Moments, 1984; Second Genesis (reissue) 1984; Atlantis, 1985; Best Of..., 1988; Introducing...; Phantom Navigator, 1987; Joy Ryder, 1988; with Weather Report: Weather Report, 1971; I Sing The Body Electric, 1972; Sweetnighter, 1973; Mysterious Traveller, 1974; Tail Spinnin', 1975; Black Market, 1976; Black Market/Heavy Weather, 1978; Mr Gone, 1978; 8.30, 1979; Night Passage, 1980; Weather Report, 1982; Procession, 1983; Domino Theory, 1984; Sportin' Life, 1985; This Is This!, 1986; Greatest Hits, 1991; with Miles Davis: In Berlin, 1964; ESP, 1965; Miles Smiles, 1967; The Sorcerer, 1967; Nefertiti, 1968; Miles In The Sky, 1968; Filles De Kilimanjaro, 1968; In A Silent Way, 1969; Bitches Brew, 1970; Live Evil, 1972; Big Fun, 1974; Water Babies, 1977; Circle In The Round, 1979; with Joni Mitchell: Don Juan's Reckless Daughter, 1977; Mingus, 1979; Wild Things Run Fast, 1982; Dog Eat Dog, 1985; Chalk Mark In A Rain Storm, 1988; Night Ride Home, 1991; Also featured on recordings by: Airto; Stanley Clarke; Don Henley; Herbie Hancock; Freddie Hubbard; Jaco Pastorius; Sanatana; Steely Dan; Joe Zawinul. Address: c/o The Jazz Tree, 648 Broadway, Suite 703, New York, NY 10012, USA.

SHPORTKO Victor, b. 30 Oct 1944, Dniepropetrovsk, Ukraine. Singer. m. Natalia Biezko, 29 Oct 1977, 1 son, 1 daughter. Education: Kiev Institute of Culture. Musical Education: Dniepropetrovsk Music Institute. Career: Tours: Canada; USA; Belgium; Poland; Czechoslovakia; Germany; Greece; Appears regularly on Ukrainian television and radio. Recordings: 3 Ukrainian cassettes. Honours: Singer Laureate International Competitions. Memberships: Ukrainian Musical Societies. Hobbies: Travel. Current Management: Nicholas Tarasinko, 3A Horkogo Street, Kiev, Ukraine. Address: 125A Horogo Street, Apartment 109, Kiev 252006, Ukraine.

SHREEVE Mark, b. 2 June 1957, Great Yarmouth, Norfolk, England. Composer; Musician (keyboards, synthesisers, guitar). Education: Studied architecture. Musical Education: Self-taught. Career: UK Electronica Festival, 1983,

1984, 1990; EMMA Festival, 1994; KLEM Festival, Netherlands, 1995. Compositions: Songs include: Touch Me, 1986; I Surrender, 1987; True Devotion, 1988 (all recorded by Samantha Fox); Recordings: Albums: Assassin, 1983; Legion, 1985; Crash Head, 1988; Nocturne, 1995; Soundtracks include: Turnaround, 1986; Buy And Cell, 1988; Honor Bound, 1989. Honours: Gold, Silver discs, UK, USA; ASCAP Awards, various songs. Membership: PRS. Hobbies: Motorcycles; Tennis; Films. Current Management: Virtual World Ltd. Address: 155 Prince George Avenue, Southgate, London N14 4TD, England.

SHRIEVE Michael, b. 6 July 1949, San Francisco, California, USA. Musician (drums). m. Cindy Weintraub, 1 May 1982, 1 son. Education: BA, San Mateo Junior College. Musical Education: BA studies with Anthony Cirome. Career: Long involvement as drummer/percussionist with Santana; Recorded with artists such as: The Rolling Stones; Steve Winwood; David Crosby; Also with experimental jazz musicians: Stomu Yamashta; Klaus Schulze; John McLaughlin; Bill Frisell; One of first to experiment with electronic drums, 1973-; Film and television compositions include: The Tempest; The Bedroom Window. Recordings: with Santana: Santana; Abraxas; Woodstock; Santana III; Caravansérail; Welcome; Lotus; Barboletta; with Steve Winwood: Automatic Man; with Stomu Yamashta: Go; with David Crosby: If Only I Could Remember My Name; with John McLaughlin: Love Devotion and Surrender; with The Rolling Stones: Emotional Rescue; Tattoo You; with Bill Frisell: Fascination; Solo: Two Doors. Honours: Melody Maker; Modern Drummer; Grammy Nomination. Memberships: BMI; NARAS; Percussive Arts Society. Hobbies: Books; Film; Computers. Current Management: CMP Records. Address: 4756 University Village Place NE #288, Seattle, WA 98105, USA.

SCHUTZBANK Carol L. Publisher; Writer; Public Relations; Marketing; Promoter; Manager. Education: Graduate, cum laude, Deans List Honoree, Temple University. Career: Senior Editor, Director, Advertising, marketing, B-Side Magazine; Coordinates concerts, Clean Water Action, non-profit environmental group; Works with Rock the Vote, Rock For Choice, promote the organizations and issues awareness; Co-producer, Delaware Valley Music Poll Wards, 1992; Currently, Member, Board of Directors, co-producer event; Worked with; Raw Ltd, promotion and Management company; Pulsations nightclub; Coordinated Metal Mondays, heavy metal concert night; The Kennel Club nightclub; The Soviet Jewry Council; The Jewish Community Relations County; Society for Industrial and Applied Mathematics; Philadelphia Music Alliance; Formed Earwig Incorporated, music resource organization; Own label; Own independent concert promotions company; Personally managed bands including: The Electric Love Muffin. Honours: Golden Poet, Silver Poet, The American Poetry Association. Membership: Executive board, Philadelphia Audiences for Arts and Culture.

SIBERIL Soïg, b. 1 Feb 1955, France. Musician (Celtic guitar). 1 son. Musical Education: Self-taught. Career: Guitarist, 20 years; Member: Sked, 1975; Kornog, 1980; Gwerz, 1980; Pennou Skoulm, 1989; Kemia, 1989; Orion, 1992; La Rouchta, 1992; Numerous concerts and festivals all over Europe and America. Recordings: 1 solo album: Digor, 1993; 15 albums with other bands, including 5 with Kornog, 3 with Gwerz. Honours: Prix Academie du Disque Charles Cros: Gwertz, 1987; Le Sours Du Scorff, 1995. Hobbies: Gardening. Address: Mesgouez, 29270 Motreff, Brittany, France.

SIBERRY Jane, b. 12 Oct 1955, Toronto, Ontario, Canada. Singer; Songwriter; Musician (piano, guitar). Education: BSc Honours, University of Guelph (Ontario). Musical Education:

Self-taught. Career: Guest at Peter Gabriel's Real World recording week, 1994; Co-wrote and performed closing title track in film: The Crow; 5 world tours; Contributing artist on Hector Zazoos project, Songs From The Cold North Seas; Wrote, performed Calling All Angels, for Wim Wender's film Until The End Of The World. Recordings: Albums: Jane Siberry, 1981; No Borders Here, 1983; The Speckless Sky, 1985; The Walking, 1987; Bound By The Beauty, 1989; When I Was A Boy, 1993; Maria, 1995; Teenager, 1997. Honours: Casby (Canadian People's Choice Award); Album and Producer of the Year, 1986; Now Magazine Songwriter Of The Year, 1995. Current Management: Bob Blumer, Bob Blumer Management. Address: 2700 Rutherford Drive, Los Angeles, CA, USA.

SIDDIQUI Khalid, b. 14 Feb 1970, Oxford, England. Vocalist; Musician (guitar, lap steel, mandolin). Education: University of East London. Career: Founded Doleboy Cowboy record label, 1990; Releases own material, other bands' material, and re-issues; UK tour, 1993; Television: Kilroy; Radio: GLR; Mark Radcliffe, BBC Radio 1; Working/production with other bands; Currently tours London only. Recordings: City Of Circles; Spend Monday Evening With; Angry Young Women Don'tcha Just Love 'Em; God's Outlaw; Man With Cock; Background Music On Paper; Various other bands / productions include: Tribute To Johan Penson, Yupe Yeah. Publications: Contributor: Alcohol And Actors - Their Uses And Abuses; Surviving Performance Poetry Vol III: Modernists; Various fanzines. Honours: Best Soundtrack (University of Westminster) Musical accompaniment (Jackson Comedy com). Membership: Pub-Orientation Rock National Organ. Hobbies: Paranormal Arbitrator; Legal Advice; B-Movies. Current Management: Doleboy Cowboy Music. Address: 14 Westbury Road, Feltham, Middlesex TW13 5HQ, England.

SIEBINGER Manfred, b. 6 Dec 1956, Salzburg, Austria. Concert Promoter. Education: Press-distribution; Advertising Agency; High School of Music. Career: Promoter, with local acts, 1984; Jazz/folk groups; Singer, songwriter; Acts produced by Broadway Musical Company, New York; Promoter, Lucio Dalla; Donovan; Gilbert Becaud; Stéphane Grappelli; Golden Gate Quartet; Paco De Lucia; Canadian Brass; Jaco Pastorius; The Dubliners; Dave Brubeck; Kris Kristofferson; Golden Earring; Blues Pumpm; Chris Barber; Pasadena Roof Orchestra; Flying Pickets, 1986-94. Hobbies: World travel; Cultures; Music; Modern art; Painting. Current Management: PO Box 165, A-5024 Salzburg, Austria.

SIEFF Adam, b. 6 Apr 1954, London, England. Jazz Manager; Record Producer; Musician (guitar); Retailer. m. Valerie Moss, 28 Oct 1975. Career: Producer, writer, guitarist, 1973-91; Jazz Department Manager, Tower Records, Piccadilly Circus, 1991-95; Jazz Manager, Sony Music, 1995. Recordings: with Edoardo Bennato: Abbi Dubbi; with Spitting Image: The Chicken Song (Number 1, UK). Publications: Writer, reviewer for Top; Blueprint. Honours: Double Platinum (Italy), 2 Gold Awards, Abbi Dubbi, Edward Bennato. Hobbies: Food; Manchester United Football Club; Cats. Address: Sony Music, 10 Great Marlborough Street, London, England.

SIFFRE Labi. Bayswater, London, England. Singer; Musician (guitar). Musical Education: Studied music harmonics. Career: Member, various soul bands in Cannes, France; Solo artiste, late 1960s-. Recordings: Albums: Labi Siffre, 1970; Singer And The Song, 1971; Crying, Laughing, Loving, Lying, 1972; So Strong, 1988; Make My Day, 1989; Singles: It Must Be Love (later recorded by Madness), 1971; Crying, Laughing, Loving, Lying, 1971; Watch Me, 1972; (Something Inside) So Strong, 1987. Current

Management: Mismanagement, 754 Fulham Road, London SW6 5SH, England.

SIIKASAARI Eerik, b. 8 Oct 1957, Kotka, Finland. Musician (bass). Musical Education: Piano, electric and acoustic bass; Oulunkylä; Diploma, Sibelius Academy. Career: Appeared with Jukkis Uotila Quartet, Middleheim Festival, Belgium, 1978; Association with Seppo Paakkunainen's Karelia, 1980-; Plays regularly with bands: Jukka Perko Quartet; Trio Töykeät; Espoo Big Band; Jukka Linkola Quintet; Perko-Pyysalo Poppoo; Concerts with Karelia and big bands in France, Switzerland, Germany, UK, US. Honours: First prize, with Trio Töykeät, Belgian jazz contest, 1988; Yrjö Award, Finnish Jazz Federation, 1995. Address: Apollonkatu 23 B 55, 00100 Helsinki, Finland.

SILAG Marc, b. 22 May 1953, New York, USA. Tour Production Manager; Artist Manager. m. Susan Brown. Education: College. Career: General Manager, Bitter End, New York, 1974; Stage Manager, Bottom Line Theatre, New York, 1975-77; Tour, Artist Manager, 1977-; Tour, Production Manager for: Michael Urbaniak; John McLaughlin; David Sanborn; Herb Alpert; Patti Labelle; Pat Metheny Group; Paul Simon; Simon and Garfunkel; Personal Manager for: Ladysmith Black Mambazo; Chris Botti; Musical contractor, The Capeman, Broadway. Recordings: Co-ordinator: Graceland, Paul Simon (New York only); Rhythm Of The Saints, Paul Simon; Various recordings with: David Sanborn; Ladysmith Black Mambazo; Chris Botti. Publications: Musician Magazine; Record Engineer and Producer. Memberships: AFM; AFTRA. Hobbies: Fly-fishing. Current Mangement: Right Side Management. Address: 1674 Broadway #4C, New York, NY 10019, USA.

SILSON Alan, b. 21 June 1951, Bradford, West Yorkshire, England. Musician (lead guitar); Vocalist. m. Angela, 11 July 1986, 1 daughter. Musical Education: Self-taught. Career: Founder member, Smokie; Television: Top Of The Pops; Old Grey Whistle Test; Television and radio appearances in Germany; Norway; Denmark; Sweden; Ireland; Australia; Recordings: Numerous albums including: Pass It Round, 1975; Midnight Cafe, 1976; Bright Lights And Back Alleys, 1977; The Other Side Of The Road, 1979; Strangers In Paradise, 1982; Boulevard Of Broken Dreams, 1990; 20 top 20 hits, including If You Think You Know How To Love Me, 1975; Living Next Door To Alice, 1976; Lay Back In The Arms Of Someone, 1977; Compositions include: Boulevard Of Broken Dreams (number 1 album, Scandinavia, 6 weeks). Honours: Silver, Gold, Platinum discs worldwide. Memberships: Musicians' Union; PRS; MCPS; PPL; BASCA. Hobbies: Recording; Swimming; DIY.

SILVERLIGHT Terry, b. 15 Jan 1957, Newark, New Jersey, USA. Musician (drums); Composer. m. Judy, 9 July 1995. Education: Princeton University. Musical Education: Piano with Olga Van Til; Drums with Morris Lang. Career: Appearances include: Rosie O'Donnell Show, with Natalie Merchant; Atlantic Records 40th Anniversary, with Roberta Flack and Peabo Bryson; New Year's Special CBS Show, with Sheena Easton; White House Special, with Roberta Flack and Marvin Hamlisch. Compositions: All That Matters, for Louise; All I Wanna Do, for Carl Anderson; Chasin' A Dream, for Nancy Wilson; Buck Rogers, for Barry Miles; Take My Love For Real, for Yasuko Agawa and Philip Ingram. Recordings: Debut solo album: Terry Silverlight; Albums as drummer with Billy Ocean: Suddenly; Sad Songs; Love Is Forever; Color Of Love; Also recorded with: Tom Jones; Anne Murray; Laura Nyro; Phil Woods; Freddie Jackson; David Matthews; Jennifer Holladay; George Benson; Mel Tormé. Publications: Author, The Featured Drummer, 1981; Contributor to magazines including: Drum Tracks; Modern

Drummer; Percussiones; Princeton Alumni Weekly; TASCAM magazine. Membership: ASCAP. Address: 422 Carrollwood Drive, Tarrytown, NY 10591, USA.

SIMARD Bernard, b. 27 Aug 1959, Valleyfield, Québec, Canada. Musician (guitar); Singer. m. 8 July 1994, 1 son, 1 daughter. Musical Education: Self-taught. Career: Member, La Bottine Souriante; Tours include USA, Canada, Europe, 1984-87; Member, Manigance; Tours of France, 1988-90; Current member, Cabestan; First part of Raymond Léveque, 1994; Television includes: Ad Lib (Québec), BBC (UK). Recordings include: with La Bottine Souriante: La Traversée de l'Atlantique, 1986; Nouvelle Manigance, 1991; Tracks also featured on Down Home, Volumes I & II, 1986; with Cabestan: Tempête Pour Sortir; St. Laurent-Sur-Oust, 1995. Membership: SOCAN. Hobbies: Sciences; Poetry.

SIMMONS Al, b. 5 Sept 1948, Winnipeg, Manitoba, Canada. Entertainer (harmonica, banjo, bugle). m. Barbara Freundl, 22 Aug 1976, 3 sons. Musical Education: Self-taught. Career: All major symphony orchestras in Canada (Victoria, Vancouver, Calgary, Edmonton, Winnipeg, London, Toronto); Toured North America: Texas, New York, California, North West Territories; Also: Singapore, Hong Kong, Australia, Japan; Television: Sesame Street; Fred Penner. Recordings: Something's Fishy At Camp Wiganishie; Celery Stalks At Midnight. Honours: Juno Nomination: Something's Fishy At Camp Wiganshie, 1993; Juno Award, Celery Sticks At Midnight, 1996. Membership: Musicians' Union, local 190; ACTRA. Hobbies: Cross country skiing; Bicycle; Beach. Current Management: Paquin Entertainment Ltd. Address: 1067 Sherwin Road, Winnipeg, Manitoba R3H 0T8, Canada.

SIMMONS Gene (Chaim Witz), b. 25 Aug 1949, Haifa, Israel. Musician (bass guitar); Singer; Actor; Songwriter. Education: ABA, Sulllivan College, SUNY, 1970; BA, Richmond College, CUNY, 1972. Career: Founder, Wicked Lester, 1972; Founder member, US rock group Kiss, 1973-; Regular UK, US, European and worldwide tours; Actor, films: The Runaway, 1984; Never Too Young To Die, 1986; Trick Or Treat (with Ozzy Osbourne); Dead Or Alive, 1986; Kiss Attack Of The Phantom; Inventor, Axe bass guitar, 1980; Established Simmons record label, 1988-. Numerous compositions for Kiss. Recordings: Albums: Kiss, 1974; Hotter Than Hell, 1974; Dressed To Kill, 1975; Alive!, 1975; Destroyer, 1976; The Originals, 1976; Rock And Roll Over, 1976; Kiss Alive II, 1977; Love Gun, 1977; Double Platinum, 1978; Dynasty, 1979; Kiss Unmasked, 1980; Music From The Elder, 1981; Creatures Of The Night, 1982; Lick It Up, 1983; Animalize, 1984; Asylum, 1985; Crazy Nights, 1987; Smashes, Thrashes And Hits, 1988; Hot In The Shade, 1989; Revenge, 1992; Kiss Alive III, 1993; Unplugged, 1996; Solo album: Gene Simmons, 1978; Singles include: Rock'N'Roll All Nite; Beth; Detroit City; I Was Made For Lovin' You; I Love It Loud; Lick It Up; Tears Are Falling; Heaven's On Fire; Crazy Crazy Nights; Reason To Live; Hide Your Heart; Forever; God Gave Rock And Roll To You, featured in film Bill And Ted's Bogus Journey, 1992; Contribution, Runaway, to album Hear'N'Aid (charity project for Ethiopian famine relief), 1986. Honours include: Footprints at Grauman's Chinese Theater, Hollywood, 1976; Gold Ticket, Madison Square Garden, 1979; Inducted into Hollywood's Rock Walk; Kiss Day proclaimed, Los Angeles, 1993; Numerous Gold and Platinum records. Current Management: Entertainment Services Unlimited, Main Street Plaza 1000, Suite 303, Voorhees, NJ 08043, USA. Address: c/o Doc McGhee, McGhee Entertainment, 8730 Sunset Blvd, Suite 175, Los Angeles, CA 90069, USA.

SIMON Carly, b. 25 Apr 1945, New York, New York, USA. Composer; Singer; Musician

(piano, guitar). m. (1) James Taylor, 3 Nov 1971, divorced 1983, 1 son, 1 daughter, (2) James Hart, 23 Dec 1987. Education: Sarah Lawrence College, 2 years. Musical Education: Studied with Peter Seeger. Career: Singer, composer, recording artist, 1971-; Appeared in film No Nukes, 1980; Television appearances include: Carly In Concert - My Romance, 1990. Compositions: Opera, Romulus Hunt; Film scores: Working Girl; Heartburn; This Is My Life; Postcards From The Edge. Recordings: 22 albums of original compositions include: Carly Simon, 1971; Anticipation, 1972; No Secrets, 1973; Hotcakes, 1974; Playing Possum, 1975; The Best Of Carly Simon, 1975; Another Passenger, 1976; Boys In The Trees, 1978; Spy, 1979; Come Upstairs, 1980; Torch, 1981; Hello Big Man, 1983; Spoiled Girl, 1985; Coming Round Again, 1987; Greatest Hits Live, 1988; My Romance, 1990; Have You Seen Me Lately?, 1991; Letters Never Sent, 1994; Clouds In My Coffee 1965-95, 1996; Film Noir, 1997; Also appeared on albums by James Taylor; Lee Clayton; Mick Jones; Nils Lofgren; Tom Rush; Jesse Colin Young; Hit singles: Nobody Does It Better; Let The River Run; You're So Vain; Coming Round Again; Anticipation; Recorded with numerous artists including Paul McCartney; Luther Vandross; Mick Jagger; Linda Ronstadt; Michael McDonald. Publications: Children's books: Amy The Dancing Bear, 1988; The Boy Of The Bells, 1990; The Fisherman's Song, 1991; The Nighttime Chauffer, 1993. Honours: Grammy, Best New Artist, 1971; Academy Award, Let The River Run, 1989; Golden Globe. Membership: Songwriters Hall Of Fame. Hobbies: Painting; Decorating houses; Arguing. Current Management: Brian Doyle, All Access Entertainment Management. Address: 425 Madison Avenue #802, New York, NY 10017, USA.

SIMON Edward, b. 27 July 1969, Comunidad Cardom, Falcon State, Venezuela. Jazz Musician (piano). m. Maria A Simon, 19 Feb 1994. Musical Education: The University of the Arts, music performance, classical piano (not completed); The Manhattan School Of Music, music performance, jazz piano (not completed). Career: Member, Bobby Watson's Horizon, 1988-92; Played with Greg Osby; Kevin Eubanks; Paquito D'Rivera; Herbie Mann; Charlie Sepulveda; Jerry Gonzalez; Currently member, The Terence Blanchard Quartet. Recordings: Albums: Solo: Beauty Within, 1994; with Kevin Eubanks: The Searcher, 1989; Promise Of Tomorrow, 1990; with Greg Osby: Mind Games, 1988; Season Of Renewal, 1989; Man-Talk, 1990; with Bobby Watson: The Inventor, 1990; Post Motown Bop, 1991; Present Tense, 1992; Midwest & Shuffle, 1993; with Herbie Mann: Caminho de Casa, 1990; with Dave Binney: Point Game, 1990; with Victor Lewis: Family Portrait, 1992; Know It Today, Know It Tomorrow, 1993; with Claudio Roditi: Two Of Swords, 1991; with Craig Handy: Split Second Timing, 1992; with Charlie Sepulveda: Algo Nuestro, 1993; with Terence Blanchard: Romantic Defiance, 1995; The Heart Speaks, 1996; with Carl Allen: The Pursuer, 1994; with Terell Stafford: Time To Let Go, 1995. Honours: Third Finalist, The Thelonious Monk International Jazz (Piano) Competition. Memberships: NARAS; BMI. Hobbies: Weight lifting; Reading. Current Management: c/o Timothy Patterson, Split Second Timing. Address: 104 W 70th Street #11-C, New York, NY 10023, USA.

SIMON Paul, b. 13 Oct 1941, Newark, New Jersey, USA. Singer; Composer. m. (1) Peggy Harper (divorced), 1 son, (2) Carrie Fisher (divorced), 1 son, (3) Edie Brickell, 30 May 1992, 1 son. Education: BA, Queens College; Postgraduate, Brooklyn Law School. Career: Duo, Simon And Garfunkel, with Art Garfunkel, 1964-71; Appearances with Garfunkel include: Monterey Festival, 1967; Royal Albert Hall, 1968; Reunion concerts: Central Park, New York, 1981; US, European tours; Solo artiste, 1972-; Apperances include: Anti-war Festival, Shea Stadium, New York, 1970; Farm Aid V, 1992;

Hurricane Relief concert, Miami, 1992; Born At The Right Time Tour; Tour, Europe and Russia; Television includes: Paul Simon Special, 1977; Paul Simon's Graceland - The African Concert, 1987; Paul Simon - Born At The Right Time, 1992; Film appearances: Monterey Pop, 1968; Annie Hall, 1977; All You Need Is Cash, 1978; One Trick Pony, 1980; Steve Martin Live, 1985. Compositions include: The Sound Of Silence; Homeward Bound; I Am A Rock; Mrs Robinson; The Boxer; Bridge Over Troubled Water; Cecilia; Slip Slidin' Away; Late In The Evening; You Can Call Me Al; The Boy In The Bubble; Graceland; Albums: with Art Garfunkel: Wednesday Morning 3AM, 1964; The Sound Of Silence, 1966; Parsley Sage Rosemary And Thyme, 1966; Simon and Garfunkel, 1967; The Graduate (film soundtrack), 1968; Bookends, 1968; Bridge Over Troubled Water, 1970; Concert In Central Park, 1981; Various compilation albums; Solo albums: The Paul Simon Songbook, 1965; Paul Simon, 1972; There Goes Rhymin' Simon, 1973; Live Rhymin': Paul Simon In Concert, 1974; Still Crazy After All These Years, 1975; Greatest Hits Etc, 1977; One-Trick Pony, 1980; Hearts And Bones, 1983; Graceland, 1986; Negotiations and Love Songs, 1971-1986, 1988; The Rhythm Of The Saints, 1990; Paul Simon's Concert In The Park, 1991; Paul Simon 1964-1993, 1993. Publications: The Songs of Paul Simon, 1972; New Songs, 1975; One-Trick Pony (screenplay), 1980; At The Zoo (for children), 1991. Honours include: Grammy awards: two for The Graduate soundtrack, 1968, six for Bridge Over Troubled Water, 1970, two for Still Crazy After All These Years, 1986, one for Graceland, 1987; Emmy Award, Paul Simon Special, NBC-TV, 1977; Inducted into Rock And Roll Hall Of Fame, with Art Garfunkel, 1990. Address: Paul Simon Music, 1619 Broadway, Suite 500, New York, NY 10019, USA.

SIMON Yves, b. 3 May 1944, Choiseul, France. Singer; Songwriter; Novelist. Education: French degree, Sorbonne University, Paris. Career: Concerts include: Olympia, Paris, 1974; Théâtre de la Ville, Paris, 1975; Japanese tours, 1977, 1983. Recordings: 9 albums include latest: Liaisons; Many soundtracks. Publications: 7 novels include latest: La Dérive des Sentiments. Honours: Prix Médicis, Littérature, 1991; Légion d'Honneur (French equivalent MBE). Membership: SACEM. Hobby: Worldwide travel. Address: c/o Barclay, 16 Rue Fossés Saint-Jacques, 75005 Paris, France.

SIMONE Nina (Eunice Waymon), b. 21 Feb 1933, Tyron, North Carolina, USA. Singer. Musical Education: Juilliard School Of Music, New York. Career: Singer, clubs, Philadelphia; Recording artist, 1959-; Active in civil rights movement, early 1960s. Recordings: Albums: Little Girl Blue, 1950; Nina Simone At The Town Hall, 1959; At Newport, 1960; Forbidden Fruit, 1961; Nina Simone At The Village Gate, 1961; Sings Ellington, 1962; Nina's Choice, 1963; Nina Simone At Carnegie Hall, 1963; Folksy Nina, 1964; In Concert, 1964; Broadway...Blues... Ballads, 1964; I Put A Spell On You, 1965; Tell Me More, 1965; Pastel Blues, 1965; Let It All Out, 1966; Wild Is The Wind, 1966; This Is, 1966; Nina Simone Sings The Blues, 1966; High Priestess Of Soul, 1967; Sweet 'N' Swinging, 1967; Silk And Soul, 1967; 'Nuff Said, 1968; And Piano, 1969; To Love Somebody, 1969; Black Gold, 1970; Here Comes The Sun, 1971; Heart And Soul, 1971; Emergency Ward, 1972; It Is Finished, 1972; Gifted And Black, 1974; I Loves You Porgy, 1977; Baltimore, 1978; Cry Before I Go, 1980; Nina Simone, 1982; Fodder On My Wings, 1982; Live At Vine Street, 1987; Live At Ronnie Scott's, 1988; Nina's Back, 1989; In Concert, 1992; Various compilations; Singles include: I Loves You Porgy; Gin House Blues; Forbidden Fruit; Don't Let Me Be Misunderstood; I Put A Spell On You; Ain't Got No - I Got Life; To Love Somebody; To Be Young Gifted And Black; My Baby Just Cares For Me.

Address: c/o Fat City Artists, 1226 17th Avenue South, Suite 2, Nashville, TN 37212, USA.

SIMONS Ed, b. 9 June 1970, England. Musician. Education: Medieval History, Manchester University. Career: Member, The Dust Brothers with Tom Rowlands; Member, Chemical Brothers. Compositions: All recorded: Exit Planet Dust, album; Dig Your Own Hole, album (No 1 UK); Block Rockin Beats; Setting Sun; Leave Home. Recordings: Song to the Siren, 1993; 14th Century Sky, EP, 1994; My Mercury Mouth, EP, 1994; Life is Sweet, 1995; Loops of Fury, EP, 1996; Setting Sun (No 1 UK), 1997; Block Rockin Beats (No 1 UK), 1997; Electronic Battle Weapons, 1997; Elektrobank, 1997. HoNours: Twice nomminated for Brit Awards; Nomination for Mercury Prize, 1997; Grammy Award, 1997. Current Management: Robert Linney. Address: 1 Cowcross Street, London EC1M 6DR, England.

SIMPSON Christopher John, b. 13 Jul 1942, Harrogate, North Yorkshire, England. Writer; Musician. m. Linda Taylor, 28 Jul 1990, 1 son, 2 daughters (previous marriage). General Education: King's College, London. Musical Education: Self-taught. Career: Formed band, Magna Carta in 1970 (arguably longest running acoustic act in world); Appearances at various clubs and festivals; Numerous television and radio appearances; Performed at The Albert Hall 4 times; Toured 52 countries over 25 years; 19 tours for the British Council. Recordings: 23 vinyl albums and 12 CDs; Albums include: Seasons; Lord Of The Ages; Airport Song; International single: Highway To Spain. Publications: Books used in teaching in Netherlands: Seasons; Lord Of The Ages. Honours: Norway Sauda Prize; Gold disc, Seasons; Lord Of The Ages. Memberships: PRS; MCPS; BASCA. Hobbies: Caving; Reading; Outdoor activities; Food and wine; Conversation. Current Management: Magnamanagement, 16 Southwood Lane, Grassington, North Yorkshire BD23 5NA, England.

SIMPSON Jim, b. 27 Jan 1938, Westminster, London, England. Music Company Executive; Record Producer; Journalist; Musician (trumpet). 1 son. Musical Education: Self-taught; Tuition with Dougie Roberts; Dennis Darlowe. Career: Played with Locomotive, 1964-69; Managed Black Sabbath, 1969-71; Recorded and toured with American Bluesmen: Lightnin' Slim; Homesick James; Doctor Ross; Snooky Pryor, through 1970s; Began Birmingham International Jazz Festival, 1985; BT British Jazz Awards, 1987; Bruce Adams/Alan Barnes Quintet, 1995. Managing Director, Big Bear Music Group. Recordings: with Locomotive: Rudi's In Love; 5 albums with King Pleasure And The Biscuit Boys; with Black Sabbath: Black Sabbath; Paranoid; with The Quads: There Must Be Thousands. Honours: British Jazz Award, Jazz CD Of The Year, 1994. Publications: Launched jazz national magazine The Jazz Rag, 1986. Hobbies: Non-League football; Belgian beers; Jazz. Current Management: Big Bear Music. Address: PO Box 944, Edgbaston, Birmingham B16 8UT, England.

SIMPSON Kerri, b. 15 November 1960, Melbourne, Australia. Education: Selftaught. Career: Performed, toured, nationally & internationally in New Orleans, Chicago, London, Barcelona, Blues, Gospel, Alternative Dance; Regular House Artist, ABC TV's Big Gig, 1989-91; International supports for Kylie Minogue, 1991; Charlie Musselwhite, 1991; The Church, 1995. Compositions: Veve; Ah Jole; Higher; Jaguar; I Wonder; Very Popular; Shed; Billy Cowboys; Cry Mercy. Recordings: Veve, 1992; The Arousing, album, 1995; Speak, album, 1996; Higher, Razor Records; Turkey Necklasso, 1996; Psy Harmonica, Vol One; Veve Remix by Ollie Olsen. Honours: 2 ARIA Nominations, 1995; Featured Artist, Fritz Radio Berlin, 1991. Memberships: MU; Australian Performing Rights Association. Current Management: Wade Management, PO Box 2187,

St Kilda, West Vic 3182, Australia. Address: PO Box 2187, St Kilda, West Vic, Australia.

SIMPSON Valerie, b. 26 Aug 1946, Bronx, New York, USA. Singer; Songwriter. m. Nickolas Ashford, 1974. Career: Performing and songwriting duo, with husband Nickolas Ashford; Worked with Marvin Gaye singing on recordings in place of Tammi Terrell; Solo artiste, 1971-73. Compositions: Co-writer with Nickolas Ashford: Never Had It So Good, Ronnie Milsap; One Step At A Time, Maxine Brown, The Shirelles; Let's Go Get Stoned, Ray Charles; Songs include: Ain't No Mountain High Enough; You're All I Need To Get By; Reach Out And Touch Somebody's Hand; Remember Me; Solid. Recordings: Solo albums: Exposed!, 1971; Valerie Simpson, 1972; with Nickolas Ashford: Keep It Comin', 1973; Gimme Something Real, 1973; I Wanna Be Selfish, 1974; Come As You Are, 1976; So So Satisfied, 1977; Send It, 1977; Is It Still Good To Ya?, 1978; Stay Free, 1979; A Musical Affair, 1980; Performance, 1981; Street Opera, 1982; High-Rise, 1983; Solid, 1984; Real Love, 1986; Love Or Physical, 1989; As producer: The Boss, Diana Ross; The Touch, Gladys Knight. Current Management: Hopsack and Silk Productions, 254 W 72nd Street, Suite 1A, New York, NY 10023, USA.

SINATRA Frank (Francis Albert), b. 12 Dec 1915, Hoboken, New Jersey, USA. Singer; Songwriter; Actor. m. (1) Nancy Barbato, 1939 (divorced), 1 son, 2 daughters; (2) Ava Gardner, 1951 (divorced); (3) Mia Farrow, 1966 (divorced); (4) Barbara Marx, 1976. Career: Singer with Harry James Big Band, 1939; Tommy Dorsey, 1940; Solo concert singer, 1940s-; Numerous film appearances, as singer and actor, include: Higher And Higher, 1943; Anchors Aweigh, 1945; It Happened In Brooklyn, 1947; From Here To Eternity, 1953; Guys And Dolls, 1955; High Society, 1956; Pal Joey, 1957; Some Came Running, 1959; Can-Can, 1960; Von Ryan's Express, 1966; The Detective, 1968; The First Deadly Sin, 1980; Who Framed Roger Rabbit (voice), 1988. Recordings: Numerous songs include: Night And Day, 1943; Nancy, 1945; Young At Heart, 1954; Love And Marriage, 1955; The Tender Trap, 1955; How Little We Know, 1956; Chicago, 1957; All The Way, 1957; High Hopes, 1959; It Was A Very Good Year, 1965; Strangers In The Night, 1966; My Way, 1969; Something Stupid (with Nancy Sinatra), 1969; Other songs include: Three Coins In The Fountain; Come Fly With Me; Fly Me To The Moon; New York, New York; Lady Is The Tramp; One For My Baby; I've Got You Under My Skin; Over 50 hit albums include: In The Wee Small Hours, 1955; Songs For Swingin' Lovers, 1956; Come Fly With Me, 1958; Only The Lonely, 1958; Nice 'N' Easy, 1960; Strangers In The Night, 1966. Honours include: Academy Award, Best Supporting Actor, From Here To Eternity, 1953; Grammy Awards; Presidential Medal Of Freedom, 1985; NAACP Life Achievement Award, 1987. Address: Sinatra Enterprises, Goldwyn Studios, 1041 N Formosa Street, Los Angeles, CA 90046, USA.

SINATRA Nancy, b. 8 June 1940, Jersey City, New Jersey, USA. Singer; Writer. Musical Education: Lessons in music, dance, drama. Career: Appearances include: Sinatra/Elvis Presley television special, 1959; Recording debut, 1961; 10 appearances, Ed Sullivan Show; Numerous TV specials including Movin' With Nancy, 1967; Sold over 8 million records worldwide; Film appearances include: Wild Angels; Speedway (with Elvis Presley), 1968. Recordings: Albums: Boots, 1966; How Does That Grab You Darlin', 1966; Nancy In London, 1966; Sugar, 1967; Country My Way, 1967; Movin' With Nancy, 1968; Nancy And Lee (with Lee Hazlewood), 1968; Nancy, 1969; Woman, 1970; Nancy's Greatest Hits, 1970; This Is Nancy Sinatra, 1971; Did You Ever (with Lee Hazlewood), 1972; All-Time Hits, 1988; Lightning's Girl - The Very Best Of Nancy Sinatra, 1988; One

More Time, 1995; Singles include: These Boots Are Made For Walkin' (International Number 1 hit); How Does That Grab You Darlin'; Sugar Town; Something Stupid, with father Frank Sinatra (Number 1, UK); You Only Live Twice (theme to James Bond film); Jackson (with Lee Hazlewood); Did You Ever (with Lee Hazlewood). Publications: Frank Sinatra My Father, 1985; Frank Sinatra - An American Legend, 1995. Current Agent: Delseter/Saleter, 27 East 67th Street, New York, NY 10021, USA; Current Management: John Dubuque, Dublen Entertainment Group, 330 Merwin Avenue, Unit # F1, Milford, CT 06460, USA.

SINFIELD Peter John, b. 27 Dec 1943, Fulham, London, England. Divorced. Education: Selftaught. Appointments: King Crimson, writer, producer, 1969-72; Roxy Music, Producer, 1973; Solo album, 1974; Greg Lake, Co-writer, co-producer, 1974-80; Songwriting with Andy Hill, Albert Hammond, Bill Livsey and others, 1981-. Compositions: King Crimson: In the Court of the Crimson King; 21st Century Schizoid Man; I Talk to the Wind; Cat Food, King Crimson with A Ross; Emerson Lake and Palmer: Karnevil 9; Pirates; Greg Lake: C'est La Vie; I Believe in Father Xmas; The Land of Make Believe, for Bucks Fizz; Rain or Shine, for Five Star; Don't Walk Away; Have You Ever Been in Love, for Leo Sayer; Keep Each Other Warm, for Barry Manilow; Peace in Our Time, for Cliff Richard; Waiting in the Wings, for Diana Ross; As Dreams Go By, for Bette Midler; Think Twice; Call the Man, for Celine Dion. Honours: Ivor Novello Awards for Best Song, Have You Ever Been in Love, 1981, Think Twice, 1992; Call The Man, 25 million album sales. Membership: PRS; BASCA Council, Chair of IT Committee. Hobbies: Cooking; Book collecting; Herbal medicine; Politics. Current Management: c/o David Rauden, Co MGR Ltd, 55 Loudoun Road, St Johns Wood, London, NW8, England.

SINGER Ray, b. 4 July 1946, Tonbridge, Kent, England. Record Producer; Film Music Supervisor; Musician (percussion). m. Janine Turkie, 20 Sept 1987, 1 son, 2 daughters. Education: London Film School. Career: Singer: Television appearances: Juke Box Jury; Thank Your Lucky Stars; Gadzooks!; As percussionist toured with David Knopfler, Germany, 1992; Tours with Cinema, guest appearance on Eastenders; As film music supervisor: Another Country; Civvies; A Perfect Spy. Recordings: Producer: Peter Sarstedt: Where Do You Go To My Lovely; Frozen Orange Juice; Child: It's Only Make Believe; Japan: Assemblage; Robin Sarstedt: My Resistance Is Low; Produced music to over 100 TV commercials. Honours: Gold records; Ivor Novello Award, Best TV Series Music for Civvies. Memberships: PRS; Musicians' Union; Equity. Hobbies: Swimming; Music; Photography. Current Management; Olav Wyper. Address: Soundtrack Music Management, 22 Ives Street, Chelsea, London SW3 2ND, England.

SINGH Tjinder. Singer; Songwriter; Musician (guitar). Career: Musician and singer, Cornershop. Recordings include: Albums: Elvis Sex Change, 1993; Hold On It Hurts, 1994; Woman's Gotta Have It, 1995; I Was Born For The Seventh Time, 1997; Hit single: Brimful Of Asha (Number 1, UK), 1998. Address: c/o Oasis Productions, 909 Hudson Street, Suite 2, Hoboken, NJ 07030, USA.

SIOUX Siouxsie (Susan Dallion), b. 27 May 1957, Bromley, Kent, England. Singer. Career: Singer, Siouxie and the Banshees, 1976-; Film appearances: Punk Rock Movie (with The Clash, Sex Pistols, Generation X), 1978; Out Of Bounds, 1986; Tours, UK, Europe, US; Concerts include: Royal Albert Hall, 1983; Lollapalooza US tour, 1991; The Ritz, New York, 1992; Heineken Festival, Leeds, 1995; Also formed The Creatures, 1981. Recordings: Singles: with the Banshees: Hong Kong Garden, 1978; The Staircase (Mystery), 1979; Playground Twist, 1979; Happy

House, 1980; Christine, 1980; Spellbound, 1981; Fire Works, 1982; Dear Prudence, 1983; Swimming Horses, 1984; Cities In Dust, 1985; This Wheel's On Fire, 1987; Peek A Boo, 1988; Kiss Them For Me, 1991; Face To Face, 1992; with the Creatures: Mad Eyed Screamers, 1981; Miss Then Girl, 1983; Right Now, 1983; Albums: with the Banshees: The Scream, 1978; Join Hands, 1979; Kaleidoscope, 1980; Once Upon A Time, 1981; A Kiss In The Dreamhouse, 1982; Nocturne, 1983; Hyena, 1984; Tinderbox, 1986; Through The Looking Glass, 1987; Peepshow, 1988; Superstition, 1992; Twice Upon A Time - The Singles, 1992; The Rapture, 1995; with the Creatures: Feast, 1983. Current Management: Mission Impossible Management, 102A Western Road, Hove, East Sussex BN3 1FA, England.

SIRACUSA Gérard, b. 6 Oct 1957, Tunis, Tunisia. Musician (drums, percussion); Composer. m. Sophie Schneider, 28 Sept 1984, 1 son, 1 daughter. Education: Higher level studies in Science. Musical Education: Gold Medal, Percussion, National Conservatory, Rueil-Malmaison, France. Career: Goah, 1974; G S Duo with André Jaume, 1975; Trios with Raymond Boni and Michel Redolfi, 1976; Blaguebolle (musical theatre), 1974-78; Groupe de Recherche et d'Improvisation Musicales de Marseille (GRIM), 1978-84; Molto Mobile, 1980; Touchers (percussion quartet), 1981-83; Solo percussionist, 1981-86; G S Quartet, 1985; G S Alma Ata Quintet, formed for Banlieues Bleues Festival, 1986-87; Ensemble Musique Vivante, 1982-87; Un Drame Musical Instantané, 1982-84; 1991-94; Solibrius, solo percussion, 1986-; Claude Barthélémy - G S Quintet/Nonet, formed for Vandoeuvre-les-Nancy Festival, 1988-91; Collectif Incidences, 1990-94; G S Trio, 1991; Pied de Poule, 1991-93; Bûcher des Silences, formed for Moers Festival, 1991-; Trio Bal(l)ade, 1993-95; Duo with ValentinClastrier, 1995; Radio: L'Heure Bleue, by Philippe Charles, France Musique, Radio France, 1992; Television: Megamix, with Valentin Clastrier, ARTE, 1994; Fête de la Musique, ARTE, 1995. Compositions: Jardins de Paille, 1982; Titchak, 1985; Kaling, 1990; Pas Oui C'Est Non, 1993; M'Arco Polo, 1989; Ballade Sur Une Autoroute Et Ses Sept Bretelles, with Jean-Marie Maddeddu, 1994; Diptères, with Daniel Petitjean, 1993; Les Matins De Blanche, 1993; Les Petits Endroits Du Corps, 1994; 3 Minutes De Gloire, 1994; Le Dîner Percutant, 1993; Special Percussion, 1997; Music for Radio France Culture: Les Chiennes, 1987; Nationalité Française, 1988; Executeur 14, 1989; L'Argent, 1994; Le long voyage vers le jour, 1997; Les demeurés, 1997. Recordings: Musique Pour 8 - L'Oc, with André Jaume, 1982; Anna S Et Autres Histoires, with Trio MRS, 1983; Jardins De Paille, 1982; Terra, Michel Doneda, 1985; Slumberland, 1986; Kind Leader, 1991; What A Time, Michael Riessler, 1991; Hérésie, with Valentin Clastrier, 1992; Crasse Tignasse, 1993; Héloïse, 1993; Jamais Tranquille, 1993; Le Bûcher Des Silences, 1994; Les Tentations d'Abelard, 1995; Honour: First Prize, Academie Charles Cros, for Le Bûcher Des Silences, 1995. Memberships: SACEM; SPEDIDAM; ADAMI; SACD. Current Management: En L'Air Association. Address: 27 Rue des Papillons, 93100 Montreuil, France.

SISSAY Lemn, b. 1967, Billinge, Manchester. Poet. Career: BBC Radio 4, Pick of the Week, 1994; Various appearances on BBC, Channel 4 and other British Stations. Compositions: Tape recordings: Blackwise, 1988; Homeland, including 2 poems, 1988; The Play, 1996. Recordings: The Flag, 1996; Are Your Listening, 1992; Move On, 1993; Earth Flower, 1993. Publications: Books: Perceptions of the Pen, 1985; Tender Finger in a Clenched List, 1988; Records: The Flag, 1996. Current Management: Lounge Records c/o Scoop Music, Oberhafeustr 1, 20097 Hamburg, Germany.

SITBON Franck, b. 15 May 1957, Paris, France. Musician (keyboards); Singer. m. Brigitte Silverio, 3 July 1982, 2 sons. Musical Education: Private piano lessons, from age 6-15. Career: Tour, West Coast of United States, 1979-81; Returned to Paris, Played at Casino De Paris with Nicole Croiselle; Tour with Bernard Lavilliers, 1986; With Jacques Higelin, 1989; Played Italy with Pino Danielle; Tours, Tahiti, New Caledonia, with Patrick Bruel, 1992; Bercy, with Patrick Bruel, 1994. Recordings: Serge Guirao: Enchanteur, 1988; Nicole Croiselle: Black and Blanche, 1990; Joelle Ursule: Comme Dans Un Film, 1993. Publications: Method Up Clavies, 1991. Memberships: SACEM; SPEDIDAM. Hobbies: Writing; Taking care of sons. Address: 34 Rue des Bordes, 94490 Ormesson, France.

SIVADIER Pierre-Michel, b. 13 Mar 1961, Le Mans, France. Composer; Musician (piano); Singer; Songwriter. Musical Education: Master classes with Richard Beirach, Daniel Goyone. Career: Played with Christian Vander, 1987-; 2 years with Louis Petrucciani; 2 years with Peter Oxley including 3 UK tours. Recordings: Albums: D'Epreuves D'Amour (as arranger, composer, pianist), 1991; Les Fous Du Large (as composer, pianist), 1994; Up To Here - Peter Oxley (as pianist), 1994; D'Amour, Fou D'Amour (composer, singer, pianist), 1995. Membership: SACEM (Société des Auteurs Compositeurs de Musique). Hobbies: Cinema; Theatre. Current Management: Seventh Records, 101 Ave J Jaurès, 93806 Epinay Cedex, France.

SIXX Nikki (Frank Carlton Serafino Ferrano), b. 11 Dec 1958, San Jose, California, USA. Musician (bass); Songwriter. Career: Member, groups: London; Christmas; Founder member, US heavy rock group Mötley Crüe, 1981-; Worldwide concerts include: Tours with: Y&T, 1981, 1982; Kiss, 1983; Ozzy Osbourne, 1984; Iron Maiden, 1984; Cheap Trick, 1986; Theatre Of Pain World Tour, 1985-86; World tours, 1987, 1989; Major concerts: US festival, 1983; Monsters of Rock Festival, Castle Donington, 1984; Moscow Music Peace Festival, 1989. Recordings: Albums: Too Fast For Love, 1981; Shout At The Devil, 1983; Theatre Of Pain, 1985; Girls Girls Girls (Number 2, US), 1987; Dr Feelgood (Number 1, US), 1989; Decade of Decadence (Number 2, US), 1991; Til Death Do Us Part, 1994; Singles: Stick To Your Gun, 1981; Looks That Kill, 1984; Too Young To Fall In Love, 1984; Smokin' In The Boys Room, 1985; Home Sweet Home, 1985; You're All I Need, 1987; Dr Feelgood, 1989; Kick Start My Heart, 1990; Without You, 1990; Don't Go Away Mad, 1990; Same Old Situation, 1990; Primal Scream, 1991. Honours: Rolling Stone Readers Poll Winners, Best Heavy Metal Band, 1991; American Music Award, Favourite Heavy Metal Album, 1991. Current Management: The Left Bank Organisation, 6255 Sunset Blvd, Ste 1111, Hollywood, CA 90028, USA.

SIXX-SCHMULEWITZ Aaron, b. 4 Aug 1947, Feldafing, Germany. Record Company Managing Director. m. Lynda M Jones, 18 Aug 1977, 1 son, 1 daughter. Education: Bachelor of Arts, University of California at Los Angeles (UCLA). Career: Record Executive with: 1973-1974, United Artists Records, European A&R Director; 1975-1977, Arista Records, Director, International Operations; 1978-, Aura Records, Music and Entertainment, Managing Director. Address: 1 Liverpool Road, London W5 5NZ, England.

SIZE Roni. Musician (Keyboard; Drums; Sequencer). 1 son. Career: Began as DJ in clubs; Formed label Full Cycle, 1993; Creative leader of Bristol-based collective Reprazent, with record deal on Talkin' Loud; Reprazent performed live at concert venues and festivals worldwide, summer 1997; 1998 forthcoming appearances at festivals includes Glastonbury, Phoenix and Reading. Recordings: With DJ Die, Music Box; Agility; Solo:

Jazz Thing; With Reprezant: Reasons for Sharing, limited edition EP, 1996; Share the Fall, single, with remixes from Way Out West and Grooverider; New Forms/Share the Fall, featuring Bahamadia. Honour: Winner, Mercury Music Prize, for album New Forms, 1997. Address: c/o Kas Mercer, Talkin' Loud, Chancellors House, Chancellors Road, London W6 9QB, England.

SJÖSTEN Lars, b. 7 May 1941, Oskarshamn, Sweden. Jazz Pianist; Composer; Arranger. m. Lilly, 24 April 1976. Education: Piano and Harmony privately. Career: Played with Dexter Gordon, Chet Baker, Lee Konitz and many more legendary jazz musicians; Played with Lars Gullin, 1960-76; Led own groups, numerous records and radio/TV programs; Tours and festivals in Scandinavia and Europe; Composing and Arranging Commissions for Big Band. Compositions: In Confidence; Denile; Thorgeirs Sang; The Inner Voice; Tidigt; Gasoline My Beloved; From Reliable Sources; The Comeback of a Tradesman; Tale of Two Trees. Recordings: Select Notes, 1981; Bells, Blues and Brotherhood, 1983; Dedicated to Lee, w Lee Konitz, 1983, 1995; Roots and Relations, 1989; Lars Sjösten Quartet in Moscow, 1990; In Confidence, 1990; I Love You So, with Rolf Ericson, 1997. Honours: Jan Johansson, 1969; Two Golden Disques, 1981, 1989; Income Guarantee, 1990; Lars Gullin Prize, 1997. Memberships: Musician's Union; Association of Swedish Jazz Musicians; Musikcentrum. Hobbies: Computing; Reading; Walks; Movies. Current Management: Musikcentrum, Chapmansgatan 4, S-11236 Stockholm, Sweden. Address: Filipstadsbacken 70, S-123 43 Farsta, Sweden.

SKAGGS Ricky Lee, b. 18 July 1954, Cordell, Kentucky, USA. Recording Artist; Musician (guitar, banjo, mandolin, fiddle). m. Sharon White, 4 Aug 1981, 2 sons, 2 daughters. Career: Member of Country Gentlemen, 1974; Boone Creek, 1975; Emmylou Harris' Hot Band, 1977; Whites, 1980; Solo artist 1980-; Host of own radio series, Simple Life With Ricky Skaggs; Television appearnces include: Host, TNN Nashville Now; Co-host, TNN Viewer's Choice Awards. Recordings: 12 US Number 1 singles, 1981-89; Albums: Waitin' For The Sun To Shine, 1981; Highways & Heartaches, 1982; Don't Cheat In Our Hometown, 1983; Country Boy, 1984; Favourite Country Songs, 1985; Live In London, 1985; Love's Gonna Get Ya!, 1986; Comin' Home To Stay, 1988; Kentucky Thunder, 1989; My Father's Son, 1991; Ricky Skaggs Portrait, 1992; Super Hits, 1993; Solid Ground, 1996. Honours include: Ralph Stanley Dove Award, 1982; 4 Grammy Awards, 1984-92; 7 Academy Country Music Awards including Best Touring Band, 1983-87; Edison Award, Netherlands, 1987; 8 Country Music Association Awards; 6 Music City News Awards; Artist Of The Decade, BBC Radio 2, UK; Best Country Guitarist, Guitar Player Readers Poll, 1987-89; Best Country Instrumentalist, Playboy Readers Poll (twice); Gospel Voice Diamond Award, 1993. Memberships: AFTRA; AFofM. Hobbies: Fishing; Photography; Vintage Clothing Stores. Current Management: RS Entertainment Inc. Address: PO Box 150871, Nashville, TN 37215, USA.

SKARBEK Sacha J, b. Epsom, Surrey, England. Producer; Musician (keyboards); Songwriter. Musical Education: BA Hons, Music, Oxford. Career: Tours: Europe, with Double Vision; UK with Jamiroquai, Original Son; UK with Sister Sledge, Fekisha; BBC Interview, with Innocent Lies; Tour, USA, What The Funk; Various concerts with Dana Brown. Recordings: Keyboard player: Seven Seconds, Youssou N'Dour and Neneh Cherry; Keyboard player: Let It Last, Carleen Anderson; Producer, writer: Desire And Somewhere, Pauline Henry; Keyboard player, writer: Album: Original Son. Hobbies: Martial arts; Tennis. Current Managment: Alan Edwards; Clem

Chan. Address: Poole Edwards, Charlotte Street, London W1, England.

SKELLERN Peter, b. 14 Mar 1947, Bury, Lancashire, England. Musician (piano); Singer; Songwriter. Musical Education: Honours graduate, Guildhall School of Music, 1968. Career: Member, March Hare (recorded as Harlan County), 1971; Wrote and performed 6 autobiographical programmes for BBC TV; Series of musical plays, Happy Endings; Host, chat show, Private Lives, 1983; Formed Oasis with Julian Lloyd Webber, Mary Hopkin, Bill Lovelady, 1984. Recordings: Peter Skellern With Harlan County, 1971; Peter Skellern, 1972; Not Without A Friend, 1973; Holding My Own, 1974; Hold On To Love, 1975; Hard Times, 1976; Skellern, 1978; Astaire, 1979; Still Magic, 1980; Happy Endings, 1981; Introducing Right From The Start, 1981; A String Of Pearls, 1982; Best Of Peter Skellern, 1985; Love Light, 1987; Singles include: You're A Lady; Love Is The Sweetest Thing, with the Grimethorpe Colliery Band. Honours include: Best MOR Album, Music Trades Association, 1979.

SKI (Dominic Oakenfull), b. 28 Jan 1971, Sevenoaks, Kent, England. Musician (keyboards, zither); Producer; Writer. Education: City University, London. Musical Education: Keith Rusling, Kent; K B Wizard, London. Career: Keyboard player, writer, producer for the K-Creative, 1991-93; Raw Stylus, 1993; Palm Skin Productions, 1993; Thats How It Is, 1994; Galliano, 1994, 1995; Solo artiste as Ski, 1993-; Writer, jingles for various radio commercials; Television appearances include Gimme 5; Top Of The Pops; Later With Jools Holland; The Beat. Recordings: Albums: QED, K-Creative, 1992; The Plot Thickens, Galliano, 1994; Marla Glen (second album), 1995; Pushing, Raw Stylus, 1995; Galliano (fourth album), 1996; Singles: Justify, Ski featuring Chesere, Realise Your True, Ski with Ife, 1994; Theme from Millenium Falcon, 1994. Publications: Fender Rhodes, A Brief History, 1994. Hobbies: Sport. Current Management: Guy Tresize. Address: GT Management, Unit B7, 8/9 Hoxton Square, London, England.

SKIFS Björn Nils Olof, b. 20 Apr 1947, Vansbro, Sweden. Singer; Performer; Composer. m. Pernilla, 20 May 1988, 2 sons. Education: College. Career: Major concert tours and television shows, 1970-; Eurovision Song Festival, 1978 and 1981; Musicals and 3 major films (screenplay, leading role): Strul, 1986; Joker, 1989; Drömåken, 1993. Recordings: 13 albums, 1967-87, including: Hooked On A Feeling (Number 1, USA, 1974); Never My Love (Top 10, USA, 1974); Michaelangelo (Number 1, Scandinavia, 1975-76). Current Management: Desert AB, Brickebergsvagen 21A, S-702 21 Orebro, Sweden.

SKINNER Harry, b. 30 Apr 1958, Barking, Essex, England. Musician (guitar); Singer; Composer; Songwriter. m. Elizabeth Vango, 4 May 1991, 1 son, 1 daughter. Education: Southampton University, 1995-97. Musical Education: RMSM, Kneller Hall, Twickenham; Bournemouth and Poole College, Poole. Career: Oboist with Rhine Staff Band RTR, 1976-81; Formed band, Manitou, touring UK, Gemany and Japan; Formed band The Producers; Appeared at Colne Blues Festival, Burnley Blues Festival, Monighan, Templebar, Shepton Mallet and at festivals throughout Europe; Live radio sessions, BBC Radio 2, 1994; Tours of UK, Germany, France, Belgium and Ireland. Recordings: Single: Tasmania, 1984; Albums: with Manitou: Manitou At The Electric Drum I And II, 1987; Looking For The Lost, 1991; with The Producers: Escape From Muswell Hell, 1991; Ain't No Love In The World, 1993; For This Night Only, 1994; Nearly Wired, 1996; Really Wired, 1996. Honour: Nominated Best British Blues Album, Ain't No Love In The World, 1993. Memberships: Musicians' Union;

Associate Member, PRS; MCPS. Hobby: Reading. Current Management: Dave Saunders, Mojo Management / Mojo Records UK. Address: 77 Haviland Road, Boscombe, Bournemouth, Dorset BH7 6HJ, England.

SKIPPER Svend, b. 22 Apr 1947, Naestved, Denmark. Musician (piano); Conductor; Composer; Arranger. m. Ghita Noerby, 15 July 1984. Musical Education: Studied piano, solfeggio, conducting, Royal Danish Conservatory, 1970-77. Career: Musical Director, all Danish theatres, Directed musicals: The Peanuts; No No Nanette; Promises Promises; Showboat; Pal Joey; Oliver; They're Playing Our Song; Chicago; My Fair Lady; Orpheus In The Underworld; Parisian Life; Beggar's Opera (Weill); Jesus Christ Superstar; Teenage Love (Finn Savery); Starting Here Starting Now; Sunday In The Park With George; Sweeney Todd; Side By Side By Sondheim; A Little Night Music; En Spurv I Tranedans (Danish vaudeville, 1880); I'm Getting My Act Together; Les Miserables, Odense and Copenhagen; Conducted all Danish symphony orchestras; Also Danish Light Music Orchestra playing jazz, rock, musicals, Indian, classical repertoire; Concerts, television and radio appearances in Denmark and Sweden; Performed with instrumentalists and singers including: Birgit Nilsson; Elizabeth Soderstroem; Anne Sofie von Otter; Indian violinist, Supramaniam; Hubert Laws; Ben Webster; Harry "Sweets" Edison; Bob Rockwell; Doug Rayney; Touring Europe with pioneer jazz/classical Skipper-Lund-Simonsen Trio (piano, flute, bass); Own recording studio, The Holtewood Studio. Compositions: Composer for Danish films, television series, songs, signatures, 8 minute comic opera, Bread; Arranger: orchestra, theatre, live and recorded music. Recordings: More than 100, including musicals: The Peanuts; Starting Here Starting Now; Oliver. Membership: Danish Conductors Society. Hobbies: Films; Afghan dogs. Address: Pindehuggervang 19, DK 2840 Holte, Denmark.

SKIRVING Mark Antony, b. 13 March 1966, Wednesday, West Midlands, USA. Vocalist; Musician (Saxophone). 1 son. Education: 40 TV appearances worldwide; Played with: BB King; Cab Calloway; Slim Gaillard; Matt (Guitar) Murphy; Steve Cropper; Donald Dunn; Eddie Floyd; Several small film appearances. Recordings: 5 albums: King Pleasure and the Biscuit Box; This Is It; Better Beware; King Pleasure and the Biscuit Boys Live at Ronnie Scotts; Blues and Rhythm Revue, vol 1. Memberships: Birmingham Jazz Festival Board; British Jazz Awards Committee. Hobby: Acting. Current Management: Jim Simpson, Big Bear Music. Address: Big Bear Music, PO Box 944, Edgbaston, Birmingham B16 8UT, England.

SKOLNICK Alex, b. 29 Sept 1968, Berkeley, California, USA. Rock Musician (guitar). Musical Education: Studied with Joe Satriani. Career: Toured and recorded with US heavy rock group Testament; Toured with Stu Hamm; Recorded with Michael Manring. Recordings: Albums with Testament: The Legacy, 1987; The New Order, 1988; Practice What You Preach; Souls Of Black; The Ritual, 1992; with Michael Manring: Thank; Compilations: Guitars That Rule The World; Guitars Practicing Musicians. Publications: Columnist for magazines: Guitar; Guitar Player; Guitar World. Membership: ASCAP. Hobbies: Reading; Writing, specially fiction. Current Management: Marcy Straw, CMA (Creative Music Alternatives); Address: Alex Skolnick, c/o CMA, 2608 Ninth Street, Berkeley, CA 94710, USA.

SKOUBY Niels, b. 5 Oct 1938, Frederiksberg, Denmark. Singer;Entertainer; Musician (guitar). m. (1) Nina Engelbrechtsen, (2) Lis Thorgård, 5 daughters. Education: Graduated from gymnasium; Airforce pilot; Teacher; Master's certificate, Navigation. Musical Education: Mainly self-taught; 6 months course for singers, Sweden.

Career: Started performing as solo artist and in duo Hella & Niels, late 1960s; Moved to Greenland, performing solo or in groups including Uillut, 1972-82; Now mainly performing in Scandinavia as solo artist, with group Skrammelårkæstret, and with duo Dorte & Niels. Composition: Den gule kat, 1966. Recording: Uillut, 1980. Publication: Co-writer, Nordisk Visebok, 1994. Honours: First Prize, Danish Amateur Grand Prix '69, 1969. Memberships: Visens Venner; Nordvisa; KODA; DJBFA. Hobbies: Sailing; Travel; Playing and singing. Address: Ravnsvej 15, DK-8400 Ebeltoft, Denmark.

SKOVBYE Kim Lind, b. 10 Jan 1955, Copenhagen, Denmark. Musician (harp, guitar, violin, bouzouki, mandolin, recorder); Composer; Songwriter. Cohabits with Anne Ostrup, 2 sons, 2 daughters. Musical Education: Private lessons from age 9; 3 years study at Danish Music Academy. Career: 10 years teaching children; 7 years, teaching music and drama, adult training college; 10 years as street musician with the juggler and singer Hermn; Several television and radio shows; Two big concerts at the Tivoli; Several shows and tours with keyboard player, Klaus Schonning, Denmark, Germany and Netherlands. Compositions: Skygge Boxer (songs), 1986; Barsebeck (songs), 1987; Scandinavia (instrumental), 1990; Heartland (instrumental), 1992; Aftermath (instrumental), 1993; Ask And Riana (children), 1994; Mountains Of Fire (song), 1995; Coming Albums: Wayfarer, 1995; Lord Of The Rings, Part 1, 1996; Film music: Holografi, 1988; Landscapes Of Childhood, 1992; The Glassheart, 1989; Song Of A Tiger, 1989. Honours: Awards from Danish Jazz Beat Folk Society. Hobby: Staying with children in summer residence in Sweden. Current Management: The New Agency. Address: Strandvejen 324, DK-3060 Espergaerde, Denmark.

SLABAK Jan, b. 24 March 1941, Kelcany, Kyjova, Czechoslovakia. Musician (Trumpet); Composer; Conductor; Band Master. m. (1) Jitka Janowskova, 18 November 1960, (2) Ivana Soutalova, 22 July 1976, 1 son, 1 daughter. Education: State Conservatoire (Academy of Music), Brno; Janacek's Academy of Music Arts, Brno. Career: State Philharmonic Orchestra, Brno; Moravanta of Jan Slabak; Many film, TV, radio appearances. Compositions: 210 compositions for brass band, published and recorded on LPs, MCs, and CDs. Publications: Hundreds of reviews and contributions, Kaoje Kdo, 1991-92; Mijosua ic Moravanka, 1997. Honours: TV Prize, 1973; Ministry of Culture, 1975; Golden Key, Cleveland, USA, 1978; 3 times Golden Disc, 1980, 1985, 1991; 1 Platinum Disc, 1995; 1 Diamond Disc, 1996. Memberships: OSA; Chair, Competition juries. Hobbies: Nature; Cottage; Garden; Dog; Small animals. Address: Sosnova 18, Brno 63700, Czech Republic.

SLASH (Saul Hudson), b. 23 July 1965, Stoke-On-Trent, Staffordshire, England. m. Renee Suran, 10 Sept 1992. Career: Member, US heavy rock group Guns'N'Roses, 1985-; International tours include: Supports to Iron Maiden, US, 1987, 1988; Mötley Crüe, US, 1987; The Cult, US, 1987; UK tour, 1988; Support to Aerosmith, US, 1988; Get In The Ring tour, with Skid Row, 1991; World tour, 1992; Major concerts include: Monsters Of Rock, Castle Donington, 1988; Farm Aid IV, 1990; Rock In Rio II, Brazil, 1991; A Concert For Life (Freddie Mercury Tribute), Wembley, 1992; National Bowl, Milton Keynes, 1993; Leader, Slash's Snakepit, 1994-. Recordings: Albums: with Guns'N'Roses: Appetite For Destruction, 1987; G'N'R Lies (mini-album), 1988; Use Your Illusion I & II (Number 1 and 2, UK and US), 1991; The Spaghetti Incident, 1993; with Slash's Snakepit: It's 5 O'Clock Somewhere, 1994; Hit singles: with Guns'N'Roses: Welcome To The Jungle, 1987; Sweet Child O'Mine (Number 1, US), 1988; Night

Train, 1989; Paradise City, 1989; Patience, 1989; Knockin' On Heaven's Door, used in film Days Of Thunder, 1990; You Could Be Mine, used in film Terminator 2, 1991; Don't Cry, 1991; Live And Let Die, 1991; November Rain, 1992; Yesterdays, 1992; Ain't It Fun, 1993; Sympathy For The Devil, used in film Interview With A Vampire, 1994; Contributor, Nobody's Child (Romanian Angel appeal), 1990; Contributor as guest musician: Black And White,Michael Jackson, 1991; Brick By Brick, Iggy Pop, 1990; Dangerous, Michael Jackson, 1991; Coneheads (film soundtrack), 1993; Tribute To Muddy Waters, 1993; Believe In Me, Duff McKagan, 1993. Honours: American Music Awards: Favourite Heavy Metal Single 1989; Favourite Heavy Metal Artist and Album, 1989; Favourite Heavy Metal Artist, 1992; Several MTV Awards; World Music Award, Best Selling Artist Of The Year, 1993; Rolling Stone and Billboard Magazine Awards. Current Management: Big FD Entertainment, 10801 National Blvd, Suite 530, Los Angeles, CA 90064, USA.

SLATER John, b. 12 Jan 1957, London, England. Artist Manager; Tour Manager. Education: 1 year Electronics at Essex University. Career: Stage Manager at Edinburgh Playhouse, 1976-77; Sound Engineer, 1977-80, Radio Presenter, BRMB Radio Birmingham, hosting and producing Indie and Rock evening show, 1980-91, with 1500 interviews, 200 sessions and 50 concert recordings; Compered Donington Monsters of Rock Festival in 1991; Currently in partnership with Danny Kenny managing various bands. Honour: Nominated for Best UK Pop Show, Sony Radio Awards, 1987. Hobby: Formula 1 Grand Prix Racing. Address: PNG Worldwide, Westminster Court, 10 Park Road North, Birmingham B6 5UJ, England.

SLEDGE Percy, b. 25 Nov 1941, Leighton, Alabama, USA. Soul Singer. Career: Singer, The Esquires Combo; Solo recording artiste. Recordings: Albums include: When A Man Loves A Woman, 1966; Warm & Tender Soul, 1966; The Percy Sledge Soul, 1967; Take Time To Know Her, 1968; I'll Be Your Everything, 1974; If Loving You Is Wrong, 1986; Percy, 1987; Wanted Again, 1987; Blue Night, 1994; Singles: When A Man Loves A Woman, 1966; It Tears Me Up, 1967; Out Of Left Field, 1967; Take Time To Know Her, 1968. Honours include: Blues Foundation Soul/Blues Album of the Year, for Blue Night, 1996; Grammy Nomination, Blue Night, 1996. Current Management: Artists International Management, 9850 Sandalfoot Blvd #458, Boca Raton, FL 33428, USA.

SLEEN Harm van, b. 31 Dec 1965, Utrecht, The Netherlands. Bass. m. Kerstin Lucia Venhuizen, 16 August 1995, 1 daughter. Education: Bass, Hilversuns Conservatory, 1989. Career: Played with various pop groups, 1980-89; Recorded Single with Burt and the Brand New Lifestyle, 1989; Played with Jaap Dekker's Jazz and Boogie Set, 1989-93; Playing with Capelino and with Mr Boogie Woogie and the Fire Sweep Blues Band. Compositions: Take Me To Swine Lane; Goodbye; Gossip; Bad Day; If You Went Away; Trouble; Lovin On My Mind; Holy Boogie; Young Boys and Girls (On the Old Side of Town). Recordings: Relite! Revelation, 1993; Capelino, Way To Go, 1997; Mr Boogie Woogie and The Fire Sweep Blues Band, Live At the Pub, 1997. Publication: Mag Die Radio War Harder?!!, 1993. Hobbies: Tape Collecting; Family. Address: Minister Talmastratt 110, 3555 GJ Utrecht, The Netherlands.

SLICK Grace, b. 30 Oct 1939, Evanstown, Illinois, USA. Singer; Songwriter; Entertainer. m. (1) Gerald Robert Slick, 26 Aug 1961 (div), 1 daughter; (2) Skip Johnson, 25 Nov 1976. Education: Finch College, 1957-58. Career: Singer of Great Society, 1965-66; Jefferson Airplane, 1966-72; Jefferson Starship (later known as Starship), 1972-. Major concerts including

Woodstock and Altamont; Most television shows, including Ed Sullivan and Johnny Carson; Recordings: Solo albums: Manhole; Dreams; Welcome To The Wrecking Ball; Software; Albums with Jefferson Airplane/Starship include: Surrealistic Pillow; Earth; Modern Times; Winds Of Change; Blows Against The Empire; Dragon Fly; Freedom At Point Zero; Nuclear Furniture; Red Octopus; Singles include White Rabbit; Somebody To Love; We Built This City On Rock'n'Roll; Nothing's Going To Stop Us Now. Publications: Grace Slick, biography by Barbara Rosa, 1978. Honours: 4 Bay Area Music Awards, Best Singer. Membership: AFofM. Hobby: Anti-vivisection. Current Management: Trudy Green, HK Management. Address: 8900 Wilshire Boulevard #300, Beverly Hills, CA 90211-1906, USA.

SLIGER Robert Earl, b. 31 Oct 1962, Detroit, Michigan, USA. Vocalist; Songwriter; Composer; Producer; Educator; Musician (guitar, piano, drums). Education: Community College of the Air Force, USA. Musical Education: USAF Chorale with Ms Martha Daige (Director), Denver, Colorado, 1980; Voice Instruction with: Bill White and Sid Wright, Austin, Texas, 1981; Tom Prebble, Spain, 1982; Mrs Gene Nice, Pensacola Civic Opera, Florida, 1985; Vaccai, Italian Opera (English); Mr And Mrs Chris Beatty, Tennessee, 1991; Thomas Appell, California, 1997. Career: Tenor/MC, USAF Air Force Chorale, 1980-81; Lead singer, background, with Star Fire, 1982; Tenor, Gospel Quartet, W Germany, 1983; Lead singer, background, with Angel Band, 1990-92; Producer, lead and background singer, with Liberty-N-Justice, 1991-93; Lost In Eden tour, with Liberty-N-Justice, 1993; Filmed 2 music videos with Liberty-N-Justice: All Your Love, 1993; We Are Family, 1993; Solo career, 1993-; Radio interview, WQFL, WGSL, Rockford, Illinois, 1995; Tenor, Mendelssohn's Elijah, Bradley Community Chorus and Chamber Orchestra, Bradley University, IL, 1996. Compositions: Songs: Christ You Share, 1991; Through The Night, 1992; You're Not Alone, 1993; LORD Jesus Christ, 1993; In Your Arms, 1993; Dr Werking's Office, 1993; Your Open Door, with Marvin Zilch, 1994; When You're Needing a Friend, with Marvin Zilch, 1994; Show The Way, 1995; Majestic, instrumental, 1995; When I Walk With You (Road to Emmaus), 1997. Recordings: with Liberty-N-Justice: Armed With The Cross, 1992; Big Guns, 1994; with Angel Band: Down To Earth, 1992; Down To Earth (remastered), 1993. Publications: How To Read The Holy Bible - The Basics, 1988. Honours: Most Valuable Player Trophy, South Sumpter High School, Florida, 1980; Good Conduct Medal, USAF, W Germany, 1983; Honor Graduate Medal, USAF, 1985; Weigel Music Award Scholarship, Tennessee Temple University, 1986. Memberships: Gospel Music Association; ASCAP. Hobbies: Golf; Tennis; Vocal exercising; Cycling; Reading; Studying. Current Management: C&R Productions. Address: PO Box 9133, Peoria, IL 61612-9133, USA.

SLIJNGAARD Ray. Rapper; Songwriter. Career: Rapper, Belgian dance music group 2 Unlimited, 1991-. Recordings: Albums: No Limits, 1993; Real Things, 1994; Hits Unlimited, 1995; Singles: Get Ready For This; No Limits; Tribal Dance; Let The Beat Control Your Body; The Real Thing; No One. Honours: MTV Award Nominations: Best Dance Act; Best Song, Let The Beat Control Your Body. Address: c/o Michel Maartens, CBA Artists, PO Box 1495, 1200 BL Hilversum, The Netherlands.

SLOANE Carol, b. 5 Mar 1937, Providence, Rhode Island, USA. Jazz Singer. m. Edward "Buck" Spurr, 30 Nov 1986. Education: Business College. Career: Professional singer from age 14, with Ed Drew's Dance Band; Tours with Larry Elgart Orchestra, 1958-60; Singer with Hendricks (Dave) Lambert and Ross Trio, 1960; Shared bills with Bill Cosby, Woody Allen, Lenny Bruce,

Richard Pryor, 1960s; Singer with Tonight Show Band, Johnny Carson's Tonight Show; Supper club work, regular public radio show, North Carolina, 1981-85; Moved to Boston, 1986; Disc jockey, WGBH, 1986-; Played Starlight Roof, Boston, 1985. Signed with Concord Jazz, 1991; Featured artist, Pre-Fujitsu/Concord Jazz Festival party, honouring Carl Jefferson (president, Concord Jazz), 1993; 10 consecutive appearances festival season, Japan. Recordings include: Albums: A Night of Ballads (duets with Don Abney), 1984; But Not For Me (with Tommy Flanagan, George Mraz, Al Foster, Frank Wess), 1986; Love You Madly, (with Richard Rodney Bennett, Kenny Barron, Kenny Burrell), 1988; The Real Thing (with Phil Woods, Grady Tate, Mike Renzi, Rufus Reid), 1989; Heart's Desire (Stef Scaggiari, John Lockwood, Colin Bailey), 1990; Concord All Stars On Cape Cod, (Scott Hamilton & Dave McKenna), 1991; Sweet & Slow (with Frank Wess, Tenor Sax), 1992; Concord Christmas (Mel Torme, Rosemary Clooney, Various Artists), 1993; When I Look In Your Eyes (with Bill Charlap, Steve Gilmore, Ron Vincent), 1994; The Songs Carmen Sang (with Phil Woods, Bill Charlap, Michael Moore, Ron Vincent), 1995. Hobbies: Cooking; Photography; Reading. Current Management: Buck Starr. Address: Spurr Marketing Group, 215 Salem St, Woburn, MA 01801, USA.

SLUSHER Michael Dennis, b. 13 Nov 1949, Oliver Springs, Tennessee, USA. Musician (trombone); Arranger; Producer. Education: Brevard Community College, 1967-69; BS, North Texas State University, 1975. Career: Musician, Elvis Presley, 1977-79; Resident musician, venues in Las Vegas, 1977-82; Producer, arranger, Take Cover Enterprises, Beverly Hills, 1983-86; Associate Producer, television and radio commercials, 1984-86; Independent producer, arranger, Seattle, 1986-; Musician with artistes including: Frank Sinatra; Sammy Davis Jr; Tony Bennett; Righteous Brothers; Tom Jones; Glen Campbell; Paul Anka; Pearl Bailey; Also played for orchestras with: Tommy Dorsey; Si Zentner; Tex Beneke; Thad Jones; Mel Lewis.

SMALE Joanne R Muroff, b. 20 June 1949, Brooklyn, New York, USA. Production, Publicity, Promotion Executive. Education: BA Psychology, University of Miami. Career: President: Joanne Smale Productions Ltd, 1980-; Vice-President, Dark Light Music Ltd; Owner, Listening House Booking Agency, 1974-80; Publicist; numerous theatre productions; music industry events; Charity and benefit events include: Rekindle The Light Festival, 1984; Arts Against Apartheid, Toronto, 1990; Industry and media organizations include: True North Records; Sam The Record Man; Began Canadian representation for events including: New Music Seminar (New York); The International Music and Media Conference (Montreux, Switzerland); American Video Conference and Awards (Los Angeles); Publicist: Road Movies, CBCTV; In The Key Of Oscar, documentary, CBCTV; Co-producer, with National Film Board, The Un-Canadians. Honours: 6 Gold, 2 Platinum albums for work with: Rough Trade; Murray McLauchlan; Bruce Cockburn. Memberships: Videofact; Vice-president, Canadian Independent Recording Producers Association (CIRPA); Canadian Independent Film Caucus (CIFC); Canadian Women In Radio And Television (CWRT). Address: Joanne Smale Productions Ltd, 51 Bulwer Street, Toronto, Ontario M5T 1A1, Canada.

SMALL Heather. Vocalist. Career: Singer, soul group, Hothouse; Lead singer, UK dance group M People, 1991-; Major concerts include: Glastonbury Festival, 1994. Recordings: Albums: Northern Soul, 1992; Elegant Slumming, 1993; Bizarre Fruit, 1994; Bizarre Fruit II, 1995; Hit singles: How Can I Love You More, 1991; One Night In Heaven, 1993; Movin' On Up, 1993; Sight For Sore Eyes, 1994; Itchycoo Park, 1995; Search

For The Hero, 1995; Open Your Heart, 1995; Love Rendezvous, 1995. Honours include: Mercury Prize, Best Album, Elegant Slumming, 1994; BRIT Awards: Best Dance Act, 1994, 1995. Current Management: RD Worldwide Management, 37 Limerston Street, London SW10 0BQ, England.

SMALL Mina, b. 14 Mar 1958, San Francisco, California, USA. Singer; Composer; Musician (violin, piano). Musical Education; Classical and jazz. Career: Concerts, entertainment, classical jazz, 1982-; Singer with pianists, jazz groups, 1984-95; Theatre production, 1989; Records for children. Compositions: 50 for jazz, folk groups, 1989-1995. Recordings: Background vocalist, O Jamai; Solo cassette, 1995. Honours: Prix de la SACEM, CREST (France), 1995. Memberships: SACEM; SACD; SPEDIDAM. Hobby: Dance. Address: 5 Rue Olivier de Sennes, 26000 Valence, France.

SMELT Adrian Michael, b. 7 Nov 1972, Huddersfield, West Yorkshire, England. Musician (drums, percussion, guitar, bass); Vocalist; Songwriter; Producer. Education: HND in Professional Sound and Video Technology, University College, Salford. Musical Education: Percussion and Vocal tuition. Career: Played Benjamin Britten's War Requiem at The Royal Albert Hall, 1985; Choir tour of Netherlands, 1985; Drummer for Bungalow, 1989-92; Various headline dates and part tours with Cud; Member, The Sexy Cyclops Love Band, 1989-; Bass player and founder member, Beech Buggy, 1992; Presenter of Radio show on Derby Reach FM, 1994. Recorded compositions: for Bungalow: Mad World; Lunar Love; Bad Taste; You're No Good, cover of Swinging Blue Jeans; Piggy Bank Love, cover of Bonzo Dog Band; Various demos. Publications: Press and Private Photography for Retford Times Newspaper. Membership: Musicians' Union. Hobbies: Production; Photography; Radio broadcasting; Film. Address: Badgers Dell, Beecher Lane, Beckingham, near Doncaster, DN10 4QL, England.

SMETS Yasnaïa Leen, b. 17 Feb 1972, Antwerp, Mortsel, Belgium. Education: Human Science. Musical Education: Music School, Mortsel, with teacher Joost Cuypers. Career: Tours, Europe, with Hybryds, 1991-; Worldwide radio broadcast in independent charts. Recordings: Music for Rituals - An Ongoing Musical Spiritual Quest; More than 10 CD releases; More than 60 hours music registered at SABAM. Publications: Pressbook, official and underground press. Honours: Soundtrack for the Aquaria of the Antwerp Zoo. Membership: SABAM (Belgian copyright organisation). Hobby: Music. Current Management: 3riort Vzw. Address: Julian Dillenstr 22, B-2018 Antwerp, Belgium.

SMITH Arthur, b. 1 Apr 1921, Clinton, South Carolina, USA. Entertainer; Composer; Musician (guitar, violin, banjo, mandolin). m Dothy Byars, 12 Apr 1941, 2 sons. Musical Education: Father a music teacher. Career: First C&W artist on National television; First television syndication, 85 markets of C&W music; Radio series produced by Sir Charles Chilton (BBC), (USA), How Was The West Was Sung; Johnny Cash Tour; The Arthur Smith Show, TV guests: Andy Griffith; Chet Atkins; Willie Nelson; Formed Gospel Country Label, 1997. Compositions: 4 albums, 24 original hymns: I Saw A Man; Shadow Of A Cross. Recordings: Guitar Boogie; Duelling Banjos. Publications: Apply It To Life; Over 300 songs. Honours: Honorary Doctor; C&W Work Hall Of Fame; NC Broadcasters Hall Of Fame. Memberships: BMI; GMA; CMA. Hobby: Fishing. Current Management: Arthur Smith Enterprises. Address: 100 Smithfield Drive, Charlotte, NC 28270-6062, USA.

SMITH Brian, b. 13 July 1936, Thornton Heath, Surrey, England. Musician (guitar, bass, banjo, mandolin, cornet). 1 daughter. Musical

Education: Self-taught. Career: Member, Johnny Howard Orchestra, 1959; Musician, Cunard liner Queen Elizabeth I, 1961; Leader, Jazz/blues group Wes Minster Five, 1962-66; Support tours to: Sonny Boy Williamson; Memphis Slim; John Lee Hooker; Rufus Thomas; Television appearances include: Ready Steady Go; Saturday Club; Musician, Andy Ross Band and cabaret musician, 1966-; Musician for: Danny Williams; Kenny Lynch; Faith Brown; Janet Brown; Vince Hill; Bruce Forsyth; Gary Wilmott; Anita Harris; Des O'Connor; Also played with Rod Stewart; Shows (pit musician), session and film work, 1970s; Currently teacher, occasional jazz performances. Recordings: Film and session work with major artists; Numerous compositions with Wes Minster Five, including Shaking The Blues. Honours: Appointed to ILEA Panel. Membership: Musicians' Union. Hobby: Collecting old London buses. Address: 6 Selcroft Road, Purley, Surrey CR8 1AD, England.

SMITH Bryan Christopher, b. 21 Dec 1954, St Albans, Hertfordshire, England. Recording Engineer; Producer; Programmer; Musician (guitar, keyboards). m. Denise, 6 July 1974, 1 son, 1 daughter. Career: Red Bus Records, 1980-82; Member, French Impression, 1984-86; Member, The Big Push, 1992-; Founded Farm Factory Studios, 1990; Support tours: Jools Holland; Cool Notes; Member, Hello, 1993. Recordings: Musician, engineer, programmer for: Move Your Skin; And Why Not; Amazing Colossal Men: Buddy's Song; Chesney Hawkes; Also recorded Jon Anderson/Frances Dunnery, 1991; Steve Harley demos, 1994. Honours: Gold disc, Chesney Hawkes: The One And Only (hit single from Buddy's Song). Membership: PRS. Hobbies: Golf; Football. Current Management: Paul Loasby, One Fifteen Management. Address: The Gallery, 28/30 Wood Wharf, Horseferry Place, London SE10 9BT, England.

SMITH Chad. Musician (drums). Career: Member, Red Hot Chili Peppers, 1988-; International concerts include: Lollapalooza Festival tour, 1992; Hollywood Rock Festival, Rio De Janeiro, 1993; Glastonbury Festival, 1993; Television appearances include: Late Night With David Letterman, NBC TV; Rapido, BBC2; The Word, C4 TV; Saturday Night Live, NBC TV; Top Of The Pops, BBC1; Also member of Honeymoon Stitch. Recordings: Albums: Mother's Milk, 1989; Blood Sugar Sex Magik, 1992; What Hits?, 1992; Contributor, The Beavis And Butthead Experience, 1993; Singles include: Give It Away; Under The Bridge; Soul To Squeeze, for film Coneheads, 1993. Honours: MTV Music Video Awards, 1992; Grammy, Best Hard Rock Song, Give It Away, 1993. Current Management: Lindy Goetz Management. Address: 11116 Aqua Vista #39, Studio City, CA 91602, USA.

SMITH Curt, b. 24 June 1961, Bath, Avon, England. Musician (bass guitar); Singer. Education: College. Career: Professional musician since age 18; Member, graduate, 1979; Member of duo Tears For Fears, 1981-90; Solo artiste, 1991-; Concert band Mayfield, first album Mayfield, 1998. Recordings: Acting Your Age, Graduate, 1979; with Tears For Fears: The Hurting, 1982; Songs From The Big Chair, 1985; Seeds Of Love, 1989; Solo album: Soul On Board, 1993; Singles include: Shout; Everybody Wants To Rule The World; Mad World; Change; Pale Shelter; I Believe; Head Over Heels. Memberships: in UK: Musicians' Union; PRS; in US: AFTRA; BMI.

SMITH Dominic, b. 29 Oct 1967, Peterborough, Cambridgeshire, England. Music Journalist; Editor. Education: Degree, English Literature, Southampton, 1990. Career: Music journalist, Big! Magazine, 1992-95; Became Editor, 1995-. Publications: Big! Magazine. Address: Big! Magazine, Mappin House, Winsley Street, London W1, England.

SMITH Geoff, b. 11 May 1966, Tynemouth, England. Songwriter; Musician (Piano). m. Nicola Walker Smith, 16 September 1989, 2 sons. Musical Education: BA, Hons, Nottingham University, 1987; MPhil, Oxford University, 1989; PhD, Huddersfield University, 1996. Recordings: Albums: Gas Food Lodging, 1993; Fifteen Wild Decembers, 1994; Black Flowers, 1997. Publications: Co-author, American Originals, 1994; Interviews with Harold Rudd, Philip Glass, Steve Reich. Honours: Debut album selected as Top 40 Album of the Year, BBC Music Magazine; Youngest Composer to be signed by Sony Classical in the history of the label. Hobby: Music. Current Management: Keith Armstrong, Kitchenware, St Thomas' Street Stables, Newcastle Upon Tyne, NE1 4LE, England. Address: Kitchenware, St Thomas' Street Stables, Newcastle Upon Tyne, NE1 4LE, England.

SMITH Harrison, b. 24 Aug 1946, Murton, County Durham, England. Musician (tenor, soprano saxophones, bass clarinet). m. Ulrike Preuss, 7 June 1986, 1 son, 1 daughter. Musical Education: Various private lessons; Help from musicians. Career: Tours: London Jazz Composers Orchestra; District Six; Free Jazz Quartet; Radio appearances with above plus: Prana; Duo with Keith Bailey; Lysis; Maranatha; Television with: District Six; Solo gigs. Recordings: with District Six: Akuzwakale, 1984; Leave My Name At The Door, 1986; To Be Free, 1987; Mgoma Yabantwana, 1989; with Free Jazz Quartet: Premonitions, 1989. Hobbies: Reading; Gardening; DIY.

SMITH Josh, b. 10 July 1979, Middletown, Connecticut, USA. Blues Musician (guitar). Musical Education: Private study, 9 years. Career: Led own band, the Rhinocats, 3 years; Opened for bands including Buddy Guy; The Fabulous T-Birds; Allman Brothers Band. Recordings: CD: Born Under A Blue Sign, 1995; Woodsheddin, 1995. Honours: Best Blues Band, State Of Florida, Florida Jam Magazine, Jammy Awards, 1994. Membership: ASCAD. Hobbies: Music; Guitar. Current Management: Dan Cohen, Musicians Exchange. Address: 8920 N W 14th St, Pembroke Pines, FL 33024, USA.

SMITH Karen M, b. 23 July 1958, Chicago, Illinois, USA. Artist Development; Record Company Executive. m. A J Smith, 5 May 1994. Education: 2 years college. Career: Currently owner, Glow In The Dark Rehearsals (rehearsal space in Chicago); Owner, record company TOW Records, Chicago; Consultant for Ex-Idols; PO! Executive Producer for: Wait For Light; S Is For Space. Honour: Gottlieb Award, Best Rehearsal Studio, 1994. Memberships: NAMM; NARAS. Hobbies: Yoga; Cinema. Address: PO Box 740, Oak Park, IL 60303, USA.

SMITH Laura, b. 18 Mar 1952, Ontario, Canada. Singer; Songwriter; Musician (Guitar). Career: Contributor: albums, Chieftains, 1997; Far Cry From Leaving, Terry Kelly, 1996. Recordings: Between the Earth and My Soul; It's A Personal Thing. Honours: ECMA Female Artist, 1996; ECMA Album, 1996; Gemini Award for Best Performance, 1997. Memberships: SOCAN; CARAS; ECMA; AVLA. Current Management: Jones and Co. Address: 5212 Sackville St, Suite 100, Halifax, NS, B3J 1K6, Canada.

SMITH Mal, b. 2 Mar 1969, Barrow-in-Furness, Cumbria, England. Singer; Actor. Career: Vocalist with: Al-Mi-Raj, 1986-87; California, 1988; Bye Bye Sanity, 1990-; Acting, stage performances include: English National Opera Tour of A Small Green Space, 1988; Simon Zealotes in Jesus Christ Superstar, 1990. Recordings: Bye Bye Sanity; Recordings for debut album at demo stage. Publications: Various poetry in anthologies. Hobbies: Writing poetry; Reading; Swimming; Theatre; Theology; Football. Current Management: SMI, 33 Mandarin Place, Grove,

Oxfordshire, England. Address: 44 Burnley Road, Dollis Hill, London NW10 1EJ, England.

SMITH Mark "Hitman", b. 20 Oct 1972, Doncaster, Yorkshire, England. Producer; Remixer; Programmer; Musician (keyboards). Education: High Melton College, Doncaster. Musical Education: Piano, Royal School of Music. Career: Producer, remixer, for Music Factory Records; Commercial Disc Jockey; Recordings: Mixes include: Rock'N'Roll Dance Party, Jive Bunny; Nolans Hitmix; Hot Chocolate Hitmix; Remixes include: Kylie Minogue; 2 Unlimited; Kelly Marie. Publications: Contributor, Mixology Magazine. Membership: Musicians' Union. Current Management: Music Factory Records Ltd. Address: 5/7 Fitzwilliam Street, Parkgate, Rotherham, South Yorks S62 5EP, England.

SMITH Mark E(dward), b. 5 Mar 1957, Salford, Manchester, England. Singer; Songwriter; Musician (guitar). m. Brix (Laura Elise Smith), divorced 1990. Career: Founder, The Fall, 1977-. Recordings: Live At The Witch Trials, 1979; Dragnet, 1979; Totale's Turns (It's Now Or Never), 1980; Grotesque (After The Gramme), 1980; Slates, 1981; Hex Enduction Hour, 1982; Room To Love, 1982; Perverted By Language, 1983; The Wonderful And Frightening World Of..., 1984; This Nation's Saving Grace, 1985; Bend Sinister, 1986; The Frenz Experiment, 1988; I Am Kurious Oranji, 1988; Seminal Live, 1989; Extricate, 1990; 458489, 1990; 458489-B Sides, 1990; Shiftwork, 1991; Code Selfish, 1992; The Infotainment Scan, 1993; Sinister Waltz, 1996; Singles: Fiery Jack; How I Wrote Elastic Man; Totally Wired; There's A Ghost In My House; Victoria. Publication: Play: Hey! Luciani. Address: c/o Permanent Records, 22-23 Brook Mews, London W2 3BW, England.

SMITH Michael, b. 19 Jan 1967, Bridport, Dorset, England. Musician (saxophone). Musical Education: City of Leeds College of Music; Guildhall School of Music and Drama, London. Career: Saxophonist, Brand New Heavies, 1990-93; Saxophone and flute, Jamiroquai; Extensive recording, worldwide touring with above acts; Television appearances include: Top Of The Pops; The Word; The Beat; MTV's Most Wanted; In-house arranger, Acid Jazz Records. Recordings: Arranger for: Corduroy; Mother Earth; James Taylor Quartet; Solo album: The Whole Thing, 1993; Recorded every release with The Brand New Heavies; Album: with Jamiroquai: Space Cowboy. Memberships: PRS; MCPS. Hobbies: Coastal walking; Backgammon. Current Management: Richard H Smith. Address: 14D Wilde Street, London WC2B 4AG, England.

SMITH Mike, b. 6 Dec 1943, London, England. Record Producer; Songwriter; Singer; Musician (keyboards). Musical Education: Trinity College, London. Career: Lead singer, keyboard player with: Dave Clark 5; Writer all songs; Writer, producer, television commercials and themes; Record producer, 2 Top 5 albums with Michael Ball. Recordings: with Michael Ball: Michael Ball; Always; One Careful Owner. Memberships: PRS; BASCA. Hobbies: Music and more music. Current Management: Graham Carpenter. Address: Pachuco Management, Priestlands, Letchmore Heath, Herts WD2 8EW, England.

SMITH Mike (Michael John), b. 16 Nov 1946, Edgware, Middlesex, England. Artist Manager; Music Publisher; Television and Film Production Company Owner. m. Sally James, 22 July 1978, 3 sons. Career: Producer, Assistant Head Light Entertainment, LWT, 1968-76; Head of A&R, Decca Records, 1976-78; General Manager, Vice President, GTO Records, 1978-80; Own companies: Yellow Balloon Productions Ltd; Mike Music Ltd; Yellow Balloon Music; Yellow Balloon Records, 1981-. Recordings: As manager or producer: Rick Wakeman; Bruce Foxton; Adam And The Ants; Billy Ocean; The Moody Blues; The Smurfs; The Dooleys; Rolf Harris. Honours: Tokyo

Music Festival Award; Award Winning Producer of London Bridge television programme; 30 Gold and Silver discs as producer, manager of established acts. Memberships: Musicians' Union; ACCA; PRS. Hobbies: Clay pigeon shooting; Classic cars; Travel; Family. Current Management: Self-managed. Address: Freshwater House, Outdowns, Effingham, Surrey KT24 5QR, England.

SMITH Patti, b. 30 Dec 1946, Chicago, Illinois, USA. Vocalist; Songwriter; Musician (guitar); Poet; Author. m. Fred "Sonic" Smith, 1 Mar 1980, 2 sons. Career: Journalist, Rock magazine, 1970; Creem magazine, 1971; Solo artiste, 1972-; Concerts include: Support to New York Dolls, 1972; Formed Patti Smith Group, 1974; UK debut, 1976; European tour, 1976; Away from music business, 8 years, sporadic appearances, 1988-; Poetry performance, New Year's Day Extravaganza, New York, with Yoko Ono, 1975. Recordings: Co-writer (with Bruce Springsteen), Because The Night, 1978; Other singles include: Gloria; Hey Joe; So You Want To Be A Rock And Roll Star; Dancing Barefoot; Albums include: Horses, 1975; Radio Ethiopia, 1976; Easter, 1978; Wave, 1979; Dream Of Life, 1988; Peace and Noise, 1997; Guest vocalist on albums: Secret Treaties, Blue Öyster Cult, 1974; Agents Of Fortune, Blue Öyster Cult, 1976; The Whole Thing Started With Rock'N'Roll, Ray Manzarek, 1975; Nervous Night, The Hooters, 1985; Contributor, film soundtrack Until The End Of The World, 1991. Publications: Poetry: Seventh Heaven, 1971; Kodak, 1972; Witt, 1973; Feb Babel, 1979; Co-author, play Cowboy Mouth (with Sam Shepherd), 1972; Woolgathering (short stories), 1993. Current Management: Rascoff/Zysblat Organization Inc., 110 W 57th Street, 3rd Floor, New York, NY 10019-3319, USA.

SMITH Paula Dawn, b. 10 Dec 1970, Chiswick, England. Musician (multi-instrumentalist); Singer; Songwriter. Education: BA Hons, English Language, Literature, Manchester University, 1990-93. Career: Solo folk artist, vocalist, harp, whistles, guitar; Member, bands: The Forest Folk; Davy Jones' Locker; Children's Film Foundation; Keyboard player, Dylan Rabbit; Clarinet, whistles, percussion with Horseplay. Recordings: with Dylan Rabbit: The Salmon Of Knowledge, 1992; Changes, 1994; Solo: Paula Smith, 1993; Shattered, 1997; Filmscores: Trash, 1994; The Children of Lir, 1996. Hobbies: Children's Literature; Hiking. Current Management: Cauldron Music. Address: 398 Hanworth Road, Hounslow, Middlesex TW3 3SN, England.

SMITH Peter Matthew, b. 23 May 1952, London, England. Musician (guitar); Vocalist; Songwriter; Bandleader. m. Marion Kielty, 29 Oct 1993. Education: BA Soc Sci (Econ Hist). Musical Education: Self-taught. Career: Professional guitarist, vocalist, songwriter, 1974-; Live work, UK and abroad; Television, radio appearances, UK and Germany. Compositions: Incidental music: Documentary, One Man In A Boat, CH4; Comment, CH4; Late Show, BBC2. Recordings: Commercial recordings with: Lee Kosmin Band; The Uprights; Pigment Pete Smith; Skiff Skats; Roma Pierre and Her Backdoormen; Errol Linton (Germany). Memberships: PRS; Musicians' Union; MCPS. Hobby: Hon Sec, Old Reptilians C.C. Current Management: Pigme International; Matters Musical; Flying Gigs; Pipeline. Address: Pigme International, 551 Watford Way, London NW7 2PU, England.

SMITH Rob(ert Kevin), b. 17 Dec 1960, West Yorkshire, England. Musician (saxophone, keyboards, percussion). m. Sarah Stone, 12 May 1990, 2 daughters. Musical Education: Nottingham University; King's College, London. Career: with Four Quartets. Appeared on HTV, 1987; Appeared at "Outside In" jazz festivals in 1988 and 1993;

Brecon Jazz Festival, 1984-1995; 2 Arctic songs with London Sinfonietta Voices, 1994; Lecturer, composition, Bath Spa University College; Musical Director, Wonderbrass, Community Jazz Orchestra. Recordings: with Heavy Quartet: Poum, 1988; A Screaming Tradition, 1989; Short Stories, 1991; with The Diggers, 1993: Imbolc; Musicals: Race, 1989; Starcross'd, 1991; Dangerous Acquintances, 1997; Carnivore, Heavy Quartet, 1995; Film score: The Confectioner, 1997. Publications: 2 articles on trip to Gambia, Taplas, 1992. Memberships: PRS; Society for Promotion of New Music. Hobbies: Listening to music; Walking; Food, wine and beer; Rugby. Current Management: HQ Enterprises, Cardiff, Wales. Address: 26 Burlington Terrace, Llandaf, Cardiff CF5 1GG, Wales.

SMITH Robert, b. 21 Apr 1959, Crawley, Sussex, England. Singer; Musician (guitar). m. Mary Poole, 13 Aug 1988. Career: Lead singer, founder, The Cure, 1978-; Live musician with Siouxsie And The Banshees, 1979, 1982-83; Regular tours worldwide with The Cure; Concerts including: Reading Festival, 1979; Elephant Fayre Festival, Cornwall, 1983; Headline act, Glastonbury Festival, 1986, 1990, 1995; Benefit concert for Greenpeace, Royal Albert Hall, 1986; Golden Rose Festival, Montreux, 1987; Great British Music Weekend, Wembley, 1991; Provided soundtrack to film Carnage Visors, 1981. Recordings: Albums include: Three Imaginary Boys, 1979 (released as Boys Don't Cry, US); 17 Seconds, 1980; Faith, 1981; Pornography, 1982; Japanese Whispers, 1984; The Top, 1984; Concert - The Cure Live, 1984; The Head On The Door, 1985; Standing On A Beach - The Singles, 1986; Kiss Me Kiss Me Kiss Me, 1987; Disintegration, 1989; Mixed Up, 1990; Entreat, 1991; Wish (Number 1, UK), 1992; Show, 1993; Paris, 1993; Wild Mood Swings, 1996; Galore - The Singles, 1997; Singles include: Boys Don't Cry, 1979 (re-released 1986); The Love Cats, 1983; The Caterpillar, 1984; In Between Days (Without You), 1985; Why Can't I Be You?, 1987; Lullaby, 1989; Love Song, 1989; Pictures Of You, 1990; Never Enough, 1990; High, 1992; Friday I'm In Love, 1993; Wrong Number, 1997. Honours: BRIT Awards: Best Music Video, 1990; Best British Group, 1991; MTV Award, Best International Video, 1992. Address: c/o Fiction Records, Charlotte House, 4 Tottenham Mews, London W1P 3PJ, England.

SMITH Ruthie Elaine Foster, b. Manchester, England. Musician (saxophones); Singer; Composer. Musical Education: BA English/Music Honours, York University. Career: Member, Stepney Sisters, one of first feminist rock bands, 1974-76; Founder member, all women's jazz band The Guest Stars; World tours, jazz festivals, clubs including Ronnie Scott's; Also played with Mervyn Africa and Bryan Abrahams in South African band District Six; Toot Sweet with Jim Dvorak; Jazz in Britain, television, tours financed by the British Council; Served on Greater London Arts Council panel, 2 years. Recordings: 3 albums with The Guest Stars; 2 recordings with District Six; Live recordings for BBC; Currently working with Blue Skies Jazz Band, featuring Frances Knight and Julia Doyle. Honours: Jazz Bursary, Arts Council of Great Britain, to compose and perform a jazz suite. Membership: Musicians' Union. Hobbies: Gardening; Colour therapy; Astrology. Address: 63 Lothair Road South, London N4 1EN, England.

SMITH Spencer John, b. 8 Feb 1967, City of London, England. Musician (drums). Career: Member, North of Cornwallis; Concerts include support to Nico; Member, East Village, 1986-1990; Recorded 4 singles; Member, Saint Etienne, 1992; Tours include: UK; Japan; Canada; USA; Europe; Television includes: Top Of the Pops (4 times); Later With Jools Holland; The Word (2 times); Festivals include: Glastonbury; Sweden; Denmark; Radio includes: Evening session, BBC Radio 1. Recordings: with East Village: 4 singles; Albums:

Dropout; Hotrod Hotel; with St Etienne: 4 singles; 1 track on album Tiger Bay. Honours: Silver Disc, So Tough. Honour: Gold Disc, Too Young To Die, 1997. Memberships: Musicians' Union; PRS. Current Management: Heavenly Management. Address: c/o Heavenly Management, 47 Frith Street, London W1V 5TE, England.

SMITH Stephen Bowden, b. 17 Oct 1946, Oxford, England. Musician (electric, string bass). Musical Education: Studied electric bass with Joe Hubbard (theory and practice). Career: Cruise ships orchestra with Geraldo's Navy, 1969-70; P&O ships Orsova, Oriana (own trio), 1972; Michel Heuser Trio, Gstaad, Switzerland, 1972; Tour with Hindukush, Switzerland, 1974; Tommy Hawkins Band, Hammersmith Palais, 1977; John Burch Trio, London Playboy Club, 1977-78; Season and UK concerts with Matt Monro, 1978; Concerts with Vera Lynn, 1980; Accompanying jazz musicians including: Red Rodney; Tal Farlow; Slim Gaillard; Red Holloway; Harold Land; Ray Alexander; Spike Robinson; Oliver Jones; Dick Morrissey; Radio, recordings, European tours, with Stutz Bear Cats, 1984; Concerts, Spanish television with Iris Williams, 1987; Tours, television, concerts, with Vince Hill, 1988; Jazz clubs, festivals, with Butchers Brew, 1993; Tour of USA with Vince Hill, 1995-96; Cruise on flagship Oriana with the Groove Company, 1997. Compositions: Severn Borsa Nova; Purple Parrot Road; Jive For The Cider Insid 'er (Inside); The Mango Tango; Rio Yeo Samba. Recording: The Session, Whisky Time, with Diana Jarrett-Harris Trio. Hobbies: Skiing; Windsurfing. Current Management: Smith. Address: 23 Westbury Crescent, Oxford OX4 3RZ, England.

SMITH Wendy, b. 31 May 1963, Middlesbrough, Cleveland, England. Vocalist; Musician; Voice Movement Therapist. Career: Member, Prefab Sprout, 1982-; Extensive tours: Europe; UK; Japan; Numerous television appearances; Practitioner of Voice Movement Therapy, trained with Paul Newham, founder of Voice Movement Therapy. Recordings: Albums: Swoon, 1984; Steve McQueen, 1985; From Langley Park To Memphis, 1987; Protest Songs, 1988; Jordan-The Comeback, 1990; Life Of Surprises: The Best Of Prefab Sprout, 1992; Numerous hit singles. Honours: 6 Gold Albums; BRIT Award Nomination. Membership: International Network of Voice Movement Therapy Associates. Current Management: Keith Armstrong, Kitchenware Records. Address: 7 The Stables, St Thomas Street, Newcastle Upon Tyne NE41 8DU, England.

SMYTH Jimmy (James Patrick). b. 22 Apr 1958, Navan, Ireland.Musician (guitar, keyboards); Vocalist; Producer. m. Jenny Newman, 22 Mar 1994. Musical Education: Father (music teacher, RIAM, Dublin). Career: Toured with: The Kinks; Thin Lizzy; Bob Dylan; Rory Gallagher; Bon Jovi; Played guitar with: Bogey Boys; Toni Childs (all world tours); Van Morrison; Paul Brady; Don Baker; Numerous television appearances worldwide, including performance at Grammy Awards Ceremony, 1989. Compositions: Co-wrote 6 songs on Toni Child's album The Womans Boat; Many songs covered. Recordings: 2 albums as singer, guitarist with The Bogey Boys; Played on over 150 major albums. Honour: Twice voted in Top 5 guitarists in Ireland, Hot Press magazine. Memberships: Musicians' Union; ASCAP; IMRO; MCPS. Hobbies: Reading; Swimming; Working out. Current Management: Bob Brimson, 2 Tynings Terrace, Bath, Avon, England. Address: Thatched Cottage East, Upper Stand, Malahide, Co. Dublin, Ireland.

SNIDER Dee, b. New York, USA. Rock Vocalist; Lyricist. Career:Founder, vocalist, US rock group Twisted Sister; Sold over 8 million albums worldwide, 1983-87; Numerous worldwide tours; Major concerts include Monsters of Rock Festival, Castle Donington; Founder member,

vocalist, Desperado, with Bernie Torme; Founder member, Widowmaker, 1991-; Television includes: Host, Heavy Metal Mania, MTV (now known as Headbangers Ball); Radio includes: Host, Dee Snider's Metal Nation, WRCN; Defendant for rock music and lyrics, US Senate hearings, 1985. Recordings: Albums: with Twisted Sister: Under The Blade, 1982; You Can't Stop Rock And Roll, 1983; Stay Hungry, 1984; Come Out And Play, 1985; Love Is For Suckers; with Widowmaker: Blood And Bullets, 1992; Stand By For Pain, 1994; Singles: with Twisted Sister: I Am; I Wanna Rock; The Kids Are Back; Leader Of The Pack; We're Not Gonna Take It; You Can't Stop Rock'N'Roll; You Want What We Got. Current Management: c/o Music For Nations Records, 333 Latimer Road, London W10 6RA, England.

SNOW Hank (Clarence Eugene), b. 9 May 1914, Brooklyn, Nova Scotia, Canada. Country Singer; Musician (guitar); Songwriter. m. Minnie, 1936, 1 son. Career: Programme on network Canadian Farm Hour, 1936; Recording artist, solely for RCA, 1936-81; Regular tours in Canada and US, 1944-; Debut on Grand Ole Opry, 1950; Formed booking agency with Colonel Parker (Elvis Presley's manager); Several songs recorded by Elvis Presley; Leader, own band the Rainbow Ranch Boys. Compositions include: I'm Moving On; A Fool Such As I; Old Shep (all three recorded by Elvis Presley). Recordings: 85 US Country hits; US Country Number 1's include: I'm Moving On; The Golden Rocket; I Don't Hurt Anymore; Let Me Go Lover; I've Been Everywhere; Numerous albums include: Hank Snow Sings, 1952; Sacred Songs, 1958; The Singing Ranger, 1959; Together Again (with Anita Carter), 1962; I've Been Everywhere, 1963; Reminiscing (with Chet Atkins), 1964; Travelin' Blues, 1966; My Nova Scotia Home, 1967; Snow By Special Request (with Chet Atkins), 1970; Lonesome Whistle, 1972; The Jimmie Rodgers Story, 1972; All About Trains (with Jimmie Rodgers), 1975; Living Legend, 1978; Mysterious Lady, 1979; Instrumentally Yours, 1979; Lovingly Yours (with Kelly Foxton), 1980; By Request, 1981; Win Some Lose Some Lonesome (with Kelly Foxton), 1981; Brand On My Heart (with Willie Nelson), 1985. Honours: Inducted into Nashville Songwriters Hall Of Fame, 1978; Inducted into Country Music Hall Of Fame, 1979.

SNOW Phoebe (Laub), b. 17 July 1952, New York City, USA. Singer. Musical Education: Piano studies, guitar. Career: Performer, New York clubs, 1970s; Solo recording artist, 1974-; Tours with Paul Simon; Played and recorded with Stan Getz, Donald Fagen and Michael McDonald. Recordings: Albums include: Phoebe Snow, 1974; Second Childhood, 1976; It Looks Like Snow, 1976; Never Letting Go, 1977; Against The Grain, 1978; Best Of 1981; Rock Away, 1981; Something Real, 1989. Address: c/o The Agency Group, 1775 Broadway, Suite 433, New York, NY 10019, USA.

SNOWBOY (Mark Cotgrove), b. 3 July 1961, Hadleigh, Essex, England. Musician (Latin percussion); Recording Artist. Education: Graphics, Southend-On-Sea Technical College. Musical Education: Private lessons (initially with Robin Jones). Career: Television appearances: A13-The Road To Somewhere (documentary on self and two other Essex musicans); Festival Of Brighton; Sampled Here and Now, documentary; The Pier; Pebble Mill; Tours: Japan, 1991, 1993; Europe, 1994; World tours with: Lisa Stansfield, including Rock In Rio, Brazil 1993; Basia; James Taylor Quartet; Producer, various bands, sessions, remixes. Recordings: Albums: with Snowboy and the Latin Section: Ritmo Snowbo, 1989; Descarga Mambito, 1992; Something's Coming, 1994; Best Of..., 1995; The World Of..., 1995; 9 singles, 1984-93; Theme tune, Artrageous, BBC2, 1993. Memberships: Musicians' Union; PRS; MCPS; BPI. Hobbies: Record collecting; Vintage British comedy; Music Hall. Current Management: Alex Hardee,

Concorde Artists. Address: Concorde House, 101 Shepherds Bush Road, London W6 7LP, England.

SNOWDEN John Robert, b. 17 Feb 1968, Darlington, County Durham, England. Musician (jazz specialist guitar, bass); Reader all styles, versatile. Musical Education: Salford College of Technology; Graduate diploma in band musicianship (performance passed with distinction). Career: Various jazz combos, Salford College Big Band, 1989; Adaptation (cruiseship MV La Palma), 1990; National Youth Jazz Orchestra, 1991; Summer season, world cruise on board QE2, backing Neil Sedaka; Vic Damone; Iris Wlliams; Doug Cameron; Jimmy Tarbuck; with Rob Charles Orchestra; London Pops Orchestra; One Hundred Years of the Great British Musical, introduced by David Jacobs, recorded by BBC Radio 2; The Sound And Style Of James Last, national tour, 1994; Mike James Sound, including A Tribute To Nat King Cole, Birmingham Town Hall, 1994; Summer season and winter season on QE2, backing top artists; John Oliver Sound summer season, 1994; Ray McVay Orchestra, Blackpool Tower Ballroom, 1995; Teaching, Wigan, Bolton Education Authorities, 1994-95; Self-employed guitar/keyboard teacher. Membership: Musicians' Union. Address: 2 St Margarets Grove, Acklam, Middlesborough, England.

SNYMAN Neil, (Jean Corneille), b. 3 Nov 1956, Bellville, South Africa. Producer; Engineer. m. 17 Dec 1977, 1 son, 1 daughter. Education: Higher National Diploma for Technicians, Electrical Engineering. Musical Education: Informally trained; Multi-instrumentalist. Career: Specialist in Zulu ethnic recordings; Four featured documentaries on our activities, all filmed, broadcast on South African television, 1994-. Recordings: Recorded Ladysmith Black Mambazo for Rugby World Cup, 1995; For album Anthems: Swing Low; Sosholoza; World In Union. Honours: SABC Artes Awards, for traditional music. Memberships: ASAMI; SAMRO. Hobbies: Beach; Sea sport; Camping. Current Management: Direct. Address: Durban Beach Studios/Eagle Records, PO Box 11112, Marine Parade 4056, South Africa.

SOARES Joao Paulo, b. 24 July 1969, Beira, Mozambique. Singer; Graphic Designer; Writer. Education: 12 years, legal education. Career: Solo artiste as Johnny, 1990; Lead singer, composer, Selva Urbana, 1994-. Recordings: Lovers (Amor Sem Fim), 1991; Island Girl (Rapariga Da Ilha), 1991; My Dreams (Meus Sonhos), 1992; Lime Light (Sonhar Bem Alto), 1993; Street Boys (Putos Da Rua), 1994; Wonderful Tonight (Esta Noire Foi Maravilhosa), 1994; Urban Jungle (Selva Urbana), 1994. Publications: World Music (Musica Do Mundo), 1993. Membership: SPA (Portuguese Authors Society). Current Management: JPP Productions. Address: Av Paulo Vi-Lote 60-2-Fte, PO Box 59-2041 Rio Maior, Portugal.

SOENEN Geert, b. 25 April 1963, Wervik, Belgium. Piano Teacher; Conductor. m. Elly Deflo, 8 October 1988. Education: Higher Degree for Chamber Music, Conservatory of Gent, Belgium; Orchestral Conducting Degree, Conservatory of Den Haag, The Netherlands. Career: Soloist, played on trumpet and piano, classical, popular and chamber music; Conductor, Accademia Amanti Dell'Arte, The Symphony Orchestra of Flanders, The Prague Philharmonic Chamber Orchestra. Compositions: Arrangements for Pitti Polak, Raymond Van Het Groenewoud, for proms with symphony orchestra. Address: A Musschestr 55, 9000 Gent, Belgium.

SOERENSEN Kim Hougaard, b. 21 May 1956, Haldum, Denmark. Composer; Lyricist; Journalist; Music Theatre Critic. Education: Journalism, Danish University, 1981. Musical Education: Self-taught, private lessons by Danish composers. Career: Keyboard player, numerous Danish pop and rockbands, 1980-1990;

Composer, lyricist, Danish National Concert musical, The Egtved Chronicle, tour, 1993. Recording: The Egtved Chronicle, 1993. Publications: Songs From The Egtved Chronicle, 1993. Honours: The Cultural Award, 1993; The VAF Foundation Award, 1993. Memberships: Danish Jazz, Folk and Rock Composers; Danish Board of Journalists. Current Management: Scoop Agency, Boelling, DK-7100 Vejle, Denmark.

SOIRAT Philippe, b. 11 Mar 1961, Menton, France. Jazz Musician (drums). Musical Education: Jazz Academy, Monaco; Centre Musical Contemporain, Nice. Career: Concerts with: J R Monterose; Warren Bernhardt; Barney Wilen; John Stubbelfield; Duke Jordan; Ray Brown; Walter Bishop Jr; Bob Mover; Alain Jean-Marie; Jacky Terrasson; Georges Cables; LaVelle; James Moddy; Lou Donaldson; Horace Parlan; Emmanuel Bex; Jimmy Gourley; Dee Dee Bridgwater; Larry Schneider; Andy Laverne; Enrico Rava; Eric Lelann; Tours: Turkey (Armen Donelian Trio), 1990; France (Lee Konitz Quartet), 1992; Vietnam, Thailand, Malaysia, Singapore (Laurent de Wilde, Ira Coleman, Eric Barret), 1993; Australia, New Zealand (Laurent de Wilde Quartet), 1995; Portugal (Carlos Barretto Quintet); Canada (Yannick Rieu Quartet); Singapore, Brunei, Poland (Laurent de Wilde Trio), 1995; Africa (Belmondo Quintet), 1996. Recordings include: What Is The Color Of Love?, Yannick Rieu Quartet; Passione, Barney Wilen Quintet; Alone Together, Georges Cables Trio; Going Up, Carlos Barretto Quintet.

SOLEM Phil. Singer; Songwriter; Musician. Musical Education: Self-taught. Career: Member, Great Buildings since late 1970s; Member, The Rembrandts, 1991-. Recordings: The Tremblers, with Peter Noone, 1980; With Great Buildings: Apart from the Crowd, 1981; Gone, with Dwight Yoakum, 1995; Testimonial Dinner, with XTC, 1995; Compilation, Friends, 1995; Disney's Music from The Park, 1996; Oneman, with Dex Dickerson, 1997; Albums with the Rembrandts: The Rembrandts, 1991; Untitled, 1992; LP, 1995; Singles: That's Just The Way It Is Baby; Johnny Have You Seen Her; I'll Be There For You (theme for television series Friends), 1995. Honours: Grammy nomination, 1995; ASCAP and BMI Awards, 1995-97; LA Music Award. Memberships: ASCAP; SAG. Current Management: Under discussion. Address: 9744 Wilshire Boulevard, Suite 305, Beverly Hills, CA 90212, USA.

SOLO Sal, b. Hatfield, England. Singer; Songwriter; Broadcaster. Career: Lead singer, Classix Nouveaux, 1979-85; Major tours, numerous hit singles in approximately 30 countries; Lead Singer, Rockets, Italy, 1984-92; Solo career, 1984-; Host, radio shows, 1988-; Recordings: Guilty, Night People, 1981; Is It A Dream, La Verité, 1982; Secret, Imperception, Under The Sun, 1983; San Damiano, Heart & Soul, 1985; Look At Christ, 1991; Another Future, 1992; Through Ancient Eyes, 1994. Publications: For God's Sake, 1993. Honours: Various Gold and Silver discs; CACLB Radio Award, 1990. Membership: Christian Music Association; Hobby: Work for Christian Church. Current Management: Falcon Stuart, 59 Moore Park Road, London SW6 2HH, England.

SOMACH Denny, b. 30 Sept 1952, Allentown, Pennsylvania, USA. Producer; Record Company Executive. m. Kathy Levinsky Somach, 25 May 1995, 2 sons, 1 daughter. Education: BA, Moravian College. Career: Radio announcer, Station WSAN, Allentown, 1971-75; Program director, 1975; Announcer, music director, Station WYSP-FM, Philadelphia, 1975-81; Record producer; Television producer: Hot Spots; USA Network, 1982-84; Rock'n'Roll Show, CBS-TV, 1982; John Debella Show, 1990; Radio producer, Psychedelic Snack, 1985-; Ticket To Ride, 1985-; Legends of Rock, 1985-; Don Kirshner's History of Rock'n'Roll, 1990; Producer, president, Denny

Somach Productions, 1979-; President, Cinema Records, 1986-; President, founder, Musicom International, 1992. Recordings: Albums produced for: Dave Mason, 1987; Patrick Moraz, 1987; Johnny Winter, 1988; Eric Johnson, 1990. Publications: Ticket To Ride, 1989. Honours: Grammy, Best Rock Instrumentalist, Eric Johnson, Cliffs Of Dover. Membership: NARAS. Hobbies: Travel; Music; Art. Address: 812 W Darby Road, Havertown, PA 19083, USA.

SOMERS Lynn Marie, b. 15 Apr 1961, Jeanette, Pennsylvania, USA. Contemporary Christian Vocalist; Puppeteer. m. Frederick A Somers, 25 May 1984, 1 daughter. Education: BA, Psychology, Asbury College, 1983; 2 Masters degrees from United Seminary, Dayton, Ohio, 1986, 1988. Musical Education: Private vocal instruction, High School, college, seminary; Piano, guitar lessons as child, youth; MA, Theological Studies, Vocal performance emphasis. Career: Television appearance, Crosslink (United Theological Seminary), 1985; Radio interviews: Canada, 1989; WAMN, Princeton, West Virginia, 1995, Off the Cuff show on WSNJ, Bridgeton, New Jersey, 1996; Programs in churches, prisons, community and retirement homes; TV appearances: 60 Live Show with WBPH, Bethlehem, Pennsylvania, 1997; Edited version of Genesis video aired on WGCB, Red Lion, Pennsylvania and ACTV, Reading, Pennsylvania, 1997; Various tours through 28 states over 13 years. Recordings: We Are The Reason, 1986; God's House/Our House, 1992; The Gift of a Child, 1997. Publications: Video: Bible Stories From Genesis, for children; Puppets and Music, 1992; Dear Jesus, I wanna talk to you...My Home is Broken, story colouring book, 1996; Lynn Somers and Friends Character Coloring Book, 1996; Hand of the Master. puppet scriptbook, 1996; Various articles in publications, including Quarter Notes. Honours: Gospel Music Trailblazer Nomination, Airplay International, 1995. Memberships: Gospel Music Association; Fellowship Of Christian Puppeteers; Christian Educators Fellowship. Hobbies: Puppetry; Creative writing; Stories and scripts; Swimming; Bible study; Theatre. Current Managment: Hand Of The Master Ministries Inc (own non-profit ministry). Address: Lynn Somers and Friends, 103 Glen Court, Ephrata, PA 17522, USA.

SOMERVILLE Jimmy, b. 22 June 1961, Glasgow, Scotland. Singer; Songwriter. Career: Founder member, Bronski Beat, 1984-85; Formed The Communards, with Richard Coles, 1985-89; Tours include: UK Wedge tour, with Paul Weller and Billy Bragg, 1986; European tour, 1986; Solo artiste, 1989-; Concerts include: Red Hot And Dance AIDS benefit concert, 1991. Recordings: Albums with Bronski Beat: The Age Of Consent, 1984; Hundreds And Thousands, 1985; with the Communards: Communards, 1986; Red, 1987; Solo albums: Read My Lips, 1990; The Singles Collection, 1984-90, 1991; Dare To Love, 1995. Hit singles with Bronski Beat: Smalltown Boy, 1984; Why?, 1984; I Feel Love, 1985; with the Communards: You Are My World, 1985; Disenchanted, 1986; Don't Leave Me This Way, (Number 1, UK), 1986; So Cold The Night, 1986; Tomorrow, 1987; Never Can Say Goodbye, 1987; For A Friend, 1988; There's More To Love, 1988; Solo singles: Comment Te Dire Adieu, 1989; You Make Me Feel, 1990; Read My Lips, 1990; To Love Somebody, 1990; Run From Love, 1991; Hurts So Good, 1995; Heartbeat, 1995; By Your Side, 1995; Safe, 1997; Dark Sky, 1997; Other recordings include: Track On Red Hot And Blue, AIDS benefit compilation, 1990; Gimme Shelter, Voice Of The Beehive (for Putting Our House In Order charity), 1993. Current Management: Solar Management, 42-48 Charlbert Street, London NW8 7BU, England.

SONDHEIM Stephen Joshua, b. 22 Mar 1930, New York, New York, USA. Composer; Lyricist. Education: BA, Williams College, 1950.

Compositions: Incidental Music: The Girls of Summer, 1956; Invitation to a March, 1961; Twigs, 1971; Lyrics: West Side Story, 1957; Gypsy, 1959; Do I Hear A Waltz?, 1965; Candide, (additional lyrics) 1973; Music and Lyrics: A Funny Thing Happened on the Way to the Forum, 1962; Anyone Can Whistle, 1964; Evening Primrose, 1966; Company, 1970; Follies, 1971; A Little Night Music, 1973; The Frogs, 1974; Pacific Overtures, 1976; Sweeney Todd, 1979; Merrily We Roll Along, 1981; Sunday in the Park With George, 1984; Into the Woods, 1987; Assassins, 1991; Passion, 1994; Anthologies: Side by Side by Sondheim, 1976; Marry Me A Little, 1980; You're Gonna Love Tomorrow, 1983; Putting It Together, 1992. Film: Stavisky, 1974; Reds, 1981; Dick Tracy, 1990. Memberships: President, Dramatists Guild, 1973-81; American Academy and Institute of Arts and Letters. Address: c/o Flora Roberts, 157 West 57th Street, New York, NY 10019, USA.

SOPPER Josef Muff, b. 10 Jan 1958, Vienna, Austria. Managing Director. m. Petra, 12 Sept 1989, 2 sons. Musical Education: 7 years at Vienna Konservatorium. Career: Managing Director of: Rockhaus, Vienna; Vom Vereinigte Österreichische Musikforderer; Rock Syndicate, Vienna.Publications: Juke Box; Rock Box; Sound Box; Austrian Musikatlas. Hobbies: Family; Football; Classical Music. Address: c/o Rockhaus, Adalbert Stifter 73, A-1200 Vienna, Austria.

SORRELL Jonathan Lindsay, b. 19 Oct 1961, Salisbury, Wiltshire, England. Composer; Record Producer; Musician (keyboards); Programmer. m. Miriam Grech, 24 June 1994. Musical Education: Piano Diploma, 1976; A Level Music, 1978; BMus Degree, 1984. Career: Chorister, St Paul's Cathedral, 1970-75; Keyboard player for Trevor Horn, 1984-85; Keyboard player, arranger for David Dundas, 1988-95; Freelance session musician, 1985-95; Composer, television and film commercials, 1986-95. Compositions: Chart Show theme, ITV; You Bet theme, LWT; Survival logo, Anglia; Star Test, CH4; Starchamber Titles; Commercials for: American Airlines; Commerical Union; BMW Cars. Recordings: Albums with artistes including: Frankie Goes To Hollywood; Tears For Fears; Def Leppard; Film music: Little Shop Of Horrors; The Bear; Lord Of The Flies; Music Box; Freddie As F.R.O.T; Television music: ITV, LWT, CH4 television logos; BBC World News; Dark City; Sleepers; White Goods. Memberships: PRS; BASCA. Hobbies: Tennis; Cooking; Films. Current Management: Jeff Wayne Music Ltd. Address: The Cottage, 26 High Street, Prestwood, Nr Great Missenden, Bucks HP16 9ED, England.

SOSSIN Stephen Mark, b. 28 Sept 1956, Hartford, Connecticut, USA. Music Producer; Musician (guitar, bass, keyboards, violin). Education: Business, Computers, Manchester College. Musical Education: Heil/Sound Engineering; Studied with Al DiMeola and Mike Ruff; Pursuing advanced degree; Special Major Programme, California University, 1997. Career: Early performing career with artists including: Mike Ruff (keyboards, songwriter, Grammy nomination), 1986; Tom Chapin (saxophone, horns), 1971-76; Established songwriter in original music scene, New England, 1975-; Founder, Vizion productions studio, world class digital recording facility, photo, video services; Began artist development programme, 1983-; Works mainly with emerging artist, custom writing for individual's voice; Founder-Producer, New Vizion Studios. Composition: Thats Why I Ran, Dianne Glynn, 1996. Recordings: with Bonnie Lynn: Embrace Of My Heart, 1993; with Dianne Glynn: I Can't Find The Words, 1995; Thats Why I Ran, 1996; Take My Hand, 1996. Publications: Listed in Mixmaster Directory; Northeast Mix Plus; Recording Industry Sourcebook; Instage; Songwriters Market. Honours: Knight Chevalier Medal; National Patriotism Medal; AFP; Capitol Records Promotional Awards. Memberships: Independent

Producer's Guild; NE; United States Naval Institute. Hobbies: Donates time to youth groups; Outdoor hiking; Reading. Current Management: John Carpino; Agent: Caroline Hayes. Address: 38 Thompson, Unit 4H, Manchester, CT 06040, USA.

SOUQUES Laurent, b. 27 Oct 1963, Paris, France. Musician (double bass); Composer. Musical Education: Conservatoire National Supérieur de Musiques et de Dance, Paris. Career: Jazz Festival, Franche Comté, 1986, 1987, 1989; Jazz Festival Suedine Bleue (Dijon), 1986; Jazz Festival Aiguillon, 1990; Jazz clubs in Paris, 1991-95; Jazz Festival Banlieue Bleue, with G Russell, Living Time Orchestra, 1993; Banlieue Bleue, G Russell, Cité de la Musique, 1995; JUC Halle That Jazz, Paris, 1995. Compositions: Film music; Syndrome de l'Espion - Zooleil, N Joyeux; Paris des Freres Tenebres, Muriel Mazieres. Recordings: Just Back From New Orleans, 1989; G Russell for Radio France, 1993, 1995; Fire Beat, Ralph Thomas Sextet, 1996. Hobbies: Sailing; Swimming. Address: 10 Rue Saint Jean, 75017 Paris, France.

SOUSA (Duane) "Beans", b. 22 July 1951. Musician (bass); Vocalist. m. Barbara Runnion, 8 Apr 1989, 1 son. Career: Bassist for major country and rock artists: Lacy J Dalton; Phoebe Snow; Larry Hosford; Studio work for major recording companies including CBS, MCA, Capitol and Shelter Records. Recordings include: Dream Baby, Lacy J Dalton; Solo album: You Don't Know. Membership: AFofM. Hobbies: Golf; Fishing; Camping. Address: 906 30th Avenue, Santa Cruz, CA 95062, USA.

SOUTH Joe (Joe Souter), b. 28 Feb 1940, Atlanta, Georgia, USA. Musician (guitar); Singer; Songwriter. Career: Session guitarist, Nashville, 1960s; Recording sessions include: Aretha Franklin; Wilson Pickett; Marty Robbins; Eddy Arnold; Bob Dylan; Simon And Garfunkel; Solo artiste, 1962-. Compositions include: Games People Play, Billy Joe Royal and Boots Randolph; Untie Me, The Tams; Down In The Boondocks, Billy Joe Royal; I Knew You When, Billy Joe Royal; These Are Not My People, Freddy Weller; Birds Of A Feather, Paul Revere And The Raiders; Hush, Deep Purple. Recordings: Albums include: Introspect, 1968; Don't It Make You Want To Go Home, 1969; Walkin' Shoes, 1970; So The Seeds Are Growing, 1971; Midnight Rainbows, 1975; Look Inside, 1976; Other recordings include: Blonde On Blonde, Bob Dylan, 1966; Sound Of Silence, Simon and Garfunkel, 1966; Aretha Arrives, Aretha Franklin, 1967; Lady Soul, Aretha Franklin, 1968.

SPACEY-FOOTE Gary Martin, b. 15 Dec 1961, Weybridge, Surrey, England. Musician (saxophone, flute, percussion, drums). m. Carrie Spacey-Foote, 17 Aug 1991. Musical Education: Self-taught saxophone and flute; Percussion, self-taught, with some tutorage with Danny Cummings. Career: 2 world tours, Joan Armatrading; Television appearnces with Bee Gees; Tom Jones; Recording, touring, with Nightrains; The Hipjoints, Maroon Town; House Of Rhythm; Jamiroquai, Kiss Of Life; Espiritu; Lionel Moyst. Recordings: with The Hipjoints: Rock Hopper; Chillin'; with Lionel Moyst Sextet: Chillin'. Memberships: Musicans' Union; PRS. Hobbies: Keeping fit; Comedy; Black and white British films; Reading. Current Management: c/o Carrie Spacey-Foote, 34 Hampden Road, Kingston on Thames, Surrey KT1 3HG, England.

SPANG-HANSSEN Simon Cato, b. 13 Apr 1955, Hellerup, Denmark. Musician (saxophonist); Composer. m. Mariane Bitran, 23 Jan 1987, 1 son. Musical Education: Mainly self-taught. Career: Tours with: John Tchicai and Strange Brothers, Scandinavia, Germany, Italy; Andy Emler's Mega-Octet, Europe; French National Jazz Orchestra, 1991-94, Europe; Leader of Quartet, Muluankh; Duo with Denis Badault, France,

Denmark, Central Africa. Recordings: Darktown Highlights; Ten By Two; Because Forever; Mardi Gras, Chez Toi. Honours: Ben Webster Prize, 1978. Membership: Union de Musicians de Jazz (Paris). Hobbies: Travel; Discovery; Food; History; Painting; Swimming. Current Management: Blue Line Productions, Mr Bourgaut, Mr Vautrot. Address: 5 Rue Leon Giraud, 75019 Paris, France.

SPARROW Edwin Harold James, b. 28 Jan 1943, Harrogate, Yorkshire, England. Musician (drums, timpani, percussion, Latin percussion). Musical Education: Piano with Miss Evelyn Gunnar; ARCM; LTCL; LLCM; Timpani with Lewis Pocock, Trinity College. Career: Many years in France, worked with top light entertainment artistes including: Johnny Hallyday; Sylvie Vartan; Charles Aznavour; Appeared in film Les Jeunes Loups, directed by Marcel Carné; Appeared with Kevin Aires; Mike Oldfield; Nico and others connected with The Velvet Underground; Gerry Rafferty, 1970s; Closely connected with Ballet Rambert; London Contemporary Dance Theatre; Contemporary Dance and Therapy in UK; Featured on: June The 1st, 1974; Bannamour, Kevin Ayres. Hobby: Photography (pictures published in Guitar Magazine, and on album cover to Requiem For A Hick, Adrian Legg). Address: Harrogate, North Yorkshire, England.

SPEAKE Martin John, b. 3 Apr 1958, Barnet, Hertfordshire, England. Musician (alto saxophone); Jazz Educator; Composer. m. Rachel Cutler, 6 Jan 1990, 1 daughter. Musical Education: A Level Music; Classical saxophone, Trinity College of Music, LTCL, FTCL diplomas. Career: Tours of West Africa, Latin America, Europe, with saxophone quartet Itchy Fingers; Tours of Indonesia, Philippines, Croatia, UK, with 7-piece Fever Pitch, own quartet, and duo with guitarist Phil Lee; Various radio and television appearances. Recordings: Albums: with Itchy Fingers: Quark; Teranga; In Our Time, Martin Speake Group; Entertainment USA, Billy Jenkins; Midnight Sun, Flora Purim and Airto Moreira. Honours: Schlitz Young Jazz Musicians Winner, with Itchy Fingers, 1986. Membership: Musicians' Union. Hobby: Tai Chi. Address: 1 Mawson House, Baldwins Gardens, London EC1N 7SD, England.

SPEAKMAN Thomas Walker, b. 23 June 1917, Ormskirk, Lancashire, England. Musician (timpanis, percussion). m. Norah Lightburn, 7 Sept 1940, 1 son. Musical Education: Pupil, C Earnshaw, BBC Welsh Orchestra; C Botteril, Mantovani. Career: Touring in variety, 1935-39; RASC Staff Band, 1939-44; Liverpool Shakespeare Theatre, 1944-45; Royal Liverpool Philharmonic with Sir Malcolm Sargent, 1945-52; Blackpool Opera House, 1952-58; Own concert Orchestra and Dance Bands, 1958-65; MD Whitby Spa, 1958; Blackpool Symphony; Various Blackpool theatres and clubs to 1975; Morris Concert Band (H Mortimer), 1975-80; Freelance with various brass bands, local societies, last minute stand-in and deputy, 1980-97. Memberships: Gold card member, Musicians' Union, Central London BCM. Hobbies: Garden; Bowls, indoor and outdoor (Secretary, Windsor and Eton, 12 years). Address: 73 Ruddlesway, Windsor, Berkshire SL4 5SG, England.

SPEARE Paul, b. 10 Dec 1955, Romford, Essex, England. Musician (saxophone, flute); Arranger; Producer; Lecturer. m. Paula Davies, 27 July 1985, 1 daughter. Musical Education: London College of Music; Birmingham Polytechnic. Career: Member, Dexy's Midnight Runners, 1980-82; Q-Tips British tour, 1982; Elvis Costello, US, UK, and European tours, 1983; Manager, Expresso Bongo Studios, Tamworth, 1985-94; Leader, Expresso Bongo Orchestra, 1988-94; Lecturer, Popular Music, Lewisham College, London, 1995-. Recordings: Singles include: Come On Eileen, Too-Rye-Ay, Dexy's Midnight

Runners, 1982; Punch The Clock, Elvis Costello, 1983; Free Nelson Mandela, Special AKA, 1984; Keep Moving, Madness, 1984; Hold Back The Night, KWS/The Tramps, 1992. Membership: Musicians' Union. Current Management: Mr R Speare. Address: 314 Upminster Road North, Rainham, Essex RM13 9RY, England.

SPEARMAN Michael, b. 26 Feb 1967, Hexham, Northumberland, England. Jazz Musician (guitar). Education: BSC (hons) Sociology and Social Research, Diploma Market Research Society (Newcastle). Musical Education: Self-taught. Career: Collaborated with artists including: Jim Mullen; John Etheridge; Support to: John Scofield; Courtney Pine; Regular bandleader; Interviewed on BBC Radio. Compositons: Original compositions in performances, from 'bop' through modal jazz and fusion to free elements and flamenco; Demos available. Publications: Articles in several sociological journals, media articles. Membership: Musicians' Union. Hobbies: Films; Books; Occasional journalism. Current Management: Julie Savill. Address: 83 Rectory Lane, Chelmsford, Essex CM1 1RF, England.

SPEARS Billie Jo, b. 14 Jan 1937, Beaumont, Texas, USA. Country Singer. Career: Country singer, 1952-; Regular recording artiste, 1964-; Television includes: Louisiana Hayride; Leader, own band, Owlkatraz. Recordings: Hits include: Blanket On The Ground; Mr Walker, It's All Over; What I've Got In Mind; Sing Me An Old-Fashioned Song; Misty Blue; I Will Survive; Numerous albums include: The Voice Of Billie Jo Spears, 1968; Mr Walker It's All Over, 1969; Miss Sincerity, 1969; With Love, 1970; Country Girl, 1970; Just Singin', 1972; Blanket On The Ground, 1974; Billie Jo, 1975; What I've Got In Mind, 1976; By Request (with Del Reeves), 1976; If You Want Me, 1977; Everytime I Sing A Love Song, 1977; Lonely Hearts Club, 1978; Love Ain't Gonna Wait For Us, 1978; I Will Survive, 1979; Standing Tall, 1980; Special Songs, 1981; Del and Billie Jo (with Del Reeves), 1982; BJ - Billie Jo Spears Today, 1983; We Just Came Apart At The Dreams, 1984; Unmistakeably, 1992. Address: c/o Joe Taylor Artist Agency, 2802 Columbine Pl., Nashville, TN 37204, USA.

SPECTOR Phil (Harvey Phillip Spector), b. 26 Dec 1940, Bronx, New York, USA. Record Producer; Composer; Musician. m. Ronnie Spector (divorced). Career: Member, The Teddy Bears; The Spectors Three; Formed Philles Records, 1961-66; Produced albums for Beatles' Apple label; Formed Phil Spector International. Compositions: Co-writer, with Ben E King, Spanish Harlem; Young Boy Blues. Recordings: As producer for artists including: LaVern Baker; Ruth Brown; Billy Storm; Twist And Shout, The Top Notes; Corrina Corrina, Ray Petersen, 1960; Pretty Little Angel Eyes, Curtis Lee; I Love How You Love Me, Paris Sisters; Work with the Crystals and the Ronettes includes: He's A Rebel, 1962; Then He Kissed Me, 1963; Be My Baby, 1963; Baby I Love You, 1963; River Deep Mountain High, 1966; Black Pearl, Sonny Charles And The Checkmates; Albums by: John Lennon; The Plastic Ono Band; Imagine; Sometime In New York City; George Harrison: All Things Must Pass; Concert For Bangladesh; Leonard Cohen: Death Of a Ladies Man, 1977; Ramones: End Of The Century, 1980; Compilations: A Christmas Gift To You, 1963; Phil Spector Wall Of Sound, Vol 1: The Ronettes, 1975; Vol 2: Bob B Soxx And The Blue Jeans, 1975; Vol 3: The Crystals, 1975; Vol 4: Yesterday's Hits Today, 1976; Vol 5: Rare Masters, 1976; Vol 6: Rare Masters, Volume 2, 1976; The Phil Spector Story, 1976; Echoes Of The Sixties, 1977; Phil Spector 1974-79, 1979; Wall Of Sound, 1981; The Early Productions, 1958-61; Twist And Shout: Twelve Atlantic Tracks Produced By Phil Spector, 1989.

SPECTOR Ronnie (Veronica Bennett Spector Greenfield), b. 10 Aug 1943, New York, USA. Singer. m. (1) Harvey Phillip (Phil) Spector, (2) Jonathan Greenfield, 16 Jan 1982, 5 children. Career: Dancer, New York, 1962-63; Lead singer, choreographer, dancer, The Ronettes (originally Ronnie and The Relatives), 1962-67; Appearances include: Group Scene '64 Tour, support to The Rolling Stones, 1964; Solo artiste, 1969-; Writer, 1988-90. Recordings: Albums: with the Ronettes: Presenting The Fabulous Ronettes, 1965; Solo albums: Siren, 1981; Unfinished Business, 1987; Hit singles: with The Ronettes: Be My Baby, 1963; Baby I Love You, 1964; The Best Part Of Breaking Up, 1964; Do I Love You, 1964; Walking In The Rain, 1964; Contributor, A Christmas Gift For You compilation album, 1963. Publications: Be My Baby (autobiography), with Vince Waldron, 1990. Honours: Gee-Gee Awards, 16 Magazine, 1963, 1964; Inducted into New York Music Hall Of Fame, 1982; Gold discs, 1963-65; Music Awards Nominations, 1987, 1988; Grammy Award, Walking In The Rain, 1964; Grammy Nomination, 1986. Current Management: GreenSpec Properties, Ste 233, 39B Mill Plain Road, Danbury, CT 06811, USA.

SPEECH (Todd Thomas), b. 1968, Milwaukee, Wisconsin, USA. Singer; Lyricist. Education: Art Institute Of Atlanta. Career: Originally known as DJ Peech; Formed gangsta rap act DLR (Disciples Of A Lyrical Rebellion), renamed Secret Society; Evolved into hip-hop act Arrested Development, 1988-; Performances include: MTV Drops The Ball '93, 1992; MTV Unplugged, 1992; Lollapalooza '93 US Tour, 1993. Recordings: Singles include: Tennessee, 1992; People Everyday, 1992; Revolution (used in film soundtrack Malcolm X), 1993; Mr Wendal, 1993; Albums: 3 Years, 5 Months And 2 Days In The Life Of..., 1993; Unplugged, 1993; Producer, Dropping H20 On The Fiber, Gumbo, 1993. Honours include: Grammy Awards: Best New Artist, Best Rap Group, 1993; Soul Train Award, Best Rap Album, 1993; 7 Atlanta Music Awards, 1993. Current Management: Entertainment Resources International Inc., 9380 SW 72nd Street, #B-220, Miami, FL 33173, USA.

SPEIDEL Paul, b. 15 Feb 1965, Kenmare, North Dakota, USA. Jazz and Blues Musician (guitar); High School Jazz Program Director. m. Adlin Quiles, 1 June 1991. Education: BA, Augustana College, 1986. Musical Education: Master Of Music, University of Northern Colorado, 1990. Career: Freelance guitarist, bassist in Chicago, Denver, Boston; Vocal performances with Grammy nominated University of Northern Colorado Vocal Jazz I; Performances with Patti Page; Gerry Beaudoin; Jeff Benedict; Terry Cooke; Ted Pilzecker; Numerous musical shows; 3 tours, Latin and Central America with the Latin Continental Singers as Instrumental Director; Currently guitarist with the Monique Weiss Quartet; Guiarist, vocalist with the Paul Speidel Band. Publications: CD reviewer in bi-monthly No Name Jazz News. Honours: Illinois State Scholar, Colorado National Scholar, Memberships: International Association of Jazz Educators; Boston Jazz Society; Boston Blues Society; Gospel Music Association; Music Educators National Conference. Hobby: Reading classic and contemporary poetry and fiction. Current Management: PSB Management. Address: 130½ Academy Avenue, Providence, RI 02908, USA.

SPEIRS Fraser, b. 4 Oct 1949, Glasgow, Scotland. Singer; Musician (harmonica). Education: Medical Illustrator, University of Glasgow. Career: Concert appearances with: Love & Money; Tam White; Carla Laula Band; Rab Noakes; Radio credits: Radio Clyde; Radio 2 Nightride, with David Pringle Band; Television credits: All Kinds Of Country, STV; Recordings: Album with: Del Amitri; Fish; The Soup Dragons; Carol Kidd; Lloyd Cole And The Commotions; Love And Money; Carol Laula; Humpff Family;

King Hash; Kindness Of Strangers; Theme tune to Your Cheatin' Heart. Membership: Musicians' Union. Hobbies: Hockey; Skiing; Travel. Address: 53 Marywood Square, Glasgow G41 2BN, Scotland.

SPENCER John B, b. 5 June 1944, West London, England. Singer; Musician (guitar); Bandleader; Record Producer; Novelist. m. Lou, 26 Feb 1966, 3 sons. Career: Pubs, clubs, concert halls, festivals, throughout Europe, 1976-; Featured, interviewed, CH4 documentary: Living With The Blues, 1990; Radio broadcasts: Andy Kershaw Show, Radio 1, several occasions; Member, bands including: John Spencer's Louts; Spencer's Alternative; John B Spencer Band; Parlour Games; The Goods; Also worked with: Martin Simpson's Flash Company; Home Service; Toured with Fairport Convention. Compositions: Songs, One More Whiskey, Will This House Be Blessed, covered and recorded by many folk artists; Cruisin' On A Saturday Night, hit in Sweden for Jerry Williams. Recordings: The Last LP, 1978; Out With A Bang, 1986; Break And Entry, 1989; Parlour Games, 1990; Sunday Best, 1992; Appeared on: True Dare Or Promise, 1988; Blues Brittanica, 1993; The Wish And The Way, 1993; Publications: Novels: The Electronic Meat Market, 1975; A Case For Charley, 1984; Charley Gets The Picture, 1985; Quake City, 1995. Memberships: Musicians' Union; PRS; MCPS. Hobbies: Crime fiction; Vegetable growing. Current Management: Jim Driver. Address: PO Box 4215, London SE23 2QD, England.

SPIDER JOHNSON (Etienne), b. 5 Oct 1963, London, England. Musician (drums, bass, guitar); Vocalist. 1 daughter. Musical Education: Disc cutting course with LTS, Denmark Street, London; Electronics at Hackney College. Career: with Potato 5: World tour, 1989; Extensive television coverage; with The Deltones: European tour, 1991; with Nutty Boys (Madness): Crunch European tour, 1991; UK tour, 1992; with Humble Souls: European tour and television coverage, 1993-94; Humble Souls and Night Trains World tour, 1994. Recordings: Do The Jerk, Potato 5, 1989; Five Alive, Potato 5, 1990; Silent River, Deltones, 1991; Crunch, Nutty Boys, 1991; Gone He's Gone, Stop Playing Around, Wendy Walker, 1991; Thoughts And Sound Paintings, 1993-94; Sleazeball, Night Trains, 1994. Honours: BPI International Reggae Award, 1992; Best Newcomer, for Wendy Walker. Memberships: MCPS; PRS. Hobbies: Sports; Films; Concerts; Travel; Reading. Current Management: Concorde International. Address: Concorde House, Shepherds Bush Road, London W12, England.

SPIES Peter Finnick, b. 20 June 1966, Copenhagen, Denmark. Composer; Musician (piano). Career: Travelled world as commercial musician; Wrote musical, Atlantis, performed at Ostre Gasvaerk Theatre, Denmark. Compositions: Atlantis (musical); Currently working on new musical: Pelle The Conqueror. Membership: DJBFA (Danish Composers Society). Hobbies: Travel; Sport.

SPINELLI Philip Antony, b. 30 Mar 1950, Newcastle-upon-Tyne, England. Musician (drums, keyboards); Vocalist. m. Biliana Mancheva, 19 Oct 1994, 1 son. Musical Education: Berklee College, Boston, USA; Masterclass with Bob Armstrong, PIT, London. Career: Founder member, Brand X; Tours with Atomic Rooster; Edwin Starr; Rick Kenton (Roxy Music); Session work with: Chris Wood (Traffic); Pino Palladino; Several UK television appearances; Performed for HM The Queen and Royal Family, Buckingham Palace. Recordings: Albums: Brand X: First album (with Phil Collins); Locust: Alpha Waves; Singles with Atomic Rooster. Membership: Performing Rights Society. Current Management: Data Sound. Address: 19 Wharfdale, Hemel Hempstead, Herts HP2 5TQ, England.

SPINETTI Henry Anthony George, b. 31 Mar 1951, Cwm, South Wales. Musician (drums). Divorced, 2 sons. Career: Tours, concerts include: Eric Clapton, 1979-82, 1993, 1995; Tina Turner, 1984, 1985, 1990; Joan Armatrading, 1972, 1990; Neil Sedaka, 1974; Andy Fairweather-Low, 1970-76; Procol Harum, 1994; Bill Wyman, 1993, 1994; Television appearances include: Top Of The Pops; Radio includes: Wembley Concert with Tina Turner, 1990. Recordings: Albums include: with Joan Armatrading: Show Some Emotion, 1977; To The Limit, 1978; Rough Mix, Townsend And Lane, 1977; City To City, Gerry Rafferty, 1978; with Eric Clapton: Just One Night, 1979; Another Ticket, 1981; All The Best, Paul McCartney; Gone Troppo, George Harrison, 1982; Willie And The Poor Boys, 1985; Film soundtracks include: Lethal Weapon; Color Of Money. Membership: Musicians' Union. Hobbies: Model aircraft; Tennis.

SPITERI Sharleen Eugenie, b. 7 November 1967, Glasgow, England. Guitar; Piano; Organ; Harmonica. Education: Selftaught. Career: Formed Texas with John McElhone, 1988. Compositions: Albums: Southside, 1989; Mothers Heaven, 1991; Ricks Road, 1993; Whore on Blonde, 1997. Recordings: Texas Southside; Texas Mothers Heaven; Texas Ricks Road; Texas White on Blonde; Jayhawks - Bad Times; Wu Tang Clan and Texas. Honours: Capital Radio, Best Female Vocal; Malta Music Prize, Best Intl. Hobbies: Climbing; Snowboarding. Address: G R Management, 974 Pollokshaw Road, Shawlands, Glasgow G41 2HA, England.

SPIZZ (Spizzman) Julian, b. 17 Sept 1968, Florence, Italy. Vocalist; Composer; Performer. Musical Education: Studies in field of experimental singing. Career: Member, Trinovox; Appearances in major German televison and radio programmes, 1994; Concerts in major German, Swiss, Austrian towns (Berlin, Bremen, Lübeck, Stuttgart, Basel, Vienna, Innsbruck), 1994-95; Soundtrack, radio play, Bavarian State radio, 1995. Recordings: Albums: Incanto, Trinovox, 1994; Voices, Trinovox; Sarband, The Bulgarian Voices, 1994; Earborn, Trinovox and Various Artists, 1995. Honours: Italian National Award, vocal artists: Quartetto Cetra (with Trinovox), 1994. Memberships: SIAE; GEMA. Hobbies: Free climbing; Motorcycling. Address: c/o Mr Ulrich Balss, Jaro Records, Bismarck 83, D-28203 Bremen 1, Germany.

SPRINGER Scott, b. 1 Apr 1959, Birmingham, Alabama, USA. Singer; Musician (guitar, bass guitar). m. Helen C Akin, 2 Aug 1980, 2 sons, 1 daughter. Career: Tour with band Halo, USA, Canada, 1989-1993; Jesus Music, 1990; 6 Christian Radio Number 1 songs, USA. Recordings: Halo; Heaven Calling; Hello Forever. Publications: CCM; Release. Membership: BMI. Hobbies: Fishing; Basketball. Current Managment: Halo Productions Inc. Address: 311 Cherokee Drive, Clanton, AL 35046, USA.

SPRINGFIELD Dusty (Mary O'Brien), b. 16 Apr 1939, Hampstead,London, England. Singer. Career: Member, the Springfields, 1961-63; Solo artiste, 1963-; Appearances include: Tour, with the Searchers, Freddie & The Dreamers; Dave Berry, 1963; UK tour with Herman's Hermits; Dave Berry; Brian Poole; Royal Variety Show, 1968; Festival Du Disque, Berlin, 1969; Film appearance, It's All Over Town, 1964; Television appearances include: Top Of The Pops; Ed Sullivan Show; The Bacharach Sound; The Sound Of Motown; Ready Steady Go!; Own UK television series, Dusty, BBC, 1966-67; It Must Be Dusty, ITV, 1968. Recordings: Albums: A Girl Called Dusty, 1964; Everything's Coming Up Dusty, 1965; Golden Hits, 1966; Where Am I Going, 1967; Dusty In Memphis, 1969; Dusty Sings Burt Bacharach And Carole King, 1975; It Begins Again, 1978; Living Without Your Love, 1979; White Heat, 1983; The Silver Collection, 1988; Reputation, 1990; A Very Fine Love, 1995; Singles: with the Springfields:

Silver Threads And Golden Needles, 1962; Island Of Dreams, 1963; Say I Won't Be There, 1963; Solo singles include: I Only Want To Be With You (first song ever featured on Top Of The Pops), 1964; Stay Awhile, 1964; I Just Don't Know What To Do With Myself, 1964; Wishin' And Hopin', 1964; Losing You, 1964; In The Middle Of Nowhere, 1965; Some Of Your Lovin', 1965; You Don't Have To Say You Love Me (Number 1, UK), 1966; Goin' Back, 1966; All I See Is You, 1966; The Look Of Love, for film Casino Royale, 1967; I Close My Eyes And Count To Ten, 1968; Son Of A Preacher Man, 1969; The Windmills Of Your Mind, from film The Thomas Crown Affair, 1969; Guest vocalist, What Have I Done To Deserve This?, Pet Shop Boys (Number 2, US), 1988; As Long As We Got Each Other, with B J Thomas, 1988; Nothing Has Been Proved, from film Scandal, 1989. Current Management: Take Out Productions, 130 W. 57th Street, Suite 13A, New York, NY 10019, USA.

SPRINGFIELD Rick (Richard Springthorpe), b. 23 Aug 1949, Sydney, Australia. Singer; Musician (guitar, piano); Actor. Career: Member, Jordy Boys; Rock House; MPD Band; Zoot; Solo artiste, 1972-; Also television actor; Guest appearances include: The Rockford Files; Wonder Woman; The Six Million Dollar Man; Leading role, General Hospital; Actor, film, Hard To Hold, 1984. Recordings: Albums include: Beginnings, 1972; Comic Book, 1974; Heroes, 1974; Wait For The Night, 1976; Working Class Dog, 1981; Success Hasn't Spoiled Me Yet, 1982; Living In Oz, 1983; Tao, 1985; Rock Of Life, 1988; Singles include: Human Touch; Speak To The Sky; Jessie's Girl; I've Done Everything For You; Don't Talk To Strangers; Love Somebody, used in film Hard To Hold; Bruce. Current Management: Ron Weisner Entertainment, 9200 Sunset Blvd, PH15, Los Angeles, CA 90069, USA.

SPRINGSTEEN Bruce, b. 23 Sept 1949, New Jersey, USA. Singer; Songwriter; Musician (guitar). m. (1) Julianne Phillips (divorced), (2) Patti Scialfa, 1 son, 1 daughter. Career: Recording artist, 1972-; Formed own band, The E-Street Band, 1974; Numerous national and worldwide tours, include: MUSE No-Nukes Concerts, 1979; The River tour, 1980; Born In The USA tour, 1984; Tunnel Of Love Express tour, 1988; Amnesty International Human Rights Now! tour, 1988; North American tour, 1992; Numerous benefit and charity concerts. Compositions: Numerous songs include: Born To Run; Blinded By The Light (also recorded by Manfred Mann); Fire (recorded by the Pointer Sisters); Because The Night (recorded by Patti Smith); Badlands; Hungry Heart; Dancing In The Dark; Born In The USA; I'm On Fire; I'm Goin' Down; Fire; Pink Cadillac; Cover Me; 57 Channels And Nothin' On; Better Days; Glory Days. Recordings: Albums: Greetings From Asbury Park, 1973; The Wild The Innocent And The E Street Shuffle, 1973; Born To Run, 1975; Darkness On The Edge Of Town, 1978; The River (Number 1, US), 1980; Nebraska, 1982; Born In The USA (Number 1, US and UK), 1984; Live 1975-85 (Number 1, US), 1986; Tunnel Of Love (Number 1, US and UK), 1987; Human Touch (Number 1, UK), 1992; Lucky Town, 1992; In Concert - MTV Plugged, 1993; Greatest Hits, 1995; The Ghost Of Tom Joad, 1995; Contributor, We Are The World, USA For Africa, 1985; Sun City, Artists Against Apartheid, 1986. Honours include: 2 Grammy Awards: Best Male Rock Vocalist, 1984, 1987; BRIT Award, Best International Solo Artist, 1986; Inducted, Rock'n'Roll Hall Of Fame, 1988; Numerous Platinum and Gold discs; Oscar, Best Original Song In A Movie, Streets Of Philadelphia, 1994. Current Management: Jon Landau Management, 40 West Elm Street, Greenwich, CT 06830, USA.

SPRUNG Roger, b. 29 Aug 1930, New York, USA. Folk Singer; Musician (5-string banjo); Teacher; Entertainer. m. Nancy, 24 May 1990, 2 daughters. Career: Tour with Kay Starr; Jimmy

Dean TV Show; An American Experience TV Show; Dean Martin TV Show; Garry Moore Show; Appearances include: Philadelphia Folk Festival; Lincoln Center, New York; Carnegie Hall, New York. Recordings: 46 including: Bluegrass Gold, Volumes 1-2, 1976; The Philadelphia Folk Festival, 1977; 44th Annual Galax Convention, 1980; Pound Ridge Fiddler's Celebration, 1981; Irish Grass, 1983; The Irish Bluegrass Connection, 1983; Southwest Winds, 1983; Let's Pick, 1988; Thyme And Beyond, 1989; Stompin' Stuff, 1990; Recordings in the Library of Congress and Smithsonian/Folkway. Honour: World Champion 5 string banjo player. Hobbies: Music; Art; Stamps; Pets. Current Management: Sprung Enterprises. Address: 7 Papoose Hill Road, Newtown, CT 06470, USA.

SPRY Bro (Crispin Luke Robinson), b. 3 Nov 1966, London, England. Musician (congas, shakers, djembs, drumkit, percussion). Separated, 2 daughters. Education: City and East London College; Kent University. Musical Education: Studied with Bobby Sanabria, USA; John Amira, USA; Bob Armstrong, UK; Robin Jones, UK. Career: First recordings with: Manassah; Soul II Soul; Yazz; Youth; Young Disciples; Signed to Polygram as part of Galliano, 1991-; Live work: Tours with Galliano include: Europe; Japan; Australia; USA; Hong Kong; Scandinavia; Marvin Gaye Tribute Concert (feauring: Al Jarreau; George Duke; Pointer Sisters; Chaka Khan; Leon Ware; Wah Wah Watson; Chuck Rainey; James Gadson), 1992; Roy Ayers, 1995; Straight No Chaser Jazz Festival, Bheki Mselku. Recordings: First and second albums: Soul II Soul; 3 albums with Galliano, include variouscompositions. Membership: Musicians' Union. Hobbies: Afro-diasporan culture; Skateboarding; Snowballing; Busting Chalwah. Current Management: Steve Baker; World Chief. Address: Worldchief Management, 132 Liverpool Road, London N1, England.

SQUIBAN Didier, b. 23 Sept 1959. Composer; Musician (piano). 2 sons. Musical Education: Musicology. Career: Musical director, Sirius (Orchestre de Jazz de Bretagne); Tours with: Dan Arbraz; John Surman; Eric Le Lann; Yann Fanch Remener; Radio France; Festival Interceltique; Zenith (Paris). Recordings: Tendances; L'Heritage Des Celtes; Enez Eusa, with Y F Kemener; Sirius; Oceanopolis. Honours: Diapason d'Or, with Enez Eusa. Current Management: L'Oz Production (France). Address: 28 Rue Augustin SACQ, 29200 Brest, France.

SQUIRE Chris, b. 4 Mar 1948, London, England. Musician (bass). Career: Founder member, UK progressive rock group Yes, 1968-; Concerts include: Support to Cream, farewell concert, Royal Albert Hall, 1968; Support to Janis Joplin, Royal Albert Hall, 1969; Montreux TV Festival, 1969; Support to The Nice, Royal Festival Hall, 1970; Reading Festival, 1975; Yesshows '91 - Round The World In 80 Dates Tour, 1991. Recordings: Albums: Yes, 1969; Time And A Word, 1970; The Yes Album, 1971; Fragile, 1971; Close To The Edge, 1972; Yessongs, 1973; Tales From Topographic Oceans, 1973; Relayer, 1974; Yesterdays, 1975; Going For The One, 1977; Tormato, 1978; Drama, 1980; Classic Yes, 1982; 90125, 1983; 9012 Live - The Solos, 1986; The Big Generator, 1987; Union, 1991; Yesstory, 1991; Open Your Eyes, 1998; Solo album: Fish Out Of Water, 1975; Singles with Yes include: Roudabout; Wonderous Stories, Going For The One; Owner Of A Lonely Heart; Leave It; It Can Happen; Cinema; Love Will Find A Way; Rhythm Of Love; Lift Me Up. Honours: Gold Ticket, Madison Square Garden, 1978; Grammy Award, Best Rock Instrumental Performance, Cinema, 1985. Current Management: Big Bear Management, 9 Hillgate Street, London W8 7SP, England.

ST JAMES Rebecca, b. 26 July 1977, Sydney, Australia. Christian Recording Artist. Musical Education: High school music group; Coaching by Norris Brannstrom. Career: Carman's Revival In The Land Tour, 1991; Bryan Duncan's Slow Revival Tour, 1995; Dove Awards, Family TV Network, 1995; Side By Side Tour, 1995. Recordings: Refresh My Heart, 1991; Rebecca St James, 1994; Remix Album, 1995; One Way (Forefront compilation), 1995. Publications: Cover stories: Brio Magazine; Campus Life. Honours: Dove Award Nomination, New Artist of Year. Memberships: BMI; GMA. Hobbies: Bike riding; Swimming; Bible-reading; Family games; Travel. Current Management: Ambassador Agency; David Smallbone Management. Address: PO Box 1741, Brentwood, TN 37024, USA.

ST JOHN Kate Elinor Margaret, b. 2 Oct 1957, London, England. Musician (oboe, saxophone); Singer; Composer; Arranger. m. Sid Griffin, 28 July 1993. Musical Education: BSc Music, City University; Oboe at Guildhall. Career: Member, Ravishing Beauties, 1981-82; Member, Dream Academy, 1983-91; Oboe/saxophone session player in many bands; Member, Channel Light Vessel, 1994; Member, Van Morrison's live and recording band, 1991-1995. Compositions include: For television: Harry Enfield's Television Show; Harry Enfield And Chums. Recordings: Albums: with Dream Academy: The Dream Academy; Remembrance Days; A Different Kind Of Weather; with Channel Light Vessel: Automatic, 1994, Excellent Spirits, 1996; Solo albums: Indescribable Night, 1995; Second Sight, 1997; Hit single: Life In A Northern Town, Dream Academy; Singer with Roger Eno: The Familiar, 1993; Co-producer, Russian artist Boris Grebenschikov, 1995. Memberships: Musicians' Union; PRS; MCPS. Hobbies: Reading; Films. Current Management: Dominic Norman-Taylor. Address: All Saints Records, PO Box 2767, London NW1 8HV, England.

ST MITCHELL Jojo, b. 21 Feb 1957, Columbia, South Carolina, USA. Recording Artist; Manager; Musician (piano, guitar, bass, saxophone, drums). m. Clara G Butler, 18 May 1993, 1 son, 1 daughter. Education: Business Administration; Marketing (6 years college). Career: Performed for March of Dimes fundraising; Performed for sick and elderly in Columbia, South Carolina; Helped fund and run entertainment holding company, music publishing, manufacturing and distribution companies. Recordings: Over 52 releases of various recording artists including: Destination Unknown; Prey For Rain; Max Hewitt; Marshall Plan Kids. Publications: The Music Business Handbook; What A Way To Go. Honours: JUNO Award, Canada; Who's Who; Smithsonian; National Audubon Society. Memberships: Broadcast Music Inc, Harry Fox Agency. Hobbies: Chess; Music; Golf; Reading; Research; Mensa. Current Management: The Amethyst Group Ltd. Address: 273 Chippewa Drive, Columbia, SC 29210-6508, USA.

ST PIERRE Conni, b. 15 Sept 1957, Lawrence, Kansas, USA. Recording Studio Manager; Record Company Executive; Music Publisher; Record Producer; Musician (multi-instrumentalist). m. Edward (Ted) St Pierre, 24 Nov 1978. Education: Stephens College, Morley College, University of London. Musical Education: Classical piano; Flute; Voice. Career: President, Tourmaline Music (record label and publisher); Manager, The Outlook recording studio; Record producer for: Theory Of Neagativity; Willie Alexander; Rebecca Martin; Vocalist, bassist, Sky Frontier; Multi-instrumentalist, Forest Floor. Recordings: with Sky Frontier: Sky Frontier; Innocent Condemned; Frontierworld; Theory Of Negativity; with Peace Corpse: The Rat Sugar; with Forest Floor: Forest Floor; with Willie "Loco" Alexander; Private WA. Hobbies: Painting; Stained glass;

Beadwork; Collage. Current Management: Tourmaline. Address: 894 Mayville Road, Bethel, ME 04217, USA.

ST PIERRE Roger, b. 8 Nov 1941, Weymouth, Dorset, England. Music Journalist; Public Relations. m. Lesley Constantine, 10 Nov 1975, divorced, 1 son, 2 daughters. Career: Entered music business, 1966; Music For Pleasure, 1966; Established St Pierre Publicity, 1968; Promoted Unicef - Peace for Christmas concert, starring John Lennon, Yoko Ono, George Harrison, Eric Clapton, Keith Moon, 1969; Press officer, Beacon Records; Worked with most major record companies and tour promoters; Worked with club owners, DJs to establish Europe's leading disco promotion service; Handled press, television and radio promotion for such artists as: James Brown; Diana Ross; B B King; Slade; Jerry Lee Lewis; Glen Campbell; The Temptations; The Drifters; Wilson Pickett. Publications: Columns for New Musical Express and Record Mirror; Founder, editor, Disco And Club International; Writer, Blues And Soul magazine, 1966-; Co-author bestselling: Rock Handbook; Encyclopaedia Of Black Music; Books on: Michael Jackson; Tina Turner; Bob Marley; Jimi Hendrix; Bon Jovi; Tom Jones; Author, more than 1200 album sleevenotes; World authority on soul and blues; Script-writer, narrator, award-winning documentary Reggae. Hobbies: Cycling; Travel. Address: 24 Beauval Road, Dulwich, London SE22 8UQ, England.

STAF Bernt Lennart, b. 14 October 1945, Stockholm, Sweden. Singer; Songwriter. m. 2 daughters. Education: Chemist, Royal Pharmaceutical Institute, Stockholm, Sweden, 1965; Trumpet in different school orchestras; Selftaught guitar. Career: Writer of theater play, Fängspel for stage and TV, 1969; Radio and TV. Compositions: Text and music for 9 LP and CD albums; Nar dimman laffat, 1970; Uingslag, 1971; Live, 1972. Recordings: Valhall, 1974; Var, our du vill, 1976; Hycklarnas Paradis, 1981; Hammenhog Airport, 1983; Bernt Staf's Basta, 1995; Klockor, 1997. Publications: Lat almatna leva, with Cornelis Vreeswijk and Fred Akerstrom, 1971. Honour: Grammy, 1971. Memberships: SKAP; STIM; YTF. Current Management: Amigo Records. Address: Vagens Gata 439 III, 13661 Haninge, Sweden.

STAFF Bryan Alastair, b. 16 May 1950, Christchurch, New Zealand. Disc Jockey; Rock Music Journalist; Photographer. Education: BA Linguistics, Auckland University. Musical Education: Commercial radio. Career: Became an announcer, age 19, commercial radio; Specialised in local music, largely ignored on radio otherwise; Formed punk label, Ripper Records, 1979-83; In Auckland continued as rock writer, reviewer, photographer to date; Ran Ripper Records which began with New Zealand's first punk album: AK79, 1979; Ripper produced 5 albums, 20 singles over next 5 years. Publications: Co-author with Sheran Ashley: The Record Years, a history of New Zealand record labels. Membership: Recording Industry Association of New Zealand. Hobbies: Photography; Writing. Address: PO Box 5154, Wellesley Street, Auckland, New Zealand.

STAFFORD Jo, b. 12 Nov 1920, Coalinga, California, USA. Singer. m. Paul Weston. Career: Member, country music act, with sisters; Freelance singer on radio with vocal group, The Pied Pipers; Appeared, radio with Tommy Dorsey, 1939-42; Solo recording artiste, 1940s-60s; Recorded spoof albums with husband as Jonathan and Darlene Edwards; Retired from public performance, 1959; Founder, own Corinthian record label. Recordings include: Singles: Little Man With A Candy Cigar; Manhattan Serenade; For You; Yes Indeed (duet with Sly Oliver); Candy (with Johnny Mercer); That's For Me; Serenade Of The Bells; Some Enchanted Evening; Tennessee Waltz; My Darling My Darling (with Gordon McRae); Whispering Hope (with Gordon McRae);

Make Love To Me; Shrimp Boats; Keep It A Secret; Jambalaya; You Belong To Me; Numerous albums, 1953-, including several with Gordon McRae.

STAGG Mark Jeffrey, b. 26 May 1961, Sheffield, Yorkshire, England. Producer; Engineer; Programmer; Remixer. Musical Education: Manchester School Of Sound Recording. Career: Member of bands: Lionrock; Pro-Gress; Much studio work include: Production: Eskimos and Egypt; Sparks; Pro-Gress; MC Tunes; Engineering: K-Klass; Lionrock; The Grio; Björk; TC 1992; Erasure; Remixing: Nitzer Ebb; The Shamen; Supreme Love Gods; Sweet Mercy. Recordings: Co-writer and engineer, Rhythm Is A Mystery, K-Klass (Top 3 Hit UK). Memberships: Musicians' Union; PRS. Hobby: Ufology. Current Management: DEF. Address: 21 Premier House, 313 Kilburn Lane, London W9 3EG, England.

STAINTON Christopher Robert, b. 22 Mar 1944, Sheffield, Yorkshire, England. Musician (bass, piano). m. Gail Ellyn Travi, 25 June 1970, 1 daughter. Career: Tours and recordings with: Joe Cocker, 1966-72, 1988-92; Concerts include: Woodstock; Tours and recordings with Eric Clapton, 1979-85, 1993-. Recordings: Albums: with Joe Cocker: With A Little Help From My Friends, 1968; Joe Cocker, 1969; Mad Dogs And Englishmen, 1971; Something To Say, 1973; with Eric Clapton: Just One Night, 1980; Money And Cigarettes, 1983; with The Who: Quadrophenia, film soundtrack, 1979; Other recordings with: Alvin Lee; Maddy Prior; Leon Russell; Spooky Tooth; Marianne Faithful; Ian Hunter; Jim Capaldi; Gary Brooker; Bryn Haworth; Stephen Bishop. Membership: PRS. Hobbies: Computers. Current Management: Roger Forrester Management. Address: 18 Harley House, Regent's Park, London NW1 5HE, England.

STALEY Layne Thomas, b. 22 Aug 1967, Bellevue, Washington, USA. Rock Vocalist. Career: Lead singer, US rock groups: Alice In Chains; Mad Season; Appearances with Alice In Chains: Clash Of The Titans, 1991; Support tour, Van Halen, 1991; Support tour, Ozzy Osbourne, 1992; Brazil, 1993; Lollapalooza, 1993. Recordings: Albums: with Alice In Chains: Facelift, 1990; Sap, 1991; Dirt, 1992; Jar Of Flies, 1994; Alice In Chains, 1995; with Mad Season: Above, 1995. Honours: MTV Award, Would. Hobbies: Drawing; Painting; Photography; Computers. Current Management: Susan Silver Management, 207½ First Avenue South, Third Floor, Seattle, WA 98104, USA.

STAN Mircea, b. 2 Oct 1943, Romania. Musician (trombone). Musical Education: 11 years study at Music High School and Conservatory in Bucharest, 1958-1969; Self-taught jazz musician. Career: Moved to Finland, 1970s; Formed own quartet, 1972; Ran several groups including: Sextet formed for Pori Festival, 1978; Trombone quartet, toured Finland, 1980s; Played in UMO (New Music Orchestra); Also in bands run by: Heikki Sarmanto; Edward Vesala; Seppo Paakunainen; Taught trombone at Sibelius Academy; Coaches amateur jazz bands. Recordings: Album: Para Los Trombones, with own sextet, late 1980s. Address: Käsityöläisenkatu 25 E, 00750 Helsinki, Finland.

STAN Ollie, b. 28 May 1969, Kronstadt, Germany. Composer; Arranger; Musician (keyboards); Producer. Musical Education: Over 10 years lessons: piano, rhythm/percussion. Career: Tour with group: Bang!, Germany, with Dr Alban; 2 Unlimited; DJ Bobo, Mega Dance Festival, 1994. Recordings: Papa Winnie: You Are My Sunshine, 1994; Go: Your Body My Body, 1994; Bang! You Know I Know, 1994; Slavik/Kemmler: Indian Spirits (Dance Mixes), 1994; Powersound & Lori Glori: Freedom Forever, 1995. Honours: Gold, prospective Platinum for: Papa Winnie. Hobbies: Beach; Cinema; Animals;

Restaurants; Sports. Address: c/o Advance Music, Ovelgönnerweg 13, D-21335 Luneburg, Germany.

STANCHEV Georgi, b. 1 June 1951, Sofia, Bulgaria. Composer; Arranger; Lyricist; Producer. m. Tsvetanca Georgieva, 3 Dec 1976, 1 son, 2 daughters. Career: Solo vocalist, guitarist, Diana Express, 1979-81; Festivals, television; Tours: USSR, Cuba, Germany, 1984; Hungary, 1987; USSR, Romania, Israel, 1988; USSR, 1989; Worked with Hungarian group The Times, recording and performing, 1986; President, Gorgia-Venice Music House; Executive, Musical Director, Peak Music Record Company. Compositions include: Soul; Whisper. Recordings: First single, 1980; Whisper, 1982; Third single, 1982; Albums: Lovers, 1983; A Handful Of Sands, 1985; Be A Star Up To The End, 1991; Venice, 1995. Honours: Best Song of Year, Soul, 1980; Prizes, Bulgarian Television, Knoque Festival, Belgium, 1982; Prize, Dresden Festival, 1983; Best Singer, Caven, Ireland, 1984; Performer's Prize, La Valeta, Malta, 1984; Grand Prize, Composer, Siofok, Hungary, 1986; Best Singer, Best Album of Year, 1991. Address: Suhodolska str, 2 bl, 122 vh A, ap4, 1373 Sofia, Bulgaria.

STANCIC Ivan (Piko), b. 7 Apr 1952, Dalj, Croatia. Musician (drums); Producer; Arranger. m. Lada Mador, 6 Feb 1987, 1 son, 2 daughters. Education: Academie of Arts, Zagreb, Croatia; Ecole Nationale Superieure des Beaux Arts, Paris. Musical Education: Guitar, timpani, Primary Musical School, Zagreb; Private Education. Career: Musician with numerous bands including: Grupa 220; Time; Parni Valjak; Call 69; La Video; Super Session Group; Steam Roller; Film; Telephone Blues Band; Idoli; El Org; Psihomodo Pop; Novak and Kopola; Le Cinema; Over 1500 concerts and tours in: Croatia; Former Yugoslavia; France; Italy; Germany; Canada; Netherlands; Russia; Slovenia; Numerous television shows and radio interviews. Recordings: Approximately 60 albums include: with Grupa 220: Slike; with Parni Valjak: Gradske Price; with Steam Roller: City Kids; with Le Cinema: Party; with Prljavo Kazaliste: Crno Bijeli Svijet; with Idoli: debut album; with Telephone Blues Band and Cal 69: Looking Back; with Bijelo Dugme: Ciribiribella; ZG Rock Forces Live, Parni Valjak, Kazalise, Flm, Psihomodo; with Film: Live In Kulusic; Zona Sumraka; Sva Cuda Svijeta; with Aerodrom: Tango Bango; with Psihomodo Pop: Godina Zmaja; Sexy Magazin; Live In Amsterdam; with Piko: Bubnjevi Na Suncu. Honours: 6 Platinum records; 12 Gold records; Over 25 Silver records; 5 national awards for painting; Porin '94, Croatian Grammy, Design. Memberships: IAA-AIAP (International Association of Art) Paris; HDLU, Artists Union of Croatia; HGU, Croatian Musicians Union; HZH, Croatian Humanitarian Stars. Hobbies: Cycling; Football; Photography. Current Management: Vladimir Mihaljek, Croatian Music Art. Address: Croatia Records, Medugorska 61, 10000 Zagreb, Croatia.

STANDAERT Luc, b. 17 Jan 1958, Ghent, Belgium. Music Publisher; Artist Manager. m. Tine Lecompte, 3 Apr 1981. Education: Architecture; Scenography. Career: Scenographer, 1979-82; Show Director, Tour Manager, 1982-88; Music Publisher, Artist Manager, 1988-; Business ventures: Tempo BVBA; Tempo Media Nv; Yellow House BVBA; Taste My Music. Compositions: Publisher of songs performed by: Arno; Dinky Toys; Francis Goya; Viktor Lazlo; Jack Radics; Jean Bosco Safari; Music for films includes: Koko Flanel; Daens; Marie. Publications: Vrije Radio In Vlaanderen, 1986. Honours: Oscar Nomination, Daens, 1993. Memberships: SABAM; URBEM; BVBI. Address: Krijgslaan 61, 9000 Gent, Belgium.

STANGER William John Nigel, b. 16 Jan 1943, Newcastle-upon-Tyne, England. Architect; Developer; Musician (saxophone, keyboards). 2 daughters. Education: Oxford University, Newcastle University, MA (Oxon), BA, BArch. Musical Education: Piano, 1947-; Saxophone, 1959-; School education and self-taught. Career: Performed with various bands in London including: Alexis Korner, John Mayall Bluesbreakers, Alan Price Set, Herbie Goins, Night Timers, 1963-66; Performed with Newcastle Big Band (with Sting), East Side Torpedoes, Little Mo, 1996-; Currently with Crosbys; Various television and radio broadcasts. Recordings: with John Mayall: Live At Klooks Kleek; with Alan Price: Any Day Now; Album with Newcastle Big Band. Memberships: ARCUK; Musicians' Union; Equity. Hobbies: Chess; Real tennis; Keep fit. Address: 51 Brandling Place South, Jesmond, Newcastle-Upon-Tyne NE2 4RU, England.

STANIC Stjepan ("Jimmy"), b. 20 Jan 1929, Zagreb, Croatia. Musician (double bass); Singer. m. Barbara, 14 Apr 1990. Education: College. Musical Education: College of Music. Career: One of best known Croatian musicians; Performed at all major concerts and humanitarian festivals in Croatia and Slovenia; Still performs all over the world including: Canada; Germany; Switzerland; Scandinavia; Austria; Russia. Recordings: 5 singles (album of popular songs called "slagers"); Albums: Glenn Rych Orchestra (1 American standards, 1 Live V Lisinski); 4 singles; Recording, dancing, American clubs all over the world; CD of jazz standards accompanied by a trio. Membership: HGU (Croatian Musical Union). Hobbies: Mountain climbing; Painting; Collecting antiques. Current Management: HGU. Address: Ivsicev prilaz 5, 41000 Zagreb, Croatia.

STANLEY Damian Mark, b. 18 Aug 1967, Nottingham, England. Producer; Writer; Engineer; Musician (keyboards). Career: Recording artist with Mad; Overview; The Deadbeats; Owner, Spacehopper Recordings and Ill Communications; Remixes: Moodswings; Whycliffe; Turntable Orchestra; Ashley Beadle; Jimi Polo; Alabama 3 (DIY Dub); Humdrum (soundtrack to film Hackers); Chrissie Hynde; Sly & Love Child; Chumbawamba; Mind the Gap & Leena Conquest; Recording artist as MAD; Overview, The Deadbeats; DIY, DEA, Love Brothers; Owner, Spacehopper Records and DIY Communications. Memberships: PRS; MCPS. Hobbies: DJ, The Garage (Nottingham); DJ, Beatroot. Address: Spacehopper, PO Box 350, Nottingham NG3 6DF, England.

STANLEY Paul (Paul Eisen), b. 20 Jan 1950, Queens, New York, USA. Singer; Musician (guitar). Career: Member, guitarist, US rock group Kiss, 1973-; Appearances include: Debut, Academy of Music, New York, 1973; Numerous tours include UK, 1976; US Dynasty Tour, 1979; Palladium, New York, 1980; US tour, with Cheap Trick, 1988; Marquee Club, 1988; US tour, 1990; Revenge '92 Tour, 1992; Concert, Palace Of Auburn Hills, Missouri, recorded for video, album, Kiss Alive III, 1992. Numerous compositions for Kiss. Recordings: Albums: Kiss, 1974; Hotter Than Hell, 1974; Dressed To Kill, 1975; Destroyer, 1976; The Originals, 1976; Rock And Roll Over, 1976; Kiss Alive II, 1977; Double Platinum, 1978; Dynasty, 19779; Kiss Unmasked, 1980; Music From The Elder, 1981; Creatures Of The Night, 1982; Lick It Up, 1983; Animalize, 1984; Asylum, 1985; Crazy Nights, 1987; Smashes Thrashes And Hits, 1988; Hot In The Shade, 1989; Revenge, 1992; Kiss Alive III, 1993; Unplugged, 1996; Solo album: Paul Stanley, 1978; Contributor, Hear'N'Aid, charity project for Ethiopian famine relief, 1986; Numerous singles include: Rock'N'Roll All Nite; Beth; Detroit Rock City; I Was Made For Lovin' You; I Love It Loud; Lick It Up; Heaven's On Fire; Tears Are Falling; Crazy Crazy Nights; Reason To Live; Hide Your Heart; Forever; God Gave Rock And Roll To You, used in film Bill And Ted's Bogus Adventure, 1992. Honours: Footprints at Grauman's Chinese Theatre, 1976; Gold Ticket, Madison Square Garden, 1979; Inducted into Hollywood's Rock Walk, 1993; Kiss Day proclaimed in Los Angeles, 1993; Numerous Gold and Platinum discs. Current Management: Entertainment Services Unlimited, Main Street Plaza 100, Suite 303, Voorhees, NJ 08043, USA. Address: c/o Doc McGhee, McGhee Entertainment, 8730 Sunset Blvd, Suite 175, Los Angeles, CA 90069, USA.

STANNERS Malcolm James, b. 27 Dec 1965, Derby, England. Sound Engineer; Programmer; Producer. Education: Selftaught Guitar; Higher Diploma, Musical Instrument Technology. Career: Sound Engineer, Programmer, Paradise Studios, London, England, 1988-89, Clients include: Boy George, Bill Wyman, Errol Brown; Films: Madame Suzatska; Incredibly Strange Picture Show; Studio Owner, 4 Real Studios, 1989-; Dance Music Producer and Artist; Co-Founder, Salt Tank, London Records. Recordings include: Singles: Ease the Pressure, 1991; Ethereal EP, 1992; 4 EPs, 1993-94; Peel Session EP, 1994; Eugina, 1996; Swell, 1996; Album: Science and Nature, 1996; Wavebreaks, 1998; Compilation Albums: Cafe Del Mar 2; Ministry of Sound; Cream; In the Mix 96; Horizons; Chill Out 2; Trance Europe Express; Essential Mix 2; Remixes: Sueno Latino; Chakra; Paul Van Dyke; Orbital; Chicane; Man With No Name; Hawkwind; TV Incidental Music: Grandstand, Euro 1996; Home Front; Eastenders; Hollyoaks; Wish You Were Here; Tomorrow's World. Honours: Reached Top 5, twice, Indie Singles Chart; Top 10, Indie Album Chart; Top 40, UK Singles Chart. Memberships: MCPS; PRS. Current Management: Doug Smith Associates, London.

STANSFIELD Lisa, b. 11 Apr 1966, Rochdale, Lancashire, England. Singer. Career: Television presenter, Razzamatazz, ITV, 1986; Formed Blue Zone, 1984; Singer, Coldcut, 1989; Solo singer, 1989-; Tours and concerts include: All Around The World Tour, 1990; Arista Records 15th Anniversary concert, 1990; Prince's Trust Rock Gala, Wembley Arena, 1990; Rock In Rio II, Brazil, 1991; Simple Truth benefit concert for Kurdish Refugees, Wembley Arena, 1991; Red Hot & Dance AIDS benefit concert, London, 1991; Amnesty International's Big 30 Concert, ITV, 1991; Dance Energy Christmas House Party, BBC2, 1992. Compositions: Tracks on own albums co-written and produced. Recordings: Albums: Affection (Number 2, UK), 1989; Real Love, 1992; So Natural, 1993; Singles include: with Coldcut: People Hold On, 1989; Solo: This Is The Right Time, 1989; All Around The World (Number 1, UK; R&B Number 1, US), 1989; Live Together, 1990; What Did I Do To You, 1990; You Can't Deny It, 1990; This Is The Right Time, 1990; Change, 1991; All Woman, 1992; Time To Make You Mine, 1992; Set Your Loving Free, 1992; Someday (I'm Coming Back), from film The Bodyguard, 1993; In All The Right Places, 1993; So Natural, 1993; Featured vocalist, Do They Know It's Christmas (reworked), Band Aid II, 1990; Contributor, Red Hot & Blue AIDS benefit record, 1990. Honours: Variety Club Of Great Britain, Recording Artist of 1989, 1990; BRIT Awards: Best Newcomer, 1990; Best Female Artist, 1992; Ivor Novello Awards: Best Contemporary Song Award, 1990; International Hit Of The Year, 1991; Nordoff-Robbins Music Therapy Charity, Best Newcomer, 1990; Rolling Stone Critics Poll Winner, Best British Female Singer, 1990; ASCAP Award, All Around The World, 1991. Current Management: Big Life Management. Address: 15 Little Portland Street, London W1N 5DE, England.

STANTON Ian, b. 28 Oct 1950, Manchester, England. Singer; Songwriter. m. Audrey Savage, 14 Feb 1994, 1 stepson. Career: Lead singer, Hard Lines, 1982-85; Major concerts: Queen's Festival, Dublin, 1991; Vancouver Folk Festival, 1992; Glastonbury Festival, 1992; Edinburgh Festival, 1993; Numerous television and radio appearances include Link Biography. Recordings: Shrinking Man (self-produced tape), 1990; Freewheelin' (self-produced tape), 1992; Rollin'

Thunder, 1995. Memberships: PRS; MCPS. Hobbies: Writing; Computers; Board and card games. Current Management: Audrey Stanton. Address: GMCDP, Carisbrooke, Wenlock Way, Gorton, Manchester, England.

STAPLES Ian Gregory, b. 9 Jun 1945, London, England. Musician (guitar, bass, keyboards). m. (1) Norma Fairclough, deceased, 1975, (2) Partner, Sue Baines, 1976, 2 daughters from first marriage. Musical Education: Isle of Man College of Art. Career: Member of: Ginger Johnson's Afrikan Drummers band, 1968, Red Square, 1970, The Cut, 1984, The Duffs, 1986, B SO Global, 1990, Omlovent, 1990 and Single Field (Jazz), 1990. Recordings: Co-writer with John Seagroatt, B SO Global, by B SO Global; Mild Landing, with Omlovent. Memberships: Musicians' Union; PRS; PPL. Hobbies: Art; Wooden Boat Restoration; Organic Smallholding. Address: Narrowboat Lichfield, The Old Wharf, Appletree Lane, Cropredy, Banbury, Oxon OX17 1PZ, England.

STAPLEY Jay, b. 13 April 1957. Musician (guitar); Producer; Writer. m. 5 June 1990, 2 daughters. Musical Education: Self-taught. Career: Session and live work, London, 1979-; 2 world tours and albums with Roger Waters (formerly of Pink Floyd); Tubular Bells II tours with Mike Oldfield; Tours and albums with Westernhagen. Recordings: 4 solo albums. Publications: Articles on technical subjects in trade press. Memberships: PRS; MCPS. Hobbies: Sailing. Address: 11 Glenthorne Road, Friern Barnet, London N11 3HU, England.

STARDUST Alvin (Bernard William Jewry), b. 27 Sept 1942, London, England. Singer. Career: Solo singer, as Shane Fenton, early 1960s; Come-back as Alvin Stardust, 1973; Chart success, 1970s-1980s; Presenter, performer, BBC TV. Recordings: Albums: It's All Happening, 1969; Good Rockin' Tonight, 1974; Greatest Hits: Alvin Stardust, 1977; I'm A Moody Guy, 1982; I Feel Like... Alvin Stardust, 1984; 20 Of The Best, 1987; Singles include: My Coo-Ca-Choo (Number 2, UK); Jealous Mind; Red Dress; You You You; Tell Me Why; Good Love Can Never Die; Pretend; I Feel Like Buddy Holly; I Won't Run Away; So Near Christmas. Address: c/o Roy Massey Management, The Fordings, Old Road, Armitage, Staffordshire WS15 4BU, England.

STARR Edwin (Charles Hatcher), b. 21 Jan 1942, Nashville, Tennessee, USA. Singer. Career: Formed vocal group Future Tones, 1957; Member, Bill Doggett Combo, Solo artist, 1965-; Motown recording artist, 1967-75; Based in UK, 1980s; Collaborations with the Style Council; Worked with Ian Levine's Motor City Records, 1989-91. Recordings: Singles include: Agent Double-O-Soul; Stop Her On Sight (SOS); 25 Miles; Stop The War Now; Funky Music Sho Nuff Turns Me On; Albums: Soul Master, 1968; 25 Miles, 1969; Just We Two, with Blinky, 1969; War And Peace, 1970; Involved, 1971; Hell Up In Harlem, 1974; Free To Be Myself, 1975; Edwin Starr, 1977; Afternoon Sunshine, 1977; Clean, 1978; HAPPY Radio, 1979; Stronger Than You Think I Am, 1980; 20 Greatest Motown Hits, 1986; Where Is The Sound, 1991; Timeless Energy, 1996. Current Management: Barry Collings Entertainments, 21a Clifftown Road, Southend-on-Sea, Essex SS1 1AB, England. Address: c/o Lilian Kyle, 118 Derby Road, Bramcote, Nottinghamshire NG9 3HP, England.

STARR Lucille, b. St Boniface, Manitoba, Canada. Entertainer; Singer; Musician (guitar, bass). m. (1) Bob Reagan, 19 Sept 1955, divorced, 1 son; (2) Bryan Cunningham, 16 Apr 1978, 1 stepson, 1 stepdaughter. Musical Education: Studied classical (voice). Career: First Grand Ole Opry Tour with Hank Snow, 1961; 4 television shows in Los Angeles; Yodelling for Cousin Pearl on Beverly Hillbillies. Recordings:

Hits include: The French Song; Jolie Jacqueline; Colinda; Yours; Crazy Arms; Pepères Mill; First Time I've Ever Been In Love; Freight Train; Leaving It Up To You; Send Me No Roses. Honours: Several Platinum and Gold records; First lady inducted in Hall Of Honour (Canada); Hall Of Fame, Canada; Street named Lucille Starr Drive in Vancouver, BC, Canada; Inducted into Walkway of Stars, Hall of Fame, Nashville, Tennessee, 1997. Memberships: AFTRA; Television Screen Actors Guild; Musicians' Union; Canadian Country Music Association. Hobby: Needlepoint. Current Management: Cardinal Records.

STARR Ringo (Richard Starkey), b. 7 July 1940, Dingle, Liverpool, England. Musician (drums). m. (1) Maureen Cox, 1965, divorced, 2 sons, 1 daughter; m. (2) Barbara Bach, 1981. Career: Member, Rory Storm And The Hurricanes, Liverpool; Member, The Beatles, 1962-70; Appearances, Hamburg, 1962; Worldwide tours, 1963-; Attended Transcendental Meditation Course, Maharishi's Academy, Rishkesh, India, 1968; Co-founder, Apple Corps Ltd, 1968; Solo artiste, 1969-; Narrator, childrens television series, Thomas The Tank Engine; Film appearances include: A Hard Day's Night; Help!; Candy; The Magic Christian. Recordings: Albums include: with The Beatles: Please Please Me, 1963; With The Beatles, 1963; A Hard Day's Night, 1964; Beatles For Sale, 1965; Help!, 1965; Rubber Soul, 1966; Revolver, 1966; Sgt Pepper's Lonely Hearts Club Band, 1967; The Beatles (White Album), 1968; Yellow Submarine, 1969; Abbey Road, 1969; Let It Be, 1970; Solo albums: Sentimental Journey, 1969; Beaucoups Of Blue, 1970; Ringo, 1973; Goodnight Vienna, 1974; Blasts From Your Past, 1975; Ringo's Rotogravure, 1976; Ringo The 4th, 1977; Bad Boy, 1977; Stop And Smell The Roses, 1981; Old Wave, 1985; StarrStruck - Ringo's Best (1976-83), 1989; Time Takes Time, 1992; Solo singles include: It Don't Come Easy; Back Off Boogaloo; Photograph; You're Sixteen; Oh My My; Snookeroo; Only You. Numerous honours with the Beatles include: BPI Awards: Best British Album (Sgt Pepper's Lonely Hearts Club Band), Best British Group, 1952-77, 1977; Inducted into Rock And Roll Hall Of Fame, 198. Current Management: David Fishof Presents, 252 W 71st Street, New York, NY 10023, USA.

STATHAM Robert, b. 4 Apr 1959, Bournemouth, Dorset, England. Musician (fretless bass guitar). Musical Education: Certificate of Advanced Studies, Jazz/Rock, Guildhall School of Music. Career: Played with John Etheridge; Dick Heckstall-Smith; Ed Jones; Paz - Keith Emerson; Theo Travis; Radio broadcasts with Paz; Ed Jones; Theo Travis; Tours with Ed Jones; Theo Travis. Compsitions: Featured on Ed Jones album; also Ed Jones radio broadcasts, Jazz Today, 1989; Recordings with: Ed Jones; Paz; Kelvin Christiane; Theo Travis; Totally Wired compilation (acid jazz). Memberships: Musicians' Union; PRS. Current Management: Self-managed. Address: 90 Bridge Lane, Golders Green, London NW11 0EL, England.

STECHER Jody (Jonathan Allan), b. 1 June 1946, Brooklyn, New York, USA. Musician (guitar, mandolin, fiddle, banjo, sarod, sursingar, oud); Vocalist; Record Producer; Composer. m. Kate Brislin, 29 July 1987. Education: BA, English, CCNY. Musical Education: 3 years with Ali Akbar Khan; 10 years, deep study with Zia Mohiuddin Dagar. Career: Tours: USA; Canada; Ireland; Scotland; England; France; Netherlands; Belgium; Switzerland; Australia; New Zealand; Hong Kong; Duets with Kate Brislin; Hank Bradley; Alasdair Fraser; Krishna Bhatt. Numerous recordings include: Going Up On The Mountain; Rasa; The Driven Bow; A Song That Will Linger; Blue Lightning; Our Town; Stay Awhile; Sleepless Nights; Heart Songs. Publications: Liner notes to many albums; Articles in music journals. Honours: Grammy Nomination, 1993; World's Champion Guitar, Union Grove, North Carolina, 1966.

Memberships: IBMA; NARAS. Hobbies: Cooking. Address: 133 Lake Street, San Francisco, CA 94118, USA.

STECKAR Marc, b. 1 June 1935, Cherbourg, France. Musician (tuba, euphonium, trombone); Composer. m. Marie Thérèse Grosbois, 1 son, 1 daughter. Musical Education: Diploma, National Superior Conservatory of Music, Paris. Career: Played with Marlene Dietrich; Sammy Davis; Nat "King" Cole; Edith Piaf; Jacques Brel; Charles Aznavour; Claude Nougaro; Michle Legrand; Johnny Hallyday; Founder, leader of Stecker Tubapack; Concerts, festivals. Recordings: 9 records with Steckar-Tubapack; Elephant Tuba Horde; Steckar Trinity; Bagdapack; Celtophonic (Marc Steckar Au Festival Interceltique Of Lorient). Hobbies: Good food; All music. Current Management: Self-managed. Address: 7 Rue des Fontenettes, F-95550 Bessancourt, France.

STEEL Casino, b. 22 Feb 1952, Trondheim, Norway. Musician; Singer; Songwriter. m. Hanne Lerdal, 2 daughters. Career: Member, The Hollywood Brats, 1972-75; The Boys, 1975-80; The Yobs, Gary Holton/Casino Steel, 1980-84; Claudia/Big Hand/Casino, 1983-86; CCCP, 1986; Scott and Steel, 1987; Solo career, 1988-94; Ian Hunter's Dirty Laundry, 1994-; Managing Director, Revolution Records, Steelworks Publishing. Honours: Norwegian Entertainer Of The Year (Holton/Steel, 1982; Norwegian Grammy, 1985. Memberships: Board of Directors: GRAMART (Recording Artists Association); NOPA (The Norwegian Society of Popular Authors); Board of Directors, GRAMO, TONO. Address: Revolution Records, PO Box 9323, Gronland, 0135 Oslo, Norway.

STEELE Kevin, b. Cleveland, Ohio, USA. Singer; Songwriter; Musician (harmonica). Musical Education: Self-taught. Career: Lead singer, US rock group Roxx Gang; Performances include: Things You've Never Done Before World Tour, 1990; US Tour, 1991; The Voodoo You Love, US Tour, 1996-97; Television and radio apperances include: Various videos, MTV; BBC TV; Z-Rock coast to coast radio broadcast. Recordings: Things You've Never Done Before; Love 'Em And Leave 'Em; The Voodoo You Love, 1996; Mojo Gurus, 1997. Hobby: Record collecting. Current Management: Brett Steele, Steele Management. Address: 7002 124th Terrace North, Largo, FL 34643, USA.

STEELE Tommy (Thomas Hicks), b. 17 Dec 1936, Bermondsey, London,England. Actor; Singer. m. Ann Donoghue, 1960, 1 daughter. Career: First stage appearance, Empire Theatre, Sunderland, 1956; First London appearance, Dominion Theatre, 1957; Major roles include: Buttons, Rodgers and Hammerstein's Cinderella, Coliseum, 1958; Tony Lumpkin, She Stoops To Conquer, Old Vic, 1960; Arthur Kipps, Half A Sixpence, Cambridge Theatre, 1963-64; The same, Broadhurst Theatre, New York, 1965; Truffaldino, The Servant Of Two Masters, Queen's, 1969; Dick Whittington, London Palladium, 1969; Meet Me In London, Adelphi, 1971; Jack Point, The Yeoman Of The Guard, City Of London Festival, 1978; The Tommy Steele Show, London Palladium, 1973; Hans Andersen, 1974, 1977; One-man show, Prince of Wales, 1979; Singing In The Rain (also director), 1983; Some Like It Hot, 1992; What A Show, Prince of Wales Theatre, 1995; Film appearances: Kill Me Tomorrow, 1956; The Tommy Steele Story; The Duke Wore Jeans; Tommy The Toreador; Light Up The Sky; It's All Happening; The Happiest Millionaire; Half A Sixpence; Finian's Rainbow; Where's Jack?; Television: Writer, actor, Quincy's Quest, 1979. Compositions: Composed, recorded, My Life My Song, 1974; A Portrait Of Pablo, 1985; Publications: Quincy, 1981; The Final Run, 1983; Rock Suite - An Elderly Person's Guide To Rock, 1987. Honour: OBE, 1979. Hobbies: Squash; Sculpture. Current Management: James Kelly,

International Artistes Ltd, 235 Regent Street, London W1R 8AX, England.

STEEN Morten Naver, b. 5 June 1964, Copenhagen, Denmark. Musician (Guitar, Sarod, Indian Guitar, Percussion); Composer; Leader. Partner, Camilla Buttingsrud, 1 son, 1 daughter. Education: Christianshavs Gymnasium, Music Line, 1981-84. Musical Education: Selftaught; The Rhythmic Conservatory, Copenhagen, 1989-95; Sitar Studies in India, 1986, 1991; Sarod and guitar studies in India, 1986, 1991, 1993. Career: Theatrical Music: Composer: Odense Theatre, Jeppe On the Mountain, 1993-94; The Royal Danish Theatre, The Reader by Arild Dorfmann, 1995; Ensemblet, Water, 1997; Composer and Leader: Odense Theatre, Mowgli, musical, 1994-95; Odense International Music Theatre, Park, dance performance, 1996; Founder and Co-Director, Ensemblet, theatre group, 1996. Honour: From Danish Cultural Ministry, 1993. Memberships: The Danish Musicians Union; Danish Jazz Musician Association. Current Management: Ensemblet, Rialtovej 10, 2300 CPH S, Denmark. Address: Rialtovej 10, 2300 CPH S, Denmark.

STEEN Uffe, b. 27 Oct 1953, Odense, Denmark. Musician (guitar); Composer; Lecturer. m. Alice Stensbo, 1 son, 1 daughter. Musical Education: Studied clarinet, Det Fynske Musikkonservatorium, Odense, 4 years. Career: Member, Uffe Steen Quartet; Jens Jefsen Trio; Shades Of Blue; Carnivalband; Tours across Germany and Scandiniavia including Notodden Blues Festival, Norway; Numerous radio appearances; Lecturer, Det Jyske Musikkonsevatorium. Recordings: with Uffe Steen Quartet: Hymn To Spring; with Jens Jefsen: Interval; Interaction; Handshaking; Come Join Us; Springtime; with Shades Of Blue: Shades Of Blue; On A Mission From Muddy Waters. Publications: Blues-For Beginners and Advanced Students (book and tapes); Jazz Guitar (books and tapes). Memberships: DMF; DJBFA. Hobbies: Computer; Family. Address: Uffe Steen, Hostrupsvej 11, 8260 Viby J, Denmark.

STEEVES Paulette, b. 25 Nov 1955, Whitehorse, Yukon Territories, British Columbia, Canada. Songwriter; Musician (guitar); Vocalist. Divorced. 2 sons, 1 daughter. Musical Education: 1 year Canadian Academy vocal music (grant from Native American Foundation). Career: Formed The Mother and Child Band, with son Jesse (banjo, washboard, singer), son Dustin (harmonica, Indian hand drums), daughter Marina (tub base, spoons, tambourine, singer); Appearances: Hamilton Festival Of Friends, 1992; Klienburg Binder Twine Festival, 1993; Festival Of The Islands, 1993, Gananoque; Ridgetown Fair, 1993; Own Honeysuckle Records label; Workshops for making home made recycled instruments. Recordings: Heart For Sale; Cotton Fields. Memberships: SOCAN; NSWA; CAIIA. Hobbies: Hiking; Camping; Nature; Horse riding. Current Management: Self-managed. Address: The Mother and Child Band, Box 442, Johnson, AR 72741, USA.

STEFANI Gwen. Vocalist. Career: Lead singer, US group No Doubt. Recordings include: Albums: No Doubt, 1993; Tragic Kingdom, 1995; Hit single: Just A Girl. Address: c/o Spark Management, 100 Wilshire Blvd #1830, Santa Monica, CA 90405, USA.

STEFL Jiri, b. 7 Nov 1968, Ivancice u Brna, Czech Republic. Musician (Bass). m. Dagmar Matouskova, 1 daughter. Career: Tibet, rock band, 1991-; Many TV, Radio and Stage Shows. Compositions: all songs on debut album, Sambala. Recordings: SP, Popelar/Miss Morning, 1992; CD/MC, Sambala, Happy Music, 1996. Contributions: Rock of Pop; Big Bang!. Memberships: Intergram; Monitor Publishing.

Hobby: Music. Addres: Jilova 41, 639 00 Brno, Czech Republic.

STEIN, b. 27 Nov 1961, Henley-on Thames, England. Tour Manager. Education: BSc, Applied Physics. Career: Manager, various tours. Membership: International Managers Forum (IMF). Hobby: Electronics. Current Management: Concord International Artists. Address: Maverick Management, 65 Donald Woods Gardens, Surbiton, Surrey KT5 9NP, England.

STEINBACH Peter, b. 4 May 1954, Vienna, Austria. Artist Manager. Education: Trades Academy. Musical Education: Clarinet and saxophone (classical). Career: Tours of Japan 1989, 1991; France, 1994; Tours: Italy; Germany; Austria; Hungary; Artist Manager for: Gergely Szücs; Bluespumpm; Wilfried; Die Spielleute; Misfit. Publications: Video for Austrian schools: One Man Show (18 original instruments from the Middle Ages). Hobbies: Horses; Harley Davidson motorcycles. Address: Favoritenstrasse 53 2/6/18, A-1100 Vienna, Austria.

STEINCKE Viggo, b. 15 Nov 1951, Viborg, Denmark. Musician (guitar, bass); Composer. Career: Several live performances on Danish radio. Recordings: with Coma: Financial Tycoon, 1977; Amoc, 1980; Love And Madness, 1986; with Colours Of Blue: Colours Of Blue, 1989; Workshop, 1994. Honours: North Jutland Country Music Award, 1991. Memberships: KODA; Danish Music Foundation. Hobbies: Dancing; Lying in bed; Archery. Current Management: Honor Agency. Address: Schleppegrellsgade 11, 9000 Aalborg, Denmark.

STEINER Fred(erick), b. 24 Feb 1923, New York, New York, USA. Composer; Conductor; Musicologist. m. Shirley Laura Steiner, 2 daughters. Musical Education: Institute of Musical Art, New York City; BM, Oberlin Conservatory of Music, Ohio, 1943; PhD, Musicology, University of Southern California, 1981. Career: Composer, Conductor, radio in New York City; Music Director, radio programme This Is Your FBI; To Los Angeles, 1947; Many other radio programmes; First TV work, Columbia Broadcasting System, 1950; First film work, 1950; Major TV credits include Andy Griffith, Danny Thomas, Gunsmoke, Have Gun Will Travel, Hogan's Heroes, Rocky and Bullwinkle Show, Movie of the Week, Rawhide, Star Trek, Twilight Zone, Hawaii Five-O, Dynasty, Amazing Stories, Tinytoons; Major film credits include: Della, First To Fight, Hercules, The Man From Del Rio, Run For The Sun, St Valentine's Day Massacre, Time Limit, Shipwreck, The Color Purple; Lecturer, History and Art of Film Music, University of Southern California, 1984-89, College of Santa Fe, 1990-93. Compositions: Perry Mason Theme; Navy Log March; Dudley Doright Theme; Five Pieces for String Trio; Tower Music for Brass and percussion; Pezzo Italiano for cello and piano; Act Without Words, for percussion ensemble; Indian Music for Viola and Piano; Transcriptions and pieces for TV and film. Recordings: King Kong, conductor, motion picture score by Max Steiner; Great American Film scores; Music from the Paramount TV Series Star Trek. Publications: Foreword, in Music on Demand (by R R Faulkner), 1983; Music for Star Trek, in Wonderful Inventions (by Iris Newsom), 1985; Fred Steiner on Film Music, in Film Score (by Tony Thomas), 1991; Interlude, in Hollywood Holyland (by Ken Darby), 1992. Contributions to: Journal of the Arnold Schoenberg Institute; Film Music Notebook; Quarterly Journal of the Library of Congress; New Grove Dictionary of American Music; Dictionary of American Biography; New Grove Dictionary of Music and Musicians; Record Album Notes. Honours include: Academy Award Nomination, 1986; City of Los Angeles Special Recognition Certificate; Award of Merit, Society for the Preservation of Film Music. Memberships include: American Motion Picture Arts and Sciences; American Musicological Society;

AFofM; ASCAP; Society of Composers and Lyricists; Board of Advisors, Society for the Preservation of Film Music. Address: 1086 Mansion Ridge Road, Santa Fe, NE 87501, USA.

STEINKE Gord, b. 11 July 1959, North Battleford, Saskatchewan, Canada. Musician (bass guitar, acoustic guitar); Songwriter. m. Deb, 7 June 1985, 1 child. Education: BA in Journalism and Communications. Career: Appeared on numerous television shows in Canada with own band Hidden Agenda; Major concerts include Classic Rock Weekend with Deep Purple, George Thorogood, Rick Derringer and Nazareth, 1997. Recordings: Larger Than Life, Inner City, 1982; Soemthing Wrong, Gord Steinke, 1997. Honour: Recognition award, International Songwriting Competition. Memberships: ACTRA; SOCAN; ARIA. Hobbies: Motorcycles; Camping. Address: PO Box 57217, 2010A Sherwood Drive, Sherwood Park, Alberta T8A 5L7, Canada.

STEPHENSON Larry Lee, b. 24 Oct 1956, Harrisonburg, Virginia, USA. Musician (mandolin, guitar). Career: 4 years with Bill Harrell and The Virginians; 5 years with The Bluegrass Cardinals; 6 years with The Larry Stephenson Band; Tours: The Middle East; Europe; Japan; Travelled USA, Canada; Appearances: Nashville Network; Grand Ole Opry; Many Bluegrass Festivals worldwide. Recordings: Albums: 5 with Bill Harrell; 3 with The Bluegrass Cardinals; 8 with The Larry Stephenson Band; Featured musician on about 25 other Bluegrass albums. Memberships: International Bluegrass Music Association; BMI, Writer and Publisher; Musicians' Union. Hobbies: Movies; Boating; Doing nothing. Current Management: PO Box 731 Antioch, TN 37011-0731, USA.

STEPHENSON Robert, b. 30 Jun 1953, Dublin, Ireland. Music Promoter; Artist Manager; Agent. Education: Belvedere College; Roscrea College; Blackrock College; Psychology, Trinity College, Dublin, Ireland. Career: Sense of Ireland Festival, London, 1980; Organiser of Irish rock festivals in London, 1986-90; Paris, 1992; Manager of bands, tour organiser, agent and promoter; Managing Director of Treasure Island Promotions, Media, Music, Discs; Acts on record label: Dr Millar; Ruby Horse. Hobbies: Music; Photography; Winter and water sports; Conversation. Address: Bartra Lodge, Harbour Road, Dalkey, Co Dublin, Ireland.

STEPHENSON Wilfredo, b. 27 February 1948, Lima, Peru, England. m. Maria, 21 June 1988, 3 sons, 2 daughters. Education: BA, Econ, Howard University, USA; Graduate Economic Studies, Stockholm University; Computer Education, NM School, Stockholm, Sweden; Piano Lessons, Lima Musical Conservatory; Selftaught Percussionist & Bass Player; Private Lessons, Diverse Known Percussionists; Sabu Martinez, Pello Elafrokan, Anga, Tata Guiness. Career: Reader, Hot Salsa, Swedish Salsa Group, toured Scandinavia, Europe & US, 1979-95; Percussionist with Aston Reymers Riivaler, 1981-86; Co-owner, Rub a Dub Records & Studios, 1988-97; Co-Producer, Rub a Dub Catalogue (19 productions with Salsa, Afro, Flamenco & World Music), 1997. Compositions: Lana Turkaleza, 1997. Recordings: Ensemble of Salsa Percussion, solo LP, 1981; Hot Salsa, 1979; Maldito Primitivo, 1985; Hot Salsa Meets Swedish Jazz, 1988; Lamowosbacuba, 1989; Ilusiones, 1992; With Friends for Friends, 1995. Honours: Swedish Grammy for Per Mernberg. Memberships: STIM; SAMI; SKAP; Swedish Socs for Musicians. Hobbies: Footbal; Computers. Address: Alkallevagen 2, 13933 Varmdo, Sweden.

STERIAN Valeriu, b. 21 Sept 1952, Rîmnicu Sárat, Romania. Singer; Musician (guitar, drums). m. Lucia Sterian, 4 Aug 1976, 1 son. Education: Psychologist. Musical Education: Music School. Career: Folk-rock group, Vali and Carmen, 1973; Lead singer, guitar, rock group, 1975-; Valeriu

Sterian and Compania de Sunet; Tours: Rumania; Bulgaria; Hungary; Poland; Russia; Norway; Germany; France; England. Recordings: Albums: Folk, 1977; Antirazbolnica, 1979; Veac XX, 1982; Nimic Fara Oameni, 1989; Noati in Norway, 1990; Vino Doamne, 1991; S-A Votat Codul Penal, 1993; Evenimentul Zilei, 1994. Publications: Vox Pop Rock, Romania. Hobbies: Billiards. Current Management: Valerian Sterian Studio, B'inisor, Compania de sunet SRL. Address: Str Ion Cîmpineanu-27, Ap 75, Sect L, Bucharest, Romania.

STES Walter, b. 24 January 1950, Heist-Aan-Zee, Belgian. Musician (Bass). Education: Law Studies, 2 years; Oriental Philology, 2 years; Classical Education, Double Bass. Career: Musical Director, Theatre Arena, Gent, 1975-85; Musical Director, Royal Ballet of Flanders, 1985-90; Leader, Blues band, Red Rooster. Recordings: Straight From the Heart, full CD; Bluesin' Up, full CD; On the Move, full CD. Address: St Anna Straat 60, 9820 Bottelare, Belgium.

STEVEN Paul (Paul Steven Pedersen), b. 17 June 1955, Denmark. Vocalist; Musician (guitar, bass, percussion); Songwriter; Composer. m. Barbara-Anne, 13 June 1987. Musical Education: Self-taught. Career: Soldier, Danish Army, 1974-80; Disc Jockey, The Locomotion, 1981-83; Member of various groups in Luxembourg, Germany and Denmark, 1984-94; Founder member, Kid Steven and the Cucumbers, 1995-. Compositions and recordings: France And The Incredible Dream, 1979; Det Regnede Osse Paa Os Igaar, 1983; The Shit Hit The Fan, 1984; Jimi And Elvis, 1995; Amsterdam, 1997. Memberships: Dansk Musiker Forbund (Danish Musicians' Union); KODA. Hobbies: Music; Listening to the radio. Current Management: Cucumber Music. Address: Toftesgaardsvej 8, Ellinge, DK-5540 Ullerslev, Denmark.

STEVENS Craig Ronald, b. 30 Sept 1959, Syracuse, New York, USA. Singer. m. Mary L Sinclair, 30 Aug 1986. Education: MS, Musical Education: BA; AAS. Career: Touring artist, session musician, RCA Canada and Wurlitzer; Contract artist, keyboardist for Thrill Of A Lifetime, Canada, 1982. Recordings: Just Another Night, 1980, 1981; Live At The Grand, 1983; Terminal Barber Shop, 1984; Risin' Child, 1994. Publications: Poems On The Road, 1983. Honours: Excellence In Music Education, 1992. Memberships: GMA; ASCAP; CAPAC (SOCAN). Current Management: Capitol Management. Address: Division St, #1300, Suite 200, Nashville, TN 37203, USA.

STEVENS Dane, b. 31 July 1942, Colchester, Essex, England. Country Singer; Songwriter; Musician (guitar). m. Kathleen Marian, 9 Apr 1985, 3 sons, 1 daughter (previous marriage). Musical Education: Self-taught. Career: 20 years, working professional; Solo ariste, working in country music clubs, major country festivals; Local radio interviews; Radio plays; Tours nationwide. Compositions: Original songs for albums; Songs recorded by The Haleys; Jolene and Barry. Recordings: Albums: TBL: New Country; Across The Miles. Honours: Best Act, Country Music Club. Membership: PRS. Current Management: Contact Direct. Address: 139 Harwich Road, Colchester, Essex CO4 3DB, England.

STEVENS Jeremy, b. 26 Oct 1967, Britain. Electronic musician. Education: BSc Psychology. Career: Audio Postcards... MASPCD1 compilation; Several underground White Label releases; Remix work for Swim records; 2 film soundtracks; Freelance remixing and projects. Hobbies: Any electronics; Sci-Fi; Comics. Address: 15369 Nicholas Street, Omaha, NE 68154, USA.

STEVENS Michael Jefry, b. 13 Mar 1951, New York, USA. Musician (piano); Composer; Educator. Education: Masters degree, Queens College, NYC. Musical Education: Masters degree, Jazz Performance. Career: Extensive tours, Italy, Spain, Germany, Denmark, with Stevens Siegel and Ferguson trio and the Lily White Band; Various other tours including David Clayton Thomas Band; Worked with: Cecil Bridgewater; Dakota Staton; Charnott Moffett; Mark Whitfield; Ira Sullivan; Harold Vick; Ralph Lalama; Billy Drewes; Mark Feldman; Pheeroan Aklaff; Leo Smith; Gerry Hemingway; Phil Haynes; Perry Robinson; Ed Schuller; Thomas Chapin; Herb Robertson; Mark Whitecage; Billy Martin; Dave Douglas; Blood Sweat And Tears; The Platters; Carlos Patato Valdez; Jeff Andrews; Frank Gambale; Jaco Pastorius; Suzanne Vega; Head, keyboard department, National Guitar Summer Workshop; Musical Director, Music Theatre Ensemble, Barnard College, 1980-84. Compositions: Music for vocal and instrumental ensembles, dance, music-theatre, film. Recordings: with Mark Whitecage And Liquid Time: Liquid Time; Live At Brandeis; with Jim Finn: Jim Finn; Talking With Angels; with Tim Ferguson Trio: Habitat; Dedication; Vagabond Blues; with The Lily White Band: Somewhere Between Truth And Fiction; with Phil Haynes/Michael Stevens: Music For Percussion And Piano; with The Mosaic Sextet: Today This Moment; Live At Brandeis; with Stevens/Siegel/Ferguson: One Of A Kind; with Mark Whitecage/Michael Jefry Stevens: Duo Improvisations; Live At Greenwich House. Honours: BMI Composers Workshop; Eurie Blake Scholar. Memberships: BMI; Minnesota Composers Forum. Hobbies: Swimming; Tennis.

STEVENS Michael William, b. 26 Jan 1957, Wisbech, Cambridgeshire, England. Artist; Musician (saxophone, keyboards). Musical Education: Birmingham School of Music, 1975-1979. Career: MD, Take That; Bill Withers; Member, LA mix; Toured as support act with: The Temptations; Dionne Warwick; Freddie Jackson. Recordings: 2 solo albums: Light Up The Night, 1988; Set The Spirit Free, 1990; Soloist on hits by: Cathy Dennis; Glen Goldsmith; Tom Jones; Eternal. Honours: ARCM; ABSM. Hobby: Sport. Address: 32 Friary Gardens, Newport Pagnell, Bucks MK16 0JZ, England.

STEVENS Mike, b. 9 Oct 1957, Sarnia, Ontario, Canada. Musician (harmonica). m. Jane Gosselin, 8 Nov 1986, 1 son. Education: Electrical Instrumentation at college. Career: First played The Grand Ole Opry, guest of Jim and Jesse, 1989; Guested over 100 times since; Tours: Canada; USA; Japan; Bahamas; Mexico. Recordings: Harmonica, 1990; Blowing Up A Storm, 1992; Life's Railway To Heaven, 1994. Publications: Mike Stevens Harmonica Techniques For Bluegrass And Beyond. Honours: Recording of the Year, Central Canada, Bluegrass, 1990; 5 times Entertainer Of The Year, Central Canada, Bluegrass; Best Selling Album, PRC, 1992; Made a Kentucky Colonel, 1994. Memberships: SOCAN; CMRAA; HFA; AFofM; NARAS; CARAS. Hobby: Physical fitness. Current Management: Jim McReynolds, 560 Zieglers Road, TN 37066, USA. Address: 1595 Blackwell Road, Sarnia, Ontario N7X 1A4, Canada.

STEVENS Paul, b. 30 June 1969, Hammersmith, London, England. Musician (guitars: electric, acoustic, classical); Electronics and Sound Engineer. Education: Chelmsford College of Further Education, Anglia Polytechnic; Musical Education: Colchester Music College, 1980-1985; Martin Smith LLCM, 1985-1994. Career: Parallel careers as musician and electronics/sound engineer; Sessions in London, Essex and Suffolk; Many live performances with bands including: Real Lives (early version of Blur); Hot Wired; Customs Men; Colours; Dream Age; Empathy; Electronics designer and demonstrator

for Trace Elliot, designed range of valve guitar amplifiers, 1994-98. Recordings: Produced solo work of guitar instrumentals, 1991; Session for U2: I Can't Help Falling In Love (remix), 1992; Producer for: Universal (EP), Empathy, 1995. Honours: HNC Electronic Engineering, 1990; Trinity School of Music, Grade 8 guitar, 1994. Memberships: Musicians' Union; Institute of Electronics and Electrical Incorporated Engineers. Hobbies: Music; Electronics; British history; Reading. Current Management: Trace Elliot. Address: 188 Baddow Road, Chelmsford, Essex CM2 9QW, England.

STEVENS Richard William, b. 17 Aug 1962, Wegberg, Germany. Musician (drums). Musical Education: Private jazz tuition, Tommy Chase, John Stevens. Career: Performed with: Dennis Bovell; Lynton Kwesi Johnson; George Clinton; Own group: Well Red; Own project: Drumhead. Recordings with: Simply Red; Joan Armatrading; Oleta Adams; Boy George. Current Management: Copasetic Records. Address: 102 Ulleswater Road, London N14 7BT, England.

STEVENS Shakin' (Michael Barratt), b. 4 March 1948, Ely, Cardiff, South Wales. Singer; Songwriter. Career: Enjoyed much success touring for many years with his band, the Sunsets; Starred in the multi-award-winning West End musical, Elvis, which ran for 19 months from 1977; Signed as solo artist with Epic Records worldwide in 1978; First UK Top 30 single, Hot Dog, charted in 1980; First European chart entry, Marie Marie, in 1980; First UK Number 1, later a major international hit, This Ole House, 1981; 38 hit singles, 36 of which were consecutive, throughout the 1980s and 1990s; UK hits: Four No.1s, three No.2s, 12 Top 5 hits, 15 Top 10 hits, 25 Top 20 hits, 30 Top 30 hits and 32 Top 40 hits; Musical collaborations include Bonnie Tyler, Roger Taylor, Hank Marvin and Albert Lee; Tours, personal appearances and television performances worldwide; Most successful hit-maker of the 1980s in the UK, with more weeks in the charts (254 in total) than any other international recording artist; His work has been covered by many artists including Eddie Raven (A Letter To You) and Sylvia (Cry Just A Little Bit), No 1 and No 9 in the Nashville charts, and Barry Manilow (Oh Julie), US hit in 1982. Recordings: Hit singles, albums and songs have sold millions of copies, earning numerous honours and awards, including many Gold and Platinum discs worldwide; Hit albums (UK): Shakin' Stevens Take One!; This Ole House; Shakin' Stevens; Shaky; Give Me Your Heart Tonight; The Bop Won't Stop; Greatest Hits; Lipstick, Powder and Paint; Let's Boogie; A Whole Lotta Shaky; There's Two Kinds Of Music - Rock'n'Roll; The Epic Years; UK hit singles include: Hot Dog; Marie Marie; This Ole House; You Drive Me Crazy; Green Door; It's Raining; Oh Julie; Shirley; I'll Be Satisfied; The Shakin' Stevens EP; It's Late; Cry Just A Little Bit; A Rockin' Good Way (To Mess Around And Fall In Love), duet with Bonnie Tyler; A Love Worth Waiting For; A Letter To You; Teardrops; Breakin' Up My Heart; Lipstick Powder And Paint; Merry Christmas Everyone; Turning Away; Because I Love You; A Little Boogie Woogie (In The Back Of My Mind); What Do You Want To Make Those Eyes At Me For?; Love Attack; I Might; The Best Christmas Of Them All; Radio. Honours include: 30 Top 30 hits in a decade, unsurpassed by any other artist; Best Musical of 1977; Best singer/performer, MIDEM; Chartmaker Award for 4 simultaneous singles in the German chart; Gold and Platinum discs worldwide; First double platinum single ever to an international artist, Sweden; Most weeks in UK charts for international recording artist, 254 weeks. Address: c/o HEC Ltd, PO Box 184, West End, Woking, Surrey GU24 9LY, England.

STEVENS Steve, b. New York, USA. Musician (guitar). Career: Lead guitarist, Billy Idol, 1981-88; Solo artiste, and leader of own group Atomic Playboys; Also worked with Michael

Jackson; Ric Ocasek; Steve Lukather; Thompson Twins. Recordings: with Billy Idol: Don't Stop, 1981; Billy Idol, 1982; Rebel Yell, 1983; Whiplash Smile, 1986; Vital Idol, 1987; Idol Songs - 11 Of The Best, 1988; Solo: Steve Steve's Atomic Playboys, 1989; Other recordings include: Bad, Michael Jackson, 1987; Lukather, Steve Lukather, 1989; Chalk Mark In A Rain Storm, Joni Mitchell, 1988; Don't Explain, Robert Palmer, 1990; Hit singles with Billy Idol include: Hot In The City; White Wedding; Without A Face; Rebel Yell; To Be A Lover; Don't Need A Gun; Sweet Sixteen; Money Money Live; Hot In The City; Other singles include: Dirty Diana, Michael Jackson. Address: c/o Weidenbaum Ryder And Co., 720 Palisade Avenue, Englewood Cliffs, NJ 07632, USA.

STEVENSON Jeffrey, b. 14 Jan 1947, Leeds, Yorkshire, England. Musician (guitar, piano); Singer; Songwriter. m. Cecile Louise McDonald, 30 Aug 1969, 2 daughters. Musical Education: Self-taught. Career: Played role of Woof, Canadian production of musical, Hair, 1970; Singer, guitarist, co-writer, television series Spider, BBC; Support to Labi Siffre in concert; Staff writer for programme Watch, BBC TV; Numerous and television radio gigs. Compositions: Over 80 titles published / recorded. Recordings: Spider; Recorded with Mary Wilde. Memberships: Musicians' Union; Songwriters Guild; PRS; MCPS. Hobbies: Supporting Leeds United Football Club; Committed Christian; Reading. Current Management: Self-managed. Address: 30 Chiswick Village, London W4 3BY, England.

STEWART Al, b. 5 Sept 1945, Glasgow, Scotland. Singer; Songwriter; Musician (guitar). m. Kristine Russell, 18 May 1991, 1 daughter. Musical Education: Self-taught. Career: Solo artist, 1967-; Appearances include: Royal Festival Hall, 1967; US tour, 1974; Cambridge Folk Festival, 1989. Recordings: Singles include: Midnight Rocks; License To Steal; Albums: Bedsitter Images, 1967; Love Chronicles (featuring Jimmy Page), 1969; Zero She Flies, 1970; Orange, 1972; Past Present And Future, 1974; Modern Times, 1975; Year Of The Cat, 1976; Time Passages, 1978; Carrots, 1980; Live/Indian Summer, 1981; Russians And Americans, 1984; Last Days Of The Century, 1988; Rock The World, 1990; Rhymes In Rooms - Al Stewart Live Featuring Peter White, 1993; Between The Wars (with Laurence Juber), 1995. Hobbies: Wine collecting; Reading history. Current Management: c/o Steve Chapman, Chapman & Co., PO Box 5549, Santa Monica, CA 90409, USA.

STEWART Dave, b. 9 Sept 1952, Sunderland, Tyne and Wear, England. Musician (guitar, keyboards); Songwriter; Composer. m. Siobhan Fahey, 1 Aug 1987. Career: Musician, Harrison and Stewart (with Brian Harrison); Longdancer; The Catch, 1977; Renamed The Tourists, 1979-80; Formed Eurythmics with Annie Lennox, 1980-89; Worldwide concerts include Nelson Mandela's 70th Birthday Tribute, Wembley, 1988; As solo artiste: Nelson Mandela Tribute concert, Wembley, 1990; Amnesty International Big 30 concert, 1991; Founder, Spiritual Cowboys, 1990-92; Vegas, with Terry Hall, 1992-93; Founder, own record label Anxious Records, 1988; Owner, The Church recording studio, 1992; Producer, session musician, for artistes including Bob Dylan; Mick Jagger; Tom Petty; Daryl Hall; Bob Geldof; Boris Grebenshikov. Compositions: All Eurythmics songs co-written with Lennox; Theme for Jute City, BBC1; Co-writer, film score Motorcycle Mystics; Co-writer with Gerry Anderson, music for children's series GFI, 1992. Recordings: Albums: with The Tourists: The Tourists; Reality Affect; Luminous Basement; with Eurythmics: In The Garden, 1982; Sweet Dreams (Are Made Of This), 1983; Touch (Number 1, UK), 1984; 1984 (For The Love Of Big Brother), film soundtrack, 1984; Be Yourself Tonight, 1985; Revenge, 1986; Savage, 1988; We

Too Are One (Number 1, UK), 1989; Eurythmics Greatest Hits (Number 1, UK), 1991; Eurythmics Live 1983-89, 1992; with the Spiritual Cowboys: Dave Stewart And The Spiritual Cowboys, 1990; with Vegas: Vegas, 1992; Solo: Greetings From The Gutter, 1994; Film soundtrack: De Kassiere, with Candy Dulfer, 1990; Hit singles include: with the Tourists: I Only Want To Be With You, 1979; So Good To Be Back Home, 1979; with Eurythmics: Sweet Dreams (Are Made Of This) (Number 1, US), 1983; Love Is A Stranger, 1983; Who's That Girl?, 1983; Right By Your Side, 1983; Here Comes The Rain Again, 1984; Sex Crime (1984), 1984; Would I Lie To You?, 1985; There Must Be An Angel (Playing With My Heart), 1985; It's Alright (Baby's Coming Back), 1986; When Tomorrow Comes, 1986; Thorn In My Side, 1986; Missionary Man, 1986; You Have Placed A Chill In My Heart, 1988; Solo: Lily Was Here, with Candy Dulfer, 1990; Contributor, Rock The World, 1990; Give Peace A Chance, Peace Choir, 1991; Videos: Eurythmics Live; Sweet Dreams; Savage. Honours: MTV Music Awards, Best New Artist Video, Sweet Dreams, 1984; BRIT Awards: Best Producer, 1986, 1987, 1990; Grammy, Best Rock Performance, Missionary Man, 1987; Ivor Novello Awards: Songwriters of the Year (with Annie Lennox), 1984, 1987; Best Song, It's Alright, 1987. Current Management: Miss Management, 16101 Ventura Blvd, Suite 301, Encino, CA 91436, USA. Address: c/o East West Records, Electric Lighting Station, 46 Kensington Court, London W8 5DP, England.

STEWART Godfrey, b. 20 June 1949, Jamaica. Musician (percussion). Career: Concerts and Ben video; Studios: Jeffrey mobile; Aquarius, Jamaica; Green Wood; Producing songs, writing, recording. Recording: One Wave Unto Another Wave. Publications: Ex-Kemps, International Music and Recording Industry. Membership: Musicians' Union. Hobbies: Cycling; Running.

STEWART Jimmy (James Otto), b. 8 Sep 1935, San Francisco, California, USA. Musician (guitar); Producer; Composer; Writer. m. Terri Tilton Street, 22 Apr 1988. Education: AA, College of San Marteo, 1957. Musical Education: BA, Chicago School of Music, 1960; Certificate, Berklee School of Music, 1964; Private studies. Career: Featured soloist with: Los Angeles Philharmonic; Dallas Symphony Orchestra; St Louis Symphony Orchestra; San Francisco Light Opera; Guitarist with artists including: Ray Charles, Stan Getz, David Grisman, Dave Grusin, Michael Jackson, Quincy Jones, Herbie Mann, Shelly Manne, Gary McFarland, Carlos Santana, Sonny Stitt, Gabor Szabo; Musical director for: Lainie Kazan; Chita Rivera; Andy Williams; Vocal coach for: Linda Ronstadt; Juice Newton; Lee Ritenour; Master class tutor at: Dick Grove School of Music; Musicians Institute of Technology; Audio/Video Institute of Technology, Hollywood; University of Southern California. Compositions include: classical pieces, music for commercials, television, films. Recordings: Solo albums include: Fire Flower, 1977; The Touch, 1986; Blues Trax, 1992; The Art, History and Style of Jazz Guitar, 1993; The Complete Jazz Guitarist, 1994; Tribute To Classical Guitar, 1995; Also recorded with artists including: Gabor Szabo (7 albums); Burt Bacharach; James Brown; Sammy Davis Jr; Neil Diamond; Barbra Streisand; Everly Brothers; Maurice Jarre; Dusty Springfield; Featured on 1200 recordings. Publications: 24 guitar books include: Mode Mania, 1992; Heavy Metal Guitar, 1992; The Art History And Style Of Jazz Guitar, 1993; The Complete Jazz Guitarist, 1994; Tribute To Classical Guitar, 1995; Numerous songbooks; contributor to Guitar Player, Recording Engineer and Producer magazine. Honours: Alabama Jazz Hall of Fame; Decade of Service, Guitar Player Magazine. Memberships: ASCAP; NARAS; IASE. Hobby: Golf. Current Management: Terri Tilton Management. Address: 7135 Hollywood Boulevard, Suite 601, Los Angeles, CA 90046, USA.

STEWART Jon Randall, b. 14 Feb 1949. Vocalist; Musician (guitar, mandolin). Career: Lead guitar, harmony, vocals for Emmylou Harris with The Nash Ramblers, 1990-95; Opening act for Mary Chapin Carpenter, 1995. Composition: Just Like You. Recordings: Albums: What You Don't Know, 1995; Emmylou Harris and The Nash Ramblers of The Ryman. Honours: Grammy Award, Emmylou Harris and The Nash Ramblers, 1992. Hobbies: Fishing; Racing. Current Management: M Hitchcock Management. Address: PO Box 159007, Nashville, TN 37215, USA.

STEWART Mark Hinton (William), b. 12 Oct 1962, Barton-On-Sea, Hampshire, England. Keyboard Player. Musical Education: BA Hons, Music, Exeter University, England. Career: Keyboard player, co-writer, rockband Cyan; Keyboards, co-writer, jazz group This Side Up; Toured with Danny Williams; Sometime member of Mo Nazam Band and Anita Kelsey Band; Co-founder, Brazilian group Sarabanda; Director, Chamber Orchestra of London. Compositions: Co-writer, all songs for Cyan; Co-writer for This Side Up. Recordings: For album with Mo Nazam; Cyan: Highway Songs, Electric Blue Lemon. Membership: Musicians' Union. Hobbies: Photography; Tennis. Current Management: Sharon Cohen Management. Address: 56 Swinley House, Redhill Street, London NW1 4BB, England.

STEWART Rod (Roderick David), b. 10 Jan 1945, Highgate, North London, England. Singer. m. (1) Alana Collins, 1970; (2) Rachel Hunter, 1990, 1 son, 2 daughters. Career: Singer with: Steampacket; Shotgun Express; Jeff Beck Group, 1967-69; Concerts include: UK tour with Roy Orbison, 1967; US tours, 1967, 1968; The Faces, 1969-75; Appearances include: Reading Festival, 1972; UK, US tours, 1972; Solo artiste, 1971-; Solo appearances include: Rock In Rio, Brazil, 1985; Vagabond Heart Tour, 1991-92. Recordings: Singles include: Reason To Believe; Maggie May; (I Know) I'm Losing You; Handbags And Gladrags; You Wear It Well; Angel; Farewell; Sailing; This Old Heart Of Mine; Tonight's The Night (Gonna Be All Right); The Killing Of Georgie (Parts 1 and 2); Get Back; The First Cut Is The Deepest; I Don't Want To Talk About It; You're In My Heart; Hot Legs; D'Ya Think I'm Sexy?; Passion; Young Turks; Tonight I'm Yours; Baby Jane; What Am I Gonna Do; Infatuation; Some Guys Have All The Luck; Love Touch; Every Beat Of My Heart; Downtown Train; Rhythm Of My Heart; This Old Heart Of Mine; Have I Told You Lately; Reason To Believe; Ruby Tuesday; You're The Star; Albums include: 2 with Jeff Beck; 4 with the Faces; Solo albums: Every Picture Tells A Story, 1971; Never A Dull Moment, 1972; Atlantic Crossing, 1975; A Night On The Town, 1976; Foot Lose And Fancy Free, 1977; Blondes Have More Fun, 1978; Foolish Behaviour, 1980; Tonight I'm Yours, 1981; Camouflage, 1984; Love Touch, 1986; Out Of Order, 1988; The Best Of, 1989; Downtown Train, 1990; Vagabond Heart, 1991; Lead Vocalist, 1992; Unplugged... And Seated, 1993; A Spanner In The Works, 1995; Numerous compilations. Honours include: BRIT Awards, Lifetime Achievement Award, 1993; First artist to top US and UK singles and album charts simultaneously, 1971. Address: c/o Stiefel Phillips Entertainment, 9720 Wilshire Blvd, Ste 400, Beverly Hills, CA 90212, USA.

STIEF Bo, b. 15 Oct 1946, Copenhagen, Denmark. Musician (bass guitar, double bass); Composer; Bandleader; Teacher. 1 son, 2 daughters. Career: Bass player, 1963-; Began as bass player for touring soloists including: Dexter Gordon; Chet Baker; John Scofield; Don Cherry; Stan Getz; Dizzy Gillespie; Member of: Entrance; Midnight Sun; Leader, own band Chasing Dreams, 1980-; Major tours, festivals throughout Europe; Also played with: Miles Davis; Toots Thielmans; Joe Henderson; Larry Coryell; Alex Riel; Clark

Terry; Archie Shepp; Yusef Lateef; Gato Barbieri; Art Farmer; Terje Rypdal; Jan Garbarek; George Russell; Astrid Gilberto; Zoot Sims; Carla Bley; AMO; Recent collaborations with: Just Friends; Palle Mikkelborg; Barbara Thompson; Ernie Watts; Jasper van't Hof Quartet. Compositions: Simple Song; Miss Julie, used for UN educational film. Recordings: Albums: with Bo Stief Chasing Dreams: Hidden Frontiers; 1987; Chasing Dreams, 1994; Also played on over 500 albums including: Aura, Miles Davis, Palle Mikkelborg, 1985; Anything But Grey, Palle Mikkelborg, 1992; Ernie Watts, Jasper van't Hof Quartet, 1993. Honours: Jazz Musician of the Year, 1988; Composers Award of Honour, DJBFA, 1990. Address: Kaermindevej 11, DK-2820 Gentofte, Denmark.

STIGERS Curtis, b. 1968, Boise, Idaho, USA. Singer; Musician (clarinet, saxophone). Musical Education: Classical training in clarinet. Career: Member, local punk and blues bands; Later played in blues groups, New York; Discovered in jazz trio; Currently solo artiste. Recordings: Album: Curtis Stigers, 1992; Singles include: Never Saw A Miracle; Contributor, Tapestry Revisited - A Tribute To Carole King, 1996. Current Management: C. Winston Simone, 1790 Broadway, 10th Floor, New York, NY 10019, USA.

STILLS Stephen, b. 3 Jan 1945, Dallas, Texas, USA. Vocalist; Musician (guitar). m. Veronique Sanson, Jan 1971. Career: Member, Au Go Go Singers; Buffalo Springfield, 1966-68; Crosby Stills and Nash, 1968-; (also as Crosby Stills Nash and Young); Manassas, 1971-74. Performances include: with Buffalo Springfield: Monterey Festival, 1967; with Crosby Stills and Nash: Woodstock, 1969; Royal Albert Hall, 1970; Festival Of Hope, New York, 1972; Wembley Stadium, 1974; Night Of The Hurricane 2 benefit concert, Texas, 1976; Last Waltz concert, San Francisco, with The Band, 1976; US tour, 1979; Anti-nuclear benefits, Madison Square Garden, 1979; No Nukes benefit concert, Hollywood Bowl, 1980; Film, No Nukes, 1980; Live Aid, Philadelphia, 1985; Amnesty International benefit, Chile, 1990; Hurricane Andrew benefit, Miami, 1992; Royal Albert Hall, 1992; Imua Hawaii, 1992. Recordings: with Buffalo Springfield: Buffalo Springfield, 1967; Stampede, 1967; Buffalo Springfield Again, 1967; with Crosby Still And Nash: Crosby Stills And Nash, 1969; Déjà Vu, 1970; 4-Way Street, 1971; So Far, 1974; Daylight Again, 1982; What Goes Around, 1983; Allies, 1983; American Dream, 1989; Live It Up, 1990; Solo albums: Stephen Stills, 1970; Stephen Stills 2, 1971; Stills, 1975; Stephen Stills - Live On Atlantic, 1976; Illegal Stills, 1976; Still Stills - The Best Of Stephen Stills, 1977; Thoroughfare Gap, 1978; with Manassas: Manassas, 1972; Down The Road, 1973; with Stills/Young: Long May You Run, 1976. Singles include: with Buffalo Springfield: For What It's Worth, 1967; Bluebird, 1967; Rock'n'Roll Woman, 1967; with Crosby Stills and Nash: Suite - Judy Blue Eyes, 1969; Woodstock, 1970; Ohio, 1970; Just A Song Before I Go, 1977; Wasted On The Way, 1982; Southern Cross, 1982; Solo: Love The One You're With, 1971. Honours include: Grammy Award, Best New Artist, Crosby Stills and Nash, 1970; Best International Group, Melody Maker Poll, 1971. Current Management: Management Network, 14930 Ventura Blvd #205, Sherman Oaks, CA 91403, USA.

STING (Gordon Matthew Sumner), 2 Oct 1951, Wallsend, Newcastle-Upon-Tyne, England. Singer; Musician (bass); Actor. m. (1) Frances Tomelty, 1 May 1976, divorced 1984, 1 son, 1 daughter; (2) Trudie Styler, 20th August 1992, 2 sons, 2 daughters. Career: School teacher, Newcastle, 1975-77; Singer, songwriter, bass player, The Police, 1977-86; Solo artiste, 1985-; Numerous worldwide tours, television and radio, with the Police and solo; actor in films: Quadrophenia, 1980; Secret Policeman's Other Ball, 1982; Brimstone And Treacle, 1982; Dune,

1984; The Bride, 1985; Plenty, 1985; Julia And Julia, 1988; Stormy Monday, 1988; The Adventures Of Baron Munchausen, 1989; Broadway Performance, Threepenny Opera, 1989. Recordings: Hit singles include: Walking On The Moon; Message In A Bottle; So Lonely; Roxanne; De Do Do Do, De Da Da Da; Every Little Thing She Does; Every Breath You Take; Invisible Sun; Can't Stand Losing You; Don't Stand So Close To Me; If You Love Somebody; Englishman In New York; If I Ever Lose My Faith In You; Fields Of Gold; Love Is Stronger Than Justice; Cowboy Song (with Pato Banton); Let The Soul Be Your Pilot; Albums: with the Police: Outlandos D'Armour, 1977; Regatta De Blanc, 1979; Zenyatta Mondatta, 1980; Ghost In The Machine, 1981; Synchronisity, 1983; Bring On The Night, 1986; Solo albums: The Dream Of The Blue Turtles, 1985; Nothing Like The Sun, 1987; The Soul Cages, 1991; Ten Summoner's Tales, 1994; Mercury Falling, 1996; Contributor, Tower Of Song (Leonard Cohen tribute), 1995. Honours include: 8 Grammy Awards (with Police and solo); Q Award, Best Album, 1994; BRIT Award, Best Male Artist, 1994. Membership: PRS. Current Management: Firstars, 1 Water Lane, Camden Town, London NW1 8NZ, England.

STIPE (John) Michael, b. 4 Jan 1960, Decatur, Georgia, USA. Singer; Songwriter; Record Producer. Career: Member, R.E.M., 1980-; International cocnerts include: Earth Day Concert, Maryland, 1989; Green World tour, 1989; A Performance For The Planet concert, 1990; European tour, 1992; Own film and video company C-OO; Own vegetarian restaurant, The Grit, Athens, Georgia. Recordings: Chronic Town (mini-album), 1982; Murmur, 1983; Reckoning, 1984; Fables Of The Reconstruction, 1985; Life's Rich Pageant, 1986; Dead Letter Office, 1987; Document, 1987; Eponymous, 1988; Green, 1988; Out Of Time, 1991; Monster, 1995; Singles: The One I Love, 1987; Stand, 1989; Orange Crush, 1989; Losing My Religion, 1991; Shiny Happy People, 1991; Near Wild Heaven, 1991; Radio Song, 1991; Drive, 1992; Man On The Moon, 1992; The Sidewinder Sleeps Tonite, 1993; Everybody Hurts, 1993; Nightswimming; Crush With Eyeliner; What's The Frequency Kenneth?; Tracks featured on film soundtracks: Batchelor Party, 1984; Until The End Of The World, 1991; Coneheads, 1993; Recordings with: Indigo Girls, 1988; Syd Straw, 1989; Billy Bragg, 1991; Neneh Cherry, 1991; Contributor, Disney compilation, Stay Awake, with Natalie Merchant, 1988; Tom's Album, 1991; I'm Your Fan (Leonard Cohen tribute), 1991; Producer, artistes including: Swell; Chickasaw Muddpuppies; Opal Fox Society; Co-producer, film Desperation Angels, with Oliver Stone. Honours: Earth Day Award, 1990; Numerous MTV Music Video Awards, Billboard Awards, 1991; BRIT Awards: Best International Group, 1992, 1993, 1995; Grammy Awards: Best Pop Performance, Alternative Music Album, Music Video, 1992; Atlanta Music Awards, 1992; IRMA Band of the Year, 1993; Rolling Stone Critics Awards, 1993; Q Awards: Best Album, 1991, 1992; Best Act In The World, 1991, 1995. Current Management: REM/Athens, 250 W Clayton Street, Athens, GA 30601, USA.

STOCK Michael, b. 3 Dec 1951, Margate, Kent, England. Songwriter; Record Producer; Musician. m. Frances Roberta, Dec 1975, 2 sons, 1 daughter. Education: University of Hull. Career: Signed first publishing deal, 1970; Member of bands: Mirage, 1976-84; Nightwork, 1981-84; Founder, partner, writing/production team Stock Aitken Waterman, 1984-93; Relocated to new studios, started new production company and Love This Records, 1994. Recordings: As writer/producer, artists include: Princess; Hazell Dean; Dead or Alive; Bananarama; Mel & Kim; Rick Astley; Kylie Minogue; Jason Donovan; Donna Summer; Cliff Richard; Sybil; WWF; Kym Mazelle; Jocelyn Brown; Nicki French; Power Rangers; Robson & Jerome. Honours: BPI Best

Producer, 1988; IVN Songwriter of Year 3 times; BMI Award, 4 times. Memberships: PRS; BASCA. Hobby: Sport. Address: c/o Love This International, Hundred House, 100 Union Street, London SE1 0NL, England.

STOCKLEY Miriam, b. Johannesburg, South Africa. Singer. m. Rod Houison, 7 Sept 1984, 1 son, 1 daughter. Musical Education: Self-taught, sight reading, harmony and vocal arrangement. Career: Backing vocalist for top recording stars: Kylie Minogue; Jason Donovan; Brian May; Deniece Williams; Cliff Richard; Chaka Khan; Freddie Mercury; Robert Plant; Paul Young; Appeared on tribute to Freddie Mercury, Brian May tour; Worked extensively with Stock, Aitken and Waterman; Television includes: Spitting Image; Kenny Everett; Beatrix Potter's Peter Rabbit theme song. Recordings: Only You, used in Fiat commercial (Number 3, UK), 1991; Second album as Adiemus, with Jenkins Ratledge (Number 3, classical charts, Gold record Germany), 1995. Honours: Sarie Award for Best South African Recording Artiste. Memberships: PRS; MCPS; GVL; PAMRA. Address: c/o Equity, Guild House, Upper St Martins Lane, London WC2H 9EG, England.

STOICA Laura, b. 10 Oct 1967, Alba-Iulia, Romania. Singer; Entertainer; Actress. m. Florin Ionescu, 31 Oct 1992. Education: Baccalaureat, Electrical Engineering; 5 year course, Diploma in Performing Arts (theatre, musical, pop music). Musical Education: Diploma, Performing Classical Music; Licence, Professional Music Interpretation. Career: Lead singer, Riff, Semnal M. to 1988; Solo artiste, 1987-; Lead singer, Laura Stoica Band, 1993-; Over 40 live appearances, national, international, television and radio; TV specials include: 5 O'Clock Tea, 1991, 1993-95; Bucharest International, 1990, 1993; Talk Show with Laura Stoica, 1993-95; Mamaia, 1991-95; Charity for Romanian children with AIDS and orphans, 1993, 1994; Radio specials include: Talk shows, 1991-95; Laura Stoica Live, 1992-95; Unplugged, 1995; Founder, President, Laura Stoica Charity Trust, 1993. Recordings include: Single: An Actor In My Life, 1992; Album: The Fire, 1994. Honours include: City Song Trophy, 1988; Mamaia Trophy, 1990, 91; Bucharest International Award, 1990; Golden Stag International Record Trophy, 1992; Pop, Rock and Show Award, 1991, 92, 93; Radio Contact Award, 1992; Bregenz International Pop Music Award, 1992. Membership: Romanian Guild of Songwriters and Composers. Hobbies: Literature; Athletics; Tennis; Watching films; Theatre; Foreign languages (English, French, Italian). Address: 48/50 Calea Victoriei, Sector 1, PO Box 26-54, 70102 Bucharest, Romania.

STOKER Richard, b. 8 Nov 1938, Castleford, Yorkshire, England. Composer; Author; Painter; Poet. m. (2) Dr Gillian Patricia Watson, 10 July 1986. Education: Huddersfield School of Music and School of Art, 1953-58; Royal Academy of Music, with Lennox Berkeley, 1958-62; Composition with Nadia Boulanger, Paris, 1962-63; Private study wiuth Britten, Fenby and Truscott; Professor of Composition, RAM, 1963-87. Career includes: Composition Teacher to Paul Patterson, qv Joe Jackson, Malcolm Singer, the late Paul Reade and others; Performing pianist on BBC Radio and Television Compositions include: Song lyrics and music, orchestral, choral, 3 overtures, chamber music, operas; Films and theatre music; Tribute to Hoagy Carmichael, with Fayarro and Earl Okin, 1981. Recordings include: Album with Susan Fazarro. Publications: Open Window-Open Door, autobiography; Words Without Music (outposts); Between the Lines; Portrait of a Towen, filmed 1983; Tanglewood, 1994; Diva - a novel, 1995; Collected Short Stories, 1997; 3 Plays; Contributions to magazines and journals; Editor, Composer Magazine, 1969-80. Honours: Mendelssohn Scholarship, 1962; Dove Prize, RAM, 1962; Associate, Royal College of Music, 1962; Associate, 1965, Fellow, 1971,

Royal Academy of Music; Justice of the Peace, 1995-; Nominated Man of the Year, American Biographical Institute, 1997. Memberships: Executive Committee, Composers' Guild, 1969-74, 1974-80; Association of Professional Composers, 1977-, Promotions Committee, 1995-; BASCA, Professional Member, 1979-95; PRS, 1962-; MCPS, 1970; Founder Member, RAM Guild, 1986-, Executive Committee, 1994-, Treasurer, 1995-; Magistrate's Association, 1995; U3A, 1993-; Founder Member, Atlantic Council of the UK, 1994; Euro-Atlantic Group, 1994-; PEN International; English PEN, 1996-. Current Management: Ricordi and Co Ltd. Address: c/o Ricordi and Co Ltd, 210 New Kings Road, London SE3 9RU, England.

STOKES Mary Teresa, b. 25 Aug 1962, Dublin, Ireland. Singer. m. Brian Palm, 14 Feb 1994. Education: BA, Psychology; MA by Research. Musical Education: 10 years classical singing, to Grade 5. Career: Formed blues band The Mary Stokes Band, 1988 (now 5-piece); Performed concerts in Ireland, Europe, USA; Backed: John Lee Hooker; Fats Domino; Carey Bell; Lowell Fulson; B B King; Radio and television appearances: Ireland; BBC; UTV; Began composing, 1993. Recordings: 3 albums; 3 singles. Honours: Smithwicks Hot Press Best Newcomer Award, 1989. Hobbies: Film; Literature; Current affairs. Current Management: Self-managed.

STOKKEBYE Peter, b. 22 August 1975, Copenhagen, Denmark. Musician. Education: Drum School, Music School, Copenhagen. Career: Played with Blink on a Tour to Seoul in South Korea; Concert with 50,000 People on Live Television; Several Radio Programs and Television Shows. Recordings: Prunes, 1996-97; Secret Garden; Standing on the Hill; Get High, 1998. Honours: Gold Record, Korea, 1997. Membership: Danish Musicians Union. Current Management: Sundance Records. Address: Nivaavaenge 196, 2990 Nivaa, Denmark.

STOLTING Arnold Hugo, b. 12 August 1969, Georgetown, Guyana. Singer; Songwriter; Producer. Education: National Institute of Broadcasting, Toronto. Career: Productions aired on Radio Worldwide; Producer for Songwriter demo tapes; Produces professional Recording Artists and involved with development of new talent; President, CEO, Canadance Music Records/Productions/Publishing. Compositions: Numerous compositions in styles of Dance, R&B, Pop, Reggae, HipHop, Rap. Recordings: Think I'm In Love, Hugo; Hey Pretty Boy, Crystal; Give It To Me Baby, Azz; In the Distance, Sona; Summatime, Blakborough. Memberships: SOCAN; CMRRA. Hobby: Helping others. Current Management: Canadance Music. Address: 36-3430 Finch Avenue E, Toronto, On M1W 2R5, Canada.

STONE Ronald William, b. 27 Mar 1959, Merseyside, England. Record Producer; Engineer; Programmer; Musician (guitar); Songwriter. Education: Art College. Career: Member, Afraid Of Mice, 1978; Backing musician for China Crisis, 1982; Formed Freeze Frame, 1984 (hits in Europe, Japan, Australia); Producer/Engineer for: Easterhouse; Throwing Muses; The Pixies; Oceanic; River City People; Audioweb; Pete Wylie; Shack; Sara Cracknell; Mansun; Christians; Live sound: Easterhouse; Jason Donovan; WOMAD 1996, 1997; Producer/soundtracks for TV/Cinema commercials: Gas; Electricity; Tea; Yves St Laurent; Consultant A&R for major record labels. Compositions: Numerous songs published. Recordings: Producer/engineer for Say Something Good, River City People; All works by Oceanic, 1991-93; Singles and album, Attack of the Grey Lantern, by Mansun (Gold Disc). Honours: 6 Nominations for Top Advertisement Soundtracks; Gold and Silver discs as producer, engineer. Current Management: TMW. Address: TMW

House, 12 Princess Terrace, Balls Road, Birkenhead, Merseyside L43 5RB, England.

STONE Tony (Anthony George), b. 21 Dec 1930, Weston-Super-Mare, England. Musician (multi-instrumentalist); Music Teacher. m. Shirley Winifred Parker, 31 Aug 1955, 3 sons. Education: Private tuition. Career: Solo keyboard player; Saxophonist with dance bands, big bands, jazz bands, orchestras, pit orchestras; Bandleader, arranger, composer, teacher; Appearances on BBC Radio and commercial television; Currently leader of New Parkway Showband, 1985-. Compositions: The Comet; Dancing; Moonrise; Freeway; Life Goes On; My Special Xmas Wish; Chocolate Cha-Cha; Eileen; Continuation Waltz; Encounters; Easy Walk; Coleford Jaunt; Marguerite; Loneliness. Membership: Musicians' Union. Address: Horfield School of Music, 22 Wellington Hill, Horfield, Bristol BS7 8SR, England.

STONEBRIDGE, b. Stockholm, Sweden. Record Producer; Songwriter. Career: Disc Jockey at own club, Stockholm; Formed Swemix, DJ service and production group, late 1980s; Formed BTB record label, 1992; Increasing success as producer and songwriter; DJ; Formed Swemix, 1986; Success as producer and songwriter. Compositions: Jacey John's Freestyle Dub, 1990; Back It Up, 1994; Satisfy My Love, 1996; Earthbeat, 1996; Boy You Knock Me Out, 1997. Recordings include: As producer: Make My Love, Shawn Christopher; Satisfy My Love, Sabrina Johnson; I Believe, 3rd Nation; Boy You Knock Me Out, Tatyana Ave and Will Smith; Show Me Love, Robin S; Make My Love, Shawn Christopher; Numerous remix credits include: Break The Chain, Motiv 8; Right Kind Of Lover, Patti Labelle; Goodbye Baby, Lulu; Show Me Love, Robin S. Honours: Best Remixer, Swedish Dance Awards, 1991, 1993, 1994, 1996; Best 12", Winter Music Conference, 1994. Memberships: STIM; ASCAP. Current Management: Big Management, New York. Address: Stonebridge Productions, Eremitvagen 6, S-11264 Stockholm, Sweden.

STONER Joel, b. 13 Jan 1964, Sewickley, Pennsylvania, USA. Recording Engineer; Producer. m. Clare B McDonald, 10 Feb 1991, 1 son. Musical Education: Berklee College of Music, Boston. Career: Recording and mixing multi-platinum albums; Music for film, television and commericals in all styles for major record labels and film companies. Publications: Contributions to professional magazines including Billboard and Mix. Address: 1567 Fair Avenue, Simi Valley, CA 93063, USA.

STORAAS Vigleik, b. 9 Feb 1963, Bergen, Norway. Musician (piano, synthesizer). m. Astrid Vasseljen, 3 Jun 1994, 1 son, 1 daughter. Education: College. Musical Education: Jazz Department, Conservatory. Career: Festival appearances with Karin Krog, John Surman and Terje Rypdal in England and Italy. Compositions: Co-wrote many compositions including Nordic Quartet. Recordings: Nordic Quartet (with John Surman, Karin Krog, Terje Rypdal), 1995; Other albums with artists including: Bjorn Alterhaug; Soyr; Norma Winstone. Memberships: Norsk Musikforbund; NJF; FNJ, Norway. Hobby: Family. Address: Bromstadekrh 21C, 7046 Trondheim, Norway.

STOREY Michael Andrew, b. 26 Oct 1936, Wakefield, Yorkshire, England. Entertainment Agent. m. Margaret Storey, 7 Jun 1965, 1 son, 1 daughter. Career: RAF Travel Agent; Entertainment Agent, 1971-; 20 years as broadcaster, BBC Radio Leeds; Vice Chairman of British Country Music Association. Memberships: British Country Music Association; Entertainment Agents Association. Hobbies: Music; Reading; Travel. Address: Mike and Margaret Storey Entertainment, 59 Knowl Road, Golcar, Huddersfield, West Yorkshire HD7 4AN, England.

STORLOKKEN Ståle, b. 19 Feb 1969, Lillehammer, Norway. Musical Education: Trondelag Musikonservatorium, 2 years Jazzline; Pedagogic studies. Career: With band Veslefrekk: Pori Jazz Festival, Finland, 1991; All jazz festivals in Norway, 1992-1995; Molde International Jazz Festival, Kongsberg Jazzfest; Mai Jazz Stavanger, Natt Jazz Bergen; Projects in Norway with Norwegian musicians. Compositions: Specially composed piece to Kongsberg, 1994; Vossa Jazz, 1995. Recordings: with Veslefrekk: Veslefrekk; with Bodega Band: En Flik Av. Memberships: FNJ (Jazz Musicians Society); NMF (Musicians Society), Norway. Hobbies: Electronics. Current Management: Jon Tvilde (Pan Jazz Production). Address: Vangsgt 8, 5700 Voss, Norway.

STORM Gary A, b. 3 Apr 1953, Porterville, California, USA. Music Talent Agent; Musician (drums). 1 son. Education: BA, Psychology, JFK University, Orinda, California. Career: Owner, Black Lotus Talent Agency. Memberships: SFVCB; ISES; MPI. Hobbies: Science Fiction; Parapsychology; Bike riding. Address: 6331 Fairmount Avenue, #362 El Cerritu, CA 94530, USA.

STORRY Richard, b. 8 Sept 1965, Ontario, Canada. Composer; Musician (guitar, keyboards). Musical Education: Royal Academy of Music. Career: Television appearances: Motormouth; Heno; S4C; Telethon; Sky; Radio broadcasts: Radio 2; Classic FM; GLR; Performed at: Coliseum; St James' Palace; Riverside Studios; Tours throughout UK with the Tetra Guitar Quartet including South Bank Centre; West End; Accompanist for West End singers and Recreation Theatre Company's The Rivals; Music Consultant and tutor for Uncle Vanya; Adjudicator, public speaker. Compositions: Musicals: A Musical Term; Arthur; Spellbyte; Kennedy. Recordings: Tetra By Arrangement; Tetra play Vivaldi's Four Seasons. Honours: GRSM (Hons); LRAM; DipRAM; Julian Bream Prize; Lady Holland Award. Memberships: PRS; BASCA; MCPS; PAMRA. Hobbies: Theatre; Long walks; Board games; Eating out. Current Management: LA Management International. Address: 52 Junction Road, Gillingham, Kent ME7 4EQ, England.

STOTZEM Jacques, b. 17 July 1959, Verviers, Belgium. Musician (acoustic guitar). 1 son. Musical Education: Self-taught. Career: Major concerts include: Guitar Festival of Liege, 1983, 1985; Inner Circle Concert, Los Angeles, USA, 1994; International Guitar Tour, Germany, 1994; Belga Jazz Festival, 1994; Clinics for: Fishman Transducers, in Europe; Direction, Fingerstyle Workshops in Europe; Concerts during the Namm Show, Los Angeles, 1996, 1997; International Jazz Festival of Montreal, Quebec, 1997; International Guitar Festival of Birkenhead, England, 1997; International Acoustic Guitar Night, Germany, 1997. Recordings: Last Thought Before Sleeping, 1982; Training, 1985; Words From The Heart, 1988; Clear Night, 1991; Straight On, 1993; Two Bridges, 1995; Different Ways, 1996; Fingerprint, 1997. Publications: Selections from Two Bridges, Straight On and Clear Night, 1996. Membership: ASIA (Association of Stringed Instrument Artisans). Hobby: Cooking. Current Management: c/o Mr Serge Szmigielski. Address: Rue Niton 13, B-4623 Magnée, Belgium.

STOVEY Martin Trevor, b. 27 Feb 1871, Bushey, Hertfordshire, England. Musician (keyboards); Songwriter; Arranger. Education: HNC Civil Engineering. Career: Kings College, Cambridge, 1990-92; Flavour of the Month at Borderline, 1993; Lindsey Wesker Show (Kiss FM). Recordings: Driftings; Oh La La; Love Season; Chosen Child; Populus. Membership: Musicians' Union. Hobby: Aviation. Current Management: Self-managed. Address: 66 Milton Drive, Borehamwood, Hertfordshire WD6 2BB, England.

STRACHAN Matthew James, b. 11 Dec 1970, London, England. Composer; Musician (piano). Musical Education: Dartington College of Arts, Devon. Career: Musical Director of stage shows: Flora The Red Menace; Godspell; You don't Have To Say You Love Me. Compositions include: Music written or arranged for television: The Detectives; The Hypnotic World of Paul McKenna; The Jasper Carrott Trial; The Ward; What's Cooking?; Scratchy & Co. Compositions for Theatre: Simpleton of the Unexpected Isles; The Good Woman of Setzuan; The Fly. Membership: PRS; FRS; MCPS. Hobbies: Songwriting; Films. Current management: Blaze Music. Address: Upper Flat, 162 George Lane, London E18 1AY, England.

STRADLIN Izzy (Jeffrey Isbell), b. Lafayette, Indiana, USA. Rock Musician (guitar). Career: Member, US heavy rock group, Guns'N'Roses, 1985-91; Regular national/international tours include: US support tours, Mötley Crüe; The Cult; Aerosmith; Get In The Ring tour, with Skid Row, 1991; Major concerts include: Monsters of Rock, Castle Donington, 1988; Farm Aid IV, 1990; Rock In Rio II, Brazil, 1991; Founder, Izzy Stradlin and The Juju Hounds, 1992-. Recordings: Albums: Appetite For Destruction (Number 1, US), 1987; G'N'R Lies (mini-album), 1988; Use Your Illusion I & II (Number 1 and 2, US and UK), 1991; with The Ju-Ju Hounds: Izzy Stradlin and the Ju-Ju Hounds, 1992; 117°, 1998; Hit singles: with Guns'N'Roses: Welcome To The Jungle, 1987; Sweet Child O'Mine (Number 1, US), 1988; Night Train, 1989; Paradise City, 1989; Patience, 1989; Knockin' On Heaven's Door used in film Days Of Thunder, 1990; You Could Be Mine used in film Terminator 2, 1991; Don't Cry, 1991; with Ju-Ju Hounds: Pressure Drop, 1992. Honours: American Music Awards: Favourite Heavy Metal Single, 1989; Favourite Heavy Metal Artist & Album, 1989; Rolling Stone and Billboard magazine awards. Address: c/o Geffen Records, 9130 Sunset Blvd, Los Angeles, CA 90069-6197, USA.

STRAHAN Derek William, b. 28 May 1935, Penang, Malaysia. Composer; Writer; Actor; Singer; Director; Producer. divorced, 1 son, 1 daughter. Education: BA, Cantab Modern Languages, Cambridge University. Career: Singer, Songwriter, topical songs, TV appearances ABCTV, This Day Tonight, ATN7 Breakfast Show, 1970; Actor, Number 96, 1974; Actor Feature Film, Fantasy, 1990; Actor, leading role, Inspector Shanahan Mysteries (Cult of Diana), 1992; Radio Presenter, Words and Music, Eastside Radio FM, 1984-98. Compositions: Concert Music: String Quartet No 1, The Key; Clarinet Quintet No 1 in D, The Princess; Rose of the Bay, song cycle, 1987; String Trio No 1 in F, 1987; Escorts Trio, 1989; China Spring Cello/Piano, 1989; Atlantis, Flute/Piano, 1990; Solo Cello Suite No 1, 1991; Voodoo Fire, Trio, 1994; Eden in Atlantis, Soprano/Flute/Piano, 1995. Recordings: All above on CD except China Spring and Solo Cello Suite No 1; Film Music: 30 documentaries including: Shell's Australia, 13 part, 1969-73; Aliens Among Us & Garden Jungle, 1974; Artisans of Australia, 4 part, 1985; Feature films, Leonora, 1985; Fantasy, 1990; Cult of Diana, 1992. Memberships: Australian Music Centre, represented composer; Fellowship, Australian Composers; APRA; Music Arrangers Guild of Australia; Australian Writers Guild; Media Entertainment and Arts Alliance. Current Management: Revolve Pty Ltd. Addres: PO Box 1003, Marrickville, NSW 2204, Australia.

STRAIT George, b. 18 May 1952, Poteet, Texas, USA. Country Singer. m. Norma, 1 daughter. Education: Agriculture, SW Texas State University. Career: Solo singer, and with own band, Ace In The Hole, formed at college; Recording artist, Nashville, 1981-; Film appearance, The Soldier. Recordings: 31 US Country Number 1 hits include: Fool Hearted Memory, 1982; Amarillo By Morning, 1983; You Look So Good In Love, 1984; Does Fort Worth Ever Cross Your Mind, 1985; Nobody In His Right Mind Would've Left Her, 1986; Am I Blue, 1987; Famous Last Words Of A Fool, 1988; Baby's Gotten Good At Goodbye, 1989; Ace In The Hole, 1989; Love Without End, 1990; I've Come To Expect It From You, 1990; Albums include: Strait Country, 1981; Strait From Your Heart, 1982; Right Or Wrong, 1983; Does Fort Worth Cross Your Mind?, 1984; Something Special, 1985; Merry Christmas Strait To You, 1986; No 7, 1987; Ocean Front Property, 1987; If You Ain't Lovin' (You Ain't Livin'), 1988; Beyond The Blue Neon, 1989; Livin' It Up, 1990; Chill Of An Early Fall, 1991; Holding My Own, 1992; Pure Country, 1992; Lead On, 1995; Strait Out Of The Box, 1996. Honours: CMA Awards: Entertainer Of The Year, 1989, 1990; Male Vocalist Of The Year, 1985, 1986; Album Of The Year, 1985; ACM Awards: Entertainer of The Year, 1990; Male Vocalist Of The Year, 1984, 1985, 1989; American Music Award: Top Country Vocalist, 1991; SRO Touring Artist Of Year, 1990. Memberships: ACM; CMA. Current Management: Erv Woolsey Compnay, 1000 18th Avenue South, Nashville, TN 37212, USA.

STRAND Arthur John Philip, b. 8 Oct 1948, Finchampstead, Berkshire, England. Musician (fretboards, lute, flamenco); Composer. Education: SE Berks College. Musical Education: Private cornet tuition; Then self-taught. Career: Six Minus Two; Sketch; Misty; Concerts, deps, sessions; BBC radio and TV (sound only); US Forces Europe tours and residencies; Songwriting, composing; Studio installation, promotion; Own record label. Compositions: 150 songs, 1964-94; 150 instrumental melodies; 4 fusion longer works, 1985; Supplied sequence for Figure of Eight on Flowers in the Dirt album, Paul McCartney. Recordings: As bassist: If Not For You, Olivia Newton-John; Figure Of Eight, from album Sequence, Paul McCartney. Publication: Poem, Time Itself Imploded, Poetry Now, 1996; Editor, Escutcheon Magazine, 1997-. Memberships: ABJM; BASCA; Musicians' Union; GISC; F/MBF; PPL; Lute Society Flamenco; MCPS; PRS; PAMRA. Hobbies: Cricket (3 clubs); Chairman, Reading Allstars, ACUS and Berks ACUS; Umpire. Current Management: Escutcheon Music. Address: Escutcheon 8 T/Music/Records, 7 Grove Close, Nine Mile Ride, Wokingham, Berkshire, England.

STRAND-HOLM Klaus, b. 6 May 1951, Praestoe, Denmark. Musician. m. Karin Maud Mortensen, 7 April 1985. Education: Selftaught. Career: Released 25 Albums and 40 Singles, Many in Danish Charts, 1969-; Appearances on Television. Recordings: Den Bedste Pige; Lad mig Vaere den; Der' Rock, Der' Pop; 60'er musik; Herstedvester; Bank 3 gange; Oresund; Herlig Herlig; Ring Ring; Ska'det vaere os to; 25 Rode Rosek. Memberships: Dansk Musiker Forbund; KODA; NCB; DPA. Address: Stadionvej 15, 4720 Praestoe, Denmark.

STRANDBERG Orjan, b. 22 August 1956, Stockholm, Sweden. Composer; Lyricist; Musician (Guitar). m. Carina Strandberg, 3 July 1981, 1 daughter. Education: Selftaught. Career: Musician, TV, 1970; Dice, progressive rockgroup, 1974; Dice, first album, 1978; Touring in Sweden and Denmark, until 1980; Signed by Peer Music as Songwriter; JetSet, new group, 2 singles released; Fulltime Composer, commercials & industry, 1980-; Responsible for Swedish script & lyrics for Walt Disney's World in Ice, 1989-. Compositions: Commercials and industrial assignments. Recordings: with Dice: Dice, album, cd, 1978; The Four Riders of the Apocalypse, album, cd, 1992; Live Dice, album, cd, 1993; with JetSet: Rock 'n' Roller Skates, single, 1980; Diamonds for My Hands, single, 1980; Producer, Arranger, All Up to You, by World Youth Choir, single, 1989. Publications: Grönsakernas Hemliga Liv (The Secret Life of Vegetables), 1986; several papers on music and copyright between 1990 and today. Honours: Several awards; Silver Screen Award, 1985. Memberships: Board Member, Swedish Society of Popular Music Composers; Board Member, Swedish Performing Rights Society; Chairman, Swedish Society of Media Composers; Swedish Artists' and Musicians Organisation. Hobbies: Spending time with the family; Drawing; Computing. Current Management: Vision & Sound AB. Address: Vision & Sound AB, Torkils väg 2, S-192 73 Sollentuna, Sweden.

STREET Karen Jane, b. 13 Dec 1959, Burton-On-Trent, England. Musician (saxophone, accordion, clarinet, flute). Musical Education: Bath College of Higher Education; Welsh College of Music and Drama. Career: Member, The Fairer Sax; Member, Saxtet (saxophone quintet); Member, Mike Westbrook Orchestra; Extensive tours; Television and radio appearances include: Wogan; Jim'll Fix It; Blue Peter; Forty Minutes; Radio 3; Nightride; Woman's Hour; Recordings: Diversions; Saxpressions; Comparing Notes; Safer Sax. Publications: Streetwise; Easy Street; Dizzy Duets; Fairer Sax Album 1 and 2; Streetbeats; All Because Of You. Hobbies: Swimming; Tennis. Address: 14 Janice Grove, Yardley Wood, Birmingham B14 4DP, England.

STREET Stephen, b. 29 March 1960, London, England. Record Producer. m. Sarah, 14 August 1987, 2 sons, 1 daughter. Education: Self-taught Guitar, Bass Keyboards. Career: Recording Engineer, Island Records, 1980s; Freelance, after working with The Smiths on 3 albums, 1980s; Co-wrote and Produced Morrissey's First Solo LP, Viva Hate, 1988; Pursued Production career, Indie Music Genre including: Blur, Sleeper, The Cranberries, Psychedelic Furs, Triffids. Compositions: with Morrissey: Viva Hate, album; Suedehead; Singles: Everyday Is Like Sunday; Last of the Famous International Playboys; Interesting Drug. Recordings: The Smith: The Queen is Dead; Strangeways Here We come; Morrissey - Viva Hate; The Cranberries - Everybody Else is Doing It; No Need to Argue; Sleeper - The It Girl; Blur - Parklife; The Great Escape; Blur. Honours: Q Magazine, Best Producer, 1995; Brit Awards Nominee, 1995, 1996, 1998. Membership: Re-Pro. Hobbies: Football; Snow Skiing. Current Management: Gailforce Management, 30 Ives Street, London, SW3 2ND, England.

STREISAND Barbra Joan, b. 24 Apr 1942, Brooklyn, New York, USA. Singer; Actress; Director; Producer; Writer; Composer; Philanthropist. m. Elliot Gould, 1963 (divorced 1971), 1 son. Career: Actress since age 15; Recording artist, 1962-; Concerts include: Support to Liberace, Hollywood Bowl, 1963; Madison Square Garden (as part of first tour for 27 years), recorded for later release, 1994; Stage performances include: Nightclub debut, Greenwich Village, 1961; New York theatre debut, Another Evening With Harry Stoones, 1961; I Can Get It For You Wholesale, 1962; Funny Girl, New York 1964, London, 1966; Film appearances: Funny Girl, 1968; Hello Dolly!, 1969; On A Clear Day You Can See Forever, 1970; The Owl And The Pussycat, 1971; What's Up Doc?, 1972; Up The Sandbox, 1972; The Way We Were, 1973; For Pete's Sake, 1974; Funny Lady, 1975; A Star Is Born (also producer), 1976; The Main Event (also producer), 1979; All Night Long, 1981; Yentl (also writer, director, producer), 1984; Nuts (also producer, composer), 1987; The Prince Of Tides (also director, producer), 1990; Television specials: My Name Is Barbra, 1965; Color Me Barbra, 1966; Belle of 14th Street, 1967; A Happening in Central Park, 1968; Musical Instrument, 1973; One Voice, 1976; Barbra Streisand - The Concert (also producer, co-director), HBO, 1994; Executive producer, Silence: The Margarete Cammermeyer Story, NBC, 1995. Recordings: Hits include: You Don't Bring Me Flowers, duet with Neil Diamond, 1978;

Enough Is Enough, duet with Donna Summer; Albums include: The Barbra Streisand Album, 1963; The Second Barbra Streisand Album, 1963; The Third Album, 1964; My Name Is Barbra, 1965; People, 1965; Color Me Barbra, 1966; Je M'Appelle Barbra, 1967; Barbra Streisand: A Happening In Central Park, 1968; What About Me?, 1969; Stoney End, 1970; Barbra Joan Streisand, 1972; Classical Barbra, 1974; The Way We Were, 1974; Lazy Afternoon, 1975; A Star Is Born, 1976; Superman, 1977; Songbird, 1978; Wet, 1979; Guilty (with Barry Gibb), 1980; Memories, 1981; Emotion, 1984; The Broadway Album, 1986; One Voice, 1986; Til I Loved You, 1989; Just For The Record, 1991; Butterfly, 1992; Back To Broadway, 1993; Barbra Streisand - The Concert (album and video), 1994; Soundtracks include: Yentl, 1983; Nuts, 1987; The Prince Of Tides, 1991. Honours: NY Critics Award, Best Supporting Actress, for I Can Get It For You Wholesale, 1962; Variety Poll Award, Best Foreign Actress, for Funny Girl, UK, 1966; Academy Awards: Best Actress, Funny Girl, 1968; Best Composition (joint winner), Evergreen, 1976; Special Tony Award, for Funny Girl, 1970; Golden Globe Awards: Best Actress, Funny Girl, 1968; Best Picture and Best Director, Yentl, 1984; 5 Emmy Awards, My Name Is Barbra, 1966; 5 Emmy Awards, 3 Cable Ace Awards, Barbra Streisand: The Concert, 1994; Peabody Awards: My Name Is Barbra, 1966; Barbra Streisand: The Concert, 1994; Grammy Awards: Best Female Vocalist, 1963, 1964, 1965, 1977, 1986; Best Songwriter (with Paul Williams), 1977; Awarded 37 Gold and 21 Platinum albums; Only artist to have US Number 1 albums over 4 decades. Address: c/o Barwood Productions, 433 N Camden Drive, Suite 500, Beverly Hills, CA 90210, USA.

STRUMMER Joe (John Mellors), b. 21 Aug 1952, Ankara, Turkey. Musician (guitar); Singer. Career: Founder member, the 101ers, 1974-76; Member, UK punk group The Clash, 1976-86; Appearances include: Support to Sex Pistols, Anarchy In The UK tour, 1976; White Riot UK tour, 1977; European Punk Festival, 1977; Anti-Nazi League Carnival, London, 1978; Kampuchea benefit concert, London, 1979; Support to The Who, farewell US tour, US, 1982; Jamaican World Music Festival, 1982; US '83 Festival, 1983; Roskilde Festival, Denmark, 1985; Regular international tours; Actor, film Straight To Hell, 1986; Compositions include: Film scores: Walker; Permanent Record; Tours with own band, the Latino Rockabilly War, 1988; Actor, Lost In Space, 1989. Recordings: Singles include: Tommy Gun, 1979; I Fought The Law, 1980; London Calling, 1980; Train In Vain (Stand By Me), 1980; Bankrobber, 1980; Should I Stay Or Should I Go?, 1982, reiussed (Number 1, UK), 1991; Rock The Casbah, 1983; Guitarist on: Down In The Groove, Bob Dylan; Vocalist, A Rainy Night In Soho, The Pogues; Albums: The Clash, 1977; Give 'Em Enough Rope, 1978; London Calling, 1979; Black Market Clash, 1980; Sandanista!, 1980; Combat Rock, 1982; Cut The Crap, 1986; The Story Of The Clash Volume 1, 1991; The Singles Collection, 1991; Solo album: Earthquake Weather, 1990; Contributor, Down In The Groove, Bob Dylan, 1988.

STUART Gareth Ian, b. 26 Mar 1963, Bracknell, Berkshire, England. Recording Engineer; Lecturer; Musician (clarinet, saxophone, guitar). m. Amanda Jane, 23 Sept 1989, 1 son. Musical Education: Guildhall School of Music (part time), CCAT, Surrey University. Career: Recording studio owner, engineer, 1986-; Partner, Zigzag Music Productions, 1992-; Sound projectionist for Tim Souster (Equalisation and trumpet concerto); Equale Brass, Chelmsford Festival, Philharmonia, Queen Elizabeth Hall; Sinetone Generator Operator for Stockhausen "Mixtur" with BBC Symphony Orchestra, Barbican. Recordings: Sin Ti Por El Alma Adentro, for album Culture Electroniques, Julio D'Escrivan; Lady Of

The Grave, Faith; Hard 2 Get, Interlude; My Guitar, Bongo Blister; Hold On Tight, Bob And The Bearcats. Publications: Articles on recording equipment, Sound On Sound, 1987-89. Honours: Clarinet (Grade 8); Alto Saxophone (Grade 8); Piano (Grade 6); GMus, Distinction; PG Dip (Tonmeister); Surrey University. Memberships: Associate APRS; Musicians' Union; MCPS. Hobbies: Recording; Songwriting; Skiing. Address: Zigzag Music Productions, Croeso, Church Lane, Hilton, Huntingdon, Cambs PE18 9NH, England.

STUART George K, b. 25 Jan 1951, Edinburgh, Scotland. Musician (drums, percussion). 1 son. Musical Education: Self-taught. Career: Tour with band Scottie, 1975; Support to Showaddywaddy, Shakin' Stevens, and Hello; German tour of American airbases, 1974 and 1976; Television appearance: Arrows, Granada TV, (with Scottie), 1976; Radio appearances with Scottie; Member, Distraction, 1993-. Recordings: with Scottie: Happy Together, 1975; Sweet Rock 'N' Roll, 1976; The Time Has Come, 1976; with West Side Strut: Nothing I Can Do, 1978. Membership: Musicians' Union. Hobbies: Music; Computers; Sport. Address: 9 Victoria Road, Victoria Park, Newton Grange, Edinburgh EH22 4NN, Scotland.

STUART Glenn Douglas, b. 8 May 1932, Elmira, New York, USA. Musician (lead trumpet). m. Laverne, 4 Nov 1981, 1 son, 2 daughters. Musical Education: BS, Ithaca College; MA New York University. Career: Played trumpet with orchestras: Tony Pastor; Richard Hayman; Noro Morales; Ralph Marterie; Vaughn Monroe; Les And Larry Elgart; Tommy Tucker; Hank Levy; Jimmy Dorsey; Stan Kenton, Don Ellis, 1965-; Tours: Canada; Bermuda; Japan; Hawaii; Europe, with Don Ellis, 1969, 1977; Jazz Festivals include: Monterey; New Port; North Sea; Montreux; Pacific; Antibes; Television, films includes: Emmy Awards Banquet; Ed Sullivan Show; Shirley Maclaine Special; Mission Impossible; French Connection I & II; Soupy Sales Special, California; Played with artists including: The Supremes; Frankie Avalon; Joe Williams; Jack Jones; Franki Valli; Chubby Checker; Cleo Laine; Johnny Mathis; Jose Feliciano; Steve Lawrence; Phyllis Diller; Pat Boone; Louis Armstrong; Paul Anka; Teaches trumpet, schools, colleges, California; Lecturer, Clinics, universities, colleges. Recordings include: Featured on album: Autumn, Don Ellis; Single: Child Of Ecstasy, Don Ellis. Publications: The Art Of Playing Lead Trumpet. Honours: Featured soloist at International Trumpet Guild, 1977. Membership: NA of Jazz Educators. Hobby: Boating, mainly sailing 30' sloop. Address: 21682 Ocean Vista Drive, Laguna Beach, CA 92677, USA.

STUART James Hamish, b. 8 Oct 1949, Glasgow, Scotland. Singer; Musician (guitar, bass); Writer. m. Lyn, 2 May, 1 son, 2 daughters. Musical Education: 3 grades piano; Self-taught guitar, bass. Career: Began recording with Dream Police, 1969; Average White Band, 1972-82; Numerous tours, television shows, 1972-82; Tours with Chaka Khan, David Sanborn, numerous writing, production credits, 1982-87; 2 world tours, 5 albums with Paul McCartney. Recordings: Pick Up The Pieces, Person To Person, A Love Of Your Own; Queen Of My Soul; Schoolboy Crush, on 8 Average White Band albums; Flowers In The Dirt; Off The Ground; Paul Is Live; Tripping The Light Fantastic; Unplugged; Albums with Paul McCartney; Atlantic Starr: If Your Heart Isn't In It; Chaka Khan: Whatcha Gonna Do For Me; David Sanborn: Love And Happiness. Honours: 3 Grammy nominations; Many Gold, Platinum records with: Average White Band; Chaka Khan; Paul McCartney. Memberships: ASCAP; AFTRA; PRS. Hobbies: Painting; Football; Food. Current Management: Ramon Hervey. Address: New York, Los Angeles, USA.

STUART Marty, b. 30 Sept 1958, Philadelphia, Pennsylvania, USA. Singer; Musician (guitar, mandolin). Career: Concerts include No Hats Tour, 1992; Television: Marty Party, TNN, 4 shows; The Music Of The Wild West, TNN Special, 1993. Recordings: Hillbilly Rock; Little Things; Tempted; Burn Me Down; Till I Found You; Western Girls (all Top 10). Honours: CMA Award, Vocal Event, with Travis Tritt, 1992; Grammy Awards: Best Vocal Collaboration, with Travis Tritt, 1993; Best Country Instrumental, with Bob Wills, 1994. Membership: Inducted into Grand Ole Opry, 1992. Hobbies: Photography; Collectables. Current Management: Rothbaum and Garner. Address: 119 17th Avenue South, Nashville, TN 37203, USA.

SUCH David, b. 29 June 1954, Cleveland, OH, USA. College Professor; Musician. Education: BA, California State University, 1978; MA, University of California, 1980; PhD, University of California, Los Angeles, 1985. Career: Visiting Assistant Professor, Folklore and Mythology Program, University of California, Los Angeles, 1986; Lecturer, California State University, Northridge, 1987-88; Lecturer, Department of Ethnomusicology and Systematic Musicology, University of California, Los Angeles, 1987-89; Lecturer, Anthropology Department, San Diego State University, 1989-91; Lecturer, Department of Anthropology and Department of Music, Mount San Antonio College, 1995-; Freelance Soloist, Recording Artist, Composer and Producer; Music for a Small Planet: Music Around the World, producer, 1995; Soloist, Qala Al-Rawi-Bedouin Honor and Women's Poetic Tradition, 1994; World Music and Beyond, producer, 1994; Music Director, AVAZ International Music and Dance Troupe, 1986, 1987; Music Director and Composer, Theater of the Ear, KPFK radio, 1981-82. Publications: Books: Avant-garde Jazz Musicians: Performing Out There, 1993; Articles: Brown, Marion; Garnet, Carlos; Hemphill, Julius; McIntyre, Ken; Tyler, Charles; The Bodhran: The Blacksheep in The Family of Traditional Irish Musical Instruments, 1985; Manifestations of Cyclic Structures in Indian Classical Music, 1982; Out There: A Metaphor of Transcendence Among New York City, 1981; Jazz in America and South Africa: Social and Musical Parallels, 1981. Honours: California State Graduate Scholarship, 1978-80; Graduate Travel and Research Grant, UCLA, 1980-81; Institute of American Cultures Research Grant, UCLA, 1983; Faculty Research and Travel Grant, UCLA, 1986. Memberships: Society for Ethnomusicology; American Anthropological Association. Address: PO Box 92, Claremont, CA 91711, USA.

SUGAR (Zacharia Hajishacalli), b. 8 July 1954, London, England. Musician (bouzouki, Cypriot flute); Producer. m. Androulla, 24 July 1977, 2 daughters. Education: BTec, Electronics. Musical Education: Master classes, bouzouki, Greece. Career: Toured with Boy George's Jesus Loves You Band; Concerts include: Town and Country; Ronnie Scott's; Royal Festival Hall; Television and radio appearances: The Word; BSB; Birds Of A Feather, BBC; Rhythms Of The World, BBC; The Green Line, CH4; Andy Kershaw Show, BBC Radio 1; Les Nuils, French TV; Cyprus TV and radio performances. Recordings: Produced and recorded 4 Greek albums for ARC Music; Bouzouki player on Mathilda May album; Yamaha instruments for sampling bouzouki for new synth; Bouzouki player on 4 tracks for Boy George; Composer, producer, Cypriot Flute Of Sugar. Publications: Cypriot Flute Of Sugar; Haji-Mike album. Memberships: Musicians' Union; PRS; MCPS. Hobbies: Music; Philosophy; Star Trek; Reading; Family. Address: 7 Bulwer Road, Edmonton, London N18 1QL, England.

SUGGS (Graham McPherson), b. 13 Jan 1961, Hastings, Sussex, England. Singer. m. Bette Bright, 1982. Career: Singer, Madness, 1977-88; Appearances include: 2-Tone Tour, UK, 1979;

Twelve Days Of Madness Tour, 1980; Far East Tour, 1981; Prince' Trust Royal Gala, 1982; Greenpeace benefit, London, 1983; Solo artiste, 1988-; Regular comedy host, Mean Fiddler Club, North London; Manager, The Farm; Film appearances: Dance Craze, 1981; Take It Or Leave It, 1981; Madstock - The Movie, 1992. Recordings: Singles: with Madness include: The Prince, 1979; One Step Beyond, 1979; My Girl, 1980; Night Boat To Cairo, 1980; Baggy Trousers, 1980; Embarrassment, 1980; Return Of The Los Palmas Seven, 1981; Grey Day, 1981; Shut Up, 1981; It Must Be Love, 1982; Cardiac Arrest, 1982; House Of Fun (Number 1, UK), 1982; Driving In My Car, 1982; Our House, 1982; Tomorrow's (Just Another Day), 1982; Wings Of A Dove, 1983; The Sun And The Rain, 1983; Michael Caine, 1984; One Better Day, 1984; Yesterday's Men, 1985; Waiting For The Ghost, 1986; Solo singles: I'm Only Sleeping, 1995; Camden Town, 1995; Cecilia, 1996; Guest vocalist, Picadilly Place, Morrisey, 1988; Albums with Madness: One Step Beyond, 1979; Absolutely, 1980 Seven, 1981; Complete Madness, 1982; The Rise And Fall, 1982; Madness, 1983; Keep Moving, 1984; Mad Not Mad, 1985; Utter Madness, 1986; Divine Madness, 1992; Madstock!, 1992; Solo album: The Lone Ranger, 1995. Honours: Singles Artists Of The Year, NME, 1980; Ivor Novello Award, Best Pop Song, 1983.

SUMEN Jimi, b. 1958, Finland. Musician (guitar). Musical Education: Self-taught. Career: Band won Finnish rock championship, 1977; Record producer, 1980s; Member, Edward Vesala's Sound and Fury. Recordings include: Paintbrush; Rock Pentsemon.

SUMMER Donna (La Donna Adrian Gaines), b. 31 Dec 1948, Dorchester, Massachusetts, USA. Singer; Songwriter; Actress. m. (1) Helmut Sommer, 1971, divorced, 1 child, (2) Bruce Sudano, 16 July 1980, 2 children. Career: Singer, various groups, Boston; Appeared in musicals, Munich, Germany, 1967-75; Also worked as model and backing singer; Solo singer, 1975-; Major appearances include: Music For UNICEF Concert, New York, 1979; 50th American Presidential Gala, 1985; American Music Awards Concert Series, Yokohama, Japan, 1991; Actress, film Thank God It's Friday, 1978; As artist, exhibition of paintings and lithographs, Beverly Hills, California, 1989. Recordings: Albums: Love To Love You Baby, 1976; A Love Trilogy, 1976; Four Seasons Of Love, 1976; I Remember Yesterday, 1977; Once Upon A Time, 1978; Greatest Hits, 1977; Live And More, 1978; Bad Girls, 1979; On The Radio, 1980; The Wanderer, 1980; Donna Summer, 1982; She Works Hard For The Money, 1983; Cats Without Claws, 1984; All Systems Go, 1977; Another Place And Time, 1989; Best Of Donna Summer, 1990; The Donna Summer Anthology, 1993; Hit singles include: Love To Love You Baby, 1976; I Feel Love (Number 1, UK), 1977; Deep Down Inside, from film The Deep, 1977; I Love You, 1978; Love's Unkind, 1978; Last Dance, 1978; MacArthur Park (Number 1, US), 1977; Heaven Knows, 1979; Hot Stuff (Number 1, US), 1979; Bad Girls (Number 1, US), 1979; Dim All The Lights, 1979; No More Tears (Enough Is Enough), duet with Barbra Streisand (Number 1, US), 1979; On The Radio, from film Foxes, 1980; The Wanderer, 1980; Love Is In Control (Finger On The Trigger), 1982; She Works Hard For The Money, 1983; Dinner With Gershwin, 1987; This Time I Know It's For Real, 1989; I Don't Want To Get Hurt, 1989; State Of Independence, 1995. Honours: Oscar, Best Original Song, Heaven Knows, 1979; Grammy Awards: Best Rhythm & Blues Vocal Performance, 1979; Best Rock Vocal Performance, 1980; Best Inspirational Performance, 1984, 1985; American Music Awards: Favourite Female Disco Artist, Disco Single, Disco Album, 1979; Favourite Female Pop/Rock Artist, Favourite Pop/Rock Single, Favourite Female Soul/R&B Artist, 1980;

Star on Hollywood Walk Of Fame, 1992. Current Management: Management Partners, 16161 Ventura Blvd, Suite 661, Encino, CA 91436, USA.

SUMMER Henry Lee, b. 7 May 1960, Evansville, Indiana, USA. Singer; Songwriter; Record Producer; Musician (multi-instrumentalist). Education: Western Wyoming University. Musical Education: Self-taught. Career: National support tours with: Stevie Ray Vaughan; Don Henley; Eddie Money; Richard Marx; .38 Special; Chicago; Cheap Trick; The Doobie Brothers; The Allman Brothers; REO Speedwagon; Also played Indiana State Fair, with John Mellencamp, 1988; Farm Aid IV, with John Mellencamp, Willie Nelson, Guns'N'Roses, Neil Young, Bonnie Raitt, Indiana, 1990; Television appearances: David Letterman; Arsenio Hall; Charlie Rose; Guest VJ-MTV, Rock Line. Recordings: Albums: Stay With Me, 1984; Time For Big Fun, 1986; Henry Lee Summer, 1988; I've Got Everything, 1989; Way Past Midnight, 1991; Slam Drunk, 1993; Tracks for various film soundtracks including Iron Eagle II and Twins. Publications: Song book collections. Honours: BMI Award, Hey Baby, 1991. Memberships: BMI; AFTRA; AFofM. Hobbies: Basketball. Current Management: James Bogard Associates. Address: 7608 Teel Way, Indianapolis, IN 46256, USA.

SUMMERS Andy (Andrew Somers), b. 31 Dec 1942, Poulton-Le-Fylde, Lancashire, England. Musician (guitar); Singer. Career: Guitarist, vocalist, The Police, 1977-1986; Numerous worldwide tours, television, radio appearances with the Police; Began solo recording career, 1987-; Live Music director, The Dennis Miller Show, US television, 1992; Writer, film scores: Weekend At Bernie; 2010. Recordings: Hit singles with The Police: Walking On The Moon; Message In A Bottle; So Lonely; Roxanne; De Do Do Do De Da Da Da; Every Little Thing She Does; Every Breath You Take; Invisible Sun; Can't Stand Losing You; Don't Stand So Close To Me; Spirits In The Material World; Sychronicity; Albums: with The Police: Outlandos D'Amour, 1977; Regatta De Blanc, 1979; Zenyatta Mondatta, 1980; Ghost In The Machine, 1981; Synchronicity, 1983; Solo albums: I Advance Masked, with Robert Fripp, 1982; XYZ, 1987; Mysterious Barricades, 1988; Golden Wire, 1989; Charming Snakes, 1990; World Gone Strange, 1991; Synaesthesia, 1995; The Last Dance Of Mr X, 1998. Honours include: Grammy Awards, with the Police. Current Management: Firstars/Talent Bank Management, Bugle House, 21A Noel Street, London W1V 3PD, England.

SUMNER Bernard (Bernard Dicken), b. 4 Jan 1956, Salford, Lancashire, England. Musician (guitar). Career: Member, Joy Division, 1977-80; Futurama Festival, Leeds, 1979; European tour, 1980; Member, New Order, 1980-; Worldwide tours including Australia; New Zealand; Far East; US; South America; Concerts include: Glastonbury Festival, 1981, 1987; Futurama Festival, 1982; San Remo Festival, 1988; Monsters Of Art tour, with PIL and Sugarcubes, 1989; Reading Festival, 1989; Electronic, 1989; Support to Depeche Mode, Los Angeles Dodgers Stadium, 1990; Cities In The Park Festival, 1991. Recordings: Albums: with Joy Division: Unknown Pleasures, 1979; Closer, 1980; Still, 1981; The Peel Sessions, 1988; Also featured on Short Circuit - Live At The Electric Circus, 1978; with New Order: Movement, 1981; Power Corruption And Lies, 1983; Low Life, 1985; Brotherhood, 1986; Substance, 1987; Technique, 1989; BBC Radio 1 Live In Concert, 1992; Republic, 1993; Substance 1987; with Electronic: Electronic, 1991; Raise the Pressure, 1996; Singles: with Joy Division: Love Will Tear Us Apart, 1980; with New Order include: Ceremony, 1981; Temptation, 1982; Confusion, 1983; Blue Monday, 1983; Thieves Like Us, 1984; Shellshock, from film soundtrack Pretty In Pink, 1986; True Faith, 1987; Touched By The Hand Of God, 1987; Fine Time,

1988; Round And Round, 1989; World In Motion, with England Football Squad (Number 1, UK), 1990; Disappointed, 1992; How Does It Feel?, 1992; Regret, 1993; World (The Price Of Love), 1993; Spooky, 1993; with Electronic includes: Getting Away With It, featuring Neil Tennant, 1984; Get the Measure, 1991; Forbidden City, 1996; For You, 1996. Current Management: Ignition, 54 Linhope Street, London NW1 6HL, England.

SUN Joe, b. 25 Sept 1943, Rochester, Minnesota, USA. Musician; Songwriter. m. Inka Sun Paulsen, 10 Oct 1965. Education: Brown School of Broadcasting, Minneapolis, 1967. Career: National promotions director, Ovation Records, Nashville, 1976-78; Recording artist, 1978-82; Touring musician, songwriter, 1987-; Actor, film Marie - A True Story, 1986. Honour: Most Promising New Country Artist, Billboard, 1979.

SUND John, b. 6 Jan 1957, Copenhagen, Denmark. Musician (guitar); Composer. Education: Self-taught. Career: Debut at age 18 as soloist with the Danish Radio Big Band, 1976; Member of Creme Fraiche Big Band, broadcasting in radio and television, 1978; Permanent member of Danish Radio Jazzgroup, including appearances at Montmarte, 1976-80; Member and Contributor to Danish Radio Workshop/Palle Mikkelborg, 1978-80; Formed own band, John Sund Group, with others including American trumpet player Tim Hagans, 1977-79; Own trio, Trigon, broadcast on DR television, 1982; Played with Bo Stief, Thomas Clausen, Alex Riel, Mads Vinding; Currently leading cross-over ensemble Special Venture. Compositions: Fusion Symphony, extended suite of 8 compositions, 1993. Recordings: with Creme Fraiche: Storyville, 1978; Solo album: John Sund and the Danish Radio Big Band: Fusion Symphony, 1995. Honour: First jazz artist to receive Jacob Gades Grant, 1977. Membership: Society of Danish Jazz, Rock and Folk Composers (DJBFA). Current Management: Special Venture Booking, Wesselsgade 18, 4 tv, 2200 Copenhagen N, Denmark.

SUNDING Per Gunnar, b. 23 Nov 1967, Lund, Sweden. Singer; Songwriter; Producer; Musician (bass). Education: Self-taught guitar and bass. Career: Formed Eggstone with Maurits Carlsson and Patrik Bartosch in 1986; Eggstone founded Tambourine Studios with Tore Johansson and Anders Nordgren in 1991; Studios used by St Etienne and the Cardigans; Founded Vibrafon Records in 1995. Recordings: with Eggstone: Albums: In San Diego, 1992; Somersault, 1994; Vive La Difference, 1997; Producer: 3 Bob Hund albums; 1 Ray Wonder album; Co-producer on Wannadies album Bagsy Me. Membership: SKAP. Current Management: Marcantonio Management. Address: Tambourine Studios, Sofielundsv. 57, 214 34 Malmö, Sweden.

SUONSAARI Klaus, b. 7 Nov 1959, Finland. Musician (drums); Composer. Musical Education: Piano lessons from age 6; Drums from age 14; Studied at Lahti Conservatory; Eastman School Of Music, Rochester, US; Berklee College of Music, Boston, US. Career: Living, working in New York, 1985-; Played with musicians including: Bob Berg; Niels-Henning Orsted-Pedersen; Ray Drummond; Tom Harrell; Mike Mainieri; Niels Lan Doky; Muhal Richard Abrams; International appearances in US; Canada; UK; Scandinavia; Central Europe. Recordings include: Latest album Inside Out, 1995. Address: Siltakatu 5, 18100 Heinola, Finland.

SURNOCK Richard William, b. 19 Oct 1932, Chicago, Illinois, USA. Musician. m. Lynn Margaret Kennaugh, 16 May 1964, 1 son, 2 daughters. Education: Los Angeles City College. Career: Musician with: Buddy Rich, 1956; Mort Sahl and Joanie Sommers, 1958; Murry Arnold,

1960; Jim McDonald Trio, 1965-; Billy Daniels, 1970; Peggy Lee, 1980; Mickey Rooney Show, 1988; Page Cavanaugh, 1990; Palisades Symphony, 1990-.

SUTCLIFFE Jess (Jeremy), b. 25 Nov 1958, London, England. Recording Engineer; Producer. m. Shari Lee Inoue, 25 July 1987, 1 son, 1 daughter. Career: Tape Operator and Assistant Engineer, London Recording Studios, 1977; Independent First Engineer, 1979; Engineer for Vangelis, 1982-86; Recording Engineer for films, records, and TV commercials; Freelance Engineer and Producer, 1987; Moved to Los Angeles, 1988. Recordings: Artists include: Vangelis; Toto; Aretha Franklin; Jon and Vangelis; Carlene Carter; Sheila E; Quincy Jones; Patti LaBelle; Willie Nelson; Patti Austin; Gary Numan; Elvis Costello; Sheena Easton; Wall of Voodoo; The Fall; Handel's Messiah; Film scores include: The Bounty; Boyz 'n the Hood. Honours: Platinum records; Grammy Winning Records. Memberships: NARAS. Current Management: Belgravia Music. Address: Belgravia Music, 22647 Ventura Boulevard, Suite 301, Woodland Hills, CA 91364, USA.

SUTTON Chris, b. 25 Dec 1960, Essex, England. Vocalist; Songwriter; Musician (piano, keyboards). m. Elaine Sutton, 1 daughter. Career: First solo album with 22, produced by Motown producer Dennis Lambert; Support to James Brown, Wembley Arena, London; 2 Top 100 singles, Germany airplay. Compositions: That's Her Way, 1994; However Long It Takes, 1994; Miracle, 1994. Recordings: That's Her Way; However Long It Takes; Album: Songs Into The Light; Recorded with Paul McCartney, George Michael and Mark Knopfler; Singer, Knee Deep in the Hoopla album, Starship. Membership: PRS. Hobby: Sport. Address: c/o BME Records, Postbox 450224, 50877 Cologne, Germany.

SUTTON Graham Paul, b. 1 Apr 1972, Stratford, London, England. Songwriter; Singer; Producer; Multi-instrumentalist. Career: Formed Bark Psychosis, 1987; Left school and home to pursue music at 16; Recorded several independently released and critically acclaimed EPs; Signed to Circa Records; Worked with: Lee Harris, Paul Webb of Talk Talk under name Orang; Also records under name Boymerang. Recordings: Albums: Bark Psychosis: Hex, 1994; Independency, compilation of previous EPs, 1994. Memberships: Musicians' Union; PRS; MCPS. Hobbies: Graphic design; Alcohol. Current Management: Mike Collins. Address: 40 Abbotsford Gardens, Woodford Green, Essex IG8 9HW, England.

SVARE Jorgen Christian, b. 28 December 1935, Copenhagen, Denmark. Musician. 2 sons, 1 daughter. Education: Selftaught. Career: Clarinet Player, Local Bands, 1950's; Founder Member, Papa Bue's Viking Jazz Band, 1956; Played and Toured Worldwide, 30 years; Club Owner, Jazz Club, Slukefter Jazzhus, Tivoli Gardens, Copenhagen, 1994-97. Composition: Slukefter Blues. Recordings: Over 60 Albums with Papa Bue. Honour: Sorens Penge, Denmark, 1996. Membership: Danish Society of Band Leaders. Address: Peder Hvitfelats Straede 11, DK-1173 Copenhagen, Denmark.

SVENNINGSSON Uno, b. 1 July 1959, Jönköping, Småland, Sweden. Singer; Songwriter. m. Carina Bihli, 11 Sept 1993, 1 son. Career: Singer, songwriter, rock group Freda, 1983-1993; Solo artist, 1994-; Numerous television and radio appearances, major Swedish programmes. Recordings; En Människa, 1984; Välkommen Hero, 1986; Tusen Eldar, 1988; Undan För Undan, 1990; Alla Behöver, 1993; Freda Samling, 1993; Uno, 1994. Honours: Swedish Grammy Award, Best Rock Group, 1991; RockBjörnen Award, Best Male Artist, 1994; The Mozart Prize, Best Male Artist, 1994. Hobbies: Reading; Films; Music. Current Management: The Record Station.

Address: The Record Station, BMG Ariola, PO Box 1026, 17221 Sundbyberg, Sweden.

SWAN Billy, b. 12 May 1942, Cape Giardeau, Missouri, Canada. Singer; Songwriter; Musician (Guitar, Bass, Keyboards). m. Marlu, 2 daughters. Career: Musical Director, Filmography: A Thing Called Love, coached River Phoenix; Wild At Heart, acted and sang; Songwriter, Willie Nelson and Kris Krisofferson; Assistant Music Director, Great Balls of Fire; As You Like It, Scored and played singing minstrel; Toured with: T Bone Burnett; Kinky Friedman and The Texas Jewboys; Billy Joe Shaver; Black Tie; Harry Dean Stanton and Kris Kristofferson. Recordings: Albums: I Can Help; Rock 'n' Roll; Billy Swan; Four; You're OK, I'm OK; I'm Into Lovin' You; Black Tie; Recent Releases: Billy Swan's Best, 1993; Vinyl Junkie Country, Undying Love, 1995; The Sun Studio Story: Rockabilly B; Lonely Weekends, 1995; Bop To Be, 1995; Billy Swan Live, 1996; Billy Swan, Choice Cuts, 1997; The Best of Billy Swan, 1997; Billy Swan - collectibles, 1997; I Can Help/Rock 'n' Roll Moon and Billy Swan/Four - See For Miles, 1997. Current Management: Dennis Muirhead, Muirhead Management, 202 Fulham Road, Chelsea, London SW10 9PJ, England. Address: Chelsea, London, SW10 9PJ, England.

SWAN Ren. Mix Engineer; Engineer. Career: Engineering work for Jon Douglas on: Salt 'N' Pepa, Champagne 7"; Michelle Gayle, Do You Know, Sensational; Remix of Clementine for Mark Owen with Grant Mitchell (3 UK charts); Working on Gary Barlow's forthcoming album with Grant and Gary; Remixed, Above the Law, The Evil That Men Do; Working on Dee Ellington (RCA) Album; Currently engineering and mixing, with Grant Mitchell, Connor Reeves Album, Wildstar/Telstar; Working with Jon Douglas on All Saints; Engineering and mixing credits include: George Michael, Older; Eternal, including: Stay, Oh Baby I, Good Thing; Michael Jackson, Wanna Be Starting Something mix; De La Soul, Ring Ring; Aswad, Close to You, 7" and 12" remix; Pet Shop Boys, Where The Streets Have No Name 7". Address: SARM Productions, SP2 Holdings Ltd, The Blue Building, 42/46 St Luke's Mews, London W11 1DG, England.

SWANSON David James, b. 15 Aug 1951, Edinburgh, Scotland. Musician (percussion). 1 daughter. Musical Education: Studied with James Catherwood privately; 1 year music course at college. Career: Played with many jazz stars including: Joe Temperley; Roy Williams; Kenny Davern; Buddy DeFranco; Tal Farlow; Louis Stewart; Tour of Middle East with Demis Roussos; Television appearances with: Tam White; Benny Waters; Healing Force; Craig McMurdo; Radio with George Chisholm; Recent tour with Herb Geller; Featured in Edinburgh Jazzfest with Alex Shaw Trio, 1997; Tutor with Fyjo and Nyjos; Member, Jack Duff Quintet. Membership: Chairman, Edinburgh Branch, Musician's Union. Hobbies: Music; Snooker; Cooking. Address: c/o Musician's Union, 1 Seafield Road East, Edinburgh, Scotland.

SWANT Doc (Barclay-Ron Swant), b. 4 Jan 1950, Eganuille, Ontario, Canada. Musician (drums, guitar). m. Sharon Jane Hill, 9 Sep 1972, 1 son. Education: College. Musical Education: Self-taught. Career: Songwriter since age 14; Actor in 2 Canadian films; Appeared on local TV shows; Sung in local pubs and at festivals. Recordings: My Nashville Country Home, Keith Bradford; Friends Of The Flag, Jack Greene; A Tennessee Saturday Night, Tommy Cash. Memberships: CCMA; BMI; International Productions. Hobbies: Hockey; Golf; Chess; Writing. Current Management: Watermain Songwriters: Four Guitar Productions. Address: 205 Romulus Priv, Ottawa, Ontario K1K 3Y2, Canada.

SWINFIELD Raymond, b. 14 Dec 1939, Sydney, Australia. Musician (saxophone, clarinet, flutes). m. Rosemarie, Sept 1970, divorced 1991. Career: Played on recordings by: Quincy Jones; Robert Farnon; Henry Mancini; Pat Williams; Ella Fitzgerald; The Beatles; Phil Woods; Michel Legrand; Kiri Te Kanawa; Stéphane Grappelli; Johnny Mercer; J J Johnson. Compositions: Sydney Suite; Rain Curtain; Caroline; Thinking On It. Recordings: Albums: Rain Curtain; The Winged Cliff; Angel Eyes. Honours: Own albums listed amongst jazz records of the Year in Gramaphone Jazz Journal magazines. Memberships: PRS; British Jazz Musicians. Address: c/o Musicians' Union, National Office, 60/62 Clapham Road, London SW9 0JJ, England.

SYKES John, b. 29 July 1959. Rock Musician (guitar); Songwriter. Career: Guitarist, UK rock groups Streetfighters; Tygers Of Pan Tang, 1980-81; Thin Lizzy, 1982-83; Concerts include: UK tour, 1982; Tours, Europe, Japan, 1983; Reading Festival, 1983; Monsters Of Rock European tour, 1983; Guitarist, Whitesnake, 1984-86; Tours, UK, Europe, 1984; US tours with Dio and Quiet Riot, 1984; Rock In Rio (largest ever rock festival), 1985. Compositions: Co-writer with David Coverdale: Still Of The Night; Is This Love?. Recordings: Albums: with Tygers Of Pan Tang: Spellbound, 1981; Crazy Nights, 1981; with Thin Lizzy: Thunder And Lightning, 1983; with Whitesnake: Slide It In, 1984; Whitesnake, (Number 2, US), 1987; Singles: with Thin Lizzy: Hollywood; Cold Sweat; Thunder And Lightning; The Sun Goes Down; with Whitesnake: Give Me More Time; Standing In The Shadow; Love Ain't No Stranger. Honours: Platinum and Gold discs. Current Management: Music Group Management. Address: 3500 West Olive, Suite 950, Burbank, CA 91505, USA.

SYLVAIN Dominique, b. 17 Nov 1959, New York, USA. Haïtian Singer; Author; Composer. 1 daughter. Education: DEA, degree in Anthropology. Musical Education: Piano, guitar, percussion, voice. Career: Concerts include: L'Espace Julien (Marseilles), 1993; Pollen France Inter, 1994; L'Opus Café (Paris); Festival d'Été de Besauçon, 1995; 2 broadcasts for France Inter radio; Television appearances: Antenne 2; RFO. Recordings: Reconnais, 1994. Honour: First Prize, Choreography and Interpretation, FFD, 1990. Memberships: SACEM; ADAMI; SACED. Current Management: Myriam Willis. Address: Axile 37 Rue Doudeauville, F-75018 Paris, France.

SYLVESTRE Frédéric, b. Angouleme, France. Musician (guitar, synthesizer guitar). Career: Played with artists including: Eddy Louiss; Martial Solal; Christian Escoudé; Marcel Azzola; Michel Graillier; Bernard Lubat; Alain Jean-Marie; Pepper Adams; Albi Cullaz; Tania Maria; Claude Cagnasso; Aldo Romano; Marc Bertaux; Jacques Vidal; Eric Le Lann; Gérard Marais; Jean-Louis Chautemps; Sacha Distel; Philip Catherine; Didier Levallet; Marcel Azzola; Jimmy Gourley; Georges Arvanitas; Luigi Trussardi. Recordings: Five Compact, Claude Cagnasso Big Band; with the Dolphin Orchestra: Prologue; Olympia Live; Rencontre; with Jacques Vidal: Premier Grand Cru; 2+; Hommages; Trio Live; Capricorne; with Martial Solal Big Band: Martial Solal Big Band Joue André Hodeir; Big Band de Guitares de Gerard Marais, Gerard Marais; Music Band, Teddy Lasry; Dolores, Jean-Marc Jafet; Gipsy Waltz, Christian Escoudé Octet; Salena Jones Sings Cole Porter; Holidays, Christian Escoudé; News Of Bop, Jacques Vidal Quintet; Trio Sur Seine, with Marcel Azzola. Hobby: Tennis. Address: 31 Rue de Fontarabie, 75020 Paris, France.

SYLVIAN David (David Batt), b. 23 Feb 1958, Beckenham, Kent, England. Singer; Musician (guitar). Career: Singer, guitarist, Japan, 1977-82; Solo artiste, 1982-; Member, Rain Tree Crow (with 3 members of Japan), 1991.

Recordings: Albums: with Japan: Adolescent Sex, 1978; Obscure Alternatives, 1978; Quiet Life, 1980; Gentlemen Take Polaroids, 1980; Assemblage, 1981; Tin Drum, 1981; Oil On Canvas, 1983; Exorcising Ghosts, 1984; Solo albums: Brilliant Trees, 1984; Alchemy, An Index of Possibilities, 1985; Gone To Earth, 1986; Secrets Of The Beehive, 1987; Plight And Premonition, with Holger Czukay, 1988; Flux and Mutability (with Holger Czukay), 1989; Weather Box, 1989; Ember Glance, The Permamence Memory (with Russell Mills), 1991; with Rain Tree Crow: Rain Tree Crow, 1991; with Robert Fripp: The First Day, 1993; Damage, (with Robert Fripp) 1994; Guest singer, Dreams Of Reason Produce Monsters, Mick Karn, 1987; Singles include: with Japan: Life in Tokyo, 1979; The Art Of Parties, 1981; Quiet Life, 1981; Ghosts, 1982; Cantonese Boy, 1982; Night Porter, 1982; Canton, 1983; Solo: Red Guitar, 1984; The Ink In The Well, 1984; Pulling Punches, 1984; Taking The Veil, 1986; Let The Happiness In, 1987; with Ryûichi Sakamoto: Forbidden Colours, from film Merry Christmas Mr Lawrence, 1983. Current Management: Opium (Arts) Ltd, 49 Portland Road, London W11 4LJ, England.

SYMES Ivan Douglas, b. 9 Feb 1961, Cuckfield, Sussex, England. Writer; Producer; Musician (keyboards, guitar). Musical Education: Self-taught. Career: Rhythm guitarist, rock band: Suspect; Guitarist, band: Times Begins; Assistant to writer, Best of British, BBC1; Rivals, BBC2; Library albums KPM; Boosey and Hawkes; Sound Design; Hot Air Fashion Show, Islington Design Centre; Film: Roadside; Queens Park Rangers, official season, 1993-94; British Open Golf Championships, 1994. Memberships: Musicians' Union. Hobbies: Writing; Reading; Concept design. Address: 10 Tythe Barn, Bolney, West Sussex RH17 5PH, England.

SZABO Richard Wayne, b. 16 Mar 1956, Newark, New Jersey, USA. Musician (trumpet); Bandleader. Education: BA, Music Education, Fairleigh Dickinson University, Madison, New Jersey, USA. Career: Played in bands of Maynard Ferguson; Buddy Rich; Ray Anthony; Sammy Kaye; Guy Lombardo; Tito Puente; Billy May; Xavier Cugat; Frank Sinatra Jr; Appeared or recorded with: Melissa Manchester; The Grass Roots; Mel Torme; Johnny Desmond; Margaret Whiting; Helen Forrest; Regis Philbin; The Four Tops; The Four Lads; The Four Aces; The Chordettes; Author (screenplay): College Inc, 1984; Traffic Vigilante, 1986; Music director, Station WPCN-AM Radio, Pennsylvania, 1988. Recordings: Manhattan At Dusk; Best Of Both Worlds; Big Bands 80s, Various Artists Vols 3 and 4; Jumpin' On The Bandstand. Honours: Listed in Who's Who in Entertainment. Memberships: Songwriters Hall Of Fame; NARAS; AFofM; AFTRA; IJAE. Hobbies: Golf; Fishing; Photography. Current Management: Al Bauman, Fame Management, 939 Kimball Street, Phildelphia, PA 19147, USA.

SZAWLOWSKI William Stephen, b. 24 Mar 1955, Montreal, Quebec, Canada. Record Producer; Engineer; Arranger; Writer. m. Margaret Lilliane Boutet, 6 Sept 1975, 2 sons. Career: Assistant recording engineer, 1974-75; Recording engineer, 1976-83; President, SCI Productions, Record Producer, 1984-90; Independent Record Producer, Engineer, Arranger, 1991-; Recordings: Producer for: Marjo; Marie-Carmen; Ray Lyell; Engineer for: April Wine; Aldo Nova; Frank Marino; Robbie Robertson; Helix; Luba; Teaze; Murray Head; Walter Rossi; Cirque du Soleil; Diane DuFresne; Kashtin; Pagliaro; Nanette Workman. Honours: 27 Gold and Platinum discs; ADISQ Award, Best Engineer, 1987. Membership: SOCAN. Hobbies: Home renovation; Cooking; Computers. Address: 7195 Mauriac Street, Brossard, Quebec J4Y 1T8, Canada.

SZCZESNIAK Mieczyslaw Wojciech, b. 9 July 1964, Kalisz, Poland. Vocalist. Musical Education: Academy of Music, Katowice. Career: Many television and radio appearances, concerts and recitals, Poland and abroad; Pop and jazz festivals include: Jazz Jamboree, Warsaw; Gospel festivals. Recordings include: Debut: Niby Nowy, 1990. Honours: Sopot Festival, 1989; Bresenz Intertalent, 1989; Golden Orpheus, 1990; Cesmè Festival, 1990; Golden Record of Nashville (FIDOF) 1990. Memberships: STOMUR (Polish Society of Pop Musicians); PSJ (Polish Society of Jazz). Address: Plac Wolnica 11/11, 31-060 Krakow, Poland.

T

TABOR June, b. 31 Dec 1947, Warwick, Warwickshire, England. Folk Singer. Career: Singer of contemporary and traditional songs; Various collaborations with: Martin Simpson; Maddy Prior (as the Silly Sisters); The Oyster Band; Hugh Warren; Nic Jones; Martin Carthy; Peter Bellamy; The Albion Band; Fairport Convention. Recordings: Albums: Airs And Graces, 1976; Ashes And Diamonds, 1977; Bees On Horseback, 1977; A Cut Above, with Martin Simpson, 1980; Abyssinians, 1983; Theme From Spy Ship, 1983; The Peel Sessions, 1986; Silly Sisters, with Maddy Prior, 1986; Aqaba, 1988; Some Other Time, 1989; No More To The Dance, with Maddy Prior, 1990;Aspects, 1990; Angel Tiger, 1992. Current Management: NE Music Management, Priory House, 55 Lawe Road, South Shields, Tyne & Wear NE33 2AL, England.

TACUMA Jamaaladeen (Rudy MacDaniel), b. 11 June 1956, Hempstead, New York, USA. Musician (double bass); Composer. Musical Education: Double bass from age 13. Career: Session musician, 1977-; Played with Charles Earland; Ornette Coleman's band Prime Time; Jeff Beck; Jayne Cortez (poet); Solo recording artiste, 1983-; Founder, own dance band Cosmetic, 1983-; Founder member, Golden Palominos; Concerts include: Recital with the Ebony String Quartet, Carnegie Hall, 1985. Recordings: Albums: Solo: Showstopper, 1983; Renaissance Man, 1984; Music World, 1987; Juke Box, 1989; Boss Of The Bass, 1993; with Cosmetic: So Tranquilizin', 1984; with Ornette Coleman/Prime Time: Dancing In Your Head, 1977; Body Meta, 1978; Of Human Feelings, 1979; Opening At The Caravan Of Dreams, 1985; In All Languages, 1987; with James Blood Ulmer: Tales Of Captain Black, 1978; As producer: (I Want To) Squeeze You Hold You, Willy De Ville, 1983. Honour: Downbeat Poll, Talent Deserving Wider Recognition (most votes ever), 1981.

TADMAN Tad (Paul Tadman), b. 19 Oct 1969, Sutton, Surrey, England. Musician (bass guitar). Education: Wimbledon School of Art. Musical Education: Mainly self-taught. Career: Member, Nutty Boys; Television appearances: TXT, ITV; The Big E, ITV; 100% programme, BBC; Radio sessions on BBC and GLR. Recordings include: It's OK I'm A Policeman, Nutty Boys (EP and video), 1992. Membership: Musicians' Union. Hobbies include: Photography; Classic Cars. Current Management: Universal, Railton Road, London SE24, England. Address: c/o PO Box 3087, London NW5 3DZ, England.

TAFFOUREAU Eric, b. France. Record Company Executive; Concert Promoter; Recording Studio Manager; Singer. Career: Reporter, photographer, music and fashion Press Agency, 1979-84; Created Entertainment industry magazine, For Ever, 1981; Tour organizer, venues across Paris, 1982; Popular television and radio celebrity; Organizer, annual Starockmania festival (charity event); Formed Valotte Records, UK, France, 1987; Manager, Chateau of Valotte recording studio, Burgundy (used by Julian Lennon and Thomas Dolby); Organizer variety of showcase concerts in London, including: Marquee Club; 100 Club; Dingwall's tour; Producer, album, Vince Taylor; Singer, The London Buses, including Number 1 and UK tour. Honours: Invited by François Mitterand to Rights of Man Evening; Invited by Jacques Chirac to Mairie De Paris, 1995, 1996. Address: Valotte Records, 138 Rue Nationale, BP 46, F-75013 Paris, France; Valotte Recording Studio, Domaine de la Garenne, F-58440 La Celle Sur Loire, France.

TAFJORD Stein Erik, b. 2 Nov 1953, Langevag, Norway. Musician (tuba). m. 1 Sept 1973-93, 3 daughters. Musical Education:

Norwegian State Academy of Music. Career: Norwegian Radio symphony Orchestra; Carla Bley Scandinavian Orchestra; Lester Bowie; David Murrey's Jazz Baltica Ensemble; The Brazz Brothers; Soloist, several TV-radio productions in Europe, USA. Recordings: Participated on approximately 120 recordings, 16 with own band. Honours: Jazz Musician of the Year, Norway, 1991. Membership: Norwegian Musicians' Union. Address: Vennersborgveien 14dj, N-0281 Oslo, Norway.

TALBOT Jamie Robert, b. 23 Apr 1960, London, England. Musician (saxophone, clarinet, flute). m. Clare, 4 Nov 1988, 1 son. Musical Education: Centre for Young Musicians, RCM (briefly). Career: Worked with: Stan Tracy; John Dankworth; Cleo Laine; Gil Evans; Ella Fitzgerald; Nelson Riddle; Frank Sinatra; Shorty Rogers; Natalie Cole. Recordings: Altitude, Jamie Talbot Sextet; Live At Ronnie Scott's, Stan Tracey; Genesis, Stan Tracey; Suddenly Last Tuesday, Clark Tracey. Address: 34 Elmers End Road, Anerley, London SE20 7SN, England.

TALGORN Frederic, b. 2 July 1961, Toulouse, France. Education: With Professors of Paris Conservatory. Career: Films: The Temp; Fortress; Le Brasier; Delta Force 2; Robottox; Edge of Sanity; Young Indiana Jones; Momty Der Spimmerratz. Compositions: Concerto for Percussions and Orchestra; Elegy for Double Bass and Strings; Vinura et San Guiness, Cantata; Concerto for Trumpet and Orchestra; Olympus for Brass Ensemble. Recordings: Vinura et San Guiness; Elegy for Double Bass and Orchestra; Olympus. Memberships: ASCAP; SACEM. Current Management: Paul Talkington (Europe); Film Music Associates (USA). Address: c/o FMI, 9465 Wilshire Boulevard, Suite 405, Beverly Hills, CA 90212, USA.

TAMINIAUX Eric, b. 13 March 1963, La Hestre, Belgium. Education: Germanic Languages College, 1981-84; 3 Years, Music School; Selftaught Guitarist. Career: First Band, 17 years old; Singer, Guitarist, Halloween, support act for various Belgian bands, 1983-94; Singer, Guitarist, Check Point Charlie, support act for French band Miossec, 1994-. Compositions: With Halloween: Somebody Else Is You, 1991; Nameless People's Hotel, 1993; With Check Point Charlie, 12 Tracks Recorded. Membership: Belgian Society of Authors, Composers and Publishers. Hobby: Fishing. Current Management: Keylight. Address: c/o Keylight, Rue Amerique 79, B-6120 Ham Sur Heure, Belgium.

TAMPIER Karel, b. 24 June 1946, Ceské, Budejovice. Composer; Songwriter. m. Jitka Tichovská, 21 June 1974, 3 daughters. Education: Piano lessons, 9 years; Selftaught Guitar, Mandolin, Keyboards. Career: Leader, Guitar, Mandolin Player, Bluegrass Group, Bobri, 1970-84; Leader, Piano - GR, Zridlo, The Source, 1979-85; Countryfuga, family group with wife and 3 daughters, 1989-93; Concerts in clubs and festivals in Czechoslovakia; About 100 songs recorded in Czech radio; 10 performances in Czech and Slovak TV; Music for Theatre. Compositions: Proc Jsem Mrtev? (Why Do I Death?); Postel (The Bed) - Song and Musical. Recordings: Bobri, 1977-80, 1994. Honours: Czech Country and Folk Festival, Porta: Main prizes for interpretation, 1978, 1979, 1980; Main prize for songwriter, 1984. Hobbies: Literature; Hiking. Current Management: Studio Pod Sítí, Na Mlynské Stoce 11, 370 01 Ceské, Budejovice, Czech Republic. Address: Staromestská 9, 37004 Ceské Budejovice, Czech Republic.

TANSLEY Darren, b. 30 Jan 1966, West Hornden, Essex, England. Musician (piano, keyboards). Career: Keyboard player, Blyth Power, 1990-95; Formed Downwarde Spiral Records, to release Blyth Power's albums, 1993; Founder, Press To Play Live booking agency,

1995; Tours with Blyth Power: UK; Europe; Former Yugoslavia; Australia. Compositions include: Title track of album Pastor Skull. Recordings: with Blyth Power: The Guns Of Castle Cary, 1991; Pastor Skull, 1993; Paradise Razed, 1995; Guest musician, Irish whistle, A Million Suns, The Killjoys, 1993. Memberships: Musicians' Union; PRS. Hobbies: Animal rights; Dungeons And Dragons. Address: 25 Mill Street, Colchester, Essex CO1 2AH, England.

TANT Jean Arthur Jozef, b. 26 Mar 1956, Ostend, Belgium. Artist Manager. m. Reynaert Rose Tant, 5 Aug 1983, 2 sons, 2 daughters. Career: Sales Department, Daikin Europe; Sales Department, Cera-Bank; Director of record shop, Podium; Director, Kras Artists; Director, Witlof Music. Membership: Financial Director, Belgian Union of Booking Agencies. Hobbies: Music; Holidays. Address: Leernsestw 168, B-9800 Deinze, Belgium.

TANT Jean-Christophe, b. 12 Feb 1962, Lille, France. Singer; Composer; Musician (guitar). Education: Degree, Plastic Arts. Musical Education: Academy of Music, Lille. Career: Performed at festivals including: Montreal; Munchen-Gladbach; Edinburgh; Lille; Jelena Gora; Jazz Valley, Paris; Singapore; Television appearances: France: FR3, M6, A2; Poland, Channel 1; Radio appearances: France Inter, Europe 2, Frequence Nord. Honour: Golden Nono (Wazemmes), France. Membership: SACEM. Current Management: Lyse Bochner.

TAPIO Jorma Ilmari, b. 6 Aug 1957, Mikkeli, Finland. Musician (alto saxophone, bass clarinet, flutes, percussion). Musical Education: Piano, private lessons, aged 6; Violin, flutes and saxophone at music school; Lessons from Pekka Pöyry, Juhani Aaltonen and Edward Vesala. Career: Member, trio Lavantairyhmä, 1980-82; Member, traditional tango band, rock groups and big bands; Own tapes for radio, television documentaries, theatre, film pieces and dance performances; Numerous tours with Krakatau; Tours, recordings, television appearances and two documentary films with Edward Vesala; Founder, own group Rolling Thunder, 1995-97; Also solo appearances. Recordings: with Krakatau: Ritual, 1988; with Edward Vesala's Sound and Fury: Lumi, 1985; Ode To The Death Of Jazz, 1989; Invisible Storm, 1991; Nordic Gallery, 1994. Current Management: Self-managed. Address: Agricolankuja 2 C 96, 00530 Helsinki, Finland.

TARDLEY Ken, b. 5 Oct 1949, Rotherham, Yorkshire, England. Musician (Dobro); Bandleader; University Lecturer. m. Lorretta Tardley, 12 Aug 1982, 1 daughter. Education: BSc Hons, Chemistry, MSC, Systems Analysis, PGCE. Musical Education: Elkins College, West Virginia, 1990, 1995. Career: Member, US band, Muleskinner, 1990-92; Member, Sound In Mind, 1985-93; Member, Generation Gap, 1992-94; Toured USA, 1994; DJ, WTHO radio, Thompson, Georgia, USA; Curator, Dalebilly Museum, Airdale Drive, Howarth. Recordings: Riding Down The Canyon, Sound In Mind, 1989; Muleskinner, 1990. Publications: Staff writer, British Bluegrass News. Honours: King of The Dalebilly Dobro Players, 1995. Membership: Founder member, British Bluegrass Music Association. Hobbies: Management Cybernetics; Real Ale. Current Managment: Loretta Tardley. Address: 65 Gledholt Bank, Huddersfield, West Yorkshire HD1 4HE, England.

TASHIAN Barry M, b. 5 Aug 1945, Oak Park, Illinois, USA. Musician (guitar); Singer; Songwriter. m. Holly Kimball, 1 Nov 1972, 2 sons. Education: 2 years college, Boston University. Musical Education: Guitar, keyboards, vocal studies since childhood. Career: Founder, leader, Barry and the Remains, 1964-66; Ed Sullivan Show; Hullaballoo; Beatles US Tour, 1966; Guitarist, singer, with Emmylou Harris, 1980-90; Toured worldwide; The

Tonight Show; David Letterman; Duet with spouse as Barry and Holly Tashian, tour: USA; Europe; Canada; Australia; Grand Ole Opry; Recorded with Nanci Griffith, Iris Dement. Compositions: 3 songs for Daniel O'Donnell, Nashville Bluegrass Band; Two Ways to Fall, title song of album by Ty England. Recordings: The Remains, 1966; 4 albums as Barry and Holly Tashian; Harmony. Honours: Indie Award, Country Album Of The Year, Straw Into Gold. Memberships: AFofM; IBMA; NARAS; AFTRA; BMI. Current Management: Tashian Music. Address: POB 150921, Nashville, TN 37215-0921, USA.

TASHIAN Holly P, b. 8 Jan 1946, New York, USA. Singer; Songwriter; Musician (guitar). m. Barry Tashian, 1 Nov 1972, 2 sons. Education: BA Psychology, 1 year graduate. Musical Education: Private lessons, violin, piano, voice. Career: As act Barry and Holly Tashian; Television: Grand Ole Opry Live; American Music Shop; Backstage Opry; Radio: Grand Ole Opry; Prairie Home Companion. Compositions: Songs recorded by Nashville Bluegrass Band and Ty England; Daniel O'Donnell; Roland White; Jody Stecher; Kate Brislin. Recordings: Albums: Trust In Me; Live In Holland; Ready For Love; Straw Into Gold; Harmony; Recordings with: Nanci Griffith; Delia Bell. Honours: NAIRD (National Association of Independent Records Distributors); Country Album of the Year, Straw Into Gold, 1995. Memberships: ASCAP; AFofM; IBMA; NARAS; Folk Alliance. Hobbies: Dogs; Cooking. Current Management: Tashian Music. Address: Tashian Music, PO Box 150921, Nashville, TN 37215, USA.

TATE Geoff. Vocalist. Career: Lead singer, US rock group Queensrÿche, 1981-. Recordings: Albums: Queen Of The Reich (EP), 1983; The Warning, 1984; Rage For Order, 1985; Operation - Mindcrime, 1988; Empire, 1990; Promised Land, 1994; Singles include: Silent Lucidity; Best I Can; Jet City Woman. Current Management: Q-Prime Inc., 729 Seventh Avenue, 14th Floor, New York, NY 10019, USA.

TAUPIN Bernie, b. 22 May 1950, Lincolnshire, England. Songwriter. Career: Long-term songwriting partnership with Elton John, 1967-. Compositions: As co-writer with Elton John: Albums with Elton John: All albums, 1969-77; Too Low For Zero, 1983; Sleeping With The Past, 1989; Two Rooms - Celebrating The Songs Of Elton John and Bernie Taupin, 1992; Numerous hits include: Don't Let The Sun Go Down On Me; Crocodile Rock; Rocket Man; Scarifice; Sorry Seems To Be The Hardest Word; Daniel; Saturday Night's Alright For Fighting; Other co-compositions include: Skyline Pigeon, Roger Cook, 1968; I Can't Go On Living Without You, 1969; Snookeroo, 1975. Honours: Ivor Novello Awards: Best Song, Daniel, 1974; Sacrifice, 1991; MTV Award, Special Recognition Trophy, 1987; Inducted into Songwriters Hall Of Fame, 1992. Current Management: Lippman Entertainment, 8900 Wilshire Blvd, Suite 340, Beverly Hills, CA 90211, USA.

TAVERNER Tony, b. 20 September 1957, London, England. Producer; Engineer. m. Ruth, 4 children. Career: Engineered Duran Duran's US No 1 single, Ordinary World and The Wedding Album, and Thank You, albums; Co-Produced & Engineered, Warren Cuccurullo's 2 solo album projects; Engineered and Produced 2 chart topping albums in Spain with Duncan Dhu; Workd with Mikel Erentxum and Diego Vasallo; Senior Engineer, Maison Rouge Studio's in London, 1977-88; Engineer with Jeff Beck, 1973-88; Teamed-up with songwriter, producer and film/TV music composer, Mike Moran, 1993-. Publications: The Woman I Love, TV series; Taggart; The Turnaround. Honours: Numerous Gold & Platinum album awards. Current Management: Soundtrack Music Management, 22 Ives Street, Chelsea, London SW3 2ND, England.

TAYLER Stephen William, b. 20 Sept 1953, High Wycombe, Buckinghamshire, England. Recording and Mixing Engineer; Producer; Programmer; Musician (various). Musical Education: New College School (Choir); Shrewsbury School (Music Scholarship); Royal College of Music (ARCH). Career: Trident Studios: House Engineer, 1974-80; Freelance engineer, musician, producer, programmer, 1980-; Worked on over 120 album projects. Recordings: Engineer / mixer for: Tina Turner; Stevie Nicks; Peter Gabriel; Bob Geldof; Rush; Howard Jones; The Fixx; Others. Honours: Numerous include: Ampex Golden Reel; 2 BASF/Studio Awards for Excellence. Memberships: Re-pro; Musicians' Union. Hobbies: Eating; Sleeping. Address: c/o Chimera Records, 41 Rosebank, Holyport Road, London SW6 6LQ, England.

TAYLOR Andy, b. 16 Feb 1961, Tynemouth, Tyne & Wear, England. Musician (guitar). m. Tracey Wilson, 29 July 1982. Career: Guitarist, Duran Duran, 1979-86; Guitarist, Power Station, 1985; Solo artiste, 1986; Concerts include: Uk tour, support to Hazel O'Connor, 1980; Edinburgh Festival, 1980; US tour, support to Blondie, 1982; MENCAP charity , concert, attended by HRH the Prince and Princess of Wales, 1983; Live Aid, Philadelphia, 1985; Television appearance, Miami Vice, NBC, 1985. Recordings: Albums: with Duran Duran: Duran Duran, 1981; Carnival, 1982; Seven And The Ragged Tiger, 1983; with Power Station: The Power Station, 1985; Solo: Thunder, 1987; Singles with Duran Duran include: Planet Earth, 1981; Girls On Film, 1981; My Own Way, 1981; Hungry Like The Wolf, 1982; Save A Prayer, 1982; Is There Something I Should Know (Number 1, UK), 1983; Rio, 1984; Union Of The Snake, 1984; New Moon On Monday, 1984; The Wild Boys, 1984; A View To Kill, Bond film theme (Number 1, US), 1985; with Power Station: Some Like It Hot, 1985; Get It On, 1985; Communication, 1985; Solo: Take It Easy, 1986; When The Rain Comes Down, 1986; Lola, 1990. Honours include: Best Group, Daily Mirror/BBC TV Nationwide/Radio 1 Awards, 1983; Grammy Awards, Best Video Short and Album, 1984; BRIT Award, Best British Music Video, Wild Boys, 1985; Ivor Novello, International Hit Of The Year, 1985; Star on Hollywood Walk Of Fame, 1993.

TAYLOR Christopher Gordon, b. 24 Nov 1966, Birmingham, England. Musician (keyboards, drums); Composer; Arranger. Career: Musical Director for Central Television: Central Weekend; Keyboards, MD, Ruby Turner, 1988-95; MD, Accompanist, many top UK cabaret artists; Musical Director for Sheila Ferguson, 1996; Musical Director for the Three Degrees and The Supremes, 1997; Oh What a Night, The Musical, Opera House. Compositions: Gardener's World, BBC, 1990; Central Weekend, Central TV, 1993; Home Run, Central TV, 1993; Sunday Supplement, Central TV, 1994; Many video soundtracks. Memberships: Musicians' Union; British Music Writers Council; PRS; MCPS. Hobbies: Jazz; Sports Cars; DIY. Current Management: Grosvenor Records. Address: 16 Grosvenor Road, Handsworth Wood, Birmingham B20 3NP, England.

TAYLOR Crispin Luke, b. 1 July 1961, London, England. Musician (drums, percussion). m. Rosamond Howe, 26 Mar 1994, 2 daughters. Musical Education: Self-taught. Career: Concerts include: Montreux Jazz Festival (twice); Nice Jazz Festival, twice; Glastonbury Festival, 4 times. Television appearances: The Word and Pebble Mill, with Seal; Top Of The Pops, with Galliano; Dance Energy and Motormouth, with Definition Of Sound. Recordings: with Galliano: The Plot Thickens; Joyful Noise Unto The Creator; with Urban Species: Spiritual Love; Listen; with Oui 3: Oui Love You; Tracks/singles: Wear Your Love Like Heaven, Definition of Sound (Number 12, UK charts); Let It Last, Carleen Anderson; Mathar, Indian Vibes; As co-writer, producer: Scratchmo,

1988; Same Feeling, Mica Paris, 1988. Honours: 2 Silver discs. Membership: PRS. Hobby: Piano. Current Management: Pump Music. Address: 9A Yerbury Road, London N19 4RN, England.

TAYLOR Gary A (Anthony), b. 18 Jan 1951, Los Angeles, California, USA. Singer; Songwriter; Musician (keyboards). 2 sons, 1 daughter. Education: 5 years college (Psychology major). Musical Education: Self-taught piano. Career: Working in studios; Began songwriting early 80's; Signed to A&M Records, 1983; Virgin Records, 1988; Written, produced records for numerous artists; Radio and television commercials; solo artist, 1988-. Compositions: Good Love (Anita Baker); I'm Coming Back (Lalah Hathaway); Square One (Ray Parker Jr); One Day At A Time (Vanessa Williams); Songs also recorded by: Grover Washington Jr; Vesta Williams; Chico Debarge; Joyce Kennedy; The Whispers; Mac Band; Jennifer Holiday; Stephanie Mills. Recordings: Albums: Compassion, 1988; Take Control, 1990; Square One, 1995. Hobbies: Gym training; People watching. Current Management: Steven Ivory. Address: 156 W 56th Street, 5th Floor, New York, NY 10019, USA.

TAYLOR Graeme David, b. 2 Feb 1954, Stockwell, London, England.Musician (guitar, mandolin, banjo, piano). m. Sue Meldon, 20 July 1974, 1 daughter. Musical Education: Music O'Level, Piano lessons to Grade 4. Career: Tours with Gryphon, Europe, USA, supporting Yes, 1971-; Many television appearances include: Jim'll Fix It; Magpie; All BBC radio channels in 1 week; Tours in Albion Band with Billy Connolly; Julie Covington; Theatre work: National Theatre productions, Lark Rise To Candleford; The Mysteries; Other theatre include: Cats; Joseph And The Technicolour Dreamcoat; Television includes: This Is Your Life with Rolf Harris. Recordings: 4 Gryphon albums include: Gryphon; Midnight Mushrumps; with Albion Band: Rise Up Like The Sun; Prospect Before Us; Home Service; Alright Jack; Many of own compositions on these recordings. Memberships: Musicians' Union; PRS. Hobbies: Cooking; Brewing; Gardening; Cycling. Current Management: London Musicians. Address: 15 Eastway, Morden, SurreySM4 4HW, England.

TAYLOR James, b. 12 Mar 1948, Boston, Massachusetts, USA. Singer; Songwriter. m. Kathryn Walker, 1985. Career: First album, produced by Peter Asher, Apple Records, London, 1968; Signed to Warner Brothers Records; Moved to California, with Peter Asher, 1969; Films: Two Lane Blacktop, 1971; No-Nukes, 1980; Tours, USA: 1971, 1974-77, 1979-87, 1990-92, 1994; Tours: Far East, Australia, 1981; Italy, 1985; Australia, Europe, Brazil, 1986; Australia, New Zealand, 1988; Europe, 1992; Far East, Australia, 1995. Concerts include: Carnegie Hall, 1975; No-Nukes Concerts, 1979; Rock In Rio, Rio De Janeiro, 1985; Festivals, Munich, Nurburgring, Berlin, Germany, 1986; Phoenix Festival, 1995; Television includes: Live In Concert, Atlanta, 1981; Working, PBS-TV, 1981. Recordings: Albums: James Taylor, 1968; Sweet Baby James, 1970; Mud Slide Slim, 1971; One Man Dog, 1972; Walking Man, 1974; Gorilla, 1975; In The Pocket, 1976; Greatest Hits, 1976; JT, 1977; Flag, 1979; Dad Loves His Work, 1981; That's Why I'm Here, 1985; Never Die Young, 1988; New Moon Shne, 1991; James Taylor (Live), 1993; In The Hands Of The Inevitable, 1995; Singles include: Carolina In My Mind, 1969; Something's Wrong, 1969; Sweet Baby James, 1970; Fire And Rain, 1970; Country Road, 1971; You've Got A Friend (by Carole King), 1971; Long Ago And Far Away (with Joni Mitchell), 1971; Don't Let Me Be Lonely Tonight, 1972; One Man Parade, 1973; Mockingbird (with Carly Simon), 1974; Walking Man, 1974; Mexico. 1975; You Make It Easy, 1976; Appeared on No-Nukes album, 6 tracks, 1979; In Harmony, Sesame Street album, 1980; Producer, guitarist, singer, (sister) Kate Taylor's single, 1977, album,

1988. Honours include: Grammy Awards, 1972, 1978. Address: Peter Asher Management, 644 N Doheny Drive, Los Angeles, CA 90069, USA.

TAYLOR Jeremy, b. Newbury, Berkshire, England. Singer; Composer; Entertainer. Education: French, Italian, Oxford University. Career: Taught at Eton College; Taught in South Africa; Wrote hit show, Wait A Minim, West End (two years) and Broadway; Worked with Sydney Carter, Spike Milligan; One man shows throughout South Africa. Recordings include: Ag Please Daddy (Number 1, South Africa), now unofficial national anthem. Current Management: Jim McPhee, Acorn Entertainments. Address: Winterfold House, 46 Woodfield Road, Kings Heath, Birmingham B13 9UJ, England.

TAYLOR (Nigel) John, b. 20 June 1960, Birmingham, Warwickshire, England. Musician (bass, guitar); Songwriter. 1 daughter. Career: Founder member, Duran Duran, 1978-; Member, Power Station, 1985; Performances include: Edinburgh Festival, 1980; UK tour, supporting Hazel O'Connor, 1980; UK tour, 1981; MENCAP charity concert, attended by HRH the Prince and Princess of Wales, 1983; Live Aid, Philadelphia, 1985; Guest appearance, Miami Vice, NBC, 1985; The Secret Policeman's Third Ball, London, 1987; An Acoustic Evening With Duran Duran, Birmingham Symphony Hall, 1993. Recordings: Albums: with Duran Duran: Duran Duran, 1981; Carnival, 1982; Seven And The Ragged Tiger, 1983; Arena, 1984; So Red The Rose, 1985; Notorious, 1987; Big Thing, 1988; Decade, 1990; Duran Duran (The Wedding Album), 1993; Thank You, 1995; with Power Station: The Power Station, 1985; Singles: with Duran Duran: Planet Earth, 1981; Girls On Film, 1981; My Own Way, 1981; Save A Prayer, 1982; Hungry Like A Wolf, 1982; Is There Something I Should Know (Number 1, UK), 1983; Rio, 1983; Union Of The Snake, 1983; New Moon On Monday, 1984; The Reflex (Number 1, UK and US), 1984; The Wild Boys, 1984; A View To A Kill, theme from Bond film (Number 1, US), 1985; Notorious, 1986; Meet El Presidente, 1987; I Don't Want Your Love, 1988; All She Wants, 1989; Do You Believe In Shame, featured in film Tequila Sunrise, 1989; Violence Of Summer (Love's Taking Over), 1990;Serious, 1990; Ordinary World, 1993; Come Undone, 1993; Too Much Information, 1993; with Power Station: Some Like It Hot, 1985; Communication, 1985; Solo: I Do What I Do, theme from film 9½ Weeks, 1986; Contributor, Do They Know It's Christmas?, Band Aid, 1984. Honours: BRIT Award, Best British Music Video, 1985; Ivor Novello Award, International Hit Of The Year, 1985; Star on Hollywood Walk Of Fame, 1993. Current Management: The Left Bank Organisation, 6255 Sunset Blvd 1111, Hollywood, CA 90028, USA.

TAYLOR John Michael, b. 24 Mar 1934, Retford, Nottinghamshire, England. Musician (trumpet, piano, keyboards, organ). Musical Education: Piano lessons, 1 year, aged 9; Trumpet lessons, 1 year, aged 12. Career: Mike Taylor Jazzmen, 1956-59; Micky Askman Ragtime Jazzband, 1959-63; Appearances: Morecomb & Wise Show; 2 appearances: Thank Your Lucky Stars; Kent Walton Show; BBC Jazz Club; Midland Allstars, 1964-66; Second City Jazzmen, 1969-75; Accompanied various American stars including: Billy Butterfield; Wild Bill Davidson; Eddie Miller; Bud Freeman; Art Hodes; Earl Warren; Kenny Daverne; John Handy; Derby Big Band, 1976-79; Burton MU Big Band, 1977-80; All That Jazz Parade band, 1984-89; Festivals: Tilburg; Giethoorn; Breda; Kassel; 2 times Ascona Jazz Festival; 3 times Upton Jazz Festival; 2 times Bude; Keswick; Edinburgh; Duke Ellington Conference, Harlem, 1985-1994; German tour; Several London Night at the Cotton Club shows with: Doc Cheetham; Benny Waters; Adelade Hall; Bertice Reading; Herb Jeffries; Juanita Brooks; Hi-Life Parade Band, 1989-; Ascona Festival; 3 times Cork Jazz Festival; 2 times Bude Festival;

Keswick Festival. Freelance musician, on piano, trumpet, with numerous groups. Membership: Musicians' Union. Hobby: Sailing. Address: 1 Redblock Field, Lichfield, Staffordshire WS14 0AB, England.

TAYLOR Jon T-Bone, b. 29 Aug 1963, London, England. Blues and Jazz Musician (guitar). Musical Education: Guildhall School Of Music. Career: Leader of Bop Brothers, 1986-; Guitarist with Tim Richards' bands Roogalator and Grooveyard; Toured with Charlie Sayles; Champion Jack Dupree; Mojo Buford; Lefty Dizz; Dick Heckstall-Smith. Recordings: Strange News, Bop Brothers, 1995; Bop Brothers....And Sisters, with Earl Green, Dana Gillespie and Ruby Turner, 1998. Membership: Musicians' Union. Current Management: Abacabe Ltd. Address: 10 Messaline Avenue, London W3 6JX, England.

TAYLOR Linda Christina, b. 27 July 1950, Cleveland, Durham, England. Singer; Songwriter; Impressionist. m. Jeff Taylor, 28 Oct 1968, 1 son. Musical Education: Piano, Professor Larman, Bedford; Voice, Jean Knight, London. Career: Backing vocals, albums: Chris Rea; Tom Jones; Celine Dion; Gary Moore; Kylie Minogue; Doctor John; Mike And The Mechanics; Julien Clerc; ABC; Paul Young; Jimmy Nail; Sting; Johnny Hallyday; Tours with: Go West; Art Of Noise; Jocelyn Brown; Marvin Gaye; EPO (Japan); Chris Rea; Impressions: Spitting Image; Prime Suspect III; Crazy Horse, Paris; Television Commercials. Compositions: Angel; Everybody Knows; Taylor Made, (solo album, 1981); Morrisey/Mullen, 1981; Cayenne, Gary Numan, Bill Sharp; Every Waking Hour; You And Me Just Started, 1981. Honours: Platinum disc, Angel, 1990; Gold discs: Chris Rea, Breathe. Memberships: Equity; Musicians' Union; PAMRA; PRS. Hobbies: Water colour painting; Fitness; Psychotherapy study. Current Management: Isobel Griffiths; Hobsons Singers; Self-managed. Address: 61 Sutherland Avenue, Maida Vale, London W9 2HF, England.

TAYLOR Mick, b. Hemstead, England. Musician (guitar). Career: Guitarist, John Mayall's Bluebreakers, 1960s; Played National Jazz and Blues Festival, 1968; Lead guitarist, Rolling Stones, 1969-75; Film: Gimme Shelter (including Altamont Concert), 1969; Recorded, toured with Bob Dylan; Currently, session player, solo artist. Recordings: Bare Wires, John Mayalls Bluesbreakers, 1968; Albums with the Rolling Stones: Let It Bleed; Get Yer Ya Ya's Out; Sticky Fingers; Exile On Main Street; Goat's Head Soup; It's Only Rock And Roll; with Bob Dylan: Infidels; Empire Burlesque; Solo: Mick Taylor, 1979; Stranger In This Town, 1990; Video with John Mayall And The Bluesbreakers, Blues Alive, 1983. Honours: Rock And Roll Hall Of Fame (with Rolling Stones); Numerous domestic and international Gold, Platinum records. Address: 156 Fifth Avenue, Suite 434, New York, NY 10010, USA.

TAYLOR Robin, b. 17 May 1956, Copenhagen, Denmark. Composer; Multi-Instrumentalist; Producer. Education: Academy for Free and Commercial Art, Copenhagen. Musical Education: Selftaught Guitar, Bass, Keyboard, Percussion. Career: Member of several local rock groups, 1970s; First radio appearance, 1978; In collaboration with keyboard player Jan Marsfeldt; Record debut, 1991; Composer, film music; Founder, jazz/rock fusion group, Taylor's Universe, 1993; Member, Avant-garde Big Band Communio Musica led by Hugh Steinmetz, 1996-97. Recordings: Solo albums: Essay, 1991; Cloze Test Terror, 1992; Taylor's Universe: Taylor's Universe, 1994; Pork, 1996; Experimental Health, expected release 1998; Communio Musica: Special Alloy, expected release, 1998. Membership: Danish Musicians' Union. Hobbies: Bulldogs; Weird Music. Current Management: Marvel of Beauty Records, Listedvej 40, 3 MF, DK-2770 Kastrup, Denmark.

TAYLOR Roger (Meddows-Taylor), b. 26 July 1949, Kings Lynn, Norfolk, England. Musician (drums); Singer; Producer. Education: Biology. Career: Drummer, Smile; Drummer, UK rock group Queen, 1970-; Founder, The Cross, 1987-; Numerous tours include: UK; US; Australia; South America; Japan; Major concerts include: Rock In Rio, Brazil, 1985; Live Aid, Wembley, 1985; Knebworth Festival, 1986; Concert For Life, Wembley, 1985. Recordings: Albums include: Queen, 1973; Queen 2, 1974; Sheer Heart Attack, 1974; A Night At The Opera, 1975; A Day At The Races, 1977; Jazz, 1978; Live Killers, 1979; The Game, 1980; Flash Gordon (soundtrack), 1981; Greatest Hits, 1981; Hot Space, 1982; The Works, 1984; The Complete Works, 1985; A Kind Of Magic, 1986; The Miracle, 1989; Innuendo, 1991; Live At Wembley '86, 1992; Made In Heaven, 1995; with the Cross: Shove It!, 1988; Solo: Fun In Space, 1981; Strange Frontier, 1984; Happiness?, 1994; Singles include: Seven Seas Of Rye, 1974; Killer Queen, 1974; Bohemian Rhapsody (Number 1, UK), 1975; Now I'm Here, 1975; You're My Best Friend, 1976; Somebody To Love, 1976; We Are The Champions, 1977; Bicycle Race, 1978; Don't Stop Me Now, 1979; Love Of My Life, 1979; Crazy Little Thing Called Love, 1979; Play The Game, 1980; Save Me, 1980; Another One Bites The Dust (Number 1, US), 1980; Flash, 1981; Under Pressure, with David Bowie (Number 1, UK), 1981; Radio Ga Ga, 1984; I Want To Break Free, 1984; It's A Hard Life, 1984; Hammer To Fall, 1984; One Vision, 1985; A Kind Of Magic, 1986; Friends Will Be Friends, 1986; I Want It All, 1989; Breakthru, 1989; Innuendo (Number 1, UK), 1991; Headlong, 1991; Too Much Love Will Kill You, 1995; Heaven For Everyone, 1995. Honours include: Britannia Award, 1976; Gold Ticket, Madison Square Gardens, 1977; American Music Award, 1981; Silver Clef Award, Nordoff-Robbins Music Therapy Centre, 1984; Ivor Novello Award, Outstanding Contribution to British Music, 1987; BRIT Awards: Outstanding Contribution to British Music, 1990; Best British Single, 1991. Current Management: c/o Jim Beach, Queen Productions, 46 Pembridge Road, London W11 3HN, England.

TAYLOR Steve, b. 9 Dec 1957, Brawley, California, USA. Recording Artist; Songwriter; Producer; Film maker. m. Debbie L Taylor, 16 Mar 1985. Education: BA Music, Colorado University, Boulder, USA. Career: Recording artist; Producer, Co-writer for Newsboys. Recordings: I Want To Be A Clone, 1983; Meltdown, 1984; On The Fritz, 1985; I Predict 1990, 1987; Chagall Guevara, 1991; Squint, 1993; Liver, 1995; Video: Squint: Movies From The Soundtrack, 1994; Producer, Co-writer, The Newsboys: Not Ashamed, 1992; Going Public, 1994; Take Me To Your Leader, 1996; Producer, Guardian: Buzz, 1995. Honours: 2 Grammy Nominations; 19 Dove Award Nominations; 3 Dove Awards; 2 Billboard Music Video Awards (as artist and director); CCM Magazine, Producer Of The Year, 1994; 1995. Current Management: Proper Management, PO Box 23069, Nashville, TN 37202, USA.

TAYLOR Steven Vernard, b. 24 Dec 1950, Norton, Virginia, USA. Producer; Director A&R, RCM Recordings. Musical Education: Bachelor Music (opera), University of Tennessee, Complete Recording Workshop, Los Angeles Valley College. Career: 16 yaers touring as vocalist, musician; Engineered for Jimmy Buffett, Michael McDonald, Jeff Berlin; Assisstant to director on Grammy winner: Boys Of Summer (Don Henley); Musical consultant for television shows: Gimme A Break; Facts Of Life; Diff'rent Strokes; One Day At A Time. Recordings: Unknown Soul (producer); Sugar Jones; Argument Clinic (producer). Honours: Commendation by Texas Governor Ann Richards for internationally aired song: Dear Mr President, Dear Mr Gorbachev (producer/promoter). Hobbies: Hiking; Swimming; Making studio magic. Address: PO Box 4735 Austin, TX 78765-4735, USA.

TAYLOR Tot, b. 15 July 1957, Cambridgeshire, England. Producer; Record Company Executive; Songwriter; Career: Founder, own Compact Organization record label; Songwriter, Producer for Mari Wilson, Virna Lindt, early 1980's. Compositions: Music for Absolute Beginners, 1986; Started Poppy Records, 1996. Recordings: Producer: Just What I Always Wanted, Mari Wilson, 1982; World Of Leather, 1995; Producer, Bachology, 1995; Released 6 albums under own name, 1981-1995; Waterland, soundtrack, 1997; Macbeth, soundtrack, 1997. Hobby: Music. Current Management: LPA. Address: PO Box 562, London N10 3LJ, England.

TAYLOR-GOOD, Karen, b. El Paso, Texas, USA. Singer; Songwriter. Career: Began as folk singer: Austin, Texas; Europe; Radio, television commercials: United Airlines; McDonalds; Heinz; Backing singer for: Willie Nelson; Merle Haggard; Randy Travis; Roy Rogers; George Jones; Now Solo artist on Mesa Records; Songwriter for Warner Chappell; Represented US, Musical Peace Mission to Soviet Union, 1988. Compositions: Songs written for: Laura Branigan; Patty Loveless; Melanie; Nana Mouskouri; Diamond Rio. Recordings: Sang on soundtracks: Best Little Whorehouse In Texas; Smokey and the Bandit; Main solo success with: How Can I Help You Say Goodbye. Honours: Best New Female, ACM; New Folk Winner, Kerrville Festival, 1992; Songwriter of Year, SESAC, 1994; Nominated for Grammy: Best Country Song, 2 CMA Awards (all for How I Can I Help You Say Goodbye); Music Video Awards, SESAC and Music Row Magazine. Memberships: Founding member, Planet Earth Project. Current Management: SESAC. Address: 55 Music Sq E, Nashville, TN 37203, USA.

TCHANDO (Salvador Embalo), b. 22 Mar 1957, Bafata, Guiné-Bissau. Composer; Musician (guitar); Singer. Education: 2nd level, Economics, Superior Economic Institute of Lisbon. Career: Guitarist, backing singer for N'kassa Kobra; Issabari; Hanne Boel; Kaba Mane; Lead singer for Zebra; Continental Heat; Kilimandjaro; Solo artiste, 1991-; Television apperances: Afrika Musika and MCM (Paris); Special "Tchando", TVE (Bissau); Radio appearances: RFT; RDN; Africa No 1; Compositions: Music for theatre in Denmark. Recordings: Albums: Solo album: Naton; with Kabe Mane: Chefo Mae Mae; Kungha; with Hanne Boel: Dark Passion. Memberships: Danish Musicians and Composer's Union; Koda. Hobbies: Films; Sports. Address: Bispeengen 11, 2 th, 2000 Frederiksberg, Denmark.

TEE Richard, b. 24 Nov 1943, Brooklyn, New York, USA. Musician (piano, keyboards); Composer; Arranger; Condcutor. Musical Education: Classical piano training; Graduate, High School of Music and Art. Career: Staff arranger, in-house pianist, Motown Records, 1962-65; Conductor, Roberta Flack, 1972-74; Musical director, Joe Cocker, 1974; Conductor, musician, Paul Simon, 1975-; Tours include Rhythm Of The Saints tour, 1991; Member, funk band Stuff, 1976. Recordings: Solo albums: Strokin', 1979; Natural Ingredients, 1980; The Bottom Line, 1985; with Stuff: Stuff, 1977; Live In Japan, 1979; Keyboard player, numerous artists including: Paul Simon; Joe Cocker; George Benson; James Brown; Aretha Franklin; Art Garfunkel; Quincy Jones; Chaka Khan; Gladys Knight; Melba Moore; Roland Kirk; Barbra Streisand; Carly Simon; Grover Washington; Van McCoy; Billy Idol; Herbie Mann; Lena Horne; Film soundtracks include: Fletch; Ice Castles. Honours: Grammy Nominations with Stuff, 1987; Spyro Gyra, 1983; Most Valuable Player, Acoustic pianist, New York chapter, NARAS, 1979-84. Memberships: ASCAP; National Academy Arts and Sciences.

TEE-BIRDD Jamaka (Richard Anthony Johnson), b. 15 Sept 1952, Kingston, Jamaica. Musician (keyboards, guitar, percussion);

Publisher. m. Celia Caiz. Education: Kingston College, 1967-71; College Of Art, Science and Technology, 1972-73. Career: Member, bands: Bare Essentials; Zap-Pow; In-Crowd; Soul Syndicate; Burning Spear; Judy Mowatt; Bunny Wailer; Boris Gardiner; Top Notch; Roots Radics; Home T; Performed on Reggae Sunsplash I-V, X, XI, reggae Sunsplash Pay Per View, 1991; Tours: USA; Europe; Africa; South America; Japan; Israel. Composition: Jamdown Rock, song used on radio and TV to advertise The First Reggae Sunsplash. Recordings: Albums: with Zap-Pow: Now; LoveHits; ZapPow; with Soul Syndicate: Harvest Uptown-Famine Downtown; Was Is And Always; Friends Of Soul Syndicate; FM, Freddie McGregor; with In-Crowd: His Majesty Is Coming; Man From New Guinea; Best Of In-Crowd; with Burning Spear: Far Over; Fittest Of The Fittest; Resistance; People Of The World; Live In Paris; Jah Kingdom; with Israel Vibration: Forever; Vibes Alive; IV; Free to ove; On the Rock; Dub-the-Rock; Live Again; IV Dub; Cry Blood, Charlie Chaplin; Party, Yellowman; World Peace Three, Radically Radics, Roots Radics; with Bare Essentials: Back-a-Yard; No Loafin'; Soca With You; with various artistes; Reggae For Kids; RORXX (Reggae On The Rockls X), Tee-Bird Showcase; Heart Monitor. Publications: Jamaka comic magazines, Jamaka serial cartoon in the Star daily newspaper. Honours: Co-arranger of The Jamaica Festival Song Competition's first and only female performed winning song Mek Wi Put Things Right. Memberships: PRS; JFM; Musicians' Union (UK). Hobbies: Badminton; Football; Amiga computing; Drawing cartoons and comics. Current Management: RAS Records. Address: 2447 Linden Lane, Silverspring, MD 20910, USA.

TEMIZ Okay, b. 11 Feb 1939, Ankara, Turkey. Musician (percussion). 1 son. Musical Education; Conservatory. Career: World tours: USA, Europe, India, with Don Cherry, Karnata Ka College of Percussions, Oriental Wind, Okay Temiz Magnetic Band. Recordings: Music For Axaba, 1974; Oriental Wind; 12 records, 1947-1986; Fis Fis Tziganes, 1992; Fish Market, 1993. Don Cherry/Bobo Stainson/Okay Temiz, 1993. Honours: Year Of The Musician, Istanbul, 1971. Membership: Swedish And Finnish Jazz Organization. Hobbies: Live with music. Current Management: Denis Leblond, 99 Avenue de Clichy, 75017 Paris, France; Orane Senly, Artalene, 15 Passage de la Main d'Or, 75001, Paris, France; Werner Oberender, PO Box 1926, 5450 Neuvied 1, Germany. .

TEMPEST Joey, b. 19 Aug 1963, Stockholm, Sweden. Singer; Songwriter. Career: Co-founder, rock group Force, 1982; Won national rock talent contest, Sweden; Recorded two albums for Swedish market; Renamed Europe, 1985-92; Solo artist, 1993-; International tours. Recordings: Albums: with Europe: Wings Of Tomorrow, 1985; The Final Countdown, 1986; Out Of This World, 1988; Prisoners In Paradise, 1991; Solo: A Place To Call Home, 1995; Hit singles include: with Europe: Carrie; The Final Countdown (Number 1, UK), 1986; Rock The Night; Cherokee; Superstitious. Current Management: Rascoff/Zysblat Organisation, 110 W 57th Street, New York, NY 10019, USA.

TEMPLIN Ray, b. 27 Jan 1947, Chicago, Illinois, USA. Musician; Actor; Writer. m. Trish, 19 May 1968, 1 son, 1 daughter. Education: 2nd year college. Musical Education: 2 years, University of Illinois. Career: 30 years professional musician, bandleader specializing in stride piano; Major jazz festivals in USA, concerts, guest artist appearances; 20 years voice-over, acting, including cartoon and television voice; 5 seasons as piano playing proprietor of Ray Templin's Bar, on Matlock (NBC). Compositions: Jam '38 A Theatrical Experience, theatrical production. Recordings: Ray Templin - Piano Man; Ray Templin - Swingology; Crazy 'Bout Fats, Ray Templin's Chicagoans. Memberships: AFM; SAG;

AFTRA; ASCAP. Hobbies: Stereo photography; Cooking; Travel. Current Management: The Bigley Agency. Address: 6442 Coldwater Canyon Avenue, Suite 211, North Hollywood, CA 91606, USA.

TEMS Michael James Anthony (Mick), b. 3 Jan 1950, London, England. Singer; Musician. Career: Member, Welsh traditional group Swansea Jack, 1973-78; Member, Welsh traditional group Calennig, 1978-; Television includes: The Folk Club, BBC Wales, 1975; Torth y Fara, 1982; Folk On The Move, HTV, 1983; Trade Winds, BBC Wales, 1985; Fastest to Frisco, BBC Wales, 1986; Evening News, Dunedin, New Zealand, 1990; Celtic Magic, HTV, 1990; Gwerin, S4C, 1995. Recordings: Solo: Gowerton Fair, 1977; with Swansea Jack, The Seven Wonders, 1978; with Calennig: Songs And Tunes From Wales, 1980; You Can Take a White Horse Anywhere, 1983; Dyddiau Gwynion Ionawr, 1985; Dwr Glan, 1990; Trade Winds, 1994; Numerous compilations, Memberships: Equity; Musicians' Union; MCPS; PAMRA; NUJ; CDdWC; COTC. Hobbies: Music; Writing; Travel; Welsh studies. Address: 1 Ty Clwyta Cottages, Cross Inn, Llantrisant, Rhondda Cynon Taf CF72 8AZ, Wales.

TENKANEN Kari, b. 20 Feb 1963, Finland. Musician (alto, soprano saxophone, clarinet). Musical Education: Mainly self-taught; Clarinet lessons age 6-10; Jazz, summer camp held by Oulunkylä Pop/Jazz Conservatoire, 1980. Career: Member, Espoo Big Band, 10 years; Small ensembles include Jani Malmi Quartet, 5 years; Founder, own quintet. Address: Mechelininkatu 15 A 15, 00100 Helsinki, Finland.

TENNANT Neil Francis, b. 10 July 1954, North Shields, Northumberland, England. Education: Degree, History, North London Polytechnic. Career: Group: Dust, 1970-71; Publishing, 1975-; Met Christopher Lowe, began writing together, founded West End, renamed Pet Shop Boys, 1981; Granada TV special: Love Me Tender, 1987; Film: It Couldn't Happen Here, 1988; Piccadilly Theatre, TV: Wogan, Top Of The Pops, 1988; Tour, Hong Kong, Japan, UK, 1989; USA: with Electronic, Dodgers Stadium; Mayan Theatre, Los Angeles; Arsenio Hall Show, TV, 1990; Performance Tour, Japan; USA; Canada; Europe, UK, Ireland, 1991; 2 weeks, Simon Bates Show, Radio One, 1991, 1992; Launched own record label: Spaghetti, 1991; Concert, Heaven nightclub, 1991; South Bank Show, 1992; Hacienda Club, Manchester, 1992; Roseland, New York, 1992; Opening Russian MTV, 1993; Producer, songwriter, artists include: Dusty Springfield, Patsy Kensit; Liza Minnelli; Boy George; Electronic. Recordings: West End Girls (Number 1), 1985; Love Comes Quickly, 1986; Suburbia, 1986; with Dusty Springfield: What Have I Done To Deserve This?, 1987; Rent, 1987; Always On My Mind (Number 1), 1987; Heart, 1988; Domino Dancing, 1988; Left To My Own Devices, 1988; It's Alright, 1989; So Hard, 1990; Being Boring, 1990; Where The Streets Have No Name, 1991; Jealousy, 1991; DJ Culture, 1991; Was It Worth It?, 1991; Can You Forgive Her?, 1993; Go West, 1993; Albums: Please, 1991; Disco, 1986; Actually, 1987; Introspective, 1988; Behaviour, 1990; Discography, 1991; Very, 1993; Relentless, 1993; Alternative Pet Shop Boys, due release 1996; Writer, singer, Electronic; Disappointed, 1991. Honours: Ivor Novello, 1987, 1988; BPI, 1987, 1988; Berolina, 1988. Address: Pet Shop Boys Partnership, 8 Pembridge Studios, 27a Pembroke Villas, London W11 3EP, England.

TENNILLE Toni, b. 8 May 1943, Montgomery, Alabama, USA. Singer. m. Daryl Dragon, 14 Feb 1974. Career: Co-writer and performer, musical Mother Earth, San Francisco, 1972; Formed duo, The Captain And Tennille, with Daryl Dragon, 1972-80; Tour with Beach Boys, 1972; Performed at White House dinner, in honour of Queen Elizabeth II, 1976; Musical variety show, The Captain And Tennille, ABC TV, 1976; Solo artiste, 1980-; Appeared in Broadway show, Stardust, 1991; Nevada Ambassador for the Arts, 1998; Stage performance in The Rainmaker. Recordings: Albums: with The Captain and Tennille: Love Will Keep Us Together, 1975; Song Of Joy, 1976; Come In From The Rain, 1977; Captain And Tennille's Greatest Hits, 1978; Dream, 1978; Make Your Move, 1980; Twenty Years of Romance, 1995; Solo albums: More Than You Know, 1984; Moonglow, 1986; All Of Me, 1987; Never Let Me Go, 1992; Things Are Swingin', 1994; Tennille Sings Big Band, 1998; Hit singles include: Love Will Keep Us Together (Number 1, US), 1975; The Way I Want To Touch You, 1975; Lonely Night (Angel Face), 1976; Shop Around, 1976; Muskrat Love, 1976; Can't Stop Dancin', 1977; You Never Done It Like That, 1978; Do That To Me One More Time (Number 1, US), 1980. Honours: Grammy Award, Record Of The Year, Love Will Keep Us Together, 1976; Juno Awards, Best International Single, Love Will Keep Us Together, Canada, 1976. Current Management: Cheri Ingram Co., 3575 Cahuenga Blvd, Suite 600, Los Angeles, CA 90068, USA.

TERMINATOR X (Norman Rogers). Rapper; Disc Jockey. Career: Member, US rap group Public Enemy, 1984-90; Concerts include: Support to the Beastie Boys, US, 1987; Support to LL Cool J, European tour, 1987; Tour Of A Black Planet, 1990; Solo artiste, 1990-; Manager, The Entourage (hip-hop club), Long Island, New York, 1986; Recordings: Albums: with Public Enemy: Yo! Bum Rush The Show, 1987; It Takes A Nation Of Millions To Hold Us Back, 1988; Fear Of A Black Planet, 1990; Muse Sick'n'Hour Mess Age, 1994; Solo: Terminator X And The Valley Of The Jeep Beets, 1991; Singles: Rebel Without A Pause; Bring The Noise; Don't Believe The Hype; Night Of The Living Baseheads; Black Steel In The Hour Of Chaos; Fight The Power, theme song for film Do The Right Thing; Welcome To The Terrordome; 911 Is A Joke; Brothers Gonna Work It Out; Want To Be Dancin'. Current Management: Malik Entertainment Management, PO Box 310, Roosevelt, NY 11575, USA.

THAIN Laurie Anne, b. 18 Feb 1955, New Westminster, British Columbia, Canada. Singer; Songwriter; Musician (guitar). Education: BA, Physical Education and Theatre. Musical Education: Self-taught. Career: Singer in fund-raising shows (North America) to benefit disabled children; Concerts, opening shows for Lee Greenwood; Gary Morris; Rita MacNeil; Pam Tillis; Worldwide tours. Recordings: Hopeless Romantic, 1984; Matters Of The Heart, 1987; Stages, 1992. Honours: Winner, Canadian National, Du Maurier Search For Stars. Memberships: Canadian Country Music Association; AFofM; Pacific Music Industry Association. Hobbies: Walking; Biking; Golf. Current Management: Self-managed. Address: Pure Pacific Music, 31905 Woodcock Crescent, Mission, British Columbia V2V 4K2, Canada.

THANGER Hakan, b. 23 October 1943, Boo, Stockholm, Sweden. El-Base; El-Guitar; Song. divorced. Career: Contributor, Swedish Eurovision Song Contest; Played and written songs and arrangements for many artists from Sweden including: Lill Babs; Jerry Williams; Family Four and others. Composition: Dagar Jag Ner I Min Källare. Recordings: More than 500 studio recordings. Memberships: STIM; SAMI; SKAP; TSO. Hobby: Music. Address: Sverkersgatan 6, 3tr, S-126 51 Stockholm, Sweden.

THEMIS John, b. 13 Oct 1954. Producer; Musician (guitar); Writer; Musical Director. m. Anne Lawrence, 14 Jan 1981, 1 son, 2 daughters. Educaton: BSc Marketing, Management. Musical Education: Self-taught. Career: UK television appearances include: Aspel; Johnathan Ross; Terry Wogan; The Big E; The Word; The Chart Show; Pebble Mill; BPM; Top Of The Pops; Jools Holland Show; Brian Conley Show; Lilley Savage Show; The Box; MTV Live; US apperances include: Tonite With Jay Leno; The Ru Paul Show; The John and Lisa Show; French apperances include: Le Nuils; Tarata; Couscous; C'est Nous; Also television in Germany; Belgium; Argentina; Russia; Chile; Japan; Concerts include: Hammersmith Odeon; Festival Hall; Ronnie Scott's; Pride Festival, Brockwell Park, 250,000 people; International concerts include: Canada, Romania, Japan; Musical director, songwriting partner, guitarist with Boy George, for 4 years; Played with Chris De Burgh, on Room In This Heart, BBC TV; Also worked with: Dannii Minogue; Lavine Hudson; Paul Young; Wendy and Lisa; Tim Rice; Nigel Kennedy; Jason Donavon; Kim Wilde; Ray Simson; London Chamber Orchestra. Recordings: As musician, producer: with Boy George; Chris de Burgh; Suggs; Blair; Cher; Evolution; Simon Climie; Lippy Lou; Malcolm MacLaren; The Grid; Billy Ray Martin; Eve Gallagher; Elton John; Pet Shop Boys; George Michael; The Beloved; Garry Kemp; Barry Manilow; Orchestral Manoeuvres In The Dark; Bad Boys Inc; Producer, Voices single, Junior Reid. Hobby: Music. Address: 46 The Limes Avenue, London N11 1RH, England.

THISTLETHWAITE Anthony Silvester, b. 31 Aug 1955, Leicester, England. Musician (saxophone, multi-instrumentalist). Career: Busking, Paris, 1979-80; Member, The Waterboys, 1982-91; The Saw Doctors, 1993-95; Moved to St Petersburg, Russia, 1995; Currently working with top Russian bands Aquarium and DDT. Recordings: with The Waterboys: The Waterboys, 1983; A Pagan Place, 1984; This Is The Sea, 1986; Fisherman's Blues, 1989; Room To Roam, 1990; Solo albums: Aesop Wrote A Fable, 1993; Cartwheel, 1995; Other recordings with Bob Dylan; Donovan; Johnny Thunders; Psychedelic Furs; World Party; Mission; Fairground Attraction: Sharon Shannon; Eddi Reader. Membership: Musicians' Union. Hobbies: Dancing; Swimming; Eating. Address: c/o Purpleteeth Productions, PO Box 2666, London W14 0ZT, England.

THOGER Torben, b. 14 Apr 1954, Aarhus, Denmark. Composer. 1 son, 1 daughter. Career: Composer, various styles, mainly symphonic rock, for musicals, multi-media films (documentaries, commercials), television and revue and cabaret shows. Major compositions: Iris-en rockmusical, 1992; DR Derude (scores), Danish Broadcasting Corporation, 1994-96; Dr Jekyll and Mr Hyde, (musical opera), 1995. recording: Den Store Bastiansen, 1997. Publications: Soenisserne, 1991; Iris-en rockmusical, 1992; Den Store Bastiansen, 1997. Membership: DJBFA (Danish Society for Jazz, Rock and Folk Composers). Current Management: Torben Thoger Music, Torup 18, 8305 Samso, Denmark.

THOMAS B(illie) J(oe), b. 7 Aug 1942, Hugo, Oklahoma, USA. Singer; Songwriter; Entertainer. m. Gloria Richardson, 9 Dec 1968, 3 daughters. Career: Lead singer, The Triumphs; Opened for acts including Roy Orbison; The Dave Clark Five; the Four Tops; Solo artiste; Toured with Dick Clark Caravan Of Stars; Regular appearances Ed Sullivan Show, nightclubs, concert halls; Became 60th member, Grand Ole Opry; B J Thomas Celebrity Theater, Tennessee Smoky Mountains, opening spring 1996. Recordings: Albums include: Peace In The Valley; Love Shines; Great American Dream; Shining; All Is Calm, All Is Bright; Throwin' Rocks At The Moon; Nightlife; Midnite Minute; I Believe; Singles include: I'm So Lonesome I Could Cry; Mama; The Eyes Of A New York Woman; Hooked On A Feeling; Raindrops Keep Fallin' On My Head (from Butch Cassidy and the Sundance Kid soundtrack); It's Only You; I Just Can't Help Believin'; No Love At All; Rock And Roll Lullabye; As Long As We Got Each Other (theme from series Growing Pains); Somebody Done Somebody Wrong; Broken Toys (adopted as theme tune by child abuse agencies); What Ever Happened To Old Fashioned Love; New Looks From And Old Lover; The Whole World's In Love When You're Lonely. Publications: Home Where I Belong; In Tune. Honours: 5 Grammy Awards; 2 Dove Awards; 5 Platinum, 11 Gold albums: Lifetime Achievement Award, U C Berkeley; Academy Award, 1970; Country Song of the Year, 1975. Memberships: AFTRA; SAG; Grand Ole Opry; AFofM; CMA; NARAS; National Songwriters' Association. Hobby: Golf. Current Management: Agent: Lee Farmer, Marathon Attractions; Manager: Michael Goldstein, Goldwest. Address: Goldwest, 9125 Otto St, Downey, CA 90240, USA.

THOMAS Daniel, b. 11 Jan 1970, Brixton, England. Musician (keyboards); Singer; Songwriter. Career: Backing vocals for: Luther Vandross; Elton John; Carleen Anderson; Deuce; Eternal; Erasure; David Essex; Jools Holland; Played keyboards for: Sir Harry Secombe (Crystal Rose Show); IDMC; Bryan Powell; Ricky Grundy; Music Director for London Community Gospel Choir and Choir Director; Also teacher of vocal techniques. Memberships: Musicians' Union; Black Gospel Association. Hobbies: Reading; Theatre; Dining; Writing Music. Current Management: Basil Meade, Choir Connexion. Address: 9 Greenwood Drive, Highams Park, London E4 9HL, England.

THOMAS David Lynn, b. 14 June 1953, Miami, Florida, USA. Singer; Writer. m. Lynne Ferguson, 1979. Career: Formed Pere Ubu, 1975; Solo career, 1982-87; Reformed Pere Ubu, 1987. Recordings: The Modern Dance, 1978; Dub Housing, 1978; Art Of Walking, 1980; Monster Walks The Winter Lake, 1985; The Tenement Year, 1987; Cloudland, 1988; Ray Gun Suitcase, 1995. Current Management: Nick Hobbs. Address: Ubu Projex, PO Box 972, London SE24 OPD, England.

THOMAS Irma (Lee), b. 18 Feb 1941, Pontchatoula, Louisiana, USA. Singer. Career: R&B singer known as The Soul Queen Of New Orleans. Recordings: Albums: Wish Somone Would Care, 1964; Take A Look, 1968; In Between Tears, 1973; Live, 1977; Soul Queen Of New Orleans, 1978; Safe With Me, 1979; Hip Shakin' Mama, 1981; The New Rules, 1986; The Way I Feel, 1988; Simply The Best, 1991; True Believer, 1992. Address: c/o Emile Jackson, PO Box 26126, New Orleans, LA 70186, USA.

THOMAS Patrice, b. 17 Mar 1961, Besancon, France. Musician (guitar). Musical Education: Diplome d'Etat Jazz. Career: Performed at festivals: Montpellier; Mulhouse; Calvi; Milan; Nancy; Concerts at Maison de Radio France, Paris; Radio and TV: TF1; Fr3; France Musique; France Culture; France Inter. Recordings: CDs: Isis; Portraits. Honours: Soloist, first prize, 9th Jazz Challenge, Paris (Défense). Membership: UMJ; Teacher, Ecole de Musique, Montbeliard. Address: Refranche, 25330 Amancey, France.

THOMAS Patrick, b. 27 July 1960, Oxford, England. Musician; Composer; Producer. Education: BA, hons, Psychology, Open University; Private Classical Piano Lessons; Studied with Mary Howell-Pryce, St Edmund Campion School, Oxford. Career: Paris with Chuck Berry, Continental Drift, 1989; London with Derek Bailey, Eugene Chadbourne, Keith Rowe, 1990; London with John Zorn, Bucket Head, Paul Lovens, 1991; Germany with Tony Oxley, Sirone, Larry Stabbins, Manfred Schoof, 1992; Glasgow with Lol Coxhill, 1993; Berlin Jazz Festival with Bill Dixon, 1994; London Jazz Cafe with Thurston Moore, Lee Renaldo, 1996; Solo, Copenhagen, 1997. Compositions: ENsemble WX7e Turntables Dialogue (with interruptions); Pulse, for drum machine and two percussionists; Reflex, for ensemble and computers. Recordings: With Tony

Oxley Quartet, Incus, 1992; Lol Coxhill, Halim Nato, 1993; One Night in Glasgow, Scatter, 1994; Company 91, 3 volumes, 1994; Mike Cooper Island Songs, 1995; Celebration Orchestra, The Enchanted Messenger, 1996; Tones of Life, Guidance, 1997; Solo Album, Remembering, 1998. Publications: Islam's Contribution to Jazz and Improvised Music, 1993; Upside Down (The Myth of Jazz History), 1998. Honours: Arts Council of Great Britain Jazz Bursary for 3 Electro-accoustic Compositions. Memberships: Performing Rights Society; London Musicians Collective. Hobbies: Watching Cricket; History. Address: 5 Saint Omer Road, Cowley, Oxford OX4 3HB, England.

THOMAS Rufus, b. 26 Mar 1917, Cayce, Mississippi, USA. Singer; Dancer; Entertainer. Career: Member, Rabbit's Foot Minstrels, vaudeville-inspired group; Performances, Memphis nightclubs; Organized talent shows; Disc Jockey, WDIA, -1974. Recordings: Albums: Walking The Dog, 1964; Do The Funky Chicken, 1970; Doing The Push And Pull Live At PJs, 1971; Did You Hear Me, 1973; Crown Prince Of Dance, 1973; Blues In The Basement, 1975; If There Were No Music, 1977; I Ain't Gettin' Older, I'm Gettin' Better, 1977; Rufus Thomas, 1980; Jump Back - A 1963-67 Retrospective, 1984; Rappin' Rufus, 1986; That Woman Is Poison, 1988; Timeless Funk, 1992; Blues Thang!, 1996; Singles include: Bear Cat, 1953; 'Cause I Love You, duet with Carla Thomas; Walking The Dog, 1963; Jump Back, 1964; All Night Worker, 1964; Sophisticated Sissy, 1967; Memphis Train, 1968; Do The Funky Chicken, 1970; (Do The) Push And Pull Part 1, 1970; Do The Funky Penguin, 1971.

THOMPSON Christopher Hamlet, b. 9 Mar 1947, Hertford,Hertfordshire, England. Musician. m. Maggie, 4 Jan 1995, 1 son. Education: BSoc Science, Teaching Certificate. Career: Professional musician, 1972-; Joined Manfred Mann's Earth Band, 1975-86; Formed own band Night, 1979; Extensive tours throughout USA, Europe: With Manfred Mann's Earth Band, 1975-86; With Night, 1979-83; Working in Europe, under own name, 1986-; with The Alan Project; Singer, TV product campaigns: Rank Xerox; Mandate; De Beers; ADT; Bayer; Tennents Pilsner; Twix; Kelloggs Cornflakes; The Daily Mail; Peugeot 205; Abbey National; Budweiser. Recordings: with Manfred Mann's Earth Band: The Roaring Silence, 1976; Watch, 1978; Angel Station, 1979; Chance, 1980; Somewhere In Africa, 1982; Live In Budapest, 1983; Criminal Tango, 1986; Singles: Blinded By The Night; Davy's On The Road Again; Solo albums: Radio Voices, 1983; High Cost Of Living, 1986; Beat Of Love, 1989; Hits in Germany with: The Challenge, 1989; The Joker, 1991; Florida Lady, 1994; Songs and vocals to albums by: The Doobie Brothers; Tina Turner; Elton John; Roger Daltrey; Jefferson Starship; Brian May; Barbara Dickson; Ozzy Osbourne. Memberships: PRS; SAG; Equity. Current Management: Horst Zwipp, Feedback Music. Address: Residenz Am Chlab, Gmuinde Str 2, D-73614 Sharndof, Germany.

THOMPSON Danny Henry, b. 4 April 1939, Teignmouth, S Devon, England. Musician (Double Bass, Trombone). m. Sylvia Thompson, 2 stepsons, 1 son. Education: Salesian College Grammar. Musical Education: Selftaught. Career: Alexis Korner, 1964-67; Roy Orbison Tour, 1964; Recording sessions, 1960s including Marianne Faithfull; String Band, Nick Drake; Co-Founded Pentangle, 1968; Own trio with John McLaughlin, 1966; Tubby Hayes Quartet, Phil Seamen Quartet, Studio Work including Rod Stewart, Kate Bush, Talk Talk, 1970s, 1980s; Formed own band, Whatever, 1989, toured, 1992-97. Compositions: Take 3 Girls Theme, Light Flight; Musing Mingus; Til Minne Au Jan; Children of the Dark; Pitfalls; New Rhythms; No Love is Sorrow; Passion to Protect, film; Swedish Dance; Fair Isle Friends. Recordings: Sweet Child Basket of Light;

Whatever; Whatever Next; Elemental; Whatevers Best; Dizrhythmia; Songhai; Solid Air; Live at Leeds, with John Martyn; The Pentangle; Industry. Publications: Video Basically Speaking. Honour: Hugo, Chicago International Film Festival. Hobbies: Tennis; Swimming; Golf; Cricket; Snooker; Diving; Abseiling. Address: 43 Mount View, Rickmansworth, Herts WD3 2BB, England.

THOMPSON Gail, b. 15 June 1958, London, England. Musician (saxophone, clarinet); Composer; Conductor. m. Tim May, 10 May 1994. Musical Education: Studied at school; Self-taught composition, conducting. Career: Tenor saxophone, West End hit show Bubbling Brown Sugar, 1977; Music teacher, South East London Technical College, 1977; Manageress, Macari's Music Shop, Charing Cross Road, 1980; Formed Jazz Funk band The Gail Thompson Approach, featured Camden Jazz Week, 1980; Founded Women In Music, 1986; Established Sax Council tuition school; Created Jazz Force, 1986; Founded the Jazz Warriors, with Courtney Pine, 1986; Played regularly with Charlie Watts Big Band, Art Blakey's Jazz Messengers; Founded Music Work Resource Centre, music school, 3,000 members; Joined Greater London Arts, The Arts Council of Great Britain advisory panels, 1987; Presented, judged Schiltz Beer, Virgin Records competition; Television: Presented jazz programmes with Russell Davis, BBC2, 1878; Sang solo with Reggae Philharmonic Orchestra, Highway, ITV, 1990-91; Travelled Africa, studying African music, 1988; Set up Frontline Productions to promote Jazz music; MC, various major jazz festivals; Reggae Philharmonic Orchestra, on Highway, ITV, 1990-91; Vocalist, panellist, The Music Game Show, Channel 4, 1992; Films: Tell Me That You Love Me, BBC1, 1991; Close My Eyes (cinema and video release), 1991. Administrator, Britain's first National Music Day with Harvey Goldsmith, 1992; Director, Jazz Services, 1992; Freelance Consultant, music schools, projects, 1992; Chairman, Arts Council Jazz Committee; ACGTS Music Panelist, 1993; Founder and Chief Executive, Turnaround Project for music media and film for the disabled; Jazz Africa appearances at Berlin Jazz Festival; Recorded live album, 1997. Compositions: Commissioned by BBC2, composition for Midland Big Band, featuring Courtney Pine, performed, televised, Royal Albert Hall; Various compositions commissioned include: Royal Opera House Covent Garden, featuring Stan Tracey, Andy Sheppard, 1989; Jazz Africa (suite), by Apples and Snakes, 1991; TV themes for Carlton TV. Recordings: Album: Gail Force Big Band; Jazz Africa Big Band. Memberships: Chairperson, Arts Council Jazz Review; Started Jazz in Women Festival, 1997. Hobbies: Running; Squash; Steam trains. Current Management: Self-managed. Address: 5 St faiths Road, West Dulwich, London SE21 8JD, England.

THOMPSON Hank (Henry William), b. 3 Sept 1925, Waco, Texas, USA. Country Singer; Songwriter; Musician (guitar, harmonica). m. Dorothy. Career: Own radio series, Hank - The Hired Hand, 1942; Funder member, the Brazos Valley Boys, 1946; Recording artiste, 1949-; First country artist recording in stereo, 1959; Tutor, School of Country Music, Claremore, Oklahoma, 1973. Recordings: Country hits include: (I've Got) A Humpty Dumpty Heart; Whoa Sailor; The Wild Side Of Life (US Country Number 1); Waiting In The Lobby Of Your Heart; Rub-A-Dub-Dub; Breakin' The Rules; Honky Tonk Girl; The Blackboard Of My Heart; Breakin' In Another Heart; She's Just A Whole Lot Like You; Oklahoma Hills; Where Is The Circus?; The Older The Violin The Sweeter The Music; Mr Honky Tonk The King Of Western Swing; Numerous albums include: Songs Of The Brazos Valley, 1953; Hank!, 1957; Songs For Rounders, 1959; Live At The Golden Nugget (first live-in-concert country album), 1961; A Six Pack To Go, 1961; Just An Old Flame, 1967; Cab Driver - A Salute To The Mills Brothers, 1972; Movin' On, 1974;

Brand New Hank, 1978; Take Me Back To Texas, 1980; Hank Thompson, 1986; Here's To Country Music, 1988; Various compilation albums. Honour: Inducted into Country Music Hall Of Fame, 1989. Address: c/o Hank Thompson Enterprises, 5 Rushing Creek Court, Roanoke, TX 76262, USA.

THOMPSON John Alexander, b. 15 Aug 1942, Philadelphia, Pennsylvania, USA. Reverend; Gospel Singer; Choir Leader; Songwriter. Career: Founder: Sunlight Jubilee Juniors, 1955; Johnny Thompson Singers, 1965; Pennsylavania District F B H Choir, 1970; Sanctificaton, 1983; Member, Philadelphia Mass Choir and Gospel Music Preservation Alliance Choir; Johnny Thompson Singers, numerous tours, Europe and Africa, including: First Gospel act to play Montreux Festival, with Bessie Griffin, 1972; First Black Gospel act to produce own video, 1980; First Gospel act behind Iron Curtain, Poland, 1981; First Black American Gospel act to play Russia, Bulgaria and Egypt; Countless television and radio appearances, Europe; Performed with numerous Gospel acts including: Marion Wlliams; Bessie Griffin; Dorthy Love-Coates; Reverend James Cleveland; Evangelist Shirley Caesar; Dorothy Norwood. Compositions include: The Creation; Stranger On The Road; Get Up My Brother; If I Perish; Hold Out; Happy On My Way; There Must Be A Reason; If You Gonna Pray; Wrote several Gospel plays; Recordings: Albums: with The Johnny Thompson Singers: I'm On My Way To Zion, 1972; Philadelphia, 1975; Live At Montreux, 1977; Lord I Belong To You, 1982; Gospel At The Opera, 1985; Gospel Christmas, 1986; Spirit Of Gospel, 1987; Swing Low Sweet Chariot, 1988; Oh Happy Day!, 1990; 25 Years, 1990; Hand In Hand, 1993; Glory Glory Hallelujah, 1995; with The Pennsylvania District F B H Choir: Look Over Your Shoulders, 1974; Live At Lausanne, 1977. Honours: Prix Mahalia Jackson, Philadelphia, 1975. Memberships: National Convention of Gospel Choirs and Choruses; Gospel Minister, Gospel Music Workshop of America; Choral Director, Wynnefield Academy, Philadelphia. Current Management: Freddy J Angstmann. Address: Fronhof 100, CH-8260 Stein am Rhein, Switzerland.

THOMPSON Keith, b. 29 Jan 1956, Worcester, England. Blues and Rock Musician (electric and acoustic guitar, harmonica, piano, bass). m. Janette Kathleen Thompson, 26 Jun 1982, 1 son, 2 daughters. Musical Education: Self-taught. Career: Tours include: Netherlands, 1989; Denmark, 1990; UK, 1992, 1993, 1994 including appearances at The Mean Fiddler, London; The Standard, London; Greenbelt Festival, Bedfordshire; Crossrhythms Festival, Devon; Crossfire Festival, Liverpool; Road Dreams music for Tortworth TV shown on Channel 4, 1991, 1992. Recordings: Against The Odds, 1991; Young Hearts, 1992; Voice From Heaven, 1994. Honour: Songwriter Of The Year, 6 Counties Festival, 1990. Memberships: Musicians' Union; PRS; MCPS. Hobbies: Family; Walking; Swimming; Films; Television. Address: 46 Libertus Road, Cheltenham, Gloucester GL51 7EP, England.

THOMPSON Linda (Linda Peters). Singer; Songwriter. m. Richard Thompson, divorced. Career: UK tour as member of folk group Albion Band, 1972; Duo with Richard Thompson, 1972-82; Appearances include: Reading Festival, 1975; Regular UK tours; Co-writer, appeared in The Mysteries, 1975; Compositions include: Co-writer (with Betsy Cook): Telling Me Lies (recorded by Emmylou Harris; Linda Ronstadt; Reba McEntire). Recordings: Albums with Richard Thompson: Henry The Human Fly, 1972; I Want To See The Bright Lights Tonight, 1974; Hokey Pokey, 1975; Pour Like Silver, 1975; First Light, 1978; Sunnyvista, 1979; Shoot Out The Lights, 1982; Solo album: One Clear Moment, 1985.

THOMPSON Richard, b. 3 Apr 1949, London, England. Singer; Songwriter; Musician (guitar). m. Linda Peters, divorced. Career: Co-founder, guitarist, folk group Fairport Convention, 1968-1971; Concerts include: Folk Meets Pop, Royal Albert Hall, 1969; Royal Festival Hall, with Joni Mitchell, 1969; Bath Festival Of Blues & Progressive Music, 1970; London Palladium, 1970; Partnership with wife, Linda, 1972-1982; Concerts include: Reading Festival, 1975; Fairport Convention reunion concert, 1980; South Yorkshire Folk Festival, 1982; Also appeared together in groups Albion Country Band; Hokey Pokey; Sour Grapes; Solo artiste, 1982-; Regular worldwide appearances include: Guitar Legends, Seville, Spain, 1991; Cropredy Festival, 1992, 1995. Recordings: Albums: with Fairport Convention: Fairport Convention, 1968; What We Did On Our Holidays, 1969; Unhalfbricking, 1969; Liege And Lief, 1970; Full House, 1970; with Linda Thompson: I Want To See The Bright Lights Tonight, 1974; Hokey Pokey, 1975; Pour Like Silver, 1975; First Light, 1978; Sunnyvista, 1979; Shoot Out The Lights, 1982; Small Town Romance, 1982; Solo albums: Henry The Human Fly, 1972; Guitar Vocal, 1976; Strict Tempo, 1981; Hand Of Kindness, 1983; Across A Crowded Room, 1985; Daring Adventures, 1986; The Marksman (soundtrack to BBC drama series), 1987; Live, Love, Larf And Loaf, 1987; Amnesia, 1988; Rumour And Sigh, 1991; Sweet Talker, 1992; Watching The Dark - The History Of Richard Thompson, 1993; You? Me? Us?, 1996; Also featured on: Love Chronicles, Al Stewart, 1969; Drunk With Passion, The Golden Palominos, 1991; The Hunter, Jennifer Warnes, 1992; 99.9°F, Suzanne Vega, 1992. Honours include: New Music Awards: Solo Artist, Songwriter of Year, Life Achievement Trophy, 1991; Q Award, Best Songwriter, 1991. Current Management: Gary Stamler, Suite 2400, 1801 Century Park East, Los Angeles, CA 90067, USA.

THOMPSON Robert E "Butch", b. 28 Nov 1943, Stillwater, Minnesota, USA. Musician (piano, clarinet). m. Mary Ellen Niedenfuer, 20 July 1991, 2 sons. Education: BA, University of Minnesota. Vareer: Clarinetist, Hall Brothers Jazz Band, 1962-94; Pianist, leader, Butch Thompson Trio in residency, National Public Radio, 1978-86; World Tours as pianist include Cairo, Egypt, 1994; 1997; European Festivals; Appearances with orchestras include: Hartford Symphony; Minnesota Orchestra; National tour of off-Broadway show, Jelly Roll, 1996-97; Major US jazz festivals, 1970-. Compositions include: Ecuadorean Memories; Yancey On My Mind. Recordings include: 7 solo CDs; Over 100 other recordings, 25 as leader or soloist. Membership: American Federation of Musicians, local 30-73. Current Management: Donna Zajonc Management. Address: C/o Dionna Zajonc Management, Box 7023, Ann Arbor, MI 48107, USA.

THOMPSON Wayne, b. 28 July 1947, Toronto, Ontario, Canada. Artist Manager; Theatrical Producer. m. Wendy Cochrane, 24 July 1971, 2 sons. Education: BA, University of Toronto, Political Science, Economics. Career: Manager for several major artists; Currently manager for: The Barra MacNeils, Sydney, Nova Scotia. Membership: Director, Pacific Music Industry Association. Address: Pacific Music Industry Association, 177 W 7 Avenue, 4th Floor, Vancouver, British Columbia V5Y 1L8, Canada.

THOMSON Colin, b. 6 Jul 1937. University Teacher; Researcher; Musician (all saxophones, piano, drums). m. Maureen Margaret Green, 1 Sep 1962, 2 sons, 2 daughters. Education: BSc, PhD, Chemistry, Leeds University. Career: Member, Eric Thomson Band, 1953-65; Colin Thomson Big Band, 1974-; Colin Thomson Jazz Quartet; Co-Director, Fife Youth Jazz Orchestra, 1975-80; Director, St Andrews Music Centre Big Band, 1992-. Publications: 130 Scientific

publications. Honours: Chairman, Association for International Cancer Research. Membership: Musicians' Union. Hobbies: Music Education and Jazz Courses in St Andrews. Address: 12 Drumcarrow Road, St Andrews KY16 8SE, Scotland.

THOMSON Kenny, b. 18 Mar 1944, Irvine, Scotland. Musician (accordion). m. Cathy Rowan, 3 Oct 1970, 2 sons. Musical Education: Studied for 3 years with Robert McF Adamson, Cumnock. Career: Played with small local bands from age 10; Started radio broadcasting with BBC Radio Scotland, 1976; Currently, leader of The Wardlaw Scottish Dance Band. Recordings: 3 recordings of Scottish Country Dances for the Royal Scottish Country Dance Society. Membership: Musicians' Union. Hobbies: Car maintenance; Hill walking. Address: 20 Walker Court, Cumnock, Ayrshire KA18 1TF, Scotland.

THORDARSON Gunnar, b. 4 Jan 1945, Holmavík, Iceland. Composer; Producer. m. Sigrun Toby Herman, 2 sons, 3 daughters. Musical Education: Mostly self-taught; Counterpoint lessons. Career: Record producer and writer, 1966-; Member, group Hljomar, 1963-69; Member, Trubrot, 1969-73; Record producer, over 100 records; Written hundreds of television commercials, music for 3 Icelandic films and scores for two musicals. Compositions: 440 songs as songwriter; Songs recorded by various artists; Work performed by Icelandic Symphony Orchestra. Recordings: Himinn Og Jörd, 1981; Borgar Bragur, 1986; Islensk Alpydulög, 1980; Reykjavikurflugur, 1986; I Loftinu, 1987; Ungir Mennà Uppleid, 1997. Publications: Film music: Pitt Fyrsta, 1994; Agnes, 1996. Honours: Honorary Prize for Service in Icelandic Music, 1997; Arts Grant from Government, 1997. Memberhsips: STEF, Iceland; FIH, Iceland. Hobbies: Horses; Reading; Films. Current Management: Self-managed. Address: Aegisgata 10, Reykjavik 101, Iceland.

THORDSEN Hanne, b. 6 Dec 1954, Copenhagen, Denmark. Singer; Composer; Writer; Actress. (1) Keld Jakobsen, (2) Lasse Aagaard Nielsen, 1988, 2 daughters. Education: As social worker and Kindergarten teacher. Musical Education: Self-taught. Career: Singer with group Knap and Nap, (mainly Irish and Scottish Folk music and some Blues); Formed folk-rock group Freja; Performed at festivals including: Roskilde, Skagen and Tonder; Television appearance in 1984 and some radio broadcasting, 1993; Currently appearing as Salene in musical Atlantis at Östre Gasvark. Recordings: Kom Nu, Freja, 1988; Participant on the album Folkemusik Til Oerne; Atlantis (album of the musical), 1995. Membership: DJBFA. Hobbies: Music; Painting; Family. Current Management: Morten Grunwald, Östre Gasvark Theatre, Denmark. Address: Gl Mejerivej 14 D, DK-3050 Humlebaek, Denmark.

THORHALLSSON Olafur Gaukur, b. 11 Aug 1930, Iceland. Musician (guitar); Composer; Conductor; Producer; Teacher. m. (1) 1 son, 4 daughters, (2) Svanhildur Jakobsdottir, 8 June 1963, 1 son, 1 daughter. Education: Classical guitar lessons; Self-taught jazz guitar; Studied composition, Music Academy of Reykjavik, 1985; Composition, 1984, Composition for films and video, 1988, Grove School of Music, Los Angeles, USA; Guitar Institute, Hollywood, 1993. Career: Musician, Bandleader, Composer and Arranger on numerous shows, stage, television and radio; Own TV show, Icelandic State Television, 1968-71; Concerts with international vocal groups include The Mills Brothers, The Platters, The Delta Rhythm Boys; Arrangements for different kinds of groups, orchestras and artists including Björk; Head of own music school (mainly guitar), 1975-; Participated on over 100 albums as composer, lyricist, arranger, conductor, producer, musician. Compositions: Music for Icelandic feature films;

Documentaries, TV shows and plays; Popular songs over 30 years. Recordings: 11 albums with own band or orchestra, 1968-94. Publications: Author of educational material including books and cassettes, mainly for guitar students. Memberships: Icelandic Musicians' Union; Performing Rights Society of Iceland; Jazzvakning. Current Management: Self-managed. Address: Sidumula 17, 108 Reykjavik, Iceland.

THORHALLSSON Robert, b. 12 Aug 1971, Husavik, Thingeyjarsysla, Iceland. Musician (trumpet, saxophone, drums, double bass, electric bass). Education: Jazz Music Graduate on electric bass; Self-taught on double bass; Tuition on trumpet and saxophone. Career: Played in shows staged on Iceland Superstar 95-96; World premiere of Jim Cartwright's Stone Free; The Beatles' Sergeant Pepper's Lonely Hearts Club Band staged by the Icelandic Symphony, 1997. Recordings: Crougie dou là, 1995; Merman, 1996; Superstar, 1995; Stone Free, music from a play, 1996; Love, live recordings from Stone Free, 1996. Publications: Superstar, 1995; Stone Free, 1996; Merman, 1996. Honours: Gold Albums, 1996, 1997; Platinum Album, 1997. Membership: Icelandic Musicians' Association (FIH). Hobby: Sport. Current Management: Self. Address: Sigluvogur 15, 104 Reykjavik, Iceland.

THORN Tracey, b. 26 Sept, 1962. Singer; Songwriter. Education: Hull University. Career: Member, trio Marine Girls; Forms duo Everything But The Girl with musician Ben Watt, 1983-; Appearances include: Regular UK tours, 1984-; World Tour, 1990, including Japan; Friends of the Earth Benefit Concerts, 1990; Red Hot and Dance AIDS Benefit Concert, 1991; UK and US Tours, 1993-95; World tour, 1996-97 including Japan and Australasia. Compositions: Writer, co-writer with Ben Watt, and Massive Attack, of own material for trio, duo and solo work. Recordings: Albums: Solo album: A Distant Shore, 1982; with Marine Girls: Beach Party, 1980; Lazy Ways, 1983; with Everything But The Girl: Eden, 1984; Everything But The Girl (US only), 1984; Love Not Money, 1985; Baby, The Stars Shine Bright, 1986; Idlewild, 1988; The Language Of Life, 1990; Worldwide, 1991; Essence And Rare (Japan only), 1992; Acoustic, 1992 (US only); Home Movies - Best Of Everything But The Girl, 1993; Amplified Heart, 1994; Walking WOunded, 1996; with Massive Attack: Protection, 1995; Guest singer, albums by Style COuncil; Go Betweens; Lloyd Cole; Adam F; Singles include: with Everything But The Girl: Each and Every One, 1984; Come On Home, 1986; I DOn't Want To Talk About It, 1988; Missing, 1995; Walking Wounded, 1996; Wrong, 1996; Contributor with Massive Attack, film soundtrack for Batman Forever, 1995. Current Management: JFD Management, 106 Dalling Road, London W6 0JA, England.

THOROGOOD George, b. 31 Dec 1952, Wilmington, Delaware, USA. Blues Musician (guitar). Career: Former baseball player; Formed own group the Destroyers, 1973-; Opened for the Rolling Stones, 1981; Appeared at Live Aid with Albert Collins, 1985. Recordings: Albums: George Thorogood And The Destroyers, 1978; Move It On Over, 1978; Better Than The Rest, 1979; More George Thorogood And The Destroyers, 1980; Bad To The Bone, 1982; Maverick, 1985; Live, 1986; Born To Be Bad, 1988; Let's Work Together, 1995. Current Management: Mike Donahue Management, PO Box 807, Lewisburg, WV 24901, USA.

THORPE Anthony John, b. 20 July 1945, London, England. Musician (guitar); Writer; Singer; Actor. m. Shirley Atherton, 14 Feb 1968, 1 son. Education: St Ignatius' College, London. Career: Guitarist, arranger, Wee Willie Harris; Tommy Steele (including West End); Guitarist, singer, Rubettes, 1970's; Guitarist, singer, The Firm, 1980's; Writer, actor, Cooger and Dark two-man show, Edinburgh Fringe; Blues Band Gas Company, John Caira Band; Also worked with Tony Crombie, Gary Boyle, Mike Walker, Tal Farlow, Jimmy Smith and Denny Laine. Recordings: 7 albums with The Rubettes; Lead vocals on two hit singles; with The Firm: Arthur Daley; Solo album: Illusions and Dangerous Prayer. Publications: Concert reviews, The Guardian, 1980s. Memberships: Musicians' Union; PRS. Hobbies: Music; Spiritual philosophy. Address: 143 Marsden Road, Burnley, Lancashire BB10 2QW, England.

THORUP Jesper, b. 9 June 1952, Copenhagen, Denmark. Composer; Singer; Musician (drums). Musical Education: Alex Riel; Hans Fülling; Ed Thigpen. Career: Dana Gillespie (UK); The Rustics (USA); Mal Waldren Trio (USA); Benny Waters (USA); Peter Thorup and Jesper Band; Paul Millins (UK); Sam Mitchel Blue Vikings (UK/Denmark); Dexter Gordon; Jackie McLean; Danish Grand Prix; Danish Radio Jazzgroup. Compositions: Composed and recorded with: Annegrete: Hvem Sir; Duggen Falder: Drops: Koernes Sang; Aorta: Havnerfunk. Honours: First prize, Best Soloist, Dunquerque International Jazz Festival, France, 1975. Memberships: DMF; DJFBA. Hobbies: Painting; Art. Address: Fabritius Alle 16, DK-2930 Klampenborg, Denmark.

THOUMIRE Simon John, b. 11 July 1970, Edinburgh, Scotland. Musician (concertina); Composer. Musical Education: Self-taught. Career: Started at 16 years old with Seannachie, 1989; Formed duo with Ian Carr; Television performance on Aly Bain's Shetland Session; First tour USA, 1990; Formed Simon Thoumire Three, 1992; Television: Aly Bains Transatlantic Sessions, 1995; Formed duo with Fergus McKenzie. Recordings: with Seannachie: Take Note, 1987; Devil's Delight, 1992; Hootz, Simon Thoumire and Ian Carr, 1990; Waltzes For Playboys, Simon Thoumire Three, 1994; Exhibit A, Simon Thoumire and Fergus MacKenzie, 1995. Honours: BBC Radio 2 Young Tradition Award, 1989; Folk Roots, Most Innovative Performance, 1989. Membership: Musicians' Union. Hobbies: Walking; Running; Music. Current Management: Hootz! Productions. Address: 17 Redford Drive, Edinburgh EH13 0BL, Scotland.

THRALE Carlos Heinrich, b. 3 Aug 1962, London, England. Musician (guitar). Education: BA Hons, Nottingham Trent University. Musical Education: ARCM, Royal College Of Music. Career: Session musician for: Mica Paris; Freeze; Dr Egg; Sugar Bullet; Radio and television commercials; Also lecturer, Course coordinator, Popular Music. Publications: Guitar Theory and Technique, video and book, EMI, 1985. Membership: Musicians' Union. Current Management: Spencer Wells. Address: 12 Grove Road, Bingham, Nottinghamshire NG13 8DY, England.

TIELENS Louis, (Country Lewis), b. 2 Aug 1942, Beringen, Belgium. Broadcaster. m. Germa Baelen, 6 Aug 1984, 1 son, 1 daughter. Education: College. Career: DJ "Country Lewis"; Retired manager, Radio Animo; Retired Station Manager, Radio Loksbergen; Producer, syndicated country music programmes; De Bazuin non-profit organization; With wife, producer, gospel programme Good News. Membership: Executive Committee, Country and Western Association, Belgium; European Country Music Disc Jockeys Association; European Country Music Association; Greater Southern Country Music Association. Hobby: Reading. Address: Pauwenlaan 23, B-3583 Paal-Beringen, Belgium.

TIERS Wharton, b. 11 Feb 1953, Philadelphia, Pennsylvania, USA. Producer; Musician (drums, keyboards, guitar); Songwriter; Engineer. Education: BA, English, Villanova University, Pennsylvania. Career: Producer, engineer, Indie records, 1980s-90s; Over 120

records produced; Member, Laurie Anderson's Band; Glenn Branca's Band; Played with: Theatrical Girls; Glorious Strangers; Played on US network. Recordings: Albums as producer: 6 albums with Sonic Youth; with Dinosaur Jr: Just Like Heaven; You're Living All Over Me; with Gumball: Special Kiss; Unsane; Urban Discipline; Biohazard; In The Meantime, Helmet; God Knows It's True, Teenage Fan Club; Anaesthesia, Dean Wareham; Primitive Origins, Prong; Headkick Facsimile, Cop Shoot Cop; Pussy Gold 5000, Pussy Galore. Hobbies: Writing; Hiking; Electronic design. Current Management: Susan Sidel Management.

TIJSSENS Michael Warren, b. 27 Mar 1961, Amersfoort, Netherlands. Lyricist; Screenwriter; Playwright. m. Dyna Justin, 26 Sept 1987, 2 sons. Education: Royal Academy of Dramatic Art; Sorbonne University. Musical Education: Self-taught. Career: Numerous roles as actor, singer, writer, director, dramatist and producer; Now writing for artists in music business; Has worked with: Bob Geldof; Rick Smith; Karl Hyde. Recordings: Joint Venture; Tropical Corridor; Blanc Nègre; Sens Unique Show; Destination Tomorrow. Publications: Rendez-Vous; Cahiers de Prospero; Theatre Public. Honours: Prix d'Honneur, Institut Radiodiffusion Suisse. Memberships: SACEM; SACD; ATLF. Current Management: Media Writers and Translators. Address: 13 Boulevard de la Marne, 77420 Champs-Sur-Marne, France.

TIKARAM Tanita, b. 12 Aug 1969, Münster, Germany. Singer; Songwriter; Musician (guitar). Career: Moved to UK, 1982; Songwriter, 1987-; Support tour, Warren Zevon, 1988; Major international tours, 1989, 1992. Recordings: Albums: Ancient Heart, 1988; The Sweet Keeper, 1990; Everybody's Angel, 1991; Eleven Kinds Of Loneliness, 1992; Lovers In The City, 1995; Singles: Good Tradition, 1988; Twist In My Sobriety, 1988; Only The Ones We Love, 1991; I Might Be Crying, 1995; The Cappuccino Songs, 1998. Address: c/o Stephen Budd Management, 109B Regents Park Road, London NW1 8UR, England.

TIKHONOV Dimitri, b. 6 August 1964, Vladivostok, Russia. Keyboard; Vocal; Composer. m. Juliette Alix, 12 August 1994, 1 son. Education: Jazz School, St Petersburg, Russia. Career: Composer, Keyboarder & Singer of the group, Nom, St Petersburg, 1987-94; Tours over Western Europe, Italy, Czechia, France, Germany, Switzerland and Hungary; Nom video demonstrated on BBC2, MTV, M6, MCM, TV channels; Solo career of composer and bass, Geneva Opera's Choir, 1995-. Compositions: Nom, Masters of the USSR; Ape's Snout, 1995; Nom, Made in Europe, 1997. Recordings: Brutto, Nom, LP, CD, 1989; To Hell With It, LP, Super Disc, 1990; Senka - Mosgaz, LP, CD, 1992, 1994; Live is Game, CD, Ultracompact, 1995; In the Name of Mind, CD, 1995, 1996; Les Sons De Carton, solo, 1997. Honours: Skotinorap, Best Alternative Video of Russia, 1993; Nina-2, Grand Prix Exotica, 1994; Ukr Blues, Best Low Budget Video, 1996. Address: Tikhonov Dimitri, 9 Rue Du Mont-Blanc, 74100 Ville-La-Grande, France.

TILBROOK Glenn, b. 31 Aug 1957, London, England. Vocalist; Musician (guitar); Songwriter. Career; Founder member, Squeeze, 1974-; Longstanding writing partnership with Chris Difford; Performances include: US tours, 1978-; Reading Rock Festival, 1978; Dalymount Festival, Dublin, 1980; Jamaica World Music Festival, 1982; Support to Fleetwood Mac, US tour, 1990; Crystal Palace Bowl, 1991; Support to Bryan Adams, UK tour, 1992. Compositions include: Co-writer, with Elvis Costello, From A Whisper To A Scream, 1981; Songs for musical, Labelled With Love, 1983. Recordings: Albums: Squeeze, 1978; Cool For Cats, 1979; Argy Bargy, 1980; East Side Story, 1981; Sweets From A Stranger, 1982;

Singles 45's And Under, 1982; Cosi Fan Tutti Frutti, 1985; Babylon And On, 1987; Frank, 1989; A Round And A Bout, 1990; Greatest Hits, 1992; Some Fantastic Place, 1993; Ridiculous, 1995; Singles include: Take Me I'm Yours, 1978; Cool For Cats, 1979; Up The Junction, 1979; Another Nail In My Heart, 1980; Pulling Mussels From A Shell, 1980; Hourglass, 1987. Current Management: Firstars, 3520 Hayden Avenue, Culver City, CA 90232, USA.

TILLIS Mel (Lonnie Melvin), b. 8 Aug 1932, Tampa, Florida, USA. Country Singer; Songwriter; Musician (guitar, fiddle). Education: University of Florida. Career: Began performing, recording, 1956-57; Toured extensively with The Statesiders, 1960s-70s; Numerous tours and television appearances; Recorded duets with Glen Campbell and Nancy Sinatra; Film apperances: WW And The Dixie Dance Kings; Smokey And The Bandit 2; Murder In Music City; Uphill All The Way; Owned several publishing companies; Also cattle breeder. Compositions include: I'm Tired; Tupelo County Jail; I Ain't Never (all hits for Webb Pirce); Lonely Island Pearl, Johnny and Jack; Heart Over Mind, Ray Price; Ten Thousand Drums, Carl Smith; Detroit City (co-written with Danny Dill) Bobby Bare, 1963; The Snakes Crawl At Night, Charley Pride, 1966; Ruby Don't Take Your Love To Town, Johnny Darrell, 1967 (Also hit for Kenny Rogers And The First Edition, 1969). Recordings: US Country Number 1 hits: I Ain't Never; Good Woman Blues; Heart Healer; I Believe In You; Coca Cola Cowboy; Southern Rains; Other hits include: Life Turned Her That Way; Stateside; These Lonely Hands Of Mine; Send Me Down To Tucson, featured in film Every Which Way But Loose; Take My Hand; Numerous albums include: Heart Over Mind, 1961; Stateside, 1966; Mr Mel, 1967; One More Time, 1970; Mel Tillis, 1972; Sawmill, 1973; M-M-Mel And The Statesiders, 1975; Are You Sincere, 1979; The Great Mel Tillis, 1979; Southern Rain, 1980; M-M-Mel Live, 1980; It's A Long Way To Daytona, 1982; After All This Time, 1983; New Patches, 1984; California Road, 1985; Four Legends (with Jerry Lee Lewis, Webb Pierce, Faron Young), 1985; Also recorded with: Glen Campbell; Nancy Sinatra; Sherry Bryce. Publications: Stutterin' Boy, The Autobiography Of Mel Tillis (with Walter Wager). Honours: Inducted into Nashville Songwriters International Hall Of Fame; 1976; CMA Entertainer Of The Year, 1976. Address: c/o Mel Tillis Enterprises, PO Box 1626, Branson, MO 65615, USA.

TILLMAN Floyd, b. 8 Dec 1914, Ryan, Oklahoma, USA. Country Singer; Songwriter; Musician (mandolin, banjo, guitar). Career: Performed as member of Adolph Hofner; Mack Clark; Blue Ridge Playboys, 1930s; Solo artiste, 1939-60; One of first country artists to use electric guitar; Now semi-retired. Compositions: It Makes No Difference Now, hit for Bing Crosby, Gene Autry; Slippin' Around, recorded by numerous artists including Ernest Tubb, Jimmy Wakeley. Recordings: Hits include: They Took The Stars Out Of Heaven (US Country Number 1); GI Blues; Drivin' Nails In My Coffin; I Love You So Much It Hurts; Albums include: Let's Make Memories, 1962; Country, 1967; Dream On, 1968; I'll Still Be Loving You, 1969; Floyd Tillman And Friends, with Willie Nelson and Merle Haggard, 1982. Honours: Inducted into Nashville Songwriters Association Hall Of Fame, 1970; Inducted into Country Music Hall Of Fame, 1984.

TILSTON Stephen Thomas Gregory, b. 26 Mar 1950, Liverpool, England. Musician (guitar); Songwriter. m. Maggie Boyle, 27 Jan 1984, 1 son, 3 daughters. Education: Trained as graphic artist. Musical Education: Self-taught. Career: Solo, also duo with Maggie Boyle; Member, Ship Of Fools, with John Renbourn; Guitarist, Ballet Rambert. Recordings: Acoustic Confusion, 1971; Collection, 1973; Songs From The Press Rehearsal, 1977, In For A Penny, 1983; Life By Misadventure, 1987; Swans At Goole, 1990; Of Moor And Mesa, 1992;

And So It Goes, 1995. Membership: British Longbow Society. Hobby: Archery. Current Management: Alan King. Address: 78 Sydenham Park, London SE26 4DP, England.

TILTON Martha Ellen, b. 14 Nov 1915, Corpus Christi, Texas, USA. Singer. m. James L Brooks, 3 May 1953, 2 sons, 1 daughter. Musical Education: Piano. Career: Carnegie Hall Concert, Benny Goodman, 1937; Philco Radio Hall Of Fame programme; Radio, with Paul Whiteman Orchestra, 4 years, mid 1940's; Alka Seltzer Program CBS, 8 years; Martha Tilton, Count Maskey Show, National Broadcasting Company, 6 years; Capitol Records; Decca Records; Two overseas tours with Jack Benny, Larry Adler; Ingrid Bergmann, during World War II: South Pacific, 1943; Germany, 1944. Honours: Academy Of Television Arts And Sciences: Most Outstanding Female Personality, 1959-60, 1960-61; For Dedication and Service to the City, City Council Los Angeles, 1983; National Academy Of Arts And Sciences, Hall Of Fame Award, 1987. Memberships: American Federation Television and Radio Artists; American Guild Of Variety Artists. Hobbies: Needlepoint. Address: 2257 Mandeville Canyon Road, Los Angeles, CA 90049, USA.

TIMKO John Patrick, b. 6 Dec 1963, Tuscola, Michigan, USA. Singer; Songwriter. Education: Delta College, University Center, Michigan. Musical Education: Self-taught. Career: Country Music Fan Fair, 1991; Ernest Tubbs Midnight Jamboree, 1992; Charlie Daniels Round-Up, 1995; Opening act for major acts including Pam Tillis, Waylon Jennings, Billy Dean, Patty Loveless and Hank Thompson, 1991-; Appeared on Tanya Tucker's video Some Kind of Trouble. Compositions: I'd Do Anything For Love. Recordings: I Can't Forget You; Nights Like This; Hillbilly Girl; Beat Of A Heart; My Old Girl's The Best Girl. Honours: Achievement Award from Independent Record Charts, 1989; CMAA American Eagle Award, 1992. Memberships: Country Music Association; Broadcast Music Inc; AMofM. Current Management: J&V Management, 143 Elmwood Road, Caro, MI 48723, USA.

TIMONEN Marko, b. 7 Sept 1966, Kiukainen, Finland. Musician (drums). Musical Education: Studied with Jukkis Uotila, Tim Ferchen. Sibelius Academy, 1986. Career: Played in Pori Big Band; Played on various tours with groups led by Jukka Perko; Pekka Luukka; Kirmo Lintinen; Drummer with Mika Mylläri Quintet and Sonja Lumme Quartet; Participated in workshops arranged by UMO and Finnish Radio. Recordings include: Portrait By Heart, Jukka Perko Quartet. Honour: Best Young Jazz Soloist, European Championships, 1990. Address: Susitie 28 F 42, 00800 Helsinki, Finland.

TINETA (Tineta Michelle Couturier), b. 24 Aug 1972, Red Deer, Alberta, Canada. Singer; Songwriter; Musician (guitar, piano, drums). Musical Education: Self-taught. Career: Solo artist, 1989-; Support act for Steve Wariner, Pam Tillis; Major concerts: Grand Ole Opry, 1989; Big Valley Jamboree, Craven, Saskatchewan; Big Valley Jamboree, Camrose, Alberta. Compositions: Slippin Away; Love On The Line; Let's Make Up; It's Rainin'; Too Bad So Sad; Walkin' That Line; That's What Love's About. Recordings: Albums: Love On The Line; Drawn To The Fire. Honours: 3 Peoples Choice Nominations, Single of Year, Writer of Year, Most Promising Artist, 1991; Vista Rising Star Nomination; Album of Year Nomination; Video of Year Nomination. Memberships: CCMA; SOCAN; CMN; CARAS; ARIA. Hobbies: Horse riding; Water activities; Songwriting. Current Management: Keith and Dawnalyn Couturier. Address: Box 5039, Drayton Valley, Alberta T7A 1R3, Canada.

TIPLER Paul. Record Producer; Engineer. Recordings: As producer, co-producer, albums include: Mars Audiac Quintet, Stereolab; Dream Of 100 Nations, Transglobal Underground; Weird's Bar & Grill, Pop Will Eat Itself; Duniya, Loop Guru; In Love With, Mambo Taxi; Chocolate Revenge, Voodoo Queens; As engineer: Eat Yourself Whole, Kingmaker; Suspira, Miranda Sex Garden; Peggy Suicide, Julian Cope; Primo, Dr Feelgood; Singles with: Kingmaker; Shriek; Fun-Da-Mental; Pop Will Eat Itself; Back To The Planet; Jah Wobble; New Fast Automatic Daffodils. Current Management: c/o Stephen Budd Management, 109B Regents Park Road, London NW1 8UR, England.

TISO Wagner, b. Tres Pontas, Minas Gerais, Brazil. Musician (piano, keyboards); Composer; Arranger; Conductor; Musical Director. m. Giselle de Andrade Goldoni, 2 daughters. Musical Education: Self-taught. Career: Soundtracks: O Guarani, Norma Bengell, 1995; A Ostra e o Vento, Walter Lima Jnr, 1997; Television: Meu Marido, Walter Lima Jnr, TV Globo; O Sorriso do Lagarto, Roberto Talma, TV Globo; Suites: Suite Tom Jobim, 1995; Cenas Brasileiras, 1995; Stage apperances: Soloist, Rhapsody In Blue, 1997; Encontro de Violoncellos, 1997; Numerous concert and festival appearances include: Montreux Jazz Festival, with Flora Purim, Airto Moreira and Ron Carter (1974), and in 1982; Festival de Música Latina, Cuba, 1983, and Paris, 1986; Festival de Música Brasileira, Rome, 1984; Jazz festivals in São Paolo, Berlin, Montmartre and Rio de Janiero; Compositions include: Coração de Estudante, for film Jango; Chorata, suite for piano and orchestra; Lenda Ao Boto; Choro de Mae; Cafezais Sem Fim. Recordings include: Wagner Tiso, 1978; Baobab, 1990; O Livro de Jó, 1993; Brazilian Scenes, 1997. Publications: Wagner Tiso Ao Vivo na Europa, 1982; Giselle, 1986; A Floresta Amazônica (Villa Lobos), 1987; Cine Brasil (original soundtracks), 1989; Wagner Tiso Ao Vivo, with Rio Cello Ensemble, 1995. Honours: Best Arranger, for Sentinela, Milton Nascimento, 1981; Best Instrumental recording, Todas as Teclas, with Cesar Camargo Mariano, 1983; Best Soundtracks: Jango, 1984; Chico Rei, 1987. Memberships: AMAR; OMB. Hobbies: Games; Reading. Current Management: Giselle de Andrade Goldoni, Tres Mineiro Produços Artisticas Ltda. Address: Rua Cesário Alvim 55/107 Bla, Humaitá, Rio De Janiero, RJ 22261-030, Brazil.

TISSENDIER Claude, b. 1 Oct 1952, Toulouse, France. Musician (saxophones, clarinet). Musical Education: 6 years Conservatoire. Career: All major jazz festivals in France; Member, Claude Bolling Band, 20 years; Leader, own band, Saxomania, 10 years. Recordings with: Benny Carter, 1988; Spike Robinson, 1989; Phil Woods, 1991; Guy Lafitte, 1993; Marlene Verplanck, 1994; Clark Terry, 1995; 20 albums with Claude Bolling, 1978-95. Honours: Sidney Bechet Prize, 1987; Best Jazz Recording Prize, 1986, 1988; Bill Coleman Prize, 1989; Django d'Or, 1996. Hobby: Cinema. Address: 5 Rue Gracieuse, 75005 Paris, France.

TITELMAN Russ, b. 16 Aug 1944, Los Angeles, California, USA. Record Company Executive; Record Producer. m. Carol Wikarska, 10 May 1978. Career: Vice-President, A&R Department, and record producer, Warner Brothers Records, New York, 1971-. Recordings include: As producer: with Randy Newman: Sail Away, 1972; Good Old Boys, 1974; Little Criminals, 1977; with Ry Cooder: Paradise And Lunch, 1973; with James Taylor: Gorilla, 1975; In The Pocket, 1976; with Rickie Lee Jones: Rickie Lee Jones, 1979; Pirates, 1981; with Paul Simon: Heart And Bones, 1983; with George Benson: 20/20, 1985; with Steve Winwood: Back In The High Life, 1986; Higher Love, 1986; with Miriam Makeba: Sangoma, 1988; with Eric Clapton: Journeyman, 1989; Also featured on recordings by: Rufus and Chaka Khan; Ladysmith Black Mambazo; Little Feat; George Harrison. Honours: Numerous Grammy Awards with: Rickie Lee Jones; Rufus and Chaka Khan; Steve Winwood; Eric Clapton. Address: c/o Warner Brothers Records, 75 Rockefeller Plaza, New York, NY 10019, USA.

TIVEY Caroline (Cara), b. 19 Feb 1959, Wellingborough, Northamptonshire, England. Musician (piano); Backing Vocalist. m. Micky Harris, 10 Oct 1988. Musical Education: Grade 8 piano, Birmingham School of Speech and Drama. Career: Worked with: Fine Young Cannibals; Everything But The Girl; Fuzzbox; Billy Bragg; The Lilac Time; Blur; Michael Stipe (REM); Numerous worldwide tours; Television appearances include: Top Of The Pops; The Tube; The Word; Hootenanny; Letterman; The Late Show; MTV. Recordings: with Everything But The Girl: Baby The Stars Shine Bright; with The Lilac Time: And Love For All; The Astronauts; The Laundry; with Billy Bragg: Workers Playtime; Don't Try This At Home; The Internationale; with Ted Chippington: She Loves You; Man In A Suitcase. Honours: Number 1 charity single with Billy Bragg, She's Leaving Home, 1988. Membership: Musicians' Union. Hobbies: Hillwalking; Swimming; Playing bridge. Address: Flat 1, 48 Somers Road, Malvern Link, Worcestershire WR14 1JB, England.

TOBIN Karen, b. Drexel Hill, Pennsylvania, USA. Singer; Songwriter; Musician (guitar). m. Tim Boyle, divorced, 2 daughters. Education: College degree in Applied Science Education. Musical Education: Vocals, Bryn Mawr Conservatory of Music. Career: Recording artist with Arista; Atlantic Records; Nashville; Video; CMT; TNN. Compositions: Co-writer, Holdin' Back The Tears, L A Cowboys; Don't Want To Give Up On Love, Sam Harris. Recordings: Album: Carolina Smokey Man. Honours: Nomination, Country Vocalist and Music Connection, 1992; Nomination, Vocalist of the Year, CCMA, 1995. Memberships: AFTRA; SAG; CMA. Hobbies: Bike riding; Hiking; Reading; Cooking; Travel; Snorkeling. Current Management: Les Oreck, Weisberg and Associates Management. Address: 4451 Canoga Drive, Woodland Hills, CA 91403, USA.

TOCANNE Bruno, b. 19 Mar 1955, Paris, France. Jazz Musician (drums); Bandleader. 2 sons. Education: Primary School Teacher studies, University. Musical Education: Private lessons with jazz drummers; Workshops with Steve Lacy. Career: Bandleader, Bruno Tocanne Réunion; Appearances include: Montreal Jazz Festival; Zagreb Jazz Festival, 1985; Belgrade Jazz Festival, 1985; Tour, Poland, 1992; TF1-France 2, France 3, 1993; Festival Radio-France, 1995; France-Musique (radio), 1995. Recordings: Albums: Hors-Sèrie, B Tocanne, S Domancich, Philippe Sellah, Michel Saulvier, 1992; Odessa, Bruno Tocanne Réunion, S Domacich, P Rogers, Erci d'Enfert; Funérals, Sophia Domanisch Trio and Paul Rogers, John Greaves, 1994. Membership: Vice-President, UMJ (Union of Jazz Musicians), 1993-. Current Management: Association Jazzland. Address: 80 Rue de Stalingrad, 78800 Houilles, France.

TOD A, b. New York, USA. Vocalist; Musician (bass). Career: Vocalist, musician, Cop Shoot Cop, 1988-; Several international tours, Japan; Europe; US; Appearances at Reading Festival, 1992, 1994; World tour, 1993. Recorded radio session for John Peel, BBC Radio 1, 1992. Recordings: Albums: Consumer Revolt, 1990; White Noise; Ask Questions Later; Release, 1994; EPs: Headkick Facsimile; Piece Man; Suck City. Address: c/o Big Cat Records, PO Box 3074, Chiswick, London W4 4ZN, England.

TODOROV Dimo. Musician (guitar). Career: Member, Concurent, 1986-; Numerous concerts, TV and radio appearances, Bulgaria. Recordings: Rock For Peace, 1988; Rock Festival In Mitchurin, 1989; The Black Sheep (rock collection), 1992;

Something Wet (best-selling album, Bulgaria), 1994; The Best Of Bulgarian Rock, 1995. Honours: First Prizes: Top Rock Band, Youth Festival, Vidin, 1989; Rock ring, Sofia, 1990; Top Rock Composition: The Cavalry, 1991; Group Of The Year, The Darik Radio Countdown, 1994. Address: 40 St Stambolov Blvd, 1202 Sofia, Bulgaria.

TOIVANEN Pekka, b. 27 Sept 1961, Finland. Musician (tenor saxophone). Musical Education: Piano from age 10; Clarinet lessons from age 12. Career: Concerts with Kulttis Big Band; Brushane Big Band; Joined jazz department, Sibelius Academy, Helsinki, 1983; Formed own quartet, 1987. Compositions: Works for big bands, include Breakfast, commissioned by UMO, 1990. Honours: Winners, Finnish Jazz Federation band competition, 1987; Second place, Karlovy Vary contest, 1988. Address: Agricolankatu 7 D 94, 00530 Helsinki, Finland.

TOLJA Davor, b. 31 May 1957, Rijeka, Croatia. Singer; Musician (keyboards); Songwriter; Arranger. Education: 4 years technical study, Rijeka University. Musical Education: 6 years piano, musical school. Career: Keyboard player, group: Vrijeme Zemlja; Leader, author, player, singer, group Denis And Denis; Currently solo singer, composer, arranger, musician, producer; Owner, small recording studio. Recordings: with Vrijeme I Zemlja: Vrijeme I Zemlja, 1979; with Denis And Denis: Cuvaj Se, 1984; Ja Sam Lazljiva, 1985; Budi Tu, 1988; Solo: Stari Macak, 1990. Honours: Gold discs for albums: Cuvaj Se; Ja Sam Lazljiva; Best Pop Album of the Year, Rock (music magazine), Cuvaj Se, former Yugoslavia, 1984; Many pop festival awards for songs and arrangements; As a Composer participated at Eurosong, Dublin, Ireland with song Probudi Me by Group ENI, 1997. Membership: CMU (Croatian Music Union). Hobby: Animal protection. Address: Strossmayerova 11, 51000 Rijeka, Croatia.

TOLLY Maria, b. 10 Feb 1933, Islington, London, England. Composer; Singer; Songwriter. m. Valeriano Rocca, 1 Mar 1958, divorced 1980, 3 sons, 1 daughter. Education: Degree Modern Languages, 1954. Musical Education: Computer Music, Electronics, Music Courses, Dartington College, 1991-95. Career: Mezzo-soprano touring with Rae Woodland, John Lawrenson, Paul Ferris, 1977; Lead singer, Ballet Rambert's Cruel Garden (Christopher Bruce, Lindsay Kemp), 1979, 1980; Composer, performer, Theatre, 1983-89; Singer, songwriter, guitarist, tours Belgium; Netherlands; USSR; Germany; Cuba; Yugoslavia, Italy, Czechoslovakia, 1985-90; Performer, composer, Compact Theatre, 1990-92; Performer, composer, Electro-acoustic concerts, 1992-95; Festivals in London and Sheffield, 1993-97; Composed electro-acoustic music for new ballet Women Unbound, performed by Conundrum Dance Company, remiered at The Place, followed by tour of the UK, 1997; Songwriter, Managing Director for Banner Theatre's new production Redemption Song, premiered in Birmingham followed by tour of the UK, 1997; Managing Director, Telling Tales new production Rise and Run touring UK, 1998. Recordings: 3 albums, original songs: Gonna Get Up, Voices, Up To Here, 1985-88; Dance drama: About Time, 1991; Musical play: Mrs Columbus Speaks Out, 1992; New works performed, Dartington Summer School; Morley College, 1993-95. Publications: Article in Women Live, used in syllabus of Women's Studies, 1989; Chapter, songwriting, Taking Reality By Surprise, Women's Press Ltd, 1990. Honour: Winner, GLC Songwriting Competition, Victor Jara Song Competition, 1983. Memberships: Equity; Sonic Arts Network; Women In Music. Hobbies: Dancing: jazz, salsa and jive; Contemporary theatre; Gardening. Address: 91 Percival Road, Enfield, Middlesex, England.

TOLONEN Jukka Jorma, b. 16 Apr 1952, Helsinki, Finland. Musician (guitar, piano); Composer. m. Liisa-Elina, 17 July 1992, 3 sons, 1 daughter. Musical Education: Piano lessons from age 8; Sibelius Academy, 1971-72. Career: Member, Tasavallan Presidentti, 1967-74; Formed Jukka Tolonen Band, 1976; Also worked with: Bill's Boogie Band (with Bill Öhström); Piirpauke; Christian Sievert and Gilberto Moreira; Several concert tours: Germany; Switzerland; England; Scandinavia; Concerts: Moscow; Estonia; Georgia; Tatarstan; Festivals include: Montreux Jazz Festival; Reading Rock Festival; Roskilde Rock Festival; Television shows, Scandinavia and Germany; Old Grey Whistle Test, England. Recordings: 9 solo albums; 8 band albums; 4 acoustic guitar duo albums. Honours: Yrjö Award, Finnish Jazz Federation, 1972. Membership: Musicians' Union (Sweden). Hobby: Skiing, once a year. Current Management: Self-managed. Address: Norra Falla, 59041, Rimforsa, Sweden.

TOMICH Michael Robert, b. 24 Feb 1948, Chiswick, London, England. Musician (bass guitar). m. Anita Kaarinä Viero, 15 Dec 1971. Education: Nescot College, Ewell, Surrey; Stafford College, Kensington. Musical Education: Acoustic guitar, Harrow School of Music. Career: Played with more than 150 different acts, 1966-83; Constant tours of UK, Europe and USA; Numerous television appearances and radio broadcasts; Acts include: Clyde McPhatter; The Isley Brothers; Bonzo Dog Doo Dah Band; The Skatalites; Joan Armatrading; Peter Banks; Bill Bruford; Heron; Karl Wallinger; Atomic Rooster; Pickettywitch; The Gods; If; The Fantastics. Recordings: Early records with: Pickettywitch; Album: Diamond of Dreams, Heron; Many session recordings. Honours: Wycombe Radio Personality, 1994. Memberships: Musicians' Union; TV DJ Association. Hobbies: Hospital radio and mobile disc jockey. Address: 10 Sandford Gardens, High Wycombe, Bucks HP11 1QT, England.

TOMMEY Glenn, b. 27 Aug 1951, Ross-On Wye, Herefordshire, England. Recording Engineer; Producer; Composer; Arranger; Musician (guitar, keyboards, drums). m. Carolyn Jane Kellett, 1 Aug 1981, 3 sons. Education: Newton Park College, Bath. Musical Education: Newton Park College, Bath; University of Bristol, Certificate in Education (Music). Career: Resident Engineer, Crescent Studios, Bath, 1974-87; Freelance Engineer, 1987-; Projects for CBS/Sony, Tokyo; Toshiba/EMI, Tokyo; Peter Garrel IV; XTC; Big Express; Stranglers; Rupert Holmes; Korgis; Currently, lecturer in music dedicated micro-technology at Bath College of Higher Education. Honours: Best Recorded Album of the Year, Precious, Hajime Mizoguchi, 1990. Membership: Musicians' Union. Hobbies: Multi-media authoring; Swimming; Electronic construction; Gigging. Address: 99 Fairfield Park Road, Fairfield Park, Bath, Avon BA1 6JR, England

TOMPKINS David Mark, b. 12 Aug 1963, Lincoln, England. Musician (double bass, bass guitar). Education: First Class Mathematics Degree, 1984; Jazz studies, 1987-90. Musical Education: Self-taught. Career: Performed with rock band Niadem's Ghost, 1984-86; Concerts includes headlining at The Marquee Club, London; Studied Jazz, 1987-90; Member of D'semble, 1990-; Played with Martin Taylor in 1993; Currently rehearsing for recording with Matt Nickson Quartet. Recordings: In Sheltered Winds, Niadem's Ghost, 1985; D'Semble, D'Semble, 1992. Honour: Featured in Best New Band Readres Poll with Niadem's Ghost, "Sounds" magazine, 1986. Membership: Musicians' Union. Hobbies: Cinema; Chess; Reading. Address: 2 Dawlish Road, Chorlton, Manchester M21 8XR, England.

TONG Des, b. 30 Apr 1951, Woking, Surrey, England. Music Producer; Musician (bass guitar). 1 son, 1 daughter. Career: Played bass guitar with

Sad Café; Producer, Time Warp for Damian; Worked with: Real Thing; Lisa Stansfield; Joe Cocker; Alvin Stardust; Cissy Stone; Ruby Turner; Engelbert Humperdinck; Inez and Charlie Foxx; The Jacksons; Music Producer for US Gold. Honour: Siver disc, Time Warp. Membership: PRS. Hobbies: Cooking; Gardening. Current Management: Cissy Stone. Address: 108 Kingsbury Road, Erdington, Birmingham B24 8QU, England.

TONG Pete. Disc Jockey; A&R Executive. Career: Became DJ aged 15; Freelance DJ on leaving school; Worked at Blues & Soul and Black Music, 1979-83; Radio broadcaster, Radio Invicta, Capital Radio and Radio London (now GLR); Radio 1; Originally on Peter Powell show, now DJ with own dance music show; Head of A&R, London/ffrr Records. Hobbies: Travel; Tennis; Swimming; Family. Address: c/o London Records, PO Box 1422, Chancellors House, Chancellors Road, London W6 9SG, England.

TONTOH Frank, b. 22 May 1964, Kumasi, Ghana. Musician (drums); Writer; Composer. Musical Education: 2 years study, piano, Trinity College of Music. Career: Member, Osibisa, for 4 years; Aztec Camera, 4 years; Tanita Tikaram, 8 months; Also played with: Tasmin Archer; Level 42; Omar; Mica Paris; Zucchero; Roachford; Courtney Pine; Jason Rebello; Edwyn Collins; Misty Oldland. Recordings: Aztec Camera: Stray; Misty Oldland: Supernatural; Kimiko Yamashita: Love And Hate; Tony Remy: 2 albums; Theme to Wired, TV programme; Kiko Veneno: 2 albums (Gold); Bachology: 1 album. Hobbies: Cinema; Restaurants; Football and other sports.

TOPAZ Rona Lisa, b. 4 Sept 1965, New York, USA. Vocalist; Actress; Songwriter; Musician (keyboards). m. 19 Feb 1988, separated, 1992. Education: Associate Applied Sciences Degree, Performing Arts, Five Towns College; City & Guilds, Theatre Skills. Career: Recording sessions for Lloyd Clarke; Gary Louca; Sebastian; No Go Productions; Friction; District Six; Kezi O'Neal; Leighton Carter; Musicals include: Destiny; Say Why; Ensemble, Un Ballo In Maschera, for Capital Opera Company; Lead vocalist, solo artist for over 100 events including: Edinburgh Festival Fringe; Highbury Festival; Glasgow Big Day Festival, 1991; Supported 4 Men And A Dog, Glasgow Mayfest, 1992; Shape Arts Festival; International Jazz Day; Fitzrovia Festival; Television includes: Highway, ITV; Kazukos Karaoke Klub, Channel 4; Plays, films. Compositions include: Lyricist, No Second Chances, recorded 1991; Recordings: Lead vocals, Visualize, 1992. Publications: Lyrics: The Divisions Are Fine, London Voices Anthology. Honours: 2nd Prize, Croydon Music Festival; Honourable Mention, Brixton Songwriting Competition. Memberships: Musicians' Union; Women In Music. Hobbies: Cooking; Reading; Writing. Current Management: Solomon Artists Management International. Address: c/o 30 Clarence Road, Southend On Sea, Essex SS1 1BD, England.

TORK Peter (Peter Halsten Thorkelson), b. 13 Feb 1944, Washington DC, USA. Musician (bass, guitar, keyboards); Singer; Actor. Career; Folk musician with Au Go Go Singers, Los Angeles; Member, The Monkees, 1966-68; 1986-89; Actor, Monkees comedy television series, 1966-68; 33 1/3 Revolutions Per Monkee, TV Special, NBC; Monkees film, Head, premier 1968; Founder, own groups: Release, 1969; The New Monks, 1981; High school teacher, Santa Monica, early 1970s; Rejoined Monkees, 1986-89. Recordings: Albums: The Monkees (Number 1, US and UK), 1966; More Of The Monkees (Number 1, US and UK), 1967; Headquarters (Number 1, US), 1967; Pisces, Aquarius, Capricorn & Jones Ltd (Number 1, UK), 1967; The Birds, The Bees & The Monkees, 1968; Then And Now, 1986; Pool It, 1987; Hit singles: Last Train

To Clarksville (Number 1, US), 1966; I'm A Believer (Number 1, US), 1966; (I'm Not Your) Steppin' Stone, 1967; A Little Bit Me, A Little Bit You, 1967; Alternate Title, 1967; Pleasant Valley Sunday, 1967; Daydream Believer (Number 1, US), 1967; Valleri, 1968. Honours: NARM Awards, Best Selling Group, Best Album, 1967; Emmy, Outstanding Comedy Series, 1967; 3 BMI Awards, 1968; Monkees Day, Atlanta, 1986; Star on Hollywood Walk Of Fame, 1989. Address: c/o Nationwide Entertainment Services, 2756 North Green Valley Parkway, Suite 449, Las Vegas, NV 89014-2100, USA.

TORMÉ Mel (Melvin Howard), b. 13 Sept 1925, Chicago, Illinois, USA. Jazz Singer; Musician (piano, drums); Actor. m. Janette Scott (divorced), 2 children. Musical Education: Studied drums from age 7. Career: Actor, radio soap operas; Singer with Buddy Rogers; Composer, arranger, musician with Chico Marx band, 1942-43; Actor, films: Higher And Higher, 1943; Pardon My Rhythm, 1944; Words And Music, 1948; Walk Like A Dragon, 1960; A Man Called Adam, 1966; The Land Of No Return; Solo singer, 1947-; Also leader, vocal group The Mel-Tones; Festival performances with George Shearing and Bill Berry, US and UK, 1990s; Co-founder, Producers Group Ltd, 1982. Recordings: Numerous albums include: California Suite, 1949; It's A Blue World, 1955; Live At The Crescendo, 1957; Tormé, 1958; Back In Town, 1959; Mel Tormé Swings Shubert Alley, 1960; Sunday In New York, 1963; Live At The Maisonette, 1974; Mel Tormé And Friends, 1981; Encore At Marty's, 1982; Reunion, 1988; Live At Fujitsu, 1992; with George Shearing: An Evening At Charlie's, 1983; A Vintage Year, 1987; Mel And George Do World War II, 1990; with Shorty Rogers: Round Midnight, 1957; with Buddy Rich: Together Again - For The First Time, 1978. Publications: The Other Side Of The Rainbow, 1970; It Wasn't All Velvet - An Autobiography, 1988. Honour: Grammy Awards: Best Male Jazz Vocal Performance, 1983, 1984. Current Management: International Ventures Inc. Address: 23734 Valencia Blvd, Ste 202, Valencia, CA 91355, USA.

TORRENCE Dean, b. 10 Mar 1940, Los Angeles, California, USA. Singer. Education: Graphics Degree. Career: Member, duo Jan And Dean (with Jan Berry), 1957-66; 1973-; Solo artiste, 1966-; Performances include: Dick Clark's Stage Show, Michigan State Fair, 1959; American Bandstand, 1959; New York, with The Animals, Chuck Berry, Del Shannon, 1964; Launched Kittyhawk Graphics, 1967; Member, Legendary Masked Surfers, 1972; California Surfer's Stomp Festival, 1973; Subject of biopic, Dead Man's Curve, 1978. Recordings: Albums: with Jan & Dean: Jan And Dean Take Linda Surfin', 1963; Surf City And Other Swingin' Cities, 1963; Drag City, 1964; Dead Man's Curve/The New Girl In School, 1964; The Little Old Lady From Pasadena, 1964; Ride The Wild Surf, 1964; Command Performance/Live In Person, 1965; Jan And Dean Meet Batman, 1966; One Summer Night - Live, 1982; Solo album: Save For A Rainy Day, 1967; Singles: with Jan And Dean include: Linda, 1963; Surf City (Number 1, US), 1963; Drag City, 1964; Dead Man's Curve, 1964; The New Girl In School, 1964; The Little Old Lady (From Pasadena), 1964; Ride The Wild Surf, 1964; Catch A Wave, 1964; Popsicle, 1966. Current Management: Bill Hollingshead Productions, 1720 North Ross Street, Santa Ana, CA 92706, USA.

TORREZ Juan Pablo, b. 17 Aug 1946, Cuba. Musician (trombone). m. Elsa Torres, 30 Dec 1988, 1 son. Career: Member, Cuban Orchestra of Modern Music, with Paquito d'Rivera, Artuo Sandoval, Chuco Valdes, 1970s; Played with: Dizzie Gillespie; Don Cherry; Gato Barbieri; Mongo Santamaria; Slide Hampton; Astor Piazzolla; Steve Gadd; Paquito D'Rivera; Arturo Sandoval; Hilton Ruiz; Cachao; Nestor Torres; Cholate Armentaros; Giovanni Hidalgo; Travels

throughout Spain; Portugal; France; Switzerland; Italy; Germany; Poland; Mexico; USA; Canada; Currently resident in Miami, USA. Recordings: Over 20 include: Trombone Man; From John To Johnny; For Elsa; Banana Split; Foot Tapping. Honours: CD trombone, prenominado, Grammy. Memberships: ITA; National Academy Recording. Hobby: Fishing. Current Management: Elsa Torres. Address: 635 SW 36 Avenue, Miami, FIL 33135, USA.

TOURE Ali Farka, b. 1939, Gourmararusse, Mali. Musician (guitar, n'jurkel, njarka); Farmer. Musical Education: Self-taught. Career: Formerly, river ambulanceman, Mali; Member, Niafunke District Troupe (music and dance group), 1960s; Sound engineer, Radio Mali, late 1960s; Professional solo artiste, 1974-; Regular tours: UK; Europe; USA; Africa; Major concerts include: US tour with Ry Cooder, 1994; West Africa, Europe, USA, 1995; Womad Festival, Reading, 1995; New Orleans Jazz Festival; London Jazz Festival; Major role against music piracy in Mali; Part-ownership, EMI Mali and Bamako recording studio. Recordings: 6 albums, France, 1980s; 4 albums on World Circuit: Ali Farka Toure, 1988; The River, 1990; The Source, 1992; Talking Timbuktu, with Ry Cooder (Number 1, Billboard World Music Charts), 1994; Radio Mali sessions 1970-80 (unreleased), 1995; As producer: Album for Lobi Traore (Album of Year, Le Monde), 1994. Honours: Grammy, Talking Timbuktu, 1994; European World Music Album of Year, Talking Timbuktu, 1994. Address: c/o World Circuit Records, 106 Cleveland Street, London W1P 5DP, England.

TOURNAS Kostas, b. 23 Sept 1949, Tripolis, Greece. Musician (guitar); Singer; Composer; Lyricist; Producer; Recording Studio Owner. m. Maria, 4 Dec 1971. Musical Education: Harmony; Synthesis; Guitar. Career: many tours, Greece and Cyprus; Club appearances; Host or guest, radio and television talk shows; Owner, City Studios, Athens. Compositions: More than 500 titles released since 1971. Recordings: Aperanta Horafia (Endless Fields); Kiries Kai Kirioi (Ladies and Gentlemen) Duets; Poll/Anthrope (Man). Publications: Kostas Tournas' Songs (sheet music and lyrics of his best). Honours: Gold, Platinum records; Lyric awards; Forhis offer in Music Award. Memberships: AEPI Greece; ETE Greece; FIA. Hobbies: Equipment for music making; Studio work; Multimedia. Address: 133 Kafkassou Street, Kipseli, Athens, 11364, Greece.

TOUSSAINT Christophe, b. 14 Feb 1959, Géradmer, Vosges, France. Luthier; Musician. 2 sons, 1 daughter. Career: Hungary, 1987-1993; Ris Orangis, 1994; Local and regional television and radio. Recordings: Terra Incognita, 1985; Io, 1989; Christophe Toussaint Playing His Mountain Dulcimer, 1993; France-Epinette des Vosages Ocora, Radio France, 1997. Honours: Master Luthier, 1989; Diplôme d'Etat Professeur d'Epinette, 1989-. Hobbies: Plektrum dulcimer maker, player. Address: 26, Route du Col, F-88120 Sapois, France.

TOUSSAINT Jean-Baptiste Nazaire, b. 27 Jul 1960, Aruba, Netherlands Antilles. Jazz Musician (tenor and soprano saxophone). Musical Education: Saxophone at Miami State, with Charles Cox; Associate degree, Berklee College of Music, Boston, USA. Career: Member, Art Blakey's Jazz Messengers, 1982-86; Concerts worldwide include: Jazz Mobile, New York, 1982; Residency, Ronnie Scott's, 1985; Concerts with John Dankworth Band, UK, 1983; Camden Jazz Festival, 1986; Teacher, Guildhall School Of Music, 1987-; Formed own bands Jean Toussaint Quartet, 1987; Nazaire, 1992; Tours of Europe and Middle East with Max Roach, 1989; Member, Julian Joseph's band, 1992-94; Also worked with Jason Rebello; Bheki Mseleku; Lenny White, UK, Europe and US, 1995; Numerous worldwide television and radio appearances, 1982-.

Recordings: Albums: with Art Blakey's Jazz Messengers: The New York Scene, 1984; Live At Kimballs, 1985; Blue Night, 1985; Solo albums: Impressions Of Coltrane, 1987; What Goes Around, 1991; Life I Want (co-produced with Jason Rebello), 1995; with Nazaire: Whose Blues, 1992; with Andy Hamilton: Silvershine, 1990; Jamaica By Night (as producer), 1994; with Julian Joseph: The Language Of Truth, 1991; Reality, 1993. Memberships: MCPS; PRS; Broadcast Music Inc. Hobbies: Art; Films (video and cinema); DIY. Current Management: Fish Krish (Agent); Self-managed. Address: c/o Fish Krish, 6 Carlton House, 319 West End Lane, London NW6 1RN, England.

TOWNEND Jon, b. 27 Dec 1960, England. Musician (guitar); Vocalist. m. Helen Louise Buckle, 22 Sep 1990. Education: King Alfred's College, Winchester; Leeds University. Musical Education: Formerly trained on the violin. Career: Came to prominence as writer and performer through the rogue folk movement of the 1980's with Punk roots band Malcolm's Interview, then indie band God's Little Monkeys; Regular early appearances at the Vancouver Folk Festival and New York Music Seminar. Recordings: Shadows (EP), 1985; Breakfast In Bedlam, seminal album, 1987; New Maps Of Hell, 1989; LIP, 1990. Membership: Musicians' Union. Hobbies: Occasional local broadcasting; Collecting and restoring stringed instruments. Current Management: Music Consultants and Management. Address: The Studio, 1 Driffield Terrace, York YO2 2DD, England.

TOWNEND Richard James Patrick, b. 4 July 1948, London, England. Musician (banjo, guitar, fiddle). Musical Education: Self-taught. Career: Formed first school bluegrass group in UK; Played at: Royal Albert Hall; Hammersmith Odeon; Cambridge Folk Festival; Appeared on BBC Radio and television Folk and Country music programmes; Also on Kaleidoscope, BBC Radio 4; Partner in Wadhurst Bluegrass Day Venture. Recordings: Make The Old Times New, with Rosie Davis, 1995; The Echo Mountain Band, 1975, (reissued 1995); Fraces on the Frets, 1997. Memberships: Musicians' Union; British Bluegrass Music Association. Hobby: Natural History. Address: 2 Fairview Cottages, Balaclava Lane, Wadhurst, East Sussex TN5 6EQ, England.

TOWNSHEND Peter Dennis Blandford, 19 May 1945, Isleworth, London, England. Musician (guitar) Composer; Publisher; Author. m. Karen Astley, 1968, 1 son, 2 daughters. Education: Ealing Art College. Career: Member, UK rock group The Who, 1964-84; Solo artiste, 1979-; Appearances include: National Jazz and Blues festival, 1965, 1966, 1969; Monterey Pop Festival, 1967; Rock At The Oval, 1972; Farewell tour, 1982-83; Live Aid, Wembley, 1985; Reunion tour, 1989; Films include: Tommy; Quadrophenia; The Kids Are Alright; Owner Eel Pie Recording Ltd, 1972-; Established Eel Pie (bookshops and publishing), 1972-; Established Meher Baba Oceanic (UK archival library), 1976-81; Editor, Faber & Faber, 1983-. Compositions include rock operas, Tommy, 1969; Quadrophenia, 1973; Numerous songs for The Who. Recordings: Albums: with The Who: My Generation, 1965; A Quick One, 1966; The Who Sell Out, 1968; Direct Hits, 1968; Tommy, 1969; Live At Leeds, 1970; Who's Next, 1971; Meaty Beefy Big And Bouncy, 1971; Quadrophenia, 1973; Odds And Sods, 1974; The Who By Numbers, 1975; The Story Of The Who, 1976; Who Are You, 1978; The Kids Are Alright (film soundtrack), 1979; Face Dances, 1981; Hooligans, 1982; It's Hard, 1982; Rarities Vols 1 and 2, 1983; The Singles, 1984; Who's Last, 1984; Who's Missing, 1987; Who's Better Who's Best, 1988; Joined Together, 1990; 30 Years of Maximum R&B, 1994; Solo albums: Who Came First, 1972; Rough Mix, 1977; Empty Glass, 1980; All The Best Cowboys Have Chinese Eyes, 1982; Scoop, 1983; White City, 1985; Another

Scoop, 1987; The Iron Man, 1989; Psychoderelict, 1993; The Best Of Pete Townshend, 1996; Hit singles include: with The Who: I Can't Explain, 1965; Anyway Anyhow Anywhere, 1965; My Generation, 1965; Substitute, 1966; I'm A Boy, 1966; Happy Jack, 1967; Pictures Of Lily, 1967; I Can See For Miles, 1967; Pinball Wizard, 1969; See Me Feel Me, 1970; Won't Get Fooled Again, 1970; Join Together, 1972; Who Are You, 1978; You Better You Bet, 1981; Contributor, Sun City, Artists Against Apartheid, 1985. Publication: Horse's Neck, 1986. Honours include: BRIT Lifetime Achievement Award, 1983; Living Legend Award, International Rock Awards, 1991; with The Who: Gold Ticket, Madison Square Garden, 1979; Ivor Novello Award, Contribution to British Music, 1982; British Phonographic Industry Award, 1983; BRIT Award, Contribution to British Music, 1988; Inducted into Rock'n'Roll Hall of Fame, 1990; Tony Award for Tommy score, 1993; Grammy Award for original cast recording Tommy, 1993; Dora Mavor Moore Award for Tommy in Toronto, 1994; Olivier Award, Tommy, London, 1997; Q Lifetime Achievement Award for The Who. Address: Box 305, Twickenham TW1 1TT, England.

TOWNSHEND Simon John, b. 10 Oct 1960, Ealing, London, England. Songwriter; Musician (guitar, piano); Vocalist. m. Janie Harris, 15 July 1978, 2 sons, 1 daughter. Career: First record contract, Warner Bros, age 14; Founder member, On The Air, with Mark Brzezicki, Tony Butler (Big Country), 1980; Solo artiste, Polygram US; Founder member, Animal Soup, with Zak Starkey; Sung part of Newsboy in Tommy, The Who; Singer, Rise, Rise on Smash The Mirror. Compositions include: Until Tomorrow; The Way It Is; Girl In New York; Ecstasy Heaven. Recordings: Solo: When I'm A Man, 1974; Janie, 1975; Turn It On, 1976; Ready For Action, 1980; I'm The Answer, 1984; Barriers, 1986; Albums: Sweet Sound, 1984 (produced by brother Pete Townshend); Moving Target, 1986. Memberships: Musicians' Union; ASCAP; PRS; PARMA. Hobby: Keen golfer (7 handicap). Current Management: Stir Management. Address: 20 Woodgrange Avenue, Ealing Common, London W5 3NY, England.

TRAASDAHL Jan Ole, b. 21 August 1958, Odense, Denmark. Associate Professor; Pianist; Composer; Educator. m. Hanne Mulvad, 21 November 1981. Education: MA, Musicology, University of Aarhus, Denmark; Studies, Berklee College of Music, Boston, 1981. Career: Performed and Recorded with many international Jazz Soloists including Thad Jones, Richard Boone and Bent Jaedig; Conducted Big Bands and Musicals; Composed Music for Big Bands, Vocal Choirs and Theatre. Recordings: Panta Rei, 1984; Stig Moller, 1994; Musam Big Band, 1995; Video, TVE Rio de Janeiro, 1995. Publication: Rhythmic Music Education, 1996. Membership: Vice President, Musicians' Union, Copenhagen, 1996. Address: Oster Farimagsgade 45A, 2100 Kobenhavn K, Denmark.

TRACEY Clark, b. 5 Feb 1961, London, England. Musician (drums); Composer; Arranger. m. Tina May, 15 June 1989, 1 son. Musical Education: Largely self-taught. Career: Toured with Stan Tracey: USA; India; Australia; Middle East; Europe; 1978-; Own group to Far East; Many television and radio appearances; Solely jazz concerts; Own group toured Far East and Europe. Compositions: Stiperstones Suite, for own quintet, 1988; Current original album: Full Speed Sideways, for own sextet; Playing In The Yard, with Charlie Rouse and Stan Tracey; Suite for Quintet at Finnish Festival, 1997. Honours: British Jazz Award, Best Drummer Category; Best Drummer Category, British Jazz Awards, 1997. Memberships: PRS; MCPS; PPL; Musicians' Union. Hobbies: Relaxing; Doing nothing. Current Management: For sextet: Bernard Lyons, 73 Eglantine Avenue, Belfast BT9 7EU, Northern Ireland; David E Jacobs, 6 Belgrove, Tunbridge

Wells, Kent, England. Address: 8 Oliver Road, Hemel hempstead, Hertfordshire HP3 9PY, England.

TRAMP Mike. b. Denmark. Vocalist; Singer. Career: Vocalist, Danish rock group Mabel; Vocalist, songwriter, White Lion, 1985-1992; Vocalist, songwriter, Freak Of Nature, 1992-; Numerous tours: UK; Europe; US. Recordings: Albums: with White Lion: Fight To Survive, 1985; Pride, 1987; Big Game, 1989; Mane Attraction, 1991; with Freak Of Nature: Freak Of Nature, 1993; Gathering Of Freaks, 1994; Also featured on Sahara, House Of Lords, 1990. Current Management: Wyatt Management Worldwide. Address: 10797 Onyx Circle, Fountain Valley, CA 92708, USA.

TRANS-X (Pascal Leguirand), b. Paris, France. Composer; Lyricist; Vocalist. Recordings: New Age albums: Minos; De Harmonia; Gregorian Waves; As Incanta: Ishtar; Voice Of The Cybicle; Dance albums: Trans-X; Living On Video/Vivre Sur Video (2 million copies sold worldwide). Honours: Best Dance Artist, Adisq-Quebec; Platinum record, Living On Video. Membership: SGAE (Spain). Current Management: Michel Huygen (Onira International).

TRAVERS Pat, b. Canada. Musician (guitar); Songwriter; Singer. Career: Member, The Band; Founder, Pat Travers Band, London, 1976-; Concerts include: Reading Rock Festival, 1976; Worked as Nicko McBain; Scott Gorham; Pat Thrall; Tommy Aldridge; Michael Shrieve. Albums: Pat Travers, 1976; Makin' Magic, 1976; Putting It Straight, 1977; Heat In The Street, 1978; Go For What You Know - Live, 1979; Crash And Burn, 1980; Radio Active, 1981; Black Pearl, 1982; Hot Shot, 1984; School Of Hard Knocks, 1990; Blues Tracks, 1992; Just A Touch, 1993; Blues Magnet, 1994; Halfway to Somewhere, 1995; Lookin' Up, 1996; King Biscuit Live, 1997; Summerdaze '97, compilation, 1997. Current Management: Don Barnard Management, PO Box 300023, Fern Park, FL 32730, USA.

TRAVIS Randy (Randy Bruce Traywick), b. 4 May 1959, Marshville,North Carolina, USA. Country Singer; Songwriter; Musician (guitar). m. Lib Hatcher (Mary Elizabeth Robertson), 1991. Career: Played local clubs with brothers; Resident, Charlotte nightclub owned by Lib Hatcher, 1977; Early recordings as Randy Traywick; Resident singer, as Randy Ray, Nashville Palace, 1992; Name changed to Randy Travis, 1985-; Joined Grand Ole Opry, 1986. Recordings: US Country Number 1 hits: On The Other Hand; Diggin' Up Bones; Forever And Ever, Amen; I Won't Need You Anymore (Always And Forever); Gone Too Long; I Told You So; Honky Tonk Moon; Deeper Than The Holler; Is It Still Over; It's Just A Matter Of Time; Hard Rock Bottom Of Your Heart; Forever Together; Look Heart No Hands; Albums: Randy Ray Live At The Nashville Palace, 1982; Storms Of Life, 1986; Always And Forever, 1987; Old 8 X 10, 1988; An Old Time Christmas, 1989; No Holdin' Back, 1989; Heroes And Friends (duets with Merle Haggard, George Jones, Loretta Lynn, Dolly Parton, Tammy Wynette and B B King), 1990; High Lonesome, 1991; Greatest Hits Vols 1 and 2, 1992. Honours include: Grammy Award, Best Country Newcomer, 1986; Male Vocalist of the Year, Country Music Association, 1988. Current Management: Lib Hatcher-Travis Management, 1610 16th Avenue S, Nashville, TN 37212, USA.

TRAVIS Theo (Theodore John), b. 7 July 1964, Birmingham, England. Musician (tenor and soprano saxophones and flute); Composer. m. Madelyn J Cohen, 24 May 1992. Education: BMus (Hons), Manchester University. Musical Education: Grade 8 flute; Saxophone to BMus Final recital standard. Career: Toured Spain with NYJO, 1985; Leader, Theo Travis Band; Also performed with: John Etheridge; Jim Mullen; John Marshall; Slim

Gaillard; Radio includes: Jazz Parade, BBC Radio 2, playing original compositions, 1993; Interview, WKCR-FM, New York; Toured Japan with Mick Karn, 1997; Arts Council Tour for improvising trio with John Marshall (drums) and Mark Wood (guitar), 1998. Compositions: Broad Street Changes Suite for jazz septet, commissioned by West Midlands Arts; Commissioned by Derby Metro Cinema to write with Dave Sturt new music for Hitchcock silent film, The Lodger. Recordings: Solo: 2 AM, 1993; View From The Edge, 1994; with The Other Side: Dangerous Days, 1995; Secret Island, 1996; with Marshall Travis Wood, Bodywork, 1998; Guest appearances: Porcupine Tree, Mick Karn and Dick Heckstall-Smith. Honours: Financial Times Best Newcomer, 1993; Best British CD, View From The Edge, 1994; Brit Jazz Awards Nomination, Rising Star, 1995, 1996. Memberships: Musicians' Union; PRS; Equity. Hobbies: Walking in Scottish Highlands; Cinema; Listening to music.Address: 20 Strathmore Gardens, Finchley, London N3, England.

TRENT Tammy, b. 11 Apr 1968, Grand Rapids, Michigan, USA. Musician (drums, percussion). m. Trent Lenderink, 18 Aug 1990. Education: 1 year college. Career: Signed to Rex Music, Brentwood, Tennessee. Recordings: Debut album, 1995; First radio single: Your Love Is 4 Always (Number 1, Christian Hits Radio charts). Membership: BMI. Hobbies: Basketball; Volleyball; Softball; Weightlifting; Dancing; Singing. Current Management: Lenderink Management. Address: 1271 House Road, Belmont, MI 49306, USA.

TRETTINE Caroline Anne Halcrow, b. 4 Sept 1958, Kingston-on-Thames, Surrey, England. Singer; Songwriter; Musician (guitar); Systems Analyst. Education: BA Hons, Bristol University, English with French. Musical Education: Self-taught songwriting, guitar. Career: Singer, writer, guitarist with Blue Aeroplanes, 1984-85; Solo artiste, tours with: Billy Bragg; Christy Moore; Radio: Radio 1 sessions for Richard Skinner; Bob Harris, 1985-95; Member, Library of Love, 1995. Compositions include: Sleep With Me; Guilty; Hope. Recordings: with Blue Aeroplanes: Action Painting EP: Le Petit Cadeau de Don Juan, 1985; Be A Devil EP, 1990. Memberships: PRS; Musicians' Union. Hobbies: Cinema; Tennis; Comedy writing. Current Management: Sincere Management. Address: Sincere Management, 421 Harrow Road, London W9, England.

TREVISAN Luciano (Fricchetti), b. 25 Sept 1959, Venice, Italy. Musical Manager; Promoter; Publisher. Musical Education: DAMS, Bologna University. Career: Involved in Cultural Association, ARCI Manager; Record Distributors until 1986; Partner in record company, Materiali Sonori; Promoter, live events; Artist manager, 1989-; Partner, Ossigeno, Music Publishing Company, 1993-. Publications: Compra O Muori (book). Honours: Gold and Platinum records for album: Na Bruta Banda by Pitura Freska; Gold Record, Gran Calma, Pitura Freska. Memberships: Publisher Member, SIAE; Partner, Evolution Music, 1995. Hobbies: Travel; Video. Current Management: Pitura Freska, Batisto Coco, Fabio Calabro, Farenheit 45l, So Vibes. Address: Via Goldoni 42/A, 30174 Mestre Venezia, Italy.

TREWAVAS Peter, b. 15 Jan 1959, Middlesbrough, Cleveland, England. Musician (bass). Career: Member, The Metros; Bassist, UK progressive rock group Marillion, 1982-; Tours, UK; Europe; North America; Concerts include: Theakston Festival, 1982; Reading Festival, 1982, 1983; Nostell Priory Festival, 1982, 1983; Glastonbury Festival, 1983; Support to Rush, New York's Radio City Music Hall, 1983; Milton Keynes Bowl, 1984; Monsters Of Rock Festival, Castle Donington, 1985; Colombian Volcano Appeal Concert, 1986; Welcome To The Garden Party, 1986. Recordings: Albums: Script For A Jester's

Tear, 1983; Fugazi, 1984; Real To Reel, 1984; Misplaced Childhood, 1985; Brief Encounter, 1986; Clutching At Straws, 1987; B-Sides Themselves, 1988; The Thieving Magpie, 1988; Holidays In Eden, 1991; A Singles Collection 1982-92, 1992; Brave, 1994; Afraid Of Sunlight, 1995; Singles include: Market Square Heroes, 1982; He Knows You Know, 1983; Garden Party, 1983; Punch And Judy, 1984; Assassing, 1984; Kayleigh (Number 2, UK), 1985; Lavender, 1985; Heart Of Lothian, 1985; Incommunicado, 1987; Sugar Mice, 1987; Warm Wet Circles, 1987; Freaks, 1988; Hooks In You, 1989; Uninvited Guest, 1989; Easter, 1990; Cover My Eyes (Pain And Heaven), 1991; No One Can, 1991; Dry Land, 1991; Sympathy, 1992. Current Management: Hit & Run Music Ltd., 30 Ives Street, London SW3 2ND, England.

TRICKY (Adrian Thaws), b. Bristol, England. Rapper; Songwriter. Career: Rapper, Wild Bunch; Solo artiste with singer Martina; Regular collaborations as singer/writer with Massive Attack; Leader, recording project Nearly God (duets with Björk, Alison Moyet, Terry Hall, Neneh Cherry), 1996; Concerts include: T In The Park Festival, Glasgow, 1995; Reading Festival, 1995. Recordings: Single: Overcome, Wild Bunch; Solo singles: Overcome, 1995; Black Steel, 1995; The Hell EP, 1995; Pumpkin, 1995; Albums: with Massive Attack: Blues Lines, 1991; Protection, 1995; Solo albums: Maxinquaye (Number 1, UK), 1995; Nearly God, 1996. Honours: Face Magazine, Best Album of the Year, Blues Lines, 1991; BRIT Award Nominations: Best Album of Year, with Massive Attack, 1991; Best Male Artist, Best Dance Act, Best Newcomer, 1996; Gold record, Maxinquaye, 1995; Nomination, Mercury Music Prize; Q Award, Best Producer, 1995 Current Management: Fruit Management. Address: Unit 104, Saga Centre, 326 Kensal Road, London W10 5BZ, England.

TRISTANO Lennie, b. 19 March 1919, Chicago, Illinois, USA. Jazz Pianist; Composer; Teacher. m. Judy Moore, 2 sons, 2 daughters. Education: American Conservatory of Music, Chicago. Career: Solo Concerts in Paris, Berlin, Stockholm, Copenhagen, Milan, 1964, Harrogate, England, 1968; Quartet with Lenny Popkin, Waterbury, 1968; Numerous Radio and Television Appearances. Recordings: The New Tristano; Pastime; Ju Ju; Descent into the Maelstrom; Live at Birdland; Live in Toronto; Continuity; Wow; Note to Note; Manhattan Studio; Concert in Copenhagen. Publications: Several articles in professional journals and magazines. Honours: Downbeat Poll Winer, 1948; National Music Award, 1976; Downbeat Hall of Fame, 1979. Memberships: ASCAP; American Federation of Musicians. Hobby: Reading. Address: c/o Connie Crothers, PO Box 615, Cooper Station, New York, NY 10276-0615, USA.

TRITT Travis, b. 1962, Maretta, Georgia, USA. Country Singer; Songwriter. m. Theresa, 12 Apr 1997 Career: Recording artiste, 1990-; Recorded, toured with Marty Stuart, included No-Hats Tour. Compositions include: Here's A Quarter (Call Someone Who Cares). Recordings include: Anymore; Lord Have Mercy On The Working Man; Albums: Country Club, 1990; It's All About To Change, 1991; T-R-O-U-B-L-E, 1992; A Travis Tritt Christmas: Loving Time Of Year, 1992; Rhythm, Country and Blues; The Restless Kind; Greatest Hits - From The Beginning, 1995. Publication: Ten Feet Tall and Bulletproof, autobiography, 1992. Current Management: Kragen and Co, 1112 N. Sherbourne Drive, Los Angeles, CA 90069, USA.

TROCMÉ Elisa Andréa, b. 21 Aug 1955, Pennsylvania, USA. Musician (counter-bass, Bb clarinets, other winds). 2 sons, 1 daughter. Education: History, French popular arts and traditions, EHESS, Paris. Education: Private lessons, workshops with B Vitet; Tamia; Steve Lacy; Michel Fano; George Bejamin; Robert Aitken; Georges Aperghis; Toru Takemitsu; Barre Phillips. Career: Instrument making with B Vitet; Music Education Program with P Maretan, Paris, 1978; Irving Plaza/BCBG, New York, 1980; Le Grand Rex; New Morning; Centre Georges Pompidou; Musée d'Art Moderne; Grand Palais dance, music, plastic arts creations; Improvised music and dance encounters, Toulouse, 1992-; Art Wars, La Mama, Theater New York, 1980; Cinema de Minuit, directed by Patricia Bardon, ProdA2, Paris, 1984; The Weapons Of The Spirits, directed by Pierre Sauvage (prize-winning documentary, Cannes, 1987; 666, Julie West video-danmce production, S Rougier, Paris, 1985. Publications: Clarinette magazine; Translations for Télérama; L'Evenement du Jeudi; L'Humanité; Melody Maker. Honour: Oscar de Mécémat (P Mariétam). Membership: ESEM (Euro Seminoar of Ethnomusicology). Hobbies: Life; People; Democracy; Cinema; Travel. Current Management: Christianne Bories. Address: 282 Route de Seysses, 31100 Toulouse, France.

TROTT Milton, b. 4 November 1958, Adelaide, South Australia. Screen Composer Film/TV (Keyboards); Creative Consultant. Education: Classical Piano, Violin, Cello, Guitar, Drums, Flute. Career: Keyboard Player/Songwriter/Producer; Numerous local bands session too; Member, Prestigious Arts Education, 1982; Team (SA Govt), Music/Multi Media, 1985; Winner, Pot Luck, TV Talent Quest, 1989; Mr Music, Theatrespots, 1986; Musician, Magick Circus, Soundtracks TV Documentaries, 1988. Compositions: Sugar is Sweet, 1982; The Greens, 1984; H20, 1983. Recordings: Music CD, Aurora Australis, 1995. Honour: Young Composers Award, 1983. Memberships: Australian Screen Composers Association; Australian Performing Right Association. Hobbies: Loosely scripted home videos, partiese, world music. Address: Post Office Aldgate, South Australia 5154.

TROTTIER Dominique, b. 17 Aug 1949, Saigon, Vietnam. Musician (clarinet). Education: Scientiste BAC, Computer DUT. Musical Education: IACP. Career: Clarinet player; Composer with many groups; Creator, The Musique Tangente Music School, 1980. Hobbies: Patchwork; Touloulou. Address: 2 Rue du Docteur Ledermann, 92310 Sèvres, France.

TROUBRIDGE Helenna, b. 30 Apr 1966, Manchester, England. Manager; Agent; Music Publisher for film and television. Partner, Linas Valaitis. Education: BSc Hons, Media Degree, Finance; Masters in Intellectual properties. Career: Live, studio audio engineer, 1988; Manager, Tour Manager, 1991; Manager, agent, artist co-ordinator, Baroness Management (Director), 1992-; Director, Business Manager, Swan Music Publishing Ltd, specialising in TV and film, 1993-; Manager, agent of composers for television and film; Music publisher, television and film; Production assisstant for television commercials with Mirage Films. Memberships: IMF; MCPS; PRS. Hobbies: Sub-aqua diving; Skiing; Golf. Address: Swan Music Publishing Ltd, Swan House, 52-53 Poland Street, London W1V 3DF, England.

TROUT Walter Cooper, b. 6 Mar 1951, Atlantic City, New Jersey, USA. Muscian (guitar, harmonica, trumpet). m. Marie Braendgaard, 2 sons. Education: College, 1 year. Musical Education: Classical trumpet, 7 years; Self-taught, guitar, harmonica. Career: Played with John Lee Hooker, Big Mama Thornton, Joe Tex, Pee Wee Crayton, 1979-80; Lead guitarist, harmonica, Canned Heat, 1984-89; Lead guitar, John Mayall's Bluesbreakers, 1984-89; Formed the Walter Trout Band, 1989-. Recordings: With Canned Heat: The Boogie Assault, 1981; Heat Brothers '84, 1984; John Mayall's Bluesbreakers: Behind The Iron Curtain, 1985; The Power Of The Blues, 1987; Chicago Line, 1988; Life In The Jungle, 1992; Walter Trout Band: Life In The Jungle, 1989; Prisoner Of A Dream, 1990; The Love That We Once Knew, 1990; No More Fish-Jokes Live, 1992; Radio Records, 1992; Transistion, 1992; Motivation Of Love, 1992; No More Fish-Jokes Live, 1992; Tremble, 1994; Still Got The Blues, 1994; Tellin' Stories, 1994; Breaking The Rules, 1995; Where Blues Meets Rock, 1995; Jeffology (tribute to Jeff Beck), 1995; Tribute To Stevie (tribute to Stevie Ray Vaughn), 1996. Honour: BBC Listeners Poll, All Time Greatest Guitarists, '93, voted # 6 of 20. Membership: ASCAP. Hobbies: Composing music; Time With family. Current Management: MPI London, 21 A Noel St, London W1V 3PD. Address: P O Box 246, Huntington Beach, CA 92648, USA.

TROWER Robin, b. 9 Mar 1945, Southend, Essex, England. Musician (guitar). Career: Founder member, The Paramounts, 1962-66; Founder member, Procul Harum, 1967-71; Solo artiste, 1971-; Formed Jude; Miami Founder, Robin Trower Band; Founder, band BLT, 1981; Pop Festival, 1968; Palm Springs Pop Festival, 1969; Toronto Rock Festival, 1969; Atlantic City Pop Festival, 1969; Isle Of Wight Festival, 1970. Recordings: Albums with Procul Harum: Procul Harum, 1967; Shine On Brightly, 1968; A Salty Dog, 1969; Home, 1970; Solo: Twice Removed From Yesterday, 1973; Bridge Of Sighs, 1974; For Earth Below, 1975; Robin Trower Live, 1976; Long Misty Days, 1976; In City Dreams, 1977; Caravan To Midnight, 1978; Victims Of The Fury, 1980; Back It Up, 1983; Beyond The Mist, 1985; Passion, 1987; Portfolio, 1987; Take What You Need, 1988. Current Management: Stardust Management, 4600 Franklin Avenue, Los Angeles, CA 90027, USA.

TRUBETSKY Tonu (Prince), b. 24 Apr 1963, Tallinn, Revala, Estonia. Singer; Composer; Poet; Writer; Actor; Video Director. m. Anu Trubetsky, 28 May 1988, 1 son, 2 daughters. Education: Diver, Engineer forces. Musical Education: Rock'n'Roll High School. Career: Lead singer, Vennaskond, 1984-; Lead singer, Felis Ultramarinus, 1986; Prince Trubetsky and JMKE, 1986; The Un Concern, 1988; Solo artist, 1993; Business venture: Vennaskond Ltd; Films: Soda (War), 1987; Hysteria (Hysterics), 1993; Videos with Vennaskond: Elagu Proudhon! (Long Live Proudhon!), 1994; Riga My Love, 1995. Recordings: with Vennaskond: Ltn. Schmidt'i Pojad (The Sons of Lieutenant Schmidt), 1991; Girl In Black, 1991; Rockpiraadid (The Rock Pirates), 1992; Usk. Lootus. Armastus (Faith. Hope. Love), 1993; Vaenlane Ei Maga (The Enemy Is Not Sleeping), 1995; Voluri Tagasitulek (Return Of The Wizard), 1994; Inglid Ja Kangelased (Angels And Heroes), 1995. Publications: Books: Pogo, 1989; Inglid Ja Kanglased (Angels And Heroes), 1992; Anarhia (Anarchy), 1994; Daam Sinises (Lady In Blue), 1994. Honours: Levijaagup, 1990; 2 Gold Records, 1993. Hobbies: Ethnography; History. Address: Vennaskond, PO Box 2225, EE-0035 Tallinn, Estonia.

TRUE Roger, b. 2 June, Greensboro, NC, USA. Country Singer; Musician (Guitar). Career: City Stage Celebration; The Lexington Barbecue Festival; Summerfield Founder's Day Celebration; Clubs: The Blind Tiger; Kilroy's; Playing, Piedmont Triad; International Country Music Fan Fair, Nashville; Starred and Sung in motion picture, The Dam. Recordings: Crazy Arms; There Stands the Glass; Your Cheatin' Heart; Walk Through This World With Me; Tonight the Bottle Let Me Down; El Paso; Before the Next Teardrop Falls; Good Hearted Woman; Take This Job and Shove It; Don't Rock the Jukebox; We'll Burn that Bridge; Friends in Low Places, many more. Honours: Most Promising Vocal of Tomorrow Third Place, North Carolina Country Music Assocation, 1993; NCCMA Award Winner. Memberships: BMI; ASCAP. Current Management: Webb Pierce

Enterprises, 1521 Clayton Avenue, Nashville, TN 37217, USA.

TRUESDALE Tommy, b. 17 Nov 1947, Annbank, Ayr, Scotland. Vocalist; Entertainer; Actor; Radio Presenter. m. Marjory, 9 Feb 1972. Musical Education: Self-taught. Career: Television appearances: One Night Stand, Scottish TV, 1965; The Best Disco In Town, Scottish TV, 1979; The Singer and The Song, BBC, 1981; Various television and radio interviews; British headliner, Great Scottish Country Music Festival, Wonderwestworld, Ayr, 1994. Recordings: Albums: C'mon Everybody, 1979; Sings Country, 1985; The Best Of T T Album, 1990; A Tree In The Meadow, 1993. Publications: Columnist, Country Music News And Roots Magazine. Honours: Scottish Country Music Fellowship Award, Top Male Vocalist, 1989, 1990. Membership: British Country Music Association. Hobbies: Walking the dog; Watching boxing, football; Listening to all types of music. Current Management: Self-managed. Address: 3 McColgan Place, Ayr KA8 9PU, Scotland.

TRUSSARDI Louis, b. 6 June 1938, Clichy, France. Musician (contrebass). m. Martine Teyssier, 31 Jan 1972, 3 sons. Musical Education: 2 years, Conservatory de Versailles. Career: Played with: Chet Baker; Kenny Clarke; Dizzy Gillespie; Stéphane Grappelli; "Philly" Joe Jones; Art Taylor; Louis Hayse; Richie Cole; Teddy Edwards; Frank Morgan; Milt Jackson; Art Simmons; Dusco Boy Kovic. Recordings: Solo album: Vendredi 14; Also recorded with: Maurice Vander; "Philly" Joe Jones; Kenny Clarke; Stéphane Grappelli; Chet Baker. Membership: SACEM. Hobbies: Piccolo bass; Classical guitar. Address: 3 Rue d'Ablis, F-78660 Prunay en Yvelines, France.

TSENOVA Julia, b. 30 July 1948, Sofia, Bulgaria. Composer; Pianist. m. Stefan Sandulov, 1 daughter. Education: Piano, Musical Academy in Sofia, 1972; Composition, 1974; Associated Professor Dean, Department of Pop and Jazz Music, 1997. Career: Pianist and Composer. Compositions: Simphony; Movement for Orchestra; Cantus Firmus a Due; That Means all Gods. Honours: Many awards for chamber, choir and children's music. Memberships: Union of Bulgarian Composers; International Society for Contemporary Music. Address: Vassil Levski 4, 1000 Sofia, Bulgaria.

TSUI Trix Ko-Chuan, b. 20 Oct 1953, Taipei, Taiwan. Musician (guitar) Concert Promoter; Disc Jockey. m. Farie Hsiu-Ching Le, 1 Dec 1979, 1 daughter. education: Graduate: World College of Journalism and Communication. Musical Education: Self-taught. Career: Concert Promoter, Stage Manager: Chick Corea's Acoustic and Electric Band; Lee Ritnour; Brecker Brothers; Peabo Bryson and Patti Austin; Stage Manager: INXS; B B King; Hard Rock Cafe, Taipei, 1992-94; Leader, guitarist: Rock City Band, 1971-80; Diplomats, 1980-1993; Now house band of Hard Rock Cafe, Taipei, Name changed back to Rock City Band, 1994-95; Radio DJ, BBC, TBC; Technical Director, Gibson and Digitech; Musical Cosultant, Taipei Communicating Arts (from the system of MIT). Recordings: Producer debut album by Miss Jade Lee: Hermits; Blindman Pop Group: Eden; Welfare Foundation's tribute single and collection of: International Family Years. Publications: Columnist for: Non-Classical Music Magazine; Audio and CD Shopper; Liberty Time newspaper. Membership: Musical Mountain Communication. Hobby: Collecting guitars. Address: 3F No 16, Alley 88, Sec 2, Pao-Fu Road, Yung-Ho, Taipei, Taiwan.

TUBRIDY Michael, b. 6 Aug 1935, County Clare, Ireland. Civil Engineer. m. Céline Kelly, 25 Sept 1961, 2 daughters. Education: University level, UCD, Dublin. Musical Education: Self-taught. Career: Longtime member, Ceoltóirí

Cualann, Castle Céilí Band, The Chieftains, including various concerts, television, radio appearances. Recordings: Various recordings with groups; Solo album: The Eagle's Whistle. Publications: Compiler of music for Irish Traditional Music. Membership: IMRO. Hobbies: Folk dancing; Astronomy. Address: 42 Woodlawn Park, Dundrum, Dublin 14, Ireland.

TUCKER Maureen, b. 1945, New Jersey, USA. Musician (drums). Career: Musician, Velvet Underground, 1965-71; Solo artiste, 1982-; Residency, Café Bizarre; House band, Andy Warhol's Factory arts collective, New York; Member, Warhol's multi-media show, The Exploding Plastic Inevitable, 1966; Concerts include: Montreal World Fair, Canada, 1967; Reunions with Velvet Underground, France, 1990; Wembley, London, 1993. Recordings: with The Velvet Underground: The Velvet Underground And Nico, 1967; White Light, White Heat, 1968; The Velvet Underground, 1969; Loaded, 1970; Various compilations and collections; Solo albums: Playing Possum, 1982; Life In Exile After Abdication, 1989; I Spent A Week There The Other Night, 1991. Honour: Inducted into Rock'n'Roll Hall Of Fame (with Velvet Underground), 1996.

TUCKER Paul, b. 1969, Cambridge, England. Musician; Songwriter. Education: Newcastle University. Career: Member, The Lighthouse Family, 1994-; Television includes: Top Of The Pops. Recordings: Album: Ocean Drive, 1995; Singles: Lifted, 1995; Ocean Drive (used for film soundtrack Jack And Sarah), 1995. Current Management: Kitchenware, 7 The Stables, St Thomas Street, Newcastle-Upon-Tyne, Tyne And Wear NE1 4LE, England.

TUCKER Tanya, b. 10 Oct 1958, Seminole, Texas, USA. Country Singer. Career: Singing at country fairs as a teenager; Recording artist, 1972-; Regular concerts include Grand Ole Opry; Film appearance: Jeremiah Johnson (with Robert Redford). Compositions include: Save Me; Leave Them Boys Alone (co-writer with Hank Williams Jr). Recordings: Hits include: Delta Dawn; Jamestown Ferry; What's Your Mama's Name?; Lizzie And The Rainman; San Antonio Stroll; Here's Some Love; I Won't Take Less Than Your Love (with Paul Davis and Paul Overstreet); Strong Enough To Bend; If It Didn't Come Easy; Dream Lover (duet with Glen Campbell); Albums: Delta Dawn, 1972; What's Your Mama's Name?, 1973; Would You Lay With Me, 1974; Lovin' And Learnin', 1975; Tanya Tucker, 1975; Here's Some Love, 1976; You Are So Beautiful, 1977; Ridin' Rainbows, 1977; TNT, 1978; Tear Me Apart, 1979; Dreamlovers, 1980; Should I Do It?, 1981; Changes, 1982; Live, 1982; Love Me Like You Used To, 1987; Strong Enough To Bend, 1988; Tennessee Woman, 1990; Greatest Hits - Encore, 1990; What Do I Do With Me, 1991; Lizzie And The Rainman, 1992; Hits, 1992; Can't Run From Yourself, 1992; Fire To Fire, 1995. Honours: CMA Female Vocalist Of Year, 1991. Address: c/o Tanya Tucker Inc., 5200 Maryland Way #202, Brentwood, TN 37027, USA.

TUDOR-POLE Edward, b. 6 December 1956, London, England. 1 son. Education: Yardley Court Tonbridge, KESW, RADA. Career: Touring & recording with own band, Ten Pole Tudor; Acting Career: Films include: the Great Rock & Roll Swindle; Absolute Beginners; Sid & Nancy Kull the Conqueror; Theatre: The Admirable Crichton; The Rocky Horror Show; The Deep Blue Sea; TV: Top of the Pops; presented The Crystal Maze. Compositions: Recorded: Who Killed Bambi (Sex Pistols); Swords of 1000 Men; Throwing the Baby Out with the Bathwater; Wunderbar; Three Bells in a Row; Ted aint Dead. Honour: Silver Disc for Swords of 1000 Men, 1981. Hobbies: Running; Reading; Riding (horses & bikes). Address: 37 Springdale Road, London N16 9NS, England.

TULLY Nigel, b. 22 July 1943, Barnsley, Yorkshire, England. Bandleader; Singer; Musician (guitar, saxophone). m. Prue Lyell, 29 Sept 1978, 1 son, 1 daughter. Education: MA Hons, Oxon. Musical Education: Private tuition specially with Pat Crumly, saxophone. Career: Bandleader, The Dark Blues, 1962-; Completed 3500 live concerts, 1995; Highlights include 21st and 40th birthday parties for HRH Prince Charles at Buckingham Palace. Recordings: Overdue, 1983; Live At Ashdown, 1985; 25 And Going For Gold, 1988; Midsummer Dance, 1992. Memberships: Fellow, British Computer Society; Liveryman, Worshipful Company of Musicians. Current Management: Dark Blues Management Ltd. Address: 30 Stamford Brook Road, London W6 0XH, England.

TUNSTALL Kate Victoria, b. 23 June 1975, Edinburgh, Scotland. Singer; Songwriter; Musician (guitar). Education: BA Drama/Music, Royal Holloway College, London University. Musical Education: Grade 8 Distinction, flautist; Grade 7 pianist. Career: Solo gigs in: 2 London university colleges, various bars around South-West London; Various work in Chicago, Illinois, Burlington, Vermont, 1993-; Cable television show in Chicago, Illinois, USA, 1995. Recordings: Bootleg CD, recorded on Nantucket Island, USA, 1995; (Unpublished) album recorded, WWSR radio station, Vermont, USA. Membership: Musicians' Union. Hobbies: Theatre work; Acting; Classical composition; Playwriting. Address: 4 West Acres, St Andrews, Fife KY16 9UD, Scotland.

TURCHI Isabelle, b. 7 June 1965, Paris, France. Musician (violin). m. Lionel Turchi, 12 July 1990, 1 son. Musical Education: B.Mus, Musicology University; Violin, Creteil National Conservatoire. Career: Major variety shows, French television; Recordings with major French singers; Orchestra, Sporting Club, Monaco; Tours, Japan, with French Pops Orchestra. Hobbies: Fashion; Sports. Address: 1 Place Pablo Picasso, 94800 Villejuif, France.

TUREK Jan, b. 19 Oct 1957, Most, Czech Republic. Composer. m. Hana Pegrímková, 26 June 1982, 1 son, 1 daughter. Education: University of Economics; Private study of classical guitar. Career: More than 40 scenic music compositions for drama and puppet shows including realisation. Compositions: There Was a Town in Prairie, 1994; The House with 7 Circles, 1995; The Royal Seconds, 1996. Recordings: Fairy Tales of Mr Fairy-Tale, 1995. Dilia, Prague. Hobbies: Economics; Playing guitar in a rock band. Current Management: F Agency, Zizkova 1616, 434 01 Most, Czech Republic. Address: J Pruchy, 2891/379, 434 01 Most, Czech Republic.

TURNER Carl, b. 2 June 1969, Wolverhampton, England. Writer; Producer; Musician (keyboards). Education: 2 years OND, Graphic Design, Stafford College; 2 years HND, Wolverhampton College. Musical Education: Self-taught. Career: 3 major UK tours; 2 major US tours; 1 major European tour; 6 appearances, Top of the Pops; Other television appearances: Hangar 17; The Big Breakfast; The Beat; The Chart Show. Recordings: Such A Feeling, 1991; Playing With Knives (Number 4, UK); 1992; I'm Gonna Get You (Number 3, UK), 1992; Took My Love, 1993. Honours: Music Week Award, Top Dance Single, 1991. Membership: Musicians' Union; PRS. Hobbies: Historic rallying; Snowboarding. Current Management: Antony Johnson. Address: BGA, Unit 1B, Hollins Business Centre, Rowley Street, Stafford ST16 3RH, England.

TURNER Geraldine Gail, b. 23 June 1950, Brisbane, Australia. Actress; Singer. m. Brian Castles-Onion, 31 Dec 1993. Education: Diploma in Education, Queensland. Musical Education: Singing, Queensland Conservatoire, two years; Classical ballet training, ten years. Career: Internationally renowned in cabaret and as Sondheim inetrpreter; Performed in Australia,

England, Canada, USA and Africa; Starred in musicals: Oliver!; Chicago; Anything Goes; Company; Sweeney Todd; A Little Night Music; Into The Woods; Ned Kelly; Guys And Dolls; Plays: Don's party; Present Laughter; Summer Of The Seventeenth Doll; Operas and operettas: La Belle Heléne; HMS Pinafore; The Mikado; Film appearances: Careful He Might Hear You; Summerfield; Numerous televiosn appearances. Recordings: The Stephen Sondheim Songbook; Torch Songs - And Some Not So Tortous; Once In A Blue Moon; Gala Night; One Life To Live; Cast albums include: Anything Goes; Chicago. Honours: Order of Australia (OAM), 1988; Green Room Awards, for Oliver!, 1984, and Anything Goes, 1989; Mo Awards, for Sweeney Todd, 1988, and Anything Goes, 1989. Memberships: Federal President, Australian Actors' Equity, four years. Hobbies: Rose gardening; Painting. Current Management: Robyn Gardiner Management, 397 Riley Street, Surry Hills, NSW 2010, Australia. Address: 33 Munni Street, Newtown, NSW 2042, Australia.

TURNER Howard, b. 24 Feb 1959, Thornage, Holt, England. Producer; Engineer; Musician (guitar); Songwriter; Studio Designer. Education: BA Hons, UEA, Norwich; PGCE, UEA, Norwich. Career: Began Raven Recording as recording studio, 1984; Producer, Engineer for Pete DeFreitas (Echo and The Bunnymen) on Sex Gods project; Developed reputation as freelance Indie/Rock producer and engineer; Sold studios, 1991; Acquired interest in Swamp Studios, 1992; Created Raven Recording Services and Studio Wizard Organization (studio design company); Major studio installations include: GWBB (London); The Cutting Rooms (Manchester); The Temple (Malta); Numerous television and radio appearances. Recordings: 4 albums as musician under name The Nivens; As producer, albums by: Jacob's Mouse; Red Harvest; Jazz Butcher; Perfect Disaster; The Pollen; Bad Manners; Close Lobsters; Girlschool; Eden; Green On Red; Other recordings for Captain Sensible and The Damned. Memberships: APRS; RePro; PRS; MCPS. Current Management: The Studio Wizard Organisation, 1 School Cottages, Billingford, Dereham, Norfolk NR20 4RF, England.

TURNER Ike (Izear) Jr, b. 5 Nov 1931, Clarksdale, Mississippi, USA. Singer; Songwriter; Musician (guitar). m. Tina Turner (Annie Mae Bullock), 1958, divorced 1978. Career: Founder, Kings Of Rhythm band; Session guitarist, on recordings by B.B.King; Howlin' Wolf; Johnny Ace; Duo, Ike & Tina Turner, 1960-78; One of most popular acts on R&B tour circuit, 1960s; ConcerUK tourts include: with Rolling Stones, 1966; Newport 69 Festival, 1969; Support to Rolling Stones, US tour, 1969; Built Bolic Sound Recording Studio, 1970. Recordings: Albums: with Ike and Tina Turner: Live! The Ike And Tina Turner Show, 1965; River Deep, Mountain High, 1966; In Person, 1969; Outa Season, 1969; The Hunter, 1969; Come Together, 1970; Workin' Together, 1971; Live At Carnegie Hall, 1971; 'Nuff Said, 1970; Feel Good, 1972; Nutbush City Limits, 1974; Solo: My Confessions, 1988; My Blues Country, 1997; Singles include: with Kings Of Rhythm: Rocket 88, 1951; with Ike and Tina Turner: It's Going To Work Out Fine, 1961; River Deep Mountain High, 1966; A Love Like Yours, 1966; I Want To Take You Higher, 1970; Proud Mary, 1971; Nutbush City Limits, 1973; Baby Get It On, 1975. Honours: Rocket 88 widely credited as first rock'n'roll record; Rock And Roll Hall Of Fame, with Tina Turner, 1991.

TURNER Joe Lynn, b. USA. Singer. Career: Vocalist, rock groups: Fandango, 1977-80; Last Kiss, 1979; One Night Stand, 1979; Cadillac, 1980; Rainbow, 1980-85; Yngwie Malmsteen, 1987-89; Deep Purple, 1990-91; Also solo recording artiste. Recordings: Albums: 4 albums with Fandango, 1977-80; with Rainbow: Difficult To Cure, 1981; Best Of, 1981; Straight Between

The Eyes, 1982; Bent Out Of Shape, 1983; Finyl Vinyl, 1986; Solo albums: Fandango, 1982; Rescue You, 1985; Nothing Changes, 1995; with Yngwie Malmsteen: Odyssey, 1988; Live In Leningrad, 1989; with Deep Purple: Slaves And Masters, 1990. Address: c/o American Talent Group, 221 W 57th Street, 8th Floor, New York, NY 10019, USA.

TURNER Lee, b. Jacksonville, Florida, USA. Musician (piano); Composer; Arranger; Music Publisher. m. Dianne Gross, 3 sons. Education: University of Florida; Southern Baptist Theological Seminary. Career: Professional pianist since high school; Studio work, Nashville and Jacksonville; Regular television and radio appearances, dances, shows and concerts; Accompanist and soloist; Appeared with The Dream Weavers, Ed Sullivan Show; Minister of music, 29 years; Director, choirs and groups, religious and secular; Owner, publishing company, TurnerSong, 1981-. Compositions include: Into The Night, The Dream Weavers. Recordings include: It's Almost Tomorrow, The Dream Weavers; Rhapsody in Stained Glass, solo piano; There's a Meetin' Here Tonight, musical; Make Every Day a Good Day!. Honours: Annual ASCAP Award, 1974-. Memberships: ASCAP; AFofM. Address: 4263 San Jose Blvd, Jacksonville, FL 32207, USA.

TURNER Marc, b. 1951, Cambridge, England. Singer; Musician (guitar). Education: University. Musical Education: Self-taught. Career: Extensive UK work; Tours, Europe; USA; Also known as The Delta Kid, and Sunshine Joe; Currently working, studying in Spain; Various radio and television appearances. Compositions: Numerous. Recordings: Albums: Shoot The Blue Moon Down, 1982; Live - Marc Turner, 1983. Membership: Musicians' Union (UK). Hobbies: Girls; Motorcycles; Having fun; Making the world a better place. Address: c/o 172 Russell Court, Woburn Place, London, England.

TURNER Nik, b. 26 Aug 1940, Oxford, England. Musician (saxophone, flute); Vocalist; Musician; Composer; Arranger; Teacher. Musical Education: Self-taught. Career: Formed Hawkwind, 1969; Television and radio appearances: Top Of The Pops, 1972; BBC Live John Peel at Paris Theatre, 1972; Tours Of Europe, 1972-76; Left Hawkwind 1976; Formed Inner City Unit/Sphynx, 1976; Nik Turner's Fantastic All Stars, 1988; Nik Turner's Space Ritual, 1994; US tours 1994, 1995; Numerous radio appearances. Recordings: with Hawkwind: 8 albums; Numerous samplers; 6 singles include: Silver Machine (Number 1, UK), 1972; with Inner City Unit: 6 albums, 3 singles; with Sphynx: 1 album, 1978; with Nik Turner's Space Ritual: 5 albums, USA, video, 1994/95. Membership: Musicians' Union. Hobbies: Reading; Swimming; Cinema; Apiary; Writing. Current Management: Money Talks Management. Address: Cadillac Ranch, Pencraig Uchaf, Cwm Bach, Whitland, Dyfed SA34 0DT, Wales.

TURNER Roger, b. 3 Feb 1946, Whitstable, Kent, England. Musician (drums, percussion). m. Sara Ljungberg, 24 July 1992, div, 1 daughter. Education: BA, English Literature, Philosophy, University of Sussex. Musical Education: Self-taught. Career: Tours: USA; Canada; Australia; Europe; Festival concerts from the Berlin Jazz Fest to Macau; BBC Midnight Oil; Television in Australia, France, UK. Recordings: I Have No Feelings, Annette Peacock; Ammo, Phil Minton; The Recedents; Solo: Blur Between; Mouth Full of Ecstasy, Phil Minton Quartet; Birthdays, with John Russell; In the Tradition, with Alan Silva and Johannes Bauer. Honours: Arts Council of Great Britain, Bursary Awards, 1980-83. Membership: London Musicians' Collective. Current Management: Fabe/Koschik. Address: 34 Lancaster Road, London W11 1QR, England.

TURNER Scott, b. 23 Aug 1931, Sydney, Nova Scotia, Canada. Producer; Writer; Publisher. Divorced, 1 son, 1 daughter. Education: BA, BSc, University of Dubuque, 1955; 1 year Graduate School, Texas Tech University. Career includes: Lead guitarist, writer for Tommy Sands and the Raiders, 1957-60; Guy Mitchell, 1960-61; Eddie Fisher, 1961-63; Joined Writer and producer, A&M Records, 1963; General Manager, Central Songs, Hollywood; Executive Producer, Country division, Liberty and Imperial Records, 1964; Independent Producer for Slim Whitman, Del Reeves and Jimmy Clanton, 1976; Composer of over 350 recorded songs including co-written songs with many leading artists; Music Director for numerous television shows; Composer of many background tracks and songs in films. Recordings: Numerous songs recorded by various artists including: Roy Clark; Nilsson; Herb Alpert; Dean Martin; Tammy Wynette; Jimmy Dean; The Del Vikings; Skeets MacDonald; Gene Vincent, including: Shutters And Boards; Please Mr Music Man; Does He Love You Like I Do; She's My Baby. Address: 524 Doral Country Drive, Nashville, TN 37221, USA.

TURNER Tina (Annie Mae Bullock), b. 26 Nov 1939, Brownsville, Tennessee, USA. Singer. Songwriter. m. Ike Turner, 1958, divorced 1978. Career: Member, Ike & Tina Turner, 1958-78; Worldwide tours include: Support to Rolling Stones, UK tour, 1966, US tour, 1969; European tour, 1971; Newport Festival, 1969; Solo artiste, 1978-; US tour, 1981; Support to Lionel Richie, UK tour, 1984; Rock In Rio Festival, Brazil, 1985; Live Aid, Philadelphia, 1985; European tour, 1985; Prince's Trust Gala, London, 1986; World tours, 1987, 1990; Record 182,000 audience attend concert, Rio De Janeiro, 1988; First woman to play Palace of Versailles, France, 1990; Film appearances: Tommy, 1974; Mad Max - Beyond Thunderdome, 1985; Life story documented in film What's Love Got To Do With It?, 1992. Compositions include: Nutbush City Limits; Recordings: Albums with Ike Turner: Live! The Ike And Tina Turner Show, 1965; River Deep, Mountain High, 1966; Outa Season, 1969; The Hunter, 1969; Come Together, 1970; Workin' Together, 1971; Live At Carnegie Hall, 1971; 'Nuff Said, 1971; Feel Good, 1972; Nutbush City Limits, 1974; Solo albums: The Acid Queen, 1975; Private Dancer, 1984; Mad Max - Beyond The Thunderdome, 1985; Break Every Rule (Number 1 in nine countries), 1986; Live In Europe, 1988; Foreign Affair (Number 1, UK), 1989; Simply The Best, 1991; What's Love Got To With It (film soundtrack), 1993; Wildest Dreams, 1996; Hit singles include: with Ike Turner: It's Gonna Work Out Fine, 1961; Poor Fool, 1962; River Deep, Mountain High, 1966; I Want To Take You Higher, 1970; Proud Mary, 1971; Nutbush City Limits, 1973; Solo: Let's Stay Together, 1983; What's Love Got To Do With It? (Number 1, US), 1984; Better Be Good To Me, 1984; Private Dancer, 1984; We Don't Need Another Hero, theme for film Thunderdome (Number 2, US), 1985; One Of The Living, 1985; It's Only Love, with Bryan Adams, 1985; Typical Male (Number 2, US), 1986; The Best, 1989; I Don't Wanna Lose You, 1989; Be Tender With Me Baby, 1990; It Takes Two, duet with Rod Stewart, 1990; Way Of The World, 1991; I Don't Wanna Fight, 1993; Goldeneye (film theme), 1995; Contributor, We Are The World, USA For Africa, 1985. Publications: I Tina (autobiography). Honours include: Grammy Awards: Record of the Year; Song of the Year; Best Female Vocal Performance; Best Female Rock Vocal, 1985; American Music Awards: Favourite Soul/R&B Female Artist, and Video Artist, 1985; Best Female Pop/Rock Artist, 1986; MTV Music Video award, 1985; Star on Hollywood Walk of Fame, 1986; Rock And Roll Hall Of Fame, with Ike Turner, 1991; World Music Award, Outstanding Contribution To The Music Industry, 1993. Address: c/o Roger Davies Management, 15030 Ventura Blvd, Suite 772, Sherman Oaks, CA 91403, USA.

TUTUNJIAN Nancy M, b. 7 Dec 1959, Needham, Massachusetts, USA. Singer; Songwriter; Actress. Education: Associated degree in Business. Musical Education: 2 years solfege to learn to read music. Career: Regional theatre; Series of concerts sponsored by WNGN-FM, New York; Numerous festival, concert appearances all over USA; Guest on Jericho cable show; Power Hour cable show; Numerous phoned radio interviews, USA; Own record company, Paraclete Records. Compositions include: Numerous contemporary Christian songs (lyrics and music); Three one-act Biblical theatre pieces (book, lyrics and music). Recordings include: Songs For The Bridegroom, 1992; Christmas Glow, 1994. Honours: Trailblazers Award, International Airplay Association; Honorary Mention Certificate; Billboard Songwriting Contest. Membership: BMI as songwriter, publisher. Hobbies: Painting; Drawing; Cooking; Hiking; Biking; Roller-blading. Current Management: Paraclete Music Ministries. Address: PO Box 473, Watertown, MA 02272-0473, USA.

TWAIN Shania. Country Singer; Songwriter. m. Robert "Mutt" Lange. Career: Regular television performances on CMT and TNN. Compositions: Songwriting partnership with Mutt Lange (husband). Recordings: Albums: Shania Twain; The Woman In Me; Come On Over; Hit single: Any Man Of Mine. Honour: CMT Europe, Rising Video Star Of The Year, 1993. Current Management: US: Jon Landau Management, 40 West Elm Street, Greenwich, CT 06830, USA; Canada: Mary Bailey Management, PO Box 546, 4 Al Wende Avenue, Kirkland Lake, Ontario P2N 3JS, Canada.

TYAS Michael, b. 21 Jun 1957, Durham City, England. Musician (bass, guitar, mandolin, dulcimer); Vocalist. m. Margaret Tyas, 26 Sep 1992, 1 daughter. Musical Education: Self-taught. Career: Worked in amateur folk groups in North East England; Joined the Whisky Priests, 1989; Professional musician, 1991-; Toured 14 European countries; Appeared on Anglia and Tyne Tees TV, BBC Radio 1 and 2, and on national radio in Belgium, Holland and Germany. Recordings: 5 albums with The Whisky Priests including 1 live album; Lyricist for one recorded song. Hobbies: Photography; Hill walking. Current Management: Whippet Promotions UK; World Music Promotions, Continental Europe. Address: Chilton, County Durham, England.

TYLER Bonnie, b. 8 June 1951, Skewen, Wales. Singer. m. Robert Sullivan, 14 July 1973. Career: Lead vocalist, local bands; Solo artiste, 1976-; First solo female artist to enter UK album charts at Number 1; Recordings: Lost In France, 1976; It's A Heartache, 1978; Natural Force, 1978; Faster Than The Speed Of Night, 1983; Total Eclipse Of The Heart, 1983; Holding Out For A Hero, 1985; Secret Dreams, 1986; Hide Your Heart, 1987; Bitterblue, 1991; The Best Of, 1993; Free Spirit, 1996. Honours: Winner, Yamaha World Song Contest, 1978; BRIT Award Nominations, Best Female Vocalist, 1984-86; Grammy Nomination, Best Female Vocalist, 1984; Winner, Best Female Vocalist, Echo, 1994; Variety Club of Great Britain, 1984. Current Management: David Aspden Management, The Coach House, Capel Leyse, Holmwood, Dorking, Surrey RH5 4LJ, England.

TYLER Stephen (Stephen Tallarico), b. 26 Mar 1948, New York, USA. Singer; Musician (harmonica). Career: Singer, US rock band Aerosmith, 1970-; Concerts include: Support to the Kinks, Mott The Hoople, 1974; Schaefer Music Festival, New York, 1975; Reading Rock Festival, 1977; California Jam Festival II, 1978; Texxas World Music Festival, 1978; Appearance as the Future Villain Band in film Sgt Pepper's Lonely Hearts Band, 1978; California Music Festival, with Van Halen, Cheap Trick, Ted Nugent, 1979; World Series Of Rock with Journey, Ted Nugent, Thin Lizzy, 1979; Monsters of Rock Festival, Castle Donington, 1990; Television includes: MTV 10 anniverary special, ABC-TV, 1991; Saturday Night Live, NBC TV, 1993. Recordings: Albums: Aerosmith, 1973; Toys In The Attic, 1975; Get Your Wings, 1975; Rocks, 1976; Draw The Line, 1978; Night In The Ruts, 1980; Greatest Hits, 1981; Rock In A Hard Place, 1982; Classic Live!, 1986; Done With Mirrors, 1986; Permanent Vacation, 1987; Pump, 1990; Pandora's Box, 1992; Get A Grip, 1993; Singles include: Dream On; Last Child; Walk This Way; Dude (Looks Like A Lady); Angel; Rag Doll; Love In An Elevator; Janie's Got A Gun; What It Takes; Livin' On The Edge; Eat The Rich; Cryin'; Amazing. Honours include: Inducted into Hollywood's Rock Walk, 1990; 3 Boston SKC Music Awards, 1990; American Music Awards, 1991; Grammy, Best Rock Performnce, 1991; Rolling Stone and Billboard magazine awards; Platinum discs. Current Management: Magus Entertainment, 584 Broadway, Suite 1009, New York, NY 10012, USA.

TYRRELL John William, b. 14 March 1961, Melbourne, Australia. Drums; Manager. Career: Manager and Drummer, Abba Tribute Band, Björn Again, 1988-; Band formed in Melbourne with partner Rod Woolley, appeared on most TV and radio shows. Recordings: A Little Respect/Stop; Santa Claus Is Coming to Town; So You Win Again; Flashdance - What a Feeling. Membership: UK Music Union. Address: 48 Fernhead Road, Maida Vale, London W9 3EW, England.

TZUKE Judie, b. 1955, London, England. Singer; Songwriter. Education: Drama. Career: Solo artiste; Songwriting partnership with Mike Paxman, 1975; Compositions include: These Are The Laws, with Mike Paxman; Give Me The Love, recorded by Elton John. Recordings: Albums: Welcome To The Cruise, 1979; Sports Car, 1980; I Am Phoenix, 1981; Road Noise, 1982; Shoot The Moon, 1983; Ritmo, 1983; Judie Tzuke, 1985; The Cat Is Out, 1985; Turning Stones, 1989; Left Hand Talking, 1991.

U

UI CHEALLAIGH Aine, b. 29 Oct 1959, Belfast, Northern Ireland. Singer; Musician (violin); Teacher. 2 sons. Education: Degree, diploma, University College Dublin. Musical Education: City Of Belfast School Of Music. Career: Many broadcasts on RTE Radio and Television; BBC Radio; Solo singer, Riverdance-The Show, by Bill Whelan. Teacher, English, Irish and Music. Recordings: Solo album: In Two Minds, 1992. Honours: Oireachtas Gold Medal, 1990, 1992. Hobbies: Singing; Traditional fiddle. Address: Ring, Co Waterford, Ireland.

UKIC Zoran, b. 31 May 1962, Split, Croatia. Musician (drums); Record Producer; Manager. m. Vesna, 30 June 1984, 1 son, 1 daughter. Career: with Daleka Obala: Faraway Coast tours, 1990, 1993-95; Zagreb Salata, D Dvornik, N Belan, Daleka Obala, 1992; Television show 7 Noc. Recordings: with Daleka Obala: Faraway Coast, 1990; Ludi Mornari Dolaze U Grad (Crazy Sailors Come On The Town); MRL, E (Dirty), 1993; Morski Pas (Shark), 1994. Publications: Blue And Green, Croatian Rock Encyclopedia. Honour: The Best Debutant, Split Festival, 1990. Membership: Croatian Musicians' Union. Hobby: Jogging. Address: Zoran Ukic, Teutina 15, 5800 Split, Croatia.

ULRICH Lars, b. 26 Dec 1955, Copenhagen, Denmark. Musician (drums). Career: Former tennis player; Compiler, New Wave of British Heavy Metal album with Geoff Barton, 1979; UK tour with Diamond Head; Member, US heavy rock group Metallica, 1981-; Worldwide tours include: Masters of Puppets world tour, 1986-87; US tour, 1988; Damaged Justice UK tour, 1989; World tours, 1991-; Also tours with Raven; Ozzy Osbourne; Twisted Sister; Motörhead; Major concerts include: Monsters Of Rock Festival, Castle Donington, 1985, 1987, 1991; German Monster Of Rock festivals, 1987; Monsters of Rock, Europe and US tours, 1988, 1991; Day On The Green, Oakland, 1991. Recordings: Albums: Kill 'Em All, 1983; Ride The Lightning, 1984; Master Of Puppets, 1986; ...And Justice For All, 1988; Metallica (Number 1, UK and US), 1991; Live Shit, 1993; Singles: Garage Days Revisited (EP), 1987; Harvester Of Sorrow, 1988; One, 1989; Enter Sandman, 1991; The Unforgiven, 1991; Nothing Else Matters, 1992; Wherever I May Roam, 1992; Sad But True, 1992; Stone Cold Crazy, track featured on Rubáiyát (Elektra's 40th anniversary compilation). Honours: Platinum and Gold discs; Grammy Awards: Best Heavy Metal Performance: One, 1989; Stone Cold Crazy, 1991; The Unforgiven, 1992; American Music Award, Favourite Heavy Metal Artist, 1993; Bay Area Music Awards: Outstanding Album, 1992; Outstanding Metal Album, Outstanding Group, Outstanding Drummer, 1993; Rolling Stone Readers Poll Winners, Best Heavy Metal Band, 1993. Current Management: Q-Prime Inc. Address: 729 7th Avenue, 14th Floor, New York, NY 10019, USA.

ULRICH Shari, b. 17 Oct 1951, Marin County, California, USA. Composer; Musician (violin, mandolin, piano, guitar); Singer; Television Host. m. 29 Apr 1989, 1 daughter. Education: 1 year college. Musical Education: Violin training, grade 3-13, otherwise self-taught. Career: Member, Pied Pumpkin String Ensemble, 1972-76; Hometown band, 1976-78; UHF (Ulrich, Bill Henderson, Roy Forbes), 1989-; Solo artist, 1978-; Composer: theme music, several Canadian television series, documentaries; Pieces for SesameStreet; Host Future Scan 1984, 1985; Host, Inside Trax, 1989-1994. Recordings; 2 albums with Pied Pumpkin, 1974, 1975; Hometown Band: Flying, 1976; Hometown Band, 1977; Solo albums: Long Nights, 1978; One Step Ahead, 1980; Talk Around Town, 1982; Every Road, 1989; with UHF: UHF,

1990; UHF II, 1994. Honours: Juno Awards, 1977, 1981. Memberships: Vice-president, Songwriters' Association of Canada, AFofM; ACTRA; SOCAN. Hobbies: Photography; Cycling. Current Management: Self-managed. Address: Box 152, Bowen Island, British Columbia V0N 1G0, Canada.

ULRIK Hans (Jensen), b. 28 Sept 1965, Copenhagen, Denmark. Musician (saxophone, flute). Musical Education: 2 years, Berklee College of Music, Boston, USA, 1984-86. Career: Founder, own band Hans Ulrik Quartet; Member, Marilyn Mazur Future Song; Tours: Europe, mostly Scandinavia; Numerous television and radio appearances. Recordings: Day After Day (with Gary Peacock, Adam Nussbaum, John Abercrombie); Strange World (with Marilyn Mazur). Honours: Best Soloist, Leverkusen International Jazz Competition, Germany, 1988. Hobby: Sports. Current Management: The Danish Jazz League. Address: Den Danske Jazzkreds, Kjeld Langes Gade 4 A, DK 1367 Copenhagen K, Denmark.

ULSTRUP Thomas Viderø, b. 31 Aug 1968, Frederiksberg, Denmark. Musician (moog synthesizers, keyboards, modified piano); Composer; Agent; Teacher. Education: Teacher's Academy of Art, Music and Multimedia; High Schools of Jazz and Rock; Private tuition. Career: Member of various experimental groups in Copenhagen, 1984-92; Solo key performances; Co-founder with Las Nissen of Gone Fishin', 1989-96; Solo, duo and trio member and recording artist; Founder of Native Music Denmark, 1997; Radio Host, Copenhagen radio-jazz show Alternative Music; Touring with The Sun Mountain Experience in the Caribbean, 1998. Compositions: 10 x Cai, 1988; Jack Daniels, 1994; Meditations, 1998. Recordings: with Gone Fishin': Gone Fishin'. 1994; Adventure: Once Upon a Time..., 1998; Alternative music: Sound Environment, 1998. Publications: Native Music Compilation Volumes I and II, 1998; Alternative Music - Soundenvironment. Honours: Gold Talent Prize, Berlingske Tidende, 1988. Memberships: Gramex; Danish Jazz and Folk Authors (DOBFA); Composers in Denmark (KODA). Hobby: Soundscapes. Current Management: Native Music. Address: H/F Grænsen 8, Finsensvej 263, DK-2720 Vaniøse, Denmark.

ULVÆUS Bjorn, b. 25 Apr 1945, Gothenburg, Sweden. Songwriter; Musician (guitar); Vocalist. m. Agnetha Fältskog, 1971 (divorced 1979). Career: Songwriter with Benny Andersson, 1966-; Duo with Andersson as The Hootennanny Singers; Partner in production with Andersson at Polar Music, 1971; Founder member, Swedish pop group Abba, 1973-82; Winners, Eurovision Song Contest, 1974; Regular international tours and concerts include: Royal Performance, Stockholm, 1976; Royal Albert Hall, London, 1977; Film appearance: Abba - The Movie, 1978; Continued writing and producing with Andersson, 1982-; Reunion Abba appearance, Swedish TV, 1986. Compositions include: Abba songs (with Benny Andersson): Ring Ring Ring; Waterloo; Honey Honey; I Do I Do I Do I Do I Do; Mamma Mia; Dancing Queen; Fernando; Money Money Money; Knowing Me Knowing You; The Name Of The Game; Take A Chance On Me; Summer Night City; Chiquitita; Does Your Mother Know?; Gimme Gimme Gimme (A Man After Midnight); The Winner Takes It All; Super Trouper; On And On And On; Lay All Your Love On Me; One Of Us; Thank You For The Music; Musical: Chess (with Tim Rice's lyrics), 1983; I Know Him So Well; One Night In Bangkok; Musical: The Immigrants, 1994. Recordings: Albums include: with Andersson: Happiness, 1971; with Abba: Waterloo, 1974; ABBA, 1976; Arrival, 1977; The Album, 1978; Voulez-Vous, 1979; Super Trouper, 1980; Various compilations. Honours include: Gold discs; Listed as biggest-selling group in pop history, Guinness Book Of Records, 1979; Best Selling Swedish

Artist Of The Year, World Music Awards, Monte Carlo, 1993. Address: Södra Brobänken 41A, Skeppsholmen, 111 49 Stockholm, Sweden.

ULVESETH Sigurd, b. 13 July 1953, Bergen, Norway. Musician (acoustic bass). m. Eli, 13 Mar 1981, 2 sons, 1 daughter. Musical Education: Mainly self-taught. Career: Many tours, different jazz groups; Appearances, radio and television shows; Own quartet featuring Adam Nussbaum, drums. Recordings: Sigurd Ulveseth Quartet: To Wisdom The Prize (with Adam Nussbaum, Knut Rüsmas, Dug Arnesen); Played on 13 other albums. Honours: Jade Prize, 1990. Membership: Norwegian Jazz Society. Current Management: Vaakleivbrotet 7, 5062 Bones, Norway.

UNDERWOOD Charles Jeremy, b. 14 Aug 1956, Leicester, England. Musician (saxophone). Education: BA Hons, Fine Art. Musical Education: Associated Board exams (Grade 8 clarinet). Career: Professional musician, 1984-; Member, John Martyn Band, 1991-; Tours: UK; Europe; USA; Glastonbury Festival; Edinburgh Festival; Bath Festival; Member, British jazz group Spirit Level, 1989-; Member, Andy Sheppard's Big-Comotion Band, also Carla Bley's Very Big Band. Recordings: with John Martyn: Couldn't Love You More, 1992; No Little Boy, 1993; with Andy Sheppard: Rhythm Method, 1993; Delivery Suite, 1994. Memberships: PRS; MCPS. Hobby: Mountaineering. Address: 9 Lucas House, Argyle Walk, Kings Cross, London WC1, England.

UOTILA Jukkis, b. 23 Aug 1960, Finland. Musician (drums); Composer. Career: Jazz concerts, 1976-; Played and recorded with artists including: Gil Evans; McCoy Tyner; Joe Henderson; Chet Baker; Moved to New York, 1980; Worked with artists including: Randy Brecker; Eliane Elias; Ted Curson; Mike Stern; Dave Samuels; Returned to Finland; Bandleader, Jukkis Uotila Band; Performed worldwide, including festivals at Montreux, Detroit, Paris; Head of Jazz Department, Sibelius Academy, Helsinki, 1986-; Bandleader, with band featuring: Mike Stern, Bob Berg, Lars Jansson, Lasse Danielsson; Tours of Scandinavia and Germany. Address: Laivurinkatu 35 B 35, 00150 Helsinki, Finland.

UPTON Eddie, b. 4 Oct 1944, Brighton, Sussex, England. Folk Singer; Musician (concertina, harmonica, percussion). Education: BA (Hons) Politics, Sussex University. Career: Full time folk performer, 1980-, specialising in traditional English songs, music and dance; Former member, Albion Dance Band and Etchingham Steam Band, both with Ashley Hutchings; Co-founder, artistic director, Folk South West, the folk development society for South West of England. Composition: Suite of song arrangements celebrating Somerset's River Parrett, 1997. Recordings include: The Prospect Before Us, Albion Dance Band; A Tale Of Ale, Various Artists; Music For Christopher Columbus and His Crew, St Georges Canlona; Solo album: First Orders; where the Parrett Winds Peaceful, 1997. Publications: Caedmon Capers - A Collection of New Folk Dances and Folk Dance Tunes. Memberships: Folklore Society; English Folk Dance and Song Society; Equity; Musicians' Union; Performing Rights Society, 1997. Hobbies: Walking; Working. Address: 2 Hayes Cottages, Stocklinch, Ilminster, Somerset TA19 9JG, England.

URBAN Stan, b. 10 Jan 1944, Dundee, Scotland. Musician (piano); Singer. m. (1) Erika Kuhnert, 3 Sep 1963, divorced 1984, 2 sons, (2) Annette Wetterberg, 29 Mar 1986, deceased 1987, 1 adopted son, (3) Evelyn Jetzschmann, 15 Apr 1996. Musical Education: Self-taught. Career: Rock'n'roll pianist; Formed own band of German musicians, following tour of Germany with Long John Baldry, 1962; Lived and played in Ibiza, late 60s to 1984; Scandinavia recommended by

Robert Plant; Tours of Scandinavia, 1981-. Recordings: Single: Little Queenie, 1982; Albums: Rock 'N' Roll Cocktail, 1982; M'Roccan Rollers, 1986; Live, 1988; Through My Door, 1992; Can't Hold On Can't Let Go, 1995; The Devil Made the Boogie, 1997. Hobbies: Classical music; Water skiing; Parachuting. Address: Skaering Sandager 18, 8250 Egå, Denmark.

URE Midge (James), b. 10 Oct 1953, Glasgow, Scotland. Singer; Songwriter; Producer. 2 daughters. Career: Member of bands: Slik; Rich Kids; Thin Lizzy (US tour only); Visage; Formed Ultravox; Also solo artist; Trustee of Live Aid; Musical Director, Prince's Trust, 1987-88; Musical Director, special 40 minute set, Nelson Mandela Concert; Directed video Monument for televison special; Director of videos for: Ultravox; Visage; Fun Boy Three; Bananarama; Phil Lynott; Monsoon; Midge Ure/Mick Karn; Midge Ure; Martha Ladley; Truth; Andrew Strong. Compositions include: Levis Adverts music, with Christopher Cross, 1983; Writer/co-writer, many hit songs; Film music: Max Headroom; Turnaround; Playboy Late Night Theme. Recordings include: Albums: with Visage: Visage, 1990; Anvil, 1982; with Ultravox: Vienna, 1980; Rage In Eden, 1981; Quartet, 1982; Lament, 1984; The Collection, 1984; U-Vox, 1986; Solo albums: The Gift, 1985; Answers, 1988; Pure, 1991; Breathe, 1996; Singles include: with Ultravox: Sleepwalk, 1980; Vienna, 1981; All Stood Still, 1981; The Thin Wall, 1981; The Voice, 1981; Reap The Wild Wind, 1982; Hymn, 1982; Visions In Blue, 1983; We Came To Dance, 1983; Dancing With Tears In My Eyes, 1984; Lament, 1984; Love's Great Adventure, 1984; All Fall Down; Contributor, producer, co-writer (with Bob Geldof), Do They Know It's Christmas?, Band Aid (Number 1, UK), 1984; Also singles with: Slik, Rich Kids, Visage and as solo artist; Produced records for: Antrix; Ronny; Cold Fish; Phil Lynott; Pete Godwyn; Modern Man; Fatal Charm; Steve Harley; Strasse; The Messengers; Rodeo; Visage; Ultravox; Michel Van Dyke. Current Management: CMO Management, Unit 32, Ransomes Dock, 35-37 Parkgate Road, London SW11 4NP, England.

URTREGER René, b. 6 July 1934, Paris, France. Musician (piano); Bandleader; Composer. m. Jacqueline Fornari, 1 son, 1 daughter from previous marriage. Musical Education: Studied classical music from age 6; Serious study after war from age 11; Promoted Charlie Parker's music from age 13. Career: Concerts and festivals throughout the world, 1953-; Starts working at 19 with Don Byas-Buck Clayton Band, 1953; Currently worked with: Dexter Gordon; Zoot Sims; Stéphane Grappelli; Allen Eager; Stan Getz; Dizzy Gillespie; J.J.Johnson; Double Six; Current trio with Pierre Michelot and Kenny Clarke; House pianist for (Nicole) Barclay Records, France, 1954-65; European tours as pianist within Miles Davis Quartet, 1956; Miles Davis Quintet, 1957; Break from jazz music, 1967-77, touring with Sacha Distel and Claude Francois; Returned to jazz ensembles, 1977; Pianist with Sonny Stitt's French tour, 1982; Concerts with Peter King, 1993; Recordings: Numerous recordings include albums with: Lionel Hampton; Chet Baker; Bobby Jaspar; Hubert Fol; Maurice Meunier; Lester Young; Kenny Clarke; Michael Hausser; Stéphane Grappelli and Stuff Smith; Film music: Ascenseur Pour L'Echafaud, within Miles Davis Quintet; Le Poulet (Oscar short film, 1965); Other albums include: Recidive, 1978; Urtreger/Michelot/Humair Trio, 1979; Collection Privée, 1981; En Direct Du Festival D'Antibes, 1981; Jazzman, 1985; Masters, 1987; Avec Chet Baker, 1989; Serena, 1990; Film: René Urtreger/Homme De Jazz, 1991; Saint Germains Des Presents, Telefilm by J.Ch.Averty, 1993. Honours: Winner, National Jazz Tournament, 1953; Prix Django Reinhardt, L'Academie Du Jazz, 1961; Prix Boris Vian, L'Academie Du Jazz, for album Jazzman, 1985; L'Ordre Des Arts and Lettres, 1988; Grand Prix,

SACEM, 1993. Hobbies: Chess; Football amateur. Current Management: Jeanne De Mirbeck, Carlyne Music. Address: c/o Carlyne Music, La Prairie, 92410 Ville D'Avray, France.

USSING Joachim, b. 9 Oct 1952, Copenhagen, Denmark. Musician (bass player); Composer. m. Henriette Rolffes Becker, 13 Feb 1989, 1 son, 1 daughter. Musical Education: Self-taught. Career: Toured Scandinavia, television appearances with: Moirana; Phantom Band; Lone Kellermann and Rockband; Jomfru Ane; Doraz; Small Talk; Big Talk; Anne Grete; Peter Abrahamsen; Peter Viskinde, from 1974-95. Recordings: First album: Terje, Jesper, Joachim, 1970 (released 1991). Honours: Platinum disc, Natten Blir Til Dag, Lone Kellermann and Rockband. Memberships: DMF; DJBFA; KODA; GRAMEX; NCB. Current Management: DMA. Address: Vendersgade 23, 1363 Copenhagen, Denmark.

V

VACHÉ Warren Webster, b. 27 Nov 1914, Brooklyn, New York, USA. Musician (string bass); Bandleader. m. 18 Sept 1948, 2 sons. Musical Education: Self-taught. Career: Worked, played with: Bobby Hackett; Wild Bill Davison; Pee Wee Russell; Max Kaminsky; 2 sons both jazz musicians: Warren Jr, cornet; Allan, clarinet; Leader, own 7-piece jazzband, The Celebratin' Seven. Tours: Germany; Switzerland; Netherlands; Also US and international jazz festivals; Recordings: Jazzology; Swingin' and Singin'; The Music of Harry Barris; The Music of Isham Jones, 1998. Publications: This Horn For Hire, biography of Pee Wee Erwin; Crazy Fingers, biography of Claude Hopkins; Back Beats and Rim Shots, Biography of Johnny Blowers, 1997: Jazz Gentry (anthology jazz articles); The Unsung Songwriters, 1998; Editor, Jersey Jazz (monthly publication, New Jersey Jazz Society), 18 years. Memberships: Life member, American Federation Musicians; Life and founding member, New Jersey Jazz Society. Founder, American Jazz Hall Of Fame; Co-founder, American Federation of Jazz Societies. Hobbies: Jazz record collecting; Stamps; Coins; Antiques. Address: 836 W Inman Avenue, Rahway, NJ 07065, USA.

VÆRING Trine-Lise, b. 2 July 1965, Copenhagen, Denmark. Vocalist; Composer; Lyricist. m. Fredrik Lundin, 16 May 1987. Education: Architecture school, 6 years. Musical Education: New School, Department of Jazz and Contemporary Music, New York, 1 year. Career: Worked with Danish modern jazz groups, 1989-; Formed own quartet featuring Bobo Stenson, Mads Vinding and Alex Riel, 1992-; Scandinavian tours, 1993-97; Live performances on Danish, Swedish and German radio with various bands; Member, People Places Times and Faces (Scandinavian all-star band and string section), 1992; Tour and Grammy nomination for album, 1994; All music by Fredrik Lundin, lyrics by Væring; Tour with own quartet in Germany, Netherlands and Belgium, 1997. Recordings: Guest appearance on Pieces Of...Fredrik Lundin Quintet (featuring Paul Bley), 1990 and on Lundin/Danemo Music for Dreamers and Dancers, 1997; People Places Times and Faces, with Fredrik Lundin (also featuring Palle Dannielsson, Audun Kleive, Kenneth Knudsen), 1994; When I Close My Eyes, with Væring, Stenson, Vinbding and Riel, 1996; Desde el Norte, with Dos Mundos Tango Orkestret and F Lundin, 1997; CD with Væring, Stenson, Vinding and Riel, 1998. Honours: Grammy Nomination, Best Jazz Release, 1994. Hobbies: Sewing; Languages. Address: Puggaardsgade 10 St tv, 1573 Copenhagen V, Denmark.

VAERNES Knut, b. 1 Apr 1954, Trondheim, Norway. Musician (guitar); Composer; Bandleader; Record Company Executive. 1 son. Education: Master of Arts. Musical Education: Master of Music. Career: 15 years as professional musician; Concerts include: All national jazz festivals; Tours in Europe; UK tour with Cutting Edge, including Ronnie Scott's, 1983; Numerous television appearances; Extensive touring; Played with Jan Garbarek, Jon Christensen, Oslo, 1982; Head of jazz record label Curling Legs. Recordings: Albums: with Cutting Edge: Cutting Edge; Our Man In Paradise; Duesenberg; Solo albums: Admisson For Guitars and Basses, 1992; Roneo, 1993; Trio, 1995; Film music, with Jan Garbarek, 1981. Membership: Musicians' Union. Hobby: Tennis. Address: Vidarsgt. 9A, N-0452 Oslo, Norway.

VAI Steve, b. 6 June 1960, Long Island, New York, USA. Musician (guitar). Musical Education: Tutored by Joe Satriani; Jazz and Classical music, Berklee College of Music, Boston. Career: Lead guitarist, Frank Zappa, 1979-84; Built own recording studio, 1984; Lead guitarist with Alcatrazz, 1985; David Lee Roth, 1986-89; Whitesnake, 1989-90; Also solo artiste; Worldwide concerts and television/radio appearances with the above include: World Series Of Rock, US; Monsters Of Rock, UK; Super Rock, Germany; Film appearance: Crossroads. Recordings: Albums include: with Frank Zappa: Tinseltown Rebellion, 1981; You Are What You Is, 1981; Shut Up And Play Yer Guitar, 1981; Ship Arriving Too Late, 1982; The Man From Utopia, 1983; Thing Fish, 1984; Jazz From Hell, 1986; Guitar, 1988; You Can't Do That On Stage Anymore, 1988; with Alcatrazz: Disturbing The Peace, 1985; with David Lee Roth: Eat 'Em and Smile, 1986; Skyscraper, 1988; with Whitesnake: Slip Of The Tongue, 1989; Solo albums: Flex-able, 1984; Passion And Warfare, 1990; Sex And Religion, 1993; Alien Love Secrets, 1995. Current Management: C Winston Simone Management, 1790 Broadway, New York, NY 10019, USA.

VAIL Frederick Scott, b. 24 Mar 1944, San Francisco, California, USA. Recording Studio Executive. m. Brenda Joyce Howard, 18 June 1972, divorced 1977. Education: California State University, 1962-64; Industrial College of the Armed Forces, 1963; Voluntary State Community College, Nashville, 1980-81. Career: Radio announcer, Sacramento, 1958-62; Frederick Vail Productions, 1962-66; Producer, sales manager, Teen-age Fair Inc, 1966-69; Artist manager, Beach Boys, 1969-71; Promotion Manager, Capital Records, 1972-73; President, Frederick Vail & Associates, 1974-80; President, General Manager, Treasure Isle Recording Studios, 1980-; Consultant, Promotion and Marketing: Waylon Jennings, 1974-75; GRT Records, 1976-78; RSO Records, 1978-79; Lecturer, numerous colleges and universities; Event producer for: Beach Boys; Glen Campbell; Righteous Brothers; Four Seasons; Dave Clark Five; The Crickets. Recordings: Producer for: BB King; Isaac Hayes; Billy Preston; Carla Thomas; Lee Atwater; Red Hot + Blue compilation. Publications: Contributing author: Beach Boys - The California Myth, 1978; Beach Boys - Heroes & Villains, 1987; Contributor to Mix Magazine. Honours: 7 Gold, 2 Platinum discs. Memeberships: NARAS, Board of Governors, 1981-83; CMA. Address: Treasure Isle Recording Studios, Nashville, Tennessee, USA.

VALDY Paul Valdemar Horsdal, b. 1 Sept 1945, Ottawa, Canada. Singer; Songwriter; Musician (guitar); Producer. m. Kathleen Mary Fraser, 13 Aug 1986, 2 sons. Education: Usgar Collegiate, St Pat's College. Musical Education: Piano lessons; Choir; Glee club; Victoria School Of Music. Career: Appearances: International Pop Song Festival, Sopot, Poland, 1975; CBC TV Super Special Simulcast, Valdy And The Hometown Band, 1976; Expo '86, Vancouver; Festival Cervantino, Mexico, 1987; Olympic Arts Festival, Calgary, '88; World's Fair, Seville, Expo '92; Royal Gala, Melbourne Music Festival, Australia, 1995. Recordings: Albums: Country Man, 1971; Landscapes, 1972; Family Gathering, 1974; Valdy And The Home Town Band, 1976; Hot Rocks, 1978; 1001, 1979; Valdy's Kid Record, 1981; Notes From Places, 1988; Heart At Work, 1993. Publication: The Best Of Valdy. Honours: 2 Juno Awards; BMI Song Of The Year, Landscapes, 1974. Membership: AFofM, local 247; NSAI; SAC; FEPRA; CARAS; CIRPA. Hobbies: Wood-butcher; Sailing; Scuba diving; Skiing; Watercolours; Golf; Billiards. Current Management: Paquin Entertainment Group. Address: 1067 Sherwin Road, Winnipeg, Manitoba R3H 0T8, Canada.

VALENTIN David Peter, b. 29 Apr 1952, USA. Recording Artist; Musician (flute). Musical Education: High School Music & Art; 1 year Bronx Community College. Career: First artist on GRP Records; 17 albums recorded. Compositions: Over 30 compositions; Film soundtracks; Ghost music, Bill Cosby Show; Title track, album with Arturo Sandoval (Grammy award-winning album). Honours: Voted Best Flute, 6 years consecutively, Jazz Iz Magazine; Grammy Nomination, Best R&B Instrumental Performance, 1985; Entertainer Of Year, NHAMAS, 1993; Vista 2000 Excellence In The Arts, 1995. Hobbies: Practicing the flute; Love. Current Management: Carl Valldejuli, Turi's Music Inc., 193 Westward Drive, Miami Springs, FL 33168, USA. Address: 154 Harding Park, Bronx, NY 10473, USA.

VALLANCE Jim, b. 31 May 1952. Songwriter. m. Rachel Paiement, 1 son. Education: 1 year university. Musical Education: Private study, piano, cello. Compositions: for Aersmith: Other Side; Ragdoll; Eat The Rich; for Bryan Adams: Heaven; Run To You; Summer Of '69; Cuts Like A Knife; for Heart: What About Love; for Joe Cocker: When The Night Comes; for Tina Turner: It's Only Love; Back Where You Started; for Glass Tiger: Don't Forget Me When I'm Gone. Honours: 4 Juno Awards, Composer of the Year, (Canadian equivalent of Grammy); 3 BMI Awards (USA); More than 50 Gold and Platinum album awards (USA, Canada, Japan, UK, Germany). Memberships: SOCAN (Canada); ASCAP (USA); Board of Directors, PROCAN, 1987-90; Board of Directors, Songwriters Association of Canada, 1990-. Current Management: Rondor Music. Address: c/o Barbara Vander Linde, Rondor Music, 360 N. La Cienega Boulevard, Los Angeles, CA 90048, USA.

VALLDEJULI Carl Cats, b. 9 Mar 1962. Recording Artist Manager. Education: Marine Biochemist, BS, MS. Musical Education: Piano; Music Theory. Career: Produced, coordinated world-wide concert tours. Recordings: Assistant and executive producer on over 10 albums including: Arturo Sandoval; Dave Valentin; Ed Calle. Honours: IAJE; NARAS; World Relief; Billboard; Grammy. Membership: Trustee NARAS. Hobbies: Skiing; Golf. Address: Quiet Storm Inc., 2830 SW Lejeune Road, Coral Gables, FL 33134-6602, USA.

VALLEJO Ramon M, b. 20 June 1963, Honduras. Singer; Musician (trombone, percussion). Musical Education: Musicianship at Cit Lit; Brass at Kensington and Chelsea College of Private Tutors. Career: Band leader, 2 Latin bands; Tours, Europe; Radio shows on news radio GLR, Jazz FM; Backing vocals for Matt Bianco; Own show in London, played with major world famous Latin players. Compositions: Numerous, all salsa, rumba, merengue rhythms. Recordings: 1 album: Shango. Memberships: Musicians' Union; PRS. Hobbies: Tennis; Amateur radio; Country walks. Current Management: RVR Promotions. Address: Mid Basement, 32 Queens Gate Gardens, London SW7 5RR, England.

VALLELY Fintan, b. 1949, Armawh, NI, USA. Flute Player; Singer; Songwriter; Writer. m. Evelyn Conlon, 2 sons. Education: BSc, Horticulture; MA, Ethnomusicology; Oral on Playing and Ethnomusicology. Career: Touring Ireland, England, Scotland, France, Italy, USA, Canada, Germany, Indonesia, Finland, Holland, Bulgaria. Compositions: Moving Statues; Man From RTE; Willie MacBride, the Parody; Resurrection Romp. Recordings: Albums: Shanachil 29019, 1979; UMFA 001, 1988; WHN 001, 1991. Publications: Timber - The Flute Tutor, 1986; Companion to Irish Traditional Music, 1998; Rake's Almanac, music directory, 1998. Honour: All Ireland Tin Whistle Award, 1967. Current Management: Bechofer Agency, 151 Barnton Park View, Edinburgh, EH5 6HH, Scotland.

VALLI Frankie (Frank Castelluccio), b. 3 May 1937, Newark, New Jersey, USA. Singer. Career: Member, Four Seasons, 1954-1977; 1980s; Solo artiste, 1958-. Recordings: Albums: with The Four Seasons: Sherry And 11 Others, 1962; Ain't That A Shame And 11 Others, 1963; The 4 Seasons Greetings, 1963; Born To Wander,

1964; Dawn And 11 Other Great Songs, 1964; Rag Doll, 1964; Entertain You, 1965; The Four Seasons Sing Big Hits By Bacharach, David And Dylan, 1966; Working My Way Back To You, 1966; Lookin' Back, 1967; Christmas Album, 1967; Genuine Imitation Life Gazette, 1969; Edizione D'Oro, 1969; Chameleon, 1972; Streetfighter, 1975; Inside You, 1976; Who Loves You, 1976; Helicon, 1977; Reunited Live, 1981; Solo, 1967; Timeless, 1968; Inside You, 1975; Close Up, 1975; Story, 1976; Frankie Valli Is The Word, 1978; The Best Of Frankie Valli, 1980; Heaven Above Me, 1981; Singles include: with the Four Seasons: Spanish Lace; Sherry; Big Girls Don't Cry (used in film soundtrack Dirty Dancing); Walk Like A Man; Dawn (Go Away); Rag Doll; The Night; Who Loves You; December 1963 (Oh What A Night), (Number 1, US and UK), 1976; East Meets West (with the Beach Boys), 1984; Solo singles include: (You're Gonna) Hurt Yourself; Can't Take My Eyes Off You; I Make A Fool Of Myself; To Give (The Reason I Live); You're Ready Now; My Eyes Adored You; Swearin' To God; Our Day Will Come; Fancy Dancer; Where Did We Go Wrong (with Chris Forde). Address: c/o International Creative Management, 8942 Wilshire Blvd, Beverly Hills, CA 90211, USA.

VAN ACHTE Tom, b. 28 November 1971, Zelzate, Belgium. Producer; Pianist; Songwriter. Education: Classical Music Masterdegree, Lemmens Institut, Leuven, Belgium; Degrees in Music Education, Piano, Composition, Trumpet; Audio Engineer, SAE, Amsterdam, Netherlands. Career: Founder, TVA Music Company, 1993; Member, Techno Group, Tehnoheadz. Compositions: Several contributions to video and movie music; all music for Tehno Headz. Membership: ZAMU, Belgium; Professional Society of Artists and Musicians. Hobby: Karate. Current Management: Conga Agency, 1 Sinteldreef, 2300 Turnhout, Belgium. Address: Dorp 23, 9968 Bassevelde, Belgium.

VAN BAVEL Boudewijn, b. 9 Jan 1952, Breda, Netherlands. Producer; Composer. 1 son. Education: Rotterdam. Musical Education: Music High, Rotterdam, 1975; Sound Engineering, 1989. Career: Producer, composer, Black Lee, Breda, Netherlands, 1973-79; Managing Director, Bo Easy Studio's, Breda, 1980-89; Managing Director, Artists and Business, Rotterdam, 1990; Managing Director, Sky Trance International (studios and Theatre), Hilversum, Netherlands, and Antwerp, Belgium, 1990-. Recordings: California Fried Scene, Black Lee, 1979; I Got To Spend More Time, Bo Easy, 1983. Hobbies: Films; Football. Current Management: Sky Trance International, Hilversum. Address: PO Box 64, 1200 AB Hilversum, Netherlands.

VAN BEST Peter, b. 15 Oct 1951, Kaatsheuvael, Netherlands. Music Publisher; Organizer; Songwriter; Singer. Musical Education: School of Music (singing, piano). Career: Castlebar International Song Contest 1986 (RTE); Cavan International Song Contest 1988; Artemare Italy 1992; Europa Song France 1992 (Radio France); Europa Song Brussels 1993; Top Artist Show Italy, 1993; Midem Showcase 1994; Invited guest 70th anniversary in Paris of Peter Ustinov, 1991. Compositions: 25 years songwriting; own compositions published worldwide. Honours: Fidof (Festival Federation) Awards, 1988, 1990. Memberships: BUMA/Stemra, BASCA, FIDOF; SENA. Hobbies: Jogging; Geography; Reading; Travel; Design; Languages. Current Management: Best Music. Address: Crispijnstraat 9, 5171 CH Kaatsheuvel, Netherlands.

VAN DORT Elizabeth (Liz), b. 3 March 1968, Melbourne, Australia. Singer; Composer. Education: Bachelor of Arts, Social Anthropology, University of Melbourne; HSC, Classical Singing; AMEB, Classical Singing Grade 7; Numerous choral and madrigal groups; piano lessons. Career: Vocalist/Comoser, Far From the Madding

Crowd, Glastonbury Festival and others; World Voices, solo show, Australia; Backing Vocalist, Invisible Opera Company Australia; What the Funk. Recordings: Far: Far From the Madding Crowd, CD; Sting and the Radio Actors, Nuclear Waste; Daevid Allen, 12 Selves, backing vocals. Memberships: APRA; AMCOS. Hobbies: Reading; Yoga. Current Management: Evolving Management, PO Box 2237, St Kilda, West Victoria, 3182, Australia. Address: PO Box 2237, St Kilda, West Victoria, 3182, Australia.

VAN DYKE Leroy Frank, b. 4 Oct 1929, Pettis County, Missouri, USA. Country Music Performer. m. Gladys Marie Daniels, 25 June 1980, 3 son, 1 daughter. Education: Graduate, Journalism, Animal Science, University of Missouri; Graduate, Reppert's School of Autioneeering. Career: Support for show by Marilyn Monroe; Tours regularly, USA and abroad; Played Las Vegas; Plays various venues, especially agricultural events (fairs, rodeos, livestock events); Television includes: Regular member, Red Foley's Ozark Jubilee, ABC-TV; Host, Leroy Van Dyke Show; Star, film, What Am I Bid?; Radio: Co-host, Country Crossroads. Recordings include: Auctioneer; Walk On By. Honours: Billboard magazine, Biggest Ever Country Hit, Walk On By, 1994. Memberships: CMA; ACM; NATD; IEBA; IAFE. Hobby: Raising mules from registered Arabian mares and mammoth jacks. Current Management: Leroy Van Dyke Enterprises, Gladys Van Dyke. Address: 29000 Highway V, Smithton, MO 65350, USA.

VAN EYNDE Johan, b. 9 July 1966, Dendermonde, Belgium. Singer; Songwriter; Musician (Guitar). Education: Selftaught Guitar; Organ lessons; Baritone lessons; Bugle lessons. Career: Concerts with Blue Blot, The Japs and Pop in Wonderland. Recording: Nacht Van De Zottegemse Rock, 1997. Publication: I'm On My Way, 1997. Memberships: SABEM. Hobbies: Football; Internet. Current Management: Make My Day, Kalkestraat 162, 3255, Buggenhout, Belgium.

VAN HALEN Alex, b. 8 May 1955, Nijmegen, Netherlands. Musician (drums). Career: Formed US rock group Van Halen, with brother Eddie, 1974-; Support tours with UFO; Santana; Black Sabbath; Regular headlining tours, US and worldwide; Major appearances include: First US tour, 1978; California Music Festival, 1979; US Festival, 1982, 1983; Monsters of Rock, Castle Donington, 1984; Monsters of Rock US tour (with Metallica, Scorpions), 1988; Texxas Jam, 1988. Recordings: Albums: Van Halen, 1978; Van Halen II, 1979; Women And Children First, 1980; Fair Warning, 1981; Diver Down, 1982; 1984, 1983; 5150 (Number 1, US), 1986; OU812 (Number 1, US), 1988; For Unlawful Carnal Knowledge (Number 1, US), 1991; Right Here Right Now, 1993; Balance, 1995; 3, 1998; Singles include: You Really Got Me, 1978; Runnin' With The Devil, 1978; Dance The Night Away, 1979; And The Cradle Will Rock, 1980; (Oh) Pretty Woman, 1982; Dancing In The Street, 1982; Jump (Number 1, US), 1984; Panama, 1984; I'll Wait, 1984; Hot For Teacher, 1984; Why Can't This Be Love, 1986; Love Walks In, 1986; Dreams, 1986; When It's Love, 1988; Finish What Ya Started, 1988; Feels So Good, 1989; Poundcake, 1991; Top Of The World, 1991; Right Now, 1992. Honours: Numerous Platinum discs; Grammy Award, Best Hard Rock Performance, 1992; American Music Award, Favourite Hard Rock Album, 1992; Band awarded Gold Ticket, Madison Square Gardens, 1988; Inducted into Hollywood Rock Walk, 1991; MTV Video Awards, 1984, 1992. Current Management: SRO Management Inc., 189 Carlton Street, Toronto, Ontario M5A 2K7, Canada.

VAN HALEN Eddie, b. 26 Jan 1957, Nijmegen, Netherlands. Rock Musician (guitar). m. 11 Apr 1981, Valerie Bertinelli, 1 son. Musical Education: Piano lessons, Pasadena City College. Career: Founded US rock group Van Halen, with

brother Alex 1974-; Support tours to UFO; Santana; Black Sabbath; Regular headlining tours, US and worldwide; Major appearances include: First US tour, 1978; California Music Festival, 1979; US Festival, 1982, 1983; Monsters Of Rock Festival, Castle Donington, 1984; Monsters Of Rock US tour (with Metallica, Scorpions), 1988; Texxas Jam, 1988. Recordings: Albums: Van Halen, 1978; Van Halen II, 1979; Women And Children First, 1980; Fair Warning, 1981; Diver Down, 1982; 1984, 1984; 5150 (Number 1, US), 1986; OU812 (Number 1, US), 1988; For Unlawful Carnal Knowledge (Number 1, US), 1991; Right Here Right Now, 1993; Balance, 1995; 3, 1998; Singles include: You Really Got Me, 1978; Running With The Devil, 1978; Dance The Night Away, 1979; And The Cradle Will Rock, 1980; (Oh) Pretty Woman, 1982; Jump (Number 1, US), 1984; Panama, 1984; I'll Wait, 1984; Hot For Teacher, 1984; Why Can't This Be Love, 1986; Dreams, 1986; Love Walks In, 1986; When It's Love, 1988; Finish What Ya Started, 1988; Feels So Good, 1989; Poundcake, 1991; Top Of The World, 1991; Right Now, 1992; Contributor, Beat It, Michael Jackson (Number 1, US), 1983; Honours: Numerous Platinum discs; Grammy Award, Best Hard Rock Performance, 1992; American Music Award, Favourite Hard Rock Album, 1992; MTV Music Video Awards, 1984, 1992; Band awarded Gold Ticket, Madison Square Gardens, 1988. Current Management: SRO Management Inc., 189 Carlton Street, Toronto, Ontario M5A 2K7, Canada.

VAN HAM Bernhard Clemens Maria Greshard, b. 21 June 1960, Darmstadt, Heggen, Germany. Musician (keyboards, piano); Composer; Arranger. Musical Education: 2 years piano studies, Heidelberg, Germany; Diploma, Jazz University, Graz, Austria. Career: Tours, concerts with VSOP; KGB; Dagmas Hellberg; Funcmac; Musical productions (piano/keyboards); Carmen Negra; La Cage Aux Folles; Rainbow Girls. Recordings: Musicals: Smoke; Glamour Boys Ltd; Recordings with Easy Band; Maler; Carl Peyer; Funkfurter; Arrangement of La Cage Aux Folles for Arnglette/Austria, 1989. Hobbies: Computers; Internet. Address: Negerlegasse 7/18, A-1020 Vienna, Austria.

VAN HOVE Fred, b. 19 February 1937, Antwerp, Belgium. Musician (Piano, Church Organ, Accordion. m. (2) Mie Van Cakenberghe, 2 Apr 1986, 3 sons. Education: Piano, Theory, Harmony, Music Academy. Career: Concerts, radio, TV, festivals, Europe, Japan, USA, Canada. Compositions: for Mixed instrument groups and improvising soloists; for Big Band and own groups: MLB III, Piano Kwartet, Nonet. Recordings: More than 50: Lust; Pyp; Suite for B...City. Honours: Cultural Ambassador of Flanders, 1996, 1997. Memberships: Wim wzw, Association for Improvised Music, Antwerp, Chairman. Current Management: Mie, St Vincentiusstr 61, B2018 Antwerp, Belgium. Address: St Vincentiusstr 61, B-2018, Antwerp, Belgium.

VAN OLDEREN Martin, b. 3 Jan 1931, Netherlands. Blues Promoter; Record Producer; Radio Broadcaster. m. Carolien Van Der Kamp, 13 Mar 1957, 1 son, 1 daughter. Career: Organised concert featuring Memphis Slim, Little Brother Montgomery, Lightning Slim, Whispering Smith, 1971; Started Chicago Blues Festival, 1970-; Organised Blues Estafette, Utrecht, 1979-81; Amsterdam Blues Festival, Meervaart, annual event; Established Oldie Blues, own blues record label reproducing 78s, 1970; Compiled archive on blues music, including 15000 photos; Writes texts for CD covers; Broadcaster, own radio programme Bluesnachten (Blues Nights), VRPO, 1972-; Personal agent for blues artists playing in Holland including: Bo Diddley; Muddy Waters; Sonny Terry; Doctor Ross; BB King. Publications: Boogie Woogie and Blues Collector. Membership: President, Dutch Blues and Boogie Organisation. Hobbies: Record collecting;

Walking; Swimming. Current Management: Martin Van Olderen Blues Promotions. Address: Maasdrielhof 175, 1106 NG Amsterdam, Zuidoost, Netherlands.

VAN POL Hans, b. 6 Aug 1955, Amsterdam, Netherlands. Personal Manager; Talent Scout. Education: Literature and Law, University of Amsterdam. Musical Education: Private singing and dancing lessons for 4 years. Career: First Gold recording as solo singer with children's choir, 1964; Singer with various rock, wave and ska bands, 1973-78; Member of Small Talk, touring through Europe, 1978-80; Member of Dutch band, Vulcano, 1980-85; Now Manager, 1985-. Recordings: 5 albums and 15 singles. Honours: 2 Gold albums; Popularity Award, 1983. Membership: Dutch Music Manager Association. Hobbies: Sailing; Biking. Address: PO Box 9010, 1006 AA Amsterdam, Netherlands.

VAN SHELTON Ricky, b. 12 Jan 1952, Grit, Virginia, USA. Country Singer; Songwriter. m. Bettye Witt, 4 Aug 1986. Career: Previous employment includes: Pipefitter; Plumber; Car salesman; Country singer, 1985-. Recordings: Hits include: US Country Number 1s include: Somebody Lied, 1987; Life Turned Her That Way, 1987; Don't We All Have The Right, 1987; I'll Leave This World Loving You; From A Jack To A King; Living Proof; Rockin' Years, with Dolly Parton, 1991; Albums: Wild-Eyed Dream, 1987; Loving Proof, 1988; Ricky Van Shelton Sings Christmas, 1989; Ricky Van Shelton III, 1990; Backroads, 1991; Don't Overlook Salvation, 1992; Greatest Hits Plus, 1992; Love And Honor, 1994. Honours: CMA Awards: Horizon Award, 1988; Male Vocalist Of Year, 1989; Nashville Network Viewer's Choice: Male Vocalist Of Year, Album Of Year, 1989. Memberships: Country Music Association; Academy of Country Music. Hobbies: Farming; Fishing. Current Management: Michael Campbell and Associates, 40 Music Square East, Nashville, TN 37203, USA.

VAN'T HOF Jasper, b. 30 June 1947, Enschade, Netherlands. Musician (piano); Composer. Education: Business School. Musical Education: 7 years, private piano teacher. Career: 25 years playing festivals and tours in Europe; 10 years teaching music at High School. Recordings: with Pork Pie: The Door Is Open, 1975; Eyeball, 1978; 3 solo albums, acoustic piano; with Archie Shepp: Mama Rose; 7 albums with Pili Pili; Duo with Bob Malach: Dinner For Two; with Charlie Mariano: Sleep My Love; with Ernie Watts: Face To Face; Solo piano concert: Solo At The Consertgebouw. Honours: Edison Award (Netherlands) for solo piano; Downbeat Poll Winner, 3 times, 1980s. Current Management: JARO Records, Uli Balls, Bremen, Germany. Address: Bismarckstr. 83, 28 Bremen, Germany.

VANCEUNEBROUCK-WERTH Richard, b. 5 April 1952, Seattle, Washington, USA. Producer; Composer; Musician (keyboards, percussion). Musical Education: Studied under electronic music pioneer Vladimir Ussachevsky, University of Utah. Career: Performed internationally with touring groups, 1970-77; Tangerine Dream's first North American tour, 1977; First performance, Seattle Symphony Orchestra, 1982; Composed film and special event soundtracks, 1980-89; First commissioned work, IBM, Paramount, Disney, 1981; National broadcasts include CTV (Canada), ABC TV; First commissioned operatic work, Seattle's Floating Opera, 1987; Produced AFFINITY Project, release new Beethoven work, 1989; Producer, composer, St Elmo's Choir; Coventry; Charles Certain; Tangerine Dream, 1989-. Recordings: with Tangerine Dream: Music From The 21st Century; with RV-Werth and S Chatelaine: AFFINITY; with Seattle Opera's Floating Opera: Seraphim Suite; with St Elmo's Choir: Syrenes; White Stocking Day; with R Kotta: Alive, Alive-O; with Coventry: Lady's Not For Burning and many others. Honours: NAMA, Best

New Age Group, 1989; Commissions: Seattle Opera; National Endowment For The Arts, Seattle, Tacoma, Vancouver BC, Edmonton, Canada Arts Commissions; Longest Requested Airplay in Soviet Union, 1991-. Memberships: ASCAP; BMI; NAMA; International Producer's Guild. Hobbies: Pioneer laser/light artist performing internationally since 1976; Film-making. Current Management: Omega Organisation International. Address: PO Box 33623-WWIM, Seattle, WA 98133-0623, USA.

VANDENBROUCQE Gérard, b. 15 May 1961, France. Musician (violin). Musical Education: Lessons with Pierre Cuuaz; J L Pino; Didier Lockwood; TV: Antenne 2; M6; Europe 1; Appearances at: Montreal Festival, 1993; SOPS, New York; Radio France Inter. Recordings: Tango, Violin Onztet. Membership: Association Jazz et Violon. Current Management: c/o JMS, 12 Rue Bouchut, 75015 Paris, France. Address: 12 Rue Lazare Carnot, 92140 Clamart, France.

VANDROSS Luther, b. 20 Apr 1951, New York, USA. Singer; Songwriter; Arranger; Producer. Career: Member, Listen My Brother (musical theatre workshop), Harlem, 1973; Session singer (recordings andcommercials), arranger, 1974-80; Leader, own group, Luther, 1976-77; Solo artiste, 1980-; Regular international concerts. Compositions include: Fascination, David Bowie; You Stopped Lovin' Me, Roberta Flack; Recordings: Albums: with Luther: Luther, 1976; This Close To You, 1977; Solo albums: Never Too Much, 1981; Forever For Always For Love, 1982; Busy Body, 1984; Give Me The Reason, 1986; Any Love, 1988; The Best Of Luther Vandross, 1989; Power Of Love, 1991; Never Let Me Go, 1993; Songs,1994; Hit singles include: The Night I Fell In Love, 1985; Give Me The Reason, from film Ruthless People, 1986; Stop To Love, 1987; There's Nothing Better Than Love, duet with Gregory Hines, 1987; Any Love, 1989; She Won't Talk To Me, 1989; Here And Now, 1990; Power Of Love/Love Power, 1991; Don't Want To Be A Fool, 1991; The Best Things In Life Are Free, duet with Janet Jackson, from film Mo' Money, 1992; Love The One You're With, 1995; Sessions as backing singer include: Young Americans, David Bowie, 1974; Songs For The New Depression, Bette Midler, 1975; Sounds And Stuff Like That, Quincy Jones, 1978; Le Freak, Chic, 1978; We Are Family, Sister Sledge, 1978; Other sessions for Ringo Starr; Carly Simon; Chaka Khan; Average White Band; Vocal arranger, No More Tears, Donna Summer and Barbra Streisand, 1979; Producer, recordings by Aretha Franklin; Dionne Warwick; Diana Ross; Whitney Houston; Contributor, Voices That Care (Red Cross charity record), 1991; The Heart Of A Hero (AIDS research benefit record), 1992. Honours include: MVP Background Singer, 1977-80; Grammy Awards: Best R&B Vocal Performance, 1991, 1992; Best R&B Song, 1992; Grammy Nomination, Best R&B Vocal, 1987; Soul Train Music Awards: Best Male R&B Album, 1987, 1992; Best Male R&B Single, 1990; American Music Awards: Favourite Soul/R&B Male Artist, 1988, 1990, 1992; Favourite Soul/R&B Album, 1992; NAACP Image Awards: Best Male Artist, 1990; Best Male Vocalist, Best Album, 1992; Luther Vandross Day, Los Angeles, 1991. Current Management: The Left Bank Organization. Address: 6255 Sunset Blvd, Ste 1111, Hollywood, CA 90028, USA.

VANGELIS (Evangelos Papathanassiou), b. 29 Mar 1943, Volos, Greece. Musician (keyboards); Composer. Education: Academy of Fine Arts, Athens. Musical Education: Studied Classical music with Aristotelis Coudourof. Career: Member, Formynx, 1960s; Member, Aphrodite's Child, with Demis Roussos; Composer, Paris, 1972; Built Nemo recording studio, London, 1974; Partnership with Jon Anderson as Jon & Vangelis, 1980-1984. Compositions: Music scores for French wildlife films, 1972; Heaven and Hell, Third Movement,

theme for Carl Sagan's TV series Cosmos, BBC1, 1981; Film scores: Chariots Of Fire; Blade Runner; Missing; Mutiny On The Bounty; City; 1492 - Conquest Of Paradise; All tracks on solo albums self-composed, played and produced. Recordings: Albums: with Aphrodite's Child: 666; Solo albums: L'Apocalypse Des Animaux, 1972; Heaven And Hell, 1976; Albedo 0.39, 1976; Spiral, 1977; Beauborg, 1978; China, 1979; Film soundtrack, Chariots Of Fire, 1981; Soil Activities, 1984; Mask, 1985; Opera Sauvage, 1987; Direct, 1988; Themes, 1989; 1492 - Conquest Of Paradise, 1992; Voices, 1995; As Jon & Vangelis: Short Stories, 1980; The Friends Of Mr Cairo, 1981; Private Collection, 1983; The Best Of Jon & Vangelis, 1984; Page Of Life, 1991; Singles include: with Aphrodite's Child: Rain And Tears; Solo: Heaven And Hell, Third Movement, 1981; Chariots Of Fire (Number 1, US), 1982; with Jon Anderson: I Hear You Know, 1980; I'll Find My Way Home, 1982; Also featured on Polar Shift charity album, 1991. Honour: Oscar, Best Original Score, Chariots Of Fire, 1982.

VANIAN Dave (David Letts), b. 12 Oct 1956. Singer. Career: Former grave digger; Vocalist, UK punk rock group, The Damned, 1976-77; Appearances include: Mont de Marsan punk festival, France, 1976; Support to the Sex Pistols, Anarchy In The UK Tour, 1976; First UK punk group to play US dates, 1977; Member, Doctors Of Madness, 1978; The Damned reformed, 1978-89; International concerts include: Christmas On Earth festival, Leeds, 1981; Member, side projects: Naz and the Nomads, 1988; Dave Vanian and the Phantom Chords, 1990; The Damned reunion tour, 1991. Recordings: Albums: with the Damned: Damned Damned Damned, 1977; Music For Pleasure, 1977; Machine Gun Etiquette, 1979; The Black Album, 1980; The Best Of, 1981; Strawberries, 1982; Phantasmagoria, 1985; Anything, 1986; Light At The End Of Tunnel, 1987; with Naz and the Nomads: Give Daddy The Knife, Cindy, 1988; Singles include: with The Damned: Love Song, 1979; Smash It Up, 1979; Grimly Fiendish, 1985; The Shadow Of Love, 1985; Is It A Dream, 1985; Anything, 1986; Eloise (Number 3, UK), 1986; Alone Again Or, 1987.

VANNELLI Joseph Anthony, b. 28 Dec 1950, Montreal, Quebec, Canada. Producer; Arranger; Musician (keyboards). Education: 3 years university. Musical Education: Private. Career: Worked with: Gino Vannelli; Gary Morris; David Meece; Kudasai; Marilyn Scott; Jimmy Haslip; Don Sebesky and The Royal Philharmonic Orchestra; Gregory Hines; Co-producer, commercials including Pontiac; Honda; Owner, recording studio; Concerts include Gino Vannelli's World Tour, 1990-1992; Television includes: Arsenio Hall Show, European television; Juno Award Show, Canada; Dick Clark Night Time; Documentary on rain forests of Costa Rica. Recordings: Crazy Life, 1973; Powerful People, 1974; Storm At Sunup, 1975; The Gist Of The Gemini, 1976; Brother To Brother, 1978; Nightwalker, 1981; Black Cars, 1985; Big Dreamers Never Sleep, 1987; Inconsolable Man, 1991; Gino Vannelli Live In Montreal, 1992; Yonder Tree, 1995. Publications: REP Magazine; Midi Magazine; Keyboard Magazine, Japan. Current Management: Diane Ricci. Address: 28205 Agoura Road, Agoura Hills, CA 91301, USA.

VANRE Etienne, b. 12 Oct 1961, Lille, France. Artists Manager. 1 son, 1 daughter. Career: Artist Manager, La Gueule du Loup; Management of Poesie Noire; TBX; The Drift. Recordings: Recordings of above artists. Address: 94 Blvd Chaumin, 49000 Angers, France.

VANROBAEYS Filip, Musician. Education: Selftaught, Fiddle, Harp, Guitar, Whistles, Badhan. Career: Member, Group The Swigshift; Dranouter Festival, 1995; Den Ekster, 1996, 1997; Labadoux Festival, 1997; Paulus Festival, 1997; Sloanthe

Festival, 1997; Gooik Festival 2002, 1997; De Brakke Grond, Amsterdam, 1997; Foleys Irish Pub, Gent; Radio 1, De Groote Boodschap; Several Regional Radio and Television Appearances. Compositions: Jumpin The Fences; Dirty Wally; Friends Sadness; Something to Fear; Shut the Pub; A Whistler's Wedding. Recordings: Tales From the Great Whiskey Book, 1996. Honours: Government Medal, Flute, 1986; 2nd Place, Youth Soloist Festival, 1986; Finale, Westtalent, 1995. Membership: Volksmuziekfederatie, Belgium. Hobby: Music. Current Management: KAFT Productions, Akkerwindelaan 20, 8791 Beveren-Leie, Belgium. Address: c/o Barrierestraat 49, 8940 Wervik, Belgium.

VARIS Francis, b. 4 Feb 1957, Clamart, France. Musician (accordion). m. Françoise Niay. Musical Education: Musicological License, Paris VIII University. Career: Tours and European jazz festivals with: American guitarist Tal Farlow, 1983; Brazilian singer Nazaré Pereira, 1985-; Saxophone player Lee Konitz, 1986-89; The Paris-Musette, Tokyo, Montreal, 1991-; Own group Bolovaris. Recordings: Cordes Et Lames, 1983; Medium Rare, with Lee Konitz, 1986; Accordeon Madness, with accordionist Kenny Kotwitz, 1989; Paris-Musette 1 and 2, 1991, 1993; Bolovaris, 1994. Honours: Grand Prix du Disque de l'Academie Charles Cros. Current Management: Alain Brisemontier. Address: Le Moulin, 49800 Sarrigné, France.

VARSANYI Juraj, b. 14 May 1961, Bratislava, Slovakia. Drums; Percussion; Cimbalom. Musical Education: People's Conservatory, Bratislava. Career: International tours; Many TV and radio shows with: Vus-Orchestra, Gravis, Knock-Out, Jully's Orchestra, Just Jazz, Bratislava Jazz Days, 1991; Burg Mautendorf Jazzkettbewerd-Aut; Hajnal Quintet, 1987; Varsanyi Habsburg-Wedding, 1993. Recordings: Vus LP, 1983; Gombitova and Gravis LP, 1986; Knock Out, LP, 1987; Gravis, LP, 1989; Varsanyi, LP, 1991; La Rubia, CD, 1995; Slovak Jazz Anthology, CD, 1992. Honours: Gorizia, International Festival Contest, 1986; 2nd Prize, Slovak Jazz Festival, 1995. Membership: Slovak Jazz Society, 1989/90-. Current Management: Slovak Jazz Society, Jaku Bouonalm 12, Bratislava, Slovakia. Address: Varsanyi Juraj, Hlavna 20, 90044 Tomasov, Slovakia.

VARTAN Sylvie, b. 15 August 1944, Iskretz, Bulgaria. m. 1) Johnny Hallyday, 1965, divorced, 1980, 1 son, 2) Tony Scotti, 1984. Education: Lycée Hélène-Boucher, Paris. Career: Singing debut in duet with Frankie Jordan (panne d'essence), national tours, 1961-, international tours, 1965-, including Paris Olympia, 1961, 1963, 1964 (with The Beatles), 1967, 1968, 1970, 1972, 1996; Palais des Congres, Paris, 1975-76, 1977-78, 1983; Palais des Sports, Paris, 1981, 1991; Casino de Paris, 1995; Las Vegas, USA, 1982, Los Angeles, USA, 1983, Atlantic City, USA, 1984 and Sofia, Bulgaria, 1990; Songs include: Tous mes copains, En ecoutant la pluie, I'm Watching, Si je chante, La plus belle pour aller danser, Quand tu es la, Par amour par pitié, 2'35 de bonheur, Le Kid, Comme un garcon, La Maritza, La chasse a l'homme, Loup, Dilindam, L'heure la plus douce de ma vie, Pour lui je reviens, Mon père, J'ai un problème (with Johnny Hallyday), Toi le garcon, Bye bye Leroy Brown, la drole de fin, Qu'est-ce qui fait pleurer les blondes?; Le temps du swing, Petit rainbow, I don't want the night to end, Nicolas, Merveilleusement desenchantee, L'amour c'est comme une cigarette, Aimer, Des heures de desir, Double exposure, Virage, Femme sous influence, C'est fatal, Qui tu es, Je n'aime encore que toi; TV appearances include: Show Smet, 1965; Jolie poupee, 1968; Sylvissima, 1970; Top a Sylvie Vartan, 1972, 1972; Top a Sylvie et Johnny, 1973; Je chante pour Swanee, 1974; Sylvie, 1975; Dancing Star, 1977; La Maritza, 1990; Sylvie sa

vie, 1994; Films: Un clair de lune a Maubeuge, 1962; D'ou viens-tu Johnny?, 1963; Cherchez l'idole, 1964; Patate, 1964; Les poneyttes, 1967; Malpertuis, 1971; Mon amie Sylvie, 1972; L'ange noir, 1994. Publications: Si je chante, 1981; Beauty Book, 1985. Honours: Triomphe des variétés award, 1970; Chevalier des Arts et des Lettres, 1985; Chevalier de l'ordre national du mérite, 1987; Chevalier de l'ordre du Cavalier de Madara, Bulgaria, 1996; Chevalier dans l'ordre de la legion d'Honneur, 1998. Address: c/o Charley Marouani, 37 rue Marbeuf, 75008, Paris, France.

VASCONCELLOS Joe, b. 9 Mar 1959, Santiago, Chile. Musician (percussion); Vocalist; Composer. m. Irene Gonzalez Peña, 1 Mar 1985. Education: College (Brazil, Ecuador, Japan, Italy). Musical Education: Conservatorio Musicale Nicolo Paganini, Genoa, Italy. Career: with Maria Creuza, musician (percussion): Tours throughout Brazil; Argentina; Uruguay; Spain; USA; As Joe Vasconcellos (singer with own band): all national territory Chile; TV appearances: Sabado Gigante, Chile. Recordings: As vocalist of Congreso: Viaje Por La Cresta del Mundo; Ha Llegado Carta; Joe Vasconcellos: Esto Es Solo Una Cancion; Verde Cerca; Toque, 1995; Major composition: Hijo Del Sol Luminoso. Honours: With Congreso: Best Group (Chile); As Joe Vasconcellos: Nominated Verde Cerca Best Record. Membership: Sociedad Chilena Del Derecho De Autor. Hobbies: Swimming; Cycling; Walking. Current Management: Galo Producciones S A. Address: Hernando De Aguirre 944 - Providencia, Santiago, Chile.

VASIK Cassandra, b. Chatham, Ontario, Canada. Musician (acoustic guitar); Entertainer. Musical Education: 3 year diploma, Fanshawe College, London, Ontario. Career: Member, Little Egypt; Moved to Toronto; Receptionist, independent record label; Member, Lost, acoustic trio; Television: Christmas With The Troops, performing to United Nations Peace Keeping Troops, Europe and Middle East, 1992; Ear To The Ground; Canada Day; Spotlight; Winterlude '93; Friday Night With Ralph Benmergui; Video, Sadly Mistaken, Number 1, Outlaws and Heroes, Much Music: Tours with: Randy Travis; The Nitty Gritty Dirt Band; Clint Black; Steve Wariner; Vince Gill; Van Shelton; Marty Stewart. Recordings: Albums: Wildflowers; Feels Like Home; Singles: It Comes Back To You; Which Face Should I Put On Tonight; Those Stars; Wildflowers; Sadly Mistaken; Fortune Smiled; Roll Like A Wheel; Almost Like You Cared. Honours: 2 JUNO Awards, Country Female Vocalist, 1991, 1993; Vista Rising Star Award, CCMA, 1992; CCMA Award, Vocal Collaboration (with Russell de Carle), 1993; Commemorative Medal for the 125th Anniversary, Confederation of Canada, 1993. Memberships: CARAS; SOCAN; CCMA; ACTRA. Hobbies: Cycling; Horse riding; Reading; Listening to music. Current Management: John W. Edwards, Renaissance Music and Entertainment. Address: 8821 Alamo Road, Brentwood, TN 37027, USA.

VÄTH Sven, b. 26 Oct 1964, Frankfurt, Germany. Disc Jockey; Recording Artist. Career: Former metal designer; Started soul club, Neu Isenburg, Germany; Became disc jockey, 1982-; Performed club dates worldwide; Opened Omen Club, Germany, 1988. Numerous recordings include The Harlequin, The Robot And The Ballet Dancer, 1993; Fusion, 1998. Hobbies: Travel; Theatre; Other cultures. Address: c/o Harthouse, Strahlenberger Str 125A, D-63067 Offenbach, Germany.

VAUGHAN Frankie, b. 3 Feb 1928, Liverpool, England. Singer; Entertainer. m. Stella, 6 June, 1951, 2 sons, 1 daughter. Career: Professional singer, 1951-; Worldwide theatre, concert, cabaret performances including: London Palladium; Talk Of The Town, London; Rainbow Grill, New York; Dunes Hotel, Las Vegas; 42nd Street, West End, 1986; UK tour, Syd Lawrence Orchestra, 1989;

Golden ShowStoppers, Blackpool, 1992. Film appearances include: These Dangerous Years; Let's Make Love; The Right Approach; It's All Over Town; Television appearances include: Host, own television series; Subject, This Is Your Life, US and UK (twice). Recordings: Hit singles include: Green Door; Garden Of Eden; Kisses Sweeter Than Wine; The Heart Of A Man; Tower Of Strength; Loop De Loop; Made Of Fire; There Must Be A Way. Honours: CBE, 1997; Freeman, City of London; Honorary Fellowship, Liverpool Polytechnic (now Liverpool John Moores University). Memberships: Patron, National Boys' Club; Deputy President, NABC-Clubs for Young People; Liveryman, Worshipful Company of Carmen; Deputy Lieutenant, Buckinghamshire, 1993. Hobbies: Golf; Fishing. Current Management: Peter Charlesworth Ltd. Address: 68 Old Brompton Road, London SW7 3LQ, England.

VAUGHN Danny, b. New York, USA. Vocalist; Lyricist. Career: Singer, rock group Waysted, 1987; Tours include Europe, supporting Iron Maiden, 1987; Singer, lyricist, rock group Tyketto, 1988-; Concerts include: L'Amour, Brooklyn; NYC Cat Club, supporting Skid Row; Numerous US State Fairs; Tours and festivals, Europe, USA, 1991-. Recordings: Albums: with Waysted: Save Your Prayers, 1987; with Tyketto: Don't Come Easy, 1990; Strength In Numbers, 1994; Also featured on Union, Yes, 1991. Address: c/o Music For Nations Records, 333 Latimer Road, London W10 6RA, England.

VEAR Anthony Craigy "Watts", b. 4 Dec 1970, Middlesbrough, England. Musician (drums, percussion). Career: At 14, 3 years working mens' clubs; Theatre premieres of: Assassins; Stephen Sondheim; Manchester; Little Shop Of Horrors; 5 tours with Cholmondelys Dance Company; World tours with: Renegade Soundwave, 1994; The Wolfgang Press, 1995; Concerts in Los Angeles with Tom Jones, 1994. Recordings: Albums include: Funky Little Demons, 1993-94; Tom Jones: The Lead And How To Swing It, 1994. Honours: Included in exhibition at New Rock and Roll Museum, Cleveland, USA. Memberships: Musicians' Union; LMC; SAL, UK. Hobby: Composition. Address: Basement Flat, 5 Gilmore Road, London SE13 5AD, England.

VEDDER Eddie (Edward Mueller), b. 23 Dec 1966, Evanston, Illinois, USA. Vocalist. Career: Lead singer, US rock group Pearl Jam, 1991-; Concerts include: Support tour, Alice In Chains, 1991; Lollapalooza Festival tour, 1992; Drop In The Park concert, Seattle, 1992; European tour, 1992; Bob Dylan 30th anniversary concert, Madison Square Garden, 1992; Band appears in film Singles, 1992; Support to Keith Richards and The Expensive Winos, 1992; Rock For Choice benefit concert, Los Angeles, 1993; Concert appearances with Neil Young. Recordings: Albums: Ten, 1992; Vs. (Number 1, US), 1993; Vitalogy, 1994; Singles include: Alive, 1992; Even Flow, 1992; Jeremy, 1992; Contributor, Singles film soundtrack, 1992; Sweet Relief album, 1993; Honours: American Music Award, Favourite New Artist, Pop/Rock and Hard Rock categories, 1993; Rolling Stone Readers Awards: Best Male Singer, Best New American Band, Best Video, 1993; 4 MTV Video Awards; Highest 1-week album sales total in history, Vs., 1993. Current Management: Curtis Management, 417 Denny Way, Ste 200, Seattle, WA 98109, USA.

VEE Bobby (Robert Velline), b. 30 Apr 1943, Fargo, North Dakota, USA. Singer. Career: Founder, US group The Shadows, 1958; Solo singer, 1960-; Worldwide appearances include: Hollywood Bowl, with Jerry Lee Lewis, Brenda Lee, The Shirelles, 1961; UK tour with The Crickets, 1962; Dick Clark's Caravan Of Stars US tour, 1963; UK tour with Dusty Springfield, The Searchers, 1964; UK tour, with Dusty Springfield, The Searchers, The Zombies, 1965; UK tour, with

Del Shannon and Brian Hyland, 1988; Annual appearances, Buddy Holly Memorial Concerts; Giants Of Rock'n'Roll, Wembley Arena, with Little Richard, Duane Eddy, 1992; Film appearances: Play It Cool, 1962; Just For Fun, 1963. Recordings: Albums: Bobby Vee, 1961; Bobby Vee Sings Hits Of The Rockin' 50s, 1961; Take Good Care Of My Baby, 1962; Bobby Vee Meets The Crickets, 1962; A Bobby Vee Recording Session, 1962; Golden Greats, 1962; Merry Christmas From..., 1962; The Night Has A Thousand Eyes, 1963; Bobby Vee Meets The Ventures, 1963; Bobby Vee Sings The New Sound From England, 1964; Come Back When You Grow Up, 1967; Just Today, 1968; Nothing Like A Sunny Day, 1972; The Bobby Vee Singles Album, 1980; Hit singles include: Devil Or Angel, 1960; Rubber Ball, 1961; More Than I Can Say, 1961; Take Good Care Of My Baby (Number 1, US), 1961; How Many Tears, 1961; Run To Him, 1961; Sharing You, 1962; A Forever Kind Of Love, 1962; The Night Has A Thousand Eyes, from film Just For Fun, 1963; Charms, 1963; Come Back When You're Grown Up, 1967. Current Management: DHM - Dave Hoffman Management. Address: PO Box 26037, Minneapolis, MN 55447, USA.

VEGA Suzanne Nadine, b. 11 July 1959, Santa Monica, California, USA. Singer; Songwriter; Musician (guitar). m. Mitchell Froom, 17 Mar 1995. Education: High School For The Performing Arts, New York; Barnard College, New York. Career: Folk singer, songwriter, 1982-; Began performing at Greenwich Village; Worldwide concerts include: Royal Albert Hall, London, 1986; Prince's Trust Benefit Concert, Wembley Arena, 1986; Carnegie Hall, New York, 1987; Cambridge Folk Festival, 1991; Woody Guthrie Tribute, Central Park, New York, 1992; Berloni Foundation concert (for leukemia patients), Modena, Italy, 1992. Recordings: Albums: Suzanne Vega, 1985; Solitude Standing, 1987; Days Of Open Hand, 1991; 99.9°F, 1992; Hit singles include: Marlene On The Wall, 1986; Luka, 1987; Tom's Diner, 1987; Book Of Dreams, 1990; 99.9°F, 1992; Blood Makes Noise, 1992; Contributions to: Deadicated (Grateful Dead tribute album), 1991; Tom's Album, 1991; Pavarotti And Friends, 1993; Tower Of Strength (Leonard Cohen tribute album), 1995. Honours: Grammy, Art Direction, 1990; Other Nominations: MTV Award, Best Female Video, Luka, 1988. Current Management: AGF Entertainment Ltd, 30 W 21st Street, New York, NY 10010, USA.

VEJSLEV Jakob, b. 25 July 1957, Copenhagen, Denmark. Musician (guitar); Composer.m. Astrid Dyssegaard, 24 July 1987, 1 son. Musical Education: Self-taught. Career: Played harmonica from age 13; Guitar, 1975-; Full-time guitarist with several groups and musicians (free jazz, fusion, latin, rock), Copenhagen, 1977-; Composed jazz, classical music, worked with own trio and duo, 1985-; Moved to Norway to work as composer, musician and music teacher, 1992-. Compositions: Flute quartet in 8 movements, 1992; Trio (trombone, violin and marimba), 1993; Piece for 10 instruments, 1994. Recordings: News: Stereo Magasin; Arranger, soloist: Håndslag Til Frank, 1987; Arranger, soloist: Til Dine Ojnes Åndmusik, 1990. Memberships: Danish Jazz, Beat and Folk Composer Association; KODA (Danish Composers Copyright Association); Norwegian Jazz Association. Hobby: Artist. Current Management: Warner Chappell. Address: Jakob Vejslev, Alfheim 1A, N-7800 Namsos, Norway.

VEJSLEV Tony, b. 25 Oct 1926, Copenhagen, Denmark. Composer; Singer; Musician (guitar). m. Benthe Kolding, 19 Oct 1954, 1 son. Education: Teacher. Musical Education: Self-taught. Career: Concerts in Denmark; Radio broadcasts, 1938-; Television appearances, 1949-. Recordings: Tony Vejslev Synger, 1983; Haandslag Til Frank, 1988; Til Dine Oejnes Aaandemusik, 1990; 50 Danske Viser Og Sange,

1993. Publications: 19 Jaegerviser 1953, 1967; 26 Viser, 1987; Fem Farum Digte, 1988; 18 Danske Sange, 1990. Honours: KODA; Dansk Musikraad; Scholarships. Membership: Danish Jazz, Beat And Folk Authors. Hobbies: Travel; Literature. Current Management: Olafssongs, Copenhagen. Address: Olafssongs, Anker Heegaardsgade 2, ST TV., 1572 Copenhagen V, Denmark.

VELGHE Rudy, b. 4 January 1960, Oudenaarde, Belgium. Violin; Nyckelharpa; Guitar; Composer; Arranger. Education: Licence Degree, History, Rug-State University Gent, Belgium. Career: Professional Musician, 1987-; Founder Member, Celtic band, Orion; Composed and arranged music for different short films and TV programmes; Performed in many shows on radio and TV/BRT, RTB, BBC, Irish Radio; Studiomusician, with many artists. Compositions: Wailing Reel; Restless Home; Shores of Marsannay; Reel of Notes. Recordings: Histoires de Rue; 1990; Blue Room; Restless Home; Dao Dezi; About to Go. Current Management: VZW Orion ASBL, 136 Chaussee De Wemmel, 1090 Brussels, Belgium.

VELKE John Arthur II (Fritz), b. 10 Sept 1930, Washington, DC, USA. Teacher; Musician (trombone); Composer; Conductor; Music Publisher. m. (1) Elizabeth Downs Waterman, 18 Aug 1956, 3 sons, 1 daughter, (2) Katherine Lee Rogus, 27 Nov 1974. Education: Piano, violin and trombone lessons; BM, 1953, MM, 1955, Catholic University of American, Washington DC; Completed coursework towards doctorate; Music Composition with William Graves and George Thaddeus Jones, Catholic University of America. Career: Trombonist, US Air Force Band, Washington DC, 1953-57; Instrumental Music Teacher, Fairfax (Virginia) Public Schools, 1957-85; Music Publisher, 1971-; Trombonist, Assistant Conductor, 1974-90, Conductor, 1991-, National Concert Band of America, Washington DC. Compositions: for band: Concertino; Quartal Piece; Fanfare and Rondo; Foray at Fairfax; Plaything; Caprice and Interlude; The Kaleidoscope; Eclectique Arabique; Melbourne Centennial March; Alexandria Citizens Band March; Others: Tommie Jack Concert March; Concerto Grosso for brass sextet and orchestra; String Quartet No 1; Suite for string orchestra. Publications: Concertino for band, 1963; Colloquy for trombone trio; Fantasia for trombone solo accompanied by six trombones, 1989; Trombone Legato Style, method book. Contributions to: Warming Up By The Clock, School Musician, 1959; Concertino for Band, Journal of Band Research, American Bandmasters' Association, 1966. Honour: Ostwald Award, for Concertino for Band, American Bandmasters' Association, 1962. Memberships: ASCAP; Association of Concert Bands; International Military Music Society. Hobby: Golf. Current Management: Nancy Sies Presents, 408 E Duncan Avenue, Alexandria, VA 22301, USA. Address: 5119 Waukesha Road, Bethesda, MD 20816-2226, USA.

VENTO Joseph, b. 16 Dec 1926, Los Angeles, California, USA. Composer; Conductor; Band Leader. Education: Composition, Film-Scoring, Psychology, University of South Califonia; Optometry, Philosophy, Fresno State College; Piano, composition, Juilliard School; Conducting, New England Conservatory of Music. Debut: Accordion Solo, Radio KFI, Los Angeles, The William Tell Overture, 10 years old, 1937. Career: Films, Counterpoint, Man's Favorite Sport, This Earth is Mine, The Competition, Guide for a Married Man, Made in Paris, Girl Happy, Those Lips Those Eyes. Compositions: The Three Suns; I Can't Forget; Our Love is Gone; City of The Angles; Sacro Sanctum; Warsaw Connection; Sarah Suite; Ole Joe, 1997; Joes Bach, 1997. Recordings: Artist Of The Three Suns, Twilight Time; Joe Vento Golden Hits, Volume I and II; Surfside Records; Bells of Christmas; The Best of Joe Vento; The Best of The Three Suns; Film

Soundtrack, True Friends. Publications: I Can't Forget, 1939; City Of The Angels, 1968; Sacro Sanctum, 1979; Love Is Gone, 1995; Edulerp III, 1995. Contributions to: Midi'ing in Music Composition, Moorpark College, 1991; Nurturing Music in the Nineties. Honour: Best Accordionist Grand Prize, 1939. Memberships: ASCAP; ASMAC; AFofM, New York and Los Angeles; NARAS; American Academy of Sciences; Disabled American Veterans, SR, CDR; Music Teachers National Association, USA. Hobbies: Oceanography; Forestry; The environment. Current Management: S V Enterprises. Address: 419 Mark Drive, Simi, CA 93065, USA.

VERA Billy, b. 28 May 1944, Riverside, California, USA. Singer; Actor; Songwriter; Producer; Music Historian. m. (1) Barbara, Jan 1966, (2) Rosalee, 30 Apr 1988, 1 son, 1 daughter. Education: 1 year, Fordham University, Bronx, New York. Musical Education: Self-taught. Career: Concerts: Peppermint Lounge, New York City, 1963; Apollo Theater, 2 times, 1968; Dick Cavett Show, 1968; Steve Allen Show, 1969; NYC Academy of Music, 13 times, 1972-75; Madison Square Garden, 1972; Howard Theater, Washington DC, 1979; Johnny Carson Show, 9 times, 1986-89; Films: Buckaroo Banzai; Blind Date; The Doors; Television: Wise Guy; Alice; Scarecrow and Mrs King; Knot's Landing. Compositions: Recorded by: Ricky Nelson: Mean Old World; Barbara Lewis: Make Me Belong To You; Dolly Parton: I Really Got The Feeling; Bonnie Raitt: Papa Come Quick. Recordings: Storybook Children, 1967; With Pen In Hand, 1968; I Can Take Care Of Myself, 1981; At This Moment, 1987. Publications: Liner notes to over 200 historical albums. Honours: Gold Prize, Tokyo Music Festival, 1981; ASCAP Award, 1987. Membership: Trustee, Rhythm and Blues Foundation. Hobbies: Record Collector. Current Management: Danny Robinson Agency for the Performing Arts. Address: 9000 Sunset Blvd, Los Angeles, CA 90048-5343, USA.

VERA Stephane, b. 11 May 1965, Paris, France. Musician (drums). Education: 1 year Right University, World Music. Musical Education: Boulogne Conservatory, Jazz-Rock School. Career: Gilbert Becaud; Dany Brillant; Jeane Manson; Vivian Reed; David Koven; I Muvrini; Karim Kacel; Eric Lelann; Ultra Marine; Angelique Kidjo; Jacky Quartz; Idrissa Diop; Yvan Dautin; Georges Macintosh. Recordings with: Dany Brillant; Jacky Quartz; Imurvine; Karim Kacel; Film: Le Nouveau Monde, 1994. Publications: Drummer's Magazine, Paris; VAC Magazine. Memberships: SACEM; SPEDIDAM; SDRM. Hobbies: Swimming; Tennis; Films; Music. Current Management: Marouani Charley, Becaud's agent; Ginibrej. Address: 27 Rue D'Herblay, 78700 Conflans, Ste Honorine, France.

VERDIER Hervé, b. 6 May 1960, Yvelines, France. Musician (contrabass). 1 son. Musical Education: Self-taught, bluegrass to ethnojazz. Career: New Morning, Petit Journal Montparnasse; Café de la Plage, instants chavirés; Festival Pornic; Caen; Montauban; Créteil; Montpellier; Ris Orangis; Jazz Week Rennes; Eaze; Abries. Recordings: Corcador, Volumes 1-3. Hobbies: Tai Chi Chuan; Cooking. Current Management: Cosmo-notes. Address: 8 bis Rue Moutard-Martin, 91460 Marcoussis, France.

VEREEN Ben. Singer; Actor; Entertainer. Career: Broadway productions include: The Chimney Man in musical, Jelly's Last Jam, 1993; Sweet Charity; Hair; Jesus Christ Superstar; Pippin; Grind; I'm Not Rappaport; A Christmas Carol, 1995; One-man show, concert tours, throughout US including Las Vegas; Atlantic City; Lake Tahoe; Also Europe; Asia; Caribbean Islands; Television includes: The Fresh Prince Of Bel Air; The Nanny; New York Undercover; Star Trek - The Next Generation; Intruders; They Are

Among Us; Silk Stockings; Own series, Tenspeed And Brownshoe, 1980; JJ Starbuck; Booker; Louis Armstrong - Chicago Style; Roots; Ben Vereen: His Roots; The Jesse Owens Story; Ellis Island; All That Jazz; Funny Lady; In demand speaker on lecture circuit; Formed organization, Celebrities For a Drug Free America, 1991; Currently developing performing arts center, Chicago. Honours include: Israel's Humanitarian Award, 1978; NAACP, Image Award, 1978; 1979; Eleanor Roosevelt Humanitarian Award, 1983; Victory Award, 1990; Tony for Best Actor, Pippin; American Guild Of Variety Artists: Entertainer Of The Year; Rising Star; Song And Dance Star; Honorary Doctorates: Emerson College, Boston; St Francis College, Brooklyn; Columbia College, Chicago. Address: C/o Stan Scotland, JKE Services, 404 Park Avenue S, 10th Floor, New York, NY 10016, USA.

VERHAEREN Gert J M, b. 30 July 1973, Neerpelt, Belgium. Singer; Songwriter; Musician (Guitar, Bass Guitar; Sequencer). Education: Selftaught, Guitar, Bass Guitar, Sequencer. Career: Main concerts with band named Ivy: 1996: Zeezicht, Antwerp, Belgium; Geuselpop Festival, Maastricht, The Netherlands; Electric Ladyland Festival, Maarheze, The Netherlands; Airpop-Festival, Heerlen, The Netherlands; 1997: Absolutely Free Festival, Genk, Belgium; with band named Supergum: 1997: Support-Act, The Paranoiacs, Overpelt, Belgium; Airplane, CD, single. Recordings: Bo(o)s(e); Goozehand; Liquid Courage. Honour: Finalist, Rock Competition, Het Licht Van Eindhoven, Eindhoven, The Netherlands, 1996. Membership: SABAM. Hobbies: Listening to lots of music; Attending concerts; Recording and mixing songs. Current Management: Boom! (JP Van), Bergensesteenweg 19, 1500 Halle, Belgium. Address: Kattestraat 17, 3900 Overpelt, Belgium.

VERITY John, b. Bradford, Yorkshire, England. Vocalist; Musician (guitar); Record Producer. m. Karen, 10 Dec 1994, 2 sons, 1 daughter (from prev. relationships). Musical Education: Self-taught. Career: Guitarist, various groups, 1960's; Leader, John Verity Band, 1969-73; Support tours with: Jimi Hendrix; Canned Heat; Janis Joplin; Lead vocalist, Argent, 1973-76; Member, Phoenix; Charlie; John Coghlan's Diesel Band; Numerous concerts worldwide, including: Fender Stratocaster 40th Anniversary Concert, Manchester, 1994; Strat Pack, Australia Day, London, Hippodrome, 1995; Built own recording studio; Full time record producer; Producer, guitarist, vocalist, Saxon; John Parr; Motörhead; Ringo Starr; Russ Ballard; Tank; The Zombies; Colin Blunstone. Recordings: Albums: with Verity/John Verity Band: John Verity Band, 1972; Interrupted Journey, 1983; Truth Of The Matter, 1985; Rock Solid, 1989; Hold Your Head Up, 1994; with Argent: Circus, 1975; Counterpoints, 1975; Hold Your Head Up, 1978; with Phoenix: Phoenix, 1976; In Full View, 1979; with Charlie: Good Morning America, 1981. Memberships: MRCS; PRS. Hobby: Music. Current Management: Verity Associates. Address: 5A Greta Heath, Burton-In-Lonsdale, via Carnforth, Lancashire LA6 3LH, England.

VERLAINE Tom (Thomas Miller), b. 13 Dec 1949, New Jersey, USA. Singer; Musician (guitar). Career: Member, The Neon Boys; Goo Goo; Founder member, Television, 1973-78; Solo artiste, 1979-; Reformed Television, 1991-; Glastonbury Festival, 1992; European Festivals, Japanese and US tours, 1992. Recordings: Albums: with Television: Marquee Moon, 1978; Adventure, 1979; The Blow Up, 1990; Television, 1993; Solo albums: Tom Verlaine, 1979; Dreamtime, 1981; Words From The Front, 1982; Cover, 1984; Flash Light, 1987; Warm And Cool, 1992; Singles: with Television: Marquee Moon, 1977; Prove It, 1977; Other recordings: Guitarist, Hey Joe, Patti Smith, 1974. Honour: Rolling Stone Magzine Critics Award, Comeback Of The Year,

Television, 1993. Current Management: Basement Music, 6 Pembridge Road, London W11 3HL, England.

VERLY François, b. 5 Apr 1958, Paris, France. Jazz Musician (piano, tablas, drums, percussion). 1 daughter. Education: BEPC-Bac D. Career: Many concerts on television and radio; World tours, jazz festivals: Canada; Mexico; Colombia; Ecuador; India; Hong Kong; Europe; East Europe; Africa; Plays with Michel Portal, David Friedman and Martial Solal. Recordings with: Andy Emler, National French Jazz Orchestra, 1986, 1987; Marc Ducret; Antoine Hervé; Padovani; Denis Badault; Fawsi Al Aiedy; Nguyen Lê. Honours: First prize, Percussion, Creteil, 1978; First Prize, piano solist, Défense, 1986. Hobbies: Nature; Ecology; Solidarity with minorities. Current Management: Dominique Jezequel. Address: Jazz Concert, 1 rue Victor Hugo, 35000 Rennes, France.

VERNER J Arif, b. 17 Feb 1950, Alabama, USA. Musician (Midi guitar synthesiser); Composer. m. Donna Tregaskis, 1981, 1 son. Education: BFA. Musical Education: Self-taught. Career: Recording Artist for Spotted Peccary Music; Owner, Infinite Sound Studio; Producer of albums, films, videos and others; Author; Technical Writer; Composer. Recordings: A Vision Beyond Light; Clear Colours; Selected New Music Series Volume 1. Publications: Contributor of articles in professional journals and magazines. Memberships: BMI; ISS. Hobbies: Theosophy; Racquetball. Current Management: Authentic Marketing, 40 Waterside Plaza, C203, New York, NY 10010, USA.

VERNEY Frannie, b. 14 May 1963, Buckinghamshire, England. Vocalist; Arranger; Composer; Musician (piano, percussion). Musical Education: Grade VIII piano, 1975; Purcell School for Young Musicians; GSMD Diploma in Jazz and Studio Music, 1994. Career: Radio appearances include: BBC Radio 5, BBC Radio Scotland, Newstalk AM; Tours throughout Europe; Repeat performances at prestigious Jazz venues throughout Britain including: Jazz Cafe, Royal Festival Hall Foyer, Bull's Head Barnes, Chicken Shed Theatre, Jazz Club Ascot, Edinburgh Festival Fringe, West Wales Jazz Festival, Vortez Jazz Club, Covent Garden Festival, Cork International Jazz Festival, Greenwich and Docklands Jazz Festival; Performs original and arranged Jazz Fusion material with her band, The Big Idea; Bandleader and Promoter of successful party band, Happy Feet, who have played all over Britain and in Europe at numerous venues including: Cumberland Hotel, London, RAC Club, Epsom, St Anton am Arlberg, Austria; Also performs as Soloist, with duos, performs, writes and arranges for smaller bands and acapella groups. Memberships: PRS; MCPS; BASCA; Musicians' Union. Hobbies: Aromatherapy; Photography; Restaurant (director); Patron of British Museum; Travel. Address: Epicurean Music, London, England.

VERNHETTES Dan (Daniel), b. 20 May 1942, Paris, France. Musician (trumpet); Vocalist. m. Lill, 1965. Musical Education: Self-taught cornet, 1959-. Career: Main early influence, King Oliver; Interest developed in trumpeters of Swing era, most recently in music from New Orleans; Founder, Jazz O'Maniacs, 1966; Cornet player, bandleader, Six Cats, 1990-93; Member, Eddie Louis' Multicolor Fanfare, 1991-93; Leader, second trumpet, Swing Feeling (30s-40s jazz orchestra), 1993; Currently, trumpet player, singer, bandleader, Vintage Jazzmen (New Orleans-style sextet); Also, member, Olivier Franc orchestra, specialising in music of Sidney Bechet. Recordings include: Various records, 1960s; Vintage Jazzmen, 1995; Swing Feeling with Screamin' Jay Hawkins and Spanky Wilson, 1995. Current Management: Bertrand Henrion. Address:

45 Rue Roger Buessard, 94200 Ivry-Sur-Seine, France.

VERNON Mike, b. 20 Nov 1944, Harrow, Middlesex, England. Record Producer; Studio Owner; Songwriter. 2 daughters. Education: Croydon College Of Art. Career: Production Assistant, then Staff Producer, Decca Record Company, 1962-66; Founder, producer, Blue Horizon Label, 1966; Editor, R&B Monthly (early Blues Fanzine); Independent record producer, 1968; Formed Indigo Records, 1992; Became Code Blue (through East/West), 1994; Artists include Sherman Robertson, The Hoax, Jay Owens, Bo Diddley, John Primer and Eric Bibb. Recordings: As producer: Singles include: with Fleetwood Mac: Albatross; Need Your Love So Bad; Man Of The World; with David Bowie: The Laughing Gnome; with Focus: Hocus Pocus; Sylvia; with Bloodstone: Natural High; with Roachford: Family Man; Albums by numerous artistes include: Level 42; John Mayall's Bluesbreakers; David Bowie; Fleetwood Mac; Focus; Ten Years After; Savoy Brown; Rocky Sharpe and The Replays; Edwin Starr; Dr Feelgood; Sherman Robertson; Jimmy Witherspoon; Climax Blues Band; Joe Cocker; Danza Invisible; Renaud Hantson. Honours: 10 Gold records; 6 Silver; WC Handy Award, 1987-88. Memberships: Musicians' Union; Associate Member, Re-Pro; PRS. Hobby: Golf. Current Management: Stephen Budd Management, 109B Regent's Park Road, London NW1 8UR, England.

VERSAILLES Fred, b. 15 June 1958, Versailles, France. Producer; Composer. m. Line Alloet, 1984, 2 daughters. Education: University of Nantere, Economics. Recordings: NTM, first single: Le Monde De Demain; Albums: Authentik; Incontrolables; Native; Paris Groove Up; Dis Bonjour A La Dame. Honours: Victoire de la Musique, France, for: Native, 1994. Membership: Co-manager, Zbing Publishing. Address: 16 Rue de Saint Denis, 95160 Montmorency, France.

VESALA Edward, b. 15 Jan 1945. Musician (percussion); Composer. Career: Member, Tuohi Quartet, Montreux Jazz Festival, 1971; Joined Jan Garbarek's trio, 1972; Played jazz workshops, festivals throughout Europe; Worked with Tomasz Stanko, Stanko-Vesala Quartet, 1974-78; Solo percussionist, Finland and Europe, including Prague and Le Mans Jazz festivals; Teacher, Helsinki Theatre College; Bandleader, current group Sound And Fury. Compositions include: Music for Shakespeare's plays; Aleksis Kivi's Seven Brothers; National epic, Kalevala. Recordings: Albums: Solo: Nan Madol; Heavy Life; with Sound And Fury: Lumi; Ode To The Death Of Jazz. Honours: Best Jazz Ensemble, (with Tuohi Quartet), Montreux Jazz Festival, 1971; Yrjö Awards, Finnish Jazz Federation, 1972, 1980. Address: Seilimäki 25 C, 02180 Espoo, Finland.

VEYS Luc. Musician (accordion, spoons). Musical Education: Classical Education Piano; Private lessons accordion; Selftaught spoons. Career: Dranouter Festival, 1995; Gooik Festival 2002, 1997; De Brakke Grond, Amsterdam, Netherlands, 1997; Labadoux Festival, 1997; Den Ekster, 1996, 1997; Paulus Festival, Ostend, 1997; Sloanthe Festival, 1997; Foleys Irish Pub, Gent; National radio (Radio 1, De Groote Boodschap) and several regional radio and television appearances. Compositions: Jumpin' the Fences - Dirty Wally; Friend's Sadness; Something To Fear; Shut the Pub; A Whistler's Wedding. Recordings: Tales From the Great Whiskey Book, CD, 1996. Honours: Government Medal for Flute, 1986; 2nd Place, Youth Soloist Festival, Flute, 1986; Finale, Westtalent, 1995. Membership: Volksmuziekfederatie, Belgium. Current Management: KAFT Producties, Akkerwindelaan 20, 8791 Beveren-Leie, Belgium.

Address: Derudder Peter, Barrierestraat 49, 8940 Wervik, Belgium.

VIBSKOV Per (Nielsen), b. 23 May 1962, Viborg, Denmark. Composer; Producer; Musician (bass). Musical Education: Self-taught. Career: Bass player with: Peyote, 1978-85; Rosegarden, 1986; Janes Rejoice, 1986-87; TAO, 1988-; Bayou Brothers, 1990-94; Bass player, arranger, programmer, producer, with Home Sweet Home, 1994-; Bass player with Luksus, 1996. Recordings: with Peyote: For Sent Igen, 1984; with Janes Rejoice: Wievs To Keep, 1987; with TAO: Senor Maski, 1995; with Home Sweet Home: Divine, 1996. Honours: Prize for application, Efterslaegten, 1994. Membership: Danish Jazz, Beat, and Folk Authors. Hobbies: Theology; Yachting. Address: Viktoriagade 10 ITV, Copenhagen V, Denmark.

VICH Michal, b. 5 Nov 1952, Prague, Czechoslovakia. Singer; Musician (guitar); High School Director. m. Vera Vichova, 3 March 1977, 1 daughter. Education: School of Economics, Prague; Prague Musical School; J Jezek Conservatoire, guitar and voice studies. Career: Musician, recital group Vpred; Member, artistic group, The Prague Five; Film music for the films of T Vorel, including: Olda's Party, 1988; Kour, musical, 1990; La Serra, opera, Prague, 1994; Songs for the Children. Compositions: Kour, film soundtrack, 1990; La Serra, opera score, 1994. Recordings: Kour, film soundtrack, 1990; La Serra, opera, 1994; Albums: Monday Tells To Tuesday, 1995; Oh, The Sails, Where Are They? (with members of the Czech Philharmonic Orchestra), 1997. Publications: Books for children: Monday Tells to Tuesday, 1995; Oh, The Sails, Where Are They?, 1996. Honour: Oh, The Sails, Where Are They? selected as one of the best books of the year, 1996. Memberships: The Protective Syndicate of Authors (Czech Republic). Hobby: Sport. Address: 252 62 Unetice 84, Okr Praha Za'pad, Czech Republic.

VICKHOFF Björn Ture, b. 9 May 1946, Växjö, Sweden. Singing Songwriter (Guitar). m. Eva-Marie Vickhoff, 1 son, 1 daughter. Education: MA, Gothenburg University. Musical Education: Individual Musician Degree, Gothenburg University. Career: Kosmiskteko, an opus for TV (music, lyrics and performance); Film music to Samtidigt enfredag; TV-Serie Music: Flykten Ekomotivet; Appearances in Scandinavian TV and radio. Compositions: Västerhar, Fantastico, Utsikt. Recordings: LP: Fiskdikt Och Fagelsang; Rnalla Stangsel; CD: Fantastico. Publication: An finns det tid, anthology with environmental songs. Honours: STIM Award; Göteborg Award; Art Society Award. Memberships: SKAP; SAMI; Musikcentrum Vast; Yrkestrubadurernas förening. Hobbies: Writing a paper in MPB-artist Sonzaquinna. Address: Björn Vickhoff, Smakullar 23, 424 70 Olofstorp, Sweden.

VIDAL Jacques Henri, b. 13 Oct 1949, Athis-Mons, France. Musician (double bass); Composer; Teacher. m. 13 Apr 1993, 1 son. Musical Education: National Versailles Academy of Music. Career: Formation of Christian Vander's group, Magma, 1970; Leader, Trijoums, 1976; Tour, France, with American drummer Philly Joe Jones, 1977; Played with guitarist Frederic Sylvestre, 1978; Jacques Vidal Quintet (Michel Graillier, piano, Florin Niculescu, violin, Frederic Sylvestre, guitar, Simon Goubert, drums), 1995; Television series as musician/actor. Compositions: Music for theatre. Recordings: Return, with Christian Escoudé and A Romano, 1979; Be Bop, Pepper Adams and B Altschul, 1979; Live A L'Olympia, J P Debarbat, 1979; A Live In Paris, Glenn Ferris, 1980; Rencontre, J P Debarbat, 1981; Music Band, Teddy Lasry, 1983; Under The Magnolias, Richard Raux, 1989; with Frederic Sylvestre: Premier Grand Cru with J L Chautemps, 1980; 2 Plus, with Eric Lelann, 1982; Hommages, with Eric Lelann, A Jean-Marie, 1983; Trio Live, S Huchard, 1986; Capricorne, 1989; As

bandleader: Bass For Ever, 1995; News Of Bop, Jacques Vidal Quintet, 1995. Memberships: SACEM; SACD; ADAMI. Address: 2 Bis Cité Popincourt, 75011 Paris, France.

VIG Butch. Record Producer; Musician (drums). Career: Record producer, various artists; Musician, with group Spooner; Founder, group Garbage. Recordings: with Garbage: Album: Garbage; Singles: Vow, 1995; Subhuman, 1995; Queer, 1995; Only Happy When It Rains, 1995; Stupid Girl, 1996; As producer: Nevermind, Nirvana; Siamese Dream, Smashing Pumpkins; Remixes for: U2; Nine Inch Nails; House Of Pain. Current Management: SOS Management, 106 Cleveland Street, London W1 5DP, England.

VIKLICKY Emil, b. 23 November 1948, Olomouc, Czech Republic. Composer; Arranger; Pianist. Education: Graduated in Mathematics, Palacky University, Olomouc, 1966-71; Berklee College of Music, Boston, USA, 1977-78; Private composition studies with Jarmo Sermila, George Crumb, Dr Václav Kucera; TV Music: Hamster in Nightgown, 1994-95; Broucci; Lucas et Lucy; TV Serials: Zmatky kluka zmatlika, Hugo z hor, Hroch, Snezny muz. Honours: Winner, Jazz Improvisation Contest, Lyon, France, 1976; 1st Prize, Monaco Competition for Jazz Composers, with Green Satin, 1976; 2nd Prize, Monaco, with Cacharel, 1985; Supraphon Prize for LP debut, In Holomoc Town, 1978; FITES prize for animated films music, 1991; 2nd Prize for Tristana, Boston, Marimolin contest of contemporary music, 1994; Special Prize of the Jury for Electroacoustic Work, Paradise Park, Prague, 1996; Annual Prize of Czech Music Council, 1996. Recordings: Lacrimosa - Má je Pomsta, 1995; Food of Love, 1995; Homage to Josip Plecnik, 1996; Okno, 1997; UV Drive, 1997; Bohemia after Dark, 1997; Confluence; Together; Homage to Joan Miro; While My Lady Sleeps; Round Midnight. Address: Letohradská 36, 170 00 Praha 7, Czech Republic.

VILAS Ricardo, b. 30 August 1949, Rio de Janeiro, Brazil. Singer; Songwriter; Musician. 2 sons, 1 daughter. Career: New Morning, Paris; Rockstore, Montepellier; Cinco Voador, Rio de Janeiro; Composer and Musical Productions for Television Globo, 1983-88. Compositions: Gabriel; Viven; Recado; Estrela da Cancas. Recordings: Duo Albums, Tecae Ricardo; Solo Albums, Ricardo Vilas. Memberships: SACEM, France; Adami, France; AMAR, Brazil. Hobbies: Music; Football. Current Management: Culture Metisse. Address: 215 Boulevard Voltaire, 75011 Paris, France.

VILLEGER André Franucin Raymond, b. 12 Aug 1945, Rosny L/Bois, France. Musician (saxophone). 1 son, 1 daughter. Musical Education: Self-taught. Career: Festivals: Nice; Antibes; Paris; Marciac; Saragosse; London; Madrid; Carthage; Bayonne; Trinidad; Fort De France. Recordings: Albums: Something To Live For, 1986; A Villeger Connections, 1991. Honours: Prix Sidney Bechet 1973 (Academie Du Jazz). Membership: Los Angeles Jazz Society. Hobbies: Gardening; Astronomy. Address: 28 Rue du Gibet, 95100 Argenteuil, France.

VINCENT Amanda, b. 20 Jan 1958, Perth, Australia. Musician (keyboards). Education: BMus, major, composition. Musical Education: University of Western Australia. Career: Tours with: Eurogliders, UK, USA, Philippines, Australia, 1980-1987; Tim Finn, Australia, New Zealand, 1986; The Thompson Twins, UK, Ireland, USA, Canada, 1987; Boy George, UK, Europe, Australia, 1987-93; Jenny Morris, UK, Europe, Australia supporting Prince, 1990; Gang Of Four, UK, USA, Canada, 1991; Billy Bragg, Australia, New Zealand, Japan, 1992; Black, UK, Turkey, 1993; Yazz, UK, 1994. Compositions include: Music for Strollers, ballet, Human Veins dance theatre, Canberra, 1980; Music, Fields of Fire, ABC TV, 1987; Music, The Collector, cinema and

television, 1994; Music for TV documentary: The Feelgood Factor, 1995. Recordings: with Tim Finn: Escapade, 1983; Les Patterson Saves The World (soundtrack), 1987; with Eurogliders: Pink Suit Blue Day, 1981; This Island, 1983; Absolutely, 1985; with Jenny Morris: Animal Magic, 1986; Body And Soul, 1987; Shiver, 1989; with Boy George: Clause 28 (single), 1988; Boyfriend, 1989; High Hat, 1988; Tense Nervous Headache, 1988; Don't Try This At Home, 1991; Spiritual High, Moodswings featuring Chrissie Hynde, (single) 1991. Honours: 1 Platinum, 2 Gold albums, 1 Gold single; Second Prize, New York Film, TV awards, video: Heaven, Euroglider (single), 1985; Best Single, Heaven, Australia, 1985. Memberships: PRS; MCPS; Musicians' Union. Hobbies: Film (studying film composition, International Film School); Psychotherapy; Writing; West African art and culture. Address: Flat 5, 15A Cricklewood Broadway, London, NW2 3JX, England.

VINCENT Eric, b. 27 June 1946, Force, France. Singer; Guitarist; Violinist. m. 4 March 1987. Education: Conservatory. Career: Performed in more than 120 countries: Brooklyn Auditorium, New York, USA; World Congress Center, Atlanta, USA; Opera Manaus, Brasil; National Folk Festival of Adelaide, Australia; Theatre Municipal Manoi, Vietnam. Compositions: CD: Un Pays Quelquepart; Luca; Harmoniques; Voyage Pour L'Immediat; Haiti Kimbe. Recordings: Operation Boule De Neige; Je Suis Fatigue. Publications: Cest Comme Ca, 1987; Iles, 1987; Reflets France, 1992; Sans Borne, 1990. Memberships: SCPP; SACEM; ADAMI; SPEDIDAM. Hobbies: Chess; Windsurf; Tennis. Address: Madura, 11 bd de la Bastille, 75012, Paris, France.

VINDING Mads, b. 7 Dec 1948, Copenhagen, Denmark. Musician (bass). Career: Professional at age 16; House bass player, Montmarte jazz club, Copenhagen; Worked with many jazz masters including: Herbie Hancock, Wayne Shorter, Stan Getz, Gary Burton, Hank Jones, Dexter Gordon, Bob Brookmeyer, Ben Webster, Benny Goodman, Dizzy Gillespie, Quincy Jones, Johnny Griffin, Eddie "Lockjaw" Davis, Gerry Mulligan, Tony Williams, Ed Thigpen, Sir Roland Hanna, Dollar Brand, Clark Terry, Monty Alexander and Toots Thielemans. Recordings: Numerous albums include: Solo albums: Danish Design, 1974; The Kingdom (Where Nobody Dies), 1997; with Ed Thigpen: Action-Re-Action, 1974; Mr Taste, 1991; with Tony Williams and Wlodek Gulgowsky, Pop-Workshop, 1974; with Kai Winding: Trombone Summit, 1980; with Doug Raney: Guitar Guitar Guitar, 1985; with Dexter Gordon and Herbie Hancock: Cinema Jazz, 1986; The Other Side Of Midnight, 1986; with Hanne Boel and Jørgen Emborg: Shadow Of Love, 1987; with Roland Hanna and Jesper Thilo: This Time It's Real, 1987; with Thomas Clausen Trio: She Touched Me, 1988; Psalm, 1995; with Sven Asmussen: Fiddler Supreme, 1989; with Thomas Clausen Trio and Gary Burton: Cafe Noir, 1991; Flowers & Trees, 1992; with Danish Radio Big Band: Endangered Species, 1993; with Trine Lise Væring: When I Close My Eyes, 1996; with Jesper Thilo: Jesper Thilo Meets Thomas Clausen, 1997; Other albums with Duke Jordan; Johnny Griffin; Ernie Wilkins; Kenny Drew; Hank Jones. Address: Bøgevej 8, DK-3500 Vœrløse, Denmark.

VINTON Bobby (Stanley Robert), b. 16 Apr 1935, Canonsburg, Pennsylvania, USA. Singer. Career: Played trumpet with The Tempos; Formed own band; Became solo singer, 1962-; Sold over 30 million records worldwide; Actor, films Surf Party; Big Jake; The Train Robbers; Numerous television appearances including host of weekly variety show, 1975-78; Major concerts include: The Biggest Show Of Stars For 1960, with Chubby Checker and Brenda Lee; Dick Clark's Caravan Of Stars, US tour, 1961; New Zealand tour with Gene Pitney, 1962; Carnegie Hall, 1974; Opened The

Bobby Vinton Blue Velvet Theater, Branson, Missouri, 1993. Recordings: US Number 1 singles: Roses Are Red; Blue Velvet; There! I've Said It Again; Numerous other hits include: Blue On Blue; My Heart Belongs To Only You; Clinging Vine; L-O-N-E-L-Y; I Love How You Love Me; Coming Home Soldier; Every Day Of My Life; My Melody Of Love; Blue Velvet (Number 2, UK), re-issued due to television commercial, 1990; Albums: Roses Are Red, 1962; Bobby Vinton Sings The Big Ones, 1963; Bobby Vinton's Greatest Hits, 1964; Tell Me Why, 1964; Bobby Vinton Sings For Lonely Nights, 1965; Satin Pillows And Careless, 1966; Please Love Me Forever, 1968; Take Good Care Of My Baby, 1968; I Love How You Love Me, 1969; Vinton, 1969; Bobby Vinton's Greatest Hits Of Love, 1970; My Elusive Dreams, 1970; Every Day Of My Life, 1972; Sealed With A Kiss, 1972; Bobby Vinton's All-Time Greatest Hits, 1972; Melodies Of Love, 1974; Bobby Vinton Sings The Golden Decade Of Love, 1975; Heart Of Hearts, 1975; The Bobby Vinton Show, 1976; The Name Of Love, 1977; Timeless, 1990; Duet with George Burns on album, As Time Goes By, 1993. Honours include: Bobby Vinton Day, Chicago, 1975; Honorary citizen, Chicago, City's Certificate of Merit, 1975; Honorary doctorate of Music, Duquesne University, 1978; Several Gold discs.

VIRTANEN Heikki, b. 4 Sept 1953, Finland. Musician (bass). Musical Education: Studied contrabass and Musicology. Career: Member, jazz-rock group, Tasavallen Presidentti, early 70s; Concerts with Juhani Aaltonen; Jarmo Savolainen; Severi Pyysalo; Jukkis Uotila, 1980s-; Bass player, Conjunto Baron (with Seppo Paakkunainen); Bassist for Olli Ahvenlahti, backing singer Vesa-Matti Loiri on Olli Ahvenlahti's compositional projects. Honour: Yrjö Award, Finnish Jazz Federation, 1987. Address: Töölöntorinkatu 7, 00260 Helsinki, Finland.

VISKINDE Peter, b. 14 Nov 1953, Copenhagen, Denmark. Musician (guitar); Composer. m. Susan Kjeldsen, 23 June 1992, 2 sons, 2 daughters. Career: Musician, 1974-; Member of groups Buffalo; Hualsospillemandene; Malurt Doraz; Also recorded as solo artist. Recordings: 2 albums with Buffalo; 2 albums with Hualsospillemandene; 7 albums with Malurt; 3 solo albums, 1986, 1993 and 1994. Membership: DJBFA. Address: Lynoby Houedgade 78, DK-2800 Lynoby, Denmark.

VITEK Pavel, b. 30 September 1962, Olomouc, Czech Republic. Singer; Actor; Composer; Lyrics Author. Musical Education: Academy of Musical Art (Faculty of Dramatic Art); Conservatoire, Musical Singing. Career: Theatre Musicals: Pop Festival, 1984; Gypsies Go To Heaven, 1986; Some Like It Hot, 1987; Dracula, 1995-; TV Films: Creation of the World, 1988; About 100 various TV shows including own recital, To Find My World, 1988; Many video clips; Radio: 1994-96; Own talk show on radio frequence 1. Compositions: Scent of Your Skin, 1992; This Time I Love You Much Better, lyrics, 1993; Garden of Wishies, 1994; Amen With You, 1995; Heaven Full of Stars, lyrics, 1995. Recordings: Albums: She's got Her Day, 1988; Scent of Your Skin, 1992; Garden of Wishies, 1994; Lucky Star, 1995; Dracula, 1996. Honours: 2nd Prize, OIRT Festival Budapest, 1988; Prize of Finland, The Midnight Sun Song Festival, 1992. Memberships: Czech Association of Authors; Intergram. Hobbies: Fine Arts; Beautiful Cars; Antique; Garden; Good Wine. Current Management: Nota Bene Musical Londy'nska' 53, Prague 2, 12000, Czech Republic. Address: Pavel Vitek, Nota Bene Musical, Londy'nska' 53, 12000 Prague 2, Czech Republic.

VLAHAVAS Nicholas, b. 21 Apr 1951, London, England. Composer; Performer. Musical Education: Studied piano, guitar, flute; Goldsmiths' College, London. Career: Self-styled wandering minstrel, and techno troubadour, travelling world,

playing worldwide, 1976-; Played: Wigmore Hall; Queen Elizabeth Hall; Radio, television appearances: Greece; France; Australia; Switzerland; Live performer, jazz to classical; No commercial recordings; Founder of own latin-jazz quintet Seventh Wave performinf on London jazz circuit. Publications: A Complete Guide To Musical Invention Through The Scale-Mode-Chord Jungle. Memberships: Musicians' Union; Jazz Services. Hobbies: Learning; Travel. Address: 369A Upper Richmond Road, London SW15 5GJ, England.

VOGNAES Stig Peter, b. 21 Dec 1957, Denmark. Musician (guitar); Composer; Lyricist. 1 son, 1 daughter. Education: Teacher. Music Education: Music, University of Aarhus, Denmark. Career: Regular guest on national radio and TV in Denmark, 1975-; Guitarist, composer and lyricist with Hancats, 1989-. Recordings: Albums with Hancats: Allright-Ja!, 1990; Hancats, 1991; Eye 2 Eye, 1992. Memberships: KODA; Gramex; DJBFA. Current Management: Danartist. Address: Danartist, Overgade 41, DK-5100 Odense C, Denmark.

VOLCKE Ivan, Musician. Education: Selftaught Guitar, Vocals, Badhan, Brass Pedals. Career: Member, Group The Swigshift; Dranouter Festival, 1995; Den Ekster, 1996, 1997; Labadoux, 1997; Paulus Festival, 1997; Sloanthe Festival, 1997; Gooik Festival 2002, 1997; De Brakke Grond, Amsterdam, 1997; Foleys Irish Pub, Gent; Radio 1 De Groote Boodschap; Several Regional Radio and Television Appearances. Compositions: Jumpin The Fences; Dirty Wally; Friends Sadness; Something to Fear; Shut the Pub; A Whistler's Wedding. Recording: Tales From the Great Whiskey Book, 1996. Honours: Government Medal, Flute, 1986; 2nd Place, Youth Soloist Festival, 1986; Finale, Westtalent, 1995. Membership: Volksmuziekfederatie, Belgium. Hobby: Music. Current Management: KAFT Productions, Akkerwindelaan 20, 8791 Beveren-Leie, Belgium. Address: c/o Barrierestraat 49, 8940 Wervik, Belgium.

VOLCY Jean-Marc, b. 29 Jan 1966, Anse Royale. Cultural Officer; Musician (Guitar; Banjo; Percussion); Singer. m. Eudoxie Volcy, 4 daughters. Education: Degree in Voice Training; Selftaught Banjo and Guitar. Career: TV appearance, RFO, Reunion Island, 1994; Festival des Flaurallis Reunion Island, 1994; Radio appearance, RFI Bamako, 1993; MBF, 1995, 1996, 1997. Compositions: Musical Director, Three, musical play, 1995, 1996, 1997. Recordings: Debut album, sound track Sanmoi Swar Lo Zil St Pierre; Oseselwa and Sega of Seychelles. Publications: Debut album, Vandreni Sen and Musique Traditionelle Des Seychelles. Honours: Winner, Grand Prix D'Afrique Decouvert Des RFI, 1993; Winner, Festival Creole Song Contest, 1993, 1996. Hobbies: Cooking; Traditional Music; Watching videos. Address: Volcy c/o NAC, National Arts Council Mahe, Seychelles.

VOLLMER Brian Joseph, b. 30 June 1955, Kitchener, Ontario, Canada. Vocalist. m. Lynda Cowgill, 10 Aug 1991, 1 daughter. Musical Education: Bel canto method of singing. Career: Vocalist, heavy rock group Helix; Several tours with Helix to Europe; Tours, North America; Appearances numerous TV shows, MTV. Recordings: Albums: White Lace And Black Leather, 1978; Breaking Loose, 1979; No Rest For The Wicked, 1982; Walking The Razor's Edge, 1984; Long Way To Heaven, 1985; Wild In The Streets, 1988; Back For Another Taste, 1990; It's A Business Doing Pleasure, 1992. Honours: 2 nominations Canadian Juno Award; Heavy Metal Video of Year, Running Wild In The 21st Century. Current Management: William Seip Management. Address: 52 Terrence Street, London, Ontario N52 1C4, Canada.

VOLPELIERE-PIERROT Dan, b. 3 Feb 1944, Mauritius. Musician (congas, percussion, drums). m. Odette Dupras, 5, Dec 1973, 1 son, 1 daughter. Musical Education: Self-taught. Career: Played with: Doris Troy, 1968-69; Jackie Lomax, Klaus Vorman, The Toffs, 1970-72; Little Brother, Abi Ofarim, Ofarim and Winter, 1972-74; Saraband, Louis Veccio, Salsa Express, 1975-79; Garudas, Kassanga, The Tom Poole Blues Band, The Wish, Well Well, 1980-84; The Jason Falloon Experience, Renegade, 1987-89; Then Jerico (London), Raman, 1985-87; Ultimate Bitch, Blue Breakers, Eso Exo, Bitter, The Touch, Soft Verge, Third Force, Panic In Detroit, Strange Brew, Cosmic Steeplechaser, Stratagem, The Crystal Unicorn, Sleez, 1990-96. Recordings include: The Big Area, Then Jerico. Membership: Musicians' Union. Hobbies: Writing songs; Learning to play keyboards; Renovating French farmhouse. Current Management: The Session Connection. Address: 110-112 Disraeli Road, London SW15 2DX, England.

VOROS George Ladislaus, b. 5 Mar 1958, Swaziland. Musician (drums); Drum Teacher. Musical Education: Grade 8 Music Theory, Royal Schools; Military Band Certificate. Career: Member, South African bands: Neil Solomon; E'Void; Wozani; Numerous South African television appearances and sessions; Worked with Jimmy James and The Vagabonds, UK; Member, Stu Page Band, UK; Television: Stars In Your Eyes; Private drum studio, The Drum Workshop, 5 years. Recordings: The Love We Can Share, World Vision (charity single); Album: Come And Dance, Wozani. Publications: Book on drums, practice and performance, endorsed by Virgil Donati, Steve White and others. Honours: Best British Country Band, Stu Page Band, 1994. Membership: Musicians' Union (registered teacher). Hobby: Tai Chi Chuan. Address: Hayter & Shone Ltd Music Publishers, 19 Grove Hill, South Woodford, London E18 2JB, England.

VRAIT-WRIGHT Silvi, b. 28 Apr 1951, Kehra, Estonia. Singer; Music Teacher; English Teacher; Actress. 1 son. Education: Tartu University, Estonia, graduate, English, Philology, Language, Literature, 1974. Musical Education: Children's Music School, piano. Career: Lead singer, Fix (Estonia), 1976-83; Solo artist, 1983-; Rock opera; Porgy And Bess (Bess) by George Gershwin; Television specials: Light And Shade; Silvi And Her Friends; Silvi Vrait Sings, Eurovision Song Contest, 1994. Recordings: Albums: Silvi Vrait, 1985; Embrace, 1988; English Children's Songs; Single: Like The Sea, 1994; Album: Cosy And Warm, 1994. Hobbies: Tallinn ZONTA club; Astrology; Painting. Current Management: Rock Hotel Management, also self-managed. Address: Astangu 22-61, EE-00035 Tallinn, Estonia.

VRIENDS Peter, b. 31 October 1963, Rotterdam, The Netherlands. Midi Instruments. Education: Self educated. Career: Co-owner, record company essential dance music; Co-owner, record company basic beat recordings; Owner and Engineer, recording studio; Producing own compositions; Producing productions for third parties, mixing great variet of dance mix albums. Compositions: Pot of Gold; Joy; Love; ; Emotional Travellogue, album. Honour: Best House Record of the Year, Benelux, Pot of Gold, 1991. Memberships: SENA; IFPI; Stermra, Buma. Hobbies: Diving (scuba); Travelling; Theater; Movies; Sports. Address: Essential Dance Music BV, Nieuwe Binnenweg 19, 3014 GB Rotterdam, The Netherlands.

VUJICA Matija, b. 19 July 1963, Metkovic, Croatia. Singer. Education: Faculty of Economics, Zagreb. Musical Education: Private piano lessons. Career: Vocalist with group Gracia, 1990-; Concerts, tours and rock festivals all over Croatia, Austria, Germany, Slovenia and Sweden; Many television and radio appearances. Recordings: Hit singles: Rolana; Zaplesimo; Albums: Gracia;

Vrijeme Snova (Time Of Dreams); Jer Tu Ima Neki Crni Vrag (Black Devil Spies Upon Us All); Dancetheria; Forte Forte. Publications: Croatian Awards: Ethno Dance Award 1994; Most Original Look, 1994. Membership: Croatian Musical Union (HGU). Hobbies: Fashion; Design. Current Management: Vladimir Mihalek, Croatian Musical Art. Address: c/o Croatian Music Art, Trnjanska 88, Zagreb, Croatia.

VUVU J L, b. 12 Dec 1968, Uige, Angola. Musician (keyboards);Songwriter. 2 sons. Education: Car mechanic. Career: Street musician in Zaire (as Abute Bango Likonga); Club musician in Angola (as Parisien J L); Tour of Zaire; Residency in Cafe Rio; Now relocated to UK as dance musician. Recordings: Debut album being recorded, own compositions. Publications: Listed in Zairians And Angolans. Membership: Musicians' Union. Current Management: Basky-Capitao, Love Life M P M. Address: 82A Plashet Road, Plaistow, London, E1 0RQ, England.

VYVÉRE Pascale, b. 31 May 1966, Brussels; Belgium. Singer; Composer; Songwriter; Musician (Piano, Accordion); Actress. Education: Fine Arts Degree; Musical Theory, Harmony, Piano, Song Writing, Singing and Performing Lessons. Career: Festivals: Botanique, Brussels, 1993, 1994, 1997; Francofolies, Spa, 1994, 1997; Festival De Marne, 1993; Chorus Des Hauts-De-Seine, 1994; Many concerts in France, Belgium and Switzerland; Roles in: Chants De Femmes, Film, R Olivier, 1994; La Voix Humaine, J Cocteau, 1996; La Dame De Chez Maxim, G Feydeau, 1996. Compositions: Words and/or music of many French songs. Recordings: Single: Solo, 1994; Contributor, album: J G Coulange, Enfin Seul, 1994; Solo album: Je Vous Attends, 1997. Honours: Prize Sentier Des Halles and Prize Adiam-92, Tremplin Chorus Hauts-De-Seine, 1993; Prize Auditeurs France-Inter/RTBF/RSR, 1994. Membership: SABAM, Brussels. Current Management: Tango, ASBL, 5 Av Des Vanneaux, 1420 Braine-L'Alleud, Belgium.

W

WADE Terri (Teresa), b. 3 Mar 1957, Staffordshire, England. Singer; Entertainer. m. David Bryan, 6 Oct 1987, 1 son. Education: College of Further Education. Career: Sang for Mecca, Top Rank Dance bands; Touring bands, session work for local studios; Career as Terri Wade, 1980-; Television: Walk on parts: Crossroads; Keynotes; Sky Star Search; New Faces, 1986; Hippodrome, London; Stringfellows to promote Single Girl; Interviewed on radio stations all over country; Performed over 1,000 live shows. Recordings: Light, 1982; Single Girl, 1985, number 11 (Gay Top 20). Honours: Best Vocalist, NSSCEP, 1986, South Skeffs, 1990. Memberships: Musicians' Union; Equity. Hobbies: Tennis; Squash; Table Tennis. Current Management: Ray Stanton Entertainments. Address: 294 Ash Bank Road, Werrington, Stoke-on-Trent ST9 OJS, England.

WAEGEMAN Geert, b. 23 September 1965, Asse, Belgium. Composer; Musician; Producer. Education: Sociology; Courses in Musicology. Career: Member of Cro Magnon, Cooperation with vocalist Anna Homler, USA and Percussionist, Pavel Fajt, Czech Republic; Composed Tunes for Belgium Radio and Television, Theatre and Audiovisuals; Worked with Bi Ma Dance Company, London, England. Compositions: Zapp, 1992; Macaronic Sines, 1995; Bull, 1997; Corne De Vache, 1997. Recordings: Zapp, 1992; Macaronic Sines, 1995; Bull, 1997; Corne De vache, 1997. Hobbies: Nature; Spiritual Literature. Address: Voorzorgstraat 17, B-3010 Kessel-Lo, Belgium.

WAGER Henrik Rickard, b. 14 Mar 1969, Manchester, England. Singer. Musical Education: Birmingham University; Birmingham Conservatoire. Career: Founder member, Brave New World, 1992-93; Ascension, 1993-94; Singer with The Flying Pickets; Performed on Warning Tour, 1994; 5 Alive In '95 Tour; Director, Inner Sactum Studio; Inner Sanctum Productions; Director of Ulum Jingle Shed. Memberships: Musicians' Union; Equity. Hobbies: Dance, modern and jazz. Current Management: Self-managed.

WAGHORN Gary, b. 9 May 1949, Chatham, Kent, England. Musician (guitar, banjo). m. Linda Evans, 15 Aug 1970, 1 daughter. Career: Lead guitarist for Bonnie Tyler; Lead guitarist, vocalist, Slack Alice; Lead guitarist, backing vocals, Mountain Child. Recordings: Album: Diamond Cut, Bonnie Tyler; 6 singles with Bonnie Tyler; Single: Night Pilots, Mountain Child. Memberships: PRS; Musicians' Union. Hobbies: Music; Reading.

WAGNER Bill (William), b. 12 Feb 1920, Warsaw, Indiana, USA. Record Producer; Trumpet Arranger. m. Vicki, 23 May 1942, 2 daughters. Education: Mechanical Engineering, Purdue University; Pilot, US Air Force. Career: Personal Manager for The Four Freshmen; Pete Christlieb; Page Cavanaugh; Si Zentner; Vicki McClure; Faunda Hinton; Michael Dees; Sandy Graham; Over 100 record dates for: Serenade In Blue, USAF Band, Washington DC. Compositions: 5 jingles (musak); Airmen Of Note, USAF Band. Recordings: Producer of over 1000 records to date with various artistes including: 23 albums, The Four Freshmen; 2 albums, Sandy Graham; 3 albums, Page Cavanaugh. Memberships: NARAS; AFTRA; AGMA. Hobbies: Bridge; Reading; Music; Golf. Address: 14343 Addison Street #221, Sherman Oaks, CA 91423, USA.

WAGONER Porter, b. 12 Aug 1930, West Plains, Missouri, USA. Country Singer; Songwriter. Career: Worked at radio station; Cast member, television series Ozark Jubilee; Recording artist, 1954; Regular member, Grand Ole Opry, 1957-; Television series with own band The Wagonmasters, 1960s-70s; Co-host with singers Norma Jean, Dolly Parton; Regular recording partnership with Dolly Parton, 1967-74; Regular tours and concerts with All-Girls Band. Recordings: 81 Country hit singles include: A Satisfied Mind (US Country Number 1); Eat Drink And Be Merry; Your Old Love Letters; Sorrow On The Rocks; Misery Loves Company (US Country Number 1); The Green Green Grass Of Home (later recorded by Tom Jones and Elvis Presley); The Cold Hard Facts Of Life; The Carroll County Accident; Duets with Dolly Parton: The Last Thing On My Mind; Just Someone I Used To Know; Daddy Was An Old Time Preacher Man; If Teardrops Were Pennies; Please Don't Stop Loving Me (US Country Number 1); Albums include: A Satisfied Mind, 1956; A Slice Of Life, 1962; Old Log Cabin For Sale, 1965; The Thin Man From West Plains, 1965; The Bottom Of The Bottle, 1968; Howdy Neighbour Howdy, 1970; The Farmer, 1973; Porter, 1977; Today, 1979; Natural Wonder, 1982; One For The Road, 1983; Porter Wagoner, 1986; with Norma Jean: Porter Wagoner Show, 1963; In Person, 1964; Live - On The Road, 1966; with Dolly Parton: Just Between You And Me, 1968; Just The Two Of Us, 1969; Always, Always, 1969; Porter Wayne And Dolly Rebecca, 1970; Once More, 1971; The Right Combination, 1972; Together Always, 1972; Love And Music, 1973; We Found It, 1973; Porter'N'Dolly, 1974; Say Forever You'll Be Mine, 1975; Porter Wagoner & Dolly Parton, 1980. Honours include: CMA Awards: Vocal Group Of The Year, 1968; Vocal Duo of the Year, 1970, 1971. Address: c/o Porter Wagoner Enterprises, PO Box 290785, Nashville, TN 37229, USA.

WAILER Bunny (Neville O'Riley Livingston), b. Kingston, Jamaica. Singer; Songwriter. Career: Harmony singer, songwriter, and occasional lead singer, reggae group Bob Marley and the Wailers, 1960s and 1970s; Solo recording artist, on own Solomonic record label, 1974-. Recordings: Albums include: with the Wailers: Catch A Fire; Burnin'; Solo albums: Blackheart Man; Protest; Struggle; In A Fathers House; Bunny Wailer Sings The Wailers; Tribute To The Hon. Robert Nesta Marley; Rock'n'Groove; Hook Line And Sinker; Roots Radics Rockers Reggae; Marketplace; Bunny Wailer Live; Roots Man Skanking; Rule Dancehall; Liberation; Gumption. Address: c/o Performers of the World, 8901 Melrose Avenue, 2nd Floor, West Hollywood, CA 90069, USA.

WAINWRIGHT III Loudon, b. 5 Sept 1946, Chapel Hill, North Carolina, USA. Singer; Songwriter; Musician (guitar). m. Kate McGarrigle, divorced 1977. Education: Studied acting, Pittsburgh. Career: Singer, folk clubs, New York and Boston, 1968; Recording artiste, 1969-; Concerts include: Support to Everly Brothers, UK; Cambridge Folk Festival, 1972; Royal Festival Hall, 1992; Television includes: Several episodes, M.A.S.H.; Episode of Soldier Soldier; Stage performances: The Birthday Party; Pump Boys And Dinettes; Own show for BBC Scotland, Loudon and Co. Compositions include: Glad To See You've Got Religion; Motel Blues; Be Careful, There's A Baby In The House; The Picture, 1992; Dreaming, 1995. Recordings: Albums: Loudon Wainwright III, 1969; Album II, 1971; Album III, 1972; Attempted Moustache, 1974; Unrequited, 1975; T-Shirt, 1976; Exam, 1978; A Live One, 1979; Fame And Wealth, 1983; I'm Alright, 1984; More Love Songs, 1986; Therapy, 1989; History; Career Moves, 1995; Grown Man, 1995; Little Ship, 1997. Honours: Grammy nominations, 1985, 1986. Current Management: Rosebud Agency, 636 Shrader Street, San Francisco, CA 94117, USA.

WAITE John, b. 4 July 1955, England. Singer; Songwriter; Musician (bass, harmonica). Career: Member, The Babys, 1976-81; Solo artiste, 1981-; Singer, Bad English, 1989-91. Recordings: Albums: with The Babys: The Babys, 1976; Broken Heart, 1977; Head First, 1978; Union Jacks, 1980; On The Edge, 1980; Anthology, 1981; Solo albums: Ignition, 1982; No Brakes, 1984; Mask Of Smiles, 1985; Rovers Return, 1987; The Essential, 1991; Temple Bar (US only), 1995; with Bad English: Bad English, 1989; Backlash, 1991; Singles: Solo: Missing You (Number 1, US); Change; with Bad English: When I See You Smile (Number 1, US). Current Management: Gold Mountain Entertainment. Address: 120 West 44th Street, Suite 704, New York, NY 10036, USA.

WAITS Tom, b. 7 Dec 1949, Pamona, California, USA. Singer; Songwriter; Musician (piano, accordion); Actor. m. Kathleen Brennan, 31 Dec 1981, 1 son, 1 daughter. Career: Recording artist, 1973-; Concerts include: Ronnie Scott's jazz club, 1976; London Palladium, 1979; The Black and White Night - Roy Orbison And Friends, 1987; Actor, films including: Paradise Alley; Wolfen; Stone Boy; One From The Heart; The Outsiders; Rumblefish; The Cotton Club; Down By Law; Cold Feet; The Fisher King; At Play In The Fields Of The Lord; Queen's Logic; Bram Stoker's Dracula; Coffee And Cigarettes. Compositions include: Ol' 55, The Eagles, 1974; Angel Wings, Rickie Lee Jones, 1983; Downtown Train, Rod Stewart, 1990; One From The Heart (film soundtrack), 1981; Co-writer (with wife), musical Frank's Wild Years, 1986; Score, Alice In Wonderland, Hamburg, 1992. Recordings: Albums: Closing Time, 1973; The Heart Of Saturday Night, 1974; Nighthawks At The Diner, 1975; Small Change, 1976; Foreign Affairs, 1977; Blue Valentine, 1978; Heartattack And Vine, 1980; One From The Heart, 1982; The Asylum Years - Bounced Check, 1983; Anthology, 1983; Swordfishtrombones, 1983; Raindogs, 1985; Frank's Wild Years, 1987; Big Time, 1988; Stay Awake, 1988; Bone Machine, 1992; Black Rider, 1993; Contributor, compilation albums: Lost In The Stars, 1984; Stay Awake, 1988; Contributor, Night On Earth (film soundtrack), 1992. Honours: Oscar Nomination, One From The Heart, 1982; Grammy Award, Best Alternative Music, Bone Machine, 1993.

WAKEFIELD MILLSAPS Wilma, b. 13 Feb 1949, Monroe Co, Tennessee, USA. Singer; Songwriter; Musician (guitar). m. Bill Millsaps, 13 Nov 1967, 1 son, 1 daughter. Musical Education: Apprenticed under Tommy Scott. Career: Travelled extensively across USA with husband Bill Millsaps and their Snowbird Mountain Band; Appears twice weekly on satellite TV on Snowbird Mountain Bluegrass. Recordings: Albums include: Legendary Friends of The Snowbird Mountain Band, with John Hartford, Uncle Josh Graves, Benny Martin, others. Publications: Bluegrass Unlimited, by Dr Ivan Tribe, 1992. Memberships: BMI; IBMA. Hobbies: Hiking; Photography; Genealogy. Current Management: Bill Millsaps. Address: PO Box 85, Robbinsville, NC 28771, USA.

WAKEMAN Adam, b. 11 Mar 1974, Windsor, Berkshire, England. Musician (keyboards); Vocalist; Musical Director. Musical Education: All 8 practical and theory Asscociated Board exams, 1993-94. Career: Toured most of Europe, America, South America, UK with Wakeman With Wakeman band alongside father, Rick, 1995; Performing Musical Director with Cirque Surreal, touring UK. Recordings: Albums include: Wakeman with Wakeman; No Expense Spared; Memories Of A Victorian Age; The Official Bootleg; Tapestries, 1995; Vignettes, 1996; Solo albums include: Soliloquy; 100 Years Overtime; Real World Trilogy, 1997; 1 track on Yes tribute album with new band Jeronimo Road. Honours: Keyboard magazine, Readers Poll in Best New Talent Category, 1994. Memberships: Musicians' Union; PRS. Hobbies: Golf; Cycling. Current Management: Jeronimo Road Management, Felmersham Hall Studios, One The Row, The High Road, Felmersham, Bedfordshire MK43

7HP, England. Address: Bajonor House, 2 Bridge Street, Peel, Isle Of Man, UK.

WAKEMAN Dusty, b. 31 Aug 1953, Houston, Texas, USA. Musician (bass guitar); Record Producer; Engineer. m. Szu Wang, 5 Apr 1986. Education: University of Texas. Musical Education: Studied with Jamie Faunt. Career: Mixer, engineer, bassist, numerous recordings, 1986-; Bassist, Michelle Shocked UK tour, 1989. Recordings: Mixer, engineer, producer, bassist on albums by: Dwight Yoakam; Rosie Flores; Lucinda Williams; Buck Owens; Michelle Shocked; Los Lobos; Jackson Browne; Wynton Marsalis; Tom Russell. Honours: 2 Grammy Awards: Cryin', Roy Orbison/kd lang, 1987; Ain't That Lonely Yet, Dwight Yoakam, 1993. Current Management: Bonnie Simmons. Address: PO Box 5895, Berkeley, CA 94705, USA.

WAKEMAN Rick, b. 18 May 1949, London, England. Musician (keyboards). Career: Member, UK progressive rock group Yes, 1971-74, 1976-80, 1990; International concerts include: Yesshows '91 - Round The World in 80 Dates tour, 1991; Film: Yessongs, 1973; Solo artiste, 1974-. Compositions include: Score for Phantom Of The Opera, 1991. Recordings: Albums: with Yes: Fragile, 1971; Yessongs, 1973; Tales From Topographic Oceans, 1973; Going For The One, 1977; Union, 1991; Yesstory, 1991; Solo albums: The Six Wives Of Henry VIII, 1973; Journey To The Centre Of The Earth, 1974; The Myths And Legends Of King Arthur And The Knights Of The Round Table, 1975; White Rock, 1976; No Earthly Connections, 1976; Criminal Record, 1977; Rhapsodies, 1979; 1984, 1981; Beyond The Planets, 1984; The Gospels, 1987; Soundtrack to 1982 World Cup film Golé!, 1983; as Anderson Bruford Wakeman Howe: Anderson Bruford Wakeman Howe, 1989. Honours include: Gold Ticket, Madison Square Garden, 1978. Current Management: BDA, Bryson House, Chiltern Road, Culceth, Warrington, Cheshire WA3 4LL, England.

WALDEN John "White Boy", b. 23 Oct 1948, London, England. Musician (harmonica); Blues singer. m. Natalie Marjory Gellineau, 26 Dec 1982, 1 son, 1 daughter. Musical Education: Self-taught; Influenced by Sonny Boy Williamson and Little Walter Jacobs. Career: Took up harmonica when child; Started to play blues aged 13 with Bespoke Tailor Unit; Several European tours with John Walden Workshop, late 1960s; Madison Blues Band, 1990s; Reformed John Walden's Blues Band, 1997. Recordings: Many sessions, soundtracks, commercials; John Walden's Blues Band, CD, 1997. Honour: Acknowledged as one of the World's best blues harmonica players; Medal Winner, European Harp (Harmonica) Festival, Trossingham, Germany, 1996. Membership: Musicians' Union. Hobbies: Music; Photography; Bonsai; Fish-keeping; Reading; Computers. Address: 90 Shooters Hill Road, Blackheath, London SE3 8RL, England.

WALDEN Myron, b. 18 Oct 1973, Miami, Florida, USA. Musician (alto saxophone) Songwriter; Arranger. Education: La Guardia High School of Music and Art; Harlem School of the Arts. Musical Education: Manhattan School Of Music. Career: Performed and recorded with Ron Carter; Benny Golson; Winard Harper; Eddie Henderson; Kevin Hays; Mulgrew Miller. Recordings: Night Watch, Winard Harper; Be Yourself, Ravi Coltrane; Akilli, Ravi Coltrane; Bop, Carl Allen and Vincent Herring. Honours: Young And Upcoming Artist, Yamaha Corporation, 1990; Saxophonist Of The Year, Harlem School Of The Arts. Current Management: c/o Preston Powell, Jazzateria Inc, 112 W 72nd Street, #2F, New York, NY 10023, USA.

WALDEN Narada Michael, b. 23 Apr 1952, Kalamazoo, Michigan, USA. Singer; Musician (drums, keyboards); Record Producer; Songwriter. m. Anukampa Coles. Education: West Michigan

University, 1970-72. Career: Drummer, with John McLaughlin, 1974-76; President, Perfection Light Productions, 1976-; Recording artist, songwriter, producer, 1976-; Board of Directors, Bay Area Music Awards, San Francisco, 1992. Recordings: Solo albums: Garden Of Love Light, 1977; I Cry, I Smile, 1978; Awakening, 1979; The Dance Of Life, 1979; Victory, 1980; Confidence, 1982; Looking At You, Looking At Me, 1983; The Nature Of Things, 1985; with John McLaughlin: Apocalypse, 1974; Visions Of The Emerald Beyond, 1975; Inner Worlds, 1976; Other recordings as musician: Teaser, Tom Bolin, 1975; Wired, Jeff Beck, 1976; My Spanish Heart, Chick Corea, 1976; Jaco Pastorius, Jaco Pastorius, 1976; Black Market, Weather Report, 1976; Loading Zone, Roy Buchanan, 1977; Velvet Darkness, Allan Holdsworth, 1977; Exposure, Robert Fripp, 1979; Oneness, Santana, 1979; Clarke Duke Project 2, Stanley Clarke, 1983; Patti Austin, Patti Austin, 1984; Teaser, Angela Bofill, 1984; Who's Zoomin' Through, Aretha Franklin, 1985; Through The Storm, Aretha Franklin, 1989; As musician and producer: Hero, Clarence Clemons, 1985; While The City Sleeps, George Benson, 1986; As producer: with Sister Sledge: Love Somebody Today, 1980; All American Girls, 1981; with Whitney Houston: Whitney Houston, 1985; I'm Your Baby Tonight, 1990. Honours: NARAS Award: Songwriter Of The Year, 1986; Grammy, 1986; ASCAP Awards: Producer of the Year; Songwriter of the Year; Publisher of the Year, 1987; Billboard Magazine: Producer of the Year, 1986, 1987.

WALDEN Natan, b. 3 November 1947, Bystrzyca, Klodska, Poland. Musician (bass, keyboards); Composer. m. Ewa Kryger-Walden, 5 January 1974, 1 son, 1 daughter. Education: MFA, Music Education, Lund University, Sweden, 1982; Music Producer Degree, Malmö Academi of Music, Sweden, 1985. Appointments: Poland: Nastolatki (Teenagers); Bassplayer with legendary singer, Niemen; USA: Live work, studio work commercials with Billy Cobham and Valerie Simpson; Sweden: Studio work, Theater-musical, Röda Orm; Animalen; Blood Brothers; TV and live works with Toots Thielemans; Nestor Marconi; Lill Babs, Eurovision Song Contest; Musical Director, many TV shows on Swedish TV; Many theme songs for TV serials, Sköna Söndag; Vem Tar Vem; Helt Apropa; In Denmark: The Most; Bassplayer in live concert versions of a musical Chees; with 3 different orchestras: Danish Radio Orchestra; Odense Symphonic Orchestra; Sonderjisk Symphonic Orchestra. Honours: Golden Rose Montreux for music prod of The Prize Finalist for Outstndng Achievement in Popular Arts; International Emmy Awards, 1987. Membership: Swedish Society of Popular Music Composers. Current Management: Wiktor Kubiak Management. Address: 14 Henrietta Str, London WC2, England.

WALDRON Tom, b. 1 Feb 1960, Illinois, USA. m. Lorraine, 2 July 1988, 1 son, 2 daughters. Education: BS, MS, Civil/Structural Engineering. Career: Lead praise and worship band, Red Hill Lutheran Church, Tustin, California; Singer at other churches. Recordings: Recording of original, contemporary Christian music. Memberships: Gospel Music Association; NACAS; BMI. Hobbies: Carpentry; Golf. Current Management: Never Thirst Again Ministries. Address: PO Box 10092, Santa Ana, CA 92711-0092, USA.

WALICKI Peter Englundh, b. 4 February 1950, Denmark. Musician (Drums, Keyboards); Songwriter; Singer. m. Hanne Jakobsen, 11 May 1974, 1 son, 1 daughter. Education: Music Teacher, Danish Music School. Career: Scool Band, 1960; Doctor Phill, 1967; Several Dance bands on DFDs, 1971; Golden Diamond, 1980; Grethe Ingmann and Sunset, 1984; A/S Rockkompagniet, 1985; Hit the Hay, 1996; A/S Rockkompagniet, 1998. Compositions: Ann Mari, 1975; Habet Er Gront, 1977; Dancing Dynamite,

1996. Recordings: Ann Mari, 1975; Habet Er Gront, 1977; A/S Rockkompagniet Several Songs, 1985-98; Nikki Hokey, 1982; Mooreen, 1982. Publication: TV Show, Rock Palazt, ZDF Germany with Joe Bank's Rock Medicine Show, 1986. Memberships: KODA; NBC; DMF. Hobbies: Composing; Computers. Current Management: Strike Records, own company. Address: Peter Englundh Walicki, Lysholm Alle 64, DK 4690, Haslev, Denmark.

WALKER Billy, b. Ralls, Texas, USA. Musician (guitar); Singer. m. Bettie, 6 Feb 1978. Career: Toured with Elvis Presley, Texas, 1954; Performances include: Hollywood Bowl; Las Vegas; Hee Haw; Nashville Now; Crook & Chase; Grand Ole Opry Show, 1960-; Music City Tonight; Yesteryear; The Nashville Network; The Statler Brothers; Jimmy Dean Show; Dick Clark's American Bandstand; Billy Walker's Country Carnival, 3 years; 32 State Fairs; Tours: Austria; Bermuda; England; Guam; Hawaii; Ireland; Italy; Japan; Korea; Philippines; Japan; Spain; Sweden; Switzerland; Germany. Recordings: Over 100 chart records; 32 Top 10 hits; Number 1 hit singles: Funny How Time Slips Away; Charlie's Shoes; Cross The Brazos At Waco; A Million And One; When A Man Loves A Woman; Sing Me A Love Song To Baby;Also: She Goes Walking Through My Mind; In Del Rio; Gone Our Endless Love; Curtains On The Window; Come A Little Bit Closer; Word Games; If I'm Losing You; Don't Stop In My World; Adam's Side (most requested wedding song, US); Latest album: Larger Than Life. Publications: Larger Than Life (autobiography), due for publication 1998. Hobbies: Golf; Fishing. Current Management: Bettie Crook, Artist Management. Address: PO Box 618, Hendersonville, TN 37077-0618, USA.

WALKER Eddie, b. 31 Oct 1948, Middlesbrough, England. Singer; Musician (guitar); Songwriter. m. Judith Ann, 22 Mar 1969, 1 son. Education: Charles Trevelyan Technical College, Newcastle. Career: Concert, folk festival and club appearances throughout UK, Germany, Belgium, Netherlands, Italy, Austria, Denmark, Slovenia, Croatia, Switzerland, Ireland, Luxembourg, Hong Kong, New Zealand; Television and radio appearances: Tyne Tees TV; BBC Radio 2; BBC Radio Scotland. Recordings: Solo albums: Everyday Man, 1977; Castle Cafe, 1981; Red Shoes On My Feet, 1983; Picking My Way, 1985; with guitarist John James: Carolina Shout!, 1990; Sidesteppin, 1993. Honours: Winner of Songwriter Competition, Stolen My Heart Away, 1982. Address: 33 The Grove, Brookfield, Middlesbrough, Cleveland TS5 8DT, England.

WALKER Junior (Autrey Dewalt II), b. 1942, Blythesville, Arizona, USA. Musician (saxophone); Vocalist. Career: Founder, Junior Walker & The All Stars, 1961-; Concerts include: Miami Pop Festival, 1968; Jazz & Blues Festival, Ann Arbor, Michigan, 1972; American Bandstand's 25th Anniversry Special, ABC TV, 1977. Recordings: Albums: Shotgun, 1965; Soul Session, 1966; Road Runner, 1966; Home Cookin', 1969; Greatest Hits, 1969; What Does It Take To Win Your Love, 1970; A Gasses, 1970; Rainbow Funk, 1971; Peace And Understanding Is Hard To Find, 1973; Sax Appeal, 1977; Whopper Bopper Show Stopper, 1977; Blow The House Down, 1981; Greatest Hits, 1982; Singles: Shot Gun (Number 1 US R&B Chart), 1965; Do The Boomerang, 1965; Shake And Fingerpop, 1965; (I'm A Roadrunner), 1966; How Sweet It Is (To Be Loved By You), 1966; Money (That's What I Want) Part 1, 1966; Pucker Up Buttercup, 1967; Shoot Your Shot, 1967; Come See About me, 1968; Hip City Pt 2, 1968; Home Cookin', 1969; What Does It Take (To Win Your Love) (Number 1 US R&B), 1969; These Eyes, 1969; Gotta Hold On To This Feeling, 1970; Do You See My Love (For You Growing), 1970; Take Me Girl, I'm Ready, 1971; Walk In The Night, 1972; Way Back Home, 1973; Guest on: Urgent, Foreigner, 1981.

WALKER Mark Robert Thomas, b. 7 March 1962, London, England. Musician (drums); Lyricist; Songwriter; Journalist. m. Claire Cooper, 6 Aug 1988, 1 son, 2 daughters. Musical Education: Taught at school by Sam Bryant (RIP). Education: BEd Hons. Career: Tours with the Tin Gods, UK, Europe; Appeared at Lausanne Festival, Switzerland, 1991; Television: Hangar 17, BBC1; Radio: Live sessions for Capital Radio and GLR with Peachey Keen and World Of Leather; TV appearances: House band drummer for the Jack Dee Show; Hangar 17; Blue Peter; This Morning; Nightfever, with Rolf Harris; Solo Performer of drum shows and clinics; UK tour with Rolf Harris, 1997-98. Recordings: St Mark's Place, World Of Leather (debut album); The Coronation Street Album; Invisible History, Martin, Okasili; Private Party, Akin; Numerous recording sessions with producers Robin Miller; Faney; Colin Fairley; Jeff Foster; Composed theme tune for Airdrum (cartoon series). Memberships: Musicians' Union; PAMRA. Hobbies: Parenthood; Cycling. Current Management: Active Entertainment Management. Address: 165 Green Lane, London SE9 3SZ, England.

WALKER Nicholas David, b. 11 June 1955, Manchester, England. Musician (saxophone). m. Melissa Howell, 1 July 1983, 1 son, 2 daughters. Musical Education: City of Leeds College of Music. Career: Musician with Captain Moonlight; Macondo; Corner Pocket; King Salsa; Baritone Madness; Played at Malta Jazz Festival; Imatra Festival, Finland; Capital Music Festival; Brighton Festival. Compositions include: Souvenir; Right Mrs Wright; Migration; Sophie. Publications: Let's Get Potting - The Alternative Pool Players Approach. Recordings: with Corner Pocket: Migration; with Jazz Devils: Out Of The Dark; with Ute: Free To Be; with King Salsa: Chango. Honours: with Macondo, joint winners, GLAA Young Jazz Musician of Year, 1981. Membership: Musicians' Union. Hobby: Family. Current Management: CPM.

WALKER Scott (Noel Scott Engel), b. 9 Jan 1944, Hamilton, Ohio, USA. Singer; Songwriter; Musician (bass). m. Mette Teglbjaerg, divorced, 1 daughter. Education: Fine Arts foundation course. Musical Education: Double bass lessons. Career: Member, The Routers, 1963; Member, Dalton Brothers, 1964; Member, Walker Brothers, 1965-67; Regular television appearances; Concerts include: UK tour with Roy Orbison and Lulu, 1966; UK tour with the Troggs, 1966; Far East tour with Yardbirds and Roy Orbison, 1967; UK tour with Jimi Hendrix, 1967; Solo artiste, 1967-; Concerts include: UK tour, 1968; Weekly show, BBC, 1969; Walker Brothers Reunion, 1975-78. Recordings: Albums: with the Walker Brothers: Take It Easy With The Walker Brothers, 1966; Portrait, 1966; Images, 1967; No Regrets, 1976; Lines, 1977; Nite Flights, 1978; After The Lights Go Out, 1990; No Regrets - The Best Of The Walker Brothers, 1992; Solo albums: Scott, 1967; Scott 2, 1968; Scott 3, 1969; Scott 4, 1970; Til The Band Comes In, 1971; The Moviegoer, 1972; Any Day Now, 1973; Stretch, 1974; We Had It All, 1974; Scott Walker Plays Jacques Brel, 1981; Climate Of Hunter, 1984; Boy Child, 1990; Tilt, 1995; Hit singles: with the Routers: Let's Go, 1963; with The Walker Brothers: Make It Easy On Yourself (Number 1, UK), 1965; My Ship Is Coming In, 1966; The Sun Ain't Gonna Shine Any More, (Number 1, UK) 1966; No Regrets, 1976; Solo: Joanna, 1968; Lights Of Cincinnati, 1969. Current Management: Negus-Fancey Co., 78 Portland Road, London W11 4LQ, England.

WALKER SMITH Nicola, b. 18 Feb 1964, Batley, West Yorkshire, England. Singer. m. Geoff Smith, 16 Sept 1989, twin sons. Musical Education: BA Hons, Music, Electronics, Keele University, 1987; MA Music Theatre, Birmingham University, 1988. Career: Worldwide concert appearances; Television and radio includes: In Tune, BBC Radio 3; Midnight Oil; Music In Our Time; The Late Show, BBC2; Other radio broadcasts worldwide. Recordings: Albums: The Garden, 1991; Gas Food Lodging, 1993; Fifteen Wild Decembers, 1995; Black Flowers, with the Geoff Smith Band, 1997; L'imboscata, with Franco Battiato, 1997. Publications: American Originals (co-author with Geoff Smith), 1994. Honours: Winston Churchill Fellowship, 1992. Hobbies: Gardening; Old English crafts. Current Management: Keith Armstrong, Kitchenware, St Thomas' Street Stables, Newcastle Upon Tyne NE1 4LE, England. Address: Ash Tree Cottage, Royd Road, Meltham, West Yorkshire HD7 3BG, England.

WALLACE Angus, b. 7 April 1968, Girlsborough, Northants, England. Education: Media Productions, School of Recording, Brixton, London, 1987. Career: Own Recording Studio, age 18. Recordings: Album tracks for: Love and Rockets; Spiritualized; The Fall; Natasha Atlas (Transglobal Underground); Live Drums, recorded for The Prodigy. Honours: Ampex Golden Reel Award, 1994; Gold Disc, world wide sales, Fiend with Violin by The Fall, 1996. Hobbies: Architecture; Travel. Current Management: GMM Management, Coton, NN6 8RF, England. Address: Far Heath, Guilsborough, Northants, NN6 8RH, England.

WALLACE Robert Andrew, b. 21 Nov 1951, Glasgow, Scotland. Musician (pipes). 1 son, 1 daughter. Career: Member, folk band Whistlebinkies, 1974-; Appeared on television and radio with RSNO, Scottish Ensemble, John Cage, Yehudi Menuhin. Recordings: 5 albums with Whistlebinkies; Solo albums: Chance Was A Fine Thing, 1982; Piper Of Distinction, 1990. Publications: Glasgow Collection Of Bagpipe Music. Honours: Gold Medal, Oban, 1985; Bratach Gorm (Blue Banner), London, 1989. Memberships: Musicians' Union; CPA; Piobaireachd Society. Hobbies: Music; Reading. Current Managment: Rick Standley, Jester Management and Promotion Ltd. Address: 41 Hamilton Drive, Glasgow G12 8DW, Scotland.

WALLEME Christophe, b. 1964. Musician (acoustic bass). Musical Education: Private lessons with M Kazoran; Hein Van de Guyn; Césarius Alvim; Training with: QUEST; Kenny Barron's rhythm section. Career: Member, PRYSM; Manuel Rocheman Trio; David Patois Trio, Quintet; Sarah Lazarus Quartet; Lois Winsberg Quintet; Jean-Pierre Como Quintet; Jean-Loup Longnon Sextet and Big Band; Played numerous clubs, Paris; Festivals, France; Played with: Tom Harrell; Ted Curson; Jean-Loup Longnon; Rick Margitza; Sylvain Beuf; Eric Barret; Richard Galliano; Philip Catherine; Christian Escoudé; N'Guyen Lee; Stephanie Crawford; Walter Davis Junior; Barry Altschul; René Urtreger; Michel Graillier; Alain Jean-Marie; Georges Arvanitas; Jacky Terrasson; Jean-Pierre Como; Denuis Badault; Bob Mover; George Brown; Aldo Romano; Teacher, EDIM, 1986-. Recordings: Bop For Sale, Ludovic de Preissac Quintet, 1989; Correspondence, Daniel Beaussier Quartet, 1990; Ciao Mon Coeur, Elizabeth Caumont, 1993; Sanscrit, Daniel Beaussier Quartet, 1993; Impro Primo, Sylvain Beuf Quartet, 1993; Cyclades, Jean-Loup Lognon Big Band, 1994; PRYSM, PRYSM, 1995; Tropic City, Manuel Rocheman Trio, 1995; Express Paris-Rome, Jean-Pierre Como Quintet, 1996; Louis Winsberg Quintet. Honours: Solist Award, La Défense National Jazz Contest, 1988; First Prize, Jazz Et Polar Contest, 1991; First Prize, La Défense National Jazz Contest, 1994. Address: 16 Rue des Eglantines, 91130 Ris-Orangis, France.

WALLER Paul, b. 1961, London, England. Record Producer; Remixer; Songwriter. 2 sons, 1 daughter. Recordings: for: Björk; Soul II Soul; Naughty By Nature; Lisa Stansfield; Baby Face. Membership: Musicians' Union. Current Management: Paul Kennedy, 1 2 One Management, PO Box 6627, London N22 4JZ, England.

WALLGREN Henrik, b. 10 September 1965, Gothenburg, Sweden. Singer Songwriter. m. Katarina Wallgren, 24 June 1988, 2 daughters. Education: Selftaught. Career: Formed ORO, 1990; For Gothenburg Film Festival: Metropolis, 1994; Total King Kong, 1996; Joined Den Fule, 1994; Solo album, 1996. Compositions: New Music to Mother Curage, 1994; New Music to Nosferatu, 1995. Recordings: Milk & Concrete, 1990; Iron-Storm, 1992; Ragamedon..2048, 1993; Quake!, 1995; Walk On By, 1996. Honours: Grammis, 1993; City of Gothenburg Prize, 1997. Membership: Swedish Composers of Popular Music. Hobby: Sailing. Current Management: Musikcentrum Väst Pjurgardsgatan 13, 414 62 GBG Sweden. Address: Pl 1039, 430 85 Branne, Sweden.

WALLIN Per Henrik Marten, b. 17 July 1946, Karlsborg, Sweden. Jazz Pianist. m. Saara, 1980, 1 son, 1 daughter. Education: Fil kand; Autodidact. Career: TV-documentary in Sweden, 1990; 10 years touring with Trio, T Hultcrantz Bass and Erik Dahlbäck Drums throughout Europe, Canada, New York and India. Compositions: Mingelin No 5; Coyote. Recordings: Blues Work; Dolphins, Dolphins, Dolphins; Deep In a Dream; 2 new records, 1998. Hobbies: Reading; Listening to music. Address: Ringu 40, 11867, Stockholm, Sweden.

WALLINGER Karl, b. 19 Oct 1957, Prestatyn, Wales. Vocalist; Musician (multi-instrumentalist); Record Producer; Arranger; Songwriter. Career: Member, groups Quasimodo; Zero Zero; Out; Invisible Body Club; Member, The Waterboys, 1983-86; Founder, World Party, 1986; Concerts include: Launch of Greenpeace - Rainbow Warriors album, with Peter Gabriel, Annie Lennox, Moscow, 1989; Reims Music Festival, France, 1990. Recordings: with The Waterboys: Singles: The Whole Of The Moon, 1985; with World Party: Ship Of Fools, 1987; Is It Like Today, 1993; All I Gave, 1993; Albums: with The Waterboys: A Pagan Place, 1984; This Is The Sea, 1985. with World Party: Private Revolution, 1987; Goodbye Jumbo, 1990; Bang!, 1993. Honours include: Q Award, Best Album, Goodbye Jumbo, 1990. Current Management: Pure Management, 39 Bolton Gardens, London SW5 0AQ, England.

WALSH Greg, b. England. Record Producer. Career: Producer for: Heaven 17; Tina Turner; Chicago; Elkie Brooks; Lucio Battisti; Ron. Honours: Grammy Nomination, Album of the Year, 1984. Current Management: Gary Davison, The Liaison and Promotion Co. Address: 70 Gloucester Place, London WH1 3HL, England.

WALSH Joe, b. 20 Nov 1947, Wichita, Kansas, USA. Singer; Musician (guitar, keyboards); Record Producer. Education: Kent (Ohio) State University. Career: Member, James Gang; Solo artiste, and with own group Barnstorm, 1971-; Member, The Eagles, 1976-81; Tour of Australia, New Zealand, Japan, 1976; 2 US tours, 1977; 2 European tours, 1977; Canadian tour, 1978; Self-nominated for Vice-President, 2 US presidential campaigns; Joined with the Eagles for the Hell Freezes Over tour and album, world tour spanning 3 years and 5 countries. Recordings: Albums: with The James Gang: Yer Album, 1969; James Gang Rides Again, 1970; Thirds, 1971; Live In Concert, 1971; with The Eagles: Hotel California (Number 1, US), 1976; The Long Run (Number 1, US), 1979; Eagles Live, 1980; Solo/with Barnstorm: Barnstorm, 1972; The Smoker You Drink..., 1973; So What, 1974; You Can't Argue With A Sick Mind, 1976; But Seriously Folks, 1978; There Goes The Neighbourhood, 1981; You Bought It, You Name It, 1983; The Confessor, 1985; Got Any Gum, 1987; Ordinary Average Guy, 1991; Songs For A Dying, 1992; Look What I Did! - The Joe Walsh Anthology,

1995; Robocop (soundtrack), 1995; Hits singles: with The Eagles: Hotel California (Number 1, US), 1977; Life In The Fast Lane, 1977; Heartache Tonight (Number 1, US), 1979: The Long Run, 1980; Seven Bridges Road, 1981. Honours: Grammy Awards: Records Of The Year, Hotel California, 1978; Best Vocal Arrangement, New Kid In Town, 1978; Best Rock Vocal Performance, Heartache Tonight, 1980; American Music Awards: Favourite Pop/Rock Album, 1977, 1981; Favourite Pop/Rock Band, 1981. Hobbies: Amateur radio; Synthesizers. Current Management: David Spero Management. Address: 1679 South Belvoir Blvd, Cleveland, OH 44121, USA.

WALSH Peter, b. England. Record Producer. Career: Producer for: Simple Minds; China Crisis; Boomtown Rats; Alphaville; The Church; Scott Walker; Peter Gabriel; Miguel Bose. Current Management: Gary Davison, The Liaison And Promotion Co. Address: 70 Gloucester Place, London W1H 3HL, England.

WALSH Steve, b. 1951, St Joseph, Missouri, USA. Vocalist; Musician (keyboards); Songwriter. Career: Member, US rock group, Kansas, 1972-80; 1986-; Also solo artiste. Recordings: Albums: with Kansas: Kansas, 1974; Songs For America, 1975; Masque, 1975; Leftoverture, 1976; Point Of No Return, 1977; Two For The Show, 1978; Monolith, 1979; Audio-Visions, 1980; Power, 1986; In The Spirit Of Things, 1988; Solo album: Schemer Dreamer. Honour: UNICEF Deputy Ambassador of Goodwill, 1978. Current Management: Entertainment Services Unltd. Address: Main Street Plaza 1000, Ste 303, Voorhess, NJ 08043, USA.

WALTER Rémy, b. 1 Sept 1964, Paris, France. Singer; Actor; Record Producer. 1 daughter. Musical Education: Exam as an arranger (SACEM). Career: Producer, 1986-; First International success: Etienne by Guesh Patti; Producer, 20 singles and 7 albums; Formed own record label; Actor in 6 films, 1979. Recordings: Albums include: Ziskakan: Kasasnicola; Rosina de Peira: Anveit; Pascal Mathieu: En Attendant Des Jours Pires; A3: Les Fous Du Large; Clément Masdonoar: Anastasia; First solo album: Face To the Ground, 1995. Honours: Clément Masdonoar: Anastasia, Best World Music Record Of Year, Le Monde, 1990. Memberships: GRAF; SACEM. Hobbies: Surfing; Snowboarding; Skateboarding. Current Management: Safta Jaffery. Address: 1 Prince Of Wales Passage, 117 Hampstead Road, London NW1 3EF, England.

WALTERS Dez, b. 1 Oct 1948, Llysfaen, North Wales. Musician (guitar, banjo); Songwriter; Vocalist. m. Margaret Keppie, 24 June 1988, 3 daughters. Musical Education: Self-taught. Career: Began, early teens in rock band; Worked playing country music in: Middle East; America; Canada; Europe; Backing musician and support act to: Billie Jo Spears; Jim Glaser; Ronnie Prophet; UK and European tours; Song in film: Too Young To Die; 3 songs appeared on STV Show, 1994, 1995; Various radio stations, UK. Compositions: Writer, most of own material. Recordings: Here's Looking At You; Wide Brimmed And Legless, 1995; Ladies Man. Honours: Nomination, Best British Country Album, Wide Brimmed And Legless, 1995; Scotland's No 1 Country Band, 1994, 1995; Various awards, country clubs nationwide. Memberships: Equity; Musicians' Union. Hobbies: Reading; Motor racing; Travel; Music (general). Current Management: Square Deal Promotions. Address: Crachan #1, Melfort House, Milliken Park Road, Kilbarchan PA10 2DB, Scotland.

WALTERS Hannelore Liesemarie (Fil), b. 31 Jan 1970, Dartford, Kent, England. Singer; Songwriter; Lyricist. Musical Education: Studied violin, aged 9-12; Currently learning piano. Career: Member, various bands from age 16; Singer, songwriter, lyricist, Back To The Planet, 6 years;

Appearances radio and television; Signed to London Records, 1993; Continuous concerts, England, Europe, 6 years; Festivals include: Glastonbury; Phoenix; Reading. Recordings: 2 cassettes, 1991; 1992; Albums: Mind And Soul Collaborators, 1993; Messages After The Bleep, 1994. Hobbies: Painting; Computers (music); Reading; Swimming. Current Agent: ICM Fairwarning. Address: 8 Roberts Road, Belvedere, Kent DA17 6NP, England.

WALTERS John Leonard, b. 16 Apr 1953, Chesterfield, Derbyshire, England. Composer; Editor. m. Clare Anderson, 25 Mar 1978, 2 daughters. Education: King's College, London. Musical Education: Private study with jazz musicians, including Neil Ardley, Bob Downes. Career: Founder, Landscape, 1974-83; Zyklus, 1987-; Founder, editor, Unknown Public, creative music quarterly; Producer: Swans Way; Mike Gibbs Orchestra; People's Century (soundtrack album). Recordings: Hit single: Einstein A Go-Go; Album: From The Tea-Room Of Mars; Before The Oil Ran Out. Publications: Unknown Public - tape and CD audio journal; Gramophone Explorations 2, 1997. Honours: GLA Young Musicians Award, 1976; Prudential Awards for the Arts, 1995. Memberships: APC; Re-Pro; Musicians' Union. Current Management: Laurence Aston, Public Production Co, PO Box 354, Reading RG2 7JB, England. Address: c/o Unknown Public, 14 Clerkenwell Green, London EC1R 0DP, England.

WANDALL Marietta, b. 21 Nov 1956, Copenhagen, Denmark. Jazz Musician (piano); Composer; Music Teacher. m. Kristian Sparre Andersen, 5 Nov 1988, 2 daughters. Musical Education: Private teachers; University of Copenhagen; Mainly self-taught. Career: Played piano, synthesizer in jazz ensembles, including Crystal Quintet (with Marylin Mazur); Concerts in Denmark, Norway, Finland; Solo pianist at several Copenhagen Jazz Festivals; Duo concerts with Chris Poole (flute); Jazz duo with Hanne Romer (saxophone), 1980-; Numerous appearances on Danish radio and television; Piano teacher in digital piano-lab. Recordings: with Hanne Romer: Akijava, 1990; Ametyst, 1994. Address: C F Richsvej, 101 C, DK-2000 Frederiksberg, Denmark.

WANGFORD Hank (Samuel Hutt), b. 15 Nov 1940, Wangford, Suffolk, England. Country Singer; Musician (guitar); Doctor. Education: Medicine, Cambridge University. Career: Formerly, doctor of medicine; Became singer, London pub circuit, 1976-; Founder, Sincere Management; Sincere Products; Presenter, 2 country music television series, Channel 4; Stage show, Radio Wang; Also Senior Medical Officer, Family Planning Clinic, London. Recordings: Chicken Rhythm; Cowboys Stay On Longer; Albums: Live Hank Wangford, 1982; Hank Wangford, 1985; Rodeo Radio, 1985; Stormy Horizons, 1990; Hard Shoulder To Cry On, 1993. Publication: Author (as Sam Hutt): Hank Wangford Vol III - The Middle Years, 1989. Current Management: FAB, 132 Liverpool Road, London N1 1LA, England.

WARD Bill, b. 5 May 1948, Birmingham, England. Musician (drums). Career: Drummer, UK heavy rock group Black Sabbath (formerly Earth), 1967-80, 1983; Concerts include: Hollywood Music Festival, 1970; Madison Square Garden, New York, 1975. Recordings: Albums: Balck Sabbath, 1970; Paranoid, 1970; Master Of Reality, 1971; Black Sabbath, Vol 4, 1972; Sabbath Bloody Sabbath, 1974; Sabotage, 1975; We Sold Our Souls For Rock'n'Roll, 1976; Technical Ecstacy, 1976; Never Say Die, 1978; Heaven And Hell, 1980; Live At Last, 1980; Born Again, 1983; Singles: Evil Woman, 1970; Paranoid, 1970; Iron Man, 1972; Never Say Die, 1978; Hard Road, 1978; Neon Knights, 1980.

WARD Donald, b. 2 Oct 1928, Spion Kop, Nottinghamshire, England. Musician (trombone,

drums, tuned percussion). m. Janet Neta Pettit, 8 Oct 1955, 2 daughters. Musical Education: Piano lessons; Brass band; Also self-taught. Career: Professional musician, 1951-; Palace Theatre Mansfield; Summer season, Parade Theatre, Skegness; Winter season, Theatre Royal, Nottingham; Scottish tour, Billy Smarts Circus; Aston Hippodrome, 1954, 1956; Ipswich Hippodrome, 1956, 1960; Dance halls, jazz clubs, theatres, teaching. Recordings: Album with Shirebrook Brass Band. Membership: Musicians' Union (Golden Card holder). Hobbies: Qualified pilot (part-owner Cessna A/C); Morgan sports cars. Address: 17 Saville Road, Skegby, Sutton-In-Ashfield, Nottinghamshire NG17 3DF, England.

WARD John Robert, b. 28 June 1964, Halesworth, Suffolk, En. Singlandger; Songwriter; Musician (guitar, bass, bodhran, harmonica). Career: Began playing in rock/pop bands, 1980; Solo singer, songwriter on folk circuit, 1985-; First television appearance, Cambridge Folk Festival, 1987; Full-time musician, 1988-; Several tours, Germany, 1992. Compositions: 3 featured on Broadside, 1989. Recordings: Albums: The Shrinking World, 1988; Water On The Stone (with acoustic band), 1992. Membership: BASCA; PRS; Musicians' Union; PPL. Hobbies: Photography; Travel; Cooking; The outdoors. Address: 7 Kevington Drive, Outlon Broad, Lowestoft, Suffolk NR32 3JL, England.

WARE Martyn. Musician; Record Producer. Career: Founder member, Human League; Founder member, Heaven 17; Worldwide tours, numerous television and concert appearances; Independent Record Producer; Recordings: Albums: All Heaven 17 albums; Council Collective EP, Paul Weller; Private Dancer, Tina Turner; The Hardline According To..., Terence Trent D'Arby; I Say I Say I Say, Erasure; Reproduction, Travelog, Human League; Singles: Let's Stay Together, Tina Turner; Sign Your Name, Dance Little Sister, Wishing Well, Terence Trent D'Arby; Always, Run To The Sun, Erasure; Lover, Back In My Life, Joe Roberts; Numerous singles with: Heaven 17; Scritti Politti; Lena Fiagbe; Alison Moyet; Urban Cookie Collective; Pauline Henry; Human League. Current Management: Stephen Budd Management. Address: 109B Regents Park Road, London NW1 8UR, England.

WARE Nicholas Stewart, b. 5 Apr 1963, Burnham, Buckinghamshire, England. Project Manager, Videoconferencing. Musical Education: O Level Music, High Wycombe Music CTRE, Baritone and alto saxophone, bass guitar. Career: Bucks Cyjo, 1982-88; Herman Nush Windtunnel Experience, 1988-89; Saxophonist, musical director, arranger, soul/blues band Straight Eight, 1990-; Bucks Symphonic Ensemble, 1990-94. Recordings: Session recording with No Fear, 1987, 1989, 1990; with Orbitone: All Day; Set Me Free; Optimism; with Straight Eight: It's A Cover Up (album), 1991. Hobbies: Motorcycling; Painting; Jiving. Current Managemnt: Self-managed. Address: 9 Rectory Court, High Wycombe, Buckinghamshire HP13 7DH, England.

WARINER Steve, b. 25 Dec 1954, Noblesville, Indiana, USA. Musician (bass); Songwriter; Singer. Career: Bass player with Dottie West; Bob Luman; Chet Atkins; Solo artiste, 1978-. Compositions include: I'm Already Taken, Conway Twitty; Several songs recorded by Bob Luman. Recordings: US Country Number 1 hits: All Roads Lead To You; Some Fools Never Learn; You Can Dream On Me; Love's Highway; Small Town Girl; Lynda; The Weekend; Duets include: The Hand That Rocks The Cradle, with Glen Campbell; That's How You Know When Love's Right, with Nicolette Larson; Albums: Steve Wariner, 1982; Midnight Fire, 1983; One Good Night Deserves Another, 1985; Life's Highway, 1985; Down In Tennessee, 1986; It's A Crazy World, 1987; I Should Be With You, 1988; I Got

Dreams, 1989; I Am Ready, 1991. Honours: CMA Vocal Event Award, Restless, 1991. Address: Steve Wariner Productions, 1103 16th Avenue S, Nashville, TN 37212, USA.

WARNES Jennifer, b. 1947, Seattle, Washington, USA. Singer. Career: Singer, 1967-; Theatre appearance, Hair, Los Angeles, 1968; Recordings: Albums: I Can Remember Everything, 1968; See Me, Feel Me, Touch Me, Heal Me, 1969; Jennifer, 1972; Shot Through The Heart, 1979; The Best Of..., 1982; Famous Blue Raincoat, 1987; Just Jennifer, 1992; The Hunter, 1992; Also featured on: The Mason Williams Ear Show, Mason Williams, 1967; Everybody's Angel, Tanita Tikaram, 1991; For Our Children, with Jackson Browne, 1991; Singles include: Right Time Of The Night, 1978; I Know A Heartache When I See One, 1979; It Goes Like It Goes, 1980; Up Where We Belong, duet with Joe Cocker, for film An Officer And A Gentleman (Number 1, US), 1982; All The Right Moves, for film All The Right Moves, 1983; (I've Had) The Time Of My Life, duet with Bill Medley, for film Dirty Dancing (Number 1, US), 1987. Honours: Oscars: It Goes Like It Goes, 1980; Up Where We Belong, 1983; (I've Had) The Time Of My Life, 1988; (all for Best Original Song); Oscar Nomination, One More Hour, 1981; Grammy Awards: Best Pop Performances, Up Where We Belong, 1983; (I've Had) The Time Of My Life, 1987. Current Management: Donald Miller, 1246 Kling Street, Studio City, CA 91604, USA.

WARO Danyel, b. 10 May 1955, Tampon, Réunion Island, France. Musician; Musical Instrument Maker. 1 son. Musical Education: Traditional. Career: Tours: Japan; Europe; West Africa; Mauritius; France; Concert for Amnesty International. Recordings: Albums: Gafourn, 1986; Batarsité, 1994. Publications: 3 libretti with musical texts. Honours: French Press honours (Télérama, Le Monde). Membership: Piros disc, Saint André, Réunion Island. Hobby: Hiking. Current Management: Pageaux Martine. Address: 34 Chemin Gréviléas Fleurimont, 97460 Saint Paul, Island de la Réunion, France.

WARREN Diane, b. 1956, California, USA. Songwriter. Education: Film Studies, Cal State University. Career: Numerous hit compositions include: If I Could Turn Back Time, Cher; Solitaire, Laura Brannigan; If You Asked Me To, Celine Dion; I Get Weak, Belinda Carlisle; Rhythm Of The Night, Debarge; Look Away, Chicago; Who Will You Run To, Heart; When I'm Back On My Feet Again, Michael Bolton; Not A Dry Eye In The House, Meat Loaf; Other compositions for: Gloria Estefan; Al Green. Numerous honours include: ASCAP Songwriter of the Year, 1990, 1991, 1993; Billboard Singles Publishers of the Year, 1990, 1993; ASCAP Voice Of Music Award, 1995.

WARWICK David, b. Lincolnshire, England. Piano; Keyboards. Education: Studied Music, York University. Career: Played in England, Belgium, Switzerland, Scandinavia, Germany on stage, radio and television. Recording: Piano Dreams, album, 1995. Honour: Awarded at York University. Memberships: GEMA; BIEM. Address: BME Records Germany, 50877 Köln, 550224, Germany.

WARWICK (Marie) Dionne, b. 12 Dec 1940, East Orange, New Jersey, USA. Singer. m. Bill Elliott, deceased, 2 sons. Education: Hartt College Of Music, Hartford, Connecticut. Music Education: Masters degree, Music. Career: Singer, gospel groups The Drinkard Singers; The Gospelaires; Solo singer, 1962-; Association with songwriters Bacharach and David, originally as demo and backing singer, 1961-72; Numerous concerts, tours and benefit shows worldwide; Television includes: Top Of The Pops; Thank Your Lucky Stars; Ready Steady Goes Live!; The Bacharach Sound; It's What's Happening Baby; The Divine Dionne Warwick; Ed Sullivan Show; Host, Solid

Gold, 1980, 1984-86; Host, A Gift Of Music, 1981; Sisters In The Name Of Love, 1986; Dionne And Friends, 1990; Actress, film Slaves, 1969. Recordings: Albums: Presenting Dionne Warwick, 1964; Make Way For Dionne Warwick, 1964; The Sensitive Sound Of Dionne Warwick, 1965; Dionne Warwick In Paris, 1966; Here Where There Is Love, 1967; On Stage And In The Movies, 1967; The Windows Of The World, 1967; Valley Of The Dolls, 1968; Promises Promises, 1969; Soulful, 1969; Dionne, 1972; From Within, 1972; Just Being Myself, 1973; Then Came You, 1975; Track Of The Cat, 1976; A Man And A Woman, with Isaac Hayes, 1977; No Night So Long, 1980; Hot, Live And Otherwise, 1981; Friends In Love, 1982; Heartbreaker, 1982; So Amazing, 1983; Without Your Love, 1985; Reservations For Two, 1987; Dionne Warwick Sings Cole Porter, 1990; Friends Can Be Lovers, 1993; Aquarela Do Brazil, 1995; Numerous compilation albums; Hit singles include: Anyone Who Had A Heart, 1964; Walk On By, 1964; A Message To Michael, 1966; Alfie, 1967; I Say A Little Prayer, 1967; Do You Know The Way To San José, 1968; This Girl's In Love With You, 1969; I'll Never Fall In Love Again, 1970; Then Came You, with The Spinners (Number 1, US), 1974; I'll Never Love This Way Again, 1979; Heartbreaker, with Barry Gibb (Number 2, UK), 1982; All The Love In The World, 1983; That's What Friends Are For (AIDS charity record), with Stevie Wonder, Gladys Knight, Elton John (Number 1, US), 1985; Featured on numerous film soundtracks including: A House Is Not A Home, 1964; What's New Pussycat?, 1965; Valley Of The Dolls, 1968; The April Fools, 1969; Slaves, 1969; The Love Machine, 1971; After You, 1980; The Woman In Red, 1984; Contributor, charity records: We Are The World, USA For Africa, 1985; Forgotten Eyes, 1990; Lift Up Every Voice And Sing, 1990. Honours: Top Selling Female Artist, NARM, 1964; Grammy Awards: Best Female Pop Vocal Performance, 1969, 1970, 1980; Best Contemporary Vocal Performance, 1971; Best Female R&B Vocal Performance, 1980; Best Pop Performance, Duo or Group, 1987; Song Of The Year, 1987; Star on Hollywood's Walk Of Fame, 1985; NAACP Key Of Life Award, 1990; CORE Humanitarian Award, 1992; Nosotros Golden Eagle Humanitarian Award, 1992; Award from City of New York for contributions to AIDS research, 1987; DIVA Award, 1992; Platinum and Gold discs. Address: c/o Brokaw Company, 9255 Sunset Blvd, Suite 804, Los Angeles, CA 90069, USA.

WARWICK Ricky, b. Belfast, Northern Ireland. Vocalist; Rock Musician (guitar). m. Vanessa Warwick. Career: Member, New Model Army; Founder member, UK heavy rock group The Almighty, 1988-; Major concerts include: Monsters Of Rock Festival, Castle Donington, UK, 1982. Recordings: Albums: with The Almighty: Blood Fire And Love, 1989; Blood Fire And Live, 1990; Soul Destruction, 1991; Powertrippin', 1993; Crank, 1995; Just Add Life, 1996; Hit single: Free 'N' Easy, 1991. Current Management: Triple T Management Co., 21 Napier Place, London W14 8LG, England.

WASHBURN Dan, b. 28 May 1956, Coburg, Ontario, Canada. Singer; Songwriter; Musician (bass). m. Jane, 15 Dec 1984, 3 sons, 1 daughter. Career: Lead singer, South Mountain, 1992; Concerts, as lead singer and bassist, South Mountain: Netherlands; Germany; Switzerland; Belgium; Canada; Appeared with: Marty Stuart; Waylon Jennings; Toby Keith; Merle Haggard; Prairie Oyster; Various television shows in above mentioned countries; Appeared, CCMA Awards Show, 1993. Recordings: Played on soundtrack for Into The Fire, 1990; South Mountain album: Where There's A Will; Session bassist, singer, many Canadian country, folk, blues albums. Memberships: AFofM; Canadian Country Music Association. Hobbies: Fishing with his children; Flying model radio-controlled airplanes. Current

Management: Savannah Music Group, Agent: Katherine Faint and Associates. Address: 768 Chamberlain Street, Peterborough, Ontario K9J 4M3, Canada.

WASHINGTON Grover Jr, b. 12 Dec 1943, Buffalo, New York, USA. Musician (saxophone); Producer; Composer; Arranger. m. Christine, 1 son, 1 daughter. Musical Education: Wurlitzer School Music, Temple University; Private lessons. Career: Musician with Four Clefs until 1963; Keith McAllister, 1963-65; 19th Army band, 1965-67; Various groups with Billy Cobham; Don Gardner's Sonotones, 1967-68; Charles Erland, 1971; Solo artiste; Member, Urban Knights; Television and personal appearances in US, Canada, Europe and Japan; Regular national anthem performances for Philadelphia Eagles (American football) and Philadelphia Tigers (basketball). Recordings: Solo albums: Soul Box, 1973; Inner City Blues, 1976; All The King's Horses, Mister Magic, 1975; I Feels So Good, 1975; A Secret Place, 1976; Soul Box Vol 1, 1976; Vol 2, 1976; Live At The Bijou, 1978; Reed Seed, 1978; Paradise, 1979; Winelight, 1980; Skylarkin', 1980; Baddest, 1981; Come Morning, 1981; Anthology, 1982; Greatest Performances, 1983; Best Is Yet To Come; Inside Moves; Time Out Of Mind, 1989; Strawberry Moon; Then And Now; Grover Washington Jr At His Best; with Urban Knights: Urban Knights, 1994; Contributor, Colour And Light - Jazz Sketches On Sondheim, 1995; Also featured on albums by: Roy Ayers; Bill Withers; Robert Flack; Eric Gale; Bob James; Alphonso Johnson; Dave Matthews. Honours: Grammy Award; Gold and Platinum discs. Current Managment: Lloyd Z Remick, Zane Management, The Bellevue, 6th Floor, Broad & Walnut, Philadelphia, PA 19102, USA.

WATERHOUSE David, b. 13 July 1936, Harrogate, Yorkshire, England. m. Naoko Matsubara, 23 December 1971, 1 son. Education: King's College, Cambridge, 1956-61; BA, Hons, 1959; MA, 1963. Appointments: Research Assistant, Cambridge Institute of Criminology, 1959-60; Assistant Keeper, Department of Oriental Antiquities, British Museum, 1961-64; Research Fellow, Center for Asian Arts, University of Washington, 1964-66; Assistant Professor, Department of East Asian Studies, University of Toronto, 1966-70; Associate Professor, 1970-75; Professor, 1975-; Senior Member, University College; Licentiate, Royal Academy of Music, 1956; Fellow, Royal Society of Canada, 1990. Publications include: Editor, Dance of India, History, Perspectives and Prospects, 1997; Contributions: Japan, Religious Music, 1980; Bagpipe, Great Highland; Scotland; Highland Pipe Bands, 1992; Actors, Artists and the Stage in Eighteenth-Century Japan and England, 1981; Towards a New Analysis of Rhythm in Music, 1982; Korean Music, Trick Horsemanship & Elephants in Tohugawa, Japan, 1986; Where Did Toragaku Come From?, 1991; The Logical Priority of Performance for the Analysis of Music, 1986; John Wilson and the Highland Bagpipe in Ontario, 1990; Hogaku Preserved: A Select List of Long-Playing Records of the National Music of Japan, 1969; An Early Illustration of the Four-Stringed Kokyu, with a Disquisition on the History of Japan's Only Bowed Musical Instrument, 1970; Hogaku Preserved II: A Second List of Long-Playing Records Issued by Japanese Record Companies of the National Music of Japan, 1976; Woodcuts by Suzuki Harumoku as a Source for the History of Japanese Dance, 1988; Buddhism and Modern Music and Dance, 1995; Chinese Music in Pre-Modern Japan, 1993; Os Primeiros Contactos dos Japonese com a Musica Ocidental, 1996; Southern Barbarian Music in Japan, 1997. Address: 324 Coral Terrace, Oakville, Ontario L6J 4C4, Canada.

WATERMAN Pete, b. 15 Jan 1947. Songwriter; Record Producer; Record Company Executive. Career: Soul disc jockey; Promoter, record producer and remixer, for artistes including Adrian Baker; Susan Cadogan; Member, group, Agents Aren't Aeroplanes, 1984; Member, songwriting and production team Stock/Aitken/Waterman (SAW), with Matt Aitken and Mike Stock, 1984-93; Founder, own PWL record label, 1988; Founder, 3 record labels, PWL America, PWL Continental, PWL Black, 1991-. Recordings: Albums: Hit Factory, 1987; Hit Factory Volume 2, 1988; Hit Factory Volume 3, 1989; The Best Of Stock Aitken And Waterman, 1990; Hit singles: As co-writer, producer: You Spin Me Round, Dead Or Alive (Number 1,UK), 1984; So Macho, Sinitta, 1986; Respectable, Mel and Kim (Number 1, UK), 1987; Never Gonna Give You Up, Rick Astley, 1987; with Kylie Minogue: I Should Be So Lucky (Number 1, 12 countries), 1988; Got To Be Certain, 1988; The Locomotion, 1988; Hand On Your Heart, 1989; Better The Devil You Know, 1990; Also recordings for: Jason Donovan; Divine; Hazell Dean; Sonia; Brother Beyond; Big Fun; Donna Summer. Address: c/o PWL Management International, 4-7 The Vineyard, off Sanctuary Street, London SE1 1QL, England.

WATERS Benny, b. 23 Jan 1902, Baltimore, Maryland, USA. Jazz Musician (saxophone). Musical Education: Boston Conservatory of Music, USA. Career: Member, Charlie Miller Band, Philadelphia; Music teacher, pupils included Harry Carney (saxophone player for Duke Ellington); Member, Jimmy Archey Band; Also played with Charlie Johnson; Fletcher Henderson; "Hot Lips" Page; Stuff Smith; Leader, own jazz quartet; Toured throughout USA, Europe; Now USA's oldest performing jazzman. Recordings: First recording with Charlie Johnson's Paradise Ten Band, 1924; 70 years of recordings; Latest recordings: Swinging Again, 1994; Statesmen Of Jazz, 1995. Publications: Autobiography: The Key To A Jazzy Life. Current Management: Russ Dantzler, Hot Jazz Management & Production, Suite 4F, 328 West 43rd Street, New York, NY 10036, USA; Catz Management, PO Box 146, Centerport, NY 11721, USA.

WATERS Roger, b. 6 Sept 1944, Great Bookham, Surrey, England. Vocalist; Musician (bass); Composer. Education: Regent Street Polytechnic, London. Career: Founder member, Pink Floyd, 1965-83; Performances include: Rome International Pop Festival, 1968; Hyde Park, London, 1968; Bath Festival, 1970; Montreux Festival, 1971; Knebworth Festival, 1975; Films: Pink Floyd Live At Pompeii, 1972; The Wall, 1982; Solo artiste, 1984-; Performance of The Wall, Berlin, 1990; Guitar Legends, Seville, Spain, 1991. Recordings: Albums: Piper At The Gates Of Dawn, 1967; A Saucerful Of Secrets, 1968; More (film soundtrack), 1969; Ummagumma, 1969; Meddle, 1971; Relics, 1971; Obscured By Clouds, 1972; The Dark Side Of The Moon (Number 1, US), 1973; Wish You Were Here (Number 1, UK and US), 1975; Animals, 1976; The Wall (Number 1, US), 1979; The Final Cut, 1983; Solo albums: Music From The Body (film soundtrack), 1970; The Pros And Cons Of Hitch Hiking, 1984; When The Wind Blows, 1986; Radio KAOS, 1987; The Wall - Live In Berlin, 1990; Amused To Death, 1992; Singles include: See Emily Play, 1967; Another Brick In The Wall (Number 1, US and UK), 1979; Run Like Hell, 1980; When The Tigers Break Free, 1982; Not Now John, 1983; Solo: 5.01 AM (The Pros And Cons Of Hitch-Hiking), 1984; Radio Waves, 1987; The Tide Is Turning (After Live Aid), 1987. Honours include: with Pink Floyd: Silver Clef Award, Nordoff-Robbins Music Therapy Centre, 1980; Ivor Novello Award, Outstanding Contribution To British Music, 1992.

WATSON Andy, b. 20 June 1958, Enfield, England. Session Musician (guitar). m. Pam Watson, 20 Aug 1983. Education: Crawley and Swindon Technical College. Musical Education: London College of Music; Royal College Of Music; Leeds College Of Music. Career: Sessions for

YTV; BBC; Channel 4; Royal Philharmonic Orchestra; West End Shows: Joseph And The Amazing Technicolour Dreamcoat; Les Miserables; Sunset Boulevard; Anything Goes; Ross Mitchell Band and Singers. Recordings: Solo album: Sweeping Statement, 1989. Publications: Author, Join The Dots column, Guitarist magazine. Honours: Associate, Royal College of Music; Graduate, Leeds College of Music. Memberships: Musicians' Union; PRS; MCPS. Current Management: Self-managed. Address: Chelmsford, Essex, England.

WATSON Bobby Jr (Robert Michael), b. 23 Aug 1953, Lawrence, USA. Musician (alto saxophone); Composer; Bandleader. Education. m. Pamela Watson, 11 Sept 1976, 1 son, 1 daughter. Musicial Education: BM, Theory and Composition, University of Miami. Career: Musical director with Art Blakey and The Jazz Messengers, 1977-81; Member, Leads Horizon, 1980-; Alto with Zahir Batin, 1980-; Alto with Art Blakey And The Jazz Messengers, 1981-; Alto with Mickey Bass Quartet, 1981-; Member, 28th Street Saxophone Quartet, 1983-; Lead alto with Panama Francis And The Savoy Sultans, 1983-; Lead alto with The Duke's Men, 1987-; Performs with Charlie Mingus Epitaph Project, 1989-; Alto with Smithsonian Jazz Masterworks Orchestra, 1982; Lead alto, Carnegie Hall Jazz Orchestra, 1992; Premiered Tailor Made big band, 1993; Tours: Brazil; Europe; Japan; Canada; North America; Caribbean; Italy; Netherlands; Scotland; Germany; England; Cyprus; Every major jazz festival in Europe; Own publishing company, Lafiya Music, 1979-; Record label, New Note Records, 1983-. Compositions: Over 100. Recordings include: As leader: Post-Motown Bop; No Question About It; The Inventor; The Year Of The Rabbit; Love Remains; Round Trip; All Because Of You; Gumbo; Jewel; Recordings with artists including: Bill Cosby; Art Blakey And The Jazz Messengers; 29th Street Quartet. Honours include: Recipient Of National Endowment Composers Grant, 1980; Downbeat Critics Poll Wins: Best Alto Saxophonist, 1989-92; Jazz Musician of the Year, 1990. Hobbies: Fishing; Bowling; Table tennis. Current Management: Timothy Patterson, Split Second Timing. Address: 104 West 70th Street, Apt 11C, New York, NY 10024, USA.

WATSON Jamie, b. 3 Jun 1954, Canada. Recording Engineer; Producer; Musician (guitar, drums, keyboards). m. Beverley Watson, 29 Mar 1990. Education: George Watsons College; Edinburgh Art College. Musical Education: Self-taught. Career: Member, Solos; Major UK tour support to The Tourists, 1979; Currently owns and runs Chamber Recording Studio in Edinburgh. Recordings: Singles: Talking Pictures, Solos; Single by Persian Rugs; Album and other records on various independent labels. Memberships: PRS; MCPS. Hobbies: Playing football; Reading; Live music. Address: 120A West Granton Road, Edinburgh EH5 1PF, Scotland.

WATSON Jeff, b. 4 Nov 1959, Sacramento, California, USA. Musician (guitar); Singer; Writer; Record Producer; Sound Engineer. Education: 2 years junior college. Career: Guitarist, US rock group, Night Ranger, 1982-91; Guitarist, Mothers Army; Television appearances include: American Bandstand (4 times); Solid Gold; Tours worldwide: 10 million albums sold. Recordings: Albums: with Night Ranger: Dawn Patrol; Midnight Madness; Seven Wishes; Big Life; Man In Motion; Live In Japan; Solo: Lone Ranger; Around The Sun; with Steve Morse: Southern Steel; with Chris Isaac: San Francisco Days; Forever Blue; with Mothers Army: Mothers Army I & II; 3 Number 1 videos with Night Ranger. Honours: Multiple Platinum and Gold albums. Memberships: BMI; AFTRA; JASRAC. Hobbies: Water skiing; Scrabble. Current Management: Bruce Cohn Management, 15140 Sonoma Hwy, Glenellen, CA 93442, USA.

Address: 120 Sunnyside, #149 Mill Valley, CA 94941, USA.

WATT Ben, b. 6 Dec 1962. Musician (guitars, keyboards); Vocalist. Songwriter. Education: Hull University. Career: Solo artiste, 1981-82; Formed duo, Everything But The Girl, with singer Tracey Thorn, 1983-; Appearances include: Regular UK tours, 1984-; World Tour 1990, including Japan; Friends of the Earth Benefit Concerts; Red Hot and Dance AIDS Benefit Concert, 1991; UK and US Tours, 1993-95; World Tour, 1996-97, including Japan and Australasia. Compositions: Writer, co-writer with Tracey Thorn, of own material for duo and solo work. Recordings: Albums: Solo album: North Marine Drive, 1983; with Everything But The Girl: Eden, 1984; Everything But The Girl (US Only), 1984; Love Not Money, 1985; Baby, The Stars Shine Bright, 1986; Idlewild, 1988; The Language Of Life, 1990; Worldwide, 1991; Essence and Rare (Japan only), 1992; Acoustic, 1992 (US only); Home Movies - Best Of Everything But The Girl, 1993; Amplified Heart, 1994; Walking Wounded, 1996; Singles include: with Everything But The Girl: Each and Every One, 1984; Come On Home, 1986; I Don't Want To Talk About It, 1988; Missing, 1995; Walking Wounded, 1996; Wrong, 1996. Current Management: JFD Management, 106 Dalling Road, London W6 0JA, England.

WATT Bobby, b. Isle of Arran, Scotland. Stonemason; Musician (guitar). 2 sons. Career: Solo work all over world; Tours of: North America, as member of Cromdale; Now live outside Toronto, Canada. Recordings: Bobby Watt; C'est Watt. Current Management: Marco Polo. Address: 3 The Lilacs, 50 Elm Grove, Hayling Island PO11 9EF, England.

WATTS Andy, b. Macclesfield, England. Musician (shawn, Flemish bagpipes, clarinet, recorders, curtal); Vocalist. Education: History of Music, Cambridge University. Musical Education: Guildhall School Of Music And Drama; Royal Conservatory, The Hague, Netherlands. Career: Recorder teacher; Freelance musician with early music groups; Musical Director, Medieval Players; Baroque and classical bassoon with: The Orchestra Of The Age Of The Enlightenment; The English Baroque Solists; The Academy Of Ancient Music; Teacher, baroque bassoon, Royal Academy of Music; Founder member, The Carnival Band, 1984-; Appearances include: Glasgow Cathedral; Birmingham Symphony Hall; Barbican Centre; Arts theatres and centres; Plays material from: Sweden; Croatia; US; Bolivia; Spain; UK; France. Recordings include: Album with Maddy Prior: Christmas Carols. Current Management: c/o Jim McPhee, Acorn Entertainments. Address: Winterfold House, 46 Woodfield Road, Kings Heath, Birmingham B13 9UJ, England.

WATTS Charlie, b. 2 June 1941, Islington, London, England. Musician (drums). Career: Member, Blues Incorporated; Member, Rolling Stones, 1962-; Numerous tours and concerts include: National Jazz & Blues Festival, 1963; First UK tour, 1963; Group Scene UK tour, 1964; Debut US tour, 1964; Free concert, Hyde Park, 1969; Free concert, Altamont Speedway, 1969; Knebworth Festival, 1976; Steel Wheels North American Tour, 1989; Films include: Ladies And Gentlemen The Rolling Stones, 1976; Let's Spend The Night Together, 1983; Co-founder, record label, Rolling Stones Records, 1971. Recordings: Albums include: The Rolling Stones, 1965; The Rolling Stones No 2, 1965; Out Of Our Heads, 1965; Aftermath, 1966; Between The Buttons, 1967; Their Satanic Majesties Request, 1967; Beggar's Banquet, 1968; Let It Bleed, 1969; Get Yer Ya-Ya's Out, 1969; Sticky Fingers, 1971; Exile On Main Street, 1972; Goat's Head Soup, 1973; It's Only Rock And Roll, 1974; Black And Blue, 1976; Some Girls, 1978; Emotional Rescue, 1980; Tattoo You, 1981; Still Life, 1982; Steel Wheels,

1989; Flashpoint, 1991; Stripped, 1995; Hit singles include: It's All Over Now; Little Red Rooster; Get Off Of My Cloud; (I Can't Get No) Satisfaction; 19th Nervous Breakdown; Ruby Tuesday; Jumping Jack Flash; Honky Tonk Women; Let's Spend The Night Together; Brown Sugar; Miss You; Start Me Up; Emotional Rescue; Harlem Shuffle; Going To A Go-Go; Paint It Balck; Angie; Undercover Of The Night; She's So Cold. Honours: with Rolling Stones include: Silver Clef, Nordoff-Robbins Therapy, 1982; Grammy Award, Lifetime Achievement Award, 1986; Inducted into Rock And Roll Hall Of Fame, 1989; Q Award, Best Live Act, 1990; Ivor Novello Award, Outstanding Contribution to British Music, 1991. Current Management: Rupert Loewenstein, 2 King Street, London SW1Y 6QL, England.

WATTS Trevor Charles, b. 26 Feb 1939, York, Yorkshire, England. Musician (alto, soprano saxophones). 2 sons, 1 daughter. Musical Education: Self-taught. Career: Founder member, Spontaneous Music Ensemble; Amalgam; Moiré Music; Toured with Drum Orchestra in New Zealand; Burma; India; Caribbean; USA; Canada; Venezuela; Mexico; Botswana; South Africa; Lesotho; Colombia; Ecuador; Bolivia; Malaysia; First group to play Burma for 10 years; Arte Television show, 1994; Collaborated with traditional musicians, Khartoum International Festival, Sudan, 1996; Collaborations with Afro-Venezuelan Barlovento musicians, 1992, 1995; Toured in Cameroon, Wst Africa. Compositions: Bracknell Festival Commission: Mr Sunshine, 1984. Recordings: with M M Drum Ork: A Wider Embrace; with Moiré Music: With One Voice; with Moiré Music Trio: Intakt, 1995. Publications; Music Outside, Ian Carr, 1973; Leonard Feathers Encyclopaedia of Jazz. Memberships: PRS; MCPS; Musicians' Union; PAMRA. Hobbies: Music; Gardening. Current Management: Europe: Uli Fild, Pestalozzistrasse 28, D-42579 Heiligenhaus-Isenbügel, Germany. Address: Moire Music, 20 Collier Road, Hastings, East Sussex TN34 3JR, England.

WAVERLY Josie, b. USA. Entertainer. Married, 2 sons. Musical Education: Church. Career: Plays 150-180 dates a year, with band: Genuine Country; Appearances with country artists including: John Michael Montgomery; Lorrie Morgan; Tracy Lawrence; Charlie Daniels; Randy Travis; Neal McCoy; John Anderson; Sawyer Brown; Doug Stone. Recordings: CD and cassette: Who Cries This Time. Honours: Citizen Of The Year. Memberships: CMA; ASCAP; BMI; NAFE. Hobbies: Baking; Dude ranches; Travel; Shops. Current Management: Nancy Carroll Agency. Address: PO Box 19468, Sarasota, FL 34276, USA.

WAY Bryan Douglas, b. 20 Jan 1953, Cornerbrook, Newfoundland, Canada. Singer; Songwriter. 1 son, 1 daughter. Education: Academic, English Literature. Musical Education: Self-taught. Career: Appearances: Oprey North; Tommy Hunter Show; Ronnie Prophet Show; Global TV; Day By Day Show; Country Music Showcase; Mountain Festival; Hiram Walker Canadian Songwriter Tour. Compositions: Goodbye To The Rain, recorded by Roger Whittaker; Your Memeory Lays Down With Me, recorded by James Owen Bush; End Of Money, written and recorded by Bryan Way, played on 70 European radio stations. Publications: Country Music News; Billboard; Canadian Composer. Memberships: CCMA (Canadian Country Music Association); NSAI (Nashville Songwriters' Association International). Hobbies: Golf; Cooking; Fine Art. Current Management: Penelope Talent Agency; Suzanne Gaudette Management; Publisher: Songcraft Communications. Address: 20 Gamble Avenue, Suite 105, Toronto, Ontario M4K 2G9, Canada.

WAY Pete. Musician (bass). Career: Founder member, UFO, 1969-83; Founder member,

Waysted, 1983-88; Rejoined UFO, 1991-; UK and worldwide tours with both bands. Recordings: Albums: with UFO: UFO, 1971; UFO 2 - Flying, 1971; Live In Japan, 1972; Phenomenon, 1974; Face It, 1975; No Heavy Pettin', 1976; Lights Out, 1977; Obsession, 1978; Strangers In The Night, 1979; No Place To Run, 1980; The Wild, The Willing And The Innocent, 1981; Mechanix, 1982; High Stakes And Dangerous Men, 1992; with Waysted: Vices, 1983; The Good The Bad The Waysted, 1985.

WAYBILL Fee (John Waldo), b. 17 Sept 1950, Omaha, Nebraska, USA. Singer. Education: Drama student. Career: Lead singer, The Tubes, 1972-; Regular international tours and concerts including: Knebworth Festival (with Frank Zappa and Peter Gabriel), 1978; KUPD U-Fest, Phoenix, 1993; Band appeared in film Xanadu, 1980. Recordings: Albums: with The Tubes: The Tubes, 1975; Young And Rich, 1976; The Tubes Now, 1977; What Do You Want From Live, 1978; Remote Control, 1979; Completion Backwards Principle, 1981; TRASH (Tubes Rarities And Smash Hits), 1982; Inside Outside, 1983; Love Bomb, 1986; Solo album, Read My Lips, 1984; Singles: White Punks On Dope, 1975; Don't Touch Me There, 1976; Prime Time, 1979; I Don't Want To Anymore, 1981; She's A Beauty, 1983; Tip Of My Tongue, 1983; The Monkey Time, 1983; Piece By Piece, 1985; Other recordings: Richard Marx, Richard Marx, 1988; Contributor, film soundtrack Nobody's Perfect, 1990. Address: c/o Geoffrey Blumenauer Artists, 11846 Balboa Blvd, Suite 204, Granada Hills, CA 91344, USA.

WAYNE Jeff, b. New York, New York, USA. Composer; Arranger. Education: Journalism Graduate. Musical Education: Juillard School of Music, New York; Trinity College of Music, London. Career: Member, The Sandpipers, 1960s; Arranger, The Righteous Brothers; Composer for TV commercials, 1970s; Producer, musical director, David Essex, 1970s. Compositions include: A Tale Of Two Cities, 1969. Recordings: War Of The Worlds, 1978; War Of The Worlds: Highlights, 1981; Spartacus, 1992; Contributor, Beyond The Planets, Rick Wakeman and Kevin Peek, 1984.

WAYNE John Phil, b. 14 July 1946, West Kensington, London, England. International Concert Musician (guitar, keyboards, bass, drums); Vocalist; Actor. Partner, Ludivine Blondin, Jan 1989, 1 daughter. Education: Radio Telegraphy for Planes and Ships (HMS). Musical Education: Private tuition, 1 year; Guitar, piano, self-taught. Career: Sideman with Wild Bill Davis; David Bowie; Tom Jones; John Littleton; Stéphane Grappelli; 5 days with Count Basie; Solo artist and Trio, 1975; Arranger, replaced Quincy Jones for a year, 1978; Conducted The Paris Opera Musicians; Solo concerts: Most international festivals and concerts (jazz); Tours: Africa; Europe; Television, radio, newspapers, magazines, worldwide; Played with: Shirley Bassey; Memphis Slim; Babik Reinhardt; Christian Escoude; Militia Battlefield; Willy Mabon; Sugar Blue; Vic Pitts; Jerome Van Jones; Bruce Grant; Sangoma Everett; Jack Greg; Yos Zoomer; Business: Longsongs Music Ltd. Recordings: Let's Rock, 1968; Nunchaku, 1974; Nostalgia, 1980; Broadway By Night, 1981; 1981 Guitar Solo, 1981; John Phil Wayne Live In Europe, 1986; Fairy Queen, 1987; Heavy Metal Of The '90's, 1991; Express X, 1992; Trio Compilation, 1995; Solo Compilations, 1995; Music for films, 1970-. Honours: Godfather of the International Monte Carlo Racing Car; Twice Best Jazz Guitarist, First Prize Jazz, USA, 1980-82. Memberships: PRS; MCPS; Musicians' Union; SACEM; SGVA; Steam Train Companies. Hobbies: CFV Touristic steam train (France); Wrestling. Current Management: Longsongs Music Ltd, 21-23 Greenwich Market, London SE10 9HZ, England.

WEAVER Blue, b. 11 Mar 1947, Cardiff, Wales. Producer; Musician (keyboards). m. Ann, 24 June, 1 daughter. Musical Education: Piano Lessons; Cardiff College of Music And Drama. Career: Keyboard player, Amen Corner, tours with artists including Jimi Hendrix, Pink Floyd, Hermans Hermits, The Nice, Status Quo, 1965-70; Member, The Stawbs, 1970-73; Also session work included: T Rex; Lou Reed; Family; Alice Cooper; Graeme Edge (Moody Blues). Member, Mott The Hoople, US tour supported by Queen, first rock band to play Broadway, 1973-74; Also played keyboards for Streetwalkers; Member, Ian Hunter/Mick Ronson Band, European tour, 1974-75; US resident, member Bee Gees, 1975-82; Keyboard player, co-producer, co-writer, 6 consecutive Number 1 records, USA; Also session work; Returned to London, 1982; Played keyboards, produced, programmed computers for artists including: Pet Shop Boys; Art Of Noise; Stevie Wonder; Miguel Boise; Duran Duran; Propaganda; The Damned; Billy Ocean; Swing Out Sister; Five Star; Own digital studio; Tutor, popular music, Westminster University, London. Compositions include: Co-wrote songs for Bee Gees; Commercials include jingles for Labatts, music for Volkswagen; Videos; Film soundtracks for Palace Pictures. Recordings with: Amen Corner; Strawbs, 1970-73; Get It On, T Rex; Mott The Hoople Live; Berlin, Lou Reed; Bee Gees, 1974-82; Keyboards on albums by: Chicago; Stephen Stills; Neil Young; McGuinn Clark Hillman; The Osmonds; John Cougar Mellencamp. Honours: Emmy, music on Calder Racetrack; BMI 2 million performance song co-written with Barry Gibb: Our Love. Memberships: PRS; BMI; BASCA; Musicians' Union; Re-Pro. Address: 12 South Parade, Bedford Park, London W4 1JU, England.

WEBB Cassell, b. 7 Nov 1948, San Antonio, Texas, USA. Recording Artist; Producer. m. Craig Leon, 18 June 1984. Musical Education: Private instruction vocal training. Career: Member, various Texas psychedelic bands including The Children; Background vocalist, 1970s; Continued with production work, 1979-; Recordings: as solo artist: Llano, 1985; Thief Of Sadness, 1987; Songs Of A Stranger, 1989; Conversations At Dawn, 1990; House Of Dreams, 1992; Co-writer, The Kosh Klub Anima, 1993. Hobbies: Antique collecting; Gardening; Living. Current Management: Safta Jaffery, SJP Management. Address: 1 Prince Of Wales Passage, 117 Hampstead Road, London NW1, England.

WEBB Eric Loder, b. 27 May 1921, Bedford, Bedfordshire, England. Musican (bass, guitar, steel guitar). m. 2 sons, 1 daughter. Musical Education: Self-taught. Career: Wartime: Ralph Readers Gang Shows; Own band: Beginners Please, 1947; BBC Radio, 1948; Showtime, BBC, 1949; Geraldo Orchestra, Bermudiana Hotel, Bermuda, 1960-70. Membership: Musicians' Union. Hobbies: Genealogy; Cycling. Current Management: Colin Bryant Entertainments, Poole, Dorset, England. Address: Cuckoo Cottage, Green Bottom, Colehill, Wimborne, Dorset BH21 2LW, England.

WEBB Peter Godfrey, b. 13 May 1940, Southampton, Hampshire, England. Musician (keyboards); Vocalist. m. Barbara, 20 Apr 1963, 2 daughters. Education: Teaching diploma. Musical Education: Self-taught. Career: Semi-professional, 1967-87; Fully professional solo artiste, 1987-; Also leader, Peter Webb Trio; Montego Bay; Bittersweet. Publications: Series of children's learning tapes set to music including Tables Disco (partnership with brother). Membership: Branch Secretary, Musicians' Union. Hobbies: Reading; Watching videos. Current Management: John Bedford Enterprises, 40 Stubbington Avenue, North End, Portsmouth PO2 0HY, England. Address: 117 Athelstan Road, Bitterne, Southampton SO19 4DG, England.

WEBB Sarah Anne, b. 1971. Vocalist. Career: Singer, D-Influence; Concerts include: Support to Prince and Michael Jackson; UK tour, 1995; Television appearances include: Later With Jools Holland (with Björk), BBC2, 1995. Recordings include: Singles: I'm The One, 1990. Midnite, 1995; Waiting, 1995; Albums: Good 4 We, 1992; Prayer And Unity, 1995; Backing vocalist on album Seal, Seal, 1991. Current Management: The Third Rail, 70 Hurlingham Road, London SW6 3RQ, England.

WEBER Eberhard, b. 22 Jan 1940, Stuttgart, Germany. Musician (double bass, violincello). m. Maja, 28 June 1968. Musical Education: Studies of violincello, double bass. Career: Professional singer, 1972; Member, Dave Pike Set; Volker Kriegel Spectrum; Eberhard Weber Colours; Collaboration with Jan Garbarek, 1982-; Member, United Jazz and Rock Ensemble until 1987; Solo performances. Recordings: The Colours of Chloe; Yellow Fields; The Following Morning; Silent Feet; Fluid Rustle; Chorus; Orchestra; Pendulum; Film and television music. Honours: German Phono Academy Awards: Artist of the Year; Record of the Year, with Colours Of Chloe, 1975. Membership: Union of German Jazz Musicians (UDJ). Current Management: Bremme and Hohensee. Address: Hauptstr 25, D-69117 Heidelberg, Germany.

WECKL Dave, b. 8 January 1960, St Louis, MO, USA. Drums. m. Joyce, 6 May 1989, 1 daughter. Education: 2 Years Jazz Studies Program, Marching Bands College. Career: Stage: Simon and Garfunkel, Paul Simon, Chick Corea, Brecker Bros, Michel Camit, Mike Stern, Dave Weckl Band; TV: Tonight Show with Chick Corea; Arsenio Hill Show with Chick Corea; Mag: On covers of Modern Drummer Jazz Is and Downbeat. Compositions: Co-writer, 4 solo records. Recordings: Chick Corea Elektric Band, 6; Robert Plant (Honey Drippers); Diana Ross (Swept Away); Dave Grusin, 2; Chick Corea Akoustic Band, 2; Dave Weckl, 4. Publications: Instructional - On Warner Bros, 1988; Back to Basics, Next Step, 1989; Working It Out, I & II, 1994; The Ultimate Play Along, I & II, 1994, 1995. Honours: Grammy, Chick Corea Akoustic Band, 1988; Best Electric Jazz Drummer, Modern Drummer, 1987-92. Hobbies: Auto/Kart Racing; Swimming. Current Management: Ron Moss Management Angency. Address: 2635 Griffith Park Boulevard, LA, CA 90039, USA.

WEEDON Bert, b. 10 May 1920, East Ham, London, England. Musician (guitar); Guitar Tutor. Career: Session musician, 1950s-; Member, touring groups of Django Reinhardt; Stéphane Grappelli; Featured soloist, Mantovani; Played with numerous artistes including: Ted Heath; Jimmy Shand; Leader, own quartet, 1956; Television appearances: Residency, 5 O'Clock Club, ITV; Subject, This Is Your Life, 1992; Radio appearances: 3 shows per week, BBC Show Band; Guitar tutor, 1950s-; Play In A Day tutor books once used by Eric Clapton, George Harrison, Pete Townsend. Recordings: Guitar Boogie Shuffle (Number 1, UK), 1959; Apache, 1960; Numerous albums include: King Size Guitar, 1960; The Romantic Guitar Of Bert Weedon, 1970; Rockin At The Roundhouse, 1971; The Gentle Guitar Of Bert Weedon, 1975; 22 Guitar Greats, 1976; Guitar Favourites, 1983; Mr Guitar, 1984; Once More With Feeling, 1988; Featured musician, hundreds of records by artists including: Marty Wilde; Cliff Richard; Adam Faith; Billy Fury; Tommy Steele; Laurie London; Alma Cogan; Dicky Valentine; Frank Sinatra; Rosemary Clooney, 1950s-. Publications: Numerous guitar tuition books, courses, videos, including: Play In A Day (2 million copies sold, most successful guitar tutor book ever); Play Every Day.

WEEKES Alan Noel, b. 25 Dec 1958, London, England. Musician (guitar); Tutor; Composer. 1 son. Guildhall School Of Music and Drama, Post graduate. Career: Founder member,

pop band La Famille; Original member, Jazz Warriors; Television appearances include: Channel 4 club mix; Black On Black; Party At The Palace; Top Of The Pops; Switch; Pebble Mill; The White Room; Late Show; Tours: Japan; West Indies; First Lucia Jazz Festival; Africa; Europe with Jazz Jamaica and Sound Advice. Composition: Composer, performer, Breath (series of music commissioned by Arts Council), Shaw Theatre, 1992; Just a Dream, album, 1996. Recordings: with Sugar Minot; Carol Thompson; Trevor Walters; Jean Adebambo; Jacky Mitto; Janet Kay; Art Blakey and Dick Heckstall-Smith; Courtney Pine; Recent recordings with: Jazz Jamaica; Byron Wallen's Sound Advice; Jazz Warriors. Membership: Musicians' Union. Hobbies: Fitness; Reading; Photography. Address: 65 Clinger Court, Hoxton Street, London N1 5DF, England.

WEEKS Clifford M., b. New York City, USA. Arranger: Composer; Musician (trombone); Educator. 1 son, 1 daughter. Education: CAGS in Educational Administration, Boston State College, 1977. Musical Education: Professional Diploma in Arranging and Composition, Berklee College of Music, 1962; Bachelor of Music, 1963, Master of Music (magna cum laude), 1975, Boston Conservatory of Music. Career: Teacher, Assistant Principal, Adminstration Assistant and Cluster Coordinator in Boston public schools; Conductor, All-City Jazz band and college jazz bands; Musical Arranger, Greater Bostonians and various professional artists. Compositions: Triptych For Tuba And Piano; Four jazz/stage band compositions. Recording: Triptych For Tuba And Piano, recorded by Karl Megules, 1975. Honours: Fellow, Boston University; Omega Man of the Year, Omega Psi Phi Fraternity, 1972. Hobbies: Athletic workouts at the gym. Address: 20 Fells Avenue, Medford, MA 02155, USA.

WEIDNER Tim. Mix Engineer; Engineer; Programmer. Career: Worked with Seal on the Spacejam Soundtrack; Working with Trevor Horn for The Art of Noise and Seal (forthcoming album). Recordings: Tina Turner, Wildest Dreams; Seal, Seal I, Seal II, Kiss From a Rose (Engineer); Prayer For the Dying (Engineer, Programmer), Future Love Paradise (Engineer); Janet Jackson and Luther Vandross, Best Things in Life Are Free (Engineer, Remixer); Mike Oldfield, Tubular Bells II (Engineer, Mixed, Programmer); Shara Nelson, I Fell (Engineer, Mixed); Brand New Heavies, Back To Love (Engineer, Mixed); Sweetback. Honour: Grammy Nomination, 1995. Address: SARM Productions, SP2 Holdings Ltd, The Blue Building, 42/46 St Luke's Mews, London W11 1DG, England.

WEISS Fredric (Fred), b. 5 May 1943, Brooklyn, New York, USA. College Professor; Record Company President. m. Sharon J Williams Weiss, 4 Jan 1986, 1 son. Education: BS Degree, Broadcasting, Emerson College; MA, University of Denver; Doctoral studies, Indiana University and Texas A&M. Career: College teaching at: San Antonio College; Trinity University; SMU and University of Maryland; Record label President and Publishing Co President; Radio station Program Director; Joint author, radio programming text book. Recordings: Album: As Label President: World Bizarre; 12" Singles: Innocent Bystander; Muzik Box; Split Image; As video director: 3 videos, The Kids; 1 video, Muzik Box; 1 video, Heyoka; 1 video, Claude Morgan/The Blast. Publications: Co-author, The Radio Format Conundrum. Honour: Broadcast Preceptor Award. Memberships: Texas Music Association; NARAS (candidate); ASCAP; Texas Association of Broadcast Educators; MEIEA. Hobbies: Listening to live and recorded music; Dancing; Biking. Address: c/o Belt Drive Records Ltd, FED Publishng Company, PO Box 101107, San Antonio, TX 78201-9107, USA.

WELCH Colin Michael, b. 9 June 1962, Wareham, Dorset, England. Jazz Musician (saxophone, clarinet). m. Susan Welch, 22 Dec 1986, 1 daughter. Education: First Class BA Hons, Graphic Design, London College of Printing. Musical Education: Various grades, clarinet. Career: Played dance bands, big bands, jazz; Moved to Kent, playing and teaching music professionally, 1987; Resident jazz musician, Broome Park Country Club, Canterbury, Kent, 1992-93; Small local jazz bands; Colin Welch Big Band, culminating in 6-piece modern jazz (swing) rock band Headgear, playing own original compositions. Recordings: Headgear (own compositions), 1994. Memberships: Musicians' Union. Hobbies: Goat-keeping; Chicken-keeping; Gardening. Address: Clap Hill House, Aldington, Nr Ashford, Kent TN25 7DG, England.

WELCH Ed, b. 22 Oct 1947, Oxford, England. Composer; Arranger; Musician (piano). m. Jane, Apr 13 1968, 2 sons, 1 daughter. Education: Trinity College London. Musical Education: Music Scholar, Trinity College of Music, London, GTCL, LTCL, Mus Ed. Career: Staff arranger, plugger, orchestrator, United Artists Music, 1967-76; Freelance composer, 1977-; Guest conductor with all major British Orchestras; Musical Director for television series. Compositions: 250 recorded songs; 3 musicals; over 200 television themes, incidentals, including: Films: The Thirty Nine Steps, 1974; The Snow Goose, 1976; Television: Shillingbury Tales, 1980; Blockbusters, 1983; Catchphrase, 1985; TV AM News, 1986; Knightmare, 1986; $64000?, 1989; Jim Henson's Animal Show (all music), 1994; The National Lottery, 1994; Wolves Witches Giants, 1995. Memberships: BASCA; PRS; Musicians' Union; BAFTA Jury. Hobbies: Cricket; Farming; Reading; Travel. Address: c/o Welcome Music Ltd, Redhills, Stokenham, Nr Kingsbridge, Devon TQ7 2SS, England.

WELCH Justin, b. 4 Dec 1972, Nuneaton, England. Musician (drums). Career: Member, Elastica; Numerous television and radio appearances; Tours: UK; USA; Canada; Europe. Recordings: Single: Be My God, Suede; Album: Elastica, 1995. Current Management: CMO Management, Unit 32, Ransomes Dock, 35-37 Parkgate Road, London SW11 4NP, England.

WELDING Paul Daniel, b. 14 May 1971, St Helens, England. Record Producer; Remixer. Musical Education: Self-taught. Career: Dance music record producer; Various radio appearances on local stations; 2 appearances on television; Remixes for major record companies and also Disc Jockey at The Opera House, Toronto, Canada. Recordings: 3 record releases: Void 1 and 2; Rebound; Various remixes including: Sounds Of Blackness; Crystal Waters; Lisa M. Membership: Musicians' Union. Hobbies: Photography; Disc Jockeying; Art. Current Management: John Slater, Ken Grogan, Deep Management. Address: 85 Central Drive, Haydock, St Helens W11 0JE, England.

WELDON Joel, b. 1958. Singer; Songwriter. m. 1986-1995, 1 son, 1 daughter. Career: Major touring artist in contemporary Christian music. Recordings: Mistaken Identity, 1985; Terror And Love, 1987; Pure Adventure, 1988; Wisdom Street, 1989; Cross The World, 1990; Catch Fire America, 1991; Rock It, 1993; Rise Up America, 1994. Current Management: BMP Artist Management: Brian A Mayes. Address: PO Box 1703, La Mirada, CA 90637, USA.

WELDON Shelly, b. 22 Sept 1960, London, England. Singer; Entertainer; Musician (piano, keyboard, guitar); Writer. Education: Pitman's College, London. Musical Education: Advanced studies with Professor Dora Zafransky, Hon Professor, Trinity College of Music. Career: 2 tours, Sweden; Swedish television and radio broadcasts, 1982, 1983; Writer, producer, presenter, Capitol Radio, 1982; Personal appearance, before HM The Sultan of Oman, 1983; Radio Tross, Amsterdam, 1984; Norwegian tour, radio broadcasts, 1985; Dorchester Hotel, London, 1987-88; Featured session singer, Heathrow Hotels, London; Winner, Alternative Eurovision Song Contest, London Newstalk Radio, with If Heaven Is A Kiss Away (own lyric), 1995; Live TV, 1996; Channel 5 TV, 1997; Talent Channel, 1997. Compositions include: Lyricist, While There's A Song To Sing (composer, Marie Francis), signature tune for tenor Wynford Evans, programmes, BBC Radio 2, 1993. Recordings include: The Touch of Love, 1983; Album: Shelly At The Sheraton, 1983; Let the Bells Ring, 1996. Honours: Presented to HRH Princess Alexandra, for highest single donation to Kingston Hospital Scanner Appeal, 1994. Memberships: British Equity; Musicians' Union; PRS. Hobbies: Philately; Writing children's stories; Walking; Dancing; Reading. Address: c/o British Equity, Guild House, Upper St Martin's Lane, London WC2H 9EG, England.

WELLER Martin William Charles, b. 28 Oct 1961, Bristol, England. Singer; Songwriter; Musician (guitar); Arranger. 1 daughter. Education: City & Guilds, Industrial heating and Welding. Musical Education: Guitar and singing lessons. Career: Support to: Benny Gallagher; Isaac Guillory; Clive Gregson; Counterfeit Stones; Tours include: UK; France; Germany; Cyprus; Television appearances include: Cable TV; London Weekend Television; Local radio includes: Eclipse; Mercury; London News Radio. Many unpublished compositions. Recordings: Singles: The Good Die Young, 1984; Maggie, 1990. Honours: Finalist, Hammersmith Rock Festival, 1985; Selected to play German Festival, 1995. Membership: Musicians' Union. Hobbies: Snooker; Golf; Badminton; Squash; Skiing; Music. Current Management: Self-managed.

WELLER Paul, b. 25 May 1958, Woking, Surrey, England. Singer; Songwriter; Musician (guitar, piano). m. Dee C Lee, Dec 1986. Career: Founder, singer, guitarist, The Jam, 1976-1982; Concerts include: Reading Festival, 1978; Great British Music Festival, 1978; Pink Pop Festival, 1980; Loch Lomond Festival, 1980; Founder, The Style Council, 1983-89; Appearances include: Miners benefit concert, Royal Albert Hall, London, 1984; Live Aid, Wembley Arena, 1985; Film: JerUSAlem, 1987; Founder, The Paul Weller Movement, 1990; Solo artiste, 1990-; UK and international tours; Phoenix Festival, 1995; T In The Park Festival, Glasgow, 1995; Own record label, Freedom High. Compositions include: My Ever Changing Moods; Shout To The Top; The Walls Come Tumbling Down; Have You Ever Had It Blue, for film Absolute Beginners; It Didn't Matter; Wanted; Sunflower; Wild Wood; The Weaver. Recordings: Albums: with the Jam: In The City, 1977; This Is The Modern World, 1977; All Mod Cons, 1978; Setting Sons, 1979; Sound Affects, 1980; The Gift, 1982; Dig The New Breed, 1982; Snap!, 1983; Greatest Hits, 1991; Extras, 1992; Live Jam, 1993; with Style Council: Introducing The Style Council, 1983; Café Bleu, 1984; Our Favourite Shop, 1985; Home And Abroad, 1986; The Cost Of Loving, 1987; Confessions Of A Pop Group, 1988; The Singular Adventures Of The Style Council, 1989; Here's Some That Got Away, 1993; Solo albums: Paul Weller, 1992; Wild Wood, 1993; Live Wood, 1994; Stanley Road, 1995. Honours include: Ivor Novello Award; BRIT Awards: Best Male Artist, 1995, 1996. Current Management: Solid Bond Management, 45-53 Sinclair Road, London W14 0NS, England.

WELLER Timothy James, b. 30 Dec 1969, Tunbridge Wells, Kent, England. Musician (drums, percussion). m. Aliza Colman, 28 Nov 1992. Education: University of London, Kings College. Musical Education: Drummers Collective (New York); Bob Armstrong (London). Career: Tours

with: McKoy; Federation; Eddie Floyd; Ashley Flowers; Colin John; Performed with: Izit; Zeke Manyika; Jerry Dammers; Roger Beaujolais; Maxi Jazz; Daniel Walker; Giles Martin. Recordings: Original soundtracks for: The Confessional (David Puttnam), 1995; Johnny And The Dead (LWT), 1995; Albums, singles with: Teenie Hodges; Zeke Manyika and Jalal; McKoy; Paul Reid. Honours: Drummer Of The Year, Joe Hubbards School, Pearl Drums, 1993. Hobby: Keep Fit. Current Management: Sound Advice Management. Address: C104, Faircharm Trading Estate, 10 Creekside, London SE8 3DX, England.

WELLINGS Clive, b. 20 Sept 1953, Burton Upon Trent, England. Musician (drums); Massage Therapist. Education: BA Hons. Musical Education: Self-taught, with help from Steve York, Paul Whiteside, Jon Hiseman. Career: Drummer for: Nasty Sandwich; Midnight Sun, Bracknell Jazz Festival, 1978; Hydra; The Fabulous Falling Angels; The Royal Monkeys; Lacewing Bomber, support to Great White, 1987; The Young Outlawz; Wild Angel; Lipstick Daggers; Twisted; Secret Society; Also various session recordings. Recordings: with Lacewing Bomber: Feelin' Electric; with The Fabulous Falling Angels: Unsung Heroes. Membership: Musicians' Union. Hobbies: Graphic art; Rambling; Photography. Current Management: 1A Musical Promotions. Address: 76 Hamilton Road, Reading, Berkshire RG1 5RD, England.

WELLINGS George, b. 13 Jan 1941, Wolverhampton, Staffordshire, England. Musician (saxophones, clarinets, flutes). m. Maureen Glenn, 23 Dec 1967, 1 daughter. Career: In backing orchestras for many American and British stars including: Johnny Mathis; Jack Jones; Four Tops; O'Jays; Englebert Humperdinck; Gene Pitney; Shirley Bassey; Matt Munro; Pat Boone; Variety artistes include: Morecombe and Wise; Bruce Forsythe; Des O'Connor. Membership: Musicians' Union. Hobbies: Golf; Fly-fishing.

WELLINGTON Sheena, b. 29 Aug 1944, Dundee, Scotland. Singer; Broadcaster; Songwriter. m. Malcolm, 20 Mar 1967, 1 son. Musical Education: Oral tradition. Career: Radio Tay presenter, 1984-93; Thistle and Shamrock USA tours, 1989, 1990; Canada, 1991; Scottish Arts Council committee member, 1992-; Barcelona Celtic Festival, 1993; Nordic Festival, 1994. Compositions: Newport Braes; Women O'Dundee. Recordings: Kerelaw, 1986; Clearsong, 1990; TBD, 1995. Honours: Leng Silver Medal. Memberships: Musicians' Union; Traditional Music and Song Association; Equity; Scottish Arts Council. Hobbies: Singing; Reading; Swimmimg. Current Management: Malcolm Wellington. Address: 6 St Andrews Road, Largoward, Fife KY9 1HZ, Scotland.

WELLS Kitty (Muriel Ellen Deason), b. 30 Aug 1919, Nashville, Tennessee, USA. Singer. m. Johnnie Wright, 30 Oct 1937, 1 son, 2 daughters. Career: Founder member, the Deason Sisters, 1935-37; Regular radio programme, Nashville; Later billed as Johnnie Wright And The Harmony Girls, then the Tennessee Mountain Boys; Took name Kitty Wells, 1943; Solo recording artist, 1949-; Became member of Grand Ole Opry, 1951; Extensive worldwide tours, 1950s-70s; Toured as The Kitty Wells And Johnny Wright Family Show, 1963-; Hosted own television show, 1969-; First UK appearance, Wembley Festival, 1974. Recordings: Over 80 country hits; US Country Number 1 singles include: It Wasn't God Who Made Honky Tonk Angels, 1952; One By One (with Red Foley), 1954; Heartbreak USA, 1961; Albums include: Solo: Country Hit Parade, 1956; After Dark, 1959; Queen Of Country Music, 1962; Kitty Wells, 1966; Country Heart, 1969; Your Love Is The Way, 1970; Pledging My Love, 1971; I've Got Yesterday, 1972; Sincerely, 1972; Yours Truly, 1973; Forever Young, 1974; with Red Foley: Golden Favourites, 1961; Together Again, 1967;

with Johnnie Wright: We'll Stick Together, 1969; Heartwarming Gospel Songs, 1972; with Roy Drusky: Kitty Wells and Roy Drusky, 1987; Various compilations. Honours include: Female Country Artiste, Billboard, 1953-65; Inducted into Country Music Hall Of Fame, 1976; Named Queen Of Country Music, 1952; First female country singer to have Number 1 record, 1952. Current Management: Wright's Enterprises, 240 Old Hickory Boulevard, Madison, TN 37115, USA.

WELLS Robert Henry Arthur, b. 7 April 1962, Stockholm, Sweden. Composer; Musician (Piano & Vocal). Engaged to Maria Sköld. Education: Adolf Fredriks Music School, 1969-78; Academy of Music, 1978-82; Private piano lessons, 1969-78. Career: Professionally working in Scandinavia & Russia, 1987-; Toured with different bands & singers, 1977-87; Featuring in major TV-shows; Played for Swedish Royalties several times. Recordings: Upp Pa Berget, 1987; The Way I Feel, 1988; Rhapsody in Rock I, 1989; Rhapsody in Rock II, 1990; Norman Vs Wells, 1991; Rhapsody in Rock III, 1993; Nordic Rhapsody, 1996; Boogie Woogie Norman & Wells, 1996. Hobbies: Golf; Jogging. Address: Gurtman & Murtha, 450 7th Avenue, New York, NY 10123, USA. Address: Wells Music AB, Box 34043, 10026 Stockholm, Sweden.

WELSFORD Andy Wells, b. 14 Mar 1959, Bristol, England. Musician (drums). 1 daughter. Education: Technical college. Musical Education: Self-taught. Career: Drummer with Meat Loaf, 1985-86; March Violets, 1987; Romeo's Daughter, 1989; Then Jerico, 1994; World tours, television and radio appearances, videos; Sessions for Roxette; Whitney Houston; John Parr; Dee Lewis; Daniel Weaver; Andy Leek. Recordings: 2 albums, Romeo's Daughter; 1 track, album, Meat Loaf; 1 album, Then Jerico. Current Management: Grahame Perkins, Session Connection, B&H Musicians. Address: 20 Clementina Road, London E10 7LS, England.

WELZ Joey (Joseph Welzant), b. 17 Mar 1940, Baltimore, Maryland, USA. Singer; Musician (piano); Record Producer; Record Company Executive. 1 son, 1 daughter. Education: Degree in Broadcasting, Harford College, 1978. Musical Education: Self-taught. Career: Pianist, Bill Haley and the Comets, 1960s-1980s; Played with Beatles; Link Wray; Roy Buchanan; Reformed Original Comets, 1981; Numerous worldwide tours and television appearances; A&R executive, Canadian American Records, 1966-70; Palmer Records, Detroit, 1971-73; Music City Records, Nashville, 1974-81; Caprice Records, Pennsylvania, 1982-4; President, Caprice International Records, 1984-; Canadian American Records, 1989-; President/owner, Rock Mill Studios, Pennsylvania, 1990-. Compositions include: Hey Little Moonbeam; Baby Let Your Head Hang Down; Candle In The Wind; Forever; Everyday For The Rest Of My Life; Universal Love; One Stormy Love; In The Middle Of The Night Time; Hey Baby; Life on Mars, 1997; Your Love Means Everything, with Amy Beth; A Ring Between Us, with Amy Beth; Rang-a-Tang Boogie. Recordings: Over 100 singles and 75 albums; Hits include: One Way Ticket; 16 Ways; Where Would I Be; Rock-A-Billy; Shake Rattle And Roll; Summertime Blues; Blue Collar Love; Last Kiss; Lonesome Traveller; Forever And A Day; Spanish Rose From Mexico; Summer Place, 1996; You Don't Own Me, 1997. Honours: 5 Grammy Nominations; Top 25 Rock Pianist, Keyboard Magazine, 3 times; One of Top Rock Pianists, DIB, London, 1971; Country Rock Pioneer Award; EIA Award, Most Promising Country Male Vocalist; CMA Award, Video of Year, 1993; Independent Country Male Vocalist of Year; Legendary Performer of Year; Songwriter of Year; Inductee and Gold Charter Member, Rock and Roll Hall of Fame. Memberships: ASCAP. Hobbies: Pool; Yo-Yos. Current Management:

Caprice International Records. Address: PO Box 808, Lititz, PA 17543, USA.

WENER Louise, b. Ilford, Essex, England. Singer; Songwriter. Education: Politics and English degree, Manchester University. Career: Lead singer, Sleeper, 1993-; Support tours with: Blur; Manic Street Preachers; Major concerts include: Heineken Festival, Leeds, 1995; T In The Park, Glasgow, 1995; Glastonbury Festival, 1995; Feile Festival, Ireland, 1995; Milton Keynes Bowl, 1995; Also toured in Japan; Television includes: Later With... Britpop Now, BBC2, 1995. Recordings: Debut album: Smart, 1995; Singles: Inbetweener; What Do I Do Now?; Vegas; Delicious. Address: c/o Geoff Wener, Big Brother Management, 15 Pratt Mews, London NW1 0AD, England.

WENNIKE Ole B, b. 15 May 1958, Copenhagen, Denmark. Musician; Composer. 1 son. Education: Selftaught. Career: Founder, Copenhagen Based The Sandmen, 1985-92, support gigs in Copenhagen for Nico, Jeffrey Lee Pierce, Long Ryders, 1985-86; USA Tour, 1989, London's Borderline, 1989; Founder, Copenhagen Based Nerve, 1995, support gigs in Copenhagen for David Bowie. Compositions: Western Blood, House in the Country, Heart of Steel, 1989; 5 mins Past Loneliness, Can't Cry No More, 1993; Slave Song, 1994. Recordings: The Sandmen Albums: Western Blood, 1988; Sleepy Head, 1993; In the House of Secrets, 1994; Nerve Album: Speedfreak Jive, 1996. Honours: Danish Grammy, 1993; Gold Record, Denmark. Hobby: Movies. Current Management: Rock-On APS. Address: Rosenörns Alle 6, 4Tv, 1634 Copenhagen V, Denmark.

WENTZEL Magni, b. 28 June 1945, Oslo, Norway. Musician (classical guitar); Jazz Vocalist. m. 28 Apr 1976, 1 son. Musical Education: Private teachers, Norway and abroad. Recordings: As guitarist: with Radio Symphony Orchestra: Concierto de Aranjuez; with Art Farmer: My Wonderful One; with Roger Kelleway and Red Mitchell: New York Nights; with Roger Kelleway and Niels H O Pedersen: Come Away With Me. Honours: Gamling Prize. Membership: Norsk Musikerferbund (Norwegian Musicians' Union). Hobbies: Reading; Biology; Astrophysics; Grammar. Current Management: Den Norske Jazzscene and Diane Mitchell. Address: Neubrggt 6 A, N-0367 Oslo, Norway.

WERMAN Thomas Erlich, b. 2 Mar 1945, Newton, Massachusetts, USA. Record Producer; Musician (guitar, percussion). m. 25 Aug 1968, 1 son, 2 daughters. Education: BA, Columbia College; MBA Columbia Business School. Career: A&R Epic Records, 1970-82; Senior Vice-President, A&R Electra Records, 1982; Independent producer, 1983-; Signed: REO Speedwagon; Ted Nugent; Cheap Trick; Molly Hatchet; Boston; The Producers; Mother's Finest. Recordings: Produced: Ted Nugent; Cheap Trick; Molly Hatchet; Twisted Sister; Jeff Beck; Poison; Mötley Crüe; Kix; LA Guns; Jason and the Scorchers; Lita Ford; Gary Myrick. Honours: 13 RIAA Platinum records, 9 Gold records. Membership: NARAS. Hobbies: Running; Golf. Address: 11818 Laurel Hills Road, Studio City, CA 91604, USA.

WERNICK Peter (Dr Banjo), b. 25 Feb 1946, New York, USA. Musician (banjo); Author; Teacher; Music Association Executive. m. Joan (Nondi) Leonard, 29 June 1974, 1 son. Education: BA, Columbia College, 1966; PhD Sociology, Columbia University, 1973. Career: Country Cooking, Ithaca, New York, 1970-76; Rambling Drifters, Denver, Colorado, 1976-78; Hot Rize, Boulder, Colorado, 1978-90; Pete Wernick's Live Five, 1992-; US and international tours with Hot Rize; Appeared on Austin City Limits; Grand Ole Opry; Nashville Now; Prairie Home Companion; President, IBMA (International Bluegrass Association). Recordings: Writer, performer, Number 1 hit songs: Ruthie; Just Like You;

Albums: Solo albums: On A Roll; Dr Banjo Steps Out; with Hot Rize: Untold Stories; Take It Home; Traditional Ties; In Concert; with Five Live: I Tell You What!. Publications: Bluegrass Banjo, 1974; Bluegrass Songbook, 1976; How to Make a Band Work, 1991; Acutab Transcriptions, Volume I, 1996. Honours: IBMA Entertainer Of The Year with Hot Rize, 1989; Grammy Nomination, Hot Rize album, 1990. Memberships: President IBMA; ASCAP; NARAS. Hobbies: Sports coaching; Basketball; Homemaking. Current Management: Keith Case Associates, Nashville, Tennessee. Address: 59 Music Square West, Nashville, TN 37203, USA.

WERTICO Paul David, b. 5 Jan 1953, Chicago, Illinois, USA. Musician (drums, percussion); Instructor. m. Barbara Ungerleider, 22 Aug 1986, 1 daughter. Education: 2 years at College; Self-taught drummer; Scholarship, Western Illinois University. Career: Member, Pat Metheny Group, 1983-; Tours include: Tour of Argentina, with Pat Metheny, Ernie Watts and Charlie Haden, 1986; Also California, Japan and Hong Kong apperances, 1988; Member, Pat's Secret Story Band, performing in 18 countries worldwide; Performed with numerous jazz artists including: Larry Coryell; Lee Konitz; Herbie Mann; Terry Gibbs; Buddy DeFranco; Lew Tabakin; Art Porter; Jaco Pastorius; Chico Freeman; Ron Carter; Alan Pasqua. Recordings include: Albums: Solo/bandleader: The Yin And The Yout; Live in Warsaw!; as co-leader: Earwax Control; Spontaneous Composition; 2 LIVE; BANG!; The Sign of Four; Union; with Pat Metheny/Pat Metheny Group: First Circle, 1984; Still Life (Talking), 1987; Letter From Home, 1989; Secret Story, 1992; The Road To You, 1993; We Live Here, 1995; Quartet; Imaginary Day, 1997; Appeared on three Pat Metheny videos; Film soundtrack The Falcon and the Snowman, with Pat Metheny; Albums with artists including: Paul Winter; Kurt Elling; John Moulder; Bobby Lewis; Ken Nordine; Ellen McIlwaine. Publications: Columnist, Drums and Drumming magazine; DRUM! magazine; Contributor, Thinking In Jazz; Instructional videos on drumming and percussion. Honours: 6 Grammy Award winning albums with Pat Metheny, (three for Best Jazz Fusion Performance, three for best Contemporary Jazz Performance); Two Grammy Award Nominations for albums with Kurt Elling; NARAS Outrageous Recording Award, 1990; NAIRD Best Rock Record Award, with Ellen McIlwaine, 1981; 4th in Electric Jazz Drummer Readers' Poll, Modern Drummer Magazine, 1997; Fusion Drummer of the Year, DRUM! Magazine Readers' Poll, 1997. Memberships: Chicago Federation of Musicians; National Academy of Recording Artists and Sciences. Hobby: Steam Locomotives. Address: 8728 North Drake, Skokie, IL 60076, USA.

WESCOMB Morley, b. 19 Sept 1938. Musician (piano). m. 1978, 2 sons, 4 daughters. Education: Royal Navy. Career: Professional musician, 30 years; Leader, Clay City Stompers, Cornwall's Premier Traditional Jazzband. Hobby: The study of ragtime. Address: 28 Church Street, Mevagissey, Cornwall, England.

WEST Cedric Herbert, b. 9 Dec 1918, Rangoon, Burma. Jazz Musician (guitar, trombone). m. Nesta May Seppings, 2 Apr 1942, 1 son, 2 daughters. Education: BS Hons, First Class. Musical Education: Self-taught; Research on jazz guitar and teaching in university degree dissertation. Career: Started as member, Teddy Weather Ford Orchestra, 1945; Returned to Burma, with small band for Ensa playing in Officer's Clubs, 1945; Came to UK, 1947; Toured on trombone with: Les Douglas; Jiver Hutchinson; Viz Lewis; Settled in London, 1950s; Led groups in night clubs; Member, BBC Dance Orchestra, 1968-1978; Numerous television and recording sessions, over 300 radio broadcasts; Did numerous broadcasts including jazz clubs. Compositions: East Meets West; Bach Goes

West; Revamped 2 part inventions and fugues for 4 guitars, bass, drums. Honours: Musicians' Union Life Member. Memberships: Musicians' Union; MRS. Hobbies: Photography. Address: 56 Castleton Road, Goodmayes, Essex, England.

WEST Harry, b. 11 Jun 1926, Lee County, Virginia, USA. Singer; Musician (mandolin, banjo, guitar, other stringed instruments) m. Jeanie West, 31 July 1951, 3 sons, 1 daughter. Career: Husband and wife vocal/instrumental duet, 1951-; Perform old time gospel and traditional songs at revivals, homecomings, festivals, fiddlers conventions and local functions including Asheville North Carolina Mountain Dance And Music Festival, 1950s-60s, also recent years; Many recordings. Address: PO Box 321, Granite Quarry, NC 28072, USA.

WEST Jeanie, b. 24 Aug 1933, Lower Homony, Buncombe County, North Carolina, USA. Singer; Musician (guitar). m. Harry West, 31 July 1951, 3 sons, 1 daughter. Career: Husband and wife vocal/instrumental duet, 1951-; Playing old gospel and traditional songs at revivals, homecomings, festivals, fiddlers conventions, local functions including Asheville North Carolina Mountain Dance and Folk Music Festival, 1950s-60s, and recent years; Many recordings. Address: PO Box 321, Granite Quarry, NC 28072, USA.

WEST Leslie (Leslie Weinstein), b. 22 Oct 1945, Queens, New York, USA. Musician (guitar). Career: Guitarist, Vagrants; Founder member, US rock group Mountain, 1968-85; Concerts include: Woodstock Festival, 1970; European tour, support to Deep Purple, 1985; Also recorded as West, Bruce, Laing (with Jack Bruce, Corky Laing), 1974; Track Nantucket Sleighride used as theme for TV series, World In Action, UK. Recordings: Albums: with Mountain; Mountain Climbing, 1979; Nantucket Sleighride, 1971; Flowers Of Evil, 1971; The Road Goes On Forever - Mountain Live, 1972; Best Of..., 1973; Twin Peaks, 1974; Avalanche, 1974; Go For Your Life, 1975; Over The Top, 1995. Address: c/o Skyline Music, PO Box 31, Lancaster, NH 03584, USA.

WEST Peter, b. 3 Aug 1955, Watford, Hertfordshire, England. Musician (guitar, bass, keyboards); Programmer; Educator. Musical Education: Self-taught. Career: Tutor, Hammonds School Of Music (Guildhall Examination Centre), 1992; Appearance on London Tonight, with Phil Mack, 1993; Performed with Hazel O'Connor, London Astoria, 1995. Recordings: Featured on: Together, World's Apart; Don't Pull Your Love, Sean Maguire; I Can't Go For That, Pauline Henry; Power And Glory (Guitar library album); The Journey, 911 (No 3, UK, 1997); Rhythm of the Night, 911. Memberships: Musicians' Union; PAMRA. Address: 1 Elm Grove, Gammons Lane, Watford, Hertfordshire WD2 6BB, England.

WESTBROOK Kate, (Katherine Jane), b. Guildford, Surrey, England. Singer; Songwriter; Librettist; Painter. m. (1) 1 son, 2 daughters, (2) Mike Westbrook, 23 Sept 1976. Education: Bath Academy of Art; Reading University; London University, Institute of Education. Musical Education: Self-taught. Career: Joined Mike Westbrook Brass Band, 1974; Mike Westbrook Orchestra, 1979; Tours: Europe; Far East; Australia; Canada; Co-author with Mike Westbrook of theatre, dance pieces including: The Ass, 1985; Pier Rides, 1986; London Bridge Is Broken Down, 1987; Played role of Anna in Seven Deadly Sins, by Brecht/Weill, with LSO, Barbican, London, 1989-90; Sang Big Band Rossini, Royal Albert Hall, Proms, 1992; Good Friday 1663, television opera, libretto by Helen Simpson, Ch4 TV, 1995; Exhibitions of paintings in USA, Europe and Australia, 1963-, Galerie Cupillard, Grenoble; Dartington Arts Gallery, Devon; John Innes Centre Gallery. Norfolk and Norwich Festival. Recordings: with Kate Westbrook

Ensemble: Revenge Suite, Bloomsbury Festival, 1985. Solo album: Goodbye Peter Lorre, 1992; with Kate Westbrook and the Skirmishers: Even/Uneven, 1994; Duo with Mike Westbrook, Stage Set, 1996; Love or Infatuation, 1997; Bar Utopia, with Mike Westbrook Orchestra, 1997. Honours: Diaspason d'Or, Goodbye Peter Lorre; Also for Love For Sale with The Westbrook Trio; Nijinska's Whistle for Spink Theatre Company. Membership: Musicians' Union. Address: Brent House, Holbeton, Nr Plymouth PL8 1LX, England.

WESTBROOK Mike (Michael John David), b. 21 Mar 1936, High Wycombe, Buckinghamshire, England. Composer; Musician (piano); Bandleader. m. Katherine Jane (Kate), 23 Sept 1976, 1 son, 1 daughter (by previous marriage). Education: NDD, Plymouth College Of Art; ATD, Hornsey College Of Art. Musical Education: Self-taught. Career: Formed first band, Plymouth Art School, 1958; Led groups including: Mike Westbrook Brass Band, 1973-; Mike Westbrook Orchestra, 1974-; The Westbrook Trio, 1982-; Kate Westbrook/Mike Westbrook Duo, 1995-; Tours: Britain; Europe; Australia; Singapore; Hong Kong; Canada; New York. Compositions: Music for: Theatre; Opera; Dance; Radio; Television; Films. Recordings/compositions include: Marching Song, 1967; Metropolis, 1969; Tyger (A celebration of William Blake), 1971; Citadel/Room 315, 1974; The Westbrook Blake, 1980; On Duke's Birthday, 1984; Love For Sale, 1986; Big Band Rossini, 1987; Off Abbey Road, 1988; Bean Rows And Blues Shots, 1991; Coming Through Slaughter, 1994; Bar Utopia, 1995; Blues For Terenzi; Cable Street Blues, 1997; Television score: Caught On A Train, 1980; Cinema: Moulin Rouge, 1990; Concert works with Kate Westbrook: The Cortege, 1979; London Bridge Is Broken Down, 1987; Measure For Measure, 1992; Music theatre with Kate Westbrook include: Mama Chicago, 1978; Westbrook Rossini, 1984; The Ass, 1985; Pier Rides, 1987; Quichotte, 1989; Good Friday 1663, (TV opera), 1995; Stage Set, 1996; Love or Infatuation, 1997. Honour: OBE, 1988. Memberships: Musicians' Union; Duke Ellington Society. Hobby: Walking by the Erme Estuary. Address: Brent House, Holbeton, Nr Plymouth, Devon PL8 1LX, England.

WESTERGAAD MADSEN Dicte (Benedicte), b. 9 Sept 1966, Denmark. Singer; Songwriter; Musician. Career: Formed band Her Personal Pain, 1989; Numerous Danish club tours, including Roskilde Festival, 1991, 1994, 1997; Popkomm, Germany, 1997; Sopot Festival, Poland, 1997; Actress in film Smukke Dreng (Beautiful Boy), 1992; Lead Actress in play by Hotel Pro Forma, 1998. Recordings: with Her Personal Pain: 6 songs on Secrets II Live, 1990; 1 song (You Can't Always Get What You Want) on Rock Love and Understanding, (Amnesty International), 1991; Songs From Cinema Cafe, 1992; Solo albums: Between Any Four Walls, 1994; Voodoo Vibe, 1996; 1 song (Machinery) on Gaa Ikke Over Sporet (Don't Pass the Trail, Danish National Railways), 1997. Honours: Grammy, Best New Name, 1992. Current Management: Aarhus Musikkontor. Address: Aarhus Musikkontor, att: Dicte, Mindegade 10, 8000 Århus C, Denmark.

WESTFALL-KING Carmen Sigrid, b. 24 Aug 1962, Burlington, Ontario, Canada. Singer; Songwriter; Musician (guitar). m. Kenny King, 27 May 1989, 1 daughter. Musical Education: Recording Arts. Career: Television apperances include: Tommy Hunter Show, CBC Canada; Global TV Network; Opened concerts for Vince Gill; Waylon Jennings; Mary Chapin Carpenter; Michelle Wright; Dan Seals; Kitty Wells. Recordings: Your Old Girlfriend; You're An Angel; I Wanna Hear It From You; Talk Around Town (all Top 10, Canada). Honours: Big Country Awards, Outstanding New Artist, 1989. Memberships: SOCAN; CCMA. Hobbies: Clothing Design; Sewing; Horses. Current Management: Jerry

Knight. Address: 1050 Barnardo Avenue, Peterborough, Ontario K9H 5X2, Canada.

WESTFIELD Steve, b. 2 May 1965, Massachusetts, USA. Singer; Songwriter; Musician (guitar). Education: University of Massachusetts. Career: Singer, songwriter, guitarist, Pajama Slave Dancers, 1981-; Singer, songwriter, guitarist, Steve Westfield Slow Band, 1993-; Tour, Europe, Sebadoit, 1995-96. Recordings: with Pajama Slave Dancers: All You Can Eat, 1982; Problems Of Sects, 1983; Blood, Sweat And Beers, 1984; Pajama Beach Party, 1984; Heavy Petting Zoo, 1985; Full Metal Underpants, 1989; It Came From The Barn, 1996; with Steve Westfield Slow Band: Mangled, 1994; Reject Me...First, 1996. Current Management: c/o Andy Doherty, 63 Endicott Street #9, Boston, MA 02113, USA.

WESTON John, b. 30 Apr 1924, London, England. Semi-retired musician (saxophone, flute). Musical Education: Private, Jack Brymer; Geoffrey Gilbert. Career: Played in Air Force, 1942, 1946; Played various hotels, theatres, freelance; Now flute, Merton band; Clarinet MX Yeomanry; Trombone, Barnes Band. Membership: Musicians' Union. Hobbies: Theatre; Coda Club. Address: 180 London Road, Twickenham TW1 1EX, England.

WESTWOOD Elizabeth Rose, 29 Nov 1963, Washington DC, USA. Musician. Education: Art School, Washington DC. Career: Singer with Westworld; Radio and television appearances includes Top Of The Pops; Tours; Currently singer in Moondogg. Recordings: Albums with Westworld: Where The Action Is; Beat Box Rock'n'Roll; Movers and Shakers. Memberships: PRS; Musicians' Union. Hobbies: Painting; Travel. Current Management: Proper Management. Address: 93 Rivington Street, London EC1, England.

WESTWOOD Tim, b. 3 Oct 1967, London, England. Disc Jockey. Career: Rap DJ for radio and clubs including: Pirate radio, LWR and Kiss FM, 1984-87; Capital FM, 1987-94; 1 FM Rap Show, BBC Radio 1, 1994-. Recordings: Owner, Justice Records; Producer, General Levi and London Posse. Honours: Sony Radio Award, Best Specialist Music Programme, 1990, 1991; Current Management: Justice Production. Address: PO Box 689, London SW6 6HW, England.

WETTON John, b. 12 June 1949, Derby, England. Singer; Songwriter; Musician (bass, keyboards). m. Jill Briggs, 10 July 1987. Education: Bournemouth College. Musical Education: Brother Robert, organist, choirmaster. Career: Member, Family, 1971-72; King Crimson, 1973-75; Roxy Music, 1975; Uriah Heep, 1976; UK, 1978-79; Solo artiste, 1980; Member, Asia, 1982-91; Solo artiste, 1991-. Recordings: with Family: Fearless, 1971; Bandstand, 1972; with King Crimson: Larks Tongues In Aspic, 1973; Starless And Bible Black, 1974; Red, 1974; USA, 1975; with Roxy Music: Viva!, 1976; with UK: UK, 1978; Danger Money, 1979; with Asia: Asia, 1982; Alpha, 1983; Astra, 1985; Then And Now, 1990; Solo album: Battle Lines, 1994. Honours: 2 Grammy Nominations; 3 ASCAP Awards; 40 Gold and Platinum discs. Memberships: PRS; National Academy Of Songwriters; ASCAP. Hobbies: Horse riding; Skiing; Reading. Current Management: Carr/Sharpe Entertainment. Address: 9320 Wilshire Blvd, Suite 200, Beverly Hills, CA 90212, USA.

WETTRE Petter, b. 11 Aug 1967, Sandefjord, Norway. Musician(saxophone). 1 son. Musical Education: Berklee College of Music, Boston, USA, 1989-92. Career: Several Norwegian tours with Nordic Jazz Quartet and Petter Wettre Quartet; Appeared at Konigsberg Jazz Festival with Petter Wettre Quartet, 1993; Oslo Jazz Festival, 1994; Recorded for Norwegian National

Broadcasting 2 times; Appeared on several TV shows including: Amandas How; Tawde P; Melody Grand Prix; Freelance musician with artists including: Shirley Bassey; Magui Wenjzel; Lilh Babs; Jon Eberson; Jon Christensen;Several commercials for Norwegian radio and TV; Also runs various clinics and workshops; Currently member of: Petter Wettre Quartet, Horns For Hire, All Stars, and Oystein Sevags. Recordings include: Works with Jan Werner; Stephen Ackles; The Stavanger Gospel Choir. Honour: Outstanding Achievement Award, Berklee College of Music. Address: Bergliotsveg 1B, 0575 Oslo, Norway.

WHARTON Darren Dean. Musician (keyboards, guitar); Vocalist; Songwriter. Career: Keyboard player with Phil Lynott, 1980; Member, Thin Lizzy, 1981-83; Concerts include: Tours of UK; Scandinavia; Europe; Japan; Reading Rock Festival, 1983; Monsters of Rock Festival, Germany, 1983; Founder member, Dare, 1987-91. Recordings: Albums with Thin Lizzy: Chinatown, 1980; Adventures Of Thin Lizzy, 1981; Renegade, 1981; Thunder And Lightning, 1983; The Boys Are Back In Town, 1983; with Dare: Out Of The Silence, 1988; Blood From Stone, 1991; with Phil Lynott: Solo In Soho, 1980.

WHEATLEY Martin Russell, b. 29 August 1958, London, England. Musician. m. Angela, 3 sons. Education: BA, Colchester College; MA, University College, London. Career: Broadcasts on Radio and Television, BBC and Commercial; Concert Appearances at the Purcell Room and Queen Elizabeth Hall; Extensive Touring of Canada, USA, including Hawaii; Specialist in acoustic fretted instruments playing in authentic early styles, jazz, blues, ragtime, Hawaiian. Recordings: New Orleans Hop Scop Blues, with Bent Persson and Alain Marquet; Charleston Mad, with Neville Dickie; Syncopated Jamboree, I Like To Do Things For You, The Henderson Project, Harlem's Arabian Nights, all with Keith Nichols. Hobbies: Cricket; Old Cars; Letterpress Printing.

WHIGFIELD (Sannie Carlson), b. Denmark. Singer. Career: Former model; Member, The Whigfield Project, 1992; Solo singer, 1993-. Recordings: Singles: Saturday Night, 1994; Another Day, 1994. Address: c/o Systematic Records, PO Box 1422, Chancellors House, Chancellors Road, London W6 9SG, England.

WHILE Christine Mills, b. 22 Dec 1955, Barrow-in-Furness, England. Singer; Musician (guitar); Songwriter. m. Joe While, 18 Oct 1974, divorced 1993, 1 son, 1 daughter. Musical Education: Self-taught. Career: Tours: Canada; Kenya; Most European countries; UK; Numerous television and radio appearances; Performed at Cambridge and Edmonton festivals. Composition: Young Man Cut Down in His Prime, co-written with Julie Matthews, 1996. Recordings: Albums: Solo album (own compositions): Look At Me Now; Blue Moon On The Rise (EP), with Julie Matthews (5 songs as co-writer); with the Albion Band: Acousticity; Albion Heart. Memberships: MCPS; PRS; Musicians' Union. Hobbies: Gardening; Films; Reading; Socialising. Current Management: Blue Moon Music. Address: 130 Central Avenue, Southport, Merseyside PR8 3ED, England.

WHITAKER Michael Whiteley, b. 26 May 1948, Ploughley, Oxfordshire, England. Musician (keyboards, harmonica, percussion); Vocalist. m. Helen, 15 Aug 1969, 2 sons. Musical Education: Newcastle College Of Arts and Technology School of Music. Career: Member of Halfbreed; European tour with Leo Sayer; British tour with Curved Air; Television and radio apppearances: Tube; Geordie Scene; In Concert, BBC Radio 1. Recordings: 4 albums; 2 releases for North East labels; 12 singles. Publications: Out Now (Rock fanzine). Memberships: PRS; Equity; Musicians' Union. Hobbies: Snooker; Supporter of Newcastle United Football Club; Reading. Current Management: Bill Dixon Agency. Address: 58

Hedley Street, Gosforth, Newcastle Upon Tyne NE3 1DL, England.

WHITE Adam Peter, b. 22 Sept 1948, Bristol, England. Journalist. Career: Reporter, news editor, Music Week, 1974-77; International Editor, Billboard, 1978-80; Managing Editor, Billboard, 1981-83; Editor-in-Chief, Billboard, 1983-85; New York Bureau Chief, Radio & Records, 1985-88; London correspondent, Rolling Stone, 1988-89; International Editor-In-Chief, Billboard, 1989-. Publications: The Billboard Book Of Gold And Platinum Hits, 1990; Co-author, The Billboard Book of No 1 Rhythm & Blues Hits, 1993. Address: Billboard, 23 Ridgmount Street, London WC1E 7AH, England.

WHITE Andrew Nathaniel III, b. 6 Sept 1942, Washington, District of Columbia, USA. Musician (saxophone, oboe, horn, bass); Recording Engineer; Composer; Arranger; Conductor; Musicologist; Lecturer; Publisher; Impresario. m. Jocelyne H J Uhl. Education: BMus Music Theory, Howard University, Washington, 1964. Career: Jazz saxophonist, JFK Quintet, 1960-64, New Jazz Trio, 1965-66; Oboist, English horn player, Center of Creative and Performing Arts, 1965-67; Principal oboe and English horn, American Ballet Theater, 1968-70; Electric bassist, Stevie Wonder and Motown Records, 1968-70; Fifth Dimension, 1970-76; Weather Report (recordings), 1970-73; The Jupiter Hair Company, 1971-; Solo debut, Carnegie Hall, 1974; Jazz saxophonist, Elvin Jones, 1980-81; Beaver Harris, 1983-. Compositions include: Concerto, 1963; Concertina, 1963; Shepherd Song, 1963; Andrew With Strings, 1987; A Jazz Concerto (5 versions), 1988. Recordings: 42 self-produced recordings. Publications include: Saxophone Transcriptions - The Works of John Coltrane, 12 vols; The Eric Dolphy Series Limited; The Charlie Parker Collection, 4 vols; The Andrew White Transcription Series; Big Band Series; Small Band Series; Andy's Song Book; Chamber Music Series; Saxophone Recital Series; Saxophone Etudes; Saxophone Trios, Quartets, Quintets; 2 Symphonies For 8 Saxophones; 4 Jazz Duets; 4 Jazz Trio Sonatas; 12 Jazz Miniatures; Books on improvisation, professionalism, practice, transcription, jazz education, self-production, Coltrane's music; 5 comedy books; Contributor, numerous articles to trade journals; Staff writer, Saxophone Journal. Honours include: Numerous study grants; Conductor, Dean Dixon Memorial Award, 1984; Washington Area Music Association Award, 1985. Memberships include: International Double Reed Society; Pi Kappa Lambda. Current Management: Andrew's Musical Enterprises Inc. Address: 4830 South Dakota Avenue NE, Washington, DC 20017, USA.

WHITE Andy, b. 28 May 1962, Belfast, Ireland. Singer; Songwriter; Guitar; Bass. m. Christine, 26 August 1995, 1 son. Education: Degree in English, Robinson College, Cambridge. Recordings: Religious Persuasion, EP, 1985; Rave on Andy White, 1986; Kiss the Big Stone, 1988; Himself, 1990; Out There, 1992; Destination Beautiful, 1994; Teenage, 1996; With Liam O Maonlai and Tim Finn as ALT: Attitude, 1995; Altitude, with ALT, 1995; Teenage, 1996; Publication: The Music of What Happens, 1998. Honour: Hot Press Irish Songwriter of the Year, 1993. Current Management: c/o Madeleine Seiler, 5 Wellington Gardens, Oakley Road, Dublin 6, Ireland. Address: Box 142, CH 9445, Switzerland.

WHITE Barry, b. 12 Sept 1944, Galveston, Texas, USA. Singer; Musician (keyboards, drums). Career: Singer with The Upfronts and The Majestics; Drummer, road manager, for Earl Nelson, 1966; Manager, producer, Love Unlimited, 1968; Solo singer (originally as Barry Lee), 1965-; Founder, own production company, Soul Unlimited Productions; Television appearances include: Late Night With David Letterman; Arsenio Hall Show; Major concerts include: First Annual Gospel

Festival, Jerusalem, 1983; Regular worldwide tours. Recordings: Albums: with Love Unlimited: Love Unlimited, 1972; Under The Influence Of..., 1974; Rhapsody In White, 1974; Together Brothers (soundtrack), 1974; Solo: I've Got So Much To Give, 1973; Stone Gon', 1974; Can't Get Enough (Number 1, US), 1974; Just Another Way To Say I Love You, 1975; Let The Music Play, 1976; Is This Whatcha Wont?, 1976; Barry White Sings For Someone Your Love, 1977; Barry White The Man, 1978; The Man, 1979; The Message Is Love, 1979; I Love To Sing The Songs I Sing, 1979; Barry White's Sheet Music, 1981; Change, 1982; Heart And Soul, 1985; The Right Night And Barry White, 1987; The Man Is Back!, 1990; Love Is The Icon, 1994; Hit singles include: with Love Unlimited: Walkin' In The Rain With The One I Love, 1972; Solo: I'm Gonna Love You Just A Little More Baby, 1973; Can't Get Enough Of Your Love Babe (Number 1, US), 1974; You're The First The Last My Everything (Number 1, UK), 1974; What Am I Gonna Do With You?, 1975; You See The Trouble With Me, 1976; It's Ecstasy When You Lay Down Next To Me, 1977; Just The Way You Are, 1979; Sho' You Right, 1987. Honours: American Music Award, Favourite Male Soul/R&B Artist, 1976; Honorary degree, Recording Arts And Sciences, UCLA, 1980. Current Management: SDM Management, 740 N La Brea Avenue, 1st Floor, Los Angeles, CA 90038, USA.

WHITE Freddie, b. 22 Sept 1951, Cobh, Cork, Ireland. Singer; Songwriter; Musician (guitar). m. Ann O'Sullivan, 31 Mar 1979, 1 son, 1 daughter. Musical Education: Self-taught. Career: Concerts: Olympia Theatre; National Concert Hall; National Stadium; Television appearances: Late Late Show; Pat Kenny Show; Kelly Show; Live At Three. Recordings: Albums: Freddie White, 1979; Do You Do, 1981; Long Distance Runner, 1985; Close To You, 1991; Straight Up, 1993. Honours: Hot Press, Best Folk Specialist, 1981. Membership: PRS. Hobby: Reading. Current Management: Madeleine Seiler. Address: 5 Wellington Gardens, Dublin 6, Ireland.

WHITE Melvyn Arthur, b. 1 Dec 1963, Norwich, England. Musician (bass guitar). m. Amanda Ross, 5 Dec 1992, 2 sons. Musical Education: Self-taught. Career: Broadland Radio, 1985; Radio Manchester, 1991; Supported Jools Holland, 1991; Member, group Law; Supported Nils Lofgren and Steve Marriott. Recordings: Only One Night Away, Gospel Truth, 1988; Jackie Dee, Law, 1990. Honours: UK Band Of Year, Runner up, with Law, 1991. Membership: Musicians Union. Hobbies: Song writing; Photography; Running. Address: 16 Marsh Road Upton, Nr Acle, Norwich, Norfolk NR13 6BS, England.

WHITE Peter, b. 20 Sept 1954, Luton, Bedfordshire, England. Musician; Composer. Musical Education: Self-taught. Career: 20 years, Al Stewart; Tours, recordings, with Basia; Solo tours, recordings, 1990-. Recordings: With Al Stewart: Year Of The Cat, 1974; Time Passages, 1978; Midnight Rocks, 1980; With Basia: Time And Tide, 1987; London Warsaw New York, 1990; The Sweetest Illusion, 1994; With Shippen Wise: Standing Outside In The Rain, 1990. Honours: BMI Adult Contemporary Song Of The Year, Time Passages, 1978. Memberships: BMI; AFofM. Hobbies: Reading biographies; Cycling. Current Management: Chapman & Co Management. Address: PO Box 15906, North Hollywood, Ca 91615, USA.

WHITE Snowy (Terence Charles), b. 3 Mar 1948, Devon, England. Musician (guitar); Vocalist. Career: Guitarist with Peter Green; Guitarist with Pink Floyd (touring band); Thin Lizzy, 1979-81; Tours, Europe, UK, Japan, US, Australia, 1979-81; Solo artiste, 1982-. Recordings: Albums: with Thin Lizzy: Chinatown, 1980; Renegade, 1981; Adventures of Thin Lizzy, 1981; Solo: White Flames, 1984; Snowy White, 1985; That Certain

Thing, 1987; Change My Life, 1991; Singles: with Thin Lizzy: Chinatown; Killers Live (EP); Solo: Bird Of Paradise.

WHITE Tony Joe, b. Oak Grove, Louisiana, USA. Songwriter. Career: Toured with rock bands including Creedence Clearwater Revival, 1970s; Toured extensively throughout Europe, including shows with Joe Cocker and Eric Clapton, 1991-92. Compositions: Rainy Night in Georgia; Produced hits for: Tina Turner, Joe Cocker, Etta James, Waylon Jennings, John Anderson, Isaac Hayes, Roy Orbison, Kris Kristofferson, Charlie Rich, Chet Atkins, Hank Williams Jr, Jessi Colter, Christine McVie, Ray Charles, Aretha Franklin and Wild Cherry. Recordings: Polk Salad Annie; For Ole Times Sake; I've Got a Thing About You, Baby; The Path of a Decent Groove; Lake Placid Blues, album. Honour: Nominated for Rhythm and Blues Album, Nashville Music Awards. Address: RD Worldwide Management BV, Keizersgracht 683, Amsterdam 1017 DW, Netherlands.

WHITE Will. Musician. Career: Member of Propellerheads, with Alex Gifford. Recordings: Album: Decksandrumsandrockandroll, 1997; Singles: On Her Majesty's Secret Service (with Shirley Bassey), 1997; Dive, 1997; Take California (EP), 1997; Spybreak (EP), 1997; History Repeating (with Shirley Bassey), 1997. Address: c/o Wall of Sound, Office 3, 9 Thorpe Close, London W10 5XL, England.

WHITEHEAD Alan, b. 24 July 1945, Oswestry, Shropshire, England. Manager; Agent; Musician (drums). m. Louise Burton (actress), 17 Dec 1978, 2 sons. Career: Drummer, Marmalade, 1967-78; 14 Hit records, Marmalade; Started own company, disco act promotion, 1979; Founder, manager, Mel and Kim (4 major hit records); dance group Body Check; robotic acts: Arbie The Robot; Adam and Eve; magician Marc Oberon; Bought out by Mecca Leisure, 1985; Current owner, largest Glamour Shows agency in Europe, including: The Sunday Sport Roadshow; The Dreamboys, 1988-; Touring girl roadshows: Europe; The Far East; Japan; Australia. Recordings: Marmalade, 14 hit songs including: Loving Things; Wait For Me Mary Ann; Ob-La-Di Ob-La-Da; Baby Make It Soon; Reflections Of My Life; Rainbow; Cousin Norman; Ra Dancer; Back On the Road; Falling Apart At The Seams. Honours: Pop Group Of The Year, 1968; Various Gold discs. Memberships: British Institute of Management; Fellow, The Agents Association. Hobbies: Tennis; Scuba-diving; Collecting American cars. Address: 10 Deacons Close, Elstree, Herts WD6 3HX, England.

WHITEHEAD Tim, b. 12 Dec 1950, Liverpool, England. Jazz Musician (saxophone). m. Linda Jones, 26 June 1978, 2 sons, 2 daughters. Musical Education: Self-taught. Career: Member, Loose Tubes (modern jazz orchestra), 1984-89; Founder, Tim Whitehead Quartet, Tim Whitehead Band; Regular recordings on BBC radio, including Appleby Jazz Festival, 1995; Numerous tours, concerts include: Brecon Jazz Festival, 1992; London Jazz Festival, 1994; PORI International Jazz Festival, Finland, 1995; Regular appearances at Ronnie Scott's Club, London; Television apperances include: Wogan, BBC TV, 1986, 1987; Bath Festival, BBC2 TV, 1987; with Loose Tubes, New Years Day, Granada TV, 1988; 30 Years of PORI, Finnish TV, 1995; Also performed, toured, broadcast with: Ian Carr's Nucleus; Graham Collier; Jim Mullen's Meantime; Breakfast Band; Woodworks; Martin Drew Quartet. Composition: Nine Sketches for Solo Saxophone, 1996. Recordings: with Tim Whitehead Band: English People, 1983; Decision, 1988; with Tim Whitehead Quartet: Authentic, 1991; Silence Between Waves, 1994, 1995; with Loose Tubes: Loose Tubes; Delightful Precipice; Open Letter; Other recordings: Water's Edge, Breakfast Band; Firedance, Richard Bailey; Pictures Of You, Harry Beckett; Aural Sculpture,

The Stranglers; Live In London, Maria Muldaur; Permission, with Pete Fairclough, Mike Walker and Dudley Phillips, 1997. Honours: Young Jazz Musician, 1977; Arts Council Commission, Silence Between Waves, GLA, 1992; Commissioned by Jazz Umbrella/Arts Council to compose Nine Sketches for Solo Saxophone for London Jazz Festival on the South Bank, 1996. Membership: Chairperson, Co-founder, Jazz Umbrella (London Jazz Musicians Cooperative). Hobbies: Painting; Parenting. Address: 5 Willowbank, Ham, Richmond, Surrey, England.

WHITEHOUSE Cedric John, b. 24 Mar 1944, Walsall, West Midlands, England. Musician (guitar). m. Peggy Whitehouse, 27 Feb 1987, 2 daughters. Musical Education: A Level Music. Career: Session guitarist, 1971-; Television shows include: Golden Shot; New Faces, 1974-80; Pebble Mill at One; Radio sessions include: BBC Radio Orchestras, 1974-76; Radio 2; Archers, 1975-76; Writing, producing artists, and television commercials, 1980-95. Recordings: About 1000 television shows as session guitarist; Current production work includes: Ruby Turner (Gershwin Album); Howard McCrary; Chaka Khan. Honours: Mecca Bandleader of the Year, 1976, 1977, 1978; Carl Alan Award, 1981. Membership: Musicians' Union. Hobbies: Horses; Music. Address: Pool House, Pirton, Worcs, England.

WHITFIELD George William, b. 29 Feb 1964, Worcester, England. Musician (accordion); Vocalist. Education: Warwick University. Musical Education: Self-taught. Career: Accordion player, vocalist with Pressgang, 1988; Solo appearances; Work with outcast band, WOB, Steve Hunt; Pressgang played 180 concerts: England (including Glastonbury Festival); Germany; Belgium; France; Wales; US (including SXSW Festival), 1994. Recordings: with Pressgang: Rogues, 1989; Albums: with Pressgang: Burning Boats, 1994; with Outcast Band: Devil's Road, 1993; Steve Hunt: Head The Heart And The Hand, 1993. Memberships: Musicians' Union; PRS. Hobby: Informal musical sessions. Current Management: Vox Pop, Reading, England; Berlin Consert, Max Biere Strasse, Berlin, Germany. Address: c/o Vox Pop, 1 Donnington Gardens, Reading, Berks, England.

WHITFIELD Mark Adrian, b. 6 Oct 1966, New York, New York, USA. Musician (guitar). 2 sons. Musical Education: BMus, Berklee College of Music, Boston. Career: Appearances include: The Tonite Show; Good Morning America; The Today Show; CNN Showbiz Today; CBS Sunday Morning. Recordings: Albums: The Marksman; Patrice; Mark Whitfield; True Blue; 7th Avenue Stroll; Forever Love. Publication: Mark Whitfield Guitar Transcriptions. Honour: Honorary Mayor of Baton Rouge, Louisiana, USA. Current Management: Paul Tannen. Address: 38 Laurel Ledge Court, Stamford, CT 06903, USA.

WHITING Glynis, b. 17 Mar 1954, London, England. Singer. Career: Lead singer: Cry Bill Tinker; Limited company; Accapella Duo; New Mosaic; Jazz Vocals: Transatlantic Breakfast Revival; Easy Living; Vocalist, dulcimer player and percussionist with Chloe's Colours; Solo singer, 1992-. Membership: Musicians' Union. Address: 7 Drakefell Road, London SE14 5SL, England.

WHITMAN Slim (Otis Dewey Whitman Jr), b. 20 Jan 1924, Tampa, Florida, USA. Singer; Musician (guitar). m. Geraldine Crist, 1941, 1 son. Career: Recording artist, 1949-; Weekly appearances on Louisiana Hayride radio show; Joined in 1955 with regular appearances on Grand Ole Opry; Film appearance, Disc Jockey Jamboree, 1957; Recorded 25th Anniverary concert, Empire Theatre, Liverpool, England, 1973; Toured with son Byron, 1977-. Recordings: Hit singles include: Love Song Of The Waterfall; Indian Love Call (Number 1, UK, 11 weeks), 1955; China Doll; Cattle Call; Tumbling Tumbleweeds;

Serenade; Happy Anniversary; Numerous albums include: Slim Whitman Sings And Yodels, 1954; Slim Whitman, 1958; Once In A Lifetime, 1961; A Lonesome Heart, 1967; Slim, 1969; 25th Anniversary Concert, 1973; The Very Best Of Slim Whitman (Number 1, UK), 1976; Home On The Range, 1977; Red River Valley (Number 1, UK), 1977; Ghost Riders In The Sky, 1978; Just For You, 1980; Songs I Love To Sing, 1980; Mr Songman, 1981; Till We Meet Again, 1981; Country Songs, City Hits, 1982; Angeline, 1984; Magic Moments (with Byron Whitman), 1990; Cow Poke, 1992. Address: c/o Tessier-Marsh Talent, 505 Canton Pass, Madison, TN 37115, USA.

WHITMORE Andrew David, b. 31 Mar 1962, Coventry, England. Producer; Musician (keyboards); Studio player. m. 27 Sept 1988, 1 son, 1 daughter. Musical Education: Grade 8 piano; Grade 5 cello; Grade 5 theory. Career: Member, Terence Trent D'Arby band, keyboard player; Now accomplished programmer, producer. Composition: Co-wrote with Peter Andre, No 1 single, Flava, 1996. Recordings: Albums: MN8 (production); East 17; Paris Paris, Malcolm McLaren; Peter Andre, 3 tracks, Natural album; Kavana Productions, 3 tracks. Memberships: PRS; MCPS. Hobbies: Diving; Water skiing; Jet skiing. Current Management: Stephen Budd Management. Address: 39 Greystoke Parr Terrace, Ealing, London W5 1JL, England.

WHITTAKER Roger, b. 22 Mar 1936, Nairobi, Kenya. Singer; Whistler; Musician (guitar); Songwriter. Education: Medicine; Biology; Biochemistry. Career: Former teacher and part-time folk singer; Recording artist, 1961-. Television includes: This And That, Ulster TV; Own series, BBC TV; Concerts include: Knokke Music Festival, Belgium, 1967; Launched UNESCO songwriting competition, 1975; Worldwide record sales exceed 40 million copies. Recordings: Singles include: Mexican Whistler (Number 1 throughout Europe), 1967; The Leavin' (Durham Town), 1969; I Don't Believe In If Anymore, 1970; New World In The Morning, 1971; The Last Farewell (over 11 million copies sold), 1975; The Skye Boat Song, with Des O'Connor, 1986; Over 70 albums, including compilations and special German language recordings, 1965-. Publication: So Far So Good, with Natalie Whittaker. Honours include: B'nai B'rith Humanitarian Award, 1975. Current Management: Tembo Entertainments. Address: 223 Regent Street, London W1R 7DB, England.

WHITWAM Jan Barry, b. 21 July 1946, Prestbury, Cheshire, England. Musician (percussion, guitar). m. Anne Patricia, 19 Jan 1987, 1 son, 1 daughter. Musical Education: 2 years drum tuition. Career: Original member, Herman's Hermits, 31 years; 75 major US tours with Herman's Hermits; 20 World tours; Numerous major concerts including Royal Command Performance; Television appearances: Top Of The Pops; Ready Steady Go (UK); Danny Kay; Dean Martin; Jackie Gleason; Merv Griffin; Ed Sullivan; Hullabaloo; Shindig (USA); Film appearances: Hold On, 1966; Mrs Brown You've Got A Lovely Daughter, 1967. Recordings: 23 hit singles, UK; 24 hit singles, USA; Best-selling records in world, 1965; 60 million records sold to date. Honours: NME Award winner; Keys to 25 cities, USA; 8 Gold albums; 9 Gold singles. Memberships: Musicians' Union; Equity. Hobbies: Golf; Sailing; Gardening; Watersports. Current Management: Barry Whitwam Management. Address: 26 South Park Road, Gatley, Cheadle, Cheshire SK8 4AN, England.

WHYTE Gordon, b. 22 May 1971, Glasgow, Scotland. Freelance Musician (keyboards, guitar, bodhran); Vocalist; Songwriter. Education: Master of Engineering (MEng), 1993; Strathclyde University, Glasgow. Career: Session work for: Rick Wakeman; Noel Richards; Ian White; Established Leader of Christian Worship for

conferences and festivals, including: Spring Harvest; Greenbelt; Carberry Festivals; Songwriting partnership with Susan Lennartson established 1994. Recordings: Debut album with Susan Lennartson: Wind Of Life, 1995. Membership: Musicians Christian Fellowship (MCF). Hobby: Exploring potential of spiritual and emotional healing through music. Current Management: Gordon Whyte. Address: 31 Dunchurch Road, Paisley PA1 3JW, England.

WICKENS Paul (Wix), b. 27 Mar 1956, Chelmsford, Essex, England. Record Producer; Musician (keyboards). m. Margo Buchanan, 31 Jan 1992. Musical Education: O and A Level Music; Piano grades. Career: Recorded with: The Pretenders; Dave Stewart; Mike And The Mechanics; Celine Dion; Nik Kershaw; Boy George; Status Quo; Alison Moyet; John Hiatt; The The; Prefab Sprout; The Kane Gang; Performed live with: Joni Mitchell; Jon Bon Jovi; Ry Cooder; The Kane Gang; The Chieftains; Bob Dylan; Jim Diamond; Worked with Paul McCartney, 2 albums, 4 world tours including Maracana Stadium, Brazil (record breaking concert), 1989-; Production credits include: The Kane Gang; Jim Diamond; The Big Dish; Freddie McGregor; Mel Garside; Carmel; Tasmin Archer, including Sleeping Satellite, Number 1, UK charts. Membership: Musicians' Union; PRS. Hobbies: Sport; Classic cars. Current Management: The Producers. Address: 45-53 Sinclair Road, London W14 ONS, England.

WICKHAM Steve, b. 28 Oct 1960, Dublin, Ireland. Musician (violin). m. Barbara Kernal, 1 Dec 1983. Musical Education: College of Music. Career: With U2, tour Ireland, European dates, 1982; Television, touring: the Waterboys, 1986-89; Touring and Television: Texas kellys, 1990-92. Recordings: Elvis Costello: Spike, 1988; Texas Kellys, 1992; Waterboys: Fisherman's Blues, 1987; Room To Roam, 1989; U2: War, 1982; Sinead O'Connor: The Lion And Lion Cobra, 1987; Karl Wallinger, World Party, 1988; Sharon Shannon, 1991. Publications: Sofa So Good, 1991. Honours: Hot Press Musician of the Year, 1986. Membership: IMRO. Hobbies: Cycling; Fishing; Golf. Current Management: John Burke. Address: PO Box 282, GPO Sligo, Ireland.

WIDMARK Anders, b. 25 November 1963, Uppsala, Sweden. Pianist; Composer. Musical Education: Royal Academy of Music, Stockholm. Career: Professional pianist, 1986-; Collaborated with Stockholm Jazz Orchestra, The Swedish Radio Jazz Orchestra, Eddie Harris, Bob Brookmeyer, Clark Terry, Rebecka Törnqvist, Bengt-Arne Wallin; Soloist, performances with Sundsvall Symphony Orchestra and Uppsala Chamber Soloists; The Uppsala Stadsteater, composing music for plays, 1 year. Recordings: Solo Albums: Sylvesters sista resa, 1991; Anders Widmark and the Soul Quartet, 1993; Holly Hannah, 1994; Freewheelin', 1995; Anders Widmark, 1996; Anders Widmark Trio - Psalmer, 1997; Contributor: Dreams, Bob Brookmeyer and Stockholm Jazz Orchestra, 1989; A Night Like This, Rebecka Törnqvist, 1993; Obsession! Live at Fasching, Egil Bop Johansen, 1994. Memberships: STIM; SKAP. Current Management: NW Produktion, Björngardsgatan 9A, 11852 Stockholm, Sweden. Current Management: NW Produktion, Björngårdsgatan 9A, S-118 52 Stockholm, Sweden.Address: Karlsborgsvagen 10, 121 50, Johanneshov, Sweden.

WIEDLIN Jane, b. 20 May 1958, Oconomowoc, Wisconsin, USA. Vocalist; Musician (guitar); Songwriter. Career: Founder member, US all-female group the Go-Gos (formerly The Misfits), 1978-84; Numerous international tours; Solo artist, 1985-93; Member, reformed Go-Gos, 1994-. Compositions include: Our Lips Are Sealed (co-writer with Terry Hall). Recordings: Albums: with the Go-Gos: Beauty And The Beat (Number

1, US), 1981; Vacation, 1982; Talk Show, 1984; Greatest, 1991; Return To The Valley Of The Go-Gos, 1994; Contributor, Tame Yourself (Animal Rights benefit album), 1991; Singles: with the Go-Gos: Our Lips Are Sealed, 1981; We Got The Beat (Number 2, US), 1982; Beauty And The Beat, 1982; Solo: Blue Kiss, 1986; Inside A Dream, 1988; Rush Hour, 1988; The Whole World Lost Its Head, 1995. Address: c/o Gold Mountain Entertainment, Los Angeles, USA.

WIENEUSKI Matthew, b. 20 Sept 1965, London, England. Composer; Filmmaker; Musician (saxophone, flute). Education: Bristol University, English degree. Career: European tour, 1993; Japan, 1994; Screenplays: Hardcore Nation; The Kabbalist of Lincoln. Compositions: D*votions; The Garden Of Earthly Delights. Recordings: Albums under D*note: Babel; Criminal Justice. Membership: PRS. Address: Dorado Records, 76 Brewer Street, London W1R 3PH, England.

WIGGS Josephine Miranda Cordelia, b. 26 Feb 1963, Letchworth, Hertfordshire, England. Musician (bass guitar); Composer. Education: BA, Hons, London; MA, Philosophy, Sussex. Musical Education: Studied cello, 6 years. Career: Bass player and backing vocalist with Perfect Disaster, 1987-1990; Bass, vocals, guitar, cello, drums, with The Breeders, 1990-; Bass player with Ultra Vivid Scene, US tour, 1990; Honey Tongue (solo project with Jon Mattock, Spacemen 3, Spiritualized), 1992-. Recordings: with Perfect Disaster: Asylum Road, 1988; Up, 1989; Heaven Scent, 1990; with Breeders: Pod, 1990; Last Splash, 1993; Nude Nudes, Honey Tongue, 1992. Publication: Breeders Digest, official Fanclub newsletter. Honours: Platinum Award for US sales, Last Splash; NME Brit Awards Best Single, for Cannonball, 1993. Hobby: Needlepoint. Current Management: Janet Billig, Manage This, 154 W. 57th St #828, New York, NY 10019, USA. Address: Fairfield House, Biggleswade, Bedfordshire SG18 0AA, England.

WILBER Bob (Robert Sage), b. 15 Mar 1928, New York City, USA. Bandleader; Composer; Arranger; Writer; Musician (clarinet, soprano, alto, tenor saxophones). m. Joanne Horton, 2 sons, 1 daughter. Education: BA, State University, New York. Musical Education: Juillard, Eastman, Manhattan schools; Teachers: Sidney Bechet; Lennic Tristano; Leon Russianoff. Career: Subbed for Sidney Bechet, Nice Festival, 1948; Also leading bands at Savoy, Storyville clubs, Boston; Played with: Bobby Hackett; Benny Goodman; Jack Teagarden; Eddie Condon; Founding member, World's Greatest Jazz Band, 1969; Began Soprano Summit with kenny Davern, 1973-1978; Reformed as Summit Reunion, 1990; Performed, recorded with jazz artists including: Duke Ellington; Billy Strayhorn; Louis Armstrong; Sidney Bechet; Performed, presented Carnegie Hall Tribute to Benny Goodman; Premiered orchestral version of Duke Ellington's Queens Suite; Toured with Bechet Legacy Band; Helped organize New York jazz Repertory Company; Director, Smithsonian Jazz Repertory Ensemble; Leads big band in Benny Goodman re-creations; Musical Director: The Cotton Club; Soloist, Pittsburgh, Baltimore, Colorado Symphony Orchestras; Recorded chamber music by Brahms, Beethoven, Mozart. Compositions: The Piscean Suite; Portraits In Jazz. Recordings: Over 1500 titles include: Saxophones on: Horns A-Plenty; Nostalgia, due release 1995. Publications: Autobiography: Music Was Not Enough, 1987. Honours: Grammy Award, music for film: The Cotton Club, 1985. Memberships: ASCAP; Rotary; Senior Statesman of Jazz. Hobbies: Tennis; Travel; Theatre; Reading. Address: Moina, Park Road, Chipping Camden, Gloucestershire GL55 6EA, England.

WILDE Danny. Singer; Songwriter; Musician. Career: Member, Great Buildings; The Rembrandts, 1991-; Also solo artiste. Recordings:

3 solo albums; Albums with The Rembrandts: Rembrandts, 1991; Untitled, 1992; LP, 1995; Singles: That's Just The Way It Is Baby; Johnny Have You Seen Her?; I'll Be There For You (theme for television series Friends), 1995. Current Management: Mogul Entertainment Group. Address: 9744 Wilshire Blvd., Suite 305, Beverly Hills, CA 90212, USA.

WILDE Kim (Smith), b. 18 Nov 1960, Chiswick, London, England. Singer. Education: Art school. Career: Backing singer to father Marty; Solo artiste, 1980-; Sold 6 million discs worldwide in 18 months, 1981-82; AIDS benefit concert, Wembley, 1987; Support to Michael Jackson, Bad world tour, 1988; Performed at World Music Awards, Monaco, 1992. Recordings: Albums; Kim Wilde, 1981; Select, 1982; Catch As Can Can, 1983; Teases And Dares, 1984; The Very Best Of Kim Wilde, 1985; Another Step, 1986; Close, 1988; Love Moves, 1990; Love Is, 1992; The Singles Collection 1981-93, 1993; Now And Forever, 1995; Hit singles include: Kids In America, 1981; Chequered Love, 1981; Water On Glass, 1981; Cambodia, 1981; View From The Bridge, 1982; Rage To Love, 1985; You Keep Me Hangin' On (Number 1, US), 1986; Another Step (Closer To You), duet with Junior, 1987; Say You Really Want Me, 1987; Rockin' Around The Christmas Tree, with Mel Smith (for Comic Relief), 1987; You Came, 1988; Never Trust A Stranger, 1988; Four Letter Word, 1988; Love Is Holy, 1992; If I Can't Have You, 1993. Contributor, Rock The World charity record, 1990; Let It Be, Ferry Aid (Zeebrugge ferry disaster benefit). Honours: BRIT Award, Best British Female Artist, 1983; Played female lead in West End production of Pete Townshend's Tommy, 1996. Current Management: Big M Productions. Address: Big M House, 1 Stevenage Road, Knebworth, Herts SG3 6AN, England.

WILDE Marty (Reginald Smith), b. 15 Apr 1939, Greenwich, London, England. m. Joyce Baker, 2 Dec 1959, 2 sons, 2 daughters. Singer. Career: Performed as Reg Patterson, and with The Hound Dogs; Changed name, with backing group The Wildcats, 1957; Television appearances include: Off The Record, 1957; Oh Boy!, ITV, 1958; Host, Boy Meets Girls, 1959; Group Scene 1964, Regular UK tours, including Group Scene 1964, with Rolling Stones, 1964; Formed the Wilde Three, vocal trio, with Justin Haywood, 1965; Rock'n'Roll Road Show, UK tour with Bert Weedon, 1977; AIDS benefit, with son Ricky and daughter Kim, Wembley, 1987; Film appearances: The Helions, 1961; What A Crazy World, 1964; Theatre: Bye Bye Birdie, London production, 1961. Compositions include: Co-writer (with Ronnie Scott), Ice In The Sun, Status Quo; Jesamine, The Casuals; Co-writer (with Ricky Wilde), Kim Wilde, 1981-. Recordings: Albums: Diversions, 1969; Good Rocking, Now And Then, 1973; Hit singles include: Endless Sleep, 1958; Donna, 1959; A Teenager In Love, 1959; Sea Of Love, 1959; Bad Boy, 1960; Little Girl, 1961; Rubber Ball, 1961; Jezebel, 1963; Solid Gold, 1994; It's Been Nice, 1996. Current Management: Big M Management. Address: Big M House, 1 Stevenage Road, Knebworth, Herts SG3 6AN, England.

WILDHORN Frank N, b. 29 Nov 1958, New York, USA. Composer; Producer. 1 son. Education: College. Career: Long-term relationship with Warner Brothers Pictures to develope and compose both musical feature-length animated films and live-action projects; Creative Director of Atlantic Theatre. Recordings: Theatrical productions of: Jekyll And Hyde; The Scarlet Pimpernel; Victor/Victoria; Svengali; The Civil War; Over 200 songs. Publications: Songbooks: Jekyll And Hyde (romantic highlights and The Gothic Musical Thriller; The Scarlet Pimpernel; Linda Eder's albums: Linda Eder; So Much More. Honours: Numerous Platinum, Gold discs; ASCAP writing

awards. Memberships: ASCAP; NAS; DGA; WGA. Hobbies: Son; Sports. Current Management: Mark Shimmel. Address: Mark Shimmel Management, 8899 Beverly Blvd, Suite #100, Los Angeles, CA 90048, USA.

WILFRIED (Scheutz), b. 24 June 1950, Bad Goisern, Austria. Singer; Actor. m. Marina, 15 Apr 1982, 1 son. Education: Trades Academy, English, French studies. Career: 3 Number 1 hits in Austria; 17 hits (studio); 1 live double LP and CD; Tours in Austria, Germany, France; About 10 films in major roles. Recordings: Run Rabbit Run; Highdelbeeren; Ziwui Ziwui; Mary Oh Mary; Ikarus; Television, film music: St Benedikt. Hobbies: Mountainbiking; Snow Boarding.

WILKIE Chris, b. 25 Jan 1973, Gateshead, England. Songwriter; Musician (Guitar). Career: Member of British popgroup, Dubstar. Compositions: Anywhere; Just A Girl; I Will Be Your Girlfriend; Can't Tell Me; It's Clear; When You Say Goodbye; Wearchest; Week In, Week Out. Recordings: Stars; Not So Manic Now; Albums: Disgraceful; Goodbye. Honour: Gold Disc for Disgraceful, album, 1996. Current Management: Stevo Pearce, Some Bizarre. Address: 124 New Bond Street, London, W1Y 9AE, England.

WILKINS Keith Allen, b. 12 Sept 1974, Farmington Hills, Michigan, USA. Musician (drums, clarinet); Lyricist. Musical Education: 4 years clarinet; 1 year drum class. Career: Studio drummer, lyricist; Wrote 2 songs with Donn Hecht, 1994; Collaborated with many musicans; Drummer in local concerts; Guest, television show Dave's Garage. Compositions: Always, 1993; Hard Promises, 1993; News For You Baby, 1993; Everytime I Cry, 1995; Could It Be You, 1996; Down by the Ocean Shore, 1996; They'll Come a' Runnin', 1996; Magic Moment, 1996; Together; Good Lovin' Gone Bad. Recordings: Music of America, 1993; Hollywood Gold, 1993; America Sings, 1995. Publications: Lock and Load, articles, 1994; Stars magazine, 1995; Jam magazine, 1994. Memberships: BMI; Nashville Songwriters Association International; SW Virginia Songwriters Association (SVSA); Memphis Songwriters Association; SGA; Florida Music Association; NAS; Songwriters of Wisconsin; Rock Out Censorship; Central Florida Musicians' Association; AFofM. Hobbies: Travel; Drawing; Writing; Going to the beach. Address: KAM Lyric Writing, 11124 64th Terrace North, Seminole, FL 33772, USA.

WILKINS Mark Thomas, b. 14 Dec 1956, Seattle, Washington, USA. Music Organization Executive. Education: BA Education, 2 teaching credentials, CSULA. Musical Education: Sherwood Oaks Experimental College, LACC, CSULA. Career: Member, Quincy Jones Workshops; Head of Promotion, Mystic Records, 1983-90; Founder, Affiliated Independent Record Labels (AIR Co), and International Record Promotion (IRP), 1990-93; Co-founder, CEO, Independent Network (Indy Net), 1993-; CEO, IMRA; AIM, ILTPA. Recordings: with Mandrill: Love Attack; with Bandit: 1 World 1 People. Publications: Soundtrack Mag; Author: Music Biz 411 (USA); 411 International (Europe, Asia); The Right Way To Run A Record Label, 1996; Forms And Contracts For Success, 1996; International Success In The Music Business, 1996. Honours: Innovations In Music. Memberships: Founder, CEO, The Independent Network; Vice President, Independent Music Association (IMA); Co-founder, Independent Music Retailer's Association (IMRA); Independent Live Talent Presenter's Association (ILTPA); Association of Independent Media (AIM). Hobbies: Computers; The law; Writing; Travel. Address: Indy Net, PO Box 241648, Los Angeles, CA 90024, USA.

WILKINSON Alan James, b. 22 Aug 1954, Ilford, Essex, England. Musician (soprano, alto, baritone saxophones). Vocalist. Partner, Gina Southgate. Education: BA Hons Degree Fine Art, Leeds Polytechnic, 1975-78. Musical Education: Self-taught; Guitar, from age 13; Saxophone, 1978-. Career: Joined Crow, with Matthew Coe (aka Xero Slingsby), drummer Paul Hession, 1978; Art Bart and Fargo with Hession (toured in Europe), 1979; Trio with Akemi Kuniyoshi and Hession, 1982; Tour, Europe with drummer Steve Hubback; Duo with Hession, played 10th Free Music Festival, Antwerp and Netherlands, 1983; Art Initiative, Eindhoven; Started Termite Club, Leeds; Derek Bailey's Company, 1987; Italy, 1988, 1993; Sound Symposium, St Johns, Newfoundland, with Hession, Wilkinson, Fell, 1994; Radio 3, Jazz Today, 1987; Mixing It, 1993; CBC: Two New Hours, 1994. Recordings: with Hession, Wilkinson, Fell: Bogey's, 1991; foom! foom!, 1992; The Horrors Of Darmstadt, 1994; The Saxophone Phenomenon, 1992; with John Law Quartet: Exploded on Impact, 1992; Live solo recordings: Seedy Boy, 1994. Publications: Featured in: Penguin Guide To Jazz On CD; Guinness Encyclopedia Of Popular Music. Honours: Several ACGB & ACE touring and study awards, 1985-95; LAB travel grant, 1994. Memberships: Musicians' Union; Director London Musicians Collective. Hobbies: Concerts; Cinema; Walking; Cycling; Socialising; Eating; Cooking; Travel. Current Management: Self-managed. Address: 36 Arbor Court, Queen Elizabeth's Walk, London N16 0QU, England.

WILKINSON Gary. Record Producer. Recordings: Records Produced and Remixed: Fire Island; Farley and Heller; The Farm; Sunscreen; Janet Jackson; Roach Motel; Jimmy Somerville; Happy Mondays; M People; Pet Shop Boys; Run DMC; U2. Current Management: One Management Ltd, 43 St Alban's Avenue, London W4 5JS, England.

WILKINSON Kevin Michael, b. 11 June 1958, Stoke On Trent, England. Musician (drums). m. Marilyn Fitzgerald, 2 daughters. Career: Worked with: China Crisis; The Waterboys; Robert Fripp; The Proclaimers; Bonnie Raitt; Squeeze; Fish; Midge Ure; Ultravox. Recordings: Albums: with China Crisis: Working With Fire And Steel; Flaunt The Imperfection; What Price Paradise; Diary Of A Hollow Horse; with The Waterboys: The Waterboys, 1983; A Pagan Place, 1984; This Is The Sea, 1986; Fisherman's Blues; Secret Life Of The Waterboys, 1994; with Robert Fripp: League Of Gentlemen; God Save The King, 1985; with The Proclaimers: Hit The Highway; with Fish: Songs From The Mirror, 1993; Suits, 1994; with Gary Clark; Whodini; Magics Wind; Squeeze; Joey Ramone. Memberships: Musicians' Union; PRS. Hobbies: Children; Horse; Sea; Music. Current Management: One Art Company. Address: One Art Company, Lancaster House, 14-16 St Marks Road, London W11 19U, England.

WILLIAM Victor Prince Sylvester, b. 28 May 147, Freetown, Sierra Leone. Musician; Singer. m. Nancy Blanche Williams, 24 Oct 1987, 1 son, 3 daughters. Career: Presented and performed own compositions on Sierra Leone radio, television; Performed at: Welsh Festival; Harambe Festival; Venues all over the UK. Recordings: First UK-released album Kabor (Welcome), released in Africa; New album to be released. Various honours for Sierra Leone musicians. Membership: Musicians' Union (UK). Hobbies: Cricket; Football; Tennis. Current Management: Rob Moye, Ireland. Address: c/o 5 Milton House, Camberwell Road, London SE5 7HZ, England.

WILLIAM-OLSSON Staffan, b. 13 Dec 1959, Gothenburg, Sweden. Jazz Musician (guitar); Composer; Arranger. 1 daughter. Career: Member, Norwegian hard-rock group Sons Of Angels, 1989-91; Tours, USA, UK, Germany; Band disbanded, 1991; Now working with Norwegian soul/jazz group The Real Thing. Recordings: Albums: with Sons Of Angels: Sons

Of Angels, 1990; with The Real Thing: The Real Thing, 1992; The Real Thing In New York, 1993; A Perfect Match, 1994. Address: Eikev 5, N-1181 Oslo, Norway.

WILLIAMS Andy (Howard Andrew), b. 3 Dec 1928, Wall Lake, Iowa, USA. Singer. Career: Member, quartet with his three brothers; Own US radio shows; Backed Bing Crosby in film Going My Way, 1944; Other film appearances: Kansas City Kitty, 1944; I'd Rather Be Rich, 1964; Worked as The Williams Brothers, with Kay Thompson (pianist, singer), 1947-48; Solo singer, 1952-; Featured artist, Tonight Show, 2 years; Own weekly variety show, 1962-71. Recordings: Albums include: Moon River & Other Great Movie Themes; Days Of Wine And Roses; The Wonderful World Of Andy Williams; Dear Heart; Born Free; Love Andy; Honey; Happy Heart; Home Loving Man; Love Story; Solitaire; The Way We Were; Reflections; Greatest Love Classics; Singles include: Canadian Sunset; Butterfly; I Like Your Kind Of Love (duet with Peggy Powers); Lips Of Wine; Are You Sincere; Promise Me Love; The Hawaiian Wedding Song; Lonely Street; The Village Of St Bernadette; Can't Get Used To Losing You; Hopeless; A Fool Never Learns; (Where Do I Begin) Love Story; Solitaire; Almost There.

WILLIAMS Brad, b. 13 Apr 1968, Clatterbridge, England. Musician (guitar, bass, keyboards); Vocalist; Producer; Programmer. Musical Education: Self-taught. Career: Musician, 17 years; Performer, 12 years; Recording artist, 10 years; Teacher, 9 years; Exodus 1992 UK tour supporting Mike Peters and The Poets of Justice; Subsequent recording and touring as guitarist in his band; Live performance, interview, regular airplay, Wirral Community Radio, 1995; Interview, Mersey Community Radio, 1995. Recordings: Over 50 original compositions by Mike Peters. Membership: Musicians' Union. Hobbies: Music; Cycling; Reading. Address: c/o Paul Brown, The Image Business Ltd, Orleans House, Edmund Street, Liverpool L3 9NG, England.

WILLIAMS Claude, b. 22 Feb 1908, Muskogee, Oklahoma, USA. Jazz Musician (violin, guitar). Career: Musician for 77 years; Played with: Charlie Parker; Lester Young; Mary Lou Williams; Oklahoma Blue Devils; The Pettifords Band; Andy Kirk; Don Byas; Buddy Tate; Lloyd Cole; Nat King Cole; Count Basie; Jay McShann; Sir Roland Hanna; Grady Tate; Ruth Brown; Bill Easley; Earl May; First recorded guitarist with Basie, 1936; Musician and bandleader, 1960s-70s; Concerts included Newport in New York; Monterey Festival; Played in Black and Blue, Paris and New York, 1980's; Worldwide tours and concerts including: Carnegie Hall; President Clinton inaugural events, 1992; Jazz festivals at New Orleans; Monterey; Newport; Jazz Triumph, Puerto Rico; Master Of The Folk Violin US Tour, 1994-95. Recordings include: Swing Time In New York; Man From Muskogee (with Jay McShann); Call For The Fiddler; Live At J's, Vols 1 & 2; Recorded and toured with Statesmen Of Jazz (including Milt Hinton, Benny Waters, Jane Jarvis), 1994-95; Featured soloist, Lincoln Center Jazz Orchestra, directed by Wynton Marsalis, 1995. Honours: Best Guitarist of Year, Downbeat, 1936; First Inductee, Oklahoma Jazz Hall of Fame; Charlie Christian Jazz Award, Black Liberated Arts Inc (only recipient ever), 1994; Distinguished Achievement Award, Amherst Univeristy, 1995. Current Management: Russ Dantzler, Hot Jazz Management. Address: Suite 4FW, 328 West 43rd Street, New York, NY 10036, USA.

WILLIAMS Deniece (Chandler). Singer. Career: Solo gospel/soul singer; Joined Stevie Wonder's backing group, Wonderlove; Recording artiste, including many duets with Johnny Mathis; Recorded first gospel album 1988. Compositions: Numerous including songs recorded by: Merry Clayton; The Emotions; The Whispers; Frankie

Valli. Recordings: Albums: This Is Niecy, 1976; I'm So Proud, 1983; Let's Hear It For Yhe Boy, 1984; Hot On The Trail, 1986; Water Under The Bridge, 1987; So Glad I Know, 1988; As Good As It Gets, 1989. Address: c/o Pyramid Entertainment Group, 89 5th Avenue, 7th Floor, New York, NY 10003, USA.

WILLIAMS Don, b. 27 May 1939, Floydada, Texas, USA. Songwriter; Singer; Musician (guitar). Career: Member, Strangers Two; Pozo-Seco Singers; Solo artiste, 1971-; Film appearances: W W And The Dixie Dancekings; Smokey And The Bandit 2. Recordings: Albums: with the Poco-Seco Singers: Time, 1966; I Can Make It With You, 1967; Shades Of Time, 1968; Solo albums: Don Williams Vols 1-3, 1973, 1974; You're My Best Friend, 1975; Harmony, 1976; Visions, 1977; Country Boy, 1977; Expressions, 1978; Portrait, 1979; I Believe In You, 1980; Especially For You, 1981; Listen To The Radio, 1982; Yellow Moon, 1983; Cafe Carolina, 1984; New Moves, 1986; Traces, 1987; One Good Well, 1989; As Long As I Have You, 1989; True Love, 1990; Currents, 1992; Various compilations; Singles include: Amanda; The Shelter Of Your Eyes; I Recall A Gypsy Woman; You're My Best Friend; Tulsa Time; Till The Rivers All Run Dry; Some Broken Hearts Never Mend; Lay Down Beside Me; I Believe In You; If I Needed You (duet with Emmylou Harris); Good Ol' Boys Like Me; An Evening with Don Williams, Best of Live, 1994; Borrowed Tales, 1995; Flatlands, 1996. Address: c/o Don Williams Productions, PO Box 160206, Nashville, TN 37216, USA.

WILLIAMS Doug, b. 22 Oct 1950, Chicago, USA. Singer; Bass Guitarist. 3 daughters. Career: Powerhouse, 1975-76; My Old School, 1985; Missing in Action; Marcia Hines Band; Renee Geyer Band; Hip Hop, 1988; Duffhead, 1990; The Black Mass, 1992; The Rockmelons, 1992; D Williams and the Black Mass, 1993. Compositions: Feel So Good, 5 Track EP, 1993; Stronger Together (The Rockmelons), lead vocals; Love is Gonna Bring You Home (The Rockmelons), lead vocals. Recordings: The Rockmelons, lead vocals; Form One Planet; My Island Home; Peter Andre; Kate Ceberano, backing vocals; Grace Knight, backing vocals; Swoop, backing vocals. Honours: Chosen to sing to President Bill Clinton, Australia, 1996. Membership: APRA, Australia. Current Management: Milly Petriella, Playworks Entertainment Management. Address: PO Box 448, Crows Nest, NSW 2065, Australia.

WILLIAMS Geoffrey, b. 25 Apr 1964, London, England. Songwriter; Singer; Musician (guitar). Compositions: Songs for Beverly Hills 90210 album; Eternal; Colour Me Badd; The Drop, album, 1997. Membership: Musicians' Union. Current Management: Hands On Management. Address: 3 Lambton Place, London W11 2SH, England.

WILLIAMS (Randall) Hank Jr, b. 26 May 1949, Shreveport, Louisiana, USA. Country Singer; Musician. m. Mary Jane Williams, 2 sons, 3 daughters. Career: Performer since aged 8; Debut appearance Grand Ole Opry, 1960; Recording debut aged 14; Recorded with father Hank Williams; Connie Francis; Toured with band, the Cheatin' Hearts; Recorded as Luke The Drifter, 1960s-70s; Career halted by mountaineering accident, 1975-77. Recordings: 64 albums include: Your Cheatin' Heart (film soundtrack), 1964; Living Proof, 1974; Hank Williams Jr And Friends, 1976; 14 Greatest Hits, 1976; One Night Stands, 1977; The New South, 1977; Family Tradition, 1979; Rowdy, 1981; Hank Live, 1987; Born To Boogie, 1987; Pure Hank, 1991; Maverick, 1992; Out Of Left Field, 1993; Hog Wild, 1995; Wham Bam Sam, 1996; Singles include: Long Lonesome Blues; Standing In The Shadows (US Country Number 1); All My Rowdy Friends (Have Settled Down), 1981; Recorded with numerous artists including: Ray Charles;

Willie Nelson; John Lee Hooker; Johnny Cash; Reba McEntire; Huey Lewis; Tom Petty; Waylon Jennings; George Jones; George Thorogood; Travis Tritt. Publication: Living Proof (with Michael Bane). Honours include: 5 Entertainer Awards for country music; Youngest songwriter to win BMI citation, age 16; Emmy, Monday Night Football theme, ABC, 1990; Grammy Award, There's A Tear In My Bear, 1990; Gold Medal, International Film and TV Festival, New York; Platinum and Gold albums. Memberships: BMI; ASCAP; NEA; CMA; NARAS; ACM; AMA; AFTRA; SAG. Current Management: Merle Kilgore Management, 2 Music Circle South, Nashville, TN 37203, USA.

WILLIAMS J Owen, b. 1 Feb 1959, Ireland. Singer; Songwriter; Musician (acoustic guitar). Musical Education: Irish traditional music. Career: Glastonbury Festival, 1992, 1993; Milan, Turin festivals, Italy, 1992, 1993; Live radio sessions for Greater London Radio (GLR); London gig residency. Recordings: Albums: Ribbonmen, 1991; Sean One Shoe, 1994. Memberships: Musicians' Union; PRS. Hobbies: History; Poetry. Current Management: Freddie Daniels, Runaway Music. Address: 18c Alwyne Place, Islington, London N1 2NL, England.

WILLIAMS Leroy Anthony, b. 4 Sept 1962, London, England. Musician (drums, percussion). 1 son. Career: Played with: Five Star; Level 42; Simple Minds; Talk Talk; Hi Tension; Aswad. Recordings: There's A Reason, Hi Tension. Membership: Musicians' Union. Hobbies: Collecting classic sports cars. Current Management: Session Connection. Address: 120 Parkfield Crescent, Harrow, Middlesex HA2 6JZ, England.

WILLIAMS Linda, b. 7 July 1947, Anniston, Alabama, USA. Musician (guitar, banjo, mouth harp); Singer; Songwriter. m. Robin Williams, 2 June 1973. Education: BA Michigan State University. Musical Education: Piano lessons. Career: Began together, 1973; Worked with Garrison Keillor's Home Companion, as semi-regulars, 1975-; Numerous appearances, Grand Ole Opry, Nashville, Tennessee; Numerous television appearances include: Austin City Limits; Disney Specials; TNN Shows; Played all major festivals in USA, Canada; 2 tours: Europe, UK. Carnegie Hall, 1987. Compositions: Songs recorded by: Emmylou Harris; Tom T Hall; George Hamilton IV; Holly Near; Tim and Molly O'Brien; The Seldom Scene. Recordings: 14 albums including latest, Devil of a Dream. Publications: Songbook Of Original Pieces, Vol 1, 1979. Honours: Peabody Award, Broadcasting, for work on a Prairie Home Companion, 1980. Memberships: Country Music Association; International Bluegrass Music Association; The Folk Alliance. Hobbies: Gardening; Listening to music; Reading; Golf. Current Management: Music Tree, George Balderose. Address: 1414 Pennsylvania Avenue, Pittsburgh, PA 15233, USA.

WILLIAMS Marcus Christian, b. 25 Oct 1965, Rochdale, England. Musician (bass guitar). Education: Art College, 1 year. Musical Education: Self-taught. Career: Tours: with Julian Cope in UK, Europe and Japan; with The Mighty Lemon Drops in UK (twice), Europe and US/Canada (3 times); with Blue Aeroplanes in UK and Europe; with The Madonnas in UK; with Kirsty MacColl in UK, US and Canada; Various appearances on television, radio and at festivals, with artists including Nick Heywood; Alison Moyet; Terry Wogan. Recordings: 4 albums with The Mighty Lemon Drops; 2 albums with Blue Aeroplanes; 1 album with Hectors House; Played on 2 Lisa Stansfield albums; Various singles and sessions. Memberships: Musicians' Union; PRS. Hobbies: Cooking; Horticulture; Reading; History; Geography; Drink. Address: 5 Dralda House, Keswick Road, London SW15 2JL, England.

WILLIAMS Mason, b. 24 Aug 1938, Abilene, Texas, USA. Composer; Writer; Performer; Musician (guitar). Singer. m. (1), 1 daughter, (2), (3) Kate, 23 Feb 1993. Education: Music major, Oklahoma City University, 3 years. Career: College student/folk singer, 1959-61; US Navy, 1962-63; Hollywood folksinger, songwriter, sideman, 1964-65; Television Writer, Smothers Brothers, Andy Williams, Glenn Campbell and Petula Clark, 1966-69; Musical performances at clubs, concerts, festivals, symphony orchestra, television, 1972-; Current concerts: Mason Williams and Friends, Symphonic Bluegrass, Of Time and Rivers Flowing, X-Mas and Pop Shows. Recordings: 3 Folk, 1960-63; 6 Folk Anthologies and Them Poems, 1963-65; 5 Warner Bros LPs, 1968-71; Classical Gas, hit single, 1968; Albums: Fresh Fish, 1978; Of Time & Rivers Flowing, 1984; Classical Gas with Mannheim Steamroller, Pop, 1987; A Gift Of Song, CD X-Mas, 1992; Of Time and Rivers Flowing, CD, 1996. Publications: The Mason Williams Reading Matter, 1969; Flavors, 1971; The FCC Report, 1969; The Music Of Mason Williams, 1992; 14 limited editions. Honours: 2 Grammys; 3 Grammy Nominations; 2 Emmy nominations; 1 Emmy; 1 Writers Guild Award, 1 Nomination; Honorary DMus, Oklahoma City University, 1995. Memberships: AFofM; AFFRA; WGAW; NARAS; NAS; SGA. Hobbies: Flyfishing; Art projects. Address: PO Box 5105, Eugene, OR 97405, USA.

WILLIAMS Melanie Joy, b. 28 Oct 1964, London, England. Singer; Songwriter. Education: Languages; English; History. Career: Television appearances: Top Of The Pops; The Word; The Beat; Lily Savage; Passion; The O-Zone. Recordings: Albums: Temper Temper; Human Cradle; Single: Ain't No Love. Honours: Siver disc (UK); Gold disc (Australia). Memberships: Musicians Union; Equity. Hobbies: Meditation; Alternative Therapies; Camping; Horseriding; Animals. Current Management: Paul Craig, Sound Management. Address: 222 Lambolle Place, London, NW3 4PG, England.

WILLIAMS Mervyn, b. 8 May 1957, St James, Jamaica. Audio Engineer. Fiancée, Kaye Troy E Janagalee, 1 son, 2 daughters. Musical Education: Aquarius recording studio, studios overseas. Career: Several tours with Burning Spear. Recordings: with Jimmy Cliff; Burning Spear; Beres Hammond. Honour: Jamaica Federation of Music (JFM). Membership: MFM. Hobbies: Dominoes; Basketball; Cricket; All sports. Address: No 3 Tunbridge Drive, Kingston 19, Jamaica, West Indies.

WILLIAMS Otis Clayborn, b. 30 Oct 1941, Texarkana, Texas, USA. Singer; Songwriter; Producer. m. 28 Jan 1982, 1 daughter. Career: Temptations; Television specials; Motown revue tours; Countless tours. Recordings: 51 albums (31 gold and platinum records). Publications: Temptations, life story written by Otis Wlliams. Honours: Rock'n'Roll Hall Of Fame; Star On Hollywood Boulevard; 31 Gold, Platinum records. Membership: ASCAP. Hobbies: Writing songs; Reading; Walking Out shopping. Current Management: Star Direction Management, William Morris. Address: 9255 Sunset Boulevard, Suite 610, Los Angeles, CA 90069, USA.

WILLIAMS Paul, aka Terry Day (David Paul Gifford Williams), b. 3 Sept 1940, Kingston, Surrey, England. Composer; Record Producer. m. Rosalind Anne Burns, 3 Sept 1965, 1 son, 2 daughters. Education: MA, Cambridge University. Musical Education: Royal College of Music; Jesus College, Cambridge. Career: BBC Senior Producer, 1980; Sony Award winner, McCartney, BBC series, 1988; Composer for film, television; Worked with Phil Manzanera on Nowomowa album, 1988; TV music, House of Gristle, BBC TV, 1994; BBC TV Out Of This World, 1994; Mysteries, BBCTV; Chairman, Spearhead Productions. Compositions: Over 1000 published

for television, films. Recordings: 19 albums. Honours: 3 Sony radio awards, 1988, 1990, 1992; Stemra Award, Netherlands, 1994. Memberships: Association of Professional Composers; PRS. Hobbies: Music; Golf; Motoring. Current Management: Les Molloy, Little Venice Music, c/o Nomis, 45-53 Sinclair Road, London W14, England. Address: The Moorings, 3 High View, Cheam, Surrey SM2 7DZ, England.

WILLIAMS Philip, b. 18 Oct 1962, England. Musician (bass guitar); Vocalist. Education: BEC in Business. Musical Education: Diploma in Jazz and Light Music, Chichester. Career: Tours and various television appearances including, Kim Wilde; Walk On Fire; Helen Hofner; Fabulous Singlettes; Curtis Stigers; Jordinaires; Greg Parker; Tony Hadley; Gary Barlow. Membership: Musicians' Union. Hobbies: Squash; Swimming. Current Management: Session Connection. Address: 62 New Road, Staines, Middlesex TW18 3DA, England.

WILLIAMS Robbie (Robert Peter), b. 13 Feb 1974, Stoke-on-Trent, Staffordshire, England. Singer. Career: Member, UK all-male vocal group Take That, 1990-95; Solo artiste, 1995-; Television includes: Take That And Party, C4, 1993; Take That Away documentary, BBC2, 1993; Take That In Berlin, 1994. Recordings: Albums: Take That And Party, 1992; Everything Changes, 1993; Greatest Hits, 1996; Solo album: Life Thru A Lens, 1997; Hit singles: with Take That: It Only Takes A Minute, 1992; I Found Heaven, 1992; A Million Love Songs, 1992; Could It Be Magic, 1993; Why Can't I Wake Up With You, 1993; Solo hit singles: Freedom, 1996; Old Before I Die, 1997; Lazy Days, 1997; South of the Border, 1997; Angels, 1997; UK Number 1 hits: Pray, 1993; Relight My Fire (with Lulu), 1993; Babe, 1993; Everything Changes, 1994; Sure, 1994; Back For Good, 1995. Publications: Numerous videos, books, magazines. Honours include: 7 Smash Hit Awards, 1992, 1 in 1996; BRIT Award, Best British Single, 1994. Memberships: Equity; Musicians' Union; MCPS; PRS; ADAMI; GVC. Hobbies: Football; Music; Backgammon. Current Management: IE Music Ltd. Address: 59A Chesson Road, London W14 9QS, England.

WILLIAMS Robert David, b. 19 Apr 1960, Redhill, Surrey, England. Singer; Songwriter; Musician (guitar). Education: BA, French, German; PGCE, English, Drama. Career: Television: All The King's Men, Granada TV; Radio broadcasts: Imagens Do Brasil, BBC World Service. Recordings: Albums: Uninvited; The Best Of Aog; Relay 1 & Relay 4. Memberships: Musicians' Union; PRS. Hobbies: Yoga. Address: 129 Inderwick Road, Crouch End, London N8 9JR, England.

WILLIAMS Robin, b. 16 Mar 1947, Charlotte, North Carolina, USA. Musician (guitar, banjo, mouth harp); Singer; Songwriter. m. Linda, 2 June 1973. Education: BA, Presbyterian College. Career: Solo artiste, 1969-73; Began with Linda (wife), 1973; Worked with Garrison Keillor's Prairie Home Companion, as semi-regulars, 1975-; Numerous appearances: Grand Ole Opry, Nashville, Tennessee; Numerous television appearances include: Austin City Limits; Disney Specials; TNN Shows; Played all major festivals in USA, Canada; Toured Europe, UK, 2 times, played Carnegie Hall, 1987. Recordings: 14 albums, lates, Devil of Dream; Songs recorded by Emmylou Harris; Tom T Hall; George Hamilton IV; Holly Near; Tim and Molly O'Brien; The Seldom Scene. Publications: Songbook original pieces, Vol I, 1979. Honours: Peabody Award for Broadcasting, for work on Prairie Home Companion, 1980. Membership: Country Music Association; International Bluegrass Music Association; The Folk Alliance. Hobbies: Gardening; Listening to music; Reading; Golf. Current Management: Music Tree. Address: 1414

Pennsylvania Avenue, Pittsburgh, PA 15233, USA.

WILLIAMS Tony, b. 12 Dec 1945, Chicago, Illinois, USA. Jazz Musician (drums). Career: Musician with Sam Rivers, 1962; Jackie McLean, 1962; Miles Davis Quartet, 1963-69; Founder, Lifetime with John McLaughlin and Larry Young; Reformed with Miles Davis, 1975. Recordings: Albums: with Lifetime: Lifetime, 1965; Spring, 1966; Emergency, 1969; Ego, 1970; Turn It Over, 1970; Old Bum's Rush, 1972; Believe It, 1976; Million Dollar Legs, 1976; The Joy Of Flying, 1979; Solo albums: Civilization, 1986; Foreign Intrigue, 1986; Angel Street, 1989; Native Heart, 1990; Once In A Lifetime; Other recordings include: with Miles Davis: In Berlin, 1966; ESP, 1965; Miles Smiles, 1967; The Sorcerer, 1967; Nefertiti, 1968; Miles In The Sky, 1968; Filles De Kilimajaro, 1968; In A Silent Way, 1969; Classics, 1975; Water Babies, 1977; Circle In The Round, 1979; Also: Stanley Clarke, Stanley Clarke, 1974; The Golden Scarab, Ray Manzarek, 1975; In Retrospect, John McLaughlin, 1976; Herbie Hancock Trio, Herbie Hancock, 1977; VSOP, Herbie Hancock, 1977; Electric Guitarist, John McLaughlin, 1978; Mr Gone, Weather Report, 1978; Live Jam, Yoko Ono, 1980; Swing Of Delight, Santana, 1980; Blues For Salvador, Santana, 1985; A Question Of Time, Jack Bruce, 1989.

WILLIAMS Victoria Ann, b. 23 Dec 1958, Shreveport, Louisiana, USA. Singer; Songwriter; Musician (guitar, dulcimer, piano, mandolin, harmonica). m. Mark Olson, 22 Dec 1993. Education: 2 years college. Musical Education: Some music theory, college; Piano aged 8-10. Career: Solo recording artiste, 1987-; Appearances include: Tonight Show with Johnny Carson; Also with Jay Leno; David Letterman with Dave Pirman; Today Show; Good Morning America; Dave Stewart Show; Politically Incorrect, Comedy Channel; MTV Host twice. Recordings: Albums: Happy Come Home, 1987; Swing The Statue, 1990; Sweet Relief (compilation of own compositions recorded by artists incuding Lou Reed, Even Dando, Pearl Jam, Soul Asylum), 1993; Loose, 1994; This Moment Live In Toronto, with the Loose Band, 1995; Gas, Food And Lodging (film soundtrack), 1995; Musings Of A Creek Dipper. Memberships: US Musicians Union; AFTRA; SAG. Hobbies: Horses and mules; Swimming; Hiking; Biking. Current Management: Danny Heaps, PO Box 23, Pioneertown, CA 92268, USA.

WILLIAMSON Astrid, b. 28 Nov 1968, Shetland Islands, Scotland. Musician (piano, guitar); Singer. Musical Education: BA Hons Music, Royal Scottish Academy. Career: UK tour with Suede; Support to Bryan Ferry; Melody Maker tour. Recordings: Debut album, recorded, produced by John Cale, 1996. Hobby: Knitting. Current Management: Nick Moore, Splash Management. Address: 328 Grays Inn Road, Kings Cross, London WC1X 8BZ, England.

WILLIAMSON Cris, b. 15 Feb 1947, Deadwood, South Dakota. Singer; Songwriter; Musician (keyboards, guitar). Education: BA, University of Denver. Musical Education: 7 years piano, 7 years voice. Career: Performances include 3, Carnegie Hall, New York (2 sell-outs); Newport Folk Festival; 25 years touring include Europe; Australia; Russia; Several documentary scores; 3 film scores; Play, Blue Fish Cove (Last Summer Of), feature song, Don't Lose Heart. Recordings: Albums: Artistry Of Cris Williamson, 1963; The World Around Cris Williamson, 1965; Cris Williamson, Ampex, 1971; The Changer And The Changed, 1974; Live Dream, 1977; Strange Paradise, 1978; Lumiere, 1981; Blue Rider, 1982; Meg & Cris at Carnegie Hall, 1983; Portrait, 1983; Prairie Fire, 1984; Snow Angel, 1985; Wolf Moon, 1988; Country Blessed, 1989; The Best Of Cris Williamson, 1990; Circle Of Friends, 1991; Postcards From Paradise, (with

Tret Fure), 1993; Between The Covers (with Tret Fure). Honours: Parents Choice Award, Lumiere, 1982; Cable Car Award, Outstanding Recording Artist, 1983; 1990; City And County Of San Francisco, State Of California Honour Award, Outstanding Performer and Musician, 1988. Memberships: AFofM; AFTRA. Hobby: Horses. Current Agent: Tam Martin, Beachfront Bookings. Address: PO Box 970, Marcola, OR 97454-0970, USA.

WILLIAMSON (John Robert) Graeme, b. Montreal, Quebec, Canada. Musician (guitar); Singer; Songwriter. m. Iris Jamieson, 10 June 1995. Education: MA, Glasgow University. Musical Education: Self-taught. Career: Frequent live television CBC (national) television and local television, 1984-85; Radio: Live concert broadcasts and tours, Canada; Retired from live performance, 1985. Compositions: Might As Well Be On Mars; Every Man And Every Woman Is A Star; Let Your Light Shine; Rubber Girl. Recordings: 3 tracks, album, 1970; Albums with Pukka Orchestra: Pukka Orchestra, 1984; Dear Harry, 1993; Palace Of Memory, 1986. Honours: Casby Award (Canada), 1984. Membership: SOCAN (Canada). Hobby: Travel. Current Management: Self-managed. Address: 38 Victoria Crescent Road, Glasgow G12 9DE, Scotland.

WILLIAMSON Harry, b. 12 May 1950, Ilfracombe, Devon, England. Composer; Musician (guitar); Producer. Divorced, 1 daughter. Education: Physics, London University. Musical Education: Chorister at Exeter Cathedral; 7th grade piano and guitar. Career: Collaborated with Anthony Phillips (Genesis), 2 albums; Worked with Gong and Mother Gong, including tours USA, Europe, 1979-; Currently part of Far From The Madding Crowd, with Australian singer Liz Van Dort. Compositions include: Nuclear Waste, featuring Sting. Recordings: with Sphynx: Xitintoday; with Anthony Phillips: Tarka (Number 1, New Music Charts), 1988; The Gypsy Suite; 12 albums with Mother Gong/Gong; Far From The Madding Crowd. Honours: Best Independent Producer, USA, 1986. Memberships: PRS; MCPS; Musicians' Union. Hobbies: Swimming; Tennis; Holistic science; Woodwork. Address: PO Box 2237, St Kilda West, Melbourne, Victoria 3182, Australia.

WILLIAMSON John Robert, b. 1 Nov 1945, Victoria, Australia. Singer; Songwriter. Career: One of Australia's leading singer/songwriters, in a career spanning over 28 years and selling over 2 million albums. Creative works: 22 albums; Designer of 4 distinctive Australian flags. Honours: 4 Golden Guitars for Album of Yr; 6 Golden Guitars for Biggest Selling Album of Year; 2 Golden Guitars for Male Vocalist of Year; 2 Golden Guitars for Song of Year; 1 Golden Guitar for Heritage Award; 1 Golden Guitar for Video Clip of Year; Indicted to Roll of Renown, 1997; From the Tamworth Songwriter's Association: Songmaker Award, 1986; Children's Song of the Year for "Bushtown" (The Lawnmower Song), 1996; Children's Song of the Year for "Kitchy Kitchy Koo", 1997; Further awards since 1986 including: NZ Professional Country Music Recording Industry's vote for Best Australian Act; 4 MO Awards for Best Male Country Performer of Previous Years; 2 MO Awards for Best Country Performer; 2 MO Awards for Most Sucessful Attraction of Year; 2 ARIA Awards for Best Australian Country Record, Variety Club Entertainer of Year; Advance Australia Award for contribution to Arts and Environment; Ambassadorship from Advance Australia Foundation; AM (Mbr of the Gen Div of the Order of Aust) for services to Australian Country Music and for stimulating conservation awareness. Memberships: Australian Conservation Foundation; Salvation Army; Bush Heritage Fund; Australian National Museum; Country Music Association of Australia; Landcare Australia.

Address: PO Box 399, Epping, NSW 2121, Australia.

WILLIS Gary Glen, b. 28 Mar 1957, Longview, Texas, USA. Musician (electric bass); Composer. m. Pamela Nichols, 11 Apr 1991. Musical Education: Kiljore Jr College; East Texas State University; North Texas State University. Career: Co-founder, co-leader of Tribal Tech, with Scott Henderson, 1983-; Annual tours: USA; Europe; South America; Performed, recorded with: Allan Holdsworth; Wayne Shorter; Hubert Laws. Recordings: Albums: Tribal Tech; Spears, 1985; Dr Hee, 1987; Nomad, 1989; Tribal Tech, 1991; Illicit, 1992; Face First, 1993; Reality Check, 1995. Publications: Instructional Video: Progressive Basics, 1991; Book: Lessons With The Greats For Bass, 1995. Hobbies: Tennis; Mountain Biking. Address: 1203 East Madison Street, Colorado Springs, CO 80907, USA.

WLLOUGHBY Brian, b. 20 Sept 1949, Glenarm, County Antrim, Northern Ireland. Musician (guitar). m. Christina Onesti, 9 Aug 1986. Education: Degree, French, Spanish and Italian. Musical Education: Self-taught. Career: Guitarist for: Mary Hopkin; Joe Brown; Roger Whittaker; New World; Brian Connolly; Jim Diamond; The Monks; The Strawbs. Recordings: Albums with: Monty Python; The Strawbs; Dave Cousins/Brian Willoughby; Numerous sessions with other artistes. Publications: Guitar reviews, Musicians Only. Honours: Gold album, The Monks. Memberships: Musicians' Union; Institute of Linguists. Hobbies: Guitar collecting; Car and motorcycle maintenance; Swimming. Address: 6 Hall Road, Isleworth, Middlesex TW7, England.

WILLOW Robin, b. 29 Dec 1948, Leeds, England. Songwriter; Singer; Musician (guitar, autoharp); Maths Tutor; Photographer; Government Officer. Education: Sign Language (Stage 1); Management, Computer; Teacher's's Certificate, 1974; BA (Open), Maths and Computer Science, 1980. Career: News Reporter, Eastern Echo, Ypsilanti, 1973; Member, Bulmershe Folk Choir, 1973-74; Member, Reading Phoenix Choir, 1974-80; Mathematics Teacher, 1974-80; Computer Programmer, Government, 1980-88; Photographer, 1982-; Director, Dragonar Music, 1984-; Mathematics Tutor, 1989-; Government Officer, 1990-; Radio appearances: LBC Donkey Carol, 1985; Live premiere, For Spain & Her Alone, Derek Jameson Show, BBC2, 1988; Astoria, Oregon, 1988; Menorca, 1988; UK, 1988; Norway, 1992; Belgium, 1995; BBC local radio, 1996. Recordings: Dragonar (Trad), 1985; Reflected In A Mirror, 1987; Dragon's Fire, 1989; Alone With You, 1993; The Bright Star, 1996. Publications: One Two Testing (article by Paul Colbert), 1985; Bunjies - Nights In The Cellar, by Peter Cadle, 1994. Memberships: Phonographic Performance Ltd; Mechanical Copyright Protection Society; British Academy of Songwriters, Composers and Authors; PRS; Musicians' Union; International Songwriters Association. Hobbies: Fencing (foil, sabre, epee); Family Historian (including One Name Research). Address: Dragonar Music, PO Box 632, London NW2 5PQ, England.

WILSON Allan, b. 5 Sept 1949, London, England. Conductor. m. 25 Jan 1986, 2 daughters. Musical Education: Royal Academy of Music; State University of New York. Musical Education: Studied trumpet, composition, conducting, London's Royal Academy of Music. Career: Teacher, Conducting, orchestral training, State University of New York; Lecture recitals, Britain; USA; Canada; Appearances as trumpet player; Specialist conductor, film soundtrack music; Film credits include: by Colin Towns: The Puppet Master; Fellow Traveller; Wolves Of Willoughby Chase; Bellman and True; Knights And Emeralds; by Chris Young: The Dark Half; Hellbound: Hellraiser II; by Basil Polidouris: Lassie; by Loek Dikker: Body Parts; Television music includes: by Colin Towns: Clarissa; Capital City; The Fifteen

Streets; Blind Justice. Recordings include: Conductor: Many film soundtracks; Classical works by Mozart, Holst, Wagner, with orchestras and ensembles such as: National Studio Orchestra; London Wind Ensemble; Munich Symphony Orchestra; Hungarian State Orchestra; The Mercury Players; Festival Brass Of London; Symphonie-Orchester Graunke. Current Management: Soundtrack Music Management. Address: 22 Ives Street, Chelsea, London SW3 2ND, England.

WILSON Ann, b. 19 June 1951, San Diego, California, USA. Singer. 1 daughter. Career: Member, groups Ann Wilson & The Daybreaks; Bordersong; The Army; Renamed White Heart; Later became Heart, 1974-; UK debut, London, 1976; Regular US and international tours with artistes including Queen; Tears For Fears; Michael Bolton; Cheap Trick; Black Crowes; Concerts include: California Jam II Festival, 1978; Bread & Roses Festival, 1981; Benefit concert for local environmental groups, Seattle, 1990; Benefit for Seattle centre for victims of child abuse, 1992; Also member of side project The Lovemongers; Performed with Alice In Chains, animal rights benefit concert, Los Angeles, 1992. Recordings: Albums: with Heart: Dreamboat Annie, 1975; Little Queen, 1977; Magazine, 1978; Dog And Butterfly, 1978; Bebe Le Strange, 1980; Private Audition, 1982; Passionworks, 1983; Heart (Number 1, US), 1985; Bad Animals, 1987; Brigade, 1990; Rock The House Live!, 1991; Desire Walks On, 1993; The Road Home, 1996; Hit singles include: Magic Man, 1976; Barracuda, 1977; Straight On, 1978; Tell It Like It Is, 1981; How Can I Refuse, 1984; What About Love?, 1985; Never, 1985; These Dreams (Number 1, US), 1986; Nothin' At All, 1986; If Looks Could Kill, 1986; Alone (Number 1, US), 1987; Who Will You Run To, 1987; There's The Girl, 1988; What About Love, 1988; All I Wanna Do Is Make Love To You, 1990; Stranded, 1990; Will You Be There (In The Morning), 1993; Solo single: The Best Man In The World, from film The Golden Child, 1987; Duet with Robin Zander: Surrender To Me, from film Tequila Sunrise, 1989; with The Lovermongers: Battle Of Evermore, from film Singles, 1992; Guest vocalist, Sap (EP), Alice In Chains, 1992. Current Management: Borman Entertainment Inc., 1250 Sixth Street, Suite 401, Santa Monica, CA 90401, USA.

WILSON Brian, b. 20 June 1942, Inglewood, California, USA. Musician (bass, keyboards); Singer; Composer. Founder member, the Beach Boys, 1961-; Retired from live performance, to concentrate on composing and recording, 1964-; Appearances include: Australian tour, 1964; Headlines Million Dollar Party, Honolulu, 1964; US tour, 1964; Established Brother Records label, 1967; Concert at International Center, Honolulu, 1967; Plays with Beach Boys, Whiskey-A-Go-Go, Los Angeles, 1970; Filmed for NBC Special, 1976; Presenter, Don Kirshner's Second Annual Rock Music Awards, Hollywood, 1976; 15th Anniversary Beach Boys show, 1976; Rejoins band for US concerts, 1989; Solo appearance, China Club, Hollywood, 1991; Documentaries include: Prime Time Live, ABC, 1991; I Just Wasn't Made For These Times, BBC, 1995. Compositions: Many hit songs include: Caroline No; Co-writer, California Girls; Good Vibrations; Fun Fun Fun. Recordings: Albums include: Surfin' Safari, 1962; Surfer Girl, 1963; Little Deuce Coupe, 1963; Shut Down Vol 2, 1964; All Summer Long, 1964; Surfin' USA, 1965; Beach Boys Party, 1966; Pet Sounds, 1966; Beach Boys Today!, 1966; Smile, 1967; Surfer Girl, 1967; Smiley Smile, 1967; Wild Honey, 1968; 15 Big Ones, 1976; The Beach Boys Love You, 1977; Solo albums: Brian Wilson, 1988; I Just Wasn't Made For These Times, 1995; Contributor, vocals for film soundtrack Shell Life; Singles include: Surfin' USA; Surfer Girl; Little Deuce Coupe; In My Room; I Get Around; When I Grow Up To Be A Man; Dance Dance Dance; Producer: Help Me Rhonda; Barbara Ann; Caroline No; Sloop John B; God Only Knows; Good Vibrations;

Wouldn't It Be Nice; Friends; Do It Again; I Can Hear Music. Honours include: Rock And Roll Hall Of Fame, 1988; Special Award Of Merit, 1988. Current Management: Elliott Lott, Boulder Creek Entertainment Corp, 4860 San Jacinto Circle West, Fallbrook, CA 92028, USA.

WILSON Cassandra, b. Jackson, Mississippi, USA. Jazz Singer. Musical Education: Listening to father, Herman B Fowlkes, jazz musician. Career: Started playing guitar aged 6; Songwriting at 12; Solo performer as folk and blues singer, turned to jazz; Regular collaborations with saxophonist Steve Coleman; Signed to Blue Note Records. Recordings: Albums include: Point Of View, 1986; Days Aweigh, 1987; Blue Skies, 1988; Jumpworld, 1990; She Who Weeps, 1991; Blue Light 'Til Dawn, 1993; New Moon Daughter, 1996; Also featured vocalist on other artist's works. Current Management: Dream Street Management, 1460 4th Street, Suite 205, Santa Monica, CA 90401, USA.

WILSON Damian Augustine Howitt, b. 11 Oct 1969, Guildford, Surrey, England. Singer; Songwriter. Recordings: Albums: with Landmarq: Solitary Witness, 1992; Infinity Parade, 1993; The Vision Pit, 1995; with Threshold: Wounded Land, 1993; with LaSalle, 1994. Honours: Best Vocalist, Classic Rock Society, 1993.

WILSON Dennis Edward, b. 22 July 1952, Greensboro, North Carolina, USA. Musician (trombone). m. Rebecca Elvert, 12 July 1986, 1 son. Musical Education: MusB in Education, Berklee College Of Music, Boston, 1974. Career: Trombonist, Musical director, Lionel Hampton Orchestra, 1974-76; Teacher, Choral director, NY schools, 1976-77; Trombonist arranger, Count Basie Orchestra, 1977-87; Music production manager, Count Basie Enterprises, 1987-; Trombonist, arranger, Frank West Orchestra, 1990-; Also arranger, conductor, Manhattan Transfer, Blee Blop Blues, 1985; Trombonist, Dizzy Gillespie Orchestra, 1988; Creator, executive producer, Count Basie Orchestra Big Band Festival. Honour: Grammy Nomination, Manhattan Transfer, 1985; Membership: National Association of Jazz Educators.

WILSON Gerald Stanley, b. 4 Sept 1918, Shelby, Mississippi, USA. Musician (trumpet, piano); Arranger; Composer; Orchestrator; Bandleader. m. Josefina Villaseñor, 4 Sept 1950, 1 son, 3 daughters. Musical Education: Cass Tech, Detroit, Michigan, USA; Private Tutorial. Career: Local bands, Detroit; Joined Jimmie Lunceford Orchestra, as trumpeter, arranger, 1939-42; Moved to Los Angeles; Arranger, trumpeter, Les Hite, Benny Carter, Phil Moore; World War II, Joined Count Basie band, trumpeter, arranger, 1948-49; Trumpeter for Dizzy Gillespie, 1949; Arranged for artists including: Ella Fitzgerald; Nancy Wilson; Ray Charles; Bobby Darin; Dinah Washington; Carmen McRae; Sarah Vaughn; Benny Goodman; Cab Calloway; The Platters; Eartha Kitt; Billy Eckstine; Jean Luc Ponty; Performed, with Al Hirt, Carnegie Hall, 1965; Musical director, Redd Foxx Variety series, 1978; Leader, composer, arranger, own orchestra; Member, faculty, UCLA; Festivals include: Chicago Jazz, 1994; Playboy Jazz, 1995. Compositions include: Royal Suite In Seven Movements; Imagine My Frustration, featured Broadway hit: Sophisticated Ladies; Piece for symphony orchestra, 1972; filmscores include: Where The Boys Are, 1960; Love Has Many Faces, 1960; Paco, 1964; Viva Tirado (recorded by El Chicano), no 1, 1968. Recordings include: Lomelin; Calafia; Jessica; Jenna; State Street Sweet, 1995. Honours: 2 Grammy nominations, 1963, 1964; American Jazz Masters Fellowship Grant, 1990; Paul Robeson Award; Music archived by Library of Congress, Washington DC. Memberships: AFM; NARAS; ASMAC; Los Angeles Jazz Society; Board Governors, National

Academy, Recording Arts and Sciences. Current Management: Self-managed.

WILSON Joe Lee, b. 22 Dec 1935, Bristow, Oklahoma, USA. Jazz Singer; Composer; Musician (guitar, piano, percussion). m. Jill Carlyon Christopher, 13 Dec 1976, 2 daughters. Musical Education: Piano lessons age 5-10; Sang Baptist Gospel church, age 5-16; Major in voice, Los Angeles Conservatory of Music, 1955; City College, 1956-58. Career: Played with: Sonny Rollins; Freddie Hubbard; Lee Morgan; Jackie MacLean; Roy Brooks; Pharoah Sanders; Frank Foster; The Collective Black Artists' Ensemble; Roy Haynes; Milt Jackson; Rashied Ali; Miles Davis; Archie Shepp; Innovator, the Jazz Loft Movement, 1973-78; Organised Live Loft Festivals; Appeared Newport New York Jazz Festival, 1973; Numerous television shows include: Showcase '68, NBC-TV; DJ, broadcasting live jazz scenes; Leader, own jazz band; Travelled to Europe; Middle East; Africa; Far East; Played Ronnie Scott's, 1978; Clubs, concerts, festivals, France, England; Humphrey Lyttelton's BBC Radio programme; Special guest, Satchmo concert, Royal Festival Hall; Tonight In Town, BBC1 TV; Performed with Dizzy Gillespie, Marciac Festival, 1986. Compositions: Nice And Easy; Come And See; The Shadow; Lyrics to Milestones; Blues Ain't Nothing; Sphirlov; Children's Suite - Makes You Feel You're Real. Recordings: Albums: Living High Off Nickels And Dimes; Mr Joe Lee Wilson In The Great City; Without A Song; What Would It Be Without You; Things Gotta Change, Archie Shepp; Secrets From The Sun; Shout For Trane; with Archie Shepp: A Touch Of The Blues; Cry Of My People; The Shadow; Acid Rain. Honours: 5 Downbeat magazine awards; ASCAP Song award; NBC Showcase winner, 1968. Hobbies: Tai Chi Chu'an; Antiques and stones; Fishing; Dowsing laylines; Cooking original recipes. Address: 41 Rue St Louis En l'Ile; 75004 Paris, France.

WILSON Mari, b. 29 Sept 1957, London, England. Singer. Musical Education: Self-taught. Career: 6 hit singles, hit album, 1981-84; Television and concert tours: UK; Europe; USA; with 12 piece band the Wilsations; Jazz/pop career includes: Regular Ronnie Scott's Clubs appearances; Theatre, television, radio, DJ on Greater London Radio; Theatre acting: Sweet Charity; Chainsaw Manicure. Recordings: Hit singles: Just What I've Always Wanted, 1982; Cry Me A River, 1983; Theme tune to Dance With A Stranger, 1984; Albums: Show People, 1983; The Rhythm Romance, 1992. Honours: Nomination, Best British Female Artist, 1982. Memberships: Musicians' Union; Equity; PRS; MCPS. Hobbies: Writing; Working out; Swimming; Spiritual reading; Cooking. Current Management: Music: Allied Agency, 9 Great Chapel Street, London W1V 3AL; Acting: Macfarlane Chard Associates, 7/8 Little Turnstile, London WC1V 7DX, England.

WILSON Mary, b. 3 June 1944, Greenville, Mississippi, USA. Singer; Entertainer. m. Pedro A Ferrer, 11 May 1973, 2 sons (1 deceased), 1 daughter. Musical Education: Glee Club and Choir in High School; Professional vocal lessons, 1970-1992. Career: Member, Supremes, 1961-77; World tours; 15 appearances on Ed Sullivan Show; Only American act with 5 consecutive number 1 hits; 12 number 1 hits; Broke record for sales; Broke racial barriers for blacks and women; Epitomized the Motown Sound. Recordings: Where Did Our Love Go, 1964; Baby Love, 1964; Come See About Me, 1964; Stop! In The Name Of Love, 1965; Back In My Arms Again, 1965; I Hear A Symphony, 1965; My World Is Empty Without You, 1965; You Can't Hurry Love, 1966; You Keep Me Hangin' On, 1966; Love Is Here And Now You're Gone, 1967; The Happening, 1967; Reflections, 1967; Love Child, 1968; I'm Gonna Make Me Love Me (with the Temptations), 1968; Someday We'll Be Together, 1969; Up The Ladder To The Roof, 1970; Stoned Love, 1970; River

Deep Mountain High (with the Four Tops), 1970; Nathan Jones, 1971; Floy Joy, 1972; Solo: Red Hot, 1979; Walk The Line, 1992; U, 1995. Publications; Dreamgirl: My Life As A Supreme, 1986; Supreme Faith: Someday We'll Be Together, 1990. Honours: Star, Hollywood Of Fame; Inductee, Rock'N'Roll Hall Of Fame, 1988; Several awards, recording, recognition from music industry; Organizations include NAACP. Hobbies: Cooking; Skiing; Tennis; Reading; Dancing; Bowling. Current Management: Duryea Entertainment. Address: 54 Danbury Road, Suite 367, Ridgefield, CT 06877, USA.

WILSON Nancy, b. 20 Feb 1937, Chillicothe, Ohio, USA. Singer. m. (1) Kenneth C Dennis, div 1969, 1 child; (2) Wiley Burton, 1974, 2 daughters. Career: Singer, touring with Rusty Bryant band, 1956-58; Singer with George Shearing; Cannonball Adderley; Solo singer, 1959-; Singer with jazz musicians including Art Farmer, 1980s; Tours: US; Europe; Australia; Japan; Far East; Television includes: Police Story; Hawaii Five-O; It's A Living; Own television series, Nancy Wilson Show, 1974-75; Red Hot And Cool, 1990-; Film appearance, The Big Score. Numerous albums include: Nancy Wilson, 1960; Hello Young Lovers, 1962; A Touch Of Today, 1966; Just For Now, 1967; Easy, 1968; Son Of A Preacher Man, 1969; Kaleidoscope, 1971; I've Never Been To Me, 1977; Godsend, 1984; Forbidden Love, 1987; Greatest Hits, 1988; The Capitol Years, 1992; If I Had My Way, 1995; Also recorded with orchestras of Billy May; Gerald Wilson; Jimmy Jones; Oliver Nelson; Contributor, Colour And Light - Jazz Sketches On Sondheim, 1995. Honours: Grammy, Best R&B Vocal; Down Beat and Playboy Jazz Poll Winner, Best Female Vocalist; NAACP Image Award, 1986; Black Achievement Award, 1990; Star on Hollywood Walk Of Fame, 1990. Address: c/o John Levy Enterprises Inc., 2810 W Charleston Blvd, Suite G-72, Las Vegas, NV 89102, USA.

WILSON Nancy, b. 16 Mar 1954, San Francisco, California, USA. Singer; Musician (guitar). m. Cameron Crowe. Career: Member, Bordersong; Solo folk singer; Member, US rock group Heart, 1974-; UK debut, London, 1976; Regular US and international tours with artists including Queen; Tears For Fears; Michael Bolton; Black Crowes; Cheap Trick; Major concerts include: California Jam II Festival, 1978; Bread And Roses Festival, Berkeley, 1981; Benefit concert for local environmental groups, Seattle, 1990; Also member, side project The Lovemongers; Film appearances: Fast Times At Ridgemount High; The Wild Life. Recordings: Albums: Dreamboat Annie, 1975; Little Queen, 1977; Magazine, 1978; Dog And Butterfly, 1978; Bebe Le Strange, 1980; Private Audition, 1982; Passionworks, 1983; Heart (Number 1, US), 1985; Bad Animals, 1987; Brigade, 1990; Rock The House Live!, 1991; Desire Walks On, 1993; The Road Home, 1996; Hit singles: Magic Man, 1976; Barracuda, 1977; Straight On, 1978; Tell It Like It Is, 1981; How Can I Refuse, 1983; What About Love?, 1985; Never, 1985; These Dreams (Number 1, US), 1986; Nothin' At All, 1986; If Looks Could Kill, 1986; Alone (Number 1, US), 1987; Who Will You Run To, 1987; There's The Girl, 1987; What About Love, 1988; All I Wanna Do Is Make Love To You, 1990; Stranded, 1990; Will You Be There (In The Morning), 1993; Duet with Mike Reno: Almost Paradise, from film Footloose, 1984; with the Lovermongers: Battle Of Evermore, from film Singles, 1992. Current Management: Borman Entertainment Inc, 1250 Sixth Street, Suite 401, Santa Monica, CA 90401, USA.

WILSON Peter (Emerson Peters), b. 28 July 1956, Newport, Isle Of Wight, England. Musician (piano); Composer; Arranger; Teacher. Musical Education: Royal Artillery Band, 1972-77; City Of Leeds College Of Music, 1977-78; Trinity College of Music, London, 1978-82. Career: Keyboards for

Helen Shapiro and Neil Reid including television and radio; Freelance pianist, ballet, dance, cocktail bands, 1982-; First keyboards for Robin Cousins tour of UK, Electric Ice, 1984; First keyboards for rock opera, Jeanne, and musical, Judy, 1985; Keyboards for Bruce Forsyth, Val Doonican, Michael Barrymore, other cabaret acts, 1985-; Teacher, Blackheath Conservatoire Of Music, 1981-83; Member, Tower Hamlets Strings Project, 1981-92; Teacher, Arts Educational College, 1983-85; Director, Greenwich Strings Project, 1993-. Compositions: Overture and suite for string orchestra; 1 Symphony for string orchestra, 2 horns and oboe; The Pirate Suite for strings and piano; 3 piano suites, 1 piano sonata and many small pieces. Publications: Stringpops; Ragtime Preludes; Go Canon Go; Palm Court Trios. Honours: 2 awards of Coventry Godfrey Gold Medal, Royal Artillery Band; Hannah Brooke Prize for piano at TCM; Scholarship at TCM, 1981-1982; LTCL, LGSM, AMusTCL. Memberships: Musicians' Union; Radio Society of Great Britain. Hobbies: Amateur radio (call sign G0NGP); Model Making; Badminton; Reading; Walking. Address: 74 Coleraine Road, Blackheath, London SE3 7PE, England.

WILSON Reuben, b. 4 Sept 1935, Mounds, Oklahoma, USA. Musician (Hammond B3 Organ). Career: Tour with Guru and Jazzmatazz II, 1995. Recordings: Ronnie's Bonnie; Inner City Blues; We're In Love; Walk On By; On Broadway; Love Bug; Groovy Situation; Blue Mode; Set Us Free; Cisco Kid; Bad Stuff; Sweet Life; Gotta Get Your Own; Straight No Chaser; On Broadway; The Lost Grooves; Giant Steps; Hot Rod; Blue Breaks Vol 2; Orange Peel; Shades Of Red; Hip Hop Bop! NY Funkies; Sampled Recordings: Hand On The Torch: I Got It Goin' On, US3; Ill Matic: Memory Lane: NAS; Inner City Blues; Tribe Called Quest. Current Management: c/o Preston Powell, Jazzateria Inc. Address: 112 W 72nd Street #2F, New York, NY 10023, USA.

WINDRICH Erik Rudolph, b. 5 Feb 1960, Netherlands. Singer; Songwriter; Musician (multi-instrumentalist). 2 daughters, 2 stepsons, 1 stepdaughter. Education: University entrance (South Africa). Career: Evoid, 1982-86; Campus tour, 1984; Operation Hunger, Ellis Park Stadium, South Africa, 1985; Gold selling debut album, 3 hit singles, 1987-90; European tours; Regional radio UK, with The Vision Thing, 1992-; Work in progress with Ear Productions. Compositions: with Evoid: Shadows; Taximan; I Am A Fadget; with The Vision Thing: Fist In The Air; Wyah; Brother Sistem. Recordings: with Evoid: Evoid; Here Comes The Rot; A Space In Which To Create; with The Vision Thing: The Vision Thing. Honours: Sarie Award, South Africa, 1984. Memberships: SAMRO; PRS; PPL; Musicians' Union; COBRA. Hobbies: Reading; Swimming; Cycling. Current Management: Sack The Management. Address: PO Box 572, Harrow, Middlesex HA1 3XA, England.

WINN Tony Ellis, b. 15 Aug 1949, Ilford, Essex, England. Singer; Songwriter; Musician (guitar, banjo). m. Rebecca Jane Stewart, 30 May 1987, 2 sons. Career: Member, 2 touring folk bands; Currently mainly solo performances at folk clubs, festivals, arts centres around UK; Appearances include: TV AM; Live local radio performances; Recordings played on local and national radio; Formed new band Mamwf, 1995. Recordings: Albums: Between Venus And Mars; Short Stories; Singles: Motorway Maniac/Rubbish; Shadows In The Night/Secretly Admiring You; Memberships: Musicians' Union; GISC. Hobbies: Amateur theatre; Gardening; Home. Current Management: Freefall Records, 21 London Road, Kelvedon, Essex CO5 9AR, England.

WINSTON George, b. 1949, Hart, Michigan, USA. Solo Musician (piano, guitar). Career: Solo piano, guitar concerts; Producer, recordings by Hawaiian slack key guitarists for Dancing Cat

Records. Recordings: Solo piano albums: Ballads and Blues, 1972; Autumn, 1980; Winter Into Spring, 1982; December, 1982; Summer, 1991; Forest, 1994; Soundtracks: The Velveteen Rabbit (solo piano with narration by Meryl Streep), 1985; Sadako And The Thousand Paper Cranes (solo guitar with narration by Liv Ullmann) 1995. Current Management: Dancing Cat Productions, Inc. Address: PO Box 639, Santa Cruz, CA 95061, USA.

WINTER Edgar, b. 28 Dec 1946, Beaumont, Texas, USA. Musician (multi-instrumentalist); Composer. m. Monica Winter, 23 Mar 1979. Musical Education: Self-taught. Career: Member, various groups: Black Plague; Johnny Winter's group (brother); Founder, White Trash, 1971; Founder, the Edgar Winter Group, 1972; Session musician with: Meat Loaf, Dan Hartman, Bette Midler, Tina Turner, 1981-. Recordings: Albums: with Johnny Winter: Second Winter, 1970; Johnny Winter And..., 1970; with White Trash: Edgar Winter's White Trash, 1971; Roadwork, 1972; with the Edgar Winter Group: They Only Come Out At Night, 1973; Shock Treatment, 1974; The Edgar Winter Group With Rick Derringer, 1975; Recycled, 1977; The Edgar Winter Album, 1979; Standing On Rock, 1981; Solo album: Entrance, 1975; Jasmine Nightdreams, 1975; Singles include: with White Trash: Keep Playin' That Rock And Roll; I Can't Turn You Loose; with the Edgar Winter Group: Frankenstein; Free Ride; Hangin' Around; River's Risin'; Easy Street. Honours: Grammy Award Nomination. Hobby: Music. Current Management: c/o Jake Hooker, Hooker Enterprises, 1325 El Hito Circle, Pacific Palisades, CA 90272, USA.

WINTER Jean-Philippe, b. 9 Sept 1953, Haguenau, France. Musician (guitar, sitar); Singer. Education: MA, Sciences. Musical Education: Self-taught. Career: Festival de Montpellier, 1986; Tours, Netherlands; UK; Slovakia; Concert, Radio France, 1993; Music for television documentaries, Canal+. Address: 2 Rue Paul Bodin, 75017 Paris, France.

WINTER Johnny (John Dawson III), b. 23 Feb 1944, Beaumont, Texas, USA. Singer; Songwriter; Musician (guitar, harmonica); Record Producer. Career: Member, various bands, including Black Plague; Gene Terry and the Downbeats; Founder, leader, own band, 1968-; Appearances include: Newport '69 Festival, 1969; Newport Jazz Festival, 1969; Texas International Pop Festival, Dallas, 1969; Atlanta International Pop Festival, 1970; Royal Albert Hall, 1970; Bath Festival, 1970; San Francisco Blues Festival, 1987; Riverwalk Blues Fest, Fort Lauderdale, 1988. Recordings: Albums: The Progressive Blues Experiment, 1969; Johnny Winter, 1969; The Johnny Winter Story, 1969; Second Winter, 1970; Johnny Winter And/Live, 1971; Nothin' But The Blues, 1977; White Hot And Blue, 1978; Raisin' Cain, 1980; Guitar Slinger, 1984; Serious Business, 1985; Third Degree, 1985; Winter Of '88, 1988; Let Me In, 1991; with Edgar Winter (brother): Entrance, 1970; White Trash, 1971; Roadwork, 1972; Jasmine Nightdreams, 1975; Together, 1976; Together Live, 1977; with Muddy Waters: Hard Again, 1977; I'm Ready, 1977; King Bee, 1980; Guest musician, Mr Lucky, John Lee Hooker, 1991.Honours: Gold disc, Johnny Winter And - Live, 1974. Memberships: BMI; Musicians' Union. Current Management: Slatus Management, 208 East 51st Street, New York, NY 10022, USA.

WINTER Paul Theodore, b. 31 Aug 1939, Altoona, Pennsylvania, USA. Musician (saxophone); Composer; Bandleader; Recording Artist. m. Chez Liley, 1 Sept 1991. Education: BA, English composition, Northwestern University. Musical Education: Private studies with John Monti, Joe Allard. Career: Concert, recording artist, 1961-; Performed 2300 concerts, 37 countries; Recorded 31 albums; Paul Winter Sextet won Intercollegiate Jazz Festival, 1961;

State Department tour, 23 Latin American countries, 1962; Founded Paul Winter Consort, 1967; Founded Living Music Records, 1980; Played numerous environmental events including Global Forum, Oxford, 1988; Global Forum, Moscow, 1990; Earth Summit, Rio, 1992; Global Forum, Kyoto, 1993. Recordings include: The Paul Winter Sextet, 1961; Jazz Meets the Bossa Nova, 1962; Jazz Premiere: Washington, 1963; NewJazz on Campus, 1963; Jazz Meets the Folk Song, 1963; The Song of Ipanema, 1963; Rio, 1963; The Winter COnsort, 1968; Something in the Wind, 1969; Road, 1970; Icarus, 1972; Common Ground, 1977; Callings, 1980; Earth Mass, 1981; Sunsinger, 1983; Concert for the Earth, 1984; Canyon, 1985; Whales Alive, 1987; Earthbeat, 1988; Wolf Eyes, 1989; Earth: Voices Of A Planet, 1990; Solstice Live, 1992; Spanish Angel, 1993; Prayer For The Wild Things, 1994; Canyon Lullaby, 1997. Honours include: Grammy Awards, 1993, 1994; Global 500 Award, United Nations; Award of Excellence from UN's Environmental Programme; Joseph Wood Krutch Medal, US Humane Society; Alumni Merit Award, Northwestern University, 1996; Honorary DHL, Juniata College; Governor's Distinguished Arts Award, State of Pennsylvania. Current Management: International Music Network, 2 Main Street, 4th Floor, Gloucester, MA 01930, USA. Address: Living Music Records, PO Box 72, Litchfield, CT 06759, USA.

WINTHER Jens, b. 29 Oct 1960, Næstved, Denmark. Musician (trumpet); Composer; Bandleader. 2 sons, 2 daughters. Musical Education: Self-taught. Career: with Ernie Wilkins: Almost Big Band, 1980; Solo trumpeter, Danish Radio Big Band, 1982-89; Lived in New York; 91 major projects (writing and playing) for Danish Radio Big Band; Own music played with WDR, SDR, big bands in Germany, Finland, Sweden, Norway. Recordings: JW/Danish Radio Big Band; with JW Group: The Planets; The 4 Elements, big band composition, 1996, CD, 1997; Pieces for symphony orchestra. Honours: International Competition of Jazz Themes in Monaco, 1st Prize, 1990, 1991, 1996, 2nd Prize, 1988, 1997. Membership: DJBFA. Hobbies: Theosophy; Diving. Address: Sotoften 6B, DK-2680 Solrod Strand, Denmark.

WINWOOD Muff (Mervyn), b. 15 June 1943, Birmingham, England. Musician (bass); Music Company Executive. Career: Folk/blues soloist; Member, Muff-Woody Jazz Band (with brother Steve); Rhythm & Blues Quartet; Member, Spencer Davis Group, 1963-67; Concerts include: National Jazz And Blues Festival, 1965, 1966; Grand Gala du Disques, Amsterdam, 1966; UK tours with: The Rolling Stones, 1965; The Who, 1966; The Hollies, 1967; Management Executive, West End Promotions; Executive, CBS Records; Currently Managing Director, Sony Soho Square (S²) Records, London. Recordings: Albums: Their First LP, 1966; The Second Album, 1966; Autumn '66, 1966; Singles include: Strong Love, 1965; Keep On Running (Number 1, UK), 1966; Somebody Help Me (Number 1, UK), 1966; Gimme Some Lovin', 1966; I'm A Man, 1967. Honour: Carl Alan Award, Most Outstanding Group, 1966. Address: c/o Sony Soho Square (S²) Records, 10 Great Marlborough Street, London W1V 2LP, England.

WINWOOD Steve, b. 12 May 1948, Birmingham, Warwickshire, England. Musician (keyboards, guitar); Vocalist. Career: Founder member, Spencer Davis Group, 1963-67; Performances include: National Jazz And Blues Festival, 1965, 1966; Grand Gala du Disques, Amsterdam, 1966; UK tours with The Rolling Stones, 1965; The Who, 1966; The Hollies, 1967; Traffic, 1967-68; Blind Faith, 1969; Concerts include: Hyde Park, 1969; Madison Square Garden, 1969; Rejoined Traffic, 1970-75; Concerts include: Zurich Rock Festival, 1968; Hollywood Festival, 1970; Headliners, Reading Festival,

1973; Solo artiste, 1977-; ARMS benefit concert, Royal Albert Hall, 1983; US tour, with Robert Cray, 1991. Recordings: Albums: with The Spencer Davis Group: Their First LP, 1966; The Second Album, 1966; Autumn '66, 1966; with Traffic: Mr Fantasy, 1968; Traffic, 1968; John Barleycorn Must Die, 1970; The Low Spark Of High Heeled Boys, 1972; When The Eagle Flies, 1974; with Blind Faith: Blind Faith (Number 1, UK and US), 1969; Solo albums: Steve Winwood, 1977; Arc Of A Diver, 1981; Talking Back To The Night, 1982; Back In The High Life, 1986; Refugees Of The Heart, 1990; Singles include: with Spencer Davis Group: Keep On Running (Number 1, UK), 1966; Somebody Help Me, 1966; Gimme Some Lovin', 1966; I'm A Man, 1967; with Traffic: Paper Sun, 1967; Hole In My Shoe, 1967; Solo include: Higher Love, 1986; The Finer Things, 1987; Valerie, 1987; Roll With It (Number 1, US), 1988; Don't You Know What The Night Can Do, 1988; Holding On, 1989; One And Only Man, 1989. Honours include: Grammy Awards: Record of the Year, Best Pop Vocal Performance, Higher Love, 1987; Gold discs. Current Management: Ron Weisner Entertainment, 9200 Sunset Boulevard, PH15, Los Angeles, CA 90069, USA.

WISE Denny, b. 12 Sept 1947, Bedford, Bedfordshire, England. Bandleader; Vocalist; Musician; Composer. m. Teresa Wise, 31 July 1982, 1 son, 1 daughter. Education: Intermediate, Leicester Collge of Art and Technology. Musical Education: Self-taught; Some piano/vocal lessons. Career: Radio appearances include: BBC; Capital Radio; Local stations; Television appearances in Germany. Recordings: Wise One; Time; with Marian Davies (of the Ladybirds): A Toast To Gilbert O'Sullivan (Denny Wise Sings). Publications: Wise One; Love In The Night; Where Did We Go Wrong. Memberships: Musicians' Union; Variety and Allied Entertainments Council. Hobbies: Music; Swimming; Sport; Reading. Current Management: Denny Wise Organisation. Address: 65 Shawley Way, Epsom Downs, Surrey KT18 5PD, England.

WISEFIELD Laurence Mark (Laurie), b. London, England. Musician (guitar, electric and acoustic, slide, banjo); Vocalist; Songwriter. m. Patricia France Rousseau, 26 May 1986. Musical Education: Self-taught. Career: Formed group Home, 1971-73; Joined Al Stewart Band, 1973; Member, group Wishbone Ash, 1974-86; Joined Tina Turner Band, 1987; Solo performance, Night of the Guitars; Tours: Joe Cocker, Night Calls tour; Tom Jones Show; Roger Chapman Band, 1991; Eros Ramazzotti, 1994; 14 month world tour with Tina Turner, Break Every Rule Tour, including live album, video, Christmas special, Live In Rio, numerous television appearances. Recordings: 3 albums with Home, 1971-73; 9 studio albums, 2 live albums, with Wishbone Ash; Live album with Tina Turner; Albums: Night Of Guitars; UNO, Roger Chapman. Honours: Platinum, Gold albums. Memberships: Musicians' Union; PRS; MCPS; PAMRA. Hobbies: Martial arts. Address: c/o Loz Ltd, 56 Forest Court, Snaresbrook, London E11 1PL, England.

WISEMAN Debbie, b. 10 May 1963, London, England. Composer; Conductor. m. Tony Wharmby, 21 Sept 1987. Education: Saturday Exhibitioner, Trinity College of Music, 1977-81; Kingsway Princeton/Morley College, 1979-81; GGSM, Guildhall School of Music and Drama, 1984. Career: Freelance composer and conductor. Compositions: Music for film and television productions including: Wilde; Tom And Viv; Haunted; Female Perversions; The Dying Of The Light; The Good Guys; The Upper Hand; The Churchills; The Second Russian Revolution; Little Napoleons; Children's Hospital; What Did You Do In The War, Auntie?; The Cuban Missile Crisis; Vet's School; The Missing Postman. Recordings: Wilde; Tom And Viv; Haunted; Special performance of original composition with The

Debbie Wiseman Collection, St John's Smith Square, London, 1989; Wilde, 1997; Featured works on BBC Radio 3 series The Music Machine and Every Note Paints A Picture. Honours: David Taylor Memorial Prize, Trinity College of Music, 1981; Television and Radio Industries Club Award for TV Theme Music of the Year (The Good Guys), 1993; Nominated for Rank Film Laboratories Award for Creative Originality, 1994; Women in Film and Television Award; Ivor Novello Award Nomination, 1996, Royal Television Society Award Nomination, 1996, for Death of Yugoslavia. Memberships: Performing Right Society; British Academy of Film and Television Arts; Musicians' Union; British Academy of Songwriters, Composers and Authors; Association of Professional Composers. Hobby: Snooker. Current Management: c/o Peters, Fraser and Dunlop, 503/4 The Chambers, Chelsea Harbour, London SW10 0XF, England.

WISNIAK Alain, b. 23 Sept 1947, Boulogne, Seine, France. Composer; Arranger; Producer. m. Mariline Raichenbach, 25 Mar 1975, 1 son, 1 daughter. Musical Education: Marguerite Long piano school; Harmony with André Hodeir. Career: Musician for sessions and tours with major French pop artists. Recordings: Show theme for television series Maguy; Producer, composer, Cerrone's Supernature album; Soundtracks for films: La Femme Publique; L'Année Des Méduses; On Peut Toujours Rever; Victoire De La Musique, 1992; Medaille De La SACEM. Memberships: Sociétaire Définitif; SACEM. Hobby: Catamaran sailing. Current Management: Tralala Music, 14 Bld Emile Augier, 75116 Paris, France. Address: 16 Rue Paira, 92190 Meudon, France.

WITHERS Bill, b. 4 July 1938, Slab Fork, West Virginia, USA. Singer; Songwriter. m. Denise Nicholas. Career: Began work with Ford, IBM, Lockheed Aircraft Corporation; Recording artiste, 1970-; Appearances include: UK tour, 1988; Summer Jazz Explosion '92, 1992; Valley Forge Music Fair, 1992; 2 tribute concerts for Eddie Kendricks, organised by Bobby Womack, California, 1992. Recordings: Albums: Just As I Am, 1971; Still Bill, 1972; Bill Withers Live At Carnegie Hall, 1973; The Best Of Bill Withers, 1975; Making Music, 1975; Naked And Warm, 1976; Menagerie, 1977; 'Bout Love, 1979; Bill Withers Greatest Hits, 1981, 1988; Watching You, Watching Me, 1985; Singles include: Ain't No Sunshine, 1971; Grandma's Hands, 1971; Lean On Me (Number 1, US), 1972; Use Me, 1972; with Grover Washington: Just The Two Of Us, 1981; with Ralph McDonald: In The Name Of Love, 1984; Lovely Day, 1988. Honours: Grammy Awards: Best R&B Song, 1982, 1988; Gold discs for: Still Bill, 1972; Menagerie, 1977; Lean On Me, 1987. Address: c/o Associated Booking Corporation, 1995 Broadway, Suite 501, New York, NY 10023, USA.

WITTER Rick, b. 23 Nov 1972, Stockport, Cheshire, England. Singer. Career: 2 Top Of The Pops appearances; Reading Festival; 4 UK tours; 3 European tours; Roskilde '95 (Denmark); Sellout Far East tours; Various appearances on music programmes; MTV live concert; Extensive press coverage. Recordings: Singles: Mark/Casino Girl; Dolphin; Speakeasy; Ocean Pie; Album: Changegiver. Honours: Gold disc, 25,000 sales: Changegiver. Memberships: PRS; Musicians' Union. Hobbies: Smoking; Sleeping; Music. Current Management: Cut Throat Management; Polydor. Address: PO Box 77, Coventry CV7 9Y2, England.

WITTMAN William, b. 16 Sept 1952, Richmond-on-Thames, Surrey, England. Record Producer. m. Barbara Solomon, 23 Aug 1975, 1 son. Career: Mixer, record producer, New York, 1978-87; RCA Records, 1987-90; CBS Records, 1990-. Recordings: As producer include: She's So Unusual, Cyndi Lauper, 1982; Steady Nerves,

Graham Parker, 1985; Calm Animals, The Fixx, 1988. Membership: NARAS.

WOBBLE Jah (John Wardle), b. London, England. Musician (bass). Career: Member, Public Image Ltd (PIL), 1978-80; Founder, Human Condition; Jah Wobble's Invaders Of The Heart. Composition: The River, Ku-cheng concerto performed by the Royal Liverpool Philharmonic Orchestra. Recordings: Albums: with PIL: Public Image Ltd, 1978; Metal Box, 1979; Second Edition, 1980; Take Me to God, 1994; Heaven and Earth, 1995; The Inspiration of William Blake; The Celtic Poets; Requiem. Current Management: c/o 30 Hertz. Address: PO Box 11177, London E2 0DS, England.

WOCKER Sebastian Nicholas Stephen, b. Islington, London, England. Singer; Songwriter; Musician (guitar). Musical Education: Music Hochschule Hamburg, New York City. Career: Began guitar, New York, aged 13; Singer, dancer, in musical Hair, Europe, 1983; Formed Yeah, 1990; Various television appearances in Germany include 3 Nach 9; Concerts include: Kaiserkeller; Marquee; Mean Fiddler; Rock Garden. Recordings: Arsenal Rap; Michel Van Dyke; Highbury Sunshine; Yeah's debut album includes songs: Woman's Love; 001; Dream; I Won't Lie; Dirty Old Man. Publications: The Evening Bastard (Yeah fan club magazine). Honour: Winner, John Lennon Talent Award, Germany, 1994. Memberships: Musicians' Union; PRS; MCPS. Hobby: Football (Arsenal Football Club). Current Management: Musical Network GmbH, Hamburg. Address: An Der Alster 29, 200099 Hamburg, Germany.

WOERNLE Peter Andreas, b. 15 Aug 1959, Tübingen, Germany. Editor; Manager. Education: Advertising Agent; Psychologist. Musical Education: 12 years classical piano; 10 years classical cello. Career: Freelance Journalist; Press Manager, Virgin Records, Germany; Editor, Press Agency, music and communication; Publisher, youth magazine Extrem. Address: Schwetzinger Strasse 20, D-68165 Mannheim, Germany.

WOIWOD Bill (William), b. 27 Oct 1919, London, England. Musician (clarinet, bass clarinet, flute, alto flute, piccolo). m. Joan Jenner, 8 July 1950. Musical Education: Trinity College; Guildhall School of Music; London College of Music. Career: Featured soloist, Edmundo Ros LA Orchestra, 26 years; 9 concert tours, Scandinavia; Royal Command Performance, 1962; State Visit of Queen, 1956; 3 seasons, Monte Carlo; 5 tours Japan, Okinawa, Singapore; 81 television appearances, including 9 abroad; 904 BBC broadcasts. Recordings: 118 for Edmundo Ros Orchestra, Decca Studios. Teacher of woodwind for: ILEA, 15 years; Havering and Essex, 10 years; Brentwood School, 12 years. Hobbies: Golf; Model making; Playing organ.

WOLANIN Vincent M, b. 13 Dec 1947, Philadelphia, Pennsylvania, USA. Producer. m. Illona Koch Dove, 27 July 1981, 2 daughters. Education: BS Philadelphia College of Textiles and Science, 1969; Grad school, Union College, 1971. Musical Education: Accordion, piano. Career; President/CEO Topnotch Entertainment Corp; Holds musical trademarks for Studiolive Sound TM, Thoughts TM, Topnotch; Founder, Topnotch Music, Records label distributed, US by MS; Former Professional Athlete; Creator, Executive Producer, Supercollossal TM Show; Head, TopNotch Management Company. Recordings: Producer, Breaking Through album, 1995; Producer, Angry Room, Lyndal's Burning; Producer, Lingerie, Natalia. Publications: Created ads for Spin Magazine, April, May, 1996. Honours: Gold CD and record, for album: Exposed, Vince Neil, Japan, 1993; Silver CD, for Breakin'Through, 1996. Memberships: NARM (national Association of Recording Merchandisers) NARAS (National academy Recording Arts/Science. Hobbies: Golf;

Racquetball (former professional). Current Management: Topnotch Entertaianment Corp, Topnotch Music and Records. Address: Box 1515, Sanibel Island, FL 33957-1515, USA.

WOLFSON Mark, b. 1 Sept 1951, Chicago, Illinois, USA. Record Producer; Sound Engineer; Songwriter. Career: Record Production, Sound Engineer, Artist Development; Clients include: Natalie Cole; Jane Child; Stone Temple Pilots; Kimberly Bass; Producer: Film soundtracks; Television music. Recordings as producer: with UB40: Something Wild; with Talking Heads: Stop Making Sense; Also producer for Jane Child; School Of Fish; Stone Temple Pilots; Natalie Cole; Sound Engineer for: Sir Mix-A-Lot; Talking Heads; Smokey Robinson; Ice-T; Natalie Cole; Thelma Houston; Phil Everly; Melle Mel; Kim Carnes; Celia Cruz; Jane Child; Michael Des Barres; Film soundtracks include: Philadelphia; Silence Of The Lambs; Point Break; Police Academy; Police Academy III; Down And Out In Beverly Hills; K2; Television commercials include: Burger King; Coors; Toyota; 7 Up; Pizza Hut; Circle K. Honours: 25 Multi-Platinum, Platinum and Gold Records. Hobbies: Travel; Horses. Address: 11684 Ventura Boulevard, Suite 134 Studio City, CA 91604, USA.

WOLLO Erik, b. 6 Jan 1961, Norway. Composer; Producer; Musician (guitar, synthesiser). 1 son. Career: Professional artist, 1980-; Rock, jazz, classical music; Music for film, theatre, ballets, multimedia; Mostly electronic/synthesiser music, also strings, woodwinds, orchestra; Producer other artists; Building own Wintergarden Studio. Compositions: Formations, 1982; Buteo Buteo, 1986; Eb Brottsjo, 1986; Solar, 1986; Windows, 1988; Pre sense, 1990; Vidder, 1992; Cairns, 1992; Music for ballet: Pyramider, 1986; Jeg Dromte, 1992; Music for theatre: Motspillerne, 1988, 1991; Aldri Verden, 1992; Fossegrimen, 1992; Abiriels Love, music for theatre, 1996; Maunushymnen, 1997. Recordings: Albums: Where It All Begins, 1983; Dreams Of Pyramids, 1984; Traces, 1985; Silver Beach, 1986; Images Of Light, 1990; Solstice, 1992; Fossegrimen, 1995; Albums with other artists: Celeste: Design By Music, 1984; Wiese/Wollo/Waring: Trio, 1984; New Music Composer's Group: In Real Time, 1992; Transit, 1996; Dimension D, Exile, 1997. Memberships: NOPA; Ny Musikk. Hobby: Mountain climbing. Current Management: Monumental Records. Address: Blomsterveien 10, 1636 Fredrikstad, Norway.

WOMACK Bobby, b. 4 Mar 1944, Cleveland, Ohio, USA. Singer;Songwriter; Musician (guitar). m. Barbara Cooke, 1965, divorced 1970. Career: Member, The Womack Brothers (later known as The Valentinos); Support to James Brown, US tour, 1962; Guitarist, Sam Cooke, 1960; Session work, 1965; Solo artiste, 1968-; Regular UK and US tours; Concerts include: New Orleans Jazz Festival, 1992. Compositions include: It's All Over Now (UK Number 1 for Rolling Stones); Numerous songs for Wilson Pickett including: 634-5789; I'm A Midnight Mover; I'm In Love. Recordings: Albums: Fly Me To The Moon, 1968; The Womack Live, 1971; Communication, 1972; Understanding, 1972; Across 110th Street, 1973; Facts Of Life, 1973; Looking For Love Again, 1974; Bobby Womack's Greatest Hits, 1974; I Don't Know What The World Is Coming to, 1975; Safety Zone, 1976; BW Goes C&W, 1976; Home Is Where The Heart Is, 1976; Pieces, 1978; Roads Of Life, 1979; The Poet, 1981; The Poet II, 1984; So Many Rivers, 1985; Womagic, 1987; The Last Soul Man, 1987; Lookin' For A Love (1968-1975), 1993; Producer, Now Look, Ron Wood, 1974; Contributor, Sun City, Artists Against Apartheid, 1985; Dirty Work, The Rolling Stones, 1986; Coast To Coast, Paul Shaffer, 1989; Nearly Human, Todd Rundgren, 1989; Guitarist on recordings by artists including: King Curtis; Ray Charles; Wilson Pickett; Joe Tex; Aretha Franklin; Dusty Springfield; Janis Joplin;

Singer, duets with Patti Labelle; Altrina Grayson; Shirley Brown; Lulu. Address: c/o Nick Cowan, Bobby Womack and Co., 9595 Wilshire Blvd #502, Beverly Hills, CA 90210, USA.

WONDER Stevie (Steveland Morris), b. 13 May 1950, Saginaw, Michigan, USA. Singer; Musician (multi-instrumentalist); Composer. m. Syreeta Wright, 1970, divorced, 3 children. Education: Michigan State School for the Blind, 1963-68. Musical Education: Self-taught harmonica, piano. Career: Motown recording artist (initially as Stephen Judkins), 1963-70; Founder, president, music publishing company, Black Bull Music Inc; Founder, Wonderdirection Records Inc; Taurus Productions; Numerous concerts include: Midem Festival, France, 1974; Night Of The Hurricane II (hurricane relief concert), Houston, 1976; Peace Sunday, Rose Bowl, 1982; Nelson Mandela's Birthday Tribute, Wembley, 1988; Film appearances include: Bikini Beach, 1964; Muscle Beach Party, 1964. Compositions include: Lovin' You, Minnie Riperton, 1975; Recordings: Hit singles include: Fingertips Part 2 (Number 1, US), 1963; Uptight (Everything's Alright), 1966; I Was Made To Love Her, 1967; For Once In My Life, 1968; My Cherie Amour, 1969; Yester-Me, Yester-You, Yesterday, 1969; Signed Sealed Delivered I'm Yours, 1970; Superstition (Number 1, US), 1973; You Are The Sunshine Of My Life (Number 1, US), 1973; Higher Ground, 1974; Living For The City, 1974; You Haven't Done Nothin' (Number 1, US), 1974; Boogie On Reggae Woman, 1975; I Wish (Number 1, US), 1977; Sir Duke (Number 1, US), 1977; Master Blaster, 1980; Lately, 1981; Happy Birthday, 1981; Ebony And Ivory, duet with Paul McCartney (Number 1, US and UK), 1982; I Just Called To Say I Love You (Number 1, US and UK), 1984; Part-Time Lover, 1985; Don't Drive Drunk, 1985; Albums include: The 12 Year Old Genius, 1963; Up Tight Everything's Alright, 1966; Down To Earth, 1967; I Was Made To Love Her, 1967; Greatest Hits, 1968; For Once In My Life, 1969; My Cherie Amour, 1969; Signed Sealed And Delivered, 1969; Greatest Hits Vol.2, 1971; Music Of My Mind, 1972; Talking Book, 1972; Innervisions, 1973; Fulfillingness' First Finale, 1974; Songs In The Key Of Life, 1976; Journey Through The Secret Life Of Plants, 1979; Hotter Than July, 1980; Woman In Red (soundtrack), 1984; Love Songs, 1984; In Square Circle, 1985; Characters, 1987; Music From The Music Jungle Fever (soundtrack), 1991; Conversation Peace, 1995; Natural Wonder, 1996; Contributor, I Feel For You, Chaka Khan, 1984; There Must Be An Angel, The Eurthymics, 1985; That's What Friends Are For, Dionne Warwick And Friends, 1986; Hallelujah!, Quincy Jones, 1992. Honours include: Numerous Grammy Awards, including Lifetime Achievement Award, 1990; Edison Award, 1973; NARM Presidential Award, 1975; Inducted into Songwriters Hall Of Fame, 1983; Numerous American Music Awards, including Special Award of Merit, 1982; Oscar, Best Song, 1984; Gold Ticket, Madison Square Garden, 1986; Soul Train Heritage Award, 1987; Inducted into Rock'n'Roll Hall Of Fame, 1989; Nelson Mandela Courage Award, 1991; IAAAM Diamond Award for Excellence, 1991; Lifetime Achievement Award, National Academy Of Songwriters, 1992; NAACP Image Award, 1992; Numerous other charity and civil rights awards. Current Management: Stevland Morris Music, 4616 Magnolia Blvd., Burbank, CA 91505, USA.

WOOD Jeffrey, b. 5 Sept 1950, Chicago, Illinois, USA. Record Producer; Recording Artist; Composer. m. Carine F Verheyen, 16 Nov 1992. Education: BA, University of Illinois. Musical Education: 12 years piano and composition, Helen Beidel. Career: Produced over 30 major recording artists including: Luka Bloom; The Housemartins; The Origin; Pauline Black. Recordings include: Twist Of Destiny; The Surrendering Room; 3 feature film soundtracks. Current Management:

Steve Moir Company. Address: 16101 Ventura Blvd, Encino, CA 91436, USA.

WOOD Katherine (Jane Margaret), b. 21 June 1965, Bromley, Kent, England. Singer; Songwriter. Musical Education: Private classical singing lessons. Career: Career: Don't Dream It's Over - Less Stress featuring Katherine Wood for Boys Own, Substance, 1990-91; Regular demos for PWL Ltd (Pete Waterman) include: Loveland demos; 6 single releases, 1994-95; Hundreds of jazz, soul, R&B concerts, 1984-; Supported Rod Stewart, Elton John, Stevie Wonder; Backing singer, Belinda Carlisle, European Tour, 1995-; Album, 1995; Lawnmower Man II session on soundtrack, plays Radio 1, Sussex, Kiss, GLR, BSBF, Choice, 1995; Single, Whole Lotta Love with Goldbug, appeared live on Top of the Pops, 1996; In choir for entire Evita soundtrack; Backing vocals for Chaka Khan on National Lottery Show; 4 tracks on Speaker album, 1997. Recordings: Single: with Voice Of Public Demand: Celebrate The World, 1995; Out Of The Blue, Wood, Henshall, Phillips; Wrote and sung theme tune for International television series Dolphin Stories. Memberships: PRS; MCPS; Musicians' Union; British Music Writers Council; PAMRA; Equity. Hobbies: Reading; Yoga; Movies; Theatre; Listening to music; Jazz and Blues; Walking in the country. Current Management: Simon Watson, Firstars Management. Address: 26B Loveridge Road, Kilburn, London NW6 2DT, England.

WOOD Michael Stefan, b. 12 Apr 1954, Hyde, Cheshire, England. Head of Music and Expressive Arts Faculty, School. m. Anita Jane, 25 May 1991. Musical Education: Music at University of Hertfordshire, recorder with Evelyn Nallen, guitar/lute, Ian Gammie. Career: Formed folk band: The Brighthelmstones, 1969; Semi finalists National Folk Rock Fest, 1972; Album, 1971; Co-founded Wilbury Jam, 1977; Folk/cabaret in band play guitars, mandolin, banjo, recorder, clarinet, violin, trombone, horn; Played Krummhorn as part of Drake Anniversary, TVS, 1988; Similar, BBC radio, 1988. Recordings: Album: Brighthelmstones, 1971; Wilbury Jam: A Good Spread, 1980; A Second Helping, 1991. Honours: Dip Mus LTCL (Performers Recorder) LLCM ALCM. Membership: Musicians' Union. Hobbies: Walking; Watching war films; Conducting orchestras. Address: 52 Chanctonbury Road, Burgess Hill, West Sussex RH15 9EY, England.

WOOD Paul (Paul Richard Woodcock), b. 16 Nov 1964, Romford, Essex, England. Vocalist. Career: Played with The Ray Ward Trio; Worked with artists including: Don Lusher; George Chisholm; Kenny Ball; Terry Lightfoot; Appeared at venues including: Pizza Express; Cafe Loire; Royal Festival Hall; Royal Ascot; Various radio and television includes: 2 hour radio broadcast from The Film Festival Hall, Cannes, France; Currently with Glenn Miller Memorial Orchestra, 1987-; Concert tours in France, Switzerland, Spain, Italy, Germany, Belgium, Austria, including Sporting Club, Monte Carlo, before Prince Rainier and Princess Caroline; Works regularly with various bands on the Continent; Played many Liberation Concerts; Spa Belgium; Toulon, France; Lille (25000 people); Nice Jazz Festivals. Recordings: 4 albums with Glenn Miller Orchestra include: Recorded Live The Sporting Club Monte Carlo; 2 albums with Lex Van Wel and His Swing Orchestra. Memberships: Musicians' Union; The Coda Club. Hobbies: Collecting antiquarian books; Model Rolls Royce's. Current Management: Lex Van Wel, Postbus 1436-5602 BK Eindhoven, Netherlands.

WOOD Ron, b. 1 June 1947, Hillingdon, London, England. Musician (guitar, bass). 1 son. Career: Musician, Jeff Beck Group, 1967-69; Concerts include: National Jazz And Blues Festival, 1967, 1968; Newport Jazz Festival, 1969; Member, The Faces, 1969-75; Reading Jazz Festival, 1972; Buxton Festival, 1974; Member,

The Rolling Stones, 1975-; US tour, 1975; Knebworth Festival, 1976; The Band's Last Waltz Farewell Concert, San Francisco, 1976; Film, Ladies And Gentlemen, The Rolling Stones, 1977; Played Knebworth Festival as The New Barbarians (with Keith Richards), 1979; Live Aid, JFK Stadium, Philadelphia, 1985; Played with Bo Diddley as the Gunslingers; Tours: North America, 1987; Japan, 1988; Germany, Italy, Spain, 1988; Sang at Bob Dylan 30th Anniversary Tribute, Madison Square Garden, 1992. Recordings: Albums with The Faces: First Step, 1970; Long Player, 1971; A Nod's As Good As A Wink...To A Blind Horse, 1971; Coast To Coast Overture And Beginners, 1974; with The Rolling Stones: Made In The Shade, 1975; Black And Blue, 1976; Love You Live, 1977; Emotional Rescue, 1980; Tattoo You, 1981; Still Life, 1982; Undercover, 1983; Dirty Work, 1986; Steel Wheels, 1989; Singles: with The Faces: Stay With Me, 1972; Cindy Incidentally, 1973; Pool Hall Richard, 1974; You Can Make Me Dance Or Sing Or Everything, 1974; with The Rolling Stones: Fool To Cry, 1976; Miss You (Number 1 US), 1978; Emotional Rescue, 1980; Start Me Up, 1981; Going To a Go-GO; Undercover Of The Night; Dancing In The Street (Number 1 UK), 1985; Mixed Emotions, 1989. Honours include: Silver Clef, Nordoff-Robbins Music Therapy, 1982; Madison Square Garden Hall Of Fame, 1984; Grammy, Lifetime Achievement Award, 1986; Ivor Novello, Outstanding Contribution To British Music, 1991. Current Management: Rupert Loewenstein, 2 King Street, London SW1Y 6QL, England.

WOOD Roy, b. 8 Nov 1946, Birmingham, England. Singer; Musician (guitar). Career: Member, Mike Sheridan and the Nightriders; Singer, guitarist, The Move, 1966-1972; Appearances include National Jazz & Blues Festival, 1966; 14-Hour Technicolour Dream, with Pink Floyd, Alexandra Palace, 1967; Isle Of Wight Festival, 1968; Founder member, Electric Light Orchestra (ELO), 1971-72; Founder, lead singer, Wizzard, 1972-75; Concerts include: London Rock'n'Roll Festival, 1972; Reading Festival, 1972; Also formed The Wizzo Band; The Helicopters; Writer, producer, various artists including Darts, 1977; Performed at Heartbeat '86 benefit concert, 1986; Cropredy Festival, 1995. Numerous compositions include: Night Of Fear; I Can Hear The Grass Grow; Blackberry Way; Hello Susie; See My Baby Jive; Recordings: UK Top 10 singles include: with The Move: Night Of Fear, 1967; I Can Hear The Grass Grow, 1967; Flowers In The Rain (first song ever played on BBC Radio 1), 1967; Fire Brigade, 1968; Blackberry Way (Number 1, UK); Hello Susie, 1969; Brontosaurus, 1970; California Man, 1972; with ELO: 10538 Overture, 1972; with Wizzard: Ball Park Incident, 1973; See My Baby Jive (Number 1, UK), 1973; Angel Fingers (Number 1, UK); I Wish It Could Be Christmas Every Day, 1973; Rock'n'Roll Winter, 1974; Are You Ready To Rock, 1975; Solo singles include: Dear Elaine; Forever; Going Down The Road; Oh What A Shame; Albums with The Move: Move, 1968; Shazam, 1970; Looking On, 1970; Message From The Country, 1971; with ELO: Electric Light Orchestra, 1972; with Wizzard: Wizzard Brew, 1973; Introducing Eddy And The Falcons, 1974; with The Wizzo Band: On The Road Again, 1977; Super Active Wizzo, 1977; Solo albums: Boulders, 1973; Mustard, 1976; Starting Up, 1987; Various compilation albums; Contributor, Arrested (album of Police covers by various artists and the Royal Philharmonic Orchestra), 1983. Address: c/o Barry Collings Enterprises, 21a Clifftown Road, Southend-on-Sea, Essex SS1 1AB, England.

WOODLEY Mark Kenneth, b. 5 Sept 1953, Brantford, Ontario, Canada. Songwriter; Musician (piano); Vocalist; Motivator. m. Elaine, 18 June 1977, 1 son, 2 daughters. Education: Leadership Training. Career: Toured through Canada, USA, UK, 1981-; National television in Canada. Recordings: Taken By Force, Image 7, 1987; More

Like You, Image 7, 1985; Breaking Ground, Listen, 1981; Edify The Church, 1991. Honours: Nominated to International Airplay Award, 1995. Memberships: SOCAN; GMA. Hobbies: Skiing; Long-distance running; Aviation. Current Management: YES International Inc. Address: 7 Painters Road, RR7, Brantford, Ontario N3T 5L9, Canada.

WOODRUFF Bob, b. 14 Mar 1961, Suffern, New York, USA. Singer; Songwriter; Musician (guitar, drums). Career: Television appearances include: Music City Tonight, Nashville Network; TNN Country News; Inside Country, Ontario, Canada; The Road, Tribune Entertainment; Country Road Frutigen, Switzerland. Recordings: Debut: Dreams And Saturday Nights; Second release due July 1996. Honours: Charleston International Film Festival Silver Award, Best Country Music Video, for Alright, 1994. Memberships: CMA; NARAS; AFTRA; AFofM. Hobbies: Reading the classics and musical biographies; Skateboarding; 1960s "muscle cars". Current Management: Jim Della Croce Management, 1229 17th Avenue South, Nashville, TN 37212, USA.

WOODS Lesley, b. 25 Jan 1958. Singer; Songwriter; Musician (guitar); Music Business Lawyer. Education: Qualified Barrister-At-Law. Career: Singer, songwriter, guitarist, Au Pairs, 1979-84; Solo artiste, songwriter, singer, guitarist, 1985-; Also Barrister-at-Law. Recordings: Albums: Playing With A Different Sex; Sense And Sensuality; Singles include: It's Obvious. Memberships: Musicians' Union; PRS; MCPS. Hobbies: Music; Films; Keeping fit. Address: 47 Banbury House, Banbury Road, London E9 7EB, England.

WOODS Phil (Philip Wells), b. 2 Nov 1931, Springfield, Massachusetts, USA. Jazz Musician (saxophone, clarinet); Composer. Musical Education: Juilliard School of Music, New York, 1948-52. Career: Musician with Dizzy Gillespie; Quincy Jones; Benny Goodman; Gene Krupa; Buddy Rich; Michel Legrand; Thelonious Monk; Charlie Barnet; Bandleader, European Rhythm Machine, 1968-73; Phil Woods Quartet, 1974-84; Leader, Phil Woods Quintet, 1984-. Compositions include: Rights Of Swing; Three Improvisations; Sonata For Alto And Piano (Four Moods); The Sun Suite; I Remember. Recordings: with Phil Woods Quintet: Gratitude; Heaven; Bop Stew; All Bird's Children; with Phil Wood's Little Big Band: Evolution; Bouquet; Flash; Real Life; Numerous albums with Jimmy Smith; Also featured on recordings by: Benny Carter; Quincy Jones; Paul Simon; Buddy Miles; Ron Carter; Billy Joel; Steve Miller Band; Bill Evans; Carly Simon; Steely Dan; Michel Legrand; Film soundtracks include: 12 Angry Men, 1957; The Hustler, 1961. Honours: 3 Grammy Awards: More Live, Benny Carter; 1982; At The Vanguard, Benny Carter, 1983; Images, Michel Legrand, 1976; Downbeat Awards: New Star Of 1956; Reader's Poll Winner, 1975-90; Golden Feather Award, Best Group, Phil Woods Quintet, 1988-90; Critics Poll Award, 1988-91; Jazz Times Critics Poll Award, Phil Woods Quintet, 1990. Membership: AFofM.

WOODVINE-WEST Joyce, b. 2 Nov 1952, England. Jazz and Blues Scat Vocalist; Latin Percussion. 1 daughter. Musical Education: WEA and Wavendon courses; Jazz club circuit. Career: Appearances: Birmingham and Edinburgh Jazz Fringe Festivals; Beaumaris Festival; National Music Day; New Vic Theatre, Stoke-on-Trent, 1994. Membership: Musicians' Union. Hobbies: Languages; Travel; Continental songs; Percussion. Current Agent: Terry Wood, Knutsford. Address: 21 Davenport Avenue, Crewe CW2 6LG, England.

WOODWARD Keren, b. 2 Apr 1961, Bristol, Somerset, England. Singer. Career: Worked at BBC; Singer, all-girl group Bananarama, 1981-;

Performances include: BRIT Awards, 1988. Recordings: Albums: Deep Sea Skiving, 1983; Bananarama, 1984; True Confessions, 1986; The Greatest Hits Collection, 1988; Please Yourself, 1993; Singles include: Really Sayin' Somethin', 1982; Na Na Hey Hey Kiss Him Goodbye, 1983; Cruel Summer, 1983; Robert De Niro's Waiting, 1984; Cruel Summer (featured in film The Karate Kid), 1984; Venus (Number 1, US), 1986; I Heard A Rumour, 1987; Love In The First Degree, 1987; I Want You Back, 1988; Nathan Jones, 1988; Help! (with comedy duo French and Saunders), 1989; Preacher Man, 1991; Long Train Running, 1991; Movin' On, 1992; More More More, 1993; with Fun Boy Three: It Ain't What You Do, It's The Way That You Do It, 1982; Contributor: Do They Know It's Christmas, Band Aid (Ethiopian famine relief), 1984; Let It Be, Ferry Aid (Zeebrugge ferry disaster benefit), 1987; Rock The World, benefit album, 1990.

WOOLEY Sheb (Shelby F), b. 10 Apr 1921, Eric, Oklahoma, USA. Actor; Musician (fiddle, harmonica, acoustic guitar); Songwriter; Comedian. m. Linda S Dotson, 30 Dec 1985, 2 daughters. Career: Over 80 major films, including: High Noon; Outlaw; Josie Wales; War Wagon; Rio Bravo; Rocky Mountain; Giant; Television appearances include: Original cast member, Hee Haw; Rawhide, 7 years; American Bandstand; Mod Squad; Murder She Wrote; Hootnanny Hoot; The Lone Ranger; Ed Sullivan Show. Recordings: Hit singles include: The Purple People Eater (100 million sales including covers); That's My Pa; Are You Satisfied; Sweet Chile; White Lightnin'; as Ben Colder: Fifteen Beers Ago; Almost Persuaded; Harper Valley PTA. Honours: CMA Comedian of the Year, 1968; 2 Golden Boot Awards; 7 Western Heritage Awards, 1966-; Second fastest selling record ever, The Purple People Eater. Memberships: ASCAP; CMA; NARAS; ROPE; ACM; AFM; SAG; AFTRA. Hobbies: Sailing; Dominos; Cards. Current Management: Linda Dotson, Circuit Rider Talent and Management. Address: 123 Walton Ferry Road, Second Floor, Hendersonville, TN 37075-3616, USA.

WOOLWAY Colin, b. 24 Jan 1959, London, England. Musician (drums); Teacher. m. Lucy MacArthur, 22 July 1995. Career: Theatre tours: Godspell; Rocky Horror Show; 1978-80; English tour with The Enid, 1984; with Suzi Quatro: 5 Australian tours, 2 Japan tours, Russian tour, constant television appearances, 1985-93; Top Clinician for Zildjan Cymbals; Clinician for Sonor Drums, teaching at Drumsense studio. Publications: Drumsense, volumes 1-3, (drum tutors); 4 musician joke books. Hobby: Cartoonist. Current Management: Hayter and Shone, Publisher. Address: Flat 8, Highview House, 1 Highview Road, Upper Norwood, London SE19 3SS, England.

WORLLEDGE Terry, b. 31 Jan 1945, Essex, England. Musician (guitar, harmonica); Singer; Songwriter. m. Jean, 10 Oct 1964, 2 daughters. Musical Education: Self-taught. Career: Member, Country Shack; Member, Jackson Queen; Numerous appearances, Wembley Country Music Festival; Television and radio appearances: BBC; ITV; Radio: BBC Radio 2; Owner, Whirligig Music (instruments and equipment supplier). Recordings: Albums include: with Country Shack: Your Country Needs You; Portrait; Which Way Is Gone?; BBC Compilation album: 20 Country Greats; with Jackson Queen: Jackson Queen (EP). Honours: British Country Music Association, Most Promising Act, 1980; Radio 2 Country Club, Best Band during 3 years as producer. Memberships: Musicians' Union; BCMA; PRS. Hobbies: Photography; Motor racing. Current Management: Self-managed. Address: 43 Chelmer Road, Chelmsford, Essex CM2 6NH, England.

WORRALL Sean, b. 6 June 1966, Leicester, England. Artist; Record Label Owner; Magazine Editor; Concert Promoter; Singer; Musician (bass player); Fashion Designer. Education: West Surrey College of Art. Career: Editor, Organ Magazine; Toured extensively; Many radio, television appearances; Several album covers, videos. Recordings: Sophie Magic, Angel Cage; Late Developer, Rhatigan; Bullseye, Cardiacs; Redoubtable, Deathblanket, Goosebumps. Publications: Organ Magazine; Organ Videozine. Honours: The Golden Bassoon for Services to Punk Rock, 1994. Membership: The Yous Family. Current Management: Self-managed. Address: Unit 205, The Old Gramophone Works, 326 Kensal Road, London W10 5BZ, England.

WORTLEY Barry George, b. 19 May 1951, Norwich, Norfolk, England. Musician (drummer, guitar); Vocalist. m. Susan Read, 4 Oct 1986, 5 sons. Musical Education: School. Career: Member: The Aytons, 1966-68; Norma And The Shade Of Pale, 1968-71; Edentree (touring comedy/showband), 1972-75; Fresh 1975-; Winner, ITV's New Faces, 1978; (name changed to Monte Carlo for last 12 of Song For Europe and Dooley's Tour Support Band, name returned to Fresh); Currently a trio working functions and summer seasons. Recordings: Valentino; Win A Few, Lose A Few; Home Again. Honours: Music Award, Ljubljana Song Festival, Yugoslavia, 1979. Membership: Musicians' Union. Hobbies: Golf; Snooker; Odd pint of real ale. Current Management: Anglia Artistes, Nicky Walker Entertainments and Leisure Services. Address: 105 Netherwood Green, Norwich, Norfolk NR1 2RJ, England.

WORTLEY J, b. 5 June 1971, Grimsby, Lincolnshire, England. Singer; Songwriter; Musician (guitar). Musical Education: Self-taught. Career: Joined Illustrious Gy, 1989; Signed to Arista Records, 1991; Toured with Squeeze in UK; Appeared: Going Live (BBC); Several ITV programmes; Played live, Steve Wright In The Afternoon, BBC Radio 1; Recently signed with MCA, as Giant Icicles. Recordings: Singles: Twenty Questions; Anytime At All; I'm Very; Album: No No No. Membership: Musicians' Union. Hobbies: Keen Footballer. Current Management: J Cooke, Fatcat Management. Address: 81 Harley House, Marylebone Road, London NW1 5HT, England.

WRAIGHT Jeffrey Charles, b. 17 Aug 1954, West Sussex, England. Musician (keyboards, bass guitar); Vocalist; Arranger; Composer; Musical Director; Company Director, Entertainments Agency and Management. Musical Education: A Level Music; Early piano lessons but mainly self taught; Studied with Cyril Winn. Career includes: Accompanied many modern jazz artists, 1973-79; Experimental free jazz workshop, Reading, 1977-79; Television broadcasts from Bracknell Jazz Festival, 2 years running, Soulstice, Funk Jazz group recording with Tony Visconti; Founder member of early Punk group Billy and the Conquerors; Joined big band on QEII, 1979, became band leader of own band on the same ship; Several television appearances; Worked with: The Batchelors; Bob Monkhouse; Tommy Dorsey Orchestra; Peter Gordeno; Joe Loss; Faith Brown; Elaine Delmar; Lorna Dallas; Started business venture in 1983 becoming Heartrate Entertainments, 1989-; Keyboard player, vocalist, arrangements for A Tribute To The Blues Brothers, London West End, 1992; Musical Director, and rewriter of show, 1994-. Recordings include: Soulstice, Tony Visconti; Several live sessions by Pendulum; Some recordings for BBC TV and Radio including several Blues Brothers appearances. Publication: Critique on the music of Miles Davis (in preparation). Honour: John Dankworth Award for Best Instrumentalist Under 25 (Piano), 1977. Hobbies: Computer Music; Computer Studies. Current Management: Heartrate Entertainments. Address: 3 Seacroft, 9 Lansdowne Road, Worthing, Sussex BN11 4NA, England.

WRAY John, b. 16 Jan 1943, Ramshaw, England. Company Director; Musician (keyboards). m. Karen Anne Western, 9 July 1986, 1 son, 1 daughter. Musical Education: Private tuition. Career: Owner, Spennymoor Variety Club; Band leader, John Ray Set; Director, Air Entertainments Agency; Producer, tours: Simply The Best; Reach Out. Recordings: Owner, Bullseye Recording Studios. Hobbies: Flying; Swimming; Cooking. Current Management: Air Entertainments. Address: 17 Clyde Terrace, Spennymoor, Co. Durham DL16 7SE, England.

WRAY Walter, b. 7 Feb 1959, Portsmouth, Hampshire, England. Singer; Songwriter; Musician (guitar). m. Joanne Redfearn, 1 Apr 1989, 1 daughter. Education: Sheffield University. Musical Education: Guitar and piano lessons, BA dual Hons, Music/English. Career: 2 albums with band Junk; Joined rock band King Swamp, 1988; 2 albums, and tours of US and Europe; Currently solo artist. Recordings: Albums: with Junk: Cuckooland, 1986; Drop City Souvenirs, 1987; with King Swamp: King Swamp, 1988; Wiseblood, 1990; Solo: Foxgloves And Steel Strings, 1992. Memberships: Musicians' Union; PRS. Hobbies: Family. Current Management: JFD Management, 106 Dalling Road, Hammersmith, London W6 0JA, England.

WRIGHT David, b. 2 Feb 1958, Colombo, Sri Lanka. Local Government Officer. m. Nicola, 4 July 1987, 1 son. Education: Degree, Environmental Sciences. Musical Education: Self-taught. Career: Solo performer and with band The Thomas Wright Affair; Live performance, BBC Radio Bristol, Somerset Sound, 1993; Canny Wizard Stage, Glastonbury, 1994, 1995; Castle Park Stage, Bristol Sound City, 1995; Mean Fiddler, Acoustic Room, London, 1996, 1997. Recordings: Self-produced albums: Fags Out Chaps We're Going In, Thomas Wright Affair, 1993; Solo demo album: Intimate, 1996. Honours: Glastonbury Festical Canny Wizard Stage, 1994, 1995; Radio 1 FM Park Stage for Bristol Sound City, 1995; Ashton Court Festival, Bristol, 1995. Memberships: PRS; Innternational Guild of Songwriters; Musicians' Union. Hobbies: Football; Tennis; Cycling. Address: PO Box 743, Bristol BS99 5GU, England.

WRIGHT Dennis, b. 12 Dec 1926, Rochdale, Lancashire, England. Musician (drums); Arranger. m. Auidrey Elsie Jones, 8 Sept 1986, 4 sons. Musical Education: George Evans arranging course; Glenn Miller booklet. Career: Played radio broadcast, 1947; Further broadcasts Rink Ballroom, Sunderland; Own trio accompanied artists at Wetherals Night Club, Sunderland, include: Bobby Bennett; Donald Peers; Mike Sarne; Lance Percival; Bertice Reading; Bill Pertwee; Frankie Vaughn (big band); Valerie Masters; Vince Hill; Lena Martell; Dorothy Squires; Dick Emery. Recordings: Newcastle broadcast, 1947; Local band, Henfield, Sussex, recorded. Hobby: Music. Current Management: Cantare, Burgess Hill. Address: Sunrise Management, Forest Green, Dorking, Surrey, England.

WRIGHT Eugene Joseph, b. 29 May 1923, Chicago, Illinois, USA. Musician (bass); Composer. (1) Jacqueline Winters, 29 May 1945, divorced 1954, 1 son, 1 daughter, (2) Phyllis Lycett, 10 Aug 1962. Education: Tilden Tech, Chicago, 1938. Career: Bandleader, Dukes of Swing Orchestra, 1943-46; Bassist with: Count Basie Orchestra; Gene Ammons/Sonny Stitt Quintet; Buddy DeFranco; Red Norvo; Arnett Cobb; Cal Tjader; Dave Brubeck; Monty Alexander, 1947-72; Billie Holiday, US and European tours, 1954; Duo, Money Tree, 1975-86; Bandleader, Eugene J Wright Ensemble, 1986-; Private music teacher, 1969-; Performed with B.B. King Blues Band, Linda Hopkins International Jazz Festival, Switzerland, 1988; Performed with Dave Brubeck Quartet, US State Dinner (for Presidents Reagan & Gorbachev), Moscow, 1988.

Publications: Bass Solos; Modern Music For Bass; Jazz Giants. Honours: Playboy Jazz Poll Award, 1964-66; Outstanding Voluntary Service Award, Los Angeles Human Relations Commission, 1988. Memberships: NARAS; AFofM. Hobbies: Gardening; Bowling; Cycling. Address: c/o Dukes of Swing Record Company, Hollywood, California, USA.

WRIGHT Finbar, b. 26 Sept 1959, Kinsale, Co Cork, Eire. Tenor singer. m. Angela, 22 Nov 1990, 1 son, 1 daughter. Education: BD; HDE. Musical Education: Studied with Ileana Cotrubas and Veronica Dunne. Career: Australian Tour, performed with Melbourne Symphony Orchestra, Spring 1994; Performed with Montserrat Caballe, Dublin, 1993; USA tour, Spring 1995. Recordings: Albums: Because; Whatever You Believe; Live Tribute To John McCormack. Honours: IRMA Best MOR Artist, 1992; IRMA Best Male Artist, 1993. Membership: PRS. Current Management: Maurice Cassidy/Elizabeth Reeves, 57th Street Ltd, 70 Lower Baggot Street, Dublin 2, Eire.

WRIGHT Michelle, b. Chatham, Ontario, Canada. Singer; Songwriter; Musician (Guitar). Musical Education: Selftaught guitar. Career: Radio: Grand Ole Opry Debut, 1992; TV: Tonight Show with Jay Leno, 1992; The Women of Country; Prime the CBC Specials, Michelle, 1991; Songs and Secrets, 1996; Co-Host, TNN Music City News Awards, 1994; Host, 1995; CCMA Awards Show; ACM and CMA Awards Shows, 1992-96. Recordings: Do Right By Me, 1988; Michelle Wright, 1990; Now and Then, 1992; The Reasons Why, 1994; The Power of Peace, 1996; Star of Wonder, 1996; For Me It's You, 1996. Honours include: Top Female Vocalist, 1989; Top Female Vocalist, 1991; Artist of the Year, 1991; Top Country Single, Take It Like a Man, 1992; Top Female Vocalist, 1993; Artist of the Year, 1993; Top Country Album, Now and Then, 1993; Top Country Single, He Would Be Sixteen, 1993; Top Female Vocalist, 1994; Top Female Vocalist, 1995; Honorary Spokesperson for Special Olympics, 1996. Memberships: National Academy of Recording Arts and Sciences, Academy of Country Music; Country Music Association; Canadian Country Music Association; Canadian Academy of Recording Arts and Sciences. Current Management: Savannah Music, 209 10th Avenue South, Suite 528, Nashville, TN 37203, USA.

WRIGHT Nod (Alexander James), b. 14 June 1966, Hertfordshire, England. Musician (drums, percussion, guitar, keyboards). Education: North Herts College. Career: Member, Fields Of The Nephilim, now known as Rubicon; Numerous European tours; 2 American tours; Reading Festival, 1987, 1988; Loralei Festival (Germany); Chart show videos; Top Of The Pops; BBC Radio Live; Drums and Percussion. Recordings: Fields Of The Nephilim Discography, 1984-91; Rubicon, 1992-95; Co-wrote, produced, albums: Dawnrazor; The Nephilim; Elizium; Revelations; What Starts Ends; Room 101. Honours: Best Album and Band, Melody Maker Readers Poll. Memberships: PRS; Musicians' Union; BPI. Hobby: Writing other material. Address: 57 Regent Street, Stotfold, Herts SG5 4EA, England.

WRIGHT Rick, b. 28 July 1943, London, England. Musician (keyboards). Career: Member, Pink Floyd, 1965-80; 1986-; Performances include: Rome International Pop Festival, 1968; Hyde Park, London, 1968; Bath Festival, 1970; Montreux Festival, 1971; Knebworth Festival, 1975; Films: Pink Floyd Live At Pompeii, 1972. Recordings: Albums: Piper at the Gates of Dawn, 1967; A Saucerful Of Secrets, 1968; More (film soundtrack), 1969; Zabriskie Point, (film soundtrack), 1969; Ummagumma, 1969; Atom Heart Mother, 1970; Relics, 1971; Meddle, 1971; Obscured By Clouds, 1972; The Dark Side Of The Moon, 1973; Wish You Were Here (Number 1, UK and US), 1975; Animals, 1976; The Wall (Number 1, US), 1979; A Momentary Lapse of Reason,

1987; The Delicate Sound Of Thunder, 1988; Shine On, 1992; The Division Bell, 1994; Pulse, 1995; Solo: Wet Dream, 1977; As Zee (with Dee Harris): Identity, 1984; Solo: Broken CHina, 1996; Singles include: See Emily Play, 1967; Another Brick In The Wall, 1979; Run Like Hell, 1980; When The Tigers Break Free, 1982; Learning To Fly, 1987; On The Turning Away, 1987; 1 Slip, 1988. Honours: Best Group Video, MTV Music Awards, 1988; Ivor Novello Award, Outstanding Contribution To British Music, 1992; Rock and Roll Hall of Fame, 1995. Current Management: Steve O'Rourke, EMKA Productions Ltd, 43 Portland Road, Holland Park, London W11 4LJ, England.

WRIGHT Steve (Simon Neale Railton), b. 6 Feb 1962, Newcastle-Upon-Tyne, England. Musician (guitar); Music Teacher; Composer; Sound Recording Engineer; Singer. Musical Education: BA Honours Music, Anglia Polytechnic University; BA Music, Open University. Career: Guitarist, songwriter with heavy metal bands Atomkraft and Blitzkrieg, 1986-88; Guitarist with Anglia Jazz Orchestra, 1990-93; Appearances: Claremont Jazz Festival; Los Angeles, 1991; Umbria Jazz Festival, with students from Berklee College of Music, 1992. Membership: Musicians' Union. Hobbies: Saturday League amateur football; Cinema; Fitness; Travel.

WRIGHT Tony, b. Bradford, Yorkshire, England. Singer. Career: Singer, UK rock group Terrovision (formerly the Spoilt Bratz), 1986-; Support tours with The Ramones; Motörhead; Television apperances include: Top Of The Pops. Recordings: Albums: Formaldehyde, 1993; How To Make Friends & Influence People, 1994; Regular Urban Survivors, 1996; Singles: Oblivion, 1994; Middleman, 1994; Pretend Best Friend, 1994; Alice What's The Matter, 1994; Some People Say, 1995; Perseverance, 1996. Current Management: JPR Management, The Power House, 70 Chiswick High Road, London W4 1SY, England.

WÜRGLER Arne Niels, b. 30 Oct 1943, Copenhagen, Denmark. Singer; Songwriter. m. Asa Didriksen, 27 May 1989, 1 daughter. Career: Singer and songwriter; President, The Danish Society for Jazz, Rock and Folk Composers. Address: Danish Society for Jazz, Rock and Folk Composers, Gråbrodretorv 16, DK-1154 Copenhagen K, Denmark.

WURSTER Bernd, b. 15 June 1960, Reutlingen, Germany. Promoter. Career: Started as promoter, 1976-; Promoting acts in many German towns, 1976; Programme for a club, Culturefactory Fäberei 4, 1993; 2 day open air in Reutlingen market place, 1994; Full-time promoter and agent, 1995. Hobbies: Music; Concerts. Address: Bernd Wurster, Konzertbüro, Gmindstr 6/1, D-72762 Reutlingen, Germany.

WYATT Robert, b. 28 Jan 1945, Bristol, England. Composer; Singer. m. Alfreda Benge, 26 July 1974, 1 son. Career: Featured in full-length profile, Catalan Television, mid-1980s; Various radio programmes, Europe, USA; Several recordings own pieces. Compositions: Heaps of Sheeps, with Alfreda Benge, 1997; September 9th; Alien; Out of Season; A Sunday in Madrid. Recordings: Matching Male/Little Red Record; Rock Bottom; Ruth Is Stranger Than Richard; Dondestan (with poems by Alfreda Benge), compilation, mid-80s; Shleep, CD, 1997; Hapless Child, with Mike Mantler and Carla Bley, 1976. Publications: MW, with J M Marchetti. Honours: Grand Prix Du Disque, Academie Charles Cros. Memberships: PRS; MCPS; Musicians' Union; PAMRA. Hobby: Sitting around in cafes. Address: Hannibal/Ryko. Address: 78 Stanley Gardens, London W3 7SN, England.

WYKES Debsey, b. 21 Dec 1960, London, England. Singer; Songwriter; Musician (bass). Career: Six years with all girl band Dolly Mixture;

Support tours with The Undertones, Bad Manners, The Jam, Dexy's Midnight Runners; Films: Dolly Mixture documentary, director Simon West, 1983; Backing vocals, St Etienne, 2 years; British tours, European tour, US tour; Television includes: Top Of The Pops; Something Else; The Word; Later With Jools Holland; The Beat; Glastonbury; Radio sessions: Dolly Mixture, John Peel session, Radio 1, 1979; Kid Jensen sessions, 1981, 1982. Recordings: 4 singles, 1980-83; Double album: Demonstration Tapes, 1983, re-released 1995; with Captain Sensible: 6 singles include: Happy Talk (Number 1, UK charts), 1982; with Coming Up Roses: I Said Ballroom (Mini-album); Various backing vocals: St Etienne; Duetted on: Who Do You Think You Are?.

WYMAN Bill (William George Perks), b. 24 Oct 1936, Lewisham, London, England. Musician (bass). m. (1) Diane Cory, 1959, divorced, 1 son, (2) Mandy Smith, 1989, divorced 1991, m. (3) Suzanne Accosta, 1993, 1 son, 1 daughter. Career: Member, The Rolling Stones, 1962-93; Owner, Ripple Records; Ripple Music; Ripple Publications; Ripple Productions; Sticky Fingers Restaurants; Numerous tours, concerts include: Rolling Stones '66 tour, 1966; Sunday Night At The London Palladium, 1967; Free concert, Altamont Speedway, 1969; Knebworth Festival, 1976; Prince's Trust charity concert, 1986; Steel Wheels North American Tour, 1989. Recordings: Albums include: The Rolling Stones, 1964; The Rolling Stones, No 2, 1965; Out Of Our Heads, 1965; Aftermath, 1966; Between The Buttons, 1967; Their Satanic Majesties Request, 1967; Beggar's Banquet, 1968; Let It Bleed, 1969; Get Yer Ya-Ya's Out, 1969; Sticky Fingers, 1971; Exile On Main Street, 1972; Goat's Head Group, 1973; It's Only Rock and Roll, 1974; Black And Blue, 1976; Some Girls, 1978; Emotional Rescue, 1980; Still Life, 1982; Primitive Cool, 1987; Steel Wheels, 1989; Flashpoint, 1991; Solo: Stone Alone; Monkey Grip; Bill Wyman; Singles include: Come On; I Wanna Be Your Man; Get Off Of My Cloud; 19th Nervous Breakdown; Let's Spend The Night Together; It's All Over Now; Little Red Rooster; (I Can't Get No) Satisfaction; Jumping Jack Flash; Honky Tonk Women; Brown Sugar; Miss You; Ruby Tuesday; Paint It Black; Going To A Go-Go; Emotional Rescue; It's Only Rock'n'Roll; Harlem Shuffle; Start Me Up; Angie; Undercover Of The Night. Publications: The Story Of A Rock And Roll Band (with Ray Coleman), 1990; Stone Alone. Honours include: Silver Clef Award, Nordoff-Robbins Music Therapy, 1982; Grammy Lifetime Achievement Award, 1986; Inducted into Rock And Roll Hall of Fame, 1989; Q Award, Best Live Act, 1990; Ivor Novello Awards, Outstanding Contribution To British Music, 1991. Address: c/o Ripple Productions, 344 Kings Road, London SW3 5UR, England.

WYNENS Davy, b. 29 March 1975, Herentals, Belgium. Musician (Drums); Film and Television Figuration. Education: Self-taught. Career: Movies: Elixir d'Anvers TV Commercial for film magazine, Teek. Address: Schittersstraat 30, 2200 Herentals, Belgium.

WYNENS Rene, b. 21 August 1954, Bouwel, Belgium. Musician (drums); Television and Film Figuration. m. Helsen Anita, 6 September 1974, 1 son. Education: Private lessons, by drummer Jan Cuyers and Academie of Music Herentals. Career: Figuration in Different Professional Movies: Brylcream Boulevard; Karakter; Elixir d'Anvers; Gastons War; Left Luggage; Different television productions for several TV stations and production houses; Drummer and Contact Person of beatgroup, Big Problem. Recordings: Album CD, Big Problem 1; Album CD, Big Problem Rockers Look Out. Memberships: Belgian Drumclub; Dutch Slagwerkkrant. Current Management: Big Problem, PO Box 27, 2200 Herentals, Belgium.

WYNNE John Peter, b. 11 Oct 1957, Germany. Composer. Education: BA (Hons, 1st).

Musical Education: Canadian Conservatory of Music. Career: C90.RT55 L1-37, Riverside Studios; Panic and Depression, Conway Hall; Radio KPFA-FM, KALX-FM, San Francisco; CKLN-FM, Toronto; CFRA-FM, Kingston, Ontario; Offnerkanal Saarland Saärbrucken, Germany; Films: Tears Before Bedtime (London Film Festival); Headgear (London Film Festival, Whitechapel Open, European Media Art Festival). Compositions: C90.RT55 L1-37 for clarinet and Quad tape; Panic and Depression, for violin, tape and live electronics; O for ondes Martenot, oboe, computer and DAT tape, James Kamotho Kimani (tape piece); The Sound of Sirens. Honours: International Jury of ISCM (International Society for Contemporary Music); ACGB Electro-acoustic Bursary. Memberships: Musicians' Union; PRS; London Musicians' Collective. Current Managment: Self-managed. Address: 108 Crampton Street, London SE17 3AE, England.

WYNNE Michael Alexander, b. West Kirby, Merseyside, England. Composer; Songwriter; Record Producer; Arranger; Musician (electric, acoustic guitars, mandolin, banjo). Education: BA, Newcastle University. Musical Education: Self-taught. Career: Part-time recording, live work, with Irish group Flynn and Wynne; Tours include Holland, Germany, Singapore; Worked in Karachi, 1989; Producer, live all-star show, and pop album, singer Mohammed Ali Shiakhi; Also film score composition; Producer, dance album, New York, 1993; Television apperance with band Posh Monkeys, UK. Compositions: Composed musical Baby and 3 Devils. Recordings: Shiakhi Speaks (Karachi); The Wise Guys (Abbey Road). Membership: Musicians' Union; PRS; BASCA. Hobbies: Active pursuits; Philosophy. Address: c/o Wilson Barca, 13-14 Dean Steet, London W1V 5AH, England.

WYNONNA (Wynonna Judd), b. 1966. Country Singer; Musician. Career: Member, Country duo, The Judds, with mother Naomi, 1984-90; Solo artiste, billed as Wynnona, 1991-; Most successful country duo, as the Judds, with 15 million album sales; Undefeated, all 3 major US Country Awards, 8 consecutive years; Co-founder, booking agency Pro-Tours, 1988. Recordings include: Singles: Had A Dream For The Heart, 1983; Mama He's Crazy, 1984; Why Not Me, 1984; Girls Night Out, 1985; Rockin' With The Rhythm Of The Rain, 1986; Let Me Tell You About Love, 1989; Love Can Build A Bridge, 1990; Albums include: with The Judds: The Judds, 1984; Why Not Me?, 1985; Rockin' With The Rhythm Of The Rain, 1986; Heartland, 1987; Greatest Hits, 1988; River Of Time, 1989; Love Can Build A Bridge, 1990; The Judds Collection, 1991; The Essential, 1996; Solo albums: Wynnona, 1992; Revelations, 1996. Honours: 7 Grammy Awards; 4 ACM Awards, Best Duet, 1984-89; 3 CMA Awards, Best Vocal Duo, 1988-91. Current Management: William Morris. Address: c/o The Judd House, 325 Bridge Street, Franklin, TN 37064, USA.

X

X (CROSS) Alan, b. 8 Mar 1958, London, England. Producer; Writer; Musician (keyboards). Education: BA; Diploma Architecture Pt III Professional. Musical Education: Grade 5 Theory; Self-taught. Career: Founder member, band Chalk; Signed to MCA Records/Publishing, 1985; Signed solo publishing deal with Warner Chappell; Now writing and producing. Recordings: Set Me Free, Clubland; So In Love/Real Deal, Judy Cheeks. Hobbies: Swimming; Photography. Current Management: XTRAX. Address: PO Box 966, London SE11 5SA, England.

XIMENES Charlson Pedro Vasconcelos, b. 8 May 1965, Sao Caitano, Pernambuco, Brazil. Performer; Songwriter; Musician (guitar, bass, drums, saxophone); Vocalist. Musical Education: Songwriting, Music in the Making, Music History, Morley College, London. Career: Radio broadcasts include: Radio Bitury; Belo Jardim; Garanhuns Difusora; 97.7 Sao Paulo, Brazil; WMRZ Radio Miami, USA; Television appearances: Belezinha The Clown TV Show; Brazil tour with Universitaria TV crew. Recordings: with Flying Squad (Esquadrilha Da Fumaça): Tora Tora Tora, 1984; with Deja Vu: Black Angel, 1987; Love Me Tonite, 1988; Collision Course, 1998. Honours: Amateur Theatre Background Music Award, Brazil, 1980; 2nd Prize, Northeastern Popular Music Festival, Belo Jardim pe, Brazil. Membership: Musicians' Union. Hobbies: Reading; Night-clubbing. Current Management: Jackie Rice. Address: 435 Devon Mansions, Tooley Street, London SE1 2XJ, England.

Y

YA Kid K (Manuela Kamosi), b. Zaire. Rapper. Career: Moved to Belgium, aged 11; Member, Antwerp-based rap group Fresh Beat; Member, Technotronik; Rapping partnership with MC Eric. Recordings: Albums: with Technotronik: Pump Up The Jam, 1990; Trip On This - Remixes, 1990; Body To Body, 1991; Singles: Pump Up The Jam (Number 2, UK); Get Up (Before The Night Is Over); This Beat Is Technotronik; Rockin' Over The Beat; with Hi Tek: Spin That Wheel, 1990. Current Management: ARS Productions. Address: Singel 5, B-2550 Kontich, Belgium.

YAMAKOSHI Brian Seiji, b. 29 Dec 1957, Chicago, Illinois, USA. Musician (koto - Japanese harp); Composer. Education: Middlesex Polytechnic, Semester At Sea, Arizona State University. Musical Education: Music theory, guitar, piano, and koto training. Career: Television appearances: Numerous in Japan; Concon C'est Nous (France); NHK Television and radio, Japan; BBC Radio. Recordings: Snowflake, Peter Gabriel; Akiko Yano, Akira Inoue; World Diary, with Tony Levin, Manu Katché, Shanker. Memberships: ASCAP; JASRAC; SACEM. Hobbies: Skiing; Swimming; Windsurfing; Reading. Current Management: Ms Naoto Tsunoi.

YANKOVIC Weird Al (Alfred), b. 23 10 1959, Lynwood, California, USA. Musician (accordion); Songwriter; Performer; Actor. Education: BA, Architecture, California Polytechnic San Luiz Obispo, California. Musical Education: Accordion lessons. Career: As Weird Al, 15 years of successful parodies of pop classics; Concert appearances; Television and radio appearances: including own Showtime and MTV specials; 3 best-selling home videos; Film: UHF, 1989. Recordings include: Ricky, 1983; Weird Al Yankovic In 3-D, 1984; Dare To Be Stupid, 1985; Polka Party, 1986; Fat (parody of Michael Jackson: Bad), 1988; Greatest Hits, 1988; Peter And The Wolf, 1988; UHF- Soundtrack, 1989; Off The Deep End, featuring the hit Smells Like Nirvana, 1992; The Food Album, 1993; Apalooza, 1993. Publications: The Authorized Al, autobiography by Al Yankovic and Tino Insana, 1985. Honours: Grammy Awards: Best Comedy Recording: Eat It, 1984; Best Video: Fat, 1988. Membership: NARAS; BMI; AFofM. Hobbies: Eating; Sleeeping; Watching television; Films; Concerts. Current Management: Jan Levey, Imaginary Entertainment. Address: 923 Westmount Drive, Los Angeles, CA 90069, USA.

YANNI (Yanni Chryssomalis), b. 1955, Kalamata, Greece. Composer; Musician (keyboards). Education: Psychology degree, Minnesota. Career: Keyboard player with US progressive rock group Chameleon; Composer, leader, own orchestra; Recent concerts include: The Acropolis, Athens, 1993; Royal Albert Hall, London, 1995. Recordings: Albums include: Keys To Imagination, 1986; Out Of Silence, 1987; Chameleon Days, 1988; Niki Nana, 1989; Reflections Of Passion, 1990; In Celebration Of Life, 1991; Dare To Dream, 1992; Yanni - Live At The Acropolis, 1993. Honours: 2 Grammy Awards. Current Management: Yanni Management, 7805 Telegraph Road, Suite, 300, Bloomington, MN 55438, USA.

YARROW Peter, b. 31 May 1938, New York, USA. Singer; Songwriter; Film and Television Producer. Career: Member, Peter Paul & Mary, 1960-; Television specials: 25th Anniversary Special, PBS, 1985; A Holiday Celebration, PBS, 1988; Peter Paul and Mommy Too, PBS, 1993; Co-founder, Kerrville Folk Festival, Texas; Founding member, board of directors, Newport Folk Festival; Television Specials, Lifelines, PBS, 1995. Compositions: Author/co-author songs include: Puff The Magic Dragon; Light One

Candle; Day Is Done; The Great Mandala; Torn Between Two Lovers. Recordings: 16 albums with Peter, Paul & Mary; 4 solo albums. Honours: Allard K Lowenstein Award (for Human Rights, Peace and Freedom); Vista Citizen Action Leadership Award; Kate Wolf Memorial Award, The World Folk Music Association; Grammy Awards, 1962, 1963, 1969; Emmy Nominations, 1979, 1993, 1996. Memberships: Board of Directors: Center for Global Education, North American Congress on Latin America, Friends of Vista. Current Management: Walk Street Management. Address: 1639 B Electric Avenue, Venice, CA 90291, USA.

YASINITSKY Gregory Walter, b. 3 Oct 1953, San Francisco,California, USA. Composer; Musician (saxophone); Educator. m. Ann Marie Kelley, 15 Jan 1977, 1 daughter. Musical Education: AA Music, College San Mateo, 1973; San Francisco State University, BM, Composition, 1976, MA, 1978; DMA, Composition, Eastman School Of Music, Rochester, New York, 1995; Composition studies: Joseph Schwantner; Wayne Peterson; Lou Harrison; Samuel Adler; Robert Morris; Saxophone studies with Ramon Ricker, Joe Henderson, Donald Carroll, James Mathieson, Jerry Vejmola. Career: Professor of Music, Co-ordinator, Jazz Studies, Washington State Univesity, 1982-; Lecturer in Music, San Jose State University, 1978-82; San Francisco State University, 1977-81; Lecturer, Jazz Studies, 1977-80; Principal saxophonist, Spokane Symphony, 1991-; Orchestral saxophonist with: San Francisco Symphony; Oakland Symphony; Cabrillo Festival Orchestra; Performances as jazz saxophonist with: Sarah Vaughan; Lionel Hampton; Stan Getz; Clark Terry; Louis Bellson; Randy Brecker; Tom Harrell; Gary Burton; Mark Isham; Art Lande; Performances, clinics, workshops throughout USA, Canada, Japan, Europe. Compositions: Over 75 works published. Publications: Articles for: Jazz Educators Journal; Band World; New Ways; Aftertouch; Saxophone Symposium. Honours: Mullen Award Excellence in Teaching, Washington State University, 1989; Jazz Fellowship, US National Endowment for the Arts, 1986; ASCAP Special Awards for Composition, 1986-. Memberships: ASCAP; IAJE; NASA; MENC. Hobby: Cooking. Address: NW 485 Robert Street, Pullman, WA 99163, USA.

YEARWOOD Trisha, b. Georgia, USA. Country Singer. Career: Sessionsinger, Nashville, 1985-; Discovered by support tours with Garth Brooks, 1991. Recordings: Singles: She's In Love With The Boy (Number 1, US Country charts), 1991; The Woman Before Me; Wrong Side Of Memphis; XXX's And OOO's (An American Girl) (Number 1, US), 1995; Albums: Trisha Yearwood, 1991; Hearts In Armor, 1992; Thinking About You, 1995; Songbook (A Collection Of Hits); Other recordings: Backing vocals, No Fences, Garth Brooks; Tower Of Strength (Leonard Cohen tribute album), 1995. Honours: First female to top US Country Charts with debut single, 1991; Platinum discs; Grammy awards. Current Management: Kragen And Co. Address: 1112 N Sherbourne Drive, Los Angeles, CA 90069, USA.

YEO Oscar (aka Port), b. 28 June 1929, London, England. Musician (drums); Vocalist; Graphic designer. m. Gay Clarke, 16 Sept 1964, 2 sons. Musical Education: Private violin tuition as child; Self-taught since. Career: Known as Port, pre-1960; Founder member, Eric Silk's Southern Jazz Band; Broadcasts include: Albert Hall, Festival Hall concerts, include Festival Of Britain, 1950-54; Freelanced music; Graphic design to 1959; Professional musician until 1963; Semi-professional, 1963-. Membership: Musicians' Union (Gold card holder). Hobbies: Walking; Dogs; Classic cars; Jazz cocnerts. Address: Bray, Berkshire, England.

YEOH Nicola Beng Ean, b. 24 May 1973, London, England. Musician (Piano); Composer;

Arranger; Band Leader. Musical Education: A Level Music, Centre Young Musicians Weekend Arts College. Career: Courtney Pine Band, 1991-94; Neneh Cherry, 1993; The Roots, 1994; Eddie Harris, 1996; Jools Holland, TV Show, Later, 1993; Arsenio Hall, show, USA, 1993; Infinitum, own band, featuring Keith Le Blanc and Michael Mondesir, Radio 3 Broadcast, 1993. Compositions: Commissioned: Six as 1, 1996; Speechmix X-ploration, 1997; Be-Bop, 1997; Entwined, for pianist Joanna MacGregor, 1997; Infinitum, Big Band, 12 piece, 1997; Common Denominator, commissioned by LAB, 1998; Two Rainbows, 1998. Recording: Red, Hot and Cool, with The Roots and Roy Ayers. Memberships: PRS; PAMRA; MU. Hobbies: Swimming; Cycling; Learning languages. Current Management: Erika Palmer, Catalyst Management. Address: 67 Dyne Road, London, NW6 7DR, England.

YETNIKOFF Walter R, b. 11 Aug 1933, Brooklyn, New York, USA. Record Company Executive. m. June Yetnikoff, 24 Nov 1957, 2 sons. Education: BA, Brooklyn College, New York Bar, 1953; LLB, Columbia University, 1956. Career: Lawyer, New York, 1958-61; Attorney, CBS Records, 1961-65; General attorney, CBS Group, 1965-69; Vice President, International Division, CBS, 1969-71; President, CBS International, 1971-75; President, CBS Group, 1975-. Membership: International Federation of Producers of Phonographs and Videograms.

YOAKAM Dwight, b. 23 Oct 1956, Pikeville, Kentucky, USA. Country Singer; Musician (guitar); Songwriter. Education: History and Philosophy, Ohio University. Career: Country singer, 1978-; Also played with Los Lobos; Concerts include: UK and US tours; Tours with Buck Owens; Farm Aid VI, Indiana, 1993. Recordings: Albums: Guitars, Cadillacs, 1986; Hillbilly Deluxe, 1987; Buenas Noches From A Lonely Room, 1988; Just Looking For A Hit, 1989; If There Was A Way, 1990; La Croix D'Amour, 1992; This Time, 1993; Gone, 1996; Under the Covers, 1997; Come on Christmas, 1997; Singles: Honky Tonk Man, 1986; Guitars, Cadillacs, 1986; Little Sister, 1987; Streets Of Bakersfield, duet with Buck Owens, (Number 1, US Country charts), 1988; Always Late (With Your Kisses), 1988; I Sang Dixie (Number 1, US Country charts), 1989; Suspicious Minds, from film soundtrack, Honeymoon In Vegas, 1992; Fast As You Can, 1993; Dwight Live, 1995. Honours: 5 Platinum discs; 1 Multi Platinum disc; 1 Gold discs; Academy Of Country Music, Best New Male Artist, 1986; Music City News Country Award, Best Vocal Collaboration, with Buck Owens, 1988. Current Management: Borman Entertainment, 1250 6th Street, Suite 401, Santa Monica, CA 90401, USA.

YOGESWARAN Manickam, b. 3 Mar 1959, Sri Lanka. Vocalist; Musician (South Indian flute, drums). Education; Accountancy (CIMA). Musical Education: Learnt by Guru-Sisya method. Career: Concert vocalist, musician, Indo-pop Music; Lead singer, Dissidenten, European tours, 1993-; Concerts include Commonwealth Institute, 1992; Paris Music Festival, 1993; Music Guimet, Paris, 1994; Music Festival, Madras, India, 1995; Visiting Lecturer for Music Workshop Skills, Goldsmith College, University of London, England. Recordings: Background score, documentary Serendipity; 7 albums, 1990-94; Singer, Duets With Automobiles (Shobana Jeyasing Dance Company); Romance With Footnotes; tamil Classics, CD. Publications: Currently compiling video: South Indian Drumming. Honours: Kalai Mamani, London Sri Murugan Temple; Suranaya Devan, Oslo Music Association; Regular Appearances in the December Music Festical, Madras, 1994-. Membership: Musicians' Union. Hobbies: Nature; Yoga; Exercise; Teaching. Address: 29 Firdene, Tolworth, Surrey KT5 9QQ, England.

YORKE Thom. Vocalist. Career: Singer, Radiohead; Also designer of record sleeves; Support to REM, US tour, 1995; Milton Keynes Bowl, 1995. Recordings: Albums: Pablo Honey, 1993; The Bends, 1995; Singles: Creep, 1993; My Iron Lung, 1994; High And Dry, 1995; Fake Plastic Trees, 1995; Just, 1995; Street Spirit (Fade Out), 1996; Contributor, Help (Bosnia Relief Album), 1995. Honours: BRIT Nomination, Best British Group, 1996. Current Management: Courtyard Management, 21 The Nursery, Sutton Courtenay, Abingdon, Oxon OX14 4UA, England.

YOUDALE Roy, b. 17 Jun 1951, London, England. Musician (Spanish guitar, panpipes, charango); College Lecturer; Basketmaker. Education: BSc in Philosophy and Sociology; MA in Applied Social Studies; Final Diploma in Spanish, Institute of Linguistics. Career: Member, Bristol based South American folk groups, Llaima and Ritmo Latino, 1984-89; Member, South American folk duo, Duende, with John Whipps, 1990-; Television and radio apperances: BBC Radio Bristol; Local cable television. Recordings: South American Explorations, Duende, 1994 (containing 9 original co-compositions with John Whipps). Publications: 2 Research papers written on Bolivian Music for the Bolivian National Museum of Ethnography and Folklore in La Paz, 1991. Memberships: Musicians' Union; MCPS. Hobby: Ki Aikido. Address: 6 Highbury Road, Horfield, Bristol BS7 0BZ, England.

YOUNG Angus, b. 31 Mar 1959, Glasgow, Scotland. Rock Musician (guitar). Career: Guitarist, heavy rock group AC/DC, 1973-; Numerous tours worldwide; Major concerts include: Reading Rock Festival, 1978; Monsters of Rock Festival, Castle Donington, 1981, 1984; European rock festivals, Hungary, Switzerland, Belgium, Germany, 1991; Concert, Moscow, 1991; Over 80 million albums sales to date. Recordings: Singles include: Rock'n'Roll Damnation, 1978; Highway To Hell, 1979; Touch Too Much, 1980; Rock'n'Roll Ain't Noise Pollution, 1980; You Shook Me All Night Long, 1980; Back In Black, 1981; Let's Get It Up, 1982; For Those About To Rock (We Salute You), 1982; Guns For Hire, 1983; Nervous Shakedown, 1984; Shake Your Foundations, 1986; Who Made Who, 1986; Heatseeker, 1988; Thunderstruck, 1990; Moneytalks, 1990; Are You Ready, 1991; That's The Way I Wanna Rock'n'Roll, 1993; Big Gun (used in film The Last Action Hero), 1993; Hard As A Rock, 1995; Albums: High Voltage, 1975; TNT, 1975; High Voltage, 1975; Dirty Deeds Done Cheap, 1976; Let There Be Rock, 1977; Powerage, 1978; If You Want Blood You've Got It, 1978; Highway To Hell, 1979; Back In Black, 1980; For Those About To Rock (We Salute You), 1981; Flick Of The Switch, 1983; Fly On The Wall, 1985; Who Made Who, 1986; Blow Up Your Video, 1988; The Razor's Edge, 1990; Live, 1992; Ballbreaker, 1995. Current Management: Hard To Handle Management, 640 Lee Road, Suite 106, Wayne, PA 19087, USA.

YOUNG David Howard, b. 27 Sep 1965, Münster, Germany. Contemporary Composer; Musician (synthesizer); Multimedia Engineer. m. Lynn Young, 16 Aug 1985, 1 son, 2 daughters. Education: Technical College. Musical Education: Self-taught over 10 years. Career: British Telecom Engineer, 1982-88; IT Music Teacher, comprehensive school; Keyboard player, VXS, 1989-91; Solo artist as Mabyus, concept artist Teknovx, 1989-. Recordings: with VXS: Intensity, 1992; with Maybus: Teknification, 1993; Miracle Of Life, 1993; with Teknovx: Feel So Right, 1994. Membership: Musicians' Union. Hobbies: Family; Virtual reality; Graphic Design; Radio-controlled aircraft; Video games. Current Management: TEK 11 Records. Address: 18 Woodside Terrace, Chopwell, Newcastle-Upon-Tyne NE17 7EQ, England.

YOUNG Jesse Colin (Perry Miller), b. 11 Nov 1944, New York City, New York, USA. Singer; Musician (guitar, bass). Career: Began as folk singer, New York; Founder member The Youngbloods, 1965-72; Appearances include: Sky River Rock Festival; Lighter Than Air Fair, 1968; Solo career, 1973-; Appeared, No Nukes, Madison Square Garden, New York, with Bruce Springsteen, Doobie Brothers, Jackson Browne, 1979. Compositions include: Get Together, recorded by Dave Clark Five, 1970. Recordings: Albums with The Youngbloods: The Youngbloods, 1967; Earth Music, 1967; Elephant Mountain, 1969; Best Of The Youngbloods, 1970; Rock Festival, 1970; Ride The Wind, 1971; Good'n'Dusty, 1971; Sunlight, 1971; High On A Ridgetop, 1972; Get Together, 1972; Solo albums: The Soul Of A City Boy, 1964; Youngblood, 1964; Song For Juli, 1973; Light Shine, 1974; Songbirds, 1974; On The Road, 1974; Love On The Wing, 1974; American Dreams, 1978. Current Management: Skyline Music, PO Box 31, Lancaster, NH 03584, USA.

YOUNG John, b. 31 May 1956, Romford, Essex, England. Musician (keyboards); Songwriter. Musical Education: Head Chorister, Liverpool Metropolitan Cathedral; Grade VIII Piano; A Level Music. Career: Tours: Uli Jon Roth - Electric Sun world tour, 1985; Robin George, UK, 1986; Roy Wood, UK, Asia, Europe, 1987-90; Paul Rodgers and Kenny Jones (billed as The Law), UK, 1991; Bonnie Tyler world tour, 1994-; Also member, MTV band, 1988. Recordings: Albums by Batisti; Steeleye Span; Various unsigned artists including own Project Cathedral, 1986-89; Crime Of Passion, John Wetton, 1994; Live album, 1995; Current projects: Brand X album and solo album. Publication: Currently making tuition video with Robin Lumley. Membership: PRS. Current Management: The Control Group. Address: Chapel Mews, 68 Crewe Road, Alsager, Cheshire ST7 2HA, England.

YOUNG Neil, b. 12 Nov 1945, Toronto, Ontario, Canada. Singer; Songwriter; Musician (guitar). m. Pegi Young, 1 son, 1 daughter. Career: Lead singer, The Squires; Co-founder, Buffalo Springfield (with Stephen Stills), 1966-69; Support to Rolling Stones, Hollywood Bowl, 1966; CAFF Charity concert, 1967; Support tours to Steve Miller Band, 1967; Iron Butterfly, 1968; Solo artiste, with own backing group, Crazy Horse, 1969-; Joined Crosby Stills and Nash, to become Crosby Stills Nash And Young, 1969-74; Tours include: US tour, 1969; Support to Rolling Stones, 1969; European tour, 1970; European tour with Booker T and the MGs, 1993; US tour with Pearl Jam, 1995; Major concerts include: Royal Festival Hall, 1973; The Last Waltz (the Band's Farewell Concert), 1976; Miami Music Festival, 1977; Live Aid, Philadelphia, 1985; Farm Aid II, 1987; Nelson Mandela - An International Tribute, Wembley, 1990; Farm Aid V, 1992; Bob Dylan's 30th Anniversary concert, Madison Square Garden, 1992; Reading Festival, 1995; Writer, director, films: Rust Never Sleeps (also recorded soundtrack), 1979; Human Highway, 1982; Subject of documentary film, Journey Through The Past, 1973. Recordings: include: 3 albums with Buffalo Springfield; with Crosby Stills Nash And Young: Deja Vu, 1970; Four Way Street, 1971; So Far, 1974 (all US Number 1's); with Stills/Young Band: Long May You Run, 1970; Solo/with Crazy Horse: Neil Young, 1969; Everybody Knows This Is Nowhere, 1969; After The Goldrush, 1970; Crazy Horse, 1971; Loose 1972; Harvest, 1972; Journey Through The Past, 1972; Time Fades Away, 1973; On The Beach, 1974; Tonight's The Night, 1975; Zuma, 1975; American Stars And Bars, 1977; Decade, 1978; Crazy Moon, 1978; Comes A Time, 1978; Hawks And Doves, 1979; Live Rust, 1980; Re-ac-tor, 1981; Trans, 1983; Everybody's Rockin', 1983; Old Ways, 1985; Landing On Water, 1986; Life, 1987; This Note's For You, 1988; American Dream, 1988; Eldorado, 1989; Freedom, 1989; Ragged Glory, 1990; Left

For Dead, 1990; Weld, 1991; Harvest Moon, 1992; Lucky Thirteen, 1993; Unplugged, 1993; Sleeps With Angels, 1994; Mirror Ball, 1995; Dead Man - Music From And Inspired By The Motion Picture, 1996. Honours include: Grammy Award, Best New Artists (with Crosby Stills Nash And Young), 1970; Melody Maker Poll Winner, Best International Group, 1971; MTV Video Award, 1989; Rolling Stone Critics Award, Best Album, 1989; Bay Area Music Award, Outstanding Album, 1993; Q Award, Best Live Act, 1993. Current Management: c/o Elliot Roberts, Lookout Management, 2644 30th Street, 1st Floor, Santa Monica, CA 90405, USA.

YOUNG Paul. Vocalist; Musician (percussion). Career: Founder member, Sad Cafe, 1976-85; Member, Mike And The Mechanics, 1986-. Recordings include: Albums: with Sad Cafe: Fanx Ta Ra, 1977; Hungry Eyes, 1977; Misplaced Ideals, 1978; Facades, 1979; Sad Cafe, 1980; Live 1981; Ole, 1981; with Mike And The Mechanics: Mike And The Mechanics, 1986; The Living Years, 1988; Word Of Mouth, 1991; Beggar On A Beach Of Gold, 1995; Hits, 1996; Singles: with Sad Cafe: Run Home Girl; Every Day Hurts; I'm In Love Again; Hungry Eyes; with Mike And The Mechanics: All I Need Is A Miracle; The Living Years; Word Of Mouth; Over My Shoulder. Current Management: Hit And Run Music. Address: 30 Ives Street, London SW3 2ND, England.

YOUNG Paul, b. 17 Jan 1956, Luton, Bedfordshire, England. Singer. m. Stacey Smith, 9 Nov 1987, 1 son, 2 daughters. Career: Formed The Streetband; Founder member, the Q Tips, 1979-82; Solo artiste, 1982-; Tours, concerts include: Live Aid, Wembley, 1985; Prince's Trust Rock Gala, with Paul McCartney, Elton John, Tina Turner, Phil Collins, 1986; Mandela Day Concert, Wembley, 1989; Sang with Queen, Wembley, 1992; World tours, 1986, 1989. Recordings: Albums include: with The Streetband: London, 1979; Dilemma, 1979; with the Q Tips: Q Tips, 1980; Live At Last, 1982; Solo albums: No Parlez, 1983; The Secret Of Association, 1985; Between Two Fires, 1986; Other Voices, 1990; From Time To Time, 1991; The Crossing, 1993; Reflections, 1994; Paul Young, 1997; Singles include: Wherever I Lay My Hat, 1983; Love Of The Common People, 1983; Every Time You Go Away (worldwide Number 1 hit), 1985. Honours: BRIT Awards: Best British Newcomer, 1984; Best British Male Artist, 1985; Best British Music Video, 1986. Hobbies: Family; Classic cars and motorbikes; Guitars. Current Management: Clive Banks. Address: CBL Management, 1 Glenthorne Mews, 115A Glenthorne Road, London W6 0LJ, England.

YURCHENCO Henrietta Weiss, b. 22 March 1916, New Haven, USA. Ethnomusicologist; Writer. m. 1) Basil Yurchenco, June 1936, div 1955, 1 son, 2) Irving Levine, 1965, divorced, 1979. Education: Student, Yale University, 1935-36; Student, piano scholarship, Mannes College Music, 1936-38. Appointments: Radio Producer, WNYC, WBAI, others, 1939-69; Writer, Critic, Teacher, Folk Music Editor, American Record Guide and Musical Am, 1959-70; Professor, Music College, City New York, 1962-86; Brooklyn College, 1966-69; New School for Social Research, 1961-68; Co-Director, Project for Study of Women in Music; Graduate, Center CUNY. Publications: Author: A Fiesta of Folk Songs from Spain and Latin America, 1967; A Mighty Hard Road: A Biography of Woody Guthrie, 1970; !Hablamos! Puerto Ricans Speak, 1971; Contributor, articles to professional journals; 11 field recordings from Mexico PR, John's Island, SC, Guatemala, Ecuador, Morocco, issued by Libr Congress, Folkways, Nonesuch, Folkways/Smithsonian, Global Village Rounder; collections in Libr Congress, Discoteca Hebrew University, Jerusalem, Arais Montana Institute, Madrid, Instituto Nacional Indigenista, Mexico City. Honours: Grants-in-Aid, American Philosophical Society, 1954, 1956, 1957, 1965, 1967, 1989;

Grants-in-Aid, CUNY Faculty Research Fund, 1970, 1983, 1987; NEH Grantee, 1984. Memberships: International Council Traditional Music, Committee on Women's Studies; Society Ethnomusicology; Society Asian Music; Sonneck Society; International Association Study of Popular Music; American Musicologists Society; Research in Folk, Tribal and Popular Music for Library of Congress, Mexico; Guatemala, Puerto Rico, Spain, Morocco, Balearic Islands, John's Island, SC, Ireland, 1941-83. Address: 360 W 22nd St New York, NY 10011-2600, USA.

Z

ZABALA Fernando, b. 19 Apr 1962, Madrid, Spain. Promoter. Education: Lawyer. Musical Education: Saxophone player. Career: Promoter in Spain for: U2; Bruce Springsteen; Whitney Houston; REM; Michael Jackson; Pink Floyd; Tina Turner; Bryan Adams; Bon Jovi; Mike Oldfield; Paul McCartney; Dire Straits; Joe Cocker; Simply Red; Keith Richards; Red Hot Chili Peppers. Publications: Guiá De La Música-El Pais, Año De Rock. Memebrship: APCI (International Concert Promoters Association). Hobbies: Skiing; Squash; Football. Address: Sold Out, Alcalá 114-6B, 28009 Madrid, Spain.

ZAMFIR Gheorghe, b. Romania. Musician (pan-pipes). Career: World's leading pan-pipe player; Recording artist, traditional folk music, 1974; Pan-pipe versions, pop, classical and religious tunes. Recordings: Numerous albums include: L'Alouette, 1978; Impressions, 1978; In Paris, 1981; Zamfir, 1981; Lonely Shepherd, 1982; Music For The Millions, 1983; Romance, 1984; Atlantis, 1985; By Candlelight, 1986; Beautiful Dreams, 1988; Images, 1989; Singles include: Doina De Jale, theme to BBC series, The Light of Experience, 1976; Theme from De Verlaten Mijn, with James Last, 1979.

ZANDER Robin, b. 23 Jan 1953, Rockford, Illinois, USA. Singer; Musician (guitar). Career: Founder member, singer, guitarist, Cheap Trick, 1969-; Concerts include: California Music Festival, 1979; Reading Festival, 1979; Montreux Rock Festival, 1988; US tour with Robert Plant, 1988; US tour with Kiss, 1988; US tour with Heart, 1990. Recordings: albums: Cheap Trick, 1977; In Color, 1977; Heaven Tonight, 1978; Cheap Trick At Budokan, 1979; Dream Police, 1979; Found All The Parts, 1980; All Shook Up, 1980; One On One, 1982; Next Positions Please, 1983; Standing On The Edge, 1985; The Doctor, 1986; Lap Of Luxury, 1988; Busted, 1990; The Greatest Hits, 1991; Solo album: Robin Zander, 1993; Singles include: I Want You To Want Me, 1979; Voices, from film soundtrack Roadie, 1980; Stop This Game, 1980; If You Want My Love, 1982; Mighty Wings, from film soundtrack Top Gun, 1986; Ghost Town, 1988; Never Had A Lot To Lose, 1990; Surrender To Me, duet with Ann Wilson, from film soundtrack Tequila Sunrise, 1990; Can't Stop Falling Into Love, 1990. Current Management: Ken Adamany Associates, 1818 Parmenter Street, Suite 202, Middleton, WI 53562, USA.

ZAPPELLINI Marino, b. 17 May 1955, Bourges, France. Musician (saxophone, flute); Composer; Actor. Education: Master of Music, University of Paris. Musical Education: Jazz Improvisation, Harmony, Berklee School of Music, Boston, USA; Music info and Midi techniques, AFDAS; Electro-acoustic music, GMEN, GRM; Jazz professional, AFDAS; Theatre production, AFDAS. Career: Professional musician, 1978-; Leader, Madzano Quartet; Actor, theatre: Du Vent Dans Les Branches De Sassafras; Actor, film: 10 Seconds; Film director and composer, films: Le Onzième Comandment; 10 Seconds; Saxophone improvisation, orchestra, with MJC Marcel Cachin de Romainville, 1988-; Administrator, Artistic director, L'association loi 1901, Big Band Paris Est; Worked with numerous artistes including: Mama Bea Tiekelski; Toure Kunda; Antoine Tome; Urban Sax; Pierre Henri; Bernard Lubat; Gérard Marais; Mico Nissim; Corazon Rebelde; Pajaro Canzani; Salif Keita; Ousmane Kouyate; Kaba Mane; Manfila Kante; Carlos Nascimiento; Gery Burtin; Organiser, tours for artists from: Africa; UK; Spain; Portugal; Italy; Producer, publisher and promoter, recordings; Agent for shows in France and internationally; Administration for Big Band Paris Est; Tours; Mozambique; Antilles; Algeria; Gabon; UK; Spain; Portugal; Switzerland;

Numerous European festivals. Recordings: Au Printemps de Bourges, Mama Bea; Mandinka Dong, Toure Kunda; L'Amour Titant, Antoine Tome; with Urban Sax: Urban Sax II; Urban Sax III; Les Noces Alchymiques, Pierre Henry; Kunga Kungaké, Kaba Mane; Madzano Live Concert; Corazon Rebelde; Pajaro Canzani; Kabe Mane. Memberships: Admin, Cultural division, SPEDIDAM; Member, Jazz Commission, SNAM. Jazz Players Union (UMJ). Hobbies: Sport; Fishing. Address: 81 Rue Saint Maur, 75011 Paris, France.

ZARBAFIAN Dariush, b. 9 May 1951, Tehran, Iran. Salarvand Fariba, 25 July 1996, 2 sons, 1 daughter. Education: PhD, Economie, University of Teheran; Apprenticeship in Iran with the Masters; Master's Degree, Postgraduate; Doctorate in Musicology. Career: Multiple concerts in France and Europe; Radio Transmission: Radio France; TV Transmission, TF1-FR3; TLT, VPRO, Holland. Recordings: Mille Images; Assemaneh. Memberships: Societe des Auteurs; Compositeurs ete Editeurs de Musique. Hobbies: Reading; Travelling. Current Management: Fariba Salarvand. Address: Zabafian Dariush, 310 Avenue De Muret, 31 300 Toulouse, France.

ZAWINUL Joe (Josef Erich), b. 7 July 1932, Vienna, Austria. Jazz Musician (piano, synthesizer); Songwriter. Musical Education: Vienna Conservatory; Berklee College of Music, Boston, 1959. Career: Local session musician, dance, radio orchestras, 1950s; House pianist for Polydor Records; Played with Hans Koller; Maynard Ferguson; Dinah Washington; Cannonball Adderley; Miles Davis, 1961-71; Formed jazz/rock group Weather Report with Wayne Shorter, 1970-86; Solo artiste, 1985-; Leader, own groups Weather Update; Zawinul Syndicate. Recordings: Solo albums: Rise & Fall, 1968; Zawinul, 1970; Dialects, 1986; with Zawinul Syndicate: The Immigrants, 1988; Black Water, 1989; with Weather Report: Weather Report, 1971; I Sing The Body Electric, 1972; Sweetnighter, 1973; Mysterious Traveller, 1974; Tail Spinnin', 1975; Black Market, 1976; Heavy Weather, 1977; Mr Gone, 1978; 8:30, 1979; Night Passages, 1980; Weather Report, 1982; Procession, 1983; Domino Theory, 1984; Sportin' Life, 1985; This Is This, 1986; Heavy Weather - The Collection, 1990; with Cannonball Adderley: Mercy Mercy Mercy, 1966; with Miles Davis: In A Silent Way, 1969; Witches Brew, 1970; Live Evil, 1972; Big Fun, 1974; Circle In The Round, 1979; Also recorded with: Tim Hardin; Eddie Harris; Quincy Jones. Honours: Mercy Mercy Mercy (as songwriter), 1967.

ZÉ Tom (Antonio José Santana Martins), b. 11 Oct 1936, Irará, Bahia, Brazil. Composer; Singer; Arranger; Actor. m. Neusa S Martins, 14 Feb 1970, 1 son. Musical Education: University of Bahia, Music School; Higher Courses, 1962-67; Studied composition and structure with Ernst Widmer; History of Music with Professor H J Koellreuter; Cello with Piero Bastianelli; Counterpoint with Yulo Brandao; Piano and Guitar studies. Career: Tropicalist Movement, 1967; MoMA, New York, Latin American Artists of 20th Century, Concert, 1993; Opened London International Festival of Theatre, Queen Elizabeth Hall, London, England, 1993; Walker Art Center, USA, 1993; Lincoln Center, New York and Avery Fisher Hall, 1996; Jazz Festivals in USA, Canada and Europe; Actor in the theatre appearing in: Arena Canta Bahia by Augusto Boal, 1965; Rock Horror Show, directed by Rubens Correia, 1975; Cinema appearances include: Sábado by Ugo Giogetti, 1994. Recordings: Sao Benedito, 1965; Tropicália, 1968; Todosos Olhos, 1973; Estudanddo o Samba, 1976; The Best Of Tom Zé, 1990; The Hips Of Tradition, 1993. Honours: Festival Composer to Composer, Telluride Institute, USA; Down Beat magazine awards: Third place (Readers Poll), Fourth place (Critics Poll), for album The Best Of Tom Zé, 1991;

Billboard Top Alternative Album, 1991; Music Festival, TV Record: First place, Golden Viola and Silver Sabiá (song Sao Sao Paulo, Meu Amor), 1968; Fourth place (song 2001); Award for best lyrics. Memberships: US: BMI; RZO; Brazil: Abramus; Fermata; Arlequim. Hobbies: Football; Mythology; Literature. Current Management: T Stowsand, Austria; Embrashow, Brazil. Address: Rua Dr Homem de Mello 717, Sao Paulo, SP 05007-002, Brazil.

ZECIC Drazen, b. 24 July 1967, Split, Croatia. m. Bozena Poljak, 29 Aug 1992, 2 daughters. Education: Hotel Management. Musical Education: Self-educated. Career: Concerts: Croatia, including Sports Arena, Split, 1993, 1994. Tours: Canada; Australia; US; Germany; Switzerland; Italy; Television: HTV-Croatia; Local television in Australia and Canada. Recordings: Zagrli Me Nocas Jace, 1990; Govore Mi Mnogi Ljudi, 1993; Boem U Dusi, 1995. Honours: Spilt Fest-Croatia, Composer I Award, 1992; Melodije Jadrana-Cro/Grand Prix, Singer, Composer, 1993; Cardinal Stepinac Fest -Croatia, Composer I Award, 1993. Memberships: Croatian Musicians' Union; HGU. Hobbies: Swimming; Sailing; Football. Address: Croatia Records, Medugorska 61, 41000 Zagreb, Croatia.

ZELENKA Karel, b. 27 May 1946, Prague, Czech Republic. Musician (Alto and Tenor Trombone). Education: Studied, Prague Conservatory and Academy of Arts, Prague, Graduated, 1976. Career: Prague Jazz Club Reduta; Berlin Jazz Club; Lucerna Hall in Prague; Warzsaw Jazz Club, Poland. Recordings: Poste Restante, CD; Prague Big Band, Lucerna Hall Roth; Anniversary Concert, CD. Membership: The Prague Big Band. Address: Cimelicka 960/7, 142 00 Prague 4, Czech Republic.

ZEPHANIAH Benjamin Obadiah Iqbal, b. 15 Apr 1958, Birmingham, England. Poet. m. Amina Iqbal, 17 Mar 1990. Career: Tours: South Africa; Australia; US; Middle East; Presenter, Crossing The Tracks, BBC TV; Resident poet, In Living Colour, BBC Radio 4. Recordings: Albums: Rasta (workers playtime), 1983; Free South Africa, 1986; Us An Dem, 1990; Crisis, 1992; Back To Roots, 1995; Belly of Beast, 1996. Publications: Books: City Psalms; Talking Turkeys. Honours: Honorary Citizen, Memphis State, Tennessee. Memberships: PRS; Equity; Musicians' Union. Hobbies: Kung-Fu; Numismatology (Notes). Current Management: Sandra Boyce Management. Address: 1 Kingsway House, Albion Road, London N16 0TA, England.

ZEVON Warren, b. 24 Jan 1947, Chicago, Illinois, USA. Singer; Musician (guitar, piano); Songwriter. Career: Folk singer, 1969; Writer for commercials; Musician with Everly Brothers and Phil Everly, 1970-73; Solo artiste, 1973-; Member, Hindu Love Gods (with members of R.E.M.), 1990. Compositions include: When Johnny Strikes Up The Band; Hasten Down The Wind; Werewolves Of London; Poor Poor Pitiful Me; Play It All Night Long. Recordings: Albums: Zevon - Wanted Dead Or Alive, 1969; Warren Zevon, 1976; Excitable Boy, 1978; Bad Luck Streak In Dancing School, 1980; Stand In The Fire, 1981; The Envoy, 1982; Sentimental Hygiene, 1987; Quiet Normal Life, 1988; Transverse City, 1989; Mr Bad Example, 1991; Learning To Flinch, 1993; Mutineer, 1995; with Don Henley; I Can't Stand Still, 1982; with Phil Everly: Star Spangled Springer, 1973; Mystic Line, 1975; with Everly Brothers: Stories We Could Tell, 1972; with Hindu Love Gods: Hindu Love Gods, 1990. Current Managment: Peter Asher Management. Address: 644 North Doheny Drive, Los Angeles, CA 90069, USA.

ZIEGLER Michael, b. 7 November 1962, Copenhagen, Denmark. Musician. 1 son, 2 daughters. Education: Selftaught. Career: Hotel Hunger Released the Album This is Where the Fun Starts in the US and Canada, 1989; Opens the Orange Stage at Roskilde Festival, 1990; EBU Rock Festival, Ireland and Berlin, 1992. Compositions: This is Where the Fun Starts, 1989; Waiting For Alice, 1992; Frankie My Dear I Dont Give A Dam, 1994; Mars Needs Guitars, 1995; Happy Hour, 1996. Recordings: This is Where the Fun Starts, 1989; Waiting for Alice, 1992; Frankie My Dear I Dont Give a Dam, 1994; Mars Needs Guitars, 1995; Happy Hour, 1996. Memberships: Danish Artists Union; DPA. Hobbies: Computers; Football. Address: Mardal Management. Address: Valdemarsgade 524 Th, 1665 Copenhagen V, Denmark.

ZIEGLER Pablo, b. 2 September 1944, Buenos Aires, Argentina. Musician (Piano); Composer; Arranger. m. Sandra Sicbert, 10 October 1977, 1 son, 1 daughter. Education: Buenos Aires University, not completed; Classical Music, Music Conservatory of Buenos Aires. Career: Astor, Piazzolla, New Tango Quintet, Piano Player, 1978-88; Montreaux Jazz Festival, North Sea Jazz Festival and Nice Jazz Festival; Summer Stage Central Park; Solo Performer: Lincoln Center, Saint Martin in in Field Cathedral. Compositions: Milonga in the Wind; La Conexion Portena Album. Recordings: with Riazzolla Quintet: Live in Montreaux; Live in Wien; Be As Zero Hour; Symphonic Tango; Los Tangueros. Honours: Arlequin 1992 National Prize; Honorary Citizen of New Orleans City. Membership: ASCAP. Hobbies: Sailing; Fishing; Scuba Diving. Current Management: Santa Fe World, Music Agency, 609 Onate Place, Santa Fe, NM 87501, USA. Address: Tucuman, 1455 8 C (CP 1050), Buenos Aires, Argentina.

ZIMMER Hans, b. 1957, Frankfurt, Germany. Film Composer. 1 daughter. Compositions: Film scores include: Green Card; Driving Miss Daisy; Pacific Heights; Backdraft; Rain Man; Regarding Henry; Thelma & Louise; My Beautiful Laundrette.

ZIMMERMANN André François, b. 19 Jan 1965, Fort de France, Martinique. Musician (piano); Composer. Musical Education: Music school; Conservatory; Sessions. Career: Appearances on TV France; Concerts as soloist, duos, trios, big bands include: Bucharest, 1990; with the Big Band de Jazz, Metabetchouan, Canada; International Festival of Brasov, Transylvania, 1990; Festivals at Mulhouse; Nitting; Avoriaz; Piano solo, St Louis, France, 1991; Teacher, School of Music, Sundgau-Alsace. Compositions: Theatre: Les Estivants, Gorki, 1986; La Mouette, Chekov, 1990; Derrière les 7 Papiers Peints, Wilfred Grote, with Haute Alsace, 1990; Un Chapeau de Paille d'Italy, Labiche, 1991; Childrens' pieces (2 selections for piano and orchestra); Music for flute and strings; Composition for regional cinema. Recordings: Album: Jazz Conceptions, music for popular songs. Hobby: Art. Address: 22 Rue de Spechbach, F-68720 Illfurth, France.

ZIMOLKA Ales, b. 7 April 1963, Jihlava, Czech Republic. Drummer. m. Lenka Zimolková, 8 October 1988. Education: Business Academy; Piano, guitar, Basic Art School; Private lessons, drums, Prague, Prague Conservatory. Career: Member, many rock group bands, 1978-89; Member of band, Harley's John, 1990-95; Member of bands, Zoo, TMA, Little Big Company, Los Vobos, 1995-; Many video and studio recordings. Recordings: Ballads L, Irish ballads, 1996; Los Vobos: Cerné Díza (Black Hole), 1996; Zoo, 1997; Zome Country albums, 1996-97; Zoo: Good Morning, 1998. Honours: 3 times Winner, Czech Radio Top 10, Harleys, 1991. Hobbies: Sport; Literature: Sleeping. Address: Jicínská 29, 130 00 Praha 3, Czech Republic.

ZLOKIC Jasna, b. 15 Mar 1955, Vela Luka, Croatia. Economist. m. Boris Zlokic, 25 June 1977, 1 son. Musical Education: Guitar lessons. Career: First public performance aged 10; Amateur career sustained until first solo album,

1980; Highly successful solo career, 1980-. Recordings: Single: Krugovi Na Vodi, 1980; Albums: Pusti Me Da Prodem, 1983; Skitnica, 1984; Ja Sam Ti Jedini Drug, 1985; Vjeruj Mi, 1986; Kad Odu Svi, 1987; Lutajuce Srce, 1988; Vrijeme Je Uz Nas, 1989; Tiho Sviraj Pjesmu Ljubavnu, 1990; Bez Predaha, 1992; Nisam Ti Se Tugo Nadala, 1994; Ja Zivjet Cu Za Dane Radosti, 1995. Honours: Zagreb Fest, Grand Prix, 1984, 1988; Split Musical Festival Award, 1982, 1984, 1987, 1993, 1994; MESAM Awards, Female Singer of the Year, 1984, 1988; Sarajevo Festival, 1988; Bratislava Festival, 1985; Madeira Festival, 1988. Membership: HGU (Hrvatska Glazbena Unija). Hobbies: Swimming; Skiing; Tennis. Current Management: Boris Zlokic. Address: Laurenciceva 8A, 41000 Zagreb, Croatia.

ZOLOTHUHIN Adrian Dimitri, b. 22 July 1970, Middlesbrough, Cleveland, England. Musician (guitar); Arranger; Producer. Musical Education: BMus (tonmeister), University of Surrey. Career: Guitarist, Kabak; Concerts: Ashcroft Theatre; Spencer House; St James' Palace; National Portrait Gallery; Guitarist, World Of Leather; Concerts: Marquee; Garage; Subterrania; Borderline; Television: What's That Noise, BBC TV; Radio: BBC GLR, various sessions. Recordings: St Mark's Place, World Of Leather, 1994; Guitar, producer: Russian Party, World Of Leather, 1994; Guitar, arranger, Blow, as solo artist on album: Bachology, 1995. Address: 110 Grove Avenue, Hanwell, London W7 3ES, England.

ZORN John, b. 2 Sept 1953, New York City, USA. Musician (saxophone, keyboards); Composer. Career: Associated with the avant garde tradition, performing with numerous artists including Wayne Horvitz and David Moss; Works performed worldwide; Compositions commissioned by groups including the New York Philharmonic Orchestra, Brooklyn Philharmonic, Bayerische Staasoper, WDR Orchestra Köln, American Composers Orchestra, Stephen Drury and The Kronos Quartet. Compositions: Christabel, 1972; Conquest Of Mexico, 1973; Mikhail Zoetrope, 1974; Lacrosse, 1977; Hockey, 1978; Fencing, 1978; The Book Of Heads, 1978; Pool, 1979; Archery, 1979; Track & Field, 1980; Locus Solus, 1982; Sebastopol, 1983; Rugby, 1983; Cobra, 1984; Xu Feng, 1985; Godard, 1985; Spillane, 1986; Hu Die, 1986; Ruan Lingyu, 1987; Hwang Chin-ee, 1988; Cat O'Nine Tails, 1988; Quê Trân, 1988; For Your Eyes Only, 1989; Bézique, 1989; Torture Garden, 1990; Grand Guignol, 1990; Dead Man, 1990; Elegy, 1991; Leng Teh'e, 1991; Carny, 1992; Memento Mori, 1992; Kristallnacht,1992; Absinthe, 1992; Angelus Novus, 1993; Masada, 1993-97; The Sand's Share, 1994; Redbird, 1995; Dark River, 1995; Aporias, 1995; Music For Children, 1996; Duras, 1996; Kol Nidre, 1996; Orchestra Variations, 1996; Etant Donnés, 1997; Shibboleth, 1997; Cycles du Nord, 1998; Rituals, 1998.

ZULFIKARPSIC Bojan, b. 2 Feb 1968, Belgrade, Serbia. Musician (piano). m. Marie Chevallier, Aug 1993, 1 son. Career: Played with: Henri Texier; Michel Portal; Leader, Bojan Z Quartet; Concerts include: Banlieues Bleues Festival; Halle That Jazz Festival; London Jazz Festival; Jazz Across The Border, Berlin; Auditorium des Halles, Paris; Radio France, 1995. Recordings: with Bojan Z Quartet: Bojan Z Quartet, 1994; with Henri Texier's Azur Quartet: Indian's Week, 1993; Mad Nomad. Honours: First prize for composition: Concours de la Defense, 1993. Current Management: Laurence Voiturier, Artalent. Address: 15 Passage de la Main d'Or, 75011 Paris, France.

ZWILGMEYER Kalle, b. 29 October 1937, Porsgrunn, Norway. Folksinger; Songwriter; Translator; Guitar. 2 daughters. Education: University Degree in History and Geography. Musical Education: Selftaught guitar. Career:

Programme Leader, numberless folksong programmes, Norwegian radio and TV; Appearances in great many radio and TV programmes, Nordic countries; Many tours in Scandinavia and as Member of Nordic groups: Polarkvartetten; Viser På Vandring; Nordenom; Kalmarunionen; Nordiska Visensemblen; 3 Vise-menn and 1 Svenske; Appearances in folkmusic festivals. Recordings: Graverende Bevis, 1987. Publications: Vise Og Gitar, 1977; Bli Dus Med Gitaren, 1978; Som Ringer I Vann, 1980; Songtexts published in more than 20 songbooks. Honour: Vispramen Storkens Minne (Swedish Folksingers Prize), 1983. Memberships: TONO; NOPA ang Gramart, Norway; DANSK, DJBEA, Denmark. Hobbies: Gathering folksingers from all Nordic countries in Skagen, Denmark (first weekend in February every year) and in Greece (May). Address: Foderstofgården 76, 3600 Frederikssund, Denmark.

APPENDIX A
RECORD COMPANIES

ANDORRA

Limitada de Producciones SL, Ciutat Consuegra 12 , 2° , 2a, Edificio Orió, Andorra La Vella. *Administrator: Joan Deltell Porta.*

ARGENTINA

AIM (Arco Iris Musical), Avda Santa Fe 4910, Piso 4°, Of. B, 1425 Buenos Aires. *Director General: Osvaldo Bermolen.*
Barca Discos Srl, Avda Sana Fe 1780, Piso 11°, Of. 1102, 1060 Buenos Aires. *Director: Elio Barbeito.*
Clan Dilo Music, Casilla Correos 123 La Plata, 1900 Buenos Aires. *President: Giorgio Di Lorenzo.*
D Cipa Diaz Colodrero, Avda Paseo Colón 524, Piso Of. 1, 1063 Buenos Aires. *Director General: María Antonia Diaz Colodrero.*
Del Cielito Records, Laprida 1898, Piso 4, Of. B, 1425 Buenos Aires. *Director: Gustavo Gauvry.*
Discos Melopea SA, Jean Jaurés 444, 1215 Buenos Aires. *President: Félix Francisco Nebbia.*
Epsa Electrical Products SAIC, México 2835, 1223 Buenos Aires. *President: Laura Roma Casella.*
Esther M Soto Ciclo 3, Estados Unidos 629, 1101 Buenos Aires. *Contact: Esther Soto.*
Kralendijk Producciones, Sánchez de Bustamente 444, Piso 5°, Dpto 1, 1173 Buenos Aires. *President: Alejandro Solignac.*
Main Records SA, Tucumán 1673, 3° 6, 1050 Buenos Aires. *President: Alejandro Amadori.*
Musidisc Europe Sudamerica SAIC, Güemes 4418, Piso 1° A, 1425 Buenos Aires. *President: Jimmy Olszevicki.*
OM Records, Colombia 1727 Valantín Alsina, 1822 Buenos Aires. *President: Oscar Meidvilla.*
Polygram Discos SA, Avda Córdoba 1345, Piso 14, 1055 Buenos Aires. *Managing Director: Rubén Aprile.*
Rave On SA, Uruguay 546 2 6, 1015 Buneos Aires. *President: Bernado Bergeret.*

AUSTRALIA

ABC Music, Level 3, John Mellion Bldg, 10a Campbell Street, Artamon, NSW 2065. *Label Manager: Terri Nielson.*
Acid Jazz Australia Pty Ltd, Suite 73, 380 Wattle Street, Ultimo, NSW 2007. *Directors: Carolyn Smee, Mark Lovett.*
Akaba Records Pty Ltd, Level 5, 14 Martin Place, Sydney, NSW 2000. *Executive Director: James R G Bell.*
J Albert & Son P/L Albert Productions, 9 Rangers Road, Neutral Bay, NSW 2089. *General Manager: Fifa Ricobono.*
Anabasis, PO Box 437, Kew, VIC 3101. *Manager: Gina Luca Veloci.*
Au-Go-Go, 349 Little Bourke Street, Melbourne, VIC 3000. *Directors: Greta Moon, Bruce Milne.*
BIB Productions Pty Ltd, 356 Swan Street, Richmond, VIC 3121. *Chief Executive Officer: Mike Brady.*
Big Rock Pty Ltd, PO Box 273, Dulwich Hill, NSW 2203. *A & R Manager: Chris Turner.*
Black Market Music, 172 Roden Street, West Melbourne, VIC 3003. *Manager: Elly Mantzaris.*
BMG Australia Ltd, 194 Miller Street, North Sydney, NSW 2060. *Managing Director: Michael Smellie.*
Broad Music Pty Ltd, 56 Winborne Road, Brookvale, NSW 2100. *Managing Director: Ken Broad.*
Bunyip Records Pty Ltd, 3 Hessel Place, Emu Heights, NSW 2750. *Managing Director: Ian B. MacLeod.*
CAAMA Music (Central Australian Aboriginal Media Association), 101 Todd Street, Alice Springs, NT 0870. *Head of Department: Richard Micallef.*
Central Station Records, 81 Market Street, South Melbourne, VIC 3205. *Managing Director: Guiseppe Palumbo.*
CMC (Christian Marketing Communications), Unit 9, 147 Marshalltown Road, Grovedale, VIC 3216. *General Manager: Alan Kennedy.*
Colossal Records, 14-16 Wilson Avenue, Brunswick, VIC 3056. *Managing Director: Domenic Loprete.*
Crash Bang! Records Pty Ltd, Suite W2/4, 42 Wattle Street, Ultimo, NSW 2007. *Label Manager: Jason Redlich.*
Creative Vibes, 8/40 Victoria Street, Potts Point, NSW 2011. *Managing Directors: Gordon Henderson, Peter Pasqual, Heidi Pasqual.*
Dino Music Pty Ltd, PO Box 242, Purmont, NSW 2009. *Managing Director: John Harper.*
Diverse System Music, PO Box 1161, Fitzroy North, VIC 3068. *Managing Director: Tony Greene.*
Dog Meat Records, GPO Box 2366 V, Melbourne, VIC 3001. *Managing Director: David Laing.*
Dolphin Music Group Pty Ltd, 23 Darvall Street, Balmain, NSW 2041. *Chairman: Barry Chapman.*
Dominator Records, 276 Morpleth Street, Adelaide, SA 5000. *Manager: Kelly Hewson.*
East West Records, 39-47 Albany Street, Crows Nest, NSW 2065. *Managing Director: Chris Hanlon.*
EMI Music Australia, 98-100 Glover Street, Cremore, NSW 2090. *Managing Director: David Snell.*
Emily Rocords, PO Box 405, Hamilton, Brisbane, QLD 4007. *Label Manager: Mark Hanlon.*
Empire Records & Publishing, 23-25A Johnston Streeet, Collingwood, VIC 3066. *Label Manager: Paul Higgins.*
Evolving Discs Distribution Australasia, PO Box 2237, St Kilda West, VIC 3182. *Director: Elizabeth Van Dort.*
Fellaheen, PO Box A537, Sydney South, NSW 2000. *A & R and Assistant Managing Director: Adam Yee.*
Festival Records Pty Ltd, 63-79 Miller Street, Pyrmont, NSW 2009. *Chairman: Allan Hely.*
GLD Music, 79-81 Buckland Street, Chippendale, NSW 2008. *Directors: Moira Bennett, Grant Calton.*
Half A Cow Records, PO Box 1100, Strawberry Hills, NSW 2012. *Owner: Nic Dalton.*
Image Music Group Pty Ltd, 19 Johnston Street, Port Melboune, VIC 3207. *Managing Director: John McDonald.*
Integrity Music Pty Ltd, 120 Herries Street, Toowoomba, QLD 4350. *Genral Manager: Mark Freeman.*
J&B Records, 39 Whiting Street, Artamon, NSW 2064. *Chairman: Brian Nicholls.*
Kriminal Rekords, Suite 314, Prudential Building, 2 Queen Street, Brisbane, QLD 4000. *CEO: Alan Maddams.*
Larrakin Entertainment Pty Ltd, Unit 4, 809-821 Botany Road, Rosebery, NSW 2018. *Managing Director: Warren Fahey.*
Lavender Music, 5/159 Arthurton Road, Northcote, VIC 3070. *Partners: Madelen Rayner, Barbara Young.*
MCA Music Entertainment Inc (Australia), PO Box 899, Crows Nest, NSW 2065. *Managing Director: Paul Krige.*
Massive Recording Co Pty Ltd, PO Box 380 Milsons Point, Sydney, NSW 2061. *Managing Director: Laurie Dunn.*
Mint Records Pty Ltd, PO Box 210, Blackheath, NSW 2785. *Contact: Charles L Naudi.*
Modern Invasion Music, Unit 2, 14 Spink Street, Gardenvale, VIC 3185. *Manager: Daniel Janecka.*
MRA Enterainment Group, 39 Gosford Street, Mt Gravatt, QLD 4122. *Managing Director: Ray Hartley.*
Mushroom Exports Pty Ltd, 55 Danks Street, Port Melbourne, VIC 3207. *Managing Director: Scott Murphy.*
Mushroom Records Pty Ltd, 9 Dundas Lane, Albert Park, VIC 3206. *Chairman: Michael Gudinski.*
Music World, PO Box 1462, Milton Centre 4064. *Managing Director: Hoghton Hughes.*
Natural Symphonies, 10 Broughton Street, Camden, NSW 2570. *Creative Director: Ian O'Hare.*
Newmarket Music, 393-395 Macaulay Road, Kensington, VIC 3031. *National Sales Manager: Len McQualter.*
New World Productions, 151 Boundary Street, Bardon, QLD 4065. *Managing Director: Andrew Watson.*
Odessa-Mama Records, 557a North Road, Ormond, VIC 3204. *Managing Director: David Faiman.*
One Movement Records, Suite 335, 410 Elizabeth Street, Surry Hills, NSW 2010. *Label Manager: Matt Hayward.*

Opulent Music Entertainment, PO Box 270, 48 David Crescent, Bundoora, VIC 3083. *Managing Director: Anthony Chidiac.*
Origin Recordings, GPO Box 3265, Sydney, NSW 2001. *Managing Director: Philip Mortlock.*
Outlaw Records, 62 Thompson Street, Darlinghurst, NSW 2010. *Director: David Caplice.*
Phonogram / Polygram Records Australia, Unit C, 110 McEvoy Street, Alexandria, NSW 2015. *Managing Director: Tim Delaney.*
Pickwick Australia Pty Ltd, 2/111 Queensbridge Street, South Melbourne, VIC 3205. *Publicity Manager: Louise Bedford.*
Possum Music Pty Ltd, 2 /27 Wongala Crescent, Beecroft, NSW 2119. *Managing Director: Philip Israel.*
Rascal Records Pty Ltd, PO Box 146, Glenside, SA 5064. *Director: Carolyn Combe.*
Ravenswood / Foghorn Records, 64 Wattle Street, Ultimo, NSW 2007. *Managing Director: Bob Armstrong.*
Red Eye Records, PO Box 689, Darlinghurst, NSW 2010. *Label Manager: Merran Morton.*
Regular Records Pty Ltd, Suite 3, 249 Darlinghurst Road, Darlinghurst, NSW 2010. *Managing Director: Martin Fabinyi.*
Republic Records, 9 Knox Street, Chippendale, NSW 2008. *Managing Director: Vicki Gordon.*
Request Records, 15 High Peak Place, Lesmurdie, WA 6076. *Proprietor: John Green.*
Roadrunner Records (Australia) Pty Ltd, 24 High Street, Northcote, VIC 3070. *Label Manager: Bob Stevenson.*
RooArt / Ra Records, 351 Crown Street, Surry Hills, NSW 2010. *Label Manager: Todd Wagstaff.*
Round Records, 42 Breaker Street, St Morris, SA 5068. *Contact: Terry Bradford.*
Rubber Records, 59 Victoria Avenue, Albert Park, VIC 3206. *Managing Director: David Vodicka.*
Rufus Records, PO Box 116, Paddington, NSW 2021. *President: Tim Dunn.*
Sandstock Music Pty Ltd, PO Box 557, Charlestown, NSW 2290. *Managing Director: Jill Gartrell.*
Servant Communications, PO Box 2020, Launceston, Tasmania 7250. *President: Kevin N Hooper.*
Shock / Shagpile / Thrust Records, 24 High Street, Northcote, VIC 3070. *Label Manager: David Williams.*
Sirius Music, 70 Toorak Road, South Yarra, VIC 3141. *Directors: Stephen Robinson, Adrian Marchesani.*
Sonart Music Vision, PO Box 691, Brookvale, NSW 2100. *Managing Director: Les Hodge.*
Sony Music Australia Ltd, 11-19 Hargrave Street, East Sydney, NSW 2010. *Managing Director: Denis Handlin.*
Terra Australia Records, Suite 223, 161 Military Road, Neutral Bay, NSW 2089. *Contact: Alex Svencis.*
Time-Life Australia Pty Ltd, Level 6, 61 Lavender Street, Milsons Point, NSW 2061. *Chairman and Managing Director: Bonita L Boezeman.*
Troy Horse Label, 408-410 King Street, Newtown, NSW 2042. *Label Manager: Richard Vidler.*
Vampire Records, PO Box 669, Epping, NSW 2121. *Managing Director: Danny Kaleda.*
Vicious Vinyl, 7B Baxter Street, Frankston, VIC 3199. *International Affairs: Andy Van.*
Virgin Records Australia Pty Ltd, 98-100 Glover Street, Cremorne, NSW 2090. *Director of Operations: Michael Manos.*
Warner Music Australia Pty Ltd, 39-47 Albany Street, Crows Nest, NSW 2065. *Chairman: Brian Harris.*
Word Australia, 142 Canterbury Road, Kilsyth, VIC 3137. *Product and Marketing Manager: Wendy Moulton.*

AUSTRIA

Aardvarks Music, Nachtigallenstr 18, A-5023 Salzburg. *Managing Director: Michael Wagner.*
ATS Records, Breitnau 220, A-4591 Molln. *Managing Director, Reinhard Brunner.*
Banananas Records, Pebalstraase 31/1, A-8700 Leoben. *Managing Director, Klaus Katzianka*
BMG/Ariola (Austria), Erlachgasse 134-140, A-1101 Vienna. *Managing Director: Harald Th. Buechel.*
Cactus Records, Nibelungering 1, A-3423 St Andrä-Wördern. *Managing Director: Hans Hartel.*
Christmas Records, Reinhard-Machold-Str 47/3, A-8075 Graz. *Director: Alexander Rehak.*
Doremi Records, Spundag 5/6, A-1210 Vienna. *Director: Emad Sayyah.*
EMI Austria, Webgasse 43, A-1060 Vienna. *Managing Director: Hans Reinisch.*
EMP, Weinitzenstraase 1, A-8045 Graz. *Managing Director: Egon Hinz.*
European Music Project, Reinhard-Machold-Str 47/3, A-8075 Hart/Graz. *Director: Alexander Rehak.*
Extraplatte GmbH, Postfach 2, A-1094 Vienna. *Managing Director: Harald Quendler.*
FIPS Records, Schöpfergasse 3, A-1120 Vienna. *General Manager: Gunther Pfeiffer.*
Frizzey Records, Hauptstrasse 13, A-6522 Prutz. *Managing Director: Friedrich Greif.*
Gash, Raaberbahngasse 21/4/5, A-1100 Vienna. *Managing Director: Edi Ehn.*
Gig Records, Fuehrichgasse 8, A-1010 Vienna. *Managing Director: Marcus Spiegel.*
Goblin Records, Dr. Theodor Kornerstrasse, A-3100 St. Polte. *Label Manager: Ingrid Mangold.*
Honk Records, PO Box 118, A-1172 Vienna. *Managing Director: Jivi Honk.*
Operator, Brauhausgasse 14, A-3003 Gablitz. *Managing Director: Erwin Kiennaust.*
PolyGram GmbH, Edelsinnstrasse 4, PO Box 85, A-1120 Vienna. *Assistant Managing Director: Ulla Pfeiffer.*
SBF Records, Molln 129, A-4591 Molln. *Managing Director: Manfred Prentner.*
Sony Music Austria, Erlachgasse 134-140, A-1101 Vienna. *Managing Director: Martin Pammer.*
Spritzendorfer & Rossori GmbH, Hietzinger Hauptstr, 94 A-1130 Wien. *Managing Director: A Spriteendorfer.*
Ton Art, Hietzinger Hauptstrasse 130, A-1130 Vienna. *Managing Director: Alexander Munkas.*
TP Records, Reinhard-Machold-Str 47/3, A-8075 Hart/Graz. *Director: Alexander Rehak.*
Video & Tontechnik, Hoechsterstrasse 47, A-6850 Dornbirn. *Managing Director: Manfred Mäser.*

BELARUS

Beloton Records, 210015, Shrader Str 8-15, Vitebsk, Belarus. *Director: Vladimir Sartchenko.*

BELGIUM

A L C Productions, Av Eugène Ysaye 47, B-1070 Brussels. *Label Manager: Alexander Louvet.*
Alora Music, Villegas de Clercamp 13, B-1853 Grimbergen. *Managing Director: Bert Burm.*
Amor Et Psyche Productions, Allee du Cloître 43, B-1050 Brussels. *Manager: Laurent Jadot.*
Arcade Music Company, Rue de Wand 209-213, B-1020 Brussels. *General Manager: Richard Dedaper.*
ARS Productions, Single 5, B-2550 Kortich. *Managing Director: Patrick Busschots.*
Baltic NV, Rederijkersstraat 82, B-2610 Wilrijk-Antwerp. *Managing Director: Ben Gyselinck.*
Big Time International, Kloosterstraat 54, B-3900 Overpelt. *Managing Director: Jos Borremans.*
BMG Ariola Belgium, François Rigasquare 30 B 8, B-1030 Brussels. *Managing Director: Derk Jolink.*
Boom! Records, 19 Steenweg op Bergen, B-1500 Halle. *Managing Director: J P Van Haesendonck.*
Byte Records, Schriekbos n5, B-2980 Zoersel. *Managing Director: Jean-Paul De Coster.*
Caracol Music Group, 5, Rue du Cheneau, B-6120 Ham-sur-Heure. *General Manager: Timothy Hagelstein.*
Carbon 7, 23 Av Général Eisenhower, B-1030 Brussels. *Director: Guy Segers.*
Clip Records, Rozemarijnstraat 12, B-9300 Aalst. *Managing Director: Joe Bogart.*
Colour Record, Begijnhoflaan 39, B-9000 Gent. *Managing Director: Marc Van Beveren.*
Commedia Vew, Fonteinstraat 19, B-8000 Bruges. *Managing Director: Chery Deryoke.*

Crammed Discs, Rue de Général Patton 43, B-1050 Brussels. *Managing Director: Marc Hollander.*
Dexon Sprl, 41 Rue Cite de L'Enfance, B-6001 Marcinelle. *Manager: Delfosse Pierre.*
Disques du Crepuscle, 15 Galerie du Roi, B-1000 Brussels. *Managing Director: Michel Duval.*
Emergency! Records, Rue Ferdinand Bernier 38, B-1060 Brussels. *Managing Director: Marc Debouvier.*
EMI Belgium, Kolonel Bourgstraat 128, B-1040 Brussels. *Managing Director: Guy Brulez.*
Franc'Amour, Rue Paul Emile Janson 9, B-1050 Brussels. *Managing Director: Christine Jottard.*
Hautregard Recording Sc, 119 Route De Veaviers, B-4650 Herue. *Public Relations: Thieray Steinbrecher.*
Insane Music, 2 Grand Rue, B-6183 Trazegnies. *Contact: Alain Neffe.*
KK / Nova Zembla Records, Krijgsbaan 240, B- 2070 Zwyndrecht. *Managing Director: Josef Verbruggen.*
Loft Records, Kloosterstraat 54, B-3900 Overpelt. *Managing Director: Jos Borremans.*
MMD SA, Rue Ferdinand Bernier 38, B-1060 Brussels. *Managing Director: Plastic Bertrand.*
Mag SA, Avenue Louise 65, B-1050 Brussels. *Managing Director: Pierre Piront.*
Mixz Productions, Berchemlei 198, B-2140 Borgerhout. *Managing Director: Koen Tillic.*
Music & Words Belgium, Europalaan 7, B-8970 Poperinge. *President: Hans Peters.*
Myron Records, Bergstraat 13, B-1560 Hoeilaart. *Managing Director: Leon Lamal.*
Parsifal bvba, Gulden Vlieslaan 67, B-8000 Bruges. *Contact: Nico A Mertens.*
Play It Again Sam, Rue de Veeweyde 90, B-1070 Brussels. *Managing Director: Jan Hublau.*
Play That Beat, Rue Fernand Bernier 38, B-1060 Brussels. *Managing Director: Marc Debouvier.*
PolyGram Belgium, Roodebeek Avenue 30, B-1040 Brussels. *Managing Director: Bert Cloeckaert.*
Private Life/ Noise Records, 13 Rue Villegas de Clercamp, B-1853 Strombeek-Bever. *Managing Director: Olivier Verhaeghe.*
Punch, Rue de Lausanne 37, B-1060 Brussels. *Managing Director: Alexandre Saboundjian.*
Pyramid International Music, Lepelhoekstraat 26, B-9100 Sint-Niklaas. *Managing Director: Marc De Coen*
Rainbow Records & Music, Herentlfa Steenweg 20A, B-2220 Heist-Op-Den Berg. *Contact: Stan Verbeeck.*
Rainland, 9 Rue Paul-Emile Janson, B-1050 Brussels. *Managing Director: Christine Jottard.*
Rox Records, Marie Henrieet Laan 71, B-1700 Dilbeck. *Managing Director: Mario Gucci.*
Sawdust Alley, Avenue Circulaire 144b, B-1180 Brussels. *Managing Director: Calvin Owens.*
Selection & B Sharp Records, 24 Gachardstreet, B-1050 Brussels. *General Manager: Pierre Pletinckx.*
Smash Productiopns/Now Discs, Charles Quint 34B-5, B-1080 Brussels. *Managing Director: Michel Nachtergaele.*
Sony Music Belgium, Evenepoelstraat 9, B-1040 Brussels. *Managing Director: Patrick Decam.*
Target Records, Oordegemsesteenweg, B-1050 Brussels. *Contact: Claudine Sarlet.*
Team For Action (T4A), Av Oscar van Goibtsnoven 45B, B-1180 Brussels. *Managing Director: Claude Martin.*
Tempo (Top Entertainment Editions). Krijgslaan G1, B-9000 Gent. *General Manager: Luc Standaert.*
Tessa Records Rock Label, Stationsstraat 36 W3, B-9160 Lokeren. *President/Owner: Marc De Block.*
3Rioart Vzw Maoisch Theater Productions, Juliaandillenstr 22, B-2018 Antwerp. *Director: Sandy Nys.*
Virgin Belgium NV, Bld Gnral Wahis 41, B-1030 Brussels. *Managing Director: Dirk De Vries.*
Warner Music Belgium, Lambermontlaan 79, B-1030 Brussels. *Managing Director: Ted Sikkink.*
Witlof Music, Leernsestweg 168, B-9800 Deinze. *Director: Jean Tamt.*

BOLIVIA

Discolandia Dueri & Cia Ltda, Potosí 920, 1° Piso, 422 La Paz. *Proprietor: Miriam Dueri.*
Producciones Gum Prodisco, Plaza Alonso de Mendoza 500, Edif. Santa Anita Of.8, 13733 La Paz. *Director General: Germán Urquidi Navric.*

BRAZIL

Caipirapirs Produçoes Artisticas Ltda, Avda Das Aguas Marinhas 157 Pg. Petrópolis, 07600-00 São Paulo. *Contact: Pablo Ossipoff.*
Estudio Eldorado Ltda, Rua Pires da Mota 820-830, 01529 São Paulo. *Executive Director: João Lara.*
Paradox Music, Rua Dr. Pinto Ferraz, 58 Vila Mariana, 04117-040 São Paulo. *Director: Silvio Arnaldo.*
Planet Music, Avda Rebouças 2315, 04501-30 São Paulo. *President: Carlos Branco.*

BULGARIA

AVA Records, 10/83 Bassanovitch Str., 9010 Varna. *Managing Director: Anatoly Vapirov.*
Balkanton Records, 6 Haidoushka Poliana Str, 1612 Sofia. *Managing Director: Georgi Vachev.*
Denis Records, 25 Shipka Str, 1504 Sofia. *Managing Director: Daniel Rizov.*
DS Music, 17 Mizia Str, 1124 Sofia. *Directors: Lubomir Velev and Ivan Vulkov.*
Kings Records, 37 Hristo Botev Bld, 1000 Sofia. *Managing Director: Valentin Markov.*
Mega Music Ltd, 2 Trapizitza Str, Sofia 1000. *Managing Director: Mrs Dora Tchernkva.*
Riva Sound Records Ltd, Fl 3, 103 Maria Luiza Blvd, 1202 Sofia. *Managing Director: Rumen Bonchev.*
Union Media Ltd, 4th Floor, 71A Evlogi Georgiev Blvd, 1142 Sofia. *President: Martin Zachariev.*

CANADA

A&M/Island Records, 1345 Denison Street, Markham, ON L3R 5V2. *Promotion: Randy Wells.*
Alert Music, 305 - 41 Britain Street, Toronto ON M5A 1R7. *Promotion: Kathy Meisler.*
Ambassador Music, DVPO 43029, Calgary, AB T2J 5C6. *A&R Manager: Wayne Chaulk.*
Attic Music Group, 102 Atlantic Avenue, Toronto, ON M6K 1X9. *President: Alexander Mair.*
Audiogram, 822 Rue Sherbrooke Est, Montreal, PQ H2L 1K4. *Chairman: Michel Belanger.*
BMG Music Canada Inc., 150 John Street, 6th Floor, Toronto, ON M5V 3C3. *Contact: David Bendeth.*
Boomtown Music, PO Box 265, Station C, Toronto, ON M6S 3P4. *Head Of A&R: Kevin Leflar.*
Botany Park Records & Music Publishing Co, 361 Walter Drive, Keswick, ON L4P 3A8. *President: Marlaine Rennocks.*
Brass Ring Productions, PO Box 1266 Station A, Kelowna, BC V1Y 7V8. *President/Personal Manager: Becky Chapman.*
Chacka Alternative Music Inc, 3155 Halpern, St Laurent, PQ H4S 1P5. *President: Bob Chacra.*
Contagious Records, PO Box 183, 905 Croydon Avenue, Winnipeg, MB R3M 3S7. *Contact: Roman Panchyshyn.*
Current/Rage Records and Mgmt, 4 Bowden Street, Toronto, ON M4K 2X2. *President: Gerry Young.*
Diffusion i Media, 4487 Adam Street, Montreal, PQ H1V 1T9. *Contact: Jean-Francois Denis.*
Distribution Fusion III, 5455 Paré #101, Montreal, PQ H4P 1P7. *National Promotions: Nadine Campbell.*
DMT Records, 11714-113th Avenue, Edmonton, AB T5G 0J8. *President: Danny Makarm.*
Duke Street Records, 121 Logan Avenue, Toronto, ON M4M 2M9. *Public Relations: Andy Hermant.*
Ed Preston Enterprises Inc, 192 Tweedsdale Crescent, Oakville, ON L6L 4P7. *President & General Manager: Ed Preston.*

EMC Records Of Canada, 189 Scugog Street, Bowmanville, ON L1C 3J9. *Contact: Paul Andrew Smith.*
EMI Music Canada, 3109 American Drive, Mississauga, ON L4V 1B2. *Public Relations: Liz McElheran.*
Festival Records, 3271 Main Street, Vancouver, BC V5V 3M6. *Public Relations: Valdine Ciwko.*
Forte Records And Productions Inc., 320 Spadina Road, Toronto, ON M5R 2V6. *Contact: Dawna Zeeman.*
Fringe Product, PO Box 670, Station A, Toronto, ON M5W 1G2. *General Manager: Angus MacKay.*
Heaven Bent Music Corp, 11 Hopewell Crescent, Hamilton, ON L8J 1P3. *General Manager: Kathie Pietron.*
Heritage Music, 311-41 Antrim Cr., Scarborough, ON M1P 4T1. *Contact: Jack Boswell.*
Hi-Bias Records Inc, 49 Beckett Avenue, Toronto, ON M6L 2B3. *Director: Nick Fiorucci.*
Hypnotic Records, 96 Spadina Avenue, 9th Floor, Toronto, ON M5V 2J6. *Contact: Daryn Barry.*
Icedrum Records, PO Box 2310, Station A, Sudbury, ON P3A 4S8. *Contact: James Hunt.*
Inner Music, 65 Front Street W, Units 116-165, Toronto, ON M5J 1E6. *Contact: Steve Holt.*
Intrepid Music, 93 Hazelton Avenue, 3rd Floor, Toronto, ON M5R 2E1. *Public Relations: Andy McLean.*
John H Lennon Music Ltd, 1235 Bay Street, Suite 400, Toronto, ON M5R 3K4. *President: John Lennon; Managing Director: Lenny Moore*
Joe-Radio, Suite 8, 299 Lesmill Road, Toronto, ON M3B 2U1. *Contact: Christine Rodway.*
Justin Time Records Inc, 5455 Paré #101, Montreal, PQ H4P 1P7. *National Promotions: Nadine Campbell.*
KSM Records, 2305 Vista Court, Coquitlam, BC V3J 6W2. *President: David London.*
LA Records, PO Box 1096 Hudson, PQ J0P 1V0. *Producer: Michael Lengies.*
LCDM Entertainment, 2-19 Victoria Avenue W, Weston ON M9N 1E3. *Public Relations/Promotion: L C DiMarco.*
Les Disques Passeport Inc, PO Box 529, Succursale Beaubien, Montreal, PQ H2G 3E2. *Public Relations: Marc Racine.*
Les Disques Rubicon, 835 A Querbes, Outremont, PQ H2V 3X1. *Contact: Gilles Bedard.*
Magnum Records, 8607 128 Avenue, Edmonton, AB T5E 0G3. *Contact: Bill Maxim.*
Margaree Sound, 225 The Lake Driveway, West Ajax, ON L1S 5A3. *President and Chief Executive Officer: Russell Daige.*
Master Factory, 11714-113th Avenue, Edmonton, AB T5G 0J8. *President: Gerry Dere.*
MCA Records Canada, 2450 Victoria Park Avenue, Willowdale, ON M2J 4A2. *Promotion: Bill Banham.*
Murder Records, 1588 Grandville Street, Halifax, NS B3J 1X1. *Promotion: Colin MacKenzie.*
Nightlife Records, 2533A Yonge Street, Toronto, ON M4P 2H9. *Contact: Joey Cee.*
Oasis Productions Limited, 76 Cadorna Avenue, Toronto, ON M4J 3X1. *Vice President: Ron Korb.*
PolyGram Records Of Canada, 1345 Denison Street, Markham, ON L3R 5V2. *Contact: Bob Ansell.*
Quantum Records, 170A Baldwin Street, Toronto, ON M5T 1L8. *Contact: Mike Alyanak.*
Quinlan Road Ltd, Box 933, Stratford, ON N5A 7M3. *Controller: Bill Bruce.*
RDR Music Group, 299 Lesmill Road, Suite 8, Toronto, ON M3B 2U1. *President: Joe Wood.*
Record Peddler Distribution, 621 Yonge St, Toronto, ON M4Y 1Z5. *President: Ben Hoffman.*
Resort Records, 14 Sumach Street, Toronto, ON M5A 1J4. *President: Joe Bamford.*
Roto Noto, 148 Erin Avenue, Hamilton, ON L8K 4W3. *Promotion: Elaine Domsy.*
Sam Cat Records, 8 Woodlands Road, St Albert, AB T8N 3L9. *Contact: Peter Jansen.*
Savannah Music Inc, 123 Applefield Drive, Scarborough, ON M1P 3Y5. *Director of Canadian Operations: Bill Carruthers.*
Scratch Records, PO Box 5381, Whitehorse, YK Y1A 4Z2. *Producer: Daniel Janke.*
Skylark Records, 3964 W 18th Avenue, Vancouver, BC V6S 1B7. *Contact: George Laverock.*
Slak Productions, 9 Hector Avenue, Toronto, ON M6G 3G2. *President: Al Kussin.*
Sony Music Entertainment Canada, 1121 Leslie Street, North York, ON M3C 2J9. *Imports Manager: John Ellis Thomson.*
Sound Solutions, 5905 Thimens, St Laurent, PQ H4S 1V8. *Public Relations/Promotion: Frank Trimarchi.*
Sparwood Music Productions, PO Box 270, Bentley, AB T0C 0J0. *Manager: Dick Damron.*
Spinner Music Group Inc, Third Floor, 68 Water Street, Vancouver, BC V6B 1A4. *President: Ken Spence; Managing Director: Wolfgang Burandt.*
Stony Plain Records, PO Box 861, Edmonton, AB T5J 2I8. *President: Holger Peterson.*
Sunnydays Records, 6263 28th Avenue, Rosemont, Montreal, PQ H1T 3H8. *Talent Search/Manager: Fadel Chidiac.*
Tembo Music Canada Inc, 284 Church Street, Oakville, ON L6J 7N2. *Contact: J. Edward Preston.*
The Sunshine Group, 275 Selkirk Avenue, Winnipeg, MB R2W 2L5. *Manager: Ness Michaels.*
Third Wave Productions Ltd, PO Box 563, Gander, NF A1V 2E1. *President: R Archibald Bonnell.*
Unidisc Music Inc, 57B Hymus Blvd, Pointe Claire, PQ H9R 4T2. *President: George Cucuzzella.*
Virgin Music Canada, Rundle House, 514 Jarvis Street, Toronto, ON M4Y 2H6. *Public Relations: Carole MacDonald.*
Warner Music Canada, 1810 Birchmount Road, Scarborough, ON M1P 2J1. *Promotion: Randy Stark.*
Windchime Records, 99 Ivy Street, Toronto, ON M4L 2H8. *Contact: Terry Watada.*

CHILE

Alerce Producciones Fonograficas SA, Jorge Washington 380 Ñuñoa, Santiago de Chile. *General Manager: Gloria Trumper.*
BMG Chile SA, Avda 11 de Septiembre 2353, 3° Piso providencia, Santiago de Chile. *General Manager: Edgardo Larrazabal.*
Calipso Records, Thompson 3450 Estación Central, Santiago de Chile. *Commercial Manager: Hugo Ascueta Norambuena.*
Ediciones Musicales Fermata Ltda, Ebro 2751, Of. 609 Las Condes 41, Santiago de Chile. *General Manager: Eliana Cisternas.*
Union Producciones SA, California 2380, Santiago de Chile. *Director General: Jorge Saint-Jean.*

COLOMBIA

Ava Limitada, Carrera 54, n. 75-45Apartado Aereo 50-804, Barranquilla. *Proprietor: Tony Fortou.*
BMG / Ariola de Colombia SA, Calle 67, n. 7-94, 12°, Santa Fe de Bogotá DC. *Director General: Francisco Villanueva.*
Codiscos, Compañia Colombiana de Discos SA, Carrera 67, n.1, Sur 92 Guayabal, 1428 Medellín. *President: César Vallejo.*
Discos Dago, C / 33AA, n. 81-25, Medelíln. *President: Dario Gómez Zapata.*
Discos Philips, Calle 13, n. 51-39, 4282 Santa Fe de Bogotá. *Commercial Manager: Martín Wowgemunt.*
G&M Es Musica, Calle 114, n. 6A-92, Of. 419, Zona D Cundinamarca, Santa Fe de Bogota. *General Manager: Javier García M.*

CROATIA

Adam Records, Anke Butorac 12, 52000 Pula. *Managing Director: Dario Matosevic.*
Crno Bijeli Svijet, Avenija M. Drzica BB, 41000 Zagreb. *Managing Director: Branko Paic.*
Croatia Records, Medjugorska 61, 10000 Zagreb. *Director of International Business Affairs: Djordje Kekic.*
Denyken Music, Senoina 1, 41000 Zagreb. *Managing Director: Denis Mujavdzic.*
Esnaf, Gunduliceva 29, 41000 Zagreb. *Managing Director: Husein Hasanefendic.*
Jazzette Records, Vukovar Ave 35, Zagreb. *Vice President: Kolya Petrovic.*
Koncept VD, Trg Bana Josipa Jelacica 5, 41000 Zagreb. *Manager: Zvonmir Bencic.*
Skalinada, Dubrovacka 23, 58000 Split. *Director: Zdenko Runjic.*

T R I P , Argentinska 3, 10000 Zagreb. *A & R Manager: Aleksandar Dragas.*
Tutico Music, Veprinkacka 16, 41000 Zagreb. *Managing Director: Zrinko Tutić.*

CUBA

Artex SA, 5a Ave, n. 8010, Miramar, Havana. *General Manager: Tony Pinelli.*
Caribe Productions Inc., Ave 17, n. 18401 Municpio Playa, Havana. *President: Federico García Antonio.*
Egrem, C/18, n. 105, Entre 1-3, Miramar, Havana. *Director General: Julio Ballester.*

CZECH REPUBLIC

BMG Ariola (Czech Republic), Hellichova 5, Prague 1. *Managing Director: Cap Petr.*
Bonton Music, Ostrov-Stvanice 858, 170 21 Prague 7. *Managing Director: Visek Pavel.*
Indies Records, Mildy Horakove 25, 602 00 Brno. *Managing Director: Pales Milan.*
Marco Music, Sokolskà 8, 70100 Ostrava 1. *Managing Director: Krasny Denek.*
Monitor-EMI Ltd, Kova'rova 39, 15500 Prague 5, Stodulky. *Managing Director: Vladimir Kocandrle.*
Popron, U Lanové Dràhy 3, Prague 1. *Managing Director: Alynsky Zdenek.*

DENMARK

BMG Genlyd Grammofon Denmark, Overgarden Neden Vandet 17/2, DK-1414 Copenhagen K. *Managing Director: Dietmar Glodde.*
Cloudland, Skt Jørgens Allé 7 O, G6 1th, DK-1615 Copenhagen. *Managing Director: Simon Sheika.*
ELAP Music A/S, Bransagervej 2-10, 9490 Pandrup. *Promotion: Steffen Lund Nielsen.*
EMI Medley Denmark, Vognmagergade 10, DK-1120 Copenhagen K. *Managing Director: Michael Ritto.*
Foenix Music APS, Sonder Alle 12, DK-8000 Aarhus C. *Managing Director: Ole Kjaer.*
Forgalet Kragen (Craw Records), Christians Brygge 3, 1219 Copenhagen K. *Administration Director: Svend Nielsen.*
Iceberg Records, Ronne Alle 78A, DK-8600 Silkeborg. *Managing Director: Manfred Zahringer.*
Kavan Music Scandinavia, Klokkestobervef 39, DK-8800 Viborg. *Manager: Karl Aage Jensen.*
Kick Music ApS, Energivej 42 B, DK-2750 Ballerup. *Managing Director: Michael Quvang.*
Klepton Records & Publishing, Langdries 4, DK-9450 Haaltert. *Managing Director: Brits Wilfried.*
Mega Scandinavia A/S, Indiakaj 1, DK-2100 Copenhagen. *Vice President: Cai Leitner; Director of A & R and Marketing: Jesper Ban.*
Olafssongs, Anker Heegaardsgade 2, ST TV, DK-1572 Copenhagen V. *Managing Director: Finn Olafsson.*
Olga Musik ApS, Boleetvej 4, DK-8680 Ry. *Managing Director: Birger Hansen.*
Olufsen Records, Knudsvej 8, DK-1903 Frederiksberg C. *Managing Director: Peter Olufsen.*
Pineapple Records ApS, Frodesgade 74, DK-6700 Esbjerg. *Managing Director: Helge Engelbrecht.*
Polygram-Sonet Denmark, Emdrupvej 115A, DK-2400 Copenhagen NV. *A&R Manager: David Rowley.*
Rock Owl Records, Tagensvej 204, DK-2400 Copenhagen. Managing Director: Kim Kofod.
Sony Music Denmark, Vognmagergade 10, DK-1120 Copenhagen. *Managing Director: Steen Sorgenfrei.*
Steeplechase Productions, PO Box 35, Slots Aleen 16, DK-2930 Klampenborg. *Managing Director: Nils Winther.*
Storyville, Dortheavej 39, DK-2400 Copenhagen NV. *Managing Director: Karl Emil Knudsen.*
Street Dance Records ApS, Vestergade 17, DK-1456 Copenhagen K. *Managing Director: Peter Larsen.*
Sundance / Stunt Music, Kongevej 47 B, DK-1610 Copenhagen V. *Managing Director: Peter Littauer.*
Virgin Denmark, Ny Vestergade 7 B, DK-1471 Copenhagen K. *Managing Director: Henriette Blix.*
Warner Music Denmark, Antoinettevej 2, DK-2500 Valby/Copenhagen. *Managing Director: Finn Work.*
Zing Zing Music Production, Kirkegaardsstraede 3, DK-9000 Aalborg. *Managing Director: Birgitte Rode.*

ECUADOR

Fabrica Ecuatoriana de Discos SA, Km. 7-1/2 Via a la Costa, 09018 56 Guayaquil. *President: Francisco Feraud Aroca.*

ESTONIA

Forte, P O Box 472, EE0090 Tallinn. *Managing Director: Mart Maripuu.*
Salumusik, Tondi 17a, Tallinn. *Managing Director: Madis Salum.*

FIJI

Procera Music Co Ltd, PO Box 10272,Suva. *Managing Director: Anilesh Chandra.*
South Pacific Recordings, PO Box 17, Nadi. *Managing Director: Ravindra Patel.*

FINLAND

Aani Records, Aholantie 43, 03150, Huhmari. *Managing Director: Tapani Rinne.*
Amigo Musik Finland, Cygnaeuksenkatu 12, 00100 Helsinki. *Managing Director: Martti Heikkinen.*
Bad Vagum, PO Box 362, 90101 Oulu. *Managing Director: Kari Heikonen.*
Bluebird Music/Blue Bubble Records, Arinatie 8, 00370 Helsinki. *Managing Director: Niko Nordström.*
Bluelight Records, PO Box 153, 00171 Helsinki. *Managing Director: Mika Myyryläinen.*
BMG/Ariola Finland, PO Box 173, Vattuniemenranta 2, 00211 Helsinki. *Managing Director: Kuusi Maija.*
EMI Finland, Arinatie 6 E, PO Box 28, 00371 Helsinki. *Managing Director: H. Puhakka.*
Evidence/Dig It/Fazer Records, PO Box 169, 02101 Espoo. *Label Manager: Pia Louhivouri.*
Flamingo, Vapaalantie 2, 01650 Vantaa. *Managing Director: Vexi Salmi.*
Gaga Goodies, PO Box 47, 13211 Hämeenlinna. *Managing Director: Kari Helenius.*
Goofin' Records, PO Box 63, 01601 Vantaa. *Managing Director: Pete Hakonen.*
Hiljaiset Levyt Records, PO Box 211, 33201 Tampere. *Managing Director: Jukka Junttila.*
Megamania Music, Hämeentie 6 A 1, 00530 Helsinki. *Managing Director: Atte Blom.*
MIPU Music, PO Box 15, 82300 Rääkkylä. *Managing Director: Heikki Kempainen.*
Olarin Musiiki, PO Box 20, 02211 Espoo. *Managing Director: Timo Närväinen.*
Poko Records, PO Box 483, 33101 Tampere. *Manager: Pertti Palkoaho.*

Polarvox, Arinatie 2 A, 00370 Helsinki. *Managing Director: Leena Juuranto.*
PolyGram Finland, Vattuniemenranta 2, PO Box 172, 00211 Helsinki. *Managing Director: Gugi Kokljuschkin.*
Pro Records, P Hesperiankatu 9 A 7, 00260 Helsinki. *Contact: Eero Koivistoinen.*
Real Art, Pursimiehenkatu 26 i, 00150 Helsinki. *Managing Director: Pasi Ervi.*
Rockadillo Records, PO Box 35, 33201 Tampere. *Managing Director: Tapio Korjus.*
Sähkö Recordings, Perämiehenkatu 11, 00150, Helsinki. *Contact: Tommi Grönlund.*
Siboney/Love Records, Hämeentie 6 A 1, 00530 Helsinki. *Managing Director: Sini Perho.*
Sony Music Finland, PO Box 12, 02171 Espoo. *Managing Director: Antti Holma.*
Spinefarm Records, Elimäenkatu 12-16 D, 5th Floor, 00510 Helsinki. *Managing Director: Riku Paakkonen.*
Strawberry Records, PO Box 17, 01351 Vantaa. *Managing Director: Pasi Kostiainen.*
Stupido Twins Records, PO Box 301, 00121 Helsinki. *Head of Public Relations: Joose Berglund.*
Syrene Music, Saarnitie 14a, 00780 Helsinki. *Contact: Jukka Linkola.*
WEA/Warner Music Finland, Melkonkatu 28 E, 00210 Helsinki. *Managing Director: Marita Kaasalainen.*
Zen Garden, PO Box 76, 00501, Helsinki. *Managing Director: Kari Hynninen.*

FRANCE

AB Disques, 144 Ave. du Pdt Wilson, F-93210 La Plaine St Denis. *Chairman: Jean-Michel Fava.*
Airplay Records, 39 Rue de la Rochefoucauld, F-92100 Boulogne. *Head Of Marketing: Jean-Michel Doue.*
Ariola, 2 Rue des Quatre Fils, F-75003,Paris. *Label Manager: Nathalie Mercenier.*
Atoll Music, 18/20 Rue du Borrego, F-75020 Paris. *Chairman: Charles Ibgui.*
Auvidis, BP 21, 47 Ave. Paul Vaillant Couturier, F-94251 Genitilly Cedex. *Chairman: Louis Bricard.*
AYAA Disques, BP 167, F-51056 Reims Cedex. *Owner: Denis Thieblemont.*
Baya, 18 Rue de Reuilly, F-75012 Paris. *Managing Director: Françis Kertekian.*
Black Et Noir Records, 4 Rue Valdemaine, F-49100 Angers. *Head Of Promotion: Paco.*
Boucherie Productions, 15 Bis Rue Du Plateau, F-75019 Paris. *Director: Natali Luc.*
Carrere Music, 27 Rue de Suresne, F-75008 Paris. *General Manager: Michael Wijnen.*
Celine Music, 44 Rue de Miromesnil, F-75008 Paris. *Contact: Vline Buggy.*
Celluloid, 50 Rue Stendahl, F-75020 Paris. *Contact: Gilbert Castro.*
Cobalt, 145 Rue De Ménilmontant, F-75020 Paris. *Managing Director: Philippa Conrath.*
Columbia / Epic Records, 131 Ave de Wagram, F-75017 Paris. *Directors: Olivier Montfort, Laurence Le Ny.*
Declic Communication, 45 Rue St Sebastien, F-75011 Paris. *Chairman: Eric Basset.*
Delabel, 3 Rue des Minimes, F-75003 Paris. *Chairman: Emmanuel de Buretel.*
Delphine Productions, 150 Bvd Haussman, F-75008 Paris. *Chairman: Paul De Senneville.*
Dixie Frog, 218 Rue du Faubourg St Denis, F-75010 Paris. *Chairman: Philippe Langlois.*
EMI France, 37 Rue Camille Desmoulins, F-92133 Issy Les Moulineaux. *Chairman: Gilbert Ohayon.*
EPM, 188 Bvd Voltaire, F-75011 Paris. *Chairman: François Dacla.*
Eric Taffoureau Productions / Valotte Records International, 138 Rue Nationale, BP No 46, F-75013 Paris. *Director: Eric Taffoureau.*
F Communications, 11 Rue de Clichy, F-75003 Paris. *Prime Minister: Eric Norand.*
FGL, 25 Boulevard Arago, F-75013 Paris. *Managing Director: Thierry Wolf.*
Francis Dreyfus Music, 26 Ave. Kléber, F-75116 Paris. *Chairman: Francis Dreyfus.*
GRRR, 134 rue d'Estienne d'Orves, 92140 Clamart, France. *Contact: Jean-Jacques Birge.*
Happy Music, 38 Rue Voltaire, F-92800 Puteaux. *Label Manager: Frédérick Giteau.*
Island / Barclay, 16 Rue des Fossés St Jacques, F-75005 Paris. *Managing Director: Pascal Negre.*
Karmel Music, 73 Rue de Turbigo, F-75003 Paris. *General Director: Edward Aprahamian.*
Larsen Records & Fanzine, 116 Rue Du Crey, F-73230 St Alban Leysse. *Contact: Denis Oliveres.*
Made In Heaven, 6 Rue Rémy de Gourmont, F-75019 Paris. *Label Manager: Mathias Jeannin.*
Mango, 20 Rue Des Fossés St Jacques, F-75005 Paris. *Chairman: Philippe Constantin.*
MCA Music Entertainment SA, 65 Rue D'Anjou, F-75008 Paris. *Assistant to the President: Vicki Rummler.*
MSI SA, Baudrin, Labastide Castel Amouroux, F-47250 Bouglon. *Contact: Pierre-Emmanuel Gilbert.*
Musea, 68 La Tinchotte, F-57117 Retonfey. *President: Bernard Gueffier.*
Musidisc, BP 190, 3/5 Rue de Albert Vatimesnil, F-92300 Levallois-Perret. *Chairman: François Grandchamp.*
Mute France, 17 Rue Soyer, F-92200 Neuilly. *Public Relations: Helene Lemoine.*
Ness Music, 35 Rue Petit, F-75019 Paris. *Director: Nessim Saroussi.*
PEM Claude Martinez, 59 Bvd Exelmans, F-75016 Paris. *Chairman: Claude Martinez.*
Phonogram, 20 Rue des Fossés St Jacques, F-75005 Paris Cedex 05. *Managing Director: Yves Bigot.*
Polydor, 22 Rue des Fossés St Jacques, F-75005 Paris. *General Manager: Bruno Gerentes.*
Polygram France, 20 Rue des Fossés St Jacques, F-75005 Paris. *Chairman: Alfredo Gangotena.*
RCA Records, 17 Rue Soyer, F-92200 Neuilly. *General Manager: Antoine Chouchani.*
Remark Records, 89 Rue de la Boétie, F-75008 Paris. *Chairman: Marc Lumbroso.*
Roadrunner, 3-5 Rue de Albert Vatimesnil, F-92300 Levallois-Perret. *Label Manager: Stéphane Saunier.*
Rosebud Records, 10/12 Rue Jean Guy, F-35000 Rennes. *Chairman: Alan Gac.*
RRose Selavy, BP 521, F-35006 Rennes Cedex. *Company Secretary: Olivier Mellano.*
Scorpio Music, 12 Avenue George V, F-75008 Paris. *President: Henri Belold.*
Sephora, La Musique De La Vie (Dept of Gam International SA), 6 Place Jean-Paul Sartre, F-51170 Fismes. *Manager: Marc Brunet.*
Sidonie, 31 Rue François 1er, F-75008 Paris. *Chairman: Christain Dulcy.*
Skydog / Kind Of Groove, 32 Av Claude Velle Faux, F-75010 Paris. *PDG: Marc Zermati.*
Sony Music France, 131 Avenue de Wagram, F-75017 Paris. *Chairman: Paul-René Albertini.*
Topomic Music, 26 Rue L M Nordmann, F-92250 La Garenne-Colombes. *President: Pierre Jaubert.*
Top Records, 17 Ave. du Président Wilson, F-75116 Paris. *Label Manager: Alain Belolo.*
Vinilkosmo, c/o Eurokka, Esperanto Rok Asocio, F-31450 Donneville. *Director: Floreal Martorell.*
Virgin France, 11 Place des Vosges, F-75004 Paris. *Chairman: Emmanuel de Buretel.*
Vogue, 2 Rue des Quatre Fils, F-75003 Paris. *Chairman: Fabrice Nataf.*
Warner Musis France / WEA Music, 102 Ave. du Prsident Kennedy, F-75116 Paris. *Chairman: Marco-Antonio Bignotti.*
XIII Bis Music Group, 34 Rue Eugene Flachat, F-75017 Paris. *Managing Director: Laurent Dreux-Leblanc; Music Director: Brian Rawling.*

GERMANY

Arcade Deutschland, Kaiser Wilhelm Ring 17, D-40505 Düsseldorf. *Managing Director: Sylvian Jonkergow.*
Ata Tak Records, Kölner Str 226 F, D-40227 Düsseldorf. *Director: Frank Fenstermacher.*
Bellaphon Records, Mainzer Landstrasse 87-89, D-60329 Frankfurt. *Chairman: Jutta Zizanovic-Riedel.*
BMG Ariola Munich, Steinhauserstrasse 1-3, D-81677 Munich. *Managing Director: Thomas Stein.*

Century Media Records, Bissenkamp 11-13, D-44135 Dortmund. *Managing Director: Robert Kampf.*
CMP Records, PO Box 1129, D-52368 Kreuzau. *Managing Director: Ulrich Kurt Rattay.*
Comma Records & Tapes, PO Box 2148, D-63243 Neu-Isenburg. *Director: Roland Bauer.*
Commissioned Music, Hauptstr. 30, D-10827 Berlin. *Managing Director: Blixa Bargeld.*
Crosscut Records, PO Box 10 65 24, D-2800 Bremen. *Managing Director: Detevv Hoegen.*
EastWest Records GmbH, Heussweg 25, D-20255 Hamburg. *Artist Marketing Director: Boris Loehe.*
EMI Records, Maarweg 149, Postfach 30 03 29, D-50825 Cologne. *Managing Director: Helmut Fest.*
Enemy Productions Inc, #2 Edward Schmid Str 28, D-81541 Munich. *President: Michael Knuth.*
Exile Records, Lintuperstr. 39, D-12305 Berlin. *Managing Director: Ted Baxter.*
Garbitowski, Metzer Str 30, D-50677 Cologne. *Owner and Director: Jürgen Garbitowski.*
Global Records, Nederlingerstr. 21, D-80638 Munich. *Managing Director: Peter Kirsten.*
Grover Records, PO Box 3072, D-48016 Münster. *Managing Assistant: Richard Jung.*
Hansa Musik Produktion, Wittelbachstr. 18, D-10707 Berlin. *Managing Director: André Selleneit.*
Hyperium Records GmbH, PO Box 910127, D-90259 Nürnberg. *General Manager: Oliver Rösch.*
Intercord, Aixhiemer Strasse 26, D-70619 Stuttgart. *International Label Manager: Peter Cadera.*
Jaro Medien GmbH, Bismarckstr. 83, D-28293 Bremen. *Managing Director: Ulrich Balss.*
Jupiter Records, Hoechlstrasse 2, D-81675 Munich. *Managing Director: Joachim Neubauer.*
Logic Records, Strahlenbergerstr. 125A, D-63067 Offenbach. *Managing Director: Matthias Martinsohn.*
M.A.D. Fuesgen/Nickel GBR, Hagelberger Str 48, D-10965 Berlin. *Owner: Ute Fuesgen.*
Messidor Musik GmbH, Kleine Bockenheimer Str 10-12, D-60313 Frankfurt. *Managing Director: Goetz Woerner.*
Modern Music, Kurfuersten Str. 23, D-10785 Berlin. *International Manager: Birgit Nielsen.*
Music Box GmbH, Rahlstedter Str 65, D-22149 Hamburg. *Managing Director: Hubertus Branzko.*
Obsession Records, Mosel Str 24, D-50674 Cologne. *President: Cordula Schütten.*
Orgasm Records, Obertor Str 6, D-35792 Löhnberg. *Label Boss: Erich Knodt.*
Perfect Beat, Industriestr. 37, D-33034 Brakel. *Managing Director: Dieter Schubert.*
Piranha Kultur & Medien Production GmbH, Carmer Str 11, D-10623 Berlin. *Managing Director: Borkowsky Akbar.*
Play It Again Sam (Germany), Spaldingstr. 74, D-20097 Hamburg. *Managing Director: Mark Chung.*
PolyGram Germany, Glockengiesserwall 3, Postfach 10 49 09, D-20095 Hamburg. *Chairman: Wolf Gramatke.*
Rough Trade Germany, Eickeler Str. 25, D-44561 Herne. *Contact: Carsten Stricker.*
Sony Music Entertainment Germany, PO Box 10 19 60, Bleichstr. 64, D-60313 Frankfurt. *Manager: Rüdiger Fliege.*
SPV GmbH, PO Box 1147, D-30537 Hannover. *General Manager: Manfred Schutz.*
Sub Pop Germany, Gruener Weg 25, D-37688 Beverungen. *Managing Director: Reinhard Holstein.*
Subway Records, Vohwinkeler Str 154, D-42329 Wuppertal. *Managing Director: Michael Schuster.*
Synthetic Product Records, PO Box 690441, D-30613 Hannover. *Contact: Lorenz Macke.*
T'Bwana Sound/Big Easy, Schleswigerstr 19, D-44145 Dortmund. *Contact: Helmut Philipps.*
TGM Musikverlag Nietsch, Green, Kleinhammer, Max Beer Str 25, D-10119 Berlin. *Chief Executive Officer: Tim Green.*
TRITT Records, Siegener Str 6, D-65936 Frankfurt. *Owner: Nils Selzer.*
TRIXX Musikproduktion GmbH, Prinzessinnen Str 16, D-10969 Berlin. *Studio Manager: Klaus Knapp.*
Verlag Plaene GmbH, Balkenstr. 17-19, D-44137 Dortmund. *Managing Director: Friedrich Liedtke.*
Vielklang Musikproduktion GmbH, Forster Str 4/5, D-10999 Berlin. *Managing Director: Joerg Fukking.*
Virgin Germany, Herzogstr. 64, D-80803 Munich. *International Label Manager: Michael Bindernagel.*
Warner Music Germany, Hallerstr. 40, D-20146 Hamburg. *Manager: Hans Barth.*
Westpark Music, PO Box 260 227, Rathenauplatz 4, D-50515 Cologne. *President: Ulli Hetscher.*

GREECE

Akti, 311 Mesogheion Street, 15231 Athens. *Head Of Promotion: Eleni Mavrovounioti.*
Ano Kato Records, PP Germanou Street 19, 54622 Salonica. *Managing Director: George Tsakalides.*
BMG Ariola Greece, Mesogheion 230 and Perikleous 1, Holargos, 15561 Athens. *Managing Director: Miltos Karatzas.*
Hitch Hyke Records, Kosma Balanou Street 5, 11636 Athens. *Managing Director: Hannelore Thospann.*
Iptamenoi Diski (Flying Discs), 24 Korytsas Street, Papagou, 15669 Athens. *Managing Director: Theo Manikas.*
Lyra, Zalokosta Street 4, 10671 Athens. *Managing Director: Panagiotis Maravelias.*
Minos - EMI, 245-247 Mesogheion Avenue, 15451 Athens. *Chairman: Makis Matsas.*
Pegasus Records, Odiseos Androutsou Street 3-5, 15772 Athens. *Managing Director: Petros Koutsoumbas.*
Penguin Ltd, 58 Lambrou Katsuni Street, 11471 Athens. *General Manager: P. Stavroski.*
Polygram Greece, Mesogheion Avenue 296, 15510 Athens. *Managing Director: Vicotr Antippas.*
Sony Music Entertainment Greece, 311 Mesogheion Street, 15231 Athens. *Managing Director: Dimitris Yarmenitis.*
Virgin Records Greece, 557 Mesogheion Avenue, 15344 Athens. *Managing Director: Yannis Petridis.*
WEA Greece, 319 Mesogheion Avenue, 15231 Athens. *Managing Director: Ion Stamboulis.*
Wipe Out Records, PO Box 80512, 18510 Piraeus. *Managing Director: Thodoris Kritharis.*

GREENLAND

ULO - Greenlandic Music, PO Box 184, DK-3911 Sisimiut. *Production Manager: Karsten Sommer.*

HONG KONG

Amo Record Corporation (IFPI), PO Box 95170, Tsim Sha Tsui Post Office, Kowloon. *General Manager: Paul Leung.*
BMG Hong Kong Ltd, 11/F Peninsula Office Tower, 18 Middle Road, Tsimshatsui, Kowloon. *Contact: Steve Beaver.*
HNH International Ltd, 8/F Kai It Bldg, 58 Pak Tai Street, Tokwawan, Kowloon. *Managing Director: Klaus Heymann.*
Polygram Records Ltd, 1503 Garley Building, 233-239 Nathan Road, Kowloon. *Managing Director: Douglas Chan.*
Rock In Records, Room A, 24/FHaven Commercial Bldg, 8 Tsing Fung Street, Causeway Bay. *General Manager: Keith Yip.*
Schtung Records Ltd, Top Floor, 2 Kennedy Road. *Managing Director: Morton Wilson.*
Sea Music, 703 Manson House, 74-78 Nathan Road, Kowloon. *Managing Director: Richard Cooper.*
Sony Music Entertainment (Hong Kong) Ltd, 4/F Acme Building, 22-28 Nanking Street, Kowloon. *Contact: Peter Chiu.*
Virgin/EMI (Hong Kong) Ltd, Room 3201-7 Shell Tower, Times Square, 1 Matheson Street, Causeway Bay. *Managing Director: Herman Ho.*
Warner Music Hong Kong Ltd, 12/f Peninsula Office Tower, 18 Middle Road, Tsimshatsui, Kowloon. *Managing Director: Paco Wong.*
Wing Hang Record Trading Co Ltd, Flat A, 21/F, Lung Shing Industrial Centre, 142-148 Texaco Road, Tsuen Wan NT. *Managing Director: Tang Ping Hang; Chief Marketing Executive: Winnie Tang.*

HUNGARY

Alt Product, 5002 Szolnok, PO Box 76. *Managing Director: Bela Pap.*
Bahia Records, Baross u 6, 1088 Budapest. *A&R Manager: Csaba Hajnoczy.*
BMG Hungary, szt Istvàn Park 16, 1137 Budapest. *Managing Director: Jànos Kallus.*
EMI - Quint Records, Terez krt. 19, 1067 Budapest. *Managing Director: Jenö Bors.*
HMK Records, Lovag u 2, 1075 Budapest. *Managing Director: Vojislav Nesic.*
Hungaroton Gong, Vörösmarty tér 1, 1051 Budapest. *A&R Managers: laszlo Benkö, Attila Hoth.*
LP Records, Bajscy Zsilinsky u 62, 1054 Budapest. *Managing Director: Norbert Lapis.*
Polygram Hungary Ltd, Steindl Imre u 12, 1054 Budapest. *Managing Director: Laszlo Kegeous.*
Newsis Records, Villàlyi ùt 107, 1118 Budapest. *Managing Director: Robert Mandel.*
Record Express Ltd, Rath György u 6, 1123 Budapest. *Managing Director: Attila Schneider.*
Rosza Records, Maros u 29, 1122 Budapest. *Managing Director: Istvan Rosza.*
Sony Music Hungary, Ponty u 7, 1011 Budapest. *Managing Director: Malcolm Carruthers.*
T3 Records, PO Box 8, 1922 Budapest. *Managing Director: Peter György*
Trottel Records, Hunyadi 4, 1011 Budapest. *Managing Director: Tamàs Rupaszov.*
Warner Music Hungary, Hüvösvölgyi ùt 54 III EP, 1021 Budapest. *Managing Director: Istvan Jooz.*

ICELAND

Bo Haldorson Productions Inc, Box 5445, 125 Reykjavik. *Owner/Director: Bo Haldorson.*
Platonic, Skeifan 17, 108 Reykjavik. *Managing Director: Hilmar Örn Hilmarsson*
Skifan Hf, Skeifan 17, 108 Reykjavik. *Managing Director: Thorvaldur Thorsteinsson.*
Smekkkeysa / Bad Taste, PO Box 710, 121 Reykjavik. *Managing Director: Asmunder Jonsson.*
Spor Hf, Nýbýlavegur 4, PO Box 320, 202 Kópavogur. *Managing Director: Steinar Berg Isleifsson.*

INDONESIA

Jeka Records, Jalan Jembatan Tiga, 38 Blok B-13, Jakarta 14440. *Director: Sofyan Ali.*
Metro Utama Raya Electronics Industry, PO Box 4920/JKTF, Jakarta 11049. *Export Manager: Miss Lisnawati.*
Polygram Records, P.T. Suara Sentral Sejati, Kapuk Utara 89, Jakarta 14460. *Managing Director: Anthony Shih.*
RIS Music Wijaya International (BMG), Mangga Dua Plaza, Komplex Agung Sedaya Blok D/11, Jakarta 10730. *Managing Director: Effendy Widjaja.*
Sony Music, PT Indo Semar Sakti, Jl Jelambar Ilir 2, Jakarta 1460. *Director: Dr Suntono.*
Tira Wahari Lestari (BASF), Tira Building 5th Floor, Jl Hr Rasuna Said Kav, B-3 Jakarta Selatan. *Sales Manager: Johannes Hardiman.*

IRELAND

Ainm Records, 5-6 Lombard Street East, Dublin 2. *Contact : Frank Stubbs.*
Aquarhythms Ltd, 15 Upper Mount Street, Dublin 2. *Label Manager: Ann Pomerantz.*
AX-S Records, 26 Mount Eagle View, Leopardstown Heights, Dublin 18. *Managing Director: Peter Jones.*
Beaumex Music, Unit 45, Western Rockway Business Centre, Lower Ballymount Road, Walkinstown, Dublin 12. *Director: Cathal Tully.*
Beautiful Records, Ballyloughan, Bagnelstown, Co. Carlow. *Managing Director: Kieran Connors.*
BMG Records Ireland, Grafton Buildings, 34 GraftonStreet, Dublin 2. *Managing Director: Freddie Middleton; Press and Promotions Officer: Kathryn Mason.*
Celtic Heartbeat Ltd, 30/32 Sir John Rogerson's Quay, Dublin 2. *Label Manager: Aisling Meehan.*
Claddagh Records, Dame House, Dame Street, Dublin 2. *Production Manager: Tom Sherlock.*
Cross Border Media Ltd, 10 Deer Park, Ashbourne, Co. Meath. *Contact: Oliver Sweeney.*
Dabble Music, The Elms, Richmond Avenue South, Dartry, Dublin 6. *Chief Executive Officer: Pete Blackbyrne.*
Danceline Records, 267 Crodaun Forest Park, Celbridge, Co. Kildare. *Contact: Peter McCluskey .*
Dara Records, Unit 4, Great Ship Street, Dublin 8. *Managing Director: Joe and Paul O'Reilly.*
Dino Entertainment, Dino House, 12 Malborough Court, Malborough Street, Dublin 1. *A&R Manager: Susan Dunne.*
EMI Records (Ireland) Ltd, EMI House, 1 Ailesbury Road, Ballsbridge, Dublin 4. *Managing Director: Willie Kavanagh.*
Goya Records, Thompson House, McCurtain Street, Cork City. *Public Relations Officer: Paul McDermott.*
Grapevine /Solid Records, Alexandra House, Earlsfort Centre, Earlsfort Terrace, Dublin 2. *Managin Director: Peter Kenny; Label Manager: Janine Nallen.*
Green Linnet Records, 17 Lower Baggot Street, Dublin 2. *Contact: Amy Garvey.*
Harmac Music Ltd, 67 Amiens Street, Dublin 1. *Managing Director: Brendan Harvey.*
Harmony Promotions Ltd, PO Box 10, Edenderry, Co. Offaly. *Managing Director: John H Pickering.*
Hazel Music, Dublin Road, Monasterevin, Co. Kildare. *Managing Director: John Kelly.*
Independent Records, The Factory, 35A Barrow Street, Dublin 4. *Contact: Dave O'Grady.*
K-Tel Ireland Ltd/Celtic Collections, 30-32 Sir John Rogerson's Quay, Dublin 2. *General Manager: Sharon Browne.*
Lodge Records, Ballinclea Road, Co. Dublin. *International Manager: Pat Dempsey.*
Lunar / Unicorn Records, 5-6 Lombard Street East, Dublin 2. *Contact: Brian Molloy, Judy Cardiff.*
MCA Records Ireland, 30-32 Sir John Rogerson's Quay, Dublin 2. *General Manager: Dave Pennefather.*
Mother Records, 30-32 Sir John Rogerson's Quay, Dublin 2. *Contact: Elva Tarpey.*
Polygram Records Ireland, 9 Whitefriars, Aungiers Street, Dublin 2. *Managing Director: Paul Keogh.*
Preplay Records, c/o The Galway Arts Centre, 47 Dominick St, Galway. *Managing Director: Philip Gray.*
Rivervalley Records Ltd, Shruthaun, Baltinglass, Co. Wicklow. *Managing Director: Fiona Joyce.*
Round Tower Music, 48 Downside, Skerries, Co. Dublin. *Director: Clive Hudson.*
RSE Records, 11 Station Road, Raheny, Dublin 5. *Directors: Raymond J Smyth, Breide P Smyth.*
Rut Records, c/o The Galway Arts Centre, 47 Dominick Street, Galway. *Managing Director: Philip Gray.*
Sony Music Ireland Ltd, Unit 2, Carriglea Industrial Estate, Naas Road, Dublin 2. *Managing Director: John Sheehan.*
Tara Music Company Ltd, 8 Anne's Lane, Dublin 2. *Managing Director: John Cook.*
Virgin Records Ireland, 1 Ailesbury Road, Ballsbridge, Dublin 4. *Public Relations: Josephine Nestor.*
Warner Music (Ireland) Ltd, Alexandra House, Earlsfort Centre, Earlsfort Terrace, Dublin 2. *Managing Director: Dennis Woods.*
Whirling Discs Ltd, Cairns Hill, Aughamore, Co. Sligo. *Managing Director: Brian McDonagh.*

ITALY

A Tempo Srl, Via Filipo Turati 12, 50136 Florence. *Managing Director: Piero Borri.*
Abraxas Srl, Via Guglielmo Marconi 106, 50131 Florence. *Managng Director: Simone Fringuelli.*
AND Recommended Records Italia, Via Decembrio 26, 20137 Milan. *Managing Director: Alberto Crosta.*

Ala Bianca Group Srl, Via G Mazzoni 34/36, 41100 Modena. *General Manager: Toni Verona.*
Artis/Cramps Records, Via False 33, 36050 Monteviale (Vicenze). *Managing Director: Alfredo Tisocco.*
Baby Records, Via Timavo 34, 20124 Milan. *Managing Director: Monica Dahl.*
Blindness Inc, Rain 10, 39040 Cortaccia. *Managing Director: Giovannetti Reinhold.*
Blu Bus, Via Consolata 5, 11100 Aosta. *Managing Director: Sergio Milani.*
BMG Ariola Italy, Via di S. Alessandro 7, 00131 Rome. *Managing Director: Franco Reali.*
Cave Canem/Spray Records, Via Saline 8/C, 65013 Marina di Citta S. Angelo. Managing Director: Belfino de Leonardis.
Clac Records, Via Salvatore di Giacomo 73, 00142 Rome. *Managers: Massimo Calabrese, Piero Calabrese.*
Contempo Records, Corso de'Tintori 6/18r, 50122 Florence. *International Label Manager: Sebastian Koch.*
EMI Italy, Via Bergamo 315, 21042 Caronno Pertusella (Milan). *International Manager: Nico Spinosa.*
Flying Records, Via R Ruggiero 16D, 80125 Naples. *Managing Director: Flavio Rossi.*
FMA Edizioni Musicali E Discografiche Srl, Via Boccaccio N 47, 20123 Milan. *President: Mario Allione.*
Interbeat, Via A Straedella 174, 00124 Rome. *International Label Manager: Luigi Fedele.*
I Soulzionisti, Largo dell'Olgiata, 15-1s 59 3/2, 00123 Rome. *Managing Director: Stefano Bonagura.*
Kaleidoscopic Music Srl, Viale Manzoni 52, Cerveteri, 00052 Rome. *Contact: Robbie Zee.*
Kindergarten Records, Via Panicale 9, 50123 Florence. *Managing Director: Fabrizio Federighi.*
Klang Records, Via Valle Viola 35, 00141 Rome. *Managing Director: Massimo Bernardi.*
L M Records Crotalo Ed Mus, Via Del Pino 71, 48100. *Managing Director: Luigi Mazzesi.*
Materiali Sonori, Via Trieste 35, 52027 S. Giovanni Valdarno. *International Label Manager: Arlo Bigazzi.*
Minus Habens Records, Via Giustino Fortunato 8/N, 70125 Bari. *Owner: Ivan Iusco.*
Musica Maxima Magnetica, PO Box 2280, 50110 Florence. *Managing Director: Luciano Duri.*
New Tone Records, Via Principi d' Acaia 28, 10138 Turin. *International Label Manager: Bepe Grepi.*
Nuova Durium Srl, Piazza Mirabello 1, 20121 Milan. *Assistant Manager: Francesco Piccarreda.*
Polygram Italia, Via Carlo Tenca 2, 20124 Milan. *Managing Director: Stefano Senardi.*
Recordthings / Zona Archives, Box 1486, 50122 Florence. *Contact: Maurizio Nannuiu.*
Reform Records, Via Cosenza 5, 20137 Milan. *Label Manager: Alberto Lapris; A&R International: Fran Siccardi.*
Robi Droli Snc, Strada Roncaglia 16, 15040 San Germano (AL). *Managing Director: Beppe Greppi.*
Sentemo Records, Via Calstorta Vecchia 21 A, 31040 Cessalto (Treviso). *International Label Manager: Paolo Boarato.*
Sony Music Italy, Via Amedei 9, 20123 Milan. *Managing Director: Franco Cabrini.*
Studiotianta-Fortuna Records, Via Cernaia 3, 14031 Calliano. *General Manager: Massimo Visentin.*
Virgin Italy, Via Porpora 26, 20131 Milan. *Managing Director: Luigi Mantovani.*
Vizio Records, Via Festaz 52, 11100 Aoste. *Managing Director: Francseco Battisti.*
Vox Pop/Crazy Mannequin, Via Bergognone 31, 20144 Milan. *Managing Director: Carlo Albertoli.*
Warner Music / WEA Italiana, Via Milani 16, 20090 Redecescio Segrate (Milan). *Managing Director: Marco Antonio Bignotti.*
Zion, Via Latini 5, 24032 Calalziocorte (BG). *Managing Director: Cameroni Slivia.*

JAPAN

BMG Victor Inc., 1-3-9 Shibuya, Shibuya-ku, Tokyo 150. *President: Osamu Sato.*
East West Japan, 3-1-2 Kita-Aoyama, Minato-ku, Tokyo 107. *President: Takashi Kamide.*
JVC Victor Entertainment Inc., 26-18 Jingu-Mae, 4-Chome, Shibuya-ku, Tokyo 150. *President: Jun Deguchi.*
MCA Victor Inc., 9F JBP Oval, 5-52-2 Jingu-Mae, Shibuya-ku, Tokyo 150. *President: Hiroyuki Iwata.*
Nippon Columbia Co. Ltd (Denon), 14-14-4 Chome, Akasaka, Minato-ku, Tokyo 107. *Director: Toshikiko Hirahara.*
Nippon Phonogram Co. Ltd, Wako Bldg, 4-8-5 Roppongi, Minato-ku, Tokyo 106. *Chief Executive: Alex Abramoff.*
Polydor / Polygram K.K., 1-8-4 Ohashi 1-Chome, Meguro-ku, Tokyo 153. *President: Takeo Kasahara.*
Pony Canyon Inc, 2-1-1 Irifune, Chuo-ku, Tokyo 104. *General Manager of International A&R: Tatsuo Ozu; Assistant General Manager: Kaz Saito.*
Shinko Music Publishing Co Ltd, 2-1 Ogawamachi, Kanda, Chiyoda-Ku, Tokyo 101. *President: Shoichi Kusano.*
Sony Music Entertainment (Japan) Inc., PO Box 5208, Tokyo International, Tokyo 100-31. *President: Shugo Matsuo.*
Toshiba-EMI Ltd, 2-2-17 Akasaka, Minato-ku, Tokyo 105. *Contact: Takeshi Otsukotsu.*
Victor Entertainment Inc (JVC), 4-26-18 Jingumae, Shibuya-Ku, Tokyo 150. *International Operations: Aya Ohi.*
Warner Music Japan Inc., 3-1-2 Kita-Aoyama, Minato-ku, Tokyo 107. *Chairman: Ryuzo Kosugi.*

KOREA

BMG (Han Kook) Music Co. Ltd, 3rd Floor, BaekRim Building, 823-33 Yuksam-dong, Kangnam-ku, Seoul. *Managing Director: Seung Doo Park.*
Columbia / Epic Music (Korea) Inc., 2nd Floor, Doosung Bldg, 77-2 Sadang-dong, Dongjak-ku, Seoul 156 090. *Managing Director: Yeouel Yoon.*
EMI-Kemongsa Music Ltd, 9th Fl, Kemongmunhwa Centre Bldg, 772 Yuksam-dong, Kangnam-ku, Seoul 135 080. *President: Lee Kwan-Choi.*
Korea Music Co., 724-43 Yuksam-dong, Kangnam-ku, Seoul 135 080. *Contact: Duk-Joo Lee.*
Nices A&R International Entertainment, Business Division, Samsung Electronics, 19th Fl, Ahtae Bldg, 1337-20, Seocho 2-dong, Seocho-Ku, Seoul 137-072. *Manager: Kwang Woo Nam.*
Polygram Ltd, 3rd Fl, Sungsoo Bldg, 284-9 2-ka Sungsoo-dong, Sungdong-ku, Seoul. *Managing Director: David Lee.*
Seoul Music Inc., 3F Jung-Nam Bldg, 721-39 Yuksam-dong, Kang-Nam-Ku, Seoul. *President: Yong-Il Lee.*
Seoul Records Inc., 2nd Floor, Hankook Glass Bldg, 45-1 Yoido-dong, Youngdeungpo-ku, Seoul 150 010. *Contact: Hong-Kyun Shin.*
Sony Music, 98519 Bangbae-dong, Seocho-ku, Seoul. *Contact: Yun Yeo Ul.*
Warner Music Korea Ltd, 5th Fl Eunsung Bldg, 601-18 Yuksum-dong, Kangnam-Ku, Seoul 135-080. *Managing Director: Jonathan S Park.*

LATVIA

Mikrofons Ltd, Muitas Iela 1, Riga, LV-1010. *Foreign Affairs Manager: Indra Nātra.*

LITHUANIA

Blue Baltic Records, Arhcitektu 79, 2049 Vilnius. *Managing Director: Algis Pigaga.*
BNA Music, Gedimino Av. 2, 2001 Vilnius. *President: Arturas Zuokas.*
Bomba, Zygimantu 6, 2001 Vilnius. *General Director: Rimas Alisauskas.*
Zona Records, Seskines 79, 2010 Vilnius. *Managing Director: Giedrus Klimkevicus.*

LUXEMBOURG

Intercommunication, 275 Rote d'Arlon, 8001 Strassen. *Manager: Alex Felten.*
Joybringer, 27 Rue Victor Hugo, 4583 Differdange. *Contact: Andre Depienne.*

MALAYSIA

BMG Malaysia Sdn Bhd, 133-1 Jalan Segambut, Kuala Lumpur 51200. *Managing Director: Frankie Cheah.*
EMI (Malaysia) Sdn Bhd, Suite 10.01 10th Floor, Exchange Square, Off Jalem Semantan, Damansara Heights, 50490 Kuala Lumpur. *Managing Director: Beh Suat Pheng.*
Musico Sdn Bhd, Rm 3901, China Insurance Bldg, 174 Jalan Tuanku Abdul Rahman, Kuala Lumpur. *President: Bob Weiss.*
Noize Records, 17 Jalan Yap Kwan Seng, Kuala Lumpur 50450. *Contact: George Lourdes.*
Polygram Malaysia Records Sdn Bhd, 83-87 Jalan Kampung Pandan, Taman Maluri, Kuala Lumpur 55100. *Managing Director: Eric Yeo.*
Sony Music Entertainment (Malaysia), C16/C17 Jalan Ampang, Utama 1/1, Taman Ampang Utama, 68000 Ampang. *Managing Director: Rick Loh.*
Warner Music Malaysia, 9th Floor, Mui Plaza, Jalan P Ramlee, 50250 Kuala Lumpur. *Managing Director: Anthony F Fernandes.*

MEXICO

Compañia Fonografica Internacional, Sanctorum 86-B. Colonia Argentina. 11230 Mexico DF. *Director General: Ignacio Morales Perea.*
Discos Continental, Poniente 75, 160 Col. 16 de Septiembre, 11810 Mexico DF. *President: Marco Antonio Luga.*
EMI Music Mexico, Rio Tigris, 33 Col. Cuauhtémac, 06500 Mexico DF. *President: Mario Ruiz.*
Maple Audiosistemas, Priv. Alberto Barocio, 3 Circuito Ingeniero, 53100 Mexico DF. *President: David Rojas de Avila.*
Musica De Mexico, Ignacio Esteva 26-A, 11850 Mexico DF. *Proprietor: Dario Antonio Zorzano.*
Organizacion Latino Internacional, Avda. Unsurgente Sur, 953 - 202 Col. Nápoles, 03910 Mexico DF. *Director General: Tony Méndez.*
Polygram Discos, Av. Miguel Angel de Quevedo 531, Colonia Romero de Torreros, 04310 Mexico DF. *Director General: Francisco Bestard.*
Producciones Fonograficas, Adolfo Prieto 1649, 1° Piso, Col. del Valle-Benito Juárez, 03100 Mexico DF. *Director General: Bernado Yancelson.*
Suite Sync De Mexico, Prolongación Tajin, 900 Col. Emperadores, 03320 Mexico DF. *Director: Gerardo Suárez.*

NETHERLANDS

Ala Bianca Benelux, Zonnelaan 13, 1217 ND Hilversum. *Managing Director: H. Lessing.*
Artists And Business, PO Box 64, 1200 AB Hilversum. *Managing Director: Boudewyn Van Bavel*
Basic Beat, Nieuwe Binnenweg 54, 3015 BB Rotterdam. *Managing Director: Ron Hofland.*
BMG The Netherlands BV, Laaporsveld 63, 1213 VB Hilversum. *Managing Director: D Sturm.*
Brinkman Records BV, Vlietberg 5-45, 6576 JB Ooy. *Managing Director: Fred Maessen.*
CNR Music Holland, Brinklaan 109, 1404 GA Bussum. *General Manager: Leon Ten Hengel.*
Count Orlok Music, PO Box 2738, 3000 CS Rotterdam. *Contact: Johnny Zuidhof.*
Djax Records, PO Box 2408, 5600 CK Eindhoven. *Managing Director: Saskia Slegers.*
EMI Music Holland BV, Bronsteenweg 49, 2101 AB Heemstede. *Managing Director: Hennie Van Kuijeren.*
Essential Dance Music BV, Nieuwe Binnenweg 19, 3014 GB Rotterdam. *Managing Directors: P Boertje & P Vriends.*
Hotsound, Pleinweg 242 A-d, 3083 EZ Rotterdam. *Managing Director: Erik Van Vliet.*
Lana Lane Records, Faas Eliaslaan 13, 3742 AR Baarn. *Managing Director: Gerry Van Der Zwaard.*
Lower East Side Records, Govert Flickstraat 285, 1073 CA Amsterdam. *Managing Director: Jeroen Flamman.*
Mascot Records, PO Box 231, 2650 AE Berkel. *Managing Director: Ed Van Zijl.*
MMS Group of Companies, PO Box 55559, 1007 NB Amsterdam. *Vice President of A&R: Jelle Bakker.*
Mukti Records, Karel Doormanlaan 16, 1403 TM Bussum. *Managing Director: Eric Van Der Brink.*
Music & Words, PO Box 1160, 3430 BD Nieuwegein. *President: Hans Peters.*
Play It Again Sam BV, Vaartweg 129 Postbus 2115, 1200 CC Hilversum. *Managing Director: Wally Van Middendorf.*
Replay Records, Herenweg 9, 2465 AA Rijnsaterwoude. *Managing Director: Aart Mol.*
Roadrunner Records, Bijdorp 2, 1181 MZ Amstelveen. *Managing Director: Cees Wessels.*
Semaphore, PO Box 213, 1740 AE Schagen. *Label Manager: Marcel Pauvort.*
Sony Music Entertainment Holland, Herenweg 115, 2105 MG Heemstede. *Label Manager: Gerard Rutte.*
Staalplaat, PO Box 11453, 1001 GC Amsterdam. *Managing Director: Geent Jan Hobijn.*
Via Records, PO Box 2277, 1200 JV Hilversum. *Label Manager: Jos Haijer.*
Virgin Benelux, Melkpad 29, 1217 KA Hilversum. *Label Manager: Remmelt Van Beyersbergen.*
Warner Music Netherlands BV, Noorderweg 68, 1221 AB Hilversum. *International Manager: Michiel Ten Veen.*
Windham Hill Europe, Oude Enghweg 24, 1217 JD Hilversum. *General Manager: Frank Van Houten.*
Zodiac Records, Rozengracht 228, 1016 SZ Amsterdam. *Managing Director: Gert Van Veen.*

NEW ZEALAND

BMG Music New Zealand Ltd, 3rd Floor, Altos House, Cnr Newton Road/Abbey Street, Newton. *General Manager: Morrie Smith.*
Deepgrooves Entertainment, PO Box 5404, Wellesley Street, Auckland. *Contact: Kane Massey.*
Edge Music Ltd, PO Box 56219, Dominion Road, Auckland. *Directors: Tim Foreman, Richard Earwaker, Rhonda Rollinson.*
EMI Music New Zealand, PO Box 864, Auckland. *Managing Director: Kerry Byrne.*
Flying Nun Records Ltd & Flying In Distribution, PO Box 677, Auckland. *General Manager: Lesley Parrs.*
Gateway Productions, PO Box 6735, Wellesley Street, Auckland. *Manager: Greg Henwood.*
Gecko Records, 38A Glenmall Place, Glen Eden, Auckland. *Manager: Andrew Dixon.*
Hark Records, 564 Victoria Street, Hamilton. *Managing Director: Grant Hislop.*
Jayrem Records Ltd, PO Box 3101,Ohope, Wakatane. *Managing Director: James Moss.*
Kiwi Pacific Records International Ltd, PO Box 826, Wellington. *Production Manager: M F Vincent.*
Metro Marketing Ltd, 45 Mackelvie Street, Ponsonby, Auckland. *Managing Director: Graeme Pethig.*
Mushroom Records, 2nd Floor, ASB Chambers, 138 Queen Street, Auckland. *Contact: Sandii Riches.*
Onset Offset, Cashel Chambers, 224 Cashel Street, Christchurch. *Contact: Emilie Dobinson.*
Pagan Records, PO Box 47-290, Ponsonby, Auckland. *Directors: Trevor Reekie, Sheryl Morris.*
Rattle Records, PO Box 4187, Auckland. *Managing Director: Keith Hill.*
Someone Up There Records, 39 Kensington Avenue, Mt Eden, Auckland 4. *Directors: Kevin and Darlene Adair.*
Sony Music Entertainment (New Zealand) Ltd, 9th Floor, 110 Symonds Street, Auckland. *Managing Director: Michael Glading.*
Sun Pacific Music Co., 49 Murdoch Road, Grey Lynn. *Managers: Michael Donnelly, Bernard Griffin.*
Tangata Records, PO Box 3679, Shortland Street, Auckland. *A&R Director: Neil Cruickshank.*
Virgin Records New Zealand, 9th Floor, Baycorp House, 15 Hopetoun Street, Ponsonby, Auckland. *Managing Director: Kerry Byrne.*
Warner Music New Zealand Ltd, 7th Floor, Babbage House, 15 Hopetoun Street, Ponsonby, Auckland. *Contact: James Southgate.*
Yellow Bike Records, PO Box 586, Palmerston North. *Co-ordinators: Claire Pannell and Dave White.*
Yellow Eye Music, 33 Fortune Street, Dalmore, Dunedin. *Partner: Simon Vare.*

NORWAY

Arne Bendiksen Records AS, Jornstadsvn. 62, Box 181, N-1360 Nesbru. *Managing Director: Arne Bendiksen.*
Blue Wolf Productions, Box 98, N-3671 Notodden. *Managing Director: Arild Reinertsen.*
Busk Records, Fredbo Alle 14, PO Box 471, N-3903 Porsgrunn. *Managing Director: Terje Welle Busk.*
CIA Producations, Waldemar Thranesgate 55 B, N-0173 Oslo. *Administration Director: Caroline Asplin.*
CNR NonStop AS, Sandakervn. 24C, N-0401 Oslo. *Managing Director: Ole Vidar Lien.*
Continental Records, Sunbyjordet 4, N-2051 Jessheim. *Managing Director: Barry Matheson.*
Crema AS, Nedre Vollgt 3, N-0158 Oslo. *Managing Director: Arve Sigvaldsen.*
Curling Legs Productions DA, PO Box 5298, Majorst UA, N-0303 Oslo. *Manager: Knut Vaerhes.*
DAT O/S, N-9520 Guovdageaidnu. *Contact: Per L Boine.*
Dbut internautics, PO Box 9415 Valerenga, N-0610 Oslo. *Director: Per Platow.*
EMI Norsk AS, Karl Johansgt. 12 J, PO Box 492 Sentrum, N-0105 Oslo. *Managing Director: Jan Ostli.*
Enjoy Records, Tidemansgt. 1, N-0266 Oslo. *Managing Director: Jimmy James.*
Fox Records, Bratabakken 6, N-1440 Droebak. *Managing Director: Morten Reff.*
Gemini Records, Nils Hansensvej 13, PO Box 13, Bryn, N-0611 Oslo. *Managing Director: Bjorn Petersen.*
Grammofon AS Electra, St. Halvardsgt. 33, N-0192 Oslo. *Managing Director: Oyvind Dalsrud.*
Grappa Records AS, Akersgata 7, N-0158 Oslo. *Managing Director: Helge Westbye.*
Heilo, PO Box 2645 Solli, N-0302 Oslo. *Manager: Halvard Kvale.*
Hot Club Records, PO Box 5202, Majorstua, N-0302 Oslo. *Managing Director/Producer: Jon Larsen.*
Hypertonia World Enterprises, PO Box 4307 Nygardstangen, N-5028 Bergen. *Manager: Jan Bruun.*
Idut, Iggaldas, N-9710 Inore, Billefjord. *General Manager: Åge Persen.*
Jeps AS, Mandalsgt. 5, N-0190 Olso. *Managing Director: Havard Hansteen.*
LA Music AS, Skolebakken 14, N-1435 Krakstad. *Managing Director: Lillian Askeland.*
Lynor AS, Bergtorasvn. 74, PO Box 4086 Kongsgard, N-4602 Kristiansand S. *Managing Director: Livar Holland.*
Majorselskapet, Rosenborggt. 19, PO Box 5949 Majorstua, N-0308 Oslo. *International Label Manager: Trond Amlie.*
MCA Music Entertainment Norway AS, Parkvn. Bd., PO Box 2702 Solli, N-0204 Oslo. *General Manager: Petter Singsaas.*
MTG-Productions, PO Box 2500, N-3003 Drammen. *Managing Director: Larry Bringssord.*
Nidelven Grammofon AS, Hogreina 432, N-7079 Flatasen. *Managing Director: Per Adlofsen.*
Nor Wave/Norsk Gram, PO Box 4603, Valentinlyst., N-7002 Trondheim. *Managing Director: Gunnar Nordvik.*
Nor-CD, Hammerstads Gate 48, N-0363 Oslo. *Managing Director: Karl Seglem.*
Norsk Lyd & Bilde/Norwegian Sound & Vision, Rute 598, N-2760 Brandbu. *Directors: Odd Erik & Eli Kristin Hagen.*
Notabene Records AS, Bogstanvn. 31 B, N-0366 Oslo. *Managing Director: Ole A Sorli.*
Odin, Tollbugt. 28, N-0157 Oslo. *Managing Director: Rolf S. Grundesen.*
Origo Sound, Ospelia 8, N-1900 Fetsund. *Managing Director: Harald Lervik.*
Olso Records, Harald Romckes Vei 37, N-0286 Oslo. *Manager: Lars Borke,*
Polygram Norway, Drammensvn. 82 B, PO Box 2645 Solli, N-0203 Oslo. *International Label Manager: Petter Singsaas.*
Prima Music AS, Storgt. 38, PO Box 4697 Sofienberg, N-0506 Oslo. *Managing Director: Bjorn Skjennum.*
Progress Records, Gregusgt. 9, N-7002 Trondheim. *Managing Director: Jens Petter Wiig.*
Rage Records, PO Box 4721 Sofienberg, N-0506 Oslo. *Managing Director: Rino Frostad.*
Rec 90, PO Box 1291, N-5001 Bergen. *Managing Director: Torfinn Andersen.*
Revolution Records, Box 6005, N-7003 Trondheim. *Managing Director: Diesel Dahl.*
Scandinavian Records, Dronningensgt. 8B, PO Box 517 Sentrum, N-0105 Oslo. *Managing Director: Kai Roger Ottesen.*
Sonet / Slagerfabriken, Drammensvg. 88 B, PO Box 2645 Solli, N-0203 Oslo. *Managing Director: Harald Tomte.*
Sony Music Norway, PO Box 134, Okern, N-0509 Olso. *Managing Director: Rune Hagberg.*
Spesial Laboratoriet, Braavallagt. 25 B, N-5500 Haugesund. *Director: Torgrim Eide.*
Truels Brodtkorb, PO Box 2645 Solli, N-0271 Oslo. *Head Of Marketing: Truels Brodtkorb.*
Tvers Forlag AS, Hasselvn. 47 Ottestad, N-2301 Hamar. *Managing Director: Arnold Borud.*
Virgin Records Norway, Karljohansgt. 12 J, N-0101 Oslo. *Managing Director: Gyro Leira.*
Voices Of Wonder, Thv. Meyersgt. 33, N-0555 Oslo. *Contact: Per Thomas Lund, Ketil Sveen.*
Warner Music Norway, Maridalsveden 87 B, N-0403 Oslo. *Label Managers: Steen Brodtkrob, Jonny Styve.*

PERU

Discos Hispanos Del Peru SA, Esquilache, 179 San Isidro, Lima 27. *General Manager: Javier Castañeda.*
Discos Independientes SA, Avda. Arenales 2586, Lima 14. *President: Samir Giha.*
El Virrey Industrias Musicales SA, Avda. República de Panamá, 355 San Isidro, Lima 1. *Director: Wilan Kafka.*
Iempsa SA, Avda. Guillermo Dansey 1247, Apdo 67, Lima 1. *Director: Nilo Marchand.*

PHILIPPINES

A&W Records, 2nd Fl, Vergel de Dios Bldg, 530 Evangelista Street, Quiapo, Manila. *General Manager: Willie J, Villar.*
BMG Records (Pilipinas) Inc, 3F, Equitable Bank Bldg, 898 Aurora Blvd, cor Stanford Sts, Cubao, Quezon City. *Managing Director: Rudy Y Tee.*
DD International Recording Corporation, 363 P Casal Street, Quiapo, Manila 1001. *Chairman-President: Demy A Quirino Jr.*
Ivory Records, 2/F Quadstar Bldg, Ortigas Avenue, Greenhills, San Juan, Metro Manila. *President: Antonio Ocampo.*
Platinum Records, Unit 15, Town & Country Arcade, Marcos Highway, Cainta, Rizal. *President: Eli Balboa.*
Solar Records Inc., 2nd Floor, Roman Santos Bdlg, Plaza Lacson, Santa Cruz, Manila. *President: Mauro Manalangsang.*
Universal Records, 135 P, Sevilla Street, Cnr 3rd Avenue, Grace Park, Kalookan City, Metro Manila. *Vice President: Ramon Chuaying.*
Warner Music Philippines Inc., 4th Fl, Ma. Danile Bldg, 470 MH Del Pilar Corner, San Andres Street, Malate, Manila. *Managing Director: Ma-an Hontiveros.*

POLAND

Abrakadabra SA, Sportoaw 5 M 36, 05-400 Otwock. *Chairman: Antoni Roszczuk.*
Artson, Nowogrodzka 49, 00-695 Warsaw. *Managing Director: Marek Pioro*
BMG International Poland, Dygasinskiego 10, 01-603 Warsaw. *Managing Director: Poitr Naglowski.*
Digiton, Aleje Jerozolimskie 29 Apt 3, 00-508 Warsaw. *Managing Director: Lyszard Marciniak.*
Elbo Phonographic Enterprise, Ul. Moniuszki 10 m 54, 00-009 Warsaw. *Managing Director: Boguslaw Borysiuk.*

Inter Sonus, Al 3 Maja 2 m 5, 00-391 Warsaw. *Managing Director: Rygzard Adamus.*
Lion Records, Rejtana 3, 01-800 Warsaw. *Managing Director: Piotr Gryglewicz.*
Loud Out Records, U. Zielna 45/30, 00-108 Warsaw. *Managing Director: Andrzej Mackiewicz .*
MJM Music, Ul. Grochowska 341 bud 28, 03-822 Warsaw. *Managing Director: Grzegorz Stabeusz.*
Polmark, Konrada 30, 01-922 Warsaw. *Managing Director: Tadeusz Krasnodebski.*
Polonia Records, Jana Pawla II 18 m 13, 00-116 Warsaw. *Managing Director: Stanislaw Sobola.*
Polskie Nagrania, Goleszowska 6, 01-249 Warsaw. *Managing Director: Aleksander Olaszewski.*
Polton Music Distribution, Ul Dantyszka 8, 02-054 Warsaw. *President: Jan Choonauci.*
PUP Metal Mind Productions, Sleligiewicza 8/21, 40-044 Katowice. *Managing Director: Tomasz Dziubinski.*
Selles Records, Ul Jagielska 43, 02-886 Warsaw. *Owner/Managing Director: Tomasz Bielski.*
Sonic sp 200, Mscislawska 6, 01-647 Warsaw. *Managing Director: Marek Proniewicz.*
Sound Pol, Bitny Warsawskiej, 1920 R 14/88, 02-366 Warsaw. *Managing Director: Kajetan Slonina.*
SPV Poland, Ul. Twardowska 3, 01-810 Warsaw. *Managing Director: Igor Kuronski.*
Veriton Records, Bobrowiecka 1, 00-278 Warsaw. *Director: Grazyna Solinska.*
Zic-Zac Music Company, Sulkowskiego 9, 01-602 Warsaw. *Managing Director: Marek Koscikiewicz.*
ZPR Inc, 13/15 Senatorska, 00-075 Warsaw. *Manager, Artistes & Marketing Department: Anna Karolicka.*

PORTUGAL

Ama Romanta, R Coelho da Rocha 46, 1 Dto, 1200 Lisbon. *Managing Director: Joao Peste.*
Ananana, Apartado 21671, 1137 Lisbon. *Managing Director: Fred Sonsen.*
Andante-Discos Musica E Som Lda, Avenida da Boavista, 1471 Loja 8, 4100 Porto. *President: Jean Pierre Jongenelen.*
BMG Ariola Portugal, Edificio Infante D. Henrique, Rua Joao Chagas 53 A, 1495 Lisbon. *Managing Director: Toze Brito.*
Dark Records, Apartado 142, 2830 Barreiro Codex. *Managing Director: Pedro Cruz.*
Discos Belter Lda, Constituiça 74, 4200 Porto. *Contact: Antonio Figueiredo.*
Discossete, Rua Dr Faria Vasconcolos 4A, 1900 Lisbon. *Managing Director: Helena Cardinalli.*
Edisom, Rua Manuel F. Andrade 6B, 1500 Lisbon. *Managing Director: Carlos Ferreira.*
Eltatu Editor, R Rodrigo Da Fonseca, 182 4E, 1070 Lisbon. *Director: Antonio Dos Santos; Label Manager: Marta Ferreira..*
EMI Portugal, Rua de Cruz dos Poias 111, 1200 Lisbon. *Managing Director: David Ferreira.*
Farol Musica, Alto Do Coutao, Armazem I, 2735 Cacem. *Chief Executive: Antonio Guimaraes.*
Fast 'N' Loud, Apartado 13037, 1019 Lisbon Codex. *Commercial Director: Filipe Marques.*
Independent Records, Rua do Jardim, 598-4405 Valadares, Porto. *Director: Francisco Pinho.*
Johnny Blue, Rua da Madalena 90 3°, 1100 Lisbon. *Director: Miguel Santos.*
Megamusica, Representação e Distribuição Lda, Apartado 13, 2775 Carcavelos. *Managing Director: José Eduardo Santos.*
Monasterium Records, PO Box 1078, 2670 Santo Antonio Dos Cavaleiros. *Managing Director: Duarte Picoto.*
Morgana Records, Apartado 845, 2840 Seixal. *Managing Director: Duarte Dionisio.*
MTM, Apartado 30072, 1321 Lisbon Codex. *Managing Director: Hugo Moutinito.*
Musica Alternativa, Pra das Roicadas n 37 RcE, 2700 Amadora. *Managing Director: Samuel Lopes.*
Polygram Portugal, R Prof. Reinaldo dos Santos, 12 D, 1500 Lisbon. *Managing Director: Rodrigo Marin.*
Sony Musica Portugal, Rua Juliao Quintinha 11, 1500 Lisbon. *Head Of Public Relations: Paolo Bismark.*
Strauss Musica e Video SA, Rua Adelaide Cabete 3A, 1500 Lisbon. *Administrator: Armando Martins.*
Vidisco, N13 1D, Av. Bombeiros Voluntarios Pontinha, 1675 Lisbon. *Managing Director: Artur Antunes.*
Warner Music Portugal Lda, Rua D Constantino de Bragança, 26, 1400 Lisbon. *International Product Coordinate: Xana Taylor.*

ROMANIA

Astra 22 Adv Ag, Str Turda 122, BL 39, ScA, Et 6, Ap 30, Sector 1, Bucharest. *President: Vertan Adriana.*
Electrecord S A, Bvd Timisoara No 94, Sector 6, 78702 Bucharest. *General Director: Grigore Petreanu.*
Romagram Music Ltd, 8 Aviator Mircea Zorileanu Str., Sector 1, 70242 Bucharest. *Chairman: Joey De Alvare.*
Tilt And Partners, 202 A Splaiul Independentei Str., Sector 6, 77208 Bucharest. *Managing Director: Guiseppe Rossi.*
Toji Productions, 9 Piata Romana, C/40, Sector 1, 70167 Bucharest. *Managing Director: Nicu Alifantis.*

RUSSIA

Alien Records, Bolshaya Serpukhovskaya 44, Moscow. *Managing Director: Oleg Kurbatkin.*
Aprelevka Sound Inc, Arbat 44, 121 002 Moscow. *Managing Director: Grigory Figlin.*
Beloton, P Brovki 15-3-38, Vitebsk, Belarus. *Managing Director: Arseni Kritski.*
Feelee Record Company, 27 Novozavadskaya str, 121 309 Moscow. *Managing Director: Igor Tonkikh.*
Gala Records, Staraya Basmannaya 27-22, 121 309 Moscow. *Director: Boris Tzigman.*
General Records, Milyutinsky Per 15/24, 101 000 Moscow. *President: Nadia Solovieva.*
Lad Records, Dimitrova 39, 117 040 Moscow. *Chairman: Felix Perepelov.*
Russky Disc, Stankevicha 8, 103 009 Moscow. *Managing Director: Jury Parol.*
SNC Records, Krymsky Val 9, 117 049 Moscow. *Managing Director: Alexey Ugrinovitch.*
St Petersburg Label, B. Sampsoniyevsky Pr. 57, 194 044 St Petersburg. *Director: Lydia Cobrina.*
Syntex, B. Spasskaya 33-10, 129 010 Moscow. *Chairman: Alexander Kutikov.*
Tau Product, PO Box 377, 117 333 Moscow. *Chairman: Andrei Bogdanov.*
Vist, Triokhprudny Per. 4, 103 031 Moscow. *General Manager: Vladimir Oletsky.*
Zolotaya Dolina Co., Ismaelovsky Proiezd 14/1/34, 105 037 Moscow. *Contact: Eugeni Grekhov.*

SINGAPORE

BMG Singapore Pte Ltd, Alexandria Distripark, Block 2, No 11-01/04, Pasir Panjang Road, Singapore. *Director: Frankie Cheah.*
EMI (Singapore), 213 Henderson Road, 04-015 Henderson Industrial Park, Singapore. *Managing Director: David Wee.*
Form Pte Ltd, Block 994, Bendemeer Road No 02-01, Singapore. *Company Director: Ang Choon Beng.*
Hype Records Pte Ltd, 221 Henderson Road, #02-04 Henderson Bldg, Singapore 159557. *Administration Manager: Melvis Yip.*
Polygram Records Pte Ltd, 23 Gentling Road, 04-01 Chevalier House, Singapore. *Managing Director: Eric Yeo.*
Sony Music Entertainment (Singapore) Pte Ltd, 601 Sims Drive, #02-07 Singapore 887382. *Managing Director: Terence Phung.*
Warner Music Singapore Pte Ltd, 10 Anson Road, No 12-06/07/08, International Plaza, Singapore. *Managing Director: Peter Lau.*

SLOVENIA

Dallas, Kersnikova 4, 61000 Ljubljana. *Managing Director: Goran Lisica.*
Front Rock, PO Box 48, 62000 Maribor. *Manager: Dujan Hedl.*
Matrix Music, Hranilniska 6, 61000 Ljubljana. *Managing Director: Primoz Pecounik.*
RTV Slovania Records & Tapes, Dalmatinova 10, 61000 Ljubljana. *Label Manager: Ivo Umek.*
Škuc-AFK, Kersnikova 4, 61000 Ljubljana. *Managing Director: Mitja Prezelj.*
Zavod Za Umetnisko in Kulturno Produkcijo, Kersnikova 4, 61000 Ljubljana. *Managing Director: Monika Skaberne.*

SOUTH AFRICA

Ahoy Records, PO Box 5984, Johannesburg 2000. *Contact: Blondie Makhene.*
BMG Records Africa (Pty) Ltd, PO Box 5894 Johannesburg 2000. *Contact: Keith Lister/Peter Vee.*
Cap Records, 134 Unie Avenue, Lyttelton 0157. *Contact: Graham Abrahams.*
CCP Record Co (Pty) Ltd, PO Box 112564, Johannesburg 2000. *Contact: Barry Guy.*
Cornerstone Records, 175 Nicolette Street, Meyerspark 0184. *Contact: Andrew Cartwright.*
CSR Records, PO Box 7578 Johannesburg 2000. *Contact: Chris Ghelakis.*
David Gresham Record Co (Pty) Ltd, PO Box 46020, Orange Grove 2119. *Owner: David Gresham.*
Eagle Records, PO Box 11112, Marine Parade 4056. *Contact: Jean Snyman.*
EMI South Africa/Virgin Records, PO Box 11254, Johannesburg 2000. *Contact: Mike Edwards.*
Gazania Records, PO Box 569, Vredendal 8160. *Contact: HC Visser.*
Gold Dust Records (Pty) Ltd, 9 9th Avenue, Houghton 2198. *Contact: Phil Hollis.*
Hit City Records, PO Box 156, Crown Mines 2025. *Contact: Jill Galankis.*
Inhouse Records, PO Box 15, Bassonia 2061. *Contact: Phillip Nel.*
Kalawa Records, 232 Louis Botha Avenue, Orange Grove 2192. *Contact: Don Laka.*
Maranatha Record Co., PO Box 32823, Glenstantia 0010. *Contact: Lukie Carleson.*
Mike Fuller Music Records (Pty) Ltd, PO Box 66254, Broadway 2020. *Proprietor: Mike Fuller.*
Natal Records, 20B Church Road, Westville, Durban 3630. *Contact: Don Clarke.*
Phase 2 Records, PO Box 48321, Roosevelt Park 2129. *Contact: Terry Fairweather.*
Rampant Records, PO Box 192, Halfway House 1685. *Contact: Greg Nefdt.*
ReaMusic Records, PO Box 96395, Brixton 2019. *Contact: Clive Risko.*
RPM Record Co (Pty) Ltd, PO Box 2807, Johannesburg 2000. *Contact: Irving Schlosberg.*
Shifty Records, PO Box 5894, Johannesburg 2000. *Contact: Lloyd Ross.*
Stave Record Productions, PO Box 1854, Pinegowrie 2123. *Contact: Robert Schroder.*
Tequila Records, PO Box 391405, Bramley, Johannesburg 2018. *Contact: David Alexander.*
To The Edge Records, PO Box 5012, Weltevreden Park 1715. *Executive Producer: Leon Retief.*
Trio Records (Pty) Ltd, PO Box 33283, Jeppsetown 2042. *Contact: Gavin Gibb.*
TSOP Record Co, 84 Retief Street, Pretoria West 0183. *Contact: MM Mpye.*
Vusa Records, PO Box 423, Milnerton 7435. *Contact: Mynie Grove.*

SPAIN

Al.Leluia Records, Rambla Catalunya 10, 08006 Barcelona. *Managing Director: Reyes Torio.*
Avispa SL, c/o Jeronima Llorente 74, 28039 Madrid. *International Department: Margarita Abrante Guerra.*
AZ Productions, Riera de Argentona, s/n, 08300 Nataro (Barcelona). *International Department: Pere-Lluis Pont.*
B-Core, Marques de Sentmenat 72, 08029 Barcelona. *Managing Director: Jordi Llansama.*
Bat Discos, SA, Sagunto 2, 28010 Madrid. *General Manager: Jorge E Gomez Diaz.*
CDR Praktik, Alcade Mostoles 41, 08026 Barcelona. *Managing Director: Ernest Casal.*
Crab Ediciones Musicales SA, Sagunto 2, 28010 Madrid. *General Manager: Jorge E Gomez Diaz.*
Disc Medi, Argentona 3-5 Bajos, 08024 Barcelona. *Director: Alex Eslava.*
El Colectivo Karma, PO Box 821, 41080 Seville. *Manager: Andrew Jarman.*
Elephant Records, PO Box 331, 28203 Las Rozas. *Managing Director: Luis Calvo.*
Esese & Co., Llacuna 162, 08018 Barcelona. *Managing Director: Sergi Solis.*
Fabrica Magnetica, Dr. Fourquet 31, 28012 Madrid. *Managing Director: Servando Carballar.*
Fonomusic Distrimusic, Garcia de Paredes 12, 28010 Madrid. *Contact: Valentin Ladredo.*
GSG - Grup de Serveis Guilleries, Granja Baró, Ctra de la Guixa, Km 2, 08500 VIC (Barcelona). *Administration: Jordi Costa; Management: Ignasi Pla; Production: Joan Capdevila.*
Goo Records, Bailen 3 1, 48003 Bilbao. *Managing Director: Estibaliz Hernandez.*
Lakota SA, Guadalmina Alta, Calle 21 Casa 631, San Pedro de Alcantara,/Marbella, 29670 Malaga. *Managing Director: Carlo Cavicchi.*
Liquid Records, Gomis 42, 08023 Barcelona. *Managing Director: Peter Eichenberg.*
More Discos / Boy Records, Industria 132, 08025 Barcelona. *Managing Director: Ana Moran.*
New Music Ediciones Musicales SL, Apartado 9.046, 28060 Madrid. *General Manager: Gerhard Haltermann.*
On The Rock - Caroline, Rossello 336, 08025 Barcelona. *Managing Director: Enric Padascoll.*
PDI, Passeig de Gracia 74 3 1, 08008 Barcelona. *International Label Manager: Gerhard Haltermann.*
Polygram Iberica, Suero de Quinones 38, 28002 Madrid. *Contact: Elena Gorostiza, Enrique Prieto.*
Por Caridad Producciones, La Palma 72 3, 28015 Madrid. *Managing Director: M. José Martin.*
Radiation Records, Nicolas Alicorta 2, 48080 Bilbao. *Managing Director: Undi Fresnedo.*
Salseta Discos, Diputacio 180 5C, 08011 Barcelona. *Managing Director: Salvador Escriva.*
Siesta Records, Sta Cruz de Marcenado 31 6, 28015 Madrid. *International Manager: Joaquin Garcia.*
Subterfuge Records, Augusto Figueroa 21 4, 28080 Madrid. *Managing Director: Carlos Galan.*
Tram Cat, Amigo 26 4, 08021 Barcelona. *Managing Director: Toni Oro.*
Urantia Records, Rossello 227, 08008 Barcelona. *Managing Director: Ramon Bertran.*
Victoria Ediciones Musicales SA, Narvaez 14, 28009 Madrid. *Managing Director: Gerhard Haltermann.*
Walkaria Records, Pl Morron 16, 10002 Caceres. *Managing Director: Victor Guillen.*
Warner Music Spain, Aribau 282-284 5 4, 08006 Barcelona. *Head Of Promotion: Lucas Holten.*

SWEDEN

Amalthea Records, PO Box 271, 18523 Waxholm. *Managing Director: Torgny Sjöö.*
Atlantis Grammofon AB, Karlbergsvagen 57, 11335 Stockholm. *Manager/Owner: Jan Hansson.*

BORG Music Int, PO Box 6082, 20011 Malmö. *Chairman: Björn Gärdsby.*
Birdsnest Records, Kolsvagatan 4, 73133 Köping. *Managing Director: Per Granberg.*
Blitz Records AB, PO Box 347, 10126 Stockholm 1. *Managing Director: Wolfgang Jedliczka.*
BMG Ariola Sweden, PO Box 1026, 17221 Sundbyberg. *Managing Director: Hans Breitholz.*
Borderline, Gamlestadsvägen 1, 41502 Gothenburg. *Managing Director: Pär Malmstedt.*
Burning Heart, Kolsvagatan 4, 73133 Köping. *Managing Director: Peter Ahlquist.*
Business Record Concept (BRC), Box 7083, 63007 Eskilstuna. *Director: Peter Rozenbachs.*
Caprice Records, PO Box 1225, 11182 Stockholm. *Managing Director: Kjell Söderqvist.*
Einnicken Records, Ihermaeniusgatan 20, 64430 Torshälla. *Financial Manager: Stefan Wistrand.*
EMI Sweden, PO Box 1289, Tritonvägen 17, 17125 Solna. *Label Manager: Per Erik Hotti.*
Empire Records, Vintergatan 2, 17230 Sundbyberg. *Managing Director: Christer Wedin.*
Energy Records AB, Vastergatan 23, 21121 Malmö. *Contact: Håkan Ehrnst.*
Fifty/Fifty Records, Box 14096, 63014 Eskilstuna. *A&R: Peter Torsén.*
Four Leaf Clover Records, PO Box 1231, 17226 Sundbyberg. *Director: Lars Samuelson.*
Frequent Frenzy Records, PO Box 6009, 10231 Stockholm. *Managing Director: Daggan Stamenkovic.*
Gazell Music AB, Tappvägen 24, Box 20055, 16102 Brommu. *Director: Dag Haeggqvist.*
Gotherburg Records, Gammlestan 2, 41507 Gothenburg. *Managing Director: John Ballard.*
H Lime Records, Kvangärdesgatan 36 B, 63355 Eskilstuna. *International Manager: Magnus Bäckström.*
Hawk Records, Box 8061, 10420 Stockholm. *Managing Director: Björn Håkanson.*
House of Kicks Distribution, Box 2140, 10314 Stockholm. *Director: Roger Reinhold.*
HSM Records, PO Box 1122, 22104 Lund. *Managing Director: Ulf Lundwall.*
Last Buzz Record Co, Husargatanis, 41122 Gothenburg. *Producer: Håkan Forshult.*
Lush Records, Landsvägsgatan 11, 41304 Gothenburg. *Owner: Ralph Stern-Pettersson.*
M&A Music Art, Simrishamnsgatan 20A, 21423 Malmö. *Managing Director: Andreas Larsson.*
Mega Records, Ske Pargatan 8, 11452 Stockholm. *Head Of Promotion: Brita Jungberg.*
MNW Independent Label Representation, Industrivägen 1, 17148 Solna. *Assistant Director: Tomas Sunmo.*
MVG Records, PO Box 271, 18523 Waxholm. *International Manager: Lina Beckmann.*
Noble Art Records, PO Box 78, 445 22 Bohus. *A&R Manager: Magnus Cornelius.*
NonStop Records, Box 7273, 40235 Gothenburg. *Managing Director: Peter Kagerland.*
Nordic Soundlab, PO Box 31, 53221 Skara. *Managing Director: Lasse Holm.*
North Of No South (NONS) Records, Sotiehemsv 45, 90738 Umeå. *Managing Director: Robert Norsten.*
Planet Records, Torggatan 15, 17154 Solna. *Chairman: Mats Olsson.*
Polygram Records Sweden, PO Box 20510, 16102 Bromma. *Managing Director: Lenart Backman.*
Rainbow Music, Höstvägen 5, 17140 Solna / Stockholm. *Managing Director: Sture Hallberg.*
Real Time Music, Wennerbergsgatan 1, 11258 Stockholm. *Manager: Allan Gutheim.*
Roligan Records, Gotabergsgatan 2, Box 53045, 40014 Gothenburg. *Managing Director: Jasper Kumberg.*
Sidelake, Trädgardsgatan 23, 85172 Sundsvall. *Managing Director: Anders Melin.*
Silence, PO Box 271, 18523 Waxholm. *Managing Director: Eva Wilke.*
Sonet Music, PO Box 20105, 16102 Bromma. *Managing Director: Börge Engen.*
Sony Music Sweden, PO Box 20037, 16102 Bromma. *Managing Director: Stefan Klinteberg.*
Step One, Katrinebergsvgen 2, 10074 Stockholm. *Managing Director: Jörgen Sigfridsson.*
Stockholm Records, PO Box 20504, 16102 Bromma. *General Manager: Eric Hasselqvist.*
Strawberry Songs, PO Box 157, 63103 Eskilstuna. *Managing Director: Hans Lindell.*
Swedish Prime Time Records, PO Box 250 32, 75025 Upsala. *Managing Director: Dag Carlsson.*
Tempo Records, PO Box 231 49, 10435 Stockholm. *Managing Director: Peter Hartzell.*
Triple / Lionheart Records, Götgatan 81, 11662 Stockholm. *Managing Director: Robert Ljunggren.*
Virgin Records Sweden, Box 1291, 17125 Solna. *Managing Director: Anders Hjelmstorp.*
Warner Music Sweden, PO Box 1228,16428 Kista. *Manager: Marten Aglander.*
Zakana Records, Skolgatan 73A, 90330 Umeå. *Managing Director: Mikael Reinholdsson.*

SWITZERLAND

Atina Records GmbH, Hafnarstrasse 23, CH-8005 Zürich. *Owner/Managing Director: Anita Tiziani.*
Black Cat, Faellendenstrase 20, CH-8124 Maur. *Managing Director: Hili Heilinger.*
BMG Ariola Switzerland, Letzigraben 89, CH-8047 Zürich. *Director: Guido Vendramini.*
Brambus Records, PO Box 44, CH-7004 Chur. *Director: Paul Rostetter.*
Dircom, Fausses-Brayes 19, CH-2000 Neuchatel. *President: Joel Desaules.*
Dirty Alternative Beat, Rue de O'Ale 35, POB 225, CH-1000 Lausanne 17. *Contact: T Leresche.*
Disques Cellier, Aiguemont 26, Rue du Bourg de Plait, CH-1605 Chexbres. *Directors: Marcel & Catherine Cellier.*
Face Music Switzerland, Dorfstrasse 29/1, CH-8800 Thalwil. *Managing Director: Urs-Albert Wethli.*
Grooveline AG, Laubenhof, CH-6300 Zug. *Managing Director: Ermin Trevisan.*
Lux-Noise, PO Box 3212, CH-5001 Aarau. *Managing Director: Michael Hediger.*
Noise Product Switzerland, CP 363, CH-1213 Petit Lancy 1. *Label Manager: Alban Chaperon.*
NSS Records, Fahrweidstr. 81 A, CH-8651 Fahrweid. *Contact: Michel F Huwiler.*
Off Course Records, PO Box 241, CH-8025 Zürich. *Managing Director: Urs Steiger.*
150 BPM Records, Steinhauserstr. 21, CH-6330 Cham. *A&R Manager: Hans Raymondaz.*
Phonag AG, Zürcherstr. 77, CH-8041 Winterthur. *Managing Director: Peter Frei.*
Pick Records, Brunnwiesenstr. 26, CH-8049 Zürich. *Chairman: Anton Peterer.*
Sony Music Switzerland, Oberneuhofstr. 6, CH-6340 Bahr. *Manager: Mirco Vaiz.*
Steinblatt Music, Via Vicari 18, CH-6900 Lugano. *Managing Director: Marco Antognini.*
Turicaphon AG, Turicaphonstrasse 31, CH-8616 Riedikon. *Managing Director: Hans Oestreicher.*
Viteka Music Production, Ringstr. 14, PO Box 173, CH-8600 Dübendorf / Zürich, *Chairman: Willy Viteka.*
Warner Music Switzerland, Avenue Chilton 70, CH-1820 Montreux. *Managing Director: Charles Nobs.*

TAIWAN

BMG Music Taiwan Inc., 99-19 Section 2, Nankang Road, Nankang District, Taipei. *Managing Director: Swee Wong.*
Chiang Huat Co. / Around The World Music, 3/F 278 Chung Hsiao East Road, Section 4, Taipei. *Producer: Ms Hsiu Hua Ho.*
Decca Records Taiwan Ltd, 12/Fl No. 112 Chung Hsiao East Road, Section 1, Taipei. *Managing Director: Denver Chang.*
EMI (Taiwan) Ltd, 2nd Floor,no.12, 10 Alley 321 Lane, Hsing-Ming Road, Taipei. *Managing Director: Hung Tik.*
K & D Music Entertainment Inc, 6F No 63, Po-Ai Road, Taipei. *Senior Managing Director: Tom Uend.*
Polygram Records Ltd, 5F 99 Nankang Road,Section 3, Taipei. *Managing Director: Michael Hwang.*

Renaissance Records Co Ltd, No 12, Lane 13, Kwang Fu South Road, Taipei. *President: Bob Chen.*
Rock Records and Tapes, 5F, No 3, Lane 240, Kwang Fu S Road, Taipei. *President: Sam C T Duann.*
Sony Music Entertainment (Taiwan) Ltd, 8th Fl, No 35, Lane 11, Kwang-Fu North Road, Taipei. *Managing Director: Matthew Allison.*

THAILAND

BMG Music, 18/F Vanissa Bdlg, Soi Chidlom, Pleonchit Road, Patumwam, Bangkok 10110. *Managing Director: Steven Tan.*
EMI (Thailand) Ltd, 1091/183 New Petchburi Road, Makkasa, Phayathai, Bangkok 10400. *General Manager: Vichart Jirathiyut.*
Giant Records, 61/123 Taveemit Soi 9, Rama IX Road, Asoke-Din Daeng, Huay-Kwang, Bangkok 10310. *Contact: Kraisak Ochareon.*
Grammy Records, 59/1 Soi Prom Pong, Sukhumvit 39, Sukhumvit Road, Prakanong, Bangkok 10110. *Managing Director: Paiboon Damrong Chaitam.*
Michael Record Co Ltd, 52/17-18 Moo 8, Orn-Nuch Road Suanluang, Suanluang, Bangkok 10250. *Managing Director: Chokechai Jaruwatee.*
Polygram (Far East Bangkok Enterprises), 21 115-116 Royal City Avenue, Rama IX Road, Huay Kwang, Bangkok 10310. *Managing Director: Jerry Sim.*
Sony Music Entertainment (Thailand) Ltd, 1091/184-5 New Petchburi Road, Payathai, Bangkok 10400. *General Manager: Peter Gan.*
Warner Music Thailand, 143 Sukhumvit 62/1, Sukhumvit Road, Prakhanong, Bangkok 10250. *Managing Director: Wasana Silpikul.*

TURKEY

Hades Records, Gazi cd, Reisul Kuttap Sk, Peken Ap 50/B, 81160 Baglarbasi, Istanbul. *Director: Volkan Olgun.*
Jazz Records, Atlamatasi Caddesi 5, Serilen, 34470 Unkapani Istanbul. *President: Yasar Demirturk.*
MMY, IMC 6, Blok 6437, 34470 Unkapani Istanbul. *President: Yesil Giresunlu.*
RKD Ltd, Ferah Sok Ferah Apt 1, 19-9, Nisinsati Istanbul. *Managing Director: Armagan Ak.*

UKRAINE

Audio Ukraine, Laboratorny Provulok 7A, 252 133 Kiev. *Managing Director: Yuri Goncharuk.*
Komora, Dav 22, NEC, Hlushkova Ave 1, 252 085 Kiev. *Interpreter: Ivan Chuigouk.*
Leva, Kostyushka Str. 18, 290 000 Lviv. *Managing Director: Igor Krytovitch.*
NAC, Gorkok Str. 47, 252 005 Kiev. *Managing Director: Volodymyr Lagodny.*

UNITED KINGDOM

A&M Records, 136-140 New Kings Road, London SW6 4LZ. *Managing Director: Osman Erlap.*
Abbey Records, 4 Newtec Place, Magdalen Road, Oxford, Oxon OX4 1RE. *Press Officer: Peter Bromley.*
Ace Records, 46-50 Steele Road, London NW10 7AS. *Managing Director: Ted Caroll.*
Acid Jazz Records, 11 Greek Street, London WC1V 5LE. *Managing Director: Edward Piller.*
Active Records, Rockfield Studios, Amberley Court, Monmouth, Gwent NP5 4ET. *Director: Kingsley Ward.*
AKR Records, Waterside Penthouse, 156 High Street, Brentford, Middx TW8 8JA. *Managing Director: Kevin Moran.*
Almo Sounds, 3 Heathmans Road, London SW6 4TJ. *Contact: Mercedes Luis Fuentes.*
Alphabet Records, 253 Camberwell New Road, London SE5 0TH. *Contact: Mark Walmesley.*
Alternative Tentacles Records, 64 Mountgrove Road, London N5 2LT. *Label Manager: Bridget Clay.*
Anagram Records, Bishops Park House, 25-29 Fulham High Street, London SW6 3JH. *Label Manager: Adam Velasco.*
Andrew Music, 6 Wykeham Crescent, Oxford OX4 3SB. *Director: Andrew Claxton.*
Anxious, Devonshire House, 2/4 The Broadway, London N8 9SN. *Managing Director: Tony Quinn.*
Arista Records, Cavendish House, 423 New Kings Road, London SW6 4RN. *General Manager: Mark Williams.*
Ariwa Sounds Ltd, 34 Whitehorse Lane, South Norwood, London SE25 6RE. *Managing Director: Neil Fraser.*
Arrival Records, 39 Leyton Road, Harpenden, Herts AL5 2JB. *Managing Director: David Blaylock.*
Astranova, Unit 306, Canalot Production Studios, 222 Kensal Road, London W10 5BN. *Director: Scott Hill.*
Atomic Records, 32 Neal Street, London WC2H 9PS. *Contact: Mick Newton.*
Avex UK, 22 Soho Square, London W1V 5FJ. *Director: Phil France.*
Awesome Records, 59 Moore park Road, London SW6 2HA. *Managing Director: Falcon Stuart.*
Back Street Records, Cadillac Ranch, Pencraig Uchaf, Cwm Bach, Whiland, Dyfed SA3 40DT, Wales. *A&R: M Menendes & Christy French.*
Bad Habits Music Group, PO Box 111, London W13 0ZH. *Managing Director: John S Rushton.*
Bearcat Records, PO Box 94, Derby DE22 1XA. *Contact: Chris Hall.*
Beatfarm Recordings, Studio C, Chelsea Studios, 416 Fulham Road, London SW6 1HP. *Owner: Marco Perry.*
Beat Goes On Records, PO Box 22, Bury St Edmunds, Suffolk IP28 6XQ. *Label Manager: Michael Gott.*
Beechwood Records, 62 Beechwood Road, South Croydon, Surrey CR2 0AA. *Contact: Chet Selwood.*
Big Cat (UK) Records Ltd, PO Box 3074, 3rd Floor, Devonshire House, Barley Mow Passage, London W4 4ZN. *Label Manager: Tim Vass.*
Big Bear Records, PO Box 944, Birmingham, West Midlands B16 8UT. *Managing Director: Jim Simpson.*
Big Life Records, 15 Little Portland Street, London W1N 5DE. *Chairman: Jazz Summers.*
Blackout Records, 253 Camberwell New Road, London SE5 0TH. *Contact: Mark Walmesley.*
Blanco Y Negro, 66 Golborne Road, London W10 5PS. *Managing Director: Geoff Travis.*
Blueprint, PO Box 5, Derwentside, Co. Durham DH9 7HR. *Label Manager: Rob Ayling.*
BMG (UK) / RCA Records, Bedford House, 69-79 Fulham High Street, London SW6 3JW. *Chairman: John Preston.*
Bobb Records, 12 Waterford Road, Ashley, New Milton, Hants BH25 5BH. *Directors: Mike & Andrea Preston.*
Brilliant Records, 19 Ford Square, London E1 2HS. *Managing Director: Frazer Henry.*
The Brothers Organisation, 74 The Archway, Station Approach, Ranelagh Gardens, London SW6 3UH. *Directors: Ian & Nick Titchener.*
BSC Records, 23 Corbyn Street, London N4 3BY. *Directors: Andy Monoyos & Gordon Ellington.*
Bulldog Records, PO Box 130, Hove, East Sussex BN3 6QU. *Director of International Operations: Steve Lewis.*
Buzz Records, 192 Glasgow Road, Perth PH2 0NA, Scotland. *Managing Director: Dave Arcari.*
Caritas Records, 28 Dalrymple Crescent, Edinburgh EH9 2NX, Scotland. *Managing Director: James Douglas.*
Carlton Records, The Waterfront, Elstree Road, Elstree, Herts WD6 3BS. *A&R Director: John Howard.*
Carrera Recordings Ltd, Westco House, Pensarn Business Park, Abergele, Clwyd LL22 7SF, Wales. *Contact : Paul White.*
Castle Communications, Unit 29, Barwell Business Park, Leatherhead Road, Chessington, Surrey KT9 2NY. *Chairman: Terry Shand.*
Chapter 22 Music, Suite 114, The Custard Factory, Gibb Street, Birmingham B9 4AA. *Contact: Rod Thomson.*
Check Records, Stewart House, Hillbottom Road, Sands Ind. Estate, High Wycombe, Bucks HP12 4HJ. *A&R Copyrite Dept: Cathrine Lee.*
Charley Records Ltd, 156-166 Ilderton Road, London SE15 1NT. *Founder: Jean Luc Young.*
Chimera Records Ltd, 41 Rosebank, Holyport Road, London SW6 6LQ. *Managing Director: Sadia Sadia.*
China Records, 111 Frithville Gardens, London W12 7JG. *Contact: Rachel Speers.*
Circle Sound Services, Circle House, 14 Waveney Close, Bicester, Oxon OX6 8GP. *Proprietor: John Willett.*
Columbia Records, 10 Great Marlborough Street, London W1V 2LP. *Managing Director: Kip Krones.*

Confidential Records, 127 Dewsbury Road, Ossett, West Yorkshire WF5 9PA. *Director: Nev Barker.*
Cooking Vinyl, 3 Park Mews, 213 Kilburn Lane, London W10 4BQ. *A&R: Neil Armstrong.*
Deconstruction, Bedford House, 69-79 Fulham High Street, London SW6 3JW. *Managing Directors: Keith Blackhurst, Pete Hadfield.*
Dedicated Records, 36A Notting Hill Gate, London W11 3JQ. *Managing Director: Doug D'Arcy.*
Demi Monde Records & Publishing, Foel Studio, Llanfair, Caereinion, Powys SY21 0DS, Wales. *Managing Director: Dave Anderson.*
Dick Bros Record Co Ltd, The Main House, Spittalrig Farm, Nr Haddington EH41 3SU, Scotland. *Contact: Jeremy Lawson.*
Director Heat Records, 20 Lanfranc Road, Worthing, West Sussex BN14 7ER. *Managing Director: Mike Pailthorpe.*
Dorado Records Ltd, 76 Brewer Street, London W1R 3PH. *Managing Director: Ollie Buckwell.*
Down To Jam Records, 112A+B Westbourne Grove, Chepstow Road, London W2 5RU. *Managing Director: Paul Moore.*
East West Records, Electric Lighting Station, 46 Kensington Court, London W8 5DP. *Managing Director: Max Hole.*
Echo Label, 13 Bramley Road. London W10 6SP. *Managing Director: Steve Lewis.*
Ember Records, PO Box 130, Hove, East Sussex BN3 6QU. *Chairman of the Board: Jeffrey Kruger.*
EMI Records Group, EMI House, 43 Brook Green, London W6 7EF. *Contact: David Hughes.*
Engine Records, 253 Camberwell New Road, London SE5 0TH. *Contact: Mark Walmesley.*
Epic Records, 10 Great Marlborough Street, London W1V 2LP. *Managing Director: Rob Stringer.*
Equator Records, 333 Latimer Road, London W10 6RA. *Director: Carol Wilson.*
Equity Records, 112A+B Westbourne Grove, Chepstow Road, London W2 5RU. *Managing Director: Paul Moore.*
Esprit Music Ltd, Unit 306, Canalot Production Studios, 222 Kensal Road, London W10 5BN. *Director: Tony Warren.*
Fair Oaks Entertainments, PO Box 19, Ulverston, Cumbria CA12 9TF. *Proprietor/Manager: J G Livingstone.*
Fat Boy Records, PO Box 130, Hove, East Sussex BN3 6QU. *Operations Manager: Peter Hazledine.*
Fellside Recordings, 15 Banklands, Workington, Cumbria CA14 3EW. *Partner: Paul Adams.*
Fire Records, 21A Maury Road, London N16 7BP. *A&R Dept: Dave Barker & Jon Eydmann.*
First Avenue Records, The Courtyard, 42 Colwith Road, London W6 9EY. *Contact: Oliver Smallman.*
FM-Revolver / Heavy Metal Records, 152 Goldthorn Hill, Penn, Wolverhampton, West Midlands WV2 3JA. *Managing Director: Paul Birch.*
Food Records, 172A Arlington Road, London NW1 7HL. *Contact: Ellie O'Ready.*
Fool's Paradise Records, PO Box 6003, London W2 2WE. *Contact: Robin T Chuter.*
4AD, 15 Alma Road, London SW18 1AA. *Managing Director: Ivor Watts-Russell.*
Funki Dred Records Ltd, 36/38 Rochester Place, London NW1 9JX. *A&R: H Browne.*
Gee Street Records Ltd, 57 Gee Street, London EC1V 3RS. *Chief Accountant: Gerard Louis; Assistant: James Howarth.*
Global Records Ltd, 171 Southgate Road, London N1 3LE. *Managing Director: Peter Knight Jr.*
Go! Discs, 72 Black Lion Lane, London W6 9BE. *Managing Director: Andy McDonald.*
Grand Records, 107A High Street, Canvey Island, Essex S58 7RF. *Contact: Ann Adley.*
Grasmere Records, Suite 3 Paramount House, 290 Brighton Road, South Croydon, Surrey CR2 6AG. *Managing Director: Bob Barratt.*
Greentrax Recordings, Cockenzie Business Centre, Edinburgh Road, Cockenzie, East Lothian EH32 0HL, Scotland. *Proprietor: Ian D Green.*
Grenquille Records, Stewart House, Hill Bottom Road, Sands Ind. Estate, High Wycombe, Bucks HP12 4HJ. *International A&R Copyright Lawyer: Keith R Phillips.*
GRP Records International, 33 Broadwick Street, London W1V 1FR. *Contact: Frank Hendricks.*
Handle Records, Handle House, 1 Albion Place, Galena Road, Hammersmith, London W6 0QT. *Chairman: David Walker.*
Harbourtown Records, PO Box 25, Ulverston, Cumbria LA12 7UN. *Managing Director: Gordon Jones.*
Hawk Records Ltd, 123-137 York Street, Belfast BT15 1AB, Northern Ireland. *Managing Director: Charlie Tosh.*
Headscope, Street End Lane, Broadoak, Heathfield, East Sussex TN21 8TU. *Partner: Ron Geesin.*
Hotshot Records, 29 St Michaels Road, Leeds LS6 3BG. *Managing Directors: D Foster and Clio Bradbury.*
Hut Records, Kensal House, 553-579 Harrow Road, London W10 4RH. *Contact: David Boyd.*
Indigo Records, 2nd Fl, Twyman House, 31-39 Camden Road, London NW1 9LF. *Contact: Colin Newman.*
Inky Blackness, 7 Mornington Terrace, Camden Town, London NW1 7RR. *Managing Director: Ian Tregoning.*
Iona Records, 27-29 Carnoustie Place, Scotland Street, Glasgow G5 8PH, Scotland. *Managing Director: Ronnie Simpson.*
IRS Records, EMI House, 443 Brook Green, London W6 7EF. *Label Manager: Richard Breeden.*
Island Records, 22 St Peter's Square, London W6 9NW. *Managing Director: Marc Marot.*
Kinetix, The Black Office, DC Warehouse, Unit 6, Industrial Park, Maple Cross WD3 2AS. *Chairman: Jon Sharp.*
Kitchenware Records, 7 The Stables, St Thomas Street, Newcastle-Upon-Tyne, Tyne & Wear NE1 4LE. *Managing Director: Keith Armstrong.*
KRL, 9 Watt Road, Hillington, Glasgow G52 4RY, Scotland. *Managing Director: Gus McDonald.*
Kufe Records Ltd, 154 Rucklidge Avenue, Harlesden, London NW10 4PR. *Managing Director: Lindel Lewis.*
L'attitude Ltd, First Floor, Ducie House, 37 Ducie Street, Manchester M1 2JW. *Directors: Andy Dodd and Elliot Rashman.*
Linn Records, Floors Road, Waterfoot, Eaglesham, Glasgow G76 0EP, Scotland. *Label Manager: Philip Hobbs.*
Lismor Recordings Ltd, 27-29 Carnoustie Place, Scotland Street, Glasgow G5 8PH, Scotland. *Managing Director: Ronnie Simpson.*
Liverpool Music House Ltd, 51-55 Highfield Street, Liverpool L3 6AA. *Director: Colin Hall.*
Logic Records, 1st Floor, 34-35 Berwick Street, London W1V 3RF. *Contact: Tony Piercy.*
London Records, PO Box 1422, Chancellors House, Chancellors Road, London W6 9SG. *Managing Director: Colin Bell.*
Love This Records Limited, Hundred House, 100 Union Street, London SE1 0NL. *Contact: Lucy Anderson.*
Luna Park, 81 Harley House, Marylebone Road, London NW1 5HT. *Contact: Russell Vaught.*
Magnum Music Group Ltd, Magnum House, High Street, Lane End, Bucks HP14 3JG. *Chairman: Nigel Molden.*
MCA Records Ltd, 139 Piccadilly, London W1V 0AX. *Deputy Managing Director: Jeff Colembo.*
Medium Productions Limited, 74 Saint Lawrence Road, Upminster, Essex RM14 2UW. *Co-Director: Debi Zornes.*
Mercury Records, Chancellors House, 72 Chancellors Road, London W6 9QB. *Managing Director: Howard Berman.*
Metro Music Productions, Metro Radio Ltd, Longriggs, Swalwell, Gateshead, Tyne & Wear NE99 1BB. *Director of Music Production: Jon Craig.*
Millennium Records, 9 Thorpe Close, Portobello Road, London W10 5XL. *Managing Director: Ralph Ruppert.*
Milltown Productions Ltd, 26 East Parade, Bradford, West Yorkshire BD1 5HD. *Producer: Ian Smith.*
Moksha, PO Box 102, London E15 2HH. *Contact: Charles Cosh.*
Moving Shadow Records, 1st & 2nd Floors, 17 St Anne's Court, Soho, London W1V 3AW. *Label Co-Ordinator: Caroline Butler.*
Mrs Casey Music, PO Box 296, Aylesbury, Bucks HP19 3TL. *Director: Steve Heap.*
Mushroom Records UK Ltd, 555 Kings Road, London SW6 2EB. *Managing Director: Gary Ashley.*
Music of Life & Living Beat Records, 20 Hanway Street, London W1P 9DD. *Managing Director: Chris France.*
Music For Nations, 333 Latimer Road, London W10 4LG. *Managing Director: Martin Hooker.*
Musidisc UK, 32 Queensdale Road, Holland Park, London W11 4SB. *Label Manager: Judith Fisher.*
Mute Records, 429 Harrow Road, London W10 4RE. *Managing Director: Daniel Miller.*
Nation Records Ltd, 19 All Saints Road, Notting Hill, London W11 1HE. *Managing Director: Katherine Canoville.*
Neat Records, 71 High Street East, Wallsend, Tyne & Wear NE 28 7RJ. *Managing Director: Dave Wood.*
Now And Then, Unit 29, Empress Ind Estate, Anderson Sreet, Wigan, Lancs WN2 2BG. *Label Manager: Mark Ashton.*
NRG Records, 49 High Street, Kingston-Upon-Thames, Surrey KT1 1LQ. *Managing Director: Robert Jones.*
Nude Records, 6 Warren Mews, London W1P 5DJ. *Managing Director: Saul Galpern.*
One Little Indian Records, 250 York Road, London SW11 3SJ. *Managing Director: Derek Birkett.*
Orionstar Limited, 34 Hill Street, Richmond, Surrey TW9 1TN. *Manager: John Martin.*
OVC Ltd, 34 Salisbury Street, London NW8 8QE. *Managing Directors: Joanne Cohen and Peter Sullivan.*
Palace Of Fun, 16 Elm View, Huddersfield Road, Halifax, Yorkshire HX3 0AE. *Managing Director: Bill Byford.*

Park Records, PO Box 651, Oxford OX2 9RB. *Managing Director: John Dagnell.*
Perfecto Records, Electric Lighting Station, 46 Kensington Court, London W8 5DP. *Contact: Spencer Baldwin.*
Performance Equities Ltd, 112 A & B Westbourne Grove, Chepstow Road, London W2 5RU. *Managing Director: Paul Moore.*
Permanent Records, 22-23 Brook Mews, London W2 3BW. *Managing Director: J. Lennard.*
PHAB Records, High Notes, Sheerwater Avenue, Woodham, Weybridge, Surrey KT15 3DS. *Contact: Phillip Bailey.*
Planet 4, Sun House, 2-4 Little Peter Street, Manchester M15 4PS. *Managing Director: Chris Joyce.*
Plankton Records, 236 Sebert Road, Forest Gate, London E7 0NP. *Senior Partner: Simon Law.*
Play It Again Sam (UK), Suite G, Tech West, 10 Warple Way, London W3 0UE. *General Manager: Peter Dodge.*
Plutonium Records, Stanley House, 15/17 Ladybridge Road, Cheadle Hulme, Greater Manchester SK8 5BL. *Press & Promotions: Zoey Faulkner.*
Pogo Records, Stewart House, Sands Ind. Estate, High Wycombe, Bucks HP12 4HJ. *A&R: Xavier Lee.*
Polly Tone Records, PO Box 124, Ruislip, Middlesex HA4 9BQ. *Director: Valerie Biro.*
PolyGram UK, PO Box 1420, 1 Sussex Place, London W6 9XS. *Chief Executive: Roger Aimes.*
Positiva, 43 Brook Green, London W6 7EF. *Contact: Dave Lambert.*
The Precious Organisation, 14-16 Spiers Wharf, Port Dundas, Glasgow, Strathcylde, Scotland. *Contact: Elliot Davis.*
President Records Limited, Exmouth House, 11 Pine Street, London EC1R 0JH. *Managing Director: David Kassner.*
Priory Records, Unit 9B, Upper Wingbury Courtyard, Wingrave, Bucks HP22 4LW. *Proprietor: Neil Collier.*
Profile Records Ltd, White Swan House, Bennett Street, London W4 2AH. *Director: Jon Sharp.*
PWL International, 222-224 Borough High Street, London SE1 1JX. *Managaing Director: Peter Price.*
Quinlan Road (UK), 1 Heathgate Place, 75/87 Agincourt Road, MW3 2NT. *General Manager: Ian Blackaby.*
R & B Division Limited, 34 Salisbury Street, London NW8 8QE. *Managing Director: Eliot M Cohen.*
Red Bus Records Ltd, 34 Salisbury Street, London NW8 8QE. *Managing Director: Eliot M Cohen.*
Red Lightnin' Ltd, The White House, The Street, North Lopham, Diss, Norfolk IP22 2LU. *Director: Peter Shertser.*
Rhubarb Records, 3rd Floor, 28 D'Arblay Street, Soho, London W1V 3FN. *Director: Dave Holmes.*
Rhythm Squad Records Ltd, PO Box 52, Ilford, Essex IG1 3JT. *Director: Ramesh Kansara.*
Riddle Records, Cadillac Ranch, Pencraig Uchaf, Cum Bach, Whitland, Dyfed SA34 0DT, Wales. *A&R: M Menendes and Christy French.*
Roadrunner Records, Tech West House, Warple Way, London W3 0UL. *General Manager: Mark Palmer.*
Rock 'n' Roll Records, 16 Grove Plce, Penarth CF64 2ND, Wales. *Director: Paul Barrett.*
Rollover Productions, 29 Beethoven Street, London W10 4LJ. *Managing Director: Seamus Morley.*
Ronnie Scott's Jazz House, Magnum House, High Street, Lane End, High Wycombe, Bucks HP14 3JG. *Managing Director: Derek Everett.*
RooArt Europe, 22a Lambolle Place, London NW3 4HP. *Contact: Paul Craig.*
RTL Music, Stewart House, Hill Bottom Road, Sands Ind. Estate, High Wycombe, Bucks HP12 4HJ. *Owner/Producer: Ron Lee.*
Rykodisc Limited, 78 Stanley Gardens, London W3 7SN. *Managing Director: Ian Moss.*
Sadia Sadia, 41 Rosebank, Holyport Road, London SW6 6LQ.
Sain, Caolfan Sain, Llandwrog, Caernarfon, Gwynedd LL54 5TG, Wales. *Managing Director: Dafydd Iwan.*
Saxology Records, 49E St Paul's Road, London N1 2LT. *Managing Director: Mike Tanousis.*
Saydisc Records, Chipping Manor, The Chipping, Wotton-Under-Edge, Glos GL12 7AD. *Partner: Gef Lucena.*
Scotdisc Music & Video, BGS Productions Ltd, Newtown Street, Kilsyth, Glasgow G65 0JX, Scotland. *Marketing Director: Dougie Stevenson.*
Seriously Groovy Music Ltd, 3rd Floor, 28 D'Arblay Street, Soho, London W1V 3FH. *Director: Dave Holmes.*
Setanta Records, PO Box 4693, London SE5 7XZ. *Contact: Keith Cullen.*
Sidestep Records Limited, 9A Dallington Street, London EC1V 0BQ. *Joint Managing Director: Heddi Greenwood.*
Some Bizarre Ltd, 124 New Bond Street, London W1Y 9AE. *Producer: Stevo.*
Sony Music Entertainment (UK), 10 Great Marlborough Street, London W1V 2LP. *Chairman: Paul Burger.*
Sony Soho Square (S²), 10 Great Marlborough Street, London W1V 2LP. *Managing Director: Muff Winwood.*
Soundman Records, Suite 32-34 Hi Tech House, 18 Beresford Avenue, Wembley, Middlesex HA0 1YP. *Head of A&R: Antonio Raggafunk; Managing Director: Raymond Wright.*
Sound of the Underground (SOUR) Records, 8 Strutton Ground, London SW1P 2HP. *Contact: Martin Love.*
Stamina Management, 47 Prout Grove, London NW10 1PU. *Managing Director: Peter Gage.*
Start Audio & Video, Suite 20A, Canada House, Blackburn Road, London NW6 1RZ. *Sales and Commercial Manager: Brian Atkinson.*
Stephen W Tayler, 41 Rosebank, Holyport Road, London SW6 6LQ. *Contact: Stephen W Tayler.*
Stone Tiger Records, PO Box 4464, London SW19 6XT. *Owner: Les Rowley.*
Strange Fruit Records, Electron House, Cray Avenue, Orpington, Kent BR5 3PN. *General Manager: Brian O'Reilly.*
Stress Records, PO Box 89, Slough, Berkshire SL1 8NA. *Manager: Nick Gordon Brown.*
Sub Pop Records, 4 Aberdeen House, 22 Highbury Grove, London N5 2OQ. *Label Manager: Lisa Paulon.*
Swoop Records, Stewart House, Hillbottom Road, Sands Ind. Estate, High Wycombe, Bucks HP12 4HJ. *A&R: Kathrine Le Matt.*
SYME International, 81 Park Road, Wath-Upon-Dearn, Rotherham, South Yorkshire LS17 6LP. *Contact: Martin Looby.*
Taurus Records (UK), 23 Blackheath Rise, Lewisham, London SE13 7PN. *Contact: Beverly Miller.*
Tembo Entertainments, PO Box 1655, London W8 5HZ. *Contact: Howard Elson.*
Theobald Dickson Productions Ltd, The Coach House, Swinhope Hall, Swinhope, Lincolnshire LN3 6HT. *Managing Director: Bernard Theobald.*
Timbre Records Ltd, 93 Brondesbury Road, London NW6 6RY. *Managing Director: Diane M Hinds.*
TKO Records Ltd, PO Box 130, Hove, East Sussex BN3 6QU. *Chairman: Jeffrey Kruger; Director of Licensing: Steve Lewis.*
Too Pure, 3A Highbury Crescent, London N5 1RN.
Trade 2, 66 Golborne Road, London W10 5PS. *Managing Director: Geoff Travis.*
Trim Top Records, 13 Winton Park, Edinburgh EH10 7EX, Scotland. *Owner: Gerry Ford.*
Triple Earth, 24 Foley Street, London W1P 7LA. *Partner: Iain Scott.*
Unexploded Persons Bureau, PO Box 6414, London N1 3SA. *Co-Ordinator: Russell Willes.*
Unity Records, John Henry Bldg, 16/24 Brewery Road, London N7 9NH. *Manager - Sales & Retail: Pepin Clout.*
Upbeat Recordings Ltd, Sutton Business Centre, Rastmoor Way, Wallington, Surrey SM6 7AH. *Contact: Beryl Korman.*
Vinyl Japan (UK) Ltd, 281 Camden High Street, London NW1 7BX. *Manager: Patrick James.*
Vinyl Solution, 231 Portobello Road, London W11 1LT. *Contacts: Rob Tennant, Alain de la Mata, Nick Brown.*
Virgin Records, Kensal House, 553-579 Harrow Road, London W10 4RH. *Chairman: Ken Berry.*
Vision Discs, PO Box 92, Gloucester GL4 8HW. *Contact: Vic Coppersmith.*
Warner Music (UK)/ WEA Records, The Warner Bldg, 28 Kensington Church Street, London W8 4EP. *Chairman: Rob Dickins.*
Warp Records Ltd, The Ballroom, Cavendish Bldgs, 210-218 West Street, Sheffield S1 4EU. *Directors: Steve Beckett and Rob Mitchell.*
Waveeffect Limited, 34 Salisbury Street, London NW8 8QE. *Managing Director: Eliot M Cohen.*
Wolf Records, 83 Brixton Water Lane, London SW2 1PH. *Managing Director: Dominique Bretmes.*
XL Recordings, 17-19 Alma Road, London SW18 1AA. *Administration Manager: Elise Theuma.*
Young Guns Productions, 95 Carshalton Park Road, Carshalton Beeches, Surrey SM5 3SJ. *Owner: Tom Jennings.*
Zarg Records, Stewart House, Hillbottom Road, High Wycombe, Bucks HP12 4HJ. *A&R Writer/Producer: Ron Dickson.*
Zomba Records, Zomba House, 165-167 Willesden High Road, London NW10 2SG. *General Manager: Andy Richmond.*
Zoo Bee Records, Suite 6, 1 Cranbourn Alley, Cranbourn Street, London WC2H 7AN. *Producer: Tim Rabjohns.*
ZTT Records, The Blue Building, 42-46 St Lukes Mews, London W11 1DG. *Contact: Claire Leadbitter.*

USA

Aarrow Records, 900 19th Avenue So, Suite 207, Nashville, TN 37212. *Owner: Kelli Steele; A&R Director: Ruth Steele.*
A & E Music Inc, 13644 S W 142 Avenue, Suite D, Miami, FL 33186. *President: Joe Granda.*
A & R Records, 900 19th Avenue So, Suite 207, Nashville, TN 37212. *Owner: Ruth Steele.*
A&M Records, 1416 N La Brea Avenue, Hollywood, CA 90028. *President: Al Cafaro.*
Alcazar Productions, PO Box 429 South, Main Street, Waterbury, VT 05676. *Vice President: Jennifer Harwood.*
Alexandria House, 3310 West End Avenue, 5th Floor, Nashville, TN 37203. *Marketing Co-Ordinator: Michelle Gust.*
All American Music Group, 808 Wilshire Blvd, Santa Monica, CA 90405. *Director, National Publicity: Sheryl Northrop.*
American Music, 1206 Decatur Street, New Orleans, LA 70116. *President: George H Buck Jr.*
American Recordings, 3500 West Olive Avenue, Suite 1550, Burbank, CA 91505.
Antithesis Records, 273 Chippewa Drive, Columbia, SC 29210-6508.
Arista Records, 6 W 57th Street, New York, NY 10019. *President: Clive Davis.*
Artan Records, PO Box 5672, Buena Park, CA 90622-5672. *Manager: Carmen Ortiz.*
Ash Music, 116 NE 136 Avenue, Portland, OR 97230. *A&R: Jason Charles.*
Asil Records, PO Box 790576, Middle Village, NY 11379-0576. *President: Dan Karpf.*
Atlantic Records, 75 Rockefeller Plaza, New York, NY 10019-6907. *Co-Chairmen: Ahmet Ertegun, Doug Morris.*
Axbar Records, PO Box 12353, San Antonio, TX 78212. *Producer/General Manager: Joe Scates.*
Audiophile, 1206 Decatur Street, New Orleans, LA 70116. *President: George H Buck Jr.*
Baker Productions, 311 2nd Avenue SW, Callman, AL 35055. *President: Charles Baker.*
Bar None Records, PO Box 1709, Hoboken, NJ 07030. *President: Tom Prendergast.*
Bell Records International, PO Box 725, Daytona Beach, FL 32115-0725. *Vice President: Charles Vickers.*
Benson Music Group Inc, 365 Great Circle Road, Nashville, TN 37228. *International Sales: Janice Cuttler.*
Biograph Records Inc, 374 Congress Street, Suite 407, Boston, MA 02210. *Vice-President: Alan Caplin.*
Black & Blue Records, Suite 152, 400 D Putnam Pike, Smithfield, RI 02917. *President: Peter Yarmouth.*
Blaster-Boxx Hits, 519 N Halifax Avenue, Dayton Beach, FL 32118. *Chief Executive Officer: Bobby Lee Cude.*
Blue Note / Manhattan / Capitol Jazz Records, 810 7th Avenue, New York, NY 10019. *President: Bruce Lundvall.*
Blowin' Smoke Records, 7438 Shoshone Avenue, Van Nuys, CA 91406-2340. *President: Larry Weisberg.*
BME Records, PO Box 76507, Washington, DC 20013. *President: Carl Bentley.*
BMG Music / RCA, 1540 Broadway, New York, NY 10036. *Chairman: Michael Dornemann.*
Broken Rekids, PO Box 460402, San Francsico, CA 94146-0402, USA. *President: JayDid*
BSW Records, PO Box 2297, Universal City, TX 78148. *President/Chief Executive Officer: Frank Wilson.*
C & S Productions, PO Box 91492, Anchorage, AK 99509-1492. *Partner: Tim R Crawford.*
Cadence Jazz Records, Cadence Building, Redwood, NY 13679. *Producer: Bob Rusch.*
Camaraderie Music Co, 238 Austin Street, Boston, MA 02136-1844. *Contact: Curt Naihersey.*
Capitol Records, 1750 N Vine Street, Hollywood, CA 90028. *President: Gary Gersh.*
Caprice International Records, Box 808, Lititz, PA 17543. *President: Joey Welz.*
Case Entertainment Group Inc (R), 102 East Pikes Peak Avenue, Suite 200, Colorado Springs, CO 80903. *Contact: Robert A Case.*
Cat's Voice Productions, PO Box 1361, Sanford, ME 04073-7361. *Owner: Tom Reeves.*
Center for The Queen of Peace, 3350 Highway 6, Suite 412, Sugar Land, TX 77478. *Director: Rafael Brom.*
Century Media Records, 1453-A 14th Street #324, Santa Monica, Ca 90404. *Label Manager: Julie Wexler.*
C E R Records, 7400 N Adams Road, North Adams, MI 49262. *President: Claude E Reed.*
Cerebral Records, 1236 Laguna Drive, Carlsbad, CA 92008. *President: Lincoln Kroll; Publisist: Carol Leno.*
Chapel Music Group Inc, 2021 Richard Jones Road, Suite 180, Nashville, TN 37215. *Director of Marketing: Heather Campbell.*
Chemistry Records Ltd, Box 68, Las Vegas, NM 87701. *President: Robert John Jones.*
Creative Improvised Music Projects, Cadence Building, Redwood, NY 13679. *Producer: Bob Rusch.*
Circle, 1206 Decatur Street, New Orleans, LA 70116. *President: George H Buck Jr.*
Clarity Recordings, PO Box 411407, San Francisco, CA 94141-1407. *President: Ed Woods.*
Confidential Records, 1013 Evelyn Avenue, Albany, CA 94706. *President: Joel Brandwein.*
Convenience, PO Box 66461, AMC O'Hare, IL 60666. *Director: John Maz.*
Cosmotone Records, 3350 Highway 6, Suite 412, Sugar Land, TX 77478. *President: Rafael Brom.*
Cude & Pickens Music, 519 North Halifax Avenue, Daytona Beach, FL 32118. *Chief Executive Officer: Bobby Lee Cude.*
Cybortravik Recording & Video Group, 8927 Claycott Drive, Dallas, TX 75243. *chief Executive Officer: David C May.*
DanceFloor Distribution/Echo USA, 95 Cedar Lane, Englewood, NJ 07631. *President: Jeffrey Collins.*
Del-Fi Records Inc, PO Box 69188, Los Angeles, CA 90069. *Owner & President: Bob Keane.*
Diva Entertainment World, 853 Broadway #1516, New York City, NY 10003. *Managing Director: Marc Krasnow.*
E & J Records, 1505 Elvis Presley Blvd, Memphis, TN 38106. *Executive Assistant: Linda Lloyd.*
East West Records America, 75 Rockefeller Plaza, New York, NY 10019-6907. *CEO: Sylvia Rhone.*
Edensong, PO Box 34, Days Creek, OR 97429. *Owner: Rick Foster.*
Elastic Records, PO Box 17598, Anaheim, CA 92817-7598. *Owner: Amin Ghashghai.*
Elektra Records, 75 Rockefeller Plaza, New York, NY 10019-6907. *Chairman: Bob Krasnow.*
Ember Records, 4501 Connecticut Avenue, NW, Suite 905, Washington, DC 20008. *Chief Executive Officer: Michael Cohn.*
EMI Records Group, 1290 6th Avenue, New York NY 10104. *CEO: Charles Koppleman.*
Enemy Productions Inc, 234 6th Avenue, Brooklyn, NY 11215. *President: Michael Knuth.*
Epic Records, PO Box 4450, New York, NY 10101-4450. *President: Dave Glew.*
Ernie Bivens Productions, 203 Gates Drive, Hendersonville, TN 37075-4961. *Owner/Producer: Ernie Bivens.*
The Eternal Song Agency, 6326 E Livingston Avenue, Reynoldsburg, OH 43068. *President: Leopold Xavier Crawford.*
FAME Recording Studios, PO Box 2527, Muscle Shoals, AL 35662. *Studio Manager: Rodney Hall.*
Feather Records, PO Box 132, Astor Station, Boston, MA 02123-0132. *Co-Owner: L Pass.*
(510) Records, 5299 College Avenue, Suite E, Oakland, CA 94618. *President: Elliot Cahn.*
Five Roses Music Group, 34A Lanier Road, Studio I, Jekyll Island, GA 31527. *President: Sammie Lee Marler.*
Flying Heart Records, 4026 NE 12th Avenue, Portland, OR 97212. *Owner: Jan Celt.*
Fox Records, PO Box 1027, Neenah, WI 54957-1027. *President: Tony Ansems.*
Frank Russell Productions, PO Box 453, Totowa, NJ 07511. *Producer: Frank Russell.*
GBS Records, 203 Gates Drive, Hendersonville, TN 37075-4961. *Owner/Producer: Ernie Bivens.*
Geffen / DGC Records, 9130 Sunset Blvd, Los Angeles, CA 90069-6197. *Chairman: David Geffen.*
Genius Records, PO Box 481052, Los Angeles, CA 90048. *Contact: Marcy Blaustein*
GHB, 1206 Decatur Street, New Orleans, LA 70116. *President: George H Buck Jr.*
Giant Records, 8900 Wilshire Blvd, Suite 200, Beverly Hills, CA 90211. *Owner: Irving Azoff.*
Glide Records, PO Box 8243, Calabasas, CA 91372. *Proprietor: Cho Paquet.*
Gotee Records, 227 Third Avenue N, Franklin, TN 37064. *Administrative Assistant: Claudia Tapia.*
Gray Dot Records, 1991 South Cobb Drive, Marietta, GA 30060. *Chief Executive Officer: Marty Bush.*

Greco Holdings Inc, Market Street Square, 33 Wilkes Barre Boulevard, Wilkes Barre, PA 18701. *President/Chief Executive Officer: Thom Greco.*
Green Monkey Records, PO Box 31983, Seattle, WA 98103. *Owner: Tom Dyer.*
Greener Pastures Records, 70 N 202, Peterborough, NH 03458-1107. *President: Wayner Green.*
Group Productions, 2890 N Monroe Avenue, Box 481, Loveland, CO 80234. *Audio Producer/Technician: Steve Saavedra.*
GRP Records, 555 W 57th Street, New york, NY 10019. *President: Larry Rosen.*
Grrr Records, 920 W Wilson, Chicago, IL 60640. *Publicity/Retail Manager: Shelley Needham.*
Hammerhead Records Inc, 41 East University Avenue, Champaign, IL 61820. *President: Todd Thorstenson.*
Hard Hat Records, 519 N Halifax Avenue, Daytona Beach, FL 32118. *Chief Executive Officer: Bobby Lee Cude.*
Heartwrite Music, PO Box 1739, Texarkana, AR 75504. *President: David Patillo.*
High Kite Productions & Publishing, 1245 Elizabeth St, Denver, CO 80206. *Producer (Owner/President): Henry "Broz" Rowland.*
Higher Octave Music, 23715 W Malibu Road, #385, Malibu, CA 90265. *Senior Vice President: Scott Bergstein.*
Hollywood Records, 500 S Buena Vista Street, Animation Bldg, Burbank, CA 91521. *CEO: Wesley Hein.*
IKON Records, 212 North 12th Street, Suite 3, Philadelphia, PA 19107. *President A&R: Vincent Krishner.*
Imaginary Records, PO Box 66, Whites Creek, TN 37189. *Proprietor: Lloyd Townsend Jr.*
Imago Recording Company, 152 W 57th Street, 44th Floor, New York, NY 10019. *President: Terry Ellis.*
Inferno Records, PO Box 28743, Kansas City, MO 64118. *Director of A&R: Mark Murtha.*
Interscope Records, 10900 Wilshire Blvd, 12th Floor, Los Angeles, CA 90024. *Label Manager: Ted Field.*
IRS Records, 3939 Lankseshim Blvd, Studio City, CA 91064. *Chairman: Miles Copeland.*
Island Records, 400 Lafayette Street, New York, NY 10003. *Chairman: Chris Blackwell.*
Jay Jay Records, 35 NE 62nd Street, Miami, FL 33138. *President: Walter E Jagiello.*
Jazzology, 1206 Decatur Street, New Orleans, LA 70116. *President: George H Buck Jr.*
Jin, PO Drawer 10, 238 E Main St, Ville Platte, LA 70586. *President: Floyd Soileau.*
Justice Music Corporation, 11586 Blix Street, North Hollywood, CA 91602. *Executive Vice President: Monte R Thomas.*
Ketter Entertainment, PO Box 740702, San Diego, CA 92174-0702. *President/Chief Executive Officer: Al Ketter.*
King of Kings, PO Box 725, Daytona Beach, FL 32115-0725. *Vice President: Charles Vickers.*
K-Tel International (USA) Inc, 2605 Fernbrook Lane North, Minneapolis, MN 55447-4736. *President and Chief Executive Officer: Mickey Elfenbein.*
L&A Records, PO Box 296, 324 Godwin Avenue, Midland Park,NJ 07432. *President: Tony Loeffler.*
LA International, PO Box 725, Daytona Beach, FL 32115-0725. *Vice President: Charles Vickers.*
Lanor Records, PO Box 233, 329 N Main Street, Church Point, LA 70525. *Owner: Lee Lavergne.*
Landmark Communications Group, PO Box 1444, Hendersonville, TN 37077. *President: Bill Anderson Jr.*
Liberty Records, 3322 West End Avenue, Nashville, TN 37203. *President: Jimmy Bowen.*
Lifesong Records, PO Box 5807, Englewood, NJ 07631. *President: Philip S Kurnit.*
Light Records, 1207 17th Avenue S, #103, Nashville, TN 37212. *General Manager: Rob Woolsey.*
Loud Cry Records, PO Box 210270, Nashville, TN 37221-0270. *Owner/President: Don Sanders.*
Maiden Music, PO Box 777, Trevilians, VA 23170. *President: Michael D Moore.*
Mail Order Jazz, 601 Virginia Avenue, Tiften, GA 31794. *Owner: Gus P Statiras.*
Maison de Soul, PO Drawer 10, 238 E Main Street, Ville Platte, LA 70586. *President: Floyd Soileau.*
Map The Planet Records, 228 West 5th Street, Kansas City, MO 64105. *Project Co-Ordinator: Joe Comparato.*
MCA Records, 70 Universal Plaza, Universal City, CA 91608. *Chairman: Al Teller.*
Mel Carter, PO Box 69646, Los Angeles, CA 90069. *Contact: Larry Kleno.*
Mercury Records, Wolrdwide Plaza, 825 8th Avenue, New York, NY 10019. *President: Ed Eckstine.*
Metal Blade Records Inc, 2345 Erringer Road, Suite 108, Simi Valley, CA 93065. *Office Manager/Mechanical Licensing: Kim Kelly.*
Metrostar Music, PO Box 5807, Englewood, NJ 07631. *General Manager: Philip S Kurnit.*
Mirror Records Inc, 645 Titus Avenue, Rochester, NY 14617. *President: Armand Schaubroeck.*
Mobile Fidelity International, PO Box 8359, Incline Village, NV 89452-8359. *President and Executive Producer: Brad S Miller.*
Monster Music, 274 Wattis Way, South San Francisco, CA 94080. *General Manager: Thad Wharton.*
Morgan Creek Music Group, 1875 Century Park East, Suite 600, Los Angeles, CA 90067. *Chairman: James Robinson.*
Motown Records, 6255 W Sunset Blvd, 17th Floor, Los Angeles, CA 90028. *CEO: Jheryl Busby.*
NAIL Inc, 231 Commercial St, NE, Salem, OR 97301-3411. *President: Mike Jones.*
101 Records, PO Box 123, Solana Beach, CA 92075. *Creative Director: Marc Wintriss.*
Pavement Music Inc, 17W703A Butterfield Road, Oakbrook Terrace, IL 60181. *President: Mark Nawara.*
Peridot Music Co, PO Box 8846, Cranston, RI 02920. *President/Owner: Amy Parravano.*
Planet Dallas Studios Inc, 3515 Dickason, Dallas, TX 75219. *General Manager: Debb Rooney.*
Platinum Gold Productions, 9200 Sunset Blvd, Suite 1220, Los Angeles, CA 90069. *Partner: Stev Cohen.*
Plug Productions, 273 Chippewa Drive, Columbia, SC 29210-6508. *Manager: Ron Sparks.*
Polydor/Atlas, 1416 N La Brea Avenue, Los Angeles, CA 90028. *Executive Assistant: Deana J Smart.*
PolyGram Group, Worldwide Plaza, 825 8th Avenue, New York, NY 10019. *President: Rick Dobbis.*
PPL-MCI Entertainment Group, 10 Universal Plaza, PO Box 8442, Universal City, CA 91618. *Managing Director: Maxx Diamond.*
Pravda Records Inc, 3823 N Southport, Chicago, IL 60613. *Managing Director: Kenneth Goodman.*
Primitech Releases, PO Box 210330, San Francisco, CA 94121. *Owner/Label Manager: Victor Krag.*
Progressive, 1206 Decatur Street, New Orleans, LA 70116. *President: George H Buck Jr.*
Projekt Records, PO Box 1591, Garden Grove, CA 92642-1591. *General Manager: Sam.*
Pulse Records, PO Box 294, Westerville, OH 43086-0294. *President/Owner: Randy Kettering.*
Punk Metal Rock Records, PO Box 410099, San Francisco, CA 94141-0099. *A&R Head: Stash Ravine.*
Quango Music Group Inc, 9744 Wilshire Blvd, #305, Beverly Hills, CA 90212. *President: George Ghiz.*
Railroad Records, PO Box 54325, Atlanta, GA 30308. *Owner: Paul Cornwell; Manager: Ann McQueen.*
Rainforest Records Inc, 8855 SW Holly Lane, Suite 110, Wilsonville, OR 97070. *Producer & Chief Executive Officer: Ray Woods.*
Rambunctious Records Inc, c/o Power, Weiss & Kurnit, LLP, 600 Madison Avenue, 22nd Floor, New York, NY 10022-1615. *President: Philip S Kurnit.*
Randolf Productions Inc, 23181 Verdugo Drive, Suite 106, Laguna Hills, CA 92653. *President: Randy Ray.*
Relativity Records, 187-07 Henderson Avenue, Hollis, NY 11423. *President: Barry Korbin.*
Rhino Entertainment, 10635 Santa Monica Blvd, Los Angeles, CA 90025. *President: Richard Foos.*
Rhythms Productions/Tom Thumb Music, PO Box 34485, Los Angeles, CA 90034-0485. *President: Ruth White.*
Rising Son Records International, PO Box 657, Housatonic, MA 01236. *Assistant: Dawn Mitchell.*
Rising Star Records, 52 Executive Park South, Suite 5203, Atlanta, GA 30329. *Owner: Barbara Taylor.*
Rock Dog Records, PO Box 3687, Hollywood, CA 90028. *Vice President of A&R: Gerry North.*
Rodell Records Inc, PO Box 93457, Hollywood, CA 90093. *President: Adam S Rodell.*
Rosebud Records, 1030 Villa Place, Nashville, TN 37212. *President/Record Producer: Fate Vanderpool.*
Rotten Records, PO Box 2157, Montclair, CA 91763. *A&R Director: Dick Shitelmeyer.*
RRRecords, 151 Paige Street, Lowell, MA 01852. *Owner: Ron.*
Rustron Music Productions, c/o The Whimsy, 1156 Park Lane, West Palm Beach, FL 33417. *Executive Director: Rusty Gordon.*
Sabre Productions, PO Box 10147, San Antonio, TX 78210. *Producer: E J Henke.*
Salexo Music Co, PO Box 18093, Charlotte, NC 28218-0093. *President: Samuel Obie.*
Schizophonic Records, 231 Commercial St, NE, Salem, OR 97301-3411. *President: Mike Jones.*

Scooter Records/Scootertunes Inc, PO Box 610166, Dallas, TX 75261. *President: Janett Bellamy; Vice-President: Gina Bellamy.*

Scotti Bros Records, 2114 Pico Blvd, Santa Monica, CA 90405. *President: Myron Roth.*

Shiro Records Inc, 8228 Sunset Blvd, #108, Los Angeles, CA 90046. *President: Shiro Gutzie.*

Sikio Marika Records, 6840 N Maple #157, Fresno, CA 93710. *Label Head: Tyrone White.*

Silent Records, 340 Bryant Street, 3rd Floor, San Francisco, CA 94107. *President: Kim Cascone.*

Songchild Producations, 117 Manor Circle, Myrtle Beach, SC 29575-7201. *Artist: Paul Skyland.*

Sony Music Entertainment / Columbia Records, 51 W 52nd Street, New York, NY 10019. *Chairman: Michael Schulhof.*

Southland, 1206 Decatur Street, New Orleans, LA 70116. *President: George H Buck Jr.*

Sovereign Records, 1501 Broadway, Suite 1310, New York, NY 10036. *President: Ruby Fisher.*

Springhollow Records, PO Box 294, Westerville, OH 43086-0294. *Owner/President: Randy Kettering.*

Swallow, PO Drawer 10, 238 E Main Street, Ville Platte, LA 70586. *President: Floyd Soileau.*

Syntonic Research Inc, 3405 Barranos Circle, Austin, TX 78731-5711. *Sales Manager: Michael Kron.*

Tar Heel Records, PO Box 1557, West Caldwell, NJ 07007-1557. *President: Tar Heel Pete; Vice President: Tony Ansems.*

Tedesco Tunes, 16020 Lahey Street, Granada Hill, CA 91344. *President: Dale T Tedesco.*

Temple Productions Ltd, 310 E Chicago Street, Elgin, IL 60120. *President: Caesar F Kalinowski.*

Terra Nova Recording Coompany, 853 Broadway, #1516, New York, NY 10003. *President: Mark Krasnow; Chief Executive Officer: Robert Mangovceff.*

Times-Square Fantasy Theatre, 519 N Halifax Avenue, Daytona Beach, FL 32118. *Chief Executive Officer: Bobby Lee Cude.*

TKO Records, 4501 Connecticut Avenue, NW, Suite 905, Washington, DC 20008. *Chief Executive Officer: Michael Cohn.*

Tranquil Technology Music, PO Box 20463, Oakland, CA 94620. *Producer: Michael Mantra.*

Trusty Tuneshop Recording Studios, 8781 Rose Creek Road, Nebo, KY 42441. *Owner/Manager: Elsie Trusty Childers.*

Virgin Records, 338 N Foothill Road, Beverly Hills, CA 90210. *President: Phil Quartararo.*

Vokes Music, Record & Promotion Co, PO Box 12, New Kensington, PA 15068-0012. *Owner/President: Howard Vokes.*

Warner / Reprise / Sire Records, 3300 Warner Blvd, Burbank, CA 91510. *Chairman: Mo Ostin.*

Worship & Praise Records Inc, PO Box 593, Times Square Station, New York, NY 10108. *President/Chief Executive Officer/Executive Producer: Minister Maharold Peoples Jr.*

Zero Hour Records, 1600 Broadway Number 701, New York, NY 10019. *Popmeister: Serge Zero.*

Zippah Recording Studio, PO Box 1790, Brookline, MA 02146. *Co-Owner/Producer: Peter Weiss.*

Zomba Enterprises Inc, 137-139 W 25th Street, New York, NY 10001. *Senior Vice President /General Manager: David Renzer.*

VENEZUELA

Discorona CA, Río a Puente Soublette, Edif. Fonodisco Apartado 5995, 1010 Caracas. *President: Evelio Cortés.*

Inversiones Rodven CA, Centro Comercial Concresa, 2° Psio, Of. 422-Prado del Este, 1080 Caracas. *President: Rodolfo Rodríguez.*

Manoca Records Venezuela SA, Avda. San Martin, PB Local 5-6, Resid. Metroplace, 1020 Caracas. *General Manager: Angelo Nigro.*

APPENDIX B
MANAGEMENT COMPANIES

ANDORRA

Espectacles Del Principat, Ctra de l'Aldosa, Botiga 2, La Massana. *Director: Joan M. Armengal.*
Limitada de Producciones SL, Cuitat Consuegra 12, 2° 2a, Edifici Orió, Andorra La Vella. *Administrator: Joan Deltell Porta.*
Rial Andorra, Avda. de Tarragona 24, Andorra La Vella. *Manager: Pascal Lair.*

ARGENTINA

Abraxas Producciones Internacionales, Avda. Callao 875, 4° Piso H, 1023 Buenos Aires. *Director General: Carlos Pity Yñurrigarro.*
Argentina Producciones, Avda. Corrientes 1628, 11G Piso Of. B, 1042 Buenos Aires. *Director: Norberto Horacio Baccon.*
CDN Producciones Iberoamericanas, Loyola 1530, 1414 Buenos Aires. *Director General: Esteba Mellino.*
Data Pop Rock Comunicacion, 25 de Mayo 758, 5° Piso, Of. E, 1002 Buenos Aires. *President: Juan Carlos Kohan.*
Esther Margarita Soto, Estados Unidos 629, 1109 Buenos Aires. *General Manager: Esther M Soto.*
Hector Cavallero Producciones, Hipólito Irigoyen 1994, Pta Baja 4, 1089 Buenos Aires: *Contact: Hector Cavallero.*
JC Producciones Srl, Rivadavia 86, 4° Piso, Of. 6, 8300 Neuquen. *President: Juan Carlos Allende.*
Juan Carlos Baglieto, Fragata Pte, Sarmiento 1663,Buenos Aires. *Manager: Eduardo Hagopian.*
Matt Hungo Srl, Tucumán 1455, 5° Piso, Of. A-B, 1050 Buenos Aires. *General Manager: Omar Alberto Lauria.*
Mediavilla Producciones Srl, Colombia, 1727 Valetin Alsina, 1822 Buenos Aires. *President: Oscar Mediavilla.*
Ohian Producciones, Aguilar 2073, 1428 Buenos Aires. *Director: Alberto Ohanian.*
Poggini & Asociados Srl, Pasteur 250, 1 Piso, Of. C, 1028 Buenos Aires. *Manager: Rodolfo Poggini.*

AUSTRALIA

Alan James Management, GPO Box 2727, Darwin, NT 0801. *Manager: Alan James.*
Andrew McManus Management, Suite 1, 3 Smail Street, Ultimo, NSW 2007. *Managing Director: Andrew McManus.*
B & S Promotions, PO Box 1481, Frankston, VIC 3199. *Partners: Bill and Sally Dettmer.*
Bernie Stahl Entertainments, Parkrise, 5th Floor, 3 Alison Street, Surfers Paradise, QLD 4217. *Managing Director: Bernie Stahl; Director: Suzanne Stahl.*
Cranium Management, PO Box 760, Leichhardt, NSW 2040. *Manager: Skip Beaumont-Edmonds.*
Entertainment Plus, Gordon Place, Suite 15/24 Little Bourke Street, Melbourne, VIC 3000. *Manager: Andrew Malouf.*
Feel Management & Tour Co-Ordination, 2/54 Bronte Road, Bondi Junction, NSW 2022. *Director: Tim Pittman.*
Gary Morris Management, The Office, PO Box 186, Glebe, NSW 2037. *Contact: Gary Morris.*
Grant Thomas Management, PO Box 176, Potts Point, NSW 2011. *Principal: Grant Thomas.*
Ideal Management P/C, PO Box 1037, Caufield North, Melbourne, VIC 3161. *Managing Director/Chief Executive Officer: Nathan D Brenner.*
International Management Group, 281 Clarence Street, Sydney, NSW 2000. *Director of Arts & Entertainment: Stephen Flint Wood.*
International Profile Management, Entertainment Place, PO Box 4, Broadway, QLD 4006. *Director: Darren Clark.*
Isaac Apel Management, 46 Caroline Street, South Yarra, VIC 3141. *Director: Amanda Michaelson.*
Jaybee's Entertainment Agency, PO Box 37, Sanctuary Place, NSW 2540. *Manager: Narrel M Brown.*
Julie Hickson Management, 25 Overend Street, Brunswick, VIC 3056. *Manager: Julie Hickson.*
Kevin Jacobsen Management, Level 1, 98 Glebe Point Road, Glebe, NSW 2037. *Managing Director: Kevin Jacobsen.*
Lighthouse Promotions, 1st Floor, Cherry Tree, 53 Balmain Street, Sandringham VIC 3121. *Director: Linda Gebar.*
Loud & Clear Management Pty Ltd, PO Box 276, Albert Park, VIC 3206. *Managing Director: Michael Roberts.*
Management Only, PO Box 1289, North Sydney, NSW 2059. *Managing Director: Gary Grant.*
Mark Bishop Management Pty Ltd, PO Box 123, Kensington, VIC 3031. *Manager: Mark Bishop.*
McLean's Artist Management, Suite 8, 4 Jacques Avenue, Bondi Beach, NSW 2026. *Managing Director: Calum McLean.*
Melke, 158 Raglan Street, Mosman, Sydney, NSW 2088. *Director: Sue Melke.*
Melody Management, PO Box 598, Coogee, NSW 2034. *Directors: Michael & Elizabeth McMartin.*
MGM (Michael Gudinski Management), 9 Dundas Lane, Albert Park, VIC 3206. *Managing Director: Michael Gudinski.*
Michael Long Management, PO Box 494, Double Bay, NSW 2028. *Manager: Michael Long.*
Mighty Management, 21 Castle Street, Randwick, Sydney, NSW 2031. *Manager: Mick Mazzone.*
MMA Management International, 351 Crown Street, Surry Hills, NSW 2010. *Manager: Sam Evans.*
Mr Walker's Company, PO Box 2197, St Kilda, VIC 3182. *Contact: Andrew Walker.*
Nationwide Entertainment Agency, 4 Jennings Road, Heathcote, NSW 2233. *Director: Kathryn Muriti.*
Oz Artist Management, PO Box 4074, Doncaster Heights, VIC 3109. *Manager: John Perosa.*
Oz-X-Press Music, 400 North Rocks Road, Carlingford, NSW 2118. *Manager: Trudi Nicholls.*
Painters & Dockers Management, Box 69, Burnley, Melbourne, VIC 3121. *Manager: Colin Buckler.*
Paisley Management, PO Box 2227, Rose Bay North, NSW 2030. *Managing Director: Kent Paisley.*
Paul Cussen Management, Suite 1, Level 2, 41 Oxford Street, Darlinghurst, NSW 2010. *Proprietor: Paul Cussen.*
Peter Rix Management Pty Ltd, PO Box 144, Milsons Point, NSW 2061. *Managing Director: Peter Rix.*
Phill Shute Management Pty Ltd, PO Box 273, Dulwich Hill, NSW 2203. *Managing Director: Phill Shute.*
Ralph Carr Management, c/o RCM International Group, 29 Balmain Street, Richmond, VIC 1321. *Managing Director: Ralph Carr.*
Richard East Management Pty Ltd, 20 Leila Street, Prahran, VIC 3181. *Managing Director: Richard East.*
Russell J White Management, PO Box 325, South Melbourne, VIC 3205. *Managing Director: Russell White.*
Servant Communications, PO BOx 2020, Launceston, Tasmania 7250. *President: Kevin N Hooper.*
Smartartists Management, PO Box 2093, St Kilda West, VIC 3182. *Manager: Michael Lynch.*
Talentworks Pty Ltd, First Floor, 222 Albert Road, South Melbourne, VIC 3205. *Chief Executive Officer: Glenn Wheatley.*
Terry Blamey Management, 329 Monatgue Street, Albert Park, VIC 3206. *Director: Terry Blamey.*
The Neil Clugston Organization, PO Box 387, Glebe, NSW 2037. *Managing Director: Neil Clugson.*
Vicki Watson Management, PO Box 9, Balmain, Sydney, NSW 2041. *Director: Vicki Watson.*
Woodruff Management, 128 Bourke Street, Woolloomooloo, NSW 2011. *Director: John Woodruff.*
WPA Management, 1st Floor, 411 George Street, Fitzroy, VIC 3065. *General Manager: Petula Bier.*

AUSTRIA

Georg Leitner Productions, Hütteldorfstrasse 259/14, A-1140 Vienna. *Proprietor: Georg Leitner.*
Hämmerle Barbara & Werner, Harderstrasse 14, A-6972 Fussach: *Managing Directors: Barbara and Werner Hämmerle.*
Milica, Liebhartstalstr 15/5, A-1160 Vienna. *Contact: Milica.*
RATZ Promotions, Vorachstrasse 65, A-6890 Lustenau. *Contact: Thomas Radovan.*
RGG Management, Favoritstr. 52.2.6.18, A-1100 Vienna. *Manager: Peter Steinbach.*
Rock Promotion, Hietzinger Hauptstrasse 36A, A-1130 Vienna. *Contact: Peter Fröstl.*
Spritzendorfer & Rossori GmbH, Hietzinger Haupstr. 94, A-1130 Vienna. *Managing Director: A Spritzendorfer.*
Stein Music Wien, Bernardgasse 39/33, A-1070 Vienna. *Managing Director: Regine Steinmetz.*
WOM, Postfach 20, A-3105 St Pölten. *Contact: Albin Wegerbauer.*

BELGIUM

Aril Private Studio, Rue de Coron 1, B-7040 Bougnies. *Managing Director: Marylin Leleu.*
ARS Management, Singel 5, B-2550 Kontich. *Managing Director: Patrick Busschots.*
Baard & Kale, Brederodestraat 40, B-2018 Antwerp. *Managing Director: Bob Campenaerts.*
Backline, Kammerstraat 19, B-9000 Ghent. *Manager: Robert Van Yper; Bookings Agents: Sandra Heylen and Lawrence Van Den Eede.*
Commedia VZW, Fonteinstraat 19, B-8000 Bruges. *Managing Director: Cherry Deryoke.*
The Foundation VZW, Fruithoflaan 124, Bus 11, B-2600 Berchem, Antwerp. *Directors: Peter Verstraeven and Bert Van Roy.*
Klepto Management, Leuvensesteenweg 54, B-3080 Tervuren. *Managing Director: Wilfried Brits.*
Kras Artists, Leernsestwg 168, B-9800 Deimze. *Director: Jean Tans.*
LN International, PB 15 Antwerpen 17, B-2018 Antwerp. *President: Luc Nuitten.*
Merlijn, Gulden Vlieslaan 67, B-8000 Brugge. *Contact: Nico A Mertens.*
Music BaM, Lelielaan 11, B-2460 Lichtaart. *Managing Director: Gert Van Dingenen.*
Paperwork, Aarischotsesteenweg 245, B-3012 Wilsele. *Manager: Johan P Berckmans.*
Swing Promotions, Beukenlaan 3, B-2970 Schilde. *Manager Wim Groos.*
Team for Action, Av Oscar van Goibtsnoven 45B, B-1180 Brussels. *Managing Director: Claude Martin.*
Tempo, Krijgslaan 61, B-9000 Ghent. *General Manager: Luc Standaert.*
Tour de Force, Rue des Archers 19-21, B-1080 Brussels. *Managing Director: Ton Van Draanen.*
TTT, Vriesenhof 22/5, B-3000 Leuven. *Managers: Rick Tubbax and Johan P Berckmans.*
UBU, Rue Van Obberghen 92, B-1140 Brussels. *Director: Patrick DuBucq.*
Western Productions, Kammerstraat 19, B-9000 Ghent. *Manager: Robert Van Yper.*

BOLIVIA

Chelo Music, Tarbo, 118 Santa Cruz, Santa Cruz De La Sierra. *Director: Sergio Serrale Justiniano.*
HR Producciones, Loayza 349, Piso 15, Dpto 1503, Edificio Loayza, La Paz. *General Manager: Nestor Horacio Rasgido.*

BRAZIL

Carlindo Soares Promoçoes Artisticas, Rua Castro Menezes 51, Rio De Janiero. RJ. *Contact: Carlindo Soares.*
Fred Rossi Eventos e Produçoes, Rua Augusta 2516, Cj 121 Cerqueira César, 01412 100 São Paulo, SP. *Director: Fred Rossi.*
MR Comunicaçao Produçao Ltda, Caixa Postal 16692, 03197 970 CEP, São Paulo. *Director: Mário Ronco.*

BULGARIA

Berti, 14 A Skobelevska Str, 5300 Gabrovo. *Managing Director: Plamen Tolev.*
Factor TC, 2 Krakra Str, 1504 Sofia. *Managing Director: Veselin Todorov.*
Mega Music Ltd, 2 Trapezitza Str, 1000 Sofia. *Managing Director: Dora Tchernkva.*
Pana 07, Kroum Popov Str, vh B, 1000 Sofia. *Managing Director: Plamen Panaiotov.*

CANADA

Amok Artist Agency, Suite 202, 243 Main Street East, Milton, ON L9T 1P1. *Contact: Lorenz Eppinger.*
Artistic Canadian Entertainers Management Association, 4544 Dufferin Street #24, Downsview, ON M3H 5X2. *President/Consultant: Raymond A Sare.*
Balmur Ltd, 2400 - 4950 Yonge Street, Toronto, ON M2N 6K1. *Contact: Tinti Moffat.*
Bamford Group, 14 Sumach Street, Toronto, ON M5A 1J4. *President: Joe Bamford.*
Brass Ring Productions, PO Box 1266 Station A, Kelowna, BC V1Y 7V8. *President/Personal Manager: Becky Chapman.*
Bruce Allen Talent, 406 - 68 Water Street, Vancouver, BC V6B 1A4. *Contact: Kim Blake.*
Childsplay Management, 112 - 725 King Street W, Toronto, ON M5V 2W9. *Contact: Kevin Leflar.*
Current/Rage Records and Management, 4 Bowden Street, Toronto, ON M4K 2X2. *President: Gerry Young.*
Donna Kay Music Inc, Ministikwan Lake, PO Box 451, Pierceland, SK S0M 2K0. *Contact: Paul S Pospisil.*
Double A Productions, 64 Desbrisay Drive, Bridgewater, NS B4V 3H6. *Manager: Ken Alexander.*
Early Morning Productions, 1365 Yonge Street #207, Toronto, ON M4T 2P7. *Manager: Barry Harvey.*
Feeling Productions Inc., 500 - 4 Place Laval, Laval, PQ H7N 5Y3. *Manager: Rene Angelil.*
Finkelstein Management Company Ltd, 301- 151 John Street, Toronto, ON M5V 2T2. *Contact: J Languedoc.*
Forte Records And Productions, 320 Spadina Road, Toronto, ON M5R 2V6. *Contact: Dawna Zeeman.*
Gangland Artists, 707 - 810 W Broadway, Vancouver, BC V5Z 1J8. *Partners: Keith Portious, Allen Moy.*
Gino Empry Entertainment, #315-120 Carlton Street, Toronto, ON M5A 4K2. *Owner: Gino Empry.*
Ground Swell Productions, 1725 Barrington Street, Halifax, NS B3J 2N7. *President: Ian McKinnon.*
Jones & Co, 1819 Granville Street, 4th Floor, Halifax, NS B3J 3R1. *President: Sheri Jones.*
Latitude 45/Arts Promotion Inc, 109 St Joseph Blvd West, Montreal, PQ H2T 2P7.
Lazy J Management, Box 182, Midale, SK S0C 1S0. *Manager: Jeannette Marie.*
LCDM Entertainment, 1995 Weston Road, Box 79564, Weston, ON M9N 3W9. *Producer/Artist/Writer: L C Di Marco.*
Lou Blair Management Inc, 407 - 68 Water Street, Vancouver, BC V6B 1A4. *Contact: Lou Blair.*
Management Trust Ltd, 219 Dufferin Street, Suite 309B, Toronto, ON M6K 3J1. *Contact: Sarah Barker-Tonge.*
Mary Bailey Management, PO Box 546, 4 Al Wende Avenue, ON P2N 3J5. *President: Mary Bailey.*
M B H Music Management, PO Box 1096, Hudson, PQ J0P 1V0. *Manager: Andy Jameson.*

Nigel Best Management, 835 Westney Road South, Suite 10, Ajax, ON L1S 3M4. *President: Nigel Best.*
Pandyamonium/William Tenn Artist Management, 67 Mowat #431, Toronto, ON M6K 3E3. *Contact: Sandy Pandya and William Tenn.*
Paquin Entertainment Group, 1067 Sherwin Road, Winnipeg, MB R3H 0T8. *President: Gilles Paquin.*
Pro Arts Management, #3 - 3611 Mavis Road, Mississauga, ON L5C 1T7. *Contact: Gil Moore.*
Productions Martin Leclerc Inc, 2220 Rue Notre-Dame Ouest #201, Montreal, PQ H3J 2V4. *Manager: Martin Leclerc.*
Popas Management Corp. (PMC), 1407 Mount Pleasant Road, Toronto, ON M4N 2T9. *Manager: Steve Propas.*
Quinlan Road, PO Box 933, Stratford, ON N5A 7M3. *Contact: Loreena McKennit.*
Radius International, PO Box 81, 260 Adelaide Street East, Toronto, ON M5A 1N0. *General Manager: Bob Stevens.*
Regal Recordings Ltd, 2421 Hammond Road, Mississauga, ON L5K 1T3. *Contact: Doreen Davey.*
Robert Luhtala Management, 869 Broadview Avenue, Toronto, ON M4K 4P9. *Manager: Robert Luhtala.*
Savannah Music Inc, 123 Applefield Drive, Scarborough, ON M1P 3Y5. *Director of Canadian Operations: Bill Carruthers.*
SEG Productions, 3611 Mavis Road, Mississauga, ON L5C 1T7. *Contact: Cliff Hunt.*
Showcana Corporation, PO Box #4689, Station C, Calgary, AB T2T 5P1. *President: Robert James Chih.*
SL Feldman & Associates, 200 - 1505 W 2 Avenue, Vancouver, BC V6H 3Y4. *Proprietor: SL Feldman.*
SRO Management, 189 Carlton Street, Toronto, ON M5A 2K7. *Contact: Bob Roper.*
Star Rise International, 6263 28th Avenue, Rosemont, Montreal, PQ H1T 3H8. *Talent Search/Manager: Fadel Chidiac.*
Swell Music Inc., 46 Mitchell Avenue, Toronto, ON M6J 1B9. *Contact: Jeff Rogers, Sandy Rogers.*
TKO Entertainment Corp., 21501 Exeter Avenue, Maple Ridge, BC V3Z 1B3. *Contact: Peter Karroll.*
United Artist Productions Worldwide, 224 Beaverbrook Street, Winnipeg, MB R3N 1M8. *Contact: Warren Brown.*
Val Haas, Suite 1002, 5 Rowntree Road, Etobicoke, ON M9V 5G9. *Manager: Val Haas.*
Vocal Image Productions, 192 Kensington Road, Charlottetown, PEI C1A 7S3. *Manager: Berni Wood.*
Ways and Means Committee, 1971 Sprice Hill Road, Pickering, ON L1V 1S6. *Contact: Michael White.*
William Seip Management, 1615 Highland Road, Kitchener, ON N2G 3W5. *Contact: William Seip.*

CHILE

Calipso, Thompson 3450, Estacóin Cantral, Santiago de Chile. *Manager: Hugo Ascueta Norambuena.*
Galo Producciones, Alameda 171, Of. 807, Santiago de Chile. *General Manager: Alfedo Saint-Jean.*
Producciones Macondo Chile Ltda, Alvarez 58 L-6, Viña Del Mar. *Manager: Alfredo Troncoso.*
Providencia Television, Pedro de Valivia 3128 Ñuñoa, Santiago de Chile. *Executive Director: Luis Venegas.*
Ricardo Suarez Daud Y Cia Ltda, La Concepción 81, Of. 405 Providencia, Santiago de Chile. *Manager: Ricardo Suarez Daud.*
Romero Campbell Producciones, Bombero Nuñez, 385 Barrio Bellavista, Santiago De Chile. *Director: Carmen Romero Quero.*
Union Producciones SA, California 2380, Santiago de Chile. *Director General: Jorge Saint-Jean.*

CROATIA

AIMP - Promotion & Management, O. Zupancica, 41000 Zagreb. *Managing Director: Damir Tiljak.*
Crno Bijeli Svijet, Avenija Marina Drzica BB, 41000 Zagreb. *Managing Director: Branko Paic.*
Music Time, Petreticev Trg 4, 41000 Zagreb. *Managing Director: Branko Knezevic.*
Suput DOO, Novska 41, 41000 Zagreb. *Managing Director: Boris Suput.*
Tutico, Veprinacka 16, 10000 Zagreb. *Director: Zrinko Tutic.*

CUBA

Agencia Promusic, Avda. 3, n.1008, Entre 10-12 Miramar, 11300 Municipo Playa, Havana. *Director General: Julio Ballester Guzmán.*
Oficina de Pablo Lilanes, Calle 11, n. 257 Entre J y I Vedado, Havana. *Director General: Orlando Hecahvarría.*

DENMARK

Buks Booking International, Gunløgsgade 15, DK-2300 Copenhagen. *Director: Thomas H Hansen.*
Hanne Wilhelm Hansen, Gothersgade 11, DK-1123 Copenhagen K. *Contact: Hanne Wilhelm Hansen.*
JP Management, Jernbanevej 22, DK-8660 Skanderborg. *Managing Director: J P Andersen.*
Mega Scandinavia A/S, Indiakaj 1, DK-2100 Copenhagen Ø. *Vice President: Cai Leitner; Director of A&R and Marketing: Jesper Ban.*
Off Beat Productions, Norsgade 26-28, DK-8000 Århus C. *Contact: Jakob Brixvold.*
PDH Dansk Musik Formidling, Ny Vestergade 7, DK-1471 Copenhagen K. *Personal Manager: Ole Dreyer.*
TG Management, Badehusvej 1, 9000 Aarborg. *Manager: John Aagaard.*
Wennick Management, Linnesgade 14A, DK-1361 Copenhagen K. *Managing Director: Kjeld Wennick.*

DOMINICAN REPUBLIC

July Mateo Y Associates, Jos Coluene, 10 Alma Rosa, Santo Domingo. *Contact: July Mateo.*
Televisa Talents SA, Lea de Castro, 153 Gazcue, Santo Domingo. *Director General: Luis Medrano.*

ESTONIA

Eesti Kontsert, Estonia pst 4, EE 0001 Tallinn. *Director: E. Mattisen.*
Estonian Jazz Fondation, PO Box 3641, EE0090 Tallinn. *Director: Tiit Lauk.*
Makaroy Muusik Management, Regati PST 1-6K, EE-0019 Tallinn. *Manager: Martti Kitsing.*

FINLAND

NEM, PO Box 220, 33201 Tampere. *Managing Director: Harri Karvinen.*
Piikkikasvi Agency, PO Box 145, 00531 Helsinki. *Managing Director: Kari Pössi.*
Rockadillo, PO Box 35, 33201 Tampere. *Managing Director: Tapio Korjus.*
Rocktops, Torkkelinkatu 4, 00500 Helsinki. *Director: Maria Tarnanen.*
Welldone, Linnankatu 11, 00160 Helsinki. *Managing Director: Risto Juvonen.*

FRANCE

Africa Music International, 15 rue Charles Gounod, F-56100 Lorient. *Contact: Lucien Bindzi.*
Agence Kathoche, 16 Rue de Marignan, F-75008 Paris. *Agent/Director: Catherine Poensin.*
Agence Sylvie Dupuy, 27 Rue Auguste Delaune, F-94800 Villejuif. *Manager: Sylvie Dupuy.*
Alpha Bravo, 64 Av Jean Jaurès, F-93500 Pantin. *Contact: Daniel Bornet.*
Bistro Production, 31 Rue St Sébastien, F-75011 Paris. *Manager: Patrice Eskenazy.*
Corida, 120 Boulevard, Rochechojart, F-75018 Paris. *Manager: Assaad Debs.*
Daniel Bornet Management, 64 Avenue Jean Jaurès, F-93500 Pantin. *Director: Daniel Bornet.*
Do Si La Ba, 159 Chemin Lanusse, F-31200 Toulouse. *Manager: Lawrence Larrouy.*
Etienne Vanke, 94 Blvd Chaumin, F-49000 Angers. *Contact: Etienne Vanke.*
Fiesta Latina Homero Cardoso, 51 Rue Mirabeau, F-94200 Ivry Sur Seine. *Promoter: Homero Cardoso.*
Gafaiti Production, 3 Rue de la Haie du Coq, F-93300 Aubervilliers. *Manager: Nourredine Gafaiti.*
Genevieve Peygrene, 62 Rue des Rondeaux, F-75020 Paris. *Director: Genevieve Peygrene.*
Infernal, 102 Blvd Henri Barbusse, F-93100 Montreuil. *Manager: Laurent Lefebvre.*
IPS Management, 11/13 Rue Montlouis, F-75001 Paris. *Manager: André Gnimagnon.*
Le Haut De L'Affiche, 2 Bis Rue Hiche, F-94130 Nogent Sur Marne. *Chairman: Claude Abihssira.*
Made in Heaven, 6 Rue Rémy de Gourmont, F-75019 Paris. *Label Manager: Mathias Jeannin.*
Marouani, Charley and Maurice, 37 Rue Marbeuf, F-75008 Paris. *Managers: Charley and Maurice Marouani.*
Martine Palmé Management, 33 Bis Rue Doudeauville, F-75018 Paris. *Artist Manager: Martine Palmé.*
Meyer Productions, 10 Rue de L'isly, F-75008 Paris. *Managers: Olivia and Christian Meyer.*
Mondial Management, 64 Bis Rue de Paris, F-93230 Romainville. *Managers: Georges Lancry, Lisette Obydol.*
Musicomedia, 21 Av. d'Italie, F-75013 Paris. *Manager: Gladys Gabison.*
RA Production, 471 Av. Victor Hugo, F-26000 Valence. *Manager: Frédéric Loison.*
Robert Bialek Conseils, 33 Rue des Jeuneurs, F-75002 Paris. *Contact: Robert Bialek.*
Salam Aleikum Amusements, 2 Rue Carpeaux, F-75018 Paris. *Director: Stephane Benhamou.*
Sixieme Sens, 2 Rue du Chemin Vert, F-14000 Caen. *Contact: Jean Michel Lebigot.*
3 Comm, 16 Bis Rue d'Odessa, F-75014 Paris. *Director: Jean-Pierre Lenoir.*
Talent Sorcier Productions, Parc d'Activité Activa, Rue de la Batterie, F-67400 Geispolshiem/Strasbourg. *Manager: Richard Walter.*
Tourrillon Sarl, 1/233 Rue Barberaisse, F-59000 Lille. *Agent: Xavier Collin.*
Utopia Spectacles, 1 Rue Niece, F-75014 Paris. *Director: Jacques Fichelle.*
VMA, 40 Rue François 1er, F-75008 Paris. *Manager: Rose Leandri.*
XIII Bis Music Group, 34 Rue Eugene Flachat, F-75017 Paris. *Managing Director: Laurent Dreux-Leblanc.*

GERMANY

Blue Star Promotion Konzertagentur GmbH, Goebenstr 3, D-28209 Bremen. *Public Relations: Michael K Grusche.*
Castor Promotions, Dragonerstr 21, D-30163 Hannover. *Contact: Elke Fleing.*
Double Trouble, Haupstr. 30, D-10437 Berlin. *Managing Director: Petra Hammerer.*
Falkland Musik Management, Herderstr. 16, D-44147 Dortmund. *Managing Director: Thomas Falke.*
Freestyle eV, Morgensterusweg 7, D-22305 Hamburg. *Head of Managing Board: Helmut Heuer.*
Fun Factory! GmbH, Hermannstadtweg 9, D-48151 Münster. *Marketing Assistant: Claudia Weiler.*
Kick Musikverlag, Burgunder Str 8, D-50677 Cologne. *Managing Director: Goetz Elbertzagen; International Manager: Lynda Hill.*
Künstlersekretariat Ott, Moltkestrasse 18, D-79098 Freiburg. *Contact: Dieter Ott.*
Line Up Co, Linden Str 52, D-50674 Cologne Centrum.
Moskito Promotion, PO Box 3072, D-48016 Münster. *Managing Director: Oswald Münnig.*
Music Arts Network, Fichtestr 16, D-60316 Frankfurt. *General Manager: Robert Lyng.*
Partysanen Music, Skalitzer Str 68, D-10997 Berlin. *Managing Director: Roma Casley.*
Paradise Management International, PO Box 2180, D-63243 Neu-Isenburg. *Managing Director: Ralf Klug.*
Playtime Management, Weidengasse 56, D-50668 Cologne. *Chairman: Jochen Sperber.*
Rudy Holzhauer Management, Bramfelder Chaussee 238C, D-22177 Hamburg. *Artist Manager: Rudy Holzhauer.*
Thats Entertainment!, Orleanstr. 76, D-31135 Hildesheim. *Managing Directors: Felix Almstadt, Joachim Friedmann.*
Thopo Music Management, Postfach 1, D-96136 Burgebrach. *Contact: Joseph Thomann.*
Triple M Management, Schaefflerstr. 5, D-80333 Munich. *Managing Director: Mario Mendrycki.*

GREECE

Halfnote Productions, Solomon 4, Aghia Paraskevi, Athens 153. *Promotions & Publicity Manager: Mary Telemachou.*
Neo Revma, 8 Ainianos Str., 10434 Athens. *Managing Director: Dimitris Helmis.*
Rock Management, PO Box 21526, 55236 Panorama, Thessaloniki. *Managing Director: Christos Tfrzides.*
Show Productions, 318 Sygrou Av., 17673 Kailthea, Athens. *Managing Director: Konstantinos Arvanitis.*

HONG KONG

Aural Fidelity, 3B Cambridge Villa, 8-10 Chancery Lane, Central Hong Kong. *Managing Director: John Powter.*
Paciwood Music and Entertainment Ltd, No.8, King Tung Street, Hammer Hill Road, Ngau Chi Wan, Kowloon.
Sea Music, 703 Manson House, 74-78 Nathan Road, Kowloon. *Managing Director: Richard Cooper.*
Spraylot Music Ltd, Suite A, 15th Floor, Ritz Plaza, 122 Austin Road, Tsim Sha Tsui, Kowloon. *Publishing Executive: Peggy Yu.*

HUNGARY

OB Art Management, PO Box 76, 5002 Szolnok. *Managing Director: Bela Pap.*
Record Express Ltd, Rath György u 6, 1123 Budapest. *Managing Director: Attila Schneider.*
Sziget Kulturális Szervezöiroda Kft. (Island Cultural Management), Lónyay u. 18/B, 1093 Budapest. *Foreign Affairs Manager: Matthew Braghiñi.*

ICELAND

Bo Haldorson Productions, Pverholt 26, 105 Reykjavik. *Managing Director: Bo Haldorson.*
Spor HF, Nýbýlavegur 4, PO Box 320, 202 Kópavogur. *Managing Director: Steinar Berg Isleifsson.*

IRELAND

Dabble Music, The Elms, Richmond Avenue South, Dartry, Dublin 6. *Chief Executive Officer: Pete Blackbyrne.*
DCG Management, 10 St Fintan's Villas, Deansgrange, Dublin. *Contact: Gerry Harford.*
Denis Desmond Promotions, Top House, Clontarf Street, Cork 1. *Managing Director: Denis Desmond.*
Pat Egan Sound Ltd, Merchant's Court, 24 Merchant's Quay, Dublin 8. *Managing Director: Pat Egan.*
Elite Music Management, Oakdale, Roscrea Road, Templemore, Co. Tipperary. *Manager: Tony O'Toole.*
Excellent Management, 137 Carrigwood, Firhouse, Dublin 24. *Director: Neil O'Shea.*
Fifty-Seventh Street Ltd, 24 Upper Mount Street, Dublin 2. *Contact: Maurice Cassidy and Elizabeth Reeves.*
Gutter Brothers Ltd, 1 Lansdowne Park, Ennis Road, Limerick. *Managing Director: Joe Clarke.*
Icebreaker Promotions, Emyvale, Co. Monaghan. *Contact: PJ McKenna.*
Connie Lynch, 11 Stockton Green, Castleknock, Dublin 15. *Manager: Connie Lynch.*
Joe McFadden Promotions, 19 Stockton Green, Castleknock, Dublin 15. *Managing Director: Joe McFadden.*
Mister T Productions, 137A Parnell Street, Dublin 1. *Director: Tonie Walsh.*
Brian Molloy, 5-6 Lombard Street East, Dublin 2. *Contact: Brian Molloy.*
Muchwood Management, 1 Killiney Court, Seafield Road, Killiney, Co. Dublin. *Manager: David O'Reilly.*
Principle Management, 30-32 Sir John Rogerson's Quay, Dublin 2. *Managing Director: Paul McGuinness; Contact Sheila Roche.*
Real Good Management Ltd, 17 Dame Court, Dublin 2. *Director: Gerard Keenan.*
RSE Promotions, 11 Station Road, Raheny, Dublin 5. *Director: Raymond J Smyth.*
Ryan Management, 6 Danieli Drive, Artane, Dublin 5. *Managers: Nicky & Roma Ryan.*
TTMAR, Rear 22 St Stephens Green, Dublin 2. *Managing Director: Dermot McEvoy.*
Underscore Management, Pellestown House, Ashtown Gate, Ashtown, Dublin 15. *Manager: Columb Farrelly.*
Upfront Management, 4 Windmill Lane, Dublin 2. *Managing Director: David Kavanagh.*
Westland Entertainment, 35 Westland Square, Dublin 2. *Contact: Lucy McColgan.*
Whirling Music Agency, Cairns Hill, Aughamore, Near Sligo. *Manager: Brian McDonagh.*

ITALY

Arci Pisa, Borgo Stretto 72, 56100 Pisa. *Managing Director: Nicola Zaccardi.*
Casi Umani, Piazza Luigi di Savoia 28, 20124 Milan. *Managing Director: Marco Conforti.*
City Medial Two, Via Premuda 30, 42100 Reggio Emilia. *Managing Director: Roberto Meglioli.*
Dell'Amore Management, Via Zeffirino Re 2, 47023 Cesena. *Art Director: Franco Dell'Amore.*
Duende Management, Via Vanchiglia 9, 10124 Turin. *Manager: Ettore Carette.*
Giancarlo Passarella, PO Box 86, 50018 Scandicci, Florence. *Contact: Giancarlo Passarella.*
IRA Transeuropa Management, Via Landucci 38, 50100 Florence. *Managing Director: Anne-Marie Pourcet.*
Lion Snc, Via Goldoni 42/A, 30174 Mestre, Venezia. *General Manager: Luciano Trevisan.*
Massimo Maggioni Management, Villoresi 24, 20143 Milan. *Manager: Massimo Maggioni.*
Mela Di Odessa, Via Gioberti 119, 58015 Orbetello (Grosseto). *Managing Director: Lora Palmerini.*
Soggiorno Obbligato Management, Via Delle Viole 17, Vialfiorta, 37020 S, Maria di Negrar (VR). *Managing Director: Diego Alvera.*
Vitola Dino Management, Via I. Goiran 8, 00195 Rome. *Managing Director: Leonardo Vitola.*
Vu Balle' Vu Management, Via Andreini 2, 40126 Bologna. *Managing Director: Giovanni Vinci.*

JAPAN

Asada Inc, Suite 303, Lions Station Plaza, 1-39-7 Sangenjaya, Setagaya-ku, Tokyo 154. *President: Hiroshi Asada.*
International Management Group, 4th Floor, Moto-Akasaka Kikutei Bldg, 7-18 Moto Akasaka 1-Chome, Minato-ku, Tokyo 107. *Contact: Kazuo Kondo.*
Shinko Music Publishing Co Ltd, 2-1 Ogawamachi, Kanda, Chiyoda-ku, Tokyo 101. *President: Shoichi Kusano.*

LATVIA

Mikrofons Ltd, Muitas Iela 1, Riga, LV-1010. *Foreign Affairs Manager: Indra Natra.*

MEXICO

AG Ediciones Musicales SA, Peter 117, Col. Narvate, 03020 Mexico, DF. *Manager: Gerado Fojo.*
Arrabal Y Compañia SA, Insurgentes Sur 2388, 5 Piso San Angle, 01000 Mexico DF. *Contact: Felipe Vega Puentes.*
Organizacion Latino Internacional, Avda. Insurgentes Sur 953-202 Col. Nápoles, 03810 Mexico DF. *Director General: Tony Méndez.*
Producciones Enrique Guzman SA, Avda. San Bernabé 781, Col. San Jerónimo, 10200 Mexico DF. *President: Enrique Guzmán.*
Producciones Musica Y Equipos SC, Manuel Acuña 3359-B, Fracc, Monraz Guadalajara, 44670 Jalisco. *Manager: J. Ulises Calleros Ramos.*
Promesa, Camino a Santa Teresa, 13 Toresa 5-1804, 14110 Mexico. *Director General: Ignacio Rodríguez Martínez.*
RAC Producciones SA, Sierra Gorda 30, 11010 Mexico DF. *Director General: Alejandro Garza.*

NETHERLANDS

ACT, Van Leeuwenhoeksingel 69, 2611 AE Delft. *Contact: A C Raven.*
Hans Van Pol Management BV, T Point Building, 25B Osdorper 6 an, 1068 LD Amsterdam. *President: Hans W Van Pol.*
Home Management, Faas Eliaslaan 13, 3742 AR Baarn. *Managers: Eric Van Eerdenburg, Geert Van Itallie.*
JB Management, Boterstraat 73, 3082 SP Schiedam. *Managing Director: Jan Beunk, Rien Rietveld.*
Mega Management, PO Box 9242, 1006 AE Amsterdam.
Mojo Management, PO Box 3121, 2601 DC Delft. *Managing Director: Paul Van Melis.*
Moonshine Management, Langeweid 7, 1831 BL Koedyk. *President: Evert Wiljrink.*
Mukti Music Management, Karel Doormanlaan 16, 1403 TM Bussum. *Managing Director: Eric Van Der Brink.*
Music World Management, PO Box 55 55 9, 1007 NB Amsterdam. *Managing Director: Paul Coops.*
Ray Derkzen, Zoutstraat 2, 5612 HW Eindhoven. *Managing Director: Ray Derkzen.*
Supersonic Management, PO Box 339, 3500 AH Utrecht. *Manager: Lizet Hobeyn.*
VIP Promotions, Lootevsgracht 38, 1016 VS Amsterdam. *Contact: G Bezuljen.*

NEW ZEALAND

Jude Walcott Management, PO Box 55, Paekakariki, Kapiti Coast. *Contact: Jude Walcott.*
McCook Management, 7 Verel Street, 2001 Hamilton. *Managing Director: Jeannie McCook.*
Noise Machine, PO Box 11-177 Wellington. *Contact Gerald Dwyer.*
Showcase Management Ltd, 140 Vanguard Street, Nelson. *Director: Mike Duffield.*
Spasim Music Management, PO Box 2901, Christchurch. *Contacts: Jeff Sim, Karen Neill.*
Spirit Management, Lister Bldg, 9 Victoria Street East, Auckland. *Manager: Daniel Keighley.*
York Street Management, PO Box 6884, Wellesley Street, Auckland. *Contact: Tanya Moore.*

NORWAY

Continental Management, PO Box 143, N-2051 Jessheim. *Managing Director: Barry Matheson.*
dbut internautics, PO Box 9415 Valerenga, N-0610 Oslo, Norway. *Director: Per Platou.*
Groovy Management, PO Box 1291, N-5001 Bergen. *Managing Director: Torfinn Andersen.*
Ha-Ha Management, Mandalsgt. 5, N-0190 Oslo. *Managing Director: Haavard Hansteen.*
Petter Sandberg A/S, Cort Adelersgt 2, N-0254 Oslo. *Contact: Jan Sollien.*
Rage Management, PO Box 4721, N-0506 Oslo. *Managing Director: Tord Naess.*
Ramalama Management and Productions, Bispegt 12, N-0191 Oslo. *Managing Director: Steinar Vikan.*
Stageway Management AS, Skuteviksboder 11, N-5035 Bergen-Sandviken. *Manager: Woll Steinar.*
TS Artist Byra, PO Box 1683, N-7002 Trondheim. *Managing Director: Terje Storli.*
Viggo Lund Management, Akersgt. 7, N-0158 Oslo. *Managing Director: Viggo Lund.*
Wildlife Productions, Ammerudhellinga 74, N-0959 Oslo. *Managing Director: Oyvind Borgso.*

PERU

Acordes Eirl, Los Paujiles 285 D, Lima 34. *Proprietor: Julie Freundt López.*
Mapa Producciones SA, Jr. Mayta Capac 1380, Jesús María. *Manager: Alfredo Samaniego.*
Pro Art SA, Diez Canseco 236, Of. 403 Miraflores, Lima 18. *Director: Jorge Ferrand Lanciotti.*

POLAND

Dzem Agency, PO Box 580, Katowice 2. *Contact: Ena Otolinsua.*
Kantaro-Art Agency, ul Powstancov 20, 70-110 Szczecin. *Owner: Witold Ianczynski.*
Polish Radio Artists Management, Woronicza 17, 00-999 Warsaw. *Director: Andrzej Haluch.*
Warsaw Artists Management Ltd, Kazimierzowska 47/5, 02-572 Warsaw. *President: Andrzej Haluch.*
ZPR Inc, United Entertainment Enterprises Inc, Senatorska 13/15, 00 075 Warsaw. *President/Chief Executive Officer: Zhigniew Benbenek; Artists & Marketing Manager: Anna Karokicka.*

PORTUGAL

Companhia das Ideas, Av. Roma n.49 5D, 1700 Lisbon. *Director: Antonio Avelar Pinho.*
Contacto, Apartado 29, 2840 Seixal. *Managing Director: Dionisio Duarte.*
Dimas Mario Management, Rua Serpa Pinto 4A, 2800 Almada. *Public Relations: Isabel Silva.*
Encore, Rua S. João da Praça 114 1, 1100 Lisbon. *Managing Director: Rui Simoes.*
Lisbon Agency, Rua Casimiero Freire 19 RC, 1900 Lisbon. *Managing Director: Luis Tomas.*
MS Management, Rua General c. da Silva 10 7, 1500 Lisbon. *Managing Director: Manuel Moura Dos Santos.*
MTM, Apartado 300 72, 1321 Lisbon Codex. *Managing Director: Hugo Moutinho.*
Regiespectáculo, Alto do Coutão, Armazem I, 2735 Cacém. *Chief Executive: António Guimarães.*
Terra De Musica, Rua Casimiero Freire 19RC, 1900 Lisbon. *Director: Francisco Morgado.*
Uniao Lisbon, Rua B. Sabrosa 84 2C, 1900 Lisbon. *Director: Antonio Cunha.*

PUERTO RICO

Producciones Norma Pujals, Ave. Condado 57, Apt. 7a, Condado Vilomar, 00907 Condado. *Manager: Norma Pujals.*
Producciones Tropical, PO Box 11673, Fernandez Juncos, 00910 San Juan. *President: Angie Garciá.*
TS Entertainment, PO Box 12004, 00922-2004 San Juan. *Directors: Lynn Santiago, Rafael Tirado.*

ROMANIA

AMMA, Scara B, Apart 73, Calea Victorei 48/50, Sector 1, 70102 Bucharest. *Manager: Aurel Mitran.*
Cartianu Ltd, 58 Aviator Traian Vasile Str, Sector 1, 78336 Bucharest. *Chairman: Radu Cartianau.*

RUSSIA

M&L Art, PO Box 28, 630 011 Novosibirisk. *Managing Director: Sergey Bugeyev.*
Rock-Azia, Pupova 96-268, Barnaul, 656062 Siberia. *Contact: Eugene Kolbashev.*
SAV Entertainment, Marhelevskogo 15/24, 101 000 Moscow. *Managing Director: Eugeny Boldin.*
SNC Management, Krymsky Val 9, 103 045 Moscow. *Managing Director: Stas Namin.*

SINGAPORE

Hype Records Pte Ltd, 221 Henderson Road, #02-04 Henderson Bldg, Singapore 159557. *Administration Manager: Melvis Yip.*
Limelite Management Services, 38B Geylang Lorong 23, Singapore 1438. *Operations Manager: Ernest Cheong.*

SLOVENIA

Buba Promotion, 40 A Moskriceva, 61000 Ljubljana. *Managing Director: David Krzisnik.*
FV Zavod Za Umetnisko in Kulturno Produkcijo, Kersnikova 4, 61000 Ljubljana. *Managing Director: Skaberne Monika.*
Škuc-AFK, Kersnikova 4, 61000 Ljubljana. *Managing Director: Mitja Prezelj.*

SPAIN

Artcelona, Regomir 3, 08002 Barcelona. *Contact: Agnes Blot.*
Attraction Management, Genova 3, 28010 Madrid. *Managing Director: Paco Lopez.*
AYA Producciones y Management, Dante 75 Bajos, 08032 Barcelona. *Managing Director: Joaquin Ascon.*
AZ Music & Management, Riera Argentona Sin, 08300 Mataro. *Managing Director: Braulio Paz Simon.*
Blac Management, Corcega 257, 08036 Barcelona. *Managing Director: Julio Cano.*
BM Management, Mejico 17, 4-4A, 08004 Barcelona. *Chairman: Monica Gutierrez.*
Caturla & Navarro, Angela de la Cruz 24, 28020 Madrid. *Directors: José Caturla, J. Emilio Navarro.*
Chihuahua Management, Sancho Davila, 1 Entreplanta, 28028 Madrid. *Managing Director: Flor Madrid.*
Crab Ediciones, Sagunto 2, 28010 Madrid. *General Manager: Jorge E Gomez Diaz.*
Diez Management, Martinez Corrochano 3, 28007 Madrid. *Chairman: Mercedes Martin.*
EMC Management, Carlos Latorre 13, 28039 Madrid. *Director: Joan A Serra.*
Grup de Serveis Guilleries, Granja Baró, Ctra de la Guixa, km 2, 08500 VIC (Barcelona). *Administration: Jordi Costa; Management: Ignasi Pla; Production: Joan Capdevila.*
Madma S L, c/ Major, 5- Urbanizacion La Rosaleda, 08727 Sant Fuuitos De Bages (Barcelona). *Contact: Felix Camprubi I Santamans.*
MCM Management, Modesto Lafuento 46 6B, 28003 Madrid. *Chairman: Isabel Burgos.*
Oniria International S L, Alzines 3, St Quirze Parc, 08192 St Quirze Del Vallès, Barcelona. *President: Michel Huygen; Manager: Antoni Brunet.*
Pino Sagliocco Presenta SL, C/ Quintana, 2 7° 9ª, 28008 Madrid. *Chairman: Pino Sagliocco.*
Posto Nove, Muntaner 494 5B, 08022 Barcelona. *Contact: Alejandro Navarro.*
RLM Productions, Jose Maria Cavero 9, CH A, 28027 Madrid. *Managing Director: Rosa Lagappigue.*
Sauma & Tumbao, Gral Oraa 37 4, 28006 Madrid. *Director: Saul Rodriguez.*
Store Music, Gran Via 28, 3C, 18010 Granada. *Managing Director: Carmen Carnicero.*
WOM Music, Dusai 6, 07001 Palma de Mallorca. *Director: Juanjo Arzubialde.*

SWEDEN

AMP, Karlsgatan 9, S-252 24 Helsingborg. *Managing Director: Hasse Jönsson.*
Feedback Management, PO Box 558, S-631 07 Eskilstuna. *Managing Director: Mats Olsson.*
Luger Production, Fredriksgatan 35, S-811 33 Sandviken. *Managing Director/Agent: Ola Broquist; Agents: Patrick Fredriksson and Morgan Johansson.*
Madhouse, PO Box 103 30, S-100 55 Stockholm. *Managing Director: Jon Gray.*
MPA Musicart, Simrishamnsgatan 20 A, S-214 23 Malmö. *Managing Director: Andreas Larsson.*
Projektbyrân, Kungsgatan 34, S-972 41 Luleå. *Managing Director: Tomas Lind.*
RMPM Management AB, Box 17180, S-104 62, Stockholm. *Managing Director: Stefan Liga.*
Siljemark Productions, Gardscagen 2, Solna S-17152. *Contact: Lasse Karlsson.*
Stockhouse, PO Box 74, S-182 71 Stocksund. *Managing Director: Mats Bokström.*
Ton Art, PL 8007, S-441 91 Alingås. *Manager: Klas Johansson.*
XTC Productions AB, Ripsavägen 59, S-124 51 Bandhagen. *Managing Director: Ulf Wahlberg.*

SWITZERLAND

Artways Productions, Rue des-deux-Gares 6B, PO Box 30, CH-1800 Vevey. *Manager: Fabrics La Luc.*
Choc Auditif Management, Route de Genève 17, Le Flon, CH-1003 Lausanne. *Manager: Dominique Rottet.*
Its Time To Management, PO Box 1344, CH-5610 Wohlen. *Manager: Jean-Luc Itten.*
Just Two Management, Hagenbuchstr. 31, CH-9000 St Gallen. *Contact: Christoph Harzenmoser.*
VIP AG Productions, Schützengasse 30, CH-8001 Zürich. *Managing Director: Urs Peter Keller.*

TAIWAN

Formosa Artist Management, 11F, 215 Fu-Hsin South Road Sec. 1, Taipei. *General Manager: Carlos Yung-Hui Lee.*

UNITED KINGDOM

Acker's International Jazz Agency, 53 Cambridge Mansions, Cambridge Road, London SW11 4RX. *Owner: Pamela Frances Sutton.*
Acorn Entertainments, Winterfold House, 46 Woodfield Road, Kings Heath, Birmingham, B13 9UJ. *Managing Director: Jim McPhee.*
Adrian Boss Promotions, 363-365 Harrow Road, London W9 3NA. *Contact: Adrian Boss.*
AGM UK, 145A Ladbroke Grove, London W10 6HJ. *Contact: Tony Meilandt.*
ARC Music Management, 63 Blenheim Terrace, London NW8 0EJ. *Contact: Alex Ruheman.*
Arctic King Management, Bank Chambers, 4-6 Church Street, Wilmslow, Cheshire SK9 1AU. *Contact: John King.*
Asgard Management, 125 Parkway, London NW1 7PS. *Contact: Paul Charles.*
Atomic Management, 32 Neal Street, London WC2H 9PS. *Contact: Mick Newton.*
Avalon Management Group Ltd, Queen's House, 1 Leicester Place, Leicester Square, London WC2H 7BP. *Company Administrator: Marc Goodson.*
Bad Habits Music Group, PO Box 111, London W13 0ZH. *Managing Director: John S Rushton.*
Bamn Management, 167 Caledonian Road, London N1 0SL. *Managing Director: Steve Finan.*
Basement Music, 6 Pembridge Road, London W11 3HL. *Managing Director: John Telfer.*
BDA Ltd, Bryson House, Chiltern Road, Culcheth, Warrington WA3 4LL. *Managing Director: Brian Durkin.*
Bedlam Management (UK) Ltd, 3rd Floor, Devonshire House, 14 Barley Mow Passage, London W4 4ZN. *Contact: Tim Vass.*
Bernard Lee Management, Moorcroft Lodge, Farleigh Common, Warlingham, Surrey CR6 9PE. *Managing Director: Bernard Lee.*
Big Advance Management, 12 Oval Road, London NW1 7DH. *Contact: Paddy Prendergast.*
Big Bear Management, PO Box 944, Birmingham B16 8UT. *Managing Director: Jim Simpson.*
Big Life Management, 15 Little Portland Street, London W1N 5DE. *Contact: Jazz Summers.*
Black Magic Management Ltd, 296 Earls Court Road, London SW5 9BA. *Managing Director: Mataya Clifford.*
Blaylock Management Ltd, 39 Leyton Road, Harpenden, Herts AL5 2JB. *Managing Director: David Blaylock.*

Blitz, Edgwarebury Farm, Edgwarebury Lane, Edgware, Middlesex HA8 8QX. *Partners: Sue Harris and Claire Powell.*
Blueprint Management, 134 Lots Road, London SW10 0RJ. *Directors: John and Matt Glover.*
Brave Management, 15 Nottingham Road, Wandsworth, London SW17 7EA. *Managing Director: Netty Walker.*
Braw Music Management, 76 Pentland Place, Edinburgh EH10 6HS. *Contact: Kenny MacDonald.*
Brian Gannon Management, PO Box 106, Rochdale, Lancashire OL16 4HW. *Managing Director: Brian Gannon.*
Brian Reza Management, 416 High Road, Harrow Weald, Middlesex HA3 6HJ. *Manager: Brian Reza.*
Brian Yeates Associates, Home Farm House, Canwell, Sutton Coldfield, West Midlands B75 5SH. *Contact: Brian and Ashley Yeates.*
Brilliant Artistes, 253 Camberwell New Road, London SE5 0TH. *Contact: Mark Walmesley.*
Brilliant Management, 20 Stamford Brook Avenue, London W6 0YD. *Contact: Dee Harrington.*
Bruno Brookes Media and Management Ltd, Denford Mill House, Lower Derford, Hungerford, Berkshire RE17 0UN. *Managing Director: Bruno Brookes.*
Buzz Records, 192 Glasgow Road, Perth PH2 0NA, Scotland. *Managing Director: Dave Arcari.*
By Eleven, 12 Tideway Yard, 125 Mortlake High Street, London SW14 8SN. *Manager: Jill Taylor.*
Caromac Music Management, Unit 104, Ducie House, 37 Ducie Street, Manchester M1 2JW. *Manager: Caroline Elleray.*
CCC (The Crucial Chemystry Corporation), PO Box 10, London N1 3RJ. *Contact: Grant Gilbert.*
Century Music Entertainment, PO Box 1008, London W3 8ZW. *President: James Little.*
Chapter 22 Music, Suite 114, The Custard Factory, Gibb Street, Birmingham B9 4AA. *Contact: Rod Thomson.*
Charmenko, 46 Spencer Road, London SE24 0NR. *Contact: Nick Hobbs.*
Clive Banks Limited, 1 Glenthorne Mews, 115A Glenthorne Road, London W6 0LT. *Managing Director: Clive Banks.*
CMC Management, 1st Floor, 50 Bonnington Square, London SW8 1TQ. *Managing Director: Chris Molloy.*
CMO Management (International) Ltd, Unit 32 Ransomes Dock, 35/37 Parkgate Road, London SW11. *Managing Director: Chris Morrison.*
Congo Music Ltd, 17A Craven Park Road, Harlesden, London NW10 8SE. *Directors: Byron Lye-Fook and Root Jackson.*
Courtyard Management, 21 The Nursery, Sutton Courtneay, Abingdon, Oxon OX14 4UA. *Managers: Bryce Edge, Chris Hufford.*
Cromwell Management, 4/5 High Street, Huntingdon, Cambs PE18 6TE. *Managing Partner: Vic Gibbons.*
Cut Throat Management, PO Box 77, Coventry, West Midlands CV7 9YZ. *Contact: Simon Lawler.*
Damage Management, 16 Lambton Place, London W11 2SH. *Managing Director: Ed Bicknell.*
David Aspden Management, The Coach House, Capel Leyse, South Holmwood, Dorking, Surrey RH5 4LJ. *Proprietor: David Aspden.*
David Harper Management, 137 Talgarth Road, London W14 9DA. *Contact: David Harper.*
David Jaymes Associates/ D-Management, Suite 223A, Canalot Studios, 222 Kensal Road, London W10 5BN. *Contact: David Jaymes.*
DEF, 21Premier House, 313 Kilburn Lane, London W9 3EG. *Owner: Eric Hale.*
Derek Block Promotions, Douglas House, 3 Richmond Buildings, London W1V 5AE. *Managing Director: Derek Block.*
Deluxe Corporation, 13Charnhill Crescent, Bristol BS17 3JU. *Administration Manager: Helen Hawken.*
Diamond Sounds Music Management, The Fox and Punchbowl, Burfield Road, Old Windsor, Berkshire SL4 2RD. *Contact: Julie Samuel.*
Direct Heat Management, 20 Lanfranc Road, Worthing, West Sussex BN14 7ER. *Managing Director: Mike Pailthorpe.*
DT Enterprises, Midnight Rock, 83 Blackburn Road, Greenhill, Herne Bay, Kent CT7 7UT. *Contact: Dave Taylor.*
Eastonia Entertainments, Eastonia House, 174 Lisnafin Park, Strabane, Co Tyrene, Northern Ireland. *Contact: Gerry Harding.*
EC1, 1 Cowcross Street, London EC1 6DE. *Contact: Alex Nightingale.*
EG Management, 63A Kings Road, London SW3 4NT. *Chairman: Sam Adler.*
Eleventh Hour Arts, 113 Cheesemans Terrace, Star Road, London W14 9XH. *Managing Director: Debbie Golt.*
Emka Productions, 43 Portland Road, London W11 4LJ. *Contact: Mr S O'Rourke.*
Equator Music, 17 Hereford Mansions, Hereford Road, London W2 5BA. *Contact: Ernest Chapman.*
Eternal Management, 55 Lark Street, Liverpool L17 8UW. *Contact: Jill Thompson.*
Europa Jazz Live, 6 Belgrove, Tunbridge Wells, Kent TN1 1YW. *Director: David E Jacobs.*
Excellent Management, 50A Waldron Road, London SW18 3TD. *Contact: Mark Wood.*
Falcon Stuart Management, 59 Moore Park Road, London SW6 2HH. *Managing Director: Falcon Stuart.*
Fexborough Ltd, 195 Sandycome Road, Kew, Surrey TW9 2EW. *Manager: John Kalinowski.*
Fine Tuning, 57 Woodhurst Road, London W3 6SR. *Managing Director: Val Jones.*
Firebirds, 11 Chavenage, Kingswood, Bristol BS15 4LA. *Director: Craig Dunn.*
First Avenue Management, The Courtyard, 42 Colwith Road, London W6 9EY. *Contact: Oliver Smallman.*
Firstars / Talent Bank Management, Bugle House, 21A Noel Street, London W1V 3PD. *Contact: Tony Brinsley.*
Forward Management, 132 Liverpool Road, London N1 1LA. *Managing Director: Rob Challice.*
Friars Management Ltd, 33 Alexander Road, Aylesbury, Buckinghamshire HP20 2NR. *Managing Director: David R Stopps.*
Fruit Management, Unit 104, Saga Centre, 326 Kensal Road, London W10 5BZ. *Managers: Caroline Killoury, Debbie Swainson.*
Gailforce Management Ltd, 30 Ives Street, London SW3 2ND. *Managing Director: Gail Colson; Co-Ordinator: Norma Bishop.*
Ganeshe Management, Ganeshe House, Ingleby Drive, Harrow, Middlesex HA1 3LE. *Managing Director: Harvey Frost.*
Garry Brown Associates (International) Ltd, 27 Downs Side, Cheam, Surrey SM2 7EH. *Chairman: Garry Brown.*
Genius Management, 89A High Road, London N22 6BB. *Contact: Bruce Ruffin.*
Gloria Butler Management, PO Box 2686, Knowle B94 5NQ. *Manager: Gloria Butler.*
GR Management, 974 Pollokshaws Road, Shawlands, Glasgow G41 2HA, Scotland. *Administration Manager: Alan Connell.*
Hal Carter Organisation, 101 Hazelwood Lane, Palmers Green, London N13 5HQ. *Managing Director: Hal Carter.*
Hall Or Nothing, 8 Poplar Mews, Oxbridge Road, London W12 7JS. *Contact: Martin Hall.*
Handle Artists Management, Handle House, 1 Albion Place, Galena Road, Hammersmith, London W6 0QT. *Chairman: David Walker.*
Harvey Lisberg Associates, Kennedy House, 31 Stamford Street, Altrincham, Cheshire WA14 1ES. *Contacts: Harvey & Philip Lisberg.*
Hit & Run Music, 30 Ives Street, London SW3 2ND. *Contact: Tony Smith.*
Holland-Ford's, 103 Lydyett Lane, Barnton, Northwich, Cheshire CW8 4JT. *Proprietor: Bob Holland-Ford.*
Hopscotch Media Management, 46 Broadwick Street, London W1V 1FF. *Director/Partner: Alfie Dosoo.*
Huge And Jolly, 56-60 Islington Park Street, London N1 1PX. *Director: Jolyon Burnham.*
Hyperactive Music Management, 1 Glenthorne Mews, 115A Glenthorne Road, Hammersmith, London W6 0LJ. *Assistant Manager: Fiona Riddick.*
ie Music Ltd, 59A Chesson Road, London W14 9QS. *Directors: Tim Clark, David Enthoven.*
Ignition Management, 8a Wyndham Place, London W1H 1PP. *Contacts: Marcus Russell, Alec McKinney.*
Interaction, 21 Douglas Road, London NW6 7RN. *Contact: Joan Marindin.*
Interceptor Enterprises, The Greenhouse, 34-38 Provost Street, London N1 7NG. *Manager: Charlie Charlton.*
Interface Management, 37 Oxford Gardens, London W4 3BN. *Contact: Douglas Kean.*
Invasion Group, 17 Gosfield Street, London W1P 7HE. *Contact: Mike Hedge.*
Jam X Management, PO Box 3836, London NW3 4XF. *Directors: Neil Burrow and Julian Able.*
James Joseph Music Management, 85 Cicada Road, Wandsworth, London SW18 2PA. *Managing Director: James Joseph.*
Jack Bruce Music, PO Box 2440, Bures, Suffolk CO8 5HY. *Manager: Margrit Seyffer.*
Jackie Khan Management, Monroe Studios, 103-105 Holloway Road, London N7 8LT. *Managing Director: Jackie Khan.*
Jef Hanlon Management Ltd, 1 York Street, London W1H 1PZ. *Director: Alice Hanlon.*
JFD Management, 106 Dalling Road, London W6 0JA. *Contact: Jasmine Daines.*
John Ford Promotions, Bradford Court, Bradford Street, Digbeth, Birmingham B12 0NS. *Owner: John Ford.*
John Henry Management, The John Henry Bldg, 16/24 Brewery Road, London N7 4NH. *Manager - Sales & Retail: Pepin Clout.*
John Osborne Management, PO Box 173, New Malden, Surrey KT3 3YR. *Contact: John Osborne.*
John Tyrrell Management Ltd, PO Box 4058, Maida Vale, London W9 3EW. *Directors: John Tyrrell and Elisa Nadal.*

Johnny Lawes Management, 18 All Saints Road, Unit 8, London W11 1HH. *Managing Director: Johnny Lawes.*

JPR Management, The Power House, 70 Chiswick High Road, London W4 1SY. *Contact: John Reid.*

Jukes Productions, 63 Sutherland Avenue, London W9 2HF. *Contact: Geoff Jukes.*

Kasevin Rodell, 6 Bowling Green Road, Cranfield, Bedfordshire MK43 0ET. *Partner: Dian Rodell.*

Kennedy Street Management, Kennedy House, 31 Stamford Street, Altrincham, Cheshire WA14 1ES. *Director: Nick Leigh.*

Kitchenware, 7 The Stables, St Thomas Street, Newcastle-Upon-Tyne, Tyne And Wear NE1 4LE. *Managing Director: Keith Armstrong.*

Lena Davis, John Bishop Associates, Cotton's Farmhouse, Whiston Road, Cogenhoe, Northants NN7 1NL. *Director: Lena Davis.*

Les Johnson Management, 55 Rockford Close, Oakenshaw South, Redditch, Worcs B98 7SZ. *Les Johnson.*

LJE, 32 Willesden Lane, London NW6 7ST. *Contact: Laurie Jay.*

M Management, 45A Longley Road, London SW17 9LA. *Managing Director: Mort Marrinan.*

Management Connection, Flat 3, Haversham Lodge, Melrose Avenue, Willesden Green, London NW2 4JS. *Managing Director: Sharon Chevin.*

Mark Dean, Electric Lighting Station, 48 Kensington Church Street, London W8 5DP. *Manager: Mark Dean.*

Maverick Management, The Old Manor House, Station Road, Thames Ditton, Surrey KT7 0NU. *Manager: Stein.*

M D O, The Dawn, Northwood Lane, Bewdley, Worcs DY2 1AS. *Contact: Mick Owen.*

Medium Productions Limited, 74 Saint Lawrence Road, Upminster, Essex RM14 2UW. *Co-Director: Debi Zornes.*

Mercenary Music Services, 143 Turks Road, Radcliffe, Manchester M26 3WW. *Production Manager: Paul Naylor.*

Milliown Productions Ltd, 26 East Parade, Bradford, West Yorkshire BD1 5HD. *Producer: Ian Smith.*

Mission Control Management Ltd, Unit 3, Brunel Lock Devt, Cumberland Basin, Bristol BS1 6SE. *Managing Director: Richard Hutchison.*

Mission Impossible Management, 102A Western Road, Hove, East Sussex. *Contact: Tim Collins.*

Modernwood Management, Cambridge House, Card Hill, Forest Row RH18 5BA. *Directors: Mark Wood & Mickey Modern.*

MoHoHo, 149 Gibson Gardens, London N16 7HH. *Manager: Ray Hogan.*

Moksha Management, PO Box 102, London E15 2HH. *Managing Director: Charles Colm.*

Money 'Talks' Management Associates, Cadillac Ranch, Pencraiguchal, Cwm Bach, Whitland, Dyfed SA34 0DT, Wales. *Manager: M Magoon.*

Motley Music Ltd, 132 Liverpool Road, Islington, London N1 1LA. *Manager: Debbie Rawlings.*

Muirhead Management, 202 Fulham Road, Chelsea, London SW10 9PJ. *Chief Executive Officer: Dennis Muirhead.*

NE Music Management, Priory House, 55 Lawe Road, South Sheilds, Tyne & Wear NE33 2AL. *Contact: Dave Smith.*

Negus-Fancey Co., 78 Portland Road, London W11 4LQ. *Contact: Charles Negus-Fancey.*

Nigel Martin-Smith Management Ltd, 41 South King Street, Manchester M2 6DE. *Managing Director: Nigel Martin-Smith.*

19 Management Ltd, Unit 32, 35-37 Parkgate Road, London SW11 4NP. *Managing Director: Simon Fuller.*

Northern Music Company, Cheapside Chambers, 43 Cheapside, Bradford, West Yorkshire BO1 4HP. *Managing Director: Andy Farrow.*

One Fifteen, Woodwharf, 28-30 Horseferry Place, London SE10 9BT. *Manager: Paul Loasby.*

140dB Management, 1 McCrone Mews, Belsize Lane, London NW3 5BG. *Contact: Ros Earls.*

One Management, 43 St Alban's Avenue, London W4 5JS. *Managing Director: Karin Clayton.*

Opal, 3 Pembridge Mews, London W11 3EQ. *Contact: James Topham.*

Opalmist Ltd, 9 Thornton Place, London W1H 1FG. *Managing Director: Lindy Benson.*

Opium (Arts), 49 Portland Road, London W11 4LJ. *Managing Director: Richard Chadwick.*

Orionstar Limited, 34 Hill Street, Richmond, Surrey TW9 1TW. *Manager: John Martin.*

Palace Of Fun, 16 Elm View, Huddersfield Road, Halifax, West Yorkshire HX3 0AE. *Managing Director: Bill Byford.*

Park Promotions, PO Box 651, Oxford OX2 9RB. *Managing Director: John Dagnell.*

Part Rock Management, Suite 318, 535 Kings Road, London SW10 0SZ. *Contact: Stewart Young.*

Paul Crockford Management, 56-60 Islington Park Street, London N1. *Contact: Paul Crockford.*

Pet Shop Boys Partnership, 8 Pembridge Studios, 27A Pembridge Villas, London W11 3EP. *Contact: Jill Wall.*

Pete Hawkins Management, 54 The Avenue, West Wickham, Kent BR4 0DY. *Managing Director: Pete Hawkins.*

PHAB, High Notes, Sheerwater Avenue, Woodham, Surrey KT15 3SD. *Contact: Philip HA Bailey.*

Planet 4, Sun House, 2-4 Little Peter Street, Manchester M15 4PS. *Managing Director: Chris Joyce.*

PNG/Worldwide, Westminster Court, 10 Park Road North, Birmingham, B6 5UJ. *Manager: John Slater.*

Polar Union, 45-53 Sinclair Road, London W14 0NS. *Contact: Sarah Thorp.*

Precious Organisation, 14-16 Spiers Wharf, Port Dundas, Glasgow, Strathclyde, Scotland. *Contact: Elliot Davis*

Pure Management, 39 Bolton Gardens, London SW5 0AQ. *Contact: Steve Fargnoli.*

Purple Palace, 34A Flower Lane, Mill Hill, London NW7 2JE. *Contact: Stephanie Kays.*

PWL Management, 4-7 The Vineyard, off Sanctuary Street, London SE1 1QL. *General Manager: Sally Atkins.*

Queen Productions, 46 Pembridge Road, London W11 3HN. *Contact: Jim Beach.*

Quickfire Management, Basement, 19 All Saints Road, London W11 1HE. *Proprietor: Katherine Canoville.*

Quinlan Road (UK), 1 Heathgate Place, 75/87 Agincourt Road, London NW3 2NT. *General Manager: Ian Blackaby.*

Raymond Coffer Management Limited, Suite 1, Hadleigh House, 96 High Street, Bushey, Herts WD2 3DE. *Managing Director: Raymond Coffer.*

Real Life, 122 Holland Park Avenue, London W11 4UA. *Contact: Paul Lilly.*

Real World, Box Mill, Box, Corsham, Wiltshire SN13 8PL. *Studio Manager: Owen Leech.*

Ricochet, 5 Old Garden Road, The Lanterns, Bridge Lane, London SW11 3AD. *Managing Director: Stephen King.*

Riviera Global, 20 Cromwell Mews, London SW7 2JY. *Contact: Jake Riviera.*

Roger Forrester Management, 18 Harley House, London NW1 5H. *Managing Director: Roger Forrester.*

Rollover Productions, 29 Beethoven Street, London W10 4LJ. *Managing Director: Seamus Morley.*

Rough Trade Management, 66 Golborne Road, London W10 5PS. *Managing Director: Geoff Travis.*

Running Dog Management, Minka, Lower Hampton Road, Sunbury, Middlesex TW16 5PR. *Management Co-ordinator: Rachel Male.*

Rupert Loewenstein. 2 King Street, London SW1Y 6QL. *Director: Clare Turner.*

Salamander & Son Music Ltd, 23 Longman Drive, Inverness IV1 1SU, Scotland. *Contact: Heather Bunting.*

Sanctuary Music (Overseas), 1st Floor Ste, The Colonnades, 82 Bishops Bridge Road, London W2 6BB. *Contact: Rod Smallwood.*

Sandcastle Productions, 236 Sebert Road, Forest Gate, London E7 0NP. *Senior Partner: Simon Law.*

Scotford Music, 13 Winton Park, Edinburgh EH10 7EX, Scotland. *Proprietor/Manager: Gerry Ford.*

Seb Shelton Management, 13 Lynton Road, London N8 8SR. *Contact: Seb Shelton.*

Serious Speakout, 42 Old Compton Road, London W1V 5PB. *Director: John Ellson.*

Sincere Management, 421 Harrow Road, London W10 4RD. *Contact: Peter Jenner.*

Solid Bond Management, Nomis Studios, 45-53 Sinclair Raod, London W14 0NS. *Manager: John Weller.*

Some Bizarre Ltd, 124 New Bond Street, London W1. *Producer: Stevo.*

SOS Management, 106 Cleveland Street, London W1Y 5DP. *Contact: Meredith Cork.*

Sound Management Associates, 22A Lambolle Place, London NW3 4HP. *Managing Director: Paul Craig.*

Soundtrack Music Management, 22 Ives Street, London SW3 2ND. *Directors: Olaf and Carolynne Wyper.*

Southwestern Management, 13 Portland Road, Street, Somerset BA16 9PX. *Director: Chris Hannam.*

So What Arts, 1st Floor, Ducie House, 37 Ducie Street, Manchester M1 2JW. *Contact: Andy Dodd.*

Splash Management & Promotions, 328 Gray's Inn Road, King's Cross, London WC1X 8BZ. *Managing Director: Nick Moore.*

Stamina Management, 47 Prout Grove, London NW10 1PU. *Managing Director: Peter Gage.*

Startrack Studio & Artist Management, 108B North Western Street, Manchester M1 2WS. *Studio Manager: Royston.*

Stephen Budd Management, 109B Regents Park Road, London NW1 8UR. *Managing Director: Stephen Budd.*

Sylvantone Promotions, 17 Allerton Grange Way, Leeds LS17 6LP. *Proprietor: Tony Goodacre.*

SYME International Management, 81 Park Road, Wath-Upon-Dearne, Rotherham, South Yorkshire S63 7LE. *Contact: Martin Looby.*
Taurus Records, 23 Blackheath Rise, Lewisham, London SE13 7PN. *Contact: Beverley Miller.*
Tender Prey Management, 4 Ivebury Court, 325 Latimer Road, London W10 6RA. *Contact: Rayner Jesson.*
Theobald Dickson Productions Ltd, The Coach House, Swinhope Hall, Swinhope, Lincolnshire LN3 6HT. *Managing Director: Bernard Theobald.*
Tiz Hay Management, 44 Oswald Close, Leatherhead, Surrey KT22 9UG. *Contact: Tiz Hay.*
TKO Management, PO Box 130, Hove, East Sussex BN3 6QU. *Contact: Steve Lewis.*
Tony Denton Promotions Ltd, 19 South Molton Lane, Mayfair, London W1Y 1AQ. *Contact: Simon Nicholls.*
Tracy Carter Management Ltd, WT House, Pilling, Preston, Lancashire PR3 6SJ. *Owner: William Tracy Carter.*
Trinifold Management, 22 Harley House, Marylebone Road, London NW1 4PR. *Managing Director: Bill Curbishley.*
TYGER, c/o 19A Bedford Road, London N15 4HA. *Head of Music: Tim Noyce.*
UK/LA Management, Bugle House, 21A Noel Street, London W1V 3PD. *Contact: Michael Cox.*
Value Added Talent (VAT), 1-2 Purley Place, London N1 1QA. *Managing Director: Dan Silver.*
Voodoo Productions, 21 Ruckholt Close, Leyton, London E10 5NX. *Contact: Rita Campbell.*
Wedge Music, 63 Grosvenor Street, London W1X 9DA. *Contact: Tony Gordon.*
Wilcox Zodiac Organisation, 1099A Finchley Road, London NW11 0QB. *Artist Manager: Bert Wilcox.*
Wildlife Management, Unit F, 21 Heathmans Road, London, SW6 4TJ. *Managing Director: Ian McAndrew.*
William Tracey-Carter Management, WT House, Pilling, Preston, Lancs PR3 6SJ. *Contact: William Tracey-Carter.*
Wolfgang Kuhle Artist Management, PO Box 425, London SW6 3TX. *Contact: Wolfgang Kuhle.*
Worldchief Ltd, 132 Liverpool Road, London N1 1LA. *Director: Steve Baker; Assistant: Susie Blyth.*
XL Talent, Studio 7, 27A Pembridge Villas, London W11 3EP. *Contact: Ian Wright.*

URUGUAY

ABT Producciones, 25 de Mayo 544, 2 Piso, Montevideo. *Director: Adolfo Brun Thielman.*
Edmundo Klinger-Garcia Rial Assoc., Avda. Garibaldi 2748, Apto. 203, Montevideo. *Director: Edmundo Klinger.*
San Martín Producciones, José Enrique Rodó 1661, Apto. 401, 11200 Montevideo. *Director: Eduardo San Martín.*

USA

Ace Productions, PO Box 292725, Nashville, TN 37229-2725. *President: Jim Case.*
Addis, Wechsler & Associates, 955 S Carrillo Drive, Los Angeles, CA 90048. *Contact: Nick Wechsler.*
AEG Management, 1025 16th Avenue S, Suite 401, Nashville, TN 37212. *CEO: Marc Oswald.*
AFG Entertainment, 30 W 21st Street, 7th Floor, New York, NY 10010- 6905. *Contact: Ronald Fierstein.*
Aggressive Entertainment, 130 W 57th Street, Suite 5A, New York, NY 10019. *Manager: Nick Moyle.*
Al Bunetta Management, Suite 102A, 33 Music Square W, Nashville, TN 37203. *Manager: Al Bunetta.*
Al Embry International, PO Box 23162, Nashville, TN 37202. *Owner/President: Al Embry.*
Alive Enterprises, PO Box 5542, Beverly Hills, CA 90211. *Contact: Shep Gordon.*
All Access Entertainment, 425 Madison Avenue, Ste 802, New York, NY 10017. *Managers: Brian Doyle, Richard Flynn, Amy McFarland.*
All Girl Productions, Animation Bldg 3B-10, S Buena Vista, Burbank, CA 91521. *Contact: Bonnie Bruckheimer.*
Alliance Artists Ltd, Ste 220, 3423 Piedmont Road NE, Atlanta, GA 30305. *Contact: Charlie Brusco.*
Allman Brothers Band, 18 Tamworth Road, Waban, MA 02168. *Manager: Bert Holman.*
American Band Management, PO Box 840607, Houston, TX 77284-0607. *President: John Blomstrom Snr.*
Amethyst Group Ltd, 273 Chippewa Drive, Columbia, SC 29210-6508. *Chairman: C G Butler.*
Andon Artists, 79 Farview Farm Road, W Redding, CT 06896. *Owner / Manager: Arma Andon.*
Angelus Entertainment, 9016 Wilshire Blvd, Suite 346, Beverly Hills, CA 90211. *Manager: Pete Angelus.*
Art Collins Management, PO Box 561, Pine Bush, NY 12566. *Manager: Art Collins.*
Artist Representative & Management, 1257 Arcade Street, St Paul, MN 55106. *Office Manager/Agent: Roger Anderson.*
Atomic Communications Group, 10553 W Jefferson Blvd, Culver City, CA 90232. *CEO: Gabriel LeConte.*
A Train Management, PO Box 29242, Oakland, CA 94604. *Contact: Al Evers.*
Barron Entertainment, 209 10th Avenue South, Suite 232, Nashville, TN 37203. *Contact: Jay Barron.*
Barry Bergman Management, 350 E 30th Street, Ste 4D, New York, NY 10016. *Manager: Barry Bergman.*
Baruck / Consolo Management, 15003 Greenleaf Street, Sherman Oaks, CA 91403. *Contact: John Baruck, Tom Consolo.*
Bet-Car Management, 307 Lake Street, San Francisco, CA 94118. *Contact: Ora Harris.*
Big FD Entertainment, 10801 National Blvd #530, Los Angeles, CA 90064. *President: Doug Goldstein.*
Bill Graham Management, PO Box 429094, San Francisco, CA 94142-9094. *Owner: Bill Graham.*
Bill Sammeth Organization, PO Box 960, Beverly Hills, CA 90213. *President: Bill Sammeth.*
Bill Thompson Management, 2051 Third Street, San Francisco, CA 94107. *Manager: Bill Thompson.*
BJM, 250 W 57th Street, Suite 603-5, New York, NY 10107. *Manager: Paul Korzilius.*
Blanton / Harrell Entertainment, 2910 Poston Avenue, Nashville, TN 37203. *Managers: Michael Blanton, Dan Harrell.*
Blowin' Smoke Management, 7438 Shoshone Avenue, Van Nuys, CA 91406-2340. *President: Larry Weisberg.*
BMP Artist Management, PO Box 1703, La Mirada, CA 90637. *Contact: Brian A Mayes.*
Bobby Roberts Co., PO Box 3007, Hendersonville, TN 37077. *President: Bobby Roberts.*
Borman Entertainment, 9220 Sunset Blvd, Suite 320, Los Angeles, CA 90069. *President: Gary Borman.*
Brock & Associates Management, 201 Seaboard Lane, Franklin, TN 37067. *President: Darlene Brock.*
Brokaw Company, 9255 Sunset Blvds, Suite 804, Los Angeles, CA 90069. *Managers: David, Sandy and Joel Brokaw.*
Brothers Management Associates, 141 Dunbar Avenue, Fords, NJ 08863.
BTB Management Group, PO Box 3509, Westport, CT 06880. *Contact: Dee Anthony, Joshua Simons.*
Budd Carr Co Inc, 9320 Wilshire Blvd, Suite #200, Beverly Hills, CA 90212. *Contact: Marni Feenberg.*
Bullet Entertainment, 120 N Victory, Suite 102, Burbank, CA 91052. *Contact: Karmen Beck, Gary Bird.*
Bust It Management, 80 Swan Way, Suite 130, Oakland, CA 94621. *CEO: Louis Burrell.*
Carr-Sharpe Entertainment Servcies, 9320 Wilshire Blvd, Suite 200, Beverly Hills, CA 90212. *Partners: Budd Carr, Wil Sharpe.*
C & M Productions Management Group, 5114 Albert Drive, Brentwood, TN 37027. *President: Ronald Cotton.*
C M S Management, 627 Main Street, Simpson, PA 18407. *Vice President - A&R: Carl Canedy.*
C Winston Simone Management, 1790 Broadway, 10th Floor, New York, NY 10019. *CEO: C Winston Simone.*
Collins Management, 5 Bigelow Street, Cambridge, MA 02139 and 584 Broadway, Suite 506, New York, NY 10012. *Chief Executive Officer: Tim Collins.*
Columbia Artists Management, 165 W 57th Street, New York, NY 10019. *President: Ronald Wilford.*
Concrete Management, 301 W 53rd Street, Suite 11-D, New York, NY 10019. *Contact: Andy Gould.*
Courage Management, 2899 Agoura Road, Suite 562, Westlake, CA 91361. *Manager: John Courage.*
Craig H Berlin CPA, 1650 Broadway, Suite 510, New York, NY 10019. *Principal: C Berlin.*
Crazed Management, 14 Tennent Road, Morganville, NJ 07751. *Manager: Jon Zazula.*
Crossfire Productions, 1209 Baylor Street, Austin, TX 78703-4123. President: Vicky Moerbe.
Curtis Management, 417 Denny Way, 2nd Floor, Seattle, WA 98109-4934. *Contact: Kelly Curtis.*

DAS Communications, 83 Riverside Drive, New York, NY 10024. *Contacts: David Sonenberg, Bernard Alexander.*
David Lefkowitz Management, 3470 19th Street, San Francisco, CA 94110. *Owner: David Lefkowitz.*
Depth Of Field Management, 1501 Broadway, Suite 1304, New York, NY 10036. *President: Darryl Pitt.*
Diamondback-Great Pyramid (Musics), PO Box 170040, San Francisco, CA 94117. *Owner: Joseph Buchwald.*
Dream Street Management, 1460 Fourth Street, Suite 205, Santa Monica, CA 90401. *Manager: Ed Gerrard.*
Dynamic Productions Inc, 11410 West Wisconsin Avenue, Wanwatosa, WI 53226. *Vice President: Arthur Greinke.*
Earth Tracks Artists, 4809 Avenue N, Suite 286, Brooklyn, NY 11234. *Managing Director: David Krinsky.*
East End Management, 8209 Melrose Avenue, 2nd Floor, Los Angeles, CA 90046. *Manager: Tony Dimitriades.*
Endangered Species Artists Management, PO Box 20469, Columbus Circle Station, New York, NY 10023-1485. *President: Fred Porter.*
ESP Management, 888 Seventh Avenue #2904, New York, NY 10106-0001. *President: Bud Prager.*
Famous Artists, 1700 Broadway, 5th Floor, New York, NY 10019. *Manager: David Zedeck.*
Firstars, 3520 Hayden Avenue, Culver City, CA 90232. *Manager: Miles Copeland.*
Fitzgerald-Hartley Company, 50 West Main Street,Ventura, CA 93001. *Managers: Larry Fitzgerlad, Mark Hartley.*
Gallin-Morey Associates, 345 N Maple Drive, Suite 300, Beverly Hills, CA 90210. *Chairman: Sandy Gallin; President: Jim Morey.*
Gold Mountain Entertainment, Suite 450, 3575 Cahuenga Blvd West, Los Angeles, CA 90068. *President: Ron Stone.*
Greco Holdings Inc, Market Street Square, 33 Wilkes Barre Boulevard, Wilkes Barre, PA 18701. *President/Chief Executive Officer: Thom Greco.*
GRRR Records, 939 W Wilson Avenue, Chicago, IL 60610. *Booking Manager: Diane Borden.*
Hallmark Direction Company, 1905 Broadway, Nashville, TN 37203. *Artist Co-Ordinator: Donna Hysmith.*
Hard To Handle Management, 640 Lee Road, Suite 106, Wayne, PA 19087. *Contact: Steve Barnett.*
Heart Music Inc, PO Box 160326, Austin, TX 78716-0326. *Promotion Director: Karen Biller.*
Heartwrite Music, PO Box 1739, Texarkana, AR 75504. *President: David Patillo.*
Herbie Herbert Management, 2051 Third Street, San Francisco, CA 94107. *Contact: Herbie Herbert.*
HK Management, 8900 Wilshire Blvd, Suite 300, Beverly Hills, CA 90211. *Manager: Howard Kaufman.*
Imani Entertainment Inc, PO Box 150-139, Brooklyn, NY 11215. *Director: Guy Anglade.*
Industrial Management, 3450 3rd St, #2A Suite 300, San Francisco, CA 94124-1402. *President: Chris Coyle.*
Issachar Management, 111 3rd Avenue, #10F, New York City, NY 10003. *President: Jack Flanagan.*
J & D Music Services Ltd, 38 West 21 Street, 5th Floor, New York, NY 10010-6906. *President: Jerome Hershman.*
Jerry Kravat Entertainment Services (JKES) Inc, 404 Park Avenue, New York, NY 10016. *Contact: Stan Scottland.*
Joe Granda Management, 13644 S W 142 Avenue, Suite D, Miami, FL 33186. *President: Joe Granda.*
Joseph Buchwald, PO Box 347008, San Francisco, CA 94134. *Contact: Joseph Buchwald.*
Ken Adamany Associates, 1818 Parmenter Street, Suite 202, Middleton, WI 53562. *Contact: Ken Adamany.*
Kragen & Co, 1112 N Sherbourne Drive, Los Angeles, CA 90069. *Contact: Ken Kragen.*
Landmark Communications Group, PO Box 1444, Hendersonville, TN 37077. *President: Bill Anderson Jr.*
Legend Artists, 120 W 44th Street, Suite 404, New York, NY 10036. *President: Joe Boyland.*
Lippman Entertainment, 8900 Wilshire Blvd, Suite 340, Beverly Hills, CA 90211-1906. *Contact: Michael and Terry Lippman.*
Lone Wolf Management, PO Box 163390, Austin, TX 78716. *President: Bill Ham.*
Lookout Management, 2644 30th Street, 1st Floor, Santa Monica, CA 90405. *Contact: Frank Gironda, Eliiot Roberts.*
Louis Levin Management, 130 W 57th Street, Suite 10B, New York, NY 10019. *President: Louis Levin.*
Madhouse Management, PO Box 15108, Ann Arbor, MI 48106. *Contact: Doug Banker.*
Management By Jaffe, 1560 Broadway, Suite 1103, New York, NY 10036. *President: Jerry Jaffe.*
Management Network, 19430 Ventura Blvd. Suite 205, Sherman Oaks, CA 91403. *Contact: Gerry Tolman.*
Mark A Abbattista, 1875 Century Park East, Seventh Floor, Los Angeles, CA 90067. *Contact: Mark 'Abba' Abbattista.*
Mark Alan, PO Box 21323, St Paul, MN 55121. *President: Mark Alan.*
Maxine S Harvard Unltd, Commerce Center, 2227 US Highway 1 #251, N Brunswick, NJ 08902. *Manager: Maxine S Harvard.*
McCraw Management, 1830 E Kane Place, Suite #3, Milwaukee, WI 53202. *Manager: Mark McCraw.*
Mc Fadden Artists, 818 18th Avenue S, Nashville, TN 37203. *Chairmen: Jack And Jo McFadden.*
McGhee Entertainment, 9145 Sunset Blvd, Los Angeles, CA 90069. *Manager: Doc McGhee.*
Metropolitan Entertainment, 7 N Mountain Avenue, Montclair, NJ 07042. *Contact: Robert Kos.*
Mirkin Management, 906½ Congress Avenue, Austin, TX 78701. *Owner: Jan Mirkin.*
Moress Nanas Entertainment, 12424 Wilshire Blvd Suite 840, Los Angeles, CA 90025. *Partner: Herb Nanas.*
Music Man Productions, 568 Snelling Avenue N, Suite 106, St Paul, MN 55104. *Owners: Paul Manske and Steve York.*
Music Umbrella, PO Box 1067, Santa Monica, CA 90406. *President/Chief Executive Officer: Glenn H Friedman.*
Niji Management, Suite 307, 18653 Ventura Blvd, Tarzana, CA 91356. *President: Wendy Dio.*
Nippy Inc., 2160 N Central Road, Fort Lee, NJ 07024-7547. *CEO: John Houston.*
Oasis Management, 3010 E Bloomfield, Phoenix, AZ 85032. *Manager: Gloria Cavalera.*
Open Door Management, 15327 Sunset Blvd, #365, Pacific Palisades, CA 90272. *President: Bill Traut.*
Overland Productions, 156 56th Street, 5thFloor, New York, NY 10019. *President: Gary Kurfirst.*
Panacea Entertainment, 2705 Glendower Avenue, Los Angeles, CA 90027. *Chairman/Chief Executive Officer: Eric Garoner.*
Patrick Rains & Associates, 1543 7th Street, 3rd Floor, Santa Monica, CA 90401. *Manager: Patrick Rains.*
Peter Asher Management, 644 N Doheny Drive, Los Angeles, CA 90069. *President: Ira Koslow.*
Pilot Management Company, PO Box 23203, Nashville, TN 37202. *President: Johnson Bell.*
Platinum Gold Productions, 9200 Sunset Blvd, Suite 1220, Los Angeles, CA 90029. *Partner: Steve Cohen.*
PPL-MCI Entertainment Group, 10 Universal Plaza, PO Box 8442, Universal City, CA 91618. *Managing Director: Maxx Diamond.*
Precision Management, 825 N King Street, Suite A-1, Hampton, VA 23669-2814. *Operations Manager: Cappriccieo M Scates.*
Premier Artist Services, 1401 University Drive, Suite 305, Coral Springs, FL 33071. *President: Eliot H Weisman.*
Premier Productions, 1909 N Spruce, Wichita, KS 67214. *Owner: Anthony Welch.*
Production Group International, 2200 Wilson Blvd, Suite 200, Arlington, VA 22201. *President: Ed Yoe.*
Q-Prime Inc, 729 Seventh Avenue, 14th Floor, New York, NY 10019. *Co-Presidents: Cliff Burnstein, Peter Mensch.*
Quango Music Group Inc, 9744 Wilshire Blvd, #305 Beverley Hills, CA 90212. *President: George Ghiz.*
Quiet Storm Inc, 103 Westward Drive, Miami Springs, FL 33166. *Contact: Carl C Valldejuli.*
Ralph Mercado Management, 568 Broadway, Suite 806, New York, NY 10012. *President: Ralph Mercado.*
REM/Athens Ltd, PO Box 8032, Athens, GA 30603. *Contact: Bertis E. Downs, W. Jefferson Holt.*
Remington Management Inc, 6602 Harbor Town, Suite 501, Houston, TX 77036. *President: Janice D Hayes.*
Rhyme Syndicate Management, 451 N Reese Pl, Burbank, CA 91506. *President: Jorge Hinojosa.*
Rick Levy Management, 1881 S Kirkman Road, 715, Orlando, FL 32811. *President: Rick Levy.*
Roger Davies Management, 15030 Ventura Blvd, Suite 772, Sherman Oaks, CA 91403. *Manager: Roger Davies.*
Ron Weisner Entertainment, 9200 Sunset Blvd PH 15, Los Angeles, CA 90069. *Manager: Ron Weisner.*
Rosebud Agency, PO Box 170429, San Francisco, CA 94117. *President: Mike Kappus.*
Ruth Blakely Management, 610 Players Court, Nashville, TN 37211. *Chief Executive Officer: Ruth Blakely.*
Siddons & Associates, 584 North Larchmont Blvd, Los Angeles, CA 90004. *President: Bill Siddons.*
Side One Management Ltd, 1026A Third Avenue, New York, NY 10021. *President: Will Botwin.*
Slatus Management, 208 E 51st Street, New York, NY 10022. *Manager: Teddy Slater.*
Stiefel Phillips Entertainment, 9720 Wilshire Blvd, 4th Floor, Beverly Hills, CA 90212. *Managers: Arnold Stiefel, Randy Phillips.*

Stilleto Entertainment, 5443 Beethoven Street, Los Angeles, CA 90066. *Partners: Edna Collison, Garry Kief, Steve Wax.*
Surface Entertainment and Management, PO Box 2935, Church Street Station, New York, NY 10008. *Contact: Pam Beninon.*
Susan Silver Management, 207 ½ First Avenue S, Ste 300, Seattle, WA 98104. *Owner: Susan Silver.*
Talent House, 7211 Santa Monica #200, Los Angeles, CA 90046. *President: Staci Slater.*
Ted Kurland Associates, 173 Brighton Avenue, Boston, MA 02134. *President: Ted Kurland.*
Ten Ten Management, 33 Music Square W, Suite 110, Nashville, TN 37203. *President: Barry Coburn.*
Thames Talent, 45 E Putnam Avenue, Greenwich, CT 06830. *Manager: Bruce Payne.*
Third Rail Entertainment, 9169 Sunset Blvd, Los Angeles, CA 90069. *Contact: Bob Cavallo.*
Top Rock Development Corporation, 6399 Wilshire Blvd, Suite 1001, Los Angeles, CA 90049. *Managers: Doug Thaler and Stephanie Gurevitz.*
Troubadour Entertainment, 5305 Barton Vale Court, Nashville, TN 37211-8404. *President: Tony Lee.*
Turi's Music, 103 Westward Drive, Miami Springs, FL 33166. *Contact: Carl C Valldejuli.*
Umpire Entertainment Enterprises, 1507 Scenic Drive, Longview, TX 75604. *President: Jerry Haymes.*
Up Front Management, 1906 Seward Drive, Pittsburg, CA 94565. *Chief Executive Officer: Charles Coke; Vice President: Terry Pitts.*
Vector Management, PO Box 128037, Nashville, TN 37212. *Manager: Ken Levitan.*
Warren Entner Management, 5550 Wilshire Blvd, Suite 302, Los Angeles, CA 90036. *President: Warren Entner.*
Westwood Entertainment Group, 1115 Inman Avenue, Suite 330, Edison, NJ 08820-1132. *General Manager: Elena Petillo.*
Wolgemath & Hyatt Inc, 8012 Brooks Chapel Road, Suite 243, Brentwood, TN 37027. *Artist Manager: John Mallory.*
Zane Management, The Bellvue, 6th Floor, Broad & Walnut Street, Philadelphia, PA 19102. *President: LLoyd Zane Remick.*

VENEZUELA

Carlos Cassina, Avda. Lecuna, Ed. El Tjar 3, Apto E Parque Central, Caracas. *Contact: Carlos Cassina.*
Fonart SA, Avda. Caurimare, Ctro Caroní MA, Of.A-26, Col. del Bello Monte, 1041 Caracas. *Vice President: Antonio Sánchez G.*
Producciones Maria Gómez, Apartado Postal 50 158, 1050 A, Caracas. *Director: Maria Gómez.*
Representaciones Billo SA, Avda. Paez, Res. Verónica 7° Piso, Apto &C, El Paraiso, Caracas. *President: Amable Frómente.*
Sonia Guedez, Multicentro Empresarial del Este, Edif. Miranda Nucleo A, 4, Of. 47-A, Caracas. *Contact: Sonia Guedez.*

APPENDIX C
AGENTS AND PROMOTERS

ARGENTINA

Abraxas Producciones Internacionales, Avda. Callao 875, 4° Piso H, 1023 Buenos Aires. *Director: Carlos Pity Yñurrigarro.*
Aisenberg & Asociados, Juncal 3361, 6° Piso Of. C, 1425 Buenos Aires. *Director: Chiche Aisenberg.*
Dario Arellano Producciones, San Gerónimo 2005, 3000 Santa Fe. *Director: Dario Arellano.*
Felix Marín & Asociados, Talcahuano 68, 6° Piso, Of. D, 1013 Buenos Aires. *Director: Felix Marín.*
Fernando Moya Producciones, Heredia 1425,1427 Buenos Aires. *Director: Fernando Moya.*
Hector Cavallero Producciones SA, Hipólito Hirigoyen 1994, PB 4, 1089 Buenos Aires. *President: Fernando Cavallero.*
Kralendijk Producciones, Sánchez de Bustamante 444, 5° Piso, Dpto 1, 1173 Buenos Aires. *President: Alejandro Solignac.*
Matt Hungo Producciones, Tucumán 1455, 5° Piso, Dtos A-B, 1050 Buenos Aires. *Director: Omar Lauria.*
Ohanian Producciones, Aguilar 2073, 1428 Buenos Aires. *Director: Alberto Ohanian.*
Rock & Pop Internacional, Zapiola 1625, 1427 Buenos Aires. *Director: Daniel Grinbank.*
TM Producciones, Nicaragua 4994,1425 Buenos Aires. *Director: Raúl Fernández.*

AUSTRALIA

Abracadabra Event Company, 186 Glen Osmond Road, Fullarton, SA 5063. *Director: Brian Gleeson.*
Adrian Bohm Presents Pty Ltd, 44 Fourth Avenue, St Peters, SA 5069. *Director: Adrian Bohm.*
A R E The Entertainment Company, 186 Glen Osmond Road, Fullarton, SA 5063. *Director: Mark Draper.*
ATA Allstar Artists Pty Ltd, 98 Glebe Point, Glebe, NSW 2037. *Directors: Tony Brady, Kevin Jacobsen.*
Australian Variety Artists, PO Box 300, Kings Cross, NSW 2011. *Agents: Dez Dalton, Suzanne Terry.*
B & S Promotions, PO Box 1481, Frankston, VIC 3199. *Partners: Bill and Sally Dettmer.*
Cheersquad, PO Box 4153, East Richmond, VIC 3121. *Contact: Wally Kempton.*
Chevy's Entertainment Booking Agency, PO Box 380W, Smithfield West, NSW 2164. *Manager/Booking Agent: Mario J Borg.*
Class Entertainment Organization Pty Ltd, PO Box 169, Sutherland, NSW 2232. *Managing Director: Ron Ragel.*
Entertainers Pty Ltd, 48 Millswood Cr, Millswood, SA 5034. *Managing Director: Ivan Tanner.*
Feel Management & Tour Co-Ordination, 2/54 Bronte Road, Bondi Junction, NSW 2022. *Contact: Tim Pittman.*
Harbour Agency Pty Ltd, 3rd Floor, 63 William Street, East Sydney, NSW 2011. *Managing Director: Sam Righi.*
Heart Beat Promotions, 10 Raggatt Street, Alice Springs, NT 0870. *Manager: Matthew Guggisberg.*
International Management Group, 281 Clarence Street, Sydney, NSW 2000. *Director of Arts & Entertainment: Stephen Flint Wood.*
Jaybee's Entertainment Agency, PO Box 37, Sanctuary Pl, NSW 2540. *Manager: Narrell M Brown.*
Lynne James & Associates, PO Box 511, Lane Cove, Sydney, NSW 2060. *Managing Director: Lynne James.*
Mario Maicho Promotions Pty Ltd, PO Box 572, North Adelaide, SA 5006. *Secretary/Tour Co-Ordinator: Margaret Rudge.*
Melke (Artist Representation & Media Co-Ordination), 158 Raglan Street, Mosman, Sydney, NSW 2088. *Director: Sue Melke.*
Michael Coppel Presents, 716-718 High Street, Armadale, VIC 3143. *Managing Director: Michael Coppel.*
Nationwide Entertainment Agency, 4 Jennings Road, Heathcote, NSW 2233. *Director: Kathryn Muriti.*
Opulent Music Entertainment, 48 David Crescent, PO Box 270, Bundoora, VIC 1083. *Managing Director: Anthony Chidiac.*
Paul Cussen Management, Suite 1, Level 2, 41 Oxford Street, Darlinghurst, NSW 2010. *Proprietor: Paul Cussen.*
Pegasus Event Management Pty Ltd, The Hills Centre, Carrington Road, Castle Hill, NSW 2154. *Managing Director: Christopher Rix.*
Phill Shute Management Pty Ltd, PO Box 273, Dulwich Hill, NSW 2203. *Managing Director: Phill Shute.*
Premier Artists Pty Ltd, 9 Dundas Lane, Albert Park, VIC 3206. *Managing Director: Frank Stivala.*
Servant Communications, PO Box 2020, Launceston, Tasmania 7250. *President: Kevin N Hooper.*
Shawthing Entertainment, Entertainment Place, PO Box 4, Broadway, QLD 4006. *Manager: John Maher.*
Sphere Organization, Suite 21/835 Pennant Hills Road, Carlingford, NSW 2118. *Director/Manager: Eric 'Chubby' Carlini.*
Sun Promotions, PO Box 192, West Ryde, Sydney, NSW 2114. *Reggae Promoter/Venue Consultant: Ted Vassell.*
Talentworks Pty Ltd, First Floor, 222 Albert Road, South Melbourne, VIC 3205. *Chief Executive Officer: Glenn Wheatley.*
Trading Post Entertainments Agency, PO Box 124, Round Corner, Sydney, NSW 2158. *Managing Director/Booking Agent: Owen Orford.*

AUSTRIA

Austrian International Artist Agency, M Felder Str. 5, A-6900 Bregenz. *Managing Director: Viktor Pamminger.*
Live Performance Service, Esteplatz 3/13, A-1030 Vienna. *President: Fritz Thom.*
MemphisMusic Concerts, Sleveringerstrasse 194, A-1190 Vienna. *Managing Director: Wolfgang Bergelt.*
Milica, Liebhartstalstr 15/5, A-1160 Vienna. *Contact: Milica.*
RATZ Promotion, Vorachstrasse 65, A-6890 Lustenau. *Contact: Thomas Radovon.*
Rock Produktion West, Bregenzerstr. 73, A-6900 Bregenz. *Managing Director: Alex Nussbaumer.*
RoCo Management, Huetteldorfer Strasse 257C, A-1140 Vienna. *Owner: Roland Colerus.*
Stein Music Wien, Bernardgasse 39/33, A-1070 Vienna. *Managing Director: Regine Steinmetz.*
Wien Concerts, Margaretenstr. 78, A-1050 Vienna. *Managing Director: Jeff Maxian.*

BELARUS

Beloton Records, Shrader Str 8-15, Viteosk 210015. *Director: Vladimir Sartchenko.*

BELGIUM

AA LN International, PO Box 15 Antwerpen 17, B-2018 Antwerp. *President: Luc Nuitten.*
Backline, Kammerstraat 19, B-9000 Ghent. *Manager: Robert Van Yper.*
Centre Culturel de la Communaute Francaise Wallonie Bruxelles le Botanique, Rue Royale 236, B-1210 Brussels. *Contact: Paul-Henri Wauters.*
CPA (Country Programmers Association), St Pieterstraat 34/2, B-2400 Mol. *President: Eric Van De Mert.*
Euro Promo Music, 5 Square de Noville, B-1080 Brussels. *Chairman: Hans Piccini.*
Foundation VZW, Fruithoflaan 124, Bus 11, B-2600 Berchem/Antwerp. *Director: Peter Verstraelen.*
Kras Artists, Leernsestwg 168, B-9800 Deinze. *Director: Jean Tants.*

Les Fruits de la Passion Asbl, Place du Nord 3, B-4000 Liege. *Administrator: Bernard Hemblenne.*
L&S Agency, PO Box 5, B-3800 Sint-Truiden 2. *Managing Director: Mark Strauven.*
Merlyn, Gulden Vlieslaan 67, B-8000 Brugge. *Contact: Nico A Mertens.*
Music BaM, lelielaan 11, B-2460 Lichtaart. *Managing Director: Gert Van Dingenen; Assistant Managing Director: Tom van Dingenen.*
Paperwork, Aarschotsesteenweg 245, B-3012 Wilsele. *Manager: Johan P Berckmans.*
Show Organisation, Drève du Prophète 23A, B-7000 Mons. *Managing Director: George Hayes.*
Swing Promotions, Beukenlaan 3, B-2970 Schilde. *Manager: Wim Groos.*
Tour de Force, Rue des Archers 19-21, B-1080 Brussels. *Managing Director: Ton Van Draanen.*
TTT, Vriesenhof 22/5, B-3000 Leuven. *Managers: Rick Tabbax and Johan P Berckmans.*
Wallonie-Bruxelles Musiques, Bl A Max 13, (Bte 6), B-1000 Brussels. *Co-Ordinator: Patrick Printz.*
Witlof, Leernsestw 168, B-9800 Deinze. *Director: Jean Tant.*

BOLIVIA

HR Producciones, Loayza 349, 15 Piso, Dpto 1503, Edifico Loazya, La Paz. *General Manager: Nestor Horacio Rasgido.*

BULGARIA

Arsis Productions, 15 Tsarigradsko Chausse Blvd, 1220 Sofia. *Chairman: Velizar Sokolov.*
Mega Music, 2 Trapesitsa Str, 100 Sofia. *Managing Director: Dora Cherneva.*
New Music Agency, Nadejda Bl 634, Apt 14, 1231 Sofia.
Sofia Music Enterprise, 15 Ivan Rilski Str, 1000 Sofia. *Managing Director: Dimitur Kovachev.*
Sofiaconcert Artistic Agency, Volov 3, 1527 Sofia. *Manager: Jeanna Mollova.*

CANADA

Am-Can International Talent Inc, 9615 Macleod Trail S, Calgary, AB T2J 0P6. *VP Director of Sales: Frank Scott.*
Amok Artist Agency, Suite 202 243 Main Street East, Milton, ON L9T 1P1. *Contact: Lorenz Eppinger.*
August Music, 4 Maple Lead Lane, Aberfoyle, ON N1H 6H9. *General Manager: Paul Embro.*
Bandstand (International Entertainment Agency), PO Box 1010, Simcoe, ON N3Y 5B3. *President: Wayne Elliot.*
Big Time Productions Ltd, 54 Duncombe Dr, Lower Level, Hamilton, ON L9A 2G2. *President/Chief Executive Officer: John Balogh Jr.*
BWL Entertainment Connection, 19 Acadia Crescent, St Catharines, ON L2P 1H7. *Contact: Bruce Lilley.*
Community Box Offices, 1234 W Hastings Street, Vancouver, BC V6E 2M4.
Concert Productions International, c/o 111 George Street, 3rd Floor, Toronto, ON M5A 2N4. *Communications Director: James Monaco.*
ESP - Elwood Saracuse Productions, 720 Spadina Avenue, #1702, Toronto, ON M5S 2T9. *President: Elwood Saracuse.*
Festival City Folk Guild, 129 Bedford Drive, Stratford, ON N5A 5J7. *Director: Beth Beech.*
Firestar Promotions Inc, PO Box 165, 1896 West Broadway, Vancouver, BC, V6J 1Y9. *President: Firestar.*
Gino Empry Entertainment, #315-120 Carlton Street, Toronto, ON M5A 4K2. *Owner: Gino Empry.*
Joanne Smale Productions Ltd, 51 Bulwer Street, Main Level, Toronto, ON M5T 1A1. *President: Joanne Smale.*
KISS Talent Referrals, 19695-56th Avenue, Langley, BC, V3A 3X7. *Manager/Agent: Shannon M Myers.*
More Than Booking, 1819 Granville Street, 4th Floor, Halifax, NS B3J 3R1. *President: Wayne O'Connor.*
Music Company Entertainment, 31 Hamlet Road, SW, Calgary, AB T2V 3C9. *President: Fred Thoutenhoofd.*
Nat Raider Productions Inc, 5799 Eldriege Avenne, Montreal, PQ H4W 2E3. *President: Nat Raider.*
Noteable Entertainment Ltd, 940 Brunette Avenue, Coquitlam, BC, V3K 1C9. *Director - Country Division: Don Buchanan.*
Productions Martin Leclerc Inc, 2220 rue Notre-Dame Ouest #201, Montréal, PQ H3J 2V4. *Manager: Martin Leclerc.*
Regal Recordings Limited, 2421 Hammond Road, Mississauga, ON L5K 1T3. *Vice President: Doreen M Davey.*
Rose Concert Productions Inc, Box 23053, London, ON N6A 5N9. *Promoter: David Rose.*
Showcana Corportation, PO Box #4689, Station "C", Calgary, AB T2T 5P1. *President: Robert James Chin.*
Siegel Entertainment Ltd, 101-1648 W 7th Avenue, Vancouver, BC, V6J 1S5. *President: Robert Siegel.*
Silverhawk Publishing, 3073 Cedarbank Road, Rural Route # Eleven, Peterborough, ON K9J 6Y3. *President: Jim Freake.*
SL Feldman & Associates Ltd, Suite 200 - 1505 West 2nd Avenue, Vancouver, BC V6H 3Y4. *President: Sam Feldment; Senior Vice President: Shaw Saltzberg.*
Sphere Entertainment, 22 Bainsford Road, Toronto, ON M4L 3N4. *President: Patricia Silver.*
Stella Black Live Music, PO Box 23, St Anne de Belle, PQ, H9X 3L4. *President: Stella Black.*
Trick Or Treat Entertainment, 1971 Spruce Hill Road, Pickering, ON L1V 1S6. *Contact: Kay White.*
Vocal Image Productions, 192 Kensington Road, Charlottetown, PEI C1A 7S3. *Manager: Berni Wood.*

CHILE

C1 Producciones Chile, Avda. Once de Septiembre 2155, Santiago de Chile. *Director: José Castellanos.*
Galo Producciones SA, Hernando de Aguirre, 944 Providencia, Santiago de Chile. *General Manager: Alfredo Saint-Jean.*
Geomusica, Paseo Poniente, 4593 El Portal de la Viña, Santiago de Chile. *Director: Claudio Cáceras.*
Prodin Chile SA, Tomas Andrews 089 Comuna de Providencia, Santiago de Chile. *Executive Director: Ernesto Claveria.*
Producciones Macondo Chile Ltda, Alvarez 58 L-6, Viña Del Mar. *Manager: Alfredo Troncoso.*
Ricardo Suárez Daud Y Cia Ltda, La Concepción 81, Of. 405 Providencia, Santiago de Chile. *Manager: Ricardo Suárez Duad.*
Romero & Campbell Producciones, Bombero Nuñez, 385 Barrio Bellavista, Santiago de Chile. *Director: Carmen Romero Quero.*
Union Producciones SA, California 2380, Santiago de Chile. *Director General: Jorge Saint-Jean.*

CROATIA

AIMP, O. Zupancica 10, 41000 Zagreb. *Managing Director: Damir Tiljak.*
BJ Promotions, D. Cesarica 11, 41000 Zagreb. *Managing Director: Borislav Jankovic.*
Best, Jarunska 88, 41000 Zagreb. *Managing Director: Mirko Kramaric.*
Croatian Music Art, Trg S, Radica 4, 41000 Zagreb. *Managing Director: Damir Gostl.*
Jazzette, Avenija Vukovar 35, 41000 Zagreb. *Manager: Kolja Petrovic.*
Promomedia Ltd, Kralja Zvonimira 82, HR - 10 000 Zabreb. *Managing Director: Marijan Crnaric.*
T R I P, Argentinska 3, 10000 Zagreb. *A&R Manager: Aleksandar Dragas.*
Urban Concert, K Tomislava 30, 42300 Čakovec, *Director: Toni Sabol.*

CZECH REPUBLIC

10:15 Promotion, Gorkeho 24, 1100 00 Prague. *Contact: Stanko Jaroslav.*
Pragokoncert, Maltezske 1, 118 13 Prague. *Managing Director: Krajcik Josef.*

DENMARK

Arte Booking, Hvidkildevej 64, DK-2400 Copenhagen NV. *Managing Director: Fimm Thorkildsen.*
Basement Productions, PO Box 394, DK-8900 Randers. *Managing Director: Peter Astrup.*
Buks Booking Int, Gunløgsgade 15, DK-2300 Copenhagen. *Director: Thomas H Hansen.*
DKB Concertpromotion Aps, Vester Soegade 44, DK-1601 Copenhagen V. *Managing Director: Steen Mariboe.*
ET Promotion, Skindergade 8, DK-1159 Copenhagen K. *Managing Director: Ole Dreyer.*
ICO, Rosenborggade 1, DK-1130 Copenhagen K. *Managing Director: Arne Worsoe.*
Infrarouge, Vesterbrogade 20 A 1, DK-1620 Copenhagen V. *Managing Director: Thomas Seifert.*
Musicline, Livjægergade, DK-2100 Copenhagen O. *Contact: Niels Christensen.*
PDH Dansk Musik Formidling, Ny Vestergade 7, Copenhagen DK-1471. *Personal Manager: Ole Dreyer.*
Rock On International, Raadhusstraede 4A, DK-1466 Copenhagen K. *Managing Director: John Rosing.*
Soren Hojberg Booking, Frodesgade 74, DK-6700 Esbjerg. *Managing Director: Soren Hojberg.*
TG Management, Badehusvej 1, 9000 Aalborg. *Manager: John Aagaard*

ECUADOR

William's Convention Center, Los Rios, 920 Y Hurtado, 11692 Guayquil. *General Manager: William San Andrés.*

ESTONIA

Estonian Country Club, Kiriku 1, EE-0103 Tallinn. *Managing Director: Ike Volkov.*
Estonian Jazz Fondation, PO Box 3641, EE-0090 Tallinn. *Director: Tiit Lauk.*
Juri Makarov, Regati Pst 1-6k, EE-0019 Tallinn. *Manager: Martti Kitsing; Managing Director: Juri Makarov.*
Raivo Pihlak, EE-2061 Purtse. *Owner: RaivoPihlak.*
Tallinn Rock Club, Sopruse Pst 219-68, EE-0034 *Tallinn. Managing Director: Anatoly Belov.*
Tartu Jazzclub, Laulupeo 25, EE-2400 Tartu. *Manager: Aadu Birnbaum.*

FIJI

Communications Fiji Ltd, 23 Stewart Street, Suva. *Managing Director: William Parkinson.*

FINLAND

NEM Booking, PO Box 220, Tampere. *Managing Director: Harri Karvinen.*
Piikikasvi Agency, PO Box 145, 00531 Helsinki. *Managing Director: Kari Pössi.*
Rockadillo, PO Box 35, 3301 Tampere. *Managing Director: Tapio Korjus.*
Rocktops, Torkkelinkatu 4, 00500 Helsinki. *Director: Maria Tarnanen.*
Welldone, Linnankatu 11, 00160 Helsinki. *Managing Director: Risto Juvonen.*

FRANCE

Agence Kathoche, 16 Rue de Marignan, F-75008 Paris. *Agent Director: Catherine Poensin.*
Alias, 17 Ave Trudaine, F-75009 Paris. *Chairman: Dominique Revert.*
Aquitania Editions - Stars, Domaine de Barry, F-33690 Sigalens. *Director: Pryl on Lataste.*
Atefact, 13 Rue du Howald, F-67000 Strasbourg. *Director: Patrick Schneider.*
Blue Line Productions, 5 Rue Leon, Giraud, F-75019 Paris. *Director: Michel Vautrot.*
Caramba! Productions, 7 Place de Seoul, F-75014 Paris. *Director: Luc Gaurichon.*
Do Si La Ba, 159 Chemin Lanusse, F-31200 Toulouse. *Manager: Lawrence Larrouy.*
Diogene Productions, Le Grand Kerven, F-29200 Brest. *Director: Jacques Abalain.*
Encore Productions, 8 Rue de Mont-Thabor, F-75001 Paris. *Director: Pascal Bernardin.*
Festirock Organisation, Parl Tertiaire Dijon Est, 2 bis Rue du Cap Vert, F-21800 Quetigny. *President: G Gras.*
Fiesta Latina Homero Cardoso, 51 Rue Mirabeau, F-94200 Ivry Sur Seine. *Promoter: Homero Cardoso.*
Francophonie Diffusion, 33 Rue du Faubourg, Saint-Antoine, F-75011 Paris. *Director: Marie Christine Bloch.*
Leon, 23 Rue des Manguiers, F-34070 Montpellier. *Managers: Philippe Maurizi and Sean Herve Michel.*
LPI/Isotope Agency, 23 Rue Gravette, F-31300 Toulouse. *Manager: Jean Philippe Morer.*
Noumatrouff/Fédération Hiéro, 57 Rue de la Mertzav, F-68100 Mulhouse. *Director: Lodet-Boisse Simon.*
Meyer Productions, 10 Rue De L'Isly, F-75008 Paris. *Managers: Olivier and Christian Meyer.*
Ripost - Le Bocal Association Ripost, 23 Route de Villeflanzy, F-41000 Villebarou-Blois. *President: Denis Tradeau.*
Salam Aleikum Amusements, 2 rue Carpeaux, F-75018 Paris. *Director: Stephane Benhamou.*
L'Usine, 115 Rue Lesage, F-51100 Reims. *President: Alain Boucheron.*
VMA, 40 Rue François 1er, F-75008 Paris. *Director: Rose Leandri.*

GERMANY

Art Concerts GmbH, Widenmayer Str 41, D-80538 Munich. *Director: Franz Abraham.*
ASS Concert & Promotion GmbH, Postfach 730225, D-22122 Hamburg. *Presidents: Michael Bisping and Diekr Schubert.*
Bizarre Productions GmbH, Buelaustr 8, D-20099 Hamburg. *Managing Director: Christopher Brosch.*
Blue Star Promotion Konzertagentur GmbH, Goebenstr 3, 28209 Bremen. *Public Relations: Michael K Grusche.*
Castor Promotions, Dragonerstr 21, 30163 Hannover. *Contact: Elke Fleing.*
Freestyle eV, Morgensternsweg 7, 22305 Hamburg. *Head of Managing Board: Helmut Heuer.*
Freibank, Ditmar Koel Str 26, D-20459 Hamburg. *Directors: Mark Chung and Klaus Maeck.*
Harde & Partner, Unter de Linde 20, D-80939 Munich. *Owner: Jasmine Harde.*

Harry Fox, Steinstr 53, D-81667 Munich. *Contact: Harry Fox.*
Heartpunch Music Publishing & Promotion, Vohwinkeler Str 154, D-42329 Wuppertal. *Managing Director: Michael Schuster.*
Hello Concerts GmbH, Schlassgrabenstr 2½, D-86150 Augsburg. *Contacts: Walter Czermak and Lothar Schlessmann.*
Karsten Jahnke Konzertfdirektion GmbH, Hallerstraße 72, D-20146 Hamburg. *Manager and Owner: Karsten Jahnke.*
Kick Musikverlag, Burgunder Str 8, D-50677 Cologne. *Managing Director: Goetz Elbertzhagen; International Manager: Lynda Hill.*
Kultur in Der Landschaft, Brückstraße 16, D-76703 Kraichtal. *Contact: Bruno Wallisch.*
Künstlersekretariat Ott, Moltkestraße 18, D-79098 Freiburg. *Contact: Dieter Ott.*
MAD Fuesgen/Nickel GBR, Hagelberger Str 48, D-10965 Berlin. *Owner: Ute Fuesgen.*
Mama Comerts & Rav, Koncert Abentur GmbH, Promenaoeplatz 11, D-80333 Munich. *Managing Director: Klaus Bönisch.*
Meduse Live Events, Karlsruher Ring 1A, D-76297 Stutensee. *Contact: Reinhard Neroth.*
Moskito Promotion, PO Box 3072, D-48016 Münster. *Managing Director: Osuald Münnig.*
Music Box GmbH, Rahlstedter Str 65, D-22149 Hamburg. *Managing Director: Hubertus Branzko.*
Musik Komh GmbH, Rottscheidter Str 6, D-42329 Wuppertal. *Head of PR Department: Andrea Zech.*
PMI Paradise Management International, PO Box 2180, D-63243 Neu-Isenburg. *Managing Director: Ralf Klug.*
Synthetic Product Records, PO Box 690441, D-30613 Hannover. *Contact: Lorenz Macke.*
Thopo Music Management, Postfach 1, D-96136 Burgebrach. *Contact: Joseph Thomann.*

GREECE

Ankh Productions, 2 Kritis Street, 15562 Athens. *Managing D irector: Athanassios Fourgiotis.*
Anosi, 20 Zan Moreas Street, 15232 Halandri Athens. *Managing Director: Nick Hassid.*
Di Di Music / Big Star Promotion Ltd, PO Box 31327, 10035 Athens. *Managing Directors: Nana Trandou and Nick Loridas.*
Half Note Productions, Solomon 4, Aghia Paraskevi, Athens 153 A1. *Promotions & Publicity Manager: Mary Telemachou.*
Rock Management, PO Box 21526, 552 36 Panorawa, Thessalonifi. *Managing Director: Christes Tfrzides.*
Show Productions, 318 Sygrou Av, 17673 Kalithea, Athens. *Public Relations: Anta Arvanti.*
Sound & Vision Music, Militiadou Str 9, 10560 Athens. *Managing Director: Dozi Panagiotopoulou.*

HONG KONG

Arena Group Ltd, 602 California Tower, 30-32 D'Aguilar Street, Central Hong Kong. *Contact: Allen Japp.*
International Management Group, 12/F Sunning Plaza, 10 Hysan Avenue, Causeway Bay. *Director: Mark Cowley.*
Sea Music, 703 Manson House, 74-78 Nathan Road, Kowloon. *Managing Director: Richard Cooper.*

HUNGARY

Krokodil Kft, Parisi u 6B, 1052 Budapest. *Managing Director: Laszlo Besnyö.*
Multimedia Ltd, Steindl Imre 4 12, 1054 Budapest. *Managing Director: Laszlo Hegedus.*
OB Art Management/Alt Product, PO Box 76, 5002 Szolnok. *Managing Director: Bela Pap.*
PG Productions, PO Box 8, 5002 Szolnok. *Managing Director: Peter Pap.*
Purple Concerts, Menyelske u.11 F/1, 1112 Budapest. *Managing Director: Marton Brady.*
Sziget Kulturális Szervezö Iroda, Lónyay U 18/B, 1093 Budapest. *Foreign Affairs Manager: Matthew Braghini.*

ICELAND

Bo Haldorson Productions Inc, Box 5445, 125 Reykjavík. *Director: Bo Haldorson.*
Smekkleysa / Bad Taste, PO Box 710, 121 Reykjavik. *Managing Director: Jonsson Asmundur.*
Spor HF, Nýbýlavegur 4, PO Box 320, 202 Kópavogur. *Managing Director: Steinar Berg Isleifsson.*

INDONESIA

Art Circle Network, Jl. Cut Meutia 5, Jakarta-Pusat. *Marketing Director: Gumilang Ramadhan.*
JEF Production, Jl. Setiabudi Tengah 29, Jakarta-Pusat. *Contact: Sofyan Ali.*
Ono Artists Promotion, Jalan Tebet Barat 1, No.23, Jakarta 12810. *Director: Rinny Noor.*

IRELAND

Ackland Productions, 35 Rehoboth Place, Dublin 8. *Director: Jody Ackland.*
AX-S Records, 26 Mount Eagle View, Leopardstown Heights, Dublin 18. *Managing Director: Peter Jones.*
Kieran Cavanagh Promotions, 56 Fitzwilliam Square, Dublin 2. *Managing Director: Kieran Cavanagh.*
Dabble Dance, The Elms, Richmond Avenue South, Dartry, Dublin 6. *Chief Executive Officer: Peter Blackbyrne.*
Denis Desmond Promotions, Top House, Clontarf Street, Cork 1. *Managing Director: Denis Desmond.*
Pat Egan Sound Ltd, Merchants Court, 24 Merchants Quay, Dublin 8. *Managing Director: Pat Egan.*
Fifty-Seventh Street Ltd, 24 Upper Mount Street, Dublin 2. *Contact: Maurice Cassidy and Elizabeth Reeves.*
Frontline Promotions, Thompson House, MacCurtain Street, Cork City. *PR Officer: Paul McDermott.*
Gutter Brothers Ltd, 1 Lansdowne Park, Ennis Road, Limerick and Unit 52, Tam Business Centre, Dominic Street, Limerick. *Managing Director: Joe Clarke.*
Harmony Promotions Ltd, PO Box 10, Edenderry, Co Offaly. *Managing Director: John H Pickering.*
Joe McFadden Promotions, 19 Stockton Green, Castleknock, Dublin 15. *Managing Director: Joe McFadden.*
Mister T Productions, 137A Parnell Street, Dublin 1. *Director: Tonie Walsh.*
Project Arts Centre, 39 East Essex Street, Dublin 2. *Contacts: Jody Ackland and Ann Marie Walsh.*
RSE Promotions, 11/13 Station Road, Raheny, Dublin 5. *Director: Raymond J Smyth.*

ITALY

Azelea Promotion, Via Gelio Cassi 36/a, 33053 Latisana (UD). *Managing Director: Ivan Tramontin.*
Big Mama, Vicolo S Francesco & Ripa, 18 00153 Rome. *Manager: Marco Tiriemmi.*
Circuito Giovani Artisti Italiani, Via Assarotti 2, 10122 Torino. *Network Secretary: Luigi Ratclif.*
City Medial Two, Via Premvda 30, 42100 Reggio Emilia. *Managing Director: Roberto Meglioli.*
Giancarlo Passarella, Via Salutati 7, 50126 Florence. *Contact: Giancarlo Passarella.*
Lion Snc, Via Goldoni 42/A, 30174 Mestre, Venezia. *General Manager: Liciano Trevisan.*

Made In Italy Productions, Piazale Clodio 8, 00195 Rome. *Managing Director: Gepino Afeltra.*
Rock Alliance Productions, Via Marrone 20, 33170 Pordenone. *Director: Corrado Rizzotto.*
Skip Agency, Via Sivori 16-23, 16136 Genova. *Managing Director: Roberto Saracco.*
Solid Rock, Passarella Giancarlo, Via Salutati 7, 50126 Florence.
Zard Iniziative, Viale Mazzini 6, 00195 Rome. *Chairman: David Zard.*

JAPAN

Global Enterprise Co Ltd, 1-15-3 Dogenzaka, Primera Dogenzaka Ste 816, Shibuya-ku, Tokyo 150. *Contact: Ohno.*
Hayashi International Promotion, Aoyama Nozu Bldg 4F, 3-31-20 Jingumae, Shibuya-ku, Tokyo 150. *Contact: Massy Hayashi.*
Min-On Concert Association, 1-32-13 Kita-Shinjuku, Shinjuku-ku, Tokyo 169. *Contact: Teruo Nakamura.*
Udo Artists Inc., 2 Miyachu Bldg, 3-8-37 Minami-Aoyama, Minato-ku, Tokyo 107. *Contact: Seijiro Udo.*

KOREA

Big CI Event, 901 Dongbuk Bldg, 45-14 Youido-dong, Youngdeungpo-ku, Seoul 150 010. *Contact: Won Bock Choi.*
Cosmos Event Promotion, 401 Seongwon Bldg, 3-1 Pil-dong, 1-ga, Jung-ku, Seoul. *Contact: Sun Chul Kang.*
Seoul Promotions, UN Mansion, Ste 2 B2, 1035 Shinsa-dong, Yongsan-ku, Seoul. *Contact: Tae-Hyun Lee.*

LUXEMBOURG

Folk Clupp Letzerverg A S B L, PO Box 2745, L-1027. *President: Marco Uhres.*
Jazz Club Luxembourg, 72 Rue de Hamm, Luxembourg. *Chairman: Guy Fonck.*
Promotion 4, BP 728, 2017 Luxembourg. *Chairman: Mike Koedinger.*
Real Music, 27 Rue Victor Hugo, 4583 Differdange. *Contact: Andre Depienne.*

MALAYSIA

Asia Entertainment Network, 2768-2769 Jalan Changkat Permata, Taman Permata, Ulu Kelang, Kuala Lumpur 53300. *Executive Chairman: Mike Bernie.*
Music City Entertainment Corp, 20 Jalan 20/101, Taman Desa Aman, Cheras, Kuala Lumpur 56100. *Managing Director: John Chacko.*

NETHERLANDS

ACT, Van Leeuwenhoeksingel 6g, 2611 AE Delft. *Contact: A C Raven.*
Best Music, Crispijnstraat 9, 5171 CH Kaatsheuvel. *Managing Director: Peter van Best.*
Buro Gogo, PO Box 7092, 9701 JB Groningen. *Contact: Igor Mönnink.*
DIBA International Concerts, PO Box 37, Westersingel 46, 8600 AA Sneek. *Managing Director: Bauke Algera.*
Music World Management, PO Box 55 55 9, 1007 NB Amsterdam. *Managing Director: Paul Coops.*
Orange Artist Promotion, Bezuidenhoutseweg 106, 2594 AZ Den Haag. *Managing Director: Dido Smit.*
Paperclip Agency, PO Box 1519, 6501 BM Nymegen. *Proprietor: Rob Berends.*
Varke International Promotions, Looiersgracht 38, 1016 VS Amsterdam. *Manager: Gerrie Bezuijen.*

NEW ZEALAND

Benny Levin Promotions Ltd, PO Box 5564, Auckland. *Contact: Louise Hunter.*
Chamber Music New Zealand, PO Box 6238, Wellington. *General Manager: Elisabeth Airey.*
Music Corporation Ltd, 15 Day Street, Newton, Auckland. *Contact: Brian Richards.*
Pacific Region Entertainment Services, PO Box 25275, Auckland 5. *Contact: Gary Bartlett, Keith Gosling.*
Real Groovy Promotions, 438 Queen Street, Auckland. *Promotions Manager: Paul Rose.*
Shawthing Entertainment NZ Ltd, 18 Steyne Avenue, Plimmerton, Wellington. *Managing Director: Philippa Browne.*
Sons of Thunder, PO Box 509, 4 Dellys Grove, Levin 5500. *Managing Director: Regan Cunliffe.*

NORWAY

Major Artist, Rosenborggaten 19, N-0308 Oslo 8. *Manager: Jan Paulsen.*
Norsk Lyd & Bilde, Ryte 598, N-2760 Brandbu. *Directors: Odd Erik & Eli Kristin Hagen.*
Petter Sandberg A/S, Cort Adelorsgt 2, N-0254 Oslo. *Contact: Jan Sollien.*
WAPL, Gamle Kongev 16, N-0743 Trondheim. *Managing Director: Kenneth Nygard.*

PANAMA

Ache Booking Agency, Calle 2, Casa 213, Zona 5, Nuevo Reparto Panamá, 6373 Panamá. *President: Pablo Yanes.*

PERU

Acordes EIRL, Los Paujiles 285 D, Lima 34. *Proprietor: Julie Freundt López.*
In & Out Artists, Avda. Larco 930, Of. 702 Miraflores, Lima 18. *President: Roberto Beaumont Frañowsky.*
Pro Art SA, Diez Canseco 236, Of. 403, Lima 18. *Director General: Jorge Ferrand Lanciotti.*

PHILIPPINES

GR Creative Management Services, 7 Washington Street, Midland Park Manor II, Greenhills, San Juan, Metro Manilla. *President: Gerlie Rodis.*
Octoarts Entertainments, 108 Panay Avenue, Quezon City, Metro Manila. *Managing Director: Orly Ilacad.*

POLAND

Dzem Agency, PO Box 580, Katowice 2. *Contact: Ena Otolinsua.*
Interart Ltd, Ul Pugeta 6, 51-628 Wroclaw. *Contact: Margaret Szablowska.*
Kantaro - Art Agency, ul Polistancov W Ucp 20, 70-110 Szczecin. *Owner: Witold Tanczyriski.*
Metal Mind Productions Sp Z 00, Szeligiewicza 8/21, 40-044 Katowice. *Managing Director: Tomasz Drivbiriski.*
Tomasz Bielski Agency, ul Krucza 49, 00509 Warsaw. *General Manager: Tomasz Bielski; Managing Director: Krzysztof Wotowiec.*
Warsaw Artists Management Ltd, Kazimierzowska 47/5, 02-572 Warsaw. *President: Andrzej Haluch.*
ZPR Inc, Senatorska 13/15, 00-075 Warsaw. *President/Chief Executive Officer: Zbigniew Benbenek; Manager Artists & Marketing Department: Anna Karolicka.*

PORTUGAL

Concertos de Portugal, Lote 23, Sub Cave Esq, Quinta de so Miguel das Encostas, 2775 Carcavelos/Parede. *Contact: Afonso Gomes.*
MTM, Apartado 30072, 1321 Lisboa Codex. *Managing Director: Hugo Moutinho.*
Regiespectáculo, Alto do Coutão-Armazém, I-2735 Cacém. *Chief Executive: António Guimarãs.*

ROMANIA

AMMA, Scara B, Apart 73, Calea Victorei 48/50 Sector 1, 70102 Bucharest. *Manager: Aurel Mitran.*
Artexim, 155 Calea Victorei, Bl. D1, Scara 8, Et 2, 71102 Bucharest. *General Manager: Mihai Constantinescu.*
Cartianu Ltd, 58 Aviator Traian Vasile Str, Sector 1, 78336 Bucharest. *Chairman: Radu Cartianu.*
Holograf Productions Srl, 26 SF Elefterie Str, Sector 5, Bucharest. *Managing Director: Horia Moculescu.*

RUSSIA

Biz Enterprises, Bolshaya Serpukhovskaya 27, 129 010 Moscow. *Managing Director: Sergey Chistoprudov.*
Fee Lee Promotion, 27 Novozavodskaya Str, 121 309 Moscow. *Managing Director: Igor Tonkikh.*
Rock-Azia, Pupova 96-268, Barnaul, 656 062 Siberia. *Contact: Eugene Kolbashev.*

SINGAPORE

International Management Group, 50 Cuscaden Road, 05-02 HPL House, Singapore 1024. *Contact: Bart Collins.*
Jasper Productions, Unit 157A, 1st Floor, Thomson Road, Singapore 1130. *Contact: Jimmy Loh.*
Top Ten Entertainment, 400 Orchard Road, 05-18A Orchard Towers, Singapore 0923. *Managing Director: Peter Bader.*

SLOVENIA

BUBA, PO Box 38, 40A Moskrićeva, 61000 Ljubljana. *Contact: Irena Povśe and David Krźiśnik.*
FV-Zavod Za Umetniško in Kulturno Produkcijo, Kersnikova 4, 61000 Ljubljana. *Managing Director: Skaberne Mónika.*
Radio Student, Cesta 27, Aprila 31, Blou 8, 61000 Ljubljana. *Music Editor: Igor Basin.*
ŠKUC - AFK, Kersnikova 4, 61000 Ljubljana. *Managing Director: Mitja Prezelj.*

SPAIN

AZ Productions, Riere de Argentona, s/n 08300 Mataro (Barcelona). *International Department: Pere-Lluis Font.*
Colectivo Promocion de Jazz, Navarro Reverter 22, 46004 Valencia. *Contact: Julio Martin.*
Diez Management, Martinez Corrochano 3, 28007 Madrid. *Chairman: Mercedes Martin.*
El Colectivo Karma, PO Box 821, 41080 Seville. *Managers: Andrew Jarman and Mapi Guedes.*
Get In Producciones, Easo 19, 20006 San Sebastian. *Director: Inigo Argomariz.*
GSG - Grup de Serveis Guilleries, Granja Baró, Ctra de la Guixa, km 2, 08500 Vic (Barcelona). *Administration: Jordi Costa; Management: Ignasi Pla; Production: Joan Capdevila.*
Munster Tourin - Espárrago Rock Productions S. L, c/ Reyes Catdlicos 25 Oficina 2 Planta, 18001 Granada. *Promotion Director: Javier Gonzalez.*
Nox Producciones, Gran Via 40, 7-2, 28013 Madrid. *Manager: Gloria Parra.*
Pino Sagliocco Presenta SL, c/ Quintana 2, 7° 9°, 28008 Madrid. *Chairman: Pino Sagliocco.*
Poste Nove, Muntaner 494 5B, 08022 Barcelona. *Contact: Alejandro Navarro.*
RLM Productions, Jose Mara Cavero 9, CH A 28027 Madrid. *Managing Director: Rosa Lagappieve.*
Store Music, Gran Via 28, 3C, 18010 Granada. *Managing Director: Carmen Carnicero.*
UADR Marketing, Residencial Coruna 21, Casa 5, 28230 Las Rozas. *Director: Carlos Lopez.*

SWEDEN

Ema Telstar, PO Box 1018, S-181 21 Lidingö. *Managing Director: Thomas Johansson.*
Energy Rekords AB, Vastergatan 23, S-211 21 Malmo. *Concert: Håkan Ehrnst.*
Fritid & Nöjen, Sandgatan 2, S-223 50 Lund. *President: Julius Malmström.*
Headline Productions, PO Box 5948, Vasatorget 1, S-700 05 Örebro. *Managing Director: Dennis Karlsson.*
Luger Production, Fredriksgatan 35, S-811 33 Sandviken. *Managing Director: Ola Broquist; Agents: Patrick Fredriksson and Morgan Johansson.*
M & A Music Art, Simrishamnsgatan 20A, S-214 23 Malmo. *Managing Director: Andreas Larsson.*
Projektbyrån, Kungsgatan 34, S-972 41 Luleå. *Managing Director: Tomas Lind.*
Release Musik & Media, Box 7144, S-402 33 Gothenburg. *Managing Director: Lotta Jansson.*
RMP Management AB, Box 17180, S-104 62 Stockholm. *Managing Director: Stefan Liga.*
Siljemark Production, Gärdsvagen 2, S-171 52 Solna. *Manager: Jonas Siljemark.*
Storsjöyran, Storgatan 28, S-831 30 Ostersund. *Managing Director: Stefan Kauppi.*
United Stage Production AB, PO Box 9174, S-200 39 Malmo. *Managing Director: Anders Larsson.*

SWITZERLAND

Artways Productions, Rue des deux Gares GB, PO Box 30, CH-1800 Vevey. *Manager: Fabrice La Luc.*
B A Rock Enterprise, Waldheimstr 17, CH-3604 Thun. *Contact: Beat Aegler.*

Jazz Willisau, PO Box CH-6130 Willisau. *Director: Niklaus Troxler.*
Joker System Agency, PO Box 325, 1000 Lausanne 17. *Managing Director: Marc Lambelet.*
L'Agence Marcel Schiess, 12 Rue du Premier Mars, **CH-2300 La-Chaux-de-Fonds.** *Contact: Marcel Schiess.*
Music Service Adi Weiss AG, Gerberngasse 38 + 42, PO Box 57, CH-3000 Bern 13. *Vice President: Roland Röthlisberger.*
Rocking Chair, PO Box 4, CH-1800 Vevey 2. *Contact: Nicola De Pinto.*
SOFA Agency, PO Box 101, CH-1707 Fribourg. *Contact: Pascal Hunkeler & Jacques Schouwey.*
Volume Agency, Quai du Cheval-Blanc 14, CH-1204 Geneva. *Managing Director: Lori Iommi.*
VIP AG Productions, Schutzengasse 30, CH-8001 Zurich. *Managing Director: Urs Peter Keller.*

THAILAND

Music Train, 186 Soi Samarnmitr, Ramkhamhaeng Road, Prakanong, Bangkok 10250. *Managing Director: Mr Raya.*
Nititad Entertainment, 1/79-80 Moo-Baan, Shinnaket Soi 10, Ngamwongwarn Road, Bangken, Bangkok 10210. *Managing Director: Vichian Usvisessivakul.*
Soco Entertainment, 21/9 Saladaeng 1 Silom, Bangkok 10500. *Chairman: Sam Armenio.*

TURKEY

Imaj Entertainment, Haci Adil Sokak -4 Aralik No 2, 80630 Levent, Istanbul. *Director: Hale Diceli Yamanoglu.*
Major Musical Productions, Ihlamurdere Cad Misirli Sk, Arda Apt, 80690 Besiktas, Istanbul. *Managing Director: Eyup Iblag.*
Most Production, Yildizcicegi Sok 7, Etiler,Istanbul. *Chairman: Mustafa Oguz.*
Pozitif, Istiklal Caddesi 1, Baro Han 611-612, 80080 Beyoglu, Istanbul. *President: Cem Yegul.*

UNITED KINGDOM

Acker's International Jazz Agency, 53 Cambridge Mansions, Cambridge Road, London SW11 4RX. *Owner: Pamela Frances Sutton.*
Adastra, 2 Star Row, North Dalton, Driffield, East Yorkshire YO25 9UR. *Owner: Chris Wade.*
Aiken Promotions Limited, Marlborough House, 348 Lisburn Road, Belfast BT9 6GH, Northern Ireland. *Contact: Peter Aiken.*
Alan James Public Relations, 253 Camberwell New Road, London SE5 0TH. *Managing Director: Alan James.*
Andrew Storr Entertainments, 2 Burn Grange Cottage, Doncaster Road, Burn Nr Selby, North Yorkshire YO8 8LA. *Partner: Phil Storr.*
Asgard Promotions Ltd, 125 Parkway, London NW1 7PS. *Joint Managing Directors: Paul Fenn & Paul Charles.*
Autonomous Talent Booking, Unit 301 Alpha Business Centre, 60 South Grove, London E17 7NX. *Contact: Mike Hinc.*
Barry Collings Entertainments, 21a Clifftown Road, Southend-on-Sea, Essex SS1 1AB. *Managing Director: Barry Collings.*
BDA Ltd, Bryson House, Chiltern Road, Culcheth, Warrington WA3 4LL. *Managing Director: Brian Durkin.*
Bernard Lee Management, Moorcroft Lodge, Farleigh Common, Warlingham, Surrey CR6 9PT. *Managing Director: Bernard Lee.*
Black Magic Management Ltd, 296 Earls Court Road, London SW5 9BA. *Managing Director: Mataya Clifford.*
Blitz, Edgwarebury Farm, Edgwarebury Lane, Edgware, Middlesex HA8 8QX. *Partners: Sue Harris and Claire Powell.*
BPR, 36 Como Street, Romford, Essex RM7 7DR. *Manager: Brian Theobald.*
Brian Rix & Associates, PO Box 100, Ashford, Kent TN24 8AR. *Operations Manager: Simon Grant.*
Brian Yeates Associates, Home Farm House, Canwell, Sutton Coldfield, West Midlands B75 5SH. *Contact: Brian and Ashley Yeates.*
Burniston Cooke Productions, 69 MacFarlane Road, London W12 7JY. *Contact: Simon Cooke.*
Buzz Records, 192 Glasgow Road, Perth PH2 0NA, Scotland. *Managing Director: Dave Arcari.*
Cadillac Promotions, Cadillac Ranch, Pencraig Uchaf, Cwm Bach, Whitland, Dyfed SA34 0DT. *Manager: M Magoon.*
Caramba, 88 Radstock Road, Reading, Berks RG1 3PR. *Events Manager: Tim Carroll.*
Concorde International Artistes, Concorde House, 101 Shpeherds Bush Road, London W6 7CP. *Managing Director: Louis Parker.*
Creeme Entertainments, East Lynne, Harper Green Road, Doe Hey, Farnworth, Bolton BL4 7HT. *Partners: Tom, Lynne and Anthony Ivers.*
Cromwell Management, 4/5 High Street, Huntingdon, Cambs PE18 6TE. *Managing Partner: Vic Gibbons.*
Dark Blues Management Ltd, 30 Stamford Brook Road, London W6 0XH. *Director of Business Development: Kate Martin.*
Dax Entertainments, 48 Fernside Road, Poole, Dorset BH15 2JJ. *Managing Director: Dave Dacosta.*
Derek Block Promotions, Douglas House, 3 Richmond Buildings, London W1V 5AE. *Managing Director: Derek Block.*
Deri Promotions, 8 Wick Lane, Felpham, Bognor Regis, West Sussex PO22 8QG. *Proprietor: R W Cooper.*
Devenish Entertainments Ltd, 8 Forthill Road, Enniskillen, Co Fermanagh BT74 6AW, Northern Ireland. *Contact: Sean McGrade.*
D F Concerts Ltd, North Lodge, Auchineden by Blanefield, Glasgow G63 9AX, Scotland. *Managing Director: Stuart Clumpas.*
DT Enterprises, Midnight Rock, 83 Blackburn Road, Greenhill, Herne Bay, Kent CT6 7UT. *Contact: Dave Taylor.*
Elsham Hall Country Park, Nr Brigg, North Lincolnshire DN20 0QZ. *Contact: Robert Elwes.*
Entertainment Agency Group, 7 Northumberland Street, Huddersfield HD1 1RL. *Entertainment Executive: Lenny Phillip.*
Europa Jazz Live, 6 Belgrove, Tunbridge Wells, Kent TN1 1YN. *Director: David E Jacobs.*
Event Production Management, Laurels Farm, Worstead, Norfolk NR28 9RW. *Contact: Richard Abel.*
Forward Agency Booking, 132 Liverpool Road, London N1 1LA. *Managing Director: Rob Challice.*
Fadermusic, Perth Road, Wood Green, London N22 5QP. *General Manager: Bengi F-B.*
Fair Oaks Entertainment, PO Box 19, Ulverston, Cumbria CA12 9TF. *Proprietor/Manager: J G Livingstone.*
Fanfare 3000, The Folly, Pinner Hill Road, Pinner, Middlesex HA5 3YQ. *Partners: Peter Richardson and Paul Baxter.*
Fish Krish, 6 Carlton House, 319 West End Lane, London NW6 1RN. *Contact: Fish Krish.*
Fiveash & Hill Publicity and Promotions, 106 Great Portland Street, London W1N 5PE. *Partner: Graeme Hill.*
Focus Marketing Communications, HMA House, 78 Durham Road, Wimbledon, London SW20 0TL. *Managing Director: Brian Oliver.*
Fool's Paradise Records, PO Box 6003, London W2 2WE. *Contact: Robin T Chuter.*
Gordon Poole Agency Ltd, The Limes, Brockley, Bristol BS19 3BB. *Managing Director: Gordon Poole.*
Greig Clifford Promotions, 23 Harsfold Road, Rustington, West Sussex BN16 2QE. *Proprietor: Grieg Clifford.*
Grosvenor Productions Ltd, The Limes, Brockley, Bristol BS19 3BB. *Contact: Gordon Poole.*
Hal Carter Organization, 101 Hazelwood Lane, Palmers Green, London N13 5HQ. *Managing Director: Hal Carter.*
Harmony Promotions Ltd, PO Box 10, Edenderry, Co Offaly, Ireland. *Managing Director: John H Pickering.*
Harvey Goldsmith Entertainments, The Glassworks, 3-4 Ashland Place, London W1M 3JH. *Managing Director: Harvey Goldsmith.*
Holland-Ford's, 103 Lydyett Lane, Barnton, Northwich, Cheshire CW8 4JT. *Proprietor: Bob Holland-Ford.*
Hopscotch Media Management, 46 Broadwick Street, London W1V 1FF. *Director/Partner: Alfie Dosoo.*
Houndog Music Entertainment Agency, 49 Arthurton Road, Spixworth, Norwich NR10 3QU. *Proprietor: Graham John Bailey.*
I A Entertainment, 44 Top Llan, Glan Conwy, Colwyn Bay, Clwyd LL28 5ND, Wales. *Proprietor: Andrew Boggie.*
Icon Agency For Session Musicians. Ducie House, Ducie Street, Piccadilly, Manchester M1 2JW. *Partner: Jess Tyrrell.*
IMC / Fair Warning, The Plaza, 535 Kings Road, London SW10 0SZ. *Managing Director: John Jackson.*
International Talent Booking (ITB), 27A Floral Street, Covent Garden, London WC2 ED9Q. *Managing Director: Barry Dickens.*
Jane Lindsey PR, Owens House, 281-283 Goswell Road, London EC1V 7NT. *Managing Director: Jane Lindsey.*
Jean Mills Entertainments, Cox Park Cottage, Cox Park, Gunnislake, Cornwall PL18 9BB. *Proprietor: Jean Mills.*
Jef Hanlon Management, 1 York Street, London W1P 1PZ. *Managing Director: Jef Hanlon.*

John Ford Productions, Bradford Court, Bradford Street, Digbeth, Birmingham B12 0NS. *Owner: John Ford.*
John Martin Promotions Ltd, 29 Hartfield Road, London SW19 3SG. *Managing Director: John Martin.*
Kasevin Rodell, 6 Bowling Green Road, Cranfield, Bedfordshire MK43 0ET. *Partner: Diana Rodell.*
Latin Touch Entertainments, Fatima Community Centre Commonwealth Avenue, London W12 7QR. *Managing Director: Orlando Rincon P.*
The Life Organisation, 62 Argyle Street, Birkenhead, Merseyside L41 6AF. *Director: J O'Connor.*
Matters Musical Limited, The Loft, Rear of 8 West Street, Dorking, Surrey RH4 1BL. *Director: Victoria Burns.*
Max Clifford Associates Limited, Top Floor, 109 New Bond Street, London W1Y 9AA. *Managing Director: Max Clifford.*
MCP Promotions Ltd, 16 Birmingham Road, Walsall, West Midlands WS1 2NA. *Directors: Maurice Jones, Tim Parsons and Stuart Galbraith.*
Mean Fiddler, 24-28A HighStreet, Harlseden, London NW10 4LX. *Managing Director: Vince Power.*
Mel Bush Enterprises, 20/22 Wellington Road, Bournemouth BH8 8JN. *Managing Director: Mel Bush.*
Mercenary Music Services, 143 Turks Road, Radcliffe, Manchester M26 3WW. *Production Manager: Paul Naylor.*
Midland Entertainment & Management Agency, PO Box 259, Coventry CV5 8YU. *Proprietor: Chrissy Price.*
Miracle Prestige International Ltd, Bugle House, 21A Noel Street, London W1V 3PD. *Managing Director: Steve Parker.*
Mission Control Agency, 63 Lant Street, London SE1 1QN. *Director: Guy Anderson.*
Money Talks Agency, Cadillac Ranch, Pencraig Uchaf, Cwm Bach, Whitland, Dyfed SA34 0DT, Wales. *Manager: M Magoon.*
Mrs Casey Music, PO Box 296, Aylesbury, Bucks HP19 3TL. *Director: Steve Heap.*
Norman Jackson Entertainment Agency Ltd, 35 Seafield Road, Arnos Grove, London N11 1BR. *Director: Ray Gould.*
NVB Entertainments, 80 Holywell Road, Studham, Dunstable, Beds LU6 2PD. *Contact: Henri Harrison and Yvonne Farrell.*
Park Records, PO Box 651, Oxford OX2 9RB. *Managing Director: John Dagnell.*
Paul Barrett Rock'n'Roll Enterprises, 16 Grove Place, Penarth, South Glamorgan CF64 2ND, Wales. *Director: Paul Barrett.*
Paul Dainty Corporation (UK) Ltd, 4 Yeomans Row, Knightsbridge, London SW3 2AH. *Vice President: Peter Lyster-Todd.*
Pendle Borough Council, Bank House, 61 Albert Road, Colne, Lancashire BB8 0PB. *Arts and Entertainment Manager: Gary Hood.*
Phil McIntyre Promotions, 15 Riversway Business Village, Navigation Way, Preston PR2 2YP. *Managing Director: Phil McIntyre.*
Pollytone Weekenders, PO Box 124, Ruislip, Middlesex HA4 9BQ. *Director: Valerie Bird.*
Pomona, 14 Oxford Place, Rochdale OL16 5LU. *Managing Director: Mark Jones.*
Primary Talent International Limited, Africa House, 64/78 Kingsway, London WC2B 6PR. *Contact: Peter Maloney.*
Prime Time, 28 Yonge Park, London N4 3NT. *Director: Maggie O'Connor.*
Profile Artists Agency, 141 Railton Road, London SE24 0LT. *Agent: Serena Parsons.*
Prostar, 106 Hillcrest Avenue, Toftwood, Dereham, Norfolk NR19 1TD. *Proprietor: Malcolm Cook.*
Public Eye Communications, Greyhound House, 16 Greyhound Road, London W6 8NX. *New Business Director: Elaine Robertson.*
Publicity Connection, Flat 3, Haversham Lodge, Melrose Avenue, Willesden Green, London NW2 4JS. *Managing Director: Sharon Chevin.*
Purple Palace, 34A Flower Lane, Mill Hill, London NW7 2JE. *Contact: Stephanie Kays.*
Pyramid Productions, Cadillac Ranch, Pencraig Uchaf, Cwm Bach, Whitland, Dyfed SA34 0DT. *Director: S M Stein.*
Raymond Gubbay Limited, 176a High Street, Barnet, Herts EN5 5SZ. *Managing Director: Raymond Gubbay.*
Real Time, 16/18 Ramillies Street, London W1V 1DL. *P R Manager: Charlie Inskip.*
Rock Hard PR, 19d Pinfold Road, London SW16 2SL. *Owner: Roland Hyams.*
Rush Release Ltd, 74 The Archway, Station Approach, Ranelagh Gardens, London SW6 3UH. *General Manager: Jo Underwood.*
Serious Speakout, 42 Old Compton Street, London W1V 5PB. *Partners: John Cumming, John Ellson, David Jones.*
Seriously Groovy Music Ltd, 3rd Floor, 28 D'Arblay Street, Soho, London W1V 3FH. *Director: Dave Holmes.*
Sharp End Promotions Ltd, Grafton House, 2-3 Golden Square, London W1R 3AD. *Director: Robert Lemon.*
Solo-ITG, 55 Fulham High Street, London SW6 3JJ. *Managing Director: John Giddings.*
Sound & Light Productions, Kerrison Hall, 28 Kerrison Road, London W5 5NW. *Director: Jan Goodwin.*
Splash Management & Promotions, 328 Gray's Inn Road, King's Cross, London WC1X 8BZ. *Managing Director: Nick Moore.*
Square Deal Promotions, 56 Kilmuir Road, Inverness IV3 6EP, Scotland. *Contact: Ann Carmody.*
Steve Allen Entertainments, 60 Broadway, Peterborough, Cambs PE1 1SU. *Proprietor: Steve Allen.*
Stone Immaculate P R, Studio 2, 8 Nursery Road, London SW9 8BP. *Contact: Chris Stone.*
Stoneyport Agency, 39 Shandon Crescent, Edinburgh EH11 1QF, Scotland. *Contact: John Barrow.*
Swamp Agency, PO Box 94, Derby DE22 1XA. *Contact: Chris Hall.*
Sylvantone Promotions, 17 Allerton Grange Way, Leeds LS17 6LP. *Proprietor: Tony Goodacre.*
Talent Factory, Regent House, 4th Floor, 89 Kingsway, London WC2B 6RH. *Managing Director: Colin Davie.*
Talk Loud P R, 90-92 Great Portland Street, London W1N 5PB.
Taurus Records, 23 Blackheath Rise, Lewisham, London SE13 7PN. *Contact: Beverley Miller.*
TKO Promotions Ltd, PO Box 130, Hove, East Sussex BN3 6QU. *Creative Director: Howard Kruger.*
Tony Denton Promotions, 19 South Molton Lane, Mayfair, London W1Y 1AQ. *Contact: Simon Nicholls.*
Upbeat Management, Sutton Business Centre, Rastmor Way, Wallington, Surrey SM6 7AH. *Contact: Beryl Korman.*
Vinyl Japan (UK) Ltd, 281 Camden High Street, London NW1 7BX. *Manager: Patrick James.*
WOMAD, The Malt House, Mill Lane, Box, Wiltshire SN14 9PN. *Managing Director: Thomas Brooman.*
Work Hard P R, 19d Pinfold Road, London SW16 2SL. *Owner: Roland Hyams.*
Zap Club, Zap Office, 7A Middle Street, Brighton BN1 1AL. *Director: Pat Butler.*

USA

Aarrow Artist/Writer Development, 900 19th Avenue South Suite 207, Nashville, TN 37212. *Owner: Kelli Steele; A&R Director: Ruth Steele.*
Abby Hoffer Enterprises, 223 1/2 E 48th Street, New York, NY 10017-1538. *President: Abby Hoffer.*
Al Embry International, PO Box 23162, Nashville, TN 37202. *Owner/President: Al Embry.*
Ambassador Artist Agency, PO Box 50358, Nashville, TN 37205. *President: Wes Yoder.*
Ambassadors Of Praise, PO Box 369, Pearland, TX 77588-0369. *President: Patricia Nedbalek.*
American Bands Management, PO Box 840607, Houston, TX 77284-0607. *President: John Blomstron Sr.*
American Famous Talent, 816 W Evergreen, Chicago, IL 60622. *President: Ric Bricamontes.*
A&R European/US Radio Record Promotions, 900 19th Avenue So Suite 207, Nashville, TN 37212. *Owners: Ruth Steele and David Steele.*
AristoMedia, 1620 16th Avenue S, Nashville, TN 37212. *President/Owner: Jeff Walker.*
Artist Representation & Management, 1257 Arcade Street, St Paul, MN 55106. *Office Manager/Agent: Roger Anderson.*
Axbar Records, PO Box 12353, San Antonio, TX 78212. *Producer/General Manager: Joe Scates.*
Barry Agency, Box 1414, Maple Grove, MN 55311. *President: Lisa A Barry.*
Bay Concerts, 1906 Seward Drive, Pittsburg, CA 94565. *Chief Executive Officer/President: Charles Coke; Vice President: Terry Pitts.*
Bennett Morgan & Associates Ltd, 1282 Route 376, Wappingers Falls, NY 12590. *President: Bennett Morgan.*
Berkeley Agency, 2608 Ninth Street, Berkeley, CA 94710. *Agent: Jim Cassell.*
Bill Hollingshead Productions Inc, 1720 N Ross Street, Santa Ana, CA 92706. *President: Bill Hollingshead.*
Blowin' Smoke, 7438 Shoshone Avenue, Van Nuys, CA 91406-2340. *President: Larry Weisberg.*
Bobby Roberts Co. Inc, PO Box 3007, Hendersonville, TN 37077. *CEO: Bobby Roberts.*
Brad Simon Organization, 122 E 57th Street, New York, NY 10022. *President: Brad Simon.*
Brentwood Music Publishing Inc, One Maryland Farms, Brentwood, TN 37027. *Vice President of Publishing: Dale Mathews.*

AGENTS AND PROMOTERS

Brothers Management Associates, 141 Dunbar Avenue, Fords, NJ 08863.
Buddy Lee Attractions, 38 Music Square East, Suite 300, Nashville, TN 37203. *President: Tony Conway.*
Cardenas Fernandez & Associates, 1254 N Wells St, Chicago, IL 60610. *President: Henry Cardenas.*
Cerebral Records, 1236 Laguna Drive, Carlsbad, CA 92008. *President: Lincoln Kroll; Publisist: Carol Leno.*
Competitive Edge Public Relations, 9 Music Sq S #240, Nashville, TN 37203. *Contact: Debbie McClure.*
Concerted Efforts Inc., PO Box 99, Newtonville, MA 02160. *Director: Paul Kahn.*
Creative Artists Agency (CAA), 3310 West End Avenue, 5th Floor, Nashville, TN 37203. *Contact: Ron Baird.*
De Leon Artists, 4031 Panama Court, Piedmont, CA 94611. *Agent : Lupe De Leon.*
DMR Booking Agency, Suite 250, The Galleries of Syracuse, Syracuse, NY 13202. *Owner: David Rezak.*
Dynamic Directions Inc, 11410 West Wisconsin Avenue, Wauwatosa, WI 53226. *Vice President: Arthur Grinke.*
Erv Woolsey Co., 1000 18th Avenue South, Nashville, TN 37212. *CEO: Erv Woolsey.*
Events International Inc, PO Box 1560, Honolulu, HI 96806. *President: David Booth.*
Famous Artist Agency, 1700 Broadway, New York, NY 10019. *President: Jerry Ade.*
Fate's House of Music, 1030 Villa Place, Nashville, TN 37212. *President: Fate Vanderpool.*
Five Roses Music Group, 34A Lanier Road, Studio I, Jekyll Island, GA 31527. *President: Sammie Lee Marler.*
Folklore Inc., 1671 Appian Way, Santa Monica, CA 90401. *Contact: Mitch Greenhill.*
Geoffrey Blumenauer Artists (GBA), 11846 Balboa Avenue, Suite 204, Granada Hills, CA 91344. *Manager: Geoffrey Blumenauer.*
General Broadcasting Service, 203 Gates Drive, Hendersonville, TN 37075-4961. *Owner: Ernie Bivens.*
Grelo Holdings Inc, Market Street Square, 33 Wilkes Barre Boulevard, Wilkes Barre, PA 18701. *President/Chief Executive Officer: Thom Grelo.*
Heartfelt Concerts, PO Box 294, Westerville, OH 43086-0294. *President/Owner: Randy Kettering.*
International Creative Management (ICM), 40 W 57th Street, New York, NY 10019. *Contact: Music Dept.*
International Creative Management (ICM), 8943 Wilshire Blvd, Beverly Hills, CA 90211. *Contact: Music Dept.*
Jackie Paul Entertainment Group Inc, 559 Wanamaker Road, Jenkintown, PA 19046. *Chief Executive Officer: Jackie Paul.*
Keith Case & Associates, 59 Music Square West, Nashville, TN 37203. *Owner: Keith Case.*
Landmark Communications Group, PO Box 1444, Hendersonville, TN 37077. *President: Bill Anderson Jnr.*
Laura Grüb Enterprises, 235-4 Lucas Lane, Voorhees, NJ 08043. *President: Laura Grüb-Geschwindt.*
Living Rock Ministries, 1225 Atlantic Avenue, Suite 3, Rochester, NY 14609. *Program and Music Director: Pastor Samme Palermo.*
Loud Cry Productions, PO Box 210270, Nashville, TN 37221-0270. *Owner/President: Don Sanders.*
Marco Music Group, 1620 16th Avenue S, Nashville, TN 37212. *President/Owner: Jeff Walker.*
Mark Alan Agency, PO Box 21323, St Paul, MN 55121. *President: Mark Alan.*
Mazur Publications, PO Box 360, East Windsor, NJ 08520. *Publicist: Michael Mazur.*
Mia Mind Music, 500½ East 84th Street, Suite #4B, New York, NY 10028-7368. *Chief Executive Officer: Steven Bentzel.*
Mirkin Management, 906½ Congress Avenue, Austin, TX 78701. *Owner: Jan Mirkin.*
Music & Entertainment Division, 2200 Wilson Blvd, Suite 200, Arlington, VA 22201. *President, Music & Entertainment Division: Ed Yoe.*
Music Man Productions, 568 Snelling Avenue, N, Suite 106, St Paul, MN 55104. *Owners: Paul Manske and Steve York.*
Nancy Carlin Associates, 411 Ferry Street, Ste 4, Martinez, CA 94553. *Agent: Nancy Carlin.*
Only New Age Music Inc, 8033 Sunset Blvd, Suite #472, Los Angeles, CA 90046. *President: Suzanne Doucet; Vice President: James Bell.*
Pal Productions Co, PO Box 80691, Baton Rouge, LA 70898. *President/General Manager: Johnny R Palazzotto.*
Plug Productions, 273 Chippewa Drive, Columbia, SC 29210-6508. *Contact: Ron Sparks.*
PPL-MCI Entertainment Group, 10 Universal Plaza, PO Box 8442, Universal City, CA 91618. *Managing Director: Maxx Diamond.*
Precision Management, 825 N King Street, Suite A-1, Hampton, VA 23669-2814. *Operations Manager: Cappriccieo M Scates.*
Premier Productions, 1909 N Spruce, Wichita, KS 67214. *Owner: Anthony Welch.*
Prince/SF Productions, 1135 Francisco Street, Suite 7, San Francisco, CA 94109-1087. *President: Ken Malucelli.*
Punk Metal Rock Records, PO Box 410099, San Francisco, CA 94141-0099. *A&R Head: Stosh Ravine.*
Remington Management Inc, 6602 Harbor Town, Suite 501, Houston, TX 77036. *President: Janice D Hayes.*
Rock Dog Records, PO Box 3687, Hollywood, CA 90028. *Vice President of A&R: Gerry North.*
Ron Rainey & Associates, 315 S Beverly Drive, Suite 206, Beverly Hills, CA 90212. *Manager: Ron Rainey.*
Rosebud Agency, PO Box 170429, San Francisco, CA 94117. *Office Manager: Terri De Salvo.*
Rustron Music Productions, c/o The Whimsy, 1156 Park Lane, West Palm Beach, FL 33417. *Executive Director: Rusty Gordon.*
Silver Star Productions Inc, 1800 Amberwood Drive, Riverview, FL 33569. *President: Margorie Sexton.*
Squad 16, 2632 Boston Road, PO Box 65, Wilbraham, MA 01095. *Contact: Tom Najemy.*
SRO Entertainment Inc, PO Box 10161, Honolulu, HI 96816. *President: Ken Rosene.*
SRO Productions Inc, 821 Marquette Avenue South, Suite 1815, Minneapolis, MN 55402. *President: Lawrence H Berle.*
Stardate Concerts Inc, 10430 Shady Trail, Suite 104, Dallas, TX 75220. *President: Randy Shelton.*
S T A R S Productions, 1 Professional Quadrangle, 2nd Floor Suite, Sparta, NJ 07871. *President: Stephen Tarkanish.*
St John Artists, PO Box 619, Neenah, WI 54957-0619. *Owner: Jon St John.*
Sunset Promotions of Chicago Inc, 9359 S Kedzie Ave, PO Box 42877, Evergreen Park, IL 60805. *President/Chief Executive Officer: Neil J Cacciottolo.*
Surface Entertainment & Management, PO Box 2935, Church St Station, New York, NY 10008. *Contact: Pam Beninon.*
Terrace Entertainment Corp, Box 68, Las Vegas, NM 87701. *President: Robert John Jones.*
Tone Zone Booking Agency, 939 W Wilson Avenue, Chicago, IL 60610. *Booking Manager: Diane Borden.*
Triage International, PO Box 448, New York, NY 10014. *Manager: Bob Weyersberg.*
Triangle Talent Inc, 10424 Watterson Trail, Louisville, KY 40299. *Agent: Gary Deusner.*
Umpire Entertainment Enterprises, 1507 Scenic Drive, Longview, TX 75604. *President: Jerry Haymes.*
Vokes Music, Record & Promotion Co, PO Box 12, New Kensington, PA 15068-0012. *President: Howard Vokes.*
William Morris Agency, 151 El Camino Drive, Beverly Hills, CA 90212. *Contact: Music Dept.*
William Morris Agency, 1350 Avenue of the Americas, New York, NY 10019. *Contact: Music Dept.*
William Morris Agency, 2100 West End Avenue, Nashville, TN 31203. *Vice President: Rick Shipp.*
Work Horse Productions, PO Box 1001, Kapaa, Hauai, HI 96746. *Owner: Michael Gregg.*

APPENDIX D
PUBLISHERS

ARGENTINA

AIM (Arco Iris Musical), Avda. Santa Fe 4910, Piso 4°, Of. B, 1425 Buenos Aires. *Director General: Osvaldo Bermolen.*
Clan Dilo Music, Casilla Correo 123 La Plata, 1900 Buenos Aires. *President: Giorgio di Lorenzo.*
Musidisc Europe Sudamerica SAIC, Güemes 4418, 1° Piso A, 1425 Buenos Aires. *President: Jimmy Olszevicki.*
Peermusic Argentina Ediciones Y Producciones SA, Rivadavia 5012, 6 Piso, 1424 Buenos Aires. *President: Elsa Villar.*

AUSTRALIA

Black Pig Publishing, PO Box 2093, St Kilda West, VIC 3182. *Managing Director: Michael Lynch.*
BMG Music Pty Ltd, 194 Miller Street, N Sydney, NSW 2060. *Managing Director: Jim Shipstone.*
Boosey & Hawkes (Australia) Pty Ltd, Unit 12/6, Campbell Street, Artarmon, NSW 2064. *Managing Director: Richard Mackie.*
Bright Spark Songs Pty Ltd, 20 Leila Street, Prahran, VIC 3181. *Contact: Tony Moran.*
Central Australian Aboriginal Media Associates Music, 101 Todd Street, Alice Springs NT 0870. *Head of Department: Richard Micallef.*
EMI Music Publishing, 1st Floor, 100 Glover Street, Cremorne, NSW 2090. *Managing Director: John Anderson.*
Festival Music Pulbishing Group, 63-79 Miller Street, Pyrmont, NSW 2009. *Managing Director: Bruce Powell.*
Grundy Music Pty Ltd, Locked Bag 526, Frenchs Forest, NSW 2086. *Snr Consultant Business Affairs: J M Fowler.*
Ideal Management P/C, PO Box 1037, Caulfield North, Melbourne, VIC 3161. *Managing Director/Chief Executive Officer: Nathan D Brenner.*
Image Music Group Pty Ltd, 19 Johnston Street, Port Melbourne, VIC 3207. *Managing Director: John McDonald.*
Immedia!, PO Box 2977, Sydney, NSW 2001. *Managing Partner: Phil Tripp.*
J Albert & Son P/L Albert Productions, 9 Rangers Road, Neutral Bay, NSW 2089. *General Manager: Fifa Reccobono.*
Leosong Music Group, 6th Floor, 350 Kent Street, Sydney, NSW 2000. *Contact: Philip Walker, Sue Boylan.*
MCA Music Pty Ltd, 23 Pelican Street, Darlinghurst, NSW 2010. *Managing Director: Peter Hebbes.*
MMA Music, 351 Crown Street, Surry Hills, NSW 2010. *CEO: C.M. Murphy.*
Mushroom Music, 9 Dundas Lane, Albert Park, VIC 3206. *Chairman: Michael Gudinski.*
Polygram Music Publishing (Australia) Pty Ltd, 122 McEvoy Street, Alexandria, NSW 2015. *Managing Director: Roger Grierson.*
Rondor Music, 78 Chandos Street, St Leonards, NSW 2065. *Managing Director: Bob Aird.*
Shock Music Publishing Pty Ltd, 24 High Street, Northcote, VIC 3070. *Publishing Manager: Sally Galwey.*
Sony Music Publishing Australia, 11-19 Hargrave Street, Easy Sydney, NSW 2010. *General Manager: Damian Trotter.*
Warner Chappell Music, 1 Cassins Avenue, North Sydney, NSW 2060. *Managing Director: John Bromell.*
Yothu Yindi Music Pty Ltd, GPO Box 2727, Darwin, NT 0801. *Manager: Alan James.*
Zomba Production Music (Australia) Pty Limited, 25 Burton Street, Glebe, NSW 2037. *Managing Director: Stuart Livingston.*

AUSTRIA

Edition Helbing, Kaplanstr. 9, A-6063 Rum. *Managing Director: Elvira Harm-Dematte.*
Edition Musica Musikverlag, Webgasse 43, PO Box 451, A-1060 Vienna. *Managing Director: Franz Wallner.*
Koch Music Publishing, Gewerbegebeit, Postfach 24, A-6600 Höfen. *Managing Director: Franz Koch.*
Meltemi Music, Hirschstettner Str 26/H 13, A-1220 Vienna. *Managing Director: Horst Bichler.*
Polygram/Antenna Musikverlag Austria, PO Box 85, Edelsinnstr. 4, A-1122 Vienna. *Chairman: Adolf Hoffmann.*
Shamrock, Altwaidhofen 37, A-3830 Waidhofen/Thaya. *Managing Director: Uwe Kranner.*
Spritzendorfer & Rossori GmbH, Hietzinger Hauptstr 94, A-1130 Vienna. *Managing Director: A Spritzendorfer.*
Stein Music Wien, Barnardgasse 39/33, A-1070 Vienna. *Managing Director: Rudi Nemeczek.*
Warner/Chappell Musikverlag GmbH, Diefenbachgasse 35, A-1150 Vienna. *Managing Director: Peter Gruber.*

BELGIUM

ALC Productions, Av Eugène Ysaye 47, B-1070 Brussels. *Label Manager: Alexander Louvet.*
Baltic NV, Rederijkesstraat 82, B-2610 Antwerp/Wilrijk. *Manager: Eric Demarbaix.*
Caracol Music Sprl Group, 5 Rue du Cheneau, B-6120 Ham-Sur-Hevre. *General Manager: Timothy Hagelstein.*
Dexon Sprl, 41 Rue Cite de L'Enfance, B-6001 Marcinelle. *Manager: Delfosse Pierre.*
Editions Confidentielles, 90 Rue de Veeweyde, B-1070 Brussels. *Professional Manager: Piet Bekaert.*
EMI Music Publishing Belgium, Eugene Plaskylaan 140 B, B-1040 Brussels. *Manager: Guy Van Handenhove.*
MMD, Rue Fernand Bernier 38, B-1060 Brussels. *Managing Director: Plastic Bertrand.*
Multi Sound Music Publishing, 24 Gachardstreet, B-1050 Brussels. *General Manager: Pierre Pletinckx.*
Prestation Music, 24 Gachardstreet, B-1050 Brussels. *General Manager: Pierre Pletinckx.*
RVY Music Publishing, Kammerstraat 19, B-9000 Ghent. *Manager: Robert Van Yper.*
T & B Music, Gulden Vlieslaan 67, B-8000 Brugge. *Contact: Nico A Mertens.*
Team For Action, Av Oscar van Goibtsnoven 45, B-1180 Brussels. *Managing Director: Claude Martin.*
Tempo (Top Entertainment Editions), Krijgslaan 61, B-9000 Ghent. *General Manager: Luc Standaert.*
Witlof Music, Leernsestwg 168, B-9800 Deinze. *Director: Jean Tant.*

BRAZIL

Caipirapirs Produçoes Artisticas Ltda, Avda. das Aguas Marinhas 157 Pg Petrópolis, 07600-000 São Paulo. *General Manager: Pablo Ossipoff.*
Estudio Eldorado Ltda, Rua Pires de Mota 820-830, 01529 São Paulo. *Executive Director: João Lara Mesquita.*
Paradox Music, Rua Dr. Pinto Ferraz 58, Vila Marina, 04117-040 São Paulo. *Director: Silvio Arnaldo Caligaris.*

BULGARIA

Arsis Publishing, 15 Tsarigradsko Chaussse Blvd, 1220 Sofia. *Chairman: Borislav Ivanchev.*
Mega Music Ltd, 2 Trapezitza Str, 1000 Sofia. *Managing Director: Dora Tchernkva.*

Music Publishing House Balkanton, 6 Haidoushka Poliana Str, 1612 Sofia. *Managing Director: Georgi Vachev.*
Union Media Ltd Record Company, 71A Evlogi Georgiev Blvd 4th Floor, 1142 Sofia. *President: Martin Zachariev.*

CANADA

Attic Music Group, 102 Atlantic Avenue, Toronto, ON M6K 1X9. *President: Alexander Mair.*
BMG Music Publishing Canada Inc, 150 John Street, 6th Floor, Toronto, ON M5V 3C3.
Botany Park Records & Music Publishing Corp, 361 Walter Drive, Keswick, ON L4P 3A8. *President: Marlaine Rennocks.*
Brass Ring Productions (Division of Manford Music Inc), PO Box 1266 Station A, Kelowna, BC, V1Y 7V8. *President/Personal Manager: Becky Chapman.*
EMI Music Publishing Canada, 300 Richmond Street W, 2nd Floor, Toronto, ON M5V 1E6.
G Man Music, 4 Bowden Street, Toronto, ON, M4K 2X2. *President: Gerry Young.*
G String Publishing, PO Box 1096, Hudson, PQ J0P 1V0. *Manager: Tanya Hart.*
Heaven Bent Music Corp, 11 Hopewell Crescent, Hamilton, ON L8J 1P3. *General Manager: Kathie Pietron.*
John H Lennon Music Ltd, 1235 Bay Street, Suite 400 Toronto, ON M5R 3K4. *Managing Director/President: Lenny Moore, John Lennon.*
Montina Music, PO Box 702, Snowdon Station, Montreal, PQ H3X 3X8. *Professional General Manager: D Leonard.*
Morning Music Limited, 5200 Dixie Road, Suite 203, Mississauga, ON L4W 1E4. *President: Mark Altman.*
Nusinfo Publishing Group Inc, 2504 Mayfair Street, Montreal, PQH4B 2C8. *President/Owner: Jehan V Valiquet.*
PolyGram Music Publishing, 1345 Denison Street, Mackham, ON L3R 5V2. *Vice-President/General Manager: John Redmond.*
Savannah Music Inc, 123 Applefield Drive, Scarborough, ON M1P 3Y5. *Director of Canadian Operations: Bill Carruthers.*
Silverhawk Publishing, 3073 Cedarbank Road, Rural Route #11, Peterborough, ON K9J 6Y3. *President: Jim Freake.*
Songcraft Communications, 20 Gamble Avenue, Suite 105, Toronto, ON M4K 2G9. *General Manager: Bryan Way.*
Sony Music Publishing, 1121 Leslie Street, Don Mills, ON M3C 2J9.
Sparwood Music Productions, PO Box 270 Bentley, AB T0C 0J0. *Manager: Dick Damron.*
Spinner Music Group Inc, Third Floor, 68 Water Street, Vancouver, BC, V6B 1A4. *President: Ken Spence; Managing Director: Wolfgang Burandt.*
Third Wave Productions Ltd, PO Box 563, Gander, NF, A1V 2E1. *President: R Archibald Bonnell.*
TMP - The Music Publisher, Suite #300, 1670 Bayview Avenue, Toronto, ON M4G 3C2. *President: Frank Davies.*
Warner/Chappell Music Canada Ltd, 85 Scarsdale Road, Unit 101, Don Mills, ON M3B 2R2. *President: Jerry Renewych; Creative Manager: Anne-Marie Smith.*

CHILE

Ediciones Musicales Fermata Ltda, Ebro 2751, Of. 609 Las Condes 41, Santiago de Chile. *General Manager: Eliana Cisternas.*

COLOMBIA

BMG Ariola de Colombia SA, Calle 67, n. 7-94, 12°, Santa Fe de Bogotá, DC. *Director: Francisco Villanueva.*
Codiscos, Carrera 67, n. 1, Sur 92 Guayabal, 1428 Medellín. *President: César Vallejo.*
Edisdago Ltda, C / 33AA, n. 81-25, Medellín. *President: Dario Gómez Zapata.*
Promotora Colombiana de Musica Ltda, Carrera 67, n. 1 Sur 92, Medellín. *Manager: Sylvia N. Arango.*

CROATIA

CMP, Medjugoska 61, 41000 Zagreb. *A&R Manager: Sinisa Skarica.*
Kinel Music, Vinogradska Cesta 3, 41000 Zagreb. *Managing Director: Mario Kinel.*
Melody, Rubesi 139 A, 51215 Kastav. *Director: Andrej Basa.*
Skalinada, Dubrovacka 23, 58000 Split. *Director: Zdenko Runjic.*
Tutico, Veprinacka 16, 10000 Zagreb. *Director: Zrinko Tutic.*

DENMARK

Cloudland, Skt Jorgensalle 7 0.6 1th, DK-1615 Copenhagen N. *Managing Director: Simon Sheika.*
ELAP Music A/S, Bransagervej 2-10, 9490 Pandrup. *Promotion: Steffen Lund Nielsen.*
EMI Music Publishing Denmark, Gladsaxevej 135, DK-2860 Soeborg. *Managing Director: John Rasmussen.*
Great Dane Music, c/o Replay Records, Frederikssundvej 60 C, DK-2400 NV Copenhagen. *Managing Director: Henrik Boetcher.*
Iceberg Music, Ronne Alie 78, DK-8600 Silkeborg. *Managing Director: Manfred Zähringer.*
Inhouse Publishing, Vognmagergade 10, DK-1120 CopenhagenK.
Klepto Records & Publishing, Langdries 4, DK-9450 Haaltert. *Managing Director: Baits Wilfried.*
Mega Scandinavia A/S. Indiakaj 1, DK-2100 Copenhagen Ø. *Vice President: Cai Leitner; Director of A&R and Marketing: Jesper Ban.*
Olafssongs/Warner Chappell Music Denmark A/S, Anker Heegaards Gade 2, DK-1572 Copenhagen V. *President: Finn Olafsson.*
Pineapple Publishing Aps, Frodesgade 74, DK-6700 Esbjerg. *Managing Director: Helge Englebrecht.*
Sundance Music, Gl. Kongevej 47 B, DK-1610 Copenhagen V. *Managing Director: Peter Littauer.*
Warner Chappell Music Denmark, Anker Heegaardsgade 2, St Tv, DK-1572 Copenhagen. *Managing Director: Finn Olafsson.*

FINLAND

Bluebird Music, Henrikities 5 C, 00370 Helsinki. *Managing Director: Niklas Nordström.*
Fazer Songs, PO Box 169, 02101 Espoo. *A&R: Raimo Henriksson.*
Flamingo Music, Vapaalantie 2, 01650 Vantaa. *Managing Director: Vexi Salmi.*
Love Kustannus, Hämeentie 6 A 4, 00530 Helsinki. *Managing Director: Sini Perho.*
Polarvox Music Publishing Oy, Arinatie 2, 00370 Helsinki. *Managing Director: Leena Juuranto.*
Poplandia Music, PO Box 483, 33101 Tampere. *Managing Director: Kari Helenius.*
Taurus Music, PO Box 33, 02431 Masala. *ManagingDirector: Antero Päiväiänen.*
Zen Master Publishing, PO Box 35, 33201 Tampere. *Managing Director: Tapio Korjus.*

FRANCE

Alpha Bravo, 64 Av Jean Jaurès, F-93500 Pantin. *Contact: Daniel Bornet.*
BMG Music Publishing France, 10 Rue Duphot, F-75001 Paris. *Director: Stéphane Berlow.*
Boucherie Productions, 15 Bis Rue du Plateau, F-75019 Paris. *Director: Natali Luc.*
Caravage, 130 Rue Marius Aufan, F-92300 Levallois-Perret. *General Manager: Jean-Paul Smets.*

Cobalt, 145 Rue de Ménilmont, F-75020 Paris. *Managing Director: Philippa Conrath.*
Editions Essex, 5 Rue Lincoln, F-75008 Paris. *Managing Director: René Boyer.*
Editions Fortin, 4 Cité Chaptal, F-75009 Paris. *Contact: Multrier Fortin.*
EMI Music Publishing France SA, 20 Rue Molitor, F-75016 Paris. *Director: Olivier Huret.*
Fairplay (Fair and Square Publishing), 10-12 Rue Richer, F-75009 Paris. *Director: Fabrice Absil.*
FKO Music, 18 Rue de Revilly, F-25012 Paris. *Managing Director: Francis Kertekian; International Dept: Grace Casta.*
Made In Heaven, 6 Rue Rémy de Gourmont, F-75019 Paris. *Label Manager: Mathias Jeannin.*
MCA Caravelle France, 35 Blvd Malesherbes, F-75008 Paris. *Chairman: Tom Arena.*
Metisse Music Sarl, 1 Villa Juge, F-75015 Paris. *Managing Director: Petra Gehrmann.*
Nouvelles Editions Meridian, 5 Rue Lincoln, F-75008 Paris. *Managing Director: René Boyer.*
Peermusic, 5 Rue Lincoln, F-75008 Paris. *Managing Director: René Boyer.*
Polygram Music, 14 Rue Curie, F-75005 Paris. *Chairman: Philippe Lerichomme.*
Promo Sonor International, 30 Rue de Saussure, F-75017 Paris. *Managing Director: Jo Pucheu.*
Rondor Music, 32 Rue Etienne Marcel, F-75002 Paris. *Director: Halit Uman.*
Salam Aleikum Amusements, 2 Rue Carpeaux, F-75018 Paris. *Director: Stephane Benhamou.*
Scorpio Music, 12 Avenue George V, F-75008 Paris. *President: Henri Belolo.*
Skydog Kind Of Groove, 32 Av Claude Vellefaux, F-75010 Paris. *Contact: Marc Zermati.*
Société d'Editions Musicales Internationales, 5 Rue Lincoln, F-75008 Paris. *Managing Director: René Boyer.*
Sony Music Publishing France, 131 Av de Wagram, F-75017 Paris. *Director: Nicolas Galibert.*
Topomic Music, 26 Rue L M Nordmann, F-92250 La Garenne-Colombes. *President: Pierre Jaubert.*
XIII Bis Music Group, 34 Rue Eugene Flachat, F-75017 Paris. *Managing Director: Laurent Dreux-Leblanc.*

GERMANY

AlphaTon Publishing GmbH, Am Haidberg 4, D-21465 Wentorf. *Contacts: Joe Rudolph and Gerd Gerdes.*
Ata Tak Records, Kölner Str 226 F, D-40227 Düsseldorf. *Director: Frank Fenstermacher.*
Blanko Musik, Clemens Str 75, D-80796 Munich. *Managing Director: Hage Hein; Assistant Managing Director: Gerhild Malorny.*
Castor Promotions, Dragonerstr 21, D-30163 Hannover. *Contact: Elke Fleing.*
Chinotto Music Gbr, Zwickauer Str 24, D-90491 Nürnberg. *Contact: Harald Strecker.*
Edition Metromania / Warner Chappell Germany, Osterstr. 36, D-30159 Hannover. *Managing Director: Frank Bornemann.*
Edition Partysanen Publishing, Skalitzer Str 68, D-10997 Berlin. *Managing Director: Rona Casley.*
EMI Music Publishing Germany GmbH, Alsterufer 1, D-20354 Hamburg. *Director: Andreas Kiel.*
Energy Productions Inc, Eduard Schmid Str 28, D-81541 Munich. *President: Michael Kruth.*
Freibank, Ditmar-Koel-Str 26, D-20459 Hamburg. *Directors: Mark Chung and Klaus Maeck.*
Fun Factory GmbH, Hermannstadtweg 9, D-48151 Münster. *Marketing Assistant: Claudia Weiler.*
Garbitowski, Metzer Str 30, D-50677 Cologne. *Owner & Director: Jürgen Garbitowski.*
Heartpunch Music Publishing & Promotion, Vohwinkeler Str 154, D-42339 Wuppertal. *Managing Director: Michael Schuster.*
Kick Musikverlag, Burgunder Str 8, D-50677 Cologne. *Managing Director: Goetz Elbertzhagen; International Manager: Lynda Hill.*
Mainhattan Music Production, Friedrich-Ebert-Str 48, D-63179 Obertshausen. *Manager: Uwe Block.*
MCA Music Entertainment Germany, Winterhuder Weg 27, D-22085 Hamburg. *Managing Director: Adrain Facklan-Wolf.*
Moderne Welt Musikproduktions & Vennoskfungs GmbH, Marienbaden Str 6/1, D-70372 Stuttgart. *Managing Director: Henning Tögel.*
Music Box GmbH, Rahlstedter Str 65, D-22149 Hamburg. *Managing Director: Hubertus Branzko.*
Musikverlag Progressive GmbH, Bramfelder Chaussee 238c, D-22177 Hamburg. *Contact: Rudy Holzhauer.*
Piranha Kultur & Medien Produkion GmbH, Carmer Str 11, D-10623 Berlin. *Managing Director: Borkowsky Akbar.*
Polygram Songs Musikverlag Germany, Glockengiesserwall 3, D-20095 Hamburg. *Managing Director: Os Van Joost.*
R D Clevère Musikverlag, PO Box 2145, D-63243 Neu-Isenburg. *Professional Manager: Tony Hermonez.*
Rolf Budde Musikverlage, Hohenzollerdamm 54 A, D-14199 Berlin. *Managing Director: Rolf Budde.*
Siegel Music Companies, Hoechlstrasse 2, D-81675 Munich. *Managing Director: Joachim Neubauer.*
t'Bwana Sound/Big Easy, Schleswigerstr 19, D-44145 Dortmund. *Contact: Helmut Philipps.*
Thopo Music Management, Postfach 1, D-96136 Burgebrach. *Contact: Joseph Thomann.*
Vielklang Musikproduktion GmbH, Forster Str 4/5, D-10999 Berlin. *Managing Director: Matthias Bröckel.*
Westpark Music, PO Box 260 227, Rathenauplatz 4, D-50515 Cologne. *President: Ulli Hetscher.*

GREECE

Di Di Music, PO Box 31327, 43 Thiras Street, 10035 Athens. *Managing Director: Nick Loridas.*
Filippos Nakas Mousikos Oikos, 13 Navarinoy Street, 10680 Athens. *Managing Director: G. Nakas.*
General Publishing Company SA, 11 Kriezotou Street, 10671 Athens. *Managing Director: Panayiotis Maravelias.*

GREENLAND

ULO - Greenlandic Music, PO Box 184, DK-3911 Sisimiut. *Production Manager: Karsten Sommer.*

HONG KONG

Blue Max Productions, 1st Floor, Kingsfield Mansion, 457-459 King's Road, North Point. *Managing Partner: Ralph Lister.*
BMG Music Publishing Hong Kong Ltd, 11/Fl, Peninsula Office Tower, 18 Middle Road, Tsimshatsui, Kowloon. *General Manager: Irene Ho.*
Cinepoly Music Publishing Co Ltd, 8/F 100 Canton Road, Tsimshatsui, Kowloon. *Publishing Executive: Sandy Sun.*
EMI Music Publishing (S E Asia) Ltd, Room 3201-7 Shell Tower, Times Square, 1 Matherson Street, Causeway Bay. *General Manager: Teresa Yiu.*
J & L Records Co, Rm 1101 Ginza Square, 567 Nathan Road, Kowloon. *General Manager: Neo Chow.*
Polygram Music Publishing Hong Kong Ltd, 8/F 100 Canton Road, Kowloon. *President: Norman Cheng.*
Song Power Limited, PO Box 95170, Tsim Sha Tsui Post Office, Kowloon. *Director-Manager: Paul Leung.*
Sony Music Publishing, 4/F Acme Building, 22-28 Nanking Street, Yaumati, Kowloon. *General Manager: Angela Hon.*
Spraylot Music Ltd, Suite A, 15th Fl, Ritz Plaza, 122 Austin Road, Tsim Sha Tsui, Kowloon. *Publishing Executive: Peggy Yu.*
Warner Music Publishing Hong Kong Ltd, Room 301-303, Corporation Square, 8 Lam Lok Street, Kowloon Bay, Kowloon. *Managing Director: Paco Wong.*

HUNGARY

Edito Musica, Vörösmarty tér 1, 1051 Budapest. *Managing Director: Istvan Homolya.*
Joker, Florian ter 4-5, 1033 Budapest. *Managing Director: Peter Rado.*

Locomusic, PO Box 27, 1281 Budapest 27. *Managing Director: Gabor Presser.*
PG Publishing, PO Box 8, 1922 Budapest.
Sonic Boom, Iskola U 1, Szentendre. *Managing Director: Ditmar Lupfer.*

ICELAND

Skifan HF, Skiefan 17, 108 Reykjavik. *Chairman: Jon Olafsson.*
Spor Publishing, Nybylavegur 4, 200 Kopavogur. *Managing Director: Steinar Berg Isleifson.*

IRELAND

Acorn Music Ltd, Roncalli, Claremont Pines, Carrickmines, Dublin 18. *Director: Brendan Graham.*
Aigle Music, 6 Danieli Drive, Artane, Dublin 5. *Contact: Nicky and Roma Ryan.*
Asdee Music, Glenageary Office Park, Glenageary, Co Dublin. *Administrator: Peter Bardon.*
Bardis Music Co Ltd, Glenageary Office Park, Glenageary, Co Dublin. *Managing Director: Peter Bardon.*
Beann Eadair Music, 48 Downside, Skerries, Co Dublin. *Director: Clive Hudson.*
Blue Dandelion Publishing, 17 Dame Court, Dublin 2. *Contact: Fran Coleman.*
Clannad Music, Film House, 4 Windmill Lane, Dublin 2. *Managing Director: David Kavanagh.*
Cló Iar -Chonnachta, Indreabhán, Conamara, Co na Gaillimhe. *Marketing and Sales Manager: Deirdre O'Toole.*
Coyle and Coyle, 30 Lower Leeson Street, Dublin 2. *Director: James Coyle.*
Danceline Music, 267 Crodaun Forest Park, Celbridge, Co Kildare. *Director: Peter McCluskey.*
Emma Music Ltd, 5/6 Lombard St, Dublin 2. *Director: Michael O'Riordan.*
The Evolving Music Company Ltd, Alexandra House, Earlsfort Centre, Earlsfort Terrace, Dublin 2. *Contact: Denis Desmond, John J Lappin.*
Foxrock Music Productions, Alexandra House, Earlsfort Centre, Earlsfort Terrace, Dublin 2. *Managing Director: John John Lappin.*
Gael Linn Music, 26 Merrion Square, Dublin 2. *Contact: Michael Ward.*
Hazel Records, Dublin Road, Monasterevin, Co Kildare. *Managing Director: John Kelly.*
Jump Music, 19 Stockton Green, Castleknock, Dublin 15. *Managing Director: Joe McFadden.*
Lunar Records, 5-6 Lombard St East, Dublin 2. *Marketing Manager: Graham Molloy.*
McGuinness/Whelan Music Publishers, 30/32 Sir John Rogerson's Quay, Dublin 2. *Managing Director: Barbara Galavan.*
Brian Molloy, 5-6 Lombard St East, Dublin 2. *Marketing Manager: Graham Molloy.*
Mother Music Ltd, 30/32 Sir John Rogerson's Quay, Dublin 2. *Managing Director: Barbara Galavan.*
Mulligan Music Ltd., 75 Sweetmount Avenue, Dundrum, Co. Dublin. *Managing Director: Brian O'Neill.*
Peer Music Ireland Ltd, The Peer Suite, 26-27 Upper Pembroke Street, Dublin 2. *Contact: Darragh Kettle.*
Raglan Music, Glenageary Office Park, Glenageary, Co Dublin. *Administrator: Peter Bardon.*
Rosette Music Ltd, 5/6 Lombard Street, Dublin 2. *Director: Michael O'Riordan.*
RSE Music Publishing, 11-13 Station Road, Raheny, Dublin 5. *Directors: Raymond J Smyth, Breide P Smyth.*
Third Floor Ltd, 70 Lower Baggot Street, Dublin 2. *Managing Director: Maurice Cassidy.*
Woodtown Music, Dame House, Dame Street, Dublin 2. *Managing Director: Jane Bolton.*

ITALY

Ala Bianca Group Srl, Via G Mazzoni 34/36, 41100 Modena. *General Manager: Toni Verona.*
BMG Italy, Via di S Alessandro 7, 00131 Rome. *Managing Director: Mario Cantini.*
Crotalo Ed Mus, Via Del Pino 71, 48100 Lido Adriano. *Managing Director: Luigi Mazzesi.*
EMI Music Publishing Italia, Via C Ravizza 43-45, 20148 Milan. *Managing Director: Antonio Marrapodi.*
FMA Edizioni Musicali E Discografiche Srl, Via Boccaccio N 47, 20123 Milan. *President: Mario Allione.*
General Rock, Viale Manzoni 52, Cerveteri, 00052 Rome. *Contact: Robbie Zee.*
Lion Snc, Via Goldoni 42/A, 30174 Mestre Venezia. *General Manager: Luciano Trevisan.*
Nuova Durium Srl, P.zza Mirabello 1, 20121 Milan. *Assistant Manager: Francesco Piccarreda.*
Polygram Italia Edizioni, Via C Tenca 2, 20124 Milan. *Managing Director: Gianfranco Rebulla.*
Sony Music Publishing (Italy), Via Amedei 9, 20123 Milan. *Chairman: Franco Cabrini.*
Sugar Music Group, Via Quintiliano 40, 20138 Milan. *International Business Affairs: Monica Dahl.*
Virgin Dicshi Edizioni Musicali, Via Porpora 26, 20131 Milan. *Managing Director: Luigi Montovani.*
Warner Chappell Music Italiana, Corso Buenos Aires 79, 20124 Milan. *Manager: Luigi Bartolotta.*

JAPAN

Columbia Music Publishing Co, 4-14-14 Akasaka, Minato-ku, Tokyo 107. *Manager: Haijime Ogura.*
EMI Music Publishing Co Ltd, Shibuya Mitake Bldg 3F, 1-19-5 Shinuya, Shibuya-ku, Tokyo 150. *Managing Director: Namahiko Sasaki.*
MCA Panasonic Music Co Ltd, KFI Bdlg 8F, 3-6-20 Kita-Aoyama, Minato-ku, Tokyo 107. *President: Nobu Yoshinari.*
Shinko Music Publishing Co Ltd, 2-1 Ogawamachi, Kanda, Chiyoda-ku, Tokyo 101. *President: Shoichi Kusano.*
Sony Music Publishing, 1-32-12 Higashi, Shibuya-ku, Tokyo 150. *General Manager: Yoshiyuki Itoh.*
Sunkyo Music Co Ltd, 87-6 Torocho 2-Chome, Omiya-City 330. *Director: Youichi Takeuchi.*
Toshiba-EMI Music Publishing Co. Ltd, 8F Inoue Akasaka Bdlg, 1-6-8 Akasaka Bldg, Minato-ku, Tokyo 107. *President: Iaso Atsumi.*
Warner Chappell Music Japan KK, Nichion Inc, Akasaka Media Bldg, 3-6 Akasaka 5-Chome, Minato-ku, Tokyo 107. *Managing Director: Manmoru Murakami.*

KOREA

Korea Music Publishing, no. 325 Nakwon Arcade, 286-4 Nakwon-dong, Jongro-ku, Seoul. *Contact: Eun-Sik Lee.*
Sony Music Entertainment (Korea) Inc, 985-19 Bangbae-dong, Seochu-ku, Seoul. *Finance Manager: Tae Hwan Chung.*
Time Recording Inc, 620 Daeha Bldg, 14-11 Yoido-dong, Youngdungpo-ku, Seoul. *President: N.W.Cho.*

LUXEMBOURG

Joybringer, 27 Rue Victor Hugo, 4583 Differdange. *Contact: Andre Depienne.*
Promotion 4, BP 728, 2017 Luxembourg. *Director: Mike Koedinger.*
Radio Music International, Villa Louvigny, 2825 Luxembourg-Ville. *Managing Director: Ray Van Cant.*
Waltzing-Parke Productions, PO Box 59, 2010 Luxembourg. *Manager: Margaret Parke; Managing Director: Gast Waltzing.*

MALAYSIA

BMG Music Publishing Sdn Bhd, 13-1 Jalan Seganmbut, Kuala Lumpur 51200. *Managing Director: Frankie Cheah.*
Polygram Records Sdn Bhd, 83-87 Jalan Kampung Pandan, Taman Maluri, Kuala Lumpur 55100. *Managing Director: Eric Yeo.*
Pustaka Muzik EMI (Malaysia), Suite 10.01, 10th Fl, Exchange Square, off Jln Semantan, Damansara Heights, Kuala Lumpur 50490. *Publishing Manager: LimCheng Hoo.*
Sony Music Publishing, C16 & C17 Jalan Ampang Utamam 1/1, off Jalan Ampang, Selangor Darul Ehsan. *Managing Director: Rick Loh.*

MEXICO

Beechwood de Mexico SA, Río Tigris 33, 06500 Mexico DF. *Director General: Antonio Fritz.*
Compaña Fonografica Internacional SA, Sanctorum 86-B Colonia Argentina, 11230 Mexico DF. *Director General: Ignacio Morales Perea.*
Editorial Musical Juventa, Ignacio Esteva 26A, 11850 Mexico DF. *Proprietor: Dario Antonio Zorzano.*
Galaxia Musical SA, Leibnitz 130, 11590 Mexico DF. *Director General: José G Cruz Ayala.*
Organizacion Latino Internacional, Avda. Insurgente Sur 953-202, Col. Nápoles, 0380 Mexico DF. *Director General: Tony Méndez.*
Polygram Discos SA, Avda. Miguel Angel de Quevedo 531, Colonia Romero de Terreros, 04310 Mexico DF. *Director General: Francisco Bestard.*
Producciones Fonograficas SA, Adolfo Prieto 1649, 1 Piso, Colonia del Valle, 03100 Benito Juárez-Mexico, DF. *Director General: Bernardo Yancelson.*
Warner Chappell Music Mexico SA, Avda. Ejercito Nacional 209, 3 Piso, Col. Verónica Anzures, 11300 Mexico DF. *Director General: Jesús Pérez Martín.*

NETHERLANDS

Best Music, Crispijnstraat 9, 5171 CH Kaatsheuvel. *Managing Director: Peter Van Best.*
Blue & White Songs, PO Box 9010, 1006 AA Amsterdam. *President: Hans W Van Pol.*
CM Songs, Herenweg 9, 2465 AA Rijnsaterwoude. *Managing Director: Aart Mol.*
Dutchy Publishing, Pampuslaan 45, 1382 JM Weesp. *Managing Director: Xavier Pilgrims de Bigard.*
EMI Music Publishing, Schapenkamp 8A, 1211 PA Hilversum. *Managing Director: Arjen Witte.*
Moonshine, Langeweid 7, 1831 BL Koedyk. *President: Evert Wiljrins.*
Mukti Music Publishing, Karel Doormanlaan 16, 1403 TM Bussum. *Director: Eric van den Brink.*
Narada Media, J Penhyweg 2, 1217 JH Hilversum. *Director of European Marketing: Jaap Hoitingh.*
Peermusic Holland bv, Larenseweg 159, 1221 CL Hilversum. *Managing Director: J H M G van Dÿl.*
Pennies From Heaven, PO Box 3121, 2601 DC Delft. *Vice President: Paul van Meelis.*
Stichting Conamus, PO Box 929, 1200 AX Hilversum or Vaartweg 32, 1217 SV Hilversum. *General Manager: J H de Mol; Press Officer: Saskia Brwning.*
Universal Songs Holland, PO Box 2305, 1200 CH Hilversum. *Managing Director: Bram Keizer.*
VIP Promotions, Looievsgracht 38, 1016 VS Amsterdam. *PD: G Bezuijen.*
Warner-Basart Music Publishers, Flevolaan 41, 1411 KC Naarden. *Managing Director: Robin Simonse.*

NEW ZEALAND

Jayrem Music, PO Box 3101, Ohope, Woorl, 110 Symonds Street, Auckland. *General Manager: Paul Ellis.*
South Pacific Music Associates Ltd, PO Box 47-088, Ponsonby, Auckland. *Manager: Clare Chambers.*
Yellow Eye Music, PO Box 6173 Dunedin North or 33 Fortune Street, Dalmore, Dunedin. *Partner: Simon Vare.*

NORWAY

Fortissimo Forlag A/S, Box 130, 1458 Fjellstrand. *Owner/Director: Trevor Ford.*
Frost Music A/S, PO Box 6062 Etterstad, 0601 Oslo. *Managing Director: Philip Kevse.*
Late Night Music, PO Box 44, Aserudun 2 Strommen, 2014 Blystadlia. *Managing Director: Tom Sennerud.*
Musikk Produksion AS, Kjelsasvn 139 D, 0491 Oslo. *Managing Director: Harald Fjeld.*
Norwegian Songs, PO Box 4329 Torshov, Sandakaervn 24C, 0402 Oslo. *Managing Director: Audun Tylden.*
Polygram Publishing Norway, PO Box 2645 Solli, Drammnesvn 88B, 0203 Oslo. *Managing Director: Stein G Johnsen.*
Rec 90, PO Box 1291, 5001 Bergen. *Managing Director: Torfinn Andersen.*
Sonet Music Norway, PO Box 26 45 Solli, Drammensvn 88 B, 0403 Oslo. *Managing Director: Terje Engen.*
Warner Chappell Music Norway, PO Box 18, Bryn, 0611 Oslo. *Contact: Odd Steenberg.*

PERU

Ediciones Musiales Hispanas, Esquilache 179, Lima 27. *General Manager: Carlos Renjipo Mercado.*

PHILIPPINES

BAMI (Bayanihan Music Philippines Inc.), PO Box AC 270, 782 Aurora Blvd, Cubao, Quezon City, Manila. *President: Florendo Garcia.*
BMG Music Philippines, 3/F Equitable Banking Corp. Bldg, 898 Aurora Blvd, Cubao, Quezon City, Manila. *Contact: Nathaniel Tan.*
DD International Recording Corp, 363 P Casal Street, Quiapo, Manila 1001. *Chairman-President: Demy A Quirino Jr.*
EMI (Eligardi Music Inc), 6/F NIDC Bldg, 259-263 Sen Gil J, Puyat Avenue, Makati, Metro Manila. *President: Eli Gardiner.*

POLAND

Polonia Records Ltd, ul Jana Pawla II 18m 13, 00-116 Warsaw. *Contact: Staniskaw Sobola.*
Polskie Nagrania, Goleszowska 6, 01-249 Warsaw. *Managing Director: Aleksander Olaszewski.*
Polskie Wydawnictwo Muzyczne (PWM), Al Krasinskiego 11A, 31-111 Krakow. *Managing Director: Jan Betkowski.*

PORTUGAL

BMG Ariola Portugal, Rua Gregório Lopes 1514/2, 1400 Lisbon.
Concertos de Portugal Lda, Apartado 13, 2775 Carcavelos. *Director: José Silva.*
EMI Songs Portugal, Praca Nuno Rodrigues do Santos 7, 1600 Lisbon.
Farol Musica, Alto do Couto, Arnazéns I, 2735 Cacém. *Directors: Antonio Guimaráes, Fernando Júrice.*
Polygram Discos SA, Rua Prof. Reinaldo dos Santos 12-D, 1500 Lisbon. *Managing Director: Rodrigo Marin.*

Sony Music Portugal, Rua Juliao Quintinha 11, 1500 Lisbon.
Vidisco Comercio E Industria de Som Lda, Avda. Bombeiros Voluntarios 13, 1675 Pontinha. *General Manager: João Pedro Jadauji.*
Warner Chappell Portugal, Rua Dr Constantino de Braganca 26A, 1400 Lisbon.

RUSSIA

Mezhdunarodnaya Kniga, Dimitrova 39, 117 049 Moscow. *Managing Director: Stanislav Ostapishin.*
Muzyka Publishers, Neglinnaya 14, 103 031 Moscow. *Managing Director: L Sidelnikov.*

ROMANIA

Contera AV, Str Turda 122, BL 39, SCA, Et 6 Ap 30, Sect 1 Bucharest. *President: Iordachescu Octavian.*

SINGAPORE

BMG Music Publishing Pte Ltd, Alexandra Distripark, Block 2, no. 11-01/04, Pasir Panjang Road, Singapore 0511. *Managing Director: Frankie Cheah .*
EMI Music Publishing Singapore Pte Ltd, 213 Henderson Road, 04-05 Henderson Industrial Estate, Singapore 0315. *CEO: David Wee.*
Fox Agency International Inc, 391 B, Orchard Road, #09-10, Tower B, Ngee Ann City, Singapore 0923. *Regional Director: Fabian Lek.*
Hype Records Pte Ltd, 221 Henderson Road, #02-04 Henderson Bldg, Singapore 159557. *Administration Manager: Melvis Yip.*
Polygram Music Publishing Pte Ltd, 23 Genting Road, 04-01 Chevalier House, Singapore 1334. *Manager: Karen Sim.*
Sony Music Publishing (Pte) Ltd, 601 Sims Drive, 02-07, Singapore 1438. *General Manager: Terence Phung.*
Warner/Chappell Music Singapore Pte Ltd, 10 Anson Road #12-06/07/08, International Plaza, Singapore 079903. *Publishing Manager: Liz Cheam.*
White Cloud Record Pte Ltd, 246 MacPherson Road, #05-01, Betime Building, Singapore 348578. *Managing Director: Heng Ser Piah.*

SLOVAKIA

CS Music, Votrubova 2, 82109 Bratislava. *Managing Director: Dusan Tlolka.*
DMC Disco Box, Ruzinovska 28, 82101 Bratislava. *Managing Director: Ivan Malovec.*
EMI/Monitor Slovakia, Radvanska 1, 81101 Bratislava. *Managing Director: Pavol Hammel.*
Musica, palisady 36, 81632 Bratislava. *Managing Director:F J Walner.*
Polygram Slovakia, Pribinova 25, 81109 Bratislava. *Managing Director: Peter Riava.*

SLOVENIA

ŠKUC-AFK, Kersnikova 4, 61000 Ljubljana. *Managing Director: Mitja Prezelj.*

SPAIN

Blanco Y Negro, Amigo 14-16, 08021 Barcelona. *Managing Director: Sito Manovent.*
Canciones del Mundo, Magallanes 25, 28015 Madrid. *Managing Director: Luis Regatero.*
Crab Ediciones Musicales SA, Sagunto 2, 28010 Madrid. *General Manager: Jorge E Gomez Diaz.*
Doctor Music Publishing, Alcala 114-6B, 28009 Madrid. *Director: Lucia Cardenes.*
Ediciones Musicales Warner Bros SA, Lopez de Hoyos 42, 28006 Madrid. *Managing Director: Inigo Zabala.*
Epoca Music, Joanot Martorell 15, 08203 Barcelona. *Managing Director: Len Roy Carvalho.*
GSG - Grup de Serveis Guilleries, Granja Baró, Ctra de la Guixa, km 2, 08500 VIC(Barcelona). *Administration: Jordi Costa; Management: Ignasi Pla; Production: Joan Capdevila.*
Huygen Corp, Alzines 3, St Quirze Parc, 08192 St Quirze del Vallès, Barcelona. *Contact: Michel Huygen.*
Neuronium Music, Calle Alzines 3, St Quirze Parc, 08192 St Quirze del Vallès, Barcelona. *Contact: Michel Huygen.*
New Music Ediciones Musicales SA, Apartado 9.046, 28060 Madrid. *General Manager: Gerhard Haltermann.*
RLM Producciones, Jose Maria Cavero 9, Ch A, 28027 Madrid. *Managing Director: Rosa Lagarrigue.*
Sintonia, Abdon Terrades 5, 28015 Madrid. *Publisher: William Clifton.*
Sonifolk Arpafolk, Fernando el Catalico 58, 28015 Madrid. *ManagingDirector: Jose de la Fuente.*
Victoria, Narvaez 14-1A, 28009 Madrid. *General Manager: Gerhard Haltermann.*
Vortex Music, Magallanes 25, 28015 Madrid. *Managing Director: Luis Regatero.*

SWEDEN

BMG Music Publishing Scandinavia, PO Box 1026, Starrbäcksgatan 1, 17121 Sundbyberg. *Managing Director: Lars Karlsson.*
EMI Music Publishing Scandinavia AB, Box 20509, 161 02 Bromma. *Contact: Nina Schrijvershof.*
Energy Records AB, Vastergatan 23, 21121 Malmö. *Contact: Håkan Ehrnst.*
Gazell Music AB, Tappvägen 24, Box 20055, 16102 Bromma. *Director: Dag Haeggqvist.*
MCA Music Sweden, PO Box 55 505, Riddargatan 23 4, 10204 Stockholm.
Misty Music AB, PO Box 10 149, 10055 Stockholm. *Managing Director: Anders Mören.*
Mixturen, Frijyrkliga Studieförbundet, Box 479, 10129 Stockholm. *Editor: Torgny Erséus.*
Out Of Time Music, Husargatan 15, 41122 Gothenburg. *Producer: Håkan Forshult.*
Real Time Music, Wennerbergsgatan 1, 11258 Stockholm. *Manager: Allan Gutheim.*
Sonet Music AB, PO Box 20504, Mariehällsvägen 35, 16103 Bromma. *Managing Director: Ingermar Bergman.*
Stockholm Records, PO Box 20504, 16102 Bromma. *General Manager: Eric Hasselqvist.*
Warner Chappell Music Scandinavia AB, Box 533, Vendevägen 85 B, 18215 Danderyd. *Managing Director: Roy Colgate.*

SWITZERLAND

Check Point Music, Rainweg 6, CH-8967 Widen. *Managing Director: Martin Scheiss.*
Dinemec Productions SA, Bld Helvétique 17, PO Box 893, CH-1211 Geneva. *Managing Director: Paul Sutin.*
Editions Cellier, Aiguemont 26, Rue du Bourg de Plait, CH-1605 Chexbres. *Contacts: Marcel and Catherine Cellier.*
Edition Helbing AG, Pfeaffikerstrasse 6, CH-8604 Volgetswil. *Managing Director: Willy Vogt.*
Edition Melodie, Brunnwiesenstrasse 26, CH-8049 Zürich. *Chairman: Anton Peterer.*
Global Music Swiss, Im Hauel 15, CH-4147 Aesch. *Public Relations: Sonja Schmidt-Montfort.*

Hyper Music, Domberweg 12, CH-4423 Hersberg. *Managing Director: P J Waserman.*
Marion Caravatti Music (MCM), Hochwachstrasse 27A, CH-8400 Winterthur. *Chairwoman: Marion Caravatti.*
Turicaphon AG, Turicaphonstrasse 31, CH-8616 Riedikon. *Managing Director: Hans Oestreicher.*
VIP AG Productions, Schützengasse 30, CH-8001 Zürich. *Managing Director: Urs Peter Keller.*
Viteka Music Publishing, Box 173, Ringstrasse 14, CH-8600 Dübendorf/Zürich. *Chairman: Willy Viteka.*
Vynil'Art Edition, PO Box 30, CH-1800 Vevey. *Contact: Heinz Dill.*

TAIWAN

BMG Music Taiwan Inc, 99-19 Section 2, Nankang Road, Nankang District, Taipei. *Publishing Manager: Victoria Kuo.*
Polygram Music Publishing Ltd, 5/F 99 Nankang Road, Section 3, Nankang Distrcit, Taipei. *Contact: Yvette Tung.*

THAILAND

BMG Music Publishing Co, 18/F Vanissa Bldg, Soi chidlom, Ploenchit Road, Patumwam, Bangkok 10110. *Managing Director: Steven Tan.*
Song Music Publishing, 1091 / 185-5 New Petchburi Road, Payathai, Bangkok 10400. *General Manager: Peter Gan.*

TURKEY

Jazz Records & Publishing, Altmatasi Caddesi 5, Serilen, 34470 Unkapani, Istanbul. *President: Yasar Demirturk.*
Topkapi Music, Mesrutiyet Caddesi 113, Ece Han Kat 2, 80050 Tepebasi, Istanbul. *Director: Mehmet Arman.*

UNITED KINGDOM

Acuff-Rose Music Ltd, 25 James Street, London W1M 6AA. *General Manager: Tony Peters.*
Amphonic Music Ltd, Kerchesters, Waterhouse Lane, Kingswood, Tadworth, Surrey KT20 6HT. *Director: Erica Dale.*
Andrew Music, 6 Wykeham Crescent, Oxford OX4 3SB. *Director: Andrew Claxton.*
Associated Music International Ltd, 34 Salisbury Street, London NW8 8QE. *Managing Director: Eliot M Cohen.*
Bad Habits Music Group, PO Box 111, London W13 0ZH. *Managing Director: John S Rushton.*
Barn Dance Publications Ltd, 62 Beechwood Road, South Croydon, Surrey CR2 0AA. *Manager: Derek Jones.*
Barry Collings Music, 15 Claremont Road, Westcliff On Sea, Essex SS0 7DX. *Managing Director: Barry Collings.*
Black Magic Management Ltd, 296 Earls Court Road, London SW5 9BA. *Managing Director: Mataya Clifford.*
BMG Music Publishing Limited, Bedford House, 69-79 Fulham High Street, London SW6 3JN. *Managing Director: Paul Curran.*
Boosey & Hawkes Music Publishers, 295 Regents Street, London W1R 8JH. *Managing Director: R A Fell.*
Brilliant Music, 19 Ford Square, London E1 2HS. *Managing Director: Frazer Henry.*
Brothers Organization, 74 The Archway, Station Approach, Ranelagh Gardens, London SW6 3UH. *Directors: Ian and Nick Titchener.*
Bucks Music Ltd, 1A Farm Place, London W8 7SX. *Managing Director: Simon Platz.*
Bulk Music Ltd, 9 Watt Road, Hillington, Glasgow G52 4RY, Scotland. *Director: Isobel Waugh.*
Bushranger Music, 86 Rayleigh Road, Hutton, Brentwood, Essex CM13 1BH. *Managing Director: Kathy Lister.*
Campbell Connelly & Co Ltd, 8/9 Frith Street, London W1V 5TZ. *Head of Copyright: Kevin White.*
Catalyst (Music Publishing) Limited, 171 Southgate Road, London N1 3LE. *Managing Director: Peter Knight Jr.*
Carlin Music Corporation, Ironbridge House, 3 Bridge Approach, London NW1 8BD. *Chief Executive: David Japp.*
Chapter 22 Music, Suite 114, The Custard Factory, Gibb Street, Birmingham B9 4AA. *Contact: Rod Thomson.*
Charly Publishing Limited, 156-166 Ilderton Road, London SE15 1NT. *Director: Jan Friedmann.*
Chrysalis Music, The Chrysalis Building, 13 Barmley Road, London W10 6SP. *Managing Director: Jeremy Lascelles.*
Clive Banks Music, 1 Glenthorne Mews, 115A Glenthorne Road, London W6 0LJ. *Contacts: Steve James, Steve Jervier and Brock Pocket.*
Congo Music Ltd, 17A Craven Park Road, Harlesden, London NW10 8SE. *Directors: Byron Lye-Fook and Root Jackson.*
Cornish Legend Music, 153 Vauxhall Street, The Barbican, Plymouth PL4 0DF, Devon. *Partner: Nick Strachan.*
Cramer Music, 23 Garrick Street, London WC2E 8AX. *Contact: Peter Maxwell.*
Cwmni Cyhoeddi Gwynn Cyf, Y Gerlan Heol Y Dwr, Penygroes, Caernarfon, Gwynedd LL54 6LR, Wales. *Contact: Wendy Jones.*
Dance Music, 7 Mornington Terrace, Camden Town, London NW1 7RR. *Managing Director: Ian Tregoning.*
Demi Monde Records & Publishing, Foel Studio, Llanfair, Caekeinion, Powys SY21 0DS, Wales. *Managing Director: Dave Anderson.*
Demon Music Ltd, Canal House, Stars Estate, Transport Avenue, Brentford, Middlesex TW8 9HF. *James Bedbrook.*
EMI Music Publishing, 127 Charing Cross Road, London WC2H 0EA. *Managing Director: Peter Reichardt.*
Endomorph Music Publishing, 29 St Michaels Road, Leeds LS6 3BG. *Managing Director: Dave Fostin.*
Equity Records, 112 A+B Westbourne Grove, Chepstow Road, London W2 5RU. *Managing Director: Paul Moore.*
Eschenbach Editions, 28 Dalrymple Crescent, Edinburgh EH9 2NY, Scotland. *Managing Director: James Douglas.*
Esprit Music Ltd, Unit 306, Canalot Production Studios, 222 Kensal Road, London W10 5BN. *Director: Tony Warren.*
Express Music (London) Ltd, The Studio, Yew Tree Farm, Charing Heath, Kent TN27 0AU. *Managing Director: S Jackson.*
Fair Oaks Entertainments, PO Box 19, Ulverston, Cumbria CA12 9TF. *Proprietor/Manager: J G Livingstone.*
Friendly Overtures Ltd, 345 West Wycombe Road, High Wycombe, Bucks HP12 4AD. *Creative Director: Michael Batory.*
Global Music Limited, 171 Southgate Road, London N1 3LE. *Managing Director: Peter Knight Jr.*
Grade One Music, 34 Salisbury Street, London NW8 8QE. *Managing Director: Eliot Cohen.*
Gramavision, 78 Stanley Gardens, London W3 7SN. *General Manager: Guy Morris; Publishing Assistant: Anne Harrison.*
Grian Music, Cockenzie Business Centre, Edinburgh Road, Cockenzie, East Lothian EH32 0HL, Scotland. *Proprietor: Ian D Green.*
Harbourtown Music, PO Box 25, Ulverston, Cumbria LA12 7UN. *Managing Director: Gordon Jones.*
Hello Cutie Music Publications, Cadillac Ranch, Pencraig Uchaf, Cwm Bach, Whitland, Dyfed SA34 0DT, Wales. *Contacts: M Menendes and Christy French.*
Hit & Run Music (Publishing) Ltd, 30 Ives Street, London SW3 2ND. *Managing Director: Jon Crawley.*
Howard Jones Music Ltd, 33 Alexander Road, Aylesbury, Bucks HP20 2NR. *Administrator: David R Stopps.*
Jermaine Springer Publishing, PO Box 8969, London SE9 4ZB. *Director: Jermaine Springer.*
John Fiddy Music, Fruit Farm House, Foxton, Cambridge CB2 6RT. *Administrator: Cheryl Kenny.*
Josef Weinberger Ltd, 12-14 Mortimer Street, London W1N 7RD. *Promotion & Marketing: Sean Gray.*
Kassner Associated Publishers Limited, Exmouth House, 11 Pine Street, London EC1R 0JH. *Managing Director: David Kassner.*
Kinetix Music, The Black Office, DC Warehouse, Unit 6, Industrial Park, Maple Cross WD3 2AS. *Chairman: John Sharp.*
Lee Music, Stewart House, Hillbottom Road, Sands Industrial Estate, High Wycombe, Bucks HP12 4HJ. *International A&R and Company Lawyer: Keith Phillips.*
Leosong Copyright Service Limited, Greenland Place, 115-123 Bayham Street, Camden Town, London NW1 0AG. *Managing Director: Ray Ellis.*
Maecenas Europe Publishers, 5 Bushey Close, Old Barn Lane, Kenley, Surrey CR8 5AU. *Sales Manager: Alan Kirk.*
Magnum Music Group Ltd, High Street, Lane End, Bucks HP14 3JG. *Chairman: Nigel Molden.*
Maran Steele Music, Ellemford Farmhouse, Duns TD11 3SG, Scotland. *Managing Director: Hunter Steele.*
MCA Music, Elsinore House, 77 Fulham Palace Road, London W6 8JA. *Managing Director: Paul Connolly.*

Mcasso Music Productions Ltd, 9 Carnaby Street, London W1V 1PG. *Producer: Lisa McCaffery.*
Metro Music Publishers Ltd, Longriggs, Swalwell, Gateshead, Tyne & Wear NE99 1BB. *Director of Music Production: Jon Craig.*
Moggie Music Limited, 101 Hazelwood Lane, Palmers Green, London N13 5HQ. *Managing Director: Hal Carter.*
Moksha Management, PO Box 102, London E15 2HM. *Managing Director: Charles Colm.*
Moving Shadow Records, 1st + 2nd Floors, 17 St Anne's Court, Soho, London W1V 3AW. *Label Co-Ordinator: Caroline Bulter.*
Muirhead Music, 202 Fulham Road, Chelsea, London SW10 9PJ. *Chief Executive Officer: Dennis Muirhead.*
Music Collection International Ltd, 36-38 Caxton Way, Watford, Hertfordshire WD1 8UF. *Marketing Director: Danny Keene.*
Park Records, PO Box 651, Oxford OX2 9RB. *Managing Director: John Dagnell.*
Patterdale Music Ltd, 62 Pont Street Mews, Knightsbridge, London SW1X 0EF. *Managing Director: Bob Barratt.*
Paul Rodriguez Music Ltd, 42 Lucerne Road, London N5 1TZ. *Managing Director: Paul Rodriguez.*
Peermusic (UK) Ltd, Peer House, 8-14 Verulam Street, London WC1X 8LZ. *Managing Director: Nigel Elderton.*
Performance Equities Ltd, 112 A+B Westbourne Grove, Chepstow Road, London W2 5RU. *Managing Director: Paul Moore.*
Phantom Publishing, 59 Moore Park Road, London SW6 2HA. *Managing Director: Falcon Stuart.*
Pink Floyd Music Publishers, 27 Noel Street, London W1V 3RD. *Director: Peter Barnes.*
Pollytone Music, PO Box 124, Ruislip, Middlesex HA4 9BB. *Director: Valerie Bird.*
PolyGram International Music Publishing, 8 St James Square, London SW1Y 4JU. *Chief Executive: David Hockman.*
Red Bus Music (International) Ltd, 34 Salisbury Street, London NW8 8QE. *Managing Director: Eliot M Cohen.*
Rive-Droite UK Ltd, 166 Upper Richmond Road, London SW15 2SH. *Music Director: Brian Rawling.*
Robert Kingston (Music) Ltd, 43 Fairfield Road, Uxbridge, Middlesex UB8 1AZ. *Managing Director: R C Kingston.*
Rondor Music, Rondor House, 10A Parsons Green, London SW6 4TW. *Managing Director: Stuart Hornall.*
R T L Music, Stewart House, Hill Bottom Road, Sands Industrial Estate, High Wycombe HP12 4HJ. *Owner and Producer: Ron Lee.*
Rykomusic Ltd, 78 Stanley Gardens, London W3 7SZ. *General Manager: Guy Morris.*
Satellite Music Limited, 34 Salisbury Street, London NW8 8QE. *Managing Director: Eliot M Cohen.*
Scotford Music, 13 Winton Park, Edinburgh EH10 7EX, Scotland. *Proprietor/Manager: Gerry Ford.*
Sea Dream Music, 236 Sebert Road, Forest Gate, London E7 0NP. *Senior Partner: Simon Law.*
Seriously Groovy Music Ltd, 3rd Floor, 28 D'Arblay Street, Soho, London W1V 3FH. *Director: Dave Holmes.*
Songs for Today Inc, PO Box 130, Hove, East Sussex BN3 6QU. *Director of Administration: Roland Rogers.*
Sony Music Publishing, 13 Great Marlborough Street, London W1V 2LP. *Managing Director: Blair McDonald.*
Soundtrack Music Publishing, 22 Ives Street, London SW3 2ND. *Contact: Olaf Wyper.*
Start Audio & Video, Suite 20A, Canada House, Blackburn Road, London NW6 1RZ. *Sales and Commercial Manager: Brian Atkinson.*
Studio G Ltd, Ridgway House, Great Brington, Northampton NN7 4JA. *Managing Director: John Gale.*
S W Music (UK), 48 Fernside Road, Poole, Dorset BH15 2JJ. *Managing Director: Dave Dacosta.*
Sylvantone Music, 17 Allerton Grange Way, Leeds LS17 6LP. *Proprietor: Tony Goodacre.*
TKO Music Publishing Ltd, PO Box 130, Hove, East Sussex BN3 6QU. *Director of Administration: Roland Rogers.*
Tonecolor Ltd, The Studio, Yew Tree Farm, Charing Heath, Kent TN27 0AU. *Managing Director: S Jackson.*
Unity Music Publishing, John Henry Bldg, 16/24 Brewery Road, London N7 9NH. *Manager - Sales & Retail: Pepin Clout.*
Universal Songs, 51 Dorlcote Road, London SW18 3RT. *Contact: Pierre Tubbs.*
Vinyl Japan (UK) Ltd, 281 Camden High Street, London NW1 7BX. *Manager: Patrick James.*
Warlock Music Ltd, 78 Stanley Gardens, London, W3 7SZ. *General Manager: Guy Morris.*
Warner Chappell Music, 129 Park Street, London W1Y 3FA. *Managing Director: Ed Heine.*
Whole Armor/Full Armor, PO Box 130, Hove, East Sussex BN3 6QU. *Director of Administration: Roland Rogers.*
Windswept Pacific, 27 Queensdale Place, London W11 4SQ. *Contact: Debbie Miles.*
Wot Films & Music, Suite 3, 44 Mortimer Street, London W1N 7DG. *Producer: Jackie Thomas.*
Zomba Music Publishers, Zomba House, 165-167 High Road, London NW10 2SG. *Managing Director: Steven Howard.*

UKRAINE

Muzychna Ukraina, Pushkinska St 32, 252 004 Kiev. *Managing Director: Mykola Lynnyk.*
Ukrainian Musical Information Centre, Richkova St 4, 252 135 Kiev. *Managing Director: Sergiy Galuzin.*

USA

Arista Music Publishing, 8370 Wilshire Blvd, 3rd Floor, Beverly Hills, CA 90211. *Contact: Judy Hicks.*
Ashleigh Publishing, PO Box 76507, Washington DC 20013. *President: Carl Bentley.*
Axbar Records, PO Box 12353, San Antonio, TX 78212. *Producer/General Manager: Joe Scates.*
Bekool Music Group, 23 Music Square East, #101, Nashville, TN 37203. *President: Pat McKool.*
Benson Music Group Inc, 365 Great Circle Road, Nashville, TN 37228. *International Sales: Janice Cuttler.*
Betty Jane/Josie Jane Music Pub Co, 7400 N Adams Road, North Adams, MI 49262. *President: Claude E Reed.*
Bivens Music, 203 Gates Drive, Hendersonville, TN 37075-4961. *Owner: Ernie Bivens.*
Bloozy Publishing, 542 Prospect Avenue #1, Brooklyn, NY 11215. *Contact: Michael Stevens.*
BMG Music Publishing, 1 Music Circle N, Nashville, TN 37203. *Contact: Henry Hurt.*
Bob Scott Frick Enterprises, 404 Bluegrass Avenue, Madison, TN 37115. *President: Bob Frick.*
Bob White Music Inc, 212 Morrison Street, McMinnville, TN 37110. *President & Chief Executive Officer: Thomas B Vaughn.*
Cactus & Winnebago Music Publishing, PO Box 1027, Neenah, WI 54957-1027. *President: Tony Ansems.*
Carl Fischer Inc, 62 Cooper Square, New York, NY 10003. *Vice President of Publishing: Lauren Keiser.*
Cat's Voice Productions, PO Box 1361, Sanford, ME 04073-7361. *Owner: Tom Reeves.*
Cavet-Vanderpool Publ/BMI, 1030 Villa Place, Nashville, TN 37212. *President: Vera Cavet Vanderpool.*
Center for The Queen of Peace, 3350 Highway 6, Suite 412, Sugar Land, TX 77478. *Director: Rafael Brom.*
Cerebral Records, 1236 Laguna Drive, Carlsbad, CA 92008. *President: Lincoln Kroll; Publicist: Carol Leno.*
Chapel Music Group Inc, 2021 Richard Jones Road, Suite 180, Nashville, TN 37215. *Director of Marketing: Heather Campbell.*
Charisma Music Publishing Co Inc, 1841 Broadway, Suite 411, New York, NY 10023. *President: Julie Lipsivs.*
Christmas and Holiday Music, 3517 Warner Blvd, Suite 4, Burbank, CA 91505-4636. *President: Justin Wilde.*
Cosmotone Records, 3350 Highway 6, Suite 412, Sugar Land, TX 77478. *President: Rafael Brom.*
Cude & Pickens Music Publishing, 519 North Halifax Ave, Daytona Beach, FL 32118. *Chief Executive Officer: Bobby Lee Cude.*
Dancefloor Distribution, 95 Cedar Lane, Englewood, NJ 07631. *President: Jeffrey Collins.*
De Stijl Music (BMI), PO Box 170206, San Francisco, CA 94117-0206.
Disney Music Publishing Group, 350 S Buena Vista Street, Burbank, CA 91521. *Vice-President: Susan Borgeson.*
Diva Entertainment World, 853 Broadway #1516, New York City, NY 10003. *Managing Director: Marc Krasnow.*
Edensong, PO Box 34, Days Creek, OR 97429. *Owner: Rick Foster.*
EMI / Virgin Music, 827 N Hilldale Avenue, West Hollywood, CA 90069. *Vice-President: Susan Collins.*
Energy Productions Inc, 234 6th Avenue, Brooklyn, NY 11215. *President: Michael Knuth.*
Eternal Song Agency, 6326 E Livingston Avenue, Reynoldsburg, OH 43068. *President: Leopold Xavier Crawford.*

FAME Recording Studios, PO Box 2527, Muscle Shoals, AL 35662. *Studio Manager: Rodney Hall.*
Faniork Music BMI, 23797 Via Irana Valencia, CA 91355. *Owner: Don Lee.*
Fiesta City Publishers, PO Box 5861, Santa Barbara, CA 93150-5861. *President: Frank E Cooke.*
Five Roses Music Group, 34A Lanier Road, Studio 1, Jekyll Island, GA 31527. *President: Sammie Lee Marler.*
Five Star Music Inc, 40 Music Square East, Nashville, TN 37203. *Contact: Guy Parker.*
Flat Town Music Co, PO Drawer 10, 238 E Main St, Ville Platte, LA 70586. *President: Floyd Soileau.*
Folklore Music, 1671 Appian Way, Santa Monica, CA 90401. *Manager: Mitch Greenhill.*
GBS Music, 203 Gates Drive, Hendersonville, TN 37075-4961. *Owner: Ernie Bivens.*
Gramophone Music Co, PO Box 921, Beverly Hills, CA 90213. *General Manager: O Berliner.*
Group Productions, 2890 N Monroe Avenue, Box 481, Loveland, CO 80234. *Contact: Steve Saavedra.*
Hall of Fame Music Co, PO Box 921, Beverly Hills, CA 90213. *General Manager: O Berliner.*
Heartbeat Music, PO Box 294, Westerville, OH 43086-0294. *President/Owner: Randy Kettering.*
Heartwrite Music, PO Box 1739, Texarkana, AR 75504. *President: David Patillo.*
Hidden Pun Music Inc, 1841 Broadway, Suite 411, New York, NY 10023. *President: Julie Lipsivs.*
High Kite Productions & Publishing, 1245 Elizabeth St, Denver, CO 80206. *Owner/President: Henry "Broz" Rowland.*
Hit & Run Music Publishing Inc, 1841 Broadway, Suite 411, New York, NY 10023. *President: Julie Lipsivs.*
Jon Music, BMI, PO Box 233, 329 N Main Street, Church Point, LA 70525. *Owner: Lee Lavergne.*
Justice Music Corporation, 11586 Blix Street, North Hollywood, CA 91602. *Executive Vice President: Monte R Thomas.*
Ketter Entertainment, PO Box 740702, San Diego, CA 92174-0702. *President/Chief Executive Officer: Al Ketter.*
Lieber & Stoller Music Publishers, 9000 Sunset Blvd, Suite 1107, Los Angeles, CA 90069. *General Manager: Randy Poe.*
Lipservices, 9 Prospect Park West, Room 14B, Brooklyn, NY 11215-1741. *President: Julie Lipsivs.*
Little Big Town Music, 803 18th Avenue South, Nashville, TN 37203. *President: Wendy Bomar.*
Loud Cry Music Pub Co, PO Box 210270, Nashville, TN 37221-0270. *Owner/President: Don Sanders.*
MCA Music Publishing, 1114 17th Avenue South, Nashville, TN 37212. *Vice President/General Manager: Stephen Day.*
Metrostar Music, PO Box 5807, Englewood, NJ 07631. *General Manager: Philip S Kurnit.*
Mia Mind Music, 500½ East 84th Street, Suite #4B, New York, NY 10028-7368. *Chief Executive Officer: Steven Bentzel.*
MNM Music Group Inc, 1410 2nd Street, Suite 300, Santa Monica, CA 90401. *President: Nick Martinelli.*
Moller Digital Publishing, 17176 Grand Avenue, Lake Elsinore, CA 92530. *Sales Manager - Marketing: Irma Moller.*
More Brand Music Publishing, BMI, PO Box 1027, Neenah, WI 54957-1027. *President: Rita Ansems.*
Music Sales Corporation, 257 Park Avenue South, 20th Floor, New York, NY 10010. *President: Barrie Edwards.*
The Music Umbrella, PO Box 1067, Santa Monica, CA 90406. *President/Chief Executive Officer: Glenn H Friedman.*
Namax Music Publishing, PO Box 24162, Richmond, VA 23224. *President: Nanette Brown.*
Pal Productions Co, PO Box 80691, Baton Rouge, LA 70898. *President: Johnny R Palazzotto.*
Pathway Music dba, PO Box 2250, Cleveland, TN 37320-2250. *Co-Ordinator of Music: Charles Towler; Copyright Supervisor: Connie Caldwell.*
Peermusic, 8159 Hollywood Blvd, Los Angeles, CA 90069. *Chief Operating Officer/Snr Vice President: Kathy Spanberger.*
Peermusic, 810 Seventh Avenue, New York, NY 10019. *Chief Operating Officer/Snr Vice President: Kathy Spanberger.*
Peridot Music Co, PO Box 8846, Cranston, RI 02920. *President: Amy Parravano.*
PKM Music, PO Box 5807, Englewood, NJ 07631. *Partner: Philip S Kurnit.*
Platinum Gold Productions, 9200 Sunset Blvd, Suite 1220, Los Angeles, CA 90069. *Partner: Steve Cohen.*
PolyGram Music Publishing Group, 825 8th Avenue, New York, NY 10019. *Creative Directors: Randy Sabiston, Dwayne Alexander.*
PPL-MCI Entertainment Group, 10 Universal Plaza, PO Box 8442, Universal City, CA 91618. *Managing Director: Maxx Diamond.*
Pravda Records Inc, 3823 N Southport, Chicago, IL 60613. *Managing Director: Kenneth Goudman.*
Pride Music Group, PO Box 120249, Nashville, TN 37212. *Administrative Director: Tamera N Petrash.*
Quango Music Group Inc, 9744 Wilshire Blvd, #305, Beverly Hills, CA 90212. *President: George Chiz.*
Rising Star Music Publishers, 52 Executive Park South, Suite 5203, Atlanta, GA 30329. *Editor: Pat Nugent.*
Rondor Music International, 360 N La Cienega Blvd, Los Angeles, CA 90048. *Manager: Candi Brown.*
Rustron Music Publishers, c/o The Whimsy, 1156 Park Lane, West Palm Beach, FL 33417. *Executive Director: Rusty Gordon.*
Set A Record Publishing, 720 North Roosevelt St, Cherokee, IA 51012. *Manager: Frank Gallagher.*
Shawnee Press Inc, 49 Waring Drive, Delaware Water Gap, PA 18327. *Director of Sales: Dennis Bell.*
Sikio Marika Records, 6840 N Maple #157, Fresno, CA 93710. *Label Head: Tyrone White.*
Single Kick Music, PO Box 8243, Calabasas, CA 91372. *Proprietor: Cho Paquet.*
Songs For Today, 15 Rolling Way, New York City, NY 10956-6912. *Chairman: Jeffrey Kruger.*
Sony Music Publishing, 666 5th Avenue, PO Box 4451, New York, NY 10101-4451. *Director of Creative Affairs: Pati deVries.*
Spencer Ministries, 2225 Amoy West Road, Mansfield, OH 44903. *Executive Director: David Conner.*
Sublime Music, 15 Rolling Way, New York City, NY 10956-6912. *Chairman: Jeffrey Kruger.*
Tedesco Tunes, 16020 Lahey Street, Granada Hills, CA 91344. *President: Dale T Tedesco.*
Terra Nova Recording Company, 853 Broadway, #1516, New York, NY 10003. *President: Marc Krasnow; Chief Executive Officer: Robert Mangovleff.*
TKO Publishing Inc, 15 Rolling Way, New York City, NY 10956-6912. *Chairman: Jeffrey Kruger.*
Tranquil Technology Music, PO Box 20463, Oakland, CA 94620. *Producer: Michael Mantra.*
TurnerSong, 4263 San Jose Blvd, Jacksonville, FL 32207-6342. *Partner: Lee Turner.*
ViRay Publishing, BMI/Kerryray Publishing, 22432 Bayberry, Mission Viejo, CA 92692. *President: Randy Ray.*
Vokes Music, Record & Promotion Co, PO Box 12, New Kensington, PA 15068-0012. *President: Howard Vokes.*
Warner Chappell Music Inc, 10585 Santa Monica Blvd, Los Angeles, CA 90025-4950. *Senior Vice-President: Rick Shoemaker.*
Westwood Entertainment Group, 1115 Inman Avenue, Suite 330, Edison, NJ 08820-1132. *General Manager: Elena Petillo.*
Wilcom Publishing, PO Box 4456, West Hills, CA 91308. *Owner: William Clark.*
Windswept Pacific Entertainment Co, 9320 Wilshire Blvd, Suite 200, Beverly Hills, CA 90212. *President: Evan R Medow.*
Winston Music Publishers, 1680 N Vine Street, Suite 318, Hollywood, CA 90028. *President: Lynne Robin Green.*
Woodrich Enterprises Inc, PO Box 38, Lexington, AL 35648. *President: Woody Richardson.*
Xmas Music, PO Box 828, Hollywood, CA 90028. *President: Randall Paul.*
Zettitalia Music International, PO Box 8224, Universal City, CA 91618. *President/Chief Executive Officer: Suzette Cuseo-Jarrett.*
Zomba Enterprises Inc, 137-139 W 25th Street, New York, NY 10001. *Snr Vice President: David Renzer.*

VENEZUELA

Distribuidora Sonografica CA, Dolores a Pte Soublette, Edif. Centro Empresarial Sur 4, Qta. Crespo. Caracas. *General Manager: Guillermo Urbano Mijares.*

APPENDIX E
FESTIVALS AND EVENTS

AUSTRALIA

Adelaide Fringe Festival
Lion Arts Centre, Cnr North Terrace & Morphett Street, Adelaide, SA 5000.
Australia's largest fringe festival, held Feb-March.
Director: Malcolm Blaycock.

Big Day Out
212 Palmer Street, East Sydney, NSW 2010.
National alternative music event, held annually in January.
Contact: The Producers.

Brisbane Biennial International Music Festival
Level 2, 75 Grey Street, South Brisbane, QLD 4101.
Next festival will take place from May to June.
Chief Executive Officer: Nicholas Heyward.

Brisbane's World Of Music Festival
120 Main Street, Kangaroo Point, QLD4169.
World Music festival, Held at end of October.
Director: Christopher Bowen.

East Coast Blues Festival
PO Box 97, Byron Bay, NSW 2481.
Festival of Blues & Roots music held each Easter for the past 6 years.
Director Co Producer: Keven Oxford.

Festival Of Perth
3 Crawley Avenue, Crawley, WA 6009.
Multi-arts festival held Feb-March.
Director: David Blenkinsop.

Highfield Music Festival
c/o B & S Promotions, Bears Choice Music & Entertainment, PO Box 1481 Frankston, VIC 3199.
Festival co-ordinators providing live to music to venues.
Partners: Bill and Sally Dettmer.

Melbourne Music Festival
62-74 Pickles Street, S Melbourne, VIC 3205.
Australia's largest contemporary music festival. Held in February.
Executive Producer: Dobe Newton.

Moomba Festival
117 Sturt Street, S Melbourne, VIC 3205.
Australia's largest outdoor festival. Held annually in mid-March.
Directors: Bob Burton, Maria Katsonis

Port Fairy Folk Festival
PO Box 991, Geelong, VIC 3220.
Nation's premier world and folk music event.
Festival Director: Jamie McKew.

Sydney Festival
Level II, 31 Market Street, Sydney, NSW 2000.
Festival Director: Anthony Steel.

Tamworth Country Music Festival
Tamworth City Council, PO Box 555, Tamworth, NSW 2340.
Annual Country Music festival held in January, incorporating the Golden Guitar Awards.

WOMAD Adelaide
King William Street, Adelaide SA 5000.
World music event as part of the International series of concerts.
Artistic Director: Rob Brookman.

AUSTRIA

Artclub Festival Imst
Postgasse 9, A-6460 Imst.
Open air rock festival.
A&R Manager: Arin Schrott.

Kultodrom
Mistelhach.
Held 14-16 June .
Contact: Otmar Biringer.

Rock At The Border
Weitaer Strasse 104, A-3950 Gmünd.
Open-air rock festival held in the second week of August.
Chairman: Gerard Simon.

Sommer Rock Festival
Hauptstrasse 140, A-7203 Wiesen.
Open-air pop and indie music festival, held on last weekend of July.
Chairman: Ewald Tartar.

Sunspalsh Festival
Hauptstrasse 140, A-7203 Wiesen.
Open-air reggae festival held on the last weekend of August.
Chairman: Ewald Tartar.

Transmitter
ImSohl 1, A-6845 Hohenems.
Avant-garde festival held in the first week of July.
Director: Bernahrd Amann.

BELGIUM

AALN International
PB 15, Antwerpen 17, B-2018 Anvers.
Jazz, blues and world music events.
Managing Director: Luc Nuitten.

Belga Jazz Festival
c/o Jazzronaute, 34 Rue Africaine, B-1050 Brussels.
Jazz and blues festival held October-November.
Manager: Jean-Michel de Bie.

Belgium Rhythm N Blues Festival
c/o Breakaway Vzw, Postbus 43, B-3990 Peer.
R'n'B festival held in July.
Managing Director: Misjel Daniels.

Boogietown Festival
Fruithoflaan 124 Bus 11, B-2600 Berchem, Antwerp.
Blues Festival held in May every year.
Directors: Peter Verstraelen and Frederic Marechal.

Dour Music Festival
10 Rue du Marché, B-7370 Dour.
Pop music festival featuring rock, pop and rap.
Managing Director: Carlo di Antonio.

European Forum of Worldwide Music Festivals
J F Willemsstraat 10
B2530 Boechout
Secretary: Patrick de Groote.

Jazz A Liege
18 Blvd d'Avroy, B-4000 Liege.
Jazz festival held in May.
Chairman: Jean-Marie Peterken

Leffinge Leuren
c/o Leernsestwg 168, B-9800 Deimze.
International festival featuring all styles of music, held in September.
Director: Jean Tant.

Marktrock
Postbus 21, B-3000 Louvain 1.
Festival of rock, pop and blues music with 10 stages.
Managing Director: Omer Hoyelaerts.

Nandrin Rock Festival
10 Rue de Fort, B-1060 Brussels
Chairman: Pilippe Decoster.

On The Rox
Kleine Gentstraat 46, B-9051 Ghent SDW.
International rock festival.
Managing Director: Chris Verleyen.

Schrikkelpop Festival
Fruithoflaan 12G, Bus 11, B-2600 Berchem, Antwerp.
Alternative Music festival held in early August.
Directors: Peter Verstraelen and Johan Pelgrims.

Sfinks Festival
J F Willemsstraat 10, B-2530 Boechout.
Annual worldwide music festival. Held July .
Director: Patrick de Groote.

Torhout-Werchter
Beverlaat 3, B-3118 Werchter.
International rock festival held on the first weekend of July.
Chairman: Herman Schueremans.

BULGARIA

Bourgas Blues Festival
Leten Teater, Studio Goresht Piasak, 8000 Bourgas.
Open-air blues festival held in August.
Director: Roumen Yanev.

Country Festival Society 'Costar'
23 Metodi Popov str, 1113 Sofia
President: Constantin Baharov.

Sofia Country Festival
23 Metodi Popov Str, 1113 Sofia.
Leading International Country Music festival.
Manager: Decho Taralezhkov.

Varna Folk Festival
Varna Municipality, Culture Dept, 43 Osmi Primorski Polk, Varna 9000.
International Folk Festival. Held in August .

Varna Jazz Festival
Varna Municipality, Culture Dept, 43 Osmi Primorski Polk, Varna 9000.
International Jazz Festival. Held July-August .

CANADA

Beaches International Jazz Festival
1976A Queen Street E, Toronto, ON M4L 1H8.
Week long festival. Held in July .
President: Lido Chilelli.

Big Valley Jamboree
1042 Winnipeg Street, Regina, SK S4R 8P8.
Country Music festival.
Executive Producer: Alan Vinet.

Calgary International Jazz Festival
PO Box 2735 Station M, Calgary, AB T2P 3C2.
Two-day outdoor event.

Canadian Music Festival
c/o Chart Toppers, 106-5397 Eglinton Avenue W, Toronto ON M9C 5K6.
Event featuring Canadian artists.

Du Maurier Ltd Downtown Jazz Festival
366 Adelaide Street E, Suite #230, Toronto, Ontario M5A 3X9.
Annual jazz festival. Held June-July .
Director of Marketing & Communications: Bob McCullough.

Du Maurier Ltd International Jazz Festival
c/o Coastal Jazz and Blues Society, 435 West Hastings Street, Vancouver, BC V6B 1L4.
Annual Jazz festival.
Executive Director: Robert Kerr

Edmonton Folk Festival
PO Box 4130, Edmonton, AB T6E 4T2.
4-day music festival held annually in August.

Festival International de Jazz de Montreal
822 Sherbrook E, Montreal, PQ H2L 1K4.
Largest Jazz festival in North America, held in July.

Folk on the Rocks
PO Box 326, Yellowknife, NWT X1A 2N7.
Three day music festival.
Treasurer: Vicki Tompkins.

JUNO Awards
c/o CARAS
124 Merton Street, 3rd Floor
Toronto, ON M4S 2Z2.
Annual awards for outstanding Canadian achievement in the field of recorded music.

Mariposa Folk Festival
786 Dundas Street E, Toronto, ON M4M 1R1.
Traditional and Contemporary Folk festival.

Mill Race Festival of Traditional Folk Music
PO Box 22148, Galt Central PO, Cambridge, ON N1R 8E3.
Festival of traditional folk music and dance.
Chair/Artistic Director: Brad McEwen.

Musicfest Canada
200, 1400 1st Street, SW, Calgary, AB T2R 0V8.
National music festival.
Executive Director: Jim Howard.

Music West
#306, 21 Water Street, Vancouver, BC V6B 1A1.
Annual music conference and festival held in May.
Producer: Maureen Jack.

Ottawa International Jazz Festival
PO Box 3104 Station D, Ottawa, ON K1P 6H7.
Jazz festival with emphasis on Canadian talent.

St Jean-Baptiste Festival
Société des mélomanes (Canada) Inc, 1056 Burnaby Street, Suite 201, Vancouver, BC V6E 1N7.
Director: Eugène Evans.

Summerfolk Music & Crafts Festival
Box 521, Oven Sound, ON N4K 5R1
Festival held the third weekend of August every year. Held in August .
Promotion Co-Ordinator: Linda Ashley.

Under The Volcano Festival of Art & Social Change
#21552, 1850 Commercial Drive, Vancouver, BC V5N 4A0.
Annual music and arts event held since 1990.
Co-Ordinating Collective Member: Irwin Oostindie.

Vancouver Folk Music Festival
Box 381, 916 W Broadway, Vancouver, BC V5Z 1K7.
Four day folk/world music festival held in Jericho Beach Park.
General Manager: Brent Gibson.

Winnipeg Folk Festival
264 Taché Avenue, Winnipeg, MB R2W 1Z9.
Folk music festival takes place during second weekend in May.
Executive Director: Pierre Guerim.

Wye Marsh Festival
Music Committee, Wye Marsh Wildlife Centre, PO Box 100, Midland, ON L4R 4K6.
Annual wildlife festival which includes a folk music component.
Contact: Music Committee.

CROATIA

B P Club Jazz Festivals
Teslina 7, Zagreb.
Two annual jazz festivals
Contact: Boško Petrović.

Croatian Festival Of Pop Music - Split
c/o Dalmaciakoncert, Trg Republike 1/11, 58000 Split.
Pop Festival held in July.
Managing Director: Ivica Vrkic.

HTF
c/o Croatian Television, Prisavlje 3, 10000 Zagreb.
National contest for Eurovision Song Contest.
Producer: Aleksandar Kostadino.

ZagrebFest
c/o Alta, Berislaviceva 9, HDS, 41000 Zagreb.
Pop Festival held in mid-December.
Managing Director: Drago Diklic.

DENMARK

Aarhus Festival
Thomas Jensens Alle, DK-8000 C Aarhus.
Festival held in the first week of September.
Administration: Ib Christiansen.

Copenhagen Jazz Festival
Kjled Langes Gade 4A, DK-1367 K Copenhagen.
Festival of Jazz, Blues and World Music held in July.
Manager: Bodil Jacobsen.

Esbjerg Open Air
SHB - Soeren Hoejberg Booking ApS, Frodesgade 74, DK-6700 Esbjerg.
One day open air festival held in August.
Managing Director: Soeren Hoejberg.

Esbjerg Rock Festival
SHB - Soeren Hoejberg Booking ApS, Frodesgade 74, DK-6700 Esbjerg.
Open air festival held on the first weekend of June.
Managing Director: Soeren Hoejberg.

Esbjerg 60's Festival
SHB - Soeren Hoejberg Booking ApS, Frodesgade 74, DK-6700 Esbjerg.
One day festival taking place in Spring.
Managing Director: Soeren Hoejberg.

Images of Africa
Copenhagen.
Held June - July .
Contact: Lene Thiesen.

Midtfyns Festival
Laessoegade 78 st, DK-5230 M Odense.
Rock, Pop and Folk Music festival held in June-July.
Managing Director: Nina Faergeremann.

Roskilde Festival
Havsteensvej 11, DK-4000 Roskilde.
Four day music festival.
General Manager: Leif Skov.

Skagen Festival
PO Box 33, DK-9990 Skagen.
Programme Director: Peer Løgsted Andersen.

Skanderborg Festival
c/o J P Management, Jernbanevej 22, DK-8660 Skanderborg
Festival of Folk, Pop, Jazz and Rock music held in August.
Managing Director: J P Andersen

Tivoli Festival
Vesterbrogade 3, DK 1630 Copenhagen V

Tønder Festival Foundation
Vestergade 80, DK-6270 Tønder.
Folk music festival since 1975.
Festival Director: Carsten Panduro.

Worldwide Music Expo - Womex
Copenhagen.
Held in October.
Contact: Organization Office: EFWMF.

ESTONIA

Ollefestival
PO Box 2907, Tallina Peapostkontor, Tatari 23, EE-0090 Tallinn.
Pop Music festival held late June-early July.
Promoter: Lauri Viikna.

Pärnu Jazz
Papiniidu 50, EE-3600 Pärnu.
International beachtown summer festival held in July.
Festival Director: Tiit Lauk.

Rock Summer Festival
PO Box 3333, Regati Pst 1-6K, EE-0019 Tallinn.
Rock festival, held in July.
Manager: Martti Kitsing.

Tartu Jazz
Laulupeo 25, EE-2400 Tartu.
International outdoor festival of traditional and modern jazz held in Mid-July.
Festival Arena Manager: Aadu Birnbaum.

Tartu Rock Festival
Laulupeo 25, EE-2400 Tartu.
Outdoor festival, mainly Estonian artists with some foreign guest musicians.
Festival Arena Manager: Aadu Birnbaum.

Tudengijazz
PO Box 3641, EE-0090 Tallinn.
International student jazz festival held in February.
Manager: Reimo Unt.

FINLAND

April Jazz Espoo
Ahertajantie 6 B, FIN-02100 Espoo.
International indoors jazz festival, with special focus on vocal and big band jazz.
Held in April.
Contact: Martti Lappaiainen.

Baltic Jazz
Kålabacksvågen 1, FIN-25900 Taalintehdas.
National and international swing and traditional jazz event held in July.
Contact: Magi Kulla.

EloJazz&Blues
Kaislatie 9 M 2, FIN-90160 Oulu.
National outdoors and indoors jazz festival held in late July, covering all styles.
Contact: Kari Kesti.

Etinosoi!
Helsinki.
Held in November .
Contact: Anu Laakkonen.

Finnish National Jazz Days
PO Box 54, FIN-00101 Helsinki.
Annual national jazz festival, involving all styles, held in a different town each year (recently held in Helsinki and Jyväskylä). Held in November.
Contact: Finnish Jazz Federation.

Global Music Centre
Mikkolantie 17, FIN-00640 Helsinki.
Director: Anu Laakkonen.

Helsinki Festival
Rauhankatu 7 E, FIN-00170 Helsinki.
Festival of Jazz, Pop, Rock, Ethnic music. Held August - September .
Artistic Director: Esa-Pekka Salonen.

Imatra Big Band Festival
PO Box 22, FIN-55101 Imatra.
National and international outdoors/indoors festival of all jazz styles with special interest in big band music. Held June - July.

Jazz at the Market Place
Vesijärvenkatu 20, FIN-15140 Lahti
National outdoor jazz festival held in mid-August.
Contact: Martti Peippo.

Jazz on the Beach
Kauppakatu 23, FIN-92100 Raahe.
National and international outdoors/indoors festival featuring all jazz styles. Held late July.
Contact: Pertti Kinnunen.

KaamosJazz (Jazz Under Northern Lights)
FIN-99695 Tankavaara.
National indoors jazz festival. Held in late November.
Contact: Kauko Lainonen.

Kainuu Jazz Spring
Kalliokatu 7, FIN-87100 Kajaani.
International indoors event with all jazz styles, held in May.
Contact: Unto Tomiainen.

Kalott Jazz & Blues, Tornio-Haaparanta (Sweden)
Hallituskatu 9, FIN-95400 Tornio.
All jazz styles and blues. National, international and Scandinavian acts. Held late June.
Contact: Tornio City Cultural Bureau.

Kaustinen Folk Music Festival
Kaustinen.
Held in July.
Contact: Jyrki Heiskanen.

Keitele Jazz
Humpinkatu 4 A, FIN-44120 Äänekoski.
All jazz styles featured in a national and international event held in July.
Contact: Kalevi Plattonen.

Kerava Jazz
Asemantie 4, FIN-04200 Kerava.
International modern and contemporary jazz festival. Held in early June.
Contact: Kerava City Cultural Bureau.

Nummirock
FIN-61910 Nummijärvi.
Rock festival held midsummer.

Pori International Jazz Festival
Eteläranta 6, FIN-28100 Pori.
All jazz, rhythm 'n' blues and rock styles. International open-air event held July.
Contact: Jyrki Kangas.

Provinssirock
PO Box 180, FIN-60101 Seinäjoki
Rock festival held in early June.

Ruisrock
Uudenmaankatu 1, FIN-20500 Turku.
Rock festival staged by the sea in Turku and has attendance figures close to 25,000. Held in mid- summer.
Contact: Turku Music Festival Foundation.

Ruska-Swing
Oy Yleisradio Ab, PL 64, FIN-98101 Kemijärvi.
National swing and traditional jazz event. Held in September.
Contact: Pekka Lintula.

Tampere Jazz Happening
Tullikamarinaukio 2, FIN-38100 Tampere.
International contemporary and modern jazz indoor festival. Held October-November.
Contact: Aila Manninen.

Turku Jazz Festival
Uudenmaankatu 1, FIN-20500 Turku.
National and international festival, with mainly contemporary jazz styles, held in March.
Contact: Rainer Koski.

Ylläs Jazz Blues
FIN-95970 Äkäslompolo.
All jazz and rhythm'n'blues styles. National and international acts featured. Held in February.
Contact: Pirkko Hietaniemi.

FRANCE

Africolor
145 Rue de Ménilmontant, F-75020 Paris.
Music festival focused on music from Western Africa and Indian Ocean. Held in December.
Artistic Director: Philippe Conrath.

Banlieues Blues
9 Avenue Berlioz, F-93270 Sevran.
Jazz and blues events throughout Paris in March and April.
Director: Jacques Pornon.

Carnavalorock
9 Rue Galis Bizoin, F-22000 St Brieuc.
Festival held in April - May.
Chairman: Sam Burlot.

Concours de Piano Jazz Martial Solal
Acanthes, 3 Rue des Couronnes, F-75020 Paris.
International jazz piano competition held in late September. First prize of 70,000 F and engagements at a number of festivals.

Festival d'Ete de Nantes
Nantes.
Held in July.
Contact: Bertrand de Laporte.

Festival International de Jazz Antibes
Office du Tourisme,11 Place de Gaulle, F-06000 Antibes.
Open-air Jazz festival held in July.
Director: Jean-Pierre Gonzalez.

Festival International de Guitares de Vittel
BP 698, Porte de la Craffe, F-54043 Nancy.
Guitar festival held in June.
Contact: Marc Leonard.

Festival "Les Allumees"
CRDC, BP 389, F-44013 Nantes.
All styles of popular music and video, DJ's party and events (dance, theatre) and soul and cyber café.
Artistic Director: Eric Boistard.

Festival National de Blues
c/o Association "Clin d'Oreille", Hotel de Ville, F-71200 Le Creusot.
Annual festival held in July in Burgundy.
President: Renee Cerruti; Artistic Director: Emilio Armilles.

Festival "Synthese"
Institut International de Musique Electroacoustique, BP 39 - 18001 Bourges Cedex.
Festival of electro-acoustic music held in the 1st week of June.

Fiesta des Suds
Latinissimo, BP 121, F-13473 Marseille.
Director: Florence Chastanier.

Jazz A Manosque
Service Culturel, Hotel de Ville, F-04100 Manosque.
10 day festival held in the 2nd fortnight in July.
Directeur: M Gerard Ollivier.

Les Nuits Atypiques
Langon.
Held July - August.
Contact: Patrick Lavaud.

Les 24 Heures de l'Insa
Amicale des élèves INSA, Bâtiment B2, Avenue de Rangueil, F-31077 Toulouse.
Annual student festival held inMay.
Contact: Guilhem Ensuque.

Musiques Métisses
Angouléme.
Held 22-26 May .
Contact: Christian Mousset.

Nice Jazz Festival
c/o Nice Jazz Productions, 7 Place de Seoul, F-75014 Paris.
Annual Jazz festival held in July.
Director: Luc Gavrichon.

Octob'rock
115 reu Lesage, F-5110 Reims.
Organizer and Promoter of concerts including the Rock Festival held in October each year.
President: Alain Boucheron.

Open Du Rock Du Dijon
Festirock Organization, Parc Tertiaire Dijon Est, 2 bis Rue du Cap Vert, F-21800 Quetigny
European discovery festival.
President: G Gras.

Pro Jazz
10 avenue des 27 Martyrs, 78400 Chatou.
President: Pierre Dieuzey

Rock 'n' Solex
c/o Amicale de Eleves INSA, 20 Avenue des Buttes de Coësmes, F-35043 Rennes Cedex.
Organizer of the Rennes two-day rock festival.
President: Nicolas Orhon.

Sa Pon de La Musique Music Expo 96
OIP, 62 Rue de Chirmesuel, F-75008 Paris.
Exhibitors of instruments, instrument makers, distributors, music schools and score editors.
Show Managers: Jessie Westeaholz and B Corbel.

GERMANY

Afrika Festival
Würzburg.
Held in May.
Contact: Stefan Oschmann.

Ålandia Jazz
Nachtigallensteg 3, D-23611 Bad Schwartau.
National/international festival includes all jazz styles. Held in July.
Contact: Christer Mörn.

Berlin Independence Days
Köpenicker Str 6, D-10997 Berlin.
Held in October.
Contacts: Michael Betz.

Freestyle eV.
Morgensternweg 7, D-22305 Hamburg.
Music festival and event organisers.
Contact: Helmut Heuer.

Heimatklänge
Berlin.
Held in July - August .
Contact: Borkowksy Akbar.

Leipziger Rockfestival
Tollweg 42, D-04289 Leipzig.
Annual rock festival held in June.
Managing Director: Edgar Bergmann.

Music Factory
Rottscheidter Str 6, D-42329 Wuppertal.
Organizer of music fairs.
Head PR Department: Andrea Zech.

Musikmesse/Pro Light + Sound
Messe Frankfurt GmbH, Ludwig-Erhard-Anlage 1, D-60327 Frankfurt.
International trade fair for musical instruments and sheet music, light, sound and event technology.
Project Manager: Wilhelm-Peter Hosenseidl.

Popkomm
Rottscheidter Str 6, D-42329 Wuppertal.
Organizer of music fairs.
Head of PR Department: Andrea Zech.

Rheinkultur
PO Box 201303, Moltskestr. 41, D-53173 Bonn.
Germany's largest open-air festival, held in late June - early July.
Producer: Burkhard Schmoll.

Tanz & Folkfest
Rudolstadt.
Held in July.
Contact: Bernhard Hanneken.

GREECE

Athens Festival
Voukourestiou 1, 10564 Athens.
International festival held in July-August.
Managing Director: Dimos Vratsanos.

Mediterranean Music Festival
2 Kritis Street, 15562 Holargos, Athens.
World Music festival held every two years.
Public Relations: Marilena Koussoulou.

HUNGARY

Diaksziget
Lonyay u 18/B, 1093 Budapest.
International festival held in July-August.
A&R Manager: Karly Gerendai.

Island Festival
c/o Sziget Kulturális Szervezõ Iroda, Ul 18/B Lónyay, 1093 Budapest.
Festival held in the 3rd week of August each year.
Foreign Affairs Manager: Matthew Braghini.

Kalaka Folk Festival
Miskolo.
Held in July.
Contact: Csaba Lökös.

Taban
Bem Rakpart 6, 1014 Budapest.
Rock, folk and blues festival.
Contact: Aranka Marka.

Womufe
Villanyi ut 107, 1118 Budapest.
World music event held in May-June in Budapest.
Contact: Robert Mandel.

IRELAND

Bacardi Unplugged Band Competition
Hot Press, 13 Trinity Street, Dublin 2.
National band competition using "unplugged" format.
Project Co-Ordinator: Jackie Hayden.

Boyle Arts Festival
Great Meadow, Boyle, Co Roscommon.
Held in last week of July to first week in August each year.
Co-Ordinator: Fergus D Ahern.

Cork Jazz Festival
18 Stephen's Lane, Upper Mount Street, Dublin 2.
Jazz festival with Irish and international acts held in October.
Contact: Jack McGouran.

Drogheda Samba Festival
The Droichead Arts Centre, Drogheda, Co Louth.
Festival of Afro-Brazilian music including performances, workshops and carnival. Held in July each year.
Contact: Kieran Gallagher.

Feakle Traditional Music Week
Maghera, Caher, Feakle, Co Clare.
Festival of traditional music, song and dance from East Clare.
Chairman: Pat Hayes.

Feile Seamus Ennis
Finglas Art Centre, Art Squad, Unit 14B Main Shopping Centre, Finglas, Dublin 11.
Workshops and summer school promoting artists past and present in traditional music.
Chairperson: Mary McDermott.

Galway Arts Festival
7 Upper Dominick Street, Galway.
Arts Festival held in July.
Manager: Fergal McGrath.

Hot Press Music Seminars
13 Trinity Street, Dublin 2.
A series of seminars explaining the basic of the music industry to musicians etc.
Seminar Co-Ordinator: Jackie Hayden.

Mary From Dungloe International Festival
Festival Office, Main Street, Dungloe, Co Donegal.
10 music festivals held late July to early August each year. Various concerts during
the year.
Festival Director: Colm Croffy.

Monaghan Jazz & Blues Festival
Arts Office, The Tourist Office, Market House, Monaghan.
Annual jazz and blues festival held on the first weekend of September. Other yearly concerts of any form of music.
Contact: Samhairle Mac Conghaill.

Sligo Arts Festival
Model Arts, The Mall, Sligo.
Arts festival held at the end of May, with world music, street events and theatre.
Contact: Danny Kirrane.

ISRAEL

Israel Festival
PO Box 4409, Jerusalem 91044.
Festival of performing arts including music, dance and theatre. Held in May - June.

ITALY

Arezzo Wave
Via Lorenzetti 31, 52100 Arezzo.
European Rock Festival held in June.
Managing Director: Mauro Valenti

Bassano Jazz
Via Sonda 21, 36061 Bassano del Grapa.
Jazz and progressive music.
Managing Director: Giovanni Mayer.

Corridonia Jazz Festival
Antonello Andreaniu di Coop Ephemeria, P'zza 30 Aprile, 62100 Macerata.
Jazz festival held in July.

Cremona Rock
c/o Centro Musicale Il Cascinetto, Via Maffi 2, 26100 Cremona.
Annual Italian rock festival in early June.

Festambiente
Via Tripoli 27, I-58100 Grosseto.
Ecological festival.
Cultural Section Resp: Michela Presta.

Magna Grecia Rock
Via Cavour, 96100 Siracuse.
International festival held annually in Sicily.

Rockin' Umbria
Via Della Viola 1, 06100 Perugia.
International music festival.
Managing Director: Sergio Piazzoli.

Voci E Suoni Del Mediterraneo
Gibellina.
Held August -September.
Contact: Pompeo Benincasa.

World Music Festival
Rome.
Held in August.
Contact: Pietro Carli.

NETHERLANDS

Befrydings Festival
Grote Kerkstraat 14, Dg11E6 Leeuwarden.
Festival programming and production.
Contact: Sjoerd Cuperus.

Benelux International Songfestival
Crispijnstraat 9, 5171 CH Kaatsheuvel.
Managing Director: Peter Van Best.

Dynamo Open Air Festival
Juliusstraat 45, 5621 GC Rotterdam.
Largest heavy rock festival in Europe.
Managing Director: M. Kanters.

Dunya Festival
Rotterdam.
Held 1-2 June .
Contact: Martin Van Ginkel.

Frysk Festival
Grote Kerkstraat 14, DG 1146 Leeuwarden.
Contact: Sjoerd Cuperus.

Metropolis Festival
PO Box 131, 3000 AC Rotterdam.
Pop festival for young up and coming bands. Held in early July.
Managing Director: Corinne Lampen.

Music and Harmony
Oude Enghweg 24, 1217 JD Hilversum.
Organizer of international musical instruments fair in Jaarbeurs-Utrecht. Held at the beginning of September .
Contact: P M v Dooren.

North Sea Jazz Festival
PO Box 87919, 2508 DH Den Haag.
Largest indoor Jazz festival in Europe.
Manager: Paul Dankmeyer.

PinkPop
PO Box 117, 6160 AC Geleen.
International Pop Festival.
Contact: Jan Smeets.

12th Music Meeting
Nijmegen.
Held in November.
Contact: Wim Westerveld.

World Roots Festival
Amsterdam.
Held in June.
Contact: Frans Goossens.

NEW ZEALAND

Bay Of Islands Jazz & Blues Festival
Box 365 Paihia Bay Of Islands.
Annual jazz and blues event, held on second weekend in August.

Fringe Festival
6 Majoribanks Street, Mt Victoria.
New Zealand's largest open-access fringe festival.
Director: Tracy Medland.

International Music Expo
PO Box 25046, St Heliers, Auckland.
Annual trade event held in September.
Contact: Rob Eady.

Mountain Rock
51 Vogel Street, Woodville.
New Zealand's largest rock event, held annually in January.
Administration: Paul Wood.

New Zealand International Festival Of The Arts
PO Box 10113, Wellington.
Laregst arts event in the country, held alternate years; Next due in March 1998.
Executive Director: Carla Van Zon.

Tarankai Festival Of The Arts
PO Box 4251, New Plymouth.
Three week long festival held on alternate years in March.
Festival Director: Roger King.

NORWAY

Førde Folk Music Festival
PO Box 395, 6801 Førde.
Held in July.
Contact: Hilde Bjorkum.

Glopperock
PO Box 222, 6860 Sandane.
Rock festival held in June.
Managing Director: Remi Tystad.

Kalvöyafestivalen
Karl Johansgaten 8, 0154 Oslo 1.
International festival at the end of June.
Manager: Paul Karlsen.

Molde International Jazz festival
Postboks 211, 3671 Notodden.
Major Jazz festival in July.
Managing Director: Einar Gjendem.

Notodden Blues Festival
PO Box 211, 3671 Notodden.
Blues festival. Held in early August.
Promoter: Espen Fjelle.

POLAND

Folk Blues Fair
Poznan.
Held in early March.
Contact: Dionizy Piatkowski.

Jazz on Odra Festival
c/o Interart Ltd, ul Pugeta 6, 51-628 Wroclaw.
Contact: Margaret Szablowska.

Odjazdy
ALMA - ART, ul Teatralna 9, 40-003 Katowice.
Festival of rock and independent music. Held in mid- November at Spodek Hall.
Director: Bogdan Marcinkowski.

Piknik Country
Grojecka 75, 01 094 Warsaw.
Country Music festival held in July.
Manager: Ewa Dabrowska.

Sopot International Music Festival
ul. Kosciuzki 61, 81703 Sopot.
International Song Contest.
Contact: Wojciech Korzeniewski.

Stage Song Festival
Arts and Culture Centre, Rynek-Ratusz 24, PL-50-101 Wroclaw.
Presentation of Polish musical theatre highlights of the season; Promoting young actors through competition; Concerts by prominent guest performers from abroad.
Artistic Director: Roman Kolakowski.

Warsaw Summer Jazz Days
E Plater 49, 0125 Warsaw.
Jazz event held in June.
Contact: Mariusz Adamiak.

Winter Rock Festival
ALMA - ART, ul Teatralna 9, 40-003 Katowice.
Rock music festival for Polish and foreign bands. 23 February at Spodek Hall,
Director: Bogdan Marcinkowski.

PORTUGAL

Encontros Musicais da Tradiçao Europeia
Colmbra, Evora Guimaraes, Oeiras.
Held in July.
Contact: Mario Alves.

Queima Das Fitas
c/o Musica no Caraçao, EDF Fnac 2, Ave Ceuta, 1300 Lisbon.
Student rock and pop festival.
A&R: Luis Montez.

ROMANIA

Golden Stag
Etaj 4, cam 412, Calea Dorobanti 101, Sector 1, Bucharest.
International music festival.
General Manager: Dumitri Morosanu.

SLOVAKIA

Rock Pop Bratislava
Jakubovo nam 12, 81499 Bratislava.
Major rock and pop festival.
Director: Pavel Danek.

SLOVENIA

Druga Godba
Ljubljana.
Held in early June.
Contact: Bogdan Benigar

Festival Ljubljana
Trg Francoske Revolucije 1-2, 61000 Ljubljana.
Open-air event from June to September.
Managing Director: Vladimir Vajda.

No Border Jam Festival
Front Rock, PO Box 48, 62000 Marilor.
International punk, HC, garage r'n'r festival held in June every year.
Manager: DoJan Hedl.

SPAIN

Barcelona Jazz Festival
Bailen 42 2-3, 08010 Barcelona.
Jazz festival in October - November.
Managing Director: Ramoneda Tito.

Donostiako Jazzaldia - Festival of Jazz, San Sebastian
c/o Reina Regente S/N, 20003 Donistia, San Sebastian.
Annual jazz festival held over 5 days in the second half of July.
Director: Miguel Martin.

Espárrago Rock Festival
c/o Reyes, Catolicos 25, Oficina 2 Planta, 18001 Granada.
Promotion Director: Javier Gonzalez.

Guitar Festival of Cordoba
Avda Gran Capitan, No 3, E-14008 Cordoba.
Concerts of Classical, Flamenco, Pop, Rock and Antique music.
Production Manager: Ana Linares Bueno.

Madrid Jazz Festival
Navarro Reverter 22, 46004 Valencia.
Jazz festival held in June and July.
A&R: Julio Martin.

Pirineos Sur
Huesca.
Held July - August.
Contact: Luis Calvo.

WOMAD in Caceres
TBA, Caceres.
Contact: Thomas Brooman.

SWEDEN

Arvikafestivalen
PO Box 99, S-67131 Arvika.
Rock and indie music festival held in July.
Manager: Niklas Stake.

Dala Rock
PO Box 12, S-77621 Hedemora.
Festival held in July, featuringSwedish and international artists.
Managing Director: Putte Brolund.

Falun Folk Music Festival
Falun.
Held in July.
Contact: Magnus Bäckström.

Festival "Sjöslaget"
c/o Projektbyrån, Kungsgatan 34, S-97241 Luleå.
Managing Director: Tomas Lind.

Gothenburg All Star Festival
World Trade Centre, Box 5264, S-40225 Gothenburg
Major rock festival with international acts.
A&R Manager: Magnus Erikson.

Hultsfred Festival
PO Box 170, 57724 Hultsfred.
Managing Director: Gunnar Lagerman.

Re Orient Festival
Stockholm
Held in June.
Contact: Jonas Elverstig.

Sommarens Sista Suck
Box 157, 631 03 Eskilstuna.
Festival Held on the last weekend in August.
Managing Director: Hans Lindell; Programme Managers: Rocco Gustafsson and Mats Olsson.

SWITZERLAND

Caribana Festival
CH des Vignettes 2B, 1299 Crans-VD.
Music festival over 4 days covering rock, folk, tropical, rap and acid jazz.
Co-Ordinator: Tony Lerch.

Estival Jazz Lugano
6992 Vernate.
Free open air jazz festival.
Promoter/Manager: Andreas Wyden.

Gurtenfestival Bern
PO Box 57, Gerberngasse 38, CH-3000 Bern 13.
Vice President: Roland Röthlisberger.

Jazz Festival Zürich
Stadthaus, 8022 Zürich.
Public Relations: Alexander Schmid.

Jazz Willisau
PO Box CH-6130 Willisau.
Festival of jazz.
Director: Niklaus Troxler.

Montreux Jazz Festival
Sentier de Collonge 3, PO Box 1451, CH-1820 Montreux.
Annual festival held in July consisting of jazz, pop, rock, blues, and soul; 2 halls and 5 off-stages; Workshops.
Artistic Director: Claude Nobs.

Openair Festival Thun
c/o Music Service Adi Weiss AG, Gerberngasse 38 + 42, PO Box 57, CH-3000 Bern 13.
Promoter of concerts and festivals.
Vice President: Roland Röthlisberger.

TURKEY

Istanbul International Jazz Festival
Istiklal Caddesi 146, Luvr Apt Beyoglu, TR-80070 Istanbul.
Jazz festival held June - July.

UNITED KINGDOM

Aberdeen Alternative Festival
10 Belmont Street, Aberdeen AB1 1JE, Scotland.
Annual arts festival held each October, combining culture of north-east Scotland with international music, comedy, drama and dance.
Director: Duncan Hendry.

Appalachian and Bluegrass Music Festival
Ulster-American Folk Park, Castletown, Omagh, Co Tyrone.
Head of Museum Services: John A Walsh.

Bath International Music Festival
Linley House, 1 Pierrepont Place, Bath BA1 1JY.
Held May - June.
Artistic Director: Tim Joss.

Belfast Folk Festival
Students Union, University Road, Belfast BT17 1PR, Northern Ireland.
Irish and international festival.
Contact: Noel Devlin.

Beverley Folk Festival
2 Star Row, N Dalton, Driffield, E Yorks YO25 9UR.
Annual festival specialising in folk, roots and related music. Held 3rd weekend in June.
Director: Chris Wade.

Birkenhead Guitar Festival of Great Britain
Dept Leisure Servcies & Tourism, Westminster House, Birkenhead, Wirral L41 5FN.
Held 9 - 17 November .
Festival Director: Ron Smith.

Birmingham International Jazz Festival
PO Box 944, Birmingham B16 8UT.
Held in early July.
Director: Jim Simpson.

Bracknell Jazz Festival
South Hill Park, Ringmead, Bracknell, Berks RG12 7PA.
Festival Director: Paul James.

Brecon Jazz
Jazz Festival Offices, Watton Chambers, Brecon, Powys LD3 7EF, Wales.
Held in August.
Festival Co-ordinator: Deborah Parry.

Bull-Sheet Music
18 The Ramblings, Chingford, London E4 6LU|
Managing Director: Irene Bull.

Bude Jazz Festival
PO Box 73, Malvern, Worcs WR13 6RQ.
Held in late August .
Organiser: John Minnion.

Cambridge Folk Festival
The Guildhall, Cambridge CB2 3QJ.
Folk festival with programme including folk, blues, country and pop.
Promotions Officer: Eddie Barcan.

!Caramba!
88 Radstock Road, Reading, Berks RG1 3PR.
Specialists in multi cultural music events from Latin American fiestas to Nepalese feasts.
Events Manager: Tim Carroll.

Cheltenham International Festival of Music
Town Hall, Imperial Square, Cheltenham, Glos GL50 1QA.
Held during July.
Festival Organiser: Kim Sargeant.

City of London Festival
Bishopsgate Hall, Bishopsgate, London EC2M 4QD.
Jazz Festival; Held in June - July .
General Manager: Alastair Hume.

Cropredy Music Festival
c/o Fairport Convention, PO Box 37, Banbury, Oxon OX16 8YN.
Organizers of the Cropredy Music Festival.
Contact: David Pegg.

Cross Rhythms
PO Box 183, Plymouth, PL3 4YN.
Annual festival.
Administrator: Jonathan Bellamy.

Edinburgh International Festival
21 Market Street, Edinburgh EH1 1BW, Scotland.
International Arts Festival of music, theatre and dance.
Managing Director: Mike Hart.

Fleadh
PO Box 1707, London NW10.
Irish and Scottish folk festival held in Finsbury Park.
Managing Director: Vince Power.

Glasgow International Jazz Festival
18 Albion Street, Merchant City, Glasgow G1 1LH, Scotland.
10 day jazz festival. Held late June - early July.
Festival Director: Derek Gorman.

Glastonbury Festival
Worthy Farm, Pilton, Shepton Mallet, Somerset.
One of UK's leading international music events, held in June.
Managing Director: Michael Eavis.

Great British Rhythm and Blues Festival
Bank House, 61 Albert Road, Colne, Lancashire BB8 0PB.
Arts and Entertainment Manager: Gary Hood.

Greenbelt Festival
The Greenhouse, Hillmarton Road, London N7 9JE.
International festival held in August.
Contact: Martin Evans.

Greenwich Festival
Festival Office, 6 College Approach, Greenwich, London SE10 9HY.
Held May - June.
Festival Co-ordinator: Sophie Elliott.

Heineken Music Big Top
Toll House Studios, Cambridge Cottages, Kew Gardens, Surrey TW9 3AY.
International events held in various UK cities throughout the summer.
Managing Director: Mike Eddowes.

International Festival of Folk Arts
Sidmouth, Devon.
Held in early August.
Contact: Steve Heap.

Jersey Jazz Festival
131 Quennevais Park, St Brelade, Jersey.
Held in April.
Contact: Ernie Roscouet.

London Cajun Music Festival
41 Gillam Way, Rainham, Essex RM13 7HS.
Festival of Cajun music and dance.
Chairman: Erling Hagland.

London Jazz Festival
c/o Serious Speakout, 42 Old Compton Street, London W1V 5PB.
Annual jazz festival held in May.
Contacts: David Jones, John Cumming, John Ellson.

Monsters Of Rock Festival
16 Birmingham Road, Walsall, West Midlands WS1 2NA.
The UK's leading Heavy Metal festival, held annually in August.
Managing Director: Maurice Jones.

Mrs Casey Music
PO Box 296, Aylesbury, Bucks HP19 3TL.
Organizers of folk festivals and events.
Director: Steve Heap.

North Wales Bluegrass Festival
Woodstock, Llanrwst Road, Glan Conwy, Glwyd LL28 5SR, Wales.
3 day international bluegrass music festival. Held in the first week of July.
Festival Director: John Les and Gill Williams.

Notting Hill Carnival
332 Ladbroke Grove, London W10 5AH.
Street carnival and international music event, held in August.
Managing Director: Elaine Spencer.

Phoenix Festival
PO Box 1707, London NW10
International indie music festival, held in Stratford in July.
Managing Director: Vince Power.

Portobello Jazz Week
c/o Eleventh Hour Arts, 113 Cheesemans Terrace, Star Road, London W14 9XH.
Managing Director: Debbie Golt.

Reading Rock Festival
PO Box 1707, London NW10.
The UK's leading rock and pop festival, held over 3 days in August.
Managing Director: Vince Power.

Soho Jazz Festival
29 Romily Street, London W1V 6HP.
Held in first week of October.
Artistic Director: Peter Boize Oates.

Stanford in the Vale Folk Festival
1 Membury Way, Grove, Wantage, Oxon OX12 0BP.

T-in-the-Park Festival
North Lodge, Auchineden by Blanefield, Glasgow G63 9AX, Scotland.
Managing Director: Stuart Clumpas.

Warwick Folk Festival
13 Styvechale Avenue, Earlsdon, Coventry CV5 6DW.
Annual festival providing concerts, dances, workshops, crafts, displays of traditional and contemporary folk arts.
Administrator: Frances Dixon.

Winchester Folk Festival
44 Peverells Wood Avenue, Chandlers Ford, Hampshire SO53 3BW.
Annual festival of traditional dance, music and song held on the last weekend in April.
Publicity Officer: Anne Sutherland.

Woburn Festival
Kilnside, Harvest Hill, Bourne End, Bucks SL8 5JJ.
Jazz Festival; Held throughout October.
Secretary: Kate Booth.

WOMAD
Mill Side, Mill Lane, Box, Wiltshire SN13 8PN.
Worldwide festival co-ordination and production. Held in July.
Artistic Director: Thomas Brooman.

UKRAINE

Beatlesmania Music Festival
Independent Artist's Agency, Ljubchenko & Co, Room 7, Mietrostrojevskaja St 5, 320128 Dniepropetrovsk.
Annual music festival.
Director: Valeri Ljubchenko.

Directorate of the All-Ukrainian Festival of Independent Music "Alternative"
Culture Foundation, Lesya Kur-Basa Str 4, 290007 Lviv.
Held in September.
Director: Youry Grekh; Vice Director: Ruslan Koshiv.

Kharkov Assemblies International Music Festival
Institute of Musicology, Soviet Ukraine Square 20 #9, 310003 Kharkov.
Director: Grigory Hansburg.

Musica Pura Europae Festival
R Eideman Str 2-16, 310112 Kharkiv.
International music festival dealing with European neofolk & independent rock music.
Manager: Sergey Myasoedev.

Rock Fest Bee
c/o Independent Artists Agency Ljubchenko & Co, Room 7, Mietrostrojevskaja St 5, 320128 Dniepropetrovsk.
Annual music festival.
Director: Valeri Ljubchenko.

Teenwave
c/o Independent Artist Agency Ljubchenko & Co,
Room 7, Mietrostrojevskaja St 5,
320128 Dniepropetrovsk.
International teenage song festival.
Director: Valeri Ljubchenko.

"Tavria Games" International Festival
36V, Lesi Ukrainki Blvd, 252133, Kiyiv.
Organizers of the "Tavria Games" International Festival since 1992.
General Director: Nikolay Bagraev.

USA

CMJ Music Marathon & Music Fest
11 Middle Neck Road, Suite 400, Great Neck, NY 11021.
3 days and 4 nights of panels, workshops and live music showcases promoting the discovery and development of new music.
Executive Producer: Joanne Abbot Green.

Cultural Initiative Inc
PO Box 1672, Washington, DC 20013-1672.
Annual Hip-hop music conference.
Director: Timothy Jones.

Foundations Forum Inc
1133 Broadway, Suite 1220, New York, NY 10010.
Annual music event since 1988 of showcases, exhibits, screenings, parties etc.
Vice President: Kevin Keenan.

Independent Label Festival
600 South Michigan Avenue, Chicago, IL 60605-.
A music industry convention featuring panels, workshops, trade show and showcases. Held in late July.
Executive Director: Leopoldo Lastre.

Independent Music Seminar
PO Box 99090, San Diego, CA 92169.
Annual independent music event.

Jazz Times Convention
7961 Eastern Avenue, #303, Silver Spring, MD 20910.
Music industry convention.
Associate Publisher: Lee Mergner.

MusicFest
231 Harrison Drive, Denver, CO 80206.
Songwriters trade event and conference.

NAIRD Convention
1000 Maplewood Drive, Suite 211, Maple Shade, NJ 08052.
Convention for Independent record labels held in May.
Contact: Holly Cass.

New Music Seminar
632 Broadway, 9th Floor, New York, NY 10012.
International music business convention.
Contact: Mark Josephson.

New Orleans Jazz & Heritage Festival
1205 N Rampart Street, New Orleans, LA 70116.

South by Southwest Music and Media Conference
PO Box 4999, Austin, TX 78765.
Annual conference held in March for members of the music industry.
Managing Director: Roland Swenson.

Songwriters Expo
PO Box 93759, Hollywood, CA 90093.
Annual Songwriters conference.
Contact: Dan Kimpel.

Talent Search America
273 Chippewa Drive, Columbia, SC 29210-6508
International songwriting and lyric writing contests.
Contact: Talent Director.

Undercurrents
PO Box 94040, Cleveland, OH 44101-6040.
Annual international music conference, trade shows and showcase.
Director: John Latimer.

APPENDIX F
ORGANISATIONS

ARGENTINA

Asociacion Argentina de Interpretes (AADI), Av. Belgrano 3655, 1210 Buenos Aires.
Asociacion de Representantes Artisticos (ADRA), Sarmiento 1848, piso 1°C, 1044 Buenos Aires.
Camara Argentina De La Musica, Tucumán 1748, 2° piso, Of 4, 1050 Buenos Aires.
Camara Argentina de Productores e Indus de Fonogramas Y Sus Reproduc (CAPIF), Avda Corrientes 1628, 5° piso H, 1042 Buenos Aires.
Consejo Argentino de la Musica, Casilla de Correo 5532, Correo Central, 1000 Buenos Aires.
Fundacion Encuentros Internacionales de Musica Contemporanea, Casilla de Correo 1008, Correo Central, 100 Buenos Aires.
Sindicato Argentino de Musicos (SADEM), Avda Belgrano 3655, 1210 Buenos Aires.
Sociedad Argentina de Autores Y Compositores de Musica (SADAIC), Lavalle 1547, 1048 Buenos Aires.
Sociedad General de Autores de la Argentina (ARGENTORES), Pacheco de Melo 1820, 1126 Buenos Aires.
Sociedad General de Autores Y Editores (SGAE), Uruguay 775, 4° A, 1015 Buenos Aires.

AUSTRALIA

Australasian Christian Broadcasters, PO Box 2020, Launceston, Tasmania 7250. *President: Kevin N Hooper.*
Australasian Mechanical Copyright Owners Society Ltd (AMCOS), 14th Floor, 56 Berry Street, North Sydney, NSW 2060. *Company Secretary: Britten Sutcliffe.*
Australasian Performing Rights Association (APRA) Ltd, Locked Bag 3665, St Leonards, NSW 2065. *CEO: Brett Cottle.*
Australian Contemporary Music Development Company Ltd (AUSMUSIC), PO Box 307, Port Melbourne, Victoria 3207. *Executive Director: Pete Steedman.*
Australian Copyright Council, 3/245 Chalmers Street, Redfern, NSW 2016. *CEO: Libby Baulch.*
Australian Entertainment Industry Association Ltd, PO Box 423, Crows Nest, NSW 2065. *President: Nigel Lampe.*
Australian Music Association Inc, PO Box 6306, St Kilda Road, Melbourne, VIC 3004. *CEO: Rob Walker.*
Australian Music Examinations Board, 3rd Floor, 175 Flinders Lane, Melbourne 3000. *National Manager: Ann Blore.*
Australian Music Manager's Forum (AMMF), PO Box 109, Surry Hills, NSW 2010. *Co-Chairpersons: Michael McMartin and John Woodruff.*
Australian Music Publishers Association, Ltd, 56 Berry Street, 14th Floor, North Sydney, NSW 2060.
Australian Music Retailers Association (AMRA), PO Box W333, Warringah Mall, NSW 2100. *Chairman: Barry Bull.*
Australian Record Industry Association (ARIA) Ltd, 9th Floor, 263 Clarence Street, Sydney, NSW 2000. *Executive Director: Emmanuel Candi.*
Australian Songwriters Association, PO Box 123, Surry Hills, VIC 3127. *President: Mike Bowen.*
Australian Women's Contemporary Music Inc, 9 Knox Street, Chippendale, NSW 2008. *President: Vicki Gordon.*
Central Australian Aboriginal Media Association (CAAMA), 99-101 Todd Street, Alice Springs, NT 0871. *General Manager: Owen Cole.*
Country Music Association of Australia (CCMA), PO Box 298, Tamworth, NSW 2340. *Chief Executive: G M Ellis.*
Export Music Australia (EMA)Ltd, 9th Floor, 263 ClarenceStreet, Sydney NSW 2000. *Co-ordinator: Donna Chapman.*
International Society for Contemporary Music (Australian Section), c/o University of Sydney Music Department, Sydney, NSW 2006.
Music Industry Advisory Council, GPO Box 9839, Canberra, ACT 2601. *Contact: Ian James.*
Musicians' Union Of Australia, Suite 506, 3 Smail Street, Ultimo, NSW 2007. *Federal Secretary: John McAuliffe.*
Musicological Society of Australia Inc, GPO Box 2404, Canberra, ACT 2601. *National Secretary: Jaki Kane.*
National Indigenous Arts Advocacy Association Inc (NIAAA), Suite 401, Level 4, 60-62 Foveaux Street, Surry Hills, NSW 2010. *Executive Director: Bronwyn Bancroft.*
Phonographic Performance Co. Of Australia (PPCA) Ltd, 9th Floor, 263 Clarence Street, Sydney, NSW 2000. *Executive Director: Emmanuel Candi.*
Push Inc, 66 Cecil Street, Fitzroy 3065. *Executive Director: Paul Sladdin.*
Society of Australian Songwriters Inc, PO Box 290, Leichardt, NSW 2040. *President: Thomas Poland.*
Songwriters, Composers and Lyricists Association Inc (SCALA), PO Box 228, Kensington Park, SA 5068. *President: Robert Childs.*
Tasmanian Music Industry Association, 145 Charles Street, Launceston, TAS 7250. *Project Officer: Kay Lincoln.*
Venue Management Association, 100 St Kilda Road, Melbourne, NSW 3004. *Membership Secretary: Shane Hewitt.*

AUSTRIA

AIM, Seitenberggasse 50-54, A-1160 Vienna. *Chairman: Frank Golischewski.*
AKM, Baumannstr. 8-10, A-1030 Vienna. *Chairman: Gerhard Wimberger.*
Art Institut Wien, PO Box 101, A-1043 Vienna. *Chairman: Gregor Jasch.*
Austria Top 30, Habsburgergasse 6-8/18, A-1010 Vienna. *Managing Director: Franz Medwenitsch.*
Austrian Music Producers (AMP), PO Box 2, A-1094 Vienna. *President: Guenter Menschik.*
Austro-Mechana, Baumannstr. 8-10, A-1030 Vienna. *Chairman: Johann Juranek.*
IFPI, Habsburgergasse 6-8/18, A-1010 Vienna. *Chairman: Franz Medwenitsch.*
IGV, Siebenbrunnengasse 20/1, A-1050 Vienna. *Chairman: Andreas Egger.*
International Music Centre (IMZ), Lothringerstr. 20, A-130 Vienna. *Chairwoman: Avril MacRory.*
LSG, Habsburgergasse 6-8/18, A-101 Vienna. *Managing Director: Paul Fürst.*
Musiker-Komponisten Autorengilde (MKAG), Hofgasse 2/13, A-1050 Vienna. *Chairman: Peter Paul Skrepek.*
Musikverleger Union, Baumannstr. 8-10, A-1030 Vienna. *Chairman: Johann Juranek.*
Österreichishe Tonmeistervereinigung, Natterergasse 4, A-2361 Laxenburg. *President: Wolfgang Fritz.*
Österreichischer Komponistenbund (ÖKM), Ungargasse 9/2, A-1030 Vienna.
Verwertungsgesellschaft Bild Und Ton (VBT), Habsburgergasse 6-8/18, A-1010 Vienna. *Managing Director: Franz Medwenitsch.*

BELGIUM

ACOD Cultuur/Sector Musiek, Fontainasplein 9-11, B-1000 Brussels. *Secretary: Laurette Muylaert.*
Artist Service Vzw/ASBL, Postbus 1, B-8460 Oudenburg. *President: Jean-Paul Steenmans.*
Association Belge du Spectacle, Ave. Bel Air 36, B-1180 Brussels. *President: Michel Halliwell.*
Association Diffusion Musique Belge (ADIBUMEL), rue d'Arlon 75-77, B-1040 Brussels. *Contact: Franz Constant.*
Association Europeene des Radio (AER), Ave. Edouard Speeckaert 53, B-1200 Brussels. *Vice-President: Benoit Sillard.*
Ateliers Chanson, rue PE Janson 9, B-1050 Brussels. *Chairman: Michel Van Muylem.*
Belgian Association of Recording Studios, rue Moorslede 77, B-1020 Brussels. *Chairman: Erwin Veraecke.*
Belgian Music Publishers Association, Fernand Neuraystraat 8, B-1060 Brussels. *President: Roland Kruger.*
Beroepsvereniging Van Belgische Impresario's (BVBI), Kammerstraat 19, B-9000 Ghent. *Secretary: Robert Van Yder.*

CMCFB, Local 4 M 24, Blvd Reyers 52, B-1044 Brussels. *Chairman: Robert Wangermee.*
Country And Western Association Belgium, Nutstraat 18, B-3830 Wellen. *Chairman: William Magnani.*
De Bazuin Vzw, Pauwenlaan 23, B-3583 Paal-Beringen. *President: Louis Tielens.*
European Forum of Worldwide Music Festivals (EFWMF), Jan Frans Willemsstraat 10, B-2530 Boechout. *Secretary: Patrick de Groote.*
European Music Office, 126 rue Franklin, B-1040 Brussels. *General Secretary: J F Michel.*
Flanders Music Service, Stationsteenweg 238B, B-2560 Nijlen. *Managing Director: Francis Thijs.*
IFPI, Place de l'Alma 3 B5, B-1200 Brussels. *Managing Director: Vincent van Nele.*
SABAM, rue d'Arlon 75-77, B-1040 Brussels.*Chairman: Victor Legley.*
Union Professionelle des Producteurs Independants (UPPI), Rue Gachard 24, B-1050 Brussels. *President: Pierre Platinckx.*
Union Royale des Editeurs de Musique, Fernand Neuraystraat 8, B-1060 Brussels. *President: Roland Kruger.*
URADEX, Rue d'Arlon 75-77, B-1040 Brussels.
Wallonie-Bruxelles Musique, Rue Marche aux Herbes 61, 4 etage, B-1000 Brussels. *Co-ordinator: Patrick Printz.*

BOLIVIA

Asociacion Boliviana de Radiodifusoras (ASBORA), Avda Sánchez Lima, 2278 Casilla 5324, La Paz.
Educacion Radiofonica de Bolivia (ERBOL), Ballivia, 1323, 4° Casilla 5946, La Paz.

BRAZIL

Associacao Brasileira de Emissoras de Radio E Televisao (ABERT), Mezanino do Hotel Nacional Salas 5 a 8, 04280, 70322 Brasilia.
Associacao Brasileira dos Produtores de Discos, Rua Sao josé 90, Gr 1406/10, 22021 Rio de Janeiro, R J.
Instituto Brasileiro de Arte e Cultura, Rua de Imprensa 16, 20030 Rio de Janeiro, R J.
Sindicato dos Músicos Profissionals do Estado de Sao Paulo, Largo Paissandu, Sao Paulo.
Sindicato Nac. de Empresas de Agenciamiento, Producao de Eventos (SINAPREM), Avda Iparanga, 877, 13°, 01039 Sao Paulo, SP.
Sociedada Brasileira de Música Contemporânea, SQS 105, Bloco B, Ap 506, 70344-020 Brasili, D F.
Sociedada Independente de Compositores & Autores Musicals, Largo Paissandú 51, 10th, 11th, and 16th floors, 01034 Sao Paulo.
Uniao Brasileira de Compositores, Rua Visconde de Inhaúma 107, 20091 Rio de Janeiro, R J.
Uniao dos Músicos do Brasil, Av Rio Branco 185, Rio de Janeiro, R J.

BULGARIA

BAZI, 15 Tsarigradsko Chausse Blvd,1220 Sofia. *Manager: Dora Cherneva.*
Jusautor, Place Bulgaria 1, 1463 Sofia. *Director General: Jana Markova.*
Musicautor, 6 Rajcho Dimchev, 1000 Sofia. *Chairman: Konstantin Dragnev.*
Podkrepa, 2 Angel Kunchev Str, 1000 Sofia. *Chairman: Asen Gargov.*
Pop-Rock Federation, Liulin Bl. 210, Vh A, 1343 Sofia. *Chairman: Chavdar Chendov.*
Union of Bulgarian Composers (SBC), Ivan Vazov Str 2, 1000 Sofia. *Chairman: Lazar Nikolov.*

CANADA

Alberta Recording Industries Association, #208, 10136-100 Street, Edmonton, AB T5J 0P1. *Executive Assistant: Charlotte Bowman.*
American Federation of Musicians of the United States & Canada, 75 The Donway West, Suite 1010, Don Mills, ON M3C 2E9. *Vice-President (for Canada): Ray Petch.*
BC Country Music Association, 177 W 7 Avenue, 4th Floor, Vancouver BC V5Y 1L8.
Black Music Association of Canada, 59 Chester Hill Road, Toronto, ON M4K 1X4. *President: Daniel Caudeiron.*
Caledonia Folk Club, 23 Buchanan Drive, Caledonia, ONN3W 1H1. *Organiser: Bill Crawford.*
Canadian Amateur Musicians, PO Box 353, Westmount, PQ H3Z 2T5. *Director General: Barry Crago.*
Canadian Academy of Recording Arts and Sciences (CARAS), 124 Merton Street, 3rd Floor, Toronto, ON M4S 2Z2. *Executive Director: Daisy Falle.*
Canadian Association for Music Therapy, c/o Wilfrid Laurier University, 75 University Avenue W, Waterloo, ON N2L 3C5. *Administrative Co-Ordinator: Lynda Tracy.*
Canadian Association of Artists' Managers, 117 Ava Road, Toronto, ON M6C 1W2.
Canadian Country Music Association (CCMA), #127-3800 Steeles Avenue West, Woadbridge, ON L4L 4G9. *Executive Director: Sheila Hamilton.*
Canadian Disc Jockey Association Inc, National Office, 3148 Kingston Road, Suite 209-300, Scarborough, ON M1M 1P4. *National President and Chief Executive Officer: Dennis E Hampson.*
Canadian Independent Record Producers Association (CIRPA), 114 Front Street W, Suite 202, Toronto, ON M5J 2L7. *Executive Director: Brian Chater.*
Canadian Music Centre, 20 St Joseph Street, Toronto, ON M4Y 1J9.
Canadian Music Publishers Association, 320 - 56 Wellesley Street W, Toronto, ON M5S 2S3.
Canadian Musical Reproduction Rights Agency Ltd, 56 Wellesley Street West, Suite 320, Toronto, ON M5S 2S4, *General Manager: David Baskin.*
Canadian Recording Industry Association, 1255 Yonge Street, Suite 300, Toronto, ON M4T 1W6. *President: Brian Robertson.*
Canadian Society for Traditional Music, Box 4232, Sta C, Calgary, Alberta, T2T 5N1. *Membership Co-Secretary: John Leeder.*
Coastal Jazz and Blues Society, 435 West Hastings Street, Vancouver, BC V6B 1L4. *Executive Director: Robert Kerr.*
Country Music Foundation of Canada, 8607 128 Avenue, Edmonton, AB T5E 0G3.
Federation of Canadian Music Festivals, 1034 Chestnut Avenue, Moose Jaw, SK S6H 1A6.
Foundation to Assist Canadian Talent on Records, 125 George Street, 2nd Floor, Toronto, ON, M5A 2N4. *Executive Director: Heather Sym.*
Georgian Bay Folk Society, Box 521, Owen Sound, ON N4K 5R1. *Promotion Co-Ordinator: Linda Ashley.*
Music Industries Association Of Canada (MIAC), 109 - 1210 Sheppard Avenue E, North York, ON M2K 1E3.
Pacific Music Industry Association, 400-177 W 7th Avenue, Vancouver, BC V5Y 1L8. *Executive Director: Ellie O'Day.*
Photo-Connect, 244-423 King Street West, Hamilton, ON L8P 4Y1. *President and Chief Executive Officer: Kirby Ellis.*
Northern Praise Ministries Inc, PO Box 61015, Oakville, ON L6J 7P5. *Founder/Administrator: Michelle Sim.*
Société des Mélomanes (Canada) Inc, 1056 Burnaby Street, Suite 201, Vancouver, BC V6E 1N7. *Director Factotum: Eugène Evans.*
Society of Composers, Authors & Music Publishers in Canada (SOCAN), 41 Valleybrook Drive, Don Mills, ON M3B 2S6.
Society for Reproduction Rights of Authors, Composers and Publishers in Canada (SODRAC), 759 Victoria Square, Suite 420, Montreal, PQ H2Y 2J7. *General Manager: Claudette Fortier.*
Toronto Downtown Jazz Society, 366 Adelaide Street SE Sutie #230, Toronto, Ontario M5A 3X9. *Director of Marketing & Communications: Barb McCullaugh.*
Toronto Musicians' Association, 101 Thorncliffe Park Drive, Toronto, ON M4H 1M2. *Secretary: Mark Tetreault.*

CHILE

Asociación de Radiodifusores de Chile (ARCHI), Pasaje Matte, 957, Of 801, Santiago de Chile.
Asociación Nacional de Compositores, Almirante Moritt 453, Santiago de Chile.

Instituto de Música, Universidad Católica de Chile, Jaime Guzman E 3 300, Santiago de Chile.
Sociedad Chilena del Derecho de Autor (SCD), San Antonio, 427, 2° piso, Santiago de Chile.

CHINA

Assocaition of Chinese Musicians, Nong Zhanguan Nan Li, No. 10, Beijing 111026.

COLOMBIA

Asociación Colombiana de Músicos Profesionales, Calles 17, No 10-16, Of 607, Bogotá, D E.
Asociación des Artistas de Colombia, Calle 13, No 9-63, Interior 104, Apdo Aéreo 24627, Bogotá, D E.
Centro de Documentación Musical-Instituto Colombiano de Cultura, Calle 11, No 5-51, 2nd Floor, Bogotá, D E.
Instituto Colombiano de Cultura-Colcultura, Calle 11, No 5-51, 2nd Floor, Santafé de Bogotá, D C.
Sociedad de Autores y Compositores de Colmbia, Carrera 19, No 40-=72, Apdo Aéreo 6482, Santafé de Bogotá, DC ZP1.

CROATIA

Croatian Authors Agency, Preradoviceva 25, 41000 Zagreb. *Manager: Zeljka Modrusac-Ranogajec.*
Croatian Composers Society, Berislaviceva 9, 41000 Zagreb. *Managing Director: Ozren Kanceljak.*
Croatian Musicians Union, PP 560, Gruška 10, 41001 Zagreb. *Chairman: Paolo Sfeci; Secretary General: Siniša Doronjga.*
Music Information Centre, Kneza Mislava 18, 41000 Zagreb. *Managing Director: Jagoda Martincevic.*

CUBA

Centro de Información y Promoción de la Música Cubana ¨Odilio Urfé¨, Calle 17 esq. a E, Vedado, Havana.
Centro de Investigación y Desarrollo de la Música Cubana, Calle G, No 505 e/21 y 23, Vedado, Havana.
Centro Nacional de Derecho de Autor, Calle Línea No 365 (altos), esp a G, Vedado, Havana.
Centro Nacional de Música de Concierto, Calle Línea No 365, esq a G, Vedado, Havana.
Centro Nacional de Música Popular, Avenida 1 ra. e/10 y 12, Playa, Havana.
Editora Musical de Cuba, San Rafael No 104, esq a Consulado, Centro Habana, Havana.
Empresa de Grabaciones y Ediciones Musicales, Campanario No 315, e/Neptuno y San Miguel, Centro Habana, Havana.
Instituto Cubano de la Música, Calle 15 No 452, esq a F Vedado, Havana.
Unión de Escritores y Artistas de Cuba (Music Section), Calle 17 No 351, esq a H, Vedado, Havana.

CZECH REPUBLIC

Association of Musicians and Musicologists, Maltézské nám. 1, 118 00 Prague 1.
Authors Association of Protection for Rights on Musical Works, Čs. armády 20, 160 56 Prague 6.
Czech Music Fund, Besední 3, 118 00 Prague 1.
Czech Music Information Centre, Besední 3, 118 00 Prague 1. *Executive Manager: Nina Vseteckova.*
Czech Music Society, Janáčkovo nábř. 59, Smíchov, 150 00 Prague 5.
Guild of Czech Composers and Concert Artists, Valdstejnske nam. 1, 100 00 Prague 1. *President: Jan Seidel.*
IFPI CR, Senovazne nam 23, 112 82 Prague 1. *Secretary and Chief Executive: Vratislav Safar.*
International Federation of Phonogram and Videogram Producers (Czechoslovak Section), Gorkého nam. 23, 112 82 Prague 1.
International Music Council (National Committee), Valdstejnske nám. 1, Prague 1.
International Society for Contemporary Music (Czechoslovak Section), Na Březince 22, 150 00 Prague 5.
Ochranny Svaz Autorsky (OSA), Cs. Armady 20, 160 56 Prague 6. *President: Petr Janda.*
Society for Jazz, Janáčkovo nábř. 59, Smíchov, 150 00 Prague 5.
Union of Authors and Interpreters, Škroupova nám 9, 130 00 Prague 3.

DENMARK

Association of Rock/Jazz Clubs in Denmark (SAMSPIL), Graven 25 A, DK-8000 Aarhus C. *Chairman: Palle Skov; Sec Leader: Rikke Sinding.*
Council of Rhythmic Music Education (RMU), Fredensvej 18, DK-2970 Hørsholm. *Secretary of Committee: Aage Hagen.*
Danish Association of Jazz and Rock Amateurs (FAJABEFA), Musiskkens Hus, Enghavavej 40 sal, DK-1674 Copenhagen V. *Contact: Jacob Kragh.*
Danish Jazz Association, Kjeld Langesgade 4A, DK-1367 Copenhagen K. *Chairman: Frans Bak.*
Danish Jazz Centre, Borupvej 66B, DK-4683 Roennede. *Managing Director: Arnvid Meyer.*
Danish Music Council, Vesterbrogade 24 4, DK-1620 Copenhagen V. *Chairman: Lars Grunth.*
Danish Music Information Centre, Gräbrødretorv 16, DK-1154 Copenhagen K. *Chairman: Jorgen Arnsted.*
Danish Rock Council (ROSA), Karetmagergaarden, Graven 25 A, DK-8000 Aarhus C. *Chairman: Gunnar Madsen.*
Danske Jazz Beat Og Folkemusik Autorer (DJBFA), Gräbrødretrov 16, 1154 Copenhagen K. *Chairman: Torben Kjaer.*
Dansk Folkemindesamling (Danish Folklore Archives), Christians Brygge 3, 1219 Copenhagen K. *Administration Director: Svend Nielsen.*
Dansk Musiker Forbund (DMF), Vendersgade 24, DK-1363 Copenhagen K. *Contact: Gert Kring.*
Den Rytmiske Konsulentitjeneste, Kjeld Langesgade 4A, DK-1367 Copenhagen K. *Chairman: Niller Wischmann.*
Foreningen Danmarks Folkeminder (Danish Folklore Society), Christians Brygge 3, 1219 Copenhagen K. *Administration Director: Svend Nielsen.*
GRAMEX, Reventlowsgade 8/1, DK-1651 Copenhagen V. *Director: Bjorn Juell-Sundbye.*
IFPI Denmark, Store Strandstraede 20 st, DK-1255 Copenhagen K. *Chairman: Stefan Fryland.*
KIM (Women In Music), c/o Conservatory of Music, Niels Brocksgade 1, DK-1574 Copenhagen V. *Chairman: Tove Krag.*
KODA, Maltegaardsvej 24, DK-2820 Gentofte. *Chairman: Henrik Lund.*
MXP - Danish Music Export and Promotion, Sondervej 56, DK-5700 Svendborg. *Music Consultant/Chief Executive Officer: Mikael Højris.*
Nordisk Copyright Bureau (NCB), PO Box 3064, DK-1021 Copenhagen K. *Administration Executive: Kurt Hviid Mikkelsen.*
Rhythmic Music Conservatory, Dr Priemesvej 3, DK-1854 Frederiksberg C. *Director: Erik Moseholm.*

ESTONIA

Estonian Jazz Foundation, PO Box 3641, Viru Str. 16, EE-0090 Tallinn. *Director: Tiit Lauk.*
Tallinn Zeppelin Club, PO Box 3526, Tallinn EE-0090. *Club Consultant: Peter Zeluiko.*
VAAP, Toompuiestee 7, EE-0101 Tallinn.

FIJI

Fiji Composers Association, PO Box 2371, Government Buildings, Suva. *Vice-President: Seru Serevi.*
Fiji Musicans' Association, PO Box 364, Loutoka. *Vice-President: Danny Costello Jr.*
Fiji Performing Right Association Limited, GPO Box 15061, 170 Renwick Road, Suva. *Chairman: Saimone Vuatalevu.*

FINLAND

AFRB, Italahdenkatu 22 BC, 00210 Helsinki.
Finnish Big Band Association, Makslahdenkatu 1 C, 02140 Espoo. *Contact: Risto Oinaala.*
Finnish Folk and Country Music Society, PO Box 181, SF-00531 Henlsinki. Contact: Jihani Aalto.
Finnish Jazz and Pop Archive, Rajasampaanranta 2, 00560 Helsinki.
Finnish Jazz Archives, Pihlajatie 43 A, 00270 Helsinki.
Finnish Jazz Federation, PO Box 54, 00101 Helsinki.
Finnish Music Information Centre, Lauttasaarentie 1, 00200 Helsinki. *Contact: Jari Muikku.*
Finnish Music Publishers Association, Runeberginkatu 15/A/12, 00100 Helsinki. *President: Raimo Henriksson.*
Finnish Musicians' Union, Uudenmaankatu 36/D/21, 00120 Helsinki. *President: Raimo Vikstrom.*
Global Music Centre, Mikkolantie 17, 00640 Helsinki. *Director: Anu Laakkonen.*
GRAMEX, Hietaniemenkatu 15/A/12, 00100 Helsinki. *Director: Jukka Niskanen.*
IFPI Finland, Runeberginkatu 15/A/12, 00100 Helsinki. *Information Officer: Paivi Ryokas.*
Musikkikustantajatorg, Hietaniemenkatu 2, 00100 Helsinki. *Managing Director: Minna Aalto-Setälä.*
Rock Musicians Association, Uudenmaankatu 36/F/34, 00120 Helsinki. *Chairman: Nissila Pekka.*
Society of Finnish Composers, Runeberginkatu 15/A/11, 00100 Helsinki.
Suomen Paikalliradioliitto, Italahdkatu 22/B-C 00210 Helsinki. *Managing Director: Kai Salmi.*
Teosto, Lauttasaarentie 1, 00200 Helsinki. *Managing Director: Jaakko Fredman.*

FRANCE

ADAMI, 10A Rue de la Paix, F-75002 Paris. *Contact: Marie-Jeanne Peraldi.*
ANARLP, PO Box 174, F-10005 Troyes Cedex. *President: Guy Capet.*
BIEM, 56 Ave Kleber, F-75116 Paris. *President: Jean Loup Tournier.*
Bureau Export de la Musique Française, 27 Rue du Docteur Lancereaux, F-75008 Paris. *Executive Director: Marie Agnes Beau.*
Centre d'Information du Rock (CIR), 211 Avenue Jean Jaures, Parc de Villete, F-75019 Paris. *Managing Director: Jean Davoust.*
Centre Information et Ressources pour les Musiques Actuelles (IRMA), 21 bis Rue de Paradis, F-75010 Paris. *Director: Bruno Boutleux.*
Centre Musical et Creatif de Nancy, 92 Grande Rue - BP 698, F-54063 Nancy Cedex. *Teaching Director: Hans J Kullock.*
Centre National d'Action Musicale (CENAM), 11-13 Rue de l'Escaut, F-75019 Paris. *Director: Dominque Ponsard.*
CISAC, 11 Rue Keppler, F-75116 Paris. *Secretary General: Jean Alexis Ziegler.*
Collectif HASK, 9 Avenue Pasteur, F-93100 Montreuil. *Contact: Hubert Dupont.*
Comite National De La Musique (CNM), 252 rue du Faubourg Saint-Honoré, F-75008 Paris. *General Secretary: J Masson Forestier.*
CSDEM, 62 Rue Blanche, F-75009 Paris. *President: Jean Davoust.*
Eurokka (Esperanto-Rok-Asocio), F-31450 Donneville. *Director: Floréal Martorell.*
FEPS, 17 Rue Brey, F-75017 Paris. *President: Roland Bertin.*
Ferarock, BP 4015, F-31028 Toulouse Cedex. *President: Françoise Duval.*
FNAMU, 41 Bis Quai de la Loire, F-75019 Paris. *Managing Director: Catherine Lesage.*
Fondation Pour La Creation Musicale (FCM), 141 Rue Lafayette, F-75010 Paris. *Director: Bruno Rony.*
French Studios Association (ASF), 30 Rue Henri Barbusse, F-75005 Paris. *Director: Jean Louis Rizet.*
Institut International de Musique Electroacoustique, BP 39 F-18001 Bourges Cedex. *Directors: Françoise Barrière and Christian Clozier; Secretary General: Catharina Kroling.*
Institut du Monde Arabe, 1 Rue des Fosses Saint-Bernard, F-75236 Paris. *Program Director for Music, Dance & Theatre: Mohamed Metalsi.*
International Confederation of Music Publishers, 47 rue de Turbigo, F-75003 Paris.
MIDEM Organization, 179 Avenue Victor Hugo, F-75116 Paris. *CEO: Xavier Roy.*
SACEM/SDRM, 225 Ave Charles de Gaulle, F-92521 Neuilly -sur-Seine Cedex. *President: Gerard Calvi.*
SCPP, 159 Charles de Gaulle, F-92200 Neuilly-sur-Seine. *President: Rene Guittan.*
SIPLACDA, 255 Rue Saint-Honoré, F-75001 Paris. *President: Joëlle Feauveau.*
SNAAL, 17 Rue Brey, F-75017 Paris. *President: Roland Bertin.*
Societie Francaise de Production (SFP), 36 rue des Alouttes, F-75019 Paris. *Director General: Jean-Pierre Rhosse.*
SPEDIDAM, 8 Rue Bremontier, F-75017 Paris. *President: Maurice Husson.*
Syndicat Francais des Artistes-Interpretes (SFA), 21 bis Rue Victor Masse, F-75009 Paris. *Executive Director: Francois Parrot.*
Syndicat National de L'Edition Phonographique (SNEP), 27 Rue du Docteur Lancereaux, F-75008 Paris. *Manager: Herve Rony.*
Syndicat National des Artistes Musiciens (SNAM), 14-16 Rue des Lilas, F-75019 Paris. *Director: Pierre Allemand.*
Syndicat National des Autuers et Composituers (SNAC), 80 Rue Taitbout, F-75442 Paris Cedex 9. *President: Antoine Duhamel.*

GERMANY

Bundesverband Der Phonographischen Wirtschaft eV (BPW), Grelckstr 36, D-20257 Hamburg 1. *Contact: Petra Denzen.*
Deutsche Bibliothek/Deutsches Musikarchiv Berlin, Box 4502 29, D-12172 Berlin. *Library Director: Dr Heinz Lanske.*
Deutsche Disc Jockey Organisation, Kaiser Friedrich Allee 1-3, D-52074 Aachen. *Contact: Klaus Quirini.*
Deutsche Landesgruppe der IFPI eV, Grelckstrasse 36, D-22529 Hamburg. *Head of Public Relations: Elmar Kruse.*
Deutsche Phono-Akademie, Grelckstr 36, D-22529 Hamburg. *Contact: Hartmuth Bender.*
Deutsche Rockmusikerverband eV, Kolberger Strasse 30, D-21339 Luenburg. *Chairman: Ole Seelenmeyer.*
Deutscher Musikverleger Verband (DMV), Friedrich Wilhelm Str. 31, D-53113 Bonn. *President: Maja Maria Reis.*
European Association of Concert Agents, Sülzgürtel 86, D-50937 Cologne. *Contact: Andreas Braun.*
GEMA, Rosenheimer Str 11, D-81667 Munich. *Chairman: Dr Reinhold.*
GVL, Heimhuder Str 5, D-20148 Hamburg. *Managing Director: Rolf Duennwald.*
Internationaler Arbeitskries für Musik eV, Postfach 410236, D-34064 Kassel.
IDKV (German Concert Promoter and Artists Agents Association), PO Box 202364, D-20216 Hamburg. *President and General Manager: Jens Michow.*
MusikKomm GmbH, Rottscheider Str. 6, D-42329 Wuppertal. *Managing Director: Uli Grossmass.*
Verband der Deutschen Konzertdirekionen eV, Liebigstrasse 39, D-80538 Munich.
Warehouse, Linden Str 52, D-50674 Cologne.
Zentrum für Musik & Kommunikations-Tech., Rottscheider Str. 6, D-42329 Wuppertal. *Managing Director: Dieter Gorny.*

GREECE

AEPI, Deligani 14, 106 83 Athens. *President: Mimis Traiforis.*
IFPI Greece, Aghia Paraskevi 63, 152 34 Halandri, Athens. *Secretary: Miltos Karadsas.*
International Music Council (Greek Section), Mitropoleos 38, 105 63 Athens. *President: Demetre Michaelides.*
Panhellenic Musicians' Union, 10 Sapfous Str, 10553 Athens. *President: T. Athineos; General Secretary: G. Lambrianidis.*

HONG KONG

Composers and Authors Society of Hong Kong (CASH) Ltd, 18/F Universal Trade Centre, 3 Arbuthnot Road, Central Hong Kong. *Contact: Leslie Ching.*
IFPI (Hong Kong Group), 22/F Gitic Centre, 28 Queen's Road East, Wanchai, Hong Kong. *Chief Secretary: Patrick Wong.*
Hong Kong Composers Guild, c/o Music Dept, Chung Chi College, Chinese University, Shatin, New Territories. *Contact: Chan Wing Wah.*
Music Publishers Association, 11/F Peninsula Office Tower, 18 Middle Road, Kowloon. *Contact: David Loiterton.*

HUNGARY

Gewerkschaft für Musik- und Tanzkünstler, Gorkij Fasor 38, Pf 8, H-1406 Budapest. *Secretary: László Gyimesi.*
Hungarian Jazz Federation, Krudy Gy u 4, H-1088 Budapest. *Contact: Karoly Csonkis.*
Hungarian Music Council, PO Box 47, H-1364 Budapest.
Hungarian Music Society, Vörösmarty tér 1, H-1051 Budapest. *President: Zsolt Durkó.*
Institute for Musicology of the Hungarian Academy of Sciences, Táncsics Mihály utca 7, H-1014 Budapest. *Assistant Director: Tibor Tallián.*
Mahasz (IFPI), Regiposta u 13, H-1052 Budapest. *Managing Director: Agnes Musinger.*
Musicians Trade Union, Gorkij Fasor 38, H-1068 Budapest. *President: Sanor Solyom Nagy.*
Society of Hungarian Commercial Radios, Steindl Ihre u 12, H-1054 Budapest. *President: Laszlo Hegeous.*

ICELAND

Association of Light Composers and Songwriters, Háteigsvegur 28, 105 Reykiavik.
Iceland Music Information Centre, Sidumuli 34, 108 Reykjavik. *Manager: Asta Hrönn.*
Icelandic Composers Society, Laufasvegur 40, 101 Reykjavik.
Icelandic Musicians' Union, Laufásvegur 40, Reykjavík. *General Secretary: Asgeir H. Steingrimsson.*
IFPI Iceland, Kringlan 4, PO Box 3360, 123 Reykjavik. *Chairman: Steinar Berg Isleifsson.*
International Society for Contemporary Music, Laufásvegur 40, 101 Reykjavík.
Jazzvakning, PO Box 31, IS-121 Reykjavik.
Reykjavík Music Society, Garoastraeti 17, 101 Reykjaík.
Society of Icelandic Musicians, Dalsel 8, Reykjavík.
STEF, Laufasvagur 40, 101 Reykjavik. *General Manager: Eirekur Tomasson.*
Union of Authors and Copyright Owners, Laufásvegur 40, 101 Reykjavík.

INDONESIA

Indonesian Society of Composers and Arrangers, Komp Mangga Dua Plaza, Blok J, no.30, Jl Mangga Dua raya, Jakarta Utara. Chairman: Sakikin Zuchra.

IRELAND

An Chomhairle Ealaion (The Arts Council), 70 Merrion Square, Dublin 2. *Music Officer: Dermot McLaughlin.*
Association of Independent Record Retailers, 5 Cope Street, Dublin 2. *President: Brian O'Kelly.*
Association of Irish Composers, Copyright House, Pembroke Row, Lower Baggot Street, Dublin 2. *Contact: Maura Eaton.*
Association of Irish Festival Events (AOIFE), Administration Office, Rear 32 Upper Main Street, Arklow, Co. Wicklow. *National Secretary: Victor Ryan.*
British Institute of Jazz Studies, 17 The Chase, Crowthorne, Berkshire RG45 6HT. *Secretary: Graham Langley.*
Cork Music Resource Co-Op, Unit 12, Thompson's Building, McCurtain Street, Cork. *Administration Director: Angela Dorcran.*
Federation of Music Collectives, The Temple Bar Music Centre, Cyred Street North, Temple Bar, Dublin 2. *Contact: Angela Dorgan.*
Folk Music Society of Ireland, 15 Henrietta Street, Dublin 1,
IFPI Ireland, 26 Merrion Square, Dublin 2. *Chairman: Paul Keogh.*
Independent Radio and Television Commission (IRTC), Marine House, Clanwilliam Place, Dublin 2. *Contact: Lynne Scanlan.*
International Managers' Forum (IMF), 35A Lower Barrow Street, Dublin 4. *Chairman: Robbie Wooton.*
International Songwriters' Association (ISA), PO Box 46, Limerick City, Limerick. *Managing Director: James Liddane.*
Irish Association of Songwriters and Composers (IASC), Ballinclea Lodge, Ballinclea Road, Killiney, Co Dublin. *Chairman: Keith Donald.*
Irish Bluegrass Music Club, 86 Barton Road East, Dublin 14. *Contact: Carol Hawkins.*
Irish Federation of Musicians and Associated Professions, 63 Lower Gardiner Street, Dublin 1. *President: Richard Glynn.*
Irish Federation of the Phonographic Industry (IFPI), 9 Whitefriars, Aungier Street, Dublin 2. *Chairman: Paul Keogh; Secretary: Riobaird MacGorian.*
Irish Music Rights Organisation Ltd (IMRO), Copyright House, Pembroke Row, Lower Baggot Street, Dublin 2. *Chief Executive Officer: Hugh Duffy.*
Irish Musicwriters and Songwriters Association (IMSA), c/o IMRO, Copyright House, Pembroke Row, Lower Baggot Street, Dublin 2.
Irish Traditional Music Archive, 63 Merrion Square, Dublin 2. *Director: Nicholas Carolan.*
Jazz Services, Rooms 518-521, 5th Floor, Africa House, 64-78 Kingsway, London WC2E 6BD. *Contact: Celia Wood.*
Mechanical Copyright Protection Society (Ireland) Ltd (MCPS), Copyright House, Pembroke Row, Lower Baggot Street, Dublin 2. *General Manager: Victor Finn.*
Music Base, 44 East Essex Street, Dublin 2. *Youth Arts Development Officer: Greg McAteer.*
Music Network, The Coach House, Dublin castle, Dublin 2. *Information and PR Manager: Ann Swift.*
Music Publishers Association of Ireland (MPAI), Copyright House, Pembroke Row, Lower Baggot Street, Dublin 2. *President: Michael O'Riordan; Secretary: John Lappin.*
Music Retailers of Ireland, 5 Cope Street, Dublin 2. *Executive Member: Brian O Kelly.*
National Entertainment Agents Council, PO Box 112, Seaford, East Sussex BN25 1DA.
Oifig an Cheoil (The Music Office), Teo Cuilin, Dingle, Co. Kerry. *Contact: Joan Maguire.*
Performing Rights Society, Copyright House, Pembroke Row, Lower Baggot Street, Dublin 2. *Contact: Paula McDermott.*
Phonographic Performance (Ireland) Ltd (PPI), PPI House, 1 Corrig Avenue, Dun Laoghaire. Co Dublin. *Chief Executive: Dick Doyle.*
Republic of Ireland Music Publishers Association (RIMPA), Copyright House, Pembroke Row, Lower Baggot Street, Dublin 2. *Secretary: John J Lappin.*

ISRAEL

Independent Musicians Union, 6 Malkei Yisrael Square, 64591 Tel Aviv. *Chairman: Dany Gottfried.*
International Music Council (Israeli Section), Ministry of Education and Culture, Devora Hanaviah Street 2, 91911 Jerusalem. *Chief Officer: Raaya Zimran.*
International Society for Contemporary Music (Israeli Section), c/o Israel Composers' League, PO Box 45068, 61450 Tel Aviv.
Israel Composers' League, PO Box 45068, 61450 Tel Aviv. *Chairman: Manachem Zur.*
Israel Music Institute (IMI), PO Box 3004, 61030 Tel Aviv. *Director: Paul Landau.*
Jerusalem Music Centre, Mishkanot Sha'ananim, Jerusalem. *Director: Benny Gal-Ed.*
Music Information Centre of Israel, PO Box 3004, 61030 Tel Aviv. *Director: Paul Landau.*
National Council for Culture and Arts, 16 Hanatziv Street, 67018 Tel Aviv. *Chief Officer: David Sinai.*
Society of Authors, Composers, and Music Publishers in Israel (ACUM), 118 Rothschild Boulevard, 61110 Tel Aviv. *Chairman: Shlomo Tanny.*
Union of Musicians, Histradut Building, 93 Arlozorof Street, 62098 Tel Aviv. *General Secretary: Aryeh Levanon.*

ITALY

AMI, via Montenapoleone 20, 20121 Milan. *Chairman: Roberto de Luca.*
Associazione dei Fonografici Italiani (AFI), via Vittor Pisani 10, 20124 Milan. *President: Guido Rignano.*
Associazione di Informatica Musicale Italiana (AIMI), c/o La Biennale di Venezia, Settore Musica, San Marco, Ca Giustinian, 30124 Venice.
Associazione Italiana Degli Editori di Musica (AIDEM), via Enrico Toti 4, 20123 Milan. *President: Maurizio Corecha.*
Associazione Italiana Operatori Musicali (ASSIOM), c/o Centro di Ricerca e Sperimentazione per la Didattica Musicale, Villa La Torraccia, via delle Fontanelle 24, 50016 San Domenico di Fiesolo (FI).
Associazione Nazionale Musicisti di Jazz (ANMJ), via Vallerozzi 77, 53100 Sienna. *Chairman: Giorgio Gaslini.*
Bluegrass & Country Music Association of Italy, PO Box 1733, 20101 Milan. *President: Maurizio Faulisi.*
CIDIM-National Music Committee of Italy (IMC-UNESCO), via Vittoria Colonna 18, 00193 Rome.
Editori Musicali Associati (EMA), Piazza del Liberty 2, 20121 Milan. *President: Adriano Solaro.*
Federazione Industria Musicale Italiana (FIMI), Largo Augusto 3, 20122 Milan. *President: Franco Reali.*
Federazione Italiana dei Compositori de Musica Contemporanea, via Cavalieri di Vittorio Veneto 34, 56121 Cascina (PI).
Federazione Italiana della Musica (FEDERMUSICA), via Vittor Piasni 10, 20124 Milan.
FILIS, Piazza Sallustio 24, 00187 Rome. *General Secretary: Massimo Bordini.*
IMAIE, Piazza Sallusto 28, 00187 Rome. *Chairman: Angeli Otello.*
International Association for the Study of Popular Music (IASPM), Italian Section, c/o "Il Giornale della Musica", corso Vittorio Emanuelle II n 198bis, 10138 Turin.
International Dance Organization (IDO), via Bronzino 117, 50142 Florence.
Istituto Italiano per la Storia della Musica, via Vittoria 6, 00187 Rome.
Italian Braodcasting Association, via della Moscova 38A, 20121 Milan. *President: Riccardo Fausone.*
Laboratorio Musicale Periferico, via Pratese 48/a, 50145 Firenze. *President: Roberto Buoni.*
SIAE, Viale della Letteratura 30, 00144 Rome. *President: Roman Vlad.*
Sindacato Musicisti Italiani (SMI), via Goito 39, 00185 Rome.
Sindacato Nazionale Musicisti (SNM), via Pinelli 100, 10144 Turin.
Società Italiana Musica Contemporanea (SIMC), via F Juvara 11, 21029 Milan
UNCLA, Galleria del Corso 4, 20122 Milan. *Secretary General: Armando Carnadelli.*
Unione Editori di Musica Italiani (UNEMI), via Teulada 52, 00195 Rome. *President: Luciano Villeville Bideri.*
Unione Nazionale Editori di Musica Italiani (UNEMI), via Teulada 52, 00195 Rome.

JAPAN

Concert Managers Association of Japan, Mitoko Bldg, 6-2-4 Akasaka, Minato-ku, Tokyo 107. *Chairman: Naoyasu Kajimoto.*
Federation Of Music Producers Japan, Jingumae Wada Bdlg, Shibuya-ku, Tokyo 150. *President: Takeshi Hosokawa.*
Japan Association of Music Enterprises, 4F Koyanagi Bldg 1-7 Ginza, Chuo-ku, Toyko 104. *Contact: Akitomo Tanabe.*
Japan Audio Society, 3F Mori Bldg, 1-14-34 Jingumae, Shibuya-ku, Tokyo 150. *Chairman: Heitaro Nakajima.*
Japan Council Of Performers Organizations (Geidankyo), 11F Tokyo Opera City Tower, 3-20-2 Nishishinjuku, Shinjuku-ku, Tokyo 163-14. *PR: Samuel Shu. Masuyama.*
Japan International League of Artists, 2-3-16-607 Shinjuku, Shinkjku-ku, Tokyo 160. *Chief Officer: Kazuhiko Hattori.*
Japanese Composers Society, Ogawa Bldg, 3-7-15 Akasaka, Minato-ku, Tokyo 107.
Japanese Society for Rights of Authors, Composers & Publishers (JASRAC), 1-7-13 Nishishimbashi, Minato-ku, Tokyo 105. *President: Ray Nakanishi.*
Music Publishers Association Of Japan, 7F Daiichi Nanou Bldg, 2-21-2 Nishi Shinbashi, Minato-ku, Tokyo 105. *President: Misa Watanabe.*
Musicians' Union of Japan, Showa Building, 2nd Floor, 4-8 Udagawa-cho, Shibuya-ku, Tokyo 150. *Secretary General: Kazuharu Sato.*
Recording Industry Association of Japan (RIAJ), 2F Kobiki Bldg, 7-16-3 Giaza, Chao-ku 104. *Deputy Manager, Copyright Dept: Jiro Imamura.*
Union Of Tokyo Music Business People, 3F Diar Inoue Bldg, 1-6-6 Akasaka, Mianto-ku, Tokyo 107. *Chairman: Masakasu Sunadoi.*

KOREA

Asian Composers League (Korean Committee), KPO Box 874, Seoul 110 062. *Director: Sung-Jae Lee.*
IFPI, 5 Floor, Kumseok Bldg, 1574-14 Seocho-dong, Seocho-ku, Seoul 137 070. *Contact: Kim Seh Won.*
Korea Music Copyright Association (KOMCA), 2-4F, Samjeon Bldg, 236-3 Nonhyeon-dong, Kangnam-ku, Seoul 135 010. *President: Seog-Wan Gim.*
Korea Performers Association, 6 Floor, Yeil B/D, 60 Chungshin-dong, Chongro-ku, Seoul. *Contact: Yun Tong Woong.*
Music Association of Korea, 1-117 Dongsoong-dong, Chongro-ku, Seoul. *President: Sang-Hyun Cho.*

LATVIA

Baltic and Soviet DJ Association, Brivibas Street 190/4, 226 012 Riga. *Contact: Ugis Polis.*

LUXEMBOURG

SACEM, 46 Rue Goethe, 1637 Luxembourg. *Contact: Pierre Neuen.*

MALAYSIA

IFPI, 137-1/139-1 1st Floor, Wisma Hiap lee, Jln Segambut, Kuala Lumpur 51200. *General Manager: Tan Ngiap Foo.*
Phonographic Performance (Malaysia), 2nd Floor, Wisma Hiap Lee, Jln Segambut, Kuala Lumpur 51200. *General Manager: Tan Ngiap Foo.*

MEXICO

AMPROFON, Francisco Petrarca No. 223-503, Chapultepec Morales, 11560 México DF.
Camara Nacional de la Industria de Radio Y Television (CIRT), Avda Horącio, 1013 Col Polanco, 11550 Mexico, DF. *President: Raul Arechina Espinoza; General Manager: César Hernández Espejo.*
Direccion de Normas de Radiodifusion, Eugenia, 197, 1° Col Vértiz Narvarte, 03020 Mexico, DF. *Director: Alfonso Amilpas.*
Direccion General de Telecomunicaciones, Lázaro Cárdenas, 567, 11°, ala norte Navarte, 03020 Mexico, DF. *Director: Carlos Lara Sumano.*
National Traditional Country Music Association of Mexico, Esq Américas, Fracc, Reforma, Veracruz.
Sociedad de Autores y Compositores de Musica (SACM), Mayorazgo 129, 03330 Mexico, DF.

NETHERLANDS

BUMA (Composers Rights Society), PO Box 725, 1180 AS Amstelveen. *Chairman: Gerard Van Laar.*
BVPOP, PO Box 63107, 1005 LC Amsterdam. *Chairman: Andrea Steinmetz.*
Center for Netherlands Music (CNM), PO Box1634, 1200 PB Hilversum. *Chief Officer: J W ten Broeke.*
Conamus Foundation, PO Box 929, Vaartweg 32, 1200 AX Hilversum. *Managing Director: John de Sol.*
Disco Mix Club (DMC) Holland, Faass Elaislaan 13, 3742 AR Baarn. *President: Alex Van Oostrom.*
Genootschap van Nederlandse Componisten (GENECO), Prof EM Meyerslaan 3, 1183 AV Amstelveen. *Chairman: Gilius van Bergeijk.*
Gong, Kerkweg 41, 3603 CL Maarssen. *Contact: Michael Lambrechsten.*
Hard Disc (Association of Hard Rock DJs), Arkplein 103, 1826 DM Alkmaar. *President: Gus Van Suntenmaartensdijk.*
International Federation of Popular Music Publishers (IFPMP), Eikbosserweg 181, 1213 RX Hilversum. *Secretary General: Cor Smit.*
Kunstenbond FNV, Arie Biemondstraat 111, 1054 PD Amsterdam. *General Secretary: Piet van Buul.*
Mega Top 50, PO Box 483, 1200 AL Hilversum. *Managing Director: Sieb Kroeske.*
Nederlandse Toonkunstenaarsbond (NTB), Herengracht 272, 1016 BW Amsterdam. *Chairman: Michiel de Sterke.*
Nederlandse Vereniging van Producenten en Importeurs (NVPI), Albertus Perkstraat 36, 1217 NT Hilversum. *Managing Director: P R C Solleveld.*
NVGD, Die Noord 3, 1452 PS Ilpendam. *Chairman: J F T Hotzenbosch.*
PALM, Vaartweg 32, 1217 SV Hilversum. *Chairman: Cees Schrama.*
Royal Society for Music History of the Netherlands (KVNM), PO Box 1514, 3500 BM Utrecht. *President: Dr J M M van Gemert; Secretary: Dr A J Wester.*
SENA, Vaartweg 51, 1211 JE Hilversum. *Co-Ordinator: Marÿke Remkes.*
SPN/Dutch Rock Music Foundation, Wibautstraat 214, 1091 GS Amsterdam. *PR Manager & International Promotion: Laurence van Haren.*
STEMRA (Mechanical Rights Society), PO Box 725, 1180 AS Amstelveen. *Chairman: Gerard Van Laar.*
UNIM, Eikbosserweg 181, 1213 JE Hilversum. *Chairman: Guus Jansen Jr.*
Vecta, PO Box 49, 1394 ZG Nederhorst Den Berg. *Chairman: M Hanson.*

NEW ZEALAND

Australasian Mechanical Copyright Owners Society Ltd (New Zealand Branch Officer) (AMCOS), PO Box 36795, Parnell, Auckland. *General Manager (NZ): Janice Giles.*
Composers Association of New Zealand (CANZ), PO Box 4065, Wellington. *President: Denise Hulford.*
Entertainment Venues of New Zealand (EVANZ), PO Box 380, Palmerston North. *Contact: Colin Dyer.*
Independent Music Producers and Performers Associations (IMPPA), PO Box 68-593, Newton, Auckland. *Chairman: Jeff Clarkson.*
New Zealand Composers Foundation Ltd, 11-13 Broderick Road, Johnsonville, Wellington. Chairman: Ashley Heenan.
New Zealand Country Music Association, PO Box 602, Wakatane. *Secretary: Linda Mita.*
New Zealand Jazz Foundation, 18 Motueka Street, Ngaio, Wellington. *President: John Crawford.*
New Zealand Music Centre, 15 Brandon Street, Wellington. *Chairman: Merwyn Norrish.*
New Zealand Music Information Bureau Inc., Carnegie Centre, 110 Moray Place, Dunedin. *Managing Director: John Kitto.*
New Zealand Musicians' Union, Private Bag 68-914, Newton, Auckland. *Secretary: Peter Shannon.*
NZ On Air, PO Box 9744, Wellington. *Programme Manager: Brendan Smyth.*
Phonographic Performances (NZ) Ltd (PPNZ), 6th Floor, Courtenay Chambers Bldg, 15 Courtenay Place, Wellington. *Chairman: Terence O'Neill-Joyce.*
Recording Industry Association of New Zealand (RAINZ), 6th Floor, Courtenay Chambers Bldg, 15 Courtenay Place, Wellington. *Chairman: Terence O'Neill-Joyce.*

NORWAY

Association of Norwegian Jazz Musicians, Tollbugt. 28, N-0157 Oslo. *Manager: Kari Rolland.*
DENIF, PO Box 365, 1701 Sarpsborg. *Chairman: Per Langsholt.*
Foreningen Norskeplateselkaper (FONO), Rosenborggate 19, 0356 Oslo. *Chairman: Jan Paulsen.*
GGF, Sandakervelen 52, 0477 Oslo. *Director: Saemund Fiskvik.*
Gramo, Osterhaus 6T, 27, 0183 Oslo. *Executive Director: Jon Martin Gran.*
IFPI Norge, Sandakervelen 52, 0477 Oslo. *Director: Saemund Fiskvik.*
Norsk Forening For Opphavsrett, PO Box 9171, 0134 Oslo.
Norsk Jazzarkiv, Toftesgate 69, 0552 Oslo. *Director: Finn Kramer-Johansen.*
Norsk Musikerforbund, Youngsgate 11, 0181 Oslo. *Managing Director: Tore Nordvik.*
Norsk Musiker Og Musikkpedagogforening (NMM), PO Box 210, 4301 Sandnes. *Manager: Harald Bjørgan.*
Norsk Rockforbund/Norwegian Rock Association, Box 8892 Youngstorget, 0028 Oslo. *Managing Director: Øystein Ronander.*
Norske Populaerautorer (NOPA), Toyenbekken 21, PO Box 9171 Gronland, 0134 Oslo. *Chairman: Sigurd Jansen.*
Norwegain Music Information Centre, Toftesgate 69, 0552 Oslo. *Contact: Hilde Holback Hanssen.*
Norwegian Society of Composers, PO Box 9171 Gronland, 0134 Oslo. *Chairman: Hakon Berge.*
Tono, PO Box 9171, Gronland, 0134 Oslo.

PHILIPPINES

Filipino Society of Composers, Authors and Publishers Inc (FILSCAP), 1365 E Rodriguez Sr Avenue, Quezon City, Metro Manila. *President: George Canseco.*
Philippine Association of the Recording Industry, 1020 Soliven Building, EDSA, San Juan, Metro Manila. *President: Danilo Olivares.*

POLAND

Association of Polish Musicians (SPAM), ul Krucza 24-26, 00 526 Warsaw. *President: Eugeniusz Sasiadek.*
Country Music Association of Poland, ul Grójecka 75, 02 094 Warsaw. *Vice-President: Jerzy Gluszyk; Contact: Ewa Dabrowska.*
IFPI Poland, ul. Czarnieckiego 5/2, 01 511 Warsaw. *Director: Bianka Kortlan.*

Polish Composers Union (ZKP), Rynek Starego Miasta 27, 00-272 Warsaw. *President: Andrzej Chodkowski.*
Polish Jazz Society, ul. Chmielna 20, 00 020 Warsaw. *Chairman: Henryk Majewski.*
Polish Music Centre, Fredry 8, 00-097 Warsaw. *Manager: Barbara Zwolska-Steszewska.*
Stomur/Association of Entertainment Musicians, ul. Lwowska 13, 00 660 Warsaw. *Chairman: Maciej Czarnecki.*
Society of Authors (ZAIKS), Hipoteczna 2, 00 950 Warsaw. *Chairman: Tadeusz Maklakiewicz.*
Union of Lyric Writers and Composers of Light Music (ZAKR), Hipoteczna 2, 00 950 Warsaw. *Chairman: Tadeusz Maklakiewicz.*
Związok Producontów Audio-Video/Polish Society of the Phonographic Industry (ZPAV), ul Kruczkowskiego 12 m 2, 00-380 Warsaw. *General Director: Andrzej Kosmala.*

PORTUGAL

Associacao Fonografica Portuguesa (AFP), Augusto das Santos, 2/2, 1000 Lisbon. *President: Daniel de Sousa.*
Conselho Portugues da Musica, Rua Rosa Araújo, 6, 3°, 1200 Lisbon.
Instituto de Comunicacoes de Portugal (ICP), Avda José Malhoa, Lote 1683, 1000 Lisbon. *Chairman: Fernando Mendes.*
Sindicato dos Musicos, Avda D. Carlos I 72-2°, 1200 Lisbon. *President: José Tristão Nunes Nogueira.*
Sociedade Portuguesa de Autores, Avda Duque de Loulé, 31, 1050 Lisbon. *President: Luiz Francisco Rebello.*

ROMANIA

Institut de Etnografie Si Folclor C Brailoiu, Str Al Obregria Nr 3, Bloc M2, Ap 73, Sector 4, 75571 Bucharest. *Contact: Constanta Cristescu.*
Union des Musiciens Professionnels, Str Franklin Nr1, Sect 1, 70149 Bucharest. *Contact: Stefan Gheorghiu.*
Union of Composers and Musicians, Calea Victorei 141, Sect 1, 70149 Bucharest. *Chairman: Adrain Iorgulescu.*

RUSSIA

International Music Council, ul. Nyezhdanova str 8, 103 009 Moscow. *Contact: Boris Dimentman.*
International Union of Musicians, ul Gertsena 14/2, 103 009 Moscow. *President: Irina Arkhipova.*
Moscow Jazz Agency (MJA), ul. Nyezhdanova str 8-10, 103 009 Moscow. *Chairman: Yurii Saulsky.*
Russian Phonographic Association, Krymsky Val 7, 117 418 Moscow. *Manager: Alexey Ugrinovich.*
Union of Composers of Russia, ul. Nyezhdanova 8, 103 009 Moscow. *Contact: Yevgeni Krivojev.*
VAAP (Copyright Agency), Bolshaya Bronnaya 6A, 103 670 Moscow. *Chairman: Nikolaj Tchetverkiov.*

SINGAPORE

Composers and Authors Society of Singapore Ltd (COMPASS), 11-A Bukit Pasoh Road, Singapore 089825. *General Manager: Edmund Lam.*
IFPI (South East Asia Ltd), 1 Marine Parade Central, #12-01 Parkway Builders' Centre, Singapore 1544. *Deputy Regional Director, S E Asia: Leong May Seey.*
Music Publishers (S) Ltd, 1 Marine Parade Central, #12-01 Parkway Builders' Centre, Singapore 1544. *Administrative Executive: Laraine Soh.*
Musicians & Singers Association, Block 3, 03-628 Rochor Centre, Rochor Road, Singapore 0718. *Chief Officer: Stephen Gomez.*
Singapore Phonogram & Videogram Association (SPVA), 1 Marine Parade Central, #12-01 Parkway Builders' Centre, Singapore 1544. *Administrative Executive: Laraine Soh.*

SLOVAKIA

Association of Country Music, Jakubovo nam 12, 81109 Bratislava. *Chairman: Peter Gaspar.*
Disco Club Mix (DMC), Klincova 12, 821 08 Bratislava. *Manager: Igor Malovec.*
Slovak Jazz Society, Jakubovo nam 12, 81109 Bratislava. *Contact: Peter Lipa.*
Slovak Music Association, Jakubovo nam 12, 81109 Bratislava. *Director: MartinSavas.*
Slovensky Ochranny Zvaz Autorsky (SOZA), Kollarovo nam 20, 81327 Bratislava. *President: Julius Kincek.*
Union of Authors and Interprets, Jakubovo nam 12, 81109 Bratislava. *Director: Jan Balaz.*

SOUTH AFRICA

Association of the South African Music Industry, PO Box 367, Randburg 2125, Johannesburg. *Chief Executive: Des Dubery.*
Dramatic, Artistic, and Literary Rights Organization Ltd (DALRO), PO Box 9292, Johannesburg. *Managing Director: Gideon Ross.*
Foundation for the Creative Arts, PO Box 91122, Auckland Park 2006. *Executive Manager: Herman Van Niekerk.*
South African Music Rights Organization Ltd (SAMRO), PO Box 9292, Johannesburg 2000. *Managing Director: Gideon Ross.*
South African Musicians Union, PO Box 5837, Johannesburg 2000. *President: Howard Belling.*
South African Recording Rights Association Ltd (SARRAL), PO Box 4378, Johannesburg 2000. *Chief Officer: George Hardie.*
South African Society of Music Teachers, PO Box 5318, Walmer 6065.

SPAIN

Adifolk, c/ Mestre Nicolau 9-5, 08021 Barcelona. *Director: Francesc Melia.*
AEDEM, Paseo de la Castellana 93, 28046 Madrid. *President: Juan Marquez.*
AFYVE/IFPI Spain, c/ Pedro Muguruza 8 entreplanta izq., 28036 Madrid. *Director General: Carlos Grande.*
AIE, c/ Principe de Vergara 9, bajo derecha, 28001 Madrid. *President: Luis Cobos.*
APEME, Hortaleza 18-5, 28004 Madrid. *President: Jose CarrerasMoysi.*
Associacio Musics de Jazz, Gran Via 410-4, 08015 Barcelona. *Secretary: Angel Periera.*
Centro para la Difusión de la Musica Contemporánea (CDMC), Santa Isabel 52, 28012 Madrid.
Instituto de Bibliografica Musical, Penulas 12, 12p 28071 Madrid. *President: Jacinto Torres Mulas.*
Sindicato Profesional de Músicos Españoles (SPME), c/Veneras 9-1°, 28013 Madrid. *General Secretary: Jacinto Berzosa Arroyo.*
Sociedad de Conciertos, Atlamira 3, 03002 Alicante. *Director: Margarita Berenger.*
Sociedad Española de Musicologica (SEM), Canos del Peral 7, 28013 Madrid. *President: Ismael Fernandez de la Cuesta.*
Sociedad General de Autores de España (SGAE), Fernando VI 4, 28004 Madrid. *President: Manuel Gutierrez Aragón.*

SWEDEN

DMC Sweden, PO Box 295, S-101 25 Stockholm. *Contact: Per Stavborg.*

Export Music Sweden (ExMS), PO Box 27 327, S-102 54 Stockholm. *General Manager: Stuart Ward.*
Folkparkenas Nöjesservice, PO Box 171 94, S-104 62 Stockholm. *Chairman: Björn Eriksson.*
Föreningen Svenska Kompositörer Av Populärmusik (SKAP), Sandhamnsgatan 79, Box 27327, S-10254 Stockholm. *Chairman: Haakan Elmguist. Contact: Ingered Lindberg.*
Föreningen Svenska Tonsättare (FST), PO Box 27 237, S-102 54 Stockholm. *Chairman: Sten Hanson.*
IFPI Sweden, PO Box 1008, S-171 21 Solna. *Chairman: Eddie Landquist.*
Nordic Copyright Bureau (NCB), Sandhammsgatan 79, PO Box 27 237, S-102 54 Stockholm. *Director: Stefan Andersson.*
Nordic Music Committee (NOMUS), Schönfeldtsgränd 1, S-111 27 Stockholm. *Secretary General: Johan Falk.*
Rockfile Sweden HB, PO Box 558, S-631 07 Eskilstuna. *Managing Director: Hans Lindell.*
Society of Swedish Composers, PO Box 27 327, S-102 54 Stockholm.
Studiefrämjandet Music & Media - Eskilstuna, PO Box 157, S-631 03 Eskilstuna. *Department Manager: Hans Lindell.*
Svensk Musik/Swedish Music Information Centre, PO Box 27 327, S-102 54 Stockholm. *Chairman: Roland Sandberg.*
Svensk Impressarieförening (SVIMP), PO Box 11206, Vinterullsorget 62, S-100 61 Stockholm. *Chairman: Asa Ingman.*
Swedish Artists' and Musicians' Interest Organization (SAMI), Döbelnsgatan 3, S-111 40 Stockholm. *Managing Director: Yngve Aaekrberg.*
Swedish Independent Record Producers (SOM), PO Box 221, S-185 23 Vaxholm. *Secretary General: Jonas Sjostrom.*
Swedish Music Publishers Association (SMFF), PO Box 27 327, S-102 54 Stockholm. *Managing Director: Carl Lindencicna.*
Swedish Musicians Union/Svenska Musiker Förbundet, PO Box 43, Tegneratan 4, S-101 20 Stockholm. *Contact: Hakan Hillerström.*
Swedish Performing Rights Society (STIM), PO Box 27 327, S-102 54 Stockholm. *General Manager: Gunnar Petri.*

SWITZERLAND

Association of Swiss Concert Agents, 7 Rue de la Fontaine, 1211 Geneva. *President: Jack Yfar.*
Association of Swiss Musicians, Avenue du Grammont 11 bis, Case Postale 177, 1000 Lausanne 13. *General Secretary: Hélène Petitpierre.*
European Association of Music Festivals, c/o Centre Européen de la Culture Villa Moynier, 122 Rue de Lausanne, 1211 Geneva. *Secretary: Dr Henry Siegwart.*
Federation of International Music Competitions, 104 Rue de Carouge, 1205 Geneva.
Fondation Suisa Pour la Musique, Rue de l'Hopital 22, PO Box 409, 2001 Neuchatel. *Chairman: Jean Balissat.*
IFPI Switzerland, Toblerstr 76a, CH-8044 Zurich. *President: Peter Vosseler.*
International Society for Contemporary Music, c/o Association of Swiss Musicians, Avenue du Grammont 11 bis, Case Postale 177, 1000 Lausanne 13.
Schweizer Zentralband Musikhandels (SZM), Zeughausgasse 9, PO Box 238, 6301 Zug. *President: Erika Hug.*
Schweizerischer Musikverband (SMV), Hotelgasse 1, 300 Bern 7. *President: Heinz Marti.*
Suisa (Performing Rights Society of Switzerland), Bellariastrasse 82, 8038 Zürich. *Manager: Fabio Hugel.*
Suisa Music Foundation (Music Information Centre), Passage Maxmililien-de-Meuron 4, PO Box 409, 2001 Neuchâtel. *Managing Director: P Liechti.*
SVMM, PO Box, 8616 Riedikon /Uster. *President: Willy Viteka.*
Swiss Association of Professional Musicians, Elisabethenstrasse 2, 4051 Basel.
Swiss Society for Musical Research, PO Box 231, 4020 Basel.
Swiss Society for Popular Music, c/o SUISA, Bellariastrasse 82, 8038 Zürich.
VSM, Zeughausgasse 9, PO Box 238, 6301 Zug. *President: Edmund Schoenberger.*
VSSF, Zeughausgasse 9, PO Box 238, 6301 Zug. *President: Daniel Baer.*

TAIWAN

ARCO (The Association of Recording Copyright Owners of ROC), 3F, No 95, Sec 4, Nanking East Road, Taipei. *Executive Director: Robin Lee.*
IFPI Members Foundation in Taiwan , 3F, No 95, Sec 4, Nanking East Road, Taipei. *Secretary General: Robin Lee.*

THAILAND

Thai Composers Association (TCA), 107-108 Siripong Road, Sao Chingcha, Samranrat, Bangkok 10200.

TURKEY

MESAM, Kuyulu Bostan Sokak Kristal Plas Apt, Nisantasi, Istanbul.
MUYAP (Muzik Yapimlari Dernegi), IMC 6, Blok 6437, 34470 Unkapani, Istanbul. *Contact: Yasar Kekeva.*

UKRAINE

Broken Barricades, Tchernovoarmiyska 17B, 252 003 Kiev. *Manager: Sergiy Kalyta.*
Directorate of the All-Ukrainian Festival of Independent Music "Alternative", Culture Foundation, Lesva Kur-Basa Str 4, 290007 Lviv. *Director: Youry Grekh; Vice-Director: Ruslan Koshiv.*
Independent Artist's Agency 'Ljubchenko & Co', Room 7, Mietrostrojevskaja St 5, 320128 Dniepropetrovsk. *Director: Valeri Ljubchenko.*
Institute of Musicology, Institute of Musicology, Soviet Ukraine Square, 20 # 9, 310003 Kharkov. *Director: Grigory Hansburg.*
Musical Information Agency IRA, PO Box 83, 326 840 Novoya Kakhovka/Kherson. *Manager: Iryna Tsygipa.*
Producers Centre Rock Akademy, Khreschatyk 6, 252 001 Kiev. *Managing Director: Mykola Drik..*

UNITED KINGDOM

Agents' Association (GB), 54 Keyes House, Dolphin Square, London SW1V 3NA. *General Secretary: Ivan Birchall.*
Alchemea - The London College of Professional Audio Engineering and Production, The Windsor Centre, 2-18 Britannia Row, The Angel Islington, London N1 8QH. *College Director: Claude Camilleri.*
American Society of Composers, Authors and Publishers (ASCAP), 8 Cork Street, London W1X 1PB. *Contact: Karen Crowley.*
Association of Music Industry Accountants (AMIA), Becket House, 1 Lambeth Road, London SE1 7EU. *Secretary: Nicki Davies.*
Association of Professional Composers (APC), 34 Hanway Street, London W1P 9DE. *Administrator: Rosemary Dixon.*
Association of Professional Recording Services Ltd (APRS), 2 Windsor Square, Reading, Berkshire RG1 2TH. *Chief Executive: Mark Broad.*
Association of United Recording Artists (Aura), Flat B, 6 Bravington Street, London W9 3AH. *Contact: Peter Jenner.*
Belfast Jazz Society, 18 Lyndhurst Drive, Belfast B13 3PA, Northern Ireland. *Administration: George Chambers.*
Black Music Industry Association, 146 Manor Park Road, Harlesden, London NW10 4JP. *Contact: Kwaku Lutterfoot.*
British Academy of Songwriters, Composers & Authors (BASCA), The Penthouse, 4 Brook Street, Mayfair, London W1Y 1AA. *Chairman: Guy Fletcher.*
British Archive of Country Music, 163 The Gateway, Marine Parade, Dover CT16 1LS, Kent. *Managing Director: David Barnes.*
British Association of Concert Agents, 26 Wadham Road, London SW15 2LR. *President: David Sigall.*
British Association of Record Dealers (BARD), Premier House, Hinton Road, Bournemouth, Dorset BH1 2EF. *Director-General/Secretary: Bob Lewis.*

British Country Music Association, PO Box 240, Harrow, Middlesex HA3 7PH. *Chairman: Jim Marshall.*
British Phonographic Industry (BPI), 25 Saville Row, London W1X 1AA. *Director-General: John Deacon;General Manager: Peter Scaping.*
Broadcast Music Incorporated (BMI), 84 harley House, Marylebone Road, London NW1 5HN. *UK Director: Christian Ulf-Hansen.*
Chart Information Network (CIN), 8 Montague Close, London SE1 9UR. *Charts Director Designate: Omar Maskatiya.*
Christian Copyright Licensing Ltd, PO Box 1339, Eastbourne, East Sussex BN21 4YF. *UK Church & Schools Representative: Chris Williams.*
Celfyddydau Mari Arts, Studio 4, Model House Craft and Design Centre, The Bullring, Llantrisant, Rhondda Cynon Taf, Wales CF72 8EB. *Co-ordinator: Mick Tems.*
Club Gwerin Llantrisant Folk Club, 1 Ty Clyta Cottages, Cross Inn, Llantrisant, Rhondda Cynon Taf, Wales CF72 8AZ. *Secretary: Mick Tems.*
Commercial Radio Companies Association (CRCA), 77 Shaftesbury Avenue, London W1V 7AD. *Chief Executive: Paul Brown.*
Community Music Ltd, Community Music House, 60 Farringdon Road, London EC1R 3BP. *Contact: Alison Tickell.*
Composers' Guild of Great Britain (CCGB), 34 Hanway Street, London W1P 9DE. *President: Sir Peter Maxwell Davies CBE.*
Concert Promoters Association (CPA), 4th Floor, Avon House, 360-366 Oxford Street, London W1N 9HA. *Chairman: Harvey Goldsmith; Secretary: Carol Smith.*
Country Music Association (CMA), 3rd Floor, 18 Golden Square, London W1R 3AG. *European Operations Co-Ordinator: Bobbi Boyce; UK/Ireland Director: David Bower.*
Cthru Music, Swallowe Cottage, Stoke House Farm, Stoke Road, Stoke Hammond MK17 9BN. *Contact: Andrew Llewellyn.*
Guild of International Songwriters and Composers (GISC), Sovereign House, 12 Trewartha Road, Parr Sands, Penzance, Cornwall TR20 9ST. *General Secretary: Carole Jones.*
Guild of Recording Producers, Directors and Engineers (Re-Pro), 68 Cleveland Gardens, Barnes, London SW13 0AH. *Contact: Jackie DaCosta.*
Incorporated Society of Musicians, 10 Stratford Place, London W1N 9AE. *Chief Executive: Neil Hoyle.*
International Artist Managers' Association (IAMA), 41a Lonsdale Road, London W11 2BY.
International Federation of the Phonographic Industry (IFPI), 54 Regent Street, London W1R 5PJ. *Chairman: David Fine; Director-General: Nic Garnett.*
International Jazz Federation, c/o Jazzwise, 2B Gleneagle Mews, London SW16 6AE. *Vice-President: Charles Alexander.*
International Managers Forum (IMF), 134 Lots Road, London SW10 0RJ. *General Secretary: James Fisher.*
International Music Markets (IMM) Ltd, 245 Old Marylebone Road, London NW1 5QT. *General Manager: Phil Graham.*
International Society of European Songwriters and Composers (SESAC), Gresham House, 53 Clarendon Road, Watford, Herts WD1 1LA. *Chairman: Wayne Bickerton.*
Jazz Action, 1 Portrush Close, Darlington, County Durham DL1 3HU. *Development Officer: Adrian Tilbrook.*
Jazz Educaton Trust, 1 Fox Glove Close, Ringmer, East Sussex BN8 5PB. *Director: Adrian Kendon.*
Jazz North West, 2A Chruch Street, Malpas, Cheshire SY14 8NZ. *Director: Nick Purnell.*
Jazz Services, 5 Dryden Street, Covent Garden, London WC2E 9NW. *Director: Chris Hodgkins; Information Officer: Celia Wood.*
Mechanical Copyright Protection Society Ltd (MCPS), Elgar House, 41 Streatham High Road, London SW16 1ER. *CEO: John Hutchinson.*
Millward Brown Market Research Ltd, Olympus Avenue, Tachbrook Park, Warwick CV34 6RJ. *Charts Director: Bob Barnes.*
Music Industries Association, 7 The Avenue, Datchet, Slough, Berks SL3 9DH. *Secretary: J A Fox.*
Music Industry Human Rights Association, 192 Chiswick Village, London W4 3DG. *Contact: Policy Office (London).*
Music Industry Research Organization (MIRO), 8th Floor, Ludgate House, 245 Blackfriars Road, London SE1 9UR. *Editor: Lee Fisher.*
Music Publishers Association (MPA), 3rd Floor, Strandgate, 18-20 York Buildings, London WC2 6JU. *Chief Executive: Sarah Foulder.*
Musicians Benevolent Fund, 16 Ogle Street, London W1P 8JB. *Secretary to the Fund: Helen Faulkner.*
Musicians' Union (MU), 60-62 Clapham Road, London SW9 0JJ. *General Secretary: Dennis Scard.*
National Entertainment Agents Council, PO Box 112, Seaford, East Sussex BN25 2DQ. *General Secretary: Chris Bray.*
Nordoff Robbins Music Therapy, 55 Fulham High Street, London SW6 3JJ. *Chairman: Andrew Miller.*
North West Composers' Association, 41 Parklands Way, Poynton, Cheshire SK12 1AL.
North-West Musicians Collective, 6c Shipquay Street, Derry, Northern Ireland BT48 6DN. *Co-Ordinators: John O'Neill and Sean Pemberton.*
Northern Ireland Musicians' Association, 525 Antrim Road, Belfast BT15 3BS. *General Secretary: Henry C. Hamilton.*
Performing Artists Media Rights Association (PAMRA), 4th Floor, 80 Borough High Street, London SE1 1LR. *Chief Executive: Ann Rawcliffe-King; Director: Benny Gallagher.*
Performing Right Society (PRS), 29-33 Berners Street, London W1P 4AA. *CEO: John Hutchinson; Membership Director: John Sweeney.*
Phonographic Performance Ltd (PPL), 1 Upper James Street, London W1R 3HG. *CEO: Charles Andrews; Managing Director: John Love.*
Radio Academy, 5 Marklet Place, London W1N 7AH. *Chief Executive: John Bradford.*
Radio Advertising Bureau (RAB), 77 Shaftesbury Avenue, London W1V 7AD. *Director: Douglas McArthur.*
Radio Authority, Holbrook House, 14 Great Queen Street, London WC2B 5DG. *Chairman: Sir Peter Gibbings; Contact: Marion Shelley.*
Regional Promoters Association (RPA), The Leadmill, 6-7 Leadmill Road, Sheffield S1 4SE.
Scottish Music Information Centre, 1 Bowmont Gardens, Glasgow G12 9LR.
South West Jazz, Exeter and Devon Arts Centre, Bradninch Place, Gandy Street, Exeter EX4 3LS. *Regional Development Officer: Kevin Buckland.*
Tour People, Flat F, 78 Deptford High Street, London SE8 4RT. *Contact: Steve Alu.*
Variety & Allied Entertainments' Council of Great Britain, 54 Keyes House, Dolphin Square, London SW1V 3NA. *Joint Secretary: Ivan Birchall.*
Video Performance Ltd (VPL), 1 Upper James Street, London W1R 3HG. *CEO: Charles Andrews.*
Welsh Jazz Society Ltd, 26 The Balcony, Castle Arcade, Cardiff, South Glamorgan CF1 2BY. *Director: Brian Hennessey.*
Whistlebinkies, 13 Lawrence Street, Glasgow G11 5HH. *Contact: Eddie McGuire.*
Women in Music, BAC, Lavender Hill, Battersea, London SW11 5TF. *Administrative Director: Lolita Ratchford.*

URUGUAY

Asociación General de Autores del Uruguay (AGADU), Canelones, 1122, 11100 Montevideo. *President: Antonio Italiano.*
Asociación Uruguay de Musicos, Calle Maldonado 983, CP 11100 Montevideo. *President: Alfonso Coronel.*
Sociedad Uruguay de Interpretes, Canelones 1090, Montevideo. *President: José Maria Lorenzo.*
Sociedad Uruguay de Música Contemporánea, Casilla de Correo 1328, Montevideo. *President: Diego Legrand.*

USA

Academy of Country Music (ACM), 6255 Sunset Blvd, Suite 923, Hollywood, CA 90028. *President: Fred Reiser.*
Affiliated Independent Record Companies (AIRC), PO Box 241648, Los Angeles, CA 90024. *President: M Wilkes.*
American Federation of Musicians, 1501 Broadway, Suite 600, New York, NY 10036. *President: Mark Massagli.*
American Federation of Television and Radio Artists (AFTRA), 260 Madison Avenue, New York, NY 10016. *Executive Director: Bruce York.*
American Mechanical Rights Agency Inc (AMRA), 333 South Tamiami Trail, Suite 295, Venice, FL 34285. *Chief Officer: Patricia Bente.*
American Musicians' Union, 8 Tobin Court, Dumont, NJ 07628. *President: Ben Intorre.*
American Society of Composers, Authors and Publishers (ASCAP), 1 Lincoln Plaza, New York,NY 10023. *President: Marilyn Bergman.*
American Society of Music Arrangers & Composers (ASMAC), PO Box 17840, Encino, CA 91416. *President: Larry Blank; Secretary: Bonnie Janafsky.*
Audio Engineering Society, 60 East 42nd Street, Lincoln Bldg, Room 2520, New York, NY 10165. *Director: Donald Plunkett.*
Black Rock Coalition, PO Box 1054, Cooper Station, New York, NY 10276. *President: Bruce Mack.*
Broadcast Music Inc (BMI), 320 W 57th Street, New York, NY 10019. *President: Frances Preston.*
Composers Guild, Box 586, Framington, UT 84025. *President: Ruth Gatrell.*
Concerts for the Environment, 126 N 3rd Street, Suite 305, Minneapolis, MN 55401. *Executive Director: Michael Martin.*
Cosmotone Records, 3350 Highway 6, Suite 412, Sugar Land,TX 77478. *Contact: Rafael Brom.*
Country Music Association (CMA), 4 Music Circle S, Nashville, TN 37203. *Executive Director: Ed Benson.*

GAVIN, 140 2nd Street, 2nd Floor, San Francisco, CA 94105. *Chief Executive Officer: David Dalton.*
Gospel Music Association, 7 Music Circle North, Nashville, TN 37203. *Executive Director: Bruce Koblish.*
Guitar and Accessories Marketing Association, 38 West 21 Street, 5th Floor, New York, NY 10010-6906. *President: Jerome Hershman.*
Guitar Foundation of America, Box 1240, Calremont, CA 91711. *General Manager: Gunnar Eisel.*
Hawaiian Academy of Recording Arts (HARA), PO Box 821, Honolulu, 96808. *Contact: Bonni Ryder.*
Independent Music Association, 10 Spruce Road, Saddle River, NJ 07456. *Contact: Don Kulak.*
Independent Network (West Coast Office), PO Box 241648 Los Angeles, CA 90024. *Chief Executive Officer: M Wilkins.*
Independent Network (East Coast Office), PO Box 609, Ringwood, NJ 07456.
Institute of Recording Arts & Sciences, PO Box 22653, Nashville, TN 37202. *Founder & Administrator: David Mathes.*
International Association of Electronic Keyboard Manufacturers, 38 West 21 Street, 5th Floor, New York, NY 10010-6906. *President: Jerome Hershman.*
Jazz Foundation of America, 1200 Broadway, Suite 7D, New York, NY 10001. *Promotions Director: Russ Dantzler.*
Long Island Songwriters' Association Inc (LISA), PO Box 395, Holbrook, NY 11741. *President/Executive Director: Erwin K Cochran.*
Mel Carter, PO Box 69646, Los Angeles, CA 90069. *Contact: Larry Kleno.*
Mexican Network International, 235-4 Lucas Lane, Voorhees, NJ 08043. *President/Founder: Laura Grüb-Geschwindt.*
Music Association of America, 224 King Street, Englewood, NJ 07631. *Executive Director: George Strum.*
Music Distributors Association, 38 West 21 Street, 5th Floor, New York, NY 10010-6906. *President: Jerome Hershman.*
Music Educators National Conference, 1806 Robert Fulton Drive, Reston, VA 22091-4348. *Excutive Director: John J Mahlmann.*
Music Publishers' Association of the United States, 711 Third Avenue, New York, NY 10017.
Musicians Contact Service, 7315 Sunset Blvd #D, Hollywood, CA 90046. *Contact: Sterling Haug.*
Nashville Entertainment Association, PO Box 121948, Nashville, TN 37212-1948. *Excutive Director: Sherry Bond.*
NAIRD, 1000 Maplewood Drive, Suite 211, Maple Shade, NJ 08052. *Executive Director: Holly Cass.*
Nashville Songwriters Association International (NSAI), 15 Music Square West, Nashville, TN 37203. *Executive Director: Pat Rogers.*
National Academy of Popular Music, 885 Second Avenue, 26th Floor, New York, NY 10017-2201. *Director: Bob Leone.*
National Academy of Recording Arts & Sciences Inc (NARAS), 2 Music Circle S, Nashville, TN 37203.
National Academy of Songwriters (NAS), 6381 Hollywood Blvd, Suite 780, Hollywood, CA 90028. *Executive Director: Dan Kirkpatrick.*
National Association of Band Instrument Manufacturers, 38 West 21 Street, 5th Floor, New York, NY 10010-6906. *President: Jerome Hershman.*
National Association of Recording Merchandisers (NARM), 11 Eves Drive, Suite 140, Marlton, NJ 08053. *Executive Vice-President: Pam Horowitz.*
National Coalition Against Censorship, 275 Seventh Avenue, New York, NY 10001. *Excutive Director: Leanne Katz.*
National Council of Music Importers and Exporters, 38 West 21 Street, 5th Floor, New York, NY 10010-6906. *President: Jerome Hershman.*
National Music Publishers' Association, 711 Third Avenue, 8th Floor, New York, NY 10017. *Public Relations Manager: Margaret O'Keeffe.*
Northern California Songwriters Association, 855 Oak Grove Avenue, Suite #211, Menlo Park, CA 94025. *Executive Director: Ian Crombie.*
Publishers' Licensing Corporation, PO Box 5807, Englewood, NJ 07631. *President: Philip S Kurnit.*
Recording Industry Association of America (RIAA), 1020 19th Street NW, Suite 200, Washington, DC 20096. *Vice President, Member Services: John H Ganoe.*
Rhythm and Blues Rock and Roll Society, PO Box 1949, New Haven, CT 06510.
Rock And Roll Hall Of Fame, 1290 Sixth Avenue, New York, NY 10104. *Executive Director: Susan Evans.*
Rock Out Censorship (ROC), PO Box 147, Jewett, OH 43986. *Co-Founder/Editor: John Woods.*
SESAC, 55 Music Square East, Nashville, TN 37203.
Songwriters Guild of America, 6430 Sunset Blvd, #1002, Hollywood, CA 90028. *West Coast Director: B Aaron Meza.*
Songwriters of Wisconsin International, PO Box 1027, Neenah, WI 54957-1027. *President: Tony Ansems.*
Talent Search America, 273 Chippewa Drive, Columbia, SC 29210-6508. *Contact: Talent Director.*
Tennessee Songwriters Association (TSA), PO Box 2664, Hendersonville, TN 37075. *Contact: Jim Sylvis.*
Tennessee Film, Entertainment and Music Commission, Rachel Jackson Bldg, 320 6th Ave, No, Nashville, TN 37243-0790. *Executive Director: Marsha Blackburn.*
Texas Music Office, Office of the Governor, PO Box 13246, Austin, TX 78711. *Director: Casey Monahan.*
Women in Music Business Association, 20 Music Square West #200, Nashville, TN 37203. *Director: Catherine Masters.*
Women In Music National Network, 31121 Mission Blvd, Suite 123, Hayward, CA 94544. *Chairperson: Karen Jackson*

VENEZUELA

Sociedad de Autores y Compositores de Venezuela, Edif Vam, Entrada Oeste 9°, Avd Andrés Bello, Caracas.